SEVEN LANGUAGE DICTIONARY

OTHER REFERENCE BOOKS FROM
RANDOM HOUSE VALUE PUBLISHING, INC.

ROGET'S DESK THESAURUS

*WEBSTER'S ENCYCLOPEDIC UNABRIDGED
DICTIONARY OF THE ENGLISH LANGUAGE*

WEBSTER'S UNIVERSAL COLLEGE DICTIONARY

WEBSTER'S CONCISE DICTIONARY

WEBSTER'S DESK DICTIONARY

*WEBSTER'S DESK SPANISH-ENGLISH
ENGLISH-SPANISH DICTIONARY*

SEVEN LANGUAGE DICTIONARY

French-English • English-French
German-English • English-German
Hebrew-English • English-Hebrew
Italian-English • English-Italian
Portuguese-English • English-Portuguese
Russian-English • English-Russian
Spanish-English • English-Spanish

Edited by David Schumaker

Gramercy Books
New York

This 2000 edition is published by Gramercy Books™, an imprint of Random House Value Publishing, Inc. 280 Park Avenue, New York, N.Y. 10017.

Gramercy Books™ and design are trademarks of Random House Value Publishing, Inc.

Random House
New York • Toronto • London • Sydney • Auckland
http://www.randomhouse.com/

Printed and bound in the United States of America.

A CIP catalogue record for this book is available from the Library of Congress.

ISBN 0-517-05795-6

9 8 7 6 5 4 3

CONTENTS

SEVEN
LANGUAGE
DICTIONARY

COMMON USAGE
DICTIONARY

French-English
English-French

BY **Ralph Weiman** FORMERLY CHIEF
OF LANGUAGE SECTION, U.S. WAR DEPARTMENT

REVISED AND ENLARGED BY **Mary Finocchiaro**
PROFESSOR OF EDUCATION, HUNTER COLLEGE, NEW YORK CITY

AND

Remunda Cadoux CHAIRMAN OF
FOREIGN LANGUAGES, CHRISTOPHER COLUMBUS HIGH SCHOOL, NEW YORK CITY

*CONTAINING OVER 20,000 BASIC TERMS WITH
MEANINGS ILLUSTRATED BY SENTENCES AND
1000 ESSENTIAL WORDS ESPECIALLY INDICATED
TOGETHER WITH A SECTION ON LETTER-WRITING*

INTRODUCTION

The French Common Usage Dictionary lists the most frequently used French words, gives their most important meanings, and illustrates their use.

1. The *basic* words are indicated by capitals.

2. Only the most important meanings are given.

3. These meanings are illustrated, wherever necessary, by means of everyday phrases and sentences. Where there is no close English equivalent for a French word or where the English equivalent has several different meanings, the context of the illustrative sentences helps to make the meaning clear.

4. Each important word is followed by the everyday expressions in which it most frequently occurs. The Common Usage Dictionary serves accordingly as a phrase book or conversation guide: it contains thousands of everyday sentences which are of practical importance (for traveling, correspondence, etc.) or which serve as illustrations of the grammatical features of current written and spoken French. The Common Usage Dictionary should, therefore, prove helpful both to beginners who are building up their vocabulary and to advanced students who want to perfect their command of colloquial French.

5. In translating the French phrases and sentences, an attempt has been made to give not a mere translation but an equivalent—that is, what an English speaker would say in the same situation. (Literal translations have been added to help the beginner.) The user is thus furnished with numerous examples of how common French expressions (particularly the very idiomatic and the very colloquial ones) can best be translated into English. This feature makes the Common Usage Dictionary especially useful for translation work.

6. The English-French part contains the most common English words and their French equivalents. By consulting the sentences given under the French word in the French-English part, the reader can observe whether the French word always translates the English one or whether it does so only in certain cases.

EXPLANATORY NOTES

Literal translations are in quotation marks.

Very colloquial words, phrases and sentences are marked *fam.* (*expression familière* "colloquial expression, colloquialism").

Certain adjectives that end in *-al* in the masculine singular and *-ale* in the feminine singular take *-aux* in the masculine plural. This plural ending is indicated in dictionary entries. However, since the feminine plural maintains, in all cases, the regular ending *-ales*, it has not been expressly indicated in the dictionary entries.

EXAMPLES:	masculine	feminine
sing.	*cordial*	*cordiale*
plu.	*cordiaux*	*cordiales*
sing.	*égal*	*égale*
plu.	*égaux*	*égales*

Other adjectives of this type include:

amical	*intégral*	*médical*	*principal*
central	*international*	*mental*	*sentimental*
commercial	*latéral*	*national*	*social*
horizontal	*loyal*	*oriental*	*spécial*
idéal	*marital*	*original*	*triomphal*
immoral			

In written French, capital letters do not generally show an accent. However, for precision's sake, we have included all appropriate accent marks on every word entry. In the sample sentences we have followed the normal French practice of omitting accents on capital letters.

French-English DICTIONARY

A *The first letter of the alphabet.*

A, AU (*contraction of* a + le), **aux** (*pl. contraction of* a + les) *to, at.*
Je vais à Paris. *I'm going to Paris.*
Traduisez-moi ça mot à mot. *Translate this for me word for word.*
Attendez-donc à plus tard. *Wait until later.*
Retrouvons-nous à la gare. *Let's meet at the station.*
A tout à l'heure. *See you in a little while.*
A demain. *See you tomorrow.* ("Until tomorrow.")
C'est la première rue à droite. *It's the first street to your (the) right.*
Il est au jardin. *He's in the garden.*
Au mois de mai. *In the month of May.*
Au revoir. *Good-by.*

abaisser *to lower; reduce.*
s'abaisser *to stoop, lower oneself.*
abandon *m. abandonment, desertion, surrender.*
abandonner *to abandon, desert, leave.*
J'abandonne la course. *I'm out of the race.*
abat-jour *m. lampshade.*
abattre *to pull down; kill; get depressed.*
On a abattu les arbres de l'allée. *They pulled down the trees in the lane.*
On a abattu le cheval. *They killed the horse.*
Elle se laisse abattre. *She lets herself get discouraged (depressed).*
abattu *adj. discouraged, depressed, downcast.*
Je l'ai trouvée très abattue. *I found her very much depressed.*
abdomen *m. abdomen.*
abeille *f. bee.*
abîmer *to damage, spoil.*
s'abîmer *to get spoiled, decay; ruin.*
S'abîmer la santé. *To ruin one's health.*
abolir *to abolish.*
abominable *adj. abominable.*
abondamment *abundantly.*
Nous en avons abondamment. *We have plenty of it.*
abondance *f. abundance.*
Il y en a en abondance. *There's plenty of it. It's very plentiful.*
Il parle avec abondance. *He speaks fluently.*
Abondance de biens ne nuit pas. *You can't have too much of a good thing.* ("Abundance of good things doesn't hurt.")
abondant *adj. abundant.*
La main-d'œuvre est abondante dans cette région. *Manpower (labor) is plentiful in this region. There is an abundant labor supply in this region.*
abonder *to be plentiful.*
Le gibier abonde dans ce pays. *Game is plentiful in this region (part of the country).*
J'abonde parfaitement dans votre sens. *I share your opinion completely. I'm in complete agreement with you.*
abonné *m. subscriber.*
Les abonnés au téléphone, au gaz, à l'électricité, etc. *Telephone subscribers; consumers of gas, electricity, etc.*
Pour tout changement d'adresse les abonnés doivent joindre 50 centimes. *For any change of address, subscribers must send* ("attach") *50 cents. (Newspaper, magazine, etc.)*
abonnement *m. subscription.*
Prendre un abonnement à un journal. *To sub-*

scribe to a newspaper.
Une carte d'abonnement. *A season ticket.*
abonner *to subscribe.*
Etes-vous abonné à cette revue? *Do you subscribe to this magazine? Are you a subscriber to this magazine?*
s'abonner *to subscribe.*
Je m'y abonnerai. *I'm going to subscribe to it.*
ABORD *m. access, approach; outskirt.*
D'abord je n'avais pas compris; mais maintenant, j'y suis. *At first, I didn't understand, but now I get it (now I've caught on).*
De prime abord. *At first sight.*
Il est d'un abord difficile. *It's difficult to get to see him. He's hard to reach.*
Les abords de la ville sont charmants. *The outskirts of the town are very nice ("charming").*
abordable *adj. accessible.*
La côte est abordable. *The coast is easy to approach.*
Leurs prix sont abordables. *Their prices are reasonable (within one's means).*
abordage *m. collision (of ships).*
Le brouillard fut la cause de l'abordage. *The fog was responsible for ("caused") the collision.*
aborder *to land; accost, address, go up to.*
Ils abordèrent dans une île. *They landed on an island.*
Le bateau aborda à quai. *The boat docked. The boat came alongside the dock.*
Il l'a abordé pour lui demander son chemin. *He went up to him to ask him the way.*
aboutir *to lead to; succeed.*
Cela n'aboutira à rien. *That won't come (lead) to anything.*
Où aboutit cette route? *Where does this road lead to?*
Il paraissait très anxieux d'aboutir. *He seemed very anxious to succeed.*
aboyer *to bark.*
abrégé *m. outline, summary.*
abréger *to abbreviate.*
Pour abréger. *In short. To be brief.*
Comment abrégez-vous ce mot? *How do you abbreviate this word?*
Il faut que j'abrège mon séjour. *I'll have to cut my stay short.*
abréviation *f. abbreviation.*
Quelques abréviations françaises (Some French abbreviations):
D. or d. Ditto. *Ditto.*
Et Cie. Et Compagnie. *And Co.*
F. Franco. *Postage prepaid. Delivery free.*
M. Monsieur. *Mr.*
Mgr. Monseigneur. *Mgr.*
Mlle. Mademoiselle. *Miss.*
MM. Messieurs. *Messrs.*
Mme. Madame. *Mrs.*
N.B. Nota bene. *N.B.*
P.S. Post-Scriptum. *P.S. Postscript.*
P. et T. Postes et Télécommunications. *Post and Telegraph Office.*
R.S.V.P. Répondez, s'il vous plaît. *Please answer.*
S.V.P. S'il vous plaît. *Please.*
T.S.F. Télégraphie sans fil. *Radio.*
T.S.V.P. Tournez s'il vous plaît. *Turn (the knob). Turn over (a page).*
abri *m. shelter.*
Mettez-vous à l'abri. *Take shelter.*
abricot *m. apricot.*

abriter *to shelter, protect.*
s'abriter *to take shelter.*
abrupt *adj. abrupt.*
ABSENCE *f. absence.*
En son absence. *In his absence.*
Mon absence a-t-elle été remarquée? *Did anyone notice my absence?*
absent *m. absent.*
Les absents ont toujours tort. *The absent are always in the wrong.*
ABSENT *adj. absent.*
Sont-ils absents? *Are they absent?*
Il est absent de Paris. *He's away from Paris. He's not in Paris now.*
s'absenter *to be absent.*
Il faut que je m'absente pour quelques instants. *I'll have to be away for a few minutes. I have to leave for a few minutes.*
S'absenter pour affaires. *To go away on business.*
S'absenter de l'école. *To stay away from school.*
absolu *adj. absolute.*
ABSOLUMENT *absolutely.*
Absolument rien. *Absolutely nothing.*
Il me le faut absolument. *I need it badly. I must have it without fail (at all costs).*
absorber *to absorb.*
s'absorber *to be absorbed.*
s'abstenir *to abstain, refrain from.*
abstrait *m. abstract.*
Il discute toujours dans l'abstrait. *He's always arguing in the abstract.*
abstrait *adj. abstract.*
absurde *adj. absurd.*
C'est absurde! *It's absurd! It's ridiculous!*
absurdité *f. absurdity.*
Vous dites des absurdités. *You're talking nonsense.*
abus *m. abuse.*
abuser *to abuse; take advantage of.*
Il a abusé de son autorité. *He abused his authority.*
Vous abusez de sa patience. *You're trying his patience. You're taking advantage of his patience.*
s'abuser *to be mistaken.*
Vous vous abusez. *You're mistaken.*
abusif (abusive *f.*) *adj. abusive.*
académie *f. academy.*
accablant *adj. oppressive, crushing.*
Il fait une chaleur accablante. *The heat is oppressive.*
accabler *to weight down, overcome, overwhelm.*
Cette chaleur vous accable. *This heat overcomes you (gets you down).*
accéder *to accede to, comply with.*
accélérateur *m. accelerator.*
Appuyer sur l'accélérateur. *To step on the gas.*
accélération *f. acceleration.*
accélérer *to quicken.*
Accélérons le pas. *Let's walk faster. Let's quicken our pace.*
accent *m. accent.*
Parler anglais avec un accent. *To speak English with an accent.*
Où se trouve l'accent tonique dans ce mot? *Where is the accent in this word?*
Accent aigu. *Acute accent.*
Accent circonflexe. *Circumflex accent.*
Accent grave. *Grave accent.*
accentuer *to accent; accentuate.*
acceptable *adj. acceptable.*

acceptation *f. acceptance.*
ACCEPTER *to accept.*
acception *f. acceptance; meaning.*
Ce mot a plusieurs acceptions. *This word has several meanings.*
Dans toute l'acception du mot. *In every sense of the word.*
accès *m. access.*
J'ai accès à leurs dossiers. *I have access to their files.*
Leur propriété est d'accès difficile. *Their estate is difficult to reach.*
Accès interdit. *No admittance.*
Il a souvent des accès de mauvaise humeur. *He often has fits of bad temper.*
accessible *adj. accessible.*
accessoire *m. accessory.*
ACCIDENT *m. accident.*
Il a eu un accident d'automobile. *He had (met with) an automobile accident.*
Nous nous sommes rencontrés par accident. *We met by accident (by chance).*
accidentel (accidentelle *f.*) *adj. accidental.*
accidentellement *accidentally.*
acclamer *to acclaim, hail, cheer.*
s'acclimater *to become acclimatized or adapted.*
accommodant *adj. accommodating.*
Ce marchand est très accommodant. *This storekeeper is very accommodating.*
accommoder *to accommodate, suit.*
L'hôtel peut accommoder quatre-vingt-dix personnes. *The hotel can accommodate ninety people.*
Cela m'accommode à merveille. *That suits me fine (to a T).*
s'accommoder *to put up with, be satisfied with.*
Il s'accommode de tout. *He's satisfied with anything. He's easy to suit (please).*
accompagner *to accompany.*
Ils l'accompagnèrent à la gare. *They took him (her) to the station.*
accompli *adj. accomplished.*
Un fait accompli. *An accomplished fact. A fait accompli.*
accomplir *to complete, finish.*
s'accomplir *to happen; be fulfilled.*
Sa prédiction s'est accomplie. *His prediction came true.*
accomplissement *m. achievement, fulfillment.*
ACCORD *m. accord, agreement.*
Parvenir à un accord. *To reach an agreement.*
D'un commun accord. *By common consent.*
Je suis d'accord. *I agree.*
D'accord, soit. *All right, agreed. ("Agreed, let it be that way.")*
D'accord, allez-y. *All right, do it (go ahead).*
accorder *to grant.*
s'accorder *to agree.*
Son récit ne s'accorde pas avec le vôtre. *His story doesn't agree with yours.*
Votre cravate ne s'accorde pas avec votre costume. *Your tie doesn't match your suit.*
accoster *to accost, address, speak to.*
accoucher *to give birth to; lie in.*
accourir *to rush up, run up.*
Ils accoururent à son secours. *They ran to his (her) help.*
accoutumer *to accustom.*
J'y suis accoutumé maintenant. *I'm used to it now.*
s'accoutumer *to accustom oneself to, get used to.*
On s'accoutume à tout. *One gets used to everything.*

accrocher *to hang up, hook.*
Accrochez votre pardessus et votre chapeau au porte-manteau. *Hang your coat and hat on the coat-rack (clothes-stand).*
accroître *to increase, augment, enlarge.*
s'accroître *to increase.*
s'accroupir *to squat.*
accueil *m. reception.*
On lui fit bon accueil. *They welcomed him warmly. They gave him a warm reception.*
Sa proposition n'a pas reçu un très bon accueil. *His (her) suggestion (proposition) was not very well received.*
accueillir *to receive, welcome.*
On accueillera favorablement votre requête. *Your request will be favorably received.*
On m'accueillit très cordialement. *They received me very cordially.*
accu(mulateur) *m. storage battery.*
accumulation *f. accumulation.*
accumuler *to accumulate.*
accusation *f. accusation, charge.*
accuser *to accuse; acknowledge.*
N'accusez jamais sans preuve. *Never accuse without proof.*
Nous vous accusons réception de votre dernière lettre. *We acknowledge receipt of your last letter.*
s'acharner *to set about (a thing) furiously, pursue relentlessly.*
La malchance s'acharne contre lui. *Ill luck pursues him relentlessly.*
ACHAT *m. purchase.*
Allez-vous faire des achats? *Are you going shopping?*
ACHETER *to buy.*
J'ai acheté cette auto bon marché. *I bought this car cheaply.*
acheteur *m. buyer, purchaser.*
ACHEVER *to complete, end, finish.*
Achevez toujours ce que vous commencez. *Always finish what you begin.*
Ne l'interrompez pas. Laissez-le achever. *Don't interrupt him. Let him finish.*
acide *noun (m.) and adj. acid.*
ACIER *m. steel.*
acompte *m. partial payment in advance, installment.*
Un acompte de dix francs. *Ten francs on account.*
ACQUÉRIR *to acquire, purchase.*
acquisition *f. acquisition, purchase.*
acquit *m. discharge, receipt, acquittal.*
Par manière d'acquit. *For form's sake.*
Par acquit de conscience. *For conscience' sake. To salve one's conscience.*
acquitter *to acquit; receipt.*
Il a été acquitté. *He was acquitted.*
Il a acquitté la facture. *He receipted the bill.*
s'acquitter *to perform; pay a debt.*
Il s'est bien acquitté de sa mission. *He carried out his mission successfully.*
Il s'est acquitté de ses dettes. *He paid off his debts.*
ACTE *m. act, action, deed.*
Ses actes furent désavoués par son chef. *His actions were repudiated by his chief.*
Une comédie en trois actes. *A comedy in three acts. A three-act play.*
Faire acte de présence. *To put in an appearance.*
L'acte est en bonne et due forme. *The deed is in proper form.*

acteur *m.* (actrice *f.*) *actor.*
actif *m. assets, credit.*
ACTIF (active *f.*) *adj. active.*
C'est un homme très actif. *He's a very active man.*
Il mène une vie active. *He leads an active life.*
ACTION *f. action; stock.*
C'est un homme d'action. *He's a man of action.*
L'action se passe en 1830. *The action takes place in 1830.*
Ces actions sont cotées à la Bourse. *These stocks are quoted on the stock exchange.*
activer *to quicken, accelerate.*
activité *f. activity.*
L'usine est en activité. *The factory is in operation.*
actualité *f. actuality.*
Les actualités au cinéma. *The newsreel.*
C'est tout à fait d'actualité. *It's the topic of the day.*
ACTUEL (actuelle *f.*) *adj. of the present time, current.*
Le gouvernement actuel. *The present government.*
Dans l'état actuel des choses. *In the present state of affairs. The way things (conditions) are now.*
actuellement *now, nowadays, at the present time.*
adaptation *f. adaptation.*
adapter *to adapt.*
s'adapter *to adapt oneself to; fit, suit.*
ADDITION *f. addition; restaurant check.*
Il y a une erreur dans l'addition. *There's a mistake in the addition.*
J'ai demandé l'addition au garçon. *I asked the waiter for the check.*
ADDITIONNEL (additionnelle *f.*) *adj. additional.*
ADDITIONNER *to add up.*
ADIEU *good-by. (In southern France, Adieu is an everyday word for good-by. In other parts of France, Adieu is used only when one doesn't expect to see someone for a long time.)*
adjacent *adj. adjacent.*
adjectif *m. adjective.*
adjoindre *to add.*
Ils lui ont adjoint un assistant. *They gave him an assistant.*
s'adjoindre *to take as an assistant, associate with.*
Il s'est adjoint un associé. *He took a partner.*
adjoint (adjointe *f.*) *noun and adj. assistant.*
Il est adjoint au directeur. *He's (the, an) assistant director.*
ADMETTRE *to admit.*
Il est généralement admis que ... *It's generally admitted that ...*
Les enfants ne sont pas admis. *Adults only. ("Children not admitted.")*
Etre admis à un examen. *To pass an examination.*
Sa requête ne fut pas admise. *His (her) request was not (has not been) granted.*
Cette affaire n'admet aucun retard. *The (this) matter admits of no delay.*
administrateur *m.* (administratrice *f.*) *administrator, director.*
administration *f. administration.*
administrer *to administer; manage.*
admirable *adj. admirable.*
Quel temps admirable! *What glorious weather!*
admiration *f. admiration.*
admirer *to admire.*

admission f. admission.
adopter to adopt.
  Le projet de loi fut adopté à l'unanimité. *The bill was adopted unanimously.*
adoption f. adoption.
adorer to adore.
adoucir to soften; smooth; sweeten.
ADRESSE f. address.
  Voici mon adresse. *Here's my address.*
  Le maire a lu une adresse au président. *The mayor read an address to the President.*
ADRESSER to address.
  Cette lettre vous est adressée. *This letter is addressed to you.*
  Adressez le paquet par la poste. *Send the parcel by mail.*
  C'est lui qui m'a adressé à vous. *He referred me to you.*
S'ADRESSER to apply to.
  S'adresser ici. *Apply here.*
  Adressez-vous à ce monsieur là-bas. *Ask that gentleman over there.*
  C'est à vous que cela s'adresse. *This is meant for you.*
ADULTE m. adult.
ADVENIR to happen, occur.
  Il advint une chose inattendue. *Something unexpected occurred.*
  Qu'en est-il advenu? *What became of it? What happened to it?*
  Advienne que pourra. *Come what may.*
  Je le ferai quoi qu'il advienne. *I'll do it, come what may. I'll do it no matter what happens.*
adverbe m. adverb.
adversaire m. adversary, opponent, rival.
adversité f. adversity.
affable adj. affable.
affaiblir to weaken.
AFFAIRE f. affair, business, matter.
  Il est dans les affaires. *He's in business. He's a businessman.*
  Il est à ses affaires. *He's at his office.*
  Comment vont les affaires? *How's business?*
  Les affaires sont les affaires. *Business is business.*
  Où en est l'affaire? *How does that matter stand?*
  Voilà mon affaire. *That's just what I want (need).*
  Il fait mon affaire. *He's the man I need.*
  Faire l'affaire de. *To meet the needs of.*
  J'ai votre affaire. *I have just the thing for you.*
  Quelle affaire! *What a mess? What a bother (trouble)!*
  Il a égaré ses affaires. *He's mislaid his things.*
  Ce n'est pas votre affaire. *That's not your concern. That's no business of yours.*
  Se tirer d'affaire. *To get out of a difficulty.*
  C'est une affaire de goût. *It's a matter of taste.*
  J'en fais mon affaire. *Leave it to me. I'll see to it. I'll take charge of it. I'll make it my business to see about it.*
affairé adj. busy.
  Il a toujours l'air affairé. *He always looks busy.*
affairement m. bustle.
  Quel affairement! *What a hustle and bustle!*
s'affaler to fall, drop.
affamé adj. hungry, famished.
affecter to affect, influence.
affection f. affection.
  Prendre quelqu'un en affection. *To take a liking to someone. To grow attached to someone.*
affectueux (affectueuse f.) adj. affectionate.

affermir to strengthen.
affiche f. poster.
afficher to post a bill.
affirmatif (affirmative f.) adj. affirmative.
affirmative f. affirmative.
  Il a répondu par l'affirmative. *He (has) replied in the affirmative.*
affirmer to affirm, assert, maintain.
  Certaines personnes affirment . . . *Some (certain people) maintain . . .*
  Il l'affirma sous serment. *He asserted it under oath.*
affliction f. affliction.
affliger to afflict, pain, grieve.
affluence f. flow, affluence, crowd.
  L'heure d'affluence. *Rush hour.*
s'affoler to fall into a panic.
  Ne vous affolez pas. *Don't get excited.*
affranchir to free.
affranchissement m. postage.
affreux (affreuse f.) adj. horrible, dreadful, frightful.
  Il fait un temps affreux. *The weather's awful.*
  J'ai un mal de tête affreux. *I have an awful headache.*
affront m. insult.
affût m. hiding-place.
  Etre à l'affût. *To be on the watch.*
AFIN DE so that, in order to.
  Il se dépêche afin de partir plus tôt. *He's hurrying so he can leave earlier.*
afin que so that, in order that.
africain noun and adj. African.
agaçant adj. annoying, irritating.
  C'est agaçant. *It's irritating (upsetting). It gets on your nerves.*
agacer to irritate, get on one's nerves.
  Ce bruit m'agace. *This noise gets on my nerves.*
ÂGE m. age, period, era.
  Quel âge avez-vous? *How old are you?*
  Il est entre deux âges. *He's middle-aged.*
  Il a pris de l'âge ces derniers temps. *He's aged a lot recently.*
  On apprend à tout âge. *It's never too late to learn. One is never too old to learn.*
  Le Moyen-Âge. *The Middle Ages.*
âgé adj. aged.
  Il est âgé de douze ans. *He's twelve years old.*
  Elle est beaucoup plus âgée que son mari. *She's much older than her husband.*
agence f. agency.
  J'ai l'agence de leur maison pour la région. *I have the agency (branch office) of their firm for this region.*
  Une agence télégraphique. *A news agency.*
  L'agence de voyage. *Travel agency.*
agenda m. notebook, diary.
agent m. agent.
  Je suis l'agent de cette firme. *I'm the agent (representative) of this firm.*
  Agents de police. *Policemen.*
aggraver to aggravate, increase the gravity of.
s'aggraver to aggravate, get worse.
  La situation s'aggrave. *The situation is growing (getting) worse.*
agile adj. agile.
AGIR to act.
  Il agit toujours de cette façon. *He always acts that way.*
  Réfléchissez avant d'agir. *Think before you act. Look before you leap.*
S'AGIR de to be a question of, a matter of.
  De quoi s'agit-il? *What's the matter? What's it a question of?*

  Je ne sais pas de quoi il s'agit. *I don't know what it's all about. I don't know what the problem (question) is.*
  Voici ce dont il s'agit. *The thing is this. This is the question (problem).*
  Il s'agit d'une forte somme. *A lot of money is involved.*
agitation f. agitation.
agiter to stir, shake.
s'agiter to be agitated, restless; fret.
agneau m. lamb.
agonie f. agony.
agrafe f. hook; clip.
agrandir to enlarge.
agrandissement m. enlargement.
agréable adj. agreeable, pleasant.
  Une soirée agréable. *A pleasant evening.*
agréer to accept.
  Veuillez agréer mes salutations empressées. *Very truly yours.*
agrément m. consent; pleasure; favor.
agriculteur m. farmer.
agriculture f. farming.
aguets m. pl. used in the following expression:
  Se tenir aux aguets. *To be on the watch. To be on one's guard.*
ah! ah! oh!
ahuri adj. flurried, confused.
AIDE f. aid, help.
  Il vint à notre aide. *He came to our aid. He helped us.*
aide m. aide, assistant.
AIDER to help.
  Aidez-moi à porter les bagages. *Help me carry the bags.*
aïe! ouch!
aïeux m. pl. ancestors.
aigle m. eagle.
aigre adj. sour; bitter.
aigu (aiguë f.) adj. sharp, acute.
  L'accent aigu. *Acute accent.*
  Elle poussa un cri aigu. *She let out a shrill cry.*
aiguille f. needle.
  Aiguille à tricoter. *Knitting needle.*
aiguiser to sharpen.
aile f. wing.
AILLEURS elsewhere, somewhere else.
  C'est moins cher ailleurs. *It's less expensive elsewhere.*
  Par ailleurs. *Besides. Otherwise.*
  D'ailleurs, il est parti. *Besides, he's gone (he's left).*
  Nulle part ailleurs. *Nowhere else.*
  Partout ailleurs. *Everywhere else.*
AIMABLE adj. amiable, kind, pleasant, likeable.
  Vous êtes bien aimable. *That's very kind (nice) of you. ("You are very kind.")*
  C'est très aimable à vous. *That's very kind of you.*
  Voulez-vous être assez aimable de me passer le sel? *Will you please pass me the salt?*
  Elle a l'air aimable. *She looks (seems to be) pleasant.*
AIMER to love, like.
  Aimer bien. *To like very much.*
  J'aimerais. *I'd like.*
  J'aime le café. *I like coffee.*
  J'aime mieux l'autre. *I like the other one better. I prefer the other.*
  Je n'aime pas ça. *I don't like that.*
aîné noun and adj. eldest, elder, senior.
AINSI so, thus, in this way.
  Et ainsi de suite. *And so on. And so forth.*

Pour ainsi dire. *So to speak.*
C'est ainsi qu'on l'appelle. *That's his name.*
S'il en est ainsi. *If that's the case.*
Est-ce bien ainsi? *Is it all right this way?*
AIR *m. air.*
Vous êtes dans un courant d'air. *You're in a draft.*
Prendre l'air. *To get some air.*
En plein air. *Out of doors, in the open air.*
Il a cinquante ans, mais il n'en a pas l'air. *He's fifty but he doesn't look it.*
Cela en a tout l'air. *It looks very much like it.*
Elle a l'air jeune. *She looks young. She has a youthful appearance.*
La maison était tout en l'air. *The house was in disorder.*
Ce sont des paroles en l'air. *It's just idle (empty) talk.*
Je connais cet air-là. *I know that tune (melody).*
aise *f. ease, comfort, convenience.*
Il était assis bien à son aise. *He was seated very comfortably.*
Mettez-vous à l'aise. *Make yourself comfortable.*
Je ne suis pas à mon aise. *I don't feel comfortable (at ease).*
J'en suis bien aise. *I'm glad of that.*
aisé *adj. easy, comfortable, well off.*
Ce n'est pas chose aisée. *It's not an easy matter.*
Une famille aisée. *A well-to-do family.*
aisément *easily.*
Cela se croit aisément. *That's easy to believe.*
ajourner *to adjourn, postpone.*
AJOUTER *to add.*
ajuster *to adjust, adapt.*
alarmant *adj. alarming.*
alarme *f. alarm.*
alarmer *to alarm.*
album *m. album, magazine.*
alcool *m. alcohol.*
alentour *around.*
alentours *m. pl. surroundings.*
Aux alentours de. *In the vicinity of.*
alerte *noun f. and adj. alert; alarm.*
alibi *m. alibi.*
aligner *to arrange in a line, line up.*
aliment *m. food.*
alimentation *f. nutrition.*
allemand *noun and adj. German.*
Pouvez-vous traduire ceci en allemand? *Can you translate this into German?*
C'est un Allemand. *He's a German.*
aller *m. going.*
Au pis aller. *At the worst.*
Un billet d'aller. *A one-way ticket.*
Un billet d'aller et retour. *A round-trip ticket.*
ALLER *to go; to feel; to suit, fit, become; to be all right.*
Où allez-vous? *Where are you going?*
Aller à pied. *To walk.*
Comment puis-je y aller? *How can I go (get) there?*
Allons chez moi. *Let's go to my house.*
Allez lentement. *Go slow.*
Etes-vous jamais allé en Amérique? *Have you ever been to America?*
Ce chemin va à Paris. *This road leads to Paris.*
Cela va sans dire. *That goes without saying.*
Allez! *Go! Go on!*
Allez-y! *Go on ahead! Go ahead! Go on!*
Allons-y! *Let's go there. Let's go! Let's get started (going)!*
Allons donc! *Nonsense! You don't really mean that! You can't really be serious!*
Allons, décidez-vous. *Come on, make up your mind.*
Cela me va. *That suits me. That's fine as far as I'm concerned.*
Ce climat ne me va pas. *This climate doesn't agree with me.*
Sa robe lui va bien. *Her dress is very becoming.*
Il va pleuvoir. *It's going to rain.*
Qu'est-ce que vous allez manger? *What are you going to (have to) eat?*
Comment ça va?—Tout va bien. *How are things?—Everything's fine.*
Comment va la santé? *How's your health?*
Comment allez-vous? *How are you?*
Je vais très bien. *I'm very well.*
Est-ce que votre pendule va bien? *Does your clock keep good time?*
Midi va sonner. *It's almost noon.*
En allant à la Côte d'Azur. *On the way to the Riviera.*
Il va y avoir une mêlée. *There's going to be a fight.*
Va pour soixante-cinq francs! *Sold for sixty-five francs!*
Vas-y! *Go there! Go ahead! Go to it!*
S'EN ALLER *to go away, leave.*
Il est temps de s'en aller. *It's time to leave.*
Allez-vous-en. *Go away.*
alliance *f. alliance; wedding ring.*
allô *hello (on telephone).*
allonger *to lengthen.*
allumage *m. ignition.*
allumer *to light.*
ALLUMETTE *f. match.*
Avez-vous une allumette? *Do you have a match?*
allure *f. gait; appearance, looks.*
Cela a beaucoup d'allure. *That looks smart.*
allusion *f. allusion, hint.*
Faire allusion à. *To allude to. To refer to. To hint at.*
ALORS *then.*
C'était la coutume alors. *It was the custom then (in those days).*
Et alors, qu'est-ce qui est arrivé? *And what happened then?*
Alors c'est dit? *Well then, it's agreed?*
Oh! Chic alors (fam.)! *Oh! that's good! That's swell!*
Ah non, alors! *I should think not! Certainly not!*
Alors là. *As for that. Well then.*
alpaga *m. alpaca.*
En alpaga. *In (of) alpaca.*
ALPHABET *m. alphabet.*
alpinisme *m. mountain climbing.*
Faire de l'alpinisme. *To go mountain climbing.*
altérer *to alter.*
alternative *f. alternative, choice.*
alterner *to alternate.*
altitude *f. altitude.*
amabilité *f. kindness.*
amateur *m. amateur; connoisseur.*
ambassadeur *(ambassadrice f.) ambassador.*
ambiance *f. atmosphere.*
ambitieux *(ambitieuse f.) adj. ambitious.*
ambition *f. ambition.*
ambulance *f. ambulance.*
ÂME *f. soul.*
Etat d'âme. *Mood.*
C'est une âme sensible. *He (she) is a sensitive person.*
améliorer *to ameliorate, improve.*

amende *f. fine.*
AMENER *to bring.*
Il prit un autobus qui l'amena juste devant l'immeuble. *He took a bus which brought him right in front of the building.*
Vous pouvez amener votre ami. *You can bring your friend along.*
amer *(amère f.) adj. bitter.*
AMÉRICAIN *noun and adj. American.*
Amérique *f. America.*
Amérique du Nord (Sud). *North (South) America.*
ameublement *m. furniture.*
ameuter *to stir up.*
AMI *m. friend.*
C'est un de mes meilleurs amis. *He's one of my best friends.*
Ce sont des amis intimes. *They're close friends.*
amical *(amicaux pl.) adj. friendly.*
amidon *m. starch.*
amiral *m. (amiraux pl.) admiral.*
AMITIÉ *f. friendship; pl. regards.*
Une amitié solide. *A strong friendship.*
Mes amitiés chez vous. *My best regards to your family.*
Si vous lui écrivez, faites-lui mes amitiés. *If you write him, give him my regards.*
AMOUR *m. love.*
amoureux *(amoureuse f.) adj. in love.*
Il en devint amoureux. *He fell in love with her.*
ample *adj. ample, spacious.*
amplement *amply.*
ampleur *f. ampleness; breadth.*
ampoule *f. electric bulb; blister.*
amusant *adj. amusing.*
amusement *m. amusement.*
amuser *to amuse.*
Ça m'amuse. *It amuses me. I find it amusing.*
S'AMUSER *to have a good time.*
Au revoir, amusez-vous bien. *Good-by, have a good time (have fun).*
Nous nous sommes bien amusés hier. *We enjoyed ourselves yesterday. We had a good time yesterday.*
AN *m. year.*
Il y a un an. *A year ago.*
J'y habite depuis vingt ans. *I've lived there for twenty years.*
Il gagne cinquante mille francs par an. *He earns fifty thousand francs a year.*
Une fois par an. *Once a year.*
analyse *f. analysis.*
analyser *to analyze.*
ancêtre *m. ancestor.*
ANCIEN *(ancienne f.) adj. ancient; former.*
Cela évoque d'anciens souvenirs. *That brings back old memories.*
Mon ancien professeur se trouvait là par hasard. *My former teacher happened to be there.*
ancre *f. anchor.*
âne *m. donkey; jackass.*
anéantir *to annihilate, destroy.*
anesthésique *m. anesthetic.*
ange *m. angel.*
ANGLAIS *noun and adj. English.*
Parlez-vous anglais? *Do you speak English?*
Comment appelez-vous ceci en anglais? *What do you call this in English? What's the English word for this?*
Il a filé à l'anglaise. *He took French leave.*
angle *m. angle.*
Angleterre *f. England.*

angoisse f. anguish.
  Angoisses de conscience. *Qualms of conscience.*
animal (animaux pl.) noun (m.) and adj. animal.
animé adj. animated, spirited, lively.
  Le dessin animé. *The cartoon (animated).*
animer to animate, enliven.
anneau m. ring.
ANNÉE f. year.
  Bonne année! *Happy New Year!*
  L'année qui vient. *The coming year. Next year.*
anniversaire m. birthday; anniversary.
ANNONCE f. announcement; advertisement.
  Ils vont mettre une petite annonce dans le
  journal. *They're going to put an ad in the
  paper.*
annoncer to announce.
annuaire m. directory, telephone book.
  L'annuaire de téléphone. *Telephone directory.*
annuel (annuelle f.) adj. annual, yearly.
annuler to annul, make void.
anonyme adj. anonymous.
  Société anonyme. *Joint-stock company.*
anormal (anormaux pl.) adj. abnormal.
antécédent noun (m.) and adj. antecedent.
antérieur adj. anterior, previous.
anticiper to anticipate.
  Avec mes remerciements anticipés. *Thanking
  you in advance (in a letter).*
antiquaire m. antiquary; antique dealer.
antique adj. antique; ancient.
antiquité f. antiquity.
  Il est marchand d'antiquités. *He's an antique
  dealer.*
antiseptique adj. antiseptic.
anxiété f. anxiety.
  J'éprouvais de l'anxiété avant son retour. *I
  was very worried before he got back. ("I
  experienced some anxiety before his
  return.")*
ANXIEUX (anxieuse f.) adj. anxious.
  Il paraissait très anxieux d'aboutir. *He seemed
  very anxious to succeed.*
AOÛT m. August.
apaiser to appease, pacify.
(en) aparté aside, in a stage whisper.
apathie f. apathy.
APERCEVOIR to perceive, observe.
  Je vous ai aperçu dans la foule. *I got a
  glimpse of you in the crowd.*
  Je l'aperçois. *I see him.*
S'APERCEVOIR to perceive, notice.
  Il ne s'aperçoit de rien. *He doesn't notice
  anything.*
  Il est parti sans qu'on s'en aperçoive. *He left
  without anyone seeing him.*
  Il s'aperçut à temps de son erreur. *He caught
  his mistake (noticed his error) in time.*
aperçu m. glimpse; brief account.
  Il m'a donné un aperçu de la situation. *He
  gave me a brief account of the situation.*
apitoyer to move to compassion.
s'apitoyer to pity.
aplatir to flatten.
aplomb m. self-assurance; impudence.
  Quel aplomb! *What impudence!*
apostrophe f. apostrophe; reproach.
APPARAÎTRE to appear.
  Soudainement il apparut. *Suddenly he appeared.*
APPAREIL m. apparatus; equipment.
  Ne quittez pas l'appareil, s'il vous plaît. *Please
  hold the wire a minute. ("Don't leave the
  telephone . . .")*

Appareil photographique. *Camera.*
  Appareil cinématographique. *Movie camera.*
apparence f. appearance.
  Sauver les apparences. *To keep up appearances.*
apparent adj. apparent.
apparition f. appearance; brief visit.
  Faire son apparition. *To make one's appearance.*
appartement m. apartment.
APPARTENIR to belong to.
  A qui appartient cet objet? *Whom does this
  (thing, object) belong to?*
appel m. call.
  Faire l'appel. *To call the roll.*
APPELER to call.
  Appelez-moi quand vous serez prêt. *Call me
  when you're ready.*
  Appelez le médecin. *Call the doctor.*
  Comment vous appelez-vous? *What's your
  name?*
  Comment l'appelle-t-on? *What's his (her)
  name?*
  Je m'appelle. *My name is.*
APPÉTIT m. appetite.
  Ça m'a coupé l'appétit. *That took away
  (spoiled) my appetite.*
  Aiguiser l'appétit. *To whet the appetite.*
  Bon appétit! *Hearty appetite!*
applaudir to applaud, cheer.
applaudissement m. applause.
appliquer to apply.
appointements m. pl. salary.
APPORTER to bring.
  Apportez-moi une tasse de thé. *Bring me a
  cup of tea.*
  Il apporta du soin à le faire. *He exercised care
  in doing it.*
appréciation f. appreciation; estimation.
apprécier to value, appreciate.
appréhender to seize; fear, dread.
  J'appréhende de la voir. *I dread seeing her.*
  J'appréhende qu'il ne soit trop tard. *I'm
  afraid it will (may) be too late.*
appréhension f. apprehension, dread.
APPRENDRE to learn.
  Il n'est pas difficile d'apprendre une langue
  étrangère. *It's not very hard to learn a
  foreign language.*
  Elle apprend à conduire. *She's learning how to
  drive.*
apprenti noun and adj. apprentice.
apprentissage m. apprenticeship.
apprêt m. preparation.
apprêter to prepare.
s'apprêter to prepare oneself, get ready.
  Elle s'apprête à sortir. *She's getting ready to go
  out.*
apprivoiser to tame.
approbation f. approbation, approval.
approchant adj. similar, approximate.
  Si vous n'avez pas ce que je veux, donnez-moi
  quelque chose d'approchant. *If you don't
  have what I want, give me something like it.*
approche f. approach, advance.
APPROCHER to approach, come near.
  N'approchez pas, il y a du danger. *Don't go
  (come) near. It's dangerous.*
  L'heure approche. *The hour is drawing near.
  It's almost time.*
  Approchez la lampe. *Bring the lamp closer.*
S'APPROCHER to approach, come near.
  Je me suis approché de lui. *I came near him.*
  Ne vous approchez pas. *Don't come any
  closer.*

approfondir to investigate, fathom.
  Approfondir une question. *To get to the root
  (bottom) of a matter.*
s'approprier to appropriate, usurp.
approuver to approve.
  Approuvez-vous ce que j'ai dit? *Do you approve
  of what I said?*
approximatif (approximative f.) adj. approximate.
approximativement approximately.
appui m. support.
  C'est grâce à leur appui que j'ai pu y parvenir.
  I was able to succeed thanks to their help.
  Voici un exemple à l'appui de ma thèse.
  *Here's an example which supports my
  argument.*
appuyer to support.
  Il m'a dit qu'il appuyerait ma demande. *He
  told me he would support my request.*
s'appuyer to lean upon, use as support.
  Appuyez-vous sur mon bras. *Lean on my arm.*
  Appuyez-vous à la rampe pour monter
  l'escalier. *Hold on to the banister going up
  the stairs.*
âpre adj. hard, rough.
APRÈS after.
  Après vous! *After you!*
  Vous avez eu raison après tout. *You were
  right after all.*
  Eh bien! Après? *Well, what next?*
APRÈS-DEMAIN m. the day after tomorrow.
  J'espère vous donner sa réponse après-demain.
  *I hope to give you his answer the day after
  tomorrow.*
APRÈS-MIDI m. (sometimes f.) afternoon.
  Il est toujours là l'après-midi. *He's always
  there in the afternoon.*
  La représentation commence à trois heures de
  l'après-midi. *The performance begins at
  three p.m.*
  Il a passé toute l'après-midi chez moi. *He
  spent all afternoon at my place.*
apte adj. apt, fit.
aptitude f. aptitude, ability.
aquarelle f. water color (painting).
araignée f. spider.
arbitraire adj. arbitrary.
arbitre m. arbitrator, umpire, referee.
arbre m. tree.
arc m. bow; arc.
arche f. arch.
architecte m. architect.
architecture f. architecture.
ardent adj. ardent.
ardeur f. ardor, fervor.
ardu adj. steep; arduous.
arête f. fish-bone.
ARGENT m. silver; money.
  Cette cuillère est en argent. *This spoon is
  made of silver.*
  Il gagne beaucoup d'argent. *He's making
  (makes) a great deal (a lot) of money.*
  Argent comptant. *Ready money. Cash.*
  Il n'en a pas pour son argent. *He didn't get
  his money's worth.*
  Le temps c'est de l'argent. *Time is money.*
  Assez (suffisamment) d'argent. *Enough money.*
argenterie f. silverware.
argument m. argument.
arithmétique f. arithmetic.
arme f. arm, weapon.
armée f. army.
armement m. armament.
armer to arm.

armistice m. *armistice.*

armoire f. *wardrobe.*

arracher *to pull out.*
Le dentiste m'a arraché une dent. *The dentist pulled my tooth out.*
Impossible de lui arracher une parole. *You can't get a word out of him.*

arrangement m. *arrangement.*

ARRANGER *to arrange; put in order.*
Arrangez toutes ces choses. *Put all these things in order.*
Soyez tranquille, je vais arranger tout ça. *Don't worry, I'll straighten everything ("all this") out.*

s'arranger *to prepare oneself; put up with.*
Arrangez-vous. *Manage as best you can. Do the best you can.*
Laissez-moi faire, et tout s'arrangera. *Leave that to me ("Let me do it") and everything will come out all right.*
Cela s'arrangera. *It will come out all right in the end.*

ARRÊT m. *stop, halt; arrest; sentence.*
Où se trouve l'arrêt de l'autobus? *Where does the bus stop? Where's the bus stop?*
Quel est le prochain arrêt? *What's the next stop?*
Il y a un mandat d'arrêt lancé contre lui. *A warrant has been issued for his arrest.*

ARRÊTER *to stop; arrest.*
Attendez que les voitures soient arrêtées. *Wait until the traffic stops.*
Ma montre est arrêtée. *My watch (has) stopped.*
Arrêtez-le! *Arrest him!*

S'ARRÊTER *to stop.*
Arrêtons-nous ici. *Let's stop here.*
Quand le prochain train arrive-t-il, et combien de temps s'arrête-t-il? *When does the next train arrive and how long does it stop?*
La pendule s'est arrêtée. *The clock stopped.*

ARRIÈRE m. *back.*
Vous trouverez ce paquet à l'arrière de ma voiture. *You'll find that package in the back of my car.*

ARRIÈRE *behind, backwards.*
Faites deux pas en arrière. *Take two steps backwards.*
Il est toujours en arrière pour ses paiements. *He's always behind in his payments.*
Pourquoi restez-vous toujours en arrière? *Why do you always remain behind?*

arrière-grand'mère f. *great-grandmother.*

arrière-grand-père m. *great-grandfather.*

arrière-petit-fils m. *great-grandson.*

arrière-petite-fille f. *great-granddaughter.*

arrivée f. *arrival.*
Nous étions là à l'arrivée du train. *We were there when the train arrived ("at the arrival of the train").*

ARRIVER *to arrive, happen.*
Ils arrivèrent trop tard. *They arrived too late.*
Le train doit arriver à midi. *The train is due at noon.*
Tâchez d'arriver de bonne heure. *Try to come early.*
Les voilà qui arrivent. *Here they come.*
Arriver à ses fins. *To attain one's ends.*
Que vous est-il arrivé? *What happened to you?*
C'est arrivé trois jours de suite. *That's happened three days in a row.*
Quoi qu'il arrive. *Come what may.*

arrogance f. *arrogance, haughtiness.*

arrondir *to round out.*

arrondissement m. *district, borough, ward (Paris).*

arroser *to water, irrigate.*

ART m. *art.*
Les beaux-arts. *The fine arts.*

ARTICLE m. *article.*
L'importation de cet article est prohibée. *The importation of this article is prohibited.*
Avez-vous lu l'article de fond du journal de ce soir? *Did you read the editorial in this evening's paper?*
Faire l'article d'un produit. *To boost a product.*

artificiel (artificielle f.) adj. *artificial.*

artisanat m. *craftsmen.*
Les produits de l'artisanat. *Handicrafts.*

artiste m. *artist.*

as m. *ace.*
As de pique. *Ace of spades.*
C'est un as au tennis. *He's a tennis ace.*

ASCENSEUR m. *elevator.*
Est-ce que cet ascenseur descend? *Is this elevator going down?*

aspect m. *aspect.*

asperge f. *asparagus.*

aspirateur m. *vacuum cleaner.*

aspirer *to inhale; aspire to.*

assaillir *to assault.*

assemblée f. *assembly, meeting.*

assembler *to assemble.*

ASSEOIR *to seat.*
Faites-donc asseoir monsieur. *Give the gentleman a seat.*
Nous sommes assis dans la quatrième rangée. *We have seats in the fourth row.*
Je suis assis dans un courant d'air. *I'm sitting in a draft.*
Il faut asseoir cette affaire sur une base solide. *We have to establish this business on a solid basis.*

S'ASSEOIR *to sit down ("to seat oneself").*
Asseyez-vous. *Sit down.*

ASSEZ *enough, quite, rather.*
Est-ce assez comme cela? *Is that enough?*
Ça va?—Assez bien, merci. *How are you? ("How are things?")—Quite well, thank you.*
En voilà assez! *That's enough!*
J'en ai assez! 1. *I have enough of it.* 2. *I'm fed up (with it).*

assidu adj. *assiduous.*

assiette f. *plate.*
Vous avez une assiette plate et une assiette creuse. *You have a dinner plate and a soup plate.*

assigner *to assign.*

assimiler *to assimilate.*

assis *seated, sitting.*
Une place assise. *Seat (bus, etc.).*

ASSISTANCE f. *assistance; attendance; audience.*
Assistance publique. *Government agency for social welfare.*
Une assistance nombreuse. *A large audience.*

assistant m. *assistant.*

ASSISTER *to assist; attend.*
Assistons ces pauvres gens. *Let's help these poor people.*
N'oubliez pas d'assister à la séance d'ouverture de la société. *Don't forget to attend the opening meeting of the society.*

association f. *association; partnership.*
L'association a été dissoute. *The partnership was (has been) dissolved.*
Association de football. *A soccer club.*

associer *to associate.*

assortiment m. *assortment.*

assortir *to match; assort.*

assurance f. *assurance, insurance.*
Agréez l'assurance de mes sentiments distingués. *Yours very truly (in a letter).*
L'assurance sur la vie. *Life insurance.*
Faire assurer. *To have (something) insured.*

assurer *to assure; insure; ascertain.*
Assurer contre l'incendie. *To insure against fire.*

atelier m. *workshop, studio.*

atmosphère f. *atmosphere.*

atome m. *atom.*

atroce adj. *atrocious.*

ATTACHER *to attach, fasten.*
Attachez-cela avec une épingle. *Fasten that with a pin.*
Attachez-le avec la corde. *Tie it with the string (cord, rope).*
Attachez tous ces paquets ensemble. *Tie all these parcels together.*
Ils sont attachés l'un à l'autre. *They're very attached to each other.*
Je n'y attache aucune importance. *I don't attach any importance to it.*

attaque f. *attack.*

attaquer *to attack.*

ATTEINDRE *to attain, reach.*
J'ai couru mais je n'ai pu l'atteindre. *I ran but I couldn't catch up with him (her).*
Les prix ont atteint un nouveau maximum. *Prices have reached a new high.*
J'ai atteint mon but. *I've reached my goal.*

ATTENDRE *to wait.*
Attendez ici. *Wait here.*
Attendez un moment. *Wait a minute.*
Il attend depuis deux heures. *He's been waiting for two hours.*
Attendez-vous une lettre? *Do you expect a letter? Are you expecting a letter?*
Le train était attendu à onze heures cinquante. *The train was expected at eleven-fifty.*
Nous attendons du monde. *We're expecting company.*
Attendre que (+ subjunctive). *To wait until.*
En attendant. *In the meantime.*
Faire attendre. *To keep (someone) waiting.*

S'ATTENDRE *to expect.*
Je ne m'attendais pas à cela. *I didn't expect that.*

attendrir *to soften, make tender.*

s'attendrir *to be moved.*
Elle s'attendrit facilement. *She's easily moved.*

attente f. *waiting.*
Dans l'attente de vous lire. *Awaiting your reply (in a letter).*
Ils sont dans l'attente de nouvelles de leur fils. *They're waiting for news from their son.*

attentif (attentive f.) adj. *attentive.*

ATTENTION f. *attention.*
Faites attention à ce qui se passe. *Pay attention to what's going on.*
Attention! *Pay attention! Look out! Watch out!*
Attention à la marche! *Watch the step!*
Attention! Peinture fraîche! *Be careful! Wet paint.*
Faites attention, vous lui faites mal. *Be careful, you're hurting him (her).*

attentivement *carefully.*
Voulez-vous relire cela attentivement? *Will you reread this carefully?*

atterrir *to land (airplane).*

attirer *to attract, draw.*
Elle attire tous les regards. *She attracts everyone's attention ("all the glances").*

Vous avez attiré sa colère. *You've made him angry.*

attitude *f. attitude.*

ATTRACTION *f. attraction.*

Paris exerce une grande attraction sur les étrangers. *Paris has a great attraction for foreigners.*

C'est l'attraction principale du spectacle. *It's the main feature of the show.*

attrait *m. attraction, charm.*

Dépourvu d'attrait. *Unattractive.*

ATTRAPER *to catch.*

Attrape! *Catch!*

Il a attrapé un rhume. *He caught a cold.*

Le peintre a attrapé la ressemblance. *The painter caught the likeness.*

Vous êtes bien attrapé. *You've been fooled (taken in).*

attrayant *adj. attractive.*

Elle est très attrayante. *She's very attractive.*

attribuer *to attribute.*

attrister *to sadden.*

AU (aux *pl.*) *See A.*

aube *f. dawn.*

AUCUN *adj. no, no one, not any.*

Je n'y ai aucun intérêt. *I haven't any interest in it.*

Aucun de ceux-ci ne me dit rien. *I don't care for any of these.*

Cela ne fait aucun doute. *There isn't any doubt about it. There's no doubt about it.*

Laissez-le dire, cela n'a aucune importance. *Let him say what he wants. It doesn't matter at all.*

Je n'ai de nouvelles d'aucun d'eux. *I haven't had any news from any of them.*

Cette mesure n'a plus aucune raison d'être. *There is no longer any justification for this measure.*

Aucun étudiant n'a réussi à l'examen. *Not one (not a single) student passed the examination.*

audace *f. audacity.*

audacieux (audacieuse *f.*) *adj. audacious.*

AU-DESSOUS *below.*

Dix degrés au-dessous de zéro. *Ten degrees below zero.*

Au-dessous de la moyenne. *Below average.*

AU-DESSUS *above.*

Au-dessus de la porte. *Above the door.*

Au-dessus de tout éloge. *Beyond all praise.*

AU-DEVANT *toward.*

Aller au-devant de quelqu'un. *To go to meet someone.*

Aller au-devant du danger. *To anticipate a danger.*

Aller au-devant des désirs de quelqu'un. *To anticipate someone's wishes.*

augmentation *f. increase; raise.*

augmenter *to increase.*

s'augmenter *to increase.*

AUJOURD'HUI *today; nowadays.*

Je n'ai rien à faire aujourd'hui. *I have nothing to do today.*

Je pars d'aujourd'hui en huit. *I'm leaving a week from today.*

Je reviendrai d'aujourd'hui en quinze. *I'll be back (in) two weeks from today.*

Quel jour du mois est-ce aujourd'hui? *What's the date?*

C'est aujourd'hui le cinq. *Today is the fifth.*

Aujourd'hui même. *Today, this very day.*

aumône *f. alms, charity.*

auparavant *formerly, earlier; first.*

Auparavant c'était tout différent. *Formerly (previously) it was completely different.*

Auparavant passez à la banque. *Go to the bank first.*

auprès *near by, close by.*

Il est toujours auprès de lui. *He's always near him.*

Agir auprès de quelqu'un. *To use one's influence with someone.*

auquel (à laquelle *f.*, auxquels *m. pl.*, auxquelles *f. pl.* to which, to whom.

Auquel de ces hommes voulez-vous parler? *To which of these men do you wish to speak?*

aurore *f. dawn.*

AUSSI *also.*

Lui aussi viendra avec nous. *He will also come with us. He, too, will come with us.*

Aussi peu que possible. *As little as possible.*

Il était tard, aussi nous ne sommes pas sortis. *It was late, so we didn't go out.*

Il est aussi grand que vous. *He's as tall as you are.*

Aussi loin que le regard peut s'étendre. *As far as the eye can reach.*

AUSSITÔT *at once, immediately.*

Aussitôt couché, je m'endors. *As soon as I get into bed, I fall asleep. I no sooner get into bed than I go off to sleep.*

Aussitôt dit, aussitôt fait. *No sooner said than done.*

Je suis désireux de partir aussitôt que possible. *I'm anxious (eager) to leave as soon as possible.*

Je m'en occuperai aussitôt que j'aurai un moment de libre. *I'll take care of it as soon as I have a free moment.*

AUTANT *as much, as many.*

S'il gagne autant que vous le dites. *If he earns as much as you say.*

Répétez votre leçon autant que vous le pouvez. *Repeat your lesson as many times as you can.*

Pour autant qu'il est en mon pouvoir. *In so far as I can. In so far as it lies within my power.*

D'autant plus. *All the more.*

AUTEUR *m. author.*

C'est le dernier livre paru de cet auteur. *This is the latest (most recent) book by this author.*

Les droits d'auteur. *Royalties.*

authentique *adj. authentic.*

AUTO *f. See also automobile.*

Savez-vous conduire une auto? *Can you drive a car?*

Voyager en auto. *To travel by car.*

autobus *m. bus.*

Quel autobus dois-je prendre pour y aller? *What bus do I (should I) take to get there?*

Un arrêt d'autobus. *A bus stop.*

autocar *m. bus, coach (outside of city).*

automatique *adj. automatic.*

AUTOMNE *m. autumn, fall.*

AUTOMOBILE *f. automobile.*

Il fut presque écrasé par une automobile. *He was almost run over by an automobile.*

autonome *adj. autonomous.*

autonomie *f. autonomy, self-government.*

autorisation *f. authorization.*

Vous avez mon autorisation. *You have my permission.*

autoriser *to authorize.*

Il m'a autorisé de le faire. *He authorized me to do it.*

autorité *f. authority.*

Il fait autorité en la matière. *He's an authority on the subject.*

Les autorités locales. *The local authorities.*

Il l'a fait de sa propre autorité. *He did it on his own initiative.*

AUTOUR *around.*

Les planètes gravitent autour du soleil. *The planets revolve ("gravitate") around the sun.*

Il y a une grande cour de récréation autour de l'école. *There's a large yard (playground) around the school.*

Ils se rangèrent autour de la table. *They gathered around the table.*

Regardez autour de vous, vous le trouverez. *Look around you. You'll find it.*

AUTRE *adj. other.*

Ceux-ci sont moins bons que les autres. *These aren't as good as the others.*

Faites-lui une autre offre. *Make him another offer.*

Traversons de l'autre côté. *Let's cross over to the other side.*

Donnez-moi autre chose. *Give me something else.*

Et avec ça, vous faut-il autre chose? *Will you need anything else (in addition to this)?*

C'est un tout autre cas. *That's an entirely different case. It's another thing entirely.*

Vous trouverez cela autre part. *You'll find that somewhere else.*

Je l'ai vu l'autre jour. *I saw him the other day.*

A une autre fois. *Until another time.*

Il passe d'une extrémité à l'autre. *He goes from one extreme to another.*

Ni l'un ni l'autre ne valent rien. *Neither one is any good.*

Il va arriver d'un jour à l'autre. *He'll arrive any day now.*

D'autre part. *On the other hand.*

En d'autres termes. *In other words.*

Rien d'autre. *Nothing else (more).*

AUTREFOIS *formerly, in former times.*

J'en ai entendu parler autrefois. *I formerly (earlier, a long time ago) heard people speak about it.*

Les beaux jours d'autrefois. *The good old days.*

AUTREMENT *otherwise.*

Autrement nous y serions allés. *Otherwise we would have gone there.*

autrui *others, other people.*

Ne faites pas à autrui ce que vous ne voudriez pas qu'on vous fît. *Do unto others as you would have others do unto you. ("Don't do to others what you would not have others do to you.")*

avalanche *f. avalanche.*

avaler *to swallow.*

avance *f. advance.*

Il est toujours en avance. *He's always ahead of time.*

Il faudra réserver vos chambres bien à l'avance. *You'll have to reserve your rooms well in advance.*

AVANCER *to advance.*

Nous avancions à peine, tant la foule était dense. *The crowd was so thick that we couldn't move ahead (advance).*

Cela ne vous avancera guère. *That won't get you very far.*

Ma montre avance de trois minutes. *My watch is three minutes fast.*

Ne lui avancez pas d'argent. *Don't advance him any money.*

Avancer une théorie. *To advance a theory.*

AVANT *before.*

Il faut que nous le voyions avant qu'il parte. *We must see him before he leaves.*

Avant tout, faites ça. *First of all, do this.*

Elle ne rentre pas de l'école avant cinq heures. *She doesn't come home from school until five.*

Ils sont partis en avant. *They've gone on ahead.*

Avant mardi. *Before Tuesday.*

Avant de manger. *Before eating.*

Avant peu. *Before long.*

Deux cents ans avant J.C. *200 B.C.*

Le pneu avant. *The front tire.*

AVANTAGE *m. advantage.*

C'est à votre avantage. *It's to your advantage.*

Vous avez l'avantage sur moi. *You have the advantage over me.*

Vous auriez avantage à. *It would be to your advantage to.*

avantageux (avantageuse f.) *adj. advantageous.*

AVANT-HIER *m. the day before yesterday.*

Je l'ai rencontré avant-hier. *I met him the day before yesterday.*

avare *m. and f. noun and adj. miser; avaricious, miserly.*

Il est très avare. *He's very miserly.*

avarice *f. avarice.*

avarié *adj. damaged.*

AVEC *with.*

Venez avec moi. *Come with me.*

Etes-vous d'accord avec moi? *Do you agree with me?*

Avec plaisir. *With pleasure. Gladly.*

Avec grand plaisir. *With great pleasure. Very gladly.*

Avec succès. *Successfully.*

AVENIR *m. future.*

Ne recommencez pas à l'avenir. *Don't do it again in the future.*

C'est un homme d'avenir. *He's a man with a bright future.*

aventure *f. adventure.*

Je vais vous raconter ma récente aventure. *I'll tell you about an experience I had recently.*

Il racontait une de ses aventures en Amérique. *He was relating an experience of his in America.*

Elle dit la bonne aventure. *She tells fortunes.*

AVENUE *f. avenue.*

averse *f. short sudden shower.*

aversion *f. aversion, dislike.*

Il l'a en aversion. *He dislikes him (her).*

avertir *to inform; warn.*

Je vous en avertirai. *I'll let you know.*

avertissement *m. information, notification; warning.*

aveu *m. admission, avowal, confession.*

Faire l'aveu de. *To admit. To confess.*

aveugle *m. and f. noun and adj. blind; blind person.*

aviateur *m. aviator.*

aviation *f. aviation.*

avide *adj. greedy, eager.*

avion *m. airplane.*

Voyager en avion. *To travel by plane.*

Envoyer par avion. *To send by air(mail).*

AVIS *m. opinion; advice; notice.*

A mon avis. *In my opinion.*

Référez-vous-en à son avis. *Be guided by his advice.*

Sauf avis contraire, j'y serai. *Unless you hear to the contrary, I'll be there.*

Avis au lecteur. *Note to the reader (in a book).*

AVISER *to inform; consider.*

Je vous en aviserai. *I'll inform you by letter.*

Avisez-moi de votre venue. *Let me know in advance if you come.*

Il y avisera. *He'll study (consider) the matter.*

Nous aviserons. *We'll think the matter over.*

avocat *m. lawyer.*

avoir *m. possessions, property.*

Voilà tout son avoir. *That's all he has.*

AVOIR *to have.*

Est-ce que vous avez des cigarettes sur vous? *Do you have any cigarettes ("on you")?*

Il fut un temps où il avait beaucoup d'argent mais maintenant il n'en a plus. *There was a time when he had a lot of money but he no longer has any.*

Il a vingt ans. *He's twenty years old.*

Il y a beaucoup de monde. *There are many people. There's a crowd.*

Qu'est-ce qu'il a? *What's the matter with him?*

Vous avez tort. *You're wrong.*

J'avais raison. *I was right.*

J'ai faim. *I'm hungry.*

Il a soif. *He's thirsty.*

Elle a peur. *She's frightened. She's afraid.*

J'ai chaud. *I'm warm.*

Avez-vous froid? *Are you cold?*

Pourquoi avoir honte? *Why be ashamed?*

Contre qui en a-t-il? *Whom does he have a grudge against?*

Merci beaucoup. —Il n'y a pas de quoi. *Thank you very much. —Don't mention it.*

J'aurais dû y aller. *I should have gone there.*

Vous aurez besoin de cela. *You'll need that.*

Il y avait beaucoup de monde dans le magasin. *There were a lot of people in the store.*

Il n'y eut rien à faire, il y alla quand même. *There was nothing we could do about it; he went there just the same.*

Après avoir reçu le chèque. *After receiving the check.*

Auriez-vous. *Would you have.*

J'ai à écrire une lettre. *I have to write a letter.*

J'ai une lettre à écrire. *I have a letter to write.*

Avoir besoin de. *To need.*

Avoir de la peine. *To grieve, be in sorrow.*

Avoir envie de. *To want to, feel like.*

Avoir l'air riche. *To look, seem, appear rich.*

Avoir l'habitude de. *To be in the habit of, be used to.*

Avoir les cheveux noirs. *To have black hair.*

Avoir lieu. *To take place, occur.*

Avoir l'occasion de. *To have the opportunity to.*

Avoir mal à la gorge. *To have a sore throat.*

Avoir mauvaise mine. *To look bad.*

En avoir assez de. *To have enough, be sick of something.*

En avoir pour: Vous en aurez pour longtemps. *It will take you a long time, you'll have a long wait.*

N'avoir qu'à. *To have only to.*

Vous n'avez qu'à demander. *You need only ask.*

avouer *to confess.*

Il a tout avoué. *He confessed everything.*

Avouez donc tout! *Come on, make a clean breast of it!*

J'ai honte d'avouer que j'ai oublié votre adresse. *I'm ashamed to confess I've forgotten your address.*

AVRIL *m. April.*

axe *m. axis.*

azur *adj. azure, blue.*

B *The second letter of the alphabet.*

badaud *m. loiterer, idler.*

BAGAGE *m. luggage, baggage.*

Vos bagages sont-ils enregistrés? *Is your baggage checked?*

Faites descendre mes bagages. *Have my bags brought down.*

Fourgon à bagages. *Baggage car.*

Bagages à main. *Hand luggage.*

Défaire les bagages. *To unpack the bags.*

bagatelle *f. trifle.*

Pour lui ce n'est qu'une bagatelle. *It's a mere trifle for him.*

bague *f. ring.*

baguette *f. stick.*

baie *f. bay.*

baigner *to bathe, wash.*

se baigner *to bathe.*

Défense de se baigner dans le lac. *No swimming in the lake.*

baignoire *f. bathtub.*

bail *m. (baux pl.) lease.*

bâillement *m. yawning.*

bâiller *to yawn.*

bain(s) *m. bath.*

Salle de bain. *Bathroom.*

baiser *m. kiss.*

baisse *f. fall, decline.*

baisser *to lower, let down.*

Baisser les yeux. *To look down. To lower one's eyes.*

Donner tête baissée dans un piège. *To rush headlong into a trap.*

se baisser *to stoop.*

Il se baissa pour le ramasser. *He stooped to pick it up.*

bal *m. ball.*

balai *m. broom.*

balance *f. balance, scales.*

Faire pencher la balance. *To turn the scales.*

balancer *to balance; swing, sway, rock; hesitate.*

balayer *to sweep.*

balcon *m. balcony.*

balle *f. ball (golf, tennis).*

ballet *m. ballet.*

ballon *m. ball (football, soccer).*

banal *adj. banal, commonplace.*

banc *m. bench.*

bandage *m. bandage.*

bande *f. band.*

Bande de cuir. *Leather strap.*

Faire bande à part. *To keep aloof.*

La bande magnétique. *Tape (recording).*

banlieue *f. suburbs.*

bannir *to banish.*

BANQUE *f. bank.*

Des billets de banque. *Bank notes.*

banquet *m. banquet.*

banquette *f. bench.*

banquier *m. banker.*

baptiser *to baptize.*

baraque *f. booth, hut.*

barbare *adj. barbarous, cruel.*

barbe *f. beard.*

Je dois me faire faire la barbe. *I have to get a shave.*

J'ai la barbe dure. *I have a tough beard.*
barre *f. bar.*
barrer *to bar.*
barrière *f. barrier, gate.*
bas *m. stocking, lower part.*
> Le bas du pantalon retroussé. *The cuffs on the trousers.*

BAS (basse *f.*) *adj. low.*
> Je l'ai acheté à bas prix. *I bought it cheap(ly).*
> Mes fonds sont bas. *My funds are low. I'm running short of money.*

BAS *adv. low.*
> Chercher quelque chose de haut en bas. *To look (search) high and low for something.*
> A bas . . . ! *Down with . . . !*
> Je vous verrai là-bas. *I'll see you over there.*

bascule *f. weighing-machine, scale.*
base *f. base; basis.*
baser *to base.*
> Sur quoi base-t-il son opinion? *On what does he base his opinion?*

bas-relief *m. bas-relief.*
bassin *m. basin; pool.*
bataille *f. battle.*
batailler *to battle.*
BATEAU *m. boat.*
BÂTIMENT *m. building.*
> Où est le bâtiment de l'administration? *Where is the administration building?*

BÂTIR *to build, erect.*
> Faire bâtir. *To have (something) built.*

bâton *m. stick; spoke.*
battement *m. beating.*
BATTRE *to beat.*
> Battre des oeufs. *To beat (up) eggs.*
> Ils ont battu des mains. *They clapped their hands. They applauded.*
> Le coeur lui bat. *His heart is beating. His heart is in his mouth.*
> Il a battu le record de l'année dernière. *He beat last year's record.*
> Ils ont battu en retraite. *They beat a retreat.*
> Il faut battre le fer pendant qu'il est chaud. *One must strike while the iron is hot.*

SE BATTRE *to fight.*
bavard(e) *m. and f. a gossip.*
bavard *adj. talkative.*
bavardage *m. gossip.*
bavarder *to chatter, gossip.*
beau *m. beauty; dandy.*
> Le beau de l'affaire. *The cream of the jest.*

BEAU (bel *before a vowel or "mute" h,* belle *f.,* beaux *m. pl.,* belles *f. pl.*) *adj. beautiful, pretty, nice.*
> Que c'est beau! *It's really very nice! How lovely!*
> Elle a une belle écriture. *She has a nice handwriting.*
> Il y a de belles maisons dans notre rue. *There are some beautiful houses on our street.*
> Les beaux-arts. *The fine arts.*
> Le temps se met au beau. *The weather is getting nice. The weather is clearing up.*
> Je l'ai rencontré un beau jour. *I ran into him one fine day. I met him unexpectedly.*
> Il a beau faire. *He's making a useless effort.*
> Il a beau faire, il échouera. *He's trying in vain (he's making a useless effort); he won't succeed (he'll fail).*
> Vous avez beau dire, je ne le crois pas. *Say what you will, I still don't believe it.*
> Ils ont beau dire et beau faire, ça m'est égal. *They can say or do what they want to; I*

don't care.
> J'aurai beau lui parler, il n'écoute personne. *There's no use of my talking to him; he won't listen to anyone.*
> J'en entends de belles sur votre compte! *I've heard some pretty stories about you! Nice things I hear about you!*
> Ah! La belle affaire! *Well, a fine thing!*
> Il fait beau. *The weather is good.*

BEAUCOUP *much; many.*
> Le malade est beaucoup plus mal. *The patient is much worse.*
> C'est beaucoup dire. *That's saying a lot.*
> Je vous remercie beaucoup. *Thanks very much. Thanks a lot.*
> Beaucoup d'entre nous. *Many of us.*
> Beaucoup d'argent. *A lot of money.*

beau-fils *m. son-in-law* (belle-fille *f. daughter-in-law*).
beau-frère *m. brother-in-law* (belle-soeur *f. sister-in-law*).
beau-père *m. father-in-law* (belle-mère *f. mother-in-law*).
beauté *f. beauty.*
bébé *m. baby.*
bec *m. beak, bill.*
bégayer *to stammer.*
beige *adj. beige.*
bel *adj. See* beau.
> C'est un bel homme. *He's a handsome man.*
> Tout cela est bel et bon, mais . . . *That's all very well but . . .*
> Il est bel et bien ruiné. *He's completely ruined.*

belge *m. and f. noun and adj. Belgian.*
belle *See* beau.
bénéfice *m. profit.*
bénéficier *to profit.*
bénir *to bless.*
berceau *m. cradle.*
berger *m. shepherd.*
bergère *f. shepherdess; easy chair.*
besogne *f. work.*
> Il abat de la besogne. *He gets through a great deal of work quickly.*

BESOIN *m. need.*
> Il a ce dont il a besoin. *He has what he needs.*
> J'en ai un besoin urgent. *I need it badly.*
> Mes chaussettes ont besoin d'être raccommodées. *My socks need darning.*
> Il est dans le besoin. *He's very poor. He's in dire need.*
> J'interviendrai si besoin est. *I'll intervene if need be (in case of need).*
> Au besoin. *If need be.*
> En cas de besoin. *In case of need.*

bétail *m. cattle.*
bête *f. animal, beast.*
bête *adj. stupid.*
bêtise *f. stupidity.*
> Quelle bêtise! *What nonsense! How silly! How stupid!*
> C'est une bêtise. *It's silly (stupid).*
> Ne perdez donc pas votre temps à ces bêtises. *Don't waste your time on that nonsense (those stupidities).*

béton *m. cement, concrete.*
BEURRE *m. butter.*
> Donnez-moi du beurre, s'il vous plaît. *Please let me have some butter.*

bibelot *m. curio, knickknack, trinket.*
bibliothèque *f. library; bookcase.*
bicyclette *f. bicycle.*
> Se promener à bicyclette. *Go bicycle riding,*

take a bicycle ride.
bidon *m. can, tin.*
BIEN *well; very, very much; comfortable.*
> Très bien! *Very well! Fine! Good!*
> C'est bien tard. *It's very late.*
> C'est bien ça! *That's right! That's it!*
> Bien entendu. *Of course.*
> Bien sûr! *Of course! Surely!*
> Bien des fois. *Many times. Many a time. Often.*
> Eh bien, quoi de neuf? *Well, what's new?*
> C'est bien de votre part d'avoir fait ça. *It was very nice of you to do that. ("It's very nice of you to have done that.")*
> Bien qu'il fasse mauvais temps, je sortirai tout de même. *Although the weather's bad, I'll go out anyway.*
> Bien de l'inspiration. *Plenty of inspiration.*
> C'était bien pire. *That was much worse.*
> Je crois bien! *I should think so!*
> On est bien ici. *It's nice here; one is comfortable here.*
> Ou bien. *Or (else).*
> Tout est bien qui finit bien. *All's well that ends well.*
> Voudriez-vous bien? *Would you please?*
> Vous feriez bien. *You'd be doing a good thing; it would be a good idea.*

bien *m. good, welfare; virtue; pl. property.*
> Le bien et le mal. *Good and evil.*
> Faire le bien. *To do good.*
> Homme de bien. *Upright man.*
> C'est pour votre bien. *It's for your own good.*
> On dit beaucoup de bien de lui. *He's very highly spoken of.*
> Ils ont des biens en France. *They have some property in France.*
> C'est un marchand de biens. *He's a real-estate agent.*

bienfaisance *f. charity.*
bienfait *m. kindness, good turn; blessing.*
BIENTÔT *soon.*
> Nous partons bientôt à la campagne. *We'll soon be leaving for the country. We're soon leaving for the country.*
> A bientôt. *See you soon.*

bienveillance *f. kindness, benevolence.*
> Il l'a fait par bienveillance. *He did it out of kindness.*

bienvenu (bienvenue *f.*) *noun and adj. welcome.*
> Vous serez toujours le bienvenu ici. *You're always welcome (the welcome one) here.*
> Ils sont bienvenus partout. *They're welcome everywhere.*
> Soyez le bienvenu! *Welcome!*

bienvenue *f. welcome.*
> Le président dit quelques paroles de bienvenue. *The president said a few words of welcome.*

bière *f. beer.*
> La bière blonde (brune). *Light (dark) beer.*

bière *f. coffin.*
bijou *m.* (bijoux *pl.*) *jewel.*
bijouterie *f. jewelry.*
bijoutier *m. jeweler.*
bilan *m. balance sheet.*
bille *f. billiard ball; small ball; marble.*
> Le stylo à bille. *Ball-point pen.*

BILLET *m. ticket (subway, train, theatre, etc.); bill.*
> Quel est le prix des billets? *How much are (the) tickets?*
> Un billet d'aller. *A one-way ticket.*
> Un billet d'aller et retour. *A round-trip ticket.*

Voulez-vous me faire la monnaie de ce billet? *Can you change this bill for me? ("Will you give me change for this bill?")*
Payez-vous sur ce billet et rendez-moi la monnaie. *Take it out of this bill and let me have the change.*
Prendre un billet. *To buy a ticket.*
biographie *f. biography.*
biologie *f. biology.*
bis *Again! Encore!*
biscuit *m. biscuit.*
Des biscuits secs. *Crackers.*
bizarre *adj. strange, odd.*
C'est bizarre! *It's strange (queer, funny)!*
blague *f. tobacco pouch; joke, hoax.*
Blague à tabac. *Tobacco pouch.*
Quelle blague! *What a joke!*
Sans blague! *No kidding! No fooling!*
Blague à part. *All joking aside.*
blaguer *to joke.*
blâme *m. blame.*
Rejeter le blâme sur quelqu'un. *To throw the blame on someone.*
blâmer *to blame.*
blanc *m. blank; linen.*
Laissez quelques lignes en blanc. *Leave a few blank lines.*
De but en blanc. *Abruptly. Point-blank.*
Vous trouverez cela au rayon de blanc. *You'll find that in the linen department.*
Regarder quelqu'un dans le blanc des yeux. *To look someone straight in the eye.*
BLANC (blanche *f.*) *adj. white.*
Vous nous servirez une bouteille de vin blanc? *Will you give ("serve") us a bottle of white wine?*
Vous avez carte blanche. *You have a free hand. You have carte blanche.*
Elle a passé une nuit blanche. *She spent a sleepless night.*
Le film en noir et blanc. *The black-and-white film.*
blanchir *to whiten.*
blanchissage *m. laundering, washing.*
Envoyez tout ça au blanchissage. *Send all that to the laundry.*
blanchisserie *f. hand laundry.*
La blanchisserie est au coin de la rue. *The laundry is on the corner ("of the street").*
blanchisseuse *f. laundress.*
blé *m. wheat.*
blessé *noun (m.) and adj. wounded.*
blesser *to wound, hurt.*
se blesser *to hurt oneself.*
blessure *f. wound.*
BLEU *noun (m.) and adj. blue.*
Bleu marine. *Navy blue.*
Des yeux bleus. *Blue eyes.*
La robe bleue. *The blue dress.*
bloc *m. block.*
En bloc. *In bulk.*
blond (blonde *f.*) *noun and adj. blond; light (beer).*
bloquer *to block; tighten.*
se blottir *to squat; nestle; snuggle down.*
Elle se blottit dans le fauteuil. *She snuggled down in the armchair.*
blouse *f. blouse; smock.*
bobard *m. lie, fib.*
Ne me racontez pas de bobards (*fam.*)! *Tell it to the Marines! Tell it to your grandmother! You expect me to believe that!*
bobine *f. spool, reel.*
bocal *m. (bocaux pl.) glass jar.*

BOEUF *m. (boeufs pl.) ox; beef.*
Vous mettez la charrue devant les boeufs. *You're putting the cart before the horse. ("You're putting the plow before the oxen.")*
Du boeuf à la mode. *Pot roast.*
Donnez-moi un filet de boeuf. *Give me a steak tenderloin.*
BOIRE *to drink.*
Que voulez-vous boire? *What would you like (to have) to drink?*
Versez-moi à boire. *Pour me a drink.*
On sert à boire et à manger. *Food and drinks are served here.*
Buvons à votre santé. *Let's drink to your health.*
bois *m. wood; woods.*
Bois de chauffage. *Firewood.*
Allons faire un tour dans le bois. *Let's go for a walk in the woods.*
boisson *f. drink.*
C'est une boisson rafraîchissante. *It's a refreshing drink.*
Un débit de boissons. *A liquor store.*
boîte *f. box.*
Je lui ai envoyé une boîte de chocolats. *I sent him a box of chocolates.*
Des boîtes de conserves. *(Tin) cans.*
Boîte à chapeau. *Hatbox.*
Boîte d'accus. *f. Storage battery.*
N'oubliez pas de mettre la lettre dans la boîte (aux lettres). *Don't forget to put the letter in the mailbox.*
Boîte de nuit. *Nightclub.*
boiter *to limp, be lame.*
bol *m. bowl, basin.*
bombarder *to bomb, shell.*
bombe *f. bomb.*
Faire la bombe. *To go on a spree. To paint the town red.*
bon *m. bond; premium; order, voucher.*
Bon de poste. *Money order.*
Bon du Trésor. *Treasury bond.*
Bon de caisse. *Cash voucher.*
Bon de livraison. *Delivery order.*
Après cent francs d'achat, vous recevrez un bon. *If you buy a hundred francs worth of merchandise you get a premium.*
BON (bonne *f.*) *adj. good.*
Est-ce bon à manger? *Is this good to eat?*
Ça sent bon. *It smells nice. It has a nice smell.*
C'est bon. *1. That's good (fine). 2. Enough said! That will do!*
Il n'est bon à rien. *He's good-for-nothing.*
Il a une bonne nature. *He's good-natured.*
A quoi bon? *What's the use? What for? What's the good of it?*
C'est un bon garçon. *He's a decent (nice) fellow.*
Bonne année! *Happy New Year!*
Bon voyage! *Bon voyage! Pleasant journey!*
Ça ne me dit rien de bon. *I don't think anything good will come of it. It looks rather bad.*
Il fait bon ici. *It's nice (comfortable) here.*
De bonne heure. *Early.*
Voici quelque chose de bon marché. *Here's something cheap.*
Bonne chance! *Good luck!*
Bon nombre de. *A number of, a good many.*
Bon séjour! *(Have a) pleasant stay!*
Le bon chemin (sens). *The right way, road (direction).*
bonbon *m. candy.*
bond *m. bound, leap.*

bondé *adj. crowded, packed.*
bondir *to bound, leap.*
Bondir d'indignation. *To be filled with indignation.*
BONHEUR *m. happiness.*
Par bonheur. *Luckily.*
Porter bonheur. *To bring luck.*
Au petit bonheur. *In a happy-go-lucky way. In a carefree way.*
boniment *m. smooth talk, eye-wash.*
Faire le boniment. *To give a sales talk.*
BONJOUR *m. Good morning. Good afternoon. Good day. Hello.*
bonne *f. maid.*
bonnet *m. cap.*
BONSOIR *m. Good evening. Good night.*
BONTÉ *f. goodness, kindness.*
Ayez la bonté de me faire savoir. *Please let me know. ("Have the goodness to . . .")*
bord *m. edge, border; shore.*
Le bord d'un verre. *The rim of a glass.*
Il est tombé par-dessus bord. *He fell overboard.*
Aller au bord de la mer. *To go to the seashore.*
A bord. *On board (ship).*
Aux bords du Rhône. *On the banks of the Rhone.*
Le dessin du bord. *Border design.*
borne *f. limit, boundary.*
Cela dépasse toutes les bornes! *That's the limit!*
bosse *f. bump.*
bossu *noun (m.) and adj. (bossue f.) hunchback.*
botte *f. boot.*
Bottin *m. French telephone directory.*
BOUCHE *f. mouth; entrance.*
Il est resté bouche bée. *He stood gaping ("with his mouth wide open").*
Où est la bouche de métro la plus proche? *Where is the nearest subway entrance?*
bouchée *f. mouthful.*
boucher *m. (bouchère f.) butcher.*
boucher *to stop, cork; block up.*
boucherie *f. butcher shop.*
bouchon *m. cork.*
boucle *f. buckle; curl.*
Boucles d'oreilles. *Earrings.*
bouder *to sulk.*
boue *f. mud, dirt.*
bouger *to move, stir.*
Ne bougez pas! *Don't move! Don't budge!*
bougie *f. candle; spark plug.*
bouillir *to boil.*
Faites bouillir l'eau. *Boil the water.*
L'eau a-t-elle bouilli? *Has the water boiled?*
Commencer à bouillir. *To come to a boil.*
bouillon *m. bubble; bouillon.*
Un bouillon de légumes. *Vegetable broth.*
boulangerie *f. bakery.*
boule *f. ball.*
boulevard *m. boulevard.*
bouleverser *to overthrow, upset.*
Il a été bouleversé par les évènements. *The events upset him.*
bouquet *m. cluster, bunch; bouquet.*
Ça c'est le bouquet (*fam.*)! *That tops everything! That's the limit!*
bouquiniste *m. secondhand bookseller.*
bourdonnement *m. humming, buzzing; dial tone (telephone).*
bourgeois *noun and adj. middle-class, bourgeois.*
Cuisine bourgeoise. *Good plain cooking.*
bourgeoisie *f. middle class.*
bourse *f. purse; stock exchange.*
bousculer *to upset; hustle.*

BOUT m. end, extremity.

D'un bout à l'autre. From beginning to end. ("From one end to the other.")

Il est à bout de patience. He's at the end of his patience. His patience is exhausted.

Au bout d'une heure. After an hour. In an hour. ("At the end of an hour.")

Joindre les deux bouts. To make ends meet.

Au bout du compte. After all. In the end.

Savoir sur le bout du doigt. To have at one's fingertips.

A tout bout de champ. Frequently. Repeatedly.

bouteille f. bottle.

boutique f. store, shop.

bouton m. button; knob.

Voulez-vous me recoudre ce bouton? Will you please sew this button on (for me)?

Ce bouton vient de sauter. This button has just come off.

Veston à deux boutons. Two-button jacket.

Où sont mes boutons de manchettes? Where are my cuff links?

Tournez le bouton, s.v.p. (s'il vous plaît). Please turn the knob.

boutonner to button.

boutonnière f. buttonhole.

bracelet m. bracelet.

branche f. branch.

branler to shake.

BRAS m. arm.

Accueillir à bras ouverts. To receive with open arms.

Ils marchaient bras dessus, bras dessous. They walked arm-in-arm.

Avoir quelque chose sur les bras. To have something on one's hands.

brave adj. (following noun) brave; (before noun) honest, good.

C'est un homme brave. He's a brave man.

C'est un brave garçon. He's a good fellow.

bravo m. bravo; applause.

brèche f. breach, gap.

BREF (brève f.) adj. brief, short.

Il a la parole brève. He always gives curt answers.

Répondre d'un ton bref. To give a curt answer.

En bref. In brief. In short.

Il a dû partir avec bref délai. He had to leave on short notice.

brevet m. patent; certificate.

bridge m. bridge (cards).

Jouer au bridge. To play bridge.

brillant adj. brilliant, shiny.

briller to shine, glitter.

Tout ce qui brille n'est pas or. All that glitters is not gold.

brin m. blade of grass; a little bit.

Un brin d'herbe. A blade of grass.

Faire un brin de causette. To have a little chat.

brique f. brick.

brise f. breeze.

briser to break (something).

se briser to break into pieces, be broken into pieces.

broche f. brooch.

brochure f. pamphlet, brochure.

broder to embroider.

bronze m. bronze.

brosse f. brush.

La brosse du peintre. Paintbrush.

La brosse à chaussures. Shoebrush.

La brosse à cheveux. Hairbrush.

La brosse à habits. Clothesbrush.

Donnez un coup de brosse a mon pardessus. Brush my coat.

brosser to brush.

brouillard m. fog.

Il fait du brouillard. It's foggy (out).

brouille f. quarrel.

se brouiller to quarrel.

brouillon m. rough draft.

BRUIT m. noise; rumor.

Le bruit m'a empêché de dormir. The noise kept me from sleeping.

En ville le bruit court qu'ils vont partir. There's a rumor in the city that they're going to leave.

Beaucoup de bruit pour rien. Much ado about nothing.

BRÛLER to burn.

se brûler to burn.

Vous vous brûlerez les doigts. You'll burn your fingers.

BRUN noun (m.) and adj. (brune f.) brown; dark (beer).

brusque adj. sudden, abrupt.

brusquement bluntly; suddenly.

Brusquement, ils l'aperçurent. Suddenly, they saw him.

brut adj. raw; gross.

Matière brute. Raw material.

Dix pour cent brut. Ten percent gross.

brutal (brutaux pl.) adj. brutal, rough, rude.

brute f. rough person, brute.

Quelle brute! What a beast!

bu drunk (p.p. of boire).

bûche f. log.

budget m. budget.

buffet m. sideboard; refreshment room.

Vous pouvez avoir quelque chose à manger au buffet de la gare. You can get something to eat in the station restaurant ("in the refreshment room of the station").

buisson m. bush.

bulle f. bubble.

bulletin m. bulletin.

Suivant le bulletin météorologique, il pleuvra demain. According to the weather report, it will rain tomorrow.

C'est le bulletin mensuel de notre association. It's the monthly bulletin of our association.

Le bulletin de vote. Ballot.

BUREAU m. office; desk.

A partir de demain, le bureau ferme à cinq heures. Beginning tomorrow, the office will close at five.

Pouvez-vous me dire où se trouve le bureau des renseignements? Can you tell me where the information bureau is?

Envoyez ceci à l'adresse de mon bureau. Send this to my business address.

Le bureau de poste se trouve à côté de la gare. The post office is next to the railroad station.

Le bureau de tabac est au coin de la rue. The tobacco store is on the corner ("of the street").

Ramassez tous ces papiers qui traînent sur votre bureau. Gather up the papers which are scattered on your desk.

buste m. bust.

but m. goal, purpose.

Je ne puis deviner son but. I can't guess (make out) his purpose (aim).

Il alla droit au but. He went straight to the point.

buvard m. blotting paper, blotter.

C The third letter of the alphabet.

Ça (contraction of cela) that.

C'est ça! That's it! That's right!

Qu'est-ce que c'est que ça? What's that?

C'est toujours ça! That's so much to the good! At least we have that!

Ça ne fait rien. That doesn't matter. That's unimportant.

Comment vont les affaires? —Comme ci, comme ça. How are things? (How's business?) —So, so.

ÇA here; that (thing, fact).

Ça et là. Here and there.

Ça ne presse pas. There's no hurry.

Ça va. It's all right, O.K.; that's enough.

Ça y est! That's it!

C'est ça. That's it, that's right.

cabine f. cabin; booth.

Une cabine de première classe. First-class cabin (on a ship).

Où se trouvent les cabines téléphoniques? Where are the telephone booths?

cabinet m. closet, small room; cabinet.

Ce cabinet sert de débarras. This closet is used for storage. This is a storage closet.

Il est dans son cabinet de travail. He's in his study.

Il a un cabinet d'avocat. He's an attorney.

Le docteur est dans son cabinet. The doctor is in his office.

Les cabinets sont au fond du couloir. The washrooms are at the end of the hall.

Le nouveau cabinet a été formé. The new cabinet has just been formed.

câble m. cable.

câbler to cable.

cacher to hide.

se cacher to hide oneself.

cachet m. seal, stamp; pill; style.

Cachet d'oblitération. Postmark.

Avez-vous un cachet d'aspirine? Do you have an aspirin?

Cela a beaucoup de cachet. That's quite stylish.

cachette f. hiding place.

En cachette. Secretly.

cadavre m. corpse; cadaver.

cadeau m. (cadeaux pl.) present, gift.

cadet (cadette f.) noun and adj. younger, youngest, junior.

Il est le cadet. He's the youngest.

Ma fille cadette. My youngest daughter.

C'est le cadet de mes soucis. That's the least of my worries.

cadre m. frame.

Cadre (pour tableaux). (Picture) frame.

cafard m. cockroach; the blues (slang).

CAFÉ m. coffee; café.

Un café nature. Black coffee.

Donnez-moi un café au lait. Give me a coffee au lait (coffee with milk).

Allons au café. Let's go to the café.

Garçon de café. Waiter.

cafetière f. coffeepot.

cage f. cage.

cahier m. notebook.

caillou m. (cailloux pl.) pebble.

caisse f. box; crate; cash register; cash-window; teller (in a bank), pay-office.

J'ai mis mon argent à la caisse d'épargne. I put my money in the savings bank.

La caisse ferme à trois heures. *The pay-office (cash-window) closes at three p.m.*
caissier (caissière *f.*) *cashier; teller (bank).*
cajoler *to cajole.*
calamité *f. calamity.*
calcul *m. calculation, arithmetic.*
calculer *to calculate.*
calendrier *m. calendar.*
câlin *noun (m.) and adj.* (câline *f.*) *caressing, winning.*
câliner *to cajole.*
calmant *noun (m.) and adj.* (calmante *f.*) *sedative; calming, soothing.*
CALME *noun (m.) and adj. calm, quiet, mild.*
Du calme! *Be quiet!*
calmer *to calm, relieve.*
se calmer *to become calm, quiet down.*
Calmez-vous. *Calm down. Compose yourself.*
La tempête s'est calmée. *The storm has blown over.*
calomnie *f. calumny, slander.*
calomnier *to slander.*
camarade *f. friend, pal.*
C'est un bon camarade. *He's a good friend. He's a pal.*
Un camarade d'école. *A schoolmate.*
cambrioleur *m. burglar, thief.*
camelote *f. trash, junk.*
caméra *f. movie camera.*
camion *m. truck.*
camp *m. camp.*
CAMPAGNE *f. country; field; campaign.*
Nous habitons la campagne à présent. *We live in the country now.*
Mener une campagne contre quelqu'un. *To conduct a campaign against someone.*
camper *to camp.*
canadien (canadienne *f.*) *noun and adj. Canadian.*
canal *m.* (canaux *pl.*) *canal.*
canapé *m. sofa; canapé.*
canard *m. duck; hoax.*
Il fait un froid de canard. *It's bitter cold.*
canari *m. canary.*
cancer *m. cancer.*
candeur *f. candor.*
candidat *m. candidate, examinee.*
candidature *f. candidacy.*
candide *adj. candid.*
caniche *m. poodle.*
canif *m. penknife.*
canne *f. stick, cane.*
canon *m. gun, cannon, barrel.*
canot *m. canoe, boat, rowboat.*
caoutchouc *m. rubber; rubber band.*
Une balle en caoutchouc. *A rubber ball.*
Mettez vos caoutchoucs. *Put on your rubbers.*
cap *m. cape* (geog.).
CAPABLE *adj. capable, able, qualified.*
Pensez-vous qu'il soit capable de faire le travail? *Do you think he's able to do the job?*
Il en est bien capable! *He's very capable of (doing) it! I wouldn't be surprised if he did it!*
capacité *f. capacity.*
cape *f. cape* (cloak).
capitaine *m. captain.*
capital *m.* (capitaux *pl.*) *capital.*
CAPITAL (capitaux *pl.*) *adj. main, chief, principal, essential.*
Ce que je vous dis là est capital! *What I'm telling you now is essential (important).*
Peine capitale. *Capital punishment.*

capitale *f. capital (of a country).*
capitulation *f. capitulation.*
capituler *to capitulate, surrender.*
caprice *m. caprice, whim.*
Avoir des caprices. *To be fickle.*
capricieux (capricieuse *f.*) *adj. capricious.*
captif (captive *f.*) *noun and adj. captive.*
capturer *to capture, seize.*
CAR *for, because, as.*
CARACTÈRE *m. character.*
caractéristique *adj. characteristic.*
carafe *f. jug.*
caramel *m. caramel.*
cardinal *m.* (cardinaux *pl.*) *cardinal.*
cardinal (cardinaux *pl.*) *adj. chief, cardinal.*
Points cardinaux. *Cardinal points.*
caresse *f. caress, endearment.*
caresser *to caress; cherish.*
carié *adj. decayed.*
carnet *m. small notebook; book of tickets; customs permit (for car).*
Carnet d'adresses. *Address book.*
Carnet de chèques. *Checkbook.*
Carnet de secondes. *Book of secondclass tickets (subway).*
carotte *f. carrot.*
carpe *f. carp.*
Il est muet comme une carpe. *He doesn't open his mouth.* ("He's as mute as a carp.")
carré *m. square.*
carré *adj. square.*
carreau *m. square; paving tile; windowpane; diamond (cards).*
carrefour *m. crossroads.*
carrément *squarely, flatly.*
carrière *f. career; track, ground.*
Soldat de carrière. *Professional (regular) soldier.*
Donner libre carrière à son imagination. *To give free rein to one's fancy.*
carrosse *m. coach, carriage.*
carrousel *m. merry-go-round.*
carrure *f. breadth.*
Il a une belle carrure. *He's well-built.*
CARTE *f. card; menu; map.*
C'est une bonne carte dans son jeu. *That's one of his strongest cards.*
Donnez-moi la carte. *May I have the menu, please.*
Une carte postale. *A postcard.*
Des cartes de visite. *Visiting cards.*
Je me suis fait tirer les cartes hier soir. *Last night I had my fortune told.*
On lui a donné carte blanche. *He was given carte blanche. They gave him a free hand.*
Jouer aux cartes. *To play cards.*
La carte d'invitation. *(Printed) invitation.*
La carte routière. *Road map.*
carton *m. cardboard.*
cartouche *f. cartridge.*
CAS *m. case, event, occasion.*
Malheureusement ce n'est pas toujours le cas. *Unfortunately that isn't always the case.*
Le cas échéant. *If that should be the case.*
C'est le cas ou jamais de le faire. *It must be done now or never.*
C'est bien le cas de le dire. *One may indeed say so.*
En tout cas. *At all events. In any case.*
En aucun cas. *On no account.*
On fait grand cas de lui. *He's highly thought of.*
Je fais peu de cas de son opinion. *I don't value his opinion very much.*
En cas d'urgence. *In case of (an) emergency.*

En ce cas-là. *In that case.*
cascade *f. cascade, waterfall.*
caserne *f. barracks.*
casier *m. registry, records, rack, compartment.*
cassé *adj. broken.*
CASSER *to break; annul; dismiss.*
Ça ne casse rien. *It's nothing special.*
se casser *to break.*
Il s'est cassé le bras. *He broke his arm.*
casserole *f. pan.*
cassette *f. casket, case.*
catalogue *m. catalogue.*
catastrophe *f. catastrophe, accident.*
catégorie *f. category.*
catégorique *adj. categorical, clear, explicit.*
Un refus catégorique. *A flat refusal.*
cathédrale *f. cathedral.*
catholique *noun and adj. Catholic, catholic.*
cauchemar *m. nightmare.*
CAUSE *f. cause, motive; lawsuit, case.*
Il n'y a point d'effet sans cause. *There is no effect without a cause.*
La partie a été reportée à cause de la pluie. *The game was postponed on account of rain.*
Et pour cause! *For a very good reason! With good reason!*
Mettre en cause la probité de quelqu'un. *To question someone's honesty.*
Questions hors de cause. *Irrelevant questions.*
J'ai obtenu gain de cause. *I won my case.*
Connaissez-vous tous les faits de la cause? *Do you know the facts of the case?*
CAUSER *to cause.*
CAUSER *to talk, converse.*
On en cause. *People are talking about it.*
causerie *f. talk; informal lecture.*
caution *f. bail; security.*
cave *f. cellar, cave.*
cavité *f. cavity.*
CE (cet *before vowels and "mute" h; cette f. ces pl.*) *adj. this, that, these, those.*
J'ai été en retard ce matin. *I was late this morning.*
Prenez ce verre-ci. *Take this glass.*
C'est ce livre-là. *It's that book.*
Cette situation est gênante. *This situation is embarrassing.*
Un de ces jours. *One of these days.*
CE (c' *before vowels*) *pron. he, she, it, this, that.*
Ce n'est pas vrai. *It's (that's) not true.*
Est-ce assez? *Is that enough?*
C'est bien. *Good.*
C'est moi. *It's I (me).*
A ce qu'il me semble. *As it seems to me.*
Voici ce dont il s'agit. *Here's the point.*
Ce qu'il a grandi! *How he's grown!*
Sur ce, il s'en alla. *Thereupon he left.*
Il tient à ce que vous veniez. *He insists on your coming.*
Pour ce qui est de cela. *For that matter.*
Qu'est-ce que c'est? *What is it?*
CECI *this.*
Que veut dire ceci? *What does this mean?*
Écoutez bien ceci. *Listen to this.*
céder *to yield, give in.*
ceindre *to gird; encircle.*
ceinture *f. belt.*
CELA *that.*
Cela n'a pas d'importance. *That doesn't matter. That's not important.*
C'est pour cela que je viens. *That's why I've come.*
C'est bien cela. *That's right. That's it.*

Cela ne vous regarde pas. *That's no business of yours.*

célèbre *adj. famous.*

célébrer *to celebrate, praise; to practice (religion).*
On célèbre tous les cultes. *All religions are practiced.*

célibataire *m. bachelor.*

cellule *f. cell.*

CELUI (celle *f.*, ceux *m. pl.*, celles *f. pl.*) *that one; those.*
Voilà celui que je préfère. *There's the one I prefer.*
Celle-ci me paraît meilleure. *This one seems better to me.*
Ceux-ci sont plus chers. *These are more expensive.*
Préféreriez-vous celui-ci? *Would you prefer this one?*
Celui-ci est meilleur que celui-là. *This one is better than that one.*
Je n'aime ni celui-ci ni celui-là. *I don't like either one. ("I don't like this one or that one.")*

cendre *f. ash, ashes.*

cendrier *m. ashtray.*

censé *adj. supposed, reputed.*
Je ne suis pas censé le savoir. *I'm not supposed to know it.*
Nul n'est censé ignorer la loi. *Ignorance of the law is no excuse. ("No one is supposed to be ignorant of the law.")*

censure *f. censorship.*

CENT *noun (m.) and adj. hundred.*
Il a cent fois raison. *He's absolutely right.*
Cinq cents francs. *Five hundred francs.*

centaine *f. about a hundred.*

centième *noun and adj. hundredth.*

centime *m. centime.*

centimètre *m. centimeter (0.394 inch).*

central (centraux *pl.*) *adj. central.*

centrale *f. station.*
Centrale électrique. *Powerhouse.*

CENTRE *m. center.*
Le centre de la France. *The center of France.*
Centre de villégiature. *Holiday resort.*
Lyon est un centre industriel et commercial. *Lyons is an industrial and commercial center.*
Au centre. *In the center.*

CEPENDANT *nevertheless, however.*
Cependant j'aurais bien voulu y aller. *Nevertheless I should like to have gone there. ("Nevertheless I would have wished to go there.")*

CERCLE *m. circle; club.*
Cercle vicieux. *Vicious circle.*
Cercle littéraire. *Literary circle. Literary club.*
Aller au cercle. *To go to the club.*

cercueil *m. coffin.*

cérémonie *f. ceremony.*
Ne faites donc pas de cérémonies. *Don't make such a fuss. Don't stand so much on ceremony.*

cérémonieux (cérémonieuse *f.*) *adj. ceremonious, formal.*

cerf *m. deer.*

cerise *f. cherry.*

cerner *to encircle, close in upon.*
Avoir les yeux cernés. *To have rings under one's eyes.*

CERTAIN *adj. certain, sure.*
De cela, j'en suis certain. *I'm certain of that.*
Je tiens ces renseignements pour certains. *I'm*

sure of this information. *("I consider this information to be certain.")*
C'est un homme d'un certain âge. *He's middle-aged.*
Un certain nombre de personnes. *A certain number of persons.*
C'est un indice certain. *It is a sure indication.*
Ce qu'il y a de certain, c'est que . . . *One thing is certain, namely . . . What is certain is that . . .*

certainement *certainly.*
Viendrez-vous?—Mais certainement. *Will you come?—Certainly.*

certains *certain people.*
Certains le disent. *Some say so. Certain people say so.*

certificat *m. certificate.*

certifier *to certify, attest.*

certitude *f. certainty.*
J'en ai la certitude. *I'm sure of it.*

cerveau *m.* (cerveaux *pl.*) *brain.*
J'ai un rhume de cerveau. *I have a cold in my head.*

cervelle *f. brain.*
Il se creuse la cervelle. *He's racking his brains.*

cesse *f. ceasing; respite.*
Sans cesse. *Ceaselessly. Continually. Constantly.*
Il le répète sans cesse. *He keeps repeating it.*

CESSER *to cease, stop.*
La pluie a cessé. *The rain (has) stopped. It's stopped raining.*
Ce chien ne cesse d'aboyer. *This dog doesn't stop barking. This dog keeps on barking.*
Cessez de crier. *Stop shouting.*
Cessez le feu! *Cease fire!*

C'EST-À-DIRE *that is to say.*

CET *See* ce.

CEUX *See* celui.

CHACUN *adj. and pron. each, each one.*
Chacun de nous pensait de même. *Each one of us thought the same.*
Cinq francs chacun. *Five francs each. Five francs apiece.*
Chacun pour soi. *Everyone for himself.*
Chacun (à) son goût. *Everyone to his taste.*
Chacun (à) son tour. *Everyone in his turn.*

chagrin *m. grief, sorrow.*
Avoir du chagrin. *To be sad.*

chagriner *to grieve, cause grief.*

se chagriner *to grieve, worry about.*

chahut *m. row, racket.*

chahuter *to make a lot of noise.*

chaîne *f. chain; channel (television).*

CHAIR *f. flesh.*

chaire *f. chair (in a university); pulpit.*

CHAISE *f. chair.*
Chaise-longue. *Chaise-longue. Lounging chair.*

chaland *m. barge.*

chalet *m. country cottage.*

CHALEUR *f. heat.*
Par une chaleur écrasante. *In stifling heat.*

chaleureux (chaleureuse *f.*) *adj. warm; ardent.*
Un accueil chaleureux. *A hearty welcome.*

se chamailler *to quarrel, bicker.*

chambarder *to upset, disturb.*

CHAMBRE *f. room; bedroom.*
La chambre des machines. *The engine room.*
Cette chambre a besoin d'être aérée. *This room needs airing.*
Faites la chambre, s'il vous plaît. *Will you please clean the room?*
Chambre sur la rue. *Room facing the front.*

Chambre sur la cour. *Room facing the back (rear).*
Chambre à louer. *Room to let.*
Chambre d'ami. *Spare (bed) room. Guest room.*
Chambre d'enfants. *Nursery.*
Musique de chambre. *Chamber music.*
La Chambre des Députés. *The Chamber of Deputies.*

chameau *m.* (chameaux *pl.*) *camel.*

chamois *m. chamois.*
Peau de chamois. *Chamois (cloth).*

CHAMP *m. field.*
Il vient d'acheter un champ adjacent au mien. *He just bought a field next to mine.*
Champ de blé. *Field of wheat.*
Le champ est libre, allez-y! *The coast is clear. Go ahead!*
Nous y sommes allés sur-le-champ. *We went there at once (right away).*
A tout bout de champ. *Repeatedly.*
Champ de courses. *Race track.*
Champ de bataille. *Battlefield.*

champagne *m. champagne.*

champêtre *adj. rural, rustic.*

champignon *m. mushroom.*

champion *m.* (championne *f.*) *champion.*

championnat *m. championship.*

CHANCE *f. luck.*
Je n'ai pas de chance. *I don't have any luck.*
Si vous réussissez vous aurez de la chance. *If you succeed you'll be lucky.*
Il a toutes les chances pour lui. *The odds are in his favor.*
La chance a tourné. *The tables are turned.*
Je vais courir la chance. *I'll take the chance.*
Elle a des chances d'arriver. *She has good chances of succeeding.*
Voyez ce que c'est que la chance! *That's what you call luck!*
Bonne chance! *Good luck!*
Pas de chance! *No luck! Rotten luck!*
Quelle chance! *What luck! What a stroke of luck!*

chancelant *adj. staggering, unsteady.*
Santé chancelante. *Delicate health.*

chanceler *to stagger, be unsteady.*
Chanceler dans sa résolution. *To waver in one's resolution.*

chanceux (chanceuse *f.*) *adj. lucky.*
C'est un hazard chanceux. *It's a stroke of luck.*

chandelle *f. candle.*
Voir trente-six chandelles. *To see stars.*
Je vous dois une fière chandelle (*fam.*). *I ought to be very grateful to you.*

CHANGE *m. change, exchange.*
Vous aurez des francs contre vos dollars au bureau de change. *You can get your dollars changed into francs at an exchange office.*
Agent de change. *Stockbroker.*
Quel est le cours du change aujourd'hui? *What is the rate of exchange today?*
Gagner au change. *To gain on the exchange.*
Le guichet de change. *(Money) exchange window.*

changeant *adj. changing, variable.*
D'humeur changeante. *Fitful.*

CHANGEMENT *m. change.*
Changement de propriétaire. *Under new management. ("Change of ownership.")*
Il vous faudrait un changement d'air. *You need a change.*

La situation est sans changement. *The situation remains unchanged.*

Changement de vitesse. *Gearshift.*

CHANGER *to change.*

Ça change tout. *That alters matters. That changes everything.*

Changez les draps. *Change the sheets.*

Il a changé de nom. *He changed his name.*

Le temps va changer. *The weather's changing.*

Changeons de conversation. *Let's change the subject.*

Pour changer. *For a change.*

On change de train pour . . . *Change here for . . .*

Faire changer l'huile. *To have the oil changed.*

se changer *to change, to change one's clothes.*

Nous devons nous changer pour le dîner. *We have to change for dinner.*

CHANSON *f. song.*

C'est toujours la même chanson. *It's always the same old story.*

chant *m. song, singing.*

chantage *m. blackmail.*

CHANTER *to sing.*

Qu'est-ce que vous me chantez (fam.)? *What sort of a story are you telling me?*

Je le ferai si ça me chante (fam.). *I'll do it if it suits me.*

chanteur *m. (chanteuse f.) singer.*

chantier *m. yard.*

Chantier de construction. *Shipyard.*

Chantier de bois. *Lumberyard.*

Mettre un bateau en chantier. *To lay the keel of a ship.*

Mettre un bâtiment en chantier. *To put up the framework of a building.*

Avoir un ouvrage sur le chantier. *To have a piece of work in hand. To have some work in progress.*

chantonner *to hum.*

chantre *m. cantor.*

chanvre *m. hemp.*

chaos *m. chaos, confusion.*

CHAPEAU *m. (chapeaux pl.) hat.*

Oter (enlever) son chapeau. *To take one's hat off.*

chapelet *m. rosary.*

chapelle *f. chapel.*

chaperon *m. hood; chaperon.*

CHAPITRE *m. chapter.*

CHAQUE *adj. each, every.*

La situation empire chaque jour. *The situation is getting (growing) worse every day.*

Chaque chose en son temps. *There's a time for everything. ("Everything in its time.")*

Chaque chose à sa place. *Everything has its place.*

char *m. chariot, wagon.*

Char d'assaut. *Tank.*

charade *f. charade.*

charbon *m. charcoal.*

Etre sur des charbons ardents. *To be on pins and needles.*

charcuterie *f. delicatessen.*

chardon *m. thistle.*

CHARGE *f. charge; burden; position; extras (rent).*

Il est à ma charge. *I'm supporting him.*

Les devoirs de ma charge. *The duties of my position.*

Le loyer est de dix mille francs plus les charges. *The rent is 10,000 francs plus extras.*

Il est revenu à la charge. *He tried again. He*

made another attempt.

Femme de charge. *Housekeeper.*

Entrer en charge. *To take up one's duties.*

Les témoins à charge. *The witnesses for the prosecution.*

La prise en charge. *Taking over (a rented car).*

chargé *m. a person entrusted with certain duties (functions, etc.).*

Le chargé d'affaires. *The chargé d'affaires.*

chargement *m. lading, loading.*

CHARGER *to load, increase; entrust; charge.*

Charger une voiture de malles. *To load a truck with trunks.*

Cela charge mon budget. *That increases my expenses.*

On m'a chargé de cette mission. *I have been entrusted with this mission.*

Je vous charge de me remplacer. *I'd like you to take my place. I choose you as my substitute.*

Il est chargé de mes intérêts. *He's taking care of my interests. I've entrusted my interests to him.*

se charger *to undertake, to take upon oneself.*

Je m'en charge. *I take it upon myself (to do it). I'll undertake it (to do it). I'll take charge of it. I'll make it my business (to do it).*

chariot *m. wagon.*

charitable *adj. charitable, kind.*

charité *f. charity, alms.*

charmant *adj. charming.*

charme *m. charm.*

charmer *to charm, delight.*

charnière *f. hinge.*

charnu *adj. fleshy, plump.*

charrette *f. cart.*

charrier *to cart, transport.*

charrue *f. plough, plow.*

charte *f. charter.*

chasse *f. hunting; pursuit.*

chasser *to chase; hunt; discharge.*

chasseur *m. hunter; bellboy.*

châssis *m. frame.*

CHAT *m. (chatte f.) cat.*

Ils s'accordent comme chien et chat. *They fight like cats and dogs.*

Il n'y avait pas un chat. *There wasn't a living creature there.*

Je donne ma langue au chat. *I give up. I can't guess.*

J'ai d'autres chats à fouetter. *I have other fish to fry.*

Les enfants jouent à chat perché. *The children are playing tag.*

Ne réveillez pas le chat qui dort. *Let sleeping dogs lie.*

La nuit tous les chats sont gris. *All cats are gray in the dark.*

châtaigne *f. chestnut.*

châtain *adj. brown (of hair).*

Elle a les cheveux châtains. *She has brown hair.*

château *m. (châteaux pl.) castle, manor.*

châtier *to punish.*

Qui aime bien châtie bien. *Spare the rod and spoil the child.*

châtiment *m. punishment.*

chatouiller *to tickle.*

chatouilleux *(chatouilleuse f.) adj. ticklish.*

CHAUD *m. heat.*

Il ne craint ni le chaud ni le froid. *He's afraid of nothing. ("He fears neither heat nor cold.")*

"Tenir au chaud." *"Keep in a warm place."*

CHAUD *adj. warm, hot.*

Faites attention, c'est chaud. *Be careful, it's hot.*

Eau chaude. *Hot water.*

Une boisson chaude. *A warm drink.*

J'ai chaud. *I'm warm.*

Cela ne me fait ni froid ni chaud. *It's all the same to me. It makes no difference to me.*

Pleurer à chaudes larmes. *To weep bitterly.*

Il fait chaud. *The weather is warm, hot.*

chaudière *f. boiler.*

chauffage *m. heating.*

Chauffage central. *Central heating.*

chauffer *to warm, heat.*

se chauffer *to warm oneself, get warm.*

chauffeur *m. chauffeur.*

chaussée *f. highway; embankment.*

Rez-de-chaussée. *Ground floor.*

chausser *to put on shoes.*

Du combien chaussez-vous? *What size shoe do you wear?*

chaussette *f. sock.*

CHAUSSURE *f. shoe.*

Une paire de chaussures. *A pair of shoes.*

Un magasin de chaussures. *A shoe store.*

Quelle est la pointure de vos chaussures? *What size shoe do you wear?*

Nettoyez mes chaussures, s'il vous plaît. *Will you please shine my shoes?*

chauve *adj. bald.*

chaux *f. lime.*

chavirer *to capsize, turn upside down.*

CHEF *m. chief, leader, head.*

Le chef de bureau. *The chief clerk.*

Ingénieur en chef. *Chief engineer.*

Le chef d'orchestre. *The orchestra leader. The conductor.*

Chef de gare. *Stationmaster.*

C'est un chef-d'oeuvre. *It's a masterpiece.*

Chef d'équipe. *Captain of a team.*

Il l'a fait de son propre chef. *He did it on his own authority.*

CHEMIN *m. way, road.*

Ce chemin va à la ville. *That road leads to the town.*

Comment avez-vous trouvé votre chemin par la ville? *How did you find your way about the town (around town)?*

Il a fait son chemin. *He's succeeded in life. He's made his way in the world.*

Il est toujours dans mon chemin. *He's always in my way.*

L'affaire est en bon chemin. *The matter is progressing nicely.*

En chemin de fer. *By train.*

Billet de chemin de fer. *Railroad ticket.*

Le bon chemin. *The right way.*

Envoyer par chemin de fer. *To send by railway.*

Voyager en chemin de fer. *To travel by train.*

Perdre son chemin. *To lose one's way, get lost.*

Rebrousser (refaire le) chemin. *To retrace one's steps, turn back, start over again.*

cheminée *f. chimney, fireplace.*

cheminer *to tramp, walk.*

CHEMISE *f. shirt; folder (for papers).*

Chemise de nuit. *Nightgown.*

chemisier *m. woman's (tailored) blouse.*

chêne *m. oak.*

chenille *f. caterpillar.*

CHÈQUE *m. check.*

Avez-vous endossé le chèque? *Did you endorse the check?*

J'ai oublié mon carnet de chèques à la maison. *I left my checkbook at home. ("I forgot my checkbook at home.")*

Toucher un chèque. *To cash a check.*

Le chèque de voyage. *Traveler's check.*

CHER (chère *f.*) *adj. dear, beloved; expensive.*

(Mon) Cher . . . *(My) Dear . . . (in a letter).*

C'est mon voeu le plus cher. *It's my most cherished desire.*

La vie est-elle chère là? *Are living expenses high there?*

Il me le payera cher! *He'll pay dearly for that!*

CHERCHER *to seek, search; try to, go and get.*

Je l'ai cherché de tous côtés. *I looked for him everywhere.*

Allez chercher un taxi, s'il vous plaît. *Please (go and) get a cab.*

Il cherche à entrer. *He's trying to get in.*

chéri (chérie *f.*) *noun and adj. beloved, darling.*

chérir *to cherish.*

chétif (chétive *f.*) *adj. puny, weak.*

CHEVAL *m.* (chevaux *pl.*) *horse.*

Monter à cheval. *To go horseback riding.*

Fer à cheval. *Horseshoe.*

Monter sur ses grands chevaux. *To get up on one's high horse.*

chevelure *f. hair.*

chevet *m. the head of the bed.*

Rester au chevet de quelqu'un. *To remain at a person's bedside. Not to leave someone's bedside.*

CHEVEU *m.* (cheveux *pl.*) *hair.*

Je désire me faire couper les cheveux. *I want to have my hair cut. I want a haircut.*

C'est tiré par les cheveux. *That's farfetched.*

Etre à un cheveu de la ruine. *To be within a hairbreadth of disaster.*

Il se fait des cheveux blancs. *He's worrying himself gray.*

A faire dresser les cheveux. *Terrifying. Enough to make one's hair stand on end.*

cheville *f. ankle; peg.*

chèvre *f. goat.*

chevreau *m. kid.*

La peau de chevreau. *Kid(skin).*

chevreuil *m. roebuck, roe; venison.*

CHEZ *at, in, at the house of.*

Venez chez nous. *Come over to our place.*

Je vous verrai chez les Durand. *I'll see you at the Durands'.*

Nous étions chez des amis. *We were at the home of some friends.*

Monsieur Durand est-il chez lui? *Is Mr. Durand at home?*

Il faut que j'aille chez le médecin. *I have to go to the doctor's.*

Achetez cela chez l'épicier. *Buy that at the grocer's.*

Il demeure chez nous. *He lives with us.*

Faites comme chez vous. *Make yourself at home.*

C'est devenu une habitude chez lui. *It's become a habit with him.*

chic *m. trick, knack, style.*

Le chic parisien. *Parisian style.*

Elle a du chic. *She has style (chic).*

Il a un chic pour faire ça. *He has a knack for that sort of thing.*

CHIEN *m. dog.*

Chien de garde. *Watchdog.*

Chien qui aboie ne mord pas. *Barking dogs seldom bite.*

Quel temps de chien (*fam.*)! *What terrible (awful) weather!*

chiffon *m. rag; scrap of paper.*

Donnez-donc un coup de chiffon à mes chaussures. *Please shine my shoes.*

Le chiffon pour les meubles. *Dustcloth.*

chiffonner *to crumple up; ruffle.*

CHIFFRE *m. figure, number.*

Des chiffres romains. *Roman numerals.*

Des chiffres arabes. *Arabic numerals.*

Voulez-vous vérifier l'exactitude de ces chiffres? *Will you please check these figures?*

Les chiffres ne concordent pas. *The figures don't agree (tally).*

chimère *f. chimera, idle fancy.*

Se forger des chimères. *To have (entertain) illusions.*

chimie *f. chemistry.*

Chine *f. China.*

chinois *noun and adj. Chinese.*

chirurgie *f. surgery.*

chirurgien *m. surgeon.*

choc *m. shock, blow, collision.*

CHOCOLAT *m. chocolate.*

Une tablette de chocolat. *A chocolate bar.*

Une glace au chocolat. *Chocolate ice cream.*

Un chocolat chaud. *A cup of hot chocolate.*

choeur *m. choir, chorus.*

Un enfant de choeur. *An altar boy; choirboy.*

choir *to fall.*

Laisser choir. *To drop.*

choisi *adj. selected, chosen.*

Un recueil de morceaux choisis. *Collection of selected pieces (poems, essays, etc.). An anthology.*

CHOISIR *to choose.*

Il n'y a pas à choisir. *There's nothing to choose from. There is no choice left.*

CHOIX *m. choice.*

Avez-vous fait votre choix? *Have you chosen (decided, made your choice)?*

Vous n'avez pas le choix. *You have no choice. You haven't any alternative. It's not up to you.*

C'est à votre choix. *It's up to you to choose. It's up to you. As you choose.*

Articles de choix. *Choice articles.*

De tout premier choix. *Of the best quality.*

chômage *m. unemployment.*

choquer *to shock, offend.*

se choquer *to be shocked, offended.*

CHOSE *f. thing.*

Tout ça, c'est la même chose. *It all ("All that") comes to the same thing.*

Je voudrais quelque chose de bon marché. *I'd like something reasonable (cheap).*

Chose curieuse, il se taisait. *Curiously enough, he didn't say anything ("he was silent").*

Chaque chose en son temps. *Everything in its proper time.*

Toutes choses étant égales, je préfère cette solution. *Other things being equal, I prefer this solution.*

Dites-lui bien des choses de ma part. *Remember me to him (her).*

Que vous a-t-il dit? —Peu de chose. *What did he tell you? —Nothing of importance. Nothing very important.*

Ce n'est pas chose aisée. *It's no easy matter.*

La chose publique. *The public welfare.*

chou *m.* (choux *pl.*) *cabbage; dearest.*

Une soupe aux choux. *Cabbage soup.*

Des choux-fleurs. *Cauliflower.*

Mon petit chou! *Dearest!*

chrétien *m.* (chrétienne *f.*) *Christian.*

chronique *f. chronicle.*

Chronique musicale. *Musical news. News about the world of music.*

chuchoter *to whisper.*

chut! *shh!*

chute *f. fall; downfall.*

CI *here.*

Par, ci, par là. *Here and there.*

Ci-gît . . . *Here lies . . .*

Comme dit ci-après. *As is said further on (hereafter).*

Ci-joint vous trouverez . . . *Enclosed (herewith) you will find . . .*

Voir ci-dessous. *See below.*

Voir carte ci-contre. *See map on opposite page.*

Ce livre-ci. *This book.*

A cette heure-ci. *At this very hour.*

Voir ci-dessus. *See above.*

cible *f. target.*

cicatrice *f. scar.*

cidre *m. cider.*

CIEL *m.* (cieux *pl.*) *sky; heaven.*

Il n'y a pas un nuage dans le ciel. *There isn't a cloud in the sky.*

A ciel ouvert. *Under the open sky.*

Tomber du ciel. *To come as a godsend (windfall).*

C'est tombé du ciel. *It's a stroke of good fortune. It's a windfall.*

Remuer ciel et terre. *To move heaven and earth.*

Le ciel m'est témoin. *Heaven is my witness.*

Aide-toi, le ciel t'aidera. *God helps those who help themselves.*

Que le ciel m'en préserve! *God forbid!*

Ciel! *Heavens!*

Bleu ciel. *Sky-blue.*

cierge *m. candle or taper used for religious purposes.*

CIGARE *m. cigar.*

CIGARETTE *f. cigarette.*

ci-inclus *enclosed (herewith).*

cil *m. eyelash.*

cime *f. summit, top.*

ciment *m. cement.*

cimetière *m. cemetery.*

CINÉMA *m. movies.*

Faire du cinéma. *To act in the movies.*

cinématographique *adj. cinematographic.*

cingler *to lash, whip.*

CINQ *noun and adj. five.*

cinquantaine *f. (about) fifty; fiftieth year.*

CINQUANTE *noun and adj. fifty.*

cinquantième *noun and adj. fiftieth.*

CINQUIÈME *fifth.*

cintre *m. curve, bend; clothes hanger.*

cirage *m. waxing; shoe polish.*

circonférence *f. circumference.*

CIRCONSTANCE *f. circumstance.*

Le tribunal a tenu compte des circonstances atténuantes. *The court took into consideration the extenuating circumstances.*

Qu'auriez-vous fait en pareille circonstance? *What would you have done in a similar case?*

Etre à la hauteur des circonstances. *To be equal to the occasion.*

Paroles de circonstance. *Words suited to the occasion.*

circuit *m. circuit.*

Cinq mètres de circuit. *Five meters in circumference.*

Mettre une ligne en court-circuit. *To short-circuit a line.*

circulaire noun (f.) and adj. *circular.*

circulation f. *circulation; traffic.*

La circulation du sang. *Blood circulation.*

Il y a très peu de circulation dans cette rue. *There is very little traffic in this street.*

Accidents de la circulation. *Traffic accidents.*

Circulation interdite. *No thoroughfare.*

circuler *to circulate, move around.*

Circulez! *Move on! Keep moving!*

Faire circuler une nouvelle. *To spread a piece of news.*

cire f. *wax.*

cirer *to wax.*

Cirer des souliers. *To shine (polish) shoes.*

cirque m. *circus.*

CISEAUX m. pl. *scissors.*

ciseler *to engrave, chisel.*

citadin (citadine f.) noun and adj. *pertaining to a city; city-dweller.*

citation f. *quoting; citation.*

cité f. *city.*

Cité ouvrière. 1. *Block of tenement houses.* 2. *Garden city for workers.*

Cité universitaire (in Paris). *University section.*

citer *to cite, quote.*

Citez-m'en un passage. *Quote a passage of it to me.*

Il a été cité à l'ordre du jour. *He has been cited for bravery.*

Il fut cité en justice. *He was summoned to court (as a witness or as a defendant).*

citerne f. *cistern, tank.*

citoyen m. (citoyenne f.) *citizen.*

citron m. *lemon.*

Citron pressé. *Lemonade.*

citronnade f. *lemonade.*

citrouille f. *pumpkin.*

civière f. *stretcher.*

civil adj. *civil.*

civilisation f. *civilization.*

civiliser *to civilize.*

civilité f. *politeness.*

clair m. *light, shine.*

Au clair de lune. *In the moonlight.*

Il a tiré l'affaire au clair. *He cleared up the matter.*

CLAIR adj. *clear, light (in color).*

C'est clair comme le jour. *It's as clear as day.*

Le temps est clair. *The weather's clear.*

J'aime cette couleur bleu clair. *I like this light blue.*

clair adv. *clear.*

Je commence à voir clair. *I'm beginning to understand.*

Voir clair dans l'esprit de quelqu'un. *To read someone's mind.*

clairement *clearly, plainly.*

clairon m. *bugle.*

clairvoyance f. *perspicacity, clear-sightedness.*

clairvoyant adj. *perspicacious, clear-sighted.*

clameur f. *clamor, uproar.*

clan m. *clan.*

clandestin adj. *clandestine, secret.*

claquer *to clap, smack, slam.*

Il claque des dents. *His teeth are chattering.*

Il a claqué la porte en partant. *He slammed the door when (as) he left.*

clarifier *to clarify.*

clarinette f. *clarinette.*

clarté f. *light, brightness.*

CLASSE f. *class.*

Une classe de français. *A French class.*

En quelle classe voyagez-vous? *What class are you traveling?*

Aller en classe. *To go to school.*

Les classes moyennes. *The middle classes.*

classement m. *classification, filing.*

classer *to classify.*

classeur m. *rack, file.*

classification f. *classification.*

classifier *to classify.*

classique noun (m.) and adj. *classic(al).*

clause f. *clause.*

clavier m. *keyboard (of a piano, organ, typewriter, etc.)*

CLÉ (clef) f. *key.*

Fermer une porte à clé. *To lock a door.*

clément adj. *clement, lenient.*

clergé m. *clergy.*

cliché m. *cliché; negative (photography).*

client m. *client, customer.*

clientèle f. *clientele, customers.*

cligner *to blink.*

Cligner de l'oeil. *To wink.*

clignoter *to twitch.*

climat m. *climate.*

clin d'oeil m. *wink.*

clinique f. *nursing home.*

cloche f. *bell.*

clocher m. *belfry; steeple.*

clochette f. *small bell.*

cloison f. *partition, interior wall.*

cloître m. *cloister.*

clôture f. *enclosure, fence; closing.*

Mur de clôture. *Enclosing wall.*

clôturer *to close.*

Clôturer la séance. *To bring the meeting to an end. To close the meeting.*

clou m. *nail.*

clouer *to nail, fix.*

Etre cloué sur place. *To be rooted to the spot. To stand stock-still. ("To be nailed to the spot.")*

cloué adj. *studded (with nails).*

Passage clouté. *Pedestrian crossing.*

club m. *club.*

coaguler *to coagulate, curdle.*

coalition f. *coalition, alliance.*

cocasse adj. *funny, comical.*

C'était tout à fait cocasse (fam.). *It was very funny (a scream).*

coche m. *stagecoach.*

Manquer le coche. *To miss the boat.*

cocher m. *coachman.*

cochon m. *pig.*

code m. *law, code.*

Code de la route. *Traffic regulations.*

coefficient m. *coefficient.*

COEUR m. *heart.*

Il a une maladie de coeur. *He has a heart condition.*

Il en a eu le coeur brisé. *It broke his heart.*

Avoir mal au coeur. *To feel nauseous.*

En avoir le coeur net. *To clear up a matter. To get to the bottom of something.*

Je vous remercie de tout coeur. *I thank you from the bottom of my heart.*

Cela me fend le coeur. *That breaks my heart.*

Partir le coeur léger. *To set out with a light heart.*

Avoir le coeur gros. *To be sad at heart.*

Si le coeur vous en dit. *If you feel like it.*

Vous le prenez trop à coeur. *You're taking it too much to heart.*

Apprendre par coeur. *To learn by heart.*

Faire contre mauvaise fortune bon coeur. *To keep a stiff upper lip. To put a good face on a bad matter.*

Rire de bon coeur. *To laugh heartily.*

Il a son bureau au coeur du quartier des affaires. *He has his office in the heart of the business section.*

coffre m. *chest, box, trunk (car).*

coffre-fort m. *safe-deposit box.*

coffret m. *small box.*

cognac m. *brandy.*

cognement m. *knocking.*

cogner *to bump.*

cohue f. *crowd, mob.*

Quelle cohue! *What a mob!*

coiffer *to do someone's hair.*

se coiffer *to do one's hair.*

Se faire coiffer. *To have one's hair done.*

coiffeur (coiffeuse f.) *barber; hairdresser.*

coiffure f. *hairdo.*

Sa nouvelle coiffure lui va bien. *Her new hairdo is very becoming (becomes her).*

Salon de coiffure. *Beauty parlor.*

COIN m. *corner.*

Il y a un kiosque à journaux au coin de la rue. *There's a newsstand on the corner.*

Je l'ai cherché dans tous les coins. *I looked for it everywhere.*

Regarder du coin de l'oeil. *To look out of the corner of one's eye. To give a side glance.*

coincer *to wedge; corner; arrest (fam.).*

coïncidence f. *coincidence.*

col m. *collar.*

Un col souple. *A soft collar.*

Un col raide. *A hard (stiff) collar.*

Un faux col. *A detachable collar.*

colère f. *anger.*

Etre en colère. *To be angry.*

colis m. *package, parcel.*

Par colis postal. *By parcel post.*

collaborateur m. (collaboratrice f.) *collaborator.*

collaboration f. *collaboration.*

collaborer *to collaborate.*

colle f. *paste, glue.*

collection f. *collection.*

collectionner *to collect, gather.*

collège m. *high school; preparatory school.*

coller *to stick, paste, glue.*

collier m. *necklace.*

colline f. *hill.*

collision f. *collision.*

colonel m. *colonel.*

colonie f. *colony.*

coloniser *to colonize.*

colonne f. *column.*

colorer *to color.*

Elle sait colorer son récit. *She knows how to color her story.*

colossal adj. *colossal.*

Une fortune colossale. *An immense fortune.*

combat m. *fight, combat, battle.*

Engager le combat. *To go into action.*

combattre *to fight, combat, battle.*

combien *how many, how much.*

C'est combien? (Combien est-ce?) *How much is it?*

Combien vous dois-je? *How much do I owe you?*

Le combien sommes-nous? *What's the date today?*

Combien y a-t-il d'ici au parc? *How far is it from here to the park?*

C'est à combien le dollar? *What's the rate of exchange for the dollar?*

combinaison f. *combination, arrangement; slip (for women).*

combiner *to combine; scheme, contrive.*

J'ai combiné un nouveau plan. *I devised (worked out) a new project.*

comble m. *summit, top.*

De fond en comble. *From top to bottom. Completely.*

Ça c'est le comble! *That's the limit! That's the last straw!*

Pour comble de malheur. *To crown everything. To add to my troubles. ("For or as the height of misfortune.")*

Faire salle comble. *To draw a full house (theatre, etc.).*

combler *to heap, fill up; load, overload.*

Vous me comblez! *You overwhelm me! You're spoiling me!*

combustible m. *fuel.*

combustible adj. *combustible.*

comédie f. *comedy, play.*

Cessez cette comédie! *Stop acting!*

comédien (comédienne f.) *actor, player (any kind of play).*

comestible noun (m.) and adj. *victuals, food; eatable.*

comité m. *committee.*

commandant m. *commanding (officer).*

commande f. *order; control.*

Passer une commande. *To place an order.*

commander *to command, order.*

Commander à quelqu'un de faire quelque chose. *To command someone to do something.*

Commander quelque chose. *To order something.*

COMME as, *like.*

Il lui a dit cela comme ami. *He told that to him as a friend.*

Il a agit comme un enfant. *He acted like a child.*

Comment ça va? —Comme ci, comme ça. *How are things? —So, so.*

A-t-il été nommé? —Non, mais c'est tout comme. *Has he been appointed? —No, but he's as good as (appointed).*

Comme il est tard! *How late it is!*

Il est très comme il faut. *He's very proper (well-bred). He's a gentleman.*

Comme cela. *Like that, that way.*

Qu'est-ce qu'il nous faut comme papiers? *What do we need in the way of documents?*

commencement m. *beginning.*

Au commencement j'ai cru qu'il plaisantait. *At first I thought he was joking.*

Dès le commencement ça m'a déplu. *I disliked it from the start.*

COMMENCER *to begin.*

Il a commencé à travailler. *He started to work.*

Pour commencer. *First of all. To begin with.*

Commencer par. *To begin with, by.*

COMMENT how.

Comment ça va? *How are you?*

Comment? *What did you say? I beg your pardon?*

Mais comment donc! *By all means!*

Comment! *What!*

Comment fait-on pour . . . *How does one go about . . .*

commentaire m. *commentary; comment.*

Ceci se passe de commentaire. *This speaks for itself. ("No comment is necessary.")*

commenter *to comment.*

commerçant m. *merchant, dealer.*

commerce m. *trade.*

commercial (commerciaux pl.) adj. *commercial.*

commettre *to commit.*

Vous avez commis une erreur. *You've made a mistake.*

commis m. *clerk.*

commissaire m. *commissary, commissioner.*

commissariat m. *commissionership used in the following expression:*

Le commissariat de police. *Police headquarters. The central police station of a precinct.*

commission f. *commission; committee, message; errand.*

Sa commission sur l'affaire est de 5%. *His commission on the deal is 5%.*

Commission d'enquête. *Board of inquiry.*

Puis-je faire une commission? *Is there any message? Can I take a message (for you)?*

Voulez-vous me faire une commission? *Would you please do (run) an errand for me?*

commissionnaire m. *commission agent; messenger.*

commode f. *chest of drawers, bureau.*

commode adj. *practical, convenient.*

C'est commode. *It's convenient (handy). It's comfortable.*

Il est très commode. *He's very pleasant (good-natured, easygoing).*

commodité f. *convenience, comfort.*

Vivre dans la commodité. *To live in comfort.*

commotion f. *commotion, shock.*

commun m. *common; commonplace; the common run:*

Cela tombe dans le commun. *It's becoming commonplace.*

COMMUN adj. *common.*

C'est très commun. *That's very common.*

Amis communs. *Mutual friends.*

Avoir des intérêts communs. *To have common interests.*

D'un commun accord. *By common consent.*

Faire cause commune avec quelqu'un. *To make common cause with someone.*

Le sens commun. *Common sense.*

Nom commun. *Common noun.*

N'avoir rien de commun avec quelqu'un. *To have nothing in common with someone.*

Lieux communs. *Commonplaces. Commonplace (trivial) remarks.*

Expression peu commune. *Unusual expression.*

Ce sont des gens très communs. *They're very common (people).*

communal (communaux pl.) adj. *communal.*

communauté f. *community.*

commune f. *smallest territorial district in France.*

communication f. *communication.*

Communication d'idées. *Exchange of ideas.*

Je me suis nis en communication avec eux. *I got in touch with them.*

Communication téléphonique. *Telephone call.*

Vous avez la communication. *Your call is ready. Here's your party.*

communion f. *communion.*

communiqué m. *communiqué, official news.*

communiquer *to communicate.*

Je lui ai communiqué votre note. *I gave him your note.*

Les chambres communiquent. *The rooms are adjoining (communicating).*

Je ne puis pas encore communiquer avec lui. *I haven't yet been able to get in touch with him.*

communisme m. *communism.*

communiste m. and f. *noun and adj. communist.*

compagne f. *(female) companion.*

COMPAGNIE f. *company.*

Dupont et Cie. (et Compagnie). *Dupont and Co.*

Je me plais en sa compagnie. *I like his company.*

Je vous tiendrai compagnie. *I'll keep you company.*

Il nous a faussé compagnie. *He left us suddenly. He deserted us. He left us in the lurch.*

compagnon m. *companion.*

Compagnon de travail. *Fellow worker.*

Compagnon d'infortune. *Companion in misfortune.*

comparable adj. *comparable.*

COMPARAISON f. *comparison.*

Hors de toute comparaison. *Beyond comparison.*

Etablir une comparaison entre deux choses. *To draw a parallel between two things.*

comparaître *to appear.*

Vous devez comparaître en personne. *You have to appear in person.*

comparatif (comparative f.) adj. *comparative.*

comparativement *comparatively.*

COMPARER *to compare.*

compartiment m. *compartment.*

Compartiment de première classe. *First-class compartment.*

C'est un compartiment de non-fumeurs. *No smoking in this compartment.*

compas m. *compass.*

compassion f. *compassion, pity.*

Faire compassion. *To arouse compassion.*

compatible adj. *compatible.*

compatir *to sympathize with.*

Je compatis à votre chagrin. *I sympathize with you in your grief.*

compatissant adj. *compassionate, sympathizing.*

compatriote m. and f. *compatriot, fellow-countryman.*

compensation f. *compensation.*

compenser *to compensate for.*

compétent adj. *competent.*

compétition f. *competition.*

complainte f. *complaint.*

complaire *to please, humor.*

Il lui complaît. *He humors him.*

se complaire *to take delight in, derive pleasure from.*

Se complaire à faire quelque chose. *To take pleasure in doing something.*

complaisance f. *complacence; kindness.*

Auriez-vous la complaisance de . . . ? *Would you be so kind as to . . . ?*

complaisant adj. *obliging, willing.*

complet m. *suit.*

Je viens de m'acheter un complet marron. *I just bought (myself) a brown suit.*

COMPLET (complète f.) adj. *full, complete.*

C'est complet. *There's no more room. It's full.*

Manque complet de. *Complete (utter) lack of.*

Un repas complet. *A full meal.*

COMPLÈTEMENT *fully, completely.*

Il est complètement ruiné. *He's completely ruined.*

COMPLÉTER *to complete, finish.*

complet-veston m. *business suit.*

complexe noun (m.) and adj. *complex.*

complication f. *complication.*
Entrer dans des complications. *To meet with complications.*

complice m. *a party to, accomplice.*

compliment m. *compliment; congratulations; regards.*
Je vous fais mes compliments. *I congratulate you. Congratulations!*
Mes compliments chez vous. *Remember me at home. Give my regards to your family.*

compliqué adj. *complicated.*

compliquer *to complicate.*

se compliquer *to become complicated, involved.*
Cela se complique. *It's getting involved (complicated).*

complot m. *plot, conspiracy.*

comploter *to plot, scheme.*

comporter *to allow; include.*
Cette règle comporte des exceptions. *This rule has exceptions.*
Je le ferai malgré les inconvénients que cela comportera. *I'll do it in spite of the difficulties which it will entail.*

se comporter *to behave.*

composer *to compose.*
Composer un numéro. *To dial a number.*

se composer *to consist of, be composed of, be made up of.*
L'appartement se compose de huit pièces et deux salles de bains. *The apartment consists of eight rooms and two bathrooms.*

compositeur m. *(compositrice f.) composer.*

composition f. *composition, essay.*

compote f. *compote, stewed fruit.*

compréhension f. *understanding.*
Avoir la compréhension facile. *To understand things right away. To have a quick mind.*

COMPRENDRE *to include; understand.*
Tout est compris. *Everything is included.*
Ce prix ne comprend pas les rectifications. *This price doesn't include alterations.*
Y compris. *Including.*
Il est facile de comprendre pourquoi. *It's easy to understand why.*
Il ne comprend pas l'anglais. *He doesn't understand English.*
Je n'y comprends rien. *I can't understand it at all. I can't make it out.*
C'est à n'y rien comprendre. *It's beyond me. I can't understand it. It doesn't make sense.*
Cela se comprend. *That's easy to understand. Naturally. Of course.*
Je peux juste à peu près me faire comprendre en français. *I can just about make myself understood in French.*
Je lui ai fait comprendre que . . . *I made it clear to him that . . .*

comprimé m. *pill.*

comprimer *to compress; curb, repress.*

compromettre *to commit; compromise.*
Ne me compromettez pas là-dedans. *Don't involve me in it.*

compromis m. *compromise.*
Mettre une affaire en compromis. *To submit an affair for arbitration.*

comptabilité f. *bookkeeping.*

comptable m. *bookkeeper, accountant.*

comptant m. *cash.*
Au comptant ou à crédit. *In cash or on credit.*
Payable au comptant. *Terms, cash.*

comptant adj. *in cash.*
Argent comptant. *Ready money. Spot cash.*
Payer comptant. *To pay cash.*

Ne prenez pas tout pour argent comptant. *Don't take everything for gospel truth.*

COMPTE m. *account; calculation; amount.*
Créditez-en mon compte. *Credit this to my account.*
Faites-vous ouvrir un compte à la banque. *Open a bank account.*
Faites le compte des recettes. *Add up the receipts.*
Tenez compte de tout ça. *Take all that into account.*
Un compte-rendu. *A report.*
Les bons comptes font les bons amis. *Short reckonings make long friends.*
J'ai un compte à régler avec lui. *I have a bone to pick with him.*
Je m'en rends compte. *I understand that. I'm aware of that.*
Son compte est bon. *Now he's in for it.*
Régler de vieux comptes. *To pay off old scores.*
Il ne doit de comptes à personne. *He is answerable to nobody.*
Elle est inquiète sur son compte. *She is worried about him.*
Pour mon compte. *As far as I'm concerned.*
En fin de compte. *After all. In the end. When all is said and done.*

compte-gouttes m. *dropper.*

COMPTER *to count.*
L'enfant est en train d'apprendre à compter. *The child is just learning how to count.*
Nous serons dix sans compter l'hôte. *We'll be ten, not counting the host.*
A compter de demain. *Counting from tomorrow.*
Puis-je compter sur vous? *Can I count (depend, rely) on you?*
Vous pouvez y compter. *You may depend upon it.*
J'avais compté sur quelque chose de mieux. *I counted on something better. I had expected something better.*
Je vous compterai cet article trente francs. *I'll charge you thirty francs for this item.*
Ça ne compte pas. *That doesn't matter. That doesn't count.*

compteur m. *meter (taxi).*

comptoir m. *counter.*

concéder *to concede, grant, admit.*
Je concède que j'ai eu tort. *I admit I was wrong.*
Je vous concède ce point. *I grant you that point.*

concentré adj. *concentrated.*

se concentrer *to concentrate.*
Se concentrer en soi-même. *To retire within oneself.*

conception f. *conception.*

concerner *to concern.*
Cela ne vous concerne pas. *That doesn't concern you.*
Est-ce que cela le concerne? *Is that any of his business?*
Pour ce qui me concerne. *As far as I'm concerned.*
Concernant. *In regard to. Regarding.*

concert m. *concert.*
Dépêchez-vous si vous ne voulez pas être en retard pour le concert. *Hurry up if you don't want to be late for the concert.*
Nous devons agir de concert. *We have to act together.*

se concerter *to consult one another.*

concession f. *concession.*

concevoir *to conceive.*

Cela se conçoit facilement. *That's easily understood.*

concierge m. and f. *janitor, superintendent.*

concilier *to reconcile, conciliate.*

concis adj. *concise, terse.*

concision f. *brevity.*

CONCLURE *to conclude.*
Conclure la paix. *To conclude peace.*
Il faut conclure maintenant. *It's time to come to a conclusion.*
Une entente a été conclue. *An understanding has been reached (arrived at).*
C'est une affaire conclue. *The matter's closed. That's settled. It's a bargain.*
Que concluez-vous de ce fait? *What do you infer (conclude) from that? What do you think that means?*

conclusion f. *conclusion.*

concorde f. *concord; harmony.*

concours m. *meeting; assistance, help; contest.*
Point de concours. *Point of convergence.*
Prêter son concours à quelqu'un. *To help someone. To collaborate with someone.*
Par le concours de. *Through the help of.*
Hors de concours. *Not competing (on account of acknowledged excellence). Beyond comparison. In a class by itself.*
Concours d'admission. *Entrance examination.*

concret *(concrète f.) adj. concrete.*

concurrence f. *competition.*

concurrent m. *competitor.*

concurrent adj. *competitive.*

condamnation f. *condemnation.*

condamner *to sentence, condemn, blame.*

condenser *to condense.*

condescendre *to condescend.*

CONDITION f. *condition.*
A condition que (de). *Provided that.*
Dans ces conditions. *Under these conditions. Under these circumstances.*
Dans les conditions actuelles. *Under present conditions.*
J'accepte mais à condition que . . . *I accept with the condition that . . .*
J'accepte à une seule condition. *I accept but on one condition.*
Les conditions étaient raisonnables. *The terms were reasonable.*
Se rendre sans condition. *To surrender unconditionally.*

conditionnel *(conditionnelle f.) adj. conditional.*

condoléance f. *condolence.*
Veuillez agréer mes sincères condoléances. *Please accept my heartfelt sympathy.*

conducteur m. *(conductrice f.) conductor.*
Un conducteur d'autobus. *A bus conductor.*

CONDUIRE *to drive; lead.*
Un permis de conduire. *A driving license.*
Savez-vous conduire? *Do you know how to drive?*
Conduire une armée. *To lead an army.*
Il la conduisit chez elle. *He took her home.*
Il conduit bien sa barque. *He manages his affairs well.*
Le cuivre conduit l'électricité. *Copper conducts electricity.*

SE CONDUIRE *to behave.*
Il ne sait pas se conduire. *He doesn't know how to behave.*
Quelle manière de se conduire! *What a way to behave! What behavior!*

conduit m. *passage, channel.*
Conduit souterrain. *Drain.*

conduite *f. conduct; command.*
Sa conduite est irréprochable. *His conduct is irreproachable (perfect).*
N'avez-vous pas honte de votre conduite? *Aren't you ashamed of your behavior?*
Changer de conduite. *To turn over a new leaf.*
Conduite d'eau. *Waterpipe.*
cône *m. cone.*
confection *f. construction; ready-to-wear clothes.*
La confection de cette machine est très chère. *This machine is very expensive to construct.*
Acheter une robe de confection. *To buy a ready-made dress.*
confectionner *to make, manufacture.*
conférence *f. conference; lecture.*
Il est en conférence avec le docteur Dupont. *He's conferring (in conference) with Dr. Dupont.*
Il a fait une conférence excellente. *He gave an excellent lecture.*
conférencier (conférencière *f.*) *lecturer.*
conférer *to confer.*
confesser *to confess.*
confession *f. confession, avowal.*
confiance *f. trust, confidence.*
J'ai entière confiance en lui. *I have complete confidence in him.*
C'est une personne de confiance. *He (she) is a trustworthy person.*
Abus de confiance. *Breach of trust.*
confidence *f. confidence; secret.*
confidentiel (confidentielle *f.*) *adj. confidential.*
A titre confidentiel. *Confidentially.*
confier *to trust, entrust; confide.*
se confier *to confide in, trust to.*
confiner *to border upon.*
confirmation *f. confirmation.*
En confirmation de votre commande, ayez l'obligeance de nous envoyer une lettre. *Please send us a letter in confirmation of your order.*
En confirmation de mon coup de téléphone de ce matin. *Confirming my telephone call of this morning.*
Confirmation d'un traité. *Ratification of a treaty.*
confirmer *to confirm.*
L'exception confirme la règle. *The exception proves the rule.*
confiscation *f. confiscation, seizure.*
confiserie *f. candy store.*
confisquer *to confiscate.*
confiture *f. jam, preserves.*
conflit *m. conflict.*
Conflit d'opinions. *Conflict of opinion.*
confondre *to confuse.*
Je confonds toujours ces deux personnes. *I always get those two people mixed up. I always mistake one for the other.*
Confondre des noms. *To confuse names. To get names confused.*
Il est confus. *He's baffled.*
Il en est confus. *He's very sorry (about it).*
se confondre *to become confused.*
Se confondre en excuses. *To apologize profusely.*
confondu *adj. confused, disconcerted, abashed.*
Je suis confondu de votre bonté. *I'm overwhelmed by your kindness. I don't know what to say (how to express my gratitude).*
Il a été confondu. *He was confused (disconcerted, abashed).*
conforme *adj. according, consistent.*

Une copie conforme à l'original. *A copy corresponding to the original.*
Leur goûts sont conformes aux nôtres. *Their tastes are similar to (agree with) ours.*
Leurs actions ne sont pas conformes à leurs principes. *Their actions (acts) aren't in conformity with their principles.*
conformément *in accordance with, in conformity with, in compliance with.*
Conformément à vos ordres. *In accordance with your instructions ("orders").*
conformer *to form, shape.*
Conformer sa conduite à ses paroles. *To suit his actions to his words.*
se conformer *to comply with.*
Il s'est conformé à ses ordres. *He complied with his instructions.*
conformité *f. conformity.*
Ses vues sont en conformité avec les miennes. *His views agree with mine.*
En conformité de (avec). *In accordance with.*
CONFORT *m. comfort.*
Une maison avec confort moderne. *A house with all modern conveniences.*
Le niveau du confort. *The standard of living.*
CONFORTABLE *adj. comfortable.*
Ce fauteuil est très confortable. *This armchair is very comfortable.*
confronter *to confront.*
confus *adj. confused; embarrassed.*
Je suis tout confus. *I'm terribly sorry. I'm very embarrassed.*
Il en est confus. *He's very sorry. He doesn't know how to apologize.*
Il est confus. *He's baffled. He doesn't know how to act (what to do).*
Vous me rendez confus. *You embarrass me.*
Des voix confuses. *Indistinct voices.*
Notions vagues et confuses. *Vague and confused ideas.*
Souvenirs confus. *Blurred memories.*
confusion *f. confusion.*
Tout était en confusion. *Everything was in confusion (in a confused state).*
Mettre tout en confusion. *To upset everything. To put everything in disorder.*
Confusion de noms. *A mistake in names.*
Etre rouge de confusion. *To blush with embarrassment.*
congé *m. leave; discharge.*
Il a obtenu un congé de huit jours. *He received (got) a week's vacation. He got a week off.*
On a donné congé au locataire. *The tenant was given notice.*
Nous avons pris congé d'eux. *We took leave of them.*
congédier *to dismiss, fire.*
Ils ont congédié la bonne. *They dismissed the maid.*
conglomération *f. conglomeration.*
congrès *m. congress, assembly, conference.*
Le congrès international des étudiants. *International Students Congress.*
conjugaison *f. conjugation.*
conjuguer *to unite; conjugate.*
conjurer *to plot; entreat; ward off.*
Ils ont conjuré sa défaite. *They plotted his defeat.*
Je vous en conjure. *I entreat (implore) you.*
Il a conjuré la ruine de son ami. *He prevented (averted, staved off) his friend's ruin.*
CONNAISSANCE *f. acquaintance; knowledge.*

Amenez vos amis et connaissances. *Bring your friends and acquaintances.*
Nous sommes en pays de connaissance. *We are with old friends.*
Enchanté de faire votre connaissance. *Glad (happy) to know you.*
Je suis très content d'avoir fait leur connaissance. *I'm very glad to have met them.*
En connaissance de cause. *With full knowledge of the facts. On good grounds.*
A ma connaissance, l'affaire n'est pas encore conclue. *To my knowledge (as far as I know), the matter isn't settled yet.*
Il n'en a pas la moindre connaissance. *He doesn't know (understand) the least thing about it. He doesn't have the slightest knowledge of the subject.*
Sans connaissance. *Unconscious.*
connaisseur *m. expert, connoisseur.*
CONNAÎTRE *to know.*
Je ne veux pas les connaître. *I don't want to meet them (to be acquainted with them).*
Je connais bien son caractère. *I know (understand) his character very well.*
Il s'y connait. *He has great experience in the matter.*
Il s'est fait connaître. 1. *He introduced himself.* 2. *He made himself known. He made a name for himself.*
Il en connaît bien d'autres. *He has many more tricks up his sleeve.*
se connaître en. *To be a connoisseur of, an expert at.*
connexion *f. connection.*
connivence *f. connivance.*
Agir de connivence avec quelqu'un. *To act in complicity with someone.*
conquérir *to conquer, capture.*
Il a conquis l'estime de ses chefs. *He won the esteem of his superiors.*
conquête *f. conquest.*
Vous avez fait sa conquête. *You've won his (her) heart.*
consacrer *to dedicate, devote.*
Je ne puis vous consacrer que quelques minutes. *I can spare you only a few minutes.*
conscience *f. conscience.*
Une conscience droite. *A clear conscience.*
Cas de conscience. *Point of conscience.*
C'est une affaire à votre conscience. *Follow your conscience.*
Par acquit de conscience. *For conscience' sake. To salve one's conscience.*
Cela lui pèse sur la conscience. *It's weighing on his conscience.*
Il travaille avec conscience. *He works conscientiously.*
Il a conscience de ses erreurs. *He's aware of his errors (mistakes).*
consciencieux (consciencieuse *f.*) *adj. conscientious.*
conscient *adj. conscious.*
Je suis conscient de la gravité de la situation. *I'm aware (conscious) of the gravity of the situation.*
consécutif (consécutive *f.*) *adj. consecutive.*
CONSEIL *m. advice, counsel; council.*
Donnez-moi un conseil. *Give me your advice.*
Je vais prendre conseil de mon avocat. *I'm going to ask the advice of my lawyer.*
Je viens sur le conseil de . . . *I've come at the advice of . . .*
Le conseil municipal. *The city council.*

La nuit porte conseil. *Sleep on it. ("Night brings counsel.")*

Passer en conseil de guerre. *To be court-martialed.*

conseiller m. *counselor, adviser.*

conseiller *to advise.*

Que me conseillez-vous de faire? *What do you advise me to do?*

consentement m. *consent, assent.*

Je vous donne mon consentement. *You have my consent. I give you my consent.*

consentir *to consent, agree.*

Il a consenti à venir. *He agreed to come.*

CONSÉQUENCE f. *consequence, result.*

Les conséquences se feront sentir sous peu. *The consequences will soon become apparent (make themselves felt).*

C'est une affaire sans conséquence. *It's an unimportant matter.*

En conséquence. *Consequently. As a result.*

conséquent adj. *consistent.*

Il n'est pas conséquent avec lui-même. *He's not consistent.*

Par conséquent. *Consequently. As a result.*

conservateur m. *keeper, guardian, commissioner.*

Conservateur d'un musée. *Curator of a museum.*

conservateur (conservatrice f.) adj. *conservative.*

conservation f. *conservation, preservation.*

Instinct de la conservation. *Instinct of self-preservation.*

conservatoire m. *conservatory.*

conserve f. *preserves.*

Boîtes de conserve. *(Tin) cans.*

Mettre en conserve. *To can.*

conserver *to preserve, keep, maintain, save (tooth).*

Conservez-le avec soin. *Take good care of it.*

Il a conservé son sang-froid. *He kept his head. He didn't lose his head.*

se conserver *to keep.*

Articles qui ne se conservent pas. *Perishable goods. ("Articles that don't keep.")*

CONSIDÉRABLE adj. *considerable.*

Une quantité considérable. *A considerable quantity.*

Elle m'a rendu un service considérable. *She did me a great favor.*

CONSIDÉRATION f. *consideration.*

Il n'a de considération pour personne. *He has no consideration for anyone.*

Je le prendrai en considération. *I'll take it into consideration.*

Agréez, Monsieur, l'assurance de ma parfaite considération. *Very truly yours (in a letter).*

CONSIDÉRER *to consider.*

Ce n'est pas à considérer. *It's not to be thought of. It's not even to be considered.*

Il faut considérer que . . . *It must be borne in mind that . . .*

Il est très considéré dans notre milieu. *He is highly thought of in our circle.*

Nous sommes considérés responsables. *We are held liable (considered responsible).*

consignation f. *consignment; deposit.*

CONSIGNE f. *orders, instructions; regulations; baggage room, check room.*

Il a manqué à la consigne. *He disobeyed orders.*

Je ne connais que la consigne. *Orders are orders. ("I don't know anything but the orders.")*

Etre de consigne. *To be on duty.*

Nous avons mis les bagages à la consigne. *We left our baggage in the check room.*

consigner *to deposit; register.*

Consigner ses bagages. *To leave one's luggage*

in the check room.

consistance f. *consistency.*

CONSISTER *to consist of.*

En quoi cela consiste-t-il? *What does it (this) consist of?*

consolation f. *consolation.*

consoler *to console, comfort.*

se consoler *to be consoled.*

Consolez-vous! *Cheer up!*

consolider *to consolidate, strengthen.*

consommateur m. *consumer.*

consommation f. *consummation; consumption; drinks.*

Payer pour les consommations. *To pay for the drinks.*

consommer *to consume, use up.*

consonne f. *consonant.*

conspirateur m. (conspiratrice f.) *conspirator.*

conspiration f. *conspiracy.*

conspirer *to conspire, plot.*

CONSTAMMENT *constantly.*

Ils se disputent constamment. *They're constantly (continually) arguing.*

constance f. *constancy, persistence.*

constant adj. *constant.*

constatation f. *establishment, verification.*

constater *to state; ascertain; verify.*

Constater un fait. *To establish a fact.*

Il constata que tout marchait mal. *He noticed that things were going badly.*

Ils étaient contents de constater de pareils progrès. *They were glad (happy) to see such rapid progress.*

Vous pouvez constater! *You can see for yourself!*

consterné adj. *astonished, dismayed, appalled.*

Il le regardait d'un air consterné. *He looked at him with an air of amazement.*

consterner *to astonish.*

Nous en fûmes consternés. *We were appalled by it (staggered by it, dismayed at it).*

constituer *to constitute, form.*

Ils constituent une société littéraire. *They're forming a literary society.*

constitution f. *constitution.*

Avoir une bonne constitution. *To have a good constitution.*

constitutionnel (constitutionnelle f.) adj. *constitutional.*

CONSTRUCTION f. *building, structure; construction.*

CONSTRUIRE *to build.*

consul m. *consul.*

consulat m. *consulate.*

consultation f. *consultation.*

Heures de consultation. *Consulting hours (at a doctor's office). Doctor's hours.*

CONSULTER *to consult.*

Il faut consulter un médecin. *You'd better (we'd better) consult a doctor.*

Consulter un dictionnaire. *To consult a dictionary.*

se consulter *to consult one another; be consulted.*

Ils se consultent. *They're deliberating. They're putting their heads together.*

consumer *to consume.*

L'incendie a tout consumé. *The fire destroyed everything.*

CONTACT m. *contact, touch.*

Il est entré en contact avec lui. *He was (got) in contact (came into contact) with him.*

J'évite tout contact avec eux. *I'm avoiding all contact with them.*

Mettre le contact. *To turn (switch) on (the light, etc.).*

Couper le contact. *To turn (switch) off.*

contagieux (contagieuse f.) adj. *contagious.*

contagion f. *contagion.*

conte m. *story, tale.*

Un conte de fées. *A fairy tale.*

contemplation f. *contemplation; meditation.*

contempler *to contemplate, ponder, look intently at.*

contemporain adj. *contemporary.*

contenance f. *countenance; capacity, extent.*

Faire bonne contenance. *To keep one's countenance. To put a good face on a bad matter. To make the best of a bad bargain. To keep smiling.*

Perdre contenance. *To be put out of countenance. To become embarrassed (flustered).*

Faire perdre contenance à quelqu'un. *To stare someone out of countenance. To embarrass someone.*

Quelle est la contenance de ce réservoir? *What's the capacity of this reservoir (tank)?*

CONTENIR *to contain.*

Que contient ce paquet? *What does this package contain?*

Ce rapport contient beaucoup d'erreurs. *This report has many mistakes in it.*

se contenir *to contain oneself, control oneself.*

Il n'a pu se contenir. *He couldn't control himself.*

content m. *sufficiency, enough of.*

Manger tout son content. *To eat one's fill.*

Il en a son content. *He's gotten enough of it. That's enough for him. He has had his fill.*

CONTENT adj. *glad, happy, satisfied, content.*

Je suis content de vous voir. *(I'm) Glad to see you.*

Etes-vous content du résultat de votre travail? *Are you pleased (satisfied) with the result of your work?*

contentement m. *contentment.*

SE CONTENTER *to be content with, satisfied with.*

J'ai dû me contenter de cela. *I had to be content (satisfied) with that. I had to content myself with that.*

Il sait se contenter de peu. *He's satisfied with little.*

CONTENU m. *contents.*

Le contenu d'une lettre. *The contents of a letter.*

Le contenu de ce paquet paraît être avarié. *The contents of this package seem damaged.*

conter *to tell, relate.*

contestation f. *dispute.*

contester *to contest, dispute.*

Je ne conteste pas ce fait. *I'm not disputing the fact.*

continent m. *continent.*

contingent m. *contingent, quota.*

CONTINU adj. *continuous.*

Une ligne continue. *A continuous (unbroken) line.*

Est-ce que le courant est alternatif ou continu? *Is the current alternating or direct?*

continuation f. *continuation.*

CONTINUEL (continuelle f.) adj. *continual.*

Un bruit continuel. *A continual noise. A noise that doesn't stop.*

continuellement *continually.*

CONTINUER *to continue.*

Continuez votre récit. *Go on with your story.*

Cela continuera longtemps. *It will last (for) a long time.*

La neige continue de (à) tomber. *It's still snowing. It keeps on snowing. The snow's still falling.*

contour *m. contour, outline.*

contourner *to go around.*

Contourner la loi. *To get around (evade) the law.*

contracter *to contract.*

Contracter une assurance. *To take out an insurance policy.*

Contracter une habitude. *To acquire a habit.*

contraction *f. contraction.*

contradiction *f. contradiction.*

Il a l'esprit de contradiction. *He's very contrary. He contradicts everything you say.*

contradictoire *adj. contradictory, opposing.*

contraindre *to compel, force.*

Il fut contraint d'obéir. *He was forced to obey.*

contrainte *f. restraint; coercion.*

Parler sans contrainte. *To speak without restraint. To speak frankly.*

CONTRAIRE *adj. opposite.*

Il est d'un avis contraire. *He's of the opposite opinion.*

Contraire à la raison. *Against all common sense.*

Sauf avis contraire. *Unless advised to the contrary.*

Au contraire. *On the contrary.*

Au contraire de. *Contrary to.*

Le lait lui est contraire. *Milk disagrees with him.*

CONTRAIREMENT *contrary; on the contrary.*

Contrairement à ce que je pensais. *Contrary to what I thought.*

contrariant *adj. trying; annoying.*

Comme c'est contrariant! *What a nuisance! How annoying!*

contrarié *adj. annoyed, upset.*

contrarier *to oppose; provoke.*

Pourquoi toujours le contrarier? *Why do you always oppose (provoke, cross) him?*

Contrarier les desseins de quelqu'un. *To interfere with someone's schemes. To thwart someone's plans.*

contrariété *f. annoyance, vexation.*

Quelle contrariété! *What a nuisance! How annoying!*

Eptouver une vive contrariété. *To be very much (highly) annoyed.*

contraste *m. contrast.*

contraster *to contrast.*

contrat *m. contract.*

Rupture de contrat. *Breach of contract.*

contravention *f. misdemeanor, police offense.*

CONTRE *against.*

Ils s'allièrent contre l'ennemi. *They made an alliance (united) against the enemy.*

Il dressa une échelle contre le mur. *He placed a ladder against the wall.*

Le pour et le contre de cette question. *The pros and cons of this question.*

Il y a du pour et du contre. *There's something to be said on both sides.*

Il se tenait tout contre lui. *He was standing very near him.*

S'assurer contre l'incendie. *To insure against fire.*

Envers et contre tous. *Against all comers.*

Il le fit à contre-coeur. *He did it reluctantly (unwillingly).*

Contre toute attente. *Contrary to all expectation.*

Livraison contre remboursement. *Cash on delivery.*

Par contre. *On the other hand.*

contrebande *f. contraband, smuggling.*

contrebandier *m. smuggler.*

contredire *to contradict.*

contrée *f. region.*

contrefaçon *f. counterfeiting.*

contrefaire *to counterfeit; imitate.*

contre-ordre *m. counter-order, countermanding.*

Sauf contre-ordre. *Unless I hear to the contrary.*

contresigner *to countersign.*

contretemps *m. wrong time; piece of bad luck.*

A contretemps. *At the wrong time.*

C'est arrivé à contretemps. *It happened at a bad moment.*

Un fâcheux contretemps. *An annoying occurrence.*

contrevenir *to contravene.*

CONTRIBUER *to contribute.*

Je contribuerai à la dépense. *I'll contribute toward the expenses.*

contribution *f. contribution, tax.*

Contributions directes. *Direct taxation.*

contrit *adj. contrite, penitent.*

D'un air contrit. *Penitently. In a contrite spirit.*

CONTRÔLE *m. control.*

Il a perdu tout contrôle sur lui-même. *He lost his self-control.*

Contrôle postal. *Postal censorship.*

contrôler *to control; check; punch (tickets).*

se contrôler *to control oneself.*

contrôleur *m. inspector; conductor (of a trolley, train, etc.).*

Contrôleur des contributions. *Inspector of taxes.*

CONVAINCRE *to convince.*

J'en suis convaincu. *I'm sure of it. I'm convinced of it.*

convaincu *adj. convinced, full of conviction, earnest.*

Parler d'un ton convaincu. *To speak with conviction.*

convalescence *f. convalescence.*

convalescent (convalescente *f.*) *noun and adj. convalescent.*

CONVENABLE *adj. suitable, becoming; decent, proper.*

Ce n'est pas très convenable. *That's not nice (proper).*

Vous devriez choisir un moment plus convenable pour y aller. *You should find a more suitable time to go there.*

Croyez-vous qu'il soit convenable que j'y aille? *Do you think it's all right (proper) for me to go there?*

Je n'ai rien de convenable à me mettre. *I haven't anything decent to put on.*

convenablement *suitably, properly, fitly.*

Faites-le convenablement. *Do it right. Do it well.*

convenance *f. suitability, fitness, convenience; decency.*

Ces conditions sont-elles à votre convenance? *Are these terms acceptable to you?*

C'était un mariage de convenance. *It was a marriage of convenience.*

CONVENIR *to suit, fit; be right, proper, agree, admit.*

Cet emploi m'aurait convenu. *This job (position) would have suited me (been just right for me).*

Il ne vous convient pas de . . . *It's not advisable (proper, suitable) for you to . . .*

Si cela vous convient. *If it's convenient for you. If it suits your convenience. If it's agreeable to you.*

Il convient de ne pas en parler. *It's not proper (right) to speak about it.*

Je conviens que j'ai eu tort. *I admit that I was wrong.*

A l'heure convenue. *At the hour agreed (fixed, set) upon.*

C'est convenu. *It's agreed. Settled.*

Convenir (à). *To suit, be suitable.*

convention *f. convention, agreement; standard.*

La convention de Genève. *The Geneva Convention.*

Les conventions sociales. *The social conventions.*

conventionnel (conventionnelle *f.*) *adj. conventional.*

conversation *f. conversation.*

Lier conversation avec quelqu'un. *To enter (get) into a conversation with someone.*

Faire tous les frais de la conversation. *To do all the talking.*

converser *to converse, talk with.*

conversion *f. conversion.*

convertir *to convert; turn into.*

se convertir *to become converted, become a convert.*

conviction *f. conviction.*

Une conviction inébranlable. *A firm (unshakable) conviction.*

Pièce de conviction. *Piece of evidence.*

convier *to invite.*

convive *m. and f. guest (at the table).*

convocation *f. convocation, convening.*

convoi *m. convoy.*

convoiter *to covet, desire.*

convoitise *f. covetousness.*

convoquer *to summon, call together.*

Avez-vous été convoqué à la réunion? *Were you asked to the meeting?*

convulsion *f. convulsion.*

coopération *f. cooperation.*

coopérer *to cooperate.*

coordination *f. coordination.*

coordonner *to coordinate, arrange.*

copie *f. copy.*

copier *to copy.*

copieux (copieuse *f.*) *adj. copious.*

coq *m. rooster.*

Fier comme un coq. *Proud as a peacock.*

coque *f. shell.*

Oeufs à la coque. *Soft-boiled eggs.*

coquet (coquette *f.*) *adj. coquettish; elegant, smart, stylish; dainty.*

coquette *f. coquette, flirt.*

coquetterie *f. coquetry, coquettishness; smartness, stylishness.*

coquillage *m. shellfish; shell.*

coquille *f. shell.*

corbeau *m.* (corbeaux *pl.*) *crow.*

corbeille *f. basket.*

Corbeille à papier. *Wastepaper basket.*

Corbeille à pain. *Bread-basket.*

Corbeille à ouvrage. *Work-basket.*

corbillard *m. hearse.*

corde *f. cord, rope.*

Corde à linge. *Clothesline.*

Corde à sauter. *Skipping rope.*

Instrument à cordes. *Stringed instrument.*

Etre au bout de sa corde. *To be at the end of one's rope.*

Usé jusqu'à la corde. *Threadbare.*

cordial (cordiaux pl.) *adj. cordial.*
　Un accueil cordial. *A hearty welcome.*
cordialement *cordially.*
　Cordialement à vous. *Sincerely yours.*
cordon *m. cord, string, band; ribbon.*
　Cordon de sonnette. *Bellrope.*
　Cordon bleu. *First-rate cook (used only of a woman).*
　Tenir les cordons de la bourse. *To hold the purse strings.*
　Cordon, s'il vous plaît! *Door, please! (Said to the concierge when you want the door opened late at night.)*
cordonnier *m. shoemaker.*
corne *f. horn.*
　Bêtes à cornes. *Horned beasts.*
　Rentrer les cornes. *To draw in one's horns.*
cornet *m. small horn, trumpet; telephone receiver.*
　Cornet de téléphone. *Telephone receiver.*
corporel (corporelle *f.*) *adj. corporal.*
　Châtiment corporel. *Corporal punishment.*
CORPS *m. body.*
　Le corps humain. *The human body.*
　Garde du corps. *Bodyguard.*
　Corps liquide. *Liquid body.*
　Lutter corps à corps avec quelqu'un. *To come to grips with someone. ("To fight body to body.")*
　Il a le diable au corps. *He's very wild. He's full of devilment. Nothing can stop him. ("He has the devil in his body.")*
　Prendre corps. *To assume shape.*
　Se donner corps et âme à quelque chose. *To be entirely devoted to something.*
corpulence *f. corpulence, stoutness.*
correct *adj. correct, exact.*
　Est-ce que c'est correct? *Is that correct?*
　Votre réponse est correcte. *Your answer is right.*
correction *f. correction, accuracy.*
　Avez-vous fait toutes les corrections nécessaires? *Did you make (have you made) all the necessary corrections?*
　Maison de correction. *Reformatory. House of Correction.*
correspondance *f. correspondence; connection, change (subway).*
　Il a ouvert sa correspondance. *He opened his mail.*
　Prendre la correspondance. *To change trains (subway).*
correspondant *m. correspondent; party (telephone).*
　Il est le correspondant étranger de ce journal. *He's the foreign correspondent of this paper.*
correspondre *to correspond, agree.*
　Je corresponds avec elle. *I correspond with her. I write to her.*
　La théorie ne correspond pas aux faits. *The theory doesn't square with the facts.*
corridor *m. corridor, passage.*
corriger *to correct.*
corroborer *to corroborate, confirm.*
corrompre *to corrupt, deprave; bribe.*
　Corrompre un témoin. *To bribe a witness.*
corrompu *adj. corrupt, depraved.*
corruption *f. corruption.*
corsage *m. bodice, body (of a dress).*
corset *m. corset.*
cortège *m. procession.*
　Cortège nuptial. *Wedding procession.*
　Cortège funèbre. *Funeral procession.*
corvée *f. forced labor; drudgery.*
　Etre de corvée. *To be on duty.*

Quelle corvée! *How tiresome! What a nuisance!*
cosmopolite *m. and f. noun and adj. cosmopolitan.*
costaud (fam.) *noun (m.) and adj. strong, strapping fellow; husky fellow.*
costume *m. suit, costume, outfit.*
　Costume de ski. *Ski outfit, ski clothes.*
cote *f. quota, quotation.*
côte *f. rib; shore.*
　Ou lui compterait les côtes, il est tellement maigre. *He's so thin you can count the bones ("the ribs").*
　Ils se tenaient côte à côte. *They were standing side by side.*
　Nous nous tenions les côtes de rire. *We split our sides laughing.*
　Le bateau a été jeté à la côte par la tempête. *The boat was cast ashore by the storm.*
　Côte d'Azur. *French Riviera.*
côté *m. side, direction.*
　C'est à côté. *It's nearby, next door.*
　C'est son côté faible. *That's his weak spot.*
　Prendre les choses par le bon côté. *To look on the bright side of things.*
　Il a mis de l'argent de côté. *He has put some money aside.*
　Ils s'en allèrent chacun de son côté. *Each went his way.*
　Répondre à côté. *To miss the point (in an answer). To give an answer that is beside the point.*
　De ce côté-ci. *On this side, in this direction.*
　De côté. *On the side (seats).*
　De l'autre côté de. *On the other side of.*
　De quel côté? *In which direction?*
　Du côté de la Sorbonne. *Toward the Sorbonne.*
côtelette *f. chop.*
cotisation *f. contribution; dues.*
se cotiser *to contribute; pay dues.*
coton *m. cotton.*
　Des bas de coton. *Cotton stockings.*
　Du coton hydrophile. *Absorbent cotton.*
　Filer un mauvais coton. *To be in a bad way.*
côtoyer *to border on, keep close to.*
COU *m. neck.*
　L'enfant se jeta au cou de sa mère. *The child hugged its mother ("threw himself on his mother's neck").*
　Prendre ses jambes à son cou. *To take to one's heels.*
　Etre dans les dettes jusqu'au cou. *To be up to one's ears in debt.*
couchage *m. bedding.*
　Le sac de couchage. *Sleeping bag.*
couche *f. bed; couch.*
　Couche de houille. *Coal-bed.*
coucher *to sleep.*
　On coucha à la belle étoile. *We slept in the open air.*
se coucher *to go to bed.*
　Il est allé se coucher tard. *He went to bed late.*
　Couche-toi. *Go to bed.*
couchette *f. berth.*
coude *m. elbow.*
　Coude à coude. *Side by side.*
　Jouer des coudes à travers la foule. *To shoulder (elbow) one's way through the crowd.*
coudoyer *to elbow, rub shoulders with.*
coudre *to sew.*
　Coudre un bouton. *To sew a button on.*
　Machine à coudre. *Sewing machine.*
coulant *adj. flowing.*
　Noeud coulant. *Slip knot.*
　Il est coulant en affaires. *He's very accommo-*

dating. He's easy to do business with.
couler *to flow; sink.*
　Faites couler l'eau. *Let the water run.*
　Le navire a coulé. *The ship sank.*
couleur *f. color.*
　Il m'en a fait voir de toutes les couleurs (fam.). *He gave me plenty of trouble.*
　Le film en couleurs. *Color film.*
couleuvre *f. garter snake.*
coulisse *f. groove; wings (theatre).*
　Porte à coulisse. *Sliding door.*
　Fenêtre à coulisse. *Sliding window.*
　Les coulisses. *The wings (in a theatre).*
　Savoir ce qui se passe dans les coulisses. *To know what's happening behind the scenes.*
couloir *m. corridor, passageway.*
COUP *m. blow; stroke.*
　Il lui a donné un coup. *He struck him.*
　Un coup de tonnerre. *A thunderclap.*
　Un coup de soleil. *Sunstroke.*
　Ce fut un coup dur pour sa famille. *It was a heavy blow to his family.*
　Donner un coup de main. *To lend (give) someone a hand. To help someone out.*
　Un coup de tête. *An impulsive act. Something done on the spur of the moment.*
　Faire quelque chose par un coup de tête. *To act on impulse (impulsively).*
　Un sale coup. *A dirty trick.*
　Tenir le coup. *To withstand the blow. To hold out.*
　Coup de téléphone. *Telephone call.*
　Il fut tué sur le coup. *He was killed on the spot.*
　Tout à coup. *All of a sudden. Suddenly. All at once.*
　Le coup de coude. *Nudge.*
　Le coup d'envoi. *Kickoff (soccer).*
　Le coup de pied. *Kick.*
　Le coup de sifflet. *Whistle (-blast).*
　Le coup-franc. *Free kick (soccer).*
　Un coup de fil. *A telephone call.*
　Un coup d'oeil. *A glance.*
　Un coup de peigne. *A quick hair-combing.*
　Les trois coups. *The three knocks (theatre).*
coupable *m. a guilty person.*
coupable *adj. guilty.*
coupe *f. cup; cutting.*
　La coupe de cheveux. *Haircut.*
coupe-papier *m. paper knife.*
couper *to cut.*
　Il lui coupa la parole. *He interrupted him.*
　Ne coupez pas. *Hold the wire. Don't hang up.*
se couper *to cut oneself.*
　Il s'est coupé le doigt. *He cut his finger.*
　Se faire couper les cheveux. *To have one's hair cut, have a haircut.*
couple *m. pair, couple.*
coupon *m. cutting; coupon.*
　Coupon de robe. *Dress length.*
　Coupon de rationnement. *Rationing stamp (coupon).*
coupure *f. cut, gash; small banknote.*
　Coupure de journal. *Newspaper clipping.*
　Donnez-moi quelques petites coupures, s'il vous plaît. *Give me some small bills, please.*
COUR *f. court; courtship; yard.*
　Cour de justice. *Court of justice.*
　Faire la cour à une jeune fille. *To court a girl.*
　Cour d'un immeuble. *Courtyard (of a building).*
COURAGE *m. courage.*
　Perdre courage. *To lose heart.*
　Prendre son courage à deux mains. *To pluck*

up courage. ("To take one's courage into one's hands").

Du courage! *Cheer up!*

Le courage lui manqua. *His courage failed him.*

courageux (courageuse f.) adj. courageous.

COURAMMENT easily, fluently; generally.

Il parle anglais couramment. *He speaks English fluently.*

Ce mot s'emploie couramment. *This word is in current use.*

COURANT noun (m.) and adj. current; running.

Eau courante. *Running water.*

Le courant d'une rivière. *The current of a river.*

La monnaie courante. *Legal tender.*

J'ai reçu votre lettre du vingt courant. *I received your letter of the 20th (of this month).*

Donnez-moi vos prix courants. *What are your prices? May I see your list of prices?*

Courant électrique. *Electric current.*

Il y a un courant d'air ici. *There's a draft here.*

Dans le courant de la semaine. *Some day this week.*

Je ne suis au courant de rien. *I don't know anything about it.*

Tenez-moi au courant. *Keep me informed.*

courbature f. stiffness, tiredness.

Avoir une courbature. *To be stiff (aching) all over.*

courbaturer to tire oneself out.

Je me sens tout courbaturé. *I feel stiff all over. My whole body aches.*

courbe f. curve.

courber to bend, curve.

se courber to bend, stoop.

COURIR to run.

Courez vite après lui. *Run after him quickly.*

Vous courez un grand risque. *You're running a great risk.*

Par le temps qui court. (Par les temps qui courent.) *Nowadays. As things are at present.*

Faire courir un bruit. *To spread a rumor.*

couronne f. wreath. crown.

couronnement m. crowning.

couronner to crown.

COURRIER m. mail; column, report (newspaper, magazine).

Y a-t-il du courrier pour moi? *Is there any mail for me?*

Faites-le-moi savoir par retour du courrier. *Let me know by return mail.*

courroie f. strap.

courroucé adj. angry.

courroux m. anger, wrath.

Etre en courroux. *To be angry.*

COURS m. course; flow; currency; rate, price.

Cours du soir. *Evening courses.*

En cours de route. *While traveling.*

Les cours d'eau navigables. *Navigable streams.*

Le cours du marché. *The market prices.*

Cette pièce n'a pas cours. *This coin is not legal (is no longer current).*

Il donne libre cours à sa joie. *His happiness is unrestrained.*

Le cours du change. *Rate of exchange.*

course f. run; race; course.

Course de chevaux. *Horse race.*

Faire des courses. *To go out shopping.*

Garçon de courses. *Errand boy.*

COURT adj. short.

Une courte phrase. *A short sentence.*

Elle a la vue courte. *She's nearsighted (shortsighted).*

Tout court. *That's all. Just that.*

De courte durée. *Short-lived.*

Rester court. *To stop short.*

Couper court. *To put an end to. To cut short.*

Elle est toujours à court d'argent. *She's always short of money.*

courtier m. broker.

courtiser to court.

courtois adj. courteous.

courtoisie f. courtesy, politeness.

COUSIN m. (cousine f.) cousin.

Cousin germain. *First cousin.*

Cousins au second degré. *Second cousins.*

coussin m. cushion.

COÛT m. cost.

Le coût de la vie. *The cost of living.*

COUTEAU m. knife.

COÛTER to cost.

Ceci coûte dix francs. *This costs ten francs.*

Il me le faut, coûte que coûte. *I must have it at any cost.*

Cela m'a coûté les yeux de la tête. *That cost me a mint of money (a small fortune). ("That cost me the eyes of the head.")*

coûteux (coûteuse f.) adj. costly, expensive.

Peu coûteux. *Inexpensive.*

COUTUME f. custom, habit.

Cette coutume existe encore. *This custom still exists.*

J'ai coutume de lire avant d'aller me coucher. *I'm in the habit of reading before going to bed.*

Comme de coutume. *As usual.*

coutumier (coutumière f.) adj. in the habit of; customary.

couture f. sewing, needlework.

Nous avons été battus à plate couture. *We were completely beaten.*

couturier m. (couturière f.) dressmaker.

couvent m. convent.

couver to hatch (eggs); brood.

couvercle m. lid, cover.

couvert m. cover; things on the table for a meal.

Sous le couvert de la nuit. *Under cover of night.*

Mettez le couvert pour le dîner. *Set the dinner table.*

Oter le couvert. *To clear the table.*

couverture f. cover; covering; blanket.

couvre-lit m. bedspread.

COUVRIR to cover.

Couvrez cette casserole. *Cover this pot.*

Elle a couvert ses plans. *She concealed (hid) her plans.*

Le bruit couvrait ma voix. *The noise drowned out my words.*

se couvrir to cover oneself; to be covered.

Couvrez-vous bien. *Dress yourself warmly.*

Se couvrir le visage. *To cover (hide) one's face.*

crabe m. crab.

crachat m. spittle.

cracher to spit.

Défense de cracher. *No spitting.*

C'est son père tout craché (fam.). *He's the spitting image of his father.*

craie f. chalk.

CRAINDRE to fear.

Il ne craint personne. *He's not afraid of anyone.*

Il n'y a rien à craindre. *There is nothing to be afraid of (to fear).*

Je ne crains pas de le dire. *I'm not afraid to say so.*

CRAINTE f. fear, dread.

Soyez sans crainte. *Have no fear.*

Surveillez-le de crainte qu'il ne s'en aille. *Watch him lest he leave.*

craintif (craintive f.) adj. timid, apprehensive.

cramoisi adj. crimson.

crampe f. cramp.

se cramponner to hold on to, clutch.

Elle se cramponnait à sa mère. *She held on to her mother.*

cran m. notch; spirit.

Cran de sûreté. *Safety-notch.*

Il ne le lâche pas d'un cran (fam.). *He won't leave him for a moment.*

Il a du cran. *He has a lot of self-assurance.*

Il manque de cran. *He has no spirit.*

crâne m. skull, cranium.

Il avait le crâne fracassé. *He had a fractured skull.*

crapeau m. toad.

craquer to crack.

Faire craquer les doigts. *To crack one's fingers.*

CRAVATE f. tie.

Avez-vous une cravate pour aller avec ce costume? *Do you have a tie to go with this suit?*

Rajustez votre cravate. *Fix your tie.*

CRAYON m. pencil.

Vous pouvez écrire au crayon ou à l'encre. *You can write in pencil or ink.*

créance f. trust, belief; credit.

Lettres de créance. *Credentials.*

créancier m. creditor.

créateur (créatrice f.) noun and adj. creator; creative.

Le Créateur. *The Creator. God.*

Créateur d'un article. *Inventor of an article.*

création f. creation.

créature f. creature.

C'est une bonne créature. *He's (she's) a nice person.*

crèche f. crib; day nursery.

crédit m. credit.

A crédit. *On credit.*

Il achète à crédit et vend comptant. *He buys on credit and sells for cash.*

créditer to credit.

crédule adj. credulous, gullible.

Ne soyez donc pas aussi crédule. *Don't believe everything you're told.*

crédulité f. credulousness.

CRÉER to create; establish.

Il s'est créé beaucoup d'ennemis. *He made many enemies for himself.*

CRÈME f. cream.

crêpe f. crape; pancake.

crépiter to crackle.

crépuscule m. twilight.

crête f. crest.

creuser to hollow out; dig; to drill (tooth).

Se creuser la tête. *To rack one's brains.*

creux (creuse f.) noun (m.) and adj. hollow.

crevaison f. puncture, flat (tire).

crevasse f. crack, split.

crève-coeur m. bitter disappointment, heartbreak.

crever to burst, break out.

Le torrent a crevé la digue. *The flood burst the dam.*

Le nuage creva. *There was a cloudburst.*

Il en crèvera de dépit (fam.). *He'll be very disappointed. ("He'll burst with spite.")*

Cela crève les yeux. *You can't help noticing it. It stares you in the face.*

Le pneu crevé. *Flat tire.*

crevette *f. shrimp.*
CRI *m. scream.*
  Pousser un cri aigu. *To scream.*
  A grands cris. *With loud cries.*
  Le dernier cri. *The latest style. The latest rage.*
    The last word.
criard *adj. shrill; gaudy.*
cribler *to riddle with bullets.*
CRIER *to cry, scream.*
  Ne criez pas si fort. *Don't shout so loud! Don't*
    yell like that!
  Il cria: "Au feu, au feu." *He cried: "Fire, fire!"*
  Sans crier gare. *Without a word of warning.*
  Il criait à tue-tête. *He cried (out) at the top*
    of his lungs. He screamed (yelled). He
    shouted as loud as possible.
  Crier misère. *To complain of poverty.*
crime *m. crime.*
criminel (criminelle *f.*) *noun and adj. criminal.*
crin *m. horsehair.*
crinière *f. mane (of a horse, lion, etc.).*
crise *f. crisis; fit; attack.*
  Crise politique. *Political crisis.*
  Une crise de nerfs. *A fit of hysterics.*
crisper *to contract, clench.*
cristal *m.* (cristaux *pl.*) *crystal.*
cristalliser *to crystallize.*
critique *m. critic.*
critique *f. criticism.*
critique *adj. critical, decisive.*
  Etre dans une situation critique. *To be in a*
    critical situation.
critiquer *to criticize.*
croc *m. canine tooth.*
crochet *m. hook; crochet.*
crocheter *to crochet.*
crochu *adj. hooked.*
crocodile *m. crocodile.*
CROIRE *to believe.*
  Croire en Dieu. *To believe in God.*
  Je vous crois! *I should say so!*
  C'est à croire. *It's credible. It's believable. It's*
    something you can believe.
  Moi, je ne le crois pas. *I don't think so. I don't*
    believe it.
  Croyez bien. (Croyez-le bien). *Depend on it.*
  Croyez bien que je suis navré. *Believe me,*
    I'm terribly sorry.
  A l'en croire, on pourrait penser qu'il est
    quelqu'un. *To listen to him you would think*
    that he's really somebody.
se croire *to believe oneself, to consider oneself.*
  Il se croyait tout permis. *He thought he could*
    do anything.
  Il se croit (un) malin. *He thinks he's clever*
    (smart).
  Cela se croit aisément. *That's easy to believe.*
croisement *m. crossing.*
  "Croisement dangereux." *"Dangerous cross-*
    roads."
croiser *to cross.*
  Les mots croisés. *Crossword puzzle.*
croisière *f. cruise.*
croissance *f. growth.*
croître *to grow; increase.*
  Mauvaise herbe croît toujours. *Ill weeds grow*
    apace.
CROIX *f. cross.*
croquer *to crunch; sketch.*
croquis *m. sketch.*
crouler *to shake; give way.*
croustillant *adj. crisp.*
croûte *f. crust.*

croyant *adj. believing.*
cru *adj. raw; crude.*
  Légumes crus. *Raw vegetables.*
cruauté *f. cruelty.*
cruche *f. pitcher; jug.*
  Tant va la cruche à l'eau qu'à la fin elle se
    casse. *The pitcher goes so often to the well*
    that at last it breaks.
cruel (cruelle *f.*) *adj. cruel.*
cruellement *cruelly, bitterly.*
crustacés *m. pl. shellfish.*
cube *m. cube.*
cubiste *m. cubist (painting).*
cueillir *to gather, pick.*
cuiller *f.* (also spelled cuillère) *spoon.*
  Cuiller à soupe. *Tablespoon.*
cuillerée *f. spoonful.*
cuir *m. leather.*
  En cuir. *In, of leather.*
CUIRE *to cook.*
  La bonne fait cuire le petit déjeuner dans la
    cuisine. *The maid is cooking breakfast in*
    the kitchen.
  Le pain cuit. *The bread is baking.*
  Les yeux me cuisent. *My eyes are smarting.*
  Il vous en cuira. *You'll smart for it. You'll be*
    sorry for it. You'll suffer for it.
CUISINE *f. kitchen; cuisine.*
  Articles de cuisine. *Cooking utensils.*
  J'adore la cuisine à la française. *I'm fond of*
    (I like) French cooking.
  Ma mère a d'excellentes recettes de cuisine.
    My mother has some excellent recipes.
  Livre de cuisine. *Cook book.*
  Elle fait bien la cuisine. *She is a good cook.*
    She cooks well.
cuisiner *to cook.*
cuisinier *m.* (cuisinière *f.*) *cook.*
cuisinière *f. cooking stove.*
cuisse *f. thigh.*
cuit *adj. cooked.*
  Bien cuit. *Well-cooked, well-done (meat).*
cuivre *m. copper.*
culbute *f. somersault.*
culbuter *to turn a somersault; upset.*
culinaire *adj. culinary.*
culminant *adj. culminating.*
culotte *f. breeches.*
culte *m. worship; cult, creed, religion.*
cultivateur *m. cultivator; farmer.*
cultivé *adj. cultured.*
cultiver *to cultivate.*
culture *f. culture.*
cumulatif (cumulative *f.*) *adj. cumulative.*
cupide *adj. greedy.*
cupidité *f. cupidity, greed.*
cure *f. treatment, cure.*
curé *m. priest.*
cure-dents *m. toothpick.*
curer *to pick, clean.*
  Se curer les ongles. *To clean one's nails.*
curieux (curieuse *f.*) *noun and adj. curious;*
    curious person.
  Un attroupement de curieux. *A crowd of in-*
    terested spectators.
  Il était curieux de le savoir. *He was curious to*
    know it.
  Il a une curieuse façon de parler. *He has a*
    curious way of speaking.
curiosité *f. curiosity.*
  Cette visite inopinée piqua sa curiosité. *That*
    unexpected visit excited his curiosity.
  Le curiosités de la ville. *The sights of the town.*

cuve *f. tank, cistern.*
cuvette *f. washbasin.*
cycle *m. cycle.*
cyclisme *m. cycling.*
  Faire du cyclisme. *To ride a bicycle.*
cycliste *adj. of cycling.*
  La course cycliste. *Bicycle race.*
cygne *m. swan.*
cylindre *m. cylinder.*
cynique *m. and f. noun and adj. cynical, cynic.*

D *The fourth letter of the alphabet.*

d' *See de.*
dada *m. hobby.*
  Chacun a son dada. *Everyone has his fad (pet*
    hobby, pet subject).
daigner *to deign, condescend.*
daim *m. buck; buckskin, suede.*
dame *f. lady.*
  Priez la dame d'entrer. *Ask the lady to come*
    in.
  Elle fait la grande dame. *She puts on airs.*
  Jeu de dames. *Checkers.*
DANGER *m. danger.*
  A l'abri du danger. *Safe.*
  Courir un danger. *To be in danger. To run a*
    risk.
  Pas de danger (fam.)! *No fear! Not very likely!*
dangereux (dangereuse *f.*) *adj. dangerous.*
danois *noun and adj. Danish.*
DANS *in.*
  Mettez-le dans votre poche. *Put it in your*
    pocket.
  Portez ce paquet dans ma chambre, s'il vous
    plaît. *Please take this parcel to my room.*
  Ce n'est pas dans mon pouvoir. *It's not within*
    my power.
  Il est dans son droit. *He's within his rights.*
  Dans l'ensemble. *On the whole. Everything*
    taken together.
  Je reviendrai dans trois jours. *I'll come back*
    in three days.
  Vous les aurez dans la journée. *You'll have them*
    the same day.
danse *f. dance, dancing.*
danser *to dance.*
darder *to dart, shoot forth.*
DATE *f. date.*
  Sa lettre porte la date du cinq juin. *The letter*
    is dated June the fifth.
  Une amitié de vieille date. *A friendship of long*
    standing. An old friendship.
dater *to date.*
  A dater de ce jour. *From today on.*
  Dater de loin. *To be of long standing.*
DAVANTAGE *more, further.*
  Je n'en dis pas davantage. *I'll say no more.*
  Je ne resterai pas davantage. *I won't stay any*
    longer.
  Bien davantage. *Much more.*
DE (d', du, des) *of, from.*
  De jour en jour. *From day to day.*
  Du matin au soir. *From morning till night.*
  De haut en bas. *From top to bottom.*
  De mal en pis. *From bad to worse.*
  Un morceau de pain. *A piece of bread.*
  Ce tableau est de Renoir. *This painting is by*
    Renoir.
  J'ai changé d'avis. *I changed my mind.*
  C'est à vous de jouer. *It's your turn to play.*
  Avez-vous du vin? *Have you any wine?*
dé *m. thimble; dice.*

débâcle f. *downfall, collapse.*
déballer *to unpack.*
débandade f. *disbanding, stampede.*
  A la débandade. *In confusion.*
débarquement m. *landing, disembarkment.*
  Quai de débarquement. *Arrival platform.*
débarquer *to land; unload.*
débarras m. *riddance.*
  Bon débarras! *Good riddance!*
débarrasser *to rid, clear up; clear (a table).*
  J'en suis enfin débarrassé. *At last I'm rid of it.*
  Débarrassez la table. *Clear the table.*
se débarrasser *to get rid of, shake off.*
  Je ne puis me débarrasser de lui. *I can't get rid of him.*
débarrer *to unbar; uncap (lens of camera).*
débat m. *debate.*
débattre *to debate, discuss.*
se débattre *to struggle.*
débit m. *(retail) store.*
  Débit de tabac. *Tobacco store.*
  Débit de vin. *Wine shop.*
débiter *to sell retail; debit.*
  Veuillez en débiter mon compte. *Please charge it to my account.*
déblayer *to clear away.*
déboire m. *disappointment, failure.*
  Avoir des déboires. *To meet with failure.*
  Il a eu des déboires dans la vie. *He's had his disappointments in life.*
déboîter *to dislocate.*
  Il s'est déboîté l'épaule en tombant. *He fell and dislocated his shoulder.*
débonnaire adj. *meek, mild.*
  Il est débonnaire. *He's good-natured.*
débordant adj. *overflowing.*
  Débordant de santé. *Bursting with health.*
  Joie débordante. *Bubbling over with joy.*
débordement m. *overflow, flood.*
déborder *to overflow.*
  Plein à déborder. *Full to overflowing.*
  Il déborde de vie. *He's full of vitality.*
  Je suis débordé de travail. *I'm swamped with work.*
déboucher *to uncork.*
débourser *to pay out (money), spend.*
  Sans rien débourser. *Without spending a penny.*
DEBOUT *upright, standing.*
  Se mettre debout. *To stand up.*
  Allons, debout! *Come on, get up!*
  Il dormait debout. *He couldn't keep his eyes open. He was asleep on his feet.*
  Il n'est pas encore debout. *He's not up yet.*
  Une histoire à dormir debout. *A dull tale.*
  Cela ne tient pas debout. *It's preposterous.*
déboutonner *to unbutton.*
débraillé adj. *untidy, slovenly.*
débrayer *to change gear.*
débris m. pl. *debris.*
  Débris d'un naufrage. *Remains of a wreck.*
débrouillard m. *a resourceful person.*
débrouillard adj. *resourceful.*
se débrouiller *to manage, get along.*
  Je me débrouille tant bien que mal. *I manage (get along) as best I can.*
  Il sait se débrouiller. 1. *He can take care of himself. He can stand on his own two feet.* 2. *He knows his way around. He knows how to get out of difficulties.*
début m. *start, beginning; debut.*
  Il n'est pas à son début. *He's not a beginner. He's no novice.*
  Elle a fait ses débuts au théâtre. *She made her debut on the stage.*
débutant m. *beginner.*
débuter *to begin.*
  Il débute à quatre cents francs par mois. *He's starting at four hundred francs a month.*
décadence f. *decadence, decline.*
décamper *to decamp, make off.*
décapotable f. *convertible (car).*
décédé m. *a deceased person.*
décédé adj. *deceased.*
décéder *to die.*
DÉCEMBRE m. *December.*
décemment *decently.*
décence f. *decency, modesty.*
  Il n'a aucune décence. *He has no modesty.*
décent adj. *decent, modest, proper.*
déception f. *deception, disappointment.*
  Il a éprouvé une cruelle déception. *He met with a sad disappointment.*
décès m. *decease; death.*
décevoir *to deceive, disappoint.*
  Cet aboutissement inattendu l'a déçu. *That unexpected outcome (result) disappointed him.*
déchaînement m. *breaking loose, outburst.*
déchaîner *to unchain, let loose.*
  Il est déchaîné (fam.). *Nothing will stop him.*
décharge f. *unloading; relief; outlet.*
  A la décharge de l'accusé. *In favor of the defendant.*
décharger *to unload; relieve.*
  Décharger sa conscience. *To relieve one's conscience.*
déchéance f. *fall, downfall.*
déchet m. *waste, refuse.*
  Déchets de viande. *Meat scraps.*
déchiffrer *to decipher.*
  Je ne sais pas déchiffrer cette lettre. *I can't read this letter.*
déchiqueter *to cut, tear.*
déchirement m. *tearing.*
  Déchirement de coeur. *Heartbreak.*
déchirer *to tear.*
  Ma jupe est déchirée. *My skirt is torn.*
  Il est déchiré par le remords. *He's torn with remorse.*
déchirure f. *tear, rip.*
déchoir *to fall.*
  Sa popularité déchoit. *His popularity is falling off.*
déchu adj. *fallen.*
décidé adj. *resolute, determined.*
  Chose décidée. *Settled matter.*
  C'est un homme très décidé. *He's very resolute.*
décidément *decidedly.*
  Décidément, je n'ai pas de chance. *I really haven't any luck.*
DÉCIDER *to decide.*
  Voilà qui décide tout! *That settles it!*
  Qu'avez-vous décidé? *What have you decided?*
  Je suis décidé à le faire. *I'm determined to do it.*
SE DÉCIDER *to make up one's mind, resolve, be decided.*
  Il a fini par se décider. *He finally made up his mind.*
  Il est long à se décider. *He is slow in making decisions. It takes him a long time to decide.*
décimal (décimaux pl.) adj. *decimal.*
décisif (decisive f.) adj. *decisive.*
  Au moment décisif. *At the crucial moment.*
  Argument décisif. *Decisive argument.*
décision f. *decision.*

déclamation f. *elocution, oratory.*
  Discours plein de déclamation. *Bombastic speech.*
déclamatoire adj. *declamatory, high-flown.*
déclamer *to declaim, recite.*
déclaration f. *declaration, proclamation.*
  Déclaration de guerre. *Declaration of war.*
  Déclaration en douane. *Customs declaration.*
déclarer *to declare; state.*
  La guerre fut déclarée. *War was declared.*
  Il déclara ses intentions. *He made his intentions known.*
  Avez-vous quelque chose à déclarer? *Have you anything to declare (at the customs)?*
déclenchement m. *starting.*
  Déclenchement d'une attaque. *Launching of an attack.*
déclencher *to start, launch.*
  Déclencher les hostilités. *To open hostilities.*
déclencheur m. *shutter release.*
déclin m. *decline, decay.*
déclinaison f. *declination; declension.*
décliner *to decline, refuse.*
décoiffé adj. *dishevelled (hair).*
décoller *to loosen, disengage.*
  Il ne décolle pas (fam.). *He won't budge from here.*
décolleté adj. *cut low in the neck (of a dress).*
décolorer *to fade, discolor.*
décombres m. pl. *debris, rubbish.*
décommander *to cancel, countermand.*
  Décommander une réunion. *To cancel a meeting.*
décomposer *to decompose, decay.*
décompte m. *deduction.*
  Faire le décompte. *To make a deduction from a sum to be paid.*
déconcerté adj. *disconcerted.*
  Il eut l'air déconcerté. *He looked abashed (put out, baffled).*
déconcerter *to disconcert, baffle.*
  Cette réponse le déconcerta. *The answer upset him (took him aback, put him out of countenance, disconcerted him).*
déconfire *to put out of countenance.*
déconfit adj. *crestfallen.*
déconseiller *to advise against.*
  Je vous déconseille de la faire. *I advise you against doing it.*
décontenancé adj. *confused, abashed.*
décontenancer *to put out of countenance, abash.*
  Il ne s'est pas décontenancé. *He wasn't put out of countenance. He didn't lose his self-assurance.*
déconvenue f. *disappointment.*
  Quelle déconvenue! *What a disappointment!*
décor m. *decorations; show; setting, scenery.*
  Changement de décor. *Change of scenery.*
  Tout cela n'est qu'une façade pour le décor. *All that's nothing but window-dressing. All that's nothing but show.*
décoratif (décorative f.) adj. *decorative, ornamental.*
décoration f. *decoration, medal.*
décorer *to decorate; confer an honor on.*
  Décorer une chambre. *To decorate a room.*
  Il a été décoré. *He received a decoration.*
découper *to slice, carve.*
  Découper de la viande. *To slice meat.*
  Découper un article dans le journal. *To cut out an article in a newspaper.*
  Découper une volaille. *To carve a fowl.*
découragement m. *discouragement.*

décourager *to discourage.*
Il m'a découragé de le faire. *He discouraged me from doing it.*
se décourager *to be disheartened.*
Il n'est pas homme à se décourager. *He's not a man to lose courage easily. He's not the sort of person to get discouraged easily.*
décousu *adj. unsewn; disconnected.*
Une conversation décousue. *A rambling conversation.*
découvert *(m.) noun and adj. uncovered; brought to light.*
Mettre quelque chose à découvert. *To uncover something. To bring something to light.*
Avoir la tête découverte. *To be bareheaded.*
découverte *f. discovery.*
DÉCOUVRIR *to discover.*
décrépit *adj. decrepit.*
décrépitude *f. decrepitude, decay.*
décret *m. decree, order.*
décréter *to decree, issue.*
décrier *to disparage, discredit.*
DÉCRIRE *to describe.*
décrocher *to unhook, take off; lift (telephone receiver).*
décroître *to decrease.*
Aller en décroissant. *To keep decreasing.*
dédaigner *to disdain, scorn.*
dédaigneux (dédaigneuse *f.*) *adj. disdainful.*
Il fait le dédaigneux. *He turns up his nose.*
dédain *m. disdain, scorn.*
Avec dédain. *Scornfully.*
DEDANS *inside, within.*
Au dehors et au dedans. *Outside and inside.*
Je l'ai mis là-dedans. *I put it in there.*
Il a tenté de me mettre dedans. *He tried to get the better of me.*
dédicacer *to dedicate; autograph.*
dédier *to dedicate.*
se dédire *to take back.*
Il s'est dédit de sa promesse. *He broke his promise.*
Je ne puis m'en dédire. *I can't go back on my word.*
dédommagement *m. indemnity, compensation.*
dédommager *to indemnify, compensate.*
déduction *f. deduction, inference.*
Faire une déduction. 1. *To deduct.* 2. *To deduce. To infer.*
Pouvez-vous me faire une déduction? *Can you give me a discount? Can you let me have it a little cheaper.*
déduire *to deduce, infer, deduct.*
défaillance *f. failing, failure.*
Moment de défaillance. *Weak moment.*
Sans défaillance. *Unflinching. Without flinching.*
défaillant *adj. failing, faltering.*
Défaillant de fatigue. *Dropping with fatigue.*
Mémoire défaillante. *Faltering memory.*
défaillir *to become weak, lose strength.*
Ses forces commencent à défaillir. *His strength is beginning to fail.*
Sans défaillir. *Without flinching.*
Elle se sentait prête à défaillir. *She felt about to faint.*
défaire *to defeat; undo.*
L'ennemi a été défait. *The enemy was beaten (defeated).*
Il défait tout ce que je fais. *He undoes all that I do.*
Défaire les bagages. *To unpack the bags.*
se défaire *to get rid of.*

Il faut vous défaire de cette habitude. *You must get out of that habit.*
Il ne veut pas s'en défaire. *He won't part with it.*
Je n'ai pu me défaire de lui. *I couldn't get rid of him.*
défait *adj. undone, loose; discomposed.*
Il avait le visage défait. *His face was drawn.*
Elle avait les cheveux défaits. *Her hair was disheveled.*
défaite *f. defeat, excuse.*
Essuyer une défaite. *To suffer a defeat.*
C'est une mauvaise défaite. *It's a poor excuse.*
DÉFAUT *m. defect, fault; deficiency.*
C'est là son moindre défaut. *That's the least of his (her) faults.*
Sa mémoire lui fait souvent défaut. *His memory often fails him.*
A défaut de mieux. *For want of something better.*
défaveur *f. disfavor, discredit.*
Tomber en défaveur. *To fall out of favor.*
défavorable *adj. unfavorable.*
Des conditions défavorables. *Unfavorable conditions.*
défectueux (défectueuse *f.*) *adj. defective, faulty.*
DÉFENDRE *to defend, protect, forbid.*
Défendre sa patrie. *To defend one's country.*
Il sait défendre son opinion. *He can hold his own.*
C'est défendu. *That's not allowed. That's forbidden.*
Je vous le défends bien. *I forbid you to do it.*
se défendre *to defend oneself.*
Il est homme à se défendre. *He's the kind of man who fights back.*
Ne vous en faites pas pour lui, il saura se défendre. *Don't worry about him; he can take care of himself.*
Il n'a pas pu s'en défendre. *He couldn't resist the temptation.*
DÉFENSE *f. fortification; prohibition.*
Les défenses de la ville. *The fortifications of the city.*
Défense de marcher sur le gazon. *Keep off the grass.*
Une défense absolue. *A strict prohibition.*
Défense de stationner ici. *No loitering. No parking.*
Défense de fumer. *No smoking.*
Défense d'afficher. *Post no bills.*
Défense d'entrer. *No admittance.*
défenseur *m. protector, defender; supporter.*
défensif (défensive *f.*) *adj. defensive.*
défensive *f. defensive.*
Se tenir sur la défensive. *To be on the defensive.*
déférence *f. deference, respect.*
déférer *to submit, refer.*
défi *m. challenge.*
Jeter un défi à quelqu'un. *To challenge someone.*
Relever un défi. *To take up a challenge.*
En défi de quelque chose. *In defiance of something.*
défiance *f. distrust, suspicion.*
déficit *m. deficit.*
défier *to defy.*
se défier *to distrust, be distrustful.*
Se défier de quelqu'un. *To distrust someone.*
défilé *m. defile, gorge, mountain pass; marching past; parade, procession.*
Défilé de mannequins. *Fashion show.*
défiler *to march past, parade.*
Les troupes défilèrent. *The troops paraded.*
défini *adj. definite.*

définir *to define, describe.*
C'est difficile à définer. *It's hard to define.*
définitif (définitive *f.*) *adj. definitive, final.*
Résultat définitif. *Final result.*
En définitive. *In short.*
définition *f. definition.*
Quelle est la définition de ce mot? *What's the definition of this word?*
définitivement *definitely, finally.*
Elle est partie définitivement. *She left for good.*
déformer *to deform, put out of shape.*
défraîchi *adj. soiled, faded.*
Des fleurs défraîchies. *Faded flowers.*
se défraîchir *to fade.*
défunt *m. deceased.*
dégagé *adj. easy, free, offhand, flippant.*
D'un air dégagé. *In an offhand manner.*
dégager *to redeem, release, clear.*
Je l'ai dégagé de sa parole. *I released him from his promise.*
se dégager *to free oneself, break loose.*
Se dégager d'une promesse. *To get out of a promise.*
Enfin la vérité se dégage. *At last the truth is coming out.*
dégât *m. damage, devastation.*
dégel *m. thaw.*
dégeler *to thaw.*
dégénéré *noun and adj. degenerate.*
dégouliner *to trickle.*
dégoût *m. disgust, loathing.*
dégoûtant *adj. disgusting.*
dégoûter *to disgust.*
Elle en est dégoûtée. *She's disgusted by it. She's sick of it.*
dégrader *to degrade, lower.*
dégraissage *m. (dry) cleaning.*
dégraisser *to remove the fat.*
Faire dégraisser. *To have (something) cleaned.*
degré *m. degree, extent.*
dégringoler *to fall, tumble down.*
Il dégringola en bas des escaliers. *He tumbled (came tumbling) down the stairs.*
déguenillé *adj. ragged, tattered.*
déguisement *m. disguise, fancy dress.*
se déguiser *to disguise oneself, put on fancy dress.*
déguster *to taste, sample.*
dehors *m. appearance, exterior.*
Personne aux dehors aimables. *Person who makes a nice appearance.*
Sous des dehors trompeurs. *Under false colors. Not to be what one pretends to be. ("Under deceitful appearances.")*
DEHORS *outside, out, out of doors.*
Il fait froid dehors. *It's cold out.*
Mettre quelqu'un dehors. *To throw (put) someone out.*
Ne pas se pencher au dehors. *Do not lean out of the window.*
En dehors de la maison. *Outside the house.*
Au dehors de ce pays. *Outside this country.*
DÉJÀ *already.*
Il est déjà là. *He's already there.*
Je l'ai déjà vu. *I've seen him before.*
DÉJEUNER *m. lunch.*
Où prend-il son déjeuner? *Where does he eat lunch?*
DÉJEUNER *to have lunch.*
Je n'ai qu'une demi-heure pour déjeuner. *I have only half an hour for lunch.*
DELÀ *beyond.*
Au delà. *Farther. Beyond.*
C'est aller au delà de mes désirs. *It's more*

than I hoped for.
Par delà les mers. *Beyond the seas.*
délabré *adj. shattered, crumbling.*
Sa santé est bien délabrée. *Her health has become greatly impaired.*
DÉLAI *m. delay, postponement, fixed time.*
Sans délai. *Without delay.*
Dans le plus bref délai. *As soon as possible.*
délaisser *to forsake, abandon.*
délassement *m. rest, relaxation.*
La pêche est mon délassement préféré. *Fishing is my favorite pastime.*
se délasser *to relax.*
délégation *f. delegation.*
délégué *m. delegate, representative.*
déléguer *to delegate.*
délibération *f. deliberation.*
délibérément *deliberately, intentionally.*
délibérer *to deliberate.*
délicat *adj. delicate.*
Une situation délicate. *A delicate situation.*
délicatesse *f. delicacy, refinement.*
Il manque de délicatesse. *He lacks refinement.*
délices *m. pl. delight, pleasure.*
délicieux (délicieuse *f.*) *adj. delicious; delightful.*
délier *to untie.*
délirant *adj. delirious, frantic.*
délire *m. delirium.*
délirer *to be delirious.*
délit *m. offense.*
Il fut pris en flagrant délit. *He was caught in the act. He was caught red-handed.*
délivrance *f. deliverance, release.*
délivrer *to free, release.*
Les prisonniers furent délivrés. *The prisoners were released.*
Délivrer une marchandise. *To deliver goods.*
déloyal (déloyaux *pl.*) *adj. unfaithful, disloyal.*
déluge *m. deluge.*
"Après nous le déluge." *When we are gone come what may.* ("After us, the deluge.")
DEMAIN *tomorrow.*
Au revoir, à demain. *See you tomorrow.* ("Goodby until tomorrow.")
Demain matin. *Tomorrow morning.*
DEMANDE *f. request, application.*
J'espère qu'on fera droit à ma demande. *I hope my request will be granted.*
Sur demande. *On request.*
DEMANDER *to ask.*
On vous demande au téléphone. *You're wanted on the telephone.*
Quand vous la verrez, demandez-lui de nous écrire. *When you see her, ask her to write to us.*
Vous m'en demandez trop! *That's asking too much of me! You expect too much from me!*
L'affaire demande à être éclaircie. *The affair needs to be cleared up.*
Je vous demande un peu! *I ask you! Did you ever!*
Demander un conseil. *To ask for advice.*
On ne demande pas mieux. *One couldn't ask for anything better.*
se demander *to wonder.*
démangeaison *f. itch.*
démanger *to itch.*
Sa langue lui démange (*fam.*). *He's itching to speak.*
se démaquiller *to remove makeup.*
La crème à démaquiller. *Cold cream, cleansing cream.*
démarcation *f. demarcation.*

démarche *f. gait, walk; proceeding, step.*
Faire des démarches. *To take steps.*
démarrer *to start, move off.*
Le moteur ne veut pas démarrer. *The motor won't start.*
Il n'en démarrera pas. *He won't budge from his position (alter his stand, change his mind).*
démarreur *m. starter (car).*
démasquer *to unmask.*
démêlé *m. dispute, quarrel.*
Avoir des démêlés avec la justice. *To be up against the law.*
démêler *to unravel, disentangle.*
Démêler un malentendu. *To clear up a misunderstanding.*
déménagement *m. moving.*
Une voiture de déménagement. *A moving van.*
Trois déménagements valent un incendie. *Three removals are as bad as a fire.*
déménager *to move, change one's residence.*
Nous avons déménagé hier. *We moved yesterday.*
se démener *to struggle, strive.*
Se démener pour réussir. *To strive hard to succeed.*
démenti *m. lie; denial.*
Donner un démenti. *To deny, to refute.*
démentir *to give the lie to, contradict, belie.*
Ses actions démentent ses paroles. *His actions belie his words.*
demeure *f. dwelling, residence.*
Il y a établi sa demeure. *He established residence there.*
Il fut évincé de sa demeure. *He was evicted from his home.*
DEMEURER *to live, reside.*
Je ne sais pas au juste où il demeure. *I don't know exactly where he lives.*
L'affaire n'en demeurera pas là. *The affair won't stop there. The matter won't rest there.*
S'il en était demeuré là. *If he had stopped there. If he hadn't gone any further.*
DEMI *half.*
Il est une heure et demie. *It is half-past one.*
Ne faire les choses qu'à demi. *To do things halfway (by halves.) To leave things half done.*
Il ne fait que des demi-journées. *He works only half a day.*
Faire demi-tour. *To turn around.*
Un demi blonde. *A half-liter of light beer.*
Une demi-douzaine de. *Half a dozen of.*
démission *f. resignation.*
Il donne sa démission. *He's resigning.*
A-t-il offert sa démission? *Has he handed in his resignation?*
démissionner *to resign.*
démobiliser *to demobilize.*
démocratie *f. democracy.*
démodé *adj. old-fashioned, out of style.*
Cette robe est démodée. *This dress is out of style.*
demoiselle *f. young lady, miss.*
Demoiselle d'honneur. *Bridesmaid.*
démolir *to demolish.*
La maison a été démolie. *The house was demolished (torn down).*
démon *m. devil, imp.*
démonétiser *to call in (of money).*
démonstratif (démonstrative *f.*) *adj. demonstrative.*
démonstration *f. demonstration, exhibition.*
Faire une démonstration. *To demonstrate.*

démonté *adj. dismounted; upset, raging.*
se démonter *to come apart; be abashed.*
Cette machine se démonte facilement. *This machine can be taken apart (comes apart, can be dismantled) easily.*
Il ne se démonte pas facilement. *He's not easily upset.*
démontrer *to demonstrate, prove.*
démoralisé *adj. demoralized.*
démoraliser *to demoralize.*
démordre *to let go, give up.*
Il n'en démordra pas d'un iota. *He won't back down an inch.*
dénaturer *to distort, misrepresent.*
dénicher *to find out, discover.*
Où a-t-il déniché cela (*fam.*)? *Where did he find that out? Where did he ferret that out? Where did he unearth that?*
dénier *to deny.*
Dénier toute responsabilité. *To disclaim all responsibility.*
dénigrer *to disparage, speak ill of.*
Il dénigre tout le monde. *He speaks ill of everyone (knocks, disparages, runs everyone down).*
dénommer *to denominate, name.*
dénoncer *to denounce, tell on.*
dénonciation *f. denunciation.*
dénoter *to denote; indicate; point out.*
Pouvez-vous dénoter la différence? *Can you tell (indicate, point out) the difference?*
Cela dénote de l'ignorance. *That shows (reveals) ignorance.*
dénouement *m. outcome, ending (play).*
dénouer *to untie, loosen.*
Dénouer une intrigue. *To untangle a plot.*
se dénouer *to be cleared up, be unraveled, be settled.*
L'affaire se dénouera en justice. *The affair will be settled ("cleared up") in court.*
denrée *f. ware, food.*
Denrées alimentaires. *Food products.*
Denrées coloniales. *Colonial products.*
dense *adj. dense, compact, thick.*
densité *f. density.*
DENT *f. tooth.*
J'ai mal aux dents. *My teeth hurt.*
Les dents de lait. *Milk teeth.*
L'enfant fait ses dents. *The child is cutting his teeth.*
Une dent cariée. *A decayed tooth.*
Armé jusqu'aux dents. *Armed to the teeth.*
N'avoir rien à se mettre sous la dent. *To have nothing to eat.*
Il a une dent contre lui. *He has a grudge against him.*
Rire à belles dents. *To laugh heartily.*
Il n'a pas desserré les dents. *He didn't say a word. He didn't open his mouth.*
Il est sur les dents. *He's on the alert. He doesn't know what to do first.*
Cela fait grincer les dents. *It's enough to make you grind your teeth (set your teeth on edge).*
Il ment comme un arracheur de dents (*fam.*). *He's a great liar.*
Il parle entre ses dents. *He mumbles.* ("He speaks between his teeth.")
dentelle *f. lace.*
dentifrice *noun (m.) and adj. dentifrice.*
La pâte dentifrice. *Toothpaste.*
La poudre dentifrice. *Toothpowder.*
L'eau dentifrice. *Mouthwash.*
dentiste *m. and f. dentist.*

dénué *adj. destitute; devoid.*
　Dénué d'intérêt. *Devoid of interest. Completely lacking in interest.*
dénuement *m. extreme poverty.*
　Etre dans le dénuement. *To be in want.*
dépareillé *adj. odd, unmatched.*
départ *m. departure.*
　Un départ inopiné. *Sudden (unexpected) departure.*
　Quelle est l'heure de départ du train? *When does the train leave?*
　Point de départ. *Starting point.*
département *m. department.*
dépasser *to surpass, go beyond, overtake.*
　Ça dépasse mes moyens. *It's beyond my means. I can't afford it.*
　Ce travail dépasse mes forces. *This work is too much for me ("beyond my strength").*
　Ça me dépasse! *That's beyond me! That beats me! That's too much for me!*
dépaysé *adj. out of one's element. out of place.*
　Il se sent tout dépaysé. *He feels out of place.*
dépêche *f. telegram.*
　Envoyer une dépêche. *To send a telegram.*
se dépêcher *to hasten, hurry.*
　Dépêchez-vous. *Hurry up.*
　Il faut qu'il se dépêche. *He has to hurry. He'd better hurry up.*
dépeindre *to depict, describe.*
dépendance *f. dependence.*
　Etre sous la dépendance de quelqu'un. *To be under someone's domination.*
dépendre *to depend, be dependent.*
　Tout dépend des circonstances. *Everything depends on the circumstances.*
　Cela ne dépend pas de nous. *That's not up to us. That doesn't depend on us.*
　Cela dépend. *That depends.*
dépens *m. costs, expense.*
　A ses frais et dépens. *At his own expense.*
　Apprendre à ses dépens. *To learn to one's cost.*
dépense *f. expense.*
　Faire des dépenses. *To incur expenses.*
　Regarder à la dépense. *To be thrifty.*
DÉPENSER *to spend.*
　Nous avons dépensé en tout à peine vingt francs. *Altogether we spent less than twenty francs.*
　Il dépense au-delà de ses revenus. *He lives beyond his means. He spends more than he makes.*
se dépenser *to exert oneself, not to spare oneself.*
dépensier (dépensière *f.*) *adj. extravagant, spendthrift.*
dépérir *to waste away, decay.*
se dépeupler *to become depopulated.*
dépit *m. spite, resentment.*
　Masquer son dépit. *To conceal one's resentment.*
　Par dépit. *Through spite. Out of spite.*
　Il a agi en dépit du bon sens. *He acted contrary to good sense. He didn't use common sense.*
dépiter *to vex, upset.*
　Je suis fort dépité. *I'm very much annoyed.*
se dépiter *to take offense, be annoyed.*
déplacement *m. displacement, traveling.*
déplacé *adj. out of place, misplaced.*
déplacer *to displace, shift, move.*
se déplacer *to change one's place, move about.*
déplaire *to be unpleasant.*
　Cela me déplaît. *I dislike that. I don't like that.*
　Ne vous en déplaise. *No offense meant. With*

all due respect to you.
déplier *to unfold.*
déplorable *adj. deplorable, lamentable.*
déplorer *to deplore, lament.*
déployer *to display, spend, exhibit.*
déposer *to put down.*
　Déposez la valise ici. *Put the suitcase down here.*
　Ils ont déposé les armes. *They've surrendered. They've laid down their arms.*
dépositaire *m. depository, trustee.*
déposséder *to dispossess, oust.*
dépôt *m. deposit; depot.*
　Un dépôt d'autobus. *A bus terminal.*
　En dépôt. *In custody. In safekeeping.*
dépouiller *to deprive, strip.*
　Dépouiller quelqu'un de ses droits. *To deprive someone of his rights.*
　Dépouiller le courrier. *To open the mail.*
dépourvu *adj. bereft, devoid of.*
　Dépourvu d'argent. *Short of cash.*
　Etre pris au dépourvu. *To be taken unaware.*
déprimé *adj. depressed.*
　Se sentir déprimé. *To feel depressed.*
DEPUIS *since.*
　J'y habite depuis vingt ans. *I've lived there twenty years.*
　Vous avez engraissé depuis un an. *You've put on weight in this last year.*
　Mon bail est expiré depuis hier. *My lease expired yesterday.*
　Depuis lors. *Since that time.*
　Depuis quand m'attendez-vous?—Peut-être depuis dix minutes. *How long have you been waiting for me?—About ten minutes. ("Probably since ten minutes.")*
député *m. deputy, delegate.*
déraciné *adj. uprooted.*
　Se sentir déraciné. *To feel like a fish out of water.*
dérailler *to be derailed; talk nonsense (fam.).*
déraisonnable *adj. unreasonable.*
dérangement *m. disturbance, trouble.*
　Causer du dérangement à quelqu'un. *To disturb someone.*
déranger *to disturb, inconvenience.*
　Si cela ne vous dérange pas. *If it doesn't inconvenience you.*
　Cela dérange tous mes plans. *That upsets (spoils) all my plans.*
　Il ne dérange jamais personne. *He never bothers anyone.*
se déranger *to inconvenience oneself, take the trouble.*
　Ne vous dérangez pas. *Don't trouble. Don't bother.*
déraper *to skid.*
déréglé *adj. out of order.*
se dérider *to cheer up.*
dérision *f. mockery.*
　Quelle dérision! *What a mockery!*
dérisoire *adj. derisive, ridiculous.*
　Vendre quelque chose à un prix dérisoire. *To sell something at a ridiculously low price.*
dérive *f. drift.*
　Aller à la dérive. *To drift.*
dériver *to derive.*
　Ce mot dérive du latin. *This word is derived from Latin.*
DERNIER (dernière *f.*) *adj. last; noun m. and f. youngest child; the last one; the latter.*
　C'est mon dernier souci. *That's the least of my worries. ("That's my last worry.")*
　C'est sa dernière carte. *It's his last card.*

C'est du dernier ridicule. *That's utterly ridiculous.*
　Il est toujours au courant des dernières nouvelles. *He always knows the latest news. He's always informed about the latest news.*
　C'est de la dernière imprudence. *Nothing could be more imprudent.*
　Etre du dernier bien avec quelqu'un. *To be on the very best terms with someone.*
　Il veut toujours avoir le dernier mot. *He must always have the last word.*
　Voilà le dernier cri. *That's the latest rage.*
　Mon petit dernier. *My youngest child.*
　Le dernier. *The latter.*
　L'année dernière. *Last year.*
dernièrement *lately.*
dérober *to steal, make away with; hide.*
　On lui a dérobé son argent. *His money has been stolen.*
se dérober *to escape, steal away, shun.*
　Se dérober à ses créanciers. *To avoid one's creditors.*
se dérouler *to unroll, unfold.*
déroute *f. rout.*
derrière *m. back, rear.*
　Les derrières d'une armée. *The rear of an army.*
DERRIÈRE *behind; back.*
　Il a certainement quelque chose derrière la tête. *He certainly has something in the back of his mind.*
　Je l'ai laissé bien loin derrière moi. *I left him (quite, very) far behind me.*
DÈS *from.*
　Dès à présent. *Henceforth.*
　Dès son retour. *On his return.*
　Dès qu'il le saura. *As soon as he knows (learns) it.*
　Dès lors. *Ever since.*
désaccord *m. disagreement, clash.*
　Ils sont toujours en désaccord. *They always disagree.*
désagréable *adj. disagreeable, unpleasant.*
　Nouvelle désagréable. *Unwelcome news.*
　Personne désagréable. *Unpleasant person.*
désapprouver *to disapprove.*
désarmement *m. disarmament, disarming.*
désarmer *to disarm.*
désarroi *m. disorder, confusion.*
　Mettre tout en désarroi. *To turn everything upside down.*
désastre *m. disaster.*
désastreux (désastreuse *f.*) *adj. disastrous.*
désavantage *m. disadvantage, drawback.*
　Avoir le désavantage. *To be at a disadvantage.*
　A son désavantage. *To his (her) disadvantage.*
désavantageux (désavantageuse *f.*) *adj. disadvantageous.*
se désavouer *to retract, go back on one's word.*
descendant *m. descendant.*
DESCENDRE *to descend, go down.*
　Lorsque vous descendrez, regardez s'il y a du courrier. *When you go downstairs, see if there is any mail.*
　Combien de marches il y a-t-il à descendre? *How many steps are there to go down?*
　Envoyez-moi quelqu'un pour descendre mes valises. *Send someone to carry down my bags.*
　A quel arrêt dois-je descendre? *At what stop (bus, streetcar) do I get off?*
　A quel hôtel êtes-vous descendu? *At what hotel are you stopping?*

Tout le monde descend! *All off! Last stop! All change!*

descente f. *slope, descent.*
Une descente rapide. *A steep slope.*
Descente de police. *Police raid.*

descriptif (descriptive f.) adj. *descriptive.*

description f. *description.*

désemparé adj. *helpless, in distress.*

déséquilibré adj. *out of balance.*

désert m. *desert.*

désert adj. *deserted.*
L'endroit était désert. *The place was deserted.*

déserter to *desert, abandon.*

déserteur m. *deserter.*

désespéré adj. *desperate.*

désespérer to *despair, give up.*
Ne désespérez pas. *Don't give up. Don't lose courage.*

désespoir m. *despair, grief, hopelessness.*
Je suis au désespoir. *I'm in despair.*
Coup de désespoir. *Act of despair.*
En désespoir de cause. *As a last resort.*

se déshabiller to *undress.*

se déshabituer to *break oneself of a habit.*

déshériter to *disinherit.*

déshonnête adj. *improper, immodest.*

déshonneur m. *dishonor, disgrace.*

déshonorant adj. *dishonorable, shameful.*

déshonorer to *dishonor, disgrace.*

désigner to *designate, point out.*
Désigner quelque chose du doigt. *To point at something.*

désillusion f. *disillusion.*

désillusionner to *disillusion.*

désintéressé adj. *disinterested; unselfish.*

se désintéresser to *lose one's interest in.*

désinvolte adj. *easy, unconstrained, unembarrassed.*

désinvolture f. *unconstraint, ease.*

désir m. *desire, wish.*

désirable adj. *desirable.*

DÉSIRER to *desire, wish.*
Je désire vous voir. *I'd like to see you.*
Que désirez-vous de plus? *What else would you like? What do you want besides?*
Je désire recommander ma lettre. *I'd like to have my letter registered.*
Cela laisse à désirer. *It's not quite satisfactory. That leaves something to be desired.*
Je n'ai plus rien à désirer. *I can't (couldn't) wish for anything else. I've nothing left to wish for.*
Elle se fait désirer. *She keeps people waiting.*
Madame désire? *What would you like, madam?*
Qu'est-ce que vous désirez? *May I help you? What would you like? What can I do for you?*

désireux (désireuse f.) adj. *desirous.*
Il est désireux de plaire. *He's anxious to please.*

se désister to *relinquish a right, waive a claim, withdraw a legal action or one's candidacy.*
Se désister d'une demande. *To waive a claim.*
Se désister d'une promesse. *To break a promise. Not to keep a promise.*

désobéir to *disobey.*

désobéissance f. *disobedience.*

désobligeance f. *unkindness, disagreeableness.*

désobliger to *offend.*

désoeuvré adj. *unoccupied, idle.*

désolation f. *desolation, grief.*

désolé adj. *desolate; very sorry.*
Je suis désolé. *I'm very sorry.*
Je suis désolé de l'entendre. *I'm sorry to hear it.*

désoler to *ravage, devastate.*

désordonné adj. *disorderly.*

désordre m. *disorder.*
Nous trouvâmes tout en désordre. *We found everything in disorder (topsy-turvy).*

désorganisé adj. *disorganized.*

désorienté adj. *bewildered.*

désormais *henceforth, from now on.*

desséché adj. *dry.*

dessein m. *design, scheme, aim.*
A dessein. *Intentionally. Designedly.*

desserer to *loosen.*

dessert m. *dessert.*

desservir to *serve; clear (the table).*

dessin m. *drawing, sketch.*
Dessin animé. *Animated cartoon.*

dessiner to *draw.*

se dessiner to *stand out, be outlined.*
Mes projets se dessinent. *My plans are taking shape.*

dessous m. *lower part, bottom.*
Un dessous de bouteille. *A coaster.*
Avoir le dessous. *To have (get) the worst of it. To be defeated.*
Le pauvre, il a eu le dessous. *The poor fellow got the worst of it (was defeated).*
Il y a là un dessous que nous ne comprenons pas. *There's something (some mystery) about it which we don't understand.*
En dessous. *Below; next smaller (size).*

DESSOUS *under, below.*
Regardez en-dessous de la chaise. *Look under the chair.*
C'est là, en-dessous. *It's there below.*
C'est au-dessous de moi. *It's beneath me. It's beneath my dignity.*
Il y a quelque chose là-dessous. *There's something behind it.*

dessus m. *top.*
Le dessus de lit. *Bedspread.*
Le dessus de la main. *The back of the hand.*
Le dessus du panier. *The cream (pick) of the crop.*
Il a gagné le dessus. *He won the upper hand.*

DESSUS *on, over, above, on top.*
Le livre se trouve au-dessus de l'étagère. *The book's on top of the bookshelf.*
Qui habite à l'étage du dessus? *Who lives on the floor above?*
Il y a beaucoup à dire là-dessus. *A lot can be said about that. There's a good deal to say (to be said) about that.*
Ils vont bras dessus, bras dessous. *They're walking arm in arm.*
Il est en dette par-dessus la tête. *He is up to his neck in debt.*
Cette nouvelle l'a mis sens dessus dessous. *The news upset him. He was bowled over by the news.*
Il a mis le doigt dessus. *He put his finger on it. He hit the nail on the head.*

destin m. *fate, destiny.*

destinataire m. *addressee, recipient.*

destination f. *destination.*
Arriver à destination. *To arrive at a destination.*
Trains à destination de Toulouse. *Trains to Toulouse.*

destinée f. *destiny.*

destiner to *destine; intend.*
Il est destiné à devenir célèbre. *He's destined to become famous.*
Ceci vous était destiné. *This was meant for you.*

se destiner to *intend to enter a profession.*
Il se destine à la médecine. *He intends to be a doctor.*

destitué adj. *deprived of, lacking.*

destruction f. *destruction.*

désunion f. *disunion, dissension.*

détaché adj. *loose; indifferent; detached.*
D'un air détaché. *In a casual manner.*

détachement m. *indifference, detachment.*

détacher to *loosen, untie; detach.*

se détacher to *get loose, be separated; stand out.*
Se détacher sur l'horizon. *To stand out against the horizon.*

DÉTAIL m. *detail; retail.*
Vendre au détail. *To sell retail.*
Prix de détail. *Retail price.*
Donner tous les détails. *To give full particulars.*

détaillé adj. *detailed.*
Un compte-rendu détaillé. *A detailed account.*

détailler to *detail, enumerate.*

déteindre to *fade, lose color.*
Déteindre au lavage. *To run (fade) in the wash.*

se détendre to *relax, loosen.*

détente f. *relaxation, loosening.*

détention f. *holding; detention.*

détériorer to *spoil.*

détermination f. *determination.*

déterminé adj. *determined, definite; resolute.*

déterminer to *determine.*
Je suis déterminé à faire cela. *I'm determined to do it.*

détestable adj. *detestable, hateful.*

détester to *hate.*
Il le déteste. *He hates him.*

détour m. *deviation, turn.*
La route fait un brusque détour. *The road makes a sharp turn.*
Faire un détour. *To make a detour.*

détourner to *divert, avert.*
Détourner l'attention de quelqu'un. *To divert someone's attention.*
Détourner les soupçons. *To avert suspicion.*

détraqué adj. *out of order.*
Ma montre est détraquée. *My watch is out of order.*
Il est un peu détraqué (fam.). *He's a little unbalanced (crazy).*

détraquer to *put out of order, spoil, ruin.*

détresse f. *distress, affliction.*
Navire en détresse. *Ship in distress.*
Sa détresse fait pitié à voir. *Her (his) plight is pitiful.*

détriment m. *detriment.*
Il l'a appris à son détriment. *He found it out to his cost.*

détruire to *destroy.*

DETTE f. *debt.*
Il a payé les dettes les plus criardes. *He paid the most pressing debts.*
Il m'a remis une reconnaissance de dette. *He gave me an I.O.U.*

deuil m. *mourning, grief.*
Prendre le deuil. *To go into mourning.*
Porter le deuil. *To be in mourning.*

DEUX noun and adj. *two.*
Il est deux heures et quart. *It is a quarter past two.*
Les enfants étaient tous deux fatigués. *Both children were tired.*
Voici le fait en deux mots. *Briefly, the matter is this. This is the matter in a nutshell ("in two words").*
Ils se ressemblent comme deux gouttes d'eau.

They're as alike as two peas in a pod ("as two drops of water").

Il l'a vu de ses deux yeux. *He saw it with his own ("two") eyes.*

Cette classe a lieu un jeudi sur deux. *This class meets on alternate Thursdays.*

Il est entre deux âges. *He's middle-aged.*

Elle regarde à deux sous. *She thinks twice before spending anything. She pinches pennies (is penny-pinching).*

A deux pas d'ici. *Right near here, nearby, very close by.*

(Tous) les deux. *Both (of them, of us).*

Toutes les deux semaines. *Every other week.*

Vous deux. *The two of you, both of you.*

DEUXIÈME *noun and adj. second.*

C'est la deuxième maison à droite. *It's the second house to your right.*

devancer *to precede.*

devant *m. front.*

Je ne suis pas encore prêt, prenez les devants. *I'm not ready yet, go on ahead*

DEVANT *before, in front of.*

Il prit un autobus qui l'amena juste devant l'immeuble. *He took a bus which brought him right in front of the building.*

Egaux devant la loi. *Equal before the law.*

Aller au-devant de ses amis. *To go to meet one's friends (as a courtesy).*

Aller au devant des ennuis. *To borrow trouble.*

Aller droit devant soi. *To go straight ahead. To follow one's nose.*

devanture *f. shopwindow.*

dévastation *f. devastation.*

dévaster *to devastate.*

déveine *f. bad luck.*

J'ai de la déveine aujourd'hui (*fam.*). *I have no luck today. My luck's bad today.*

développement *m. development.*

développer *to develop.*

Faire développer. *To have developed (film).*

DEVENIR *to become.*

Devenir grand. *To grow tall. To grow up.*

Il devient vieux. *He's growing (getting) old.*

Que devenez-vous ces jours-ci? *What are you doing these days?*

J'ai failli en devenir fou. *It nearly drove me mad.*

Que va-t-il devenir? *What is to (will) become of him?*

Je ne sais que devenir. *I don't know which way to turn. I don't know what to do next.*

Qu'il est devenu gras! *How fat he's gotten! He's certainly gotten fat!*

Devenir blanc de rage. *To turn white with anger.*

Il en devint amoureux. *He fell in love with her.*

se dévêtir *to undress, strip.*

déviation *f. deviation.*

dévier *to deviate, diverge.*

deviner *to guess.*

Vous avez deviné juste. *That's right. You've guessed right.*

devinette *f. riddle.*

dévisager *to stare.*

devise *f. motto; currency.*

Des devises étrangères. *Foreign bills.*

devoir *m. duty, obligation.*

C'est son devoir. *It's his (her) duty.*

Faire son devoir. *To do one's duty.*

Payer ses devoirs à quelqu'un. *To pay one's respects to someone.*

Mon fils a beaucoup de devoirs à faire. *My son has a lot of homework to do.*

DEVOIR *to owe; have to; must.*

Il me doit beaucoup d'argent. *He owes me a lot of money.*

Je crois devoir rentrer à la maison. *I believe I'll have to go home.*

Il doit y avoir quelqu'un. *Someone must be there.*

Il devait lui écrire. *He was supposed to write to him.*

Il devrait lui écrire. *He ought to write to him.*

Tout doit finir. *Everything is bound to come to an end.*

Nous devons le faire. *We must do it.*

Il doit y aller. *He has to go there.*

devoirs *m. pl. homework.*

dévorer *to devour, eat greedily.*

dévot *adj. devout, pious.*

dévotion *f. devotion.*

dévoué *adj. devoted, faithful.*

Votre tout dévoué. *Yours very truly.*

dévouement *m. devotion; self-sacrifice.*

dévouer *to dedicate, consecrate.*

Dévouer son énergie à une cause. *To devote one's energy to a cause.*

se dévouer *to devote oneself.*

dextérité *f. dexterity, skill.*

diable *m. devil.*

C'est un pauvre diable. *He's a poor devil.*

C'est un assez bon diable. *He's not a bad fellow.*

Il tire le diable par la queue. *He lives from hand to mouth. He's hard up.*

Que diable voulez-vous en faire (*fam.*)? *What on earth do you want to do with it?*

Ce n'est pas le diable. *It's not so very difficult.*

diagonale *f. diagonal.*

dialogue *m. dialogue.*

diamant *m. diamond.*

diapositif *m. transparency, slide (photography).*

dicter *to dictate, suggest.*

Dictez-moi. j'écrirai. *Dictate ("to me") and I'll take it down ("I'll write").*

DICTIONNAIRE *m. dictionary.*

diète *f. diet.*

DIEU *m. God.*

Dieu sait ce qu'il en sera! *God knows what will come of it!*

Que Dieu me soit en aide! *So help me God!*

Pour l'amour de Dieu! *For goodness' sake!*

Grâce à Dieu, je n'y suis pas allé. *Thank heavens I didn't go.*

C'est une punition du bon Dieu. *It's a judgment of God.*

diffamer *to defame, slander.*

DIFFÉRENCE *f. difference.*

Cela fait une grande différence. *That makes a lot of difference.*

différend *m. disagreement.*

DIFFÉRENT *adj. different.*

Celui-ci est bien différent de l'autre. *This one is quite different from the other one.*

DIFFÉRER *to differ.*

DIFFICILE *adj. difficult, hard.*

C'est un problème difficile. *It's a difficult problem.*

Il est difficile. *He's a difficult person.*

DIFFICULTÉ *f. difficulty.*

Il fait naître des difficultés. *He creates (he's always creating) difficulties.*

Ils se sont heurtés à de sérieuses difficultés. *They encountered serious obstacles.*

digérer *to digest, swallow.*

digne *adj. worthy.*

Je l'en trouve digne. *I consider him worthy of*

it. I think he deserves it.

Cela est bien digne de lui. *That's just like him.*

dignité *f. dignity.*

digression *f. digression.*

dilapider *to waste, squander.*

dilater *to dilate, expand.*

dilemme *m. dilemma.*

diligence *f. diligence, application.*

Faire diligence. *To hurry.*

diligent *adj. diligent, industrious.*

diluer *to dilute.*

DIMANCHE *m. Sunday.*

Le(s) dimanche(s). *On Sundays.*

dimension *f. dimension, size.*

diminuer *to lessen, diminish.*

Diminuer les prix. *To reduce prices.*

Diminuer à vue d'oeil. *To diminish visibly.*

diminutif (diminutive *f.*) *adj. diminutive.*

diminution *f. diminishing, reduction.*

dinde *f. turkey.*

dindon *m. turkey.*

dîner *m. dinner.*

dîner *to dine.*

Nous dînerons en tête à tête. *We'll have dinner alone (just the two of us, privately).*

Qui dort dîne. *Sleeping makes one forget one's hunger.*

diplomatique *adj. diplomatic.*

diplôme *m. diploma.*

diplômer *to grant a diploma to.*

DIRE *to say.*

L'art de bien dire. *The art of speaking well.*

Dites-donc, quand viendrez-vous chez nous? *Well, when will you come to our place?*

Aussitôt dit, aussitôt fait. *No sooner said than done.*

Que dites-vous de cela? *What do you think of that?*

On dirait qu'il va faire beau aujourd'hui. *It looks as if it will be a beautiful day.*

Alors, c'est dit? *Then it's settled?*

Il lui a fait dire de venir. *He sent him word to come.*

Que voulez-vous dire? *What do you mean?*

Que veut dire cette attitude? *What is the meaning of your attitude?*

Je veux dire que . . . *I mean that . . .*

A vrai dire. *To tell the truth.*

Soit dit entre nous. *Between ourselves.*

Non, je ne tiens pas à y aller, cela ne me dit rien. *No, I don't feel like going there. The idea doesn't appeal to me. It doesn't appeal to me.*

Quand je vous le disais! *I told you so!*

C'est-à-dire. *That is (to say), I (you) mean, in other words.*

Comme on dit. *As they say.*

Entendre dire (que). *To hear (that).*

Il n'y a pas à dire. *There's no doubt.*

Il m'a dit de partir. *He told me to leave.*

Je dirais. *I'd say.*

se dire *to be said, call oneself.*

Cela se dit, mais ne s'écrit pas. *That's said but it's never written.*

Il se dit votre ami. *He calls himself your friend.*

Cela se dit tout bas. *That should be whispered. That shouldn't be said aloud.*

DIRECT *adj. direct, straight.*

Impôts directs. *Direct taxes.*

Train direct. *Express train.*

Complément direct. *Direct object (grammar).*

directement *directly.*

directeur *m.* (directrice *f.*) *director.*

DIRECTION f. direction; management.
  Changer de direction. 1. To change the management. 2. To change direction. To go in another direction.
directrice f. directress.
diriger to direct; lead, rule.
se diriger (vers) to head for, make for (a place).
discernement m. perception; discernment.
discerner to discern, distinguish.
  Discerner le bien du mal. To tell right from wrong.
discipline f. discipline.
discipliner to discipline.
discorde f. discord, strife.
discours m. speech.
  Prononcer un discours. To make a speech.
discret adj. discreet.
discrètement discreetly.
discrétion f. discretion, tact.
discussion f. discussion.
  La discussion s'envenima. The discussion became bitter.
  Une discussion orageuse. A stormy discussion (debate).
DISCUTER to discuss, argue.
  Nous avons discuté pendant des heures entières. We argued for hours on end.
  Il n'y a pas à discuter. There's no question about it.
DISPARAÎTRE to disappear.
  Mon livre a disparu. My book has disappeared.
dispenser to dispense; exempt.
  Je vous dispense de ces observations. You may keep those remarks to yourself.
se dispenser to excuse oneself from.
se disperser to disperse, scatter.
disponible adj. available, at one's disposition.
  Il a peu d'argent disponible. He doesn't have very much money available (at his disposal).
DISPOSER to dispose, arrange; have at one's disposal.
  Vous pouvez disposer librement de mon appartement. You can make (free) use of my apartment.
  Il dispose de grands moyens d'action. He possesses (has at his disposal) considerable resources ("means of action").
  Il est mal disposé à mon égard. He's not well-disposed toward me.
disposition f. disposal, disposition.
  Je suis tout à votre disposition. I am entirely at your disposal. I'm at your complete disposal.
dispute f. dispute, quarrel.
disputer to dispute, contest.
se disputer to quarrel.
  Ne vous disputez pas. Don't quarrel.
disque m. disc, record.
  Microsillon, stéréo, de 33 tours. Microgroove, stereo, 33 r.p.m.
disséminer to sow, scatter, disseminate.
dissension f. dissension, discord.
dissoudre to dissolve, disperse.
dissuader to dissuade.
DISTANCE f. distance; interval.
  A peu de distance. At a short distance.
  Tenez-vous à distance. Keep at a distance.
distant adj. distant; aloof.
distinct adj. distinct.
distinctement distinctly.
distinctif (distinctive f.) adj. distinctive.
  Trait distinctif. Distinguishing feature. Char-

acteristic.
distinction f. distinction.
  On doit faire une distinction entre ces deux choses. One must make a distinction (distinguish) between these two things.
  Sans distinction. 1. Indiscriminately. Without (any) discrimination. 2. Without distinction. Undistinguished.
  Un homme sans distinction. An undistinguished man.
distingué adj. distinguished.
distinguer to distinguish, discriminate.
se distinguer to distinguish oneself.
distraction f. amusement; inattention.
  Les distractions sont-elles coûteuses ici? Are the amusements here expensive?
  Il est sujet à des distractions. He's frequently very absent-minded.
distraire to divert; distract, amuse.
  Venez avec nous, cela vous distraira. Come with us. It will cheer you up (it will be a pleasant change for you).
distrait adj. absent-minded.
distribuer to distribute, give out.
distribution f. distribution.
divaguer to digress, wander.
divan m. divan, sofa.
DIVERS adj. various, several, different.
  Il fabrique des objets divers. He manufactures various kinds of articles.
  A diverses reprises. Several times.
  Faits divers. News items.
diversion f. diversion, change.
diversité f. diversity, difference.
divertir to divert; entertain.
se divertir to amuse oneself.
  Il a l'air de se divertir. He seems to be enjoying himself.
divertissement m. entertainment.
dividende m. dividend.
divin adj. divine, holy.
diviser to divide.
division f. division.
divorce m. divorce.
divorcer to divorce.
divulguer to divulge, reveal.
DIX noun and adj. ten.
DIX-HUIT noun and adj. eighteen.
DIX-HUITIÈME noun and adj. eighteenth.
DIXIÈME noun and adj. tenth.
DIX-NEUF noun and adj. nineteen.
DIX-NEUVIÈME noun and adj. nineteenth.
DIX-SEPT noun and adj. seventeen.
DIX-SEPTIÈME noun and adj. seventeenth.
dizaine f. about ten.
docile adj. docile, submissive.
DOCTEUR m. doctor.
  Docteur en médecine. Doctor. Physician, M.D.
document m. document.
documenter to document, supply information about.
se documenter to gather documentary evidence.
DOIGT m. finger.
  Mon doigt me fait mal. My finger hurts.
  Savoir quelque chose sur le bout des doigts. To have something at one's fingertips.
  Doigt de pied. Toe.
  Il se met le doigt dans l'oeil. He's fooling (deceiving) himself. He is grossly (entirely) mistaken.
  Il s'en mord les doigts. He's sorry he did it. He regrets having done it. He's repentant (now).

Il lui obéit au doigt et à l'oeil. He's at his beck and call.
  Mon petit doigt me l'a dit. A little bird told me.
  Il était à deux doigts de la ruine. He came near being ruined. He was on the very brink of ruin. He came within an ace of being ruined.
dollar m. dollar.
domaine m. domain; estate.
  Ce n'est pas de mon domaine. That's not within my province.
domestique m. servant.
domestique adj. domestic.
  Animal domestique. Domestic animal.
domicile m. residence.
  Quel est votre domicile personnel? What is your home address?
  Il a élu son domicile chez son père. He established legal residence at the home of his father.
domination f. domination.
dominer to dominate, rule.
  Dominer ses scrupules. To overcome one's scruples.
se dominer to control oneself.
  Il ne sait pas se dominer. He has no self-control.
dommage m. damage; wrong.
  Payer les dommages-intérêts. To pay the damages.
  C'est dommage. It's a pity (a shame). It's too bad.
dompter to tame; overcome.
don m. gift.
  Le don des langues. A gift for languages.
  Il a le don de l'à-propos. He has the knack of always saying the right thing.
DONC so, therefore, indeed, accordingly.
  Notre travail est fini, donc nous pouvons partir. Our work is finished, so (therefore, consequently) we can go (leave).
  Il n'a pas dit non, donc je pense qu'il est d'accord. He didn't say no, so (therefore) I think he agrees.
  Vous aviez donc oublié? So you forgot, didn't you?
  Pensez donc! Just think!
  Allons donc! Nonsense! You don't really mean that. You can't really be serious.
  Dites donc. Say! Say there!
  Dites donc, ça suffit! Look here, that's enough.
  Mais comment donc? But how?
  Qu'y a-t-il donc? What's the matter anyhow?
DONNER to give.
  Donnez-moi le menu, s'il vous plaît. May I have the menu, please?
  Donnez-moi la main. Give me your hand.
  Cet arbre donne des prunes. This tree yields plums.
  Donnez-moi un acompte. Pay me a part. Let me have a down payment.
  Il m'a donné à entendre que . . . He intimated that . . . ("He gave me to understand that . . .")
  Donnez-nous de vos nouvelles. Let's hear from you.
  Le chien lui donna un coup de patte. The dog clawed (scratched) him.
  Il donne du fil à retordre. He gives one a lot of trouble. He's not easy to manage (he puts up a lot of resistance).
  Je vous donnerai un coup de main. I'll lend (give) you a hand. I'll help you.
  Il a donné à côté. He missed (his aim).

Pourquoi lui avez-vous donné le change? *Why did you put him on the wrong scent (mislead him)?*

Les fenêtres de la maison donnent sur le parc. *The windows (of the house) face the park.*

Il me donne gain de cause. *He sides with me. He decides in my favor.*

C'est à vous à donner. *It's your turn to deal the cards.*

Ce n'est pas donné à tout le monde. *That's not given to everyone (to be able to do something). Not everybody can do it.*

On lui a donné l'éveil. *They put him on his guard.*

Donner satisfaction à quelqu'un. *To please someone.*

Donner des ennuis à quelqu'un. *To cause someone trouble.*

Donner un coup de fil à. *To call, ring up (telephone).*

Donner un coup d'oeil à. *To glance, take a look at.*

se donner *to give oneself, devote oneself.*

Donnez-vous la peine d'entrer. *Will you please come in?*

Il se donne pour noble. *He passes himself off as a nobleman.*

Se donner une entorse. *To sprain, twist one's ankle.*

DONT *whose; of whom, of which.*

Le monsieur dont j'ai oublié le nom. *The gentleman whose name I've forgotten.*

Nous nous sommes arrêtés à un village dont j'ai oublié le nom. *We stopped at a village the name of which I've forgotten.*

C'est un homme dont il faut se méfier. *He's a man you can't trust (you have to be careful of).*

Voici ce dont il s'agit. *This is what it's all about.*

doré *adj. gilded.*

dorénavant *from now on, henceforth.*

DORMIR *to sleep.*

Je n'ai pas dormi de la nuit. *I didn't sleep all night.*

Il dormait comme un loir. *He was sleeping like a top.*

Il dort debout. *He can't keep his eyes open.*

Laissez dormir cetter affaire jusqu'à lundi. *Let the matter rest (wait) until Monday.*

DOS *m. back.*

J'ai mal au dos. *My back aches.*

Il n'a rien à se mettre sur le dos. *He hasn't a shirt to his back.*

Il m'a mis cela sur le dos. *He gave me the responsibility.*

Il se met tout le monde à dos. *He turns everybody against him.*

Il me tourne le dos. *He turns his back on me.*

Il est toujours sur mon dos. *He's always at my side telling me what to do.*

Il a bon dos. *They put all the blame on him. They blame him for everything.*

J'en ai plein le dos (fam.). *I'm fed up with it.*

dose *f. dose, share.*

dossier *m. back; record; file.*

Le dossier d'une chaise. *The back of a chair.*

Apportez les dossiers de l'affaire X. *Bring the files on the X case.*

dot *f. dowry.*

douane *f. customs; customhouse; duty.*

Droits de douane. *Custom duties.*

Bureau de douane. *Customhouse.*

La déclaration en douane. *Customs declaration.*

Passer à la douane. *To clear, go through customs.*

Le poste de douane. *Customs house.*

douanier *m. customs officer.*

double *adj. double.*

Mot à double sens. *Ambiguous word.*

Fermer une porte à double tour. *To double-lock a door.*

doubler *to double.*

Le prix de la viande a doublé. *The price of meat has doubled.*

Défense de doubler. *No passing on this road.*

doublure *f. lining.*

DOUCEMENT *slowly, gently.*

Allez-y (plus) doucement. *Act prudently. Go easy.*

Doucement, ne nous échauffons pas. *Take it easy, let's not get excited.*

Ça va tout doucement. *Things are so-so. Things aren't too bad.*

douceur *f. sweetness, softness.*

douche *f. shower.*

Prendre une douche. *To take a shower.*

doué *adj. gifted.*

Il est doué pour la musique. *He has a gift for music.*

douillet (douillette *f.*) *adj. soft, overdelicate.*

DOULEUR *f. pain, ache; grief.*

Cette médicament adoucira votre douleur. *This medicine will relieve your pain.*

Elle est abîmée dans sa douleur. *She is overwhelmed by grief.*

douloureux (douloureuse *f.*) *adj. painful.*

DOUTE *m. doubt.*

Avoir des doutes au sujet de quelque chose. *To doubt something. To have doubts about something.*

Cela est hors de doute. *There is no question about it.*

Il n'y a pas l'ombre d'un doute. *There is not a shadow of a doubt.*

Sans doute. *Of course. Doubtlessly.*

DOUTER *to doubt.*

Je doute qu'il accepte. *I don't think he'll accept. I doubt whether he'll accept.*

se douter *to suspect; think.*

Je m'en doutais bien. *I thought so. I thought (guessed) as much.*

Il ne se doutait de rien. *He suspected nothing. He had no inkling (of what was going on, etc.). He hadn't the slightest suspicion (notion, idea).*

douteux (douteuse *f.*) *adj. doubtful.*

DOUX (douce *f.*) *adj. soft, gentle, easy.*

Il est doux comme un mouton. *He's as gentle as a lamb.*

C'est doux au toucher. *It feels soft (to the touch).*

Il n'a pas la main douce. *He's rough. He doesn't use kid gloves.*

Filer en douce. *To leave on the sly. To steal away.*

Elle lui fait les yeux doux. *She's making eyes at him (looking sweet at him).*

Il fait doux. *The weather is mild.*

DOUZAINE *f. dozen.*

DOUZE *noun and adj. twelve.*

DOUZIÈME *noun and adj. twelfth.*

dramatique *adj. dramatic.*

L'art dramatique. *The drama.*

Situation dramatique. *Dramatic situation.*

dramatiser *to dramatize.*

drame *m. drama.*

drap *m. sheet; cloth.*

Ce drap est à raccommoder. *This (bed) sheet has to be mended.*

Les voilà dans de beaux draps. *They're in a fine pickle. They're in a fine mess.*

drapeau *m.* (drapeaux *pl.*) *flag.*

dresser *to erect.*

Il dresse l'oreille. *He's on the alert. ("He pricks up his ears.")*

On lui avait dressé un piège. *They had set a trap for him.*

Dresser un acte de décès. *To make out a death certificate.*

DROIT *m. right; law; duty.*

La force prime le droit. *Might is right.*

Il a reconnu mon droit. *He recognized my claim.*

C'est mon droit. *It's my privilege.*

Il a droit à la retraite. *He's entitled to a pension.*

Droits d'entrée. *Import duties.*

Droits de sortie. *Export duties.*

Le droit d'inscription. *Registration fee.*

Le droit d'entrée est cher. *The entrance fee is expensive.*

Droits de succession. *Inheritance tax.*

Il fait son droit à Paris. *He's studying law in Paris.*

Le droit des gens. *International law.*

Le droit d'aînesse. *Birthright.*

DROIT *adj. right, straight.*

Une ligne droite. *A straight line.*

Tenez-vous droit. *Stand (up) straight.*

Aller droit au fait. *To go straight to the point.*

C'est le bras droit du patron. *He's the boss's right-hand man.*

DROITE *f. right hand.*

Elle était assise à ma droite. *She sat on my right.*

Tenir sa droite. *To keep to the right.*

DRÔLE *adj. funny, amusing.*

Comme c'est drôle! *How strange!*

Cela m'a fait un drôle d'effet. *It gave me a funny feeling.*

Quelle drôle d'idée! *What a funny idea!*

C'est un drôle de personnage (fam.). *He's a queer fellow.*

Ce fromage a un drôle d'aspect. *This cheese doesn't look right.*

DU *See de. from the, of the, some.*

Je veux du pain. *I'd like some bread.*

Il revient de la Côte d'Azur. *He just came back from the Riviera.*

Pas du tout. *Not at all.*

dû *m. due.*

Il réclame son dû. *He claims his due.*

dû (due *f.*) *adj. due, owed.*

L'acte est en bonne et due forme. *The deed is in proper form.*

duquel (de laquelle *f.*, desquels *m. pl.*, desquelles *f. pl.*) *of which, whom.*

Duquel s'agit-il? *Which one is it a question of?*

DUR *adj. hard, rough.*

Ce lit est trop dur. *This bed is too hard.*

Oeufs durs. *Hard-boiled eggs.*

Il est dur d'oreille. *He's hard of hearing.*

Il a la tête dure. *He's thick-headed (stubborn).*

Travailler dur. *To work hard.*

DURANT *during.*

Durant sa vie. *During his lifetime.*

Durant son voyage, il est tombé malade. *He became sick during his trip.*

Je l'ai attendu trois heures durant. *I waited for him three whole hours.*

durcir *to harden.*

durée f. duration.
De courte durée. *Short-lived.*
La durée de la guerre. *The duration of the war.*
DURER to last.
J'ai peur que cela ne dure pas. *I'm afraid it won't last.*
dureté f. *hardness.*
dynamite f. *dynamite.*
dysenterie f. *dysentery.*

E *The fifth letter of the alphabet.*
EAU f. (eaux pl.) *water.*
Cours d'eau. *Waterway.*
Il tombe de l'eau. *It's raining.*
Jet d'eau. *Fountain.*
C'est une goutte d'eau dans la mer. *It's like a drop in the ocean. It's a drop in the bucket.*
Il revient sur l'eau. *He's making a new start in business. He's getting on his feet again.*
eau-de-vie f. *brandy.*
eau-forte m. (eaux-fortes pl.) *etching.*
ébahi adj. *amazed, dumbfounded.*
ébaucher to *sketch.*
éblouir to *dazzle.*
éblouissant adj. *dazzling.*
ébranlement m. *shock, concussion.*
ébranler to *shake.*
L'explosion ébranla la maison. *The explosion shook the house.*
Sa raison en fut ébranlée. *His mind was unsettled by it.*
écaille f. *scale, shell; tortoise shell.*
écart m. *deviation; digression.*
Il se tient à l'écart. *He keeps in the background.*
écarter to *separate; move aside.*
Ecarter les obstacles. *To brush the obstacles aside.*
s'écarter to *move aside; diverge; deviate.*
échafaud m. *scaffold.*
échafaudage m. *scaffolding.*
échancrer to *indent, notch.*
échancrure f. *indentation, groove.*
échange m. *exchange.*
En échange de. *In exchange for.*
Faire un échange. *To exchange.*
échanger to *exchange.*
échantillon m. *sample.*
échapper to *escape, overlook.*
Il a échappé à la mort. *He escaped death.*
Il laissa échapper toute l'histoire. *He blurted out the whole story.*
Nous l'avons échappé belle. *We had a narrow escape.*
s'échapper to *escape.*
écharpe f. *scarf.*
s'échauffer to *become overheated, warm up.*
échéance f. *date; term (of payment).*
Payable à l'échéance. *Payable at maturity.*
échéant adj. *falling due.*
Le cas échéant. *In that case.*
échec m. *failure, defeat.*
Subir un échec. *To suffer defeat. To meet with failure.*
échecs m. pl. *chess.*
Faisons une partie d'échecs. *Let's play a game of chess.*
échelle f. *ladder; scale.*
échelon m. *step (of a ladder).*
Monter par échelons. *To rise by degrees.*
échelonner to *space out, spread out.*
échevelé adj. *dishevelled.*
écho m. *echo.*

Faire écho. *To echo.*
échoir to *fall to one's lot.*
Le devoir m'échut de le lui dire. *It fell to me to tell him.*
échouer to *fail.*
Mon plan a échoué. *My plan failed.*
Il a échoué à son examen. *He failed in his examination.*
éclaboussement m. *splashing.*
éclabousser to *splash.*
éclaboussure f. *splash.*
éclair m. *lightning, flash.*
Il a passé comme un éclair. *He shot by like lightning.*
Vif comme l'éclair. *Quick as lightning. Quick as a flash.*
Ce fut un éclair de génie. *It was a stroke of genius.*
éclairage m. *lighting, illumination.*
Eclairage des rues. *Street lighting.*
éclaircir to *clear up, clarify, explain.*
s'éclaircir to *clear up, become brighter; lighten (color).*
Le temps s'éclaircit. *The weather's clearing up.*
éclairer to *light, illuminate.*
Cette lampe n'éclaire pas. *This lamp gives a poor light.*
éclat m. *burst; glitter.*
Son mariage se fit sans éclat. *His (her) marriage took place quietly. He (she) had a quiet wedding.*
Une action d'éclat. *A brilliant feat.*
Partir d'un éclat de rire. *To burst into laughter. To burst out laughing.*
éclatant adj. *loud, ringing.*
éclater to *split, burst.*
Un incendie éclata. *A fire broke out.*
Eclater de rire. *To burst into laughter. To burst out laughing.*
ÉCOLE f. *school, schoolhouse.*
Se rendre à l'école. *To go to school.*
Maître d'école. *Schoolteacher.*
écolier m. (écolière f.) *schoolboy, schoolgirl.*
éconduire to *show to the door.*
écono me adj. *thrifty.*
ÉCONOMIE f. *economics; thrift; pl. savings.*
Economie politique. *Political economy.*
Par économie de temps. *To save time.*
Faire des économies. *To save money. To put money aside.*
économique adj. *economical.*
économiser to *save.*
Economiser pour l'avenir. *To save up for the future.*
écorce f. *bark; rind, peel.*
écorcher to *peel off, graze.*
Il écorche le français. *He murders French.*
écossais noun and adj. *Scotch.*
écouler to *flow out, run out.*
Faire écouler l'eau. *To drain off the water.*
écoute f. *listening-place.*
Se tenir aux écoutes. *To keep one's ears open. To eavesdrop.*
ÉCOUTER to *listen to.*
Maintenant je suis tout à vous, je vous écoute. *"Now I'm at your disposal; I'm listening."*
Ecoutez! *Look here! I'll tell you what!*
Ecoutez-moi. *Take my advice. Listen to me.*
J'écoute. *Number, please? (telephone).*
écran m. *screen.*
écrasant adj. *crushing.*
écraser to *crush, run over.*
Vous allez vous faire écraser. *You'll be run*

over *(you'll get yourself run over).*
Je suis écrasé de travail. *I'm swamped with work.*
s'écraser to *collapse.*
s'écrier to *cry out, exclaim.*
ÉCRIRE to *write.*
Je lui ai écrit un mot. *I dropped him a line.*
J'écris toujours toutes mes lettres à la machine. *I always type my letters.*
Machine à écrire. *Typewriter.*
Comment écrit-on ce mot en français? *How do you write (spell) this word in French?*
écriteau m. *poster, notice.*
ÉCRITURE f. *handwriting.*
Il a une belle écriture. *He has good handwriting.*
ÉCRIVAIN m. *writer.*
s'écrouler to *collapse, fall to pieces.*
Tous leurs plans s'écroulèrent. *All their plans collapsed.*
écume f. *foam.*
écureuil m. *squirrel.*
écurie f. *stable.*
édifice m. *building.*
édifier to *erect; edify, enlighten.*
Il m'a édifié sur cette affaire. *He enlightened me about the matter.*
éditer to *publish.*
éditeur m. *publisher.*
édition f. *publication, edition.*
Edition épuisée. *Out of print.*
Maison d'édition. *Publishing house.*
éditorial (éditoriaux pl.) adj. *editorial.*
ÉDUCATION f. *education; breeding, manners.*
Ils ont reçu une excellente éducation. *They received an excellent education.*
C'est un homme sans éducation. *He's an illbred person. He's a boor.*
Il n'a pas d'éducation. *He has no breeding.*
effacé adj. *unobtrusive, retiring.*
Manières effacées. *Retiring manners.*
effacer to *erase, obliterate.*
s'effacer to *fade, wear away, stand aside.*
Les souvenirs s'effacent vite. *Memories fade rapidly.*
effaré adj. *frightened, dismayed.*
s'effarer to *be frightened, startled.*
effaroucher to *startle.*
effectif (effective f.) adj. *effective.*
effectivement *effectively; in reality, actually.*
Cela est arrivé effectivement. *It really (actually) happened.*
effectuer to *effect, carry out.*
Effectuer une réconciliation. *To bring about a reconciliation.*
effervescence f. *effervescence.*
effervescent adj. *effervescent.*
EFFET m. *impression, effect.*
Prendre effet. *To take effect. To go into effect.*
Il me fait l'effet d'un ignorant. *He strikes me as being very ignorant.*
A cet effet. *To this end.*
Mon conseil a produit l'effet voulu. *My advice had the desired effect.*
Cela fait de l'effet. 1. *That is effective.* 2. *That has the right effect. That looks well. That attracts attention.*
En effet. *As a matter of fact.*
Sans effet. *Ineffective.*
Il a manqué son effet. *He failed to make the impression (he was supposed to).*
effets m. pl. *possessions, belongings.*
Faites vos effets. *Pack up your things.*

Ces effets ont été portés. *These clothes have been worn.*
efficace adj. *effective, adequate.*
efficacité f. *effectiveness.*
effigie f. *effigy.*
effiler *to taper.*
effleurer *to touch lightly.*
s'effondrer *to fall in, break down.*
Le plafond s'effondra. *The ceiling collapsed.*
s'efforcer *to endeavor, strive.*
EFFORT m. *effort.*
Malgré tous nos efforts. *Despite all our efforts.*
Faire un effort sur soi-même. *To exercise self-control.*
effrayer *to frighten.*
effroi m. *fright, terror, fear.*
effronté adj. *brazen-faced, shameless.*
effronterie f. *impudence.*
effroyable adj. *frightful.*
effusion f. *effusion, overflowing.*
Avec effusion. *Effusively.*
EGAL (égale, égales f., égaux m. pl.) noun and adj. *equal.*
Sous ce rapport, il est sans égal. *In that respect he has no equal.*
C'est égal! N'importe! *It doesn't matter! Never mind!*
Ça m'est bien égal. *I don't care. It's all the same to me.*
Tout cela lui est bien égal. *All that's the same to him. All that makes no difference to him. He's indifferent to all that.*
Cela vous est-il égal que je ferme la porte? *Do you mind if I shut the door?*
ÉGALEMENT *equally; also.*
J'irai également. *I'll go too. I'll also go.*
égaler *to equalize, equal.*
égaliser *to equalize.*
égalité f. *equality, evenness.*
ÉGARD m. *regard.*
N'ayez aucune crainte à cet égard. *Have no fear on that score.*
Avoir des égards. *To be considerate.*
Eu égard aux circonstances. *All things considered. Considering the circumstances.*
Il a manqué à sa parole à mon égard. *He didn't keep his word to me.*
Qu'avez-vous à dire à son égard? *What do you have to say concerning (about) him?*
égarer *to mislay, lose.*
J'ai égaré ma montre. *I mislaid my watch.*
s'égarer *to get lost.*
Je me suis égaré. *I got lost.*
égayer *to cheer up.*
église f. *church.*
égoïsme m. *egoism, selfishness.*
égoïste m. and f. noun and adj. *egoist; selfish.*
Agir en égoïste. *To act selfishly.*
Une personne égoïste. *A selfish person.*
égorger *to butcher, slaughter.*
égout m. *drain, sewer.*
égoutter *to drain.*
Faire égoutter des légumes. *To strain vegetables.*
égratigner *to scratch.*
élan m. *spring, bound; outburst; impulse.*
D'un seul élan. *At one bound.*
Elan de l'imagination. *Flight of the imagination.*
élancé adj. *tall and slim.*
s'élancer *to rush, spring.*
Il s'élança à sa poursuite. *He dashed after him.*
élargir *to widen, stretch.*

élastique m. and f. noun and adj. *elastic.*
élection f. *election.*
électricité f. *electricity.*
électrophone m. *record player, phonograph.*
élégance f. *elegance.*
élégant adj. *elegant; stylish.*
élément m. *element.*
Il est dans son élément. *He's in his element.*
élémentaire adj. *elementary.*
éléphant m. *elephant.*
élevage m. *breeding, raising (of animals).*
élévation f. *elevation; rise.*
élève m. and f. *student, pupil.*
élevé adj. *high; brought up, reared.*
Bien élevé. *Well-bred.*
Mal élevé. *Ill-bred.*
élever *to bring up; raise, erect.*
Elever des enfants. *To rear (raise) children.*
On lui a élevé un monument. *They erected a monument to him.*
s'élever *to rise, arise.*
éliminer *to eliminate.*
élire *to elect.*
élite f. *elite.*
ELLE (elles pl.) *she; it; her.*
Vous pouvez vous fier à elle. *You can trust her. You can have confidence in her.*
Chez elle. *At her house.*
Chacune d'elles. *Each of them.*
elle-même *herself.*
elles-mêmes (f. pl.) *themselves.*
éloge m. *praise.*
Adresser des éloges à quelqu'un. *To praise someone.*
Faire l'éloge de quelqu'un. *To sing someone's praises.*
élogieux (élogieuse f.) adj. *laudatory, flattering.*
Il parla de lui en termes élogieux. *He spoke highly of him.*
éloigné adj. *far, distant, remote.*
Le plus éloigné. *The furthermost.*
Avenir peu éloigné. *Near future.*
Rien n'est plus éloigné de mes intentions. *Nothing is further from my intentions.*
Parent éloigné. *Distant relative.*
éloignement m. *absence, removal.*
éloigner *to move away.*
Eloigner les soupçons. *To avert suspicion.*
Eloigner une pensée. *To dismiss a thought.*
s'éloigner *to move off, withdraw.*
S'éloigner de tout le monde. *To shun everybody.*
éloquence f. *eloquence.*
éloquent adj. *eloquent.*
émail m. *enamel.*
émancipation f. *emancipation.*
émanciper *to emancipate.*
s'émanciper *to gain one's freedom.*
émaner *to emanate, issue forth.*
emballage m. *packing, wrapping.*
Papier d'emballage. *Wrapping paper.*
emballer *to pack.*
s'emballer *to be carried away.*
Ne vous emballez pas! *Keep cool!*
S'emballer pour quelque chose. *To be keen on something.*
embarcadère m. *pier.*
embargo m. *embargo.*
embarquement m. *embarking.*
embarquer *to take on board; involve.*
Ce sont eux qui l'ont embarqué dans cette affaire. *They're the ones who got him involved in that affair.*
s'embarquer *to go on board, start upon.*

Ils s'embarquèrent à Marseille. *They embarked at Marseilles.*
embarras m. *obstacle; difficulty, trouble.*
Se trouver dans l'embarras. *To be in difficulties.*
Se tirer d'embarras. *To get out of a difficulty.*
Faire des embarras. *To be fussy (particular).*
Je n'ai que l'embarras du choix. *I have too much to choose from.*
embarrassant adj. *cumbersome; perplexing.*
Une situation embarrassante. *An embarrassing position.*
embarrassé adj. *perplexed, embarrassed.*
embarrasser *to embarrass.*
Il n'est jamais embarrassé. *He's never at a loss.*
Que cela ne vous embarrasse pas. *Don't let that trouble you (bother you, put you out). Have no fear on that score.*
Il est embarrassé d'un rien. *He makes a mountain out of a molehill.*
Cette question m'embarrasse. *That question puzzles me.*
embaucher *to hire.*
embellir *to embellish; grow more beautiful.*
Comme elle a embelli! *How beautiful she's become!*
embêtant adj. (fam.). *boring; annoying.*
embêter (fam.). *to annoy.*
s'embêter (fam.). *to be bored.*
emblée *used only in the following phrase:*
D'emblée. *At once. Right away.*
emblème m. *emblem.*
embonpoint m. *stoutness, weight.*
embouteillage m. *traffic jam, tie-up.*
embranchement m. *branching off; branch.*
embrasser *to embrace, kiss.*
N'embrassez pas trop à la fois. *Don't undertake too much at once. Don't try to do too many things at the same time.*
Embrasser une autre religion. *To adopt another religion.*
embrayage m. *clutch (car).*
embrouiller *to entangle; confuse.*
s'embrouiller *to get confused.*
embûche f. *ambush, snare.*
embuscade f. *ambush, snare.*
émeraude f. *emerald.*
émerveillé adj. *amazed, filled with wonder.*
émetteur (émettrice f.) adj. *broadcasting.*
émettre *to emit, issue; express.*
Emettre une opinion. *To express an opinion.*
émeute f. *riot, outbreak.*
émigrant m. *emigrant.*
émigration f. *emigration.*
émigré m. *refugee.*
émigrer *to emigrate, migrate.*
éminence f. *eminence.*
éminent adj. *eminent.*
émissaire m. *emissary.*
émission f. *emission, issue; radio broadcast.*
emmagasiner *to store (goods).*
emmêler *to entangle, mix up.*
emmener *to lead away, take out.*
émoi m. *agitation, excitement.*
émotion f. *emotion, stir.*
émotionner *to move, stir (emotionally), thrill.*
s'émotionner *to be moved, stirred, roused; get excited.*
émouvant adj. *moving, touching.*
émouvoir *to move, rouse.*
Elle était émue jusqu'aux larmes. *She was moved to tears.*
empaqueter *to pack, make into a parcel.*
s'emparer *to take hold of.*

empêchement *m. hindrance, impediment, bar.*
EMPÊCHER *to prevent, keep from.*
    Empêchez-les de faire cela. *Prevent (keep) them from doing that.*
    Il faut souffrir ce que l'on ne peut empêcher. *What can't be cured must be endured.*
    Qu'est-ce qui vous a empêché de venir? *What kept you from coming?*
s'empêcher *to refrain from.*
empereur *m. emperor.*
empesé *adj. stiff, starched.*
empeser *to starch.*
    Faire empeser. *To have (something) starched.*
empester *to infect.*
emphase *f. pomposity, bombast.*
empiéter *to encroach upon, infringe.*
empiler *to stack.*
empire *m. empire.*
empirer *to get worse.*
emplacement *m. site, location.*
emplette *f. purchase.*
    J'ai fait des emplettes. *I've been shopping.*
EMPLOI *m. employment, function.*
    Mode d'emploi. *Directions for use.*
    Il est apte à tous les emplois. *He's well qualified for every occupation.*
    Etre sans emploi. *To be out of work.*
employé *m. employee.*
EMPLOYER *to use.*
    Ils ont employé tous les moyens. *They've tried everything. They've tried all possible means.*
empocher *to pocket.*
empoigner *to grasp, seize.*
empoisonnement *m. poisoning.*
empoisonner *to poison.*
    Elle empoisonne sa vie. *She makes life unbearable for him (her).*
emportement *m. transport, anger.*
EMPORTER *to carry away.*
    Le vent a emporté mon chapeau. *The wind blew my hat away.*
    Emportez tout cela. *Take all that away.*
    Il a été emporté par la fièvre thyphoïde. *He died of typhoid. He was carried off by typhoid.*
    Restez calme, ne vous laissez pas emporter. *Remain calm, don't lose control of yourself.*
    L'emporter sur quelqu'un. *To get the best of someone.*
    Il fut emporté par l'enthousiasme. *He was carried away by enthusiasm.*
s'emporter *to run away; fly into a passion.*
    Les chevaux se sont emportés. *The horses ran away.*
    Il s'emporta. *He flew into a rage.*
empreindre *to imprint.*
empreinte *f. impression, print.*
    Empreintes digitales. *Fingerprints.*
empressé *adj. eager, zealous.*
empressement *m. eagerness, readiness.*
    Mettre beaucoup d'empressement à faire quelque chose. *To be more than willing to do something.*
s'empresser *to hurry, hasten.*
emprise *f. expropriation; influence.*
    Il a beaucoup d'emprise sur lui. *He has a lot of influence over him.*
emprisonnement *m. imprisonment.*
emprisonner *to imprison.*
emprunt *m. borrowing, loan.*
emprunter *to borrow.*
ému *adj. moved, touched.*
EN *into, in, to, within.*

    Aller en ville. *To go into town.*
    Venir en auto. *To come by car.*
    Aller en Amérique. *To go to America.*
    En son honneur. *In his honor.*
    En été. *In the summer.*
    Il est né en 1912. *He was born in 1912.*
    En son absence. *In his absence.*
    En vacances. *On vacation.*
    Montre en or. *Gold watch.*
    De mal en pis. *From bad to worse.*
    De jour en jour. *From day to day.*
    On apprend en vieillissant. *We learn as we grow older.*
    Voyager en auto (avion, bateau, chemin de fer, taxi, voiture). *To travel by auto (plane, boat, railway, taxi, car).*
    En deux jours. *In (within) two days.*
EN *some, any; of him, of her, of it, of them; from there.*
    En avez-vous? *Do you have any (of it, of them)?*
    En voulez-vous? *Do you want some (of it, of them)?*
    A-t-il de l'argent? —Oui, il en a. *Does he have any money? —Yes, he has some.*
    Donnez-en à Jean. *Give some to John.*
    Avez-vous besoin de mon livre? —Oui, j'en ai besoin. *Do you need my book? —Yes, I need it.*
    Ont-ils des livres? —Ils en ont beaucoup. *Do they have any books?—They have many of them.*
    Vient-il de Paris? —Il en vient directement. *Is he coming from Paris? —He's coming directly from there.*
    Qu'en pensez-vous? *What do you think of (about) it?*
    S'en aller. *To go away.*
    S'en faire. *To worry.*
    Ne t'en fais pas. *Don't worry.*
encadrer *to frame.*
enceinte *f. enclosure, walls.*
enceinte *adj. pregnant.*
encercler *to encircle.*
enchaînement *m. linking-up; connection.*
enchaîner *to chain; link; connect.*
enchanter *to enchant, charm.*
    Je suis enchanté de vous revoir. *I am delighted to see you again.*
    Ça ne m'enchante pas. *It doesn't appeal to me.*
    Permettez-moi de vous presenter à M. Lardieu.—Enchanté. *I'd like to introduce you to Mr. Lardieu.—Glad to know you.*
enchère *f. bid.*
    Vente aux enchères. *Auction sale. Sale by auction.*
enchevêtré *adj. tangled, involved.*
enchevêtrer *to entangle; ravel.*
enclin *adj. inclined, apt.*
encolure *f. neck-opening.*
encombre *m. hindrance.*
    Nous sommes arrivés sans encombre. *We arrived without difficulty.*
encombrement *m. obstruction; crowd.*
encombrer *to encumber.*
ENCORE *yet, still.*
    Quoi encore? *What else?*
    Encore une fois. *Once more.*
    Attendons encore un peu. *Let's wait a little longer.*
    Hier encore je lui ai parlé. *I spoke to him only yesterday.*
    Il n'est pas encore là. *He hasn't come yet.*

encourageant *adj. encouraging.*
encouragement *m. encouragement.*
encourager *to encourage.*
encourir *to incur.*
encre *f. ink.*
encrier *m. inkwell.*
encyclopédie *f. encyclopedia.*
endormi *adj. asleep.*
endormir *to put to sleep.*
s'endormir *to fall asleep.*
    Elle s'est endormie de fatigue. *She was so tired that she fell asleep.*
ENDROIT *m. place.*
    Quel joli endroit! *What a beautiful place!*
    Cette pièce est très amusante par endroits. *This play is very amusing in places.*
    L'endroit faible. *The weak spot.*
    Il a mal agi à mon endroit. *He didn't act well toward me. He didn't treat me right.*
enduire *to smear, cover.*
endurance *f. endurance.*
endurcir *to harden.*
endurer *to endure, bear.*
énergie *f. strength, energy.*
énergique *adj. energetic.*
énervant *adj. irritating.*
énervé *adj. irritated, exasperated, on edge.*
énerver *to get on someone's nerves, upset someone.*
s'énerver *to become irritated, exasperated; get nervous.*
enfance *f. childhood.*
enfant *m. child.*
enfantillage *m. childishness.*
enfantin *adj. childish.*
enfer *m. hell.*
enfermer *to lock up, lock away.*
ENFIN *at last, finally, after all.*
    Il y est enfin arrivé, il le mérite bien. *He finally succeeded—he certainly deserves to.*
    Je suis heureux d'être reçu enfin à mon examen. *I'm glad I finally passed that examination.*
enflammer *to inflame.*
enfler *to swell.*
enfoncer *to drive in, push in.*
s'enfoncer *to penetrate, go deep into.*
enfouir *to bury in the ground.*
s'enfuir *to flee.*
engagé *adj. Stuck, jammed (mechanism).*
engagement *m. obligation; pledge; pawning.*
engager *to pledge, promise, bind; engage; urge.*
    Cela n'engage à rien. *That's not binding.*
s'engager *to enlist, pledge.*
engin *m. engine.*
englober *to include, take in.*
engloutir *to swallow; engulf.*
s'engouffrer *to be engulfed.*
engourdi *adj. numb.*
engourdir *to make numb.*
engourdissement *m. numbness.*
engraisser *to fatten; gain weight.*
enivrer *to go to one's head, intoxicate.*
enjamber *to step over, stride.*
enjeu *m. (enjeux pl.) stake.*
enjoindre *to enjoin; to order.*
enlacer *to entwine, clasp.*
enlever *to remove, wipe off, clear away.*
    Enlevez toutes ces choses. *Remove all these things. Take all these things away.*
ennemi *noun (m.) and adj. enemy.*
ENNUI *m. nuisance, trouble, bother.*
    Il lui a causé beaucoup d'ennuis. *He caused him a lot of trouble.*

Cela a amené des ennuis. *That caused all sorts of trouble.*

Je regrette si je vous ai causé un ennui quelconque. *I'm sorry if I caused you any inconvenience.*

Mourir d'ennui. *To be frightfully bored.*

Quel ennui! *What a nuisance!*

ennuyer *to bore, bother.*

Cela vous ennuierait-il d'attendre un peu? *Would you mind waiting a little?*

Je suis très ennuyé. *I'm very much worried. I have a lot of trouble (a lot of worries).*

s'ennuyer *to be bored.*

ennuyeux (ennuyeuse f.) adj. *boring, tedious.*

énorme adj. *enormous.*

énormément *enormously, extremely.*

Je le regrette énormément. *I'm extremely sorry.*

énormité f. *enormousness; enormity.*

s'enquérir *to inquire.*

enquête f. *inquiry.*

Faire une enquête. *To hold an inquiry.*

enragé adj. *rabid, mad.*

enrager *to enrage, fume.*

enregistrer *to register.*

s'enrhumer *to catch a cold.*

s'enrichir *to grow (get) rich.*

s'enrôler *to enlist.*

enroué adj. *hoarse, husky.*

enrouler *to roll up, wind.*

enseigne f. *sign; token.*

Nous sommes tous logés à la même enseigne. *We're all in the same boat.*

enseignement m. *teaching, education.*

enseigner *to teach.*

ENSEMBLE noun m. and adv. *together, whole.*

L'ensemble du travail est bon. *The work is good on the whole.*

Vue d'ensemble. *General view. All-round picture.*

Etre bien ensemble. *To be on good terms.*

Ils sont arrivés ensemble. *They arrived together.*

ensevelir *to bury.*

ensoleillé adj. *sunny, sunlit.*

ensorceler *to bewitch.*

ENSUITE *then, afterwards.*

Allons d'abord déjeuner, ensuite nous irons au musée. *Let's first have lunch; afterwards we'll go to the museum.*

Et ensuite? *And what else? And then what?*

s'ensuivre *to follow, ensue.*

entamer *to begin, start.*

Il entama la conversation. *He opened the conversation.*

entasser *to heap up.*

ENTENDRE *to hear, understand.*

J'entends un bruit. *I hear a noise.*

Il entend mal. *He's hard of hearing (he doesn't hear well).*

Elles ne veulent pas en entendre parler. *They won't hear of it. They refuse to consider it.*

Il n'y entend rien. *He can't make it out.*

Il ne veut rien entendre. *He won't listen.*

J'ai entendu dire que . . . *I've heard it said that . . .*

Faire entendre raison à quelqu'un. *To bring someone to reason.*

A l'entendre. *To listen to him. From what he says.*

Faites commes vous l'entendez. *Do what you think best. Do it your own way. Do it any way you please.*

Vous entendez tout de travers. *You misunderstand the whole thing. You've got every-*

thing wrong.

Je n'entends pas que vous fassiez cela. *I won't allow you to do that. I won't hear of your doing that.*

Il n'y entend pas malice. *He means well. He doesn't mean any harm.*

C'est entendu. *That's settled. It's a bargain. Agreed. All right. Very well, it's a deal.*

Bien entendu. *Of course.*

S'ENTENDRE *to be audible; understand; agree.*

On ne s'entend pas ici. *There's so much noise you can't hear anything. You can't hear yourself talk here.*

Ils s'entendent à demi-mot. *They know at once what the other is going to say.*

Lui et moi nous finissons toujours par nous entendre. *We always agree in the end.*

Ils ne s'entendent pas bien. *They don't get along well together.*

Cela s'entend. *It goes without saying.*

Il s'entend aux affaires. *He's a born businessman. He has a good business head.*

entente f. *understanding; agreement; meaning.*

Ils arrivèrent à une entente. *They reached an agreement.*

Mot à double entente. *Word with a double meaning.*

enterrement m. *burial.*

enterrer *to bury.*

entêté adj. *stubborn.*

s'entêter *to be stubborn.*

enthousiasme m. *enthusiasm.*

enthousiasmer *to make someone enthusiastic.*

s'enthousiasmer *to become enthusiastic.*

J'en ai été enthousiasmé. *I was very enthusiastic about it.*

ENTIER (entière f.) adj. *entire, whole.*

La famille entière alla en promenade. *The whole family went for a walk.*

Ce savon se vend dans le monde entier. *This soap is sold all over the world.*

entièrement *entirely, wholly.*

entorse f. *sprain, strain.*

entourer *to surround, encircle.*

entr'acte m. *intermission (theatre).*

s'entraider *to help one another.*

entrain m. *heartiness, spirit.*

Il a de l'entrain. *He's full of energy. He's full of life.*

entraînement m. *training.*

entraîner *to draw along, sweep away; involve; train for sports.*

ENTRE *between, among.*

Tout est fini entre nous. *It's all over between us.*

Nous sommes entre amis. *We are among friends.*

Parler entre les dents. *To mumble.*

Il est entre bonnes mains. *He's in good hands.*

ENTRÉE f. *entrance.*

Entrée interdite. *No admittance.*

Entrée libre. *Admission free.*

Droit d'entrée. *Import duty.*

entrefaite f. (usually in the pl.) *meantime.*

Il arriva sur ces entrefaites. *He arrived in the meantime.*

entremise f. *intervention.*

entreprendre *to undertake, attempt.*

entreprise f. *enterprise, undertaking.*

Entreprise commerciale. *Business concern.*

ENTRER *to enter, come in.*

Entrez. *Come in.*

Défense d'entrer. *No admittance.*

Entrez dans cette chambre-ci. *Go into this room.*

Entrer à l'école. *To enter (begin) school.*

Entrer à l'université. *To enter the university.*

Entrer en fonctions. *To take up one's duties.*

Il ne m'était pas entré dans l'idée que . . . *It never entered my mind that . . .*

entresol m. *mezzanine.*

entretenir *to keep up, maintain, entertain, support.*

entretien m. *upkeep; conversation.*

Frais d'entretien. *Cost of maintenance.*

J'ai eu un entretien avec elle. *I had a talk with her.*

entrevoir *to catch a glimpse of.*

Je n'ai fait que l'entrevoir. *I only caught a glimpse of him (her).*

entrevue f. *interview.*

énumérer *to enumerate.*

envahir *to invade.*

enveloppe f. *envelope.*

envelopper *to wrap up, surround.*

envergure f. *spread, span.*

De grande envergure. *Far-reaching.*

envers m. *wrong side, back.*

Mettre sa robe à l'envers. *To put on one's dress inside out.*

envers *toward, to.*

Envers et contre tous. *Against everyone. Against all comers.*

ENVIE f. *envy; wish.*

Par envie. *Through jealousy.*

Cela vous donne envie de rire. *It (that) makes you want to laugh. It's enough to make you laugh.*

Elle mourait d'envie d'y aller. *She was dying to go there.*

Avec envie. *Longingly.*

J'en ai envie. *I'd like to have it. I feel like it.*

Je n'ai pas envie d'y aller. *I don't feel like going there.*

envier *to envy, covet.*

envieux (envieuse f.) adj. *envious.*

environ *around; nearly.*

Il doit être environ cinq heures. *It must be about five o'clock.*

J'ai environ cent francs. *I have about a hundred francs.*

environs m. pl. *vicinity; neighborhood.*

Il habite dans les environs de Paris. *He lives near Paris. He lives in the vicinity of Paris.*

envisager *to face; consider.*

envoi m. *parcel.*

Nous avons reçu son envoi. *We received his parcel.*

s'envoler *to fly away.*

envoyé m. *envoy, delegate.*

ENVOYER *to send.*

Il a envoyé chercher le médecin. *He sent for the doctor.*

Elle vous envoie ses meilleures amitiés. *She sends you her best regards.*

Envoyez-moi un mot. *Drop me a line.*

Je vous envoie toutes mes pensées affectueuses. *Affectionately yours (in a letter).*

Envoyez-le promener (fam.). *Send him about his business.*

épais (épaisse f.) adj. *thick, dense, heavy.*

épaisseur f. *thickness; depth; density.*

épanchement m. *pouring out; effusion.*

épancher *to pour out.*

s'épanouir *to open out; beam.*

épargne f. *saving, thrift.*

Caisse d'épargne. *Savings bank.*

épargner *to spare; save.*

éparpiller *to scatter, disperse.*

épars *adj. scattered, dispersed; dishevelled.*
  Cheveux épars. *Dishevelled hair.*
épatant *adj. wonderful, stunning.*
  C'est épatant (*fam.*)! *That's wonderful! That's swell!*
épater *to astound, amaze.*
épaule *f. shoulder.*
épée *f. sword.*
épeler *to spell.*
éperdu *adj. distressed, dismayed.*
éperdument *desperately.*
épeuré *adj. frightened.*
épice *f. spice.*
épicerie *f. grocery store.*
épicier *m. grocer.*
épidémie *f. epidemic.*
épidémique *adj. epidemic.*
épier *to watch, spy upon.*
épilepsie *f. epilepsy.*
épilogue *m. epilogue.*
épinard *m. spinach.*
épine *f. thorn, spine; obstacle.*
épineux (épineuse *f.*) *adj. thorny, ticklish.*
épingle *f. pin.*
  Une épingle à nourrice. *A safety pin.*
épisode *m. episode.*
éploré *adj. weeping.*
éplucher *to peel, clean, sift.*
épluchure *f. piece of peel.*
éponge *f. sponge.*
époque *f. period, time.*
épouse *f. wife.*
épouser *to marry.*
épouvantable *adj. dreadful, appalling, frightful.*
épouvante *f. fright, terror.*
épouvanter *to terrify, dismay.*
époux *m. husband.*
s'éprendre *to fall in love.*
épreuve *f. proof, test, trial, ordeal; print (photography).*
éprouver *to try; experience.*
  J'éprouve du plaisir à vous voir. *I'm very happy to see you.*
  Eprouver une perte. *To suffer a loss.*
  Je l'ai éprouvé par moi-même. *I went through the same experience myself.*
épuisement *m. draining off; exhaustion.*
épuiser *to exhaust.*
  Il a épuisé ma patience. *He exhausted my patience.*
  Ce livre est épuisé. *That book is out of print.*
équilibre *m. equilibrium, balance.*
équilibrer *to balance.*
équipage *m. crew.*
équipe *f. team.*
  Chef d'équipe. *Foreman.*
  L'esprit d'équipe. *Team spirit.*
équiper *to equip.*
équivalent *noun (m.) and adj. equivalent.*
équivoque *adj. equivocal.*
éreintement *m. exhaustion.*
éreinter *to exhaust.*
s'éreinter *to tire oneself out.*
ériger *to erect.*
errant *adj. wandering, roving.*
errer *to wander, go astray; err, make a mistake.*
  Nous avons erré toute la nuit. *We wandered around the whole night.*
  Tout le monde peut errer. *Anyone is likely to make a mistake.*
erreur *f. mistake, error.*
erroné *adj. erroneous, wrong, mistaken.*
éruption *f. eruption.*

escadre *f. squadron.*
escale *f. call, stop.*
  Vol sans escale. *Nonstop flight.*
escalier *m. staircase, stairs.*
escargot *m. snail.*
esclavage *m. slavery.*
esclave *m. and f. slave.*
escompte *m. discount, rebate.*
  A l'escompte. *At a discount.*
escompter *to discount.*
escorte *f. escort; convoy.*
escorter *to escort; convoy.*
escrime *f. fencing.*
escroc *m. swindler, crook.*
escroquer *to steal, swindle.*
espace *m. area, space.*
espacé *adj. far-apart.*
Espagne *m. Spain.*
  En Espagne. *In, to Spain.*
espagnol *noun (m.) and adj. Spanish.*
espèce *f. species, kind, sort.*
  L'espèce humaine. *Mankind.*
  Une espèce de. *A sort of.*
espérance *f. hope.*
espérer *to hope, expect.*
espiègle *adj. mischievous.*
espièglerie *f. prank.*
espion *m. spy.*
espoir *m. hope.*
ESPRIT *m. spirit, mind; sense, wit.*
  Il se met l'esprit à la torture. *He's racking his brains.*
  Quand est-ce que cette idée vous est venue à l'esprit? *When did you get that idea?*
  Il a de l'esprit. *He's witty (clever).*
  Avez-vous perdu l'esprit? *Have you lost your senses?*
  C'est un esprit léger. *He's a superficial person.*
  Avoir l'esprit des affaires. *To have a good business head.*
  Présence d'esprit. *Presence of mind.*
  Etat d'esprit. *State of mind.*
esquisse *f. sketch.*
esquisser *to sketch, outline.*
esquiver *to elude; dodge.*
s'esquiver *to slip off.*
essai *m. attempt, trial.*
  C'était son coup d'essai. *It was his first attempt.*
  Prendre à l'essai. *To take on approval.*
  Mettre à l'essai. *To put to the test.*
  Essai de vitesse. *Speed test.*
  Faire un essai. *To try (something) out.*
essayage *m. fitting; testing.*
  Le salon d'essayage. *Fitting room.*
ESSAYER *to try, try on.*
  Laissez-moi essayer. *Let me try.*
  Essayer une robe. *To try on a dress.*
essence *f. essence; gas.*
  Vérifier le niveau d'essence. *To check the gas gauge.*
essentiel *m. essential.*
  L'essentiel. *The main point.*
essentiel (essentielle *f.*) *adj. essential.*
essoufflé *adj. out of breath.*
essouffler *to put out of breath.*
s'essouffler *to be out of breath.*
essuie-main *m. hand towel.*
essuyer *to wipe; to suffer, undergo (a loss, blow, etc.).*
  Essuyer la vaisselle. *To dry the dishes.*
  Essuyez votre figure. *Wipe your face.*
  Essuyer un refus. *To meet with a refusal.*
  Essuyer une perte. *To suffer a loss.*
estimation *f. estimation, appraising.*

estime *f. esteem, regard.*
estimer *to estimate, value.*
estomac *m. stomach.*
  J'ai mal à l'estomac. *I have a stomachache.*
estrade *f. platform, stage.*
estropié *adj. crippled, disabled.*
estropier *to cripple.*
ET *and.*
  Deux et deux. *Two and two.*
  Je n'ai pas faim. Et vous? *I'm not hungry. How about you?*
étable *f. stable.*
ÉTABLIR *to establish, set up; lay down, settle.*
  Son père l'a établi à Paris. *His father started him in business in Paris.*
  Etablir un prix. *To fix a price.*
  On ne put établir son identité. *They couldn't identify him.*
s'établir *to establish oneself.*
  Il s'est établi à son compte. *He's in business for himself.*
établissement *m. establishment, premises.*
  Etablissement de charité. *Charitable institution.*
étage *m. floor, flight, story.*
étagère *f. rack, shelf.*
étain *m. tin.*
étalage *m. display, shopwindow.*
étaler *to spread out, unfold; show off.*
étancher *to quench; stanch.*
étang *m. fish pond; pool.*
étape *f. stage, halting-place, lap (of race).*
ÉTAT *m. state, condition.*
  Il y a du mieux dans son état. *There is some improvement in his health.*
  Il est en état de payer. *He's in position to pay.*
  Il était en état de légitime défense. *It was a case of legitimate self-defense.*
  Faire grand état de quelque chose. *To make a lot of fuss about something.*
  Ses états de service sont bons. *His record is satisfactory.*
  Un état lucratif. *A well-paid job.*
  Les bureaux de l'état. *Government bureaus.*
  Les Etats-Unis *m. pl. The United States.*
  Aux Etats-Unis. *In (to) the United States.*
ÉTÉ *m. summer.*
  été *been.*
éteindre *to put out, extinguish; cancel.*
s'éteindre *to die out.*
étendre *to spread out, stretch out; extend, expand.*
s'étendre *to extend, stretch.*
étendue *f. expanse, extent.*
éternel (éternelle *f.*) *adj. eternal.*
éternité *f. eternity.*
éternuer *to sneeze.*
étincelant *adj. sparkling.*
étinceler *to sparkle.*
étincelle *f. spark.*
étiquette *f. label, tag; etiquette.*
étoffe *f. material.*
étoile *f. star.*
étonnant *adj. amazing; wonderful.*
étonnement *m. amazement; surprise.*
étonner *to surprise, amaze.*
étouffer *to suffocate; deaden; stifle; hush up.*
étourderie *f. thoughtless action; blunder.*
étourdi *adj. careless, thoughtless.*
étourdissement *m. dizziness; shock.*
étrange *adj. strange; foreign.*
étranger *m. (étrangère f.) foreigner; abroad.*
  Vivre à l'étranger. *To live abroad.*
  Il y a beaucoup d'étrangers à Paris. *There are*

many foreigners in Paris.

étranger (étrangère f.) adj. foreign.

étrangler to strangle.

être m. being, creature.

Un être humain. A human being.

Le bien-être. Well-being.

ÊTRE to be.

Etre fatigué. To be tired.

Etre à l'heure. To be on time.

C'est vrai. It's true.

A qui est ceci? To whom does this belong?

Qu'est-ce que c'est? What is it?

Il est à Paris. He is in Paris.

Il est arrivé hier. He arrived yesterday.

J'y suis. I understand. I get it.

Vous n'y êtes pas. You don't understand.

Ainsi soit-il. So be it.

Etant donné votre refus. Given your refusal.

Ça y est! That's it!

C'est, ce sont. It (he, she, this, that) is; they are.

étreindre to clasp, embrace.

étreinte f. embrace.

étrennes f. pl. New Year's gift.

étroit adj. narrow, limited.

étroitesse f. narrowness.

ÉTUDE f. study.

L'étude des langues. The study of languages.

Ce notaire a vendu son étude. That notary has sold his practice.

A l'étude. Under consideration (of a project, etc.).

Il y fit ses études de droit. He studied law there.

étudiant m. (étudiante f.) student.

Etudiant en médecine. Medical student.

étudier to study.

étui m. case, sheath.

Etui à cigarettes. Cigarette case.

eu had.

EUX they, them.

eux-mêmes (m. pl.) themselves.

évacuer to evacuate.

évadé m. escaped prisoner.

s'évader to escape, get away.

évaluation f. evaluation.

évaluer to value, estimate.

s'évanouir to faint.

évanouissement m. fainting spell.

s'évaporer to evaporate.

évasif (évasive f.) adj. evasive.

évasion f. escape, flight.

éveil m. alarm, awakening.

éveillé adj. lively, wide-awake.

éveiller to wake, arouse.

Cela éveilla mon attention. That aroused my attention.

Le bruit m'éveilla. The noise woke me up.

s'éveiller to wake up.

événement m. event.

Le cours des événements. The course of events.

Cela fera événement. That will cause quite a stir.

éventuel (éventuelle f.) adj. possible, likely to happen.

éventuellement possibly, on occasion.

évêque m. bishop.

évidemment evidently; naturally.

Evidemment, il faut y aller. Of course, we have to go.

évidence f. evidence, conspicuousness.

En évidence. Conspicuous.

Mettre en évidence. To make evident.

évident adj. evident.

évier m. kitchen sink.

éviter to avoid, prevent.

évoluer to develop, evolve.

évolution f. evolution.

évoquer to evoke.

EXACT adj. exact, true, correct.

C'est exact. It's a fact.

Il n'est jamais exact. He is never on time.

exactement exactly.

exactitude f. correctness, accuracy.

exagérer to exaggerate.

exalter to exalt, extol.

s'exalter to grow excited, enthusiastic.

examen m. examination.

examiner to examine, investigate.

exaspération f. exasperation.

exaspérer to exasperate.

s'exaspérer to become exasperated.

exaucer to fulfill, grant.

excéder to exceed.

EXCELLENT adj. excellent.

excentricité f. eccentricity.

excentrique m. and f. noun and adj. eccentric.

excepté excepting, besides.

exception f. exception.

Sans exception. Without exception.

exceptionnel (exceptionnelle f.) adj. exceptional.

excès m. excess, intemperance.

excessif (excessive f.) adj. excessive.

exciter to excite, stir up, arouse.

exclamation f. exclamation.

Point d'exclamation. Exclamation mark.

s'exclamer to exclaim, cry out.

exclure to exclude.

exclusion f. exclusion.

exclusivement exclusively.

exclusivité f. exclusiveness.

excursion f. excursion, tour.

excusable adj. excusable.

excuse f. excuse, apology, pretense.

EXCUSER to excuse.

Excusez-moi. Excuse me. Pardon me.

S'EXCUSER to apologize.

Je m'excuse, cela m'est sorti de la tête. I'm sorry. It slipped my mind.

exécuter to perform, carry out, execute.

exécution f. execution, performance; enforcement.

Mettre un projet en exécution. To carry out a plan.

exemplaire m. pattern; sample.

En double exemplaire. In duplicate.

EXEMPLE m. example.

Donner l'exemple. To set the example.

Suivre l'exemple de quelqu'un. To follow someone's example.

Que ceci vous serve d'exemple. Let this be a lesson (warning) to you.

Supposons à titre d'exemple. Let's suppose for argument's sake.

Joindre l'exemple à la parole. To suit the action to the word.

Etre un exemple de vertu. To be a model of virtue.

Par exemple! Really! How do you like that!

Ça, par exemple, c'est trop fort. That, really, is too much.

Par exemple. For example.

exempt adj. exempt.

Exempt de droits. Duty-free.

exercer to exercise, practice, exert.

s'exercer to drill, practice.

exercice m. exercise, practice.

Exercice d'une profession. Practice of a profession.

Faire l'exercice. To drill.

exhaler to exhale; give vent to.

exhiber to show, produce.

exhibition f. exhibition.

exigeant adj. exacting, demanding.

Elle est exigeante. She's too hard to please.

exigence f. exactingness; exigence.

Satisfaire les exigences. To meet the requirements.

exiger to exact, require.

Qu'exigez-vous encore de moi? What more do you expect (want) from me?

L'honneur l'exige. Honor demands it.

exil m. exile.

exilé noun and adj. exile; exiled.

exiler to exile.

existence f. existence; life.

Moyens d'existence. Means of subsistence.

exister to exist, live.

expansion f. expansion.

expatrier to expatriate.

expédier to send off, forward; ship.

expéditeur m. (expéditrice f.) shipper.

expédition f. expedition; shipment.

expérience f. experience.

Faire une expérience. To experience. To have an experience.

expert m. and f. noun and adj. expert.

expiation f. expiation.

expier to expiate, atone for.

expiration f. expiration.

expirer to expire; die.

explication f. explanation.

expliquer to explain.

s'expliquer to understand.

Je ne m'explique pas comment il a pu le faire. I can't understand how he was able to do it.

exploit m. exploit, feat, achievement.

exploitation f. exploitation.

exploiter to exploit, take advantage of; improve.

explorer to explore, search.

explosion f. explosion.

Faire explosion. To blow up.

exportateur m. exporter.

exportation f. export.

exporter to export.

exposé m. statement, report.

Faire l'exposé de. To give an account of.

exposer to show, state; expose, endanger.

Exposer sa vie. To risk one's life.

exposition f. exhibition; exposition, account.

Salle d'exposition. Showroom.

exprès on purpose, purposely.

C'est un fait exprès. It was done on purpose.

exprès (expresse f.) adj. express.

Par exprès. Special delivery.

expression f. expression.

exprimer to express.

exquis adj. exquisite.

extase f. ecstasy, rapture.

s'extasier to go into raptures.

extension f. extension, extent.

s'exténuer to wear oneself out.

extérieur noun (m.) and adj. exterior.

A l'extérieur. Outside.

extérieurement externally.

exterminer to exterminate, annihilate.

extra m. extra.

extraire to extract, draw out.

extrait m. extract.

extraordinaire adj. extraordinary.

extravagance f. extravagance.

extravagant adj. extravagant.
extrême m. extreme, utmost.
extrêmement extremely.
extrémité f. extremity.
exubérance f. exuberance.
exubérant adj. exuberant, immoderate.

F   The sixth letter of the alphabet.

fable f. fable.
fabricant m. manufacturer; mill owner.
fabrication f. manufacture.
fabrique f. factory; manufacture.
    La marque de fabrique. The trade-mark.
    C'est le prix de fabrique. It's the cost price.
fabriquer to manufacture.
    Il fabrique des autos. He manufactures cars.
    Qu'est-ce que vous êtes en train de fabriquer (fam.)? What are you doing? What are you up to?
fabuleusement fabulously.
fabuleux (fabuleuse f.) adj. fabulous.
façade f. front, facade.
face f. face.
    Face à face. Face to face.
    Il faut considérer ce problème sur toutes ses faces. We must consider this problem in all its aspects.
    Pile ou face. Heads or tails.
    Regardez en face. Look on the opposite side.
    Ma maison fait face à la poste. My house faces the post office.
facétieux (facétieuse f.) adj. facetious.
fâché adj. offended, vexed, angry.
fâcher to offend, displease.
    Vous le fâcherez en faisant cela. You will offend him (make him angry) by doing that.
    Soit dit sans vous fâcher. I hope you won't feel offended by what I say. Please don't take offense (at what I'm going to say).
se fâcher to take offense; get angry.
    Il s'est fâché tout rouge. He lost his temper completely. He flared up.
    Il se fâche pour un rien. He takes offense at the least little thing.
    Ne vous fâchez pas. Don't get angry.
fâcheux (fâcheuse f.) adj. annoying.
    Un incident fâcheux. An awkward incident.
FACILE adj. easy.
    C'est plus facile à dire qu'à faire. It's easier said than done.
    Il est facile à vivre. He's easy to get along with.
FACILEMENT easily.
facilité f. facility, ease.
    Il fait tout avec facilité. He does everything with ease.
    Facilités de payements. Easy terms.
faciliter to facilitate, make easy.
FAÇON f. manner.
    De façon à. So as to.
    D'une façon ou d'une autre. Some way or other. One way or another.
    En aucune façon. By no means.
    De cette façon, je vous attends demain. Then I'll expect you tomorrow.
    De toute façon, je vous verrai demain. Anyhow, I'll see you tomorrow.
    Ne faites pas tant de façons. Don't stand on ceremony.
    C'est sa façon de parler. That's his way of speaking. That's the way he speaks.
    Je vais lui dire ma façon de penser. I'll give him a piece of my mind.

    Sans façon. Simply. Informally. Without any fuss.
    Je n'aime pas la façon de cette robe. I don't like the cut (make) of this dress.
    Qu'est-ce que c'est que ces façons? What sort of manners are these? What kind of behavior is this? Is this the way to behave?
façonner to work, shape.
facteur m. factor; postman.
    Il est important de prendre tous ces facteurs en considération. It's important to take all these factors into consideration.
    A quelle heure vient la facteur? What time does the postman come?
faction f. sentry duty.
facture f. bill, invoice.
facultatif (facultative f.) adj. optional.
faculté f. faculty.
    La faculté de droit. The law faculty.
    Il a encore toutes ses facultés. He's still in posession of all his faculties.
fade adj. insipid.
FAIBLE adj. weak.
faiblesse f. weakness.
faiblir to weaken.
faïence f. pottery.
faillir to fail, err; be on the point of; go bankrupt.
    En cela, il a failli. He failed in that.
    Elle a failli tomber. She came near falling. She almost fell.
faillite f. bankruptcy.
FAIM f. hunger.
    Assouvir sa faim. To satisfy one's hunger.
    J'ai une faim de loup. I'm terribly hungry.
    Je mourais de faim. I was starved.
fainéant noun and adj. lazy, idle.
FAIRE to do, make.
    Que faites-vous demain? What are you doing tomorrow?
    Il a fait cette radio lui-même. He built this radio himself.
    Faites comme vous voudrez. Do as you like.
    Faites-le-moi voir. Show it to me. Let me see it.
    Il a fait son devoir. He did his duty.
    Il a fait son chemin. He made his way in the world.
    Il a fait beaucoup d'argent l'an passé. He made a lot of money last year.
    Il fait ses études à Londres. He's studying in London.
    Qu'est-ce que vous voulez que j'y fasse? What can I do about it?
    Vous pouvez faire usage de ma voiture. You can use my car.
    Faire une promenade. To go for a walk.
    Toute réflexion faite. All things considered.
    Il ne sait que faire. He doesn't know what to do.
    Il n'y a rien à faire. There's nothing to be done.
    Qu'est-ce que ça fait? What does it matter?
    Ça ne fait rien. It doesn't matter. It doesn't make any difference.
    Deux et deux font quatre. Two and two are four.
    Il fait nuit. It's dark (night).
    Il n'en fait qu'à sa tête. He does as he pleases.
    Il lui a fait dire de venir. He sent him word to come.
    Faites-le entrer. Show him in.
    Cela fait soixante-douze francs. That's seventy-two francs.
    Comment fait-on pour . . . How does one go about . . .
    Elle ne fait que parler. She does nothing but talk.

    Faire bon voyage. To have a good trip.
    Faire de l'alpinisme. To go mountain climbing.
    Faire de son mieux. To do one's best.
    Faire des photo(graphie)s. To take photos (pictures).
    Faire des repas légers. To take light meals.
    Faire des sports d'hiver. To practice (engage in) winter sports.
    Faire dix minutes de marche. To walk for ten minutes.
    Faire du cyclisme. To ride a bicycle.
    Faire du ski (nautique). To go (water-)skiing.
    Faire l'affaire de. To meet the needs of.
    Faire la connaissance de. To make the acquaintance of.
    Faire la quête. To take up a collection (church).
    Faire la queue. To stand on line.
    Faire le plein (d'essence). To fill up (with gasoline).
    Faire mal. To hurt.
    Faire mieux de. To do better to.
    Faire partie de. To be part of.
    Faire salle comble. To draw a full house (theatre).
    Faire signe à. To motion to.
    Faire une commission. To take, deliver a message.
    Faire un essai. To try (something) out.
    Faire un prix global. To make a total price.
    Faire un tour (un voyage). To take a trip.
    Faire une tournée. To go on tour (theatre).
    Fait à la main. Handmade.
    Il fait beau (chaud, doux, du soleil, du vent, frais, froid, mauvais). The weather is fine (warm, mild, sunny, windy, cool, cold, bad).
    Pourquoi faire? What for?
    Tout à fait. Quite, entirely, altogether.
s'en faire to worry.
    Ne t'en fais pas. Don't worry.
se faire to be made; be done; get used to.
    Il se fait du mauvais sang. He worries himself sick.
    Il se fit naturaliser Américain. He became a naturalized American citizen.
    On se fait à tout. One gets used to everything.
    Il se fait tard. It's getting late.
    Comment se fait-il qu'elle ne soit pas ici? How come she's not here?
    Cela ne se fait pas. People don't do that. That's not done.
faire faire to have done.
    Faire faire le graissage. To have a lubrication job done.
se faire faire to have something done or made for oneself.
    Se faire faire les ongles (une mise en plis). To have one's nails done (one's hair set).
faiseur m. (faiseuse f.) maker.
    Un faiseur de projets. A schemer.
    C'est un faiseur! He's a bluffer!
FAIT m. fact; act.
    Un fait accompli. A fait accompli. An accomplished fact. A thing already done.
    Il était bien au courant du fait. He was well aware of the fact.
    Allons au fait. Let's come to the point.
    Je vais vous mettre au fait. I'll acquaint you with the matter.
    Ces faits sont assez rares. These occurrences are rather rare. These things seldom happen (occur).
    Si fait, si fait. Yes, indeed.
    Au fait. By the way.

fait *done, made.*

faîte *f. top, summit.*

falaise *f. cliff.*

FALLOIR *to be necessary.*

Nous avons tout ce qu'il nous faut. *We've everything we need.*

Merci, c'était juste ce qu'il me fallait. *Thanks a lot, that's just what I needed.*

Il s'en est fallu de peu pour que je réussisse. *I nearly succeeded.*

Il faut que vous y alliez. *You must go there.*

Il faut avouer que c'est un peu de notre faute. *We must admit that it's partly our fault.*

Il fallait voir ça, ça valait mille! *You ought to have seen it, it was worth a fortune!*

Il faudra que j'y aille. *I'll have to go there.*

Vous l'avez fait? —Il a bien fallu. *Did you do it?—I didn't have any choice. I had to.*

C'est un jeune homme comme il faut. *He's a well-bred young man.*

Combien de temps faudra-t-il? *How much time (how long) will it take?*

Il ne faut pas tout croire. *You mustn't believe everything.*

S'il le faut. *If necessary.*

Tout ce qu'il vous faut. *Everything you need.*

fameusement *famously; awfully.*

FAMEUX (fameuse *f.*) *adj. famous.*

familiariser *to familiarize.*

familiarité *f. familiarity.*

familier *m. close friend, a friend of the family.*

Il est un des familiers de la maison. *He's a friend of the family.*

familier (familière *f.*) *adj. familiar.*

Très vite le nouveau système lui devint familier. *He soon became accustomed to the new system.*

Ce visage m'est familier. *I've seen that face before.*

familièrement *familiarly.*

FAMILLE *f. family.*

Toute ma famille était là. *My whole family was there.*

Quel est votre nom de famille? *What's your last name?*

Ils ont un air de famille. *They have (bear) a family resemblance.*

famine *f. starvation.*

fanatique *m. and f. noun and adj. fanatic, fan.*

Un fanatique du cinéma. *A movie fan.*

se faner *to wither, fade.*

fanfaron *m.* (fanfaronne *f.*) *boaster.*

Il fait le fanfaron. *He's bragging.*

fange *f. mud.*

fantaisie *f. fancy, imagination; humor, whim, caprice.*

fantastique *adj. fantastic.*

fantôme *m. ghost.*

farce *f. joke.*

fard *m. make-up for the face.*

Il l'a dit sans fard. *He said it plainly.*

fardeau *m.* (fardeaux *pl.*) *burden.*

se farder *to put on make-up.*

farine *f. flour.*

Ce sont des gens de la même farine. *They're birds of a feather.*

farouche *adj. wild, savage.*

fasciner *to fascinate.*

fastidieux (fastidieuse *f.*) *adj. tedious, dull, wearisome.*

fat *noun (m.) and adj. conceited, vain.*

fatal *adj. fatal.*

fatalité *f. fate, fatality, calamity.*

fatigant *adj. tiring.*

fatigue *f. fatigue, weariness.*

Tomber de fatigue. *To be dead tired. ("To drop with fatigue.")*

Je suis mort de fatigue. *I'm dead tired.*

Habits de fatigue. *Working clothes.*

fatigué *adj. tired.*

fatiguer *to tire, wear out.*

fatuité *f. self-conceit.*

faubourg *m. suburb, outlying part of a city.*

se faufiler *to slip in or out of a place.*

fausser *to falsify, distort.*

Fausser une clé. *To bend a key.*

Fausser une serrure. *To tamper with a lock.*

fausseté *f. falsehood; falseness.*

FAUTE *f. lack, need; mistake; fault.*

Faire faute. *To be lacking.*

Il leur a fait faute. *He let them down.*

Sans faute. *Without fail.*

Je viendrais sans faute. *I'll come without fail.*

Il parle français sans faute. *He speaks French without any mistakes.*

Corrigez mes fautes, s'il vous plaît. *Please correct my mistakes.*

Il est en faute. *He made a mistake. He's guilty.*

Ce n'est pas (de) sa faute. *It's not his fault.*

A qui la faute? *Whose fault is it?*

Faire une faute. *To make a mistake.*

Faute d'orthographe. *Spelling mistake.*

Faute de jugement. *A mistake in judgment. An error of judgment.*

Faute d'inattention. *A slip.*

Faute de mieux. *For want of something better.*

fauteuil *m. armchair.*

Le fauteuil d'orchestre. *Orchestra seat.*

fautif (fautive *f.*) *adj. faulty.*

FAUX (fausse *f.*) *adj. false.*

Il fait fausse route. *He took the wrong road. He is on the wrong track.*

C'est un faux bonhomme. *He's a hypocrite.*

Il a fait un faux-pas. *He committed a faux-pas (an error of conduct). He made a mistake (blunder).*

Un faux numéro. *Wrong number (telephone).*

FAVEUR *f. favor, good will.*

Une faveur insigne. *A special favor.*

Cette mode a pris faveur. *This fashion is in vogue.*

Un billet de faveur. *A free ticket. A free pass.*

favorable *adj. favorable.*

favorablement *favorably.*

favori (favorite *f.*) *noun and adj. favorite.*

favoriser *to be partial to.*

fécond *adj. fruitful, fertile.*

fédération *f. federation.*

fée *f. fairy.*

féerique *adj. fairylike, enchanting.*

feindre *to pretend, feign.*

feinte *f. pretense.*

félicitation *f. congratulation.*

féliciter *to congratulate.*

Permettez-moi de vous féliciter. *Allow me to congratulate you.*

se féliciter *to be pleased with something.*

femelle *f. female.*

féminin *adj. feminine.*

FEMME *f. woman, wife.*

fendre *to split.*

FENÊTRE *f. window.*

fente *f. crack, slit, slot.*

La fente latérale. *The side slash (man's suit jacket).*

FER *m. iron.*

Partez-vous par chemin de fer? *Are you going by train?*

Voulez-vous donner un coup de fer à ma cravate, je vous prie. *Please press my tie.*

ferme *f. farm.*

ferme *adj. firm, steady.*

fermement *firmly.*

FERMER *to close, shut.*

Fermez la porte. *Close (shut) the door.*

Fermer une lettre. *To seal a letter.*

J'ai fermé l'eau (le gas). *I turned off the water (the gas).*

Il n'a pu fermer l'oeil de la nuit. *He couldn't sleep a wink last night.*

On ferme. *It's closing time.*

fermeté *f. firmness, hardness.*

fermeture *f. closing.*

Heure de fermeture. *Closing time.*

Une fermeture éclair. *A zipper.*

fermier *m.* (fermière *f.*) *farmer.*

féroce *adj. ferocious.*

ferraille *f. scrap iron.*

fertile *adj. fertile, fruitful.*

fertilité *f. fertility.*

fervent *noun and adj. enthusiast; fervent.*

ferveur *f. fervor.*

fessée *f. spanking.*

festin *f. feast.*

festival *m.* (festivaux *pl.*) *festival.*

FÊTE *f. holiday; name day; festivity.*

Que lui offrirez-vous pour sa fête? *What will you give him for his name day?*

Ce n'est pas tous les jours fête. *Christmas comes but once a year. We'll make this an occasion.*

On lui fera fête. *We'll give him a hearty welcome.*

Ce serait une fête de les voir. *It would be a treat to see them.*

La fête bat son plein. *The festival is at its height. The celebration is in full swing.*

fêter *to celebrate.*

FEU *m. fire, heat, flame; traffic light.*

Voulez-vous me donner du feu, s'il vous plaît? *May I have a light, please?*

Au feu! *Fire!*

Jeter de l'huile sur le feu. *To add fuel to the fire.*

C'est un feu de paille. *It's only a flash in the pan.*

Il n'y voit que du feu. *He doesn't see the trick.*

J'en mettrais ma main au feu. *I could swear to it.*

Il a le visage en feu. *His face is flushed.*

Feu de camp. *Campfire.*

Le feu passe au rouge. *The traffic light changes to red.*

feu *adj. late, deceased.*

feuille *f. leaf, sheet.*

feuilleter *to turn over the pages of a book, leaf through a book.*

feuilleton *f. feuilleton, serial.*

feutre *m. felt.*

Un chapeau de feutre. *A felt hat.*

FÉVRIER *m. February.*

fiançailles *f. pl. engagement.*

fiancé *m.* (fiancée *f.*) *fiancé.*

se fiancer *to become engaged.*

fiasco *m. fiasco.*

ficeler *to tie up.*

ficelle *f. string.*

fiche *f. slip; file.*

fiction *f. fiction.*

fidèle *adj. faithful.*

fidélité *f. faithfulness.*
La haute fidélité. *High fidelity.*

fier (fière *f.*) *adj. proud.*
Etre fier de quelqu'un. *To be proud of someone.*
Il est fier comme Artaban. *He's as proud as Lucifer.*
J'ai eu une fière peur. *I was really frightened.*

se fier *to trust.*
Il ne fait pas bon se fier à lui. *He's not to be trusted. Don't depend on him.*
Fiez-vous à moi. *Leave it to me.*

fierté *f. pride, vanity.*

fièvre *f. fever.*

fiévreux (fiévreuse *f.*) *adj. feverish.*

figer *to congeal, set.*
Il resta figé sur place. *He was rooted to the spot.*

figue *f. fig.*

figure *f. form, shape; face, looks.*
Il fait bonne figure. *He cuts a good figure. He makes a good impression.*
Il fait triste figure. *He cuts a sorry figure.*
Il a fait longue figure. *He pulled a long face.*
Sa figure ne me revient pas. *I don't like his looks.*
Je ne savais trop quelle figure faire. *I didn't know how to look (what countenance to assume).*
Il le lui a jeté à la figure. *He threw it up to him. He insulted him.*

figurer *to appear, figure in.*
Il n'a pas voulu que son nom figure dans l'affaire. *He didn't want his name to appear in the matter.*

se figurer *to imagine.*
S'il se figure cela, il s'abuse. *If he imagines that, he is only deceiving (fooling) himself.*
Ne vous figurez pas que les alouettes vont vous tomber toutes rôties dans la bouche. *Don't expect a fortune to drop into your lap.*
Figurez-vous que vous êtes aux Indes. *Imagine yourself in India.*

FIL *m. thread, wire.*
Donnez-moi du fil et une aiguille. *Give me some thread and a needle.*
Du fil de fer barbelé. *Barbed wire.*
Donnez du fil à retordre. *To cause a lot of trouble.*
Ce rasoir a perdu son fil. *This razor has lost its edge.*
Sa vie ne tenait qu'à un fil. *His life hung by a thread.*
Cette malice est cousue de fil blanc. *This trick is too obvious.*
De fil en aiguille. *One thing led to another.*
Il tient le fil de l'intrigue. *He knows all about the intrigue.*
Donnez-moi un coup de fil. *Give me a ring.*
Qui est au bout du fil? *Who's speaking (telephone)?*

file *f. row, line.*

filer *to spin; to follow; leave.*
Filer du lin. *To spin flax.*
Il a filé à l'anglaise. *He took French leave.*
Le train filait le long du fleuve. *The train was running along the river.*
Le bateau file quinze noeuds à l'heure. *The boat makes fifteen knots an hour.*
Le voleur est filé par la police. *The thief is being shadowed by the police.*
Allez, filez (fam.)! *Get out! On your way!*

filet *m. net.*
Auriez-vous l'obligeance de descendre le sac jaune du filet? *Would you mind taking down the yellow bag from the rack?*

FILLE *f. daughter; girl.*
Il n'a des yeux que pour sa fille. *His daughter is the apple of his eye.*
Comment écrit-on votre nom de jeune fille? *How do you spell your maiden name?*
C'est une vieille fille. *She's a spinster (old maid).*

filleul *m.* (filleule *f.*) *godchild.*

film *m. 'film, movie, picture.*
Le film en couleurs (en noir et blanc). *Color (black-and-white) film.*
Le grand film. *Main feature.*

filtre *m. filter, strainer.*

FILS *m. son.*
Il est le fils de son père. *He resembles his father. He's a chip off the old block.*
Il est le fils de ses oeuvres. *He is a self-made man.*

FIN *f. end.*
Mettre fin à. *To put an end to. To stop.*
Tirer à sa fin. *To come to an end.*
Ça n'a pas de fin. *There's no end to it.*
Sans fin. *Endless. Endlessly.*
Il a mené cette affaire à bonne fin. *He brought the affair to a successful conclusion.*
A cette fin. *To that end. For that purpose.*
A la fin. *In the end.*
A la fin des fins. *In the end. When you come down to it.*
A la fin du compte. *In the end. When all is said and done. To make a long story short.*
Payable fin courant. *Payable at the end of the current month.*
Qui veut la fin veut les moyens. *Where there's a will, there's a way.*
Ceci se passait vers fin 1930. *This happened toward the end of 1930.*

FIN *adj. fine, refined; slender; subtle.*
C'est un fin gourmet. *He's a real gourmet.*
Il n'est pas fin. *He's not shrewd.*
Bien fin qui m'y prendra. *(No one will) Catch me doing that!*
C'est trop fin pour moi. *That's too subtle for me. I don't get the joke.*
Il a l'oreille fine. *He has a good ear.*
Ils jouent au plus fin. *They're trying to outsmart each other.*

final *adj. final.*

finalement *finally.*

finance *f. finance; cash, ready money.*
Etre à court de finance. *To be short of cash.*

financier *m. financier.*

financier (financière *f.*) *adj. financial.*

finesse *f. finesse, fineness, shrewdness, wit.*
Elle a beaucoup de finesse. *She has a lot of wit.*
Il entend finesse à tout ce qu'on dit. *He gives a malicious slant to everything you say.*

FINIR *to end, finish.*
Il finit par nous dire ce que nous voulions savoir. *In the end he told us what we wanted to know.*
Quand il s'y met, il n'en finit plus. *Once he starts, he never stops.*
C'est fini entre eux. *It's all over between them.*
Il a fini par y arriver. *He finally succeeded.*
Tout est bien que finit bien. *All's well that ends well.*

fisc *m. the treasury.*

Les agents du fisc. *Tax collectors.*

fiscal (fiscaux *pl.*) *adj. fiscal.*

fixation *f. fixing.*

fixe *adj. fixed.*
Un prix fixe. *A fixed price.*

fixement *fixedly, steadfastly.*
Regarder quelque chose fixement. *To stare at something.*

fixer *to fix.*
Fixer les yeux sur quelqu'un. *To stare at someone.*
Maintenant je suis fixé. *Well, now I know what's what. That settles it.*
Nous y avons fixé notre résidence. *We have settled (set up residence) there.*

se fixer *to settle, set up residence.*

flacon *m. flask.*

flageolet *m. kidney bean.*

flagrant *adj. flagrant.*
En flagrant délit. *In the very act. (Caught) Red-handed.*

flair *m. scent.*
Cet homme a du flair. *This man has a gift for finding things out.*

flairer *to scent, smell.*

flamand *noun and adj. Flemish.*

flambant *adj. blazing.*

flambeau *m.* (flambeaux *pl.*) *torch.*

flamber *to flame, flame up.*

flamboyant *adj. flaming.*

flamboyer *to blaze.*

flamme *f. flame.*

flanc *m. flank, side.*

flanelle *f. flannel.*
Un costume de flanelle grise. *A gray flannel suit.*

flâner *to lounge about, be idle.*

flashcube *m. flashcube.*

flatter *to flatter.*

se flatter *to delude oneself, imagine.*

flatterie *f. flattery, compliment.*

flatteur *m.* (flatteuse *f.*) *flatterer.*

flatteur (flatteuse *f.*) *adj. flattering.*

fléau *m.* (fléaux *pl.*) *plague, curse.*

flèche *f. arrow.*

fléchir *to bend; yield, give way; move, touch.*
Se laisser fléchir. *To relent. To yield. To give in.*

flegmatique *adj. phlegmatic.*

flegme *m. phlegm; coolness, imperturbability.*
Il est d'un grand flegme. *He's very cool.*

flemme *f.* (fam.) *laziness.*
Il a la flemme de le faire. *He's too lazy to do it.*

flétrir *to wither, fade.*

fleur *f. flower.*

fleurir *to bloom.*

fleuriste *m. florist.*

fleuve *m. river.*

flexible *adj. flexible.*

flocon *m. flake.*

flot *m. wave.*

flottant *adj. floating.*

flotte *f. fleet.*

flotter *to float.*

flou *adj. soft, fluffy (of hair); blurred.*

fluctuation *f. fluctuation.*

fluet (fluette *f.*) *adj. thin, delicate.*

fluide *noun (m.) and adj. fluid.*

flûte *f. flute.*

flux *m. flow.*
Un flux de paroles. *A flow of words.*

fluxion *f. fluxion.*

foi *f. faith, trust, belief.*
J'ai foi en lui. *I have faith in him.*

On ne peut ajouter foi à ce qu'il dit. *You can't believe (rely upon) what he says.*

Il n'a ni foi ni loi. *He follows neither law nor gospel.*

Ma foi, tant pis. *Well, never mind.*

Etre de bonne foi. *To be sincere.*

foie *m. liver.*

Mal au foie. *Liver complaint.*

foin *m. hay.*

foire *f. fair.*

La foire de Lyon. *The Lyons Fair.*

FOIS *f. time, turn.*

Deux fois. *Twice.*

Je l'ai vue une fois avec lui. *I once saw her with him.*

Je vous raconterai ça une autre fois. *I'll tell you about it some other time.*

Maintes et maintes fois. *Again and again. Many times.*

Il y a regardé à deux fois avant de commencer. *Before he started, he thought about it twice.*

Une fois n'est pas coutume. *Once does not make a habit.*

Une bonne fois. *Once for all.*

Des fois qu'il viendrait vous voir (fam.). *In case he should come to see you.*

Une fois par semaine (jour, an, mois). *Once a week (day, year, month).*

Une fois arrivé, vous . . . *Once you arrive, you . . .*

foison *m. plenty, abundance.*

foisonner *to abound.*

folâtre *adj. playful.*

folichon (folichonne *f.*) *adj. playful.*

folie *f. madness, extravagance.*

Faire des folies. *To squander money.*

folle *See* fou.

follement *madly.*

fomenter *to foment, excite, stir up.*

foncé *adj. dark (of a color).*

Vert foncé. *Dark green.*

foncer *to dash, rush.*

foncier (foncière *f.*) *adj. based on land; fundamental.*

foncièrement *fundamentally, essentially, basically.*

fonction *f. function, duty, office.*

Faire fonction de. *To act as.*

Entrer en fonctions. *To take up one's duties.*

fonctionnaire *m. civil servant.*

fonctionner *to work, to operate, to function.*

Cette machine ne fonctionne pas. *This machine doesn't work.*

Le métro ne fonctionne plus. *The subway trains aren't running.*

FOND *m. bottom, back, rear; background.*

De fond en comble. *From top to bottom.*

Au fond. *At bottom. Basically. On the whole. In the main. After all.*

Le fond d'une boutique. *The back of a shop.*

On ne peut faire fond sur lui. *One can't depend on him. You can't rely on him.*

A fond de train. *At full speed.*

Au fond du coeur il était très fier de ce qu'il avait fait. *Deep down ("at the bottom of his heart"), he was very proud of what he had done.*

Je l'ai trouvé au fin fond de mon tiroir. *I found it at the very bottom of my drawer.*

Il faut aller au fond de cette affaire. *We must get to the root of that matter.*

Il connaît l'histoire à fond. *He has a thorough knowledge of history.*

Un article de fond. *An editorial.*

fondamental *adj. fundamental.*

fondateur *m.* (fondatrice *f.*) *founder.*

fondation *f. foundation.*

fondé *m. agent, proxy.*

Fondé de pouvoir. *Agent.*

fondé *adj. well-founded, justified.*

Ses soupçons ne sont pas fondés. *His suspicions are groundless (have no basis).*

fondement *m. foundation, base.*

Une rumeur sans fondement. *An unfounded rumor.*

fonder *to found, establish.*

fondre *to melt.*

fonds *m. funds, capital.*

Etre en fonds (fam.). *To be in funds.*

fontaine *f. spring, fountain.*

fonte *f. melting.*

forçat *m. convict.*

Il mène une vie de forçat. *He works very hard. He slaves (away).*

FORCE *f. strength, force.*

Il est à bout de force. *He's exhausted.*

Il n'a pas la force de parler. *He's too weak to speak.*

Il est un joueur de tennis de première force. *He's a first-rate tennis player.*

Il cria de toutes ses forces. *He shouted with all his might.*

Il le fera de gré ou de force. *He'll have to do it whether he wants to or not. He'll have to do it willy-nilly.*

Vous n'êtes pas de sa force. *You're no match for him.*

Ici les fermiers sont la force du pays. *Here the farmers are the backbone of the country.*

Par force. *Under compulsion.*

Il entra par force dans la maison. *He forced his way into the house.*

Les agents de la force publique. *The police force.*

Les forces aériennes. *Air force.*

De force égale. *Evenly matched.*

force *adj. a great deal, many.*

Il reçut force compliments. *He received many compliments.*

forcément *under compulsion, necessarily, forcibly.*

forcené *m. and f. madman, madwoman.*

forcené *adj. frantic, mad.*

forcer *to force, break open.*

On dut forcer la porte. *They had to force the door.*

On lui a forcé la main. *They forced his hand.*

Ne forcez pas votre talent. *Don't overestimate your ability. Don't try to do things that are beyond your ability.*

forêt *f. forest.*

forfait *m. contract; crime.*

Travailler à forfait. *To work on a contract basis. To work for a fixed fee.*

Il a commis un forfait. *He committed a crime.*

forge *f. forge.*

forger *to forge.*

Cette lettre a été forgée. *This letter has been (is) forged.*

forgeron *m. blacksmith.*

formalité *f. formality, red tape.*

format *m. format.*

Format de poche. *Pocket size.*

formation *f. formation.*

FORME *f. form, shape; etiquette, manners.*

En bonne et due forme. *In due and proper form.*

Il l'a fait pour la forme. *He did it for form's sake.*

Prendre forme. *To take shape.*

Etre en forme. *To be in form.*

Sous toutes les formes. *In all aspects.*

formel (formelle *f.*) *adj. formal.*

formellement *formally, expressly, explicitly.*

former *to form, create.*

se former *to form, to take form.*

formidable *adj. formidable; wonderful, tremendous, unbelievable.*

J'ai une idée formidable. *I have a brilliant idea.*

C'est formidable tout de même! *That's really something!*

Vous êtes formidable! *You're the limit!*

formulaire *m. printed form.*

formule *f. formula, printed form.*

formuler *to formulate.*

fort *m. strong point; fort, fortress.*

C'est son fort. *That's his forte. That's his strong point. That's what he does (knows) best.*

FORT *adj. strong; loud.*

C'est un esprit fort. *He has a strong mind.*

Parlez plus fort, s'il vous plaît. *Please speak louder.*

Il a trouvé plus fort que lui. *He found his match.*

J'aurai fort à faire en cela. *I'll have a great deal to do (in that). That will give me a lot of work (trouble).*

Ça ne marche pas fort. 1. *I'm not feeling too well.* 2. *It's not going too well.*

C'est trop fort! *That's too much!*

C'est plus fort que moi. *I can't help it.*

forteresse *f. fortress.*

fortifiant *m. tonic.*

fortification *f. fortification.*

fortifier *to strengthen; fortify.*

fortune *f. fortune, chance, fate; wealth.*

Un coup de fortune. *A stroke of luck.*

Il a amassé une grande fortune. *He made a fortune.*

Ils ont perdu leur fortune. *They lost all their money.*

Faire contre mauvaise fortune bon coeur. *To make the best of a bad job. To put a good face on a bad matter.*

fortuné *adj. fortunate, lucky.*

fosse *f. pit, hole.*

fossé *m. ditch.*

fossette *f. dimple.*

fou (folle *f.*) *noun and adj. mad, insane.*

Elle est folle de joie. *She's overjoyed ("mad with joy").*

Etre fou de quelqu'un. *To be crazy (mad) about someone.*

foudre *f. lightning.*

foudroyer *to crush, overwhelm.*

fouet *m. whip, rod.*

fouetter *to whip.*

fougue *f. spirit, passion.*

fougueux (fougueuse *f.*) *adj. impetuous.*

fouiller *to dig, investigate, search.*

fouillis *m. mess.*

foulard *m. scarf.*

foule *f. crowd.*

fouler *to tread; sprain.*

Se fouler le poignet. *To sprain one's wrist.*

foulure *f. sprain.*

four *m. oven.*

La pièce fit four. *The play was a flop.*

fourbe *m. rogue, cheat.*

fourberie *f. cheating, deceit.*

fourbu *adj. overtired.*

Je suis fourbu (fam.). *I'm dead tired.*

fourche *f. fork, point of bifurcation.*
fourchette *f. fork.*
fourmi *f. ant.*
fourmiller *to swarm.*
fourneau *m. (fourneaux pl.) furnace.*
fournir *to furnish.*
fournisseur *m. supplier.*
fourniture *f. supplies, material.*
fourreur *m. furrier.*
fourrure *f. fur.*
foyer *m. hearth.*
fracas *m. crash; fracas, uproar.*
fracasser *to smash.*
fraction *f. fraction.*
fracture *f. fracture.*
fracturer *to fracture.*
fragile *adj. fragile.*
fragilité *f. fragility.*
fragment *m. fragment.*
fraîcheur *f. coolness.*
frais *m. pl. expenses; efforts.*
   A grands frais. *At a great cost (expense).*
   Il en est pour ses frais. *He had all that trouble*
     for nothing.
   Ne vous mettez pas en frais pour moi. *Don't*
     put yourself out for me.
   Les frais de retour. *Charge for returning*
     (rented car).
frais (fraîche *f.*) *adj. cool, fresh.*
   Pas frais. *Stale.*
   Mettre au frais. *To put in a cool place.*
   De fraîche date. *Recent.*
   Il fait frais. *The weather is cool.*
fraise *f. strawberry.*
framboise *f. raspberry.*
franc *m. franc.*
franc (franche *f.*) *adj. frank, loyal; genuine.*
   Franc comme l'or. *As frank (open) as a child*
     ("as gold").
   Jouer franc jeu. *To play fair. To be fair and*
     square. To be on the level.
français *m. French (language).*
   En français. *In French.*
FRANÇAIS *adj. French.*
Français *m. Frenchman.*
FRANCE *f. France.*
franchement *frankly, openly.*
franchir *to cross.*
   L'avion a franchi l'Atlantique en un temps
     record. *The plane crossed the Atlantic in*
     record time.
franchise *f. frankness; exemption.*
franco *free.*
   Livré franco. *Delivery free of charge.*
franc-parler *m. candor, frankness.*
frange *f. fringe.*
frapper *to strike; surprise.*
   Frapper à la porte. *To knock at the door.*
   Cette remarque m'avait frappé. *I was struck*
     by that remark.
fraternel (fraternelle *f.*) *adj. fraternal.*
fraternité *f. fraternity.*
fraude *f. fraud.*
frauder *to smuggle.*
fraudeur *m. smuggler.*
se frayer *to clear a way for oneself.*
   Se frayer un passage. *To clear a way for*
     oneself.
frayeur *f. fright, fear, terror.*
fredonner *to hum.*
frein *m. brake; curb.*
frêle *adj. weak, frail.*
frémir *to vibrate, quiver.*

Ça me fait frémir quand j'y pense. *It gives*
   me the shivers to think of it.
frémissement *m. quiver, shudder.*
frénésie *f. frenzy.*
fréquent *adj. frequent.*
fréquenter *to frequent, keep company with.*
FRÈRE *m. brother.*
   Beau-frère. *Brother-in-law.*
frétiller *to wriggle.*
friandise *f. dainty, delicacy.*
friction *f. friction, rubbing.*
frileux (frileuse *f.*) *adj. chilly, sensitive to cold.*
friper *to rumple.*
fripon *m.* (friponne *f.*) *rogue.*
frire *to fry.*
frise *f. frieze.*
friser *to curl, wave.*
frisson *m. shiver.*
frissonner *to shiver, shudder.*
frite *f. French fried potato.*
friture *f. fried food.*
frivole *adj. frivolous.*
frivolité *f. frivolity.*
FROID *noun (m.) and adj. cold; coldness.*
   Il fait froid aujourd'hui. *It's cold today.*
   Cela ne me fait ni chaud ni froid. *It's all the*
     same to me. It makes no difference to me
     one way or the other.
   Il n'a pas froid aux yeux. 1. *He's very de-*
     termined. 2. *He's not at all shy.*
froidement *coldly.*
froideur *f. coldness.*
froisser *to crease, rumple; hurt (one's feelings).*
fromage *m. cheese.*
froncer *used in the following expression:*
   Froncer les sourcils. *To frown.*
front *m. forehead; front.*
frontière *f. border, frontier.*
frottement *m. rubbing.*
frotter *to rub.*
fructueux (fructueuse *f.*) *adj. fruitful.*
fruit *m. fruit.*
frustrer *to frustrate.*
fugitif *m.* (fugitive *f.*) *fugitive, runaway.*
fuir *to flee; avoid; leak.*
fuite *f. flight, evasion.*
fumée *f. smoke.*
fumer *to smoke, fume.*
fumier *m. manure.*
funèbre *adj. mournful, dismal.*
funérailles *f. pl. funeral rites.*
funeste *adj. deadly, fatal.*
fur *m. used in the following expression:*
   Au fur et à mesure. *Gradually. Proportionately.*
     In proportion (as). As soon (as). As far (as).
     In succession.
fureur *f. fury.*
   Il s'est mis en fureur. *He flew into a rage.*
   Cette pièce fait fureur. *This play is a hit.*
furie *f. fury, rage.*
furieusement *furiously.*
furieux (furieuse *f.*) *adj. furious, enraged.*
furtif (furtive *f.*) *adj. furtive.*
furtivement *furtively.*
fuselage *m. fuselage.*
fusil *m. gun.*
fusiller *to shoot.*
fusion *f. fusion, melting.*
futile *adj. futile, trifling.*
futilité *f. futility.*
futur *noun (m.) and adj. future.*
fuyard *m. fugitive.*

G *The seventh letter of the alphabet.*

gâcher *to spoil, make a mess of.*
gâchis *m. slush; mess; wet mortar.*
gaffe *f. blunder.*
gage *m. pledge, deposit, security.*
   Mettre en gage. *To pawn.*
   En gage d'amitié. *In token of friendship.*
gager *to wager, bet.*
gagne-pain *m. livelihood.*
gagner *to gain, earn, win, save (time); reach.*
   Il gagne son pain. *He just about makes a living.*
   C'est autant de gagné! *So much to the good!*
   Il a gagné la porte. *He reached the door. He*
     got to the door.
   Gagné par le sommeil. *Overcome by sleep.*
gai *adj. gay, cheerful.*
gaiement *gaily.*
gaieté *f. mirth.*
gaillard *m. jolly fellow, daring fellow.*
gaillard *adj. strong, vigorous.*
gain *m. gain, profit; success.*
gala *m. gala; celebration.*
galant *adj. gallant, courteous.*
galanterie *f. courtesy, politeness.*
galerie *f. gallery.*
galet *m. pebble.*
galoche *f. rubber; pl. rubbers, overshoes.*
galon *m. stripe.*
galop *m. gallop.*
gamin *m.* (gamine *f.*) *youngster.*
gamme *f. scale; range.*
gant *m. glove.*
garage *m. garage.*
garant *m. surety, bail.*
garantie *f. guarantee; security, pledge.*
garantir *to guarantee; certify.*
GARÇON *m. boy; bachelor; fellow; waiter.*
   C'est un bon garçon. *He's a good fellow.*
   C'est un vieux garçon. *He's an old bachelor.*
   Garçon, l'addition, s'il vous plaît. *Waiter, the*
     check, please.
garde *f. guard, defense.*
   Etre sur ses gardes. *To be on one's guard.*
garde *m. guard, attendant.*
GARDER *to keep.*
   Il garde le lit. *He's confined to bed.*
   Il garde la chambre. *He stays (is staying) in*
     his room.
   Voulez-vous garder cet enfant? *Will you take*
     care of (watch) this child?
   Je le garderai comme souvenir. *I'll keep it as*
     a souvenir.
   Il n'a pas pu garder le sérieux. *He couldn't*
     keep a straight face.
   Garder rancune. *To bear a grudge against.*
   Dieu m'en garde! *God forbid!*
se garder *to beware; watch out; keep from.*
   Gardez-vous de tomber. *Watch out you don't*
     fall. Take care not to fall.
   Je m'en garderai bien. *I'll take good care not*
     to do that.
gardien *m.* (gardienne *f.*) *guardian, warden.*
gare *f. railroad station.*
   Où se trouve la gare? *Where's the station?*
   Par la gare (par chemin de fer). *By railway.*
gare! *Look out! Out of the way!*
se gargariser *to gargle.*
garni *m. furnished rooms.*
garnir *to furnish; adorn, decorate.*
garnison *f. garrison.*
garniture *f. ornaments, trimmings.*
   La garniture d'intérieur. *Upholstery (car).*

gars *m. fellow.*

gaspillage *m. waste, squandering.*

gaspiller *to waste, squander.*

gâté *adj. spoiled.*
Un enfant gâté. *A spoiled child.*

gâteau *m.* (gâteaux *pl.*) *cake.*

gâter *to spoil, soil; waste.*

se gâter *to go wrong, get bad, spoil.*
Les affaires se gâtent. *Business is taking a turn for the worse. Business is getting bad.*
Le temps se gâte. *It's getting cloudy. It's going to rain.*

GAUCHE *m. and f. noun and adj. left side; left; awkward.*
Aller à gauche. *To go to the left.*
Il emprunte à droite et à gauche. *He borrows left and right.*
Il a dû se lever du pied gauche. *He got up on the wrong side of the bed.*
Il est gauche. *He's very awkward (clumsy).*
La Rive Gauche. *The Left Bank (Paris).*
La toile de gauche. *The canvas on the left.*

gaucherie *f. awkwardness.*

gaz *m. gas.*

gaze *f. gauze.*

gazette *f. gazette, news sheet.*

gazeux (gazeuse *f.*) *adj. effervescent.*
Eau gazeuse. *Soda water.*

gazon *m. grass, lawn.*

géant *noun (m.) and adj. giant.*

gelée *f. frost.*

geler *to freeze.*

gémir *to groan, moan.*

gémissement *m. groan, moan.*

gênant *adj. annoying.*
Ça a dû être gênant. *That must have been awkward.*

gencive *f. gums (of the mouth).*

gendarme *m. gendarme.*

gendre *m. son-in-law.*

gêne *f. uneasiness; inconvenience.*
Il est sans gêne. *He has a free and easy (offhand) manner. He doesn't stand on ceremony.*
Cela ne me cause aucune gêne. *It doesn't inconvenience me in the least.*
Ils sont dans la gêne. *They're in (great) difficulties.*

gêné *adj. uneasy, embarrassed.*

GÊNER *to inconvenience; prevent, hinder.*
Sa présence me gênait pour parler librement. *His presence prevented me from speaking freely.*
Cela vous gêne-t-il? *Does it bother you? Is it in your way?*
Il est gêné dans ses affaires. *His affairs are not quite in order.*

SE GÊNER *to inconvenience oneself, trouble oneself.*
Je ne me suis pas gêné pour le lui dire. *I made no bones about telling him so.*
Ne vous gênez pas! *Make yourself at home!*

général *m. general.*

GÉNÉRAL *adj. general.*
. En général. *Generally. In general.*

généralement *generally.*

généraliser *to generalize.*

génération *f. generation.*

généreusement *generously.*

généreux (généreuse *f.*) *adj. generous.*

générosité *f. generosity.*

génial (géniaux *pl.*) *adj. inspired, full of genius.*
Une idée géniale. *A brilliant idea.*

génie *m. genius.*

genou *m.* (genoux *pl.*) *knee.*

GENRE *m. kind, class; gender.*
Quel genre de livres aimez-vous? *What kind of books do you like?*
C'est plus dans mon genre. *That's more in my line.*
Ce genre de maladie est courant ici. *This type of illness is quite common here.*
C'est de très mauvais genre. *It's very bad form.*
Se donner un genre. *To pose. To give oneself airs.*

GENS *m. pl. people, persons.*
Ce sont des gens bien. *They're nice people.*
Beaucoup de jeunes gens y vont. *A lot of young people go there.*

GENTIL (gentille *f.*) *adj. kind, nice.*
Ils ont tous été très gentils. *They were all very nice.*
C'est gentil à vous de penser à moi. *It's kind of you to remember me.*

gentillesse *f. graciousness.*
Auriez-vous la gentillesse de fermer la fenêtre? *Would you be kind enough to close the window? Would you be so kind as to close the window?*

gentiment *kindly, pleasantly.*

géographie *f. geography.*

géologie *f. geology.*

géométrie *f. geometry.*

gérance *f. management.*

gérant *m.* (gérante *f.*) *manager.*

gerbe *f. sheaf.*

gercer *to chap.*
Mains gercées. *Chapped hands.*

gerçure *f. chap, crack.*

gérer *to manage, take care of.*

germain *adj. used in the following expression:*
Cousin germain. *First cousin.*

germe *m. germ.*

germer *to germinate.*

gérondif *m. gerund.*

geste *m. gesture; action.*

gesticuler *to gesticulate*

gibier *m. game (animals).*

gifle *f. slap in the face.*

gifler *to slap.*

gigot *m. leg of lamb.*

gilet *m. vest.*

gîte *m. home, lodging.*

glace *f. ice; ice cream.*

glacer *to freeze.*

glacial *adj. icy.*

glacière *f. icebox.*

glissant *adj. slippery.*

glisser *to slide; slip out; pass over.*
Il lui en a glissé un mot. *He gave him a hint (about it).*

global *adj. global, total.*

globe *m. globe.*

gloire *f. glory, fame.*

glorieux (glorieuse *f.*) *adj. glorious.*

glorifier *to praise.*

glouton (gloutonne *f.*) *adj. gluttonous.*

gloutonnerie *f. greediness.*

gluant *adj. sticky.*

goguenard *adj. sneering.*

gomme *f. eraser.*

gonflé *adj. swollen.*

gonfler *to swell.*

gorge *f. throat; gorge; groove.*
Mal à la gorge. *A sore throat.*

gorgée *f. mouthful.*

gorille *m. gorilla.*

gosier *m. throat.*

gosse *m.* (fam.) *kid, brat.*

gouache *f. gouache (painting).*

gourmand *adj. greedy.*

gourmet *m. gourmet.*

GOÛT *m. taste, flavor, liking.*
C'est une affaire de goût. *It's a matter of taste.*
Il y prend goût. *He's taken a liking to it.*
Je lui trouve un petit goût salé. *It tastes a little too salty to me.*

goûter *m. five-o'clock tea.*

goûter *to taste, appreciate; to have tea.*

goutte *f. drop; gout.*
Il n'y entend pas goutte. *He doesn't understand the least thing about it.*
Je n'y vois pas goutte. *I can't see at all. I can hardly see.*

gouttière *f. gutter.*

gouvernante *f. governess.*

gouvernement *m. government.*

gouverner *to govern.*

gouverneur *m. governor.*

grâce *f. mercy; thanks; grace.*
Grâce à Dieu! *Thank God!*
Faire quelque chose de bonne grâce. *To do something readily (willingly, with good grace).*
Il est dans les bonnes grâces du patron. *He's in the boss's good graces.*

gracieux (gracieuse *f.*) *adj. graceful, courteous.*

grade *m. rank, grade.*

grain *m. grain; bit; bead.*

graine *f. seed.*

graissage *m. greasing, lubrication.*

graisse *f. grease, fat.*

graisser *to grease; bribe.*

graisseux (graisseuse *f.*) *adj. greasy.*

grammaire *f. grammar.*

gramme *m. gram.*

gramophone *m. phonograph.*

GRAND *adj. great, large, tall.*
C'est un grand homme sec. *He's a tall thin man.*
Elle est aussi grande que moi. *She's as tall as I.*
Grand-père (mère). *Grandfather (mother).*
Ma grande soeur. *My big (older) sister.*
Grand froid. *Severe cold.*
Au grand jour. *Publicly. In public.*
De grande taille. *Of large size.*

grand'chose *much.*
Ce n'est pas grand'chose. *It's not very important. It doesn't matter.*

grandeur *f. size, greatness.*

grandiose *adj. grandiose.*

grandir *to grow, increase.*

grand-père *m. grandfather.*

grappe *f. bunch.*

gras (grasse *f.*) *adj. fat, oily, greasy.*

gratification *f. gratuity, tip, bonus.*

gratin *m. gratin (covered with bread crumbs and grated cheese and then baked).*
Des pommes de terres au gratin. *Potatoes au gratin.*

gratis *free of charge.*
Entrée gratis. *Admission free.*

gratte-ciel *m. skyscraper.*

gratter *to scratch.*

gratuit *adj. free.*
Entrée gratuite. *Admission free.*

gratuitement *without charge.*

grave *adj. grave, serious.*

gravement *seriously.*

graver to engrave, carve.
gravier m. gravel.
gravir to climb.
gravité f. gravity.
gravure f. engraving, print.
gré m. pleasure, gratitude.
  Je lui en sais un gré infini. *I'm very grateful to him for that.*
  Elle n'en fait qu'à son gré. *She does as she pleases.*
  Bon gré mal gré. *Willy-nilly. Whether one likes it or not.*
grec (grecque f.) noun and adj. Greek.
grêle f. hail.
grêle adj. slender, slim.
grêler to hail.
grelotter to shiver with cold.
grenier m. garret, attic.
grenouille f. frog.
grève f. strike.
  Se mettre en grève. *To go on strike.*
gribouiller to scribble.
grief m. grievance.
  Le seul grief que j'aie. *The only objection I have.*
  Il a un grief contre moi. *He has a grievance against me.*
griffe f. claw.
griffoner to scribble.
grignoter to nibble.
gril m. broiler.
grille f. iron gate.
griller to toast, broil.
  Pain grillé. *Toast.*
grimace f. grimace.
grimper to climb.
grincement m. grinding.
grincer to grind.
grincheux (grincheuse f.) adj. grumpy.
grippe f. grippe, flu; dislike.
  Avoir la grippe. *To have the grippe.*
  Elle m'a pris en grippe. *She's taken a dislike to me.*
gris adj. gray.
grogner to groan, grunt.
grognon adj. grumbling.
grondement m. roaring; rumbling.
gronder to roar; scold.
groom m. bellboy.
gros m. mass; wholesale.
  En gros et au détail. *Wholesale and retail.*
  Le gros de l'armée n'est pas encore passé. *The main body of the army hasn't passed yet.*
  Voici, en gros, ce que j'ai compris. *Here is roughly what I understood.*
GROS (grosse f.) adj. stout, fat, thick, big, coarse.
  Une grosse corde. *A thick rope.*
  Il est trop gros. *He's too fat (stout).*
  Gros rire. *Loud laugh.*
grossier (grossière f.) adj. coarse, rude.
grossièreté f. coarseness; rudeness.
grossir to enlarge, increase; grow bigger, gain weight.
grotesque adj. absurd, ridiculous.
grotte f. cave.
grouillement m. swarming.
grouiller to swarm.
groupe m. group.
groupement m. group, association.
grouper to group.
guenille f. old rag.
GUÈRE not much, only a little, hardly, scarcely.
  Je ne l'aime guère. *I don't really like him (her).*

Il ne la voit guère. *He hardly ever sees her.*
Je ne suis guère content. *I'm hardly satisfied. I'm not at all satisfied.*
Il n'y a guère plus de trois ans. *It's barely more than three years ago.*
Est-il ruiné? —Il ne s'en faut guère. *Is he bankrupt? —Pretty nearly.*
guérir to heal, get well.
guérison f. recovery.
guerre f. war.
guet m. watch, lookout.
  Il a l'oeil et l'oreille au guet. *He keeps his eyes and ears open.*
  Il fait le guet. *He's keeping watch. He's on the alert.*
guet-apens m. ambush.
guetter to watch.
gueule f. mouth (used only of animals).
guichet m. ticket window.
guide m. guide, guidebook.
guider to lead.
guidon m. handlebar.
guigne f. bad luck.
guignol m. Punch and Judy show.
guillemets m. pl. quotation marks.
guillotine f. guillotine.
guillotiner to guillotine.
guise f. manner, way.
  Il n'en fait qu'à sa guise. *He does just as he pleases.*
  A votre guise! *As you please!*
guitare f. guitar.
guitariste m. guitar player, guitarist.
guttural (gutturaux pl.) adj. guttural.
gymnastique f. physical training.

H *The eighth letter of the alphabet.*

Note: Words marked with a dot have an aspirate "h." Aspirate-h nouns take the complete singular article (le or la) instead of l' (i.e., le héros). The plural article les has no liaison with its noun.

habile adj. clever, skillful, able, competent.
habileté f. skillfulness.
habillé adj. dressed; dressy.
habiller to dress, clothe.
S'HABILLER to dress.
  Elle est en train de s'habiller. *She's getting dressed.*
habit m. coat; full dress; pl. clothes.
habitant m. (habitante f.) inhabitant, resident.
habitation f. dwelling.
HABITER to inhabit, dwell in, live.
  Où habitez-vous maintenant? *Where are you living now? Where do you live now?*
habits m. pl. clothes.
HABITUDE f. habit.
  D'habitude ils arrivent toujours en retard. *They're generally late.*
  Venez comme d'habitude. *Come as usual.*
habitué m. and f. person who frequents a place, regular customer.
habituel (habituelle f.) adj. habitual, usual, customary.
habituellement habitually, usually.
s'habituer to get used to.
  On s'y habitue peu à peu. *One gradually gets used to it.*
• **hache** f. axe.
• **hacher** to chop.
• **hagard** adj. haggard.
• **haie** f. fence.
• **haillon** m. rag.
  Il est en haillons. *He's in rags and tatters.*

• **haine** f. hatred.
• **haineux** (haineuse f.) adj. hateful.
• **haïr** to hate.
haleine f. breath.
  Je suis hors d'haleine. *I'm out of breath.*
  Elle a lu ce livre tout d'une haleine. *She read that book in one sitting.*
  Il nous a tenus en haleine. *He kept us in suspense.*
  C'est un récit de longue haleine. *That's a long-winded story.*
• **haletant** adj. panting.
• **haleter** to pant.
hallucination f. hallucination.
halluciner to hallucinate.
• **halte** f. halt.
  Halte là! *Stop there!*
hameçon m. fishhook.
• **hanche** f. hip.
• **handicap** m. handicap.
• **hangar** m. hangar.
• **hanter** to haunt.
• **hantise** f. obsession.
• **harangue** f. harangue.
• **haranguer** to harangue.
• **harasser** to harass, tire out.
• **harceler** to annoy, bother, pester.
• **hardi** adj. bold.
• **hardiesse** f. boldness, daring.
• **hareng** m. herring.
• **hargneux** (hargneuse f.) adj. peevish, surly.
• **haricot** m. bean.
harmonie f. harmony.
harmonieux (harmonieuse f.) adj. harmonious.
• **harnais** m. harness.
• **harpe** f. harp.
• **HASARD** m. risk, peril, chance.
  Je l'ai rencontré par hasard. *I met him by accident.*
  Le hasard fit que j'ai réussi. *I succeeded by mere luck.*
  Il court le hasard de perdre gros. *He runs the risk of losing heavily.*
  Il ne faut rien laisser au hasard. *It's best to leave nothing to chance.*
se • **hasarder** to risk.
• **hasardeux** (hasardeuse f.) adj. hazardous, risky.
• **hâte** f. hurry, speed.
  Je l'ai écrit à la hâte. *I wrote it in a hurry.*
  J'ai hâte de le revoir. *I'm eager to see him again. I can't wait to see him again.*
• **hâter** to hasten, hurry up.
  Hâtez-vous! *Hurry up!*
• **hâtivement** hastily.
  Il s'habilla hâtivement. *He dressed in a hurry.*
• **hausse** f. rise.
• **hausser** to raise, lift up.
  se • **hausser** to raise oneself.
• **HAUT** noun (m.) and adj. top, summit; high.
  Aller en haut. *To go upstairs.*
  Allez voir là-haut si vous le trouvez. *See if you can find it up there.*
  A marée haute. *At high tide.*
  La haute mer. *The high seas.*
  Penser tout haut. *To think aloud.*
  Voir plus haut. *See above.*
• **hautain** adj. haughty.
• **hauteur** f. height.
• **haut-parleur** m. loudspeaker.
hebdomadaire adj. weekly.
héberger to shelter.
hébété adj. dazed.
  Un regard hébété. *A bewildered expression.*

hébreu (hébraïque f.) noun and adj. Hebrew.
hectare m. hectare.
• **hein** what?
hélas alas.
hémisphère m. hemisphere.
herbe f. grass, herb.
héréditaire adj. hereditary.
hérédité f. heredity.
héritage m. inheritance.
hériter to inherit.
héritier m. (héritière f.) heir.
héroïne f. heroine.
héroïque adj. heroic.
• **héros** m. hero.
hésitation f. hesitation, wavering.
hésiter to hesitate.
HEURE f. hour; time.
    D'heure en heure la situation empirait. *The situation was growing worse every hour.*
    Je serai prête dans une demi-heure. *I'll be ready in half an hour.*
    Mettez votre montre à l'heure. *Set your watch.*
    A dix heures tapant. *At ten sharp.*
    A la bonne heure! *Excellent! Good! Fine!*
    Il l'a fait sur l'heure. *He did it right away.*
    Tout à l'heure. *Right away. In a moment.*
    Bon, à tout à l'heure. *Good, see you later.*
    A neuf heures quinze du matin. *At 9:15 A.M.*
    A quelle heure? *At what time?*
    A sept heures et demie. *At 7:30.*
    A vingt et une heures. *At 9:00 P.M.*
    Cent kilomètres à l'heure. *A hundred kilometers an hour.*
    De (très) bonne heure. *(Very) early.*
    L'heure d'affluence. *Rush hour.*
    L'heure d'arrivée (de départ). *Arrival (departure) time.*
    Payer par heure. *To pay by the hour.*
    Quelle heure est-il? *What time is it?*
    Se faire réserver une heure. *To make an appointment (hairdresser, etc.).*
    A l'heure. *On time.*
heureusement happily, luckily, fortunately.
HEUREUX (heureuse f.) adj. happy, lucky, fortunate.
• **heurt** m. shock, blow.
• **heurter** to knock against, collide (with); hurt someone's feelings.
• **hideux** (hideuse f.) adj. hideous, frightful.
HIER m. yesterday.
    Il y est allé hier soir. *He went there last night.*
• **hiérarchie** f. hierarchy.
hilarité f. hilarity.
hirondelle f. swallow (bird).
• **hisser** to hoist.
HISTOIRE f. history, story, tale.
    Un cours d'histoire. *A history course.*
    Raconter une histoire. *To tell a story.*
    Histoire de rire. *For the fun of it. Just for fun.*
historien m. historian.
historique adj. historical.
hiver m. winter.
    Faire des sports d'hiver. *To practice, engage in winter sports.*
• **hocher** to shake (one's head), nod.
• **homard** m. lobster.
homicide m. homicide.
hommage m. homage, respect.
HOMME m. man.
    Un homme comme il faut. *A well-bred man. A gentleman.*
    Un brave homme. *A nice fellow.*
    Un homme de tous métiers. *A jack-of-all-trades.*

honnête adj. honest, loyal, polite.
honnêtement honestly.
honnêteté f. honesty.
HONNEUR m. honor.
    C'est beaucoup d'honneur pour moi. *It is a great honor to me.*
    Il a agi en tout bien tout honneur. *He acted honestly. He acted with the best intentions.*
    Elle fait les honneurs de la maison. *She's doing the honors ("of the house").*
    Parole d'honneur! *On my word of honor!*
    On a donné une réception en son honneur. *They gave a party for him.*
    Le diplôme d'honneur. *Certificate of honor.*
honorable adj. honorable.
honorablement honorably.
honoraires m. pl. fees (professional man).
honorer to pay honor; do credit to.
• **honte** f. shame, disgrace, confusion.
    N'avez-vous pas honte de faire cela? *Aren't you ashamed to do that?*
    J'ai honte de vous faire attendre. *I'm sorry to make you wait. I'm sorry to keep you waiting.*
    Il fait honte à sa famille. *He's the black sheep of the family.*
    Quelle honte! *How disgraceful!*
• **honteusement** disgracefully.
• **honteux** (honteuse f.) adj. ashamed.
    Il en a été tout honteux. *He was very ashamed about (of) it.*
hôpital m. hospital.
• **hoquet** m. hiccup.
horaire m. timetable.
horizon m. horizon.
horizontal (horizontaux pl.) adj. horizontal.
horloge f. clock.
horloger m. watchmaker.
hormis except, save.
    Ils étaient tous là hormis trois. *They were all there but three.*
horreur f. horror, dread.
    Juste ciel! Quelle horreur! *Heavens! How awful!*
    Il me fait horreur. *He horrifies me. I find him repulsive.*
    J'ai horreur de. *I loathe. I have a horror of.*
horrible adj. horrible.
horrifier to horrify.
• **HORS** out of, outside, beside.
    Hors d'usage. *No longer used.*
    C'est hors de pair. *It's beyond comparison.*
    Ici tout est hors de prix. *Everything is terribly expensive here.*
    Il est hors de lui. *He's beside himself.*
    C'est tout à fait hors de question. *It's altogether out of the question.*
• **hors-d'oeuvre** m. hors-d'oeuvre.
hospice m. poorhouse; charitable institution.
hospitalier (hospitalière f.) adj. hospitable.
hospitalité f. hospitality.
hostile adj. hostile.
hostilité f. hostility; pl. hostilities.
hôte m. (hôtesse f.) host.
HÔTEL m. hotel.
    Ils sont descendus à l'hôtel. *They stopped at the hotel.*
    L'hôtel de ville. *The city hall.*
hôtellerie f. inn.
• **houille** f. coal.
    Houille blanche. *Water power.*
• **houleux** (houleuse f.) adj. heavy, surging.
• **houppe** f. puff.
• **housse** f. cover.
• **huer** to boo.

huilage m. lubrication.
huile f. oil.
    La peinture à l'huile. *Oil painting.*
• **HUIT** noun and adj. eight.
    Huit jours. *A week.*
• **huitaine** f. about eight.
• **HUITIÈME** noun and adj. eighth.
huître f. oyster.
humain adj. human.
    Le genre humain. *Mankind.*
humanité f. humanity.
humble adj. humble.
humblement humbly.
humeur f. humor, disposition, temper, mood.
    Avec humeur. *Crossly.*
    Il est d'une humeur massacrante. *He's as cross as can be.*
    Elle était de bonne humeur. *She was in a good mood.*
humide adj. damp, wet.
humidité f. humidity.
humiliant adj. humiliating.
humiliation f. humiliation.
humilier to humiliate.
humilité f. humility.
humour m. humor.
• **hurlement** m. howl.
• **hurler** to yell, scream.
hygiène f. hygiene.
hygiénique adj. hygienic.
hymne m. hymn.
hypnotiser to hypnotize.
hypnotisme m. hypnotism.
hypocrisie f. hypocrisy.
hypocrite m. and f. noun and adj. hypocrite; hypocritical.
hypothèque f. mortgage.
hypothèse f. hypothesis, assumption.
hystérie f. hysteria.
hystérique adj. hysterical.

    I   *The ninth letter of the alphabet.*

ICI here, in this place; now, this time.
    Par ici la sortie. *This way out.*
    Il fait bon ici. *It's comfortable (nice) here.*
    A combien d'ici est l'école? *How far is the school from here?*
    Je ne suis pas d'ici. *I'm a stranger here.*
    Jusqu'ici. *Up to here. Up to now.*
    D'ici là. *Between now and then. In the meanwhile. Until then.*
    D'ici peu. *Before long.*
    Je dois quitter New York d'ici une semaine. *I have to leave New York within a week.*
    Ici Charles Lewis. *This is Charles Lewis speaking (on telephone).*
    Par ici. *This way.*
idéal noun (m.) and adj. (idéal, idéales f.) ideal. (The m. plural of the adjective is idéaux; the plural of the noun is usually idéaux, though the form idéals sometimes occurs.)
idéalisme m. idealism.
idéaliste m. and f. idealist.
idée f. idea, conception, plan.
    Quelle drôle d'idée! *What a funny idea!*
    Une idée fixe. *An obsession.*
    Se faire des idées. *To imagine things.*
    Faites à votre idée. *Do as you see fit (think right).*
    L'idée me vient que . . . *It occurs to me that . . . The thought occurs to me that.*
    Elle a des idées noires. *She has the blues.*

identification f. *identification.*
identifier *to identify.*
identique *adj. identical.*
identité f. *identity.*
Les pièces d'identité. *Identification (papers).*
idiome m. *language, dialect.*
idiot (idiote f.) *noun and adj. idiot; idiotic, stupid.*
Si vous êtes assez idiot pour le faire (*fam.*). *If you're stupid enough to do it.*
idolâtrer *to worship, idolize.*
idole f. *idol.*
ignoble *adj. vile, base.*
ignominie f. *shame, disgrace.*
ignominieux (ignominieuse f.) *adj. disgraceful.*
ignorance f. *ignorance.*
ignorant *adj. ignorant, illiterate.*
ignorer *to be ignorant of, be unaware.*
Il ignorait tout ce qui s'était passé. *He didn't know anything about what had taken place. He knew nothing of what had happened.*
Je n'ignore pas que. *I'm not unaware that.*
IL *he, it.*
Faites-le monter quand il viendra. *Send (show) him up when he comes.*
Il pleut. *It's raining.*
Il est tard. *It's late.*
Il y a une erreur. *There's a mistake.*
Il y a longtemps. *A long time ago.*
Il y en a d'autres. *There are others.*
île f. *island.*
illégal (illégaux pl.) *adj. illegal.*
illégitime *adj. illegitimate, unlawful.*
illicite *adj. unlawful.*
illimité *adj. boundless.*
illisible *adj. illegible.*
illogique *adj. illogical.*
illumination f. *illumination.*
illusion f. *illusion, delusion.*
s'illusionner *to delude oneself.*
illustration f. *illustration.*
illustre *adj. illustrious, renowned.*
illustrer *to illustrate; explain.*
s'illustrer *to become famous.*
image f. *image, picture, likeness.*
imaginaire *adj. imaginary.*
imagination f. *imagination; fancy.*
imaginer *to imagine, conceive.*
s'imaginer *to imagine, believe.*
Il ne faut pas vous imaginer que . . . *You mustn't imagine (believe) that . . .*
imbécile *adj. fool.*
imbécilité f. *stupidity.*
imbiber *to soak.*
imbu *adj. imbued.*
Il est imbu de lui-même. *He's conceited. He's impressed with his own importance.*
imitateur m. (imitatrice f.) *imitator.*
imitation f. *imitation, copy.*
imiter *to imitate.*
immaculé *adj. immaculate.*
immatriculation f. *matriculation, registration.*
immatriculer *to matriculate, register.*
immédiat *adj. immediate.*
immédiatement *immediately.*
immémorial (immémoriaux pl.) *adj. immemorial.*
immense *adj. huge.*
immerger *to immerse.*
IMMEUBLE m. *building.*
immigrant m. *immigrant.*
immigration f. *immigration.*
immigré m. *immigrant.*
immigrer *to immigrate.*

imminent *adj. imminent.*
immobile *adj. motionless.*
Un visage immobile. *Immobile features.*
Rester immobile. *To stand still.*
immobilier (immobilière f.) *adj. immovable, real.*
Biens immobiliers. *Real estate.*
Agence immobilière. *Real estate agency.*
immobilité f. *immobility.*
immodéré *adj. immoderate.*
immodeste *adj. immodest.*
immonde *adj. filthy.*
immoral (immoraux pl.) *adj. immoral.*
immortalité f. *immortality.*
immortel (immortelle f.) *adj. immortal.*
immunité f. *immunity.*
impair *adj. odd.*
Un nombre impair. *An odd number.*
impardonnable *adj. unpardonable.*
imparfait *adj. imperfect, unfinished.*
impartial (impartiaux pl.) *adj. impartial.*
impasse f. *blind alley; difficulty.*
impassible *adj. impassive.*
impatience f. *impatience.*
impatient *adj. restless, impatient.*
impatienter *to exhaust someone's patience.*
Il m'impatiente. *He makes me lose my patience.*
s'impatienter *to grow impatient.*
impayable *adj. priceless, very funny.*
Il est impayable dans ce rôle. *He's perfect (excellent, very funny) in that part. He's tops in that role.*
impeccable *adj. impeccable, faultless.*
impénétrable *adj. impenetrable, inscrutable.*
impératif *noun (m.) and adj.* (impérative f.) *imperative.*
imperceptible *adj. imperceptible.*
imperfection f. *imperfection, incompletion.*
impérialisme m. *imperialism.*
impérieux (impérieuse f.) *adj. imperative.*
Il est impérieux que j'y aille. *It's absolutely necessary for me to go there.*
imperméable m. *raincoat.*
imperméable *adj. impermeable.*
impertinence f. *impertinence.*
impertinent *adj. impertinent, fresh.*
impétueux (impétueuse f.) *adj. impetuous.*
impétuosité f. *impulsiveness.*
impitoyable *adj. pitiless.*
implacable *adj. implacable, relentless.*
implicite *adj. implicit.*
impliquer *to involve.*
Il y est impliqué. *He's involved (mixed up) in it.*
implorer *to implore, beseech, beg.*
impoli *adj. impolite.*
Il a été impoli envers nous. *He was rude to us.*
impolitesse f. *impoliteness, rudeness.*
impopulaire *adj. unpopular.*
IMPORTANCE f. *importance.*
Je n'y attache aucune importance. *I don't attach any importance to it (that). I don't consider it important.*
Cela n'a aucune importance. *It doesn't matter at all.*
IMPORTANT *adj. important.*
importation f. *importation; pl. imports.*
importer *to import.*
IMPORTER *to matter.*
N'importe. *Never mind. It's not important.*
N'achetez pas n'importe quoi. *Don't buy just anything at all.*
N'importe quand. *No matter when.*
Faites-le n'importe comment. *Do it some way or other.*

Mais qu'importe? *But what of it? What difference does it make?*
N'importe qui vous le dira. *Anyone will tell you.*
N'importe où. *Anywhere.*
N'importe quel(le). *Any . . . at all.*
importun *adj. importunate, tiresome, bothersome, unwelcome.*
importuner *to bother.*
imposant *adj. imposing.*
imposer *to impose; inflict; levy, tax.*
Il a imposé des conditions. *He imposed conditions.*
Prix imposé par le fabricant. *Retail price set by the manufacturer.*
Son âge impose le respect. *His age commands respect.*
Imposer une punition. *To inflict (a) punishment.*
s'imposer *to impose oneself.*
impossibilité f. *impossibility.*
IMPOSSIBLE *noun (m.) and adj. impossible.*
Il tente l'impossible. *He attempts the impossible.*
Je ferai l'impossible pour vous. *I'll do my utmost to help you. I'll do anything for you.*
Il est impossible (*fam.*). *He's impossible.*
imposteur m. *impostor.*
imposture f. *imposture.*
impôt m. *tax.*
Impôt sur le revenu. *Income tax.*
impotence f. *impotence, helplessness.*
impotent *adj. helpless.*
impraticable *adj. impracticable.*
impression f. *impression.*
L'impression d'ensemble. *The general impression.*
Il a fait impression. *He made quite an impression.*
impressionnant *adj. impressive.*
impressionner *to impress.*
impressionniste *impressionist (painting).*
imprévu *adj. unexpected.*
Des difficultés imprévues. *Unforeseen difficulties.*
imprimer *to print.*
imprimerie f. *printing plant.*
imprimés m. pl. *printed matter.*
imprimeur m. *printer.*
improbabilité f. *improbability, unlikelihood.*
improbable *adj. unlikely.*
impromptu *adj. impromptu.*
impropre *adj. incorrect.*
Une expression impropre. *An incorrect expression.*
improviser *to improvise.*
(à l') improviste *unexpectedly.*
Il est venu à l'improviste. *He came unexpectedly.*
imprudence f. *imprudence.*
imprudent *adj. imprudent, incautious.*
impuissance f. *impotence; powerlessness.*
impuissant *adj. powerless.*
impulsif (impulsive, f.) *impulsive.*
impur *adj. impure; foul.*
imputer *to impute.*
inaccessible *adj. inaccessible.*
inaccoutumé *adj. unaccustomed, unusual.*
inachevé *adj. unfinished.*
inactif (inactive f.) *adj. inactive.*
inadmissible *adj. inadmissible.*
inanimé *adj. lifeless.*
inaperçu *adj. unseen.*
Il passa inaperçu. *He escaped notice.*
inapte *adj. unfit.*

inaptitude f. unfitness.
inattentif (inattentive f.) adj. inattentive.
inattention f. lack of attention, heedlessness.
inauguration f. inauguration.
inaugurer to inaugurate.
incalculable adj. incalculable.
incapable adj. incapable.
incapacité f. incapacity.
incassable adj. unbreakable.
incendie m. fire.
incendier to set on fire.
incertain adj. uncertain, doubtful.
incertitude f. incertitude, doubt.
incessamment incessantly; at once, right away.
　Il parle incessamment. He speaks constantly.
　Il arrivera incessamment. He'll be here right away.
incident m. incident, occurrence.
incinérer to burn to ashes.
incision f. incision.
inciter to incite, instigate.
incliner to bend; incline toward.
　Incliner la tête. To bend one's head.
　Incliner à faire quelque chose. To feel inclined to do something.
　Elle incline pour la couleur bleue. She likes blue. Blue is her favorite color.
s'incliner to slant, slope; bow to, yield to, submit to.
　S'incliner devant les faits. To bow to the inevitable.
inclus adj. included, enclosed.
　Ouvert toute la semaine, dimanche inclus. Open daily and Sundays. ("Open all week, including Sundays.")
　Ci-inclus. Enclosed herewith.
incognito incognito.
incohérence f. incoherence.
incohérent adj. incoherent.
incomber to be incumbent on; devolve on.
incommode adj. inconvenient, uncomfortable, unhandy.
　Cette chaise est très incommode. This chair is very uncomfortable.
　Un homme incommode. An unpleasant man.
incommoder to inconvenience, trouble.
　Cela vous incommoderait-il de remettre notre rendez-vous? Would it inconvenience you to postpone our appointment?
incomparable adj. incomparable, matchless.
incompatible adj. incompatible.
incompétence f. incompetency.
incompétent adj. incompetent.
incompréhensible adj. incomprehensible.
incompréhension f. lack of understanding.
inconcevable adj. inconceivable.
incongru adj. incongruous, out of place.
inconnu m. stranger.
inconnu adj. unknown.
　Ce lieu m'est inconnu. This place is unfamiliar to me.
inconscient adj. unconscious.
inconséquent adj. inconsistent.
inconsidération f. lack of consideration, thoughtlessness.
inconsolable adj. inconsolable.
incontestable adj. undeniable.
inconvenance f. impropriety.
inconvénient m. inconvenience, disadvantage, objection.
　Il n'y a pas d'inconvénient à cela. There's no objection to that.
　Je n'y vois pas d'inconvénient. I see no objection to that.

Il a évité un inconvénient. He avoided a difficulty.
incorporer to incorporate.
incorrect adj. incorrect.
　C'est incorrect. It isn't true.
incrédule adj. incredulous.
incrédulité f. incredulity.
incriminer to accuse, indict.
incroyable adj. incredible.
incruster to encrust.
inculpé m. defendant.
inculper to indict, charge.
incurable adj. incurable.
indécence f. indecency.
indécent adj. indecent.
indécis adj. uncertain, undecided; indistinct.
indécision f. indecision.
indéfini adj. indefinite.
indélicatesse f. indelicacy, tactlessness.
indemne adj. uninjured, unharmed, safe and sound.
indemnité f. indemnity.
indépendance f. independence, freedom.
indépendant adj. independent.
indication f. indication.
　A titre d'indication. For your guidance.
　J'ai suivi les indications données. I did as directed.
indice m. sign, mark.
indifférence f. indifference.
indifférent adj. indifferent.
　Ça m'est indifférent. I don't care (either) one way or the other. It's all the same to me.
　Il m'est indifférent. He's nothing to me. I don't care about him.
　Ils ont parlé de choses indifférentes. They talked about the weather.
indigence f. poverty, want.
indigent adj. poor, destitute.
indignation f. indignation.
indigne adj. unworthy.
indigner to rouse indignation.
　Cela m'indigne. It makes my blood boil.
s'indigner to become indignant.
indiquer to indicate.
　Pouvez-vous m'indiquer la rue de Rivoli? Could you please tell me how to get to Rivoli Street?
　Cela indique sa bêtise. It only shows his stupidity.
indirect adj. indirect.
indiscret (indiscrète f.) adj. indiscreet.
indiscrétion f. indiscretion.
　Sans indiscrétion, qu'est-il arrivé? If you don't mind my asking, what happened?
indispensable adj. indispensable.
indisposer to indispose.
individu m. fellow.
　C'est un drôle d'individu. He's a funny (queer) fellow.
　C'est un misérable individu. He's an awful (miserable) person. He's a scoundrel.
　Quel sale individu (fam.)! What a nasty fellow!
individuel (individuelle f.) adj. individual.
indocile adj. disobedient.
indolent adj. indolent, indifferent, apathetic.
indu adj. undue, not right.
　Rentrer à une heure indue. To come home very late.
induire to induce, lead, infer.
　Induire en erreur. To mislead.
　Induire en tentation. To lead into temptation.
indulgence f. indulgence, leniency.

indulgent adj. indulgent, lenient.
industrie f. industry; skill.
　L'industrie minière. The mining industry.
　Un chevalier d'industrie. A confidence man. A swindler.
　Il vit d'industrie. He lives by his wits.
industriel m. manufacturer.
industriel (industrielle f.) adj. industrial.
industrieux (industrieuse f.) adj. busy.
inébranlable adj. unshakable.
inédit adj. unpublished.
inégal (inégaux pl.) adj. unequal, uneven.
inégalité f. lack of equality.
inepte adj. inept, foolish, stupid, absurd.
inerte adj. inert, dull.
inévitable adj. inevitable, unavoidable.
inévitablement inevitably.
inexact adj. inaccurate.
inexactitude f. inaccuracy.
inexorable adj. inexorable.
inexpérience f. inexperience.
infaillible adj. infallible.
infanterie f. infantry.
infatuer to infatuate.
infect adj. filthy, foul.
infecter to infect, taint.
infection f. infection.
inférieur adj. inferior.
infériorité f. inferiority.
infidèle adj. unfaithful, faithless.
infidélité f. faithlessness.
infime adj. lowest, extremely trifling.
infini adj. infinite, boundless.
infiniment infinitely, extremely.
　Je regrette infiniment, mais je ne peux pas venir cet après-midi. I'm terribly sorry but I won't be able to come this afternoon.
infirme m. and f. noun and adj. cripple; infirm, crippled.
infirmière f. nurse.
infliger to inflict.
INFLUENCE f. influence; authority.
INFLUENCER to influence.
INFORMATION f. information, news; inquiry.
　Je vous envoie ceci pour votre information. I'm sending you this for your information.
　Informations de la dernière heure. Latest bulletins (news).
　Nous avons pris des informations sur lui. We made inquiries about him.
s'informer to inquire, investigate.
　Il s'est informé de votre santé à plusieurs reprises. He asked (inquired) about your health several times.
infortune f. misfortune, calamity.
infortuné adj. unfortune, ill-fated.
s'ingénier to tax one's ingenuity, contrive.
ingénieur m. engineer.
ingénieux (ingénieuse f.) adj. ingenious, clever.
ingrat adj. ungrateful.
ingratitude f. ingratitude.
ingrédient m. ingredient.
inhabile adj. inapt, unskilled.
inhabitable adj. uninhabitable.
inhumain adj. inhuman.
inhumer to bury.
inimaginable adj. unimaginable.
inimitié f. enmity, hatred.
ininflammable adj. uninflammable.
inintelligence f. lack of intelligence.
ininterrompu adj. uninterrupted.
initial (initiale, initiales, f., initiaux m., pl.) noun (f.) and adj. initial.

initiation *f. initiation, introduction.*
initiative *f. initiative.*
initier *to initiate, teach.*
injure *f. insult, abuse.*
injurier *to insult, call names.*
injuste *adj. unjust.*
injustice *f. injustice, unfairness.*
innocence *f. innocence.*
innocent *adj. innocent; simple, foolish.*
    Aux innocents les mains pleines. *The fools have all the luck. Fortune is kind to fools.*
innombrable *adj. numberless.*
inoculer *to inoculate.*
inoffensif (inoffensive *f.*) *adj. harmless.*
inondation *f. flood.*
inonder *to flood.*
inopiné *adj. unexpected.*
inouï *adj. unheard of; wonderful, extraordinary.*
inquiet (inquiète *f.*) *adj. uneasy, restless, worried.*
    Je suis très inquiet à son sujet. *I'm very worried about him (her).*
inquiéter *to worry (someone), alarm, make uneasy.*
s'inquiéter *to worry.*
    Ne vous inquiétez pas pour cela. *Set your mind at rest (at ease) about that. Don't worry about that. Don't let that worry you.*
    Il n'y a vraiment pas lieu de s'inquiéter. *There is no reason to worry. There's really no cause for concern (for alarm).*
inquiétude *f. anxiety, restlessness, uneasiness.*
insanité *f. insanity.*
inscription *f. inscription, registration.*
inscrire *to write down; register.*
    Inscrivez tout ce que je vais dire. *Write down everything I'm going to say.*
s'inscrire *to write down one's name, register, matriculate.*
inscrit *adj. inscribed; registered, indicated, shown.*
insensé *adj. insane, mad, rash.*
insensible *adj. insensible, indifferent (to), unmoved (by).*
inséparable *adj. inseparable.*
insérer *to insert.*
insidieux (insidieuse *f.*) *adj. insidious.*
insigne *m. emblem.*
insigne *adj. distinguished, remarkable.*
insinuation *f. insinuation.*
insinuer *to insinuate.*
insistance *f. insistence.*
insister *to insist.*
    Il a spécialement insisté sur ce point. *He laid stress on that point.*
insolence *f. insolence.*
insolent *adj. insolent, rude.*
insomnie *f. insomnia.*
insouciance *f. unconcern.*
insouciant *adj. careless, unconcerned.*
inspecter *to inspect.*
inspecteur *m. inspector.*
inspection *f. inspection, survey.*
inspiration *f. inspiration, suggestion.*
    Sous l'inspiration du moment. *On the spur of the moment.*
inspirer *to inhale; inspire.*
instabilité *f. instability.*
instable *adj. unstable, unsteady, fickle.*
installation *f. installation.*
installer *to install.*
instamment *eagerly, earnestly.*
    Prier instamment. *To beg. To entreat. To request earnestly.*
instance *f. entreaty, solicitation, request.*
    Etre en instance de départ pour. *To be on the point of leaving for.*
    Se rendre aux instances de quelqu'un. *To yield to someone's entreaties.*
INSTANT *m. instant, moment.*
    Je suis à vous dans un instant. *I'll be with you in a moment.*
    Un instant! *Just a minute!*
    Il va arriver d'un instant à l'autre. *He'll be here any minute.*
instantané *m. snapshot.*
instantanément *instantaneously.*
instar *used in the following expression:*
    A l'instar de. *Like. After the fashion of. In imitation of.*
instigateur *m.* (instigatrice *f.*) *instigator.*
instigation *f. instigation.*
instiller *to instill.*
instinct *m. instinct.*
    L'instinct de conservation. *The instinct of self-preservation.*
instinctif (instinctive *f.*) *adj. instinctive.*
instituer *to institute.*
institut *m. institute.*
instituteur *m.* (institutrice *f.*) *schoolteacher in elementary school.*
institution *f. institution; boarding school.*
instruction *f. instruction; education.*
    Manquer d'instruction. *To lack education.*
    Suivez les instructions données. *Follow the directions (instructions).*
INSTRUIRE *to instruct, teach; inform.*
instruit *adj. well-educated, well-informed.*
instrument *m. instrument, tool.*
INSU *m. unawareness.*
    A l'insu de. *Unknown to. Without the knowledge of.*
    Il l'a fait à l'insu de ses parents. *He did it without his parents' knowledge.*
    Pourquoi l'avez-vous fait à mon insu? *Why did you do it behind my back?*
insubordination *f. insubordination.*
insubordonné *f. insubordinate.*
insuccès *m. failure.*
insuffisance *f. insufficiency, deficiency, incompetence.*
insuffisant *adj. insufficient, incompetent.*
insulte *f. insult.*
insulter *to insult.*
insupportable *adj. unbearable.*
s'insurger *to rebel, revolt.*
insurrection *f. insurrection.*
intact *adj. intact.*
intarissable *adj. inexhaustible.*
intégral (intégraux *pl.*) *adj. integral, entire.*
intégrité *f. integrity.*
intellectuel (intellectuelle *f.*) *noun and adj. intellectual.*
intelligemment *intelligently.*
intelligence *f. intelligence.*
    Etre d'intelligence avec. *To have an understanding with. To be in league with. To be hand in glove with.*
intelligent *adj. intelligent, clever.*
intempérance *f. intemperance.*
intense *adj. intense.*
intensité *f. intensity.*
INTENTION *f. intention, purpose.*
    Vous vous méprenez sur ses intentions. *You're mistaken about his intentions.*
    Avez-vous l'intention d'y aller? *Do you intend to go there?*
    Il l'a fait avec intention. *He did it on purpose.*
intercéder *to intercede.*

intercepter *to intercept.*
interdire *to forbid.*
    C'est interdit. *That's not allowed. That's prohibited.*
    Les chiens sont interdits. *No dogs allowed.*
interdit *adj. forbidden; confused.*
    Entrée interdite sous peine de poursuite. *No admittance under penalty of law.*
    Passage interdit. *No thoroughfare.*
    Elle demeura tout interdite. *She stood there completely confused (at a loss for words, speechless).*
INTÉRESSANT *adj. interesting.*
INTÉRESSER *to interest, concern; give a share.*
    En quoi tout cela vous intéresse-t-il? *How does all that concern you?*
    On l'a intéressé dans l'affaire. *He'll receive his share of the profits.*
INTÉRÊT *m. interest, share.*
    Les intérêts du prêt s'accumulent. *The interest on the loan is accruing.*
    J'ai intérêt à en acheter. *It's to my interest to buy some of it.*
    Il y aurait intérêt à. *It would be desirable (to our advantage) to.*
    Porter intérêt à quelqu'un. *To take an interest in someone.*
    Il paiera des dommages-intérêts. *He'll pay damages.*
intérieur *m. inside; home; home life.*
    Nous avons rendez-vous à l'intérieur du restaurant. *We're meeting inside the restaurant.*
    Ils n'ont pas d'intérieur à eux. *They have no home life.*
intérieur *adj. interior.*
intérim *m. interim.*
interloquer *disconcert.*
    Il en resta tout interloqué (*fam.*). *He was completely disconcerted. He was taken aback. He was speechless.*
intermède *m. medium; interlude.*
    Par l'intermède de. *By means of. Through the medium (agency) of.*
intermédiaire *noun (m.) and adj. intermediary; intermediate.*
interminable *adj. interminable, endless.*
internat *m. boarding school.*
international (internationaux *pl.*) *adj. international.*
interne *m. boarder (at school); intern (hospital).*
interner *to intern.*
interpeller *to call upon.*
interprétation *f. interpretation.*
interprète *m. interpreter.*
interpréter *to interpret.*
interrogation *f. interrogation.*
    Point d'interrogation. *Question mark.*
interrogatoire *m. interrogatory.*
interroger *to examine, question.*
interrompre *to interrupt.*
    Excusez-moi de vous interrompre, mais on vous appelle au téléphone. *Pardon me for interrupting you, but you're wanted on the phone.*
    J'ai dû interrompre mes leçons d'anglais lorsque mon professeur est parti. *I had to discontinue my English lessons when my teacher left.*
interruption *f. interruption.*
interurbain *adj. interurban, long-distance (telephone).*
    Un appel interurbain. *Long-distance telephone call.*

intervalle *m. interval.*
intervenir *to intervene, interfere.*
intervention *f. interference.*
interview *m. and f. interview.*
intestin *m. intestine; pl. intestines.*
intimation *f. notification of an order.*
intime *adj. intimate, private.*
 Un ami intime. *An intimate (very close) friend.*
intimider *to intimidate.*
intimité *f. intimacy.*
intituler *to entitle.*
intolérable *adj. intolerable, unbearable.*
intolérance *f. intolerance.*
intolérant *adj. intolerant.*
intonation *f. intonation.*
intoxication *f. poisoning.*
intransigeance *f. intransigence, uncompromising-*
 ness.
intransigeant *adj. uncompromising, intolerant.*
intrépide *adj. dauntless, bold.*
intrigant *m. intriguer, schemer, wire-puller.*
intrigue *f. intrigue, plot (of a book, etc.).*
intriguer *to plot; puzzle.*
 Cette affaire l'intrigue beaucoup. *This case*
 (matter) puzzles him a lot.
introduction *f. introduction.*
INTRODUIRE *to introduce.*
 Il a introduit beaucoup de réformes. *He in-*
 troduced numerous reforms.
 Il fut introduit au salon. *He was shown into*
 the living (parlor) room.
introuvable *adj. not to be found.*
 Cet article est introuvable. *This article is hard*
 to find (not to be found).
intrus *m. intruder.*
intuition *f. intuition.*
inutile *adj. useless.*
invalide *m. and f. noun and adj. invalid, cripple.*
invariable *adj. invariable.*
invasion *f. invasion.*
invective *f. invective.*
inventaire *m. inventory.*
inventer *to invent, devise.*
invention *f. invention.*
inverse *m. reverse, opposite.*
 Il fait toujours l'inverse de ce qu'on lui demande. *He always does the opposite of what*
 you ask him.
inverse *adj. reverse, contrary, opposite.*
 En sens inverse. *In the opposite direction.*
inversibles *m. pl. film (for transparencies).*
invincible *adj. invincible, unconquerable.*
invisible *adj. invisible.*
invitation *f. invitation.*
 Une carte d'invitation. *(Printed) invitation.*
invité *m. guest.*
inviter *to invite.*
involontaire *adj. involuntary.*
involontairement *involuntarily.*
invoquer *to call upon.*
invraisemblable *adj. unlikely, hard to believe.*
 Une histoire invraisemblable. *A tall story.*
invulnérable *adj. invulnerable.*
iode *m. iodine.*
 Teinture d'iode. *Tincture of iodine.*
ironie *f. irony.*
ironique *adj. ironical.*
irréfléchi *adj. thoughtless, hasty, rash.*
irrégulier (irrégulière *f.*) *adj. irregular.*
irrémédiable *adj. irremediable.*
irréparable *adj. irreparable.*
irréprochable *adj. irreproachable.*
irrésistible *adj. irresistible.*

irrespectueux (irrespectueuse *f.*) *adj. disrespectful.*
irresponsable *adj. irresponsible.*
irrévocable *adj. irrevocable.*
irrigation *f. irrigation.*
irriguer *to irrigate.*
irritable *adj. irritable.*
irritant *adj. irritating.*
irriter *to irritate, annoy, anger.*
irruption *f. irruption, violent entry.*
 Faire irruption dans une salle. *To burst into a*
 room.
islamique *adj. Islamic.*
isolement *m. isolation, loneliness; insulation.*
isoler *to isolate, separate.*
israélite *m. and f. noun and adj. Jew, Jewish.*
issu *adj. born of, descended from.*
issue *f. issue, way out.*
Italie *f. Italy.*
italien (italienne *f.*) *noun and adj. Italian.*
item *ditto; likewise, also.*
itinéraire *m. itinerary, route.*
ivoire *m. ivory.*
ivre *adj. drunk.*
ivresse *f. drunkeness, intoxication; enthusiasm.*
ivrogne *m. drunkard.*

J *The tenth letter of the alphabet.*

jadis *formerly, once.*
jaillir *to gush (out), spurt, burst forth.*
jalousie *f. jealousy, envy.*
jaloux (jalouse *f.*) *adj. jealous.*
JAMAIS (with ne) *never.*
 Je n'y ai jamais été. *I've never been there.*
 Jamais de la vie! *Never! Not on your life!*
jambe *f. leg.*
 Il a pris ses jambes à son cou (*fam.*). *He took*
 to his heels.
jambon *m. ham.*
JANVIER *m. January.*
japonais (japonaise *f.*) *noun and adj. Japanese.*
jaquette *f. jacket of a woman's suit.*
jardin *m. garden.*
jardinier *m.* (jardinière *f.*) *gardener.*
jargon *m. jargon; slang; incorrect language.*
jarretière *f. garter.*
jaser *to chatter.*
jaunâtre *adj. yellowish.*
jaune *adj. yellow.*
 Jaune paille. *Straw-yellow, straw-colored.*
jaunir *to turn yellow.*
JE *I.*
jersey *m. woolen material.*
jet *m. throw, throwing; gush; jet; ray.*
 Un jet d'eau. *A fountain.*
jetée *f. jetty, pier.*
jeter *to throw.*
jeton *m. token (game).*
jeu *m.* (jeux *pl.*) *game; play.*
 Etre en jeu. *To be at stake.*
 Un jeu de mots. *A pun.*
 Un jeu d'esprit. *A witticism.*
 Le jeu des acteurs. *Acting.*
 Les jeux d'eau. *Fountains (playing).*
 Les jeux de lumière. *Lighting (theatre).*
JEUDI *m. Thursday.*
 Le(s) jeudi(s). *On Thursdays.*
à jeun *fasting.*
 Prenez ce médicament à jeun. *Take this medi-*
 cine on an empty stomach.
JEUNE *adj. young; junior.*
 Jeune homme. *Young man.*
 Jeune fille. *Young lady.*

 Dubois jeune. *Dubois, Jr.*
jeûne *m. fast.*
jeûner *to fast.*
jeunesse *f. youth.*
joaillerie *f. jewelry.*
joie *f. joy.*
joindre *to join, unite.*
se joindre *to join; join in.*
joint *adj. joined, connected; enclosed, attached.*
joli *m. used in the following expression:*
 C'est du joli (*fam.*)! *That's a fine thing!*
JOLI *adj. pretty.*
 Une jolie femme. *A pretty woman.*
joliment *nicely.*
 Il nous a joliment trompés. *He really (cer-*
 tainly) took us in (fooled us).
jonction *f. junction.*
joue *f. cheek.*
jouer *to play.*
 Jouer au bridge (au tennis). *To play bridge*
 (tennis).
 Jouer du piano (de la flûte, de la clarinette).
 To play the piano (the flute, the clarinet).
se jouer *to make game of; make light of.*
 Il se joue de tout le monde. *He makes game*
 of everybody.
 Se jouer des difficultés. *To overcome difficulties*
 with the greatest ease. To make light of
 difficulties.
jouet *m. toy.*
joueur *m.* (joueuse *f.*) *player, gambler.*
joufflu *adj. chubby.*
joug *m. yoke.*
jouir *to enjoy, rejoice in.*
 Il jouit d'une bonne santé. *He enjoys good*
 health.
 Il sait jouir de la vie. *He knows how to enjoy*
 life.
jouissance *f. enjoyment.*
JOUR *m. day, daytime; daylight.*
 Quel jour sommes-nous? *What's today?*
 Je le vois tous les jours. *I see him every day.*
 De nos jours. *In our time. Nowadays. These*
 days.
 Sur ses vieux jours. *In his old age.*
 Il fait jour. *It's daylight.*
 Au petit jour. *At daybreak.*
 Jeter le jour dans. *To throw light on.*
 Du jour au lendemain. *Overnight. From one*
 day to the next.
 Ils vivent au jour le jour. *They live from hand*
 to mouth.
 A un de ces jours. *See you one of these days.*
 So long.
 Mettre un compte à jour. *To bring an account*
 up to date.
 Ces jours-ci. *These days.*
 Huit (quinze) jours. *One week (two weeks).*
 Payer par jour. *To pay by the day.*
 Plusieurs fois par jour. *Several times a day.*
journal *m.* (journaux *pl.*) *newspaper; diary.*
 Le marchand de journaux. *Newsvendor.*
journalier (journalière *f.*) *adj. daily.*
 Un travail journalier. *A daily task.*
journalisme *m. journalism.*
journaliste *m. journalist.*
journée *f. day.*
 Payé à la journée. *Paid by the day.*
 Dans la journée. *During the day.*
 Vous les aurez dans la journée. *You'll have them*
 the same day.
jovial *adj. jovial, jolly.*
joyau *m.* (joyaux *pl.*) *jewel.*

joyeux (joyeuse f.) adj. merry, jolly.
jubiler to be jubilant, rejoice, exult.
judiciaire adj. judicial.
Une enquête judiciaire. An official inquest.
judicieux (judicieuse f.) adj. judicious, sensible.
juge m. judge.
jugement m. judgment, sentence.
juger to judge.
À en juger par. Judging by.
JUILLET m. July.
JUIN m. June.
jumeau (jumelle, jumelles f., jumeaux pl.) noun and adj. twin.
jumelles f. pl. binoculars, opera glasses.
jupe f. skirt.
jurer to swear.
juridiction f. jurisdiction.
juridique adj. juridical, judicial.
juron m. oath, swear-word.
jury m. jury.
jus m. juice.
Le jus de fruits. Fruit juice.
JUSQUE till, until, as far as.
Jusqu'ici. Up to here. Up to now.
Jusque là. Up to there. Up to then.
Du matin jusqu'au soir. From morning till night.
Jusqu'-où allez-vous? How far are you going?
Jusqu'à un certain point, il a raison. He's right up to a certain point.
Attendez jusqu'après la fin du mois. Wait till the end of the month.
Jusqu'à quel âge avez-vous vécu à Paris? How old were you when you left Paris? ("Up to what age did you live in Paris?")
JUSTE adj. just, fair, exact.
Un homme juste. An upright man.
Rien de plus juste. Nothing could be fairer.
C'est juste ce qu'il me faut. It's just what I want (need).
Quelle est l'heure juste? What is the correct time?
Je ne sais au juste s'il est parti. I don't know for sure whether he left.
Son vêtement est trop juste. His coat is too tight.
Comme de juste. Of course.
justement exactly.
C'est justement ce que je vous disais. That's exactly what I was telling you.
justesse f. exactness, accuracy.
La justesse d'une opinion. The soundness of an opinion.
Il est arrivé de justesse. He arrived just in time.
justice f. justice, jurisdiction; courts of justice.
justification f. justification.
justifier to justify.
se justifier to justify oneself.
juvénile adj. juvenile.
juxtaposer to place side by side.

K The eleventh letter of the alphabet.

képi m. cap, kepi.
kilo m. (abbreviation of kilogramme) kilogram.
kilométrage m. distance in kilometers (cf. mileage).
kilomètre m. kilometer.
kiosque m. stand; newsstand.
klaxon m. automobile horn.

L The twelfth letter of the alphabet.

l' See le.
la See le.
LÀ there, to there.
Ça et là. Here and there.
Il est allé là. He went there.
LÀ-BAS over there.
Regardez là-bas. Look over there.
labeur m. labor, toil.
laboratoire m. laboratory.
laborieux (laborieuse f.) adj. laborious, industrious.
labour m. plowing.
labourage m. plowing.
labourer to plow.
laboureur m. plowman.
labyrinthe m. labyrinth.
lac m. lake.
lacer to lace, tie.
Lacez vos souliers. Tie your shoelaces.
lacet m. lace.
lâche m. coward.
lâche adj. loose; cowardly.
lâchement in a cowardly way.
lâcher to loosen, relax, release.
lâcheté f. cowardice.
lâcheur m. (lâcheuse f.) quitter.
lacune f. gap; blank.
là-dessus on that, on it, thereupon.
laid adj. ugly.
laideur f. ugliness.
laine f. wool.
En laine. In, of wool.
laisse f. leash.
LAISSER to leave.
Laissez ça là. Leave it (that) there.
Laissez-moi tranquille. Let me alone.
Laissez donc! Please don't trouble yourself. Don't bother.
Laissez voir. Let's see, let me see (it).
Vous me la laissez à 60 francs? Will you give it to me for 60 francs?
se laisser to let oneself, allow oneself.
Elle se laisse abattre. She lets herself get depressed. She lets herself get discouraged.
Je ne me suis pas laissé faire. I didn't let myself be taken in.
Ils ne se le laisseront pas dire deux fois. They won't have to be told twice.
laisser-aller m. taking things easy, slackness, neglect, listlessness.
Il est d'un laisser-aller incroyable! He's unbelievably negligent (careless, sloppy)!
laisser-faire m. non-interference, non-intervention.
laisser-passer m. pass.
LAIT m. milk.
Café au lait. Coffee (with milk).
Dents de lait. First teeth. Milk teeth.
Soeur de lait. Foster sister.
laiterie f. dairy.
laitier m. (laitière f.) dairyman, dairywoman.
laiton m. brass.
laitue f. lettuce.
lambeau m. (lambeaux pl.) scrap, shred.
Mes vêtements sont en lambeaux. My clothes are in rags.
Mon pardessus tombe en lambeaux. My overcoat is falling to pieces.
lame f. blade, plate, sheet, wire.
Lame de rasoir. Razor blade.
lamentable adj. deplorable, pitiful.
lamentation f. lamentation.
se lamenter to lament.

lampe f. lamp.
lampe-éclair f. flashbulb.
lance f. spear.
lancer to throw, fling; emit; issue (a warrant, etc.).
se lancer to rush, dash.
LANGAGE m. language.
langoureux (langoureuse f.) adj. languishing; languid; yearning, pining.
langouste f. rock lobster.
LANGUE f. tongue; language.
langueur f. languor.
languide adj. languid, weary, listless.
languir to languish, pine.
languissant adj. languid; languishing.
lanterne f. lantern.
lapider to lapidate, stone.
lapin m. rabbit.
laps m. lapse (time).
lapsus m. lapse, error, slip.
larcin m. larceny, petty theft.
lard m. pork fat.
large m. breadth, width; open sea.
large adj. broad, wide; extensive; generous.
largesse f. liberality.
largeur f. width; broadness.
larme f. tear.
larmoyant adj. weeping, tearful.
larron m. robber, thief.
larynx m. larynx.
las (lasse f.) adj. tired, weary; disgusted, fed up.
Je suis très las. I'm very tired.
Je suis bien las de cela. I'm sick and tired of that.
lasser to tire, fatigue, bore.
se lasser to tire, grow weary.
latéral (latéraux pl.) adj. lateral.
latin noun and adj. Latin.
latitude f. latitude.
laurier m. laurel; glory.
lavabo m. washbasin, washstand; lavatory, washroom.
lavage m. washing.
laver to wash, bathe.
SE LAVER to wash oneself.
laverie f. machine laundry.
lavette f. washcloth.
layette f. layette.
LE (la f., les pl., l' before vowels and "mute" h) the.
Le livre. The book.
La lettre. The letter.
L'homme. The man.
Les hommes. The men.
LE (la f., les pl., l' before vowels and "mute" h) him, her, it.
Faites-le tout de suite! Do it right away.
Je la vois assez souvent. I see her quite often.
Je l'ai commandé. I ordered it.
Je le veux. I want it.
lécher to lick.
leçon f. lesson.
Etudiez vos leçons. Study your lessons.
Il lui a fait la leçon. He lectured him. He gave him a lecture.
lecteur m. (lectrice f.) reader.
lecture f. reading.
légal (légaux pl.) adj. legal.
légalité f. legality.
légation f. legation.
légendaire adj. legendary, fabulous.
légende f. legend.
LÉGER (légère f.) adj. light (in weight).
légèrement lightly.

légèreté f. *lightness.*
légion f. *legion.*
   La légion d'honneur. *The Legion of Honor.*
   La Légion Étrangère. *The Foreign Legion.*
législatif (législative f.) adj. *legislative.*
législation f. *legislation.*
législature f. *legislature, legislative body.*
légitime adj. *legitimate, justifiable.*
legs m. *legacy.*
léguer *to bequeath.*
légume m. *vegetable.*
LENDEMAIN m. *the next day.*
LENT adj. *slow.*
LENTEMENT *slowly.*
lenteur f. *slowness.*
lentille f. *lentil.*
LEQUEL (laquelle f., lesquels m. pl., lesquelles
   f. pl.) *who, which one.*
   Je ne sais lequel choisir. *I don't know which
     one to choose.*
   Laquelle voulez-vous? *Which one do you want?*
lessive f. *washing.*
lessiver *to wash (clothes, etc.).*
leste adj. *nimble.*
lestement *briskly, nimbly.*
léthargie f. *lethargy.*
LETTRE f. *letter.*
   La lettre recommandée. *Registered letter.*
LEUR *their; to them.*
   Cela leur appartient. *That belongs to them.*
levain m. *yeast.*
levant m. *Levant.*
levée f. *removal, collecting; trick (in cards).*
   La levée postale. *Mail collection.*
lever m. *rising, getting up.*
   A quelle heure est le lever du rideau? *(At) what
     time does the curtain go up?*
   Le lever du soleil. *Sunrise.*
LEVER *to raise, lift.*
   Lever la tête. *To raise one's head. To look up.*
   Il n'est pas encore levé. *He isn't up yet. He
     hasn't gotten up yet.*
   La séance a été levée à trois heures. *The meet-
     ing was adjourned at three o'clock.*
SE LEVER *to get up.*
   Je dois me lever de bonne heure demain matin.
     I have to get up early tomorrow morning.
   Le vent se lève. *The wind is rising.*
levier m. *lever.*
lèvre f. *lip.*
   Il l'a dit du bout des lèvres. *He said it half-
     heartedly.*
   Je l'ai sur le bord des lèvres. *I have it on the
     tip of my tongue.*
   Du rouge à lèvre. *Lipstick.*
lézard m. *lizard.*
liaison f. *joining, binding.*
liasse f. *bundle.*
libéral (libéraux pl.) adj. *liberal.*
libéralité f. *liberality, generosity.*
libération f. *liberation.*
libérer *to set free.*
liberté f. *liberty, freedom.*
libraire m. *bookseller.*
librairie f. *bookshop.*
LIBRE adj. *free.*
   Etes-vous libre ce soir? *Are you free tonight?*
   .Il n'a pas un moment de libre. *He hasn't a
     free moment. He hasn't a minute to himself.*
   Libre à vous. *Do it if you wish. It's up to you.*
   Avez-vous une chambre libre? *Do you have
     a vacant room?*
   Avoir du temps libre. *To have some free time.*

librement *freely.*
licence f. *license, permission.*
   Il a passé sa licence de droit. *He received a
     law degree.*
   La licence d'exportation. *Export license.*
lie f. *dregs.*
liège m. *cork.*
lien m. *tie, bond.*
lier *to bind, tie.*
LIEU m. (lieux pl.) *place.*
   Au lieu de. *In place of. Instead of.*
   En premier lieu. *In the first place.*
   Avoir lieu. *To take place.*
   Tenir lieu de. *To take the place of.*
   Lieu commun. *Commonplace. Trite saying.*
   Etre sur les lieux. *To be on the spot.*
lieutenant m. *lieutenant.*
lièvre m. *hare.*
LIGNE f. *line, row, rank.*
   La ligne est occupée, raccrochez. *The line is
     busy, hang up (telephone).*
   Suivez la ligne du chemin de fer. *Follow the
     railroad track.*
   Cette question vient en première ligne. *This
     question is of primary importance.*
   Prenez cela en ligne de compte. *Take that
     into account. Take that into consideration.*
   Ecrivez-moi quelques lignes. *Drop me a few
     lines.*
   A la ligne. *New paragraph (in dictating).*
   En ligne. *In line, lined up.*
ligue f. *league.*
lime f. *file.*
limer *to file.*
limitation f. *limitation, restriction.*
limite f. *limit.*
limiter *to bound.*
Limoges m. *Limoges porcelain.*
limonade f. *lemon drink (carbonated).*
limpide adj. *limpid, clear.*
lin m. *flax; linen.*
linge m. *linen; laundry.*
lingerie f. *linen manufacture; linen room; lingerie.*
linguiste m. and f. *linguist.*
lion m. *lion.*
liqueur f. *liquor, liqueur.*
liquidation f. *liquidation; clearance sale.*
liquide adj. *liquid.*
liquider *to liquidate.*
LIRE *to read.*
   Avez-vous jamais lu ce livre? *Have you ever
     read this book?*
   Je sais lire en français mais je ne sais pas le
     parler. *I can read French but I can't speak
     it.*
lisible adj. *legible.*
lisiblement *legibly.*
lisse adj. *smooth, polished.*
liste f. *list.*
LIT m. *bed; layer.*
   Garder le lit. *To stay in bed.*
LITRE m. *liter (measure).*
littéraire adj. *literary.*
littéral adj. *literal.*
   Sens littéral. *Literal meaning.*
littéralement *literally.*
littérature f. *literature.*
livide adj. *livid.*
livraison f. *delivery.*
LIVRE m. *book.*
livrer *to deliver.*
se livrer *to give way to; devote one's attention to.*
livret m. *small book; bankbook.*

local m. (locaux pl.) *premises.*
local (locaux pl.) adj. *local.*
localité f. *locality, place, spot.*
locataire m. *tenant.*
location f. *hiring, renting.*
   Prix de location. *Rent.*
   Location de livres. *Lending library.*
   Bureau de location. *Box office.*
locomotive f. *locomotive, engine.*
locution f. *expression, phrase.*
loge f. *lodge; loge, box.*
logement m. *lodging, housing.*
loger *to reside; put up, accommodate.*
logique adj. *logical; f. logic.*
logiquement *logically.*
logis m. *home, house.*
   Il garde le logis. *He stays at home.*
LOI f. *law.*
LOIN *far.*
   Les voyez-vous là-bas au loin? *Do you see them
     over there in the distance?*
   Loin de là. *Far from it.*
   De loin en loin. *At long intervals.*
   Cet artiste ira loin. *This artist will go far.*
   Ne pas voir de loin. *To lack foresight.*
lointain m. *distance.*
   On peut le voir dans le lointain. *You can see
     it in the distance.*
loisir m. *leisure.*
   A ses moments de loisir. *In his spare time.*
long m. and f. *long.*
   Le long de la Seine. *Along the Seine.*
   Il s'est promené le long de la rivière. *He walked
     along the river.*
   au long de. *Alongside of. Along.*
   A la longue. *In the long run.*
   Etendu de tout son long (fam.). *Lying at full
     length.*
   Se promener de long en large. *To walk to and
     fro.*
   Cinq mètres de long. *Five meters long.*
LONG (longue f.) adj. *long.*
   Avoir la vue longue. *To be farsighted.*
   En longue. *Lengthwise.*
   De longues années. *Many years.*
longitude f. *longitude.*
LONGTEMPS *a long time.*
   Il y a longtemps que je l'attends. *I've been
     waiting for him a long time.*
longuement *for a long time.*
longueur f. *length, duration.*
loque f. *rag.*
   En loques. *In rags.*
lorgnette f. *opera glasses.*
lorgnon m. *lorgnette.*
LORS *then.*
   Dès lors. *From that time.*
   Depuis lors. *Since then.*
LORSQUE *when.*
   Lorsque j'ai voulu m'en aller . . . *When I
     wanted to go . . .*
lot m. *lot, share, prize.*
loterie f. *lottery.*
lotion (pour les cheveux) f. *(hair) lotion.*
louable adj. *laudable, praiseworthy.*
louange f. *praise.*
louche adj. *cross-eyed; squinting; shady, suspicious.*
loucher *to be cross-eyed.*
LOUER *to praise; rent, lease.*
   Il le loua. *He praised him.*
   Louer une voiture à l'heure. *To hire a car by
     the hour.*
   Chambres à louer. *Rooms to let. Rooms for rent.*

loup *m. wolf.*
  J'ai une faim de loup. *I have a ravenous appetite.* ("*I have the hunger of a wolf.*")
  Il est connu comme le loup blanc. *Everybody knows him.*
loupe *f. magnifying glass.*
LOURD *adj. heavy.*
  Ça pèse lourd. *It's heavy. It weighs a lot.*
  Il fait lourd aujourd'hui. *It's sultry (close, humid) out today.*
  J'ai la tête lourde. *My head feels heavy.*
  Il a fait une lourde erreur. *He made a grave mistake.*
lourdaud *adj. awkward, clumsy.*
loyal (loyaux *pl.*) *adj. honest, fair.*
loyauté *f. honesty.*
loyer *m. rent.*
lu (*have*) *read.*
lubie *f. whim.*
lucide *adj. clear.*
lucratif (lucrative *f.*) *adj. profitable.*
lueur *f. gleam.*
lugubre *adj. dismal, gloomy.*
LUI *him, her, it.*
  Je me souviens de lui. *I remember him.*
  Lui aussi me l'a dit. *He also told it to me.*
lui-même *himself.*
LUMIÈRE *f. light.*
  Il n'y a pas assez de lumière. *There isn't enough light.*
  Les jeux de lumière. *Lighting (theatre).*
lumineux (lumineuse *f.*) *adj. bright.*
lunatique *m. and f. noun and adj. eccentric person, capricious.*
LUNDI *m. Monday.*
LUNE *f. moon.*
lunettes *f. pl. glasses.*
lustre *m. gloss, luster, brilliance; chandelier.*
luthérien (luthérienne *f.*) *noun and adj. Lutheran.*
lutte *f. fight.*
lutter *to wrestle, struggle.*
luxe *m. luxury, splendor.*
luxueux (luxueuse *f.*) *adj. luxurious, sumptuous.*
lycée *m. secondary school.*
lycéen *m.* (lycéenne *f.*) *pupil attending the lycée.*

M *The thirteenth letter of the alphabet.*

MA *See* mon.
  Ma soeur va au lycée. *My sister goes to the lycée.*
macabre *adj. macabre, gruesome.*
  Un humour macabre. *Grim humor.*
macadam *m. macadam.*
macaron *m. macaroon.*
mâcher *to chew.*
  Mâchez votre nourriture. *Chew your food.*
  Il ne mâche pas ses mots. *He doesn't mince words.*
  Son frère lui a mâché tout son travail. *His work has been prepared for him by his brother.*
machin *m. what's-his-name; what-do-you-call-it, thingumajig, thingumbob.*
  C'est machin qui l'a dit. *What's-his-name said so.*
  Qu'est-ce que c'est que ce machin-là? *What's that gadget?*
machinal (machinaux *pl.*) *adj. mechanical; instinctive.*
machinalement *mechanically, instinctively.*
MACHINE *f. machine, engine.*
  Une machine infernale. *A bomb.*
  La machine à écrire. *Typewriter.*

La machine à coudre. *Sewing machine.*
  Machine à vapeur. *Steam engine.*
  Les machines. *The machinery.*
  Faites machine en arrière. *Reverse the engine.*
  À la machine. *By machine.*
machiner *to plot.*
  Machiner la perte de quelqu'un. *To plot someone's ruin.*
  Qu'est-ce qu'il machine encore? *What else is he up to? What's he up to now?*
machinerie *f. machinery.*
mâchoire *f. jaw.*
  Il s'est cassé la mâchoire. *He broke his jaw.*
mâchonner *to chew with difficulty; mumble.*
maçon *m. mason.*
maçonnerie *f. masonry.*
MADAME *f.* (mesdames *pl.*) *Madam, Mrs.*
  Si madame permet. *If madam will permit.*
  Pardon, madame. —Du tout, monsieur. *I beg your pardon, madam. —Not at all.*
  Eh bien, mesdames, nous ferions mieux d'entrer. *Well, ladies, we'd better go in.*
  Comment va madame votre mère? *How's your mother?*
  Madame est servie. *Dinner is served.*
  Mme (*abbreviation of* madame). *Mrs.*
MADEMOISELLE *f.* (mesdemoiselles *pl.*) *Miss.*
  Bonne nuit, mademoiselle. *Good evening, Miss.*
  Mlle (*abbreviation of* mademoiselle). *Miss.*
  Comment va mademoiselle votre soeur? *How is your sister?*
MAGASIN *m. store, shop.*
  Ce magasin est bien monté. *This store's well stocked.*
  Elle court les magasins. *She goes from one shop to another. She makes the rounds of the stores.*
  Il tient un magasin d'épicerie. *He has a grocery store.*
  Un magasin de nouveautés. *A novelty shop.*
  Le grand magasin. *The department store.*
magazine *m. magazine.*
magicien *m.* (magicienne *f.*) *magician.*
magie *f. magic; charm.*
  La magie noire. *Black magic.*
  La magie de son sourire. *The charm of her smile.*
magique *adj. magic.*
magistral (magistraux *pl.*) *adj. magisterial, masterly.*
magistrat *m. magistrate.*
magistrature *f. magistracy; the bench.*
  La magistrature assise. *The judges. The bench.*
magnanime *adj. magnanimous, generous.*
  C'est une personne magnanime. *He's (she's) very magnanimous.*
magnanimité *f. magnanimity.*
magnétique *adj. magnetic.*
  La bande (le ruban) magnétique. *The tape.*
magnétisme *m. magnetism; hypnotism.*
magnétophone *m. tape recorder.*
magnificence *f. magnificence, splendor.*
  La magnificence de la réception a ébloui les invités. *The splendor of the reception dazzled the guests.*
  Telle magnificence n'avait jamais été vue. *Such splendor (magnificence) had never been seen before.*
MAGNIFIQUE *adj. magnificent, splendid.*
  Il fait un temps magnifique. *It's a glorious day.*
  Un repas magnifique. *An excellent (a wonderful) meal.*
mahométan *noun and adj. Mohammedan.*
MAI *m. May.*

maigre *adj. lean, thin.*
  Elle est maigre comme un clou. *She's as thin as a rail.*
  Ses appointements sont maigres. *His salary is low.*
  Un jour maigre. *A fast day. A day of fasting.*
  Une majorité de cinq voix, c'est maigre. *A majority of five votes—that's not very much.*
maigrir *to grow thinner, lose weight.*
  Elle a maigri et pâli. *She's grown thinner and paler.*
maille *f. stitch.*
  Tricoter deux mailles à l'envers et deux à l'endroit. *Purl two, knit two.*
maille *f. an old copper coin.*
  Il n'a ni sou ni maille. *He hasn't a penny to his name.*
  Il a eu maille à partir avec lui. *He had a bone to pick with him.*
maillot *m. tights.*
  Un maillot de bain. *A bathing suit.*
MAIN *f. hand.*
  J'ai mal aux mains. *My hands hurt. My hands are sore.*
  Il a les mains nettes dans cette affaire. *His hands are clean in this affair.*
  Je m'en lave les mains. *I wash my hands of it.*
  Il a eu la main heureuse. *1. He was lucky. 2. He had a lucky hand (in cards).*
  Elle lui a accordé sa main. *She agreed to marry him.* ("*She gave him her hand.*")
  On a mis la dernière main à ce travail. *They put the finishing touches on this piece of work.*
  L'argent ne lui tient pas dans les mains. *He's (she's) a spendthrift.*
  Ils vont la main dans la main. *They always agree with each other.* ("*They always go hand in hand.*")
  Je lui ai payé cette somme de la main à la main. *I paid this sum to him in person (in cash and without receipt).*
  Il s'est défendu les armes à la main. *He offered armed resistance.*
  Il n'y va pas de main morte. *He goes at it tooth and nail.*
  Donner un coup de main. *To lend a hand. To help.*
  Il fait sentir sa main. *He exercises his authority. He makes his authority felt.*
  Nous avons tout de première main. *We buy from the producer.*
  Je l'ai acheté de seconde main. *I bought it secondhand.*
  J'ai quelqu'un sous la main. *I have someone I can use. I have someone who can help me.*
  Ils ont agi sous main. *They've acted secretly. They've acted in an underhanded manner.*
  Il fut pris la main dans le sac. *He was caught in the act. He was caught red-handed.*
  Ils en sont venus aux mains. *They came to blows over it.*
  On le lui a remis en mains propres. *It was delivered to him personally.*
  C'était préparé de longue main. *It was provided for long in advance.*
  On lui a mis le marché en mains. *He was told to take it or leave it.*
  Il a mis la main à la pâte. *He joined in to help. He lent a hand.*
  Il dépense son argent à pleines mains. *He spends his money freely.*
  C'est fait de main de maître. *It has the touch of the master.*

J'en mettrais ma main au feu. *I could swear to it.*

Il a un poil dans la main. *He's very lazy. ("Hair grows in the palm of his hands.")*

Il a fait des pieds et des mains pour réussir. *He did everything in his power to succeed.*

Il a le coeur sur la main. 1. *He's generous (open-hearted).* 2. *He wears his heart on his sleeve.*

Fait à la main. *Handmade.*

Laver à la main. *To wash by hand.*

main-d'oeuvre f. *manpower.*

La main-d'oeuvre est abondante dans la région. *Manpower is plentiful in this region. There is an abundant labor supply in this region.*

maint adj. *many a.*

Je le lui ai dit maintes fois. *I told it to him many a time (many times).*

maintenance f. *maintenance.*

MAINTENANT *now.*

Que devons-nous faire maintenant? *What shall we do now?*

Elle a bonne mine maintenant. *She looks well now.*

A vous maintenant. *It's your turn now.*

Maintenant même. *Right now.*

MAINTENIR to *maintain.*

Il maintient ce qu'il a dit. *He maintains (sticks to) what he said.*

Maintenir l'ordre. *To preserve order.*

Maintenir les prix bas. *To keep prices down.*

se maintenir *to keep oneself; keep up, last.*

Il se maintient dans les bonnes grâces du patron. *He keeps in his boss's favor.*

Vous croyez que cela va se maintenir? *Do you think it's going to last long?*

maintien m. *maintenance; behavior.*

MAIRE m. *mayor.*

Le maire et ses adjoints. *The mayor and his deputies.*

Monsieur le Maire. *Mr. Mayor.*

MAIRIE f. *city hall.*

Pourriez-vous me dire où se trouve la mairie? *Can you tell me where City Hall is?*

MAIS but.

Mais certainement! *(But) Of course! Why, certainly!*

Mais oui! *Why, certainly! Why, of course!*

Mais si! *(denies or contradicts a previous negative statement) But it's so. But it's true. I tell you yes. Yes, indeed!*

Mais non! *Of course not! I should say not! No, indeed!*

Je le ferai, mais il faut que vous m'aidiez. *I'll do it but you'll have to help me.*

J'accepte, mais à charge de revanche. *I accept but on condition that you let me do the same for you sometime.*

Mais qu'avez-vous donc? *Why, what's the matter (with you)? Why, what's the trouble?*

Non seulement . . . mais encore . . . *Not only . . . but also . . .*

maïs m. *corn.*

MAISON f. *house.*

Meubler une maison. *To furnish a house.*

A la maison. *At home.*

Il est de la maison. *He's one of the family.*

Cette maison se spécialise dans ces machines. *This firm specializes in these machines.*

Maison René Dubois. *The firm of René Dubois.*

On a fait maison nette. *They made a clean sweep of all the employees.*

MAÎTRE m. (maîtresse f.) *master; teacher.*

Son père est allé voir son maître. *His father went to see his teacher.*

En France, les avocats sont appelés "maître." *In France, lawyers are addressed as "maître."*

Ce fut un coup de maître. *It was a masterly stroke.*

Il parle en maître. *He speaks with authority.*

Il ne faut pas le blâmer, il n'est pas maître de ses actes. *There's no point blaming him (throwing the blame on him); he's not responsible for his actions (for what he does).*

maîtresse adj. *chief, principal.*

Une oeuvre maîtresse. *Masterwork.*

maîtriser to *master; overcome; overpower.*

Maîtrisez votre envie de rire. *Keep a solemn face. Try to keep from laughing.*

Deux hommes ont essayé de le maîtriser. *Two men tried to overpower him.*

majesté f. *majesty.*

Il a des allures pleines de majesté. *He has a very stately bearing.*

majestueux (majestueuse f.) adj. *stately, majestic.*

La majeure partie du temps il est au bureau. *Most of the time he's at the office.*

Son fils est majeur depuis deux mois. *His son came of age two months ago.*

Ceci est un cas de force majeure. *It's a case of absolute necessity.*

major m. *major.*

majorité f. *majority; coming of age.*

Je me rallie au point de vue de la majorité. *I side with the majority.*

La majorité absolue. *Absolute majority.*

Il a atteint sa majorité. *He came of age.*

majuscule adj. *capital letter.*

Ce mot ne s'écrit pas avec une majuscule. *This word isn't capitalized.*

MAL m. (maux pl.) *evil, wrong.*

Discerner le bien du mal. *To tell right from wrong.*

C'est peut-être un bien pour un mal. *Perhaps it's a blessing in disguise.*

Elle a eu du mal à le retenir à la maison. *She had trouble keeping him home.*

J'ai mal partout. *I ache all over.*

Je l'ai dit sans penser à mal. *I didn't mean any harm by it. I didn't mean any offense.*

J'ai mal à la gorge. *I have a sore throat.*

J'ai mal aux dents. *I have a toothache. My teeth hurt.*

Cette dent me fait mal. *This tooth hurts me.*

J'ai un mal de tête affreux. *I have a frightful headache.*

Il avait le mal du pays. *He was homesick.*

Mal au coeur. *Nausea, upset stomach.*

mal adj. *bad.*

Bon gré mal gré. *Willy-nilly.*

MAL adv. *bad, badly.*

Il a pris très mal la chose. *He took the thing very badly.*

Il y avait pas mal de monde. *There was quite a crowd there. There were a good many people there.*

Ce titre s'adapte mal au roman. *That title doesn't suit (isn't appropriate to) the novel.*

malade m. or f. *patient.*

Comment va le malade aujourd'hui? *How's the patient today?*

MALADE adj. *sick, ill.*

Alors qu'il était malade. *When he was ill.*

Il est tombé malade hier. *He was taken ill yesterday.*

Il en est malade. *He's very upset about it. It's made him sick.*

maladie f. *sickness.*

Il sort de maladie. *He's just getting over (recovering from) his illness.*

maladif (maladive f.) adj. *sickly.*

maladresse f. *blunder.*

Il a commis une maladresse. *He made a blunder.*

maladroit adj. *awkward, clumsy.*

Il est maladroit. *He's clumsy.*

Il a la main maladroite. *His fingers are all thumbs.*

malaise m. *discomfort; uncomfortableness; uneasiness.*

Il a un léger malaise. *He's slightly indisposed.*

malappris m. *ill-bred person.*

Ne fréquentez pas ces malappris. *Don't go around with those ill-bred people.*

malchance f. *ill luck, bad luck.*

La malchance s'acharne après eux. *They're very unlucky. They have very bad luck. ("Bad luck pursues them relentlessly.")*

Par malchance, je n'étais pas là. *As ill luck would have it, I wasn't there.*

maldonne f. *misdeal.*

Il y a maldonne. *It's a misdeal. The cards haven't been dealt right.*

mâle m. *male.*

Mâle ou femelle. *Male or female.*

mâle adj. *male, masculine, virile.*

C'est un enfant mâle. *It's a boy.*

Une voix mâle. *A manly voice.*

malédiction f. *curse.*

malentendu m. *misunderstanding.*

Il y a un malentendu en cela. *There's some misunderstanding there.*

malfaire to *do ill, do mischief.*

malfaisant adj. *mischievous; injurious.*

malfaiteur m. *thief.*

MALGRÉ *in spite of, notwithstanding.*

Malgré tout. *In spite of everything.*

Malgré tous ses défauts, nous l'aimons bien quand même. *In spite of all his faults we still like him very much.*

MALHEUR m. *unhappiness; bad luck; calamity.*

Il m'est arrivé un malheur. *Something terrible happened to me.*

Jouer de malheur. *To be unlucky.*

Pour comble de malheur. *To crown one's troubles.*

A quelque chose malheur est bon. *It's an ill wind that blows no good.*

Le grand malheur! *That's nothing much to complain about. That's not such a great tragedy.*

malheureusement *unfortunately.*

MALHEUREUX (malheureuse f.) adj. *unhappy; unfortunate; wretched, poor.*

Il est très malheureux. *He's very unhappy.*

Il a la main malheureuse. *He's unlucky.*

malhonnête adj. *dishonest; rude.*

Un malhonnête homme. *A dishonest man.*

Des paroles malhonnêtes. *Rude words.*

malhonnêtement *dishonestly; rudely.*

malhonnêteté f. *dishonesty; rudeness.*

malice f. *spite, mischief, slyness; trick.*

Par malice. *Maliciously. Through spite.*

D'un air plein de malice. *With a sly grin.*

Il lui a fait une malice. *He played a trick on him.*

malicieux (malicieuse f.) *adj. malicious.*

malin (maligne f.) *adj. clever, sly, shrewd, malicious; malignant.*
C'est un malin. *He has his wits about him. He's a shrewd fellow. He knows a trick or two. He has a trick or two up his sleeve. He knows what's what.*
Ce n'est pas malin! *That's not so clever! That's not very difficult! That's easy enough!*
Une fièvre maligne. *A malignant fever.*

malingre *adj. puny, weak.*

malle f. *trunk.*
Il fait sa malle. *He's packing his trunk.*

malpropre *adj. unclean; indecent.*

malpropreté f. *dirt, dirtiness, uncleanliness.*

malsain *adj. unhealthy, unwholesome.*

malséant *adj. unbecoming, improper.*

maltraiter *to mistreat.*

malveillance f. *malevolence; spite.*

malveillant *adj. malevolent, ill-disposed, evil-minded.*

malvenu *adj. unwelcome.*

maman f. *mother, ma, mom.*

manche m. *handle, holder.*

manche f. *sleeve.*
Aux manches courtes. *With short sleeves, short-sleeved.*

manchette f. *cuff; wristband (shirt).*

mandat m. *mandate; warrant; money order.*

mandataire *adj. mandatory; proxy, attorney.*

mandat-carte m. *a money order in the form of a postcard.*

mandat-poste m. *postal money order.*

mander *to inform; write to say; to send word; send for.*
On l'a fait mander. *He was sent for.*

manège m. *riding school; merry-go-round; maneuver.*

MANGER *to eat.*
Que désirez-vous manger? *What would you like to eat?*
Il donne à manger. *He has (keeps) a restaurant.*
La salle à manger était très grande. *The dining room was very large.*
Il mange ses mots. *He clips his words.*
Manger de tout. *To eat everything, anything, all sorts of things.*

mangeur m. (mangeuse f.) *eater, one who eats.*
Un mangeur de livres. *A bookworm.*

maniable *adj. easy to handle.*

maniaque *adj. eccentric, crotchety.*

manie f. *mania, passion, hobby.*

maniement m. *handling.*

manier *to handle, use.*
Savoir manier la parole. *To know how to handle words.*
Il manie bien la langue. *He expresses himself well.*
Il a bien manié l'affaire. *He handled the deal very well.*

MANIÈRE f. *manner, way, fashion.*
D'une manière ou d'une autre il faut le faire. *It has to be done one way or another (by hook or by crook).*
Il a de très bonnes manières. *He has very good manners.*
En aucune manière. *By no means. In no manner (way).*

maniéré *adj. affected.*

maniérisme m. *mannerism.*

manifestation f. *manifestation, demonstration.*

manifeste *adj. evident, clear.*

manifester *to make clear.*

Il a manifesté ses intentions. *He made his intentions clear.*

manigance f. *trick.*

manipuler *to manipulate, handle.*

manivelle f. *handle.*

mannequin m. *mannequin, model, dummy.*

manoeuvre f. *action, maneuver.*

manoeuvrer *to manage, drill.*

MANQUE m. *want, lack.*
Manque de goût. *Lack of taste.*
C'est un manque d'égards. *That shows lack of respect (consideration).*

manqué *adj. unsuccessful; would-be.*
Un peintre manqué. *A would-be painter.*
C'est un garçon manqué. *She ought to have been a boy. She's a tomboy.*

manquement m. *omission, lack.*

MANQUER *to miss; lack; be wanting.*
Le temps me manque. *I haven't enough time. I haven't much time.*
Ne manquez pas de venir. *Don't fail to come. Be sure to come.*
Elle a manqué de se noyer. *She almost drowned. She barely escaped drowning.*
Il manque à sa parole. *He breaks his word. He doesn't keep his word.*
Vous nous manquez. *We miss you.*

mansarde f. *garret, attic.*

manteau m. (manteaux pl.) *coat.*

manucure m. *manicure.*

manuel (manuelle f.) *adj. manual.*

manufacture f. *manufacture; making; factory.*

manufacturer *to make, manufacture.*

manuscrit m. *copy; manuscript.*

maquillage m. *make-up.*

se maquiller *to put make-up on.*

marais m. *marsh, swamp.*

maraude f. *plundering.*

marbre m. *marble.*

MARCHAND(E) m. *or f. merchant, storekeeper.*

marchand *adj. saleable; having to do with trade.*
Un navire marchand. *A merchant ship. A merchantman.*

marchandage m. *bargaining; haggling.*

marchander *to bargain, haggle.*

marchandise f. *goods, merchandise.*

MARCHE f. *walk, movement; progress; step; march.*
Faites marche arrière; la rue est barrée. *Back up. The road is blocked.*
Il y a vingt minutes de marche. *It's a twenty-minute walk from here.*
Quelque marches plus bas. *A few steps farther down.*
Marches militaires. *Military marches.*
Faire dix minutes de marche. *To walk for ten minutes.*

MARCHÉ m. *market; marketing; bargain.*
Faire le marché. *To do the marketing.*
Par-dessus le marché. *Besides (that). In addition (to that).*
Cet article est bon marché. *This article is very cheap.*
Meilleur marché. *Cheaper, less expensive.*
Le Marché aux Puces. *Flea Market.*

marchepied m. *running board.*

MARCHER *to walk; progress; work (of machines).*
Marchons plus vite. *Let's walk faster.*
L'affaire marche bien, je crois. *I believe the business (matter, affair) is coming along nicely.*
Cette machine ne marche pas. *This machine doesn't work.*

La pendule marche-t-elle? *Is the clock going?*
Qu'est-ce qui ne marche pas? *What's wrong? What's the matter?*

MARDI m. *Tuesday.*
Mardi Gras. *Shrove Tuesday.*

marécage m. *marsh.*

marée f. *tide.*

margarine f. *margarine.*

marge f. *margin, border.*

MARI m. *husband.*

mariage m. *marriage.*

se marier *to marry, get married.*

marin m. *sailor, seaman.*

marin *adj. marine, nautical.*
Il a le pied marin. *He has good sea legs.*

marionnette f. *marionette, puppet.*

marital (maritaux pl.) *adj. marital.*

maritime *adj. maritime.*

marmelade f. *marmalade.*

marmite f. *saucepan, pot.*

marmotter *to mumble.*

marotte f. *whim, hobby.*
Chacun a sa marotte. *Everyone has his hobby (whim, fad). Everyone has a weakness for something.*

marque f. *mark; scar; stamp; brand.*
Une marque d'affection. *A mark of affection.*
Une marque d'estime. *A token of esteem.*
Une liqueur de marque. *A very fine liquor. A liquor of superior quality.*

marquer *to mark, stamp.*
Ma montre marque midi. *It's noon by my watch.*

marron m. *chestnut.*

marronnier m. *chestnut tree.*

MARS m. *March.*

marteau m. *hammer.*

martial *adj. martial.*

martyr m. *martyr.*

martyre m. *martyrdom.*

martyriser *to make a martyr of, persecute.*

mascarade f. *masquerade; pretense.*

masculin *noun (m.) and adj. masculine, manly.*

masque m. *mask, face, countenance.*

masqué *adj. disguised.*

masquer *to conceal.*

massacrant *adj. cross.*
Il est d'une humeur massacrante. *He's very cross (in an awful mood, in a vile temper).*

massacre m. *massacre, slaughter.*

massacrer *to massacre, slaughter.*

massage m. *massage.*

masse f. *mass, heap, lump.*
En masse. *By bulk. In great quantity.*
Les masses. *The masses.*

massif (massive f.) *adj. massive, bulky, solid.*

massue f. *club.*

match (de football) m. *(football) game, match.*

matelas m. *mattress.*

matelot m. *sailor.*

mater *to break someone in.*
Il a finalement été maté. *He was finally broken in.*

matériaux m. pl. *materials.*

matériel m. *equipment; implements.*

maternel (maternelle f.) *adj. maternal, motherly.*

mathématiques f. pl. *mathematics.*

MATIÈRE f. *matter, subject matter; theme; cause; contents.*
En matière de. *In matters of.*
Entrer en matière. *To broach a subject.*
La table des matières. *The table of contents.*

MATIN m. *morning.*

Comment cela s'est-il passé ce matin? *How did it go this morning?*
Demain matin. *Tomorrow morning.*
Le samedi matin. *On Saturday morning(s).*
Neuf heures du matin. *Nine A.M.*
matinal (matinaux pl.) *adj. early rising.*
   Vous êtes bien matinal aujourd'hui. *You certainly got up early today. You're certainly up early today!*
MATINÉE *f. morning.*
   Y a-t-il un train pour Paris dans la matinée? *Is there a train for Paris in the morning?*
maudire *to curse.*
maudit *adj. accursed.*
MAUVAIS *adj. bad.*
   Des mauvaises nouvelles. *Bad news.*
   Passer un mauvais quart d'heure. *To spend an uncomfortable quarter of an hour.*
   Il parle un mauvais français. *He speaks (a) broken French.*
   Il a très mauvaise mine. *He doesn't look well at all. He looks quite ill.*
   Le mauvais sens. *The wrong direction.*
maximum *m. maximum, highest point.*
mayonnaise *f. mayonnaise.*
ME (m' before vowels) *me, to me, myself.*
   Ça ne me plaît pas. *I don't like that.*
   Je me lave les mains. *I'm washing my hands.*
méchanicien *m. mechanic.*
méchanique *noun (f.) and adj. mechanics; mechanical.*
   Par pure méchanceté. *Out of pure spite.*
méchanceté *f. wickedness, malice, spite.*
méchant *adj. wicked; naughty; sorry, disagreeable.*
   Il n'est pas si méchant qu'il en a l'air. *He's not as bad as he looks.*
   Un méchant enfant. *A naughty child.*
   Une méchante affaire. *An unpleasant business.*
   Elle portait ce méchant manteau. *She was wearing that shabby coat.*
mèche *f. wick.*
   Il a vendu la mèche. *He let the cat out of the bag.*
   Eventer la mèche. *To discover a plot.*
méconnaissable *adj. unrecognizable.*
méconnaître *to disregard, slight.*
mécontent *adj. displeased, dissatisfied.*
   Il est très mécontent de lui. *He's very displeased with him.*
   Il n'a pas sujet d'être mécontent. *He has no reason to be dissatisfied.*
médaille *f. medal.*
MÉDECIN *m. doctor, physician.*
médecine *f. medicine (profession).*
médical (médicaux pl.) *adj. medical.*
médicament *m. medicine.*
médiocre *adj. mediocre.*
médiocrité *f. mediocrity.*
médire *to slander.*
méditation *f. meditation.*
méditer *to meditate; plot.*
méfait *m. misdeed.*
méfiance *f. distrust.*
se méfier *to be suspicious, mistrust, be on one's guard against.*
   Il ne se méfie de rien. *He doesn't suspect anything.*
mégarde *f. inadvertence.*
   Il l'a fait par mégarde. *He didn't mean to do it. He didn't do it purposely. He did it by mistake.*
MEILLEUR *adj. better, best; preferable.*
   Celui-là est meilleur. *That one is better.*

Mon meilleur ami. *My best friend.*
mélancolie *f. melancholy, sadness.*
mélancolique *adj. melancholy.*
mélange *m. mixture.*
mélanger *to mix.*
mêlée *f. mêlée, scramble, free-for-all.*
mêler *to mix.*
   Il est mêlé à une mauvaise affaire. *He got himself involved (mixed up) in an unpleasant affair ("in a bad business").*
   Mêlez les cartes. *Shuffle the cards.*
se mêler *to be mixed; get mixed up in.*
   Mêlez-vous de ce qui vous regarde. *Attend to (mind) your own business.*
mélodie *f. melody.*
mélodieux (mélodieuse f.) *adj. melodious.*
melon *m. cantaloupe.*
membre *m. member; limb.*
MÊME *noun and adj. same, the same.*
   C'est la même chose. *It's the same thing.*
   Je le ferai moi-même. *I'll do it myself.*
   Cela revient au même. *It amounts to the same thing.*
   C'est la bonté même. *He (she) is very kind ("is kindness itself").*
   Aujourd'hui même. *Today, this very day.*
   Dans Paris même. *Within Paris itself.*
   Moi-même, lui-même, soi-même. *Myself, himself, oneself.*
MÊME *even, also.*
   Même s'il pleut, nous irons. *We'll go even if it rains.*
   Même lui était d'accord. *Even he agreed.*
   Il n'est même pas venu nous voir. *He didn't even come to see us.*
   Vous auriez pu me le dire, tout de même! *Still, you could have told me!*
   Vous auriez tout de même pu le faire. *You still could have done it.*
   Nous devrons le faire, tout de même. *We'll have to do it anyway.*
   Etre à même de. *To be able to. To be in a position to.*
mémoire *f. memory.*
menace *f. threat.*
menacer *to threaten.*
ménage *m. housekeeping; household; married couple.*
   Avez-vous fait le ménage? *Have you finished (done) the housework?*
   Le jeune ménage est très heureux. *The newlyweds are very happy.*
ménager *to economize, be careful of; treat with respect; arrange, bring about.*
   Vous devez ménager votre santé. *You ought to take care of yourself (of your health).*
   Ménager quelqu'un. *To spare someone. To be considerate of someone.*
   Il ne ménage pas assez ses expressions. *He's not careful enough about his speech.*
   Elle lui ménageait une surprise. *She prepared a surprise for him. She had a surprise in store for him.*
ménagère *f. housekeeper.*
mendiant *m. beggar.*
mendier *to beg, ask for alms.*
MENER *to lead.*
   Où mène ce chemin? *Where does this road lead?*
   Cela ne mènera à rien. *That won't lead to anything.*
   Mener une affaire à bien. *To bring a matter to a successful conclusion.*
mensonge *m. lie.*

mensuel (mensuelle f.) *adj. monthly.*
mensuellement *monthly.*
mental (mentaux pl.) *adj. mental.*
mentalité *f. mentality, way of looking at things.*
menteur *m. (menteuse f.) liar.*
mention *f. mention.*
   Faire mention de. *To mention.*
mentionner *to mention.*
mentir *to lie.*
menton *m. chin.*
menu *m. menu.*
   Donnez-moi le menu, s'il vous plaît. *May I please have the menu?*
menu *adj. small.*
   Chaque semaine il reçoit de l'argent pour ses menus plaisirs. *Every week he receives some pocket money.*
menuisier *m. carpenter.*
se méprendre *to make a mistake, be mistaken about.*
   Il s'est mépris sur mes intentions. *He misunderstood my intentions.*
   Quant à son but, il n'y a pas à s'y méprendre. *There can be no mistake about his purpose (object).*
mépris *m. contempt.*
méprise *f. mistake.*
   Il l'a fait par méprise. *He did it by mistake.*
mépriser *to despise.*
MER *f. sea.*
   Par mer. *By sea.*
   Cette année nous n'allons pas à la mer. *We're not going to the seashore this year.*
   Les bananes viennent d'outre-mer. *Bananas come from overseas.*
mercerie *f. haberdashery.*
MERCI *f. thanks; mercy.*
   C'est bon, merci. *That will do, thank you.*
   Dieu merci, il est sain et sauf! *Thank God, he's all right!*
   Etre à la merci de. *To be at the mercy of.*
   Sans merci. *Without mercy. Merciless.*
   Il a accordé merci aux prisonniers. *He showed mercy to the prisoners.*
   Merci (bien, beaucoup). *Thank you (very much).*
MERCREDI *m. Wednesday.*
   Le mercredi des cendres. *Ash Wednesday.*
MÈRE *f. mother.*
   Ma mère est sortie. *Mother isn't in. Mother's gone out.*
   La mère Durand fait son marché (fam.). *Old Mrs. Durand is doing her marketing.*
   La maison mère se trouve 12 rue Caumartin. *The main office is at 12 Caumartin Street.*
mérite *m. merit, worth.*
mériter *to deserve.*
merveille *f. wonder, miracle.*
   Ça va? —Ça va à merveille. *How are things? —Fine! Couldn't be better.*
MERVEILLEUX (merveilleuse f.) *adj. wonderful, excellent.*
mésaventure *f. misadventure, misfortune.*
mésinterpréter *to misinterpret, misconstrue.*
mesquin *adj. stingy, petty.*
   Elle est mesquine. *She's stingy.*
   Elle a l'esprit mesquin. *She's very petty.*
   C'est très mesquin de sa part. *That's very cheap of him (her).*
message *m. message.*
   Portez ce message à monsieur Dubois. *Take this message to Mr. Dubois.*
messagerie *f. transport service.*
messe *f. (eccles.) mass.*

MESURE f. measure.
Prendre la mesure de quelque chose. To measure (take the measurement of) something.
Il prit toutes les mesures nécessaires. He took all the necessary measures.
Je vous aiderai dans la mesure du possible. I'll help you as much as I can.
Il est en mesure de le faire rapidement. He's prepared to do it quickly.
Le parlement a approuvé la mesure. Parliament ratified the bill.
Au fur et à mesure. Gradually. In proportion (to). In the measure that. In succession. As soon as. As fast as.
Au fur et à mesure que vous recevrez de la marchandise, envoyez-la moi. As you get the goods in, send them to me.
Battre la mesure. To beat time.
Ce costume a été fait sur mesure. This suit was made to order.
mesurer to measure.
se mesurer to measure oneself against someone.
métal m. (métaux pl.) metal.
métallurgie f. metallurgy.
métaphore f. metaphor, image.
méthode f. method, way, custom.
méticuleux (méticuleuse f.) adj. meticulous.
MÉTIER m. trade, employment.
Quel est son métier? What's his trade?
Il est menuisier de son métier. He's a carpenter by trade.
MÈTRE m. meter.
métro (**politain**) m. subway (Paris).
METTRE to put.
Mettez ça ici. Put that here.
Mettre la dernière main à quelque chose. To put the finishing touches on something.
Je n'ai plus rien à me mettre. I don't have a thing left to wear.
Je ne peux pas mettre la main sur mon chapeau. I can't find my hat.
Nous y avons mis deux heures. We spent two hours on it, it took us two hours.
SE METTRE to place oneself, sit down; begin, set about.
Allons nous mettre à table. Let's sit down to dinner (lunch, breakfast, etc.). ("Let's sit down to the table.")
Se mettre au lit. To go to bed. To get into bed.
Ils se sont mis à rire. They all started to laugh.
Le temps se met au beau. The weather's getting nice.
Mettons-nous au travail. Let's begin (get down) to work.
Mets-toi ici. Stand here.
MEUBLE m. piece of furniture.
Les meubles de style. Period furniture.
meubler to furnish.
meunier m. miller.
meurtre m. murder.
meurtrier (meurtrière f.) adj. murderous, deadly.
Une arme meurtrière. A deadly weapon.
meute f. pack (of dogs, etc.).
mezzanine f. mezzanine.
mi-chemin halfway.
Ce restaurant se trouve à mi-chemin de Bordeaux. This restaurant is halfway to Bordeaux.
micmac m. underhand intrigue; mess.
Il y a un micmac là-dedans. There's something fishy about it.
Quel micmac (fam.)! What a mess!

(à) **mi-côte** halfway.
Ils sont descendus de bicyclettes à mi-côte. Halfway up the hill they got off their bicycles.
micro m. microphone.
Il parle au micro. He speaks on the air (radio).
microbe m. microbe.
microscope m. microscope.
microsillon m. microgroove (record).
MIDI m. noon; the South of France.
Il est près de midi. It's nearly noon. It will soon be noon.
Il part demain dans le Midi. He's leaving tomorrow for the South (South of France).
miel m. honey.
mielleux (mielleuse f.) adj. honeyed.
MIEN m. (mienne f.) mine.
A qui appartient ce livre? —C'est le mien. Whose book is this? —It's mine.
miette f. crumb.
MIEUX better.
Tant mieux. So much the better.
J'aimerais mieux pas. I'd rather not.
Vous aimez mieux rester ou partir? Would you rather stay or go?
Mieux vaut tard que jamais. Better late than never.
Le mieux est de ne pas en parler. The best thing is to say nothing about it. It's best not to talk about it.
Cela (ça) vaudrait mieux. That would be better.
Faire de son mieux. To do one's best.
Je ferais mieux d'attendre. I'd better wait.
Mieux vaut les faire réparer. It's better to have them repaired.
On ne demande pas mieux. One couldn't ask for anything better.
mignon (mignonne f.) adj. dainty, cute.
migraine f. headache.
mijoter to simmer.
mil thousand. See mille.
En l'an mil neuf cent quarante-deux. During the year 1942. In 1942.
MILIEU m. middle; environment; sphere.
Mettez cette table au milieu de la chambre. Put this table in the middle of the room.
Couper par le milieu. To cut in half.
Il n'appartient pas à notre milieu. He doesn't belong to our circle.
militaire m. soldier.
militaire adj. military.
MILLE adj. thousand.
Merci mille fois. Thanks very much. ("Thanks a thousand times.")
millier m. about a thousand.
Des milliers de choses. Thousands of things.
million m. million.
millionnaire m. and f. noun and adj. millionaire.
mince adj. thin, slender.
mine f. look, bearing.
Vous avez bonne mine. You look well (fine).
Il a fait mine de ne pas me voir. He pretended not to see me.
Avoir mauvaise mine. To look bad.
mine f. mine.
Une mine de fer. An iron mine.
mineur m. miner.
mineur adj. under age.
Il est mineur. He's under age. He's a minor.
miniature f. miniature.
minime adj. small, tiny.
minimum m. minimum.
ministère m. ministry.

Le Ministère de la Guerre. The War Department.
ministre m. minister.
minois m. face, pretty face.
minorité f. minority.
minuit m. midnight.
minuscule adj. tiny.
Un salon minuscule. A tiny living room.
Des lettres minuscules. Lower case (letters).
MINUTE f. minute.
Faites-le à la minute. Do it right away.
Attendez une minute, je viens. Wait a minute, I'm coming.
Minute! Wait a minute! Just a minute! In a minute!
minutieux (minutieuse f.) adj. meticulous; careful.
miracle m. miracle.
mirage m. mirage.
mirobolant (fam.) adj. astounding.
miroir m. mirror.
miroiter to flash, glitter, reflect light.
mise f. putting, manner of dressing.
Ce n'est pas de mise. It's not proper.
Mise en action. Realization.
Cette affaire a été mise au point. This matter was clarified and settled.
Mise en vigueur. Enforcement. Putting into effect.
Mise en vente. Sale (in a store).
Mise en plis. Hair setting.
misérable adj. miserable.
misère f. misery.
miséricorde f. mercy.
mission f. mission.
mitaine f. mitten.
mi-temps f. half-time (sports).
mitrailler to shoot with a machine gun.
mitrailleuse f. machine-gun.
(à) **mi-voix** under one's breath.
Il parle à mi-voix. He speaks under his breath.
mixte adj. mixed.
mixture f. mixture.
mobile adj. mobile, movable.
mobilier m. furniture.
mobilisation f. mobilization.
mobiliser to mobilize.
MODE f. fashion; custom; millinery.
Ce n'est plus à la mode. This has gone out of fashion. It (this) is no longer fashionable.
Magasin de modes. Millinery store.
modèle m. model, pattern, design.
modeler to model, shape.
modération f. moderation.
modéré adj. moderate.
modérer to moderate.
MODERNE adj. modern.
modeste adj. modest, unassuming.
modestie f. modesty.
modifier to modify.
modiste f. milliner.
moëlle f. marrow.
moeurs f. pl. manners; morals.
Autres temps, autres moeurs. Manners change with the times.
Un certificat de bonne vie et moeurs. A certificate of good character.
MOI me.
C'est moi. It's me (I).
C'est à moi. It's mine.
Asseyez-vous près de moi. Sit near me.
Donnez-le-moi. Give it to me.
Moi-même. Myself.

MOINDRE adj. less; the least.
Je n'ai pas le moindre doute à ce sujet. I don't doubt that in the least. I haven't the least doubt about it.
Il a choisi le moindre de deux maux. He chose the lesser of the two evils.
C'est très gentil de votre part d'avoir fait ça. —Mais non, c'est bien la moindre des choses. That's very kind of you. —Not at all. It's nothing.
Le moindre bruit le dérange. The least noise disturbs him.

moine m. monk.

MOINS m. less; fewer.
Il est une heure moins le quart. It's a quarter to one. ("It's an hour less a quarter.")
Pas le moins du monde. Not at all. Not in the least.
Au moins. At least.
A moins que. Unless.

MOIS m. month.

moisir to become moldy.

moisson f. harvest.

moissonner to reap.

moite adj. moist.

MOITIÉ f. half.
Voulez-vous la moitié de cette pomme? Do you want half of this apple?
Ne faites pas les choses à moitié. Don't do things halfway.

molaire f. molar.

mollesse f. softness; flabbiness.

moment m. moment.
Il sera là dans un moment. He'll be there in a moment.
C'est le bon moment. Now is the time.
On l'attend d'un moment à l'autre. We expect him any moment now.
Du moment que ça ne vous intéresse pas. Since it doesn't interest you.
C'est le moment de . . . It's the moment to, it's time to . . .
En ce moment. (Just) now, at this moment.
Par moments. At times, occasionally.
(Pas) pour le moment. (Not) for the moment.

momie f. mummy.

MON m. (ma f., mes pl.) my.
Mon père et ma mère sont en voyage. Both Dad and Mother are away.
Mes livres ne sont pas ici. My books aren't here.

monarchie f. monarchy.

monarque m. monarch.

monastère m. monastery.

mondain adj. worldly, fashionable.

mondanités f. pl. society news.

MONDE m. world, universe; people, crowd.
Il court le monde. He travels all over the world.
Elle a mis au monde une fille. She gave birth to a daughter.
Il n'y avait pas grand monde. There weren't many people there (present).
Nous attendons du monde. We're expecting company.
Tout le monde en parle. Everyone is talking about it.
Le beau monde. Society. The fashionable set.
Je ne le ferais pour rien au monde. I wouldn't do it for anything in the world.
Partout au monde. Everywhere in the world.
Que de monde! What a crowd!

monétaire adj. monetary.

MONNAIE f. coin; small change; currency.
Avez-vous de la petite monnaie? Have you

any small change?
La monnaie de ce pays. The currency of this country.

monnayeur m. one who coins (mints) money.
Faux monnayeur. Counterfeiter.

monocle m. monocle.

monologue m. monologue, soliloquy.

monopole m. monopoly.

monopoliser to monopolize.

monotone adj. monotonous.

monotonie f. monotony.

MONSIEUR m. (messieurs pl.) Mr.
Bonjour, monsieur Dupont. Hello, Mr. Dupont. Good day, Mr. Dupont.
Qui est ce monsieur? Who is that gentleman?
Monsieur chose. Mister what's-his-name?
Dites à ces messieurs d'entrer. Ask the (these) gentlemen to come in.
Monsieur 'dame. Sir, madam (addressing a man and woman together).
Le monsieur. Man, gentleman.

monstre m. monster.

monstrueux (monstrueuse f.) adj. monstrous, huge.

mont m. mountain, mount.

montagne f. mountain.

montant m. total, sum total, amount.

montant adj. rising.
La marée montante. The rising tide.

MONTER to go up.
Le train va partir, vous feriez mieux de monter dedans. You'd better get on the train—it's about to leave.
Monter à l'échelle. To climb the ladder.
Il est monté en grade. He has been promoted. He has risen in grade.
Le vin lui est monté à la tête. The wine went to his head.
Monter la tête à quelqu'un. To get someone worked up. To work on someone's feelings.
se monter to provide oneself; amount to; get excited.
Il s'est bien monté pour son voyage. He provided himself with everything he needed for his trip.
A combien se monte la facture? What does the bill amount to?
Il se monte la tête. He's getting himself (all) worked up (excited).

MONTRE f. watch; show.
J'ai cassé ma montre. I broke my watch.
Il a fait montre d'un grand courage. He displayed great courage.

montre-bracelet f. wristwatch.

MONTRER to show.
Montrez-le-moi. Show it to me.
Montrer du doigt quelque chose à quelqu'un. To point out something to someone.
se montrer to appear.
Il se montra à la fenêtre. He appeared at the window.
Il s'est montré sous son vrai jour. He showed himself in his true colors (in his true light).
Il s'est montré très gentil. He was very nice.

monture f. setting, mounting, frame.

monument m. monument.

se moquer to laugh at, make fun of, ridicule.
Il s'est bel et bien moqué de nous. He certainly made us look like fools.
Je m'en moque comme de l'an quarante. I don't give a hang. I don't care a straw about it.
En tout cas il s'en moque. Anyway, he doesn't care.

C'est se moquer du monde! That's the height of impertinence! That's taking people for fools!

moqueur (moqueuse f.) adj. mocking, jeering, derisive.

moral noun (m.) and adj. morale f. morale, mind, spirit; moral.
Remontez-lui le moral. Encourage him. Help his morale.
Un conte moral. A story with a moral.

morale f. morality, ethics.
Il lui a fait la morale pendant deux heures. He lectured him (gave him a lecture) for two hours.

moralement morally.

moralité f. morality; moral.
Sa moralité est douteuse. His honesty (morality) is questionable.
La moralité de cette histoire. The moral of this (the) story.

moratorium m. moratorium.

morbide adj. morbid.

MORCEAU m. (morceaux pl.) piece.
Prenez un morceau de pain. Take a piece of bread.
Le vase a été mis en morceaux. The vase broke into pieces.
Il a vendu sa voiture pour un morceau de pain. He sold his car for a song (for next to nothing).
Un morceau pour piano à quatre mains. A four-hand piano piece.

morceler to cut up in small pieces.

mordant adj. mordant, biting, caustic.
Paroles mordantes. Biting (cutting) words.

mordicus stoutly.
Il le nia mordicus. He denied it stoutly.
Il a défendu son opinion mordicus. He defended his position tooth and nail.

mordiller to nibble.

mordre to bite.

se mordre to bite.
Il s'en mord les doigts. He regrets what he did.
Il s'en mord la langue. He regrets what he said.

morgue f. pride, haughtiness, arrogance.

morgue f. morgue.

moribond m. moribund, dying.

morne adj. gloomy, dismal, dull.

morose adj. morose, gloomy.

mors m. bit (of a bridle).

morsure f. bite.

mort m. dead person, casualty.

MORT f. death.
Il a vu la mort de près. He nearly died. He came very near dying.
Un silence de mort. Dead silence.

MORT adj. dead.

mortalité f. mortality, death rate.

mortel (mortelle f.) adj. mortal.

morte-saison f. slack season.

mortifier to mortify; humiliate.

mortuaire adj. mortuary.

mosquée f. mosque.

MOT m. word.
Traduisez-moi ça mot à mot. Translate that for me word for word.
Je vais vous envoyer un mot à ce sujet. I'll let you know about it. I'll drop you a line about it.
Mots d'esprit. Witticisms. Witty remarks.
Un bon mot. A pun.
Il ignore le premier mot de la biologie. He doesn't know the first thing about biology.

Pour vous dire tout en deux mots. *To be brief.* *("To tell you everything in two words.")*

Il a toujours le mot pour rire. *He's always cracking jokes (telling funny stories). He's fond of a joke.*

Laisser un mot. *To leave a message.*

Les mots croisés. *Crossword puzzle.*

moteur *m. motor, engine.*

Un moteur électrique. *An electric motor.*

Un moteur Diesel. *A Diesel engine.*

Un moteur à vapeur. *A steam engine.*

moteur (motrice *f.*) *adj. motive, propulsive, driving (power).*

motif *m. motive, cause.*

Pour quel motif? *On what ground? For what reason?*

Sans motif. *Without a motive. Without any reason (cause).*

Avoir un motif pour faire quelque chose. *To have a motive for doing something.*

Pour des motifs de jalousie. *Out of jealousy. ("For reasons of jealousy.")*

Leurs motifs sont bons. *Their motives are good.*

Sous aucun motif. *On no account.*

motion *f. motion.*

motiver *to motivate.*

Sur quoi motivez-vous votre décision? *On what do you base your decision?*

Ce discours a motivé beaucoup de critiques. *This speech led to (caused) a lot of criticism.*

motocyclette *f. motorcycle.*

mou (mol *before a vowel or "mute"* h, molle *f.* moux *m. pl.*, molles *f. pl.*) *adj. soft.*

Un lit mou. *A soft bed.*

Un chapeau mou. *A felt hat.*

Une personne molle. *A spineless person.*

Temps mou. *Humid (close, sticky) weather.*

mouche *f. fly.*

Agaçant comme une mouche. *Very irritating.*

Quelle mouche vous pique (*fam.*)? *What's the matter with you? What's wrong with you? What's come over you?*

C'est une fine mouche. *He's (she's) a sly one.*

Faire d'une mouche un éléphant. *To make a mountain out of a molehill.*

Elle a pris la mouche. *She was offended.*

se moucher *to blow one's nose.*

mouchoir *m. handkerchief.*

moudre *to grind.*

moue *f. pout.*

Elle fait la moue. *She's pouting.*

mouiller *to soak, wet.*

Leurs vêtements étaient tout mouillés. *Their clothes were all wet (soaked).*

moulage *m. casting.*

moule *m. mold.*

mouler *to cast, mold, shape.*

moulin *m. mill.*

Un moulin à café. *A coffee mill.*

mourant *m.* (mourante *f.*) *a dying person; adj. dying.*

mourir *to die.*

Il est mort avant-hier. *He died the day before yesterday.*

Mourir de rire. *To die with laughter.*

Mourir de froid. *To perish from cold.*

Je m'ennuie à mourir. *I'm bored to death.*

mousse *f. moss.*

mousseline *f. muslin.*

mousser *to foam.*

Faites mousser cette crème. *Whip (up) the cream.*

moustache *f. mustache.*

moustique *m. mosquito.*

moutarde *f. mustard.*

mouton *m. sheep.*

Revenons à nos moutons. *Let's get back to the subject (to the point).*

mouvement *m. movement, motion, impulse.*

Mettre en mouvement. *To start. To put in motion.*

Etre en mouvement. *To be in motion.*

Ils ont souvent des mouvements de colère. *They often have fits of anger (angry moods).*

Une symphonie en trois mouvements. *A symphony in three movements.*

Elle l'a fait de son propre mouvement. *She did it of her own accord.*

mouvementé *adj. animated.*

mouvoir *to move.*

Le bateau est mû à la vapeur. *This boat is driven by steam.*

Il est mû par l'intérêt. *He's acting out of self-interest. ("He's motivated by interest.")*

Mû par la pitié. *Moved by pity.*

moyen *m. means.*

Voies et moyens. *Ways and means.*

La fin justifie les moyens. *The end justifies the means.*

Il a employé les grands moyens. *He took extreme measures.*

Au moyen de . . . *By means of . . .*

Il n'en a pas les moyens. *He hasn't the means. He can't afford it.*

moyen (moyenne *f.*) *adj. mean, middle, medium.*

Le Moyen Âge. *The Middle Ages.*

Le Français moyen. *The average Frenchman.*

moyennant *provided that.*

moyenne *f. average, medium.*

En moyenne. *On the average.*

muer *to molt, cast, slough off (of animals); break (of voice).*

muet (muette *f.*) *adj. mute, speechless.*

Un film muet. *A silent film.*

Etre sourd-muet. *To be deaf and dumb.*

Muet comme la tombe. *As silent as the grave.*

mugir *to low; bellow.*

mugissement *m. lowing; roaring.*

mulâtre *m.* (mulâtresse *f.*) *mulatto.*

mule *f. mule.*

multiplication *f. multiplication.*

multiplier *to multiply.*

se multiplier *to multiply.*

Leurs difficultés se sont multipliées. *Their difficulties increased as they went along.*

multitude *f. multitude.*

Il adressa la multitude. *He addressed the crowd.*

J'ai reçu une multitude de cartes de Noël. *I received lots (loads) of Christmas cards.*

municipal (municipaux *pl.*) *adj. municipal.*

se munir *to provide oneself.*

Se munir de provisions. *To provide oneself with food. To take along provisions.*

Munissez-vous de monnaie. *Take some small change along.*

munition *f. ammunition.*

mur *m. wall.*

mûr *adj. ripe, mature, matured.*

muraille *f. high, defensive wall.*

mural (muraux *pl.*) *adj. mural.*

mûrir *to ripen; mature.*

murmure *m. murmur, whispering.*

murmurer *to murmur, whisper.*

muscle *m. muscle.*

museau *m. muzzle, snout.*

musée *m. museum.*

Le musée (d'art). *The (art) museum.*

muselière *f. muzzle.*

muser *to idle, dawdle.*

musical (musicaux *pl.*) *adj. musical.*

music-hall *m. music hall.*

musicien *m.* (musicienne *f.*) *musician.*

musique *f. music.*

La musique de chambre. *Chamber music.*

mutilation *f. mutilation.*

mutilé *m. mutilated; disabled.*

C'est un mutilé de guerre. *He's a disabled war veteran.*

mutiler *to maim.*

se mutiner *to mutiny.*

mutuel (mutuelle *f.*) *adj. mutual.*

myope *adj. myopic, shortsighted.*

myopie *f. myopia.*

mystère *m. mystery.*

Il a résolu le mystère. *He solved the mystery.*

Il fait grand mystère de tout. *He makes a great mystery out of everything.*

Il n'en fait pas mystère. *He makes no secret of it (no mystery about it).*

mystérieux (mystérieuse *f.*) *adj. mysterious.*

mystifier *to mystify, hoax.*

mythe *m. myth, legend.*

mythologie *f. mythology.*

N *The fourteenth letter of the alphabet.*

nacre *f. mother-of-pearl.*

nage *f. swimming; perspiration.*

A la nage. *By swimming.*

Il est tout en nage. *He's bathed in perspiration.*

nageoire *f. fin.*

nager *to swim.*

Sait-il nager? *Does he know how to swim?*

Il sait nager. 1. *He can swim.* 2. *He can manage (take care of himself, get along).*

Ils nagent dans l'opulence. *They're swimming in wealth. They're rolling in riches.*

nageur *m.* (nageuse *f.*) *swimmer.*

naguère *not so long ago.*

naïf (naïve *f.*) *adj. naive, artless; silly.*

Avoir un air naïf. *To look innocent (naive).*

Quel naïf! *What a fool! What a simpleton!*

nain *m.* (naine *f.*) *dwarf.*

naissance *f. birth, beginning.*

Elle donna naissance à un fils. *She gave birth to a son.*

Il est Français de naissance. *He's French by birth.*

Cette rumeur a pris naissance récemment. *This rumor sprang up recently.*

NAÎTRE *to be born.*

Il est né coiffé. *He was born with a silver spoon in his mouth.*

Lucienne Durand, née Legroux. *Lucienne Durand, née Legroux (i.e. whose maiden name was Legroux).*

Cela fit naître des soupçons. *That made people suspicious. That aroused suspicion.*

Faire naître le mépris. *To breed contempt.*

Je ne suis pas né d'hier. *I wasn't born yesterday.*

naïvement *naively.*

J'ai pensé naïvement qu'ils tiendraient leur promesse. *I naively thought they would keep their promise.*

naïveté *f. naïvete.*

Elle a eu la naïveté de le croire. *She was naive enough to believe that.*

nantir *to secure, provide.*
  Il l'a nanti de vêtements. *He provided him with clothes.*
nantissement *m. pledge, security.*
naphtaline *f. naphthaline.*
nappe *f. tablecloth.*
narcotique *m. narcotic.*
narguer *to scorn, sneer.*
narine *f. nostril.*
narquois *adj. sly.*
  Un sourire narquois. *A sly smile.*
  Une remarque narquoise. *A sly (ironical, bantering) remark.*
narrateur *m.* (narratrice *f.*) *narrator.*
narration *f. narration.*
nasal (nasaux *pl.*) *adj. nasal.*
nasillard *adj. nasal.*
natal (nataux *pl.*) *adj. native.*
  Son pays natal. *His native country.*
natalité *f. birthrate.*
natation *f. swimming.*
natif (native *f.*) *adj. native.*
nation *f. nation.*
national (nationaux *pl.*) *adj. national.*
nationalisme *m. nationalism.*
nationalité *f. nationality.*
  Quelle est votre nationalité? *What nationality are you?*
naturalisation *f. naturalization.*
naturaliser *to naturalize.*
NATURE *f. nature.*
  La nature l'a bien partagée. *She's very talented.*
  Une nature-morte. *A still-life painting.*
  Elle est d'une nature douce. *She has a nice disposition.*
  Payer en nature. *To pay in kind.*
  Un café nature. *Black coffee.*
  Tout cela n'est certainement pas de nature à nous rassurer. *That's certainly not very reassuring.*
  Contre nature. *Unnatural.*
naturel *m. naturalness; native disposition.*
  Ça a été peint au naturel. *It's painted from life. It's a very realistic painting.*
  Voir les choses au naturel. *To see things as they are.*
  Etre d'un bon naturel. *To have a good disposition.*
  Etre d'un mauvais naturel. *To be ill-natured.*
  Un heureux naturel. *A cheerful disposition.*
NATUREL (naturelle *f.*) *adj. natural.*
  Histoire naturelle. *Natural history.*
  Les sciences naturelles. *The natural sciences.*
  Mort naturelle. *Natural death.*
  Elle est très naturelle. *She's very unaffected.*
  Son explication m'a paru très naturelle. *His explanation seemed very straightforward (honest, reasonable) to me.*
  De grandeur naturelle. *Life-size.*
  Il trouve ça tout naturel. *He takes it for granted.*
  Ce vêtement est en soie naturelle, non pas en soie artificielle. *This garment is made of real silk, not rayon.*
NATURELLEMENT *naturally.*
  Ses cheveux bouclent naturellement. *Her hair is naturally curly.*
  A-t-il été fâché lorsqu'il l'apprit? —Naturellement! *Was he angry when he heard about it? —Naturally!*
  Naturellement je le ferai. *Naturally I'll do it. Of course I'll do it.*
naufrage *m. shipwreck, wreck.*

  Il fit naufrage au port. *He fell just short of success (of his goal). He failed just when it looked as though he'd succeed. He failed with his goal in sight. ("He was shipwrecked in sight of the harbor.")*
nauséabond *adj. nauseous, foul.*
nausée *f. nausea, nauseousness.*
naval *adj. naval.*
navet *m. turnip.*
navette *f. shuttle.*
  Il fait la navette entre Paris et Tours. *He travels back and forth between Paris and Tours.*
navigateur *m. navigator.*
navigation *f. navigation, sailing.*
naviguer *to sail.*
  Naviguer au long cours. *To be a merchant seaman.*
  Il a navigué sur toutes les mers. *He's sailed the seven seas.*
  Il navigue à l'aventure. *He tramps about (goes from one place to another as the fancy takes him).*
  Ici il faut naviguer avec prudence. *We must tread lightly here (proceed with caution).*
NAVIRE *m. ship.*
  Le navire faisait eau. *The ship had sprung a leak.*
  Navire de guerre. *A warship.*
  Un navire à vapeur. *A steamer.*
navrant *adj. heart-rending.*
  C'est une histoire navrante. *It's a heart-rending story.*
navrer *to distress.*
  Je suis navré, mais je ne puis accepter votre invitation. *I'm terribly sorry but I can't accept your invitation.*
  J'ai été navré d'apprendre la grande perte que vous venez de subir. *I was very sorry to hear of your loss (the loss you have just suffered).*
NE (n' before vowels and "mute" h) *not, no.*
  Je ne sais pas. *I don't know.*
  Je n'ai que cent mille francs. *I have only 100,000 francs.*
  Il n'accepte aucune observation. *He doesn't like to be criticized. He never accepts any criticism.*
  Je crains qu'il ne revienne plus. *I'm afraid he won't come back (again).*
  Ils ne tarderont guère à venir. *It won't be long before they'll be here (come).*
  Il est plus intelligent qu'il n'en a l'air. *He's more intelligent than he looks.*
  Il agit autrement qu'il ne parle. *His actions don't agree with his words. He speaks one way and acts another. ("He acts otherwise than he speaks.")*
  Ne . . . à peine. *Hardly, scarcely.*
  Ne . . . jamais. *Never.*
  N'est-ce pas? *Isn't that so?*
  Il m'a prié de ne pas parler. *He begged me not to speak.*
  Ne . . . point. *Not at all.*
  Elle ne fait que parler. *She does nothing but talk.*
  Ne . . . rien. *Nothing.*
  Ne . . . ni . . . ni . . . . *Neither . . . nor . . .*
  N'importe où. *Anywhere.*
  N'importe quelle banque. *Any bank.*
NÉANMOINS *however, nevertheless.*
  Néanmoins je le ferai. *Nevertheless I'll do it.*
NÉANT *m. nothing, nought, nothingness.*
  Néant. *None. Nothing to report (in filling out a form).*

  Le néant de la gloire. *The emptiness of glory.*
  Il est sorti du néant. *He rose from obscurity.*
  Réduire quelque chose à néant. *To reduce to nothing (nought). To annihilate.*
nébuleux (nébuleuse *f.*) *adj. cloudy; nebulous.*
nécessaire *m. what is necessary, necessity.*
  Il n'a que le strict nécessaire. *He only has the bare necessities.*
  Elle se prive du nécessaire pour ses enfants. *For the sake of her children she deprives herself even of necessities.*
  Nous faisons le nécessaire. *We're doing whatever is necessary. We're taking all necessary measures.*
  Un nécessaire à ouvrage. *A sewing kit.*
  Un nécessaire de toilette. *A toilet case.*
NÉCESSAIRE *adj. necessary.*
  C'est nécessaire. *It (this) is necessary.*
  Il est nécessaire que vous le fassiez. *It's necessary that you do it.*
  Des mesures nécessaires. *Necessary measures.*
  Il s'est rendu nécessaire à son patron. *He made himself indispensable to his boss.*
NÉCESSITÉ *f. necessity; need.*
  Denrées de première nécessité. *Essential foodstuffs.*
  Faire quelque chose par nécessité. *To be compelled to do something. To do something out of necessity.*
  Se trouver dans la nécessité de faire quelque chose. *To find oneself obliged to do something.*
  Il est de toute nécessité de le faire. *It's absolutely essential that it be done.*
  La nécessité est mère de l'invention. *Necessity is the mother of invention.*
  Nécessité n'a pas de loi. *Necessity knows no law.*
  Faire de nécessité vertu. *To make a virtue of necessity.*
nécessiter *to necessitate.*
  Ceci va nécessiter notre départ. *This will oblige (make it necessary for) us to leave.*
néfaste *adj. unlucky, evil.*
négatif (négative *f.*) *adj. negative.*
négligeable *adj. negligible.*
négligence *f. neglect, negligence; mistake; carelessness.*
  Négligence à faire quelque chose. *Carelessness in doing something.*
  Par négligence. *Through carelessness. Through an oversight.*
négligent *adj. careless.*
  Ne soyez pas si négligent. *Don't be so careless.*
  D'un air négligent. *Carelessly. Nonchalantly. Casually.*
négliger *to neglect.*
se négliger *to neglect oneself.*
négoce *m. trade, business.*
négociation *f. negotiation.*
négocier *to negotiate.*
nègre *m.* (négresse *f.*) *Negro.*
  Il travaille comme un nègre. *He works like a slave.*
NEIGE *f. snow.*
neiger *to snow.*
néon *m. neon.*
  Une enseigne au néon. *A neon sign.*
NERF *m. nerve; tendon; vigor, energy.*
  Elle a ses nerfs aujourd'hui. *She's nervous (jumpy, jittery, irritable) today.*
  Il me tape sur les nerfs (*fam.*). *He exasperates me.*

Ce bruit vous agace les nerfs. *That noise irritates (gets on) one's nerves.*

nerveux (nerveuse *f.*) *adj. nervous.*

nervosité *f. nervousness, irritability.*

net (nette *f.*) *adj. clean, neat; net.*

C'est clair et net. *There's no doubt about it. It's very clear.*

Il le lui a refusé tout net. *He refused him flatly.*

Je veux en avoir le coeur net. *I want to know the truth about it. I want to get to the bottom of it.*

Quel a été votre bénéfice net? *What was your net profit?*

J'ai reçu mille francs net. *I received a clear 1,000 francs.*

Il veut en avoir le coeur net. *He wants to get to the bottom of it. He wants to clear the matter up.*

nettement *clearly.*

netteté *f. neatness, cleanliness, clearness.*

nettoyage *m. cleaning.*

Nettoyage à sec. *Dry cleaning.*

nettoyer *to clean, sweep.*

Faire nettoyer à sec. *To have something dry-cleaned.*

neuf *m. what is new; novelty.*

Quoi de neuf? *What's new?*

NEUF (neuve *f.*) *adj. new.*

NEUF *noun and adj. nine.*

neutralité *f. neutrality.*

neutre *adj. neutral.*

NEUVIÈME *noun and adj. ninth.*

neveu *m. nephew.*

névralgie *f. neuralgia.*

névrose *f. neurosis.*

NEZ *m. nose.*

Saigner du nez. *To bleed from the nose. To have a nosebleed.*

Parler du nez. *To talk through one's nose.*

Il ne voit pas plus loin que le bout de son nez. *He can't see any further than the end of his nose.*

Il lui a ri au nez. *He laughed in his face.*

Elle a le nez retroussé. *She has a turned-up nose.*

NI *nor.*

Ni celui-ci, ni celui-là. *Neither this one, nor that one.*

niais *adj. simple, foolish.*

niaiserie *f. foolishness.*

niche *f. dog kennel; trick.*

se nicher *to build a nest, nestle.*

nid *m. nest.*

nièce *f. niece.*

nier *to deny.*

nigaud *adj. simpleton.*

niveau *m. level.*

Vérifier le niveau d'essence. *To check the gas gauge.*

noble *m. and f. noble; nobleman or noblewoman.*

noble *adj. noble.*

noblesse *f. nobility.*

noce *f. wedding.*

Ils sont partis en voyage de noces. *They left for their honeymoon.*

Il a fait la noce. *He went on a spree.*

noceur *m.* (noceuse *f.*) *dissipated person.*

Noël *m. Christmas.*

Le Père Noël. *Santa Claus.*

noeud *m. knot, bow.*

NOIR *noun (m.) and adj.* (noire *f.*) *black.*

Elle est vêtue de noir. *She's dressed in black.*

Voir tout en noir. *To see the dark side of everything.*

Il a l'oeil au beurre noir. *He has a black eye.*

C'est ma bête noire. *It's my pet aversion.*

Il est dans la misère noire. *He's in dire poverty.*

noirceur *f. blackness; slander.*

noircir *to blacken.*

noix *f. walnut, nut.*

NOM *m. name; noun.*

Votre nom ne lui revient pas. *He doesn't recall your name.*

Il l'a fait en mon nom. *He did it on my behalf.*

Son nom de famille est Durand. *His surname is Durand.*

Un nom de guerre. *A pseudonym. An assumed name. A pen name.*

Se faire un nom. *To win (make) a name for oneself.*

NOMBRE *m. number.*

Un bon nombre de gens sont du même avis. *A good many people are of the same opinion.*

Ils sont au nombre de dix. *They're ten in number.*

Compter quelqu'un au nombre de ses amis. *To count someone as one of (among) one's friends.*

nombreux (nombreuse *f.*) *adj. numerous.*

C'est un de ses nombreux admirateurs. *He's one of his many admirers.*

nomination *f. appointment.*

nommer *to name, call; appoint.*

Peut-il nommer la personne qui lui a dit cela? *Can he name the person who told him that?*

Il vient d'être nommé directeur. *He was just named director.*

NON *no, not.*

Je pense que non. *I think not.*

Mais non! *(But) No! Certainly not!*

nonchalance *f. nonchalance.*

nonchalant *adj. nonchalant.*

NORD *noun (m.) and adj. north.*

L'Amérique du Nord. *North America.*

Il ne perd pas le nord, celui-là. *He's never at a loss. ("He never loses his bearings.")*

Le pôle nord. *The North Pole.*

normal (normaux *pl.*) *adj. normal.*

Elle n'est pas dans son état normal. *She isn't her usual self.*

NOS *See notre.*

nostalgie *f. nostalgia.*

notable *adj. notable, important.*

notaire *m. notary.*

note *f. note; remark, observation; bill.*

Il y a une note dans le journal à ce sujet. *There is a notice in the paper about that.*

Prendre note de quelque chose. *To take note (notice) of something. To bear something in mind.*

Prendre des notes. *To take notes.*

L'explication se trouve dans les notes au bas de la page. *The explanation is given ("is found") in the footnotes.*

Le docteur envoya sa note. *The doctor sent his bill.*

C'est un mauvais élève. Il ne récolte que des mauvaises notes. *He's a poor student. He only gets bad marks.*

Le pianiste a fait une fausse note. *The pianist hit a wrong note.*

noter *to notice, note; to mark.*

Notez bien que je n'en suis pas certain! *Mind, I'm not sure about it!*

Ce sont des choses à noter pour plus tard. *These are things to watch for later on.*

Avez-vous noté l'adresse? *Did you mark down the address?*

J'ai noté le passage d'un trait rouge. *I marked that passage in red.*

notice *f. notice, short account.*

Notice biographique. *Biographical sketch.*

notifier *to notify.*

notion *f. notion, idea.*

notoriété *f. notoriety.*

NÔTRE (le nôtre *m.*, la nôtre *f.*, les nôtres *m. and f.*) *ours.*

NOTRE (notre *f.*; nos *pl.*) *adj. our.*

Notre chose à nous. *Our own thing.*

nouer *to knot, tie.*

nourrir *to feed, nourish.*

nourriture *f. food.*

NOUS *we, us.*

nous-mêmes *ourselves.*

NOUVEAU (nouvel *m. used before a vowel or "mute" h*, nouvelle *f.*, nouveaux *m. pl.*, nouvelles *f. pl.*) *adj. new.*

Je ne suis pas encore installé dans mon nouvel appartement. *I'm not settled yet in my new apartment.*

C'est la nouvelle mode. *That's the latest fashion.*

De nouveau. *Again, once more.*

nouveauté *f. newness, novelty.*

NOUVELLE *f. a piece of news, information; short story; pl. news.*

Demander des nouvelles de la santé de quelqu'un. *To ask after someone's health.*

De qui tenez-vous cette nouvelle? *Who gave you that information? Who told you the news?*

Il a écrit des nouvelles pour les journaux. *He's written short stories for the newspapers.*

Il aura de mes nouvelles! *He'll hear from me!*

Pas de nouvelles, bonnes nouvelles. *No news is good news.*

nouvelliste *m. short-story writer.*

NOVEMBRE *m. November.*

novice *m. novice.*

novocaïne *f. novocaine.*

noyau *m. stone (of a fruit).*

noyer *to drown.*

se noyer *to drown oneself.*

nu *adj. naked, bare, undressed.*

Il est sorti nu-tête. *He went out bareheaded.*

nuage *m. cloud.*

nuance *f. shade, hue, nuance.*

nue *f. high cloud.*

On le porte jusqu'aux nues. *They praise him to the skies.*

nuire *to harm, injure.*

Il cherche à me nuire auprès d'eux. *He's trying to put me in bad with them. He's trying to hurt me in their opinion.*

nuisible *adj. harmful, injurious.*

NUIT *f. night, darkness.*

A la nuit tombante. *At nightfall.*

Bonne nuit. *Good night.*

Elle a passé une nuit blanche. *She had a sleepless night.*

nul (nulle *f.*) *adj. no one; nobody; null.*

A l'impossible nul n'est tenu. *No one can be expected to do the impossible.*

Nul et non avenu. *Null and void.*

Nulle part. *Nowhere.*

nullité *f. invalidity; emptiness; nonentity.*
NUMÉRO *m. number; edition (publication).*
  Vous m'avez donné un faux numéro. *You gave me the wrong number.*
  Je lui ai donné votre numéro de téléphone. *I gave him your telephone number.*
numéroter *to number.*
nuptial *(nuptiaux pl.) adj. bridal.*
nuque *f. the nape of the neck.*
nutrition *f. nutrition.*

  O *The fifteenth letter of the alphabet.*

obéir *to obey, be obedient.*
  Je lui obéis. *I obey him (her).*
  J'y obéis. *I obey it.*
obéissance *f. obedience.*
obéissant *adj. obedient.*
obèse *adj. fat, stout.*
obésité *f. obesity.*
obituaire *noun (m.) and adj. obituary.*
objecter *to object.*
  Je n'y objecte pas. *I don't object to it. I have no objection (to raise).*
objectif *m. objective, aim, goal; lens (camera).*
  Atteindre son objectif. *To attain one's object (goal).*
objectif *(objective f.) adj. objective.*
objection *f. objection.*
OBJET *m. object, thing, article, purpose.*
  Emballez ces objets. *Pack up these things.*
  Dans cet objet. *With this end in view.*
  Objet direct. *Direct object (grammar).*
obligation *f. obligation.*
obligatoire *adj. obligatory, compulsory.*
obligeance *f. kindness.*
  Auriez-vous l'obligeance de sonner? *Would you mind ringing the bell?*
obliger *to oblige, compel; please.*
  Je suis obligé de vous quitter. *I'm obliged (I have) to leave you.*
  Le devoir m'y oblige. *Duty compels me to do it.*
  Vous l'avez obligé, il vous en est reconnaissant. *You've been of service to him; he's very grateful ("for it").*
oblique *adj. oblique.*
oblitérer *to obliterate.*
obscène *adj. obscene.*
obscur *adj. dark, dim, gloomy.*
  Il fait obscur ici. *It's dark here.*
  Il est de naissance obscure. *He comes from an obscure family. ("He is of obscure birth.")*
obscurcir *to obscure, dim.*
s'obscurcir *to grow dim, become cloudy.*
obscurité *f. obscurity, darkness.*
obséder *to obsess.*
obsèques *f. pl. funeral.*
observation *f. observation, lookout; remark, hint.*
observatoire *m. observatory.*
observer *to observe, examine, look at; remark, notice.*
  Observez strictement votre régime. *Keep strictly to your diet.*
  On vous observe, prenez garde. *Be careful, you're being watched.*
  Comme vous me l'avez fait observer. *As you pointed out to me.*
obsession *f. obsession.*
obstacle *m. obstacle.*
obstiné *adj. obstinate, stubborn.*
s'obstiner *to be obstinate, persist in.*

obstruer *to obstruct.*
obtenir *to obtain.*
obtus *adj. dull.*
  Il a l'esprit obtus. *He's dull-witted.*
obus *m. shell (artillery).*
OCCASION *f. occasion, opportunity; reason, motive; bargain.*
  Nous avons rarement l'occasion d'y aller. *We rarely have occasion to go there.*
  Profiter de l'occasion. *To take advantage of the opportunity.*
  A l'occasion. *If need be. On occasion. When the opportunity occurs.*
  Je le vois par occasion. *I see him from time to time.*
  D'occasion. *Secondhand, used.*
occasionner *to cause.*
Occident *m. Occident, West.*
occidental *(occidentaux pl.) adj. occidental, western.*
occupation *f. occupation, pursuit, employment, work.*
  Armée d'occupation. *Army of occupation.*
  Si mes occupations me le permettent, je viendrai. *I'll come if my work permits.*
  Il est sans occupation. *He's out of work.*
occuper *to occupy, take up; preoccupy; reside in; busy.*
  L'ennemi a occupé la ville. *The enemy occupied the town.*
  Toutes les places sont occupées. *There aren't any vacant seats. All the seats are taken.*
  Occuper une place importante dans le gouvernement. *To hold an important position in the government.*
  La ligne est occupée. *The (telephone) line is busy.*
s'occuper *to busy oneself with, take care of, be engaged in:*
  Est-ce qu'on s'occupe de vous? *Are you being waited on? Is someone waiting on you?*
  Voulez-vous être assez aimable de vous occuper de moi? *Would you mind waiting on me?*
  Je m'en occuperai. *I'll see to it.*
  Il s'occupe de tout. *He's attending to everything.*
océan *m. ocean.*
OCTOBRE *m. October.*
octroyer *to grant.*
oculiste *m. oculist.*
odeur *f. odor, scent.*
odieux *(odieuse f.) adj. odious, hateful.*
odorat *m. sense of smell.*
OEIL *m. (yeux pl.) eye, sight.*
  Loin des yeux, loin du coeur. *Out of sight, out of mind.*
  Il n'a pas froid aux yeux. 1. *He's very determined.* 2. *He's not at all shy.*
  Cela saute aux yeux. *It's as clear as daylight. It's so obvious it almost hits you in the eye. It stares you in the face.*
  Cela lui crève les yeux. *It's right before his eyes.*
  Elle le voit d'un mauvais oeil. *She looks unfavorably upon it.*
  Cela coûte les yeux de la tête. *It costs a mint of money. It costs a small fortune.*
  Il ne dort que d'un oeil. *He sleeps with one eye open. He's always on the alert.*
  Il ne peut en croire ses yeux. *He can't believe his eyes.*
  Il y tient comme à la prunelle de ses yeux.

  He values it as the apple of his eye.
  Jetez un coup d'oeil sur son travail. *Take a look at his work.*
OEUF *m. egg.*
  Comment préférez-vous vos oeufs: à la coque, brouillés ou sur le plat? *How do you like your eggs—boiled, scrambled or fried?*
OEUVRE *f. work.*
  Il faut les voir à l'oeuvre! *You should see them at work!*
  Il est fils de ses oeuvres. *He's a self-made man.*
  Il a mis tous les moyens en oeuvre. *He left no stone unturned.*
  Ses oeuvres ont beaucoup de succès. *His works are very popular.*
  Oeuvres de bienfaisance. *Works of charity.*
  A l'oeuvre on connaît l'artisan. *A carpenter is known by his chips. A man is known by what he does. The proof of the pudding is in the eating.*
  Chef-d'oeuvre. *Masterpiece.*
  Oeuvre maîtresse. *Masterwork.*
offense *f. offense.*
offenser *to offend, shock.*
s'offenser *to be offended.*
  Il s'offense d'un rien. *He takes offense at the least thing.*
office *m. duty, functions.*
  Faire office de secrétaire. *To act as a secretary.*
  C'est mon office de . . . *It's my duty to . . .*
  Il m'a rendu un mauvais office. *He did me a bad turn.*
  Office divin. *Religious service.*
officiel *(officielle f.) adj. official.*
officier *m. officer.*
officieux *(officieuse f.) adj. officious; unofficial, informal.*
  Commission officieuse. *Informal commission.*
offrande *f. offering.*
offre *f. offer, tender.*
  Voici ma dernière offre. *Here's my last offer.*
  Il lui a fait des offres de service. *He offered to help him.*
offrir *to offer, present; give a present.*
  Il lui a offert une montre pour son anniversaire. *He gave him (her) a watch for his (her) birthday.*
s'offrir *to propose oneself, offer.*
s'offusquer *to be offended, shocked.*
oie *f. goose.*
  Bête comme une oie. *Silly as a goose.*
oignon *m. onion.*
oindre *to rub with oil.*
oiseau *m. (oiseaux pl.) bird.*
oisif *(oisive f.) adj. idle.*
oisiveté *f. idleness.*
olive *f. olive.*
ombrage *m. shade; offense.*
ombrageux *(ombrageuse f.) adj. touchy, easily offended.*
ombre *f. shade, shadow, spirit, obscurity, shelter, cover.*
  Mettons-nous à l'ombre. *Let's get out of the sun. Let's get in the shade.*
  Il n'y a pas l'ombre de vérité en cela. *There isn't a bit (shred, shadow) of truth in that.*
  Il a été mis à l'ombre. *He was put in jail.*
omelette *f. omelet.*
omettre *to omit.*
omission *f. omission.*

ON *one, we, people, they.*
  On ne sait jamais. *One never knows.*
  On dit que . . . *It's said that . . . People say that . . .*
  On m'a volé ma montre. *My watch has been stolen. Someone stole (has stolen) my watch.*
  Où va-t-on? *Where are we going?*
  On sonne. *Someone's ringing.*
oncle *m. uncle.*
onde *f. wave.*
ondoyer *to wave, undulate.*
onduler *to undulate.*
ongle *m. fingernail, toenail.*
  Il est artiste jusqu'au bout des ongles. *He's an artist to his fingertips. He's every inch an artist.*
  Il le sait sur l'ongle. *He knows it perfectly.*
  Il se ronge les ongles. *He's very impatient. ("He is biting his nails.")*
onguent *m. ointment, unguent, salve.*
ONZE *noun and adj. eleven.*
ONZIÈME *noun and adj. eleventh.*
opéra *m. opera.*
opération *f. operation, performance.*
opérer *to operate.*
opérette *f. operetta.*
opiniâtre *adj. obstinate.*
s'opiniâtrer *to be stubborn, obstinate; cling to an opinion.*
opinion *f. opinion.*
opportun *adj. timely, opportune.*
opportunité *f. opportunity.*
opposé *noun (m.) and adj. (opposée f.) opposite; adverse.*
  C'est tout l'opposé! *It's quite the contrary (opposite, reverse)!*
opposer *to oppose.*
s'opposer *to oppose, object to.*
opposition *f. opposition.*
oppresser *to oppress.*
oppression *f. oppression.*
opprimer *to oppress.*
opter *to choose.*
optimisme *m. optimism.*
optimiste *m. optimist.*
optimiste *adj. optimistic.*
option *f. option, choice.*
optique *adj. optic.*
opulence *f. opulence, wealth.*
opulent *adj. opulent, wealthy.*
OR *m. gold.*
  Une bague en or. *A gold ring.*
  C'est de l'or en barre. *It's as good as gold.*
  Il a un coeur d'or. *He has a heart of gold.*
  C'est une affaire d'or! *It's a gold mine!*
or *now, but.*
  Or ça. *Now then.*
  Or donc . . . *Well then . . .*
oracle *m. oracle.*
orage *m. storm.*
orageux (orageuse *f.*) *adj. stormy.*
oraison *f. oration.*
oral (oraux *pl.*) *adj. oral.*
ORANGE *noun (f.) and adj. orange (fruit).*
orange *noun (m.) and adj. orange (color).*
orateur (oratrice *f.*) *orator.*
orbite *f. orbit.*
orchestre *m. orchestra.*
  Un chef d'orchestre. *An orchestra leader.*
  A l'orchestre. *In the orchestra (seats).*
  Le fauteuil d'orchestre. *Orchestra seat.*
ordinaire *m. usual way.*

D'ordinaire. *Usually. As a rule.*
  Cela sort de l'ordinaire. *That's unusual.*
  Faites-le comme à l'ordinaire. *Do it as usual. Do it the usual way.*
  Plus qu'à l'ordinaire. *More than usual.*
  Au-dessus de l'ordinaire. *Out of the ordinary.*
  C'est un homme au-dessus de l'ordinaire. *He's an unusual man.*
  Par avion ou ordinaire? *Airmail or regular?*
ORDINAIRE *adj. ordinary, common.*
  En temps ordinaires. *In ordinary times.*
  C'est un homme ordinaire. (Il est très ordinaire.) *He's very ordinary (common, vulgar).*
  Il a répondu avec sa politesse ordinaire. *He answered with his usual politeness.*
ordonnance *f. order; ordonnance, regulation; prescription.*
  Il a rendu une ordonnance. *He issued an order.*
  Une ordonnance de police. *A police regulation.*
  Le docteur a donné une ordonnance au malade. *The doctor gave the patient a prescription.*
ordonner *to order, set in order.*
ORDRE *m. order.*
  Un numéro d'ordre. *A serial number.*
  Remettez de l'ordre dans vos affaires. *Tidy up your belongings. Put your things in order.*
  Passons à l'ordre du jour. *Let's proceed with the order of the day.*
  De premier ordre. *First rate.*
  Payez à l'ordre de. *Pay to the order of.*
ordure *f. dirt; pl. garbage.*
OREILLE *f. ear, hearing.*
  Il a de l'oreille. *He has a musical ear.*
  Ça lui entre par une oreille et ça lui sort par l'autre. *It goes in one ear and out the other.*
  Faire la sourde oreille. *To turn a deaf ear.*
  Vous pouvez dormir sur vos deux oreilles. *You've nothing to worry about. You can sleep soundly.*
  Il ne s'est pas fait tirer l'oreille. *He didn't have to be asked twice. He didn't have to be coaxed.*
  L'oreille fine. *Acute hearing.*
oreiller *m. pillow.*
orfèvrerie *f. goldsmith's work.*
organe *m. organ (of the body).*
organisation *f. organization.*
organiser *to organize.*
organisme *m. organism.*
orge *f. barley.*
orgue *m. organ (mus.).*
orgueil *m. pride, arrogance.*
  Rabaisser l'orgueil de quelqu'un. *To take someone down a peg or two.*
  Il y a mis son orgueil. *He took pride in doing it.*
orgueilleux (orgueilleuse *f.*) *adj. proud, arrogant.*
Orient *m. Orient, East.*
oriental (orientaux *pl.*) *adj. oriental.*
orientation *f. orientation.*
  Il a perdu le sens de l'orientation. *He lost his sense of direction.*
orienter *to orient.*
orifice *m. aperture.*
originaire *adj. originating.*
  Il est originaire de Tours. *He comes from Tours.*
original (originaux *pl.*) *adj. original.*

originalité *f. originality, oddity.*
origine *f. origin, source, birth.*
  Dès l'origine. *From the outset.*
ornement *m. ornament.*
orner *to adorn, trim.*
ornière *f. rut.*
  Il est sorti de l'ornière. *He got out of the rut.*
orphelin *m.* (orpheline *f.*) *orphan.*
orphelinat *m. orphanage.*
orthographe *f. spelling.*
  Des fautes d'orthographe. *Spelling mistakes.*
OS *m. bone.*
  Ils ont été trempés jusqu'aux os. *They were soaked to the skin ("to the bones.")*
  Il n'a que les os et la peau. *He's only skin and bones.*
osciller *to oscillate.*
oser *to dare.*
  Si j'ose m'exprimer ainsi. *If I may take the liberty of saying so.*
osseux (osseuse *f.*) *adj. bony.*
ostentation *f. ostentation, show.*
otage *m. hostage.*
ÔTER *to take away, take off.*
  Oter les taches de graisse. *To remove grease stains.*
  Tenez, ôtez-moi cela de là. *Here, take this away.*
  Il lui a ôté son chapeau. *He raised his hat to him (her).*
OU *or.*
  Ou . . . ou . . . *Either . . . or . . .*
  Ou (bien). *Or (else).*
OÙ *where.*
  Où serez-vous? *Where will you be?*
  Où allons-nous? *Where are we going?*
  Où en sont les choses? *How do matters stand? What's the situation?*
  N'importe où. *Anywhere.*
  Où vous voudrez. *Wherever you wish.*
ouate *f. cotton.*
ouater *to pad; line.*
oubli *m. forgetting, neglect.*
OUBLIER *to forget.*
  J'ai oublié de lui demander. *I forgot to ask him.*
  J'ai oublié mes gants chez vous. *I forgot my gloves at your house.*
s'oublier *to forget oneself.*
OUEST *m. west.*
OUI *yes, so, indeed.*
  Mais oui! *Why certainly! Of course!*
ouie *f. hearing.*
ouragan *m. hurricane.*
ourlet *m. hem.*
ours *m. bear.*
outil *m. tool.*
outiller *to supply, equip.*
outrage *m. insult.*
outrager *to insult.*
outrageusement *insultingly.*
outrance *f. excess.*
  A outrance. *To excess. To the bitter end. Beyond all measure.*
  Ils se battirent à outrance. *They fought desperately.*
OUTRE *beyond.*
  Outre measure. *Beyond measure.*
  Outre cette somme. *In addition to that sum.*
  Il passa outre. *He went on.*
outrepasser *to overstep, go beyond, exceed.*
OUVERT *adj. open, frank, sincere.*
  Le musée est-il ouvert aujourd'hui? *Is the museum open today?*

Il parle à coeur ouvert. *He speaks very frankly (openly).*

ouvertement *openly, frankly.*

ouverture *f. opening; overture.*

L'ouverture d'un crédit. *The opening of an account.*

Il a profité de la première ouverture pour y aller. *He seized the first opportunity to go there.*

OUVRAGE *m. work, performance.*

Il abat de l'ouvrage comme quatre. *He does a great deal of work. ("He works for four.")*

Ils se sont mis à l'ouvrage. *They set to work.*

Il a du coeur à l'ouvrage. *He works with a will.*

Un ouvrage d'art. *A work of art.*

Ouvrages publics. *Public works.*

Un bel ouvrage. *A nice piece of work.*

ouvreuse *f. usherette.*

ouvrier *m. workman, artisan.*

OUVRIR *to open; begin.*

Ouvrez la fenêtre. *Open the window.*

Ils ont ouvert des négociations. *They opened (began) negotiations.*

Ouvrir l'appétit. *To sharpen the appetite.*

s'ouvrir *to open.*

ovale *adj. oval.*

oxygène *noun and adj. oxygen.*

P *The sixteenth letter of the alphabet.*

pacifier *to pacify, appease.*

pacifique *adj. pacific, peaceful, peaceable.*

pacifiste *m. pacifist.*

pacotille *f. cheap wares.*

pacte *m. pact, contract.*

pactiser *to make an agreement, come to terms, compromise.*

pagaille *f. disorder.*

Tout était en pagaille. *Everything was in disorder.*

page *f. page.*

En première page. *On the front page.*

paiement *See payement.*

paillasse *f. straw mattress.*

paillasson *m. doormat.*

paille *f. straw.*

Jaune paille. *Straw-yellow, straw-colored.*

paillette *f. spangle.*

PAIN *m. bread, loaf.*

Donnez-moi du pain et du vin. *Give me some bread and wine.*

Ça se vend comme des petits pains. *It's selling like hot cakes.*

Je l'ai eu pour une bouchée de pain. *I got it for almost nothing (for a song).*

Il ne vaut pas le pain qu'il mange. *He isn't worth his salt.*

pair *noun (m.) and adj. equal, even.*

Il est sans pair. *He's without a peer.*

Un écrivain hors de pair. *An incomparable writer.*

Il marche de pair avec son époque. *He keeps abreast of the times.*

Une domestique engagée au pair. *A maid receiving room and board but no salary.*

Un nombre pair. *An even number.*

paire *f. pair, couple.*

Je voudrais une paire de gants. *I'd like a pair of gloves.*

Les deux font la paire. *They are two of a kind.*

paître *to graze.*

paix *f. peace.*

Il a cédé pour avoir la paix. *He gave in just to have peace.*

Fichez-moi la paix (fam.)! *Let me alone! Don't bother me!*

palais *m. palace; palate.*

Le Palais de Justice. *Law Courts.*

pâle *adj. pale.*

palette *f. palette.*

palier *m. landing of a flight of stairs.*

pâlir *to turn pale.*

palissade *f. fence.*

palmier *m. palm tree.*

palper *to feel.*

palpitation *f. palpitation.*

palpiter *to palpitate.*

se pâmer *to faint; be enraptured.*

pamplemousse *m. grapefruit.*

panier *m. basket.*

Un panier à papiers. *A wastepaper basket.*

panique *f. panic.*

panne *f. breakdown.*

L'auto est en panne. *The car broke down.*

Avoir une panne d'essence (une panne sèche). *To be, run out of gasoline.*

La panne d'allumage. *Ignition trouble.*

La panne de moteur. *Engine trouble.*

panneau *m. (panneaux pl.) panel; trap.*

Le panneau de la porte. *The door panel.*

Il a donné dans le panneau. *He fell into the trap.*

panorama *m. panorama.*

panoramique *adj. panoramic.*

pansement *m. bandage.*

panser *to bandage.*

pantalon *m. pants, trousers.*

pantelant *adj. panting, gasping.*

pantomine *f. pantomime, dumb show.*

pantoufle *f. slipper.*

papa *m. daddy, father.*

pape *m. pope.*

paperasses *f. pl. old wastepaper, scribbled papers; red tape.*

papeterie *f. stationery store.*

PAPIER *m. paper; document.*

Papier à lettres. *Writing paper.*

Papier d'emballage. *Wrapping paper.*

Vos papiers sont en règle. *Your papers are in order.*

Il est dans ses petits papiers (fam.). *He stands well (is in good) with him.*

Rayez cela de vos papiers. *Don't count on any such thing.*

papillon *m. butterfly.*

papotage *m. gossip.*

papoter *to gossip.*

paquebot *m. liner.*

Pâques *m. pl. Easter.*

paquet *m. package, parcel, bundle.*

PAR *by, by means of, across, through.*

Par contre. *On the other hand.*

Par ici. *This way.*

Par la suite. *In the course of time.*

A en juger par. *Judging by.*

Par la gare (chemin de fer), avion, bateau. *By, via railway, air(mail), ship.*

Par exemple. *For example, for instance.*

Par exprès. *Special delivery.*

Par moments. *At times, occasionally.*

Par une chaleur écrasante. *In stifling heat.*

Par un si beau dimanche. *On such a beautiful Sunday.*

Payer par heure (jour, semaine). *To pay by the hour (day, week).*

Une fois par semaine (jour, mois, an). *Once a week (day, month, year).*

parachute *m. parachute.*

parade *f. parade.*

parader *to parade.*

paradis *m. paradise.*

paradoxe *m. paradox.*

paragraphe *m. paragraph.*

PARAÎTRE *to appear; be published.*

Vous paraissez être tout chose. *You seem out of sorts (not yourself, out of spirits).*

Un sourire parut sur ses lèvres. *A smile came to his lips.*

Il laisse trop paraître ses sentiments. *He betrays his feelings too much.*

A ce qu'il paraît. *Apparently.*

Quand ce livre paraîtra-t-il? *When will the book appear (be published)?*

Oui, paraît-il. *Yes, so it seems.*

parallèle *m. and f. noun and adj. parallel.*

paralyser *to paralyze.*

paralysie *f. paralysis.*

paralytique *m. and f. noun and adj. a paralytic; paralyzed.*

parapet *m. parapet.*

paraphrase *f. paraphrase.*

parapluie *m. umbrella.*

parasite *m. parasite, sponger.*

parasol *m. parasol.*

paratonnerre *m. lightning rod.*

parc *m. park.*

parcelle *f. particle.*

PARCE QUE *because, on account of.*

Je n'y ai pas été parce que j'étais fatigué. *I didn't go because I was tired.*

J'ai dû partir parce qu'il se faisait tard. *I had to leave because it was getting late.*

parchemin *m. parchment.*

parcimonie *f. stinginess.*

parcimonieux (parcimonieuse f.) *adj. stingy.*

parcourir *to travel through, run through.*

Il a parcouru le monde dans tous les sens. *He has been all over the world.*

J'ai parcouru le journal. *I glanced at (had a look at) the paper.*

Un frisson me parcourut. *A shiver ran up and down my spine.*

parcours *m. course, distance covered.*

Effectuer le parcours. *To cover the distance.*

PAR-DESSOUS *under.*

PAR-DESSUS *over.*

pardessus *m. overcoat.*

PAR-DEVANT *in front of.*

PARDON *m. pardon.*

Je vous demande pardon. *I beg your pardon. Pardon me.*

Pardon? *I didn't quite catch that. What did you say?*

pardonnable *adj. pardonable, excusable.*

PARDONNER *to pardon, forgive.*

Pardonnez-moi. *Pardon me.*

PAREIL (pareille f.) *adj. like, similar.*

En pareil cas. *In such cases. In a similar case.*

Un pareil travail. *A similar job. A job of this sort.*

pareille *f. the like.*

Je n'ai jamais vu la pareille. *I never saw the like.*

Ne manquez pas de lui rendre la pareille. *Be sure to pay him back in his own coin.*

pareillement *likewise; in the same manner.*

Et moi pareillement. *And so do I. (And so am I, etc.).*

parent m. relative; pl. parents.
parenté f. relationship.
parenthèse f. parenthesis.
parer to adorn.
paresse f. laziness.
paresseux (paresseuse f.) adj. lazy, idle.
PARFAIT adj. perfect; finished.
   Parfait sous tous les rapports. Perfect in every respect.
   Parfait! Fine! Good!
   Voilà qui est parfait! That's wonderful! That's perfect!
   C'est un parfait raseur (fam.). He's a terrible bore.
parfaitement perfectly; exactly.
   Parfaitement, c'est ce que j'ai dit. Exactly. That's just what I said.
PARFOIS sometimes.
parfum m. perfume.
se parfumer to use perfume.
pari m. bet.
paria m. outcast.
parier to bet.
parité f. equality.
parjure f. perjury.
parlement m. parliament.
parlementer to negotiate, parley.
PARLER to talk.
   Vous parlez trop vite. You speak (you're speaking) too fast.
   On parle de vous. People are talking about you.
   Parlez-vous sérieusement? Are you serious?
   Parlez-moi de votre voyage. Tell me about your journey (trip).
se parler to speak to each other.
   Ils ne se parlent plus. They are no longer on speaking terms.
parloir m. parlor.
PARMI among.
paroi f. partition wall.
paroisse f. parish.
PAROLE f. word, speech.
   Avoir la parole. To have the floor.
   La parole est à lui. It's his turn to speak.
   Ce sont des paroles en l'air. It's just idle talk. It's all talk. It's just a lot of talk.
   Parole d'honneur. Word of honor. I give you my word of honor.
   Tenir sa parole. To keep one's word.
   Rendre sa parole à quelqu'un. To release someone from a promise.
parquet m. floor.
parrain m. godfather.
parsemer to strew.
PART f. share, portion, part.
   Il s'attribua la meilleure part. He took the best part for himself. ("He assigned the best part to himself.")
   Il n'est pas là, il a dû partir quelque part. He isn't there. He must have gone somewhere.
   Dites-leur bien des choses aimables de notre part. Give them our best regards.
   Ça c'est un cas à part. That's quite another question.
   Et à part ça, quoi de neuf? Apart from that, what else is new?
   C'est de la part de qui? Who's calling? (telephone).
   Nulle part. Nowhere.
partage m. share, division.
   Nous en avons fait le partage. We divided it equally.
partager to share, divide, distribute.

Partager en deux. To divide in two.
   Voulez-vous partager notre dîner? Will you share our dinner? Will you have a bite with us?
partenaire m. partner.
parterre m. flower bed.
parti m. party, side; decision.
   Un parti politique. A political party.
   J'en ai pris mon parti. I have made up my mind.
   Parti pris. Preconceived notion. Prejudice.
   Tirer bon parti de quelque chose. To turn something to good advantage.
   Il a pris parti pour lui. He sided with him.
   Il ne sait quel parti prendre. He doesn't know what to do.
partial (partiaux pl.) adj. partial.
partialité f. partiality.
participation f. participation.
participe m. participle.
participer to take part, participate in.
particulier (particulière f.) adj. particular; private.
   Je n'ai rien de particulier à vous dire. I've nothing special to tell you.
   J'ai des raisons particulières pour ne pas y aller. I have personal reasons for not going there.
particulièrement particularly, in particular.
PARTIE f. part, game.
   La plus grande partie de la journée. The greater part of the day.
   En grande partie. To a great (large) extent. In a large measure.
   Faire partie de. To belong to. To be a member of.
   Il s'en est fallu de peu que je n'aie gagné la partie. I came very near winning the game.
   Perdre la partie. To lose the game.
   Partie nulle. Game that ends in a draw.
   C'est une partie remise. The pleasure is only deferred.
   Voulez-vous être de la partie? Will you join us? Will you be one of us?
PARTIR to start; leave.
   A partir de demain. Starting from tomorrow. Beginning tomorrow.
   Il est parti pour Paris. He left for Paris.
   Partir en France. To leave for France.
   Il partit d'un éclat de rire. He burst out laughing.
   Votre raisonnement part d'un principe faux. The basis of your argument is wrong. ("Your argument is based on a wrong foundation.")
   Il est parti de rien. He rose from nothing.
   Il a maille à partir avec lui. He has a bone to pick with him.
partisan m. partisan; advocate of, one in favor of.
partition f. partition.
PARTOUT everywhere.
parure f. set.
   Une parure de diamants. A set of diamonds.
parvenir to reach.
   Votre lettre m'est enfin bien parvenue. Your letter finally reached me.
   Il est parvenu à ses fins. He achieved his purpose. He attained his end.
   Parvenir à entrer. To manage to get in.
   Il parviendra à le faire. He'll succeed in doing it. He'll manage to do it.
PAS m. step; pace; footprint.
   Accélérons le pas. Let's walk faster.
   Il a fait un faux pas. He stumbled. He made a blunder.
   Il n'y a qu'un pas. It's only a few steps away.

Il habite à deux pas d'ici. He lives a few steps away.
   A pas de loup. By stealth. Stealthily.
   Il l'a tiré d'un mauvais pas. He got him out of a fix.
   Il n'y a que le premier pas qui coûte. Getting started is the only hard part. The beginning is the only difficulty.
   Le Pas de Calais. The straits of Dover.
PAS not.
   Pourquoi pas? Why not?
   Pas moi. Not I.
   Pas si bête. I'm not such a fool. I'm not that much of a fool.
   Ne·... pas. Not.
   Non pas. Not.
   Pas du tout! Not at all! No indeed!
   Pas pour le moment. Not for the moment.
   Pas que je sache. Not that I know (of).
passable adj. passable, fairly good.
   Le dîner était passable. The dinner was fairly good.
passade f. short stay.
passage m. passage.
   Passage interdit au public. No thoroughfare.
   On avait barré le passage. They blocked the way.
   Le passage clouté. Pedestrian crossing.
passager m. (passagère f.) passenger.
passager (passagère f.) adj. fleeting, transitory.
passant m. passerby.
passe f. pass.
   Le mot de passe. Password.
   Il est dans une passe difficile. He's in a difficult situation. He's in a tight corner (spot).
passé m. past, past things.
   Dans le passé. In the past.
passe-partout m. passkey.
passeport m. passport.
PASSER to pass.
   Il passa sur le quai. He passed on to the platform.
   Passez me voir quand vous aurez le temps. Look me up when you have time.
   J'ai passé l'été dernier à la même plage. I spent last summer at the same beach.
   On ne passe pas. No thoroughfare.
   Ils sont passés maîtres dans cet art. They are past masters in that art.
   Comme le temps passe! How (quickly) time flies!
   Passons maintenant à un autre chapitre, voulez-vous? Let's change the subject (drop the matter), shall we?
   Cette pièce passa à la télévision. This play is shown on television.
   Je passerai au bureau. I'll stop in at the office.
   Je te passerai les mots croisés. I'll give you the crossword puzzle.
   On peut passer? Can we go through?
   Passer l'après-midi (la nuit). To spend the afternoon (the night).
   Passer à la douane. To clear, go through customs.
   Passer par le portillon automatique. To go through the automatic gate.
   Passer par un magasin. To stop at a store.
   Passez à la caisse. Go to the cashier's desk.
   Passez-moi le 48.62.57 à Bordeaux. Connect me with 48.62.57 (telephone) in Bordeaux.
   "Passez piétons." "Pedestrians Walk" (traffic sign).
   Regarder passer les gens. To watch the people passing by.
SE PASSER to happen; do without.

Cela se passe couramment tous les jours. *It (that) takes place (happens) every day.*
Qu'est-ce qui se passe? *What's going on?*
Il faudra vous en passer. *You'll have to do without (dispense with) it.*
Je ne puis m'en passer. *I can't do without it.*
passerelle f. *footbridge, bridge (on a ship), gangway.*
passif m. *debts, liabilities; passive (grammar).*
L'actif et le passif. *Assets and liabilities.*
passif (passive f.) adj. *passive; on the debit side.*
passion f. *passion.*
passionnant adj. *thrilling.*
Une histoire passionnante. *A thrilling story.*
passionner to *excite.*
passoire f. *strainer.*
pasteur m. *pastor.*
patauger to *splash and flounder.*
pâte f. *paste; dough.*
pâté m. *patty; block; blot.*
Un pâté de maisons. *A block of buildings.*
J'ai fait un pâté. *I made a blot.*
patelin m. *small locality.*
patente f. *patent.*
patenté adj. *licensed.*
paternel (paternelle f.) adj. *paternal.*
paternité f. *fatherhood.*
pâteux (pâteuse f.) adj. *pasty, doughy, sticky, viscous, clammy.*
pathétique adj. *pathetic.*
pathos m. *affected pathos, bathos.*
patience f. *patience.*
Je suis à bout de patience. *("I'm at the end of my patience.") My patience is at an end. I've lost patience.*
patient adj. *patient.*
patin m. *skate.*
Des patins à roulettes. *Roller skates.*
Des patins à glace. *Ice skates.*
patinage m. *skating.*
patiner to *skate.*
pâtir to *suffer.*
Il a pâti la faim. *He suffered hunger.*
pâtisserie f. *pastry; pastry shop.*
patrie f. *native country.*
patrimoine m. *inheritance.*
patriote m. and f. *patriot.*
patriote adj. *patriotic.*
patriotisme m. *patriotism.*
patron m. *patron; employer, boss; pattern.*
Il est bien vu de son patron. *His employer (boss) thinks well of him.*
J'aime ce patron. *I like this pattern.*
patronage m. *patronage.*
patrouille f. *patrol.*
patrouiller to *patrol.*
patte f. *paw.*
pâturage m. *pasture.*
pâturer to *pasture.*
paume m. *palm.*
paupière f. *eyelid.*
pause f. *pause.*
pauvre adj. *poor.*
pauvrement *poorly.*
pauvreté f. *poverty.*
pavé m. *pavement.*
pavillon m. *pavilion; flag.*
payable adj. *payable.*
payant adj. *paying.*
Entrée payante. *No free admission.*
paye f. *pay.*
C'est le jour de paye, aujourd'hui. *Today's payday.*

payement m. *payment.*
payer to *pay.*
Il le paya de la même monnaie. *He paid him back in his own coin.*
Payez-lui son dû. *Give him his due.*
Faire payer les frais. *To have the expenses paid.*
PAYS m. *country.*
Voir du pays. *To travel.*
Elle a le mal du pays. *She's homesick.*
Il est en pays de connaissance. *He feels at home. He's among friends.*
paysage m. *landscape; scenery.*
paysan m. *peasant.*
peau f. *skin; peel.*
Il n'a que les os et la peau. *He's just skin and bone.*
Il a sauvé sa peau. *He saved his own skin.*
pêche f. *peach.*
pêche f. *fishing.*
péché m. *sin.*
pêcher to *fish.*
pécher to *sin.*
pécuniaire adj. *pecuniary, having to do with money.*
pédant m. and f. *noun and adj. pedant, pedantic.*
peigne m. *comb.*
Donner un coup de peigne. *To run the comb through the hair.*
peigner to *comb.*
peignoir m. *dressing gown.*
peindre to *paint, portray.*
PEINE f. *punishment; pain; trouble.*
On lui a remis sa peine. *He was pardoned.*
Entrée interdite sous peine d'amende. *No admittance under penalty of law.*
Rien ne peut adoucir sa peine. *Nothing can relieve her sorrow.*
Cela me fait de la peine. *I feel sorry about that.*
Votre absence m'a mis en peine. *Your absence got me into (caused me a lot of) trouble.*
A grand'peine. *With much difficulty. With great difficulty.*
Ce n'est pas la peine. *It's not worth while. It's not worth the trouble.*
Il a peine à se soutenir. *He can hardly stand up (keep on his feet).*
Je le connais à peine. *I hardly know him.*
J'ai peine à croire que ce soit vrai. *I can hardly believe that's true.*
Il a de la peine à rester éveillé. *He can hardly remain awake.*
Avoir de la peine. *To grieve, be in sorrow.*
Ne vous donnez pas la peine. *Don't trouble.*
peintre m. *painter.*
peinture f. *painting; paint; picture.*
La peinture à l'huile. *Oil painting.*
péjoratif (péjorative f.) adj. *disparaging.*
pêle-mêle *pell-mell, in disorder, helter-skelter.*
peler to *peel.*
pèlerin m. *pilgrim.*
pèlerinage m. *pilgrimage.*
pelle f. *shovel.*
pellicule f. *film.*
Le rouleau de pellicules. *Roll of film.*
pelote f. *ball.*
pelouse f. *lawn.*
pelure f. *peel, skin.*
pénalité f. *penalty.*
penalty m. *penalty (soccer).*
penaud adj. *crestfallen.*
Il en est resté tout penaud. *He looked sheepish.*
penchant m. *slope; inclination, bent.*
Il est sur le penchant de sa ruine. *He's on the brink of ruin.*

Elle a un penchant pour la danse. *She likes to dance.*
pencher to *incline, bend, lean.*
se pencher to *lean.*
Ne vous penchez pas à la fenêtre. *Don't lean out of the window.*
PENDANT *during, while.*
J'ai été en Angleterre pendant huit jours. *I was in England for a week.*
Pendant que vous y êtes . . . *While you're on the subject . . . While you're at (about) it . . .*
pendre to *hang.*
Pendez ce tableau au mur. *Hang this picture on the wall.*
pendule f. *clock.*
pénétrer to *penetrate.*
pénible adj. *painful, difficult.*
Il m'est pénible de devoir dire cela. *It's painful for me (I hate) to have to say this.*
péniblement *painfully.*
péninsule f. *peninsula.*
pénitence f. *penitence; punishment.*
pensée f. *thought.*
Elle est absorbée dans ses pensées. *She's absorbed in her thoughts.*
Je l'ai fait avec la pensée que . . . *I did it with the thought in mind that . . .*
PENSER to *think, consider, intend.*
Y pensez-vous! *What an idea!*
Vous n'y pensez pas! *You don't mean it! You don't intend to do it!*
Ça me fait frémir quand j'y pense. *It gives me the shivers just to think about it.*
Quand pensez-vous faire un voyage au Canada? *When do you expect to take a trip to Canada? When are you planning to go to Canada?*
Faites-moi penser à cela. *Remind me of that.*
Qu'est-ce que vous pensez d'elle? *What's your opinion of her?*
Pensez donc! *Just imagine! Just think of it!*
Je pense à lui. *I'm thinking of him (her).*
J'y pense. *I'm thinking of it.*
Nous pensions louer une voiture. *We were thinking of renting a car.*
penseur m. *thinker.*
pensif (pensive f.) adj. *pensive.*
pension f. *pension; boardinghouse; board.*
Je suis en pension chez Mme. Dupont. *I'm boarding at Mrs. Dupont's.*
La pension est-elle bonne ici? *Is the food good in this boardinghouse? "Is the board good here?")*
Elle a mis son fils en pension. *She sent her son to a boarding school.*
pensionnaire m. *boarder.*
pensionnat m. *boarding school.*
pente f. *slope, descent.*
pénurie f. *scarcity, dearth.*
pépin m. *pit, kernel.*
perçant adj. *piercing.*
percer to *pierce.*
PERDRE to *lose.*
Nous n'avons pas de temps à perdre. *We have no time to lose.*
Vous ne perdez rien pour attendre. *You'll lose nothing by waiting.*
Ne perdez donc pas votre temps à ces bêtises. *Don't waste your time on that nonsense.*
Perdre la raison. *To go mad. To lose one's mind (reason).*
Il courait à perdre haleine. *He ran until he was out of breath.*

PÈRE *m. father.*
M. Dupont père. *Mr. Dupont, senior.*
Il est bien le fils de son père. *He's a chip off the old block.*
perfection *f. perfection.*
A la perfection. *Perfectly.*
perfectionner *to perfect, improve.*
perfide *adj. perfidious, deceiving.*
perfidie *f. perfidy, treachery.*
perforer *to perforate.*
péril *m. danger, hazard.*
Faites-le à vos risques et périls. *Do it at your own risk.*
Il l'a aidé au péril de sa vie. *He helped him at the risk of his life.*
Mettre en péril. *To endanger. To imperil. To jeopardize.*
périlleux (périlleuse *f.*) *adj. perilous, risky.*
période *f. period, age.*
périodique *noun (m.) and adj. periodic; periodical.*
péripétie *f. adventure.*
périr *to perish.*
perle *f. pearl.*
permanence *f. permanence.*
permanent *adj. permanent.*
PERMETTRE *to permit.*
Permettez-moi de vous présenter à ma soeur. *Allow me to introduce you to my sister.*
Permettez que je vous accompagne. *May I go along with you? May I accompany you? ("Allow me to accompany you.")*
Vous permettez? — Faites donc! *May I? — Of course!*
Me permettez-vous de fumer? *Do you mind my smoking? Do you mind if I smoke?*
Cet argent lui permit de faire un long voyage. *That money enabled him to take a long trip.*
Il se croyait tout permis. *He thought he could do anything.*
Permis à vous de ne pas me croire. *You're free to believe me or not.*
Permettez! 1. *Excuse me! Allow me!* 2. *Wait a minute! Not so fast!*
Si madame permet. *If madame will permit.*
se permettre *to allow oneself, take the liberty.*
Il se permet beaucoup trop de choses. *He takes too many liberties.*
Si je peux me permettre de vous faire une observation. *If I may take the liberty of remarking.*
Je ne peux pas me le permettre. *I can't afford it.*
permis *m. license, permit.*
permission *f. permission; leave, furlough.*
Vous avez ma permission. *You have my permission.*
Demander la permission. *To ask permission.*
Il est en permission. *He's on leave (on furlough).*
pernicieux (pernicieuse *f.*) *adj. pernicious.*
perpendiculaire *adj. perpendicular.*
perpétuel (perpétuelle *f.*) *adj. perpetual, everlasting, endless.*
perpétuellement *perpetually.*
perpétuité *f. perpetuity.*
Prison à perpétuité. *Life imprisonment.*
perplexe *adj. puzzled.*
perquisition *f. search.*
Un mandat de perquisition. *A search warrant.*
La police a fait une perquisition chez lui. *The police searched his house.*
perquisitionner *to make a search.*
perroquet *m. parrot.*
perruque *f. wig.*
persécuter *to persecute.*
persécution *f. persecution.*
persévérance *f. perseverance.*
persévérer *to persevere, persist.*
persistance *f. persistence.*
persister *to persist.*
personnage *m. person; distinguished person; a somebody; character (play).*
personnalité *f. personality.*
PERSONNE *f. person, individual.*
La personne dont je vous ai parlé . . . *The person I spoke to you about . . .*
Les enfants ne sont admis qu'accompagnés par de grandes personnes. *Children must be accompanied by adults.*
Une personne de marque. *A man of note. An important (outstanding) man.*
PERSONNE *anyone, anybody, no one, nobody.*
Heureusement, personne n'a été blessé dans l'accident. *Fortunately, no one was hurt (injured) in the accident.*
Je n'y suis pour personne. *I'm not at home to anybody.*
Personne n'est venu. *Nobody came. No one came.*
Qui est venu? —Personne. *Who came? —No one.*
personnel *m. staff, personnel.*
personnel (personnelle *f.*) *adj. personal.*
personnellement *personally.*
personnifier *to personify; impersonate.*
Elle est la bonté personifiée. *She's kindness itself.*
perspective *f. perspective.*
perspicace *adj. perspicacious, shrewd.*
perspicacité *f. perspicacity, insight.*
persuader *to persuade, convince.*
Il est persuadé qu'il réussira. *He imagines (he's sure, convinced) he'll succeed.*
Nous sommes persuadés que vous nous aiderez. *We feel confident that you'll help us.*
persuasif (persuasive *f.*) *adj. persuasive.*
persuasion *f. persuasion.*
perte *f. loss.*
Profits et pertes. *Profit and loss.*
A perte de vue. *As far as the eye can reach.*
Il raisonne toujours à perte de vue. *He never stops arguing.*
pertinent *adj. pertinent, relevant.*
perturbation *f. perturbation, disturbance.*
pervers *adj. perverse, depraved, wicked.*
pervertir *to corrupt.*
pesant *adj. heavy, weighty.*
peser *to weigh.*
Combien cela pèse-t-il? *How much does it (this) weigh?*
Pesez bien vos paroles. *Weigh your words carefully.*
peste *f. plague.*
pétard *m. firecracker.*
pétillement *m. crackling, sparkling.*
pétiller *to crackle.*
Le bois pétille. *The wood is crackling.*
Elle pétille d'esprit. *She's very witty.*
PETIT *adj. small.*
Un petit bout, s'il vous plaît. *A little bit, please.*
Petit à petit. *Bit by bit. Little by little.*
Ne faites pas la petite bouche. *Don't mince matters. Don't beat about the bush.*
La petite monnaie. *Small change.*
PETIT DÉJEUNER *m. breakfast.*
pétition *f. petition.*
pétrifier *to petrify.*
pétrin *m. kneading-trough.*
Eh bien, il est dans un beau pétrin (*fam.*). *Well, he's in a fine mess (fix).*
pétrole *m. petroleum, oil.*
Une lampe à pétrole. *A kerosene lamp.*
pétulance *f. petulance, liveliness.*
PEU *m. a little; a few.*
J'en ai peu. *I have a few. I've got a few.*
Peu à peu. *Little by little.*
Ce chapeau est un peu juste. *This hat is a little too tight.*
Faites voir un peu. *Just show me.*
Ne vous inquiétez donc pas pour si peu de chose. *Don't let such trifles disturb you.*
Il y a un peu plus de trois semaines. *A little over three weeks ago.*
Je vous demande un peu! *I ask you! How do you like that!*
Mais pourquoi, je vous demande un peu! *But why, I'd like to know.*
Ce n'est pas peu dire. *That's saying a good deal.*
En peu de mots, voilà l'histoire. *Here's the story in a nutshell ("in a few words").*
Un tout petit peu. *Just a little bit.*
peuple *m. people, nation.*
PEUR *f. fear, fright, terror.*
Il a peur. *He's afraid.*
Il en a été quitte pour la peur. *He got off with just a fright.*
Il en est presque mort de peur. *He nearly died of fright. It nearly frightened him to death.*
J'ai peur qu'il ne vienne pas. *I'm afraid he won't (mayn't) come.*
De peur que. *For fear that.*
peureux (peureuse *f.*) *adj. easily frightened.*
PEUT-ÊTRE *maybe, perhaps.*
phare *m. lighthouse.*
pharmacie *f. pharmacy, drugstore.*
pharmacien *m. pharmacist, druggist.*
phénomène *m. phenomenon.*
philosophe *m. philosopher.*
philosophie *f. philosophy.*
photo *f. photo.*
photographe *m. photographer.*
photographie *f. photography.*
Le magasin de photographie. *Camera shop.*
photographier *to photograph, take a snapshot.*
photographique *adj. photographic.*
Un appareil photographique. *A camera.*
phrase *f. sentence.*
physionomie *f. face.*
physique *f. physics.*
physique *adj. physical.*
pianiste *m. and f. pianist.*
piano *m. piano.*
Jouer du piano. *To play the piano.*
pic *m. pick; peak.*
PIÈCE *f. piece; room; play; coin.*
Il l'a mis en pièces. *He broke it to pieces.*
Des pièces de rechange. *Spare parts.*
Ça rafraîchira la pièce. *That will cool the room.*
Cette pièce est très courue. *This play is very popular.*
Il lui rendra la monnaie de sa pièce. *He'll pay him back in the same coin.*
Les pièces d'identité. *Identification papers.*
PIED *f. foot.*
Mon pied a glissé et je suis tombé. *My foot slipped and I fell.*
Un coup de pied. *A kick.*
A pied. *By foot. On foot.*

Combien y a-t-il à pied d'ici à la gare? *How long does it take to walk from here to the station?*

Doigt de pied. *Toe.*

Sur la pointe des pieds. *On tiptoe.*

Ne vous laissez pas marcher sur les pieds. *Don't let people take advantage of you (step all over you).*

Il était armé de la tête aux pieds. *He was armed to the teeth.*

On l'a mis au pied du mur. *He was cornered. He was with his back to the wall. They had him with his back to the wall.*

Il a mis l'affaire sur pied. *He got the business started.*

Il a dû se lever du pied gauche. *He must have gotten up on the wrong side of the bed.*

Le tour (la promenade) à pied. *Walk, stroll.*

piège m. *trap, snare.*

PIERRE f. *stone, flint, rock.*

Il a un coeur de pierre. *He has a heart of stone.*

Il est merciless (heartless).

L'âge de pierre. *The Stone Age.*

Il gèle à pierre fendre. *It's freezing (out).*

Une pierre à briquet. *A flint (for a lighter).*

piété f. *piety.*

piétiner to *trample, stamp.*

piéton m. *pedestrian.*

piètre adj. *paltry, poor.*

C'est un piètre nageur. *He's a poor swimmer.*

pieux (pieuse f.) adj. *pious, devout.*

pigeon m. *pigeon.*

pile f. *heap; reverse (of coin).*

Une pile de livres. *A pile of books.*

Pile ou face. *Heads or tails.*

pilier m. *pillar.*

pillage m. *pillage, looting.*

piller to *plunder.*

pilote m. *pilot.*

piloter to *pilot; to lead, guide, show around; to show someone the way.*

pilule f. *pill.*

pince f. *grip; pincers.*

pinceau m. (pinceaux pl.) *paintbrush.*

pincer to *pinch.*

ping-pong m. *ping-pong.*

pipe f. *pipe.*

pique m. *spade (cards).*

pique-assiette m. *sponger.*

piquer to *prick, stitch; excite, pique, nettle.*

Les moustiques m'ont piqué cette nuit. *I was bitten up by mosquitoes last night.*

Cela piqua sa curiosité. *That aroused his curiosity.*

Elle a été piquée au vif par ces paroles. *She was greatly piqued (nettled) at this remark.*

se piquer to *pride oneself; pretend.*

Il se pique de son savoir. *He likes to think he knows it all.*

piqûre f. *sting; injection.*

PIRE m. adj. *worst; worse.*

Le pire c'est que . . . *The worst part is . . . The worst is that . . . .*

Ce qu'il y a de pire . . . *What's worse . . .*

C'était bien pire. *That was much worse.*

PIS *worse.*

Il met les choses au pis. *He assumes the worst.*

En mettant les chose au pis, on ne perdra pas tout. *If worst comes to worst, we won't lose anything.*

Chaque jour cela va de mal en pis. *It gets worse daily. Everyday it goes from bad to worse.*

piscine f. *swimming pool.*

piste f. *track.*

Etre à la piste. *To be on the track of.*

Nous faisons fausse piste. *We're on the wrong track.*

pistolet m. *pistol, gun.*

piston m. *piston.*

Il a du piston. *He has pull.*

piteux (piteuse f.) adj. *pitiful, sorry.*

Ils sont revenus dans un piteux état. *They came back in a very sorry condition.*

Il fait une assez piteuse figure. *He cuts a pretty sorry figure.*

PITIÉ f. *pity.*

Il me fait pitié. *I feel sorry for him.*

Il l'a pris en pitié. *He took pity on him.*

Quelle pitié! *What a pity!*

pitoyable adj. *pitiable, wretched.*

pitoyablement *woefully.*

pittoresque adj. *picturesque, quaint.*

pivot m. *pivot.*

Un point de pivot dans l'histoire. *A turning point in history.*

pivoter to *pivot.*

placard m. *poster; cupboard.*

PLACE f. *place, spot; seat.*

Il ne peut pas rester en place. *He can't stand still.*

Je vais essayer d'avoir des places. *I'll try to get seats.*

A votre place, je n'accepterais pas. *If I were in your place, I wouldn't accept.*

Je ne voudrais pas être à sa place. *I wouldn't like to be in his shoes (place).*

Je viens à la place de mon frère. *I've come instead of my brother.*

Faites place! *Make room!*

Remettre quelqu'un à sa place. *To put someone in his place. To take someone down a peg or two.*

Il est sans place. *He's out of a job.*

Une place assise. *Seat (bus).*

On fait tout sur place. *Everything is done on the premises.*

placement m. *placing; investment.*

Bureau de placements. *Employment agency.*

Il a fait un placement avantageux. *He made a good investment.*

PLACER to *place.*

Placez cela sur la table. *Put that on the table.*

Cet article est difficile à placer. *This article (item) is hard to sell.*

Impossible de placer un mot! *It's impossible to get a word in edgewise!*

Placer son argent à l'intérêt. *To invest one's money at interest.*

plafond m. *ceiling.*

plage f. *beach.*

plaider to *plead.*

plaie f. *wound.*

plaindre to *pity.*

Elle est bien à plaindre. *You really have to feel sorry for (pity) her.*

se plaindre to *complain.*

Il est toujours en train de se plaindre. *He's always complaining.*

Je vois ce dont vous vous plaignez. *I see what you're complaining of.*

plaine f. *plain.*

plainte f. *complaint.*

Formulez vos plaintes par écrit. *State your complaints in writing.*

plaintif (plaintive f.) adj. *plaintive.*

plaire to *be pleasant, please.*

Ça ne me plaît pas. *I don't like that.*

Plaît-il? *I didn't quite catch that. Will you please say that again?*

S'il vous plaît. *Please.*

Comme il vous plaira. *As you please. As you wish.*

se plaire to *like, enjoy.*

Il s'y plaît. *He likes it there.*

Il se plaît à contrarier les gens. *He takes pleasure in contradicting people.*

plaisant adj. *pleasant, agreeable.*

plaisanter to *joke.*

Vous plaisantez! *You're joking! You don't really mean it!*

Il ne plaisante jamais en affaires. *He takes his business matters very seriously. ("He never trifles about business.")*

plaisanterie f. *joke.*

Il entend la plaisanterie. *He can take a joke.*

Il l'a fait par plaisanterie. *He did it in jest (as a joke).*

Tourner une chose en plaisanterie. *To laugh a thing off.*

PLAISIR m. *pleasure, amusement; consent.*

Train de plaisir. *Excursion train.*

C'était plaisir de l'entendre. *It was a pleasure to hear him.*

Faire plaisir à quelqu'un. *To please someone.*

Voulez-vous me faire un plaisir? *Will you please do me a favor?*

Je le ferai avec plaisir. *I'll be glad to do it.*

plan m. *plan, design, scheme.*

Leurs plans échouèrent. *Their plans failed (fell through).*

Il m'a laissé en plan (fam.). *He left me in the lurch.*

Le premier plan. *Foreground (painting).*

planche f. *board, plank; shelf.*

plancher m. *floor.*

planer to *soar.*

planète f. *planet.*

plante f. *plant; sole of the foot.*

planter to *plant.*

plaque f. *plate, sheet.*

plastique adj. *plastic.*

plat m. *dish.*

Ce plat est bien assaisonné. *This dish (food) is well seasoned.*

Il a mis les pieds dans le plat. *He made a blunder. He put his foot in it.*

Quel est le plat-du-jour? *What's the special on today's menu? What's today's special?*

plat adj. *flat, plain, dull.*

Il a les pieds plats. *He has flat feet.*

Plat comme une galette. *As flat as a pancake.*

Elle a les cheveux plats. *She has straight hair.*

Un pneu à plat. *Flat tire.*

plateau m. *tray.*

platine m. *platinum.*

platitude f. *platitude.*

plâtre m. *plaster.*

plausible adj. *plausible.*

plein m. *full part; height.*

Le plein de la mer. *High tide.*

La fête bat son plein. *The festival is at its height.*

PLEIN adj. *full, filled, complete.*

Plein de monde. *Crowded.*

Observation pleine d'esprit. *Witty remark.*

Il est plein de vie. *He's full of life.*

En plein air. *In the open air, out of doors.*

Faire le plein (d'essence). *To fill up (with gasoline).*

pleur *m. tear.*
pleurard *adj. whining.*
pleurer *to cry, weep.*
pleurnicher *to whimper.*
pleutre *m. coward.*
pleuvoir *to rain.*
Il recommence à pleuvoir. *It's starting to rain again.*
Pleuvoir à verse. *To pour.*
Les lettres de félicitation pleuvèrent. *Congratulatory notes poured in.*
pli *m. fold, crease.*
Une mise en plis. *A hair-setting.*
plier *to fold, bend.*
Il plia son journal. *He folded his paper.*
Il plia bagage et partit. *He packed (up) and left.*
Tout plie devant lui. *He carries all before him.*
plomb *m. lead.*
plomber *to fill (tooth).*
plombier *m. plumber.*
plongeon *m. dive; diving; plunge.*
Faire une plongeon. *To dive.*
plonger *to plunge, dive.*
se plonger *to plunge.* ·
ployer *to bend, bow.*
plu *pleased.*
PLUIE *f. rain.*
Une pluie torrentielle. *A heavy rain. A heavy downpour.*
Parler de la pluie et du beau temps. *To talk about the weather.*
plume *f. feather, quill; pen.*
plumeau *m. (plumeaux pl.) feather duster.*
plupart *f. the greater part.*
La plupart d'entre eux sont d'accord avec moi. *Most of them agree with me.*
La plupart du temps. *Generally. Most of the time.*
pluriel *m. plural.*
PLUS *more, most, farther, further.*
Je ne lui en donnerai plus. *I won't give him any more.* .
Elle a tout au plus vingt ans. *She is twenty at most.*
Plus j'essaye moins je réussis. *The more I try the less I succeed.*
Vous auriez pu venir plus tôt. *You might have come sooner.*
En plus. *Extra, additional.*
Ne . . . plus. *No longer, no more.*
Plus de trois minutes. *More than three minutes.* ·
PLUSIEURS *several, many, some.*
Plusieurs fois. *Several times.*
Plusieurs personnes. *Several people.*
J'en ai plusieurs. *I have several (of them).*
PLUTÔT *sooner, rather.*
Il fait plutôt froid. *It's rather cold.*
Plutôt que. *Rather than.*
Plutôt mourir! *I'd sooner die!*
pneu *m. tire.*
pneu(matique) *m. express letter (Paris).*
pneumonie *f. pneumonia.*
poche *f. pocket.*
Format de poche. *Pocket-sized.*
poêle *f. frying pan.*
poésie *f. poetry.*
poète *m. poet.*
poétique *adj. poetical.*
poids *m. weight, heaviness, gravity, burden.*
poignant *adj. poignant, heart-gripping.*
poignard *m. dagger.*
poignée *f. handful.*
poignet *m. wrist.*

poil *m. hair, fur.*
poinçonner *to punch.*
poing *m. fist.*
POINT *m. point; period.*
Point de vue. *Point of view.*
Mettre au point. *To perfect.*
Jusqu'à un certain point je suis d'accord. *Up to a certain point, I agree.*
Sur ce point. *On that score.*
Point. *Period.*
Deux points. *Colon.*
Point virgule. *Semicolon.*
Point d'interrogation. *Question mark.*
Point d'exclamation. *Exclamation mark.*
Le point du jour. *Dawn.*
POINT *no, not, not at all.*
Peu ou point. *Little or none at all.*
Je n'en veux point. *I don't want that at all. I don't like that at all.*
Ce n'est point de mon ressort. *It's not at all in my province.*
pointe *f. point.*
Sur la pointe des pieds. *On tiptoe.*
pointiller *to dot.*
pointilliste *m. pointillist (painting).*
pointu *adj. sharp, pointed.*
pointure *f. size (shoes, socks, stockings, gloves, hats).*
poire *f. pear.*
pois *m. pea.*
Des petits pois. *Green peas.*
poison *m. poison.*
poisson *m. fish.*
poitrine *f. chest.*
poivre *m. pepper.*
pôle *m. pole.*
poli *adj. polite.*
police *f. police.*
police *f. policy.*
poliment *politely.*
polir *to polish; refine.*
polisson (polissonne *f.*) *adj. naughty child.*
politesse *f. politeness.*
politicien (politicienne *f.*) *noun and adj. politician.*
politique *f. politics, policy.*
politique *adj. political.*
poltron (poltronne *f.*) *adj. cowardly.*
POMME *f. apple.*
Ces pommes sont aigres. *These apples are sour.*
Pommes de terre frites. *French-fried potatoes.*
pompe *f. pomp, ceremony.*
pompe *f. pump.*
pompeux (pompeuse *f.*) *adj. pompous.*
pompier *m. fireman.*
ponctuel (ponctuelle *f.*) *adj. punctual.*
ponctuer *to punctuate.*
pondre *to lay (eggs).*
pont *m. bridge.*
populaire *adj. popular; vulgar.*
population *f. population.*
porc *m. pig; pork.*
Côtelettes de porc. *Pork chops.*
porcelaine *f. porcelain.*
pore *m. pore.*
port *m. harbor, port, shelter; bearing; carrying.*
Ils sont arrivés à bon port. *They arrived safe and sound.*
Faire naufrage au port. *To fail with one's goal in sight. To be shipwrecked in port (in sight of the harbor).*
Franco de port. *Postage prepaid. Delivery free.*
Elle a un port de reine. *She has a very stately appearance (bearing).*

portant *adj. bearing, carrying.*
Il n'est pas bien portant. *His health is poor.*
Il a tiré sur lui à bout portant. *He shot at him point-blank.*
PORTE *f. door.*
Fermez la porte. *Close the door.*
porte-bagages *m. luggage rack (car).*
porte-bonheur *m. good-luck charm.*
porte-cigare *m. cigar holder; pl. cigar case.*
porte-cigarette *m. cigarette holder; pl. cigarette case.*
porte-clefs *m. pl. key ring.*
portefaix *m. porter.*
portefeuille *m. wallet; briefcase; portfolio.*
portemanteau *m. coat-stand; coat-hanger.*
porte-mine *m. automatic pencil.*
porte-monnaie *m. purse.*
porte-parole *m. spokesman.*
PORTER *to bear, carry; wear.*
Je ne peux pas porter ce paquet, il est trop lourd. *I can't carry this package—it's too heavy.*
Toutes deux portaient des jupes bleues. *Both were wearing blue skirts.*
SE PORTER *to be worn; to go; to be (of health).*
C'est tout ce qui se porte en ce moment. *That's the latest fashion. Everyone's wearing that now.*
Il se porta à son secours. *He went to his aid.*
Je ne m'en porte pas plus mal. *I'm none the worse for it.*
Comment vous portez-vous? *How are you?*
Je me porte à ravir. *I'm in excellent health.*
porteur *m. bearer; porter.*
Payable au porteur. *Payable to bearer.*
Un porteur portait leurs valises. *A porter carried their suitcases.*
portière *f. carriage door, car door.*
portillon (automatique) *m. (automatic) gate (subway).*
portion *f. portion, helping.*
portrait *m. portrait, picture.*
pose *f. attitude, posture; exposure (photography).*
pose-mètre *m. exposure meter, light meter.*
POSER *to place, lay down; pose; ask (a question).*
Posez le paquet sur la table. *Put this package on the table.*
Il pose. *He's very affected. He shows off.*
Je vais vous poser une question. *I'm going to ask you a question.*
Ce problème qui se pose à nous est ardu. *We have a difficult problem before us.*
poseur (poseuse *f.*) *adj. person who poses, affected person.*
position *f. position.*
posséder *to possess, own.*
possession *f. possession, property.*
possibilité *f. possibility.*
POSSIBLE *adj. possible.*
Est-ce qu'il vous sera possible de venir avec nous? *Will it be possible for you to come with us?*
postal *adj. postal.*
La carte postale. *Postcard.*
POSTE *f. post office; mail.*
Le bureau de poste. *The post office.*
Vous trouverez la poste dans la première rue à droite. *The post office is on the first street to your right.*
La poste aérienne. *Airmail.*
Le bureau des P et T (Postes et Télécommunications). *Post office.*
La poste restante. *General delivery.*

poste m. *post, station.*

Le poste de douane. *Customs station, customs house.*

postérieur adj. *posterior.*

postérité f. *posterity.*

posthume adj. *posthumous.*

post-scriptum m. *postscript.*

posture f. *posture.*

pot m. *jug, can, jar.*

Sourd comme un pot. *As deaf as a post.*

Ne tournez pas autour du pot! *Don't beat around the bush!*

potable adj. *drinkable; good enough.*

L'eau est potable. *The water is drinkable.*

Le travail est potable. *The work is fairly good.*

potage m. *soup.*

poteau m. (poteaux pl.) *post, stake.*

potence f. *gallows.*

potentiel (potentielle f.) adj. *potential.*

potin m. *gossip; row, rumpus.*

Elles font des potins. *They're gossiping.*

Il fait du potin. *He's raising a rumpus.*

potion f. *potion, medicine.*

poubelle f. *garbage can.*

pouce m. *thumb.*

poudre f. *powder, dust, gunpowder.*

poudrer to *powder.*

pouffer to *burst out.*

Il pouffa de rire (fam.). *He burst out laughing.*

poule f. *hen, fowl.*

poulet m. *chicken.*

poulie f. *pulley.*

pouls m. *pulse.*

poumon m. *lung.*

poupée f. *doll.*

POUR *for, for the sake of, on account of, on the part of, toward.*

Faites cela pour moi. *Do it for me (for my sake).*

J'en ai pour un mois. *It will take me a month.*

Le pour et le contre. *The pros and cons.*

Pour ainsi dire. *As it were. So to speak.*

Comment fait-on pour . . . *How does one go about . . .*

Pour commencer. *To begin with.*

Pour toujours. *Forever.*

S'arranger (avec quelqu'un) pour . . . *To arrange (with someone) to . . .*

Pour que. *So that, in order that.*

pourboire m. *tip.*

pour-cent m. *percentage.*

pourcentage m. *percentage.*

pourchasser to *pursue.*

pourparler m. *negotiation.*

Entrer en pourparlers. *To enter into negotiations.*

POURQUOI *why.*

Pourquoi pas? *Why not?*

C'est pourquoi je vous demande d'y aller. *That's why I ask (I'm asking) you to go there.*

Pourquoi faire? *Why? What for?*

pourrir to *rot, decay.*

pourriture f. *rotting, decay, rot.*

poursuite f. *pursuit, lawsuit.*

poursuivre to *pursue.*

POURTANT *however, yet, still.*

Il habite la France depuis peu de temps et pourtant il parle très bien le français. *He's been in France for only a short while, yet he speaks French very well.*

Il a beaucoup de talent et pourtant il n'a jamais rien fait. *He's talented, yet he's never managed to achieve anything. Though he's very talented, he's never accomplished anything.*

Pourtant vous progressez, cela ne fait pas de doute. *Still you're progressing, there's no doubt of that.*

Pourtant j'aurais bien voulu la voir. *Still I should like to have seen her.*

Pourtant vous avez raison. *You're right, nevertheless.*

C'est comme ça pourtant. *Believe it or not.*

pourvoir to *provide.*

pourvu que *provided that.*

Je viendrai pourvu que je finisse mon travail. *I'll come provided I finish my work.*

Pourvu qu'il revienne vite. *I hope he'll return very soon.*

Pourvu que nous puissions monter! *I only hope we can get on!*

pousser to *push, shove; to grow (hair, etc.).*

Poussé par la pitié. *Prompted by pity.*

Il lui a poussé la main. *He forced his hand.*

L'herbe pousse très vite. *The grass grows very quickly.*

poussière f. *dust.*

poutre f. *beam.*

POUVOIR m. *power, ability, authority.*

Pouvoir d'achat. *Purchasing power.*

Il a un grand pouvoir sur lui. *He has a great influence over him.*

Il exerce un pouvoir. *He has power of attorney.*

POUVOIR to *be able, have power, be allowed.*

Je ne peux (puis) pas venir. *I can't come.*

Cela se peut bien. *It's quite possible.*

On n'y peut rien. *There's nothing that can be done. It can't be helped.*

Si vous ne pouvez pas, dites-le. *If you can't, say so.*

Pouvez-vous m'indiquer où se trouve la poste? *Can you tell me where the post office is?*

Je n'en peux plus. *I'm exhausted.*

Vouloir c'est pouvoir. *Where there's a will there's a way.*

En quoi pourrais-je vous servir? *What can I do for you?*

En quoi puis-je vous être utile? *What can I do for you?*

Est-ce que je peux? *May I?*

Pourriez-vous . . . *Could you . . .*

se pouvoir to *be possible.*

Il se peut qu'il soit parti. *He may have gone (left). It's possible that he's gone.*

Ça se peut. *That's possible.*

prairie f. *meadow.*

pratique f. *practice, performance.*

pratique adj. *practical.*

Il a beaucoup de sens pratique. *He has a great deal of common sense. He's very practical.*

pratiquer to *practice; carry out; make; play (sports).*

Voilà comment il faut pratiquer. *This is how the thing is done. This is the way you have to go about it.*

Pratiquer sa religion. *To practice one's religion.*

pré m. *meadow.*

préalable m. *first of all.*

Au préalable, allez-lui parler. *First of all, go (to) speak to him.*

précaire adj. *precarious.*

précaution f. *precaution.*

précédent adj. *preceding.*

Il m'a téléphoné le jour précédent. *He called me up the day before.*

précéder to *precede; take precedence.*

C'est dans le chapitre qui précède. *It's in the preceding chapter. It's in the chapter before this one.*

précepteur m. (préceptrice f.) *family tutor.*

prêcher to *preach.*

précieux (précieuse f.) adj. *precious, costly; affected.*

précipice m. *precipice.*

précipiter to *precipitate, hurl, throw down, plunge; hurry, hasten.*

Précipiter ses pas. *To hurry along.*

Il ne faut rien précipiter. *Never do things in a hurry. You mustn't hurry things. Let things take their course.*

se précipiter to *rush down; rush on; hurry.*

précis adj. *precise, accurate, concise.*

A vingt et une heures précises. *At exactly 9:00 P.M.*

précisément *precisely.*

préciser to *specify.*

précision f. *precision, accuracy.*

précoce adj. *precocious.*

précocité f. *precociousness.*

précurseur m. *forerunner, precursor.*

prédécesseur m. *predecessor.*

prédestiné adj. *predestined.*

prédiction f. *prediction.*

prédilection f. *predilection, preference.*

prédire to *predict, foretell.*

prédominant adj. *prevailing.*

prédominer to *prevail.*

préface f. *preface.*

préférable adj. *preferable.*

préféré adj. *favorite.*

préférence f. *preference.*

De préférence. *Preferably.*

PRÉFÉRER to *prefer.*

Laquelle préférez-vous? *Which (one) do you prefer?*

préjudice m. *prejudice, damage, harm.*

préjugé m. *presumption; prejudice.*

se prélasser to *enjoy comfort, lounge around; take things (life) easy.*

prélever to *deduct.*

préliminaire adj. *preliminary.*

prélude m. *prelude.*

prématuré adj. *premature.*

préméditation f. *premeditation.*

préméditer to *premeditate.*

PREMIER (première f.) adj. *first; former (of two).*

A la première occasion. *At the first opportunity.*

Matières premières. *Raw materials.*

Le premier rôle. *The leading role.*

En première. *In first class.*

En première page. *On the front page.*

Le premier plan. *Foreground (painting).*

Les quatre premières places. *The first four seats.*

se prémunir to *provide oneself.*

Il se prémunit d'argent. *He provided himself with money. He took enough money along.*

PRENDRE to *take, grasp, seize, catch; to have (food, drink).*

Prenez-en. *Take some.*

Prenez tout cela en considération. *Take all that into consideration.*

Je sais comment le prendre. *I know how to manage him (deal with him).*

Où avez-vous pris cela? *Where did you get that idea?*

Il se laissa prendre. *He let himself be caught.*

Je vous prendrai en passant. *I'll call for you (pick you up) on my way.*

Qu'est-ce qui le prend? *What's the matter with him? What's come over him? What's gotten into him?*

Qu'est-ce que vous allez prendre! *You're in for it!*

Il a pris du poids. *He has gained weight.*
Prendre un billet. *To buy, get a ticket.*
Prendre la correspondance. *To change trains
(subway).*
Prendre des renseignements. *To get information.*
se prendre *to be caught; set about.*
Il s'est pris d'amitié pour lui. *He took a liking
to him.*
Il s'y est bien pris. *He set about it the right way.*
Il s'en est pris à lui. *He blamed him. He picked
on him.*
prénom m. *Christian name, first name.*
préoccupation f. *preoccupation.*
préoccuper *to absorb one's thought, engross one's
mind, preoccupy.*
Ses affaires le préoccupent. *He's engrossed in
his business.*
se préoccuper *to give one's attention to, see to a
matter, trouble oneself about.*
préparatifs m. pl. *preparations.*
préparation f. *preparation.*
préparer *to prepare, to make ready.*
Faire préparer une ordonnance. *To have a prescription filled.*
se préparer *to get ready.*
Je m'étais préparé à partir. *I had gotten ready
to leave.*
Un orage se prépare. *A storm is gathering (brewing).*
prépondérant adj. *preponderant.*
PRÈS *near,*
Versailles est près de Paris. *Versailles is near
Paris.*
Tout près. *Quite near. Close by.*
De près et de loin. *Near and far.*
A peu près. *Nearly. Almost. About.*
Il y avait à peu près vingt personnes. *There
were about twenty people.*
Il y a près de deux ans. *Nearly two years ago.*
prescription f. *prescription.*
prescrire *to prescribe.*
présence f. *presence, attendance.*
Il l'a dit en ma présence. *He said it in my
presence.*
Je ferai acte de présence. *I'll put in an ap-
pearance.*
présent m. *gift; present (time).*
A présent. *Just now, at present.*
présent adj. *present.*
présentable adj. *presentable.*
présentation f. *presentation.*
Payable à présentation. *Payable on demand.*
Lettre de présentation. *Letter of introduction.*
présenter *to present, offer, introduce; deliver.*
se présenter *to present oneself, appear, occur.*
L'affaire se présente bien. *The business (affair,
deal) sounds very promising.*
Une difficulté s'est présentée. *A difficulty arose.*
Si jamais le cas se présente. *If the case ever
arises (comes up).*
Il s'est présenté chez elle. *He called on her.*
préservation f. *preservation.*
préserver *to preserve.*
présidence f. *presidency, chairmanship.*
président m. *president, chairman.*
présidentiel (présidentielle f.) adj. *presidential.*
présider *to preside.*
présomption f. *presumption.*
présomptueux (présomptueuse f.) adj. *presumptuous.*
PRESQUE *almost, nearly, all but.*
C'est presque fini. *It's almost finished.*

Il a presque réussi. *He almost succeeded.*
Je ne le vois presque jamais. *I hardly ever see
him.*
Je l'ai eu pour presque rien. *I got it for almost
nothing (for a song).*
pressant adj. *pressing, urgent.*
C'est un cas pressant. *It's an urgent case.*
presse f. *haste; crowd; press.*
Il n'y a pas de presse. *There's no hurry.*
La presse quotidienne. *The daily press.*
pressentiment m. *foreboding.*
pressentir *to have a foreboding.*
presser *to squeeze; hasten; hurry.*
Ça ne presse pas. *There's no hurry.*
Je suis très pressé. *I'm in a great hurry.*
C'est une affaire qui presse. *It's an urgent matter.*
Un citron pressé. *Lemonade.*
se presser *to hurry.*
Pressez-vous! *Hurry up!*
pressing m. *(dry) cleaner.*
pression f. *pressure.*
prestige m. *prestige.*
présumer *to presume, suppose.*
prêt m. *loan.*
prêt (à) *ready (to).*
prétendre *to pretend; maintain; aspire to.*
Il prétend que ce n'est pas vrai. *He maintains
that it isn't true.*
Prétendre à faire quelque chose. *To aspire to do
something.*
prétentieux (prétentieuse f.) adj. *pretentious.*
prétention f. *pretention; claim.*
PRÊTER *to lend.*
Pouvez-vous me prêter un livre? *Can you lend
me a book?*
se prêter *to lend itself.*
Cet appartement se prête à nos besoins. *This
apartment is suited to (suits) our needs.*
prétexte m. *pretext, pretense.*
prêtre m. *priest.*
preuve f. *proof, evidence.*
prévaloir *to prevail.*
prévenant adj. *obliging, nice.*
prévenir *to anticipate; notify in advance; forestall,
ward off; warn.*
Prévenir les désirs de quelqu'un. *To anticipate
someone's wishes.*
Prévenez-moi d'avance. *Let me know in advance.*
En cas d'accident, prévenez ma famille. *In case
of accident, notify my family.*
Prévenir une maladie. *To ward off a sickness.*
prévision f. *anticipation; forecast.*
Contre toute prévision. *Contrary to all expectations.*
prévoir *to forecast, foresee, look forward to.*
Il a prévu tout ce qui est arrivé. *He foresaw
everything that happened.*
La réunion prévue pour demain n'aura pas lieu.
*The meeting scheduled for tomorrow will
not take place.*
C'était à prévoir. *That was to be expected.*
prévoyance f. *forethought, precaution.*
prier *to pray, beg.*
Entrez, je vous en prie. *Please come in.*
Puis-je ouvrir la fenêtre?—Je vous en prie. *May
I open the window?—Please do. Of course.*
Il aime se faire prier. *He likes to be coaxed.*
prière f. *prayer, request, petition.*
primaire adj. *primary, elementary.*
prime f. *premium, bonus.*
prime adj. *first, early.*
De prime abord. *At first. At first sight.*

primitif (primitive f.) adj. *primitive.*
prince m. *prince.*
principal m. *principal thing.*
Le principal est de réussir. *The main thing is to
succeed.*
principal (principaux pl.) adj. *principal, chief, head.*
principauté f. *principality.*
principe m. *principle; basis; rule.*
C'est un de ses principes. *It's one of his principles.*
En principe je ne le fais pas. *As a rule I don't do
it.*
PRINTEMPS m. *spring.*
priorité f. *priority.*
pris adj. *caught.*
Se trouver pris. *To be (get) caught.*
prise f. *taking, capture.*
La prise de vue. *Shot (photography).*
La prise en charge. *Taking over (rented car).*
prison f. *prison.*
prisonnier m. *prisoner.*
privation f. *privation, hardship.*
privé adj. *private.*
priver *to deprive.*
Je ne vous en prive pas? *Can you spare it?*
privilège m. *privilege.*
privilégié adj. *privileged.*
PRIX m. *price, cost; prize, reward.*
Il faut à tout prix que nous le fassions. *We have
to do it at any cost.*
Articles de prix. *Expensive goods (merchandise).*
Le prix de rachat. *Resale price.*
Le prix global. *Total price.*
probabilité f. *probability.*
PROBABLE adj. *probable, likely.*
PROBABLEMENT *probably.*
PROBLÈME m. *problem, puzzle.*
procédé m. *process; behavior.*
procéder *to proceed.*
procédure f. *procedure.*
procès m. *lawsuit, trial.*
procession f. *procession.*
procès-verbal m. *(official) report, written report of
proceedings, minutes of a meeting, record (of
evidence).*
PROCHAIN adj. *next, coming.*
La semaine prochaine. *Next week.*
La prochaine fois. *Next time.*
prochainement *shortly, soon.*
proche adj. *near, close at hand, approaching.*
proclamation f. *proclamation.*
proclamer *to proclaim.*
procurer *to procure, obtain, acquire.*
Pouvez-vous me procurer cela? *Can you get
that for me?*
procureur m. *attorney.*
Procureur général. *Attorney General.*
Procureur de la République. *District attorney.*
prodigalité f. *prodigality, lavishness.*
prodige m. *marvel, wonder, prodigy.*
prodigieux (prodigieuse f.) adj. *prodigious, wonderful.*
prodigue adj. *prodigal, lavish.*
prodiguer *to squander, be lavish, give freely.*
production f. *production.*
produire *to produce.*
Quel effet a-t-elle produit sur lui? *What impression did she make on him?*
Cela n'a produit aucun effet. *It had no effect.*
Produire un titre. *To show one's title deeds.*
produit m. *produce; product; production.*
Il importe des produits étrangers. *He imports
foreign products.*

Il est dans les produits alimentaires. *He's in the food business.*
profane *adj. profane.*
profaner *to profane, desecrate, violate, defile.*
professer *to profess.*
professeur *m. and f. teacher, professor.*
profession *f. profession; declaration.*
professionel (professionnelle *f.*) *adj. professional.*
professorat *m. professorship.*
profil *m. profile.*
profit *m. profit, gain, advantage.*
Profits et pertes. *Profit and loss.*
Faites-en votre profit. *Make the best of it.*
profitable *adj. profitable, advantageous.*
profiter *to profit, benefit; grow.*
PROFOND *adj. deep; dark.*
profondément *profoundly, deeply.*
profondeur *f. depth; profundity.*
profusion *f. profusion.*
programme *m. program.*
progrès *m. progress.*
progresser *to progress.*
progressif (progressive *f.*) *adj. progressive.*
prohiber *to prohibit.*
prohibition *f. prohibition.*
proie *f. prey.*
projet *m. project, scheme, design.*
prologue *m. prologue.*
prolonger *to prolong.*
promenade *f. walk, stroll; ride.*
Faire une promenade (à pied, en voiture). *To take (a walk or stroll, a ride).*
promener *to take (out) for a walk.*
Faire promener un chien. *To take a dog out for a walk.*
Il l'a envoyé promener. *He sent him packing.*
se promener *to go for a walk, ride.*
Se promener à bicyclette (à cheval). *To go bicycle (horseback) riding.*
promesse *f. promise.*
promettre *to promise.*
promotion *f. promotion.*
prompt *adj. prompt, quick, sudden, swift.*
Il est très prompt. *He's very prompt.*
Avoir la répartie prompte. *To be quick at repartee.*
Avoir l'esprit prompt. *To have a quick mind. To have a ready wit. To catch on quickly.*
promptement *promptly.*
Il a répondu promptement. *He answered promptly.*
promptitude *f. promptness.*
promulguer *to promulgate, issue.*
pronom *m. pronoun.*
prononcer *to pronounce.*
Comment le prononcez-vous? *How do you pronounce it?*
Est-ce que je le prononce bien? *Do I pronounce it right? Am I pronouncing it right?*
se prononcer *to declare.*
prononciation *f. pronunciation.*
propagande *f. propaganda.*
propager *to propagate, spread.*
prophète *m. prophet.*
prophétie *f. prophecy.*
propice *adj. propitious, favorable.*
proportion *f. proportion; dimensions.*
Toutes proportions gardées. *Due allowance being made.*
propos *m. purpose; talk.*
A propos, est-ce que vous venez avec nous? *By the way, are you coming with us?*
Vous arrivez bien à propos. *You've come just*

in time.
Il est à propos. *It's desirable.*
Mal à propos. *At the wrong time.*
A propos de . . . *Speaking of . . .*
proposer *to propose, offer.*
se proposer *to intend.*
Que se propose-t-elle de faire? *What does she intend to do?*
proposition *f. proposition, offer, proposal.*
PROPRE *adj. own; clean, neat.*
A sa propre surprise. *To his own surprise.*
Ses propres paroles. *His own words. His very words.*
Le sens propre d'un mot. *The right meaning of a word.*
Biens propres. *Personal property.*
Un propre à rien. *A good-for-nothing.*
Pas propre. *Not clean. Dirty.*
propreté *f. cleanliness, neatness.*
propriétaire *m. proprietor, landlord.*
propriété *f. property.*
prose *f. prose.*
prospère *adj. prosperous.*
prospérer *to prosper.*
prospérité *f. prosperity, success.*
protecteur (protectrice *f.*) *noun and adj. protector; protective.*
protection *f. protection.*
protéger *to protect.*
protestant *m. Protestant.*
protestation *f. protestation.*
protester *to protest.*
protocole *m. protocol.*
prouesse *f. prowess.*
prouver *to prove, show.*
provenir *to proceed, result.*
proverbe *m. proverb.*
providence *f. providence.*
province *f. province.*
Une vie de province. *Country life.*
provision *f. provision, stock.*
provisoire *adj. provisional, temporary.*
Un emploi provisoire. *A temporary job.*
provocant *adj. provoking.*
provocation *f. provocation.*
provoquer *to provoke, stir up.*
proximité *f. proximity.*
prudemment *prudently, discreetly.*
prudence *f. prudence.*
prudent *adj. prudent, cautious.*
prune *f. plum.*
pruneau *m. prune.*
prunier *m. plum tree.*
pseudonyme *m. pseudonym.*
psychiatre *m. psychiatrist.*
psychiatrie *f. psychiatry.*
psychologie *f. psychology.*
psychologique *adj. psychological.*
Au moment psychologique. *At the psychological moment.*
psychologue *m. psychologist.*
pu *been able.*
public *m. the public.*
Il l'a fait en public. *He did it publicly.*
publicité *f. publicity, advertising.*
publier *to publish, make public.*
puce *f. flea.*
Le Marché aux Puces. *Flea Market.*
pudeur *f. modesty.*
puéril *adj. puerile, childish.*
PUIS *then, afterwards; besides.*
Nous mangerons d'abord, puis nous irons au théâtre. *First we'll eat, then we'll go to the*

theatre.
Il est venu une fois nous voir, puis on ne l'a plus jamais revu. *He came to see us once and then we never saw him again.*
Et puis? *What's next? What then?*
PUISQUE *since, as.*
Puisqu'il ne vient pas, commençons sans lui. *Since he isn't coming, let's start without him.*
Je n'y suis pas allé puisque vous me l'avez déconseillé. *I didn't go since you had advised me not to.*
puissance *f. power.*
puissant *adj. powerful.*
puits *m. well.*
punir *to punish.*
punition *f. punishment.*
pupille *m. ward, minor in charge of a guardian.*
pupitre *m. desk.*
pur *adj. pure.*
purée *f. purée, mash.*
Purée de pommes de terre. *Mashed potatoes.*
purement *purely.*
pureté *f. purity.*
purge *f. purgative.*
purification *f. purification.*
purifier *to purify.*
putride *adj. putrid.*
pyjama *m. pajamas.*

Q *The seventeenth letter of the alphabet.*

quadruple *m. quadruple, fourfold.*
quai *m. platform (train); wharf; embankment.*
Je vous retrouverai sur le quai (d'une gare). *I'll meet you on the platform (of a railroad station).*
qualifier *to qualify.*
qualité *f. quality.*
QUAND *when.*
Quand viendrez-vous? *When will you come?*
Venez n'importe quand. *Come (at) any time.*
Quand même, vous n'auriez pas dû le faire. *Nevertheless you shouldn't have done it.*
Quand je vous le disais! *Didn't I tell you so!*
QUANT À *as for, as to.*
Quant à moi. *As for me.*
Quant à cela. *As for that.*
QUANTITÉ *f. quantity, abundance.*
QUARANTAINE *f. about forty.*
QUARANTE *noun and adj. forty.*
quarantième *noun and adj. fortieth.*
quart *m. quarter.*
Il est une heure moins le quart. *It's a quarter to one.*
Les trois quarts du temps, il ne fait rien. *Most of the time he does nothing.*
quartier *m. quarter, neighborhood.*
Coupez cette pomme en quartiers. *Cut this apple into quarters.*
J'habite dans ce quartier-ci. *I live in this neighborhood.*
QUATORZE *noun and adj. fourteen.*
QUATORZIÈME *noun and adj. fourteenth.*
QUATRE *noun and adj. four.*
Venez vers les quatre heures. *Come about four o'clock.*
Je demeure à quatre pas d'ici. *I live close by.*
Je me tenais à quatre pour ne pas éclater de rire. *It was all I could do to keep from laughing.*
quatre-vingt-cinq *eighty-five.*
QUATRE-VINGTIÈME *noun and adj. eightieth.*
QUATRE-VINGTS *noun and adj. eighty.*
QUATRIÈME *noun and adj. fourth.*

QUE *that, which.*
Je pense que c'est vrai. *I think that it's true.*
Je pense que non. *I think not.*
Les objets que vous voyez ici lui appartiennent. *The things which you see here belong to him.*
Ce que. *That which, what.*
QUE *than, that, as, what.*
Il est plus grand que sa soeur. *He's taller than his sister.*
Ne . . . que. *Only.*
Elle ne fait que parler. *She does nothing but talk.*
Que c'est ennuyeux! *How boring that is! What a bore!*
Que de monde! *What a crowd!*
Que de richesses! *What riches!*
QUEL (quelle *f.*) *adj. which, which one, what.*
Quel livre voulez-vous? *Which book do you want?*
Quel est son nom? *What's his name?*
Quelle heure est-il? *What time is it?*
Quel que soit le résultat, je le ferai. *Whatever the outcome may be, I'll do it.*
Quel âge avez-vous? *How old are you?*
Quelle est sa nationalité? *What is his nationality?*
Quel luxe! *What (a) luxury!*
QUELCONQUE *adj. any.*
Un livre quelconque. *Any book.*
Il est très quelconque. *He's very ordinary (common).*
C'est très quelconque. *It's very ordinary (common).*
QUELQUE *adj. some, any.*
Quelques amis sont venus hier soir. *Some friends came last night.*
Je l'ai vu il y a quelques jours. *I saw him a few days ago.*
J'ai vu quelque chose d'amusant. *I saw something amusing.*
Quelques-uns. *Some (things, people).*
A quelque chose malheur est bon. *It's an ill wind that blows nobody good.*
Quelque chose de meilleur (de différent). *Something better (different).*
QUELQUEFOIS *sometimes.*
Je le vois quelquefois. *I see him sometimes.*
QUELQUE PART *somewhere.*
QUELQU'UN *someone, somebody.*
querelle *f. quarrel.*
quereller *to quarrel.*
QU'EST-CE QUE *what.*
Qu'est-ce que c'est? *What's this? What is it?*
Qu'est-ce que c'est que cela? *What's that?*
QUESTION *f. question.*
Poser une question. *To ask a question.*
Sortir de la question. *To be beside the point.*
La personne en question. *The person in question.*
Il n'en est pas question. *It's out of the question.*
questionner *to question.*
quête *f. search; collection.*
Faire la quête. *To take up a collection (church).*
queue *f. tail; line.*
Il fait la queue. *He's waiting in line. He's waiting for his turn.*
A la queue leu leu. *One behind the other.*
Une histoire sans queue ni tête. *A senseless, disconnected story.*
Un piano à queue. *A grand piano.*
QUI *who, whom, which, that.*
Qui est-ce? *Who is he? Who is it?*
Qui désirez-vous voir? *Whom do you want to see?*

A qui est-ce? *Whose is this? To whom does this belong?*
A qui le tour? *Whose turn is it?*
quiconque *whoever.*
Quiconque veut venir. *Whoever wants to come.*
quille *f. ninepin.*
quincaillerie *f. hardware store.*
QUINZAINE *f. about fifteen.*
Dans une quinzaine. *In two weeks ("fifteen days").*
Une quinzaine (d'années). *About fifteen (years).*
QUINZE *noun and adj. fifteen.*
D'aujourd'hui en quinze. *Two weeks from today.*
QUINZIÈME *noun and adj. fifteenth.*
quittance *f. receipt.*
quitte *adj. free, out of debt; to be quits with.*
Etre quitte de dettes. *To be out of debt.*
Il en est quitte pour la peur. *He escaped with a good fright.*
Il en est quitte à bon marché. *He got off cheaply.*
Il est quitte envers vous. *He owes you nothing. He's even with you.*
QUITTER *to leave.*
Quitter la chambre. *To leave the room.*
A quelle heure quittez-vous votre travail? *At what time do you leave work?*
Il a quitté Paris. *He left Paris.*
Il a quitté prise. *He let go.*
Quitter ses habits. *To take off one's clothes.*
Ne le quittez pas des yeux. *Keep your eyes on him.*
Ne quittez pas. *Hold on, just a moment (telephone).*
qui-vive *m. alert.*
Il est sur le qui-vive. *He's on the alert.*
QUOI *what, which.*
Quoi? Vous dites? *What did you say?*
A quoi pensez-vous? *What are you thinking about?*
A propos de quoi? *What's it in regard to? What's it about?*
Avez-vous de quoi écrire? *Do you have anything to write with?*
N'importe quoi. *No matter what. Anything.*
Merci. —Il n'y a pas de quoi. *Thanks. —Not at all.*
En quoi pourrais-je vous servir? *What can I do for you?*
En quoi puis-je vous être utile? *What can I do for you?*
QUOIQUE *although, though.*
Je serai là quoique je puisse être en retard. *I'll be there although I may be a little late.*
Quoiqu'il en soit. *Be that as it may.*
quotidien (quotidienne *f.*) *adj. daily.*
quotidien *m. daily newspaper.*

R *The eighteenth letter of the alphabet.*

rabâcher *to repeat over and over again, keep harping on.*
rabais *m. reduction in price, discount.*
Il l'a eu au rabais. *He got it at a reduced price.*
rabaisser *to lower, reduce.*
se rabaisser *to lower oneself.*
rabat-joie *m. wet blanket.*
rabattre *to beat down; reduce.*
Il lui faudra en rabattre. *He'll have to lower his pretentions (come down a peg or two).*
Il n'en rabattra pas un sou. *He won't take a cent off. He won't reduce his price a cent.*

se rabattre *to fall back on.*
rabbin *m. rabbi.*
raccommodage *m. darning.*
raccommoder *to darn, repair; reconcile.*
Mes chaussettes ont besoin d'être raccommodées. *My socks need darning.*
se raccommoder *to make up, settle one's differences.*
raccourci *m. short cut.*
raccourcir *to shorten.*
Je viens de raccourcir ma nouvelle robe. *I just shortened my new dress.*
Les jours raccourcissent. *The days are growing shorter.*
Son tricot a raccourci. *His sweater shrank.*
raccrocher *to hang up again.*
Raccrochez et refaites votre numéro. *Hang up and dial again.*
se raccrocher *to clutch, hold.*
Elle se raccroche toujours à cette espérance. *She still clings to that hope.*
race *f. race; breed.*
rachat *m. buying back.*
Le prix de rachat. *Resale price.*
racheter *to buy back, redeem.*
racine *f. root, origin.*
râclée *f. thrashing, licking.*
râcler *to scrape.*
racontar *m. idle tale.*
RACONTER *to tell, relate.*
Raconter une histoire. *To tell a story.*
Qu'est-ce que vous racontez là? *What are you talking about?*
C'est ce qu'on raconte. *That's what people say.*
radeau *m. raft.*
radiateur *m. radiator.*
radieux (radieuse *f.*) *adj. radiant, beaming, shining.*
radio *f. radio.*
radiodiffuser *to broadcast.*
radiographie *f. X-ray picture.*
radiographier *to X ray.*
radis *m. radish.*
radotage *m. twaddle, nonsense.*
radoter *to talk nonsense.*
se radoucir *to grow milder.*
Le temps a l'air de s'être radouci. *The weather seems to have become milder.*
rafale *f. squall.*
raffermir *to strengthen, fortify.*
se raffermir *to grow stronger, improve.*
Sa santé se raffermit de jour en jour. *Her health is improving every day.*
raffiné *adj. refined, subtle.*
raffiner *to refine.*
Raffiner du sucre. *To refine sugar.*
Vous raffinez! *You're too subtle!*
raffoler *to be very fond of.*
Il en raffole. *He's crazy about it.*
rafler *to sweep off, carry away.*
rafraîchir *to refresh, cool, freshen.*
Rafraîchir la mémoire de quelqu'un. *To refresh someone's memory.*
se rafraîchir *to get cooler.*
Le temps se rafraîchit. *It's getting cooler.*
rafraîchissement *m. refreshment.*
rage *f. rage.*
Il est fou de rage. *He's very angry. He's in a rage.*
Accès de rage. *Fit of madness.*
J'ai une violente rage de dents. *I have a terrible toothache.*
Cela fait rage. *It's quite the rage.*
rager *to rage.*
ragoût *m. stew.*

raide *adj. stiff, tight.*
Des cheveux raides. *Straight hair.*
Ça c'est un peu raide! *That's a little too much!*
raideur *f. stiffness.*
se raidir *to stiffen, become stiff.*
raie *f. line, stripe; part (in hair).*
rail *m. rail.*
railler *to mock, make fun of.*
raillerie *f. banter.*
raisin *m. grapes.*
Des raisins secs. *Raisins.*
RAISON *f. reason.*
Les raisons qu'il a données ne tiennent pas debout. *The reasons he gave don't make sense.*
Sans rime ni raison. *Without cause. Without rhyme or reason.*
Il lui a donné raison. *He backed him up. He sided with him. He said he was right.*
A raison de. *At the rate of.*
Il est revenu à la raison. *He came to his senses.*
Avez-vous perdu votre raison? *Are you out of your mind?*
Avoir raison. *To be right.*
raisonnable *adj. reasonable.*
Il m'a fait des prix raisonnables. *He gave me a fair price. The prices he asked were reasonable.*
raisonnement *m. reasoning, reason.*
Son raisonnement est sain. *His argument (reasoning) is sound.*
Pas de raisonnement! *Don't argue!*
raisonner *to argue; reason.*
Raisonnez moins et travaillez davantage. *Argue less and work more.*
Elle raisonne comme un enfant. *She reasons like a child.*
rajeunir *to grow young again.*
Vous rajeunissez tous les jours. *You look younger every day.*
Cette robe vous rajeunit. *That dress makes you look younger.*
rajustement *m. readjustment.*
ralentir *to slow down.*
Ralentissez, vous roulez trop vite. *Slow down, you're going too fast.*
"Ralentir!" *"Drive slowly!" "Slow down!"*
rallonge *f. extension-leaf.*
rallonger *to lengthen.*
rallumer *to relight; revive.*
ramasser *to gather up, collect, pick up.*
Ramassez vos papiers. *Pick up (collect) your papers.*
Il ramassa sa monnaie et partit. *He picked up his money and left.*
rame *f. oar.*
rameau *m. (rameaux pl.) twig.*
ramener *to bring back, bring home, restore.*
Il l'a ramené chez lui. *He brought him (her) back to his house.*
Il a ramené sa famille de la campagne. *He brought his family back from the country.*
Pouvez-vous me ramener chez moi? *Can you take me home?*
On l'a ramené à la vie. *They revived him.*
ramer *to row.*
ramification *f. ramification.*
ramifier *to ramify, branch out.*
se ramollir *to soften.*
rampe *f. banister.*
ramper *to crawl, creep; crouch.*
rance *adj. rancid.*
rancir *to grow rancid.*

rancœur *f. rancor, bitterness.*
Il lui tient rancœur. *He bears him a grudge. He has a grudge against him.*
rançon *f. ransom.*
rançonner *to set a ransom; cheat, exploit.*
On vous a rançonné dans cet hôtel-là. *They cheated you in that hotel.*
rancune *f. spite, grudge.*
Il lui en garde rancune. *He's bearing him a grudge. He has a grudge against him.*
Sans rancune! *No hard feelings! Let bygones be bygones!*
Par rancune. *Out of spite.*
rang *m. row, line, rank.*
Nous étions assis au premier rang. *We sat in the first row.*
Il a le rang de ministre. *He has the rank of minister.*
Tenir le premier rang. *To hold first place.*
Tenir son rang. *To live up to one's position.*
rangée *f. row, line.*
ranger *to put in order, arrange.*
Rangez vos livres par rang de taille. *Arrange your books by size.*
Faites ranger les curieux. *Keep (hold) the crowd back.*
se ranger *to side with; fall in line.*
Ils se rangèrent tous en ligne. *They all fell into line. They all lined up.*
Rangez-vous! *Get out of the way! Make way!*
Elle se rangea à mon avis. *She sided with me.*
ranimer *to revive; liven up.*
rapatriement *m. repatriation.*
rapatrier *to repatriate.*
râpé *adj. grated; shabby.*
Ses vêtements sont tout râpés. *His clothes are shabby.*
rapetisser *to reduce, shrink.*
rapide *m. express train.*
rapide *adj. rapid.*
rapidité *f. swiftness, rapidity.*
rappel *m. recall; repeal.*
rappeler *to recall, call back (telephone).*
L'ambassadeur a été rappelé. *The ambassador was recalled.*
Rappelez-moi à son bon souvenir. *Give him my regards. Remember me to him.*
SE RAPPELER *to remember, recollect.*
Je ne me le rappelle pas. *I don't recall it.*
Il se les rappelle. *He remembers them.*
Je me rappelle votre nom. *I remember your name.*
rapport *m. relation; report.*
Voulez-vous me faire un rapport sur la question? *Will you give me a report on the matter?*
Sous ce rapport, nous ne sommes pas d'accord. *In this respect we don't agree.*
Etre en mauvais rapports avec quelqu'un. *To be on bad terms with someone.*
rapporter *to bring back.*
Rapportez un pain. *Bring back a loaf of bread.*
Ne manquez pas de me rapporter les livres. *Be sure to return these books to me.*
Tout cela ne lui a rapporté que des ennuis. *All it brought him was a lot of trouble.*
Ça ne rapporte rien. *It doesn't pay.*
Ce placement rapporte trois pour cent. *This investment bears 3 percent interest.*
se rapporter *to refer.*
Cela se rapporte à autre chose. *That refers to something else.*
Je m'en rapporte à vous. *I leave it to you. I*

take your word for it.
RAPPROCHER *to bring nearer, bring together.*
Rapprochez votre chaise de la table. *Move your chair nearer (to) the table.*
raquette *f. racket.*
Une raquette de tennis. *A tennis racket.*
rare *adj. rare.*
Un livre rare. *A rare book.*
Vous devenez rare! *You're (you've become) quite a stranger!*
rarement *rarely.*
ras *adj. close-cropped, close-shaven, smooth, bare, flat.*
Faire table rase. *To make a clean sweep.*
Ils étaient en rase campagne. *They were in the open country.*
raser *to shave.*
Se faire raser. *To have oneself shaved, get a shave.*
se raser *to shave oneself.*
rasoir *m. razor.*
La lame de rasoir. *Razor blade.*
se rassasier *to eat one's fill.*
rassemblement *m. gathering, assembly, crowd.*
se rassembler *to get together, assemble, gather.*
se rasseoir *to sit down again.*
rassis *adj. stale.*
rassurer *to reassure.*
se rassurer *to regain one's self-assurance, feel reassured.*
rat *m. rat.*
râtelier *m. a set of false teeth.*
rater *to fail; miss.*
Il a raté son examen. *He flunked his exam.*
Il s'en est fallu de peu que je rate le train. *I came very close to missing the train. I almost missed the train.*
rattacher *to tie up again.*
se rattacher *to join, adhere to.*
rattraper *to catch up, overtake.*
J'ai dû courir pour le rattraper. *I had to run to catch up with him.*
Allez-y, je vous rattraperai. *Go (on) ahead, I'll catch up to you.*
Il va falloir rattraper le temps perdu. *You'll have to make up for lost time.*
se rattraper *to recover.*
rature *f. erasing, crossing out, scratching out.*
raturer *to cross out, scratch out.*
rauque *adj. harsh, hoarse.*
ravage *m. ravage, havoc.*
ravager *to ravage, spoil, ruin.*
L'orage a ravagé la région. *The storm ravaged the region.*
ravaler *to swallow again.*
Il dut ravaler ses mots. *He had to retract his words.*
ravir *to ravish, carry off; enrapture, delight.*
Je suis ravi de vous voir. *I'm delighted to see you.*
A ravir. *Admirably. Wonderfully well.*
Jouer du piano à ravir. *To play the piano very well.*
ravissant *adj. delightful, lovely.*
Elle est ravissante. *She's lovely.*
rayer *to cross out.*
Rayez ce mot. *Cross this word out.*
rayon *m. ray; radius; department (of a store); shelf.*
Des rayons de soleil. *Sunbeams.*
Où se trouve le rayon des chemises? *Where is the shirt department?*
rayonner *to radiate, shine.*
rayure *f. stripe.*

réaction f. reaction.
réagir to react.
réalisation f. realization.
réaliser to realize, fulfill.
réaliste adj. realistic.
réalité f. reality.
En réalité. In reality. As a matter of fact.
rebelle adj. rebellious.
se rebeller to rebel.
rébellion f. rebellion.
rebord m. edge, brim.
rebours m. wrong way.
A rebours. Against the grain. The wrong way. Backwards.
Au rebours de ce que j'ai dit. Contrary to what I said.
Il prend tout à rebours. He misconstrues everything.
reboutonner to rebutton.
rebrousser to retrace.
Il a rebroussé chemin. He retraced his steps.
rebut m. rebuff.
recacheter to seal again.
récemment lately.
récent adj. recent.
récepteur m. telephone receiver.
réception f. reception; hotel (reception) desk.
Il nous ont fait bonne réception. They gave us a warm welcome (reception).
Accuser réception d'une lettre. To acknowledge receipt of a letter.
recette f. receipt, return; recipe.
Les recettes du jour. The day's receipts. The money taken in during the day.
La pièce fait recette. The play is drawing well. The play is a box-office success.
Le garçon de recettes est venu encaisser la facture. The collector came to collect the bill.
receveur m. receiver; collector; conductor (bus).
RECEVOIR to receive.
Recevoir des ordres. To receive orders.
Recevoir un cadeau. To receive a present.
Nous avons bien reçu votre lettre. We are in receipt of your letter.
Recevoir quelqu'un à bras ouverts. To welcome someone with open arms.
Recevoir un mauvais accueil. To receive a cold welcome.
Il reçoivent beaucoup. They do a good deal of entertaining. They entertain a lot.
Se faire recevoir avocat. To be called to the bar.
rechange m. change.
Une roue de rechange. A spare wheel.
La pièce de rechange. Spare part.
Le pneu de rechange. Spare tire.
recharger to reload.
Recharger un appareil. To reload a camera.
réchaud m. portable stove.
réchauffer to warm up again; revive.
recherche f. research, investigation; studied elegance.
Des recherches scientifiques. Scientific research.
Mis avec recherche. Dressed with meticulous care.
recherché adj. in demand; select; mannered (painting).
rechercher to seek again, look for again; seek after.
Rechercher un mot dans le dictionnaire. To look up a word in the dictionary.
Tout le monde le recherche. He's very much sought after. People like his company.
rechute f. relapse.
réciproque adj. reciprocal, mutual.

récit m. tale; recital, narration.
Faites-moi le récit de ce qui s'est passé. Give me an account of what took place (happened).
réciter to recite, tell, relate.
réclamation f. claim, complaint, protest.
réclame f. advertisement, publicity.
réclamer to claim, require.
Il en réclame la moitié. He claims half of it.
Réclamer des soins. To require care.
récolte f. harvest, crop.
récolter to harvest.
recommandation f. recommendation, advice.
Une lettre de recommandation. A letter of recommendation.
J'ai suivi ses recommandations. I followed his advice.
recommander to recommend, register.
Faites recommander cette lettre. Have this letter registered. Register this letter.
recommencer to start again.
récompense f. reward; recompense.
récompenser to reward.
réconciliation f. reconciliation.
réconcilier to reconcile.
reconduire to drive back; take home.
réconfort m. comfort, relief.
réconforter to comfort, help.
reconnaissance f. recognition; gratitude; reconnaissance.
Ils ont pour vous beaucoup de reconnaissance. They're very grateful to you.
Il lui a témoigné de la reconnaissance. He showed his gratitude to him.
Avec reconnaissance. Gratefully. Thankfully. With thanks.
reconnaissant adj. grateful, thankful.
Je vous suis reconnaissant de m'avoir aidé. I'm very grateful to you for having helped me.
Je vous serais très reconnaissant si vous pouviez le faire. I would be very grateful to you if you could do it.
reconnaître to recognize.
Je l'ai reconnu de suite. I recognized him right away.
Je vous reconnais bien là. That's just typical of you. It's (that's) just like you.
se reconnaître to know (recognize) each other.
Ils ne se sont pas reconnus. They didn't recognize one another.
Je ne m'y reconnais plus. I'm completely at a loss. I'm completely confused.
reconsidérer to reconsider.
record m. record.
Il détient le record. He holds the record.
se recoucher to go to bed again.
recoudre to sew again, sew back on.
recourir to run again; turn to, resort to.
recours m. recourse.
J'ai recours à vous pour . . . I am applying to you for . . .
recouvrir to cover over, recover.
Recouvert (de). Upholstered (with, in).
récréation f. recreation, amusement; pastime.
se récrier to cry out.
récrimination f. recrimination.
récrire to rewrite.
recrue f. recruit.
rectangle m. rectangle.
rectifier to rectify, correct.
rectification f. adjustment.
reçu m. receipt.
Voilà votre reçu. Here's your receipt.

Au reçu de votre lettre. Upon receipt of your letter.
recueil m. collection.
se recueillir to collect oneself.
reculer to draw back, go backwards; put off; delay.
(à) reculons backwards.
Marcher à reculons. To walk backwards.
récupérer to recover.
rédacteur m. staff member of newspaper or magazine.
Le rédacteur en chef. The editor.
Le rédacteur-gérant. The managing editor.
rédaction f. writing; editing; editorial staff.
rédiger to draw up, write; edit.
Cet article a été rédigé par le rédacteur en chef. This article was written by the editor.
redire to say again.
redoubler redouble, increase.
Redoubler d'efforts. To redouble one's efforts.
redoutable adj. redoubtable, terrible, dreadful.
redouter to dread, fear.
redresser to straighten out, put to rights, reform.
réduction f. reduction.
réduire to reduce.
Edition réduite. Abridged edition.
réel (réelle f.) adj. real.
réellement really.
refaire to do over.
Ça doit être refait. It must be done over. That has to be redone.
Vous avez été refait. You were tricked.
Refaire le chemin. To start over again, retrace one's steps.
référence f. reference.
Donner des références. To give references.
réfléchir to reflect.
Réfléchissez-y. Think it over.
C'est tout réfléchi! My mind is made up! I've decided!
réflexion f. reflection.
réforme f. reform.
réformer to reform.
refouler to drive back.
Il a été refoulé. He was driven back.
Elle a refoulé ses larmes. She checked her tears.
refrain m. refrain.
refroidir to cool; to discourage.
Dépêchez-vous, le dîner va se refroidir. Hurry up, the food's getting cold.
refuge m. refuge, shelter.
se réfugier to seek refuge, seek shelter.
refus m. refusal, denial.
refuser to refuse.
Il a refusé de le voir. He refused to see him.
Il a été refusé à l'examen. He failed the examination.
regagner to regain.
régal m. feast, treat.
Quel régal! How delicious (of food)!
se régaler to treat oneself, give oneself a treat.
regard m. look, glance.
Attirer tous les regards. To attract attention.
Suivre du regard. To follow with one's eyes.
Au regard de. In comparison with. With regard to.
REGARDER to look at.
Regardez ça. Look at that.
Il ne regarde pas à l'argent. Money is no object to him.
Il ne regarde que ses intérêts. He cares only about his own interest.
Cela ne me regarde pas. That doesn't concern me.
Regarde donc! Just look!

régime *m. diet; administration.*
  Elle suit un régime. *She's on a diet.*
  Le régime de ce pays. *The administration of this country.*
région *f. region.*
règle *f. rule; ruler.*
  Il est de règle de. *It's customary to.*
  En règle générale. *As a general rule.*
  En règle. *In order, O.K.*
règlement *m. ruling, regulation.*
réglementaire *adj. according to regulation, correct.*
régler *to rule (paper); arrange, adjust.*
  Une affaire réglée. *A matter that has been settled.*
  Régler un compte. *To settle an account.*
  Régler une montre. *To set a watch.*
se régler *to be guided by.*
  Je me réglerai sur lui. *I'll follow his example. I'll go (I'll be guided) by what he says.*
règne *m. reign.*
régner *to reign, prevail.*
regret *m. regret, sorrow.*
  A mon grand regret. *To my great regret. Much to my regret.*
  A regret. *With regret.*
  J'en suis au regret. *I'm sorry.*
regrettable *adj. deplorable, regrettable.*
regretter *to regret, be sorry.*
  Je regrette de ne pouvoir accepter. *I'm sorry I can't accept.*
régularité *f. regularity.*
régulier (régulière *f.*) *adj. regular.*
rehausser *to raise up, heighten, enhance.*
rein *m. kidney.*
reine *f. queen.*
réinstaller *to reinstall, re-establish.*
réintégrer *to reinstate, restore.*
rejeter *to reject, throw back.*
  Il a rejeté son offre. *He rejected his offer.*
  Il a rejeté la faute sur lui. *He put the blame on him.*
rejoindre *to join again, reunite.*
se réjouir *to rejoice.*
  Je me réjouis de vous revoir. *I'm very glad to see you again.*
relâche *m. respite.*
  Travailler sans relâche. *To work without stopping.*
  Il y a relâche ce soir. *There's no performance tonight.*
relâcher *to loosen.*
relatif (relative *f.*) *adj. relative.*
relation *f. relation, acquaintance.*
  Il a de belles relations. *He has good connections.*
reléguer *to relegate.*
relever *to raise again; point out.*
  Il relève de maladie. *He's just getting over his illness.*
  Il a relevé des fautes. *He pointed out some mistakes.*
se relever *to get up again, rise again.*
relier *to bind.*
religion *f. religion.*
religieux (religieuse *f.*) *adj. religious.*
relire *to read again, reread.*
reliure *f. binding.*
reluire *to shine, be bright.*
remarquable *adj. remarkable.*
remarque *f. remark, notice.*
  Ligne de remarque. *Noteworthy.*
  Une remarque piquante. *A stinging remark.*
remarquer *to remark; notice.*

Je n'avais pas remarqué. *I hadn't noticed. I didn't notice.*
Partout où il va, il se fait remarquer. *Wherever he goes he makes himself conspicuous (attracts attention).*
remboursable *adj. refundable.*
rembourser *to repay, refund.*
remède *m. remedy; cure.*
remédier *to remedy.*
remerciement *m. thanks.*
  Une lettre de remerciement. *A letter of thanks. A thank-you note.*
remercier *to thank; dismiss.*
  Je vous en remercie. *Thanks. Thank you (for it).*
  Je vous remercie beaucoup. *Thanks a lot.*
  Je vous remercie de votre amabilité. *Thank you for your kindness.*
remettre *to put back, put back again, put on again.*
  Il a remis son chapeau sur la tête. *He put his hat on again.*
  L'air de la mer l'a remis complètement. *The sea air restored him completely.*
  Remettez cette lettre en mains propres. *Deliver this letter to the addressee only.*
  Il l'a remis à sa place. *He put him in his place. He took him down a peg or two.*
se remettre *to start again, recover.*
  Se remettre à. *To start again. To set about again.*
  Il s'est remis au travail. *He started to work again.*
  Se remettre d'une maladie. *To recover from an illness.*
  Il a eu une rechute, il a dû se remettre au lit. *He had a relapse and had to go back to bed again.*
  Il se remet à sa place. *He's going back to his seat.*
  Je m'en remets à vous. *I leave it to you.*
  Remettez-vous-en à moi. *Leave it to me.*
remise *f. putting back.*
  Faire une remise en état. *To put into shape, overhaul (car).*
remonter *to go up again.*
  Remonter à sa chambre. *To go up to one's room again.*
remords *m. remorse.*
remplacer *to replace, substitute.*
remplir *to fill up; fulfill; fill out (form).*
  Remplir d'allégresse. *To cheer up. To make happy. ("To fill with joy.")*
  Remplir son devoir. *To fulfill one's duty.*
remporter *to take back; obtain.*
  Il a remporté le premier prix. *He carried off the first prize.*
  Remporter la victoire. *To win a victory.*
remue-ménage *m. bustle.*
remuer *to move, stir.*
  Ne remuez pas tant. *Don't move around so much.*
  Remuer ciel et terre. *To move heaven and earth.*
renard *m. fox.*
rencontre *f. meeting, encounter.*
RENCONTRER *to meet, come across.*
  Je l'ai rencontré il y a à peu près dix jours. *I met him about ten days ago.*
  Il a rencontré beaucoup de difficultés. *He encountered many difficulties.·*
se rencontrer *to meet; be found.*
  Nous nous rencontrons ce soir. *We're meeting tonight. We'll meet tonight.*
rendement *m. output.*

RENDEZ-VOUS *m. appointment.*
  Prenons rendez-vous pour demain matin. *Let's make an appointment for tomorrow morning.*
  Fixer un rendez-vous. *To make an appointment, date.*
se rendormir *to go to sleep again.*
RENDRE *to give back, return.*
  Rendre un livre. *To return a book.*
  Rendre de l'argent. *To pay back money.*
  Rendre visite à quelqu'un. *To return someone's call.*
  Rendre la monnaie d'une pièce d'un franc. *To give change for a franc.*
  Rendre service à quelqu'un. *To do someone a favor.*
  Vous m'avez rendu un grand service. *You've done me a great service (favor).*
  La lettre l'a rendue heureuse. *The letter made her happy.*
se rendre *to surrender, yield; go (to a place).*
  L'ennemi s'est rendu. *The enemy surrendered.*
  Il se rend ridicule. *He's making himself ridiculous.*
  Se rendre compte de quelque chose. *To realize (understand) something.*
  Il s'y est rendu hier soir. *He went there last night.*
renfermer *to lock up again; contain.*
renfort *m. reinforcement.*
renier *to disown.*
renifler *to sniffle.*
renom *m. reputation.*
  Un avocat de grand renom. *A very well-known lawyer.*
renommée *f. fame.*
renoncer *to renounce.*
renouveler *to renew.*
RENSEIGNEMENT *m. (piece of) information; pl. information.*
  Ce renseignement m'a été très utile. *This piece of information was very useful to me.*
  Fournir des renseignements sur quelque chose. *To give (furnish) information about something.*
  Le service des renseignements. *Information (telephone).*
  Prendre des renseignements. *To get information.*
renseigner *to give information.*
se renseigner *to make inquiries.*
rente *f. yearly income.*
rentrée *f. reentering, reopening.*
RENTRER *to go in, go or come home.*
  Il est l'heure de rentrer. *It's time to go home.*
  Ils rentrèrent à la maison. *They returned home.*
  Rentrer dans les bonnes grâces de quelqu'un. *To regain favor with someone. To get into someone's good graces again.*
  Il eut envie de rentrer sous terre. *He was terribly embarrassed.*
renverse *f. reversal.*
  Il tomba à la renverse. *He fell on his back.*
renverser *to overthrow; overturn, upset, knock down.*
renvoyer *to return, send back; dismiss, fire.*
  Si ce livre ne vous plaît pas, renvoyez-le moi. *If you don't like the book, send it back to me.*
  Il a été renvoyé. *He was fired.*
répandre *to pour, spill; spread.*
  Répandre des larmes. *To shed tears.*
  Elle répandit la nouvelle. *She spread the news.*

se répandre *to spread.*

L'eau se répandit sur la table. *The water spread (ran) all over the table.*

Il se répandit en excuses. *He apologized profusely.*

Le bruit se répand que. *A rumor is being spread that. It's being rumored that.*

réparation *f. repair; reparation.*

réparer *to repair, mend.*

L'auto vient d'être réparée. *The car has just been repaired.*

Réparer les dégâts. *To make good the damage.*

Faire réparer. *To have (something) repaired, fixed.*

répartie *f. repartee.*

repas *m. meal.*

Faire des repas légers. *To take light meals.*

REPASSER *to pass again, call again; iron.*

Quand repassera-t-il? *When will he call again (stop by again)?*

Repassez cette chemise, je vous prie. *Will you please iron this shirt?*

Une planche à repasser. *An ironing board.*

Faire repasser. *To have (something) ironed.*

repentir *m. remorse.*

se repentir *to repent.*

RÉPÉTER *to repeat; rehearse.*

Veuillez répéter ce que vous avez dit. *Will you please repeat what you said?*

répétition *f. repetition.*

répit *m. respite.*

replier *to fold again.*

réplique *f. retort, repartee.*

Argument sans réplique. *Unanswerable argument.*

Il lui donna la réplique. *He gave him the cue.*

Obéir sans réplique. *To obey without a word.*

répliquer *to retort, answer back.*

Ne répliquez pas! *Don't answer back!*

RÉPONDRE *to answer.*

Il n'a rien répondu. *He didn't answer.*

Cela ne répond pas à nos besoins. *That doesn't answer our needs.*

Je lui réponds. *I answer him, her.*

J'y réponds. *I answer it.*

RÉPONSE *f. answer, reply.*

REPOS *m. rest, quiet, peace.*

Il vous faut prendre du repos. *You need some rest.*

Mettez-vous l'esprit en repos. *Set your mind at rest.*

C'est un placement de tout repos. *It's a safe investment.*

reposer *to put back again; rest, repose.*

Ici repose. *Here lies.*

se reposer *to rest; rely on.*

repousser *to push away, repulse, drive back; reject.*

reprendre *to take back, get back; resume.*

Reprenons à partir de la page 10. *Let's start again on page 10.*

On ne m'y reprendra plus, croyez bien. *You can be sure they won't catch me at it again.*

Reprendre la parole. *To begin talking again.*

Reprenez vos places. *Return to your seats.*

représaille *f. reprisal.*

représentant *m. representative, delegate.*

REPRÉSENTATION *f. exhibition; performance.*

La représentation commence à trois heures de l'après-midi. *The performance begins at 3 P.M.*

J'ai la représentation de cette maison. *I have the agency for this firm. I represent this firm.*

représenter *to represent.*

se représenter *to imagine.*

Représentez-vous ma surprise! *Imagine my surprise!*

réprimande *f. rebuke.*

réprimander *to rebuke.*

réprimer *to repress.*

REPRISE *f. recapture; resumption; pickup (of rented car).*

A deux reprises. *Twice.*

A plusieurs reprises. *Several times. Over and over again. Many times.*

réprobateur (réprobatrice *f.*) *adj. reproachful.*

reproche *m. reproach.*

reprocher *to reproach.*

se reprocher *to reproach oneself.*

république *f. republic.*

répugnance *f. repugnance.*

répugner *to be repugnant, repulsive.*

réputation *f. reputation, fame, character.*

requête *f. request.*

réquisition *f. requisition.*

rescousse *f. rescue.*

Venir à la rescousse. *To come to the rescue.*

réseau *m. net; system.*

Le réseau de chemins de fer. *The railway system.*

réservation *f. reservation.*

réserve *f. reserve, reservation.*

RÉSERVER *to reserve.*

Il faudra réserver vos chambres bien à l'avance. *You'll have to reserve your rooms well in advance.*

Tous droits réservés. *All rights reserved.*

Se faire réserver une heure. *To make an appointment (hairdresser, etc.).*

réservoir *m. tank (gasoline).*

résidence *f. residence.*

résider *to reside.*

résignation *f. resignation.*

se résigner *to be resigned, resign oneself.*

résistance *f. resistance, opposition.*

Faire résistance. *To offer resistance.*

Eprouver une résistance. *To meet with resistance.*

Le ragoût est la pièce de résistance. *The main dish is the stew.*

résister *to resist.*

résolu *adj. resolute, determined.*

résolution *f. resolution.*

résonner *to resound, ring.*

résoudre *to resolve, solve.*

Résoudre un problème. *To solve a problem.*

Il a résolu de partir. *He resolved (made up his mind) to leave.*

Cela ne résout pas la question. *That doesn't solve the problem.*

RESPECT *m. respect.*

Tenir en respect. *To respect. To hold in respect.*

Manquer de respect à quelqu'un. *To lack respect for someone.*

Respect de soi. *Self-respect.*

Veuillez bien présenter mes respects à madame votre mère. *Please give my regards to your mother.*

respecter *to respect.*

respectueux (respectueuse *f.*) *adj. respectful, deferential.*

respiration *f. respiration, breathing.*

respirer *to breathe.*

resplendir *to shine, glitter.*

resplendissant *adj. resplendent, shining.*

responsabilité *f. responsibility.*

responsable *adj. responsible, answerable.*

ressemblance *f. likeness.*

ressembler *to be like, look like.*

Cela y ressemble beaucoup. *It's very much like it. It resembles it a lot.*

se ressembler *to look alike.*

Ils se ressemblent comme deux gouttes d'eau. *They're as alike as two peas in a pod. They resemble each other like two drops of water.*

Qui se ressemble s'assemble. *Birds of a feather flock together.*

ressentiment *m. resentment.*

ressentir *to feel.*

ressort *m. spring; elasticity; resort.*

ressortir *to bring out.*

Faire ressortir le sens d'une phrase. *To bring out the meaning of a sentence.*

ressource *f. resource, expedient; pl. means.*

C'est un homme de ressources. *He's a resourceful man.*

En dernière ressource je le lui demanderai. *I'll ask him as a last resort.*

restant *adj. remaining.*

La poste restante. *General delivery.*

restaurant *m. restaurant.*

RESTE *m. remains, rest.*

Le reste de la famille. *The rest of the family.*

Le reste de la soirée. *The rest of the evening.*

Du reste. *Besides. Moreover.*

RESTER *to remain, stay.*

Je resterai là quelques jours. *I'll stay there a few days.*

Il nous reste encore quelques sous. *We still have a few pennies left.*

restriction *f. restriction.*

résultat *m. result, consequence.*

résulter *to result.*

Qu'en est-il résulté? *What was the outcome? What was the result?*

résumé *m. summary, synopsis.*

résumer *to sum up, recapitulate.*

Résumons. *Let's sum up.*

Voilà toute l'affaire résumée en un mot. *That's the whole thing in a nutshell.*

rétablir *to re-establish, restore.*

RETARD *m. delay, slowness.*

Je suis en retard. *I'm late.*

retarder *to delay, be slow.*

Ma montre retarde de vingt minutes. *My watch is twenty minutes slow.*

RETENIR *to keep back, hold back; retain, reserve.*

Retenez-le. *Hold him back.*

Retenir sa colère. *To restrain (curb) one's anger.*

Elle ne retient rien. *She can't remember anything.*

Qu'est-ce qui vous retient? *What's keeping you?*

J'ai retenu deux places pour ce soir. *I reserved two seats for this evening.*

retentir *to resound.*

retenue *f. reserve, moderation, caution, restraint.*

retirer *to draw back; retract.*

J'ai retiré mon argent. *I drew out my money.*

Retirer ses paroles. *To retract one's words.*

retomber *to fall again, have a relapse.*

retouche *f. alteration.*

RETOUR *m. return.*

Il est de retour. *He's back. He returned.*

Un billet d'aller et retour. *A round-trip ticket.*

Je vous répondrai par retour de courrier. *I'll answer you by return mail.*

Les frais de retour. *Charge for returning (rented car).*

retourner *to turn again, turn back, return.*
  Il est retourné en arrière. *He turned back. He went back. He returned.*
  Retourner sur ses pas. *To retrace one's steps.*
  Je vous retourne votre livre. *I'm returning your book.*
se retourner *to turn around.*
  Je n'ai même pas eu le temps de me retourner. *I didn't even have time to look around.*
retraite *f. retreat, shelter, retirement pension.*
retrécir *to shrink; become narrow.*
retroussé *adj. turned-up.*
  Elle a le nez retroussé. *She has a turned-up nose.*
  Le bas du pantalon retroussé? *Cuffs on the trousers?*
retrouver *to find again, recover, recognize.*
  Je n'ai pas pu retrouver cet endroit. *I couldn't find that place again.*
  Je l'ai retrouvé l'autre jour dans un café. *I ran into him the other day in a café.*
  Je vous retrouverai ce soir. *I'll see you again this evening.*
se retrouver *to find one another again, meet; recognize.*
  Retrouvons-nous à la gare. *Let's meet at the station.*
  A la fin nous nous sommes retrouvés. *At last we found each other.*
réunion *f. meeting, reunion.*
réunir *to reunite, join together; gather.*
se réunir *to meet, gather together.*
RÉUSSIR *to succeed.*
  Il n'a pas réussi à l'avoir. *He failed to get it.* ("*He didn't succeed in getting it.*")
  Il n'a pas réussi le coup. *He didn't bring it off.*
  Cela lui a mal réussi. *It turned out badly for him.*
revanche *f. revenge; return.*
  En revanche. *On the other hand. In return.*
rêvasser *to daydream.*
rêve *m. dream.*
réveil *m. awakening, waking.*
  A son réveil. *When he awoke.*
réveille-matin *m. alarm clock.*
réveiller *to wake, wake up, arouse.*
  Réveillez-moi à huit heures. *Wake me at eight.*
SE RÉVEILLER *to wake up.*
  Il faisait grand jour quand nous nous sommes réveillés. *It was broad daylight when we woke.*
  Son courage se réveilla. *His courage revived.*
réveillon *m. Christmas Eve or New Year's Eve party.*
  Le réveillon de Noël. *Christmas Eve.*
  Le réveillon du jour de l'an. *New Year's Eve.*
révélation *f. revelation, disclosure.*
révéler *to reveal, betray.*
revendiquer *to lay claim to.*
revendre *to resell.*
REVENIR *to return, come back.*
  Quand revenez-vous? *When will you return? When are you coming back?*
  Je n'en reviens pas. *I can't get over it.*
  Il revient de loin. *He has been at death's door.*
  Ça revient au même. *That comes to the same thing. That amounts to the same thing.*
  Il est revenu sur ses pas. *He retraced his steps.*
  Il est revenu sur sa promesse. *He went back on his promise.*
  Maintenant ça me revient. *Now I remember. Now it comes back to me.*
  Sa tête ne me revient pas. *I don't like his looks.*
  Cela (ça) revient moins cher. *That's cheaper.*

That comes to less.
revenu *m. income.*
rêver *to dream.*
révérence *f. reverence.*
  Avec révérence. *Reverently.*
  Faire une révérence. *To curtsy.*
rêverie *f. reverie, daydreaming; daydream.*
revers *m. reverse, back.*
  Eprouver des revers. *To suffer a loss. To meet with reverses.*
  Les revers d'un veston. *The lapels of a coat.*
  Le revers d'une robe. *The wrong side of a dress.*
reviser *to revise.*
révision *f. revision, reconsideration.*
revivre *to come to life again.*
REVOIR *m. meeting again.*
  Au revoir. *Good-by.*
revoir *to see again, meet again.*
  Je l'ai revu l'autre jour. *I saw him again the other day.*
révolte *f. revolt.*
se révolter *to revolt.*
révolution *f. revolution.*
révoquer *to repeal, annul.*
revue *f. review, magazine.*
  Les troupes ont été passées en revue. *The troops passed in review.*
  Je lis cette revue chaque semaine. *I read this magazine every week.*
rez-de-chaussée *m. ground floor.*
rhumatisme *m. rheumatism.*
rhume *m. cold.*
  Attraper un rhume. *To catch a cold.*
  J'ai un rhume. *I have a cold.*
ricaner *to sneer.*
riche *adj. rich.*
richesse *f. riches; wealth.*
  Que de richesses! *What riches!*
ride *f. wrinkle.*
rideau *m. (rideaux pl.) curtain, screen.*
ridicule *adj. ridiculous.*
ridiculiser *to ridicule.*
RIEN *m. trifle.*
  C'est un rien. *It's a mere trifle.*
  Il se fâche pour un rien. *He gets angry at the least little thing.*
  Il faut y ajouter un rien de sel. *It needs just a trifle more salt.*
RIEN *anything; nothing.*
  Je n'ai rien dit. *I didn't say anything.*
  Qu'est-ce que vous avez dit?—Rien. *What did you say?—Nothing.*
  Je n'ai rien à lire ce soir. *I have nothing to read tonight.*
  Si cela ne vous fait rien. *If you don't mind.*
  Rien d'autre. *Nothing else.*
rigide *adj. rigid.*
rigolo (rigolote *f.*) *adj. comical.*
rigoureux (rigoureuse *f.*) *adj. rigorous.*
rigueur *f. rigor, strictness, severity.*
  A la rigueur. *Strictly speaking.*
  C'est de rigueur. *It's compulsory.*
rime *f. rhyme.*
rincer *to rinse.*
RIRE *m. laughter.*
RIRE *to laugh.*
  Ils éclatèrent de rire. *They burst out laughing. They burst into laughter.*
  C'est à mourir de rire. *It's too funny for words.* ("*It's enough to make you die laughing.*")
  Rire tout bas. *To laugh to one's self.*
  Il a ri jaune. *He laughed out of the other side of his face.*

risque *m. risk, chance.*
  Je ne veux pas prendre ce risque. *I don't want to take the chance (risk).*
  Vous le faites à vos risques et périls. *You do it at your own risk.*
risquer *to risk.*
  Qui ne risque rien, n'a rien. *Nothing ventured, nothing gained.*
rivage *m. bank, side.*
rival *m. (rivaux pl.) rival.*
rivalité *f. rivalry.*
rive *f. bank (of stream, pond, or lake).*
  La Rive Gauche. *Left Bank (Paris).*
rivière *f. river, stream.*
riz *m. rice.*
robe *f. dress, gown.*
  La robe de soie. *Silk dress.*
robinet *m. tap, faucet.*
robuste *adj. robust.*
rocher *m. rock, cliff.*
rôder *to prowl.*
roi *m. king.*
rôle *m. role, part.*
romain (romaine *f.*) *noun and adj. Roman.*
roman *m. novel.*
romantique *adj. romantic.*
rompre *to break; interrupt.*
  Rompre des relations. *To break off relations.*
  Il rompit la conversation. *He interrupted the conversation.*
rond *m. round; ring, circle.*
rond *adj. round.*
ronfler *to snore.*
ronger *to gnaw.*
rose *f. rose.*
rose *adj. pink.*
rosée *f. dew.*
rossignol *m. nightingale; (colloq.) piece of junk, "lemon."*
rôti *m. roast.*
rôtir *to roast.*
roue *f. wheel.*
rouge *m. red color; redness; rouge.*
  Un bâton de rouge. *Lipstick.*
ROUGE *adj. red; ruddy.*
rougir *to turn red, blush.*
rouille *f. rust.*
rouleau *m. roll.*
  Le rouleau (de pellicules). *Roll (of film).*
rouler *to roll, roll up; drive.*
  Il roula la feuille de papier soigneusement. *He carefully rolled up the sheet of paper.*
  Rouler à toute vitesse. *To drive at full speed.*
roulette *f. small wheel.*
  Ça marche comme sur des roulettes. *It's going like clockwork.*
ROUTE *f. road, highway.*
  Où aboutit cette route? *Where does this road lead to?*
  En route! *Let's be off!*
  Frais de route. *Traveling expenses.*
routier *adj. of roads.*
  La carte routière. *Road map.*
routine *f. routine.*
roux (rousse *f.*) *adj. red-haired, russet.*
royaliste *m. and f. noun and adj. royalist.*
royaume *m. kingdom, realm.*
ruban *m. ribbon; band.*
  Le ruban magnétique. *Tape recording.*
rubis *m. ruby.*
rubrique *f. column (newspaper).*
  La rubrique sportive. *Sports section.*
rude *adj. rough, harsh.*

RUE f. street.

Quelle est le nom de cette rue? *What's the name of this street?*

Au bout de la rue, tournez à droite. *Turn right at the end of the street.*

Une telle occasion ne court pas les rues. *You don't get this opportunity every day.*

se ruer *to rush, dash.*

ruine f. *ruin.*

Il était à deux doigts de sa ruine. *He was on the very brink of (verge of) ruin. He came within an ace of being ruined.*

Ça tombe en ruines. *It's falling to pieces.*

ruiner *to ruin, destroy, spoil.*

Sa santé est ruinée. *His health is ruined.*

Il est bel et bien ruiné. *He's completely ruined.*

se ruiner *to ruin oneself.*

Il s'est ruiné la santé. *He ruined his health.*

ruisseau m. (ruisseaux pl.) *stream.*

ruisselant adj. *streaming.*

ruisseler *to stream down.*

rumeur f. *rumor.*

rupture f. *rupture; breaking-off.*

Une rupture définitive. *A final break.*

rural (ruraux pl.) adj. *rural.*

ruse f. *ruse, trick.*

ruser *to use craft.*

russe m. and f. noun and adj. *Russian.*

rustique adj. *rustic.*

rustre m. *boor.*

S *The nineteenth letter of the alphabet.*

SA See son.

Où se trouve sa lettre? *Where is his (her) letter?*

Où se trouve sa bague? *Where is his (her) ring?*

sable m. *sand, gravel.*

sabotage m. *sabotage.*

saboteur m. *saboteur.*

SAC m. *bag, sack, pouch, pocketbook.*

L'affaire est dans le sac. *It's as good as settled. It's as good as done. It's a cinch. ("It's in the bag.")*

Il a été pris la main dans le sac. *He was caught red-handed.*

Mettre une ville à sac. *To sack a town.*

sacré adj. *sacred, holy.*

sacrement m. *sacrament.*

Le sacrement de mariage. *Sacrament of marriage.*

sacrifice m. *sacrifice.*

sacrifier *to sacrifice.*

sage m. *a wise man, a learned man.*

sage adj. *well-behaved (of children).*

Soyez sage! *Be good! Behave yourself! (Said to a child.)*

L'enfant est sage comme une image. *The child is very good (obedient).*

Une petite fille sage. *A good little girl.*

sagesse f. *wisdom, good behavior.*

saignant adj. *rare (of meat).*

saigner *to bleed.*

sain adj. *sound, healthy.*

saint adj. *holy, sacred.*

SAISIR *to seize.*

Je ne saisis pas. *I don't quite get (understand) it.*

Pardonnez-moi, je n'ai pas bien saisi votre nom. *Pardon me, I didn't quite catch your name.*

On a saisi ses biens. *His property was attached.*

SAISON f. *season.*

salade f. *salad.*

salaire m. *salary; wages.*

sale adj. *dirty.*

saler *to salt.*

saleté f. *dirt.*

salière f. *saltcellar.*

salir *to dirty, soil; defame.*

salle f. *hall, room.*

Une grande salle. *A large hall.*

Salle à manger. *Dining room.*

Salle de bains. *Bathroom.*

Salle d'attente. *Waiting room.*

Faire salle comble. *To draw a full house (theatre).*

La salle de concert. *Concert hall.*

salon m. *parlor, living room.*

Le salon d'essayage. *Fitting room.*

Le salon des dames (salon de beauté). *Beauty parlor.*

saluer *to pay one's respects, greet, take one's hat off to someone.*

salut m. *salvation, safety.*

salutation f. *salutation, greeting.*

Agréez mes sincères salutations (in a letter). *Best regards. ("Accept my kind regards.")*

SAMEDI m. *Saturday.*

sandale f. *sandal.*

sandwich m. *sandwich.*

SANG m. *blood.*

Il a le sang chaud. *He's quick-tempered.*

Bon sang ne peut mentir. *Blood will tell.*

Il se fait du mauvais sang. *He worries a lot.*

sang-froid m. *sang-froid, composure, coolness, self-control.*

sanglant adj. *bloody, blood-covered.*

sanglot m. *sob.*

sangloter *to sob.*

sanitaire adj. *sanitary.*

SANS *without.*

Sans amis. *Without friends. Friendless.*

Sans fin. *Without end.*

Sans blague! *No kidding! You're joking!*

Sans cesse. *Ceaselessly. Without stopping. Without a halt.*

Sans arrêt. *Without stopping.*

Il répète les mêmes mots sans arrêt. *He keeps repeating the same thing.*

Sans doute. *No doubt. Doubtless. Probably.*

Sans doute il viendra. *He'll probably (doubtlessly) come.*

Retrouvez-moi sans faute à six heures. *Meet me without fail at six o'clock.*

Bien entendu, cela va sans dire. *Of course, that goes without saying.*

Ne vous absentez pas sans le dire. *Don't leave without telling someone.*

N'y allez pas sans qu'on vous le dise. *Don't go unless you're told to.*

sans-façon m. *offhandedness, overfamiliarity; bluntness.*

C'est un sans-façon. *He has no manners. He's too familiar (too free and easy in his ways).*

C'est d'un sans-façon! *That's going a bit too far!*

sans-gêne m. *overfamiliarity, unceremoniousness, cheek, nerve.*

Votre ami est d'un sans-gêne. *Your friend is too familiar (takes too many liberties). Your friend is too free-and-easy (happy-go-lucky).*

sans-souci m. and f. *careless (easygoing) person.*

SANTÉ f. *health.*

Est-elle en bonne santé? *Is she in good health?*

Il respire la santé. *He looks the picture of health.*

A votre santé! *Here's to you! ("Your health!")*

saoul adj. *drunk.*

sarcasme m. *sarcasm, sarcastic remark.*

sarcophage m. *sarcophagus.*

sardine f. *sardine.*

satellite m. *satellite, follower.*

satin m. *satin.*

satire f. *satire.*

satisfaction f. *satisfaction.*

Il me donne satisfaction. *I'm satisfied with him.*

A la satisfaction de tous. *To everyone's satisfaction.*

satisfaire *to satisfy.*

satisfaisant adj. *satisfactory.*

Le résultat fut très satisfaisant. *The result was very satisfactory.*

satisfait adj. *satisfied.*

Etes-vous satisfait de son travail? *Are you satisfied with his work?*

sauce f. *sauce, gravy.*

sauf (sauve f.) adj. *safe, unharmed.*

Nous en sommes sortis sains et saufs. *We came out of it safe and sound.*

SAUF *save, except.*

Nous les avons tous trouvés, sauf trois. *We found all of them except three.*

Tout le monde était là sauf lui. *Everybody was here except him.*

Sauf avis contraire. *Unless I (you) hear to the contrary.*

saumon m. *salmon.*

saut m. *leap, jump.*

sauter *to jump, leap; omit; come off.*

Vous avez sauté tout un paragraphe. *You've skipped a paragraph.*

Cela saute aux yeux. *It's as plain as can be. It's very conspicuous. It's very obvious. ("It leaps to the eye.")*

Il a sauté sur l'offre. *He leaped at the offer.*

Ce bouton vient de sauter. *This button has just come off.*

sautiller *to hop.*

sauvage adj. *savage, wild.*

sauvegarder *to safeguard.*

sauver *to save, rescue.*

Ils sont soucieux de sauver les apparences. *They're anxious to keep up appearances.*

se sauver *to save oneself, to take refuge; to leave.*

Il se sauva à toutes jambes. *He ran away as fast as his legs could carry him.*

Il est tard, je me sauve. *It is late. I have to be going (I must be off).*

Sauve qui peut! *Every man for himself!*

sauvetage m. *rescue.*

Un bateau de sauvetage. *A lifeboat.*

savant m. *learned man, scholar.*

savant adj. *learned.*

SAVOIR m. *knowledge, erudition, learning.*

Il se targue de son savoir. *He boasts of his knowledge.*

Il n'a pas de savoir-vivre. 1. *He doesn't know how to live.* 2. *He doesn't know how to behave.*

Il ne manque pas de savoir-faire. *He knows how to handle people. He has his wits about him.*

SAVOIR *to know.*

Je ne sais pas. *I don't know.*

Je ne le sais pas. *I don't know it.*

Je n'en sais rien. *I don't know anything about it.*

Savez-vous l'anglais? *Do you know English?*

Savez-vous l'heure qu'il est? *Do you know what time it is?*

Que désirez-vous savoir? *What do you want to know? What would you like to know?*

Faites-lui savoir que nous viendrons demain. *Inform him that we're coming tomorrow.*
Je ne sais pas pourquoi il est venu. *I don't know why he came (he's come).*
Pas que je sache. *Not that I know of. Not to my knowledge.*
Pour autant que je sache. *As far as I know.*
Un je ne sais quoi. *An indefinable something (quality).*
Comme vous devez le savoir. *As you must know.*
SAVON m. *soap.*
savourer to *taste, relish, enjoy (food, etc.).*
savoureux (savoureuse f.) adj. *tasty.*
scandale m. *scandal.*
scandaleux (scandaleuse f.) adj. *scandalous.*
scandaliser to *shock.*
scarlatine f. *scarlet fever.*
sceau m. (sceaux pl.) *seal.*
scélérat m. *villain, scoundrel, rascal.*
scellé m. *seal.*
scène f. *scene, stage (theatre).*
sceptique adj. *sceptical.*
sceptre m. *scepter.*
scie f. *saw.*
science f. *science.*
Sciences appliquées. *Applied sciences.*
Homme de science. *Scientist.*
scintillant adj. *scintillating.*
scintiller to *scintillate; sparkle, twinkle.*
scolaire adj. *pertaining to school.*
L'année scolaire commence le premier octobre. *The school year begins October 1st.*
scrupule m. *scruple.*
scrupuleux (scrupuleuse f.) adj. *scrupulous.*
scruter to *scrutinize; to examine closely.*
scrutin m. *ballot.*
sculpter to *sculpture.*
sculpteur m. *sculptor.*
sculpture f. *sculpture.*
SE *himself, herself, itself, oneself, themselves.*
Il se lave les mains. *He's washing his hands.*
Il se lève. *He's getting up.*
Ce mot se prononce ainsi. *That word is pronounced this way.*
Il se marie demain. *He's getting married tomorrow.*
La ville se voit d'ici. *The city can be seen from here.*
séance f. *meeting.*
La séance est levée. *The meeting is adjourned.*
SEC (sèche f.) adj. *dry.*
Faire nettoyer à sec. *To have (something) dry cleaned.*
sécher to *dry.*
séchoir m. *hair dryer.*
SECOND adj. *second.*
SECONDAIRE adj. *secondary.*
SECONDE f. *second; second class.*
Attendez une seconde! *Wait a second!*
Je serai là dans une seconde. *I'll be there in a minute.*
Un carnet de secondes. *A book of second-class tickets.*
secouer to *shake.*
secours m. *help, assistance.*
Au secours! *Help!*
Ils accoururent à son secours. *They ran to his aid. They came running to help him.*
Sortie de secours. *Emergency exit.*
secousse f. *shock, jolt.*
secret m. *secret.*
Je ne suis pas du secret. *I'm not in on the secret.*

C'est le secret de Polichinelle. *It's an open secret.*
secrétaire m. *writing desk.*
secrétaire f. *secretary.*
secteur m. *sector.*
section f. *section.*
sécurité f. *security.*
En sécurité. *In safety.*
sédition f. *sedition.*
séduire to *seduce; entice, attract, tempt.*
séduisant adj. *seductive, tempting, fascinating.*
Un sourire séduisant. *A bewitching smile.*
Une offre séduisante. *A tempting offer.*
seigneur m. *lord, nobleman.*
SEIZE noun and adj. *sixteen.*
SEIZIÈME noun and adj. *sixteenth.*
séjour m. *stay, visit.*
Un séjour de dix jours. *A ten-day visit.*
Il a fait un court séjour à Paris. *He stayed in Paris for a short time.*
Il faut que j'abrège mon séjour. *I'll have to cut my stay short. I'll have to leave earlier than I intended.*
Bon séjour! (Have a) *pleasant stay!*
séjourner to *stay, remain.*
SEL m. *salt.*
Voudriez-vous me passer le sel? *Would you mind passing me the salt?*
selle f. *saddle.*
SELON *according to.*
Selon ce qu'il dit. *According to what he says.*
Selon lui, vous avez tort. *According to him, you're wrong.*
Faites selon vos désirs. *Do as you wish.*
C'est selon. *That depends.*
Chacun vit selon ses moyens. *Everyone lives according to his means.*
SEMAINE f. *week.*
La semaine prochaine. *Next week.*
Le semaine dernière. *Last week.*
Payer par semaine. *To pay by the week.*
Toutes les deux semaines. *Every other week.*
Une fois par semaine. *Once a week.*
SEMBLABLE adj. *alike, similar.*
A-t-on jamais vu rien de semblable? *Did you ever see such a thing!*
Rien de semblable! *Nothing of the sort!*
semblant m. *semblance, appearance.*
Il fait semblant de ne pas comprendre. *He pretends not to understand.*
SEMBLER to *seem, appear.*
Ceci semble très peu. *This seems very little.*
Il me semble que c'est plutôt cher. *It seems to me that it's rather expensive.*
A ce qu'il me semble c'est plutôt injuste. *It seems to me that's rather unfair.*
C'est ce qui lui semble. *It's just as he thought.*
SEMELLE f. *sole.*
semer to *sow.*
semestre m. *semester.*
SENS m. *sense; opinion; direction.*
Le sens figuré. *Figurative sense.*
Une expression à double sens. *A double-entendre. An ambiguous expression.*
Il perdit ses sens. *He lost consciousness.*
Le bon sens. *Good sense.*
Cela n'a pas de sens commun. *That's absurd. That doesn't make sense.*
Il n'a pas de sens. *He has no common sense.*
Sens dessus-dessous. *Upside down.*
Attention, c'est une rue à sens unique. *Look out! This is a one-way street.*

Le bon (mauvais) sens. *The right (wrong) direction.*
sensation f. *sensation.*
sensé adj. *sensible, judicious.*
sensible adj. *sensitive.*
Il parle d'une manière sensible. *He speaks in a very sensitive way.*
C'est une âme sensible. *She's a sensitive person ("soul").*
Il est très sensible à la critique. *He's very sensitive to criticism.*
Il est sensible à l'adulation. *He's open to flattery. He's influenced by flattery.*
sentence f. *sentence.*
Il a reçu la sentence de mort. *He received the death sentence. He was sentenced to death.*
sentier m. *footpath.*
sentiment m. *feeling, sensation.*
Il n'a aucun sentiment. *He has no feeling.*
Nous partageons vos sentiments. *We share your views. We feel the way you do.*
Je voudrais savoir votre sentiment là-dessus. *I'd like to know what you think about it.*
Il est animé de bons sentiments. *He's well-meaning. His intentions are good.*
sentimental (sentimentaux pl.) adj. *sentimental.*
sentinelle f. *sentry.*
SENTIR to *perceive, feel; smell.*
On sent un courant d'air. *There's a draft. You can feel a draft.*
Il ne peut pas les sentir. *He can't stand them.*
Cela sent bon. *That smells nice.*
Cela ne sent pas bon. *I don't like the looks of it. It doesn't seem promising.*
se sentir to *feel.*
Elle ne se sent pas bien. *She doesn't feel well.*
Elle se sent faible. *She feels faint.*
Les effets se font encore sentir. *The effects are still being felt.*
séparation f. *separation.*
séparer to *separate, divide.*
SEPT noun and adj. *seven.*
SEPTEMBRE m. *September.*
SEPTIÈME noun and adj. *seventh.*
serein adj. *serene, calm.*
sérénité f. *serenity.*
sergent m. *sergeant.*
série f. *series, mass.*
Fait en série. *Mass production. ("Mass-produced.")*
Article hors série. *Specially manufactured article. Article made to order.*
sérieusement *seriously.*
SÉRIEUX (sérieuse f.) adj. *serious.*
Etes-vous sérieux? *Are you serious?*
C'est un jeune homme peu sérieux. *He's an irresponsible young man. He's not very serious.*
A demain les affaires sérieuses. *Let's enjoy ourselves today; business tomorrow.*
C'est bien autrement sérieux. *It's (that's) far more serious.*
serment m. *oath.*
sermon m. *sermon.*
serpent m. *snake.*
serré adj. *tight.*
On est un peu serré ici. *We're a little bit crowded in here.*
Il a le coeur serré. *He has a heavy heart.*
serrer to *press, squeeze, crush.*
Serrez-lui la main. *Shake hands with him.*
Cela serre le coeur. *That's heart-rending.*
Serrer les dents. *To clench one's teeth.*

Serrer les rangs. *To close ranks.*
Jouer serré. *To be cautious. To play a cautious game. To play the cards close to the chest.*
serrure *f. lock.*
serrurier *m. locksmith.*
servante *f. maid, servant.*
service *m. service; help.*
Qu'y a-t-il pour votre service? *What can I do for you?*
Faites-moi ce service. *Do me a ("this") favor.*
Service militaire. *Military service.*
Chef de service. *Departmental head.*
A votre service. *At your service.*
serviette *f. napkin; towel; briefcase.*
Une serviette de toilette. *A (hand or face) towel.*
Une serviette éponge. *A Turkish towel.*
servir *to serve.*
On sert à boire et à manger. *Food and drink served here.*
Madame est servie. *Dinner is ready.*
Elle sert à table. *She waits on (the) table.*
Que cela vous serve de leçon. *Let that be a lesson to you.*
En quoi pourrais-je vous servir? *What can I do for you?*
Servir la messe. *To serve mass.*
se servir *to help oneself.*
Servez-vous. *Help yourself.*
Comme je n'avais pas de ciseaux je me suis servi d'un couteau. *Since I didn't have a pair of scissors, I used a knife.*
serviteur *m. servant.*
servitude *f. servitude, slavery.*
SES *See son.*
seuil *m. threshold.*
SEUL *adj. only, sole, single; alone.*
Mon seul et unique désir. *My only wish.*
Il aime rester seul. *He likes to be alone.*
SEULEMENT *only.*
Non seulement . . . mais encore . . . *Not only . . . but also . . .*
sévère *adj. severe, austere.*
sévérité *f. severity.*
sexe *m. sex.*
shampooing *m. shampoo.*
SI *if, whether; suppose that.*
Si on faisait une promenade? *How about taking a walk?*
Si on voulait la revendre? *Suppose we wanted to sell it back?*
SI *so.*
Ne parlez pas si haut. *Don't talk so loud.*
Il pleuvait si fort que nous ne pûmes sortir. *It rained so hard that we couldn't go out.*
Par un si beau dimanche. *On such a beautiful Sunday.*
SI *yes (in answering a negative question).*
N'avez-vous pas d'argent? —Si, j'en ai. *Don't you have any money? —Yes, I do.*
N'est-il pas encore parti? —Si, il est parti. *Hasn't he left yet? —Yes, he has.*
sidéré *adj. dumbfounded.*
Il en resta tout sidéré. *He was completely dumbfounded.*
siècle *m. century.*
siège *m. siege; seat.*
siéger *to be seated.*
SIEN *(sienne f.) his, hers, its.*
Ce n'est pas mon livre, c'est le sien. *It's not my book; it's his.*
Il a fait des siennes. *He's up to his old tricks again.*

sieste *f. nap, siesta.*
siffler *to whistle; hiss.*
sifflet *m. whistle; hiss.*
signal *m. signal.*
signaler *to point out.*
J'ai signalé l'erreur à son attention. *I drew his attention to the error.*
signature *f. signing, signature.*
signe *m. sign.*
Faire signe. *To make a sign. To signal. To gesture. To motion.*
Faire signe que oui. *To nod assent.*
signer *to sign.*
Signez ici. *Sign here.*
signification *f. meaning.*
SIGNIFIER *to mean.*
Qu'est-ce que ça signifie? *What does that mean?*
Qu'est-ce que ce mot signifie? *What does this word mean? What's the meaning of this word?*
SILENCE *m. silence.*
silencieux *(silencieuse f.) adj. silent.*
silhouette *f. silhouette, outline.*
similarité *f. similarity, likeness.*
SIMPLE *adj. simple.*
C'est simple comme bonjour. *As easy as falling off a log. As simple as ABC. As easy as anything.*
Un simple soldat. *A private.*
simplement *(tout simplement) simply; just, only.*
Ce sont des gens simples. *They're very simple people.*
simplicité *f. simplicity.*
simuler *to simulate, sham, pretend.*
sincère *adj. sincere.*
sincérité *f. sincerity.*
singe *m. monkey.*
singulier *(singulière f.) adj. singular; strange.*
Voici autre chose de plus singulier. *Here's something else that's even stranger.*
sinistre *adj. sinister.*
SINON *otherwise.*
sirop *m. syrup.*
sitôt *so soon.*
situation *f. situation.*
SIX *noun and adj. six.*
SIXIÈME *noun and adj. sixth.*
ski *m. ski, skiing.*
Faire du ski. *To ski.*
slip *m. pair of (man's) shorts, bathing trunks.*
sobre *adj. sober, temperate, serious.*
sobriété *f. sobriety.*
sobriquet *m. nickname.*
social *(sociaux pl.) adj. social.*
socialisme *m. socialism.*
socialiste *m. and f. noun and adj. socialist.*
société *f. society.*
Il ne fréquente que la haute société. *He moves only in the best circles.*
La société fait un appel de capital. *The company is increasing its capital.*
Il s'affilia à une société sportive. *He joined an athletic club.*
J'ai eu le plaisir de sa société. *I have had the pleasure of his company.*
La Société Nationale des Chemins de Fer Français (S.N.C.F.). *French National Railways.*
SOEUR *f. sister.*
sofa *m. sofa.*
SOI *himself, herself, itself.*
Cela va de soi. *That goes without saying. Of course.*
Il n'a pas dix minutes à soi. *He hasn't ten*

minutes to himself.
Chacun pour soi. *Every man for himself.*
Il ne pense qu'à soi. *He thinks only of himself.*
Soi-disant. *Would-be.*
Un chez soi. *A home.*
soi-même *oneself.*
soie *f. silk.*
SOIF *f. thirst.*
J'ai soif. *I'm thirsty.*
soigner *to look after, take care of.*
Il faut bien les soigner. *We must take good care of them.*
SOIN *m. care.*
Prenez soin de ne pas réveiller les enfants. *Take care not to wake the children.*
Aux bons soins de. *In care of.*
Ce travail est fait sans soin. *This work is carelessly done.*
Elle a beaucoup de soin. *She's very tidy.*
Il est aux petits soins pour elle. *He shows her a lot of attention.*
SOIR *m. evening.*
A ce soir. *See you tonight. Until tonight.*
soirée *f. evening; party.*
soit *so be it; either . . . or . . .*
Je viendrai soit demain soit jeudi. *I'll come either tomorrow or Thursday.*
Vous venez avec moi? — Soit. *Are you coming with me? — All right.*
soixantaine *f. about sixty.*
SOIXANTE *noun and adj. sixty.*
soixante-dix *(-douze) seventy (seventy-two).*
soixantième *noun and adj. sixtieth.*
sol *m. ground.*
soldat *m. soldier.*
solde *m. sale.*
solde *f. pay.*
SOLEIL *m. sun.*
Il fait du soleil. *The weather is sunny.*
solennel *(solennelle f.) adj. solemn.*
solide *adj. solid, strong.*
Il est solide au poste. *He's strong. He's hale and hearty.*
Asseoir sur une base solide. *To establish on a solid basis.*
Il n'est pas solide sur ses jambes. *His legs are weak.*
solidifier *to solidify.*
solidité *f. solidity.*
solitaire *adj. solitary.*
solitude *f. solitude.*
solliciter *to entreat, beseech, ask earnestly.*
solution *f. solution.*
sombre *adj. dark, gloomy, somber.*
Il y fait sombre comme dans un four. *It's pitch-black. ("It's as black as an oven.")*
Une robe bleu sombre. *A dark-blue dress.*
sombrer *to sink.*
sommaire *m. summary, table of contents.*
sommaire *adj. summary, concise.*
Un repas sommaire. *A quick meal. A snack.*
sommation *f. summons.*
somme *m. nap.*
SOMME *f. sum.*
La somme s'élève à deux cent dix francs. *The total amounts to 210 francs.*
En somme. *On the whole. Finally. After all. In the end.*
SOMMEIL *m. sleep.*
J'ai sommeil. *I'm sleepy.*
Le sommeil le gagne. *He's becoming very sleepy.*
sommeiller *to doze.*

sommer *to summon.*
sommet *m. summit.*
somptueux (somptueuse *f.*) *adj. sumptuous.*
son *m. sound.*
SON (sa *f.*, ses *pl.*) *adj. his, hers, its.*
  Il veut son livre. *He wants his book.*
  Où est sa lettre? *Where's his (her) letter?*
  Il cherche ses gants. *He's looking for his gloves.*
  Des sons bruyants. *Noise.*
songe *m. dream.*
  En songe. *In a dream.*
  J'ai fait un drôle de songe. *I had a strange dream.*
songer *to dream; daydream.*
  Songer à partir. *To think of leaving. To plan (intend) to leave.*
  Nous songeons avec regret à votre départ. *We're sorry that you're leaving.*
sonner *to ring.*
  On sonne. *Someone is ringing.*
  Vous avez le temps de déjeuner avant que la cloche ne sonne. *You have time for lunch before the bell rings.*
sonnerie *f. ringing.*
sonnette *f. bell.*
sonore *adj. sonorous, resonant.*
sorcier *m.* (sorcière *f.*) *sorcerer; witch.*
sordide *adj. sordid, squalid, mean.*
sornette *f. nonsense, idle talk.*
sort *m. lot, fate.*
  Les hommes sont rarement contents de leur sort. *People are seldom satisfied with their lot.*
  On l'abandonna à son sort. *He was left to his fate.*
  Le sort en est jeté. *The die is cast.*
SORTE *f. manner, way.*
  Toutes sortes de. *All kinds of.*
  De toute sorte. *Of every kind.*
  De telle sorte que. *In such a way that.*
  En quelque sorte. *In some way. In a way. In some degree.*
  D'aucune sorte. *Certainly not.*
  Ne parlez pas de la sorte. *Don't speak like that (that way).*
  Il parle avec un accent de sorte qu'il est difficile de le comprendre. *He speaks with such an accent that it's hard to understand him.*
sortie *f. exit.*
  Par ici la sortie. *Exit (through here).*
SORTIR *to go out.*
  Il vient de sortir. *He just went out. He just left.*
  Vous sortez de la question. *You're getting away from the point.*
  Sortez les mains de vos poches. *Take your hands out of your pockets.*
sottise *f. foolishness.*
  Il ne fait que des sottises. *He's always doing something foolish. He's always making some blunder.*
  Il est en train de débiter des sottises. *He's talking nonsense.*
SOU *m. penny.*
  Nous étions sans le sou. *We were without a penny.*
  Il n'a pas un sou vaillant. *He hasn't a penny to his name.*
  Il n'a pas pour deux sous de courage. *He hasn't any courage.*
souche *f. stump; stock.*
  Venir de bonne souche. *To come of good stock.*
  Une souche. *A stub (of a ticket).*

SOUCI *m. worry, care.*
  Il n'a aucun souci. *He has no worries.*
  C'est le cadet de mes soucis. *That's the least of my worries.*
se soucier *to concern oneself, bother with.*
soucieux (soucieuse *f.*) *adj. anxious.*
  Il est soucieux de faire son devoir. *He's anxious to do his duty.*
  Il est peu soucieux de le revoir. *He isn't very eager to see him again.*
SOUDAIN *suddenly.*
  Soudain, ils entendirent un bruit. *Suddenly they heard a noise.*
SOUDAINEMENT *suddenly.*
  Une idée lui vint à l'esprit soudainement. *Suddenly he got an idea.*
souffle *m. breath.*
souffler *to breathe, blow.*
soufflet *m. slap.*
souffrance *f. suffering.*
  Malgré ses souffrances. *In spite of his troubles.*
  Cette affaire est en souffrance. *The matter has been postponed (is being held in abeyance).*
souffrant *adj. unwell.*
  Il paraît souffrant. *He seems to be unwell. He seems to be suffering (in pain).*
souffrir *to suffer.*
  Cela ne souffrira aucune difficulté. *There won't be the slightest difficulty.*
  Je ne peux pas la souffrir. *I can't bear the sight of her.*
souhait *m. wish, desire.*
  A souhait. *According to one's wishes. To one's liking.*
souhaiter *to wish.*
  Je vous souhaite un bon anniversaire. *(I wish you a) Happy Birthday!*
souiller *to soil.*
soulagement *m. relief, alleviation (of pain).*
soulager *to ease, relieve, alleviate.*
  Il fut soulagé. *He was relieved. His mind was set at ease.*
soulever *to raise, lift; rouse, stir up.*
  Il ne pouvait pas soulever le paquet, c'était trop lourd. *He couldn't lift the package; it was too heavy.*
  Cela me soulève le coeur. *That makes me sick. That makes me nauseous.*
soulier *m. shoe.*
  Lacez vos souliers. *Tie your shoelaces.*
  Il est dans ses petits souliers. *He's uneasy.*
souligner *to underline.*
se soumettre *to submit.*
  Il a dû se soumettre à leur décision. *He had to abide by their decision.*
soumission *f. submission; surrender.*
soupçon *m. suspicion; a little bit.*
  Rien ne justifiait ces soupçons. *Nothing justified these suspicions.*
  Est-ce que vous voulez encore un peu de vin? —Juste un soupçon. *Do you want a little more wine? —Just a little bit more. Just a drop more.*
soupçonner *to suspect.*
soupe *f. soup.*
SOUPER *to have supper.*
  Allons souper. *Let's have supper.*
  Cette fois-ci j'en ai soupé (fam.)! *This time I'm fed up with it!*
soupir *m. sigh.*
soupirer *to sigh.*
souple *adj. flexible, pliant.*
  Un bois souple. *Pliant wood.*

  Un esprit souple. *A versatile mind.*
  Un prix souple. *A price that is not fixed (that can be changed).*
  Il est souple comme un gant. *He's easy to manage.*
source *f. source.*
  Je le tiens de bonne source. *I have it on good authority (from a good source).*
  Eau de source. *Spring water.*
sourcil *m. eyebrow.*
sourciller *to frown, wince.*
sourd *adj. deaf.*
  Il est sourd comme un pot. *He's as deaf as a post.*
  Il fait la sourde oreille. *He turns a deaf ear.*
sourdine *f. mute.*
  En sourdine. *In secret. On the sly.*
souriant *adj. smiling.*
SOURIRE *m. smile.*
SOURIRE *to smile; attract.*
  Il sourit tout le temps. *He's always smiling.*
  Je dois avouer que l'idée me sourit. *I must admit that the idea attracts me (that I like the idea).*
souris *f. mouse.*
sournois *adj. sly.*
SOUS *under, beneath.*
  Regardez sous la table. *Look under the table.*
  C'est sous ce tas de papiers. *It's under this pile of papers.*
  Cet acteur est connu sous le nom de Durand. *The stage name of this actor is Durand. ("This actor is known under the name of Durand.")*
  Sous-directeur. *Assistant director.*
souscription *f. subscription.*
souscrire *to subscribe.*
  Souscrire un chèque au porteur. *To make a check payable to bearer.*
sous-entendu *m. double meaning.*
  Il le lui a fait comprendre par sous-entendus. *He hinted at it.*
sous-louer *to sublet.*
sous-main *m. blotter.*
soussigné *adj. undersigned.*
  Je, soussigné. *I, the undersigned.*
sous-sol *m. basement.*
soustraction *f. subtraction.*
soustraire *to subtract.*
  Soustrayez dix de vingt. *Subtract ten from twenty.*
  Il a soustrait dix francs au cent qu'il me devait. *He took off ten francs from the 100 he owed me.*
soutenir *to support, hold up; maintain.*
  Si on ne l'avait pas soutenu, il serait tombé. *If we hadn't held him up, he would have fallen.*
  Il soutenait que je m'étais trompé. *He insisted (maintained) that I was mistaken.*
  J'ai toujours soutenu son point de vue. *I've always supported his point of view.*
se soutenir *to support oneself.*
  Il peut à peine se soutenir sur ses jambes. *He can hardly keep on his feet.*
soutenu *adj. sustained.*
souterrain *m. underground.*
souvenir *m. remembrance.* ◆
  En souvenir de. *In memory of.*
  Son souvenir m'est resté. *I still remember him.*
SE SOUVENIR *to remember.*
  Il se souvient toujours de vous. *He still remembers you.*

Je m'en souviens comme si ça m'était arrivé hier. *I can remember it as though it were yesterday.*

Je me souviens de votre nom. *I remember your name.*

SOUVENT *often.*
Est-ce que ceci arrive souvent? *Does this often happen?*
Je vais souvent chez lui. *I often go to his home.*

souverain *m. sovereign.*

souverain *adj. supreme.*
Un remède souverain. *A sure remedy.*
Il a un souverain mépris pour eux. *He has great contempt for them.*

spacieux (spacieuse *f.*) *adj. spacious.*

SPÉCIAL (spéciaux *pl.*) *adj. special.*
Un train spécial. *A special train.*
C'est une occasion spéciale. *It's a special occasion.*
Affectez cette dépense au compte spécial. *Put that expense on the special account.*

spécialiser *to specialize.*

se spécialiser *to specialize.*

spécialiste *m. and f. noun and adj. specialist; technician.*

spécialité *f. specialty.*
C'est une des spécialités de la maison. *This is one of the specialties of the house (in a restaurant).*

spécifier *to specify, be specific.*
Spécifiez! *Be specific!*

spécimen *m. specimen.*

spectacle *m. spectacle, show.*
Spectacle pour grandes personnes seulement. *Adults only.*

spectateur *m.* (spectatrice *f.*) *spectator; pl. audience.*

spectre *m. ghost.*

spéculateur *m. speculator.*

spéculer *to speculate.*

sphère *f. sphere; field, element.*
Là, il est hors de sa sphère. *He's out of his element there.*

spirituel (spirituelle *f.*) *adj. witty.*

spleen *m. spleen.*

splendide *adj. splendid.*
C'est splendide! *That's wonderful!*
Il fait un temps splendide, n'est-ce pas? *The weather's lovely, isn't it?*

spontané *adj. spontaneous.*

sport *m. sport.*
Faire des sports d'hiver. *To practice (engage in) winter sports.*

sportif (sportive *f.*) *adj. pertaining to sports.*

square *m. enclosed public garden.*

squelette *m. skeleton.*

stable *adj. stable, permanent.*
Un emploi stable. *A permanent position (job).*

stand *m. stand.*

station *f. standing, station, resort, stand.*
Il se tient là en station derrière la porte. *He's standing posted there behind the door.*
Une station balnéaire. *A seashore resort.*
La station de ski. *Ski resort.*
La station-service. *Service station.*
La tête de station. *Taxi stand.*

stationner *to stop.*
Défense de stationner! *No parking! No loitering!*

statue *f. statue.*

stature *f. stature.*

statut *m. statute, bylaw.*

sténo *shorthand. See* sténographie.

sténographie *f. shorthand.*

stéréo(phonique) *adj. stereo(phonic).*

stérile *adj. sterile, barren.*

stimuler *to stimulate, spur on.*

stock *m. stock (in trade).*

store *m. window shade.*

stratagème *m. stratagem, trickery.*

strict *adj. strict.*

strictement *strictly.*

structure *f. structure.*
Une structure imposante. *An imposing structure. A huge building.*

studieux (studieuse *f.*) *adj. studious.*

studio *m. studio.*

stupéfaction *f. amazement.*
Imaginez-vous ma stupéfaction! *Imagine my amazement (surprise)!*

stupéfait *adj. amazed.*
J'en suis resté tout stupéfait. *I was completely dumbfounded.*

stupeur *f. stupor.*
Il fut frappé de stupeur. *He was dumbfounded.*

stupide *adj. stupid.*

stupidité *f. stupidity.*

style *m. style.*
Les meubles de style. *Period furniture.*

styler *to train.*
Votre domestique est bien stylée. *Your maid is well-trained.*

stylo *f.* (fountain) *pen.*
Le stylo à bille. *Ball-point pen.*

su *m. knowledge.*
Au su et au vu de tout le monde. *In public. Publicly.*
Il l'a fait au su de tout le monde. *He did it publicly.*

su *knowledge.*

suave *adj. suave.*

subconscient *adj. subconscious.*

subdiviser *to subdivide.*

SUBIR *to undergo.*
Il a subi une grave opération. *He underwent a serious operation.*
Il n'est pas homme à subir un affront. *He isn't one to overlook an insult.*
Il a subi un grand choc. *He received a great shock.*

subitement *suddenly.*

subjonctif (subjonctive *f.*) *noun (m.) and adj. subjunctive.*

subjuguer *to subdue, subjugate.*

sublime *adj. sublime.*

submerger *to submerge.*

subordonner *to subordinate.*

subside *m. subsidy.*

subsidiaire *adj. subsidiary, additional.*

subsistance *f. maintenance, subsistence.*
Il gagne juste assez pour sa subsistance. *He earns just enough for his subsistence.*

subsister *to subsist; continue to exist, remain.*
Ce contrat subsiste toujours. *This contract still holds.*

substance *f. substance.*
En substance. *In substance.*
Certaines substances fermentent sous l'action de l'eau ou de la chaleur. *Certain substances ferment under the action of water or heat.*
Un argument sans substance. *An argument without any weight.*
La substance d'un article. *The gist of an article.*

substituer *to substitute.*

substitution *f. substitution.*

subterfuge *m. subterfuge.*

subtil *adj. subtle.*

subvenir *to provide.*
Subvenir aux besoins de quelqu'un. *To provide for someone's needs.*

succéder *to succeed, follow after, take the place of.*
Il succéda à son père. *He succeeded his father.*

succès *m. success.*
Avec succès. *Successfully.*
La pièce a eu un succès fou. *The play was a great success.*
J'ai essayé sans succès. *I tried in vain.*
Rien ne réussit comme le succès. *Nothing succeeds like success.*

successeur *m. successor.*

succession *f. succession.*
Il a recueilli la succession de son père. *He inherited his father's money.*
Il a pris sa succession. *He took over his business.*
Droits de succession. *Inheritance taxes.*

succinct *adj. succinct, concise.*

succomber *to succumb, yield to.*
Il a succombé à la tentation. *He yielded to temptation.*
Succomber sous le poids de quelque chose. *To sink under the weight of something.*
Je succombe de sommeil. *I'm dead tired. I can't keep my eyes open.*
Succomber sous le nombre. *To yield to superior numbers. To be overpowered by numbers.*

succulent *adj. juicy.*
Un repas succulent. *An appetizing meal.*

succursale *f. branch.*
Cette banque a une succursale rue de Rivoli. *This bank has a branch on Rivoli Street.*

sucer *to suck.*

SUCRE *m. sugar.*
Aimez-vous beaucoup de sucre dans votre café? *Do you like a lot of sugar in your coffee?*
Elle est tout sucre et tout miel. *She's all honey.*

sucrier *m. sugar bowl.*

SUD *noun (m.) and adj. south.*

suer *to sweat, perspire.*

sueur *f. perspiration, sweat.*

SUFFIRE *to be sufficient.*
Cela suffit. *That's enough.*
Est-ce que cela suffit? *Is that enough?*
Il suffit. *It's enough.*
Une fois suffit, n'y revenez plus. *Once is enough. Don't try it again.*
Il suffit qu'on lui dise de faire quelque chose pour qu'il fasse le contraire. *All you have to do is tell him to do something and he does the opposite. You have only to tell him to do something for him to do the opposite.*

suffisamment *sufficiently.*
Suffisamment d'argent. *Enough money.*

SUFFISANT *adj. sufficient.*
Ce n'est pas suffisant. *It's not enough.*

suffoquer *to suffocate.*

suffrage *m. suffrage.*

SUGGÉRER *to suggest.*
Pouvez-vous suggérer quelque chose d'autre? *Can you suggest anything else?*
Il a suggéré que nous attendions encore un mois. *He suggested that we wait another month.*

SUGGESTION *f. suggestion.*
Puis-je offrir une suggestion? *May I make a suggestion?*
Je crois que nous devrions adopter toutes ses suggestions. *I think we should adopt all of his suggestions.*

suicide m. suicide.

se suicider to commit suicide.

suie f. soot.

SUITE f. (act of) following, sequence; pursuit; what follows; consequence, result.

Revenez tout de suite. *Come back right away.*

Cinq fois de suite. *Five times in succession.*

Et ainsi de suite. *And so forth. And so on. Et cetera.*

Tout ce qu'on peut faire, c'est attendre la suite. *All we can do is to wait and see what happens.*

Comme suite à votre lettre du dix courant. *In reference to your letter of the tenth of this month.*

Il n'a pas de suite dans les idées. *He's inconsistent.*

La suite au prochain numéro. *To be continued in the next issue.*

La suite des événements. *The sequence (course) of events.*

Suite d'orchestre. *Suite for orchestra.*

Par suite de sa maladie il a dû partir dans le Midi. *Because of his illness he had to leave for the South.*

suisse m. and f. noun and adj. Swiss.

suivant (suivante f.) noun and adj. following, next.

Le suivant! *Next!*

Au suivant! *Next, please!*

Prenez le suivant. *Take the next one.*

SUIVANT following, in conformance with, according to.

J'agirai suivant la décision que vous prendrez. *I'll act according to your decision.*

Suivant le journal, le cabinet démissionera demain. *According to the newspaper, the cabinet will resign tomorrow.*

SUIVRE to follow.

Partez maintenant, je vous suis dans un moment. *You leave now. I'll follow you in a minute.*

Il le suit de près. *He's close on his heels.*

Son accent est si prononcé que j'ai beaucoup de mal à le suivre. *He has such a thick accent that it's hard for me to follow him.*

Oui, je vous suis. *Yes, I follow you.*

Il suit un cours de philosophie. *He attends a philosophy class. He's taking a course in philosophy.*

A suivre. *To be continued.*

A faire suivre. *Please forward.*

N'oubliez pas de suivre l'affaire. *Don't forget to follow the matter up.*

Une conséquence suit l'autre. *One thing leads to another.*

Il suit de là que . . . *It follows from this that . . .*

se suivre to follow in order.

Que s'en est-il suivi? *What came of it? What was the result?*

Cela posé, il s'en suit que nous nous étions trompés. *Once that is granted, it follows that we must have been mistaken.*

Les jours se suivent et ne se ressemblent pas. *There is no telling what tomorrow will bring.*

SUJET m. subject.

Quelle est le sujet de ce livre? *What's the subject of this book?*

Assez sur ce sujet. *That's enough about that (matter).*

Il n'a qu'une connaissance superficielle du sujet. *He has only a very superficial knowledge of the subject.*

Mauvais sujet. *A good-for-nothing. A rascal.*

Il était inquiet à son sujet. *He was worried about him (her).*

Au sujet de votre ami, il est revenu me voir hier. *As for your friend, he came back to see me yesterday.*

J'ai tout sujet de croire que c'est ainsi. *I have every reason to believe that it's so.*

sujet (sujette f.) adj. subject to, inclined to, liable, exposed.

Elle est sujette aux maux de têtes. *She's subject to headaches.*

Super m. special ("Super") gasoline.

superbe adj. superb.

Il fait un temps superbe. *The weather is magnificent.*

Elle a un teint superbe. *She has a beautiful complexion.*

supercherie f. deceit, fraud.

superficie f. surface, area.

superficiel (superficielle f.) adj. superficial.

superflu adj. superfluous.

Il serait superflu d'en dire plus long. *It would be superfluous to say any more.*

supérieur adj. superior.

supériorité f. superiority.

superlatif noun (m.) and adj. (superlative f.) superlative.

superstitieux (superstitieuse f.) adj. superstitious.

superstition f. superstition.

suppléer to take the place of; supply.

Il s'est fait suppléer par un jeune homme. *He found a young man to replace him.*

Suppléez-nous de marchandise aussitôt que possible. *Supply us with more merchandise as soon as possible.*

supplément m. supplement, extra.

On paye un supplément pour le vin. *You have to pay extra for the wine.*

supplémentaire adj. supplementary.

Faire des heures supplémentaires. *To work overtime.*

On lui a demandé de rédiger un article supplémentaire. *They asked him to write an additional article.*

suppliant adj. pleading, suppliant.

supplication f. entreaty, plea.

supplice m. punishment, torture, agony.

supplier to beseech.

Je vous en supplie! *I beg of you! Please!*

support m. support, pillar, prop.

supportable adj. bearable, tolerable.

supporter to support; bear, suffer, put up with.

Je ne peux pas la supporter. *I can't stand her.*

supposer to suppose.

supposition f. supposition.

supprimer to suppress, cancel, abolish.

suprématie f. supremacy.

suprême adj. supreme, highest.

sur adj. sour.

SUR on, upon, above.

Mettez-le sur la table. *Put it on the table.*

Ne vous accoudez pas sur la table. *Don't lean on the table.*

Il a écrit un livre sur les Etats-Unis. *He wrote a book about the United States.*

Cette table a deux mètres sur cinq. *This table is two meters by five.*

Il était sur le point de partir. *He was just about to leave.*

Il arriva sur ces entrefaites. *He arrived just at that moment.*

Revenez sur vos pas. *Retrace your steps.*

Je n'ai pas d'argent sur moi. *I have no money on (with) me.*

SÛR adj. certain.

J'en suis sûr. *I'm certain about it.*

Il est toujours sûr de son fait. *He always knows what he's talking about.*

Bien sûr, j'ai compris. *Of course, I understood.*

Soyez sûr que je ne l'oublierai pas de sitôt. *You may be sure that I won't forget it so soon.*

Il est sûr de son affaire. 1. *He's sure to succeed.* 2. *He's sure to get what he deserves. He's sure to get his.*

surcharger to overload, overburden.

surchauffer to overheat.

surcouper to overtrump (cards).

surcroît m. addition.

Par surcroît. *In addition.*

Il a peur de faire un surcroît d'effort. *He's afraid to exert himself ("make an extra effort.")*

SÛREMENT surely.

Il va sûrement échouer. *He'll surely fail. He's sure to fail.*

Qui va lentement va sûrement. *Slow and sure wins the race.*

surenchère f. higher bid.

surestimer to overestimate.

sûreté f. safety.

Ne vous en faites pas, il est en sûreté. *Don't worry, he's safe.*

La Sûreté. *The Criminal Investigation Department.*

surface f. surface, area.

Il n'approfondit rien, il s'arrête toujours à la surface des choses. *He never examines anything carefully. He never goes below the surface.*

Quelle est la surface de ce terrain? *What's the area of this piece of land?*

surgir to spring up; appear.

Une voile surgit à l'horizon. *A sail appeared on the horizon.*

Faire surgir un souvenir. *To evoke a memory.*

surhumain adj. superhuman.

Un effort surhumain. *A superhuman effort.*

sur-le-champ at once, immediately.

Faites-le sur-le-champ. *Do it right away.*

surlendemain m. the day after.

Nous connaîtrons le résultat le surlendemain. *We'll know the outcome the day after tomorrow.*

surmener to overwork.

se surmener to overwork oneself.

surmontable adj. surmountable, that can be overcome.

Des difficultés surmontables. *Surmountable obstacles. Difficulties that can be overcome.*

surmonter to rise higher; surmount.

Il a surmonté tous ses ennuis. *He overcame all his difficulties.*

surnaturel (surnaturelle f.) adj. supernatural.

surnom m. nickname.

surpasser to surpass.

surpeuplé adj. overpopulated.

surplus m. surplus, excess.

Vous pouvez garder le surplus. *You may keep the remainder (what's left over).*

Au surplus, ayez la bonté de me taper deux lettres. *In addition, please type two letters for me. Will you also type two letters for me, please?*

surprenant adj. amazing, surprising.

SURPRENDRE *to surprise.*
Je ne suis pas du tout surpris. *I'm not at all surprised.*
Qu'il vous ait joué ce coup ne me surprend pas du tout. *I'm not at all surprised that he played that trick on you.*
Je l'ai surpris en flagrant délit. *I caught him in the act.*
L'orage nous a surpris. *The storm overtook us.*
SURPRISE *f. surprise.*
A ma grande surprise. *To my great surprise. Much to my surprise.*
Quelle bonne surprise! *What a pleasant surprise!*
Il nous a tous eu par surprise! *He took us all by surprise.*
surréaliste *adj. surrealistic.*
sursaut *m. jump; start.*
Il s'est éveillé en sursaut. *He awoke with a start.*
sursauter *to jump up; start (up).*
Il sursaute chaque fois qu'on ouvre la porte. *He jumps up every time the door opens.*
Pour un rien, elle sursaute. *She gets excited about the least little thing.*
sursis *m. respite.*
On lui a accordé un sursis. *He was granted an arrest of judgment.*
SURTOUT *above all, particularly, especially.*
Surtout, revenez à temps. *Be sure to come back on time. Above all, get back in time.*
Il lui a surtout demandé de ne pas en parler. *He especially asked him not to speak about it.*
Surtout n'allez pas là-bas. *Be sure not to go there.*
Surtout ne le laissez pas faire cela. *Whatever you do, don't let him do that.*
surveillance *f. supervision.*
surveillant *m. watchman; proctor, monitor (in a school).*
surveiller *to keep an eye on, watch.*
survenir *to arrive unexpectedly.*
Il survint une tempête. *A heavy storm suddenly arose.*
survivant *m. survivor.*
survivre *to survive.*
susceptible *adj. susceptible.*
Je pense que ceci est susceptible de vous intéresser. *I think this may be of interest to you.*
susciter *to stir up, raise up, instigate, rouse, create, give rise to, cause.*
susdit *noun (m.) and adj. aforesaid.*
suspect (suspecte *f.*) *noun and adj. suspect.*
suspecter *to suspect.*
suspendre *to suspend.*
Le chandelier est suspendu au plafond. *The chandelier is suspended from the ceiling.*
A cause de la grève le travail a été suspendu. *Work has been suspended because of the strike.*
suspens *m. suspense.*
Ne nous tenez pas en suspens. *Don't keep us in suspense.*
suspension *f. suspension, cessation.*
suspicion *f. suspicion.*
svelte *adj. slender, slim.*
S.V.P. *(abbreviation of s'il vous plaît) Please.*
Sonnez S.V.P. *Please ring the bell.*
R.S.V.P. *R.S.V.P. Please answer.*
syllabe *f. syllable.*
symbole *m. symbol.*

symbolique *adj. symbolic.*
symétrie *f. symmetry.*
symétrique *adj. symmetrical.*
sympathie *f. sympathy.*
J'éprouve beaucoup de sympathie envers elle. *I've a great deal of sympathy for her.*
Il s'aliéna les sympathies de tous. *He lost everybody's sympathy. He alienated everybody.*
sympathique *adj. congenial, likeable, pleasant.*
C'est un homme très sympathique. *He's a very congenial (pleasant, nice, likeable) fellow.*
Il m'est très sympathique. *I like him a lot.*
sympathiser *to sympathize.*
symphonie *f. symphony.*
symphonique *adj. symphonic.*
symptôme *m. symptom.*
synagogue *f. synagogue.*
syncope *f. fainting spell; syncopation (music).*
syndicat *m. (trade) union.*
synonyme *adj. synonymous.*
syntaxe *f. syntax.*
système *m. system.*
Le système métrique. *Metric system.*
Le système nerveux. *The nervous system.*
Le système digestif. *The digestive system.*
Il s'habitua rapidement au système nouveau. *He rapidly became accustomed to the new system.*
Il me tape sur le système (*fam.*). *He gets on my nerves.*
Par système. *Systematically.*

T *The twentieth letter of the alphabet.*

ta *See ton.*
tabac *m. tobacco.*
TABLE *f. table.*
Mettre la table. *To set the table.*
Mettons-nous à table. *Let's sit down to eat.*
Une table de quatre couverts, s'il vous plaît. *A table for four, please.*
Une table alphabétique. *An alphabetical list.*
Table des matières. *Table of contents.*
tableau *m. picture, painting.*
Le tableau noir. *Blackboard.*
Le cadre pour tableaux. *Picture frame.*
tablier *m. apron.*
tabouret *m. stool.*
tache *f. spot, stain.*
Une tache de vin. *A wine stain.*
Une tache de naissance. *Birthmark.*
Des taches de rousseur. *Freckles.*
Faire une tache. *To make a stain.*
TÂCHE *f. job, task.*
Une tâche difficile. *A difficult task.*
Mettez-vous à la tâche. *Get down to work.*
Il prit à tâche de terminer le travail. *He made it his business to finish the work. He made it his job to get the work finished.*
Un ouvrage à la tâche. *Piecework.*
Ouvrier à la tâche. *A worker who does piecework.*
TACHER *to spot.*
TÂCHER *to try.*
Tâchez d'y aller. *Try to go there.*
Tâchez d'arriver de bonne heure. *Try to come early.*
Tâchez de ne pas oublier. *Try not to forget.*
Je tâcherai. *I'll try.*
tacite *adj. tacit, implied.*
taciturne *adj. taciturn, silent.*
tact *m. tact.*

taie *f. case, pillowcase.*
Une taie d'oreiller. *A pillowcase.*
taille *f. cutting; height; waist; size (dresses, suits, coats, shirts).*
C'est un homme de taille moyenne. *He's a man of average height.*
Elle a une taille mince. *She's slender.*
Quelle est votre taille? *What size do you wear? What's your size?*
Il est de taille à se défendre. *He's capable of taking care of himself (defending himself).*
tailler *to sharpen.*
Taillez votre crayon. *Sharpen your pencil.*
On m'a taillé de la besogne. *I have my work cut out for me.*
tailleur *m. tailor; (woman's) suit.*
Son tailleur a beaucoup de chic. *Her suit is very smart.*
taire *to say nothing of, keep quiet about, suppress.*
se taire *to be silent.*
Taisez-vous! *Keep quiet! Shut up!*
Vous n'avez plus qu'à vous taire. *You'd better not say anything. You'd better keep quiet.*
Qui se tait consent. *Silence gives consent.*
talc *m. talc, talcum powder.*
talent *m. talent, skill.*
talon *m. heel.*
tambour *m. drum.*
tamis *m. sieve.*
tampon *m. plug, stopper.*
TANDIS QUE *while, whereas.*
Il lisait tandis que je travaillais. *He was reading while I worked.*
Il peut y aller tandis que nous devons rester ici. *He's able to go there whereas we have to stay here.*
tangible *adj. tangible.*
tanné *adj. sunburnt.*
TANT *so much.*
Ne m'en donnez pas tant. *Don't give me so much.*
J'ai tant de travail à faire! *I've so much work to do!*
Je le lui ai répété tant de fois. *I've repeated it to him so many times.*
Tant de monde. *So many people. Such a crowd.*
Si vous réussissez, tant mieux. *So much the better if you succeed.*
Tant pis! *Too bad! So much the worse.*
Nous l'avons fait tant bien que mal. *We did it as well as we could.*
Vous m'en direz tant! *You don't say so!*
tante *f. aunt.*
tantôt *in a little while, by and by; shortly, soon.*
A tantôt. *See you later.*
tapage *m. racket, noise.*
taper *to tap, strike, beat; type.*
Tapez cette lettre à la machine. *Type this letter.*
tapis *m. rug, carpet.*
tapisserie *f. tapestry.*
Faire tapisserie. *To be a wallflower.*
tapissier *m. upholsterer.*
taquin (taquine *f.*) *noun and adj. teasing; a person who likes to tease.*
taquiner *to tease.*
TARD *late.*
Il est rentré tard. *He came home late.*
Il était plus tard qu'on ne le croyait. *It was later than we thought.*
A plus tard. *See you later.*
Mieux vaut tard que jamais. *Better late than never.*

Il n'est jamais trop tard pour bien faire. *It's never too late to mend.*

tarder *to delay.*

Sans tarder. *Without any delay.*

Il me tarde de la revoir. *I can't wait to see her again.*

se targuer *to boast of, take pride in, plume oneself on.*

tarif *m. rate, scale of prices, price list.*

Demi-tarif. *Half-fare (for a child).*

Quels sont vos tarifs? *What are your prices?*

Tarif des lettres. *Postal rate.*

Un paquet affranchi au tarif des lettres. *A package sent as first-class mail.*

tarte *f. tart, pie.*

tas *m. pile, heap.*

Un tas de papiers. *A pile of papers.*

Regardez en-dessous ce tas de lettres. *Look under this pile of letters.*

Un tas de foin. *A haystack.*

TASSE *f. cup.*

Voulez-vous encore une tasse de café? *Do you want another cup of coffee?*

Donnez-moi une demi-tasse. *Give me a demi-tasse.*

se tasser *to crowd together.*

tâter *to feel, handle, touch.*

tâtonner *to feel one's way, grope.*

(à) tâtons *gropingly.*

Il nous faut y aller à tâtons, il n'y pas de lumière. *There's no light. We'll have to grope our way in the dark.*

taureau *m. bull.*

Prendre le taureau par les cornes. *To take the bull by the horns.*

taux *m. rate of interest.*

Au taux de 4%. *At the rate of 4%.*

taverne *f. tavern.*

taxe *f. tax.*

taxer *to tax.*

taxi *m. cab, taxi.*

En taxi. *By taxi.*

te *you, to you.*

technique *f. technique.*

technique *adj. technical.*

teindre *to dye.*

Se teindre les cheveux. *To tint, dye one's hair.*

teint *m. complexion.*

Avoir le teint clair. *To have a clear complexion.*

teinte *f. tint; touch.*

Demi-teinte. *Half-tint.*

Une légère teinte d'ironie. *A slight touch of irony.*

teinture *f. dye.*

TEL (telle *f.*) *adj. such.*

Une telle chose ne se voit pas tous les jours. *You don't see that sort of thing every day.*

Un tel garcon ira loin. *A boy (fellow) of this sort will go far.*

De tels moyens ne s'emploient pas. *Such means can't be used.*

De telle sorte que. *In such a way that (as to).*

Tel père, tel fils. *Like father, like son.*

télécommunications (*f.*) *telecommunications.*

Le bureau des P et T (Postes et Télécommunications). *Post office.*

TÉLÉGRAMME *m. telegram.*

télégraphie *f. telegraphy.*

Télégraphie sans fil (T.S.F.). *Radio.*

télégraphier *to telegraph.*

TÉLÉPHONE *m. telephone.*

Passez-moi l'annuaire du téléphone. *Please hand me the telephone book.*

Donnez-moi un coup de téléphone, n'est-ce pas? *Give me a ring, won't you?*

Le téléphone automatique. *Dial telephone.*

Parler au téléphone. *To speak on the telephone.*

téléphoner *to telephone.*

téléphonique *adj. telephonic.*

La cabine téléphonique. *Telephone booth.*

téléphoniste *m. and f. telephone operator.*

télévision *f. television.*

TELLEMENT *so much.*

Elle a tellement changé! *She changed so much!*

Il a tellement regretté de n'avoir pas pu venir. *He was so sorry he couldn't come.*

Il était tellement pressé qu'il a oublié sa clé. *He was so much in a hurry that he forgot his key.*

téméraire *adj. bold.*

témérité *f. temerity, boldness.*

témoignage *m. evidence.*

Vous serez appelé en témoignage. *You'll be called as a witness.*

Un faux témoignage. *A false witness. False evidence.*

En témoignage d'estime. *As a token of esteem.*

témoigner *to bear witness.*

témoin *m. witness.*

Je vous prends en témoin. *I call you to witness.*

Je tiens à vous parler sans témoins. *I'd like to speak to you privately.*

tempe *f. temple (of the head).*

tempérament *m. temperament.*

Il est actif par tempérament. *He's very active (by nature).*

température *f. temperature.*

tempête *f. storm.*

temple *m. temple, Protestant church.*

temporaire *adj. temporary.*

temporairement *temporarily.*

TEMPS *m. time; weather.*

C'était le bon vieux temps! *Those were the good old days!*

Je ne me sens pas très bien ces derniers temps. *I haven't been feeling very well lately.*

La plupart du temps. *Most of the time.*

Vous arrivez juste à temps. *You've come just in time.*

Dans le temps. *Formerly.*

Dans son temps. *In due course.*

Nous nous voyons toujours de temps en temps. *We still see one another from time to time.*

Entre temps. *Meanwhile.*

Tout ces choses prennent du temps. *All these things take time.*

En même temps. *At the same time.*

Par le temps qui court rien n'est surprenant. *Nothing is surprising nowadays.*

Que faire pour tuer le temps? *What shall we do to kill time?*

Le temps a l'air de se mettre au beau. *It looks as though the weather is going to be nice.*

Quel temps abominable! *What awful weather!*

De tous les temps. *Of all time.*

tenace *adj. obstinate.*

ténacité *f. tenacity, tenaciousness.*

tenailles *f. pl. pliers.*

tendance *f. tendency.*

tendon *m. tendon.*

tendre *adj. tender.*

Cette viande n'est pas assez tendre. *This meat isn't tender enough.*

Elle a le coeur trop tendre. *She's too tender-hearted.*

tendre *to stretch; hold out; put forth.*

Tendre la main. 1. *To lend a helping hand.* 2. *To beg alms.*

Quand j'ai eu besoin de lui, il m'a tendu la main. *When I needed him, he lent me a helping hand.*

Il lui tendit la main. *He held out his hand to him.*

A quoi tendent ces paroles? *What are you driving at?* ("What do these words mean?")

tendrement *tenderly, affectionately.*

tendresse *f. tenderness, affection.*

Elle fit preuve d'une grande tendresse. *She showed great affection.*

TENIR *to hold.*

Tenez ce livre, je vous prie. *Please hold this book.*

Je tiens cela de bonne source. *I have it on the best authority.*

Tenir compte de quelque chose. *To take something into consideration (account).*

Je tiens à vous dire que . . . *I have to (must) tell you that . . .*

Il ne tient qu'à vous de le faire. *It's up to you to do it.*

Il le tiendra au courant des résultats. *He will keep him posted about the results.*

Tenir sa promesse. *To keep one's word.*

Tenir tête à. *To resist.*

Tenir lieu de. *To act as.*

Tiens, je n'aurais jamais cru cela. *Well, I would never have believed that.*

Tenez, le voilà! *Look, there he is!*

Tenez, prenez-le. *Here, take it.*

Tenez, c'est pour vous. *Here, this is for you.*

Cela lui tient au coeur. *He's set his heart on it.*

Tenez ferme! *Hold fast! Hold out! Stick it out to the end!*

Je n'y tiens pas. *I don't particularly care about it. I don't particularly care to. I don't care for it. I would rather not.*

Votre raisonnement ne tient pas debout. *Your argument doesn't hold.*

Qu'à cela ne tienne. *Never mind that. Don't let that be an obstacle. That need be no objection.*

Si vous y tenez. *If you insist (on it).*

SE TENIR *to stay; keep from; refrain from.*

Se tenir chez soi. *To stay home.*

Tenez-vous debout. *Stand up.*

Tenez-vous tranquille. *Keep quiet.*

Ils se tenaient les côtes de rire. *They split their sides laughing.* ("They held their sides laughing.")

Se tenir sur ses gardes. *To be on one's guard.*

Maintenant vous savez à quoi vous en tenir. *Now you know how things stand.*

Il s'en tient à ce qu'il dit. *He maintains what he said.*

tennis *m. tennis.*

tension *f. tension.*

tentant *adj. tempting.*

tentatif (tentative *f.*) *adj. tentative.*

tentation *f. temptation.*

tentative *f. attempt.*

La tentative a échoué. *The attempt failed.*

Après plusieurs tentatives. *After several attempts.*

tente *f. tent.*

tenter *to try; tempt.*

Je vais encore une fois tenter la chance. *I'm going to try my luck once again.*

Cela me tente. *That tempts me. That attracts me.*

J'ai été tenté de le faire. *I was tempted to do it.*

tenu adj. kept.
Une maison bien tenue. A well-kept house.
tenue f. holding.
La tenue des livres. Bookkeeping.
Ces enfants ont beaucoup de tenue. These children are well brought up. These children are well-behaved.
Il a de la tenue. He has very good (dignified) manners. He's well-bred. He has a sense of decorum.
Voyons, ayez de la tenue. Come on, behave yourself.
En tenue de soirée seulement (in an invitation). Formal dress.
En grande tenue. In evening dress. In formal dress.
terme m. term, boundary.
Il a mené cette affaire à bon terme. He brought this deal to a successful conclusion.
Il a avoué en termes propres. He admitted (it) in so many words.
Ménager ses termes. To mince words.
Etes-vous en bons termes avec eux? Are you on friendly terms with them?
Mettre un terme à. To put an end to.
Nous l'avons acheté à terme. We bought it on the installment plan.
Louer une maison pour un terme. To rent a house for four months.
Aux termes de . . . By the terms of . . .
terminaison f. termination, ending; end, conclusion.
TERMINER to finish.
Avez-vous terminé? Have you finished? Are you through?
C'est à peu près terminé. It's almost (just about) finished.
terminus m. terminus; end of the line (bus, etc.).
terne adj. dull.
Une couleur terne. A dull color.
ternir to tarnish, stain.
terrain m. ground.
Terrains à vendre. Plots of land (building plots) for sale. Lots for sale.
Il a acheté un terrain. He bought a piece of ground.
Il perd du terrain chaque jour. He's losing ground every day.
Là, il est sur son terrain. There, he's in his element. He's at home there.
Sonder le terrain. To see how the land lies. To sound (someone) out.
Tâter le terrain. To feel one's way. To see how the land lies.
terrasse f. terrace; pavement in front of a sidewalk café.
TERRE f. earth, land.
Sa terre lui rapporte un petit revenu. His land yields him a small income.
Remuer ciel et terre. To move heaven and earth.
Ne jetez pas de papier par terre. Don't throw any paper on the ground.
Un tremblement de terre. An earthquake.
Etre terre à terre. To be commonplace. To be vulgar. To be matter-of-fact. To be of the earth; earthy.
terreur f. fear.
Il fut pris de terreur. He was terror-stricken.
terrible adj. terrible, dreadful.
Quelque chose de terrible vient de lui arriver. Something dreadful just happened to him.
Un enfant terrible. A little devil.

terriblement terribly.
Je suis terriblement gênée. I'm terribly embarrassed.
terrifier to terrify.
territoire m. territory.
testament m. testament, will.
TÊTE f. head; mind.
Il a mal à la tête. He has a headache.
Il a perdu la tête. 1. He lost his head. 2. He lost his mind.
Quel est votre tour de tête? What size hat do you wear?
Crier à tue-tête. To scream at the top of one's lungs.
Donner tête baissée dans quelque chose. To rush headlong into something.
Elle fait la tête. She's sulking.
Il leur a tenu tête. He held his own against them.
J'en ai par-dessus la tête de toutes ses histoires. I'm fed up with all his (her) stories.
Elle se casse la tête. She's racking her brain.
Je ne sais où donner la tête. I don't know which way to turn.
Il se l'est mis dans la tête. He took it into his head to do it.
Avoir en tête. To have in the back of one's mind.
Se monter la tête. To get excited.
Il n'en fait qu'à sa tête. He does just as he pleases.
Un coup de tête. A sudden rash act. An impetuous (impulsive) act.
Il a pris la tête de la procession. He headed the procession.
Un tête à tête. A private conversation.
La tête de station. Taxi stand.
La tête me tourne. My head is spinning.
têtu adj. stubborn.
texte m. text.
textile m. textile.
thé m. tea.
THÉÂTRE m. theatre.
Etes vous allé au théâtre hier soir? Did you go to the theatre last night?
Un coup de théâtre. An unexpected sensational event.
Il veut faire du théâtre. He wants to go on the stage.
théière f. teapot.
thème m. theme.
théorie f. theory.
thermomètre m. thermometer.
thermos m. thermos bottle.
thèse f. thesis.
tic m. nervous twitch.
ticket m. ticket (bus).
tic-tac m. tick-tock.
tiède adj. lukewarm.
tiédeur f. warmth, lukewarmness.
TIEN (tienne f.) yours.
Est-ce que c'est le tien? Is that yours?
Il faut y mettre du tien. You must contribute your share.
Tu as encore fait des tiennes! You've been up to your old tricks again!
tiers m. a third.
tiers (tierce f.) adj. third.
Une tierce personne. A third party.
tige f. stem.
tigre m. tiger.
timbale f. metal drinking cup.
TIMBRE m. postage stamp; bell.

Avez-vous du papier à lettre, une enveloppe et un timbre? Do you have some writing paper, an envelope, and a stamp?
Le timbre a sonné. The bell rang.
timide adj. timid, shy.
timidité f. timidity.
tintamarre m. racket, noise.
Quel tintamarre! What a racket!
tinter to ring, toll, knell.
tir m. shooting.
tirade f. tirade, speech.
tirage m. drawing; impression (print); circulation.
Le tirage de la loterie nationale. The drawing of the national lottery.
Un tirage assez élevé. A fairly wide circulation.
Tirage à part. Separate reprint (an article).
Edition à tirage limité. Limited edition.
tirailler to bother, pester.
tiré adj. drawn.
Il est tiré à quatre épingles. He's spick and span.
Un visage tiré. A drawn face. Drawn features.
tire-bouchon m. corkscrew.
tirelire f. money box.
TIRER to draw, pull; print (photography).
Il sait tirer avantage de tout. He knows how to turn everything to his advantage (to derive profit from everything, to turn everything to account).
Elle s'est fait tirer les cartes. She had her fortune told.
Il l'a tiré d'erreur. He undeceived him. He opened his eyes.
Tirer les oreilles de quelqu'un. To pull someone's ears.
Il se fait tirer l'oreille. He's very reluctant. He has to be coaxed.
Tirer à la courte paille. To draw straws.
Tirer à blanc. To fire a blank.
Faire tirer un cliché. To have a negative printed.
se tirer to get out of.
tiroir m. drawer.
tisane f. infusion of camomile or barley.
tisser to weave.
tissu m. material.
titre m. title.
Il l'a reçu titre gratuit. He received it free.
tituber to stagger.
titulaire m. and f. noun and adj. head, chief; pertaining to a title, titular.
toast m. toast.
toc m. imitation jewelry; fake, sham, anything trashy.
C'est du toc (fam.). 1. It's imitation jewelry. 2. It's faked. It's a fake.
tocsin m. alarm.
tohu-bohu m. hurly-burly.
TOI you (familiar). See tu.
Ils sont à tu et à toi. They are on the most familiar terms.
Qui est là, c'est toi? Who's there? Is that you?
toi-même yourself (familiar).
toile f. linen; cloth; canvas (painting).
Draps de toile. Linen sheets.
toilette f. act of washing, dressing; dressing-up; washstand, dressing table; washroom.
Vous voulez faire un brin de toilette avant de sortir? Do you want to wash up a bit before going out?
Une toilette ravissante. A striking dress.
Les articles de toilette. Toilet accessories (articles).
Où se trouve la toilette? Where is the washroom?

toiser *to eye.*
Il l'a toisé avec dédain. *He looked him up and down contemptuously.*
toit *m. roof.*
tolérable *adj. tolerable, bearable.*
tolérance *f. tolerance.*
tolérant *adj. tolerant.*
tolérer *to tolerate.*
Je ne peux pas tolérer cet individu. *I can't stand that fellow.*
tomate *f. tomato.*
tombe *f. grave.*
tombeau (tombeaux *pl.*) *m. tomb.*
Il me mettra au tombeau. *He'll be the death of me.*
tombée *f. fall.*
A la tombée du jour. *At nightfall.*
A la tombée de la nuit. *At nightfall.*
TOMBER *to fall.*
Les feuilles commencent à tomber. *The leaves are starting to fall.*
Il tombe de l'eau. *It's raining.*
Tomber des nues. *To be astounded.*
On entendrait tomber une épingle. *You could hear a pin drop.*
Le projet est tombé à l'eau. *The project fell through. Nothing came of the project.*
Je tombe de sommeil. *I'm dead tired.*
Il est tombé malade. *He became sick.*
Il en est tombé amoureux. *He fell in love with her.*
tombola *f. charity lottery.*
tome *m. volume.*
Le tome premier n'est pas trouvable. *Volume one is missing (can't be found).*
ton *m. tone.*
Il changera bientôt de ton. *He'll soon change his tune.*
Prenez-le d'un ton un peu moins haut. *Come down a peg or two. Get off your high horse.*
Ses plaisanteries sont de très mauvais ton. *His jokes are in very bad taste.*
TON (ta *f.*, tes *pl.*) *your (familiar).*
Où est ton couteau? *Where's your knife?*
Ta sœur m'a téléphoné. *Your sister phoned me.*
Où sont tes livres? *Where are your books?*
tondeuse *f. (hair-) clippers.*
tondre *to clip.*
Tondre les cheveux. *To clip one's hair.*
tonique *adj. tonic.*
tonne *f. ton.*
tonneau (tonneaux *pl.*) *barrel.*
tonner *to thunder.*
tonnerre *m. thunder.*
torche *f. torch.*
torchon *m. dish towel.*
tordre *to twist, wring.*
Tordez ces vêtements. *Wring these clothes out.*
se tordre *to twist.*
Se tordre de rire (*fam.*). *To split one's sides laughing.*
torpeur *f. torpor.*
torpille *f. torpedo.*
torrent *m. torrent.*
Il pleut à torrent. *It's raining in torrents.*
Un torrent d'injures. *A stream of insults.*
Un torrent de larmes. *A flood of tears.*
torrentiel (torrentielle *f.*) *adj. torrential.*
Une pluie torrentielle. *A torrential rain.*
torride *adj. torrid; scorching.*
La zone torride. *The torrid zone.*
Il y faisait une chaleur torride. *The heat was scorching.*

torse *m. torso.*
TORT *m. wrong; error, fault.*
Vous avez tort. *You're wrong.*
Il est difficile de savoir qui a tort et qui a raison dans ce cas. *It's hard to know in this case who's right and who's wrong.*
Les absents ont toujours tort. *The absent are always in the wrong.*
Taisez-vous. Vous parlez à tort et à travers. *Keep quiet. You're talking nonsense.*
Vous lui avez fait beaucoup de tort. *You've done him a great deal of harm. You've wronged him.*
torticolis *m. stiff neck.*
tortue *f. turtle.*
Lent comme une tortue. *Slow as a snail ("as a turtle").*
torture *f. torture.*
Il a mis son esprit à la torture. *He racked his brain.*
torturer *to torture.*
TÔT *soon; early.*
Tôt ou tard. *Sooner or later.*
Il faudra quand même que vous le fassiez, tôt ou tard. *You'll have to do it sooner or later anyway.*
Nous avons l'habitude de nous réveiller tôt. *We're used to (accustomed to) getting up early.*
Pouvez-vous venir plus tôt? *Can you come earlier?*
Le plus tôt possible. *As soon as possible.*
total (totaux *pl.*) *noun (m.) and adj.* (totale *f.*) *total.*
Faites le total. *Add it up. Get the total.*
Le total s'élève à près de dix mille francs. *The whole sum amounts to 10,000 francs.*
totalement *totally.*
totalité *f. totality.*
En totalité. *As a whole.*
touchant *m. touching, pathetic.*
TOUCHER *to touch; to cash (check).*
N'y touchez pas! *Don't touch that!*
On ne touche pas! *Hands off! Don't touch!*
En ce qui touche cette affaire . . . *As far as this question is concerned . . .*
Ça lui a touché le cœur. *That affected (moved) him (her). ("It touched his [her] heart.")*
Je vais lui toucher un mot. *I'll mention it to him. I'll have a word with him about it. I'll drop him a hint (about it).*
se toucher *to border on each other.*
touffe *f. tuft, clump, wisp.*
touffu *adj. bushy, thick.*
Cheveux touffus. *Bushy hair.*
Bois touffus. *Thick woods.*
TOUJOURS *always; still.*
Il vient toujours trop tôt. *He always comes too early.*
Je suis toujours content de vous voir. *I'm always glad to see you.*
Essayez toujours! *Keep trying!*
Se trouve-t-il toujours à Paris? *Is he still in Paris?*
Toujours est-il que je ne l'ai plus jamais revu. *The fact remains that I never saw him again.*
Comme toujours. *As always, as usual.*
Pour toujours. *Forever.*
toupet *m. toupee; nerve (fam.).*
Quel toupet! *What nerve!*
Il en a du toupet! *He has some nerve!*
tour *f. tower.*
TOUR *m. turn; tour; stroll; trick.*

Faire un tour. *To take a walk.*
A chacun son tour. *Every dog has his day.*
Fermer à double tour. *To double-lock.*
A tour de rôle. *In turn.*
En un tour de main. *In the twinkling of an eye.*
Quel est votre tour de tête? *What size hat do you wear?*
Son sang n'a fait qu'un tour. *It gave him a dreadful shock.*
Un tour de cartes. *A card trick.*
Jouer un mauvais tour à quelqu'un. *To do someone a bad turn. To play someone a dirty trick.*
Le tour à pied. *Walk, stroll.*
Un disque de 33 tours. *33 r.p.m. record.*
Votre tour dans la queue. *Your place in the line.*
tourbillon *m. whirlwind.*
tourisme *m. touring.*
Bureau de tourisme. *Travel bureau. Travel agency.*
touriste *m. tourist.*
tourment *m. torment.*
Il a fait le tourment de ma vie. *He has been the bane of my existence.*
Les tourments de la faim. *Hunger pangs.*
tourmente *f. storm.*
tourmenter *to torment.*
Il le tourmente sans arrêt. *He keeps tormenting him.*
Cet incident le tourmente. *This incident worries him.*
tournant *m. turning.*
Les tournants de l'histoire. *The turning points of history.*
J'ai pris le mauvais tournant. *I took the wrong turn.*
tournée *f. tour (theatre); round.*
La tournée d'un agent de police. *A policeman's beat.*
Il a payé une tournée à tout le monde. *He bought a round of drinks for everyone.*
Faire une tournée. *To go on tour.*
tournemain *f. jiffy.*
Il l'a fait en un tournemain. *He did it in a jiffy (in the twinkling of an eye, before you could say Jack Robinson).*
TOURNER *to turn.*
Quand vous arrivez devant votre hôtel, tournez à gauche. *When you come to your hotel, turn to the left.*
L'affaire a mal tourné. *The deal fell through.*
Ma tête me tourne. *I feel giddy. My head's swimming.*
Il tourne autour du pot. *He's beating around the bush.*
Elle lui a tourné la tête. *He became infatuated with her. ("She turned his head.")*
Il l'a tourné en ridicule. *He made fun of him. He made him look ridiculous.*
Tourner le dos à quelqu'un. *To give someone the cold shoulder.*
tournoi *m. tournament.*
tournure *f. shape, figure; turn, cast, appearance.*
La tournure d'une phrase. *The construction of a sentence. Sentence-construction.*
Ses affaires ont pris une bien mauvaise tournure. *His affairs took a turn for the worse.*
TOUS (plural of tout) *all.*
Ils sont tous partis. *They've all left.*
Tous les deux. *Both.*
tousser *to cough.*

TOUT (toute *f.*, toutes *f. pl.*, tous *m. pl.*) *adj. and pron. all, any, every.*
Tous les jours. *Every day.*
Tout au moins. *At the very least.*
Tout à fait. *Entirely.*
Tout le monde est là. *Everybody's there.*
Elles sont toutes parties à la campagne. *They all left for the country.*
J'ai laissé toutes mes affaires à Paris. *I've left all my things in Paris.*
Rien du tout. *Nothing at all.*
Pas du tout. *Not at all.*
Voilà tout. *That's all.*
Par-dessus tout. *Above all.*
A tout à l'heure! *See you later!*
Tout d'un coup. *Suddenly.*
De tous les temps. *Of all time.*
Tous les deux. *Both (of them, of us).*
Tous les trois. *All three (of them, of us).*
Toute la journée. *The whole day, all day long.*
Toutes les deux semaines. *Every other week.*
Toutes sortes de. *All kinds of.*
Manger de tout. *To eat all sorts of things.*
Tout ce qu'il vous faut. *Everything you need.*
Tout ce qui peut intéresser une femme. *Everything that could interest a woman.*
Tout est bien qui finit bien. *All's well that ends well.*
tout *m. the whole thing; the entire amount.*
(Mais) pas du tout! *Not at all! No indeed! Certainly not!*
tout, toute *adv. very, quite, entirely, completely.*
Mes gencives sont tout enflées. *My gums are all swollen.*
Tout à fait. *Quite, entirely, altogether.*
Tout à l'heure. *Presently, in a little while; a little while ago.*
Tout de suite. *Right away, immediately.*
Tout droit. *Straight ahead.*
Tout près d'ici. *Right near here.*
Tout simplement. *(Quite) simply; just, only.*
Un tout petit peu. *Just a little bit.*
Vous avez la gorge toute rouge. *Your throat is all red.*
TOUTEFOIS *nevertheless.*
Toutefois je ne suis pas d'accord avec vous. *Nevertheless, I don't agree with you.*
Toutefois ce n'est pas une raison pour que vous vous fâchiez. *That's still no reason for you to get angry.*
toux *f. cough.*
trac *m. fear.*
J'ai le trac (*fam.*). *I'm afraid. I have cold feet.*
tracas *m. worry.*
Il a eu des tracas dernièrement. *He's been very worried lately.*
tracasser *to bother, pester.*
Il l'a tracassé du matin au soir. *He bothered him from morning till night.*
Ne vous tracassez pas. *Don't worry. Don't let it worry you.*
trace *f. track; footprint.*
Il suit les traces de son père. *He's following in his father's footsteps.*
Ce poème lui a laissé une trace profonde. *The poem made a deep impression on him.*
tracer *m. to trace.*
Tracer une carte. *To trace a map.*
Il faut tracer une ligne de conduite. *We must lay down (work out) a policy.*
tradition *f. tradition.*
C'est une vieille tradition. *It's an old tradition.*
traditionnel (traditionnelle *f.*) *adj. traditional.*

traducteur *m.* (traductrice *f.*) *translator.*
traduction *f. translation.*
traduire *to translate.*
trafic *m. traffic.*
Durant les heures d'affluence il y a beaucoup de trafic ici. *During rush hours there's a lot of traffic here.*
Les heures de fort trafic. *Busy hours. Peak hours.*
Les heures de faible trafic. *Slack hours.*
trafiquer *to trade in, deal in.*
tragédie *f. tragedy.*
tragique *noun (m.) and adj. tragic.*
Il prend tout au tragique. *He takes everything too seriously.*
trahir *to betray.*
trahison *f. treachery, betrayal.*
TRAIN *m. train; rate.*
J'ai manqué le train. *I missed the train.*
Le train doit arriver à midi. *The train is due at noon.*
Il a mené l'affaire à bon train. *He brought the deal to a successful conclusion.*
Au train où vous allez vous n'aurez pas encore fini dans dix ans. *At the rate you're going, you'll never finish.*
Il a mis l'affaire en train. *He prepared the deal. He got the deal started.*
Ils mènent grand train. *They live in grand style.*
A fond de train. *At full speed.*
Il est en train d'écrire des lettres. *He's busy writing letters.*
Il est en train de partir. *He's ready (about) to leave.*
Il est en train de s'habiller. *He's getting dressed.*
Elle est en train de préparer le dîner. *She's preparing dinner.*
traîne *f. train (of a dress).*
traîneau *m. sleigh.*
traîner *to drag; be scattered around.*
L'affaire traîne en longueur. *The matter (affair, business) is taking a long time ("is dragging out.")*
Il laisse tout traîner. *He leaves everything lying about. He leaves things scattered about.*
Ne laissez pas traîner vos vêtements. *Don't leave your clothes lying about.*
Ramassez toutes les choses qui traînent. *Pick up everything that's scattered about.*
se traîner *to crawl along.*
traintrain *m. routine.*
Les choses vont leur traintrain. *Things are taking their course (moving slowly).*
traire *to milk.*
trait *m. used in the following expressions:*
Il a bu tout d'un trait. *He gulped it down. ("He drank it in one swallow.")*
Des traits réguliers. *Regular features.*
Un trait de génie. *A stroke of genius.*
Cela a trait à ce qu'on vient de dire. *That refers to what has already been said.*
Un trait d'union. *A hyphen.*
traite *f. stretch; draft, bill.*
Durant leur voyage ils ont fait 500 km. d'une traite. *During their trip they made 500 kilometers at a stretch.*
Ils l'ont fait tout d'une traite. *They did it straight off the bat.*
Accepter une traite. *To accept a note (draft).*
traité *m. treaty, treatise.*
traitement *m. treatment, salary.*
Le traitement d'une maladie. *The treatment of*

a disease.
Son traitement n'est pas très élevé. *His salary isn't very high.*
Il a subi des mauvais traitements. *He was mistreated. He was harshly treated.*
traiter *to treat.*
Il a traité cette affaire à la légère. *He treated the matter lightly. He didn't take the matter to heart.*
Traiter quelqu'un d'égal à égal. *To treat someone as an equal.*
Il l'a traité d'imbécile. *He called him a fool.*
traître *m. traitor.*
traître *adj. treacherous.*
Il ne m'en a pas dit un traître mot. *He didn't mention it to me. He didn't tell me the first thing (a single word) about it.*
trajet *m. journey.*
J'ai fait une partie du trajet en auto. *I drove part of the way.*
Ce n'est pas un long trajet. *It isn't a long trip.*
Un trajet de quatre heures. *A trip that takes four hours. A four-hour trip.*
trame *f. plot.*
tramer *to weave.*
tramway *m. trolley car, streetcar.*
Est-ce que le tramway s'arrête ici? *Does the trolley stop here?*
tranchant *m. edge.*
Epée à deux tranchants. *Two-edged sword.*
tranchant *adj. cutting, sharp.*
tranche *f. slice.*
Couper du pain en tranches. *To slice a loaf of bread.*
Une tranche de jambon. *A slice of ham.*
trancher *to cut, slice.*
Tranchons là. (Tranchons la question.) *Let's drop the subject.*
Il tranche sur tout. *He's very dogmatic.*
tranchée *f. trench.*
TRANQUILLE *adj. tranquil, calm.*
Tenez-vous tranquille. *Keep still. Keep quiet.*
Restez tranquille. *Keep still. Keep quiet.*
Maintenant j'ai l'esprit tranquille. *Now my mind is at ease.*
Les enfants sont très tranquilles. *The children are very quiet.*
Laissez-moi tranquille. *Let me alone.*
C'est un homme très tranquille. *He's a very calm person.*
tranquillement *quietly, calmly.*
tranquilliser *to calm.*
se tranquilliser *to calm down, to feel calmer, to be easier in one's mind.*
tranquillité *f. tranquillity.*
transaction *f. transaction.*
transatlantique *noun (m.) and adj. transatlantic.*
Une chaise transatlantique. *A deck chair.*
transcription *f. transcription; transcript.*
transcrire *to transcribe.*
transe *f. anxiety.*
transférer *to transfer.*
transformation *f. transformation.*
transformer *to change.*
transfusion *f. transfusion.*
transi *adj. chilled, numb.*
Transi de froid. *He's numb with cold. He's frozen.*
Transi de peur. *He's petrified (with fear). He's frightened to death.*
transit *m. transit.*
Un visa de transit. *A transit visa.*
transitaire *m. forwarding agent.*

transition f. transition.
transmettre to transmit.
transparent adj. transparent.
transpercer to pierce; penetrate.
transpiration f. perspiration.
transpirer to perspire.
transport m. transport; transportation.
  Frais de transport. Freight charges.
  Avec transport. Enthusiastically.
transporter to transport.
  Il fut transporté à l'hôpital. He was carried to
    the hospital.
  Etre transporté de joie. To be beside oneself
    with joy.
trappe f. trap, pitfall.
traquer to track down.
TRAVAIL m. (travaux pl.) work.
  Un travail difficile. A difficult job.
  Au travail maintenant! Get to work! Let's get
    to work!
  Il faut se mettre au travail. We must get down
    to work.
  Le Ministère du Travail. Ministry of Labor.
    Labor Department.
  Les travaux publics. Public works.
  Condamné aux travaux forcés. Condemned to
    hard labor.
TRAVAILLER to work.
  Ils travaillent trop. They work too hard (much).
  Il travaille à l'heure. He works by the hour.
  Quelque chose la travaille. Something is prey-
    ing on her mind.
se travailler to worry.
travailleur m. worker, industrious person.
travailleur (travailleuse f.) adj. industrious.
TRAVERS m. breadth, width.
  A travers. Across.
  A travers champ. Across country.
  Passez au travers de ce champ. Go through
    this field.
  Elle fait tout de travers. She does everything
    wrong.
  Il l'a regardé de travers. He gave him a black
    look.
  Vous avez tout compris de travers. You've
    misunderstood everything.
traversée f. crossing.
  Avez-vous fait une bonne traversée? Did you
    have a good crossing?
TRAVERSER to cross.
  Traversons. Let's cross over to the other side.
  Elle a traversé la rue. She crossed the street.
  Une idée lui a traversé l'esprit. An idea flashed
    through his (her) mind.
travesti adj. disguise.
  Un bal travesti. A fancy dress ball.
travestir to disguise.
trébucher to stumble.
trèfle m. clover; clubs (cards).
TREIZE noun and adj. thirteen.
TREIZIÈME noun and adj. thirteenth.
tremblement m. trembling.
  Une tremblement de terre. An earthquake.
trembler to tremble, shake.
trempe f. stamp; quality.
  Un homme de sa trempe. A man of his caliber.
tremper to soak.
  J'étais trempé jusqu'aux os. I was soaked to
    the skin ("bones").
tremplin m. springboard.
trentaine f. about thirty.
TRENTE noun and adj. thirty.
  Il est six heures trente. It's six-thirty.

J'ai vu trente-six chandelles. I saw stars. ("I
  saw thirty-six candles.")
J'en ai assez de faire ses trente-six volontés.
  I'm tired of catering to his whims.
Il n'y a pas trente-six façons de le faire. There
  are no two ways about it.
Vous me l'avez déjà répété trente-six fois.
  You've repeated it to me a hundred ("thirty-
  six") times.
trentième noun and adj. thirtieth.
trépigner to stamp one's feet.
TRÈS very.
  Très bon. Very good.
  Très bien. Very well.
  Très peu. Very little.
  C'est très joli. It's very pretty.
  J'ai très froid. I'm very cold.
  De très bonne heure. Very early.
trésor m. treasure.
trésorerie f. treasury.
trésorier m. (trésorière f.) treasurer.
tressaillir to start, give a start, quiver.
tresse f. braid.
tresser to weave.
trêve f. truce.
triangle m. triangle.
tribu f. tribe.
tribunal m. (tribunaux pl.) tribunal, court.
tribut m. tribute.
tricher to cheat.
tricherie f. cheating; trickery.
tricheur m. (tricheuse f.) cheat, trickster.
tricot m. sweater; knitting.
tricoter to knit.
trier to sort, sort out.
  Aujourd'hui je vais trier mes lettres. Today I'll
    sort my correspondence.
trimbaler (fam.) to drag.
trimestre m. three-month period.
trinquer to clink glasses.
trio m. trio.
triomphal (triomphaux pl.) adj. triumphal.
triomphe m. triumph.
triompher to triumph.
  Il a triomphé de toutes les difficultés. He over-
    came every difficulty.
triple adj. triple.
tripoter to paw, handle; meddle with, mess about,
  play with; speculate with.
  Ne tripotez pas mes affaires. Don't tamper with
    (mess around with) my things.
  Il tripote l'argent des autres. He speculates
    with other people's money.
TRISTE adj. sad.
  Elle a l'air triste. She looks sad.
  Je fus bien triste d'apprendre que . . . I was
    very sorry to hear that . . .
  Il lui a fait triste mine. He received him with-
    out enthusiasm.
tristesse f. melancholy, sadness.
  Avec tristesse. Sadly.
trivial (triviaux pl.) adj. trivial.
trivialité f. triviality, triteness; vulgarity.
  Trève de trivialités! Enough nonsense! Let's
    get serious!
TROIS noun and adj. three.
  Les trois quarts du temps. Most of the time.
    ("Three quarters of the time.")
  Diviser en trois. To divide into three parts.
  Le trois juillet. July third.
  Tous les trois. All three (of them, of us).
  Trois fois par jour. Three times a day.
TROISIÈME noun and adj. third.

trombe f. whirlwind.
  Il est entré en trombe. He came bursting in.
trompe-l'oeil m. deceptive appearance; deception,
  sham.
  Ces promesses ne sont qu'un trompe-l'oeil.
    These are empty promises.
  Cette nouvelle loi n'est qu'un trompe-l'oeil.
    This new law is just so much window-
    dressing (camouflage, bluff).
tromper to deceive.
  C'est ce qui vous trompe. This is where you're
    mistaken. This is what fools you.
  Il se laisse tromper par les apparences. He's
    taken in by appearances.
  Tromper la vigilance de quelqu'un. To elude
    the vigilance of someone.
SE TROMPER to be mistaken.
  Vous vous trompez. You're mistaken.
  Je me suis trompé sur ce sujet. I was mistaken
    about that.
  Il est facile de se tromper dans un cas pareil.
    It's very easy to make a mistake in a case of
    this sort.
  A moins que je ne me trompe, c'est l'endroit
    même. Unless I'm mistaken, this is the very
    spot.
  Il n'y a pas à s'y tromper. There's no mistake
    about it.
tromperie f. deceit; delusion.
trompette f. trumpet.
  Il partit sans tambour ni trompette. He left
    quietly (without any fuss).
trompeur (trompeuse f.) noun and adj. deceitful,
  deceptive.
  Les apparences sont trompeuses. Appearances
    are deceptive.
  A trompeur, trompeur et demi. Set a thief to
    catch a thief.
tronc m. trunk.
  Le tronc de l'arbre. The trunk of a tree.
trône m. throne.
TROP too.
  Trop tôt. Too early.
  Trop tard. Too late.
  N'allez pas trop loin. Don't go too far.
  Il était de trop. He was unwelcome. ("He was
    one too many.")
  C'en est trop! This is too much! This is the
    last straw!
  Bien trop cher. Much too expensive.
  Trop longtemps. Too long.
trophée f. trophy.
trot m. trot.
trotter to trot.
  Elle est toujours à trotter. She's always on the
    go.
  Cette chanson me trotte dans la tête. That tune
    keeps running through my head.
trottoir m. sidewalk.
trou m. hole, opening.
trouble noun (m.) and adj. confusion, disorder.
  Etat de trouble. State of agitation. Agitated
    state.
  Cause de trouble. Disturbing factor.
  Des troubles de vision. Trouble with one's
    eyesight. Eye trouble.
  Il lui a jeté le trouble dans l'esprit. He made
    him uneasy.
  Il a une âme trouble. His mind is uneasy.
  Il a une vision trouble. He has poor vision.
  Pêcher dans l'eau trouble. To fish in troubled
    waters.
trouble-fête m. kill-joy, wet blanket.

troubler *to stir up; disturb.*
    Cette situation est troublée. *The situation is confused.*
    Troubler le bonheur de quelqu'un. *To mar someone's happiness.*
    Troubler l'ordre public. *To disturb the peace.*
    Elle est toute troublée. *She's flustered (confused, upset). She's all excited.*
se troubler *to become cloudy; to get dim, blurred; to get confused.*
    Le temps commence à se troubler. *It's getting cloudy (overcast).*
    L'orateur se troubla. *The speaker became confused (lost the thread of his speech).*
    Sans se troubler. *Unruffled.*
    Sans se troubler il continua son travail. *He continued his work calmly.*
troupe *f. troop, troops.*
troupeau *m.* (troupeaux *pl.*) *flock.*
trousse *f. bundle, package; case, kit; pl. heels.*
    Une trousse d'outils. *A tool kit.*
    Une trousse de toilette. *A case for toilet articles.*
    Il était à ses trousses. *He was at his heels.*
trousseau *m.* (trousseaux *pl.*) *bunch (of keys); outfit, trousseau.*
    Un trousseau de clés. *A bunch of keys.*
    Elle achète son trousseau. *She's buying her trousseau.*
trouvaille *f. lucky find.*
    Notre bonne est une trouvaille. *Our maid's a treasure.*
TROUVER *to find; to think, consider.*
    L'avez-vous trouvé? *Did you find it?*
    Vous trouverez le bureau au bout du couloir. *You will find the office at the end of the corridor.*
    Venez me trouver jeudi. *Come to see me Thursday.*
    Ne trouvez-vous pas qu'il a tort? *Don't you think (agree) he's wrong?*
    Elle est jolie, vous ne trouvez pas? *She's pretty, don't you think?*
    Vous trouvez? *You think so? Do you think so?*
    Je le trouve sympathique. *I find him very pleasant (likeable, nice).*
    Je lui trouve mauvaise mine. *I don't think he looks well.*
    Trouver plaisir à. *To take pleasure in.*
SE TROUVER *to be; to feel.*
    Où se trouve la poste? *Where is the post office?*
    Il se trouvait dans le besoin. *He was in need.*
    Mon ancien professeur se trouvait là par hasard. *My former teacher happened to be there.*
    Il se trouva que je ne pouvais pas y aller. *It so happened that I couldn't go there.*
    Je me trouve mieux. *I feel better.*
truc *m. knack; whatsis, gimmick.*
    Avoir le truc pour faire quelque chose. *To have a knack for doing something.*
    Il a trouvé le truc. *He got the knack.*
    Il connaît les trucs du métier. *He knows all the tricks of the trade.*
truite *f. trout.*
truqueur *m.* (truqueuse *f.*) *faker, humbug, trickster, swindler.*
T.S.F. (télégraphie sans fil) *radio ("wireless").*
TU *you (familiar).*
    Où vas-tu? *Where are you going?*
    Que dis-tu? *What are you saying?*
tube *m. tube.*
tuberculose *f. tuberculosis.*

tuer *to kill.*
    J'ai failli être tué. *I came very near being killed.*
    Tuer le temps. *To kill time.*
    L'ennui le tue. *He's bored to death.*
se tuer *to kill oneself.*
    Il se tue au travail. *He's working himself to death.*
tue-tête *used in the following expression:*
    Crier à tue-tête. *To shout at the top of one's lungs.*
tuile *f. tile.*
    Quelle tuile (*fam.*)! *What bad luck!*
tumeur *f. tumor.*
tumulte *m. tumult; hustle and bustle.*
    En tumulte. *In an uproar. In confusion.*
    Un tumulte d'applaudissements. *Thunderous applause. A thunder of applause.*
tunnel *m. tunnel.*
turbulent *adj. turbulent, wild.*
turque *m. and f. noun and adj. Turkish.*
tutelle *f. guardianship.*
tuteur *m.* (tutrice *f.*) *guardian.*
se tutoyer *to be on familiar terms, to use "tu" to one another.*
tuyau *m.* (tuyaux *pl.*) *pipe.*
tweed *m. tweed.*
    En tweed. *In, of tweed.*
tympan *m. eardrum.*
type *m. type; fellow.*
    Le vrai type anglais. *The typical Englishman.*
    C'est un drôle de type (*fam.*). *He's a strange fellow.*
    J'ai connu un type qui . . . (*fam.*). *I once knew a fellow who . . .*
typhoïde *adj. typhoid.*
typique *adj. typical.*
tyran *m. tyrant.*
tyrannie *f. tyranny.*
tyranniser *to tyrannize.*

U *The twenty-first letter of the alphabet.*
ulcère *m. ulcer.*
ultérieur *adj. ulterior; subsequent.*
    Il a été élu dans une séance ultérieure. *He was elected at a later meeting.*
    Attendez les ordres ultérieurs. *Wait for further orders.*
ultérieurement *later on, subsequently.*
    Marchandises livrables ultérieurement. *Goods to be delivered later. Goods for future delivery.*
    Cette partie du contrat a été ajoutée ultérieurement. *This part of the contract was added subsequently.*
ultimatum *m. ultimatum.*
ultra- *ultra-.*
UN (une *f.*) *adj. and pron. one.*
    Ils arrivèrent un à un. *They arrived one by one.*
    Vous ne pouvez les distinguer l'un de l'autre. *You can't tell (distinguish) one from the other. You can't tell which is which.*
    Un de ces jours. *One of these days.*
    L'un et l'autre. *Both (of them).*
    Ni l'un ni l'autre. *Neither (of them).*
unanime *adj. unanimous.*
unanimité *f. unanimity.*
uni *adj. united, smooth, even, plain.*
unifier *to unify.*
    Ces deux industries furent unifiées. *These two industries were consolidated.*

Unifiez vos idées. *Organize your ideas.*
uniforme *noun (m.) and adj. uniform.*
    Une couleur uniforme. *A solid color.*
    Il vit une vie uniforme. *He leads an uneventful life.*
union *f. union.*
unique *adj. unique, sole.*
    Son unique plaisir. *His one (sole) pleasure.*
    Il est fils unique. *He's an only son.*
    Rue à sens unique. *One-way street.*
uniquement *solely.*
unir *to unite, join.*
    Ces faits sont étroitement unis. *These facts are closely connected.*
    Unir le geste à la parole. *To suit the action to the word.*
    Les Etats-Unis. *The United States.*
unisson *m. unison.*
    Chanter à l'unisson. *To sing in harmony.*
    Ses goûts sont à l'unisson des miens. *His tastes are similar to mine.*
unité *f. unity; unit.*
univers *m. universe.*
universel (universelle *f.*) *adj. universal, worldwide.*
universitaire *adj. pertaining to a university.*
université *f. university, college.*
urbain *adj. urban.*
urgence *f. urgency.*
    Il y a urgence à ce que ce soit fait immédiatement. *It's most important that this be done immediately.*
    En cas d'urgence. *In case of emergency.*
urgent *adj. urgent, pressing.*
    J'en ai un besoin urgent. *I need it urgently.*
    Il a du travail urgent à fair. *He has some urgent work to finish.*
USAGE *m. use; custom.*
    Faites usage d'un antiseptique. *Use an antiseptic.*
    Pour l'usage externe. *For external use only.*
    C'est un article à son usage. *This is for his personal use.*
    Usage personnel. *Personal use.*
    Ce costume est hors d'usage. *This suit is worn out.*
    Un mot hors d'usage. *An obsolete word.*
    Des phrases d'usage. *Polite (conventional) expressions.*
    Selon l'usage. *According to custom.*
    Il est d'usage de. *It's customary to.*
    Usages locaux. *Local customs.*
    Il manque d'usage. *He lacks breeding.*
usé *adj. worn-out.*
    Un costume usé. *A worn-out suit. An old suit.*
user *to use; wear out.*
    Il a usé son pardessus. *His overcoat is worn out. He wore his coat out.*
    Il a usé ses yeux à force de lire sans avoir assez de lumière. *He spoiled his eyes by reading in poor light.*
    Il a usé de moyens peu honnêtes. *He used (resorted to) dishonest means.*
    User de force. *To use force.*
    User de son droit. *To avail oneself of one's rights. To take advantage of one's rights.*
    Il a usé de tous les artifices pour réussir. *He used every trick in order to succeed.*
    Est-ce ainsi que vous en usez avec eux? *Is that how you deal with them?*
s'user *to wear out.*
    Sa vue s'use de plus en plus. *His eyesight is growing worse.*

usine f. factory, plant.

Un ouvrier d'usine. A factory worker.

ustensile m. utensil.

usuel (usuelle f.) adj. usual, common.

Une expression usuelle. A common expression.

usuellement usually.

usure f. usury; wear.

Cette étoffe résiste bien à l'usure. This material wears well.

usurper to usurp.

UTILE adj. useful.

En quoi puis-je vous être utile? What can I do for you? Can I be of any help to you?

Est-ce que cela pourra vous être utile? Can this be of any use to you? Can you use this?

C'est un homme utile à connaître. He's a useful man to know.

Je le ferai en temps utile. I'll do it in due time.

utiliser to utilize.

utilité f. utility.

Ceci est d'une grande utilité. This has many uses. This is very useful.

Sans utilité. Useless.

V The twenty-second letter of the alphabet.

vacance f. vacancy; pl. vacation.

Où partez-vous en vacances cette année? Where are you going for your vacation this year?

Les grandes vacances finissent le premier octobre. The summer vacation ends October first.

vacant adj. vacant, unoccupied.

vacarme m. noise; uproar, hubbub.

Ils font du vacarme. They're making a racket.

vacciner to vaccinate.

vache f. cow.

vacillant adj. unsteady.

vaciller to be unsteady, waver, vacillate.

Il vacille sur ses jambes. He's unsteady on his legs.

Je ne m'en rappelle plus bien; ma mémoire vacille sur ce sujet. I can't recollect it very clearly; my memory is uncertain on that point.

Il vacille entre les deux solutions. He's hesitating between the two solutions. He can't make up his mind which solution to choose.

va-et-vient m. coming and going.

vagabond adj. vagabond, vagrant.

vague f. wave.

Les vagues étaient très hautes. The waves were very high.

Une vague de chaleur. A heat wave.

vague adj. vague, indefinite.

Sa réponse fut très vague. His answer was very vague.

Une couleur vague. An indefinite color.

Un regard vague. A vacant glance.

Je ne sais pas ce qu'il est, quelque vague acteur, je crois. I don't know what he is—some sort of actor, I believe.

vaguement vaguely.

vaillance f. bravery.

vaillamment valiantly.

vaillant adj. brave, spirited.

Elle n'a pas un sou vaillant. She hasn't a penny.

vain adj. vain.

De vaines promesses. Empty promises.

Elle est très vaine. She's very vain.

En vain. In vain. Vainly.

vaincre to conquer.

Ils furent vaincus. They were defeated.

Il a vaincu sa frayeur. He overcame his fear.

Il a dû s'avouer vaincu. He had to admit defeat.

vainqueur m. conqueror, victor.

vaisseau m. (vaisseaux pl.) vessel.

vaisselle f. plates and dishes.

Faire la vaisselle. To do the dishes.

valable adj. valid.

Ces billets ne sont valables que pour deux mois. These tickets are good for only two months.

Une excuse valable. A valid excuse.

valet m. valet.

Le valet de pique. The jack of spades.

Il a une âme de valet. He's very servile.

VALEUR f. value; pl. bonds, securities.

C'est un bijou de valeur. It's a very valuable jewel.

C'est un homme de valeur. He's very capable. He's a man of great abilities.

Cela n'a pas grande valeur. It isn't worth much.

Attacher beaucoup de valeur à quelque chose. To attach a great deal of importance to something. To set great store by something.

Ces renseignements sont sans aucune valeur. This information is completely valueless.

Mettre en valeur. To set off to best advantage.

Il sait mettre ses connaissances en valeur. He knows how to show off his knowledge.

Mettre une propriété en valeur. To improve the value of a property.

Il a mis ce mot en valeur. He emphasized that word.

Ces valeurs sont d'un bon rapport. These securities yield a good return.

Un colis avec valeur déclarée. A registered parcel.

valeureux (valeureuse f.) adj. brave, courageous.

validité f. validity.

La validité de ce passeport est d'un an. This passport is valid for a year.

La validité d'un argument. The validity of an argument.

valise f. valise, suitcase.

Portez cette valise en haut. Carry this suitcase upstairs.

J'ai déja fait mes valises. I've already packed my bags.

vallée f. valley.

La vallée de la Loire. The Loire Valley.

VALOIR to be worth.

Cela ne vaut rien. It's (that's) not worth anything. It's (that's) worthless.

Cela ne vaut pas grand'chose. That's not very important. That's not worth very much.

Il ne vaut pas mieux que son prédécesseur. He's no better than his predecessor.

Ça vaudrait mieux. That would be better. That would be more advisable.

Il vaudrait mieux rester ici pour le moment. It would be better to stay here for the moment.

Autant vaut retourner à la maison. We may as well go home.

Il sait se faire valoir. He knows how to make the most of himself.

Je trouve que cela vaut le coup. I think it's worth trying.

Cela ne vaut pas la peine. It isn't worth while.

Mieux vaut tard que jamais. Better late than never.

Ce n'est rien qui vaille. It's not worth anything. It's not something of value.

Mieux vaut les faire réparer. It's better to have them repaired.

valse f. waltz.

valser to waltz.

vanille f. vanilla.

vanité f. vanity.

vaniteux (vaniteuse f.) adj. vain, conceited.

vanter to praise.

se vanter to boast.

Il se vante de son succès. He boasts about his success.

Ce n'est pas quelque chose dont je me vanterais. That's nothing to brag about. I wouldn't boast about anything of that sort.

vapeur f. steam, vapor.

Vapeur d'eau. Steam.

Bateau à vapeur. Steamer.

vaquer to be in recess; devote one's attention to.

Il vaque à ses occupations. He attends (devotes himself) to his business.

variable adj. variable, changeable.

Un temps variable. Changeable weather.

Il est d'humeur variable. He's very moody. His moods keep changing.

variation f. variation.

Variation de temps. Changes in the weather.

VARIER to vary, change.

Les opinions varient à ce sujet. Opinions vary on this subject.

Ce tissu varie en qualité. This cloth varies in quality.

Le temps varie. The weather is changing.

variété f. variety.

Il n'y a pas grande variété ici. There's very little variety here (in a store, restaurant, etc.).

vase m. vase.

vaseline f. vaseline.

vaste adj. vast, spacious.

vaudeville m. vaudeville.

vau-l'eau used in the following expressions:

A vau-l'eau. Downstream. Adrift.

Tout va à vau-l'eau. Everything is going to ruin.

Aller à vau-l'eau. To come to nothing.

se vautrer to sprawl.

VEAU m. (veaux pl.) calf.

Un rôti de veau. Roast veal.

vécu have lived.

vedette f. star.

C'est une des dernières vedettes. He's (she's) one of the recent stars (movies, theatre).

Une vedette à moteur (or une vedette). A motorboat; patrol boat.

végétation f. vegetation; pl. adenoids.

végéter to vegetate.

véhémence f. vehemence.

véhément adj. vehement.

véhicule m. vehicle.

veille f. the state of being awake; day or evening before.

La veille des élections. The day before election.

Je l'ai vu la veille au soir. I saw him last night.

La veille de Noël. Christmas Eve.

Il est à la veille de la ruine. He's on the brink of ruin.

VEILLER to stay up; watch over.

Elle a veillé très tard. She sat up very late.

Veiller aux intérêts de quelqu'un. To look after someone's interests.

Il veillera sur lui. *He'll look after him. He'll take care of him.*

Veillez à ce que mes ordres soient exécutés. *See to it that my orders are carried out.*

veilleur m. *watcher, night watchman.*

veilleuse f. *night light.*

Lumière en veilleuse. *Dim light. Light turned low.*

Il a mis l'électricité en veilleuse. *He dimmed the lights.*

Mettez vos phares en veilleuse. *Dim your headlights.*

VEINE f. *vein; luck.*

Il s'est coupé une veine. *He cut a vein.*

Il a de la veine. *He is lucky. He has luck.*

Ça a été un coup de veine. *It was a stroke of luck.*

Pas de veine! *Rotten luck!*

Il est en veine de plaisanterie. *He's in a humorous (joking) mood.*

vélo m. (fam.) *bicycle.*

vélocité f. *velocity.*

velours m. *velvet.*

vendange f. *grape harvest.*

vendeur m. (vendeuse f.) *person who sells; salesman, salesgirl; storekeeper.*

VENDRE to *sell.*

Ce magasin vend de tout. *This store sells (carries) everything.*

Maison à vendre. *House for sale.*

Cela se vend beaucoup. *That sells very well.*

VENDREDI m. *Friday.*

vénéneux (vénéneuse f.) adj. *poisonous (of plants).*

vénérable adj. *venerable.*

vénération f. *veneration, respect.*

vénérer to *revere, respect.*

vengeance f. *revenge.*

venger to *avenge.*

se venger to *get revenge.*

venimeux (venimeuse f.) adj. *poisonous.*

venin m. *venom.*

VENIR to *come.*

Venez avec nous. *Come with us.*

Quand pensez-vous venir? *When do you expect to come?*

Faites-le venir. *Have him come. Ask him to come. Get him to come.*

Il l'a fait venir. *He sent for him.*

Le voilà qui vient! *Here he comes!*

Je viens le voir. *I've come to see him.*

Il vient de sortir. *He just went out (left). He's just gone out.*

Où voulez-vous en venir? *What are you driving at?*

Maintenant je vous vois venir. *Now I see what you're driving at.*

D'où vient-il que vous n'alliez plus là? *How come you don't go there anymore?*

Il en était venu à sa fin. *He was at the end of his rope.*

Il me vient à l'idée que. *It occurs to me that.*

VENT m. *wind.*

Il fait du vent aujourd'hui. *It's windy today.*

Un coup de vent. *A gust of wind.*

Il est entré en coup de vent. *He dashed in.*

Il a jeté la paille au vent. *He trusted to luck.*

Regarder de quel côté souffle le vent. *To see how the land lies.*

Quel bon vent vous amène? *What lucky chance brings you here?*

Qui sème le vent récolte la tempête. *He that sows the wind shall reap the whirlwind.*

Il en a eu vent. *He got wind of it.*

Il a donné vent à sa colère. *He gave vent to his anger.*

VENTE f. *sale.*

Marchandise de bonne vente. *Goods that sell well.*

La vente ne va pas. *Business is slow.*

Hors de vente. *No longer on sale.*

Mise en vente. *For sale.*

En vente. *On sale.*

En vente à. *On sale at.*

ventilateur m. *ventilator, electric fan.*

VENTRE m. *belly, stomach.*

Il a mal au ventre (fam.). *He has a stomachache.*

Ventre affamé n'a point d'oreilles. *A hungry man doesn't listen to reason. ("A hungry stomach has no ears.")*

venu m. *one who comes.*

Le premier venu. *The first one who comes.*

Le dernier venu. *The last one who comes.*

venue f. *coming, arrival.*

Votre venue lui fera beaucoup de plaisir. *He'll be very happy (pleased) if you come. ("Your coming will give him a great deal of pleasure.")*

Avisez-moi de votre venue. *Let me know in advance when you'll arrive. ("Notify me in advance of your arrival.")*

Après plusieurs allées et venues . . . *After going back and forth several times . . .*

ver m. *worm.*

Un ver de terre. *An earthworm.*

Ver à soie. *Silkworm.*

véracité f. *veracity, truthfulness.*

verbal (verbaux pl.) adj. *verbal, oral.*

verbalement *verbally.*

VERBE m. *verb; tone of voice.*

Un verbe régulier. *A regular verb.*

Avoir le verbe haut. *To be dictatorial.*

verdict m. *verdict.*

verdir to *turn green.*

verdure f. *greenery.*

verge f. *rod, staff, switch.*

Gouverner avec une verge de fer. *To rule with a rod of iron.*

Il est sous la verge de son frère aîné. *He's under his older brother's thumb.*

Verge d'or. *Goldenrod.*

verger m. *orchard.*

verglas m. *sleet.*

véridique adj. *veracious, true.*

vérification f. *verification.*

vérifier to *verify, adjust.*

Vérifier une référence. *To verify (check) a reference.*

Vérifier la tension artérielle. *To take one's blood pressure.*

Vérifiez si tout est prêt. *Make sure that everything is ready.*

Il faut vérifier les suffrages. *The votes have to be counted and checked.*

Ma montre a besoin d'être vérifiée. *My watch needs adjusting.*

véritable adj. *real.*

C'est un véritable diamant, et non pas du toc. *It's a real diamond, not an imitation.*

Il n'a fait que glisser sur le véritable sujet. *He barely touched on the real subject.*

Ce fut une véritable surprise. *It was a real surprise.*

Il a été un véritable ami. *He has been a true (real) friend.*

véritablement *truly, really.*

VÉRITÉ f. *truth.*

La vérité pure et simple. *The pure and simple truth.*

Dites la vérité. *Tell the truth.*

Ce que je vous dis là, c'est la vérité. *What I'm telling you is a fact (the truth).*

La vérité finit toujours par se découvrir. *Truth will out.*

En vérité ça ne me dit rien. *To tell the truth it doesn't appeal to me.*

Je lui ai dit ses quatre vérités. *I told him a few home truths.*

vermine f. *vermin.*

vernir to *varnish.*

Les peintures viennent d'être vernies. *The paintings have just been varnished.*

Il a verni son récit. *He colored his story.*

vérole f. *pox.*

La petite vérole. *Smallpox.*

VERRE m. *glass.*

Boire dans un verre. *To drink from a glass.*

Mettre sous verre. *To keep under glass.*

Articles de verre. *Glassware.*

Papier de verre. *Sandpaper.*

J'ai pris un verre avec lui. *I had a drink with him.*

Vous voulez boire un petit verre? *Would you like a drink (of liquor)?*

verrou m. *bolt.*

vers m. *verse.*

VERS prep. *toward.*

Allons vers cette maison-là. *Let's go toward that house.*

Le voilà! Il vient vers nous. *There he is! He's coming toward us.*

Nous en reparlerons vers la fin de l'année. *We'll talk about it again toward the end of the year.*

Venez vers les deux heures. *Come about two.*

Il sera là vers trois heures. *He'll be there around three.*

(à) verse *pouring, emptying.*

A verse. *In torrents.*

La pluie tombe à verse. *It's pouring. It's raining in torrents. The rain's coming down in sheets. It's raining buckets. It's raining cats and dogs.*

versé adj. *experienced, versed in.*

VERSER to *pour; to deposit (money).*

Verser de l'eau. *To pour (some) water.*

Verser du café. *To pour (some) coffee.*

Versez-lui à boire. *Pour him a drink. Fill his glass.*

Verser une faible lumière. *To shed a dim light.*

Il a versé son argent à la banque. *He deposited his money at the bank.*

version f. *version.*

verso m. *back, reverse.*

Voir au verso. *See the reverse side.*

La réponse est écrite au verso. *The answer is written on the back.*

vert m. *green.*

VERT adj. *green.*

Légumes verts. *Green vegetables. Greens.*

Fruits verts. *Unripe fruit.*

Haricots verts. *String beans.*

Vert d'envie. *Green with envy.*

La verte jeunesse. *Callow youth.*

Vert clair (foncé). *Light (dark) green.*

vertical (verticaux pl.) adj. *vertical.*

vertige m. *dizziness, giddiness.*

Il fut pris de vertige. *He became dizzy.*

Cela m'a donné le vertige. *It made me dizzy.*

vertu f. *virtue, courage.*
Les quatre vertus cardinales. *The four cardinal virtues.*
Vivre dans la vertu. *To lead a good life.*
En vertu du contrat. *Under the terms of the contract.*
Faire de nécessité vertu. *To make a virtue of necessity.*
Plantes qui ont la vertu de guérir. *Plants that have healing properties.*
vertueux (vertueuse f.) *adj. virtuous.*
verve f. *zest, animation.*
Plein de verve. *Full of life. In lively spirits.*
Parler avec verve. *To speak in a lively manner.*
L'orateur était en verve aujourd'hui. *The speaker was in form today.*
veste f. *coat or jacket of a woman's suit.*
vestiaire m. *cloakroom.*
vestibule m. *hall, lobby.*
vestige m. *vestige, trace, remains.*
veston m. *coat, jacket (man's).*
Le complet-veston. *Business suit.*
Le veston à deux boutons. *Two-button jacket.*
vêtement m. *garment; pl. clothes.*
vétérinaire m. *veterinary.*
vêtir *to clothe, dress.*
Chaudement vêtu. *Warmly dressed.*
se vêtir *to be dressed in, put on.*
véto m. *veto.*
veuf *noun (m.) and adj. widower; widowered.*
veuve *noun (f.) and adj. widow, widowed.*
vexation f. *vexation.*
vexer *to vex, annoy.*
Ça le vexe. *That annoys him.*
Cela me vexe d'apprendre que . . . *I'm very sorry to hear that . . .*
viager m. *life interest.*
Il a placé son argent en viager. *He invested his money in a life annuity.*
viager (viagère f.) *adj. for life.*
Une rente viagère. *An income for life.*
VIANDE f. *meat.*
vibrant *adj. vibrating.*
vibrer *to vibrate.*
vice m. *vice.*
vice- *vice-.*
Vice-président. *Vice-president.*
vice versa *vice versa.*
vicieux (vicieuse f.) *adj. vicious; incorrect use of a word or expression.*
Un chien vicieux. *A vicious dog.*
Cercle vicieux. *A vicious circle.*
Une locution vicieuse. *An incorrect expression.*
Usage vicieux d'un mot. *The wrong use of a word.*
vicissitude f. *vicissitude.*
victime f. *victim.*
victoire f. *victory.*
victorieux (victorieuse f.) *adj. victorious.*
victuaille f. *usually pl. victuals.*
vide m. *empty space, void.*
Regarder dans le vide. *To stare into space.*
VIDE *adj. empty.*
J'ai l'estomac vide. *I'm hungry.*
Un appartement vide. *An empty apartment.*
Tête vide. *Empty-headed.*
Paroles vides de sens. *Meaningless words. Words without any sense.*
Des phrases vides. *Empty words.*
Il est revenu les mains vides. *He came back empty-handed.*
vider *to empty, clear out.*

Videz vos verres! *Drink!* ("*Empty your glasses.*")
Il fut forcé de vider les lieux. *He was compelled to vacate the premises.*
VIE f. *life.*
Plein de vie. *Full of life.*
Pour la vie. *For life.*
Sans vie. *Lifeless.*
Prix de la vie. *Cost of living.*
Comment gagne-t-il sa vie? *What does he do for a living?*
Jamais de la vie! *Never! It's out of the question!*
vieil *See* vieux.
vieillard m. *old man.*
vieille f. *old woman.*
vieillerie f. *old things, old rubbish, old clothes; old-fashioned idea.*
vieillesse f. *old age.*
vieillir *to grow old.*
vieux m. *old man.*
Mon vieux. *My friend. Old chap.*
VIEUX (vieil *before masculine nouns beginning with a vowel or "mute" h,* vieille f., vieilles f. pl.) *adj. old.*
De vieilles habitudes. *Old habits.*
Ça, c'est une vieille histoire. *That's an old story.*
Une vieille fille. *An old maid.*
Un vieux beau. *An old dandy.*
Ses parents sont vieux jeu. *His parents are old-fashioned.*
Un vieil homme. *An old man.*
VIF (vive f.) *adj. alive, living.*
Chair vive. *The quick. Living flesh.*
Vous l'avez blessé au vif. *You've wounded him to the quick.*
Elle a la langue vive. *She has a sharp tongue.*
Elle a l'humeur un peu vive. *She's short-tempered.*
Ils marchèrent à vive allure. *They walked at a brisk pace.*
La discussion était très vive. *The discussion was very lively.*
Un vert très vif. *Intense green. Very green.*
Il est vif comme la poudre. *He's very excitable. He flares up easily.*
A vif. *Exposed (nerve).*
vigie f. *lookout.*
Il est de vigie. *He's on the lookout.*
vigilance f. *vigilance.*
vigilant *adj. vigilant.*
vigne f. *vine; vineyard.*
vigoureux (vigoureuse f.) *adj. vigorous.*
vigueur f. *vigor, strength.*
Cette loi a été mise en vigueur. *This law is now in force.*
vil *adj. vile; cheap.*
Je l'ai acheté à vil prix. *I bought it for a song (dirt-cheap).*
Une vile calomnie. *A vile calumny.*
vilain *adj. nasty, villainous.*
Ce sont de vilaines gens. *They're a bad lot.*
Il lui joua un vilain tour. *He played a mean trick on him.*
C'est une vilaine affaire. *It's an ugly (bad) business.*
Un vilain incident. *An ugly incident.*
Il fait vilain. *The weather's nasty.*
vilenie f. *meanness.*
Il lui a fait des vilenies. *He played a mean trick on him.*
villa f. *villa.*
village m. *village.*

VILLE f. *town, city.*
Pouvez-vous m'indiquer comment je peux aller à la ville la plus proche? *Can you tell me how to get to the nearest town?*
Nous irons en ville cet après-midi faire des emplettes. *We're going to town this afternoon to do some shopping.*
Habiter hors de la ville. *To live out of town.*
Nous dînons en ville ce soir. *We're dining out tonight.*
villégiature f. *a stay in the country.*
Ils sont partis en villégiature. *They went to a summer resort.*
VIN m. *wine.*
Une bouteille de vin blanc. *A bottle of white wine.*
Une bouteille de vin rouge. *A bottle of red wine.*
vinaigre m. *vinegar.*
VINGT *noun and adj. twenty.*
A vingt et une heures. *At 9:00 P.M.*
vingtaine f. *about twenty.*
VINGTIÈME *noun and adj. twentieth.*
violation f. *violation.*
violemment *violently.*
violence f. *violence.*
violent *adj. violent.*
violer *to violate.*
VIOLET (violette f.) *adj. purple.*
violon m. *violin.*
vipère f. *viper.*
Elle a une langue de vipère. *She has a venomous tongue.*
virage m. *turning.*
Faites attention au virage. *Be careful, there's a curve in the road.*
virgule f. *comma.*
Point virgule. *Semicolon.*
viril *adj. manly, virile.*
vis f. *screw.*
visa m. *visa.*
Le visa d'entrée. *Entrance visa.*
VISAGE m. *face.*
Il a un visage aux traits accentués. *His face has strongly marked features.*
Il a le visage en feu. *His face is very red.*
Toute vérité a deux visages. *There are two sides to every question.* ("*Every truth has two aspects.*")
Faire bon visage à quelqu'un. *To smile at someone.*
Faire mauvais visage à quelqu'un. *To frown at someone.*
vis-à-vis *opposite.*
Ils sont assis vis-à-vis l'un de l'autre. *They're sitting facing each other.*
Ses sentiments vis-à-vis de moi. *His feelings toward me.*
Vis-à-vis de moi il a toujours été très chic. *He has always been nice to me.*
Son respect vis-à-vis de lui diminuait chaque jour. *He respected him less and less.* ("*His respect toward him decreased every day.*")
viser *to aim; to visé, stamp (passport).*
Il a visé juste. *His aim was good. He hit the mark.*
A quoi vise tout cela? *What's the purpose of this? What's the object of this?*
Il a visé à ce but. *That was his goal (object, purpose).*
Je ne vise personne. *I'm not referring (alluding) to anyone in particular.*
Cette accusation le vise. *That accusation is directed against him.*

Elle vise toujours à l'effet. *She's always trying to create an impression.*

visible *adj. visible; easy to read.*
C'est très visible. *It's very conspicuous.*
Monsieur n'est pas visible. *Mr. X is not at home.*
Il ne sera pas visible avant deux heures. *He won't be able to see anyone before two o'clock.*
Ces objets d'art ne sont pas visibles. *These objects of art aren't open (accessible, on display) to the public.*

vision *f. vision.*
Sa vision n'est pas bonne. *He has poor vision.*
Il en a eu une vision momentanée. *He had (got) a glimpse of it.*
Une vision nette de quelque chose. *A clear view of something.*

VISITE *f. visit.*
Aller en visite. *To go visiting. To pay a call.*
Faire des visites. *To go visiting.*
Il lui a rendu visite. *He called on her.*
Qu'est-ce qui me vaut votre visite? *To what do I owe your visit?*
Une carte de visite. *A visiting card.*
Heures de visite. *Visiting hours.*
La visite des bagages. *Baggage inspection.*
La visite guidée (avec guide). *Guided tour.*
La visite-conférence. *Lecture tour.*

VISITER *to visit, examine.*
Visiter un malade. *To visit a patient.*
J'ai visité toutes les pièces. *I have been into every room.*
La douane a visité les malles. *The customs officials inspected the trunks.*
Faire visiter. *To show (someone) around.*

visiteur *m. (visiteuse f.) visitor.*
visser *to screw.*
vital (vitaux *pl.*) *adj. vital, essential.*
vitalité *f. vitality.*
VITE *swift, fast, quickly.*
Venez vite! *Come quickly!*
Faites vite! *Hurry up!*
Faites-le aussi vite que possible. *Do it as quickly as possible.*

vitesse *f. speed.*
A toute vitesse. *At full speed.*
Je vais expédier mon travail à toute vitesse. *I'm going to rush through my work. I'm going to get my work done as fast as possible.*
Il a expédié le colis en grande vitesse. *He sent the parcel by express.*
Changer de vitesse. *To change gears.*
Le changement de vitesse automatique. *Automatic transmission.*

vitre *f. pane (of glass).*
vitrine *f. shop window, showcase.*
vivace *adj. long-lived.*
Une haine vivace. *An undying hatred.*
Un préjugé vivace. *A deep-rooted prejudice.*
vivacité *f. vivaciousness, vivacity, liveliness; promptness.*
vivant *m. living being; lifetime.*
Les vivants et les morts. *The living and the dead. The quick and the dead.*
Du vivant de son père il n'aurait jamais osé. *He wouldn't have dared during his father's lifetime.*
En son vivant la maison était toujours remplie de monde. *During his lifetime the house was always full of company.*
C'est un bon vivant. 1. *He enjoys life. He*

knows how to live. 2. *He's easygoing. He's a jolly fellow.*

vivant *adj. alive, living.*
Une langue vivante. *A living (modern) language.*
Pas une âme vivante. *Not a living soul.*
Il n'y a pas un homme vivant qui s'en souvient. *There isn't a man alive who remembers it.*
Il est le portrait vivant de son grand-père. *He's the living image of his grandfather.*

vivement *quickly, briskly, vigorously.*
Il entra vivement dans le magasin. *He hurried into the store.*
Sa mort les a vivement affligés. *They were deeply affected by his death.*
Il le ramassa vivement. *He snatched it up.*
Il a répondu vivement. *He answered warmly (with feeling).*
Vivement, on est en retard! *Hurry up, we're late!*

vivoter *to keep body and soul together.*
Ça va? —On vivote. *How are you getting along? —I just barely manage.*
Voilà deux ans qu'ils vivotent. *For two years now they've barely kept body and soul together.*

VIVRE *to live.*
Vivre au jour le jour. *To live from day to day. To live from hand to mouth.*
Il n'a pas besoin de travailler pour vivre. *He doesn't have to work for a living.*
On peut vivre à très bon marché ici. *One can live very cheaply here.*
Ils vivent à Lyon. *They live in Lyons.*
Il fait bon vivre ici. *Life is pleasant here.*
Je n'ai pas rencontré âme qui vive. *I didn't meet a living soul.*
Il se laisse vivre. *He takes life easy.*
Il est commode à vivre. *He's easy to get on with.*
Qui vivra verra. *Live and learn. Time will tell.*
Vive la république! *Long live the Republic!*
vivres *m. pl. provisions, supplies.*
vocabulaire *m. vocabulary.*
vocation *f. vocation.*
vociférer *to shout, bawl, yell.*
voeu *m. (voeux pl.) vow; wish.*
Il est resté fidèle à son voeu. *He kept his vow.*
Son voeu a été accompli. *His wish was fulfilled.*
Tous mes voeux. *My best wishes.*
Mes voeux vous accompagnent. *My best wishes.*
Il a fait voeu de se venger. *He vowed vengeance.*
vogue *f. fashion.*
Ce chanteur est en vogue. *That singer is popular.*
La mode en vogue. *The prevailing fashion.*
C'est la vogue actuellement. *It's the latest rage. It's the rage at present.*
voguer *to row; sail.*
VOICI *here is, here are.*
Voici le livre. *Here's the book.*
Voici, monsieur. *Here you are, sir.*
En voici un autre. *Here's another one.*
Nous y voici. *Here we are. We've arrived.*
Je l'ai vu voici deux ans. *I saw him two years ago.*
Voici ce qu'il m'a dit. *Here's what he told me.*
Mon ami que voici vous le dira. *My friend here will tell you.*
Qu'est-ce qui vous est arrivé? —Voici. *What*

happened to you?—This is what happened.*
Voici . . . qui arrive. *Here comes . . .*
Vous voici. *Here you are.*
VOIE *f. way, road.*
Voie publique. *Public thoroughfare.*
Par voie de Paris. *Via Paris.*
Par voie de mer. *By sea.*
Voie ferrée. *Railroad track.*
Ligne à une voie. *Railroad line with a single track.*
Voie d'eau. *Waterway.*
Vous n'êtes pas dans la bonne voie. *You aren't on the right track.*
Il était en voie de guérison. *He was getting better. His health was improving.*
Etre en voie de réussir. *To be on the road to success.*
Obtenir par la voie de la persuasion. *To get by persuasion.*
Vous vous engagez dans une voie très dangereuse. *You're entering upon a very dangerous course.*
Ne vous en faites plus, l'affaire est en bonne voie. *Don't worry about it anymore, the affair (matter) is going well.*
VOILÀ *there is, there are.*
Le voilà. *Here he comes.*
Voilà tout. *That's all.*
A la bonne heure! Voilà ce qu'il y a de bon. *Good! That's one comfort.*
Voilà près d'un mois. *It's now nearly a month.*
Voilà ce qu'il m'a demandé. *That's what he asked me.*
Il est revenu voilà quatre ans. *He came back four years ago.*
En voilà un qui fera son chemin! *That fellow will go far.*
En voilà une idée! *What an idea!*
Voilà! *There! There you are!*
voile *f. sail.*
voile *m. veil.*
Prendre le voile. *To take the veil.*
voiler *to veil.*
voilette *f. veil of a woman's hat.*
VOIR *to see.*
Que voyez-vous? *What do you see?*
Je ne peux pas le voir d'ici. *I can't see it from here.*
Je le vis partir. *I saw him leave.*
Voulez-vous voir si c'est fini? *Will you please see if it's finished?*
Je l'ai vu de mes propres yeux. *I saw it with my own eyes.*
Je verrai. *I'll see about it.*
C'est ce que nous verrons. *That remains to be seen.*
Il voit de loin. *He has foresight.*
Il fit voir son manuscrit à un ami. *He showed his manuscript to a friend.*
Nous avons été les voir. *We went to visit them.*
Il a vu rouge. *He saw red.*
Venez me voir quand vous serez à New York. *Look me up ("come to see me") when you're in New York.*
A le voir on dirait qu'il est très jeune. *To judge by his looks you'd say he's very young.*
Je le vois venir. *I see what he's driving at (what he's trying to do).*
Enfin, vous voyez où je veux en venir. *At any rate you understand just what I'm driving at.*

Cela n'a rien à voir à l'affaire. *That is entirely beside the point. That has nothing to do with the matter.*

Il n'a rien à voir là-dedans. *He has nothing to do with it.*

A ce que je vois, il n'a pas changé. *As far as I can see, he hasn't changed.*

Il s'est fait bien voir de son patron. *He gained the favor of his boss (chief, employer).*

Je ne peux pas le voir. *I can't stand him. I can't bear the sight of him.*

Il est bien vu de tout le monde. *He is highly esteemed by everybody.*

Vous n'y pensez pas, voyons! 1. *Come on, you don't really mean that!* 2. *Come on, you wouldn't really do it!*

Voyons, la dernière fois que je l'ai vu, c'était en 1942. *Let's see, the last time I saw him was in 1942.*

Voir c'est croire. *Seeing is believing. ("To see is to believe.")*

Laissez voir. *Let's see, let me see (it).*

se voir *to see oneself; see one another; be apparent or obvious.*

On s'y voit comme dans une glace. *You can see yourself there as in a mirror.*

Ils ne se voient plus. *They don't see each other anymore.*

Cela se voit. *That's obvious.*

Cela se voit tous les jours. *That happens every day. That's an everyday occurrence. You see that every day.*

voisin *m. neighbor.*

C'est mon voisin. *He's my neighbor. He's a neighbor of mine.*

Bon avocat, mauvais voisin. *A good lawyer makes a bad neighbor.*

voisin *adj. neighboring, adjacent, adjoining.*

Deux chambres voisines. *Two adjoining rooms.*

voisinage *m. proximity; vicinity, neighborhood.*

Tout le voisinage en parle. *The whole neighborhood is talking about it.*

voiture *f. car (subway, train); automobile.*

Ranger sa voiture. *To park one's car.*

Attention aux voitures. *Watch out for the cars.*

Nous sommes allés à Paris en voiture. *We drove down to Paris.*

Voiture d'enfant. *Baby carriage.*

En voiture! *All aboard!*

Voiture d'occasion. *Used car, secondhand car.*

Voyager en voiture. *To travel by car.*

VOIX *f. voice; vote.*

Il parle à haute voix. *He speaks in a loud voice.*

N'élevez pas la voix. *Don't raise your voice!*

De vive voix. *Viva voce. Orally.*

La voix du peuple. *Public opinion.*

Il a voix au chapitre. *He has a say in the matter.*

Il lui a donné sa voix. *He voted for him.*

vol *m. flight.*

vol *m. theft.*

volage *adj. fickle.*

volaille *f. poultry.*

volant *m. steering wheel.*

Au volant. *At the wheel.*

volcan *m. volcano.*

volée *f. flight.*

voler *to fly.*

Entendre voler une mouche. *To hear a pin drop.*

voler *to steal.*

Il ne l'a pas volé (fam.)! *He got what he deserved!*

volet *m. shutter.*

voleur *m. (voleuse f.) thief.*

volontaire *adj. voluntary.*

volontairement *voluntarily.*

volonté *f. will.*

A volonté. *At will.*

Prenez-en à volonté. *Take as much as you want.*

Il le fait à volonté. *He does it when he feels like it.*

Elle fait ses quatre volontés. *She does just as she pleases.*

Une volonté de fer. *An iron will.*

Faire acte de bonne volonté. *To show (prove) one's goodwill.*

Il l'a fait de sa propre volonté. *He did it of his own accord (of his own free will).*

Les dernières volontés. *Last will and testament.*

VOLONTIERS *gladly, with pleasure.*

Très volontiers. *With pleasure.*

Il consentit volontiers à le faire. *He readily consented to do it.*

Pouvez-vous m'indiquer comment je peux me rendre à cette adresse? —Volontiers. *Could you please tell me how to get to this address? —I'd be glad to.*

Je mangerais volontiers un dessert. *I could do with a dessert. I'd like very much to have some dessert.*

On croit volontiers que . . . *One would like to believe that . . .*

volte-face *f. turning around.*

Il fit volte-face. *He turned around.*

volubilité *f. volubility.*

volume *m. volume.*

volumineux *(volumineuse f.) adj. bulky, voluminous.*

vomir *to vomit.*

vomissement *m. vomiting.*

voracité *f. voracity.*

vos *See votre.*

vote *m. vote, voting.*

Droit de vote. *Right to vote. Franchise.*

Bulletin de vote. *Ballot.*

Le vote d'une loi. *Passage of a law.*

Loi en cours de vote. *Bill before the House.*

voter *to vote.*

VOTRE *(vos m. and f. pl.) adj. your.*

Mettez votre chapeau. *Put your hat on.*

Faites votre choix. *Select (choose) what you want. Take your choice.*

Est-ce que ce sont vos livres? *Are those your books?*

Vos chemises sont prêtes. *Your shirts are ready.*

VÔTRE *(la vôtre f., les vôtres m. and f. pl.) yours.*

Ce n'est pas la mienne, c'est la vôtre. *It isn't mine; it's yours.*

Son travail est aussi bien que le vôtre. *His work is as good as yours.*

Vous avez encore fait des vôtres. *You've been up to some of your old tricks again.*

A la vôtre! *To yours! (i.e. to your health, as a toast).*

vouer *to vow; dedicate.*

se vouer *to devote oneself.*

VOULOIR *to want.*

Je veux sortir me promener. *I want to go out for a walk.*

Vous voulez venir? *Do you want to come?*

Si vous voulez, vous pouvez revenir demain. *If you like you can come back tomorrow.*

Il veut dix mille francs pour sa voiture. *He wants ten thousand francs for his car.*

Que voulez-vous dire? *What do you mean?*

Qu'est-ce que cela veut dire? *What does that mean?*

Que voulez-vous? 1. *What do you want? What can I do for you?* 2. *It can't be helped. What can you expect? What's to be done?*

Que me voulez-vous? *What do you want of me?*

Je veux bien. *I'd be glad to. I'm willing to. I have no objection.*

Je ne veux pas. *I don't want to.*

Vous l'avez bien voulu! *You asked for it!*

Je vous prie de vouloir bien m'attendre quelques instants. *Would you be good enough to wait for me for a few seconds?*

Il lui en veut. *He bears him a grudge. He has a grudge against him.*

Il faut savoir ce que l'on veut. *One has to make up one's mind.*

Je voudrais y aller. *I'd like to go there.*

Je voulais vous écrire là-dessus. *I meant to write you about it.*

Veuillez me faire savoir. *Please let me know.*

Veuillez faire ceci. *Please do this.*

Qu'il le veuille ou non, il faut qu'il le fasse. *Whether he wants to or not, he has to do it.*

Vouloir c'est pouvoir. *Where there's a will, there's a way.*

Veuillez agréer, Monsieur, à l'assurance de ma plus parfaite considération. *Very truly yours.*

Où vous voudrez. *Wherever you wish.*

Tu veux? *How about it? Would you like to?*

Voudriez-vous (bien) . . . *Would you . . .*

voulu *have wanted.*

VOUS *you.*

Vous désirez? *What would you like?*

Ce chapeau est à vous. *That's your hat.*

Faites comme chez vous. *Make yourself at home.*

Vous dites? *I beg your pardon? What did you say?*

De vous à moi. *Between you and me. Between the two of us.*

Vous deux. *You two, the two of you.*

vous-même(s) *yourself, yourselves.*

voûte *f. vault, arch.*

voûter *to vault, arch over.*

se voûter *to become round-shouldered or bent, stoop, be bent with age.*

VOYAGE *m. trip.*

Quand pensez-vous être de retour de votre voyage? *When do you expect to be back from your trip?*

Voyage de noces. *Honeymoon.*

Il est en voyage. *He's traveling.*

Bon voyage! *Pleasant journey!*

VOYAGER *to travel.*

J'aimerais voyager. *I'd like to travel.*

Voyager en train. *To travel by train.*

VOYAGEUR *m. (voyageuse f.) traveler, passenger.*

voyageur *(voyageuse f.) adj. traveling.*

Commis voyageur. *Traveling salesman.*

Pigeon voyageur. *Carrier pigeon.*

voyant *adj. showy, gaudy.*

Une couleur voyante. *A showy color.*

voyou *m. good-for-nothing.*

vrac *m. loose.*

Il a acheté des livres en vrac. *He bought a job lot of books.*

vrai *m. truth.*

Le vrai de l'affaire, c'est que . . . *The truth of the matter is that . . .*

Est-elle revenue pour de vrai? *Did she really come back?*

A vrai dire . . . *To tell the truth . . .*

VRAI *adj. true.*

Ma foi, c'est vrai! *It's really true!*

C'est un vrai bohème. *He's a real bohemian.*

Aussi vrai que je m'appelle Jacques. *As sure as my name is Jack.*

Tu le veux, vrai? *You want it, don't you?*

Vous me téléphonerez, pas vrai? *You'll phone me, won't you?*

VRAIMENT *really.*

Vraiment? *Really? Is that so?*

Vraiment, je ne pensais plus le revoir. *I really never expected to see him again.*

Vraiment, vous n'auriez pas dû vous donner tant de mal. *You really shouldn't have put yourself to all that trouble.*

J'ai appris quelque chose de vraiment drôle. *I just heard something really funny.*

vraisemblable *adj. probable, likely, credible.*

C'est très vraisemblable. *It's very probable (likely).*

Une histoire vraisemblable. *A story that sounds true.*

vu *seen, regarded.*

Etre bien vu. *To be respected.*

Mal vu. *Held in poor esteem.*

Ni vu ni connu (*fam.*). *Nobody will be any the wiser.*

Au vu et au su de tous. *Openly. To everybody's knowledge. As everybody knows.*

Vu que. *Since. Whereas. Seeing that.*

VUE *f. sight.*

Il a perdu la vue. *He lost his sight.*

Je ne le connais que de vue. *I only know him by sight.*

Il y a une très belle vue d'ici. *There's a very nice view from here.*

Nous nous sommes complètement perdus de vue. *We completely lost touch with one another.*

A première vue. *At first sight. Offhand.*

Mettre bien en vue. *To display prominently.*

Une vue saine. *A sound viewpoint.*

Il parle à perte de vue. *He talks endlessly.*

Il doit avoir quelque chose en vue. *He must have something in view.*

Avoir des vues sur quelque chose. *To have something in view (in mind). To have de-*

signs on something. *To aim (be aiming) at something.*

Prise de vue. *Shot (photography).*

vulgaire *adj. vulgar; common.*

Un remarque vulgaire. *A vulgar remark.*

L'opinion vulgaire. *Public opinion.*

Le français vulgaire. *French slang.*

vulgarité *f. vulgarity.*

vulnérable *adj. vulnerable.*

W *The twenty-third letter of the alphabet.*

wagon *m. carriage, coach.*

Un wagon-restaurant. *A dining car.*

Un wagon-lit. *A sleeper.*

Wagon de marchandises. *Freight car.*

watt *m. watt.*

Une ampoule de cinquante watts. *A fifty-watt bulb.*

w.-c. *water closet, toilet.*

week-end *m. weekend.*

Les Durand sont partis en week-end. *The Durands left for the weekend.*

whisky *m. whisky.*

Y *The twenty-fifth letter of the alphabet.*

Y *there, to there.*

Allez-y! 1. *Go there.* 2. *Go right ahead!*

Nous nous y sommes perdus. *We got lost there.*

Revenons-y. *Let's go back there.*

La vie y est très chère. *Life there is very expensive.*

Merci.—Il n'y a pas de quoi. *Thank you. —Not at all. Don't mention it.*

Il y a cinq personnes ici. *There are five people here.*

Il y avait beaucoup de monde. *There were a lot of people.*

Il y a quatre ans. *Four years ago.*

Il y a longtemps. *A long time ago.*

Il y a peu de temps. *A short while ago.*

Y a-t-il des lettres pour moi? *Are there any letters for me?*

J'y suis accoutumé maintenant. *I'm used to it now.*

Ah, j'y suis! *Oh, now I understand!*

Je n'y suis pas du tout. *I'm all at sea.*

Pendant que vous y êtes, donnez-moi un couteau. *While you're at it, get me a knife.*

Ça y est! *It's done! That's it!*

Je n'y suis pour rien. *I have nothing to do with it. I have no part in it.*

Il y a deux jours que j'ai mal aux dents. *I've had a toothache for two days.*

Il y en a d'autres. *There are others.*

J'y obéis. *I obey it.*

J'y pense. *I'm thinking about it.*

J'y réponds. *I answer it.*

J'y suis. *I understand, I get it.*

Nous y avons mis deux heures. *It took us two hours, we spent two hours on it.*

Y compris. *Including.*

yacht *m. yacht.*

yeux (*s. oeil*) *m. eyes.*

Coûter les yeux de la tête. *To cost a fortune.*

J'ai mal aux yeux. *My eyes hurt.*

Z *The twenty-sixth letter of the alphabet.*

zèle *m. zeal.*

Brûler de zèle pour quelque chose. *To be very enthusiastic about something.*

Faire du zèle. *To show a lot of zeal (earnestness, enthusiasm).*

zélé *adj. zealous.*

zéro *m. zero.*

Le thermomètre est à zéro. *The thermometer is at zero.*

C'est un zéro. *He's of no account. He's a nonentity.*

Toute sa fortune a été réduite à zéro. *His fortune was reduced to nothing.*

zeste *m. peel.*

Le zeste d'une orange. *Orange peel.*

Cela ne vaut pas un zeste. *It isn't worth a straw.*

zézayer *to lisp.*

zigzag *m. zigzag.*

Il fait des zigzags. *He's staggering along.*

zinc *m. zinc.*

zone *f. zone.*

La zone torride. *The torrid zone.*

C'est un peintre de seconde zone. *He's a second-rate painter.*

zoo *m. zoo.*

zut *darn it.*

Zut alors! *Darn it!*

Zut, j'ai raté mon coup. *Darn it, I missed ("my shot").*

GLOSSARY OF PROPER NAMES

Alain	*Allan*	**Claire**	*Clara*	**Hélène**	*Helen*	**Monique**	*Monique*
Alexandre	*Alexander*	**Claude**	*Claude*	**Henri**	*Henry*	**Olivier**	*Oliver*
Alice	*Alice*	**Claudine**	*Claudine*	**Hubert**	*Hubert*	**Paul**	*Paul*
André	*Andrew*	**Colette**	*Colette*	**Jacques**	*Jack*	**Pauline**	*Pauline*
Anne	*Anna, Ann(e)*	**Daniel**	*Daniel*	**Jean**	*John*	**Pierre**	*Peter*
Antoine	*Anthony*	**Denis**	*Dennis*	**Jeanne**	*Jane*	**Raymond**	*Raymond*
Arthur	*Arthur*	**Denise**	*Denise*	**Julien**	*Julian*	**René**	*Rene*
Berthe	*Bertha*	**Dominique**	*Dominic*	**Léon**	*Leo*	**Robert**	*Robert*
Blanche	*Blanche*	**Édouard**	*Edward*	**Lucien**	*Lucian*	**Roger**	*Roger*
Camille	*Camille*	**François**	*Francis*	**Marc**	*Mark*	**Solange**	*Solange*
Catherine	*Catherine*	**Frédéric**	*Frederick*	**Marguerite**	*Margaret*	**Suzanne**	*Susan*
Cécile	*Cecilia*	**Georges**	*George*	**Marie**	*Mary*	**Victor**	*Victor*
Charles	*Charles*	**Gérard**	*Gerald*	**Marthe**	*Martha*	**Yvonne**	*Yvonne*
Christine	*Christine*	**Gustave**	*Gustavus*	**Maurice**	*Maurice*		
Christophe	*Christopher*	**Guy**	*Guy*	**Michel**	*Michael*		

GLOSSARY OF GEOGRAPHICAL NAMES

Afrique f. *Africa.*
Alger m. *Algiers.*
Algérie f. *Algeria, Algiers.*
Allemagne f. *Germany.*
(les) Alpes f. pl. *the Alps.*
Alsace f. *Alsace.*
Amérique f. *America.*
   l'Amérique du Nord *North America*
   l'Amérique du Sud *South America.*
   l'Amérique Centrale *Central America.*
   les Etats-Unis d'Amérique *the United States of America.*
Angleterre f. *England.*
Anvers m. *Antwerp.*
(l')Argentine f. *Argentina, the Argentine.*
Asie f. *Asia.*
(l')Atlantique m. *the Atlantic.*
Australie f. *Australia.*
Autriche f. *Austria.*
Belgique f. *Belgium.*
Bordeaux m. *Bordeaux.*
Brésil m. *Brazil.*
Bretagne f. *Brittany.*
   la Grande Bretagne *Great Britain.*
Britanniques (Îles) adj. *the British Isles.*

Bruxelles f. *Brussels.*
Chine f. *China.*
Danemark m. *Denmark.*
Douvres m. *Dover.*
Dunkerque m. *Dunkirk.*
Écosse f. *Scotland.*
Égypte f. *Egypt.*
Espagne f. *Spain.*
(les) États-Unis m. pl. *the United States.*
Europe f. *Europa; Europe.*
Genève f. *Geneva.*
Grèce f. *Greece.*
(la) Havane f. *Havana.*
(le) Hâvre m. *Le Havre.*
Hollande f. *Holland.*
Hongrie f. *Hungary.*
Inde f. *India.*
Indochine f. *Indo-China.*
Irlande f. *Ireland.*
Islande f. *Iceland.*
Italie f. *Italy.*
Japon m. *Japan.*
Londres m. *London.*
Lyon m. *Lyons.*
Maroc m. *Marocco.*

Marseille m. *Marseilles.*
(la) Méditerranée f. *the Mediterranean (Sea).*
Moscou f. *Moscow.*
Normandie f. *Normandy.*
Norvège f. *Norway.*
Océanie f. *Oceania.*
(les) Pays-Bas m. pl. *the Netherlands.*
Pérou m. *Peru.*
Perse f. *Persia.*
Pologne f. *Poland.*
Prusse f. *Prussia.*
Pyrénées f. pl. *Pyrenees.*
Roumanie f. *Rumania.*
Russie f. *Russia.*
Scandinavie f. *Scandinavia.*
Sibérie f. *Siberia.*
Sicile f. *Sicily.*
Suède f. *Sweden.*
Suisse f. *Switzerland.*
Syrie f. *Syria.*
Tanger m. *Tangier.*
Terre-Neuve f. *Newfoundland.*
Tunisie f. *Tunis.*
Venise f. *Venice.*
Vienne f. *Vienna.*

French-English DICTIONARY

A

a (an) un, une.
abandon (to) abandonner.
abbreviate abréger.
abreviation abréviation f.
ability talent m.
able adj. capable.
able (be) pouvoir.
abolish abolir.
about à propos de; autour de (around).
    What's it about? De quoi s'agit-il?
above au-dessus, en haut, dessus.
abroad à l'étranger.
absence absence f.
absent absent.
absolute absolu.
absorb absorber.
abstain from s'abstenir de.
abstract abstrait.
absurd absurde.
abundant abondant.
abuse abus m.
abuse (to) abuser.
academy académie f.
accent accent m.
accent (to) accentuer.
accept accepter.
acceptance acceptation f.
accident accident m.
accidental accidentel.
accidentally accidentellement.
accommodation arrangement m.
accommodate accommoder.
accompany accompagner.
accomplish accomplir.
accord accord m.
according (to) selon, suivant, d'après.
account récit m., compte m.
accuracy exactitude f., justesse f.
accurate juste, exact.
accuse accuser.
ache douleur f.
ache (to) faire mal à.
achieve accomplir.
achievement accomplissement m.
acid acide, aigre.
acid acide m.
acknowledge reconnaître, convenir.
acknowledgment aveu m.; accusé de réception m.
acquaintance connaissance f.
acquire acquérir.
acre acre f.
across à travers.
act acte m.
act (to) agir.
action action f.
acting jeu m.
active actif.
activity activité f.
actor acteur m., comédien m.
actual réel, effectif.
actually effectivement.
acute aigu.
adapt adapter.
add ajouter, additionner.
addition addition f.
address adresse f.
address (to) adresser.
addressee destinataire m.
adequate suffisant.
adjective adjectif m.
adjoining voisin.

administer administrer, distribuer.
admiral amiral m.
admiration admiration f.
admire admirer.
admission entrée f.
admit reconnaître, avouer; admettre; recevoir.
admittance entrée f.
    No admittance. Défense d'entrer. Entrée interdite.
adopt adopter.
adult adulte noun and adj.
advance progrès m.
advance (to) avancer.
advantage avantage m.
adventure aventure f.
adverb adverbe m.
advertise annoncer, afficher.
advertisement annonce f., affiche f., réclame f.
advice conseil m.
advise conseiller.
affair affaire f.
affect intéresser; affecter.
affected affecté.
affection affection f.
affectionate affectueux.
affirm affirmer.
affluence affluence f.
afloat à flot.
afraid effrayé.
African africain.
after ensuite, après.
afternoon après-midi m.
afterwards après.
again encore, de nouveau.
against contre.
age âge m., époque f.
age (to) vieillir.
agency agence f.
agent agent m.
aggravate aggraver.
ago il y a.
    five years ago il y a cinq ans.
agree consentir à. être d'accord.
agreeable agréable.
agreed entendu, d'accord.
agreement pacte m., accord m.
agricultural agricole.
agriculture agriculture f.
ahead en avant.
aid aide f.
aid (to) aider.
    first aid les premiers soins.
    first-aid station station de secours.
aim but m.
aim (to) viser.
air air m.
airmail par avion.
airplane aéroplane m., avion m.
aisle passage m., allée f.
alarm alerte f., alarme f.
album album m.
alike pareil, semblable.
alive vivant, vif.
all tous, tout, toute, toutes.
    all right entendu, parfait.
alley allée f.
allow permettre.
allowed permis.
ally allié m.
almost presque.
alone seul.
along le long de.
alpaca alpaga m.

already déjà.
also aussi.
alter changer.
alternate (to) alterner.
alternately alternativement.
although bien que, quoique.
altitude élévation f.
always toujours.
amazed émerveillé, étonné.
amazed (be) être étonné.
amazement étonnement m.
amazing étonnant.
ambassador ambassadeur m.
ambitious ambitieux.
amend amender, corriger.
amends réparation f.
America Amérique f.
American américain.
among parmi.
amount somme f.
amount (to) revenir.
ample ample.
amuse amuser.
amusement amusement m.
amusing drôle.
analyze analyser.
ancestor ancêtre m.
anchor ancre f.
ancient ancien.
and et.
anecdote anecdote f.
anesthetic anesthésique.
angel ange m.
anger colère f.
anger (to) mettre en colère, fâcher.
angry en colère, courroucé, fâché.
    get angry se fâcher.
animal animal noun and adj.
animate animer.
animated animé.
annex annexe f.
annihilate anéantir.
anniversary anniversaire m.
announce annoncer.
annoy contrarier, ennuyer.
annual annuel.
annul annuler.
anonymous anonyme.
another un autre, une autre.
answer réponse f.
answer (to) répondre.
anterior antérieur (à).
anticipate anticiper, devancer.
antique antique.
anxiety anxiété f.
anxious inquiet.
any quelque.
anybody n'importe qui, personne.
anyhow n'importe comment.
anyone n'importe qui.
anything n'importe quoi; quelque chose.
anyway n'importe comment.
anywhere n'importe où.
apart à part.
apartment appartement m.
apiece pièce, par tête.
apologize s'excuser.
apparent manifeste.
appeal (to) en appeler à, plaire.
appear apparaître.
appearance apparition f., air m.
appease apaiser.
appendix appendice m.

appetite appétit m.
applaud applaudir.
applause bravo m., applaudissement m.
apple pomme f.
application application f. (*diligence*), demande f., (*request*).
apply avoir rapport à (*be suitable*); solliciter (*apply for*); s'adresser à (*apply to*); appliquer (*administer*).
appoint désigner, nommer.
appointment rendez-vous m.; désignation f.
appreciate apprécier.
appreciation appréciation f.
approach abords m. pl., approche f.
appropriate convenable adj.
approval approbation f.
approve approuver.
April avril m.
apron tablier m.
arbitrary arbitraire.
arcade arcade f.
architect architecte m.
architecture architecture f.
ardent ardent.
area surface f.
argue discuter.
argument argument m.
arise se lever.
arm bras m.
  firearms arme f.
arm (to) armer.
armchair fauteuil m.
army armée f.
around autour de, alentour.
arouse soulever, éveiller.
arrange arranger.
arrangement disposition f.
arrest arrestation f.
arrest (to) arrêter.
arrival arrivée f.
arrive arriver.
art art m.
article article m.
artificial adj. artificiel.
artist artiste m.
artistic artistique.
as comme.
  as . . . as . . . aussi . . . que . . .
as for quant à.
as it were pour ainsi dire.
as little as aussi peu que.
as long as tant que.
as much autant.
as much as autant que.
as soon as dès que.
ascertain constater.
ash cendre f.
ashamed honteux.
aside de côté, à part, (en) aparté.
ask demander.
asleep endormi.
aspire aspirer à.
assault assaut m.
assemble réunir; rassembler.
assembly assemblée f.; congrès m.
assign assigner.
assist aider à.
assistance aide f.
assistant adjoint m.
associate associé m.
assume assumer, supposer.
assurance assurance f.
assure assurer.

astonish étonner.
astonishing étonnant.
astounded stupéfait.
at à.
  at first d'abord.
  at last enfin.
  at once aussitôt.
  at the home of chez.
  at the place of business of chez.
  at the same time à la fois.
athlete athlète m.
athletic athlétique, sportif.
athletics sports m. pl.
atmosphere atmosphère f.
attach attacher.
attack attaque f.
attack (to) attaquer.
attain atteindre.
attempt essai m., tentative f.
attempt (to) essayer, tenter.
attend assister à.
attention attention f.
attic mansarde f.
attitude attitude f.
attorney avocat m., avoué m.
attract attirer.
attraction attraction f., attrait m.
attractive séduisant.
audience audience f., auditoire m.
August août m.
aunt tante f.
author auteur m.
authority autorité f.
authorize autoriser.
automatic automatique.
automobile automobile f., auto f., voiture f.
autumn automne m. and f.
avenue avenue f.
average moyenne f.
  on the average en moyenne.
avoid éviter.
awake éveillé.
awake (be) être éveillé.
awake (to) réveiller, s'éveiller.
award récompense f.
award (to) accorder.
aware (be) se rendre compte de.
away absent.
  go away s'en aller.
awful affreux.
awhile pendant quelque temps.
awkward maladroit.
azure azur.

B

baby bébé m.
back dos m. (*body*); arrière m., derrière m., fond m.
background fond m.
backwards (en) arrière.
bacon lard fumé m.
bad mauvais.
badge insigne f.
bag sac m.
baker boulanger m.
bakery boulangerie f.
balance équilibre m.; solde m.
bald chauve.
ball balle f.
ball-point pen stylo à bille m.
balloon ballon m.
banana banane f.
band troupe f. (*troop*); lien m. (*tie*); orchestre m.

(*orchestra*); ruban m.
bandage pansement m.
banister rampe f.
bank banque f.; bord m., rive f. (*river*).
  the Left Bank la Rive Gauche.
bank note billet de banque m.
bankruptcy banqueroute f.
banquet banquet m.
bar barre f.
barber coiffeur m.
bare nu, dégarni.
bargain occasion f.
  secondhand car voiture d'occasion.
barge chaland m.; péniche f.
barn grange f.
barrel tonneau m.
barren stérile.
bas-relief bas-relief m.
base bas, vil.
basin bassin m.
basis base f.
basket panier m.
bath bain m.
bathe baigner.
battery accu(mulateur) m.
battle bataille f., combat m.
be être.
  be ahead of devancer.
  be hungry avoir faim.
  be right avoir raison.
  be sleepy avoir sommeil.
  be sorry regretter.
  be thirsty avoir soif.
  be to blame être coupable.
  be wrong avoir tort.
beach plage f.
beaming radieux, rayonnant.
bean haricot m.
bear (to) porter, soutenir.
beat (to) battre; frapper (*strike*).
beautiful beau, belle.
beauty beauté f.
beauty parlor salon de beauté m., salon des dames, m.
because parce que.
because of à cause de.
become devenir.
becoming convenable; seyant.
bed lit m.
bedclothes couvertures f. pl.
bedding couchage m.
bedroom chambre à coucher f.
beef boeuf m.
beer bière f.
beet betterave f.
before avant (que).
beg mendier, supplier.
beggar mendiant m.
begin commencer.
beginning commencement m., début m.
behave se conduire.
behavior conduite f., tenue f.
behind en arrière, derrière.
Belgian belge.
belief croyance f.
believe croire.
bell cloche f.
belong appartenir.
below en-dessous, en bas, sous.
belt ceinture f.
bench banc m.
bend plier; courber, se pencher.
beneath dessous.

benefit bénéfice m., bienfait m.
benefit (to) bénéficier.
beside de plus, à part.
besides en outre.
best le meilleur.
bet pari m.
bet (to) parier.
betray trahir.
better meilleur, mieux.
between entre.
beware of se garder de, prendre garde à.
beyond plus loin, au delà de, hors de.
bicycle bicyclette f.
    bicycle race course cycliste f.
bid (to) ordonner, inviter, offrir.
big grand, gros.
bill facture f.; addition f. (*restaurant*); note f.
    bill of fare menu m.
billion milliard m.
bind lier.
biology biologie f.
bird oiseau m.
birth naissance f.
birthday anniversaire m.
biscuit biscuit m.
bishop évêque m.
bit (a) un peu.
bit morceau m.
bite morsure f., piqûre f.
bite (to) mordre.
bitter amer.
bitterness amertume f.
black noir.
blackbird merle m.
blade lame f.
blame blâme m.
blame (to) blâmer.
blank en blanc.
blanket couverture f.
bleed saigner.
bless bénir.
blessing bénédiction f.
blind adj. aveugle.
    a blind man un aveugle.
blind (to) aveugler.
block bloc m.
block (to) encombrer.
blond adj. blond.
    a blond un blond.
blood sang m.
blotter buvard m.
blouse blouse f., chemisier m. (*woman's tailored*).
blow coup m.
blue bleu, azur.
blush rougeur f.
blush (to) rougir.
board pension f. (*food*); planche f. (*plank*).
boardinghouse pension de famille.
boast se vanter.
boat bateau m., barque f., canot m.
body corps m.
boil (to) bouillir.
boiler chaudière f.
bold hardi.
bond lien m.
bone os m.
boo (to) huer.
book livre m.
    book of tickets carnet m.
booking location f.
booklet carnet m.
bookseller libraire m.; bouquiniste m. (*second-hand*).

bookstore librairie f.
border frontière f., limite f. (*boundary*).
bored (be) s'embêter, s'ennuyer.
boring ennuyeux, embêtant.
born (be) naître.
borough arrondissement m. (*Paris*).
borrow emprunter.
both les deux.
bother ennui m.
bother (to) se tracasser; (se) déranger; ennuyer.
    Don't bother! Ne vous dérangez pas!
bottle bouteille f.
bottom adj. dernier, le plus bas.
bottom bas m., fond m.
bough rameau m.
bounce (to) bondir.
boundary borne f., frontière f.
boundless illimité.
bowl écuelle f.
box boîte f., caisse f.
box office bureau de location m.
boy garçon m.
bracelet bracelet m.
braid natte f., tresse f.
brain cerveau m., cervelle f.
brake frein m.
branch branche f.
brave brave, courageux.
bread pain m.
breadth travers m.
    across à travers.
break (to) briser, rompre, casser.
    break out éclater.
breakdown panne f. (*mechanical*).
    engine trouble panne de moteur.
breakfast petit déjeuner m.
    have breakfast prendre le petit déjeuner.
breath souffle m., respiration f.
breathe respirer.
breeze brise f.
bribe (to) corrompre.
brick brique f.
bride mariée f.
bridge pont m.; bridge m. (*cards*).
brief bref.
bright clair.
brighten s'éclaircir.
brilliant éclatant.
bring apporter, amener.
bring together rapprocher.
bringing up éducation f.
British britannique.
broad large.
broil griller.
broken cassé.
bronze bronze m.
brook ruisseau m.
broom balai m.
brother frère m.
brother-in-law beau-frère m.
brown brun.
bruise (to) meurtrir.
brush brosse f.
brute brute f.
bubble bulle f.
buckle boucle f.
bud bourgeon m.
budget budget m.
buffet (dresser) buffet m.
build construire, bâtir.
building construction f.; bâtiment m.
bulletin bulletin m.
bundle paquet m.

burden charge f.
bureau bureau m.
burn (to) brûler.
burst éclat m.
burst (to) éclater.
bus autobus m.; autocar m. (*outside city*).
bush buisson m.
bushel boisseau m.
business affaire f.
businessman homme d'affaires m.
bust buste m.
busy occupé.
but mais.
butcher boucher m.
butcher shop boucherie f.
butter beurre m.
button bouton m.
buy (to) acheter; prendre.
    buy a ticket prendre un billet.
buyer acheteur m.
buzzing bourdonnement m.
by par; à.
    by and by sous peu.
    by then d'ici là.

C

cab taxi m.
cabbage chou m.
cabin cabine f.
cabinet cabinet m.
cable câble m.
cage cage f.
cake gâteau m.; pain m. (*of soap*).
calendar calendrier m.
calf veau m.
call appel m., cri m.; visite f.
call (to) convoquer, appeler.
    call back rappeler.
    call forth évoquer.
    call out s'écrier.
calm calme.
camera appareil photographique m.; appareil ciné-matographique (*movie*).
camera shop magasin de photographie m.
camp camp m.
campfire feu de camp m.
camp (to) camper.
can boîte de conserve f.; bidon m.
can pouvoir (*be able*).
Canadian canadien.
cancel annuler.
candidate candidat m.
candle bougie f.
cantor chantre m.
canvas toile f. (*painting*).
cap casquette f.
capacity capacité f.
capital adj. capital.
capital capitale f. (*city*); capital m. (*money*).
capricious capricieux.
captain capitaine m.
captive captif.
capture (to) capturer.
car tramway m. (*streetcar*); voiture f.; wagon m.
carbon paper papier carbone m.
card carte f.
care soin m.
    in care of aux bons soins de (*in a letter*).
    take care of soigner, prendre soin de.
care (to)
    care about se soucier.
    care for aimer.
    care to avoir envie.

I don't care. Ça m'est égal.
career carrière f.
careful soigneux.
careless négligent.
cares soucis m.; ennuis m.
caretaker concierge m. f.
carpenter menuisier m.; charpentier m.
carpet tapis m.
carry porter.
carry off emporter.
carry out exécuter.
cartoon (animated) dessin animé.
carve découper; sculpter.
carved sculpté.
case cas m.; étui m. (*container*); caisse f.
    in that case dans ce cas.
cash argent comptant m.
cash register caisse f.
cash (to) toucher.
cashier caissier m.
cask tonneau m.
castle château m.
cat chat m.
catastrophe catastrophe f.
catch attraper.
category catégorie f.
Catholic catholique.
cattle bétail m.
cause raison f., cause f.
cause (to) causer.
cavalry cavalerie f.
cavity cavité f.
cease cesser.
ceiling plafond m.
celebrate célébrer; fêter.
cellar cave f.
cement ciment m.
cemetery cimetière m.
cent sou m., centime m.
center centre m.
centimeter centimètre m.
central central.
century siècle m.
cereal céréale f.
ceremony cérémonie f.
certain certain, sûr adj.
certainly certainement.
certainty certitude f.
certificate certificat m.
chain chaîne f.
chain (to) enchaîner.
chair chaise f.; chaire f.
chairman président m.
chalk craie f.
challenge défi m.
challenge (to) défier.
champion champion m.
chance hasard m., chance f.
change change m., transformation f., changement
    m.; correspondance f. (*subway*).
change (to) changer.
chapel chapelle f.
chapter chapitre m.
character caractère m.; personnage m. (*in play*).
characteristic caractéristique noun and adj.
charge droit m.
charge (to) charger.
charitable charitable.
charity charité f.
charm charme m., grâce f.
charm (to) enchanter, charmer.
charming charmant, ravissant, délicieux.
charter charte f.

chase (to) poursuivre; chasser (*drive out*).
chat (to) bavarder.
cheap bon marché.
cheat (to) tricher, tromper.
check chèque m.
check (to) vérifier.
cheek joue f.
cheer (to) acclamer, encourager.
cheerful gai.
cheese fromage m.
chemical chimique.
chemist chimiste m.
chemistry chimie f.
cherish chérir.
cherry cerise f.
chest poitrine f. (*body*); coffre m. (*box*).
    chest of drawers commode f.
chestnut marron m., châtaigne f.
chew mâcher.
chicken poulet m.
chief adj. principal; maîtresse.
    masterwork oeuvre maîtresse f.
chief chef m. (*head*).
child enfant m., gosse m.
chime carillon m.
chimney cheminée f.
chin menton m.
china porcelaine f.
Chinese chinois.
chip jeton m.
chocolate chocolat m.
    chocolate bar tablette de chocolat.
choice adj. de choix.
choice choix m.
choir choeur m.
choke étrangler; étouffer.
choose choisir.
chop côtelette f. (*cut of meat*).
Christian chrétien noun and adj.
Christmas Noël f.
church église f., temple m. (*Protestant*).
cigar cigare m.
cigarette cigarette f.
cinematographic cinématographique.
circle cercle m.
circular circulaire m.
circulation circulation f.; tirage m. (*newspaper*).
circumstances circonstances f. pl.
citizen citoyen m.
city ville f.
city hall hôtel de ville.
civil civil.
civilization civilisation f., culture f.
civilize civiliser.
claim demande f., droit m.
claim (to) prétendre, réclamer, revendiquer.
clamor clameur f.
clap (to) applaudir.
clarinette clarinette f.
class classe f.
classic(al) classique.
classify classifier, classer.
clause clause f.
clean propre.
clean (to) nettoyer, degraisser.
    have (something) cleaned faire degraisser.
cleaning nettoyage m.
cleanliness propreté f.
clear clair, lucide.
clear (to) éclaircir; desservir (*a table*).
clearly clairement, ouvertement.
clerk employé de bureau m.
clever habile, adroit, intelligent.

climate climat m.
climb grimper.
clip agrafe f. (*paper clip*).
clip (to) attacher.
clippers tondeuse f.
cloak pèlerine f.
clock horloge f.
close auprès, tout près (*near*).
close (to) fermer.
closed fermé.
closet armoire f.
cloth étoffe f., toile f., tissu m.
clothe habiller.
clothes vêtement m., habits m. pl.
    clothes hanger cintre m.
cloud nuage m.
cloudy nuageux.
clover trèfle m.
club cercle m.; club m.
coach autocar m. (*outside city*).
coal charbon m.
coarse grossier.
coast côte f.
coat manteau m.; veste f., veston m. (*of suit*).
cocoa chocolat chaud m.
code code m.
coffee café m.
coffeepot cafetière f.
coffin cercueil m.
coin pièce f.
cold froid adj.
cold cream crème à démaquiller.
coldness froideur f.
collaborate collaborer.
collar col m.; collier m. (*dog*).
collect réunir, assembler.
collection collection f.; quête f. (*in church*).
collective collectif.
college université f.
colonial colonial.
colony colonie f.
color couleur f.
color (to) colorer.
column colonne f.; rubrique f. (*newspaper, maga-*
    zine).
comb peigne m.
comb (to) peigner.
combination combinaison f.
combine combiner.
come venir.
    come back revenir.
    come by again repasser.
    come off sauter.
comedy comédie f.
comet comète f.
comfort confort m.
comfort (to) consoler, rassurer.
comfortable confortable, à l'aise.
comma virgule f.
command commandement m.
command (to) commander.
commander commandant m.
commerce commerce m.
commercial adj. commercial.
commission commission f.
commit commettre.
common commun, ordinaire.
communicate communiquer.
communication communication f.
community communauté f.
companion camarade m. and f., compagnon m.,
    compagne f.
company (guests) monde m., invités m. pl.

company (firm) compagnie f.
compare comparer.
comparison comparaison f.
compete faire concurence.
competition concurrence f.
complain se plaindre.
complaint plainte f.
complete complet.
complex adj. complexe.
complexion-teint m.
complicate compliquer.
complicated compliqué.
compliment compliment m.
compose composer.
composer compositeur m.
composition composition f.
compromise compromis m.
compromise (to) compromettre.
comrade camarade m.
conceit amour-propre m.
conceive concevoir.
concentrate concentrer.
concern maison f. (business); affaire f.; importance f.; anxiété f.
concern (to) concerner.
concert concert m.
concierge gardien m.
concrete concret adj.
condemn condamner.
condense condenser.
condition condition f., état m.
conduct conduite f.
conduct (to) conduire, diriger (music).
conductor conducteur m.; receveur m. (on train, bus, etc.).
confess avouer.
confession aveu m.
confidence confidence f., confiance f.
confident confident.
confidential confidentiel.
confirm confirmer.
confirmation confirmation f.
congenial sympathique.
congratulate féliciter.
congratulation félicitation f.
connect unir, mettre en contact.
connection association f., relations f. pl.; correspondance f. (subway).
conquer conquérir.
conquest conquête f.
conscience conscience f.
conscientious consciencieux.
conscious conscient.
consent consentement m.
consent (to) consentir.
conservative conservateur noun and adj.
consider considérer.
considerable considérable.
consideration réflexion f.; considération f.
consist (of) consister de.
consistent conséquent.
constant constant.
constantly constamment.
constitution constitution f.
constitutional constitutionnel.
consul consul m.
contagious contagieux.
contain contenir.
container récipient m.
contemporary contemporain.
contempt mépris m.
contend concourir.
content (be) être content, être satisfait.

content (to) satisfaire, contenter.
content(s) contenu m.
continent continent m.
continual continuel.
continue continuer.
contract contrat m.
contract (to) contracter.
contractor entrepreneur m.
contradict contredire.
contradiction contradiction f.
contradictory contradictoire.
contrary adj. contraire.
    contrary to contrairement.
contrary contraire m.
    on the contrary au contraire.
contrast contraste m.
contrast (to) contraster.
contribute contribuer.
contribution contribution f.
control contrôle m., autorité f.
control (to) gouverner, maîtriser, contrôler.
controversy polémique f.
convenience convenance f.
convenient commode.
convention réunion f., convention f.
conversation conversation f.
converse converser, causer.
convert (to) convertir.
convertible décapotable f. (car).
convict (to) convaincre, condamner.
conviction conviction f.
convince convaincre.
cook cuisinière f.
cook (to) cuire.
cooked cuit.
cool frais.
cool (to) refroidir.
copy exemplaire m., copie f.
copy (to) copier.
cork bouchon (stopper); liège m. (material).
cork (to) boucher.
corn maïs m.
corner coin m.; recoin m. (nook).
corporation corporation f.
correct correct, exact.
correct (to) corriger.
correction correction f.
correspond correspondre.
correspondence correspondance f.
correspondent correspondant m.
corresponding correspondant.
corrupt corrompre.
corruption corruption f.
cost coût m.
cost (to) coûter.
costly coûteux.
costs frais m. pl.
costume costume m.
cottage chaumière f.
cotton coton m. (cotton thread, cotton material); ouate f. (medicine).
couch canapé m.
cough toux f.
cough (to) tousser.
count comte m.
count (to) compter.
counter comptoir m. (store); guichet m.
countersign (to) contresigner.
countess comtesse f.
countless innombrable.
country province f.; campagne f.; patrie f. (fatherland).
country house maison de campagne f.

countryman compatriote m. and f.; campagnard m.
couple couple m.
courage courage m.
course cours m.
court tribunal m.
courteous courtois.
courtesy courtoisie f.
courtyard cour f.
cousin cousin m.
cover couvercle m.
cover (to) couvrir.
    cover over recouvrir.
cow vache f.
crack fente f.
crack (to) craquer, fendre.
cradle berceau m.
craftsmen artisanat m.
crash fracas m.
crazy fou.
cream crème f.
    cleansing cream crème à démaquiller.
create créer.
creature créature f.
credit crédit m.
creditor créancier m.
creed culte m.
cricket grillon m.
crime crime m.
criminal criminel m.
crisis crise f.
crisp croustillant.
critic critique m.
crooked de travers.
crop moisson f.
cross adj. maussade, de mauvaise humeur.
cross croix f.
cross (to) croiser; rayer.
crossing passage m., traversée f.
    pedestrian crossing passage clouté.
crossroads carrefour m.
crossword puzzle mots croisés m. pl.
crouch accroupir.
crow corbeau m.
crowd foule f., affluence f.
    rush hour l'heure d'affluence.
crowd (to) encombrer.
crowded rempli de monde, encombré (streets, etc.); bondé.
crown couronne f.
crown (to) couronner.
cruel cruel.
cruelty cruauté f., barbarie f.
crumb miette f.
crumbling effondrement m.
crushing écrasant.
crust croûte f.
crutch béquille f.
cry cri m.
cry (to) pleurer.
cubist cubist m.
cuff manchette f.
cult culte m.
cunning ruse f., artifice m.
cup tasse f.
cupboard placard m.
cure cure f.
cure (to) guérir.
curio bibelot m.
curiosity curiosité f.
curious curieux.
curl (to) boucler.
current adj. courant.
current cours m.

curtain rideau m.
curve courbe f.
cushion coussin m.
custom usage m.
customary habituel.
customer client m.
customhouse douane f.
customs official douanier m.
customs permit carnet m.
cut (to) couper.

D

dagger poignard m.
daily quotidien.
   daily newspaper quotidien m.
dainty délicat.
dairy laiterie f.
dam barrage m.
damage dommage m.
damage (to) endommager, avarier.
damp humide.
dance danse f.
dance (to) danser.
danger danger m.
dangerous dangereux.
Danish danois n. and adj.
dark noir, foncé.
darkness obscurité f.
dash se précipiter.
date date f.
date (to) dater.
daughter fille f.
dawn aurore f., aube f.
day jour m., journée f.
   day after tomorrow après-demain m.
   day before veille f.
   day before yesterday avant-hier m.
dazzle éblouir.
dead mort.
deaf sourd.
deal opération f., affaire f.
dealer vendeur m., marchand m.
dear cher, coûteux (*expensive*).
death mort f.
debarkation débarquement m.
debatable discutable.
debate discussion f.
debate (to) discuter.
debris débris m. pl.
debt dette f.
debtor débiteur m.
decanter carafe f.
decay décadence f., ruine f.
decay (to) se gâter, dépérir.
decayed carié.
   a decayed tooth une dent cariée.
deceased défunt.
deceit déception f.
deceive tromper.
December décembre m.
decent comme il faut, respectable.
decide décider.
decidedly décidément.
decision décision f.
decisive décisif.
deck pont m.
declare déclarer.
decline décadence f.; baisse f.
decline (to) décliner; baisser.
declaration déclaration f.
   customs declaration déclaration en douane.
decoration décor m.

decrease réduction f.
decrease (to) diminuer.
decree ordonnance f.; arrêt m.
dedicate consacrer.
deed acte m., exploit m.
deep profond.
deeply profondément.
deer cerf m.
defeat défaite f.
defeat (to) vaincre.
defect défaut m.
defend défendre.
defense défense f.
defiance défi m.
define définir, déterminer.
definite défini.
definitely décidément.
defy défier.
degree degré m.
delay retard m.
delay (to) tarder.
delegate délégué m.
delegate (to) déléguer.
deliberate adj. délibéré.
deliberate (to) délibérer.
deliberately délibérément.
delicacy délicatesse f.
delicate délicat.
delicious délicieux.
delight joie f.
delight (to) ravir.
delighted enchanté.
delightful ravissant.
deliver remettre, livrer.
deliverance délivrance f.
delivery livraison f.
demand demande f.
demand (to) réclamer, exiger.
demonstrate démontrer.
demonstration démonstration f., manifestation f.
denial dénégation f.
denounce dénoncer.
dense dense.
density densité f.; épaisseur f.
dental dentaire.
dentifrice dentifrice noun m. and adj.
dentist dentiste m.
denial refus m., démenti m.
deny nier, démentir.
department département m.; rayon m. (*of store*).
   in the dress department au rayon des robes.
department store grand magasin m.
departure départ m.
depend dépendre.
dependence dépendance f.
dependent adj. dépendant (de).
deplore déplorer.
deposit dépôt m.
deposit (to) verser (*money*).
depot dépôt m.
depress abattre, déprimer.
depression abattement m. (*mood*).
deprive priver (de).
depth profondeur f., fond m.
deputy adjoint m.
deride tourner en dérision.
derive dériver de; provenir de.
descend descendre.
descendant descendant m.
descent descente f.
describe décrire.
description description f.
desert désert m.

desert (to) abandonner.
deserve mériter.
design dessein m.
design (to) dessiner.
designed (for) destiné à.
desirable désirable.
desire désir m., envie f.
desire (to) désirer.
desirous désireux.
desk bureau m.; guichet m.
desolate solitaire, désolé.
desolation désolation f.
despair désespoir m.
despair (to) désespérer.
desperate désespéré.
despise mépriser.
despite en dépit de.
despondent abattu.
dessert dessert m.
destination destination f.
destiny destin m.
destitute indigent.
destroy détruire.
destruction destruction f.
detach détacher.
detail détail m.
detailed minutieux.
detain retenir.
detect découvrir.
determination détermination f.
determine déterminer.
detest détester.
detour détour m.
detract from déprécier, dénigrer.
detriment détriment m.
develop développer.
development développement m.
device expédient m.
devil diable m.
devise combiner.
devoid of dépourvu de.
devote dévouer.
devour dévorer.
dew rosée f.
dial cadran m. (*clock*).
dial (to) composer (*telephone*).
dial telephone téléphone automatique m.
dial tone bourdonnement m.
dialect dialecte m.
dialogue dialogue m.
diameter diamètre m.
diamond diamant m.
diary journal m.
dictate dicter.
dictionary dictionnaire m.
die mourir.
diet régime m.
differ différer.
difference différence f.
different différent.
difficult difficile.
difficulty difficulté f.
dig creuser, fouiller.
digest digérer.
dignity dignité f.
dim sombre.
dimension dimension f.
diminish diminuer.
dinner dîner m.
dine dîner.
dip (to) plonger, tremper.
diploma diplôme m.
diplomacy diplomatie f.

diplomat diplomate m.
direct adj. direct, droit, précis, net.
direct (to) diriger.
direction direction f.; administration f.; sens m.
directions indications f. pl.
director directeur m.
directory annuaire m.; almanach m.
dirt saleté f.
dirty sale.
disability incapacité f.
disable rendre incapable (de).
disabled invalide.
disadvantage désavantage m.
disagree ne pas être d'accord, différer.
disagreeable désagréable.
disagreement désaccord m.
disappear disparaître.
disappearance disparition f.
disappoint décevoir.
disapprove désapprouver.
disaster catastrophe f., désastre m.
disastrous funeste, désastreux.
discharge congé m. (from a position, etc.); coup de feu (of gun), décharge f.
discharge (to) congédier (a person); décharger (a gun).
discipline discipline f.
disclaim désavouer, renier.
disclose découvrir, révéler.
disclosure découverte f.; révélation f.
discomfort malaise m.
discontent mécontentement m.
discontented mécontent (de).
discontinue discontinuer.
discord discorde f.
discount escompte m.
discourage décourager.
discouragement découragement m.
discover découvrir.
discovery découverte f.
discreet discret.
discretion discrétion f.
discuss discuter.
discussion discussion f.
disdain dédain m.
disdain (to) dédaigner.
disease maladie f.
disgrace déshonneur m., honte f.
disguise déguisement m.
disgust dégoût m.
disgust (to) dégoûter.
disgusted dégoûté.
disgusting dégoûtant.
dish plat m.
dishonest malhonnête.
disk disque m.
dislike aversion f.
dislike (to) ne pas aimer.
dismay consterner.
dismiss renvoyer, congédier.
dismissal renvoi m.
disobey désobéir.
disorder désordre m.
disown renier, désavouer.
dispense dispenser.
display exposition f., étalage m.
display (to) montrer.
displease déplaire.
displeasure déplaisir m.
disposal disposition f.
dispose disposer.
disprove refuter.
dispute dispute f.

dispute (to) disputer.
dissolve dissoudre.
distance distance f.
    distance covered parcours m.
    distance in kilometers kilométrage m.
distant lointain.
distinct clair, distinct (de).
distinction distinction f.
distinguish distinguer.
distort déformer.
distract distraire.
distress détresse f.
distress (to) affliger.
distribute distribuer.
distribution distribution f.
district quartier m., arrondissement m. (Paris).
distrust défiance f., méfiance f.
distrust (to) se méfier de.
disturb déranger; ennuyer.
disturbance désordre m.; agitation f.
ditch fossé m.
dive (to) plonger.
divide partager, diviser.
divine divin.
division division f.
divorce divorce m.
divorce (to) divorcer.
dizziness vertige m.
dizzy frappé de vertige.
do faire.
dock quai m. (pier).
doctor médecin m.
doctrine doctrine f.
document document m.
dog chien m.
dollar dollar m.
dome dôme m.
domestic domestique noun and adj
dominate dominer.
done fait.
door porte f.; portière f. (car).
doorkeeper concierge m. f.
dose dose f.
dot point m.
double double noun m. and adj.
doubt doute m.
doubt (to) douter.
doubtful douteux, indécis.
doubtless sans doute.
dough pâte f.
down en bas.
downwards en bas.
dozen douzaine f.
draft projet m.; traite f. (bank); enrôlement m. (military).
draft (to) élaborer (draw up); conscrire.
drag traîner.
drain vider, dessécher.
drama drame m.
dramatic dramatique.
draw dessiner.
draw back reculer.
drawer tiroir m.
drawing dessin m.
    animated cartoon dessin animé.
    border design dessin du bord.
drawing room salon m.
dread crainte f., terreur f.
dread (to) redouter, craindre.
dreaded redoutable.
dream rêve m.
dream (to) rêver.
dreamer rêveur m.

dress robe f.
dress (to) habiller, s'habiller.
dressmaker couturière f.
drill (to) creuser (tooth).
drink boisson f.
drink (to) boire.
drip dégoutter.
drive aller en voiture, conduire (car); pousser (force).
driver chauffeur m.
drop goutte f.
drop (to) laisser tomber (allow to fall); baisser; abandonner.
drown noyer, se noyer.
drug drogue f.
druggist pharmacien m.
drugstore pharmacie f.
drum tambour m.
drunk ivre.
dry sec.
dry (to) sécher.
dry cleaner pressing m.
dry cleaning dégraissage m., nettoyage à sec m.
dryness sècheresse f.
duchess duchesse f.
due dû.
duke duc m.
dull terne (color); bête (stupid).
dumb muet (deaf and dumb); stupide, bête (stupid).
during pendant.
dust poussière f.
dust (to) épousseter.
dusty poussiéreux.
duty douane f. (customs), impôt m.; devoir m. (obligation).
dwell demeurer.
dwelling demeure f.
dye teinture f.
dye (to) teindre.

E

each chaque, chacun.
    each other se, l'un l'autre.
    each time chaque fois.
eager ardent.
eagle aigle m.
ear oreille f.
early de bonne heure, tôt.
earn gagner.
earnest sérieux.
earnestly instamment.
earth terre f.
ease aise f.
ease (to) soulager.
easily facilement.
east est m.
Easter Pâques m. pl.
eastern oriental.
easy facile.
easy chair bergère f.
eat manger.
echo écho m.
economical économe (person), économique (thing).
economize faire des économies.
economy économie f.
edge bord m.
edition édition f., numéro m. (publication).
editor rédacteur m.
editorial article de tête m.
education éducation f.
effect effet m.
effect (to) effectuer.

effective efficace.
efficiency efficacité f.
effort effort m.
egg oeuf m.
egoism égoïsme m.
eight huit.
eighteen dix-huit.
eighteenth dix-huitième.
eighth huitième.
eightieth quatre-vingtième.
eighty quatre-vingts.
either ou.
   either one l'un ou l'autre.
elastic élastique noun m. and adj.
elbow coude m.
elder aîné.
elderly d'un certain âge.
eldest plus âgé.
elect choisir, élire.
election élection f.
elector électeur m.
electric(al) électrique.
electricity électricité f.
elegant élégant.
element élément m.; facteur m.
elementary élémentaire.
elephant éléphant m.
elevator ascenseur m.
eleven onze.
eleventh onzième.
eliminate éliminer.
eloquence éloquence f.
eloquent éloquent.
else autrement, sinon (otherwise).
   someone else quelqu'un d'autre.
   somewhere else ailleurs.
elsewhere ailleurs.
elude éluder, éviter.
embankment quai m. (river).
embark embarquer, s'embarquer.
embarrass embarrasser.
embarrassing gênant.
embarrassment embarras m.
embassy embassade f.
embody incarner.
embroidery broderie f.
emerge surgir.
emergency circonstance critique f.
eminent éminent.
emotion émotion f.
emperor empereur m.
emphasis emphase f.
emphasize appuyer sur, mettre en relief.
emphatic énergique.
empire empire m.
employee employé m.
employer patron m.
employment emploi m.
empty vide.
empty (to) vider.
enable mettre à même de, donner le moyen de.
enamel émail m.
enclose entourer, joindre.
enclosed ci-inclus, ci-joint.
encourage encourager.
encouragement encouragement m.
end bout m., fin f.; but m. (aim).
end (to) finir, aboutir (result), terminer.
endeavor effort m.
endeavor (to) s'efforcer de.
ending dénouement m. (play or story).
endorse endorser, confirmer.
endure supporter.

enemy ennemi m.
energetic énergique.
energy énergie f.
enforce imposer.
engage engager, s'engager à.
engaged couple fiancés m.
engagement engagement m.
engine machine f.
engineer ingénieur m.
England Angleterre f.
English anglais noun and adj.
engrave graver.
engraving gravure f.
enjoy s'amuser, jouir.
enjoyment jouissance f.
enlarge élargir.
enlargement agrandissement m.
enlist enrôler, s'enrôler.
enormous énorme.
enormously énormément.
enough assez, suffisament.
enrich enrichir.
enter entrer.
entertain recevoir, amuser.
entertainment amusement m.
enthusiasm enthousiasme m.
enthusiastic enthousiaste.
entire entier.
entitle intituler (title), donner droit à (give one
   the right to).
entrance entrée f.
entrust confier à.
enumerate énumérer.
envelope enveloppe f.
envious envieux.
envy envie f., jalousie f.
envy (to) envier.
episode épisode m.
equal égal.
equal (to) égaler.
equality égalité f.
equilibrium équilibre m.
equip équiper, munir de.
equipment équipement m. (outfit).
equity équité f.
era ère f.
erase effacer.
eraser gomme f.
erect droit.
erect (to) dresser, ériger, fonder.
err errer, se tromper.
errand course f., commission f.
error erreur f., tort m.
escalator escalier roulant m.
escape fuite f.
escape (to) échapper.
escort escorter.
especially spécialement.
essay essai m., composition f. (school).
essence essence f.
essential essentiel, indispensable.
establish établir.
establishment établissement m.
estate biens m. pl., propriété f.
esteem estime f.
esteem (to) estimer.
esthetic esthétique.
estimate appréciation f., évaluation f. (value).
estimate (to) évaluer, apprécier.
estimation jugement m.
etching eau-forte f.
eternal éternel.
eternity éternité f.

ether éther m.
European européen noun and adj.
evade esquiver, éluder.
evasion évasion f.
eve veille f.
   on the eve of à la veille de.
even adj. uni, égal, pair (number).
even adv. même.
evening soir m.
   Good evening! Bonsoir!
   yesterday evening hier soir.
   tomorrow evening demain soir.
event événement m.
ever jamais, toujours.
every chaque, tous.
   every day tous les jours.
everybody tout le monde.
everything tout.
everywhere partout.
evidence évidence f.
evident évident.
evidently évidemment.
evil adj. mauvais.
evil mal m.
evoke évoquer.
evolve développer.
exact précis, exact.
exactly exactement.
exaggerate exagérer.
exaggeration exagération f.
exalt exalter.
exaltation exaltation f.
examination examen m.
examine examiner.
example exemple m.
exceed dépasser.
excel exceller à.
excellence excellence f.
excellent excellent.
except sauf.
except (to) excepter.
exception exception f.
exceptional exceptionnel.
exceptionally exceptionnellement.
excess excès m.
excessive excessif.
exchange échange m.
   exchange window guichet de change m.
exchange (to) échanger.
excite exciter, agiter.
excitement excitation f., agitation f.
exclaim s'écrier.
exclamation exclamation f.
exclamation mark point d'exclamation.
exclude exclure.
exclusive exclusif.
excursion excursion f., tour m.
excuse excuse f.
excuse (to) excuser.
   Excuse me. Excusez-moi.
execute exécuter, effectuer.
execution exécution f.
exempt exempt (de).
exercise exercice m.
exercise (to) exercer.
exert exercer, mettre en oeuvre.
exertion effort m.
exhaust épuiser.
exhaustion épuisement m.
exhibit (to) exhiber, exposer.
exhibition exposition f.
exile proscrit m., exilé m.
exile (to) exiler.

exist exister.
existence existence f.
exit sortie f.
expand amplifier, étendre.
expansion expansion f.
expansive expansif.
expect attendre.
expectation attente f., espérance f.
expedition expédition f.
expel expulser.
expense frais m., dépense f.
expensive coûteux.
experience expérience f.
experience (to) éprouver.
experiment expérience f.
expert expert m.
    to be expert at se connaître en.
expire expirer.
explain expliquer.
explanation explication f.
explanatory explicatif.
explode faire explosion, éclater.
exploit exploit m.
exploit (to) exploiter.
explore explorer.
explosion explosion f.
export exportation f.
export (to) exporter.
expose exposer.
exposed à vif (nerve).
exposure pose f. (photography).
exposure meter pose-mètre m.
express express (train) noun m. and adj., exprès.
    by express par exprès.
express (to) exprimer.
expression expression f.
expressive expressif.
expulsion expulsion f.
exquisite exquis.
extend étendre.
extensive vaste.
extent étendue f.
    to some extent jusqu'à un certain point.
exterior noun m. and adj. extérieur.
exterminate exterminer.
external extérieur, externe.
extinct étient.
extinction extinction f.
extinguish éteindre.
extra en plus, supplémentaire.
extract extrait m.
extract (to) extraire.
extraordinary extraordinaire.
extravagance extravagance f.
extravagant extravagant.
extreme noun m. and adj. extrême.
extremely extrêmement.
extremity extrémité f.
eye oeil (pl. yeux) m.
eyebrow sourcil m.
eyeglasses lunettes f. pl.
eyelid paupière f.

F

fable fable f.
fabric étoffe f., tissu m.
face figure f., face, f.
face (to) faire face à.
facilitate faciliter.
facility facilité f., aisance f.
fact fait m.
    in fact en effet.

factory fabrique f.
faculty faculté f.
fade se faner.
fail
    without fail sans faute.
fail (to) manquer (à), faillir.
faint évanouissement m.
faint (to) s'évanouir.
fair droit, juste.
faith foi f.
faithful fidèle adj.
fall chute f.; automne m. and f.
fall (to) tomber.
false faux.
fame réputation m., renomée f.
familiar familier.
family famille f.
famine famine f.
famous fameux, célèbre.
fan éventail m.
    electric fan ventilateur.
    sports fan supporter m., fanatique m.
fanatic adj. fanatique.
fanatic fanatique m.
fancy fantaisie f.; caprice m.
fantastic fantastique.
far loin.
farce farce f.
fare prix de la place m., prix du voyage m., tarif m.
farm ferme f.
farmer fermier m.
farming agriculture f.
farther plus éloigné; plus loin.
farthest le plus éloigné.
fashion mode f.; manière f.
fashionable à la mode, chic.
fast vite, solide.
fasten attacher.
fat adj. gros, gras.
fat graisse f.
fatal fatal.
fate destinée f.
father père m.
father-in-law beau-père m.
faucet robinet m.
fault faute f., défaut m., tort m.
favor service m., faveur f.
    Could (will) you do me a favor? Voulez-vous me rendre un service?
favor (to) favoriser.
favorable favorable.
favorite adj. favori, préféré.
fear crainte f., peur f.
fear (to) craindre.
fearless intrépide.
feather plume f.
feature trait m., caractéristique f.
February février m.
federal fédéral.
fee honoraires m. pl., droit m.
feeble faible.
feed nourrir.
feel (to) éprouver, sentir; tâter (touch).
feel like (to) avoir envie de.
    I feel like laughing. J'ai envie de rire.
feeling sensibilité f.; sensation f.; sentiment m.
fellow bonhomme m., gars m.
fellowship camaraderie f.; bourse f. (school).
fellow worker collègue m. and f., confrère m.
female femelle f.
feminine féminin noun m. and adj.
fence clôture f., barrière f.
fencing escrime f.

ferocious féroce.
ferry bac m.
fertile fertile.
fertilize féconder, fertiliser.
fertilizer engrais m.
fervent ardent.
fervor ferveur f., ardeur f.
festival fête f.
fetch aller chercher, apporter.
fever fièvre f.
few peu.
fiber fibre f.
fiction romans m. pl.
fidelity fidélité f.
    high fidelity haute fidélité.
field champ m.
fierce cruel, violent.
fiery ardent.
fifteen quinze.
    about fifteen une quinzaine.
    two weeks quinze jours.
fifteenth quinzième.
fifth cinquième.
fiftieth cinquantième.
fifty cinquante.
fig figue f.
fight lutte f.; mêlée f.
fight (to) combattre.
figure forme f. (form); chiffre m. (number).
file lime f. (tool); dossier m. (papers).
fill remplir; plomber (tooth).
film pellicule f.; film m.; inversibles m. pl. (for transparencies).
    color film film en couleurs m.
filthy sale.
final décisif, définitif, final.
finance finance f.
financial financier.
find (to) trouver.
    find oneself se retrouver.
fine adj. beau; fin (not coarse).
    Fine! Très bien!
fine amende f.
finger doigt m.
fingernail ongle m.
finish (to) finir; terminer, compléter.
fire feu m.; incendie m.
fireplace cheminée f.; foyer m.
firm adj. ferme; constant (character).
firm maison f. (business).
first adj. premier.
    for the first time pour la première fois.
first adv. d'abord, tout d'abord.
    at first d'abord, tout d'abord.
fish poisson m.
fish (to) pêcher.
fisherman pêcheur m.
fist poing m.
fit convenable, propre à.
fit (to) convenir, adapter.
fitness à-propos m., aptitude f.
fitting essayage m.
    fitting room salon d'essayage.
five cinq.
fix fixer.
flag drapeau m.
flame flamme f.
flank flanc m.
flank (to) flanquer.
flash of lightning éclair m.
flashbulb lampe-éclair f.
flashcube flashcube m.
flat plat; fade (taste).

flat tire pneu crevé m., crevaison. f.
flatter flatter.
flattery flatterie f.
flavor goût m., saveur f.; bouquet m.
flea puce f.
Flea Market Marché aux Puces m.
fleet flotte f.
flesh chair f.
flexibility souplesse f.
flexible souple, flexible.
flight vol m. (*in air*), fuite f. (*rout*).
fling (to) jeter.
flint caillou m., pierre à briquet f.
float flotter.
flood inondation f.
flood (to) inonder.
floor plancher m.; étage m. (*story*).
flourish prospérer.
flow affluence f.
flow (to) couler.
flower fleur f.
fluid fluide.
flute flûte f.
    play the flute jouer de la flûte.
fly mouche f.
fly (to) voler.
foam écume f.
foam (to) écumer.
fog brouillard m.
fold pli m.
fold (to) plier.
foliage feuillage m.
follow suivre.
    follow one another se suivre.
following suivant.
fond (be) aimer.
fondness tendresse f.
food nourriture.
fool imbécile noun and adj.
foolish sot.
foot pied m.
football football m.
footstep pas m.
for pour.
    for example par exemple.
    for the first time pour la première fois.
    for the most part pour la plupart.
    for the present pour le moment.
forbid défendre.
force force f.
force (to) obliger.
ford gué m.
foreground premier plan m.
forehead front m.
foreign étranger.
foreigner étranger m.
foresee prévoir.
forest forêt f.
forget oublier.
forgetfulness oubli m.
forgive pardonner.
forgiveness pardon m.
fork fourchette f.
form forme f.; fiche f.; formulaire m. (*printed*).
form (to) former.
formal formel, cérémonieux.
formality formalité f.
format format m.
formation formation f.
former ancien; précédent.
formerly autrefois.
formula formule f.
forsake renoncer à.

fort fort m.
fortunate heureux.
fortunately heureusement.
fortune fortune f.
fortieth quarantième.
forty quarante.
forward en avant.
forward (to) faire suivre.
forwarding agent transitaire m.
foster nourrir.
foul sale, impur.
found trouvé.
found (to) fonder.
foundation fondation f.
founder fondateur m.
fountain fontaine f.
four quatre.
fourteen quatorze.
fourteenth quatorzième.
fourth quatrième.
fowl volaille f. (*poultry*).
fox renard m.
foyer foyer m.
fragment fragment m.
fragrance parfum m.
fragrant parfumé.
frail fragile.
frame cadre m.
frame (to) encadrer.
franc franc m.
frank franc.
frankness franchise f.
free libre, gratuit.
free (to) libérer; débarasser.
freedom liberté f.
freeze glacer, geler.
freight chargement m.
French français noun and adj.
French fried potato frite f.
French Riviera Côte d'Azur, f.
frequent fréquent.
frequent (to) fréquenter.
frequently fréquemment.
fresh frais.
friction friction f.
Friday vendredi m.
friend ami m.
friendly amical.
friendship amitié f.
frieze frise f.
frighten effrayer.
frightening effrayant.
fringe frange f.
frivolity frivolité f.
frivolous frivole.
frog grenouille f.
from de; dès, depuis.
front devant, de devant.
frontier frontière f.
fruit fruit m.
fry (to) frire.
frying pan poêle à frire f.
fuel combustible m.
fugitive fugitif noun and adj.
fulfill accomplir.
full plein.
fully abondamment.
fun amusement m.
    have fun s'amuser.
funny amusant, drôle.
function fonction f.
function (to) fonctionner.
fund fonds m. pl.

fundamental fondamental noun and adj.
funds fonds m. pl.
funny drôle.
fur fourrure f.
furious furieux.
furnace four m.
furnish garnir, meubler (*a room*).
furniture meubles m. pl., mobilier m.
furrow sillon m.
further ultérieur, plus lointain, supplémentaire.
fury rage f.
future adj. futur.
future avenir m.
    in the future à l'avenir.

G

gadget truc m.
gaiety gaieté f.
gain gain m.
gain (to) gagner.
gallant brave.
gallery galerie f.
gallop galop m.
gamble (to) jouer.
game jeu m., partie f.
garage garage m.
garden jardin m.
gardener jardinier m.
garlic ail m.
garment vêtement m.
gas gaz m.
gasoline essence f. (*for car*).
gate porte f.; barrière f.; portillon m.
    automatic gate portillon automatique (*subway*).
gather réunir, cueillir.
gay gai.
gem pierre précieuse f.
gender genre m.
general adj. général.
    in general en général.
general général m.
general delivery poste restante f.
generality généralité f.
generalize généraliser.
generation génération f.
generosity générosité f.
generous généreux.
genius génie m.
gentle doux.
gentleman monsieur m.
    Gentlemen. Messieurs.
    Ladies and gentlemen. Mesdames et messieurs.
gentleness douceur f.
gently doucement.
genuine authentique.
geographical géographique.
geography géographie f.
germ germe m.
German allemand noun and adj.
gesture geste m.
get obtenir, recevoir.
    get along se débrouiller.
    get off descendre.
ghastly hagard.
giant colosse m., géant m.
gift don m., cadeau m.
gifted doué.
gilded doré.
girl fille f.
give donner.
    give back rendre, remettre.

give up abandonner.
glad heureux, content.
gladly volontiers.
glance coup d'oeil m.
glance (to) entrevoir.
glass verre m.
    looking glass glace f., miroir m. (*small*).
    drinking glass verre m.
gleam lueur f.
gleam (to) luire.
glitter éclat m.; scintillation f.
glitter (to) briller, étinceler.
global global.
globe globe m.
gloomy lugubre.
glorious glorieux.
glory gloire f.
glove gant m.
glow chaleur f. (*heat*), lumière f. (*light*).
go (to) aller.
    go away partir, s'en aller.
    go back retourner, rentrer, reculer.
    go by again repasser.
    go down descendre.
    go forward avancer.
    go out sortir.
    go to bed se coucher.
    go to meet aller à la rencontre.
    go to sleep s'endormir.
    go up monter.
    go with accompagner.
    take oneself se rendre.
goal-keeper gardien de but m.
goalie gardien de but m.
God Dieu m.
gold or m.
golden d'or, en or.
goldsmith's work orfèvrerie f.
golf golf m.
good bon, bien.
    Good afternoon! Bonjour!
    Good evening! Bonsoir!
    Good morning! Bonjour!
    Good night! Bonsoir! Bonne nuit!
good-by au revoir, adieu.
goodness bonté f.
goods marchandise f.
goodwill bonne volonté f.
goose oie f.
gorgeous ravissant.
gossip commérage m.; bavard m. (*person*); potins m. pl.
gossip (to) potiner, bavarder.
gouache gouache f.
govern gouverner.
grace grâce f.
graceful gracieux.
grade grade m.
grain grain m.
grammar grammaire f.
grand grandiose, majestueux.
    Grand! Magnifique! Epatant!
grandchild petit-fils m.
granddaughter petite-fille f.
grandeur grandeur f.
grandfather grand-père m.
grandmother grand'mère f.
grandson petit-fils m.
grant concession f.
grant (to) accorder.
    Granted! D'accord!
grape raisin m.
grapefruit pamplemousse m.

grasp (to) saisir, comprendre (*understand*).
grass herbe f.
grasshopper sauterelle f.
grateful reconnaissant.
gratis gratuit.
gratitude reconnaissance f.
grave adj. grave, sérieux.
grave tombe f.
gravel gravier m.
gray gris.
grease graisse f.
greasing graissage m.
great grand (*of a person*); énorme (*size*).
greatness grandeur f.
greedy avide, gourmand.
Greek grec.
green vert.
greet saluer, accueillir.
greeting salutation f., accueil m.
grief peine f.
grieve affliger, attrister.
grin (to) ricaner.
grind moudre.
groan gémissement m.
groan (to) gémir.
grocer épicier m.
grocery store épicerie f.
grope tâtonner.
gross grossier, brut.
ground terre f.
group groupe m.
group (to) grouper.
grouping groupement m.
grow croître, grandir; pousser (*vegetation*).
growth croissance f.
grudge rancune f.
    hold a grudge against en vouloir à.
gruff rude, brusque.
guard garde m.
guard (to) garder.
guardian tuteur m., gardien m.
guess conjecture f.
guess (to) deviner, conjecturer.
    guess right deviner juste.
guide guide m.
guide (to) guider, piloter.
guidebook guide m.
guilt faute f.
gum gencive f. (*of the teeth*).
gun fusil m.
gush jet m.

H

habit habitude f.
    to be in the habit of avoir l'habitude de.
habitual habituel.
hail grêle f.
hair cheveu m., cheveux m. pl.
hair (to do someone's) coiffer.
hair clippers tondeuse f.
hairdo coiffure f.
hairdresser coiffeur m.
half demi, moitié.
    half-liter of light beer demi blonde m.
    half a dozen demi-douzaine f.
half-hour demi-heure f.
half-time mi-temps f. (*sports*).
hall salle f.
ham jambon m.
hammer marteau m.
hand main f.
hand (to) passer, remettre.

handbag sac à main m.
handful poignée f.
handkerchief mouchoir m.
handle anse f., poignée f.
handle (to) manier, manoeuvrer.
handsome beau, belle.
handy adroit (*person*), commode (*easy to handle*).
hang pendre, suspendre.
    hang up raccrocher (*telephone receiver*).
happen arriver, se passer.
happening événement m.
happiness bonheur m.
happy heureux, content.
harbor port m., asile m. (*refuge*).
hard difficile (*difficult*); dur (*not soft*).
harden endurcir.
hardly guère, à peine.
hardness dureté f.
hardship privation f., épreuve f.
hardware quincaillerie f.
hardware store quincaillerie f.
hardy robuste, vigoureux.
hare lièvre m.
harm mal m.
harm (to) nuire, faire tort à.
harmful nuisible.
harmless inoffensif.
harmonious harmonieux.
harmony harmonie f.
harsh âpre.
harvest récolte f., moisson f.
haste hâte f.
hasten se hâter, se dépêcher.
hat chapeau m.
hate haine f.
hate (to) détester, haïr.
hateful odieux.
hatred haine f.
haughty hautain.
have avoir.
have to devoir.
haven asile m., refuge m.
hay foin m.
he il.
head tête f. (*part of body*); chef m. (*chief*); chevet m. (*of bed*).
head for se diriger vers.
headache mal de tête m.
heading rubrique f. (*newspaper, magazine*).
heal guérir; se guérir; se cicatriser (*wound*).
health santé f.
healthy sain.
heap tas m.; pile f.
heap up entasser.
hear entendre.
    hear about entendre parler de.
    hear that entendre dire que.
hearing ouïe f.
heart coeur m.
heat chaleur f.
heaven ciel m.
    Heavens! Mon Dieu! Ciel!
heavy lourd.
hedge haie f.
heed (to) faire attention à.
heel talon m.
height hauteur f.; comble m.
heir héritier m.
hello allô.
helm gouvernail m.
help aide f., secours m.
help (to) aider.
helper aide noun and adj.

helpful utile.
hem ourlet m.
hen poule f.
henceforth désormais.
her la, lui, son, sa, ses.
herb herbe f.
herd troupeau m.
here ici.
 Here! Tenez! Tiens!
herewith ci-joint.
hero héros m.
heroic héroïque.
heroine héroïne f.
herring hareng m.
herself elle-même.
hesitate hésiter.
hide (to) cacher, dissimuler.
hideous hideux.
high haut.
higher supérieur.
hill colline f.
him le, lui.
himself lui-même.
hind de derrière.
hinder empêcher, gêner.
hinge gond m.
hint allusion f.
hint (to) faire allusion à, insinuer.
hip hanche f.
hire (to) louer, engager.
 for hire à louer.
hiring location f.
his son, sa, ses, à lui, le sien, la sienne, les siens,
 les siennes.
hiss sifflet m.
hiss (to) siffler.
historian historien m.
historic historique.
history histoire f.
hoarse rauque.
hoe houe f.
hold prise f.
hold (to) tenir.
hole trou m.
holiday jour de fête m.; congé m.; jour férié m.,
 jour de vacances m.
holiness sainteté f.
hollow creux.
holy saint.
homage hommage m.
home maison f.
 home town ville natale f.
homework devoirs m. pl.
honest honnête.
honesty honnêteté f.
honey miel m.
honor honneur m.
honor (to) honorer.
honorable honorable.
hood capuchon m.
hoof sabot m.
hook crochet m.
hope espoir m.
hope (to) espérer.
hopeful plein d'espoir.
hopeless sans espoir, désespéré.
horizon horizon m.
horizontal horizontal.
horn trompe f.; corne f.
horrible horrible.
horror horreur f.
horse cheval m.
horseback (on) à cheval.

hosiery bonneterie f.
hospitable hospitalier.
hospital hôpital m.
host hôte m.
hostess hôtesse f.
hostile hostile.
hot chaud.
hotel hôtel m.
hour heure f.
house maison f.
household ménage m.
housekeeper ménagère f.
how comment.
 how much combien de.
 how many combien de.
 how long combien de temps.
 how often combien de fois.
 How beautiful! Que c'est beau!
 How are you? Comment allez-vous?
however cependant.
howl hurlement m.
howl (to) hurler.
human humain.
humane humain.
humanity humanité f.
humble humble.
humid humide.
humiliate humilier.
humility humilité f.
humming bourdonnement m.
humor humeur f.
hundred cent.
hundredth centième.
hunger faim f.
hungry (be) avoir faim.
hunt chasse f.
hunt (to) chasser.
hunter chasseur m.
hurry hâte f.
 be in a hurry être pressé.
hurry (to) se hâter, se presser, se dépêcher.
hurt (to) faire mal.
husband mari m.
hush (to) calmer, étouffer (a scandal).
hyphen trait d'union m.
hypocrisy hypocrisie f.
hypocrite hypocrite m. and f.
hypothesis hypothèse f.

I

I je.
ice glace f.
icy glacial.
idea idée f.
ideal idéal noun m. and adj.
idealism idéalisme m.
idealist idéaliste m. and f.
identical identique.
identification papers pièces d'identité f.
idiot noun m. and adj. imbécile.
idle oisif.
idleness oisiveté f.
if si.
ignition allumage m.
ignoble ignoble.
ignorance ignorance f.
ignorant ignorant.
ignore refuser de connaître, ne tenir aucun compte
 de.
ill mal; malade.
illness maladie f.
illusion illusion f.

illustrate illustrer.
illustration illustration f.
image image f.
imaginary imaginaire.
imagination imagination f.
imagine s'imaginer, se figurer.
imitate imiter.
imitation imitation f.
immediate immédiat.
immediately tout de suite, aussitôt, immédiatement.
immigration immigration f.
imminent imminent.
immobility immobilité f.
immoral immoral.
immorality immoralité f.
immortal immortel.
immortality immortalité f.
impartial impartial.
impatience impatience f.
impatient impatient.
imperfect défecteux.
impertinence impertinence f.
impertinent impertinent.
impetuosity impétuosité f.
impetuous impétueux.
impious impie.
import importation f.
import (to) importer.
importance importance f.
important important.
imposing imposant.
impossible impossible.
impress (to) impressionner.
impression impression f., empreinte f.
 be under the impression that avoir l'impression que.
impressionist impressioniste.
impressive impressionnant.
imprison emprisonner.
improve améliorer.
improvement amélioration f., mieux m., progrès m.
improvise improviser.
imprudence imprudence f.
imprudent imprudent.
impulse impulsion f., inspiration f.
impulsive impulsif.
impure impur.
in dans, en.
inadequate insuffisant.
inaugurate inaugurer.
incapable incapable.
incapacity incapacité f.
inch pouce m.
incident incident m.
include renfermer.
included compris.
including y compris.
income rente f., revenu m.
incomparable incomparable.
incompatible incompatible.
incompetent incompétent.
incomplete incomplet.
incomprehensible incompréhensible.
inconvenience incommodité f.
inconvenient inconvénient, pas pratique.
incorrect inexact.
increase augmentation f.
increase (to) augmenter.
incredible incroyable.
incur encourir, contracter.
indebted endetté.
indecision indécision f.

indecisive indécis.
indeed en effet, vraiment.
independence indépendance f.
independent indépendant.
index index m., table des matières f.
index finger index m.
indicate indiquer.
indicated inscrit.
indicative indicatif m.
indifference indifférence f.
indifferent indifférent.
indignant indigne.
indignation indignation f.
indirect indirect.
indirectly indirectement.
indiscretion indiscrétion f.
indispensable indispensable.
individual individu m.; individuel adj.
individualist(ic) individualiste.
indivisible indivisible.
indolence indolence f.
indolent indolent.
indoors à la maison.
    go indoors rentrer.
induce persuader, occasionner.
induct installer; initier.
indulge avoir de l'indulgence; s'adonner.
indulgence indulgence f.
indulgent indulgent, complaisant.
industrial industriel.
industrious appliqué, laborieux.
industry industrie f.; application f.
inexhaustible inépuisable.
inexplicable inexplicable.
inexpressible inexprimable.
infallible infaillible.
infamous infâme.
infancy enfance f.
infant petit enfant m.
infantry infanterie f.
infection infection f.
infer conclure.
inference déduction f.
inferior inférieur.
infernal infernal.
infinite infini.
infinity infinité f.
inflate gonfler.
inflict infliger.
influence influence f.
influence (to) influencer.
inform informer, prévenir, faire savoir.
information information f.; renseignements m. pl.
ingenious ingénieux.
ingenuity ingéniosité f.
ingratitude ingratitude f.
inhabit habiter.
inhabitant habitant m.
inherit hériter.
inheritance héritage m.
inhuman inhumain.
initial adj. initial.
initial initiale f.
initiate commencer, initier.
initiation initiation f.
initiative initiative f.
injection piqûre f.
injurious nuisible.
injury blessure f.
injustice injustice f.
ink encre f.
inkwell encrier m.
inland intérieur m.

inn auberge f.
innate inné.
innkeeper aubergiste m.
innocence innocence f.
innocent innocent.
inquire demander, se renseigner.
inquiry recherche f.; enquête f.
inscribed inscrit.
inscription inscription f.
insect insecte m.
insensible insensible.
inseparable inséparable.
inside dedans.
inside intérieur m.
insight pénétration f.
insignificant insignifiant.
insincere peu sincère.
insinuate insinuer.
insist insister.
insistantly instamment.
insistence insistance f.
insoluble insoluble.
inspect inspecter.
inspection inspection f.
inspiration inspiration f.
install installer.
installment acompte m., versement m.
instance exemple m.
instant instant m.
instantaneous instantané.
instantly à l'instant.
instead of au lieu de.
instigate provoquer, inciter à.
instinct instinct m.
instinctive instinctif.
institute institut m.
institute (to) instituer.
institution institution f.
instruct instruire.
instruction instruction f.
instructions indications f. pl.
instructor instituteur m., institutrice f., instructeur m.
instrument instrument m.
insufficiency insuffisance f.
insufficient insuffisant.
insult insulte f.
insult (to) insulter, injurier.
insuperable insurmontable.
insurance assurance f.
insure assurer.
integral intégral.
intellect intelligence f.
intellectual intellectuel m.
intelligence intelligence f.
intelligent intelligent.
intelligently intelligemment.
intend se proposer de.
intense intense.
intensity intensité f.
intention intention f.
interest intérêt m.
    take an interest in s'intéresser à.
interest (to) intéresser.
interesting intéressant.
interfere intervenir, gêner.
interference intervention f.
interior noun. m. and adj. intérieur.
intermediate intermédiaire.
intermission entr'acte m.
international international.
interpose interposer.
interpret interpréter.

interpretation interprétation f.
interpreter interprète m.
interrupt interrompre.
interruption interruption f.
interurban interurbain (*telephone*).
interval intervalle m.
interview entrevue f., interview f.
interview (to) avoir une entrevue, interviewer.
intimacy intimité f.
intimate intime.
intimidate intimider.
into dans, en.
intolerable intolérable.
intolerance intolérance f.
intolerant intolérant.
intonation intonation f.
intrigue intrigue f.
introduce présenter, amener.
introduction introduction f. (*book*); initiation f.
intuition intuition f.
invade envahir.
invariable invariable.
invasion invasion f.
invent inventer.
invention invention f.
inventor inventeur m.
invert renverser, intervertir.
invest placer (de l'argent), investir.
investment placement m.
invisible invisible.
invitation invitation f.
invite inviter.
invoice facture f.
invoke invoquer.
involuntary involontaire.
involve impliquer.
iron fer m.
iron (to) repasser.
    have (something) ironed faire repasser.
irony ironie f.
irregular irrégulier.
irreparable irréparable.
irresistible irrésistible.
irritate irriter.
irritation irritation f.
Islamic islamique.
island île f.
isolate isoler.
issue sortie f., résultat m., issue f.
issue (to) émettre, distribuer; sortir, jaillir.
it il.
Italian italien noun and adj.
item détail m.
itinerary itinéraire m.
its son.
it's c'est, il est.
    It's late. Il est tard.
    It's here. C'est ici.
itself lui-même, elle-même, se, même.
ivory ivoire f.
ivy lierre m.

J

jacket veste f.; veston m.
    business suit complet-veston.
    two-button jacket veston à deux boutons.
    woman's jaquette f.
jam confiture f.
jammed engagé (*mechanism*).
January janvier m.
Japanese japonais.
jar vase m.

jaw mâchoire f.
jealous jaloux.
jealousy jalousie f.
jelly confiture f., gelée f.
jewel bijou m.
Jewish israélite.
job tâche f., travail m., emploi m.
join allier, attacher; rejoindre.
joint joint m., jointure f., articulation f.
joke plaisanterie f.
joke (to) plaisanter, blaguer.
jolly joyeux, gai.
journal journal m.
journalism journalisme m.
journalist journaliste m.
journey voyage m.
joy joie f.
joyous joyeux.
judge juge m.
judge (to) juger.
judgment jugement m.
judicial (court) judiciaire.
juice jus m.
July juillet m.
jump saut m.
jump (to) sauter.
June juin m.
junior cadet; plus jeune.
just juste adj.
just (to have) venir de.
    Nous venons d'arriver. We have just arrived.
justice justice f.
justify justifier.

K

keen piquant, aigu.
keep garder.
    keep back retenir.
    keep from empêcher (prevent); s'abstenir (refrain).
    keep quiet se taire.
    keep in mind tenir compte de quelque chose, se souvenir de quelque chose.
    Keep still! Restez tranquille!
keeper gardien m.
kernel noyau m.
kettle bouilloire f.
key clef, clé f.
kick coup de pied m.
kick (to) donner un coup de pied.
kid chevreau m.
    kidskin la peau de chevreau.
kill tuer.
kilometer kilomètre m.
kin parenté f.
kind adj. bon, bienveillant, aimable, gentil.
kind sorte f., genre m.
kindly aimable.
    Will you kindly . . . Voulez-vous avoir la bonté de . . . Seriez-vous assez aimable pour . . .
kindness bonté f., amabilité m.
king roi m.
kingdom royaume m.
kiss baiser m.
kiss (to) embrasser.
kitchen cuisine f.
kite cerf-volant m.
knee genou m.
kneel s'agenouiller.
knickknack bibelot m.
knife couteau m.
knight chevalier m.

knit tricoter.
knock coup m.
knock (to) frapper.
knocking cognement m.
knot noeud m.
know savoir (have knowledge of); connaître (be acquainted with).
    be expert in se connaître en.
knowledge connaissance f.
known connu.

L

label étiquette f.
labor travail m.
laboratory laboratoire m.
lace dentelle f.
lack manque m.
lack (to) manquer.
lady dame f., madame f.
    Ladies. Dames.
    Ladies and gentlemen. Mesdames et messieurs.
lake lac m.
lamb agneau m.
lame boiteux.
lamp lampe f.
land terre f.
land (to) débarquer (ship), aterrir (airplane).
landing débarquement m.
landscape paysage m.
language langage m.
languish languir.
languor langueur f.
lantern lanterne f.
lap étape f. (of race).
large gros, grand.
last dernier.
    last night hier soir.
last (to) durer.
lasting durable.
latch loquet m.
late tard, tardif.
lately dernièrement.
lateral latéral.
Latin latin.
latter celui-ci, celle-ci, ceux-ci, celles-ci.
laugh (to) rire.
laughter rire m.
laundering blanchissage m.
laundress blanchisseuse f.
laundry blanchisserie f.
lavish prodigue.
lavish (to) prodiguer.
law loi f.
lawful légal.
lawn pelouse f.
lay (to) poser, déposer; pondre (hen).
layer couche f.
lazy paresseux.
lead plomb m. (metal).
lead (to) conduire, emmener, mener.
leader chef m.
leadership direction f., conduite f.
leaf feuille f. (tree).
leak fuite f.
lean (to) appuyer.
leap saut m.
leap (to) sauter.
learn apprendre.
learned adj. savant.
learning érudition f.
least (le) moins, moindre m.
    at least au moins.

leather cuir m.
leave permission f.; congé m.
leave (to) abandonner (desert); laisser (quit); léguer (bequeath).
lecture conférence f., semonce f. (reprimand).
    lecture tour visite-conférence f.
left gauche noun m. and f. and adj.
    to the left à gauche.
leg jambe f.
legal légal.
legend légende f.
legislation législation f.
legislator législateur m.
legislature législature f.
legitimate légitime.
leisure loisir m.
lemon citron m.; rossignol m. (colloq.).
    buy a lemon acheter un rossignol.
lemon drink limonade f. (carbonated).
lemonade citron pressé m.
lend prêter.
length longueur f., durée f.
lengthen allonger.
lens objectif m. (camera).
less moins.
lesson leçon f.
let laisser, permettre (permit); louer (rent).
    for let à louer.
    to let alone laisser tranquille.
letter lettre f.
    express letter pneu(matique) m. (Paris).
level niveau m.
liable responsable, susceptible.
liar menteur m.
liberal libéral.
liberty liberté f.
library bibliothèque f.
license licence f., permission f., permis m.
    driver's license or permit permis de conduire.
lick (to) lécher.
lie mensonge m. (falsehood).
lie (to) coucher, être couché; mentir (tell a falsehood).
    lie down se coucher.
lieutenant lieutenant m.
life vie f.
lift (to) lever, soulever; décrocher (telephone receiver).
light adj. clair; blond.
light lumière f.
light (to) allumer.
light (up) éclairer.
light meter pose mètre m.
lighten alléger; éclaircir (color).
lighthouse phare m.
lighting éclairage m.
lightning éclair m.
likable sympathique.
like pareil; semblable à, comme.
like (to) aimer; vouloir.
    Would you like to go? Voudriez-vous venir?
likely probable.
liking gré m.
likeness ressemblance f.
likewise pareillement.
liking penchant m.; goût m.
limb membre m.
limit limite f.
limit (to) confiner, borner.
Limoges porcelain Limoges m.
limp (to) boiter.
line ligne f.; queue f.
line up (to) aligner; doubler.

stand in line faire la queue.
linen toile f., linge m., lin m.
linger s'attarder.
lining doublure f.
link chaînon m. (*chain*).
link (to) lier.
lion lion m.
lip lèvre f.
liquid liquide noun m. and adj.
liquor liqueur f.
list liste f.
listen écouter.
liter litre m.
literary littéraire.
literature littérature f.
little petit; peu de.
live vivant.
live (to) vivre.
lively vivant, gai, animé, vif.
liver foie m.
load charge f. (*cargo*); fardeau m.
load (to) charger.
loan emprunt m., prêt m.
loan (to) prêter.
local local.
locate situer.
location endroit m., site m.
lock serrure f.
lock (to) fermer à clef.
locomotive locomotive f.
log bûche f.
logic logique f.
logical logique.
loneliness solitude f.
lonely solitaire.
long long, longtemps.
 a long time longtemps.
 before long sous peu.
 long ago autrefois, jadis.
long-distance interurbain (*telephone*).
 a long-distance call un appel interurbain.
longing grande envie f.
look regard m., air m., aspect m.
look (to) regarder.
 Look out! Attention! Prenez garde!
 Look! Tiens!
loose lâche.
loosen desserrer.
lord maître m., seigneur m.
lose perdre.
 lose one's way s'égarer.
loss perte f.
lost perdu.
lot (a) beaucoup.
 a lot of money beaucoup d'argent.
 a lot of people beaucoup de monde.
lotion lotion f.
 hair lotion lotion pour les cheveux.
loud fort, bruyant.
 Speak louder. Parlez plus fort (haut).
love amour m.
love (to) aimer.
lovely charmant, délicieux, ravissant.
low bas.
lower (to) baisser, abaisser.
low-necked décolleté.
loyal loyal.
loyalty loyauté f., fidélité f.
lubrication graissage m.
luck chance f.
lucky heureux, qui porte bonheur.
luggage bagages m. pl.
 luggage rack. porte-bagage (*car*).

luminous lumineux.
lump morceau m., bloc m., tas m.
lung poumon m.
luxe, abondance f.
 de luxe de luxe.
luxurious luxueux.
luxury luxe m.

M

machine machine f.
machine laundry laverie f.
mad fou.
madam madame f.
made fait.
madness folie f.
magazine magazine m., revue périodique f., album m.
magistrate magistrat m.
magnetic magnétique.
magnificent magnifique, formidable.
maid bonne f. (*servant*).
mail courrier m.
main principal.
main road grande route f.
main street grand-rue f.
maintain maintenir, soutenir.
maintenance entretien m., maintien m.
majesty majesté f.
majority majorité f.
make (to) faire.
male mâle.
malice méchanceté f.
man homme m.
 men messieurs.
manage gérer, mener, venir à bout de, se débrouiller.
management gérance f.
manager gérant m.; directeur m.
manicure manucure m.
mankind humanité f.
manner manière f.
mannered recherché (*painting*).
manners politesse f.; manières f. pl.
manufacture fabrication f., manufacture f.
manufacture (to) fabriquer.
manufacturer industriel m., fabriquant m.
manuscript manuscrit m.
many beaucoup.
map carte f., plan m.
March mars m.
march marche f.
march (to) marcher.
margin marge f.
marine marine f.
mark marque f.
mark (to) marquer.
market marché m.
marriage mariage m.
marry épouser.
marvel merveille f.
marvelous merveilleux.
masculine mâle; masculin.
mask masque m.
mask (to) masquer.
mason maçon m.
mass masse f. (*quantity*); messe f. (*church*).
mast mât m.
master maître m.
master (to) dominer.
masterpiece chef d'oeuvre m., oeuvre maîtresse f.
match allumette f.; match m. (*sports*), parti m. (*marriage*).
match (to) assortir.

material matière f., étoffe f.
maternal maternel.
mathematics mathématiques f. pl.
matter affaire f., chose f., matière f., propos, m.
matter (to) importer.
mattress matelas m.
mature mûr.
maximum maximum m.
May mai m.
may pouvoir (*to be able*).
mayor maire m.
me me, moi.
meadow prairie f.
meal repas m.
mean moyenne f.
mean (to) vouloir dire.
meaning sens m.
means moyen m., moyens m. pl. (*resources*).
meanwhile (in the) en attendant, sur ces entrefaites.
measure mesure f.; comble m. (*heaped*).
measure (to) mesurer.
meat viande f.
mechanic mécanicien m.
mechanical mécanique.
mechanically mécaniquement; machinalement.
medal médaille f.
meddle se mêler de.
mediate intervenir.
medical médical.
medicine (*science*) médecine f.
mediocre médiocre.
mediocrity médiocrité f.
meditate méditer.
meditation méditation f.
medium adj. moyen.
medium intermédiaire m.; milieu m.
meet (to) rencontrer.
 meet again retrouver.
meeting rencontre f.; réunion f.; meeting m. (*political*).
melt fondre.
member membre m.
memorize apprendre par coeur.
memory mémoire f.; souvenir m.
menace (to) menacer.
mend (to) raccommoder, réparer, arranger
mental mental.
mention mention f.
mention (to) mentionner.
menu carte f.
merchandise marchandise f.
merchant marchand m., négociant m.
merciful clément.
merciless impitoyable.
mercury mercure m.
mercy pitié f., miséricorde f.
merit mérite m.
merry joyeux, gai.
message message m.
messenger messager m.
metal métal m.
metallic métallique.
meter mètre m.
 taxi meter compteur m.
method méthode f.
metropolis métropole f.
microgroove microsillon m.
microphone microphone m.
middle adj. moyen.
middle milieu m., moyen m.
 in the middle of au milieu de.
 Middle Ages Moyen Âge m.

midnight minuit m.
might force f., puissance f.
mighty fort, puissant.
mild doux.
mildness douceur f.
military militaire.
milk lait m.
milkman laitier m.
mill moulin m.
miller meunier m.
million million m.
millionaire millionnaire noun m. and adj.
mind esprit m.
mind (to) faire attention à, s'inquiéter de.
mine mine f. (coal or steel).
mine à moi, le mien, la mienne, les miens, les miennes.
miner mineur m.
mineral minéral m.
minimum minimum m.
minister ministre m., pasteur m. (Protestant).
ministry ministère m.
mink vison m.
minor mineur m. (age).
minority minorité f.
minute minute f.
    Just a minute! Un instant!
    Wait a minute! Attendez un instant!
    Any minute now. D'un moment à l'autre.
miracle miracle m.
mirror miroir m.
miscellaneous divers.
mischief espièglerie f.
mischievous espiègle.
misdemeanor délit m.
miser avare m.
miserable misérable.
miserably misérablement.
misery misère f.
misfortune malheur m.
mishap accident m.
misprint faute d'impression f.
Miss mademoiselle f.
miss (to) manquer.
mission mission f.
missionary missionnaire m.
mist brouillard m.
mistake faute f.
mistake (to) se tromper.
    to be mistaken se tromper.
Mister monsieur m.
mistrust méfiance f.
mistrust (to) se méfier.
mistrustful méfiant.
misunderstand comprendre mal.
misunderstanding malentendu m.
misuse abus m.
misuse (to) abuser de.
mix mêler.
mixture mélange m.
mob foule f.
mobile mobile.
mobility mobilité f.
mobilization mobilisation f.
mobilize mobiliser.
mock se moquer de.
mockery moquerie f.
mode mode f.
model modèle noun m. and adj.
model (to) modeler.
moderate modéré.
moderate (to) modérer.
moderation modération f.

modern moderne.
modest modeste.
modesty modestie f.
modification modification f.
modify modifier.
moist moite.
moisten humecter.
molar molaire f.
moment moment m.
    Just a moment! Un instant!
    any moment now d'un moment à l'autre.
monarchy monarchie f.
monastery monastère m.
Monday lundi m.
money argent m., monnaie f.
    small change petite monnaie.
money order mandat m.
    postal money order mandat-poste.
monk moine m.
monkey singe m.
monologue monologue m.
monopoly monopole m.
monotonous monotone.
monotony monotonie f.
monster monstre m.
monstrosity monstruosité f.
monstrous monstrueux.
month mois m.
monthly mensuel.
monument monument m.
monumental monumental.
mood humeur f.
moody de mauvaise humeur.
moon lune f.
moonlight clair de lune m.
mop balai m.
moral moral, adj.
morale moral m.
moralist moraliste m.
morality moralité f.
morals morale f.
more (de)plus, davantage.
morning matin m.
morsel morceau m.
mortal mortel m.
mortal adj. mortel, fatal.
mortgage hypothèque f.
mortgage (to) hypothéquer.
mosque mosquée f.
mosquito moustique m.
most la plupart de; le plus de; le plus.
mostly la plupart de temps, pour la plupart.
moth mite f.
mother mère f.
mother-in-law belle-mère f.
motion mouvement m., signe m.
motionless immobile.
motivate motiver.
motive motif m.
motor moteur m.
motor (to) aller en auto.
mount mont m. (hill).
mount (to) monter.
mountain montagne f.
mountain climbing alpinisme m.
mountainous montagneux.
mourn se lamenter.
mournful triste, lugubre.
mourning deuil m.
mouse souris f.
mouth bouche f.; embouchure f. (of a river).
movable mobile.
move mouvement m.

move (to) remuer, se mouvoir, bouger; déménager (household).
movement mouvement m.
movie camera appareil cinématographique m., caméra f.
movies cinéma m.
moving touchant (emotionally).
Mr. monsieur, M.
Mrs. madame, Mme.
much beaucoup.
    very much grand-chose.
mud boue f.
muddy boueux.
mule mule f.
multiple multiple noun m. and adj.
multiply multiplier.
multitude multitude f.
mumble marmotter.
municipal municipal.
municipality municipalité f.
munitions munitions f. pl.
murder meurtre m.
murder (to) assassiner.
murmur murmure m.
murmur (to) murmurer.
muscle muscle m.
museum musée m.
mushroom champignon m.
music musique f.
musical musical.
musician musicien m.
must devoir, falloir.
mustard moutarde f.
mute muet noun and adj.
mutter murmure m.
mutter (to) murmurer.
mutton mouton m.
my mon, ma, mes.
myself moi-même.
mysterious mystérieux.
mystery mystère m.

N

nail ongle m. (finger); clou m.
nail (to) clouer.
naive naïf.
naked nu.
name nom m.
    first name prénom m.
    last name nom de famille m.
    What is your name? Comment vous appelez-vous?
    My name is. Je m'appelle.
name (to) nommer.
nameless sans nom.
namely c'est à dire.
nap somme m.
nape nuque f.
napkin serviette f.
narrow étroit.
narrow (to) restreindre.
nasty désagréable.
nation nation f.
national national.
nationality nationalité f.
nationalization nationalisation f.
nationalize nationaliser.
native indigène m.
natural naturel.
naturally naturellement.
naturalness naturel m.
nature nature f.

human **nature** la nature humaine.
still **life** nature(s) morte(s).
naughty méchant.
nautical nautique.
go **water-skiing** faire du ski nautique.
naval naval.
navy marine f.
near près de, auprès de, prochain, proche.
nearly presque.
neat net.
neatness netteté f.
necessarily de nécessité, forcément, de force.
necessary nécessaire.
necessary (to be) falloir.
necessity nécessité f.
neck cou m.
necklace collier m.
necktie cravate f.
need besoin m.
be in **need** of avoir besoin de.
need (to) avoir besoin de.
needle aiguille f.
needless inutile.
needy nécessiteux.
negative adj. négatif.
negative cliché m. (*photography*).
neglect négligence f.
neglect (to) négliger.
negotiate négocier, traiter.
negotiation négociation f.
Negro nègre m.
neighbor voisin m.
neighborhood voisinage m.
neither non plus; ni l'un, ni l'autre; ni.
neither one ni l'un, ni l'autre.
neither . . . **nor** ni . . . ni.
neon néon m.
neon sign enseigne au néon.
nephew neveu m.
nerve nerf m.
nervous nerveux.
nest nid m.
net filet m.
neutral neutre.
neuter neutre noun and adj.
never jamais.
nevertheless néanmoins, quand même.
new nouveau, neuf.
news nouvelle f., actualités, f. pl.
society **news** mondanités f. pl.
newspaper journal m.
newsstand kiosque m.
next suivant, prochain, ensuite.
nice gentil, agréable.
nickname surnom m.
niece nièce f.
night nuit f., soir m.
nightgown chemise de nuit f.
nightingale rossignol m.
nightmare cauchemar m.
nine neuf.
nineteen dix-neuf.
nineteenth dix-neuvième.
ninetieth quatre-vingts-dixième.
ninety quatre-vingt-dix.
ninth neuvième.
no non.
no longer ne plus.
No Smoking. Défense de fumer.
nobility noblesse f.
noble noble noun and adj.
nobody personne f.
noise bruit m.

noisy bruyant.
nominate nommer, désigner.
nomination nomination f., désignation f.
none ne . . . point, ne . . . aucun.
nonsense bêtise f.
noon midi m.
nor ni, non plus.
neither . . . **nor** ni . . . ni.
normal adj. normal.
north nord m.
North America Amérique du Nord f.
northern du nord.
northwest nord-ouest m.
nose nez m.
nostril narine f.
not ne . . . pas.
note note f., billet m.
note (to) noter.
notebook carnet m.
nothing rien.
notice avis m.
Notice to the public. Avis au public.
notice (to) remarquer.
notify avertir.
notion idée f.
noun nom m.
nourish nourrir.
nourishment nourriture f.
novel adj. nouveau.
novel roman m.
novelty nouveauté f.
November novembre m.
novocaine novocaïne f.
now maintenant.
now and then de temps en temps.
nowadays de nos jours.
nowhere nulle part.
nude adj. nu.
nude nu m. (*painting*).
nuisance peste f., ennui m.
null nul.
numb engourdi.
number numéro m.
number (to) compter.
numbered numéroté.
numerous nombreux.
nun religieuse f.
nurse bonne d'enfant f., infirmière f.
nursery chambre d'enfants f.
nut noix f.

O

oak chêne m.
oar rame f.
oat avoine f.
oath serment m.
obedience obéissance f.
obedient obéissant.
obey obéir.
object objet m., but m.
object (to) s'opposer a.
objection objection f.
I see no **objection** to it. Je n'y vois pas d'inconvénient.
objectionable répréhensible.
objective objectif noun m. and adj.
objectively objectivement.
objectivity objectivité f.
obligation obligation f.
obligatory obligatoire.
oblige obliger.
obliging serviable.

oblique oblique.
obscure obscur.
obscurity obscurité f.
observation observation f.
observatory observatoire m.
observe observer.
observer observateur m.
obstacle obstacle m.
obstinacy obstination f.
obstinate obstiné, têtu.
obvious évident.
obviously évidemment.
occasion occasion f.
occasion (to) occasionner.
occasionally de temps en temps.
occupation métier m., occupation f.
occupied occupé.
occupy occuper.
occur arriver, se trouver.
occurrence occurence f.
ocean océan m.
October octobre m.
odd impair (*number*); dépareillé (*not matched*);
bizarre (*strange*).
odds avantage m.; différence f.
odor odeur f.
of de, en.
off de.
offend offenser.
offense injure f., offense f., délit m.
offensive adj. injurieux.
offensive offensive f.
offer offre f.
offer (to) offrir.
offering offrande f.
office bureau m.; fonction f.
officer officier m.
official adj. officiel.
official fonctionnaire m.
often souvent.
oil huile f.
oil painting peinture à l'huile.
old vieux.
my **friend, old chap** mon vieux.
old age vieillesse f.
old man vieillard m.
olive olive f.
olive oil huile d'olive.
ominous de mauvais augure.
on sur.
once une fois, autrefois.
at **once** tout de suite.
all at **once** tout à coup.
once in a while de temps en temps.
once a year une fois par an.
one un (*numeral*).
one pron. on, vous, soi, celui, celle, etc.
one's son, sa, ses.
oneself soi-même, se.
onion oignon m.
only seul, simple, unique, seulement.
open adj. ouvert.
open (to) ouvrir, s'ouvrir.
opening ouverture f.
opera opéra m.
opera glasses jumelles f. pl.
operate opérer.
operation opération f.
opinion opinion f.
opponent adversaire m.
opportune opportun.
opportunity occasion f.
oppose s'opposer à., résister.

opposite en face de, opposé.
opposition opposition f.
oppress opprimer.
oppression oppression f.
optimism optimisme m.
optimistic optimiste.
or ou.
    either . . . or ou . . . ou.
oral verbal.
orange orange f.
orator orateur m.
oratory art oratoire.
orchard verger m.
orchestra orchestre m.
ordeal épreuve f.
order ordre m.
    in order to afin de.
    put in order ranger.
    in order that afin que, pour que.
order (to) ordonner, commander.
ordinarily d'ordinaire.
ordinary banal, ordinaire.
organ organe m. (*body*); orgue m. (*music*).
organization organisation f.
organize organiser.
Orient Orient m.
oriental oriental noun and adj.
origin origine f.
original original.
originality originalité f.
originate créer.
ornament ornement m.
orphan orphelin m.
ostentation ostentation f.
other autre.
ouch! aïe!
ought devoir.
ounce once f.
our(s) notre, nos.
ourselves nous-mêmes.
out dehors, hors de.
outcome conséquence f.; dénouement m.
outdo surpasser.
outer extérieur m.
outlast survivre à.
outlaw proscrit m.
outlaw (to) proscrire.
outlay dépense f.
outlet issue f.; débouché m.
outline contour m., silhouette f.
outline (to) ébaucher, esquisser.
outlook perspective f.
output rendement m., production f.
outrage outrage m.
outrageous atroce; indigne.
outside dehors, hors.
oval ovale noun m. and adj.
oven four m.
over dessus.
overcoat pardessus m.
overcome surmonter, subjuguer.
overflow déborder.
overlook négliger; pardonner.
overpower accabler, subjuguer.
overrule rejeter.
overrun envahir.
overseas outre-mer.
oversight inadvertance f.
overtake rattraper.
overthrow renverser.
overwhelm accabler.
owe devoir.
own adj. propre.

own (to) posséder.
owner propriétaire m.
ox boeuf m.
oxygen oxygène m.
oyster huître f.

P

pace pas m.
pace (to) arpenter.
    pace up and down arpenter de long en large.
pacific pacifique.
pack (to) emballer.
package colis m., emballage m., paquet m.
packed bondé.
page page f.
pain douleur f., peine f.
pain (to) faire mal.
painful douloureux.
paint peinture f.
paint (to) peindre.
painter peintre m.
painting peinture f.
pair paire f.
pale pâle.
pamper gâter.
pamphlet brochure f.
pan poêle f.
pancake crêpe f.
pane vitre f.
panel panneau m.
pang angoisse f.
panic panique f.
panorama panorama m.
panoramic panoramique.
pants pantalon m.
paper papier m.
parachute parachute m.
parade parade f.
paragraph paragraphe m.
parellel parallèle f.
paralysis paralysie f.
paralyze paralyser.
parcel paquet m., colis m., emballage m.
parcel post colis postal.
pardon pardon m.
pardon (to) pardonner.
parent père m., mère f.; parent m.
parenthesis parenthèse f.
Parisian parisien noun and adj.
park parc m.
park (to) stationner (*a car*).
parliament parlement m.
part partie f.; endroit m.
    in hair raie f.
part (to) diviser, se séparer.
partial partiel, partial.
partially avec partialité; en partie.
participate participer (à).
particular particulier.
particularity particularité f.
particularly particulièrement.
partner associé m.; partenaire m. and f.
party parti m.
    party telephone correspondant m.
pass laisser-passer m.
pass (to) dépasser; passer.
passage passage m., allée f., traversée f.
passenger voyageur m.
passing passager.
passion passion f.
passive passif.
passport passeport m.

past prep. au delà de (*beyond*).
    half-past seven sept heures et demie.
    past ten o'clock dix heures passées.
past adj. passé, dernier.
    the past year l'année dernière, l'an passé.
past passé m.
    in the past dans le passé.
paste pâte f.
pastry pâtisserie f.
pastry shop pâtisserie f.
patch pièce f.
patch (to) rapiécer.
patent brevet d'invention m.
paternal paternel.
path allée f., sentier m.
pathetic pathétique.
patience patience f.
patient adj. patient.
patient malade m. and f.
patriot patriote m. and f.
patriotism patriotisme m.
patron patron m.
patronize protéger.
pattern modèle m., dessin m.
pause pause f.
pause (to) faire une pause.
pave paver.
pavement pavé m., trottoir m.
paw patte f.
pay salaire m.
pay (to) payer, regler (*check*).
payable payable.
payment payement m.
pea pois m.
peace paix f.
peaceful paisible.
peach pêche f.
peak cime f.
pear poire f.
pearl perle f.
peasant paysan m.
pebble caillou m.
peculiar particulier.
pecuniary pécuniaire.
pedal pédale f.
pedant pédant m.
pedestrian piéton m.
peel pelure f.
peel (to) peler.
pen plume f.
penalty peine f., penalty m. (*soccer*).
pencil crayon m.
penetrate pénétrer.
peninsula péninsule f.
penitence pénitence f.
penny sou m.
pension pension f.
people peuple m., gens m. pl.
pepper poivre m.
perceive apercevoir.
percent pour cent.
percentage pourcentage m.
perfect parfait.
    Perfect! Parfait! Très bien!
perfect (to) rendre parfait.
perfection perfection f.
perfectly parfaitement.
perform accomplir, exécuter.
performance accomplissement m.; représentation f.
perfume parfum m.
perfume (to) parfumer.
perhaps peut-être.

peril péril m.
period période f.; point m. (*punctuation*).
periodical périodique m.
perish périr.
permanent permanent.
permission permission f.
permit permis m.
permit (to) permettre.
perplex embrouiller.
persecute persécuter.
persecution persécution f.
perseverance persévérance f.
persist persister.
person personne f.
personal personnel.
personality personnalité f.
perspective perspective f.
persuade persuader, convaincre.
pertaining appartenant.
petty petit.
pharmacist pharmacien m.
pharmacy pharmacie f.
phenomenon phénomène m.
philosopher philosophe m.
philosophical philosophique.
philosophy philosophie f.
phonograph électrophone m.
photograph photographie f.
     take a photograph prendre une photographie.
photographer photographe m.
phrase locution f.
physical physique.
physician médecin m.
piano piano m.
pick (to) cueillir, choisir.
pick up ramasser.
pickup reprise f. (*rented car*).
picnic pique-nique m.
picture image f., tableau m.
     take a picture prendre une photographie.
picturesque pittoresque.
pie tarte f.
piece morceau m.; partie f.; pièce f.
pig cochon m.
pigeon pigeon m.
pile tas m.
pile (to) empiler, entasser.
pill pillule f., cachet m., comprimé m.
pillar pilier m.
pillow oreiller m.
pilot pilote m.
pilot (to) piloter.
pin épingle f.
pinch (to) pincer.
pink adj. rose.
pious pieux.
pipe pipe f. (*for smoking*); tuyau m., tube m.
pitiful pitoyable.
pity pitié f., dommage m.
     What a pity! Quel dommage!
place lieu m., endroit m.
     to take place avoir lieu.
place (to) mettre.
placing mise f.
plain adj. simple.
plain plaine f.
plan plan m., projet m.
plan (to) projeter.
plane plan m.; avion m. (*airplane*).
plant plante f.
plant (to) planter.
plaster plâtre m.
plate assiette f.

platform estrade f.; plate-forme f.; quai m. (*train*).
platter plat m.
play jeu m.; pièce de théâtre f.
play (to) jouer; pratiquer (*sports*).
player comédien m. (*theatre*).
plea requête f.
plead plaider.
pleasant agréable.
please (to) plaire, complaire.
     (if you) please s'il vous plaît.
pleased content.
pleasure plaisir m.
pledge garantie f., gage m.
pledge (to) garantir.
plenty abondance f.
plot complot m., intrigue f.
plot (to) comploter, conspirer.
plow charrue f.
plow (to) labourer.
plum prune f.
plunder (to) piller.
plural pluriel m.
plus plus.
pocket poche f.
     pocket size format de poche.
poem poème m.
poet poète m.
poetic poétique.
poetry poésie f.
point point m.; pointe f.
point (to) indiquer.
pointed pointu.
pointillist pointilliste m. (*painting*).
poise savoir-faire m.
poison poison m.
poison (to) empoisonner.
poisoning empoisonnement m.
polar polaire.
police police f.
policeman agent de police m.
policy politique f.
polish vernis m.; cirage m.
polish (to) polir, cirer.
polite poli.
politely poliment.
politeness politesse f.
political politique.
politics politique f.
pond étang m.
poor pauvre.
popular populaire.
population population f.
port port m.
porter porteur m., concierge m. f.
portrait portrait m.
pose pose, f.
position position f.; situation f. (*job*).
positive positif.
possess posséder.
possession possession f.
possibility possibilité f.
possible possible.
post poteau m.; poste f.
postage affranchissement m.
     postage stamp timbre m.
postal postal
     postal service service poste(s) f.
postcard carte postale f.
poster affiche f.
posterity postérité f.
post office poste f.
pot pot m.
potato pomme de terre f., frite f. (*French fried*).

pottery faïence f.
pound livre f.
pour verser.
poverty pauvreté f.
powder poudre f.
power pouvoir m., puissance f.
powerful puissant.
practical pratique.
practice habitude f., pratique f., exercise m.
practice (to) pratiquer.
praise éloge m.
praise (to) louer.
prank espièglerie f.
pray prier.
prayer prière f.
preach prêcher.
precaution précaution f.
precede précéder.
preceding précédent noun m. and adj.
precept précepte m.
precious précieux.
precise précis.
precision précision f.
predecessor prédécesseur m.
preface préface f.
prefer préférer.
preference préférence f.
prejudice préjugé m.
preliminary préliminaire, préalable.
prepare préparer.
prescribe prescrire.
prescription ordonnance f.
presence présence f.
present adj. actuel, présent.
present don m.; présent m.
     make a present faire cadeau, faire présent.
present (to) offrir, présenter.
preserve (to) préserver, conserver.
preside présider.
president président m.
press presse f.
press (to) presser, serrer.
     press clothes repasser des vêtements.
pressing pressant.
pressure pression f.
prestige prestige m.
presume présumer.
pretend prétendre, prétexter.
pretext prétexte m.
pretty adj. joli.
pretty adv. assez.
     pretty soon assez tôt.
     pretty nearly presque.
prevail prévaloir.
prevent empêcher, éviter.
prevention empêchement m.; précautions f. pl.
previous antérieur, précédent.
     the previous year l'année précédente.
prey proie f.
price prix m.
pride orgueil m.
priest prêtre m.
principal principal; maîtresse.
principle principe m.
print épreuve f. (*photography*).
print (to) imprimer; tirer.
     to have a negative printed faire tirer un cliché.
printed matter imprimés m. pl.
prison prison f.
prisoner prisonnier m.
private particulier, privé, confidentiel.
privilege privilège m.
prize prix m.

prize (to) attacher beaucoup de prix à.
probable probable.
probably probablement, sans doute.
problem problème m.
procedure procédé m.
proceed avancer, procéder, provenir de.
process procédé m., développement m.
procession cortège m., procession f.
proclaim proclamer.
produce (to) produire.
product produit m.
production production f.
productive productif.
profession profession f.
professional professionnel.
professor professeur m.
profile profil m.
profit profit m.; bénéfice m., bénéfices m. pl.
profit (to) profiter.
profits bénéfices m. pl.
profoundly profondément.
program programme m.
progress progrès m.
progress (to) faire des progrès.
prohibit défendre.
prohibition défense f.
project projet m.
project (to) projeter.
promise promesse f.
promise (to) promettre.
prompt prompt.
promptness promptitude f.
pronoun pronom m.
pronounce prononcer.
proof preuve f.
proper comme il faut.
property propriété f.; biens m. pl., terres f. pl.
proportion proportion f.
proposal proposition f.
propose proposer.
prosaic prosaïque.
prose prose f.
prospect prospective.
prosper prospérer.
prosperity prospérité f.
prosperous prospère.
protect protéger.
protection protection f.
protector protecteur m.
protest protestation f.
protest (to) protester.
Protestant protestant.
proud fier.
prove prouver.
proverb proverbe m.
provide pourvoir, fournir.
provided that pourvu que.
province province f.; ressort m. (*sphere of action*).
provision provision f., précaution f.
provoke provoquer, irriter.
proximity proximité f.
prudence prudence f.
prudent prudent.
prudently prudemment.
prune pruneau m.
psychological psychologique.
psychology psychologie f.
public public noun m. and adj.
publication publication f., revue f.
publish publier (*edict, etc.*); éditer (*book, paper*).
publisher éditeur m.
pull (to) tirer.
pulpit chaire f., tribune f.

pulse pouls m.
pump pompe f.
pump up gonfler.
puncture pneu crevé m., crevaison f.
punish punir.
punishment punition f.
pupil élève m.; prunelle f. (*eye*).
purchase achat m.
purchase (to) acheter
pure pur.
purity pureté f.
purpose but m., propos m.
purse porte-monnaie m. (*change purse*).
pursue poursuivre.
pursuit poursuite f.
push (to) pousser, enfoncer (*button*).
put mettre, poser, placer.
    put away mettre de côté.
    put back remettre.
    put off remettre.
    put on mettre.
putting mise f.
    hair setting mise en plis.
putting back remise f.
    put into shape, overhaul (*car*) faire une remise
    en état.
puzzle perplexité f., énigme f.
puzzle (to) embarrasser.

Q

quaint bizarre.
qualify qualifier.
quality qualité f.
quantity quantité f.
quarrel querelle f.
quarter quart m.; quartier m.
queen reine f.
queer bizarre.
quench étancher, éteindre.
quest quête f.
question question f.
question (to) interroger.
quick rapide, vif.
quickly rapidement.
    Come quickly! Venez vite!
quiet adj. calme, tranquille.
    Keep quiet! Restez tranquille! Taisez-vous!
quiet (to) calmer.
quit quitter.
quite tout à fait, assez.
    quite good assez bon.
quote citer.

R

rabbi rabbin m.
rabbit lapin m.
race course f.; race f. (*ethnic*).
radiator radiateur m.
radio radio f.
rag lambeau m. (*tatter*); chiffon m.
rage rage f.
ragged (en) haillons.
rail rail m.
railroad chemin de fer m.
rain pluie f.
rain (to) pleuvoir.
rainbow arc-en-ciel m.
rainy pluvieux.
raise augmentation f.
raise (to) lever, élever.
raisin raisin sec m.

rake râteau m.
rally (to) rallier.
range portée f., étendue f.
range (to) ranger; varier de., à.
rank grade m., rang m.
ransom rançon f.
rapid rapide.
rapidity rapidité f.
rapidly rapidement.
rapture transport m., saisissement m.
rash téméraire (*reckless*).
rat rat m.
rate vitesse f. (*of speed*); taux m. (*of interest*);
    cours m.
    rate of exchange cours du change m.
rate (to) évaluer.
rates tarif m. (*fare*).
rather plutôt.
    rather than plutôt que.
    rather good assez bon.
    I'd rather go j'aimerais mieux y aller.
ration ration f.
rational raisonable.
rave délirer.
raw cru.
ray rayon m.
razor rasoir m.
    razor blade lame de rasoir.
reach étendue f.; portée f.
reach (to) arriver à, atteindre; s'étendre.
react réagir.
reaction réaction f.
read lire.
reading lecture f.
ready prêt.
real réel, véritable.
realistic réaliste.
realization réalisation f.
realize réaliser, comprendre.
really en vérité, vraiment, réellement, véritable-
    ment.
    Really! Vraiment!
rear (from the) de derrière.
rear (to) élever (*children*).
reason raison f.
reason (to) raisonner.
reasonable raisonnable.
reasoning raisonnement m.
reassure rassurer.
rebel rebelle noun and adj.
rebel (to) se révolter.
rebellion rébellion f.
recall rappel m.
recall (to) rappeler, se rappeler.
receipt recette f.; quittance f., reçu m.
receive recevoir; accueillir.
receiver récepteur m. (*telephone*).
recent récent.
reception réception f., accueil m.
recess trêve f. (*time*).
reciprocal réciproque.
recite réciter.
recognize reconnaître.
recoil reculer.
recollect se souvenir.
recollection souvenir m.
recommend recommander.
recommendation recommandation f.
reconcile réconcilier.
reconstitute reconstituer.
record dossier m. (*file*); disque m. (*phonograph*).
record player électrophone m.
recover retrouver; se remettre (*health*); recouvrir.

recruit recrue f.
rectangle rectangle m.
red rouge.
red tape formalité f.
reddish brown roux.
redeem racheter.
redouble redoubler.
reduce réduire.
reduction réduction f.
reed roseau m.
refer référer, se rapporter à.
reference allusion f., référence f.
referring se rapportant à.
refine raffiner, épurer.
refinement raffinement m.
reflect refléter, réfléchir.
reflection reflet m., réflexion f.
reform réforme f.
reform (to) se réformer.
refrain refrain m.
refrain (to) s'abstenir.
refresh rafraîchir.
refreshment rafraîchissement m.
refuge refuge m.
    take refuge prendre refuge, se réfugier.
refund remboursement m.
refund (to) rembourser.
refundable remboursable.
refusal refus m.
refuse (to) refuser.
refute réfuter.
regard égard m., estime f.
    in regard to en ce qui concerne.
regime régime m.
regiment régiment m.
region région f.
register registre m.
register (to) enregistrer, se faire inscrire.
registered immatriculé (car); inscrit.
regret regret m.
regret (to) regretter.
regrettable regrettable.
regular régulier, ordinaire.
regulate régler.
regulation réglement m.
rehearsal répétition f.
rehearse répéter.
reign règne m.
reign (to) régner.
reinforce renforcer.
reject rejeter.
rejoice réjouir, se réjouir.
rejoin rejoindre.
relapse rechute f.
relate raconter.
relation parent m. (relative).
relationship rapport m.; parenté f.
relative adj. relatif.
relative parent m.
relax se délasser, se relâcher, se détendre.
relaxation détente f.
release délivrance f.
release (to) libérer, décharger.
relent s'attendrir.
relentless impitoyable.
relevant pertinent.
reliable digne de confiance.
reliance confiance f.
relic relique f.
relief soulagement m.; secours m.
relieve soulager; relever (duty).
religion religion f., culte m.

religious religieux; divin.
relinquish abandonner.
relish saveur f. (flavor).
relish (to) savourer.
reload recharger.
reluctance répugnance f.
reluctant peu disposé à.
rely upon compter sur.
remain rester.
remainder restant m., reste m.
remaining restant.
remake (to) refaire.
remark observation f., remarque f.
remark (to) remarquer, faire remarquer.
remarkable remarquable.
remedy remède m.
remember se rappeler, se souvenir.
remembrance souvenir m.
remind rappeler.
remorse remords m.
remote reculé adj.
removal enlèvement m. (taking away).
remove (to) enlever, supprimer.
remove makeup se démaquiller.
renew renouveler.
rent loyer m.
rent (to) louer.
rental location f.
reopening rentrée f.
repair réparation f.
repair (to) réparer.
repeat répéter.
repent se repentir.
repetition répétition f.
replace remplacer.
replacement rechange m.
reply réponse f.
reply (to) répondre.
report rapport m., compte rendu m. (of a meeting).
report (to) rapporter, faire un rapport.
represent représenter.
representation représentation f.
representative représentant m.
repress réprimer.
reprimand réprimande f.
reprimand (to) réprimander.
reprisal représaille f.
reproach reproche m.
reproach (to) reprocher.
reproduce reproduire.
repurchase rachat m.
    retail price prix de rachat.
reputation réputation f.
request demande f., requête f.
request (to) demander, prier, solliciter.
require exiger, avoir besoin de, demander.
rescue délivrance f.; secours m.
rescue (to) délivrer, secourir.
research recherche f.
resemble ressembler (à).
resent être froissé de.
resentment ressentiment m.
reservation réserve f., arrière-pensée f., réservation f.
reserve réserve f.
reserve (to) réserver, retenir (rooms, seats).
reside demeurer.
residence lieu de séjour m., résidence f., demeure f.
resign donner sa démission.
    resign oneself se résigner.
resignation démission f., résignation f.

resist résister.
resistance résistance f.
resolute résolu.
resolution résolution f.
resolve décider, résoudre.
resort recours m., ressource f.
resort (to) avoir recours à.
resource ressource f.
respect respect m.
respect (to) respecter.
respectful respectueux.
respective respectif.
respite répit m.
responsibility responsabilité f., charge f.
responsible responsable.
rest repos m.; reste m.
rest (to) se reposer.
restaurant restaurant m.
restless inquiet, agité.
restoration restauration f.
restore rendre, remettre.
restrain contenir, réprimer.
restraint contrainte f.
restrict restreindre.
restriction restriction f.
result résultat m.
result (to) résulter de.
resume reprendre.
retail détail m.
    retail price prix de rechat m.
retail (to) vendre au détail (sell retail).
retain retenir.
retaliate user de représailles.
retaliation représailles f. pl.
retire se retirer.
retirement retraite f.
retrace rebrousser.
retract rétracter.
retreat retraite f.
retrieve recouvrir.
return retour m., rentrée f.
return (to) revenir, rendre; renvoyer; rentrer.
    return home rentrer à la maison.
reveal révéler.
revelation révélation f.
revenge vengeance f., revenge f.
revenue revenu m.
reverence révérence f.
reverend révérend.
reverse contraire noun m. and adj., inverse noun m. and adj.
reverse (to) intervertir; annuler (decision).
revert revenir.
review revue f.
review (to) revoir, analyser, passer er. revue.
revise réviser.
revision révision f.
revive faire revivre, ranimer, réveiller (memories).
revoke révoquer.
revolt révolte f.
revolt (to) se révolter.
revolution révolution f.
revolve tourner.
reward récompense f.
reward (to) récompenser.
rhyme rime f.
rib côte f.
ribbon ruban m.
rice riz m.
rich riche.
richness richesse f.
rid (get) débarasser.

get rid of something se débarasser de quelque chose.
riddle énigme f., devinette f.
ride promenade f.; trajet m. (*length of*).
ride (to) monter; se promener.
ridiculous ridicule.
rifle fusil m.
right adj. droit, exact, vrai, juste.
right droit m.; bien m.
  have a right to avoir le droit de.
  to the right à droite.
right away instantanément, tout de suite.
righteous juste.
righteousness justice f.
rightful légitime.
rigid raide.
rigor rigueur f.
rigorous rigoureux.
ring anneau m., bague f
ring (to) sonner.
ringing sonnerie f.
rinse (to) rinser.
riot émeute f.
ripe mûr.
ripen mûrir.
rise hausse f.
rise (to) se lever, augmenter.
risk risque m.
risk (to) risquer.
rite rite m.
ritual rituel m.
rival rival noun and adj.
rivalry rivalité f.
river rivière f., fleuve m.
Riviera Côte d'Azur f. (*French*).
road chemin m., route f.
road map carte routière f.
roads (of) routier.
roar rugissement m.
roar (to) rugir; hurler.
roast rôti m.
roast (to) rôtir.
rob voler, piller.
robber bandit m., brigand m.
robbery vol m.
robe robe f.
robust robuste.
rock rocher m., roc m.
rock (to) balancer.
rocky rocheux.
rod baguette f.
roll rouleau m., petit pain m. (*bread*).
roll (to) rouler, enrouler.
Roman romain.
romantic romantique.
romanticism romantisme m.
roof toit m.
room chambre f.; place f. (*space*).
  There's no room. Il n'y a pas de place.
  make room for faire place à.
root racine f.
rope corde f.
rose rose f.
rot (to) pourrir.
rough rude, grossier.
round adj. rond.
round adv. en rond, tout autour.
round n. tournée f., tour m.
round off arrondir.
rouse réveiller, provoquer.
rousing émouvant.
rout tumulte m.; déroute f.
rout (to) mettre en déroute.

route route f., parcours m.
routine routine f.
rove parcourir, errer.
row rang m.; vacarme m. (*tumult*).
row (to) ramer.
rowboat canot m.
royal royal.
royalist royaliste.
rub (to) frotter.
rubber caoutchouc m.
rubbish décombres m. pl; blague f. (*nonsense; bunk*).
rude brusque, commun, vulgaire, impoli.
ruffle ride f.
ruffle (to) chiffonner.
rugby rugby m.
ruin ruine f.
ruin (to) ruiner.
rule règle f., domination f., autorité f.
rule (to) gouverner; régler (*lines*).
ruler gouverneur; règle (*for lines*).
rumor rumeur f.
run (to) courir.
  run away fuir.
rural rural.
rush foule f., ruée f.
rush (to) se précipiter.
russet roux.
Russian russe.
rust rouille f.
rust (to) rouiller.
rustic rustique.
rusty rouillé.
rye seigle m.

S

sack sac m.
sacrament sacrement m.
sacred sacré.
sacrifice sacrifice m.
sacrifice (to) sacrifier.
sacrilege sacrilège m.
sad triste.
sadden attrister.
saddle selle f.
sadness tristesse f.
safe sain et sauf, sûr, certain.
safe (be) être en sûreté.
safe-deposit box coffre-fort m.
safely sain et sauf.
safety sécurité f., sûreté f.
sail voile f.
sail (to) naviguer.
saint saint m.
sake (for the sake of) pour l'amour de.
salad salade f.
salary appointements m. pl.
sale vente f.
salesman vendeur.
saleswoman vendeuse.
salt sel m.
salt (to) saler.
salute salut m.
salute (to) saluer.
salvation salut m.
same même.
  all the same tout de même.
sample échantillon m.
sanctuary sanctuaire m.
sand sable m.
sandal sandale f.
sandwich sandwich m.
sandy sablonneux.

sane sain d'esprit.
sanitary sanitaire.
sap sève f.
sarcasm sarcasme m.
sarcastic sarcastique.
sarcophagus sarcophage m.
sardine sardine f.
satiate rassasier.
satin satin m.
satisfaction satisfaction f.
satisfactory satisfaisant.
satisfy contenter, satisfaire.
saturate saturer.
Saturday samedi m.
sauce sauce f.
saucer soucoupe f.
sausage saucisse f.
savage sauvage, brutal.
save faire des économies (*money*); sauver (*rescue*).
  save time gagner du temps.
savings économies f.; épargne f.
savior sauveur m.
saxophone saxophone m.
  play the saxophone jouer de saxophone.
say! tiens!
say (to) dire.
scales balance f.
scalp cuir chevelu m.
scan scruter.
scandal scandale m.
scanty peu abondant.
scar cicatrice f.
scarce rare.
scarcely à peine.
scare (to) effrayer.
scarf écharpe f.
scatter répandre, éparpiller.
scene scène f.
scenery paysage m. (*landscape*), décor m. (*theatre*).
schedule liste f., horaire m.
scheme dessein m., plan m.
scholar savant m.
school école f.
science science f.
scientific scientifique.
scientist homme de science m.
scissors ciseaux m. pl.
scold gronder.
scope envergure f.
scorn mépris m.
scorn (to) mépriser.
scornful méprisant, dédaigneux.
scrape gratter.
scratch égratignure f.
scratch (to) gratter.
scream cri m.
scream (to) crier.
screen écran m.
screw vis f.
scribble (to) griffonner.
scruple scrupule m.
scrupulous scrupuleux.
scrutinize scruter.
sculpted sculpté.
sculpture sculpture f.
sea mer f.
seal sceau m., cachet m.
seal (to) sceller, cacheter.
seam couture f.
search recherche f.
search (to) chercher, fouiller.
seashore plage f.
seasickness mal de mer m.

season saison f.
season (to) assaisonner (*flavor*).
seat siège m., place f.
seat (to) faire asseoir.
seated assis.
second adj. second (*numeral*).
second deuxième; seconde f. (*time*).
second (to) appuyer.
secondary secondaire.
secondhand d'occasion.
secret secret noun m. and adj.
secretary secrétaire m. and f.
sect secte f.
section section f.; rubrique f. (*newspaper, maga-zine*).
   sports section rubrique sportive.
secure adj. en sûreté, sûr.
secure (to) mettre en sûreté; obtenir, fixer.
security garantie f., sûreté f.
see voir.
seed graine f., semence f.
seek chercher, rechercher.
seem sembler, paraître.
seize saisir.
seldom rarement.
select adj. recherché.
select (to) choisir.
selection choix m.
-self -même.
   myself moi-même.
selfish égoïste.
selfishness égoïsme m.
sell vendre.
   sell again revendre.
seller vendeur m. vendeuse f.
semi- demi-.
semicolon point et virgule m.
senate sénat m.
senator sénateur m.
send envoyer, expédier.
   send back renvoyer.
   send for faire venir..
sender expéditeur m.
senior aîné m.
sensation sensation f.
sense sens m.
senseless insensé.
sensibility sensibilité f.
sensible sensé, raisonnable.
sensitive sensible.
sensitiveness sensibilité f.
sentence phrase f. (*grammar*); jugement m.
sentiment sentiment m.
sentimental sentimental.
separate adj. séparé, à part.
separate (to) séparer.
separately séparément.
separation séparation f.
September septembre m.
serene serein.
sergeant sergent m.
series série f.
serious sérieux, sobre.
seriously sérieusement.
sermon sermon m.
servant domestique m. and f.
serve servir.
service service m.; office m.
   religious service office divin.
session séance f.
set adj. fixe, résolu, prescrit.
set assortiment m., service m.
set (to) mettre, placer.

setting décor m. (*stage*).
settle (to) arranger, régler, fixer, s'établir.
settlement accord m., colonie f.
seven sept.
seventeen dix-sept.
seventeenth dix-septième.
seventh septième.
seventieth soixante-dixième.
seventy soixante-dix.
several plusieurs.
   several times à plusieurs reprises.
severe sévère.
severity sévérité f.
sew coudre.
   sew back on recoudre.
sewer égout m.
sewing machine machine à coudre f.
sex sexe m.
shabby usé.
shade ombre f.
shade (to) ombrager.
shadow ombre f.
shady ombragé.
shake (to) secouer, agiter; serrer (*hands*); hocher (*head*).
shallow pèu profond.
sham adj. faux.
sham (to) simuler.
shame honte f.
shame (to) faire honte à.
shameful honteux.
shameless éhonté.
shampoo shampooing m.
shape forme f.
shape (to) former.
shapeless informe.
share part f.; action f. (*business*).
share (to) partager.
shareholder actionnaire m.
sharp adj. aigu.
sharp dièse m. (*music*).
sharpen aiguiser.
shatter fracasser.
shave (to) raser.
she elle.
shed hangar m.
shed (to) verser, répandre.
sheep mouton m.
sheer pur.
sheet feuille f. (*paper*); drap m. (*bedsheet*).
shelf rayon m., étagère f.
shell coquille f.
shelter abri m.
shelter (to) abriter.
shepherd berger m.
shield bouclier m.
shield (to) protéger.
shift déplacement m.; équipe f. (*of workmen*).
shift (to) déplacer, changer de place.
shine briller.
ship navire m., vaisseau m.
ship (to) expédier.
shipment expédition f.; envoi m.
shirt chemise f.
shiver frisson m.
shiver (to) frissonner.
shock choc m.
shock (to) choquer, scandaliser.
shoe soulier m., chaussure f.
shoemaker cordonnier m.
shoot tirer.
shooting tir m.
shop boutique f.

shore rive f.
short court.
shorten abréger, raccourcir.
shorthand sténographie f.
shorts slip m. (*men's*).
shot coup m.
shoulder épaule f.
shout cri m.
shout (to) crier.
shove (to) pousser.
shovel pelle f.
show spectacle m.
show (to) montrer.
show around piloter.
shower averse f., douche f.
shown inscrit.
shrill criard.
shrimp crevette f.
shrink rétrecir.
shrub buisson m.
shun éviter.
shut adj. fermé.
shut (to) enfermer, fermer.
shutter release déclencheur m. (*camera*).
shy timide.
sick malade.
sickness maladie f.
side côté m., bord m.
sidewalk trottoir m.
siege siège m.
sigh soupir m.
sigh (to) soupirer.
sight vue f.
sign signe m., enseigne f.
sign (to) signer.
signal signal m.
signature signature f.
significance signification f.
significant significatif.
signify signifier.
silence silence m.
silence (to) faire taire.
silent silencieux.
silent (to be) se taire.
silk soie f.
silken de soie.
silly sot.
silver argent m.
silvery argentin.
similar semblable.
similarity similitude f.
simple simple.
simplicity simplicité f.
simply simplement.
simulate simuler.
simultaneous simultané.
sin péché m.
sin (to) pécher.
since depuis; puisque.
sincere sincère.
sincerely sincèrement.
   Yours sincerely. Votre tout dévoué.
sincerity sincérité f.
sinew tendon m.
sing chanter.
singer chanteur m., chanteuse f.
single seul; célibataire (*unmarried*).
singular singulier, remarquable.
sinister sinistre.
sink évier m. (*kitchen*).
sink (to) (s') enfoncer, couler, sombrer.
sinner pécheur m.
sip (to) boire à petits coups, siroter.

sir monsieur.
    Thank you, sir. Merci, monsieur.
sister soeur f.
sister-in-law belle-soeur f.
sit s'asseoir, être assis.
site emplacement m.
sitting assis.
situation situation f.
six six.
sixteen seize.
sixteenth seizième.
sixth sixième.
sixtieth soixantième.
sixty soixante.
size taille f., grandeur f., pointure f. (*shoes, stockings, socks, gloves, hats*).
skate (to) patiner.
skates patins m. pl.
skeleton squelette m.
skeptic sceptique m. and f.
sketch croquis m.
ski ski m.
    water-skiing ski nautique.
skid (to) déraper.
skill adresse f.
skillful adroit.
skin peau f.
skirt jupe f.
skull crâne m.
sky ciel m.
sky-blue bleu ciel.
slander calomnie f.
slap soufflet m.
slate ardoise f.
slaughter massacre m.
slave esclave m. and f.
slavery servitude f., esclavage m.
sled, sledge luge f., traîneau m.
sleep sommeil m.
sleep (to) dormir.
sleeping bag sac de couchage m.
sleeve manche f.
slender mince, svelte.
slice tranche f.
slide diapositif m. (*photography*).
slide (to) glisser.
slight mince, moindre.
slight (to) dédaigner.
slip combinaison f.; fiche f. (*of paper*).
slip (to) glisser.
slipper pantoufle f.
slippery glissant.
slit fente f.
slope pente f.; piste f. (*ski*).
slot fente f.
slovenly malpropre, négligent.
slow lent.
slowness lenteur f., retard m.
late en retard.
slumber sommeil m.
slumber (to) sommeiller.
sly malin, rusé.
small petit.
smart élégant, habile, chic.
smash (to) briser.
smear tache f.
smear (to) enduire.
smell odeur f., odorat m.
smell (to) sentir, flairer.
smile sourire m.
smile (to) sourire.
smoke fumée f.
smoke (to) fumer.

smooth lisse, uni.
smother étouffer.
smuggle faire passer en contrebande.
smuggler contrebandier, m.
snake serpent m.
snapshot instantané m.
snatch arracher, saisir.
sneer (to) ricaner.
sneeze (to) éternuer.
snore (to) ronfler.
snow neige f.
snow (to) neiger.
so (thus) ainsi.
    and so on ainsi de suite.
    so much si, tellement, tant.
    so many tant de.
    so that afin que, pour que.
soak tremper.
soap savon m.
sob sanglot m.
sober sobre.
sociable sociable.
social social.
society société f.
sock chaussette f., socquette f.
socket orbite f.
sofa canapé m.
soft bas, doux, mou.
soften amollir, adoucir.
softly doucement.
soil (to) salir, souiller.
soldier soldat m.
sole semelle f. (*shoe*); plante f. (*foot*).
solemn solennel.
solemnity solennité f.
solicit solliciter.
solid solide, massif.
solitary solitaire.
solitude solitude f.
soluble soluble.
solution solution f.
solve résoudre.
some quelque, quelques.
somebody quelqu'un.
somehow d'une manière ou d'une autre.
someone quelqu'un.
something quelque chose.
sometime un jour.
sometimes parfois, quelquefois.
somewhat quelque peu.
somewhere quelque part.
son fils m.
song chanson f., chant m.
son-in-law gendre m.
soon bientôt, tôt.
soot suie f.
soothe calmer.
sore plaie f.
sorrow douleur f.
sorry triste, fâché.
    be sorry about regretter.
sort sorte f., genre m.
sort (to) trier, classer.
sought-after recherché.
soul âme f.
sound adj. sain.
sound son m.
sound (to) sonner.
soup soupe f., potage m.
sour aigre.
source origine f., source f.
south sud m.
South America Amérique de Sud f.

southern méridional, du sud.
southwest sud-ouest m.
sovereign souverain m.
sow (to) semer.
space espace m., emplacement m.
space (to) espacer.
spacious vaste, spacieux.
spade bêche f.; pique m. (*cards*).
Spain Espagne m.
Spanish espagnol.
spare adj. disponible.
spare (to) épargner.
spark étincelle f.
sparkle (to) étinceler.
sparrow moineau m.
speak parler.
speaker orateur m.
special spécial, particulier.
specialty spécialité f.
specific spécifique.
specify spécifier.
spectacle spectacle m.
spectator spectateur m.
speculate spéculer.
speech parole f., discours m.
speed vitesse f.
speedy rapide.
spell charme m.
spell (to) épeler.
spelling orthographe f.
spend dépenser.
sphere sphère f.
spice épice f.
spider araignée f.
spill répandre, renverser.
spin filer.
spirit esprit m.
spirited animé.
spiritual spirituel.
spit (to) cracher.
spite dépit m., rancune f.
spite (to) contrarier.
spiteful rancunier.
splash (to) éclabousser.
splendid splendide.
    Splendid! Epatant!
    That's splendid! A la bonne heure!
splendor splendeur f.
split fendre, partager, se diviser.
spoil gâter.
sponge éponge f.
spontaneous spontané.
spoon cuillère f., cuiller f.
spoonful cuillerée f.
sport sport m.
spot tache f.
sprain entorse f.
sprain (to) fouler.
    se fouler le poignet to sprain one's wrist.
spread (to) étendre, répandre.
spring printemps m. (*season*), saut m. (*leap*), ressort m. (*machine*), source f. (*water*).
spring (to) sauter, jaillir. provenir de.
sprinkle asperger, parsemer de.
sprout germer, pousser.
spry alerte.
spur (to) pousser à.
spurn dédaigner.
spy espion m.
spy (to) épier.
squadron escadron m.
squander gaspiller.
square carré noun m. and adj.

squeeze (to) serrer, presser.
squirrel écureuil m.
ssh! chut!
stabilize stabiliser.
stable écurie f.
stable adj. étable.
stack pile f.
stack (to) empiler.
stadium stade m.
staff bâton m. (*stick*); personnel m.
stage scène f., estrade f., étape f.
stain tache f.
stain (to) tacher.
stairs escalier m.
stammer bégayer.
stamp timbre m. (*postage*).
stand position f.
stand (to) être debout, supporter.
star étoile f.
starch amidon m.
starch (to) empeser.
   have (something) starched faire empeser.
starched empesé.
stare (to) regarder fixement.
start (to) commencer, tressaillir.
start over again refaire.
   retrace one's steps refaire le chemin.
starter démarreur m. (*car*).
starve mourir de faim.
state état m., situation f.
state (to) déclarer.
stately plein de dignité.
statement déclaration f.
station gare f. (*railroad*); poste, m.
   first-aid station station de secours f.
statistics statistique f.
statue statue f.
statute statut m.
stay séjour m. (*visit*).
stay (to) rester.
steady ferme, stable, sûr.
steak bifteck m.
steal voler.
steam vapeur f.
steamer vapeur m., paquebot m.
steel acier m.
steep adj. raide.
steeple clocher m.
steer (to) diriger.
stem tige f.
stenographer sténo-dactylo f.
stenography sténographie f.
step pas m.; marche f. (*stair*).
step (to) marcher.
stereophonic stéréo(phonique).
sterile stérile.
stern adj. sévère.
stew ragoût m. (*meat*).
stew (to) étuver.
stick bâton m.
stick (to) coller.
stiff raide; empesé.
stiffen raidir.
stiffness raideur f.
stifling écrasant.
still adj. immobile, calme, tranquille.
   Keep still! Restez tranquille!
still adv. encore, toujours, quand même.
still life nature(s) morte(s) f.
stimulate stimuler.
stimulus stimulant m.
sting piqûre f.
sting (to) piquer (*of an insect*).

stinginess mesquinerie f.
stingy mesquin.
stir (to) agiter.
stitch point m. (*sewing*), maille f. (*knitting*).
stock marchandises f. pl. (*goods*); valeurs f. pl. (*finance*).
stocking bas m.
stomach estomac m.
stone pierre f.
stool tabouret m.
stop halte f., arrêt m.
stop (to) arrêter, s'arrêter, cesser.
storage battery accu(mulateur) m., boîte d'accus f.
store magasin m., boutique f.
stork cigogne f.
storm orage m.
story histoire f.
stout gros.
stove fourneau m., poêle m.
straight droit.
straighten redresser.
strain tension f., effort m.
strange curieux, étrange.
stranger étranger m., inconnu m.
strap courroie f.
straw paille f.
strawberry fraise f.
straw-colored jaune paille.
stream courant m., ruisseau m. (*small river*).
street rue f.
strength force f.
strengthen fortifier.
strenuous énergique.
stress force f., pression f.
stretch étendue f.
stretch (to) étendre, tendre.
strict strict.
stride enjambée f.
stride (to) marcher, enjamber.
strife lutte f.
strike grève f. (*workmen*).
strike (to) battre, frapper.
string ficelle f.
strip (to) dépouiller.
stripe bande f., galon m.
strive s'efforcer de.
stroke coup m.
stroll tour m., promenade f.
stroll (to) faire un tour.
strong fort, puissant.
structure structure f.
struggle lutte f.
struggle (to) lutter, se débattre.
stubborn opiniâtre.
stuck engagé.
studded with nails clouté.
   pedestrian crossing passage clouté.
student étudiant m., étudiante f.
studious studieux.
study étude f., cabinet de travail m. (*room*).
stuff étoffe f.
stuff (to) bourrer, remplir.
stumble (to) trébucher.
stump souche f.
stun étourdir.
stunt tour m.
stupendous prodigieux.
stupid stupide.
stupidity stupidité f.
stupor stupeur f.
sturdy vigoureux.
stutter (to) bégayer.
style style m., modèle m.

stylish chic.
subdue subjuguer.
subdued sobre.
subject sujet m., propos m.
subject (to) assujettir, exposer à.
subjective subjectif.
subjugate subjuguer.
subjunctive subjonctif.
sublime sublime.
submission soumission f.
submissive soumis.
submit soumettre.
subordinate subordonné.
subordinate (to) subordonner.
subscribe souscrire, s'abonner à.
subscription souscription f., abonnement m.
subside s'apaiser.
subsidy subvention f.
subsist exister, subsister de.
substance substance f.
substantial substantiel.
substantiate prouver.
substantive substantif m.
substitute substitut m.
substitute (to) remplacer, substituer à.
substitution substitution f.
subtle subtil.
subtract soustraire.
subtraction soustraction f.
suburb faubourg m.
subway métro(politain) m. (*Paris*).
succeed réussir, succéder à.
success succès m.
successful heureux.
succession succession f.
successor successeur m.
such tel.
sudden soudain.
suddenly tout à coup.
sue poursuivre (*in law*).
suffer souffrir.
suffering souffrance f.
suffice suffire.
sufficient suffisant.
sufficiently suffisamment.
sugar sucre m.
suggest suggérer, proposer.
suggestion suggestion f.
suicide suicide m.
suit costume m. (*clothes*); complet-veston m.; tailleur m. (*woman's*); procès m. (*law*).
suit (to) convenir à, adapter à.
suitable convenable.
sulk bouder.
sullen maussade.
sum somme f.
summary résumé m.; sommaire m.
summer été m.
summit sommet m., cime f., comble m.
summon sommer, convoquer.
sumptuous somptueux.
sum up résumer.
sun soleil m.
sunbeam rayon de soleil m.
Sunday dimanche m.
sundry divers.
sunny ensoleillé.
sunrise lever du soleil m.
sunset coucher du soleil m.
sunshine soleil m.
superb superbe.
superficial superficiel.
superfluous superflu.

superintendent gérant m.
superior supérieur.
superiority supériorité f.
superstition superstition f.
supervise surveiller.
supper souper m.
supplement supplément m.
supplementary supplémentaire.
supply provision f.
supply (to) fournir.
support appui m.
support (to) appuyer, supporter.
suppose supposer.
suppress supprimer, réprimer.
supreme suprême.
sure sûr.
surety certitude f.
surface surface f.
surgeon chirurgien m.
surgery chirurgie f.
surmount surmonter.
surname nom de famille m.
surpass surpasser.
surplus surplus m.
surprise surprise f.
surprise (to) surprendre.
surrealistic surréaliste.
surrender abandon m., reddition f.
surrender (to) rendre, se rendre, renonce à.
surround entourer.
surroundings environs m. pl.
survey examen m.
survey (to) examiner, arpenter (land).
survive survivre.
susceptibility susceptibilité f.
susceptible susceptible.
suspect suspect m.
suspect (to) soupçonner.
suspense incertitude f.
suspension suspension f.
suspicion soupçon m.
suspicious suspect.
sustain soutenir.
swallow (to) avaler.
swamp marais m.
swan cygne m.
sway (to) balancer.
swear jurer.
sweat sueur f.
sweat (to) suer.
sweep (to) balayer.
sweet doux.
sweetness douceur f.
swell (to) gonfler, enfler.
swift rapide.
swim (to) nager.
swindler escroc m.
swing (to) osciller, se balancer.
Swiss suisse.
switch interrupteur m. (electricity).
swollen enflé.
sword épée f.
syllable syllabe f.
symbol symbole m.
symbolic symbolique.
symbolize symboliser.
symmetrical symétrique.
symmetry symétrie f.
sympathetic sympathique, compatissant.
sympathize compatir à.
sympathy sympathie f.
symphonic symphonique.
symptom symptôme m.

synagogue synagogue f.
syrup sirop m.
system système m.
systematic systématique.

T

table table f.
   table of contents sommaire m.
tablecloth nappe f.
tacit tacite.
tacitly tacitement.
taciturn taciturne.
tact tact m.
tactfully avec tact.
tail queue f. (animal).
tailor tailleur m.
take prendre.
   take again reprendre.
tale conte m., histoire f.
talent talent m.
talk causerie f.; conversation f.
talk (to) parler.
talkative bavard.
tall grand.
tame soumis, apprivoisé.
tangle (to) enchevêtrer.
tank réservoir m.; char d'assaut m. (mil.).
tape bande f., ruban m.
   tape recorder magnétophone m.
tapestry tapisserie f.
tar goudron m.
tardy lent, tardif.
target cible f.
tariff tarif m.
tarnish (to) se ternir.
tarry séjourner; tarder.
task tâche f.
taste goût m., gré m.
taste (to) goûter.
tax impôt m., taxe f.
taxi taxi m.
tea thé m.
teach enseigner.
teacher instituteur m., institutrice f., professeur m.
team équipe f. (sports).
tear larme f.
tear (to) déchirer, se déchirer.
tease (to) taquiner.
teaspoon cuillère à café f.
technical technique.
technique technique f.
tedious ennuyeux.
telecommunications télécommunications f.
telegram télégramme m.
telegraph télégraphe m.
telegraph (to) télégraphier.
telegraphic télégraphique.
telephone téléphone m.
   telephone booth cabine telephonique f.
   telephone call communication f.
telephone operator téléphoniste f.
telephone (to) téléphoner.
television télévision f.
tell dire.
temper colère f.; tempérament m.
temperance tempérance f.
temperate sobre; tempéré (climate).
temperature température f.
tempest tempête f.
temple temple m.
temporary provisoire, temporaire.

tempt tenter.
temptation tentation f.
ten dix.
tenacious tenace.
tenacity ténacité f.
tenant locataire m.
tend soigner; tendre à.
tendency tendance f.
tender tendre.
tennis tennis m.
tense adj. tendu.
tense temps m. (grammar).
tension tension f.
tent tente f.
tenth dixième.
tepid tiède.
term terme m.
terminate terminer.
terrace terrasse f.
terrible terrible.
terrific épatant, formidable.
terrify épouvanter.
territory territoire m.
terror terreur f.
test épreuve f.
test (to) mettre à l'épreuve.
testify témoigner, attester.
testimony témoignage m.
text texte m.
textbook manuel m.
than que.
thank remercier.
thanks merci m., remerciements m. pl.
that (those pl) demons. adj. ce, cet, cette, ces.
   that man cet homme, cet homme-là.
that demons. pron. celui, celle, ceux, celles.
   that is c'est à dire.
   That's it. C'est cela.
that relative pron. qui, que.
that conj. que.
   so that pourvu que.
   in order that pour que.
thaw dégel m.
the le, la, les.
theatre théâtre m.
their leur, leurs.
theirs le leur, la leur, les leurs, à eux, à elles.
them les, leur, eux, elles, se.
theme thème m.
themselves se, eux-mêmes m., elles-mêmes f.
then alors, puis, donc.
theoretical théorique.
theoretically théoriquement.
theory théorie f.
there là, voilà; y.
   there is (there are) il y a.
thereafter après cela.
therefore donc.
thereupon là-dessus.
thermometer thermomètre m.
these ces; ceux, celles.
thesis thèse f.
they ils, elles, eux.
thick épais.
thicken épaissir.
thickness épaisseur f.
thief voleur m.
thigh cuisse f.
thimble dé m.
thin mince, maigre.
thing chose f.; object m.
think penser, croire.
third tiers m.

third adj. troisième.
thirst soif f.
thirteen treize.
thirty trente.
this ce, cet, cette.
    this one celui-ci, celle-ci.
thorn épine f.
thorough (à) fond, complet, achevé, minutieux.
though quoique.
thought pensée f.; idée f.
thoughtful pensif; attentif.
thoughtless étourdi.
thousand mil, mille, millier.
thrash battre.
thread fil m.
thread (to) enfiler (needle).
threat menace f.
threaten menacer.
three trois.
threshold seuil m.
thrift économie f.
thrifty économe.
thrill tressaillement m.
thrill (to) faire frémir, émouvoir.
thrilling saisissant.
thrive prospérer, croître.
thriving prospère.
throat gorge f.
throb (to) palpiter.
throne trône m.
throng foule f.
through par, à travers.
throughout d'un bout à l'autre; partout.
throw jeter, lancer.
    throw back rejeter.
thumb pouce m.
thunder tonnerre m.
thunder (to) tonner.
thunderbolt foudre f.
Thursday jeudi m.
thus ainsi.
thwart contrarier.
ticket billet m. (subway, train, theatre); ticket m. (bus).
    ticket collector receveur m. (bus).
    ticket office bureau de location m.
    ticket window guichet m.
tickle chatouiller.
ticklish chatouilleux.
tide marée f.
tidiness ordre m.
tidy propre, rangé.
tie lien m. (bond); cravate (necktie).
tie (to) lier, attacher (bind).
tiger tigre m.
tight serré.
tile carreau m., tuile f.
till (to) labourer.
till jusqu'à; jusqu'à ce que.
    till now jusqu'à présent.
tilt (to) pencher.
timber bois m.
time temps m.; heure f. (hour).
    from time to time de temps en temps.
    in time à temps.
    What time is it? Quelle heure est-il?
    to have a good time bien s'amuser.
    on time à l'heure.
timetable horaire m.
timid timide.
timidity timidité f.
tin étain m.; bidon m.
tinkle tinter.

tint (to) teindre.
    tint one's hair teindre les cheveux.
tiny tout petit.
tip bout m. (end); pourboire m. (money).
tip (to) donner un pourboire (give a tip).
tip over renverser.
tire pneu m. (car).
tire (to) fatiguer, se fatiguer.
tired fatigué.
tireless infatigable.
tiresome fâcheux.
tissue tissu m.
title titre m.
to à, en, envers, vers, pour.
toad crapaud m.
toast pain grillé m.; toast m.
tobacco tabac m.
tobacco store débit de tabac m.
today aujourd'hui.
toe doigt de pied m., orteil m.
together ensemble.
toil travail m.
toil (to) travailler.
toilet toilette f.; w.-c. m.
token témoignage m.; jeton m. (coin).
tolerable supportable; passable.
tolerance tolérance f.
tolerant tolérant.
tolerate tolérer.
toll (to) tinter, sonner.
tomato tomate f.
tomb tombeau m.
tomorrow demain.
ton tonne f.
tone ton m.
tongs tenailles f. pl.
tongue langue f.
tonight ce soir.
too trop (too much); aussi (also).
tool outil m., instrument m.
tooth dent f.
    have a toothache avoir mal aux dents.
toothbrush brosse à dents f.
toothpaste pâte dentifrice f.
toothpick cure-dent m.
tooth powder poudre dentifrice f.
top sommet m., dessus m.
topic sujet m.
torch torche f.
torment tourment m.
torture supplice m., torture f.
toss (to) jeter; s'agiter.
total total noun m. and adj.
totally totalement.
touch toucher m.; touche f.
touch (to) toucher.
touching touchant.
touchy susceptible.
tough dur, rude.
tour voyage m., tour m., tournée f.
tour (to) visiter, voyager.
tourist touriste m.
    tourist agency un bureau de tourisme, un bureau de voyage.
tournament tournoi m.
toward vers, envers, pour.
towel essuie-main m., serviette f.
    hand towel essuie-main m., serviette de toilette.
    face towel serviette de toilette.
    bath towel serviette de bain.
    Turkish towel serviette éponge.
tower tour f.
town ville f.

town hall hôtel de ville m., mairie f.
toy jouet m.
trace trace f.
trace (to) tracer, retrouver.
track traces f. pl.; voie f. (railroad); piste f.
trade commerce m.; métier m.
    trade union syndicat. m.
tradition tradition f.
traditional traditionnel.
traffic circulation f.
tragedy tragédie f.
tragic tragique.
trail trace f., piste f.
trail (to) traîner.
train train m.
train (to) s'entraîner, élever.
training entraînement m.; éducation f.
traitor traître m.
trample piétiner.
tranquil tranquille.
tranquillity tranquillité f.
transaction transaction f. (commerce).
transfer transfert m.
transfer (to) transférer.
transition transition f.
transitory transitoire.
translate traduire.
translation traduction f.
translator traducteur m., traductrice f.
transmission transmission f.
transmit transmettre.
transparency diapositif m. (photography).
transparent transparent.
transport transport m.
    transport service messagerie f.
transport (to) transporter.
transportation transport m.
transverse transverse.
trap piège m.
trap (to) prendre au piège.
trash camelote f.
travel voyage m.
travel (to) voyager.
traveler voyageur m.
    traveler's check chèque de voyage m.
tray plateau m.
treacherous traître.
treachery trahison f.
treason trahison f.
treasure trésor m.
treasurer trésorier m.
treasury trésorerie f.
treat fête f.
treat (to) traiter.
treatment traitement m.
treaty traité m.
tree arbre m.
tremble trembler.
trembling tremblement m.
tremendous immense, formidable.
trench tranchée f.
trend tendance f.
trial épreuve f.; procès m.; essai m.
triangle triangle m.
tribe tribu f.
tribulation tribulation f.
tribunal tribunal m.
tribune tribune f.
tribute tribut m.
trick tour m., niche f.
trick (to) tromper.
trifle bagatelle f.
trifling insignifiant.

trim (to) orner, parer.
trimming décor m., garniture f.
trinket bibelot m.
trip voyage m.; parcours m.
    take a trip faire un voyage.
trip (to) trébucher.
triple triple.
triumph triomphe m.
triumph (to) triompher.
triumphant triomphant.
trivial trivial, insignifiant.
troop troupe f.
trophy trophée f.
trot trot m.
trot (to) trotter.
trouble difficulté f., souci m.
trouble (to) déranger, inquiéter.
    Don't trouble yourself! Ne vous dérangez pas!
trousers pantalon m.
truck camion m.
true vrai; fidèle; véritable.
truly vraiment; véritablement.
    Yours truly. Agréez, Monsieur (Madame), mes
        meilleures salutations.
trump atout m.
trump (to) couper (avec l'atout).
trumpet trompette f.
trunk malle f.
trunks slip m. (*men's bathing*).
trust confiance f.
trust (to) avoir confiance en; confier à.
trusting confiant.
trustworthy digne de confiance.
truth vérité f.
truthful sincère.
truthfully sincèrement.
truthfulness sincérité f.
try essai m.
try (to) essayer, tâcher.
    Try to come. Tâchez de venir.
    Try to be on time. Tâchez d'être à l'heure.
tube tube m.
tumble (to) tomber, s'effondrer.
tumult tumulte m.
tune air m.
tune (to) accorder.
tunnel tunnel m.
turf gazon m.
turkey dindon m., dinde f.
Turkish turque.
turmoil tumulte m.
turn tour m.
turn (to) tourner.
    Turn left. Prenez la première à gauche.
    turn back rebrousser.
    turn up rebrousser.
    retrace one's steps. rebrousser chemin.
turned-up retroussé.
    turned-up nose nez retroussé.
turnip navet m.
tweed tweed m.
twelfth douzième.
twelve douze.
twentieth vingtième.
twenty vingt.
twenty-five vingt-cinq.
twenty-four vingt-quatre.
twenty-six vingt-six.
twice deux fois.
twilight crépuscule m.
twin jumeau m., jumelle f.
twist entorse f.
twist tordre.

two deux.
type type m.
type (to) taper à la machine.
typewriter machine à écrire f.
tyranny tyrannie f.
tyrant tyran m.

U

ugliness laideur f.
ugly laid.
ulterior ultérieur.
ultimate dernier.
ultimately à la fin.
umbrella parapluie m.
umpire arbitre m.
unable to incapable de; être dans l'impossibilité
    de.
unanimity unanimité f.
unanimous unanime.
unanimously à l'unanimité.
unaware (to be) ignorer.
unawares (au) dépourvu, à l'improviste.
unbar débarrer.
unbearable insupportable.
unbelievable incroyable.
unbutton déboutonner.
uncap débarrer (*lens of camera*).
uncertain incertain.
uncertainty incertitude f.
unchangeable immuable.
uncle oncle m.
uncomfortable mal à l'aise (*person*); peu con-
        fortable (*thing*).
uncommon rare.
unconscious sans connaissance.
unconsciously sans le savoir.
uncouth grossier.
uncover découvrir.
undecided indécis.
undefinable indéfinissable.
undeniable incontestable.
under sous, de dessous, au-dessous de.
undergo subir.
underground souterrain.
underhand adj. clandestin, sournois.
underhand adv. sous main.
underline souligner.
underneath en dessous.
understand comprendre.
understanding adj. compréhensif.
understanding entente f., chose convenue f.; com-
        préhension f.
undertake entreprendre.
undertaker entrepreneur de pompes funèbres m.
undertaking entreprise f.
undesirable peu désirable.
undignified peu digne.
undo défaire.
undress se déshabiller (*undress oneself*).
uneasiness malaise m.; gêne f.
uneasy inquiet.
unemployed chômeurs m. pl.; sans travail adj.
unequal inégal.
uneven inégal.
uneventful tranquille, sans événements.
unexpected inattendu, soudain.
unexpectedly à l'improviste.
unfailing infaillible.
unfair injuste, déloyal.
unfaithful infidèle.
unfamiliar peu connu.
unfavorable peu propice, défavorable.

unfit incapable de, peu propre à.
unfold déplier; exposer (*explain*).
unforeseen imprévu.
unforgettable inoubliable.
unfortunate malheureux.
unfortunately malheureusement.
ungrateful ingrat.
unhappily malheureusement.
unhappiness malheur m.
unhappy malheureux.
unharmed sain et sauf.
unhealthy insalubre.
unheard (of) inouï.
unhesitatingly sans hésiter.
unhoped for inespéré.
unhurt sain et sauf.
uniform uniforme noun m. and adj.
uniformity uniformité f.
uniformly uniformément.
unify unifier.
unimportant peu important.
unintentional involontaire.
unintentionally involontairement.
uninviting peu engageant.
union union f.
unique unique.
unison unisson m.
unit unité f.
unite unir.
united uni.
United States Etats-Unis m.
unity unité f.
universal adj. universel.
universe univers m.
university université f.
unjust injuste.
unjustifiable injustifiable.
unkempt inculte.
unkind peu aimable.
unknown inconnu noun and adj.
unknown to à l'insu de.
unlawful illégal, illicite.
unless à moins que, à moins de.
unlikely improbable.
unlimited illimité.
unload décharger.
unluckily malheureusement.
unmask démasquer.
unmistakably incontestablement.
unnecessary pas nécessaire, inutile.
unoccupied inoccupé; libre.
unofficial non officiel.
unpack déballer, défaire les bagages.
unpleasant désagréable.
unpublished inédit.
unquestionably incontestablement.
unravel démêler.
unreal irréel.
unreasonable déraisonnable.
unrecognizable méconnaisable.
unreliable douteux (*news*); sur qui on ne peux pas
        compter (*person*).
unrest agitation f.
unrestrained libre.
unrestricted sans restriction.
unroll dérouler.
unsafe dangereux.
unsatisfactory peu satisfaisant.
unsatisfied mécontent.
unscrupulous sans scrupule.
unseemly inconvenant.
unseen adj. inaperçu.
unselfish désintéressé.

unspeakable inexprimable.
unsteady instable.
unsuccessful infructueux.
unsuitable peu propre à.
unthinkable inimaginable.
untidy malpropre (person); en désordre (thing).
untie dénouer.
until jusqu'à, jusqu'à ce que.
    until now jusqu'à présent, jusqu'ici.
untiring infatigable.
untrimmed sans garniture.
untrue faux.
untrustworthy indigne de confiance.
untruth mensonge m.
unusual extraordinaire, rare, peu commun.
unwarranted injustifié.
unwell indisposé.
unwholesome malsain.
unwilling peu disposé à.
unwise imprudent.
unworthy indigne.
unyielding inflexible.
up en haut de.
upheaval soulèvement m.
uphold soutenir, appuyer.
upholstered (with) recouvert de.
upkeep entretien m.
upon sur.
upper supérieur.
upright droit, honnête.
uprising soulèvement m.
uproar vacarme m.
upset bouleversement m.
upset (to) bouleverser.
upside down sens dessus dessous.
upstairs en haut.
upward en haut.
urge (to) prier, faire valoir.
urgency urgence f.
urgent urgent.
urgently instamment.
us nous.
use usage m., emploi m.
use (to) se servir de.
    use up user.
    wear away user.
    wear out user.
used d'occasion.
    used car voiture d'occasion.
used to habitué à.
useful utile.
useless inutile.
usherette ouvreuse f.
usual ordinaire, usuel.
usually habituellement, d'habitude, d'ordinaire.
usurp usurper.
utensil ustensile m.
utility utilité f.
utilize utiliser.
utmost le plus.
utter le plus grand; absolu.
utter (to) prononcer.
utterance expression f.
utterly tout à fait.

V

vacant vide.
vacation vacances f. pl.
vague vague.
vain vain, vaniteux.
    in vain en vain.
valiant vaillant.

valid valide, valable.
validity validité f.
valise valise f.
valley vallée f.
valuable de valeur.
value valeur f.
value (to) estimer, évaluer.
valued estimé.
valve soupape f.
vanilla vanille f.
vanish disparaître.
vanity vanité f.
vanquish vaincre.
vapor vapeur f.
variable variable.
variance désaccord m.
variation variation f.
varied varié.
variety variété f.
various divers.
varnish (to) vernir.
vary varier, différer sur.
vase vase m.
vast vaste.
vault voûte f.
veal veau m.
vegetable légume m.
vehemence véhémence f.
vehement véhément.
vehicle véhicule m.
veil voile m., voilette f.
veil (to) voiler.
vein veine f.
velocity vitesse f.
velvet velours m.
venerable vénérable.
venerate vénérer.
veneration vénération f.
vengeance vengeance f.
venom venin m.
ventilation ventilation f.
ventilator ventilateur m.
venture (to) risquer, se hasarder à.
verb verbe m.
verdict verdict m.
verge bord m.
    on the verge of à deux doigts de.
verge (to) pencher vers.
verification vérification f.
verify vérifier.
versatile aux talents variés.
versatility souplesse d'esprit f.
verse vers m., strophe f.
version version f.
vertical vertical.
very très, même.
    very much grand-chose.
vessel vaisseau m.
vest gilet m.
vex ennuyer.
via via.
vibrate retentir, vibrer.
vice vice m.
vice-president vice-président m.
vice versa vice versa.
vicinity voisinage m.
victim victime f.
victor vainqueur m.
victorious victorieux.
victory victoire f.
victuals victuailles f. pl.
view vue f.
view (to) voir, envisager.

vie with rivaliser avec.
vigor vigueur f.
vigorous vigoureux.
vile vil.
village village m.
villain scélérat m.
vindicate défendre.
vindictive vindicatif.
vine vigne f.
vinegar vinaigre m.
violence violence f.
violent violent.
violet violette f.; violet adj.
violin violon m.
virile viril.
virtue vertu f.
virtuous vertueux.
visa visa m.
    entrance visa visa d'entrée.
visibility visibilité f.
visible visible.
visibly visiblement.
vision vision f., vue f.
visit visite f.
    guided tour visite guidée (avec guide).
visit (to) visiter.
visitor visiteur m.
visual visuel.
visualize se représenter.
vital vital.
vitality vitalité f.
vivacious vif.
vivid vif.
vocabulary vocabulaire m.
vocal vocal.
vocation vocation f.
vogue vogue f.
voice voix f.
voice (to) exprimer.
void vide; nul.
volubility volubilité f.
voluble doué de volubilité.
volume volume m.
voluminous volumineux.
voluntary volontaire.
vote voix f.
vote (to) voter.
vouch for répondre de.
vow voeu m.
vow (to) vouer, jurer.
vowel voyelle f.
vulgar vulgaire.
vulnerable vulnérable.

W

wag (to) hocher, agiter.
wager pari m.
wager (to) parier.
wages salaire m.
waist taille f.
wait (to) attendre.
waiter garçon m.
wake (to) éveiller, s'éveiller.
walk démarche (gait) f.; promenade f., marche f.;
    allée f.
    go for a walk se promener, faire une promenade.
walk (to) aller à pied, marcher, se promener.
wall mur m.
wallet portefeuille m.
walnut noix f.
wander errer.
want besoin m., manque m.

want (to) avoir envie de; vouloir.
war guerre f.
warble gazouiller.
ward pupille f. (*person*); salle f. (*hospital*); arrondissement m. (*Paris*).
wardrobe garde-robe f., armoire f.
ware, wares marchandises f. pl.
warehouse magasin m.
warfare guerre f.
wariness prudence f.
warm chaud.
     be warm avoir chaud.
warm (to) chauffer.
warmth chaleur f.
warn prévenir, avertir.
warning avertissement m.
warrant autorisation f.; mandat m.
warrant (to) garantir; justifier.
warrior guerrier m.
wary prudent.
wash lessive f.
wash (to) laver.
washing machine machine à laver f.
washroom lavabo m., toilette f.
waste gaspillage m., perte f.
waste (to) gaspiller.
watch montre f. (*timepiece*); garde f. (*guard*).
watch (to) observer.
watchful vigilant.
water eau f.
water (to) arroser.
water color aquarelle f.
water skiing ski nautique m.
waterfall chute d'eau f.
waterproof adj. imperméable.
wave vague f. (*sea*); onde f. (*physics*); ondulation f. (*hair*).
wave (to) onduler, agiter.
waver vaciller, balancer.
wax cire f.
way chemin m.; façon f., manière f.; trajet m. (*length of*).
we nous.
weak faible.
weaken affaiblir.
weakly faiblement.
weakness faiblesse f.
wealth richesse f.
wealthy riche.
weapon arme f.
wear porter.
weariness fatigue f.
weary las.
weather temps m.
weave tisser.
wedding noces f. pl.
wedge coin m.
Wednesday mercredi m.
weed mauvaise herbe f.
week semaine f.
weekend week-end m.
weekly hebdomadaire.
weep pleurer.
weigh peser.
weight poids m.
welcome bienvenu.
     Welcome! Soyez le bienvenu (la bienvenue).
     You're welcome. il n'y a pas de quoi (*answer to "Thank you"*).
welcome (to) accueillir.
welfare bien-être m.
well puits m.
well! eh bien! tiens!

west ouest m.
western occidental.
wet mouillé.
whale baleine f.
wharf quai m.
what ce que, ce dont; qu'est-ce qui, qu'est-ce que, quoi.
     What is it? Qu'est-ce que c'est?
     What? Comment? Vous dites?
whatever quoi que, quelque, quel que.
wheat blé m.
wheel roue f.; volant m.
     at the wheel au volant.
when lorsque, quand.
whenever toutes les fois que.
where où.
wherever partout où.
whether si, soit que.
whew! ouf!
which que, quel, qui, dont; lequel, laquelle, ce qui, ce que; quel, quelle.
whiff bouffée f.
while pendant que, tandis que.
     Wait a while. Attendez une minute.
whim caprice m.
whimper pleurnicher.
whine gémissement m.
whine (to) gémir.
whip fouet m.
whip (to) fouetter.
whirlwind tourbillon m.
whisper chuchotement m.
whisper (to) chuchoter.
whistle sifflet m.
whistle (to) siffler.
white blanc.
who qui, qui est-ce qui.
whoever quiconque.
whole tout, toute, entier.
whole (the) tout m., totalité f.
wholesale en gros.
wholesome sain.
whom que.
whose dont, de qui.
why pourquoi.
     Why not? Pourquoi pas?
wicked méchant.
wide large.
widen élargir, s'élargir.
widow veuve f.
widower veuf m.
width largeur f.
wife femme f.
wig perruque f.
wild sauvage.
wilderness désert m.
wildness état sauvage m.
wile ruse f.
will volonté f.
will (to) vouloir.
willful volontaire.
willing bien disposé.
willingly volontiers.
win gagner.
wind vent m.
wind (to) enrouler.
windmill moulin m.
window fenêtre f.; guichet m.
windy venteux.
wine vin m.
wing aile f.
wink clin d'oeil m.
winner gagnant m.

winter hiver m.
wipe essuyer.
wire dépêche f., télégramme m.; fil de fer (*metal*) m.
wire (to) télégraphier.
wisdom sagesse f.
wise sage.
wish désir m.
wish (to) désirer, vouloir; souhaiter.
wit esprit m.
witch sorcière f.
with avec.
withdraw (se)retirer.
withdrawal retraite f.
wither se flétrir.
within dedans.
without sans.
witness témoin m.
witness (to) être témoin de.
witty spirituel.
woe malheur m.
wolf loup m.
woman femme f.
wonder merveille f.; étonnement m.
wonder (to) se demander, être étonné de.
wonderful merveilleux.
     Wonderful! Merveilleux!
wood bois m.
woods bois m.
woodwork boiserie f.
wool laine f.
woolen de laine.
word mot m.
     word for word mot à mot.
work travail m., devoir m., oeuvre f.
work (to) travailler.
worker ouvrier m.
workman ouvrier m.
work of art objet d'art m.
workshop atelier m.
work yard chantier m.
world monde m.
worldliness mondanité f.
worldly mondain.
worm ver m.
worry ennui m., souci m.
worry (to) se tracasser, s'inquiéter, s'en faire.
     Don't worry! Ne vous inquiétez pas! Ne vous en faites pas! Ne vous tracassez pas! Ne t'en fais pas!
worse pire m.
worship culte m.
worship (to) adorer.
worst pis.
worth valeur f.
worth (to be) valoir.
worthless sans valeur; indigne.
worthy digne.
wound blessure f.
wound (to) blesser.
wounded blessé.
wrap (to) envelopper; emballer.
wrapping emballage m.
wrath courroux m.
wrathful courroucé.
wreath couronne f.
wreck naufrage m. (*ship*); ruine f.; accident m. (*train wreck, etc.*).
wreck (to) ruiner, démolir, saboter.
     be wrecked (*of a ship*) faire naufrage.
wrestle lutter.
wrestler lutteur m.
wrestling lutte f.
wretched misérable.

wring tordre.
wrinkle ride f.
wrinkle (to) rider.
wrist poignet m.
write écrire.
writer écrivain m.
writing écriture f.
in writing par écrit.
written écrit; par écrit.
wrong adj. faux.
wrong mal m., tort m.
be wrong avoir tort.
What's wrong? Qu'est-ce qui ne marche pàs?
wrong (to) faire tort à.

X

X-ray picture radio(graphie) f.
X ray (to) radiographier.

Y

yard yard m., cour f.
yarn fil m.
yawn bâillement m.
yawn (to) bâiller.
year an m., année f.
yearly annuel adj.; annuellement adv.
yearn for soupirer après.
yearning désir m.
yeast levure f.
yell (to) hurler.
yellow jaune.
yes oui, si.
yesterday hier.
yet encore; néanmoins.
yield (to) produire, donner; céder, consentir.
yielding accommodant.
yoke joug m.

yolk jaune m. (egg).
you vous.
young jeune.
young lady demoiselle f., jeune fille f.
your votre, vos; ton, ta, tes (familiar).
yours à vous; à toi (familiar).
yourself vous-même, vous-mêmes pl.; toi-même (familiar).
youth jeunesse f.
youthful jeune.
youthfulness jeunesse f.

Z

zeal zèle m.
zealous zèlé.
zero zéro m.
zone zone f.
zoo jardin zoölogique m.
zoology zoölogie f.

GLOSSARY OF PROPER NAMES

Adolph	Adolphe	Charlotte	Charlotte	Gregory	Grégoire	Maurice	Maurice
Adrian	Adrien	Daniel	Daniel	Gustavus	Gustave	Michael	Michel
Albert	Albert	David	David	Guy	Guy	Miriam	Miriam
Alexander	Alexandre	Donald	Donald	Harry	Henri	Paul	Paul
Alfred	Alfred	Edith	Édith	Henry	Henri	Peter	Pierre
Alice	Alice	Edmund	Edmond	Hubert	Hubert	Ralph	Ralph
Allan	Alain	Edward	Édouard	Hugh	Hughes	Richard	Richard
Andrew	André	Eleanor	Éléonore	Irene	Irène	Robert	Robert
Anita	Anne	Emily	Émilie	Jane	Jeanne	Ruth	Ruth
Anthony	Antoine	Evelyn	Eveline	Jerome	Jérôme	Silvia	Sylvie
Arnold	Arnaud	Ferdinand	Ferdinand	Joan	Jeanne	Theresa	Thérèse
Arthur	Arthur	Frances	Françoise	Judith	Judith	Thomas	Thomas
Beatrice	Béatrice	Francis	François	Julian	Julien	Vincent	Vincent
Bernard	Bernard	Frederick	Frédéric	Lawrence	Laurent	Vivian	Viviane
Bertram	Bertrand	Gabriel	Gabriel	Lewis	Louis	William	Guillaume
Blanche	Blanche	George	Georges	Lillian	Liliane		
Carol	Caroline	Gertríde	Gertrude	Lucy	Lucie		
Charles	Charles	Gilbert	Gilbert	Mary	Marie		

GLOSSARY OF GEOGRAPHICAL NAMES

Africa Afrique f.	Dover Douvres m.	Moscow Moscou f.
Algeria Algérie f.	Dunkirk Dunkerque m.	New Zealand Nouvelle-Zélande f.
Algiers Alger m.	Egypt Égypte f.	Normandy Normandie f.
Alps Alpes f. pl.	England Angleterre f.	Norway Norvège f.
Alsace Alsace f.	Europe Europe f.	Pacific adj. and noun Pacifique.
America Amérique f.	Geneva Genève f.	Persia Perse f.
North America l'Amérique du Nord.	Genoa Gênes f.	Poland Pologne f.
Central America l'Amérique Centrale.	Greece Grèce f.	Prussia Prusse f.
South America l'Amérique du Sud.	Hague (La) Haye.	Pyrenees Pyrénées f. pl.
Antwerp Anvers m.	Hamburg Hambourg m.	Rheims Reims m.
Argentina Argentine f.	(Le) Havre (Le) Hâvre.	Rhine Rhin m.
Asia Asie f.	Holland Hollande f.	Rhineland Rhénanie f.
Atlantic noun and adj. Atlantique.	Hungary Hongrie f.	Rumania Roumanie f.
Australia Australie f.	Iceland Islande f. \	Russia Russie f.
Austria Autriche f.	India Inde f.	Scotland Écosse f.
Bermudas Bermudes f. pl.	Indo-China Indochine f.	Siberia Sibérie f.
Bordeaux Bordeaux m.	Ireland Irlande f.	Sicily Sicile f.
Brazil Brésil m.	Italy Italie f.	Spain Espagne f.
Brittany Bretagne f.	Japan Japon m.	Sweden Suède f.
Brussels Bruxelles f.	Jugoslavia Yougoslavie f.	Switzerland Suisse f.
Canada Canada m.	Lisbon Lisbonne f.	Tunis Tunisie f.
Chile Chili m.	London Londres m.	Turkey Turquie f.
China Chine f.	Lyons Lyon m.	United States États-Unis m. pl.
Corsica Corse f.	Marseilles Marseille m.	Venice Venise f.
Czechoslovakia Tchécoslovaquie f.	Mexico Mexique m.	Vienna Vienne f.
Denmark Danemark m.		Wales Pays de Galles m.

LETTER WRITING

1. FORMAL INVITATIONS AND ACCEPTANCES

FORMAL INVITATIONS

Monsieur et madame de Montour vous prient de leur faire l'honneur d'assister à un bal, donné en l'honneur de leur fille Marie-José, le dimanche huit avril à neuf heures du soir.

> *M. et Mme. de Montour*
> *35 Avenue Hoche*
> *Paris xvi ème.*

R.S.V.P.

Mr. and Mrs. de Montour request the pleasure of your presence at a ball given in honor of their daughter, Marie-José, on Sunday evening, April the eighth, at nine o'clock.

> Mr. and Mrs. de Montour
> 35 avenue Hoche
> Paris xvi ème.

R.S.V.P.

R.S.V.P. stands for *Répondez s'il vous plaît.* Please answer.

NOTE OF ACCEPTANCE

Monsieur et madame du Panier, vous remercient de votre aimable invitation à laquelle ils se feront un plaisir de se rendre.

Mr. and Mrs. du Panier thank you for your kind invitation and will be delighted to come.

2. THANK-YOU NOTES

> *le 14 mars 1956*

Chère Madame,

Je tiens à vous remercier de l'aimable attention que vous avez eue en m'envoyant le charmant présent que j'ai reçu. Ce tableau me fait d'autant plus plaisir qu'il est ravissant dans le cadre de mon studio.

Je vous prie de croire à l'expression de mes sentiments de sincère amitié.

> *Renée Beaujoly*

> March 14, 1956

Dear Mrs. Duparc,

I should like to thank you for the delightful present you sent me. The picture was all the more welcome because it fits in so beautifully with the other things in my studio.

Thank you ever so much.

> Sincerely yours,
> Renée Beaujoly

3. BUSINESS LETTERS

M. Roger Beaumont
2 rue Chalgrin
Paris

> *le 6 novembre 1955*
> *M. le rédacteur en chef*
> *"Vu"*
> *3 Blvd. des Capucines*
> *Paris*

Monsieur,

Je vous envoie ci-inclus mon chèque de 120 frs., montant de ma souscription d'un abonnement d'un an à votre publication.

Veuillez agréer, Monsieur, mes salutations distinguées.

> *Roger Beaumont*

ci-inclus un chèque

> 2 Chalgrin Street
> Paris
> November 6th, 1955

Circulation Department
"Vu"
3 Blvd. des Capucines
Paris

Gentlemen:

Inclosed please find a check for 120 francs to cover a year's subscription to your magazine.

> Sincerely yours,
> Roger Beaumont

Inc.

Dupuis Aîné
3 rue du Quatre-Septembre
Paris.

le 30 septembre 1955
Vermont et Cie.
2 rue Marat
Bordeaux
Gironde

Monsieur,

En réponse à votre lettre du dix courant, je tiens à vous confirmer que la marchandise en question vous a été expédiée le treize août par colis postal.

Veuillez agréer, Monsieur, mes salutations distinguées,

Henri Tournaire

db/ht

3 Quatre-Septembre St.
Paris
September 30, 1955

Vermont and Co.
2 Marat Street
Bordeaux
Gironde

Gentlemen:

In reply to your letter of the 10th of this month, I wish to confirm that the merchandise was mailed to you parcel post on August the 13th.

Sincerely yours,
Henri Tournaire

db/ht

4. INFORMAL LETTERS

le 5 mars 1955

Mon cher Jacques,

Ta dernière lettre m'a fait grand plaisir.

Tout d'abord laisse-moi t'annoncer une bonne nouvelle: je compte venir passer une quinzaine de jours à Paris au commencement d'avril et je me réjouis à l'avance à l'idée de te revoir ainsi que les tiens qui je l'espère, se portent bien.

Colette vient avec moi et se fait une grande joie à l'idée de connaître enfin ta femme, de cette manière nous pourrons laisser nos deux femmes potiner un après-midi et nous pourrons rester ensemble comme nous faisions au lycée. Les affaires marchent bien en ce moment, espérons que ça con-

tinuera. Tâche de ne pas avoir trop de malades au mois d'avril, enfin il est vrai que ces choses-là ne se commandent pas.

Toute ma famille se porte bien, heureusement.

J'ai pris l'apéritif avec Dumont l'autre jour, qui m'a demandé de tes nouvelles. Son affaire marche très bien.

J'allais presque oublier le plus important, peux-tu me réserver une chambre au Grand Hôtel pour le cinq avril, je t'en saurais fort gré.

J'espère avoir le plaisir de te lire très bientôt.

Mes respects à ta femme et pour toi une amicale poignée de main,

ton ami,
André

March 5th, 1955

Dear Jack,

I was very happy to receive your last letter.

First of all, I've some good news for you. I expect to spend two weeks in Paris at the beginning of April and I'm looking forward to the prospect of seeing you and your family, all of whom I hope are well.

Colette's coming with me; she's delighted to be able at last to meet your wife. That way we shall be able to let our two wives gossip and we can spend the afternoon talking together as we used to at school. Business is pretty good right now. Let's hope it will keep up. Try not to get too many patients during the month of April, though I suppose that's a little difficult to arrange.

I had cocktails with Dumont the other day and he asked about you. His business is going well.

I almost forgot the most important thing. Can you reserve a room for me at the Grand Hotel for April the fifth? You'll be doing me a great favor.

I hope to hear from you soon. My best regards to your wife.

Yours,
Andrew

Paris, le 3 avril 1955

Ma Chérie,

J'ai bien reçu ta lettre du trente et je suis heureuse de savoir que ta fille est tout à fait remise.

Rien de bien nouveau ici, sauf que Pierre me donne beaucoup de mal, enfin toi aussi tu as un fils de cet âge-là, et tu sais ce que je veux dire!

L'autre jour, j'ai rencontré Mme Michaud dans la rue, Dieu qu'elle a vieilli! Elle est méconnaissable!

Ma femme de chambre vient de me quitter, les domestiques deviennent insupportables à Paris, tu as bien de la veine d'être à la montagne pour encore un mois.

Nous avons vu ton mari l'autre soir, il est venu dîner à la maison; il se porte bien et voudrait bien te voir de retour.

Que fais-tu de beau toute la journée à Chamonix? Y-a-t-il encore beaucoup de monde là-bas? Il paraît que les de Villneque sont là. A Paris tout le monde parle des prochaines fiançailles de leur fille.

Nous sommes allés à une soirée l'autre soir chez les Clergeaud, cette femme ne sait pas recevoir, je m'y suis ennuyée à mourir.

Voilà à peu près tous les derniers potins de Paris, tu vois que je te tiens bien au courant, tâche d'en faire autant.

Embrasse bien Françoise pour moi.

Meilleurs baisers de ton amie,

Monique

Paris, April 3rd, 1955

Darling,

I received your letter of the 30th and I'm happy to learn that your daughter has completely recovered.

Nothing new here, except that Peter is giving me a lot of trouble. You have a son of the same age, so you know what I mean.

The other day I ran into Mrs. Michaud in the street. My, how she's aged! She's unrecognizable!

My chambermaid just left me; servants in Paris are becoming impossible. You're lucky to be staying in the mountains for another month.

We saw your husband the other night—he had dinner at our house. He's well and is looking forward to your coming home.

What do you do all day long in Chamonix? Is it still very crowded? It seems that the de Villneques are there. In Paris, the future engagement of their daughter is the talk of the town.

The other evening we went to a dull party given by the Clergeauds. She doesn't know how to entertain and I was bored to death.

That's about all of the latest Paris gossip. You see how well I keep you posted—try to do the same.

Give my love to Frances.

Love,

Monique

5. FORMS OF SALUTATIONS AND COMPLIMENTARY CLOSINGS

SALUTATIONS

Formal

Monsieur l'Abbé,	Dear Reverend:
Monsieur le Député,	Dear Congressman:
Monsieur le Maire,	Dear Mayor (Smith):
Cher Professeur,	Dear Professor (Smith):
Cher Maître, (Mon cher Maître,)	Dear Mr. (Smith): (Lawyers are addressed as "Maître" in France.)
Monsieur,	Dear Sir:
Messieurs,	Gentlemen:
Cher Monsieur Varnoux,	My dear Mr. Varnoux:
Chère Madame Gignoux,	My dear Mrs. Gignoux:

Informal

Mon Cher Roger,	Dear Roger,
Ma Chère Denise,	Dear Denise,
Chéri,	Darling (*m.*),
Chérie,	Darling (*f.*),
Mon Chéri,	My darling (*m.*),
Ma Chérie,	My darling (*f.*),

COMPLIMENTARY CLOSINGS

Formal

1. *Agréez, je vous prie, l'expression de mes salutations les plus distinguées.*
   ("Please accept the expression of my most distinguished greetings.") Very truly yours.

2. *Veuillez agréer l'expression de mes salutations distinguées.*
   ("Will you please accept the expression of my distinguished greetings.") Very truly yours.

3. *Veuillez agréer, Monsieur, mes salutations empressées.*
   ("Sir, please accept my eager greetings.") Yours truly.

4. *Veuillez agréer, Monsieur, mes sincères salutations.*
   ("Sir, please accept my sincere greetings.") Yours truly.

5. *Agréez, Monsieur, mes salutations distinguées.*
   ("Sir, accept my distinguished greetings.") Yours truly.

6. *Votre tout dévoué.*
   ("Your very devoted.") Yours truly.

Informal

1. *Je vous prie de croire à l'expression de mes sentiments de sincère amitié.*
   ("Please believe in my feelings of sincere friendship.")
   Very sincerely.

2. *Meilleures amitiés.*
   ("Best friendship.") Sincerely yours.

3. *Amicalement.*
   ("Kindly.") Sincerely yours.

4. *Mes pensées affectueuses* (or *amicales*).
   ("My affectionate *or* friendly thoughts.") Sincerely.

5. *Une poignée de main amicale.*
   ("A friendly handshake.") Sincerely.

6. *Je te serre la main.*
   ("I shake your hand.") Sincerely.

7. *Affectueusement.*
   Affectionately.

8. *Très affectueusement.*
   ("Very affectionately.") Affectionately yours.

9. *Je vous prie de bien vouloir transmettre mes respects à Madame votre mère.*
   Please give my regards to your mother.

10. *Transmets mes respects à ta famille.*
    Give my regards to your family.

11. *Rappelle-moi au bon souvenir de ta famille.*
    Remember me to your family.

12. *Embrasse tout le monde pour moi.*
    ("Kiss everybody for me.") Give my love to everybody.

13. *Je t'embrasse bien fort.* ⎫
    Millions de baisers. ⎭ Love.

6. FORM OF THE ENVELOPE

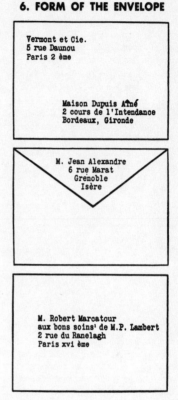

Vermont et Cie.
5 rue Daunou
Paris 2 ème

Maison Dupuis Aîné
2 cours de l'Intendance
Bordeaux, Gironde

M. Jean Alexandre
6 rue Marat
Grenoble
Isère

M. Robert Marcatour
aux bons soins[1] de M.P. Lambert
2 rue du Ranelagh
Paris xvi ème

[1]"In care of." Sometimes written as in English: C/o.

COMMON USAGE
DICTIONARY

German-English
English-German

BY **Genevieve A. Martin** AND
Theodor Bertram

BASED ON THE METHOD DEVISED BY
RALPH WEIMAN
FORMERLY CHIEF OF LANGUAGE SECTION,
U. S. WAR DEPARTMENT

---

*CONTAINING OVER 15,000 BASIC TERMS WITH
MEANINGS ILLUSTRATED BY SENTENCES AND
1000 ESSENTIAL WORDS ESPECIALLY INDICATED*

INTRODUCTION

The German Common Usage Dictionary lists the most frequently used German words, gives their most important meanings and illustrates their use.

1. The *basic* words are indicated by capitals.

2. Only the most important meanings are given.

3. These meanings are illustrated, wherever necessary, by means of everyday phrases and sentences. Where there is no close English equivalent for a German word or where the English equivalent has several different meanings, the context of the illustrative sentences helps to make the meanings clear.

4. Each important word is followed by the everyday expressions in which it most frequently occurs. The Common Usage Dictionary serves accordingly as a phrase book or conversation guide: it contains thousands of everyday sentences which are of practical importance (for traveling, correspondence, etc.) or which serve as illustrations of the grammatical features of current written and spoken German. The Common Usage Dictionary should, therefore, prove helpful both to beginners who are building up their vocabulary and to advanced students who want to perfect their command of colloquial German.

5. In translating the German phrases and sentences an attempt has been made to give not a mere translation but an equivalent — that is, what an English speaker would say in the same situation. (Literal translations have been added to help the beginner.) The user is thus furnished with numerous examples of how common German expressions (particularly the very idiomatic and the very colloquial ones) can best be translated into English. This feature makes the Common Usage Dictionary especially useful for translation work.

6. The English-German part contains the most common English words and their German equivalents. By consulting the sentences given under the German word in the German-English part the reader can observe whether the German word always translates the English one or whether it does so only in certain cases.

EXPLANATORY NOTES

Literal translations are in parentheses.

Gender is indicated by *m.* for masculine, *f.* for feminine and *n.* for neuter.

Case is indicated by *nom.* for nominative, *gen.* for genitive, *dat.* for dative, *acc.* for accusative.

German-English DICTIONARY

A

AB 1. *adv.* off, down, away from, from.
ab heute from today.
ab und an now and then.
ab und zu to and fro, now and then.
von hier ab from here.
von nun ab henceforth.
2. *separable prefix (implies a movement down or away, imitation, appropriation, deterioration, destruction).*
Das Flugzeug stürzte ins Meer ab. The plane fell down into the sea.
The church is a hundred meters away from the river.
Einige alte Häuser werden abgebaut. Some old houses will be demolished.
Er hat ihm tausend Mark abgeschmeichelt. He got a thousand marks from him by flattery.
Ich schreibe meine Aufgabe ab. I copy my homework.
Abart *f.* variety.
abbeissen to bite off.
sich die Nägel abbeissen to bite one's nails.
abbezahlen to pay off.
abbiegen to turn off.
Abbild *n.* copy, image.
abbinden to unbind.
Abbitte *f.* apology.
abbrechen to break up, interrupt, deduct, gather.
Blumen abbrechen to gather flowers.
die Arbeit abbrechen to cease work.
abdanken to dismiss, abdicate.
Der Fürst hat abgedankt. The prince has abdicated.
abdrehen to turn off, switch off.
Drehen sie das Radio ab! Turn off the radio!
abdrucken to print.
ABEND *n.* evening.
diesen Abend this evening.
Es wird Abend. It is getting dark.
heute Abend tonight.
Abenteuer *n.* adventure.
auf Abenteuer ausgehen to look for adventure.
abenteuerlich adventurous.
Abenteurer *m.* adventurer.
ABER but, however, anyway.
Ich wollte ausgehen aber das Wetter war zu schlecht. I wanted to go out but the weather was too bad.
Das Kind wollte spielen, die Mutter aber wollte nicht. The child wanted to play but the mother did not want to.
Der König aber ... as for the king ...
Nein aber! I say!
Nun aber! But now!
tausend und aber tausend thousands and thousands.
abermals again, once more.
abfahren to set off, depart.
Der Zug fährt um drei Uhr ab. The train leaves at three.
Sie fuhr übel ab. She got the worst of it.
Abfahrtsort *m.* place of departure.
abfinden to settle, come to an agreement.
abführen to lead away, carry away.
Abführung *f.* removal.
Abgabe *f.* tax, tribute, delivery.
abgabenfrei tax free.
abgabenpflichtig taxable.
Abgang *m.* departure, exit.
ABGEBEN to give, supply, deliver, pay taxes.
sich mit etwas abgeben to occupy oneself with a matter.
Wir können die Waren zu diesem Preis nicht abgeben. We cannot supply the merchandise on these terms.
abgehen to depart, go off.
Er lässt sich nichts abgehen. He denies himself

nothing.
von seinem Vorhaben nicht abgehen to persist in one's plans.
abgemacht agreed.
abgewinnen to win from.
abgewöhnen to disaccustom, give up.
Ich habe mir das Rauchen abgewöhnt. I have given up smoking.
Abgrund *m.* abyss, precipice.
abhalten to hold off, restrain.
Lassen Sie sich nicht abhalten. Don't let me stop you.
abhängen to unhang, hang up (phone), disconnect.
abhängig sloping, dependent on.
abheben to lift off, uncover, become detached.
Die helle Gestalt hebt sich auf dem dunkeln Hintergrunde vorteilhaft ab. The light figure is brought into relief against the dark background.
Abhilfe *f.* relief.
abholen to get, collect.
Das Taxi wird mich abholen. The taxi will pick me up.
Abkunft *f.* descent, origin.
ablenken to divert, distract.
ablesen to pick up, read off.
abliefern to deliver.
ABMACHEN to remove, loosen, agree, settle.
Abgemacht! Agreed!
abnehmen to take off, gather, pick up (phone).
Er nimmt seinen Hut ab. He takes off his hat.
Abneigung *f.* dislike, antipathy.
Abort *m.* lavatory.
abräumen to take away, remove.
ABREISE *f.* departure.
eine unvorhergesehene Abreise an unexpected departure.
Absage *f.* refusal.
absagen to refuse, to cancel, call off.
eine Gesellschaft absagen lassen to call off a party.
Falls Sie mir nicht absagen, komme ich. Unless you call it off, I'll come.
Abscheu *m.* aversion, horror.
abscheulich horrible, abominable, nasty.
Das war abscheulich von ihm. It was very nasty of him.
ABSCHIED *m.* departure.
Abschied nehmen to take leave.
Ich werde Abschied von Ihnen nehmen. I am going to leave you.
Den Abschied bekommen to be dismissed.
Der Offizier hat seinen Abschied genommen. The officer has been placed on the retired list.
abschreiben to copy, to deduct.
abseits prep. (gen.) aside, apart, away from.
ABSICHT *f.* intention, purpose, view.
in der Absicht with the intention.
Er tat es in böser Absicht. He did it with a malicious intention.
absichtlich on purpose.
Abstand *m.* distance, interval.
Er nahm Abstand von seiner Erbschaft. He gave up his inheritance.
Absturz *m.* fall, crash.
Er wurde bei einem Flugzeugabsturz getötet. He was killed in a plane crash.
ABTEIL *n.* compartment, division, section.
Abteil erster Klasse *n.* first-class compartment.
Nichtraucherabteil *n.* non-smoking compartment.
Abteilung *f.* department (in a store).
Schuhabteilung *f.* shoe department.
abtrocknen to dry off, wipe.
das Geschirr abtrocknen to dry the dishes.
abwärts downward.
abwechseln to vary, change, alternate.
abwesend absent.
Abwesenheit *f.* absence.
abzahlen to pay off.

abziehen to retain, take off, subtract.
Der Arbeitgeber zieht die Steuer vom Einkommen ab. The employer retains taxes from the salary.
Abzugskanal *m.* sewer.
ach! Ah! Oh!
ACHT eight.
heute in acht Tagen A week from today.
achtmal eight times.
ACHTE eighth.
achten to esteem, regard, respect.
ACHTUNG *f.* esteem.
Achtung! Beware! Attention!
achtungsvoll respectful.
ACHTZEHN eighteen.
ACHTZEHNTE eighteenth.
ACHTZIG eighty.
ACHTZIGSTE eightieth.
ACKER *m.* field, soil.
Ackerbau *m.* agriculture.
ackern to plough.
Ackersmann *m.* ploughman.
addieren to add up.
Adel *m.* nobility, aristocracy.
Ader *f.* vein.
Adjektiv *n.* adjective.
adlig noble.
ADRESSE *f.* address.
Hier ist meine Adresse. Here is my address.
adressieren to address.
Adverb *n.* adverb.
Affe *m.* monkey.
Affekt *m.* excitement.
affektiert affected.
Agent *m.* agent.
ahnen to have a presentiment.
Es ahnt mir Unglück. I have a presentiment of evil.
Ich habe keine Ahnung. I don't have the slightest idea.
ähnlich similar, like.
ähnlich sehen to look alike
Ähnlichkeit *f.* similarity, resemblance.
Akademie *f.* academy, university.
Akten *pl.* deeds, documents.
Aktie *f.* share, stock.
aktiv active.
Akzent *m.* accent, stress.
Alarm *m.* alarm.
Alkohol *m.* alcohol, liquor.
ALL (aller, alle, alles) entire, whole, every, each, any.

all die Leute	everybody.
all und jeder	each and every.
alle Tage	every day.
auf alle Fälle	in any case.
ohne allen Grund	for no reason at all.

ALLEIN alone, single, solitary, apart, lonesome.

Ich bin allein.	I am lonesome.
Sie lebt allein.	She lives alone.

allerart diverse.
allgemein universal.
Alphabet *n.* alphabet.
ALS when, than, as, like.
Als Bismarck starb. When Bismarck died.
Sie ist grösser als ihr Bruder. She is taller than her brother.
als ob as if, as though
Er tut als ob er die Antwort kenne. He acts as if he knew the answer.
so bald als as soon as
ALSO so, thus, in this way.
"Also sprach Zarathustra.." "Thus spoke Zarathustra..."
ALT old, aged, ancient.
alte Sprachen ancient languages (classics)
altehrwürdig venerable.
altgläubig orthodox.

altmodisch old-fashioned.

eine alte Junger an old maid.

ALTER n. age, old age, antiquity.

Mittelalter n. Middle Ages.

älter older, elder, senior.

Altertum n. antiquity.

Altertumshändler m. antique dealer.

älteste oldest.

am (an dem) on, at.

Amerikaner m. —in f. American.

amerikanisch American.

AMT n. office, charge, board.

In compound words, the suffix amt designates a government office:

das Auswärtige Amt the Foreign Office.

Polizeiamt n. police station

Zollamt n. customs.

in Amt und Würden stehen to be a person of position.

amüsant amusing.

AMÜSIEREN to amuse.

sich amüsieren to enjoy oneself.

Ich habe mich in der Gesellschaft sehr amüsiert. I enjoyed myself at the party.

AN 1. prep. (dat. when answering question, Wo?; acc. when answering question, Wohin?, and depending on the idiom).

an die Arbeit gehen to go to work.

an der Arbeit sein to be at work.

an der Donau on the Danube.

an und für sich in itself.

Er starb an seinen Wunden. He died of his wounds

Es ist an mir. It is my turn.

Ich gehe an die Tür. I go to the door.

Ich weiss, was an der Geschichte dran ist. I know what the story is.

soviel an mir liegt as far as I am concerned.

2. separable prefix. (implies movement closer to the speaker, proximity, contact. attraction, climbing, beginning).

Der Hund ist angebunden. The dog is tied.

Der Tag bricht an. The day begins.

Er behielt seine Schuhe an. He kept his shoes on.

Er zieht seine Jacke an. He puts his coat on.

Ich steige langsam den Berg hinan. I climb the mountain slowly.

anbehalten to keep on.

Ich will meinen Mantel anbehalten. I'll keep my coat on.

anbieten to offer, volunteer.

Anblick m. sight, view.

Andenken n. memory, souvenir.

zum Andenken an meine Eltern. In memory of my parents.

ANDER other, another, different, next.

am anderen Morgen the next morning.

anderer Meinung sein to be of a different opinion.

ein andermal another time.

einen Tag um den andern every other day.

etwas anderes another thing, something different.

nichts anderes als nothing but.

unter anderem among other things.

anderenfalls otherwise.

anderseits on the other side.

andeuten to indicate.

Anerbieten n. offer, proposal.

Anfall m. attack, fit.

Herzanfall m. heart attack.

Anfang m. beginning, start.

anfangen (to) begin, start.

von Anfang, bis zu Ende from beginning to end.

Anfrage f. inquiry.

anfragen to inquire.

anfreunden (sich) to become friends.

angemessen suitable, accurate.

Angesicht n. face, countenance.

von Angesicht zu Angesicht face to face.

angesichts considering, in view of.

Angewohnheit f. habit, custom.

angrenzen to border.

Angriff m. attack.

in Angriff nehmen to set about.

Angst f. anxiety.

ängstigen to frighten.

sich ängstigen vor to be afraid of.

sich ängstigen um to feel anxious about.

anhaben to wear, have on.

Ich kann ihm nichts anhaben. I cannot find any weak spot in him.

anhalten to stop, pull up.

anhören to listen to.

Anker m. anchor.

anklagen to accuse.

ankleiden to dress.

anklopfen to knock at.

ANKOMMEN to arrive, approach, reach.

Es kommt darauf an, ob Sie Zeit haben. It depends on whether you have time.

Wir müssen es darauf ankommen lassen. We have to take a chance on it.

ANKUNFT f. arrival.

anmelden to announce, notify, report.

Anmut f. grace, charm.

anmutig graceful, charming.

Annahme f. acceptance, assumption.

annehmen to accept, receive, assume, take care of.

anpassen to fit, suit, adapt.

anprobieren to try on.

anrechnen to charge.

zu viel anrechnen to overcharge.

Ich rechne Ihnen Ihre Hilfe hoch an. I appreciate your help very much.

Anrede f. address.

anreden to address, accost.

Der Schutzmann redete mich an. The policeman called me.

anregen to incite, stimulate, excite.

Ansage f. announcement, notification.

ansagen to announce, notify.

anschauen to look at, contemplate.

anschaulich evident, clear.

Anschrift f. address (letter).

anschuldigen to accuse.

ANSEHEN to look at, consider, regard.

dem Ansehen nach to all appearances.

im Ansehen stehen to be esteemed.

vom Ansehen kennen to know by sight.

Ansicht f. view, sight, opinion.

nach meiner Ansicht according to my opinion.

Ansichtskarte f. picture postcard.

Ansprache f. speech, address.

Ar spruch m. claim, pretension.

Anspruch haben auf to be entitled to.

Anstand m. manners, decency, etiquette.

ohne Anstand without hesitation.

anständig decent, respectable.

ANSTATT (statt)

1. prep. (gen.) instead of; also conj.

Statt eines Regenschirmes nahm er einen Stock. Instead of an umbrella, he took a stick.

Anstatt seine Arbeit zu tun, geht er spazieren. Instead of doing his work, he takes a walk.

anstrengen (sich) to strain, exert.

anstrengend tiring, trying, exacting.

ANTWORT f. answer.

ANTWORTEN to answer.

anvertrauen to entrust, confide.

Anwalt m. lawyer, attorney.

anwesend present.

Anwesenheit f. presence.

Anzahl f. quantity, amount.

anzahlen to pay on account.

Anzeige f. notice, advertisement.

anzeigen to notify, report, announce.

Ich halte es für angezeigt. I consider it advisable.

ANZUG m. suit, dress.

anzüglich suggestive, personal.

Anzüglichkeit f. suggestive remark.

anzünden to light the fire, set fire to.

APFEL m. apple.

in den sauern Apfel beissen to swallow a bitter pill.

APFELSINE f. orange.

Apotheke f. pharmacy.

Apotheker m. pharmacist.

Apparat m. apparatus, appliance, telephone.

Bleiben Sie am Apparat! Hold the wire!

Appetit m. appetite.

applaudieren to applaud.

APRIL m. April.

Äquator m. equator.

ARBEIT f. work, job.

ARBEITEN to work, manufacture.

arbeitsfähig able-bodied

arbeits unfähig unfit for work

Arbeiter m. (—in, f.) worker, laborer.

Arbeiterstand m. working class.

Arbeitgeber m. employer.

Arbeitnehmer m. employee.

arbeitsam industrious, diligent.

Architekt m. architect.

Architektur f. architecture.

arg bad, mischievous.

Sie dachte an nichts Arges. She meant no harm.

Ärger m. Annoyance, anger, worry.

ärgerlich annoying, angry.

ärgern to annoy, irritate, bother.

Argument n. argument.

Aristokrat m. aristocrat.

Aristokratie f. aristocracy.

aristokratisch aristocratic.

ARM m. arm.

ARM poor

Armband n. bracelet.

Armbanduhr f. wrist watch.

Ärmel m. sleeve.

Armlehne f. arm of chair.

Armut f. poverty.

Arrest m. arrest.

ART f. kind, manner, way, type.

artig good, well-behaved.

Artikel m. article.

Arznei f. medicine (drug).

Arzneikunde f. pharmacy (profession of).

Ast m. branch (tree).

Atem m. breath, suspense.

Dieser Kriminalroman halt uns in Atem. This detective story keeps us in suspense.

atemholen to take breadth.

atemlos breathless.

atemraubend breath-taking.

Der Film war atemraubend. The movie was breath-taking.

Athlet m. athlete.

atmen to breathe.

AUCH also, too even.

was auch whatever.

wer auch whoever.

wo auch wherever.

Was auch geschieht, Sie sind verantwortlich.
Whatever happens, you are responsible.

Wer auch kommen mag, ich bin nicht zu Hause.
Whoever comes, I am not home.

Wo auch immer er auftauchen mag, man wird
ihn erkennen.
Wherever he appears, he will be recognized.

AUF 1. prep. (dat. when answering question,
Wo?; acc. when answering question, Wohin?,
and depending on the idiom) on, upon, at, in.
to, for, during.

Er kommt auf die Strasse hinab. He comes
down to the street.

Ich kaufe Gemüse auf dem Markt. I buy
vegetables at the market.

Ich traf sie auf dem Ball. I met her at the ball.

Ich fahre auf das Land. I drive to the country.

Sie wohnen auf oliesem Schloss. They
live in that castle.

Die Jäger gehen auf die Jagd. The hunters go
hunting.

Der Tag folgt auf die Nacht. The day follows
the night.

alle bis auf einen all except one.

auf der Rückfahrt von Wien during the return
from Vienna.

auf Deutsch in German.

auf einmal suddenly.

auf keinen Fall in no case.

auf Wiedersehen! Good-bye!

Liebe auf den ersten Blick love at first sight.

2. adv. up, upwards.

auf und ab up and down.

3. Conj. auf dass in order to.

auf dass nicht for fear that.

4. Separable prefix (implies motion upward or
outward, opening, completion).

Ich setze meinen Hut auf. I put my hat on.

Die Sonne geht auf. The sun is rising.

Bitte, machen Sie das Fenster auf. Please
open the window.

aufbewahren to keep, preserve, stock.

Aufbewahrung f. preservation, storage.

aufbrauchen to use up.

aufeinander one on top of the other.

Aufenthalt m. stay, residence.

aufessen to eat up.

Auffassung f. conception, interpretation.

Aufgabe f. task, duty, problem.

aufgeben to commission, order, lose, give up,
resign, check, send.

die Hoffnung aufgeben to lose hope.

ein Telegramm aufgeben to send a telegram.

aufhängen to hang up.

aufheben to pick up, rise, abolish.

aufheitern to cheer up.

aufklären to clear, explain.

Aufklärung f. explanation.

aufmachen to open, unlock, undo.

Aufmachung f. make up.

aufmerken to pay attention, attend.

aufmerksam attentive.

Aufmerksamkeit f. attention.

Aufnahme f. taking up, admission, enrollment,
snapshot.

aufnahmefähig receptive.

Aufnahmeprüfung f. entrance examination.

aufnehmen to lift, take up, admit, photograph,
record (a voice).

aufpassen to adapt, fix, pay attention.

Aufgepasst! Attention!

Aufpasser m. watcher, spy.

aufräumen to arrange, put in order, clean.

aufrecht upright, straight.

aufregen to stir up, excite.

aufregend exciting, seditious.

Aufregung f. excitement, agitation.

Aufsatz m. main piece, top, ornament,
article (newspaper).

aufschliessen to unlock.

Aufschluss m. opening up, explanation, information.

Aufschluss über eine Sache geben to give
some information about something.

aufschreiben to write down.

Aufsehen n. sensation, attention.

Er erregt Aufsehen. He attracts attention.

Aufstand m. tumult, revolt.

AUFSTEHEN stand up, rise, get up.

aufstehen gegen to rebel against.

Stehen Sie auf! Get up!

aufstellen to set up, erect, draw up, nominate.

Eine Behauptung aufstellen to make
a statement.

Auftrag m. commission, instruction.

im Auftrage von by order of.

einen Auftrag ausführen to execute
a commission.

auftragen to carry up, serve up, draw, charge.

Er hat mir viele Grüsse an Sie aufgetragen.
He sends you his regards. ("He charged me
with many greetings for you.")

aufwachen to awake.

aufwachsen to grow up.

Aufwand m. expenditure, expense.

aufwärts upwards.

Er schwimmt den Fluss aufwärts. He swims
upstream.

aufwecken to awaken.

aufziehen to bring up, raise, wind a watch, pull
up, tease.

Einen aufziehen to make fun of somebody.

Aufzug m. procession, parade, attire, outfit, act
(play), elevator.

AUGE n. eye.

Er versuchte mir Sand in die Augen zu
streuen. He tried to deceive me ("throw
dust into my eyes").

gute Augen haben to have good eyesight.

grosse Augen machen to look very surprised.

Ich habe kein Auge zugemacht. I did not
sleep a wink.

unter vier Augen privately ("between
four eyes").

Wir haben ihn aus den Augen verloren. We
lost sight of him.

Augenarzt m. oculist.

Augenblick m. moment.

im Augenblick for the moment.

augenblicklich immediately.

Augenbraue f. eyebrow.

Augenlid n. eyelid.

Augenwimper f. eyelash.

AUGUST m. August.

Auktion f. auction sale.

AUS 1. prep. (dat.) out, out of, for, from, in, upon.

Aus den Augen, aus dem Sinn. Out of sight,
out of mind.

Er kommt aus dem Theater. He comes out of
the theater.

Er hat es aus Liebe getan. He did it for love.

Meine Uhr ist aus Gold. My watch is made of
gold.

Sie stammt aus Paris. She is a native of
Paris.

2. adv. out, over, up.

von hier aus from here.

von mir aus for my part.

3. separable prefix. Implies the idea of
motion out (in this case also combines with
hin or her), achievement.

Die Vorstellung ist aus. The performance
is over.

Ich gehe aus dem Speisezimmer hinaus. I go
out of the dinning room.

ausbessern to repair.

ausbilden to form, develop, cultivate, educate,
train.

ausbleiben to stay away, fail to appear, escape.

Ihre Strafe wird nicht ausbleiben. You will
not escape punishment.

Ausblick m. outlook, prospect.

ausbrechen to break out, vomit.

in Tränen ausbrechen to burst into tears.

Ausbruch m. outbreak, eruption, escape.

Ausdauer f. perseverance, assiduity.

ausdauern to hold out, outlast, endure.

ausdehnen to expand, prolong.

ausdenken to invent, conceive, imagine.

Ausdruck m. expression, phrase.

ausdrücken to squeeze, express.

sich kurz und klar ausdrücken to express
oneself briefly and to the point.

auseinander apart, separately.

ausführen to take out, export, realize.

ausführlich adj. detailed, full; in detail, fully.

Erzählen Sie mir alles ausführlich. Tell me
everything in detail.

ausfüllen to fill out, stuff.

Ausgabe f. delivery, edition, issue, publication.

Ausgang m. way out, exit, end.

ausgeben to give out, deliver, issue, deal (cards).

ausgehen to go out, come out, run out, proceed,
start from, end.

frei ausgehen to go free.

ihm geht die Geduld aus. He is losing his
patience.

Wie wird diese Sache ausgehen? How will
this matter end?

AUSGEZEICHNET excellent, distinguished.

ausgleichen to make even, equalize, settle,
arrange, compensate.

aushalten to bear, suffer, support, hold out, last.

Aushang m. notice (posted); poster.

aushängen to hang out, post a notice.

Aushilfe f. aid (temporary); assistant.

auskleiden to undress.

auskommen to manage, get along.

Es ist schwer mit ihm auszukommen. It is
difficult to get along with him.

Ich komme nicht mit dem Papier aus. I can't
manage with the paper. (I don't have enough
of it.)

Auskunft f. information, intelligence.

Auskunftei f. information bureau.

auslassen to leave out, omit, let out.

Auslese f. choice, selection.

auslesen to select, choose, read through.

ausmachen to put out, constitute, come to,
settle, amount.

Das macht nichts aus. It does not matter.

Ausmass n. measurement, scale, proportion.

mit solchem Ausmass to such an extent.

ausmessen to measure, survey.

Ausnahme f. exception.

ohne Ausnahme without exception.

auspacken to unpack.

Ausrede f. excuse, pretense.

ausreden to finish speaking, excuse.

einem etwas ausreden to dissuade somebody
from something.

ausrichten to execute, deliver, obtain.

Haben Sie es ihm ausgerichtet? Did you give
him the message?

Ausruf m. cry, exclamation.

ausrufen to cry out, admonish, proclaim.

ausruhen to rest.

Aussage f. statement, assertion, declaration,
evidence.

aussagen to affirm, declare, give evidence.

ausschalten to cut out, switch off.

Schalten Sie den Motor aus! Switch off
the motor!
ausscheiden to separate, withdraw.
ausschiffen to disembark, land.
ausschliessen to exclude.
ausschliesslich exclusive.
ausschmücken to decorate, adorn.
ausschneiden to cut out, snipe.
AUSSEHEN to look out, appear.
Aussehen n. look, air.
aussen on the outside, abroad, without.
von aussen from the outside.
aussenden to send out.
AUSSER 1. prep. (dat.) out of, out, besides.
ausser der Jahreszeit out of season
ausser sich beside oneself.
2. with gen. out of.
ausser Landes out of the country.
3. conj. except, unless, but.
Ausser Sonntags, gehe ich jeden Tag in
die Schule. I go to school every day except
Sunday.
ausserdem besides, moreover.
aussetzen to set out, put out, offer, bequeath.
auszusetzen haben to find fault with.
Aussicht f. view, prospect.
aussinnen to plan, plot, scheme.
aussöhnen to reconcile.
aussondern to separate, select.
Aussprache f. pronunciation, accent.
aussprechen to pronounce, express.
aussuchen to seek out, search.
Austausch m. exchange.
austauschen to exchange.
Auster f. oyster.
austragen to deliver, distribute.
austreten to tread under, trample, retire.
Ausverkauf m. clearance sale.
ausverkaufen to sell out, clear off (a shop).
Auswahl f. choice, assortment, selection.
auswählen to choose, select.
Auswanderer m. emigrant.
auswandern to emigrate.
Auswanderung f. emigration.
auswärtig foreign, abroad.
Ausweg m. way out.
ausweichen to avoid, evade, shun.
Ausweis m. certificate, document, identity card.
ausziehen to undress, pull out, extract,
move, remove.
Auszug m. departure, extract, removal.
Auto n. automobile, car.
Autobahn n. parkway.
Autobus m. bus.
Axt f. axe.

B

Bach m. brook.
BACKEN to bake, fry.
Bäcker m. baker.
Backobst n. dried fruit.
Backofen m. oven.
Backpulver n. baking powder.
BAD n. bath, spa.
Badeanstalt f. baths, swimming pool.
Badeanzug m. bathing suit.
Badehose f. bathing shorts.
Bademantel m. bathrobe.
Badeort m. spa.
Badetuch n. bath towel.
Badewanne f. bathtub.
Badezimmer n. bathroom.
BAHN f. track, road, way, railway.
Bahnarbeiter m. railway man.
Bahnbeamte m. railroad official.
Bahngleis n. track.
BAHNHOF m. station.

Bahnsteig m. platform.
Bahnübergang m. railroad crossing.
Balance f. balance, equilibrium.
balancieren to balance.
BALD soon, shortly.
bald. ., bald. .. sometimes. . ., sometimes. . .
bald darauf soon after.
Balkon m. balcony.
Ball m. ball, dance.
Ballett n. ballet.
Ballon m. balloon.
Band n. ribbon.
Bande f. band, gang.
bändigen to tame, to break.
Bandmass n. tape measure.
BANK f. 1. bench, seat.
durch die Bank all, without exception.
auf die lange Bank schieben to postpone,
delay.
2. bank.
Geld auf der Bank haben to have money
in the bank.
Bankanweisung f. check.
Bankbeamte m. bank clerk.
BAR bare, naked, devoid of.
barfuss barefoot.
Bär m. bear.
Bargeld n. cash.
bar zahlen to pay cash.
barmherzig merciful.
Barmherzigkeit f. mercy.
Baron m. (—in, f.) Baron (ess).
Bart m. beard, whiskers.
BAU m. building, construction, edifice, frame.
Bauch m. belly, stomach.
BAUEN to build, construct, cultivate.
Luftschlösser bauen to build castles
in the air.
Bauer m. peasant.
Bauernhof m. farm.
Bauernvolk n. countryfolk.
baufällig dilapidated.
BAUM m. tree, pole.
Baumschule f. nursery (trees).
Baumwolle f. cotton.
Baustein n. brick.
beabsichtigen to intend.
beachten to observe, notice.
Beachtung f. consideration, attention.
beachtenswert noteworthy.
Beamte m. official, civil servant.
Zollbeamte m. customs officer.
beängstigen to alarm.
beanspruchen to claim, demand.
beanstanden to object, reject.
beantworten to answer, reply.
beaufsichtigen to supervise.
beben to tremble.
vor Angst beben to tremble with fear.
Becher m. cup, goblet, dice box.
bedacht thoughful, considerate.
bedanken to thank.
Bedarf m. need, requirement.
bedauerlich deplorable, regrettable.
bedecken to cover.
Der Himmel ist bedeckt the sky
is overcast.
bedenken to think, think over, reflect, ponder.
sich eines andern bedenken to change one's
mind.
bedenklich doubtful.
Bedenkzeit f. time for reflection.
Bedienung f. service.
einschliesslich der Bedienung service
included.
bedürfen to need, require.
Bedürfnis n. need, want necessity.
beeindrucken to impress.

beerdigen to bury.
Beerdigung f. funeral.
befassen to occupy.
Er befasst sich mit Politik. He is in politics.
Befehl m. order, command.
befehlen to order, command.
befestigen to fasten, fortify.
befolgen to obey.
befreien to free, liberate.
Befreier m. liberator.
Befreiung f. liberation.
befreunden to befriend.
sich befreunden mit to become friends with.
befriedigen to satisfy, content.
befriedigend satisfying.
Befriedigung f. satisfaction, gratification.
Befund m. state, condition, report.
befürchten to apprehend, fear.
Befürchtung f. apprehension, fear.
befürworten to recommend.
begabt gifted.
begeben (sich) to set about.
begegnen to meet, encounter.
begeistern to inspire, fill with enthusiasm.
begeistert inspired, enthusiastic.
Begeisterung f. inspiration, enthusiasm.
Beginn m. beginning.
BEGINNEN to begin, start.
beglaubigen to attest, certify.
begleiten to accompany.
nach Hause begleiten to see (someone) home.
begründen to found, to prove.
Behaglichkeit f. comfort.
behalten to keep, retain, remember.
Behalten Sie das Kleingeld! Keep the change!
behandeln to handle, deal with.
beharren to persist, remain firm.
beharren auf to insist on.
behaupten to maintain, assert, affirm.
Behelf m. help, expedient.
behelfen (sich) to manage, do without.
BEI 1. prep. (dat.) at, by, near, with, because of,
in case of.
bei der Hand by hand.
Bei Feuer, müssen wir die Feuerwehr rufen. In
case of a fire, we must call the fire department.
Bei ihrem Charakter wird sie unglücklich
werden. With (because of) her character, she
will be unhappy.
bei Tage by day.
bei weitem by far.
beim Metzger at the butcher's.
Er arbeitet bei Licht. He works by light.
Hast du Geld bei dir? Do you have any money
on you?
Ich kaufe meine Kleider bei Engels. I buy my
clothes at Engels.
Meine Schwester wohnt bei mir. My sister lives
with me.

Beichte f. confession.
beichten to confess.
BEIDE both.
wir beide both of us.
einer von beiden one of the two.
keiner von beiden neither of them.
beiderseits on both sides, mutually.
BEIFALL m. approval, approbation, applause.
beifolgend herewith, enclosed.
beiläufig accidental, casual; incidentally.
beilegen to add, enclose.
Beileid n. sympathy.
Beileid bezeigen to console somebody.
beim (bei dem) at, by.
BEIN n. leg, bone.
sich kein Bein ausreissen to take it easy.

Er ist immer auf den Beinen. He's always on his feet.

beinahe nearly, almost.

beipflichten to agree with, assent to.

beisammen together.

beiseite aside, apart.

BEISPIEL n. example.

zum Beispiel for example.

Das ist ein schlechtes Beispiel. This is a bad example.

beispiellos unheard of.

beissen to bite.

Der Hund beisst nicht. The dog does not bite.

beistehen to help, stand by.

beistimmen to agree with.

Beitrag m. contribution, subscription.

bejahen to answer in the affirmative, assent, accept.

bejammern to lament.

bejammernswert deplorable, lamentable.

bekämpfen to combat, fight, struggle.

BEKANNT well-known, acquainted.

bekannt machen mit to introduce to.

Bekannte m. acquaintance, friend.

Bekanntmachung f. publication, announcement, notice.

bekennen to confess, admit, profess.

sich schuldig bekennen to plead guilty.

beklagen to complain, lament.

BEKOMMEN to get, receive, catch, agree with.

Das ist nicht mehr zu bekommen. You can't get that any more.

Es bekommt mir nicht. It does not agree with me.

bekräftigen to confirm, corroborate.

belächeln to smile at.

belachen to laugh at.

belästigen to molest, trouble.

beleben to animate, revive.

Beleg m. proof, evidence, illustration.

BELEGEN to cover, reserve.

Ich möchte einen Platz belegen. I want to reserve a seat.

belegte Brötchen sandwiches.

eine Vorlesung belegen to enroll for a course.

belehren to enlighten, instruct.

eines Besseren belehren to correct.

beleidigen to offend, insult.

beliefern to supply.

belohnen to reward.

Belohnung f. reward.

belügen to lie (falsify).

belustigen to amuse, entertain.

Belustigung f. amusement.

bemerkbar noticeable, perceptible.

bemerken to notice, observe, remark.

bemerkenswert noticeable, noteworthy.

Bemerkung f. remark, observation.

bemitleiden to pity, be sorry for.

bemitleidenswert deplorable.

benachrichtigen to inform, advise.

Benachrichtigung f. information, advice.

benachteiligen to prejudice.

Benachteiligung f. prejudice, injury.

benehmen to behave.

Benimm dich nicht wie ein kleines Kind! Don't behave like a child!

beneiden to envy.

benommen confused, dizzy.

benötigen to require.

benutzen to use, employ, utilize.

beobachten to observe, watch.

heimlich beobachten to shadow.

BEQUEM suitable, convenient, lazy.

Sei nicht so bequem! Don't be so lazy!

bequemen to condescend, comply, submit.

Bequemlichkeit f. convenience.

beraten to advise.

Berater m. adviser.

beratschlagen to deliberate.

berechnen to calculate, estimate.

bereden to talk over, persuade.

Beredsamkeit f. eloquence.

Bereich m. & n. reach, range, area, zone.

BEREIT ready, prepared.

bereit halten to keep ready.

bereitwillig willing, ready.

Bereitwilligkeit f. willingness.

bereuen to repent, regret.

BERG m. mountain, hill.

über alle Berge sein to be out of the woods.

Mir standen die Haare zu Berge. My hair stood on end.

Bergmann m. miner.

berichten to report.

berichtigen to correct, amend, settle (a bill).

Berichtigung f. correction, amendment.

berücksichtigen to consider.

Berücksichtigung f. consideration, regard.

BERUF m. profession, occupation.

beruflich professional.

berufstätig working.

beruhigen to quiet, calm.

Beruhigung f. reassurance, comfort.

BERÜHMT famous, celebrated.

Berühmtheit f. fame, celebrity.

besänftigen to soften, appease, soothe.

beschädigen to damage, injure, harm.

beschäftigen to occupy, engage, employ.

Beschäftigung f. occupation.

beschäftigungslos unemployed, out of work.

Bescheid m. answer, information.

Bescheid geben to inform.

Ich habe ihm gehörig Bescheid gesagt. I told him off.

bescheiden modest, moderate.

Bescheidenheit f. modesty.

bescheinen to shine upon.

bescheinigen to certify, attest.

Bescheinigung f. certificate, receipt.

beschleunigen to hasten, accelerate.

beschränken to limit, confine, restrict.

Beschränkung f. limitation, restriction.

beschreiben to write upon, describe.

Beschreibung f. description.

beschuldigen to accuse.

Beschuldigung f. accusation.

Beschwerde f. hardship, trouble, complaint.

beschweren (sich) to complain.

Beschwerdebüro n. complaint department.

beschwichtigen to calm, pacify, appease.

Besen m. broom.

besetzen to trim, occupy, set.

Es ist alles besetzt! All seats are occupied!

Besetzt! Occupied! Busy!

Besetzung f. occupation, cast.

Die Besetzung ist aussergewöhnlich gut. The cast is outstanding.

besichtigen to view, inspect, visit.

Besichtigung f. view, inspection.

besiegen to conquer, beat, defeat.

besinnen to consider, reflect.

sich eines Besseren besinnen to think better of.

besinnlich contemplative, thoughtful.

Besitz m. possession, property, estate.

besorgen to take care of, fetch, procure, provide.

Besorgnis f. fear, alarm.

Besorgung f. care, management.

Besorgungen machen to go shopping.

besprechen to discuss, talk over, criticize, review.

BESSER better.

umso besser so much the better.

bessern to improve, recover.

sich bessern to improve oneself.

Besserung f. recovery, improvement.

Gute Besserung! I hope you will get well soon!

best(er-es) best.

beständig constant, permanent, steady; constantly, all the time.

Beständigkeit f. constancy, stability.

bestätigen to confirm, ratify.

bestechen to bribe, corrupt.

bestechlich corruptible.

Bestechung f. corruption.

Besteck n. one setting of silver.

bestellen to arrange, order, tell, cultivate.

Waren bestellen to order goods.

zu sich bestellen to send for.

BESTIMMEN to decide, fix, intend, define, induce.

bestimmen über to dispose of.

bestimmt! agreed!

Bestimmtheit f. certainty, precision.

bestrafen to punish.

Bestrafung f. punishment.

BESUCH m. visit, company, attendance.

BESUCHEN to visit, attend.

Besucher m. visitor, spectator, audience.

beteiligen to give a share, take part, take an interest.

beteiligt sein to participate.

Beteiligung f. share, participation.

betonen to stress, accent, emphasize.

Betonung f. stress, emphasis.

beträchtlich considerable.

betreffen to concern.

was mich betrifft so far as I am concerned.

betreten to tread on.

Betreten des Rasens verboten! Keep off the grass!

Betrieb m. management, plant, factory.

in Betrieb sein to be working.

ausser Betrieb not working, closed

in Betrieb setzen to set in motion.

betrinken to get drunk.

betrüben to grieve, distress.

Betrug m. deception, fraud, swindle.

betrügen to deceive, defraud, trick.

BETT n. bed.

das Bett hüten to be confined in bed.

früh zu Bett gehen to go to bed early.

Bettdecke f. blanket, bedspread.

betteln to beg.

Bettlaken n. sheet.

Bettler m. beggar.

Bettwäsche f. bed linen.

beugen to bend, bow.

beunruhigen to disturb, alarm, upset.

beurlauben to grant leave, take leave.

beurlaubt absent on leave.

Beutel m. bag, purse.

bevollmächtigen to empower, authorize.

BEVOR before.

bewachen to watch over.

bewältigen to master.

bewegen to move, stir.

Beweggrund m. motive.

Was war der Beweggrund des Verbrechens? What was the motive of the crime?

beweglich movable, mobile, quick, lively.

BEWEGUNG f. movement, agitation, motion.

Einer politischen Bewegung angehören to belong to a political party.

Beweis m. proof, evidence.

beweisen to prove, demonstrate.

Beweisführung f. demonstration.

bewerben to apply for, compete.

Bewerber m. applicant, candidate.
Bewerbung f. application, courtship.
bewilligen to consent, concede.
bewusst conscious.
    sich einer Sache bewusst sein to be
    conscious or aware of something.
bewusstlos unconscious.
BEZAHLEN to pay.
    sich bezahlt machen to pay for itself (be
    lucrative).
bezaubernd charming.
bezichtigen to charge with.
Bezug m. covering, cover, case.
    in Bezug auf in regard to.
    Bezug nehmen auf to refer to.
    unter Bezugnahme auf with reference to.
Bibel f. Bible.
Bibliothek f. library.
Bibliothekar m. librarian.
Biene f. bee.
Bier n. beer.
BIETEN to offer.
    sich alles bieten lassen to put up with
    everything.
BILD n. image, picture, illustration, portrait,
    likeness.
BILDEN to form, shape, educate.
    Der Präsident hat ein neues Kabinett
    gebildet. The president has formed a new
    cabinet.
    die bildenden Künste fine arts.
Bildseite f. face, head (coin).
Bildung f. formation, constitution.
billig just, reasonable, fair, moderate.
binden to bind, tie.
BIS until, as far as, about.
    zwei bis drei Pfund. About two or
    three pounds.
    bis an (acc.) up to.
    bis in alle Ewigkeit till the end of time.
    bis auf (acc.) except for.
    Mir gefällt der Film bis auf das Ende. I like
    the film except for the ending.
    alle bis auf einen all except one.
    bis auf weiteres until further notice.
    bis zu (dat.) (down) to.
    von dem Kopf bis zu den Füssen from head
    to foot.
    bis jetzt so far.
    bisher till now.
    bisweilen sometimes.
Bischof m. bishop.
bisschen a bit, a little, a while.
    Das ist ein bisschen stark. That's going a
    bit too far.
    Er kam ein bisschen spät. He came a little late.
Bissen m. bite, mouthful.
Bitte f. request, prayer.
BITTE please. bitte, bitte schön, bitte sehr.
    (In response to a request: Here you are.
    In response to thanks: You are welcome; don't
    mention it.)
    Wie, bitte? I beg your pardon?
BITTEN to ask, beg, implore.
    Ich bitte um Entschuldigung. I beg your
    pardon, I am sorry.
bitter bitter.
blamieren to expose to ridicule.
    sich blamieren to make a fool of oneself.
BLATT n. leaf, petal, blade, sheet.
    sich kein Blatt vor den Mund nehmen to
    speak plainly.
Blattern f. smallpox.
blättern to leaf through the pages of a book.
Blatternimpfung f. smallpox vaccination.

BLAU blue.
Blech n. tin.
Blei n. lead.
BLEIBEN to stay, remain, keep, last.
    bleiben lassen to leave alone.
    Das bleibt unter uns. That's between you
    and me.
    Es bleibt dabei Agreed.
    sich gleich bleiben to remain the same.
    stehen bleiben to stop, stand still.
bleibend permanent, lasting.
bleich pale, faded, faint.
bleichen to bleach.
Bleistift m. pencil.
blenden to blind, dazzle.
BLICK m. glance, look, gaze.
    auf den ersten Blick at first sight.
    Er warf ihm einen bösen Blick zu. He gave
    him a dirty look.
blind blind, false.
    ein blinder Alarm a false alarm.
Blindheit f. blindness.
blinken to glitter, glimpse, twinkle, signal.
Blitz m. lightening, flash.
blitzen to lighten, flash, sparkle.
Block m. block, log, pad, stocks.
blond blond, fair.
BLOSS bare, naked, uncovered; merely, only.
    Ich tue es bloss Ihnen zu gefallen. I am only
    doing it to please you.
blühen to bloom.
BLUME f. flower.
    Lasst Blumen sprechen! Say it with flowers!
Blumenkohl m. cauliflower.
Bluse f. blouse.
BLUT n. blood, race, parentage.
blutarm anemic.
Blutdruck m. blood pressure.
bluten to bleed.
Blutprobe f. blood-test.
Blutvergiftung f. blood-poisoning.
Boden m. floor, ground, soil, attic.
Bogen m. bow, curve, arch.
BOHNE f. bean.
    grüne Bohnen string beans.
    weisse Bohnen dried beans.
Bombardement n. bombardment.
bombardieren to bomb.
Bombe f. bomb.
    Atombombe f. atomic bomb.
Bonbon m. & n. candy.
BOOT n. boat.
    Bootsfahrt f. boatride.
Börse f. purse, stock exchange.
Börsenmakler m. stockbroker.
bösartig ill-natured, wicked, malicious.
BÖSE bad, angry, evil.
boshaft malicious, mischievous.
Bote m. messenger.
Botschaft f. news.
Botschafter m. ambassador.
boxen to box.
Brand m. burning, fire, conflagration.
    in Brand geraten to catch fire.
Brandschaden m. damage by fire.
BRATEN m. roast.
    Brathuhn n. roast chicken.
    Bratkartoffeln pl. fried potatoes.
    Bratapfel m. baked apple.
BRATEN to roast, grill, fry.
Brauch m. usage, use, custom.
brauchbar useful, practicable.
BRAUCHEN to use, employ, need.
    Wie lange werden Sie noch brauchen? How
    much more time will it take you?

Brauhaus n. brewery, tavern.
BRAUN brown.
Brause f. shower, douche, spray.
brausen to storm, rage, roar, rush.
    sich abbrausen to take a shower.
Braut f. fiancee.
    Brautführer m. best man.
    Brautjungfer, f. bridesmaid.
    Brautkleid n. wedding dress.
    Brautpaar n. engaged couple.
Bräutigam m. bridegroom.
brav good, honest, excellent.
BRECHEN to break, pick.
    Er spricht ein gebrochenes Deutsch. He
    speaks broken German.
BREIT broad, wide, flat.
    weit und breit high and low.
Breite f. breadth, width, latitude.
Bremse f. brake.
bremsen to put the brakes on.
BRENNEN to burn, brand, bake, roast.
    darauf brennen to be anxious.
    Es brennt in der Stadt. There is a fire in town.
Brett n. board, plank, shelf, stage.
    am schwarzen Brett on the board.
BRIEF m. letter.
Briefkasten m. letter-box.
Briefmappe f. attaché case.
Briefmarke f. stamp.
Briefpapier n. stationery.
Brieftasche f. wallet, pocket-book.
Briefträger m. mailman.
Briefumschlag m. envelope.
Brille f. glasses.
BRINGEN to bring, fetch, carry, put, take.
    dazu bringen to induce to.
    Er hat sich ums Leben gebracht. He's
    committed suicide.
    es zu etwas bringen to achieve something.
    Ich werde das in Ordnung bringen. I'll
    straighten that out.
    um etwas bringen to deprive of.
britisch British.
BROT n. bread.
    Brötchen roll.
    sein Brot verdienen to earn one's living.
Brötchen n. roll.
Bruch m. break, fracture, fraction.
Bruchteil m. fraction.
BRÜCKE f. bridge (also dental).
    Er hat alle Brücken hinter sich abgebrochen.
    He has burnt his bridges behing him.
BRUDER m. brother.
    Bruderschaft f. fraternity.
Brunnen m. spring, well, fountain.
Brust f. breast, chest, bosom.
Bube m. boy, jack of cards.
BUCH n. book.
Buchdeckel m. cover, binding.
Buchführung f. bookkeeping.
Buchhaltung f. bookkeeping.
Buchhändler m. bookseller.
Buchhandlung f. bookshop.
Büchse f. can.
Buchstabe m. letter, character.
Buchumschlag m. jacket (book).
Bügelbrett n. ironing board.
Bügeleisen n. iron (for pressing).
bügeln to press
Bühne f. stage, platform.
Bund m. league, confederation.
Bündel m. bundle.
bunt colored, lively, gay.
    Das ist mir zu bunt. I'm fed up with it.

Burg *f.* castle, citadel.
Bürge *f.* bail.
bürgen to guarantee, vouch for.
Bürger *m.* citizen, townsman.
Bürgerkrieg *m.* civil war.
Bürgermeister *m.* mayor.
Bürgersteig *m.* pavement.
BÜRO *n.* office.
Bürobote *m.* office boy.
bürokratisch bureaucratic.
Bursch *m.* youth, lad, fellow.
Burschenschaft *f.* students' association.
Bürste *f.* brush.
bürsten to brush.
Busch *m.* bush.
Busse *f.* penitence, repentance.
    Busse tun to do penance.
büssen to suffer for, expiate.
Büste *f.* bust.
Büstenhalter *m.* brassiere.
BUTTER *f.* butter.
Butterbrot *n.* slice of bread and butter.

C

Café *n.* café.
Cello *n.* cello.
Cellist *m.* cellist.
Champagner *m.* champagne.
Charakter *m.* character, disposition.
charakteristisch characteristic.
Chauffeur *m.* chauffeur.
Chef *m.* head, boss, chief.
Chemie *f.* chemistry.
chemisch chemical.
Chinese *m.* Chinese (person).
chinesisch Chinese.
Chirurg *m.* surgeon.
Chor *m.* choir, chorus.
Choral *m.* chorale.
Chorgesang *m.* choir singing.
Choristin *f.* chorus-girl.
Chorknabe *m.* choir-boy.
Christ *m.* Christian.
Christenheit *f.* Christendom.
Christentum *f.* Christianity.
Chronik *f.* chronicle.
Cousin *m.* (Vetter *m.*) cousin (man).
Cousine *f.* (Kusine) cousin (woman).
Creme *m.* cream (cosmetic).

D

DA 1. *adv.* there, here.
    2. *conj.* when, because, as, since.
    da sein to be present.
    da stehen to stand near, stand by.
DABEI near, near by, close to, moreover.
    dabei bleibt es there the matter ends.
dableiben to stay, remain.
Dach *n.* roof.
    unter Dach und Fach safe.
Dachkammer *f.* attic.
DADURCH through it, by it, thereby.
    dadurch dass through the fact that.
    Er ist dadurch berühmt geworden. That made
    him famous.
DAFÜR for that, for it, instead of it.
    dafür sein to be in favor of.
    Ich kann nichts dafür. It is not my fault.
DAGEGEN 1. *adv.* against it.
    nichts dagegen haben to have no objection.
    2. *conj.* on the other hand.
DAHEIM at home.
DAHER from there.
    Ich komme gerade daher. I am just coming
    from there.

DAHIN to there.
    bis dahin by then.
    Ich gehe sofort dahin. I am going there
    right now.
dahinten behind.
damalig then, of that time.
Dame *f.* lady, queen (cards), checkers.
    eine Partie Dame spielen to play a game of
    checkers.
DAMIT 1. *adv.* with it, by it.
    Was wollte er damit sagen? What does he mean
    by that?
    2. *conj.* so that, in order to.
    Ich sage es noch einmal damit Sie es nicht
    vergessen. I say it once more so that you won't
    forget it.
    damit nicht for fear that.
Dämmerlicht *n.* dusk.
Dämmerung *f.* twilight, dawn.
Dampf *m.* vapor, steam.
Dampfbad *n.* steam bath.
dämpfen to damp, tone down, extinguish, steam
    (cooking).
Dämpfer *m.* steamer.
DANACH afterwards, after that, thereafter.
    Es sieht danach aus. It looks like it.
daneben 1. *adv.* near it, next to it, close by.
    2. *conj.* besides, moreover, at the same time,
    also.
DANK *m.* thanks, gratitude, reward.
    Gott sei Dank! Thank God!
    zum Dank as a reward.
DANKBAR grateful, thankful.
DANKE! thank you!
    Danke schön! Thank you very much!
DANKEN to thank.
    Nichts zu danken. Not at all, don't mention it.
DANN then, thereupon.
    dann und wann now and then.
DARAN (dran) at it, of that, in it, in that.
    Ich glaube daran. I believe in it.
    nahe daran sein to be near, on the point of.
    Wer ist dran? Whose turn is it?
DARAUF (drauf) on, upon it, after that, thereupon.
    darauf aus sein to be out to, aim at.
    Es kommt darauf an. It all depends.
    Ich lege keinen Wert darauf. I'm not interested
    in it.
DARAUS (draus) of it, of that, from this, from that.
    Daraus ist nichts geworden. Nothing came of it.
darbieten to offer, present.
Darbietung *f.* entertainment, performance.
DAREIN (drein) into it, therein.
DARIN (drin) in it, in that.
    Es ist nichts darin. There is nothing to it.
darlegen to explain.
Darlegung *f.* explanation, exposition.
Darlehen *n.* loan.
DARÜBER (drüber) 1. *adv.* over it, above it,
    about it.
    Darüber besteht kein Zweifel. There is no doubt
    about that.
    darüber hinaus beyond that.
    2. *conj.* meanwhile.
DARUM (drum) round it, for it, about it.
    Ich kann mich nicht darum kümmern. I can't
    take care of that.
DARUNTER (drunter) under it, underneath, among
    them, by that.
    Was verstehen Sie darunter? What do you mean
    by that?
DAS 1. *neuter article (nom. and acc.).* the.
    2. *demons. pron.* that.
    3. *rel. pron.* which, that.
    das jenige das the one which.

    dasselbe the same.
dasein to exist, be present.
Dasein *n.* existence, life.
    Kämpf für das Dasein struggle for life.
DASS *conj.* that.
    dass doch if only.
Datum *n.* date.
Dauer *f.* length, duration.
    auf die Dauer for long.
DAUERN to last, continue
    lange dauern to take a long time.
Dauerwelle *f.* permanent wave.
Daumen *m.* thumb.
DAVON for it, from this, from that, of it, of that.
    Was halten Sie davon? What do you think of it?
    Geben Sie mir ein Paar davon. Give me a pair
    of them.
    Das hängt davon ab. It depends.
DAVOR in front of it, of it, of that.
    Sie stehen direkt davor. They stand right in
    front of it.
DAZU to it, for it, for that purpose.
    Es ist schon zu spät dazu. It is already too late
    for that.
    dazu gehören to belong to it.
    dazu tun to add to.
dazwischen in between.
Decke *f.* cover, blanket.
Deckel *m.* cover, lid.
DECKEN to protect, cover, guard, secure.
Deckung *f.* cover, shelter, protection.
    in Deckung gehen to take cover.
Defekt *m.* defect, deficiency.
Degen *m.* sword.
DEIN (*poss. adj. fam. form.*) your.
DEIN(er, e, es) (*poss. pron. fam. form.*) yours.
DEM *dat. sing. of der and das* to the, to this, to
    whom, to which.
    demnach then.
    demnächst soon, shortly.
    demzufolge accordingly.
    Wie dem auch sei be that as it may.
Demokrat *m.* democrat.
Demokratie *f.* democracy.
Demut *f.* humility.
demütig humble.
demütigen to humiliate.
Demütigung *f.* humiliation.
DEN *acc. sing. of der; dat. pl. of die.* the, this,
    to them, whom, that.
DENEN *dat. pl. of die (rel. pron.)* to whom, to
    which.
DENKEN to think, intend, mean.
    Was denke. Sie zu tun? What do you intend to do?
    denken an to remember, think of.
    sich denken to imagine.
    Das kann ich mir schon denken. I can
    well imagine.
Denker *m.* thinker.
DENN for, because, then.
    es sei denn, dass unless.
dennoch nevertheless.
deponieren to deposit.
DER 1. *masc. article (nom.)* the; *fem. (gen. & dat.)*
    of the, to the; *pl. (gen.)* of the.
    2. *demons. pron.* this.
    3. *rel. pron.* which, who, that.
    derjenige der the one who, he who.
    derselbe the same.
DEREN *gen. fem. and pl. of die, (rel. pron.)* whose.
DES *gen. sing. of der and das of the.*
DESHALB therefore, for that reason.
DESSEN *gen. sing. of der and das pron.* whose.
Detektiv *m.* detective.
deuten to point out, explain, interpret.

deutlich distinct, clear; distinctly, clearly.
Deutlichkeit f. distinctness, clearness.
DEUTSCH German.
DEUTSCHE m. & f. German (person)
DEUTSCHLAND n. Germany.
Deutung f. interpretation, explanation.
Devise f. foreign bill, motto.
DEZEMBER m. December.
Dialekt m. dialect.
Diamant m. diamond.
Diät f. diet.
    Diät leben to diet.
DICH acc. of du. (fam. form) you.
DICHT thick, dense, tight, close.
dichten to compose, write poetry, invent.
Dichter m. poet.
Dichtung f. poetry, fiction.
DICK thick, stout, fat.
    Er ist dick geworden. He got fat.
Dickkopf m. blockhead.
DIE 1. fem. article (nom. and acc.), the.
    pl. article (nom. and acc.), the.
    2. demons. pron. this.
    3. rel. pron. who, which, that.
    diejenige die she who, the one which.
    dieselbe the same.
DIEB m. thief, burglar.
    Halten Sie den Dieb! Stop the thief!
DIENEN to serve.
    Womit kann ich dienen? Can I help you?
Diener m. servant.
Dienerin f. maid.
dienlich serviceable.
Dienst m. service, duty, situation, employment.
    ausser Dienst off duty.
    zu Diensten stehen to be at a person's
    disposal.
DIENSTAG m. Tuesday.
Dienstbotenzimmer n. servant's room.
diensteifrig zealous.
Dienstmädchen n. maid.
Dienststelle f. headquarters.
DIES(er,-e,-es) this, that.
DIESMAL this time.
DIESSEITS (gen.) on this side.
Diktat n. dictation, treaty.
DING n. thing, object.
    guter Dinge sein to be in high spirits.
    vor allen Dingen first of all.
Diplom n. diploma, certificate.
Diplomatie f. diplomacy.
diplomatisch diplomatic.
DIR dat. of du (fam. form) you, to you.
direkt direct
Direktor m. director.
Dirigent m. conductor.
dirigieren to conduct, direct.
diskret discreet, tactful.
Diskretion f. discretion.
diskutieren to discuss.
Distanz f. distance.
DOCH however, anyway, nevertheless, but, still,
    yet; surely, of course, yes(in answer to a nega-
    tive question); indicates a well-known fact.
    Willst du nicht kommen? Doch. Won't you
    come? Of course.
    Habe ich doch gewusst, dass er schwer krank
    war. I knew (very well) he was very ill.
    Ich werde doch gehen. I will go anyhow.
    Ja doch! of course.
    Sie werden doch zugeben, dass er recht hatte.
    But you will admit he was right.
    Und doch ist es nicht so traurig, wie Sie
    denken. And still it is not so sad as you think.
DOKTOR m. doctor.

den Doktor machen to take the degree of doctor.
Doktorarbeit f. thesis for doctorate.
Dokument n. document.
dokumentieren to prove.
Dolch m. dagger.
dolmetschen to interpret.
Dolmetscher m. interpreter.
Dom m. cathedral.
Donner m. thunder.
    vom Donner gerührt thunderstruck.
donnern to thunder.
Donnerschlag m. thunderbolt.
DONNERSTAG m. Thursday.
Donnerwetter n. thunderstorm.
    Donnerwetter! Good heavens!
doppeldeutig ambiguous.
Doppelpunkt m. colon.
doppelt double.
    Doppelbett, n. double bed.
    Doppelzimmer, n. room with twin beds.
DORF n. village.
Dorn m. thorn.
DORT there, yonder.
    dorther from there.
    dorthin there, that way, over there.
Dose f. box, can, dose, amount.
DRAHT m. wire, cable, line.
drängen to push, press, hurry, urge.
    Nicht drängen! Do not push!
draussen outside, outdoors, abroad.
drehen to turn, rotate, revolve.
DREI three.
Dreieck n. triangle.
DREISSIG thirty.
DREISSIGSTE thirtieth.
DREIZEHN thirteen.
DREIZEHNTE thirteenth.
dringen to enter, get in, penetrate.
    dringen auf to insist on.
dringend urgent.
DRITTE third.
Droge f. drug.
Drogerie f. chemist's shop.
drüben over there, yonder.
Druck m. pressure, compression.
    in Druck gehen to go to press.
drucken to print.
Druckknopf m. push button.
Drukfehler m. misprint.
Dschungel f. jungle.
DU pers. pron. fam. form. you.
    auf du und du stehen to be on intimate terms.
Duft m. scent, smell, fragrance.
DUFTEN to smell sweet, be fragrant.
duftig sweet-smelling, fragrant.
dulden to endure, bear, suffer.
dumm stupid, dull, ignorant.
    Sei nicht so dumm! Don't be so stupid!
    Es wurde mir zu dumm. I got sick and
    tired of it.
Dummheit f. stupidity, blunder.
Dummkopf m. stupid fellow, dunce.
düngen to fertilize.
Dünger m. fertilizer, manure.
dunkel dark, gloomy, vaguely.
    Ich erinnere mich dunkel... I vaguely
    remember...
Dunkelheit f. darkness, obscurity.
dunkeln to get dark.
DÜNN thin, weak, rare.
DURCH 1. prep. (acc.) through, across, by, by
    means of, because of.
    Durch den Krieg wurden viele Städte
    zerstört. Many cities were destroyed because
    of the war.

Er bestand die Prüfung durch viel Arbeit.
He passed the examination by working hard.
(through much work.)
Er schickt es durch die Post. He sends it
by post.
Ich ging durch den Wald. I walked through
the forest.
die ganze Zeit durch all the time.
durch und durch through and through.
2. prefix.
a) inseparable. through, across, around.
Die Milchstrasse durchzieht den Himmel. The
milky way goes across the sky.
b) separable. implies the idea of accomplishment.
Ich lese das Buch durch. I read the book to
the end.
durcharbeiten to work through, study thoroughly.
durchaus thoroughly, absolutely.
    durchaus nicht not at all, not in the least.
durcheinander confusedly, in disorder.
durchfahren to drive through.
Durchfahrt f. thoroughfare, passage.
    Keine Durchfahrt! No thoroughfare!
durchfechten to fight out.
durchfinden to find one's way through.
durchführbar to carry out, accomplish, execute.
Durchführung f. accomplishment, execution,
Durchführung f. accomplishment, execution,
    performance.
Durchgang m. passageway.
    Kein Durchgang! No trespassing!
durchgehen to go through, pass through, run away.
durchhalten to hold out, carry through.
durchmachen to go through, suffer.
    Sie haben viel durchgemacht. They have gone
    through a lot.
Durchmesser m. diameter.
durchnehmen to work through, go over.
Durchreise f. journey through, passing through,
    transit.
durchreisen to travel through, cross.
Durchreisevisum n. transit visa.
durchschauen to look through.
Durchschlag m. collander, strainer, carbon copy.
durchschlagend powerful.
Durchschlagpapier n. carbon paper.
durchschneiden to cut through.
durchsetzen to achieve.
durchsuchen to search through.
Durchsuchung f. search, police raid.
durchtrieben cunning, sly, artful.
Durchzug m. march through, passage through.
DÜRFEN to be allowed to, be permitted.
    Darf ich, bitte? May I, please?
    Darf ich um den nächsten Tanz bitten? May I
    have the next dance?
    Darf man hier rauchen? Is smoking allowed here?
dürftig poor, needy, indigent.
DÜRR dry, parched, dried, lean, skinny.
    dürres Holz dry wood.
DÜRRE f. dryness, drought.
Durst m. thirst.
    Das macht Durst. That makes (one) thirsty.
dürsten to be thirsty, long for, crave.
durstig thirsty.
Dusche f. shower-bath.
duschen (sich) to take a shower.
Dutzend n. dozen.
    dutzendmal dozens of times.

E

Ebbe f. ebb, low tide.
    die Ebbe und die Flut the ebb and flow.
EBEN even, flat, smooth.

eben erst just now.
eben deshalb for that very reason.
ebenfalls likewise, too, also.
ebenmässig symmetrical, proportional.
ebenso just as, just so, quite as.
zu ebener Erde on the ground floor.
Ebene f. plain.
ebnen to level, smooth.
Echo n. echo.
ECHT genuine, true, real, legitimate.
Echtheit f. legitimacy.
Ecke f. corner, angle.
eckig triangular, cornered.
edel noble, well-born, generous.
Efeu n. ivy.
Effekt m. effect, stocks.
Effekthascherei f. showing off.
effektvoll effective.
Egoismus m. egoism.
Egoist m. egoist.
egoistisch egoistic.
egozentrisch egocentric.
EHE before, until.
ehemals formerly.
eher sooner, rather.
Ehe f. matrimony, marriage.
Ehefrau f. wife, spouse.
Ehegatte m. husband.
Ehepaar n. married couple.
ehelich matrimonial, conjugal.
Ehescheidung f. divorce.
Ehescheidungsklage f. divorce suit.
Eheschliessung f. marriage.
EHRE f. honor, reputation, respect.
Meine Ehre steht auf dem Spiel. My honor
is at stake.
ehren to honor.
ehrenamtlich honorary.
Ehrenbezeigung f. mark of respect.
Ehrenwort n. word of honor.
ehrerbietig respectful.
Ehrerbietung f. deference, respect.
Ehrfurcht f. respect, awe, reverence.
Ehrgefühl n. sense of honor, self-respect.
Ehrgeiz m. ambition.
ehrgeizig ambitious.
Ehrlichkeit f. honesty.
Ehrlosigkeit f. dishonesty, infamy.
Ei n. (pl. Eier) egg.
Eigelb n. egg yolk.
Eiweiss n. egg white.
Rühreier scrambled eggs.
Spiegeleier fried eggs.
Weiche Eier soft-boiled eggs.
Eiche f. oak.
Eichhörnchen n. squirrel.
Eifer m. zeal, ardor.
Eifersucht f. jealousy.
eifersüchtig jealous.
eifrig eager, keen, zealous.
EIGEN own, proper, particular, special, choosy.
Er ist sehr eigen im Essen. He is very fussy
about his food.
eigenartig odd, peculiar, strange, queer.
eigensinnig stubborn, obstinate.
eigentlich real, actual; actually, really, exactly,
just, as a matter of fact, indeed.
Was heisst das eigentlich? What does it
actually mean?
Eigentum n. property.
eigentümlich queer, odd, peculiar.
eignen (sich) to be suited, qualified.
EILE f. hurry, haste, speed.
Es hat keine Eile. There's no hurry about it.
Eile mit Weile. Haste makes waste.

EILEN (sich) to hurry.
Das eilt sehr. This is very urgent.
Das eilt nicht. There's no hurry.
eilig fast, hasty.
es eilig haben to be in a hurry.
Eilzug m. fast train, express.
EIN, eine, ein 1. indefinite article. a, an.
2. number. one.
3. pron. one.
Eines Tages some day.
ein für allemal once for all.
4. separable prefix (implies the idea of
entrance or reduction in volume).
Die Lehrerin trat in das Schulzimmer ein.
The teacher (fem.) entered the classroom.
Läuft dieser Stoff ein? Does this material
shrink?
EINANDER each other, one another.
Wir haben einander jahrelang nicht gesehen.
We have not seen each other for years.
einarbeiten to get used to, familiarize with.
einatmen to inhale.
Einbahnstrasse f. one-way street.
einbiegen to turn into.
Biegen Sie in diese Strasse ein. Turn into
this street.
einbilden to imagine, fancy, think, believe.
Einbildung f. imagination, conceit, presumption.
einbrechen to break open, through.
Heute Nacht ist ein Deibe bei ihm eingebrochen.
Last night a thief broke into his house.
Einbrecher m. burglar.
Einbruch m. house-breaking, burglary.
EINDRUCK m. impression.
Er tut es bloss, um Eindruck zu machen. He
does it only to show off.
EINFACH simple, plain, single; simply, plainly,
elementary.
einfache (Fahrt) one-way (ticket).
Einfall m. falling down, collapse, idea, whim.
Wie kommen Sie auf den Einfall? What gave
you the idea?
einfältig simple.
Einfluss m. influence.
einflussreich influential.
Einfuhr f. importation, import.
einführen to introduce, import, inaugurate.
Einführung f. importation.
Einfuhrzoll m. import duty.
Eingabe f. petition, memorial.
EINGANG m. entrance.
Kein Eingang. No entrance.
Verbotener Eingang! Keep out!
eingeben to give, administer, inspire.
eingebildet imaginary.
Eingebung f. inspiration.
Eingemachte n. preserves, jam.
eingestehen to admit, confess.
eingewöhnen to accustom.
Einhalt m. stop.
Einhalt gebieten to put a stop to.
einhalten to observe, follow, keep to, meet.
Wird er den Termin einhalten? Will he meet
the deadline?
Einhaltung f. observance.
Einheit f. unity, union, unit.
einheitlich uniform.
einholen to bring in, collect, gather, make up.
einholen gehen to go shopping.
einig in agreement, united, unanimous.
einigemal several times.
einigen to come to terms, unite, unify.
Einig (-er, -e, -es) some, any, a few.
einigermassen to some extent, somewhat.
Einigkeit f. harmony.

Einigung f. agreement.
einjagen to alarm, frighten.
EINKAUF m. purchase, buying.
EINKAUFEN to buy, purchase, shop.
Einkaufspreis, m. cost price.
Einkommen n. income.
Einkommensteuer f. income tax.
einladen to invite.
EINLADUNG f. invitation.
Einlass m. entrance, admission.
einlassen to admit, let in.
einleben to settle down, familiarize oneself.
einleiten to begin, initiate, introduce, institute.
Einleitung f. introduction.
einmachen to preserve.
Einmachglas n. preserves jar.
EINMAL once, formerly.
auf einmal all at once.
Es war einmal...Once upon a time there was...
noch einmal once more.
einmengen to meddle with, interfere.
einmütig unanimous.
Einnahme f. occupation, capture, conquest.
einnehmen to engage, occupy, receive, collect,
captivate.
einnehmend captivating.
einordnen to arrange, classify, file.
einpacken to wrap up.
einpflanzen to plant, inculcate.
einrahmen to frame.
einreden to persuade, talk someone into.
einreichen to hand in, deliver, present.
einreihen to insert, include, arrange.
Einreise f. entry into a country.
Einreiseerlaubnis f. permit to enter a country.
einrichten to arrange, prepare, manage,
furnish.
sich einrichten to plan.
Einrichtung f. furniture.
EINS one, the same.
Es kommt auf eins hinaus. It comes to the
same thing.
EINSAM lonely, solitary, lonesome.
Einsamkeit f. loneliness, solitude.
einschläfern to lull to sleep.
einschalten to insert, put in.
einschenken to pour in.
einschlafen to fall asleep.
einschlagen to drive in (nail), break, wrap up.
Schlagen Sie mir das, bitte, ein. Will you
please wrap that for me?
einschliessen to lock up, enclose.
einschliesslich inclusive.
Einschreibebrief m. registered letter.
einschreiben to enter, note down, register.
einschreiten to intervene, proceed.
einschüchtern to intimidate.
EINSEITIG one-sided, partial.
einsetzen to put it, insert.
sich einsetzen für to speak on behalf of.
Einspruch m. protest, objection.
Einspruch erheben to object to, protest
against.
EINST once, one day.
einstmals once, formerly.
einstweilen meanwhile, for the present.
einstweilig temporary.
einsteigen to get in.
Nach Düsseldorf einsteigen! (Passengers) to
Düsseldorf, all aboard!
einstellen to put on, adjust, stop, cease.
Arbeit einstellen to strike.
Betrieb einstellen to close down.
sich einstellen auf to be prepared.

Einstellung f. adjustment, enlistment, attitude.
  Ich verstehe Ihre Einstellung nicht. I don't understand your attitude.
einstimmen to join in.
einstimmig unanimous.
einstudieren to study, rehearse.
einteilen to divide, plan, distribute.
Einteilung f. division, distribution, arrangement.
eintönig monotonous.
Eintönigkeit f. monotony.
Eintracht f. harmony, union, concord.
eintreffen to arrive, happen.
  Was ich befürchtete, ist eingetroffen. What I was afraid of has happened.
EINTRETEN to go in, enter.
  Bitte, treten Sie ein! Won't you come in, please!
  eintreten für to stand up for.
  eintreten in to join.
EINTRITT entrance, entry.
  Eintritt verboten! No admission!
  Eintritt frei! Admission free!
Eintrittsgeld n. admission fee.
Eintrittskarte f. ticket.
EINVERSTANDEN agreed.
  einverstanden sein to agree.
Einverständnis n. agreement, consent.
Einwand m. objection, protest.
einwandfrei faultless, perfect.
Einwanderer m. immigrant.
einwandern to immigrate.
Einwanderung f. immigration.
einwechseln to change money.
einwenden to object.
einwilligen to consent.
Einwilligung f. consent.
Einwurf m. slit, slot.
Einzahl f. singular.
einzahlen to pay in.
Einzahlung f. payment.
EINZELN individual, particular, separate, single.
  Kann man jeden Band einzeln kaufen? Can I buy each volume separately?
  jeder einzelne each and every one.
einziehen to pull in, draw, move in.
  Sie sind schon in ihre neue Wohnung eingezogen. They have already moved into their new apartment.
EINZIG only, sole, unique.
  einzig und allein solely, entirely.
  Er ist das einzige Kind. He is the only child.
Einzug m. entry, entrance, moving in.
EIS n. ice, ice cream.
  Eisbahn, f. rink.
  Eisschrank, m. refrigerator.
  eisig icy.
EISEN n. iron.
  zum alten Eisen werfen to junk.
Eisenbahn f. railway.
  Eisenbahnwagen, m. railway car.
Eisenwaren pl. hardware.
eisern(er-e,-es) of iron, inflexible.
  der eiserne Vorhang the iron curtain.
  Er hat einen eisernen Willen. He has an iron will.
eitel vain, conceited, idle.
Eitelkeit f. vanity, conceit.
Elefant m. elephant.
elegant elegant.
Eleganz f. elegance.
Elektriker m. electrician.
elektrisch electric.
elektrisieren to electrify.

Elektrizität f. electricity.
Element n. element.
elementar elementary.
Elend n. misery, misfortune, distress.
elend miserable, ill; miserably.
Elfenbein n. ivory.
ELFTE eleventh.
Ellenbogen m. elbow.
elterlich parental.
ELTERN pl. parents.
elternlos orphan.
Emigrant m. emigrant.
Empfang m. receipt, reception.
EMPFANGEN to receive, welcome.
Empfänger m. receiver, addressee.
empfänglich susceptible.
Empfangnahme f. receipt (paper).
empfehlen to recommend.
empfinden to experience, feel, perceive.
empfindlich sensitive.
Empfindlichkeit f. sensitiveness.
empören to rouse, excite, shock.
Empörung f. rebellion.
ENDE n. end, result, conclusion, extremity.
  am Ende in the end, after all.
  Ende gut, alles gut. All is well that ends well.
  letzten Endes finally.
  zu Ende führen to finish.
  zu Ende gehen to come to an end.
ENDEN to end, finish, stop, die.
Endergebnis n. final result.
endgültig final, definite.
endlos endless.
Endstation f. terminus.
Energie f. energy.
energisch energetic, vigorous.
ENG narrow, tight, close, intimate.
  engherzig narrow-minded.
engagieren to engage.
Engel m. angel.
Engländer m. Englishman.
Engländerin f. Englishwoman.
Englisch n. English.
  auf Englisch in English.
Enkel m. 1. ankle.
  2. grandson.
Enkelkind n. grandchild.
Enkeltochter f. (Enkelin) granddaughter.
entbehren to be without, lack, miss.
entbehrlich superfluous, spare.
Entbehrung f. privation, want.
entdecken to discover, find out, detect.
Entdecker m. discoverer.
Entdeckung f. discovery.
Ente f. duck.
entehren to dishonor.
enteignen to expropriate, dispossess.
Enteignung f. expropriation.
enterben to disinherit.
entfalten to unfold, develop, display.
entfernen to remove, take away, depart.
  sich entfernen to leave.
entfernt far off, far away, distant.
  nicht im entferntesten not in the least.
Entfernung f. distance.
entfliehen to run away, escape.
entfremden to estrange, alienate.
Entfremdung f. estrangement, alienation.
entführen to carry off, elope.
Entführung f. abduction, elopement, kidnapping.
entgegen toward, opposed to, contrary to.
entgegen arbeiten to work against, counteract.

entgegengehen to go to meet, face.
entgegengesetzt opposite.
entgegenhalten to object, contrast.
entgegenkommen to come to meet.
  auf halbem Weg entgegenkommen to meet halfway.
entgegenkommend obliging, kind, helpful.
entgegennehmen to accept, receive.
entgegensehen to look forward to, expect.
entgegensetzen (entgegenstellen) to oppose, contrast.
entgegentreten to advance toward, oppose.
entgegnen to reply, answer.
Entgegnung f. reply.
entgehen to escape, elude.
enthalten to contain, hold, include.
  enthalten sein to be included.
entkommen to escape.
entladen to unload, discharge.
Entladung f. discharge.
entlassen to dismiss.
Entlassung f. dismissal.
entledigen to get rid of, perform, execute.
entmutigen to discourage, dishearten.
entnehmen to take from, gather, understand.
enträtseln to solve, decipher.
entrüsten to provoke, irritate, make angry.
Entrüstung f. anger, indignation.
entsagen to renounce, abandon.
  dem Thron entsagen to abdicate.
entschädigen to compensate.
Entschädigung f. compensation.
Entscheid m. answer.
entscheiden to decide, make up one's mind.
  Entscheiden Sie das. You decide that.
entscheidend decisive, critical.
Entscheidung f. decision, judgment, sentence. award.
entschieden decided, firm, resolute.
Entschiedenheit f. determination, certainty.
entschliessen to decide, make up one's mind.
  Ich habe mich anders entschlossen. I've changed my mind.
Entschlossenheit f. determination.
Entschluss m. resolution, decision.
entschuldbar excusable.
ENTSCHULDIGEN to excuse.
  Entschuldigen Sie, bitte! Please excuse me!
  Ich bitte vielmals um Entschuldigung. I am awfully sorry.
  sich entschuldigen to apologize.
entschwinden to vanish, disappear.
entsetzen to dismiss from, relieve, frighten.
entsetzlich terrible, dreadful.
entsinnen to remember, recollect, recall.
entspannen to relax.
Entspannung f. relaxation, rest, recreation.
entstehen to arise, originate.
Entstehung f. rise, origin, formation.
entstellen to distort, misrepresent.
enttäuschen to disappoint.
Enttäuschung f. disappointment.
ENTWEDER...ODER either...or.
entwerfen to draw up, design.
entwerten to depreciate, cancel.
ENTWICKELN to develop, explain.
  einen Film entwickeln to develop a film (photographic).
Entwicklung f. development.
Entwicklungsjahre pl. adolescence.
entwürdigen to degrade, disgrace.
Entwurf m. sketch, draft.
entziehen to deprive of, take away from, withdraw.

entzücken to delight, charm, enchant.
entzückend charming, delightful.
entzwei in two, torn, broken.
entzweien to estrange, alienate.
Episode f. episode.
Epoche f. epoch, era.
ER he.
   er selbst himself.
erarbeiten (sich) to get through hard work.
erbarmen to feel pity, have mercy.
erbärmlich pitiful, miserable.
erbarmungslos merciless, pitiless.
Erbe m. heir.
Erbe n. heritage, inheritance.
erben to inherit.
Erbfolge f. succession.
erblassen to turn pale.
erblicken to catch sight of, perceive.
erbrechen to break open, vomit.
Erbschaft f. inheritance, legacy.
Erbse f. pea.
Erbstück n. heirloom.
Erbteil n. portion of inheritance.
Erdbeben n. earthquake.
Erdbeere f. strawberry.
Erdboden m. ground, soil, earth.
ERDE f. earth, ground, soil.
   auf der Erde on earth.
Erdgeschoss n. ground floor.
   zu ebener Erde on the ground floor.
Erdkunde f. geography.
erdolchen to stab.
Erdteil m. continent.
ereignen to happen, occur, pass.
   Wann hat sich das ereignet? When did that happen?
Ereignis n. event, occurrence, incident.
erfahren to learn, experience.
Erfahrung f. experience, information.
   Wo kann ich das erfahren? Where can I get this information?
   aus Erfahrung by experience.
   erfahrungsgemäss from experience.
erfinden to find out, discover, invent.
Erfinder m. inventor.
Erfindung f. invention.
Erfolg m. success, result, outcome.
erfolgen to result, follow.
erfolglos unsuccessful, fruitless.
erfolgreich successful.
erforderlich necessary, requisite.
erforschen to explore, investigate.
Erforschung f. exploration, investigation.
ERFREUEN to give pleasure, gladden, be pleased, rejoice.
erfreulich delightful, gratifying, satisfactory.
erfreulicherweise fortunately.
ERFREUT glad, pleased, delighted.
   Sehr erfreut (in social introductions). How do you do? (Delighted.)
erfrieren to die of cold, freeze to death.
erfrischen to refresh.
Erfrischung f. refreshment.
ergänzen to complete, restore.
Ergänzung f. completion, restoration.
ergeben to produce, yield, result in.
ergeben devoted.
   Ihr ergebener yours faithfully.
ergiebig productive.
ergreifen to seize, take hold of.
ergreifend moving, touching.
ergriffen moved, touched.
Ergriffenheit f. emotion.
erhalten to receive, obtain, preserve.
Erhalter m. supporter.
erhältlich obtainable.
Erhaltungszustand m. condition, state of preservation.

erheben to raise, lift up, collect.
erhebend elevating, impressive.
erheblich considerable.
Erhebung f. raising, elevation, revolt.
erhitzen to heat, warm.
erholen to recover, get better.
Erholung f. recovery, rest, recreation.
ERINNERN to remind.
   Erinneren Sie mich später daran. Remind me about it later.
   sich erinnern an to remember, recall.
   Ich kann mich nicht mehr daran erinnern. I can't remember it any more.
Erinnerung f. remembrance, recollection, memory.
   Erinnerung wachrufen to evoke memories.
   zur Erinnerung in memory of.
erkälten to chill.
   sich erkälten to catch a cold.
erkämpfen to win by fighting.
erkennbar recognizable.
ERKENNEN to recognize, perceive, realize.
   zu erkennen geben to show, indicate.
   sich zu erkennen geben to make oneself known.
erkenntlich recognizable, grateful.
Erkenntnis f. knowledge, perception, understanding.
ERKLÄREN to explain, account for, declare.
ERKLÄRUNG f. explanation, interpretation, declaration.
erkranken to fall ill, be taken ill.
Erkrankung f. illness.
erkundigen to inquire, make inquiries.
Erkundigung f. inquiry.
ERLAUBEN to allow, permit, presume.
   Erlauben Sie, bitte! Allow me, please!
Erlaubnis f. permission, leave, license.
erleben to experience.
Erlebnis n. event.
erledigen to carry through, wind up, dispatch.
   erledigt sein to be dead tired.
erleichtern to facilitate, ease, relieve.
Erleichterung f. facilitation, relief.
erlogen false, untrue, fabricated.
erlösen to save, redeem, deliver.
Erlösung f. redemption, release, deliverance.
ermächtigen to empower, authorize.
Ermahnung f. exhortation, admonition.
ermässigen to reduce, abate.
   Ermässigte Preise reduced prices.
ermöglichen to make possible, enable.
ermorden to murder, assassinate.
Ermordung f. murder, assassination.
ermüden to tire out, weary.
Ermüdung f. fatigue, weariness.
ermutigen to encourage.
ernähren to nourish, feed, support.
Ernährung f. nourishment, food, support, maintenance.
ernennen to nominate, appoint.
Ernennung f. nomination, appointment.
erneuern to renew, renovate, replace.
Erneuerung f. renewal, renovation.
erniedrigen to humiliate, depress.
Erniedrigung f. humiliation, degradation.
ERNST serious, severe, grave; seriously.
   Sie nimmt die Sache ernst. She takes the matter seriously.
   ernst meinen to be serious about something.
Ernst m. seriousness, earnestness, gravity.
   Ernst machen mit to put into practice.
   Ernstfall, m. emergency.
Ernte f. harvest, crop.
Erntearbeit f. harvesting.
ernten to harvest.
erobern to conquer, capture.
eröffnen to open, start, disclose.
erörtern to discuss.
Erörterung f. discussion.
erpressen to extort, blackmail.

Erpressung f. extortion, blackmail.
erraten to guess.
erregbar excitable, irritable.
erregen to excite, stir up.
Erregung f. excitement, agitation.
erreichbar attainable, within reach.
erreichen to reach, attain, get.
ERSATZ m. substitute, equivalent, spare.
   Ersatzreifen m. spare tire.
   Ersatzteil m. spare part.
erschaffen to create, produce.
Erschaffung f. creation.
erscheinen to appear, come out.
Erscheinung f. appearance, figure, apparition.
erschiessen to shoot; to kill by shooting.
Erschiessung f. execution by gunfire.
erschöpfen to exhaust.
   erschöpfend exhaustive.
Erschöpfung f. exhaustion.
erschrecken to frighten.
erschrocken frightened.
erschüttern to shake, upset, shock.
   Die Nachricht hat uns erschüttert. We were shocked by the news.
erschweren to make more difficult, aggravate.
ersetzen to replace, compensate, restore.
ersparen to save, economize.
ERST first, at first, only.
   der erste beste the first that comes.
   eben erst just now.
   erst als not till.
   erst recht nicht certainly not.
   Zum ersten, zum zweiten, zum dritten! Going, going, gone!
Erstaufführung f. opening night.
erstaunen to astonish.
erstaunlich astonishing.
erstenmal (zum) for the first time.
erstens firstly.
erstgeboren first-born.
ersticken to suffocate.
erstmalig first, for the first time.
Ertrag m. produce, yield, profit, returns.
erträglich bearable, endurable.
ertränken to drown.
ertrinken to be drowned.
erübrigen to save, spare.
erwachen to awake.
erwachsen to grow up.
   die Erwachsenen the grown-ups, adults.
erwägen to consider, weigh.
erwähnen to mention.
ERWARTEN to wait for, await, expect.
Erwartung f. expectation, hope.
   in Erwartung Ihrer Antwort looking forward to your reply.
erwartungsvoll expectant, full of hope.
erweitern to widen, expand.
Erweiterung f. widening, expansion.
Erwerb m. acquisition, gain, profit.
erwerben to acquire, gain.
erwerbslos unemployed, out of work.
Erwerbslosenunterstützung f. unemployment relief.
ERZÄHLEN to tell, relate, narrate.
Erzählung f. story, tale, narrative.
erzeugen to breed, produce, procreate.
Erzeugnis n. product.
   Deutsches Erzeugnis. Made in Germany.
Erzeugung f. procreation, production.
erziehen to raise, educate, train.
erzieherisch educational.
Erziehung f. education, upbringing.
Erziehungswesen n. educational system.
erzürnen to get angry.
erzwingen to force, extort.
ES it.
essbar edible.

ESSEN to eat, dine.
Essen n. food, dinner, meal.
Essenszeit f. mealtime.
Essig m. vinegar.
Esslöffel m. tablespoon.
Esswaren pl. provisions, victuals.
Esszimmer n. dining room.
Etage f. floor.
Etagenwohnung f. flat.
ETWA nearly, about, by chance.
ETWAS some, something, any, anything, a bit, somewhat.
EUCH acc. and dat. of ihr (fam. form pl.) you, to you.
EUER poss. adj. (fam. pl. form) your.
EUER(ER, -E, -ES) poss. pron. (pl. fam. form) yours.
euerseits on your part.
euresgleichen like you, of your kind.
euretwegen for your sake, on account of you.
Europa n. Europe.
evakuieren to evacuate.
evangelisch Protestant.
Evangelium n. Gospel.
EWIG eternal, forever, all the time.
Ewigkeit f. eternity.
exakt exact.
Examen n. examination.
Examenarbeit f. thesis, paper.
examinieren to examine.
Excellenz f. Excellency.
Exemplar n. sample.
exemplarisch exemplary.
exerzieren to drill.
Existenz f. existence.
existieren to exist, live.
Experiment n. experiment.
experimentieren to experiment.
Export m. export.
Exporteur m. exporter.
exportieren to export.
Extrablatt n. special edition.
Extrakt m. extract.
exzentrisch eccentric.

F

Fabel f. fable, story, plot.
fabelhaft fabulous.
Fabrik f. factory, mill, plant.
Fabrikanlage f. plant.
Fabrikant m. manufacturer.
Fabrikarbeiter m. factory worker.
Fabrikat n. product (manufactured).
Fabrikation f. making.
fabrizieren to manufacture.
Fach n. compartment, shelf, drawer.
  Was ist Ihr Fach? What's your line?
Fächer m. fan.
Fachkenntnis f. technical knowledge.
Fachmann m. expert, specialist.
Fackel f. torch.
Faden m, thread.
  an einem Faden hängen to hang by a thread.
FÄHIG able.
  fähig sein to be able, capable.
Fähigkeit f. capability.
Fahne f. flag, banner.
Fahnenflucht f. desertion.
Fahnenflüchtige m. deserter.
Fahrbahn f. road, track.
fahrbar passable, navigable.
Fähre f. ferry.
FAHREN to drive, ride, go, travel.
  Fahren Sie rechts! Keep to the right!
  Fahrendes Volk n. tramps.
  mit dem Schiff fahren to sail.
  spazieren fahren to go for a ride.
Fahrer m. driver.

Fahrgast m. passenger.
Fahrgeld n. fare.
Fahrkarte f. ticket (transportation).
Fahrkartenschalter m. ticket window.
fahrlässig careless, negligent.
Fahrlässigkeit f. carelessness, negligence.
Fahrplan m. timetable.
  fahrplanmässig on schedule.
Fahrrad n. bicycle.
Fahrschein m. transportation ticket (bus).
Fahrstrasse f. highway.
Fahrstuhl m. lift, elevator.
  Fahrstuhlführer, m. elevator boy, attendant.
FAHRT f. ride, journey, trip.
  Hin-und Rückfahrt round trip.
  in voller Fahrt at full speed.
  Was kostet die Fahrt, bitte? How much is the fare, please?
Fahrzeug n. vehicle, vessel.
Fakultät f. faculty.
FALL m. fall, drop, case, accident.
  auf jeden Fall, auf alle Fälle in any case.
  auf keinen Fall! On no account!
  Gesetzt den Fall dass... Supposing that...
Falle f. trap.
FALLEN to fall.
  fallen lassen to let fall, drop.
  im Felde fallen to be killed in action.
  in den Rücken fallen to attack from behind.
  in Ohnmacht fallen to faint.
  Das Fest fällt auf einen Sonntag. The holiday falls on a Sunday.
  Das fällt nicht weiter ins Gewicht. That is of no further consequence.
falls in case, in the event.
Fallschirm m. parachute.
FALSCH wrong, incorrect, false.
  Sie hat falsche Zähne. She has false teeth.
  Das Geld ist falsch. The money is counterfeit.
  falsch verstehen to misunderstand.
fälschen to falsify, forge.
Fälscher m. forger.
Falschheit f. falseness, falsehood.
Falschspieler m. cheat (at cards).
Fälschung f. forgery.
Falte f. pleat, fold, wrinkle.
falten to fold.
familiär familiar, intimate.
FAMILIE f. family.
Familienname m. last name.
Fanatiker m. fanatic.
Fang m. catch, capture, prey.
fangen to catch, capture.
FARBE f. color, paint.
  farbenblind color blind.
färben to color, dye.
  sich die Haare färben to dye one's hair.
farbig colored.
farblos colorless, pale.
Fasching m. carnival.
Fass n. barrel, cask.
  Das schlägt dem Fass den Boden aus. That's the last straw.
Fassade f. front (of a building).
FASSEN to catch, seize, hold, apprehend, grasp, comprehend.
  Fassen Sie sich kurz! Make it short!
  ins Auge fassen to consider.
Fassung f. setting, composure.
  aus der Fassung bringen to upset, disconcert.
fast almost, nearly.
faul lazy, rotten, lazy.
  Das ist eine faule Sache. This is a shady business.
faulen to rot, be lazy.
Faulheit f. laziness.
Faulpelz m. idler, lazybones.
Faust f. fist.

  auf eigene Faust on one's own responsibility.
  faustdick hinter den Ohren haben to be sly.
Fausthandschuh m. mitten; boxing glove.
FEBRUAR m. February.
FEDER f. pen, feather.
  Federhalter m. penholder.
  federleicht light as a feather.
Federvieh n. poultry.
Fee f. fairy.
feenhaft fairylike.
fegen to sweep.
Fehl m. blame.
fehl wrong.
  fehl am Platze sein to be out of place.
Fehlbetrag m. deficit.
FEHLEN to miss, make a mistake, lack, be absent.
  es an nichts fehlen lassen to spare no pains.
  Sie werden mir sehr fehlen. I'll miss you very much.
  Was fehlt Ihnen? What's the matter with you?
FEHLER m. fault, defect, mistake, blunder.
  Das ist mein Fehler. That is my fault.
Fehlgriff m. mistake.
Fehlschlag failure.
Feier f. festival, celebration, ceremony, party.
feierlich solemn, festive, ceremonious.
Feierlichkeit f. solemnity, ceremony.
feiern to celebrate.
  Sie feiern ihre goldene Hochzeit. They are celebrating their golden anniversary.
Feierstunde f. leisure hour, festive hour.
Feiertag m. holiday.
feige cowardly.
Feigheit f. cowardice.
feil for sale, mercenary.
  feil bieten to offer for sale.
  feil halten to have for sale.
FEIN fine, thin, delicate, refined, distinguished, elegant.
Feind m. enemy.
feindlich hostile.
feinfühlig sensitive.
Feingefühl n. tact.
Feinheit f. fineness, grace, elegance, refinement, subtlety.
Feinschmecker m. gourmet.
FELD n. field, plain, ground, square.
  Schlachtfeld, n. battlefield.
Feldstecher m. binoculars.
Feldzug m. campaign.
Fell n. skin, hide, coat, fur (animals).
  Diese Katze hat ein schönes Fell. This cat has a beautiful fur.
Fels m. rock, cliff.
  felsenfest firm as a rock.
felsig rocky, craggy.
FENSTER n. window.
Fensterbank f. window-sill.
Fensterflügel m. window-sash.
Fensterrahmen m. window-frame.
Fensterscheibe f. window pane.
Ferien pl. holidays, vacation.
FERN far, distant, remote.
  von fern from afar, from a distance.
Ferne f. distance.
ferner further, furthermore, besides.
Ferngespräch n. long-distance phone call.
Fernglas n. binoculars, field glass.
fernmündlich by telephone, over the telephone.
  Das Telegramm wurde mir fernmündlich durchgegeben. The telegram was given to me over the phone.
Fernsehen n. television.
Fernsprechbuch n. telephone directory.
Fernsprecher m. telephone.
Fernsprechstelle f. telephone booth.
FERTIG ready, ready-made, finished, done.

fertigbringen to bring about, accomplish.
sich fertig machen to get ready.
Werden Sie damit fertig werden? Will you
be able to manage this by yourself?
FEST n. festival, feast.
FEST firm, hard, rigid, steady, solid, stiff,
stable, firmly, stiffly, fully.
eine feste Stellung a permanent post.
fester Schlaf sound sleep.
festbinden to tie, bind, fasten.
Festessen n. banquet.
festfahren to get stuck.
Festhalle f. banqueting hall.
festhalten to hold tight.
festigen to make firm.
Festigkeit f. solidity, firmness.
festlegen to fix, lay down, invest.
festlich festive, solemn.
Festlichkeit f. festivity.
festmachen to fasten, attach, fix, settle.
Festnahme f. arrest, seizure.
festsetzen to fix, set, settle.
Der Preis wird auf hundert Mark festgesetzt.
The price has been fixed at one hundred
marks.
festsitzen to be stuck, fit tightly.
Festspiel n. festival performance.
Feststellung f. statement, determination,
identification.
Festtag m. holiday, feast.
Festung f. fortress, stronghold.
FETT fat, plump, fertile, rich, greasy.
Fett n. grease, fat.
fettig fatty, greasy.
Fetzen m. rag, scrap.
FEUCHT damp, humid, muggy.
FEUER n. fire, firing, bombardment.
Feuer! Fire!
Feuer fangen to catch fire.
Feuer geben to give a light.
feuerfest fireproof.
Feuergefahr f. danger of fire.
feuergefährlich inflammable.
Feuerlöscher m. fire-extinguisher.
Feuerung f. fuel.
Feuerversicherung f. fire insurance.
Feuerwache f. fire station.
Feuerwerk n. firework.
Feuerzeug n. lighter.
Fieber n. fever, temperature.
Fieber messen to take the temperature.
fieberhaft feverish.
Fiebermesser n. thermometer.
fiebern to be feverish, have a temperature.
Fieberthermometer n. clinical thermometer.
Fieberwahn m. delirium.
Figur f. figure, form, shape.
Filiale f. branch.
FILM m. film, picture, movie.
Filmaufnahme f. shooting of film.
filmen to film.
Filmstreifen m. filmstrip.
Filter m. filter.
filtern to filter, strain.
Filz m. felt.
filzig stingy.
Finanz f. finance.
Finanzamt n. revenue office.
finanziell financial.
finanzieren to finance, support.
FINDEN to find, discover, meet with, think,
consider.
Finder m. finder.
findig clever, ingenious.
Findigkeit f. cleverness.
FINGER m. finger.
Fingerabdruck m. fingerprint.
Fingerfertigkeit f. dexterity, skill.

Fingerhut m. thimble.
Fingerspitze f. tip of the finger.
Fingerspitzengefühl n. flair.
Fingerzeig m. hint, tip.
finster dark, gloomy, obscure.
Finte f. feint, trick.
Firma f. firm, business.
FISCH m. fish.
FISCHEN to fish.
Fischer m. fisherman
Fischerei f. fishing, fishery.
Fischgräte f. fish-bone.
Fischhändler m. fishmonger.
FLACH flat, plain, level.
Fläche f. surface, plain, area.
Flachland n. flat country, plain.
Flagge f. flag.
flaggen to deck with flags.
Flamme f. flame.
FLASCHE f. bottle.
Flaschenbier n. bottled bier.
Flaschenhals m. neck of a bottle.
Flaschenöffner m. bottle opener.
flatterhaft fickle, inconsistent.
Flatterhaftigkeit f. fickleness.
flattern to flutter, wave.
FLECK m. place, spot, stain.
vom Fleck kommen to get on, make headway.
Flecken m. spot, stain.
fleckenlos spotless.
fleckig spotted, stained.
Flegel m. boor, impertinent person.
flegelhaft rude, insolent.
Flegeljahre pl. teens.
flehen to implore, beseech.
flehentlich fervent.
FLEISCH n. flesh, meat, pulp.
Fleischbrühe f. meat broth.
Fleischer m. butcher.
fleischig fleshy, plump.
fleischlos meatless.
FLEISS m. diligence, industry.
mit Fleiss on purpose.
fleissig diligent, industrious.
flicken to patch, mend, repair.
Flieder m. lilac.
Fliege f. fly.
FLIEGEN to fly, rush.
in die Luft fliegen to blow up.
Flieger m. airman, aviator, pilot.
Fliegeralarm m. air raid alarm.
fliehen to run away, flee.
fliessen to flow, run.
fliessendes Wasser running water.
fliessend sprechen to speak fluently.
flink quick, agile, nimble.
Flinte f. shotgun, rifle.
die Flinte in das Korn werfen to give up.
Flirt m. flirtation.
flirten to flirt.
Flitter m. tinsel.
Flitterwochen pl. honeymoon.
Floh m. flea.
Flöte f. flute.
flöten to play the flute.
flott afloat, floating.
Flotte f. fleet, navy.
Fluch m. curse, imprecation.
fluchen to curse, swear.
Flucht f. flight, escape.
flüchten to flee, escape.
flüchtig careless, passing, superficial.
Er ist nur ein flüchtiger Bekannter. He is only
a passing acquaintance.
Flüchtling m. fugitive.
FLUG m. flight (aerial).
Flugblatt n. pamphlet.
Fluggast m. air passenger.

Flughafen m. airport.
Flugplatz m. airfield.
Flugwesen n. aviation, aeronautics.
Flugzeug n. airplane.
Flugzeugführer m. pilot.
Flugzeugträger m. aircraft carrier.
Flur f. field, meadow.
Flur m. hall, corridor.
FLUSS m. river.
flüssig liquid, fluid.
Flüssigkeit f. fluidity.
Flusslauf m. course of a river.
flüstern to whisper.
Flut f. tide, flood.
fluten to stream, flow.
FOLGE f. sequence, succession.
Folge leisten to comply with.
Folgeerscheinung f. consequence, effect.
FOLGEN to follow, succeed, obey, mind.
daraus folgt hence follows.
folgendermassen as follows.
folgern to infer, conclude, deduce.
Folgerung f. inference, conclusion, deduction.
folglich consequently.
folgsam obedient, docile.
Folgsamkeit f. obedience, docility.
Folter f. torture.
foltern to torture.
fordern to demand, ask, claim, require.
Forderung f. demand, claim, challenge.
Form f. form, shape.
Formalität f. formality.
Format n. size, weight, importance.
Formel f. formula.
formell formal.
formen to form, shape.
förmlich formal, ceremonious, regular.
Formlosigkeit f. formlessness, shapelessness.
Formular n. form.
formulieren to formulate, define.
formvollendet perfect in form.
forschen to investigate, search.
Forschung f. inquiry, investigation.
Förster m. forester, gamekeeper.
FORT adv. and separable prefix (implies movement
away from speaker, or continuation). away, off,
gone, on (going on).
in einem fort on and on.
und so fort and so forth.
fortan henceforth, from this time.
Fortbildung f. further study.
fortfahren to drive away, remove, continue.
Bitte, fahren Sie fort! Please go on!
fortführen to lead away, go on, continue.
fortgehen to go away.
fortgesetzt continuous, incessant.
fortschreiten to advance, proceed, make progress.
Fortschritt m. progress.
fortschrittlich progressive.
fortsetzen to continue, carry on, pursue.
Fortsetzung f. continuation, pursuit.
Fortsetzung folgt to be continued.
Fracht f. freight.
Frachtdampfer m. freighter.
FRAGE f. question, inquiry, problem.
das ist noch die Frage that remains to be seen.
eine Frage stellen to ask a question.
ohne Frage undoubtedly.
FRAGEN to ask, inquire.
fragen nach to ask for.
nichts danach fragen not to care about
something.
sich fragen to wonder.
Es fragt sich, ob es der Mühe wert ist. It is a
question whether it is worth the trouble.
Fragezeichen n. question mark.
fraglich in question, questionable, doubtful.
fraglos unquestionable.

FRAU *f.* woman, wife, Mrs.
  gnädige Frau Madam.
  Ihre Frau Gemahlin your wife.
Frauenarzt *m.* gynecologist.
FRÄULEIN *n.* young lady, girl, Miss.
fraulich womanly.
frech impudent, insolent.
Frechheit *f.* impudence, insolence.
FREI free, vacant, open, liberal, spontaneous,
  frank; freely, frankly, at ease.
  die freie Zeit leisure, spare time.
  Es ist mein freier Tag. This is my day off.
  Ist dieser Platz frei? Is this seat taken?
  unter freiem Himmel, im Freien outside, in the
  open air.
Freibillet *n.* complimentary ticket.
Freidenker *m.* freethinker.
freien to court, woo.
Freier *m.* suitor.
freigeben to set free, release, open (to the public).
freigebig liberal, generous.
Freigebigkeit *f.* liberality, generosity.
Freigeist *m.* freethinker.
freihalten to hold, treat.
Freiheit *f.* freedom.
freilassen to release, set free.
Freilassung *f.* release.
Freimut *m.* frankness, candor.
freimütig frank, candid.
freisprechen to acquit, absolve.
Freispruch *m.* acquittal.
Freistelle *f.* scholarship, free place.
FREITAG *m.* Friday.
freiwillig voluntary, spontaneous.
Freiwillige *m.* volunteer.
FREMD strange, foreign, unknown, exotic.
  fremdes Gut other people's property.
fremdartig strange, odd.
FREMDE *m.* foreigner, tourist, foreign country.
  in der Fremde abroad.
Fremdenführer *m.* tourist guide.
Fremdenverkehr *m.* tourist traffic.
Fremdsprache *f.* foreign language.
Fremdwort *n.* foreign word.
Fressen *n.* animal food, feed.
fressen to eat (animals), feed.
FREUDE *f.* joy, delight, pleasure, cheer.
  Freude haben an to enjoy, delight in.
  freudestrahlend beaming with joy.
freudelos joyless, cheerless.
freudig joyful, cheerful.
freuen to please, delight.
  sich freuen to be pleased, rejoice.
  Es freut mich sehr, Sie kennenzulernen. I am
  very glad to meet you.
  sich freuen auf to look forward to.
FREUND *m.* **-in** *f.* friend.
FREUNDLICH friendly, kind, obliging, pleasant.
Freundlichkeit *f.* friendliness.
Freundschaft *f.* friendship.
freundschaftlich friendly, serviceable.
FRIEDE *m.* peace.
Friedensbruch *m.* breach of peace.
Friedensvertrag *m.* peace treaty.
Friedhof *m.* churchyard, cemetery.
friedlich peaceful.
friedliebend peace-loving.
frieren to freeze, be cold, get cold.
  Mich friert (es). I am cold.
FRISCH fresh, bright, lively, new.
  auf frischer Tat in the very act of.
  frisch gestrichen wet paint.
  frische Eier fresh eggs.
  frische Wäsche clean linen.
FRISÖR *m.* barber, hairdresser.
frisieren to fix one's hair.
  sich frisieren lassen to have one's hair done.
Frisur *f.* hairdressing, hairdo.

froh glad, happy.
frohgemut cheerful.
FRÖHLICH merry, happy.
  Fröhliche Weihnachten! Merry Christmas!
Fröhlichkeit *f.* cheerfulness.
Frohsinn *m.* cheerfulness.
fromm pious, religious, godly.
Front *f.* front (military).
Frosch *m.* frog.
Frost *m.* frost, cold, chill.
frösteln to shiver, feel chilly.
FRUCHT *f.* fruit, crop, produce.
fruchtbar fruitful, fertile.
Fruchtbarkeit *f.* fruitfulness, fertility.
fruchtbringend fruit-bearing, productive, fertile.
fruchten to bear fruit, to have effect.
Fruchtsaft *m.* fruit juice.
FRÜH early in the morning.
  heute früh this morning.
  morgen früh tomorrow morning.
Frühe *f.* morning, dawn.
  in aller Frühe very early.
früher earlier, sooner, former.
  früher oder später sooner or later.
frühestens at the earliest.
FRÜHLING *m.* Spring.
FRÜHSTÜCK *n.* breakfast.
frühstücken to breakfast.
Fuchs *m.* fox.
fügen to join, put together, add, submit.
fügsam yielding, submissive.
Fügung *f.* dispensation, coincidence.
fühlbar tangible, perceptible.
FÜHLEN to feel, sense, be sensitive to.
  sich gut fühlen to feel well.
FÜHREN to lead, conduct, direct, handle, carry.
  Wer führt? Who is ahead?
  Er führt immer das grosse Wort. He is always
  bragging.
  Er führt etwas im Schilde. He is up to
  something.
Führer *m.* leader, driver, pilot, guidebook.
Führerschein *m.* driving license.
Führung *f.* leadership, command, direction,
  management, behavior, conduct.
Führungszeugnis *n.* reference, certificate.
FÜLLEN to fill, stuff.
  sich füllen to fill up.
  Das Stadion füllt sich langsam. The stadium
  is slowly filling up.
Fund *m.* finding.
Fundament *n.* foundation.
fundieren to lay a foundation.
FÜNF five.
FÜNFTE fifth.
FÜNFZEHN fifteen.
FÜNFZEHNTE fifteenth.
FÜNFZIG fifty.
FÜNFZIGSTE fiftieth.
Funk *m.* wireless, radio (communications medium).
Funke *m.* spark.
funkeln to sparkle.
Funker *m.* telegraphist.
Funkspruch *m.* radiogram.
FÜR *prep.* (*acc.*) for, by, to.
  ein für allemal once for all.
  Er Schritt für Schritt vorwärts. He
  walks forward step by step.
  Ich arbeite für mich. I work for myself.
  Ich habe Karten für das Theater. I have
  tickets for the theater.
  Stück für Stück piece by piece.
  Tag für Tag day by day.
  was für ein? what kind of?
FURCHT *f.* fear, fright, dread, anxiety.
furchtbar awful, horrible, terrible; awfully, terribly.
fürchten to fear.
fürchterlich terrible, horrible, frightful.

furchtlos fearless, intrepid.
Furchtlosigkeit *f.* fearlessness, intrepidity.
furchtsam timid, nervous.
Furchtsamkeit *f.* timidity.
Fürst *m.* (**-in** *f.*) prince(ss).
Fürwort *n.* pronoun.
FUSS *m.* foot, base, bottom.
  auf eigenen Füssen stehen to be independent.
  auf freien Fuss setzen to set at liberty.
  Er lebt auf grossem Fuss. He is living in
  grand style.
  Ich stehe mit ihm auf gutem Fuss. I am on good
  terms with him.
  zu Fuss on foot.
Fussball *m.* soccer.
Fussbank *f.* footstool.
Fussgänger *m.* pedestrian.
  nur für Fussgänger for pedestrians only.
Fussspur *f.* footprint.
Fussstapfe *f.* footstep.
Fusstritt *m.* kick.
Futter *n.* 1. food, feed (animals). 2. sheath, lining.
Futterseide *f.* silk for lining.

G

Gabe *f.* present, gift, talent.
Gabel *f.* fork.
gähnen to yawn, gape.
GANG *m.* walk, stroll, walk, aisle, course, gear,
  hall, errand.
  in Gang setzen to start, set.
  in vollem Gang in full swing.
Gans *f.* goose.
Gänseblümchen *n.* daisy.
GANZ all, whole, entire, complete; in full, wholly,
  entirely, thoroughly, altogether.
  die ganze Stadt the whole town.
  ganz anders quite different.
  ganz besonders more especially.
  ganz gleich all the same, no matter.
  ganz und gar wholly.
  ganz und gar nicht not at all.
  im ganzen on the whole.
  im grossen und ganzen on the whole.
  von ganzem Herzen with all my heart.
GAR done, cooked through; fully, very, quite, even.
  gar kein... no... whatsoever.
  gar nicht not at all.
  gar nichts nothing at all.
Garage *f.* garage.
Garderobe *f.* wardrobe, cloakroom.
Garderobenmarke *f.* check (cloakroom).
Garderobennummer *f.* check (cloakroom).
Gardine *f.* curtain.
Garn *n.* yarn, thread.
garnieren to trim, garnish.
Garnitur *f.* trimming, outfit.
garstig nasty, ugly.
GARTEN *m.* garden.
Gartenhaus *n.* summer house.
Gartenlaube *f.* garden house (pavilion).
Gärtner *m.* gardener.
Gas *n.* gas.
Gashahn *m.* gas tap.
Gasleitung *f.* gas pipes, gas supply.
Gasse *f.* narrow street, alley.
GAST *m.* visitor, guest.
gastfreundlich hospitable.
Gastfreundschaft *f.* hospitality.
Gastgeber *m.* host.
Gasthaus *n.* inn, hotel.
Gasthof *m.* inn, hotel.
gastlich hospitable.
Gastspiel *n.* guest performance.
Gastwirt *m.* innkeeper.
Gasuhr *f.* gas meter.
Gatte *m.* husband.
Gattin *f.* wife.

Gaumen m. palate.
Geächtete m. outlaw.
Gebäck n. pastry, cookie.
Gebärde f. gesture, movement.
gebärden (sich) to behave, conduct oneself.
Gebäude n. building, structure, edifice.
GEBEN to give, present, produce, yield.
    Das gibt mir zu denken. That makes me wonder.
    es gibt there is, there are.
    gegeben werden to play (in theater).
    Was wird heute im Theater gegeben? What's playing tonight at the theater?
Gebet n. prayer.
Gebiet n. district, territory, area, field.
gebieten to order, command.
Gebirge n. mountain chain.
gebirgig mountainous.
Gebiss n. set of teeth, denture.
Gebot n. order, command, law.
Gebrauch m. use, customs, rites.
gebrauchen to use, make use of.
gebräuchlich usual, in use.
Gebühr f. duty, tax, fee, rate.
gebühren to be due, proper.
gebührenfrei tax-free.
gebührenpflichtig taxable.
gebührlich suitable, proper.
GEBURT f. birth, origin, extraction.
Geburtshelferin f. midwife.
Geburtsjahr n. year of birth.
Geburtsschein m. birth certificate.
Geburtstag m. birthday.
Gedächtnis n. memory, remembrance.
    aus dem Gedächtnis from memory.
GEDANKE m. thought, idea.
    sich Gedanken machen to worry.
    Wie kommen Sie auf den Gedanken? What gives you that idea?
gedankenlos thoughtless.
Gedankenlosigkeit f. thoughtlessness.
Gedeck n. cover (at table), set of table linens.
gedeihen to grow, develop, succeed.
gedenken to intend, think of.
Gedenkfeier f. commemoration.
Gedicht n. poem.
gediegen pure, solid.
Gedränge n. crowd, throng.
gedruckt printed.
Geduld f. patience, endurance.
gedulden (sich) to have patience.
geduldig patient.
Gefahr f. danger, risk.
gefährden to endanger, expose to danger.
gefährlich dangerous, perilous.
gefahrlos safe, secure, without danger.
gefahrvoll dangerous, perilous.
GEFALLEN to please, suit.
    Das gefällt mir. I like that.
    sich gefallen lassen to submit, put up with.
gefällig pleasant, agreeable.
Gefangene m. prisoner, captive.
    Kriegsgefangene m. prisoner of war.
Gefangenschaft f. captivity, confinement.
Gefangensetzung f. capture, arrest.
Gefängnis n. prison, jail.
Gefäss n. container, receptacle.
gefasst composed, collected, calm.
    sich gefasstmachen auf to be prepared for.
Geflügel n. birds, poultry, fowl.
Geflüster n. whispering.
Gefolge n. suite, entourage.
GEFÜHL n. feeling, sentiment, sense, emotion, sensation.
gefühllos numb, heartless.
Gefühllosigkeit f. numbness, heartlessness.
gefühlvoll tender, sentimental.
gegebenenfalls eventually, possibly.
GEGEN prep. (acc.) against, about, around,

toward, for, to, compared with.
    Die Soldaten kämpfen gegen den Feind. The soldiers fight against the enemy.
    Er schwamm gegen den Strom. He swam against the current.
    Es ist gegen neun Uhr. It is about nine o'clock.
    gegen voriges Jahr compared with last year.
    gegeneinander against each other.
    Waren gegen Geld tauschen to exchange goods for money.
GEGEND f. country, region, district.
Gegenseite f. opposite side.
gegenseitig reciprocal, mutual.
Gegenstand m. subject.
gegenstandlos pointless.
Gegenteil n. contrary, opposite.
    im Gegenteil on the contrary.
gegenüber opposite.
Gegenwart f. present, presence.
gegenwärtig present.
Gegenwert m. equivalent.
Gegner m. opponent, adversary, enemy.
Gehalt n. content.
Gehalt m. salary.
gehaltlos worthless.
gehaltvoll valuable, substantial.
gehässig spiteful, malicious.
Gehässigkeit f. spite, malice.
geheim concealed, hidden, clandestine.
GEHEIMNIS n. secret, mystery.
geheimnisvoll mysterious.
Geheimpolizei f. secret police.
GEHEN to go, walk, pass, move, leave; run, work (machinery).
    an die Arbeit gehen to go to work.
    Das geht nicht. That won't do.
    Es geht mir gut, danke. I am fine, thank you.
    Es geht nichts über gutes Bier. There is nothing like good beer.
    Es geht um Tod und Leben. It is a matter of life and death.
    gehen auf (nach) to face on, look out on.
    gehen lassen to let go, give up.
    sich gehen lassen to let oneself go.
    Wie geht es Ihnen? How are you?
Gehilfe m. assistant, clerk, helper.
Gehirn n. brain.
GEHÖR n. hearing; ear (mus.).
gehorchen to obey.
GEHÖREN to belong to, be owned by.
    Das gehört nicht zur Sache. That's beside the point.
    Dazu gehört Zeit. That takes time.
gehorsam obedient.
Geige f. violin.
geigen to play the violin.
GEIST m. spirit, genius, mind.
geistesabwesend absent-minded.
Geistesgegenwart f. presence of mind.
geisteskrank of unsound mind, insane.
geistesschwach feeble-minded.
geistig spiritual, intellectual, mental.
geistlich religious, spiritual.
geistlos spiritless, lifeless, dull.
geistreich ingenious, spiritual, witty.
Geiz m. stinginess, avarice.
geizig avaricious, stingy.
Geizkragen m. miser.
Gelände n. country, countryside.
Geländer n. railing, banister.
gelangen to reach, arrive, attain to.
gelassen calm, collected.
Gelassenheit f. calmness, composure.
geläufig fluent, familiar, current.
gelaunt disposed.
    gut gelaunt in good humour.
    schlecht gelaunt cross, bad-tempered.

Geläute n. chime, ringing of bells.
GELB yellow.
gelblich yellowish.
Gelbsucht f. jaundice.
GELD n. money.
    Bargeld , n. cash.
    Kleingeld, n. change.
Geldentwertung f. inflation.
Geldschein m. paper money.
Geldschrank m. safe.
Geldstück n. coin.
Geldtasche f. purse.
Gelee m. jelly.
gelegen 1. situated.
    2. convenient.
    Er kam gerade zu gelegener Zeit. He came just at the right time.
Gelegenheit f. opportunity, occasion, chance.
Gelegenheitskauf m. bargain.
gelegentlich occasional, accidental.
gelehrig docile, teachable.
Gelehrigkeit f. docility.
Gelehrsamkeit f. learning, erudition.
gelehrt learned, scholarly, erudite.
Gelehrte m. scholar, savant.
Geleise n. track.
Geleit n. escort, convoy.
geleiten to accompany, escort, convoy.
Geleitwort n. motto.
Gelenk n. joint, articulation.
Geliebte m. & f. lover, mistress, beloved.
gelingen to succeed, manage.
gelten to matter, mean, be worth, have influence, be valid.
    Das gilt nicht. That does not count.
    gelten als to be considered as.
Geltungstrieb m. desire to dominate.
gemächlich comfortable.
Gemahl m. husband.
Gemahlin f. wife.
gemäss suitable.
GEMEIN ordinary, general, low, vulgar, common.
    der Gemeine the private soldier.
    Es war gemein von ihm. It was mean of him.
    gemeinhaben mit to have in common with.
Gemeinde f. community, congregation, parish, municipality.
Gemeinheit f. vulgarity, basness, bad trick.
gemeinnützig beneficial to the community.
Gemeinschaft f. community.
    in Gemeinschaft mit together with.
GEMÜSE n. vegetables.
Gemüsehändler m. greengrocer.
Gemüt n. soul, mind, heart, feelings.
gemütlich good-natured, cozy.
Gemütlichkeit f. comfort, coziness.
GENAU close, tight, exact, accurate.
    Er nimmt es sehr genau. He is very particular.
    Nehmen Sie es nicht zu genau! Don't take it too literally!
Genauigkeit f. exactness, accuracy, precision.
General m. general.
genesen to recover, get better.
Genesung f. recovery, convalescence.
genial full of genius.
Genialität f. originality.
Genick n. nape (of neck).
Genie n. genius.
genieren to trouble, inconvenience, bother.
geniessbar eatable, drinkable.
geniessen to eat, enjoy, have the benefit of.
Genosse m. companion.
GENUG sufficient, enough.
Genugtuung f. satisfaction, compensation.
Geographie f. geography.
GEPÄCK n. luggage, baggage.
Gepäckabfertigung f. luggage office, cloakroom.

Gepäckannahme m. luggage counter.
Gepäckaufbewahrung f. luggage counter.
Gepäckausgabe f. luggage office.
Gepäckschein n. receipt for registered baggage.
Gepäckstück n. bag, parcel.
Gepäckträger m. porter.
GERADE direct, upright, straight, honest; just,
   exactly, directly.
   nun gerade now more than ever.
   geradeaus straight on.
Gerät n. tool, implement, utensil.
geraten to succeed, turn out well.
   aneinander geraten to come to blows.
   Ihm gerät nichts. He never succeeds in any-
   thing.
   in Brand geraten to catch fire.
geräumig roomy, spacious.
Geräusch n. noise.
geräuschlos noiseless.
geräuschvoll noisy.
GERECHT just, fair, equitable.
Gerechtigkeit f. justice, righteousness,
   fairness.
Gerede n. talk, humor.
Gereiztheit f. irritation.
Gericht n. dish, course, judgment.
   Jüngstes Gericht. Last Judgment.
   vor Gericht in court.
Gerichtshof m. court of law.
gering small, little, unimportant.
   nicht im geringsten not in the least.
   geringfügig unimportant.
Gerippe n. skeleton.
GERN gladly, with pleasure, readily, easily.
   gern essen to like (to eat something).
   Gern geschehen! Don't mention it!
   gern haben to like (a person or object).
   gern tun (or any verb of action) to like (to do
   something).
   Ich esse gern Eisbein mit Sauerkraut. I like
   pig's knuckles with sauerkraut.
   Sie hat ihn gern.   She likes him.
   Tanzen Sie gern? Do you like to dance?
Geruch m. smell, scent, odor.
geruchlos odorless.
Gerücht n. rumor, report.
Gerüst n. scaffold, stage.
GESANG m. song, singing.
Gesanglehrer m. singing teacher.
GESCHÄFT n. business, transaction,
   commerce, commercial firm, store.
geschäftlich commercial.
Geschäftsführer m. manager.
Geschäftsmann m. business man.
geschäftsmässig commercial.
Geschäftsviertel n. shopping district.
Geschäftszeit f. office hours.
GESCHEHEN to happen, occur, be done.
   Es geschieht ihm recht. It serves him right.
   Es ist um mich geschehen. I am done for.
   geschehen lassen to allow, permit.
Geschenk n. present, gift.
GESCHICHTE f. story, history.
Geschichtsbuch n. history book.
Geschick n. fate, destiny.
geschickt clever, capable.
Geschirr n. crockery, dishes, china.
GESCHLECHT n. sex, gender, kind, species, race,
   family, stock.
geschlechtlich sexual.
GESCHMACK m. taste, flavor.
   Geschmack finden an to like.
geschmacklos insipid, in bad taste.
Geschmacklosigkeit f. bad taste.
geschmackvoll tasteful.
Geschrei n. shouting, screaming, clamor.
Geschwätz n. idle talk.
geschwätzig talkative.

geschwind quick, fast, swift, prompt, speedy.
Geschwindigkeit f. quickness, rapidity.
   Geschwindigkeitsgrenze 60 km. Speed limit
   60 kilometers.
Geschwister pl. brother(s) and sister(s).
Geselle m. fellow, companion, journeyman.
Geselligkeit f. sociability, social life.
GESELLSCHAFT f. society, association, company.
   (jemanden) Gesellschaft leisten to keep
   (someone) company.
   in Gesellschaft socially.
Gesellschafter m. partner.
Gesellschaftsanzug m. evening clothes.
Gesellschaftskleidung f. evening clothes.
   Gesellschaftskleidung erwünscht. Evening
   dress requested.
Gesellschaftsspiel n. party game.
Gesetz n. law, statute.
Gesetzbuch n. code.
gesetzlich legal, lawful.
gesetzwidrig unlawful, illegal.
GESICHT n. vision, sight, hallucination.
   appearance, face.
   Das steht Ihnen gut (zu Gesicht). It is very
   becoming to you.
   Gesichter schneiden to make faces.
   Sie lachte übers ganze Gesicht. She was all
   smiles.
Gesichtszug m. feature.
Gesinnung f. mind, way of thinking.
gesinnungslos unprincipled.
gesinnungstreu loyal.
Gesinnugswechsel m. change of opinion.
gesittet well-mannered.
gespannt stretched, strained.
Gespenst n. ghost.
gespenstig ghostly.
Gespött n. mockery, derision.
GESPRÄCH n. talk, conversation, discourse.
gesprächig talkative.
Gesprächsstoff m. topic of conversation.
Gestalt f. form, figure, shape, build, frame,
   manner, fashion.
gestalten to form.
Geständnis n. confession.
gestehen to confess, admit.
Gesträuch n. shrubs, bushes, shrubbery.
Gesuch n. application, petition, request.
GESUND healthy, well, sound, natural.
   gesunder Menschenverstand common sense.
Gesundheit f. health.
   Gesundheit! God bless you!
gesundheitlich hygienic, sanitary.
gesundheitshalber for the sake of health.
Getränk n. drink, beverage.
Getreide n. grain.
Getreidehalm m. corn stalk.
Getreidespeicher m. granery.
Getümmel n. bustle, tumult.
Gewächs n. plant.
gewachsen equal to.
   Er ist der Arbeit gewachsen. He is equal
   to the task.
   Er ist seinem Gegner gewachsen. He is a
   match for his opponent.
Gewächshaus n. conservatory (greenhouse).
gewagt risky.
Gewähr f. security, surety.
gewähren to grant.
   jemanden gewähren lassen to let a person
   do as he pleases.
GEWALT f. power, authority, force, violence.
   in der Gewalt haben to have command of,
   master.
   mit aller Gewalt with all one's might.
   sich in der Gewalt haben to have self-control.
Gewaltherrschaft f. despotism.
gewaltsam violent.

gewalttätig brutal, violent.
gewandt agile, skillful, clever.
gewärtig expecting, expectant.
Gewebe n. weaving, web, tissue, fabric.
Gewehr n. rifle, weapon.
Gewerbe n. trade, business, profession.
Gewerbeschein m. trade license.
Gewerbeschule f. trade, technical school.
gewerbsmässig professional.
Gewicht n. weight.
   ins Gewicht fallen to weigh with.
gewichtig weighty, important.
Gewinn m. winning.
Gewinnanteil m. dividend.
gewinnbringend profitable, lucrative.
GEWINNEN to gain, earn, win, produce,
   extract.
   es über sich gewinnen to bring oneself to.
Gewinner n. winner.
gewinnsüchtig greedy (for victory).
Gewirr n. confusion, mess.
GEWISS certain, sure, fixed; certainly, indeed,
   of course, no doubt.
   Gewiss! Surely!
   In gewissem Sinne hat er recht. In a sense
   he is right.
gewissenlos unscrupulous.
gewissermassen to some extent, so to speak, as
   it were.
Gewissheit f. certainty.
Gewitter n. thunderstorm.
gewittern to thunder.
Gewitterregen m. deluge.
GEWÖHNEN to accustom.
   sich an etwas gewöhnen to get used to
   something.
Gewohnheit f. habit.
gewöhnlich usual, ordinary, common.
gewöhnt accustomed.
Gewölbe n. vault.
Gewühl n. turmoil, crowd.
Gewürz n. spice, seasoning, condiment.
gewürzig spiced.
geziert affected.
giessen to pour, water, spill.
Gift n. poison.
giftig poisonous, venomous.
Gipfel m. summit, peak, top.
Gipfelpunkt m. limit.
Giraffe f. giraffe.
Gitter n. railing, fence, grating.
Glanz m. brightness, glamour.
glänzen to shine, glitter, gleam.
glänzend shining, lustrous.
Glanzleistung f. (top) record.
glanzvoll brilliant, splendid, glorious.
GLAS n. glass, jar, pitcher.
gläsern of glass, vitreous.
GLATT even, smooth, slippery, flat; smoothly,
   slippery.
Glatteis n. slippery ice.
Glauben m. faith, confidence, trust, belief.
GLAUBEN to believe, trust, think, suppose.
   Sie können ihm aufs Wort glauben. You can
   take his word for it.
glaubhaft credible, likely, probable.
gläubig believing, faithful.
gläublich credible, likely.
glaubwürdig credible, reliable, authentic.
Glaubwürdigkeit f. credibility, authenticity.
GLEICH same, similar, alike, even, level, direct,
   equal, like, equivalent; equally, just, at
   once, immediately.
   es einem gleich tun to rival a person.
   Es ist mir gleich. It is all the same to me.
   gleich darauf immediately afterwards.
   Gleich und gleich gesellt sich gern. Birds of a
   feather flock together.

gleichberechtigt entitled to the same rights.

GLEICHEN to be equal, resemble.

gleichfalls likewise.

gleichförmig uniform.

gleichgesinnt congenial.

Gleichgewicht n. equilibrium, balance, poise.

gleichgültig indifferent, unconcerned.

Gleichgültigkeit f. indifference.

Gleichheit f. equality, identity, similarity.

gleichmässig proportional.

Gleichstrom m. direct current.

gleichviel no matter, just the same.

gleichwertig equivalent.

gleichzeitig simultaneous.

Gletscher m. glacier.

Glied n. limb, member.

gliedern to articulate, arrange, classify.

glitzern to glitter, glisten, twinkle.

Globus m. globe.

Glocke f. bell, clock.

Glockenspiel n. chime.

Glockenturm m. steeple.

GLÜCK n. fortune, good luck, prosperity.

    etwas auf gut Glück tun to take a chance on something.

    Glück haben to be lucky.

    Glück im Spiel, Unglück in der Liebe. Lucky at cards, unlucky in love.

    Glück wünschen to congratulate.

    Viel Glück! Good luck! Many happy returns!

glucken to succeed, be lucky.

GLÜCKLICH fortunate.

    Glückliche Reise! Have a pleasant trip!

glücklicherweise fortunately.

Glücksfall m. chance.

Glücksspiel n. game of chance.

Glückwunsch m. congratulations, good wishes.

Glühbirne f. electric bulb.

glühen to glow.

glühend glowing, fervent.

Glühwurm m. glowworm.

Glut f. glow, heat.

Gnade f. favor, mercy.

    auf Gnade und Ungnade at discretion.

Gnadengesuch n. petition for clemency.

GNÄDIG merciful, gracious.

    gnädige Frau Madam.

GOLD n. gold.

golden gold, of gold, golden.

Goldgrube f. gold mine.

goldig shining like gold.

    jedes Wort auf die Goldwaage legen to weigh one's words carefully.

Golf m. golf.

gönnen to wish well, allow, permit; not to begrudge.

Gönner m. patron.

Gotik f. Gothic.

GOTT m. God.

    Gott sei Dank! Thank God!

    leider Gottes unfortunately.

    Um Gottes willen! For Heaven's sake!

Götterdämmerung f. twilight of the Gods.

Gottesdienst m. public worship, service (church).

göttlich divine, godlike.

Grab n. tomb, grave.

Grabstein m. tombstone.

Grad m. degree.

Graf m. count.

Gräfin f. countess.

Gram m. sorrow, grief.

grämen to grieve, worry.

Gramm n. gram. (1,000 grams equal 1 kilogram.)

Grammatik f. grammar.

GRAS n. grass.

grässlich terrible, horrible.

Gräte f. fish-bone.

Gratulant m. congratulator, well-wisher.

gratulieren to congratulate.

GRAU gray.

grauen to be afraid, shudder, dread.

    Es graut mir vor. I am afraid.

grauenhaft horrible, ghastly.

grauenvoll awful, dreadful.

Grauhaar n. gray hair.

grausam cruel.

Grausamkeit f. cruelty.

grausig gruesome, ghastly.

Grazie f. grace, charm.

graziös gracious.

greifbar tangible, palpable.

greifen to seize, grasp, catch, touch, strike.

    ineinander greifen to interlock.

Greis m. old man.

Greisenalter n. old age.

Greisin f. old woman.

Grenze f. frontier, boundary, limit.

grenzenlos boundless, infinite.

Grenzverkehr m. traffic at or across the frontier, frontier trading.

Griff m. grip, grasp, hold, catch.

Grimm m. anger, rage.

grimmig furious, grim.

Grippe f. grippe.

grob clumsy, thick, rough, coarse.

Grobheit f. coarseness, rudeness.

Groll m. resentment, anger.

grollen to be resentful, angry.

GROSS big, tall, large, great, huge, grand.

    die grossen Ferien the summer vacation.

    gross tun to boast.

    gross ziehen to bring up.

    grosse Kinder grown-up children.

    grosser Buchstabe capital letter.

    im grossen und ganzen on the whole.

grossartig great, grand.

GRÖSSE f. size, dimension, largeness, tallness, celebrity, star.

Grosseltern pl. grandparents.

Grosshandel m. wholesale trade.

grossjährig of age.

Grossmacht f. great power.

grossmütig generous, magnanimous.

Grossmutter f. grandmother.

grosspurig arrogant.

Grossstadt f. big town.

Grossstädter m. inhabitant of a large town.

grösstenteils for the most part, largely.

Grossvater m. grandfather.

grosszügig generous, on a large scale.

Grün n. green, verdure.

GRÜN green (adj.).

    im Grünen in country surroundings.

    vom grünen Tisch aus only in theory.

GRUND m. ground, bottom, cause, reason.

    im Grunde after all.

    auf den Grund gehen to investigate.

    Aus welchem Grunde? For what reason?

Grundbesitz m. real estate.

gründen to found, establish, promote.

Grundgedanke m. fundamental idea.

Grundlage f. foundation.

grundlegend fundamental.

gründlich thorough, solid, profound.

Gründlichkeit f. thoroughness, solidity.

Grundsatz m. principle.

grundsätzlich fundamental.

Grundstück n. piece of land, lot.

Gründung f. foundation, establishment.

grünen to grow green, sprout.

Gruppe f. group, sectio...

GRUSS m. greeting; salute (military).

GRÜSSEN to greet, salute.

    grüssen lassen to send one's regards.

gültig valid, available, good, current.

Gültigkeit f. validity; currency (monetary).

Gummi m. rubber, eraser.

Gummiabsatz m. rubber heel.

Gummiband n. rubber band.

Gummimantel m. raincoat.

Gummischuh m. galosh.

Gunst f. kindness, favor.

    zu Gunsten von in favor of.

günstig kind, favorable.

Gurke f. cucumber.

Gürtel m. belt, girdle.

Gusstein m. sink.

Gut n. property, good, estate, farm.

GUT good, pleasant, kind, full; well, pleasantly, kindly.

    es gut haben to be well off.

    Gute Besserung! I hope you get well soon!

    Guten Morgen! Good morning!

    kurz und gut in short.

    Schon gut! All right!

Gutachten n. expert opinion, estimate.

Gutachter m. assessor, surveyor.

gutartig good-natured.

Güte f. kindness.

Güterzug m. freight train.

gutgelaunt in a good temper, in good spirits.

gutgläubig credulous.

Guthaben n. balance, credit.

gutheissen to approve, sanction.

gutherzig kind-hearted.

gütig kind, good.

gutmachen to make amends for.

gutmütig good-natured.

Gutmütigkeit f. good nature.

Gutsbesitzer m. landowner, gentleman farmer.

Gutschein m. token, voucher.

gutwillig willing, voluntary.

Gymnasialbildung f. classical education.

Gymnasiast m. high-school boy.

Gymnasium n. high-school.

Gymnastik f. gymnastics.

H

HAAR n. (Haare pl.) hair.

    sich die Haare machen to do one's hair.

    Haare auf den Zähnen haben to stand up (to opponents).

    um ein Haar nearly, narrowly.

    kein gutes Haar an einem lassen to pull a person to pieces.

    sich in die Haare geraten to come to blows.

    Lassen Sie sich darüber keine grauen Haare wachsen! Don't let that give you gray hair!

haaren to shed hair (animals).

Haarnadel f. hairpin.

Haarspalterei f. hair-splitting.

Haarwasser n. hair tonic.

Habe f. property, belongings.

    Hab und Gut good and chattel.

    habhaft werden to obtain possession.

HABEN to have, own, possess, get.

    Den wievielten haben wir heute? What is the date today?

    nichts auf sich haben to be of no consequence.

    Recht haben to be right.

    unter sich haben to be in charge of.

    Was hast du? What is the matter with you?

    zu haben sein to be obtainable.

Habgier f. greed, avarice.

habgierig greedy, avaricious.

Habseligkeiten pl. belongings.

hacken to chop, mince.

Hafen m. port, harbor.

Hafenstadt f. seaport.

Haft f. custody, arrest, detention.

haftbar responsible, liable.

haften to stick to, cling to.

    haften für to answer for (bear the responsibility).

Häftling m. prisoner.
haftpflichtig liable, responsible.
   mit beschränkter Haftung with limited
   liability.
Haftung f. liability, responsibility.
Hagel m. hail.
Hagelschlag m. hailstorm.
HAHN m. rooster, cock.
Hai m. shark.
Haken m. hook, mark.
HALB half.
   auf halbem Wege midway, halfway.
   ein halbes Pfund half a pound.
   halb durchgebraten medium done (meat).
   halb so viel half as much.
   halb zwei half past one.
halbieren to halve, bisect.
Halbinsel f. peninsula.
Halbmond m. crescent moon, half-moon.
Halbwelt f. demi-monde.
Hälfte f. half.
   Kinder zahlen die Hälfte. Children pay half
   price.
Halle f. hall, hangar.
HALS m. neck, throat.
   Es hängt mir schon zum Hals heraus. I am
   sick and tired of it already.
   Hals über Kopf headlong.
   um den Hals fallen to embrace.
Halsband n. necklace.
halsbrecherisch dangerous.
Halsschmerzen pl. sore throat.
Halstuch n. scarf.
Halt m. stop, halt, hold, footing.
   Halt! Stop!
haltbar lasting, durable.
Haltbarkeit f. durability.
HALTEN to hold, support, observe, keep,
   celebrate, last, stop, endure, continue,
   follow.
   an sich halten to restrain oneself.
   Er hält sich für sehr klug. He thinks he is
   very clever.
   halt machen to stop.
   halten für to consider, think.
   es halten mit to side with.
   Halten Sie sich rechts! Keep to the right!
   halten von to think of.
   schwer halten to be difficult.
   sein Wort halten to keep one's word.
   viel halten auf to think highly of.
   Was halten Sie von ihr? What do you think
   of her?
Haltestelle f. stop, station.
haltlos without support, unsteady, unprincipled.
Haltung f. behavior, attitude, self-control.
Hammer m. hammer.
HAND f. hand, palm.
   auf Händen tragen to spoil.
   bei der Hand sein to be ready.
   die Hand im Spiel haben to have a finger in
   the pie.
   einem die Hand geben to shake hands with
   someone.
   Hand und Fuss haben to be to the purpose.
   mit Händen und Füssen with might and main
   (tooth and nail).
   unter der Hand secretly.
   von der Hand gehen to work well.
   von der Hand weisen to decline.
   zur Hand handy.
Handarbeit f. manual work, labor.
HANDEL m. trade, business, affair.
   Handel treiben to trade.
   handelseinig werden to come to terms.
handeln to act, do.
   handeln mit to trade with.
   handeln von to deal with.

   sich handeln um to be about, be a matter of.
Handelskammer f. chamber of commerce.
Handfertigkeit f. manual skill.
Handfesseln f. handcuffs.
Handgelenk n. wrist.
Handgemenge f. hand-to-hand fighting.
Handgepäck n. hand luggage.
handgreiflich obvious, manifest.
   handgreiflich werden to use one's fists.
handhaben to handle, manage.
Handkoffer m. suitcase.
Händler m. trader, dealer.
handlich handy.
Handlung f. act, action, deed, business.
Handlungsweise f. way of acting, method of
   dealing.
Handschrift f. handwriting.
Handschuh m. glove.
Handstreich m. surprise attack.
Handtasche f. handbag.
Handtuch n. towel.
Handwerk n. handicraft, trade.
   einem das Handwerk legen to stop a
   person's activities.
hängen to hang, suspend, fix, attach.
   hängen bleiben to be caught.
hänseln to tease.
Harm m. grief, sorrow, insult, injury.
harmlos harmless.
Harmlosigkeit f. harmlessness, innocence.
Harmonie f. harmony.
harmonieren to harmonize, agree.
HART hard, firm, solid.
   hartherzig hard-hearted.
   harthörig hard of hearing.
Härte f. hardness, roughness, cruelty,
   severity.
hartnäckig obstinate, stubborn.
Hase m. hare.
Hasenbraten m. roast hare.
Hass m. hate, hatred.
hassen to hate.
hässlich ugly, nasty.
Hässlichkeit f. ugliness.
Hast f. hurry, haste.
hastig hurried, hasty.
Haube f. hood, cap.
   unter die Haube bringen to marry off.
Hauch m. breath, slight breeze.
hauchen to breathe.
Haufen m. heap, pile.
häufen to heap, pile, accumulate.
häufig frequent, abundant.
HAUPT n. chief, head.
Hauptbahnhof m. main station.
Hauptmann m. captain.
Hauptperson f. principal person, leading
   character (theater).
Hauptpostamt n. general post office.
Hauptquartier n. headquarters.
Hauptsache f. main thing.
hauptsächlich principal.
Hauptstadt f. capital.
Hauptverkehrszeit f. rush hours.
Hauptwort n. substantive, noun.
HAUS n. house, home, building.
   das Haus bestellen to put one's affairs in
   order.
   das Haus hüten to be confined to the house.
   nach Hause gehen to go home.
   von Haus aus originally.
   zu Hause at home.
Hausgestellte m. & f. servant.
Hausarbeit f. housework.
Hausaufgabe f. homework.
Häuschen n. small house.
Hausflur m. hall, corridor.
Hausfrau f. housewife.

Haushalt m. household.
haushalten to keep house, to economize.
Haushälterin f. housekeeper.
Hausherr m. master.
Hauslehrer m. private tutor.
häuslich domestic.
Häuslichkeit f. family life, domesticity.
Hausmeister m. janitor.
Hausschuh m. slipper.
Haussuchung f. police raid.
Haustier n. domestic animal.
Haustüre f. front door.
Hauswirt m. landlord.
HAUT f. skin, hide, coat.
   aus der Haut fahren to lose one's patience.
   sich seiner Haut wehren to defend oneself.
Hautfarbe f. complexion.
heben to lift, raise.
Heer n. army.
Hefe f. yeast.
Heft n. handle, notebook, pamphlet, number.
heften to pin, fasten, stitch, fix.
heftig violent, strong.
Heftigkeit f. violence, vehemence, intensity.
heikel delicate, ticklish, difficult.
HEIL unhurt, intact, safe, cured.
heilbar curable.
heilen to cure.
heilig holy, godly, sacred.
   Heiligabend Christmas Eve.
heilkräftig curative.
Heilmittel n. remedy.
heilsam curative.
Heilsarmee f. Salvation Army.
Heilung f. healing, cure.
Heilverfahren n. medical treatment.
HEIM n. home.
heim homeward.
Heimat f. native country, homeland.
heimatlos homeless.
Heimatstadt f. home town.
Heimkehr (—kunft) f. homecoming.
heimlich secret, private, comfortable; secretly,
   privately.
Heimsuchung f. trial, misfortune.
Heimtücke f. malice.
heimtückisch malicious, insidious.
Heimweg m. way home, return.
Heimweh n. homesickness.
   Heimweh haben to be homesick.
HEIRAT f. marriage.
heiraten to marry, get married.
Heiratsantrag m. proposal.
heiser hoarse.
   heiser sein to be hoarse, have a sore throat.
Heiserkeit f. hoarseness, sore throat.
HEISS hot.
HEISSEN to call, name, be called.
   das heisst that is.
   es heisst they say.
   Ich heisse Anna. My name is Ann.
   Wie heisst das auf Englisch? What is that
   called in English?
heiter gay, cheerful.
Heiterkeit f. brightness, clearness, serenity,
   cheerfulness.
heizbar with heating.
heizen to heat.
Heizkissen n. electric pad.
Heizkörper m. radiator.
Heizung f. heating, firing, radiator.
Held m. hero.
HELFEN to support, help, assist.
   Ich kann mir nicht helfen. I can't help it.
Helfer m. helper, assistant.
Helfershelfer m. accomplice ("helper's helper")
HELL bright, shining, clear, light, fair, pale,
   sheer.

Helle f. clearness, brightness.
hellhörig keen of hearing.
Helm m. helmet.
HEMD n. shirt.
Hemdbrust f. shirt front, dicky.
hemmen to check, stop, hinder, restrain.
Hemmung f. inhibition, check, stoppage, restraint.
hemmungslos free, unrestrained.
HER 1. adv. here, from, since, ago.
   von Alters her of old, long ago.
   2. separable prefix (implies the idea of a movement toward the speaker)
   Kommen Sie her! Come here!
herab down, downward.
herablassen to lower, let down, condescend.
Herablassung f. condescension.
herabsehen to look down upon.
herabsetzen to lower, degrade, reduce (price).
Herabsetzung f. lowering, degradation; reduction (price).
heran on, up, near, along.
heranbilden to train, educate.
herankommen to come near.
   die Dinge an sich herankommen lassen to bide one's time.
heranwachsen to grow up.
HERAUF up, upwards.
heraufgehen to go up.
   Kommen Sie herauf! Come up!
HERAUS out, from within.
   Sie kommen heraus. They are coming out.
herausbekommen to get back (money); find out.
   auf eins herauskommen to be all one.
herausnehmen to take out, extract.
herausstellen to turn out, appear.
herbei here, near, hither.
herbeischaffen to bring near, procure, produce.
HERBST m. autumn.
herbstlich autumnal.
Herd m. hearth, fireplace.
Herdplatte f. hot plate.
HEREIN in.
   Kommen Sie herein! (Herein!) Come in!
   Hier herein, bitte! This way, please!
hereinfallen to be taken in, disappointed.
herkommen to come near, approach, originate.
Herkunft f. origin, descent.
HERR m. master, gentleman, lord, sir, Mr.
   Meine Damen und Herren Ladies and gentlemen.
   Ist der Herr Doktor zu sprechen? Can I see the doctor?
   eigener Herr sein to stand on one's own feet.
   Herr werden to master, overcome.
   Herr im Hause sein to be the master of the house.
herrichten to arrange.
herrisch imperious, dictatorial.
Herrschaft f. power, rule, command, master and mistress (of an estate).
herrschen to rule, govern, prevail, exist.
Herrscher m. ruler, tyrant, dictator.
herrschsüchtig fond of power, tyrannical.
herüber across, to this side.
herüberkommen to come over.
HERUM around, round, near, about.
   rundherum all around.
herumdrehen to turn round.
herumführen to lead.
herumreichen to hand around.
herumtreiben (sich) to run around.
HERUNTER down, off.
herunterkommen to come down.
   Komm gleich herunter! Come down right away!
heruntersetzen to lower.
hervor out, forth.
hervorbringen to produce, yield.
hervorheben to make prominent.
hervorragen to stand out, project.

hervorragend prominent, excellent.
hervortun (sich) to distinguish oneself.
HERZ n. heart, feeling, mind, courage.
   ans Herz legen to recommend to someone's care.
   ins Herz schliessen to become fond of.
   sich ein Herz fassen to take courage.
   sich zu Herzen nehmen to take to heart.
   unter dem Herzen tragen to be expecting a child.
   von Herzen gern with the greatest pleasure.
   Was haben Sie auf dem Herzen? What's on your mind?
herzleidend suffering from heart trouble.
herzlich hearty, cordial.
   mit herzlichen Grüssen with kindest regards.
herzlos heartless.
Herzschlag m. heart beat, heart failure.
Heu n. hay.
Heufieber n. hay fever.
Heuchelei f. hypocrisy.
heucheln to feign, pretend.
Heuchler m. hypocrite.
HEUTE today.
   heute abend tonight.
   heute früh; heute morgen this morning.
   heute vor acht Tagen a week ago.
   heutzutage nowadays.
Hexe f. witch.
HIER here.
   hier und da here and there.
hierauf hereupon.
hierdurch through this, this way, thereby.
hierher here, hither.
hierherum hereabout.
hiermit herewith, with this.
hiernach after this, thereupon.
hierüber over here, about this.
hiervon hereof, from this.
hierzu to this, moreover.
hierzulande in this country.
HILFE f. help, assistance, support, relief.
   Hilfe leisten to help, assist.
   erste Hilfe first aid.
hilflos helpless.
hilfreich helpful, charitable.
hilfsbedürftig indigent, needing help.
HIMMEL m. sky, heaven.
   aus allen Himmeln fallen to be bitterly disappointed.
Himmelsrichtung f. quarter, direction, point of compass.
himmlisch heavenly, celestial.
HIN 1. adv. there, thither.
   hin und her to and fro.
   hin und her überlegen to turn over in one's mind.
   hin und wieder now and then.
   2. separable prefix (implies the idea of a movement away from the speaker).
   Gehen Sie hinaus. Go out.
hinab down, downward.
HINAUF up, upward.
   hinaufarbeiten to work one's way up.
   Er geht die Treppe hinauf. He goes up the stairs.
HINAUS out, outside, past.
   darüber hinaus beyond that.
   Ich schicke die Kinder hinaus. I am sending the children outside.
hinausgehen to go out.
hinauskommen to come out.
   auf eins hinauskommen to come to the same thing.
hinausschieben to defer, postpone, put off.
hinauswerfen to throw out, expel.
   hoch hinauswollen to aim high.
hinausziehen to draw out, put off.
Hinblick m. look at or toward.

   im Hinblick auf with regard to.
hinbringen to take, bring, carry.
hinderlich in the way, hindering, obstructive.
hindern to prevent, hinder, hamper.
hindurch through, throughout, across.
HINEIN in, into.
   Ich gehe in das Zimmer hinein. I go into the room.
hineingehen to go into.
hinführen to convey, carry, drive to.
Hinfahrt f. trip there.
hinfallen to fall down.
hinfällig frail, weak.
   hinfällig werden to fail, come to nothing.
hinfort henceforth, in the future.
Hingabe f. surrender, devotion.
hinhalten to put off.
hinlänglich sufficient, adequate.
hinnehmen to take, accept.
hinsehen to look at.
hinsetzen to set down, sit down.
hinsichtlich with regard to.
hinstellen to place, put down, lie down.
hinten behind, in the rear, at the back.
HINTER 1. prep. (dat. when answering question, Wo?; acc. when answering question, Wohin? and depending on the idiom) behind, back, after.
   Hinter dem Haus ist eine Garage. There is a garage behind the house.
   Sie hat schon viel hinter sich. She has been through a lot.
   hinter sich bringen to get over, cover.
Hinterbliebene m. & f. survivor.
hintereinander one after the other.
   zwei Tage hintereinander two days running.
Hintergedanke m. underlying thought, unacknowledged motive.
Hintergrund m. background.
Hinterhalt m. ambush.
hinterhältig malicious, devious.
hinterher behind, afterwards.
hinterlassen to leave, leave behind.
   Hat er keine Nachricht für mich hinterlassen? Hasn't he left a message for me?
hinterlegen to deposit.
Hinterlist f. artifice, fraud, trick.
hinterlistig artful, cunning.
Hinterrad n. backwheel.
hinters hinter das.
   ins Hintertreffen geraten to be handicapped.
Hinüber over, across, over there, to the other side.
HINUNTER down, downward, downstairs.
   Sie geht die Treppe hinunter. She walks down the stairs.
Hinweg m. way there.
hinweg away, off.
hinwegkommen (über) to get over.
hinwegsetzen (über) to disregard.
Hinweis m. indication, hint, reference, direction.
hinweisen to show, indicate, refer.
hinwerfen to throw down.
hinzu to, near, there.
hinzufügen to add.
hinzuziehen to include, consult.
Hirn n. brain.
Hitze f. heat.
hitzig hot, hot-headed.
HOCH high, tall, lofty, great, noble.
   Es geht hoch her. Things are getting pretty lively.
   Hände hoch! Hands up!
   hoch anrechnen to value greatly.
   Hoch lebe ...! Long live ...!
   hochleben lassen to toast.
hochachten to esteem, respect.
Hochachtung f. esteem, respect.
   hochachtungsvoll yours faithfully.

Hochbetrieb m. intense activity.
Hochdeutsch n. high German, standard German.
hochhalten to cherish, raise.
Hochhaus n. skyscraper.
hochherzig high-minded, magnanimous.
Hochmut m. pride, arrogance.
hochmütig arrogant, proud.
Hochschule f. university, college.
Hochsommer m. midsummer.
Hochspannung f. high tension.
    Vorsicht! Hochspannung! Caution! High tension
    wires!
HÖCHST highest, utmost, extreme, maximum; very,
    extremely.
Hochstapelei f. swindling.
Hochstapler m. swindler.
höchstens at best, at most.
Höchstgeschwindigkeit f. top speed, speed limit.
Höchstgrenze f. limit.
Höchstleistung f. maximum output, record
    performance.
höchstwahrscheinlich most likely.
hochtrabend high-sounding.
Hochverrat m. high treason.
Hochzeit f. wedding, marriage.
Hochzeitsreise f. honeymoon trip.
HOF m. yard, court, farm.
    den Hof machen to pay court to.
HOFFEN to hope.
hoffentlich it is to be hoped.
Hoffnung f. hope.
    sich falsche Hoffnungen machen to have
    illusions.
hoffnungslos hopeless.
hoffnungsvoll hopeful.
HÖHE f. height, altitude, latitude, top, summit,
    amount.
    auf der Höhe sein to be up to date, to be in
    top form.
    auf der Höhe von at the altitude of.
    aus der Höhe from on high.
    Das ist die Höhe. That is the limit.
    in (der) Höhe von in the amount of.
Höhensonne f. ultraviolet light.
höher higher, superior.
HOHL hollow, concave, dull.
Höhle f. hole, cave.
Hohlraum m. empty space, cavity.
Hohn m. scorn, sneer, mockery, insult.
höhnen to mock, defy.
höhnisch scornful, sneering.
HOLEN to get, take, fetch.
    sich Rat holen to consult.
HÖLLE f. hell.
höllisch hellish, infernal.
HOLZ n wood, timber, lumber.
hölzern wooden.
Honig m. honey.
horchen to listen, lend an ear, listen in, spy.
    Es horcht jemand. Somebody is listening in.
HÖREN to hear, listen, attend, obey, understand.
    schwer hören to be hard of hearing.
Horizont m. horizon.
Horn m. horn, bugle.
Horoskop n. horoscope.
    ein Horoskop stellen to cast horoscope.
Hörspiel n. radio play.
Hose f. trousers, pants.
    Sie hat die Hosen an. She wears the pants.
Hosenträger pl. suspenders.
Hotel n. hotel, inn.
hübsch pretty, charming, nice.
Huf m. hoof.
Hügel m. hill.
HUHN n. hen.
    gebratenes Hühnchen roast chicken.
    junges Huhn young chicken.
Huld f. grace, favor, charm.

huldigen to pay homage.
Humor m. sense of humor.
humoristisch humorous.
HUND m. dog.
Hundert n. hundred.
    zu Hunderten by hundreds.
HUNDERT one hundred (adj.)
HUNGER m. hunger.
    Hunger haben to be hungry.
Hungerkur f. reducing diet.
hungern to be hungry, starve.
Hungersnot f. famine.
hungrig hungry.
husten to cough.
    Hustensirup, m. cough syrup.
HUT m. hat.
    unter einen Hut bringen
    to reconcile.
hüten to guard, keep, beware.
    das Zimmer hüten to be confined to one's
    room.
Hütte f. hut.

ICH I, self, ego.
Ideal n. ideal.
Idealist m. idealist.
Idee f. idea, notion.
identifizieren to identify.
identisch identical.
IHM dat. of er, es (pers. pron., masc. and neut.)
    to him, to it.
IHN acc. of er (pers. pron., masc.) him, it.
IHNEN (Ihnen) dat. of sie (pers. pron. pl.) to them.
IHNEN (Ihnen) dat. of Sie (pers. pron. sing.
    polite form) to you.
IHR dat. of sie (pers. pron. fem.) to her, to it.
IHR (Ihr) poss. adj. (fem. and pl.) her, its, their.
IHR (Ihr) poss. adj. (sing. polite form) your.
IHR(ER, -E, -ES) poss. pron. (fem. and pl.)
    hers, its, theirs.
    poss. pron. (sing. polite form) your.
ihretwegen on her (its, their) account, for
    her sake.
Ihretwegen on your account, for your sake.
illustrieren to illustrate.
imitieren to imitate.
IMMER always, ever.
    auf immer forever.
    immer mehr more and more.
    immer wieder again and again.
    immerfort continually, constantly.
    wer auch immer whoever.
immerhin for all that, still, nevertheless.
immerzu all the time, continually.
impertinent impertinent, insolent.
imponieren to impress.
Import m. imports, importation.
Impuls m. impulse.
impulsiv impulsive.
IN prep. (dat. answering question, Wo?; acc.
    answering question, Wohin?) in, into, to, at.
    Die Besucher gehen in die Oper. The spec-
    tators go to the opera.
    Der Lehrer sitzt in dem Zimmer. The teacher is
    sitting in the room.
    Der Lehrer tritt in das Zimmer ein. The teacher
    goes into the room.
    Der Sänger singt in der Oper. The singer sings
    at the opera.
    Goethe wurde in Frankfurt geboren. Goethe was
    born in Frankfort.
    im Februar in February.
    im Kreise in a circle.
Inbegriff m. embodiment, essence.
inbegriffen including inclusive, included.
INDEM while, by, on, since.
indirekt indirect.

indiskret indiscreet, tactless.
Indiskretion f. indiscretion.
Industrie f. industry.
Industrielle m. manufacturer, producer.
Infektionskrankheit f. infectious disease.
infolge in consequence of, as a result of.
    infolgedessen because of that, consequently,
    hence.
Ingenieur m. engineer.
Inhaber m. holder, proprietor, occupant.
Inhalt m. contents, area, extent, volume, capacity.
inhaltlich with regard to the contents.
Inhaltsangabe f. summary, table of contents.
inhaltsleer empty, meaningless.
inhaltsreich full of meaning, significant.
Inhaltsverzeichnis n. contents, table of contents,
    index.
inmitten in the midst of.
innen within, inside, in.
INNER interior, internal, inner.
innerhalb within, inside.
innerlich inward, internal, interior.
innig hearty, intimate.
Innigkeit f. cordiality, intimacy.
ins in das.
insbesondere particularly.
Inschrift f. inscription, legend.
Insekt n. insect.
INSEL f. island.
Inserat n. advertisement.
inserieren to advertise.
insgesamt all together, collectively.
insofern in so far, as far as that goes.
insoweit in so far.
Instandhaltung f. upkeep.
inständig instant, urgent.
Instinkt m. instinct.
instruieren to instruct, brief.
Instrument n. instrument.
intelligent intelligent.
Intelligenz f. intelligence, understanding, intellect.
interessant interesting.
Interesse n. interest, advantage.
interessieren to interest.
international international.
interviewen to interview.
Inventar n. inventory, stock.
investieren to invest.
inzwischen in between, in the meantime.
IRGEND any, some.
    wenn irgend möglich if at all possible.
irgendetwas something.
irgendjemand somebody.
irgendwann sometime.
irgendwie somehow.
irgendwo somewhere.
irgendwoher from some place or other.
irgendwohin to somewhere or other.
ironisch ironical.
irre astray, wrong, confused, insane.
    irre werden an to lose confidence in.
IRRE f. wandering, mistaken course.
    in die Irre gehen to lose one's way, go astray.
    Irre machen to confuse.
irren to err, wander, lose one's way, be mistaken,
    be wrong.
    sich irren to be mistaken.
    Irren ist menschlich. To err is human.
Irrenanstalt f. lunatic asylum.
irritieren to irritate.
Irrsinn m. madness, insanity.
irrsinnig mad, insane.
Irrtum m. error, mistake.
    Sie sind im Irrtum. You are mistaken.
irrtümlich erroneous, wrong.
Italiener m. Italian (person).
Italienisch n. Italian (language).
italienisch Italian.

J

JA yes, really, indeed, certainly.
  Da sind Sie ja! So there you are!
  Sie wissen ja, dass ich nicht gehen kann.
  But you know that I can't go.
  ja sogar even.
Jacke f. jacket.
Jackenkleid n. lady's suit.
JAGD f. hunt, pursuit, hunting, shooting.
  auf die Jagd gehen to go hunting.
Jagdschein m. hunting license.
jagen to chase, pursue.
Jäger m. hunter, huntsman, sportsman.
jäh sudden, quick, steep.
JAHR n. year.
  ein halbes Jahr six months.
Jahrestag m. anniversary.
Jahreswende f. New Year, turn of the year.
JAHRESZEIT f. season.
jahrhundert n. century.
jährlich yearly, annual.
Jahrmarkt m. fair.
Jahrtausend n. thousand years, millennium.
Jahrzehnt n. decade.
Jähzorn m. sudden anger, violent temper.
jähzornig hot-tempered, irascible.
Jammer m. misery, wailing.
  Was für ein Jammer! What a pity!
jammern to lament, wail, moan.
JANUAR m. January.
Japaner m. Japanese (person).
japanisch Japanese (language).
jauchzen to exult, shout, rejoice.
JAWOHL of course, indeed.
JE each, ever, at all times.
  je zwei two at a time.
  Sie erhielten je ein Pfund. They received a
    pound each.
  je nach according to.
  je nachdem according as.
  Je eher umso (desto) besser. The sooner, the
    better.
jedenfalls at all events, in any case.
JEDER (jede, jedes) every, each, either, any.
jedermann everyone, everybody.
jederzeit at any time, always.
jedesmal every time.
  jedesmal wenn whenever, as often as.
jedoch however, nevertheless.
jeher von jeher at all times, from times
    immemorial.
jemals at any time.
jemand somebody, someone.
JENER (jene, jenes) that, that one, the former,
    the other.
  jenseitig opposite, on the opposite side.
JENSEITS 1. *adv.* beyond, on the other side,
    yonder.
  2. *prep.* (*gen.*) that side, on the other side.
jetzig present, actual.
JETZT now, at present.
Joch n. yoke.
Jod n. iodine.
Journalist m. journalist.
Jubel m. rejoicing, jubilation.
Jude m. Jew.
jüdisch Jewish.
JUGEND f. youth, young people.
Jugendfreund m. friend of youth.
jugendlich youthful.
Jugendliche m. & f. young boy or girl.
Jugendliebe f. first love.
Jugendzeit f. youth, young days.
JULI m. July.
JUNG young, youthful.
Junge m. boy, lad.
jungenhaft boyish.

jünger younger.
Jungfrau f. virgin, maid, maiden.
  alte Jungfer old maid.
Junggeselle m. bachelor.
Jüngling m. young man.
JUNI m. June.
Jura pl. law.
  Jura studieren to study law.
Jurist m. law-student, lawyer.
Justiz f. administration of the law.
Juwel n. jewel.
Juwelier m. jeweler.

K

Kabarett n. cabaret.
Kabine f. cabin.
Kachel f. glazed tile.
KAFFEE m. coffee.
Kaffeekanne f. coffee-pot.
Käfig m. cage.
kahl bald, bare, naked.
kahlköpfig bald-headed.
Kai m. wharf.
Kaiser m. emperor.
Kalb n. calf.
Kalbfleisch n. veal.
  Kalbsbraten m. roast veal.
Kalender m. calendar.
kalkulieren to calculate.
KALT cold, indifferent.
kaltblütig cold-blooded.
Kälte f. coldness, indifference.
Kamel n. camel.
Kamera f. camera.
Kamerad m. friend, comrade, fellow.
Kameradschaft f. fellowship, comradeship.
Kamin m. chimney, fireplace.
Kamm m. comb.
kämmen to comb.
Kammer f. small room, chamber (government).
Kammermusik f. chamber music.
KAMPF m. fight, combat, conflict, struggle.
  Kampf ums Dasein struggle for a living.
KÄMPFEN to fight.
Kanal m. canal, sewer.
Kanarienvogel m. canary bird.
Kandidat m. candidate.
kandidieren to be a candidate.
Kaninchen n. rabbit.
Kanne f. jug, pot, pitcher.
Kanone f. cannon.
Kante f. edge, corner.
kantig edged, angular.
Kantine f. canteen, mess.
Kanzel f. pulpit.
Kapelle f. chapel, band.
Kapital n. capital.
Kapitalanlage f. investment.
Kapitalismus m. capitalism.
Kapitalist m. capitalist.
kapitalkräftig wealthy.
Kapitän m. captain.
Kapitel n. chapter.
kapitulieren to capitulate.
Kaplan m. chaplain.
kaputt broken, ruined, out of order.
Karfreitag m. Good Friday.
Karikatur f. caricature.
Karneval m. carnival.
Karotte f. carrot.
Karriere f. career, gallop.
KARTE f. card, ticket, map, menu.
  Karten legen to tell one's fortune.
Kartenspiel n. card game, pack of cards.
KARTOFFEL f. potato.
  Kartoffelpüree n. mashed potatoes.
  Bratkartoffeln pl. fried potatoes.

  Kartoffelsalat, m. potato salad.
Karton m. cardboard, box.
Karwoche f. Passion Week.
KÄSE m. cheese.
Kaserne f. barracks.
Kasse f. cash-box.
  Zahlen Sie, bitte, an der Kasse. Please pay
    the cashier.
Kassenschein m. receipt.
kassieren to receive money.
Kassierer m. cashier.
Kastanie f. chestnut.
Kasten m. box, chest, mailbox.
Katalog m. catalog.
Katastrophe f. catastrophe.
katastrophal catastrophic.
Katholik m. Roman Catholic.
katholisch Roman Catholic. (*adj.*)
Katze f. cat.
kauen to masticate, chew.
  Kaugummi, n. chewing-gum.
KAUF m. buy, purchase.
  mit in Kauf nehmen to put up with.
KAUFEN to buy, purchase.
  sich etwas kaufen to buy oneself something.
Käufer m. buyer.
Kaufhaus n. store, warehouse, department store.
Kaufladen m. store, shop.
Kaufmann m. shopkeeper, merchant.
KAUM hardly, scarcely, barely.
Kavalier m. cavalier, gentleman.
keck bold, daring, impudent.
Keckheit f. boldness.
Kegel m. ninepin.
kegeln to bowl.
Kehle f. throat.
Kehlkopf m. larynx.
KEHREN turn, to sweep.
  sich kehren an to pay attention to; to mind.
  kehrtmachen to face about, turn back.
KEIN *adj.* no, not one, not any.
KEIN (ER,-E,-ES) *pron.* none, neither.
  keiner von beiden neither of them.
keinerlei of no sort.
KEINESWEGS on no account, not at all.
Kelch m. cup, goblet, chalice.
Keller m. cellar.
KELLNER m. (-in f.) waiter, (waitress).
KENNEN to know, be acquainted with.
  kennenlernen to meet, become acquainted
    with.
Kenner m. connoisseur.
Kennkarte f. identity-card.
kenntlich recognizable, distinguishable.
KENNTNIS f. knowledge, information.
  in Kenntnis setzen to inform.
  zur Kenntnis nehmen to take note of.
Kennzeichen n. identification.
Kern m. kernel, corn, seed, stone (fruit).
Kerze f. candle, sparking plug.
Kessel m. boiler, kettle.
Kette f. chain, necklace.
Kettenhund m. watch dog.
keuchen to pant, puff.
Keuchhusten m. whooping cough.
Keule f. club, leg (of lamb, etc.).
keusch pure, modest, chaste.
Keuschheit f. modesty, purity, chastity.
Kiefer m. jaw.
Kilogramm n. kilogram (2.204 pounds).
Kilometer m. kilometer (.621 miles).
Kilometerzähler m. mileage recorder.
KIND n. child.
  kleines Kind baby (infant).
  von Kind auf from childhood on.
Kindergarten m. kindergarten, nursery school.
Kinderlähmung f. infantile paralysis.

kinderlos childless.
Kindermädchen n. nursemaid.
Kinderstube f. nursery.
Kinderwagen m. baby carriage.
Kindheit f. childhood.
kindisch childish.
kindlich childlike, filial.
Kinn n. chin.
Kino n. cinema, picture show, movies.
Kirche f. church, service.
Kirchhof m. cemetery.
Kirchturm m. church steeple.
Kirsche f. cherry.
Kissen n. cushion, pillow.
Kissenbezug m. cover, pillow-case.
Kiste f. box, chest, case.
kitzeln to tickle.
kitzlig ticklish.
Kloge f. lament, complaint.
klagen to lament, complain, sue.
Kläger m. plaintiff.
kläglich lamentable, deplorable.
klamm numb, stiff, tight.
klammern to fasten, clasp, cling to.
Klang m. sound, tone, ringing of bell.
Klangfarbe f. timbre.
klanglos soundless.
klangvoll sonorous.
Klappstuhl m. camp stool or chair.
Klapptisch m. folding table.
Klaps m. slap.
KLAR clear, limpid, pure, plain, evident.
    klar und deutlich distinctly, plainly.
    klar zum Gefecht ready for action.
    klar legen (stellen) to clear up, explain.
    sich klar darüber sein to realize.
Klarinette f. clarinet.
Klarinettist m. clarinetist.
KLASSE f. class, form, order.
Klassenlehrer m. class-teacher.
Klassenzimmer n. classroom.
Klassik f. classical art, classical period.
Klatsch m. smack, crack, gossip.
klatschen to clap, lash, applaud.
    Beifall klatschen to applaud.
Klavier n. piano.
Klavierspieler m. pianist.
kleben to stick, glue.
Klee m. clover, shamrock.
KLEID n. dress, frock, gown.
    die Kleider, pl. garments.
kleiden to dress, clothe, suit, become.
    Er ist immer gut gekleidet. He is always well-dressed.
Kleiderbügel m. coathanger.
Kleiderbürste f. clothes brush.
Kleiderschrank m. wardrobe.
Kleidung f. dress, clothes, clothing.
KLEIN little, small, tiny, minor.
    klein schneiden to cut in pieces.
    klein schreiben to write with small letters.
    von klein auf from infancy on.
KLEINGELD n. change (monetary).
kleingläubig of little faith.
Kleinholz n. sticks, firewood.
Kleinkram m. trifle.
Kleinstadt f. small provincial town.
kleinstädtisch provincial.
klettern to climb.
Klima n. climate.
klimatisch climatic.
klimmen to climb.
Klingel f. bell.
klingeln to ring.
Klinke f. doorknob; handle.
klipp snapping sound, snap of the fingers.
    klipp und klar quite clear.
klirren to clink, jingle.

klopfen to beat, knock, tap.
Kloster n. monastery, convent.
Klub m. club.
Klubsessel m. lounge chair, easy chair.
KLUG intelligent, sensible, clever.
    Ich werde nicht klug daraus. I can't figure it out.
Klugheit f. intelligence.
Klumpen m. lump.
KNABE m. boy, lad.
Knall m. bang, detonation, crack.
knapp narrow, tight, close, poor.
    knapp werde to run short of.
Knappheit f. narrowness, conciseness.
Knecht m. servant, farmhand, slave.
Knechtheit f. servitude, slavery.
kneifen to pinch, nip.
Kneipe f. tavern, public house.
Knie n. knee.
Kniehosen pl. breeches, shorts.
knistern to rustle, crackle.
KNOCHEN m. bone.
knöchern of bone, bony.
Knopf m. button, knob, head.
knöpfen to button.
Knopfloch n. buttonhole.
Knospe f. bud.
knospig full of buds.
Knoten m. knot.
knurren to growl, rumble.
knusprig crisp.
Koch m. cook.
Kochbuch n. cookbook.
KOCHEN to cook, boil.
Kochgeschirr n. pots and pans.
Köchin f. cook.
Kochlöffel m. ladle.
Kochtopf m. saucepan, pot, casserole.
Koffer m. trunk, bag, suitcase.
Kognak m. cognac, brandy.
Kohl m. cabbage.
Kohle f. coal, carbon.
    auf Kohlen sitzen to be on tenterhooks.
Kohleneimer m. coal bucket.
Koje f. cabin, berth.
Kollege m. colleague.
Kolonialwaren pl. groceries.
Kolonialwarenhandlung f. grocery store.
Komiker m. comedian.
komisch comical.
Komma n. comma.
kommandieren to command, order.
KOMMEN to come, arrive, get, result, happen, occur.
    Das kommt davon. That's the result.
    Das kommt nicht in Frage. This is out of the question.
    Es kommt darauf an. It depends.
    kommen lassen to send for.
    kommen sehen to foresee.
    nicht dazu kommen to have no time to.
    Wann komme ich an die Reihe? When will it be my turn?
    Wie kommt es, dass how is it that.
    zu sich kommen to recover.
kommend next.
    kommende Woche next week.
Kommentar m. commentary.
Kommode f. commode.
Komödiant m. comedian, actor, hypocrite.
Komödie f. comedy.
Kompass m. compass.
komplett complete; completely.
Kompliment n. compliment.
komponieren to compose.
Komponist m. composer.
Konditor m. pastry cook.
Konditorei f. pastry-shop, cafe.
Konfekt n. candy, chocolates, sweets.

Konfektion f. ready-made clothes.
Konferenz f. conference.
Konfession f. confession.
Konflikt m. conflict.
KÖNIG m. king.
königlich royal.
Konkurrent m. rival.
Konkurrenz f. competition.
konkurrieren to be in competition with, compete.
Konkurs m. bankruptcy.
KÖNNEN to be able to, be possible, understand.
    Das kann sein. It may be.
    Das kann nicht sein. It is impossible.
    Ich kann nicht mehr. I am exhausted.
    Er kann nichts dafür. It is not his fault.
konsequent consistent.
Konsequenz f. consistency.
konservativ conservative.
Konservatorium n. academy of music.
Konserve f. canned goods.
konstruieren to construct.
Konstrukteur m. constructor.
Konsul m. consul.
Konsulat n. consulate.
Kontinent m. continent.
Konto n. account (financial).
Kontoauszug m. statement (account).
Kontrakt m. contract.
Kontrast m. contrast.
Kontrolle f. control.
Kontrolleur m. controller.
kontrollieren to control.
Konversationslexikon n. encyclopedia.
Konzert n. concert.
KOPF m. head, brains, intellect, heading.
    auf den Kopf stellen to turn upside down.
    aus dem Kopf by heart.
    einem den Kopf waschen to give a person a dressing-down.
    Es ist mir über den Kopf gewachsen. It was too much for me.
    im Kopf behalten to remember.
    Kopf oder Schrift heads or tails.
    nicht auf den Kopf gefallen sein to be no fool.
    sich den Kopf zerbrechen to rack one's brains.
    sich etwas aus dem Kopf schlagen to dismiss something from one's mind.
    sich in den Kopf setzen to take into one's head.
    über den Kopf waschen to be too much for.
    vor den Kopf stossen to hurt, offend.
Kopfarbeit f. brain work.
Kopfkissen n. pillow.
Kopfsalat m. lettuce.
kopfscheu timid.
Kopfschmerzen pl. headache.
    Ich habe Kopfschmerzen. I have a headache.
Kopfweh n. headache.
Korb m. basket.
    Hahn im Korbe sein to be cock of the walk.
Kork m. cork, stopper.
    Korkzieher m. corkscrew.
Korn n. grain.
    aufs Korn nehmen to aim at.
KÖRPER m. body.
körperlich bodily, physical.
Körperpflege f. physical culture, care of the body.
Körperwärme f. body heat.
korrekt correct.
Korrespondenz f. correspondence.
Korridor m. corridor.
korrigieren to correct.
Kosmetik f. cosmetics.
Kost f. food, board.
kostbar precious, costly, valuable.
Kostbarkeit f. preciousness, object of valor.
Kosten f. costs, expenses.
    auf seine Kosten kommen to recover expenses, be satisfied with the deal.

KOSTEN to cost, require, taste.
Kostenanschlag *m.* estimate.
kostenlos free.
kostenpflichtig liable for the cost.
Kostenpunkt *f.* expenses.
köstlich precious, valuable, delicious.
kostspielig expensive.
Kostüm *n.* costume, tailored suit.
Kostümfest *n.* fancy dress ball.
Kotelett *n.* cutlet, chop.
Krabbe *f.* shrimp, crab.
Krach *m.* crash, noise, quarrel.
    mit Ach und Krach with difficulty, just barely.
KRAFT *f.* strength, energy, power.
    ausser Kraft setzen to annul, abolish.
    Das geht über meine Kräfte. That's too much for me.
    in Kraft treten to come into force, effect.
    nach besten Kräften to the best of one's ability.
    zu Kräften komme. to regain one's strength.
kräftig robust, strong.
kraftlos weak, feeble.
Kragen *m.* collar.
KRANK ill, sick.
    sich krank lachen to split one's sides (with laughter).
    krank werden to be taken ill.
Kranke *m.* patient.
Krankenauto *n.* ambulance.
Krankenhaus *n.* hospital.
Krankenschwester *f.* nurse.
Krankheit *f.* illness, disease.
Kranz *m.* wreath, garland.
kraus crisp, curly.
    die Stirne krausziehen to knit one's brow.
Kraut *n.* cabbage.
Krawatte *f.* necktie.
Krebs *m.* crawfish, cancer.
Kredit *f.* credit.
KREIS *m.* circle, social group.
    einen Kreis ziehen to describe a circle.
    sich im Kreise drehen to turn around, rotate.
kreisen to circle, revolve, circulate.
Kreislauf *m.* circulation, course, revolution.
KREUZ *n.* cross; clubs (cards).
    das Kreuz schlagen to cross oneself.
    das Rote Kreuz the Red Cross.
    kreuz und quer in all directions.
Kreuzung *f.* crossing.
    Eisenbahnkreuzung. Railroad crossing.
Kreuzverhör *n.* cross-examination.
Kreuzworträtsel *n.* crossword puzzle.
kriechen to creep, crawl.
KRIEG *m.* war.
    im Krieg in wartime.
    Krieg führen to make war.
Kriegsgefangene *m.* prisoner of war.
Kriegsschauplatz *m.* theater of war.
Kriminalpolizei *f.* criminal investigation department.
Kriminalroman *m.* detective-story.
Kritik *f.* criticism.
Kritiker *m.* critic.
kritiklos uncritical, undiscriminating.
kritisch critical.
kritisieren to criticize.
Krone *f.* crown.
Kronleuchter *m.* chandelier.
Krug *m.* pitcher, jar.
Krümel *n.* crumb.
krümeln to crumble.
krumm crooked, curved, bent.
krümmen to bend.
Krümmung *f.* curve.
Krüppel *m.* cripple.
Krystall *n.* crystal.
KÜCHE *f.* kitchen, cooking.
Kuchen *m.* cake, pastry.

Kuchenbäcker *m.* pastry-cook.
Küchenherd *m.* stove.
Kugel *f.* bullet, ball, globe, sphere.
Kuh *f.* cow.
    Er ist bekannt wie eine bunte Kuh. He is well-known everywhere ("like a colorful cow").
KÜHL cool, fresh, chilly.
Kühlanlage cold storage plant.
Kühle *f.* coolness, freshness.
kühlen to cool.
Kühler *m.* radiator (car).
Kühlschrank *m.* refrigerator.
Kühlung *f.* cooling, freshness.
kühn bold, daring, audacious.
Kühnheit *f.* boldness, audacity.
Kulisse *f.* wing.
kultivieren to cultivate.
Kultur *f.* culture.
Kummer *m.* grief, sorrow.
kummervoll sad, sorrowful.
Kunde *f.* customer, client, news.
Kundgebung *f.* demonstration.
kundig well-informed, experienced.
kündigen to give notice.
Kundschaft *f.* intelligence.
künftig in the future.
KUNST *f.* art.
Kunstausstellung *f.* art exhibition.
Kunstgalerie *f.* art gallery.
kunstgerecht correct.
Kunsthandel *m.* fine art trade.
Kunsthändler *m.* art dealer.
Künstler *m.* artist.
künstlich artificial, false.
Kunstmaler *m.* painter.
Kunstseide *f.* artificial silk.
Kunststoff *m.* plastics.
Kunststück *n.* feat, trick.
KUR *f.* treatment, cure.
Kurgast *m.* visitor, patient.
Kurhaus *n.* casino.
kurios odd, strange.
Kurort *m.* health resort.
Kurs *m.* course, rate of exchange.
Kurve *f.* curve, bend, turn.
    Gefährliche Kurve! Dangerous curve!
KURZ short, brief, abrupt; in short, briefly.
    den Kürzern ziehen   to be the loser.
    in kurzem   soon, shortly.
    kurz darauf   shortly after.
    kurz oder lang   sooner or later.
    kurz und bündig   concisely, briefly.
    kurz und gut   in short.
    vor kurzem   recently.
    zu kurz kommen   to come off badly.
Kürze *f.* shortness, brevity.
kürzen to shorten, abridge.
kurzgefasst concise.
Kurzgeschichte *f.* short story.
kürzlich lately, recently.
Kurzschrift *f.* shorthand.
kurzsichtig shortsighted.
Kürzung *f.* shortening, abbreviation.
Kuss *m.* kiss.
    Mit Grüssen und Küssen With love and kisses.
küssen to kiss.
Küste *f.* coast, shore.
Kuvert *n.* envelope, cover, wrapping.

L

Laborant *m.* laboratory assistant.
Laboratorium *n.* laboratory.
lächeln to smile.
    höhnisch lächeln to sneer.
Lachen *n.* laugh, laughter.
LACHEN to laugh.

lächerlich laughable, ridiculous.
    lächerlich machen to ridicule.
lachhaft ridiculous.
Laden *m.* shop, store, shutter.
Ladeninhaber *m.* shopkeeper.
Ladenschluss *m.* closing time.
Ladentisch *m.* counter.
Lage *f.* situation, position, site, condition, storage.
Lager *n.* bed, couch, layer, support.
Lageraufnahme *f.* inventory.
Lagergeld *n* storage fee.
Lagerhaus *n.* warehouse.
lagern to lie down, camp.
lahm lame, paralyzed.
Laie *m.* layman.
Laken *n.* sheet.
LAMPE *f.* lamp, light.
Lampenfieber *n.* stagefright.
Lampenschirm *m.* lamp-shade.
LAND *n.* land, mainland, ground.
    an Land gehen to land, go ashore.
    aufs Land gehen to go to the country.
    ausser Landes gehen to go abroad.
landen to land, put ashore.
Landesbrauch *m.* national custom.
Landesfarben *pl.* national colors.
Landessprache *f.* national language.
Landestracht *f.* national costume.
Landesverrat *m.* high treason.
Landesverweisung *f.* expulsion, banishment, exile.
Landhaus *n.* country house.
Landkarte *f.* map.
Landschaft *f.* landscape, scenery.
landschaftlich provincial.
Landstrasse *f.* highway, highroad.
Landung *f.* landing, disembarkation.
Landwirtschaft *f.* farming, agriculture.
landwirtschaftlich agricultural.
LANG long, tall.
    auf lange Sicht long-dated.
    auf die lange Bank schieben to put off.
    den lieben langen Tag the livelong day.
    einen Tag lang for a day.
    Es dauert lange. It takes long.
    über kurz oder lang sooner or later.
langatmig long-winded, lengthy.
Länge *f.* length, duration.
    der Länge nach lengthwise.
    in die Länge ziehen to drag on, spin out
langen to suffice, last, be enough.
    langen nach to reach for.
Längengrad degree of longitude.
länger longer.
    Je länger, je lieber. The longer, the better.
    schon länger for some time.
Langeweile *f.* boredom.
langfristig long-dated.
LÄNGS *prep. (gen.)* along.
    Der Weg läuft längs des Stromes. The road runs along the river.
langsam slow, tardy.
    Langsam fahren! Slow down!
Langsamkeit *f.* slowness.
längst long ago, long since.
    schon längst for a very long time.
    am längsten the longest.
    längstens at the latest, at the most.
langweilen to bore.
    sich zu Tode langweilen to be bored to death.
langwierig lengthy.
Lärm *m.* noise, din, row.
LASSEN to let, allow, permit, suffer, omit, abandon.
    aus dem Spiel lassen to leave out of the question.
    Das muss man ihm lassen. One must credit him with that.
    es beim alten lassen to let things remain as they are.
    holen lassen to send for.

Lass das! Don't!

Lass nur! Never mind!

Ich habe den Wagen waschen lassen. I had the car washed.

machen (waschen, reinigen, richten, usw.) lassen to have made (washed, cleaned, fixed, etc.),

mit sich reden lassen to be reasonable.

sein Leben lassen to lose one's life.

sich sagen lassen to be told, take advice.

sich Zeit lassen to take time.

warten lassen to keep waiting.

lässig lazy, idle, indolent.

Last f. load, weight, burden, charge.

lästig troublesome, annoying, irksome.

Lastwagen m. cart, truck, van.

Laterne f. lantern, lamp.

Laub f foliage, leaves.

Laubwald n. forest.

Laubwerk n. foliage.

Lauer f. ambush.

lauern to wait for.

Lauf m. race, course, run, current.

in vollem Lauf at full gallop.

freien Lauf lassen to give vent to.

Laufbahn f. career.

LAUFEN to run, flow, go on.

laufen lassen to let things go.

auf dem laufenden sein to be up to date, abreast.

laufend running.

Laufjunge m. errand-boy.

Laune f. mood, whim.

guter Laune sein to be in good mood.

launisch moody.

Laut m. sound, tone.

LAUT 1. adj. loud, noisy, audible.

laut werden to become known, get about.

2. prep. (gen.) according to, in accordance with

laut Befehls by order.

laut Rechnung as per account.

lauten to sound.

läuten to ring, toll.

lautlos silent.

Lautlosigkeit f. silence.

Lautsprecher m. loudspeaker.

lauwarm lukewarm.

LEBEN n. life, lifetime, living.

am Leben bleiben to survive.

am Leben sein to be alive.

auf Leben und Tod a matter of life and death.

einem Kind das Leben schenken to give birth to a child.

ins Leben rufen to originate, start.

LEBEN to live, be alive, dwell, stay.

lebendig living, lively.

Lebendigkeit f. liveliness, animation.

Lebensgefahr f. danger, risk of one's life.

lebensgefährlich highly dangerous.

Lebenslage f. position.

lebenslänglich for life, perpetual.

Lebenslauf m. curriculum vitae, background.

Lebensmittel n. food, provisions.

lebensmüde tired of life.

Lebensraum m. living space.

Lebensunterhalt m. livelihood, living.

Lebenswandel m. life, conduct.

Lebensweise f. mode of life.

Leber f. liver.

lebhaft lively, vivacious.

Leck n. leak.

lecken to lick.

LEDER n. leather.

LEER empty, vacant, blank, idle.

mit leeren Händen with empty hands.

Leere f. emptiness, void, vacuum.

leerlauf m. neutral (gear).

leeren to empty.

LEGEN to put, lay, place, lie down, calm down.

Lehne f. back of chair.

lehnen to lean against, rest upon.

sich lehnen to lean back.

Lehnstuhl m. armchair.

Lehramt n. teacher's post.

Lehrberuf m. teaching profession.

Lehrbuch n. text book.

Lehre f. instruction, precept, advice, warning.

LEHREN to teach, instruct.

LEHRER m. (= in, f.) teacher.

Lehrfach n. teaching profession.

lehrhaft didactic.

Lehrjahre pl. years of apprenticeship.

lehrreich instructive.

Leib m. body, belly, womb.

Leibgericht n. favorite dish.

Leibschmerzen m. pl. stomach-ache, colic

Leiche f. corpse.

LEICHT easy, light, slight, mild, careless, frivolous; easily.

etwas leicht nehmen to take it easy.

leicht möglich very probable.

leichtfertig thoughtless, frivolous.

Leichtfertigkeit f. thoughtlessness, frivolity.

leichtgläubig credulous.

Leichtsinn m. carelessness, thoughtlessness.

leichtsinnig careless, thoughtless.

LEID n. grief, sorrow, pain, harm.

Er tut mir leid. I am sorry for him.

Es tut mir leid. I am sorry about it.

sich ein Leid antun to commit suicide.

zu meinem Leidwesen to my regret.

leiden to suffer, bear, endure, stand.

leiden können, leiden mögen to like.

Sie leidet schwer darunter. It's making her very miserable.

Leidenschaft f. passion.

leidenschaftlich passionately.

leidenschaftslos dispassionate.

leider unfortunately.

leider nicht unfortunately not.

Leihbibliothek f. lending library.

leihen to lend.

Leine f. leash.

Leinwand f. linen, screen.

leise soft, gentle, dim.

mit leiser Stimme in a low voice.

Leiste f. strip.

leisten to perform, carry out, accomplish.

es sich leisten können to be able to afford something.

leistungsfähig capable, fit, efficient.

Leistungsfähigkeit f. capacity for work, efficiency, power.

leiten to lead, conduct, manage, direct.

Leiter m. leader, manager, principal, head.

Leitung f. direction, management, guidance, line, pipe.

Leitungswasser tap water.

Lektion f. lesson (in a book).

lenkbar docile, tractable.

lenken to direct, conduct, drive, steer.

lernbegierig anxious to learn.

LERNEN to learn, study.

Lesebuch n. reader (book).

LESEN to read, lecture.

lesenswert worth reading.

Leser m. reader (person).

leserlich legible.

LETZT last, latest, final, extreme.

in letzter Zeit lately, recently.

letzte Neuheit latest novelty.

letzten Endes after all.

letzten Sonntag last Sunday.

letztes hergeben to do one's utmost.

zu guter Letzt finally, in the end.

letztens lately, of late.

Leuchte f. lamp, light.

leuchten to light, shine, beam, glow.

Leuchter m. candlestick.

Leuchtturm m. lighthouse.

Leuchtuhr f. luminous clock or watch.

Leuchtzifferblatt n. luminous dial.

leugnen to deny, disavow.

LEUTE pl. people, persons, folk.

Leutnant m. second lieutenant.

leutselig affable.

Lexikon n. dictionary.

LICHT n. light, candle, illumination.

Bitte, machen Sie das Licht an. Please turn on the light.

Licht anzünden to turn on the light.

Licht auszünden to turn off the light.

in ein falsches Licht setzen to misrepresent.

Mir ging ein Licht auf. It dawned on me.

licht

am lichten Tage in broad daylight.

lichte Augenblicke sane moments.

lichtempfindlich sensitive to light.

lichten to thin out, clear (forest).

Lichterglanz m. brightness.

Lichtpause f. photostatic copy.

Lichtreklame f. luminous sign, illuminated advertisement.

LIEB dear, nice, beloved, agreeable.

Es ist mir lieb. I am glad.

es wäre mir lieb I should like.

Liebchen n. darling, love, sweetheart.

LIEBE f. love, affection, charity.

aus Liebe for love.

mir zu Liebe for my sake.

LIEBEN to love, like, be in love.

liebenswürdig amiable, kind.

Liebenswürdigkeit f. amiability, kindness.

lieber dearer, rather.

Liebeserklärung f. declaration of love.

Liebesgeschichte f. love story.

Liebespaar n. lovers, couple.

liebgewinnen to grow fond of.

liebhaben to love.

Liebhaber m. (= in f.) lover; amateur.

Liebhaberei f. fancy, liking; hobby.

liebkosen to caress, fondle.

Liebkosung f. caress, petting.

lieblich lovely, charming.

Liebling m. darling, favorite.

Liebreiz m. charm, attraction.

Liebschaft f. love affair.

Liebste m. & f. dearest, beloved, lover, sweetheart.

LIED n. song, air.

Liederbuch n. song-book, hymn-book.

liederlich slovenly, immoral, dissolute.

lieferbar available.

Lieferfrist f. term of delivery.

liefern to deliver, yield, produce.

Lieferung f. delivery, supply.

Lieferzeit f. time (or term) of delivery.

LIEGEN to lie, rest, be situated, stand.

Das liegt an mir. It is my fault.

Mir liegt daran. I am interested in the matter.

Mir liegt nichts daran. I don't care for it.

liegenlassen to leave.

Likör m. liqueur, cordial.

Limonade f. lemonade.

lindern to soften, ease, soothe.

Linderung f. relief.

Linie f. line, descent, branch (of a family).

in erster Linie first of all.

LINK left, wrong side of a cloth, reverse of a coin.

linkisch award, clumsy.

LINKS to the left, on the left.

Gehen Sie nach links! Go to the left!

Sie liess ihn ganz links liegen. She gave him the cold shoulder.
linkshändig left-handed.
Linnen n. linen
Linse f. lentil.
Lippe f. lip.
Lippenstift m. lipstick.
List f. cunning, craft.
Liste f. list, roll, catalogue.
listig cunning, crafty, sly, astute.
Liter m. liter (1.056 quarts).
literarisch literary.
Literatur f. literature, letters.
Litfasssäule f. billboard.
Lizenz f. license, permit.
Lob n. praise.
loben to praise.
lobenswert praiseworthy.
lobpreisen to praise.
Loch n. hole, gap.
Locke f. lock, curl.
locken to entice, allure.
Löffel m. spoon.
　　Esslöffel, m. tablespoon.
Loge f. box (theater).
Logik f. logic.
logisch logical.
Lohn m. compensation, reward, wages.
Lohnempfänger m. wage-earner.
lohnen to reward.
　　Es lohnt sich. It is worth while.
Löhnung f. pay.
lokal local, suburban.
Lokomotive f. engine (of a train).
Los n. lot, chance.
LOS
　1. *adv.* loose, slack, free.
　　Hier ist viel los. There's plenty going on here.
　　Mit ihm ist nicht viel los. He is not up to much.
　　Was ist los? What's up?
　2. *separable prefix (implies the idea of separation or quick movement).*
　　Du kannst die Hunde loskoppeln. You can untie the dogs.
　　Eins, zwei, drei, los! One, two, three, go!
losbinden to untie, unloosen.
löschen to put out, extinguish.
losgehen to set out, become loose, go off.
loskommen to get away.
loswerden to get rid of.
Löwe m. lion.
LUFT f. air, breath, breeze.
　　aus der Luft greifen to invent.
　　frische Luft schöpfen to take the air.
　　in die Luft sprengen to blow up.
　　keine Luft bekommen not to be able to breathe.
luftdicht air-tight.
lüften to air.
luftig airy, breezy.
Luftkrankheit f. airsickness.
　　luftkrank sein to be airsick.
Luftkurort m. health resort.
luftleer airless.
　　luftleerer Raum vacuum
Luftpost f. air mail.
Luftraum m. atmosphere.
Lüge f. lie, untruth, falsehood.
lügen to lie (falsify).
Lunge f. lung.
Lungenentzündung f. pneumonia.
Lupe f. magnifying glass.
Lust f. pleasure, joy, delight, inclination, lust.
　　Lust haben to be inclined to.
lustig gay, funny, jolly.
　　sich lustig machen to make fun of.
Lustspiel n. comedy.

Luxus m. luxury.
Lyrik f. lyrics.

M

Machart f. style, description, kind, sort.
MACHEN to make, do, manufacture, cause, amount to.
　　Das lässt sich machen. That is feasible.
　　Das macht nichts. That does not matter.
　　Was macht Ihre Erkältung? How is your cold?
MACHT f. strength, might, power, authority.
mächtig strong, mighty, powerful.
machtlos powerless.
MÄDCHEN n. girl, servant.
　　Mädchen für alles general servant.
mädchenhaft girlish, maidenly.
Mädchenname m. maiden name.
Magen m. stomach.
　　Ich habe einen verdorbenen Magen. I have an upset stomach.
Magenverstimmung f. stomach upset.
mager thin, scanty.
Magerkeit f. leanness, skimpiness.
mähen to mow, cut, reap.
MAHL n. meal.
mahlen to grind, mill.
Mahnbrief m. request to pay.
mahnen to remind, admonish, exort.
Mahnung f. reminder, warning.
MAI m. May.
Maiglöckchen n. lily of the valley.
Mais m. corn, maize.
Major m. major.
MAL n. 1. landmark, monument, mark.
　　2. time, turn.
　　dieses Mal for once.
　　ein für alle Mal once and for all.
　　mit einem Mal suddenly.
　　zum ersten Mal for the first time.
mal times, once, just.
　　Danke vielmals thank you very much.
　　Viermal drei ist zwölf. Three times four is twelve.
malen to paint, portray, represent.
　　sich malen lassen to have one's portrait made.
Maler m. painter.
malerisch pictorial, picturesque.
MAN one, they, people, you.
　　man hat mir gesagt, dass.... I was told that....
　　Man sagt so. So they say.
MANCHE many, some.
manch(er,-e,-es) many a.
mancherlei various, diverse.
manchmal sometimes.
Mangel m. need, want, absence, lack.
　　aus Mangel an for want of.
mangelhaft faulty, defective.
mangeln to want, be wanting.
　　es mangelt mir an I am short of.
Manier f. manner, style.
manierlich polite, civil, mannerly.
MANN m. man; husband.
　　mit Mann und Maus with every soul.
　　wenn Not am Mann ist if the worst comes to the worst.
Mannesalter n. manhood.
mannhaft manly.
männlich male, manly.
Manschette f. cuff.
Manschettenknopf m. sleeve link.
MANTEL m. coat.
Mappe f. document case, writing case.
Märchen n. fairy tale.
märchenhaft fabulous, legendary.
Marine f. navy.
Mark f. mark (coin).
markant characteristic, striking.
Marke f. mark, sign, postage stamp, token.
MARKT m. market, market place.

Markthalle f. market-hall.
Marktplatz m. market place.
Marmelade f. jam.
Marmor m. marble.
Marmorplatte f. marble slab.
Marsch m. march.
marschieren to march.
MÄRZ m. March.
Marzipan m. & n. marzipan.
MASCHINE f. machine, engine, typewriter.
　　auf der Maschine schreiben to typewrite.
Maske f. mask, disguise.
Maskenball m. fancy dress ball.
Maskerade f. masquerade.
MASS n. measure, dimension, size, degree, proportion, moderation.
　　in hohem Mass in a high degree.
　　Mass nehmen to measure.
　　Masse und Gewichte pl. weights and measurements.
　　nach Mass gemacht made to measure.
Massarbeit f. made to measure (to order).
MASSE f. crowd, mass, quantity.
massenhaft in large quantities, wholesale.
massgebend standard.
massgeblich standard.
masshalten to observe moderation, keep within limits.
mässig reasonable, moderate, poor, mediocre.
mässigen to observe moderation, restrain.
Mässigkeit f. moderation, frugality.
masslos boundless, without limit.
Massregel f. measure, step.
Massstab m. yard, measure, scale.
Material n. material, substance.
materialisieren to materialize.
materialistisch materialistic.
Mathematik f. mathematics.
Matratze f. mattress.
Matrose m. sailor.
matt weak, soft, dull; mate(chess).
　　mattsetzen to mate (chess).
Mauer f. wall.
mauern to build with stones.
Maultier n. mule.
Maurer m. mason, bricklayer.
Maus f. mouse.
Mechanik f. mechanics.
Mechaniker m. mechanic.
mechanisch mechanical.
Medikament n. medicament.
Medizin f. medicine, remedy.
Mediziner m. medical student.
MEER n. sea, seashore.
Meerenge f. channel.
Meeresspiegel m. sea-level.
Mehl n. flour.
Mehlspeise f. pudding.
MEHR more.
　　desto mehr all the more.
　　immer mehr more and more.
　　je mehr...desto mehr...the more.
　　mehr als more than.
　　nicht mehr no more, any more, any longer.
　　nie mehr never again.
　　nur mehr only, nothing but.
　　um so mehr als... all the more as.
Mehrbetrag m. surplus.
mehrere several.
mehreres several things.
mehrfach manifold, numerous.
Mehrheit f. majority.
mehrmals several times, again and again.
Mehrzahl f. majority, plural.
Meile f. mile (1.609 kilometers).
MEIN poss. adj. my.
MEINEN to mean, think, believe, suppose.
　　Was meinen Sie damit? What do you mean by that?

Was meinen Sie dazu? What do you think about it?

Wie meinen Sie? I beg your pardon?

MEIN(er,-e-es) *poss. pron.* mine.

meinerseits for my part, as far as I am concerned.

meihesgleichen my equals, people like me.

meinethalben for my sake, for all I care.

meinetwegen for my sake, for me, on my account, as far as I am concerned.

meinetwillen (um—) for my sake.

MEINUNG *f.* meaning, opinion, view.

einem die Meinung sagen to give someone a piece of one's mind.

meiner Meinung nach to my mind, in my opinion.

meist most, mostly.

die meisten most people.

MEISTENS mostly.

MEISTER *m.* master.

Meisterschaft *f.* championship.

Meistersinger *m.* mastersinger.

Meisterstück *n.* masterpiece.

Meisterwerk *n.* masterpiece.

Meldeamt *n.* registration office.

melden to report, announce, inform, apply.

Meldezettel *m.* registration form.

Meldung *f.* news, announcement, advice, notification.

melken to milk.

Melodie *f.* melody, tune.

Menge *f.* quantity, amount, lots, multitude.

in Mengen in abundance, plenty of.

mengen to mix, meddle, interfere.

MENSCH *m.* man, human being, person.

Es kam kein Mensch. Not a soul came.

seit Menschengedenken within the memory of man; immemorial.

Was für ein Mensch ist er? What sort of a person is he?

Menschenalter *n.* generation.

menschenmöglich humanly possible.

Menschheit *f.* human race.

menschlich human.

Menschlichkeit *f.* human nature.

merkbar noticeable.

merken to perceive, notice, observe, note.

sich nichts merken lassen to appear to know nothing.

merklich noticeable.

Merkmal *n.* characteristic, sign, mark.

merkwürdig characteristic, strange, peculiar, remarkable.

merkwürdigerweise strangely enough, strange to say.

Merkwürdigkeit *f.* strangeness, peculiarity.

Messe *f.* mass; fair; mess (officers').

MESSEN to measure, survey, take the temperature (of a patient).

m' Blicken messen to eye.

sich messen mit to compete with.

sich nicht messen können mit to be no match for.

MESSER *n.* knife.

Messergriff *m.* knife handle.

Messerstich *m.* stab (with a knife).

Messing *n.* brass.

Metall *n.* metal.

Meter *m. & n.* meter (39.37 inches).

Metermass *n.* tape-measure.

Methode *f.* method.

Metzger *m.* butcher.

Metzgerei *f.* butcher's shop.

Meuterei *f.* mutiny.

MICH *acc. of ich (pers. pron)* me, myself.

Miene *f.* expression (facial), air, countenance.

gute Miene zum bösen Spiel machen to put up a brave show.

MIETE *f.* rent, lease.

Die Miete ist fällig. The rent is due.

zur Miete wohnen to be a tenant.

mieten to rent.

Mieter *m.* tenant.

mietfrei rent free.

Mietshaus *n.* apartment house.

Mietvertrag *m.* lease.

Mikrofon *n.* microphone.

Mikroskop *n.* microscope.

mikroskopisch microscopic.

MILCH *f.* milk.

Milchgeschäft *n.* dairy.

Milchgesicht *n.* baby face.

Milchglas *n.* opalescent glass.

Milchladen *m.* dairy.

Milchstrasse *f.* Milky Way.

Milchzahn *m.* milk tooth.

MILD mild, soft, gentle, mellow, kind, charitable.

Milde *f.* gentleness, kindness.

mildern to soften, extenuate.

Mildemde Umstände extenuating circumstances.

mildtätig kind, generous.

Militär *n.* army, service.

Militärdienst *m.* active service.

militärisch military.

Militarismus *m.* militarism.

MILLIARDE *f.* billion.

MILLION *f.* million.

Millionär *m.* millionaire.

MINDER less, minor, inferior.

minderbemittelt of moderate means.

Minderheit *f.* minority.

minderjährig minor (age).

minderjährig sein to be a minor.

Minderjährigkeit *f.* minority (age).

minderwertig inferior.

Minderwertigkeitsgefühl *n.* inferiority complex.

MINDEST least.

nicht im mindesten not in the least, by no means.

mindestens at least.

Mindestlohn *m.* minimum wage.

Mine *f.* mine.

Mineral *n.* mineral.

Minister *m.* minister.

Ministerium *n.* ministry.

Ministerpräsident *m.* prime minister.

MINUTE *f.* minute.

minutenläng for several minutes.

MIR *dat. of ich (pers. pron.)* to me, me, myself.

mischen to blend, mix, meddle, shuffle (cards).

sich mischen to interfere.

Mischung *f.* blend, mix.

missachten to disregard, disdain.

Missachtung *f.* disregard, disdain.

missbilligen to disapprove.

Missbilligung *f.* disapproval.

missbrauchen to misuse, abuse.

missen to do without.

Misserfolg *m.* failure.

Missetat *f.* misdeed, crime.

Missetäter *m.* criminal.

missfallen to displease.

Missgeschick *n.* bad luck, misfortune.

missglücken to fail.

missgönnen to grudge.

missgünstig envious, jealous.

misstrauen *n.* distrust, mistrust.

misstrauen to distrust, mistrust.

misstrauisch suspicious.

missvergnügt displeased.

missverstehen to misunderstand.

MIT *prep. (dat.)* with, at, by.

Der Patient hat mit gutem Appetit gegessen. The patient has eaten with a good appetite.

mit anderen Worten in other words.

mit der Post by post.

mit der Zeit gradually.

Mit fünf Jahren spielte er schon Klavier. At the age of five, he already played the piano.

Wir sind mit der Eisenbahn gereist. We traveled by train.

2. *separable prefix (implies accompaniment or participation).*

Kommen Sie mit? Are you coming along?

mitarbeiten to collaborate, cooperate, contribute.

Mitarbeiter *m.* collaborator.

Mitbesitzer *m.* joint proprietor.

mitbringen to bring along.

Mitbürger *m.* fellow citizen.

miteinander with each other, together, jointly.

mitempfinden to sympathize with.

Mitgefühl *n.* sympathy.

Mitgift *f.* dowry.

Mitglied *n.* member.

mitkommen to accompany, come along, keep up.

Mitleid *n.* sympathy, pity, mercy.

Mitleidenschaft *f.* compassion.

in Mitleidenschaft ziehen to affect.

mitleidig compassionate.

mitleidlos pitiless.

mitmachen to take part in, go through.

Sie hat sehr viel mitgemacht. She went through a lot.

mitnehmen to take along, affect.

Ihr Tod hat ihn sehr mitgenommen. Her death affected him deeply.

mitschuldig implicated (in a crime).

Mitschuldige *m. & f.* accomplice.

mitspielen to join in a game; to accompany (music).

MITTAG *m.* noon, midday; south.

zu Mittag essen to have lunch.

Mittagessen *n.* lunch.

mittags at noon.

Mittagspause *f.* lunch hour.

MITTE *f.* middle, centre, mean, medium.

Er ist Mitte Dreissig. He is in his middle thirties.

goldene Mitte golden mean.

mitteilen to impart, communicate.

Mitteilung *f.* information, communication, intelligence.

Mittel *n.* means; remedy, cure, medicine.

Er ist ohne irgendwelche Mittel. He is penniless.

Mittelalter *n.* Middle Ages.

Mitteleuropa *n.* Central Europe.

mittellos without means.

mittelmässig average, mediocre.

Mittelmeer *n.* Mediterranean.

Mittelstand *m.* middle class.

MITTEN midway, in the middle of.

mitten auf (in) in the midst of.

mittendrin right in the middle of.

mittendurch right across, right through.

MITTERNACHT *f.* midnight.

mitternachts at midnight.

mittlerweile meanwhile, in the meantime.

MITTWOCH *m.* Wednesday.

mitunter sometimes, now and then.

Mitwelt *f.* our age, our generation.

Mitwisser *m.* confidant, one in on the secret.

MÖBEL *n.* piece of furniture.

Möbel *pl.* furniture.

Möbelhändler *m.* furniture dealer.

Möbelstück *n.* piece of furniture.

möblieren to furnish.

Mode *f.* fashion.

Modell *n.* model, pattern, mold.

modern modern.

Modeschau *f.* fashion show.

modisch fashionable.

MÖGEN to want, wish, be able, be allowed; to like, care for.

Das mag ich nicht. I don't like that.

Das mag sein that may be so.

Er ist faul, er mag nicht lernen. He is lazy, he does not want to learn.

Ich möchte nicht. I don't want to.

Ich möchte wissen. I'd like to know.

wie dem auch sein mag be that as it may.

lieber mögen to prefer.

Ich möchte lieber auf dem Land leben. I'd rather live in the country.

möglich possible, practicable, feasible, likely.

alles mögliche all sorts of things, everything possible.

möglichst wenig as little as possible.

möglichst schnell as quickly as possible.

Nicht möglich! It can't be!

sein möglichstes tun to do one's utmost.

möglicherweise possibly, perhaps.

Möglichkeit f. possibility, chance.

Mole f. pier.

Moment m. moment.

Einen Moment! One moment!

Momentaufnahme f. snapshot.

Monarchie f. monarchy.

MONAT m. month.

monatelang for months.

monatlich monthly.

Mönch m. monk.

MOND m. moon.

Mondschein m. moonlight.

Monolog m. monologue.

MONTAG m. Monday.

Moor n. swamp.

Moos n. moss.

Mop m. mop.

moppen to mop.

Moral f. morality, morals, moral.

moralisch moral.

moralisieren to moralize.

Mord m. murder.

Selbstmord, m. suicide.

Mordanschlag m. murderous attack.

Mörder m. murderer.

MORGEN m. morning, dawn, daybreak; the following day.

früh morgens early in the morning.

Guten Morgen. Good morning.

heute morgen this morning.

morgens in the morning.

morgen tomorrow.

morgen früh tomorrow morning.

morgen in acht Tagen a week from tomorrow.

Morgen ist auch ein Tag. Tomorrow is another day.

Morgengrauen n. dawn of the day, break of the day.

morgenländisch from the Middle East.

Morgenrock m. robe.

Motor m. motor, engine.

Motorboot m. motor boat.

Motorpanne f. engine trouble.

Motorrad n. motorcycle.

Motte f. moth.

Mücke f. mosquito (gnat).

Mückenstich m. mosquito bite.

MÜDE tired, weary.

müde werden to get tired.

Müdigkeit f. weariness, fatigue.

MÜHE f. labor, toil, effort.

sich Mühe geben to take pains.

der Mühe wert worth while.

mit Müh und Not only just, barely.

Mühe machen to give troubles.

mühelos easy, effortless.

mühevoll laborious, difficult.

Mühle f. mill.

Müller m. miller.

MUND m. mouth.

den Mund halten to keep one's mouth shut.

den Mund vollnehmen to brag.

Er ist nicht auf den Mund gefallen. He has a ready tongue.

nach dem Mund reden to flatter.

Sie leben von der Hand in den Mund. They live from hand to mouth.

Mundwinkel m. corner of the mouth.

Munition f. ammunition.

munter wide-awake, alive, gay.

Münze f. coin, medal.

Sie nimmt alles für bare Münze. She takes everything at its face value.

mürrisch morose, sullen.

Museum n. museum.

Musik f. music.

musikalisch musical.

Muskel m. muscle.

Muskelkater m. stiffness and soreness.

MÜSSEN to have to, be obliged to, must, ought to.

Alle Menschen müssen sterben. All human beings must die.

Man müsste es ihr eigentlich sagen. Somebody really ought to tell her.

Sie müssen nicht, wenn Sie nicht wollen. You don't have to if you don't want to.

Muster n. sample, model, design, pattern.

mustergültig exemplary, perfect.

musterhaft exemplary, standard.

mustern to examine.

Musterung f. examination.

MUT m. courage, fortitude, state of mind.

jemandem den Mut nehmen to discourage someone.

Mut fassen to summon up courage.

Mut machen to encourage.

mutig brave.

mutlos despondent.

MUTTER f. mother

Muttermal n. birthmark.

Muttersprache f. mother tongue.

Mütze f. cap.

N

NACH 1. *prep. (with dat.)* after, toward, according to, like, past, by, in.

dem Namen nach kennen to know by name.

der Sage nach according to the legend.

Der Vater schickt die Kinder nach Hause. The father sends the children home.

einer nach dem andren one after another, one at a time.

Es ist zehn nach fünf. It is ten after five.

Es sieht nach Schnee aus. It looks like snow.

Gehen Sie nach links. Turn left.

meiner Meinung nach in my opinion.

Nach dem Essen ruht er sich aus. He rests after meals.

nach und nach little by little.

2. *adv.* after, toward, according to.

3. *separable prefix (implies coming after, following, imitation).*

Der Schutzmann lief dem Dieb nach. The policeman ran after the thief.

Kannst du diese Arbeit nachmachen? Can you copy this work?

nachahmen to imitate.

nachahmenswert worthy of imitation.

Nachahmung f. imitation.

Nachbar m. neighbor.

Nachbarschaft f. neighborhood.

nachdem *conj.* after.

Nachdem er sie verlassen hatte, weinte sie. After he left, she cried.

nachdenken to reflect, think.

nachdenken über to think over.

nachdenklich thoughtful.

Nachdruck m. stress, emphasis, reprint, reproduction.

Nachdruck verboten. Reproduction forbidden.

nachdrücklich strong, emphatic.

nacheifern to emulate.

nachforschen to inquire into, investigate.

Nachfrage f. inquiry, demand.

nachgeben to yield, give way.

nachgehen to follow, investigate, inquire.

Nachgeschmack m. after-taste.

nachher afterwards, later.

Nachhilfe f. aid, help, coaching.

Nachkomme m. descendant.

nachkommen to come later, follow on.

Nachkriegszeit f. postwar period.

nachlässig negligent, careless.

Nachlässigkeit f. negligence, carelessness.

nachlaufen to run after.

nachlesen to look up (in a book).

nachmachen to imitate, copy, counterfeit, duplicate.

NACHMITTAG m. afternoon.

nachmittags afternoons, in the afternoon.

Nachnahme f. cash on delivery.

Nachname m. surname.

nachprüfen to test, check, verify.

Nachricht f. news, information, account, report, message.

Ist eine Nachricht für mich da? Is there a message for me?

nachsagen to repeat after.

nachsehen to revise, check, examine.

nachsenden to send after.

Nachsicht f. indulgence.

nachsichtig (–sichtsvoll) indulgent, lenient.

nächst nearest, next, closest, following.

prep. (dat.) next to, next after.

Nächstenliebe f. love for one's fellow men; charity.

NACHT f. night.

bei Nacht, des Nachts at night.

über Nacht during the night.

über Nacht bleiben to stay overnight.

zu Nacht essen to eat supper.

Nachteil m. disadvantage, loss, damage, injury.

im Nachteil sein to be at a disadvantage.

Nachthemd n. nightgown.

Nachtigall f. nightingale.

Nachtisch m. dessert.

Nachtrag m. supplement.

nachtragen to add.

nachträglich additional, further.

Nachweis m. proof, evidence.

nachweisen to prove.

Nachwirkung f. after-effect.

Nachwuchs m. after-crop, rising generation.

Nacken m. nape of the neck.

nackt naked, nude, bare, plain.

Nadel f. needle, pin.

NAGEL m. nail.

an den Nagel hängen to give up.

den Nagel auf den Kopf treffen to hit the nail on the head.

Nagelfeile f. nail file.

Nähe f. nearness, proximity, vicinity.

in der Nähe near to, close at hand.

NAHE near, close to, imminent, approaching.

nahe daran sein to be about.

zu nahe treten to hurt one's feelings, offend.

nahen to draw near, approach.

nähen to sew, stitch.

näher nearer, closer, more intimate, further.

Nähere n. details, particulars.

Näherin f. seamstress.

nähern to bring near, place near.

nahestehen to be closely connected, be friends with.

Nähgarn n. sewing thread.

Nähmaschine f. sewing machine.

Nähnadel f. sewing needle.

Nährboden m. fertile soil.

nähren to feed, nurse, nourish.

sich nähren von to live on.
Nahrung *f.* nourishment, food.
Nahrungsmittel *pl.* food, foodstuffs.
NAME *m.* name, appellation, character.
  dem Namen nach by name.
  im Namen (with gen.) on behalf of.
namenlos nameless.
Namenstag *m.* saint's day, name day.
nämlich namely, same, very.
Narbe *f.* scar.
Narkose *f.* anesthetic.
Narr *m.* fool, jester.
  zum Narren halten to make a fool of.
narren to fool.
NASE *f.* nose.
  Der Zug fuhr mir vor der Nase weg. I missed
  the train by a hair.
  Sie schlug ihm die Tür vor der Nase zu. She
  slammed the door in his face.
NASS wet, damp.
  Die Strasse ist nass. The street is wet.
  Bei Nässe glatt. Slippery when wet.
  nass werden to get wet.
Nation *f.* nation.
national national.
Nationalhymne *f.* national anthem.
NATUR *f.* nature, disposition, constitution.
Naturalismus *m.* naturalism.
naturalistisch naturalistic.
Naturgeschichte *f.* natural science.
natürlich natural, unaffected.
  Natürlich! Of course!
Natürlichkeit *f.* naturalness, simplicity.
Naturschutzgebiet *n.* national park.
naturtreu lifelike.
Nebel *m.* fog, mist, haze.
nebelhaft nebulous.
nebelig (neblig) misty, foggy.
Nebelregen *m.* drizzle.
Nebelwetter *n.* foggy weather.
NEBEN 1. *prep. (dat. when answering question,*
  Wo?, acc. when answering question,
  Wohin?). next, next to, beside, among,
  besides.
  2. *adv.* next to, beside, among.
  Setzen Sie sich neben mich! Sit down next
  to me!
  Er sass neben dem Mädchen. He was
  seated next to the girl.
  neben anderen Dingen among other things.
nebenan next door.
Nebenanschluss *m.* extension (telephone).
nebenbei on the side, by the way, adjoining.
  nebenbei bemerkt (gesagt) by the way,
  incidentally.
Nebenberuf *m.* additional occupation, side-line.
Nebenbuhler *m.* rival.
Nebenbuhlerschaft *f.* rivalry.
nebeneinander next to each other, side by side.
Nebeneingang *m.* side entrance.
Nebeneinnahme *f.* additional income.
Nebenerzeugnis *n.* by-product.
Nebenfluss *m.* tributary.
Nebengebäude *n.* additional building, annex.
Nebengeräusch *n.* static (radio).
nebenher (nebenhin) by the side of.
Nebenkosten *f.* incidentals, extra.
Nebenlinie *f.* branch, secondary railroad line.
Nebenmensch *m.* fellow-creature.
Nebenperson *f.* secondary character (theater).
Nebenrolle *f.* secondary part (theater).
Nebensache *f.* matter of secondary importance.
nebensächlich unimportant, immaterial.
Nebensatz *m.* subordinate clause (grammar).
Nebenstrasse *f.* side-street.
Nebenzimmer *n.* next room.
necken to tease.
Neffe *m.* nephew.

Negative *n.* negative.
Neger *m.* (-in, *f.*) Negro.
negieren to deny.
NEHMEN to take, accept, receive.
  Abschied nehmen to say good-bye.
  Anstoss nehmen to object.
  es sich nicht nehmen lassen to insist on
  something.
  es genau nehmen to be pedantic.
  etwas zu sich nehmen to eat something.
  genau genommen strictly speaking.
  Nehmen Sie Platz! Sit down!
  sich in Acht nehmen to be careful.
Neid *m.* envy, jealousy.
neidisch jealous, envious.
Neige *f.* slope, decline.
  auf die Neige gehen to be on the decline,
  come to an end.
neigen to incline, bow.
  geneigt sein to be inclined.
Neigung *f.* slope, declivity, inclination, taste.
NEIN no.
Nektar *m.* nectar.
Nelke *f.* carnation.
NENNEN to name, call, mention.
  ein Ding beim rechten Namen nennen to call a
  spade a spade.
nennenswert worth mentioning.
Nennwort *n.* noun.
Nerv *m.* nerve.
  auf die Nerven fallen to drive mad.
Nervenheilanstalt *f.* mental hospital.
nervenkrank neurotic, neurasthenic.
Nervenschwäche *f.* nervous debility,
  neurasthenia.
nervös nervous.
Nervosität *f.* nervousness.
Nerz *m.* mink.
Nest *n.* nest.
NETT nice, neat, pretty.
Netz *n.* net, network.
NEU new, fresh, recent, modern, latest.
  Was gibt's Neues? What's new?
Neubau *m.* new building, reconstruction.
neuerdings recently, lately.
Neuerung *f.* innovation.
Neugier *f.* curiosity.
neugierig curious.
Neuheit *f.* novelty.
Neuhochdeutsch *n.* modern high German.
Neuigkeit *f.* news.
NEUJAHR *n.* New Year.
  Glückliches Neujahr! Happy New Year!
neulich recently, the other day.
NEUN nine.
NEUNTE ninth.
NEUNZEHN nineteen.
NEUNZEHNTE nineteenth.
NEUNZIG ninety.
NEUNZIGSTE ninetieth.
neutral neutral.
Neuzeit *f.* modern times.
neuzeitlich modern.
NICHT not.
  auch nicht not even.
  ganz und gar nicht not in the least.
  gar nicht not at all.
  nicht einmal not even.
  nicht mehr no longer, no more.
  Nicht wahr? Isn't it?
  noch nicht not yet.
Nichtachtung *f.* disregard.
Nichte *f.* niece.
NICHTS nothing, not anything.
  gar nichts nothing at all.
  Es macht nichts. It doesn't matter.
  Ich will nichts mehr davon hören. I don't

  want to hear another word about that.
  mir nichts, dir nichts quite coolly.
  nichts als nothing but.
  nichts anderes nothing else.
nichtsdestoweniger nevertheless.
nichtssagend meaningless, insignificant.
Nichtstuer *m.* idler.
Nichtstun *n.* idling.
nie never,
  fast nie hardly ever.
NIEDER down, low, mean.
  auf und nieder up and down.
niedergeschlagen downhearted, depressed.
Niedergeschlagenheit *f.* depression.
Niederlage *f.* defeat, warehouse.
niedertreten to trample.
niedrig low, inferior, humble.
NIEMALS never.
NIEMAND nobody.
Niere *f.* kidney.
nimmer never.
nimmermehr nevermore, by no means.
nirgends nowhere.
nirgendwo nowhere.
NOCH still, yet, besides.
  noch dazu in addition.
  noch ein another.
  noch einmal once more.
  noch einmal so so twice as.
  noch etwas something else.
  noch immer still.
  noch nicht not yet.
  noch nie never before.
  weder....noch neither...nor.
nochmals once again.
Norden *m.* North.
  nach Norden in the direction of the North.
nordisch northern, nordic.
nördlich northern.
nordöstlich northeastern.
Nordpol *m.* North Pole.
Nordsee *f.* North Sea.
Norm *f.* standard, rule.
normal normal.
NOT *f.* distress, want.
  mit Not only just, narrowly.
  ohne Not without real cause.
  seine liebe Not haben mit to have a hard
  time with.
  zur Not if need be.
Notar *m.* notary.
notariell attested by a notary.
Notausgang *m.* emergency exit.
Notbehelf *m.* expedient.
Notbremse *f.* emergency brake.
Note *f.* note (music, bank, dipl.); mark (school);
  (-n,*pl.*, music).
Notfall *m.* emergency.
notgedrungen compulsory, forced.
nötig necessary, needful.
  nötig haben to need.
nötigenfalls if need be.
notleidend poor, distressed.
Notlüge *f.* white lie.
notwendig necessary.
Notwendigkeit *f.* necessity.
Novelle *f.* short story, short novel.
NOVEMBER *m.* November.
nüchtern empty, sober, insipid.
Nüchternheit *f.* emptiness, sobriety, insipidity.
null null.
  null und nichtig null and void.
Null *f.* zero.
numerieren to number.
  numerierte Platz *m.* reserved seat.
NUMMER *f.* number, part, ticket, size, issue.
  Seine Nummer ist besetzt. His line is busy.
  Welche Nummer tragen Sie? What size do you wear?

die letzte Nummer the last issue (magazine).
NUN now, well, then.
von nun an henceforth, from now on.
NUR only, sole, merely, just, possibly.
nur mehr still more.
Nur zu! Go on!
wenn nur if only.
wer nur immer whoever.
Nuss /. nut.
Nussbaum m. walnut tree.
Nussknacker m. nutcracker.
nutzbar useful, necessary.
nutzbringend profitable.
Nutzen m. profit, benefit.
nützen to be of use, be profitable, serve.
Es nützt nicht! It's no use!
nützlich useful.
Nützlichkeit /. usefulness, utility.
nutzlos useless.
Nutzlosigkeit /. uselessness, futility.
Nylon n. nylon.

O

OB whether, if.
Wir möchten wissen ob sie kommen. We want
to know whether they are coming.
als ob as if, as though.
OBEN above, up, upstairs, on top.
auf....oben at the top of.
dort oben up there.
nach oben upwards.
oben auf on top of.
von oben bis unten from top to bottom.
von oben herab behandeln to treat in a
condescending manner.
obendrein into the bargain, in addition.
ober upper, supreme, above.
das obere Bett the upper berth.
Ober m. waiter.
Herr Ober! Waiter!
Oberbefehlshaber m. commander-in-chief.
Oberfläche /. surface, area.
oberflächlich superficial, superficially.
oberhalb upstairs, above.
Oberhemd n. shirt.
Oberkellner m. headwaiter.
Oberkörper m. upper part of the body.
Oberlippe /. upper lip.
Oberst m. colonel.
oberst highest, top.
Oberstleutnant m. lieutenant colonel.
obgleich although.
Oboe /. oboe.
Obrigkeit /. authority.
obschon although.
Obst n. fruit.
Obstgarten m. orchard.
Ochs m. ox.
öde dull, empty.
ODER or.
oder aber instead.
entweder oder either or.
Ofen m. stove, furnace.
offen open, free, vacant, frank, sincere.
auf offener Strecke on the road.
offen gestanden frankly.
offenbar obvious, evident.
Offenbarung /. disclosure, revelation.
Offenheit /. frankness, sincerity.
offenherzig frank, sincere.
offensichtlich obvious, apparent.
öffentlich public.
Öffentlichkeit /. publicity.
offiziell official.
Offizier m. officer.
öffnen to open, dissect.
Öffnung /. opening, gap, dissection.
OFT often, frequently.

öfter more often
je öfter... desto the more...the more.
des öfteren frequently.
öfters quite often.
oftmals often, frequently.
OHNE prep. (acc.) without, but, for, except.
Er ging ohne ein Wort zu sagen. He left
without saying a word.
ohne dass without (conj.)
ohne dass er mich angeredet hatte without his
having spoken to me.
ohne weiteres right off.
ohne zu without (before verb).
ohne zu antworten without answering.
ohnehin besides, apart.
Ohnmacht /. faintness, unconsciousness, faint.
ohnmächtig powerless, unconscious, helpless.
ohnmächtig werden to faint.
OHR n. ear, hearing.
die Ohren steif halten to keep one's courage.
ganz Ohr sein to be all ears.
Ohrring m. earring.
OKTOBER m. October.
ÖL n. oil.
Ölbaum m. olive tree.
Ölbild n. oil painting.
ölen to oil, lubricate.
Ölfarbe /. paint.
ölig oily.
Olive /. olive.
Omelette n. omelet.
ONKEL m. uncle.
OPER /. opera, opera house.
Operation /. operation.
Operette /. operetta.
Opfer n. sacrifice, martyr, victim.
opfern to sacrifice.
Opferung /. sacrifice.
Optiker m. optician.
Optimismus m. optimism.
optimistisch optimistic.
Orange /. orange.
Orchester n. orchestra.
Orden m. order, decoration.
ordentlich in order, neat, tidy.
ordnen to put in order, arrange.
ORDNUNG /. order, arrangement.
Das finde ich ganz in Ordnung. I think it is
quite all right.
In Ordnung bringen to settle, straighten out.
Ist alles in Ordnung? Is everything all right?
nicht in Ordnung out of order.
Organ n. organ (body).
organisieren to organize.
organisch organic.
Organist m. organist.
Orgel /. organ (music).
original original.
ORT m. place, spot, locality.
Wir fanden alles wieder an Ort und Stelle. We
found everything back in place.
örtlich local.
Osten m. East, Orient.
nach Osten in the direction of the
East.
Osterfest n. Easter.
Ostern n. East.
Österreicher m. Austrian.
österreichisch Austrian.
östlich eastern.
Ostsee /. Baltic sea.
ostwärts eastward.
Ozean m. ocean.

P

Paar n. pair, couple.
paar few, some, even, matching.
ein paar a few, several.

ein paarmal several times.
paaren to pair, couple.
Pächter m. farmer, tenant, householder.
Päckchen n. small parcel.
packen to seize, grasp, pack.
packend thrilling, absorbing.
Paddelboot n. canoe.
paddeln to paddle.
Paket n. parcel.
Paketannahme /. parcel-receiving office.
Pakt m. pact, agreement.
Palast m. palace.
Palme /. palm.
panieren to bread.
Panik /. panic.
Panne /. breakdown, trouble (motor).
Pantoffel m. slipper, mule.
unter dem Pantoffel stehen to be henpecked.
Pantoffelheld m. henpecked husband.
Panzer m. armor, tank.
panzern to armor, plate.
Papagei m. parrot.
PAPIER n. paper, identification paper, document.
zu Papier bringen to write down, put on paper.
Papierbogen m. sheet of paper.
Papiergeld n. paper money.
Papierhandlung /. stationery store.
Papierkorb m. wastepaper basket.
Pappe /. cardboard.
Papst m. Pope.
Parade /. parade, review.
Paradies n. paradise.
paradiesisch paradisiacal.
parallel parallel.
Parfum n. perfume.
PARK m. park, grounds.
parken to park.
Parkverbot! No parking!
Parkplatz m. parking place.
Parlament n. parliament.
Parodie /. parody.
Partei /. party, faction, tenant, side.
Partei nehmen für to take the side of.
Parterre n. ground floor.
Partie /. part, section.
Partner m. partner.
Partnerschaft /. partnership.
Pass m. pass, passage, passport.
Passagier m. passenger.
Passamt n. passport division.
Passant m. passer-by.
PASSEN to fit, suit, be convenient, be suitable.
zu einander passen to match, harmonize.
PASSEND suitable, convenient.
passieren to go through, pass, cross, happen.
Was ist passiert? What happened? (What's
the trouble?)
passiv passive.
Passkontrolle /. examination of passport.
Pastete /. pie, pastry.
Pastor m. pastor, minister, clergyman.
Pate m. godfather.
Patenkind n. godchild.
Patent n. letters patent.
Patentamt n. patent office.
patentieren to patent.
pathetisch pathetic.
Patient m. patient.
Patin /. godmother.
Patriot m. patriot.
patriotisch patriotic.
Pauke /. kettledrum.
Pause /. pause, interval, break, rest (music).
pausieren to pause.
Pech n. pitch, bad luck.
pechschwarz pitch-black.
Pechsträhne /. run of ill luck.
Pechvogel m. unlucky person.

Pedal n. pedal.
Pedant m. pedant.
pedantisch pedantic.
Pein f. pain, agony, torture.
peinigen to torment, harass.
Peiniger m. tormentor.
Peinigung f. torment, torture.
peinlich painful, embarrassing.
Peinlichkeit f. painfulness; carefulness, embarrassment.
Peitsche f. whip, lash.
Pellkartoffeln pl. potatoes in their jackets.
PELZ m. fur, pelt, skin, hide, fur coat.
Pelzhändler m. furrier.
Pelzmantel m. fur coat.
Pension f. pension; boarding-house.
    Er erhält eine Pension. He receives a pension.
    in Pension sein to board.
Pensionat n. boarding-school.
pensionieren to pension off.
per a, per.
    per Post by post.
    per Adresse care of.
Periode f. period.
Perle f. pearl, bead.
perlen to sparkle.
Perlenkette f. pearl necklace, string of pearls.
PERSON f. person, personage, character (theater).
    in Person in person.
Personal n. staff, employees, personnel.
Personalbeschreibung f. personal description of a person.
Personalien pl. particulars about a person.
Personenaufzug m. passenger elevator.
Personenkraftwagen m. motor-car.
Personenzug m. passenger train.
persönlich personal; personally.
Persönlichkeit f. personality.
Perücke f. wig.
pessimistisch pessimistic.
Pest f. plague, pestilence, epidemic.
Petersilie f. parsley.
Pfad m. path.
Pfadfinder m. (-in, f.) boy (girl) scout.
Pfahl m. pole, stake, pile, post.
Pfand m. pledge, security, forfeit.
pfänden to seize, take in pledge.
Pfandhaus n. pawnshop.
Pfandleiher m. pawnbroker.
Pfandschein m. pawn ticket.
Pfanne f. pan.
Pfannkuchen m. pancake.
Pfarrer m. priest, pastor, minister.
Pfarrgemeinde f. parish.
Pfau m. peacock.
PFEFFER m. pepper.
Pfefferkuchen m. spiced cakes, gingerbread.
Pfefferminz m. & f. peppermint.
pfeffern to season with pepper.
Pfeife f. whistle, pipe.
pfeifen to whistle, pipe.
Pfeil m. arrow.
Pfeiler m. pillar, post.
PFERD n. horse.
Pfiff m. whistle, whistling, trick.
Pfingsten n. & f. Pentecost, Whitsuntide.
Pfirsich m. peach.
PFLANZE f. plant.
pflanzen to plant.
Pflanzenkunde f. botany.
Pflaster n. plaster, pavement.
Pflasterstein m. paving-stone.
PFLAUME f. plum.
    gedörrte Pflaume f. prune.
Pflaumenmus n. plum jam.
PFLEGE f. care, attention, nursing.

Pflegeeltern pl. foster parents.
Pflegekind n. foster child.
pflegen to care for, cherish, nurse, cultivate.
PFLICHT f. duty, obligation.
Pflichteifer m. zeal.
Pflichtgefühl n. sense of duty.
pflichtgemäss conformable to one's duty.
pflücken to pick, gather, pluck.
Pflug m. plough.
pflügen to plough.
Pförtner m. gatekeeper.
Pfote f. paw.
Pfui! Shame!
Pfund n. pound.
Pfütze f. puddle.
Phänomen n. phenomenon.
Phantasie f. imagination, fancy.
phantasieren to daydream, imagine.
Phantast m. dreamer, visionary.
phantastisch fantastic, fanciful.
Philosoph m. philosopher.
Philosophie f. philosophy.
philosophieren to philosophize.
Photoapparat m. camera.
Photograph m. photographer.
Photographie f. photography.
photographieren to photograph.
Physik f. physics.
Pianist m. pianist.
Piano n. piano.
Picknick n. picnic.
Pietät f. reverence, piety.
pietätlos irreverent.
Pikkoloflöte f. piccolo.
Pilger m. pilgrim.
pilgern to go on a pilgrimage.
Pille f. pill.
Pilot m. pilot.
Pilz m. mushroom.
    Giftpilz, m. poisonous mushroom.
Pinsel m. brush, paintbrush.
pinseln to paint.
Pirat m. pirate.
Pistole f. pistol.
Plage f. plague.
plagen to plague, torment.
    sich plagen to struggle, overwork oneself.
Plakat n. placard, poster.
    Keine Plakate. Post no bills.
Plakatsäule f. sign post.
Plan m. plan, map, design; intention.
planen to plan, scheme.
Planet m. planet.
planlos without any fixed plan.
planmässig according to plan; methodical.
Planung f. planning, plan.
Planwirtschaft f. economic planning.
Plastik f. plastic art, sculpture.
plastisch plastic.
Platin n. platinum.
plätschern to splash.
PLATT flat, level, insipid, dull.
Plattdeutsch n. Low German.
Platte f. plate, tray; record (phonograph)
    kalte Platte cold meats.
PLATZ m. place, spot, room, seat; square (street).
    Platz machen to make room.
    Bitte, nehmen Sie Platz. Please have a seat.
    am Platz sein to be opportune.
Platzanweiser m. (in,-f.) usher.
Plätzchen n. little place; cookie.
platzen to burst, explode, crack.
Platzmangel m. lack of space.
Plauderei f. chat, small talk, conversation.
PLAUDERN to chat, talk, gossip.
PLÖTZLICH sudden; suddenly.
plump heavy, shapeless, tactless, clumsy.
Plumpheit f. shapelessness, heaviness,

    clumsiness.
plumpsen to plump down.
Plunder m. trash.
plündern to plunder, pillage.
Plünderung f. plundering, sack.
Plural m. plural.
Pöbel m. mob, populace.
pöbelhaft vulgar, low.
pochen to knock, beat, throb.
Pocken f. pl. smallpox.
Pockenimpfung f. smallpox vaccination.
Podium n. platform, rostrum.
Poesie f. poetry.
Poet m. poet.
poetisch poetical.
Pol m. pole.
polar polar, arctic.
Polarforscher m. polar explorer.
Pole m. Pole (native of Poland).
polieren to polish.
Politik f. politics, policy.
Politiker m. politician.
politisch political.
politisieren to talk politics.
Politur f. polish.
POLIZEI f. police.
    Rufen Sie die Polizei! Call the police!
Polizeiamt n. police-station.
Polizeiaufsicht f. police control.
polizeilich m. police officer.
polizeilich of the police.
Polizeistreife f. police raid.
Polizeistunde f. curfew.
polizeiwidrig contrary to police regulations.
Polizist m. policeman, constable.
polnisch Polish.
Polster n. cushion, pillow, bolster, pad.
Polstermöbel pl. upholstered furniture.
Polstersessel m. easy chair.
Polsterung f. upholstery, padding, stuffing.
Pomade f. pomade.
Pomp m. pomp.
pomphaft pompous, magnificent.
pompös pompous, magnificent.
populär popular (political).
Pore f. pore.
porös porous.
Portemonnaie n. purse.
Portion f. portion, helping, ration, order.
Porto n. postage.
portofrei postfree, prepaid.
portopflichtig liable to postage fee.
Porträt n. portrait, likeness.
porträtieren to portray, paint a portrait.
Porträtmaler m. portrait painter.
Porzellan n. porcelain, china.
Porzellanservice n. set of china.
positiv positive.
Posse f. farce, trick.
POST f. post, mail, post office.
Postamt n. post office.
Postanweisung f. money order.
Postbeamte m. post-office clerk.
Postbote m. postman.
Posten m. post, situation.
    auf dem Posten sein to feel well.
Postkarte f. postcard.
postlagernd general delivery.
postlich postal.
Postschliessfach n. post-office box.
postwendend by return mail.
Pracht f. splendor.
Prachtausgabe f. deluxe edition.
prächtig magnificent, splendid, lovely.
prachtvoll splendid, gorgeous, magnificent.
prahlen to brag, boast.
Prahlerei f. boasting, bragging.
prahlerisch boastful, ostentatious.

praktisch clever, handy, useful.
    Praktischer Arzt general practitioner.
praktizieren to practice (a profession).
prall blazing, tight, tense.
    in der prallen Sonne in the full glare of the sun.
Prämie f. premium.
prämieren to award a prize to.
Präposition f. preposition.
präsentieren to present.
Präsident m. president.
Präsidium n. chair, presidency
prassen to feast, revel.
präzis precise, exact, punctual.
Präzision f. precision.
predigen to preach.
Prediger m. preacher, minister.
Predigt f. sermon, lecture.
PREIS m. price, cost, rate, praise.
    um jeden Preis at any cost.
    um keinen Preis not at any price.
    zum festem Preis at fixed price.
Preisangabe f. quotation of prices.
Preisausschreiben n. prize competition.
Preisbewerber m. competitor.
Preiselbeere f. cranberry.
preisen to praise, extol, glorify.
Preiserhöhung f. rise in prices.
Preisgabe f. surrender, abandonment.
preisgeben to surrender, give up, abandon,
    sacrifice.
Preislage f. price range.
Preisrichter m. arbiter, judge.
Preissturz m. fall in prices.
Preisträger m. prize-winner.
Preistreiberei f. forcing up of prices.
preiswert reasonable, cheap.
Premiere f. first night.
Presse f. press.
Pressestimme f. press comment, review.
Priester m. priest.
Prima f. highest class of secondary school.
prima prime, first-rate.
primitiv primitive.
Prinz m. (—essin, f.) prince(ss).
Prinzip n. principle.
    aus Prinzip as a matter of principle.
prinzipiell on principle.
PRIVAT private, privately.
Privatrecht n. civil law.
Probe f. trial, experiment, test, probation;
    rehearsal (theater).
    auf die Probe stellen to put to the test.
    Probe ablegen to give proof of.
Probeabzug m. proof.
proben to rehearse.
probeweise on approval, on trial.
Probezeit f. time of probation.
probieren to try, taste.
    Darf ich das anprobieren? May I try this on?
Problem n. problem.
problematisch problematic.
Produkt n. product.
Produktion f. production.
Produzent m. producer, manufacturer.
produzieren to produce, show off, exhibit.
Professor m. professor.
Professur f. professorship.
Prognose f. forecast.
Programm n. program.
Projekt n. project.
Projektionsapparat m. projector.
Proklamation f. proclamation.
Prokura f. procuration, power of attorney.
prolongieren to prolong.
Promenade f. promenade.
Propaganda f. propaganda.
Prophet m. prophet.
prophetisch prophetic.

prophezeien to prophesy.
Prophezeiung f. prophecy.
Proportion f. proportion.
Prosa f. prose.
Prosit! To your health!
Prospekt m. prospect.
Protest m. protest.
    Protest erheben to protest.
Protestant m. Protestant.
protestantisch Protestant.
Protestantismus m. Protestantism.
protestieren to protest.
Protokoll n. ticket (police); protocol.
Proviant m. provision.
Provinz f. province.
provinziell provincial.
Provision f. provision, brokerage.
Prozent n. per cent.
Prozentsatz m. percentage.
prozentual expressed as percentage.
PROZESS m. lawsuit, process, proceedings, trial.
    im Prozess liegen to be involved in a law suit.
    kurzen Prozess machen mit to dispose of
    quickly.
prozessieren to be involved in a lawsuit.
Prozession f. procession.
PRÜFEN to test, investigate, inspect, examine.
Prüfer m. examiner.
Prüfling m. examinee.
PRÜFUNG f. investigation, examination.
    eine Prüfung ablegen to take an examination.
Prunk m. splendor, ostentation.
prunkvoll gorgeous, splendid.
Psychiater m. psychiatrist.
Psychiatrie f. psychiatry.
psychisch psychic.
Psychologe m. psychologist.
Psychologie f. psychology.
psychologisch psychological.
Psychopath m psychopath.
Publikum n. public.
Pudel m. poodle.
pudelnass drenched, soaked.
Puder m. toilet powder.
pudern to powder.
Puls m. pulse.
Pulsschlag m. pulse-beat.
Pult n. desk.
Pulver n. powder, gunpowder.
Pulverfass n. powder barrel.
    auf dem Pulverfass sitzen to sit on top of a
    volcano.
PUNKT m. point, dot, spot.
    der springende Punkt the salient point.
    Punkt ein Uhr at one o'clock sharp.
pünktlich on time, punctual, prompt.
Pünktlichkeit f. punctuality.
Puppe f. doll, puppet.
Putz m. trimming, ornament, dress.
putzen to clean, polish.
Putzfrau f. charwoman.
Putzlappen m. duster, flannel, polishing cloth.
Pyjama n. & m. pajamas.

Q

Quadrat n. square.
Quäker m. Quaker.
Qual f. torment, torture, pain.
quälen to torment, worry, torture, bother.
Quäler m. tormentor.
Quälerei f. tormenting, torture.
Quälgeist m. nuisance (person).
qualifizieren to qualify.
Qualität f. quality.
qualitativ qualitative.
Qualitätsware f. high-class article.
Qualm m. dense smoke.
qualmen to smoke (chimney).

qualmig smoky.
qualvoll very painful, agonizing.
Quarantäne f. quarantine.
    unter Quarantäne stellen to quarantine.
Quecksilber n. mercury.
Quelle f. spring, fountain.
quellen to gush, well, flow.
Quellwasser n. spring water.
quer cross, lateral, oblique; across, obliquely.
    kreuz under quer all over.
querfeldein across country.
Querschnitt m. cross-section.
Querstrasse f. crossroad.
Quertreiberei f. intrigue.
quetschen to squeeze, smash.
Quetschung f. contusion.
Quetschwunde f. bruise.
quietschen to scream, squeal.
quittieren to receipt.
Quittung f. receipt.
Quote f. quota, share.

R

Rabatt m. discount.
Rabbiner m. rabbi.
Rache f. revenge.
rächen to revenge, avenge.
    sich rächen take revenge, get revenge.
    Deine Faulheit wird sich an dir rächen.
    You will have to suffer for your laziness.
Rachsucht f. thirst for revenge.
rachsüchtig revengeful.
RAD n. wheel, bicycle.
radfahren to cycle.
Radfahrer m. cyclist.
Radfahrweg m. cycle track.
Radiergummi m. eraser.
Radierung f. etching.
Radio n. radio.
Radreifen m. bicycle tire.
raffiniert refined.
Rahm m. cream.
Rahmen m. frame.
Rakete f. rocket.
Rampe f. ramp, platform; limelight.
ramponieren to damage.
RAND m. edge, brim, border, margin.
    ausser Rand und Band sein to be out of hand.
    Schreiben Sie es an den Rand! Write it in the
    margin!
Randbemerkung f. marginal note.
Rang m. rank, order, quality, class.
    den Rang ablaufen to get the better of.
    ersten Ranges first class, first rate.
    erster Rang first balcony, dress circle.
    zweiter Rang second balcony, upper circle.
Rangabzeichen n. badge of rank.
Rangordnung f. order of precedence.
Rangstufe f. degree.
rar rare, scarce.
Rarität f. rarity, curiosity.
rasch quick, swift, speedy.
rascheln to rustle.
rasen to rave, rage, speed.
rasend raving, raging.
    rasend machen to make mad.
Raserei f. raving, fury, rage.
Rasierapparat m. safety razor.
    elektrischer Rasierapparat electric razor.
rasieren to shave.
    sich rasieren to shave (oneself).
    sich rasieren lassen to get shaved.
Rasierklinge f. razor blade.
Rasiermesser n. razor.
Rasierpinsel m. shaving brush.
Rasierzeug n. shaving things.
Rasse f. race, breed.

rassig thoroughbred.
rassisch racial.
Rast f. resting, recreation, rest, repose.
rasten to rest.
rastlos restless, indefatigable.
Rastlosigkeit f. restlessness.
RAT m. counsel, advice, consultation, remedy.
  Rat schaffen to devise means.
  um Rat fragen to ask advice.
  zu Rat ziehen to consult.
Rate f. installment.
raten to advise, guess, solve.
ratenweise by installments.
Ratgeber m. adviser.
Ration f. ration.
rationell rational; economical.
ratlos at a loss, helpless.
Ratlosigkeit f. helplessness, perplexity.
Ratschlag m. counsel, advice.
ratschlagen to deliberate.
Rätsel n. riddle, enigma, puzzle.
  Es ist mir ein Rätsel. It puzzles me.
rätselhaft mysterious, enigmatic.
Ratte f. rat.
Raub m. robbery, plundering.
  auf Raub ausgehen to go on the prowl.
rauben to rob, plunder.
Räuber m. robber, thief.
Raubmord m. murder and robbery.
Raubtier n. beast of prey.
Raubvogel m. bird of prey.
Rauch m. smoke.
RAUCHEN to smoke.
  Rauchen Verboten! No Smoking!
Raucher m. smoker.
räuchern to smoke, cure, fumigate.
Räucherwaren pl. smoked meats and fish.
Rauchtabak m. tobacco.
Rauchzimmer n. smoking room.
RAUH uneven, rough, raw, hoarse, harsh.
Rauheit f. roughness, harshness.
RAUM m. place, room, space.
  Raum geben to give way, indulge.
räumen to clear away, remove, clean, evacuate.
Rauminhalt m. volume, capacity.
räumlich relating to space, spatial.
Räumlichkeit f. room, premises, space.
Raummangel m. lack of room.
Räumung f. removal, evacuation.
Raupe f. caterpillar.
Raupenschlepper m. caterpillar tractor.
Rausch m. drunkenness, intoxication, frenzy.
rauschen to rustle, rush, roar.
Rauschgift n. narcotic.
Reaktion f. reaction.
Rebe f. grape, vine.
Rebell m. rebel.
rebellieren to rebel.
Rechen m. rake.
Rechenmaschine f. calculating machine.
Rechenschaft f. account.
Rechenschieber m. slide rule.
RECHNEN to count, reckon,
  calculate.
RECHNUNG f. sum, account, bill, calculation.
  auf eigene Rechnung at one's own risk.
  auf Rechnung setzen to charge, put to one's
  account.
  in Rechnung ziehen to take into account.
  laut Rechnung as per invoice.
  Meine Rechnung, bitte. Please bring me the
  check.
  Sind Sie auf Ihre Rechnung gekommen? Did
  you get your money's worth? (Was it worth
  while?)
Rechnungsprüfer m. auditor.
RECHT n. right, privilege, title, claim, law.
  alle Rechte vorbehalten all rights reserved.

an den Rechten kommen to meet one's match.
  mit vollem Recht for good reasons.
  nach dem Rechten sehen to see to things.
  Recht behalten to be right in the end.
  Recht geben to agree with.
  Recht haben to be right.
  Recht sprechen to administer justice.
  von Rechts wegen by rights, according to the
  law.
  zu Recht bestehen to be valid.
RECHT right, all right, right-hand, correct,
  proper, genuine, lawful.
  Das ist mir recht. That's all right with me.
  Das ist nur recht und billig. That's only fair.
  die rechte Hand the right hand.
  erst recht all the more now, now more than
  ever.
  Es geschieht ihm recht. It serves him right.
  es recht machen to suit, please.
  Man kann es nicht allen recht machen. You
  cannot please everybody.
  schlecht und recht not bad.
  zur rechten Zeit in time.
Rechte f. right hand.
Rechteck n. rectangle.
rechteckig rectangular.
rechterhand on the right hand.
rechtfertigen to justify.
  sich rechtfertigen to justify oneself.
Rechtfertigung f. justification.
rechthaberisch dogmatic.
rechtlich just, lawful, legitimate.
Rechtlichkeit f. integrity, honesty.
rechtmässig lawful, legitimate.
RECHTS to the right, on the right.
  Biegen sie rechts ab! Turn to the right!
  nach rechts to the right.
  Nehmen Sie die erste Strasse rechts. Take the
  first turn to your right.
  Rechts Halten! Keep to the right!
  Rechts um! Right turn!
Rechtsanspruch m. legal claim.
Rechtsanwalt m. lawyer, counsel.
Rechtsbeistand m. legal adviser.
rechtschaffen honest, upright; very, extremely.
Rechtschreibung f. spelling.
Rechtsfall m. lawsuit.
Rechtsgelehrte m. jurist.
rechtsgültig legal, valid.
Rechtspruch m. verdict.
rechtsungültig illegal, invalid.
rechtsverbindlich legally, binding.
Rechtsweg m. legal proceedings, law.
rechtswidrig illegal.
Rechtswissenschaft f. jurisprudence.
rechtzeitig in good time.
recken to stretch, extend.
Redakteur m. editor.
Redaktion f. editors, editorial staff.
redaktionell editorial.
REDE f. talk, discourse, speech, conversation,
  rumor.
  Davon ist keine Rede! That's out of the
  question!
  Davon ist nicht dir Rede! That's not the point!
  eine Rede halten to make a speech.
  in die Rede fallen to interrupt.
  nicht der Rede wert not worth mentioning.
  Rede stehen to answer for.
  Wovon ist die Rede? What is it all about?
  zur Rede stellen to call to account.
Redefluss m. flow of words.
Redefreiheit f. freedom of speech.
redegewandt fluent, eloquent.
REDEN to talk, speak, converse, make a speech.
  begeistert reden to rave, enthuse.
  mit sich reden lassen to listen to reason.
  nicht zu reden von to say nothing of.

von sich reden machen to cause a stir.
Redensart f. phrase, idiom, nonsense.
Redner m. orator, speaker.
redselig talkative.
reduzieren to reduce.
Reederei f. steamship company.
Referenz f. reference.
reformieren to reform.
Regal n. shelf.
rege active, brisk.
Regel f. rule, regulation, principle.
  in der Regel as a rule.
regelmässig regular, proportional.
regeln to arrange, regulate.
  geregelt regular, well ordered.
regelrecht regular, correct, proper.
REGEN m. rain, shower.
  Auf Regen folgt Sonnenschein. The calm follows
  the storm. ("After rain follows sunshine.")
Regenbogen m. rainbow.
regendicht waterproof.
Regenmantel m. raincoat.
Regenschirm m. umbrella.
Regenzeit f. rainy season.
Regie f. production (theater); administration,
  management.
regieren to rule, govern, reign.
Regierung f. government, reign, rule.
Regierungsbeamte m. government official.
Regiment n. regiment, government.
Regisseur m. stage manager.
Register n. register, index, table of contents.
registrieren to register.
REGNEN to rain.
  Es regnet in Strömen. It's raining cats and dogs.
regnerisch rainy.
regsam active, agile, quick.
Regsamkeit f. agility, activity, quickness.
Regung f. movement.
Reh n. deer.
Rehbraten m. roast venison.
Reibeisen n. grater.
reiben to rub, grate, grind.
  wundreiben (sich) to chafe.
REICH rich, wealthy, well off, plentiful,
  abundant.
Reich n. empire, kingdom.
  Deutsche Reich n. Germany.
  Österreich n. Austria.
reichen to give, present, hand.
reichhaltig full, rich, abundant.
Reichhaltigkeit f. fullness, richness.
reichlich plentiful, abundant, copious.
Reichsautobahn f. state road.
Reichtum m. wealth, abundance.
Reichweite f. range, reach.
Reif m. frost.
REIF ripe, mature, mellow.
Reifen m. tire.
reifen to ripen, mature.
Reifenpanne f. flat tire, blowout.
Reifenschaden m. flat tire, blowout.
Reifeprüfung f. final comprehensive examination.
Reifezeugnis n. final certificate, diploma.
reiflich maturely, carefully.
REIHE f. row, range, series, sequence.
  ausser der Reihe out of one's mind.
  der Reihe nach successively, in rotation.
  Er ist an der Reihe. It is his turn.
Reihenfolge f. succession, sequence.
reihenweise in rows.
reihum in turns, by turns.
Reim m. rhyme.
reimen to rhyme.
REIN clean, plain, sheer, pure, genuine, tidy.
  aus reinem Trotz out of sheer obstinacy.
Reinfall m. failure, let down.
Reingewinn m. net profit.

Reinheit *f.* purity, pureness.
REINIGEN to clean, cleanse, purify.
Reinigung *f.* cleaning, cleansing.
Reinigungsanstalt *f.* cleaner's.
reinlich clean, neat, tidy.
Reinlichkeit *f.* cleanliness, neatness, tidiness.
Reis *m.* rice.
REISE *f.* trip, journey, voyage.
Glückliche Reise! Have a nice trip!
Reisebüro *n.* tourist office.
Reiseführer *m.* guidebook.
REISEN to travel.
REISENDE *m.* passenger, traveler.
Reisescheck *m.* traveler's check.
reissen to tear, pull, drag.
an sich reissen to seize, hold up, snatch up.
in Stücke reissen to tear to pieces.
sich reissen um to fight for.
reissend ravenous, rapid, torrential.
reissende Strom *m.* torrent.
Reissverschluss *m.* zipper.
reiten to ride a horse.
Reiter *m.* horseman, cavalryman.
Reithose *f.* riding pants.
Reitschule *f.* riding school.
REIZ *m.* charm, attraction; irritation; incentive.
reizbar sensitive, irritable.
reizen to irritate, excite, provoke, tempt.
reizend charming.
reizlos unattractive.
reizvoll charming, attractive.
REKLAME *f.* publicity, advertisement.
Reklame machen to advertise.
rekonstruieren to reconstruct.
Rekord *m.* record, competition.
Rekrut *m.* recruit.
Rektor *m.* university president.
relativ relative, relating to.
Religion *f.* religion.
religiös religious.
Rennbahn *f.* racecourse.
RENNEN to run, race.
Rennfahrer *m.* racing cyclist.
Rennstall *m.* racing stable.
renovieren to renovate, redecorate.
Rentamt *n.* revenue office.
Rente *f.* revenue, pension.
Reparation *f.* reparation.
Reparatur *f.* repair.
Wegen Reparatur geschlossen. Closed for repairs.
Reparaturwerkstätte *f.* repair shop.
Reportage *f.* commentary, eye-witness account.
repräsentieren to represent.
Republik *f.* republic.
Republikaner *m.* Republican.
republikanisch republican.
Reserve *f.* reserve.
Reserverad *n.* spare wheel.
reservieren to reserve.
Respekt *m.* respect.
respektabel respectable.
respektieren to respect.
respektlos without respect, irreverent.
respektvoll respectful.
Rest *m.* rest, remains, remnant.
restaurieren to repair, restore (work of art).
Restbestand *m.* remainder, residue.
restlos complete, without anything left over.
Resultat *n.* result, answer.
retten to save, preserve, rescue, deliver.
Rettung *f.* rescue, saving, escape.
Rettungsboot *n.* lifeboat.
Rettungsring *m.* lifebelt.
Reue *f.* repentance.
reuen to repent, regret.
Es reut mich. I regret.

reumütig repentant, penitent.
Revier *n.* hunting ground, district.
Polizeirevier *n.* district police station.
Revolte *f.* revolt, insurrection.
Revolution *f.* revolution.
revolutionär revolutionary.
Revolver *m.* revolver.
Rezept *n.* recipe, prescription.
rezitieren to recite.
Rheumatismus *m.* rheumatism.
rhythmisch rhythmical.
Richter *m.* judge.
RICHTIG right, correct, true, real, straight.
Das ist nicht sein richtiger Name. That's not his real name.
Meine Uhr geht richtig. My watch is right.
Richtig! Quite right!
Richtigstellung *f.* rectification.
Richtung *f.* direction, line, course, tendency.
riechen to smell.
Riemen *m.* strap.
Riese *m.* giant.
riesenhaft gigantic, colossal.
Rind *n.* ox, cow, cattle.
Rinde *f.* bark, rind of cheese, crust.
Rinderbraten *m.* roast beef.
Rindfleisch *n.* beef.
Ring *m.* ring, circle.
ringen to struggle, wrestle.
Ringkampf *m.* wrestling match.
Ringkämpfer *m.* wrestler, athlete.
Ringrichter *m.* umpire.
rings round, around.
ringsum (-her) all around.
Rinne *f.* gutter, channel.
rinnen to flow, run.
Rinnstein *m.* gutter.
Rippe *f.* rib.
riskant risky.
riskieren to risk.
Riss *m.* tear, hole, gap, crack.
Ritter *m.* knight, cavalier.
Rittergut *n.* estate, manor.
ritterlich chivalrous, gallant.
Rivale *m.* rival.
Rock *m.* coat(man's); skirt.
rodeln to sled.
Rodelschlitten *m.* sled.
roden to root out, clear (forest, garden).
ROH raw, crude, coarse, rare (steak).
Rohmaterial *n.* raw material.
Rohr *n.* pipe, oven.
Röhre *f.* tube, valve.
Rolle *f.* roll, cylinder; part (theater).
aus der Rolle fallen to misbehave.
die Rollen verteilen to cast (a play).
Rollenbesetzung *f.* cast.
Roller *m.* rolling sea.
Rollmops *m.* herring.
Rollschuh *m.* rollerskate.
Rollschuh laufen to rollerskate.
Rollstuhl *m.* wheelchair.
Rolltreppe *f.* escalator.
Roman *m.* novel, fiction.
Romanschriftsteller *m.* novelist.
Romantik *f.* romanticism.
Romantiker *m.* romanticist.
romantisch romantic.
röntgen to X-ray.
Röntgenaufnahme *f.* X-ray photograph.
Röntgenbild *n.* X-ray photograph.
Röntgenstrahlen *pl.* X-rays.
rosa pink, rose-colored.
Rose *f.* rose.
Rosenkohl *m.* Brussels sprouts.
Rosine *f.* raisin.
Rost *m.* 1. rust.
2. grate.

Rostbraten *m.* roast beef.
rösten to roast, grill, toast.
Rostfleck *m.* ironmold.
rostfrei stainless.
rostfreier Stahl stainless steel.
rostig rusty.
ROT red, ruddy.
rot werden to blush.
rotblond auburn.
Röte *f.* red, redness, blush.
Rotkohl *m.* red cabbage.
Rotstift *m.* red pencil.
Rotwein *m.* red wine.
Rübe *f.* sugar beet.
die rote Rübe the red beet.
Rubin *m.* ruby.
Rückantwort *f.* reply.
Rückblick *m.* glance back, retrospect.
RÜCKEN *m.* back, rear.
den Rücken kehren to turn one's back.
in den Rücken fallen to attack from the rear.
Rücken gegen Rücken back to back.
rücken to move, push, move away.
Rückendeckung *f.* rear, cover, protection.
rückerstatten to refund.
Rückfahrkarte *f.* return ticket.
Rückfahrt *f.* return trip.
Rückfall *m.* relapse.
rückfällig relapsing.
Rückflug *m.* return flight.
Rückfrage *f.* query, search back.
Rückgabe *f.* return.
Rückgang *m.* decline, falling off.
rückgängig retrogressive.
rückgängig machen to cancel
Rückgrat *n.* spine, backbone.
Rückhalt *m.* reserve, support.
rückhaltlos unreserved, without reserve.
Rückkehr *f.* return.
Rückkunft *f.* return.
Rücklehne *f.* back (of chair).
Rückmarsch *m.* retreat.
Rückporto *n.* return postage.
Rückreise *f.* return trip.
Rückschlag *m.* reverse, setback, reaction.
Rückschritt *m.* step back, relapse.
Rückseite *f.* back, reverse side.
Rücksicht *f.* regard, consideration.
rücksichtslos inconsiderate, reckless.
rücksichtsvoll considerate.
Rücksitz *m.* back seat.
Rücksprache *f.* discussion, consultation.
Rücksprache nehmen to discuss, talk over.
Rückstand *m.* arrears, residue.
rückständig backward, old-fashioned.
Rückstrahler *m.* rear reflector.
Rücktritt *m.* retirement, resignation.
Rückwand *f.* back wall.
rückwärts backwards; back.
Rückwärtsgang *m.* reverse gear.
Rückweg *m.* way back, return.
rückwirkend retroactive, retrospective.
Rückwirkung *f.* reaction, retroaction.
Rückzahlung *f.* repayment.
Rückzug *m.* withdrawal, retreat.
Ruder *n.* oar, rudder, helm.
ans Ruder kommen to come into power.
Ruderboot *n.* rowboat.
rudern to row.
Ruf *m.* reputation, cry, call.
im Rufe stehen to be reputed, generally considered as.
RUFEN to call, shout.
Soll ich sie rufen lassen? Shall I send for her?
wie gerufen kommen to come at the right moment.
Rufname *m.* Christian name.
Rüge *f.* censure, reprimand.

rügen to censure, reprimand.

RUHE f. rest, repose, calm.
Angenehme Ruhe! Sleep well!
in aller Ruhe very calmly.
Lassen Sie mich in Ruhe! Leave me alone!
Nichts bringt ihn aus der Ruhe. Nothing upsets him.
Ruhe! Silence! Quiet!
sich zur Ruhe setzen to retire.
zur Ruhe gehen to go to bed.

ruhelos restless.

RUHEN to rest, sleep, stand still.
ruhen auf to rest on, be based on.

Ruhestätte f. resting-place.

Ruhestellung f. at-ease position (standing).

Ruhestörer m. brawler, rioter.

RUHIG still, quiet, silent, calm, composed.
Bleiben Sie ruhig sitzen! Don't get up!
Sei ruhig! Be quiet!

Ruhm m. fame, glory.

rühmen to praise.
sich rühmen to boast, brag.

rühmlich glorious, praiseworthy.

ruhmlos inglorious, obscure.

Rührei n. scrambled egg.

rühren to move, touch, stir.

rührend touching, moving, pathetic.

rührig active, quick.

rührselig sentimental, emotional.

Rührung f. emotion, feeling.

Ruine f. ruin.

ruinieren to ruin.

RUND round, circular, plump.
rund heraus flatly.
rund (her)um all around.

Rundblick m. panorama.

RUNDE f. circle, lap, beat.
die Runde machen to make a round.

runden to make round, round.

Rundfahrt f. circular tour.

Rundfrage f. inquiry, questionnaire.

RUNDFUNK m. radio, wireless, broadcasting.
im Rundfunk gehört heard over the radio.

Rundfunkgerät n. wireless set.

Rundfunkhörer m. listener (radio).

Rundgang m. round (military), stroll.

rundlich round, rounded.

Rundschreiben n. circular letter.

Rundung f. rounding, curve.

Russ m. soot.

Russe m. (Russin f.) Russian (person).

russig sooty.

russisch Russian.

Russische n. Russian (language).

rüsten to arm, prepare for war.

rüstig strong, robust, vigorous.

Rüstung f. preparation, equipment, armor.

Rutsch m. slide, glide, landslip.

rutschen to slide, slip, skid.

rutschig slippery.

S

Saal m. large room, hall.

Saat f. seed.

Säbel m. saber.

sabotieren to sabotage.

Sachbearbeiter m. expert.

sachdienlich relevant, pertinent.

SACHE f. thing, subject, business, case, cause, point, subject.
bei der Sache sein to pay attention.
gemeinsame Sache machen to make common cause with.
zur Sache to the point.

Sachen pl. things, clothes.
seine sieben Sachen all one's belongings.

sachgemäss appropriate, suitable.

Sachkunde f. expert knowledge.

sachkundig expert, competent.

Sachlage f. state of affairs.

sachlich factual, essential, objective.

Sachlichkeit f. reality, objectivity.

Sachschaden m. damage to property.

sachte soft, gentle, slow.

Sachverhalt m. facts of the case.

Sack m. sack, bag, pocket, purse.

Sackgasse f. blind alley, dead end.

säen to sow.

Saft m. juice, liquid, sap.
Apfelsinensaft m. orange juice.

saftig juicy, succulent.

saftlos dry.

Sage f. legend, tale.

Säge f. saw.

SAGEN to say, tell, mean.
Das hat nichts zu sagen. That does not matter.
Das ist leichter gesagt als getan. That's easier said than done.
Er hat es mir ins Ohr gesagt. He whispered it in my ear.
Gesagt, getan. No sooner said than done.
man sagt they say.
sagen lassen to send word.
sage und schreibe precisely.
sich etwas gesagt sein lassen to be warned.
unter uns gesagt between you and me.
Was sagen Sie dazu? What do you say to that?
Was wollen Sie damit sagen? What do you mean by that?

sagenhaft legendary, fabulous, mythical.

Sägewerk n. sawmill.

Sahne f. cream.

Saison f. season (social).

Saisonausverkauf m clearance sale.

Saite f. string, chord.

Saiteninstrument n. stringed instrument.

Salat m. salad.
grüner Salat lettuce.

Salbe f. salve, ointment.

salben to anoint.

Salmiakgeist m. ammonia.

Salon m. drawing room.

salutieren to salute.

SALZ m. salt.

salzen to salt, season.

Salzgurke f. pickled cucumber.

salzhältig containing salt.

salzig salted, salty.

Same m. seed.

SAMMELN to collect, gather, accumulate.

Sammelplatz m. assembly.

Sammelstelle f. assembly.

Sammler m. collector.

Sammlung f. collection.

SAMSTAG m. Saturday.

Samt m. velvet.

samt together with.
samt und sonders one and all.

sämtlich altogether, all of them.

Sanatorium n. sanatorium.

SAND m. sand.

Sandale f. sandal.

Sandboden m. sandy soil.

sandig sandy.

SANFT soft, tender, delicate, gentle, smooth.

Sanftheit f. softness.

sänftigen to soften, appease.

Sanftmut f. gentleness.

sanftmütig gentle, meek.

Sänger m. (-in, f.) singer.

Sanitäter m. medical aid (person).

Sardelle f. anchovy.

Sardine f. sardine.

Sarg m. coffin.

sarkastisch sarcastic.

Satiriker m. satirist.

satirisch satirical.

SATT full, satisfied, saturated.
Ich habe es satt. I've enough of it, I'm fed up with it.
nicht satt werden never to be tired of.

Sattel m. saddle.
in allen Sätteln gerecht sein to be good at everything.

satteln to saddle.

sättigen to satisfy, saturate.

Satz m. set, clause, sentence (grammar); proposition (philo.); phrase (music); sediment.

Satzbau m. sentence structure.

Satzzeichen n. punctuation mark.

sauber clean, neat, tidy.

Sauberkeit f. tidiness, cleanliness.

säuberlich clean, neat.

säubern to clean, clear.

Säuberung f. cleaning.

Sauce f. sauce, gravy.

SAUER sour, acid, pickled.

Sauerbraten m. sauerbraten.

Sauerkraut m. sauerkraut.

säuerlich acid, acidulous.

säuern to acidify.

Sauerstoff m. oxygen.

Sauerstoffgerät n. oxygen apparatus.

saugen to suck, absorb.

säugen to suckle, nurse.

Säugling m. infant, baby.

Säule f. pillar, column.

Saum m. edge, border, hem.

Säure f. acid, sourness, tartness, acidity.

säurehaltig containing acid.

Saxophon n. saxophone.

schäbig shabby, worn out.

Schäbigkeit f. shabbiness.

Schach n. chess.
Schach bieten to defy.

Schachbrett n. chessboard.

Schachfeld n. square of a chessboard.

schachmatt checkmate.

Schachpartie f. chess game.

Schachtel f. box.

SCHADE too bad.
Es ist schade! It is a pity!
Wie schade! What a pity!
zu schade für too good to.

Schaden m. damage, harm, injury, bias.
Durch Schaden wird man klug. You learn by your mistakes.
zu Schaden kommen to suffer damage.

SCHADEN to hurt, damage, injure, prejudice.
Es schadet nichts. It doesn't matter.

Schadenersatz m. compensation.

Schadenfreude f. malicious joy.

schadenfroh rejoicing over another's misfortune.

schadhaft damaged, defective, dilapidated.
sich schadlos halten to get even with.

schädlich harmful, bad.

Schaf n. sheep.

Schäfchen n. lamb.
sein Schäfchen ins Trockene bringen to feather one's nest.

Schäfer m. shepherd.

Schäferhund m. sheep-dog.

schaffen to create, produce, accomplish, make, do.
einem zu schaffen machen to give trouble.
sich zu schaffen machen to be busy.
wie geschaffen für as though cut out for.

schaffend creative, working.

Schaffner m. conductor, (train) guard.

Schal m. shawl, scarf.

Schale f. skin, peel, rind, shell.

schälen to peel, shell, bark, skin.

Schalk m. rogue.

schalkhaft roguish.

Schall m. sound.

schalldicht soundproof.

Schalleffekt m. sound effect.

schallen to sound, resound.

Schalllehre f. acoustics.

Schallplatte f. record (phonograph).

Schaltanlage f. switch, gear.

schalten to deal with, use, direct, change gears.

Schalter m. switch, ticket-window.

Schaltjahr n. leap year.

Schaltung f. gear change, connection.

Scham f. shame, modesty.

schämen (sich) to be ashamed.

Schamgefühl n. sense of shame.

schamhaft modest, bashful.

schamlos shameless, impudent.

Schamlosigkeit f. shamelessness, impudence.

schamrot blushing red.

Schamröte f. blush.

schandbar infamous.

Schande f. shame, disgrace.

schänden to spoil, disfigure, dishonor, rape.

schändlich shameful, disgraceful.

Schändlichkeit f. infamy.

Schandtat f. crime, misdeed.

SCHARF sharp, keen, harsh, pointed, piercing, acute, strong, quick.

 Behalten Sie ihn scharf im Auge! Keep a sharp eye on him!

 Ich bin nicht so scharf darauf. I am not so keen on that.

Scharfblick m. penetrating glance.

Schärfe f. sharpness, rigor, acuteness.

schärfen to sharpen.

scharfkantig sharp-edged.

Scharfsicht f. keenness of sight, perspicacity.

scharfsichtig keen-sighted, penetrating.

Scharlach m. scarlet fever.

SCHATTEN m. shadow, shade, spirit, phantom.

 in den Schatten stellen to overshadow.

 Sie folgt mir wie ein Schatten. She follows me like a shadow.

Schattenseite f. shady side.

schattieren to shade.

schattig shady.

Schatz m. treasure.

Schatzamt n. treasury.

Schatzanweisung f. treasury bond.

schätzen to value, estimate, judge.

schätzenswert estimable.

Schatzmeister m. treasurer.

Schätzung f. estimate, taxation.

schätzungsweise approximately.

SCHAU f. sight, view, show, exhibition.

 zur Schau stellen to exhibit, display.

Schauder m. shudder, shivering, horror, terror, fright.

schauen to see, behold, gaze, view.

Schauer m. horror, terror, awe, thrill.

schauerlich awful.

schauern to shudder, shiver.

 mich schaudert bei I shudder at.

Schauerroman m. thriller.

Schaufel f. shovel, scoop.

schaufeln to shovel.

Schaufenster n. show-window.

Schaukasten m. show case.

Schaukel f. swing.

schaukeln to swing, rock.

Schaukelstuhl m. rocking chair.

schaulustig curious.

SCHAUSPIEL n. spectacle, scene, play, drama.

Schauspieler m. (–in, f.) actor (actress).

Schauspielkunst f. dramatic art.

Schaustellung f. exhibition.

Schaustück n. specimen.

Schaum m. foam.

zu Schaum schlagen to beat up.

schäumen to foam.

schaumig foamy, frothy.

Scheck m. check.

Scheckbuch n. check book.

Scheckformular n. blank check.

Scheckinhaber m. bearer.

Scheibe f. (window) pane, disk, slice, target.

Scheibenwischer m. window-wiper.

Scheide f. boundary, limits, frontier.

scheiden to separate, divide, part, divorce.

 sich scheiden lassen to get a divorce.

Scheidewand f. partition.

Scheidung f. separation, divorce.

Scheidungsklage f. divorce suit.

SCHEIN m. appearance, air, look; shine; ticket; receipt.

 Der Schein trügt. Appearances are deceiving.

scheinbar apparent.

Scheinbild n. phantom, illusion.

SCHEINEN to shine; seem; look.

scheinheilig hypocritical.

Scheintod m. suspended animation.

Scheinwerfer m. reflector, search light, headlight (car).

Scheitel m. top, crown, summit.

scheitern to fail.

Schelle f. door bell, little bell.

Schema n. order, arrangement, model.

schematisch systematic, mechanical.

Schenkel m. thigh.

schenken to give, present with, grant.

 geschenkt bekommen to get as a present.

Schenker m. donor.

Schenkung f. donation, gift.

Schere f. scissors.

Scherz m. joke, jest, pleasantry.

scherzen to joke, make fun of.

scherzhaft joking.

Scherzwort n. joke.

SCHEU shy, timid.

 scheu werden to shy.

scheuen to avoid, shun.

 sich scheuen to shy away.

scheuern to scrub, rub, clean, chafe.

Schicht f. layer, bed, coat, shift.

Schichtwechsel m. change of shift.

Schick m. elegance, smartness, chic.

SCHICKEN to send, dispatch.

 schicken nach to send for.

 sich schicken in to put up with.

schicklich proper, decent.

Schicksal n. fate, destiny, lot.

Schiebefenster n. sash-window.

SCHIEBEN to move, push, shove.

 schieben auf to lay the blame on.

Schiebetür f. sliding door.

Schiebung f. profiteering.

Schiedsrichter m. umpire.

schief oblique, crooked, askance.

Schiefer m. slate, splinter.

Schieferdach n. slate roof.

Schiene f. rail, track, splint.

schiessen to shoot, flash, fire.

SCHIFF n. boat, ship, vessel.

 zu Schiff on board, by boat.

schiffbar navigable.

Schiffbruch m. shipwreck.

Schiffchen n. small boat, shuttle.

schiffen to ship, sail.

Schiffer m. sailor.

Schiffsbesatzung f. crew.

Schiffskörper m. hull.

Schiffsladung f. cargo.

Schiffswerft m. wharf, dock.

Schild n. shield, coat of arms, sign.

 im Schilde führen to have something up one's sleeve.

schildern to relate, describe.

Schilderung f. description.

Schimmel m. mold, mildew.

schimmelig moldy.

Schimmer m. glitter.

schimmern to glitter, gleam.

Schimpf m. disgrace, insult.

schimpfen to kick, gripe, scold.

 schimpfen mit to scold.

schimpflich disgraceful.

Schimpfwort n. invective.

SCHINKEN m. ham.

 Eier mit Schinken ham and eggs.

Schirm m. umbrella, shelter, lampshade.

Schlacht f. combat, battle.

schlachten to slaughter, kill, butcher.

Schlächter m. butcher.

Schlachtfeld n. battlefield.

Schlachthaus n. slaughterhouse.

Schlachtschiff n. battleship.

SCHLAF m. sleep.

 im Schlaf liegen to be asleep.

Schlafanzug m. pajamas.

Schläfchen n. nap.

SCHLAFEN to sleep.

 schlafen gehen to go to bed.

Schlafenszeit m. bedtime.

schlaff slack, loose, relaxed.

Schlaffheit f. laxity.

Schlafkrankheit f. sleeping sickness.

schlaflos sleepless.

Schlaflosigkeit f. insomnia.

Schlafmittel m. narcotic.

schläfrig sleepy.

Schlafsaal m. dormitory.

Schlafwagen m. sleeping-car.

Schlafwandler m. sleepwalker.

Schlafzimmer n. bedroom.

SCHLAG m. blow, stroke, striking (clock).

 zwei Fliegen auf einen Schlag treffen to kill two birds with one stone.

Schlagader f. artery.

Schlaganfall m. stroke, fit.

SCHLAGEN to beat, knock, hit, strike, throb.

 sich schlagen to fight.

 sich geschlagen geben to give up.

 schlagen nach to take after.

 eine geschlagene Stunde a whole hour.

schlagfertig quick at repartee.

Schlagfertigkeit f. quickness at repartee.

Schlagsahne f. whipped cream.

Schlagwort n. slogan.

Schlagzeile f. headline.

Schlagzeug n. percussion instrument.

Schlamm m. mud, ooze.

schlammig muddy, oozy.

Schlange f. snake.

 Schlange stehen to make a line.

Schlangenbiss m. snake bite.

schlank slim, slender.

Schlankheit f. slimness, slenderness.

schlapp weak, tired, limp, flabby.

 schlapp machen to collapse.

schlau sly, cunning.

Schlauberger m. sly fox.

Schlauch m. hose, tube.

Schlauheit f. slyness, cunning.

Schlaukopf m. sly fox.

SCHLECHT bad, poor, inferior, ill, wicked.

 mir ist schlecht I feel sick.

 schlecht machen to run down.

 schlecht und recht somehow.

 schlecht werden to spoil (food).

schlechtgelaunt in a bad temper.

Schlechtigkeit f. badness, wickedness.

schleichen to creep, drag, sneak.

 sich davon schleichen to steal away.

 wie die Katze um den heissen Brei

schleichen to beat around the bush
("to creep like the cat around the hot roast").
schlicht simple, plain, even.
schlichten to make simple, smooth.
Schlichtheit f. simplicity.
Schliesse f. clasp, fastening.
SCHLIESSEN to close, lock, shut, break up.
in die Arme schliessen to embrace.
geschlossen enclosed.
Schliessfach n. locker.
schliesslich final, finally, after all.
Schliessung f. closing.
schlimm bad, sore.
schlimmstenfalls if the worst comes to the
worst.
Schlinge f. knot, loop.
sich aus der Schlinge ziehen to get out of a
difficulty.
Schlips m. necktie (coll.).
Schlitten m. sled, sleigh.
Schlittenfahrt f. sleigh driving.
Schlittschuh m. skate.
Schlittschuh laufen to skate.
Schlittschuhläufer m. skater.
SCHLOSS n. castle, lock.
Schlosser m. locksmith.
Schluck m. gulp, draught.
Schluckauf m. hiccup.
schlucken to gulp, swallow.
Schlucker m. hiccup.
armer Schlucker poor wretch.
Schlummer m. slumber.
schlummern to slumber.
Schlüpfer m. panties.
SCHLUSS m. closing, shutting, conclusion.
Schlüssel m. key, code.
Schlüsselbund m. bunch of keys.
Schlüsselloch m. keyhole.
Schlusslicht n. tail light.
Schlusswort n. summary, last word.
Schmach f. disgrace, dishonor, humiliation.
schmachten to languish.
schmachvoll disgraceful, humiliating.
schmackhaft tasty, savory.
schmähen to abuse.
schmählich disgraceful.
SCHMAL narrow, thin, slender, poor.
Hier ist Schmalhans Küchenmeister. We are
on short rations here.
schmälern to diminish, lessen.
Schmalz n. drippings.
SCHMECKEN to taste, try.
Es schmeckt gut. It tastes good.
Es schmeckt mir nicht. I don't like it.
schmecken nach to taste of.
Wie schmeckt's? How do you like it?
Schmeichelei f. flattery.
schmeichelhaft flattering.
Schmeichelkatze f. wheedler.
schmeicheln to flatter.
Schmeichler m. flatterer.
schmeichlerisch flattering.
schmelzen to melt.
SCHMERZ m. pain, ache, hurt, sorrow.
SCHMERZEN to hurt, pain, grieve.
Schmerzensgeld n. smart money, compensation.
schmerzerfüllt deeply affected.
schmerzhaft painful.
schmerzlich grievous, sad.
schmerzlos painless.
schmerzstillend soothing.
Schmetterling m. butterfly.
Schmied m. blacksmith.
Schmiede f. forge.
schmieden to forge, hammer.
schmiegen to bend.
schmiegsam flexible, supple.
Schmiegsamkeit f. flexibility.

schmieren to spread, grease, smear.
Schminke f. rouge, paint, make up.
schminken to make up, paint the face.
Schmöker m. bad novel, trashy book.
schmollen to sulk.
Schmorbraten stewed steak.
SCHMUCK m. jewelry, ornament, decoration.
schmücken to decorate, adorn.
Schmuckstück n. piece of jewelry.
Schmuggel m. smuggling.
schmuggeln to smuggle.
schmunzeln to grin.
Schmutz m. dirt, mud.
schmutzen to dirty.
Schmutzfleck m. stain, spot.
schmutzig dirty.
Schnabel m. beak, bill.
schnarchen to snore.
schnaufen to breathe heavily, pant.
Schnecke f. snail.
wie eine Schnecke kriechen to go at a
snail's pace.
SCHNEE m. snow.
Schneeball m. snowball.
Schneefall m. snowfall.
Schneeflocke f. snowflake.
Schneeglöckchen n. snowdrop.
Schneekette f. non-skid chain (automobile).
Schneeschuh m. ski.
Schneetreiben n. blizzard.
schneeweiss snow-white.
SCHNEIDEN to cut, carve.
sich schneiden to cut oneself.
schneidend sharp, bitter.
Schneider m. tailor.
schneien to snow.
SCHNELL quick, fast, swift, prompt, speedy.
Schnelligkeit f. rapidity, velocity.
Schnellzug m. express train.
Schnippchen n. snap of the fingers.
ein Schnippchen schlagen to play a trick.
Schnitt m. cut, cutting, incision.
der goldene Schnitt A medial section.
Schnittblumen pl. cut flowers.
Schnittmuster n. cut pattern.
Schnittwunde f. cut.
schnitzen to carve, cut.
Schnupfen m. (head) cold.
schnupfen to take snuff.
Schnur f. string, cord.
über die Schnur hauen to kick over the traces.
Schnurrbart m. moustache.
schnurren to hum, buzz, purr.
schnurstracks immediately.
Schock m. shock.
Schokolade f. chocolate.
SCHON already, all right, very, yet, even,
indeed, certainly.
Schon gut! All right!
Wenn schon! So what!
SCHÖN beautiful, handsome, fine, nice, fair, noble.
Danke schön (Schönen Dank).   Thanks.
Das wäre noch schöner!   That's all we
                              need!
die Schönen Künste   the fine arts.
schön tun   to flatter.
Schönen Gruss an   Best regards to
Ihre Frau.   your wife.
Schönsten Dank.   Many thanks.
sich schön machen   to smarten
                              oneself.
schonen to spare, save, look after.
schonend careful, considerate.
Schöngeist m. wit; esthete.
schöngeistig esthetical.
Schönheit f. beauty.
Schönheitsmittel n. cosmetic.
Schönheitspflege f. beauty treatment.

Schonung f. indulgence.
schonungslos pitiless.
schöpfen to draw, create.
Schöpferkraft f. creative, power.
Schöpflöffel m. strainer.
Schornstein m. chimney, funnel.
Schoss m. lap.
Schotte m. Scotsman.
schottisch Scottish.
schräg diagonally.
Schräge f. slant, slope.
Schramme f. scratch, scar.
schrammen to scratch.
Schrank m. wardrobe.
Schranke f. fencing, enclosure, gate.
sich in Schranken halten to keep within bounds.
schrankenlos boundless, without limits.
Schrankkoffer m. wardrobe trunk.
Schraube f. screw, propeller, bolt.
schrauben to screw, turn, wheel.
Schraubenschlüssel m. wrench.
Schraubenzieher m. screwdriver.
SCHRECK (EN) m. scare, fright, fear, dread, horror.
in Schrecken setzen to terrify.
schrecken to frighten.
Schreckgespenst n. terrible vision.
schreckhaft timid, easily frightened.
schrecklich terrible, awful.
Schreckschuss m. false alarm.
Schrei m. scream, cry.
SCHREIBEN to write, spell.
auf der Maschine schreiben to type.
sage und schreibe precisely.
Schreiberei f. writing, correspondence.
Schreibfehler m. slip of the pen.
Schreibmappe f. writing case, portfolio, blotter.
Schreibmaschine f. typewriter.
Schreibpapier n. note paper.
Schreibstube f. office.
Schreibwaren pl. stationery.
Schreibwarengeschäft n. stationery store.
Schreibwarenhändler m. stationer.
Schreibwarenhandlung f. stationery store.
SCHREIEN to scream, shout, yell.
schreiend loud, gaudy.
Schreier m. shouter, bawler.
Schreiner m. carpenter, cabinetmaker.
Schreinerei f. cabinetmaker's.
SCHRIFT f. writing, handwriting, script.
schriftlich in writing, written.
Schriftführer m. secretary (association or politics).
Schriftsteller m. writer (author).
SCHRITT m. step, stride.
auf Schritt und Tritt everywhere, all the time.
Schritt fahren! Drive slowly!
Schritt für Schritt step by step.
Schritt halten to keep pace with.
schrubben to scrub.
Schrubber m. scrubber.
schrumpfen to shrink, contract.
Schrumpfung f. shrinking, contraction.
Schubfach n. drawer.
Schublade f. drawer.
schüchtern bashful, timid.
Schüchternheit f. bashfulness, timidity.
Schuft m. scoundrel.
SCHUH m. shoe.
einem etwas in die Schuhe schieben to put
the blame on someone.
Schuhanzieher m. shoehorn.
Schuhkrem f. shoe-polish.
Schuhmacher m. shoemaker.
Schuhputzer m. bootblack.
Schuhriemen m. shoelace.
Schuhsohle f. sole of a shoe.
Schuhwichse f. boot polish.
Schularbeit f. lesson, homework.
Schulbesuch m. attendance at school.

Schulbildung /. schooling, education.
SCHULD /. obligation, debt, cause, blame.
  in jemandes Schuld stehen to have an
  obligation.
  Schuld sein to be guilty of.
  Schulden machen to make debts.
  Schuld geben to accuse.
schuldbewusst guilt-conscious.
Schuldbrief m. bond.
schulden to owe.
Schuldenmacher m. contractor of debts.
schuldig owing, due, obliged, guilty.
  Dank Schuldig sein to be indebted.
  Geld schuldig sein to owe money.
  keine Antwort schuldig bleiben never to be
  at a loss for an answer.
Schuldigkeit /. duty, obligation.
schuldlos innocent.
Schuldner m. debtor.
Schuldschein m. bond, promissory note.
SCHULE /. school, academy, courses.
  die Schule schwänzen to cut classes.
  Schule machen to find followers.
schulen to school, train, teach.
Schüler m. student, pupil.
Schulferien pl. m. (-in /.) school holidays.
schulfrei having a holiday.
Schulfreund m. school friend.
Schulgeld n. school fees.
Schulmappe /. schoolbag, satchel.
Schulmeister m. schoolmaster, teacher.
schulmeistern to teach school, censure.
Schulstunde /. school lesson.
Schulter /. shoulder.
Schulung /. school training.
Schulzeugnis n. school certificates.
Schuppe /. scale (fish).
Schürze /. apron.
Schuss m. shot, report, round.
schussbereit ready to shoot.
Schusswaffe /. firearm.
Schussweite /. range.
Schusswunde /. bullet wound.
schütteln to shake.
schütten to pour in.
SCHUTZ m. shelter, protection, refuge.
  im Schutz der Nacht under cover of the night.
  in Schutz nehmen to defend.
  Schutz suchen to take shelter.
Schütze m. rifleman, private soldier.
schützen to protect.
  sich schützen to protect oneself.
Schutzengel m. guardian angel.
Schutzhaft /. protective custody.
Schutzimpfung /. vaccination.
schutzlos defenseless, unprotected.
Schutzmann m. policeman.
Schutzpockenimpfung /. vaccination against smallpox.
Schutztruppe /. colonial force, occupation forces.
SCHWACH weak, frail, faint, feeble.
Schwäche /. weakness, debility.
schwächen to weaken.
Schwächheit /. weakness, feebleness.
schwächlich weak, delicate.
Schwächlichkeit /. delicacy, infirmity.
Schwachsinn m. imbecility.
schwachsinnig imbecile.
Schwager m. brother-in-law.
Schwägerin /. sister-in-law.
Schwalbe /. swallow.
Schwamm m. sponge, mushroom.
Schwan m. swan.
schwanger pregnant.
Schwank m. prank, short anecdote, farce.
schwanken to rock, toss, sway.
Schwankung /. variation.
Schwanz m. tail, end.
Schwarm m. crowd, multitude.

schwärmen to swarm, riot.
Schwärmer m. enthusiast, fanatic.
Schwärmerei /. enthusiasm.
schwärmerisch enthusiastic, fanatic.
Schwarte /. rind, skin.
SCHWARZ black, dark, dirty, gloomy.
  ins Schwarze treffen to hit the bull's eye.
  schwarz auf weiss in black and white.
  Sie sieht immer alles schwarz. She always
  sees the dark side of things.
Schwarzbrot n. black bread.
Schwarze m. Negro.
Schwarzhandel m. black market.
Schwarzwald m. Black Forest.
Schwatz m. chat, talk.
Schwatzbase /. chatterbox.
schwatzen to chatter, gossip.
Schwätzer m. (-in /.) gossip.
schwatzhaft talkative.
Schwatzhaftigkeit /. loquacity.
Schwebe /. suspense.
  in der Schwebe sein to be undecided.
Schwebebahn /. suspension railway.
schweben to be suspended, pending.
  auf der Zunge schweben to have on the tip
  of the tongue.
  in Gefahr schweben to be in danger.
Schwede m. Swede.
schwedisch Swedish.
Schwefel m. sulphur.
Schweigen n. silence.
schweigsam silent, taciturn.
Schweigsamkeit /. taciturnity.
Schwein n. pig, hog.
Schweinebraten m. roast pork.
Schweinefleisch n. pork.
Schweiss m. sweat, perspiration.
Schweisstropfen m. bead of perspiration.
Schweizer m. Swiss.
schweizerisch Swiss.
schwelgen to feast, celebrate.
Schwelle /. threshold.
schwellen to swell, rise, grow.
Schwellung /. swelling, tumor, growth.
SCHWER heavy, hard, difficult, serious, strong;
  heavily, seriously, strongly.
  etwas schwer nehmen to take something
  to heart.
  schwer fallen (halten) to be difficult.
schwerblütig melancholy.
schwerfällig heavy, clumsy.
Schwerfälligkeit /. heaviness, clumsiness.
Schwergewicht n. heavyweight.
schwerhörig hard of hearing.
Schwerhörigkeit /. deafness.
Schwerkraft /. force of gravity.
Schwerkriegsbeschädigte m. disabled soldier.
schwerlich hardly, scarcely, with difficulty.
Schwermut /. melancholy, sadness.
schwermütig melancholy, sad.
Schwerpunkt m. center of gravity.
Schwert n. sword.
Schwerverbrecher m. criminal, gangster.
schwerwiegend serious, grave.
SCHWESTER /. sister, hospital nurse.
schwesterlich sisterly.
Schwiegereltern pl. parents-in-law.
Schwiegermutter /. mother-in-law.
Schwiegersohn m. son-in-law.
Schwiegertochter /. daughter-in-law.
Schwiegervater m. father-in-law.
schwierig difficult.
Schwierigkeit /. difficulty.
Schwimmanstalt /. swimming-pool.
SCHWIMMEN to swim, float, sail.
Schwimmhose /. swimming shorts.
Schwimmweste /. life jacket.

Schwindel m. swindle; dizziness.
Schwindelanfall m. fit of dizziness.
schwindeln to swindle, cheat; be dizzy.
  Mir schwindelt. I feel dizzy.
Schwindler m. swindler.
schwindlig dizzy.
schwingen to swing, sway, oscillate, vibrate.
Schwingung /. oscilliation.
Schwips m. Smack! Slap!
  einen Schwips haben to be tipsy.
schwören to swear, take an oath.
schwül sulty, muggy.
Schwung /. swing (push), vault.
  in Schwung bringen to set going.
schwungvoll energetic.
Schwur m. oath.
  Schwur leisten to take an oath.
SECHS six.
SECHSTE sixth.
SECHZEHN sixteen.
SECHZEHNTE sixteenth.
SECHZIG sixty.
SECHZIGSTE sixtieth.
See m. lake.
SEE /. sea, seaside.
  an die See gehen to go to the seaside.
  in See stechen to put to sea.
Seebad n. seaside resort.
seefest seaworthy.
  Seefest sein to be a good sailor.
Seegang m. heavy sea, swell.
Seehund m. seal.
seekrank seasick.
  seekrank sein to be seasick.
Seekrankheit /. seasickness.
SEELE /. soul, mind, spirt.
  jemandem aus der Seele sprechen to express
  a person's thoughts.
  Sie sind mit Leib und Seele dabei. They are
  in it with heart and soul.
seelisch spiritual, mental, emotional.
Seemann m. sailor.
Seemeile /. nautical mile (1.852 kilometers).
Seenot /. distress (at sea).
Seewasser n. sea-water.
Segel n. sail, canvas.
Segelboot n. sailboat.
Segelflugzeug n. glider.
segeln to sail.
Segelschiff n. sailboat.
Segen m. blessing.
segnen to bless.
SEHEN to see, look, behold, contemplate.
  darauf sehen to watch carefully.
  gut sehen to have good eyesight.
  Ich kenne sie nur vom Sehen. I know her only
  by sight.
  schlecht sehen to have poor eyesight.
  sehen nach to look after.
sehenswert worth seeing, remarkable.
Sehenswürdigkeit /. point of interest.
Sehkraft /. eyesight.
Sehne /. sinew, ligament.
SEHNEN to long, yearn for.
sehnlich ardent, longing.
Sehnsucht /. longing, yearning.
sehnsüchtig longing, yearning.
SEHR very; very much.
  Bitte sehr. You are quite welcome.
seicht shallow.
SEIDE /. silk.
Seidenpapier n. tissue paper.
Seidenraupe /. silkworm.
seidig silky.
Seife /. soap.
Seifenflocken pl. soapflakes.
Seifenpulver n. soap powder.
Seil n. rope, line.

Seilbahn f. cable.
Sein n. being.
SEIN to be, exist.
   es sei denn, dass unless.
SEIN poss. adj. his, her, its.
SEIN(ER, -E, -ES) poss. pron. his, hers.
   die Seinen one's own people.
seinetwegen because of him, for his sake.
SEIT prep. (with dat.) since, for.
   Ich warte seit einer Stunde. I have been
   waiting for an hour.
   seit kurzer Zeit lately.
   seit meiner Ankunft since my return.
   Seit Wann? Since when?
seitdem conj. since, since that time.
SEITE f. side, page, party, member.
   auf die Seite aside, away.
   auf die Seite gehen to step aside.
   Schwache Seite weakness.
   Seite an Seite side by side.
   zur Seite stehen to stand by, help.
Seitenflügel m. side aisle, wing.
Seitenstrasse f. side street.
Seitenzahl f. number of pages.
seither since then.
seitlich lateral, collateral.
seitwärts sideways, aside.
Sekt m. champagne.
Sekretär m. (–in f.) secretary.
SEKUNDE f. second (time, music, fencing).
Sekundenzeiger m. second hand (on clocks).
selbe (der, die, das) same.
selber self.
   ich selber myself.
SELBST 1. adj. or pron. self.
   Ich habe es selbst getan. I did it myself.
   Das versteht sich von selbst. That goes
   without saying.
   2. adv. even.
   Ich habe alles zu Hause gelassen, selbst
   mein Geld. I left everything at home, even
   my money.
selbständig independent.
Selbstbeherrschung f. self-control.
selbstbewusst self-assured.
Selbstbewusstsein n. self-assurance.
Selbsterhaltung f. self-preservation.
Selbsterkenntnis f. self-knowledge.
selbstgefällig self-satisfied, complacent.
Selbstgefühl n. self-respect.
Selbstgespräch m. monologue, soliloquy.
selbstherrlich autocratic.
Selbstkostenpreis m. cost price.
selbstlos unselfish, disinterested.
Selbstlosigkeit f. unselfishness.
Selbstmörder m. suicide.
selbstredend self-evident, obvious.
Selbstsucht f. selfishness, egoism.
selbstsüchtig selfish, egoistic.
SELBSTVERSTÄNDLICH evident.
Selbstvertrauen n. self-confidence.
selbstzufrieden self-satisfied.
selig blessed.
Seligkeit f. happiness, bliss.
Sellerie f. celery.
SELTEN rare, unusual.
Seltenheit f. rarity, scarcity.
SELTSAM strange, unusual, odd.
Selterwasser n. soda-water.
Semester n. term, session.
Seminar n. training college.
Senat m. senate.
senden to send, broadcast, transmit.
Sender m. transmitter.
Senderaum m. studio.
Sendung f. mission, transmission.
Senf m. mustard.
Senkel m. lace (shoe).

senken to lower, dip, sink.
   sich senken to settle.
sensationell sensational.
Sensationslust f. desire to cause a sensation.
Sentimentalität f. sentimentality.
SEPTEMBER m. September.
Serie f. series, issue.
Service n. service set.
Servierbrett n. tray.
servieren to serve, wait at a table.
Serviette f. table napkin.
Sessel m. armchair.
sesshaft settled, established.
SETZEN to put, set, place, fix, erect, put up,
   sit down.
   alles daran setzen to risk everything.
   gesetzt den Fall, dass suppose that.
   in Freiheit setzen to set free.
   Setzen Sie sich! Sit down!
   sich etwas in den Kopf setzen to get an idea
   into one's head.
   sich in Verbindung setzen mit to get in
   touch with.
   unter Druck setzen to put pressure on.
Seuche f. epidemic.
seufzen to sigh.
sezieren to dissect.
SICH oneself, himself, herself, itself, yourself,
   yourselves, themselves, each other, one
   another.
   sich selbst itself, oneself, etc.
SICHER secure, safe, certain, positive, surely.
   aus sicherer Hand on good authority.
   seiner Sache sicher sein to be certain of a
   thing.
   sicher gehen to be on the safe side.
   sicher stellen to put in safe keeping.
   sicher wissen to know for certain.
Sicherheit f. safety, security.
   in Sicherheit bringen to secure.
   Sicherheit leisten to give security.
sicherheitshalber for safety's sake.
Sicherheitsnadel f. safety-pin.
Sicherheitsschloss n. safety-lock.
sicherlich surely, certainly.
sichern to protect.
Sicherung f. protection.
SICHT f. sight, visibility.
   sichtbar visible, apparent.
sichten to sight; to sift, sort.
SIE (sie) pers. pron. 3rd pers. sing. (fem., nom. &
   acc.); 3rd pers. pl. (m., f., n., nom. & acc.)
   she, her, it; they, them.
SIE (Sie) pers. pron. 2nd pers., polite form (nom. &
   acc.) you.
Sieb n. collander, strainer.
sieben to sift, strain.
SIEBEN seven.
SIEBENTE seventh.
SIEBZEHNTE seventeenth.
SIEBZIG seventy.
siebzigst seventieth.
siech sickly, ailing, infirm.
siedeln to settle, colonize.
SIEG m. victory, triumph.
Siegel n. seal.
Sieger m. victor, winner.
siegesgewiss certain or confident of
   victory.
siegreich victorious.
Signal n. signal.
Signalhupe f. siren.
signalisieren to signal.
Signatur f. mark, sign, characteristic.
Silbe f. syllable.
Silber n. silver.
Silberpapier n. silver paper.
Silversterabend m. New Year's Eve.

SINGEN to sing.
Singstimme f. singing voice, vocal part.
sinken to sink, drop, fall.
SINN m. sense, faculty, mind, understanding,
   intellect.
   anderen Sinnes werden to change one's mind.
   in gewissem Sinn in a way, in a sense.
   im Sinn haben to intend.
   sich etwas aus dem Sinn schlagen to dismiss
   a thing from one's mind.
Sinnbild n. symbol, emblem, allegory.
sinnbildlich symbolic.
sinnen to think, reflect, meditate.
sinnlich sensual, sensuous, material.
sinnlos senseless, absurd.
Sinnlosigkeit f. senselessness, foolishness.
sinnreich sensible, clever.
Sippschaft f. kinship, relatives.
Sirene f. siren.
Sitte f. custom, habit.
Sittengesetz n. moral law, moral code.
Sittenlehre f. moral, philosophy, ethics.
sittenlos immoral, dissolute.
sittlich moral.
sittsam modest.
Sittsamkeit f. modesty.
SITZ m. seat, residence.
SITZEN to sit, fit, adhere.
   etwas auf sich sitzen lassen to put up with.
   sitzen bleiben to remain seated.
   sitzen lassen to leave.
Sitzgelegenheit f. seating accommodation.
Sitzplatz m. seat.
Skandal m. scandal.
Skelett n. skeleton.
skeptisch sceptical.
Ski m. ski.
   skilaufen to ski.
Skiläufer m. skier.
Skispringen n. ski-jumping.
Skizze f. sketch.
skizzieren to sketch.
Sklave m. slave.
sklavisch slavish, servile.
Skrupel m. scruple.
SO so, thus, in this way, like that, anyhow.
   Ach so! Oh, I see!
   So? Is that so? Indeed? Really?
   so...auch however.
   so bald als as soon as.
   so ... doch yet, nevertheless.
   so ein such a.
   so etwas a thing like that.
   so gut wie as if, practically.
   so oder so this way or that way.
   so...so though...yet.
   so wie as, the way.
Sock f. sock.
Sockenhalter m. garter (man's).
sodann then.
sodass so that.
soeben just, just now.
sofern so far as.
sofort immediately, at once.
sogar even.
sogenannt so-called.
sogleich at once, immediately.
Sohle f. sole.
sohlen to resole.
SOHN m. son.
solange so, as long as.
SOLCH such, the same.
   solch ein such a.
Soldat m. soldier.
Solist m. soloist.
SOLLEN ought, shall, to have to, must, be
   supposed to, be said to.
   Du sollst nicht töten. Thou shalt not kill.

Di Schüler sollen fleissig sein. Students must be industrious.

Er soll ein Millionär sein. They say he is a millionaire.

Sollte er nicht zu Hause sein? Is it possible that he is not at home?

Sollte er telefonieren? Should he telephone?

Was soll das heissen? What is the meaning of that?

Was soll es bedeuten? What does that mean?

somit consequently.

SOMMER m. summer.

Sommernachtstraum m. Midsummer Night's Dream.

Sommerfrische f. health-resort.

Sommersprosse f. freckle.

Sonderausgabe f. special edition.

SONDERBAR strange, peculiar.

sonderbarerweise strange to say.

sondergleichen unequaled, unique.

Sonderling m. strange character.

Sondermeldung f. special announcement.

SONDERN but (in a negative sentence).

Ich wollte nicht ausgehen, sondern zu Hause bleiben. I did not want to go out but to stay home.

nicht nur....sondern auch not only....but also.

Sie war nicht nur schön, sondern auch gut. She was not only beautiful but kind as well.

SONNABEND m. Saturday.

SONNE f. sun.

Sonnenaufgang m. sunrise.

Sonnenblume f. sunflower.

Sonnenbrand m. sunburn.

Sonnenbrille f. sunglasses.

Sonnenstrahl m. sunbeam.

Sonnenuntergang m. sunset.

sonnig sunny.

SONNTAG m. Sunday.

sonntags on Sunday.

SONST else, moreover, besides, otherwise, formerly.

Sonst noch etwas? Anything else?

sonst jemand anybody else.

sonst nichts nothing else.

sonst niemand? No one else?

sonst und jetzt formerly and now.

Was konnte ich sonst tun? What else could I do?

Wenn es sonst nichts wäre! If that were all it was!

wie sonst as usual.

sonstwie in some other way.

sonstwo elsewhere.

Sopran m. soprano.

SORGE f. grief, sorrow, anxiety, worry, trouble, care.

einem Sorgen machen to worry someone.

sich Sorgen machen to worry.

Sorge tragen to see about something.

SORGEN to care for, look after, take care of, provide.

sich sorgen um to be concerned about.

sorgen für to look after.

Sorgenkind n. delicate child.

sorgenvoll worried.

Sorgfalt f. carefulness, care, accuracy.

sorgfältig careful, painstaking.

sorglich careful.

sorglos carefree, careless.

Sorglosigkeit f. light-heartedness.

SORTE f. kind, sort, brand, grade.

sortieren to sort, arrange.

Souffleur m. prompter.

SOVIEL as much as, so far as.

soweit as far as.

sowenig as little as.

sowie as soon as.

sowieso anyway, anyhow.

sozial social.

Sozialismus m. Socialism.

Sozialist m. Socialist.

sozialistisch socialistic.

Sozialwissenschaft f. sociology.

Sozius m. partner.

spähen to be on the look out, patrol.

Spalier bilden to line.

Spalt m. crack, slot, gap.

spalten to split, divide.

sich spalten to split.

Spaltholz n. firewood sticks.

Spange f. buckle, brooch.

Spanier m. (–in f.) Spaniard.

spanisch Spanish.

Spanische n. Spanish (language).

Spanne f. short space of time, margin.

SPANNEN to put up, stretch, pull, tighten.

gespannt sein to be anxious, curious.

Ich bin auf die Antwort gespannt. I am curious to know the answer.

spannend fascinating, absorbing, thrilling.

Spannung f. tension, strain, suspense, voltage.

Sparbüchse f. money-box (piggy bank).

Spareinlage f. savings deposit.

Spargel m. asparagus.

Sparkasse f. savings bank.

spärlich scarce, frugal, thin.

Spärlichkeit f. scarcity.

SPARSAM economical, thrifty.

Sparsamkeit f. economy, thrift.

Spass m. joke, fun.

spassen to joke.

Spassmacher m. joker.

SPÄT late, belated, backward.

Besser spät als nie. Better late than never.

zu spät kommen to be late.

Wie spät ist es? What time is it?

Spaten m. spade.

später later, afterwards.

späterhin later on.

spätestens at the latest.

Spatz m. sparrow.

SPAZIEREN to walk about, stroll.

spazieren gehen to go for a walk.

Spazierfahrt f. drive.

Spaziergang m. walk.

Spaziergänger m. walker, stroller.

Speck m. bacon.

Speckschwarte f. rind of bacon.

Spediteur m. mover, shipper, forwarding agent.

Speicher m. storage room.

speichern to store.

SPEISE f. food, meal.

Speiseeis n. ice cream.

Speisekarte f. menu.

Speisenfolge f. menu.

Speisesaal m. dining room.

Speisewagen m. dining car.

Spekulant m. speculator.

spekulieren to speculate.

Spende f. gift, present, donation.

spenden to dispense, bestow, administer.

Spender m. giver, donor, benefactor.

spendieren to pay for.

Sperre f. gate, closing, barrier.

sperren to close, shut, block, barricade.

ins Gefängnis sperren to put in prison.

Sperrguthaben n. blocked account.

Sperrholz n. plywood.

Spesen f. pl. charges, expenses.

Spezialarzt n. specialist.

spezialisieren to specialize.

speziell special, particular.

spezifisch specific.

spezifizieren to specify.

Spiegel m. mirror.

Spiegelbild n. reflected image.

spiegelglatt smooth as a mirror.

spiegeln to shine, glitter.

sich spiegeln to be reflected.

SPIEL n. game, deck of cards, playing, play, sport, touch (music).

auf dem Spiel stehen to be at stake.

aufs Spiel setzen to risk.

Lassen Sie mich aus dem Spiel. Leave me out of this.

leichtes Spiel haben to have no difficulties.

seine Hand im Spiel haben to have a finger in the pie.

sein Spiel treiben mit to make game of.

Spieldose f. musical box.

SPIELEN to play, act, perform, gamble, pretend.

Was spielt man heute abend? What's playing tonight?

Spielerei f. trifle.

Spielplan m. program, repertory.

Spielsachen pl. toys.

Spielverderber m. kill-joy.

Spielzeug n. toy.

Spiess m. lance, spear, pike.

Spiessbürger m. bourgeois.

Spinat m. spinach.

Spinne f. spider.

spinnen to spin.

Spinngewebe n. cobweb.

Spinnrad n. spinning wheel.

Spion m. spy.

Spionage f. spying, espionage.

Spionageabwehr f. counterespionage.

spionieren to spy.

Spiritus m. spirits, alcohol.

SPITZ pointed, sharp, acute, caustic.

Spitze f. point, tip (tongue), top, head, lace, sarcasm.

etwas auf die Spitze treiben to carry to extremes.

SPITZEN to sharpen, point.

seine Ohren spitzen to prick one's ears.

Spitzenleistung f. record, maximum.

Spitzenlohn m. maximum pay.

Spitzentanz m. toe-dance.

spitzfindig pointed, sharp, sarcastic, subtle.

Spitzfindigkeit f. subtlety.

spitzig pointed, sharp, sarcastic.

Spitzname m. nickname.

Splitter m. splinter, chip.

splittern to splinter, split.

spontan spontaneous.

Sporn m. spur.

Sport m. sport.

Sport treiben to go in for sports.

Sportfunk m. radio sports news.

Sportler m. sportsman.

sportlich sporting, athletic.

Sportname m. nickname.

Spott m. mockery, ridicule.

Spöttelei f. chaff, raillery.

spötteln to laugh, sneer at.

spotten to mock, make fun, defy.

spöttisch mocking, scoffing, sarcastic.

SPRACHE f. language, speech, talk.

mit der Sprache herausrücken to come out with something.

zur Sprache bringen to bring up a subject.

zur Sprache kommen to be mentioned.

Sprachfertigkeit f. fluency.

sprachgewandt fluent.

sprachkundig proficient in languages.

Sprachlehre f. grammar.

sprachlich linguistic.

sprachlos speechless.

Sprachschatz m. vocabulary.

Sprachschnitzer m. blunder, mistake.

Sprachstörung f. speech defect.

SPRECHEN to speak, talk, say, converse, discuss.
Der herr Doktor ist nicht zu sprechen. The doctor is busy.
gut zu sprechen sein auf to be kindly disposed to.
Ich bin für niemanden zu sprechen. I am in to no one.
sich herumsprechen to be whispered about town.
Sie sprechen nicht miteinander. They are not on speaking terms.
Sprechen Sie Deutsch? Do you speak German?
Sprechen Sie langsam, bitte. Please speak slowly.
Wen wünschen Sie zu sprechen? Whom do you want to see?
Sprecher m. speaker.
Sprechstunde f. office hours, office (doctor).
Sprechstundenhilfe f. doctor's receptionist.
Sprechweise f. diction.
Sprechzimmer n. consulting room.
sprengen to burst, blow up, blast, spray.
Sprengung f. blowing up.
Sprichwort n. proverb.
Springbrunnen m. fountain.
SPRINGEN to jump, skip, spring, play.
Das ist der springende Punkt. That is the crucial point.
in die Augen springen to be obvious.
spritzen to spray, splash, sprinkle.
spröde reserved, shy.
Sprosse f. rung (ladder).
Sprössling m. sprout, shoot, offshoot.
Spruch m. aphorism, saying.
spruchreif ripe for decision.
sprudeln to bubble up.
sprühen to spark.
Sprühregen m. drizzle, drizzling rain.
SPRUNG m. leap, jump, crack.
Es ist nur ein Sprung von meinem Haus. It is only a stone's throw from my house.
Ich war auf dem Sprung auszugehen. I was just going to leave.
Sprungschanze f. ski-jump.
spucken to spit.
Spucken Verboten! No spitting!
Spuk m. ghost.
Spülbecken n. washtub.
spülen to rinse.
Spülwasser n. dishwater.
Spund m. plug, stopper.
SPUR f. trace, trail, track, footprint.
einem auf die Spur kommen to be on a person's tracks.
Keine Spur! Not in the least!
spüren to feel perceive, experience.
spüren nach to track, follow.
spurlos trackless.
Spürsinn m. shrewdness.
Spürsinn haben to have a flair.
STAAT m. state, government, pomp, parade, show.
in vollem Staat in full dress.
Staat machen to show off.
staatlich public, political.
Staatsaktion f. political event.
Staatsangehörige m. & f. subject, national.
Staatsangehörigkeit f. nationality, citizenship.
Staatsanwalt m. public prosecutor.
Staatsdienst m. civil service.
Staatsmann m. statesman, politician.
staatsmännisch statesmanlike.
Stab m. stick, rod, bar, staff.
den Stab brechen über to condemn.
stabil stable.
stabilisieren to stabilize.
Stachel m. thorn, prickle, sting, spur.
Stachelbeere f. gooseberry.
Stacheldraht m. barbed wire.
Stadion n. stadium, arena.

Stadium n. phase, stage.
STADT f. town, city.
Stadtbahn f. city railway.
stadtbekannt known all over town.
Städter m. townsman.
Stadtgespräch n. talk of the town.
städtisch municipal, urban.
Stadtteil m. quarter (of a town).
Stahl m. steel.
stählern steely.
Stahlguss m. steel.
Stall m. stable.
Stamm m. stem, root, trunk.
Stammbaum m. genealogical tree.
stammeln to stammer.
stammen to spring from, come from.
Stammgast m. regular customer.
Stammhalter m. eldest son.
stämmig sturdy, strong, vigorous.
stampfen to stamp, mash, crush.
Stand m. standing position.
einen schweren Stand haben to have a tough job.
guten Stand haben to be in good condition.
Standbild n. statue.
Ständchen n. serenade.
Standesamt n. registrar's office.
Standesbeamte m. registrar.
Standesehe f. marriage for position or rank.
standesgemäss in accordance with one's rank.
Standesgericht n. court martial.
Standesunterschied m. difference of class.
standhaft steady, constant.
standhalten to hold firm.
ständig permanent.
Standort m. station, position.
Standpunkt m. point of view.
Standuhr f. grandfather's clock.
Stange f. pole, bar, perch.
eine Stange Gold a bar of gold.
von der Stange ready-made.
Stanze f. stanza.
stanzen to stamp.
STARK strong, stout, considerable, hard.
Das ist denn doch zu stark! That is too much!
stark auftragen to exaggerate, boast.
Stärke f. strength, force, vigor, intensity, energy, violence.
stärken to strengthen, fortify, starch, confirm.
Starkstrom m. power current.
Starkstromleitung f. power-circuit.
starr stiff, hard, paralyzed.
starren vor Staunen to be dumbfounded.
starren to stare, be numb.
starrköpfig stubborn.
Starrsinn m. obstinacy.
Start m. start.
Startbahn f. runway.
starten to start.
startklar ready for the take off.
Station f. station, stop, ward.
freie Station free board and lodging.
Stationsarzt m. resident physician.
Stationsvorsteher m. station master.
Statistik f. statistics.
statistisch statistical.
STATT f. place.
an Kindesstatt annehmen to adopt a child.
STATT (anstatt) prep. (gen.) instead of.
stattfinden to take place.
stattgeben to permit, allow.
statthaft admissible, legal.
stattlich stately, magnificent, imposing.
Stattlichkeit f. dignity, magnificence.
Statue f. statue.
Staub m. dust, powder.
in den Staub ziehen to depreciate.

Staub wischen to dust.
stauben to be dusty.
staubig dusty.
Staublappen m. duster.
Staubsauger m. vacuum-cleaner.
staunen to be surprised.
STECHEN to stick, bite, sting.
sich stechen to prick oneself.
in die Augen stechen to take one's fancy.
Stechfliege f. horse-fly.
Steckdose f. wall-plug, socket.
STECKEN to stick, pin up, fasten, fix, plant, stuff.
Dahinter steckt etwas. There is something behind this.
in Brand stecken to set fire.
steckenbleiben to be stuck.
Steckenpferd n. hobby, pet project.
Stecker m. plug.
Stecknadel f. pin.
STEHEN to stand, stop, be, suit, become.
gut stehen to be becoming. (Rot steht ihr. Red is becoming to her.)
gut stehen mit to be on good terms with
geschrieben stehen to be written.
stehenbleiben to stop, remain standing.
stehend standing, stationary, permanent.
stehenden Fusses at once.
stehenlassen to leave (standing).
Stehlampe f. floor lamp.
STEHLEN to steal, rob, take away.
steif stiff.
Steig m. path.
STEIGEN to climb, go up, ascend, rise, increase.
zu Kopf steigen to go to one's head.
steigend growing, increasing.
steigern to raise, increase, intensify.
sich steigern in to intensify, work up.
Steigerung f. raising, increase, gradation, climax.
steil steep, precipitous.
Steilhang m. steep slope.
STEIN m. stone, rock, jewel.
Das hat den Stein ins Rollen gebracht. That started the ball rolling.
Das ist nur ein Tropfen auf den heissen Stein. That's only a drop in the bucket.
einen Stein im Brett haben bei to be in favor with.
Mir fällt ein Stein vom Herzen! I feel so relieved!
Stein des Anstosses stumbling block.
Stein und Bein schwören to swear by all the gods.
Steinbruch m. quarry.
steinern of stone.
steinhart as hard as stone.
steinig stony, rocky.
Steinobst n. stone-fruit.
steinreich very wealthy.
Steinzeit f. Stone Age.
STELLE f. spot, place, position, situation, passage.
auf der Stelle on the spot.
offene Stelle vacancy.
von der Stelle kommen to make progress.
zur Stelle sein to be present.
an Stelle von instead of.
STELLEN to put, place, set, arrange, regulate, provide, furnish.
auf den Kopf stellen to turn upside down.
auf sich selbst gestellt sein to be dependent on oneself.
eine Bedingung stellen to make a condition.
eine Frage stellen to ask a question.
Er ist sehr gut gestellt. He is very well off.
sich stellen to stand.
kalt stellen to put in a cool place.
sich gut stellen mit to be on good terms with.

sich stellen zu to behave toward.
zur Verfügung stellen to place at one's
disposal.
Stellengesuch n. application for a position.
stellenlos unemployed.
Stellennachweis m. employment reference.
Stellenvermittlung f. employment agency.
STELLUNG f. position, situation, stand, job.
Stellung nehmen zu to express one's opinion.
Stellungnahme f. opinion, comment.
Stellungsgesuch n. application for a position.
stellungslos unemployed.
Stellungswechsel m. change of position.
Stellvertreter m. representative.
Stempel m. stamp, postmark.
Stempelkissen n. ink-pad.
stempeln to stamp, mark.
stenografieren to write in shorthand.
stenografisch stenographic.
Stenogramm n. shorthand.
Stenogramm aufnehmen to take down in
shorthand.
Stenotypist m. (–istin, f.) stenotypist.
Steppdecke f. quilt.
Sterbebett n. deathbed.
Sterben n. death.
im Sterben liegen to be dying.
STERBEN to die.
sterblich mortal.
sterblich verliebt madly in love.
Sterblichkeit f. death rate.
steril sterile.
sterilisieren to sterilize.
Stern m. star.
Sternbild n. constellation.
Sterndeuter m. astrologer.
Sternschnuppe f. shooting-star.
stets always, forever.
Steuer n. rudder, helm, steering wheel.
Steuer f. tax.
steuerfrei tax-free.
steuern to steer, pilot, drive.
steuerpflichtig subject to taxation.
Steuerrad n. steering wheel.
Steuerzahler m. taxpayer.
Stich m. sting, prick, stitch.
im Stich lassen to forsake.
Stichtag m. fixed day.
Stichwort n. catchword, cue.
Stiefbruder m. stepbrother.
Stiefmutter f. stepmother.
Stiefmütterchen n. pansy.
Stiefschwester f. stepsister.
Stiefsohn m. stepson.
Stieftochter f. stepdaughter.
Stiefvater m. stepfather.
Stiel m. handle, stick, stem.
Stier m. bull.
Stierkämpfer m. bullfighter.
Stift m. pencil, crayon.
stiften to donate; to found, establish.
Stifter m. founder; donor.
Stiftung f. foundation.
Stil m. style, manner.
stilgerecht in good style, taste.
STILL still, quiet, silent, secret.
Seien Sie still! Be quiet!
STILLE f. silence, calm, quietude, peace.
im Stillen secretly.
in aller Stille privately, secretly.
stillen to quiet, appease, satisfy, quench, nurse.
stillhalten to keep still.
Stilleben n. still life (art).
stilllegen to shut down, close, discontinue.
stillschweigen to be silent.
stillschweigend silent.
Stillstand m. standstill, stop.
stillstehen to stand still, stop.

Still gestanden! Attention!
stilvoll in good style, taste.
Stimmabgabe f. vote, voting.
stimmberechtigt entitled to vote.
STIMME f. voice, part, comment, vote.
Stimme abgeben to vote.
STIMMEN to tune, vote, be correct, impress
someone, influence someone's mood.
Das stimmt! That is correct!
Werden Sie für oder dagegen stimmen? Are
you going to vote for or against?
Stimmrecht n. right to vote.
STIMMUNG f. tuning, pitch, key, mood, humor,
impression, atmosphere.
Stimmung machen für to create a mood for, to
make propaganda for.
Stimmungsmensch m. moody person.
stimmungsvoll impressive.
Stimmzettel m. ballot.
Stirn f. forehead, front, impudence.
die Stirn runzeln to frown.
einem die Stirne bieten to show a bold front.
Stock m. stick, rod, cane, floor (story).
über Stock und Stein up hill and down dale.
Welcher Stock? What floor?
stockdumm utterly stupid.
stocken to stop, stand still.
ins Stocken geraten to get tied up.
stockfinster pitch-dark.
Stockfisch m. dried cod.
Stockwerk n. story, floor.
Stoff m. matter, substance.
stöhnen to groan.
stolpern to stumble, trip over.
stolz proud.
stopfen to darn, fill, stuff.
Stopfgarn n. darning thread.
Stopfnadel f. darning needle.
stoppen to stop.
Stoppuhr f. stop-watch.
Stöpsel m. stopper, cork.
stöpseln to cork.
Storch m. stork.
STÖREN to disturb, trouble, inconvenience.
Nicht stören! Do not disturb!
störrisch stubborn.
Störung f. disturbance, upset.
geistige Störung mental disorder.
Stoss m. push, poke, pile, jerk, shock.
stossen to push, shove, hit, kick, knock.
stossen auf to run into.
Stossseufzer m. deep sigh, groan.
Stossstange f. bumper.
stottern to shutter, stammer.
Strafanstalt f. penitentiary.
strafbar liable to punishment.
Strafe f. punishment, penalty, fine.
bei Strafe von on pain of.
strafen to punish.
Straferlass m. amnesty.
straff stretched, tense, tight, strict.
straffällig punishable.
straffen to tighten.
sträflich criminal, punishable.
straffrei exempt from punishment, unpunished.
Strafgefangene m. convict.
Strafgericht n. criminal court.
Strafporto n. extra postage, surcharge.
Strafpredigt f. reprimand.
Strafprozess m. criminal case.
strafwürdig punishable.
STRAHL m. ray, beam, stream.
strahlen to radiate, beam, shine.
stramm tight, close.
stramm stehen to stand at attention.
STRAND m. seashore, beach, strand.
Strandbad n. seaside, resort.
stranden to run around or ashore.

Strandschuhe pl. beach shoes.
STRANG m. rope, cord, track.
am gleichen Strang ziehen to act in concert.
über die Stränge schlagen to kick over the
traces.
wenn alle Stränge reissen if the worst comes to
the worst.
zum Strang verurteilen to condemn to the
gallows.
Strapaze f. fatigue.
strapazieren to tire, enervate.
STRASSE f. street, highway, road.
an der Strasse by the wayside.
auf der Strasse in the street.
Strassenarbeiter m. roadman.
Strassenbahn f. tramway.
Strassenfeger m. street cleaner.
sträuben to ruffle up, bristle.
Strauch m. shrub, bush.
streben to endeavor, aspire, aim at.
Streber m. climber, careerist.
Strecke f. distance, way, route, tract.
auf freier Strecke on the road.
strecken to stretch, extend, stretch out.
die Waffen strecken to lay down arms.
sich strecken to stretch.
Streich m. stroke, blow.
einem einen Streich spielen to play a trick on
a person.
streichen to spread, rub, strike, erase, cancel,
paint, wander, stroll, migrate.
Frisch gestrichen! Wet paint!
Streichholz n. match.
Streichmusik f. string music.
Streichquartett n. string quartet.
Streife f. patrol, raid.
streifen to touch lightly, stripe, brush, wander.
Streik m. strike.
in den Streik treten to go on strike.
streiken to strike.
STREIT m. fight, quarrel, dispute.
streitbar valiant.
streiten to fight, quarrel.
Streitfall m. quarrel, controversy.
Streitfrage f. matter in dispute.
einem etwas streitig machen to contest a
person's right to a thing.
STRENG strict, stern, severe.
streng genommen strictly speaking.
Strenge f. severity, strictness.
strengläubig orthodox.
streuen to strew, scatter, spread.
Strich m. dash, stroke, line, compass point.
Machen wir einen Strich darunter. Let's put an
end to that.
nach Strich und Faden thoroughly.
Strichpunkt m. semicolon.
Strick m. cord, rope.
wenn alle Stricke reissen if everything else
fails.
stricken to knit.
Stroh n. straw.
Strohhalm m. straw (for drinking).
STROM m. large river, stream, current.
Es regnet in Strömen. It's pouring.
stromabwärts downstream.
stromaufwärts upstream.
strömen to stream, flow, pour.
Strömung f. current, stream.
Stromzähler electric meter.
Strudel m. whirlpool.
Strumpf m. stocking, sock.
Strumpfband n. garter.
Strumpfhalter m. garter (woman's)
struppig bristly, unkempt.
STUBE f. room, chamber, living room.
Stubenhocker m. stay-at-home.
stubenrein house-broken.

STÜCK n. piece, play, extract, morsel.
　aus einem Stück all of a piece.
　aus freien Stücken of one's own free will.
　ein starkes Stück a bit stiff.
　ein Stück Arbeit a stiff job.
　ein Stück mitnehmen to give a lift.
　Er hält grosse Stücke auf ihn. He thinks a lot of him.
　in allen Stücken in every respect.
stückweise piece by piece, by the piece.
Student m. (—in, f.) student.
Studie f. study, sketch (art).
studieren to study.
Studium n. study, university education.
Stufe f. step, stair, level.
　auf gleicher Stufe mit on a level with.
stufenweise by degrees, gradually.
STUHL m. chair, seat.
stumm dumb, silent, mute.
Stummheit f. dumbness.
stumpf blunt, obtuse, dull.
　mit Stumpf und Stiehl root and branch.
Stumpfsinn m. stupidity.
stumpfsinnig stupid, dull.
STUNDE f. hour; lesson, period.
stundenlang for hours.
Stundenplan m. timetable.
Stundenzeiger m. hour-hand.
stündlich hourly.
Stundung f. delay of payment.
STURM m. storm, gale.
stürmen to take by storm.
stürmisch stormy, impetuous.
Sturz m. fall, crash, tumble, overthrow, collapse.
　zum Sturz bringen to overthrow.
stürzen to overthrow, throw down, fall down, plunge into, crash.
　Nicht stürzen! Handle with care!
Stütze f. stay, support, help.
stutzen to trim, cut short, stop short.
stützen to support, base, prop up.
Stutzer m. dandy.
Stützpfeiler m. pillar, support.
Stützpunkt m. base, strong point.
Subjekt n. subject.
Substantiv n. substantive, noun.
Substanz f. substance.
substrahieren to subtract.
Suche f. search, quest.
　auf die Suche gehen to go in search of.
　auf der Suche nach in search of.
SUCHEN to look for, try, seek.
　das Weite suchen to run away.
　nach Worten suchen to be at a loss for words.
　Sie hat hier nichts zu suchen. She has no business here.
Sucht f. passion, rage.
Süden m. south.
Südfrüchte pl. tropical fruits.
südlich southern, (to the) south.
Südpol m. south pole.
Sühne f. expiation.
sühnen to expiate.
Summe f. sum, amount.
summieren to add up.
Sumpf m. swamp.
Sünde f. sin.
Sünder m. (—in f.) sinner.
sündhaft sinful.
sündigen to sin.
Suppe f. soup, broth.
suspendieren to suspend.
SÜSS sweet, fresh, lovely.
Süsse f. sweetness.
süsslich sweetish, mawkish.
Symbol n. symbol.
symbolisch symbolical.
Sympathie f. sympathy.

sympathisch nice, likable, congenial.
Symphonie f. symphony.
Symptom n. symptom.
Synagoge f. synagogue.
System n. system.
Szene f. scene.
Szenerie f. scenery, settings.

T

Tabak m. tobacco.
Tabelle f. table, index, schedule.
Tablett n. tray.
Tablette f. tablet.
Tadel m. reprimand, blame.
tadellos excellent, perfect.
tadeln to blame, find fault.
TAFEL f. board, blackboard, bar, plate, table.
　die Tafel aufheben to rise from table.
TAG m. day, daylight; life (one's days).
　alle acht Tage every week.
　alle Tage every day.
　am Tag during the day, in the daytime.
　an den Tag bringen to bring to light.
　auf ein paar Tage for a few days.
　auf seine alten Tage in his old age.
　bei Tage in the daytime.
　den ganzen Tag all day long.
　dieser Tage one of these days.
　einen um den andern Tag every other day.
　eines Tages some day.
　Er lebt in den Tag hinein. He lives from hand to mouth.
　Guten Tag! Good morning!
　in acht Tagen in a week.
　Tag aus, Tag ein day in, day out.
　Tag für Tag day by day.
　unter Tage arbeiten to work underground.
　vierzehn Tage two weeks.
　vor acht Tagen a week ago.
Tagebuch n. diary.
tagelang for days.
Tagesgesprach n. topic of the day.
Tageszeitung f. daily paper.
Tagewerk n. day's work.
taghell as light as day.
täglich daily.
tagsüber during the day.
Tagung f. conference, meeting.
Taille f. waist.
Takt m. time measure (music).
Taktgefühl n. tact.
Taktik f. tactics.
taktisch tactical.
taktlos tactless.
Taktlosigkeit f. tactlessness, indiscretion.
Taktstock m. baton.
taktvoll tactful, discreet.
Tal n. valley.
Talent n. talent, ability.
talentiert talented.
talentvoll talented.
Talk m. talcum powder.
Talsperre f. river dam.
talwärts downhill.
Tank m. tank (car).
tanken to fill up (car).
Tanne f. fir tree.
Tannenadeln pl. fir needles.
Tannenbaum m. fir tree.
Tannenzapfen m. fir cone.
Tante f. aunt.
Tanz m. dance, ball.
　Darf ich um den nächsten Tanz bitten? May I have the next dance?
TANZEN to dance.
Tänzer m. (—in f.) dance partner.

Tapete f. wallpaper.
Tapezier m. paperhanger, upholsterer.
tapezieren to paper.
tapfer brave, gallant.
Tapferkeit f. bravery, gallantry.
Tarif m. rate, tariff.
tarifmässig in accordance with the tariff.
tarnen to camouflage, disguise.
Tarnung f. camouflage.
TASCHE f. pocket, bag, purse.
　jemandem auf der Tasche liegen to be a financial drain on a person.
Taschenbuch n. pocketbook.
Taschendieb m. pickpocket.
Taschenlampe f. flashlight.
Taschenmesser n. pocket knife.
Taschentuch n. handkerchief.
Taschenuhr f. pocket-watch.
TASSE f. cup.
　eine Tasse Kaffee a cup of coffee.
Taste f. key (music and typewriter).
tasten to touch, feel.
TAT f. deed, act, fact, achievement, feat.
　auf frischer Tat in the very act.
　in der Tat indeed, as a matter of fact.
tatenlos inactive, idle.
Täter m. perpetrator.
tätig active.
　tätig sein to be active.
Tätigkeit f. activity, job.
tatkräftig energetic.
Tatsache f. fact.
tatsächlich real, actual.
Tau m. dew.
Tau n. rope.
taub deaf, empty, hollow.
Taube f. pigeon.
Taubheit f. deafness.
taubstumm deaf and dumb.
Taubstumme m. deaf-mute.
tauchen to dive, dip, plunge.
Taucher m. diver.
tauen to thaw.
Taufe f. baptism, christening.
　aus der Taufe heben to be godfather (or godmother).
taufen to baptize.
taugen to be of use.
Taugenichts m. good-for-nothing.
Tauglichkeit f. fitness, suitability.
Tausch m. exchange.
tauschen to exchange, swap.
täuschen to delude, deceive, disappoint.
　Mich können Sie nicht täuschen. You can't fool me.
　sich täuschen to be mistaken, fool oneself.
　sich täuschen lassen to let oneself be fooled.
Täuschung f. deception.
TAUSEND thousand.
tausendmal a thousand times.
Tauwetter n. thaw.
Taxe f. tax, rate, duty.
Taxi n. taxi.
　ein Taxi holen to call a cab.
taxieren to appraise, value.
Technik f. technology.
technisch technical.
Tee m. tea.
Teelöffel m. teaspoon.
Teer m. tar.
Teich m. pond.
Teig m. dough.
TEIL m. & n. part, share, portion.
　ich für mein Teil as for me.
　sich sein Teil denken to have one's own ideas.
　zum Teil partly.
　zum grössten Teil for the most part.

teilbar divisible.

Teilchen n. particle.

TEILEN to divide, share, distribute, deal out.
geteilte Gefühle mixed feelings.
geteilter Meinung sein to be of a different opinion.
sich teilen in to divide, split.

Teilhaber m. partner, participant.

Teilhaberschaft f. partnership.

Teilnahme f. participation, condolences.
Meine aufrichtige Teilnahme my sincere condolences.

teilnahmslos indifferent.

teilnahmsvoll sympathetic.

teilnehmen to take part in.

Teilnehmer m. participant, subscriber.

teilweise partial.

Teilzahlung f. part-payment, installment.

TELEFON n. telephone.

Telefonanruf m. telephone call.

Telefonbuch n. telephone directory.

TELEFONIEREN to telephone.

telefonisch telephonic, by telephone.

Telefonist m. (-in, f.) telephone operator.

Telefonnummer f. telephone number.

Telefonzelle f. telephone booth.

Telefonzentrale f. telephone exchange.

Telegrafie f. telegraphy.

TELEGRAFIEREN to telegraph.

telegrafisch by telegram.

TELEGRAMM n. telegram.

Telegrammformular n. telegraph form.

Teller m. plate.

Temperament n. temperament, character, disposition.

Temperatur f. temperature.

Temperaturschwankungen pl. variations in temperature.

Tempo n. time, measure, speed.

Tendenz f. tendency, inclination.

Tennis n. tennis.

Tennisplatz m. tennis court.

Tennisschläger m. tennis racket.

Tenor m. tenor.

Teppich m. carpet.

Termin m. deadline.

Terrasse f. terrace.

Territorium n. territory.

Testament n. testament.

TEUER expensive, high, costly.

Teuerung f. dearness, scarcity, high cost of living.

Teufel m. devil.
Den Teufel an die Wand malen. Speak of the devil and there he is.

teuflisch devilish, diabolical.

Text m. text, libretto.
aus dem Text kommen to lose the thread.

Textbuch n. words, libretto.

Textilien pl. textiles.

Textilwaren pl. textiles.

THEATER n. theater, stage.

Theaterbesuch m. playgoing.

Theaterbesucher m. playgoer.

Theaterdirektor m. manager of a theater.

Theaterkasse f. box office.

theatralisch theatrical.

Theke f. counter, bar.

Thema n. theme, subject.

Theologe m. theologian.

Theoretiker m. theoretician.

Thermometer n. thermometer.

Thermometerstand m. thermometer reading.

Thron m. throne.

Thronbesteigung f. accession to the throne.

TIEF deep, low, deeply, far.
Das lässt tief blicken. That tells a tale.
in tiefer Nacht late at night.

Tiefe f. depth, profundity.

tiefgründig deep, profound.

tiefliegend sunken.

Tiefsee f. deep sea.

tiefsinnig profound, pensive, melancholy.

Tiefstand m. lowness, low level.

TIER n. animal, beast.

Tierarzt m. veterinary.

Tiergarten m. zoo.

Tiger m. tiger.

Tinte f. ink.
in der Tinte sitzen to be in a mess.

Tintenfass n. inkwell.

Tintenfleck m. blot, ink spot.

TISCH m. table.
bei Tisch during the meal.
Bitte, zu Tisch! Dinner is ready!
Er ist gerade zu Tisch gegangen.
He has just gone out to lunch.
reinen Tisch machen to make a clean sweep.
unter den Tisch fallen to be ignored.

Tischdecke f. tablecloth.

Tischler m. cabinet-maker.

Tischplatte f. table top.

Tischrede f. after-dinner talk.

Tischtennis n. table tennis, ping-pong.

Tischtuch n. tablecloth.

Tischzeit f. dinner-time.

Titel m. title, claim.

Titelbild n. frontispiece.

Titelblatt n. title page.

Titelhalter m. title-holder.

Toast m. toast.

toasten to drink toasts.

toben to rage, rave.

Tobsucht f. raving madness.

tobsüchtig raving mad.

TOCHTER f. daughter.

TOD m. death, decease.
des Todes sein to be doomed.

Todesanzeige f. death notice.

Todeskampf m. death agony.

Todesstrafe f. capital punishment, death penalty.

Todestag m. death anniversary.

todkrank very ill.

tödlich fatal, deadly, mortal.

todmüde dead tired.

Toilette f. toilet, dress, dressing table, lavatory.
Toilette machen to dress, get dressed.

tolerant tolerant.

toll mad, insane, raving, awful.

tölpisch clumsy.

Ton m. sound, note, stress, accent.

tönen to sound, resound.

Tonfall m. musical intonation.

Tonfilm m. sound film.

Tonkunst f. music, musical art.

Tonleiter f. scale.

tonlos soundless, voiceless.

Tonne f. barrel, ton.

Tönung f. shading.

Topf m. pot.

Tor n. gate.

Tor m. fool.

Torheit f. foolishness, folly.

töricht foolish, silly.

Torte f. layer cake.

tosen to rage, roar.

TOT dead, dull.
tote Zeit dead season.
toter Punkt deadlock.

totarbeiten (sich) to kill oneself with work.

Tote m. dead person, deceased.

TÖTEN to kill.
sich töten to commit suicide.
sich totlachen to die laughing.

Totenbett n. deathbed

totenbleich deadly pale.

totenstill still as death.

Tötung f. killing, slaying.

Tour f. tour, excursion.
in einer Tour without stopping.

Tournee f. tour (theater).

Trab m. trot.
im Trab quickly.

Tracht f. dress, costume.

trachten to strive, seek after.
einem nach dem Leben trachten
to make an attempt on a person's life.

traditionell traditional.

Trage f. barrow, litter.

TRAGEN to carry, bear, wear, take, endure, suffer, produce.
die Schuld tragen an to carry the blame for.
Sie trägt Trauer. She is in mourning.

TRÄGER m. porter.

Tragfähigkeit f. capacity.

Tragfläche f. wing of aircraft.

Tragflügel m. wing of aircraft.

Tragik f. tragic (art).

tragisch tragic.

Tragödie f. tragedy.

trainieren to train.

Träne f. tear.

Trank m. drink.

tränken to water, soak.

transpirieren to perspire.

Transport m. transport.

Traube f. grape, bunch of grapes.

Traubenlese f. grape harvest.

Traubenmost m. grape juice.

trauen to marry, give in marriage, join, trust, rely.
Ich traue ihm alles zu. I believe him capable of everything.
sich trauen lassen to get married.

Trauer f. sorrow, grief, affliction.

Traueranzeige f. announcement of a death.

Trauermarsch m. funeral march.

trauern to mourn, grieve.

Trauerspiel n. tragedy.

Traufe f. gutter.
vom Regen in die Traufe out of the frying pan into the fire.

träufeln to drop.

traulich intimate, cosy.

TRAUM m. dream, fancy, illusion.
Träume sind Schäume. All dreams are lies.

träumen to dream.

Träumer m. dreamer.

träumerisch dreamy.

traumhaft dreamlike.

TRAURIG sad, sorrowful, mournful.

Traurigkeit f. sadness.

Trauschein m. marriage certificate.

Trauung f. marriage ceremony.

Trauzeuge m. witness to a marriage.

TREFFEN to meet, hit, strike, affect, touch, fall upon.
Alle nötigen Vorbereitungen sind getroffen worden. All the necessary arrangements have been made.
sich getroffen fühlen to feel hurt.
sich gut treffen to be lucky.
sich treffen to meet.
Vorsichtsmassregeln treffen to take all the necessary precautions.

treffend to the point.

Treffer m. target, luck, winning ticket, prize.

trefflich excellent, admirable.

Trefflichkeit f. excellence.

treiben to drive, set in motion, float, drift.
Wintersport treiben to practice winter sports.

Treibhaus n. conservatory.

trennbar sparable, divisible.

TRENNEN to separate, divide, dissolve.

getrennt leben to live separately.
sich trennen to part.
sich trennen von to part from.
Trennung *f.* separation.
Treppe *f.* stairway, stairs.
Treppenabsatz *m.* landing.
Treppengeländer *n.* banisters, railing.
Tresor *m.* treasury.
TRETEN to step, tread, walk, go.
in jemandes Fusstapfen treten
to follow one's footsteps.
in Kraft treten to go into effect.
in Verbindung treten to get in touch.
mit Füssen treten to trample under foot.
zu nahe treten to hurt one's feelings.
TREU faithful, true, loyal.
treubrüchig faithless, perfidious.
Treue *f.* fidelity, faithfulness, loyalty.
treuherzig frank, naive.
treulich faithfully.
treulos unfaithful.
Treulosigkeit *f.* faithlessness.
Tribüne *f.* tribune.
Trieb *m.* sprout, shoot, motive power.
trinkbar drinkable.
TRINKEN to drink, absorb.
Trinker *m.* drunkard.
Trinkgeld *n.* tip.
Trinkspruch *m.* toast.
Tritt *m.* step, footstep.
Trittbrett *n.* running board.
Triumph *m.* triumph, victory.
triumphieren to triumph.
trocken dry, arid, dull.
im Trockenen sein to be under cover.
Trockenmilch *f.* dry milk.
trocknen to dry up.
Trommel *f.* drum.
trommeln to beat the drum.
Trompete *f.* trumpet.
Trompeter *m.* trumpeter.
Tropen *pl.* tropics.
tropfen to drop, drip.
tropfenweise by drops, drop by drop.
TROST *m.* comfort.
trostbedürftig in need of consolation.
trösten to comfort, console, cheer up.
sich trösten to cheer up.
tröstlich consoling, comforting.
trostlos discouraged.
Trostlosigkeit *f.* despair, hopelessness.
trostreich comforting, consoling.
Trottoir *m.* pavement.
TROTZ *prep.* (*gen.*) in spite of.
Trotz der Kälte ging ich jeden Tag spazieren.
In spite of the cold, I took a walk every day.
Trotz *m* obstinacy, stubbornness, defiance.
jemandem zum Trotz in defiance of someone.
Trotz bieten to defy.
trotzdem nevertheless, anyway, although.
Trotzdem es sehr kalt ist, werde ich
spazieren gehen. Although it is very cold, I
shall take a walk.
trotzen to defy, be obstinate.
trotzig defiant.
trüb dark, sad, gloomy.
trüben to dim, trouble, spoil.
Der Himmel trübt sich. The sky is clouding
over.
Trübsal *f.* affliction.
trübselig sad, gloomy, dreary.
trübsinnig melancholy.
trügen to deceive.
trügerisch deceitful.
Truhe *f.* chest, trunk.
Trümmer *f.* ruins, debris.
in Trümmer gehen to be shattered.

Trumpf *m.* trump.
trumpfen to trump.
Trunk *m.* drink.
Trunkenheit *f.* drunkenness.
Truppe *f.* troop, company.
Truthahn *m.* turkey.
Tube *f.* tube.
tuberkulös tuberculous.
TUCH *n.* cloth, fabric, shawl.
tüchtig good, able, fit, qualified, competent,
efficient.
Tüchtigkeit *f.* fitness, ability, efficiency.
Tücke *f.* malice, spite.
tückisch malicious, spiteful.
TUGEND *f.* virtue.
tugendhaft virtuous.
tugendsam virtuous.
Tulpe *f.* tulip.
Tumult *m.* tumult, commotion.
TUN to do, make, act, perform, execute.
Das tut nichts. That does not matter.
des Guten zu viel tun to overdo something.
Er tut nur so. He is only pretending.
Es tut mir leid. I am sorry.
es zu tun bekommen mit to have trouble with.
Haben Sie sich weh getan? Did you hurt
yourself?
Mir ist darum zu tun. It is very important for
me.
tun als ob to pretend.
Tun Sie als ob Sie zu Hause wären. Make
yourself at home.
Wir haben viel zu tun. We are very busy.
tunlich feasible, practicable.
Tunnel *m.* tunnel.
tupfen to dot, touch lightly, dab.
TÜR *f.* door, doorway,
vor der Tür stehen to be imminent.
Türgriff *m.* doorknob.
Türklinke *f.* latch (handle).
Turm *m.* tower, steeple.
Turmuhr *f.* church clock.
Turnen *n.* gymnastics.
turnen to do gymnastics.
Turnhalle *f.* gymnasium.
Turnier *n.* tournament.
Tusche *f.* India ink.
Tüte *f.* paper bag.
typisch typical.
Tyrann *m.* tyrant.
tyrannisieren to tyrannize.

U

Übel *n.* evil, ailment, misfortune, inconvenience.
ÜBEL evil, wrong, bad, ill.
Das ist nicht übel. That is not bad.
Mir ist übel. I feel sick.
übel daran sein to be in a bad way.
übelgelaunt cross, grumpy.
übelgesinnt evil-minded.
Übelkeit *f.* nausea.
übelnehmen to mind.
übelnehmerisch touchy, susceptible.
Übelstand *m.* inconvenience, drawback.
Übeltäter *m.* evil-doer, criminal.
üben to exercise, practise.
ÜBER 1. *prep.* (*dat. when answering question,
Wo?; acc. when answering question, Wohin?,
and depending on the idiom*) higher, while,
concerning, via.
den Winter über the whole winter long.
Er schwamm über den See. He swam across
the lake.
Er zog sich die Decke über den Kopf. He
pulled the blanket over his head.
Ich wundere mich über ihre Einstellung. I am
surprised at her attitude.

Sie sprach über ihre Sorgen. She spoke about
her sorrows.
über Bord overboard.
Über der Erde ziehen Wolken. Clouds are
floating above the earth.
über kurz oder lang sooner or later.
über und über over and over.
Seine Liebe geht ihr über alles. She places
his love above everything.
überall all over.
von Berlin über Strassburg nach Paris from
Berlin to Paris via Strassburg.
2. *adv.* wholly, completely, in excess.
3. *prefix.*
a) *separable* (*when meaning* above).
Das Flugzeug fliegt über dem Ozean. The
airplane flies above the ocean.
b) *inseparable* (*in all uses where it does not
mean* above.)
Er übersetzt ein Gedicht von Schiller. He
translates a poem by Schiller.
überaltert too old.
überanstrengen to overwork, overstrain.
überarbeiten to review, go over.
sich überarbeiten to overwork oneself.
überbelichten to overexpose (photo).
überbieten to excel, surpass.
Überblick *m.* perspective, summary, survey.
überblicken to survey, sum up.
überdachen to roof.
überdauern to outlast.
überdies besides, moreover.
Überdruss *m.* boredom, satiety, disgust.
zum Überdruss werden to become a bore.
überdrüssig tired of, sick of, bored with.
Übereifer *m.* excess zeal.
übereignen to transfer, assign, convey.
übereilen to rush, hurry, precipitate.
sich übereilen to be in a great hurry.
Übereilen Sie sich nicht! Don't rush!
Übereilung *f.* hastiness, rush.
übereinkommen to agree.
Übereinkunft *f.* agreement, arrangement.
übereinstimmen to agree, coincide.
Übereinstimmung *f.* agreement, conformity.
überessen to overeat.
überfahren to overrun (signal) run over.
Überfahrt *f.* crossing.
Überfall *m.* holdup.
überfallen to hold up.
überfällig overdue.
Überfallkommando *n.* flying squad (police).
überfliegen to fly over, skim through.
überfliessen to overflow, run over.
überflügeln to surpass, outstrip.
Überfluss *m.* abundance, profusion.
im Überfluss abundantly.
zum Überfluss unnecessarily.
überflüssig superfluous, unnecessary.
überfordern to overcharge.
Überfracht *f.* excess freight, overweight.
überführen to convey, transport.
Überführung *f.* conveying, transfer.
überfüllen to overload, crowd.
Überfüllung *f.* overloading.
Übergabe *f.* delivery, surrender.
Übergang *m.* passage, crossing.
übergeben to hand over, deliver.
übergehen (*separable prefix*) to cross, pass over.
übergehen (*inseparable prefix*) to pass by, omit.
Das Geschäft ist in andere Hände
übergegangen. This store has changed hands.
Übergewicht *n.* overweight, excess weight.
das Übergewicht bekommen to lose one's
balance.
übergiessen to spill.
Überhandnahme *f.* increase.

überhandnehmen to increase, spread.
Überhang *m.* curtain, hangings.
überhangen to hang over.
ÜBERHAUPT in general, altogether.
    überhaupt nicht not at all.
überheben to save, spare, exempt.
überheblich presumptuous.
Überhelichkeit *f.* presumption, arrogance.
überholen to pass (car), surpass, overhaul.
überholt outdated.
überhören to miss, ignore.
Überkleid *n.* overdress, overall.
überkochen to boil over.
überladen to overload.
überlassen to leave, give up, cede.
überlasten to overload.
überlaufen to run over, boil over, desert.
Überläufer *m.* deserter.
überleben to survive, outlive.
    sich überlebt haben to be outdated.
Überlebende *m.* survivor.
überlegen to reflect, consider.
    sich überlegen to think over, consider.
überlegen *adj.* superior.
    Ich habe es mir anders überlegt. I've changed my mind.
    überlegen sein to be better than.
Überlegenheit *f.* superiority.
überliefern to deliver, transmit.
Überlieferung *f.* delivery, tradition, surrender.
überlisten to outwit.
ÜBERMACHT *f.* superiority, predominance.
Übermass *n.* excess.
    im Übermass to excess, excessive.
übermässig excessive, immoderate.
Übermensch *m.* superman.
übermenschlich superhuman.
übermitteln to transmit.
Übermittlung *f.* transmission.
ÜBERMORGEN the day after tomorrow.
übermüden to overtire.
Übermüdung *f.* over-fatigue.
Übermut *m.* high spirits.
übermütig to be in high spirits.
übernachten to stay overnight, spend the night.
Übernahme *f.* taking over.
übernatürlich supernatural.
übernehmen to take over, seize.
    sich übernehmen to overstrain oneself.
überordnen to set over.
überraschen to surprise.
Überraschung *f.* surprise.
überreden to persuade.
überreichen to hand over, present.
überreif overripe.
Überrest *m.* remainder.
überrumpeln to surprise, take by surprise.
Überrumpelung *f.* surprise, sudden attack.
überschätzen to overrate, overestimate.
überschauen to overlook, survey.
Überschlag *m.* estimate.
überschlagen to estimate; to skip.
überschneiden to intersect, overlap.
überschreiten to cross, exceed, overstep.
Überschreitung *f.* crossing, excess, transgression.
Überschrift *f.* heading, title.
Überschuh *m.* overshoe, galosh.
Überschuss *m.* surplus, excess.
überschüssig in excess.
überschwemmen to inundate.
Überschwemmung *f.* inundation, flood.
Übersee *f.* overseas.
übersehen to survey, overlook.
übersenden to send, transmit.
Übersender *m.* sender.
Übersendung *f.* transmission.

übersetzen to pass across.
ÜBERSETZEN to translate.
Übersetzer *m.* translator.
Übersetzung *f.* translation.
Übersicht *f.* view, review, summary.
übersichtlich clear, visible.
Übersichtlichkeit *f.* clearness, lucidity.
übersinnlich transcendental.
überspannen to stretch over, span.
überspannt eccentric.
Überspanntheit *f.* eccentricity.
überspitzt too subtle.
überspringen to jump across.
überstehen to endure, come through.
überstrahlen to shine upon, outshine.
überströmen to overflow.
Überstunden *pl.* overtime.
    Überstunden machen to work overtime.
ÜBERSTURZEN to rush, hurry, act hastily.
    Überstürzen Sie sich nicht! Don't rush yourself!
übertragbar transferable.
übertragen to transfer, give up, entrust with, transmit, broadcast.
Übertragung *f.* transfer, transcription, transmission.
übertreffen to excell, surpass.
übertreiben to exaggerate.
Übertreibung *f.* exaggeration.
übertreten to go over, change over, violate.
Übertretung *f.* violation, transgression.
übertrumpfen to outdo.
übervölkert overpopulated.
übervorteilen to take advantage.
überwachen to watch over, supervise.
Überwachung *f.* observation, surprise.
überwältigen to overwhelm.
Überwältigung *f.* overwhelming.
überweisen to transfer, remit.
    telegraphisch überweisen to send a cable.
Überweisung *f.* transfer, remittance.
überwiegen to outweigh.
überwiegend preponderant, predominant.
überwinden to overcome.
Überwindung *f.* overcoming, conquest.
Überzahl *f.* numerical superiority, majority.
überzählig surplus.
überzeugen to convince.
Überzeugung *f.* conviction, belief.
    der Überzeugung sein to be convinced.
überziehen to cover, re-cover; to overdraw (bank account).
    das Bett überziehen to change the sheets.
üblich usual, customary.
U-Boot *n.* submarine.
ÜBRIG left over, remaining, other.
    das Übrige the rest.
    ein übriges tun to do more than necessary.
    Haben Sie ein paar Minuten für uns übrig? Can you spare us a few minutes?
    im übrigen otherwise.
    nichts übrig haben für to care little for.
    übrig bleiben to be left over.
    übrig lassen to leave.
    zu wünschen übrig lassen to leave much to be desired.
ÜBRIGENS besides, by the way.
ÜBUNG *f.* exercise, practice, drill.
UFER *n.* shore, bank (river).
UHR *f.* hour, clock, watch.
    nach der Uhr sehen to look at the time.
    um halb fünf at half past five.
    Um wieviel Uhr? At what time?
    Wieviel Uhr ist es? What time is it?
Uhrmacher *m.* watchmaker.
Uhrzeiger *m.* clock hand.
UM 1. *prep. (acc.).* at, about, around, because of, for the sake of, for, up.

    Der Zug verlässt Düsseldorf um drei Uhr. The train leaves Düsseldorf at three o'clock.
    einer um den anderen one after the other.
    Ihre Zeit ist um. Your time is up.
    Tag um Tag every day, day after day.
    Wir ängstigen uns um sie. We worry about her.
    Wir sitzen um den Tisch. We sit around the table.
    Um Himmels willen! For God's sake!
    um jeden Preis at any cost.
    um keinen Preis not at any price.
    um so besser all the better.
    um zwei Jahre älter two years older.
    2. *Adv.* around.
    um und um around.
    um herum all around.
    3. *Conj.* (um...zu). in order to.
    Um den Frieden zu erhalten, dankt der Prinz ab. The prince abdicates in order to preserve peace.
    4. *Prefix.* a) *inseparable (implies the meaning of around).*
    Gärten umgeben das Schloss. The castle is surrounded by gardens.
    b) *separable. (implies the meaning of to upset, to transform).*
    Er warf den Stuhl um. He overturned the chair.
umadressieren to redirect a letter.
umändern to change, alter.
Umänderung *f.* change, alteration.
umarbeiten to remodel.
Umarbeitung *f.* remodeling.
umarmen to embrace, hug.
Umarmung *f.* embrace, hug.
Umbau *m.* rebuilding, reconstruction.
umbinden to tie round, put on.
umblättern to turn over.
umblicken to look about.
umdrehen to turn, turn round.
Umdrehung *f.* turning round.
umfahren to drive around.
Umfahrt *f.* circular tour.
umfallen to topple over.
Umfang *m.* circumference, extent, size.
umfangreich comprehensive, extensive.
umfassen to clasp, embrace, enclose.
umfassend comprehensive, extensive, complete, full.
umformen to transform, remodel.
Umfrage *f.* inquiry.
Umgang *m.* association, relations.
umgänglich sociable.
Umgangsformen *pl.* manners.
Umgangssprache *f.* colloquial speech.
umgeben to surround.
Umgebung *f.* surroundings, environs.
Umgegend *f.* neighborhood, vicinity.
UMGEHEN to go around, circulate, haunt, evade.
    umgehend antworten to answer by return.
umgekehrt opposite, reverse, contrary.
umgestalten to alter, transform, reform.
umgraben to dig up.
umgruppieren to regroup.
Umhang *m.* cape, shawl.
UMHER around, about, here and there.
umherblicken to glance around, look around.
umhin about.
    Ich kann nicht umhin. I can't help (refrain from).
umhüllen to wrap, cover, veil.
Umkehr *f.* return, change.
UMKEHREN to turn back, turn around, turn upside down, invert, reverse.
Umkehrung *f.* inversion, reversal.
umkleiden to change clothes.
Umkreis *m.* circle, circuit.
umkreisen to revolve, circle around.

Umkreisung *f.* encirclement.
Umlauf *m.* rotation, revolution, circulation.
    in Umlauf setzen to circulate.
umleiten to divert (traffic).
Umleitung *f.* detour.
    Strassenbau! Umleitung! Road under repair!
    Detour!
umliegend surrounding, neighboring.
umpflanzen to transplant.
umreissen to outline, sketch.
Umriss *m.* sketch, outline, contour.
Umsatz *m.* sale, turnover.
umschalten to switch over.
Umschalter *m.* switch, commutator.
UMSCHLAG *m.* envelope, cover, wrapper, hem,
    compress, change.
umschlagen to fell, knock down, put on, change.
umschliessen to enclose.
umschwärmen to swarm around.
Umschwung *m.* change, revolution.
umsehen to look back, round.
    Sie sehen sich nach einer neuen Wohnung
    um. They are looking for a new apartment.
Umsicht *f.* circumspection, prudence, caution.
umsichtig cautious, prudent.
umsonst gratis, for nothing; in vain.
UMSTAND, *m.* circumstances, fact.
    ohne Umstände without ceremony.
    mildernde Umstände extenuating circum-
    stances.
    sich Umstände machen to put oneself out.
    Sie ist in anderen Umständen. She is ex-
    pecting a baby.
    Umstände machen to make a fuss.
    unter allen Umständen in any case, by all
    means.
    unter keinen Umständen on no account.
    unter gewissen Umständen in certain circum-
    stances.
umständlich laborious.
Umsteige fahrschein *m.* transfer-ticket.
    einen Umsteige fahrschein verlangen to ask
    for a transfer.
umsteigen to change trains.
umstimmen to tune to another pitch.
umstritten disputed, controversial.
Umsturz *m.* downfall, revolution.
umstürzen to throw down, overturn.
Umtausch *m,* exchange.
umtauschen to change for.
umtun to drape around.
umwechseln to exchange, change (money).
Umweg *m.* detour.
Umwelt *f.* surroundings, environment.
umwenden to turn, turn over.
umwerben to court.
umwickeln to wrap up.
umziehen to change clothes.
Umzug *m.* procession.
unabhängig independent.
Unabhängigkeit *f.* independence.
unabkömmlich indispensable.
unablässig incessant.
unabsehbar incalculable.
unabsichtlich unintentional.
unabwendbar inevitable.
unachtsam careless.
unangebracht out of place.
unangefochten undisputed.
unangemessen inadequate, improper.
unangenehm unpleasant, disagreeable.
unannehmbar unacceptable.
Unannehmlichkeit *f.* inconvenience, trouble.
Unansehnlichkeit *f.* plainness.
unanständig improper, indecent.
unappetitlich unappetizing, uninviting.
Unart *f.* bad behavior, rudeness.
unartig naughty.

unauffindbar undiscoverable.
unaufgefordert unasked.
unaufhaltsam inevitable, impetuous.
unaufhörlich incessant, incessantly.
unaufmerksam inattentive.
unaufrichtig insincere.
unausbleiblich unfailing, certain.
unausführbar impracticable, not feasible.
unaussprechlich inexpressible.
unausstehlich intolerable, unbearable.
unbarmherzig unmerciful, pitiless, brutally.
Unbarmherzigkeit *f.* mercilessness.
unbeabsichtigt unintentional, undesigned.
unbeachtet unnoticed.
unbeanstandet not objected to, unopposed.
unbeantwortet unanswered.
unbedachtsam inconsiderate, thoughtless.
unbedenklich harmless.
unbedeutend insignificant, trifling.
unbedingt unconditional, absolute.
    Sie müssen unbedingt dabei sein. You must
    be there whatever may happen.
unbeeinflusst unprejudiced.
unbefangen impartial, unprejudiced.
Unbefangenheit *f.* impartiality; facility.
unbefriedigend unsatisfactory, unsatisfactorily.
unbefriedigt unsatisfied.
unbefugt incompetent.
unbegabt not gifted, not clever.
unbegreiflich inconceivable.
unbegrenzt unbounded, unlimited.
unbegründet unfounded, groundless.
Unbehagen *n.* discomfort.
unbehaglich uncomfortable.
unbehelligt undisturbed.
unbehilflich helpless.
unbehindert unrestrained.
unbeholfen clumsy.
UNBEKANNT unknown.
    Er ist hier unbekannt. He is a stranger
    here.
unbekümmert unconcerned.
unbeliebt unpopular.
unbemerkt unnoticed.
UNBEQUEM uncomfortable, inconvenient.
Unbequemlichkeit *f.* discomfort.
unberechenbar incalculable.
unberechtigt unauthorized, unjustified.
unberührt untouched, intact, innocent.
unbeschädigt undamaged, uninjured.
unbescheiden immodest, insolent.
unbeschreiblich indescribable.
unbeschwert light.
unbesehen without inspection, hesitation.
unbesiegbar invincible.
Unbesonnenheit *f.* indiscretion, imprudence.
unbesorgt unconcerned.
    Seien Sie unbesorgt. Don't worry.
unbeständig unstable, unsteady.
unbestechlich incorruptible.
unbestimmt undetermined, undefined, indefinite.
unbestreitbar indisputable.
unbeträchtlich inconsiderable.
unbeugsam inflexible, stubborn.
unbewandert inexperienced.
unbeweglich motionless.
unbewohnt uninhabited.
unbewusst unconscious.
unbezahlbar priceless.
unbezwingbar invincible.
unbrauchbar useless, of no use.
UND and.
    und so weiter and so forth.
Undank *m.* ingratitude.
undankbar ungrateful.
Undankbarkeit *f.* ingratitude.
undenkbar unconceivable.
undeutlich indistinct, vague.

undicht leaky.
Unding *n.* absurdity, impossibility.
unduldsam intolerant.
undurchdringlich impenetrable.
uneben uneven, rough.
unebenbürtig inferior.
unecht not genuine, false, improper, artificial.
unehelich illegitimate.
unehrbar indecent, immodest.
unehrenhaft dishonorable.
unehrlich dishonest.
uneigennützig unselfish.
uneinig disunited.
Uneinigkeit *f.* discord, disagreement.
uneins divided.
    uneins sein to disagree.
unempfindlich insensible.
UNENDLICH infinite, endless, infinitely.
    unendlich lang endless.
unentbehrlich indispensable.
unentgeltlich free of charge.
unentschieden undecided.
unentschlossen irresolute.
unentschuldbar inexcusable.
unerbittlich inexorable.
unerfahren inexperienced.
unerforschlich impenetrable.
unerfreulich unpleasant, unsatisfactory.
unerfüllbar unrealizable.
unerhört unheard of, insolent.
unerklärlich inexplicable.
unerlaubt illicit, unlawful.
unermesslich boundless, infinite.
unermüdlich untiring.
unerreichbar inaccessible.
unerreicht unequaled.
unerschrocken fearless.
unerschütterlich imperturbable.
unersetzlich irreplaceable.
unerträglich unbearable, intolerable.
unerwartet unexpected.
unerwünscht undesired, unwelcome.
unerzogen uneducated, ill-bred.
UNFÄHIG incapable, unable.
Unfähigkeit *f.* inefficiency.
Unfall *m.* accident.
Unfallversicherung *f.* insurance against accidents.
unfehlbar certainly, surely.
unfreiwillig involuntary.
unfreundlich unfriendly, unpleasant.
unfruchtbar unproductive, sterile.
Unfug *m.* wrong, mischief, nonsense.
ungebildet uneducated.
ungebührlich indecent, improper.
ungebunden unbound, unrestrained.
ungedeckt uncovered (also for a check).
ungeduldig impatient, impatiently.
ungeeignet unsuitable, unfit.
UNGEFÄHR approximately, about, nearly.
    von ungefähr by chance.
ungefährlich harmless.
ungehalten angry.
Ungeheuer *n.* monster.
ungeheuer huge, enormous, vast, monstrous.
ungehorsam disobedient.
ungekünstelt unaffected, simple.
ungelegen inconvenient.
ungelernt unskilled.
ungemütlich uncomfortable.
ungeniert free and easy.
ungeniessbar inedible, unbearable.
ungenügend insufficient.
ungepflegt neglected, untidy.
UNGERECHT unjust.
ungerechtfertigt unjustified.
Ungerechtigkeit *f.* injustice.
UNGERN unwillingly, reluctant.
ungeschehen undone.

Ungeschick n. misfortune.
Ungeschicklichkeit f. awkwardness.
ungeschickt awkward, clumsy.
ungesetzlich illegal.
ungestört undisturbed.
ungestüm impetuous.
ungesund unhealthy.
ungetreu faithless.
ungewiss uncertain.
Ungewissheit f. uncertainty.
ungewöhnlich unusual, strange.
ungewohnt unaccustomed, unfamiliar.
ungezogen ill-bred, naughty.
Unglaube m. disbelief.
ungläubig incredulous.
unglaublich incredible.
ungleich unequal, unlike.
UNGLÜCK n. misfortune, bad luck, accident.
unglücklich unfortunate, unlucky.
unglücklicherweise unfortunately.
Unglücksvogel m. unlucky person.
Ungnade f. disgrace, displeasure
    in Ungnade fallen bei to displease someone.
ungültig void, invalid.
    für ungültig erklären to annul.
ungut
    Nichts für ungut. No harm meant.
Unheil n. mischief, harm, disaster.
unheilbar incurable, irreparable.
unheilvoll disastrous.
unheimlich sinister.
unhöflich impolite, rude.
Uniform f. uniform.
UNIVERSITÄT f. university, college.
unkenntlich unrecognizable.
Unkenntnis f. ignorance.
unklar not clear.
unklug imprudent, unwise.
Unkosten pl. expenses.
Unkraut n. weeds.
unleserlich illegible.
unliebenswürdig unamiable, unkind.
unlogisch illogical.
unmässig immoderate, disproportionate.
unmenschlich inhuman.
Unmenschlichkeit f. inhumanity, cruelty.
unmerklich imperceptible.
unmittelbar immediate.
UNMÖBLIERT unfurnished.
unmodern old-fashioned, antiquated.
UNMÖGLICH impossible.
Unmöglichkeit f. impossibility.
unmoralisch immoral.
unmündig minor
    unmündig sein to be a minor.
unnachsichtig strict, severe.
unnahbar unapproachable, inaccessible.
unnatürlich unnatural, affected.
UNNÖTIG unnecessary, needless.
unordentlich disorderly, untidy.
UNORDNUNG f. disorder.
    in Unordnung bringen to mess up.
unparteiisch impartial.
unpassend inappropriate.
unpässlich indisposed, ailing.
unpersönlich impersonal.
unpraktisch impractical.
unpünktlich unpunctual.
Unrecht n. injustice.
    im Unrecht in the wrong.
    Unrecht haben to be wrong.
    zu Unrecht unlawfully, unjustly.
UNRECHT wrong, unjust, unfair.
unredlich dishonest.
unregelmässig irregular.
unreif unripe.
unrein unclean.
    ins Unreine schreiben to make a rough copy.

Unruhe f. uneasiness.
Unruhen pl. riots.
unruhig restless, uneasy.
Unruhstifter m. agitator.
UNS acc. and dat. of the pers. pron. wir; reflexive
    and reciprocal pron.: us, to us, ourselves,
    each other.
unsachlich subjective, personal.
unsagbar unspeakable.
unsauber dirty, filthy.
Unsauberkeit f. dirt, filth.
unschädlich harmless.
    unschädlich machen to render harmless,
    neutralize, disarm.
unschätzbar invaluable.
unscheinbar insignificant, plain homely.
unschlüssig wavering, irresolute.
UNSCHULDIG innocent.
unselbständig helpless, dependent.
UNSER Poss. adj. our.
UNSER (er-e -es) Poss. pron. ours.
unsereins people like us.
unsererseits as for us, for our part.
unseresgleichen people like us.
unserethalben for our sakes, on our behalf.
unseretwegen for our sakes.
unseretwillen for our sakes.
UNSICHER unsafe, uncertain, unsteady.
Unsicherheit f. insecurity, uncertainty.
Unsinn m. nonsense.
Unsitte f. bad habit, abuse.
unsterblich immortal.
unstet changeable, unsteady.
unsympathisch unpleasant.
untätig inactive.
untauglich useless; unfit (sports, army).
UNTEN below, beneath, underneath.
    von oben bis unten from top to bottom, from
    head to foot.
UNTER 1. Prep. (dat. when answering question,
    Wo?; acc. when answering question, Wohin?,
    and depending on the idiom): under underneath,
    below, beneath, among, during, by.
    Ich habe meine Schuhe unter das Bett gestellt.
    I put my shoes under the bed.
    Ich sass unter den Zuschauern.
    I sat among the spectators.
    Unter anderem hat sie mir gesagt ...
    Among other things, she told me ...
    unter freiem Himmel in the open air.
    unter uns gesagt between us.
    unter vier Augen privately ("under four eyes").
    2. Prefix.
    a) separable (when meaning under).
    Die Sonne geht im Westen unter.
    The sun sets in the West.
    b) inseparable when not meaning under.
    Wir unterhielten uns über die Ferien.
    We talked about the holidays.
unterbauen to lay a foundation.
unterbelichten to underexpose (photo).
Unterbewusstsein n. sub-conscious.
unterbieten to undersell.
UNTERBRECHEN to interrupt, disconnect, cut off.
    Fräulein, wir sind unterbrochen worden.
    Operator, we have been cut off.
Unterbrechung f. interruption.
unterbringen to put up, accommodate, place.
unterdessen meanwhile, in the meantime.
unterdrücken to oppress, suppress.
Unterdrückung f. repression, oppression.
untereinander among ourselves, reciprocally.
Unterernährung f. malnutrition.
Unterführung f. underpass.
Untergang m. setting, going down, destruction,
    fall; decline.
    der Sonnenuntergang the sunset.
Untergebene m. & f. subordinate.

UNTERGEHEN to go down, set, sink.
Untergrundbahn f. subway.
unterhalb below.
Unterhalt m. maintenance, living.
UNTERHALTEN to support, maintain, keep up.
    sich gut unterhalten to have a good time.
    sich unterhalten to converse, talk.
unterhandeln to negotiate.
Unterhemd n. vest.
Unterhosen pl. shorts, drawers.
unterirdisch underground.
Unterkleidung f. underwear.
unterkommen to find accommodations, find a situation.
Unterkunft f. accommodation.
Unterlage f. foundation, support, evidence, pad.
Unterlass m. stopping
    ohne Unterlass incessantly.
unterlassen to omit, neglect, fail to.
unterlegen to lay under, put under.
unterliegen to be defeated.
Unterlippe f. lower lip.
Untermieter m. subtenant.
UNTERNEHMEN to undertake, attempt.
unternehmend enterprising.
Unternehmer, m. contractor.
Unternehmung f. enterprise, undertaking.
unterordnen to subordinate, submit.
Unterordnung f. subordination.
unterreden to converse, confer with.
Unterredung f. talk, conference.
UNTERRICHT m. instruction, teaching, education,
    lesson.
unterrichten to teach, instruct.
Unterrock m. slip, petticoat.
unterschätzen to underestimate, underrate.
unterscheiden to distinguish, differentiate,
    discriminate,
    sich unterscheiden to differ.
Unterscheidung f. distinction, discrimination.
UNTERSCHIED m. difference.
    ohne Unterschied alike.
unterschiedlich different, distinct.
unterschiedslos indiscriminately.
unterschlagen to embezzle.
Unterschlagung f. embezzlement.
unterschreiben to sign.
Unterschrift f. signature.
Unterseeboot n. submarine.
unterstehen to stand under, be subordinate.
    sich unterstehen to dare.
unterstützen to support, aid, assist.
Unterstützung f. support, aid, relief.
untersuchen to examine, investigate.
Untersuchung f. examination, investigation.
Untertasse f. saucer.
Untertitel m. subtitle (movie).
Unterwäsche f. underwear.
unterwegs on the way.
unterweisen to instruct.
Unterweisung f. instruction.
Unterwelt f. underworld.
unterwerfen to subjugate.
unterwürfig submissive.
unterzeichnen to sign, ratify.
Unterzeichner m. signatory.
Unterzeichnung f. signature, ratification.
untragbar not transferable, not negotiable; unbearable.
untrennbar inseparable.
UNTREU untrue, unfaithful.
untröstlich disconsolate.
Untugend f. vice, bad habit.
unübersehbar immense, vast.
unübertrefflich unequaled.
ununterbrochen continuously.
unverantwortlich irresponsible.
unverbesserlich incorrigible.
unverbindlich not obligatory, without obligation.
unverdient undeserved.

unverdorben unspoilt, pure.
unvergänglich imperishable, immortal.
unvergleichlich imcomparable.
unverheiratet unmarried.
unverhofft unexpected.
unverkennbar unmistakable.
unverletzt unhurt, uninjured.
unvermeidlich inevitable.
Unvermögen n. inability, incapacity.
unvermutet unexpected.
unvernünftig unreasonable.
unverrichtet unperformed.
    unverrichteter Sache unsuccessfully.
unverschämt impudent, fresh.
unversehens unexpectedly.
unversehrt intact, safe.
unverständlich unintelligible, incomprehensible.
unverwüstlich indestructible, inexhaustible.
unverzeihlich unpardonable.
unverzollt duty unpaid.
unverzüglich immediate.
unvollkommen imperfect.
unvollständig incomplete, defective.
unvorhergesehen unforeseen.
UNVORSICHTIG careless.
unvorteilhaft unprofitable, unbecoming.
unweiblich unwomanly.
unweit not far off, near.
Unwesen n. mischief, abuse.
    sein Unwesen treiben to be up to one's tricks.
unwesentlich unessential, immaterial.
    Das ist ganz unwesentlich. That does not
    matter.
Unwetter n. storm, hurricane.
unwiderruflich irrevocable
unwiderstehlich irresistible.
Unwille m indignation.
unwillkommen unwelcome.
unwillkürlich instinctively, involuntarily.
unwirksam ineffective, inefficient.
unwirtlich inhospitable, dreary.
unwirtschaftlich uneconomic.
unwissend ignorant.
UNWOHL not well, indisposed.
Unwohlsein n. indisposition.
unwürdig unworthy.
Unzahl f. endless number.
unzählig countless.
unzeitgemäss inopportune, out of season.
unzerbrechlich unbreakable.
unzivilisiert uncivilized, barbarian.
unzufrieden dissatisfied.
unzulänglich inadequate.
unzulässig forbidden.
unzureichend insufficient.
unzuverlässig unreliable.
unzweideutig unequivocal, unambiguous.
unzweifelhaft undoubted, indubitable.
üppig luxuriant, abundant, voluptuous.
Üppigkeit f. luxury.
uralt very old, ancient.
Uraufführung f. first performance, opening night.
Ureinwohner m. original inhabitant.
Urgrosseltern pl. great-grandparents.
Urkunde f. deed, document, record.
Urkundenfälscher m. forger of documents.
urkundlich documentary, authentic.
Urlaub m. leave, furlough, vacation.
    der bezahlte Urlaub the paid vacation.
URSACHE f. cause, reason.
    Keine Ursache! Don't mention it!
Ursprung m. source, origin.
ursprünglich original, primitive.
URTEIL n. judgment, decision, sentence, opinion.
urteilen to judge, pass a sentence, give an opinion.
urteilsfähig competent to judge.
urteilslos without judgment.
Urteilsspruch m. sentence, verdict.

V

Vagabund m. vagabond.
Vanille f. vanilla.
Variante f. variant.
Variation f. variation.
Varieté n. music-hall.
variieren to vary.
Vase f. vase.
Vaselin n. vaseline.
VATER m. father.
Vaterhaus n. home.
Vaterland n. native land, fatherland.
vaterländisch national, patriotic.
vaterlandsliebend patriotic.
väterlicherseits on the father's side.
vaterlos fatherless.
Vaterstadt f. native town.
vegetarisch vegetarian.
Veilchen n. violet.
Vene f. vein.
Ventil n. valve.
verabreden to agree upon, make an agreement.
    verabredet sein to have a date or appointment.
Verabredung f. agreement, engagement; appointment.
verabreichen to give, dispense.
verabscheuen to detest.
verabschieden to dismiss, discharge.
    sich verabschieden to say good-bye.
verachten to despise, scorn, disdain.
verächtlich contemptuous, disdainful.
Verachtung f. contempt, scorn, disdain.
verallgemeinern to generalize.
veraltet old, obsolete.
veränderlich variable, unstable.
VERÄNDERN to change, alter, vary.
Veränderung f. change, alteration, variation.
verängstigt intimidated.
veranlagt inclined.
    gut veranlagt sein to be talented.
Veranlagung f. talent.
veranlassen to cause.
Veranlassung f. reason, suggestion.
veranschlagen to estimate.
    zu hoch veranschlagen to overrate.
veranstalten to arrange, organize, set up.
Veranstaltung f. arrangement, organization.
verantworten to answer for, account for.
verantwortlich responsible.
VERANTWORTUNG f. responsibility.
    auf seine Verantwortung at his own risk.
    zur Verantwortung ziehen to call to account.
verantwortungslos irresponsible.
verarbeiten to use, work up, manufacture.
Verarbeitung f. manufacturing.
Verband m. bandage, association.
verbannen to banish, exile.
Verbannung f. banishment, exile.
VERBESSERN to improve, correct.
Verbesserung f. improvement, correction.
verbeugen to bow.
Verbeugung f. bow.
verbiegen to bend, twist.
verbieten to forbid.
    Rauchen verboten! No smoking!
    Strengstens verboten! Strictly forbidden!
verbinden to tie, bind, bandage, connect,
    combine, join.
    Fräulein, Sie haben mich falsch verbunden!
    Operator, you gave me the wrong number!
    sich verbinden to unite.
    sich zu Dank verbunden fühlen to feel
    indebted to.
verbindlich obligatory, courteous.
Verbindlichkeit f. obligation.
VERBINDUNG f. union, combination.
    sich in Verbindung setzen mit to get in
    touch with.

verblüffen to disconcert.
verblüffend amazing.
Verblüffung f. stupefaction, amazement.
verbluten to bleed to death.
verborgen hidden, concealed, secret.
Verborgenheit f. concealment, retirement,
    seclusion.
Verbot n. prohibition, ban.
verboten prohibited, forbidden.
Verbrauch m. consumption.
verbrauchen to consume, use.
Verbraucher m. consumer.
Verbrechen n. crime.
    ein Verbrechen vergehen to commit a crime.
Verbrecher m. criminal.
verbrecherisch criminal.
verbreiten to spread, diffuse.
verbrennen to burn, cremate.
    sich verbrennen to burn oneself.
Verbrennung f. burning, combustion.
verbringen to spend, pass time.
verbunden obliged.
verbürgen to guarantee.
Verdacht m. suspicion.
verdächtig suspicious.
verdächtigen to distrust.
Verdächtigung f. insinuation, false charge.
verdammen to condemn.
verdammenswert damnable.
Verdammnis f. damnation.
Verdammung f. condemnation.
verdanken to owe something.
Verderb m. ruin.
Verderben n. ruin, destruction.
    jemanden ins Verderben stürzen to ruin a
    person.
VERDERBEN to spoil, ruin.
    Ich möchte es mir nicht mit ihm verderben. I
    don't want to displease him.
    sich den Magen verderben to upset one's
    stomach.
Verderber m. corrupter.
verderblich pernicious.
verdienen to earn, gain, deserve, merit.
Verdienst m. gain, profit.
Verdienst n. merit.
verdienstlich deserving.
verdienstvoll deserving.
verdient deserving.
    sich verdient machen um to deserve well of.
Verdikt n. verdict.
verdingen (sich) to take a situation.
verdolmetschen to interpret.
verdoppeln to double.
verdorben spoilt.
verdrängen to displace, push aside.
verdrehen to twist, sprain.
    einem den Kopf verdrehen to turn one's head.
verdummen to grow stupid.
verdünnen to thin, dilute.
Verdünnung f. attenuation, rarefaction, dilution.
verdunsten to evaporate.
Verdunstung f. evaporation.
verdursten to die of thirst.
veredeln to ennoble, improve, refine, finish.
verehren to respect, worship, adore.
Verehrer m. worshipper.
Verehrung f. respect.
vereidigen to swear in, put on oath.
Vereidigung f. swearing in, taking of an oath.
Verein m. union, association.
vereinbar compatible, consistent.
Vereinbarung f. agreement.
vereinfachen to simplify.
vereinigen to join, unite, reconcile.
    die Vereinigten Staaten von Amerika. The
    United States of America.

vereisen to turn to ice.
vereiteln to frustrate, thwart.
verelenden to sink into poverty.
vererben to bequeath, transmit, hand down.
verewigen to perpetuate, immortalize.
Verfall m. decay, ruin.
 im Verfall geraten to go to ruin, decay.
verfallen to decline, go to ruin, grow weaker, expire.
 einem verfallen to become dependent on a person.
 verfallen lassen to let go to waste.
 verfallene Züge sunken features.
verfassen to compose, write.
Verfasser m. author, writer.
Verfassung f. state, condition.
verfechten to stand up for.
verfliegen to fly away, disappear, vanish.
verfolgen to follow, pursue, prosecute.
 heimlich verfolgen to shadow.
 gerichtlich verfolgen to prosecute.
Verfolgung f. pursuit, prosecution.
verfügbar available.
verfügen to arrange, decree, obtain.
 verfügen über to dispose of, have at one's disposal.
 zur Verfügung stellen to place at one's disposal.
verführen to induce, prevail upon, seduce.
Verführer m. tempter, seducer.
verführerisch tempting, seductive.
Verführung f. temptation.
Vergangenheit f. past; past tense (grammar).
vergänglich transitory, perishable.
Vergaser m. carburetor.
vergeben to give away, dispose of, confer, forgive.
vergebens in vain, vainly.
Vergebung f. pardon, forgiveness.
vergelten to pay back, repay, retaliate.
Vergeltung f. return, recompense.
VERGESSEN to forget, neglect.
vergesslich forgetful.
Vergesslichkeit f. forgetfulness.
vergiften to poison.
Vergiftung f. poisoning.
Vergleich m. comparison, agreement, arrangement.
VERGLEICHEN to compare, check, settle.
VERGNÜGEN n. pleasure, joy, fun.
vergnügen (sich) to amuse, enjoy oneself.
VERGNÜGT pleased, glad.
 Ich komme mit Vergnügen. I'll be delighted to come.
 Viel Vergnügen! Have a good time!
 Vergnügungsreise, f. pleasure trip.
vergnügungssüchtig pleasure-seeking.
vergraben to bury, hide in the ground.
vergrössern to enlarge, magnify.
Vergrösserung f. enlargement.
Vergünstigung f. privilege.
Verhältnis n. relation, ratio, love-affair.
verhältnismässig relative, proportional.
verhasst hated, hateful, odious.
verheimlichen to conceal, keep secret.
verheiraten to marry off.
verherrlichen to glorify.
Verherrlichung f. glorification.
verhindern to hinder, prevent.
Verhinderung f. hindrance, draw-back.
Verhör n. examination.
verhören to examine, interrogate.
verhungern to die of hunger.
verirren to lose one's way, go astray.
VERKAUF m. sale.
VERKAUFEN to sell.
 billiger verkaufen to undersell.
 zu verkaufen for sale.
VERKÄUFER m.(—in, f.) sales person.

verkäuflich for sale.
VERKEHR m. traffic, circulation, communication, trade.
verkehren to associate, transform, convert, change, run (buses).
 verkehren mit to associate with, see a good deal of.
Verkehrsampel f. signal light.
Verkehrsschutzmann m. traffic policeman.
Verkehrsunfall m. traffic-accident.
verkehrt wrong, backwards, upside down, absurd.
 verkehrt gehen to go the wrong way.
verkennen to fail to recognize, mistake, misunderstand, undervalue.
verkleiden to disguise, camouflage.
Verkleidung f. disguise, camouflage.
verkommen to be ruined, become bad, degenerate.
Verkommenheit f. depravity, degeneracy.
verkörpern to personify, incarnate, embody.
Verlag m. publication, publishing firm.
verlangen to demand, desire, require.
 auf Verlangen by request, on demand.
 verlangen nach to long for.
verlängern to extend, prolong.
Verlängerung f. extension, prolonging.
Verlass m. trustworthiness.
 Auf ihn ist kein Verlass. He cannot be relied on.
VERLASSEN to leave, abandon, desert.
verlegen embarrassed, self-conscious, confused.
 um etwas verlegen sein to be at a loss for.
 um Geld verlegen sein to be short of money.
Verlegenheit f. embarrassment, difficulty.
Verleger m. publisher.
verleihen to lend out, confer, bestow, grant.
verletzbar vulnerable, susceptible.
verletzen to hurt, injure, offend.
Verletzung f. injury, offense, violation.
verleugnen to deny, injure, offend.
Verleugnung f. denial, denunciation.
verleumden to calumniate, slander.
Verleumder m. slanderer.
verleumderisch slanderous.
Verleumdung f. slander, defamation, libel.
VERLIEBEN (sich) to fall in love.
verliebt in love.
 Sie ist verliebt bis über die Ohren. She is head over heels in love.
VERLIEREN to lose, waste, disappear.
 An ihm ist nicht viel verloren. He's no great loss.
 Ich habe keinen einzigen Augenblick zu verlieren. I don't have a single moment to lose.
verloben (sich) to get engaged.
Verlobte m. & f. fiancé(e).
Verlobung f. engagement.
Verlust m. loss, waste, escape.
vermehren to increase.
Vermehrung f. increase.
vermieten to rent, let, hire out.
Vermieter m. landlord.
vermissen to miss.
vermuten to suppose, presume, suspect.
vermutlich presumable, probable.
vernachlässigen to neglect.
Vernachlässigung f. neglect.
verneigen to bow.
Verneigung f. bow.
vernichten to annihilate, destroy.
Vernichtung f. annihilation, destruction.
VERNUNFT f. reason, understanding, intelligence, good sense, judgment.
 Vernunft annehmen to listen to reason.
 zur Vernunft bringen to bring to one's senses.
veröffentlichen to publish.
Veröffentlichung f. publication.
verordnen to order, decree.

Verordnung f. order, decree, prescription.
verpacken to pack up, wrap up.
Verpackung f. packing up, wrapping up.
verpfänden to pawn, mortgage.
verpflegen to feed, board.
Verpflegung f. feeding, board, food.
 Zimmer mit Verpflegung. Room and board.
verpflichten to oblige, bind, engage.
 sich verpflichten to commit (bind) oneself.
 verpflichtet sein to be under obligation.
Verpflichtung f. obligation, duty, engagement.
Verrat m. treason, betrayal.
verraten to betray, disclose, reveal.
Verräter m. traitor.
verräterisch treacherous.
verrechnen to reckon up, charge, account; miscalculate.
Verrechnung f. settling of an account, reckoning.
verreisen to go away.
 verreist sein to be away.
verrichten to execute, perform, accomplish.
 die Hausarbeit verrichten to do the housework.
Verrichtung f. execution, performance, function, work.
VERRÜCKT crazy, mad.
Vers m. verse, stanza.
versagen to deny, refuse; fail, miss.
VERSAMMELN to assemble, bring together, gather.
 sich versammeln to gather.
versäumen to neglect, omit, miss.
Versäumnis f. n. neglect, omission.
verschenken to give away.
verschicken to send away, dispatch, evacuate.
Verschickung f. dispatch, transportation, evacuation.
VERSCHIEDEN different from, distinct, various.
verschlafen to oversleep, sleepy.
verschlimmern to aggravate.
Verschlimmerung f. deterioration.
verschlissen worn out, threadbare.
verschlucken to swallow the wrong way.
Verschluss m. lock, fastener, clasp, seal, plug, zipper.
verschmachten to languish.
verschonen to spare, exempt from.
verschönern to beautify, embellish, adorn.
Verschönerung f. embellishment.
verschreiben to prescribe, order in writing, write for.
 sich verschreiben to make a mistake in writing.
verschwägert related by marriage.
verschwenden to waste, lavish.
Verschwender m. spendthrift, extravagant person.
verschwenderisch wasteful, extravagant.
verschwiegen discreet, close.
Verschwiegenheit f. secrecy, discretion.
verschwistert like brothers and sisters, closely united.
Versehen n. mistake, oversight.
VERSEHEN to provide, furnish, supply with; to overlook.
 ehe man sich's versieht unexpectedly, suddenly.
 sich versehen to make a mistake.
versehentlich by mistake.
VERSETZEN to displace, transfer, pledge, pawn.
 den Verstand verlieren to go out of one's mind.
 Just put yourself in my place.
Versetzung f. transfer, moving up.
VERSICHERN to insure, affirm.
Versicherung f. insurance.
versöhnen to reconcile, conciliate.
Versöhnung f. reconciliation.
versorgen to provide, supply.
Versorger m. support, breadwinner.
Versorgung f. supply.
verspätet late.
Verspätung f. delay, lateness.
 Verspätung haben to be late.
verspielen to lose, gamble away.
VERSPRECHEN to promise.

Ich habe mich nur versprochen.
It was only a slip of the tongue.
sich etwas versprechen von to expect much of.
Versprechung *f.* promise.
VERSTAND *m.* mind, sense, brain, intellect.
  den Verstand verlieren to go out of one's mind.
  zu Verstand kommen to arrive at the age of discretion.
verständig intelligent, sensible, wise.
verständigen to inform, notify.
  sich verständigen to come to an understanding with.
verständlich understandable, clear, comprehensible.
  sich verständlich machen to make oneself understood.
Verständlichkeit *f.* intelligibility, clearness.
Verständnis comprehension, understanding.
  Verständnis haben für to appreciate.
verständnislos unappreciative, stupid.
verständnisvoll understanding, appreciative.
Versteck *n.* hiding place.
verstecken to hide, conceal.
versteckt hidden, concealed.
  versteckte Absichten ulterior motives.
VERSTEHEN to understand, comprehend, know.
  falsch verstehen to misunderstand.
  Ich verstehe nicht! I don't understand!
  sich verstehen to understand each other.
  sich von selbst verstehen to go without saying.
  Was verstehen Sie darunter? What do you understand by that?
  zu verstehen geben to give to understand.
versteifen to stiffen.
  sich versteifen auf to insist on.
versteigern to sell at auction.
Versteigerung *f.* auction.
verstellbar adjustable.
verstellen to change order or position, block, disguise.
  sich verstellen to put on an act.
Verstellung *f.* dissimulation, disguise, hypocrisy.
versteuern to pay duty on.
verstimmen to annoy, upset.
Verstimmung *f.* ill humor, bad temper.
Versuch *m.* experiment, trial.
VERSUCHEN to try, attempt, taste, sample.
  es versuchen mit to give a trial to, to put to the test.
Versuchung *f.* temptation.
vertagen to adjourn.
vertauschen to exchange.
verteidigen to defend.
Verteidiger *m.* defender, advocate, attorney.
Verteidigung *f.* defense.
verteilen to distribute, dispense, assign.
Verteilung *f.* distribution.
Vertrag *m.* contract, treaty, agreement.
VERTRAGEN to carry away, bear, stand, endure, tolerate, digest.
  ich kann diese Speise nicht vertragen.
  This food does not agree with me.
  sich vertragen to get along.
  sich wieder vertragen to settle one's differences.
Vertrauen *n.* confidence.
vertrauen to trust.
vertrauensvoll confident.
vertrauenswürdig trustworthy.
vertraulich confidential.
vertraut familiar.
  im Vertrauen in confidence, confidentially.
  im Vertrauen auf relying on, trusting to.
  sich vertraut machen to become familiar.
Vertraute *m. f.* intimate friend.
vertreten to represent, substitute for; to sprain.
Vertreter *m.* representative, substitute.
VERTRETUNG *f.* representation, replacement.

eine Vertretung übernehmen to take the place of, represent.
vertrösten to put off, console.
verunglücken to have an accident.
verurteilen to sentence, condemn.
Verurteilung *f.* sentence, condemnation.
vervielfältigen to multiply, duplicate, reproduce.
verwahren to keep, put away.
verwaisen to become an orphan.
verwaist orphaned, deserted.
verwandt related, similar, allied.
Verwandte *m.* relation, relative.
Verwandtschaft *f.* relationship, relations.
verwechseln to take for, mistake for.
Verwechslung *f.* mistake, confusion.
verweigern to deny, refuse.
Verweigerung *f.* denial, refusal.
Verweis *m.* reproof, reprimand, reference.
Verweisung *f.* exile, banishment.
VERWENDEN to use, utilize, employ, expend.
  sich verwenden für to put in a good word for.
  verwenden auf to put in on, spend on.
Verwendung *f.* use, utilization, application.
verwirklichen to realize, materialize.
Verwirklichung *f.* realization, materialization.
Verwöhnung *f.* spoiling, pampering.
verwunderlich astonishing, surprising.
verwundern to surprise.
Verwunderung *f.* surprise, astonishment.
verzagen to lose heart, despair.
VERZEIHEN to pardon, forgive, excuse.
  Verzeihen Sie! Excuse me!
verzeihlich excusable.
VERZEIHUNG *f.* pardon, excuse.
  Ich bitte Sie um Verzeihung! Please excuse me!
Verzicht *m.* resignation, renunciation.
verzichten to renounce, resign, give up.
verzinsen to pay interest on.
verzögern to delay.
verzollen to pay duty on.
  Haben Sie etwas zu verzollen? Have you anything to declare?
Verzollung *f.* payment of duty, clearance.
verzweifeln to despair.
verzweifelt desperate, despairing.
Verzweiflung *f.* despair, desperation.
  zur Verzweiflung bringen to drive one mad.
Veto *n.* veto.
  Veto einlegen to veto a thing.
VETTER *m.* cousin.
Vieh *n.* cattle.
Viehhändler *m.* cattle dealer.
VIEL much, a great deal, a lot of.
  ein bisschen viel a little too much.
  in vielem in many respects.
  noch einmal so viel as much again.
  viele many.
  sehr viele many (people).
  Viel Glück! Lots of luck!
  Viel Vergnügen! Have a good time!
vielerlei many kind of.
VIELLEICHT perhaps.
vielseitig many-sided, versatile.
VIER four.
  zu vieren, zu viert four of us.
Viereck *n.* square.
viereckig square, quadrangular.
VIERTE fourth.
VIERTEL *n.* quarter, fourth.
  Es ist viertel vor zwei. It is a quarter to two.
vierteljährlich quarterly.
Viertelstunde *f.* a quarter of an hour.
viertelstündlich every quarter of an hour.
VIERZEHN fourteen
  vierzehn Tage two weeks.
VIERZEHNTE fourteenth.
VIERZIG forty.

VIERZIGSTE fortieth.
Viola *f.* viola.
Violine *f.* violin.
virtuos masterly.
Virtuose *m.* virtuoso.
Virtuosität *f.* virtuosity.
Vision *f.* vision.
Visite *f.* visit.
Visitenkarte *f.* visiting-card.
Vitrine *f.* show-case.
VOGEL *m.* bird.
  den Vogel abschiessen to carry off the prize.
Vogelscheuche *f.* scarecrow.
Vokabel *f.* word.
Vokabelschatz *m.* vocabulary (range).
VOLK *n.* people, nation, crowd.
  das arbeitende Volk the working classes.
  das gemeine Volk the mob.
  der Mann aus dem Volk the man in the street.
Volksabstimmung *f.* plebiscite.
Volkslied *n.* folk song.
Volksschule *f.* elementary or primary school.
volkstümlich national, popular.
  volkstümliche Preise popular prices.
Volksversammlung *f.* public meeting.
Volkswagen *m.* people's car.
VOLL 1. *adj. & adv.* full, filled, complete, whole, entire; fully, completely.
  aus vollem Herzen from the bottom of the heart.
  aus voller Kehle at the top of one's voice.
  den Mund voll nehmen to boast.
  Die Rechnung ist voll bezahlt. The bill is paid in full.
  in voller Fahrt at full speed.
  Man kann ihn nicht für voll nehmen.
  One cannot take him too seriously.
  2. Prefix.
  a) separable (meaning to fill)
  Sie giesst die Gläser voll. She fills up the glasses.
  b) inseparable (meaning to accomplish, finish).
  Er vollführte eine gute Leistung.
  He executed a good performance.
Vollbart *m.* beard.
vollblütig full-blooded.
vollbringen to finish, accomplish, complete.
Volldampf *m.* full steam.
völlig complete, entire, quite.
volljährig of age.
Volljährigkeit *f.* majority (of age).
VOLLKOMMEN perfect, complete.
Vollkommenheit *f.* perfection.
Vollkraft *f.* full vigor.
Vollmacht *f.* full power, power of attorney.
Vollmilch *f.* unskimmed milk.
Vollmond *m.* full moon.
vollständig complete.
vollzählig complete, full, completely, absolutely.
VON 1. *prep. (dat.).* from, by, with, of, on, upon, about.
  Amerika wurde von Kolumbus entdeckt.
  America was discovered by Columbus.
  Der Platz war voll von Menschen.
  The place was full of people.
  ein Gedicht von Heine a poem by Heine.
  eine Feder von Gold a gold pen.
  von heute ab from today on.
  Von meinem Fenster sehe ich auf den Garten.
  From my window I see the garden.
  2. *adv.*: apart, separate.
  von einander apart.
  von klein auf from childhood (on).
  von mir aus as far I am concerned.
  von selbst by itself, automatically.
  von Nutzen sein to be needful, necessary.
VOR 1. *prep. (dat. when answering question, Wo?; acc. when answering question, Wohin?, and depending on the idiom).* before, in front of, ahead of, for, with, against, from.

Das Bild ist vor mir. The picture is in front of me.

Es ist ein viertel vor elf. It is a quarter to eleven.

Ich werde sie vor ihm warnen. I will warn her against him.

nach wie vor as usual.

nicht vor not until.

vor acht Tagen a week ago.

vor allem above all, first of all.

vor der Klasse before class.

vor Hunger sterben to die of hunger.

Vor ihm müssen Sie sich in Acht nehmen. With him, you must be on your guard.

vorzeiten formerly

vorab above all.

2. *separable prefix (implies movement forward, presentation, demonstration).*

Der Lehrer las ein Gedicht vor. The teacher read a poem aloud.

Die Soldaten rückten vor. The soldiers moved forward.

Wir bereiten uns auf die Prüfung vor. We prepare ourselves for the examination.

vorahnen to have a presentiment.

Vorahnung f. presentiment.

voran ahead, before.

vorangehen to precede.

mit gutem Beispiel vorangehen to set a good example.

Voranschlag m. estimate.

Voranzeige f. preliminary advertisement.

Vorarbeit f. preliminary work.

Vorarbeiter m. foreman.

VORAUS in front of, ahead of.

etwas voraus haben vor to have an advantage over a person.

im Voraus in advance.

weit voraus way ahead.

vorausgehen to lead the way, precede.

voraussetzen to presuppose, assume.

Voraussetzung f. supposition, assumption.

voraussichtlich presumable, probable.

Vorbehalt m. reservation, proviso.

ohne Vorbehalt unconditionally

unter Vorbehalt aller Rechte all rights reserved.

vorbehalten to keep in reserve, withhold.

sich vorbehalten to reserve to oneself.

vorbehaltlos unconditional.

vorbei by, along, past, over, gone.

vorbeireden (aneinander) to be at cross-purposes.

vorbereiten to prepare, make ready.

Vorbereitung f. preparation.

vorbeugen to hinder, prevent.

Vorbeugungsmassregel f. preventive measure.

Vorbild n. model, pattern, standard.

vorbildlich model, ideal.

Vorbildung f. preparatory training, education.

vorder fore, forward, anterior.

Vordergrund m. foreground.

Vorderhaus n. front part of the house.

vordringlich urgent.

voreilig hasty.

Voreiligkeit f. precipitation, rashness.

voreingenommen prejudiced.

Voreingenommenheit f. prejudice.

vorenthalten to keep back, withhold.

Vorfall m. occurrence, event.

vorfallen to occur, happen, take place.

Vorfreude f. joy of anticipation.

vorführen to demonstrate, produce.

Vorführung f. demonstration.

Vorgang m. occurrence.

Vorgänger m. predecessor.

VORGEHEN to go on, go forward, go first, lead, take place, occur, act, be of special importance.

Gehen Sie schon vor! Go right ahead!

Vorgeschichte f. previous history.

Vorgeschmack m. foretaste.

Vorgesetzte m. & f. chief, boss

VORGESTERN the day before yesterday.

vorhaben to have on, wear, to intend, plan.

Haben Sie morgen etwas vor?

Do you have any plans for tomorrow?

Vorhang m. curtain.

vorher before, beforehand, in advance, previously.

vorherrschen to predominate, prevail.

vorherrschend predominant, prevailing.

Vorjahr n. preceding year.

Vorkenntnis f. previous knowledge.

vorkommen to come forward, occur, happen.

Es kommt Ihnen nur so vor.

You are just imagining that.

Vorkommnis n. occurrence, event.

Vorlage f. model, pattern, copy.

vorlassen to give precedence to.

vorläufig preliminary.

Vorleger m. mat, rug.

vorlesen to read aloud.

Vorlesung f. lecture, recital.

vorletzt one before the last.

Vorliebe f. predilection, preference.

vormachen to put, place before, impose on someone, fool.

vormerken to make a note of, put down.

sich vormerken lassen to book.

Vormittag m. morning ("before noon").

Vormund m. guardian.

Vormundschaft f. guardianship.

VORN in front, in front of.

nach vorn forward.

nach vorne heraus wohnen to live in the front part of a house.

von vorn from the front.

von vorn anfangen to start afresh.

von vorn herein from the first.

Vorname m. Christian name.

vornehm of high rank, noble, distinguished.

Vornehmheit f. distinction, high rank.

vornehmlich principally, chiefly, especially.

Vorort m. suburb.

Vorplatz m. court, hall, vestibule.

Vorrang m. precedence, priority.

Vorrat m. store, stock, provision.

vorrätig in stock, on hand.

nicht mehr vorrätig out of stock.

Vorratskammer f. storeroom, pantry.

vorsagen to dictate, say, prompt.

Vorsatz m. purpose.

Vorschlag m. proposal, proposition.

vorschlagen to propose, offer.

vorschreiben to set a copy.

Vorschrift f. copy, direction.

vorschriftmässig according to instructions.

vorsehen to provide for, consider, take care.

Vorsehung f. providence.

VORSICHT f. foresight, caution, prudence.

Vorsicht! Take care! Beware!

Vorsicht Stufe! Mind the step!

vorsichtig cautious, prudent.

vorsichtshalber as a precaution.

Vorsichtsmassregel f. precaution, measure.

Vorsitz m. presidency, chairman.

den Vorsitz führen to preside in the chair.

Vorspeise f. hors d'oeuvre, relish.

vorsprechen to pronounce, recite.

vorsprechen bei to call on.

Vorsprung m. projection, projecting part.

Vorstadt f. suburb.

Vorstand m. board of directors.

vorstellen to place before, put in front of, demonstrate, introduce, represent, act.

sich etwas vorstellen to imagine something.

sich vorstellen to introduce oneself.

vorstellig adj.

vorstellig werden to present a case, petition.

VORSTELLUNG f. introduction, presentation, performance, picture.

Wann fängt die Vorstellung an? When does the performance start?

Vorstellungsvermögen n. imagination.

Vorteil m. advantage, profit.

VORTEILHAFT advantageous, favorable.

vorteilhaft aussehen to look one's best.

Vortrag m. reciting, delivery, execution, lecture.

vortragen to carry forward, recite, declaim, execute, perform.

vortrefflich excellent, admirable, splendid.

Vortrefflichkeit f. excellence.

vorüber past, over, by, along.

vorübergehen to go by, pass.

Vorurteil n. prejudice.

vorurteilslos unprejudiced.

Vorverkauf m. booking in advance (theater); advance sale.

vorvorgestern three days ago.

Vorwand m. pretext, pretense, excuse.

VORWÄRTS forward, onward, on.

Vorwärts! Go on! Go ahead!

vorwärtsgehen to go on, advance, progress.

vorwärtskommen to get on, advance, prosper.

vorwärtskommend predominant.

Vorwurf m. reproach.

Vorwürfe machen to blame.

vorwurfsvoll reproachful.

vorzeigen to show, produce, exhibit, display.

vorzeitig premature, precocious.

vorziehen to draw forward, prefer.

Vorzimmer n. antechamber.

Vorzug m. preference, superiority.

vorzüglich excellent, superior, first-choice.

Vorzüglichkeit f. excellency, superiority.

Vorzugspreis m. special price.

W

WAAGE (Wage) f. balance, scales.

einem die Waage halten to be a match for.

sich die Waage halten to counterbalance each other.

wagerecht horizontal level.

WACH awake, alive, brisk.

Wachdienst m. guard duty.

Wache f. guard, watch, sentry.

WACHEN to be awake, remain awake.

wachen über to watch over.

Wachs n. wax.

wachsam vigilant, watchful.

Wachsamkeit f. vigilance.

WACHSEN to grow, increase, extend.

ans Herz wachsen to grow fond of.

einem gewachsen sein to be a match for one.

einer Sache gewachsen sein to be equal to a task.

Wachstum n. growth, increase.

Wacht f. guard, watch.

Wächter m. watchman, guard.

Waffe f. weapon, arm.

Waffel f. wafer, waffle.

Waffeleisen n. waffle-iron.

Waffenschein m. gun-license.

Waffenstillstand m. armistice.

WAGEN m. car, automobile, railroad car, cab, wagon.

wagen to venture, risk, dare.

gewagt daring, risky, perilous.

Wagnis n. risk.

WAHL f. choice, selection, election.

in engere Wahl kommen to be on the short list.

seine Wahl treffen to make one's choice.

vor die Wahl stellen to let one choose.

wahlberechtigt entitled to vote.

WÄHLEN to choose, select, pick out, elect, dial.

Wähler m. elector, selector.

wählerisch particular, fastidious.

Wahlkampf m. election, contest.

wahllos indiscriminately.

Wahlstimme f. vote.

Wahn m. delusion, illusion.

Wahnsinn m. insanity, madness, craziness.

wahnsinnig insane, mad.

WAHR true, sincere, genuine, real, proper, veritable.
etwas nicht wahr haben wollen not to admit a thing.
Nicht wahr? Isn't it? Don't you think so?
so wahr ich lebe as sure as I live.
wahr werden to come true.

WÄHREND 1. *prep. (gen.):* during, for, in the course of.
Während des Winters verleben wir unsere Ferien in den Bergen. During the winter we spend our vacations in the mountains.
2. *conj.* while.
Sie kam während Sie weg waren. She came while you were out.

WAHRHEIT f. truth.
Ich habe ihm gehörig die Wahrheit gesagt. I really gave him a piece of my mind.

wahrheitsgetreu truthful, true.

wahrheitslebend truthful.

wahrnehmbar perceptible, noticeable.

wahrsagen to tell fortunes, prophesy.

Wahrsagerin f. fortune teller.

WAHRSCHEINLICH probable, likely.

Wahrscheinlichkeit f. probability.

Währung f. standard, currency.

Waise f. & m. orphan.

Waisenhaus n. orphanage.

Wal m. whale.

WALD m. forest, woodland.

waldig woody.

Waldung f. woodland, wood.

Wall m. rampart, dike.

Walnuss f. walnut.

Walze f. roller, barrel.

walzen to walz.

Walzer m. waltz.

WAND f. wall, partition.

Wandel m. change, alteration.
Handel und Wandel trade, commerce.

wandelbar perishable; changeable, fickle.

wandern to wander.

Wanderschaft f. trip, tour, travels.

Wanderung f. excursion, trip, hike, migration.

Wandgemälde n. mural painting, fresco.

Wandschrank m. cupboard.

Wankelmut m. inconsistency, fickleness.

WANN when.
wann immer whenever.
dann und wann now and then.

Wanne f. tub, bath.

Wannenbad n. tub bath.

WARE f. article, goods, merchandise.

Warenhaus n. department store.

Warenprobe f. sample.

WARM warm.
Ist es Ihnen warm genug? Are you warm enough?
warm stellen to keep hot.

Wärme f. heat, warmth.

WÄRMEN to warm, heat.

Wärmflasche f. hot-water bottle.

warnen to warn, caution.

Warnung f. warning.

Warnungssignal n. danger signal.

WARTEN to wait, attend to, nurse.
warten auf to wait for.
warten lassen to keep waiting.

Wärter m. attendant.

Wartesaal m. waiting-room.

Wartezimmer n. doctor's waiting room.

WARUM why, for what reason.

WAS what, whatever, that which, which, that.
Ach was! Nonsense!
Nein so was! Well, I never!
was ... auch immer no matter what, whatever.
was für ein what sort of, what a.

Waschbecken n. wash basin.

WÄSCHE f. wash; linen, underclothing.
in die Wäsche geben to send to the laundry.
grosse Wäsche haben to have washing day.
schmutzige Wäsche soiled linen, dirty clothes.

waschecht fast color.

Wäschegeschäft n. haberdashery, lingerie store.

Wäscheklammer f. clothespin.

Wäscheleine f. clothesline.

waschen to wash.

Wäscherei f. laundry.

WASSER n. water.
fliessendes Wasser running water.
ins Wasser fallen to end in smoke.
mit allen Wassern gewaschen sein to be cunning.
sich über Wasser halten to keep one's head above water.
zu Wasser und zu Lande by land and sea.

Wasserball m. water polo.

Wasserbehälter m. reservoir, tank.

wasserdicht waterproof.

Wasserfall m. waterfall.

Wasserfarbe f. water-color.

Wasserflugzeug n. sea plane.

Wasserglas n. glass, tumbler.

wasserhältig containing water.

wässerig watery.
einem den Mund wässerig machen to make a person's mouth water.

Wasserkanne f. watering-can.

Wasserleitung f. water supply, water pipes, faucet, sink.

Wasserspiegel m. water-surface.

Wasserstiefel pl. rubber boots.

Wasserstrahl m. jet of water.

Watte f. wadding, cotton-wool.

weben to weave.

Weber m. weaver.

Wechsel m. change, alteration, succession, turn.
gezogener Wechsel draft.

Wechselgeld n. change (money).
Bitte, zählen Sie ihr Wechselgeld nach. Please count your change.

Wechselkurs m. rate of exchange.

WECHSELN to change, exchange, alternate, shift.
seinen Wohnort wechseln to move away.
den Besitzer wechseln to change ownership.

wechselseitig reciprocal, mutual, alternate.

WECKEN to wake, awaken.

Wecker m. alarm-clock.

weder neither.
weder...noch neither...nor.

WEG m. way, path, road, street, walk.
am Weg by the roadside.
auf gütlichem Weg in a friendly way.
auf halbem Weg halfway.
aus dem Weg gehen to make way for, stand aside.
in die Wege leiten to prepare for.
seiner Wege gehen to go one's way.
sich auf den Weg machen to set out.

WEG 1. *adv.* away, off, gone, lost, disappeared.
Hände weg! Hands off!

Ich muss weg. I must go.
2. *separable prefix (implies a motion away from the speaker).*
Er warf das alte Buch weg. He threw the old book away.
Geh weg! Go away!

wegbleiben to stay away, be omitted.

wegbringen to take away, remove.

WEGEN *prep. (gen.):* because of, for the sake of, owing to.
Wegen des Krieges konnte ich nicht von Europa zurückkommen. Because of the war, I could not come back from Europe.

wegfahren to drive off, away.

weggehen to go away, depart, leave.

weglegen to put away.

wegnehmen to take away, carry off, confiscate, occupy.

Wegweiser m. signpost.

wegwerfen to throw away.

wegwerfend disparaging, contemptuous.

WEH sore, aching, painful.
weh tun to ache, to hurt.

wehleidig plaintive.

Wehmut f. sadness, melancholy.

wehmütig sad, melancholy.

Wehrdienst m. military service.

wehren to hinder, forbid, arrest, defend.
sich seiner Haut wehren to defend one's life.

wehrfähig able-bodied.

wehrlos unarmed, defenseless, weak.

Wehrmacht f. armed forces.

Wehrpflicht f. conscription.

wehrpflichtig liable to military service.

Weib n. woman.

weibisch effeminate.

weiblich female, feminine, womanly.

Weiblichkeit f. womanhood, femininity.

WEICH soft, mold, mellow, tender, smooth.
weiches Ei soft-boiled egg.

weichen to retreat, give in, yield; soften, soak.

weichherzig soft-hearted.

weichlich soft, flabby, weak.

weigern to refuse.

Weigerung f. refusal.

Weihe f. consecration, initiation, inauguration.

weihen to consecrate, dedicate, devote.

WEIHNACHTEN pl. Christmas.

weihnachtlich of Christmas.

Weihnachtsabend m. Christmas Eve.

Weihnachtsbaum m. Christmas tree.

Weihnachtslied n. Christmas carol.

WEIL because, since.

WEILE f. while, space of time.
Damit hat es gute Weile. There is no hurry.
Eile mit Weile. Haste makes waste.

WEIN m. wine, vine.

Weinberg m. vineyard.

WEINEN to weep, cry.

Weinessig m. wine vinegar.

Weinfass n. wine cask.

Weinkarte f. winelist.

Weinlese f. vintage.

Weinprobe f. wine-tasting.

Weinrebe f. vine.

Weinstock m. vine.

Weintraube f. grape, bunch of grapes.

WEISE f. manner, way, tune.
auf diese Weise in this way.
in der Weise, dass in such a way that, so that.

WEISEN to show, refer, direct, point out, point at.

Weisheit f. wisdom, prudence.

weismachen to make one believe, hoax.

WEISS white, blank, clean.
Weisser Sonntag Sunday after Easter.

weissagen to predict, prophesy.

Weissager m. (-in, f.) prophet.

WEIT distant, far, vast, loose, wide, big.
    bei weitem by far, by much.
    beit weitem nicht by no means.
    es weit bringen to get on well, be successful.
    nicht weither sein not to be worth much.
    von weitem from a distance.
    weit gefehlt quite wrong.
    weit und breit far and wide.
    weit voraus way ahead.
    weit weg far away.
    wenn alles so weit ist when everything is
    ready.
weitab far away.
weitaus by far.
Weitblick m. foresight.
Weite f. width, size, extent, distance, length.
WEITER further, farther, more, else, additional.
    bis auf weiteres until further notice.
    des weiteren furthermore.
    nichts weiter nothing more.
    niemand weiter no one else.
    Nur weiter! Go on!
    ohne weiteres immediately.
    und so weiter and so on.
    was weiter what else.
    wenn's weiter nichts ist if that's all there
    is to it.
Weitere n. rest, remaining part.
weiterführen to continue, carry on.
weitergeben to pass on to.
Weiterreise f. continuation of a trip.
weitgehend far-reaching, full, much.
weither from afar.
weitläufig distant, wide, extensive, roomy.
weitschweifig detailed, tedious.
weitsichtig far-sighted.
Weizen m. wheat, corn.
WELCH (ein) what (a)
    Welch ein Zufall! What a coincidence!
WELCH(-ER, -E, -ES) 1. inter. pron. & adj. what,
    who, whom, which.
    2. rel. pron. what, which, that, who, whom.
Welle f. wave, surge.
    Wellen schlagen to rise in waves.
Wellenlinie f. wavy line.
Wellenreiter m. surf-rider.
WELT f. world, universe, people.
    alle Welt everybody, everyone in the world.
    auf der Welt on earth.
    auf die Welt kommen to come into the world,
    be born.
    aus der Welt schaffen to put out of the way.
    in der ganzen Welt on earth.
    in die Welt setzen (zur Welt bringen) to give
    birth to.
Weltall n. universe.
Weltanschauung f. world outlook.
weltbekannt world-famous.
weltfremd secluded, solitary.
Weltmann m. man of the world.
Weltmeister m. world champion.
Weltraum m. space, universe.
Weltuntergang m. end of the world.
WEM dat. of wer. to whom.
WEN acc. of wer. whom.
Wende f. turn, turning point.
wenden to turn, turn around.
    Bitte wenden! Please turn over!
Wendepunkt m. turning point.
WENIG little, few, a few.
    ein wenig a little, a bit.
WENIGER less, fewer, minus.
    immer weniger less and less.
    nichts weniger als anything but.
    vier weniger eins four minus one.
wenigst (er,-e,-es) least.
wenigstens at least.

WENN if, in case of, when.
    auch wenn even if.
    immer wenn whenever.
    Rufen Sie mich an wenn Sie kommen wollen.
    Call me when you want to come.
    selbst wenn even if, supposing that.
    wenn auch (wenn gleich, wenn schon) although.
    Wenn das nur wahr wäre! If it were only true!
    wenn nur provided that.
    Wenn schon! What of it!
    wenn Sie kommen könnten If you could come.
WER inter. pron. who, what.
    wer anders who else.
    wer auch immer whoever.
    Wer da? Who is it?
werben to recruit; to court, propose (marriage).
WERDEN 1. to become, turn out, prove, happen.
    Was soll aus ihr werden? What's to become
    of her?
    2. aux. verb to form future and passive.
    shall, will, is, are.
werfen to throw, cast, toss.
WERK n. work, labor, production, performance, deed.
    ans Werk! Go to it!
    ins Werk setzen to set going.
    zu Werk gehen to begin.
Werkstatt f. workshop.
Werktag m. working day.
werktags on weekdays.
werktätig active
    die werktätige Bevolkerung working classes.
Werkzeug m. utensil.
WERT worth, valuable, worthy, honored, esteemed.
    im Werte von at a price of.
    nichts wert sein to be no good.
Wertangabe f. declaration of value.
Wertgegenstünde pl. valuables.
wertlos worthless.
Wertpapier n. security, bond.
Wertsachen pl. valuables.
wertvoll valuable, precious.
Wesen n. creature, soul, personality.
wesentlich essential, substantial.
WESSEN gen. of wer. whose? whose.
Weste f. waistcoat, vest.
Westen m. the West, Occident.
    nach Westen west (direction).
westlich western, occidental.
westwarts westwards.
Wette f. bet, wager.
    eine Wette eingehen to make a bet.
    um die Wette laufen to race someone.
wetteifern to emulate; to vie.
wetten to bet, wager.
WETTER n. weather.
    Alle Wetter! My word!
    Heute ist das Wetter wunderschön!
    The weather is wonderful today!
Wetterbericht m. meteorological report.
Wetterlage f. weather conditions.
Wettkampf m. match, contest, prize fighting.
Wettstreit m. competition, match.
WICHTIG important.
    sich wichtig machen to act important.
WIDER 1. prep. (acc.) against, contrary to, versus.
    Wider meinen Willen against my will.
    2. inseparable prefix. (con-,re-, anti-, contra-)
widerhallen to echo, resound.
widerlegen to refute.
Widerlegung f. refutation.
widerlich repulsive, disgusting.
Widerrede f. contradiction.
widerrufen to revoke, withdraw, retract, cancel.
Widersacher m. adversary.
widersetzen (sich) to oppose, resist.
widerspiegeln to reflect, mirror.
Widerstand m. resistance, opposition.

Widerwille m. repugnance, disgust.
widerwillig reluctant, unwilling.
widmen to dedicate.
Widmung f. dedication.
WIE how, as, such, like.
    so . . . wie as . . . as.
    wie auch immer however.
    Wie bitte? What did you say?
    wie dem auch sei be that as it may.
    Wie geht es Ihnen? How are you?
    wie gesagt as has been said.
WIEDER 1. adv. again, anew, back, in return for.
    hin und wieder now and then.
    immer wieder again and again.
    2. prefix.
    a) inseparable. In verb wiederholen (to repeat).
    b) separable (implies the idea of repetition or
    opposition).
wiederbekommen to get back, recover.
wiederbeleben to revive, reanimate.
Wiederbelebungsversuch m. attempt at resuscitation.
wiederfinden to find, recover.
wiedererkennen to recognize.
wiedererlangen to get back.
wiedererobern to reconquer.
Wiedergabe f. return; reproduction, recital (work of art).
wiedergeben to give back, return.
Wiedergutmachung f. reparation.
WIEDERHOLEN to repeat, renew, reiterate, fetch,
    bring back.
Wiederholung f. repetition, reiteration.
    im Wiederholungsfalle if it should happen again.
wiederhören to hear again.
    auf Wiederhören! Good-bye! (radio, tel.).
WIEDERSEHEN to see again, meet again.
    auf Wiedersehen! Good-bye! So long!
Wiege f. cradle.
wiegen to rock, move to, shake, sway.
Wiese f. meadow.
wieso why.
WIEVIEL how much.
    Der wievielte ist heute? What date is today?
wieviele how many.
WILD wild, rough, angry, furious, savage, untidy.
Wild n. game (hunting).
Wildbraten m. venison.
Wilddieb m. poacher.
Wildente f. wild duck.
Wildleder n. deerskin, suede.
Wildnis f. wilderness, desert.
WILLE m. will, way, determination, purpose.
    aus freiem Willen voluntarily.
    guter Wille good intention.
    letzter Wille last will.
willenlos lacking will power, irresolute.
Willenlosigkeit f. lack of will power.
Willenskraft f. will power.
willfahren to gratify, grant, please.
Willkommen n. welcome, reception.
Willkür f. discretion, arbitrariness.
willkürlich arbitrary, despotic.
WIND m. wind, breeze.
    bei Wind und Wetter in storm and rain.
    guter Wind fair wind.
    in den Wind reden to talk in vain.
    in den Wind schlagen to disregard.
    vor dem Wind segeln to run before the rain.
Windel f. baby's diaper.
Windelkind n. infant.
windeln to swaddle.
winden to wind.
windig windy, breezy.
Windstille f. calm.
Wink m. sign, nod, wink.
Winkel m. corner, angle, secret spot.
winken to wave, nod, wink.
WINTER m. winter.

im Winter in winter.
Winterfrische *f.* winter resort.
Winterschlaf *m.* hibernation.
Wintersport *m.* winter sports.
winzig tiny, diminutive.
Winzigkeit *f.* tininess.
Wirbel *m.* whirlpool, eddy.
Wirbelknochen *m.* vertebra.
wirbeln to whirl.
Wirbelsäule *f.* spine.
Wirbelsturm *m.* tornado, hurricane.
wirken to act, do, work, produce.
WIRKLICH real, actual, true, genuine.
Wirklichkeit *f.* reality, actuality.
wirksam active, effective.
Wirkung *f.* action, working, operation.
wirkungslos ineffectual, inefficient.
wirkungsvoll effective, striking.
Wirt *m.* host, proprietor, landlord.
wirtlich hospitable.
Wirtschaft *f.* housekeeping, economy, tavern, public house.
die Wirtschaft führen to keep house.
wirtschaften to manage.
Wirtschaftsgeld *n.* housekeeping money.
Wirtschaftslage *f.* economic situation.
Wirtschaftsprüfer *m.* general adviser, accountant.
Wirtshaus *n.* inn, public house.
WISSEN *n.* knowledge, learning.
meines Wissens as far as I know.
nach bestem Wissen und Gewissen most conscientiously.
wider besseres Wissen against one's better judgment.
WISSEN to know, be aware of, understand, be acquainted with.
Ich weiss nicht. I don't know.
nicht dass ich wüsste not that I am aware of.
Wissenschaft *f.* science, knowledge.
Wissenschaftler *m.* scientist, scholar.
wissenswert worth knowing, interesting.
Witwe *f.* widow.
Witwer *m.* widower.
Witz *m.* wittiness, witticism, wit, joke, pun.
witzig witty.
WO where, in which; when.
wo auch immer wherever.
woanders elsewhere.
wobei whereat, whereby, in which, upon which.
WOCHE *f.* week.
diese Woche this week.
heute in einer Woche a week from today.
Wochenende *n.* weekend.
wochenlang for weeks.
wochentags on weekdays.
Wochenschau newsreel; weekly publication.
wöchentlich weekly.
wodurch by which, whereby, how.
wofür for which, for what.
WOHER from where, from what place?
Woher wissen Sie das? How do you know that?
WOHIN to where, to what place?
WOHL *n.* welfare, prosperity, good health.
sich wohl fühlen to feel well.
WOHL well, all right, probably, presumably, very likely, indeed.
Ich verstehe wohl. I can well understand.
Leben Sie wohl! Good-bye!
wohl oder übel willy nilly.
Zum Wohl! To you! (a toast)
Wohlbehagen *n.* comfort, ease.
wohlbekannt well-known, familiar.
Wohlfahrt *f.* welfare.
Wohlgeruch *m.* fragrance, sweet, perfume.
wohlhabend wealthy, well-off.
Wohlklang *m.* harmony, melody.
wohlschmeckend tasty, palatable.
Wohlstand *m.* well-being, wealth, fortune.

wohltuend comforting, pleasant.
wohlverdient well-deserved, merited.
WOHNEN to live, dwell, reside, stay.
zur Miete wohnen to live as a tenant, rent-payer.
wohnhaft living, dwelling.
wohnlich comfortable, cozy.
WOHNUNG *f.* house, dwelling, residence, flat.
Wohnviertel *n.* residential district.
Wohnzimmer *n.* sitting-room.
Wolf *m.* wolf.
Wolke *f.* cloud.
aus allen Wolken fallen to be thunderstruck.
Wolkenbruch *m.* cloudburst.
Wolkenkratzer *m.* skyscraper.
WOLLE *f.* wool.
WOLLEN to want, wish, will, desire, like, mean.
Das will etwas heissen. That means something.
Das will was heissen. That's really something.
Er mag wollen oder nicht. Whether he likes it or not.
Wie Sie wollen. As you like.
WOMIT with what, by which, with which.
Womit kann ich dienen? What can I do for you?
womöglich if possible.
WORAN whereon, by what.
woran liegt es? how is it that?
WORAUF on what, upon which.
WORAUS of what, out of which.
WORIN in which, in what.
WORT *n.* word, expression, saying, promise.
aufs Wort gehorchen to obey implicitly.
das grosse Wort führen to brag.
das Wort ergreifen to begin to speak.
das Wort führen to be spokesman.
einen beim Wort nehmen to take one at one's word.
Er hat sein Wort gebrochen. He broke his promise.
Ich habe kein Wort davon gewusst.
I did not know a thing about it.
ins Wort fallen to interrupt, cut short.
mit anderen Worten in other words.
Sie macht viele Worte. She talks too much.
ums Wort bitten to ask for the floor.
zu Wort kommen lassen to let one speak.
Wörterbuch *n.* dictionary.
Wortschatz *m.* vocabulary.
wortwörtlich word for word.
WORÜBER of what, about which, whereof.
WORUNTER among what, which.
WOVON about what, which.
WOVOR of what, for what, before what, which.
WOZU before what, of what, for what, which.
wund sore, wounded.
Wunde *f.* wound.
Wunder *n.* wonder, miracle.
sein blaues Wunder erleben to be amazed.
WUNDERBAR wonderful, marvelous.
Wunderbar! Wonderful! Splendid!
wunderbarerweise strange to say.
Wunderkind *n.* child prodigy.
wunderlich strange, odd.
WUNDERN to astonish, surprise.
sich wundern to be surprised, wonder.
wunderschön beautiful, lovely, exquisite.
WUNSCH *m.* wish, desire, request.
auf Wunsch by request, if desired.
Haben Sie noch eine Wunsch?
Is there anything else you'd like?
nach Wunsch as one desires.
WÜNSCHEN to wish, desire, long for.
Glück wünschen to congratulate (wish luck).
Was wünschen Sie? May I help you?
Würde *f.* dignity, honor, title, rank.
in Amt und Würden holding a high office.
würdelos undignified.
würdevoll dignified.

würdig worthy, deserving of, respectable.
würdigen to value, appreciate.
nicht eines Wortes würdigen not to say a word.
Würfel *m.* die, cube.
Der Würfel ist gefallen. The die is cast.
würfeln to play dice.
Würfelspiel *n.* dice game.
Würfelzucker *m.* lump of sugar.
würgen to choke, strangle.
Wurm *m.* worm.
Wurst *f.* sausage.
Würze *f.* seasoning, spice, flavor.
Wurzel *f.* root.
würzen to season.
würzig spicy.
wüst waste, deserted, desolate, wild, dissolute.
Wüste *f.* desert.
Wüstling *m.* libertine, dissolute person.
WUT *f.* rage, fury.
in Wut geraten to fly into a rage.
wüten to rage, be furious.
wütend enraged, furious.

X

xmal ever so often, any number of times.

Y

Y the twenty-fifth letter of the alphabet.

Z

zagen to be afraid, hesitate.
zähe tough, tenacious, stubborn.
ZAHL *f.* figure, number, numeral.
zahlbar payable, due.
zahlen to pay.
ZÄHLEN to count, number, calculate.
gezählt numbered.
Zahlkarte *f.* money-order form.
zahllos countless, innumerable.
zahlreich numerous.
Zahltag *m.* pay-day.
Zahlung *f.* payment.
zahlungsfähig solvent.
zahm tame, domestic.
zähmen to tame, break in.
ZAHN *m.* tooth.
ein schlechter Zahn a bad tooth.
die Zähne putzen to brush the teeth.
einem auf den Zahn fühlen to sound a person.
künstliche Zähne artificial teeth.
Zahnarzt *m.* dentist.
Zahnbürste *f.* toothbrush.
Zahnfleisch *n.* gum.
Zahnfüllung *f.* filling.
zahnlos toothless.
Zahnpasta *f.* toothpaste.
Zahnschmerzen *pl.* toothache.
Zahnstein *m.* tartar.
Zahnstocher *m.* toothpick.
Zahnweh *n.* toothache.
Zange *f.* pincers.
Zank *m.* quarrel.
zanken to quarrel.
zänkisch quarrelsome.
zanksüchtig quarrelsome.
ZART tender, soft, delicate, fragile, frail.
zartfühlend tactful, sensitive.
Zartgefühl *n.* delicacy of feeling.
Zartheit *f.* tenderness, delicacy.
Zauber *m.* magic, charm, spell.
Zauberei *f.* magic, witchcraft.
Zauberflöte *f.* magic flute.
zauberhaft magical, enchanting.
zaubern to practice magic, conjure.
zaudern to hesitate, delay.
Zaun *m.* hedge, fence.
Streit von Zaune brechen to pick a quarrel.

Zebra n. zebra.

Zehe f. toe.

Zehenspitze f. point of the toe.

auf Zehenspitzen gehen to tiptoe.

ZEHN ten.

zehnfach tenfold.

ZEHNTE tenth.

Zeichen n. sign, signal, token, brand.

zum Zeichen dass as a proof that.

Zeichensetzung f. punctuation.

Zeichensprache f. sign language.

ZEICHNEN to draw, design, mark.

ZEICHNUNG f. drawing, sketch, design.

Zeigefinger m. forefinger, index.

ZEIGEN to show, point at, point out, exhibit, display.

Zeiger m. hand of the clock, pointer.

ZEIT f. time, duration, period, epoch, season.

Damit hat es Zeit. There is no hurry.

die freie Zeit leisure, spare time.

Es ist an der Zeit. It is high time.

höchste Zeit high time.

in der letzten Zeit lately.

in jüngster Zeit quite recently.

Lassen Sie sich Zeit! Take your time!

mit der Zeit gradually.

Zeit seines Lebens during life.

zu gleicher Zeit at the same time.

zur rechten Zeit in the nick of time.

zur Zeit at present.

Zeit ist Geld. Time is money.

Zeitalter n. age, generation.

zeitgemäss timely, seasonable.

Zeitgenosse m. contemporary.

zeitgenössisch contemporary.

ZEITIG early, timely, mature, ripe.

zeitlebens for life.

Zeitpunkt m. time, moment.

Zeitschrift f. journal, periodical, magazine.

ZEITUNG f. newspaper, paper.

Zeitungsausschnitt m. press cutting.

Zeitungskiosk m. newsstand.

Zeitungsnotiz f. notice, item, paragraph.

Zeitungsstand m. newsstand.

Zeitungsverkäufer m. news vendor.

Zeitvertreib m. pastime, amusement.

Zeitwort n. verb.

Zelle f. cell, booth.

Zelt n. tent, canopy.

Zement m. cement.

Zentimeter m. & n. centimeter (.3937 inch).

Zentrale f. central office, station, telephone exchange.

Zentralheizung f. central heating.

ZENTRUM n. center.

zerbrechen to break, smash.

sich den Kopf zerbrechen to rack one's brains.

zerbrechlich fragile.

Zerbrechlichkeit f. fragility, brittleness.

Zeremonie f. ceremony.

zerreissbar tearable.

zerreissen to tear, lacerate.

zerren to drag, pull.

zerschmettern to crush, destroy.

zerstören to destroy, demolish, devastate, ruin.

Zerstörer m. destroyer, devastator.

Zerstörung f. devastation, demolition, destruction.

zerstreuen to disperse, scatter, dissipate, divert.

zerstreut absent-minded.

Zerstreuung f. dispersion, distraction, amusement.

Zerwürfnis n. disagreement, quarrel.

Zettel m. slip, note, label, ticket, poster, bill.

Zeug n. stuff, material, cloth, fabric, utensils, things.

sich ins Zeug legen to set to work.

Zeuge m. witness.

zeugen to testify, bear witness, give evidence.

Zeugenaussage f. evidence, deposition.

Zeugenvernehmung f. hearing of witnesses.

Ziege f. goat.

Ziegel m. brick, tile.

Ziegelstein m. brick.

ZIEHEN to pull, draw, haul, tug, tow, extract, move, migrate, weigh.

den Kürzeren ziehen to get the worst of it.

nach sich ziehen to have consequences.

Er zieht den Hut. He tips his hat.

zur Rechenschaft ziehen to call to account.

Ziehung f. drawing of lottery.

Ziel n. goal.

sich ein Ziel setzen to aim at.

zielbewusst systematic, methodical.

zielen to aim.

ziellos aimless.

Zielscheibe f. target.

Zielscheibe des Spottes sein to be a laughing stock.

ziemen to become, be suitable.

ZIEMLICH rather, pretty, fairly, quite, considerable.

so ziemlich about, pretty much.

ziemlich viele quite a few.

Zierde f. ornament, decoration.

zieren to decorate, adorn, embellish.

zierlich elegant, graceful, delicate.

Ziffer f. figure, cipher.

Zifferblatt n. dial, face.

ZIGARETTE f. cigarette.

Zigarettenetui n. cigarette-case.

Zigarettenspitze f. cigarette-holder.

Zigarre f. cigar.

Zigarrenkiste f. cigar-box.

Zigeuner m. gypsy.

ZIMMER n. room, apartment, chamber.

Zimmerdecke f. ceiling.

Zimmermädchen n. chambermaid.

Zimmermann m. carpenter.

zimperlich supersensitive, prudish, affected.

Zimt m. cinnamon.

Zinn n. tin, pewter.

Zins m. tax, duty, rent; interest.

auf Zinsen ausleihen to lend money at interest.

mit Zins und Zinseszins in full measure.

Zinseszins m. compound interest.

Zinsfuss m. rate of interest.

Zirkel m. circle, compasses.

Zirkus m. circus.

Zitat n. quotation.

Zitrone f. lemon.

Zitronenlimonade f. lemonade.

Zitronenpresse f. lemon-press.

Zitronensaft m. lemon juice.

zittern to tremble, shake, quiver, shiver.

zivil civil, reasonable, moderate.

in Zivil in plain clothes.

Zivilbevölkerung f. civilian population.

Zivilisation f. civilization.

zivilisieren to civilize.

Zivilist m. civilian.

zögern to hesitate, delay, linger.

ZOLL m. duty, toll, tariff, customs.

Zoll m. inch.

Zollabfertigung f. customs inspection.

ZOLLAMT n. customhouse.

Zollbeamte m. customhouse officer.

zollfrei free of duty.

Zollgebühr f. duty.

Zöllner m. customs collector.

zollpflichtig subject to customs.

Zollschranke f. customs barrier.

Zollstock m. yardstick.

Zollverschluss m. customs seal.

Zone f. zone.

Zopf m. braid, pigtail.

Zorn m. anger, rage, wrath.

zornig angry.

ZU 1. prep. (dat.). to, at, by, near, beside, for, with, in front of, on.

Die Deutschen essen immer Kartoffeln zum Fleisch. Germans always eat potatoes with meat.

Er war nicht zu Hause. He was not at home.

Ich gehe zu meiner Tante. I am going to my aunt's.

Setzen Sie sich zu mir. Sit down by me.

Wenn es friert, wird das Wasser zu Eis. When it freezes, water turns to ice.

Wir essen Eier zum Frühstück. We eat eggs for breakfast.

zu Fuss, zu Pferd on foot, on horseback.

zu meinem Erstaunen to my surprise.

zum König gekrönt werden to become a king.

zum Teil partly.

zum "Weisses Rössl!" at the "White Horse" (inn).

2. adv. too (more than enough), toward.

zu viel too much.

3. before infinitive to.

Si wussten nicht was zu tun. They did not know what to do.

4. Separable prefix (implies direction toward the speaker, increase, continuation, closing, confession).

Sie liefen dem Walde zu. They ran toward the forest.

Der Verbrecher gab es zu. The criminal confessed.

Ich darf nicht mehr zunehmen. I must not gain more weight.

Mach die Tür zu! Close the door!

Nur zu! Come on!

Zubehör m. & n. accessories, trimmings, belongings.

zubereiten to prepare, cook, mix.

Zubereitung f. preparation.

Zucht f. breeding, training, education; breed, race, stock.

züchten to breed, grow, cultivate, train.

züchtig chaste, modest.

züchtigen to punish, correct, chastise.

zucken to flash.

mit den Achseln zucken to shrug one's shoulders.

ZUCKER m. sugar.

Zuckerguss m. icing.

zuckerhaltig containing sugar.

zuckerkrank diabetic.

zuckern to sugar, sweeten.

Zuckerwerk n. confectionery, sweets.

zudem besides, moreover.

zudrücken to shut, close.

ein Auge zudrücken to be indulgent.

zuerst at first, in the first place.

Zufahrt f. Drive.

Zufall m. chance, accident, occurrence.

durch Zufall by accident.

zufällig casual, by accident, by chance.

zufällig tun to happen to do.

zufälligerweise by chance.

Zuflucht f. refuge, shelter.

seine Zuflucht nehmen zu to take refuge with.

ZUFRIEDEN satisfied, content.

sich zufrieden geben to rest content with.

zufrieden lassen to let alone, leave in peace.

Zufriedenheit f. contentment, satisfaction.

zufriedenstellen to content, satisfy.

zufriedenstellend satisfactory.

ZUG m. train; drawing, draft; procession, march, impulse; feature, characteristic.

Er liegt in den letzten Zügen. He is breathing his last.

Zug um Zug without delay, uninterruptedly.

Wann kommt der Schnellzug aus Berlin an? When does the express train from Berlin arrive?

Zugabe f. extra, addition, encore.
Zugang m. entrance, door, access.
zugänglich accessible, open to.
zugeben to add, allow, permit.
Zügel m. bridle, rein.
zügellos unbridled, unrestrained.
Zugeständnis n. concession, admission.
Zugluft f. draught, current of air.
zugunsten in favor of, for the benefit of.
zugute (halten) to allow for, take into consideration, give credit for.
　　zugute kommen to come in handy, be an advantage to.
Zuhilfenahme f. (unter Zuhilfenahme von) with the help of.
zuhören to listen to.
Zuhörer m. hearer, listener.
Zuhörerschaft f. audience.
ZUKUNFT f. future.
zukünftig future.
zulächeln to smile at.
Zulage f. addition, raise.
zulangen to hand, give.
zulässig admissible, permissible.
Zulassung f. admission, permission.
ZULETZT finally, ultimately.
　　zuletzt kommen to arrive last.
zuliebe (tun) to do for someone's sake.
　　einem zuliebe tun to please someone.
zumachen to close, shut, fasten; to hurry.
zumal especially, particularly.
zumindest at least.
zumuten to expect of.
　　sich zu viel zumuten to attempt too much.
Zumutung f. unreasonable demand, imputation.
zunächst first, first of all, above all.
zünden to catch fire, inflame, arouse enthusiasm.
zunehmen to grow, increase, get fuller.
zuneigen to lean forward, incline.
Zuneigung f. liking, affection, sympathy, inclination.
ZUNGE f. tongue.
　　Das Wort liegt mir auf der Zunge. I have the word on the tip of my tongue.
　　eine belegte Zunge a fuzzy tongue.
　　eine feine Zunge haben to be a gourmet.
zurechnungsfähig responsible, of sound mind.
Zurechnungsfähigkeit f. responsibility.
zurecht right, in order, in time.
zurechtfinden to find one's way about.
zurechtsetzen (einem den Kopf zurechtsetzen) to bring one to reason.
Zurechtweisung f. reprimand, reproach.
ZURÜCK 1. adv. back, backwards, late, behind.
　　2. separable prefix (implies the idea of a return motion; back).
　　Wir kamen erst um elf Uhr zurück. We only came back at eleven.
zurückbeben to start back, recoil.
zurückbehalten to keep back, retain.
zurückbekommen to get back, recover.
zurückbleiben to stay behind.
zurückbringen to bring back.
zurückfahren to drive back, return.
zurückfordern to reclaim.
zurückgehen to go back, return, retreat, decrease, decline.
zurückgezogen retired, secluded, lonely.
Zurückgezogenheit f. retirement.
zurückhalten to hold back, delay, detain.
zurückhaltend reserved.
zurückkehren to return, go back, come back.
zurücklassen to leave behind.
zurücknehmen to take back, withdraw.
zurücksetzen to put back, replace, reduce, neglect.
Zurücksetzung f. neglect.
zurückstellen to put back, replace, reserve, put aside.

zurücktreten to step back, withdraw, resign.
zurückversetzen to put back, restore.
　　sich in eine Zeit zurückversetzen to go back (in imagination) to a time.
zurückweisen to send away, send back, repulse.
zurückzahlen to pay back, repay.
Zurückzahlung f. repayment.
zurückziehen to draw back, take back.
Zuruf m. acclamation, shout, call.
zurufen to call to, shout to.
Zusage f. acceptance, promise.
ZUSAGEN to promise, please, appeal.
　　einem etwas auf den Kopf zusagen to tell a person plainly.
ZUSAMMEN together, altogether.
zusammenfassen to sum up, summarize.
zusammenfassend comprehensive.
zusammengehören to belong together, match, be correlated.
Zusammenhalt m. holding together.
Zusammenhang m. connection.
zusammenhangslos disconnected.
Zusammenkunft f. meeting, reunion, assembly.
Zusammenspiel n. playing together, teamwork.
Zusammenstoss m. collision, clash.
zusammenstossen to smash, collide.
zusammentreffen to meet each other, coincide.
zusammenzählen to count up, add up.
zusätzlich additional.
ZUSCHAUER m. spectator.
Zuschauerraum m. theater auditorium.
Zuschlag m. addition, increase in price.
zuschlagpflichtig liable to additional payment.
zuschliessen to lock, lock up.
Zuschrift f. letter, communication.
zuschulden adv.
　　sich etwas zuschulden kommen lassen to be guilty of doing something.
zusehen to look on, watch for, wait.
zusehends visibly, noticeably.
zusichern to assure of, promise.
Zusicherung f. insurance.
zuspitzen to point, sharpen.
zusprechen to encourage.
　　Trost zusprechen to comfort, console.
Zuspruch m. consolation, encouragement.
ZUSTAND m. state, condition, position, situation.
　　zustande bringen to do, get done.
zuständig belonging to, responsible, authorized, competent.
Zuständigkeit f. competence.
zustimmen to consent, agree.
Zustimmung f. consent.
Zustrom m. influx, crowd, multitude.
zutrauen to believe (one) capable of.
zutraulich confiding, trusting.
zutreffend correct.
ZUTRITT m. admission, entrance.
　　Zutritt verboten! No admittance!
zuverlässig reliable, trustworthy.
Zuversicht f. confidence, trust.
zuversichtlich confident.
ZUVIEL too much.
zuvor before, previously, formerly.
zuvorkommen to come first.
zuvorkommend obliging.
Zuvorkommenheit f. politeness, kindness.
ZUWEILEN sometimes, now and then, occasionally.
zuwider offensive, repugnant.
zuwider (sein) to be repugnant.
　　Das ist mir zuwider. I hate it.
zuzahlen to pay extra.
zuziehen to draw together, call, invite, consult.
zuzüglich including, plus.
Zwang m. compulsion, constraint, pressure.
　　sich Zwang antun to restrain oneself.
　　sich keinen Zwang antun to be quite free and easy.

zwanglos free and easy.
Zwanglosigkeit f. freedom, ease.
Zwangslage f. condition of constraint.
　　sich in einer Zwangslage befinden to be under compulsion.
zwangsläufig necessarily, inevitably.
ZWANZIG twenty.
Zwanziger m. figure 20, a 20-year old.
　　in den Zwanzigern sein to be in one's twenties.
ZWANZIGSTE twentieth.
ZWAR indeed, although.
　　und zwar in fact, namely.
ZWECK m. purpose, design, aim, object, end, goal.
　　keinen Zweck haben to be of no use.
　　Zu welchem Zweck? Why? What for?
zwecklos useless.
Zwecklosigkeit f. uselessness, aimlessness.
zweckmässig expedient.
ZWEI two.
　　zu zweien by pairs, two by two.
zweideutig ambiguous.
zweierlei of two kinds, different.
zweifach twofold, double.
ZWEIFEL m. doubt, suspicion.
zweifelhaft doubtful.
zweifellos doubtless, indubitable.
zweifeln to doubt, question, suspect.
Zweifelsfall m. im Zweifelsfall in case of a doubt.
zweifelsohne without doubt, doubtless.
Zweig m. branch.
Zweigstelle f. branch office.
Zweikampf m. duel.
zweimal twice.
zweireihig double-breasted.
zweischneidig two-edged, ambiguous.
Zweisitzer m. two-seater.
ZWEITE second, next.
　　zu zweit two by two.
zweitens secondly, in the second place.
Zwerg m. dwarf.
Zwieback m. rusk, biscuit.
Zwiebel f. onion, bulb (plant).
Zwielicht n. twilight, dusk.
Zwietracht f. discord.
Zwilling m. twin.
zwingen to compel, force, get through, finish.
zwingend forcible.
zwinkern to blink.
Zwirn m. thread, sewing-cotton.
ZWISCHEN prep. (dat. when answering question, Wo?; acc. when answering question, Wohin?, and depending on the idiom). among, between.
　　Zwischen den Städten Duisburg und Köln liegt Düsseldorf. Between the cities of Duisburg and Cologne lies Düsseldorf.
　　zwischen drei und vier between three and four.
Zwischenbemerkung f. digression.
Zwischendeck n. lower deck.
zwischendurch through, in the midst of.
Zwischenfall m. incident, episode.
Zwischenlandung f. intermediate landing or stop (flight).
Zwischenpause f. interval, break.
Zwischenraum m. space, gap, interval.
Zwischenzeit f. interval.
　　in der Zwischenzeit in the meantime.
zwitschern to twitter.
ZWÖLF twelve.
ZWÖLFTE twelfth.
Zyklus m. cycle, course, series.
Zylinder m. cylinder.
Zyniker m. cynic.
zynisch cynical.
Zynismus m. cynicism.

GLOSSARY OF PROPER NAMES.

Albrecht Albert.
Alfred Alfred.
Andreas Andrew.
Anne Ann.
Anton Anthony.
August August.
Barbara Barbara.
Bernhard Bernard.
Bertha Bertha.
Eduard Edward.
Elisabeth (Else) Elizabeth.
Emilie Emily.
Emma Emma.
Erich Eric.
Ernst Ernest.
Eugen Eugene.
Franz Frank.
Franziska Frances.
Friedrich Frederick.

Fritz Fred.
Genoveva. Genevieve.
Georg George.
Gertrud (Trudchen) Gertrude.
Gretchen Margaret.
Gustav Gustave.
Heinrich Henry.
Helene Helen.
Ilse Elsie.
Jakob James.
Johann John.
Johanna Jane, Joan.
Josef Joseph.
Karl Charles.
Katharina (Kätchen) (Käthe) Katherine (Kate).
Klaus Nicholas.
Lotte Charlotte.
Ludwig Lewis.
Luise Louise.

Maria Mary.
Martha Martha.
Michael Michael.
Minna Wilhelmina.
Moritz Maurice.
Otto Otto.
Paul Paul.
Paula Paula.
Peter Peter.
Richard Richard.
Robert Robert.
Rosa Rose.
Rüdiger Roger.
Rudolph Ralph.
Susanne Susan.
Theodor Theodore.
Therese Theresa.
Thomas Thomas.
Wilhelm William.

GLOSSARY OF GEOGRAPHICAL NAMES

Aachen n. Aix-la-Chapelle.
Afrika n. Africa.
Ägypten n. Egypt.
Alpen pl. Alps.
Amerika n. America.
    die Vereinigten Staaten pl. the United States.
    Nord Amerika n. North America.
    Süd Amerika n. South America.
    Mittel-Amerika n. Central America
Antwerpen n. Antwerp.
Asien n. Asia.
Atlantik m. (der Atlantische Ozean) Atlantic (the
    Atlantic Ocean).
Australien n. Australia.
Belgien n. Belgium.
Berlin n. Berlin.
Bonn n. Bonn.
Brasilien n. Brazil.
Brüssel n. Brussels.
Dänemark n. Denmark.
Deutschland n. Germany.
Europa n. Europe.
Frankfurt n. Frankfort.
Frankreich n. France.
Griechenland n. Greece.
Haag (der) The Hague.
Hamburg n. Hamburg.
Holland n. Holland.
Indien n. India.
Irland n. Ireland.

Italien n. Italy.
Japan n. Japan.
Jugoslavien n. Yugoslavia.
Kanada n. Canada.
London n. London.
Mexico n. Mexico.
Moskau n. Moscow.
München n. Munich.
Norwegen n. Norway.
Nürnberg n. Nuremberg.
Österreich n. Austria.
Polen n. Poland.
Portugal n. Portugal.
Preussen n. Prussia.
Rhein m. Rhine.
Rheinland n. Rhineland.
Rumänien n. Rumania.
Russland n. Russia.
Saar f. Saar.
Sachsen n. Saxony.
Schlesien n. Silesia.
Schottland n. Scotland.
Schweden n. Sweden.
Schweiz f. Switzerland.
Stille Ozean (der) Pacific Ocean.
Tschechoslovakei f. Czechoslovakia.
Türkei f. Turkey.
Ungarn n. Hungary.
Wien n. Vienna.

English-German DICTIONARY

A

a (an) ein, eine.
abandon (to) verlassen.
abbreviate (to) abkürzen.
abbreviation abkürzung, /.
ability Fähigkeit, /.
able fähig.
able (to be) können.
abolish (to) abschaffen.
about ungefähr; um (acc.) (around).
above über.
abroad im Ausl.. d.
absence Abwesenheit, /.
absent abwesend.
absolute unbedingt.
absorb (to) aufsaugen
abstain (to) sich enthalten.
abstract abstrakt.
absurd unvernünftig.
abundant reichlich.
abuse Missbrauch, m.
academy Akademie, /.
accent Akzent, m.
accent (to) betonen.
accept (to) annehmen.
acceptance Annahme, /.
accident Unfall, m.; Zufall, m. (chance).
accidental zufällig.
accidentally nebenbei.
accommodate (to) unterbringen.
accommodation Unterkunft, /.
accompany (to) begleiten.
accomplish (to) vollführen.
accord Übereinstimmung, /.
according to zu (dat.); zufolge dem.
account Rechnung, /.; Konto, n. (balance).
    on no account auf keinen Fall.
    to pay the account die Rechnung bezahlen.
accuracy Genauigkeit, /.
accurate genau, richtig, akkurat.
accuse (to) anklagen, beschuldigen.
accustom (to) gewöhnen.
ace Ass, n.
ache Schmerz, m.
ache (to) schmerzen.
achieve (to) vollbringen.
achievement Vollbringung, /.; Leistung (result).
acid sauer
acknowledge (to) anerkennen.
acknowledgment Anerkennung, /.
acquaintance Bekannte, m. & /.
acquire (to) erwerben.
across gegenüber.
act Handlung, /.; Akt, m. (of a play); Gesetz, n. (law).
active tätig.
activity Tätigkeit, /.
actor Schauspieler, m.
actress Schauspielerin, /.
actual wirklich.
acute akut.
adapt (to) anpassen.
add (to) zufügen.
addition Zusatz, m.; Addition, /. (math.).
    in addition to Zusätlich zu (dat.).
address Adresse, /.; Anschrift, /.; Ansprache, /.; Anrede, /. (speech).
address (to) adressieren; anreden, ansprechen, sich wenden an (speech).
adequate angemessen.
adjective Eigenschaftswort, n.
adjoining angrenzend.
administer (to) verwalten.
admiral Admiral, m.
admiration Bewunderung, /.
admire (to) bewundern.
admission Eintritt, m.
admit (to) einlassen; zugeben (concede).

admittance Zutritt, m.
    no admittance Zutritt verboten.
adopt (to) adoptieren (child); annehmen (idea).
adult Erwachsene(r) noun, m. & /.; erwachsen (adj.).
advance (to) vorangehen (lead); steigen (price).
    in advance im Voraus.
advantage Vorteil, m.
adventure Abenteuer, n.
adverb Adverb, n.
advertise (to) anzeigen; Reklame machen.
advertisement Anzeige, /.; Reklame, /.
advice Rat, m.
advise (to) raten.
affair Geschäft, n. (business); Sache, /. (thing).
affect (to) betreffen.
affected geziert, affektiert (pretentious); gerührt (moved).
affection Zuneigung, /.
affectionate herzlich, zärtlich, liebevoll.
affirm (to) bestätigen, bekräftigen.
affirmation Bestätigung, /.; Bekräftigung, /.
afloat schwimmend.
afraid ängstlich.
after nach (dat.).
afternoon Nachmittag, m.
afterward nachher.
again wieder.
against gegen (acc.); wider (acc.).
age Alter, n. (also old age); Epoche, /. (history).
agency Vertretung, /.
agent Agent, m.
aggravate (to) verschlimmern; ärgern (annoy).
ago vor (dat.).
    three days ago vor drei Tagen.
agree (to) übereinstimmen.
agreeable angenehm.
agreed abgemacht.
agreement Übereinstimmung, /.; Vertrag, m. (contract).
agricultural landwirtschaftlich.
agriculture Landwirtschaft, /.
ahead voran, voraus.
aid Hilfe, /.
    first aid Erste Hilfe.
aid (to) helfen.
aim Ziel, n.; Zweck, m.
aim (to) erreichen; zielen (shooting).
air Luft, /.
air force Luftwaffe, /.
air mail Luftpost, /.
airfield Flugplatz, m.
airplane Flugzeug, n.
airport Flughafen, m.
aisle Seitenschiff, n.
alarm Alarm, m.
alarm clock Wecker, m.
alcohol Alkohol, m.
alike gleich, ähnlich.
all ganz, alles.
    all right in Ordnung, bestimmt.
    not at all keineswegs.
alliance Verbindung /.; Allianz, /. (pact).
allow (to) erlauben, gestatten.
allowed gestattet.
ally Verbündete, m.
almost fast, beinahe.
alone allein.
along entlang.
already schon, bereits.
also auch.
altar Altar, m.
alter (to) ändern, verwandeln.
alternate abwechselnd.
alternate (to) abwechseln.
although obwohl, obgleich.
altitude Höhe, /.
altogether zusammen; gänzlich (wholly).
always immer

amaze (to) erstaunen.
amazement Verwunderung, /.
ambassador Botschafter, m.
ambassadress Botschafterin, /.
ambitious ehrgeizig.
amend (to) berichtigen.
American Amerikaner (noun, m.); amerikanisch (adj.).
among mitten; unter (dat. or acc.).
amount Betrag, m.
ample geräumig.
amuse (to) amüsieren.
amusement Unterhaltung, /.
amusing amüsant.
analyze (to) analysieren.
ancestors Vorfahren, pl.
anchor Anker, m.
ancient alt.
and und.
anecdote Anekdote, /.
angel Engel, m.
anger Ärger, m.
angry ärgerlich, bös.
animal Tier, n.
animate (to) beleben.
annex Nebengebäude, n.
annihilate (to) vernichten.
anniversary Hochzeitstag, m.
announce (to) ansagen.
announcement Anzeige, /.
annoy (to) ärgern.
annual jährlich.
annul (to) annullieren; ungültig machen.
anonymous anonym.
another ein anderer.
answer Antwort, /.
answer (to) antworten.
anterior vorhergehend.
anticipate (to) vorhersehen (foresee); erwarten (expect).
antique altertümlich, antik.
anxiety Unruhe, /.
anxious unruhig.
any etwas (some); irgend ein (whatever).
anybody irgendjemand.
anyhow sowieso.
    anyway irgendwie.
anything irgendetwas.
anywhere irgendwo.
apart abseits.
apartment Wohnung, /.
apiece jeder; jedes Stück.
apologize (to) sich entschuldigen.
apparent scheinbar.
appeal (to) gefallen.
appear (to) erscheinen.
appearance Erscheinung, /.
appease (to) besänftigen.
appendix Anhang, m.
appetite Appetit, m.
applaud (to) applaudieren; klatschen.
applause Applaus, m.
apple Apfel, m.
application Antrag, m. (request); Gewissenhaftigkeit, /.(diligence).
apply(to) sich bewerben (for a job); auftragen (use).
appoint (to) ernennen.
appointment Verabredung, /.
appreciate (to) schätzen.
appreciation Anerkennung, /.
appropriate angemessen.
approve (to) genehmigen.
April April, m.
apron Schürze, /.
arbitrary eigenwillig.
arcade Arkade, /.
architect Architekt, m.; Baumeister, m.
architecture Architektur, /.
ardent feurig, glühend.

area Gebiet, n.
argue (to) verhandeln, diskutieren.
argument Wortwechsel, m.
arise (to) aufsteigen; aufstehen (get up).
arm Arm, m.
    firearms Waffen, pl.
arm (to) bewaffnen.
army Heer, n.; Armee, f.
around herum, um (acc.).
arouse (to) erregen (revolt); erwecken (suspicion);
    aufwecken (wake up).
arrange (to) ordnen.
arrangement Ordnung, f.(order); Anordnung, f.
    (preparation).
arrest Verhaftung, f.
arrest (to) verhaften.
arrival Ankunft, f.
arrive (to) ankommen.
art Kunst, f.
article Artikel, m.
artificial künstlich.
artist Künstler, m.
artistic künstlerisch.
as als (when); so (as much); da (because).
    as . . . . as   so . . . . wie.
    as long as   so lange wie.
    as soon as   sobald.
    as to   mit Bezug auf (business);
                  was...anbetrifft.
    as well   sowohl, auch.
    as yet   bis jetzt.
ascertain (to) feststellen.
ash Asche, f.
ashamed beschämt; verschämt (shy).
aside beiseite, abseits.
ask (to) fragen.
asleep schlafend.
aspire (to) sich sehnen.
aspirin Aspirin, f.
assault Angriff, m.
assemble (to) versammeln.
assembly Versammlung, f. (congress);
    Gesellschaft, f.
assign (to) zuteilen.
assist (to) beistehen.
assistant Gehilfe, m.
associate (to) vereinigen.
assume (to) annehmen.
assurance Versicherung, f.
assure (to) versichern.
astonish (to) erstaunen.
astound (to) verblüffen.
asylum Asyl, n.
at an, in (dat. or acc.); bei, zu (dat.).
    at home zu Hause.
    at first zuerst.
    at last endlich.
    at once sofort.
    at times zuweilen.
athlete Athlet, m.
athletics Gymnastik, f.
atmosphere Atmosphäre, f.
attach (to) anhängen.
attain (to) erreichen.
attempt (to) versuchen.
attend (to) beiwohnen.
attendant Gehilfe, m.
attention Aufmerksamkeit, f.
attic Dachkammer, f.
attitude Haltung, f.; Einstellung, f. (mental).
attorney Anwalt, m.
attract (to) anziehen.
attraction Anziehung, f.
attractive schön, anziehend.
audience Zuhörer, pl.
August August, m.
aunt Tante, f.
author Autor, m.

authority Autorität, f.
authorize (to) ermächtigen.
automatic automatisch.
automobile Auto, n.
autumn Herbst, m.
available verügbar.
average Durchschnitt, m.
avoid (to) vermeiden.
awake wach.
awake (to) wecken; erwachen (oneself).
award Belohnung, f.
award (to) zuerkennen.
aware gewahr.
away fort, weg.
    to go away weggehen.
awful furchtbar.
awkward ungeschickt.

B

baby Kind, n.
back Rücken (noun, m.) (body); zurück (adv.).
background Hintergrund, m.
backwards rückwärts.
bacon Speck, m.
bad schlecht.
badge Marke, f.
bag Beutel, m.
baggage Gepäck, n.
baker Bäcker, m.
bakery Bäckerei, f.
balance Gleichgewicht, n.
balcony Balkon, m.
ball Ball, m.
balloon Ballon, m.
banana Banane, f.
band Band, n.; Musikkapelle, f.
bandage Verband, m.
banister Treppengeländer, n.
bank Bank, f.
bank note Banknote, f.
bankruptcy Bankrott, m.
banquet Bankett, n.
bar Barre, f. (metal); Bar, f. (for drinks).
barber Frisör, m.
bare bloss, bar.
barefoot barfuss.
barge Barke, f. Lastschiff, n.
barn Scheune, f.
barrel Fass, n.
barren unfruchtbar.
basin Becken, n.
basis Grundlage, f.
basket Korb, m.
bath Bad, n.
bathroom Badezimmer, n.
bathe (to) baden.
battle Schlacht, f.
bay Bucht, f.
be (to) sein.
    to be hungry hungrig sein.
    to be right   Recht haben.
    to be thirsty Durst haben.
    to be tired   müde sein.
    to be wrong Unrecht haben.
beach Strand, m.
bean Bohne, f.
bear (to) aushalten.
beard Bart, m.
beat (to) schlagen.
beautiful schön, wunderschön.
beauty Schönheit, f.
beauty parlor Schönheitssalon, m.
because weil.
become (to) werden.
becoming passend, vorteilhaft.
bed Bett, n.

beef Rindfleisch, n.
beer Bier, n.
beet Rübe, f.
before vor (dat. or acc.); bevor (conj.).
beg (to) betteln.
beggar Bettler, m.
begin (to) beginnen, anfangen.
beginning Anfang, m.
behave (to) sich betragen, sich benehmen.
behavior Verhalten, n.
behind hinter (dat. or acc.).
belief Glaube, m.
believe (to) glauben.
bell Glocke, f.
belong (to) gehören.
below unter (dat. or acc.).
belt Gürtel, m.
bench Bank, f.
bend (to) biegen.
beneath unten; unter (dat. or acc.).
benefit Vorteil, m.
beside neben (dat. or acc.).
besides ausserdem.
best beste (der, die, das) (adj.); am besten (adv.).
bet Wette, f.
bet (to) wetten.
betray (to) verraten.
better besser.
between zwischen (dat. or acc.).
beware (to) sich hüten.
    Beware! Achtung!
beyond jenseits (gen.).
bicycle Fahrrad, n.
bid (to) bieten; befehlen (order).
big gross.
bill Rechnung, f.
    bill of fare Speisekarte, f.
billion Billion, f.
bind (to) binden.
bird Vogel, m.
birth Geburt, f.
birthday Geburtstag, m.
biscuit Zwieback, m.
bishop Bischof, m.
bit Stück, n.; Gebiss, n. (horse).
bite Biss, m.
bite (to) beissen.
bitter bitter.
bitterness Bitterkeit, f.
black schwarz.
blade Klinge, f. (razor); Blatt, n. (grass).
blame Schuld, f.; Tadel, m.
blame (to) tadeln.
blank unbeschrieben (page); verwundert (expression).
blanket Decke, f.
bleed (to) bluten.
bless (to) segnen.
blessing Segnung, f.; Segen, m.
blind blind.
block Block, m.
block (to) versperren.
blood Blut, n.
blotter Loschpapier, n.
blouse Bluse, f.
blow Schlag, m.
blow (to) blasen; putzen (nose).
blue blau.
blush (to) erröten.
board Brett, n. (plank); Verpflegung, f. (food).
boarding house Pension, f.
boast (to) prahlen.
boat Boot, n.
body Körper, m.
boil (to) kochen, sieden.
boiler Kessel, m.
bold kühn.
bomb Bombe, f.
    atom bomb. Atombombe, f.

bond Aktie, *f.* (stock).
bone Knochen, *m.*
book Buch, *n.*
bookseller Buchhändler, *m.*
bookstore Buchhandlung, *f.*
border Grenze, *f.*
boring langweilig.
born geboren.
borrow (to) borgen, leihen,
both beide.
bother (to) ärgern, plagen, bemühen.
   Don't bother! Bemühen Sie sich nicht!
bottle Flasche, *f.*
bottle opener Flaschenöffner, *m.*
bottom Boden, *m.*
bounce (to) aufspringen.
bowl Schale, *f.*
box Schachtel, *f.*
boy Junge, *m.;* Knabe, *m.*
bracelet Armband, *n.*
braid Borte, *f.;* Zopf, *m.* (hair).
brain Gehirn, *n.*
brake Bremse, *f.*
branch Ast, *m.* (tree); Filiale, *f.* (business).
brave tapfer.
brassiere Büstenhalter, *m.*
bread Brot, *n.*
break (to) brechen; lösen (engagement).
breakfast Frühstück, *n.*
   have breakfast frühstücken.
breath Atem, *m.*
breathe (to) atmen.
breeze Wind, *m.;* Brise, *f.*
bribe (to) bestechen.
brick Backstein, *m.*
bride Braut, *f.*
   bridegroom Bräutigam, *m.*
bridge Brücke, *f.*
brief kurz.
bright hell, klar.
brighten (to) erheitern; sich aufklären (weather).
brilliant glänzend.
bring (to) bringen.
bring up (to) erziehen.
British britisch.
broad weit, breit.
broil (to) braten.
broken zerbrochen.
brook Bach, *m.*
broom Besen, *m.*
brother Bruder, *m.*
brother-in-law Schwager, *m.*
brown braun.
bruise (to) quetschen.
brush Bürste, *f.*
bubble Blase, *f.*
buckle Schnalle, *f.*
bud Knospe, *f.*
budget Budget, *n.*
build (to) bauen.
building Gebäude, *n.*
bulletin Bulletin, *n.*
bundle Bündel, *n.*
burn (to) brennen.
burst (to) bersten.
bus Autobus, *m.* Omnibus, *m.*
bush Busch, *m.*
business Geschäft, *n.*
businessman Geschäftsmann, *m.*
busy beschäftigt.
but aber; sondern (neg.).
butcher Metzger, *m.*
butcher shop Metzgerei, *f.*
butter Butter, *m.*
button Knopf, *m.*
buy (to) kaufen.
buyer Käufer, *m.*
by von (dat.); durch (acc.); neben (dat. & acc.)
   (close to); um (acc.) (time).

C

cab Taxi, *n.*
cabbage Kohl, *m.;* Kraut, *m.*
cable Kabel, *n.*
cage Käfig, *m.*
cake Kuchen, *m.*
calendar Kalender, *m.*
calf Kalb, *n.*
call Ruf, *m.*
call (to) rufen; anrufen; telefonieren (telephone);
   heissen (name).
calm ruhig.
camera Kamera, *f.*
camp Lager, *n.*
camp (to) lagern.
can Büchse, *f.;* Dose, *f.*
can (to be able) können.
can opener Büchsenöffner, *m.*
cancel (to) rückgängig machen, annulieren.
candidate Kandidat, *m.*
candle Kerze, *f.*
candy Bonbons, *pl.*
cap Mütze, *f.*
capital Hauptstadt, *f.* (city); Kapital, *n.* (finance).
capricious launisch; eigensinning (temperamental).
captain Hauptmann, *m.* (army); Kapitän, *m.* (navy).
captive Gefangene, *m.*
capture (to) fangen; einnehmen.
car Wagen, *m.*
carbon paper Durchschlagpapier, *n.*
card Karte, *f.*
care Sorge, *f.* (anxiety); Sorgfalt, *f.* (caution).
   care of   bei
   take care of pflegen
care (to) sich sorgen.
   care about sich kümmern.
   care for (to like) gern haben.
   I don't care. Das ist mir gleich.
career Laufbahn, *f.*
careful vorsichtig, sorgfältig.
careless nachlässig, sorglos.
caress Liebkosung, *f.*
carpenter Zimmermann, *m.*
carpet Teppich, *m.*
carry (to) tragen.
carve (to) schnitzen.
case Fall, *m.;* Aktentasche, *f.* (container).
   in case im Falle.
cash Bargeld, *n.*
   to pay cash bar zahlen.
cash (to) einlösen, kassieren.
cashier Kassierer, *m.*
castle Schloss, *n.*
cat Katze, *f.*
catch (to) fangen.
category Kategorie, *f.*
cathedral Dom, *m.*
Catholic katholisch.
cattle Vieh, *n.*
cause Grund, *m.;* Ursache, *f.*
cause (to) verursachen.
cavalry Reiterei, *f.*
cease (to) aufhören.
ceiling Decke, *f.*
celebrate (to) feiern.
cellar Keller, *m.*
cement Zement, *m.*
cemetery Kirchhof, *m.;* Friedhof, *m.*
center Zentrum, *n.*
central zentral.
central heating Zentralheizung, *f.*
century Jahrhundert, *n.*
cereal Getreide, *n.* (grain); Mehlspeise, *f.* (prepared).
ceremony Zeremonie, *f.*
certain gewiss.
certainty Gewissheit, *f.;* Sicherheit, *f.*
certificate Zeugnis, *n.*
chain Kette, *f.*

chair Stuhl, *m.*
chairman Vorsitzende, *m.;* Präsident, *m.*
chalk Kreide, *f.*
challenge Herausforderung, *f.*
challenge (to) herausfordern.
champion Meister, *m.*
   world champion Weltmeister, *m.*
chance Zufall, *m.*
change Veränderung, *f.;* Kleingeld, *n.* (money).
change (to) ändern; wechseln (money).
chapel Kapelle, *f.*
chapter Kapitel, *n.*
character Charakter, *m.*
characteristic charakteristisch.
charge (to) beladen; berechnen (price).
charitable wohltätig.
charity Wohltätigkeit, *f.*
charming reizend.
chase (to) jagen.
chat (to) plaudern.
cheap billig.
cheat (to) betrügen.
check Scheck, *m.;* Rechnung, *f.* (in a restaurant).
check (to) kontrollieren; aufgeben (baggage).
cheek Wange, *f.*
cheer (to) aufheitern.
cheerful heiter, freudig, fröhlich.
cheese Käse, *m.*
chemical chemisch.
cherish (to) schätzen.
cherry Kirsche, *f.*
chest Brust, *f.;* Kiste, *f.* (box).
   chest of drawers Kommode, *f.*
chestnut Kastanie, *f.*
chew (to) kauen.
chicken Huhn, *n.;* Hühnchen, *n.*
chief Leiter, *m.*
chief (adj.) haupt–.
chime Glockenspiel, *n.*
chimney Schornstein, *m.*
chin Kinn, *n.*
china Porzellan, *n.*
chip Span, *m.;* Splitter, *m.*
chocolate Schokolade, *f.*
choice Wahl, *f.*
choir Chor, *m.*
choke (to) ersticken.
choose (to) auswählen.
chop Kotelett, *n.*
Christmas Christ (noun, *m.*); christlich (adj.).
Christmas Weihnachten, *f.*
church Kirche, *f.*
cigar Zigarre, *f.*
cigarette Zigarette, *f.*
circle Kreis, *m.*
circular rund.
circulate (to) kreisen.
circumstances Umstände, *pl.*
citizen Bürger, *m.*
city Stadt, *f.*
city hall Rathaus, *n.*
civil zivil.
civilization Zivilisation, *f.*
civilize (to) zivilisieren.
claim Forderung, *f.*
claim (to) fordern.
clamor Geschrei, *n.*
clap (to) klatschen.
class Klasse, *f.*
classify (to) klassifizieren.
clause Klausel, *f.*
clean rein, sauber.
clean (to) reinigen.
cleaners Reinigungsanstalt, *f.*
cleanliness Reinlichkeit, *f.*
clear klar.
clerk Angestellte, *m.*
clever klug, schlau.
climate Klima, *n.*

climb (to) klimmen, steigen (stairway); besteigen (mountain).
clip Klammer, *f.*
clip (to) beschneiden (cut); zusammenfügen (attach).
clock Uhr, *f.*
close nahe.
close (to) zumachen, schliessen.
closed geschlossen.
closet Schrank, *m.*
cloth Tuch, *n.*
clothes Kleider, *pl.*
cloud Wolke, *f.*
cloudy bewölkt.
clover Klee, *m.*
club Klub, *m.;* Keule, *f.* (cards).
coal Kohle, *f.*
coarse roh.
coast Küste, *f.*
coat Mantel, *m.* (overcoat); Anzug, *m.* (suit).
code Gesetzbuch, *n.* (law); Code, *m.*
coffee Kaffee, *m.*
coffin Sarg, *m.*
coin Münze, *f.*
cold kalt.
coldness Kälte, *f.*
collaborate (to) zusammenarbeiten.
collar Kragen, *m.;* Halsband, *n.* (dog).
collect (to) sammeln.
collection Sammlung, *f.*
collective gesamt.
college Universität, *f.*
colonial kolonial.
colony Kolonie, *f.*
color Farbe, *f.*
color (to) färben.
column Spalte, *f.;* Kolonne, *f.* (military); Säule, *f.* (arch).
comb Kamm, *m.*
comb (to) kämmen.
combination Verbindung, *f.*
combine (to) verbinden.
come (to) kommen.
    come back zurückkommen.
comedy Komödie, *f.*
comet Komet, *m.*
comfort Behaglichkeit, *f.;* Trost, *m.* (moral).
comfort (to) trösten.
comfortable bequem.
comma Komma, *n.*
command Befehl, *m.*
command (to) befehlen.
commander Befehlshaber, *m.*
commercial geschäftsmässig.
commission Kommission, *f.;* Offizierspatent, *m.*
commit (to) begehen.
common gemein, gewöhnlich.
communicate (to) mitteilen.
communication Mitteilung, *f.*
community Gemeinde, *f.*
companion Genosse, *m.*
company Gesellschaft, *f.* (social); Kompanie, *f.* (military).
compare (to) vergleichen.
comparison Vergleich, *m.*
compete (to) konkurrieren.
competition Konkurrenz, *f.;* Tournier, *n.* (sports).
complain (to) sich beklagen.
complaint Klage, *f.*
complete vollenden.
complex Komplex, (noun, *m.*); verwickelt (adj.).
complexion Gesichtsfarbe, *f.*
complicate (to) verwickeln, komplizieren.
complicated verwickelt, kompliziert.
compliment Kompliment, *n.*
compose (to) komponieren.
composer Komponist, *m.*
composition Komposition, *f.*

compromise Kompromiss, *m.;* Vergleich, *m.*
compromise (to) einen Kompromiss machen, kompromittieren.
conceit Einbildung, *f.*
conceited eingebildet.
conceive (to) ersinnen.
concentrate (to) konzentrieren.
concern Angelegenheit, *f.* (matter); Sorge, *f.* (anxiety); Geschäft, *n.* (business).
concern (to) betreffen.
concert Konzert, *n.*
concrete konkret.
condemn (to) verurteilen, verdammen.
condense (to) kondensieren.
condition Zustand, *m.*
conduct Benehmen, *n.*
conduct (to) führen; dirigieren (music).
conductor Führer, *m.* (guide); Schaffner, *m.* (vehicle); Dirigent, *m.* (music).
confess (to) gestehen; beichten (church).
confession Geständnis, *n.;* Beichte, *f.* (church).
confidence Vertrauen, *n.*
confident vertrauend, vertrauensvoll.
confidential vertraulich.
confirm (to) bestätigen.
confirmation Bestätigung, *f.*
congratulate (to) gratulieren.
congratulations Glückwunsch, *m.*
connect (to) verbinden.
connection Verbindung, *f.*
conquer (to) erobern, besiegen.
conquest Eroberung, *f.;* Sieg, *m.*
conscience Gewissen, *n.*
conscientious gewissenhaft.
conscious bewusst.
consent Einwilligung, *f.*
conservative konservativ.
consider (to) betrachten (look); bedenken (think).
considerable beträchtlich.
consideration Betrachtung, *f.*
consist of (to) bestehen (aus – dat.).
consistent übereinstimmend.
constant beständig.
constitution Verfassung, *f.;* Gesundheit, *f.* (health).
constitutional verfassungsmässig.
consul Konsul, *m.*
contagious ansteckend.
contain (to) enthalten.
container Behälter, *m.*
contemporary Zeitgenosse, (noun, *m.*); zeitgenössisch (adj.).
content zufrieden.
content (to) befriedigen.
contents Inhalt, *m.;* Gehalt, *m.*
continent Kontinent, *m.*
continual fortwährend.
continue (to) fortfahren.
contract Vertrag, *m.*
contractor Unternehmer, *m.*
contradict (to) widersprechen.
contradiction Widerspruch, *m.*
contradictory widersprechend.
contrary Gegenteil (noun, *n.*); entgegengesetzt (adj.). on the contrary im Gegenteil.
contrast Gegensatz, *m.*
contrast (to) abstechen.
contribute (to) beitragen.
contribution Beitrag, *m.*
control Kontrolle, *f.*
control (to) kontrollieren.
controversy Meinungsverschiedenheit, *f.*
convenience Bequemlichkeit, *f.*
convenient passend; bequem (practical).
convent Kloster, *n.*
convention Versammlung, *f.*
conversation Gespräch, *n.;* Unterhaltung, *f.*
converse (to) sich unterhalten.
convert (to) verwandeln.

convict (to) verurteilen.
conviction Verurteilung, *f.*
convince (to) überzeugen.
cook Koch, *m.;* Köchin, *f.*
cook (to) kochen.
cool kühl.
cool (to) kühlen.
copy Kopie, *f.*
cork Kork, *m.*
corkscrew Korkenzieher, *m.*
corn Mais, *m.*
corner Ecke, *f.*
corporation Körperschaft, *f.*
correct richtig.
correct (to) berichtigen, korrigieren.
correction Berichtigung, *f.*
correspond (to) korrespondieren.
correspondence Briefwechsel, *m.*
correspondent Korrespondent, *m.*
corresponding entsprechend.
corrupt (to) verderben.
corruption Verdorbenheit, *f.*
cost Kosten, *f.*
costume Kostüm, *n.*
cottage Häuschen, *n.*
cotton Baumwolle, *f.;* Watte, *f.* (pharmacy).
couch Sofa, *n.*
cough Husten, *m.*
count Graf, *m.* (nobility); Zählung, *f.*
count (to) zählen.
counter Ladentisch, *m.*
countess Gräfin, *f.*
countless zahllos.
country Land, *n.;* Vaterland, *n.* (fatherland).
countryman Landsmann, *m.*
couple Paar, *n.*
courage Mut, *m.*
course Lauf, *m.* (direction); Kursus, *m.* (studies).
court Gericht, *n.*
courteous zuvorkommend.
courtesy Höflichkeit, *f.*
courtyard Hof, *m.*
cousin Vetter, *m.;* Cousine, *f.*
cover Decke, *f.*
cow Kuh, *f.*
crack Riss, *m.*
crack (to) knacken.
cradle Wiege, *f.*
crash Zusammenbruch, *m.*
crazy verrückt.
cream Sahne, *f.*
create (to) schaffen.
creature Geschöpf, *n.;* Wesen, *n.*
credit Kredit, *m.*
creditor Gläubiger, *m.*
crime Verbrechen, *n.*
crisis Krise, *f.*
crisp knusperig.
critic Kritiker, *m.*
critical kritisch.
criticize (to) kritisieren.
crooked krumm.
crop Ernte, *f.*
cross Kreuz, *n.*
crossing Übergang, *m.*
crossroads Strassenkreuzung, *f.*
crouch (to) sich ducken.
crow Krähe, *f.*
crowd Menge, *f.*
crowd (to) überfüllen.
crowded überfüllt.
crown Krone, *f.*
crown (to) krönen.
cruel grausam.
cruelty Grausamkeit, *f.*
crumb Krume, *f.*
crumble (to) zerbröckeln.
crust Kruste, *f.*

crutch Krücke, *f.*
cry Ruf, *m.*; Geschrei, *n.*
cry (to) weinen (weep); schreien (shout).
cuff Manschette, *f.*
cunning gerissen.
cup Tasse, *f.*
cure Heilung, *f.*
curiosity Neugier, *f.*
curious neugierig.
curl Locke, *f.*
current Strom (noun, *m.*); laufend (adj.).
curtain Vorhang, *m.*
curve Kurve, *f.*
cushion Kissen, *n.*
custom Sitte, *f.*
customary gebräuchlich.
customer Kunde, *m.*
customhouse Zollamt, *m.*
customs official Zollbeamter, *m.*
cut Schnitt, *m.*
cut (to) schneiden.

D

dagger Dolch, *m.*
daily täglich.
dainty zierlich.
dairy Milchgeschäft, *n.*
dam Damm, *m.*
damage Schaden, *m.*
damage (to) beschädigen.
damp feucht.
dance Tanz, *m.*
dance (to) tanzen.
danger Gefahr, *f.*
dangerous gefährlich.
dark dunkel.
darkness Dunkelheit, *f.*
dash (to) sich beeilen.
date Datum, *n.*; Verabredung, *f.* (meeting).
daughter Tochter, *f.*
dawn Morgendämmerung, *f.*
day Tag, *m.*
    day after tomorrow übermorgen.
    day before yesterday vorgestern.
    yesterday gestern.
dazzle (to) blenden.
dead tot.
deaf taub.
deal Teil, *m.*; Geschäft, *n.* (business).
deal (to) ausgeben (cards).
dealer Händler, *m.*; Geber, *m.* (cards).
dear lieb; teuer (*also* expensive).
death Tod, *m.*
debate Debatte, *f.*
debt Schuld, *f.*
debtor Schuldner, *m.*
decanter Karaffe, *f.*
decay Verfall, *m.* (ruin); Fäulnis, *f.* (rot).
decay (to) verfallen, verfaulen.
deceased verstorben.
deceit Falschheit, *f.*
deceive (to) betrügen.
December Dezember, *m.*
decent anständig.
decide (to) entscheiden.
decided entschieden.
decision Entscheidung, *f.*; Entschluss, *m.*
decisive entscheidend.
deck Deck, *n.*
declare (to) erklären.
decline Abnahme, *f.*; Fall, *m.*
decline (to) verfallen, abweisen; deklinieren (grammar).
decrease Abnahme, *f.*; Verminderung, *f.*
decrease (to) abnehmen, vermindern.
decree Verordnung, *f.*
dedicate (to) widmen.

deed Tat, *f.*
deep tief.
deer Hirsch, *m.*
defeat Niederlage, *f.*
defeat (to) besiegen.
defect Fehler, *m.*
defend (to) verteidigen.
defense Verteidigung, *f.*
defiance Trotz, *m.*
define (to) definieren.
definite bestimmt.
defy (to) trotzen.
degree Grad, *m.*
delay Verzögerung, *f.*
delay (to) aufhalten.
delegate Delegierter, *m.*
delegate (to) delegieren.
deliberate (to) erwägen.
deliberately absichtlich.
delicacy Delikatesse, *f.*
delicate zart.
delicious köstlich.
delight Freude, *f.*
delighted erfreut.
deliver (to) liefern.
deliverance Befreiung, *f.*
delivery Ablieferung, *f.*
demand Forderung, *f.*; Nachfrage, *f.* (business).
demand (to) fordern.
democracy Demokratie, *f.*
demonstrate (to) demonstrieren.
demonstration Kundgebung, *f.*; Demonstration, *f.*
denial Verleugnung, *f.*
denounce (to) denunzieren.
dense dicht.
density Dichte, *f.*
dentist Zahnarzt, *m.*
deny (to) ableugnen, verleugnen.
departure Abreise, *f.*
department Abteilung, *f.*
depend (to) abhängen.
dependent abhängig.
deplore (to) beweinen.
deposit Anzahlung, *f.*
depress (to) niederdrücken.
depression Depression, *f.*
deprive (to) berauben, entziehen.
depth Tiefe, *f.*
deride (to) verlachen, verhöhnen.
derive (to) ableiten.
descend (to) abstammen.
descendant Nachkomme, *m.*
descent Abstieg, *m.*; Abstammung, *f.* (family).
describe (to) beschreiben.
description Beschreibung, *f.*
desert Wüste, *f.*
desert (to) verlassen.
deserve (to) verdienen.
design Zeichnung, *f.* (drawing); Absicht, *f.* (intention).
designer Zeichner, *m.*
desirable wünschenswert.
desire (to) wünschen.
desire Wunsch, *m.*
desirous begierig.
desk Pult, *n.*
desolate trostlos.
despair Verzweiflung, *f.*
despair (to) verzweifeln.
desperate verzweifelt.
despise (to) verachten.
despite trotz (gen.).
dessert Nachtisch, *m.*
destiny Schicksal, *n.*
destroy (to) zerstören.
destruction Zerstörung, *f.*
detach (to) lösen.
detail Einzelheit, *f.*

detain (to) aufhalten.
detect (to) entdecken.
detective Detektiv, *m.*
detective story Kriminalgeschichte, *f.*; Detektivroman, *m.*
determination Entschlossenheit, *f.*
determine (to) bestimmen.
detest (to) verabscheuen.
detour Umweg, *m.*
detract (to) abziehen.
detrimental schädlich.
develop (to) entwickeln.
development Entwicklung, *f.*
device Kunstgriff, *m.*
devil Teufel, *m.*
devise (to) ersinnen.
devoid bar (gen.); ohne (acc.)
devote (to) widmen
devour (to) verschlingen.
dew Tau, *m.*
dial Zifferblatt, *n.* (clock).
dial (to) wählen.
dialect Dialekt, *m.*
dialogue Dialog, *m.*
diameter Durchmesser, *m.*
diamond Diamant, *m.*
diary Tagebuch, *n.*
dictate (to) diktieren.
dictation Diktat, *n.*
dictionary Wörterbuch, *n.*
die (to) sterben.
diet Diät, *f.*
differ (to) sich unterscheiden.
difference Unterschied, *m.*
different verschieden.
difficult schwierig.
difficulty Schwierigkeit, *f.*
dig (to) graben.
digest (to) verdauen.
dignity Würde, *f.*
dim trübe.
dimension Dimension, *f.*; Mass, *n.*
diminish (to) vermindern.
dining room Speisesaal, *m.*
dinner Abendessen, *n.*
dine (to) essen, speisen.
dip (to) senken, (ein)tauchen.
diplomacy Diplomatie, *f.*
diplomat Diplomat, *m.*
direct direkt.
direct (to) den Weg zeigen (show the way).
direction Richtung, *f.*
director Direktor, *m.*
directory Adressbuch, *n.*
dirt Schmutz, *m.*
dirty schmutzig.
disability Unfähigkeit, *f.*
disabled unfähig.
disadvantage Nachteil, *m.*
disagree (to) uneinig sein.
disagreeable unangenehm.
disagreement Meinungsverschiedenheit, *f.*
disappear (to) verschwinden.
disappearance Verschwinden, *n.*
disappoint (to) enttäuschen.
disapprove (to) missbilligen, ablehnen.
disaster Unglück, *n.*; Katastrophe, *f.*
disastrous unheilvoll.
discharge Entlassung, *f.* (dismissal); Abfeuern, *n.* (gun).
discharge (to) entlassen (person); abfeuern (firearm).
discipline Zucht, *f.*
disclaim (to) bestreiten.
disclose (to) enthüllen.
disclosure Enthüllung, *f.*
discomfort Unbehaglichkeit, *f.*
disconnect (to) trennen.

discontent unzufrieden.
discontinue (to) aufhören.
discord Zwietracht, /.
discount Skonto, m. (financial); Rabatt, m.
discourage (to) entmutigen.
discouragement Entmutigung, /.
discover (to) entdecken.
discovery Entdeckung. /.
discreet diskret, vorsichtig.
discretion Klugheit, /.; Urteil, n.
discuss (to) besprechen, erörtern.
discussion Erörterung, /.; Diskussion, /.
disdain Verachtung, /.
disdain (to) verschmähen, verachten.
disease Krankheit, /.
disgrace Schande, /. (shame); Ungnade, /.
disguise Verkleidung, /.
disguise (to) verkleiden.
disgust Ekel, m.
disgust (to) (an)ekeln.
disgusted ekelhaft, angeekelt.
dish Speise, /. (food); Schüssel, /. (plate).
dishonest unehrlich.
disk Scheibe, /.
dislike Widerwille, m.
dislike (to) nicht mögen.
dismiss (to) entlassen.
dismissal Entlassung, /.
disobey (to) nicht gehorchen.
disorder Unordnung, /.
dispense (to) verteilen.
display Entfaltung /. (unfold); Schau, /. (exposition).
displease (to) missfallen.
displeasure Missfallen, n.
disposal Verfügung, /.
dispose (to) anordnen, verfügen.
dispute Streit, m.
dispute (to) streiten.
dissolve (to) auflösen.
distance Entfernung, /.
distant entfernt.
distinct deutlich.
distinction Auszeichnung, /.; Unterschied, m. (difference).
distinguish (to) unterscheiden.
distort (to) verdrehen.
distract (to) verwirren.
distress Not, /.
distress (to) betrüben.
distribute (to) verteilen.
district Distrikt, m.
distrust Misstrauen, n.
distrust (to) misstrauen.
disturb (to) stören.
disturbance Störung, /.
ditch Graben, m.
dive (to) tauchen.
divide (to) verteilen.
divine göttlich.
division Teilung, /.
divorce (to) scheiden.
divorced geschieden.
dizziness Schwindel, m.
dizzy schwindlig.
do (to) tun, machen.
dock Dock, n.
doctor Arzt, m.
doctrine Lehre, /.
document Urkunde, /. Dokument, n.
dog Hund, m.
doll Puppe, /.
dome Kuppel, /.
domestic Häuslich; einheimisch (native).
domestic animal Haustier, n.
dominate (to) beherrschen.
door Tür, /.
dose Dosis, /.

dot Punkt, m.
double doppelt.
doubt Zweifel, m.
doubt (to) zweifeln.
doubtful zweifelhaft.
doubtless ohne Zweifel.
dough Teig, m.
down unter (dat. or acc.); hinunter, herunter.
dozen Dutzend, n.
draft Wechsel, m. (money); Zeichnung, /. (drawing).
drag (to) schleppen.
drain (to) entwässern.
drama Drama, m.
draught Zug, m.
draw (to) zeichnen.
draw back (to) schleppen.
drawer Schublade, /.
drawing-room Gesellschaftszimmer, n.: Salon, m.; Wohnzimmer, n.
dread Furcht, /.
dread (to) fürchten.
dreadful furchtbar, schrecklich.
dream Traum, m
dream (to) träumen.
dreamer Träumer, m.
dress Kleid, n.
dress (to) sich anziehen.
dressmaker Schneiderin, /.
drink Getränk, n.
drink (to) trinken.
drip (to) tropfen.
drive (to) fahren.
driver Chauffeur, m.
drop Fall, m.; Tropfen, m. (liquid).
drown (to) ertrinken.
drug Droge, /.
drugstore Apotheke, /.; Drogerie, /.
drum Trommel, /.
drunk betrunken.
dry trocken.
dry (to) trocknen.
dryness Trockenheit, /.
duchess Herzogin, /.
duck Ente, /.
due Gebühr, /.
duke Herzog, m.
dull trüb (weather); matt (color); dumpf (sound).
dumb stumm; dumm (stupid).
    deaf and dumb taubstumm.
during während (gen.).
dust Staub, m.
dust (to) abstäuben.
dusty staubig.
Dutch holländisch.
duty Pflicht, /.; Dienst, m. (service); Zoll, m. (customs).
dwarf Zwerg, m.
dwell (to) wohnen.
dye Farbe, /.
dye (to) färben.

                            E

each jeder.
    each other einander.
    each time jedesmal.
eager eifrig.
eagle Adler, m.
ear Ohr, n.
early früh.
earn (to) verdienen.
earnest ernst.
earth Erde, /.
ease Bequemlichkeit, /. (comfort); Ruhe, /. (calm); Linderung, /. (relief); Leichtigkeit, /. (facility).
ease (to) lindern, erleichtern.
easily leicht.
east Osten, m.

Easter Ostern, pl.
eastern östlich.
easy leicht.
eat (to) essen.
echo Echo, n.
echo (to) widerhallen.
economical wirtschaftlich; sparsam.
economize (to) sparen.
edge Schneide, /. (blade); Rand, m. (rim).
edition Ausgabe, /.; Auflage, /.
editor Redakteur, m.
editorial Leitartikel (noun, m.); redaktionell (adj.).
education Bildung, /.
effect Wirkung, /.
effective wirkungsvoll.
efficiency Leistungsfähigkeit, /.
effort Anstrengung, /.; Bestreben, n. (endeavor).
egg Ei, n. (Eier, pl.)
egoism Egoismus, m.; Selbstsucht, /.
eight acht.
eighteen achtzehn.
eighteenth achtzehnte.
eighth achte.
eightieth achtzigste.
eighty achtzig.
either oder.
    either...or   entweder...oder.
elastic elastisch.
elbow Ellbogen, m.
elder älter.
elderly älterer, ältlich.
eldest Älteste, m. & /.
elect (to) erwählen.
election Wahl, /.
elector Wähler, m.
electrical elektrisch.
electricity Elektrizität, /.
elegant elegant.
element Element, n.
elementary elementar.
elephant Elefant, m.
elevator Aufzug, m.
eleven elf.
eleventh elfte.
eliminate (to) ausscheiden.
eloquence Beredsamkeit, /.
eloquent beredt.
else ander, anders; sonst (otherwise).
    anyone else   irgend ein anderer.
    elsewhere   anderswo.
    everybody else   jeder andere.
    nobody else   sonst niemand.
    someone else   ein anderer.
elude (to) ausweichen.
embark (to) (sich) einschiffen.
embarrass (to) in Verlegenheit bringen.
embarrassing unangenehm, beschämend.
embarrassment Verlegenheit, /.
embassy Botschaft, /.
embody verkörpern.
embrace (to) umarmen.
embroidery Stickerei, /.
emerge (to) herauskommen.
emergency Notfall, m.
eminent hervorragend.
emotion Aufregung, /.
emperor Kaiser, m.
emphasis Nachdruck, m.
emphasize (to) betonen.
emphatic nachdrücklich.
empire Reich, n.
employee Angestellte, m. or /.
employer Arbeitgeber, m.
employment Arbeit, /.; Beschäftigung, /.
empty leer.
enable (to) befähigen.
enamel Email, n.
enclose (to) einschliessen.

enclosure Anlage, *f.* (letter); Einzäunung, *f.* (fence).
encourage (to) ermutigen.
encouragement Ermutigung, *f.*
end Ende, *n.*
end (to) enden, aufhören.
endeavor Bestreben, *n.;* Bemühung, *f.*
endeavor (to) sich bemühen.
endorse (to) unterzeichnen.
endure (to) ertragen.
enemy Feind, *m.*
energy Energie, *f.*
enforce (to) durchsetzen.
engage (to) anstellen.
engaged beschäftigt (busy); verlobt (affianced).
engagement Verabredung, *f.* (appointment);
   Beschäftigung, *f.* (business); Verlobung, *f.*
   (marriage)
engine Maschine, *f.;* Lokomotive, *f.* (train).
engineer Ingenieur, *m.*
English englisch.
engrave (to) eingravieren.
enjoy (to) geniessen, amüsieren.
   enjoy oneself sich amüsieren.
enjoyment Vergnügen, *n.*
enlarge (to) vergrössern.
enlist (to) anwerben.
enormous ungeheuer.
enough genug.
enter (to) hineingehen.
   Enter! Herein!
entertain (to) unterhalten.
entertainment Unterhaltung, *f.*, Schau, *f.* (show).
enthusiasm Begeisterung, *f.*
enthusiastic begeistert.
entire ganz.
entitle (to) berechtigen.
entrance Eingang, *m.*
entrust (to) anvertrauen.
enumerate (to) aufzählen.
envelope Umschlag, *m.*
envious neidisch.
envy Neid, *m.*
envy (to) beneiden.
episode Episode, *f;* Begebenheit, *f.*
equal gleich.
equal (to) gleichen.
equality Gleichheit, *f.*
equator Äquator, *m.*
equilibrium Gleichgewicht, *n.*
equip (to) ausrüsten.
equipment Ausrüstung, *f.*
era Zeitalter, *n.*
erase (to) ausstreichen.
eraser Gummi, *m.*
erect (to) errichten.
err (to) sich irren.
errand Auftrag, *m.*
error Irrtum, *m.*
escalator Rolltreppe, *f.*
escape Flucht, *f.*
escape (to) entlaufen.
escort (to) begleiten, eskortieren.
especially besonders.
essay Aufsatz, *m.*
essence Essenz, *f.* (extract); Wesen, *n.*
essential wesentlich.
establish (to) errichten, gründen.
establishment Gründung, *f.*
estate Vermögen, *n.* (wealth); Gut, *n.* (land).
esteem Achtung, *f.*
esteem (to) schätzen.
estimate Kostenanschlag, *m.* (cost); Schätzung, *f.*
   (appraise).
estimate (to) veranschlagen.
eternal ewig.
eternity Ewigkeit, *f.*
European Europäer (noun, *m.*); europäisch. (adj.).

evade (to) entfliehen.
evasion Ausflucht, *f.*
eve Vorabend, *m.*
even eben (adj.); sogar. (adv.)
evening Abend, *m.*
   good evening! Guten Abend!
evening clothes Gesellschaftsanzug, *m.*
evening dress Abendkleid, *n.* (woman's).
event Ereignis, *n.*
ever je, jemals.
every jeder
   everybody jedermann.
   everything alles.
   everywhere überall.
evidence Beweis, *m.*
evident offenbar.
evil Übel (noun, *n.*); schlecht (adj.).
evoke (to) hervorrufen.
evolve (to) herausarbeiten, sich entwickeln.
exact genau.
exaggerate (to) übertreiben.
exaggeration Übertreibung, *f.*
exalt (to) erheben.
exaltation Erhebung, *f.*
examination Prüfung, *f.*
examine (to) prüfen.
example Beispiel, *n.*
exceed (to) überschreiten.
excel (to) übertreffen.
excellence Vortrefflichkeit, *f.*
excellent vortrefflich, ausgezeichnet
except ausgenommen; ausser (dat.).
except (to) ausnehmen.
exception Ausnahme, *f.*
exceptional aussergewöhnlich.
exceptionally ausnahmsweise.
excess Übermass, *n.*
excessive übermässig.
exchange Tausch, *m.*
exchange (to) wechseln.
excite (to) aufregen.
excitement Aufregung, *f.*
exclaim (to) ausrufen.
exclamation Ausruf, *m.*
exclude (to) ausschliessen.
exclusive ausschliesslich.
excursion Ausflug, *m.*
excuse Verzeihung, *f.*
excuse (to) verzeihen, entschuldigen.
   Excuse me Verzeihung! (Entschuldigung!)
execute (to) ausführen (carry out); hinrichten (put
   to death).
execution Ausführung, *f.* (of plan or idea);
   Hinrichtung *f.* (of person).
exempt (to) befreien.
exercise Übung, *f.*
exercise (to) üben.
exert (to) sich anstrengen.
exertion Anstrengung, *f.*
exhaust (to) erschöpfen.
exhaustion Erschöpfung, *f.*
exhibit (to) ausstellen.
exhibition Ausstellung, *f.*
exile Verbannung, *f.*
exile (to) verbannen.
exist (to) existieren.
existence Existenz, *f.*
exit Ausgang, *m.*
expand (to) ausdehnen.
expansion Ausdehnung, *f.*
expensive teuer.
experience Erfahrung, *f.*
experience (to) erfahren.
experiment (to) experimentieren.
expert Fachmann, *m.*
expire (to) verscheiden, ablaufen.
explain (to) erklären.

explanation Erklärung, *f.*
explanatory erklärend.
explode (to) explodieren.
exploit Heldentat, *f.*
exploit (to) ausnützen.
explore (to) erforschen.
explosion Explosion, *f.*
export (to) ausführen, exportieren.
export Ausfuhr, *f.;* Export, *m.*
expose (to) aussetzen.
express Schnellzug, *m.*
express (to) ausdrücken.
expression Ausdruck, *m.*
expressive ausdrucksvoll.
expulsion Ausstossung, *f.*
exquisite vorzüglich.
extend (to) verlängern, ausdehnen.
extensive ausgedehnt.
extent Weite, *f.* (distance); Verlängerung, *f.* (time).
exterior Äussere (noun, *n.*); äusserlich (adj.).
exterminate (to) ausrotten.
external äusserlich, auswärtig.
extinction Erlöschen, *n.*
extinguish (to) erlöschen.
extra extra.
extraordinary aussergewöhnlich.
extravagant verschwenderisch.
extreme äusserst.
eye Auge, *n.*
eyebrow Augenbraue, *f.*
eyeglasses Brille, *f.*
eyelash Wimper, *f.*
eyelid Augenlid, *n.*
eyesight, Gesicht, *n.;* Sehkraft, *f.*

F

fable Fabel, *f.*
face Gesicht, *n.*
face (to) unter die Augen treten, gegenüberstehen
facilitate (to) erleichtern.
facility Leichtigkeit, *f.*
fact Tatsache, *f.*
   in fact in der Tat.
   as a matter of fact im übrigen.
factory Fabrik, *f.*
faculty Fähigkeit, *f.* (ability); Fakultät, *f.* (school).
fade (to) welken.
faded verschossen (color).
fail (to) fehlen; unterlassen (neglect); durchfallen
   (exam).
   without fail ganz gewiss.
failure Misserfolg, *m.*
faint (to) ohnmächtig werden.
fainting spell Ohnmacht, *f.*
fair schön (weather); hell (complexion); ehrlich
   (just).
   fair play ehrliches Spiel.
faith Glaube, *m.* (religion); Treue, *f.*
faithful treu.
fall Fall, *m;* Sturz, *m;* Herbst, *m.* (autumn).
fall (to) fallen, stürzen.
false falsch.
fame Ruhm, *m.*
familiar vertraut.
family Familie, *f.*
famine Hungersnot, *f.*
famous berühmt.
fan Fächer, *m.* Ventilator, *m.* (ventilator).
fancy Neigung, (noun, *f.*); bunt (adj.).
fantastic fantastisch.
far weit, fern.
force Posse, *f.*
fare Fahrpreis, *m.*
farewell Abschied, *m.*
   Farewell! Lebe wohl!
farm Bauernhof, *m.*

farmer Landwirt, m.
farming Landwirtschaft, f.
farther weiter, ferner.
fashion Mode, f.
fashionable elegant, modisch, modern.
fast schnell.
fasten (to) befestigen.
fat Fett (noun, n.); fett, dick (adj.).
fatal tödlich, fatal.
fate Schicksal, n.
father Vater, m.
father-in-law Schwiegervater, m.
faucet Knopf; m.; Hahn, m.
fault Fehler, m.
favor Gunst, f.
    Do me a favor. Tun Sie mir einen Gefallen.
favor (to) begünstigen.
favorable günstig.
favorite Günstling, m.; Liebling, m.; lieblings (adj.).
fear Furcht, f.
fear (to) fürchten.
fearless furchtlos.
feather Feder, f.
feature (Gesichts)zug, m.; Merkmal, n.; Film, m. (movie).
February Februar, m.
federal Bundes.
federation Verband, m.
fee Gebühr, f.
feeble schwach.
feed (to) füttern.
feel (to) fühlen.
feeling Gefühl, n.
fellow Kamerad, m.
fellowship Kameradschaft, f.; Gemeinschaft, f.
female weiblich.
feminine fraulich.
fence Zaun, m.
fencing Fechten, n.
fender Kotflügel, m.
ferocious wild.
ferry Fähre, f.
fertile fruchtbar.
fertilize (to) befruchten.
fertilizer Düngemittel, n.; Dünger, m.
fervent inbrünstig.
fervor Inbrunst, f.
festival Fest, n.
fetch (to) holen.
fever Fieber, n.
few wenige.
    a few ein paar.
fiction Dichtung, f.
field Acker, m.; Feld, n.
fierce wild.
fiery feurig.
fifteen fünfzehn.
fifteenth fünfzehnte.
fifth fünfte.
fiftieth fünfzigste.
fifty fünfzig.
fig Feige, f.
fight Kampf, m.
fight (to) kämpfen.
figure Figur, f.; Ziffer (number).
file Feile, f. (tool); Ablage, f. (office).
fill (to) füllen.
filling (tooth) Füllung, f.
film Film, m.
filthy schmutzig.
final endgültig.
finance Finanz, f.
finance (to) finanzieren.
financial finanziell.
find (to) finden.
fine Geldstrafe (noun, f.); fein (adj.) (opp. of coarse); schön (adj.) (elegant).

finger Finger, m.
finish (to) beenden.
fire Feuer, n.
fireman Feuerwehrmann, m.
fireplace Kamin, m.
firm Firma, (noun, f.); fest, stark (adj.).
first erster.
    at first zuerst.
fish Fisch, m.
fish (to) fischen.
fisherman Fischer, m.
fishing Fischen, n.
fist Faust, f.
fit Anfall, (noun, m.); passend (adj.) (becoming); tauglich (adj.) (capable).
fitness Tauglichkeit, f.
five fünf.
fix (to) reparieren.
flag Fahne, f.
flame Flamme, f.
flank Seite, f.
flash Blitz, m. (lightning).
flashlight Blitzlicht, n.
flat flach.
flatter (to) schmeicheln.
flatterer Schmeichler, m.
flattery Schmeichelei, f.
flavor Aroma, n.
fleet Flotte, f.
flesh Fleisch, n.
flexibility Biegsamkeit, f.
flexible biegsam.
flight Flug, m.
fling (to) werfen.
flint Kieselstein, m.
float (to) treiben.
flood Überschwemmung, f.
flood (to) überschwemmen.
floor Boden, m.; Stock, m. (story).
flourish (to) blühen.
flourishing blühend.
flow (to) strömen.
flower Blume, f.
fluid flüssig.
fly Fliege, f.
fly (to) fliegen.
foam Schaum, m.
fog Nebel, m.
fold Falte, f.
fold (to) falten.
foliage Laubwerk, n.
follow (to) folgen.
following folgend.
fond zärtlich, liebevoll.
fondness Zärtlichkeit, f.
food Essen, n.
fool Narr, m.
foolish töricht, lächerlich.
foot Fuss, m.
football Fussball, m.
footstep Schritt, m.
for für (acc.); zu (dat.); wegen (gen.) (on account of); denn (because).
    as for me was mich betrifft.
    for a year während eines Jahres.
    for example zum Beispiel.
    word for word Wort für Wort.
forbid (to) verbieten.
force Kraft, f.
force (to) zwingen.
ford Furt, f.
foreground Vordergrund, m.
forehead Stirn, f.
foreign fremd, ausländisch.
foreigner Fremder, m; Ausländer, m.
forest Wald, m.
forget (to) vergessen.

forgetfulness Vergesslichkeit, f.
forget-me-not Vergissmeinnicht, n.
forgive (to) vergeben, verzeihen.
forgiveness Vergebung, f.
fork Gabel, f.
form Form, f.
formal offiziell, formell.
formation Bildung, f.
former fruher; erster (as opposed to latter).
formerly vormals.
formula Formel, f.
forsake (to) verlassen.
fort Festung, f.
fortieth vierzigste.
fortunate glücklich.
fortunately glücklicherweise.
fortune Vermögen, n.; Glück, n. (luck).
forty vierzig.
forward vorwärts.
forward (to) absenden.
foster (to) pflegen.
foul faul.
found (to) gründen.
foundation Gründung, f.
founder Gründer, m.
fountain Brunnen, m.
fountain pen Füllfeder, f.
four vier.
fourteen vierzehn.
fourteenth vierzehnte.
fourth vierte.
fowl Geflügel, n.
fox Fuchs, m.
fragile zerbrechlich.
fragment Bruchstück, n.
fragrance Duft, m.
fragrant duftig.
frail zart.
frame Rahmen, m.
frame (to) rahmen.
frank aufrichtig, freimütig.
frankness Offenheit, f.
free frei.
freedom Freiheit, f.
freeze (to) frieren.
freight Fracht, f.
French französisch.
frequent häufig.
frequently oft, oftmals.
fresh frisch.
friction Reibung, f.; Friktion, f. (hair).
Friday Freitag, m.
fried gebraten.
friend Freund, m.
friendly freundlich.
friendship Freundschaft, f.
frighten (to) erschrecken.
frightening schrecklich. erschreckend.
fringe Rand, m.
frivolity Leichtsinn, m.
frog Frosch, m.
from von, aus (dat); nach (dat.) (according to).
    from morning till night von früh bis spät.
    from time to time von Zeit zu Zeit.
    from top to bottom von oben bis unten.
front Vorderseite, f.; Front, f. (military).
frozen gefroren.
fruit Frucht, sing. f.; Obst, coll., n.
fry (to) braten.
    fried eggs Spiegeleier, pl.
    fried potatoes Bratkartoffeln, pl.
frying pan Bratpfanne, f.
fuel Brennstoff, m.
fulfill (to) erfüllen.
full voll.
fully voll.
fun Scherz, m; Spass, m.

to have fun sich amüsieren.
to make fun sich lustig machen.
function Funktion, f.
function (to) funktionieren.
fund Fonds, m.
fundamental grundlegend; wesentlich.
funeral Begräbnis, n.
funny komisch.
fur Pelz, m.
furious wütend, rasend.
furnace Ofen, m.
furnish (to) möblieren.
furniture Möbel, f.
furrow Furche, f.
further weiter.
fury Wu, f.
future Zukunft (noun, f.); zukünftig (adj.).

G

gaiety Fröhlichkeit, f.
gain Gewinn, m.
gain (to) gewinnen.
gallant tapfer, ritterlich.
gallery Galerie, f.
gallop Galopp, m.
gamble (to) spielen.
game Spiel, m.
garage Garage, f.
garbage Abfälle, pl.
garden Garten, m.
gardener Gärtner, m.
garlic Knoblauch, n.
gas Gas, n.
gasoline Benzin, n.
gate Tor, n.
gather (to) sammeln.
gay lustig.
gear Getriebe, n.
gem Edelstein, m.
general General, m. (military); allgemein (adj.).
generality Allgemeinheit, f.
generalize (to) verallgemeinern.
generation Geschlecht, n.
generosity Freigebigkeit, f.; Grossmut, f.
(magnanimity).
generous grosszügig.
genius Genie, n.
genteel fein, vornehm.
gentle artig, vornehm, sanft.
gentleman Herr, m.
gentleness Sanftheit, f.
genuine echt.
geographical geographisch.
geography Geographie, f.
germ Keim, m.
German Deutscher (noun, m.); deutsch (adj.).
gesture Gebärde, f.
get (to) bekommen, erwerben, holen (fetch);
werden (become);
get down hinunterkommen.
get off absteigen.
get up aufstehen.
ghastly grässlich.
ghost geist, m.
giant Riese, m.
gift Geschenk, n.
gifted begabt.
girl Mädchen, n.
give (to) geben.
to give back zurückgeben.
glad froh.
gladly gern.
glance Blick, m.
glass Glas, n.
looking glass Spiegel, m.

glasses Brille, f.
gleam Schein, m.; Schimmer, m.
gleam (to) scheinen.
glitter Glanz, m; Glitzen, n.
globe Kugel, f.
gloomy düster.
glorious glorreich.
glory Ruhm, m.
glove Handschuh, m.
glow Glut, f.; Glühen, n.
glue Leim, m.
go (to) gehen.
to go away weggehen.
to go back zurückgehen.
to go in hineingehen.
to go out herausgehen, ausgehen.
to go to bed zu Bett gehen.
God Gott, m.
godchild Patenkind, n.
godfather Pate, m.
godmother Patin, f.
gold Gold, n.
golden golden.
golf Golf, m.
good gut.
Good afternoon! Guten Tag!
Good evening! Guten Abend!
Good morning! Guten Morgen!
Good night! Gute Nacht!
good-bye Auf Wiedersehen!
good-looking gut aussehend.
goodness Güte, f.
goods Waren, pl.
goodwill guter Wille, m.
goose Gans, f.
gossip Klatsch, m.
gossip (to) klatschen.
govern (to) regieren.
grace Gnade, f.; Anmut, f. (charm).
graceful anmutig.
grade Grad, m.
grain Korn, n.
grammar Grammatik, f.
grand grossartig.
grandchild Enkelkind, n.
granddaughter Enkelin, f.
grandfather Grossvater, m.
grandmother Grossmutter, f.
grandson Enkel, m.
grant Bewilligung, f.; Schenkung, f.
grant (to) bewilligen.
grape Weintraube, f.
grapefruit Pompelmuse, f.
grasp Griff, m.
grasp (to) greifen.
grass Gras, n.
grateful dankbar.
gratitude Dankbarkeit, f.
grave Grab, (noun, n.); ernst (adj.).
gravy Sauce, f.
gray grau.
grease Fett, n.
great gross.
greatness Grösse, f.
greedy gierig, gefrässig.
green grün.
greet (to) grüssen.
greeting Gruss, m.
grief Kummer, m.
grieve (to) sich grämen.
grin (to) grinsen.
grind (to) mahlen.
groan Stöhnen, n.
groan (to) stöhnen.
grocer Kolonialwarenhändler, m.
grocery store Kolonialwarenladen, m.
gross grob.

ground Boden, m.
group Gruppe, f.
group (to) gruppieren.
grow (to) wachsen; bauen (crops).
growth Gewächs, n.
grudge Groll, m.
guaranteed garantiert.
guess Vermutung, f.
guess (to) raten.
guide Führer, m.
gum Zahnfleisch, n. (teeth).
chewing gum Kaugummi, n.
gun Gewehr, n.
gush Erguss, m.
gush (to) hervorströmen.

H

habit Gewohnheit, f.
habitual gewöhnlich.
hail Hagel, m.
hair Haar, n.
hairdo Frisur, f.
hairdresser Frisör, m.
hairpin Haarnadel, f.
half halb.
hall Halle, f.; Saal, m. Diele, f.
ham Schinken, m.
hammer Hammer, m.
hand Hand, f.
hand (to) reichen.
handbag Handtasche, f.
handful Handvoll, f.
handkerchief Taschentuch, n.
handle Griff, m.
handle (to) tun.
handsome stattlich.
handy handlich.
hang (to) hängen.
happen (to) geschehen.
happiness Glück, n.
happy glücklich.
harbor Hafen, m.
hard hart.
harden (to) härten.
hardly kaum.
hardness Härte, f.
hardware Eisenwaren, pl.
hardware store Eisenwarengeschäft, n.
hardy abgehärtet.
hare Hase, m.
harm Schaden, m.
harm (to) schädigen.
harmful schädlich.
harmless harmlos.
harmonious harmonisch.
harmony Harmonie, f.
harsh barsch.
harvest Ernte, f.
haste Eile, f.
hasten (to) eilen.
hat Hut, m.
hate Hass, m.
hate (to) hassen.
hateful gehässig.
hatred Hass, m.
haughty stolz.
have (to) haben.
haven Hafen, m.
hay Heu, n.
he er.
head Kopf, m. (of a person); Chef, m. (of a firm);
Haupt, n. (of a government).
headache Kopfschmerzen, pl.
heal (to) heilen.
health Gesundheit, f.

healthy gesund.

heap Haufen, m.

heap (to) (auf)häufen.

hear (to) hören.

hearing Gehör, n.

heart Herz, n.

heaven Himmel, m.

heavy schwer.

hedge Hecke, f.; Zaun, m.

heel Ferse, f. (of the foot); Absatz, m. (of a shoe).

height Höhe, f.

heir Erbe, m.

hell Hölle, f.

helm Ruder, n.

help Hilfe, f.

help (to) helfen.

helpful behilflich.

hem Saum, m.

hen Huhn, n.; Henne, f.

her ihr (pers. pr., dat.; poss. adj.); sie (pers. pr., acc.).

herb Kraut, n.

herd Herde, f.

here hier.

herewith hiermit.

hero Held, m.

heroic heldenhaft, heroisch.

heroine Heldin, f.

herring Hering, m.

hers ihr(er, -e, -es).

herself sie (ihr) selbst; sich.

hesitate (to) zögern.

hide (to) verstecken.

hideous scheusslich.

high hoch.

higher höher.

hill Hügel, m.

him ihn (acc.); ihm (dat.).

himself er (ihm, ihn) selbst; sich.

hinder (to) hindern.

hint Wink, m.

hint (to) andeuten.

hip Hüfte, f.

hire (to) mieten.

his sein (poss. adj.); sein(er, -e, -es) (pron.).

hiss (to) zischen.

historian Geschichtsschreiber, m.

historical historisch.

history Geschichte, f.

hoarse heiser.

hoe Hacke, f.

hold Halt, m.

hold (to) halten.

hole Loch, n.

holiday Feiertag, m.

holidays Ferien, pl.

holy heilig.

homage Huldigung, f.

home Heim, n.

honest ehrlich.

honesty Ehrlichkeit, f.

honey Honig, m.

honeymoon Flitterwochen, pl.

honor Ehre, f.

honor (to) ehren.

honorable ehrenvoll.

hood Kapuze, f.; Dach, n. (car).

hoof Huf, m.

hook Haken, m.

hope Hoffnung, f.

hope (to) hoffen.

hopeful hoffnungsvoll.

hopeless hoffnungslos.

horizon Horizont, m.

horizontal horizontal.

horn (auto) Hupe, f.

horrible schrecklich.

horse Pferd, n.

horseback (on) zu Pferde.

hosiery Strümpfe, f.

hospitable gastfrei.

hospital Krankenhaus, n.

host Gastgeber, m.; Wirt, m.

hostess Gastgeberin, f.; Wirtin, f.

hostile feindlich.

hot heiss.

hotel Hotel, n.; Gasthof, m.

hour Stunde, f.

house Haus, n.

household Haushalt, m.

housekeeper Haushälterin, f.

housemaid Hausmädchen, n.

how wie

    How are you? Wie geht's?

however dennoch.

howl Heulen, n.

howl (to) heulen.

human menschlich.

humane human.

humanity Menschlichkeit, f.

humble demütig.

humid feucht.

humiliate erniedrigen, demütigen.

humility Demut, f.

humor Humor, m.

hundred hundert.

hundredth hundertste.

hunger Hunger, m.

hungry hungrig.

hunt Jagd, f.

hunter Jäger, m.

hurricane Orkan, m.

hurry Eile, f.

    Hurry up! Beeilen Sie sich!

hurt (to) verwunden; verletzen.

husband Mann, m.; Gatte, m.

hush (to) schweigen.

hyphen Bindestrich, m.

hypocrite Heuchler, m.

I ich.

ice Eis, n.

ice cream Eis, n.

icy eisig.

idea Idee, f.; Einfall, m.

ideal Ideal, (noun, n.); ideal (adj.).

idealism Idealismus, m.

idealist Idealist, m.

identical identisch.

identity Identität, f.

idiot Idiot, m.

idle müssig.

idleness Müssigkeit, f.

if wenn, ob.

ignoble unedel.

ignorance Unwissenheit, f.

ignorant unwissend.

ignore (to) ignorieren.

ill krank.

illegal gesetzwidrig, ungesetzlich.

illness Krankheit, f.

illusion Täuschung, f.

illustrate (to) illustrieren.

illustration Abbildung, f.

image Einbildungskraft, f.; Ebenbild, n.; Bild, n.

imagination Fantasie, f.

imagine (to) sich einbilden.

imitate (to) nachahmen.

imitation Nachahmung, f.

immediate unmittelbar.

immediately sogleich, sofort.

immigrant Immigrant, m.

imminent bevorstehend.

immobility Unbeweglichkeit, f.

immoral unmoralisch.

immorality Unsittlichkeit, f.

immortal unsterblich.

immortality Unsterblichkeit, f.

impartial unparteiisch.

impassible gefühllos.

impatience Ungeduld, f.

imperfect Vergangenheit (noun, f.) (in grammar); unvollkommen (adj.).

impertinence Unverschämtheit, f.

impetuosity Ungestüm, n.

import Einfuhr, f.; Import, m.

import (to) einführen, importieren.

important wichtig.

imported importiert.

importer Importeur, m.

impossible unmöglich.

impress (to) Eindruck machen.

impression Eindruck, m.

imprison (to) einsperren.

improve (to) verbessern.

improvement Verbesserung, f.

improvise (to) improvisieren.

imprudence Unvorsichtigkeit, f.

imprudent unklug.

impulse Antrieb, m.

impure unrein.

in in (dat.).

inadequate unzulänglich.

inaugurate (to) eröffnen.

incapable unfähig.

incapacity Unfähigkeit, f.

inch Zoll, m.

incident Vorfall, m.

include (to) einschliessen.

included eingeschlossen.

income Einkommen, n.

income tax Einkommensteuer, f.

incomparable unvergleichlich.

incompatible unvereinbar.

incompetent untauglich; unzulänglich.

incomplete unvollständig.

inconvenient lästig, unbequem.

incorrect unrichtig.

increase Erhöhung, f.

increase (to) sich vermehren, erhöhen.

incredible unglaublich.

indebted verschuldet; verpflichtet.

indecision Unentschlossenheit, f.

indeed tatsächlich.

independence Unabhängigkeit, f.

independent unabhängig.

index Inhaltsverzeichnis, n.

index finger Zeigefinger, m.

indicate (to) zeigen.

indicative Indikativ (noun, m.) (in grammar); anzeigend (adj.).

indifference Gleichgültigkeit, f.

indifferent gleichgültig.

indigestion Verdauungsstörung, f.

indignant entrüstet.

indignation Entrüstung, f.

indirect indirekt.

indiscreet indiskret.

indiscretion Unbedachtsamkeit, f.

indispensable unentbehrlich.

individual einzeln.

indolent träge.

indoors im Hause.

induce (to) veranlassen.

indulge (to) sich hingeben.

indulgence Nachsichtigkeit, f.

indulgent nachsichtig.

industrial industriell.

industrious fleissig.

industry Industrie, f.

inefficient unfähig.

infancy Kindheit, f.

infant kleines Kind, *n.*
infantry Infanterie, *f.*
infection Infektion, *f.*
inferior minderwertig.
infernal höllisch.
infinite unendlich.
infinity Unendlichkeit, *f.*
influence Einfluss, *m.*
influence (to) beeinflussen.
inform (to) benachrichtigen.
information Auskunft, *f.;* Nachricht, *f.* (news).
ingenious geistig.
ingenuity Scharfsinn, *m.*
inhabit (to) bewohnen.
inhabitant Einwohner, *m.*
inherit (to) erben.
inheritance Erbgut, *n.*
inhuman unmenschlich.
initial Anfangsbuchstabe, *m.*
initiate (to) einweihen.
initiative Initiative, *f.*
injection Einspritzung, *f.*
injury Verletzung, *f.*
injustice Ungerechtigkeit, *f.*
ink Tinte, *f.*
inkwell Tintenfass, *n.*
inland Binnenland, *n.*
inn Gasthof, *m.*
innkeeper Gastwirt, *m.*
innocent unschuldig.
innocence Unschuld *f.*
inquire (to) sich erkundigen.
inquiry Erkundigung, *f.;* Auskunft, *f.*
insane geisteskrank.
inscription Inschrift, *f.*
insect Insekt, *n.*
insensible unempfindlich.
inseparable unzertrennlich.
inside drinnen.
insight Einsicht, *f.*
insignificant unbedeutend.
insincere unaufrichtig.
insinuate (to) andeuten.
insist (to) bestehen auf.
insistence Beharren, *n.*
inspect (to) besichtigen.
inspection Besichtigung, *f.*
inspiration Inspiration, *f.*
install (to) einstellen, installieren.
installment Rate, *f.;* Teilzahlung, *f.*
instance Beispiel, *n.;* Fall, *m.*
instant Augenblick, *m.*
instantly sofort.
instead of anstatt (gen.).
institute (to) herbeiführen.
institution Anstalt, *f.*
instruct (to) unterrichten.
instructor Lehrer, *m.*
instruction Anweisung, *f.;* Unterricht, *m.* (teaching).
instrument Instrument, *n.*
insufficient ungenügend.
insult Beleidigung, *f.*
insult (to) beleidigen.
insurance Versicherung, *f.*
insure (to) versichern.
intact unversehrt.
intellectual intellektuell.
intelligence Intelligenz, *f.*
intelligent intelligent.
intend (to) beabsichtigen.
intense intensiv.
intensity Heftigkeit, *f.*
intention Absicht, *f.*
interest Interesse, *n.*
interesting interessant.
interfere (to) sich einmischen.
interior Innere, *n.*
intermediate mittel.

intermission Pause, *f.*
international international.
interpret (to) interpretieren, übersetzen; deuten (emotion).
interpreter Dolmetscher, *m.*
interrupt (to) unterbrechen.
interval Pause, *f.;* Zwischenzeit, *f.*
interview Interview, *n.*
intimacy Vertrautheit, *f.*
intimate vertraut.
into in (dat. or acc.).
intolerant unduldsam.
intonation Tonfall, *m.*
introduce (to) vorstellen.
introduction Vorstellung, *f.*
intuition Einfühlungsgabe, *f.*
invade (to) einfallen.
invent (to) erfinden.
invention Erfindung, *f.*
inventor Erfinder, *m.*
invert (to) umkehren, umdrehen.
invest (to) investieren; anlegen (money).
investment Kapitalanlage, *f.*
invisible unsichtbar.
invitation Einladung, *f.*
invite (to) einladen.
invoice Faktura, *f.*
invoke (to) anrufen.
involve (to) verwickeln.
iodine Jod, *n.*
Irish irländisch.
iron Eisen, *n.* (metal); Bügeleisen, *n.* (for ironing).
iron (to) bügeln.
irony Ironie, *f.*
irregular unregelmässig.
irresistible unwiderstehlich.
irritate (to) reizen, ärgern.
island Insel, *f.*
isolate (to) absondern, isolieren.
issue Ausgabe, *f.*
it es.
Italian Italiener (noun, *m.*); italienisch (adj.).
itch (to) jucken.
its sein (poss. adj.); sein(er, -e, -es), (poss. pron.).
itself es (ihm) selbst, sich.
ivory Elfenbein, *n.*
ivy Efeu, *n.*

J

jacket Jacke, *f.*
jail Gefängnis, *n.*
jam Marmelade, *f.*
January Januar, *m.*
Japanese Japaner (noun, *m.*); japanisch (adj.).
jar Krug, *m.*
jaw Kiefer, *m.*
jealous eifersüchtig.
jealousy Eifersucht, *f.*
jelly Gelee, *n.*
jewel Juwel, *m.*
jeweler Juwelier, *m.*
Jewish jüdisch.
job Arbeit, *f.*
join (to) binden.
joint Gelenk, *n.*
joke Witz, *m.;* Scherz, *m.;* Spass, *m.*
joke (to) scherzen.
jolly lustig.
journalist Journalist, *m.*
journey Reise, *f.*
joy Freude, *f.*
joyous freudig.
judge Richter, *m.*
judge (to) urteilen.
judgment Urteil, *n.*
judicial gerichtlich.
juice Saft, *m.*
July Juli, *m.*

jump Sprung, *m.*
jump (to) springen.
June Juni, *m.*
junior jünger.
jungle Dschungel, *m.*
just recht (fair); gerecht (justice); gerade (recent).
justice Gerechtigkeit, *f.*
justify (to) rechtfertigen.

K

keen scharf.
keep (to) halten (retain); hindern (hinder).
    keep off abhalten.
    keep on fortfahren.
    keep up aufrechterhalten.
kernel Kern, *m.*
kettle Kessel, *m.*
key Schlüssel, *m.*
kick Fusstritt, *m.*
kick (to) ausschlagen.
kidneys Nieren, *pl.*
kill (to) töten.
kin Blutsverwandtschaft, *f.*
kind Art (noun, *f.*); gütig (adj.).
kindly freundlich.
kindness Güte, *f.;* Freundlichkeit, *f.*
king König, *m.*
kingdom Königreich, *n.*
kiss Kuss, *m.*
kiss (to) küssen.
kitchen Küche, *f.*
kite Drache, *m.*
knee Knie, *n.*
kneel (to) knieen.
knife Messer, *n.*
knight Ritter, *m.*
knit (to) stricken.
knock Schlag, *m.;* Hieb, *m.* (beating); Klopf, *m.;* Griff, *m.* (door).
knock (to) klopfen, schlagen, hauen, stossen; anklopfen (door).
knot Knoten, *m.*
know (to) wissen (have knowledge of); kennen (be acquainted with).
knowledge Kenntnis, *f.*

L

label Zettel, *m.*
labor Arbeit, *f.*
laboratory Laboratorium, *n.*
laborer Arbeiter, *m.*
lace Spitze, *f.* (ornamental); Senkel, *m.* (of a shoe).
lack Mangel, *m.*
lack (to) mangeln.
lady Dame, *f.*
lake See, *m.*
lamb Lamm, *n.*
lame lahm.
lamp Lampe, *f.*
land Land, *n.*
land (to) landen.
landscape Landschaft, *f.*
language Sprache, *f.*
languish (to) schmachten.
languor Schlaffheit, *f.*
lantern Laterne, *f.*
large gross
last letzt.
    last year voriges Jahr.
last (to) dauern.
lasting dauernd.
latch Klinke, *f.* (knob); Drücker.
late spät.
lately kürzlich.
latter letzter.
laugh (to) lachen.

laughter Gelächter, n.
lavish freigebig.
lavish (to) überhäufen.
law Gesetz, n.; Recht, n. (code).
lawful rechtmässig.
lawn Rasenplatz, m.
lawyer Rechtsanwalt, m.
lay (to) legen.
layer Schicht, f.
lazy faul.
lead Blei, n.
lead (to) führen.
leader Führer, m.
leadership Führung, f.
leaf Blatt, n.
leak Leck, n.
lean (to) lehnen.
leap (to) springen.
leap Sprung, m.
learn (to) lernen.
learned gelehrt.
learning Gelehrsamkeit, f.
least wenigste.
  at least mindestens.
leather Leder, n.
leave (to) verlassen (abandon); weggehen (on foot);
  wegfahren (by vehicle).
lecture Vortrag, m.
left linke.
  to the left links.
leg Bein, n.
  leg of lamb Hammelkeule, f.
legal gesetzmässig.
legend Sage, f.
legislation Gesetzgebung, f.
legislator Gesetzgeber, m.
legitimate legitim.
leisure Freizeit, f.
lemon Zitrone, f.
lemonade Limonade, f.
lend (to) leihen.
length Länge, f.
lengthen (to) verlängern.
less weniger.
lesson Stunde, f.; Lektion, f. (in book).
let (to) lassen; gestatten (allow); vermieten (rent).
letter Buchstabe, m. (alphabet); Brief, m.
  (correspondence).
level Niveau, n.
liable haftbar.
liar Lügner, m.; Lügnerin, f.
liberal liberal.
liberty Freiheit, f.
library Bibliothek, f.
license Erlaubnis, f.
lick (to) lecken.
lie Lüge, f.
lie (to) lügen (falsify); liegen (rest).
lieutenant Leutnant, m.
life Leben, n.
lift (to) heben.
light Licht (noun, n.); leicht (adj.).
light (to) anzünden.
  to light up erleuchten.
lighten (to) erhellen (brightness); erleichtern
  (weight).
lighter Feuerzeug, n.
lighthouse Leuchtturm, m.
lighting Beleuchtung, f.
lightning Blitz, m.
like wie (as); ähnlich (similar).
like (to) gern haben, mögen, gefallen.
  I'd like to ich möchte.
likely wahrscheinlich.
likeness Ähnlichkeit, f.
likewise gleichfalls.
liking Vorliebe, f.
limb Glied, n.

limit Grenze, f.
limit (to) begrenzen.
limp hinken.
line Linie, f.
line up (to) sich anstellen.
linen Wäsche, f. (household); Leinwand, f.
  (fabric).
linger (to) weilen.
lingerie Damenwäsche, f.
lining Futter, n.
link Glied, n.
link (to) verbinden.
lion Löwe, m.
lip Lippe, f.
lipstick Lippenstift, m.
liquid Flüssigkeit (noun, f.); flüssig (adj.).
liquor Alkohol, m.; Likör, m. (liqueur).
list Liste, f.
literary literarisch.
literature Literatur, f.
little klein.
  a little ein wenig.
live lebend.
live (to) leben.
lively lebhaft, lebendig.
liver Leber, f.
load Last, f. (burden); Ladung, f. (cargo).
load (to) laden.
loan (ver)leihen.
lobby Vorhalle, f.
local lokal.
locate (to) orientieren, finden.
location Platz, m; Gegend, f.
lock Schloss, n.
lock (to) zuschliessen.
locomotive Lokomotive, f.
log Klotz, m.
logic Logik, f.
logical logisch.
loneliness Einsamkeit, f.
lonely einsam.
long lang.
  long ago vor langer Zeit; längst.
  a long time lange.
long (to) sehnen.
longer länger.
longing Sehnsucht, f.
look Blick, m.
look (to) schauen; aussehen (appear).
  Look! Sehen Sie her!
  Look out! Passen Sie auf!
  to look forward entgegensehen; sich freuen
  auf (rejoice).
loose lose.
loosen (to) lösen.
lose (to) verlieren.
loss Verlust, m.; Schaden, m.
lost verloren.
lot (a) viel (much).
loud laut.
love Liebe, f.
love (to) lieben.
lovely schön, reizend.
low niedrig.
lower (to) niederholen.
loyal treu.
loyalty Treue, f.
luck Glück, n.
lucky glücklich.
luggage Gepäck, n.
luminous leuchtend.
lump Klumpen, m.
lunch Mittagessen, n.
lung Lunge, f.
luxurious prächtig.
luxury Luxus, m.

M

machine Maschine, f.
mad verrückt.
madam gnädige Frau.
made gemacht.
madness Wahnsinn, m.
magazine Zeitschrift, f.
magistrate Magistrat, m.
magnificent prachtvoll.
maid Dienstmädchen, n. (servant).
mail Post, f.
main haupt—
  the main thing die Hauptsache.
maintain (to) erhalten; unterhalten (support).
maintenance Unterhalt, m.
majesty Majestät, f.
major Major, m.
majority Mehrheit, f.
make (to) machen.
man Mann, m.; Mensch, m. (human being).
manage (to) führen, verwalten.
management Leitung, f.
manager Leiter, m.
manicure Maniküre, f.
mankind Menschheit, f.
manner Art, f.; Weise, f.
manners Bildung, f.
manufacture Fabrikation, f.
manufactured hergestellt.
many viele.
map Karte, f.
marble Marmor, m.
March März, m.
march Marsch, m.
march (to) marschieren.
margin Rand, m.
marine Marine, f.
mark Kennzeichen, n.
mark (to) markieren.
market Markt, m.
marketplace Marktplatz, m.
marriage Heirat, f.
married verheiratet.
marry (to) heiraten, sich verheiraten; trauen
  (perform the ceremony).
  to marry off verheiraten.
marvel Wunder, n.
marvel (to) sich wundern.
marvelous wunderbar.
masculine männlich.
mask Maske, f.
mask (to) maskieren.
mason Maurer, m.
mass Masse, f.; Messe, f. (church).
massage Massage, f.
master Meister, m.
master (to) meistern.
masterpiece Meisterwerk, n.; Meisterstück, n.
match Streichholz, n. (incendiary); Gleiche, n.
  (comparative).
match (to) zusammenpassen.
material Material, n.
maternal mütterlich.
mathematics Mathematik, f.
matter Angelegenheit, f. (affair); Stoff, m.
  (substance).
  What's the matter? Was ist los?
mattress Matratze, f.
mature erwachsen.
May Mai, m.
may dürfen (to be allowed); mögen (to be likely).
mayor Bürgermeister, m.
me mich (acc.); mir (dat.).
meadow Wiese, f.
meal Mahl, n.
mean übel (unkind).
mean (to) meinen (to be of the opinion); bedeuten

(to signify).

What does it mean? Was bedeutet das?

meaning Bedeutung, *f.* (significance).

means Mittel, *n.*

meanwhile inzwischen.

measure Mass, *n.*

measure (to) messen.

meat Fleisch, *n.*

mechanic Mechaniker, *m.*

mechanical mechanisch.

medal Medaille, *f.* (jewel); Orden, *m.*

medical ärztlich.

medicine Medizin, *f.* (science); Arznei, *f.*

(medication).

mediocre mittelmässig.

mediocrity Mittelmässigkeit, *f.*

meditate (to) grübeln, sinnen, nachdenken.

meditation Nachdenken, *n.*

medium mittel.

meet (to) treffen.

Pleased to meet you Sehr erfreut Sie

kennenzulernen.

meeting Versammlung, *f.*

melon Melone, *f.*

melt (to) schmelzen.

member Mitglied, *n.*

memorize (to) auswendig lernen.

memory Gedächtnis, *n.*

mend (to) reparieren.

mental geistig.

mention (to) erwähnen.

menu Speisekarte, *f.*

merchandise Ware, *f.*

merchant Kaufmann, *m.*

merciful barmherzig.

merciless unbarmherzig.

mercury Quecksilber, *n.*

mercy Barmherzigkeit, *f.*

merit Verdienst, *n.*

merit (to) verdienen.

merry fröhlich, heiter, lustig.

message Nachricht, *f.*

messenger Bote, *m.*

metal Metall, *n.*

metallic metallisch.

method Methode, *f.*

Mexican Mexicaner (noun, *m.*); mexikanisch (adj.).

microphone Mikrofon, *n.*

middle Mitte, *f.*

middle age mittleres Alter, *n.*

Middle Ages Mittelalter, *n.*

midnight Mitternacht, *f.*

midway halbwegs.

might Macht, *f.*

mighty mächtig.

mild leicht, mild, sanft.

mildness Milde, *f.*

mile Meile, *f.*

military militärisch.

milk Milch, *f.*

milkman Milchhändler, *m.*

milky way Milchstrasse, *f.*

mill Mühle, *f.*

miller Müller, *m.*; Müllerin, *f.*

milliner Modistin, *f.*

million Million, *f.*

millionaire Millionär, *m.*

mind Verstand, *m.*; Sinn, *m.*

mind (to) beachten (to pay heed); aufpassen (*also*

to watch over).

mine Grube, *f.* (coal).

mine (poss. pr.) mein(er, -e, -es).

miner Bergmann, *m.*

mineral mineralisch.

mineral Mineral, *n.*

minister Minister (state), *m.*; Geistliche, *m.*

(church).

ministry Ministerium, *n.* (state); Amt, *n.* (church).

mink Nerz, *m.*

minor jüngere.

minority Minderheit, *f.*

minute Minute, *f.*

Just a minute! Einen Augenblick!

Wait a minute! Warten Sie einen Augenblick!

Any minute now! Jeden Augenblick!

miracle Wunder, *n.*

mirror Spiegel, *m.*

miscellaneous gemischt, verschieden.

mischief Unfug, *m.*

mischievous boshaft.

miser Geizhals, *m.*

miserly geizig.

misfortune Unglück, *n.*

Miss Fräulein, *n.*

miss (to) versäumen.

mission Mission, *f.*

mist Nebel, *m.*

mistake Fehler, *m.*

mistaken irrtümlich.

You are mistaken. Sie sind im Irrtum.

Mister Herr.

mistrust (to) misstrauen.

misunderstand (to) missverstehen.

misunderstanding Missverständnis, *n.*

misuse (to) missbrauchen.

mix (to) mischen.

mixture Mischung, *f.*

mob Pöbel, *m.*

mobile beweglich.

mobilization Mobilmachung, *f.*

mobilize (to) mobilisieren.

mock (to) verspotten.

mockery Gespött, *n.*

mode Mode, *f.*

model Modell, *n.*

moderate mässigen.

moderation Mässigkeit, *f.*

modern modern.

modest bescheiden.

modesty Bescheidenheit, *f.*

modification Veränderung, *f.*

modify (to) verändern.

moist feucht.

moisten anfeuchten.

moment Augenblick, *m.*; Moment, *m.*

Just a moment Einen Augenblick.

monarchy Monarchie, *f.*

monastery Kloster, *n.*

Monday Montag, *m.*

money Geld, *n.*

monk Mönch, *m.*

monkey Affe, *m.*

monologue Monolog, *m.*

monotonous eintönig.

monotony Eintönigkeit, *f.*

monster Ungeheuer, *n.*

monstrous ungeheuer.

month Monat, *m.*

monthly monatlich.

monument Denkmal, *n.*

monumental monumental.

mood Stimmung, *f.*; Laune, *f.* (temper).

moody launisch.

moon Mond, *m.*

moonlight Mondschein, *m.*

mop Mop, *m.*

moral Moral, *f.*

morality Sittlichkeit, *f.*

more mehr.

moreover darüber hinaus.

morning Morgen, *m.*

morsel Bissen, *m.*

mortal sterblich.

mortality Sterblichkeit, *f.*

mortgage Hypothek, *f.*

mortgage (to) verpfänden.

mosquito Mücke, *f.*

most am meisten.

most of die meisten.

mostly meistens.

moth Motte, *f.*

mother Mutter, *f.*

mother-in-law Schwiegermutter, *f.*

motion Bewegung, *f.*

motionless bewegungslos.

motivate (to) beweisen, begründen.

motor Motor, *m.*

mount Hügel, *m.*

mountain Berg, *m.*

mountainous bergig.

mourn (to) trauern.

mournful traurig.

mourning Trauer, *f.*

mouse Maus, *f.*

mouth Mund, *m.*

move (to) bewegen.

movement Bewegung, *f.*

movies Kino, *n.*

moving rührend.

much viel.

How much? Wieviel?

mud Schlamm, *m.*

muddy schlammig.

mule Maultier, *n.*

multiply (to) multiplizieren.

multitude Menge, *f.*

mumble (to) murmeln.

municipal städtisch.

munition Munition, *f.*

murder Mord, *m.*

murder (to) ermorden.

murderer Mörder, *m.*

murmur (to) murren.

muscle Muskel, *m.*

museum Museum, *n.*

mushroom Pilz, *m.*

music Musik, *f.*

musical musikalisch.

musician Musiker, *m.*

must müssen.

mustache Schnurrbart, *m.*

mustard Senf, *m.*

mute stumm.

mutton Hammelfleisch, *n.*

my mein.

myself ich (mich, mir) selbst.

mysterious geheimnisvoll.

mystery Geheimnis, *n.*

N

nail Nagel, *m.*

nail (to) nageln.

naive harmlos, naive.

naked nackt.

name Name, *m.*

first name Vorname, *m.*

last name Zuname, *m.*

What is your name? Wie heissen Sie?

namely nähmlich.

nap Schläfchen, *n.*

napkin Serviette, *f.*

narrow eng.

nasty garstig.

nation Nation, *f.*

national national.

nationality Nationalität, *f.*

native Eingeborene, *m.*, *f.*, *n.*

native country Heimat, *f.*

natural natürlich.

naturally natürlich.

nature Natur, *f.*

naughty unartig.

naval see-.

navy Flotte, *f.*
near nah.
nearly beinahe.
neat nett, ordentlich.
neatness Niedlichkeit, *f.*; Sauberkeit, *f.*
necessary notwendig.
necessity, Notwendigkeit, *f.*
neck Hals, *m.*
necklace Halsband, *n.*
necktie Krawatte, *f.*; Schlips, *m.* (colloquial).
need Not, *f.*; Bedürfnis, *f.*
need (to) brauchen.
needle Nadel, *f.*
needless unnötig.
needy dürftig, bedürftig.
negative Negativ, *m.*
neglect Vernachlässigung, *f.*
neglect (to) vernachlässigen.
negotiate (to) unterhandeln.
negotiation Unterhandlung, *f.*
Negro Neger, *m.*
neighbor Nachbar, *m.*
neighborhood Nachbarschaft, *f.*
neither kein(er,-e,-es).
    neither...nor weder...noch.
nephew Neffe, *m.*
nerve Nerv, *m.*
    What a nerve! So eine Frechheit!
nervous nervös.
nest Nest, *n.*
net Netz, *n.*
neuter Neutrum, *n.*
neutral neutral.
never niemals, nie.
    Never mind! Das macht nichts!
nevertheless trotzdem; auf alle Fälle.
new neu.
news Nachrichten, *pl.*
newspaper Zeitung, *f.*
next nächst.
nice nett.
nickname Spitzname, *m.*
niece Nichte, *f.*
night Nacht, *f.*
nightgown Nachthemd, *n.*
nightmare Alpdrücken, *n.*
nine neun.
nineteen neunzehn
ninety neunzig.
ninth neunte.
no nein; kein (adj).
    no longer nicht mehr.
    no matter ungeachtet (gen.)
nobility Adel, *m.*
noble adlig.
nobody niemand.
noise Geräusch, *n.*
noisy geräuschvoll.
nominate (to) ernennen.
nomination Ernennung, *f.*
none kein(e, -er, -es).
nonsense Unsinn, *m.*
noon Mittag, *m.*
nor noch.
normal normal.
north Norden, *m.*
northern nordisch, nördlich.
northeast Nordosten, *m.*
northwest Nordwesten, *m.*
nose Nase, *f.*
nostril Nasenloch, *n.*
not nicht.
note Note, *f.*
note (to) notieren.
notebook Notizbuch, *n.*
nothing nichts.
notice Benachrichtung, *f.*
notice (to) bemerken

notify (to) benachrichtigen.
notion Idee, *f.*; Begriff, *m.*
noun Name, *m.*
nourish (to) nähren.
nourishment Nahrung, *f.*
novel Roman, *m.*
novelty Neuheit, *f.*
November November, *m.*
now jetzt.
    now and then. dann und wann; manchmal.
nowadays heutzutage.
nowhere nirgendwo.
nude nackt, bloss.
nuisance Unfug, *m.*
null null.
    null and void null und nichtig.
numb gefühllos.
number Nummer, *f.*
numerous zahlreich.
nun Nonne, *f.*
nurse Krankenschwester, *f.* (for the sick);
    Kindermädchen (for children).
nursery Kinderstube, *f.* (children); Gärtnerei, *f.*
    (trees)
nursery rhyme Kinderlied, *n.*
nut Nuss, *f.*
nutcracker Nussknacker, *m.*

O

oak Eiche, *f.*
oar Ruder, *n.*
oat Hafer, *m.*
oath Eid, *m.*
obedience Gehorsam, *m.*
obedient gehorsam.
obey (to) gehorchen.
object (to) einwenden, dagegen sein.
objection Einwand, *m.*
objective objektiv.
objectively sachlich.
obligation Verpflichtung, *f.*
oblige (to) verpflichten.
obliging gefällig.
obscure verdunkelt; verworren (meaning).
obscurity Dunkelheit, *f.*
observation Beobachtung, *f.*
observatory Sternwarte, *f.*
observe (to) beobachten.
obstacle Hindernis, *n.*
obstinacy Eigensinn, *m.*
obstinate eigensinnig.
obvious klar.
obviously offenbar, deutlich.
occasion Gelegenheit, *f.*
occasional gelegentlich.
occasionally zuweilen.
occupation Beschäftigung, *f.*
occupy (to) besitzen; besetzen (military).
occur (to) vorkommen (an event); einfallen
    (a thought).
occurrence Vorfall, *m.*
ocean Ozean, *m.*
October Oktober, *m.*
odd ungerade (uneven); sonderbar (unusual).
odor Geruch, *m.*
of von (dat.); aus (dat.) (made of).
    of course natürlich.
off fort, weg.
    off and on ab und zu.
offend (to) beleidigen.
offense Beleidigung, *f.*
offensive beleidigend.
offer (to) anbieten.
offering Gabe, *f.*
office Büro, *n.*
official offiziell.

often oft, oftmals.
oil Öl, *n.*
old alt.
olive Olive, *f.*
olive oil Olivenöl, *n.*
on auf (dat. or acc.); an (dat. or acc.) (date).
once einmal; vormals, einst (formerly).
    at once   sofort.
    once in a while manchmal.
    once more   noch einmal.
one ein(er, -e, -es).
one (pr.) man.
oneself sich, sich selbst.
onion Zwiebel, *f.*
only nur.
open offen.
open (to) öffnen.
opener Öffner, *m.*
opening Öffnung, *f.*
opera Oper, *f.*
operate (to) operieren.
operation Operation, *f.*
opinion Meinung, *f.*
opponent Gegner, *m.*
opportune gelegen.
opportunity Gelegenheit, *f.*
oppose (to) sich widersetzen.
opposite gegenüber.
opposition Widerstand, *m.*
oppress (to) unterdrücken.
oppression Unterdrückung, *f.*
optician Optiker, *m.*
optimism Optimismus, *m.*
optimistic optimistisch.
or oder.
orange Apfelsine, *f.*
orange juice Apfelsinensaft, *m.*
orator Redner, *m.*
orchard Obstgarten, *m.*
orchestra Orchester, *n.*
ordeal Prüfung, *f.*
order Ordnung, *f.* (neatness); Bestellung, *f.*
    (commercial); Befehl, *m.* (command); Orden, *m.*
    (decoration).
    out of order   kaputt.
    to put in order in Ordnung bringen.
order (to) ordnen (regulate); bestellen (commercial);
    befehlen (command).
ordinary gewöhnlich.
organ Orgel, *f.* (music); Organ, *n.* (anatomy).
organization Organisation, *f.*
organize (to) organisieren.
Orient Orient, *m.*
oriental orientalisch.
origin Ursprung, *m.* (source); Herkunft, *f.* (descent).
original original.
originality Originalität, *f.*
ornament Ornament, *n.*
orphan Waisenkind, *n.*
orthodox orthodox.
other anderer.
ought (to) sollen.
ounce Unze, *f*
our unser.
ours unser(er, -e, -es).
out aus (dat.); hinaus.
    out of   ausser (dat.)
outcome Folge, *f.*; Ergebnis, *n.*
outdo (to) übertreffen.
outdoors im Freien.
outer äusser.
outlast überdauern.
outlaw Geächtete, *m.*
outlaw (to) ächten.
outlay Auslage, *f.*
outlet Auslass, *m.*; Absatz, *m.* (market)
outline Umriss, *m.*
outlook Aussicht, *f.*

output Produktion, f.; Leistung, f. (machine).
outrage Schandtat, f.
outrageous schändlich.
outside Aussenseite (noun, f.); draussen (outdoors);
    ausserhalb (besides).
oval oval.
oven Ofen, m.
over über (acc.); vorbei (finished).
    over and over   wieder und wieder.
overboard über Bord.
overcoat Mantel, m.
overcome (to) überwinden.
overflow (to) überfliessen.
overlook (to) übersehen.
overrun überrennen.
overseas übersee.
overthrow umstürzen.
overwhelm (to) überwältigen.
owe (to) schulden.
owl Eule, f.
own eigen.
own (to) besitzen (possess); bekennen (admit).
owner Eigentümer, m.
ox Ochse, m.
oxygen Sauerstoff, m.
oyster Auster, f.

P

pace Schritt, m.
pace (to) schreiten.
pacific friedlich.
pack Kartenspiel, n. (cards).
pack (to) einpacken.
package Paket, n.
page Seite, f.
pain Schmerz, m.
pain (to) schmerzen.
painful schmerzhaft.
painless schmerzlos.
paint Farbe, f.
paint (to) malen (art); anstreichen (a wall).
painter Maler, m. (artist); Anstreicher (workman).
painting Gemälde, n.
pair Paar, n.
pajamas Pyjama, m.
palace Palast, m.
pale blass.
palm Palme, f.
pamphlet Broschüre, f.
pan Pfanne, f.
pancake Pfannkuchen, m.
pane Scheibe, f.
panel Füllung, f.; Liste, f. (persons).
panic Panik, f.
panorama Panorama, n.
panties Schlüpfer, m.
pants Hose, f.
paper Papier, n.
parachute Fallschirm, m.
parade Parade, f.
paragraph Paragraph, m.; Absatz, m.
parallel parallel.
paralysis Lähmung, f.
paralyzed gelähmt.
parcel Paket, n.
pardon Verzeihung, f.
pardon (to) vergeben.
parenthesis Klammer, f.
parents Eltern, pl.
Parisian Pariser, m.
park Park, m.
park (to) parken.
parliament Parlament, n.
parrot Papagei, m.
parsley Petersilie, f.
part Teil, n. (share); Ersatzteil (machinery).
part (to) teilen; sich trennen (separate);
    scheiteln (hair).

partial teilweise.
partiality Vorliebe, f.
particular besonder(er, -e, -es).
particularly besonders.
partner Partner, m.
party (political) Partei, f.; Gesellschaft, f.
    (society).
pass Ausweis, m.
pass (to) durchgehen, vorbeigehen; passen (cards);
    bestehen (exam).
passage Durchgang, m.; Überfahrt, f. (travel).
passenger Passagier, m.
passion Leidenschaft, f.
passionately leidenschaftlich.
passive Passiv, n.
passport Pass, m.
past Vergangenheit (noun, f.); vorbei, vorige
    (time); nach (on the clock).
    ten past six   zehn nach sechs.
paste Kleister, m.
paste (to) kleistern.
pastry Gebäck, n.
pastry shop Konditorei, f.
patch Flicken, m.
patch (to) flicken.
patent Patent, n.
paternal väterlich.
path Weg, m.
pathetic pathetisch.
patience Geduld, f.
patient Patient (noun, m.); geduldig (adj.).
patriot Patriot, m.
patriotic patriotisch.
patron Gönner, m.
patronage Gönnerschaft, f.
patronize (to) unterstützen.
pattern Muster, n.
pause Pause, f.
pave (to) pflastern.
pavement Pflaster, n.
paw Pfote, f.
pay Lohn, m.; Löhnung, f.; Sold, m. (military).
pay (to) zahlen.
payment Bezahlung, f.
pea Erbse, f.
peace Frieden, m.
peaceful friedlich.
peach Pfirsich, m.
peak Gipfel, m.
peanut Erdnuss, f.
pear Birne, f.
pearl Perle, f.
peasant Bauer, m.
pebble Kieselstein, m.
peculiar sonderbar.
pedal Pedal, n.
pedantic pedantisch.
pedestrian Fussgänger, m.
peel Rinde, f.; Schale, f.
peel (to) schälen.
pen Feder, f.
    fountain pen   Füllfeder, f.
penalty Strafe, f.
pencil Bleistift, m.
penetrate (to) durchdringen.
peninsula Halbinsel, f.
penitence Reue, f.
pension Pension, f. ·
people Leute, pl.
pepper Pfeffer, m.
peppermint Pfefferminz, m.
per pro.
perceive (to) wahrnehmen.
percentage Prozentsatz, m.
perfect vollkommen.
perfection Vollkommenheit, f.
perfectly gänzlich.
perform (to) verrichten; aufführen (theater or

    surgery).
performance Vorstellung, f.
perfume Parfüm, n.
perfume (to) parfümieren.
perhaps vielleicht.
period Periode, f.
periodical periodisch.
permanent ständig.
permission Erlaubnis, f.
permit Erlaubnisschein, m.
permit (to) erlauben.
peroxide Hyperoxyd, n.
perpetual immerwährend.
perplex verwirren.
persecute (to) verfolgen.
persecution Verfolgung, f.
perseverance Ausdauer, f.
persist (to) beharren.
person Person, f.
personal persönlich.
personality Persönlichkeit., f.
perspective Perspektive, f.
perspiration Schweiss, m.
persuade (to) überreden.
pertaining gehören (zu).
petrol Petroleum, n.
petticoat Unterrock, m.
petty kleinlich.
pharmacist Apotheker, f.
pharmacy Apotheke, f.
phenomenon Phänomen, n.
philosopher Philosoph, m.
philosophical philosophisch.
philosophy Philosophie, f.
phonograph Plattenspieler, m.
photograph Fotografie, f.
photograph (to) aufnehmen.
photographer Fotograf, m.
phototast Lichtpause, f.
phrase Frase, f.
physical körperlich.
physician Arzt, m; Doktor, m.
piano Klavier, n.
pick (to) pflücken.
pick up (to) aufheben.
picnic Piknik, n.
picture Bild, n.
picturesque malerisch.
pie Torte, f.
piece Stück, n.
pier Mole, f.
pig Schwein, n.
pigeon Taube, f.
pile Haufen, m.
pile (to) aufhäufen.
pilgrim Pilger, m.
pill Pille, f.
pillar Säule, f.
pillow Kissen, n.
pilot Pilot, m.
pin Stecknadel, f.
pinch (to) kneifen.
pink rosa.
pious fromm.
pipe Pfeife, f. (tobacco); Rohr, n. (plumbing).
pirate Seeräuber, m.; Pirat, m.
pistol Pistole, f.
pitiful mitleidig.
pity Mitleid, n.
place Platz, m.; Stelle, f. (spot, situation);
    Ort, m. (locality).
    take place   stattfinden.
place (to) stellen.
plain Ebene (noun, f.); einfach (adj.).
plan Plan, m. (project); Grundriss, m.
plan (to) ausdenken.
plane Flugzeug, n.
planet Planet, m.

plant Pflanze, f.
plant (to) pflanzen.
plaster Verputz, m.
plastic Kunststoff (noun, m.); plastisch (adj.).
plate Teller, m.
platform Bahnsteig, m. (station).
platter Platte, f.
play Spiel, n.; Stück, n. (theater).
play (to) spielen.
plea Gesuch, n.
plead (to) plädieren.
pleasant angenehm.
please bitte.
please (to) gefallen.
pleasure Vergnügen, n.
pledge Pfand, n.
plenty genug (enough); reichlich (abundance).
plot Verschwörung, f. (conspiracy); Handlung, f. (of a story).
plot (to) anstiften.
plow Pflug, m.
plow (to) pflügen.
plum Pflaume, f.
plumber Klempner, m.
pneumonia Lungenentzündung, f.
pocket Tasche, f.
poem Gedicht, n.
poet Poet, m.
poetic poetisch.
poetry Dichtung, f.
point Punkt, m.; Spitze, f.
point (to) spitzen.
pointed spitz.
poise Gleichgewicht, n.
poison Gift, m.
poison (to) vergiften.
poisonous giftig.
polar pol–.
pole Pol, m.
police Polizei, f.
policeman Schutzmann, m.; Polizist, m.
policy Politik, f.; Police, f. (insurance).
Polish polnisch.
polish Glanz, m.
polish (to) glänzend machen; polieren.
polite höflich.
politeness Höflichkeit, f.
political politisch.
pond Teich, m.
pool Pfuhl, m.
poor arm.
Pope Papst, m.
popular volkstümlich.; beliebt (liked).
population Bevölkerung, f.
pork Schweinefleisch, n.
port Hafen, m.
porter Träger, m.
portrait Bild, n.
Portuguese Portugiese (noun, m.); portugiesisch (adj.).
position Stellung, f. (job); Lage, f. (site).
positive bestimmt.
possibility möglicherweise.
possible möglich.
post Post, f.; Stelle, f. (job).
postage Porto, n.
postcard Postkarte, f.
poster Plakat, n.
posterity Nachwelt, f.
post office Postamt, n.
pot Topf, m.
potato Kartoffel, f.
pound Pfund, m.
pour (to) giessen.
poverty Armut, f.
powder Pulver, n.; Puder, m. (cosmetic).
powder (to) pudern.
power Macht, f.

powerful mächtig.
practical praktisch.
practice (to) üben.
praise Lob, n.
praise (to) loben.
prank Prank, m.; Streich, m.
pray (to) beten.
prayer Gebet, n.
preach (to) predigen.
preacher Prediger, m.
precaution Vorsicht, f.
precede (to) vorangehen.
preceding vorangehend.
precept Vorschrift, f.; Beispiel, n. (example).
precious kostbar.
precise genau; steif (formal).
precision Genauigkeit, f.
predecessor Vorgänger, m.
preface Vorwort, n.
prefer (to) vorziehen.
preference Vorzug, m.
pregnant schwanger.
prejudice Vorurteil, n.
preliminary einleitend.
preparation Vorbereitung, f.
prepare (to) vorbereiten.
prepay (to) vorauszahlen.
prescribe (to) verschreiben.
prescription Rezept, n.
presence Gegenwart, f.; Anwesenheit, f.
present Gegenwart, f. (grammar); Geschenk, n. (gift); anwesend (adj.).
preserve (to) erhalten; konservieren (food).
preserves Konserven, f.; Eingemachte, n.
preside (to) präsidieren.
president Präsident, m.
press Presse, f.
press (to) drücken; bügeln (clothes).
pressing dringend.
pressure Druck, m.; Andrang, m. (blood–).
prestige Prestige, n.; Ansehen, n.
presume (to) vermuten.
pretend (to) vorgeben.
pretext Vorwand, m.
pretty hübsch, nett.
prevail (to) vorherrschen.
prevent (to) verhindern.
prevention Verhinderung, f.
previous frühere.
prey Raub, m.
price Preis, m.
pride Stolz, m.
priest Priester, m.
prince Prinz, m.
principal haupt– (adj.).
principle Grundsatz, m.
print (to) drucken.
prison Gefängnis, n.
prisoner Gefangene, m.
private privat.
privilege Vorrecht, n.
prize Preis, m.
prize (to) schätzen.
probable wahrscheinlich.
problem Problem, n.
procedure Verfahren, n.
proceed (to) fortschreiten.
process Verfahren, n; Prozess, m.
procession Prozession, f.
proclaim (to) bekanntmachen.
produce (to) erzeugen.
product Erzeugnis, n.
production Erzeugung, f.; Produktion, f.
productive fruchtbar.
profession Beruf, m.
professional berufsmässig.
professor Professor, m; Lehrer, m. (school).
profile Profil, n.

profit Gewinn, m.
profit (to) gewinnen.
program Programm, n.
progress Fortschritt, m.
progress (to) vorwärtskommen.
progressive fortschrittlich.
prohibit (to) verbieten.
prohibition Verbot, n.
project Projekt, n.
project (to) hervorstehen.
promise (to) versprechen.
prompt schnell.
pronoun Fürwort, n.
pronounce (to) aussprechen.
pronunciation Aussprache, f.
proof Beweis, m.
propaganda Propaganda, f.
proper passend; anständig (decent).
property Eigentum, n.
proportion Verhältnis, n.
proposal Vorschlag, m.
propose (to) vorschlagen.
prose Prosa, f.
prospect (to) Aussicht, f.
prosper (to) gedeihen.
prosperity Wohlstand, m.
prosperous gedeihlich, blühend.
protect (to) schützen.
protection Schutz, m.
protector Beschützer, m.
protest Einspruch, m.
protest (to) protestieren.
Protestant Protestant, m.
proud stolz.
prove (to) probieren.
proverb Sprichwort, n.
provide (to) versorgen.
provided that vorausgesetzt dass.
province Provinz, f.
provincial provinziell.
provision Provision, f.
provoke (to) herausfordern, reizen.
proximity Nähe, f.
prudence Vorsicht, f.
prudent klug, vorsichtig.
prune Backpflaume, f.
psychological psychologisch.
psychology Psychologie, f.
public Publikum (noun, n.); öffentlich (adj.).
publication Herausgabe, f. (literary); Veröffent- lichung, f. (notification)
publish (to) herausgeben (book); veröffentlichen (announcement).
publishing house Verlag, m.
publisher Verleger, m.
pull (to) ziehen.
pump Pumpe, f.
punish (to) bestrafen.
punishment Strafe, f.
pupil Schüler, m.; Schülerin, f.
purchase (to) kaufen.
purchase Einkauf, m.
pure rein.
purity Reinheit, f.
purple Purpur, m.
purpose Absicht, f.
purse Geldtasche, f.
pursue (to) verfolgen.
push (to) stossen.
put (to) legen (lay); setzen (set); stellen (place).
	put down aufschreiben.
	put off aufschieben.
	put on anziehen.
	put up aufstellen.
puzzle Rätsel, n.
puzzle (to) verwirren.

Q

quaint seltsam.
qualify berechtigen.
quality Qualität, f.
quantity Quantität, f.
quarrel Streit, m.
quarter Viertel, n.
queen Königin, f.
queer seltsam.
quench (to) löschen.
question Frage, f.
question (to) fragen.
quick schnell.
quiet ruhig.
quit (to) verlassen.
quite ganz.
quote (to) anführen.

R

rabbit Kaninchen, n.
race Rennen, n. (contest); Rasse, f. (species).
radiator Heizkörper, m.
radio Radio, n.
rag Fetzen, m.
rage Wut, f.
ragged zerlumpt.
rail Schiene, f.
railroad Eisenbahn, f.
railroad car Eisenbahnwagen, m.
rain Regen, m.
rain (to) regnen.
rainbow Regenbogen, m.
raincoat Regenmantel, m.
rainy regnerisch.
raise (to) erhöhen.
raisin Rosine, f.
rake Rechen, m.
rank Rang, m.
rapid schnell.
rapidly schnell.
rapture Entzücken, n.
rash Hautausschlag (noun, m.) (skin); hastig (adj.).
rat Ratte, f.
rate Kurs, m. (exchange); Verhältnis, n.
rate (to) schätzen.
rather ziemlich, lieber, eher.
ration Ration, f.
rational vernünftig.
rave (to) schwärmen.
raw roh.
ray Strahl, m.
razor Rasiermesser, n.
razor blade Razierklinge, f.
reach (to) erreichen.
reach Bereich, m; Reichweite, f.
react (to) rückwirken, reagieren.
read (to) lesen.
reading Lesen, n.; Lektüre f.
ready fertig.
real wirklich.
realization Verwirklichung, f.
realize (to) verwirklichen.
really wirklich.
rear Hintergrund (noun, m.); hinter (adj.).
rear (to) grossziehen.
reason Grund, m. (cause); Vernunft, f. (intelligence).
reason (to) besprechen.
reasonable vernünftig.
reasoning Schlussfolgerung, f.
reassure (to) beruhigen.
rebel Rebell, m.
rebel (to) sich auflehnen.
rebellion Empörung, f.
recall (to) sich erinnern (memory); zurückrufen (to summon back).

receipt Quittung, f.
receive (to) empfangen
receiver Empfänger, m.
recent neu.
recently neulich.
reception Empfang, m.
recess Nische, f.
reciprocal gegenseitig.
recite (to) aufsagen; rezitieren (drama).
recognize (to) erkennen.
recollect (to) sich erinnern.
recollection Erinnerung, f.
recommend (to) empfehlen.
recommendation Empfehlung, f.
reconcile (to) versöhnen.
record Ordner, m.
    phonograph record (Schall)platte, f.
recover (to) sich erholen.
recruit Rekrut, m.
recruit (to) rekrutieren.
red rot.
Red Cross Rote Kreuz, n.
redeem (to) erlösen.
reduce (to) herabsetzen; abnehmen (weight).
reduction Nachlass, m.
reed Schilf, m.
reef Riff, n.
refer (to) sich beziehen.
reference Bezugnahme, f.
referring to bezugnehmen auf.
refine (to) verfeinern.
refinement Bildung, f.
reflect (to) zurückstrahlen
reflection Widerschein, m. (image); Überlegung, f. (thoughts).
reform Besserung, f.
reform (to) sich bessern.
refrain (to) sich enthalten.
refresh (to) erfrischen.
refreshment Erfrischung, f.
refrigerator Kühlschrank, m.
refuge Zufluchtsort, m.
    take refuge flüchten.
refugee Flüchtling, m.
refund Rückzahlung, f.
refund (to) zurückzahlen.
refusal Verweigerung, f.
refuse (to) ablehnen, verweigern.
refute (to) widerlegen.
regard Ansehen, n.
regardless unbeachtet.
regime Regime, n.
regiment Regiment, n.
register (to) eintragen (membership); einschreiben (letter).
regret Bedauern, n.
regret (to) bedauern.
regular regelmässig.
regulate regulieren.
regulation Vorschrift, f.
rehearsal Probe, f.
rehearse (to) Probe halten.
reign Regierung, f.
reign (to) regieren.
reinforce (to) verstärken.
reject (to) verwerfen.
rejoice (to) sich freuen.
relapse Rückfall, m.
relate (to) erzählen.
relation Verwandtschaft, f.
relationship verwandtschaftliche Beziehung, f.
relative Verwandte, m.
relax (to) entspannen.
relaxation Entspannung, f.
release Befreiung, f.
release (to) freilassen.
reliable zuverlässig.
relic Überbleibsel, n.; Relique, f.; (religious).

relief Erleichterung, f.; Linderung, f. (of pain).
relieve (to) erleichtern, lindern.
religion Religion, f.
religious religiös.
relinquish (to) aufgeben.
relish (to) munden.
relish Geschmack, m.
reluctance Widerwille, n.
reluctant widerwillig.
rely (to) sich verlassen.
remain (to) bleiben.
remainder Rest, m.
remark Bemerkung, f.
remark (to) bemerken.
remarkable bemerkenswert.
remedy Arznei, f. (medicine); Hilfsmittel, n. (cure).
remember (to) sich erinnern.
remembrance Erinnerung, f.
remind (to) mahnen.
remorse Reue, f.
remote entfernt (distance); rückständig (antiquated).
removal Beseitigung, f.
remove (to) entfernen.
renew (to) erneuern.
renewal Erneuerung, f.
rent Miete, f.
rent (to) mieten.
repair Reparatur, f.
repay (to) zurückzahlen.
repeat (to) wiederholen.
repent (to) bereuen.
repetition Wiederholung, f.
reply Antwort, f.
reply (to) antworten.
report Bericht, m.; Zeugnis, n.
report (to) berichten.
reporter Reporter, m.
represent (to) vertreten.
representation Vertretung, f.
representative Vertreter, m.
repress (to) unterdrücken.
repression Unterdrückung, f.
reprimand Verweis, m.
reprimand (to) tadeln.
reprisal Gegenmassregel, f.
reproach Vorwurf, m.
reproach (to) vorwerfen.
reproduce (to) reproduzieren.
reproduction Reproduktion, f.
republic Republik, f.
reputation Ruf, m.; Ansehen, n
request Bitte, f.
request (to) bitten.
require (to) benötigen.
requirement Bedarf, m.
rescue (to) retten.
research Forschung, f.
resent (to) verübeln.
resentful empfindlich.
resentment Verdruss, m.
reservation Reservation, f.
reserve (to) reservieren.
reservoir Behälter, m.
residence Wohnstätte, f.
resident Bewohner, m.
resign (to) aufgeben.
resignation Rücktritt, m.
resist (to) widerstehen.
resistance Widerstand, m.
resolute entschlossen.
resolution Beschluss, m.
resolve (to) sich entschliessen (decide); lösen (problem).
resort Kurort, m. (health); Luftkurort, m. (vacation); Zuflucht, f. (recourse).
resource Hilfsmittel, n.
respect Achtung, f.

respectful ehrfürchtig, achtungsvoll.
respective bezüglich.
responsibility Verantwortlichkeit, f.
responsible verantwortlich.
rest Ruhe, f.
rest (to) ruhen.
restaurant Restaurant, n.
restless unruhig.
restoration Wiederherstellung, f.
restore (to) wiederherstellen, restaurieren.
restrain (to) zurückhalten.
restraint Zurückhaltung, f.
restrict (to) beschränken.
restriction Einschränkung, f.
result Resultat, n.
result (to) folgen.
resume (to) wiederaufnehmen, wieder anfangen.
retail Einzelverkauf, m.; Kleinhandel, m.
retail (to) im Kleinhandel verkaufen.
retain (to) behalten.
retaliate (to) vergelten.
retaliation Vergeltung, f.
retire (to) sich zurückziehen.
retirement Zurückgezogenheit, f.
retract widerrufen; zurückziehen.
retreat Rückzug, m.
retreat (to) sich zurückziehen.
return Rückkehr, f.
return (to) zurückkehren.
reveal (to) offenbaren, enthüllen.
revelation Offenbarung, f.
revenge Rache, f.
revenge (to) rächen.
revenue Einkommen, n.
reverence Ehrerbietung, f.
reverend ewürdig.
reverse Rückseite, f.
reverse (to) umkehren.
review (to) betrachten; mustern (inspect);
    rezensieren (critical).
review Überblick, m. Parade, f. (army);
    Revue, f. (theater), Rezension, f.
revise (to) revidieren, (critique).
revive neubeleben.
revival Wiederbelebung, f.
revoke (to) widerrufen.
revolt Aufstand, m.
revolt (to) sich empören.
revolution Revolution, f.
revolve (to) sich drehen.
reward Belohnung, f.
reward (to) belohnen.
rhyme Reim, m.
rhyme (to) reimen.
rib Rippe, f.
ribbon Band, n.
rice Reis, m.
rich reich.
richness Reichtum, m.
rid (to get) loswerden.
riddle Rätsel, n.
ride Fahrt, f.
ridiculous lächerlich.
rifle Gewehr, n.
right richtig (correct); rechts (position).
    all right ganz gut.
righteous gerecht.
rigid steif, fest, starr.
rigor Strenge, f.
rigorous streng, scharf, hart.
ring Ring, m.
    wedding ring Ehering, m.
ring (to) ringen.
rinse (to) spülen, ausspülen.
riot Aufruhr, f.; Schwelgerei, f. (army).
ripe reif.
ripen (to) reifen.
rise Steigung, f.

rise (to) aufstehen (get up); steigen (increase,
    mount); aufgehen (sun).
risk Gefahr, f.
risk (to) riskieren.
rite Ritus, m.
ritual rituell.
rival Rivale, m.
rivalry Mitbewerbung, f.; Konkurrenz, f.
river Fluss, m.
roach Schabe, f.
road Weg, m.
roar (to) brüllen.
roast Braten, m.
roast (to) braten.
rob (to) rauben.
robber Räuber, m.
robbery Diebstahl, m.
robe Morgenrock, m.
robust stark, rüstig.
rock Felsen, m.
rock (to) wiegen.
rocky felsig.
rocket Rakete, f.
rod Rute, f.
roll Rolle, f. (cylinder); Brötchen, n. (bread).
roll (to) rollen.
Roman Römer (noun, m.); römisch (adj.).
romantic romantisch.
roof Dach, n.
room Zimmer, n. (of a house); Raum, m. (space).
    There is no room. Da ist kein Platz.
roomy geräumig.
root Wurzel, f.
rope Seil, n.
rose Rose, f.
rot (to) faulen; vermodern.
rough rauh (coarse); roh (crude); stürmisch
    (stormy).
round Runde (noun, f.); rund (adj.).
round um (acc.); herum.
rouse (to) aufwecken; erzürnen (anger).
routine Routine, f.; Erfahrung, f.
row Reihe, f.
row (to) rudern.
royal königlich.
rub (to) reiben.
rubber Gummi, m.
ruby Rubin, m.
rude grob.
ruffle (to) verwirren.
ruin Ruine, f.
ruin (to) ruinieren.
rule Regel, f.
rule (to) regieren, beherrschen.
ruler Lineal, n.
rum Rum, m.
rumor Gerücht, n.
run (to) rennen, laufen.
    run away weglaufen.
rural ländlich.
rush (to) Sturz, m.; Andrang, m. (crowd).
Russian Russe (noun, m.); russisch (adj.)
rust (to) verrosten.
rusty rostig.
rye Roggen, m.

S

sacred heilig.
sacrifice Opfer, n.
sacrifice (to) opfern.
sacrilege Entweihung, f.
sad traurig.
sadden (to) trauern.
saddle Sattel, m.
sadness Traurigkeit, f.
safe Schliessfach (noun, n.) (of a bank);
    wohlbehalten (adj.) (in safekeeping);
    sicher (adj.) (secure).

safety Sicherheit, f.
sail (to) segeln.
sail Segel, n.
sailor Matrose, m.
saint Heilige, m. & f.
    patron saint Schutzheilige, m. & f.
sake (for the—of) um (gen.) willen.
salad Salat, m.
salami Salami, f.
salary Gehalt, n.
sale Verkauf, m.; Ausverkauf, m. (bargain).
saleslady Verkäuferin, f.
salesman Verkäufer, m.
salmon Lachs, m.
salt Salz, n.
salute Gruss, m.
salute (to) grüssen.
salvation Rettung, f.
Salvation Army Heilsarmee, f.
same der (die-, das-). selbe
    the same as derselbe wie.
    all the same es spielt keine Rolle.
sample Muster, n.
sanctuary Zufluchtsort, m.
sand Sand, m.
sandal Sandale, f.
sandwich Butterbrot, n.
sandy sandig.
sanitary hygienisch.
sap Saft, m.
sapphire Saphir, m.
sarcasm Sarkasmus, m.
sarcastic sarkastisch.
sardine Sardine, f.
satiate (to) sättigen.
satin Seidenatlas, m.
satisfaction Befriedung, f.
satisfactory zufriedenstellend.
satisfy (to) befriedigen.
saturate (to) durchtränken.
Saturday Samstag, m.
sauce Sauce, f.
saucer Untertasse, f.
sausage Wurst, f.
savage wild.
save (to) sparen (hoard); retten (rescue).
saving Ersparnis, f.
savior Erretter, m.
Savior Heiland, m.
say (to) sagen.
scale Schuppe, f.; Tonleiter, f. (music).
scales Massstab, m.; Waage, f.
scalp Skalp, m.
scan (to) überblicken.
scandal Skandal, m.
scanty knapp, dürftig.
scar Narbe, f.
scarce knapp.
scarcely kaum.
scare (to) erschrecken.
scarf Schal, m.
scarlet scharlachrot.
scattered verstreut.
schedule Stundenplan, m. (time).
scheme Schema, n.; Entwurf, m.
scholar Gelehrte, m & f.
school Schule, f.
schoolteacher Lehrer, m.; Lehrerin, f.
science Wissenschaft, f.
scientific wissenschaftlich.
scientist Wissenschaftler, m.
scissors Schere, f.
scold (to) schelten.
scorn Verachtung, f.
scorn (to) verachten.
scornful verächtlich.
Scottish schottisch.
scrape (to) kratzen; schaben (vegetables).

scraper Schaber, m.
scratch Schramme, f.
scratch (to) kratzen.
scream Schrei, m.
scream (to) schreien.
screen Schirm, m.
   movie screen Leinwand, f.
screw Schraube, f.
scribble (to) kritzeln.
scruple Skrupel, m.
scrupulous gewissenhaft.
scrutinize (to) prüfen.
sculptor Bildhauer, m.
sculpture Bildhauerei, f.
sea Meer, n.
seal Siegel, n.; Seehund, m. (animal).
seal (to) siegeln.
seam Naht, f.
search Suche, f.; Untersuchung, f. (customs).
search (to) suchen; untersuchen.
seashore Seeküste, f.
seasickness Seekrankheit, f.
season Jahreszeit, f.; Saison, f. (events).
seat Sitz, m.
seat (to) setzen; stellen.
second zweit(er, -e, -es).
secret Geheimnis, noun, n.; geheim (adj.).
secretary Sekretär, m.; Sekretärin, f.
sect Sekte, f.
section Teil, m.
secure sicher.
secure (to) sichern.
security Sicherheit, f.
see (to) sehen.
seed Samen, m.
seek (to) suchen.
seem (to) scheinen.
seize (to) ergreifen, fassen.
seldom selten, rar.
select (to) wählen.
selection Auswahl, f.
selfish selbstsüchtig.
selfishness Selbstsucht, f.
sell (to) verkaufen.
semicolon Semikolon, n.
senate Senat, m.
senator Senator, m.
send (to) senden.
senior Ältere.
sensation Gefühl, n. (feeling); Sensation, f. (excitement).
sense Sinn, m.
senseless sinnlos.
sensibility Vernünftigkeit, f.
sensible vernünftig.
sensitive empfindlich.
sensitivity Empfindlichkeit, f.
sensual wollüstig.
sensuality Wollust, f. Sinnlichkeit, f.
sentence Urteil, n. (legal); Satz, m. (grammar).
sentiment Gefühl, n.
sentimental sentimental.
sentimentality Sentimentalität, f.
separate einzeln.
separate (to) trennen.
separately besonders.
separation Trennung, f.
September September, m.
serene heiter.
sergeant Sergeant, m.
series Serie, f.
serious ernst.
seriousness Ernst, m.
servant Diener, m.
serve (to) dienen.
service Dienst, m.; Gottesdienst, m. (church).
session Sitzung, f.
set festgelegt.
set Sammlung, f. (collection); Untergang, m. (sun);

Satz, m. (series); Service, n. (dishes).
set (to) setzen; stellen (clock).
settle (to) begleichen (accounts); erledigen (conclude).
settlement Begleichung, f.; Erledigung, f. Siedlung f. (houses).
seven sieben.
seventeen siebzehn.
seventeenth siebzehnte.
seventh siebte.
seventieth siebzigste.
seventy siebzig.
several mehrere.
   several times mehrmals.
severe streng (stern, rigorous); hettig (pain).
severity Strenge, f.
sew (to) nähen.
sewer Abzugskanal, m.
sex Geschlecht, n.
shabby schäbig.
shade Schatten, m.
shadow Schatten, m.
shady schattig.
shake (to) schütteln; zittern (tremble).
   handshake Händedruck, m.
shallow seicht.
shame Schande, f. (disgrace); Scham, f. (modesty).
shameful schändlich.
shameless schamlos.
shampoo Shampoo, n.
shape Form, f.
share Teil, m.; Anteil, m.; Aktie, f. (stock).
share (to) teilen.
shareholder Aktionär, m.
sharp scharf.
sharpen schärfen.
shave (to) sich rasieren.
she sie.
shed (to) vergiessen (spill); abwerfen (discard).
sheep Schaf, n.
sheer rein, lauter.
sheet (Bett)laken, n. (linens); Blatt, n. (paper).
shelf Brett, n.
shell Muschel, f.; Geschoss, n. (artillery).
shelter Unterkunft, f.; Luftschutzraum, m (air raids).
shelter unterstellen (from exposure); schützen (from danger).
shepherd Schäfer, m.;
shield Schild, n.
shield (to) schützen.
shift Schicht, f. (workers).
shift (to) schieben.
shine (to) scheinen; putzen (shoes).
ship Schiff, n.
ship (to) senden, befördern.
shipment Verladung, f.; Verschiffung, f.; Beförderung, f.
shirt Hemd, n.
shiver Schauer, m.
shiver (to) (er)schauern.
shock Schlag, m. (blow); Stoss, m.
shock (to) anstossen (scandalize); erschüttern.
shoe Schuh, m.
shoemaker Schuhmacher, m.
shoot (to) schiessen.
shop Laden, m.; Geschäft, n.
short kurz.
shorten (to) kürzen.
shorthand Kurzschrift, f.; Stenographie, f.
shorts Unterhosen, pl. (men's).
shot Schuss, m.
shoulder Schulter, f.
shout Schrei, m.
shout (to) schreien.
shovel Schaufel, f.
show Vorstellung, f. (play); Ausstellung, f. (exhibition).
show (to) zeigen.

shower Schauer, m. (rain); Dusche, f. (shower-bath).
shrill schrill.
shrimp Krabbe, f.
shrink (to) einlaufen.
shrub Strauch, m.
shrubbery Gebüsch, n.
shun (to) meiden.
shut geschlossen.
shut (to) schliessen.
shy schüchtern.
sick krank.
sickness Krankheit, f.
side Seite, f.
sidewalk Bürgersteig, m.
siege Belagerung, f.
sigh Seufzer, m.
sigh (to) seufzen.
sight Aussicht, f.; Anblick, m.
sign Zeichen, n.
sign (to) zeichnen.
signal Signal, n.
signal (to) signalisieren.
signature Unterschrift, f.
significance Bedeutung, f.
significant bezeichnend.
signify (to) bezeichnen (indicate); bedeuten (mean).
silence Schweigen, n.
silent still, schweigend.
silk Seide, f.
silken seiden.
silly ausgelassen, dumm.
silver Silber, n.
silvery silbern.
similar ähnlich.
similarity Ähnlichkeit, f.
simple einfach.
simplicity Einfachheit, f.
simply nur (only).
simulate (to) erheucheln, vortäuschen.
simultaneous gleichzeitig.
sin Sünde, f.
sin (to) sündigen.
since seit (dat.); da, weil (because).
sincere aufrichtig.
sincerity Aufrichtigkeit, f.
sing (to) singen.
singer Sänger, m.; Sängerin, f.
single einzeln; ledig (unmarried).
singular einzigartig; seltsam (strange).
sinister unheilvoll.
sink Gussstein, m.; Ausguss, m.
sink (to) sinken.
sinner Sünder, m.; Sünderin, f.
sip (to) nippen.
sip Schluck, m.
sir Herr, m.
sister Schwester, f.
sister-in-law Schwägerin, f.
sit (to) sitzen (be seated); sich setzen (sit down).
site Lage, f.; Bauplatz, m.
situation Lage, f.
six sechs.
sixteen sechzehn.
sixteenth sechzehnte.
sixth sechste.
sixtieth sechzigste.
sixty sechzig.
size Grösse, f.
skate Schlittschuh, m.
skate (to) Schlittschuh laufen.
skeleton Gerippe, n.
sketch Skizze, f.
sketch (to) skizzieren.
skill Geschicklichkeit, f.
skillful geschickt, kundig.
skin Haut, f.
skirt Rock, m.
skull Schädel, m.

sky Himmel, m.
skyscraper Wolkenkratzer, m.
slander (to) verleumden.
slap Klaps, m.
slate Schiefer, m.
slaughter (to) schlachten.
slave Sklave, m.; Sklavin, f.
slavery Sklaverei, f.
sleep Schlaf, m.
sleep (to) schlafen.
sleeve Ärmel, m.
sleigh Schlitten, m.
slender schlank.
slice Schnitte, f.
slice (to) in Scheiben schneiden.
slide (to) schleifen, gleiten.
slight gering.
slip entschlüpfen.
slip Fehler, m. (mistake); Unterrock, m. (lingerie).
slope Abhang, m.
slot Einwurf, m.; Schlitz, m. (mail).
slow langsam.
slumber Schlummer, m.
slumber (to) schlummern.
sly schlau.
small klein.
smart elegant (clothes); gescheit (clever).
smash (to) zerschmettern.
smear (to) schmieren.
smell Geruch, m.
smell (to) riechen.
smile Lächeln, n.
smile (to) lächeln.
smoke Rauch, m.
smoke (to) rauchen.
smooth glatt.
smother (to) ersticken.
smuggle (to) schmuggeln.
snail Schnecke, f.
snake Schlange, f.
snapshot (Moment)aufnahme, f.
snatch (to) ergreifen.
sneer (to) (ver)hönnen.
sneeze (to) niessen.
snore (to) schnarchen.
snow Schnee, m.
snowstorm Schneesturm, m.
so so.
    and so on   und so weiter
soak (to) einweichen; durchnässen (drench).
soap Seife, f.
sob Schluchzen, n.
sob (to) schluchzen.
sober nüchtern.
social gesellschaftlich.
society Gesellschaft, f.
sock Sock, m.
soda Sodawasser, n.
soft weich.
soften (to) erweichen, aufweichen.
soil (to) beschmutzen.
soil Erde, f.; Boden, m.
soiled schmutzig.
soldier Soldat, m.
sole Sohle, f.
solemn feierlich.
solemnity Feierlichkeit, f.
solicit (to) bitten; nachsuchen.
solid fest.
solitary einsam (lonely); einzeln (one).
solitude Einsamkeit, f.
solution Lösung, f.
solve lösen.
some einige (a few); etwas (partial).
somebody jemand.
somehow irgendwie.
something etwas.
sometimes zuweilen.

somewhat etwas.
somewhere irgendwo.
son Sohn, m.
song Lied, n.
son-in-law Schwiegersohn, m.
soon bald.
soot Russ, m.
soothe (to) besänftigen; lindern (pain).
sore Geschwür (noun, n.); wund, schmerzhaft (adj.); empfindlich, verärgert (annoyed).
        sore throat   Halsschmerzen, pl.
sorrow Kummer, m.
sorry bekümmert.
    I am sorry.   Es tut mir leid.
sort Sorte, f.
sort (to) sortieren.
sound Laut, m.
sound (to) lauten.
soup Suppe, f.
sour sauer.
source Quelle, f. (spring); Ursprung, m. (origin).
south Süden, m.
southeast Südost, m.; Südosten, m.
southern Süd–; südlich.
southwest Südwest, m.; Südwesten, m.
sovereign Herrscher, m.
sow (to) säen.
space Raum, m.; Zwischenraum, m. (space between).
spacious (ge)räumig.
spade Spaten, m.; Pik, n. (cards).
Spanish spanisch.
spare spärlich.
spare (to) entbehren.
spark Funke, m.
sparkle (to) funkeln, glänzen.
sparrow Sperling, Spatz, m.
speak (to) sprechen.
special besonders, extra.
specialty Spezialität, f.
specific eigen, spezifisch, genau.
specify (to) spezifizieren.
spectacle Schauspiel, n.
spectator Zuschauer, m.
speculate (to) spekulieren.
speech Sprache, f.; Rede, f.
speed Geschwindigkeit, f.
speedy schnell.
spell Zauber, m. (charm).
spell (to) buchstabieren, schreiben.
spelling Buchstabieren n.
spend (to) ausgeben.
sphere Sphäre, f.
spice Gewürz, n.
spice (to) würzen.
spicy würzig.
spider Spinne, f.
spill (to) verschütten.
spin (to) spinnen.
spine Rückgrat, n.
spirit Geist, m.
spiritual geistig.
spit (to) spucken.
spite Bosheit, f.
    in spite of   trotz (gen.), trotzdem (gen. or dat.).
splash (to) (be)spritzen.
splendid prachtvoll.
    Splendid!   Wunderbar!
splendor Pracht, f.; Glanz, m.
split Spalt, m.
split (to) spalten.
spoil (to) verderben; verwöhnen (child).
sponge Schwamm, m.
spontaneous spontan.
spoon Löffel, m.
spoonful Löffelvoll, m.
sport Sport, m.
spot Fleck, m. (stain); Stelle, f. (place).
spread (to) verbreiten; bestreichen (on bread).

spring Frühling, m. (season); Sprung, m. (jump); Quelle, f. (source).
spring (to) springen.
sprinkle sprenkeln.
sprout Sprössling, m.
spur Sporn, m.
spur (to) anspornen.
spurn (to) verschmähen.
spy Spion, m.
spy (to) spionieren.
squadron Schwadron, f.
square Quadrat, n.
squeeze (to) (aus)drücken.
squirrel Eichhörnchen, n.
stabilize (to) stabilisieren.
stable fest (adj.); stabil.
stack Stoss, m. (wood).
stack (to) aufstapeln.
stadium Stadion, n.
staff Stab (military), m.; Personal, n. (business).
stage Bühne, f. (theater).
stain Fleck, m.
stain (to) (be)flecken.
stairs Treppe, f.
stammer (to) stottern.
stamp Briefmarke, f.; Stempel, m.
stand Stand, m.
    Stand still!   Stillgestanden!
star Stern, m.
starch Stärke, f.
stare (to) starren.
start Anfang, m.
start (to) beginnen, anfangen.
starve (to) (ver)hungern.
state Staat, m. (country); Zustand, m. (condition).
state (to) angeben.
stately stattlich.
statement Erklärung, f.; Aufstellung, f. (account).
stateroom Kabine, f.
station Bahnhof, m. (railroad); Stellung, f. (position).
statistics Statistik, f.
statue Statue, f.
stay Aufenthalt, m.
stay (to) bleiben.
steady fest.
steak Beefsteak, n.
steal (to) stehlen.
steam Dampf, m.
steamer Dampfer, m.
steel Stahl, m.
steep steil.
steer (to) steuern.
stem Stiel, m.
stenographer Stenotypistin, f.
stenography Kurzschrift, f.; Stenographie, f.
step Schritt, m.; Stufe, f. (stairs).
step (to) schreiten.
sterilized sterilisiert.
stern ernst.
stew Ragout, n.
stew (to) schmoren.
steward Steward, m.
stick Stock, m.
stick (to) stecken; ankleben (paste).
stiff steif.
stiffen (to) (ver)steifen; verstärken.
stiffness Steifheit, f.
still still, ruhig (adj.); jedoch, noch (adv.)
still (to) stillen.
stimulant Anregungsmittel, n.
stimulate (to) anregen.
sting Stich, m.
sting (to) stechen.
stinginess Geiz, m.
stingy geizig.
stir (to) rühren, bewegen.
stirrup Steigbügel, m.

stitch Stich, m.; Masche, f.
stitch (to) heften; nähen (sew).
stock Warenbestand, m.; Stamm, m.
stocking Strumpf, m.
stomach Magen, m.
stone Stein, m.
stool Schemel, m.
stop Haltestelle, f.
stop (to) halten.
    Stop! Halt!
store Laden, m.; Warenhaus, n.
stork Storch, m.
storm Sturm, m.
story Geschichte, f.
stove Ofen, m.
straight gerade.
    straight on gerade aus.
straighten gerade machen, aufrichten.
strain Anstrengung, f.
strange seltsam, sonderbar.
stranger Ausländer, m; Fremde, m.
strap Riemen, m.
straw Stroh, n.; Strohhalm, m. (for drinking).
strawberry Erdbeere, f.
stream Strom, m.
street Strasse, f.
streetcar Strassenbahn, f.
strength Kraft, f.
strengthen verstärken; kräftigen.
strenuous angestrengt.
stress Druck, m; Betonung, f. (accentuation).
stretch Strecke, f.
stretch (to) strecken.
strict streng.
stride Schritt, m.
string Bindfaden, m.
strip (to) streifen; entkleiden (of clothes).
stripe Streifen, m.
strive (to) streben.
stroke Schlag, m.; Zug, m. (pen).
stroll Spaziergang, m.
stroll (to) spazierengehen.
strong stark.
structure Bau, m.
struggle Kampf, m.
struggle (to) kämpfen.
stubborn hartnäckig.
student Schüler, m. · Schülerin, f.; Student, m. & f.
studio Studio, n.
studious lernbegierig, lerneifrig.
study Studium, n.
study (to) studieren.
stuff Stoff, m.
stuff (to) stopfen.
stumble (to) stolpern.
stump Stumpf, m.
stun (to) betäuben.
stunt Sensation, f.
stupendous fantastisch.
stupid dumm.
stupidity Dummheit, f.
stupor Betäubung, f.
sturdy kräftig.
stutter (to) stottern.
style Stil, m.
subdue (to) unterwerfen.
subject Angelegenheit, f.; Fach, n. (school).
subjugate (to) beherrschen.
subjunctive Konjunktiv, m.
sublime erhaben.
submission Unterwerfung, f.
submissive unterwürfig.
submit (to) unterwerfen.
subordinate untergeordnet.
subordination Unterordnung, f.
subscribe (to) abonnieren.
subscription Abonnement, n.
subsist (to) bestehen.

substance Substanz, f.
substantial beträchtlich.
substitute (to) ersetzen.
substitution Ersatz, m.
subtle scharfsinnig, fein, spitzfindig.
subtract abziehen.
subtraction Abzug, m.
suburb Vorstadt, f.
subway Untergrundbahn, f.
succeed (to) nachfolgen; gelingen (achieve).
success Erfolg, m.
successful erfolgreich.
succession Nachfolge, f.
successor Nachfolger, m.
such solch.
    Such a scandal! Solch ein Skandal!
sudden plötzlich.
sue (to) verklagen.
suffer (to) leiden.
suffering Leiden, n.
sufficient genügend.
sugar Zucker, m.
suggest (to) andeuten, vorschlagen.
suggestion Anregung, f.
suicide Selbstmord, m.
suit Anzug, m.; Kostum, n. (lady's).
suitable passend.
sulk (to) schmollen.
sullen mürrisch.
sum Summe, f.
summary Auszug, m.
summer Sommer, m.
summit Gipfel, m.
summon (to) vorladen; einberufen.
sumptuous prächtig, kostbar.
sum up (to) abkürzen, zusammenfassen.
sun Sonne, f.
sunbeam Sonnenstrahl, m.
Sunday Sonntag, m.
sunny sonnig.
sunrise Sonnenaufgang, m.
sunset Sonnenuntergang, m.
sunshine Sonnenschein, m.
superb herrlich.
superficial oberflächlich.
superfluous überflüssig.
superintendent Inspektor, m.
superior Vorgesetzte, m. & f.
superiority Überlegenheit, f.
superstition Aberglaube, m.
supervise (to) beaufsichtigen.
supper Abendessen, n.
supplement Nachtrag, m.; Beilage, f.
supplementary ergänzend.
supply (to) versorgen.
support stütze, f.; Unterstützung, f.
support (to) (unter)stützen.
suppose (to) vermuten, annehmen.
suppress (to) unterdrücken.
supreme höchst, oberst.
sure gewiss, sicher.
surety Sicherheit, f.
surface Oberfläche, f.
surgeon Chirurg, m.
surgery Chirurgie, f.
surname Zuname, m.; Nachname, m.
surpass übertreffen.
surprise Überraschung, f.
surprise (to) überraschen.
surrender Übergabe, f.
surrender (to) aufgeben, übergeben.
surroundings Umgebung, f.
survey Übersicht, f.; Vermessung, f.
survey (to) besichtigen, vermessen.
survive (to) überleben.
susceptibility Empfänglichkeit, f.
susceptible empfänglich.
suspect (to) verdächtigen.

suspense Ungewissheit, f.; Spannung, f.
suspicion Verdacht, m.
suspicious verdächtig.
sustain (to) ernähren.
swallow Schluck, m. (gulp); Schwalbe, f. (bird).
swallow (to) verschlucken.
swamp Sumpf, m.
swan Schwan, m.
swear (to) schwören.
sweat Schweiss, m.
sweat (to) schwitzen.
sweep (to) kehren; fegen.
sweet süss.
sweetness Süsse, f.
swell (to) (an)schwellen.
swift schnell, rasch.
swim (to) schwimmen.
swindle (to) schwindeln.
swindler Schwindler, m.
swing (to) schwingen.
Swiss Schweizer (noun, m.); schweizerisch (adj.).
switch Schalter, m.
sword Schwert, n.
syllable Silbe, f.
symbol Symbol, n.
symbolic symbolisch.
symbolize symbolisieren.
symmetrical symmetrisch.
sympathetic mitfühlend.
sympathize (to) mitfühlen.
sympathy Sympathie, f.; Verständnis, n.
symptom Symptom, n.
syrup Sirup, m.
system System, n.
systematic systematisch.

               T

table Tisch, m.
tablecloth Tischtuch, n.
tacit stillschweigend.
taciturn schweigsam.
tact Takt, m.
tactful taktvoll.
tactless taktlos.
tail Schwanz, m.
tailor Schneider, m.
take (to) nehmen.
tale Erzählung, f.
talent Talent, n.; Begabung, f.
talk Gespräch, m.
talk (to) reden, plaudern.
talkative gesprächig.
tall hoch; gross (people).
tame zahm.
tame (to) zähmen.
tangle (to) verwickeln.
tank Tank, m.
tapestry Wandteppich, m.
tar Teer, m.
tardy spät.
target (Ziel)scheibe, f.
tarnish (to) trüben.
task Aufgabe, f.
taste Geschmack, m.
taste (to) schmecken.
tax Steuer, f.
taxi Taxi, n.
tea Tee, m.
teach (to) unterrichten.
teacher Lehrer, m.; Lehrerin, f.
team Gruppe, f.; Mannschaft, f. (sports).
tear Träne, f.(teardrop); Riss, m. (rip).
tear (to) (zer)reissen.
tease (to) necken.
teaspoon Teelöffel, m.
technical technisch.
technique Technik, f.

tedious langweilig, ermüdend.
telegram Telegramm, n.
telegraph (to) telegrafieren.
telephone Telefon, n.
    telephone operator Telefonistin, f.
telephone (to) telefonieren, anrufen.
tell (to) sagen.
temper Laune, f.
temperate gemässig, mässig.
temperature Temperatur, f.
tempest Sturm, m.
temple Tempel, m.; Schläfe, f. (head).
temporary vorübergehend.
tempt (to) versuchen, verlocken.
temptation Versuchung, f.
ten zehn.
tenacious zäh.
tenacity Zähigkeit, f.
tenant Mieter, m.
tend (to) sich neigen zu.
tendency Neigung, f.
tender zart, empfindlich.
tennis Tennis, n.
tense gespannt.
tense Zeitform, f. (grammar).
tension Spannung, f.
tent Zelt, n.
tenth Zehntel (noun, n.) (fraction); zehnt (adj.).
tepid lauwarm.
term Ausdruck, m.
terrace Terrasse, f.
terrible schrecklich.
terrify (to) (er)schrecken.
territory Gebiet, n.
terror Schrecken, m.
test Prüfung, f.
test (to) prüfen.
testify (to) bezeugen.
testimony Zeugnis, n.
text Text, m.
textbook Lehrbuch, n.
than als.
thank (to) danken.
    Thank you! Danke schön!
thankful dankbar.
that das (demonstrative);der,die,das, welch(er,-e,-es)
    (relative); dass, damit (conjunction).
thaw Tauwetter, n.
thaw (to) tauen.
the der, die, das.
theater Theater, n.
their ihr.
theirs ihr(er, -e, -es).
them sie (acc.); ihnen (dat.).
theme Thema, n.
themselves sie (ihnen) selbst, sich.
then dann.
theory Theorie, f.
there dort.
    there is, there are es gibt.
thereafter danach.
thereby dadurch.
therefore deshalb, daher.
thereupon darauf.
thermometer Fiebermesser, m.
these diese.
thesis These, f.
they sie.
thick dick.
thief Dieb, m.
thigh Schenkel, m.
thimble Fingerhut, m.
thin dünn.
thing Sache, f.; Ding, n.
think (to) denken.
third dritte.
thirst Durst, m.
thirteen dreizehn.

thirteenth dreizehnte.
thirtieth dreissigste.
thirty dreissig.
this dieser.
thorn Dorn, m.
thorough gründlich, gänzlich.
though zwar, obwohl, obgleich.
thought Gedanke, m.
thoughtful nachdenklich.
thoughtless rücksichtslos.
thousand tausend.
thrash (to) dreschen.
thread Faden, m.
threat Drohung, f.
threaten (to) drohen.
three drei.
threshold Schwelle, f.
thrift Sparsamkeit, f.
thrifty sparsam.
thrill Schauer, m.; Begeisterung, f.
thrill (to) schauern.
thrilling ergreifend, begeisternd.
thrive (to) gedeihen.
thriving ergreifend.
throat Kehle, f.; Hals, m.
throb (to) schlagen.
throne Tron, m.
throng Menge, f.
through durch (acc.); durchaus.
throughout durchaus.
throw (to) werfen.
thumb Daumen, m.
thunder Donner, m.
thunder (to) donnern.
Thursday Donnerstag, m.
thus so.
thwart (to) vereiteln.
ticket Karte, f.; Fahrkarte, f. (train).
ticket window Schalter, m.
tickle (to) kitzeln.
ticklish kitzlig.
tide Flut, f. (high); Ebbe, f. (low).
tidiness Ordentlichkeit, f.
tidy ordentlich.
tie Band, n.;(bond); Krawatte, f.
    (necktie).
tie (to) binden.
tiger Tiger, m.
tight eng.
tile Ziegel, m. (roof); Kachel, f. (wall); Fliese, f.
    (kitchen).
till bis.
    till now bisher.
tilt (to) kippen.
timber Bauholz, n.
time Zeit, f.
    from time to time von Zeit zu Zeit.
    on time pünktlich.
    to have a good time sich vergnügen,
    sich amüsieren.
    what time is it? Wie spät ist es?
timid zaghaft, furchtsam.
timidity Furchtsamkeit, f.
tin Zinn, n.
tinkle (to) klingeln.
tiny winzig.
tip Spitze, f. (end); Trinkgeld, n.
    (money).
tip (to) Trinkgeld geben.
tire Reifen, m.
tire (to) ermüden.
tired müde.
tireless unermüdlich.
tiresome langweilig.
title Titel, m.
to zu (with infinitive); nach, zu (dat);
    an (dat. or acc.).
toad Kröte, f.

toast Toast, m.
tobacco Tabak, m.
today heute.
toe Zehe, f.
together zusammen.
toil (to) schwer arbeiten.
toilet Toilette, f.
token Andenken, n; Münze, f. (coin).
tolerable erträglich.
tolerance Toleranz, f.; Duldung, f.
tolerant duldsam.
tolerate (to) dulden.
toll (to) läuten.
tomato Tomate, f.
tomb Grab, n.
tomorrow morgen.
ton Tonne, f.
tone Ton, m.
tongs Zange, f.
tongue Zunge, f.
tonight heute abend.
too auch (also); zu (excessive).
tool Werkzeug, n.
tooth Zahn, m.
toothbrush Zahnbürste, f.
toothpaste Zahnpasta, f.
toothpick Zahnstocher, m.
toothpowder Zahnpulver, n.
top Gipfel, m.; Oberst, n.
topic Gesprächsstoff, m.; Thema, n.
torch Fackel, f.
torment Qual, f.
torment (to) quälen.
torture Folter, f.
torture (to) foltern.
toss (to) werfen.
toss Wurf, m.
total Gesamtsumme, f.; gesamt (adj.).
totally gänzlich.
touch (to) berühren.
touching rührend.
touchy empfindlich.
tough hart.
tour Reise, f.; Rundreise, f.
tour (to) herumreisen, bereisen.
tourist Tourist, m.
tournament Turnier, n.
toward zu, nach (dat.); gegen (acc.).
towel Handtuch, n.
tower Turm, m.
town Stadt, f.
toy Spielzeug, n.
trace Spur, f.
trace (to) zeichnen (drawing); nachspüren.
track Spur, f.
trade Handel, m.
tradition Überlieferung, f.
traditional herkömmlich, überliefert.
traffic Verkehr, m.
tragedy Tragödie, f.
tragic tragisch.
trail Fährte, f.
train Zug, m.
train (to) erziehen.
training Erziehung, f.
traitor Verräter, m.
trample (to) niedertreten.
tranquil ruhig.
tranquillity Ruhe, f.
transaction Verhandlung, f.; Transaktion, f.
transfer (to) übertragen.
transit Durchgang, m.
transition Übergang, m.
transitory vergänglich.
translate (to) übersetzen.
translation Übersetzung, f.
translator Übersetzer, m.
transmission Übersendung, f.

transmit (to) übersenden.
transparent durchsichtig.
transport Transport, m.
transport (to) transportieren.
transportation Beförderung, f.
trap Falle, f.
trap (to) fangen, ertappen.
trash Plunder, m.
travel Reise, f.
travel (to) reisen.
traveler Reisende, m. & f.
tray Tablett, n.
treacherous treulos.
treachery Treulosigkeit, f.
treason Verrat, m.
treasure Schatz, m.
treasurer Schatzmeister, m.
treasury Schatzamt, n.
treat Bewirtung, f.
treat (to) behandeln.
treatment Behandlung, f.
treaty Vertrag, m.
tree Baum, m.
tremble (to) zittern.
trembling Zittern, n.
tremendous ungeheuer.
trench Graben, m.; Schützengraben, m. (military).
trend Neigung, f.
trial Probe, f.
triangle Dreieck, n.
tribe Stamm, m.
tribunal Tribunal, n.
tribune Tribüne, f.
tribute Abgabe, f.
trick Kniff, m.
trifle Kleinigkeit, f.
trifling kleinlich (petty); gering (minor).
trim (to) besetzen (sewing); stutzen (hair).
trimming Verzierung, f.; Besatz, m. (clothes).
trip Fahrt, f.
trip (to) stolpern.
triple dreifach.
triumph Triumph, m.
triumph (to) siegen.
trivial geringfügig.
trolley car Strassenbahnwagen, m.
troop Truppe, f.
trot Trab, m.
trot (to) traben.
trouble Unannehmlichkeit, f.
trousers Hose, f.
truck Lastwagen, m.
true wahr.
truly wahrhaftig; aufrichtig.
trump Trumpf, m.
trump (to) trumpfen.
trumpet Trompete, f.
trunk Koffer, m.
trust Vertrauen, n.
trust (to) trauen.
trustworthy zuverlässig.
truth Wahrheit, f.
truthful wahrhaft.
truthfully aufrichtig.
truthfulness Aufrichtigkeit, f.
try (to) versuchen, probieren.
tube Rohr, n.
tumble (to) stürzen.
tumult Aufruhr, m.
tune Melodie, f.
tune (to) stimmen.
tunnel Tunnel, m.
turf Rasen, m.
turkey Truthahn, m.
turmoil Aufruhr, f.; Unruhe, f.
turn (to) drehen.
　　turn back zurückkehren.
　　Turn left. Biegen Sie links ein.

turnip weisse Rübe, f.
twelfth zwölfte.
twelve zwölf.
twentieth zwanzigste.
twenty zwanzig.
twice zweimal.
twilight Zwielicht, n.
twin Zwilling (noun, m.); doppelt (adj.).
twist (to) drehen.
two zwei.
type Modell, n.
type (to) mit der Schreibmaschine schreiben.
typewriter Schreibmaschine, f.
tyranny Tyrannei, f.
tyrant Tyrann, m.

U

ugliness Hässlichkeit, f.
ugly hässlich.
ultimate letzt.
umbrella (Regen)schirm, m.
umpire Schiedsrichter, m.
unable to unfähig.
unanimity Einmütigkeit, f.
unanimous einstimmig.
unawares unversehens.
unbearable unerträglich.
unbelievable unglaublich.
unbutton (to) aufknöpfen.
uncertain unsicher.
uncertainty Unsicherheit, f.
unchangeable unveränderlich.
uncle Onkel, m.
uncomfortable unbequem.
uncommon ungewöhnlich.
unconscious bewusstlos.
unconsciousness Ohnmacht, f.
uncouth ungebildet.
uncover (to) aufdecken.
undecided unentschieden.
undefinable undefinierbar.
undeniable unleugbar.
under unter (dat. or acc.).
undergo (to) durchmachen; erleiden (suffer).
underground Untergrund (noun, n.);
　　unterirdisch (adj.)
underline (to) unterstreichen.
underneath unten.
understand (to) verstehen.
understanding Verständnis, n.; Einverständnis, n.
undertake (to) unternehmen.
undertaker Leichenbestatter, m.
underwear Unterwäsche, f.
undesirable unerwünscht.
undignified würdelos.
undo (to) aufmachen; auflösen (untie).
undress (to) sich ausziehen.
uneasy beunruhigt.
uneasiness Beunruhigung, f.
unemployed arbeitslos.
unequal ungleich; unvergleichlich.
uneven uneben.
uneventful öde.
unexpected unerwartet.
unfair ungerecht.
unfaithful untreu.
unfavorable ungünstig.
unforgettable unvergesslich.
unfortunate unglücklich.
unfortunately unglücklicherweise.
ungrateful undankbar.
unhappily leider.
unhappy unglücklich.
unharmed unverletzt.
unhealthy ungesund.
unheard (of) unerhört.
uniform Uniform (noun, f.); gleichförmig (adj.).

uniformity Gleichförmigkeit, f.
uniformly gleichförmig.
unify (to) vereinigen.
unimportant unwichtig.
unintentional unabsichtlich.
union Vereinigung, f.; Verband, m.
universal universal.
universe Weltall, n.
university Universität, f.
unjust ungerecht.
unkind unfreundlich.
unknown unbekannt.
unlawful ungesetzlich.
unless es sei denn dass.
unlike unähnlich, anders als.
unlikely unwahrscheinlich.
unlimited unbeschränkt.
unload (to) abladen, ausladen.
unluckily unglücklicherweise.
unnecessary unnötig.
unoccupied unbesetzt; unbeschäftigt.
unpack (to) auspacken.
unpleasant unangenehm.
unpublished unveröffentlicht.
unquestionably fraglos.
unravel (to) lösen.
unreal unwirklich.
unreasonable unvernünftig.
unreliable unzuverlässig.
unrestrained ungezwungen.
unroll (to) abwickeln, entrollen.
unsafe unsicher.
unsatisfactory unbefriedigend.
unsatisfied unbefriedigt.
unscrupulous bedenkenlos, skrupellos.
unselfish selbstlos.
unsteady unbeständig.
unsuccessful erfolglos.
unsuitable unpassend.
untidy unordentlich.
untie (to) lösen; aufbinden.
until bis, an, zu (dat.).
　　until now bisher.
untrue unwahr; untreu (faithless).
unusual ungewöhnlich.
unwell unwohl.
unwholesome ungesund.
unwilling widerwillig.
unwise unklug.
unworthy unwürdig.
up auf (dat. or acc.).; aufwärts; oben.
uphold (to) stützen.
upkeep Instandhaltung, f.
upon auf, über (dat. or acc.).
upper ober.
upright aufrecht.
uprising Aufstand, m.
upset beunruhigt.
upset (to) umkehren; aufregen (distress).
upside down drunter and drüber.
upstairs oben.
upward steigend, aufwärts.
urge (to) dringen, drängen.
urgent dringend.
us uns.
use Gebrauch, m.; Verwendung, f. (utility).
use (to) gebrauchen; verwenden.
used to (to be) gewöhnt sein.
useful nützlich.
useless nutzlos.
usual gewöhnlich.
utensil Werkzeug, n.; Gerät, n.
utility Nützlichkeit, f.
utilize (to) nutzbar machen.
utmost äusserst.
　　to the utmost aufs äusserste.
utter (to) äussern, aussprechen.
utterly durchaus.

V

vacant frei.
vacation Ferien, pl.
vaccination Impfung, f.
vaccination certificate Impfschein, m.
vaguely unbestimmt.
vain eitel.
   in vain vergebens, umsonst.
valiant tapfer.
valid gültig.
validity Gültigkeit, f.
valley Tal, n.
valuable wertvoll.
value Wert, m.
value (to) schätzen.
valued geschätzt.
valve Ventil, n.
vanilla Vanille, f.
vanish (to) verschwinden.
vanity Eitelkeit, f.
vanquish (to) besiegen.
vapor Dampf, m.
variable veränderlich.
variation Abweichung, f.; Variation, f.
varied verschieden.
variety Abwechslung, f.; Mannigfaltigkeit, f.
various verschieden.
varnish (to) lackieren.
vary (to) verschieden.
vase Vase, f.
vast ungeheuer.
vault Gewölbe, n.
veal Kalbfleisch, n.
vegetable Gemüse, n.
vehicle Fahrzeug, n.
veil Schleier, m.
veil (to) verschleiern.
vein Ader, f. (body and mineral); Laune, f. (luck).
velvet Samt, m.
venerable ehrwürdig.
venerate (to) verehren.
veneration Verehrung, f.
vengeance Rache, f.
ventilation Lüftung, f.
ventilator Ventilator, m.; Entlüftung, f.
venture (to) wagen.
verb Zeitwort, n.
verdict Urteil, n.
verge Rand, m.
   on the verge of am Rand (gen).
verification Bestätigung, f.
verify (to) bestätigen.
verse Vers, m.; Dichtung, f. (poetry).
version Version, f. (translation); Darstellung, f. (account).
very sehr.
vest Weste, f.
veterinarian Tierarzt, m.
vice Laster, n.
vice-president Vizepräsident, m.
vice versa umgekehrt.
vicinity Nähe, f.; Nachbarschaft, f.
victim Opfer, n.
victor Sieger, m.
victorious siegreich.
victory Sieg, m.
view Aussicht, f.; Ansicht, f. (opinion).
vigorous kräftig.
vile abscheulich.
village Dorf, n.
vine Weinstock, m.
vinegar Essig, m.
vineyard Weingarten, m.
violence Gewalttätigkeit, f.; Heftigkeit, f.
violent gewaltig, heftig.
violet Veilchen, n.
violet violett.

violin Geige, f.
violinist Geiger, m.
virtue Tugend, f.
virtuous tugendhaft.
visible sichtbar.
vision Sehen, n.; Erscheinung, f. (ghost).
visit Besuch, m.
visit (to) besuchen.
visitor Besucher, m.
visualize (to) sich vorstellen.
vital lebens-; vital.
vitality Lebenskraft, f.
vivacious lebhaft.
vivacity Lebhaftigkeit, f.
vivid lebendig.
vocabulary Wortschatz, m.
vocal stimmlich, stimmhaft.
vocation Beruf, m.
vogue, Mode, f.
voice Stimme, f.
void Leere (noun, f.); leer (empty); ungültig (invalid).
volcano Vulkan, m.
volume Umfang, m.
voluntary freiwillig.
vote (to) stimmen.
vote Stimme, f.
vow Gelübde, n.
vow (to) geloben.
vowel Vokal, m.
vulgar gemein, niedrig.
vulnerable verwundbar.

W

wager Wette, f.
wager (to) wetten.
wages Gehalt, n.
waist Taille, f.
wait (to) warten.
   waiting room Wartezimmer, n.
waiter Kellner, m.; Kellnerin, f.
wake (to) aufwecken.
wake up (to) erwachen.
walk Spaziergang, m.
walk (to) gehen.
   take a walk spazierengehen.
wall Wand, f.
wallet Brieftasche, f.
walnut Walnuss, f.
wander wandern.
wanderer Wanderer, m.
want Mangel, m.; Not, f. (poverty).
want (to) wollen.
war Krieg, m.
ward Saal, m. (hospital).
wardrobe Kleiderschrank, m.
ware Ware, f.
warehouse Warenhaus, n.
warm warm.
warm (to) wärmen.
warmth Wärme, f.
warn (to) warnen.
warning Warnung, f.
warrior Krieger, m.
wash (to) waschen.
washroom Waschraum, m.
washstand Waschbecken, n.
waste Verschwendung, f.
waste (to) verschwenden.
watch Uhr, f.
watch (to) wachen.
watchful wachsam.
water Wasser, n.
waterfall Wasserfall, m.
waterproof wasserdicht.
wave Welle, f.
wave (to) schwenken; winken; wellen (hair).

wax Wachs, n.
way Weg, m. (road); Weise, f. (manner).
we wir.
weak schwach.
weaken (to) schwächen.
weakness Schwachheit, f.
wealth Reichtum, m.
wealthy reich.
weapon Waffe, f.
wear (to) tragen.
weariness Müdigkeit, f.; Langweile, f.
weary müde.
weather Wetter, n.
weave (to) weben.
wedding Hochzeit, f.
Wednesday Mittwoch, m.
weed Unkraut, n.
week Woche, f.
weekend Wochenende, n.
weekly wöchentlich.
weep (to) weinen.
weigh (to) wiegen.
weight Gewicht, n.
welcome Empfang, m.
welfare Wohlfahrt, f.
well gut.
well Brunnen, m.
   oil well Ölquelle, f.
west west; Westen, m.
westwards westwärts.
wet nass, feucht.
whale Walfisch, m.
what was; welch(er, -e, -es) (which).
   what kind of was für ein.
whatever was auch.
wheat Weizen, m.
wheel Rad, m.
when wenn, als; wann (interrogative).
whenever so oft wie.
where wo; wohin (whereto).
whereas da, nun.
wherever überall wo.
whether ob.
which der (die, das); welch(-er, -e, -es).
   which one welch(-er, -e, -es).
while Weile (noun, f.); indem, während (conj.).
whim Laune, f.; Einfall, m.
whip Peitsche, f.
whisper (to) flüstern.
whistle Pfeife, f.
whistle pfeifen.
white weiss.
who der (die, das), welch(er, -e, -es) (pron.); wer (inter. pron.).
whoever wer auch immer.
whole Ganze (noun, n.), ganz (adj.).
wholesale Grosshandel, m.
wholesome heilsam, gesund.
whose dessen (deren); wessen (inter.).
why warum.
wicked böse.
wide breit.
widen (to) breiten, erweitern.
widow Witwe, f.
widower Witwer, m.
width Weite, f. Breite, f.
wife Frau, f.
wig Perücke, f.
wild wild.
wilderness Wildnis, f.
will Wille, m.; Testament, n. (legal).
will (to) wollen.
willing gewillt.
willingly gern.
win (to) gewinnen.
wind Wind, m.
wind (to) winden.
window Fenster, n.

windy windig.
wine Wein, m.
wing Flügel, m.
wink Blinzeln, n.; Augenzwinkern, n.
wink (to) blinzeln, zwinkern.
winner Sieger, m.
winter Winter, m.
wipe (to) wischen; ausrotten (wipe out).
wire Draht, m.
wire (to) kabeln.
wisdom Weisheit, f.
wise weise.
wish Wunsch, m.
wish (to) wünschen.
wit Witz, m.; Geist, m.
witch Hexe, f.
with mit (dat.).
withdraw (to) zurückziehen; abheben.
wither (to) verwelken.
within drinnen.
without ohne (acc.).
witness Zeuge, m.
witness (to) bezeugen.
witticism Witz, m.
witty witzig, geistreich.
woe Weh, n.
wolf Wolf, m.
woman Frau, f.
wonder Wunder, n.
wonder (to) sich wundern, sich fragen.
wonderful wunderbar.
wood Holz, n.
woods Wald, m.
woodwork Holzwerk, n.
wool Wolle, f.
word Wort, n.
    word by word Wort für Wort.
work Arbeit, f.
    work of art Kunstgegenstand, m.
work (to) arbeiten.

worker Arbeiter, m.
workshop Werkstatt, f.
world Welt, f.
wordly weltlich.
worried besorgt.
worry Sorge, f.; Plage, f.
worry (to) besorgen; plagen
    Don't worry Sorgen Sie sich nicht!
    (Machen Sie sich keine Sorgen!)
worse schlechter.
worship (to) anbeten.
worst schlechtest.
worth Wert, m.
worthless wertlos.
worthy würdig.
wound Wunde, f.
wound (to) verwunden.
wounded verwundet.
wrap (to) einschlagen, (ein)wickeln.
wrath Zorn, m.
wreath Kranz, m.
wreck Wrack, n. Schiffbruch, m.
wreck (to) zertrümmern, scheitern.
wrestle (to) (aus)wringen.
wrestler Ringkämpfer, m.
wrestling Ringkampf, m.
wretched elend, erbärmlich.
wring (to) ringen.
wrist Handgelenk, n.
write (to) schreiben.
writer Schreiber, m.; Schriftsteller, m.
writing Schreiben, n.; Schrift, f. (work).
    in writing in Schrift, schriftlich.
wrong unrecht, falsch.
    You are wrong. Sie haben Unrecht.

X

X-ray Röntgenstrahlen, pl.

Y

yacht Yacht, f.
yard Hof, m. (courtyard).
yarn Garn, n.
yawn Gähnen, n.
yawn (to) gähnen.
year Jahr, n.
yearly jährlich.
yearn (to) sich sehnen.
yearning Sehnen, n.; Sehnsucht, f.
yeast Hefe, f.
yell (to) schreien.
yellow gelb.
yes ja, doch.
yesterday gestern.
yet noch (also besides); doch, dennoch (however).
yield (to) aufgeben (give up); erzeugen (produce).
yoke Joch, n.
yolk (Ei) Dotter, n. (of an egg).
you Sie, du (familiar sing.); ihr (familiar pl.);
    Sie, dich, euch (acc.); Ihnen, dir, euch (dat.).
young jung.
    young lady junge Dame, f.; Fräulein, n.
your Ihr, dein, ihr.
yours Ihr(-er, -e, -es); dein(-er, -e, -es).
yourself Sie (Ihnen) selbst; du (dich, dir) selbst;
    ihr (euch)
youth Jungend, f.

Z

zeal Eifer, m.
zealous eifrig.
zebra Zebra, n.
zero Null, f.
zipper Reissverschluss, m.
zone Zone, f.
zoo Tierpark, m.; Zoo, m.
Zoology Zoologie, f.

GLOSSARY OF PROPER NAMES

Albert Albrecht.
Alfred Alfred.
Andrew Andreas.
Ann Anna.
Anthony Anton.
August August.
Barbara Barbara.
Bernard Bernhard.
Bertha Bertha.
Charles Carl.
Charlotte Lotte.
Edward Eduard.
Elisabeth Elisabeth, Else.
Elsie Ilse.
Emily Emilie.
Eric Erich.
Ernest Ernst.

Eugene Eugen.
Frances Franziska.
Frank Franz.
Frederick Friedrich.
Fred Fritz.
George Georg.
Gertrude Gertrud, Trudchen.
Gustave Gustav.
Helen Helene.
Henry Heinrich.
Jane Johanna.
John Johann, Hans.
Joseph Josef.
Katherine Katharina,
    Käthchen, Käthe.
Lewis Ludwig.

Louise Luise.
Margaret Gretchen, Margareta.
Martha Martha.
Mary Maria.
Maurice Moritz.
Michael Michael.
Nicolas Nikolaus, Klaus.
Otto Otto.
Paul Paul.
Peter Peter.
Ralph Rudolf, Rolf.
Roger Rüdiger.
Susan Susanne.
Theodore Theodor.
Theresa Therese.
Thomas Thomas.
William Wilhelm.

GLOSSARY OF GEOGRAPHICAL NAMES

Africa Afrika, n.
Aix-la-Chapelle Aachen, n.
Alps Alpen, pl.
America Amerika, n.
    North America Nordamerika, n.
    Central America Zentralamerika, n., Mittelamerika, n.
    South America Südamerika, n.
Antwerp Antwerpen, n.
Arabia Arabien, n.
Asia Asien, n.
Atlantic Atlantik, m.
Australia Australien, n.
Austria Österreich, n.
Belgium Belgien, n.
Berlin Berlin, n.
Bonn Bonn, n.
Brazil Brasilien, n.
Brussels Brüssel, n.
Canada Kanada, n.
China China, n.
Czechoslovakia Tschechoslovakei, f.

Denmark Dänemark, n.
Egypt Ägypten, n.
England England, n.
Europe Europa, n.
France Frankreich, n.
Frankfort Frankfurt, n.
Germany Deutschland, n.
Hamburg Hamburg, n.
Greece Griechenland, n.
Hague Haag, m.
Holland Holland, n.
Hungary Ungarn, n.
India Indien, n.
Ireland Irland, n.
Italy Italien, n.
Japan Japan, n.
Jugoslavia Jugoslavien, n.
London London, n.
Mexico Mexico, n.
Moscow Moskau, n.

Munich München, n.
Norway Norwegen, n.
Nüremberg Nürnberg, n.
Pacific Ocean Stille Ozean, m.
Poland Polen, n.
Portugal Portugal, n.
Prussia Preussen, n.
Rhine Rhein, m.
Rhineland Rheinland, n.
Russia Russland, n.
Saar Saar, f.
Saxony Sachsen, n.
Scotland Schottland, n.
Silesia Schlesien, n.
Spain Spanien, n.
Sweden Schweden, n.
Switzerland Schweiz, f.
Turkey Türkei, f.
United States die Vereinigten Staaten, pl.
Vienna Wien, n.

COMMON USAGE DICTIONARY

Hebrew-English

English-Hebrew

BY **Samuel Steinberg**

BASED ON THE METHOD DEVISED BY
RALPH WEIMAN
FORMERLY CHIEF OF LANGUAGE SECTION
U. S. WAR DEPARTMENT

Prepared in co-operation with The Seminary School
of Jewish Studies of The Jewish Theological Seminary

Containing over 12,000 basic terms with meanings illustrated
by sentences and 1000 essential words especially indicated

INTRODUCTION

The *Hebrew Common Usage Dictionary* lists the most frequently used Hebrew words, gives their most important meanings, and illustrates their use.

1. The *basic* Hebrew words are indicated by the use of a • to their right.

2. Only the most important meanings are given.

3. These meanings are illustrated, wherever necessary, by means of everyday phrases and sentences.

4. Each important word is followed by the everyday expressions in which it most frequently occurs. The *Common Usage Dictionary* serves accordingly as a phrase book or conversation guide: it contains thousands of everyday sentences which are of practical importance (for traveling, correspondence, etc.), or which serve as illustrations of the grammatical features of spoken Hebrew. The *Common Usage Dictionary* should, therefore, prove helpful both to beginners who are building up their vocabulary and to advanced students who want to perfect their command of contemporary Hebrew.

5. In translating the Hebrew phrases and sentences, an attempt has been made to give not a mere translation but an equivalent—that is, what an English speaker would say in the same situation. (Literal translations have been added to help the beginner.)

6. The English-Hebrew part contains the most common English words and their Hebrew equivalents. By consulting the sentences given under the Hebrew word in the Hebrew-English part, the reader can observe how the word is used in practical cases.

7. After each verb, there are two forms in the parentheses: the third-person masculine singular, in both past and future tenses.

A short history of the Hebrew language:

A. Classical Hebrew. The Hebrew of the Bible shows evidence of a long period of development, with an extensive vocabulary and a complex grammatical system. Generally, the language of the Bible is relatively consistent, although there must have been changes during the millenium covered by this literature. This consistency may be due to the editors who determined the final form of the Hebrew Scriptures. How the language was pronounced in those days we have no way of knowing, although there is internal evidence that there were distinct tribal dialects (Judges XII: 5,6). In the later books of the Bible we find that the language has been greatly influenced by Aramaic, and some chapters are written entirely in this language.

B. Mishnaic Hebrew. Post-Biblical Hebrew (as it appears in one of the chief literary documents of the period—the Mishna) while it uses many of the words of the Bible, shows the influence of Aramaic and popular usages. It contains many words which do not appear in Biblical literature, and borrows many words from Aramaic, Greek and other languages. Its grammar is not as literary as that of the Bible.

C. Medieval Hebrew. In the course of the centuries following the destruction of the Second Temple (70 C. E.), Hebrew ceased to be a spoken language, and was used as a literary medium. Medieval Hebrew is not uniform but

varies with the country in which it was written and the subject matter it deals with.

D. Modern Hebrew. During the Nineteenth Century, there was a Hebrew literary revival. The Hebrew writers returned to Biblical Hebrew, but found it inadequate to express their ideas. Through their struggles, Modern Hebrew evolved. The revival of Hebrew as a spoken tongue less than one hundred years ago also demanded new expressions. This new idiom is based on the language of the Bible, both in vocabulary and grammar. There are many borrowings from Mishnaic and Medieval Hebrew. Thousands of new words have been coined or borrowed from other modern languages.

Nature of the language. Hebrew is a consonantal language. The basic meaning of a word is determined by the consonants. The nuances are determined by the prefixes and suffixes, and the choice of vowels. In the case of verbs these additions determine the conjugation, the tense, the number and the gender. For example, the three consonants ל (l), מ (m), ד (d) form a root whose meaning is related to learning or teaching. A few of the possible variations are listed below

Hebrew	Phonetic pronunciation	meaning
למד	LaMaD	he learned
למד	LiMeD	he taught
למוד	LiMooD	teaching
למידה	L'MiDah	learning
מלמד	m'LaMeD	teacher
למדן	LaMDan	scholar
תלמיד	taLMiD	pupil
תלמוד	taLMooD	study
התלמד	hitLaMeD	he taught himself

As these forms are the basis upon which the conjugation is built, they provide an added help to the learner.

EXPLANATORY NOTES

POINTING: Hebrew newspapers and books are written without vowels. Therefore as an aid in reading, the ו and the י are often used to indicate the vowels וֹ וּ and ‏ַ‏. This has led to the ו and י being retained even in pointed writing: מוּתָר for מֻתָר ; מְגִילָה for מְגִלָּה; אָדוֹם for אָדֹם.

In this dictionary the most common form of the words in question has been used.

VERBS, NOUNS, AND ADJECTIVES: The present tense of a verb may also be used to indicate the *person* who performs the act, and the adjective describing it, as well:

I go up	אֲנִי עוֹלֶה
The one who goes up (the immigrant)	הָעוֹלֶה
The rising moon	הַיָרֵחַ הָעוֹלֶה

ADJECTIVES: Many adjectives may be translated into Hebrew thru the use of שֶׁל :

intestinal (of the intestines)	שֶׁל הַמֵעַיִם
peaceful (of peace)	שֶׁל שָׁלוֹם
oral (of the mouth)	שֶׁל הַפֶּה

Many adjectives which in English begin with *un* or *in* are best translated by the use of a negative or the phrase "that cannot be."

impossible (not possible)	אִי־אֶפְשָׁרִי
indescribable (that cannot be described)	שֶׁאִי אֶפְשָׁר לְתָאֵר אוֹתוֹ

The following abbreviations have been used:

masculine	ז' – זָכָר
feminine	נ' , – נְקֵבָה
plural	ר' – רַבִּים
masculine plural	ז"ר
feminine plural	נ"ר
masculine and feminine	זו"נ

In the plurals of nouns, sometimes none of the vowels of the singular appear as in סֵפֶר (SeFeR) a book; סְפָרִים (S'FaRim) books.

DIALECTS. There are a variety of dialects used today in the pronunciation of Hebrew. This stems from the fact that for many years those who spoke Hebrew were dispersed in many lands and were influenced by the native tongues of those lands. The two best known are the Ashkenazic (Germanic) and the Sephardic (Spanish). The primary differences are as follows:

symbol	Ashkenazic	Sephardic
ת	s	t
ו	oh	aw (as in law)
ָ	aw (as in law)	a (as in father)
ֵ	ai (as in rain)	e (as in ten)

The Sephardic dialect is used in Israel today. This is the pronunciation used in this course. Even in the Sephardic there are minor variations in the pronunciation of some of the letters, particularly the ח and the ע which are pronounced gutturally by Israelis of Spanish and Oriental backgrounds.

Hebrew-English DICTIONARY

א

father;head	●אָב, ז.(רי אָבוֹת)
grandfather	אָב זָקֵן, ז.
stepfather	אָב חוֹרֵג, ז.
papa	●אַבָּא, ז.
to get lost	אבד (אָבַד,יֹאבַד)
to lose; to destroy	אִבֵּד (אַבֵּד, יְאַבֵּד)
I lost the book.	אָבַד לִי הַסֵּפֶר.
He lost the book.	הוּא אִבֵּד אֶת הַסֵּפֶר
loss	אֲבֵדָה, נ.
destruction	אַבַּדּוֹן, ז.
lost	אָבֵד
woe!	אֲבוֹי!
watermelon	אֲבַטִּיחַ, ז.
springtime	אָבִיב, ז.
poor man	אֶבְיוֹן, ז.
knight	אַבִּיר, ז.
knighthood	אַבִּירוּת, נ.
to mourn	אבל (אָבַל, יֶאֱבַל)
mourner	אָבֵל, ז.
mourning	אֵבֶל, ז.; אֲבֵלוּת, נ.
but	●אֲבָל
stone	אֶבֶן, נ.(רי אֲבָנִים)
blister	אֲבַעְבּוּעָה, נ.
to wrestle	אבק (הֵאָבֵק) (נֶאֱבַק, יֵאָבֵק)
dust	אָבָק, ז.
buttonhole	אֶבֶק, ז.
powder	אַבְקָה, נ.
member; part	אֵבֶר, ז.
union	אֲגֻדָּה, נ.
The union went out on strike.	הָאֲגֻדָּה יָצְאָה לִשְׁבִיתָה.
legend	אַגָּדָה, נ.
thumb	אֲגוּדָל, ז.
nut	אֱגוֹז, ז.
lake	אֲגַם, ז.

pear	אַגָּס, ז.
fist	אֶגְרוֹף, ז.
mist, vapor	אֵד, ז.
Mister (Mr.), possessor	●אָדוֹן, ז.
Good morning, Mr. Levi.	בֹּקֶר טוֹב, אָדוֹן לֵוִי.
about	●אוֹדוֹת (עַל)
The story is about the war.	הַסִּפּוּר הוּא עַל אוֹדוֹת הַמִּלְחָמָה.
polite	אָדִיב
politeness	אֲדִיבוּת, נ.
powerful	אַדִּיר
indifferent	אָדִישׁ
indifference	אֲדִישׁוּת, נ.
red	●אָדֹם
to get red	אדם(אָדַם, יֶאְדַּם)
man; person	אָדָם,בֶּן-אָדָם,ז.
He's a good person.	הוּא אָדָם טוֹב.
God created man in his image.	אֱלֹהִים בָּרָא אֶת הָאָדָם בְּצַלְמוֹ.
earth	אֲדָמָה, נ.
redhaired	אַדְמוֹנִי
measles	אַדֶּמֶת, נ.
on the contrary	אַדְּרַבָּה
to love, to like	●אהב (אָהַב, יֶאֱהַב)
The child loved the mother.	הַיֶּלֶד אָהַב אֶת הָאֵם.
I like to play tennis.	אֲנִי אוֹהֵב לְשַׂחֵק טֶנִיס.
love	●אַהֲבָה, נ.
alas!	אֲהָהּ!
tent	אֹהֶל, ז.
or	●אוֹ
goose	אַוָּז, ז.
drake	בַּר-אַוָּז, ז.
oh!	●אוֹי!
enemy	אוֹיֵב, ז.
air	אֲוִיר, ז.
The air is clear.	הָאֲוִיר צַח.
What's the weather?	מַהוּ מֶזֶג הָאֲוִיר?

airplane	אֲוִירוֹן, ז.
perhaps	●אוּלַי
hall	●אוּלָם, ז.
penknife	אוֹלָר, ז.
craftsman	אוּמָן, ז.
handicraft	אוּמָנוּת, נ.
wheel	אוֹפָן, ז.
bicycle	אוֹפַנַּיִם, ז.
treasure	אוֹצָר, ז.
light	●אוֹר, ז.
guest	אוֹרֵחַ, ז.
sign; miracle	אוֹת, ז.
letter	●אוֹת, נ.
The first letter is aleph.	הָאוֹת הָרִאשׁוֹנָה הִיא "א".
me,you,him	●אוֹתִי,אוֹתְךָ,אוֹתוֹ
I saw him.	רָאִיתִי אוֹתוֹ.
then	אָז
warning	אַזְהָרָה, נ.
belt	אֵזוֹר, ז.
to listen	(אָזַן) הֶאֱזִין (הַאֲזֵן, יַאֲזִין)
ear	אֹזֶן, נ.(רי אָזְנַיִם)
citizen	אֶזְרָח, ז.
citizenship	אֶזְרָחוּת, נ.
brother	●אָח, ז.
stepbrother	אָח חוֹרֵג, ז.
one	●אֶחָד, ז.
everyone	●כָּל אֶחָד
some	●אֲחָדִים
union	אִחוּד, ז.
brotherhood	אַחֲוָה, נ.
backward	אָחוֹר
lateness	אִחוּר, ז.
sister, relative, nurse	●אָחוֹת, נ.
stepsister	אָחוֹת חוֹרֶגֶת,נ.
to hold	אָחַז(אָחַז, יֹאחַז)
possession	אֲחֻזָּה, נ.
holding	אֲחִיזָה, נ.
to be late	●אִחֵר(אַחֵר, יְאַחֵר)

grandmother	אֵם זְקֵנָה, נ.
stepmother	אֵם חוֹרֶגֶת, נ.
A Jewish center of population	עִיר וָאֵם בְּיִשְׂרָאֵל
if	אִם●
If so, I'll go.	אִם כֵּן, אֵלֵךְ.
God willing	אִם יִרְצֶה הַשֵּׁם
mama, mommy	אִמָּא, נ.●
bath	אַמְבָּט, ז. אַמְבַּטְיָה, נ.●
nation	אֻמָּה, נ.●
trust; faith	אֵמוּן, ז.
religion; faith	אֱמוּנָה, נ.
courageous	אַמִּיץ
saying	אֲמִירָה, נ.
unfortunate	אֻמְלָל
truly; amen	אָמֵן
artist	אָמָן, ז.
trade; art	אֻמָּנוּת, נ.
indeed	אָמְנָם, אֻמְנָם
Is it possible?	הַאֻמְנָם?
courage	אֹמֶץ, ז.
to encourage	אִמֵּץ(אַמֵּץ, יְאַמֵּץ)
middle	אֶמְצַע, ז.
the middle one; means	אֶמְצָעִי, ז.
The end justifies the means.	הַמַּטָּרָה מַצְדִּיקָה אֶת הָאֶמְצָעִים.
to say	אָמַר(אֱמֹר, יֹאמַר)
this proves...	זֹאת אוֹמֶרֶת...
What do you plan to do?	מָה אַתָּה אוֹמֵר לַעֲשׂוֹת?
last night	אֶמֶשׁ, ז.●
truth	אֱמֶת, נ.●
to verify	אִמֵּת(אַמֵּת, יְאַמֵּת)
where to?	אָן, לְאָן, אָנָה?●
Where are you going?	לְאָן אַתָּה הוֹלֵךְ?
how long?	עַד אָן, עַד אָנָה?
where to?	אָנָה?
we	אֲנוּ, אֲנַחְנוּ
man	אֱנוֹשׁ, ז.
sigh	אֲנָחָה, נ.

Is there a clock here? (there is)	הֲיֵשׁ פֹּה שָׁעוֹן?
None.	אֵין
There is no clock here.	אֵין פֹּה שָׁעוֹן.
I have no money.	אֵין לִי כֶּסֶף.
where?	אֵיפֹה?●
man	אִישׁ, ז.(רִי אֲנָשִׁים)●
peasant	אִישׁ שָׂדֶה, ז.
pupil (of the eye)	אִישׁוֹן, ז.
personality	אִישִׁיּוּת, נ.
but	אַךְ
disappointment	אַכְזָבָה
cruel	אַכְזָר, אַכְזָרִי
eating	אֲכִילָה, נ.
to eat	אָכַל(אֱכֹל, יֹאכַל)●
food	אֹכֶל, ז.●
inn	אַכְסַנְיָה, נ.●
saddle	אֻכָּף, ז.
What do I care?	(אִכְפַּת) מָה אִכְפַּת לִי?●
peasant; farmer	אִכָּר, ז.●
agriculture	אִכָּרוּת, נ.
don't	אַל●
Don't speak.	אַל תְּדַבֵּר.
immortality	אַל-מָוֶת, ז.
to	אֶל●
He went to the market.	הוּא הָלַךְ אֶל הַשּׁוּק.
God	אֵל, אֱלֹהִים●
these	אֵלֶּה, אֵלּוּ●
if	אִלּוּ
idol	אֱלִיל, ז.
mute	אִלֵּם, ז.(נ.אִלֶּמֶת)
widower	אַלְמָן, ז.(נ.אַלְמָנָה)
unknown	אַלְמוֹנִי
thousand	אֶלֶף, ז.●
mother	אֵם, נ.●
The mother of all life.	אֵם כָּל חַי.
parting of the ways	אֵם הַדֶּרֶךְ, נ.

Please, don't be late.	בְּבַקָּשָׁה, לֹא לְאַחֵר.
another	אַחֵר, ז.
after	אַחַר, אַחֲרֵי
I'll go in the afternoon.	אֵלֵךְ אַחַר הַצָּהֳרַיִם.
He will come afterwards.	הוּא יָבוֹא אַחַר כָּךְ.
responsible	אַחְרָאִי
last	אַחֲרוֹן●
responsibility	אַחֲרָיוּת, נ.
end	אַחֲרִית, נ.
one	אַחַת●
all the same	אַחַת הִיא
all at once	בְּבַת אַחַת
how much more so	עַל אַחַת כַּמָּה וְכַמָּה
slowly	אַט, לְאַט●
little by little	לְאַט לְאַט
left-handed	אִטֵּר (אִטֵּר יַד יְמִינוֹ)
noodles	אִטְרִית, נ.
island	אִי, ז.●
where?	אֵי, אַיֵּה●
Where is my book?	אַיֵּה הַסֵּפֶר שֶׁלִּי?
hatred	אֵיבָה, נ.
which	אֵיזֶה, ז.(נ.אֵיזוֹ)●
Which do you want?	אֵיזֶה אַתָּה רוֹצֶה?
how?	אֵיךְ, אֵיכָה?●
quality	אֵיכוּת, נ.
ram	אַיִל, ז.
gazelle	אַיֶּלֶת, נ.
morning star	אַיֶּלֶת הַשַּׁחַר, נ.
tree	אִילָן, ז.(רִי אִילָנוֹת)
to threaten	אִיֵּם(אַיֵּם, יְאַיֵּם)
frightful, terrible	אָיֹם, ז.(אֲיֻמָּה, נ.)
fright	אֵימָה, נ.
when?	אֵימָתַי?
no; there is not	אַיִן, אֵין●

we	אֲנַחְנוּ
I	אֲנִי, אָנֹכִי
ship	אֳנִיָּה, נ.
to complain; to murmur	אנן(הִתְאוֹנֵן, יִתְאוֹנֵן)
groan	אֲנָקָה, נ.
misfortune	אָסוֹן, ז.(רי אֲסוֹנוֹת)
He had an accident.	קָרָה לוֹ אָסוֹן.
It's a great tragedy.	זֶה אָסוֹן גָּדוֹל.
forbidden	אָסוּר
no smoking	אָסוּר לְעַשֵּׁן
no parking	הַחֲנָיָה אֲסוּרָה
harvest	אָסִיף, ז.
prisoner	אָסִיר, ז.
storehouse	אָסָם, ז.
to gather	אסף (אָסַף, יֶאֱסֹף), אַסֵּף (אִסֵּף, יְאַסֵּף)
to assemble	הֵאָסֵף, הִתְאַסֵּף
harvest; compilation; meeting	אֹסֶף, ז., אֲסֵפָה, נ.
to bind; to forbid	אסר (אָסַר, יֶאֱסֹר)
nose	אַף, ז.
even	אַף עַל פִּי
nevertheless	אַף עַל פִּי כֵן
to bake	אפה(אָפָה, יֹאפֶה)
pea	אָפוּן, ז.
guardian	אַפּוֹטְרוֹפּוֹס, ז.
dark	אָפֵל, ז.
darkness	אֲפֵלָה, נ.
even	אֲפִלוּ
not even once	אֲפִלוּ פַּעַם אַחַת לֹא
even though you give me everything	אֲפִלוּ אִם תִּתֵּן לִי הַכֹּל
manner	אֹפֶן, ז.
fashion	אָפְנָה, נ.
according to the latest fashion	לְפִי הָאָפְנָה הָאַחֲרוֹנָה
nought	אֶפֶס, ז.
to restrain oneself	אפק (הִתְאַפֵּק, יִתְאַפֵּק)

horizon	אֹפֶק, ז.
gray	אָפֹר
ashes	אֵפֶר, ז.
chicken	אֶפְרֹחַ, ז.
possible	אֶפְשָׁר
impossible	אִי אֶפְשָׁר
possibility	אֶפְשָׁרוּת, נ.
finger	אֶצְבַּע, נ.
shelf	אִצְטַבָּה, אִצְטַבָּא, נ.
nobleman	אָצִיל, ז.
nobility	אֲצִילוּת, נ.
near	אֵצֶל
The park is near my house.	הַגַּן הוּא אֵצֶל בֵּיתִי.
to collect	אצר(אָצַר, יֶאֱצֹר)
pistol, revolver	אֶקְדָּח, ז.
climate	אַקְלִים
to lurk	ארב (אָרַב, יֶאֱרֹב)
chimney	אֲרֻבָּה, נ.
locust	אַרְבֶּה, ז.
four	אַרְבַּע, נ. אַרְבָּעָה, ז.
forty	אַרְבָּעִים
to weave	ארג (אָרַג, יֶאֱרֹג)
cloth	אֶרֶג, ז.
chest	אַרְגָּז, ז.
stable	אֻרְוָה, נ.
closet;coffin	אָרוֹן, ז(רי אֲרוֹנוֹת)
clothes closet	אֲרוֹן בְּגָדִים
book case	אֲרוֹן סְפָרִים
Holy Ark	אֲרוֹן הַקֹּדֶשׁ
damned	אָרוּר
cedar	אֶרֶז, ז.
rice	אֹרֶז, ז.
way	אֹרַח, ז.
meal	אֲרוּחָה, נ.
breakfast	אֲרוּחַת הַבֹּקֶר
lunch	אֲרוּחַת הַצָּהֳרַיִם
dinner	אֲרוּחַת הָעֶרֶב
caravan	אֹרְחָה, נ.

lion	אֲרִי, אַרְיֵה, ז.
weaving	אֲרִיגָה, נ.
long	אָרֹךְ
at length	אֲרֻכּוֹת
length	אֹרֶךְ
poison	אֶרֶס, ז.
earth; country	אֶרֶץ, נ.(רי אֲרָצוֹת)
the land(Israel)	הָאָרֶץ
manners	דֶּרֶךְ אֶרֶץ
abroad	חוּץ לָאָרֶץ
fire	אֵשׁ, נ.
Give me a light.	תֵּן לִי אֵשׁ.
waterfall	אֶשֶׁד, ז.
woman; wife	אִשָּׁה, נ.(רי נָשִׁים)
confirmation	אִשּׁוּר, ז.
bunch of grapes	אֶשְׁכּוֹל, ז (רי אֶשְׁכּוֹלוֹת)
grapefruit	אֶשְׁכּלִית
to accuse	אשם (הֶאֱשִׁים)
guilty	אָשֵׁם
guilt	אָשָׁם, ז. אַשְׁמָה, נ.
rubbish	אַשְׁפָּה, נ.(רי אַשְׁפּוֹת)
happiness	אֹשֶׁר, ז.
that	אֲשֶׁר
the man who came	הָאִישׁ אֲשֶׁר בָּא
that I spoke of	אֲשֶׁר עָלָיו דִּבַּרְתִּי
happy	אַשְׁרֵי
you	אַתָּה, נ. אַתְּ, ז.
hoe	אֵת, ז.
with	אֵת, אֶת
Come with me.	בּוֹא אִתִּי.
she-donkey	אָתוֹן
you(pl.)	אַתֶּם, ז. אַתֶּן, נ.
yesterday	אֶתְמוֹל
citron	אֶתְרוֹג, ז.

ב

in	בְּ
explanation	בָּאוּר, ז.

●בֵּאֵר(בֵּאֵר,יְבָאֵר)	to explain
בְּאֵר	well
בגד (בָּגַד, יִבְגֹּד)	to be treacherous
בֶּגֶד	coat
בְּגָדִים	clothing
בֶּגֶד יָם	bathing suit
בִּגְלַל	because of
בַּגְרוּת,נ.	maturity
בַּד,ז.	linen
לְבַד	alone
מִלְּבַד	except
בדד(הִתְבּוֹדֵד, יִתְבּוֹדֵד)	to isolate oneself
בָּדָד,לְבָדָד	solitary
ברח (בָּדַח,יִבְדַּח) בִּדֵּחַ (בִּדַּח,יְבַדַּח)	to amuse
בַּדְחָן	buffoon
בַּדְחָנוּת,נ.	buffoonery
בְּדִידוּת,נ.	loneliness
בְּדִיחָה,נ.	joke
בְּדִיקָה,נ.	examination
בדל (הִבָּדֵל)	to be separated
הִבְדִּיל (הִבְדִּיל, יַבְדִּיל)	to separate
בְּדֹלַח,ז.	crystal
בֶּדֶק,ז.	repair
בדק (בָּדַק,יִבְדֹּק)	to examine
הָרוֹפֵא בָּדַק אֶת הַחוֹלֶה.	The doctor examined the patient.
בֹּהוּ,ז.	emptiness
●בָּהִיר	clear, bright
בהל (הִבָּהֵל) (נִבְהַל, יִבָּהֵל)	to get frightened
הִבְהִיל (הִבְהִיל, יַבְהִיל)	to frighten
בֶּהָלָה	terror, bewilderment confusion
בְּהֵמָה,נ.	cattle
בַּהֲמִיּוּת,נ.	bestiality
בֹּהֶן,ז.(ר׳ בְּהוֹנוֹת)	thumb
●בוא (בָּא, יָבוֹא)	to come, to enter; to appear,to arrive
בּוֹא בַּיָּמִים	to grow old
בָּא כֹּחַ	representative
בָּא אֶל אֲבוֹתָיו	died
בּוֹגֵד,ז.	traitor
בּוֹגֵר,ז.	adult
הוּא מוֹרֶה לְבוֹגְרִים.	He teaches adults.
הוּא בּוֹגֵר הַגִּמְנַסְיָה.	He is a graduate of the Gymnasium.
בּוֹדֵד	solitary
בּוּז,ז.	contempt
●בּוּל,ז.	postage stamp
בּוֹר,ז.(ר׳ בּוֹרוֹת)	pit
בּוּר	ignorant
בּוּרְגָּנִי	bourgeois
בּוּרוּת,נ.	ignorance
בּוֹשׁ (בּוֹשׁ, יֵבוֹשׁ)	to be ashamed
עַד בּוֹשׁ	to the last
בּוּשָׁה,בֹּשֶׁת,נ.	shame
בִּזְבֵּז(בִּזְבֵּז,יְבַזְבֵּז)	to waste
בזה(בָּזָה,יִבְזֶה)	to despise, disdain
בָּזוּי	despised
בזז (בָּזַז,יָבֹז)	to plunder
בִּזָּיוֹן,ז.	disdain
●בָּחוּר,ז.	young man;bachelor
●בַּחוּרָה,נ.	young woman
בְּחִינָה,נ.	examination,test
עָמַדְתִּי לַבְּחִינָה.	I took the examination.
עָמַדְתִּי בַּבְּחִינָה.	I passed the examination.
בְּחִירָה,נ.	choice
בְּחִירוֹת,נ״ר	election
בחן (בָּחַן,יִבְחַן)	to examine
הִבְחִין (הִבְחִין, יַבְחִין)	to distinguish
●בחר (בָּחַר, יִבְחַר)	to choose,to select, to prefer
בָּחַר אוֹתִי	chose me
בָּחַר בִּי	chose me
בָּחַר לוֹ	chose for himself
בַּחֲרוּת	youth
●בטא (בִּטֵּא, יְבַטֵּא)	to express, to utter
●בָּטוּחַ	secure;sure
●בִּטּוּי,ז.	expression
בִּטּוּל,ז.	suppression; cancellation
●בטח (בָּטַח,יִבְטַח)	to trust
אֲנִי בָּטוּחַ כִּי זֶה נָכוֹן.	I am sure it is correct.
הִבְטִיחַ (הִבְטִיחַ,יַבְטִיחַ)	to assure, to promise
בֶּטַח,ז.בִּטְחָה,נ.	surety,assurance; security
בֶּטַח,לָבֶטַח	surely
בִּטָּחוֹן,ז.	confidence
בטל (בָּטֵל,יִבְטַל)	to be idle
בִּטֵּל (בִּטֵּל,יְבַטֵּל)	to annul
בָּטֵל,ז.	void
הוֹלֵךְ בָּטֵל,ז.	idle
בַּטָּלָה	idleness
בַּטְלָן,ז.	loafer
בֶּטֶן,נ.	belly;body;bowels
בִּטְנָה,נ.	lining
●בִּי	in me
בִּיאָה,נ.	entrance
בִּיאַת הַשֶּׁמֶשׁ	sunset
בִּיב,ז.	channel
בִּימָה,נ.	pulpit;stage
●בִּין (בָּן,יָבִין)	to understand
הֵבִין (הֵבִין, יָבִין)	to understand; to explain
אֲנִי מֵבִין.	I understand.
זֶה לֹא מוּבָן.	It's not clear (understood).
●בֵּין	between
בֵּין אָדָם לַחֲבֵרוֹ	laws controlling man's behavior towards his fellow man
בֵּין אָדָם לַמָּקוֹם	laws controlling man's relationship to God.
בֵּינוֹ וּבֵין עַצְמוֹ	by himself
בֵּין-כָּךְ וּבֵין-כָּךְ	anyhow
בֵּין הַשְּׁמָשׁוֹת	twilight
בִּינָה,נ.	intelligence
בֵּינוֹנִי	mediocre

meanwhile	●בֵּינָתַיִם
egg	●בֵּיצָה, נ. (ר׳ בֵּיצִים)
capital city	בִּירָה, נ.
to put to shame	בִּיֵּשׁ (בִּיֵּשׁ, יְבַיֵּשׁ)
bashful	בַּיְשָׁן, ז.
house	●בַּיִת, ז. (ר׳ בָּתִּים)
court	בֵּית דִּין, ז.
hospital	בֵּית חוֹלִים, ז.
factory	בֵּית חֲרֹשֶׁת, ז.
prison	בֵּית כֶּלֶא, ז.
synagogue	● בֵּית כְּנֶסֶת, ז.
toilet	בֵּית כִּסֵּא, ז.
school	●בֵּית מִדְרָשׁ, בֵּית סֵפֶר, ז.
sanctuary	בֵּית מִקְדָּשׁ, ז.
the Temple in Jerusalem	בֵּית הַמִּקְדָּשׁ, ז.
drug store	בֵּית מִרְקַחַת
court	בֵּית מִשְׁפָּט
cemetery	בֵּית עוֹלָם, בֵּית קְבָרוֹת, ז.
domestic	בֵּיתִי
to weep, to mourn	בכה (בָּכָה, יִבְכֶּה) בַּכָּה (בָּכָּה, יְבַכֶּה)
firstborn	●בְּכוֹר, ז.
first fruits	בִּכּוּרִים, ז"ר
Shevuoth (feast of first fruits)	חַג הַבִּכּוּרִים, ז.
weeping	בְּכִי, בֶּכִי, ז. בְּכִיָּה, נ.
lamenter	בַּכְיָן, ז.
to prefer	בִּכֵּר (בִּכֵּר, יְבַכֵּר)
birthright, privilege	בְּכוֹרָה, נ.
confusion	בִּלְבּוּל, ז.
to confuse	בִּלְבֵּל (בִּלְבֵּל, יְבַלְבֵּל)
to get confused	הִתְבַּלְבֵּל (הִתְבַּלְבֵּל, יִתְבַּלְבֵּל)
to wear out	בָּלָה (בָּלָה, יִבְלֶה)
to waste or pass time	●בִּלָּה זְמַן
How did you enjoy it?	אֵיךְ בִּלִּיתָ?
I had a good time.	בִּלִּיתִי יָפֶה.
fright	בֶּהָלָה, נ.

to project	בלט (בָּלַט, יִבְלֹט)
without	●בְּלִי
with no end to it	עַד בְּלִי דַי
without limit	בְּלִי גְבוּל
without doubt	בְּלִי סָפֵק
projection	בְּלִיטָה, נ.
swallowing	בְּלִיעָה, נ.
wicked	בְּלִיַּעַל (אִישׁ-, בֶּן-)
to swallow	בלע (בָּלַע, יִבְלַע)
besides	בִּלְעֲדֵי
There was no one there besides me.	לֹא הָיָה שָׁם אִישׁ בִּלְעָדַי.
investigator, detective	בַּלָּשׁ, ז.
except, not, only, beside, without	בִּלְתִּי
altar	בָּמָה, נ.
high places (of idol worship)	בָּמוֹת
son	בֵּן, ז. (ר׳ בָּנִים)
man	בֶּן אָדָם, ז. (ר׳ בְּנֵי אָדָם)
friend of the family	בֶּן בַּיִת, ז. (ר׳ בְּנֵי בַּיִת)
ally	בֶּן בְּרִית
of the same age	בֶּן גִּיל, ז. (ר׳ בְּנֵי גִיל)
contemporary	בֶּן דּוֹר, ז. (ר׳ בְּנֵי דוֹר)
one of a couple	בֶּן זוּג, ז.
youngest son	בֶּן זְקוּנִים, ז.
brave man	בֶּן חַיִל, ז.
provincial	בֶּן כְּפָר, ז. (ר׳ בְּנֵי כְּפָר)
townsman	בֶּן כְּרַךְ, ז. (ר׳ בְּנֵי כְּרַךְ)
prince	בֶּן מֶלֶךְ, ז. (ר׳ בְּנֵי מֶלֶךְ)
learned man	בֶּן תּוֹרָה, ז.
cultured man	בֶּן תַּרְבּוּת, ז.
builder	בַּנַּאי, ז.
to build	בנה (בָּנָה, יִבְנֶה)
The building proceeded well.	הַבִּנְיָן הִתְקַדֵּם יָפֶה.
building	בִּנְיָן, ז.
It was a beautiful building.	הַבִּנְיָן הָיָה יָפֶה.

basis, foundation	בָּסִיס, ז.
to found, to base	בִּסֵּס (בִּסֵּס, יְבַסֵּס)
through, for	בַּעַד
I brought a book for you.	הֵבֵאתִי סֵפֶר בַּעַדְךָ.
through	מִבַּעַד לְ-
cleaning away	בִּעוּר, ז.
to stamp	בעט (בָּעַט, יִבְעַט)
husband; possessor	בַּעַל, ז.
married	בַּעַל אִשָּׁה
house owner	בַּעַל בַּיִת, ז. (ר׳ בַּעֲלֵי בָּתִּים)
living creature	בַּעַל חַי, ז.
cripple	בַּעַל מוּם, ז. (ר׳ בַּעֲלֵי מוּם)
artisan	בַּעַל מְלָאכָה, ז. (ר׳ בַּעֲלֵי מְלָאכָה)
miracle worker	בַּעַל נֵס, ז.
to burn	בער (בָּעַר, יִבְעַר)
swamp	בִּצָּה, נ.
onion	בָּצָל, ז.
dough	בָּצֵק, ז.
drought	בַּצֹּרֶת, נ.
bottle	בַּקְבּוּק, ז.
examination; visit	בִּקּוּר, ז.
experienced, versed	בָּקִי
expertness	בְּקִיאוּת, נ.
valley	בִּקְעָה, נ.
to criticize	בִּקֵּר (בִּקֵּר, יְבַקֵּר)
cattle	בָּקָר, ז.
calf	בֶּן בָּקָר, ז.
morning; dawn	●בֹּקֶר, ז. (ר׳ בְּקָרִים)
Good morning.	בֹּקֶר טוֹב.
in the morning	בַּבֹּקֶר
criticism	●בִּקֹּרֶת, נ.
to seek; to desire; to ask	●בִּקֵּשׁ (בִּקֵּשׁ, יְבַקֵּשׁ)
He sought his uncle.	הוּא בִּקֵּשׁ אֶת הַדּוֹד.
He asked his uncle to come.	הוּא בִּקֵּשׁ מֵהַדּוֹד לָבוֹא.
request	●בַּקָּשָׁה, נ.

although	אַף עַל גַב
tax-collector	גַּבַּי, ז.
to collect taxes	גבה (גָּבָה, יִגְבֶּה)
high; elevated	גָּבֹהַ
haughty	גְּבַהּ לֵב
height	גֹּבַהּ, ז.
eyebrow	גַּבָּה, נ.
boundary	גְּבוּל, ז.
strong; hero	גִּבּוֹר, גִּבּוֹר חַיִל, ז.
strength, courage	גְּבוּרָה, נ.
cheese	גְּבִינָה, נ.
goblet	גָּבִיעַ, ז.
master; rich man	גְּבִיר, ז.
mistress; rich lady; madam	גְּבִירָה, נ.
humpback, humpbacked	גִּבֵּן, ז.
hill	גִּבְעָה, נ.
to be strong; to be powerful	גבר (גָּבַר, יִגְבַּר)
to be victorious	הִתְגַּבֵּר (הִתְגַּבֵּר, יִתְגַּבֵּר)
male	גֶּבֶר, ז.
Mrs. Miss, Mistress	גְּבֶרֶת, נ.
roof	גַּג, ז.
troupe	גְּדוּד, ז.
big, great	גָּדוֹל
education; breeding	גִּדּוּל, ז.
kid, goat	גְּדִי, ז.
to grow up	גדל (גָּדַל, יִגְדַּל)
greatness, size	גֹּדֶל, ז.
greatness	גְּדֻלָּה, גַּדְלוּת, נ.
one-armed man	גִּדֵּם, ז.
to cut off; to fell; to break	גדע (גָּדַע, יִגְדַּע)
fence, hedge	גָּדֵר, נ.
hurdle	גְּדֵרָה, נ.
ironing	גִּהוּץ, ז.
to iron	גהץ (גִּהֵץ, יְגַהֵץ)
baby bird	גּוֹזָל, ז.
nation; gentile	גּוֹי, ז.

I bought it for you.	קָנִיתִי זֹאת בִּשְׁבִילְךָ.
cooking; ripening; maturing	בִּשּׁוּל, ז.
cooked	בָּשׁוּל
ripe	בָּשֵׁל
to ripen	בשל (בָּשַׁל, יִבְשַׁל)
to cook	בִּשֵּׁל (בִּשֵּׁל, יְבַשֵּׁל)
fragrance, perfume	בֹּשֶׂם, ז.
perfume	בְּשָׂמִים, ז.
to announce	בשר (בִּשֵּׂר, יְבַשֵּׂר)
flesh, meat	בָּשָׂר, ז.
mortal	בָּשָׂר וָדָם, ז.
blood relation	שְׁאֵר בָּשָׂר, ז.
good news	בְּשׂוֹרָה, נ.
shame	בֹּשֶׁת, נ.
daughter	בַּת, נ. (רִ' בָּנוֹת)
at once	בְּבַת אַחַת
They all laughed at once.	כֻּלָּם צָחֲקוּ בְּבַת אַחַת.
smile	בַּת צְחוֹק, נ.
echo; voice from heaven	בַּת קוֹל, נ.
virgin	בְּתוּלָה

ג

proud	גֵּא
to rise; to be haughty	גאה (גָּאָה, יִגְאֶה)
to boast	הִתְגָּאָה (הִתְגָּאָה, יִתְגָּאֶה)
proud, haughty, arrogant	גֵּאֶה
haughtiness	גַּאֲוָה, נ.
haughty	בַּעַל גַּאֲוָה
majesty; pride; genius	גָּאוֹן, ז.
to redeem	גאל (גָּאַל, יִגְאַל)
redeemer	גּוֹאֵל, ז.
redemption	גְּאֻלָּה, נ.
back	גַּב, ז.
My back hurts.	גַּבִּי כּוֹאֵב.
upon	עַל גַב

please	בְּבַקָּשָׁה
son; pure, clean; expert, skilled	בַּר, ז.
man of sense	בַּר דַעַת, ז.
Bar Mitzvah	בַּר מִצְוָה
authority	בַּר סַמְכָא, ז.
to create	ברא (בָּרָא, יִבְרָא)
creation of the world	בְּרֵאשִׁית
swan	בַּרְבּוּר, ז.
hail	בָּרָד, ז.
blessed	בָּרוּךְ
Welcome!	בָּרוּךְ הַבָּא!
clear, certain	בָּרוּר
clearly, certainly	בָּרוּר
clearness	בֵּרוּר, ז.
tap	בֶּרֶז, ז.
The water came out of the tap.	הַמַּיִם יָצְאוּ מִן הַבֶּרֶז.
iron	בַּרְזֶל, ז.
railroad	מְסִלַּת בַּרְזֶל, נ.
to run away; to fly	ברח (בָּרַח, יִבְרַח)
to bring in contraband	הִבְרִיחַ מִן הַמֶּכֶס
healthy; well-fed	בָּרִיא
creation; world	בְּרִיאָה, נ.
health	בְּרִיאוּת, נ.
creation; creature	בְּרִיָּה, בְּרִיָּה, נ.
fleeing	בְּרִיחָה, נ.
convenant; alliance	בְּרִית, נ. (רִ' בְּרִיתוֹת)
circumcision	בְּרִית (מִילָה)
to bless	ברך (בֵּרֵךְ, יְבָרֵךְ)
knee	בֶּרֶךְ, נ. (רִ' בִּרְכַּיִם)
blessing	בְּרָכָה, נ.
pond	בְּרֵכָה, נ.
lightning; shine, glitter	בָּרָק, ז.
to select; to clear	ברר (בֵּרֵר, יְבָרֵר)
choice	בְּרֵרָה, נ.
for	בִּשְׁבִיל

body;corpse — גְוִיָּה,נ.
parchment — גְוִיל,ז.
exile — גוֹלָה,נ.
color,dye,shade — ●גַוָּן,ז.
monotonous — חַדְגוֹנִי
multicolored,varied — רַבְגוֹנִי
to die — גוע (גָוַע,יִגְוַע)
body — גוּף
pronoun — מִלַּת הַגּוּף
corpse — גוּפָה,נ.
to dwell — ●גוּר (גָר,יָגוּר)
Where do you live? — אֵיפֹה אַתָּה גָר?
baby lion,baby dog — גּוּר,ז.
lot, destiny — גּוֹרָל,ז.
block — גּוּשׁ,ז.
cashier,treasurer — גִּזְבָּר,ז.
balcony — גְּזוּזְטְרָה,נ.
to shear — גזז (גָּזַז,יָגֹז)
shearing — גְּזִיזָה,נ.
hewn stone — גָּזִית,נ.
to rob — גָּזַל (גָּזַל,יִגְזֹל)
plunder — גְּזֵלָה,נ.
robber — גַּזְלָן,ז.
robbery — גַּזְלָנוּת,נ.
to exaggerate — גַּזֵּם (גִּזֵּם,יְגַזֵּם) הִגְזִים (הִגְזִים,יַגְזִים)
You're exaggerating. — אַתָּה מַגְזִים.
exaggeration — גּוּזְמָה,נ.
to cut down; to order — גזר (גָּזַר,יִגְזֹר)
carrot — גֶּזֶר,ז.
judgment — גְּזַר,גְּזַר דִּין,ז.
decree — גְּזֵרָה,נ.
figure — גִּזְרָה,נ.
She has a lovely figure. — יֵשׁ לָהּ גִּזְרָה יָפָה.
(glowing) coal — גַּחֶלֶת,נ.
divorce — גֵּט,ז.
valley — גַּי,גַּיְא,גֵּיא,זו"נ (ר' גֵּאָיוֹת)

tendon — גִּיד,ז.
age, joy — ●גִּיל,ז.
joy — גִּילָה,נ.
to mobilize — גַּיֵּס (גִּיֵּס,יְגַיֵּס)
brother-in-law — גִּיס,ז.
limestone, chalk — גִּיר,ז.
to convert (to the Jewish faith) — גַּיֵּר (גִּיֵּר,יְגַיֵּר)
to convert oneself (to the Jewish faith) — הִתְגַּיֵּר (יִתְגַּיֵּר)
wave — גַּל,ז.
rolling — גִּלְגּוּל,ז.
to roll — גַּלְגֵּל (גִּלְגֵּל,יְגַלְגֵּל)
The children rolled the balls. — הַיְלָדִים גִּלְגְּלוּ אֶת הַכַּדּוּרִים.
to roll — הִתְגַּלְגֵּל (הִתְגַּלְגֵּל,יִתְגַּלְגֵּל)
He rolled to the bottom of the hill. — הוּא הִתְגַּלְגֵּל לְתַחְתִּית הָהָר.
wheel — גַּלְגַּל,ז.
skull — גֻּלְגֹּלֶת,נ.
to uncover, to emigrate — גלה (גָּלָה,יִגְלֶה), גַּלֵּה
to banish — הַגְלֵה (הִגְלָה,יַגְלֶה)
to uncover oneself — הִתְגַּלָּה (הִתְגַּלָּה, יִתְגַּלֶּה)
shaving,shave — ●גִּלּוּחַ,ז.
I want a shave and a haircut. — אֲנִי רוֹצֶה גִּלּוּחַ וְתִסְפֹּרֶת.
clear,open — גָּלוּי
uncovering,laying bare;revelation — גִּלּוּי,ז.
announcement — גִּלּוּי דַּעַת,ז.
revelation — גִּלּוּי שְׁכִינָה,ז.
post card — גְּלוּיָה,נ.
exile — גָּלוּת,נ.
to shave — ●גַּלֵּחַ (גִּלֵּחַ,יְגַלֵּחַ)
The barber shaved me. — הַסַּפָּר גִּלֵּחַ אוֹתִי.
to shave oneself — ●הִתְגַּלֵּחַ (הִתְגַּלֵּחַ,יִתְגַּלֵּחַ)
I shaved myself. — הִתְגַּלַּחְתִּי.
priest — גַּלָּח,ז.
ice cream — גְּלִידָה,נ.
sheet — ●גִּלָּיוֹן,ז.

Give me a sheet of paper. — תֵּן לִי גִּלָּיוֹן שֶׁל נְיָר.
cylinder;district — גָּלִיל,ז.
district;rolling — גְּלִילָה,נ.
to roll,turn, move away — גלל (גָּלַל,יָגֹל)
to roll — הִתְגּוֹלֵל (הִתְגּוֹלֵל, יִתְגּוֹלֵל)
because of — (גלל) בִּגְלַל
idiot — גֹּלֶם,ז.
solitary — גַּלְמוּד,ז.
also — ●גַּם
even if — ●גַּם אִם
to stammer — גַּמְגֵּם (גִּמְגֵּם,יְגַמְגֵּם)
dwarf — גַּמָּד,ז.
weaned — גָּמוּל
reward — גְּמוּל,ז.
finished, complete — ●גָּמוּר
The meal is finished. — הָאֲרוּחָה גְּמוּרָה.
favor; loan — גְּמִילוּת חֶסֶד, -חֲסָדִים,נ.
flexible,pliant — גָּמִישׁ
suppleness — גְּמִישׁוּת,נ.
to ripen, to recompense,to wean,to do good — גמל (גָּמַל,יִגְמֹל)
camel — ●גָּמָל,ז.
camel driver — גַּמָּל,ז.
to finish,to cease, to end — ●גמר (גָּמַר,יִגְמֹר)
end — גֶּמֶר,גְּמָר,ז.
The term (studies) ends next week. — גְּמַר הַלִּמּוּדִים הוּא כְּעוֹד שָׁבוּעַ.
garden — ●גַּן,ז.
zoo — ●גַּן חַיּוֹת,ז.
vegetable garden — גַּן יְרָקוֹת,ז.
paradise — גַּן עֵדֶן,ז.
to steal, to purloin — גנב (גָּנַב,יִגְנֹב)
to steal in — הִתְגַּנֵּב (הִתְגַּנֵּב,יִתְגַּנֵּב)
thief — גַּנָּב,ז.
theft — גְּנֵבָה,נ.

glue	דֶּבֶק, ז.
devotion	דְּבֵקוּת, נ.
to speak	דַּבֵּר (דִּבֶּר, יְדַבֵּר)
I spoke to David.	דִּבַּרְתִּי אֶל דָּוִד.
He persuaded the boy.	הוּא דִּבֵּר עַל לֵב הַיֶּלֶד.
thing; affair; speech; word	דָּבָר, ז.
about	כְּדָבַר-, עַל דְּבַר-
history	דִּבְרֵי הַיָּמִים, ז"ר
something	דְּבַר מַה
It's nothing.	אֵין דָּבָר.
pestilence	דֶּבֶר, ז.
raft	דֹּבְרָה, נ.
speaker	דַּבְרָן, ז.
honey	דְּבַשׁ, ז.
camel's hump	דַּבֶּשֶׁת, נ.
fish	דָּג, ז. דָּגָה, נ.
to tickle	דִּגְדֵּג (דִּגְדֵּג, יְדַגְדֵּג)
hatching	דְּגִירָה, נ.
flag	דֶּגֶל, ז.
sample; pattern	דֻּגְמָה, נ.
grain; rye	דָּגָן, ז.
cornflower	דְּגָנִיָה, נ.
dot(in a letter)	דָּגֵשׁ, ז.
breast;tap;nipple	דַּד, ז.
faded	דֵּהֶה
to be shocked, to be startled	דהם (הִדְהַם) (נִדְהַם, יִדְהַם)
to gallop	דהר (דָּהַר, יִדְהַר)
gallop	דְּהָרָה, נ.
to fish	דוג (דָּג, יָדוּג)
fishing	דֻּגָה, נ.
kettle	דּוּד, ז.
uncle, friend	דּוֹד, ז.
dollar	דּוֹלָר, ז.
silence	דּוּמִיָה, נ.
quietly	דּוּמָם
mineral	דּוֹמֵם, ז.
to judge	דון, דין (דָּן, יָדוּן)

threshing floor	גֹּרֶן, נ. (ר' גְּרָנוֹת)
deduction;deficit	גֵּרָעוֹן, ז.
kernel,grain	גַּרְעִין, ז.
to chase out; to divorce	גרש (גֵּרֵשׁ, יְגָרֵשׁ), גֹּרַשׁ (גֹּרַשׁ, יְגֹרַשׁ)
rain	גֶּשֶׁם, ז.
It's raining.	גֶּשֶׁם יוֹרֵד.
materialism; corporality	גַּשְׁמִיּוּת, נ.
bridge	גֶּשֶׁר, ז.
to build a bridge; to connect	גשר (גָּשַׁר, יִגְשֹׁר)
to feel	גשש (גָּשַׁשׁ, יְגַשֵּׁשׁ)
to wrestle	הִתְגּוֹשֵׁשׁ (הִתְגּוֹשֵׁשׁ, יִתְגּוֹשֵׁשׁ)
wine press	גַּת, נ.

ד

to languish; to weep	דאב (דָּאַב, יִדְאַב)
to grieve	הִדְאִיב (הִדְאִיב, יַדְאִיב)
distress; sorrow	דְּאָבָה, נ.
to be anxious	דאג (דָּאַג, יִדְאַג)
Don't worry.	אַל תִּדְאַג.
anxiety, care	דְּאָגָה, נ.
post office	דֹּאַר, ז.
air mail	דֹּאַר אֲוִיר
bear	דֹּב ז"ן (ר' דֻּבִּים)
There never was such a thing.	לֹא דֻּבִּים וְלֹא יַעַר.
cherry	דֻּבְדְּבָן, ז.
calumny, slander	דִּבָּה, נ.
sticking together; evil spirit	דִּבּוּק, ז.
speech, word	דִּבּוּר, ז.
immediately	תּוֹךְ כְּדֵי דִבּוּר
bee	דְּבוֹרָה, נ.(ר' דְּבוֹרִים)
palace	דְּבִיר, ז.
pressed fig	דְּבֵלָה, נ.
to stick to; to join	דבק (דָּבַק, יִדְבַּק)

deceit	גְּנֵבַת דַעַת, נ.
to blame	גנה (גִּנָּה, יְגַנֶּה)
blame	גְּנוּת, נ.
to hide	גנז (גָּנַז, יִגְנֹז)
gardener	גַּנָּן, ז.
thick;rough;vulgar	גַּס
vulgarity	גַּסוּת
yearning	גַעֲגוּעִים,ז"ר
I yearn for my homeland. I am homesick.	אֲנִי מָלֵא גַעֲגוּעִים לְאַרְצִי.
to scold; to address harshly	גער (גָּעַר, יִגְעַר)
scolding	גְּעָרָה, נ.
volcano	גַּעַשׁ (הַר גַּעַשׁ, ז.)
vine	גֶּפֶן, נ.
cotton	צֶמֶר גֶּפֶן, ז.
The doctor asked for cotton.	הָרוֹפֵא בָּקֵשׁ צֶמֶר גֶּפֶן.
match	גַּפְרוּר, ז.
Give me a cigarette and a match.	תֵּן לִי סִיגַרְיָה וְגַפְרוּר.
sulphur	גָּפְרִית
spark	גֵּץ, ז.
proselyte;stranger, foreigner	גֵּר, ז.
stocking	גֶּרֶב, ז. (ר' גַּרְבַּיִם)
throat	גַּרְגֶּרֶת, נ.
to scratch	גרד (גָּרַד, יִגְרֹד), גֵּרֵד (גֵּרֵד, יְגָרֵד)
to scratch oneself	הִתְגָּרֵד (הִתְגָּרֵד, יִתְגָּרֵד)
place of execution	גַּרְדּוֹם, ז.
to provoke	גרה (גֵּרָה, יְגָרֶה)
excitement,stimulus	גֵּרוּי, ז.
throat	גָּרוֹן, ז.
poor,inferior	גָּרוּעַ
The performance was very poor.	הַהַצָּגָה הָיְתָה גְּרוּעָה מְאֹד.
driving out;divorcing	גֵּרוּשׁ, ז.
axe	גַּרְזֶן, ז.
to draw lots	גרל (הִגְרִיל) (הִגְרִיל, יַגְרִיל)
to cause	גרם (גָּרַם, יִגְרֹם)

דּוֹנַג, ז.	wax
●דַּוְקָא	precisely, only, but
לָאו דַּוְקָא	not necessarily
דור (דָּר, יָדוּר)	to dwell
דּוֹר, ז.	generation
●דַּוָּר	postman
דוש (דָּשׁ, יָדוּשׁ)	to thresh
דחה (דָּחָה, יִדְחֶה)	to push; to postpone
דְּחוּי, ז.	delaying; respite; rejection
דָּחוּס	thick
דָּחוּק	pressed, forced
דְּחִיָּה, נ.	delay
דְּחִיפָה, נ.	push
דְּחִיקָה, נ.	pressing
דַּחְלִיל, ז.	scarecrow
דחף (דָּחַף, יִדְחֹף)	to push
הִדָּחֵף (נִדְחַף, יִדָּחֵף)	to push oneself
דחק (דָּחַק, יִדְחַק)	to press
דְּחָק, דֹּחַק, ז.	oppression; distress
●דַּי	enough
דַּי וְהוֹתֵר	more than enough
●יוֹתֵר מִדַּי	too much
מִדֵּי יוֹם בְּיוֹמוֹ	every day
דַּיָּג, ז.	fisherman
דְּיוֹ, נ.	ink
דִּיּוּק, ז.	precision
●בְּדִיּוּק	precisely
תָּבוֹא בְּשֵׁשׁ בְּדִיּוּק.	Come at six sharp.
דְּיוֹתָה, נ.	inkstand
דִּין, ז.	court sentence; law; judgment
בֵּית דִּין	court
●עוֹרֵךְ דִּין, ז.	lawyer
דִּין וְחֶשְׁבּוֹן	account; report
קִבַּלְנוּ דִּין וְחֶשְׁבּוֹן עַל הָאֲסֵפָה.	We received a report on the meeting.
דַּיָּן, ז.	judge

●דַּיְסָה, נ.	porridge, cereal
דַּיְקָן, ז.	punctual; pedant
דַּיְקָנוּת, נ.	punctuality
דַּיָּר, ז.	lodger
●דִּירָה, נ.	lodgings; apartment
דַּיִשׁ, ז.	time of threshing
דִּישָׁה, נ.	threshing
דכא (דִּכָּא, יְדַכֵּא) דכה (דִּכָּה, יְדַכֶּה)	to oppress
דַּל	poor
דלג (דָּלַג, יִדְלֹג)	to jump; to skip; to leap; to hop
דלה (דָּלָה, יִדְלֶה)	to draw(water); to raise
דִּלּוּג, ז.	jump; skipping
דַּלּוּת, נ.	poverty
דְּלִי, ז.	bucket; pail
דַּלַּעַת, נ.	gourd
●דלק (דָּלַק, יִדְלַק)	to burn ; to pursue
הִדְלִיק (הִדְלִיק, יַדְלִיק)	to kindle
בְּבַקָּשָׁה לְהַדְלִיק אֶת הָאוֹר.	Please turn on the light.
אִי אֶפְשָׁר לְהַדְלִיק אֶת הַמְּכוֹנָה.	I can't start the motor.
דֶּלֶק, ז.	fuel
דְּלֵקָה, נ.	fire
דַּלֶּקֶת, נ.	fever, inflammation
●דֶּלֶת, נ.	door
דָּם, ז.	blood
דָּמִים	money
דְּמֵי קְדִימָה	deposit
דִּמְדּוּמִים, ז"ר	twilight
דמה (דָּמָה, יִדְמֶה)	to resemble
הוּא דּוֹמֶה לְאָחִיו.	He resembles his brother.
דִּמָּה (דִּמָּה, יְדַמֶּה)	to compare
כִּמְדֻמֶּה	as it seems
כִּמְדֻמֶּה לִי שֶׁזֶּה נָכוֹן.	It seems right to me.
דְּמוּת, נ.	likeness, image
דִּמְיוֹן, ז. ר' דִּמְיוֹנוֹת	resemblance; fancy

יֵשׁ דִּמְיוֹן גָּדוֹל.	There's a great resemblance.
יֵשׁ לוֹ דִּמְיוֹן.	He has imagination.
דִּמְיוֹנִי	imaginary
דְּמָמָה, נ.	silence
דֹּמֶן, ז.	dung
דִּמְעָה, נ.	tear
●דֵּעָה, דַּעַת, נ.	knowledge; opinion
אֲנַחְנוּ בְּדֵעָה אַחַת.	We agree.
מַה דַּעְתְּךָ?	What's your opinion?
דַּף, ז.	board; sheet; page
דְּפוּס, ז.	print; form
דְּפִיקָה, נ.	knocking, beating
דפס (הִדְפִּיס) (הִדְפִּיס, יַדְפִּיס)	to print
●דפק (דָּפַק, יִדְפֹּק)	to knock, to beat
דֹּפֶק, ז.	pulse
דַּק, ז.	thin
●דִּקְדּוּק, ז.	precision; grammar
דִּקְדֵּק, ז.	to be exact, to watch carefully
●דַּקָּה, נ.	minute
דְּקִירָה, נ.	sting; puncture
דֶּקֶל, ז.	date palm
דקר (דָּקַר, יִדְקֹר)	to pierce
דָּרְבָן, ז.	spur; sting
דַּרְגָּה, נ.	step
דַּרְדַּר, ז.	thistle
●דָּרוֹם, ז.	south
●דְּרוֹמִי, ז.	southern
דְּרוֹר, ז.	freedom
דְּרוּשׁ, ז.	sermon
דְּרִישָׁה, נ.	exploring; demand
דרך (דָּרַךְ, יִדְרֹךְ)	to step; to stamp; to bend(the bow)
הִדְרִיךְ (הִדְרִיךְ, יַדְרִיךְ)	to lead
●דֶּרֶךְ, זו"נ (ר' דְּרָכִים)	way, mode
●דֶּרֶךְ	through
דֶּרֶךְ אֶרֶץ	manners
דֶּרֶךְ הַמֶּלֶךְ	highway

for instance	דֶּרֶךְ מָשָׁל
He did it as it should be done.	הוּא עָשָׂה זֹאת כְּדַרְכּוֹ.
to explore; to demand	●דרש (דָּרַשׁ, יִדְרֹשׁ)
lecture, sermon	דְּרָשָׁה, נ.
preacher	דַּרְשָׁן, ז.
grass	דֶּשֶׁא, ז.
fat	דֶּשֶׁן, ז.
religion	דָּת, נ.
religious	דָּתִי, ז.

ה

the	●הַ-
is it?	●הַ-
hurrah!	הָאָח
illumination	הָאָרָה, נ.
friendliness welcome	הֶאָרַח פָּנִים
bringing	הֲבָאָה, נ.
difference	●הֶבְדֵּל, הַבְדֵּל, ז.
It makes no difference.	אֵין הֶבְדֵּל.
separation	הַבְדָּלָה, נ.
let us!	הָבָה
glance	הַבָּטָה, נ.
promise	●הַבְטָחָה, נ.
vanity	הֶבֶל, ז.
understanding	●הֲבָנָה, נ.
expression	הַבָּעָה, נ.
convalescence	הַבְרָאָה, נ.
sound, pronunciation	הֲבָרָה, נ.
smuggling	הַבְרָחָה, נ.
picking up	הַגְבָּהָה, נ.
limiting; definition	הַגְבָּלָה, נ.
strengthening	הַגְבָּרָה, נ.
legend; saying	הַגָּדָה, נ.
enlargement	הַגְדָּלָה, נ.
definition	הַגְדָּרָה, נ.
rudder	הֶגֶה, ז.

correction; marginal note	הַגָּהָה, נ.
proper; worthy	הָגוּן, ז.
exaggeration	הַגְזָמָה, נ.
thought; logic	הִגָּיוֹן, ז.
logical	הֶגְיוֹנִי
emigration	הֲגִירָה, נ.
suitably, seemly; proper	(הגן) כַּהֹגֶן
defense; militia	הֲגָנָה
casting lots	הַגְרָלָה, נ.
offering; bringing near	הַגָּשָׁה, נ.
echo	הֵד, ז.
mutual	הֲדָדִי
It's a mutual love.	זֹאת אַהֲבָה הֲדָדִית.
splendid	הָדוּר, ז.
idiot; ignorant	הֶדְיוֹט, ז.
lighting, illumination	הַדְלָקָה, נ.
footstool	הֲדֹם, ז.
myrtle	הֲדַס, ז.
to push	הדף (הָדַף, יֶהְדֹּף)
printing	הַדְפָּסָה, נ.
latch, clasp	הֶדֶק, ז.
splendor, glory	הָדָר, הֶדֶר, ז.; הֲדָרָה, נ.
gradation	הַדְרָגָה, נ.
gradually	בְּהַדְרָגָה
direction	הַדְרָכָה, נ.
alas!	הָהּ, הוֹ, הוֹי!
he	הוּא
transport	הוֹבָלָה, נ.
glory; majesty	הוֹד, ז.
confession; thanks	הוֹדָאָה, הוֹדָיָה, נ.
thanks to	הוֹדוֹת לְ-
Thanks to David, we got tickets.	הוֹדוֹת לְדָוִד קִבַּלְנוּ כַּרְטִיסִים.
announcement	●הוֹדָעָה, נ.
present tense	●הֹוֶה, ז.
being, existence	הֱוָיָה, נ.

proof	הוֹכָחָה, נ.
folly	הוֹלֵלוּת, נ.
riches; property	הוֹן, ז.
deceit	הוֹנָאָה, נ.
addition	הוֹסָפָה, נ.
appearance	הוֹפָעָה, נ.
The violinist's last appearance was made last night.	הַהוֹפָעָה הָאַחֲרוֹנָה שֶׁל הַכַּנָּר הָיְתָה אֶמֶשׁ.
expense; edition; carrying out	●הוֹצָאָה, נ.
I had many expenses.	הָיוּ לִי הוֹצָאוֹת רַבּוֹת.
It's a new edition.	זֹאת הוֹצָאָה חֲדָשָׁה.
teaching; meaning	הוֹרָאָה, נ.
letting down	הוֹרָדָה, נ.
parents	הוֹרִים, ז"ר
occasion	●הִזְדַּמְּנוּת, נ.
I'll come at the first opportunity.	אָבוֹא כַּהִזְדַּמְּנוּת הָרִאשׁוֹנָה.
invitation, order	הַזְמָנָה, נ.
damage, injury	הֶזֵּק, ז.
returning	הַחֲזָרָה, נ.
absolutely	(הֶחְלֵט) בְּהֶחְלֵט
decision	הַחְלָטָה, נ.
improvement	הֲטָבָה, נ.
she	●הִיא, נ.
hurrah!	הֵידָד!
to be, to exist, to become	●היה (הָיָה, יִהְיֶה)
It never existed.	לֹא הָיָה וְלֹא נִבְרָא.
I intended to write to you.	הָיָה בְּדַעְתִּי לִכְתֹּב אֵלֶיךָ.
He became a man.	הוּא הָיָה לְאִישׁ.
as	הֱיוֹת
well	הֵיטֵב
palace; temple	הֵיכָל, ז.
where?	הֵיכָן?
it means	הַיְנוּ
beating	הַכָּאָה, נ.
denial	הַכְחָשָׁה, נ.

resignation	הִסְתַּלְּקוּת, נ.
hiding	הֶסְתֵּר, ז.
transport	הַעֲבָרָה, נ.
absence	הֶעְדֵּר, ז.
impudence	הֵעָזָה, נ.
hiding	הַעֲלָמָה, נ.
bestowal	הַעֲנָקָה, נ.
note, comment	הֶעָרָה, נ.
I have a comment on this.	יֵשׁ לִי הֶעָרָה בְּעִנְיָן זֶה.
valuation	הַעֲרָכָה, נ.
adoration	הַעֲרָצָה, נ.
copy; translation	הַעְתָּקָה, נ.
reverse; contrary; conversion	●הִפּוּךְ, ז.
turning over	הֲפִיכָה, נ.
to overturn	הָפַךְ (הָפַךְ, יַהֲפֹךְ)
reverse, opposite	●הֵפֶךְ
quite the contrary	לְהֵפֶךְ
dropping	הַפָּלָה, ז.
loss	הֶפְסֵד, ז.
interruption	●הֶפְסֵק, ז. הַפְסָקָה, נ.
distribution, circulation	הֲפָצָה, נ.
no man's property	הֶפְקֵר, ז.
licentiousness	הֶפְקֵרוּת, נ.
separation; analysis	הַפְרָדָה, נ.
exaggeration	הַפְרָזָה, נ.
difference	הֶפְרֵשׁ, ז.
separation	הַפְרָשָׁה, נ.
abstraction	הַפְשָׁטָה, נ.
performance	●הַצָּגָה
première	הַצָּגַת בְּכוֹרָה
excuse; defense; vindication	הִצְטַדְּקוּת, נ.
distinction	הִצְטַיְּנוּת, נ.
catching cold	הִצְטַנְּנוּת, נ.
rescue	הַצָּלָה, נ.
success, luck	הַצְלָחָה, נ.
Good luck!	בְּהַצְלָחָה!
suggestion	הַצָּעָה, נ.

further	(הֲלֹן) לְהַלָּן
See below.	רְאֵה לְהַלָּן.
sheltering over-night	הֲלָנָה, נ.
joke	הֲלָצָה, נ.
they	הֵם, הֵמָּה
noise; multitude, mob	הָמוֹן, ז.
vulgar	הֲמוֹנִי
postal order; check	●הַמְחָאָה, נ.
noise	הֶמְיָה, נ.
noise	הֲמֻלָּה, נ.
recommendation	הַמְלָצָה, נ.
invention	הַמְצָאָה, נ.
continuation	הֶמְשֵׁךְ, ז.
here	●הֵן, הֵנָּה
come here	בּוֹא הֵנָּה
they	הֵן
enjoyment; use	הֲנָאָה, נ.
engineering; geometry	הַנְדָּסָה, נ.
behold!	●הִנֵּה!
Here is a book.	הִנֵּה סֵפֶר.
to enjoy; to utilize	(הנה) הֶהֱנָה, הֵהָנוֹת
I enjoyed the performance very much.	נֶהֱנֵיתִי מְאֹד מִן הַהַצָּגָה.
conduct; guiding; performance	הַנְהָגָה, נ.
management	הַנְהָלָה, נ.
relief; reduction	הֲנָחָה, נ.
supposition; postulate; hypothesis; proposition	הַנָּחָה, נ.
hush!	הַס!
explanation	הַסְבָּרָה, נ.
quarantine; bracket; shutting in	הֶסְגֵּר, ז.
consent	הֶסְכֵּם, ז. הַסְכָּמָה, נ.
obituary	הֶסְפֵּד, ז.
provision	הַסְפָּקָה, נ.
heating	הַסָּקָה, נ.
removing	הֲסָרָה, נ.
organization	הִסְתַּדְּרוּת, נ.
observation	הִסְתַּכְּלוּת, נ.

disgrace	הַכְלָמָה, נ.
preparation	הֲכָנָה, נ.
bringing in; income	הַכְנָסָה, נ.
hospitality	הַכְנָסַת-אוֹרְחִים, נ.
subjection; humbleness	הַכְנָעָה, נ.
humbly	בְּהַכְנָעָה
recognition	הַכָּרָה, נ.
gratefulness, gratitude	הַכָּרַת טוֹבָה, הוֹדָיָה, נ.
Please meet my friend.	כְּבַקָּשָׁה לְהַכִּיר אֶת חֲבֵרִי.
proclamation	הַכְרָזָה, נ.
necessity	הֶכְרֵחַ, ז.
necessary	הֶכְרֵחִי
necessity	הֶכְרֵחִיּוּת, נ.
preparation, fitness	הַכְשָׁרָה, נ.
dictation	הַכְתָּבָה, נ.
crowning	הַכְתָּרָה, נ.
indeed	הֲלֹא, הֲלוֹא
farther; out!	●הָלְאָה
dressing	הַלְבָּשָׁה, נ.
birthday	●הֻלֶּדֶת יוֹם הֻלֶּדֶת, ז.
loan	הַלְוָאָה, נ.
heaven grant; may it be so	הַלְוַאי, הַלְוַי
this one	הַלָּז, הַלָּזֶה, הַלָּזוּ
walking; conduct	הֲלִיכָה, נ.
to walk	●הָלַךְ (הָלַךְ, יֵלֵךְ)
to lead	הוֹלִיךְ
to walk to and fro	הִתְהַלֵּךְ
He walked to the park.	הוּא הָלַךְ אֶל הַגַּן.
He strolled in the park.	הוּא הִתְהַלֵּךְ בַּגַּן.
round trip	●הָלוֹךְ וָשׁוֹב
law	הֲלָכָה, נ.
properly	כַּהֲלָכָה
to praise	הִלֵּל (הִלֵּל, יְהַלֵּל)
to boast	הִתְהַלֵּל (הִתְהַלֵּל, יִתְהַלֵּל)
praise	הַלֵּל, ז.
to strike down; to fit	הָלַם (הָלַם, יַהֲלֹם)

parallelism	הַקְבָּלָה, נ.
preface	הַקְדָּמָה, נ.
consecration	הַקְדָּשָׁה, נ.
reducing	הַקְטָנָה, נ.
relief	הֲקָלָה, נ.
raising	הֲקָמָה, נ.
circumference	הֶקֵּף, ז.
walking around;credit	הַקָּפָה, נ.
dictation	הַקְרָאָה, נ.
offering; nearing	הַקְרָבָה, נ.
comparison, analogy	הֶקֵּשׁ, ז.
listening;attention	הַקְשָׁבָה, נ.
mountain	הַר, ז.
much, many	הַרְבֵּה
to kill	הָרַג (הָרַג, יַהֲרֹג)
slaughter	הֶרֶג, ז. הֲרֵגָה,נ.
habit	הֶרְגֵּל, ז.
feeling	הַרְגָּשָׁה, נ.
pregnant woman	הָרָה, נ.
thought	הִרְהוּר, ז.
comfort, relief	הַרְוָחָה, נ.
expansion	הַרְחָבָה, נ.
removal	הַרְחָקָה, נ.
wetting	הַרְטָבָה, נ.
lo! well!	הֲרֵי!
slaughter	הֲרִיגָה, נ.
pregnancy	הֵרָיוֹן, ז.
destruction	הֲרִיסָה, נ.
nodding	הַרְכָּנָה, נ.
to destroy	הָרַס (הָרַס, יַהֲרֹס)
destruction	הֶרֶס, ז.
moment	הֶרֶף-עַיִן
lecture	הַרְצָאָה, נ.
authorization	הַרְשָׁאָה, נ.
improvement,betterment	הַשְׁבָּחָה, נ.
attaining;conception	הַשָּׂגָה, נ.
inspection; super-intendence	הַשְׁגָּחָה, נ.
equation	הַשְׁוָאָה, נ.
destruction	הַשְׁחָתָה, נ.

intellect; enlightenment	הַשְׂכָּלָה, נ.
throwing away; projection	הַשְׁלָכָה, נ.
completion	הַשְׁלָמָה, נ.
extermination	הַשְׁמָדָה, נ.
supposition,hypothesis	הַשְׁעָרָה, נ.
degradation	הַשְׁפָּלָה, נ.
influence	הַשְׁפָּעָה, נ.
irrigation	הַשְׁקָאָה, נ.
opinion; looking	הַשְׁקָפָה, נ.
intercession	הִשְׁתַּדְּלוּת, נ.
perfecting	הִשְׁתַּלְמוּת, נ.
evolution; link; chain	הִשְׁתַּלְשְׁלוּת, נ.
association	הִתְאַחֲדוּת, נ.
harmony, accord; concord	הִתְאָמָה, נ.
effort	הִתְאַמְּצוּת, נ.
solitude	הִתְבּוֹדְדוּת, נ.
assimilation	הִתְבּוֹלְלוּת, נ.
strengthening	הִתְגַּבְּרוּת, נ.
revelation	הִתְגַּלּוּת, נ.
realization	הִתְגַּשְּׁמוּת, נ.
formation	הִתְהַוּוּת, נ.
sarcasm	הִתּוּל, ז.
union	הִתְחַבְּרוּת, נ.
innovation	הִתְחַדְּשׁוּת, נ.
obligation	הִתְחַיְּבוּת, נ.
beginning	הַתְחָלָה, נ.
rivalry,competition	הִתְחָרוּת, נ.
settlement	הִתְיַשְּׁבוּת, נ.
denial	הִתְכַּחֲשׁוּת, נ.
to ridicule	הִתֵּל (הִתֵּל, יְהַתֵּל)
enthusiasm	הִתְלַהֲבוּת, נ.
linking	הִתְלַכְּדוּת, נ.
diligence, per-severance	הִתְמָדָה, נ.
resistance	הִתְנַגְּדוּת, נ.
collision	הִתְנַגְּשׁוּת, נ.
conduct	הִתְנַהֲגוּת, נ.
assault, attack	הִתְנַפְּלוּת, נ.

justification	הִתְנַצְּלוּת, נ.
assault	הִתְנַקְשׁוּת, נ.
waking up	הִתְעוֹרְדוּת, נ.
swooning	הִתְעַלְפּוּת, נ.
gymnastics	הִתְעַמְּלוּת, נ.
boasting	הִתְפָּאֲרוּת, נ.
resignation	הִתְפַּטְּרוּת, נ.
outbreak	הִתְפָּרְצוּת, נ.
spreading	הִתְפַּשְּׁטוּת, נ.
development;evolution	הִתְפַּתְּחוּת, נ.
progress	הִתְקַדְּמוּת, נ.
approach	הִתְקָרְבוּת, נ.
catching cold	הִתְקָרְדוּת, נ.
joining	הִתְקַשְּׁרוּת, נ.
permission; solution; solving	הַתֵּר, ז.
warning	הַתְרָאָה, נ.
excitement	הִתְרַגְּזוּת, נ.
irritability; excitement	הִתְרַגְּשׁוּת, נ.
rise	הִתְרוֹמְמוּת, נ.
widening	הִתְרַחֲבוּת, נ.
keeping away	הִתְרַחֲקוּת, נ.
negligence	הִתְרַשְּׁלוּת, נ.

ו

and	וְ-, וַ-, וֶ-, וִ-
sure, certain	וַדַּאי, וַדִּי
surely	כַּוַּדַּאי
to confess	וִדָּה (הִתְוַדָּה) (הִתְוַדֵּה, יִתְוַדֶּה)
confession	וִדּוּי, ז.
hook	וָו, ז.
curtain	וִילוֹן, ז.(רי וִילָאוֹת)
discussion	וִכּוּחַ, ז.
to discuss	וִכַּח (הִתְוַכֵּחַ) (הִתְוַכֵּחַ, יִתְוַכֵּחַ)
meeting;commitee	וַעַד, ז.
commission	וַעֲדָה, נ.
rose	וֶרֶד, ז.
rosy	וָרֹד, ז.

privilege	זְכוּת, נ.
purity	זַכּוּת, נ.
privilege, merit	זְכִיָּה, נ.
concession	זִכָּיוֹן, ז.
remembrance	זְכִירָה, נ.
to remember	●זכר(זָכַר,יִזְכֹּר)
to recall	הִזָּכֵר(נִזְכַּר,יִזָּכֵר)
to remind	הַזְכִּיר(הִזְכִּיר,יַזְכִּיר)
male	●זָכָר, ז.
memory, remembrance	זֵכֶר, זִכָּרוֹן, ז.
maleness	זַכְרוּת, נ.
forget-me-not	זִכְרִיָּה, נ.
to drip	זלג(זָלַג,יִזְלֹג)
disdain	זִלְזוּל, ז.
to disdain	זִלְזֵל(זִלְזֵל,יְזַלְזֵל)
buzzing	זִמְזוּם, ז.
to buzz	זִמְזֵם(זִמְזֵם,יְזַמְזֵם)
nightingale	זָמִיר, ז.
spring	עֵת הַזָּמִיר, נ.
time	●זְמַן, ז.
as long as	●כָּל זְמַן
It happened a long time ago	הַדָּבָר הָיָה מִזְּמַן.
They came on time	הֵם בָּאוּ בַּזְּמַן.
between terms, vacation	בֵּין הַזְמַנִים
to invite	●(זמן) הִזְמֵן (הִזְמִין, יַזְמִין)
temporary	זְמַנִּי, ז.
to sing; to play (an instrument)	זָמַר(זָמַר, יְזַמֵּר)
song; singing	זֶמֶר,ז. זִמְרָה,נ.
musical instruments	כְּלֵי זֶמֶר, ז.
tail	זָנָב, ז.(רי זְנָבוֹת)
to abandon	(זנח) הַזְנֵחַ (הִזְנִיחַ,יַזְנִיחַ)
sweat	זֵעָה, נ.
trembling	זַעֲזוּעַ, ז.
to startle	זִעֲזֵעַ(זִעֲזֵעַ,יְזַעֲזֵעַ)
small	זָעִיר, ז.

They are a charming couple.	הֵם זוּג נֶחְמָד.
Give me a pair of shoes.	תֵּן לִי זוּג נַעֲלַיִם.
Two is an even number.	שְׁתַּיִם מִסְפָּר זוּג.
to pair	זָוַג (זִוֵּג,יְזַוֵּג)
marriage; pairing	זִוּוּג, ז.
to stir	זוז (זָז,יָזוּז)
reptile	זוֹחֵל,ז.(רי זוֹחֲלִים)
corner, angle	זָוִית, נ.
cheap	●זוֹל
It's a cheap price.	זֶה מְחִיר זוֹל.
cheap	●כָּזוֹל
I bought the coat cheaply.	קָנִיתִי אֶת הַבֶּגֶד בְּזוֹל.
glutton	זוֹלֵל, ז.
gluttony	זוֹלְלוּת, נ.
except	זוּלַת, זוּלָתִי
sauce	זוּם, ז.
prostitute	זוֹנָה, נ.
to sneeze	זוֹרֵר(זוֹרֵר,יְזוֹרֵר)
to creep	זחל(זָחַל,יִזְחַל)
arming	זִיּוּן, ז.
armory	בֵּית זִיּוּן, ז.
projection	זִיז, ז.
to arm	זֵיֵּן (זִיֵּן,יְזַיֵּן)
to arm oneself	הִזְדַּיֵּן (הִזְדַּיֵּן, יִזְדַּיֵּן)
weapon	זַיִן, ז.
forger	זַיְפָן, ז.
forgery	זַיְפָנוּת, נ.
sparkle	זִיק, ז.
arena	זִירָה, נ.
olive; olive tree	זַיִת, ז.(רי זֵיתִים)
clear, pure	זַךְ
pure water	מַיִם זַכִּים
innocent	זַכַּאי, ז.
to be worthy	זכה(זָכָה,יִזְכֶּה)
glass	זְכוּכִית, נ.
magnifying glass	זְכוּכִית מַגְדֶּלֶת,נ.

to renounce	וַתֵּר(וִתֵּר,יְוַתֵּר)
liberal; open handed; indulgent	וַתְרָן
liberality	וַתְרָנוּת, נ.
wolf	זְאֵב, ז.
this one	●זֹאת, נ.
and yet	●בְּכָל זֹאת
fly	זְבוּב, ז.
fertilizing	זִבּוּל, ז.
to sacrifice	זבח(זָבַח,יִזְבַּח)
sacrifice; feast	זֶבַח, ז.
manure	זֶבֶל, ז.
to fertilize	זִבֵּל(זִבֵּל,יְזַבֵּל)
dung-carrier	זַבָּל, ז.
glazier	זַגָּג, ז.
glazing	זְגוּג, ז.
villain	זֵד, ז.
insolence	זָדוֹן, ז.
wickedly	בְּזָדוֹן
this one	●זֶה, ז.
from here	מִזֶּה
to gild	זהב(הַזְהֵב)(הִזְהִיב,יַזְהִיב)
gold	זָהָב, ז.
sonnet	שִׁיר זָהָב
that is	זֶהוּ
golden	זָהֹב
identity	זֶהוּת, נ.
careful	●זָהִיר, ז.
carefulness	זְהִירוּת, נ.
dirt	זֻהֲמָה, נ.
to be careful	●זהר(הִזָּהֵר)(נִזְהַר,יִזָּהֵר)
Look out!	הִזָּהֲרוּ!
to warn	הִזְהִיר
luster, shine	זֹהַר, ז.
that, which	זוֹ
to flow	זוב(זָב,יָזוּב)
pair	●זוּג, ז.(רי זוּגוֹת)

society, company	●מֶחְבְּרָה, נ.
social	חַבְרוּתִי, ז.
It's a social problem.	זֹאת בְּעָיָה חַבְרוּתִית.
pamphlet	חֹבֶרֶת, נ.
to tie up; to bandage; to put on(a hat)	חבש(חָבַש, יַחְבֹּש)
holiday	●חַג, ז.
to celebrate	חָגַג (חָגַג, יָחֹג)
girdle	חֲגוֹר, ז. חֲגוֹרָה, נ.
festival	חֲגִיגָה, נ.
to gird	חָגַר (חָגַר, יַחְגֹּר)
lame	חִגֵּר, ז.
sharp	חַד, ז.
The pencil is sharp.	הָעִפָּרוֹן חַד
to sharpen	חדד(חִדֵּד, יְחַדֵּד)
to be glad	חדה(חָדָה, יֶחֱדֶה)
to gladden	חִדָּה(חִדָּה, יְחַדֶּה)
sharpening; joke	חִדּוּד, ז.
joy	חֶדְוָה, נ.
innovation; news	חִדּוּש, ז.
modern	חָדִיש, ז.
to stop	חדל (חָדַל, יֶחְדַּל)
The rain stopped.	הַגֶּשֶם חָדַל.
to penetrate	חדר(חָדַר, יַחְדֹּר)
room	●חֶדֶר, ז.
dining room	חֲדַר הָאֹכֶל, ז.
living room	חֲדַר הָאוֹרְחִים, ז.
bedroom	חֲדַר הַמִּטוֹת, ז.
bath room	חֲדַר שֶׁמּוֹש
to renew; to invent	חִדֵּש (חִדֵּש יְחַדֵּש)
month	●חֹדֶש, ז.
first of the month	●רֹאש חֹדֶש, ז.
new	●חָדָש, ז.
What's new?	מַה חָדָש?
news	חֲדָשָׁה, נ.
monthly	חָדְשִׁי
debt	חוֹב, ז.(רי חוֹבוֹת)
lover	חוֹכֵב, ז.

ח	
to hide oneself	חבא (הֶחְבָּא) (נֶחְבָּא, יֵחָבֵא)
to hide	הֶחְבִּיא(הֶחְבִּיא, יַחְבִּיא)
to endear; to like	●חבב (חִבֵּב, יְחַבֵּב)
to be loved	הִתְחַבֵּב (הִתְחַבֵּב, יִתְחַבֵּב)
love	חִבָּה, נ. חִבּוּכ, ז.
affectionately	בְּחִבָּה
embrace	חִבּוּק, ז.
addition; essay	חִבּוּר, ז.
conjunction	מִלַּת הַחִבּוּר, נ.
society, club	חֶבְרָה, נ.
wound	חַבּוּרָה, נ.
to beat	חבט (חָבַט, יַחְבֹּט)
beloved, lovely	●חָבִיב, ז.
He is a charming boy.	הוּא בָּחוּר חָבִיב.
I like him	הוּא חָבִיב עָלַי
bundle, parcel	●חֲבִילָה, נ.
bandage	חֲבִישָׁה, נ.
barrel	חָבִית, נ.(רי חָבִיּוֹת)
scrambled eggs	חֲבִיתָה, נ.
to hurt	חבל (חָבַל, יַחְבֹּל)
to ruin	חִבֵּל(חִבֵּל, יְחַבֵּל)
it's a pity	●חֲבָל
It's a pity you didn't see the movie.	חֲבָל שֶׁלֹּא רָאִיתָ אֶת הַסֶּרֶט.
rope	חֶבֶל, ז.
destruction	חַבָּלָה, נ.
destroyer	חַבְּלָן, ז.
lily	חֲבַצֶּלֶת, נ.
to embrace	חבק (חָבַק, יַחְבֹּק) חִבֵּק (חִבֵּק, יְחַבֵּק)
to join	חבר (חָבַר, יֶחְבֹּר)
to compose	חִבֵּר(חִבֵּר, יְחַבֵּר)
association	חֶבֶר, ז.
friend	●חָבֵר, ז.(רי חֲבֵרִים)
friend	●חֲבֵרָה, נ. חֲבֵרוֹת

It was a city in miniature.	זֹאת הָיְתָה עִיר בִּזְעֵיר אַנְפִּין.
to be angry	זעם (זָעַם, יִזְעַם)
anger	זַעַם, ז.
anger, rage	זַעַף, ז.
to cry	זעק (זָעַק, יִזְעַק)
crying	זְעָקָה, נ.
pitch, tar	זֶפֶת, נ.
to pitch	זפת (זִפֵּת, יְזַפֵּת)
the youngest son	זְקוּנִים (בֶּן-, יֶלֶד-), ז.
upright	זָקוּף, ז.
distillation	זִקּוּק, ז.
to grow old	●זקן (זָקֵן, יִזְקַן) הִזְדַּקֵּן (הִזְדַּקֵּן, יִזְדַּקֵּן)
old man	●זָקֵן, ז.
beard	זָקָן, ז.
old woman	זְקֵנָה, נ.
old age	זִקְנָה,נ. זְקֻנוֹת, נ.
strange; foreign	זָר, ז.
garland	זֵר, ז.
arm; strength	זְרוֹעַ, נ.
strangeness	זָרוּת, נ.
to stimulate	זרז(זֵרֵז, יְזָרֵז)
to hurry	הִזְדָּרֵז(הִזְדָּרֵז, יִזְדָּרֵז)
to shine; to rise (sun)	זרח(זָרַח, יִזְרַח)
eager, zealous; alert	זָרִיז
eagerness	זְרִיזוּת, נ.
sunrise	זְרִיחָה, נ.
sowing	זְרִיעָה, נ.
sprinkling; throwing	זְרִיקָה, נ.
to stream	זרם(זָרַם, יִזְרֹם)
stream	זֶרֶם, ז.
to sow	זרע (זָרַע, יִזְרַע)
seed; sowing; posterity	זֶרַע, ז.
to throw	זרק(זָרַק, יִזְרֹק)
little finger	זֶרֶת, נ.

חוֹבָה, נ.	duty
חוֹבֵל, ז.	sailor
חוּג, ז.	circle
חוֹגֵג	festive
חוּד, ז.	point
לְחוּד	separately
חַוָּה, נ.	village, settlement
חַוַּת דַּעַת, נ.	opinion
●חוֹזֶה, ז.	prophet; agreement
הוּא חָתַם עַל חוֹזֶה לִשְׁלֹשָׁה חֳדָשִׁים.	He signed a lease for three months.
חוּט, ז.	thread
חוּט הַשִּׁדְרָה, ז.	spine
חוֹטֵא, ז.	sinner
●חוֹל, ז.(ר׳ חוֹלוֹת)	sand
חוֹל	secular
חוֹל הַמּוֹעֵד, ז.	intermediate days of a holiday period
●חוֹלֶה	ill
אֲנִי חוֹלֶה.	I am ill.
חוּלְיָה, נ.	link; vertebra
חוֹלָנִי	sickly
●חוּם	brown
חוֹמָה, נ.	wall
חוס (חָס, יָחוּס)	to spare
●חוּץ	outside
נָסַעְתִּי לְחוּץ לָאָרֶץ.	I traveled abroad.
נֵצֵא הַחוּצָה.	Let's go outside.
חִוֵּר, ז.	pale
חוֹר, ז.	hole
חוּרְבָּה, נ.	ruin
חוש (חָשׁ, יָחוּשׁ)	to feel
אֲנִי חָשׁ בְּרֹאשִׁי.	My head hurts.
הֵחִישׁ(הֵחִישׁ, יָחִישׁ)	to hurry, to urge
חוּשׁ, ז.	sense
חוּשׁ הַשְּׁמִיעָה שֶׁלּוֹ מְצוּיָן.	His (sense of) hearing is excellent.
חוֹתָם, ז.	seal
חזה (חָזָה, יֶחֱזֶה)	to see
חָזֶה, ז.	breast
חָזוֹן, ז.	vision, prophecy
חִזּוּק, ז.	strengthening
חִזָּיוֹן, ז.(ר׳ חֶזְיוֹנוֹת)	vision; play
חֲזִיר, ז.	pig
חֲזִית, נ.	front
●חַזָּן, ז.	cantor
חַזָּנוּת, נ.	cantorate
חזק(חָזַק, יֶחֱזַק)	to be strong
חִזֵּק(חִזֵּק, יְחַזֵּק)	to strengthen
הִתְחַזֵּק (הִתְחַזֵּק, יִתְחַזֵּק)	to become strong
●חָזָק	strong
חֹזֶק, ז.	strength
(חָזְקָה) בְּחָזְקָה	by force
חֲזָקָה, נ.	occupying; taking
●חזר (חָזַר, יַחֲזֹר)	to return; to repent
הֶחֱזִר (הֶחֱזִיר, יַחֲזִיר)	to give back
חָזַר עַל הַפְּתָחִים	to beg
חֲזָרָה, נ.	repetition; turning back
בַּחֲזָרָה	back
נָתַתִּי לוֹ אֶת סִפְרוֹ בַּחֲזָרָה.	I gave his book back to him.
חֲזֶרֶת, נ.	lettuce, salad
חטא (חָטָא, יֶחֱטָא)	to sin
חֵטְא, ז. חַטָּאָה, נ.	sin
חַטָּא, ז.	sinner
חטב(חָטַב, יַחְטֹב)	to fell, to cut
חִטָּה, נ.(ר׳ חִטִּים)	wheat
חֲטִיפָה, נ.	snatching
חֹטֶם, ז.	nose
חטף(חָטַף, יַחְטֹף)	to snatch
●חַי	living
מַיִם חַיִּים	running water
בַּעַל-חַי	living creature
לְחַיִּים!	To health!
חַיֵּב (חִיֵּב, יְחַיֵּב)	to pronounce guilty
הִתְחַיֵּב(הִתְחַיֵּב, יִתְחַיֵּב	to pledge
●חַיָּב	guilty; obliged
אֲנִי חַיָּב לוֹ חֲמִשָּׁה דוֹלָרִים.	I owe him five dollars.
חִידָה, נ.	riddle
חַיְדַק, ז.	microbe
חיה(חָיָה, יִחְיֶה)	to live
הֶחֱיָה(הֶחֱיָה, יְחַיֶּה)	to revive
חַיָּה, נ.	beast, animal
חִיּוּב	guilt; affirmative
בְּחִיּוּב	positively
●חִיּוּבִי, ז.	positive
קִבַּלְתִּי תְּשׁוּבָה חִיּוּבִית.	I received a positive answer.
חִיּוּת, נ.	life, living
חַיָּט, ז.(נ. חַיֶּטֶת)	tailor
●חַיִּים, ז״ר	life
●חַיָּל	soldier
חַיִל, ז.	strength; army
בֶּן חַיִל, ז.	hero
חֵיל הָאֲוִיר	air force
חֵיל הַיָּם	navy
חֵיל רַגְלִי	infantry
חִיל, ז.	quake
חִיצוֹן, חִיצוֹנִי	exterior
חֵיק, ז.	bosom; pocket
חֵירוּת, נ.	freedom
חִישׁ	quickly
חֵךְ, ז.	palate
●חִכָּה(חִכָּה, יְחַכֶּה)	to wait
חַכֵּה רֶגַע.	Wait a moment.
חַכָּה, נ.	fish hook
חִכּוּךְ, ז.	scratching
חֲכִירָה, חֲכִירוּת, נ.	lease
חכך (הִתְחַכֵּךְ) (הִתְחַכֵּךְ, יִתְחַכֵּךְ)	to scratch; to rub
●חכם(חָכַם, יֶחְכַּם)	to be clever
חִכֵּם(חִכֵּם, יְחַכֵּם)	to teach
הִתְחַכֵּם (הִתְחַכֵּם, יִתְחַכֵּם)	to become wise
●חָכָם	wise, clever
תַּלְמִיד חָכָם, ז.	scholar
חָכְמָה, נ.	wisdom; science

to rent; to lease	חכר (חָכַר, יַחְכֹּר)
to milk	חלב (חָלַב, יַחְלֹב)
milch cow	חוֹלֶבֶת, נ.
milk	●חָלָב, ז.
grease	חֵלֶב, ז.
white of egg;protein	חֶלְבּוֹן, ז.
to be sick	●חלה(חָלָה, יֶחֱלֶה)
I became ill a week ago.	חָלִיתִי לִפְנֵי שָׁבוּעַ.
I was ill a week.	הָיִיתִי חוֹלֶה שָׁבוּעַ.
white loaf	חַלָּה, נ.
rust	חֲלוּדָה, נ.
dream	חֲלוֹם, ז.(ר׳ חֲלוֹמוֹת)
window	●חַלּוֹן, ז.(ר׳ חַלּוֹנוֹת)
exchange	חִלּוּף, ז.
vanguard; pioneer	●חָלוּץ, ז.
division;difference; separation	חִלּוּק, ז.
division	חֲלוּקָה, נ.
weak	חָלוּשׁ
to decide	●חלט (הֶחְלַט) (הֶחְלִיט, יַחְלִיט)
sickness	חֳלִי, ז.
milking	חֲלִיבָה, נ.
flute	חָלִיל, ז.
God forbid!	חָלִילָה!
to repeat again	חָזֹר חֲלִילָה
suit(of clothes)	●חֲלִיפָה, נ.
alternately	חֲלִיפוֹת
weakness	חֲלִישָׁה, נ.
space	חָלָל, ז.
to dream	חלם(חָלַם, יַחֲלֹם)
yolk	חֶלְמוֹן, ז.
flint	חַלָּמִישׁ, ז.
to take off; to free	חלץ (חָלַץ, יַחֲלֹץ)
blouse	●חֻלְצָה, נ.
to divide; to dispute	חלק (חָלַק, יַחֲלֹק)
to divide	●חִלֵּק(חִלֵּק, יְחַלֵּק)

to be divided	הִתְחַלֵּק (הִתְחַלֵּק, יִתְחַלֵּק)
part, lot	●חֵלֶק, ז.
smooth	חָלָק
allotment	חֶלְקָה, נ.
to be weak	חלשׁ (חָלַשׁ, יֶחֱלַשׁ)
to weaken	הֶחֱלִישׁ(הֶחֱלִישׁ, יַחֲלִישׁ)
weak; weakling	חַלָּשׁ, ז.
weakness	חֻלְשָׁה, נ.
father-in-law	חָם, ז.
warm	●חַם, חָם
I feel warm.	חַם לִי.
heat	●חֹם, ז.
He has a high temperature.	יֵשׁ לוֹ חֹם גָּבוֹהַּ.
butter	●חֶמְאָה, נ.
to desire	חמד(חָמַד, יַחְמֹד)
grace	חֶמֶד, ז.
desire, grace	חֶמְדָּה,נ.
sun	חַמָּה, נ.
summer	יְמוֹת הַחַמָּה, ז״ר
darling	●חָמוּד, ז.
She is a darling girl.	הִיא יַלְדָּה חֲמוּדָה.
heating	●חִמּוּם, ז.
fermenting	חִמּוּץ, ז.
donkey	חֲמוֹר, ז.
severe	חָמוּר
mother-in-law	חָמוֹת, נ.
warm	חָמִים
warmth	חֲמִימוּת, נ.
slightly sour	חָמִיץ
fifth	●חֲמִישִׁי, ז.
fifth part	חֲמִישִׁית, נ.
to take pity	חמל(חָמַל, יַחְמֹל)
pity	חֶמְלָה, נ.
to warm	חמם(חַם, יָחֹם), חִמֵּם(חִמֵּם, יְחַמֵּם), הֵחַם(הֵחַם, יָחֵם)
to warm oneself	הִתְחַמֵּם (הִתְחַמֵּם, יִתְחַמֵּם)
to rob	חמס (חָמַס, יַחְמֹס)

plunder; violence	חָמָס, ז.
hot desert wind	חַמְסִין
fermented food	חָמֵץ, ז.
vinegar	חֹמֶץ, ז.
acid	חֻמְצָה, נ.
sulphuric acid	חֻמְצַת גָּפְרִית
oxygen	חַמְצָן, ז.
to turn aside, to slip away	חמק(חָמַק, יַחְמֹק) הִתְחַמֵּק(הִתְחַמֵּק, יִתְחַמֵּק)
pitch, asphalt	חֵמָר, ז.
clay;material;body	חֹמֶר, ז.
donkey driver	חַמָּר, ז.
material	חָמְרִי, ז.
materialism	חָמְרִיּוּת, נ.
five	●חָמֵשׁ,נ. חֲמִשָּׁה, ז.
fifty	●חֲמִשִּׁים
charm	●חֵן, ז.
She is full of charm.	הִיא מְלֵאָה חֵן.
thanks	חֵן חֵן
to please	●מָצָא חֵן
I liked the movie.	הַסֶּרֶט מָצָא חֵן בְּעֵינַי.
to camp	חנה (חָנָה, יַחֲנֶה)
education	חִנּוּךְ, ז.
gracious	חַנּוּן, ז.
shopkeeper; grocer	●חֶנְוָנִי, ז(נ. חֶנְוָנִית)
hypocrisy	חֲנֻפָּה, נ.
shop	●חֲנוּת, נ.
to embalm; to put forth buds	חנט (חָנַט, יַחְנֹט)
resting; camp	חֲנָיָה, נ.
apprentice	חָנִיךְ, ז.
gums	חֲנִיכַיִם, ז״ר
mercy	חֲנִינָה, נ.
lance	חֲנִית, נ.
to educate	חנך(חָנַךְ, יַחְנֹךְ) חִנֵּךְ(חִנֵּךְ, יְחַנֵּךְ)
consecration;Hanukkah	חֲנֻכָּה, נ.
for nothing; undeserved	●חִנָּם, לְחִנָּם

חנן(חָנַן,יֶחֱנַן)	to be merciful
חנף(חָנַף,יֶחֱנַף)	to flatter
הֶחֱנִף(הֶחֱנִיף,יַחֲנִיף)	to flatter
חָנֵף, ז.	flatterer,hypocrite
חנק(חָנַק,יֶחֱנַק)	to strangle
חֶנֶק, ז.	strangling
חַנְקָן, ז.	nitrogen
חַס וְשָׁלוֹם! חַס וְחָלִילָה!	God forbid!
חַסָּה	lettuce
חסד (הִתְחַסֵּד) (הִתְחַסֵּד, יִתְחַסֵּד)	to be pious
חֶסֶד, ז.	favor; grace
חסה(חָסָה,יֶחֱסֶה)	to find shelter
חִסּוּר,ז.	decrease;substraction
חָסוּת, נ.	shelter
חָסִיד	pious
חֲסִידָה, נ.	stork
חֲסִידוּת, נ.	piety
חסל(חָסַל,יַחְסֹל)	to cease
●חסר(חָסַר,יֶחְסַר)	to be wanting, to lack
חִסֵּר(חִסֵּר,יְחַסֵּר) הֶחְסִיר(הֶחְסִיר,יַחְסִיר)	to take off, to subtract
●חָסֵר, ז.	wanting, less
חֹסֶר, ז.	lack, need
חֶסְרוֹן(חִסָּרוֹן),ז. (ר' חֶסְרוֹנוֹת)	defectiveness; loss
●חוֹף, ז.(ר' חוֹפִים)	coast
חֻפָּה, נ.	canopy; marriage ceremony
חִפּוּשׂ, ז.	looking for
חִפּוּשִׁית, נ.	beetle
חפז(חָפַז,יַחְפֹּז), הֵחָפֵז(נֶחְפַּז,יֵחָפֵז)	to hurry
חִפָּזוֹן, ז.	hurry
חֲפִיפָה,נ.	shampoo, head-washing
חֲפִירָה,נ.	digging;excavating
חֹפֶן,ז.(ר' חָפְנַיִם)	handful
חפף(חָפַף,יָחֹף)	to cover; to wash(the head)
חפץ(חָפֵץ,יַחְפֹּץ)	to want
חָפֵץ, ז.	desiring,wanting
חֵפֶץ, ז.	desire, object
חפר (חָפַר, יַחְפֹּר)	to dig; to be ashamed
חפש(חָפַשׂ,יַחְפֹּשׂ) חִפֵּשׂ(חִפֵּשׂ,יְחַפֵּשׂ)	to search
הִתְחַפֵּשׂ(הִתְחַפֵּשׂ, יִתְחַפֵּשׂ)	to disguise oneself
●חֹפֶשׁ, ז.	liberty; vacation
חָפְשִׁי	free
חֵץ, ז.(ר' חִצִּים)	arrow
חצב(חָצַב,יַחְצֹב)	to hew, to hew out
חַצָּב, ז.	stonemason
חצה(חָצָה,יֶחֱצֶה)	to halve
חָצוּף, ז.	impertinent
●חֲצוֹת, נ.	half; midnight
חֲצִי	half
בַּחֲצִי	in the middle
לַחֲצִי	in halves
חָצִיר	hay
חֻצְפָּה	impertinence
חָצָץ, ז.	gravel
חֲצֹצְרָה, נ.	trumpet
חֹק, ז.(ר' חֻקִּים)	law
לִבְלִי חֹק	without limit
חֹק וְלֹא יַעֲבֹר	an unbreakable law
חִקָּה(חִקָּה,יְחַקֶּה)	to imitate
חִקּוּי, ז.	imitation
חֲקִירָה, נ.	examination; exploration
חַקְלָאוּת, נ.	agriculture
חַקְלַאי, ז.	farmer
חקק(חָקַק,יָחֹק)	to engrave
חקר(חָקַר,יַחְקֹר)	to investigate, to explore
חֵקֶר, ז.	exploration
חֵקֶר הַמִּקְרָא	Biblical research
חַקְרָן, ז.	investigator
חָרֵב(חָרֵב,יֶחֱרַב)	to dry up; to be ruined
●הֶחֱרִיב(הֶחֱרִיב, יַחֲרִיב)	to ruin, to destroy
חָרֵב	dry; waste
חֹרֶב, ז.	drought; waste
חֶרֶב,נ.(ר' חֲרָבוֹת)	sword
חָרְבָּה,חֻרְבָּה, נ.	ruin
חֲרָבָה, נ.	dryness
●חֻרְבָּן, ז.	destruction
זֶה הָיָה בִּשְׁנַת 200 אַחֲרֵי חֻרְבַּן בַּיִת שֵׁנִי.	It was in the year 200 after the destruction of the Second Temple.
חרד(חָרַד,יֶחֱרַד)	to tremble
הֶחֱרִיד(הֶחֱרִיד, יַחֲרִיד)	to frighten
חָרֵד	fearful; God-fearing;orthodox
חֲרָדָה, נ.	terror
חַרְדָּל, ז.	mustard
חרה(חָרָה,יֶחֱרֶה)	to be angry
הִתְחָרָה(הִתְחָרָה,יִתְחָרֶה)	to compete
חָרוּז, ז.	verse; rhyme; string of pearls
חֵרוּם, ז.	state of war; emergency
חֲרוּמַף	flat-nosed
●חָרוֹן, ז.	anger
חֵרוּף, ז.	insult
חָרוּץ	diligent,sharp
חֵרוּת, נ.	freedom
חרז(חָרַז,יַחֲרֹז)	to string; to rhyme
חרט (הִתְחָרֵט) (הִתְחָרֵט, יִתְחָרֵט)	to repent
חֶרֶט, ז.	stylus,chisel
חֲרָטָה, נ.	repentance
חַרְטוֹם, ז.	beak; muzzle
חֳרִי (-אַף), ז.	wrath
חָרִיף	spicy;clever;sharp
חֲרִיפוּת,נ.	acuteness,cleverness
חֲרִיצוּת, נ.	diligence
חָרִישׁ,ז. חֲרִישָׁה,נ.	ploughing
חֵרֶם, ז.	destruction; ban; excommunication
חֶרְמֵשׁ, ז.	sickle
חֶרֶס, ז.	clay
כְּלִי חֶרֶס	earthen vessel
חַרְסִינָה, נ.	porcelain

to drown somebody	הַטְבֵּעַ(הִטְבִּיעַ, יַטְבִּיעַ)
nature; quality; character	טֶבַע, זו"נ
natural science	יְדִיעַת הַטֶּבַע, נ.
natural	טִבְעִי, ז.
naturalness	טִבְעִיּוּת, נ.
ring	טַבַּעַת, נ.
roasting	סִגּוּן, ז.
to roast	סִגֵּן(סִגֵּן, יְסַגֵּן)
clean, pure	טָהוֹר
to clean	טִהַר(טִהֵר, יְטַהֵר)
to clean oneself	הִטָּהֵר(הִטַּהֵר, יִטָּהֵר)
to be good	טוֹב(טוֹב, יִיטַב)
to do good	הֵטִיב(הֵטִיב, יֵיטִיב)
good	טוֹב
kindhearted	טוֹב לֵב
good-looking	טוֹב מַרְאֶה
leaders	טוֹבֵי הָעִיר
holiday	יוֹם טוֹב
kindness; favor	טוֹבָה, נ.
to fly	טוּס(טָס, יָטוּס)
They flew to Israel.	הֵם טָסוּ לְיִשְׂרָאֵל.
peacock	טַוָּס, ז.
form; copy	טוֹפֶס, ז.
Give me a form to fill out.	תֵּן לִי טוֹפֶס לְמַלֵּא.
row, line	טוּר, ז.
dampness; moss	טַחַב, ז.
to grind	טָחַן(טָחַן, יִטְחַן)
mill	טַחֲנָה, נ.
nature, character	טִיב, ז.
walk	טִיּוּל, ז.
to cover with mortar	טִיַּח(טִיַּח, יְטַיַּח)
whitewash	טִיחַ, ז.
mud, clay	טִיט, ז.
to walk; to take an excursion	טִיֵּל(טִיֵּל, יְטַיֵּל)
beginner	טִירוֹן, ז.

to desire	חשק(חָשַׁק, יַחְשֹׁק)
desire	חֵשֶׁק, ז.
I don't feel like doing it.	אֵין לִי חֵשֶׁק.
rim of a wheel	חִשֻּׁק, ז.
to fear	חשש(חָשַׁשׁ, יַחְשֹׁשׁ)
fear	חֲשָׁשׁ, ז., חֲשָׁשָׁה, נ.
suspicious	חַשְׁשָׁן
cat	חָתוּל, ז.
piece	חֲתִיכָה, נ.
signature; subscription; finish	חֲתִימָה, נ.
undermining	חֲתִירָה, נ.
to cut	חתך(חָתַךְ, יַחְתֹּךְ)
to seal; to subscribe; to sign	חתם(חָתַם, יַחְתֹּם)
A lease must be signed.	צָרִיךְ לַחְתֹּם עַל חוֹזֶה
to marry	חתן(הִתְחַתֵּן)(הִתְחַתֵּן, יִתְחַתֵּן)
groom; fiancé; son-in-law	חָתָן, ז.
father-in-law	חוֹתֵן, ז.
marriage	חֲתֻנָּה, נ.
mother-in-law	חוֹתֶנֶת, נ.
to undermine	חתר(חָתַר, יַחְתֹּר)

ס

to sweep	טאטא(טִאטֵא, יְטַאטֵא)
immersion	טְבּוּל, ז.
middle	טַבּוּר, ז.
to slaughter	טבח(טָבַח, יִטְבַּח) טַבֵּחַ(טִבַּח, יְטַבֵּחַ)
butchery	טֶבַח, ז.
butcher; cook	טַבָּח, ז.
slaughtering	טְבִיחָה, נ.
immersion; baptism	טְבִילָה, נ.
to immerse; to bathe	טבל(טָבַל, יִטְבֹּל)
to immerse, to baptize	טִבֵּל(טִבֵּל, יְטַבֵּל) (הִטְבִּיל, יַטְבִּיל)
table; board	טַבְלָה, נ.
to drown	טבע(טָבַע, יִטְבַּע)

winter	חֹרֶף, ז.
disgrace	חֶרְפָּה, נ.
to grind (one's teeth)	חרק(חָרַק, יַחֲרֹק שִׁנַּיִם)
potsherd	חֶרֶשׂ, ז.
soft	חֶרֶשׁ
softly	חֶרֶשׁ
to plough	חרש(חָרַשׁ, יַחֲרֹשׁ)
to keep quiet	הֶחֱרַשׁ(הֶחֱרִישׁ, יַחֲרִישׁ)
deaf	חֵרֵשׁ
wood, thicket	חֹרֶשׁ, ז. חֻרְשָׁה, נ.
deafness	חֵרְשׁוּת, נ.
manufacture	חֲרֹשֶׁת, נ.
factory	בֵּית חֲרֹשֶׁת, ז.
to engrave	חרת(חָרַת, יַחֲרֹת)
secretly	חֲשַׁאי(בַּחֲשַׁאי)
to think, to calculate	חשב(חָשַׁב, יַחְשֹׁב)
What do you think?	מַה אַתָּה חוֹשֵׁב?
I intend to travel in the summer.	אֲנִי חוֹשֵׁב לִנְסֹעַ בַּקַּיִץ.
to calculate	חִשֵּׁב(חִשֵּׁב, יְחַשֵּׁב)
arithmetic; account, bill	חֶשְׁבּוֹן, ז. (רִ' חֶשְׁבּוֹנוֹת)
Waiter, please give me the bill.	מֶלְצָר, בְּבַקָּשָׁה תֵּן לִי אֶת הַחֶשְׁבּוֹן.
Take into account that a hundred people will be there.	תָּכִיא בְּחֶשְׁבּוֹן שֶׁיִּהְיוּ מֵאָה אִישׁ.
to suspect	חשד(חָשַׁד, יַחְשֹׁד)
suspicion	חֶשֶׁד, חֲשָׁד, ז.
esteemed	חָשׁוּב
It's an important matter.	זֶה עִנְיָן חָשׁוּב.
suspected	חָשׁוּד
importance	חֲשִׁיבוּת, נ.
to spare; to save	חשך(חָשַׂךְ, יַחְשֹׂךְ)
to be dark	חשך(חָשַׁךְ, יֶחְשַׁךְ)
to get dark	הֶחְשִׁיךְ(הֶחְשִׁיךְ, יַחְשִׁיךְ)
darkness	חֹשֶׁךְ, ז., חֲשֵׁכָה, נ.
electricity	חַשְׁמַל, ז.
to electrify	חַשְׁמֵל(חִשְׁמֵל, יְחַשְׁמֵל)

dry	יָבֵשׁ
dry land;continent	יַבָּשָׁה,יַבֶּשֶׁת,נ.
grief; affliction	יָגוֹן, ז.
exertion	יְגִיעָה, נ.
exhausted, weary	יָגֵעַ
handle	יָד, נ.(רי יָדוֹת)
hand	יָד, נ.(רי יָדַיִם)
by force	בְּחֹזֶק יָד
at once	מִיָּד
profession	מִשְׁלַח יָד
near	עַל יָד
He came to a decision.	הוּא בָּא לִידֵי הַחְלָטָה.
He did his duty.	הוּא יָצָא יְדֵי חוֹבָתוֹ.
immediately	חֵכֶף וּמִיָּד
well-known	יָדוּעַ
as everyone knows	כַּיָּדוּעַ
friend	יָדִיד, ז.
friendship	יְדִידוּת, נ.
knowledge, tidings	יְדִיעָה, נ.
to know	ידע(יָדַע, יֵדַע)
to announce	הוֹדֵעַ(הוֹדִיעַ,יוֹדִיעַ)
to convert to Judaism	יְהֵד (יִהֵד, יְיַהֵר)
to become a Jew	הִתְיַהֵד(הִתְיַהֵד,יִתְיַהֵד)
Judaism	יַהֲדוּת, נ.
Jew	יְהוּדִי
haughty	יָהִיר
haughtiness	יְהִירוּת, נ.
diamond	יַהֲלֹם, ז.
jubilee	יוֹבֵל, ז.
woman in confinement (for child-bearing)	יוֹלֵדָה,נ.
day	יוֹם, ז.(רי יָמִים)
every day	כָּל יוֹם
all day	כָּל הַיּוֹם
today	הַיּוֹם
holiday	יוֹם טוֹב
time will tell	יָמִים יַדַּבְּרוּ

of no importance; tasteless	טָפֵל
blank(of application)	טֹפֶס
to climb	טַפֵּס(טִפֵּס, יְטַפֵּס)
stupid person	טִפֵּשׁ, ז.
stupidity	טִפְּשׁוּת, נ.
busy	טָרוּד
bother	טֹרַח, ז. טִרְחָה, נ.
fresh	טָרִי
not yet, before	טֶרֶם
to tear	טרף(טָרַף, יִטְרֹף)
prey	טֶרֶף, ז.
forbidden food	טְרֵפָה, נ.
parlor	טְרַקְלִין, ז.
rocks	טְרָשִׁים, ז"ר
blurring	טִשְׁטוּשׁ, ז.
to blur	טַשְׁטֵשׁ(טִשְׁטֵשׁ, יְטַשְׁטֵשׁ)

י

proper	יָאֶה
despair	יֵאוּשׁ, ז.
Don't despair.	אַל יֵאוּשׁ.
suitable	(יָאוּת)כִּיָאוּת
river; lake; Nile	יְאֹר, ז.
to despair	יאש(הֶן אַשׁ)(נוֹ אַשׁ, יֶן אַשׁ) (הִתְיָאֵשׁ,הִתְיַאֵשׁ,יִתְיָאֵשׁ)
produce	יְבוּל, ז.
The orchard produce was excellent this year.	יְבוּל הַפַּרְדֵּסִים הָיָה מְצֻיָּן הַשָּׁנָה.
drying	יִבּוּשׁ, ז.
Draining the swamp took a year.	יִבּוּשׁ הַבִּצָּה אָרַךְ שָׁנָה.
to lead, to transport	(יכל)הוֹבֵיל(הוֹבִיל,יוֹבִיל)
wart	יַבֶּלֶת, נ.
brother-in-law	יָבָם, ז.
sister-in-law	יְבָמָה, נ.
to get dry	יבש(יָבֵשׁ, יִיבַשׁ)
to put to shame; to dry	הוֹבֵשׁ(הוֹבִישׁ, יוֹבִישׁ)
to dry up	הִתְיַבֵּשׁ(הִתְיַבֵּשׁ,יִתְיַבֵּשׁ)

ceremony	טֶכֶס, ז.
strategy	טַכְסִיס, ז.
dew	טַל, ז.
to mend	טָלָא(טָלָא, יִטְלָא)
shred	טְלַאי, ז.
lamb	טָלֶה, ז.(רי טְלָאִים)
spotted; mended	טָלוּא
covered with dew	טָלוּל
wrap;prayer shawl	טַלִּית, נ.
to profane	טַמֵּא(טִמֵּא, יְטַמֵּא)
unclean	טָמֵא
uncleanness	טֻמְאָה, נ.
hidden	טָמוּן
hidden	טָמִיר
to hide	טמן(טָמַן, יִטְמֹן)
tray	טַס, ז.
to mistake	טעה(טָעָה, יִטְעֶה)
mistake, error	טָעוּת, נ.
by mistake	בְּטָעוּת
writer's error	טָעוּת סוֹפֵר
typographical error	טָעוּת הַדְּפוּס
tasteful	טְעִים
to taste	טעם(טָעַם,יִטְעַם)
taste	טַעַם, ז.
words that make sense	דְּבָרִים שֶׁל טַעַם
for no reason	בְּלֹא טַעַם
There's no accounting for tastes.	עַל טַעַם וְרֵיחַ אֵין לְהִתְוַכֵּחַ.
to load; to claim	טען(טָעַן, יִטְעַן)
claim; objection	טַעֲנָה, נ.
children	טַף, ז.
drop	טִפָּה, נ.
nursing	טִפּוּל, ז.
type	טִפּוּס, ז.
handbreadth	טֶפַח, ז.
dripping	טִפְטוּף, ז.
parasite	טְפִיל, ז.
to occupy oneself with; to nurse	טַפֵּל(טִפֵּל, יְטַפֵּל)

ostrich	יַעֲנָה, בַּת יַעֲנָה,נ.
to advise	יעץ(יָעַץ,יִיעַץ)
to consult	הִתְיָעֵץ(הִתְיָעֵץ,יִתְיָעֵץ)
forest	יַעַר, ז.
forester	יַעֲרָן, ז.
to beautify	יָפָה(יִפָּה,יְיַפֶּה)
to adorn oneself	הִתְיַפָּה (הִתְיַפָּה, יִתְיַפֶּה)
beautiful	יָפֶה
good	יָפֶה
adornment	יִפּוּי, ז.
authorization	יִפּוּי כֹּחַ, ז.
to sigh	יפח(הִתְיַפֵּחַ)(הִתְיַפַּח,יִתְיַפַּח)
beauty	יֹפִי, ז.
to appear	יפע(הוֹפִיעַ) (הוֹפִיעַ, יוֹפִיעַ)
to go out	יצא(יָצָא, יֵצֵא)
to carry out, to spend	הוֹצִיא(הוֹצִיא, יוֹצִיא)
to go mad	יָצָא מִדַּעְתּוֹ
exception	יוֹצֵא מִן הַכְּלָל
to publish	הוֹצִיא לָאוֹר
olive-oil	יִצְהָר, ז.
couch	יָצוּעַ, ז.
creature	יָצוּר, ז.
going out;exodus	יְצִיאָה, נ.
balcony	יָצִיעַ, ז.
casting	יְצִיקָה, נ.
creature	יָצִיר, ז.
creation	יְצִירָה, נ.
to make a bed; to propose	יצע(הִצַּע) (הִצִּיעַ,יַצִּיעַ)
to pour,to cast	יצק(יָצַק,יִצֹּק)
to create	יצר(יָצַר,יִיצֵר)
impulse	יֵצֶר, ז.
wine press	יֶקֶב, ז.
being, creation	יְקוּם, ז.
dear, precious	יַקִּיר
to wake	יקץ(הֵקֶץ)(הֵקִיץ,יָקִיץ)
to be dear	יקר(יָקַר,יִיקַר)
to revere	הוֹקַר(הוֹקִיר,יוֹקִיר)

to be convinced	יכח(הֻכַּח) (נוֹכַח,יִוָּכַח)
to convince	הֹכִיחַ(הוֹכִיחַ, יוֹכִיחַ)
to argue with	הִתְוַכֵּחַ (הִתְוַכַּח, יִתְוַכַּח)
to be able	יכל(יָכֹל,יוּכַל)
so to speak	כִּבְיָכֹל
possibility	יְכֹלֶת, נ.
to bear	ילד(יָלְדָה,תֵּלֵד)
to be born	הִוָּלֵד(נוֹלַד,יִוָּלֵד)
to beget	הוֹלִיד(הוֹלִיד,יוֹלִיד)
a child, a boy	יֶלֶד, ז.
a girl	יַלְדָּה, נ.
childhood	יַלְדוּת, נ.
to wail	ילל(יָלַל,יְיֵלל)
wailing	יְלָלָה, נ.
bag,satchel; compilation	יַלְקוּט, ז.
sea	יָם, ז.
Mediterranean Sea	הַיָּם הַגָּדוֹל, הַיָּם הַתִּיכוֹן
Dead Sea	יָם הַמֶּלַח
bay	לְשׁוֹן יָם, נ.
right	יָמִין, ז.
right	יְמָנִי
to suck	ינק(יָנַק,יִינַק)
to nurse	הֵנִיק(הֵינִיק,יֵינִיק)
owl	יַנְשׁוּף, ז.
to found	יסד(יָסַד,יִיסַד)
foundation	יְסוֹד,ז. (רי יְסוֹדוֹת)
thorough; basic	יְסוֹדִי
torture	יִסּוּרִים, ז"ר
jasmine	יַסְמִין, ז.
to add	יסף(יָסַף,יְיֵסַף) הוֹסִיף(הוֹסִיף,יוֹסִיף)
to punish	יסר(יִסַּר,יְיַסֵּר)
to determine	יעד(יָעַד,יִיעַד)
to meet	הוֹעַד(נוֹעַד,יִוָּעֵד)
afforestation	יִעוּר, ז.
to be useful	יעל(הוֹעַל) (הוֹעִיל,יוֹעִיל)
because	יַעַן

Middle Ages	יְמֵי הַבֵּינַיִם
birthday	יוֹם הֻלֶּדֶת
daily	יוֹמִי
by day	יוֹמָם
diary	יוֹמָן, ז.
pigeon	יוֹנָה, נ.(רי יוֹנִים)
suckling baby	יוֹנֵק, ז.
mammals	יוֹנְקִים, ז"ר
creator	יוֹצֵר, ז.
first rains	יוֹרֶה, ז.
heir	יוֹרֵשׁ, ז.
heir to the throne	יוֹרֵשׁ עֶצֶר, ז.
inhabitant	יוֹשֵׁב, ז.
chairman	יוֹשֵׁב רֹאשׁ, ז.
more	יוֹתֵר
particularly	בְּיוֹתֵר
the most...	הַיוֹתֵר...
too much	יוֹתֵר מִדַּי
undertaking	יָזְמָה, נ.
to join	יחד(יָחַד,יְיַחֵד)
together	יַחַד, יַחְדָּו
unity;monotheism	יִחוּד, ז.
especially	בְּיִחוּד
descent; noble birth; relation	יִחוּס, ז.
sole, single	יָחִיד, ז.
solitude	יְחִידוּת, נ.
to hope	יחל(יָחַל(יִחֵל,יְיַחֵל)
to derive from, to be related	יחס(הִתְיַחֵס) (הִתְיַחֵס,יִתְיַחֵס)
descent; relation	יַחַס, ז.
in relation	כְּיַחַס
preposition	מִלַּת הַיַּחַס, נ.
person of noble birth	יַחְסָן, ז.
aristocracy	יַחְסָנוּת, נ.
barefoot	יָחֵף
wine	יַיִן, ז.(רי יֵינוֹת)
Wine goes in, secrets come out.	נִכְנַס יַיִן, יָצָא סוֹד.
whiskey	יַיִן שָׂרוּף, ז.

כ

like, as	-כְּ
as wise as Solomon	חָכָם כִּשְׁלֹמֹה
to feel pain	כאב(כָּאַב, יִכְאַב)
What hurts?	מַה כֹּאֵב לְךָ?
pain	כְּאֵב, ז.
stomachache	כְּאֵב בֶּטֶן
headache	כְּאֵב רֹאשׁ
here	כָּאן
here	לְכָאן
from here	מִכָּאן
to be heavy	כבד(כָּבֵד, יִכְבַּד)
to have the honor	הֻכְבַּד(נִכְבַּד, יֻכְבַּד)
to honor	כִּבֵּד(כִּבֵּד, יְכַבֵּד)
to have the honor	הִתְכַּבֵּד(הִתְכַּבֵּד, יִתְכַּבֵּד)
heavy	כָּבֵד
liver	כָּבֵד, ז.
weight	כֹּבֶד, ז.
seriousness	כֹּבֶד רֹאשׁ
heaviness	כְּבֵדוּת, נ.
to be extinguished	כבה(כָּבָה, יִכְבֶּה)
to extinguish, to quench	כִּבָּה(כִּבָּה, יְכַבֶּה)
the light went out	כָּבָה הָאוֹר
he put out the light	הוּא כִּבָּה אֶת הָאוֹר
honoring	כִּבּוּד, ז.
honor	כָּבוֹד, ז.
riches	כְּבוּדָּה, נ.
extinguishing	כִּבּוּי, ז.
washing	כִּבּוּס, ז. כְּבִיסָה, נ.
conquest;preserving	כִּבּוּשׁ, ז.
preserves	כְּבוּשׁ, ז.
mighty	כַּבִּיר
road	כְּבִישׁ, ז.
cable	כֶּבֶל, ז.
to wash	כבס(כָּבַס, יִכְבֹּס)

to set; to populate	הוֹשֵׁב(הוֹשִׁיב, יוֹשִׁיב)
to settle; to think over	הִתְיַשֵּׁב(הִתְיַשֵּׁב, יִתְיַשֵּׁב)
to preside	יָשַׁב רֹאשׁ
settlement, populated district	יִשּׁוּב, ז.
a civilized person	אָדָם מִן הַיִּשּׁוּב
Jewish population of Israel	הַיִּשּׁוּב
deliberation	יִשּׁוּב הַדַּעַת, ז.
help	יְשׁוּעָה, נ.
being	יְשׁוּת, נ.
sitting;Talmud school	יְשִׁיבָה, נ.
desert	יְשִׁימוֹן, ז.
old	יָשִׁישׁ
to sleep	ישׁן(יָשַׁן, יִישַׁן)
to grow obsolete	הִתְיַשֵּׁן(הִתְיַשֵּׁן, יִתְיַשֵּׁן)
sleeping	יָשֵׁן, ז.
old	יָשָׁן
to be helped	ישׁע(הוּשַׁע)(נוֹשַׁע, יִוָּשַׁע)
to help	הוֹשֵׁעַ(הוֹשִׁיעַ, יוֹשִׁיעַ)
help	יֶשַׁע, ז.
to be straight; to be pleasing; to be righteous	ישׁר(יָשַׁר, יִישַׁר)
to straighten	יִשֵּׁר(יִשֵּׁר יְיַשֵּׁר)
to straighten	הִיְשִׁיר(הִיְשִׁיר, יַיְשִׁיר)
to become straight	הִתְיַשֵּׁר(הִתְיַשֵּׁר, יִתְיַשֵּׁר)
straight, correct, honest	יָשָׁר
straightness,honesty	יֹשֶׁר, ז.
honestly	בְּיֹשֶׁר
wedge;peg	יָתֵד, נ.(רי יְתֵדֹת)
orphan	יָתוֹם, ז.(ני יְתוֹמָה)
mosquito	יַתּוּשׁ, ז.
to remain	יתר(הִוָּתֵר)(נוֹתַר, יִוָּתֵר)
to leave	הוֹתֵר(הוֹתִיר, יוֹתִיר)
surplus	יֶתֶר, ז.
more than that	יֶתֶר עַל כֵּן
advantage	יִתְרוֹן, ז.

to become expensive	הִתְיַקֵּר(הִתְיַקֵּר, יִתְיַקֵּר)
dear, costly	יָקָר
rare	יְקַר הַמְּצִיאוּת
expensive	בְּיֹקֶר
this is expensive	זֶה בְּיֹקֶר
to fear	ירא(יָרֵא, יִירָא)
fearful, afraid	יָרֵא
fear	יִרְאָה, נ.
reverence	יִרְאַת הַכָּבוֹד, נ.
to go down	ירד(יָרַד, יֵרֵד)
to put down	הוֹרֵד(הוֹרִיד, יוֹרִיד)
to grow poor	יָרַד מִנְּכָסִים
to shoot	ירה(יָרָה, יִירֶה)
to teach	הוֹרֵה(הוֹרָה, יוֹרֶה)
low; degraded	יָרוּד
inheritance	יְרֻשָּׁה, נ.
moon	יָרֵחַ, ז.
month	יֶרַח, ז.
monthly	יַרְחוֹן
fair	יָרִיד, ז.
descent;degradation	יְרִידָה, נ.
shooting	יְרִיָּה, נ.
curtain,parchment	יְרִיעָה, נ.
thigh	יָרֵךְ, נ.(רי"ז יְרֵכַיִם)
descendant	יוֹצֵא יָרֵךְ, ז.
to spit; to be green	ירק(יָרַק, יִירַק)
green	יָרֹק
vegetables	יָרָק, יֶרֶק, ז.(רי יְרָקוֹת)
greenish	יְרַקְרַק
to inherit	ירשׁ(יָרַשׁ, יִירַשׁ)
being	יֵשׁ, ז.
there is, there are	יֵשׁ
I desire	יֵשׁ אֶת נַפְשִׁי
there are those who say...	יֵשׁ אוֹמְרִים...
There's plenty.	יֵשׁ וָיֵשׁ.
to sit, to sit down; to inhabit	ישׁב(יָשַׁב, יֵשֵׁב)
He did no work.	הוּא יָשַׁב בָּטֵל.

already	●כְּבָר
recently	זֶה לֹא כְּבָר
a long time ago	מִכְּבָר
sieve	כְּבָרָה, נ.
sheep	כֶּבֶשׂ, ז.
to subdue, to conquer; to preserve	כבש(כָּבַשׁ, יִכְבַּשׁ) כַּבֵּשׁ(כִּבֵּשׁ, יְכַבֵּשׁ)
sheep	כִּבְשָׂה, נ.
furnace	כִּבְשָׁן, ז.(רי כִּבְשׁוֹנוֹת)
jug	כַּד, ז.
worthy	●כְּדַאי
Jerusalem is worth visiting.	כְּדַאי לְבַקֵּר אֶת יְרוּשָׁלַיִם
It doesn't pay to talk to him.	לֹא כְּדַאי לְדַבֵּר אֵלָיו.
ball	כַּדּוּר, ז.
globular	כַּדּוּרִי
for, so that	כְּדֵי , בִּכְדֵי
roundness	כַּדְּרוּת, נ.
so	כֹּה
to and fro	כֹּה וָכֹה
meanwhile	עַד כֹּה וְעַד כֹּה
dark, dim	כֵּהֶה
priesthood, office	כְּהֻנָּה, נ.
to minister; to officiate	כהן (כִּהֵן, יְכַהֵן)
priest	כֹּהֵן, ז.(נ. כֹּהֶנֶת)
high priest	הַכֹּהֵן הַגָּדוֹל, ז.
laundress	כּוֹבֶסֶת, נ.
hat	●כּוֹבַע, ז.
hatter	כּוֹבָעִי, ז.
direction	●כִּוּוּן, ז.
Go in this direction to the corner.	לֵךְ בַּכִּוּוּן הַזֶּה עַד הַפִּנָּה.
burn	כְּוִיָּה, נ.
star	כּוֹכָב, ז.
planet	כּוֹכָב לֶכֶת
comet	כּוֹכַב שָׁבֵט, ז.
fixed star	כּוֹכַב שֶׁבֶת
to contain	כול(הֵכִיל)(הֵכִיל, יָכִיל)
to prepare	כון(הֵכִין)(הֵכִין, יָכִין)

to direct	כון(כִּוֵּן, יְכַוֵּן)
to get ready	הִתְכַּוֵּן(הִתְכַּוֵּן, יִתְכַּוֵּן)
to intend	הִתְכַּוֵּן(הִתְכַּוֵּן, יִתְכַּוֵּן)
intention, devotion	כַּוָּנָה, נ.
shelves	כּוֹנָנִית, נ.
glass	●כּוֹס, נ.(רי כּוֹסוֹת)
unbeliever	כּוֹפֵר, ז.
furnace	כּוּר, ז.
bookbinder	כּוֹרֵךְ, ז.
winegrower	כּוֹרֵם, ז.
beehive	כַּוֶּרֶת, נ.
to tell a lie	כזב(כָּזַב, יִכְזַב)
to confute; to disappoint	הַכְזָב (הִכְזִיב, יַכְזִיב)
lie	כָּזָב, ז.
liar	כַּזְבָן, ז.
vigor, strength	●כֹּחַ, ז.(רי כֹּחוֹת)
representative	בָּא כֹחַ, ז.
to deny	כחד(כִּחֵד, יְכַחֵד)
blue	●כָּחֹל
to grow lean	כחש(כָּחַשׁ, יִכְחַשׁ)
that; because	●כִּי
but; unless	כִּי אִם
even though	אַף כִּי
lance	כִּידוֹן, ז.
because	כֵּיוָן
miser	כֵּילַי, ז.
pocket; bag	●כִּיס, ז.
loss	חֶסְרוֹן כִּיס, ז.
how	כֵּיצַד
hearth	כִּירָה, נ. כִּירַיִם, ר"ז
so, thus	●כַּךְ, כָּכָה
after	●אַחַר כַּךְ
Either way, I shall lose.	בֵּין כַּךְ וּבֵין כַּךְ אֲנִי אַפְסִיד.
loaf; cake	כִּכָּר, נ.(רי כִּכָּרוֹת)
every; all	●כָּל
everything, all	●הַכֹּל
all	●כָּל
everyone who	●כָּל הַ-

so much	●כָּל כַּךְ
the least	כָּל שֶׁהוּא
to imprison	כלא(כָּלָא, יִכְלָא)
prison	כֶּלֶא, ז.
mixture	כִּלְאַיִם, ז"ר
dog	כֶּלֶב, ז.(נ. כַּלְבָּה)
dog	כְּלַבְלַב, ז.
to be over, to be finished	כלה(כָּלָה, יִכְלֶה)
to finish	כַּלָּה(כִּלָּה, יְכַלֶּה)
end, destruction	כָּלָה, נ.
wholly	כָּלָה
bride	כַּלָּה, נ.
cage	כְּלוּב, ז.
something	כְּלוּם
nothing	●לֹא כְּלוּם
that means	כְּלוֹמַר
vessel, tool	כְּלִי,ז.(רי כֵּלִים)
arms	כְּלֵי זַיִן
silver vessels	כְּלֵי כֶסֶף
kidney	כִּלְיָה,נ.(רי כְּלָיוֹת)
remorse	מֻסַּר כְּלָיוֹת
destruction	כְּלָיָה,נ. כִּלָּיוֹן, ז.
completely; perfectly	כָּלִיל
to nourish; to contain	כִּלְכֵּל(כִּלְכֵּל, יְכַלְכֵּל)
maintenance; economy; economics	כַּלְכָּלָה, נ.
to include; to unite; to generalize	כלל(כָּלַל, יִכְלֹל)
totality; rule	כְּלָל, ז.
in general	בִּכְלָל
inclusive	עַד וְעַד בִּכְלָל
exclusive	עַד וְלֹא עַד בִּכְלָל
general	כְּלָלִי, ז.
shame	כְּלִמָּה, נ.
towards	כְּלַפֵּי
how much? how many?	●כַּמָּה?
How much does it cost?	בְּכַמָּה זֶה עוֹלֶה?
how long	כַּמָּה זְמַן
like, as	●כְּמוֹ

atonement	כַּפָּרָה, נ.
countryman, villager	כַּפְרִי, פַּרְי, ז.
atonement	כִּפּוּרִים, ז"ר
to tie	כפת(כָּפַת, יִכְפֹּת)
button;bud	כַּפְתּוֹר, כַּפְתֹּר, ז.
to button	כִּפְתֵּר(כִּפְתֵּר, יְכַפְתֵּר)
pillow	כַּר, ז.
cock's comb	כַּרְבֹּלֶת, נ.
cabbage;cherub	כְּרוּב, ז.
cauliflower	כְּרוּבִית, נ.
proclamation	כָּרוֹז, ז.
to proclaim	כרז(הִכְרִיז)(הִכְרִיז,יַכְרִיז)
to force	כדח(הַכְרִיחַ)(הִכְרִיחַ,יַכְרִיחַ)
against my will	(כֹּרַח)עַל כָּרְחִי
ticket	כַּרְטִיס, ז.
wrapping,binding	כְּרִיכָה, נ.
divorce	כְּרִיתָה, כְּרִיתוּת,נ.
to roll; to wrap; to bind	כרך(כָּרַךְ, יִכְרֹךְ)
volume	כֶּרֶךְ, ז.
I read the first volume.	קָרָאתִי אֶת הַכֶּרֶךְ הָרִאשׁוֹן.
city	כְּרַךְ, כְּרָךְ, ז.
leap	כִּרְכּוּר, ז.
to hop	כִּרְכֵּר(כִּרְכֵּר, יְכַרְכֵּר)
vineyard	כֶּרֶם, ז.
belly	כֶּרֶס, ז.
to gnaw	כִּרְסֵם(כִּרְסֵם,יְכַרְסֵם)
potbellied	כְּרַסְתָן, ז.
to kneel	כרע(כָּרַע,יִכְרַע)
to subdue; to decide	הִכְרִיעַ(הִכְרִיעַ,יַכְרִיעַ)
shinbone	כֶּרַע, נ(רי כְּרָעַיִם)
magic	כִּשּׁוּף, ז.
to stumble	כשל(כָּשַׁל,יִכְשַׁל)
to lead astray	הִכְשִׁיל(הִכְשִׁיל,יַכְשִׁיל)
magician	כַּשָּׁף, ז.
to be fit	כשר(כָּשֵׁר,יִכְשַׁר)
to prepare	הִכְשִׁיר(הִכְשִׁיר,יַכְשִׁיר)

garment	כְּסוּת, נ.
pretext	כְּסוּת עֵינַיִם, נ.
silly	כְּסִיל
silliness	כְּסִילוּת, נ.
money; silver	כֶּסֶף, ז.
to yearn for	כסף(הִכָּסֵף)(נִכְסַף,יִכָּסֵף)
to silver	הִכְסִיף(הִכְסִיף,יַכְסִיף)
silvery; financial	כַּסְפִּי
mercury	כַּסְפִּית, נ.
pillow; quilt	כֶּסֶת, נ.
ugliness	כֹּעַר, ז.
cake	כַּעַךְ, ז.
to be angry	כעס(כָּעַס,יִכְעַס)
to make angry	הִכְעִיס(הִכְעִיס,יַכְעִיס)
anger	כַּעַס, ז.
ill-tempered person	כַּעֲסָן, ז.
to become ugly	כער(הַכֵּעַר)(הִכְעִיר,יַכְעִיר)
hand;spoon	כַּף,נ.(רי"ז כַּפַּיִם, רי כַּפּוֹת)
weighing pan (for scale)	כַּף מֹאזְנַיִם
sole of the foot	כַּף רֶגֶל
cliff	כֵּף, ז.
to force	כפה(כָּפָה,יִכְפֶּה)
vault;top;skullcap	כִּפָּה, נ.
ungrateful	כְּפוּי טוֹבָה
doubled, folded; multiplied	כָּפוּל
atonement	כִּפּוּר, ז.
lion cub	כְּפִיר, ז.
denial;unbelieving	כְּפִירָה,נ.
to multiply	כפל(כָּפַל, יִכְפֹּל) הִכְפִּיל(הִכְפִּיל,יַכְפִּיל)
multiplication	כֶּפֶל, ז.
twice as much	כִּפְלַיִם
to bend	כפף(כָּפַף,יִכְפֹּף)
to deny	כפר(כָּפַר,יִכְפֹּר)
to atone	כִּפֵּר(כִּפֵּר,יְכַפֵּר)
village	כְּפָר, ז.
ransom	כֹּפֶר, ז.

hidden	כָּמוּס, ז.
quantity	כַּמּוּת, נ.
gentile priest	כֹּמֶר, כֹּמֶר, ז.
honest	כֵּן, ז.
yes	כֵּן
therefore	לָכֵן
if so	אִם כֵּן
afterwards	אַחֲרֵי כֵן
nevertheless	אַף עַל פִּי כֵן
wrong	לֹא כֵן
louse	כִּנָּה, נ.(רי כִּנִּים)
to name	כנה(כִּנָּה,יְכַנֶּה)
nickname	כִּנּוּי, ז.
suffixes	כִּנּוּיִים, ז"ר
gathering	כִּנּוּס, ז.
gathering; gang	כְּנוּפִיָה, נ.
violin	כִּנּוֹר, ז.
entrance	כְּנִיסָה, נ.
to roll up; to set up	כנן(כִּנֵּן,יְכַנֵּן)
to collect, to assemble	כנס(כָּנַס,יִכְנֹס) כִּנֵּס(כִּנֵּס,יְכַנֵּס)
to bring in	הִכְנִיס(הִכְנִיס,יַכְנִיס)
to assemble; to shrink	הִתְכַּנֵּס(הִתְכַּנֵּס,יִתְכַּנֵּס)
gathering	כְּנֶסֶת, כֶּנֶס, נ.
The Knesset is Israel's parliament.	הַכְּנֶסֶת הִיא הַפַּרְלָמֶנְט שֶׁל יִשְׂרָאֵל.
synagogue	בֵּית הַכְּנֶסֶת
to be subjected, to submit	כנע(הִכָּנַע)(נִכְנַע,יִכָּנַע)
to subject	הִכְנִיעַ(הִכְנִיעַ,יַכְנִיעַ)
merchant;Canaanite	כְּנַעֲנִי, ז.
wing; edge	כָּנָף,נ.(רי כְּנָפַיִם)
violinist	כַּנָּר
chair	כִּסֵּא,ז.(רי כִּסְאוֹת)
toilet	בֵּית הַכִּסֵּא, ז.
to cover	כסה(כָּסָה,יִכְסֶה) כִּסָּה(כִּסָּה,יְכַסֶּה)
to cover oneself	הִתְכַּסָּה(הִתְכַּסָּה,יִתְכַּסֶּה)
cover	כְּסוּי, ז.

הֵם הִכְשִׁירוּ אֶת הַקַּרְקַע לִנְטִיעָה. — They prepared the soil for planting.

כָּשֵׁר — approved

(כֹּשֶׁר) שְׁעַת הַכֹּשֶׁר — suitable time; fitness

כִּשְׁרוֹן, ז. (ר׳ כִּשְׁרוֹנוֹת) — talent

כַּשְׁרוּת, נ. — fitness

כַּת, כִּתָּה, נ. — party;sect;class

●כתב (כָּתַב, יִכְתֹּב) — to write

הִכְתִּיב (הִכְתִּיב, יַכְתִּיב) — to dictate

כְּתָב, ז. — writing

כְּתָב יָד, ז. — manuscript

כְּתָב עֵת — a periodical

כְּתֻבָּה, נ. — marriage contract

כַּתְּבָן, ז. — writer

●כְּתֹבֶת, נ. — address,inscription

כְּתִיבָה, נ. — writing

●כֹּתֶל, ז. — wall

הַכֹּתֶל הַמַּעֲרָבִי — the Western Wall, the Wailing Wall

כֶּתֶם, ז. — spot;pure gold

כָּתֹם, ז. — yellow

כֻּתְנָה, נ. — cotton

●כֻּתֹּנֶת, כְּתֹנֶת, נ. — shirt

כָּתֵף, נ. — shoulder

כֶּתֶר, ז. — crown

כתר (הִכְתִּיר) (הִכְתִּיר, יַכְתִּיר) — to crown; to surround

ל

●לְ- — to

●לֹא, לוֹא — no, not

אִם לֹא — if not

וְלֹא עוֹד אֶלָּא — not only this, but

לֹא כְלוּם — nothing

לאה (הִלָּאֵה) (נִלְאָה, יִלְאֶה) — to get tired

הֶלְאָה (הֶלְאָה, יַלְאֶה) — to make tired

לֵאוּת, נ. — weariness

●לְאֹם, ז. — nation

לְאֻמִּי, ז. — national

בֵּין לְאֻמִּי — international

לְאֻמִּיּוּת, נ. — nationalism

לֵב, לֵבָב, ז. (ר׳ לִבּוֹת, לְבָבוֹת) — heart

שִׂים לֵב! — Pay attention!

דִּבַּרְתִּי עַל לִבּוֹ. — I persuaded him.

בְּלֵב וָלֵב — insincerely

●לְבַד — alone

לְבַדִּי, לְבַדְּךָ — by myself etc.

לַבָּה, נ. — flame; lava

לבה (לִבָּה, יְלַבֶּה) — to blow

לִבּוּן, ז. — making red-hot; whitewashing;cleaning

לְבוּשׁ, נ. — garment

לָבִיא, ז. — lion

לְבִיאָה, לְבִיָּה, נ. — lioness

לְבִישָׁה, נ. — dressing

לבן (הִלְבֵּן) (הִלְבִּין, יַלְבִּין) — to be white; to whiten

הִתְלַבֵּן (הִתְלַבֵּן, יִתְלַבֵּן) — to become clean

●לָבָן, ז. — white

לְבָנִים, ז״ר — linen

לֹבֶן, ז. — whiteness

לְבָנָה, נ. — moon

לְבֵנָה, נ. (ר׳ לְבֵנִים) — brick

●לבש (לָבַשׁ, יִלְבַּשׁ) — to put on

הִלְבִּישׁ (הִלְבִּישׁ, יַלְבִּישׁ)

הִתְלַבֵּשׁ (הִתְלַבֵּשׁ, יִתְלַבֵּשׁ) — to dress oneself

לִגְיוֹן, ז. — legion

לְגִימָה, נ. — mouthful

לִגְלֵג (לִגְלֵג, יְלַגְלֵג) — to mock

לִגְלוּג, ז. — mockery

לִגְמְרֵי, לְגַמְרֵי — completely

לֵדָה, נ. — birth

לַהַב, ז. לֶהָבָה, לַהֶבֶת, נ. — flame, blade

להב (הִלְהֵב) (הִלְהִיב, יַלְהִיב) — to inspire

הִתְלַהֵב (הִתְלַהֵב, יִתְלַהֵב) — to be inspired

לַהַג, ז. — silly talk

לָהוּט, ז. — passionate

להט (הִתְלַהֵט) (הִתְלַהֵט, יִתְלַהֵט) — to grow hot

לַהַט, ז. — edge (sword); strong heat

לַהֲקָה, נ. — group, company

לוּ, לוּא — if; oh that

לוה (לָוָה, יִלְוֶה) — to borrow

הִלְוָה (הִלְוָה, יַלְוֶה) — to lend

לֹוֶה, ז. — debtor

●לוּחַ, ז. (ר׳ לוּחוֹת) — blackboard; board; calendar; timetable

לְוָיָה, נ. — escort; burial

לִוְיָתָן, ז. — whale

לוּל, ז. — poultry house

לוּלֵא, לוּלֵי — if not

לוּלָב, ז. — palm leaf

לוּן, לִין (לָן, יָלִין) — to stay overnight

הִתְלוֹנֵן (הִתְלוֹנֵן, יִתְלוֹנֵן) — to complain

לוץ (הִתְלוֹצֵץ) (הִתְלוֹצֵץ, יִתְלוֹצֵץ) — to joke

לוש (לָשׁ, יָלוּשׁ) — to knead

לְזוּת (-שְׂפָתַיִם), נ. — slander

לֵחַ, ז. — freshness;juice

לַח, ז. — wet, damp

לְחוּד — separately

●לַחוּת, נ. — humidity,dampness

לְחִי, לֶחִי, נ. (ר׳ לְחָיַיִם) — cheek; jawbone

●לְחַיִּים! — Your health!

לְחִיצָה, נ. — pressing

לְחִישָׁה, נ. — whispering

בִּלְחִישָׁה — softly

לַחְלוּחִית, נ. — dampness

לחם (לָחַם, יִלְחַם) — to fight; to eat (bread)

הִלָּחֵם (נִלְחַם, יִלָּחֵם) הַלְחֵם (הִלְחִים, יַלְחִים) — to solder

●לֶחֶם, ז. — bread

אֲנִי רוֹצֶה פַּת לֶחֶם. — I want a piece of bread.

לַחְמָנִיָּה, נ. — roll

לַחַן, ז. — melody

לחץ (לָחַץ, יִלְחַץ) — to press

לַחַץ, ז. — oppression

לחש (לָחַשׁ, יִלְחַשׁ) — to whisper

הִתְלַחֵשׁ (הִתְלַחֵשׁ, יִתְלַחֵשׁ) — to whisper

לַחַשׁ, ז. — whispering

בְּלַחַשׁ — softly

(לט) בַּלָּט, בַּלָּאט — secretely

לְטָאָה, נ. — lizard

לְטִיפָה, נ. — fondling

לְטִישָׁה, נ. — sharpening

לטש (לָטַשׁ, יִלְטֹשׁ) — to sharpen

●לַיִל, לַיְלָה, ז. (ר׳ לֵילוֹת) — night

הַלַּיְלָה — tonight

חֲצוֹת הַלַּיְלָה midnight
לֵיל יָרֵחַ a moonlit night
לִילָךְ,ז. lilac
לִינָה,נ. night's lodging
לֵיצָן,ז. mocker
לֵיצָנוּת,נ. derision
לַיִשׁ,ז. lion
לִישָׁה,נ. kneading
לכד (לָכַד, יִלְכֹּד) to conquer, to capture
הִלָּכֵד (נִלְכַּד, יִלָּכֵד) to be conquered, to be captured
הִתְלַכֵּד (הִתְלַכֵּד, יִתְלַכֵּד) to join firmly
לְכִידָה,נ. conquest, capture
לִכְלוּךְ,ז. soiling
לִכְלֵךְ (לִכְלֵךְ, יְלַכְלֵךְ) to soil
לְכַתְּחִילָה from the start
●למד (לָמַד, יִלְמַד) to learn
●לִמֵּד (לִמֵּד, יְלַמֵּד) to teach
הִתְלַמֵּד (הִתְלַמֵּד, יִתְלַמֵּד) to get used to
לַמְדָן,ז. learned man
●לָמָּה? why? what for?
לָמָּה לִי כֶּסֶף? Why do I need money?
לִמּוּד,ז. learning
לְמַעַן in order that
לְמַפְרֵעַ ahead
●לָנוּ us
תֵּן לָנוּ קָפֶה וְעוּגוֹת. Give us coffee and cakes.
לֹעַ,ז. gullet; abyss
לעג (לָעַג, יִלְעַג) to deride
לַעַג,ז. mockery
לֹעֵז,ז. foreign
לַעַז,ז. foreign language
בְּלַעַז, לַעֲזִית in a foreign language
לְעֵיל above
כָּתוּב לְעֵיל. It is written above (previously).
לְעִיסָה,ז. chewing
לְעֻמַּת opposite; towards
לעס (לָעַס, יִלְעַס) to chew
לְפִי according, because

לְכָל אֶחָד לְפִי צְרָכָיו. To each according to his needs.
לַפִּיד,ז. torch
לְפִיכָךְ therefore
●לִפְנֵי before
לִפְנֵי הַצָּהֳרַיִם A.M.
●לְפָנִים once, formerly
לִפְנִים within
לֶפֶת,נ. turnip, dessert
לֵץ,ז. mocker
לָצוֹן,ז. mockery
לקה (הִלְקָה) (הִלְקָה, יַלְקֶה) to whip, to punish
●לָקוֹחַ,ז. (ר' לָקוֹחוֹת) customer
לִקּוּט,ז. collection
לִקּוּי,ז. defect; eclipse
●לקח (לָקַח, יִקַּח) to take; to buy
יִצְחָק לָקַח אֶת רִבְקָה לְאִשָּׁה. Isaac married Rebecca.
הוּא לָקַח אֶת לֵב הַשּׁוֹמְעִים. He enchanted the listeners.
הִתְלַקֵּחַ (הִתְלַקֵּחַ, יִתְלַקַּח) to flare up
לֶקַח,ז. instruction
לקט (לָקַט, יִלְקֹט); לִקֵּט (לִקֵּט, יְלַקֵּט) to gather
לֶקֶט,ז. gleaning
לְקִיחָה,נ. taking
לְקִיטָה,נ. gathering
לְקִיקָה,נ. licking
לקק (לָקַק, יִלְקֹק) לִקֵּק (לִקֵּק, יְלַקֵּק) to lick
לַקְקָן,ז. (נ. לַקְקָנִית) greedy
לִקְרַאת towards
לְשַׁד,ז. juice
●לָשׁוֹן זו"נ (ר' לְשׁוֹנוֹת) tongue; expression
לְשׁוֹן יָם,נ. gulf
לְשׁוֹן הָרָע,נ. calumny
לִשְׁכָּה,נ. office; room
לשן (הַלְשֵׁן) (הִלְשִׁין, יַלְשִׁין) to denounce

מ

●מִ, מֶ- from

●מְאֹד very, much
עַד מְאֹד exceedingly
●מֵאָה,נ. hundred
מְאוּם, מְאוּמָה something; anything
לֹא מְאוּמָה, אֵין מְאוּמָה nothing
מֵאוּן,ז. refusal
מָאוּס,ז. loathsome
מָאוֹר,ז. light; lamp
מְאֹרָע,ז. (ר' מְאוֹרָעוֹת) happening, event
מְאֻזָּן horizontal
מַאֲזָן,ז. balance sheet
מֹאזְנַיִם,ז. scales
הַחֶנְוָנִי שָׁקַל אֶת הַבָּשָׂר בְּמֹאזְנַיִם. The shopkeeper weighed the meat on the scales.
●מְאֻחָר late
מֵאֵימָתַי? since when
●מַאֲכָל,ז. food
עֵץ מַאֲכָל,ז. fruit tree
מַאֲכֶלֶת,נ. butcher's knife
●מַאֲמָר,ז. speech; decree; article
מַאֲמָר מֻסְגָּר parenthetical remark
מַאֲמָר רָאשִׁי editorial
מָאֵן (מֵאֵן, יְמָאֵן) to refuse
מְאֻנָּךְ vertical
מאס (מָאַס, יִמְאַס) to despise
מַאֲסָר,ז. prison
מַאֲפֶה,ז. pastry
מַאֲפִיָּה,נ. bakery
מַאֲפֵרָה,נ. ash tray
מַאֲרָב,ז. ambush
מְאָרֵחַ hospitable
●מְאֻשָּׁר happy
●מָאתַיִם two hundred
מַבְהִיל terrifying
מַבְהִיק shining
מֻבְהָק clear; shining
מָבוֹא,ז. (ר' מְבוֹאוֹת) entrance; preface
מְבוֹא הַשֶּׁמֶשׁ,ז. sunset
מָבוֹי,ז. passage
מְבוּכָה,נ. consternation

What's bothering you?	מַה לְךָ?	Shield of David, sexagram	מָגֵן דָּוִד	flood	מַבּוּל,ז.
Why should I speak?	מַה לִי לְדַבֵּר?	unbecoming	מְגֻנֶּה	fountain	מַבּוּעַ,ז.
something	מַשֶּׁהוּ	touch	מַגָּע,ז.	examination	מִבְחָן,ז.
with what?	●בַּמֶּה?	boot	מַגָּף,ז.	to take an examination	עָמֹד לְמִבְחָן
suitable, proper	מֵהֻגָּן	plague	מַגֵּפָה,נ.	to pass an examination	עָמֹד בְּמִבְחָן
emigrant	מְהַגֵּר,ז.	drawer	מְגֵרָה,נ.	selection	מִבְחָר,ז.
edition	מַהֲדוּרָה,נ.	defect	מִגְרַעַת,נ.	first-rate	מֻבְחָר
circumcised;mixed	מָהוּל	rake	מַגְרֵף,ז. מַגְרֵפָה,נ.	cooking-spoon	מַבְחֵשׁ,ז.
confusion, disturbance	מְהוּמָה,נ.	grater	מְגֵרֶת,נ.	look; prospect expression	מַבָּט,ז.
nature, quality	מָהוּת,נ.	pasture; building plot	מִגְרָשׁ,ז.	trust; object of reliance	מִבְטָא,ז.● מִבְטָח,ז.
prompt, quick	מָהִיר●	desert (ר' מִדְבָּרִיּוֹת)	מִדְבָּר,ז.●		
hurry; promptness	מְהִירוּת,נ.●	oases	נְאוֹת מִדְבָּר	expert	מֵבִין,ז.●
going; distance	מַהֲלָךְ,ז.●	wild	מִדְבָּרִי	structure	מִבְנֶה,ז.
It's a three-hour walk.	זֶה מַהֲלָךְ שֶׁל שָׁלֹשׁ שָׁעוֹת.	to measure (מַד,מָדַד,יָמֹד,יָמְדָד)	מדד	fortress	מִבְצָר,ז.
stroke	מַהֲלֻמָה,נ.	to measure (מִדֵּד,יְמַדֵּד)	מַדֵּד	critic; censor	מְבַקֵּר,ז.●
to hesitate,to be late	הִתְמַהְמֵהַ (הִתְמַהְמֵהַ) (יִתְמַהְמֵהַּ)	measure	מִדָּה,נ.	wire, telegram	מִבְרָק,ז.●
engineer	מְהַנְדֵּס,ז.	rigorous justice	מִדַּת הַדִּין,נ.	I sent a wire to my uncle.	שָׁלַחְתִּי מִבְרָק לְדוֹדִי.
overthrow; revolution	מַהְפֵּכָה,נ.	mercy	מִדַּת הָרַחֲמִים,נ..	brush	מִבְרֶשֶׁת,נ.
to hurry	מַהֵר (מִהֵר,יְמַהֵר)	tit for tat	מִדָּה כְּנֶגֶד מִדָּה	cook	מְבַשֵּׁל,ז.
fast, quick	מַהֵר, מְהֵרָה	quarrel	מָדוֹן,ז.	collection	מַגְבִּית,נ.
leader; guide	מוֹבִיל,ז.	why?	●מַדּוּעַ?	hat	מִגְבַּעַת,נ.
sense	מוּבָן,ז.	pile of wood	מְדוּרָה,נ.	towel	מַגֶּבֶת,נ.●
What's the meaning of the word?	מַה מּוּבַן הַמִּלָּה?	thermometer	מַדְחֹם,ז.●	tower	מִגְדָּל,ז.●
Is everything understood?	הַכֹּל מוּבָן?	enough	(מַדַּי) לְמַדַּי	lighthouse	מִגְדָּלוֹר,ז.
of course	כַּמּוּבָן	measuring	מְדִידָה,נ.	magnifying glass	מַגְדֶּלֶת,נ.
surveyor	מוֹדֵד,ז.	politician	מְדִינַאי,ז.	jam (preserves)	מִגְדָּנִית,נ.
acquaintance	מוֹדָע,ז.	country, state	מְדִינָה,נ.	pressing iron	מַגְהֵץ,ז.
advertisement	מוֹדָעָה,נ.●	exact	מְדֻיָּק●	multicolored	מְגֻוָּן,ז.
banana	מוֹז,ז.	apparent	מְדֻמֶּה●	terror	מָגוֹר,ז.
tavern-keeper	מוֹזֵג,ז.	It seems to me.	כִּמְדֻמֶּה לִי.	dwelling	מָגוּר,נ.
strange; queer	מוּזָר	quarrel	מְדָנִים ז"ר	ridiculous	מְגֻחָךְ
absolute	מֻחְלָט,ז.	knowledge, science	מַדָּע,ז.	preacher	מַגִּיד,ז.
staff	מוֹט,ז. (ר' מוֹטוֹת)	scientific	מַדָּעִי	proofreader	מַגִּיהַּ,ז.
good;it is better	מוּטָב	shelf	מַדָּף,ז.	sickle	מַגָּל,ז.
ready	מוּכָן	printer	מַדְפִּיס,ז.	whip	מַגְלֵב,ז.
shopkeeper	מוֹכֵר	grammarian, pedantic	מְדַקְדֵּק,ז.	roll; parchment; the Book of Esther	מְגִלָּה,נ.
to circumcise	מָגֹל (מָל, יָמֹל)●	step, grade	מַדְרֵגָה,נ.	pus	מֻגְלָה,נ.
		guide, leader	מַדְרִיךְ,ז.	shaven	מְגֻלָּח
		treading, footstep	מִדְרָךְ,ז.	aim, purpose; tendency	מְגַמָּה,נ.
		sidewalk	מִדְרָכָה,נ.		
		treading	מִדְרָס,ז.	shield; shelter	מָגֵן,ז.
		interpretation	מִדְרָשׁ,ז.		
		what?	●מַה?מָה?		

frying pan	מַחֲבַת,נ. (ר' מַחֲבַתִּים)	savior	אֵין מִלָּה בְּשָׁבִיל הַמּוּשָׂג הַזֶּה,	opposite	מוּל,מוֹל
			There is no word	The park	הַגַּן מוּל בֵּיתִי.
pointed	מְחֻדָּד,ז.		for this concept.	is opposite my house.	
to wipe	מחה (מָחָה,יִמְחֶה)	savior	מוֹשִׁיעַ,ז.	birth	מוֹלָד,ז.
to protest		reins	מוֹשְׁכוֹת,נ"ר	birth;native land	מוֹלֶדֶת,נ. ●
compass	מְחוּגָה,נ.	ruler	מוֹשֵׁל,ז.	blemish,defect	מוּם,ז.
district	מָחוֹז,ז. (ר' מְחוֹזוֹת)	to die	מות (מֵת,יָמוּת)	expert	מֻמְחֶה,ז.
corset	מָחוֹךְ,ז.	to kill	הֵמִית (הֵמִית,יָמִית)	apostate	מוּמָר,ז.
dance	מָחוֹל,ז. (ר' מְחוֹלוֹת)	death	מָוֶת,ז. (ר' מִיתוֹת)	numerator	מוֹנֶה,ז.
lawgiver	מְחוֹקֵק,ז.	a condemned man	אִישׁ מָוֶת	taxi	מוֹנִית ●
vision	מַחֲזֶה,ז. (ר' מַחֲזוֹת) ●	deserving death	בֶּן מָוֶת	institute	מוֹסָד,ז.
performance, scene		Angel of Death	מַלְאַךְ הַמָּוֶת	appendage	מוּסָף,ז.
needle	מַחַט,נ. (ר' מְחָטִים)	altar	מִזְבֵּחַ,ז. (ר' מִזְבְּחוֹת)	ethics; reproof	מוּסָר,ז.
applause	מְחִיאַת כַּפַּיִם (מְחִיאָה)	temper	מֶזֶג,ז.	moral	מוּסָרִי
obliged	מְחֻיָּב	weather	מֶזֶג הָאֲוִיר ●	morality	מוּסָרִיּוּת,נ.
means of life	מִחְיָה,נ.	to pour	מזג (מָזַג,יִמְזֹג)	term;holiday	מוֹעֵד,ז.
forgiveness	מְחִילָה,נ.	dirty	מְזֹהָם	little,trifle	מוּעָט
partition	מְחִצָּה,נ.	traveling bag	מִזְוָדָה,נ. ●	useful	מוֹעִיל
erasing	מְחִיקָה,נ.	doorpost	מְזוּזָה,נ. ●	counsel	מוֹעֵצָה,נ.
price	מְחִיר,ז. ●	food	מָזוֹן,ז. (ר' מְזוֹנוֹת)	miracle;proof	מוֹפֵת,ז.
to forgive	מחל (מָחַל,יִמְחֹל)	bandage	מָזוֹר,ז.	exemplary;model	מוֹפְתִי
dairy	מַחְלָבָה,נ.	pier	מֵזַח,ז.	exit	מוֹצָא,ז.
sickness	מַחֲלָה,ז. מַחֲלָה,נ.	intentionally	בְּמֵזִיד (מֵזִיד)	Saturday	מוֹצָאֵי שַׁבָּת
corkscrew	מַחְלֵץ,ז.	damaging;	מַזִּיק,ז.	night after dark	
class;division	מַחְלָקָה,נ.	evil spirit		publisher	מוֹצִיא (-לָאוֹר)
quarrel	מַחֲלֹקֶת,נ.	secretary	מַזְכִּיר,ז.	solid	מוּצָק
teakettle	מֵחַם,ז.	planet;	מַזָּל,נ. (ר' מַזָּלוֹת)	hearth	מוֹקֵד,ז.
compliment	מַחְמָאָה,נ.	fate; luck		early; preceding	מֻקְדָּם ●
delight	מַחְמָד,ז.	fork	מַזְלֵג,ז. (ר' מַזְלְגוֹת) ●	stumbling block;	מוֹקֵשׁ,ז.
because	מֵחֲמַת	song; psalm	מִזְמוֹר,ז.	snare	
camp	מַחֲנֶה זו"נ (ר' מַחֲנוֹת)	cash	מְזֻמָּן,ז. ●	to change	מור (הֵמַר) (הֵמִיר,יָמִיר)
educator	מְחַנֵּךְ,ז.	singer	מְזַמֵּר,ז.		
shelter	מַחֲסֶה, ז.	cupboard;	מִזְנוֹן,ז. ●	to change	הֵמִיר דָּת
muzzle	מַחְסוֹם,ז.	refreshment room		one's faith	
lack;want;need	מַחְסוֹר,ז.	east	מִזְרָח,ז. ●	terror, awe	מוֹרָא,ז.
storehouse	מַחְסָן,ז.	eastern	מִזְרָחִי,ז. ●	slope	מוֹרָד,ז.
rough	מְחֻסְפָּס	mattress	מִזְרָן,ז.	rebel	מוֹרֵד,ז.
quarry	מַחְצָב,ז. מַחֲצֵבָה,נ.	sowing	מִזְרָע,ז.	teacher	מוֹרָה,ז. ●
half	מֶחֱצָה,מַחֲצִית,נ.	sowing machine	מִזְרָעָה,נ.	guide	מוֹרֵה דֶּרֶךְ
mat	מַחְצֶלֶת,נ.	brain	מֹחַ,ז. (ר' מֹחוֹת)	heritage	מוֹרָשׁ,ז. מוֹרָשָׁה,נ.
to erase	מחק (מָחַק,יִמְחַק)	to clap	מחא (מָחָא,יִמְחָא)	delegate	מֻרְשֶׁה,ז.
eraser	מַחַק,ז.	to protest		seat,	מוֹשָׁב,ז. מוֹשָׁבָה,נ.
exploration, research	מֶחְקָר,ז.	protest	מְחָאָה,נ.	colony	(ר' מוֹשָׁבוֹת)
		churn	מַחְבֵּצָה,נ.	conception	מֻשָּׂג,ז.
tomorrow	מָחָר,ז. ●	author	מְחַבֵּר,ז.	I have	אֵין לִי מֻשָּׂג.
plough	מַחֲרֵשָׁה,נ.	copybook	מַחְבֶּרֶת,נ. ●	no idea.	

morrow	מָחֳרָת,נ.●
the day after tomorrow	מָחֳרָתַיִם●
thought	מַחֲשָׁבָה,נ.
relative (נ. מְחֻתֶּנֶת) by marriage	מְחֻתָּן,ז.
underground	מַחְתֶּרֶת,נ.
broom	מַטְאֲטֵא,ז.
kitchen	מִטְבָּח,ז.●
slaughterhouse	מִטְבְּחַיִם (בֵּית ה-) ז"ר
coin	מַטְבֵּעַ, זו"נ (ר' מַטְבְּעוֹת)
bed	מִטָּה,נ.●
stick;clan	מַטֶּה,ז. (ר' מַטּוֹת)
downward	מַטָּה
spinning	מַטְוֶה,ז.
pendulum	מְטֻלְטֶלֶת,נ.
treasure	מַטְמוֹן,ז.
plantation	מַטָּע,ז. מַטָּעָה,נ.
dainties(food)	מַטְעַמִּים,ז"ר
handkerchief;shawl	מִטְפַּחַת,נ.●
rain	מָטָר,ז.
purpose	מַטָּרָה,נ.
umbrella	מִטְרִיָּה,נ.●
who?	מִי?●
soon	מִיָּד●
classification	מִיּוּן,ז.
particular;separate	מְיֻחָד,ז.
well-born	מְיֻחָס,ז.
the best	מֵיטָב,ז.
circumcision	מִילָה,נ.
water	מַיִם, ז"ר●
flowing water	מַיִם חַיִּים
salt water	מֵי מֶלַח
watery	מֵימִי
kind, genus; sex; heretic	מִין,ז.●
like	כְּמִין
to sort, to classify	מִיֵּן (מִיֵּן,יְמַיֵּן)
heresy	מִינוּת,נ.
wet nurse	מֵינֶגֶת,נ.
juice	מִיץ,ז.●
settled	מְיֻשָּׁב
plain	מִישׁוֹר,ז.
straightforwardness	מֵישָׁרִים, ז"ר

death	מִיתָה,נ.
unnatural death	מִיתָה מְשֻׁנָּה
string;sinew	מֵיתָר,ז.
pain	מַכְאוֹב,ז.
laundry	מִכְבָּסָה,נ.
press	מִכְבֵּשׁ,ז.
stroke;wound	מַכָּה,נ.
institute;foundation	מָכוֹן,ז.
The Weizmann Institute is in Rehoboth.	מָכוֹן וַיְצְמָן הוּא בִּרְחוֹבוֹת.
machine	מְכוֹנָה,נ.
mechanic	מְכוֹנֵן,ז.
ugly	מְכוֹעָר
paintbrush	מַכְחוֹל,מִכְחָל,ז.
sale	מְכִירָה,נ.
college	מִכְלָלָה,נ.
food	מַכֹּלֶת,נ.
grocery store	חֲנוּת מַכֹּלֶת
treasure	מִכְמָן,ז.
trousers	מִכְנָסַיִם,ז"ר
duty,tax	מֶכֶס,ז.
customhouse	בֵּית הַמֶּכֶס,ז.
cover	מִכְסֶה,ז. (ר' מִכְסָאוֹת)
to sell	מָכַר (מָכַר,יִמְכֹּר)●
to devote oneself	הִתְמַכֵּר (הִתְמַכֵּר,יִתְמַכֵּר)
acquaintance	מַכָּר,ז.
mine	מִכְרֶה,ז. (ר' מִכְרוֹת)
stumbling block	מִכְשׁוֹל,ז.
tool, instrument	מַכְשִׁיר,ז.
magician	מְכַשֵּׁף,ז.
letter	מִכְתָּב,ז.●
I wrote a letter to my brother.	כָּתַבְתִּי מִכְתָּב לְאָחִי.
letter of recommendation	מִכְתַּב הַמְלָצָה
desk	מִכְתָּבָה
to be full	מָלֵא (מָלֵא,יִמְלָא)
to fill	מִלֵּא (מִלֵּא,יְמַלֵּא)
substitute	מִלֵּא מָקוֹם
full	מָלֵא●
angel	מַלְאָךְ,ז.
work	מְלָאכָה,נ.
artificial	מְלָאכוּתִי
garment	מַלְבּוּשׁ,ז.

word	מִלָּה,נ.(ר' מִלִּים)
word for word	מִלָּה בְּמִלָּה
preposition	מִלַּת יַחַס
conjunction	מִלַּת קִשּׁוּר
filling	מִלּוּא,ז.
creditor	מַלְוֶה,ז.
loan	מִלְוֶה,ז. מִלְוָה,נ.
salted	מָלוּחַ●
herring	דג מָלוּחַ
dominion;monarchy	מְלוּכָה,נ.
inn, hotel	מָלוֹן,ז. (ר' מְלוֹנוֹת)
dictionary	מִלּוֹן,ז.
salt	מֶלַח,ז.●
to salt	מלח (מָלַח,יִמְלַח)
sailor	מַלָּח,ז.
battle,war	מִלְחָמָה,נ.
mortar;cement	מֶלֶט,ז.
to escape	מלט (הִמָּלֵט)(נִמְלַט,יִמָּלֵט)
to save	מִלֵּט (מִלֵּט,יְמַלֵּט)
salting	מְלִיחָה
parable,phrase	מְלִיצָה,נ.
to reign	מלך (מָלַךְ,יִמְלֹךְ)
to take counsel	הִמָּלֵךְ (נִמְלַךְ,יִמָּלֵךְ)
to set on the throne	הִמְלִיךְ (הִמְלִיךְ,יַמְלִיךְ)
king	מֶלֶךְ,ז.●
queen	מַלְכָּה,נ.
kingdom	מַלְכוּת,נ.
teacher	מְלַמֵּד,ז.
cucumber	מְלַפְפוֹן,ז.
waiter	מֶלְצַר,ז.●
Waiter, the menu,please!	מֶלְצַר, תָּפְרִיט בְּבַקָּשָׁה!
spring rain	מַלְקוֹשׁ,ז.
tongs	מֶלְקָחַיִם,ז"ר
informer	מַלְשִׁין,ז.
denunciation	מַלְשִׁינוּת,נ.
money	מָמוֹן,ז. (ר' מָמוֹנוֹ)
bastard	מַמְזֵר,ז.
handkerchief	מִמְחָטָה,נ.
from itself	מֵמֵּילָא
kingdom	מַמְלָכָה,נ.
appointed	מְמֻנֶּה

sufficient	מַסְפִּיק●
That's enough!	מַסְפִּיק!
Not enough!	לֹא מַסְפִּיק!
There's enough bread.	יֵשׁ מַסְפִּיק לֶחֶם.
doubtful	מְסֻפָּק●
I doubt that it is so.	אֲנִי מְסֻפָּק אִם הַדָּבָר כֵּן
The whole matter is in doubt.	כָּל הָעִנְיָן מְסֻפָּק.
number	מִסְפָּר, ז.
scissors	מִסְפָּרַיִם, ז"ר
result,consequence	מַסְקָנָה, נ.
to deliver, to denounce	מסר (מָסַר, יִמְסֹר)
comb	מַסְרֵק, ז. (ר' מַסְרְקוֹת)
tradition	מַסֹרֶת, נ.
hiding place	מִסְתּוֹר, ז.
laboratory	מַעְבָּדָה, נ.
density	מַעֲבֶה, נ.
passage	מַעֲבָר, ז.
circle	מַעְגָּל, ז.
delicacies	מַעֲדַנִּים, ז"ר
hoe	מַעְדֵּר, ז.
shelter	מָעוֹז, ז.
minority	מִעוּט, ז.
dwelling	מָעוֹן, ז. מְעוֹנָה, נ.
flight	מָעוּף, ז.
money	מָעוֹת, נ.
to be small	מעט (מָעַט, יִמְעַט)
to lessen	מַעֵט (מִעֵט, יְמַעֵט) הַמְעֵט (הִמְעִיט, יַמְעִיט)
little	מְעַט●
little by little	מְעַט מְעַט
almost	כִּמְעַט
wrap;covering	מַעֲטֶה, ז.
tunic;envelope	מַעֲטָפָה, נ.
intestines	מְעִי, ז. (ר' מֵעַיִם)
overcoat	מְעִיל, ז.
raincoat	מְעִיל גֶּשֶׁם
deceit	מְעִילָה, נ.
intestines	מֵעַיִם, ז"ר
spring,fountain	מַעְיָן, ז.
digested	מְעֻכָּל
deceit	מַעַל, ז.
from above	מַעַל (מִמַּעַל)

lock	מַנְעוּל, ז.
orchestra leader	מְנַצֵּחַ, ז.●
pierced	מְנֻקָּב
portion,lot	מְנָת, נ.
upon condition that	עַל מְנָת
tribute,tax	מַס, ז. (ר' מִסִּים)
income tax	מַס הַכְנָסָה
gathering,circle	מְסִבָּה, נ.
fit,able	מְסֻגָּל
He is not fit for hard work.	הוּא אֵינוֹ מְסֻגָּל לַעֲבוֹדָה קָשָׁה.
locksmith	מַסְגֵּר, ז.
frame	מִסְגֶּרֶת, נ.
foundation	מַסָּד, ז.
compositor	מְסַדֵּר, ז.
order	מִסְדָּר, ז.
corridor	מִסְדְּרוֹן, ז.
trade	מִסְחָר, ז.
store,shop	בֵּית מִסְחָר
delivery	מְסִירָה, נ.
devotion	מְסִירוּת, נ.
self-sacrifice	מְסִירַת נֶפֶשׁ, מְסִירוּת נֶפֶשׁ
curtain	מָסָךְ, ז.●
When does the curtain rise?	מָתַי עוֹלֶה הַמָּסָךְ?
veil,mask	מַסֵּכָה, נ.
conventional	מֻסְכָּם
dangerous	מְסֻכָּן, ז.
It's a dangerous experiment.	זֶה נִסּוּי מְסֻכָּן.
He is seriously sick.	הוּא חוֹלֶה מְסֻכָּן.
poor man	מִסְכֵּן, ז.
poverty	מִסְכֵּנוּת, נ.
highway	מְסִלָּה, נ.
railroad	מְסִלַּת בַּרְזֶל
nail	מַסְמֵר, ז.
strainer	מִסְנֶנֶת, נ.
journey	מַסָּע, ז.
support, arm (of a chair)	מִסְעָד, ז.
restaurant	מִסְעָדָה, נ.●
wailing	מִסְפֵּד, ז.
fodder	מִסְפּוֹא, ז.

inventor	מַמְצִיא, ז.
average	מְמֻצָּע
essential	מַמָּשׁ●
There's nothing to it.	אֵין בּוֹ מַמָּשׁ.
essentially	מַמָּשׁ●
reality	מַמָּשׁוּת, נ.
essential,concrete	מַמָּשִׁי
It's a real problem.	זֹאת בְּעָיָה מַמָּשִׁית.
government	מֶמְשָׁלָה, נ.●
sweets	מַמְתַּקִּים, ז"ר
from	מִן●
from then	מִן הַיּוֹם הַהוּא
immediately	מִיָּד
from here	מִכָּאן
never	מֵעוֹלָם
from the midst of	מִתּוֹךְ
melody	מַנְגִּינָה, נ.
musician	מְנַגֵּן, ז.●
to count	מנה (מָנָה, יִמְנֶה)
to appoint	מִנָּה (מִנָּה, יְמַנֶּה)
part,portion	מָנָה, נ.●
I want a portion of meat.	אֲנִי רוֹצֶה מָנָה שֶׁל בָּשָׂר.
custom	מִנְהָג, ז.
leader	מַנְהִיג, ז.
director	מְנַהֵל, ז.
quietness;late	מָנוֹחַ, ז.
appointment	מִנּוּי, ז.
ugly	מְנֻוָּל, ז. (נ. מְנֻוֶּלֶת)
escape	מָנוֹס, ז. מְנוּסָה, נ.
lever, crane	מָנוֹף, ז.
lamp,candlestick	מְנוֹרָה, נ.
convent	מִנְזָר, ז.
gift	מִנְחָה, נ. (ר' מְנָחוֹת)
share	מְנָיָה, נ.
counting	מְנִיָּה, נ.
where from?	מִנַּיִן?
number;counting	מִנְיָן, ז.
prevention	מְנִיעָה, נ.
fan	מֵנִיף, ז. מְנִיפָה, נ.
well-behaved	מְנֻמָּס
experienced	מְנֻסֶּה
to prevent; to refuse;to hinder	מנע (מָנַע, יִמְנַע)

little	מֵצַר ,ז.
watchtower	מִצְפֶּה ,ז.
conscience	מַצְפּוּן ,ז.
to suck	מָצַץ (מצץ, יִמֹץ)
distress,boundary, strait	מֵצַר ,ז.
leper	מְצֹרָע ,ז.
parallel	מַקְבִּיל
hammer	מַקֶּבֶת ,נ.
drill	מַקְדֵּחַ ,ז.
early	מֻקְדָּם
He came early.	הוּא בָּא מֻקְדָּם.
temple	מִקְדָּשׁ ,ז.
the Temple in Jerusalem	בֵּית הַמִּקְדָּשׁ
choir	מַקְהֵלָה ,נ.
meeting	מִקְוֶה ,ז.
place	מָקוֹם ,ז. (ר' מְקוֹמוֹת)
instead	בִּמְקוֹם
anyway	מִכָּל מָקוֹם
source;stem	מָקוֹר ,ז.
beak	מַקּוֹר ,ז.
original	מְקוֹרִי
originality	מְקוֹרִיּוּת
accuser	מְקַטְרֵג ,ז.
pipe	מְקֹטֶרֶת ,נ.
cane, stick	מַקֵּל ,ז. (ר' מַקְלוֹת)
shower	מִקְלַחַת ,נ.
refuge	מִקְלָט ,ז.
purchase;cattle	מִקְנֶה ,ז.
charm	מִקְסָם ,ז.
corner;profession	מִקְצוֹעַ ,ז.
a little	מִקְצָת ,נ.
reading,Holy Writ	מִקְרָא ,ז.
opera glass	מִקְרֶבֶת ,נ.
happening	מִקְרֶה ,ז.
It was an interesting happening.	הָיָה זֶה מִקְרֶה מְעַנְיֵן.
by chance	מִקְרִי
cold storage; refrigerator	מַקְרֵר ,ז.
bitter	מַר
view; appearance	מַרְאֶה ,ז. (ר' מַרְאוֹת)
looking glass	מַרְאָה ,נ.

refuge	מִפְלָט ,ז.
monster	מִפְלֶצֶת ,נ.
ruin,defeat	מַפָּלָת ,נ.
because	מִפְּנֵי
	לֹא יָכֹלְתִּי לָבוֹא מִפְּנֵי הַגֶּשֶׁם.
I could not come because of the rain.	
coddled	מְפֻנָּק
deed	מִפְעָל ,ז. מִפְעָלָה ,נ.
numbering;mustering	מִפְקָד ,ז.
commander	מְפַקֵּד ,ז.
well-known,famous	מְפֻרְסָם ,ז.
bay	מִפְרָץ ,ז.
sail	מִפְרָשׂ ,ז.
key	מַפְתֵּחַ ,ז. (ר' מַפְתְּחוֹת)
engraver	מְפַתֵּחַ ,ז.
threshold	מִפְתָּן ,ז.
to find	מָצָא (מצא, יִמְצָא)
	לֹא מָצָא יָדָיו וְרַגְלָיו.
He was confused.	
to be, to find oneself	הִמָּצֵא (נמצא, יִמָּצֵא)
to deliver,to invent	הִמְצִיא (המציא, יַמְצִיא)
situation	מַצָּב ,ז.
What is the situation?	מַה הַמַּצָּב?
He is in an unfortunate position.	מַצָּבוֹ אֻמְלָל.
What is the state of your health?	מַה מַצַּב בְּרִיאוּתְךָ?
I am in a good mood.	יֵשׁ לִי מַצַּב רוּחַ טוֹב.
statue;memorial	מַצֵּבָה ,נ.
painter's brush	מַצְבּוֹעַ ,ז.
unleavened bread	מַצָּה ,נ.
fort	מְצוּדָה ,נ.
command;good deed	מִצְוָה ,נ.
usual	מָצוּי
depth	מְצוּלָה ,נ.
distress	מָצוֹק ,ז.
siege;distress	מָצוֹר ,ז.
forehead	מֵצַח ,ז.
find;bargain	מְצִיאָה ,נ.
reality	מְצִיאוּת ,נ.
lucky	מֻצְלָח
turban,cap	מִצְנֶפֶת ,נ.

ascent	מַעֲלֶה ,ז.
step;preference; degree	מַעֲלָה ,נ.
	הַחֹם עָלָה בְּשָׁלֹשׁ מַעֲלוֹת.
The temperature rose three degrees.	
up,above	מַעֲלָה ,לְמַעֲלָה
excellent	מְעֻלֶּה
elevator	מַעֲלִית ,נ.
post,standing,rank	מַעֲמָד ,ז.
in the presence	בְּמַעֲמַד-
burden	מַעֲמָסָה ,נ.
depth	מַעֲמָק ,ז.
address	מַעַן ,ז.
answer	מַעֲנֶה ,ז.
interesting	מְעַנְיֵן
hindrance	מַעֲצוֹר ,מַעֲצָר ,ז.
cubic	מְעֻקָּב
balcony;railing	מַעֲקֶה ,ז.
mixed	מְעֹרָב
sociable	מְעֹרָב עִם הַבְּרִיּוֹת
west	מַעֲרָב ,ז.
western	מַעֲרָבִי
cave	מְעָרָה ,נ.
appraiser	מַעֲרִיךְ ,ז.
admirer	מַעֲרִיץ ,ז.
act	מַעֲרָכָה ,נ.
first act	מַעֲרָכָה רִאשׁוֹנָה
deed;work; occupation;tale	מַעֲשֶׂה ,ז.
What are you doing here?	מַה מַעֲשֶׂיךָ כָּאן?
practical	מַעֲשִׂי
tale	מַעֲשִׂיָּה ,נ.
chimney	מַעֲשֵׁנָה ,נ.
tenth;tithe	מַעֲשֵׂר ,ז.
copyist,translator	מַעְתִּיק ,ז.
tablecloth;map	מַפָּה ,נ.
bellows	מַפּוּחַ ,ז.
accordion	מַפּוּחִית ,נ.
disappointment	מַפָּח ,ז. (מַפַּח נֶפֶשׁ)
fattened	מְפֻטָּם
eminent	מֻפְלָג
party	מִפְלָגָה ,נ.
defeat	מַפָּלָה ,נ.

appearance	מַרְאִית-עַיִן, נ.
upper end	מְרַאֲשׁוֹת, נ"ר
carpet	מַרְבַד, ז.
greater number	מַרְבִּית, נ.
square,quadrangle	מְרֻבָּע, ז.
manger	מֵרְבֵּק, ז.
rest	מַרְגּוֹעַ, ז.
spy	מְרַגֵּל, ז.
foot (end)	מַרְגְּלוֹת, נ"ר
pearl	מַרְגָּלִית, נ.
to rebel	מרד (מָרַד,יִמְרֹד)
rebellion	מֶרֶד, ז.
to oppose	מרה (מָרָה,יִמְרֶה)
bitterness	מָרָה, נ.
melancholy	מָרָה שְׁחוֹרָה, נ.
height	מָרוֹם, ז.
high society	מָרוֹם עַם הָאָרֶץ
race	מֵרוֹץ,מְרוּצָה, נ.
bitter herbs / horse-radish	מָרוֹר, ז.
dominion	מֶרוּת, נ.
to rub	מרח (מָרַח,יִמְרַח)
space	מֶרְחָב, ז.
bath	מֶרְחָץ, ז.
distance	מֶרְחָק, ז.
to pluck out	מרט (מָרַט,יִמְרֹט)
quarrel	מְרִיבָה, נ.
rebellion	מְרִידָה, נ.
slightly bitter	מָרִיר
bitterness	מְרִירוּת, נ.
timidity	מֹרֶךְ, ז.
chariot	מֶרְכָּב, ז. מֶרְכָּבָה, נ.
center	מֶרְכָּז, ז.
City Hall	הָעִירִיָה בְּמֶרְכַּז הָעִיר.
is in the center of the city.	
fraud, deceit	מִרְמָה, נ.
pasture	מִרְעֶה, ז.
cure	מַרְפֵּא, ז.
terrace	מִרְפֶּסֶת, נ.
elbow	מַרְפֵּק, ז.
energy	מֶרֶץ, ז.
atomic energy	מֶרֶץ אַטוֹמִי
content	מְרֻצֶּה
awl	מַרְצֵעַ, ז.
to polish	מרק (מָרַק,יִמְרֹק)
soup	מָרָק, ז.
ointment	מִרְקַחַת
drugstore	בֵּית מִרְקַחַת
delegate	מֻרְשֶׁה, ז.
madam,Mrs.	מָרַת, נ.
Good morning, Mrs. Cohen.	בֹּקֶר טוֹב,מָרַת כֹּהֵן.
cellar	מַרְתֵּף, ז.
bearing; prophecy; burden	מַשָּׂא, ז. (ר' מַשָּׂאוֹת)
trade	מַשָּׂא וּמַתָּן
longing,ideal	מַשָּׂא נֶפֶשׁ, ז.
well	מַשְׁאָב, ז.
pump	מַשְׁאֵבָה, נ.
praiseworthy	מְשֻׁבָּח
crisis	מַשְׁבֵּר, ז.
wave,surf;crisis	מִשְׁבָּר, ז.
faulty	מֻשְׁבָּשׁ
error	מִשְׁגֶּה, ז.
overseer	מַשְׁגִּיחַ, ז.
crazy	מְשֻׁגָּע
to draw out	משה (מָשָׁה,יִמְשֶׁה)
a trifle	מַשֶּׁהוּ
Give me something sweet.	תֵּן לִי מַשֶּׁהוּ מָתוֹק.
oar	מָשׁוֹט, ז.
file	מְשׁוֹף, ז.
saw	מַשּׂוֹר, ז.
singer;poet	מְשׁוֹרֵר, ז.
joy	מָשׂוֹשׂ, ז.
feeling,touching	מִשּׁוּשׁ, ז.
to anoint	משח (מָשַׁח,יִמְשַׁח)
ointment;polish	מִשְׁחָה, נ.
whetstone	מַשְׁחֶזֶת, נ.
destroyer	מַשְׁחִית, ז.
play;game	מִשְׂחָק, ז.
theater	בֵּית מִשְׂחָק, ז.
playground	מִגְרַשׁ מִשְׂחָקִים
actor	מְשַׂחֵק, ז.
order	מִשְׂטָר, ז.
police	מִשְׁטָרָה, נ.
silk	מֶשִׁי, ז.
anointed;Messiah	מָשִׁיחַ, ז.
anointing	מְשִׁיחָה, נ.
drawing	מְשִׁיכָה, נ.
to draw,	משך (מָשַׁךְ,יִמְשֹׁךְ)
to continue	המשה (הִמְשָׁה,הִמְשִׁיךְ, יַמְשִׁיךְ)
duration	מֶשֶׁךְ, ז.
during	בְּמֶשֶׁךְ
I was in Tel Aviv last week.	הָיִיתִי בְּתֵל אָבִיב בְּמֶשֶׁךְ הַשָּׁבוּעַ שֶׁעָבַר.
couch	מִשְׁכָּב, ז.
bedroom	חֲדַר הַמִּשְׁכָּב, ז.
pledge;pawn	מַשְׁכּוֹן, ז.
wise;enlightened	מַשְׂכִּיל
dwelling;tabernacle	מִשְׁכָּן, ז.
salary	מַשְׂכֹּרֶת, נ.
to rule	משל (מָשַׁל,יִמְשֹׁל)
proverb,fable;example	מָשָׁל, ז.
for example	לְמָשָׁל
Book of Proverbs	מִשְׁלֵי
sending	מִשְׁלוֹחַ,מְשְׁלָח, ז.
delegate	מִשְׁלַח, ז.
mission; delegation	מִשְׁלַחַת, נ.
perfect	מֻשְׁלָם
triangle;threefold	מְשֻׁלָּשׁ, ז.
apostate	מֻשְׁמָד, ז.
feeling,touching	מִשְׁמוּשׁ, ז.
meaning	מַשְׁמָע, ז. מַשְׁמָעוּת, נ.
discipline, obedience	מִשְׁמַעַת, נ.
lane	מִשְׁעָל, ז.
support,prop	מִשְׁעָן, ז. מַשְׁעֵנָה,מִשְׁעֶנֶת, נ.
family	מִשְׁפָּחָה, נ.
judgment,sentence	מִשְׁפָּט, ז.
court	בֵּית מִשְׁפָּט
prejudice	מִשְׁפָּט קָדוּם
funnel	מַשְׁפֵּךְ, ז.
management;holding	מֶשֶׁק, ז.
drink	מַשְׁקֶה, ז. (ר' מַשְׁקָאוֹת)
beam of the doorway	מַשְׁקוֹף, ז.
weight	מִשְׁקָל, ז.
eyeglasses	מִשְׁקָפַיִם
telescope	מִשְׁקֶפֶת, נ.
office	מִשְׂרָד, ז.
Immigration Office	מִשְׂרַד הָעֲלִיָּה
The office will open at eight.	הַמִּשְׂרָד יִפָּתַח בִּשְׁמוֹנֶה.

office;job	מִשְׂרָה, נ.
He holds a high office.	יֵשׁ לוֹ מִשְׂרָה גְבוֹהָה.
servant	מְשָׁרֵת, ז.
to feel	מֹשֵׁשׁ (מִשֵּׁשׁ, יְמֹשׁ) (מִשֵּׁשׁ, יְמַשֵּׁשׁ)
feast	מִשְׁתֶּה, נ. (ר' מִשְׁתָּאוֹת)
tree nursery	מַשְׁתֵּלָה, נ.
mutual,joint	מְשֻׁתָּף
dead	מֵת, ז.
prudent;composed	מָתוּן
sweet	מָתוֹק
to stretch	מָתַח (מָתַח, יִמְתַּח)
when?	מָתַי?
consideration	מְתִינוּת, נ.
sweetness	מְתִיקוּת, נ.
metal	מַתֶּכֶת, נ.
diligent	מַתְמִיד, ז.
to wait	מָתַן (הַמְתֵּן)(הִמְתִּין, יָמְתִּין)
present,gift	מַתָּן, ז. מַתָּנָה, נ.
loins	מָתְנַיִם, ז"ר
to be sweet	מָתַק (מָתַק, יִמְתַּק)
to sweeten	הִמְתִּיק (הִמְתִּיק, יַמְתִּיק)
reformed,corrected	מְתֻקָּן
permitted,allowed	מֻתָּר
translator, interpreter	מְתֻרְגָּם, מְתֻרְגְּמָן, ז.
gift,present	מַתָּת, נ.

נ

please	נָא
leather bottle	נֹאד, ז.
pleasant;suitable	נָאֶה
beautiful	נָאוָה
sermon;utterance	נְאֻם, ז.
enlightened	נָאוֹר
oasis	נְאוֹת (-מִדְבָּר), ז.
to speak	נָאַם (נָאַם, יִנְאַם)
faithful,reliable	נֶאֱמָן
reliability	נֶאֱמָנוּת, נ.
to commit adultery	נָאַף (נָאַף, יִנְאַף)
to groan	נָאַק (נָאַק, יִנְאַק)
groan	נְאָקָה, נ.

to prophesy	נָבָא (נִבָּא, יְנַבֵּא)
prophecy	נְבוּאָה, נ.
prophetic	נְבוּאִי
hollow	נָבוּב
bewildered	נָבוֹךְ
abuse	נִבּוּל, ז.
obscene speech	נִבּוּל פֶּה, ז.
sensible	נָבוֹן
to bark	נָבַח (נָבַח, יִנְבַּח)
elected	נִבְחָר
parliament	בֵּית הַנִּבְחָרִים
to look	נָבַט (הִבִּיט, יַבִּיט)
prophet	נָבִיא, ז.
barking	נְבִיחָה, נ.
to wither	נָבַל (נָבַל, יִבֹּל)
to violate	נִבֵּל (נִבֵּל, יְנַבֵּל)
villain	נָבָל, ז.
corpse	נְבֵלָה, נ.
disgrace	נַבְלוּת, נ.
to wipe	נָגַב (נָגַב, יִנְגֹּב)
to wipe oneself	הִתְנַגֵּב (הִתְנַגֵּב, יִתְנַגֵּב)
South; drought	נֶגֶב, ז.
to tell to say	נָגַד (הִגִּיד)(הִגִּיד, יַגִּיד)
Please tell me...	בְּבַקָּשָׁה לְהַגִּיד לִי...
to oppose;to contradict	הִתְנַגֵּד (הִתְנַגֵּד, יִתְנַגֵּד)
against	נֶגֶד
according to	כְּנֶגֶד
from in front	מִנֶּגֶד
splendor;Venus	נֹגַהּ, ז.
melody	נִגּוּן, ז.
leader,rich man	נָגִיד, ז.
wealth	נְגִידוּת, נ.
music;accent playing	נְגִינָה, נ.
touching	נְגִיעָה, נ.
approach	נְגִישָׁה, נ.
oppression	נְגִישָׂה, נ.
to play	נִגֵּן (נִגֵּן)(נִגֵּן, יְנַגֵּן)
to touch	נָגַע (נָגַע, יִגַּע)
interested	נוֹגֵעַ בְּדָבָר

carpenter	נַגָּר, ז.
to oppress	נָגַשׂ (נָגַשׂ, יִגֹּשׂ)
to approach	נִגַּשׂ (נִגַּשׂ, יִגַּשׂ)
to bring	הִגִּישׁ (הִגִּישׁ, יַגִּישׁ)
to volunteer; to give freely	נָדַב (נָדַב, יִדֹּב) (הִתְנַדֵּב, יִתְנַדֵּב)
donation	נְדָבָה, נ.
generous	נַדְבָן
generosity	נַדְבָנוּת, נ.
to wander	נָדַד (נָדַד, יִדֹּד)
dowry	נְדוּנְיָה, נ.
generous	נָדִיב
generosity	נְדִיבוּת, נ.
to shake; to rock;to swing	נָדַד (נִדְנֵד, יְנַדְנֵד)
swing;rocking chair	נַדְנֵדָה, נ.
shaking	נִדְנוּד, ז.
to vow	נָדַר (נָדַר, יִדֹּר)
vow	נֶדֶר, ז.
to drive	נָהַג (נָהַג, יִנְהַג)
to introduce a custom	הִנְהִיג (הִנְהִיג, יַנְהִיג)
to behave, to be in the habit	הִתְנַהֵג (הִתְנַהֵג, יִתְנַהֵג)
driver	נֶהָג
to lead	נָהַל (נָהַל, יְנַהֵל)
to flow; to stream	נָהַר (נָהַר, יִנְהַר)
stream,river	נָהָר, ז.
to wander	נָד (נָד, יָנוּד)
to shake	הִתְנוֹדֵד (הִתְנוֹדֵד, יִתְנוֹדֵד)
dwelling	נָוֶה, ז.
disgrace	נָוֻל, ז.
liquid	נוֹזֵל, ז.
to rest	נָח (נָח, יָנוּחַ)
to put down	הִנִּיחַ (הִנִּיחַ, יַנִּיחַ)
pleasant,convenient	נוֹחַ
He is well liked.	הוּא נוֹחַ לַבְּרִיּוֹת.
He is easily angered.	הוּא נוֹחַ לִכְעֹס.
curved,inclined	נוֹטֶה
beauty	נוֹי, ז.
to slumber	נָם (נָם, יָנוּם)
slumber	נְגֻמָה, נ.

נוס (נָס, יָנוּס) to flee
נוע (נָע, יָנוּעַ) to move, wander
נוֹף, ז. landscape, top
נוֹצָה, נ. feather
נוֹצְרִי, ז. Christian
●נוֹרָא, ז. terrible
נוֹשֵׂא, ז. subject
מַהוּ נוֹשֵׂא הַשִּׂיחה? What's the subject of conversation?
נוֹתָר, ז. left over
נָזִיד, ז. soup
נְזִילָה, נ. flowing
נְזִיפָה, נ. reproof
נָזִיר, ז. monk; hermit
נְזִירוּת, נ. abstinence
נזל (נָזַל, יָזַל) to flow
●נַזֶּלֶת, נ. cold
קָרָאתִי לָרוֹפֵא כִּי יֵשׁ לִי נַזֶּלֶת. I called the doctor because I have a cold.
נזף (נָזַף, יִזֹּף) to reprove
נֶזֶק, ז. damage, loss
●נזק (הַזֵּק) (הִזִּיק, יַזִּיק) to damage
נזר (הִנָּזֵר)(נִזַּר, יִנָּזֵר) to abstain
נֵזֶר crown
●נָחוּץ necessary
נְחוֹשָׁה, נ. copper
נָחִיל, ז. swarm
נְחִיצוּת, נ. necessity
נְחִירַים, ז"ר nostrils
●נחל (נָחַל, יִנְחַל) to inherit; to take into possession
הַנְחֵל (הִנְחִיל, יַנְחִיל) to bequeath
נַחַל, ז. river
נַחֲלָה, נ. possession; inheritance
נחם (הִנָּחֵם)(נִחַם, יִנָּחֵם) to repent; to console oneself
נַחֵם (נִחַם, יְנַחֵם) to console
נֶחָמָה, נ. consolation
נַחַר, ז. נַחֲרָה, נ. snoring
נחש (נָחַשׁ, יְנַחֵשׁ) to guess
נָחָשׁ, ז. snake
נַחְשׁוֹל, ז. storm (on the sea)

נְחֹשֶׁת, נ. copper
●נַחַת, נ. rest, pleasure
נַחַת רוּחַ, נ. amusement
בְּנַחַת quietly
נַחְתֹּם, ז. baker
●נטה (נָטָה, יִטֶּה) to bend; to decline
הַטֵּה (הִטָּה, יַטֶּה) to incline, to turn off
נְטִיָּה, נ. inclination, inflection
נְטִילָה, נ. taking
נְטִילַת יָדַיִם, נ. washing hands
נְטִיעָה, נ. planting; plant; plantation
נְטִיפָה, נ. dripping
נטל (נָטַל, יִטֹּל) to lift up, to take
הֵטֵל (הִטִּיל, יַטִּיל) to throw
הֵטֵל בֵּיצִים to lay eggs
נֵטֶל, ז. burden
נטע (נָטַע, יִטַּע) to plant
נֶטַע, ז. plant
נֶטֶף, ז. drop
נטר (נָטַר, יִטֹּר) to watch; to resent
נִיב (-שְׂפָתַים) expression
נִיד, ז. movement
נִיחוֹחַ delightful
נִימָה, נ. thread; hair; string
נִיצוֹץ, ז. spark
נְיָר, ז. (ר' נְיָרוֹת) paper
תֶּן לִי נְיָר וְעִפָּרוֹן. Give me paper and pencil.
נְכָא, ז. (ר' נְכָאִים) depression
נְכָאת (בֵּית נְכָאת), ז. museum
נִכְבָּד respected
נֶכֶד, ז. grandson, posterity
נכה (נָכָה)(הִכָּה, יַכֶּה) to beat
הִכּוֹת שָׁרָשִׁים to strike root
נָכֶה crippled
●נָכוֹן ready, correct
לַנָכוֹן, אַל נָכוֹן right
נֹכַח opposite
נְכֹחָה, נ. straightness
נְכִי, ז. paralysis

נִכָּיוֹן, ז. reduction, discount
נוֹכֵל, ז. swindler
נכל (נִכֵּל, יְנַכֵּל) הִתְנַכֵּל (הִתְנַכֵּל, יִתְנַכֵּל) to be cunning; to defraud
נְכָסִים, ז"ר property
יָרַד מִנְּכָסָיו to grow poor
●(נכר) הַכֵּר (הִכִּיר, יַכִּיר) to recognize
בְּבַקָּשָׁה לְהַכִּיר אֶת חֲבֵרִי. Please meet my friend.
אֲנִי מַכִּיר אוֹתוֹ. I know him.
נִכָּר evident
לֹא נִכָּר כִּי הוּא הָיָה חוֹלֶה. It's not evident that he was ill.
נֵכָר, ז. strange land
נָכְרִי strange, alien
נָמוּךְ low
נִמּוּס, ז. manners
נָמֵל, ז. harbor
נְמָלָה, נ. (ר' נְמָלִים) ant
נמנם (נִמְנֵם, יְנַמְנֵם) to slumber
נִמְצָע, ז. impossible
נָמֵר, ז. tiger
נֶמֶשׁ, ז. freckle
נַנָּס, ז. dwarf
נֵס, ז. flag; miracle
נִסְבָּה, נ. reason, motive
נסג (נָסַג, יִסַּג) to retreat
נסה (נָסָה)(נִסָּה, יְנַסֶּה) to try
נִסָּיוֹן, ז. (ר' נְסָיוֹנוֹת) trial; examination; experience
עָמַד בַּנִּסָּיוֹן passed the test
בַּעַל נִסָּיוֹן man of experience
נָסִיךְ, ז. prince
נְסִיכוּת, נ. dukedom
●נְסִיעָה, נ. journey
נסך (נָסַךְ, יִסֹּךְ) to anoint; to pour out
●נסע (נָסַע, יִסַּע) to travel
נִסְתָּר hidden
נִסְתָּרוֹת, נ"ר secret
נְעוּרִים, ז"ר youth
הַנְּעוּרִים עוֹבְרִים מַהֵר. Youth passes swiftly.
נְעִילָה, נ. locking, putting on boots

●נָעִים,ז. pleasant
נָעִים מְאֹד. It's a pleasure.
נְעִים זְמִירוֹת יִשְׂרָאֵל. Sweet singer of Israel (King David)
נְעִימָה,נ. melody,charm
נְעִימוּת,נ. pleasure
●נַעַל,נ. (ר' נְעָלַיִם) shoe
נעל (נָעַל,יִנְעַל) to put on boots
נֹעַם,ז. loveliness
נעם (הִנְעֵם)(הִנְעִים,יַנְעִים) to make pleasant
נַעַר,ז. lad
נֹעַר,ז. youth
מִנֹּעַר from childhood
נַעֲרָה,נ. girl,maid
נַעֲרוּת,נ. youth
נִפּוּחַ,ז. swelling
נָפוּחַ,ז. swollen
נפח (נָפַח,יִפַּח) to blow
הִתְנַפֵּחַ (הִתְנַפַּח,יִתְנַפַּח) to swell; to be haughty
נֶפַח,ז. volume
נֶפַח הַכַּד הוּא לִיטֶר. The volume of the pitcher is one liter.
נַפָּח,ז. smith
נֵפְט,ז. petroleum
נְפִיל,ז. giant
נְפִילָה,נ. fall
נפל (נָפַל,יִפֹּל) to fall
נָפַל לִבּוֹ. He became discouraged.
נָפַל לַמִּשְׁכָּב. He became ill.
נָפַל עַל פָּנָיו. He prostrated himself.
נָפַל רוּחוֹ. He lost heart.
הִפִּיל (הִפִּיל,יַפִּיל) to cause to fall;to miscarry
הִתְנַפֵּל (הִתְנַפֵּל, יִתְנַפֵּל) to attack, to throw oneself
נֵפֶל,ז. miscarriage
●נִפְלָא wonderful
נפץ (נָפַץ,יָפוּץ) to scatter
נִפֵּץ (נִפֵּץ,יְנַפֵּץ) to dash to pieces
נֶפֶץ,ז. fragment
נְפוּצוֹת,נ"ר Diaspora

נפש (הִנָּפֵשׁ)(נָפַשׁ,יִנָּפֵשׁ) to rest,to relax
נֶפֶשׁ,נ.(ר' נְפָשׁוֹת) soul; person; life
נֹפֶשׁ,ז. rest
נַפְשִׁי spiritual
נִצָּב,ז. handle;firm;upright
נִצָּה,נ. bud,blossom
נִצּוּל,ז. exploitation
נִצַּח (נִצַּח,יְנַצַּח) to be victorious,to direct
נֶצַח,ז. eternity
לָנֶצַח forever
נִצָּחוֹן,ז.(ר' נִצְחוֹנוֹת) victory
נִצְחִי eternal
נִצְחִיּוּת,נ. eternity
נְצִיב,ז. governor,column
וַתְּהִי נְצִיב מֶלַח. She (Lot's wife) became a column of salt.
נצל (הִנָּצֵל) (נִצַּל, יִנָּצֵל) to be saved
נִצֵּל (נִצֵּל,יְנַצֵּל) to exploit
הִצִּיל (הִצִּיל,יַצִּיל) to save
הִתְנַצֵּל (הִתְנַצֵּל,יִתְנַצֵּל) to justify oneself
נִצָּן,ז. flower
נצץ (נָצַץ,יָנֹץ) to sparkle
נַצְרוּת,נ. Christianity
נקב (נָקַב,יִנְקֹב) to pierce, to specify
נִקֵּב (נִקֵּב,יְנַקֵּב) to pierce
נֶקֶב,ז. hole
●נְקֵבָה,נ. female,woman
נִקְבָּה,נ. tunnel
נְקֵבוּת,נ. femininity
נקד (נָקַד,יִנְקֹד) נִקֵּד (נִקֵּד, יְנַקֵּד) to make points
נְקֻדָּה,נ. point
נִקָּה (נִקָּה,יְנַקֶּה) to clean
נִקּוּד,ז. vowel pointing
נִקּוּי,ז. cleaning
●נָקִי clean;innocent
הַבַּיִת נָקִי. The house is clean.
הוּא נְקִי מִפֶּשַׁע. He is innocent of any crime.

לְשׁוֹן נְקִיָּה euphemism (clean tongue)
נְקִי כַּפַּיִם innocent (clean hands)
נִקָּיוֹן,ז. נְקִיּוּת,נ. purity
נָקִיק,ז. crevice
נְקַלָּה,נ. ease
עַל נְקַלָּה easily
נקם (נָקַם,יִקֹּם) to revenge
נָקָם,ז.נְקָמָה,נ. revenge
נַקְנִיק,ז. sausage
נקע (נָקַע,יֵקַע) to be dislocated
נקף (הִקִּיף)(הִקִּיף,יַקִּיף) to surround
נִקֵּר (נִקֵּר,יְנַקֵּר) to peck; to hollow out
נִקְרָה,נ. hollow
●נֵר,ז. (ר' נֵרוֹת) candle
נֵר תָּמִיד Eternal Light
נִרְפֶּה negligent
נַרְתִּיק,ז. case
נשא (נָשָׂא,יִשָּׂא) to lift; to carry; to marry; to forgive
הַסַּבָּל נָשָׂא אֶת הָאַרְגָּז. The porter carried the trunk.
יַעֲקֹב נָשָׂא אֶת רָחֵל. Jacob married Rachel.
נשב (נָשַׁב,יִשֹּׁב) to blow
(נשג) הִשִּׂיג (הִשִּׂיג,יַשִּׂיג) to attain,to object
נִשְׂגָּב elevated
נשה (נָשָׁה,יִשֶּׁה) to forget; to demand payment
נֹשֶׁה,ז. creditor
נִשּׁוּק,ז. kissing
●נָשִׂיא,ז. president
נְשִׁיכָה,נ. biting
נְשִׁימָה,נ. breath
בִּנְשִׁימָה אַחַת at once
נְשִׁיקָה,נ. kiss
נשך (נָשַׁךְ,יִשֹּׁךְ) to bite
נֶשֶׁךְ,ז. usury
נשם (נָשַׁם,יִשֹּׁם) to breathe
נְשָׁמָה,נ. soul;breath

He arranged the books. — הוּא סָדַר אֶת הַסְּפָרִים.

order,section — סֶדֶר, ז.

Laws of Nature — סֵדֶר בְּרֵאשִׁית

agenda — סֵדֶר הַיּוֹם

Everything is in order. — הַכֹּל בְּסֵדֶר.

one after another — כְּסֵדֶר

steward;organizer; usher — סַדְרָן, ז.

moon — סַהַר, ז.

prison — סֹהַר, בֵּית הַסֹּהַר, ז.

species,sort — סוּג, ז.

secret — סוֹד, ז. (ר' סוֹדוֹת)

shawl — סוּדָר, ז.

to converse — סוּחַ (סָח, יָסוּחַ)

merchant — סוֹחֵר, ז. (נ. סוֹחֶרֶת)

agent;manager — סוֹכֵן, ז.

agency — סוֹכְנוּת, נ.

sole (shoe) — סוּלְיָה, נ.

blind — סוּמָא, ז. (נ. סוּמָה)

horse — סוּס, ז.

walrus — סוּס הַיָּם, ז.

mare — סוּסָה, נ.

to end — סוּף (סָף, יָסוּף)

reed — סוּף, ז.

end — סוֹף, ז.

at the end — לָסוֹף, בְּסוֹף, לְבַסּוֹף

finally — סוֹף סוֹף

infinity — אֵין סוֹף

storm — סוּפָה, נ.

author,writer — סוֹפֵר, ז.

to turn off; to come in — סוּר (סָר, יָסוּר)

to remove — הֵסִיר (הֵסִיר, יָסִיר)

to drag — סָחַב (סָחַב, יִסְחַב)

rag — סְחָבָה, נ.

roundabout — סָחוֹר

merchandise — סְחוֹרָה, נ.

to squeeze — סָחַט (סָחַט, יִסְחַט)

squeezing — סְחִיטָה, נ.

to trade — סָחַר (סָחַר, יִסְחַר)

dizziness — סַחַרְחֹרֶת, נ.

slap — סְטִירָה, נ.

to slap — סָטַר (סָטַר, יִסְטֹר)

fence — סְיָג, ז.

He walked around the house. — הוּא הָלַךְ מַסְבִיב לַבַּיִת.

surrounding — סְבִיבָה, נ.

The surroundings are beautiful. — הַסְּבִיבָה יָפָה.

top — סְבִיבוֹן, ז.

The boy played with the top. — הַיֶּלֶד שִׂחֵק בַּסְּבִיבוֹן.

to get enmeshed — סבך (הִסְתַּבֵּךְ)(הִסְתַּבֵּךְ, יִסְתַּבֵּךְ)

to suffer — סבל (סָבַל, יִסְבֹּל)

I suffer in the heat. — אֲנִי סוֹבֵל מִן הַחֹם.

I cannot stand him. — אֵינֶנִּי יָכֹל לִסְבֹּל אוֹתוֹ.

suffering — סֵבֶל, סֹבֶל, ז.

porter — סַבָּל, ז.

tolerant — סַבְלָן

patience — סַבְלָנוּת, נ.

to soap — סבן (כִּבֵּן, יְסַבֵּן)

to explain — סבר (הִסְבִּיר)(הִסְבִּיר, יַסְבִּיר)

to be friendly — סֵבֶר פָּנִים

friendliness — סֵבֶר פָּנִים, ז.

closing — סְגִירָה, נ.

to make fit — סגל (סִגֵּל, יְסַגֵּל)

to fit oneself — הִסְתַּגֵּל (הִסְתַּגֵּל, יִסְתַּגֵּל)

violet (color) — סֶגֶל, ז.

substitute — סֶגֶן, ז.

style — סִגְנוֹן, ז.

to close — סגר (סָגַר, יִסְגֹּר)

to close oneself in — הִסָּגֵר (נִסְגַּר, יִסָּגֵר)

to deliver — סגר (סִגֵּר, יְסַגֵּר)

rain,shower,storm — סַגְרִיר, ז.

rainy day — יוֹם סַגְרִיר

order;prayer book — סִדּוּר, ז.

ordinal — סִדּוּרִי, ז.

sheet — סָדִין, ז.

anvil — סַדָּן, ז.

to cleave — סדק (סָדַק, יִסְדֹּק)

cleft — סֶדֶק, ז.

to arrange — סדר (סָדַר, יְסַדֹּר) סִדֵּר (סִדֵּר, יְסַדֵּר)

twilight, evening; ball (dance) — נֶשֶׁף, ז.

a dance — נֶשֶׁף רִקּוּדִים

an artistic evening — נֶשֶׁף אָמָנוּתִי

to kiss — נשק (נָשַׁק, יִשַּׁק)

weapons — נֶשֶׁק, ז.

eagle — נֶשֶׁר, ז.

young eagle — בֶּן נֶשֶׁר, ז.

to fall off — נשר (נָשַׁר, יִשַּׁר)

The leaves fell off the tree. — הֶעָלִים נָשְׁרוּ מִן הָעֵץ.

operation;analysis, cutting — נִתּוּחַ, ז.

to cut;to operate; to analyze — נתח (נִתַּח, יְנַתַּח)

slice — נֵתַח, ז.

a slice of meat — נֵתַח בָּשָׂר

path — נָתִיב, ז. נְתִיבָה, נ.

subject — נָתִין, ז.

He is a British subject. — הוּא נָתִין שֶׁל אַנְגְּלִיָה.

citizenship — נְתִינוּת, נ.

to give — נתן (נָתַן, יִתֵּן)

yielded fruit — נָתַן פְּרִי

agreed — נָתַן יָד

Would that..! — מִי יִתֵּן..!

to be given — הִנָּתֵן (נִתַּן, יִנָּתֵן)

ס

old man; grandfather — סָב, סַבָּא, ז.

old woman; grandmother — סָבָה, נ. סַבְתָא

to move round; to surround — סבב (סָבַב, יָסֹב)

to cause to surround — סִבֵּב (סִבֵּב, יְסַבֵּב)

to turn away; to cause;to sit at table — הֵסֵב (הֵסֵב, יָסֵב)

cause — סִבָּה, נ.

turn — סָבוּב, ז.

interlacing — סָבוּךְ, ז.

soap — סַבּוֹן

round — סָבִיב

lime	סִיד ,ז.
to whitewash	כִּיֵד (סִיֵד,יְסַיֵד)
whitewasher	סַיָד ,ז.
whitewashing	סִיוּד ,ז.
finishing	סִיּוּם ,ז.
help	סִיּוּעַ ,ז.
visit,tour	סִיּוּר ,ז.
wholesale merchant	סִיטוֹן ,ז.
to finish	סִיֵם (סִיֵם,יְסַיֵם)
China	סִין ,ז.
apron	סִינָר ,ז.
to help	סִיֵּעַ (סִיֵּעַ,יְסַיֵּעַ)
party	סִיעָה,נ.
sword	סַיִף ,ז.
pot;thorn	סִיר ,ז.
to tour	סִיֵּר (סִיֵר,יְסַיֵר)
boat	סִירָה,נ.
sum	סַךְ ,ז.
total;result	סַךְ הַכֹּל
thicket;hut	סֻכָּה,נ.
hope	סִכּוּי,ז.
roofing	סִכּוּךְ
sum	סְכוּם,ז.
knife	סַכִּין,נ.
to cover; to shelter,to protect	סכך (סַךְ,סָכַךְ,יָסֹךְ)
roof	סְכָךְ,ז.
awning	סְכָכָה,נ.
to observe	סכל (הִסְתַּכֵּל)(הִסְתַּכֵּל,יִסְתַּכֵּל)
silly	סָכָל
silliness	סֶכֶל,ז. סִכְלוּת,נ.
to sum up	סִכֵּם (סִכֵּם,יְסַכֵּם)
to agree	הִסְכִּים (הִסְכִּים,יַסְכִּים)
I agree.	אֲנִי מַסְכִּים.
to endanger	סִכֵּן (סִכֵּן,יְסַכֵּן)
danger	סַכָּנָה,נ.
There is no danger.	אֵין כָּל סַכָּנָה.
danger of life	סַכָּנַת נְפָשׁוֹת
quarrel,argument	סִכְסוּךְ,ז.
to ensnare	סִכְסֵךְ (סִכְסֵךְ,יְסַכְסֵךְ)
to close	סָכַר (סָכַר,יִסְכֹּר)
dam	סֶכֶר
sugar	סֻכָּר
basket	סַל,ז.

forever	סֶלָה
to forgive	סלח (סָלַח,יִסְלַח)
Forgive me. Excuse me.	סְלַח לִי.
one who forgives	סַלְחָן,סַלְחָן,ז.
forgiveness	סְלִיחָה,נ.
Pardon!	סְלִיחה!
spool	סְלִיל,ז.
rampart	סֹלְלָה,נ.
ladder	סֻלָּם,ז. (רי סֻלָּמוֹת)
curling;trill	סִלְסוּל,ז.
to trill; to curl;to fondle	סִלְסֵל (סִלְסֵל,יְסַלְסֵל)
rock	סֶלַע,ז.
to pervert	סִלֵּף (סִלֵּף,יְסַלֵּף)
to remove; to pay out	סִלֵּק (סִלֵּק,יְסַלֵּק)
to go away; to die	הִסְתַּלֵּק (הִסְתַּלֵּק,יִסְתַּלֵּק)
beetroot	סֶלֶק,ז.
fine flour	סֹלֶת,נ.
medicine,poison	סַם,ז.
life-giving drug	סַם חַיִּים
poison	סַם מָוֶת
near;leaning	סָמוּךְ
alley	סִמְטָה,נ.
authorization	סְמִיכָה,סְמִיכוּת,נ.
to lean on, depend on	סמך (סָמַךְ,יִסְמֹךְ)
I'm depending on you.	אֲנִי סוֹמֵךְ עָלֶיךָ.
to rely	הִסְתַּמֵּךְ (הִסְתַּמֵּךְ,יִסְתַּמֵּךְ)
reliance	סֶמֶךְ,ז.
reliable person	בֶּן סֶמֶךְ,ז.
symbol	סֵמֶל,ז.
to mark	סִמֵּן (סִמֵּן,יְסַמֵּן)
sign	סִמָּן,ז.
a good omen	סִמָּן טוֹב
to nail	סמר (סָמַר,יִסְמֹר)
rag	סְמַרְטוּט,ז.
squirrel	סְנָאִית,נ.
sandal	סַנְדָּל,ז.
shoemaker	בַּנְדְּלָר,ז.
Sanhedrin (upper court)	סַנְהֶדְרִיָה,סַנְהֶדְרִין,נ.
swallow	סְנוּנִית,נ.

blindness	סַנְוֵרִים,ז"ר
chin	סַנְטֵר,ז.
defender (legal)	סָנֵיגוֹר,ז.
defense (legal)	סָנֵיגוֹרְיָה,נ.
branch	סָנִיף
There is a branch bank in Jaffa.	יֵשׁ סָנִיף שֶׁל הַבַּנְק בְּיָפוֹ.
to strain	סִנֵּן (סִנֵּן,יְסַנֵּן)
fin	סְנַפִּיר,ז.
to support, to feed	סָעַד (סָעַד,יִסְעַד)
support	סַעַד,ז.
meal;banquet	סְעוּדָה,נ.
twig;paragraph	סָעִיף,ז.
to storm	סָעַר (סָעַר,יִסְעַר)
storm	סַעַר,ז. סְעָרָה,נ.
threshold,sill	סַף,ז.
to absorb	ספג (סָפַג,יִסְפֹּג)
blotting paper	נְיָר סוֹפֵג,ז.
to mourn	סָפַד (סָפַד,יִסְפֹּד)
to hold a funeral sermon	הִסְפִּיד (הִסְפִּיד,יַסְפִּיד)
couch	סַפָּה,נ.
sponge	סְפוֹג,ז.
spongy	סְפוֹגִי
ceiling	סִפּוּן,ז.
satisfaction	סִפּוּק,ז.
story;haircutting	סִפּוּר,ז.
ship	סְפִינָה,נ.
sapphire	סַפִּיר,ז.
counting	סְפִירָה,נ.
cup	סֵפֶל,ז.
sailor	סַפָּן,ז.
bench	סַפְסָל,ז.
to strike; to clap hands	ספק (סָפַק,יִסְפֹּק)
to be content,	הִסְתַּפֵּק (הִסְתַּפֵּק,יִסְתַּפֵּק)
doubt	סָפֵק,ז.
undoubtedly	בְּלִי סָפֵק
There is no doubt.	אֵין סָפֵק.
scepticism	סַפְקָנוּת,נ.
to count	סָפַר (סָפַר,יִסְפֹּר)
to tell	סִפֵּר (סִפֵּר,יְסַפֵּר)
to cut one's hair	הִסְתַּפֵּר (הִסְתַּפֵּר,יִסְתַּפֵּר)

book — סֵפֶר, ז.
The Book of Books (Bible) — סֵפֶר הַסְּפָרִים
scholar — יוֹדֵעַ סֵפֶר, ז.
People of the Book (the Jews) — עַם הַסֵּפֶר
barber — סַפָּר, ז.
literature — סִפְרוּת, נ.
library — סִפְרִיָּה
librarian — סִפְרָן, ז.
stoning — סְקִילָה, נ.
glance,review — סְקִירָה, נ.
to stone — סקל (סָקַל, יִסְקֹל)
to clear away stones — סִקֵּל (סִקֵּל, יְסַקֵּל)
curiosity — סַקְרָנוּת, נ.
to refuse — סרב (סֵרֵב, יְסָרֵב)
to knit — סרג (סָרַג, יִסְרֹג)
a ruler — סַרְגֵּל, ז.
My ruler is 12 inches long. — הַסַּרְגֵּל שֶׁלִּי הוּא 12 אִינְטְשׁ.
refusal — סֵרוּב, ז.
stench — סִרָחוֹן, ז.
to scratch — סרט (סָרַט, יִסְרֹט)
ribbon;film — סֶרֶט, ז.
We saw an interesting film. — רָאִינוּ סֶרֶט מְעַנְיֵן.
crayfish,cancer — סַרְטָן, ז.
knitting — סְרִיגָה, נ.
scratch — סְרִיטָה, נ.
eunuch — סָרִיס, ז.
combing — סְרִיקָה, נ.
to castrate; to pervert — סרס (סֵרֵס, יְסָרֵס)
to comb — סרק (סָרַק, יִסְרֹק)
autumn — סְתָו, סְתָיו, ז.
closed;uncertain — סָתוּם, ז.
shutting;filling — סְתִימָה, נ.
contradiction — סְתִירָה, נ.
to close up — סתם (סָתַם, יִסְתֹּם)
to destroy; to contradict — סתר (סָתַר, יִסְתֹּר)
to hide — הִסְתִּיר (נִסְתַּר, יַסְתֵּר)
הִסְתַּתֵּר (הִסְתַּתֵּר, יִסְתַּתֵּר)
hiding place — סֵתֶר, ז.
secretly — בְּסֵתֶר, ז.

secret — דְּבַר סֵתֶר, ז.

ע

cloud;thick,dense — עָב, ז.
to serve; to work;to worship — עבד (עָבַד, יַעֲבֹד)
I work in an office. — אֲנִי עוֹבֵד בְּמִשְׂרָד.
He is an idol worshipper. — הוּא עוֹבֵד אֱלִילִים.
to tan, to elaborate — עִבֵּד (עִבֵּד, יְעַבֵּד)
They worked out an excellent plan. — הֵם עִבְּדוּ תָּכְנִית יָפָה.
to cause to work — הֶעֱבִיד (הֶעֱבִיד, יַעֲבִיד)
slave — עֶבֶד, ז.
fact — עֻבְדָּה, נ.
slavery — עַבְדוּת, נ.
thick,dense — עָבֶה, ז.
tanning,elaborating — עִבּוּד, ז.
work,ministry — עֲבוֹדָה, נ.
agriculture — עֲבוֹדַת הָאֲדָמָה
idolatry — עֲבוֹדָה זָרָה, נ.
for — עֲבוּר
because of;for — בַּעֲבוּר
for me, for you — בַּעֲבוּרִי, בַּעֲבוּרְךָ
thickness — עֳבִי, ז.
embryo — עֻבָּר, ז.
to pass; to trespass — עבר (עָבַר, יַעֲבֹר)
to take across — הֶעֱבִיר (הֶעֱבִיר, יַעֲבִיר)
past tense — עָבַר, ז.
flank,side — עֵבֶר, ז.
from the other side — מֵעֵבֶר
He came from the other side of the river. — הוּא בָּא מֵעֵבֶר הַנָּהָר.
trespass,sin — עֲבֵרָה, נ.
wrath — עֶבְרָה, נ.
Hebrew — עִבְרִי, ז.
sinner — עַבַרְיָן, ז.

Hebrew — עִבְרִית
tomato — עַגְבָנִיָה, עַגְבָנִית, נ.
custard;cake — עֻגָה, נ.
circle — עִגּוּל, ז.
earring — עָגִיל, ז.
round — עָגֹל
calf — עֵגֶל, ז.
heifer — עֶגְלָה, נ.
cart — עֲגָלָה, נ.
driver — עֶגְלוֹן, ז.
anchor — עֹגֶן, ז.
until — עַד
soon — עַד מְהֵרָה
forever — לְעַד
witness — עֵד, ז.
congregation — עֵדָה, נ.
hoeing — עִדּוּר, ז.
testimonial; certificate — עֵדוּת, נ.
ornament — עֲדִי, ז.
still — עֲדַיִן
not yet — עֲדַיִן לֹא
tender — עָדִין
tenderness — עֲדִינוּת, נ.
better;preferable — עָדִיף
hoeing — עֲדִירָה, נ.
delight — עֵדֶן, ז.
paradise — גַּן עֵדֶן, ז.
surplus — עֹדֶף, ז.
תֵּן לִי אֶת הָעֹדֶף בְּכֶסֶף קָטָן.
Give me my change in small coins.
to hoe — עדר (עָדַר, יַעְדֹר)
to be lacking — הֶעְדֵּר (נֶעְדַּר, יֵעָדֵר)
lentil — עֲדָשָׁה, נ. (ר' עֲדָשִׁים)
flute;organ — עֻגָב, ז.
to testify;to warn — עוד (הֵעִיד, יָעִיד)
to take heart — הִתְעוֹדֵד (הִתְעוֹדֵד, יִתְעוֹדֵד)
more — עוֹד
not yet — עוֹד לֹא
in a little while — עוֹד מְעַט
again — עוֹד פַּעַם
to sin — עוה (עָוָה, יַעֲוֶה)

to twist	עָוָה (עָוָה, יַעֲוֶה)
perverting	עִוּוּת,ז.
to dare	(עוז) הֵעֵז (הֵעֵז, יָעֵיז)
convulsions	עֲוִית,נ.
wrong	עָוֶל,ז.
baby	עֹגֶל,ז.
sacrifice	עוֹלָה,נ.
wrong	עַוְלָה,נ.
child	עוֹלֵל,ז.
world	עוֹלָם,ז.
forever	לְעוֹלָם
world to come	עוֹלָם הַבָּא
cemetery	בֵּית עוֹלָם,ז.
eternal	עוֹלָמִי
eternally	עוֹלָמִים,עוֹלָמִית
sin	עָוֹן,ז. (ר' עֲווֹנוֹת)
term;time	עוֹנָה,נ.
to fly	עוּף (עָף, יָעוּף)
to soar	הִתְעוֹפֵף (הִתְעוֹפֵף, יִתְעוֹפֵף)
to waken	עוּר (עָר, יָעוּר)
to wake; to stir up	עוֹרֵר (עוֹרֵר, יְעוֹרֵר)
to wake; to remark	הֵעִיר (הֵעִיר, יָעִיר)
to waken;to be excited	הִתְעוֹרֵר (הִתְעוֹרֵר, יִתְעוֹרֵר)
skin	עוֹר,ז. (ר'עוֹרוֹת)
to blind	עִוֵּר (עִוֵּר, יְעַוֵּר)
to become blind	הִתְעַוֵּר (הִתְעַוֵּר,יִתְעַוֵּר)
blind	עִוֵּר
crow	עוֹרֵב,ז.
blindness	עִוָּרוֹן,ז.
lawyer	עוֹרֵךְ דִּין
to bend; to pervert	עָוָה (עָוָה,יַעֲוֶה)
strong	עַז
impudent	עַז פָּנִים
goat	עֵז,נ.
strength	עֹז,ז.
devil	עֲזָאזֵל,ז.
to leave	עָזַב (אָזַב, יַעֲזֹב)
inheritance	עִזָּבוֹן,ז.
desolation; disorder	עֲזוּבָה,נ.

impertinence	עַזּוּת,נ. (-פָּנִים, -מֵצַח)
abandoning	עֲזִיבָה,נ.
to help	עָזַר (עָזַר, יַעֲזֹר)
help	עֵזֶר,ז., עֶזְרָה,נ.
first aid	עֶזְרָה רִאשׁוֹנָה
temple court	עֲזָרָה,נ.
women's court	עֶזְרַת נָשִׁים,נ.
pen	עֵט,ז.
to wrap	עטה (עָטָה, יַעֲטֶה)
adorning	עִטּוּר,ז.
sneeze	עָטוּשׁ,ז., עֲטִישָׁה,נ.
udder	עָטִין,ז.
wrapping	עֲטִיפָה,נ.
bat	עֲטַלֵּף,ז.
to wrap	עָטַף (עָטַף, יַעֲטֹף)
to encircle	עָטַר (עָטַר, יַעֲטֹר)
to crown	עָטַר (עָטַר,יַעֲטֹר) הֶעֱטִיר (הֶעֱטִיר,יַעֲטִיר)
crown	עֲטָרָה,נ.
ruins	עִי,ז.
study;theory	עִיּוּן,ז.
theoretical	עִיּוּנִי
kite	עַיִט,ז.
eye	עַיִן,נ. (ר' עֵינַיִם)
an eye for an eye	עַיִן תַּחַת עַיִן
like,similar	כְּעֵין
in the presence of	לְעֵינֵי
I liked it. (It found favor in my eyes.)	הַדָּבָר מָצָא חֵן בְּעֵינַי.
tired	עָיֵף
to get tired	עיף (עָיֵף, יִיעַף)
weariness	עֲיֵפוּת,נ.
town	עִיר,נ. (ר' עָרִים)
capital city	עִיר הַבִּירָה
The Holy City (Jerusalem)	עִיר הַקֹּדֶשׁ
small town,hamlet, village	עֲיָרָה,נ.
townsman	עִירוֹנִי,עִירָנִי,ז.
township	עִירִיָּה,נ.
nakedness;naked	עֵירֹם,ז.
to hinder	עָכַב (עָכַב, יְעַכֵּב)
to stay; to be prevented	הִתְעַכֵּב (הִתְעַכֵּב,יִתְעַכֵּב)

spider	עַכָּבִישׁ,ז.
spider web	קוּרֵי עַכָּבִישׁ,ז"ר
mouse	עַכְבָּר
hindrance	עִכּוּב,ז.
immediately	בְּלִי עִכּוּב
digestion	עִכּוּל,ז.
muddy	עָכוּר
to digest	עִכֵּל (עִכֵּל, יְעַכֵּל)
now	עַכְשָׁו,עַכְשָׁיו
on,upon	עַל, עַל
through	עַל יְדֵי
so,that is why	עַל כֵּן
orally	עַל פֶּה
on the surface	עַל פְּנֵי
in any case	עַל כָּל פָּנִים
yoke	עֹל,ז.
to insult	עלב (עָלַב,יַעֲלֹב) הֶעֱלִיב (הֶעֱלִיב,יַעֲלִיב)
insult	עֶלְבּוֹן,עַלְבּוֹן,ז.
to ascend	עלה (עָלָה, יַעֲלֶה)
to climb	
to raise; to carry up	הֶעֱלָה (הֶעֱלָה, יַעֲלֶה)
leaf	עָלֶה,ז.
miserable	עָלוּב
gifted person	עִלּוּי,ז.
apt	עָלוּל
hiding	עִלּוּם,ז.
anonymous	בְּעָלוּם שְׁמוֹ
youth	עֲלוּמִים, ז"ר
leech	עֲלוּקָה,נ.
merry	עָלֵז,ז.
darkness	עֲלָטָה,נ.
going up;ascent;loft	עֲלִיָּה,נ.
topmost,upper	עֶלְיוֹן
gaiety	עֲלִיזוּת,נ.
accusation;deed	עֲלִילָה,נ.
gaiety	עֲלִיצוּת,נ.
to vanish	עלם (הֶעֱלֵם)(נֶעֱלַם,יֵעָלֵם)
to hide; to hush up	הֶעֱלִים (הֶעֱלִים,יַעֲלִים)
to vanish	הִתְעַלֵּם (הִתְעַלֵּם, יִתְעַלֵּם)
young man	עֶלֶם,ז.
young lady	עַלְמָה,נ.

עלף, הִתְעַלֵּף (הִתְעַלֵּף, יִתְעַלֵּף)
to faint

nation,people עַם, ז.●

עַם הָאָרֶץ, ז. (ר' עַמֵי הָאָרֶץ)
ignorant

with עִם

nevertheless עִם כָּל זֶה

at dark;at sunset עִם חֲשֵׁכָה

to stand עמד (עָמַד, יַעֲמֹד)●

to place הֶעֱמִיד (הֶעֱמִיד, יַעֲמִיד)

He stood הוּא עָמַד אֵצֶל הַבַּיִת.
near the house.

הוּא עָמַד עַל דַּעְתּוֹ.
He insisted.

Where אֵיפֹה עוֹמֵד הָאוֹטוֹבּוּס?
does the bus stop?

place,situation עֲמִדָּה, נ.

with me עִמָּדִי

pillar,page עַמּוּד, ז.

loaded עָמוּס

standing עֲמִידָה, נ.

starch עֲמִילָן, ז.

sheaf עָמִיר, ז.

friend עָמִית, ז.

to toil עמל (עָמַל, יַעֲמֹל)

to make עָמֵל (עָמֵל, יַעֲמֹל)
tired,to drill

to הִתְעַמֵּל (הִתְעַמֵּל, יִתְעַמֵּל)
drill; to exercise

hard-working עָמֵל

hard work עָמָל, ז.

popular עֲמָמִי, ז.

public school בֵּית סֵפֶר עֲמָמִי

popularity עֲמָמִיּוּת, נ.

to bear עמס (עָמַס, יַעֲמֹס)

הֶעֱמִיס (הֶעֱמִיס, יַעֲמִיס)
to burden

to deepen עמק (הֶעֱמִיק, יַעֲמִיק)(הֶעֱמַק)

deep עָמֹק●

depth עֹמֶק, ז. עֲמָקוּת, נ.

valley עֵמֶק, ז.●

The Valley(Jezreel) הָעֵמֶק

sheaf עֹמֶר, ז.

grape עֵנָב, ז. (ר' עֲנָבִים)●

pleasure,enjoyment עֹנֶג, ז.●

---

with pleasure בְּעֹנֶג

ענג (הִתְעַנֵּג)(הִתְעַנֵּג, יִתְעַנֵּג)
to enjoy

delicate עָנֹג

to answer; ענה (עָנָה, יַעֲנֶה)●
to testify

Answer the עֲנֵה עַל הַשְּׁאֵלָה.
question.

to be הֵעָנֶה (נַעֲנָה, יֵעָנֶה)
answered

to torture עִנָּה (עִנָּה, יְעַנֶּה)

הִתְעַנָּה (הִתְעַנָּה, יִתְעַנֶּה)
to suffer;to fast

humble עָנָו

humbleness עֲנָוָה, נ.

torture עִנּוּי, ז.

poor עָנִי●

poverty עֹנִי, ז.

tie עֲנִיבָה, נ.●

אֲנִי רוֹצֶה עֲנִיבָה שְׁחוֹרָה.
I want a black tie.

poverty עֲנִיּוּת, נ.

affair עִנְיָן, ז.●

עִנְיֵן (עִנְיֵן, יְעַנְיֵן)●
to interest

It's very זֶה מְעַנְיֵן מְאֹד.
interesting.

cloud עָנָן, ז.●

to cover עִנֵּן (עִנֵּן, יְעַנֵּן)●
(with clouds)

branch עָנָף, ז.●

thick with branches עָנֵף

giant עֲנָק, ז.●

gigantic עֲנָקִי

to punish ענש (עָנַשׁ, יַעֲנֹשׁ)

punishment עֹנֶשׁ, ז.

dough עִסָּה, נ.

busy עָסוּק●

juice עָסִיס, ז.

to occupy עסק (עָסַק, יַעֲסֹק)

הֶעֱסַק (הֶעֱסִיק, יַעֲסִיק)
to busy

הִתְעַסֵּק (הִתְעַסֵּק, יִתְעַסֵּק)
to be busy

occupation,business עֵסֶק, ז.

active עַסְקָן

---

eyelash עַפְעַף, ז. (ר' עַפְעַפִּים)

earth;ashes;dust עָפָר, ז.

young deer עֹפֶר, ז.

gazelle;lovely girl עָפְרָה, נ.

pencil עִפָּרוֹן, ז.●

lead עֹפֶרֶת, נ.

tree עֵץ, ז.●

עצב (עָצַב, יַעֲצֹב) הָעֶצֶב
to grieve הֶעֱצִיב (הֶעֱצִיב, יַעֲצִיב)
הִתְעַצֵּב (הִתְעַצֵּב, יִתְעַצֵּב)
to grieve

nerve,grief עֶצֶב, ז.

sorrowful עָצֵב●

affliction עִצָּבוֹן, ז. עַצֶּבֶת, נ.

counsel,advice עֵצָה, נ.●

grieved,sad עָצוּב●

numerous עָצוּם

flowerpot עָצִיץ, ז.

constipation; עֲצִירָה, נ.
keeping back

to be עצל (הֶעֱצַל, יֵעָצֵל)(נֶעֱצַל, יֵעָצֵל)
lazy הִתְעַצֵּל (הִתְעַצֵּל, יִתְעַצֵּל)

lazy עָצֵל

laziness עַצְלָה, עַצְלוּת, נ.

lazy עַצְלָן, ז.

to close; עצם (עָצַם, יַעֲצֹם)
to get strong

essence,bone עֶצֶם, נ.

me,you עֶצֶם (עַצְמִי, עַצְמְךָ)

I'll go by myself. אֵלֵךְ בְּעַצְמִי.

power עֹצֶם, ז. עָצְמָה, נ.

substance עַצְמוּת, נ.

to keep back עצר (עָצַר, יַעֲצֹר)

heir to the עֶצֶר (יוֹרֵשׁ-), ז.
throne

reign;curfew עֹצֶר, ז.

assembly; עֲצָרָה, עֲצֶרֶת, נ.
feast day

to deceive; עקב (עָקַב, יַעֲקֹב)
to follow closely

heel עָקֵב, ז.

because עֵקֶב

tearing out עֵקּוּר, ז.

curve;bend עֲקֻמָּה, נ.

roundabout ways עֲקִיפִים, ז"ר

sting עֲקִיצָה, נ.

tortuous	עֲקַלָּתוֹן
curved	עָקֹם
to sting	עָקַץ (עָקַץ, יַעֲקֹץ)
sting	עֹקֶץ
barren	עָקָר
main point;principle	עִקָּר,ז.
root	
not at all	לֹא כָל עִקָּר
scorpion	עַקְרָב
barren	עֲקָרָה
chief	עִקָּרִי
crooked	עָקֵשׁ
crookedness	עַקְשׁוּת
stubborn	עַקְשָׁן
stubborness	עַקְשָׁנוּת,נ.
awake	עֵר,ז.
temporary	עֲרָאִי
pleasant	עָרֵב
eve,evening	עֶרֶב,ז.
twilight	בֵּין הָעַרְבַּיִם
willow;steppe	עֲרָבָה,נ.
mixing;confusion	עִרְבּוּב,ז.
confusion	עִרְבּוּבְיָה,נ.
pledge	עֵרָבוֹן,ז.
bail	עַרְבוּת,נ.
rubbers	עַרְדָּלִים,ז"ר
mixture	עֵרוּב,ז.
garden bed	עֲרוּגָה,נ.
nakedness	עֶרְוָה,נ.
cunning	עָרוּם,עָרֹם
naked	עָרוּם
editing;arranging	עֲרִיכָה,נ.
cradle	עֲרִיסָה,נ.
tyrant	עָרִיץ,ז.
tyranny	עֲרִיצוּת,נ.
loneliness	עֲרִירוּת,נ.
lonely	עֲרִירִי
to set in order	עָרַךְ(עָרַךְ, יַעֲרֹךְ)
to prepare,to edit	
argued (in court)	עָרַךְ מִשְׁפָּט
edited a newspaper	עָרַךְ עִתּוֹן
set a table	עָרַךְ שֻׁלְחָן
to value	הֶעֱרִיךְ (הֶעֱרִיךְ, יַעֲרִיךְ)
worth, value;	עֵרֶךְ,עֵרֶךְ,ז.
order	
approximately	בְּעֵרֶךְ

uncircumcised	עָרֵל
foreskin	עָרְלָה,נ.
to	עָרַם (הֶעֱרִים,יַעֲרִים)
act cunningly	
cunning	עֹרֶם,ז. עָרְמָה,נ.
heap	עֲרֵמָה,נ.
cunning	עַרְמוּמִית,נ.
chestnut	עַרְמוֹן,ז.
wide-awake	עֵרָנִי
complaint,appeal	עִרְעוּר,ז.
to complain	עִרְעֵר (עִרְעֵר, יְעַרְעֵר)
to appeal	
to drip	עָרַף (עָרַף, יַעֲרֹף)
neck	עֹרֶף,ז.
stubborn	קְשֵׁה עֹרֶף
fog	עֲרָפֶל,ז.
vein	עֹרֶק,ז.
bed	עֶרֶשׂ,נ. (ר' עֲרָשׂוֹת)
moth	עָשׁ,ז.
grass	עֵשֶׂב,ז.
to do,to make	עָשָׂה (עָשָׂה, יַעֲשֶׂה)
succeeded	עָשָׂה חַיִל
did a good deed	עָשָׂה חֶסֶד
yielded fruit	עָשָׂה פְּרִי
made	עָשׂוּי
smoking	עָשָׁן,ז.
doing	עֲשִׂיָּה,נ.
rich	עָשִׁיר
riches	עֲשִׁירוּת,נ.
tenth	עֲשִׂירִי
to smoke	עָשֵׁן (עָשַׁן) עָשֵׁן,יֶעְשַׁן (עֲשַׁן)
to smoke	יְעַשֵּׁן
No smoking.	אָסוּר לְעַשֵּׁן.
to rob	עָשַׁק (עָשַׁק, יַעֲשֹׁק)
robbery	עֹשֶׁק,ז.
to get rich	עָשַׁר (הֶעֱשִׁיר, יַעֲשִׁיר)
riches	עֹשֶׁר,ז.
ten	עֶשֶׂר,עֲשָׂרָה
twenty	עֶשְׂרִים
ten	עֲשֶׂרֶת
time	עֵת,נ.
at any time	בְּכָל עֵת
now	כָּעֵת
24 hours	מֵעֵת לְעֵת
meanwhile	לְעֵת עַתָּה

frequently	לְעִתִּים קְרוֹבוֹת
now	עַתָּה
just now	זֶה עַתָּה
newspaper	עִתּוֹן,ז.
journalist	עִתּוֹנַאי,ז.
press	עִתּוֹנוּת,נ.
timely	עִתִּי
future	עָתִיד,ז.
in the future	לֶעָתִיד לָבוֹא
future	עֲתִידוֹת,נ"ר
ancient	עַתִּיק
antiquity	עַתִּיקֻת
	עתק (הֶעְתִּיק,יַעֲתִּיק)
to move;to copy;to translate	
abundance	עֲתָרֶת,נ.

פ

side;edge	פֵּאָה,נ.
wig	פֵּאָה נָכְרִית,נ.
because	מִפְּאַת
to decorate	פֵּאֵר (פֵּאֵר, יְפָאֵר)
to boast	(הִתְפָּאֵר,יִתְפָּאֵר)
glory	פְּאֵר,ז.
faulty	פָּגוּם,ז.
dagger	פִּגְיוֹן,ז.
defectiveness	פְּגִימָה,נ.
meeting	פְּגִישָׁה,נ.
to damage	פָּגַם (פָּגַם,יִפְגֹּם)
damage	פְּגָם,ז.
to meet;	פָּגַע (פָּגַע,יִפְגַּע)
to touch	
ill-luck;adventure	פֶּגַע,ז.
to lag behind	פִּגֵּר (פִּגֵּר,יְפַגֵּר)
cadaver	פֶּגֶר,ז.
vacation	פַּגְרָה,נ.
to meet	פָּגַשׁ (פָּגַשׁ,יִפְגֹּשׁ)
I met him in the park.	פָּגַשְׁתִּי אוֹתוֹ בַּגַּן.
to meet	הִפָּגֵשׁ (נִפְגַּשׁ,יִפָּגֵשׁ)
We met each other in the park.	נִפְגַּשְׁנוּ בַּגַּן.
to redeem	פָּדָה (פָּדָה,יִפְדֶּה)
to be redeemed	הִפָּדֶה (נִפְדָּה,יִפָּדֶה)

Right column

redeeming	פְּדוּת,נ.,פְּדָיָה
ransom	פְּדִיָה,נ. פִּדְיוֹן,ז.
forehead	פַּדַּחַת,נ.
mouth	פֶּה,ז. (ר' פִּיוֹת)
unanimously	פֶּה אֶחָד
by heart	עַל פֶּה
according to	עַל פִּי
though	אַף עַל פִּי
because	לְפִי שֶׁ-
here	פֹּה
from here	מִפֹּה
so far	עַד פֹּה
yawn	פִּהוּק,ז.
to yawn	פִּהֵק (פִּהֵק,יְפַהֵק)
cross-eyed	פּוֹזֵל
to blow	פּוּחַ (פָּח,יָפוּחַ)
to blow; to fan	הָפֵם (הֵפִים,יָפִים)
eye-paint	פּוּךְ,ז.
bean	פּוֹל,ז.
publicity	פּוּמְבִּי,ז.
publicly	בְּפוּמְבִּי
inn	פּוּנְדָּק,ז.
final authority	פּוֹסֵק,ז.
worker	פּוֹעֵל,ז.
My father is a factory worker	אָבִי פּוֹעֵל בְּבֵית חֲרֹשֶׁת.
to scatter	פּוּץ (פָּץ,יָפוּץ)
to scatter; to disperse	הָפֵץ (הֵפִיץ,יָפִיץ)
to burst, to explode	הִתְפּוֹצֵץ (הִתְפּוֹצֵץ,יִתְפּוֹצֵץ)
lot	פּוּר,ז.
accident; punishment	פּוּרְעָנוּת,נ.
redemption	פּוּרְקָן,ז.
criminal; sinner	פּוֹשֵׁעַ,ז.
lukewarm	פּוֹשָׁרִים
pure gold	פָּז,ז.
scattering	פִּזּוּר,ז.
absent-mindedness	פִּזּוּר הַנֶּפֶשׁ
hasty	פָּזִיז
haste	פְּזִיזוּת,נ.
to squint	פָּזַל (פָּזַל,יִפְזַל)
liturgic song; refrain	פִּזְמוֹן

Middle column

to waste; to scatter	פַּזֵּר (פִּזֵּר,יְפַזֵּר)
to be scattered	הִתְפַּזֵּר (הִתְפַּזֵּר,יִתְפַּזֵּר)
squanderer	פַּזְרָן,ז. פַּזְרָנִית,נ.
extravagance	פַּזְרָנוּת,נ.
sheet metal; trap	פַּח,ז.
to be afraid	פַּחַד (פָּחַד,יִפְחַד)
to frighten	הִפְחֵד (הִפְחִיד,יַפְחִיד)
fear	פַּחַד,ז.
pasha	פֶּחָה,ז.
low; small	פָּחוּת
less	פָּחוֹת
less or more	פָּחוֹת אוֹ יוֹתֵר
at least	לְפָחוֹת
at least	לְפָחוֹת,לְכָל הַפָּחוֹת
coal	פֶּחָם,ז.
carbon paper	נְיָר פֶּחָם
carbon	פַּחְמָן,ז.
pit	פַּחַת,נ.(ר' פְּחָתִים)
to decrease	פָּחַת (הִפְחִית,יַפְחִית)
liberation	פְּטוֹר,ז.
bill of divorcement	גֵּט פִּטּוּרִים,ז.
guiltless	פָּטוּר,ז.
death	פְּטִירָה,נ.
hammer	פַּטִּישׁ,ז.
babble, chatter	פִּטְפּוּט,ז.
to chatter	פִּטְפֵּט (פִּטְפֵּט,יְפַטְפֵּט)
babbler	פַּטְפְּטָן
chatter	פַּטְפְּטָנוּת
to set free	פָּטַר (פָּטַר,יִפְטֹר)
to say good-by; to die	הִפָּטֵר (נִפְטַר,יִפָּטֵר)
to dismiss; to declare exempt	פִּטֵּר (פִּטֵּר,יְפַטֵּר)
to resign	הִתְפַּטֵּר (הִתְפַּטֵּר,יִתְפַּטֵּר)
mushroom	פִּטְרִיָה,נ.
poetry; liturgic poetry	פִּיּוּט,ז.
appeasing, soothing	פִּיּוּס
soot	פִּיחַ,ז.
poet	פַּיְטָן,ז.

Left column

elephant	פִּיל,ז.
concubine	פִּילֶגֶשׁ,פִּלֶגֶשׁ,נ.(ר' פִּלַגְשִׁים)
to appease	פַּיֵּס (פִּיֵּס,יְפַיֵּס)
flask	פַּךְ,ז. (ר' פַּכִּים)
to be wonderful; to be impossible	פָּלָא (נִפְלָא,יִפָּלֵא)
to astonish	הַפְלֵא (הִפְלִיא,יַפְלִיא)
to wonder	הִתְפַּלֵּא (הִתְפַּלֵּא,יִתְפַּלֵּא)
I'm surprised at you.	אֲנִי מִתְפַּלֵּא עָלֶיךָ.
wonderful	נִפְלָא
marvels	נִפְלָאוֹת,נ"ר
wonder	פֶּלֶא,ז.
brook; part	פֶּלֶג,ז.
division	פְּלֻגָּה,נ.
steel	פְּלָדָה,נ.
parting	פִּלּוּג,ז.
a certain person	פְּלוֹנִי,ז.
piece	פֶּלַח,ז.
field laborer; peasant	פַּלָּח,ז.
worship	פֻּלְחָן,פֶּלְחָן,ז.
miracle	פְּלִיאָה,נ.
fugitive	פָּלִיט,ז.
criminal	פְּלִילִי
criminal court	בֵּית מִשְׁפָּט פְּלִילִי
district	פֶּלֶךְ,ז.
to judge; to think	פִּלֵּל (פִּלֵּל,יְפַלֵּל)
to pray	הִתְפַּלֵּל (הִתְפַּלֵּל,יִתְפַּלֵּל)
candlestick	פָּמוֹט,ז.
lest	פֶּן
spare time	פְּנַאי
to turn	פָּנָה (פָּנָה,יִפְנֶה)
to remove; to clean	פִּנָּה (פִּנָּה,יְפַנֶּה)
corner	פִּנָּה,נ.
empty, free	פָּנוּי
Is this place free?	הַאִם הַמָּקוֹם פָּנוּי?
coddling	פָּנוּק,ז.

detail	פְּרָט, ז.
specially	בִּפְרָט
private	פְּרָטִי
fruit	פְּרִי, ז.
to nourish;to support	פִּרְנֵס (פִּרְנֵס, יְפַרְנֵס)
to support oneself	הִתְפַּרְנֵס (הִתְפַּרְנֵס, יִתְפַּרְנֵס)
livelihood	פַּרְנָסָה, נ.
prize	פְּרָס, ז.
publication;publicity	פִּרְסוֹם, ז.
to announce	פִּרְסֵם (פִּרְסֵם, יְפַרְסֵם)
to become known	הִתְפַּרְסֵם (הִתְפַּרְסֵם, יִתְפַּרְסֵם)
to disturb	פָּרַע (הִפְרִיעַ)(הִפְרִיעַ, יַפְרִיעַ)
pogrom	פְּרָעוֹת, נ"ר
butterfly	פַּרְפַּר
to break through;to flow over	פָּרַץ (פָּרַץ, יִפְרֹץ)
to rush in	הִתְפָּרֵץ (הִתְפָּרֵץ, יִתְפָּרֵץ)
breach;defeat	פֶּרֶץ, ז.
to protect	עָמַד בַּפֶּרֶץ
face	פַּרְצוּף, ז.
joint;limb;chapter, lecture	פֶּרֶק
to separate;to explain	פָּרַשׁ (פָּרַשׁ, יִפְרֹשׁ)
plain,common	פָּשׁוּט, ז.
to take off	פָּשַׁט (פָּשַׁט, יִפְשֹׁט)
to undress	הִתְפַּשֵּׁט (הִתְפַּשֵּׁט, יִתְפַּשֵּׁט)
simplicity	פַּשְׁטוּת, נ.
sin,crime	פֶּשַׁע, ז.
to compromise	פִּשֵּׁר (פִּשֵּׁר, יְפַשֵּׁר)
meaning	פֵּשֶׁר, ז.
compromise	פְּשָׁרָה, נ.
slice of bread	פַּת, נ.
suddenly	פִּתְאֹם
sudden	פִּתְאֹמִי
proverb	פִּתְגָּם, ז.
to open	פָּתַח (פָּתַח, יִפְתַּח)
to develop;to engrave;to unite	פִּתַּח (פִּתַּח, יְפַתַּח)

compensation	פִּצּוּי, ז.
peeling;splitting	פִּצּוּל, ז.
to crack	פָּצַח (פָּצַח, יִפְצַח)
to wound	פָּצַע (פָּצַע, יִפְצַע)
wound	פֶּצַע, ז.
bomb	פְּצָצָה, נ.
to count;to command;to visit	פָּקַד (פָּקַד, יִפְקֹד)
order	פְּקֻדָּה, נ.
The officer gave an order.	הַקָּצִין נָתַן פְּקֻדָּה.
deposit	פִּקָּדוֹן, ז.(ר'פִּקְדוֹנוֹת)
care,inspection	פִּקּוּחַ, ז.
lifesaving	פִּקּוּחַ נֶפֶשׁ, ז.
to open	פָּקַח (פָּקַח, יִפְקַח)
He opened his eyes.	הוּא פָּקַח אֶת עֵינָיו.
clever;seeing	פִּקֵּחַ, ז.
official,employee	פָּקִיד, ז.
to burst	פָּקַע (פָּקַע, יִפְקַע) הִתְפַּקֵּעַ (הִתְפַּקֵּעַ, יִתְפַּקֵּעַ)
doubt;scruple	פִּקְפּוּק, ז.
stopper,cork	פְּקָק
steer,bull	פַּר, ז.
wild	פֶּרֶא, ז.
suburb	פַּרְבָּר, פַּרְוָר, ז.
to take leave	פָּרַד (הִפָּרֵד)(נִפְרַד, יִפָּרֵד)
to separate	הִפְרִיד (הִפְרִיד, יַפְרִיד)
mule	פֶּרֶד, ז. פִּרְדָּה, נ.
orchard	פַּרְדֵּס, ז.
orchard owner	פַּרְדְּסָן, ז.
to be fertile;to multiply	פָּרָה (פָּרָה, יִפְרֶה)
to fertilize	הִפְרָה (הִפְרָה, יַפְרֶה)
cow	פָּרָה, נ.
parting	פֵּרוּד, ז.
small copper coin	פְּרוּטָה, נ.
piece	פְּרוּסָה, נ.
crumbs	פֵּרוּרִים, ז"ר
explanation	פֵּרוּשׁ, ז.
expressly	בְּפֵרוּשׁ
flower,blossom	פֶּרַח, ז.
to specify;to change money	פָּרַט (פָּרַט, יִפְרֹט)

intention;turn	פְּנִיָה, נ.
face	פָּנִים, ז"ר
formerly	לְפָנִים
in his presence	בְּפָנָיו
in his absence	שֶׁלֹּא בְּפָנָיו
anyway	עַל כָּל פָּנִים
separately	בִּפְנֵי עַצְמוֹ
interior	פְּנִים, ז.
inside	בִּפְנִים
inner	פְּנִימִי
pearls	פְּנִינִים
lantern	פָּנָס, ז.
to coddle	פִּנֵּק (פִּנֵּק, יְפַנֵּק)
notebook	פִּנְקָס, ז.
stripe	פַּס, ז.
sculpture	פֶּסֶל, ז.
verse;sentence	פָּסוּק, ז.
Passover	פֶּסַח, ז.
lame	פִּסֵּחַ, ז.
idols	פְּסִילִים, ז"ר
step	פְּסִיעָה, נ.
He walked with long strides.	הוּא הָלַךְ בִּפְסִיעוֹת גְּדוֹלוֹת.
to declare as useless;to carve	פָּסַל (פָּסַל, יִפְסֹל)
idol,image	פֶּסֶל, ז.
sculptor	פַּסָּל, ז.
leavings	פְּסֹלֶת, נ.
piano	פְּסַנְתֵּר, ז.
to stride, to step	פָּסַע (פָּסַע, יִפְסַע)
small	פָּעוּט
action	פְּעֻלָּה, נ.
active	פָּעִיל
activity	פְּעִילוּת, נ.
to act	פָּעַל (פָּעַל, יִפְעַל)
action;work;verb	פֹּעַל, ז.
step; time	פַּעַם, נ. (ר' פְּעָמִים)
once	פַּעַם
this time	הַפַּעַם
from time to time	מִפַּעַם לְפַעַם
sometimes	לִפְעָמִים
bell	פַּעֲמוֹן, ז.
gape	פָּעַר (פָּעַר, יִפְעַר)
to open	פָּצָה (פָּצָה, יִפְצֶה)

הִתְפַּתֵּחַ (הִתְפַּתֵּחַ, יִתְפַּתֵּחַ) to develop	
פֶּתַח, ז. opening; doorway	
פֶּתִי, ז. fool	
פְּתִיחָה, נ. opening	
פֶּתַע (-פֶּתְאֹם) suddenly	
פֶּתֶק, ז. פִּתְקָה, נ. note	
מַה כָּתוּב בַּפֶּתֶק? What is written in the note?	
פָּתֹר (פָּתַר, יִפְתֹּר) to interpret; to solve	
פִּתְרוֹן, ז. interpretation; solution	

צ

צֹאן, נ. sheep	
צָבָא, ז.(ר' צְבָאוֹת) army	
צָבָא קֶבַע regular army	
אִישׁ צָבָא soldier	
צָבוּעַ hypocritical; colored	
צִבּוּר, ז. community; public	
שְׁלִיחַ צִבּוּר, ז. cantor	
צִבּוּרִי, ז. communal	
צְבִי, ז. stag	
צָבַע (צָבַע, יִצְבַּע) to paint, to dye	
הִצְבִּיעַ (הִצְבִּיעַ, יַצְבִּיעַ) to vote; to lift a finger	
צֶבַע, ז. color, dye	
צַבָּע, ז. painter; dyer	
צַד, ז. (ר' צְדָדִים) side	
הַצִּדָּה aside	
מִצִּדִּי as far as I am concerned	
צְדָדִי incidental	
צַדִּיק, ז. righteous	
צֶדַע, ז. צְדָעָה, נ. temple	
צָדַק (צָדַק, יִצְדַּק) to be just	
צָדַקְתָּ you were right	
הִצְדִּיק (הִצְדִּיק, יַצְדִּיק) to declare right	
הִצְטַדֵּק (הִצְטַדֵּק, יִצְטַדֵּק) to justify oneself	
אֲנִי מִצְטַדֵּק. I apologize.	
צֶדֶק, ז. justice	

צְדָקָה, נ. justice, charity	
צָהֹב yellow	
צְהַבְהַב, ז. yellowish	
צֹהַר (הִצְהִיר, יַצְהִיר)(הִצְהֵר) to declare, to proclaim	
צָהֳרַיִם noon	
אַחֲרֵי הַצָּהֳרַיִם P.M.	
לִפְנֵי הַצָּהֳרַיִם A.M.	
צַו, ז. command	
צַוָּאָה, נ. testament	
צַוָּאר, ז. neck	
צִוָּה (צִוָּה, יְצַוֶּה) to command	
צִוּוּי, ז., order; imperative	
צוֹלֵעַ, ז. lame	
צוּם (צָם, יָצוּם) to fast	
צוֹם, ז. fast day	
צוֹמֵחַ, ז. vegetation	
צוֹנֵן, ז. cold	
צוֹנְנִים cold water	
צוּף, ז. honeycomb	
צוֹפֶה, ז. prophet; scout	
צוּר, ז. rock	
צוּרָה, נ. picture; looks; form	
צַוָּארוֹן, ז. collar	
צוֹרֵף, ז. goldsmith	
צַח clear; fresh	
הוּא מְדַבֵּר עִבְרִית צָחָה. He speaks a beautiful Hebrew.	
צְחוֹק, ז. laughter	
צִחְצַח (צִחְצַח, יְצַחְצַח) to polish	
צָחַק (צָחַק, יִצְחַק) to laugh	
צִי, ז. ship; fleet	
צַיִד, ז. hunt	
צַיָּד, ז. hunter	
צֵידָה, נ. provisions	
צִיּוּן, ז. mark; gravestone	
צִיּוֹנִי, ז. Zionist	
צִיּוֹנִיּוּת, נ. Zionism	
צִיּוּר, ז. picture, painting	
צִיֵּן (צִיֵּן, יְצַיֵּן) to mark	
הִצְטַיֵּן (הִצְטַיֵּן, יִצְטַיֵּן) to excel	
מְצֻיָּן excellent	
צִיץ, ז. blossom	
צִיר, ז. hinge; delegate; messenger	

צַיֵּר (צִיֵּר, יְצַיֵּר) to paint	
רֶמְבְּרַנְט צִיֵּר בְּהוֹלַנְדִיָּה. Rembrandt painted in Holland.	
צַיָּר, ז. painter	
שָׁגָל צַיָּר גָּדוֹל. Chagall is a great painter.	
צֵל, ז. (ר' צְלָלִים) shadow	
צָלַב (צָלַב, יִצְלֹב) to nail to the cross	
הִצְטַלֵּב (הִצְטַלֵּב, יִצְטַלֵּב) to make the sign of the cross	
צְלָב, ז. cross	
נוֹסְעֵי הַצְּלָב, נוֹשְׂאֵי הַצְּלָב, ז"ר Crusaders	
צָלוּל clear	
צָלַח (הִצְלִיחַ, יַצְלִיחַ) to succeed	
צַלַּחַת, נ. dish	
צָלִי, ז. roast meat	
צֶלֶם, ז. image, idol	
צַלָּם, ז. photographer	
צִלֵּם (צִלֵּם, יְצַלֵּם) to photograph	
הִצְטַלֵּם (הִצְטַלֵּם, יִצְטַלֵּם) to be photographed	
הוּא צִלֵּם אוֹתִי. He photographed me.	
הִצְטַלַּמְתִּי. I had my picture taken.	
צָלַע (צָלַע, יִצְלַע) to limp	
צֵלָע, נ. rib; side	
צִלְצוּל, ז. ringing	
צִלְצֵל (צִלְצֵל, יְצַלְצֵל) to ring	
צָמֵא (צָמֵא, יִצְמָא) to be thirsty	
אֲנִי צָמֵא מְאֹד. I am very thirsty.	
צָמָא, ז. thirst	
צִמּוּק, ז. raisin	
צָמַח (צָמַח, יִצְמַח) to grow	
צֶמַח, ז. plant	
צָמִיד, ז. bracelet	
צֶמֶר, ז. wool	
צֶמֶר גֶּפֶן, ז. cotton	
צְנוֹן, ז. radish	
צָנוּעַ modest	
צִנּוֹר, ז. canal; pipe	
צְנִימִים, ז"ר toast	

turban;headdress — צָנִיף, ז.

to catch cold;to be cooled — •צנן (הִצְטַנֵּן)(הִצְטַנֵּן, יִצְטַנֵּן)

He caught cold, and so will not come. — הוּא הִצְטַנֵּן וְלָכֵן לֹא יָבוֹא.

flask;jar — צִנְצֶנֶת, נ.

to march — צעד (צָעַד, יִצְעַד)

step — צַעַד, ז.

veil,shawl — צָעִיף, ז.

young — •צָעִיר, ז.

toy — צַעֲצוּעַ, ז.

to scream — צעק (צָעַק, יִצְעַק)

screaming — צְעָקָה, נ.

to worry — •צָעַר (צָעַר, יִצְעַר)

The children worried the mother. — הַיְלָדִים צָעֲרוּ אֶת הָאֵם.

to be worried;to be sorry — •הִצְטַעֵר (הִצְטַעֵר, יִצְטַעֵר)

I am sorry that I won't see the film. — אֲנִי מִצְטַעֵר שֶׁלֹּא אֶרְאֶה אֶת הַסֶּרֶט.

worry; pain — צַעַר, ז.

the difficulties of raising children — צַעַר גִּדּוּל בָּנִים

north — •צָפוֹן, ז.

northern — •צְפוֹנִי

crowded — צָפוּף

bird — צִפּוֹר, נ. (ר' צִפֳּרִים)

whistle — צְפִירָה, נ.

We heard the train-whistle. — שָׁמַעְנוּ אֶת הַצְּפִירָה שֶׁל הָרַכֶּבֶת.

whistling — צִפְצוּף, ז.

to whistle, to chirp — צפצף (צִפְצֵף, יְצַפְצֵף)

The bird is chirping. — הַצִּפּוֹר מְצַפְצֶפֶת.

frog — צְפַרְדֵּעַ, נ. (ר' צְפַרְדְּעִים)

nail — צִפֹּרֶן, ז.

I cut my nails. — גָּזַזְתִּי אֶת הַצִּפָּרְנַיִם.

narrow; sorry — •צַר

I'm very sorry. — צַר לִי מְאֹד.

trouble;suffering; distress — צָרָה, נ.

hoarse — צָרוּד

necessary — •צָרִיךְ

It's not necessary to speak. — לֹא צָרִיךְ לְדַבֵּר.

barrack,hut — צְרִיף, ז.

to need — •צרך (צָרַךְ, יִצְרַךְ)

I need a pencil. — אֲנִי צָרִיךְ עִפָּרוֹן.

I needed his help. — הִצְטָרַכְתִּי לְעֶזְרָתוֹ.

I do not have to return to the doctor. — לֹא אֶצְטָרֵךְ לָשׁוּב לָרוֹפֵא.

need — צֹרֶךְ, ז.

There is no need for an introduction. — אֵין כָּל צֹרֶךְ בְּהַקְדָּמָה.

community needs — צָרְכֵי צִבּוּר

Sabbath needs (wine,candle,hallah,etc.) — צָרְכֵי שַׁבָּת

bundle — צְרוֹר, ז.

ק

stomach — קֵבָה, נ.

fixed — •קָבוּעַ

I'll come at the fixed time. — אָבוֹא בַּשָּׁעָה הַקְּבוּעָה.

The price is set. — הַמְּחִיר קָבוּעַ.

gathering;assembly; collective settlement — קִבּוּץ, ז.

collection,group; collective settlement — •קְבוּצָה, נ.

burial — קְבוּרָה, נ.

cube — קֻבִּיָּה, נ.

to receive — קִבֵּל (קִבֵּל, יְקַבֵּל)

I received a letter from my uncle. — קִבַּלְתִּי מִכְתָּב מִדּוֹדִי.

It's an accepted matter. — זֶה דָּבָר מְקֻבָּל.

receipt;reception — •קַבָּלָה, נ.

contractor — קַבְּלָן, ז.

fixed time — קֶבַע, ז.

to collect — קבץ (קָבַץ, יִקְבֹּץ) קִבֵּץ (קִבֵּץ, יְקַבֵּץ)

to assemble — הִתְקַבֵּץ (הִתְקַבֵּץ, יִתְקַבֵּץ)

compilation — קֹבֶץ, ז.

beggar — קַבְּצָן, ז.

to bury — קבר (קָבַר, יִקְבֹּר)

grave — •קֶבֶר

Rachel's tomb — קֶבֶר רָחֵל

cemetery — בֵּית הַקְּבָרוֹת, ז.

ancient — קָדוּם

prejudice — מִשְׁפָּט קָדוּם, ז.

holy — •קָדוֹשׁ

God — הַקָּדוֹשׁ בָּרוּךְ הוּא, ז.

consecrating — קִדּוּשׁ, ז.

martyrdom (Sanctification of the Holy Name) — קִדּוּשׁ הַשֵּׁם

marriage ceremony — קִדּוּשִׁים (קִדּוּשִׁין) ז"ר

fever — קַדַּחַת, נ.

east, east wind — קָדִים, ז.

forward — קָדִימָה

prayer for the dead — קַדִּישׁ, ז.

ancient times;east — קֶדֶם, ז.

in days of old — בִּימֵי קֶדֶם

before — קֹדֶם

first of all — קֹדֶם לַכֹּל

eastward — קֵדְמָה

progress — קִדְמָה, נ.

ancient — קַדְמוֹן, קַדְמוֹנִי

ancient (primitive) man — הָאָדָם הַקַּדְמוֹן

pot — קְדֵרָה, נ.

to be holy — קדש (קָדַשׁ, יִקְדַּשׁ)

to dedicate, to consecrate — הִקְדִּישׁ (הִקְדִּישׁ, יַקְדִּישׁ)

to purify oneself — הִתְקַדֵּשׁ (הִתְקַדֵּשׁ, יִתְקַדֵּשׁ)

holiness — קֹדֶשׁ, ז.

the Holy Land — אַדְמַת הַקֹּדֶשׁ

Holy Writ — כִּתְבֵי הַקֹּדֶשׁ, ז"ר

the Holy of Holies — קֹדֶשׁ הַקֳּדָשִׁים

holiness — קְדֻשָּׁה, נ.

blunt — קֵהֶה

to assemble — קהל (הִקְהִיל)(הִקְהִיל, יַקְהִיל)

community;assembly — קָהָל, ז.

community — קְהִלָּה,נ.

cord;line — קַו,ז.

to hope — קִוָּה (קִוָּה,יְקַוֶּה)

אֲנִי מְקַוֶּה כִּי תּוּכַל לָבוֹא.
I hope you will be able to come.

voice — קוֹל,ז.(ר' קוֹלוֹת)

echo — בַּת קוֹל,נ.

obeyed — שָׁמַע בְּקוֹל

I got up from the chair. — קַמְתִּי מִן הַכִּסֵּא.

I got up in the morning. — קַמְתִּי בַּבֹּקֶר.

to get up — קוּם (קָם,יָקוּם)

to raise — הֵקִים (הֵקִים,יָקִים)

to revolt — הִתְקוֹמֵם (הִתְקוֹמֵם, יִתְקוֹמֵם)

story (of a building); stature — קוֹמָה,נ.

monkey — קוֹף,ז.

thorn;splinter — קוֹץ,ז.

beam, rafter — קוֹרָה,נ.

prosecutor — קַטֵּגוֹר,ז.

inferior,small — קָטֹן, קָטָן

to be small — קָטֹן (קָטַן,יִקְטַן)

to belittle;to make smaller — הִקְטִין (הִקְטִין,יַקְטִין)

to grow less — הִתְקַטֵּן (הִתְקַטֵּן,יִתְקַטֵּן)

cripple — קִטֵּעַ,ז.

fragment — קֶטַע,ז.

to pluck — קָטַף (קָטַף,יִקְטֹף)

steam engine — קַטָּר,ז.

diameter — קֹטֶר,ז.

vomit — קִיא,ז.

to vomit — קִיא (הֵקִיא,יָקִיא)

existence — קִיּוּם,ז.

steam — קִיטוֹר,ז.

to fulfil; to affirm — קִיֵּם (קִיֵּם,יְקַיֵּם)

existing — קַיָּם,ז.

rising — קִימָה,נ.

toothpick;splinter — קֵיסָם,ז.

summer — קַיִץ,ז.

extreme — קִיצוֹן

---

wall — קִיר,ז.(ר' קִירוֹת)

light,easy — קַל

frivolous — קַל דַּעַת

a little while — שָׁעָה קַלָּה

thin — קָלוּשׁ

ease — קַלּוּת

frivolity — קַלּוּת דַּעַת,נ.

to take in — קָלַט (קָלַט,יִקְלֹט)

absorption; taking root — קְלִיטָה,נ.

curse — קְלָלָה,נ.

features (face) — קְלַסְתֵּר,ז.

parchment — קְלָף,ז.

peel — קְלִפָּה,נ.

cards — קְלָפִים,ז"ר

spoiling — קִלְקוּל,ז.

to spoil — קִלְקֵל (קִלְקֵל,יְקַלְקֵל)

to get spoiled — הִתְקַלְקֵל (הִתְקַלְקֵל,יִתְקַלְקֵל)

flour — קֶמַח,ז.

to fold — קָמַט (קָמַט,יִקְמֹט)

fold;wrinkle — קֶמֶט,ז.

a handful — קֹמֶץ,ז.

stingy — קַמְצָן

greed;stinginess — קַמְצָנוּת,נ.

teapot — קֻמְקֻם,ז.

nest — קֵן,ז.

to envy — קָנָא (קָנָא,יְקַנֵּא)

I envy you. — אֲנִי מְקַנֵּא בְּךָ.

to be envious — הִתְקַנֵּא (הִתְקַנֵּא,יִתְקַנֵּא)

envy — קִנְאָה,נ.

fanaticism — קַנָּאוּת,נ.

fanatic — קַנַּאי,ז.

to buy — קָנָה (קָנָה,יִקְנֶה)

purchase — קְנִיָּה,נ.

acquisition;possession — קִנְיָן,ז.

fine;punishment — קְנָס,ז.

jug — קַנְקַן,ז.

charm,magic — קֶסֶם,ז.

inkstand — קֶסֶת,נ.

dish — קְעָרָה,נ.

plate — קְעָרִית,נ.

freezing — קִפָּאוֹן,ז.

hot-tempered person; pedant — קַפְּדָן,ז.

---

cashier;money box — קֻפָּה,נ.

Pay at the cashier's. — תְּשַׁלֵּם בַּקֻּפָּה.

spring — קְפִיץ,ז.

The spring was broken. — הַקְּפִיץ נִשְׁבַּר.

jumping — קְפִיצָה,נ.

to fold — קָפַל (קָפַל,יְקַפֵּל)

fold — קֶפֶל,ז.

box — קֻפְסָה,נ.

to jump — קָפַץ (קָפַץ,יִקְפֹּץ)

to jump — קִפֵּץ (קִפֵּץ,יְקַפֵּץ)

end — קֵץ,ז.

rhythm — קֶצֶב,ז.

butcher — קַצָּב,ז.

border;end — קָצֶה,ז. קָצָה,נ. (ר' קְצָווֹת)

summary — קִצּוּר,ז.

in short — בְּקִצּוּר

prince;rich man; leader;officer — קָצִין,ז.

cutlet — קְצִיצָה,נ.

harvest — קָצִיר,ז.

harvesting — קְצִירָה,נ.

foam;anger — קֶצֶף,ז.

to harvest — קָצַר (קָצַר,יִקְצֹר)

to shorten — קִצֵּר (קִצֵּר,יְקַצֵּר)

short — קָצָר

The story is very short. — הַסִּפּוּר קָצָר מְאֹד.

shorthand — קַצְרָנוּת,נ.

a little — קְצָת,נ.

cold — קַר

I'm cold. — קַר לִי.

cold — קֹר,ז.

to call; to read;to convoke — קָרָא (קָרָא,יִקְרָא)

to dictate — הִקְרָא (הִקְרִיא,יַקְרִיא)

to get near — קָרַב (קָרַב,יִקְרַב)

to bring near;to offer — הִקְרִיב (הִקְרִיב,יַקְרִיב)

to approach — הִתְקָרֵב (הִתְקָרֵב,יִתְקָרֵב)

battle — קְרָב,ז.

interior — קֶרֶב,ז.

interest	רבִּית,נ.
teacher	רַבָּן (ר' רַבָּנָן),ז.
rabbinate	רַבָּנוּת,נ.
quarter	רֶבַע,ז.
quarter of an hour	רֶבַע שָׁעָה
quarter after six (o'clock)	שֵׁשׁ וָרֶבַע
spying	רִגּוּל,ז.
to tremble, to rage	רגז (רָגַז,יִרְגַּז)
to excite	הִרְגִּיז (הִרְגִּיז,יַרְגִּיז)
to get excited	הִתְרַגֵּז (הִתְרַגֵּז,יִתְרַגֵּז)
anger; excitement	רֹגֶז,ז. רָגְזָה,נ.
passionate	רַגְזָן
common,usual	רָגִיל
It's a common occurence.	זֶה דָּבָר רָגִיל.
to accustom	רגל (הֻרְגַּל)(הִרְגִּיל,יַרְגִּיל)
to get used to	הִתְרַגֵּל (הִתְרַגֵּל,יִתְרַגֵּל)
It's necessary to get used (to it).	צָרִיךְ לְהִתְרַגֵּל.
foot	רֶגֶל,נ. (ר' רַגְלַיִם)
times	רֶגֶל,נ. (ר' רְגָלִים)
by foot	בָּרֶגֶל
on foot	רַגְלִי
minute,moment	רֶגַע,ז.
Wait a moment.	חַכֵּה רֶגַע.
to feel	רגש (הֻרְגַּשׁ)(הִרְגִּישׁ,יַרְגִּישׁ)
How do you feel?	אֵיךְ אַתָּה מַרְגִּישׁ?
to be moved	הִתְרַגֵּשׁ (הִתְרַגֵּשׁ,יִתְרַגֵּשׁ)
feeling	רֶגֶשׁ,ז.
persecution	רְדִיפָה,נ.
ambition	רְדִיפָה אַחֲרֵי כָּבוֹד,נ.
to fall asleep	רדם (הֵרָדֵם)(נִרְדַּם,יֵרָדֵם)
to pursue, to chase	רדף (רָדַף,יִרְדֹּף)
furnishing	רִהוּט,ז.

You can get in touch with me by telephone.	אַתָּה יָכֹל לְהִתְקַשֵּׁר אִתִּי בַּטֶּלֶפוֹן.
knot,conspiracy	קֶשֶׁר,ז.
rainbow,bow	קֶשֶׁת,נ.

ר

to see	ראה (רָאָה,יִרְאֶה)
to be seen;to seem	הֵרָאֶה (נִרְאָה,יֵרָאֶה)
to show	הֶרְאָה (הֶרְאָה,יַרְאֶה)
to look like	הִתְרָאֶה (הִתְרָאָה,יִתְרָאֶה)
worthy	רָאוּי
mirror	רְאִי,ז.
seeing	רְאִיָּה,נ.
appearance;appointment	רְאָיוֹן,ז.
I have an appointment at six.	יֵשׁ לִי רְאָיוֹן בְּשֵׁשׁ.
beginning;top;head	רֹאשׁ,ז.
from the start	מֵרֹאשׁ
New Year's Day	רֹאשׁ הַשָּׁנָה
initials	רָאשֵׁי תֵּבוֹת
chairman	יוֹשֵׁב רֹאשׁ
first	רִאשׁוֹן,ז.
at first	רִאשׁוֹנָה
principal	רָאשִׁי
principal article (editorial)	מַאֲמָר רָאשִׁי
beginning	רֵאשִׁית,נ.
teacher;Rabbi	רַב,ז.
enough	רַב
multitude,majority	רֹב,ז.
mostly	לָרֹב
ten thousand	רְבָבָה,נ.
jam	רִבָּה,נ.
I eat bread and jam.	אֲנִי אוֹכֵל לֶחֶם בְּרִבָּה.
increase	רִבּוּי,ז.
square	רִבּוּעַ,ז.
gentlemen (vocative)	רַבּוֹתַי
sir;a rabbi	רַבִּי,ז.
quarter	רְבִיעִית,נ.
the fourth	רְבִיעִי,ז.

relationship	קִרְבָה,נ.
sacrifice	קָרְבָּן,ז.
to happen	קרה (קָרָה,יִקְרֶה)
What happened?	מַה קָּרָה?
relation;near	קָרוֹב,ז.
It's very near.	זֶה קָרוֹב מְאֹד.
He is my relation.	הוּא קָרוֹב שֶׁלִּי.
approximately	בְּקָרוֹב
cart	קָרוֹן,ז. (ר' קְרוֹנוֹת)
bald-headed	קֵרֵחַ
ice	קֶרַח,ז.
baldness	קָרַחַת,קָרְחָה,נ.
chalk	קַרְטוֹן,ז.
reading,calling	קְרִיאָה,נ.
town	קִרְיָה,נ.
tearing	קְרִיעָה,נ.
winking	קְרִיצָה,נ.
cool	קָרִיר
coolness	קְרִירוּת,נ.
horn;fund;edge	קֶרֶן,נ.
rhinoceros	קַרְנַף,ז.
ankle	קַרְסֹל,ז.
to tear	קרע (קָרַע,יִקְרַע)
tear;fragment	קֶרַע,ז.
to wink	קרץ (קָרַץ,יִקְרֹץ)
floor;soil	קַרְקַע,זו"נ (ר' קַרְקָעוֹת)
to cool	קרר (קָרַר,יְקָרֵר)
to catch cold; to get cold	הִתְקָרֵר (הִתְקָרֵר,יִתְקָרֵר)
board	קֶרֶשׁ,ז.
stubble,straw	קַשׁ,ז.
to listen,to obey	קשב (הֻקְשַׁב)(הִקְשִׁיב,יַקְשִׁיב)
to be hard	קשה (קָשָׁה,יִקְשֶׁה)
difficult,hard	קָשֶׁה
cucumber	קִשּׁוּא,ז.
adornment	קִשּׁוּט,ז.
to decorate	קשט (קִשֵּׁט,יְקַשֵּׁט)
to adorn oneself	הִתְקַשֵּׁט (הִתְקַשֵּׁט,יִתְקַשֵּׁט)
to tie	קשר (קָשַׁר,יִקְשֹׁר) (קֻשַּׁר,יְקֻשַּׁר)
to communicate	הִתְקַשֵּׁר (הִתְקַשֵּׁר,יִתְקַשֵּׁר)

English	Hebrew
friendship	רֵעוּת,נ.
beloved (fem.)	רַעְיָה,נ.
idea	רַעְיוֹן,ז. (ר' רַעְיוֹנוֹת)
poison	רַעַל,ז.
thunder	רַעַם,ז.
mane	רַעְמָה,נ.
fresh;verdant	רַעֲנָן
	רכא (רָפָא,יִרְפָּא) רָפָא
to cure	רִפֵּא,יְרַפֵּא
to get healed,to get well	הִתְרַפֵּא (הִתְרַפֵּא,יִתְרַפֵּא)
weak	רָפֶה
medicine	רְפוּאָה,נ.
healing	רִפּוּי,ז.
mud	רֶפֶשׁ,ז.
barn	רֶפֶת,נ.
runner	רָץ,ז.
to wish	רצה (רָצָה,יִרְצֶה)
God willing	אִם יִרְצֶה הַשֵּׁם
will	רָצוֹן,ז.
as you like	כִּרְצוֹנְךָ
willingly	בְּרָצוֹן
satisfied	שְׂבַע רָצוֹן
strap	רְצוּעָה,נ.
to kill	רצח (רָצַח,יִרְצַח)
murder	רֶצַח,ז. רְצִיחָה,נ.
seriousness	רְצִינוּת,נ.
serious	רְצִינִי
It's a serious matter.	זֶה דָּבָר רְצִינִי.
He is gravely ill.	הוּא חוֹלֶה רְצִינִי.
glowing coal; pavement;floor	רִצְפָּה,נ.
only,but	רַק
spittle,saliva	רֹק,ז.
to dance; to jump	רקד (רָקַד,יִרְקֹד)
dancer	רַקְדָן,ז.
temple (of head)	רַקָּה,נ.
dance	רִקּוּד,ז.
dancing	רְקִידָה,נ.
to mix(ointment); to preserve (fruit)	רקח (רָקַח,יִרְקַח)
sky;vault	רָקִיעַ,ז.
to embroider	רקם (רָקַם,יִרְקֹם)
embroidery	רִקְמָה,נ.

sauce	רֹטֶב,ז.
to quarrel	ריב (רָב,יָרִיב)
quarrel	רִיב,ז.(ר' רִיבוֹת)
odor	רֵיחַ,ז.(ר' רֵיחוֹת)
to smell	ריח (הֵרִיחַ)(הֵרִיחַ,יָרִיחַ)
running	רִיצָה,נ.
empty	רֵיק
emptiness	רֵיקוּת,נ.
emptiness	רֵיקָנִיּוּת,נ.
softness	רֹךְ,ז.
soft	רַךְ
to ride	רכב (רָכַב,יִרְכַּב)
train	רַכֶּבֶת,נ.
railroad station	תַּחֲנַת הָרַכֶּבֶת
concentration	רִכּוּז,ז.
softening	רִכּוּךְ,ז.
property	רְכוּשׁ,ז.
softness	רַכּוּת,נ.
to concentrate	רכז (רִכֵּז,יְרַכֵּז)
to concentrate oneself	הִתְרַכֵּז (הִתְרַכֵּז,יִתְרַכֵּז)
riding	רְכִיבָה,נ.
to acquire	רכש (רָכַשׁ,יִרְכֹּשׁ)
high	רָם
deceit	רַמָּאוּת,נ.
swindler	רַמַּאי,ז.
to deceive	רמה (רִמָּה,יְרַמֶּה)
height	רָמָה,נ.
pomegranate	רִמּוֹן
to hint	רמז (רָמַז,יִרְמֹז)
hint	רֶמֶז,ז.
hint;winking	רְמִיזָה,נ.
reptile	רֶמֶשׂ,ז.
singing;rejoicing	רִנָּה,נ.
bridle	רֶסֶן,ז.
bad	רַע
friend	רֵעַ,ז.
evil	רֹעַ
to be hungry	רעב (רָעֵב,יִרְעַב)
I'm hungry.	אֲנִי רָעֵב.
hunger	רָעָב,ז.
to tremble	רעד (רָעַד,יִרְעַד)
trembling	רַעַד,ז. רְעָדָה,נ.
to graze	רעה (רָעָה,יִרְעֶה)
evil	רָעָה

to furnish	רַהֵט (רָהַט,יְרַהֵט)
furniture	רָהִיטִים,ז"ר
gun	רוֹבֶה,ז.
wind; spirit;mood	רוּחַ,זו"נ (ר' רוּחוֹת)
breath of life	רוּחַ חַיִּים
spirit of wisdom	רוּחַ חָכְמָה
space, profit	רֶוַח,ז.
release	רְוָחָה,נ.
spiritual	רוּחָנִי
spirituality	רוּחָנִיּוּת,נ.
rider,horseman	רוֹכֵב,ז.
shepherd	רוֹעֶה,ז.
physician	רוֹפֵא,ז.
dentist	רוֹפֵא שִׁנַּיִם
to run	רוץ (רָץ,יָרוּץ)
to run to and fro	הִתְרוֹצֵץ (הִתְרוֹצֵץ,יִתְרוֹצֵץ)
murderer	רוֹצֵחַ,ז.
bachelor	רַוָּק,ז.
apothecary	רוֹקֵחַ,ז.
secret	רָז,ז.
lean	רָזֶה
leanness	רָזוֹן,ז.
to be wide	רחב (רָחַב,יִרְחַב)
to extend	הִרְחִיב (הִרְחִיב,יַרְחִיב)
wide,extensive	רָחָב,ז.
width,extent	רֹחַב,ז.
street	רְחוֹב,ז. (ר' רְחוֹבוֹת)
Allenby Street	רְחוֹב אַלֶנְבִּי
charitable	רַחוּם
far,distant	רָחוֹק
distance	רִחוּק,ז.
washing	רְחִיצָה,נ.
to have pity	רחם (רָחַם,יְרַחֵם)
womb	רֶחֶם,ז.
pity	רַחֲמִים,ז"ר
pity	רַחְמָנוּת,נ.
to wash	רחץ (רָחַץ,יִרְחַץ)
I washed my hands.	רָחַצְתִּי אֶת הַיָּדַיִם.
to wash oneself	הִתְרַחֵץ (הִתְרַחֵץ,יִתְרַחֵץ)
I bathed. (I washed myself.)	הִתְרַחַצְתִּי.

permitted — רַשַאי

רשה (הַרְשָׁה,יַרְשֶׁה) to permit, to allow

notes, sketch — רָשׁוּם,ז.

permit — רְשׁוּת,נ.

permit, list — רִשָׁיוֹן,ז.(ר' רִשְׁיוֹנוֹת)

list — רְשִׁימָה,נ.●

to record — רשם (רָשַׁם,יִרְשֹׁם)

impression — רֹשֶׁם,ז.

זֶה עָשָׂה עָלַי רֹשֶׁם כַּבִּיר. It made a great impression on me.

official — רִשְׁמִי

(רשע) הַרְשִׁיעַ,יַרְשִׁיעַ) to do evil; to accuse

viciousness — רֶשַׁע,ז.

sinner — רָשָׁע,ז.

net — רֶשֶׁת,נ.

to boil — רתח (רָתַח,יִרְתַּח)

to boil — הִרְתִּיחַ,יַרְתִּים)

hot-tempered — רַתְחָן,ז.

boiling — רְתִיחָה,נ.

to harness — רתם (רָתַם,יִרְתֹּם)

harness — רִתְמָה,נ.

ש

that — שֶׁ●

אֲנִי יוֹדֵעַ שֶׁאַתָּה בָּרִיא. I know that you are healthy.

to draw water, to attract — שאב (שָׁאַב,יִשְׁאַב)

magnet — אֶבֶן שׁוֹאֶבֶת,נ.

to roar — שאג (שָׁאַג,יִשְׁאַג)

roar — שְׁאָגָה,נ.

pit; hell — שְׁאוֹל,ז.

tumult — שָׁאוֹן,ז.

disgust — שָׁאַט (-נֶפֶשׁ)

drawing (water) — שְׁאִיבָה,נ.

striving — שְׁאִיפָה,נ.

to ask; to borrow — שאל (שָׁאַל,יִשְׁאַל)●

שָׁאַלְתִּי שְׁאֵלָה. I asked a question.

שָׁאַלְתִּי מִמֶּנּוּ סֵפֶר. I borrowed a book from him.

---

to lend — הִשְׁאִיל (הִשְׁאִיל,יַשְׁאִיל)

הִגֹּא הִשְׁאִיל לִי סֵפֶר. He lent me a book.

request; question — שְׁאֵלָה,נ.●

untroubled — שַׁאֲנָן

to remain — שאר (הִשְׁאֵר)(נִשְׁאַר,יִשָׁאֵר)●

to leave over — הִשְׁאִיר (הִשְׁאִיר,יַשְׁאִיר)

rest, remains — שְׁאָר,ז.

old; grandfather — שָׂב

captured — שָׁבֻי

week — שָׁבוּעַ,ז.(ר' שָׁבֻעוֹת)

vow, oath — שְׁבוּעָה,נ.

mistake — שִׁבּוּשׁ,ז.

captivity — שְׁבוּת,ז.

to praise; to improve; to ameliorate — שַׁבַּח (שָׁבַּח,יְשַׁבֵּחַ)

improvement; praise — שֶׁבַח,ז.

tribe; stick, staff — שֵׁבֶט,ז.

captivity — שְׁבִי

path — שְׁבִיל,ז.

for the sake of; for — בִּשְׁבִיל●

הַסֵּפֶר הַזֶּה בִּשְׁבִיל דָּוִד. This book is for David.

עָשִׂיתִי זֹאת בִּשְׁבִילוֹ. I did it for his sake.

seventh — שְׁבִיעִי

breaking — שְׁבִירָה,נ.

rest; strike — שְׁבִיתָה,נ.

ear of corn — שִׁבֹּלֶת,נ.(ר' שִׁבֳּלִים)

oats — שִׁבֹּלֶת שׁוּעָל,נ.

to get full — שבע (שָׂבַע,יִשְׂבַּע)

to satiate — הִשְׂבִּיעַ (הִשְׂבִּיעַ,יַשְׂבִּיעַ)

satiated — שָׂבֵעַ,ז.

satisfied — שְׂבַע רָצוֹן

satiation — שָׂבַע,ז.שָׂבְעָה,נ.

to swear — שבע (הִשָּׁבַע)(נִשְׁבַּע,יִשָׁבַע)

to cause to swear — הִשְׁבִּיעַ (הִשְׁבִּיעַ,יַשְׁבִּיעַ)

seven — שֶׁבַע,ז.שִׁבְעָה,נ.

seventy — שִׁבְעִים●

seven times — שִׁבְעָתַיִם

to break — שׁבר (שָׁבַר,יִשְׁבֹּר)

---

to be broken — הִשָּׁבֵר (נִשְׁבַּר,יִשָׁבֵר)

breakage; provision — שֶׁבֶר,ז.

receipt — שֹׁבֶר,ז.

fractions — שְׁבָרִים,ז"ר

to make a mistake — שבש (שָׁבַשׁ,יְשַׁבֵּשׁ)

to keep the Sabbath; to rest — שבת (שָׁבַת,יִשְׁבֹּת)

ceasing; sitting — שְׁבִתָה,נ.

sabbatical year; week; Sabbath — שַׁבָּת,נ.

rest — שַׁבָּתוֹן,ז.

to make a mistake — שגה (שָׁגָה,יִשְׁגֶּה)

I made a mistake. — שָׁגִיתִי.

to supervise; to watch — שגח (הִשְׁגִּיחַ)(הִשְׁגִּיחַ,יַשְׁגִּיחַ)

mistake — שְׁגִיאָה,נ.

to go mad — שגע (הִשְׁתַּגֵּעַ,יִשְׁתַּגֵּעַ)

madness — שִׁגָּעוֹן,ז.

breast — שַׁד,ז.

field — שָׂדֶה,ז"ון (ר' שָׂדוֹת)

match, proposed marriage — שִׁדּוּךְ,ז.

God Almighty — שַׁדַּי,ז.

to propose a match — שַׁדֵּךְ (שַׁדֵּךְ,יְשַׁדֵּךְ)

matchmaker — שַׁדְכָן,ז.

matchmaking — שַׁדְכָנוּת,נ.

to try, to endeavor — שדל (הִשְׁתַּדֵּל)(הִשְׁתַּדֵּל,יִשְׁתַּדֵּל)●

אֶשְׁתַּדֵּל לָבוֹא. I'll try to come.

אִם תִּשְׁתַּדֵּל,תַּצְלִיחַ. If you will try (exert yourself), you will succeed.

row — שְׁדֵרָה,נ.

backbone — חֹגֶט הַשִּׁדְרָה,ז.

lamb — שֶׂה,ז.

vanity; lie — שָׁוְא,ז.

in vain — לַשָּׁוְא

to return — שוב (שָׁב,יָשׁוּב)●

אֲנִי אָשׁוּב בְּעוֹד שָׁעָה. I'll return in an hour.

to give back; to answer — הֵשִׁיב (הֵשִׁיב,יָשִׁיב)

English	Hebrew
again	שׁוב
mischievous, naughty	שׁוֹבָב, שׁוֹבֵב, ז.
receipt	שׁוֹבֵר, ז.
to be like; to be equal; to be worth	שׁוה (שָׁוָה, יִשְׁוֶה)
They are equal in weight.	הֵם שָׁוִים בַּמִּשְׁקָל.
How much is it worth?	כַּמָּה זֶה שָׁוֶה?
to compare	הִשְׁוָה (הִשְׁוָה, יַשְׁוֶה)
worth; equal; like	שָׁוֶה, ז.
equality	שִׁוּיִי, ז.
equal rights	שִׁוּוּי זְכֻיוֹת, ז.
equal weight (balance)	שִׁוּוּי מִשְׁקָל
to row; to wander	שׁוט (שָׁט, יָשׁוּט)
whip	שׁוֹט, ז.
fool	שׁוֹטֶה, ז.
policeman	שׁוֹטֵר, ז.
equality	שִׁוָּיוֹן, ז.
indifference	שִׁוְיוֹן נֶפֶשׁ, ז.
hem, margin; bottom	שׁוּל, שׁוּלַיִם, ז.
fat	שֻׁמָּן, ז.
I like meat without fat.	אֲנִי אוֹהֵב בָּשָׂר בְּלִי שֻׁמָּן.
watchman, guard	שׁוֹמֵר, ז.
enemy	שׂוֹנֵא, ז.
fox	שׁוּעָל, ז.
doorkeeper	שׁוֹעֵר, ז.
judge	שׁוֹפֵט, ז.
ram's horn	שׁוֹפָר, ז. (ר' שׁוֹפָרוֹת)
market	שׁוּק, ז. (ר' שְׁוָקִים)
thigh	שׁוֹק, ז.
ox	שׁוֹר, ז. (ר' שְׁוָרִים)
line; row; avenue	שׁוּרָה, נ.
lily; rose	שׁוֹשָׁן, ז. שׁוֹשַׁנָּה, נ.
partner	שֻׁתָּף, ז.
plum	שְׁזִיף
bribe	שֹׁחַד, ז.
to swim	שׂחה (שָׂחָה, יִשְׂחֶה)
dark; brown	שָׁחֹם
consumptive	שַׁחֲנֶף
black	שָׁחֹר, ז.

to slaughter	שׁחט (שָׁחַט, יִשְׁחַט)
armpit	שֶׁחִי, ז.
swimming	שְׂחִיָּה, נ.
slaughter	שְׁחִיטָה, נ.
to thread	שׁחל (הִשְׁחִיל, יַשְׁחִיל)
consumption	שַׁחֶפֶת, נ.
to play; to mock	שׂחק (שָׂחַק, יִשְׂחַק)
to laugh	
to amuse; to play	שִׂחֵק (שִׂחֵק, יְשַׂחֵק)
performer	שַׂחְקָן
dawn	שַׁחַר, ז.
liberation	שִׁחְרוּר, ז.
black	שְׁחַרְחַר
morning	שַׁחֲרִית, נ.
to set free	שִׁחְרֵר (שִׁחְרֵר, יְשַׁחְרֵר)
to be set free; to liberate oneself	הִשְׁתַּחְרֵר (הִשְׁתַּחְרֵר, יִשְׁתַּחְרֵר)
flat	שָׁטוּחַ, ז.
overwhelmed	שָׁטוּף, ז.
nonsense	שְׁטוּת, נ.
surface	שֶׁטַח, ז.
superficial	שִׁטְחִי
superficiality	שִׁטְחִיּוּת, נ.
carpet, rug	שָׁטִיחַ, ז.
rinsing, washing	שְׁטִיפָה, נ.
Satan; adversary	שָׂטָן, ז.
current; velocity	שֶׁצֶף, ז.
bond; bill; document	שְׁטָר, ז. (ר' שְׁטָרוֹת)
promissory note	שְׁטַר חוֹב, ז.
gift	שַׁי, ז.
grey hair; old age	שֵׂיבָה, נ.
return	שִׁיבָה, נ.
conversation	שִׂיחָה, נ.
rowing, boating	שַׁיִט, ז.
system	שִׁיטָה, נ.
belonging	שַׁיָּךְ, ז.
To whom does it belong?	לְמִי זֶה שַׁיָּךְ?
relation	שַׁיָּכוּת, נ.
to put	שִׂים (שָׂם, יָשִׂים)
putting	שִׂימָה, נ.
to sing	שׁיר (שָׁר, יָשִׁיר)

song; poem	שִׁיר, ז.
caravan	שַׁיָּרָה, נ.
poetic	שִׁירִי
marble	שַׁיִשׁ, ז.
to lie down	שׁכב (שָׁכַב, יִשְׁכַּב)
He lay down to sleep early.	הוּא שָׁכַב לִישׁוֹן מֻקְדָּם.
layer	שִׁכְבָה, נ.
childless	שַׁכּוּל
childlessness	שִׁכּוּלִים, ז"ר
settlement, quarter	שְׁכוּנָה, נ.
drunkard	שִׁכּוֹר, ז.
to forget	שׁכח (שָׁכַח, יִשְׁכַּח)
I forgot.	שָׁכַחְתִּי.
to be forgotten	הִשָּׁכַח (נִשְׁכַּח, יִשָּׁכַח)
to make forget	הִשְׁכִּיחַ (הִשְׁכִּיחַ, יַשְׁכִּיחַ)
forgetting	שְׁכִחָה, נ.
forgetful	שַׁכְחָן
lying down	שְׁכִיבָה, נ.
knife	שַׂכִּין, ז.
divine spirit	שְׁכִינָה, נ.
hireling	שָׂכִיר, ז.
rent; wages	שְׂכִירוּת, נ.
intelligence	שֵׂכֶל, ז.
perfection	שִׁכְלוּל, ז.
intelligent	שִׂכְלִי
to perfect	שִׁכְלֵל (שִׁכְלֵל, יְשַׁכְלֵל)
to rise early	שׁכם (הִשְׁכִּים, יַשְׁכִּים)
shoulder	שְׁכֶם, ז.
to dwell	שׁכן (שָׁכַן, יִשְׁכֹּן)
neighbor	שָׁכֵן, ז.
neighborhood	שְׁכֵנוּת, נ.
to convince	שִׁכְנֵעַ (שִׁכְנֵעַ, יְשַׁכְנֵעַ)
to get drunk	שׁכר (הִשְׁתַּכֵּר, יִשְׁתַּכֵּר)
pay, wages	שֵׂכָר, ז.
beer	שֵׁכָר
rent	שְׂכַר דִּירָה
to hire	שׂכר (שָׂכַר, יִשְׂכֹּר)
to lease, to let	הִשְׂכִּיר (הִשְׂכִּיר, יַשְׂכִּיר)

English	Hebrew
What's new?	מַה נִּשְׁמַע?
to announce	הִשְׁמִיעַ (הִשְׁמִיעַ, יַשְׁמִיעַ)
hearing	שֶׁמַע ז.
to watch	שָׁמַר (שָׁמַר, יִשְׁמֹר)
to preserve	שִׁמֵּר (שִׁמֵּר, יְשַׁמֵּר)
to be careful	הִשָּׁמֵר (נִשְׁמַר, יִשָּׁמֵר)
to be preserved	הִשְׁתַּמֵּר (הִשְׁתַּמֵּר, יִשְׁתַּמֵּר)
sun	שֶׁמֶשׁ ז. (ר' שְׁמָשׁוֹת)
The sun set.	הַשֶּׁמֶשׁ בָּא.
The sun rose.	הַשֶּׁמֶשׁ עָלָה.
The sun rose.	הַשֶּׁמֶשׁ זָרַח.
dusk,twilight	בֵּין הַשְּׁמָשׁוֹת
to serve	שִׁמֵּשׁ (שִׁמֵּשׁ, יְשַׁמֵּשׁ)
to use	הִשְׁתַּמֵּשׁ (הִשְׁתַּמֵּשׁ, יִשְׁתַּמֵּשׁ)
servant	שַׁמָּשׁ ז.
windowpane	שִׁמְשָׁה נ.
sunshade	שִׁמְשִׁיָּה נ.
ivory;tooth	שֵׁן נ. (ר' שִׁנַּיִם)
artificial tooth	שֵׁן תּוֹתֶבֶת נ.
dentist	רוֹפֵא שִׁנַּיִם
to hate	שָׂנֵא (שָׂנֵא, יִשְׂנָא)
hatred	שִׂנְאָה נ.
year	שָׁנָה נ. (ר' שָׁנִים)
two years	שְׁנָתַיִם
sleep	שֵׁנָה נ.
change,alteration	שִׁנּוּי ז.
second	שֵׁנִי ז.
Monday	יוֹם שֵׁנִי
second	שְׁנִיָּה נ.
Sixty seconds in a minute.	שִׁשִּׁים שְׁנִיּוֹת בְּדַקָּה.
two	שְׁנַיִם ז. שְׁתַּיִם נ.
again	שֵׁנִית
yearly	שְׁנָתִי
to subdue	שִׁעְבֵּד (שִׁעְבֵּד, יְשַׁעְבֵּד)
subjection	שִׁעְבּוּד ז.
hour;time	שָׁעָה נ.
while	בְּשָׁעָה שֶׁ-
at any hour	בְּכָל שָׁעָה
a while	שָׁעָה קַלָּה
wax	שַׁעֲוָה נ.

complete	שָׁלֵם
perfection	שְׁלֵמוּת נ.
perfectly	בִּשְׁלֵמוּת
three	שְׁלֹשָׁה ז. שָׁלֹשׁ נ.
diarrhea	שִׁלְשׁוּל ז.
day before yesterday	שִׁלְשׁוֹם
chain	שַׁלְשֶׁלֶת נ.
there	שָׁם
You will find him there.	תִּמְצָא אוֹתוֹ שָׁם.
noun;name	שֵׁם ז. (שֵׁמוֹת)
in honor of the Lord	לְשֵׁם שָׁמַיִם
for its own sake	לִשְׁמָהּ
God	הַשֵּׁם
good reputation	שֵׁם טוֹב
first name	שֵׁם פְּרָטִי
left	שְׂמֹאל ז.
left,right	שְׂמֹאל, יָמִין
left	שְׂמָאלִי ז.
there	שָׁמָּה
Go (to) there.	לֵךְ שָׁמָּה.
rumor	שְׁמוּעָה נ.
use	שִׁמּוּשׁ ז.
useful	שִׁמּוּשִׁי
to be glad	שָׂמַח (שָׂמַח, יִשְׂמַח)
to gladden	שִׂמַּח (שִׂמַּח, יְשַׂמַּח)
glad	שָׂמֵחַ
joy	שִׂמְחָה נ.
blanket	שְׂמִיכָה נ.
heaven;skies	שָׁמַיִם ז"ר
God-fearing	יְרֵא שָׁמַיִם
for the sake of God	לְשֵׁם שָׁמַיִם
eighth	שְׁמִינִי
eighth part	שְׁמִינִית נ.
hearing	שְׁמִיעָה נ.
watching	שְׁמִירָה נ.
dress	שִׂמְלָה נ.
waste	שְׁמָמָה נ.
to be fat	שָׁמֵן (שָׁמֵן, יִשְׁמַן)
fat (adj.)	שָׁמֵן ז.
oil,fat	שֶׁמֶן ז.
eight	שְׁמֹנָה ז. שְׁמֹנֶה נ.
eighty	שְׁמֹנִים
cream	שַׁמֶּנֶת נ.
to hear	שָׁמַע (שָׁמַע, יִשְׁמַע)

Apartment to let	דִירה להשׂכיר
to earn	הִשָּׂכֵר (הִשְׂתַּכֵּר, יִשְׂתַּכֵּר)
drunkenness	שִׁכָּרוֹן ז. שִׁכְרוּת נ.
of	שֶׁל
mine	שֶׁלִּי
your	שֶׁלְּךָ
rung (of a ladder)	שָׁלָב ז.
snow	שֶׁלֶג ז.
skeleton	שֶׁלֶד ז.
flame	שַׁלְהֶבֶת נ.
quiet	שָׁלֵו, שָׁלִיו ז.
peace	שַׁלְוָה נ.
greeting;peace	שָׁלוֹם ז.
How are you?	מַה שְׁלוֹמְךָ?
paying	שִׁלּוּם ז.
trinity	שִׁלּוּשׁ ז.
to send; to stretch out	שָׁלַח (שָׁלַח, יִשְׁלַח)
to cast out	שָׁלַח (שָׁלַח, יִשְׁלַח)
table	שֻׁלְחָן ז. (ר' שֻׁלְחָנוֹת)
to rule	שָׁלַט (שָׁלַט, יִשְׁלֹט)
sign;shield	שֶׁלֶט ז.
On the sign is written, "No Smoking."	עַל הַשֶּׁלֶט כָּתוּב: אָסוּר לְעַשֵּׁן.
power;rule	שִׁלְטוֹן ז.
messenger	שָׁלִיחַ ז.
cantor	שְׁלִיחַ צִבּוּר ז.
mission	שְׁלִיחוּת נ.
ruler	שַׁלִּיס ז.
ruling	שְׁלִיסָה נ.
negation	שְׁלִילָה נ.
negative	שְׁלִילִי
I received a negative answer.	קִבַּלְתִּי תְּשׁוּבָה שְׁלִילִית.
adjutant	שָׁלִישׁ ז.
a third	שְׁלִישׁ ז.
third	שְׁלִישִׁי
to throw	שָׁלַךְ (הִשְׁלִיךְ, יַשְׁלִיךְ)
to pay	שִׁלֵּם (שִׁלֵּם, יְשַׁלֵּם)
to complete;to conciliate	הִשְׁלִים (הִשְׁלִים, יַשְׁלִים)
to perfect oneself	הִשְׁתַּלֵּם (הִשְׁתַּלֵּם, יִשְׁתַּלֵּם)

cough — שָׁעוּל, ז.

clock — שָׁעוֹן, ז.

bean — שְׁעוּעִית, נ.

measure — שָׁעוּר, ז.

lesson — שִׁעוּר, ז.

hairy — שָׂעִיר

to cough — (הִשְׁתַּעֵל)(הִשְׁתַּעֵל, יִשְׁתַּעֵל)

whooping cough — שַׁעֶלֶת, נ.

to be bored — (הִשְׁתַּעְמֵם)(הִשְׁתַּעְמֵם, יִשְׁתַּעְמֵם)

boredom — שִׁעְמוּם, ז.

to lean — שָׁעַן (הִשָּׁעֵן)(נִשְׁעַן, יִשָּׁעֵן)

watchmaker — שָׁעָן, ז.

to value, to suppose — שָׁעַר (שִׁעֵר)(שָׁעַר, יְשַׁעֵר)

gate — שַׁעַר, ז.

doorkeeper — שֹׁעֵר, ז.

hair — שֵׂעָר, ז. שַׂעֲרָה, נ.

to play with — שַׁעֲשֵׁעַ (הִשְׁתַּעֲשֵׁעַ)(הִשְׁתַּעֲשֵׁעַ, יִשְׁתַּעֲשֵׁעַ)

lip;language;speech — שָׂפָה, נ. (ז' שְׂפָתַיִם, ר' שְׂפָתוֹת, שָׂפוֹת)

judgment — שִׁפּוּט, ז.

slave;servant — שִׁפְחָה, נ.

to judge — שָׁפַט (שָׁפַט, יִשְׁפֹּט)

to be sentenced — הִשָּׁפֵט (נִשְׁפַּט, יִשָּׁפֵט)

outpouring — שְׁפִיכָה, נ.

to pour out — שָׁפַךְ (שָׁפַךְ, יִשְׁפֹּךְ)

to overflow — הִשְׁתַּפֵּךְ (הִשְׁתַּפֵּךְ, יִשְׁתַּפֵּךְ)

mean,low — שָׁפָל, ז.

meanness — שִׁפְלוּת, נ.

mustache — שָׂפָם, ז.

rabbit — שָׁפָן, ז.

abundance — שֶׁפַע, ז.

to influence — שֶׁפַע (הִשְׁפִּיעַ)(הִשְׁפִּיעַ, יַשְׁפִּיעַ)

pipe — שְׁפוֹפֶרֶת, נ.

to rub — שִׁפְשֵׁף (שִׁפְשֵׁף, יְשַׁפְשֵׁף)

sack — שַׂק, ז.

to be diligent — שָׁקַד (שָׁקַד, יִשְׁקֹד)

almond — שָׁקֵד, ז.

diligent — שַׁקְדָן

to water, to irrigate — שָׁקָה (הִשְׁקָה)(הִשְׁקָה, יַשְׁקֶה)

drink — שִׁקְנִי, ז.

weighing — שִׁקּוּל, ז.

considering — שִׁקּוּל הַדַּעַת, ז.

transparent — שָׁקוּף

to be quiet — שָׁקַט (שָׁקַט, יִשְׁקֹט)

to calm down,to soothe — הִשְׁקִיט (הִשְׁקִיט, יַשְׁקִיט)

quiet — שֶׁקֶט, ז.

quiet — שָׁקֵט

setting of the sun — שְׁקִיעָה, נ.

to weigh — שָׁקַל (שָׁקַל, יִשְׁקֹל)

How much does it weigh? — כַּמָּה זֶה שׁוֹקֵל?

shekel (coin) — שֶׁקֶל, ז.

to set; to sink — שָׁקַע (שָׁקַע, יִשְׁקַע)

to invest; to sink — הִשְׁקִיעַ (הִשְׁקִיעַ, יַשְׁקִיעַ)

to settle — הִשְׁתַּקַּע (הִשְׁתַּקַּע, יִשְׁתַּקַּע)

to lie — שָׁקַר (שָׁקַר, יִשְׁקֹר)

lie — שֶׁקֶר, ז.

sovereign;officer — שַׂר, ז.

singer — שָׁר, ז.

heat — שָׁרָב, ז.

uniform — שְׂרָד (בִּגְדֵי שְׂרָד)

princess — שָׂרָה, נ.

shoelace — שְׂרוֹךְ, ז.

sleeve — שַׁרְוָל, שַׁרְווּל, ז.

service — שֵׁרוּת, ז.

to make incisions;to scratch — שָׂרַט (שָׂרַט, יִשְׂרֹט)

drawing — שִׂרְטוּט, ז.

to draw; to line — שִׂרְטֵט (שִׂרְטֵט, יְשַׂרְטֵט)

remainder — שָׂרִיד, ז.

whistling — שְׁרִיקָה, נ.

muscle — שְׁרִיר, ז.

to burn — שָׂרַף (שָׂרַף, יִשְׂרֹף)

angel — שָׂרָף, ז.

fire — שְׂרֵפָה, נ.

reptile — שֶׁרֶץ, ז.

to whistle — שָׁרַק (שָׁרַק, יִשְׁרֹק)

to uproot — שֵׁרֵשׁ (שֵׁרֵשׁ, יְשָׁרֵשׁ)

to take root — הִשְׁרִישׁ (הִשְׁרִישׁ, יַשְׁרִישׁ)

to take root — הִשְׁתָּרֵשׁ (הִשְׁתָּרֵשׁ, יִשְׁתָּרֵשׁ)

basis,root — שֹׁרֶשׁ, ז.

chain — שַׁרְשֶׁרֶת, נ.

joy — שָׂשׂוֹן, ז.

sixth — שִׁשִּׁי, ז.

Friday — יוֹם שִׁשִּׁי

sixty — שִׁשִּׁים

sixth part — שִׁשִּׁית, נ.

buttocks — שֵׁת, ז.

to drink — שָׁתָה (שָׁתָה, יִשְׁתֶּה)

drinking — שְׁתִיָּה, נ.

sapling — שְׁתִיל, ז.

two — שְׁתַּיִם, נ.

silence — שְׁתִיקָה, נ.

to plant — שָׁתַל (שָׁתַל, יִשְׁתֹּל)

to urinate — שָׁתַן (הִשְׁתִּין)(הִשְׁתִּין, יַשְׁתִּין)

urine — שֶׁתֶן, ז.

to let share — שִׁתֵּף (שִׁתֵּף, יְשַׁתֵּף)

to participate — הִשְׁתַּתֵּף (הִשְׁתַּתֵּף, יִשְׁתַּתֵּף)

partner — שֻׁתָּף, ז.

partnership — שֻׁתָּפוּת, נ.

to be silent — שָׁתַק (שָׁתַק, יִשְׁתֹּק)

silent person — שַׁתְקָן, ז.

ת

desire — תַּאֲבָה, נ.

appetite — תֵּאָבוֹן, ז.

with good appetite — לְתֵאָבוֹן, בְּתֵאָבוֹן

passion — תַּאֲוָה, נ.

symmetry — תְּאוּם, ז.

twins — תְּאוֹמִים, ז"ר

description — תֵּאוּר, ז.

fig — תְּאֵנָה, נ. (ר' תְּאֵנִים)

to describe — תֵּאֵר (תֵּאֵר, יְתָאֵר)

description;shape — תֹּאַר, ז.

adverb — תֹּאַר הַפֹּעַל

adjective — תֹּאַר הַשֵּׁם

date — תַּאֲרִיךְ, ז.

English	Hebrew
garment	תִּלְבֹּשֶׁת,נ.
to hang up; to suspend	תלה (תָּלָה,יִתְלֶה)
hanging	תָּלוּי
It depends on you.	זֶה תָּלוּי בְּךָ.
steep	תָּלוּל,ז.
hanging	תְּלִיָּה,נ.
hangman	תַּלְיָן,ז.
furrow,garden bed	תֶּלֶם,ז.
teaching;Talmud	תַּלְמוּד,ז.
pupil	תַּלְמִיד,ז.
curls	תַּלְתַּלִּים,ז.ר.
simple;guiltless; pious;complete	תָּם,ז.
innocence	תֹּם,ז.
to wonder	תמה (תָּמַה,יִתְמַה)
stupefaction	תִּמָּהוֹן,ז.
yesterday as before	תְּמוֹל שִׁלְשׁוֹם
picture	תְּמוּנָה,נ.
exchange	תְּמוּרָה,נ.
always	תָּמִיד
constancy	תְּמִידוּת,נ.
constant	תְּמִידִי
astonishment, amazement	תְּמִיהָ,תְּמִיהָה,נ.
relief;support	תְּמִיכָה,נ.
innocent;whole	תָּמִים,ז.
innocence; simplicity	תְּמִימוּת,נ.
to support	תמך (תָּמַך,יִתְמֹך)
essence	תַּמְצִית,נ.
palm,date	תָּמָר,ז.
condition	תְּנַאי,ז.
on condition that	בִּתְנַאי שֶׁ-
injunction	צַו עַל תְּנַאי
produce	תְּנוּבָה,נ.
lobe of the ear	תְּנוּך (-אֹזֶן),ז.
slumber	תְּנוּמָה,נ.
movement	תְּנוּעָה,נ.
There was a great deal of traffic in the street.	הָיְתָה תְּנוּעָה רַבָּה בָּרְחוֹב.
swinging	תְּנוּפָה,נ.
oven	תַּנּוּר,ז.

Law of Moses, Pentateuch	תּוֹרַת מֹשֶׁה, הַתּוֹרָה
The Written Law	תּוֹרָה שֶׁבִּכְתָב
The Oral Law	תּוֹרָה שֶׁבְּעַל פֶּה
resident,inhabitant	תּוֹשָׁב,ז.
cannon	תּוֹתָח,ז.
band,orchestra	תִּזְמֹרֶת,נ.
bandage	תַּחְבֹּשֶׁת,נ.
boundary	תְּחוּם,ז.
feeling	תְּחוּשָׁה,נ.
(weather) forecast	תַּחֲזִית
resurrection	תְּחִיָּה,נ.
to begin	תחל (הֵחֵל)(הִתְחִיל,יַתְחִיל)
beginning	תְּחִלָּה,נ.
at first	בַּתְּחִלָּה
station	תַּחֲנָה,נ.
under	תַּחַת
lower	תַּחְתּוֹן,ז.
underwear	תַּחְתּוֹנִים
bottom;subway	תַּחְתִּית,נ.
journey,tour	תִּיּוּר,ז.
middle	תִּיכוֹן,ז.
Mediterranean	הַיָּם הַתִּיכוֹן
right away	תֵּיכָף,תֵּיכֶף וּמִיָּד
south;Yemen	תֵּימָן,ז.
suckling,infant	תִּינוֹק,ז.
brief case	תִּיק,ז.
traveler,tourist	תַּיָּר,ז.
goat	תַּיִשׁ,ז.
parrot	תֻּכִּי,ז.
sky-blue	תָּכֹל,ז.
sky-blue	תְּכֵלֶת,נ.
purpose,end	תַּכְלִית,נ.
content	תֹּכֶן,ז.
What are the contents of the story?	מָה הַתֹּכֶן שֶׁל הַסִפּוּר?
it might happen	(תכן) יִתָּכֵן
plan;program	תָּכְנִית,נ.
curriculum	תָּכְנִית לְמּוּדִים
strategy	תַכְסִיסֵי מִלְחָמָה,ז"ר
covering	תַּכְרִיך,ז.
shroud	תַּכְרִיכִים,ז"ר
jewelry	תַּכְשִׁיט,ז.
heap;hill	תֵּל,ז.

What's today's date?	מַה הַתַּאֲרִיךְ הַיּוֹם?
box;ark	תֵּבָה,נ.
mailbox	תֵּבַת דֹּאַר
grain,produce	תְּבוּאָה,נ.
understanding	תְּבוּנָה,נ.
earth	תֵּבֵל,נ.
straw	תֶּבֶן,ז.
model	תַּבְנִית,נ.
to summon; to demand	תבע (תָּבַע,יִתְבַּע)
fire	תַּבְעֵרָה,נ.
cooked food	תַּבְשִׁיל,ז.
discovery	תַּגְלִית,נ.
recompense	תַּגְמוּל,ז.
frequent,constant	תָּדִיר
emptiness	תֹּהוּ,ז.
depth, bottom (of the sea)	תְּהוֹם,ז"ו(ר' תְּהוֹמוֹת)
praise	תְּהִלָּה,נ.
procession	תַּהֲלוּכָה,נ.
revolution	תַּהְפּוּכָה,נ.
accuser	תּוֹבֵעַ,ז.
grief	תּוּגָה,נ.
thanks	תּוֹדָה,נ.
many thanks	תּוֹדָה רַבָּה
gratefully	בְּתוֹדָה
interior	תּוֹךְ,תָּוֶךְ,ז.
inside	בְּתוֹךְ
into	לְתוֹךְ
therefore	מִתּוֹךְ כַּךְ
worm	תּוֹלָע,ז. תּוֹלַעַת,נ.
addition	תּוֹסֶפֶת,נ.
abomination	תּוֹעֵבָה,נ.
use	תּוֹעֶלֶת,נ.
What's the use? What's the advantage?	מַה הַתּוֹעֶלֶת?
consequence	תּוֹצָאָה,נ.
issues,results	תּוֹצָאוֹת,נ"ר
score (results of the game)	תּוֹצָאוֹת הַמִּשְׂחָק
production	תּוֹצֶרֶת,נ.
column;line;turn	תּוֹר
Stand in line!	עֲמֹד בַּתּוֹר!
Now it's my turn.	עַכְשָׁו תּוֹרִי.
religion;doctrine; law	תּוֹרָה,נ.

translation	●תַּרְגּוּם,ז.	tasteless	תָּפֵל	consolation	תַּנְחוּמִים,ז"ר
exercise	תַּרְגִּיל,ז.	prayer	●תְּפִלָּה,נ.	whale	תַּנִּין,ז.
	●תִּרְגֵּם (תִּרְגֵּם,יְתַרְגֵּם)	to grasp	(תָּפַס,יִתְפֹּס)	fermenting	תְּסִיסָה,נ.
to translate		to drum	(תָּפַף,יְתֹף)	haircut;hairdressing	תִּסְפֹּרֶת,נ.
interpreter,	תֻּרְגְּמָן,ז.	function	תַּפְקִיד,ז.	to stray	(תָּעָה,יִתְעֶה)
translator		to sew	(תָּפַר,יִתְפֹּר)	to mislead	(הִתְעָה,יַתְעֶה)
spinach	תֶּרֶד,ז.	to stitch	תִּפֵּר (תִּפֵּר,יְתַפֵּר)	attestation;diploma	תְּעוּדָה
sound sleep	תַּרְדֵּמָה,נ.	menu	תַּפְרִיט	channel	תְּעָלָה,נ.
joyful shouting;	תְּרוּעָה,נ.	to catch	(תָּפַשׂ,יִתְפֹּשׂ)	propaganda	תַּעֲמוּלָה,נ.
alarm		to climb	(תִּפֵּשׂ,יְתַפֵּשׂ)	pleasure	●תַּעֲנוּג,ז.
medicine	תְּרוּפָה,נ.	hope	תִּקְוָה,נ.	with pleasure	בְּתַעֲנוּג
excuse;answer	תֵּרוּץ,ז.	correction	תִּקּוּן,ז.	fasting	תַּעֲנִית,נ.
shutter	תְּרִיס,ז.	epoch	תְּקוּפָה,נ.	razor	תַּעַר,ז.
dozen	●תְּרֵיסָר,ז.	blowing of a horn	תְּקִיעָה,נ.	exhibition	●תַּעֲרוּכָה,נ.
mast	תֹּרֶן,ז.	strong	תַּקִּיף,ז.	industry	תַּעֲשִׂיָּה,נ.
cock	תַּרְנְגֹל,ז.	to improve;	תִּקֵּן (תִּקֵּן,יְתַקֵּן)	drum	תֹּף,ז.
hen	תַּרְנְגֹלֶת,נ.	to correct		decoration	תַּפְאוּרָה,נ.
sketch	תַּרְשִׁים,ז.	improvement	תַּקָּנָה,נ.	splendor	תִּפְאָרָה,תִּפְאֶרֶת,נ.
answer;repentance	תְּשׁוּבָה	to blow a	(תָּקַע,יִתְקַע)	orange	תַּפּוּז,ז.
help	תְּשׁוּעָה,נ.	horn,to stick into		apple	●תַּפּוּחַ,ז.
desire	תְּשׁוּקָה,נ.	to assail;	(תָּקַף,יִתְקֹף)	potato	תַּפּוּחַ אֲדָמָה,ז.
ninth	תְּשִׁיעִי,ז.	to overpower		orange	תַּפּוּחַ זָהָב,ז.
ninth part	תְּשִׁיעִית,נ.	violence	תֹּקֶף,ז.	occupied	●תָּפוּס
payment	●תַּשְׁלוּם,ז.	budget	תַּקְצִיב,ז.	This	הַמָּקוֹם הַזֶּה תָּפוּס.
nine	●תֵּשַׁע,תִּשְׁעָה,ז.	ceiling	תִּקְרָה,נ.	place is occupied.	
ninety	●תִּשְׁעִים	civilization;	תַּרְבּוּת,נ.	apprehension;	תְּפִיסָה,נ.
		culture;taming		grasping	
		cultured	בֶּן תַּרְבּוּת	sewing	תְּפִירָה,נ.

English-Hebrew DICTIONARY

A

abandon (to)	עָזַב
abbreviate (to)	קָצֵר
abbreviation	קִצוּר
ability	יְכֹלֶת
able (to be)	יָכֹל
able-bodied	בָּרִיא
aboard	עַל, בְּ-
abolish (to)	בִּטֵּל
about	סָבִיב, עַל, בְּעֵרֶךְ
about the end of the month.	בְּעֵרֶךְ בְּסוֹף הַחֹדֶשׁ
What's it about?	עַל מַה זֶה?
above	מֵעַל
above all	יוֹתֵר מִכֹּל
abroad	חוּץ לָאָרֶץ
absence	חֶסֶר
absent	חָסֵר
absent-minded	מְפֻזָּר
absolute	מֻחְלָט
absorb (to)	קָלַט
abstain from (to)	נִמְנַע מִ-
abstract	מֻפְשָׁט
absurd	מְגֻחָךְ
abundance	רֹב
abundant	רַב
abuse	גִּדּוּף
abuse (to)	גִּדֵּף
academic	אֲקָדֵמִי
academy	אֲקָדֶמְיָה
accelerate (to)	מִהֵר
accelerator	מֵחִישׁ
accent	טַעַם, נְגִינָה
accent (to)	הִטְעִים
accept (to)	קִבֵּל
accident	מִקְרֶה, אָסוֹן
accidental	מִקְרִי
accidentally	בְּמִקְרֶה
acclimated (to be)	הִתְאַקְלֵם, יִתְאַקְלֵם
accommodate (to)	סִגֵּל, הִתְאִים
accommodation	הַתְאָמָה
accompaniment	לִוּוּי
accompany (to)	לִוָּה
accomplish(to)	הוֹצִיא לַפֹּעַל
accord	הֶסְכֵּם
according to	לְפִי
account	חֶשְׁבּוֹן
on account of	מִפְּנֵי
accuracy	דִּיּוּק
accurate	מְדֻיָּק
accuse (to)	הֶאֱשִׁים
accustom (to)	הִרְגִּיל
ace	יְחִידָה, אַלּוּף
ache	כְּאֵב
headache	כְּאֵב רֹאשׁ
ache (to)	כָּאַב
It hurts me.	כּוֹאֵב לִי
achieve(to)	הִשִּׂיג
achievement	הֶשֵּׂג
acid (adj.)	חָמוּץ
acid (n.)	חֻמְצָה
acknowledge (to)	הוֹדָה
acquaintance	מַכִּיר
acquire (to)	רָכַשׁ
across	מֵעֵבֶר
act	מַעֲשֶׂה
act (to)	שִׂחֵק
(to) act as	לְשַׁמֵּשׁ
action	פְּעֻלָּה
activity	פְּעִילוּת
actor	שַׂחְקָן
actual	מַמָּשִׁי
acute	חַד, חָרִיף
adapt (to)	הִסְתַּגֵּל
add (to)	חִבֵּר
addition	חִבּוּר
in addition to	נוֹסָף לְ-
address	כְּתֹבֶת
address (to)	פָּנָה אֶל
adequate	מַסְפִּיק
adhesive	דֶּבֶק
adjective	תֹּאַר הַשֵּׁם
adjoining	מְחֻבָּר
adjoining rooms	חֲדָרִים סְמוּכִים
administer (to)	נִהֵל
administration	הַנְהָלָה
admiration	הַעֲרָצָה
admire (to)	הֶעֱרִיץ
admission	כְּנִיסָה
ticket of admission	כַּרְטִיס כְּנִיסָה
admit (to)	הִכְנִיס
admittance	כְּנִיסָה
Free admittance.	כְּנִיסָה חָפְשִׁית
No admittance.	הַכְּנִיסָה אֲסוּרָה
adolescent (n.)	מִתְבַּגֵּר
adopt (to)	אִמֵּץ
adopted child	יֶלֶד מְאֻמָּץ
adorable	חִנָּנִי
adult	בּוֹגֵר
advance	הִתְקַדְּמוּת
in advance	לְמַפְרֵעַ
advance (to)	הִתְקַדֵּם
advantage	יִתְרוֹן
adventure	הַרְפַּתְקָה
adverb	תֹּאַר הַפֹּעַל
advertise (to)	פִּרְסֵם
advertisement	פִּרְסֹמֶת
advice	עֵצָה
advise (to)	יָעַץ
affair	עֵסֶק, עִנְיָן
affected	מְלָאכוּתִי
affection	חִבָּה
affectionate	מָלֵא חִבָּה
affirm (to)	אִשֵּׁר
afloat	צָף
afraid	מְפַחֵד
after	אַחֲרֵי

afternoon	אַחֲרֵי הַצָּהֳרַיִם	alive	חַי	amuse (to)	כִּנַּח
afterward(s)	אַחֲרֵי-כֵן	all (n.)	כֹּל	amusement	הֲנָאָה
again	עוֹד פַּעַם	all (adj.)	כָּל	amusing	מְבַדֵּחַ
never again	לְעוֹלָם לֹא	all day	כָּל הַיּוֹם	analyze (to)	נִתַּח
against	נֶגֶד	alley	סִמְטָה	ancestor	אָב
age	גִיל	alliance	בְּרִית	anchor	עֹגֶן
of age	מְבֻגָּר	allow (to)	הִרְשָׁה	ancient	עָתִיק
under age	קָטָן	allowed	מֻתָּר	and	וְ-
age (to)	הִזְקִין	ally	בֶּן-בְּרִית	anecdote	סִפּוּר
agency	סוֹכְנוּת	almost	כִּמְעַט	angel	מַלְאָךְ
agent	סוֹכֵן	alone	יְחִידִי	anger	כַּעַס
aggravate (to)	הִרְגִּיז	along	לְאֹרֶךְ, עַל-יַד	angle	זָוִית, פִּנָּה
aggressive	תּוֹקֵף	all along	כָּל הָעֵת הַהִיא	angry	כּוֹעֵס
agnostic	כּוֹפֵר	along the side	לְאֹרֶךְ הַצַּד	(to) get angry	כָּעַס
ago		(to) go along	הִסְכִּים	animal	חַיָּה
five years ago	לִפְנֵי חָמֵשׁ שָׁנִים	aloud	בְּקוֹל	animate (to)	הֶחֱיָה
long ago	מִזְּמַן	alphabet	אָלֶף בֵּית	ankle	קַרְסוֹל
agree (to)	הִסְכִּים	already	כְּבָר	annihilate (to)	הָרַס
agreeable	נוֹחַ	also	גַם	anniversary	יוֹם הַשָּׁנָה
agreement	הַסְכָּמָה, הֶסְכֵּם	altar	מִזְבֵּחַ	announce (to)	הוֹדִיעַ
as per agreement	לְפִי הַהֶסְכֵּם	alter (to)	שִׁנָּה	annoy (to)	הִרְגִּיז
agricultural	חַקְלָאִי	alteration	שִׁנּוּי	annual	שְׁנָתִי
agriculture	חַקְלָאוּת	alternately	זֶה אַחַר זֶה	annul (to)	בִּטֵּל
ahead	קָרָאשׁ	although	לַמְרוֹת	anonymous	אַלְמוֹנִי
aid	עֶזְרָה	altitude	גֹּבַה	another	אַחֵר
first aid	עֶזְרָה רִאשׁוֹנָה	aluminum	אֲלוּמִינְיוּם	in another hour	בְּעוֹד שָׁעָה
aid (to)	עָזַר	always	תָּמִיד	answer	תְּשׁוּבָה
aim	מַטָּרָה	amaze (to)	הִפְלִיא	answer (to)	עָנָה
aim (to)	כִּוֵּן	amazed (to be)	הִתְפַּלֵּא	anthem	הִמְנוֹן
air	אֲוִיר	amazement	הִתְפַּלְּאוּת	anticipate (to)	הִקְדִּים
air mail	דֹּאַר אֲוִיר	ambassador	שַׁגְרִיר	antique	עַתִּיקָה
airplane	מָטוֹס	ambitious	חָרוּץ	anti-Semite	אַנְטִי-שֵׁמִי
aisle	שְׁגָרָה	ambush	מַאְרָב	anxiety	דְּאָגָה
alarm (to)	עוֹרֵר פַּחַד	amend (to)	שִׁנָּה, תִּקֵּן	anxious	דּוֹאֵג
alarm clock	שָׁעוֹן מְעוֹרֵר	amends	תַּשְׁלוּמֵי נֶזֶק	any	אֵיזֶה
alcohol	אַלְכֹּהֹל	American	אֲמֵרִיקָנִי	anybody	מִי שֶׁהוּא
alert	עֵר	among	בֵּין	anyhow	בְּכָל אֹפֶן
alien	זָר	amount	סְכוּם	anything	מַשֶּׁהוּ
alike	דּוֹמֶה	ample	דַּי, מַסְפִּיק	anywhere	בְּכָל מָקוֹם שֶׁהוּא

apart	לְבַד	arm	זְרוֹעַ	assimilation	הִתְבּוֹלְלוּת
apartment	דִּירָה	arm in arm	שְׁלוּבֵי זְרוֹעַ	assist (to)	עָזַר
apologize (to)	בִּקֵּשׁ סְלִיחָה	armistice	כְּרִית שָׁלוֹם	assistance	עֶזְרָה
apparent	בָּרוּר	army	צָבָא	associate	שֻׁתָּף
apparently	כַּנִּרְאֶה	around	מִסָּבִיב	associate (to)	הִשְׁתַּתֵּף
appeal (to)	בִּקֵּשׁ	arouse (to)	עוֹרֵר	assume (to)	קִבֵּל עַל עַצְמוֹ
appear (to)	הוֹפִיעַ	arrange (to)	סִדֵּר	assurance	הַבְטָחָה
appearance	צוּרָה	arrangement	סִדּוּר	self-assurance	בִּטָּחוֹן עַצְמִי
appease (to)	פִּיֵּס	arrest	עֲצִירָה	assure (to)	הִבְטִיחַ
appendix	נִסְפָּח	arrest (to)	עָצַר	astonish (to)	הִפְלִיא
appetite	תֵּאָבוֹן	arrival	כְּנִיסָה	astounded	מֻפְתָּע
applaud (to)	מָחָא כַּף	arrive (to)	הִגִּיעַ	astounding	מַפְתִּיעַ
applause	מְחִיאַת כַּפַּיִם	art	אָמָנוּת, אֻמָּנוּת	asylum	מִקְלָט
apple	תַּפּוּחַ	artery	עוֹרֵק	at	בְּ, אֵצֶל
application	תַּקְלִישׁ	article	דָּבָר	at first	בָּרִאשׁוֹנָה
apply (to)	הִגִּישׁ בַּקָּשָׁה	artificial	מְלָאכוּתִי	at last	לְבַסּוֹף
appoint (to)	מִנָּה	artist	אָמָן	at once	מִיָּד
appointment	מִנּוּי	artistic	אָמָנוּתִי	at the same time	בְּאוֹתוֹ זְמָן
appreciate (to)	הֶעֱרִיךְ	as	כְּמוֹ	at that time	בַּזְּמָן הַהוּא
appreciation	הַעֲרָכָה	as...as...	כְּמוֹ...	at two o'clock	בְּשָׁעָה שְׁתַּיִם
approach (to)	הִתְקָרֵב	as if	כְּאִלּוּ	at work	בַּעֲבוֹדָה
appropriate	מַתְאִים	as long as	כָּל זְמַן שֶׁ-	We were at David's.	הָיִינוּ אֵצֶל דָּוִד.
approval	הַסְכָּמָה	as soon as	כַּאֲשֶׁר		
approve (to)	הִסְכִּים, אִשֵּׁר	as well	כְּמוֹ כֵן	athlete	אַתְלֵט
approximately	בְּעֶרֶךְ	ascertain (to)	הוֹכִיחַ	athletic	אַתְלֵטִי
April	אַפְרִיל	Asia	אַסְיָה	athletics	אַתְלֵטִיקָה
apron	סִנָּר	ash	אֵפֶר	atmosphere	אֲוִירָה
Arab	עֲרָבִי	ashamed	בּוֹשׁ	atom	אָטוֹם
Arabic	עֲרָבִית	ash tray	מַאֲפֵרָה	atomic	אָטוֹמִי
arbitrary	קָשֶׁה עֹרֶף	aside	הַצִּדָּה	attach (to)	חִבֵּר
architect	אַדְרִכָל	ask (to)	שָׁאַל	attack (to)	הִתְקִיף
architecture	אַדְרִכָלוּת	asleep	יָשֵׁן	attain (to)	הִשִּׂיג
ardent	נִלְהָב	(to) fall asleep	נִרְדָּם	attempt	נִסָּיוֹן
area	שֶׁטַח	aspire (to)	קִוָּה	attempt (to)	נִסָּה
argue (to)	רָב	aspirin	אַסְפִּרִין	attend (to)	בִּקֵּר
argument	רִיב	assassin	רוֹצֵחַ	(to) attend to	טִפֵּל בְּ-
arid	יָבֵשׁ	assault	הַתְקָפָה	attention	תְּשׂוּמֶת-לֵב
arise (to)	קָם	assemble (to)	אָסַף	attic	עֲלִיָּה
ark	אֲרוֹן	assign (to)	נָתַן חֵלֶק	attitude	יַחַס
				attorney	עוֹרֵךְ דִּין

attract (to)	מָשַׁךְ	badly	רַע	battle	מִלְחָמָה
attraction	מְשִׁיכָה	bag	שַׂק	bay	מִפְרָץ
attractive	מוֹשֵׁךְ אֶת הַלֵּב	baggage	חֲפָצִים	be (to)	הָיָה
audacity	חֻצְפָּה	bake (to)	אָפָה	(to) be ahead	הָיָה רִאשׁוֹן
audience	קָהָל	baker	אוֹפֶה	(to) be hungry	הָיָה רָעֵב
August	אוֹגוּסְט	bakery	מַאֲפִיָּה	(to) be right	צָדַק
aunt	דּוֹדָה	balance	שִׁוּוּי מִשְׁקָל	(to) be sorry	הִצְטַעֵר
austerity	צֶנַע	balcony	יָצִיעַ	(to) be thirsty	הָיָה צָמֵא
authentic	אֲמִתִּי	bald	קֵרֵחַ	(to) be wrong	טָעָה
author	סוֹפֵר	ball	כַּדּוּר	(to) be tired	הָיָה עָיֵף
authority	רָשׁוּת	balloon	כַּדּוּר פּוֹרֵחַ	beach	שְׂפַת הַיָּם
authorize (to)	הִרְשָׁה	banana	בַּנָנָה	beaming	קוֹרֵן
automatic	אוֹטוֹמָטִי	band	חֲבוּרָה	bean	פּוֹל
automobile	מְכוֹנִית	bandage	תַּחְבּוֹשֶׁת	bear (to) (carry)	נָשָׂא
autumn	סְתָו	banister	מַעֲקֶה	(endure, suffer)	סָבַל
available	נִמְצָא	bank	בַּנְק	(support)	נָשָׂא
average	מְמֻצָּע	bank note	שְׁטָר כֶּסֶף	(to) bear a grudge	נָטַר
avoid (to)	נִמְנַע מִ-	bankruptcy	פְּשִׁיטַת הָרֶגֶל	(to) bear children, etc.	יָלְדָה
awake	עֵר	(to) go bankrupt	פָּשַׁט אֶת הָרֶגֶל	(to) bear fruit, etc.	נָשָׂא פְּרִי
awaken (to)	הִתְעוֹרֵר	banquet	מִשְׁתֶּה	(to) bear in mind	זָכַר
award	פְּרָס	bar	מוֹט	beast	בְּהֵמָה
away	הָלְאָה	barber	סַפָּר	beat (to) (strike)	הִכָּה
(to) go away	הָלַךְ לוֹ	barbershop	מִסְפָּרָה	(heart)	דָּפַק
awe	יִרְאָה	bare	עָרֹם	(in a game)	נִצַּח
awful	נוֹרָא	bargain	מְצִיאָה	(to) beat a drum	תָּפַף
awhile	לְרֶגַע	barge	סִירָה	beautiful	יָפֶה
		bark (to)	נָבַח	beauty	יֹפִי
		barn	אָסָם	because	כִּי
B		barrel	חָבִית	because of	מִפְּנֵי
		barren	עָקָר	become (to)	הָיָה לְ-
baby	תִּינוֹק	base (n.)	בָּסִיס	(to) become accustomed	הִתְרַגֵּל
bachelor	רַוָּק	bashful	בַּיְשָׁן	bed	מִטָּה
back (part of the body)	גַּב	basin	קְעָרָה	bedroom	חֲדַר הַמִּטּוֹת
behind one's back	מֵאֲחוֹרֵי הַגַּב	basket	סַל	beef	בְּשַׂר בָּקָר
back door	דֶּלֶת אֲחוֹרִית	bastard	מַמְזֵר	beefsteak	אֻמְצָה
(to) go back	שָׁב	bath	אַמְבַּטְיָה	beer	בִּירָה
background	רֶקַע	bathe (to)	רָחַץ	beet	סֶלֶק
backwards	אֲחוֹרַנִּית	bathing suit	בֶּגֶד יָם	before	לִפְנֵי
bad	רַע	bath tub	אַמְבַּטְיָה	beg (to)	הִתְחַנֵּן, בִּקֵּשׁ נְדָבוֹת
badge	סֵמֶל				

beggar	מְבַקֵּשׁ נְדָבוֹת	birthday	יוֹם הֻלֶּדֶת	rowboat	סִירַת שַׁיִט
begin (to)	הִתְחִיל	biscuit	כִּסְקְוִיט	body	גּוּף
beginning	הַתְחָלָה	bishop	הֶגְמוֹן	boil (to)	רָתַח
behave (to)	הִתְנַהֵג יָפֶה	bit	רֶסֶן	boiler	דּוּד
behavior	הַנְהָגָה	bit (a)	חֲתִיכָה	bold	אַמִּיץ
behind	מֵאָחוֹר	bite	נְשִׁיכָה	bomb	פְּצָצָה
Belgian	בֶּלְגִּי	bite (to)	נָשַׁךְ	atomic bomb	פְּצָצָה אַטוֹמִית
belief	אֱמוּנָה	bitter	מַר	bond	קֶשֶׁר
believe (to)	הֶאֱמִין	bitterness	מְרִירוּת	bone	עֶצֶם
bell	פַּעֲמוֹן	black	שָׁחוֹר	book	סֵפֶר
belly	בֶּטֶן	blade	לַהַב	bookseller	מוֹכֵר סְפָרִים
belong (to)	שַׁיָּךְ לְ-	blame	אַשְׁמָה	bookstore	חֲנוּת סְפָרִים
below	לְמַטָּה	blame (to)	הֶאֱשִׁים	boot	מַגָּף
belt	חֲגוֹרָה	blank (n.)	חָלָל	booth	כִּיתָן
bench	סַפְסָל	blank (adj.)	חָסֵר, רֵיק	border	גְּבוּל
bend (to)	כָּפַף	blanket	שְׂמִיכָה	boring	מְשַׁעֲמֵם
beneath	מִתַּחַת	bleed (to)	שָׁתַת דָּם	born (to be)	נוֹלַד
benefit	תּוֹעֶלֶת	blemish	פְּגָם	borrow (to)	שָׁאַל
benefit (to)	הוֹעִיל	bless (to)	בֵּרַךְ	bosom	חֵיק
berry	תּוּת	blessing	בְּרָכָה	both	שְׁנֵיהֶם
beside	עַל יָד	blind	עִוֵּר	bother	טִרְדָּה
besides	חוּץ מִן	blind (to)	עִוֵּר	bother (to)	הִטְרִיד
best	הַטּוֹב	blister	אֲבַעְבּוּעָה	bottle	בַּקְבּוּק
bet	הִתְעָרְבוּת	block	קֻפְיָה	bottle opener	מַפְתֵּחַ
bet (to)	הִתְעָרֵב	block (to)	עָצַר	bottom	תַּחְתִּית
betray (to)	בָּגַד	blood	דָּם	bottom (adj.)	נָמוּךְ
better	יוֹתֵר טוֹב	bloom	פָּרַח	bounce (to)	קָפַץ
between	בֵּין	blotter	סוֹפֵג	boundary	גְּבוּל
beyond	מֵעֵבֶר לְ-	blouse	חֻלְצָה	boundless	אֵין סוֹפִי
Bible	תַּנַ"ךְ	blow	מַכָּה	bowl	קְעָרָה
bicycle	אוֹפַנַּיִם	blow (to)	נָשַׁף	box	קוּפְסָה, תֵּבָה
big	גָּדוֹל	blue	כָּחוֹל	boy	יֶלֶד
bill	חֶשְׁבּוֹן	blush	אֹדֶם	bracelet	צָמִיד
bill of fare	תַּפְרִיט	blush (to)	הִתְאַדֵּם	braid	מִקְלַעַת
billion	בִּלְיוֹן	board (of wood)	קֶרֶשׁ	brain	מֹחַ
bind (to)	קָשַׁר	boarding house	אַכְסַנְיָה	brake	מַעֲצוֹר
biography	בִּיאוֹגְרָפְיָה	boast (to)	הִתְאַמֵּר	branch	עָנָף
bird	צִפּוֹר	boat	סִירָה	brandy	יַיִ"שׁ
birth	לֵידָה	sailboat	סִירַת מִפְרָשׂ	brave	אַמִּיץ

bread	לֶחֶם
break (to)	שָׁבַר
(to) break out	הִתְפָּרֵץ
breakfast	אֲרוּחַת בֹּקֶר
breast	שַׁד, שָׁדַיִם
breath	נְשִׁימָה
breathe (to)	נָשַׁם
breeze	רוּחַ
bribe (to)	שִׁחֵד
brick	לְבֵנָה
bride	כַּלָּה
bridegroom	חָתָן
bridge	גֶּשֶׁר
brief	קָצָר
bright	בָּהִיר
brighten (to)	הֵאִיר
brilliant	נוֹצֵץ
bring (to)	הֵבִיא
bring together (to)	אִחֵד
bring up (to)	גִּדֵּל
British	בְּרִיטִי
broad	רָחָב
broadcast	שִׁדֵּר
broil (to)	צָלָה
broiled	צָלוּי
broken	שָׁבוּר
brook	נַחַל
broom	מַטְאֲטֵא
brother	אָח
brother-in-law	גִּיס
brown	חוּם
bruise (to)	נָקַף
brush	מִכְרֶשֶׁת
brute	חַיָּה
bubble	בַּעְבּוּעַ
bucket	דְּלִי
buckle	אַבְזָם
bud	צִיץ
budget	תַּקְצִיב

buffet	מִזְנוֹן
bug	יַחוּשׁ
build (to)	בָּנָה
building	בִּנְיָן
bull	פַּר
bulletin	עָלוֹן
bundle	חֲבִילָה
burial	קְבוּרָה
burn (to)	שָׂרַף
burst (to)	הִתְפַּקַּע
bury (to)	קָבַר
bus	אוֹטוֹבּוּס
bush	שִׂיחַ
business	עֵסֶק
businessman	בַּעַל עֵסֶק
busy	עָסוּק
but	אֲבָל
butcher	קַצָּב
butcher shop	אִטְלִיז
butter	חֶמְאָה
button	כַּפְתּוֹר
buy(to)	קָנָה
buyer	קוֹנֶה
by (near)	עַל יָד
by and by	בְּקָרוֹב, עוֹד מְעַט
by day	בַּיּוֹם
by then	עַד אָז
by and large	בְּדֶרֶךְ כְּלָל
by hand	בַּיָּד
by that time	עַד אָז
by the way	דֶּרֶךְ אַגַּב
by virtue of	בִּזְכוּת
Finish it by Sunday.	תִּגְמֹר עַד יוֹם א'.
Send it by airmail.	שְׁלַח אוֹתוֹ בְּדֹאַר אֲוִיר.

C

cab (taxi)	מוֹנִית
cabbage	כְּרוּב

cab driver	נֶהָג
cabinet	חֵכָה
cablegram	כְּבֶלְגְּרָמָה
cafe	קָפֶה
cage	כְּלוּב
cake	עֻגָּה
calendar	לוּחַ
calf	עֵגֶל
call	קְרִיאָה
call (to)	קָרָא
(to) call (summon)	קָרָא
(to) call in a loud voice	קָרָא בְּקוֹל
(to) call a meeting	קָרָא לַאֲסֵפָה
(to) call forth	עוֹרֵר
(to) call back	הֵשִׁיב
(to) call out	הִכְרִיז, צָעַק
(to) call on (someone)	בִּקֵּר
calm	שֶׁקֶט
camel	גָּמָל
camera	מַצְלֵמָה
camp	מַחֲנֶה
camp (to)	חָנָה
can (able)	יָכוֹל
can	פַּח
cancel (to)	בִּטֵּל
candidate	מֻעֲמָד
candle	נֵר
cap	כּוֹבַע
capacity	קִבּוּל
capital (n.)	בִּירָה, מָמוֹן
capital (adj.)	רָאשִׁי
capricious	עַקֵשׁ
captain	רַב חוֹבְלִים
captive	שָׁבוּי
capture (to)	שָׁבָה
car	מְכוֹנִית
carbon paper	נְיָר פֶּחָם
card	כַּרְטִיס

game of cards	קְלָפִים	cement	מֶלֶט	charm	חֵן
care	טִפּוּל	cemetery	בֵּית קְבָרוֹת	charm (to)	קָסַם
in care of (c/o)	אֵצֶל	center	מֶרְכָּז	charming	נֶחְמָד
(to) take care	נִזְהַר	central	מֶרְכָּזִי	chase (to)	רָדַף
(to) take care of	טִפֵּל בְּ-	century	מֵאָה	chat (to)	שׂוֹחֵחַ
care (to)	טִפֵּל	cereal	דַּיְסָה	cheap	זוֹל
I don't care	לֹא אִכְפַּת לִי	ceremony	טֶקֶס	cheat (to)	רִמָּה
career	קַרְיֶרָה	certain	וַדַּאי	check (banking)	הַמְחָאָה
careful	זָהִיר	certainty	וַדָּאוּת	(chess)	שַׁחְמָט
careless	קְלֵי זָהִיר	certificate	תְּעוּדָה	(control)	בְּדִיקָה
caress	לְטִיפָה	birth certificate	תְּעוּדַת לֵידָה	(in a restaurant)	חֶשְׁבּוֹן
carp	קַרְפ	chain	שַׁרְשֶׁרֶת	(restraint)	מַעְצוֹר
carpenter	נַגָּר	chain (to)	כָּבַל	(verification)	אִשּׁוּר
carpet	מַרְבַד, שָׁטִיחַ	chair	כִּסֵּא	check (to)	עָצַר
carry (to)	נָשָׂא	chairman	יוֹשֵׁב רֹאשׁ	cheek	לְחִי
(to) carry out	מִלֵּא	chalk	גִּיר	cheer (to)	שִׂמַּח
carve (to)	חָרַת	champagne	שַׁמְפַּנְיָה	cheerful	שָׂמֵחַ
case	עִנְיָן	champion	אַלּוּף	cheese	גְּבִינָה
in that case	אִם כֵּן הַדָּבָר	chance	מִקְרֶה	chemical	כִימִי
cash	כֶּסֶף	by chance	בְּמִקְרֶה	chemist	כִימַאי
cashier	גִּזְבָּר, קֻפַּאי	happening by chance	קָרָה בְּמִקְרֶה	cherish (to)	שָׁמַר
cast (to)	זָרַק	(opportunity)	הִזְדַּמְנוּת	cherry	דֻּבְדְּבָן
cat	חָתוּל	(probability)	אֶפְשָׁרוּת	chest	חָזֶה
catch (to)	תָּפַשׂ	(risk)	הִסְתַּכְּנוּת	chest of drawers	שִׁדָּה
(to) catch cold	הִתְקָרֵר	change	שִׁנּוּי	chew (to)	לָעַס
(to) catch (on) fire	נִדְלַק	change (to)	שִׁנָּה	chicken	תַּרְנְגֹל
(to) catch up	הִשִּׂיג	chapel	בֵּית תְּפִילָה	chief	רֹאשׁ
category	מִין, סוּג	chapter	פֶּרֶק	chief (adj.)	רָאשִׁי
Catholic	קַתוֹלִי	character	אֹפִי	child	יֶלֶד
cattle	בָּקָר	characteristic	אָפְיָנִי	chime	פַּעֲמוֹנִים
cause	סִבָּה	charge		chimney	אֲרֻבָּה
cause (to)	גָּרַם	(load,quantity of powder, electricty,fuel,etc.)	מִטְעָן	chin	סַנְטֵר
cavalry	פָּרָשִׁים	(accusation)	הַאֲשָׁמָה	China	סִין
cave	מְעָרָה	(attack)	הַתְקָפָה	chip	קִיסָם
cease (to)	פָּסַק	(bookkeeping)	חִיּוּב	chocolate	שׂוֹקוֹלָד
ceiling	תִּקְרָה	(order)	הַקָּפָה	choice	בְּחִירָה
celebrate (to)	חַג	(price)	מְחִיר	choir	מַקְהֵלָה
celebration	חֲגִיגָה	charitable	נָדִיב	choke (to)	חָנַק
cellar	מַרְתֵּף	charity	צְדָקָה	choose (to)	בָּחַר

chop (to)	חָטַב	closed	סָגוּר	(to) come back	שָׁב
Christian	נוֹצְרִי	closure	סְגִירָה	(to) come by	הִשִּׂיג
Christmas	חַג הַמוֹלָד	cloth	אָרִיג	(to) come down	יָרַד
church	כְּנֵסִיָּה	clothe (to)	הִלְבִּישׁ	(to) come in	נִכְנַס
cigar	סִיגָרָה	clothes	בְּגָדִים	(to) come near	הִתְקָרֵב
cigarette	סִיגָרִיָה	clothes hanger	קוֹלָב	(to) come out	יָצָא
cinnamon	קִנָּמוֹן	cloud	עָנָן	comedy	קוֹמֶדְיָה
circle	עִגּוּל	cloudy	מְעֻנָּן	comet	שָׁבִיט
circular	עָגֹל	club	מַקֵּל, אֲגֻדָּה	comfort	נֶחָמָה
circulation	סַפּוּכ	coal	פֶּחָם	comfort (to)	נִחֵם
circumcise (to)	מָהַל	coarse	גַּס	comfortable	נוֹחַ
circumcision	בְּרִית	coast	חוֹף	comma	פְּסִיק
circumstances	מִסְפּוֹת	coat	בֶּגֶד, מְעִיל	command	צִוּוּי
circus	קִרְקָס	cocoa	קַקָאוֹ	command (to)	צִוָּה, פָּקַד
citizen	אֶזְרָח	code	סֵפֶר חֻקִים	commander	מְפַקֵּד
city	עִיר	coffee	קָפֶה	commemorate (to)	הִנְצִּיר
city hall	עִירִיָה	coffee with cream	קָפֶה לָבָן	commerce	מִסְחָר
civil	אֶזְרָחִי	coffin	אָרוֹן	commercial	מִסְחָרִי
civilization	תַּרְפּוֹת	coin	מַטְבֵּעַ	commission	וַעֲדָה
claim	דְרִישָׁה	cold	קַר	common	פָּשׁוּט
claim (to)	תָּבַע	I am cold	קַר לִי	communicate (to)	הוֹדִיעַ
clamor	רַעַשׁ	coldness	קֹר	communication	תַּחְבּוּרָה
clap (to)	מָחָא פַּף	collaborate (to)	שִׁתֵּף עֲבוֹדָה	community	קְהִילָה
class	מַחְלָקָה	collar	צַוָּארוֹן	company	חֶבְרָה
classify (to)	מִיֵן	collect (to)	אָסַף	compare (to)	הִשְׁוָה
clause	סָעִיף	collection	אֹסֶף	comparison	הַשְׁוָאָה
clean	נָקִי	collective	קִבּוּצִי	compete (to)	הִתְחָרָה
clean (to)	נָקָה	college	מִכְלָלָה	competition	הִתְחָרוּת
cleanliness	נִקָּיוֹן	colonial	שֶׁל מוֹשָׁבוֹת	complain (to)	הִתְאוֹנֵן
clear	צָלוּל	colony	מוֹשָׁבָה	complaint	הִתְאוֹנְנוּת
clearly	בְּרוּר	color	צֶבַע	complete	שָׁלֵם
clerk	פָּקִיד	color (to)	צָבַע	complex (adj.)	מֻרְכָּב
clever	פִּקֵחַ	column	עַמּוּד	complexion	גּוֹן עוֹר
climate	אַקְלִים	comb	מַסְרֵק	complicate (to)	סִבֵּךְ
climb (to)	טִפֵּס	comb (to)	סָרַק	complicated	מְסֻבָּךְ
clip (to)	קִצֵץ	combination	צֵרוּף	compliment	מַחֲמָאָה
clock	שָׁעוֹן	combine (to)	צֵרֵף	compose (to)	חִבֵּר
close (adj.)	קָרוֹב	come (to)	בָּא	composer (music)	מַלְחִין
close (to)	סָגַר	(to) come about	הָיָה	composition	חִבּוּר

comprehend (to)	הֵכִין	consent (to)	הִסְכִּים	control (to)	שָׁלַט
compromise	פְּשָׁרָה	conservative	שַׁמְרָנִי	controversy	וִכּוּחַ
compromise (to)	פִּשֵּׁר	consider (to)	שָׂם לֵב	convalescence	הַחְלָמָה
comrade	חָבֵר	considerable	הַרְבֵּה	convenience	נוֹחִיּוּת
conceal (to)	הִסְתִּיר	consideration	הִתְחַשְּׁבוּת	at your convenience	כְּפִי נוֹחֲלְךָ
conceit	גַּאֲוָה	consist (to)	מֻרְכָּב מִן	convenient	נוֹחַ
concentrate (to)	הִתְרַכֵּז	consistent	עָקִיב	convention	וְעִידָה
concern	דְּאָגָה	console (to)	נִחֵם	conversation	שִׂיחָה
concern (to)	נָגַע	consonant	עִצּוּר	converse (to)	שׂוֹחֵחַ
concert	קוֹנְצֶרְט	conspicuous	בּוֹלֵט	convert (to)	הָפַךְ
conclusion	הַחְלָטָה, סוֹף	constant	תָּדִיר	convict (to)	חִיֵּב בַּדִּין
concrete (adj.)	מֻחְשִׁי	constitution	חֻקָּה	conviction	חִיּוּב
condemn (to)	גִּנָּה	constitutional	חֻקָּתִי	convince (to)	שִׁכְנֵעַ
condense (to)	קִצֵּר	construct (to)	בָּנָה	cook	טַבָּח
condition	תְּנַאי	consul	שַׁגְרִיר	cook (to)	בִּשֵּׁל
conduct	הִתְנַהֲגוּת	contagious	מִדַּבֵּק	cookie	עֻגִיָּה
conduct (to)	נָהַג	contain (to)	הֵכִיל	cool	קָרִיר
conductor	נָהָג	container	כְּלִי	cool (to)	קֵרֵר
conference	וְעִידָה	contemporary	בֶּן זְמָן	copper	נְחשֶׁת
confess (to)	הוֹדָה	contend (to)	טָעַן	copy	הֶעְתֵּק
confession	וִדּוּי	content (n.)	תֹּכֶן	copy (to)	הֶעְתִּיק
confidence	בִּטָּחוֹן	contented	שָׂמֵחַ, שְׂבַע-רָצוֹן	cord	חֶבֶל
confident	בָּטוּחַ	contest	הִתְחָרוּת	cork	פְּקָק
confidential	סוֹדִי	continent (n.)	יַבֶּשֶׁת	cork (to)	סָתַם
confirm (to)	אִשֵּׁר	continual	תְּמִידִי	corkscrew	מַחְלֵץ
confirmation	אִשּׁוּר	continue (to)	הִמְשִׁיךְ	corn	תִּירָס
confuse (to)	בִּלְבֵּל	contract	חוֹזֶה	corner	פִּנָּה
confusion	בִּלְבּוּל	contractor	קַבְּלָן	corporation	חֶבְרָה
congratulate (to)	בֵּרַךְ	contradict (to)	סָתַר	corpse	פֶּגֶר
congratulation	בְּרָכָה	contradiction	סְתִירָה	correct	נָכוֹן
congregation	קְהִלָּה	contradictory	סוֹתֵר	correct (to)	תִּקֵּן
conjugation	נְטִיָּה	contrary	גֶּנֶד	correction	תִּקּוּן
connect (to)	חִבֵּר	on the contrary	לְהֶפֶךְ	correspond (to)	הִתְכַּתֵּב
connection	חִבּוּר	contrary (adj.)	סוֹתֵר	correspondence	חִלּוּף מִכְתָּבִים
conquer (to)	כָּבַשׁ	contrast	נִגּוּד	correspondent (newspaper)	כַּתָּב
conquest	כִּבּוּשׁ	contrast (to)	הִשְׁוָה	corresponding	מַקְבִּיל
conscience	מַצְפּוּן	contribute (to)	תָּרַם	corrupt	לְשַׁחֵת
conscientious	בַּעַל מַצְפּוּן	contribution	תְּרוּמָה	corruption	הַשְׁחָתָה
conscious	עֵר	control	שְׁלִיטָה	cost	מְחִיר

at any cost	בְּכָל מְחִיר	creation	יְצִירָה	cup	גָּבִיעַ, סֵפֶל
it costs	זֶה עוֹלֶה	creative	יוֹצֵר	cure	תְּרוּפָה
costume	תִּלְבֹּשֶׁת	creature	בְּרִיָה	cure (to)	רִפֵּא
cottage	צְרִיף	credit	הַקָּפָה	curiosity	סַקְרָנוּת
cotton	צֶמֶר גֶּפֶן	creditor	נוֹשֶׁה	curious	סַקְרָן
couch	סַפָּה	crib	עֲרִיסָה	curl	תִּלְתַּל
cough	שִׁעוּל	cricket	צְרָצַר	curl (to)	תִּלְתֵּל
cough (to)	הִשְׁתַּעֵל	crime	פֶּשַׁע	current (n.)	זֶרֶם
council	וַעַד	criminal	פּוֹשֵׁעַ	current (adj.)	מְקֻבָּל
count (to)	סָפַר	crisis	מַשְׁבֵּר	curse	קְלָלָה
counting	סְפִירָה	crisp	פָּרִיךְ	curtain	מָסָךְ
counter (adj.)	נֶגְדִּי	critic	מְבַקֵּר	curve	עָקֹם
counterfeit	מְזֻיָּף	criticism	בִּקֹּרֶת	cushion	כַּר
countless	אֲשֶׁר לֹא יִמָּנֶה	crooked	עָקֹם	custom	מִנְהָג
country	מְדִינָה, אֶרֶץ	crop	יְבוּל	customary	נָהוּג
countryman	בֶּן-אָרֶץ	cross	צְלָב	customer	קוֹנֶה
couple	זוּג	cross (to)	עָבַר	customhouse	בֵּית-הַמֶּכֶס
courage	אֹמֶץ	(to) cross one's mind	עָלָה עַל הַדַּעַת	customs official	פָּקִיד-הַמֶּכֶס
course	מַהֲלָךְ	(to) cross out	מָחַק	cut	חֲתָךְ
of course	כַּמּוּבָן	crossing	פְּנִיָה	cut (to)	חָתַךְ
court	בֵּית דִּין	crossroads	פָּרָשַׁת דְּרָכִים		
courteous	אָדִיב	crouch (to)	רָבַץ	**D**	
courtesy	נִמּוּס, אֲדִיבוּת	crowd	קָהָל	dagger	פִּגְיוֹן
courtship	חֲזִירָה	crowd (to)	דָּחַק	daily	יוֹמִי
courtyard	חָצֵר	crude	גַּס	dainty	עָדִין
cousin	בֶּן-דּוֹד	cruel	אַכְזָר	dairy	מַחְלָבָה
cover (to)	כִּסָּה	cruelty	אַכְזָרִיּוּת	dairy products	תּוֹצֶרֶת חָלָב
covering	מִכְסֶה	cruise	סִיּוּל בָּאֳנִיָּה	dam	סֶכֶר
cow	פָּרָה	crumb	פֵּרוּר	damage	נֶזֶק
coward	מוּג לֵב	crumble (to)	פֵּרֵר	damage (to)	הִזִּיק
crack	סֶדֶק	crust	קְרוּם	damp	רָטֹב
crack (to)	פָּקַע	crutch	קַב	dance	רִקּוּד
cradle	עֲרִיסָה	cry	קְרִיאָה	dance (to)	רָקַד
crash	נֶפֶץ	cry (to)	בָּכָה	danger	סַכָּנָה
crash (to)	נֻפַּץ	cucumber	מְלָפְפוֹן	dangerous	מְסֻכָּן
crawl	זָחַל	cultural	תַּרְבּוּתִי	dark	חָשׁוּךְ
crazy	מְשֻׁגָּע	culture	תַּרְבּוּת	darkness	חֹשֶׁךְ
cream	שַׁמֶּנֶת	cunning	עָרְמוּמִי	dash (to)	הִשְׁלִיךְ
create (to)	בָּרָא			date	תַּאֲרִיךְ

daughter	פַּת	declaration	הַצְהָרָה	deliverance	גְּאֻלָּה
daughter-in-law	פַּלָה	declare (to)	הוֹדִיעַ	delivery	מְסִירָה
dawn	שַׁחַר	decline (to) (refuse)	מֵאֵן	demand	דְּרִישָׁה
day	יוֹם	decorate (to)	קִשֵּׁט	demand (to)	דָּרַשׁ
all day	כָּל הַיּוֹם	decrease	הַקְטָנָה	democracy	דֶמוֹקְרָטִיָה
day after tomorrow	מָחָרָתַיִם	decrease (to)	הִקְטִין	demonstrate (to)	הוֹכִיחַ
day by day	מִיּוֹם לְיוֹם	decree	צַו	demonstration	הוֹכָחָה
day before yesterday	שִׁלְשׁוֹם	dedicate (to)	חָנַךְ	denial	הַכְחָשָׁה
every day	כָּל יוֹם	deduction	הַפְחָתָה	denounce (to)	הֶאֱשִׁים
daydream	חֲלוֹם פָּהָקִיץ	deed	מַעֲשֶׂה	dense	סָמִיךְ
dazzle (to)	סִנְוֵר	deep	עָמֹק	density	סְמִיכוּת
dead	מֵת	deer	צְבִי	dental	שֵׁנִי
deaf	חֵרֵשׁ	defeat	כִּשָּׁלוֹן	dentifrice	אַבְקַת שְׁנַיִם
deaf and dumb	חֵרֵשׁ-אִלֵּם	defeat (to)	נִצַּח	dentist	רוֹפֵא שְׁנַיִם
deal	עֵסֶק	defect	מוּם	deny (to)	הִכְחִישׁ
dealer	סוֹחֵר	defend (to)	הֵגֵן	department	מַחְלָקָה
dear	יָקָר	defense	הֲגָנָה	department store	חֲנוּת כָּל בּוֹ
death	מָוֶת	defiance	מֶרֶד	depend (to)	סָמַךְ
debatable	מֻטָל בְּסָפֵק	define (to)	הִגְדִּיר	dependence	סְמִיכָה
debate	וִכּוּחַ	definite	מֻחְלָט	dependent (adj.)	תָּלוּי
debate (to)	הִתְוַכֵּחַ	deformed	בַּעַל מוּם	deplore (to)	הִצְטַעֵר עַל
debris	חֲרָבוֹת	defraud (to)	רִמָּה	deposit	פִּקָּדוֹן
debt	חוֹב	defy (to)	הִתְנַגֵּד לְ-	deposit (to)	הִפְקִיד
debtor	בַּעַל חוֹב	degree	מַעֲלָה, מַדְרֵגָה	depot (railway)	תַּחֲנָה
decade	עָשׂוֹר	delay	עִכּוּב	depress (to)	מֵעִיק
decanter	בַּקְבּוּק	delay (to)	עִכֵּב	depression	שֶׁקַע
decay	רִקָּבוֹן	(linger)	הִתְעַכֵּב	deprive (to)	מָנַע מִן
decay (to)	רָקַב	(defer)	דָּחָה	depth	עֹמֶק
deceased	מֵת	delegate	צִיר	derive (to)	גָּזַר
deceit	מִרְמָה	delegate (to)	נָתַן כֹּחַ לְ-	descend (to)	יָרַד
deceive (to)	רִמָּה	deliberate (adj.)	מָחוּן	descendant	צֶאֱצָא מִן
December	דֶצֶמְבֶּר	deliberate (to)	שָׁקַל בְּשִׁקּוּלוֹ	descent	יְרִידָה
decent	הָגוּן	deliberately	בְּמַחְשָׁבָה תְּחִילָה	describe (to)	תֵּאֵר
decide (to)	הֶחֱלִיט	delicacy	עֲדִינוּת	description	תֵּאוּר
decidedly	בְּהֶחְלֵט	delicate	עָדִין	desecrate (to)	חִלֵּל
decipher (to)	פִּעֲנֵחַ	delicious	טָעִים	desert	מִדְבָּר
decision	הַחְלָטָה	delight	עֹנֶג	desert (to)	עָזַב
decisive	מַחְלִט	delight (to)	עִנֵּג	desertion	עֲזִיבָה
deck	סִפּוּן	deliver (to)	הֵבִיא	deserve (to)	זָכָה

design	תָּכְנִית	devour (to)	אָכַל	director	מְנַהֵל
design (to)	עָשָׂה תָּכְנִית	devout	אָדוּק	directory	סֵפֶר
desirable	רָצוּי	dew	טַל	dirt	רֶפֶשׁ
desire	רָצוֹן	diagonal	אֲלַכְסוֹן	dirty	מְלֻכְלָךְ
desire (to)	רָצָה	diagram	דִיאַגְרָמָה	disability	חֻלְשָׁה
desk	מַכְתֵּבָה	dial	חוּגָה	disabled	בַּעַל מוּם
desolate	שָׁמֵם	dialect	מִבְטָא	disagree (to)	חָלַק עַל
desolation	שְׁמָמָה	dialogue	דּוּ-שִׂיחַ	disagreement	מַחֲלֹקֶת
despair	יֵאוּשׁ	diameter	קֹטֶר	disappear (to)	נֶעֱלַם
despair (to)	הִתְיָאֵשׁ	diamond	יַהֲלֹם	disappoint (to)	אִכְזֵב
desperate	יֵאוּשִׁי	diary	יוֹמָן	disappointment	אַכְזָבָה
despise (to)	בָּז	dictate (to)	הִכְתִּיב	disapprove (to)	הִתְנַגֵּד
despite	לַמְרוֹת	dictator	רוֹדָן	disaster	אָסוֹן
despondent	נוֹאָשׁ	dictionary	מִלּוֹן	discharge	פִּטּוּרִים
dessert	לִפְתָּן , פַּרְפֶּרֶת	die (to)	מֵת	discharge (to)	פִּטֵּר
destiny	גוֹרָל	diet	מָזוֹן	disciple	תַּלְמִיד
destitute	עָנִי	differ (to)	נִבְדַּל	discipline	מִשְׁמַעַת
destroy (to)	הֶחֱרִיב	difference	הֶבְדֵּל , הַבְדֵּל	disclaim (to)	הִכְחִישׁ
destruction	חֻרְבָּן	different	שׁוֹנֶה	disclose (to)	גִּלָּה
detach (to)	הִפְרִיד	difficult	קָשֶׁה	disclosure	גִּלּוּי
detail	פְּרָט	difficulty	קֹשִׁי	discomfort	אִי-מְנוּחָה
detain (to)	עִצֵּר	dig (to)	חָפַר	discontent	אִי-רָצוֹן
detect (to)	גִּלָּה	digest (to)	עִכֵּל	discontented	מָרְגָּז
detention	עֲצִירָה	digestion	עִכּוּל	discontinue (to)	הִפְסִיק
deteriorate (to)	הֻגְרַע	dignified	אֲצִילִי	discord	רִיב
determination	הַחְלָטָה	dignity	כָּבוֹד	discount	נִכָּיוֹן
determine (to)	הֶחֱלִיט	dilute (to)	מָהַל	discourage (to)	רִפָּה יָדֵי
detest (to)	שָׂנֵא	dim	כֵּהֶה	discouragement	רִפְיוֹן יָדַיִם
detour	דֶּרֶךְ עֲקִיפִין	dimension	מֵמַד	discover (to)	גִּלָּה
detract from (to)	גָּרַע מִן	diminish (to)	הִפְחִית	discovery	גִּלּוּי
detriment	נֵזֶק	dimple	גֻּמָּה	discreet	זָהִיר
devastation	הֶרֶס	dine (to)	סָעַד	discretion	זְהִירוּת
develop (to)	פִּתֵּחַ	dining room	חֲדַר אֹכֶל	discrimination (racial)	הַפְלָיָה
development	פִּתּוּחַ	dinner	אֲרוּחַת הָעֶרֶב	discuss (to)	נָשָׂא וְנָתַן
device	הַמְצָאָה	dip (to)	טָבַל	discussion	מַשָׂא וּמַתָּן
devil	שֵׁד	diplomacy	מְדִינָאוּת	disdain	בּוּז
devise (to)	הִמְצִיא	diplomat	מְדִינָאִי	disdain (to)	בָּז
devoid of	חָסֵר	direct (to)	כִּוֵּן	disease	מַחֲלָה
devote (to)	הִקְדִּישׁ	direction	כִּוּוּן	disgrace	חֶרְפָּה

disguise	הִתְחַפְּשׂוּת	ditch	קְצָעָה	dozen	תְּרֵי־שַׂר , תְּרֵי־סַר
disgust	גֹּעַל נֶפֶשׁ	dive (to)	צָלַל	draft (air)	רוּחַ פְּרָצִים
disgusting	מְעוֹרֵר גֹּעַל נֶפֶשׁ	divide (to)	חָלַק	(bank)	הַמְחָאָה
dish	צַלַּחַת	divine	אֱלֹהִי	(sketch, outline)	שִׂרְטוּט
dishonest	בִּלְתִּי יָשָׁר	division	חֲלֻקָּה	draft (to)	שִׂרְטֵט
disinfectant	מְחַטֵּא	divorce	גֵּרוּשִׁים	drag (to)	סָחַב
disinterested	בִּלְתִּי מְעֻנְיָן	divorce (to)	גֵּרֵשׁ	drain (to)	יִבֵּשׁ
dislike	שִׂנְאָה	dizziness	סְחַרְחֹרֶת	drama	מַחֲזֶה
dislike (to)	שָׂנֵא	dizzy	סְחַרְחַר	draw (to)(with a pencil)	צַיֵּר
disloyal	בּוֹגֵד	do (to)	עָשָׂה	(curtains)	סָגַר
dismiss (to)	פִּטֵּר	to do without	הִסְתַּדֵּר	(salary)	קִבֵּל מַשְׂכֹּרֶת
dismissal	פִּטּוּרִים	Do come.	תָּבוֹא	(lottery, etc.)	הִפִּיל גּוֹרָל
disobey (to)	מָרָה	Do you believe?	הַאִם אַתָּה מַאֲמִין?	(money,liquids,etc.)	הוֹצִיא
disorder	אִי־סֵדֶר	How do you do?	מַה שְׁלוֹמְךָ?	(to) draw back	נָסוֹג, הֵשִׁיךְ אָחוֹר
dispense (to)	חִלֵּק	That will do.	זֶה דַי.	(to) draw up	הֵכִין
display	הַצָּגָה	dock	מֵזַח	drawback	מִגְרַעַת
display (to)	הִצִּיג	doctor	רוֹפֵא	drawer	מְגֵרָה
displease (to)	הִכְעִיס	doctrine	תּוֹרָה	drawing room	חֲדַר הָאוֹרְחִים
dispute	רִיב	document	תְּעוּדָה	dread	פַּחַד
dispute (to)	רָב	dog	כֶּלֶב	dread (to)	פָּחַד
disqualify (to)	פָּסַל	dogmatic	דּוֹגְמָטִי	dreaded	נוֹרָא
disrespect	אִי־כָּבוֹד	dome	כִּפָּה	dream	חֲלוֹם
dissolve (to)	הֵמִיס	domestic	בֵּיתִי	dream (to)	חָלַם
distance	מֶרְחָק	dominant	שׁוֹלֵט	dreamer	חוֹלֵם
distant	רָחוֹק	dominate (to)	מָשַׁל	dress	שִׂמְלָה
distinct	מְיֻחָד	doom	גּוֹרָל	dress (to)	לָבַשׁ
distinction	הֶבְדֵּל, הֶכְרֵל	door	דֶּלֶת	(to) get dressed	הִתְלַבֵּשׁ
distinguish (to)	הִבְדִּיל	next door	בִּשְׁכֵנוּת	(to) dress a wound	חָבַשׁ
distort (to)	עִוֵּת	dose	מָנָה	dressmaker	תּוֹפֶרֶת
distract (to)	הֵסִיחַ אֶת הַדַּעַת	dot	נְקֻדָּה	drill	מַקְדֵּחַ
distress	צָרָה	double	כָּפוּל	drink	מַשְׁקֶה
distress (to)	צִעֵר	doubt	סָפֵק	drink (to)	שָׁתָה
distribute (to)	חִלֵּק	doubt (to)	הָיָה מְסֻפָּק	drip (to)	נָטַף
distribution	חֲלֻקָּה	doubtful	מְסֻפָּק	drive (to)(a car,etc.)	נָהַג
district	מָחוֹז	doubtless	בְּלִי־סָפֵק	(a nail)	תָּקַע
distrust	אִי־אֵמוּן	dough	בָּצֵק	(to) drive away	גֵּרֵשׁ
distrust (to)	חָשַׁד	down(n.)	נוֹצָה	driver	נֶהָג
disturb (to)	הִפְרִיעַ	down (adv.)	לְמַטָּה	droop (to)	נָבַל
disturbance	הַפְרָעָה	doze (to)	נִמְנֵם	drop	טִפָּה

drop (to) (let go)	הִפִּיל	(of corn)	שִׁבֹּלֶת	eggplant	חָצִיל
(fall in drops)	טִפְטֵף	early	מֻקְדָּם	egoism	אַנֹכִיּוּת
(release, let fall)	הִפִּיל	earn (to)	הִרְוִיחַ	Egypt	מִצְרַיִם
(to) drop a subject	עָזַב	earnest	רְצִינִי	eight	שְׁמוֹנָה
(to) drop in on	בָּקַר	earth	אֶרֶץ	eighteen	שְׁמוֹנָה עָשָׂר
drought	בַּצֹּרֶת	ease	קַלּוּת	eighteenth	הַשְּׁמוֹנָה עָשָׂר
drown (to)	טָבַע	at ease	נֹחַ	eighth	שְׁמִינִי
drug	מִרְקַחַת	with ease	בְּקַלּוּת	eighty	שְׁמוֹנִים
druggist	רוֹקֵחַ	ease (to)	הֵקֵל	either..	אוֹ
drugstore	בֵּית מִרְקַחַת	easily	בְּקַלּוּת	either...or..	אוֹ...אוֹ...
drum	תֹּף	east	מִזְרָח	either one	אוֹ זֶה אוֹ זֶה
drunk	שִׁכּוֹר	Easter	פַּסְחָא	elaborate	מְסֻבָּךְ
dry	יָבֵשׁ	eastern	מִזְרָחִי	elastic	גָּמִישׁ
dry (to)	יִבֵּשׁ	easterner	מִזְרָחִי	elbow	מַרְפֵּק
dryness	יֹבֶשׁ	eastward	מִזְרָחָה	elder	בְּכוֹר
due	מַגִּיעַ	easy	קַל	elderly	זָקֵן
dull	קֵהֶה	eat (to)	אָכַל	eldest	הַבְּכוֹר
dumb	אִלֵּם	eccentric	אֶקְצֶנְטְרִי	elect (to)	בָּחַר
duplicate (to)	הֶעְתִּיק	echo	הֵד	election	בְּחִירוֹת
duration	מֶשֶׁךְ	economical	כַּלְכָּלִי	elector	בּוֹחֵר
during	בְּמֶשֶׁךְ	economize (to)	חָשַׂךְ	electric(al)	חַשְׁמַלִּי
dust	אָבָק	economy	כַּלְכָּלָה	electricity	חַשְׁמַל
dust (to)	אִבֵּק	edge	שָׂפָה	elegant	נָאֶה
dusty	אֲבָקִי	(of a blade)	לַהַב	element	יְסוֹד
Dutch	הוֹלַנְדִי	(of a stream, etc.)	גָּדָה	elementary	יְסוֹדִי
duty	חוֹבָה	(of a table, a book)	קָצֶה	elephant	פִּיל
dwarf	גַּמָּד	edition	מַהֲדוּרָה	elevator	מַעֲלִית
dwell (to)	גָּר	editor	עוֹרֵךְ	eleven	אַחַד עָשָׂר
dwelling	בַּיִת, מְגוּרִים	editorial	מַאֲמָר רָאשִׁי	eleventh	הָאַחַד עָשָׂר
dye	צֶבַע	education	חִנּוּךְ	eliminate (to)	הִשְׁמִיט
dye (to)	צָבַע	effect	מְסוּבָּב	eloquence	יְפִי הַדִּבּוּר
		effect (to)	גָּרַם	eloquent	יְפֵה הַדִּבּוּר
E		effective	פּוֹעֵל	else	אַחֵר
each	כָּל אֶחָד	effeminate	נָקְבִּי	or else	אַחֶרֶת
each other	זֶה אֶת זֶה	efficiency	יְעִילוּת	someone else	מִשֶּׁהוּ אַחֵר
each time	כָּל פַּעַם	effort	נִסָּיוֹן	elsewhere	בְּמָקוֹם אַחֵר
eager	לָהוּט	egg	בֵּיצָה	elude (to)	הִשְׁתַּמֵּט
eagle	נֶשֶׁר	hard-boiled egg	בֵּיצָה שְׁלוּקָה	embark (to)	הִפְלִיג
ear (organ of hearing)	אֹזֶן	scrambled eggs	בֵּיצִיָה	embarrass (to)	הֵבִיא בִּמְבוּכָה

embarrassment	מְבוּכָה	energetic	בַּעַל מֶרֶץ	epidemic	מַגֵּפָה
embassy	שַׁגְרִירוּת	energy	מֶרֶץ	episode	מִקְרֶה
embezzle (to)	מָעַל	enforce (to)	הִכְרִיחַ	epoch	תְּקוּפָה
embitter (to)	מֵרַד	engage (to)	הָיָה עָסוּק כְּ-	equal	שָׁוֶה
emblem	סֵמֶל	(a room,etc.)	שָׂכַר	equal (to)	שָׁוָה
embody (to)	הִגְשִׁים	(in a conversation)	שׂוֹחֵחַ	equality	שִׁוְיוֹן
embroider (to)	רָקַם	engagement (promise of marriage)	אֵרוּשִׂים	equilibrium	שִׁוּוּי מִשְׁקָל
embroidery	רִקְמָה	(date)	רֵאָיוֹן	equip (to)	צִיֵּד
emerge (to)	הוֹפִיעַ	(employment for a stated time)	חוֹזֶה	equipment	צִיּוּד
emergency	חֵרוּם	engine	מְכוֹנָה	era	תְּקוּפָה
emigrant	מְהַגֵּר, יוֹרֵד	engineer	מְהַנְדֵּס	erase (to)	מָחַק
emigrate (to)	הִגֵּר, יָרַד	English	אַנְגְּלִי	eraser	מוֹחֵק
eminent	נִכְבָּד	engrave (to)	חָרַת	erect	יָשָׁר
emotion	רֶגֶשׁ	enjoy (to)	נֶהֱנָה	erect (to)	הֵקִים
emperor	קֵיסָר	enjoyment	הֲנָאָה	err (to)	טָעָה
emphasis	הַדְגָּשָׁה	enlarge (to)	הִגְדִּיל	errand	שְׁלִיחוּת
emphasize (to)	הִדְגִּישׁ	enormous	עָצוּם	error	טָעוּת
emphatic	מָדְגָּשׁ	enough	דַּי, מַסְפִּיק	escape	מָנוֹס
empire	מַמְלָכָה	enrich (to)	הֶעֱשִׁיר	escape (to)	פָּרַח
employ (to)	שָׂכַר	en route	בַּדֶּרֶךְ	escort	בֶּן לְוָיָה
employee	שָׂכִיר	enter (to) (a house,etc.)	נִכְנַס	escort (to)	לִוָּה
employer	נוֹחֵן עֲבוֹדָה	(in a register,etc.)	רָשַׁם	especially	בְּיִחוּד
employment	עֲבוֹדָה	(into a conversation)	פָּתַח בְּשִׂיחָה.	essay	חִבּוּר
empty	רֵיק			essence	תַּמְצִית
empty (to)	הֵרִיק	entertain (to)	שִׁעֲשַׁע	essential	עִקָּרִי
enable (to)	הִרְשָׁה	entertainment	שַׁעֲשׁוּעִים	establish (to)	יִסֵּד
enamel	אֲמָל	enthusiasm	הִתְלַהֲבוּת	establishment	מוֹסָד
enchant (to)	הִקְסִים	enthusiastic	מִתְלַהֵב	estate	נְכָסִים
enclose (to)	שָׂם כְּ-	entire	פְּלִיל	esteem	הוֹקָרָה
encore	עוֹד פַּעַם	entrance	כְּנִיסָה	esteem (to)	הוֹקִיר
encourage (to)	עוֹדֵד	entrust (to)	הִבְטִיחַ	esthetic	אֶסְתֵּטִי
encouragement	עִדּוּד	entry	כְּנִיסָה	estimate	אֹמֶד
end	סוֹף	enumerate (to)	סָפַר, מָנָה	estimate (to)	הֶאֱמִיד
end (to)	גָּמַר	envelope	מַעֲטָפָה	estimation	הַאֲמָדָה
endeavor	נִסָּיוֹן	envious	מְקַנֵּא	eternal	נִצְחִי
endeavor (to)	נִסָּה	environment	סְבִיבָה	eternity	נֶצַח
endorse (to)	אִשֵּׁר	envy	קִנְאָה	ether	אֶתֶר
endure (to)	סָבַל	epic	אֶפִּי	etiquette	נִמּוּס
enemy	אוֹיֵב			eulogy	הֶסְפֵּד

European	אֵירוֹפִי	evidence	עֵדוּת	exempt	פָּטוּר
evacuate (to)	הֵרִיק	evident	בָּרוּר	exercise	תַּרְגִּיל
evade (to)	הִתְחַמֵּק	evil	רֹע	exert (to)	הִתְאַמֵּץ
evaluate (to)	הֶעֱרִיךְ	evil (adj.)	רַע	exertion	הִתְאַמְּצוּת
evaporate (to)	הִתְאַדָּה	evoke (to)	עוֹרֵר	exhale (to)	נָשַׁף
evasion	הַעֲרָמָה	evolve (to)	הִתְפַּתַּח	exhaust (to)	נִצֵּל
eve	עֶרֶב	exact	מְדֻיָּק	exhaustion	אֲפִיסַת כֹּחוֹת
on the eve of	בְּעֶרֶב	exaggerate (to)	הִגְזִים	exhibit (to)	הִצִּיג
even	שָׁוֶה	exaggeration	הַגְזָמָה	exhibition	תַּעֲרוּכָה
(not odd)	זוּג	exalt (to)	שִׂגֵּב	exile	גָּלוּת
(level)	חָלָק	exaltation	הִתְרוֹמְמוּת	exile (to)	גָּלָה
even (adv.)	אֲפִילוּ	examination	בְּחִינָה	exist (to)	הִתְקַיֵּם
even as	כְּמוֹ	(to) take an examination	נִבְחַן	existence	קִיּוּם
even if	אֲפִילוּ אִם	examine (to)	בָּחַן	exit	יְצִיאָה
even so	בְּכָל זֹאת	example	דֻּגְמָה	expand (to)	הִתְפַּשֵּׁט
even that	גַּם זֹאת	exasperate (to)	הִרְגִּיז	expansion	הִתְפַּשְּׁטוּת
not even that	אֲפִילוּ לֹא זֹאת	exceed (to)	עָבַר	expansive	מִתְפַּשֵּׁט
evening	עֶרֶב	excel (to)	הִצְטַיֵּן	expect (to)	קִוָּה
yesterday evening	אֶמֶשׁ	excellence	הִצְטַיְּנוּת	expectation	תִּקְוָה
Good evening!	עֶרֶב טוֹב!	excellent	מְצֻיָּן	expedition	מִשְׁלַחַת
event	מִקְרֶה	except	מִלְּבַד	expel (to)	גֵּרֵשׁ
eventual	סוֹפִי	except (to)	הוֹצִיא מִן הַכְּלָל	expense	הוֹצָאָה
ever	בְּכָל עֵת	exception	יוֹצֵא מִן הַכְּלָל	expensive	יָקָר
(always)	תָּמִיד	exceptional	יוֹצֵא מִן הַכְּלָל	experience	נִסָּיוֹן
(never)	לְעוֹלָם לֹא	excess	עֹדֶף	experience (to)	הִרְגִּישׁ
as ever	כְּתָמִיד	exchange	הַחְלָפָה	experiment	נִסָּיוֹן
ever so much	עַרְבָּה יוֹתֵר	excited (to be)	הִתְרַגֵּשׁ	expert	מֻמְחֶה
ever since	מִיּוֹם	excitement	הִתְרַגְּשׁוּת	expire (to)	מֵת
every	כָּל	exclaim (to)	קָרָא	explain (to)	בֵּאֵר
every bit	הַכֹּל	exclamation	קְרִיאָה	explanation	בֵּאוּר
every day	כָּל יוֹם	exclamation mark	סִמָּן קְרִיאָה	explode (to)	הִתְפּוֹצֵץ
every other day	כָּל יוֹמַיִם	exclude (to)	הוֹצִיא מִן הַכְּלָל	exploit	עֲלִילָה
every one	כָּל אֶחָד	exclusive	מְיֻחָד	exploit (to)	נִצֵּל
every once in a while	מִפַּעַם לְפַעַם	excursion	טִיּוּל	explore (to)	חָקַר
every time	כָּל פַּעַם	excuse	אֲמַתְלָה	explosion	הִתְפּוֹצְצוּת
everybody	הַכֹּל	excuse (to)	סָלַח	export	יִצּוּא
everyone	כָּל אֶחָד	Excuse me.	סְלַח לִי.	export (to)	יִצֵּא
everything	כָּל דָּבָר	execute (to)	הוֹצִיא לַפֹּעַל	expose (to)	גִּלָּה
everywhere	בְּכָל מָקוֹם	execution	הוֹצָאָה לַפֹּעַל	express	אֶקְסְפְּרֶס

express (to)	הִפִּיעַ	factual	עֻבְדָתִי	by far	כְּהַרְבֵּה
expression	הַבָּעָה	faculty (school)	חֶבֶר הַמּוֹרִים	far away	רָחוֹק מְאֹד
expressive	מַבִּיעַ	fad	שִׁגָּעוֹן	so far	עַד פֹּה
expulsion	גֵרוּשׁ	fade (to)	דָהָה	As far as I'm concerned.	לְדַיְדִי.
exquisite	עָדִין	fail		How far?	מַה הַמֶרְחָק?
extend (to)	הוֹשִׁיט	without fail	כְּלִי עֶפְבּ	farce	מַהֲתַלָּה
extensive	רָחָב	fail (to) (in an under- taking, on an exam)	נִכְשַׁל	fare	מְחִיר
extent	שִׁעוּר	(in health)	חָלָה	farm	חַוָּה
to some extent	קִמְדָּה יְדוּעָה	(to) do something	לֹא הוֹצִיא לַפֹּעַל.	farmer	אִכָּר
exterior	חִיצוֹנִיּוּת	failure (fault, defect)	חִסָּרוֹן	farming	אִכָּרוּת
exterminate (to)	אִבֵּד	(bankruptcy)	פְּשִׁיטַת רֶגֶל	farther (adj.)	יוֹתֵר רָחוֹק
external	חִיצוֹנִי	faint	חַלָשׁ	farthest	הֲרָחוֹק פִּיוֹתֵר
extinct	נִכְחָד	faint (to)	הִתְעַלֵּף	fashion	אָפְנָה
extinction	הַכְחָדָה	fair (adj.)	בָּהִיר	fashionable	כָּאָפְנָה
extinguish (to)	כִּבָּה	(hair)	צָהִיר	fast (adj.)	מָהִיר
extra (adj.)	מְיֻתָּר	(clear)	בָּהִיר	fast (to)	צָם
extract (to)	הוֹצִיא	(just)	צוֹדֵק	fasten (to)	חִבֵּר
extraordinary	יוֹצֵא מִגֶּדֶר הָרָגִיל	(moderate)	בֵּינוֹנִי	fat	שָׁמֵן
extravagance	בַּזְבּוּז	fair play	יֹשֶׁר	fatal (incurable)	אָנוּשׁ
extravagant	מְבַזְבֵּז	fair weather	מֶזֶג, אֲוִיר יָפֶה	fate	גוֹרָל
extreme	קִיצוֹנִי	faith	אֱמוּנָה	father	אָב
extremely	הַרְבֵּה מְאֹד	faithful	נֶאֱמָן	father-in-law	חוֹתֵן
extremity	קָצֶה	faithfulness	אֱמוּן	fatigue	לֵאוּת
eye	עַיִן	fake	מְזֻיָּף	faucet	בֶּרֶז
eyebrow	גַּבָּה	fall	מַפָּלָה	fault	אָשָׁם
eyeglasses	מִשְׁקָפַיִם	fall (to)	נָפַל	favor	טוֹבָה
eyelid	עַפְעַף	false	שֶׁקֶר	favor (to)	נָטָה חֶסֶד
		fame	שֵׁמַע	favorable	מוֹעִיל
F		familiar	רָגִיל	favorite	מֻחְמָד
fable	מָשָׁל	family	מִשְׁפָּחָה	fear	פַּחַד
fabric	פַּד	famine	רָעָב	fear (to)	פָּחַד
face	פָּנִים	famous	יָדוּעַ	fearless	חֲסַר פַּחַד.
face (to)	פָּנָה	fan	מְנִיפָה	feather	נוֹצָה
facial	שֶׁל הַפָּנִים	electric fan	מְנִיפַת חַשְׁמָל	feature	פַּרְצוּף
facilitate (to)	הֵקֵל	fanatic	קַנָּאִי	February	פֶבְּרוּאָר
facility	קַלּוּת	fancy (adj.)	יָפֶה	federal	מְמְשַׁלְתִּי
fact	עֻבְדָה	fantastic	דִמְיוֹנִי	fee	תַּשְׁלוּם
in fact	בֶּאֱמֶת	far	רָחוֹק	feeble	חַלָשׁ
factory	בֵּית חֲרֹשֶׁת			feed (to)	הֶאֱכִיל

feel (to)	הַרְגִּישׁ	figure	צוּרָה	The dress fits you well.	הַשִּׂמְלָה הוֹלֶמֶת אוֹתָךְ.
(to) feel well	הַרְגִּישׁ טוֹב	file(for nails,etc.)	מַשׁוֹר	fitness	כֹּשֶׁר
feeling (sentiment)	הַרְגָּשָׁה	(for papers,cards,etc.)	תִּיק	five	חֲמִשָּׁה
(sensitiveness)	רְגִישׁוּת	file (to)	נִסֵּר	fix (to)	תִּקֵּן
fellow	חָבֵר	fill (to)	מִלֵּא	flag	דֶּגֶל
fellowship	חֲבֵרוּת	film	סֶרֶט	flame	לֶהָבָה
fellow student	תַּלְמִיד חָבֵר	filthy	מְלֻכְלָךְ	flank	אֲגַף
fellow worker	חָבֵר לַעֲבוֹדָה	final	סוֹפִי	flannel	פְלָנֶל
female	נְקֵבָה	finance	כְּסָפִים	flap	רַשׁ
feminine	נְקֵבִי	financial	כַּסְפִּי	flash	נִצְנֵץ
fence	גָּדֵר	find (to)	מָצָא	flashlight	פָּנָס
ferocious	אַכְזָרִי	(to) find out	גִּלָּה	flat	דִּירָה
ferry	מַעְבָּרָה	fine (n.)	קְנָס	flat (adj.)	שָׁטוּחַ
ferry boat	מַעְבָּרָה	fine (adj.)	מְצֻיָּן	flatter (to)	הֶחֱנִיף
fertile	פּוֹרָה	Fine!	יָפֶה!	flattery	חֲנִיפָה
fertilize (to)	זִבֵּל	finger	אֶצְבַּע	flavor	טַעַם
fertilizer	זֶבֶל	finish (to)	גָּמַר	fleet (n.)	צִי
fervent	נִלְהָב	fire	אֵשׁ	flesh	בָּשָׂר
fervor	הִתְלַהֲבוּת	fire (to) (burn)	הִדְלִיק	flexibility	גְּמִישׁוּת
festival	חֲגִיגָה	(a gun)	יָרָה	flexible	גָּמִישׁ
fetch (to)	הֵבִיא	(an employee)	פִּטֵּר	flight	בְּרִיחָה
fever	חֹם	firearms	נֶשֶׁק	fling (to)	זָרַק
few	מְעַט	fireman	מְכַבֶּה-אֵשׁ	flint	חַלָּמִישׁ
a few	מְעַטִים	fireplace	אָח	float (to)	צָף
a few days	יָמִים אֲחָדִים	firm (n.)	חֶבְרָה	flood	מַבּוּל
fiber	סִיב	firm (adj.)	חָזָק	flood (to)	שָׁטַף
fiction	סִפְרֹת	first (adj.)	רִאשׁוֹן	floor	רִצְפָּה
field (military)	שָׂדֶה	for the first time	בַּפַּעַם הָרִאשׁוֹנָה	flourish (to)	שָׂגָה
(specialty)	מִקְצוֹעַ	at first	בָּרִאשׁוֹנָה	flow (to)	נָזַל
fierce	אַכְזָרִי	fish	דָּג	flower	פֶּרַח
fiery	פּוֹעֵר	fish (to)	דָּג	fluid	נוֹזֵל
fifteen	חֲמִשָּׁה-עָשָׂר	fisherman	דַּיָּג	fly	זְבוּב
fifteenth	הַחֲמִשָּׁה עָשָׂר	fist	אֶגְרוֹף	fly (to)	עָף
fifth	חֲמִישִׁי	fit (seizure)	הַתְקָפָה	foam	קֶצֶף
fiftieth	הַחֲמִישִּׁים	fit (adj.)	מַתְאִים	foam (to)	קָצַף
fifty	חֲמִישִּׁים	fit (to)(a dress,etc.)	הִתְאִים	focus	מוֹקֵד
fig	תְּאֵנָה	(to) fit into	נִכְנַס	fog	עֲרָפֶל
fight	קְטָטָה	It fits badly.	זֶה לֹא מַתְאִים.	fold	קִפּוּל
fight (to)	נִלְחַם	That would fit the case.	זֶה מַתְאִים.	fold (to)	קִפֵּל

foliage	עֳפִי	former	קוֹדֵם	freight train	רַכֶּבֶת הוֹבָלָה
follow (to)	עָקַב	formerly	לְפָנִים	French	צָרְפָתִי
following	דַּלְקֵמָן	formula	נוּסְחָה	frequent	תָּכוּף
fondness	חִבָּה	forsake (to)	עָזַב	frequently	לְעִתִּים קְרוֹבוֹת
food	אֹכֶל	fort	מְצוּדָה	fresh	טָרִי
fool	טִפֵּשׁ	fortieth	הָאַרְבָּעִים	friction	חִכּוּךְ
foolish	טִפְּשִׁי	fortunate	בַּר-מַזָּל	Friday	יוֹם שִׁשִּׁי
foot	רֶגֶל	fortunately	כַּמָזָל	friend	חָבֵר, יָדִיד
football	כַּדּוּר רֶגֶל	fortune	מַזָּל	(to) be friends with	הִתְיַדֵּד עִם
footstep	צַעַד	forty	אַרְבָּעִים	friendly	יְדִידוּתִי
for	בִּשְׁבִיל	forward	קָדִימָה	friendship	יְדִידוּת
for example	לְמָשָׁל	forward (to)	הֶקָרִים	frighten (to)	הִפְחִיד
for the first time	בַּפַּעַם הָרִאשׁוֹנָה	foster (to)	פִּלְפֵּל	frightening	מַפְחִיד
for the most part	כָּעֵקֶר	found (to)	יָסַד	fringe	צִיצִית
for the present	לְעֵת עַתָּה	foundation	יְסוֹד	frivolity	קַלּוּת רֹאשׁ
for the time being	לְעֵת עַתָּה	founder	מְיַסֵּד	frog	צְפַרְדֵּעַ
This is for her.	זֶה כִּשְׁבִילָהּ.	fountain	מִזְרָקָה	from	מִן
forbid (to)	אָסַר	four	אַרְבָּעָה	front (in front of)	לְפָנֵי
force	כֹּחַ	fourteen	אַרְבָּעָה עָשָׂר	fruit	פְּרִי
force (to)	הִכְרִיחַ	fourteenth	הָאַרְבָּעָה עָשָׂר	fry (to)	טִגֵּן
ford	מַעְבָּר	fourth	רְבִיעִי	frying pan	מַחֲבַת
forearm	זְרוֹעַ	fowl	עוֹף	fuel	דֶּלֶק
forecast	תַּחֲזִית	fox	שׁוּעָל	fugitive	פָּלִיט
forefinger	אֶצְבַּע	fraction	שֶׁבֶר	fulfill (to)	קִיֵּם
forehead	מֵצַח	fracture	שֶׁבֶר	full	מָלֵא
foreign	זָר	fragment	חֲתִיכָה	fully	כַּשָּׁלֵמוּת
foreigner	זָר	fragrance	רֵיחַ	fun	עֹנֶג
foreman	מְפַקֵּחַ	fragrant	מֵרִיחַ	(to) have fun	הִתְעַנֵּג
forest	יַעַר	frail	רָפֶה	function	תַּפְקִיד
foreword	הַקְדָּמָה	frame	מִסְגֶּרֶת	fund	קֶרֶן
forget (to)	שָׁכַח	frank	גָּלוּי	fundamental	יְסוֹדִי
forgetfulness	שִׁכְחָה	frankness	גְּלוּי לֵב	funds	כְּסָפִים
forgive (to)	סָלַח	freak	מִפְלֶצֶת	funnel	מַשְׁפֵּךְ
forgiveness	סְלִיחָה	freckle	נֶמֶשׁ	funny	מַצְחִיק
fork	מַזְלֵג	free	חָפְשִׁי	fur	פַּרְוָה
form	צוּרָה	free (to)	שִׁחְרֵר	furious	זוֹעֵם
form (to)	יָצַר	freedom	חֹפֶשׁ	furnace	כּוּר
formal	פוֹרְמָלִי	freeze (to)	קָפָא	furnish (to)	סִפֵּק
formation	יְצִירָה	freight	הוֹבָלָה	furniture	רָהִיטִים

furrow	תֶּלֶם	generosity	נְדִיבוּת	glamour	קֶסֶם
further	יוֹתֵר רָחוֹק	generous	נָדִיב	glance (to)	הֵעִיף עַיִן
fury	זַעַם	genitals	אֶבָרֵי הַמִּין	glass	זְכוּכִית
futile	חַסַר תּוֹעֶלֶת	genius	גָּאוֹן	drinking glass	כּוֹס
future	עָתִיד	gentile	גּוֹי	glasses (eyeglasses)	מִשְׁקָפַיִם
in the future	כֶּעָתִיד	gentle	רַךְ	looking glass	רְאִי
		gentleman	אָצִיל	glitter	נִצְנוּץ
G		gentleness	רֹךְ	glitter (to)	נִצְנֵץ
gaiety	עֲלִיזוּת	genuine	אֲמִתִּי	globe	כַּדּוּר
gain	רֶוַח	geographic(al)	גִּיאוֹגְרָפִי	gloomy	אָפֵל
gain (to)	הִרְוִיחַ	geography	גִּיאוֹגְרָפִיָה	glorious	נֶהְדָּר
gall (impudence)	חוּצְפָּה	germ	חַיְדַּק	glory	הָדָר
gallant	אָרִיב	German	גֶּרְמָנִי	glove	כְּסָיָה
gallery	יָצִיעַ	gesture	תְּנוּעָה	glue	דֶּבֶק
gallop (to)	דָּהַר	get (to)	קִבֵּל	go (to)	הָלַךְ
galosh	מַגָּף	(to) get ahead	הִתְקַדֵּם	(to) go away	הָלַךְ לוֹ, עָזַב
gamble (to)	שִׂחֵק	(to) get away	נִמְלַט	(to) go back	שָׁב
game	מִשְׂחָק	(to) get back	שָׁב	(to) go down	יָרַד
gang	כְּנוּפִיָה	(to) get home	שָׁב הַבַּיְתָה	(to) go forward	הִתְקַדֵּם
gap	פֶּרֶץ	(to) get in	נִכְנַס	(to) go in	נִכְנַס
garage	מוּסָךְ	(to) get married	הִתְחַתֵּן	(to) go out	יָצָא
garbage	פְּסֹלֶת	(to) get off	יָרַד	(to) go to sleep	הָלַךְ לִישֹׁן
garden	גַּן	(to) get on	עָלָה	(to) go up	עָלָה
gardener	גַּנָּן	(to) get out	יָצָא	(to) go with	הָלַךְ עִם, לָוָה
gargle (to)	גִּרְגֵּר	(to) get up	הֵקִיץ	goal	מַטָּרָה
garlic	שׁוּם	Get down!	רֵד!	God	אֱלֹהִים
garter	בְּרִית	Get up!	קוּם!	god	אֵל
gas	גַּז	giant	עֲנָק	godparent	סַנְדָּק
gate	שַׁעַר	gift	מַתָּנָה	gold	זָהָב
gather (to)	אָסַף	gifted	בַּעַל כִּשְׁרוֹנוֹת	golden	זָהֹב
gathering	אֲסֵפָה	girdle	חֲגוֹרָה	good	טוֹב
gauze	גָּזָה	girl	יַלְדָּה	good!	טוֹב!
gay	עַלִּיז	give (to)	נָתַן	Good morning.	בֹּקֶר טוֹב.
gem	אֶבֶן טוֹבָה	(to) give a gift	נָתַן מַתָּנָה	Good night.	לַיְלָה טוֹב.
gender	מִין	(to) give back	הֵשִׁיב	good-by	שָׁלוֹם
general (adj.)	כְּלָלִי	(to) give in	נִכְנַע	goodness	טוֹב
generality	כְּלָלִיּוּת	(to) give up	הִתְיָאֵשׁ	goods	סְחוֹרָה
generalize (to)	כָּלַל	glad	שָׂמֵחַ	good will	רָצוֹן טוֹב
generation	דּוֹר	gladly	כְּשִׂמְחָה	goose	אַוָּז

gossip	רְכִילוּת	greedy	חוֹמֵד , חַמְדָן	habitual	רָגִיל
govern (to)	מָשַׁל	Greek	יְוָנִי	hail	בָּרָד
governess	מַדְרִיכָה	green	יָרֹק	hair	שֵׂעָר
government	מֶמְשָׁלָה	greet (to)	קִבֵּל אֶת פְּנֵי.	hairbrush	מִבְרֶשֶׁת
governor	מוֹשֵׁל	greeting	קַבָּלַת פָּנִים	haircut	תִּסְפֹּרֶת
grace	חֵן	grief	עֶצֶב	hairdo	תִּסְרֹקֶת
graceful	מְלֵא חֵן	grieve (to)	הִתְאַבֵּל	hair dye	צֶבַע
grade	מַדְרֵגָה	grin (to)	חִיֵּךְ	hairpin	סִכַּת שֵׂעָר
grain	תְּבוּאָה	grind (to)	טָחַן	hairy	שָׂעִיר
grammar	דִקְדוּק	groan (to)	נֶאֱנַק	half(n.)	חֵצִי
grand	נֶהְדָּר	grocer	בַּעַל מַכֹּלֶת	half (adj.)	חֲצִי
Grand!	נֶהְדָּר!	grocery store	חֲנוּת מַכֹּלֶת	half and half	חֲצִי חֲצִי
grandchild	נֶכֶד	groom	חָתָן	half hour	חֲצִי שָׁעָה
grand daughter	נֶכְדָּה	gross	גַּס	hall	אוּלָם
grandfather	סָב	ground	קַרְקַע	hammer	פַּטִּישׁ
grandmother	סָבָה	group	קְבוּצָה	hand	יָד
grandson	נֶכֶד	group (to)	חִלֵּק לִקְבוּצוֹת	hand made	מְלֶאכֶת יָד
grant	מַתָּן	grouping	קִבּוּץ	(of a watch)	מָחוֹג
grant (to)	נָתַן	grow (to)	גָּדַל , צָמַח	by hand	בְּיָד
grape	עֵנָב	(to) grow old	הִזְדַּקֵּן	in hand	בַּיָּד
grapefruit	אֶשְׁכּוֹלִית	(to) grow better	הִשְׁתַּפֵּר	offhand	כְּלִי הֲכָנָה
grasp (to)	אָחַז	(to) grow worse	הוּרַע	on the other hand	מִצַּד שֵׁנִי
grass	עֵשֶׂב	growth	גִּדּוּל	hand (to)	נָתַן
grateful	אֲסִיר תּוֹדָה	grudge	טִינָה	handbag	אַרְנָק
gratitude	הַכָּרַת תּוֹדָה	guard	שׁוֹמֵר	handful	מְלֹא הַיָּד
grave	קֶבֶר	guard (to)	שָׁמַר	handicap	מִכְשׁוֹל
grave (adj.)	רְצִינִי	guardian	אֶפּוֹטְרוֹפּוֹס	handkerchief	מִטְפַּחַת
gravel	חָצָץ	guess	נִחוּשׁ	handle	יָדִית
graveyard	בֵּית קְבָרוֹת	guess (to)	נִחֵשׁ	handle (to)	מִשְׁמֵשׁ
gravy	רֹטֶב	guide	מוֹרֶה דֶּרֶךְ	handsome	יְפֵה-תֹּאַר
gray	אָפֹר	guilt	אַשְׁמָה	handwriting	כְּתַב יָד
grease	חֵלֶב	guilty	אָשֵׁם	handy	יָעִיל
great	גָּדוֹל	gum	גֻּמִּי	hang (to)	תָּלָה
a great deal	הַרְבֵּה	gun	רוֹבֶה	happen (to)	קָרָה
a great man	אָדָם גָּדוֹל	gush	שָׁפַךְ	happening	מִקְרֶה
a great many	הַרְבֵּה			happiness	אֹשֶׁר
Great!	נִפְלָא!		H	happy	מְאֻשָּׁר
greatness	גְדוּלָה	habit	הֶרְגֵּל	harass (to)	הִרְגִּיז
greed	סַמְכָּנוּת	(to) be in the habit of	רָגִיל	harbor	נָמֵל

hard	מְקְשֶׁה	heap	עֲרֵמָה	heritage	יְרוּשָׁה
hard luck	מַזָּל רַע	heap (to)	עָרַם	hero	גִּבּוֹר
hard work	עֲבוֹדָה קָשָׁה	hear (to)	שָׁמַע	heroine	גְּבוֹרָה
harden (to)	הִקְשָׁה	(to) hear from	שָׁמַע מִן	herring	דָּג מָלוּחַ
hardly	בְּקוֹשִׁי	hearing	שְׁמִיעָה	hers	שֶׁלָּהּ
hardness	קְשִׁי	heart	לֵב	herself	בְּעַצְמָהּ
hardship	מְצוּ	by heart	בְּעַל פֶּה	hesitant	מְהַסֵּס
hardware	כְּלֵי מַתֶּכֶת	heart and soul	בְּלֵב שָׁלֵם	hesitate	פִּקְפֵּק
harm	רָעָה	(to) take to heart	שָׂם לֵב	hide (n.)	עוֹר
harm (to)	הִזִּיק	hearty	לְבָבִי	hide (to)	הֶחְבִּיא
harmful	מַזִּיק	heat	חֹם	hideous	אָיֹם
harmless	בִּלְתִּי מַזִּיק	heaven	שָׁמַיִם	high	גָּבוֹהַּ
harmonious	מַתְאִים	heavy	כָּבֵד	hill	גִּבְעָה
harmony	הַתְאָמָה	Hebrew	עִבְרִית	him	אוֹתוֹ
harsh	קָשֶׁה	hedge	מְשֻׂכָה	to him	לוֹ
harvest	קָצִיר	heed (to)	שָׂם לֵב	himself	בְּעַצְמוֹ
haste	מְהִירוּת	heel	עָקֵב	hinder (to)	עִכֵּב
hasten (to)	מִהֵר	hell	אֲבַדּוֹן	hinge	צִיר
hat	כּוֹבַע	hello	שָׁלוֹם	hint	רֶמֶז
hatch (to)	דָּגַר	help (to)	עָזַר	hint (to)	רָמַז
hate	שִׂנְאָה	helper	עוֹזֵר	hip	יָרֵךְ
hate (to)	שָׂנֵא	helpful	מוֹעִיל	hire (to)	הִשְׂכִּיר
hateful	שָׂנוּא	hem	שָׂפָה	his	שֶׁלּוֹ
hatred	שִׂנְאָה	hen	תַּרְנְגֹלֶת	hiss (to)	לָחַשׁ
haughty	גֵּאֶה	henceforth	מֵעַתָּה	historian	הִסְטוֹרְיוֹן
have (to)	הָיָה לְ-	her (pron.)	לָהּ, אוֹתָהּ	historic	הִסְטוֹרִי
(to possess)	הָיָה	to her	אֵלֶיהָ	history	דִּבְרֵי-הַיָּמִים, הִסְטוֹרְיָה
(to) have in mind	הָיָה בְּדַעְתּוֹ	her (adj.)	שֶׁלָּהּ	hit (to)	הִכָּה
(to) have to	הָיָה צָרִיךְ	herb	עֵשֶׂב	hoard	אוֹצָר
haven	מִקְלָט	herd	עֵדֶר	hoarse	צָרוּד
hay	שַׁחַת	here	פֹּה, הֵנָּה	hoe	מַעְדֵּר
hazard	סַכָּנָה	around here	בַּסְּבִיבָה	hold	אֲחִיזָה
haze	עֲרָפֶל	near here	קָרוֹב לְפֹה	hold (to)	הֶחְזִיק
he	הוּא	Come here.	בֹּא הֵנָּה.	(in one's hands, arms, etc.)	הֶחְזִיק
head	רֹאשׁ	Here!	הִנֵּה!	(to grasp)	אָחַז
headache	כְּאֵב רֹאשׁ	Here it is.	הִנֵּה זֶה.	(to contain, to have capacity for)	הֵכִיל
heal (to)	רִפֵּא	heredity	תּוֹרָשָׁה	(to) hold back	מָנַע
health	בְּרִיאוּת	heresy	כְּפִירָה	(to) hold a meeting	הִתְאַסֵּף
healthy	בָּרִיא	herewith	בָּזֶה		

(to) hold one's tongue	שָׁתַק	hot	חַם	husband	בַּעַל
(to) hold a conversation	שׂוֹחֵחַ	hotel	מָלוֹן	hush	שֶׁקֶט
hole	חוֹר	hour	שָׁעָה	hygiene	הִגִּיֵנָה
holiday	חַג	house	בַּיִת	hymn	הַמְנוֹן
holiness	קְדֻשָּׁה	household	מִשְׁפָּחָה	hyphen	מָקָף
hollow	חָלוּל	housekeeper	בֶּן מֶשֶׁק	hypocrisy	צְבִיעוּת
holy	קָדוֹשׁ	housemaid	מְשָׁרֶתֶת	hypocrite	צָבוּעַ
homage	כָּבוֹד	housework	עֲבוֹדַת בַּיִת	hypothesis	הַנָּחָה
home	בַּיִת	how	אֵיךְ		
at home	בַּבַּיִת	how long	כַּמָּה זְמַן	I	
homely	מְכֹעָר	how many	כַּמָּה		
honest	כֵּן	how much	כַּמָּה	I	אֲנִי
honesty	כֵּנוּת	How are you?	מַה שְׁלוֹמְךָ?	ice	קֶרַח
honey	דְּבַשׁ	How beautiful!	מַה יָּפֶה!	ice cream	גְּלִידָה
honor	כָּבוֹד	however	בְּכָל זֹאת	icy	קָרֹחַ
honor (to)	כִּבֵּד	howl	יְלָלָה	idea	רַעְיוֹן
honorable	מְכֻבָּד	howl (to)	יִלֵּל	ideal (n.)	מִשְׂאַת נֶפֶשׁ
hood	שַׁבִּיס	hug	חִבּוּק	ideal (adj.)	אִידְאָלִי
hoof	פַּרְסָה	huge	עָצוּם	idealism	אִידֵאָלִיּוּת
hook	וָו	hum (to)	זִמְזֵם	idealist	אִידֵאָלִיסְט
hop (to)	נִתֵּר	human	אֱנוֹשִׁי	identical	זֵהֶה
hope	תִּקְוָה	humane	אֱנוֹשִׁי	identification	זִהֵּי
hope (to)	קִוָּה	humanity	אֱנוֹשִׁיּוּת	identity	זֵהוּת
hopeful	מָלֵא תִקְווֹת	humble	עָנָו	idiom	נִיב
hopeless	נוֹאָשׁ	humid	לַח	idiot	אִדְיוֹט
horizon	אֹפֶק	humiliate (to)	הִשְׁפִּיל	idle	בָּטֵל
horizontal	אָפְקִי	humility	עֲנָוָה	idleness	בַּטָּלָה
horn	שׁוֹפָר	humor	לָצוֹן	idol	פֶּסֶל
horrible	אָיֹם, נוֹרָא	hundred	מֵאָה	if	אִם
horrify (to)	הִבְעִית	hundredth	הַמֵּאָה	ignoble	שָׁפָל
horror	אֵימָה	hunger	רָעָב	ignorance	בּוּרוּת
horse	סוּס	hungry (to be)	רָעֵב	ignorant	בּוּר
hosiery	גַּרְבַּיִם	hunt	צַיִד	ignore (to)	הִתְעַלֵּם מִן
hospitable	מַכְנִיס אוֹרְחִים	hunt (to)	צָד	ill	חוֹלֶה
hospital	בֵּית חוֹלִים	hunter	צַיָּד	(to) become ill	חָלָה
hospitality	הַכְנָסַת אוֹרְחִים	hurry	מְהִירוּת	illness	מַחֲלָה
host	מְאָרֵחַ	(to) be in a hurry	מִהֵר	illusion	דִּמְיוֹן
hostess	מְאָרַחַת	hurry (to)	מִהֵר	illustrate (to)	הִסְבִּיר
hostile	עוֹיֵן	hurt (to)	הִכְאִיב	illustration	הַסְבָּרָה
				image	צֶלֶם

imaginary	דמיוני	impudent	חצוף	indifference	אדישות
imagination	דמיון	impulse	דחיפה	indifferent	אדיש
imagine (to)	דמה	impure	בלתי נקי	indignant	כועס
imitate (to)	חקה	in	ב-	indignation	כעס
imitation	חקוי	inadequate	חסר	indirect	עקם
immediate	מידי	inasmuch as	מכיון ש-	indiscreet	אי זהיר
immediately	מיד	inaugurate (to)	הכניס למשרה	indiscretion	אי זהירות
immigrant	מהגר	incapable	שאינו מסגל	indispensable	הכרחי
immigrant to Israel	עולה	incapacity	אי-יכלת	individual	יחיד
imminent	קרוב	incense	קטרת	individual (adj.)	יחידי
immobility	חסר תנועה	inch	זרת	indivisible	בלתי-מתחלק
immoral	בלתי מוסרי	incident	מקרה	indolence	עצלות
immorality	פריצות	incline	שפוע	indolent	עצל
immortal	נצחי	inclination	נטיה	indoors	בבית
immortality	אלמות	include (to)	כלל	indorse (to)	חתם על
immune	מחסן	included	כלול	induce (to)	פתה
impartial	חסר משוא פנים	income	הכנסה	induct (to)	הכניס
impatience	אי-סבלנות	income tax	מס הכנסה	indulge (to)	פנק
impatiently	בלי סבלנות	incomparable	שאין כמוהו	indulgence	פנוק
imperfect	פגום	incompetent	בלתי מכשר	indulgent	מפנק
impertinence	חוצפה	incomplete	בלתי משלם	industrial	תעשיתי
impertinent	חצוף	incomprehensible	בלתי-מובן	industrious	מתמיד
impetuosity	פזיזות	inconvenience	אי-נוחיות	industry	תעשיה
impetuous	פזיז	inconvenient	אי-נוח	ineffective	חסר תוצאות
impious	חסר יראה	incorrect	בלתי-נכון	inevitable	הכרחי
import	יבוא	increase	הוספה	inexcusable	שאין לסלוח
import (to)	הביא מחוץ לארץ	increase (to)	הוסיף	inexhaustible	בלתי-פוסק
importance	חשיבות	incredible	שאין להאמין לו	inexplicable	שאין לבארו
of the utmost importance	ממדרגה ראשונה	indebted	חיב	inexpressible	שאין לבטאו
important	חשוב	indecision	הסוס	infallible	שאינו שוגה
imposing	מהדר	indecisive	מהסס	infamous	נבזה
impossible	אי אפשרי	indeed	אמנם	infancy	ילדות
impress (to)	עשה רשם	indefinite	בלתי מדיק	infant	תינוק
impression	רשם	independence	עצמאות	infantry	חיל רגלי
imprison (to)	אסר	independent	עצמאי	infatuation	חבה
improve (to)	הטיב	index	מפתח	infect (to)	הרביק
improvement	הטבה	index finger	אצבע	infection	הרעלה
imprudence	חסר חכמה	indicate (to)	הראה	infer (to)	בא לידי מסקנה
imprudent	חסר חכמה	indicative	מראה	inference	הקש

inferior	פָּחוּת	inquiry	שְׁאֵלָה	insult	עֶלְבּוֹן
infernal	שֶׁל אֲבַדּוֹן	insane	מְשֻׁגָּע	insult (to)	הֶעֱלִיב
infinite	אֵין סוֹפִי	inscription	כְּתֹבֶת	insuperable	שֶׁאֵין לַעֲלוֹת עָלָיו
infinity	אֵין סוֹף	insect	חֶרֶק	insurance	בִּטּוּחַ
inflict (to)	גָּרַם כְּאֵב	insensible	חֲסַר רֶגֶשׁ	insure (to)	הִבְטִיחַ
influence	הַשְׁפָּעָה	inseparable	בִּלְתִּי־נִפְרָד	intact	שָׁלֵם
influence (to)	הִשְׁפִּיעַ עַל	inside	בְּתוֹךְ	integral	אִינְטֶגְרָל
inform (to)	הוֹדִיעַ	insidious	מִרְמֶה	integration	אִינְטֶגְרַצְיָה
information	הוֹדָעָה	insight	הֲבָנָה	integrity	יֹשֶׁר
infuriate (to)	הִכְעִיס	insignificant	חֲסַר עֵרֶךְ	intellect	שֵׂכֶל
ingenious	שָׁנוּן	insincere	כּוֹזֵב	intellectual	שִׂכְלִי
ingenuity	חָכְמָה	insinuate (to)	הִתְגַּנֵּב	intelligence	שֵׂכֶל
ingenuous	תָּמִים	insist (to)	הִתְעַקֵּשׁ	intelligent	חָכָם
ingratitude	כְּפִיַּת טוֹבָה	insistence	הִתְעַקְּשׁוּת	intend (to)	כִּוֵּן
inhabit (to)	שָׁכַן	insoluble	בַּל יִמַּס	intense	עַז
inhabitant	שׁוֹכֵן	insomnia	אִי שֵׁנָה	intensity	עֹז
inherit (to)	יָרַשׁ	inspect (to)	בִּקֵּר, בָּדַק	intention	כַּוָּנָה
inheritance	יְרֻשָּׁה	inspection	בְּדִיקָה	interest	עִנְיָן
inhibition	עִכּוּב	inspiration	הַאֲצָלָה	interesting	מְעַנְיֵן
inhuman	בִּלְתִּי־אֱנוֹשִׁי	install (to)	חָנַךְ	interfere (to)	הִפְרִיעַ
initial	רִאשׁוֹן	installment	תַּשְׁלוּם חֶלְקִי	interference	הַפְרָעָה
initiate (to)	הִכְנִיס לְ־	instance	מָשָׁל	interior	פְּנִים
initiative	יָזְמָה	for instance	לְמָשָׁל	intermediate	בֵּינוֹנִי
inject (to)	הִכְנִיס	instant	רֶגַע	intermission	הַפְסָקָה
injurious	מַזִּיק	instantaneous	רִגְעִי	intermittent	בִּרְוָחִים
injury	פֶּצַע	instantly	מִיָּד	international	בֵּין לְאֻמִּי
injustice	אִי־צֶדֶק	instead of	בִּמְקוֹם	interpose (to)	חָצַץ
ink	דְּיוֹ	instigate	הֵסִית	interpret (to)	תִּרְגֵּם
inkwell	דְּיוֹתָה	instinct	יֵצֶר	interpretation	תִּרְגּוּם
inland	בִּפְנִים הָאָרֶץ	instinctive	יִצְרִי	interpreter	מְתַרְגֵּם
inlet	מִפְרָץ	institute	מָכוֹן	interrupt (to)	הִפְסִיק
inn	אַכְסַנְיָה	institute (to)	כּוֹנֵן	interruption	הַפְסָקָה
innate	מִלֵּדָה	institution	מוֹסָד	interval	הֶפְסֵק
inner	פְּנִימִי	instruct	לִמֵּד	interview	רִאָיוֹן
innkeeper	בַּעַל אַכְסַנְיָה	instruction	לִמּוּד	intestines	מֵעַיִם
innocence	תֹּם	instructor	מוֹרֶה	intimacy	קִרְבָה
innocent	תָּמִים	instrument	כְּלִי	intimate	קָרוֹב
innumerable	אֵין מִסְפָּר	insufficient	בִּלְתִּי מַסְפִּיק	intimidate (to)	הִפְחִיד
inquire (to)	שָׁאַל	insulation	בִּדּוּד	into	לְתוֹךְ

intolerable	מָשֶׂה מִנְשׂוֹא	irritation	גרוּי	jolly	עַלִיז
intolerance	אִי סַבְלָנוּת	island	אִי	journal	עִתּוֹן
intolerant	שֶׁאֵינוֹ סַבְלָן	isolate (to)	הבדיל	journalism	עִתּוֹנָאוּת
intonation	הַטְעָמָה	Israel	יִשְׂרָאֵל	journalist	עִתּוֹנָאִי
introduce (to)	הִצִּיג	issue	יציאה	journey	נְסִיעָה
introduction	הַצָּגָה	it	זֶה	joy	שִׂמְחָה
letter of introduction	מִכְתָּב הַמְלָצָה	it is	זֶה	joyous	שָׂמֵחַ
intuition	הָאָרָה	It's here.	זֶה פֹּה.	judge	שׁוֹפֵט
invade (to)	פָּלַשׁ	It's late.	זֶה מְאָחָר.	judge (to)	שָׁפַט
invalid (n.)	חַלָּשׁ	Italian	אִיטַלְקִי	judgment	מִשְׁפָּט
invalid (adj.)	בָּטֵל	itch	גרוּי	judicial	מִשְׁפָּטִי
invariable	בִּלְתִּי מִשְׁתַּנֶּה	item	פְּרָט	juice	מִיץ
invasion	פְּלִישָׁה	its	שֶׁלּוֹ	July	יוּלִי
invent (to)	הִמְצִיא	itself	בְּעַצְמוֹ	jump	קְפִיצָה
invention	הַמְצָאָה	ivy	קִיסוֹס	jump (to)	קָפַץ
inventor	מַמְצִיא			June	יוּנִי
invert (to)	הָפַךְ			junior	קָטָן
invest (to)	הִשְׁקִיעַ	**J**		just	רַק, אַךְ
investigate (to)	חָקַר			just now	פָּעַת
investment	הַשְׁקָעָה	jacket (short coat)	מְעִיל	justice	צֶדֶק
invigorating	מְעוֹרֵר	(covering, casing)	קְלִיפָּה	justify	הִצְדִּיק
invisible	סָמוּי	jail	בֵּית אֲסוּרִים	juvenile	שֶׁל נַעַר
invitation	הַזְמָנָה	jam	רִבָּה		
invite (to)	הִזְמִין	January	יָנוּאָר		
invoke (to)	הִתְפַּלֵּל	Japan	יָפָן	**K**	
involuntary	בְּעַל כָּרְחוֹ	jar (container)	צִנְצֶנֶת	keen	חַד
involve (to)	סִבֵּךְ	jaw	לְחִי	keep (to)	שָׁמַר, הֶחֱזִיק
iodine	יוֹד	jealous	מְקַנֵּא	(to) keep away	הִתְחֵק מִן
Iran	אִירָן	jealousy	קִנְאָה	(to) keep back (retain)	עָצַר, חָשַׂךְ
Iraq	עִירָק	jelly	קְרִישׁ	(to) keep from (hinder)	שָׁמַר מִן, מָנַע
iron	בַּרְזֶל, מגהץ	jest	הֲלָצָה	(to) keep from (refrain)	נִמְנַע
iron (to)	גִּהֵץ	Jew	יְהוּדִי	(to) keep in mind	זָכַר, שָׁמַר
irony	לַעַג	jewel	תַּכְשִׁיט	(to) keep one's hands off	לֹא נָגַע
irregular	לֹא יָשָׁר	job	עֲבוֹדָה	(to) keep one's word	קִיֵּם אֶת דְּבָרָיו
irreparable	שֶׁאֵין לוֹ תַּקָּנָה	join (to) (unite)	אִחֵד		
irresistible	בַּל יְנֻצַּח	(an organization)	הָיָה לְחָבֵר בְּ-	(to) keep quiet	שָׁתַק
irrigate (to)	הִשְׁקָה	(to put together)	חִבֵּר	(to) keep track of	הִתְחַקָּה עַל
irritable	רַגְזָן	joint	פֶּרֶק		
irritate	גֵּרָה	joke	הֲלָצָה	kernel	גַּרְעִין
		joke (to)	הִתְלוֹצֵץ		

kerosene	נֵפְט			late	מְאֻחָר
kettle	דּוּד, קֻמְקוּם	**L**		lately	מִקָּרוֹב
key	מַפְתֵּחַ	label	פֶּתֶק	later	מְאֻחָר מִן
keyhole	חוֹר לְמַפְתֵּחַ	labor	עָמָל	latest	הָאַחֲרוֹן
kick	בְּעִיטָה	laboratory	מַעְבָּדָה	latter	אַחֲרוֹן
kick (to)	בָּעַט	lace	שְׂנָץ	laugh	צְחוֹק
kid	גְּדִי	lack	מַחְסוֹר	laugh at (to)	צָחַק
kidnap (to)	חָטַף	lack (to)	חָסֵר	laughter	צְחוֹק
kidney	כִּלְיָה	lacquer	לַכָּה	laundry	מִכְבָּסָה
kill (to)	הָרַג	ladder	סֻלָּם	lavatory	חֲדַר רַחֲצָה
kind (n.)	סוּג, מִין	ladle	מַצֶּקֶת	lavish	בַּזְבְּזָנִי
a kind of	מִין	lady	גְּבִירָה	lavish (to)	בִּזְבֵּז
nothing of the kind	לְגַמְרֵי לֹא	the lady of the house	גְּבֶרֶת הַבַּיִת	law	חֹק
kind (adj.)	טוֹב לֵב	Ladies!	גְּבִירוֹתַי!	lawful	חֻקִּי
kindergarten	גַּן יְלָדִים	lag (to)	פִּגֵּר	lawyer	עוֹרֵךְ דִּין
kindly	טוֹב לֵב	lake	אֲגַם	lay (to)	הִשְׁכִּיב, הִנִּיחַ
will you kindly?	בְּטוּבְךָ?	lamb	שֶׂה	(to) lay away (aside, by)	חָסַךְ
kindness	חֶסֶד	lame	פִּסֵּחַ	(to) lay hands on ..	שָׁלַח יָד בְּ..
king	מֶלֶךְ	lamp	מְנוֹרָה	(to) lay hold of	אָחַז
kingdom	מַמְלָכָה	land	אֶרֶץ	(to) lay off (to fire)	פִּטֵּר
kiss	נְשִׁיקָה	land (to)	נָחַת	(to) lay the blame on	הֶאֱשִׁים
kiss (to)	נָשַׁק	landlord	בַּעַל בַּיִת	layer	שִׁכְבָּה
kitchen	מִטְבָּח	landscape	נוֹף	lazy	עָצֵל
kite	דַּאָה	language	לָשׁוֹן, שָׂפָה	lead	הִתְחָלָה
knack	כִּשָּׁרוֹן	languish (to)	חָלַשׁ	lead (to)	נָהַג
knee	בֶּרֶךְ	languor	חֻלְשָׁה	leader	מַנְהִיג
on one's knees	כּוֹרֵעַ בֶּרֶךְ	lanky	סָחוּשׁ	leadership	נְהִיגָה
kneel (to)	כָּרַע	lantern	פָּנָס	leaf	עָלֶה
knife	סַכִּין	lap	חֵיק	leak (to)	דָּלַף
penknife	אוֹלָר	lapel	רַשׁ	lean (to)	נִשְׁעַן
knit (to)	סָרַג	large	גָּדוֹל	leap	קְפִיצָה
knock	דְּפִיקָה	last (adj.)	אַחֲרוֹן	leap (to)	קָפַץ
knock (to)	דָּפַק	at last	לְבַסּוֹף	learn (to)	לָמַד
knot	קֶשֶׁר	last month	בַּחֹדֶשׁ שֶׁעָבַר	learned	מְלֻמָּד
know (to)	יָדַע	last night	אֶמֶשׁ	learning	לִמּוּד
knowledge	יְדִיעָה	lastly	לְאַחֲרוֹנָה	lease (to)	חָכַר
known	יָדוּעַ	last (to)	הִתְקַיֵּם	least	הַפָּחוֹת
		lasting	קַיָּם	at least	לְפָחוֹת
		latch	בְּרִיחַ	leather	עוֹר

leave	חֹפֶשׁ	liberty	חֹפֶשׁ	linen	פִּשְׁתָּה
leave (to)	עָזַב	library	סִפְרִיָּה	linger (to)	הִתְמַהְמֵהַּ
(quit)	הִתְפַּטֵּר	license	רִשָּׁיוֹן	lining	בִּטְנָה
(desert)	עָרַק	lick (to)	לָקַק	link	קֶשֶׁר
(go out)	יָצָא	lid	מִכְסֶה	link (to)	קָשַׁר
(go away)	עָזַב	lie	שֶׁקֶר	lion	אֲרִי
(to) leave behind	עָזַב	lie (to)	שִׁקֵּר	lip	שָׂפָה
(to) leave out	הִשְׁמִיט	lie down (to)	שָׁכַב	liquid	נוֹזֵל
lecture	הַרְצָאָה	lieutenant	סֶגֶן	liquor	מַשְׁקֶה
left	שְׂמֹאל	life	חַיִּים	list	רְשִׁימָה
left hand	יַד שְׂמֹאל	lifeboat	סִירַת הַצָּלָה	listen (to)	שָׁמַע
left-handed	אִטֵּר	lifeguard	מַצִּיל	literary	סִפְרוּתִי
to the left	שְׂמֹאלָה	lift (to)	הֵרִים	literature	סִפְרוּת
leg	רֶגֶל	light (n.)	אוֹר	little	קָטָן, מְעַט
legal	חֻקִּי	light (adj.)	קַל, בָּהִיר	a little	מְעַט
legend	אַגָּדָה	light complexion	בְּהִיר עוֹר	little boy	יֶלֶד
legislation	חֹק	light reading	קְרִיאָה קַלָּה	little by little	לְאַט לְאַט
legitimate	חֻקִּי	light-headed	קַל רֹאשׁ	very little	מְעַט מְאֹד
leisure	פְּנַאי	lighten (to)	הֵקַל	live (adj.)	חַי
lemon	לִימוֹן	light up (to)	הֵאִיר	live (to)	חָיָה
lemon juice	מִיץ לִימוֹן	lighthouse	מִגְדַּלּוֹר	lively	מָלֵא חַיִּים
lemonade	מֵי לִימוֹן	lighting	הָאָרָה	liver	כָּבֵד
lend (to)	הִשְׁאִיל	lightly	בְּקַלּוּת	load	מִטְעָן
length	אֹרֶךְ	lightning	בָּרָק	load (to)	טָעַן
lengthen (to)	הֶאֱרִיךְ	like	כְּמוֹ	loaf	כִּכָּר
lens	עֲדָשָׁה	like (to)	אָהַב	loan	הַלְוָאָה
less	פָּחוֹת	Would you like to go?	הַתִּרְצֶה לָלֶכֶת?	loan (to)	הִלְוָה
lesson	שִׁעוּר	likely	כִּנְרְאֶה	lobe	תְּנוּךְ
let (to)	נָתַן	likeness	דִּמְיוֹן	local	מְקוֹמִי
"To let"	"לְהַשְׂכִּיר"	likewise	גַּם כֵּן	locate (to)	מָצָא
(to) let alone	עָזַב	liking	חִבָּה	location	מָקוֹם
letter	מִכְתָּב, אוֹת	limb	אֵבֶר	lock	מַנְעוּל
lettuce	חַסָּה	limit	גְּבוּל	lock (to)	נָעַל
level (adj.)	יָשָׁר	limit (to)	הִגְבִּיל	locomotive	קַטָּר
lever	מָנוֹף	limp (n.)	צְלִיעָה	log	קוֹרָה
liable	אַחְרַאי	limp (adj.)	רָפֶה	logic	הִגָּיוֹן
liar	שַׁקְרָן	limp (to)	צָלַע	logical	הִגָּיוֹנִי
libel (to)	הוֹצִיא לַעַז	line	קַו	loneliness	בְּדִידוּת
liberal	נָדִיב			lonely	בּוֹדֵד

long	אֹרֶךְ, אֲרֻכּוֹת	lover	אוֹהֵב	maintain (to)	הֶחֱזִיק
all day long	כָּל הַיּוֹם	loving	אוֹהֵב	majesty	הוֹד מַלְכוּת
a long time	זְמַן אָרֹךְ	low	נָמוּךְ	major	עִקָּרִי
a long time ago	לִפְנֵי זְמַן רַב	lower (to)	הוֹרִיד	majority	רֹב
as long as	כְּאֹרֶךְ	lowly	שָׁפֵל	make (to)	עָשָׂה, יָצַר, בָּרָא
before long	עוֹד מְעַט	loyal	נֶאֱמָן	(to) make a good salary	הִשְׂתַּכֵּר יָפֶה
how long?	כַּמָּה זְמַן?	loyalty	אֱמוּן	(to) make a living	הִתְפַּרְנֵס
how long ago?	לִפְנֵי כַּמָּה זְמַן?	luck	מַזָּל	(to) make a mistake	טָעָה
long ago	מִזְמַן	lucky	בַּר-מַזָּל	(to) make a stop	עָצַר
long distance	דֶּרֶךְ אֲרֻכָּה	luggage	מִטְעָן	(to) make friends	הִתְיַדֵּד
not long ago	לֹא מִזְמַן	lukewarm	פּוֹשֵׁר	(to) make fun of	צָחַק בְּ-
It's five inches long.	אָרְכּוֹ חֲמִשָּׁה אִינְטְשׁ.	luminous	מֵאִיר	(to) make happy	שִׂמַּח
		lump	דְּבַלּוּל	(to) make haste	מִהֵר
longing	חֵשֶׁק	lunatic	מְשֻׁגָּע	(to) make headway	הִתְקַדֵּם
look	מַבָּט	lunch	אֲרוּחַת צָהֳרַיִם	(to) make into	הָפַךְ לְ-
look (to)	הִבִּיט	lung	רֵיאָה	(to) make known	הוֹדִיעַ
Look out!	הִזָּהֵר!	lust	תַּאֲוָה	(to) make no difference	לֹא שִׁנָּה דָבָר
(to) look after	דָּאַג לְ-	luxe (de)	מְהֻדָּר	(to) make one's mind up	הֶחְלִיט
(to) look alike	דָּמוּ	luxurious	שֶׁל מוֹתָרוֹת	(to) make out	הֵכִין
(to) look into	בָּדַק	luxury	מוֹתָרוֹת	(to) make possible	אִפְשֵׁר
(to) look like snow	נִרְאֶה יֵרֵד שֶׁלֶג			(to) make ready	הֵכִין
(to) look out	נִזְהַר			(to) make room	פִּנָּה מָקוֹם
(to) look over	עָבַר עַל	M		(to) make sad	הֶעֱצִיב
Look!	הַבֵּט!	machine	מְכוֹנָה	(to) make sick (annoy)	מַטְרִיד
loose	רָפֶה	sewing machine	מְכוֹנַת תְּפִירָה	(to) make tired	עִיֵּף
loosen (to)	הִרְפָּה	mad	מְשֻׁגָּע		
lord	אָדוֹן	madam	גְּבֶרֶת	male	זָכָר
lose (to)	אִבֵּד	madness	שִׁגָּעוֹן	malice	טִינָה
loss	אֲבֵדָה	magazine	סְתָב-עֵת	malignant	מַזִּיק
lost	אָבֵד	magic	כִּשּׁוּף	man	אִישׁ
lot (n.)	פּוּר	magician	מְכַשֵּׁף	manage (to)	נִהֵל
a lot	הַרְבֵּה	magnet	מַגְנֵט	management	הַנְהָלָה
a lot of money	הַרְבֵּה כֶּסֶף	magnificent	נֶהְדָּר	manager	מְנַהֵל
a lot of people	הַרְבֵּה אֲנָשִׁים	magnify (to)	הִגְדִּיל	mankind	אֱנוֹשִׁיּוּת
loud	בְּקוֹל	maid	עַלְמָה	manner	אֹפֶן
love	אַהֲבָה	mail	דֹּאַר	good manners	נִמּוּסִים
love (to)	אָהַב	main	רָאשִׁי	manufacture	חָרֹשֶׁת
loveliness	יֹפִי	main road	כְּבִישׁ רָאשִׁי	manufacture (to)	יָצַר
lovely	יָפֶה	main street	רְחוֹב רָאשִׁי	manufacturer	יַצְרָן
				manuscript	כְּתַב יָד

many	הַרְבֵּה	mathematics	מַתֵּימָטִיקָה	(a bill, etc.)	פָּרַע
map	מַפָּה	matter	חֹמֶר	(to get together, assemble)	הִתְאַסֵּף
marble	שַׁיִשׁ	(thing)	דָּבָר	meeting	פְּגִישָׁה
March	מֶרְץ	(question)	עִנְיָן	melody	לַחַן
march (n.)	מִצְעָד	an important matter	דָּבָר חָשׁוּב	melt (to)	הֵמִיס
march (to)	צָעַד	What's the matter?	מַה יֵּשׁ	member	חָבֵר
margin	שׁוּל	mattress	מִזְרָן	memorize (to)	לָמַד בְּעַל פֶּה
marine	יַמִּי	mature	מְבֻגָּר	memory	זִכָּרוֹן
mark	סִמָּן	matzoth	מַצּוֹת	mend (to)	תִּקֵּן
mark (to)	סִמֵּן	maximum	מַקְסִימוּם	mental	שִׂכְלִי
market	שׁוּק	May	מַאי	mention	הַזְכָּרָה
maroon	חוּם	may	יָכֹל	mention (to)	הִזְכִּיר
marriage	נִשּׂוּאִים	mayor	רֹאשׁ עִיר	menu	תַּפְרִיט
marrow	לְשַׁד	me	אוֹתִי	merchandise	סְחוֹרָה
marry (to)	נָשָׂא	meadow	שָׂדֶה	merchant	סוֹחֵר
marsh	בִּצָּה	meal	אֲרוּחָה	merciful	רַחְמָן
martyr	קָדוֹשׁ	mean (adj.)	אַכְזָר	merciless	אַכְזָר
marvel	פֶּלֶא	mean (to)	הִתְכַּוֵּן	mercury	כַּסְפִּית
marvelous	מַפְלִיא	meaning	מוּבָן	mercy	רַחְמָנוּת
masculine	גַּבְרִי, זָכָר	means	אֶמְצָעִים	merit	זְכוּת
mash (to)	פָּתַשׁ	meanwhile	בֵּינְתַיִם	merry	עַלִּיז
mask	מַסְוֶה	measure	מִדָּה	mess	בִּלְבּוּל
mask (to)	הִתְחַפֵּשׂ	measure (to)	מָדַד	message	יְדִיעָה
mason	בַּנַּאי	meat	בָּשָׂר	messenger	שָׁלִיחַ
masquerade	נֶשֶׁף מַסֵכוֹת	mechanic	מְכוֹנַאי	metal	מַתֶּכֶת
mass	חֹמֶר	mechanically	מְכָנִית	metallic	מַתַּכְתִּי
massacre	טֶבַח	medal	מֶדַלְיָה	meter (measurement)	מֶטֶר
mast	תֹּרֶן	meddle (to)	הִתְעָרֵב	(for gas, electricity, etc.)	שָׁעוֹן
master	אָדוֹן	mediate (to)	תִּוֵּךְ	method	שִׁטָה
master (to)	שָׁלַט בְּ-	medical	רְפוּאִי	metropolis	עִיר וָאֵם
mat	מַחְצֶלֶת	medicine	רְפוּאָה	mezuza	מְזוּזָה
match	גַּפְרוּר	mediocre	בֵּינוֹנִי	microphone	מַגְבִּיר קוֹל
(to light with)	גַּפְרוּר	mediocrity	בֵּינוֹנִיּוּת	middle (n.)	אֶמְצַע
(sport)	הִתְחָרוּת	meditate (to)	הָגָה	about the middle of March	בְּאֶמְצַע מֶרְץ
(a pair)	זוּג	meditation	הָגוּת	in the middle of the night	בַּחֲצוֹת הַלַּיְלָה
(marriage)	זִוּוּג	meek	עָנָו	middle (adj.)	אֶמְצָעִי, בֵּינוֹנִי
match (to)	הִתְאִים	meet (to)	פָּגַשׁ	middle-aged	בְּגִיל בֵּינוֹנִי
material (n.)	חֹמֶר	(to come across)	פָּגַשׁ		
maternal	אִמְהִי	(to know)	הִכִּיר		

middle-class	מַעֲמָד בֵּינוֹנִי
Middle Ages	יְמֵי הַבֵּינַיִם
midnight	חֲצוֹת
might	עֹז
mild	מָתוּן
mildew	יֵרָקוֹן
mildness	מְתִינוּת
mile	מִיל
military (adj.)	צְבָאִי
milk	חָלָב
milkman	חַלְבָּן
mill	טַחֲנָה
miller	טוֹחֵן
million	מִלְיוֹן
millionaire	בַּעַל מִלְיוֹן
mind	שֵׂכֶל
mind (to)	שָׁמַר
mine	מִכְרֶה
mine (pr.)	שֶׁלִּי
miner	כּוֹרֶה
minimum	מִינִימוּם
minister	צִיר, שַׂר, כֹּהֵן
ministry	כְּהֻנָּה
minor (adj.)	קָטָן
minority	מִעוּט
minus	פָּחוֹת
minute (n.)	דַּקָּה
any minute now	מִיָּד
Just a minute!	רַק רֶגַע!
Wait a minute.	חַכֵּה רֶגַע.
miracle	נֵס
mirror	רְאִי
miscarriage	הַפָּלָה
miscellaneous	שׁוֹנוֹת, שׁוֹנִים
mischief	קִלְקוּל
mischievous	מְחַבֵּל
miser	כִּילַי
miserable	אֻמְלָל
misery	צַעַר

misfortune	אָסוֹן
mishap	צָרָה
misprint	שַׁעוּת הַדְּפוּס
Miss (unmarried girl or woman)	גְּבֶרֶת
miss (to)	הֶחֱטִיא
mission	שְׁלִיחוּת
missionary	מִיסִיוֹנֶר
mist	עֲרָפֶל
mistake	שַׁעוּת
mistake (to)	שָׁעָה
Mister	מַר, אָדוֹן
Mr. Levi	מַר לֵוִי
mistrust	חֲשָׁד
mistrust (to)	חָשַׁד
mistrustful	חַשְׁדָּנִי
misunderstanding	אִי-הֲבָנָה
mix (to)	עִרְבֵּב
mixer	מְעָרֵב
mixture	תַּעֲרֹבֶת
mob	אֲסַפְסוּף
mobility	תְּנוּעָה
mobilization	גִּיּוּס
mobilize (to)	גִּיֵּס
mock (to)	לִגְלֵג
mockery	לִגְלוּג
mode	אֹפֶן
model	דֻּגְמָה
model (to)	הִרְגִּים
moderate	מְמֻצָּע
moderate (to)	מִתֵּן
moderation	מְתִינוּת
modern	חָדִישׁ
modest	עָנָו
modesty	עֲנָוָה
modification	שִׁנּוּי
modify (to)	שִׁנָּה
moist	רָטֹב
moisten (to)	הִרְטִיב

mold	דְּפוּס
moment	רֶגַע
any moment now	כָּרֶגַע
Just a moment.	רַק רֶגַע.
monarchy	מַלְכוּת
monastery	מִנְזָר
Monday	יוֹם שֵׁנִי
money	כֶּסֶף
monkey	קוֹף
monologue	שִׂיחַת יָחִיד
monopoly	מוֹנוֹפּוֹלִין
monotonous	חַדְגּוֹנִי
monotony	חַדְגּוֹנִיּוּת
monster	מִפְלֶצֶת
monstrosity	מִפְלֶצֶת
month	חֹדֶשׁ
last month	בַּחֹדֶשׁ שֶׁעָבַר
next month	בַּחֹדֶשׁ הַבָּא
monthly	חָדְשִׁי
monument	מַצֵּבָה
mood	מַצַּב-רוּחַ
moody	קוֹדֵר
moon	יָרֵחַ
honeymoon	יֶרַח הַדְּבַשׁ
moonlight	אוֹר הַיָּרֵחַ
moral (adj.)	מוּסָרִי
moralist	בַּעַל מוּסָר
morality	מוּסָר
more	יוֹתֵר
more or less	פָּחוֹת אוֹ יוֹתֵר
no more	דַּי
once more	עוֹד פַּעַם
the more ... the better	כָּל הַמּוֹסִיף... הֲרֵי זֶה מְשֻׁבָּח
moreover	יֶתֶר עַל כֵּן
morning	בֹּקֶר
this morning	הַבֹּקֶר
moron	מוֹרוֹן
mortal	אֱנוֹשִׁי
mortgage	מַשְׁכַּנְתָּא

mortgage (to)	מִשְׁכֵּן	multiple (adj.)	מֻפְגָּל	name	שֵׁם
Moslem	מֻסְלְמִי	multiply (to)	הִכְפִּיל	first name	שֵׁם פְּרָטִי
mosquito	יַתּוּשׁ	multitude	הָמוֹן	last name	שֵׁם הַמִּשְׁפָּחָה
most	הַגָּדוֹל בְּיוֹתֵר	mumble (to)	מִלְמֵל	What is your name?	מַה שִׁמְךָ
at most	לְכָל הַיּוֹתֵר	municipal	עִירוֹנִי	My name is...	שְׁמִי...
for the most part	בְּעִקָּר	municipality	עִירִיָּה	name (to)	כִּנָּה
most of us	רֻבֵּנוּ	munitions	נֶשֶׁק	nameless	חֲסַר שֵׁם
mostly	בְּעִקָּר	murder	רֶצַח	namely	כְּלוֹמַר
moth	עָשׁ	murder (to)	רָצַח	nap (a short sleep)	שֵׁנָה קַלָּה
mother	אֵם	murmur	לַחַשׁ	napkin	מַפִּית
mother-in-law	חוֹתֶנֶת	murmur (to)	לָחַשׁ	narcotic	מַרְדִּים
motion	תְּנוּעָה	muscle	שְׁרִיר	narrow	צַר
motionless	מְחֻסַּר תְּנוּעָה	museum	מוּזֵיאוֹם	narrow (to)	צִמְצֵם
motivate (to)	הֵנִיעַ	mushroom	פִּטְרִיָּה	nasal	חָטְמִי
motive	מֵנִיעַ	music	זִמְרָה, מוּסִיקָה	nasty	מָאוּס
motor (n.)	מָנוֹעַ	musical	מוּסִיקָלִי	nation	עַם, לְאוֹם
motto	סִסְמָה	musician	מְנַגֵּן	national	לְאֻמִּי
mount	גִּבְעָה	muslin	מוּסְלִין	nationality	לְאֻמִּיּוּת
mount (to)	עָלָה	must (have to)	צָרִיךְ	nationalization	הַלְאָמָה
mountain	הַר	mustard	חַרְדָּל	nationalize (to)	הִלְאִים
mountainous	הַרְרִי	mute	אִלֵּם	native (n.)	אֶזְרָח
mourn (to)	סָפַד	mutiny	מֶרֶד	native (adj.)	טִבְעִי
mournful	עָצוּב	mutter	מִלְמוּל	natural	טִבְעִי
mourning	אֵבֶל	mutter (to)	מִלְמֵל	naturally	בְּאֹפֶן טִבְעִי
mouse	עַכְבָּר	mutton	בְּשַׂר כֶּבֶשׂ	naturalness	טִבְעִיּוּת
mouth	פֶּה	mutual	הֲדָדִי	nature	טֶבַע
movable	נַיָּד	my	שֶׁלִּי	human nature	טֶבַע הָאָדָם
move (to)	הֵנִיעַ	myself	עַצְמִי	naughty	רַע
movement	תְּנוּעָה	mysterious	מִסְתּוֹרִי, סוֹדִי	nauseous	מַבְחִיל
movies	קוֹלְנוֹעַ	mystery	סוֹד	naval	יַמִּי
moving	נָע	mystic	מֻפְלָא	navel	טַבּוּר
mow (to)	קָצַר	myth	מִתּוֹס	navigation	סַפָּנוּת
Mr.	מַר, אָדוֹן			navy	צִי
Mrs.	מָרַת, גְּבֶרֶת	**N**		near	קָרוֹב
much	הַרְבֵּה			nearly	פִּמְעַט
mucous	רִירִי	nail	מַסְמֵר, צִפֹּרֶן	nearsighted	קְצַר רְאִיָּה
mud	בּוֹץ	nail (to)	סָמַר	neat	מְסֻדָּר
muddy	מְזֹהָם	naïve	תָּמִים	necessarily	בְּהֶכְרֵחַ
mule	פֶּרֶד	naked	עָרֹם	necessary	הֶכְרֵחִי

necessity	צֹרֶךְ
neck	צַוָּאר
necklace	עֲנָק
necktie	עֲנִיבָה
need	צֹרֶךְ
needle	מַחַט
needless	בִּלְתִּי-נָחוּץ
needy	דַל
negative (n.)	שְׁלִילָה
negative (adj.)	שְׁלִילִי
neglect	הַזְנָחָה
neglect (to)	הִזְנִיחַ
negligent	רַשְׁלָן
negotiate (to)	נָשָׂא וְנָתַן
negotiation	מַשָּׂא וּמַתָּן
Negro	כּוּשִׁי
neighbor	שָׁכֵן
neighborhood	שְׁכוּנָה
neither	לֹא זֶה
neither one	אַף אֶחָד לֹא
neither... nor	לֹא... וְלֹא...
nephew	בֶּן אָח
nerve	עֲצָב
What a nerve!	אֵיזוֹ חֻצְפָּה!
nervous	עַצְבָּנִי
nest	קֵן
net	רֶשֶׁת
net (adj.)	נָקִי
neurotic	עַצְבִּי
neuter	סְתָמִי
neutral	נֵיטְרָלִי
never	לְעוֹלָם לֹא
nevertheless	בְּכָל זֹאת
new	חָדָשׁ
news	חֲדָשׁוֹת
newsdealer	מוֹכֵר עִתּוֹנִים
newspaper	עִתּוֹן
next	אַחַר כָּךְ, הַבָּא
nice	נָאֶה

nickname	כִּנּוּי
niece	בַּת-אָח
night	לַיְלָה
nightgown	כְּסוּת לַיְלָה
nightmare	סִיּוּט
nine	תִּשְׁעָה
nineteen	תִּשְׁעָה עָשָׂר
nineteenth	הַתִּשְׁעָה עָשָׂר
ninety	תִּשְׁעִים
ninth	תְּשִׁיעִי
no	לֹא, אֵין
by no means	בְּשׁוּם אוֹפֶן לֹא
no longer	יוֹתֵר לֹא, אֵינוֹ עוֹד
no matter	אֵין דָּבָר
no matter how much	לֹא חָשׁוּב כַּמָּה
no one	אַף אֶחָד
no other	אֵין אַחֵר
No admittance.	הַכְּנִיסָה אֲסוּרָה.
No smoking.	אָסוּר לְעַשֵּׁן.
noble (adj.)	אָצִיל
nobody	אַף אֶחָד לֹא
nod	נִעְנֵעַ רֹאשׁ
noise	רַעַשׁ
noisy	מַרְעִישׁ
nominate (to)	הִצִּיעַ
nomination	הַעֲמָדָה
none	אַף אֶחָד לֹא
nonsense	שְׁטוּת
noodles	אִטְרִיּוֹת
noon	צָהֳרַיִם
nor	אַף לֹא
neither... nor	לֹא... וְלֹא...
normal (adj.)	נוֹרְמָלִי
north	צָפוֹן
northeast	צָפוֹן-מִזְרָח
northern	צְפוֹנִי
northward	צָפוֹנָה
northwest (n.)	צָפוֹן-מַעֲרָב
nose	אַף

nostril	נְחִיר
not	לֹא
notary	נוֹטַרְיוֹן
note	תָּו
note (to)	רָשַׁם
noted	רָשׁוּם
nothing	אֶפֶס
notice	הוֹדָעָה
notice (to)	שָׂם לֵב
notify (to)	הוֹדִיעַ
notion	מֻשָּׂג
notorious	מְפֻרְסָם
noun	שֵׁם עֶצֶם
nourish (to)	זָן
nourishment	מָזוֹן
novel (n.)	סִפּוּר
novel (adj.)	חָדָשׁ
novelty	חִדּוּשׁ
November	נוֹבֶמְבֶּר
now	עַכְשָׁו
now and then	לִפְעָמִים
nowadays	בַּיָּמִים הָאֵלֶּה
nowhere	בְּשׁוּם מָקוֹם לֹא
nude	עֵירֹם
nudge (to)	דָּחַף
nuisance	דָּבָר מַרְגִּיז
null	בָּטֵל
numb	קָפוּא
number	מִסְפָּר
number (to)	סָפַר
nurse	אָחוֹת רַחֲמָנִיָּה
nursery	חֲדַר יְלָדִים
nut (for eating)	אֱגוֹז
(for a screw)	אֹם

O

oar	מָשׁוֹט
oasis	נְוֵה
oat	שִׁבֹּלֶת שׁוּעָל

oath	שְׁבוּעָה	oculist	רוֹפֵא עֵינַיִם	on my arrival	מִשֶּׁהִגַּעְתִּי
obedience	צַיְּתָנוּת	odd	מְשֻׁנֶּה	on my part	מִצִּדִּי
obedient	צַיְּתָן	odor	רֵיחַ	on my word	עַל דְּבָרָתִי
obey (to)	שָׁמַע	of	שֶׁל	on Saturday	בְּשַׁבָּת
object	דָּבָר	of course	בְּוַדַּאי	on that occasion	אָז
object (to)	הִתְנַגֵּד	off		on the (an) average	בְּאֹפֶן מְמֻצָּע
objection	הִתְנַגְּדוּת	a day off	יוֹם חֹפֶשׁ	on the contrary	לְהֶפֶךְ
objective (n.)	מַטָּרָה	off and on	לְסֵרוּגִים	on the left	לִשְׂמֹאל
objectively	בְּאֹפֶן אוֹ בְּיֶקְסְטִי בִּי	off the coast	עַל יַד הַחוֹף	on the table	עַל הַשֻּׁלְחָן
objectivity	אוֹ בְּיֶקְטִיבִיּוּת	off the track	יָרַד מִן הַמַּסְלוּל	on the train	בָּרַכֶּבֶת
obligation	חוֹבָה	ten miles off	מֶרְחָק שֶׁל עֲשָׂרָה מִילִין	on the whole	בְּדֶרֶךְ כְּלָל
obligatory	מְחַיֵּב	(to) take off	פָּשַׁט	on time	בַּזְּמַן
oblige (to)	כָּפָה	Take it off the table.	הוֹרֵד מִן הַשֻּׁלְחָן.	once	פַּעַם
oblique	אֲלַכְסוֹנִי	Take your hat off.	הָסֵר אֶת הַכּוֹבַע.	all at once	בְּבַת אַחַת
obnoxious	נִתְעָב			at once	מִיָּד
obscene	גַּס	The meeting is off.	הָאֲסֵפָה בֻּטְלָה.	once a year	פַּעַם בְּשָׁנָה
obscure	אָפֵל	The cover is off.	הַמִּכְסֶה הֻגְדַּר.	once in awhile	מִפַּעַם לְפַעַם
obscurity	אֲפֵלָה	offend (to)	הֶעֱלִיב	one (pron.)	אֶחָד
observant	פִּקֵּחַ	offense	עֶלְבּוֹן	one (adj.)	אֶחָד
observation	תַּצְפִּית	offensive (adj.)	מַעֲלִיב	oneself	עַצְמוֹ
observatory	מִצְפֶּה	offer	הַצָּעָה	onion	בָּצָל
observe (to)	הִסְתַּכֵּל	offer (to)	הִצִּיעַ	only	רַק
observer	מִסְתַּכֵּל	offering	הַצָּעָה, קָרְבָּן	open (adj.)	פָּתוּחַ
obsolete	בָּטֵל	offhand	כִּלְאַחַר יָד	in the open	בַּגָּלוּי
obstacle	מִכְשׁוֹל	office (a building, a room, etc.)	מִשְׂרָד	open (to)	פָּתַח
obstinacy	עַקְשָׁנוּת	(position)	מִשְׂרָה	opening	פֶּתַח
obstinate	עַקְשָׁן	officer	קָצִין	opera	אוֹפֵּרָה
obstruct (to)	אָטַם	official	פָּקִיד	operate (to) on	נִתַּח
obstruction	מַעֲצוֹר	often	לְעִתִּים קְרוֹבוֹת	operation	נִתּוּחַ
obvious	בָּרוּר	oil	שֶׁמֶן	opinion	דֵּעָה
obviously	בִּבְרִירוּת	old	זָקֵן	opponent	מִתְנַגֵּד
occasion	הִזְדַּמְּנוּת	old age	זִקְנָה	opportune	בָּא בְּעִתּוֹ
occasionally	לִפְעָמִים	old man	זָקֵן	opportunity	הִזְדַּמְּנוּת
occupation	מִקְצוֹעַ	He is two years old.	הוּא בֶּן שְׁנָתַיִם.	oppose (to)	הִתְנַגֵּד
occupy (to)	תָּפַס	olive	זַיִת	opposite	הֵפֶךְ
occur (to)	קָרָה	olive oil	שֶׁמֶן זַיִת	opposition	הִתְנַגְּדוּת
occurrence	מִקְרֶה	on	עַל	oppress (to)	לָחַץ
ocean	אוֹקְיָנוֹס	on credit	בְּהַקָּפָה	oppression	לַחַץ
October	אוֹקְטוֹבֶּר	on foot	בְּרֶגֶל	optician	אוֹפְּטִיקָן

optimism	אוֹפְּטִימִיּוּת
optimist	אוֹפְּטִימִיסְט
optimistic	אוֹפְּטִימִיסְטִי
option	בְּרִירָה
or	אוֹ
either...or	אוֹ...אוֹ
oral	בְּעַל פֶּה
orange (n.)	תַּפּוּחַ זָהָב
orator	נוֹאֵם
orchard	פַּרְדֵּס
orchestra	תִּזְמֹרֶת
ordeal	מִבְחָן
order	סֵדֶר
in order to	כְּדֵי לְ-
(to) put in order	סִדֵּר
order (to)	פָּקַד
ordinary	פָּשׁוּט
organ	עֻגָּב
organization	הִסְתַּדְּרוּת
organize (to)	אִרְגֵּן
Orient (the)	מִזְרָח
oriental	מִזְרָחִי
origin	מוֹצָא
original	מְקוֹרִי
originality	מְקוֹרִיּוּת
originate (to)	יָצַר
originator	מְחַדֵּשׁ
ornament	עֲדִי
orphan	יָתוֹם
orthodox	אָדוּק
ostentation	הִתְהַדְּרוּת
other	אַחֵר
ought	צָרִיךְ
our(s)	שֶׁלָּנוּ
ourselves	בְּעַצְמֵנוּ
out	חוּץ, מִחוּץ
out of breath	בְּחֹסֶר נְשִׁימָה
out of date	מְיֻשָּׁן
out of doors	בַּחוּץ
out of order	לֹא בְּסֵדֶר
out of place	לֹא בִּמְקוֹם
out of print	לֹא בִּדְפוּס
out of respect for	מִתּוֹךְ כָּבוֹד
out of season	לֹא בְּעוֹנָה
out of style	לֹא בָּאָפְנָה
out of work	מְחֻסַּר עֲבוֹדָה
outcast	מְנֻדֶּה
outcome	תּוֹצָאָה
outdo (to)	הִשִּׂיג
outer	חִיצוֹן
outlay	הוֹצָאָה
outlet	מוֹצָא
outline	תָּכְנִית
outline (to)	רָשַׁם תָּכְנִית
outlook	סִכּוּי
output	תּוֹצֶרֶת
outrage	נְבָלָה
outrageous	נִתְעָב
outside	בַּחוּץ
outward	הַחוּצָה
oval	סְגַלְגַּל
oven	תַּנּוּר
over	עַל, מֵעַל
(to) be over	נִגְמַר
all over	בְּכָל מָקוֹם
all the world over	בְּכָל הָעוֹלָם
over again	עוֹד פַּעַם
over and over	חוֹזֵר
overcoat	אַדֶּרֶת
overcome (to)	כָּבַשׁ
overflow (to)	הֵצִיף
overhead	מִמַּעַל
overnight	בֶּן לַיְלָה
overpower (to)	נִצַּח
overrule (to)	בִּטֵּל
overseas	מֵעֵבֶר לַיָּם
overshoes	מַגָּפַיִם
oversight	הֶסַּח הַדַּעַת
overtake (to)	הִשִּׂיג
overthrow (to)	הָפַךְ
overwhelm (to)	הֵמַם
owe (to)	הָיָה חַיָּב
own	שֶׁל עַצְמוֹ
owner	בַּעַל
ox	שׁוֹר
oxygen	חַמְצָן
oyster	צְדָפָה

P

pace (speed)	מְהִירוּת
pacifist	אוֹהֵב שָׁלוֹם
pack (to)	אָרַז
package	חֲבִילָה
pact	בְּרִית
pad	מִרְפָּד
page	דַּף
paid	מְשֻׁלָּם
pain	כְּאֵב
pain (to)	הִכְאִיב
painful	מַכְאִיב
paint	צֶבַע
Wet paint.	צֶבַע טָרִי.
paint (to)	צָבַע
painter	צַבָּע, צַיָּר
painting	צִיּוּר
pair	זוּג
pale	חִוֵּר
pamphlet	חוֹבֶרֶת
pan	מַחֲבַת
pancake	לְבִיבָה
pane	שִׁמְשָׁה
panic	בֶּהָלָה
panorama	מַרְאֶה כְּלָלִי
pants	מִכְנָסַיִם
paper	נְיָר
paprika	פַּפְּרִיקָה
parachute	פַּרְשׂוּט

parade	תַּהֲלוּכָה	past (n.)	עָבָר, אָחֲרֵי	pearl	פְּנִינָה
paragraph	סָעִיף	half-past seven	שֶׁבַע וָחֵצִי	peasant	אִכָּר
parallel	מַקְבִּיל	past ten o'clock	אַחֲרֵי עֶשֶׂר	pebble	אֶבֶן
paralysis	שִׁתּוּק	the past year	הַשָּׁנָה שֶׁעָבְרָה	peculiar	מְשֻׁנֶּה
paralyze (to)	שִׁתֵּק	paste	דֶּבֶק	pedal	דַּוְשָׁה
parcel	חֲבִילָה	paste (to)	הִדְבִּיק	pedantic	קַפְּדָנִי
pardon	סְלִיחָה	pastry	תּוּפִינִים	pedestrian	הוֹלֵךְ בָּרֶגֶל
pardon (to)	סָלַח	pastry shop	חֲנוּת תּוּפִינִים	peel	קְלִיפָּה
parenthesis	סוֹגְרַיִם	patch	טְלַאי	peel (to)	קִלֵּף
parents	הוֹרִים	patch (to)	טָלָא	pen	עֵט
park	גַּן	patent (adj.)	גָּלוּי	fountain pen	עֵט נוֹבֵעַ
park (to)	חָנָה	paternal	אַבְהִי	penalty	עֹנֶשׁ
No parking.	הַחֲנָיָה אֲסוּרָה.	path	מְסִלָּה	pencil	עִפָּרוֹן
parkway	כְּבִישׁ	pathetic	נוֹגֵעַ לַלֵּב	penetrate (to)	חָדַר
parliament	בֵּית מְחוֹקְקִים	patience	סַבְלָנוּת	peninsula	חֲצִי-אִי
parlor	טְרַקְלִין	patient (adj.)	סַבְלָן	penitence	תְּשׁוּבָה
part	חֵלֶק	patriotic	פַּטְרִיוֹטִי	pension	קִצְבָּה
a great (large) part of	חֵלֶק גָּדוֹל	patriotism	פַּטְרִיוֹטִיּוּת	people	אֲנָשִׁים, עַם
part of speech	חֵלֶק דִּבּוּר	patron	תּוֹמֵךְ	pepper	פִּלְפֵּל
for one's part	מִצִּדּוֹ	patronize (to)	תָּמַךְ בְּ-	perceive (to)	הִרְגִּישׁ
(to) do one's part	עָשָׂה חֶלְקוֹ	pattern	תַּבְנִית	percent	אָחוּז לְמֵאָה
part (to)	נִפְרַד	pause	הַפְסָקָה	percentage	אָחוּזִים
partial	חֶלְקִי	pause (to)	הִפְסִיק	perfect	שָׁלֵם
partially	בְּמִקְצָת	pavement	מִדְרָכָה	perfect (to)	הִשְׁלִים
particular (n.)	פְּרָט	paw	רֶגֶל	perfection	הַשְׁלָמָה
particular (adj.)	מְיֻחָד	pawn	מַשְׁכּוֹן	perfectly	בִּשְׁלֵמוּת
particularity	דִּיּוּק	pawnbroker	מַלְוֶה בְּמַשְׁכּוֹן	perform (to)	פָּעַל, הִצִּיג
particularly	בְּיִחוּד	pay	תַּשְׁלוּם	performance (of a machine)	פְּעֻלָּה
partition	מְחִיצָה	pay (to)	שִׁלֵּם	(theater)	הַצָּגָה
partly	בְּמִקְצָת	(to) pay in cash	שִׁלֵּם בִּמְזֻמָּנִים	perfume	בֹּשֶׂם
partner	שֻׁתָּף	(to) pay a call	בִּקֵּר	perfume (to)	בִּשֵּׂם
party (social)	נֶשֶׁף	(to) pay attention	שָׂם לֵב	perhaps	אוּלַי
pass	מַעֲבָר	payment	תַּשְׁלוּם	peril	סַכָּנָה
pass (to)	עָבַר	pea	אֲפוּן	period	עֵת
passage	דֶּרֶךְ	peace	שָׁלוֹם	periodical	כְּתַב עֵת
passenger	נוֹסֵעַ	peaceful	שָׁקֵט	perish (to)	אָבַד
passion	תְּשׁוּקָה	peach	אֲפַרְסֵק	permanent	תָּדִיר
passive	סָבִיל	peak (summit, climax)	פִּסְגָּה	permission	רְשׁוּת
passport	דַּרְכּוֹן	pear	אַגָּס	permit	רִשָּׁיוֹן

permit (to)	הַרְשָׁה	pier	מַעֲגָנָה	(to) play a part	שִׂחֵק תַּפְקִיד
perplex (to)	פִּלְבֵּל	pig	חֲזִיר	(to) play a game	שִׂחֵק מִשְׂחָק
persecute (to)	רָדַף	pile	עֲרֵמָה	(to) play a joke	הִתֵּל
persecution	רְדִיפָה	pile (to)	עָרַם	player	שַׂחְקָן
perseverance	הַתְמָדָה	pill	גְּלוּלָה	playful	עַלִּיז
persist (to)	הִתְמִיד	pillar	עַמּוּד	playwright	כּוֹתֵב מַחֲזוֹת
person	אִישׁ	pillow	כַּר	plea	בַּקָּשָׁה
personal	אִישִׁי	pilot (airplane)	טַיָּס	plead (to)	בִּקֵּשׁ
personality	אִישִׁיּוּת	pin	סִכָּה	(to) plead with	הִתְחַנֵּן לִפְנֵי
perspective	פֶּרְסְפֶּקְטִיבָה	pinch (to)	צָבַט	pleasant	נָעִים
perspiration	זֵעָה	pink	וָרֹד	please (to)	הִשְׂבִּיעַ
perspire (to)	הִזִּיעַ	pioneer	חָלוּץ	please, if you please	בְּבַקָּשָׁה
persuade (to)	פִּתָּה	pious	חָסִיד	I'm pleased	אֲנִי שְׂבַע-רָצוֹן
pertaining	נוֹגֵעַ לְ-	pipe (for liquids)	צִנּוֹר	pleased	שְׂבַע-רָצוֹן
pessimist	פֶּסִּימִיסְט	(for smoking)	מִקְטֶרֶת	pleasure	עֹנֶג
petty	פָּעוּט	pity	רַחֲמִים	pledge	הַבְטָחָה
pharmacist	רוֹקֵחַ	What a pity!	חֲבָל!	pledge (to)	הִבְטִיחַ
pharmacy	בֵּית מִרְקַחַת	place	מָקוֹם	plenty	שֶׁפַע
phenomenon	תּוֹפָעָה	in my place	בִּמְקוֹמִי	plot	קֶשֶׁר
philanthropy	נַדְבָנוּת	in place	בַּמָּקוֹם	plow	מַחֲרֵשָׁה
philosopher	פִּילוֹסוֹף	(to) lose one's place	אָבַד אֶת הַמָּקוֹם	plow (to)	חָרַשׁ
philosophical	פִּילוֹסוֹפִי	(to) take place	קָרָה, הִתְקַיֵּם	plum	שְׁזִיף
philosophy	פִּילוֹסוֹפִיָה	place (to)	שָׂם	plunder	שָׁלַל
photograph	צֶלֶם	plain (adj.)	פָּשׁוּט	plural	רַבִּים
(to) take a photograph	הִצְטַלֵּם	plaintiff	תּוֹבֵעַ	plus	וְעוֹד
phrase	מִבְטָא	plan	תָּכְנִית	pneumonia	דַּלֶּקֶת הָרֵאָה
physical	גַשְׁמִי	plan (to)	תִּכְנֵן	pocket	כִּיס
physician	רוֹפֵא	plane	מִישׁוֹר	pocketbook	אַרְנָק
piano	פְּסַנְתֵּר	planet	כּוֹכַב לֶכֶת	poem	שִׁיר
pick (to)	נָקַר	plant	צֶמַח	poet	מְשׁוֹרֵר
(to choose)	בָּחַר	plant (to)	נָטַע	poetic	שִׁירִי
(to) pick a quarrel	חִרְחֵר	plaster	טִיחַ	poetry	שִׁירָה
I have a bone to pick	יֵשׁ לִי טַעֲנָה	plate (for food)	צַלַּחַת	point	נְקֻדָּה
(to) pick up (with the fingers)	הֵרִים	(sheet metal; printing)	לוּחַ	point (to)	הִצְבִּיעַ
pickle	מְלָפְפוֹן חָמוּץ	(photography)	טַבְלָה	pointed	מְחֻדָּד
picnic	טִיּוּל זִיג	platform	בָּמָה	poison	רַעַל
picture	תְּמוּנָה	play	מַחֲזֶה	poison (to)	הִרְעִיל
picturesque	צִיּוּרִי	play (to)	שִׂחֵק	poisoning (n.)	הַרְעָלָה
piece	חֲתִיכָה	(to) play an instrument	נָגֵן	polar	קֹטְבִּי

pole	מוֹט	power	כֹּחַ	(to) be present	נָכַח
police	מִשְׁטָרָה	electric power	כֹּחַ חַשְׁמַל	present (to)	הִצִּיג
policeman	שׁוֹטֵר	horsepower	כֹּחַ סוּס	preserve (to)	שָׁמַר
policy	שִׁטָה	power of attorney	כֹּחַ יִפּוּי	preside (to)	יָשַׁב בְּרֹאשׁ
Polish	פּוֹלָנִי	the great powers	הַמַעֲצָמוֹת הַגְדוֹלוֹת	president	נָשִׂיא
polish (to)	צִחְצַח	powerful	אַדִיר	press	מַכְבֵּשׁ
polite	נִמוּסִי	practical	מַעֲשִׂי	(machine)	מְכוֹנַת דְפוּס
politeness	נִמוּסִים	practice	מִנְהָג	(printing plant)	דְפוּס
political	פּוֹלִיטִי	practice (to)	הִתְאַמֵן	the press	הָעִתּוֹנוּת
politics	פּוֹלִיטִיקָה	praise	תְהִלָה	press (to)	כָּבַשׁ
pond	בְּרֵכָה	praise (to)	הִלֵל	(clothes)	גִהֵץ
poor	עָנִי	prank	לָצוֹן	(to urge)	הִפְצִיר
popular	הֲמוֹנִי	pray (to)	הִתְפַּלֵל	pressing	נֶחֱץ
population	אֻכְלוּסִיָה	prayer	תְפִלָה	pressure	לַחַץ
port	נָמֵל	preach (to)	הִטִיף	prestige	פְּרֶסְטִיג'
porter	סַבָּל	precaution	זְהִירוּת תְחִילָה	presume (to)	הֵנִיחַ
portrait	צִיוּר	precede (to)	הִקְדִים	pretend (to)	הֶעֱמִיד פָּנִים
position	מַצָב	preceding	קוֹדֵם	pretext	אֲמַתְלָה
positive	וַדַאי	precept	מִצְוָה	pretty (adj.)	יָפֶה
possess (to)	קָנָה	precious	יָקָר	pretty (adv.) (quite)	כִּמְעַט
possession	קִנְיָן	precise	מְדֻיָק	pretty nearly	כִּמְעַט
possibility	אֶפְשָׁרוּת	predecessor	קוֹדֵם	pretty soon	עוֹד מְעַט
possible	אֶפְשָׁרִי	preface	הַקְדָמָה	prevail (to)	הִשְׁפִּיעַ עַל
post	דֹאַר	prefer (to)	בָּכַר	prevent (to)	מָנַע
postage	מְחִיר מִשְׁלוֹחַ	preference	בִּכּוּר	prevention	מְנִיעָה
postage stamp	בּוּל	pregnancy	הֵרָיוֹן	previous	קוֹדֵם
post card	גְלוּיָה	pregnant	הָרָה	the previous year	אֶשְׁתָּקַד
poster	מוֹדָעָה	prejudice	מִשְׁפָּט קָדוּם	prey	טֶרֶף
posterity	זֶרַע	preliminary	מַבוֹאִי	price	מְחִיר
post office	בֵּית דֹאַר	preparation	הֲכָנָה	pride	גַאֲוָה
pot	סִיר	prepare (to)	הֵכִין	priest	כֹּהֵן
potato	תַפּוּחַ אֲדָמָה	prescribe (to)	צִוָה	prime (adj.)	רִאשׁוֹן
poultry	עוֹפוֹת	presence	מַעֲמָד	principal (adj.)	רָאשִׁי
pound	לִטְרָה	present (n.)	מַתָּנָה	principal (n.)	מְנַהֵל
pour (to)	שָׁפַךְ	(to) give a present	נָתַן מַתָּנָה	principle	עִקָרוֹן
It's pouring.	גֶשֶׁם יוֹרֵד.	present (adj.)	הוֶֹה	print (to)	הִדְפִּיס
poverty	עֹנִי	at present	עַכְשָׁו, כָּעֵת	printing	דְפוּס
powder	אָבָק	present-day	שֶׁל הַיוֹם	prison	בֵּית אֲסוּרִים
face powder	פּוּדְרָה	the present month	הַחֹדֶשׁ	prisoner	אָסִיר

private	פְּרָטִי	property	רְכוּשׁ	publisher	מוֹצִיא לָאוֹר
privilege	זְכוּת	proportion	יַחַס	pull (to)	מָשַׁךְ
prize	פְּרָס	proposal	הַצָּעָה	(to) pull off	הֵסִיר
prize (to)	הוֹקִיר	propose (to)	הִצִּיעַ	(to) pull up	עָקַר
probable	שֶׁיִּתָּכֵן	proprietor	בַּעַל	(to) pull through	הִשְׁחִיל
probably	וַדַּאי	prosaic	שָׁכִיחַ	pulpit	בָּמָה
problem	בְּעָיָה	prose	פְּרוֹזָה	pulse	דֹּפֶק
procedure	תַּהֲלִיךְ	prosecute (to)	תָּבַע לְדִין	pump	מַשְׁאֵבָה
proceed (to)	הִתְחִיל	prosecution	תְּבִיעָה	punish (to)	עָנַשׁ
process	תַּהֲלִיךְ	prospect	סִכּוּי	punishment	עֹנֶשׁ
procession	תַּהֲלוּכָה	prosper (to)	שִׂגְשֵׂג	pupil	תַּלְמִיד
proclaim (to)	הִכְרִיז	prosperity	שֶׁפַע	puppet	בֻּבָּה
produce (to)	יָצַר	prosperous	מַצְלִיחַ	purchase	קְנִיָּה
product	תּוֹצֶרֶת, מוֹצָר	prostrate	מִשְׁתַּחֲוֶה	purchase (to)	קָנָה
productive	פּוֹרֶה	protect (to)	הֵגֵן	pure	טָהוֹר
profane	חֻלּוֹנִי	protection	הֲגָנָה	purify (to)	טִהֵר
profession	מִקְצוֹעַ	protector	מָגֵן	purity	טֹהַר
professional	מִקְצוֹעִי	protest	מֶחָאָה	purple	אַרְגָּמָן
professor	פְּרוֹפֶסוֹר	protest (to)	מָחָה	purpose	מַטָּרָה, כַּוָּנָה
profile	פְּרוֹפִיל	proud	גֵּאֶה	for the purpose	כְּדֵי
profit	רֶוַח	prove (to)	הוֹכִיחַ	on purpose	בְּכַוָּנָה
profit (to)	הִרְוִיחַ	proverb	מָשָׁל	to no purpose	לַשָּׁוְא
profits	רְוָחִים	provide (to)	סִפֵּק	With what purpose?	לְאֵיזוֹ מַטָּרָה?
program	תָּכְנִית	provided that	בִּתְנַאי שֶׁ-	purse	אַרְנָק
progress	הִתְקַדְּמוּת	province	מָחוֹז	pursue (to)	רָדַף
progress (to)	הִתְקַדֵּם	provision	צֵידָה	pursuit	רְדִיפָה
progressive	מִתְקַדֵּם, פְּרוֹגְרֶסִיבִי	provoke (to)	גֵּרָה	push (to)	דָּחַף
prohibit (to)	אָסַר	proximity	קִרְבָה	put (to)	שָׂם
prohibition	אִסּוּר	prude	צָנוּעַ	(to) put away	חָסַךְ, הִנִּיחַ
project	מְשִׂימָה	prudence	מְתִינוּת	(to) put in order	סִדֵּר
promise	הַבְטָחָה	prune	שָׁזִיף מְיֻבָּשׁ	(to) put off	דָּחָה
promise (to)	הִבְטִיחַ	psalm	מִזְמוֹר	(to) put on clothes	לָבַשׁ
promotion	הִתְקַדְּמוּת	psychic	פְּסִיכִי	(to) put on weight	הִשְׁמִין
prompt	מָהִיר	psychological	פְּסִיכוֹלוֹגִי	(to) put out a light, etc.	כִּבָּה
promptness	דַּיְקָנוּת	psychology	פְּסִיכוֹלוֹגְיָה		
pronoun	מִלַּת הַגּוּף	public (n.)	קָהָל, צִבּוּר	(to) put out a book, etc.	הוֹצִיא לָאוֹר
pronounce (to)	בִּטֵּא	public (adj.)	עֲמָמִי	(to) put up for sale	הֶעֱמִיד לִמְכִירָה
proof	הוֹכָחָה	publication	הוֹצָאָה לָאוֹר		
proper	מַתְאִים	publish (to)	הוֹצִיא לָאוֹר	(to) put up with	סָבַל

(to) put to bed	הִשְׁכִּיב
(to) put to sleep	הִרְדִּים
(to) put together	אָחֵד
Put on your hat!	חֲבֹשׁ אֶת הַכּוֹבַע!
puzzle	חִידָה
puzzle (to)	הִפְלִיא

Q

quaint	פְּלִתִּי-מְצֻגֶּי
quake	רָעַד
qualification	סְגֻלָּה
quality	אֵיכוּת
quantity	כַּמּוּת
quarrel	רִיב
quarrel (to)	רָב
quarter	רֶבַע
queen	מַלְכָּה
queer	מְשֻׁנֶּה
quench (to)	כִּבָּה
question	שְׁאֵלָה
out of the question	לֹא בָּא בְּחֶשְׁבּוֹן
question mark	סִמָן שְׁאֵלָה
without any question	בְּלִי סָפֵק
(to) ask a question	שָׁאַל שְׁאֵלָה
What's the question?	מָה הַשְּׁאֵלָה?
question (to)	שָׁאַל
quick	מָהִיר
quickly	בִּמְהִירוּת
Come quickly!	מַהֵר!
quiet (adj.)	שָׁקֵט
Keep quiet!	שְׁקֹט!
quiet (to)	הִשְׁקִיט
quit (to)	הִתְפַּטֵּר
quite	לְגַמְרֵי
quite good	דַּי טוֹב
quote (to)	צִטֵּט

R

rabbi	רַב, רַבִּי
rabbinical	רַבָּנִי
race (contest)	הִתְחָרוּת
race (people)	גֶּזַע
radiant	מַזְהִיר
radio	רַדְיוֹ
radish	צְנוֹן
rag	סְמַרְטוּט
rage	זַעַם
ragged	בָּלוּי
rail	פַּס
railroad	מְסִלַּת בַּרְזֶל
railroad station	תַּחֲנַת רַכֶּבֶת
rain	גֶּשֶׁם
rainbow	קֶשֶׁת
rainy	גָּשׁוּם
raise	הַעֲלָאָה
raise (to) (prices, salary)	הֶעֱלָה
raise (animals, a crop)	גִּדֵּל
(to) raise an objection	הִתְנַגֵּד
raisin	צִמּוּק
rake	מַגְרֵפָה
rally (to)	קִבֵּץ
range	רֶכֶס
range (to)	שׁוֹטֵט
rank (n.)	שׁוּרָה
ransom	פִּדְיוֹן
rap (to)	דָּפַק
rapid	מָהִיר
rapidity	מְהִירוּת
rapidly	מַהֵר
rapture	הִתְפַּעֲלוּת
rare	נָדִיר
rat	עַכְבָּר
rate	מִדָּה, אָחוּז
at any rate	בְּכָל אֹפֶן
at the rate of	לְפִי שֶׁעוּר שֶׁל
rate of interest	רִבִּית
rate of exchange	שַׁעַר חֲלִיפִין
first rate	מִמַּדְרֵגָה רִאשׁוֹנָה
rate (to)	אָמַד
rather	מֻטָּב שֶׁ-
rather good	דַּי טוֹב
rather than	מֻטָּב שֶׁ...מִן...
I'd rather go.	מֻטָּב שֶׁאֵלֵךְ.
ration	מָנָה
rational	שִׂכְלִי
rattle (to)	קִשְׁקֵשׁ
rave (to)	הִשְׁתּוֹלֵל
raw (meat)	חַי
ray	קֶרֶן
razor	תַּעַר
razor blade	תַּעַר
reach	הַשָּׂגָה
reach (to)	הִשִּׂיג
react (to)	הֵגִיב
reaction	תְּגוּבָה
reactionary (adj.)	נָסוֹג
read (to)	קָרָא
reader	קוֹרֵא
readily	בִּמְהִירוּת
ready	מוּכָן
real	מַמָּשִׁי
reality	מְצִיאוּת
realization	הַגְשָׁמָה
realize (to)	הִרְגִּישׁ, מִמֵּשׁ
(to) realize a danger	הִכִּיר סַכָּנָה
(to) realize a profit	הִרְוִיחַ
really	בֶּאֱמֶת
reap (to)	קָצַר
rear (n.)	אָחוֹר
rear (adj.)	אֲחוֹרִי
reason	סִבָּה, הִגָּיוֹן
reasonable	צוֹדֵק
rebel	מוֹרֵד
rebel (to)	מָרַד
rebellion	מֶרֶד
rebellious	מַרְדָּנִי
recall (to)	זָכַר

receipt	קַבָּלָה	redolent	רֵיחָנִי	regular	סָדִיר
receive (to)	קִבֵּל	reduce (to)	הִפְחִית	regulate (to)	סִדֵּר
receiver	מְקַבֵּל	reduction	הַפְחָתָה	regulation	סִדּוּר, חֹק
recent	חָדָשׁ	redundant	עוֹדֵף	rehabilitate (to)	שִׁקֵּם
reception	קַבָּלָה	reed	קָנֶה	rehearsal	חֲזָרָה
recession	נְסִיגָה	reel	סְלִיל	rehearse (to)	חָזַר
reciprocate	גָּמַל	reel (to)	פָּרַה	reign	מִמְשָׁל
recite (to)	דִּקְלֵם	referee	שׁוֹפֵט	reign (to)	מָשַׁל
reckless	בִּלְתִּי זָהִיר	reference (in a book)	מַרְאֵה מָקוֹם	reinforce (to)	חִזֵּק
recklessly	בְּאִי-זְהִירוּת	(for a job)	הַמְלָצָה	reject (to)	דָּחָה
reckon (to)	חָשַׁב	refine (to)	זִקֵּק	rejection	דְּחִיָּה
recline (to)	הֵסֵב	refined	עָדִין	rejoice (to)	שָׂמַח
recognition	הַכָּרָה	refinement	עֲדִינוּת	relapse	נְסִיגָה
recognize (to)	הִכִּיר	reflect (to)	חָשַׁב	relate (to) (tell)	סִפֵּר
recollect (to)	זָכַר	reflection (thought)	מַחְשָׁבָה	relation	יַחַס
recollection	זִכָּרוֹן	(in mirror)	בְּבוּאָה	(kinship)	קִרְבָה
recommend (to)	הִמְלִיץ	reflex (adj.)	מֻחְזָר	(be connected with)	קָשׁוּר לְ-
recommendation	הַמְלָצָה	reform (to)	הֵטִיב דַּרְכּוֹ	everything relating to	הַכֹּל הַנּוֹגֵעַ לְ-
recompense	תַּשְׁלוּם	refrain	פִּזְמוֹן	in relation to	בְּיַחַס
reconcile (to)	הִשְׁלִים	refrain (to)	נִמְנַע	relationship	קִרְבָה
reconciliation	הַשְׁלָמָה	refreshment	מַטְעָם	relative (n.)	קָרוֹב
record (phonograph)	תַּקְלִיט	refrigerator	מְקָרֵר	relative (adj.)	יַחֲסִי
(sports)	שִׂיא	refuge	מִקְלָט	relax (to)	רָפָה
(voucher,etc.)	תְּעוּדָה	(to) take refuge	מָצָא מִקְלָט	relaxation	רִפְיוֹן, נֹפֶשׁ
on record	רָשׁוּם	refugee	פָּלִיט	release	שִׁחְרֵר
record (to)	רָשַׁם	refund (to)	הֶחֱזִיר	relent	נֶעְתַּר
records	רְשִׁימוֹת	refusal	סֵרוּב	relentless	אַכְזָרִי
recover (to)	הִבְרִיא	refuse (to)	סֵרַב	relevant	שַׁיָּךְ
recovery	הַבְרָאָה	refute (to)	סָתַר	reliable	מְהֵימָן
recreation	בִּדּוּר	regard	חִבָּה	reliance	אֵמוּן
recruit	טִירוֹן	in regard to	בְּנוֹגֵעַ לְ-	relic	שָׂרִיד
rectangle	מַלְבֵּן	in this regard	בְּמוּבָן זֶה	relief	רְוָחָה
rectify (to)	תִּקֵּן	without any regard to	בְּלִי שִׂים לֵב לְ-	relieve (to)	הֵקֵל
recuperate (to)	הֶחֱלִים	regime	מִשְׁטָר	religion	דָּת
recuperation	הַחְלָמָה	region	אֵזוֹר	religious	דָּתִי
red	אָדֹם	register	רְשִׁימָה	relinquish (to)	נָטַשׁ
reddish	אֲדַמְדַּם	register (to)	נִרְשַׁם	relish	טַעַם
redeem (to)	פָּדָה	regret	צַעַר	relish (to)	נֶהֱנָה
redemption	פִּדְיוֹן	regret (to)	הִצְטַעֵר	reluctance	אִי-רָצוֹן

reluctant	חֲסַר רָצוֹן
rely upon (to)	סָמַךְ עַל
remain (to)	נִשְׁאַר
remainder	שְׁאֵרִית
remark	הֶעָרָה
remark (to)	הֵעִיר
remarkable	נִפְלָא
remedy	תְּרוּפָה
remember (to)	זָכַר
I don't remember.	אֵינִי זוֹכֵר.
Remember me to him.	דְּרִישַׁת שָׁלוֹם מִמֶּנִּי.
remembrance	מַזְכֶּרֶת
remind (to)	הִזְכִּיר
reminder	מַזְכֶּרֶת
remnant	שְׁאֵרִית
remorse	חֲרָטָה
remote	רָחוֹק
removal	הֲסָרָה
remove (to) (a stain, etc.)	הֵסִיר
(to take to another place)	הֶעֱבִיר
(from a job)	פִּטֵּר
renew (to)	חִדֵּשׁ
renounce (to)	וִתֵּר בְּ-
rent	שְׂכַר דִּירָה
rent (to)	שָׂכַר
repair	תִּקּוּן
repair (to)	תִּקֵּן
reparation	שִׁלּוּם
repeat (to)	חָזַר
repent (to)	הִתְחָרֵט
repentance	תְּשׁוּבָה
repertoire	אוֹצָר
repetition	חֲזָרָה
replica	הֶעְתֵּק
reply	תְּשׁוּבָה
reply (to)	הֵשִׁיב
report	דִּין וְחֶשְׁבּוֹן
reporter	עִתּוֹנָאִי
represent (to)	הִצִּיג
representation	הַצָּגָה
representative (n.)	בָּא כֹּחַ
repress (to)	דִּכֵּא
reprimand	נְזִיפָה
reprimand (to)	נָזַף
reproach	הוֹכָחָה
reproach (to)	הוֹכִיחַ
reproduce (to)	הֶעְתִּיק
reprove (to)	הוֹכִיחַ
reptile	רֶמֶשׂ
republic	רֶפּוּבְּלִיקָה
repulsive	דּוֹחֶה
reputable	הָגוּן
reputation	שֵׁם
request	בַּקָּשָׁה
request (to)	בִּקֵּשׁ
require (to)	דָּרַשׁ
rescue	הַצָּלָה
rescue (to)	הִצִּיל
research	מֶחְקָר
resemble (to)	דָּמָה
resent (to)	כָּעַס עַל
resentment	תַּרְעֹמֶת
reservation	שְׁמִירָה
reserve (to)	שָׁמַר
reservoir	מִקְוֶה
resign (to)	הִתְפַּטֵּר
resignation	הִתְפַּטְּרוּת
resist (to)	הִתְנַגֵּד
resistance	הִתְנַגְּדוּת
resolute	תַּקִּיף
resolution	הַחְלָטָה
resolve (to)	הֶחְלִיט
resort	אֶמְצָעִי
resort (to)	אָחַז בְּאֶמְצָעִי
resource	מָקוֹר
respect (esteem, regard)	כָּבוֹד
in this respect	בְּמוּבָן זֶה
in (with) respect to	בְּהִתְחַשֵּׁב עִם
with due respect	בְּכָבוֹד
respect (to)	כִּבֵּד
respectful	מְכַבֵּד
respite	רְוָחָה
responsibility	אַחְרָיוּת
responsible	אַחְרַאי
rest	מְנוּחָה
rest (to)	נָח
restaurant	מִסְעָדָה
restful	מַרְגִּיעַ
restless	חֲסַר מְנוּחָה
restoration	הֲשָׁבָה
restore (to)	הֵשִׁיב
restrain (to)	עָצַר
restraint	מַעְצוֹר
restrict (to)	הִגְבִּיל
restricted	מֻגְבָּל
restriction	הַגְבָּלָה
result	תּוֹצָאָה
result (to)	יָצָא
resume (to)	הִמְשִׁיךְ
retail	קִמְעָא
retain (to)	הֶחְזִיק
retaliate (to)	הֵשִׁיב גְּמוּל
retaliation	נְקָמָה
retire (to)	מָשַׁה יָדוֹ מִן
retirement	פְּרִישָׁה
retract (to)	חָזַר בּוֹ
retraction	בִּטּוּל
retreat	נְסִיגָה
retrench (to)	הִקְטִין
retribution	גְּמוּל
return	שִׁיבָה, חֲזָרָה
in return	תְּמוּרָה
return trip	הָלוֹךְ וָשׁוֹב
Many happy returns.	רַב בְּרָכוֹת.
return (to)	שָׁב
(to go or come back)	חָזַר

(to give back)	הֵשִׁיב	riddle	חִידָה	(of a bell)	צִלְצוּל
(to) return a book	הֵשִׁיב סֵפֶר	ride	רְכִיבָה	ring (to)	צִלְצֵל
(to) return a favor	הֵשִׁיב טוֹבָה	ride (to)	רָכַב	rinse	שָׁטַף
(to) return home	שָׁב הַבַּיְתָה	ridge (n.)	חָרִיץ	riot	פְּרָעוֹת
reveal (to)	גִלָּה	ridicule	לַעַג	ripe	בָּשֵׁל
revelation	גִלּוּי	ridiculous	מְגֻחָךְ	ripen (to)	הִתְבַּשֵּׁל
revelry	הוֹלְלוּת	rifle	רוֹבֶה	rise	קִימָה
revenge	נְקָמָה	right (n.)	צֶדֶק, יָמִין	rise (to) (stand up, get up)	קָם
revenue	הַכְנָסָה	by right	לְפִי הַצֶּדֶק	(to move upward)	עָלָה
revere (to)	הֶעֱרִיץ	(to) have a right to	יֵשׁ לוֹ הַזְּכוּת	(the sun)	זָרַח
reverence	יִרְאָה	(to) be in the right	צָדַק	(to rebel)	מָרַד
reverend	נִכְבָּד	to the right	יְמִינָה	(prices, salary)	עָלָה
reverent	מַעֲרִיץ	Right!	נָכוֹן!	risk	סַכָּנָה
reversal	הִפּוּךְ	right	יְמָנִי	risk (to)	סִכֵּן
reverse	הֵפֶךְ	(correct)	נָכוֹן	rite	טֶקֶס
reverse (to)	הָפַךְ	(fit)	מַתְאִים	ritual	פֻּלְחָן
revert (to)	הֵסַב לְאָחוֹר	(just)	צוֹדֵק	rival	יָרִיב, מִתְחָרֶה
review	חֲזָרָה	all right	בְּסֵדֶר	rivalry	הִתְחָרְגוּת
review (to)	חָזַר	right away	מִיָּד	river	נָהָר
revise (to)	חִדֵּשׁ	right hand	יַד יָמִין	road	דֶּרֶךְ
revision	חִדּוּשׁ	right here	פֹּה	roar	שְׁאָגָה
revive (to)	הֶחֱיָה	right now	עַכְשָׁו	roar (to)	שָׁאַג
revoke (to)	בִּטֵּל	right in the middle	בְּדִיּוּק בָּאֶמְצַע	roast	צָלִי
revolt (to)	מָרַד			roast (to)	צָלָה
revolution	מֶרֶד, מַהְפֵּכָה	right or wrong	נָכוֹן אוֹ לֹא	rob (to)	גָּזַל
revolutionary	מַהְפְּכָנִי	the right man	הָאִישׁ הַנָּכוֹן	robber	גַּזְלָן
revolve (to)	הִסְתּוֹבֵב	the right time	הַשָּׁעָה בְּדִיּוּק	robbery	גְּזֵלָה
reward	גְּמוּל	(to) be right	צָדַק	robe	אִצְטַלָּה
rhetoric	מְלִיצָה	Is this right?	הַאִם זֶה נָכוֹן?	robust	חָזָק
rheumatic	שִׁגְרוֹנִי	It's right.	זֶה נָכוֹן.	rock	סֶלַע
rheumatism	שִׁגָּרוֹן	It's not right.	זֶה לֹא נָכוֹן.	rock (to)	נִדְנֵד
rhubarb	חָמִיץ	righteous	צַדִּיק	rocky	סַלְעִי
rhyme	חָרוּז	righteousness	צֶדֶק	rod	מַטֶּה
rib	צֵלָע	rightful	צוֹדֵק	roe	אַיָּלָה
ribbon	סֶרֶט	rigid	קָשֶׁה	role	תַּפְקִיד
rice	אֹרֶז	rigor	קֹשִׁי	roll	מְגִלָּה
rich	עָשִׁיר	rigorous	קָשֶׁה	roll (to)	גָּלַל
richness	עֹשֶׁר	rind	קְלִיפָּה	Roman	רוֹמִי
rid (to get)	הִתְפַּטֵּר מִן	ring (for finger)	טַבַּעַת	romantic	רוֹמַנְטִי

romanticism	רוֹמֶנְטִיּוּת	rule	מִמְשָׁל	sacrifice (to)	הִקְרִיב
roof	גַּג	rule (to)	מָשַׁל	sacrilege	חִלּוּל
room	חֶדֶר	(to draw lines)	שִׂרְטֵט	sad	עָצוּב
(space)	מָקוֹם	(to govern)	שָׁלַט	sadden (to)	הֶעֱצִיב
inside room	חֶדֶר פְּנִימִי	(to establish a rule) קָבַע חֹק		saddle	אֻכָּף
There's no room for doubt.	אֵין מָקוֹם לְסָפֵק.	(to) rule over	שָׁלַט עַל	sadness	עֶצֶב
There's not enough room.	אֵין דַּי מָקוֹם.	ruler	מוֹשֵׁל	safe (adj.)	שָׁמוּר
(to) make room for	פִּנָּה מָקוֹם	rummage	שִׁירַיִם	(from danger)	בָּטוּחַ
There's no room.	אֵין מָקוֹם.	rumor	שְׁמוּעָה	(from risk)	בָּטוּחַ
root	שֹׁרֶשׁ	run (to)	רָץ	(unhurt)	שָׁלֵם
rope	חֶבֶל	(a watch, a machine, etc.)	פָּעַל	safe and sound	בָּרִיא וְשָׁלֵם
rose	שׁוֹשַׁנָּה	(to) run across	פָּגַשׁ	safe trip	דֶּרֶךְ צְלֵחָה
rot (to)	הִרְקִיב	(to) run away	בָּרַח	safe (to be)	בָּטוּחַ
rotten	רָקוּב	(to) run into	פָּגַשׁ	safeguard	שְׁמִירָה
rouge	אֹדֶם	(to) run over (a liquid)	נִשְׁפַּךְ	safely	בִּבְטָחָה
rough (adj.)	מְחֻסְפָּס	(to) run over by car, etc.		safety	בִּטָּחוֹן, מִבְטָח
round (adj.)	עָגֹל		צָבַר עַל	safety razor	תַּעַר מִבְטָח
a round table	שֻׁלְחָן עָגֹל	(to) run up and down	הִתְרוֹצֵץ	safety zone	אֵזוֹר מִבְטָח
round numbers	מִסְפָּרִים עֲגֻלִּים	(to) run wild	הִתְפָּרַע	safety bolt	בָּרִיחַ מִבְטָח
round trip	הָלוֹךְ וָשׁוֹב	rupture	שֶׁבֶר	Sahara	סַחֲרָה
round (adv.)	סָבִיב	rural	כַּפְרִי	sail	מִפְרָשׂ
all year round	כָּל הַשָּׁנָה	rush	חִפָּזוֹן	sail (to)	הִפְלִיג
round (n.)	סִבּוּב	rush (to)	מִהֵר	sailor	מַלָּח
round off	עִגֵּל	(to) rush in	פָּרַץ	saint	קָדוֹשׁ
route	דֶּרֶךְ	Russian	רוּסִי	sake	מַעַן
routine	שִׁגְרָה	rust	חֲלוּדָה	for my sake	לְמַעֲנִי
row (rank, file)	שׁוּרָה	rustic	כַּפְרִי	for the sake of	לְמַעַן
(brawl)	רַעַשׁ	rusty	חָלוּד	salad	סָלָט
row (to)	חָתַר	ruthless	אַכְזָרִי	salary	מַשְׂכֹּרֶת
royal	מַלְכוּתִי	rye	שִׁפּוֹן	sale	מְכִירָה
rub (to)	שִׁפְשֵׁף			salesman	זַבָּן
rubber	גּוּמִי	**S**		salt	מֶלַח
rubbers (overshoes)	עַרְדָּלַיִם	Sabbath	שַׁבָּת	salt (to)	מָלַח
rubbish	אַשְׁפָּה	saccharin	סַכָּרִין	salty	מָלוּחַ
rude	גַּס	sack	שַׂק	salute (in army)	הַצְדָּעָה
rug	שָׁטִיחַ	sacrament	סַקְרָמֶנְט	salute (to)	הִצְדִּיעַ
ruin	חֻרְבָּן	sacramental	קָדוֹשׁ	salvation	גְּאוּלָה
ruin (to)	הֶחֱרִיב	sacred	קָדוֹשׁ	salve	מִשְׁחָה
		sacrifice	קָרְבָּן	same	אוֹתוֹ

all the same	בְּכָל זֹאת	scaffold	זָקִיף	(for windows,etc.)	וִילוֹן
sample	דוּגְמָה	scald (to)	צָרַב	(movies)	מָסָךְ
sanctify	קִדֵּשׁ	scales	מֹאזְנַיִם	(of smoke)	מָסָךְ
sanction	אִשּׁוּר	scallion	בָּצָל אַשְׁקְלוֹן, כְּצַלְצַל	(of fire)	מָסָךְ
sanctuary	מִשְׁכָּן	scalp	קַרְקֶפֶת	screw	פֶּלֶג
sand	חוֹל	scan (to)	הִסְתַּכֵּל	screwdriver	מַבְרֵג
sandal	סַנְדָּל	scandal	נְבָלָה	scribe	סוֹפֵר
sandwich	סַנְדְּוִיץ	scanty	מִצְמָץ	scripture	כִּתְבֵי הַקֹּדֶשׁ
sandy	מָלֵא חוֹל	scapegoat	שָׂעִיר לַעֲזָאזֵל	scroll	מְגִלָּה
sane	שָׁפוּי	scar	צַלֶּקֶת	scrub (to)	מָרַק
sanitary	בְּרִיאוּתִי	scarce	נָדִיר	scruple	הֶסֵּס
sanitation	שְׁמִירַת הַבְּרִיאוּת	scarcely	כִּמְעַט שֶׁ-	scrupulous	קַפְּדָנִי
sap	מִיץ	scare (to)	הִפְחִיד	scrutinize (to)	בָּחַן
sarcasm	לַעַג	scarf	סוּדָר	sculpture	פִּסּוּל
sarcastic	לוֹעֵג	scatter (to)	פִּזֵּר	scum	קֶצֶף
sardine	סַרְדִּין	scene	חִזָּיוֹן	sea	יָם
sash	אַבְנֵט	scenery	תְּפְאוֹרָה	seal	חוֹתָם
satan	שָׂטָן	schedule	רְשִׁימָה	seal (to)	חָתַם
satchel	מִזְוָדָה	scheme	תַּחְבּוּלָה	seam	תֶּפֶר
satin	סַטֶן	scholar	תַּלְמִיד חָכָם	search (act of looking for)	חִפּוּשׂ
satire	סַטִירָה	scholarship	לַמְדָנוּת		
satisfaction	שְׂבִיעַת רָצוֹן	school	בֵּית סֵפֶר	(scrutiny, investigation)	חֲקִירָה
satisfactory	מַשְׂבִּיעַ-רָצוֹן	science	מַדָּע	(for concealed weapons,etc.)	מִשּׁוּשׁ
satisfy (to)	הִשְׂבִּיעַ	scientific	מַדָּעִי		
saturated	רָוֶה	scientist	אִישׁ מַדָּע	in search of	מְחַפֵּשׂ
Saturday	שַׁבָּת	scissors	מִסְפָּרַיִם	search (to) (for)	חִפֵּשׂ, בִּקֵּשׁ
sauce	רֹטֶב	scold (to)	גָּעַר	(to explore)	חִפֵּשׂ, בִּקֵּשׁ
saucer	קַעֲרִית	scope	הֶקֵּף	(to investigate, to inquire)	חָקַר
sauerkraut	כְּרוּב כָּבוּשׁ	scorn	בּוּז	(to) search a house,etc.	חִפֵּשׂ
sausage	נַקְנִיק	scorn (to)	בָּז	seashore	חוֹף
savage	פֶּרֶא	scornful	מָלֵא בּוּז	seasickness	חֳלִי יָם
save (prep.)	חוּץ מִן	scout	צוֹפֶה	season (at the year)	עוֹנָה
save (to) (a person)	הִצִּיל	scowl	מַבָּט קוֹדֵר	in season	בָּעוֹנָה
(to) save money	חָסַךְ	scratch	סָרִיטָה	season (to)	תִּבֵּל
savings	חִסָּכוֹן	scratch (to)	סָרַט	seasoning	תְּבָלִים
savior	גּוֹאֵל	scream	צְעָקָה	seat	מוֹשָׁב
say (to)	אָמַר	scream (to)	צָעַק	seat (to)	הוֹשִׁיב
saw (n.)	מַשּׂוֹר	screen (a portable partition)	מָסָךְ	second	שְׁנִיָּה
scab (on a wound)	גֶּלֶד			wait a second!	חַכֵּה שְׁנִיָּה!

second (adj.)	שֵׁנִי	selfish	אָנֹכִי, אָנֹכִיּוּתִי	set (adj.)	קָבוּעַ
on second thought	אַחֲרֵי הִתְחַשְּׁבוּת	selfishness	אָנֹכִיּוּת	set (to)	שָׁקַע
second class	מַחְלָקָה שְׁנִיָּה	sell (to)	מָכַר	(to) set aside money	חָסַךְ
second to none	אֵין שֵׁנִי לוֹ	semi-	חֲצִי	(to) set free	שִׁחְרֵר
secondary	שְׁנִיִּי	semi circle	חֲצִי עִגּוּל	(to) set in order	סִדֵּר
secret	סוֹד	Semite	שֵׁמִי	(to) set on fire	הִדְלִיק
secretary	מַזְכִּיר	senate	מוֹעֵצָה	(to) set to work	הֶעֱסִיק
sect	כַּת	send (to)	שָׁלַח	settle (to)	יִשֵּׁב
section	חֵלֶק	(to) send away	גֵּרֵשׁ	settlement (a small village)	מוֹשָׁבָה
secular	חוּלָנִי	(to) send back	הֶחֱזִיר	(adjustment of an account etc.)	יִשּׁוּב, סִדּוּר
secure (adj.)	בָּטוּחַ	(to) send in	שָׁלַח		
secure (to)	הִבְטִיחַ	(to)send word	מָסַר	(colonization)	הִתְיַשְּׁבוּת
security	בִּטָּחוֹן	senile	שֶׁל זִקְנָה	seven	שִׁבְעָה
seduce (to)	פִּתָּה	senior	בְּכוֹר	seventeen	שִׁבְעָה-עָשָׂר
see (to)	רָאָה	sensation	רֶגֶשׁ	seventeenth	הַשִּׁבְעָה עָשָׂר
(to) see about	דָּאַג	sense	חוּשׁ	seventh	שְׁבִיעִי
(to) see one's way clear	רָאָה דַּרְכּוֹ	senseless	חֲסַר רֶגֶשׁ	seventy	שִׁבְעִים
(to) see someone home	לִוָּה	sensibility	רְגִישׁוּת	several	אֲחָדִים
(to) see someone off	נִפְרַד מִן	sensible	נָכוֹן	several times	פְּעָמִים אֲחָדוֹת
(to) see the point	הֵבִין	sensitive	רָגִישׁ	severe	מַקְפִּיר
(to) see to	דָּאַג לְ-	sensual	חוּשָׁנִי	severity	הַקְפָּדָה
Let's see.	נִרְאֶה.	sentence	מִשְׁפָּט	sew (to)	תָּפַר
See?	מֵבִין?	sentiment	רֶגֶשׁ	sewer	בִּיב
seed	זֶרַע	sentimental	רַגְּשָׁי	sex	מִין
seek (to)	חִפֵּשׂ	separate	נִפְרָד	shabby	בָּלוּי
seem (to)	נִדְמָה	separate (to)	הִפְרִיד	shade	צֵל
segregate (to)	הִבְדִּיל	separately	לְבַד	shadow	צֵל
segregation	הַבְדָּלָה	separation	פְּרִידָה	shady	מוּצָל
seize (to)(apprehend)	תָּפַשׂ	September	סֶפְּטֶמְבֶּר	shaggy	שָׂעִיר
(to comprehend)	הֵבִין	series	סִדְרָה	shake (to) (tremble)	רָעַד
(to grasp)	אָחַז	serious	רְצִינִי	(to) shake hands	לָחַץ יָד
(to take possession of)	לָכַד	sermon	דְּרָשָׁה	(to) shake one's head	נִעְנַע
seldom	לְעִתִּים רְחוֹקוֹת	servant	עֶבֶד, מְשָׁרֵת	shallow	שִׁטְחִי
select (to)	בָּחַר	serve (to)	שֵׁרֵת	shame	בּוּשָׁה
selection	בְּחִירָה	(to) serve notice	הוֹדִיעַ	shame (to)	בִּיֵּשׁ
self	עֶצֶם	(to) serve the purpose	סִפֵּק אֶת הַצֹּרֶךְ	shameful	מְבַיֵּשׁ
self-confidence	בִּטָּחוֹן עַצְמִי	service	שֵׁרוּת	shameless	בְּלִי-בּוּשָׁה
self-evident	מוּבָן מֵאֵלָיו	session	מוֹשָׁב	shampoo	חֲפִיפָה
				shape	צוּרָה

shape (to)	צָר	shock (to)	זְעֲזֵעַ	shrink (to)	הִתְכַּוֵּץ
shapeless	חֲסַר צוּרָה	shoe	נַעַל	shroud	תַּכְרִיכִים
share	חֵלֶק, מְנָיָה	shoemaker	סַנְדְּלָר	shrub	שִׂיחַ
share (to)	חָלַק	shoot (to)	יָרָה	shudder (to)	חָרַד
shareholder	בַּעַל מְנָיָה	shooting	יְרִיָּה	shun (to)	הִתְרַחֵק מִן
sharp (adj.)	חַד	shop	חֲנוּת	shut (adj.)	סָגוּר
a sharp answer	תְּשׁוּבָה חֲרִיפָה	shore	חוֹף	shut (to)	סָגַר
a sharp pain	כְּאֵב חוֹדֵר	short (not long,brief)	קָצָר	(to) shut in	הִסְגִּיר
at two o'clock sharp	בְּשָׁעָה שְׁתַּיִם בְּדִיּוּק	(not tall)	נָמוּךְ	(to) shut out	נָעַל כַּפָּנַי
sharp-edged	חַד	(of goods)	חָסֵר	(to) shut up(to be quiet)	שָׁתַק
sharp-pointed	חַד	a short time ago	לִפְנֵי זְמַן קָצָר	shutter	תְּרִיס
sharp-witted	חָרִיף	for short	לְשֵׁם קִצּוּר	shy	בַּיְשָׁנִי
sharpen (to)	חִדֵּד	in short	בְּקִצּוּר	sick	חוֹלֶה
shave (to)	הִתְגַּלֵּחַ	in a short while	עוֹד מְעַט	sickness	מַחֲלָה
she	הִיא	short cut	קִצּוּר	side	צַד
shed	דִּיר	short story	סִפּוּר	side by side	זֶה עַל יַד זֶה
shed (to)	נָשַׁר	(to) be short	חָסַר	on this side	בְּצַד זֶה
sheep	צֹאן	shortage	מַחְסוֹר	(the) wrong side out	הָפוּךְ
sheer (adj.)	גָּמוּר	shorten (to)	קִצֵּר	sidewalk	מִדְרָכָה
sheet	סָדִין	shorthand	קַצְרָנוּת	siege	מָצוֹר
sheik	שֵׁיךְ	shortly	בְּקָרוֹב	sieve	כְּבָרָה
shelf	אִצְטַבָּא	shot	יְרִיָּה	sigh	אֲנָחָה
shell	קְלִיפָּה	shoulder	כָּתֵף	sigh (to)	נֶאֱנַח
shelter	מַחְסֶה	shout	צְעָקָה	sight	רְאִיָּה, מַרְאֶה
shepherd	רוֹעֶה	shout (to)	צָעַק	at first sight	בִּרְאִיָּה רִאשׁוֹנָה
shield	מָגֵן	shove (to)	דָּחַף	What a sight!	אֵיזֶה מַרְאֶה!
shield (to)	הֵגֵן	shovel	אֵת	sight-seeing	תִּיּוּר
shift	חֲלִיפָה	show (appearance;theatre;spectacle)	הַצָּגָה	sign	סִמָּן
shift (to)	הֶחֱלִיף	(exibition)	תַּעֲרוּכָה	sign (to)	חָתַם
shin	שׁוֹק	(ostentation)	הִתְיַהֲרוּת	signal	אוֹת
shine	בְּרַק	show window	חַלּוֹן רַאֲוָה	signature	חֲתִימָה
shine (to)	הִבְרִיק	show (to)	הִצִּיג	significance	מַשְׁמָעוּת
ship	אֳנִיָּה	(to) show off	הִתְיַהֵר	signify (to)	הֶרְאָה
ship (to)	שָׁלַח	(to) show someone in	הֵרָאָה אֶת הַדֶּרֶךְ	signpost	צִיּוּן, שֶׁלֶט
shipment	מִשְׁלָח	(to) show up	גִּלָּה	silence	שֶׁקֶט
shirt	כֻּתֹּנֶת	shower	מִקְלַחַת	silence (to)	הִשְׁקִיט
shiver	רְעָדָה	shrew	מְרֻשַּׁעַת	silent	שֶׁקֶט
shiver (to)	רָעַד	shrill	חַד	silk	מֶשִׁי
shock	זַעֲזוּעַ			silly	טִפְּשִׁי

silver	כֶּסֶף	size	גֹּדֶל	slippery	חֲלַקְלַק
similar	דּוֹמֶה	skate (to)	הֶחֱלִיק	slope	מִדְרוֹן
similarity	דִּמְיוֹן	skates	מַחֲלִיקַיִם	slop	שׁוֹפָכִים
simple	פָּשׁוּט	skeleton	שֶׁלֶד	sloppy	רַשְׁלָנִי
simplicity	פַּשְׁטוּת	skeptic(al)	סַפְקָן	slot	סֶדֶק
simply	פָּשׁוּט	sketch	רֶשֶׁם	slovenly	רַשְׁלָנִי
simulate (to)	הֶעֱמִיד פָּנִים	skewer	שִׁפּוּד	slow	אִטִּי
sin	חֵטְא	skill	אֻמָּנוּת	slowness	אִטִּיּוּת
sin (to)	חָטָא	skillet	מַחֲבַת	slumber	שֵׁנָה
since (adj. prep.)	מֵאָז	skillful	מְאֻמָּן	slumber (to)	יָשֵׁן
since (conj.)	מִפְּנֵי שֶׁ-	skin	עוֹר	sly	עָרוּם
sincere	יָשָׁר, נֶאֱמָן	skip (to)	דִּלֵּג	small	קָטָן
sincerely	בֶּאֱמֶת	skirt	חֲצָאִית	smart	חָכָם
sincerity	יֹשֶׁר	skull	קָדְקֹד	smash (to)	שָׁבַר
sinful	חוֹטֵא	skullcap	כִּפָּה	smear	כֶּתֶם
sing (to)	שָׁר	sky	שָׁמַיִם	smear (to)	מָרַח
singer	שָׁר	slab	טַבְלָה	smell	רֵיחַ
single	יָחִיד	slack (adj.)	נִרְפֶּה	smell (to)	הֵרִיחַ
(unmarried)	רַוָּק	slam (n.)	דְּפִיקָה	smile	חִיּוּךְ
not a single word	אַף מִלָּה לֹא	slander	לַעַז	smile (to)	חִיֵּךְ
single room	חֶדֶר לְיָחִיד	slang	עֲגָה	smoke	עָשָׁן
singular	יָחִיד	slant	שִׁפּוּעַ	smoke (to)	עִשֵּׁן
sinister	רַע	slap	סְטִירָה	smoker	מְעַשֵּׁן
sink	כִּיּוֹר	slat	פַּס	smoking	עִשּׁוּן
sink (to)	הִטְבִּיעַ	slate	צִפְחָה	smooth	חָלָק
sinner	חוֹטֵא	slaughter	רֶצַח	smother (to)	הֶחֱנִיק
sip (to)	גָּמַע	slave	עֶבֶד	smuggle (to)	הִבְרִיחַ
sir	אָדוֹן	slavery	עַבְדּוּת	snake	נָחָשׁ
Thank you, Sir!	תּוֹדָה, אָדוֹן	sleep	שֵׁנָה	snapshot	צִלּוּם
sister	אָחוֹת	sleep (to)	יָשֵׁן	snatch (to)	חָטַף
sister-in-law	גִּיסָה	sleeve	שַׁרְווּל	sneeze (to)	הִתְעַטֵּשׁ
sit (to)	יָשַׁב	slender	דַּק	snore (to)	נָחַר
site	מָקוֹם	slice	נֵתַח	snow	שֶׁלֶג
situation	מַצָּב	slide (to)	הֶחֱלִיק	snow (to)	יָרַד שֶׁלֶג
six	שִׁשָּׁה	slight (adj.)	רָזֶה	snug	מְחֻרְפָּק
sixteen	שִׁשָּׁה עָשָׂר	slight (to)	זִלְזֵל	so (thus)	כָּךְ
sixteenth	הַשִּׁשָּׁה עָשָׂר	slime	פּוּץ	and so forth, and so on	וְכוּלֵי
sixth	שִׁשִּׁי	slimy	מְצִי	at so much a meter	כָּל מֶטֶר עוֹלֶה
sixty	שִׁשִּׁים	slipper	סַנְדָּל		

if so	אִם כֵּן
so-called	הַמְכֻנֶּה
so much (many)	הַרְבֵּה
so-so	כַּךְ, כָּכָה
so that	כְּדֵי שֶׁ-
I hope so.	אֲנִי מְקַוֶּה 'שֶׁכַּךְ.
Isn't that so?	לֹא כֵן?
I think so.	דַעְתִּי כַּךְ.
That is so.	זֶה כַּךְ.
soak (to)	סָפַג
soap	סַבּוֹן
sob	הִתְיַפְּחוּת
sober	פִּכֵּחַ
sociable	חַבְרוּתִי
social	חֶבְרָתִי
society	חֶבְרָה
sock	גֶּרֶב
socket	צָמִיד
soda (drinking)	גָּזוֹז
sofa	סַפָּה
soft	רַךְ
soften (to)	רִכֵּךְ
soil (to)	לִכְלֵךְ
soldier	חַיָּל
sole (n.)	סֻלְיָה
solemn	פָּכָד
solemnity	כֹּבֶד רֹאשׁ
solicit (to)	הִפְצִיר
solid	מוּצָק
solitary	בּוֹדֵד
solitude	בְּדִידוּת
solution (answer)	פִּתָּרוֹן
solve (to)	פָּתַר
some	אֲחָדִים
at some time or other	פַּעַם
some of his books	אֲחָדִים מִסְפָרָיו
some two hundred	כְּמָאתַיִם
Bring me some cigars.	הָבֵא לִי כַּמָּה סִיגָרוֹת.
I have some left.	יֵשׁ לִי עוֹד אֲחָדִים.
Some (people) think so.	יֵשׁ חוֹשְׁבִים כַּךְ.
somebody	מִישֶׁהוּ
somehow	אֵיךְ שֶׁהוּא
someone	מִישֶׁהוּ
something	מַשֶּׁהוּ
sometime	פַּעַם אַחֶרֶת
sometimes	לִפְעָמִים
somewhat	מְעַט
somewhere	אֵי שָׁם
son	בֵּן
song	שִׁיר
son-in-law	חָתָן
soon	בְּקָרוֹב
soot	פִּיחַ
soothe (to)	פִּיֵּס
sore (n.)	פֶּצַע
sorrow	עֶצֶב
sorry	עָצוּב
(to) be sorry about	הִתְעַצֵּב עַל
I am sorry.	אֲנִי מִצְטַעֵר.
sort	מִין
sort (to)	מִיֵּן
soul	נֶפֶשׁ
sound (n.)	קוֹל
sound (to)	הִשְׁמִיעַ קוֹל
soup	מָרָק
sour	חָמוּץ
source	מָקוֹר
south	דָּרוֹם
southeast	דָּרוֹם מִזְרָח
southern	דְּרוֹמִי
southward	דָּרוֹמָה
southwest	דָּרוֹם-מַעֲרָב
sovereign	שַׁלִּיט
Soviet	סוֹבְיֶט
sow (to)	זָרַע
space	מֶרְחָב
spacious	מְרֻוָּח
spade	מַעְדֵּר
span	זֶרֶת
Spanish	סְפָרַדִּי
spare (adj.)	נוֹסָף
spare (to)	חָמַל עַל
(to forgive)	סָלַח
(to save)	חָמַל
(to) be sparing	חָסַךְ
I have time to spare.	יֵשׁ לִי פְּנַאי.
They spared his life.	חָמְלוּ עַל חַיָּיו.
spark	נִיצוֹץ
sparkle (to)	נָצַץ
spasm	עֲוִית
speak (to)	דִּבֵּר
(to) speak for	דִּבֵּר בְּשֵׁם
(to) speak for itself	הֵעִיד עַל עַצְמוֹ
(to) speak one's mind	גִּלָּה דַעְתּוֹ
(to) speak out	הִגִּיד פֶּה מָלֵא
(to) speak to	דִּבֵּר אֶל
(to) speak up	דִּבֵּר בְּקוֹל
speaker	מְדַבֵּר
special	מְיֻחָד
special delivery	מִשְׁלוֹחַ מְיֻחָד
special delivery stamp	פּוּל לְמִשְׁלוֹחַ מְיֻחָד
specialty	סְגֻלָּה
specific	מְדֻיָּק
specify (to)	פֵּרֵשׁ
spectacle	רַאֲוָה
spectator	צוֹפֶה
speculate (to)	שִׁעֵר
speculation	סַפְסָרוּת
speech	נְאוּם
speed	מְהִירוּת
speedy	מָהִיר
spell	קֶסֶם
spell (to)	אִיֵּת

How do you spell..?	אֵיךְ כּוֹתְבִים...?	spread (to)	פָּרַשׂ	(stall)	בֵּיתָן
spelling	אִיּוּת	spring	קָפִיץ	(newsstand)	קִיוֹסְק
sphere	כַּדּוּר	spring (season)	אָבִיב	stand (to)	עָמַד
spice	סַם	spring (to)	קָפַץ	(to resist)	עָמַד נֶגֶד
spider	עַכָּבִישׁ	sprinkle (to)	הִזָּה	(to set something on end)	הֶעֱמִיד
spill (to)	שָׁפַּךְ	sprout (to)	נָבַט		
spin (to)	טָוָה	spry	זָרִיז	(to stop moving)	עָצַר
spine	חוּט שִׁדְרָה	spur (to)	דִּרְבֵּן	(to) stand by	עָמַד לְיָד
spinster	פְּתוּגָלָה זְקֵנָה	spurn (to)	מָאַס	(to) stand in line	עָמַד בַּתּוֹר
spirit	רוּחַ	spy	מְרַגֵּל	(to) stand in the way	עָמַד בַּדֶּרֶךְ
spiritual	רוּחָנִי	spy (to)	רִגֵּל	(to) stand one's ground	עָמַד עַל עֶמְדּוֹ
spit (to)	יָרַק	squander (to)	כָּזְבֵּז		
spite	טִינָה	square (adj.)	מְרֻבָּע	(to) stand on one's feet	עָמַד עַל רַגְלָיו
spiteful	שׁוֹמֵר טִינָה	squat	גוּץ		
splash (to)	הִתִּיז	squeak	צְרִיחָה	(to) stand out(be pro- minent, conspicuous)	בָּלַט
splendid	נֶהְדָּר	squeeze (to)	לָחַץ		
splendor	הָדָר	squint (to)	פָּזַל	(to) stand pain,etc.	סָבַל
splinter	קֵיסָם	stab (to)	דָּקַר	(to) stand still	עָמַד בְּלִי נוֹעַ
splinter (to)	נִפֵּץ	stabilize (to)	יִצֵּב		
split (to)	בָּקַע	stable (adj.)	קָבוּעַ	(to) stand the test	עָמַד בַּבְּחִינָה
(to divide)	חִלֵּק	stack	עֲרֵמָה		
(to) split the difference	חִלֵּק אֶת הַהֶפְרֵשׁ	stadium	אִצְטַדְיוֹן	(to) stand together	עָמְדוּ יַחַד
		staff (baton, pole, rod, stick)	מַטֶּה	(to) stand up for	עָמַד לְיָמִין
(to) split one's sides with laughter	הִתְפַּקַּע מִצְּחוֹק	(body of officers)	צֶוֶת	I am standing.	אֲנִי עוֹמֵד.
		(personnel)	סֶגֶל	I can't stand him.	אֵינִי יָכוֹל לִסְבֹּל אוֹתוֹ.
(to) split up	נִפְרְדוּ	editorial staff	מַעֲרֶכֶת		
(to) split hairs	הִתְפַּלְפֵּל	stage	בָּמָה	Stand back!	הִתְרַחֵק!
spoil (to) (damage)	קִלְקֵל	stain	כֶּתֶם	Stand up!	קוּם!
(to rot)	הִתְקַלְקֵל	stain (to)	צָבַע, הִכְתִּים	standard (flag)	נֵס
(to) get spoiled	הִתְקַלְקֵל	stairs	מַדְרֵגוֹת	standard of living	רָמַת הַחַיִּים
sponge	סְפוֹג	stale	יָשָׁן	standard price	מָחִיר קָבוּעַ
spontaneous	סְפּוֹנְטָנִי	stammer	גִּמְגּוּם	standstill	קִפָּאוֹן
spool	סְלִיל	stammer (to)	גִּמְגֵּם	star	כּוֹכָב
spoon	כַּף	stamp (for letters)	בּוּל	start (beginning)	הַתְחָלָה
spoonful	מְלֹא כַּף	(for documents)	חוֹתָם	(departure)	יְצִיאָה
sport	סְפּוֹרְט	stand	מַעֲמָד	(of a car, an engine)	הַדְלָקָה
spot	כֶּתֶם	(a piece of furniture)	כַּן	start (to)(begin)	הִתְחִיל
sprain	נְקִיעָה	(platform)	בָּמָה	(an engine,etc.)	הִדְלִיק
sprain (to)	נָקַע			(to) start out	יָצָא
				starve (to)	רָעַב
				state	מַצָּב
				state (to)	הִגִּיד

stately	מְפֹאָר
statement (declaration)	הַצְהָרָה, גִּלּוּי דַעַת
(of an account)	חֶשְׁבּוֹן
(report)	דִין וְחֶשְׁבּוֹן
stateroom	תָּא
station	תַּחֲנָה
statistics	סְטַטִיסְטִיקָה
statue	פֶּסֶל
statute	חֹק
stay	שְׁהִיָּה
stay (to) (tarry)	שָׁהָה
(to put off)	דָחָה
(to) stay away	הִתְרַחֵק
(to) stay in	נִשְׁאַר בְּ-
(to) stay in bed	נִשְׁאַר בַּמִּטָּה
He's staying at the hotel.	הוּא מִשְׁתַּכֵּן בַּמָּלוֹן.
steady	קָבוּעַ
steak	אֻמְצָה
steal (to)	גָנַב
steam	קִיטוֹר
steamship	אֳנִית קִיטוֹר
steel	פְּלָדָה
steep	תָּלוּל
steeple	מִגְדָּל
steer (to)	הִנְהִיג
stem	קָנֶה
stenographer	קַצְרָן
step	צַעַד
(stair)	מַדְרֵגָה
step by step	לְאַט-לְאַט
(to) be in step	הָלַךְ בְּצַעַד
step (to)	צָעַד, דָרַךְ
(to) step aside	סָר הַצִּדָּה
(to) step back	נָסוֹג
(to) step down (decrease)	הִמְעִיט
(to) step in (take part)	הִשְׁתַּתֵּף
(to) step on	דָרַךְ
(to) step out	יָצָא
stepbrother	אָח חוֹרֵג
stepchild	יֶלֶד חוֹרֵג
stepdaughter	בַּת חוֹרֶגֶת
stepfather	אָב חוֹרֵג
stepmother	אֵם חוֹרֶגֶת
stepsister	אָחוֹת חוֹרֶגֶת
stepson	בֵּן חוֹרֵג
sterile	עָקָר
sterilized	טָהוֹר
stern (adj.)	קָשֶׁה
stew	תַּבְשִׁיל
stew (to)	בִּשֵּׁל
stick	מַקֵּל
stick (to)	דָבַק
(to fasten)	חִבֵּר
(to glue)	הִדְבִּיק
(to keep on)	נִדְבַּק
(to stab)	דָקַר
(to thrust)	דָחַף
(to) stick out (one's head)	הוֹצִיא רֹאשׁ
(to) stick up for	עָמַד לִימִין
stiff	לֹא גָמִישׁ
(formal)	פוֹרְמָלִי
(not natural in manner)	מְלָאכוּתִי
(strong)	חָזָק
stiffen (to)	הִקְשָׁה
stiffness	קֹשִׁי
still (adj.)	נָח, שָׁקֵט
still life	חַיִּים דוֹמְמִים
still water	מַיִם שְׁקֵטִים
(to) stand still	עָמַד פְּשֻׁקְטָ
Be still!	שְׁקֹט!
Keep still!	שְׁקֹט!
still (adv.)	עוֹד
stimulate (to)	עוֹרֵר
stimulus	גֵּרוּי
sting	עֲקִיצָה
sting (to)	עָקַץ
stingy	כַּלַּי
stir (to)	בָּחַשׁ
stitch	תֶּפֶר
stock (supply of goods)	מְלַאי
(share)	מְנָיָה
stock company	חֶבְרַת מְנָיוֹת
stock market	בּוּרְסָה
stocking	גֶּרֶב
stomach	קֵבָה
stone	אֶבֶן
stool	שְׁרַפְרַף
stop	עֲצִירָה
stop (to)	עָצַר
(to stay)	עָצַר
(to) stop over	שָׁהָה
Stop!	עֲמֹד! עֲצֹר!
Stop a minute.	הַפְסֵק לְדַקָּה.
Stop that, now!	הַפְסֵק מִיָּד!
store	חֲנוּת
storm	סְעָרָה
story	סִפּוּר
stove	תַּנּוּר
straight	יָשָׁר
straighten (to)	יִשֵּׁר
strain	מְתִיחָה
strain (to) (make an effort)	הִתְאַמֵּץ
(the eyes, etc.)	עִיֵּף
(through a strainer)	סִנֵּן
strange	זָר
stranger	זָר
strangle (to)	חָנַק
strap	רְצוּעָה
strategy	טַכְסִיס
straw	קַשׁ
strawberry	תּוּת שָׂדֶה
stream	זֶרֶם
street	רְחוֹב
strength	כֹּחַ

strengthen (to)	חַזֵּק	stumble (to)	נִכְשַׁל	successful	מַצְלִיחַ
strenuous	מְרֻצֶּי	stump	גֶּזַע	succession	חֲלִיפָה
stress (force,pressure)	לַחַץ	stun (to)	הָמַם	successor	יוֹרֵשׁ
(accent)	נְגִינָה	stunt	פֶּלֶא	such	כֵּן, כָּזֶה
(importance)	הַדְגָּשָׁה	stupendous	נִפְלָא	suck (to)	יָנַק
(strain)	מָתִיחֻת	stupid	טִפְּשִׁי	suction	יְנִיקָה
stretch	מְתִיחָה	stupidity	טִפְּשׁוּת	sudden	פִּתְאוֹמִי
stretch (to)	מָתַח	sturdy	חָסִין	suddenly	פִּתְאֹם
strict	מַקְפִּיד	stutter (to)	גִּמְגֵּם	sue (to)	תָּבַע
stride	פְּסִיעָה	style	סִגְנוֹן	suffer (to)	סָבַל
stride (to)	פָּסַע	subdue(to)	הִכְנִיעַ	suffering	סֵבֶל
strife	תִּגְרָה	subject	נוֹשֵׂא	sufficient	מַסְפִּיק
strike	שְׁבִיתָה	subjective	סוּבְּיֶקְטִיבִי	suffocate (to)	נֶחְנַק
strike (to)	הִכָּה	subjugate (to)	כָּבַשׁ	sugar	סֻכָּר
(to) strike against	שָׁבַת	subjunctive	תְּנַאי	suggest (to)	הִצִּיעַ
(to) strike a match	הִצִּית	sublime	נִשְׂגָּב	suggestion	הַצָּעָה
(to) strike at	הִכָּה	submission	הַכְנָעָה	suicide	אִבּוּד לָדַעַת
(to) strike home	קוֹלֵעַ	submissive	נִכְנָע	suit (of clothes)	חֲלִיפָה
(to) strike (cross) out	מָחַק	submit (to)	נִכְנַע	(court)	מִשְׁפָּט
(to) strike one as funny	הִצְחִיק	subordinate	מִשְׁנֶה	suit (to)(be suitable)	הִתְאִים
string	חגט	subscribe (to)	חָתַם עַל	(to be becoming)	הָלַם
strip	פַּס	subscription	חֲתִימָה	(to please or satisfy)	מָצָא חֵן
strip (to)	פָּשַׁט, חָשַׂף	subside (to)	שָׁכַך	suitable	מַתְאִים
stripe	פַּס	subsidiary	צְדָדִי	sullen	קוֹדֵר
strive (to)	הִשְׁתַּדֵּל	subsidy	תְּמִיכָה	sum	סְכוּם
stroke	הַכָּאָה	subsist (to)	הִתְפַּרְנֵס	summary	סִכּוּם
stroll	טִיּוּל	substance	תֹּכֶן	summer	קַיִץ
stroll (to)	טִיֵּל	substantial	מַמָּשִׁי	summit	פִּסְגָּה
strong	חָזָק	substantive	מַמָּשִׁי	summon (to)	הִזְמִין
structure	מִבְנֶה	substitute	מְמַלֵּא מָקוֹם	sumptuous	מְהֻדָּר
struggle	קְרָב	substitute (to)	מִלֵּא מָקוֹם	sum up (to)	סִכֵּם
struggle (to)	הִתְלַבֵּט	substitution	מִלּוּא מָקוֹם	sun	שֶׁמֶשׁ
stubborn	עַקְשָׁנִי	subtle	דַּק	sunbeam	קֶרֶן שֶׁמֶשׁ
student	תַּלְמִיד	subtract (to)	הֶחְסִיר	Sunday	יוֹם רִאשׁוֹן
studious	חָרוּץ	subtraction	חֶסְגֵּר	sunken	שָׁקוּעַ
study	לִמּוּד	suburb	פַּרְוָר	sunny	בָּהִיר
study (to)	לָמַד	subway	תַּחְתִּית	sunrise	זְרִיחָה
stuff	חֹמֶר	succeed (to)	הִצְלִיחַ	sunset	שְׁקִיעָה
stuff (to)	מִלֵּא	success	הַצְלָחָה	sunshine	זֹהַר

sunstroke	מַכַּת שֶׁמֶשׁ	susceptible	רָגִישׁ	Syria	סוּרְיָה
superb	נֶהְדָּר	suspect	חָשׁוּד	syrup	עָסִיס
supercilious	יָהִיר	suspect (to)	חָשַׁד	system	שִׁטָּה
superficial	שִׁטְחִי	suspension	תְּלִיָה	systematic	שִׁטָתִי
superfluous	מְיֻתָּר	suspicion	חֲשָׁד		
superintendent	מְפַקֵּח	suspicious	חָשׁוּד	T	
superior	גָּבוֹהַּ	sustain (to)	כִּלְכֵּל	table	שֻׁלְחָן
superiority	יִתְרוֹן	swallow (to)	בָּלַע	tablecloth	מַפָּה
superlative	מַמְדְּרֵגָה רִאשׁוֹנָה	swamp	בִּצָּה	tablespoon	כַּף
superstition	אֱמוּנָה תְּפֵלָה	sway (to)	נַעֲנַע	tablet	טַבְלָה
supper	אֲרוּחַת עֶרֶב	swear	נִשְׁבַּע	tacit	שׁוֹתֵק
supplement	מוּסָף	sweat	זֵעָה	tacitly	בִּשְׁתִיקָה
supplementary	נוֹסָף	sweat (to)	הִזִּיעַ	taciturn	שַׁתְקָנִי
supply	מְלַאי	sweater	סְוֶדֶר	tact	הַבְחָנָה
supply (to)	סִפֵּק	sweep (to)	טִאטֵא	tactfully	בְּהַבְחָנָה
support	תְּמִיכָה	sweet (adj.)	מָתוֹק	tail	זָנָב
support (to)	תָּמַךְ	sweetheart	אוֹהֵב	tailor	חַיָּט
suppose (to)	הִנִּיחַ	sweetness	מֹתֶק	take (to)	לָקַח
supposition	הַשְׁעָרָה	swell (to)	נָפַח	(to grasp)	אָחַז
supreme	עֶלְיוֹן	swelling	נְפִיחָה	to take a bath	הִתְרַחֵץ
sure	בָּטוּחַ	swift	מָהִיר	to take a bite	נָשַׁךְ
surety	עֵרָבוֹן	swim (to)	שָׂחָה	to take account of	לָקַח בְּחֶשְׁבּוֹן
surface	שֶׁטַח	swindler	רַמַּאי	to take advantage of	נִצֵּל
surgeon	מְנַתֵּחַ	swing (to)	נִדְנֵד	to take advice	קִבֵּל עֵצָה
surgery (operation)	נִתּוּחַ	switch (change, shift)	שִׁנּוּי	to take after	דוֹמֶה
surmount (to)	הִתְגַּבֵּר עַל	(electric)	מְתֶג	to take a liking to	אָהַב
surname	שֵׁם מִשְׁפָּחָה	(railroad)	מַעֲבִיר	to take a nap	הִתְנַמְנֵם
surpass (to)	עָלָה עַל	sword	חֶרֶב	to take an oath	נִשְׁבַּע
surplus	עוֹדֶף	syllable	הֲבָרָה	to take apart (a machine)	פֵּרַק
surprise	הַפְתָּעָה	symbol	סֵמֶל	to take a picture	צִלֵּם
surprise (to)	הִפְתִּיעַ	symbolic	סִמְלִי	to take a step	פָּסַע
surrender	כְּנִיעָה	symbolize (to)	סִמֵּל	to take a trip	נָסַע
surrender (to)	נִכְנַע	symmetrical	סִמֶטְרִי	to take a walk	טִיֵּל
surround (to)	הִקִּיף	symmetry	סִמֶטְרִיָה	to take away	הֵסִיר
surroundings	סְבִיבָה	sympathetic	מְשַׁתֵּף צַעַר	to take back	הֵשִׁיב
survey	מְדִידָה, מִסְקָר	sympathy	הִשְׁתַּתְּפוּת בְּצַעַר	to take care	נִזְהַר
survey (to)	מָדַד, סָקַר	symptom	סִמָּן	to take care of	שָׁמַר
survive (to)	נִשְׁאַר בַּחַיִּים	synagogue	בֵּית כְּנֶסֶת	to take chances	הִסְתַּכֵּן
susceptibility	רַגְשָׁנוּת	synopsis	סִפּוּג	to take down (lower)	הוֹרִיד

to take effect	יָצָא לַפֹּעַל	tax	מַס	tenth	עֲשִׂירִי
to take from (subtract)	חָסַר	taxi	מוֹנִית	tepid	פּוֹשֵׁר
to take into consideration	הִתְחַשֵּׁב	tea	תֵּה	term	תְּקוּפָה
to take it easy	לֹא הִתְאַמֵּץ	teach (to)	לִמֵּד	terrace	מִרְפֶּסֶת
to take leave	נִפְרַד	teacher	מוֹרֶה	terrible	נוֹרָא
to take note	רָשַׁם	team	קְבוּצָה	terrify (to)	הִרְעִית
to take notice	שָׂם לֵב	tear (to)	קָרַע	territory	גָּלִיל
to take off (a plane)	הִמְרִיא	tease (to)	גֵּרָה	terror	בְּעָתָה
to take out	הוֹצִיא	teaspoon	כַּפִּית	terrorist	קִרְיוֹן
to take part	הִשְׁתַּתֵּף	technical	טֶכְנִי	test	בְּחִינָה
to take place	הִתְקַיֵּם	tedious	מְשַׁעֲמֵם	test (to)	בָּחַן
to take refuge	נִמְלַט	telegram	מִבְרָק	testify (to)	הֵעִיד
to take to heart	שָׂם לֵב	telegraph	טֶלֶגְרַף	testimony	עֵדוּת
to take up a subject	לָמַד	telegraphic	טֶלֶגְרָפִי	text	פָּתוּב
to take upon oneself	קִבֵּל עַל עַצְמוֹ	telephone	טֶלֶפוֹן	textbook	סֵפֶר לִמּוּד
		telephone (to)	טִלְפֵּן	than	מֵאֲשֶׁר
Take my word for it.	הַאֲמֵן לִי.	tell (to)	סִפֵּר	thank (to)	הוֹדָה
tale	סִפּוּר	temper	מֶזֶג	thankful	אֲסִיר תּוֹדָה
talent	כִּשָּׁרוֹן	temperament	מֶזֶג	thanks	תּוֹדָה
talk (to)	דִּבֵּר	temperance	בֵּינוֹנִיּוּת	that (pron.)	אֲשֶׁר, שֶׁ
talkative	פַּטְפְּטָנִי	temperate	בֵּינוֹנִי	that is	זֹאת אוֹמֶרֶת
tall	גָּבוֹהַּ	temperature	חֹם	That's it.	זֶה הוּא.
Talmud	תַּלְמוּד	tempest	סַעַר	that (adj.)	הַהוּא
tame	בֵּיתִי	temple	הֵיכָל, מִקְדָּשׁ	thaw	נְמִיסָה
tang	רֵיחַ חָרִיף	temporary	זְמַנִּי	thaw (to)	נָמֵס
tangent	מַשָּׁק	tempt (to)	נִסָּה	the	הַ-
tangerine	מַנְדָּרִינָה	temptation	נִסָּיוֹן	theater	תֵּאַטְרוֹן
tangle (to)	סִבֵּךְ	ten	עֲשָׂרָה	theft	גְּנֵבָה
tank	גִּגִּית	tenacious	מַדְבֵּק	their	שֶׁלָּהֶם
tap	דְּפִיקָה	tenant	דַּיָּר	theirs	שֶׁלָּהֶם
tapestry	שָׁטִיחַ	tend (to)	נָטָה	them	אוֹתָם
tar	זֶפֶת	tendency	נְטִיָּה	theme	נוֹשֵׂא
tardy	מְפַגֵּר	tender (adj.)	רַךְ	themselves	כְּעַצְמָם
target	מַטָּרָה	tennis	טֶנִיס	then (adv.)	אָז
tarnish(to)	כָּהָה	tense	זְמַן	theoretical	רַעְיוֹנִי
tart (adj.)	חָרִיף	tense (adj.)	מָתוּחַ	theory	תֵּאוֹרְיָה, הַנָּחָה
task	תַּפְקִיד	tension	מְתִיחוּת	there	שָׁם
taste	טַעַם	tent	אֹהֶל	there is	יֵשׁ
taste (to)	טָעַם	tentative	נִסָּיוֹנִי	there are	יֵשׁ

over there!	שָׁם!
thereafter	אַחֲרֵי כֵן
thereupon	אָז
thermometer	מַדְחֹם
these	אֵלֶּה
thesis	מֶחְקָר
they	הֵם
thick	עָבֶה
thicken (to)	עִבָּה
thickness	עֳבִי
thief	גַּנָּב
thigh	יָרֵךְ
thimble	אֶצְבָּעוֹן
thin	רָזֶה
thing	דָּבָר
think (to) (believe)	חָשַׁב
as you think fit	לְפִי רַאֲתְךָ
(to) think it over	הִתְחַשֵּׁב
(to)think nothing of	הָיָה קַל בְּעֵינָיו
(to) think of	זָכַר
I think so.	.אֲנִי חוֹשֵׁב כָּךְ
third	שְׁלִישִׁי
thirst	צָמָא
thirteen	שְׁלֹשָׁה עָשָׂר
thirteenth	הַשְּׁלֹשָׁה עָשָׂר
thirty	שְׁלוֹשִׁים
this	זֶה
thorn	קוֹץ
thorough	שָׁלֵם
those	הָהֵם
though	אֲפִילוּ
thought	מַחְשָׁבָה
thoughtful	חוֹשֵׁב
thoughtless	חֲסַר מַחְשָׁבָה
thousand	אֶלֶף
thread	חוּט
thread (to)	הִשְׁחִיל
threat	אִיּוּם
threaten (to)	אִיֵּם

three	שְׁלֹשָׁה
threshold	מִפְתָּן
thrift	חִסָּכוֹן
thrifty	חַסְכָנִי
throat	גָּרוֹן
throb (to)	דָּפַק
throng	הֲמוֹן
through	דֶּרֶךְ
(to) be through	גָּמַר
throughout	כֻּלּוֹ
throw	זְרִיקָה
throw (to) (a ball, a stone, etc.)	זָרַק
(to) throw away	זָרַק
(to) throw light on	הֵאִיר
(to) throw out	הִשְׁלִיךְ
thumb	בֹּהֶן
thunder	רַעַם
thunder (to)	רָעַם
thunderbolt	חָזִיז
Thursday	יוֹם חֲמִישִׁי
thus	כָּךְ
tick (to)	לְקַלֵּק
ticket	כַּרְטִיס
ticket window	קֻפָּה
tickle (to)	דִּגְדֵּג
tide	גֵּאוּת
tidy	נָקִי, מְסֻדָּר
tie	קֶשֶׁר
tie (to)	קָשַׁר
tiger	נָמֵר
tight	מָדֹק
tile	לְבֵנָה
till	עַד
till (to)	חָרַשׁ
tilt	נְטִיָּה
timber	עֵצִים
time	זְמָן
a long time ago	לִפְנֵי זְמָן רַב

any time	בְּכָל עֵת
at the proper time	בַּזְּמָן הַנָּכוֹן
at the same time	כְּאוֹתוֹ זְמָן
at this time	כָּעֵת
at this time (of the day	בְּשָׁעָה זוֹ
at times	לִפְעָמִים
for the time being	לְעֵת עַתָּה
from time to time	מִפַּעַם לְפַעַם
in an hour's time	בְּעוֹד שָׁעָה
in time	בִּזְמָן
one at a time	אֶחָד אֶחָד
on time	בִּזְמָן
some time ago	לִפְנֵי כַּמָּה זְמָן
spare time	פְּנַאי
the first time	פַּעַם רִאשׁוֹנָה
time and again	פַּעַם אַחַר פַּעַם
(to) have a good time	לְבַלּוֹת
Be on time.	בּוֹא בִּזְמָן.
Have a good time!	תְּבַלֶּה בִּנְעִימִים!
timely	בִּזְמָן
timetable	לוּחַ
timid	פַּחְדָּנִי
timidity	פַּחְדָּנוּת
tin	בְּדִיל
tiny	זָעִיר
tip (point,end)	קָצֶה, חֹד
(gratuity)	הַעֲנָקָה
(secret information)	גִּלּוּי סוֹד
tip (to)	הֶעֱנִיק
(to warn)	הִזְהִיר
(to give a tip)	הֶעֱנִיק
(to slant)	הִטָּה
(to) tip over	הָפַךְ
tire	צְמִיג
tire (to)	עִיֵּף
tired	עָיֵף
tireless	כְּלִי לֵאוּת
tiresome	מְיַגֵּעַ

title	שֵׁם	torch	לַפִּיד	trample (to)	דָרַךְ
to	אֶל	torment	יִסּוּרִים	tranquil	שָׁקֵט
toast (bread)	צָנִים	torture (to)	עָנָה	tranquillity	שֶׁקֶט
tobacco	טַבָּק	toss (to)	הִשְׁלִיךְ	transaction	עֵסֶק
tobacco store	חֲנוּת טַבָּק	total (n.)	סַךְ הַכֹּל	transfer	הַעֲבָרָה
today	הַיוֹם	totally	לְגַמְרֵי	transfer (to)	הֶעֱבִיר
toe	אֶצְבַּע	touch	נְגִיעָה	transition	מַעֲבָר
together	יַחַד	touch (to)	נָגַע	transitory	חוֹלֵף
toil	עָמָל	touching	נוֹגֵעַ	translate (to)	תִּרְגֵּם
toilet	בֵּית שִׁמוּשׁ	tough	קָשֶׁה	translation	תִּרְגּוּם
toilet paper	נְיָר שִׁמוּשׁ	tour	סִיּוּר	translator	מְתַרְגֵּם
token	אוֹת	tour (to)	סִיֵּר	transmission	מְסִירָה
tolerable	שֶׁאֶפְשָׁר לָנָשָׂא	tourist	תַּיָּר	transmit (to)	מָסַר
tolerance	סַבְלָנוּת	tourist agency	סוֹכְנוּת תַּיָּרִים	transparent	שָׁקוּף
tolerant	סַבְלָנִי	tow(to)	מָשַׁךְ	transport	הוֹבָלָה
tolerate (to)	סָבַל	toward	לִקְרַאת	transport (to)	הוֹבִיל
toll	מַס	towel	מַגֶּבֶת	transportation	הַעֲבָרָה
toll (to)	צִלְצֵל	tower	מִגְדָל	transverse	אֲלַכְסוֹנִי
tomato	עַגְבָנִיָה	town	עִירָה	trap	פַּח
tomb	קֶבֶר	town hall	עִירִיָה	trap (to)	לָכַד
tomorrow	מָחָר	toy	צַעֲצוּעַ	trash	פְּסֹלֶת
ton	טוֹן	trace	זֵכֶר	travel	נְטִיעָה
tone	צְלִיל	trace (to)	עָקַב	travel (to)	נָסַע
tongs	מֶלְקָחַיִם	track	מַסְגֵּל	travel agency	סוֹכְנוּת נְסִיעוֹת
tongue	לָשׁוֹן	trade	מִסְחָר	traveler	נוֹסֵעַ
tonic (medicine)	מַבְרִיא	trade-mark	חוֹתֶמֶת	tray	טַס
tonight	הַלַּיְלָה	trade-union	אֲגוּדָה מִקְצוֹעִית	treacherous	בּוֹגֵד
too	גַם כֵּן	tradition	מָסוֹרָה	treachery	בְּגִידָה
too much	יוֹתֵר מִדַי	traditional	מְסָרְתִּי	tread (to)	פָּסַע
tool	מַכְשִׁיר	traffic	תְּנוּעָה	treason	בְּגִידָה
tooth	שֵׁן	tragedy	טְרָגֶדְיָה	treasure	מַטְמוֹן, אוֹצָר
toothache	כְּאַב שִׁנַּיִם	tragic	טְרָגִי	treasurer	גִזְבָּר
toothbrush	מִבְרֶשֶׁת שִׁנַּיִם	trail	שֹׁבֶל	treasury	אוֹצָר
toothpaste	מִשְׁחַת שִׁנַּיִם	trail (to)	עָקַב	treat (to)(well,badly)	הִתְנַהֵג
toothpick	קֵסָם	train	רַכֶּבֶת	(with food,drinks,etc.)	כִּבֵּד
		freight train	רַכֶּבֶת מַשָׂא	(a patient)	טִפֵּל
toothpowder	אַבְקַת שִׁנַּיִם	train (to)	אִמֵּן	treatment	טִפּוּל
top	רֹאשׁ	training	אִמוּן	treaty	חוֹזֶה
topic	נוֹשֵׂא	traitor	בּוֹגֵד	tree	עֵץ

tremble (to)	רָעַד	trousers	מִכְנָסַיִם	(to) turn down (to refuse)	סֵרֵב
trembling	רְעִידָה	truce	הֲפוּגָה	to turn into	הָפַךְ לְ-
trembling (adj.)	רוֹעֵד	truck	אוֹטוֹ מַשָּׂא	to turn off	סָגַר
tremendous	עָצוּם	true	אֲמִתִּי	to turn one's back on	הֵסֵב גַּבּוֹ
trench	חֲפִירָה	truly	בֶּאֱמֶת		
trend	נְטִיָּה	yours truly	שֶׁלְּךָ בֶּאֱמֶת	to turn over	הָפַךְ
trespass (to)	פָּשַׁע	trumpet	חֲצוֹצְרָה	(to hand over)	מָסַר
trial	בְּחִינָה	trunk	אַרְגָּז	(to transfer)	הֶעֱבִיר
triangle	מְשֻׁלָּשׁ	trust	אֵמוּן	(to tumble)	הִתְהַפֵּךְ
tribe	שֵׁבֶט	trust (to)	הֶאֱמִין	(to turn sour (milk, etc.)	הֶחֱמִיץ
tribulation	צָרָה	trusting	מַאֲמִין		
tribunal	בֵּית דִּין	trustworthy	נֶאֱמָן	to turn to	פָּנָה לְ-
tribute	מַס	truth	אֱמֶת	(to) turn up (to appear)	הוֹפִיעַ
trick	תַּכְסִיס	truthful	אֲמִתִּי		
trick (to)	רִמָּה	truthfully	בֶּאֱמֶת	to turn upside down	הָפַךְ עַל פָּנָיו
trifling	מְצֹעָר	try	נִסָּיוֹן		
trim (to)	קִשֵּׁט	try (to)	נִסָּה, הִשְׁתַּדֵּל	turnip	לֶפֶת
trimming	קִשּׁוּט	Try to come.	הִשְׁתַּדֵּל לָבוֹא.	tutor	מוֹרֶה פְּרָטִי
trinket	עֲדִי	Try to be on time.	הִשְׁתַּדֵּל לָדַיֵּק.	tweezers	מַלְקֵטֶת
trio	שְׁלִישִׁיָּה			twelve	שְׁנֵים עָשָׂר
trip	נְסִיעָה	tube	צִנּוֹר	twenty	עֶשְׂרִים
trip (to)	הִכְשִׁיל	Tuesday	יוֹם שְׁלִישִׁי	twenty-five	עֶשְׂרִים וַחֲמִשָּׁה
triple	מְשֻׁלָּשׁ	tumor	גָּרוּל	twenty-four	עֶשְׂרִים וְאַרְבָּעָה
triumph	נִצָּחוֹן	tumult	שָׁאוֹן	twice	פַּעֲמַיִם
triumphant	מְנַצֵּחַ	tune	לַחַן	twilight	דִּמְדּוּמִים
trivial	קַל	tune (to)	כִּוֵּן	twin	תְּאוֹם
trolley car	חַשְׁמַלִּית	tunnel	מִנְהָרָה	twist	קְלִיעָה
trophy	מַזְכֶּרֶת	turban	תַּרְבּוּשׁ	two	שְׁנַיִם
tropical	טְרוֹפִּי	turkey	תַּרְנְגוֹל הֹדוּ	type	טִפּוּס
trot	דְּהָרָה	Turkey	טוּרְקִיָּה	typewriter	מְכוֹנַת כְּתִיבָה
trot (to)	דָּהַר	Turkish	טוּרְקִי	tyranny	עֲרִיצוּת
trouble (bother)	טִרְחָה	turmoil	מְהוּמָה	tyrant	עָרִיץ
(difficulty)	קֹשִׁי	turn	סִבּוּב		
(disagreement)	צָרוֹת	turn (to) (revolve)	כָּבַב	**U**	
(distress)	צַעַר	(to become pale, etc.)	הָפַךְ לְ-	ugliness	כִּעוּר
(worry)	צָרוֹת	(to change direction)	הָפַךְ פָּנָיו	ugly	מְכֹעָר
				ulcer	כִּיב
trouble (to)	הִטְרִיחַ	to turn against	הִתְנַגֵּד	ulterior	נִסְתָּר
Don't trouble yourself.	אַל תִּטְרַח.	to turn around	הִסְתּוֹבֵב	ultimate	סוֹפִי
troupe	לַהֲקָה	to turn back	חָזַר	ultimately	לְבַסּוֹף

ultimatum	אוּלְטִימָטוּם	undoubtedly	בְּלִי סָפֵק	unite (to)	אִחָה
umbrella	מִטְרִיָּה	undress (to) (oneself)	הִתְפַּשֵּׁט	united	מְאֻחָדִים
umpire	שׁוֹפֵט	uneasiness	אִי מְנוּחָה	United States	אַרְצוֹת הַבְּרִית
unanimity	פֶּה אֶחָד	uneasy	חֲסַר מָנוּחָה	unity	אַחְדּוּת
unanimously	פֶּה אֶחָד	unemployed	בָּטֵל	universal	עוֹלְמִי
unbearable	כָּבֵד מִנְּשׂא	unemployment	בַּטָּלָה	universe	עוֹלָם
unbelievable	שֶׁלֹּא יֵאָמֵן	unequal	לֹא שָׁוֶה	university	אוּנִיבֶרְסִיטָה
unbutton (to)	הִתִּיר	uneven	לֹא חָלָק	unjust	לֹא צוֹדֵק
uncalled-for	מְיֻתָּר	unexpected	בִּלְתִּי צָפוּי	unkempt	פָּרוּעַ
uncertain	מְסֻפָּק	unexpectedly	לְפֶתַע	unkind	רַע לֵב
uncertainty	סָפֵק	unfailing	נֶאֱמָן	unknown	בִּלְתִּי-יָדוּעַ
unchangeable	בִּלְתִּי מְשֻׁנֶּה	unfair	לֹא צוֹדֵק	unlawful	בִּלְתִּי-חֻקִּי
uncivilized	חֲסַר תַּרְבּוּת	unfaithful	בּוֹגֵד	unless	אִם לֹא
unconditional	מֻחְלָט	unfamiliar	זָר	unlikely	מְסֻפָּק
unconscious	חֲסַר הַכָּרָה	unfavorable	לֹא רָצוּי	unlimited	בִּלְתִּי מֻגְבָּל
unconsciously	בְּלִי דַעַת	unfit	לֹא מַתְאִים	unload (to)	פָּרַק
uncouth	גַּס	unfold (to)	פָּרַשׂ	unluckily	בְּלִי מַזָּל
uncover (to)	גִּלָּה	unforeseen	בִּלְתִּי צָפוּי	unmistakably	בְּלִי סָפֵק
uncultivated (field)	בָּר	unforgettable	שֶׁלֹּא יִשָּׁכַח	unnecessary	מְיֻתָּר
undecided	מְסֻפָּק	unfortunate	אֻמְלָל	unoccupied	רֵיק
undeniable	שֶׁאֵין לְהַכְחִישׁ	ungrateful	כְּפוּי טוֹבָה	unofficial	בִּלְתִּי רַשְׁמִי
under	תַּחַת	unhappily	בְּלִי שִׂמְחָה	unpleasant	לֹא נָעִים
under the table	תַּחַת הַשֻּׁלְחָן	unhappiness	אִי שִׂמְחָה	unquestionably	בְּלִי כָּל סָפֵק
undergo (to)	סָבַל	unhappy	אֻמְלָל	unravel (to)	פָּתַח
underground (adj.)	מִתַּחַת לָאֲדָמָה	unhealthy	לֹא בָּרִיא	unreal	מְדֻמֶּה
undergound (n.)	מַחְתֶּרֶת	unheard (of)	בִּלְתִּי נִשְׁמַע	unreasonable	לֹא הֶגְיוֹנִי
underhanded	עָרוּם	unhesitatingly	בְּלִי הֶסּוּס	unrecognizable	בִּלְתִּי מֻכָּר
underline (to)	הִטְעִים	unhoped for	בִּלְתִּי מְקֻוֶּה	unreliable	פּוֹחֵז
underneath	מִתַּחַת	uniform (n.)	מַדִּים	unrest	חֹסֶר מָנוּחָה
understand (to)	הֵבִין	uniformity	שִׁוְיוֹן	unrestricted	בִּלְתִּי מֻגְבָּל
understanding	הֲבָנָה	uniformly	כְּצוּרָה אַחַת	unroll (to)	גָּלַל
undertake (to)	קִבֵּל עַל עַצְמוֹ	unify (to)	אִחֵד	unsafe	מְסֻכָּן
undertaker	קַבְרָן	unimportant	לֹא חָשׁוּב	unscrupulous	חֲסַר עֶקְרוֹנִים
undertaking	נִסָּיוֹן	unintentional	בִּלְתִּי מְכֻוָּן	unseemly	לֹא נָאֶה
underwear	תַּחְתּוֹנִים	unintentionally	בְּלִי כַּוָּנָה	unseen (adj.)	סָמוּי
undesirable	בִּלְתִּי רָצוּי	uninviting	דּוֹחֶה	unspeakable	שֶׁאֵין לְבַטֵּא
undignified	חֲסַר כָּבוֹד	union	אֶגֶד, אֲגוּדָה	unsteady	רוֹפֵף
undisturbed	שׁוֹקֵט	unique	מְיֻחָד	unsuccessful	בִּלְתִּי מֻצְלָח
undo (to)	בִּטֵּל	unit	יְחִידָה	unsuitable	לֹא מַתְאִים

unthinkable	לֹא יְשֹׁעַר	urgent	דָחוּק, תָּכוּף	vapor	אֵד
untidy	פָּרוּעַ	us	אוֹתָנוּ	variable	מְשֻׁתַּנֶּה
untie (to)	הִתִּיר	use	שִׁמּוּשׁ	variation	שִׁנּוּי
until	עַד	use (to)	הִשְׁתַּמֵּשׁ בְּ-	varied	מְגֻוָּן
until now	עַד עַכְשָׁו	used to	הָיָה רָגִיל	variety	גִּוּוּן
untrue	שֶׁקֶר	useful	שִׁמּוּשִׁי	various	שׁוֹנֶה
untruth	שֶׁקֶר	useless	חֲסַר תּוֹעֶלֶת	varnish	לַכָּה
unusual	נָדִיר	usher	סַדְרָן	varnish (to)	לִכֵּךְ
unwell	לֹא בָּרִיא	usual	רָגִיל	vary (to)	שִׁנָּה
unwilling	מְמָאֵן	usually	עַל פִּי רֹב	vase	כַּד
unwise	לֹא חָכָם	usury	נֶשֶׁךְ	vast	רָחָב
unworthy	לֹא כְּדַאי	utensil	כְּלִי	vault	כִּפָּה
up	עַל, לְמַעְלָה	utility	תּוֹעֶלֶת	veal	בְּשַׂר עֵגֶל
up and down	לְמַעְלָה וּלְמַטָה	utilize (to)	הִשְׁתַּמֵּשׁ בְּ-	vegetable	יָרָק
(to) go up	עָלָה	utter (to)	בִּטֵא	vehemence	עֹז
up to (capable of doing)	מוּכָן	utterly	לְגַמְרֵי	vehicle	רֶכֶב
She's not up yet.	הִיא טֶרֶם קָמָה.			veil	צָעִיף
The time is up.	הַזְּמַן עָבַר.		V	veil (to)	כִּסָּה
This side up (on cases).	צַד זֶה לְמַעְלָה.	vacancy	מָקוֹם פָּנוּי	vein	וָרִיד
Up there!	שָׁם לְמַעְלָה!	vacant	רֵיק	velocity	מְהִירוּת
What's up?	מַה יֵשׁ?	vacation	חֹפֶשׁ	velvet	קְטִיפָה
upheaval	מַהְפְּכָה	vaccinate (to)	הִרְכִּיב אֲבַעְבּוּעוֹת	venerable	זָקֵן, נִכְבָּד
uphold (to)	סָעַד	vacuum	חָלָל	venerate (to)	כִּבֵּד
upkeep	פַּרְנָסָה	vague	סָתוּם	veneration	כָּבוֹד
upon	עַל	vain	יָהִיר	vengeance	נְקָמָה
upper	עֶלְיוֹן	in vain	לַשָּׁוְא	venom	רַעַל
upright	זָקוּף	valiant	גִּבּוֹר	ventilation	אָוְרוּר
uprising	הִתְקוֹמְמוּת	valid	שָׁרִיר	ventilator	מְאַוְרֵר
uproar	שָׁאוֹן	validity	תֹּקֶף	venture	נִסָּיוֹן
upset	נֶהְפָּךְ	valley	עֵמֶק	verb	פֹּעַל
upset (to)	הָפַךְ	valuable	יָקָר	verdict	פְּסַק דִּין
upside down	רֹאשׁ לְמַטָה	value	עֵרֶךְ	verge	שָׂפָה
upstairs	לְמַעְלָה	value (to)	הֶעֱרִיךְ	verification	אֲמִתּוּת
up-to-date	עַדְכָּנִי	valued	יָקָר	verify (to)	אִמֵּת
uptown	מַעְלֵה הָעִיר	valve	שַׁסְתּוֹם	versatile	רַבְצְדָדִי
upward	מַעְלָה	vandal	מַשְׁחִית	versatility	רַבְצְדָדִיּוּת
urge (to)	הִפְצִיר	vanilla	וָנִילָה	verse	חָרוּז
urgency	דֹחַק	vanish (to)	נֶעֱלַם	version	נֻסְחָה
		vanquish (to)	כִּבֵּשׁ	vertebra	חֻלְיָה

vertical	מְאֻנָּךְ	vision	רְאִיָה	(to) wait on (in a store, etc. to serve)	שֵׁרֵת
very	מְאֹד	visit	בִּקּוּר	Wait!	חַכֵּה!
vessel	כְּלִי	visit (to)	בִּקֵּר	Wait for me!	חַכֵּה לִי!
vest	חֲזִיָה	visitor	מְבַקֵּר	waiter	מֶלְצַר
veterinarian	רוֹפֵא בְּהֵמוֹת	visual	נִרְאֶה	wake (to)	עוֹרֵר
veto	וֵטוֹ	visualize (to)	רָאָה בְּדִמְיוֹן	walk	טִיּוּל
vex (to)	הִרְגִּיז	vital	חִיּוּנִי	walk (to)	הָלַךְ
via	דֶּרֶךְ	vitality	חִיּוּנִיּוּת	(to) go for a walk	הָלַךְ לְטַיֵּל
vibrate (to)	נָעֲנַע	vivacious	עַלִּיז	wall	חוֹמָה
vice-president	סְגַן-נָשִׂיא	vivid	מַזְהִיר	wallet	אַרְנָק
vice-versa	לְהֶפֶךְ	vocabulary	מִלּוֹן	walnut	אֱגוֹז
vicinity	קִרְבָה, קִרְבַת מָקוֹם	vocal	קוֹלִי	waltz	וַלְס
vicious	כָּלְתִּי מְרֻסָּן	vocation	מִשְׁלַח יָד	wander (to)	תָּעָה
victim	קָרְבָּן	vogue	מוֹדָה	want	חֹסֶר
victor	מְנַצֵּחַ	voice	קוֹל	want (to) (need, desire)	רָצָה
victory	נִצָּחוֹן	void	חָלָל	war	מִלְחָמָה
victuals	מָזוֹן	volt	וֹולְט	ward	חָנִיךְ
view	רְאִיָה, הַשְׁקָפָה	volubility	שֶׁטֶף דִּבּוּר	wardrobe	אֲרוֹן בְּגָדִים
view (to)	הִשְׁקִיף	voluble	דַּבְּרָנִי	ware(s)	סְחוֹרָה
vigor	אוֹן	volume	נֶפַח	warehouse	מַחְסָן
vigorous	חָזָק	voluminous	רַב	warfare	מִלְחָמָה
vile	מֻשְׁחָת	voluntary	מֵרָצוֹן	warm	חַם
village	כְּפָר	volunteer	מִתְנַדֵּב	I am warm.	חַם לִי.
villain	רָשָׁע	vomit (to)	הֵקִיא	warm (to)	חִמֵּם
vindicate (to)	הִצְדִּיק	vote	הַצְבָּעָה	warmth	חֹם
vindictive	נוֹטֵר	vote (to)	הִצְבִּיעַ	warn (to)	הִזְהִיר
vine	גֶּפֶן	vow	שְׁבוּעָה, נֶדֶר	warning	הַזְהָרָה
vinegar	חֹמֶץ	vow (to)	נִשְׁבַּע, נָדַר	warrant	סַמְכָה
vineyard	כֶּרֶם	vowel	תְּנוּעָה	warrant (to)	הִצְדִּיק
violence	אֲלִימוּת	vulgar	גַּס	wart	יַבֶּלֶת
violent	אַלִּים			wary	זָהִיר
violet (adj.)	סָגֹל			wash	כְּבִיסָה
violin	כִּנּוֹר	**W**		wash (to)	רָחַץ, כִּבֵּס
violinist	כַּנָּר	wager	הִתְעָרְבוּת	washroom	חֲדַר רַחְצָה
virgin	בְּתוּלָה	wager (to)	הִתְעָרֵב	waste (to)	בִּזְבֵּז
virile	גַּבְרִי	wages	שָׂכָר	waste (n.)	אָבְדָן
virtue	מַעֲלָה	wagon	עֲגָלָה	watch	שָׁעוֹן
virtuous	מֻסָּרִי	waist	מָתְנַיִם	watch (to)	שָׁמַר
visible	נִרְאֶה	wait (to)	חִכָּה	(to) watch out	נִזְהַר

(to) watch one's step	נִזְהַר	weakness	חֻלְשָׁה	where	אֵיפֹה, אַיֵּה
(to) watch over	שָׁמַר	wealth	עֹשֶׁר	(to what place?)	לְאָן?
watchful	שַׁמְרָנִי	wealthy	עָשִׁיר	wherever	בְּכָל מָקוֹם
water	מַיִם	wean (to)	גָּמַל	which	אֵיזֶה
watermelon	אֲבַטִּיחַ	weapon	כְּלִי זַיִן	while (n.)	עֵת, זְמַן
waterproof	טָרִיש	wear (to)	לָבַש	Wait a while!	חַכֵּה מְעַט!
wave (radio,etc.)	גַּל	(to) wear down	שָׁחַק	whim	קַפְּרִיסָה
(hair)	תִּלְתּוּל	weariness	יְגִיעָה	whine (to)	יִלֵּל
wave (to)	נוֹפֵף	weary	יָגֵעַ	whip	שׁוֹט
(to signal by waving)	רָמַז	weather	מֶזֶג אֲוִיר	whip (to)	הִצְלִיף
(to) wave in the air	הֵנִיף	weave (to)	אָרַג	whisper	לַחַשׁ
(to) wave one's hand	הֵנִיעַ	web (spider)	קוּרִים	whisper (to)	לָחַשׁ
waver (to)	הִתְנוֹדֵד	wedding	חֲתֻנָּה	whistle	שְׁרִיקָה
wax	שַׁעֲוָה	Wednesday	יוֹם רְבִיעִי	whistle (to)	שָׁרַק
way	דֶּרֶךְ	week	שָׁבוּעַ	white	לָבָן
(manner)	אֹפֶן	week end	סוֹף הַשָּׁבוּעַ	who	מִי
all the way	כָּל הַדֶּרֶךְ	weekly	שְׁבוּעִי	whoever	כָּל מִי
any way	בְּכָל אֹפֶן	weep (to)	בָּכָה	whole (the)	הַכֹּל
by the way	אַגַּב	weigh (to)	שָׁקַל	whole (adj.)	כָּל
by way of	דֶּרֶךְ	weight	מִשְׁקָל	wholesale	סִיטוֹנוּת
in no way	כְּשׁוּם אֹפֶן	welcome (n.)	קַבָּלַת פָּנִים	wholesome	בָּרִיא
in some way or other	בְּאֵיזֶה אֹפֶן שֶׁהוּא	Welcome!	בָּרוּךְ הַבָּא!	whom	אֲשֶׁר אוֹתוֹ
in such a way	בְּאֹפֶן כָּזֶה	You're welcome!	בְּבַקָּשָׁה!	whose	אֲשֶׁר שֶׁלּוֹ
in this way	בְּאֹפֶן זֶה	welfare	שָׁלוֹם	why	מַדּוּעַ
this way	לְכַאן	well (adv.)	טוֹב, הֵיטֵב	Why not?	מַדּוּעַ לֹא?
(to) give way	נָסוֹג	Well!	וּבְכֵן!	wicked	רָשָׁע
(to) have (get) one's way	הִשִּׂיג מְבֻקָּשׁוֹ	west	מַעֲרָב	wide	רָחָב
under way	פֻּדָּרָה	western	מַעֲרָבִי	widen (to)	הִרְחִיב
way in	כְּנִיסָה	westerner	מַעֲרָבִי	widow	אַלְמָנָה
way off	רָחוֹק	westward	מַעֲרָבָה	widower	אַלְמָן
way out	יְצִיאָה	wet	רָטֹב	width	רֹחַב
ways and means	דְּרָכִים, אֶמְצָעִים	what	מַה	wife	אִשָּׁה
Get out of the way.	צֵא מִן הַדֶּרֶךְ.	What?	מַה?	wig	פֵּאָה נָכְרִית
we	אֲנַחְנוּ	What is it?	מַה זֶה?	wild	בָּר, פֶּרֶא
weak	חַלָּשׁ	whatever	כָּל אֲשֶׁר	wilderness	יְשִׁימוֹן, מִדְבָּר
weaken (to)	הֶחֱלִישׁ	wheat	חִטָּה	wildness	פְּרָאוּת
weakling	חַלָּשׁ	wheel	גַּלְגַּל	wile	מִרְמָה
weakly	בְּחֻלְשָׁה	when?	מָתַי?	will	רָצוֹן
		whenever	כַּאֲשֶׁר	willful	עַקְשָׁנִי

willing	מֵאוֹדּ רָצוֹן	wood	עֵץ	wrist	פֶּרֶק הַיָּד
willingly	בְּרָצוֹן	wooden	מֵעֵץ	write (to)	כָּתַב
wilt (to)	נָבַל	woods	חֹרְשָׁה	writer	כּוֹתֵב
win (to)	זָכָה	wool	צֶמֶר	writing	כְּתִיבָה
wind	רוּחַ	woolen	צַמְרִי	in writing	בִּכְתָב
wind (to)	כָּרַךְ	word	מִלָּה	written	כָּתוּב
window	חַלּוֹן	work	עֲבוֹדָה	wrong (n.) (injustice)	עָוֶל
windy	סוֹעֵר	work (to)	עָבַד	(harm)	רָעָה
wine	יַיִן	worker	עוֹבֵד, פּוֹעֵל	wrong (adj.)	לֹא נָכוֹן
wing	כָּנָף	work of art	מְלֶאכֶת מַחֲשֶׁבֶת	wrong (to)	הֵרַע לְ-
wink	קְרִיצָה	workshop	בֵּית עֲבוֹדָה		
winner	זוֹכֶה	world	עוֹלָם	**X**	
winter	חֹרֶף	worm	תּוֹלַעַת		
wipe (to)	נָגַב	worry	דְּאָגָה	X-ray	קֶרֶן אֶקְס
wire	תַּיִל	worry (to)	דָּאַג		
wire (to)	קָשַׁר	Don't worry.	אַל תִּדְאַג.	**Y**	
wisdom	חָכְמָה	worse	גָּרוּעַ		
wise	חָכָם	worship	עֲבוֹדָה	yarn	מַטְוֶה
wish	בַּקָּשָׁה	worship (to)	עָבַד	yawn	פִּהוּק
wistful	נִכְסָף	worst	הַגָּרוּעַ בְּיוֹתֵר	yawn (to)	פִּהֵק
wit	בִּינָה	worth	עֵרֶךְ	year	שָׁנָה
witch	מְכַשֵּׁפָה	worthless	חֲסַר עֵרֶךְ	yearly	שְׁנָתִי
with	עִם	worthy	רָאוּי	yearn for (to)	עָרַג
withdraw (to)	נָסַג	wound	פֶּצַע	yearning	עֵרָגוֹן
withdrawal	נְסִיגָה	wound (to)	פָּצַע	yeast	שְׁמָרִים
wither (to)	נָבֵל	wounded	פָּצוּעַ	yell (to)	צָעַק
within	פְּנִימָה	wrap (to)	עָטַף	yellow	צָהֹב
without	בְּלִי	wrath	חֵמָה	yes	כֵּן
witness	עֵד	wrathful	מָלֵא חֵמָה	yesterday	אֶתְמֹל
witty	חָרִיף	wreath	זֵר	yet	עוֹד
woe	יָגוֹן	wreck (of a boat)	אֳנִיָּה שְׁבוּרָה	yield	יְבוּל
Woe is me!	אוֹי לִי!	wreck (to)	שָׁבַּר	yield (to)	נָתַן פְּרִי
wolf	זְאֵב	wrench (tool)	מַפְתֵּחַ	yoke	עֹל
woman	אִשָּׁה	wrestle (to)	נֶאֱבַק	yolk	חֶלְמוֹן
womb	רֶחֶם	wrestler	מִתְאַבֵּק	you	אַתָּה, אַתְּ, אַתֶּם, אַתֶּן
wonder	פֶּלֶא	wrestling	הַאָבְקוּת	young	צָעִיר
wonder (to)	הִתְפַּלֵּא	wretched	עָלוּב	young lady	בַּחוּרָה
wonderful	נִפְלָא	wring (to)	סָחַט	young man	בָּחוּר
Wonderful!	פְּלָאֵי פְּלָאִים!	wrinkle	קֶמֶט	your(s)	שֶׁלְּךָ

yourself	כְּעַצְמְךָ	zealot	קַנַּאי	Zionist	צִיּוֹנִי
youth	נֹעַר	zealous	קַנָּאִי	zone	אֵזוֹר
youthful	צָעִיר	zero	אֶפֶס	zoo	גַּן חַיּוֹת
		zigzag (adj.)	עֲקַלְקַל	zoology	זְאוֹלוֹגְיָה
Z		zinc	אָבָץ		
zeal	קַנָּאוּת	Zionism	צִיּוֹנוּת		

COMMON USAGE DICTIONARY

Italian-English
English-Italian

BY **Genevieve A. Martin** AND
Mario Ciatti
BASED ON THE METHOD DEVISED BY
RALPH WEIMAN
FORMERLY CHIEF OF LANGUAGE SECTION,
U. S. WAR DEPARTMENT

CONTAINING OVER 15,000 BASIC ENTRIES WITH
MEANINGS ILLUSTRATED BY SENTENCES AND
1000 ESSENTIAL WORDS ESPECIALLY INDICATED

INTRODUCTION

The Italian Common Usage Dictionary lists the most frequently used Italian words, gives their most important meanings and illustrates their use.

1. The *basic* words are indicated by capitals.

2. Only the most important meanings are given.

3. These meanings are illustrated, wherever necessary, by means of everyday phrases and sentences. Where there is no close English equivalent for an Italian word or where the English equivalent has several different meanings, the context of the illustrative sentences helps to make the meanings clear.

4. Each important word is followed by the everyday expressions in which it most frequently occurs. The Common Usage Dictionary serves accordingly as a phrase book or conversation guide: it contains thousands of everyday sentences which are of practical importance (for traveling, correspondence, etc.) or which serve as illustrations of the grammatical features of current written and spoken Italian. The Common Usage Dictionary should, therefore, prove helpful both to beginners who are building up their vocabulary and to advanced students who want to perfect their command of colloquial Italian.

5. In translating the Italian phrases and sentences an attempt has been made to give not a mere translation but an equivalent — that is, what an English speaker would say in the same situation. (Literal translations have been added to help the beginner.) The user is thus furnished with numerous examples of how common Italian expressions (particularly the very idiomatic and the very colloquial ones) can best be translated into English. This feature makes the Common Usage Dictionary especially useful for translation work.

6. The English-Italian part contains the most common English words and their Italian equivalents. By consulting the sentences given under the Italian word in the Italian-English part the reader can observe whether the Italian word always translates the English one or whether it does so only in certain cases.

EXPLANATORY NOTES

Literal translations are in parentheses.

Very colloquial words, phrases and sentences are marked *colloq*.

Italian-English DICTIONARY

361

NOTE: To help the student pronounce words in which the stress is not on the expected syllable, we have purposely added some accent marks which are not required in Italian writing. More complete information on pronunciation is given in the manual.

A

A, AD (used in front of words beginning with vowels) *to, at.* Also:
  al (contraction of *a* plus *il*).
  allo (contraction of *a* plus *lo*; used in front of words beginning with z, s followed by a consonant, and gn).
  alla (contraction of *a* plus *la*).
  ai (plural; contraction of *a* plus *i*).
  alle (plural; contraction of *a* plus *le*).
  agli (plural; contraction of *a* plus *gli*).
  alle tre *at three o'clock.*
  andare a piedi *to go on foot.*
  cucinare all' italiana *to cook in the Italian way.*
  A domani. *See you tomorrow. (Until tomorrow.)*
  Andiamo al cinema! *Let's go to the movies!*
  È andato allo stadio. *He went to the stadium.*
  È la prima strada a destra. *It's the first street on the right.*
  Hai dato la mancia ai facchini? *Did you tip the porters?*
  Io vado a Roma. *I'm going to Rome.*
  Mi preparo ad andar via. *I'm getting ready to leave (go away).*
  Questi libri appartengono agli studenti. *These books belong to the students.*
  Siamo andati alla fiera. *We went to the fair.*
  Ti condurrò alle corse. *I'll take you to the races.*

abbaiare *to bark.*
abbandonare *to abandon.*
abbandono *abandonment, desertion.*
abbassare *to lower; to reduce.*
abbasso *down, downstairs.*
abbastanza *enough, rather.*
abbattere *to throw down; to demolish; to pull down; to fell; to bring down.*
  Egli ha abbattuto un aeroplano nemico. *He brought down an enemy plane.*
  Hanno abbattuto gli alberi del giardino. *They felled the trees in the garden.*
  La minima cosa lo abbatte. *The least thing depresses him.*
abbattersi *to get disheartened; to get depressed.*
  Non bisogna abbattersi così facilmente. *One should not get discouraged so easily.*
abbattuto *dejected, downhearted.*
  L'ho trovato molto abbattuto. *I found him very downhearted.*
abbazia *abbey.*
abbellimento *improvement, embellishment.*
abbellire *to improve; to make more beautiful.*
abbigliamento *clothes.*
abbisognare *to be in need of; to need.*
  Egli abbisogna di tutto. *He is in need of everything.*
  Ti abbisogna qualcosa? *Do you need anything?*
abboccamento *interview, talk.*
abbominevole *abominable.*
abbonamento *subscription.*
  Egli ha un biglietto d'abbonamento ferroviario. *He has a season train ticket.*
  Ho un abbonamento a questa rivista. *I have a subscription to this magazine.*

abbondante *abundant.*
  La mano d'opera è abbondante in questa regione. *There is an abundant labor supply in this region.*
abbondanza *abundance; plenty.*
  V'e un' abbondanza di limoni in Sicilia. *There is an abundance of lemons in Sicily.*
abbondare *to abound; to be plentiful.*
  La selvaggina abbonda in questo paese. *Game is plentiful in this country.*
abbordare *to board (a ship); to accost (a person).*
  Mi ha abbordato scortesemente. *He accosted me rudely.*
abbottonare *to button.*
abbozzo *sketch.*
abbracciare *to embrace.*
abbraccio *embrace, hug.*
abbreviamento *abbreviation; abridgment (of a text).*
abbreviare *to make shorter; to abbreviate.*
abbreviazione, f. *abbreviation.*
  Qualche abbreviazione italiana (Some Italian abbreviations):
  mons. *monsignore* Mgr.
  N.B. (nota bene) *N.B.*
  P.T. (Poste e Telegrafi) *post and telegraph office.*
  sig. *signore* Mr.
  sig.a *signora* Mrs.
  sig.na *signorina* Miss.
abbronzare *to become suntanned.*
abbrustolito *toasted.*
abbuiare *to darken.*
abdicare *to abdicate.*
abete, m. *fir tree.*
abietto *base, abject.*
abile *able, skillful.*
abilità *ability, capability.*
abisso *abyss.*
abitabile *habitable.*
ABITANTE, m. *inhabitant.*
abitare *to live; to dwell.*
abitazione, f. *habitation, house.*
ABITO *suit, dress.*
abituale, m. & f. adj. *habitual, usual.*
abituarsi *to get used to.*
ABITUATO *accustomed; used to.*
abitudine, f. *habit, custom.*
abolire *to abolish.*
abolizione, f. *abolition.*
aborrire *to abhor.*
abrasione, f. *abrasion.*
abusare *to take advantage of.*
  Egli abusa della mia pazienza. *He is taking advantage of my patience.*
abuso *abuse.*
  Egli fa abuso di tabacco. *He smokes too much.*
accademia *academy.*
  Accademia di Belle Arti. *Academy of Fine Arts.*
accademicamente *academically.*
accademico *academician.*
academico, adj. *academic.*
ACCADERE *to happen.*
  Che cos'è accaduto? *What happened?*
  È accaduta una disgrazia. *An accident has happened.*
  Mi è accaduto d'incontrarlo. *I happened to meet him.*
  Non accade mai. *It never happens.*
accaldarsi *to become excited (nervous).*
accampamento *camp, camping.*
accampare *to camp; to encamp (military).*
  I soldati si sono accampati ai piedi della collina. *The soldiers have encamped at the foot of the hill.*

accanimento *obstinacy, persistence.*
ACCANTO *beside, near, by.*
  La chiesa si trova accanto al cimitero. *The church is near the cemetery.*
  Le fanciulle camminano una accanto all'altra. *The girls are walking side by side.*
  Siedi accanto a me. *Sit by me.*
accappatoio *robe; —da bagno* *bathrobe;* *—da toletta* *dressing robe.*
accarezzare *to caress; to fondle; to cherish.*
  accarezzare un'idea *to cherish an idea.*
  Il bimbo accarezza il suo cane. *The boy is caressing his dog.*
accartocciare *to wrap up.*
accatastare *to heap up.*
accattare *to beg.*
accattone, m. *beggar.*
accecare *to blind.*
accedere *to accede; to enter.*
accelerare *to accelerate; to hasten.*
  Dobbiamo accelerare il passo. *We must hasten (quicken our steps).*
accelerato *accelerated; (as a noun) local train.*
acceleratore, m. *accelerator.*
  Premi l'acceleratore. *Step on the gas. (Press the accelerator.)*
ACCENDERE *to light; to kindle; to turn on.*
  Accende la luce. *He turns the light on.*
  Accendi il fuoco nel camino. *Light a fire in the fireplace.*
  Ho acceso la candela. *I lit the candle.*
accendersi *to light up; to ignite; to get excited.*
accendi-sigaro *cigarette lighter.*
accennare *to hint; to point out.*
accenno *hint, nod.*
accentare *to accent.*
accentato *accented.*
  L'ultima sillaba è accentata. *The stress is on the last syllable.*
  accento *accent, stress.*
  Egli ha un leggiero accento. *He has a slight accent.*
accentuare *to emphasize; to accent.*
accerchiamento *encircling, surrounding.*
accerchiare *to surround; to encircle.*
  La casa è accerchiata. *The house is surrounded.*
accertare *to ascertain; to verify.*
accertarsi *to make certain.*
  Me ne voglio accertare. *I want to make sure of it.*
acceso *alight, aflame.*
  La folla è accesa d'ira. *The crowd is in a fit of rage.*
  La luce è accesa nel corridoio. *The light is on in the hall.*
accessibile *accessible.*
ACCESSO *access, admission, attack, fit.*
  Egli ha avuto un accesso di rabbia. *He had a fit of rage.*
accessorio *accessory.*
accettabile, m. & f. adj. *acceptable.*
ACCETTARE *to accept.*
  Accetti le mie scuse. *Accept my apology.*
  Ho accettato il suo invito. *I accepted his invitation.*
  Le condizioni furono accettate da tutti. *Everyone agreed to the conditions.*
  Non posso accettare questo dono. *I can't accept this gift.*
acciaio *steel.*
accidentale *accidental.*
ACCIDENTE, m. *accident.*
  E' morto in un accidente automobilistico. *He died in an automobile accident.*

Accidenti! *The devil!*

acc:gliato *gloomy, frowning.*

accingersi *to get ready.*

Mi accingo a partire. *I'm preparing to leave.*

acciocchè *that; in order that.*

acciottolato *pavement.*

acciuga *anchovy.*

acciuffare *to catch; to grasp.*

acclamare *to acclaim.*

acclamazione, f. *acclamation.*

acclimatarsi *to become acclimated.*

ACCLUDERE *to enclose.*

Accludo una fotografia di mio figlio. *I am enclosing a snapshot of my son.*

Non si dimentichi di accludere la fattura. *Don't forget to enclose the bill.*

accluso *enclosed.*

accoccolarsi *to squat; to crouch.*

accoglienza *reception, welcome.*

Mi han fatto una cordiale accoglienza. *They welcomed me warmly.*

accogliere *to receive; to welcome.*

Andiamo ad accogliere gli ospiti. *Let us go and receive the guests.*

Egli fu accolto male. *He was not welcome. (He was poorly received.)*

accollarsi *to take upon oneself; to assume.*

Mi sono accollato questa responsabilità. *I assumed this responsibility.*

accollato *highnecked.*

accoltellare *to stab.*

accolto *received.*

accommiatarsi *to say good-bye.*

accomodabile, m. & f. adj. *adjustable.*

ACCOMODARE *to mend; to repair; to suit; to settle; to fix.*

Bisogna far accomodare questa lampada. *This lamp must be repaired.*

Questo non mi accomoda. *This doesn't suit me.*

Ti accomoderò io! *I'll fix you up!*

accomodarsi *to sit down; to make oneself comfortable.*

accompagnamento *accompaniment (musical).*

ACCOMPAGNARE *to accompany.*

Il pianista lo accompagnò magnificamente. *The pianist accompanied him magnificently.*

Mi ha accompagnato a casa. *Ile saw me home.*

accompagnatore, m. *accompanist (musical).*

accomunare *to join; to unite.*

acconciare *to put in order; to adorn.*

accondiscendente *condescending.*

accondiscendere *to condescend.*

acconsentire *to allow; to consent; to agree.*

Chi tace acconsente. *Silence gives consent.*

accontentare *to content; to please.*

accontentarsi *to be content.*

Mi accontento facilmente. *I'm easily pleased.*

ACCONTO *account.*

Egli mi ha dato una somma in acconto. *He gave me some money on account.*

accoppiare *to couple.*

accoppiarsi *to couple.*

Sono bene accoppiati. *They make a fine couple.*

accorare *to grieve.*

accorciare *to shorten.*

accorciarsi *to become shorter.*

D'inverno le giornate si accorciano. *In winter the days become shorter.*

accorciatoia *short-cut.*

accordabile *allowable; tunable (music).*

ACCORDARE *to grant; to accord; to tune.*

Devo fare accordare il pianoforte. *I must have the piano tuned.*

Ti posso accordare solo dieci minuti di tempo. *I can give you only ten minutes' time.*

accordar(si) *to come to an agreement.*

Dopo lunga discussione si sono finalmente accordati. *After lengthy discussion they finally came to an agreement.*

ACCORDO *agreement, accord, harmony.*

D'accordo! *Agreed!*

Gianna e Maria sono venute ad un accordo. *Jean and Mary reached an agreement.*

In casa nostra regna un perfetto accordo. *There is complete harmony in our home.*

Siamo perfettamente d'accordo. *We are in complete agreement.*

Si è stabilito un accordo fra i due. *An agreement was reached between the two.*

accorgersi *to take notice; to become aware of.*

Mi sono accorto d'aver lasciato l'ombrello nel treno. *I noticed I'd left my umbrella in the train.*

accorrere *to run up; to run.*

accortezza *shrewdness, sagacity.*

accorto *careful, clever.*

accostare *to approach; to put beside.*

accreditare *to credit.*

La somma gli fu accreditata. *The sum was credited to him.*

accreditato *reliable, accredited.*

accrescere *to increase.*

accrescimento *increase.*

ACCUDIRE *to attend; to take care of.*

Devo accudire alle mie faccende. *I must attend to my duties.*

ACCUMULARE *to accumulate; to amass.*

Egli ha accumulato una gran fortuna. *He amassed a fortune.*

accuratamente *accurately, carefully.*

accuratezza *accuracy, care.*

accurato *accurate, careful.*

accusa *charge, accusation.*

ACCUSARE *to accuse; to charge.*

Egli fu accusato ingiustamente. *He was unjustly accused.*

accusato, noun & adj. *accused; defendant (legal).*

L'accusato fu rimesso in libertà. *The defendant was freed.*

accusatore, m. *accuser.*

acerbamente *bitterly, sharply.*

acerbezza *sourness, unripeness.*

acerbo *unripe.*

acero *maple.*

acetato *acetate.*

aceto *vinegar.*

acetone, m. *acetone.*

acidità *sourness, acidity.*

acido *acid, sour.*

ACQUA *water.*

acqua di mare *sea water.*

acqua dolce *fresh water.*

acqua minerale *mineral water.*

acqua ossigenata *peroxide.*

un bicchier d'acqua *a glass of water.*

acquaforte, f. *etching.*

acquaio *sink.*

acquario *aquarium.*

acquavite, f. *brandy.*

acquazzone, m. *shower (of rain).*

acquedotto *aqueduct.*

acquarello *water color.*

acquietare *to quiet; to appease.*

acquirente, m. *buyer.*

acquistare *to buy; to acquire.*

acquisto *purchase.*

Vado a fare degli acquisti in città. *I'm going shopping in town.*

acre *acrid.*

acro *acre.*

acrobata, m. *acrobat.*

acutamente *acutely, shrewdly.*

acuto *acute, sharp, keen.*

ad *see A.*

adagiare *to lay; to place.*

adagio *slowly.*

adattarsi *to suit; to conform; to submit.*

ADATTO *qualified for; suitable; right.*

Non sono adatto per questo impiego. *I am not qualified for this position.*

Quest' abito non è adatto per me. *This suit is not right for me.*

addestrare *to train.*

ADDIO *good-bye, farewell.*

addirittura *really, quite, completely.*

additare *to point at; to point out.*

addizionale *additional.*

ADDIZIONARE *to add; to sum up.*

addizione, f. *addition.*

A scuola i bambini imparano a fare l'addizione. *In school children learn to add.*

addobbare *to decorate; to furnish.*

addolcire *to sweeten; to soften.*

addolcirsi *to become sweet.*

ADDOLORARE *to grieve.*

addolorato *sorry, grieved.*

addome, m. *abdomen.*

addomesticare *to tame.*

addormentare *to put to sleep.*

ADDORMENTARSI *to fall asleep.*

Mi sono addormentato sul divano. *I fell asleep on the divan.*

addossare *to lay on; to throw on.*

Mi hanno addossato la colpa di questo incidente. *They blamed me for this incident.*

addossarsi *to take upon oneself; to saddle oneself with.*

Mi sono addossato un sacco di lavoro. *I saddled myself with a lot of work.*

addosso *upon; on; on one's back.*

Buttati addosso un vestito e vieni. *Throw some clothes on and come.*

Gli furono tutti addosso. *They all fell on him.*

addotto *alleged.*

addurre *to allege.*

adeguatamente *adequately.*

Furono adeguatamente compensati. *They were adequately repaid.*

ADEGUATO *adequate.*

adempiere *to accomplish.*

adempimento *accomplishment.*

aderire *to adhere to.*

adesione, f. *adherence, assent.*

adesivo *adhesive.*

ADESSO *now.*

Vogliamo uscire adesso? *Shall we go out now?*

adiacente *adjacent, adjoining.*

adirato *angry.*

adocchiare *to eye.*

ADOLESCENTE noun & adj. *adolescent.*

ADOPERARE *to use; to make use of.*

La farina si adopera per fare il pane. *Flour is used to make bread.*

adorare *to adore.*

adorazione, f. *adoration.*

adornamento *ornament.*

adornare *to adorn.*

ADOTTARE *to adopt; to pass.*

È stato adottato un nuovo sistema. *A new system was adopted.*

Hanno adottato un bambino dell'orfanatrofio. *They adopted one of the boys from the orphanage.*

Le nuove leggi furono adottate. *The new laws were passed.*

adottivo *adopted.*

adozione, f. *adoption.*

adulare *to flatter.*

adulatore, m. *flatterer.*

adulazione, f. *adulation, flattery.*

ADULTO *adult.*

adunanza *meeting.*

adunare *to assemble.*

AEREO, adj. *of the air; airy.*

ferrovia aerea *elevated railway.*

forze aeree *air force.*

linea aerea *air line.*

posta aerea *air mail.*

AEREO *aircraft, airplane.*

aerodromo *aerodrome.*

aeroplano *airplane.*

aeroporto *airport.*

afa *sultriness; sultry weather.*

affabile *affable, kind.*

affaccendato *busy.*

AFFACCIARSI *to present oneself; to appear.*

Si è affacciato al balcone. *He appeared at the balcony.*

Un pensiero mi si affaccia alla mente. *A thought is occurring to me (is presenting itself to my mind).*

affamare *to starve.*

affamato *starving, hungry.*

affannare *to pant; to make uneasy.*

affannarsi *to be anxious.*

affanno *difficulty of breathing (panting); uneasiness.*

Fu colto da un affanno improvviso. *He was struck by a sudden anxiety.*

AFFARE, m. *business, affair.*

Gli affari sono affari. *Business is business.*

Non sono affari tuoi. *It's none of your business.*

Si tratta d'un affare spiacevole. *It's an unpleasant affair.*

affascinante *charming, fascinating.*

affascinare *to charm; to enchant; to bewitch.*

affascinato *fascinated, charmed.*

affaticare *to weary; to fatigue.*

affaticato *fatigued, weary.*

AFFATTO *not at all.*

Affatto! *Not at all!*

Non sono affatto stanco. *I'm not at all tired.*

affermare *to affirm; to state; to say.*

affermativa *affirmative.*

affermativamente *affirmatively.*

affermativo, adj. *affirmative.*

affermazione, f. *affirmation, statement.*

afferrare *to seize; to catch.*

affettare *to cut into slices; to affect.*

AFFETTO *affection.*

AFFETTUOSAMENTE *affectionately.*

affettuoso *affectionate.*

affezionarsi *to become attached to.*

affezionato *affectionate, fond.*

affidamento *assurance.*

non dare affidamento *not to be dependable.*

non fare affidamento su di *not to rely on.*

affidare *to commit; to trust.*

affidare alla memoria *to learn by heart; to commit to memory.*

Mi affido a te. *I trust you. (I entrust myself to you.)*

affilare *to sharpen.*

affiliare *to affiliate.*

affinare *to refine.*

affinchè *in order that.*

affisso *bill, poster, placard.*

affittare *to let; to lease.*

stanza da affittare *room to let.*

affitto *rent, lease.*

affliggente *distressing.*

affliggere *to distress; to sadden.*

afflitto *afflicted.*

affogare *to suffocate; to drown.*

affollato *crowded.*

affondare *to sink.*

affrancare *to stamp.*

Questa lettera non è affrancata. *This letter is not stamped.*

affrancatura *postage.*

AFFRETTARE *to hasten; to hurry.*

affrettare il passo *to quicken the pace.*

affrettato *hurried, hasty.*

affrontare *to meet.*

agente, m. *agent.*

AGENZIA *agency, branch.*

agenzia di navigazione *shipping agency.*

agenzia di viaggio *travel agency.*

agevolare *to aid; to help.*

agevolazione, f. *concession, facilitation.*

aggettivo *adjective.*

aggiornare *to adjourn; to post up; to date.*

aggiungere *to add.*

aggiungersi a *to join.*

aggiunta *addition.*

aggiustare *to arrange; to fix.*

aggrapparsi *to cling to.*

aggravare *to aggravate.*

La situazione si è aggravata. *The situation grew more serious.*

aggredire *to assault.*

aggressivo *aggressive.*

agguato *ambush.*

agiatezza *comfort, wealth.*

agiato *wealthy.*

agio *leisure, opportunity.*

a tutto agio *at one's convenience.*

Non ho agio di farlo. *I have no time to do it.*

AGIRE *to act; to behave.*

Questo non è modo d'agire. *This is no way to behave.*

AGITARE *to shake; to wave.*

agitarsi *to get excited; to toss.*

Mi agito inutilmente. *I'm needlessly anxious.*

agitato *excited, agitated.*

mare agitato *rough sea.*

agitazione, f. *anxiety, restlessness.*

aglio *garlic.*

agnello *lamb.*

ago *needle.*

agonìa *agony, torment.*

agonizzare *to agonize.*

agricolo *agricultural.*

agricoltore, m. *farmer.*

agricoltura *farming, agriculture.*

agro *sour, bitter.*

agrodolce *bittersweet.*

agrumi *citrus fruits.*

aiutante, m. *assistant, helper, mate.*

AIUTARE *to help.*

aiuto *aid, assistance.*

Aiuto! *Help!*

ala *wing.*

alba *dawn.*

albeggiare *to dawn.*

alberare *to plant with trees.*

alberare una nave *to mast a vessel.*

alberatura *masting.*

albergare *to lodge; to be lodged.*

albergatore, m. *hotel-keeper.*

ALBERGO *hotel, inn.*

scendere ad un albergo *to put up at an hotel.*

albero *tree; mast (of a ship).*

albicocca *apricot.*

albore, m. *whiteness.*

primi albori *dawn.*

alcova *alcove.*

alcuno *some, none (with negative sentences); any (with interrogative).*

alcuni giornali *some newspapers.*

Avete alcuni amici? *Do you have any friends?*

Non ne ho alcuno. *I haven't any. I have none.*

alfabeto *alphabet.*

alfine *at last.*

alienare *to alienate.*

alimentare, adj. *alimentary.*

generi alimentari *foodstuffs, groceries.*

alimentare, verb *to feed.*

alimentarsi *to feed on; to nourish oneself.*

ALIMENTO *food.*

allacciare *to lace, to link.*

allagamento *inundation, flood.*

ALLARGARE *to widen; to enlarge; to broaden.*

allarmante *alarming.*

allarmare *to alarm.*

ALLARME, m. *warning, alarm.*

segnale d'allarme *warning signal.*

allato *on the side of; alongside.*

alleanza *alliance.*

fare alleanza con *to ally oneself to.*

ALLEGGERIRE *to lighten; to relieve.*

alleggerire la pena *to relieve the suffering.*

allegramente *cheerfully, gaily.*

allegrezza *cheerfulness, joyfulness.*

ALLEGRÌA *gaiety.*

allegro *gay, cheerful.*

allenamento *training.*

allenare *to train.*

Si è allenato per l'incontro. *He trained himself for the match.*

allenatore, m. *trainer.*

allentare *to relax; to loosen.*

allentare la stretta *to relax the hold.*

terreno allentato *soft ground.*

allergico *allergic.*

allestire *to prepare.*

allevamento *breeding, rearing.*

allevamento di bestiame *cattle breeding.*

ALLEVARE *to rear; to breed.*

allevare un bambino *to raise a child.*

allevatore, m. *breeder.*

alleviare *to alleviate; to mitigate.*

allievo, m; **allieva,** f. *pupil.*

allodola *lark, skylark.*

ALLOGGIARE *to lodge.*

alloggiare in un albergo *To lodge at an hotel.*

alloggiare truppe *to quarter soldiers.*

alloggio *lodging.*

prendere alloggio *to put up at.*

vitto e alloggio *room and board.*

ALLONTANARE *to remove.*

allontanarsi da *to go away from.*

allontanarsi dall'argomento *to digress; to stray from the subject.*

ALLORA *then.*

d'allora in poi *from that time on.*

fin d'allora *since then.*
allorchè *when, whenever.*
àlluce, m. *big toe.*
alludere *to allude (to); to hint.*
 Non alludevo a lui. *I wasn't referring to him.*
alluminio *aluminum.*
ALLUNGARE *to lengthen.*
 allungare il passo *to quicken one's pace.*
 allungare il vino coll'acqua *to dilute wine with water.*
 allungare la mano *to extend one's hand.*
allungato *lengthened, diluted.*
allusione, f. *allusion, hint.*
 fare allusione a *to hint at.*
alluvione, f. *alluvion; flood deposit.*
alquanto *somewhat; a good deal.*
altamente *highly.*
altare, m. *altar.*
ALTERARE *to alter; to change.*
 alterarsi *to get angry.*
alterazione, f. *change, alteration.*
alterigia *pride.*
ALTEZZA *height; width (of material).*
altipiano *plateau.*
altitudine, f. *altitude.*
ALTO *high; lofty; loud (voices).*
 ad alta voce *in a loud voice.*
 dall'alto della montagna *from the mountain top.*
 in alto *on high.*
altoparlante, m. *loud-speaker.*
altresì *also, too.*
ALTRETTANTO *as much as; so much; equally.*
 altrettanto lontano *as far as; equally far.*
 Altrettanto a lei. *The same to you.*
 Ne ho altrettanti. *I have as many.*
ALTRIMENTI *differently, otherwise, or, else.*
ALTRO *other.*
 dell'altro *some more.*
 l'un l'altro *each other.*
 l'uno o l'altro *one or the other.*
 ne l'uno, ne l'altro *neither one.*
 qualche cos'altro *something else.*
 quest'altra settimana *next week.*
 senz'altro *immediately; at once.*
 tutt'altro *not at all; anything but.*
 un altro *another.*
ALTROVE *elsewhere.*
ALTRUI *another's; of others.*
 la casa altrui *other people's homes.*
altura *height.*
alunno, m.; alunna f. *pupil.*
alveare, m. *beehive.*
ALZARE *to raise; to lift.*
 alzarsi *to get up; to rise.*
 alzarsi in piedi *to stand up.*
alzata *lifting; raising.*
 l'alzata del sole *the rising of the sun.*
alzato *up.*
 È alzato? *Is he up?*
amabile *lovable, amiable.*
amaca *hammock.*
amante, m. & f. *lover, admirer.*
amaramente *bitterly.*
AMARE *to love.*
amareggiare *to embitter; to grieve.*
 amareggiarsi *to fret.*
amarezza *bitterness.*
AMARO *bitter, harsh.*
 amaro digestivo *bitters.*
ambasciata *embassy, message.*
 fare un'ambasciata *to bring a message.*
ambasciatore, m. *ambassador; ambasciatrice, f. ambassadress.*

ambedue *both.*
ambire *to desire ardently.*
ambidestro *ambidextrous.*
ambizione, f. *ambition.*
ambizioso *ambitious.*
ambulante *ambulating, itinerant.*
ambulanza *ambulance.*
ameno *agreeable, pleasant, amusing.*
americano *American.*
amichevole *friendly.*
amichevolmente *in a friendly manner.*
amicizia *friendship.*
AMICO, m.; AMICA, f. *friend.*
amido *starch.*
 dar l'amido a *to starch.*
ammaestrare *to train.*
AMMALARE; AMMALARSI *to become ill.*
AMMALATO *ill.*
ammassare *to amass.*
ammasso *heap, mass.*
ammazzare *to kill.*
 ammazzarsi *to kill oneself.*
ammesso *admitted.*
AMMETTERE *to acknowledge; to admit.*
 Ammetto il mio errore. *I admit my mistake.*
AMMINISTRARE *to manage; to administer.*
 amministrare la giustizia *to administer justice.*
 amministrare un'azienda *to manage a business.*
amministrativo *administrative.*
amministratore, m. *administrator.*
amministrazione, f. *administration.*
 consiglio d'amministrazione *board of directors.*
AMMIRARE *to admire.*
ammiratore, m.; ammiratrice, f. *admirer.*
ammirazione, f. *admiration.*
ammissibile *admissible, permitted.*
AMMISSIONE, f. *admission.*
 esame d'ammissione *entrance examination.*
 tassa d'ammissione *entrance fee.*
ammobiliare *to furnish (a home).*
AMMODO, adv. *nicely; adj. nice, good.*
 una persona ammodo *a nice person.*
ammogliare *to marry.*
 ammogliarsi *to get married; (man) to take a wife.*
ammogliato *married (man).*
ammonire *to warn.*
ammontare, m. *sum.*
ammontare *to reach (a figure); to amount.*
 A quanto ammonta la somma? *What is the sum? How large is the sum?*
ammorbidire *to soften.*
 ammorbidirsi *to become soft.*
amo *fishing hook.*
AMORE, m. *love, affection.*
 amor proprio *self-esteem.*
 fortunato in amore *lucky in love.*
 per amor del cielo *for heaven's sake.*
 per amore o per forza *by hook or by crook.*
 È un amore. *It's a darling. It's adorable.*
amoreggiare *to flirt.*
amoroso *loving.*
ampiamente *amply, sufficiently.*
 ampiamente ricompensato *amply rewarded.*
ampio *ample, wide.*
ampolla *cruet.*
ampolliera *cruet stand.*
amputare *to amputate.*
anagrafe, f. *register of births, deaths and marriages.*
analfabeta *illiterate, adj. & noun.*
analfabetismo *illiteracy.*
analisi, f. *analysis.*
 analisi del sangue *blood test.*

 in ultima analisi *after all.*
analizzare *to analyse.*
ANCHE *also, too.*
 anche se *even though; even if.*
 quand'anche *even though.*
 Anche questo finirà. *This too shall end.*
àncora *anchor.*
 gettar l'àncora *to cast anchor.*
 levar l'àncora *to weigh anchor.*
ANCORA *yet, still.*
 Ancora qui? *Still here?*
 Non sono andato ancora. *I haven't gone yet.*
ancorare *to anchor.*
ANDARE *to go.*
 a lungo andare *in the long run.*
 andare a cavallo *to go horseback riding.*
 andare a piedi *to go on foot.*
 andare di fretta *to be in hurry.*
 andare in auto *to go by car.*
 Come va? *How are you?*
 Come va questa faccenda? *How is this matter?*
 Come vanno gli affari? *How is business?*
 Come vanno le tue cose? *How is everything with you?*
 Il mio orologio va avanti. *My watch is fast.*
 Il tuo orologio va indietro. *Your watch is slow.*
 Quest' orologio va male. *This watch is not right.*
ANDATA *departure, going.*
 biglietto d'andata *one-way ticket.*
 biglietto d'andata e ritorno *round-trip ticket.*
 viaggio d'andata *outward journey.*
andatura *gait.*
androne, m. *lobby, corridor.*
ANELLO *ring (jewelry); link (chain).*
 anello nuziale *wedding ring.*
 l'anello più debole della catena *the weakest link in the chain.*
anfibio *amphibious (adj.); amphibian (noun).*
anfiteatro *amphitheatre.*
angelico *angelic.*
angelo *angel.*
ANGOLO *angle, corner.*
 l'angolo della strada *street corner.*
anguilla *eel.*
angusto *narrow.*
 una camera angusta *a narrow room.*
ANIMA *soul, spirit.*
 con tutta l'anima *with all one's heart.*
 senz' anima *without spirit.*
 Non c'è anima viva... *There's not a soul...*
animale m. *animal.*
 animale feroce *wild animal.*
animare *to animate.*
 animarsi *to become animated; to get excited; to take courage.*
ANIMO *mind.*
 avere in animo di... *to intend to...*
 farsi animo *to take heart.*
 mettere l'animo in pace *to set one's mind at rest.*
 mettersi in animo di *to make up one's mind to.*
 Animo! *Come on! Take heart!*
anitra *duck.*
annebbiamento *dimming, clouding, obscuring.*
annebbiare *to fog; to dim.*
annebbiarsi *to become foggy; to grow dim.*
 La vista mi si sta annebbiando. *My eyesight is growing dim.*
 Si è annebbiato il tempo. *The weather has become foggy.*
annegare *to drown.*
annerire *to blacken; to darken.*
 annerito dal sole *sunburnt.*

annesso *annexed, attached.*
annessi e connessi *appendages.*
annientare *to annihilate.*
ANNIVERSARIO *anniversary.*
anniversario di nascita *birthday.*
anniversario di nozze *wedding anniversary.*
ANNO *year.*
anni fà *years ago.*
anno di nascita *year of birth.*
capodanno *New Year's Day.*
di anno in anno *from year to year.*
essere avanti negli anni *to be on in years.*
il primo dell'anno *New Year's Day.*
per anni e anni *for years and years.*
tanto all'anno *so much a year.*
Buon Anno! *Happy New Year!*
annodare *to knot.*
annodare relazioni *to form connections.*
ANNOIARE *to annoy; to weary.*
annoiare la gente *to bore people.*
annoiato *bored, weary.*
annotare *to note; to annotate.*
annotazione, f. *note, annotation.*
annottare *to grow dark.*
annoverare *to count; to number.*
Ti annovero fra i miei amici. *I number you among my friends.*
ANNUALE *yearly, annual.*
annualmente *annually.*
annullamento *annulment.*
annullare *to annul; to cancel.*
annunziare *to announce.*
annunziatore, m.; **annunziatrice,** f. *announcer.*
annunzio *announcement, advertisement.*
annuvolato *cloudy.*
anonimo *anonymous.*
società anonima *joint-stock company.*
anormale *abnormal.*
anormalità *abnormality.*
ansante *panting; out of breath.*
ansare *to pant.*
ansia *anxiety.*
ansiosamente *anxiously.*
ansioso *anxious, desirous.*
Sono ansioso di vederti. *I'm anxious to see you.*
antenato *ancestor.*
antenna *antenna (animal & radio).*
anteriore *previous, fore.*
le ruote anteriori dell'automobile *the front wheels of the auto.*
antiaereo *anti-aircraft.*
antichità *antiquity, antique.*
ANTICIPO *anticipation, deposit, advance.*
arrivare in anticipo *to arrive ahead of time.*
Ho ricevuto un anticipo sullo stipendio. *I got an advance on my salary.*
ANTICO *ancient, old.*
gli antichi *people of old.*
in antico *in ancient times.*
antimeridiano *a.m.; before noon.*
le undici antimeridiane *eleven a.m.*
ANTIPASTO *hors d'oeuvre.*
antipatia *dislike.*
antipatico *disagreeable, unpleasant.*
ANZI *on the contrary; rather.*
anzianità *seniority, age.*
ANZIANO *aged, old, senior.*
ANZICHE *rather than.*
Preferisco pernottare all'albergo anziché fare il viaggio di notte. *I'd rather stay the night at the hotel than travel through the night.*
anzidetto *afore-mentioned; above mentioned.*
ANZITUTTO *first of all; above all.*

La salute anzitutto. *Health above all.*
ape, f. *bee.*
aperitivo *aperitif.*
APERTAMENTE *openly, frankly.*
Mi ha detto apertamente quello che pensava di me. *He told me frankly what he thought of me.*
APERTO *open.*
apertura *opening.*
apostrofo *apostrophe.*
appagare *to satisfy; to please.*
appagarsi di poco *to be pleased with little.*
appannare *to dim; to obscure.*
apparecchiare *to prepare.*
apparecchiare la tavola *to set the table.*
APPARENTE *apparent.*
apparentemente *seemingly.*
APPARENZA *appearance.*
Non si può giudicare dall'apparenza. *One can't judge from appearances.*
APPARIRE *to appear; to seem.*
apparire improvvisamente *to appear suddenly.*
apparire stanco *to seem tired.*
apparizione, f. *apparition.*
APPARTAMENTO *flat, apartment.*
Si affitta appartamento. *Apartment to let.*
appartarsi *to withdraw.*
appartenente *belonging to.*
APPARTENERE *to belong to; to be a member of.*
Appartengo alla Società Figli d'Italia. *I belong to the Sons of Italy club.*
Questo libro mi appartiene. *This book is mine (belongs to me).*
appassionare *to interest; to impassion.*
La lettura di questo libro mi appassiona. *This book interests me.*
appassionato *passionate; fond of; partial.*
giudizio appassionato *a biased judgment.*
appassionato della musica *fond of music.*
appassire *to wither; to fade.*
appassito *faded, withered.*
appello *call, appeal.*
APPENA *hardly; scarcely; as soon as.*
Erano appena usciti. *They had just left.*
Riesco appena a camminare. *I can hardly walk.*
Siamo appena in tre. *We are only three (people).*
Verrò appena posso. *I'll come as soon as I can.*
APPENDERE *to hang up.*
APPETITO *appetite, hunger.*
avere appetito *to be hungry.*
appianare *to settle; to soothe; to level.*
applaudire *to applaud; to cheer.*
applauso *applause.*
applicabile *applicable.*
APPLICARE *to apply; to enforce.*
applicare il freno *to apply the brake.*
applicare una legge *to enforce a law.*
applicarsi *to apply oneself; to devote oneself.*
applicazione, f. *application.*
appoggiare *to lean; to lay; to rest; to back; to support.*
appoggiare al muro *to rest against the wall.*
appoggiato *leaning.*
appoggiatoio *support, rest.*
appoggio *support, aid, rest.*
apporre *to affix.*
APPOSTA *on purpose; just for.*
È stato fatto apposta. *It was done on purpose.*
L'ho conservato apposta per te. *I saved it just for you.*
L'ho fatto apposta per indispettirlo. *I did it just to spite him.*
APPRENDERE *to learn; to hear.*

apprendere facilmente *to learn easily.*
apprendere una notizia *to hear a piece of news.*
apprendista, m. *apprentice.*
apprensione, f. *apprehension, fear.*
essere in apprensione *to be apprehensive.*
APPRESSO *near by; close to; then; after.*
Che cosa viene appresso? *What comes next?*
la casa appresso alla mia *the house next to mine.*
APPREZZARE *to appreciate.*
Ho apprezzato molto la sua cortesia. *I appreciated his courtesy very much.*
apprezzato *esteemed.*
approdare *to land; to get ashore.*
approdo *landing, landing-place.*
APPROFITTARE *to profit (by); to take advantage of.*
approfittare dell'occasione *to take the opportunity.*
approfittare troppo *to abuse.*
appropriarsi *to appropriate.*
appropriato *appropriate, proper.*
appropriazione, f. *appropriation.*
appropriazione indebita *embezzlement.*
APPROSSIMATIVAMENTE *approximately.*
approssimativo *approximate.*
APPROVARE *to approve.*
approvare una legge *to pass a law.*
approvazione, f. *approval.*
APPUNTAMENTO *appointment.*
Ho un'appuntamento alle tre. *I've an appointment at three.*
APPUNTARE *to sharpen; to pin; to note.*
appunto *note, remark.*
APPUNTO, PER L'APPUNTO *precisely; just so; just.*
Per l'appunto! *Exactly!*
Stavo appunto per partire. *I was just about to leave.*
aprile *April.*
pesce d'aprile *April fool's joke.*
APRIRE *to open.*
Apri la porta. *Open the door.*
La porta si è aperta. *The door opened.*
aquario *aquarium.*
aquila *eagle.*
aranceto *orange grove.*
arancia *orange.*
spremuta d'arancia *orange juice.*
succo d'arancia *orange juice.*
aranciata *orangeade.*
arare *to plough.*
aratro *plough.*
arazzo *piece of tapestry.*
arazzi *tapestry.*
arbitro *arbiter, arbitrator.*
fare da arbitro *to referee.*
arcata *arcade.*
arcato *arched.*
architetto *architect.*
architettura *architecture.*
arcivescovo *archbishop.*
arco *bow, arch.*
strumento ad arco *string instrument.*
arcobaleno *rainbow.*
ardente *burning, ardent.*
amore ardente *ardent love.*
fiamma ardente *burning flame.*
ARDERE *to burn; to be on fire.*
Ardo dal desiderio... *I'm very desirous...*
ardimento *boldness, daring, impudence.*
ARDIRE *to dare; to have the courage to; to have the impudence.*

arditamente *boldly.*
arditezza *boldness.*
ardito *bold, fearless.*
area *area.*
  area fabbricabile *building ground.*
arena *arena.*
argentare *to silver.*
argentato *silvered, silverplated.*
argenteria *silver plate.*
ARGENTO *silver.*
ARGOMENTO *subject, topic.*
  argomento in discussione *subject under discussion.*
  entrare in argomento *to broach the subject.*
  trattare l'argomento *to treat a subject.*
ARIA *air.*
  all'aria aperta *in the open air.*
  aver l'aria di *to look like.*
  buttar per aria *to fling; to upset.*
  darsi delle arie *to give oneself airs.*
  in aria *in the air.*
  per via aerea *by air.*
aridamente *aridly, dryly.*
aridità *aridity, aridness, dryness.*
arido *arid, dry.*
  terreno arido *barren land.*
aristocratico *aristocratic.*
aristocrazia *aristocracy.*
aritmetica *arithmetic.*
ARMA *weapon.*
  arma da fuoco *firearm.*
  arma tagliente *sharp weapon.*
  deporre le armi *to lay down arms; (fig.) to give up.*
armadio *wardrobe closet.*
armare *to arm.*
armarsi *to arm oneself.*
armato *armed.*
  armato di coraggio *armed with courage.*
  cemento armato *reinforced cement.*
armistizio *armistice.*
armonia *harmony.*
armoniosamente *harmoniously.*
armonioso *harmonious.*
AROMA m. *flavor, fragrance.*
arrabbiarsi *to get angry.*
  arrabbiarsi per un nonnulla *to get angry over nothing.*
arrabbiato *enraged.*
arredare *to furnish.*
arrendersi *to surrender; to surrender oneself.*
  Mi arrendo al suo miglior giudizio. *I surrender to your better judgment.*
arrestare *to arrest; to stop.*
  arrestarsi a metà frase *to stop in the middle of a sentence.*
  Fu arrestato e condannato. *He was arrested and condemned.*
arretrato *behindhand; in arrears.*
  essere arretrato *to be behind.*
  Ho molto lavoro arretrato. *I am behind in my work.*
arricchire *to enrich; to make rich.*
  arricchirsi *to become rich.*
arricchito *newly rich; profiteer.*
arricciare *to curl.*
  arricciare il naso *to frown.*
arricciato *curled.*
ARRIVARE *to arrive.*
  arrivare a destinazione *to reach one's destination.*
  arrivare a tempo *to arrive on time.*
  arrivare in ritardo *to arrive late.*

  arrivare sano e salvo *to arrive safely.*
ARRIVO *arrival.*
  all'arrivo *on the arrival.*
  gli ultimi arrivi *the latest supplies.*
  l'ora d'arrivo *the hour of arrival.*
arrogante *arrogant.*
arroganza *arrogance.*
arrossire *to blush; to turn red.*
arrostire *to roast.*
ARROSTO *roast.*
arruffare *to disorder; to upset.*
arrugginire *to rust; to make rusty.*
  arrugginirsi *to become rusty.*
arrugginito *rusty.*
ARTE f. *art, cunning.*
  ad arte *on purpose.*
  belle arti *fine arts.*
articolo *article.*
  articolo di fondo *editorial.*
artista *artist, m. & f.*
artistico *artistic.*
ascendere *to ascend; to amount to.*
  La somma ascende a tre milioni. *The sum reaches three millions.*
ASCENSORE, m. *elevator.*
ascesa *ascent.*
ascia *axe.*
asciugamano *towel.*
ASCIUGARE *to dry; to dry up; to wipe.*
  asciugare all'aria *to dry in the air.*
asciutto *dry.*
ASCOLTARE *to listen; to hear.*
  ascoltare la radio *to listen to the radio.*
  Ascoltami bene. *Listen to me carefully.*
ascoltatore, m.; **ascoltatrice**, f. *listener.*
ascolto *listening.*
  dare ascolto a *to heed; to listen to.*
  stare in ascolto *to be listening.*
ASILO *asylum, shelter, refuge.*
  asilo infantile *kindergarten; nursery school.*
  chiedere asilo *to seek shelter.*
asino *ass; donkey;* **asina** *she-donkey.*
asparago; asparagi, pl. *asparagus.*
ASPETTARE *to wait for.*
  aspettare con ansia *to look forward to.*
  non mi aspettavo di *I didn't expect.*
  Lo aspetto da un momento all'altro. *I expect him any minute.*
  Ti aspetterò alla stazione. *I'll wait for you at the station.*
  Vi aspetto alle tre. *I expect you at three.*
ASPETTO *look, aspect.*
  a primo aspetto *at first sight; at first.*
  aver l'aspetto di un signore *to look like a gentleman.*
  sotto tutti gli aspetti *from every point of view.*
  un aspetto serio *a serious mien.*
aspirapolvere, m. *vacuum cleaner.*
aspro *harsh, sharp.*
  con voce aspra *in a harsh voice.*
  vino aspro *sharp wine.*
assaggiare *to taste; to try; to test.*
assai *very much; enough.*
assalire *to assail; to assault; to attack.*
assassinare *to assassinate.*
assassino *assassin.*
asse, m. *board, plank, axis.*
assegnamento *reliance, allotment.*
  Non fare assegnamento su di me. *Don't count on me.*
assegnare *to assign; to allot.*
  Gli fu assegnato il primo premio. *He was given first prize.*

  Questo posto mi è stato assegnato. *This place was assigned to me.*
ASSEGNO *check, allowance.*
  in assegno *C.O.D.*
  pagare con un' assegno *to pay by check.*
  Ho ricevuto il mio assegno mensile. *I received my monthly allowance.*
assennato *wise, judicious.*
assentarsi *to absent oneself.*
  Mi son dovuto assentare per ragioni di malattia. *I had to absent myself on account of illness.*
assenso *assent.*
ASSENTE *absent.*
  assente da casa *away from home.*
  assente dal lavoro *away from work.*
  assente dalla scuola *absent from school.*
ASSENZA *absence, lack.*
  fare troppe assenze dalla scuola *to be absent from school too often.*
ASSERIRE *to assert; to declare; to affirm.*
  asserire il contrario *to say the opposite.*
asserzione, f. *assertion, declaration.*
assetato *thirsty.*
assettato *in order; tidy.*
ASSICURARE *to assure; to secure; to insure.*
  Ho assicurato la mia casa contro gli incendi. *I insured my home against fire.*
  Mi ha assicurato che sarebbe venuto. *He assured me he would come.*
ASSICURARSI *to make sure; to insure oneself.*
  Mi sono assicurato per cinquemila dollari. *I took out a five thousand dollar policy.*
  Mi voglio assicurare che la porta sia chiusa. *I want to make sure the door is closed.*
assicurazione, f. *insurance.*
  polizza d'assicurazione *insurance policy.*
assistente *assistant, noun & adj.*
assistenza *assistance, aid, help.*
ASSISTERE *to assist; to aid; to nurse; to be present.*
  I forti assistono i deboli. *The strong help the weak.*
  La cerimonia fu assistita da molti. *Many were present at the ceremony.*
  L'infermiera assiste l'ammalato. *The nurse is assisting the patient.*
asso *ace.*
associare *to associate; to take into partnership.*
associazione, f. *association.*
ASSOLUTAMENTE *absolutely, completely.*
ASSOLUTO *absolute, complete.*
  autorità assoluta *complete authority.*
assolvere *to absolve; to forgive.*
ASSOMIGLIARE *to look like; to be like; to resemble; to compare.*
  Ha assomigliato la fanciulla ad una statua. *He compared the girl to a statue.*
  Si assomigliano come due gocce d'acqua. *They are as alike as two drops of water.*
assopirsi *to get drowsy.*
assorbente *absorbing.*
  carta assorbente *blotting paper.*
assorbire *to absorb.*
ASSORTIMENTO *assortment.*
assortito *assorted.*
assorto *absorbed.*
  assorto nello studio *absorbed in studying.*
ASSUMERE *to assume; to take on.*
  Mi sono assunto questa incombenza. *I took on this task.*
assurdo *absurd.*
asta *lance, spear, pole.*
  vendita all'asta *auction sale.*

ASTENERSI *to abstain.*
Mi astengo dal bere. *I abstain from drinking.*
astio *hatred.*
aver astio contro qualcuno *to bear someone a grudge.*
astratto *abstract.*
astuccio *box, case.*
astutamente *cunningly.*
astuto *cunning, astute.*
astuzia *astuteness, cunning, trick.*
atleta, m. *athlete.*
atletica *athletics.*
atletico *athletic.*
atmosfera *atmosphere.*
atomico *atomic.*
bomba atomica *atomic bomb.*
atrio *lobby.*
ATTACCARE *to attack; to assail; to attach; to stick; to paste.*
ATTACCO *attack, juncture, connection, touch.*
attacco elettrico *electric connection (outlet).*
un'attacco d'influenza *a touch of influenza.*
atteggiamento *attitude, behaviour.*
ATTENDERE *to wait; to await; to expect.*
Bisogna attendere. *We have to wait.*
attenersi *to conform.*
attento *attentive.*
attenzione, f. *attention.*
ATTESA *waiting, expectation.*
sala d'attesa *waiting room.*
attestare *to testify; to bear witness.*
attimo *instant, moment.*
ATTIRARE *to attract; to draw attention.*
attirarsi *to draw upon oneself.*
ATTITUDINE, f. *disposition, inclination.*
ATTIVITÀ *activity.*
essere in attività di servizio *to be on active duty.*
attivo *active.*
ATTO *act, deed, certificate.*
all'atto pratico *in practice.*
atto di nascita *birth certificate.*
nell'atto di *in the act of.*
prendere atto di *to take note of.*
primo atto *first act.*
attore, m. *actor;* **attrice,** f. *actress.*
ATTORNO *about, around, round.*
ATTRAENTE *attractive, charming.*
ATTRARRE *to attract.*
attrarre attenzione *to attract attention.*
attrarre folla *to attract a crowd.*
attratto *attracted.*
ATTRAVERSARE *to cross.*
attraversare la strada *to cross the street.*
attraversare un fiume a nuoto *to swim across a river.*
attraversare un paese in automobile *to drive across a country.*
ATTRAVERSO *across, through.*
Abbiamo trovato una barricata attraverso la strada. *We found a barricade across the road.*
Siamo passati attraverso lo stretto di Messina. *We passed through the Strait of Messina.*
attrazione, f. *attraction.*
numero d'attrazione *starring act (theatrical).*
attrezzo *implement, tool.*
ATTRIBUIRE *to attribute.*
attrito *friction.*
ATTUALE *actual, real, current, present.*
attualità *reality; topic of the day.*
audace *bold, rash.*
audizione, f. *audition.*
AUGURARE *to wish; to bid.*

augurare la buona notte *to bid goodnight.*
Mi auguro di poterlo fare. *I hope to be able to do it.*
augurio *wish, omen.*
essere di buon'augurio *to presage good luck.*
Auguri di felice Natale. *Wishes for a happy Christmas.*
Porga i miei auguri a sua moglie. *Extend my wishes to your wife.*
aula *hall, room.*
aula scolastica *classroom.*
AUMENTARE *to increase; to augment; to raise.*
aumentare di volume *to increase in volume.*
aumentare le tasse *to increase the taxes.*
aumentare lo stipendio *to raise the salary.*
AUMENTO *increase, raise, rise.*
un aumento del due per cento *a two percent rise.*
aurora *sunrise, dawn.*
aurora boreale *aurora borealis.*
austero *austere, strict.*
autentico *authentic, real.*
AUTISTA, m. *driver, chauffeur.*
AUTO *motor car.*
autobiografia *autobiography.*
AUTOBUS, m. *bus.*
autocarro *motor-lorry.*
autocorriera *motor-coach.*
automobile f. *automobile.*
AUTORE, m. *author.*
autorimessa *garage.*
AUTORITÀ *authority.*
AUTORIZZARE *to authorize.*
autorizzato *authorized.*
non essere autorizzato a *to be not entitled to; to be not authorized to.*
autorizzazione, f. *authorization.*
autunno *fall, autumn.*
AVANTI *ahead, before.*
avanti a me *before me.*
avanti Cristo *before Christ.*
avantieri *the day before yesterday.*
da ora in avanti *from this time forward; from now on.*
essere molto avanti *to be ahead; to be far advanced.*
il giorno avanti *the preceding day.*
Avanti! *Forward! Come in! (in answer to a knock).*
Il mio orologio è avanti. *My watch is fast.*
avanzare *to advance; to be left over.*
avanzo *remnant, remainder.*
Ne ho d'avanzo. *I've more than enough.*
avaro, adj. *avaricious; (as noun) miser.*
avena *oats.*
farina d'avena *oatmeal.*
AVERE *to have.*
aver caldo *to be warm.*
avercela con qualcuno *to bear a grudge against somebody.*
aver dolore a *to feel a pain in.*
aver fame *to be hungry.*
aver freddo *to be cold.*
aver paura *to be afraid.*
aver ragione *to be right.*
aver sete *to be thirsty.*
aver sonno *to be sleepy.*
aver torto *to be wrong.*
aver trent'anni *to be thirty years old.*
Che cosa avete? *What's the matter with you?*
avo *grandfather.*
i miei avi *my ancestors.*
avvelenare *to poison.*
avvelenamento *poisoning.*

avvenimento *event, incident.*
AVVENIRE, m. *future.*
in avvenire *in the future.*
avvenire *to happen.*
avventura *adventure.*
avverbio *adverb.*
avversario *opponent.*
AVVERTIRE *to warn; to caution; to inform.*
avviarsi *to set out.*
AVVICINARE *to approach; to draw near.*
avvicinarsi *to draw nearer.*
avvilire *to humiliate.*
avvilito *discouraged, humiliated.*
AVVISO *notice, advice, opinion.*
avviso pubblicitario *poster, advertisement.*
essere d'avviso *to be of the opinion.*
avvocato *lawyer.*
AZIONE, f. *action; share (stock).*
azoto *azote.*
azzardo *hazard, risk.*
giuocar d'azzardo *to gamble.*
azzurro *blue, azure.*

B

baccano *noise, hubbub.*
bacchetta *rod, baton.*
bacchetta magica *magic wand.*
baciare *to kiss.*
bacile, m. *wash-basin.*
BACIO *kiss.*
baco *silkworm, worm, beetle.*
BADARE *to mind.*
Bada a te! *Beware!*
Io bado alle mie faccende. *I mind my own business.*
Non ci badare. *Pay no attention.*
baffi, m. pl. *whiskers.*
BAGAGLIO *luggage, baggage.*
bagnare *to wet;* **bagnarsi** *to wet oneself; to get soaked.*
bagnino *bathing attendant.*
BAGNO *bath.*
camera da bagno *bathroom.*
costume da bagno *bathing suit.*
farsi un bagno *bathe oneself.*
baia *bay.*
balbettare *to stutter; to lisp.*
balbettare delle scuse *to stammer excuses.*
balcone, m. *balcony.*
balena *whale.*
baleno *lightning, flash.*
È arrivato in un baleno. *He arrived in a flash.*
balia *nurse (children's).*
balla *bale.*
BALLARE *to dance.*
ballo *dance, dancing, ball.*
lezione di ballo *dancing lesson.*
balocco *toy.*
balzare *to bound; to start.*
bambina *little girl; child.*
BAMBINO *little boy; child.*
bambagia *cotton (surgical).*
bambola *doll.*
banana *banana.*
banca *bank.*
biglietto di banca *bank-note.*
bancarotta *bankruptcy.*
banchiere *banker.*
banco *bank, counter, bench.*
banco di lavoro *workbench.*
banco di scuola *school desk.*
banconota *bank-note.*
banda *band, gang.*

bandiera *flag, banner.*
  bandiera a mezz'asta *half-mast flag.*
bar *bar.*
baracca *hut.*
barattolo *pot, tin.*
barba *beard.*
  farsi la barba }
  radersi la barba } *to shave.*
barbabietola *beet.*
barbieria *barbershop.*
barbiere, m. *barber.*
BARCA *boat.*
  barca a remi *rowboat.*
  barca a vela *sailboat.*
barile, m. *barrel.*
  averne a barili *to have a great quantity of (by the barrelful).*
barzelletta *joke.*
BASE, f. *base, basis.*
  base navale *naval base.*
  in base a *on the basis of.*
BASSO, adj. *low, short; (noun) base, bass.*
  a bassa voce *in a soft voice.*
  alti e bassi *ups and downs.*
  un' azione bassa *a base deed.*
BASTARE *to suffice; to be enough.*
  basti dire che *suffice it to say.*
  Basta! *Enough! That will do!*
bastone, m. *stick; cane; club.*
  il bastone della mia vecchiaia *the staff of my old age.*
  l'asso di bastoni *the ace of clubs.*
battaglia *battle, fight.*
  campo di battaglia *battlefield.*
battello *boat.*
  battello a vapore *steamboat.*
battente, m. *leaf of a door; shutter.*
BATTERE *to beat; to strike; to knock.*
  battersi a duello *to duel.*
  battere alla porta *to knock at the door.*
  battere la grancassa (colloq.) *to advertise; to call attention to (to beat the drum).*
  senza battere ciglio *without batting an eyelash.*
battito *beat.*
battuto *beaten.*
  Mi ha battuto lealmente. *He beat me fairly.*
baule, m. *trunk.*
bavero *collar.*
bazar, m. *bazaar.*
beato *happy.*
belga *Belgian (also noun.)*
bellezza *beauty.*
  Che bellezza! *How wonderful! (What beauty!).*
BELLO *fine, beautiful, handsome.*
benchè *though, although.*
benda *bandage.*
BENE, m. *good, welfare.*
  beni mobili ed immobili *personal property and real estate.*
  per il bene di tutti *for the good of all.*
  voler bene a *to like; to love.*
BENE, adv. *well.*
  fare le cose per bene *to do things well.*
  star bene di salute *to be in good health.*
  stare abbastanza bene *to be fairly well off.*
benedetto *blessed.*
benedire *to bless.*
benedizione, f. *blessing, benediction.*
BENEFICIO *benefit, advantage, profit.*
benessere, m. *comfort, well-being.*
beni, m. pl. *property.*
benino *fairly well; rather well.*
BENISSIMO *very well; quite well.*

Benissimo! *Fine!*
bensì *but.*
BENVENUTO *welcome.*
  Desidero darti il benvenuto. *I wish to welcome you.*
benzina *gasoline.*
BERE *to drink.*
  Bevo alla tua salute! *I drink your health!*
berretto *cap.*
bersaglio *target.*
bestemmia *oath, curse.*
BESTIAME, m. *cattle.*
  tanti capi di bestiame *so many head of cattle.*
bestia *beast.*
bevanda *drink.*
BIANCHERIA *linen.*
  biancherìa da tavola *table linen.*
  biancherìa personale *lingerie.*
BIANCO *white, noun & adj.*
  bianco d'uovo *white of the egg.*
  lasciare in bianco *to leave blank.*
biasimare *to blame; to find fault with.*
bibita *drink.*
biblioteca *library.*
BICCHIERE, m. *glass.*
bicicletta *bicycle.*
  andare in bicicletta *to ride a bicycle.*
bietola *beet.*
biglietterìa *ticket office.*
BIGLIETTO *ticket, note, card.*
  biglietto d'ammissione *ticket (admission).*
  biglietto di andata e ritorno *round-trip ticket.*
  biglietto di banca *bank note.*
  biglietto di visita *visiting card.*
bilancia *scales.*
bilanciare *to balance.*
BILANCIO *balance; balance sheet.*
  bilancio consuntivo *final balance.*
  bilancio dello stato *budget.*
  bilancio preventivo *estimate.*
  mettere in bilancio *to place in balance.*
binario *track, rail.*
biondo *blond, fair.*
BIRRA *beer.*
bisbigliare *to whisper.*
biscotto *biscuit, cooky.*
bisnomo *great-grandfather.*
BISOGNARE *to be necessary; to have to.*
  Bisogna affrettarsi. *We must hurry.*
  Bisogna che egli lo faccia. *He must do it.*
  Bisognava saperlo prima. *We should have known sooner.*
  Mi bisogna un pò di zucchero. *I need a little sugar.*
BISOGNO *want, need, poverty.*
  aver bisogno di *to need.*
bistecca *beefsteak.*
  bistecca ai ferri *broiled steak.*
bisticciarsi *to quarrel.*
bivio *crossroad.*
bloccare *to block; to blockade.*
blocco *blockade.*
  togliere il blocco *to remove the blockade.*
blu *blue.*
BOCCA *mouth.*
  bocca da incendio *fire-plug.*
  bocca del cannone *muzzle.*
boccone, m. *mouthful, morsel.*
bolla *bubble.*
bollire *to boil.*
bollito, adj. *boiled; (as a noun) boiled meat.*
bollo *stamp, seal.*
  bollo dell'ufficio postale *postmark.*

bomba *bomb.*
  a prova di bomba *bombproof.*
bonario *gentle, meek.*
BONTA *goodness, kindness.*
  avere la bontà di *to have the kindness (of).*
  bontà d'animo *kindheartedness.*
BORDO *board (naut.); border, margin.*
  andare a bordo *to go aboard.*
borghese, m. *civilian.*
  agente in borghese *plainclothes policeman.*
borgo *village.*
BORSA *purse, bag.*
  borsa di studio *scholarship.*
  borsa nera *black market.*
  Borsa Valori *Stock Exchange.*
borsetta *handbag.*
bosco *woods.*
botte *barrel, cask.*
BOTTEGA *shop.*
bottegaio *shopkeeper.*
BOTTIGLIA *bottle.*
BOTTONE, m. *button.*
  attaccare un bottone *to sew a button.*
  attaccare un bottone a *to buttonhole (somebody).*
bozzetto *sketch; rough model.*
braccialetto *bracelet.*
BRACCIO, m. braccia, pl. *arms (of the body).*
  accogliere a braccia aperte *to greet with open arms.*
  aver le braccia legate *to have one's hands tied.*
  bracci *arms (of a stream).*
  braccio di mare *strait.*
  con le braccia incrociate *with folded arms; idle.*
  offrire il braccio *to offer assistance.*
  prendere in braccio *to take in one's arms.*
bramare *to crave for.*
BRAVO *clever, skillful, honest, brave, good.*
  Bravo! *Well done!*
BREVE *short, brief.*
  fra breve *shortly; in a little while.*
  in breve *in brief.*
  in breve tempo *in a short time.*
brevetto *patent.*
  ufficio brevetti *patent office.*
brillante *brilliant, glittering.*
brillare *to sparkle.*
brindare *to toast (drink to the health of).*
brindisi, m. *a toast.*
brio *spirits, mettle.*
brodo *broth.*
  Lascialo bollire nel suo brodo. *Let him stew in his own juice.*
bromuro *bromide.*
bronzatura *bronzing.*
  bronzatura del sole *sun tan.*
BRUCIARE *to burn; to be on fire; to set fire to.*
  bruciarsi *to burn oneself.*
bruciatura *burning, burn, scorch.*
bruno, adj. *dark, brown.*
brutto *ugly, bad.*
buca *hole.*
  buca delle lettere *mailbox.*
bucare *to pierce; to puncture.*
bucato *washing, wash.*
  fare il bucato *to do the washing.*
bucatura *puncture (of a tire).*
buccia *skin, peel.*
buco *hole.*
bue *ox.*
  bistecca di bue *beefsteak.*
buffo *comic, funny.*
bugìa *falsehood, lie.*
  dire una bugìa *to tell a lie.*

bugiardo; bugiarda, f. *liar.*
BUIO *dark,* adj. & noun.
  al buio *in the dark.*
  buio pesto *pitch dark.*
  fare un salto nel buio *to leap into the dark.*
  nel buio della notte *in the dark of night.*
buono, noun *bond, bill.*
  buono del tesoro *treasury bond; treasury bill.*
  buono di guerra *war bond.*
BUONO, adj. *good.*
  colle buone *in a kind manner.*
  levarsi di buon' ora *to rise early.*
  un pranzo alla buona *a simple meal.*
  Alla buon' ora. *At last.*
  C' è voluto del buono e del bello per convincerlo.
    It took a great deal to convince him.
  È un buon' a nulla. *He's a good-for-nothing.*
  È un poco di buono. *He's not much good.*
burla *trick.*
  fare una burla *to play a trick.*
  per burla *in jest.*
BURRO *butter.*
BUSSARE *to knock.*
  Hanno bussato alla porta. *Someone knocked on
    the door.*
busta *envelope.*
buttare *to throw.*
  buttare tutto per aria *to upset; to mess.*
  Buttalo via! *Throw it away!*

C

cabina *cabin, stateroom.*
  cabina da bagno *dressing room (beach).*
  cabina telefonica *telephone booth.*
cacào *cocoa.*
caccia *hunting, hunt.*
  andare a caccia *to go hunting.*
  cane da caccia *hunting dog.*
  fucile da caccia *hunting rifle*
  licenza da caccia *game license.*
cacciare *to go hunting.*
cacciatore, m. *hunter.*
cacciavite, m. *screw-driver.*
cacio *cheese.*
CADERE *to fall.*
  cadere dalle nuvole *to be greatly surprised.*
  cadere in ginocchio *to fall to one's knees.*
  il cadere della notte *nightfall.*
  il cadere del sole *sunset.*
caduta *fall, downfall.*
caduto, *fallen.*
CAFFE m. *coffee, café.*
cagione, f. *cause, reason.*
calamaio *inkwell.*
calare *to lower; to let down.*
  calare l'ancora *to drop anchor.*
calcagno *heel.*
calcio *kick.*
  dare un calcio *to kick.*
  giuoco del calcio *football.*
caldaia *boiler.*
CALDO *heat, warmth;* (as adj.) *warm.*
  aver caldo *to be warm.*
  ondata di caldo *heat wave.*
callo *corn (on the toe).*
CALMA *calm, stillness, composure.*
calmare *to calm; to soothe.*
calore, m. *warmth, ardour.*
calunnia *slander.*
calvo *bald.*
CALZA *stocking.*
  fare la calza *to knit.*
calzatura *footwear.*

calzettina *sock.*
calzolaio *shoemaker.*
calzolerìa *shoestore.*
CALZONI *trousers.*
cambiale, f. *bill of exchange; promissory note.*
cambiamento *change.*
cambiare *to change.*
  cambiare idea *to change one's mind.*
  cambiare in meglio *to change for the better.*
  cambiarsi *to change (one's clothes).*
cambiavalute, m. *money-changer.*
CAMBIO *change.*
  in cambio di *in exchange for.*
  leva di cambio *gear lever.*
  prima di cambio *first gear.*
CAMERA *chamber, room.*
  camera da bagno *bathroom.*
  camera da letto *bedroom.*
  Camera di Commercio *Chamber of Commerce.*
cameriera *maid.*
cameriere, m. *servant, valet.*
CAMICIA (camicetta) *shirt.*
  camicia da notte *nightgown.*
  in maniche di camicia *in shirtsleeves.*
  È nato colla camicia. *He was born lucky.*
camino *chimney.*
CAMMINARE *to walk.*
  camminare in punta di piedi *to tip-toe.*
campagna *country, campaign.*
  casa di campagna *country home.*
  fare una campagna contraria a *to campaign
    against.*
campana *bell (church).*
campanello *bell.*
campanile, m. *church steeple.*
campeggiare *to camp.*
campidoglio *capitol.*
campione, m. *sample, champion.*
  campione dei pesi massimi *heavyweight
    champion.*
  Prendi questo come campione. *Take this as
    a sample.*
campo *field, ground.*
  campo di battaglia *battlefield.*
  campo di giuoco *playground.*
  ospedale da campo *field hospital.*
camposanto *cemetery.*
CANALE, m. *channel.*
  Canale di Suez *Suez Canal.*
CANCELLARE *to erase; to rub out.*
  cancellare dalla memoria *to forget.*
cancro *cancer.*
candela *candle.*
CANE, m. *dog;* **cagna,** f. *bitch.*
  lasciar stare i cani che dormono *to let sleeping
    dogs lie.*
cannone, m. *cannon.*
cantare *to sing.*
cantiere, m. *yard.*
  cantiere navale *shipyard.*
canto *song, corner.*
canzone, f. *song.*
capace *able, capable.*
capello *hair.*
  capelli biondi *blonde hair.*
  capelli scuri *dark hair.*
  farsi tagliare i capelli *to get a haircut.*
  fin sopra i capelli *up to his ears.*
capelluto *hairy.*
  cuoio capelluto *scalp.*
CAPIRE *to understand.*
  capire male *to misunderstand.*
  capirsi a vicenda *to understand each other.*

  Mi lasci capir bene. *Let me get things straight.*
capitale, f. *capitol.*
capitale, m. *capital (money).*
capitale, adj. *main.*
  pena capitale *capital punishment.*
capitano *captain.*
capitolo *chapter.*
capo *head, leader.*
capolavoro *masterpiece.*
capovolgere *to upset; to overturn.*
  capovolgersi *to capsize.*
cappella *chapel.*
CAPPELLO *hat.*
CAPPOTTO *overcoat.*
capra *goat.*
capriccio *whim, fancy, caprice.*
  fare i capricci *to get out of hand.*
capriccioso *capricious, freakish.*
caramente *dearly.*
CARATTERE, m. *character, disposition.*
  a caratteri grandi *in bold type.*
  Ha un carattere docile. *He has a mild disposi-
    tion.*
caratteristica *characteristic, feature.*
caratteristico, adj. *characteristic, typical.*
CARBONE, m. *coal, carbon.*
  carbone fossile *pit coal.*
  miniera di carbone *coal mine.*
  carta carbone *carbon paper.*
carcere, m. *prison, jail.*
carezza *caress.*
carezzare *to caress.*
CARICARE *to load.*
  caricare l'orologio *to wind one's watch.*
  caricare un fucile *to load a gun.*
CARICO *burden, cargo, load, charge.*
  polizza di carico *bill of lading.*
  È arrivato un carico di arance. *A load of
    oranges has arrived.*
  Non ne faccia carico a me. *Don't accuse me of
    it.*
carino *nice, cute, pretty.*
carità *charity.*
caritatevole *charitable.*
carnagione f. *complexion.*
CARNE, f. *meat, flesh.*
  in carne ed ossa *in flesh and blood.*
CARO *dear, expensive.*
  a caro prezzo *dearly.*
  mia cara amica *my dear friend.*
  Queste scarpe sono troppo care. *These shoes
    are too expensive.*
carriera *career.*
  andar di carriera *to walk swiftly.*
carro *truck, wagon, cart.*
  Non bisogna mettere il carro avanti ai buoi. *One
    shouldn't place the cart before the horse.*
CARTA *paper.*
  carta assorbente *blotter.*
  carte da giuoco *playing cards.*
  carta da lettere *stationery.*
  carta geografica *map.*
  carta velina *tissue paper.*
cartoleria *stationery store.*
cartolina *post card.*
CASA *house, home.*
  a casa mia *at my house.*
  andar di casa in casa *to go from door to door.*
  casa colonica *farmhouse.*
  casa di salute *nursing home.*
  donna di casa *housewife.*
  essere in casa *to be at home.*
casalingo *domestic, homely.*

cascare *to fall.*
caschi il mondo *come what may.*
CASO *case.*
in caso di disgrazia *in case of accident.*
per puro caso *by mere chance.*
se per caso *if by chance.*
CASSA *case, box.*
cassa da morto *coffin.*
cassa di risparmio *savings bank.*
cassaforte, f. *safe.*
caseggiato *block; row of houses.*
cassettone, m. *chest of drawers.*
cassetta *box, small box.*
cassetta postale *mailbox.*
castagna *chestnut.*
CASTELLO *castle.*
castello di poppa *quarterdeck.*
castello di prua *forecastle.*
fare castelli in aria *to build castles in Spain (in air).*
castigare *to chastise.*
catasta *stack.*
categoria *category.*
catena *chain, bondage.*
cattedra *desk, chair.*
cattivo *bad.*
cattolico *Catholic, noun & adj.*
cattura *capture.*
catturare *to capture; to seize.*
caucciù m. *raw rubber.*
CAUSA *cause, reason.*
causa giudiziaria *lawsuit.*
per causa mia *on account of me (because of me).*
Sono arrivati in ritardo a causa del temporale.
They arrived late because of the storm.
CAUSARE *to cause; to be the cause of.*
cauto *prudent, wary.*
cavalcare *to ride horseback.*
cavallo *horse;* **cavalla** *mare.*
a cavallo *on horseback.*
andare a cavallo *to ride horseback.*
cento cavalli vapore *100 horsepower.*
corse di cavalli *horse races.*
cavaturaccioli, m. *corkscrew.*
cavare *to excavate; to get.*
cavo *hollow, cable.*
cedere *to give up; to cede.*
cedere il posto *to give up one's seat.*
Cedo le armi! *I surrender!*
celebrare *to celebrate.*
celere *rapid, swift.*
celerità *rapidity, swiftness.*
celia *jest, joke.*
cemento *cement.*
cemento armato *reinforced cement.*
celibe, m. *bachelor.*
CENA *supper.*
CENARE *to have supper.*
cenere, f. *ash, ashes.*
centesimo, adj. *hundreth.*
centesimo *the hundreth part of.*
centesimo di dollaro *one cent.*
cento *hundred.*
per cento *per cent.*
centrale *central.*
centro *center.*
cera *wax, look, aspect.*
avere brutta cera *to look ill.*
cerca *search, quest.*
andare in cerca di *to look for.*
CERCARE *to look for; to try.*
Cercherò di farlo stasera. *I'll try to do it tonight.*

Cerco mia sorella. *I'm looking for my sister.*
cerchia *circle, sphere.*
cerchio *hoop, circle.*
formare un cerchio *to form a circle.*
cereale, m. *cereal.*
cerimonia *ceremony.*
CERTAMENTE *certainly.*
Certamente! *Of course!*
certezza *certainty.*
certificato *certificate.*
CERTO *certain, sure.*
una certa persona *a certain party.*
certuni *some; some people.*
cervello *brain.*
senza cervello *brainless.*
CESSARE *to cease.*
cestino *small basket; wastebasket.*
CHE, rel. pron. *that, which, who, whom.*
Non c'è di che. *Don't mention it.*
CHE, adj. *what, which.*
CHE, adv. *when.*
checchè *whatever.*
checchè si dica *whatever they say.*
CHI *who, whom.*
A chi tutto, a chi niente ... *Some have too much, some too little ...*
Chi è? *Who is it?*
Di chi è questo cappello? *To whom does this hat belong?*
CHIAMARE *to call.*
chiamare aiuto *to call for help.*
chiamare al telefono *to telephone.*
Chiamiamo pane il pane e vino il vino. *Let's call a spade a spade.*
Come si chiama? *What's your name?*
Lo mando a chiamare. *I'll send for him.*
Mi chiamo Maria. *My name is Mary.*
chiamata *call.*
chiarire *to clarify; to explain.*
chiarire un dubbio *to dispel a doubt.*
CHIARO, adj. *clear, light, evident.*
colore chiaro *a light color.*
Una cosa è chiara. *One thing is evident.*
chiaro *light, brightness.*
chiaro di luna *moonlight.*
mettere le cose in chiaro *to explain things; to make things clear.*
chiasso *noise, uproar.*
chiave, f. *key.*
chiudere a chiave *to lock.*
chiave inglese *monkey-wrench.*
tener sotto chiave *to keep under lock and key.*
chicchessìa *anyone; whoever it may be.*
chiedere *to ask.*
chiedere aiuto *to ask for help.*
chiedere il permesso di *to request permission to.*
chiedere in prestito *to borrow.*
chiedere scusa *to beg pardon.*
chiesa *church.*
Vado in chiesa. *I'm going to church.*
chimica *chemistry.*
chimico *chemist.*
chinare *to bend.*
chiodo *nail.*
chitarra *guitar.*
CHIUDERE *to close; to shut.*
chiudere a catenaccio *to bolt.*
chiudere la porta a chiave *to lock the door.*
chiudersi a chiave *to lock oneself in.*
chiudersi in casa *to shut oneself off (at home).*
chiunque *whoever, whomever, anyone, anybody.*
chiunque venga *whoever should come.*

di chiunque sia *whoever it is.*
Dallo a chiunque ti piaccia. *Give it to whomever you like.*
chiuso *closed, shut.*
chiusura *closing.*
chiusura lampo *zipper.*
CI adv. *here, there.*
CI pron. *us; to us; each other; one another; it; of it.*
Ci comprendiamo. *We understand each other.*
Ci dia la ricevuta. *Give the receipt to us.*
Ci vede? *Do you see us?*
Non ci penserei nemmeno. *I wouldn't even think of it.*
ciascuno *each; each one.*
cibo *food.*
cicatrice, f. *scar.*
cicatrizzarsi *to heal up.*
La ferita si sta cicatrizzando. *The wound is healing.*
cicogna *stork.*
cieco *blind.*
vicolo cieco *blind alley.*
cielo *sky.*
cifra *sum; figure (number).*
ciglio (le ciglia, f. pl.) *eyelash.*
senza batter ciglio *without blinking.*
ciliegia *cherry.*
cima *top, summit.*
arrivare in cima alla montagna *to reach the top of the mountain.*
cinema *movies.*
cinghia *strap, belt.*
cinquanta *fifty.*
cinquantesimo *fiftieth.*
cinque *five.*
cinquecento *five hundred.*
cintola *waist, belt.*
cintura *belt.*
CIÒ *this, that, it.*
Ciò non importa. *It doesn't matter.*
Tutto ciò mi preoccupa. *All this worries me.*
cioccolata (cioccolato) *chocolate.*
CIOÈ *that is; namely.*
cipolla *onion.*
cipria *face-powder.*
CIRCA *about; as to; concerning.*
circa cento lire *about a hundred lire.*
circolare *to circulate.*
circolazione, f. *circulation, traffic.*
Circolazione in Senso Unico. *One-way Traffic.*
Circolazione Vietata. *No Through Traffic.*
circolo *circle.*
circondato *surrounded.*
circostanza *circumstance.*
circuito *circuit.*
corto circuito *short circuit.*
citare *to quote; to sue.*
città *city.*
cittadino *citizen.*
CLASSE, f. *class.*
cliente, m. *customer.*
clima, m. *climate.*
clinica *hospital.*
cocchiere, m. *coachman; cab driver.*
cocomero *watermelon.*
coda *tail.*
COGLIERE *to catch; to seize; to gather.*
cogliere l'occasione *to take the opportunity.*
cognata *sister-in-law.*
cognato *brother-in-law.*
cognome, m. *surname.*
nome e cognome *first and second name.*

coincidenza coincidence; train connection.
COLAZIONE, f. meal.
  fare colazione to eat breakfast.
  prima colazione breakfast.
  seconda colazione lunch.
colei she; that woman.
colla glue.
collana necklace.
collare, m. collar.
collega, m. colleague.
collegio college.
collera anger, rage.
  andare in collera to become angry.
colletto collar.
collo neck.
  andare a rotta di collo to go headlong.
  Ha un braccio al collo. His arm is in a sling.
colloquio conversation, interview.
  avere un lungo colloquio con to have a long
    conversation with.
colmare to fill up.
colonia colony.
coloniale colonial.
colonizzazione, f. colonization.
colonna column.
colonnato colonnade.
colorare to color.
COLORE, m. color.
  perdere colore to fade.
coloro they, those.
colpa fault.
  Non dare la colpa a me. Don't blame me.
  Non è colpa tua. It's not your fault.
colpevole guilty.
colpire to strike; to hit; to hurt.
COLPO blow, stroke, shot.
  colpo di vento a gust of wind.
  sparare un colpo to fire a shot.
  un colpo alla testa a blow on the head.
  un colpo di sole a sunstroke.
  Sento dei colpi alla porta. I hear a knocking at
    the door.
coltello knife.
colto educated, learned.
colui he; that one.
comandante, m. commander.
comando command, order.
comare, f. godmother.
COME as, like, how, as soon as.
  bella come il sole as beautiful as the sun.
  un libro come il mio a book like mine.
  Come mi vide, mi venne incontro. As soon as
    he saw me, he came towards me.
  Com' è triste! How sad it is!
  Come va? How goes it? How are you?
cominciare to begin.
commedia comedy.
commerciale commercial.
COMMERCIO commerce.
  Camera di Commercio Chamber of Commerce.
commessa, f.; commesso m. clerk.
  commesso di negozio salesclerk.
COMMETTERE to commit.
commiato leave.
commissione, f. commission, errand.
commosso moved, touched.
commozione, f. emotion.
COMMUOVERE to move; to touch.
  commuoversi to be moved.
COMODITÀ comfort.
  le comodità della propria casa the comforts of
    one's own home.
comodo comfortable.

COMPAGNÌA company.
  compagnìa edilizia construction company.
  fare compagnìa a to keep someone company.
compagno, (compagna, f.) companion, mate.
  compagno di scuola schoolmate.
  compagno in affari partner in business.
compare, m. crony, godfather.
COMPERARE to buy.
compiacenza obligingness.
compiangere to pity; to lament.
COMPIERE to accomplish; to fulfill; to perform.
  compiere il proprio dovere to do one's duty.
compito task.
compleanno birthday.
COMPLETAMENTE completely.
COMPLETARE to complete; to finish.
  completare gli studi to finish school.
complicare to complicate.
  Non complichiamo le cose! Let's not complicate
    matters!
complimento compliment.
  fare un complimento a to compliment someone.
COMPORRE to compose; to compound; to consist.
compositore, m. (compositrice, f.) composer.
composizione, f. composition.
COMPOSTO compound, composed, settle.
  interesse composto compound interest.
  Stai composto! Behave!
COMPRARE to buy.
COMPRENDERE to understand; to comprise; to
  include.
  Non comprendo l'Italiano. I don't understand
    Italian.
  Un pranzo comprende molte pietanze. A meal
    consists of many dishes.
COMPRESO understood, comprehended, included.
  tutto compreso everything included.
compromettere to compromise.
  compromettersi to compromise oneself.
COMUNE common, mutual.
  di comune accordo mutually agreed.
  l'uomo comune the common man.
comune, m. town, municipality.
COMUNICARE to communicate; to inform.
  Le comunicherò la mia decisione. I will inform
    you of my decision.
COMUNICAZIONE, f. communication, message.
  comunicazione telefonica telephone call.
  mettere in comunicazione to put a telephone
    call through.
  togliere la comunicazione to hang up.
COMUNQUE however; at any rate.
CON with; to; by; by means of.
  con piacere with pleasure.
  Andiamo con l'automobile. Let's go by car.
  Con mio grande dolore... To my great sorrow...
concedere to concede; to grant; to allow.
  concedere il permesso to grant permission.
concepire to conceive; to understand.
CONCERNERE to concern; to regard.
  È un affare che non mi concerne. It's a matter
    that doesn't concern me.
concerto concert.
concetto concept.
conclusione, f. conclusion.
  in conclusione to conclude.
concluso concluded.
concorrente, m. competitor.
concorso competition.
condannare to condemn; to blame.
condire to season.
condizione, f. condition.
  in pessime condizioni in very bad shape.

condotta behavior
condurre to conduct; to ??; to take.
  condurre all'altare to carry (to take to the altar).
condursi to behave.
confarsi to fit; to suit.
conferenza lecture, conference.
conferma confirmation.
confermare to confirm.
confessare to confess; to acknowledge; to admit.
confezionare to manufacture.
confidente confident, trusting.
confidenza confidence.
  essere in confidenza to be on intimate terms
    with.
confondere to confuse.
conforto comfort.
congedare to dismiss.
congedarsi to take leave.
congedo leave; leave of absence; discharge
  (soldiers).
congelato frozen.
congratularsi to congratulate.
congratulazione, f. congratulation.
  Congratulazioni! Congratulations!
coniglio rabbit.
connotato feature.
CONOSCENZA knowledge, acquaintance.
  essere a conoscenza di una cosa to have
    knowledge of something.
  fare la conoscenza di to make the acquaintance
    of.
  perdere la conoscenza to lose consciousness.
CONOSCERE to know; to meet.
  Lieto di averla conosciuto. Pleased to have
    met you.
conosciuto well-known.
conquistare to conquer.
consapevole aware (of).
conscio conscious, aware.
consegna delivery.
consegnare to deliver; to consign.
consenso consent.
CONSENTIRE to consent; to allow.
conservativo conservative.
considerare to consider.
considerazione, f. consideration.
considerevole considerable.
consigliare to advise.
consigliabile advisable.
consiglio advice, counsel.
consistere to consist; to be composed of.
consolare to console.
consolato consulate.
consolazione, f. consolation, solace.
  trovar consolazione to find consolation.
console, m. consul.
consonante, f. consonant.
constare to consist of; to be evident.
consultare to consult.
  consultare un medico to consult a doctor.
consumare to consume; to waste.
consumo consumption.
  per mio uso e consumo for my private use.
contabile, m. accountant, bookkeeper.
contadino/ contadina, f. peasant.
CONTANTE, adj. ready, current; (as noun,
  masc.) current.
  denaro contante ready cash.
  in contanti cash.
CONTARE to count; to rely; to number; to intend.
  Conti pure su di me. You may count on me.
  Quando conta di partire? When do you intend
    leaving?

Non conta! *It doesn't matter!*
contatto *contact, touch.*
contenere *to contain; to hold.*
contenersi *to contain oneself; to restrain oneself.*
contegno *behavior, conduct.*
CONTENTEZZA *happiness, joy.*
contento *glad, pleased.*
contenuto *contents.*
continente, m. *continent.*
continuare *to continue; to go on with; to keep on.*
Continua a nevicare. *It is still snowing.*
continuatamente *continuously.*
continuo *continuous, uninterrupted.*
una pioggia continua *a constant rain.*
CONTO *account, calculation, bill.*
chiedere il conto al cameriere *to ask the waiter for the bill.*
chiudere un conto *to close an account.*
conto in banca *bank account.*
in conto *on account.*
pagare il conto *to pay the bill.*
rendere conto di *to account for.*
rendersi conto *to realize.*
tener conto di *to take into account.*
CONTRADDIRE *to contradict.*
contraddizione, f. *contradiction.*
contrariamente *contrarily; on the contrary.*
contrarietà *contrariety, difficulty, disappointment.*
CONTRARIO *contrary.*
contrarre *to contract.*
contratto *contract.*
contravvenzione, f. *infraction, fine.*
contribuire *to contribute.*
contributo *contribution.*
CONTRO *against; in spite of.*
contro voglia *unwillingly.*
dire il pro ed il contro *to state the pro and con.*
controllare *to control.*
controllarsi *to control oneself.*
controllo *control.*
controversia *controversy.*
CONVENIENTE *convenient.*
convenienza *convenience.*
CONVENIRE *to assemble; to admit.*
Bisogna convenirne! *We must admit it!*
conversare *to converse.*
conversazione, f. *conversation.*
convertire *to convert.*
CONVINCERE *to convince.*
convinto *convinced.*
convinzione, f. *conviction.*
coperta *cover, coverlet.*
coperta imbottita *quilt.*
sotto coperta *below deck.*
coperto *covered, overcast; (as noun) cover.*
al coperto *sheltered.*
cielo coperto *cloudy sky.*
mettere un' altro coperto a tavola *to set another place at the table.*
copia *copy.*
brutta copia *rough copy.*
copiare *to copy; to imitate.*
COPPIA *couple, a pair.*
coppia di sposini *a pair of newlyweds.*
coprire *to cover; to drown out.*
coraggio *courage.* .
prendere coraggio *to summon up courage.*
corda *rope, cord.*
corda vocale *vocal cords.*
strumento a corda **stringed** *instrument.*

coricarsi *to go to bed; to lie down.*
cornice f. *frame.*
corno *horn.*
corno dell'abbondanza *horn of plenty.*
coro *chorus.*
corona *crown.*
corona di margherite *a wreath of daisies.*
corona ducale *ducal coronet.*
coronare *to crown.*
essere coronato dal successo *to be successful.*
CORPO *body, corps.*
corporazione, f. *corporation.*
corredo *equipment, outfit.*
corredo da sposa *trousseau.*
correggere *to correct.*
CORRENTE, f. *current, stream.*
corrente d'aria *draft.*
seguire la corrente *to swim with the tide.*
correntemente *currently, easily.*
parlare correntemente *to speak fluently.*
CORRERE *to run.*
corretto *correct, proper.*
agire in modo corretto *to behave properly.*
correzione, f. *correction.*
corriere, m. *messenger.*
corrispondente m. *correspondent.*
corrispondente di un giornale *newspaper correspondent.*
corrispondenza *correspondence.*
corrispondere *to correspond; to reciprocate; to pay.*
la somma corrisposta *the amount paid.*
corrugare *to wrinkle; to corrugate.*
corrugare la fronte *to frown.*
corsa *race; short trip.*
fare una corsa *to rush; to dash over.*
corsìa *ward (hospital).*
CORSO *course.*
l'anno in corso *the present year.*
nel corso degli eventi *in the course of events.*
prendere un brutto corso *to take a turn for the worse.*
corte, f. *court.*
cortèo *procession.*
cortese *polite, courteous.*
CORTESIA *politeness, kindness.*
cortile, m. *courtyard, yard.*
CORTO *short, brief.*
essere a corto di denaro *to be short of money.*
Taglia corto! *Make it brief! Cut it short!*
COSA *thing.*
cosa da niente *trifle.*
prima di ogni altra cosa *first of all.*
Cos'è successo? *What happened?*
coscia *thigh.*
coscienza *conscience.*
perdere coscienza *to lose consciousness.*
riprendere coscienza *to come to one's senses.*
COSÌ *so, thus.*
così ebbe fine... *and so ended...*
Sono così contenta. *I am so happy.*
cosicchè *so that.*
costa *coast.*
sulla costa del Pacifico *on the coast of the Pacific.*
COSTARE *to cost.*
qualunque cosa costi *whatever the cost.*
Costa troppo! *It's too expensive!*
Quanto costa? *How much is it?*
costata *chop.*
costata di agnello *lamb chop.*
costituzione, f. *constitution, foundation.*
essere di costituzione forte *to be strong.*

costo *cost, price.*
a costo di *at the risk of.*
costo di spedizione *shipping cost.*
costoro *those people; they.*
costringere *to compel; to force.*
costruire *to build; to construct.*
costruzione, f. *construction.*
costui *this man.*
costume, m. *custom, habit.*
costume da bagno *bathing suit.*
di cattivi costumi *of bad habit.*
cotone, m. *cotton.*
COTTO *cooked.*
ben cotto *well done.*
poco cotto *rare.*
troppo cotto *overcooked.*
cravatta *necktie.*
creare *to create; to establish.*
credere *to believe.*
credere a *to believe in.*
Credo che sia vero. *I believe it's true.*
Non credo! *I don't think so.*
Non ti credo! *I don't believe you.*
credito *credit.*
comprare a credito *to buy on credit.*
creditore, m. **(creditrice**, f.) *creditor.*
crema *cream.*
crescere *to grow; to increase; to rear.*
un figlio cresciuto *a grown son.*
crimine, m. *crime.*
crisi, f. *crisis.*
crisi finanziaria *financial crisis.*
una crisi di nervi *a fit of hysterics.*
cristallo *crystal, glass.*
criticare *to criticize.*
critico *critic.*
critico, adj. *critical.*
un momento critico della sua vita *a difficult period in his (her) life.*
croccante *crisp.*
crocchio *circle, group.*
croce, f. *cross.*
a occhio e croce *roughly.*
farsi il segno della croce *to make the sign of the cross.*
crocevia, m. *crossroads.*
crociera *cruise.*
crollare *to collapse.*
crosta *crust.*
crudele *cruel.*
crudo *raw.*
cuccetta *berth.*
CUCCHIAÌNO *teaspoon.*
CUCCHIAIO *tablespoon.*
cucina *kitchen, cooking.*
occuparsi della cucina *to take care of the cooking.*
cucinare *to cook.*
cucire *to sew.*
macchina da cucire *sewing machine.*
CUI *whom; whose; to whom; which; of which; to which.*
culla *cradle.*
cultura *cultivation, culture, learning.*
un'uomo di cultura *a man of learning.*
CUOCERE *to cook.*
cuocere a fuoco lento *to simmer.*
cuoco, m. **(cuoca**, f.) *cook.*
CUORE, m. *heart;* **cuori**, m. pl. *hearts (playing cards).*
con tutto il cuore *with all one's heart.*
prendere a cuore *to take to heart.*
senza cuore *heartless.*

CURA *care.*

essere sotto la cura di un medico *to be under a doctor's care.*

fare una cosa con cura *to do something carefully.*

prendersi la cura di *to take the trouble to.*

CURARE *to take care of; to nurse.*

non curarsene *not to mind; not to take heed of.*

curiosità *cusiosity.*

per curiosità *out of curiosity.*

togliersi la curiosità *to satisfy one's curiosity.*

curioso *curious, odd.*

una folla di curiosi *a crowd of curious bystanders.*

un avvenimento molto curioso *a very odd occurrence.*

curva *curve, bend.*

cuscino *pillow.*

cute, f. *skin.*

D

da *from, by, at, to, since.*

dallo scorso mese *since last month.*

da lunedì in poi *from Monday on.*

da quando *since.*

da quando l'ho conosciuto *from the time I met him.*

fin dalla prima volta *from the very first time.*

venire da *to come from.*

Da dove vieni? *Where do you come from? Where are you coming from?*

Lo conosco da poco. *I have known him a short while.*

Vado da Maria. *I'm going to Mary's.*

daccapo *again; once again.*

Ho dovuto rifare tutto daccapo. *I had to do the whole thing over again.*

Incominciamo daccapo. *Let's start from the beginning.*

dacché *since.*

daino *deer, suede.*

d'altronde *on the other side; moreover.*

DANARO (danaro) *money.*

DANNO *damage, injury, harm.*

a mio danno *to my disadvantage.*

recare danno a *to cause injury to.*

risarcire i danni *to indemnify.*

dappertutto *everywhere.*

cercare dappertutto *to search everywhere.*

DARE *to give.*

dare cattivo esempio *to set a bad example.*

dare il buongiorno *to say good morning.*

dare luogo a *to give rise to.*

dare nell'occhio *to attract attention.*

darsi a *to devote oneself to.*

Mi ha dato dell'imbecille. *He called me an imbecile.*

Mi ha dato un gran da fare. *He caused me a great deal of work.*

Può darsi! *Perhaps! That might be so!*

Quanti anni mi date? *How old do you think I am?*

Questa finestra da sul guardino. *This window opens onto the garden.*

DATA *date.*

in data del 5 maggio *dated the 5th of May.*

dattilografare *to typewrite.*

dattilografo (dattilografa, f.) *typist.*

davanti *before; in front of.*

davanzo, d'avanzo *enough of; too much.*

DAVVERO *really, indeed, truly.*

DAZIO *excise duty.*

debito *due; (as a noun) debt.*

in tempo debito *in due time.*

debole *weak, feeble.*

avere un debole per *to have a weakness for.*

decedere *to die.*

decenza *decency.*

decidere *to decide.*

decimo *tenth.*

decisamente *decidedly.*

decisione, f. *decision.*

decisivo *decisive.*

una svolta decisiva *a turning point.*

declinare *to decline.*

decrescere *to reduce.*

DEDICARE *to dedicate.*

dedicarsi *to dedicate oneself.*

dedurre *to subtract; to deduct; to infer.*

definire *to define; to settle.*

definire i termini d'un contratto *to settle the terms of a contract.*

definire una parola *to give the meaning of; to define a word.*

definitivo *definitive, definite.*

DEGNARE *to deem worthy.*

Non ti degno di uno sguardo. *I don't consider you worthy of notice.*

degnarsi *to deign.*

degno *worthy of; deserving.*

degno di fiducia *trustworthy.*

degno di miglior fortuna *deserving of better luck.*

deliberare *to deliberate; to resolve upon.*

deliberare a lungo *to deliberate at length.*

deliberatamente *deliberately.*

delicato *delicate.*

delitto *crime.*

deliziare *to delight.*

deliziarsi a *to delight in.*

delizioso *delightful, delicious.*

deludere *to disappoint; to delude.*

delusione, f. *disappointment.*

denaro *money.*

DENTE, m. *tooth.*

dente del giudizio *wisdom tooth.*

dente per dente *an eye for an eye.*

mal di denti *toothache.*

dentista, m. *dentist.*

dentro *in, within.*

da dentro *from within.*

in dentro *inwards.*

denunciare *to denounce.*

deodorante, m. *deodorant.*

deperire *to decline.*

DEPORRE *to lay; to lay down.*

deposito *deposit.*

deridere *to ridicule.*

derivare *to derive.*

derisione, f. *derision, ridicule.*

descrivere *to describe.*

descrivere l'accaduto *to describe what happened.*

descrizione, f. *description.*

desiderabile *desirable.*

desiderare *to wish; to desire.*

desiderio *desire, wish.*

esprimere un desiderio *to express a desire.*

desinare *to dine.*

desolato *desolate, disconsolate.*

desolazione, f. *desolation.*

DESTARE *to wake; to awaken; to wake up.*

destare sentimenti buoni *to awaken kind feelings.*

destarsi presto al mattino *to wake early in the morning.*

destinato *destined, appointed.*

destinato ad un glorioso avvenire *destined to have a glorious future.*

l'ora destinata *the appointed hour.*

destinazione, f. *destination.*

arrivare a destinazione *to reach one's destination.*

destino *destiny.*

DESTO *awake.*

Sono desto dalle sette. *I've been awake since seven o' clock.*

DESTRA *right; right side.*

voltare a destra *to turn to the right.*

DESTRO *right, dextrous.*

ambidestro *ambidextrous.*

la mano destra *the right hand.*

determinare *to determine.*

determinazione, f. *determination.*

detestare *to hate.*

detrarre *to deduct; to subtract.*

detrimento *detriment.*

dettaglio *detail.*

negoziante al dettaglio *retailer.*

vendita al dettaglio *retail.*

DETTARE *to dictate.*

dettare leggi *to lay down the law.*

DETTO *said; above mentioned.*

Detto, fatto. *No sooner said than done.*

Non è detto che sia vero! *It is not necessarily true!*

devotissimo *very truly.*

DI *of.*

di cattivo umore *in a bad humor.*

di faccia *facing.*

di giorno *in the daytime.*

di male in peggio *from bad to worse.*

scuola di canto *singing school.*

diaccio *icy, frozen.*

un vento diaccio *an icy wind.*

dialetto *dialect.*

dialogo *dialogue.*

diamante, m. *diamond.*

diametro *diameter.*

diario *diary, journal.*

diavolo *devil.*

dicembre *December.*

DICHIARARE *to declare.*

dichiarare il falso *to make a false declaration.*

dichiararsi *to declare oneself.*

DICHIARAZIONE, f. *declaration.*

diciannove *nineteen.*

diciannovesimo *nineteenth.*

diciassette *seventeen.*

diciassettesimo *seventeenth.*

diciottesimo *eighteenth.*

diciotto *eighteen.*

dieci *ten.*

dieta *diet.*

DIETRO *behind.*

da dietro *from behind.*

di dietro *in back of.*

DIFENDERE *to defend.*

difendere una causa *to defend a case.*

difendersi *to defend oneself.*

difesa *defense.*

legittima difesa *self-defense.*

difetto *defect, flaw.*

difettoso *defective.*

differente *different.*

differenza *difference.*

DIFFICILE *difficult.*

essere di difficile contentatura *to be hard to please.*

difficoltà *difficulty.*

aver difficoltà a   *to have difficulty in.*
diffidare   *to mistrust.*
diffidenza   *distrust, mistrust.*
diffondere   *to spread.*
diga   *dam.*
digerire   *to digest.*
digestione, f.   *digestion.*
digiuno   *fast.*
essere digiuno di   *not to know; to ignore.*
stare a digiuno   *to fast.*
DIGNITÀ   *dignity.*
dignitoso   *dignified.*
dilagare   *to overflow.*
dileguarsi   *to disappear suddenly.*
diletto   *delight.*
diluvio   *flood.*
un diluvio di pioggia   *a flood of rain.*
un diluvio di posta   *a flood of mail.*
dimagrire   *to grow thin.*
dimensione, f.   *dimension, size.*
DIMENTICARE   *to forget.*
dimettere   *to dismiss; to remove.*
dimettersi da una carica   *to resign from office.*
diminuire   *to diminish.*
diminuzione, f.   *reduction.*
diminuzione di stipendio   *reduction in salary.*
dimissione, f.   *resignation.*
chiedere le dimissioni di   *to ask for someone's resignation.*
dare le dimissioni   *to resign.*
dimora   *dwelling, residence.*
DIMOSTRARE   *demonstrate; to show.*
dimostrare buon senso   *to display good sense.*
dimostrarsi   *to prove oneself.*
non dimostrare la propria età   *not to show one's age.*
dimostrazione, f.   *demonstration, display.*
dimostrazione d'affetto   *a display of affection.*
DINANZI   *before; in front of.*
dinanzi alla legge   *in the eyes of the law.*
diniego   *denial, refusal.*
DINTORNO   *around, round, about.*
i dintorni   *the surrounding area.*
nei dintorni di   *in the general vicinity of.*
dipanare   *to wind; to unravel.*
dipartimento   *department.*
dipendente, noun & adj.   *dependent.*
DIPENDERE   *to depend.*
Dipende da te.   *It depends on you.*
dipingere   *to paint; to depict.*
dipinto dal vero   *painted from life.*
Lo ha dipinto come un' eroe.   *He depicted him as a hero.*
diplomatico   *diplomat; (as adj.) diplomatic.*
diplomazìa   *diplomacy.*
DIRE   *to say; to tell.*
a dire di   *according to.*
detto e fatto   *said and done.*
dire il vero   *to speak the truth.*
dire male di qualcuno   *to speak ill of someone.*
per così dire   *so as to say.*
sentire dire   *to hear it said; to hear about.*
Come dice?   *What did you say? I beg your pardon?*
Ho detto!   *I have spoken!*
direttamente   *directly.*
direttissimo   *express train.*
diretto   *direct, straight.*
essere diretto a   *to be headed towards; to be bound for.*
treno diretto   *a fast train.*
un appello diretto   *a direct appeal.*
direttore, m.; **direttrice,** f.   *director.*
direzione, f.   *direction, management.*

in direzione giusta   *in the right direction.*
in direzione apposta   *in the opposite direction.*
La direzione dell' impresa è stata affidata a me.   *The management of the enterprise was entrusted to me.*
dirigere   *to direct; to manage.*
dirigere un'azienda   *to manage a business.*
Le sue parole erano dirette a me.   *His words were addressed (directed) to me.*
dirigersi   *to go towards.*
dirimpetto   *opposite; across from.*
dirimpetto alla banca   *opposite the bank.*
la casa dirimpetto alla mia   *the house across from mine.*
Si sono sedute una dirimpetto all'altra.   *They sat face to face.*
DIRITTO   *right.*
diritto di nascita   *birthright.*
non avere il diritto di   *not to have the right to.*
diritto, adj.   *right, straight, honest.*
a mano diritta (destra)   *on the right hand.*
dirottamente   *without restraint.*
piangere dirottamente   *to cry unrestrainedly.*
piovere dirottamente   *to rain in torrents.*
DISACCORDO   *disagreement, discord.*
essere in disaccordo con   *to disagree with.*
V'è disaccordo fra i due.   *There is discord between the two.*
disagio   *discomfort.*
sentirsi a disagio   *to feel uncomfortable.*
vivere fra i disagi   *to live a life of privations.*
disapprovare   *to disapprove.*
disastro   *disaster, calamity.*
disastroso   *disastrous.*
discendente, adj.   *descendant, descending (also m. & f. noun).*
DISCENDERE   *to descend; to descend from.*
discendere da una famiglia italiana   *to descend from an Italian family.*
Discendo subito.   *I'll come right down.*
discesa   *descent, fall.*
I prezzi sono in discesa.   *The prices are falling.*
La strada è in discesa.   *The street slopes downward.*
disciplina   *discipline.*
disciplinato   *disciplined, obedient.*
un attore disciplinato   *a disciplined actor.*
un bambino disciplinato   *an obedient boy.*
disco   *disc, recording.*
disco sul ghiaccio   *ice hockey.*
un disco di Caruso   *a recording by Caruso.*
discordia   *discord, dissension.*
discorso   *speech, talk.*
entrare in discorso con   *to engage in conversation with.*
fare un lungo discorso   *to make a long speech.*
discosto   *distant, far.*
poco discosto   *not far.*
discreto   *discreet, moderate.*
discrezione, f.   *discretion.*
discussione, f.   *discussion, debate.*
discutere   *to discuss; to debate.*
disdegno   *disdain, contempt.*
disdire   *to annul; to retract.*
disdire un appuntamento   *to cancel an appointment.*
disdirsi   *to recant; to retract one's statements.*
DISEGNARE   *to draw; to design.*
disegno   *drawing, design.*
disfare   *to undo.*
disfare il letto   *to open (turn down) a bed.*
disfare una cucitura   *to rip a seam.*
disfare una valigia   *to unpack a valise.*

disfarsi   *to get rid of.*
disgelare   *to thaw.*
disgelo   *thaw.*
disgiungere   *to disunite; to divide.*
disgiungersi   *to separate.*
DISGRAZIA   *misfortune, accident.*
disgustare   *to disgust; to shock.*
disgustarsi   *to take a dislike to.*
disgusto   *disgust, loathing.*
disgustoso   *disgusting, loathsome, disagreeable.*
disillusione, f.   *disillusion, disenchantment.*
disimpegnare   *to disengage; to free.*
disimpegnare la marcia   *to release the clutch.*
disimpegnarsi   *to free oneself; to disengage oneself.*
disinteressatamente   *disinterestedly, altruistically.*
DISINTERESSE   *disinterestedness, unselfishness.*
disinvolto   *easy, free, self-possessed.*
disobbedienza   *disobedience.*
disobbedire   *to disobey.*
disoccupato   *unemployed.*
DISONESTO   *dishonest.*
disonore, m.   *dishonor, disgrace.*
portare disonore alla propria famiglia   *to bring disgrace upon one's family.*
DISOPRA   *on, upon, over, above.*
al disopra di ogni altra cosa   *above all else.*
il piano disopra   *the upper floor; the floor above.*
Vado disopra.   *I'm going upstairs.*
disordine, m.   *disorder, confusion.*
disotto   *under, below.*
dispari   *odd, uneven.*
numeri dispari   *odd numbers.*
disparte   *apart.*
chiamare in disparte   *to call aside.*
tenersi in disparte   *to stand aside.*
disperare   *to despair.*
fare disperare   *to drive to despair.*
disperato   *desperate, hopeless.*
una misura disperata   *a desperate measure.*
un caso disperato   *a hopeless case.*
disperazione, f.   *despair.*
disperso   *dispersed, scattered.*
andare disperso   *to get lost, to get scattered.*
dispetto   *vexation, spite.*
fare una cosa per dispetto   *to do something for spite.*
fare un dispetto a   *to vex someone.*
dispettoso   *spiteful.*
dispiacere, m.   *sorrow, regret.*
con molto dispiacere   *with great sorrow.*
dare un dispiacere a   *to cause sorrow to.*
dispiacere   *to displease.*
Mi dispiace doverti dire.   *I'm sorry to have to tell you.*
Il suo modo d'agire dispiace a tutti.   *His behavior displeases everyone.*
Non mi dispiace.   *I don't dislike it.*
disponibile   *available, vacant.*
DISPORRE   *to place; to arrange; to dispose of.*
Disponili in fila.   *Place them in a row.*
Ne puoi disporre come vuoi.   *You may dispose of them as you wish.*
DISPOSIZIONE, f.   *arrangement, disposition.*
la disposizione dei fiori   *the flower arrangement.*
Sono a vostra disposizione.   *I'm at your disposal.*
DISPOSTO   *disposed, inclined, willing.*
disposto in ordine alfabetico   *arranged in alphabetical order.*

Non è disposto agli studi. *He is not inclined to study.*

Non sono disposta a farlo. *I am not willing to do it.*

disprezzare *to despise; to hold in contempt.*

disprezzo *contempt.*

disputa *dispute, quarrel.*

dissenso *difference of opinion.*

dissolvere *to dissolve; to melt.*

distaccare *to detach.*

distaccarsi *to detach oneself; to come off.*

Il francobollo si è distaccato dalla busta. *The stamp came off the envelope.*

distacco *detachment, separation.*

Il distacco fra madre e figlia fu doloroso. *The separation between mother and daughter was painful.*

distanza *distance.*

a grande distanza da *at a great distance from.*

tenere una persona a distanza *to keep a person at arm's length.*

Qual'è la distanza fra Roma e Napoli? *What is the distance between Rome and Naples?*

distesa *extent, expanse.*

distinguere *to distinguish.*

distinguersi *to distinguish oneself.*

distinzione, f. *distinction.*

fare distinzione fra una cosa e l'altra *to distinguish between one thing and the other.*

senza distinzione alcuna *without any discrimination.*

distrarre *to distract.*

distrarre dagli studi *to distract from one's studies.*

Voglio distrarmi un pò. *I want to relax a little.*

DISTRETTO *district.*

DISTRIBUIRE *to distribute.*

distribuire la posta *to deliver the mail.*

distribuzione, f. *distribution.*

distribuzioni *mail deliveries.*

disturbare *to trouble; to disturb.*

disturbo *trouble, annoyance.*

DISUGUALE *unequal.*

DITO (le dita, f. pl.) *finger.*

dito del piede *toe.*

DITTA *concern, firm.*

divano *divan, couch, sofa.*

DIVENIRE (diventare) *to become; to grow.*

diventare pallido *to become pale.*

diventare pazzo *to go insane.*

diventare vecchio *to grow old.*

Siamo diventati amici. *We became friends.*

DIVERSO *different, some, several.*

da diverso tempo *for some time now.*

diverse volte *several times.*

Egli è molto diverso da me. *He is very unlike me.*

divertente *amusing, entertaining.*

divertimento *amusement, recreation.*

divertire *to amuse; to entertain.*

divertirsi *to amuse oneself; to enjoy oneself.*

dividere *to divide; to part; to separate.*

dividere a metà *to divide in half.*

Si è diviso da sua moglie. *He separated from his wife.*

divieto *prohibition.*

Divieto d'Affisione *No Posting.*

Divieto di Sosta *No Parking.*

divino *divine, splendid.*

divisa *uniform, dress.*

divisione, f. *division.*

divorare *to eat up; to devour.*

divorziare *to divorce.*

divorzio *divorce.*

dizionario *dictionary.*

doccia *shower.*

farsi una doccia *to take a shower.*

docile *docile, submissive.*

documento *document.*

dodicesimo *twelth.*

dodici *twelve.*

dogana *customs.*

doganiere, m. *custom-house officer.*

DOLCE *sweet.*

acqua dolce *fresh water.*

dolci *sweets.*

dolcezza *sweetness.*

DOLENTE *sorry, grieved.*

Sono dolente di dovervi informare ... *I am sorry to have to inform you ...*

DOLERE *to ache; to be grieved; to regret.*

Gli duole averti fatto male. *He regrets having hurt you.*

Mi duole la schiena. *My back hurts.*

Mi duole vederti infelice. *It grieves me to know that you are unhappy.*

DOLORE, m. *pain, ache, sorrow.*

con molto dolore *with great sorrow.*

dolor di testa *headache.*

Ho un dolore alla spalla. *I have a pain in the shoulder.*

dolorosamente *painfully, sorrowfully.*

domanda *question.*

fare domanda *to apply.*

DOMANDARE *to ask; to request.*

domandare scusa *to beg one's pardon.*

domandare un piacere *to ask a favor.*

Mi domando perchè. *I wonder why.*

domani *tomorrow.*

DOMATTINA *tomorrow morning.*

domenica *Sunday.*

domestica *servant (female);* **domestico** *(male).*

domestico *domestic, tame.*

un animale domestico *a tame animal.*

un prodotto domestico *a domestic product.*

domicilio *domicile, residence.*

dominare *to dominate.*

dominarsi *to control oneself.*

DONARE *to give; to present; to become; to donate.*

Ha donato il suo patrimonio a istituti di beneficenza. *He donated his patrimony to charitable institutions.*

Quest'abito non mi dona. *This outfit is not becoming to me.*

donato *given, presented.*

caval donato *gift horse.*

dondolare *to rock; to sway.*

DONNA *woman.*

donna di casa *housewife.*

donna di quadri *queen of diamonds.*

donna di servizio *woman-servant.*

prima donna *prima donna (first woman).*

DONO *gift.*

fare dono di *to make a present of.*

DOPO *after.*

dopodomani *the day after tomorrow.*

dopo pranzo *afternoon.*

il giorno dopo *the following day.*

poco dopo *a little later.*

doppiamente *doubly.*

DOPPIO *double.*

a doppio giro di chiave *double lock.*

a doppio petto *double-breasted.*

pagare il doppio *to pay twice as much.*

un arma a doppio taglio *a double-edged blade.*

DORMIRE *to sleep.*

dormire come un ghiro *to sleep like a log (a top).*

DORSO *back.*

dose, f. *dose.*

una buona dose di giudizio *a great deal of common sense.*

una piccola dose *a small dose.*

dote, f. *dowry.*

dotto *learned.*

DOTTORE *doctor.*

dottoressa *lady doctor.*

dottrina *doctrine.*

DOVE *where.*

Dov'è? *Where is it? Where is he? Where is she?*

Dove siamo? *Where are we?*

DOVERE *to be obliged to; to have to; to owe.*

Deve essere tardi. *It must be late.*

Devo andar via. *I must go.*

Dobbiamo partire al più presto. *We must leave at the earliest possible.*

Dovrebbe arrivare da un momento all'altro. *It should arrive any moment.*

DOVERE, m. *duty.*

credersi in dovere di *to feel obliged to.*

fare il proprio dovere *to do one's duty.*

È mio piacevole dovere... *It is my pleasant duty ...*

DOVUNQUE *wherever, anywhere.*

dovunque volgo lo sguardo *wherever I look.*

seguire dovunque *to follow anywhere.*

DOZZINA *dozen.*

a dozzine *by the dozen.*

mezza dozzina *half-dozen.*

dramma, m. *drama.*

drizzare *to straighten.*

drizzarsi *to straighten oneself.*

Drizzati! *Stand straight!*

droga *drug.*

dubbio *doubt.*

senza dubbio *doubtless.*

duce, m. *chief.*

DUE *two.*

a due a due *two by two.*

due per volta *two at a time.*

due volte tanto *twice as much.*

tagliare in due *to cut in two.*

duecento *two hundred.*

dunque *then, consequently.*

DURANTE *during.*

DURARE *to last; to continue.*

La tempesta dura da parecchio. *The storm has lasted for quite a while.*

Non può durare molto. *It can't last long.*

Tutto dura finchè può. *Everything comes to an end.*

durata *duration.*

di breve durata *of short duration.*

durezza *hardness, harshness.*

DURO *hard.*

dal cuore duro *hard-hearted.*

E

E, ED *and.*

ebbene *well!*

ebreo *Jew.*

eccellente *excellent.*

eccellenza *excellence.*

eccèllere *to excel.*

eccessivamente *excessively.*

eccessivo *excessive.*

ECCETTO *except.*

eccettuare *to except.*

eccezionale *exceptional, unusual.*
un caldo eccezionale *unusual heat.*
eccezionalmente *exceptionally.*
eccezione, f. *exception.*
eccezione fatta per *except for.*
fare eccezione per *to make an exception for.*
in via di eccezione *as an exception.*
eccitare *to excite.*
eccitazione, f. *excitement.*
ECCO *here, there, that's.*
ecco fatto *all done.*
Ecco! *llere!*
Eccomi! *llere I am!*
eco, f. *echo.*
economia *economy.*
fare economia *to economize.*
economico *economic, thrifty.*
economizzare *to economize.*
edera *ivy.*
edicola *newsstand.*
edificio *building.*
edilizia *building industry.*
edito *published.*
editore, m. *editor.*
casa editrice *publishing house.*
edizione, f. *edition.*
educare *to educate.*
educazione, f. *education.*
effettivo *effective, actual.*
effetto *effect, consequence, impression.*
effetti personali *personal effects.*
fare effetto su *to have an effect on.*
senza effetto *of no effect.*
effettuare *to effect; to put into effect.*
efficace *effective.*
efficienza *efficiency.*
EGLI *he.*
egoismo *selfishness.*
egoista, m. *selfish; (as noun) selfish person.*
egregio *exceptional, remarkable.*
eguale *equal.*
dare eguale importanza *to give the same importance.*
egualità *equality.*
elastico *elastic, noun & adj.*
elefante, m. *elephant.*
eleganza *elegance.*
elegante *elegant.*
eleggere *to elect; to appoint.*
elementare *elementary.*
elemento *element.*
elemosina *alms.*
elencare *to make a list of.*
elenco *list.*
elenco telefonico *phone book.*
elettore, m. *elector.*
elettricità *electricity.*
elettrico *electric.*
luce elettrica *electric light.*
treni elettrici *electric train.*
elevare *to elevate; to raise.*
elezione, f. *election.*
elica *propeller.*
eliminare *to eliminate.*
elogiare *to praise.*
elogio *praise.*
fare l'elogio di una persona *to sing someone's praises.*
senza tanti elogi *without much ceremony.*
eludere *to elude; to evade.*
eludere la sorveglianza *to escape surveillance.*
emergente *emergent.*
EMERGENZA *emergency.*

emergere *to emerge.*
emesso *given out; put forth.*
emettere *to emit; to send forth.*
emicrania *headache.*
emigrante, m. & f. *emigrant.*
emigrare *to emigrate.*
eminente *eminent.*
emozionante *moving.*
emozione, f. *emotion.*
emporio *market.*
energia *energy.*
energia atomica *atomic energy.*
energico *energetic, vigorous.*
enfasi, f. *emphasis.*
enigma, m. *enigma, riddle.*
enorme *enormous.*
enormemente *enormously.*
entrambi *both.*
ENTRARE *to enter; to come in.*
entrare dalla porta *to come in through the door.*
entrare in carica *to take office.*
entrare in vigore *to go into effect.*
Che cosa c'entra? *What has that to do with it?*
Entrate pure. *Come right in.*
entrata *entrance.*
ENTRO *within, in.*
entro ventiquattr'ore *within twenty-four hours.*
entusiasmo *enthusiasm.*
entusiastico *enthusiastic.*
enumerare *to enumerate.*
epidermide, f. *skin.*
episodio *episode.*
un episodio triste della sua vita *a sad episode in her life.*
un romanzo a episodi *a serial.*
època *era, period.*
EPPURE *yet; and yet; nevertheless.*
Eppure si muove! *And yet it turns! (Galileo.)*
equilibrio *balance.*
perdere l'equilibrio *to lose one's balance.*
equipaggiamento *equipment.*
equipaggiare *to equip.*
equipaggio *crew.*
equo *equitable, fair.*
ERBA *grass, herb.*
erbaccia *weed.*
in erba *in embryo.*
erbivendolo *greengrocer.*
erede, m. & f. *heir.*
eredità *inheritance.*
lasciare in eredità *to bequeath.*
ereditare *to inherit.*
erigere *to erect; to build.*
erigere un monumento *to erect a monument.*
erigersi *to set oneself up as.*
eròe *hero; erolna *heroine.**
eroico *heroic.*
errato *wrong, incorrect.*
È errato dire... *It is incorrect to say...*
errore, m. *error, mistake.*
errore di stampa *misprint.*
essere in errore *to be mistaken.*
per errore *by mistake.*
esagerare *to exaggerate.*
esagerazione, f. *exaggeration.*
esame, m. *examination, inspection.*
esame di ammissione *entrance exam.*
superare un esame *to pass an exam.*
ESAMINARE *to examine; to inspect.*
esatto *exact.*
esaudire *to grant; to fulfill.*
esaudire una richiesta *to grant a request.*
esaurimento *exhaustion.*

esaurimento nervoso *nervous breakdown.*
esaurire *to exhaust.*
esaurirsi *to exhaust oneself; to be sold out (theater).*
esausto *exhausted.*
esca *bait.*
esclamare *to exclaim.*
esclamazione, f. *exclamation.*
escludere *to exclude.*
esclusione, f. *exclusion.*
esclusivo *exclusive.*
rappresentante esclusivo *sole representative.*
escluso *left out.*
esecuzione, f. *execution, performance.*
mettere un piano in esecuzione *to put a plan into action.*
un esecuzione al pianoforte *the performance of a piece of music on the piano.*
eseguire *to execute; to accomplish.*
ESEMPIO *example, instance.*
dare un cattivo esempio *to set a bad example.*
per esempio *for instance.*
esentare *to exempt; to exonerate.*
esequie, f. pl. *funeral.*
esercitare *to exercise; to practice; to exert.*
esercitare influenza *to exert influence.*
esercitare una professione *to practice in a given profession.*
esercitarsi *to train oneself; to exercise.*
esercito *army.*
esercizio *exercise.*
essere fuori esercizio *to be out of practice.*
fare degli esercizi *to do some exercises.*
esibire *to exhibit; to show.*
esibirsi in pubblico *to show oneself in public.*
esibizione, f. *exhibition, show.*
esibizione di quadri *a painting exhibition.*
esiliare *to exile.*
esilio *exile.*
esimere *to exempt.*
esimersi da un impegno *to free oneself of an engagement.*
esistente *existent, existing.*
tutte le creature esistenti sulla terra *all creatures living on earth.*
esistenza *existence.*
un'esistenza monotona *a monotonous existence.*
esitare *to hesitate.*
esitazione, f. *hesitation.*
senza esitazione *unhesitatingly.*
èsito *result.*
L'èsito fu buono. *The result was good.*
Quale fu l'èsito? *What was the result?*
espandere *to expand.*
espansione, f. *expansion.*
espansivo *expansive.*
espatriare *to banish.*
espellere *to expel.*
esperienza *experience.*
esperimento *experiment.*
fare un experimento *to make an experiment.*
esperto *expert, skilled.*
esplodere *to explode.*
esplorare *to explore.*
esplorare ogni possibilità *to explore all possibilities.*
esplosione, f. *explosion.*
ESPORRE *to expose; to exhibit.*
esporre al ridicolo *to expose to ridicule.*
ESPORTARE *to export.*
esportazione, f. *exportation.*
esposizione, f. *exhibition.*
espressione, f. *expression.*

espressivo *expressive.*
ESPRESSO *express.*
  treno espresso *express train.*
  un caffè espresso *a cup of coffee (Italian style).*
esprimere *to express.*
  esprimere i propri sentimenti *to express one's*
  sentiments.
  esprimersi *to express oneself.*
espulsione, f. *expulsion.*
ESSA *she, it.*
ESSE, f. *they.*
essenziale *essential.*
ESSERE *to be.*
  essere disposto a *to be willing to.*
  essere in cattiva salute *to be in poor health.*
  essere in grado di *to be able to.*
  essere per; essere sul punto di *to be on the*
  point of; about to.
  essere pronto a *to be ready to.*
  se non fosse per te *if it were not for you.*
  Che cos' è? *What is it?*
  Di chi è questo libro? *Whose book is this?*
  Non c' è di che. *You are welcome.*
  Può essere. *That may be.*
  Quant' è? *How much is it?*
  Sia lodato Iddio! *May the Lord be praised!*
ESSERE, m. *being, creature.*
  un' essere spregevole *a base creature.*
  un' essere umano *a human being.*
ESSI, m. *they.*
essiccare *to dry; to dry up.*
ESSO *he, it.*
EST *east.*
  ad est *to the east.*
èstasi, f. *ecstasy.*
ESTATE, f. *summer.*
  una notte d'estate *a summer's night.*
estendere *to extend.*
estensione, f. *extension, surface.*
esteriore *exterior, outward.*
esterno *external, outside.*
ESTERO *foreign.*
  all' estero *abroad.*
  Ministero degli Esteri *State Department.*
  Ministro degli Esteri *Secretary of State.*
esteso *extensive.*
estinguere *to extinguish.*
estinto *extinguished, extinct.*
  una specie estinta *an extinct species.*
estivo *summery.*
  abiti estivi *summer clothes.*
  giornata estiva *summer day.*
  vacanza estiva *summer vacation.*
ESTRANEO *stranger.*
estrarre *to extract; to draw out.*
estratto *extract, certificate.*
  estratto di nascita *birth certificate.*
estrazione, f. *extraction, drawing.*
estremamente *extremely.*
estremo *extreme, adj. & noun.*
  L'Estremo Oriente *The Far East.*
esuberante *exuberant, over-flowery.*
ETÀ *age.*
  avere la stessa età *to be the same age.*
  dimostrare la propria età *to show one's age.*
  essere di età maggiore *to be of age.*
  mezza età *middle age.*
ètere, m. *ether.*
eternità *eternity.*
  Ho atteso un' eternità. *I waited for ages.*
eterno *eternal, everlasting.*
etichetta *label.*
evadere *to evade; to escape.*

Evangelo *Gospel.*
evasione, f. *evasion, escape.*
  evasione dal carcere *escape from prison.*
EVENTO *event.*
  lieto evento *blessed event.*
evidente *evident, apparent.*
evidenza *evidence.*
evitare *to avoid.*
evo *age.*
  Medio Evo *Middle Ages.*
evocare *to evoke.*
  evocare tristi memorie *to evoke sad memories.*
evolvere *to evolve.*
  una persona molto evoluta *a very modern person.*
EVVIVA *Hurray!*
ex- *ex-.*
  ex-combattente *ex-service man.*
  ex-moglie *ex-wife.*

F

fa *ago.*
  molto tempo fa *a long while ago.*
  poco tempo fa *a short while ago.*
fabbrica *factory.*
  marca di fabbrica *trademark.*
fabbricare *to build; to manufacture.*
fabbricato *building.*
  tassa sui fabbricati *real estate tax.*
fabbricazione, f. *manufacture.*
faccenda *business matter.*
FACCHINO *porter.*
FACCIA *face.*
  avere una faccia tosta *to be impudent; to be*
  bold.
  aver la faccia lunga *to have a long face.*
  di faccia *facing.*
  faccia a faccia *face to face.*
facciata *facade, front, page.*
  la facciata del palazzo *the front of the building.*
  la facciata di un libro *the flyleaf of a book.*
FACILE *easy.*
  di facile contentatura *easily pleased.*
  di facili costumi *of easy virtue.*
  facile alla collera *easily angered.*
  fare le cose troppo facili *to make things too*
  easy.
FACILITÀ *facility, ease, easiness.*
  facilità di parola *fluency of speech.*
facilitare *to facilitate.*
facilmente *easily.*
facoltà *faculty, authority.*
  aver facoltà di scelta *to be able to choose.*
  nelle sue piene facoltà mentali *completely*
  sane.
fagiolino *string bean.*
fagiolo *bean.*
fagotto *bundle.*
  far fagotto e andare *to pack up and go.*
falciare *to mow; cut down.*
falco *hawk.*
falegname, m. *carpenter.*
fallimento *failure, bankruptcy.*
  dichiarare fallimento *to declare bankruptcy.*
fallire *to fail; to go bankrupt.*
fallo *fault, defect.*
falsare *to alter; to falsify; to distort.*
falso, noun *falsehood.*
  testimoniare il falso *to bear false witness.*
falso, adj. *false.*
  moneta falsa *counterfeit.*
  un falso amico *a false friend*
fama *fame, reputation.*
  goder fama di *to have the reputation of.*

FAME, f. *hunger.*
  aver fame *to be hungry.*
  morir di fame *to die of hunger.*
FAMIGLIA *family.*
  rimanere in famiglia *to remain in the family.*
familiare *familiar.*
famoso *famous.*
fanale, m. *headlight.*
  fanale di coda *tail-light.*
fanatico, adj. & noun *fanatic, fanatical.*
fanciulla *girl, maid.*
fanciulezza *childhood.*
fanciullo *boy.*
fango *mud.*
fannullone, m. *idler; lazy person.*
fantasìa *fantasy, imagination.*
fantastico *fantastic.*
fantino *jockey.*
FARE *to do; to make.*
  far bene *to do well (good).*
  far cadere *to let drop; to drop.*
  far conoscenza *to make the acquaintance.*
  fare attenzione *to pay attention.*
  fare finta *to make believe.*
  fare il sordo *to pretend to be deaf.*
  fare l'avvocato *to be a lawyer.*
  fare lo stupido *to be stupid.*
  fare presto *to hurry.*
  fare una doccia *to take a shower.*
  fare una passeggiata *to take a walk.*
  far impazzire *to drive someone crazy.*
  far l'amore con *to make love to.*
  far paura a *to frighten.*
  far piangere *to make somebody cry.*
  farsi fare (una cosa) *to have (something) made.*
  far vedere una cosa *to show something.*
  Che cosa fai? *What are you doing?*
  Fa caldo! *It's warm!*
  Fa male! *It hurts!*
  Mio fratello si fa tagliare i capelli. *My brother*
  has his hair cut.
  Non fa niente. *It doesn't matter.*
  Non sappiamo cosa farci. *We cannot help it.*
  Si sta facendo scuro. *It's getting dark.*
farfalla *butterfly.*
farina *flour.*
farmaceutico *pharmaceutical.*
farmacìa *drugstore.*
farmacista *druggist.*
faro *beacon, lighthouse.*
farsa *farce.*
fascia *girdle.*
fasciare *to bandage; to swathe.*
fascicolo *issue (of a magazine); file.*
fascino *charm.*
fascio *bundle.*
fastidio *trouble, annoyance.*
  Mi da fastidio. *It bothers me.*
fastidioso *troublesome, annoying.*
fata *fairy.*
fatale *fatal.*
fatica *labor, weariness.*
faticare *to labor.*
faticosamente *laboriously; with difficulty.*
fato *fate.*
fattezze, f. pl. *features.*
FATTO *fact, deed, event.*
  È successo un fatto straordinario. *An extraord-*
  inary event took place.
  Non sono fatti vostri. *It's none of your affair.*
FATTO, adj. *done, made.*
  ben fatto *well made; well done.*
  detto fatto *no sooner said than done.*

fatto su misura *made to order.*
notte fatta *nighttime.*
Tutto fatto! *All done!*
fattorìa *farm.*
fattorino *messenger.*
fattorino telegrafico *telegraph messenger.*
fattura *invoice, bill.*
favella *speech.*
perdere la favella *to lose one's speech.*
sciogliere la favella *to loosen one's tongue.*
favola *tale, fable.*
favore, m. *favor.*
a favore di *in favor of.*
fare un favore *to do a favor.*
Per favore. *Please.*
favorire *to favor; to give.*
Favorisca! *Enter!*
Mi favorisca il burro per piacere. *Please hand me the butter.*
favorito *favorite.*
FAZZOLETTO *handkerchief.*
fazzoletto da collo *scarf.*
febbraio *February.*
febbre, f. *fever.*
aver la febbre *to have a fever.*
febbre alta *high fever.*
febbre del fieno *hay fever.*
fecondo *fertile, fruitful.*
FEDE, f. *faith, belief.*
aver fede in *to have faith in.*
fede di nascita *birth certificate.*
giurare fede a *to swear allegiance to.*
in buona fede *in good faith.*
portare la fede al dito *to wear a wedding ring.*
fedele *faithful, true.*
fedeltà *faithfulness.*
federa *pillowcase.*
federale *Federal.*
fegato *liver.*
aver fegato *to have courage.*
felice *happy.*
felicemente *happily.*
felicità *happiness.*
FEMMINA *female.*
femminile *feminine, womanly.*
genere femminile *feminine gender.*
fendere *to cleave; to split.*
fenomeno *phenomenon.*
feriale *of work.*
giorno feriale *weekday, workday.*
FERIRE *to wound.*
ferirsi *to be wounded.*
ferita *wound.*
una ferita aperta *an open wound.*
fermaglio *clasp.*
FERMARE *to stop; to fasten.*
fermare un bottone *to fasten a button.*
fermarsi in aria *to stop in mid-air.*
fermata *stop.*
FERMO *firm, still.*
con mano ferma *with a firm hand.*
ferma in posta *general delivery.*
punto fermo *period.*
stare fermo *to stand still.*
feroce *ferocious, savage.*
ferro *iron, tool.*
ferro da stiro *iron (for pressing).*
i ferri del mestiere *the tools of the trade.*
FERROVÌA *railway, railroad.*
ferrovìa sotterranea *subway.*
fertile *fertile.*
fertilizzante *fertilizer.*
fervido *fervent, ardent.*

fervore, m. *ardor, fervor.*
festa *feast.*
festa da ballo *dance.*
far festa *to make merry.*
festeggiare *to celebrate.*
festival, m. *festival.*
fetta *slice.*
tagliare a fette *to slice.*
fiaba *fable.*
fiacco *weary, dull.*
fiaccola *torch.*
fiamma *flame.*
FIAMMIFERO *match.*
fianco *side.*
fiasco *flask, failure.*
fare fiasco *to fail.*
un fiasco di vino *a flask of wine.*
fiatare *to breathe.*
FIATO *breath.*
bere tutto d'un fiato *to gulp down.*
Lasciami prendere fiato. *Let me catch my breath.*
fibbia *buckle.*
ficcare · *to drive in; to set in.*
fico *fig.*
fidanzamento *engagement, betrothal.*
fidanzare *to betroth.*
fidanzarsi *to become engaged.*
fidanzata *fiancée.*
fidanzato *fiancé.*
fidare *to trust.*
Mi fido di te. *I trust you. I have faith in you.*
fidato *trustworthy, faithful.*
fiducia *confidence, trust.*
un posto di fiducia *a position of trust.*
fiducioso *confident, hopeful.*
fieno *hay.*
fiera *fair; wild beast.*
fiero *bold, proud.*
figlia *daughter.*
FIGLIO *son.*
essere figlio a *to be the son of.*
figliuolo *son.*
figura *figure; appearance.*
fare bella figura *to cut a fine figure.*
Non fa figura. *It doesn't look well.*
fila *line, row.*
fare la fila *to make the line.*
in fila *in line.*
film, m. *film.*
filo *thread, blade.*
dare del filo da torcere *to cause great trouble.*
fil di ferro *wire.*
filo del discorso *thread of discourse.*
per filo e per segno *in every detail.*
un filo d'erba *a blade of grass.*
filobus, m. *trolley-bus.*
filosofìa *philosophy.*
filosofo *philosopher.*
finale *final.*
finanza *finance.*
finanziario *financial.*
FINCHÈ *till; until; as long as.*
Bisogna aspettare finchè arrivi. *We must wait until he arrives.*
finchè vivo *as long as I live.*
FINE, f. *end.*
lieto fine *happy ending.*
porre fine a *to put an end to.*
sino alla fine *to the very end.*
fine, m. *purpose.*
A che fine? *To what purpose?*
fine, adj. *fine, thin.*

FINESTRA *window.*
fingere *to pretend.*
FINIRE *to finish; to end.*
FINO A *until; as far as.*
andare fino a *to go as far as.*
fino a ieri *up until yesterday.*
fino a stasera *until tonight.*
finora *till now; to the present moment.*
Finora non è arrivato nessuno. *Nobody has arrived yet (until now).*
finto *false, pretended.*
FIORE, m. *flower.*
fiore artificiale *artificial flower.*
nel fiore degli anni *in the prime of life.*
Gli alberi sono in fiore. *The trees are blossoming.*
fiori, f. *clubs (playing cards).*
fiorire *to blossom; to bloom; to flourish.*
firma *signature.*
FIRMARE *to sign.*
fischiare *to hiss; to whistle.*
Mi fischiano gli orecchi. *My ears are buzzing.*
fischio *whistle, hissing.*
fisico *physical.*
fissare *to fix; to fasten; to reserve.*
fissare con una spilla *to pin; to fasten with a pin.*
fissare la data *to set the date.*
fissare qualcuno collo sguardo *to stare at someone.*
fissare un posto *to reserve a place.*
Si è fissato che non gli voglio bene. *He is convinced that I don't care for him.*
fisso *fixed, permanent, steady.*
a prezzi fissi *at fixed prices.*
impiego fisso *permanent employment.*
FIUME, m. *river.*
fiuto *scent, smell.*
fluido *fluid, adj. & noun.*
flotta *fleet.*
focolare, m. *hearth, fireside.*
fodera *lining.*
foderare *to line.*
foderato *lined.*
foderato di pelle *lined in leather.*
foggia *fashion, manner, way.*
FOGLIA *leaf.*
foglio *sheet (of paper).*
fogna *sewer.*
folla *crowd.*
folle *mad, insane.*
follìa *insanity.*
folto *thick.*
capelli folti *thick hair.*
fondamentale *fundamental.*
fondamento (fondamenta, pl. f.) *foundation.*
senza fondamento *unfounded, groundless.*
fondare *to found.*
fondatore, m. *founder.*
FONDO *bottom, fund.*
articolo di fondo *leading article (newspaper).*
da cima a fondo *from top to bottom.*
fondo cassa *cash fund.*
in fondo a *at the bottom of.*
in fondo alla strada *at the end of the street.*
senza fondi *without funds.*
fonografo *phonograph.*
fontana *fountain.*
fonte, f. *fountain, source.*
una fonte d'acqua fresca *a spring of fresh water.*
una fonte di guadagno *a source of income.*
forbici, f. pl. *scissors.*
forcella *hairpin.*

FORCHETTA fork.
foresta forest.
forfora dandruff.
forma form, shape.
  a forma di shaped like.
formica ant.
formaggio cheese.
formale formal.
FORMARE to form; to mold.
formazione, f. formation.
formula formula.
fornace, f. furnace.
fornire to supply; to furnish.
  fornirsi di tutto to supply oneself with everything.
forno oven.
  mettere al forno to put in the oven.
FORSE perhaps, maybe.
FORTE strong.
  correre forte to run fast.
  essere forte to be strong.
  parlare forte to speak loudly.
fortezza fortress.
fortuna fortune, luck.
  aver fortuna to be lucky.
  far fortuna to make a fortune.
  per fortuna fortunately.
  senza fortuna without luck.
fortunato fortunate, lucky.
FORZA strength, force.
  a forza di by dint of.
  farsi forza to muster one's courage.
  mettersi in forza to build up one's strength.
  per amore o per forza willing or unwilling.
  per forza by force.
forzare to force; to break open.
  Ha forzato la porta. He broke down the door.
  Non mi forzare a farlo. Don't force me to do it.
  Qualcuno ha forzato la serratura. Someone picked the lock.
fossa hole, pit, grave.
fosso ditch.
  fare un fosso to dig a ditch.
fotografare to photograph.
fotografia photograph, photography.
  fare una fotografia to take a photograph.
  M'interesso di fotografia. I'm interested in photography.
FRA among, between.
  fra le nuvole in the clouds.
  fra moglie e marito between husband and wife.
  fra non molto in a short while.
  fra una cosa e l'altra between one thing and the other.
  trovarsi fra amici to be among friends.
fracasso uproar; noisy quarrel.
fragile fragile, frail.
fragola strawberry.
fragrante fragrant.
frammento fragment.
francese French, noun & adj.
franco frank, open.
  franco a bordo free on board.
  Mi ha parlato franco. He spoke frankly to me.
francobollo stamp, postage.
frangia fringe.
frantumare to shatter.
  Questo bicchiere si è frantumato. This glass is shattered.
frase, f. sentence, phrase.
  frase musicale a musical phrase.
FRATELLO brother.
frattanto meanwhile.

freddamente coldly.
freddezza coolness, indifference.
FREDDO cold.
  aver freddo to be cold.
  essere freddo con qualcuno to be cold towards someone.
  prendere freddo to catch cold.
  Fa freddo. It's cold.
fregare to rub.
frenare to brake; to restrain; to repress.
  frenare un impulso to repress an impulse.
  Ho fatto appena a tempo a frenare. I applied the brakes just in time.
  Mi sono frenato a stento. I was barely able to restrain myself.
freno brake.
  applicare il freno to apply the brakes.
  mettere freno a to restrain.
  senza freno unrestrained.
frequentare to attend; to frequent.
  frequentare la scuola to attend school.
frequente frequent.
freschezza freshness, coolness.
fresco, noun coolness.
  mettere al fresco to put in a cool spot.
  stare al fresco to stay in a cool place.
FRESCO, adj. fresh, cool.
  acqua fresca fresh water.
  pesce fresco fresh fish.
FRETTA haste.
  andar di fretta to be in a hurry.
  in fretta hastily.
friggere to fry.
frigorifero refrigerator.
frittata omelette.
fritto fried.
frittura fry.
  frittura di pesce fish-fry.
frivolo frivolous.
frode, f. fraud.
FRONTE, f. forehead.
  a fronte alta with head held high.
fronte, m. front.
  di fronte a facing, opposite.
  fare fronte alle spese to pay one's expenses.
  fronte di battaglia battlefront.
frugare to search; to poke.
frusta whip.
frustare to whip.
frutta fruit.
frutteto orchard.
fucile, m. gun.
fuga flight, escape.
  darsi alla fuga to take flight.
fuggire to run away; to escape.
fuliggine, f. soot.
fulmine, m. thunderbolt.
  un colpo di fulmine love at first sight (a thunderbolt).
  un fulmine a ciel sereno a bolt out of the blue.
fumare to smoke.
  Vietato fumare! No smoking!
fumo smoke.
fune, f. rope.
funerale, m. funeral.
fungo mushroom.
  ai funghi with mushrooms.
funzionare to work; to function.
funzione, f. function.
fuoco fire.
  accendere il fuoco to light the fire.
  fuochi artificiali fireworks.
FUORCHÈ except.

tutti fuorchè lui all except him.
FUORI out, outside.
  andar fuori to go out.
  essere fuori di sè to be beside oneself.
  essere fuori pratica to be out of practice.
  fuoribordo outboard.
  fuori mano out of the way.
  fuori pericolo out of danger.
  fuori uso out of use.
furbo sly, crafty.
furia fury, rage.
  È andato su tutte le furie. He fell into a rage.
  Ho furia. I'm in a hurry.
furibondo raging, furious.
furto theft.
  furto a mano armata armed robbery.
futuro future, noun & adj.
  in futuro in the future.

G

gabbia cage.
gabinetto cabinet; small closet; toilet.
gagliardo vigorous.
gaiezza gaiety.
gaio gay.
gala gala.
galla afloat.
galleria gallery.
gallina hen.
gallo cock.
gamba leg.
gambero crab.
gambo stalk, stem.
gancio hook.
garanzia guarantee, security.
gara competition.
garbare to please; to be to one's liking.
garofano carnation.
gas, m. gas.
gassosa carbonated drink.
gatto cat.
gelare to freeze.
gelo frost.
gelosia jealousy.
gemello twin, cuff-link.
gemito groan.
gemma gem.
generale, m. general; (also adj.).
generalmente generally; in general.
generazione, f. generation.
GENERE, m. gender, kind.
  di genere maschile of masculine gender.
  di ogni genere of all kinds.
  generi alimentari foodstuffs.
genero son-in-law.
generoso generous.
genio genius, taste.
  Non va a mi genio. It's not to my liking.
genitori, m. pl. parents.
gennaio January.
gente, f. people.
genti, f. pl. peoples.
gentile kind.
gentilezza kindness.
genuino genuine.
geografia geography.
geografico geographical.
  carta geografica map.
gerente, m. manager.
germe, m. germ, shoot.
germogliare to bud; to flower; to sprout.
gesso chalk.
gesta, f. pl. deeds.

gestione, f. *management.*

gestire *to manage.*

gesto *gesture.*

GETTARE *to throw; to fling.*

gettare via *to throw away.*

gettarsi *to fling oneself.*

gettone, m. *token.*

ghermire *to clutch.*

ghiaccio *ice.*

ghiaia *gravel.*

ghiotto *gluttonous, greedy.*

ghirlanda *garland.*

GIÀ *already.*

già fatto *already done.*

giacca *jacket.*

giacchè *as, since.*

giacere *to lie (to recline).*

giallo *yellow, noun & adj.*

giallo d'uovo *egg yolk.*

giammai *never.*

giardiniere, m. *gardener.*

giardino *garden.*

gigante, m. *giant.*

giglio *lily.*

ginnasio *high school.*

ginocchio *knee.*

in ginocchio *on one's knees.*

giocare *to play.*

giocare a carte *to play cards.*

giocattolo *toy.*

giogo *yoke.*

gioia *joy.*

gioiello *jewel.*

GIORNALE, m. *newspaper.*

giornale quotidiano *daily newspaper.*

giornaliero, adj. *daily.*

giornalista, m. *journalist, newspaperman.*

giornalmente, adv. *daily.*

giornata *day.*

giornata di festa *holiday.*

giornata lavorativa *workday.*

GIORNO *day.*

di giorno *in the daytime.*

giorno per giorno *day by day.*

il giorno seguente *the following day.*

un giorno dopo l'altro *day after day.*

giovane, m. *a young man;* f. *a young woman;* (as adj.) *young.*

giovanile *youthful.*

giovanòtto *young man.*

giovedì *Thursday.*

gioventù, f. *youth.*

giovanezza *youth.*

giramento *turning, revolving.*

giramento di testa *dizzy spell.*

girare *to turn; to travel.*

fare girare la testa *to turn one's head.*

girare intorno a se *to rotate.*

giro *turn, spin.*

fare il giro del mondo *to go round the world.*

fare un giro intorno al parco *to take a walk around the park.*

in giro *in circulation.*

un giro d'ispezione *an inspection tour.*

gita *trip, outing.*

GIÙ *down.*

andare giù per le scale *to go down the stairs.*

camminare in su ed in giù *to pace; to walk up and down.*

su per giù *more or less.*

giudicare *to judge.*

giudice, m. *judge.*

giudizio *judgment, sense.*

dente del giudizio *wisdom tooth.*

mettere giudizio *to get wise; to become wiser.*

secondo il giudizio di *according to the judgment of.*

giungere *to arrive.*

giungere in fondo *to reach the end.*

Siamo appena giunti. *We have just arrived.*

giuoco *game.*

giuramento *oath.*

prestar giuramento *to take an oath.*

venir meno ad un giuramento *to break an oath.*

giurare *to swear.*

giustamente *justly.*

giustificare *to justify.*

giustificazione, f. *justification.*

giustizia *justice.*

la mano della giustizia *the arm of justice.*

giusto *right, just.*

GLI { 1. *the,* definite article, (masc. pl.). 2. *to him.*

Gli sono grato. *I am grateful to him.*

globo *globe.*

gloria *glory.*

glorioso *glorious.*

gobbo *hunchback.*

goccia *drop.*

gocciolare *to drip.*

GODERE *to enjoy.*

godere buona salute *to enjoy good health.*

Godo nel vederti. *I am pleased to see you.*

godimento *enjoyment.*

goffo *awkward.*

GOLA *throat.*

aver la gola arsa *to be thirsty.*

aver mal di gola *to have a sore throat.*

Mi fa gola. *It tempts me.*

gomito *elbow.*

gomma *gum, rubber, tire.*

una gomma forata *a flat tire.*

gondola *gondola.*

gonfiare *to inflate.*

gonfiarsi *to swell.*

gonfio *swollen, inflated.*

avere il cuore gonfio *to be heavy-hearted.*

gonna *gown, skirt.*

governante, f. *governess.*

governante, m. *ruler.*

governare *to govern.*

governo *government.*

gradevole *agreeable, pleasant.*

un gusto gradevole *a pleasant taste.*

gradino *step.*

GRADIRE *to accept; to find agreeable.*

Gradisca i miei più cordiali saluti. *Accept my most cordial greeting.*

grado *degree, extent.*

cinque gradi sotto zero *five degrees below zero.*

essere in grado di *to be in a position to.*

fino a questo grado *to this extent.*

graffiare *to scratch.*

GRANDE *great, big.*

a grandi passi *with long steps; swiftly.*

a gran velocità *at great speed.*

farsi grande *to get big; to grow tall.*

in grande *on a large scale.*

grandezza *greatness.*

grandine, f. *hail.*

grandioso *grand.*

grano *grain, corn.*

con un grano di sale *with a grain of salt.*

un grano di sabbia *a grain of sand.*

un grano d'uva *a grape.*

granturco *corn.*

grappolo *bunch.*

grasso *fat, grease;* (as adj.) *greasy.*

grato *grateful.*

grattare *to scratch.*

grave *grave, heavy.*

gratuito *free.*

gravemente *gravely, seriously.*

Egli è gravemente ammalato. *He is seriously ill.*

grazia *grace, favor.*

colpo di grazia *final stroke; coup de grace.*

fare una grazia *to grant a favor.*

grazie a *thanks to.*

GRAZIE *Thank you.*

grazioso *graceful, pretty.*

gridare *to cry out; to shout.*

Non c'è bisogno di gridare. *There's no need to shout.*

grido *cry, shout.*

grigio *gray.*

grillo *cricket.*

grosso *big, bulky.*

gruccia *crutch.*

gruppo *group.*

GUADAGNARE *to earn; to gain.*

guadagnare terreno *to gain ground.*

guadagnarsi da vivere *to earn a livelihood.*

guadagnarsi la stima di qualcuno *to earn someone's respect.*

guadagnar tempo *to gain time.*

guadagno *profit, gain.*

guaio *misfortune, difficulty.*

guancia *cheek.*

voltare l'altra guancia *to turn the other cheek.*

guanciale, m. *pillow.*

guanto *glove.*

calzare come un guanto *to fit like a glove.*

un paio di guanti *a pair of gloves.*

GUARDARE *to look.*

guardarsi dal *to guard against; to refrain from.*

guardarsi negli occhi *to stare into each other's eyes.*

senza guardare nessuno in faccia *without looking.*

Me ne guarderei bene! *I wouldn't dare!*

guardaroba, m. *wardrobe, cloakroom.*

guardia *guard.*

guardiano *watchman, keeper, guard.*

guardiano notturno *night watchman.*

guarire *to recuperate; to get well; to cure.*

guarnire *to trim.*

guarnito *trimmed.*

guerra *war.*

guarnizione, f. *trimming.*

guastare *to spoil.*

GUIDARE *to guide; to drive.*

guidare un' automobile *to drive a car.*

Si lasci guidare da me. *Allow me to guide you.*

guida *guide, guidebook.*

guscio *shell (egg).*

GUSTO *taste.*

di buon gusto *in good taste.*

gusto amaro *bitter taste.*

provare gusto in *to take pleasure in.*

una persona di gusto *a person of good taste.*

Non è di suo gusto. *It's not to his liking.*

H

hotel, m. *hotel.*

I

i *the,* (m. pl.).

i ragazzi *the boys.*

idea *idea.*
cambiare idea *to change one's mind.*
ideale, m. *ideal; (also adj.).*
idealismo *idealism.*
idealista, m. *idealist: (as adj.) idealistic.*
identico *identical.*
idiota, m. *idiot; (as adj.) idiotic.*
identificare *to identify.*
idoneo *fit, suitable.*
IERI, m. *yesterday.*
ieri l'altro *the day before yesterday.*
ieri mattina *yesterday morning.*
ieri sera *last night.*
igiene, f. *hygiene.*
ignobile *ignoble.*
ignorante *ignorant.*
ignoranza *ignorance.*
ignorare *to ignore.*
ignoto *unknown.*
di autore ignoto *by an unknown author.*
Milite Ignoto *Unknown Soldier.*
il *the, (m. sing.).*
illegale *illegal.*
illeso *uninjured, safe.*
illusione, f. *illusion.*
illuminare *to light up.*
illustrare *to illustrate.*
illustrazione, f. *illustration.*
imballare *to pack; to wrap.*
imbarazzante *embarrassing.*
una situazione imbarazzante *an embarrassing situation.*
imbarazzo *embarrassment, difficulty.*
imbarazzo finanziario *financial difficulties.*
mettere in imbarazzo *to embarrass.*
imbarcare *to ship.*
imbarcarsi *to embark.*
imbattersi *to meet with.*
imboccare *to feed.*
imbottire *to stuff; to pad.*
imbrattato *dirty.*
imbrogliare *to cheat.*
imbroglio *complication, tangle, trick.*
imbronciato *sullen.*
imitare *to imitate.*
imbucare *to mail a letter.*
imitazione, f. *imitation.*
IMMAGINARE *to imagine.*
Non riesco ad immaginare. *I can't imagine.*
Si immagini! *Just imagine!*
immaginario *imaginary.*
immaginazione, f. *imagination.*
immagine, f. *image.*
immedesimarsi *to identify oneself with.*
immediatamente *immediately.*
immediato *immediate.*
immenso *huge.*
imminente *imminent.*
immigrare *to immigrate.*
immigrante, m. & f. *immigrant.*
immobilità *immobility.*
immortale *immortal.*
immortalità *immortality.*
impaccare *to pack.*
impacciare *to impede: to embarrass.*
impacciato *constrained, uneasy.*
impallidire *to turn pale.*
imparare *to learn.*
imparare a memoria *to learn by heart.*
imparare una lingua *to learn to speak a language.*
imparentato *related.*
imparziale *impartial.*
impasto *mixture.*

IMPAZIENTE *impatient.*
impazienza *impatience.*
attendere con impazienza *to look forward to; to await anxiously.*
impedimento *prevention.*
impedire *to hinder; to obstruct.*
impazzire *to go crazy.*
IMPEGNARE *to engage; to pawn.*
impegnare un anello *to pawn a ring.*
impegnarsi a fare qualcosa *to pledge oneself to do something.*
Sono già impegnato per quella sera. *I am already engaged for that evening.*
impegno *engagement, obligation.*
impensato *unexpected.*
imperfetto *imperfect.*
impero *empire.*
IMPERMEABILE, m. *raincoat: (as adj.) water-proof.*
impertinente *insolent, impertinent.*
impeto *vehemence.*
impertinenza *impertinence.*
impetuosamente *impetuously.*
impetuoso *impetuous.*
carattere impetuoso *a violent character.*
impianto *installation, establishment.*
impiccare *to hang.*
impiegare *to employ.*
impiegato *employee; (as adj.) employed.*
impiego *employment.*
cercare impiego *to look for a job.*
implicare *to involve.*
impolverato *dusty.*
imporre *to impose.*
importante *important.*
importanza *importance.*
dare importanza a *to attach importance to.*
Non ti dare tanta importanza. *Don't give yourself so many airs.*
importare *to matter; to be of consequence.*
impossibile *impossible.*
imposta *duty, tax.*
IMPRESA *enterprise, undertaking.*
impressionare *to impress.*
Non ti impressionare. *Don't be alarmed.*
impressione, f. *impression.*
fare una brutta impressione *to impress unfavorably.*
Non mi ha fatto impressione alcuna. *It made no impression on me.*
imprevisto (impreveduto) *unforeseen; (also noun).*
se tutto procede senza imprevisti *if things proceed without complications.*
imprigionare *to imprison.*
imprimere *to impress; to stamp.*
impronta *impression, print.*
improvisamente *suddenly.*
imprudente *imprudent.*
imprudenza *imprudence.*
impulso *impulse.*
seguire il proprio impulso *to follow one's instinct.*
impurità *impurity.*
imputare *to impute; to accuse.*
IN *in, into.*
in casa *at home; in the home.*
In che modo? *In what way?*
inabile *unable.*
inadatto *unsuitable.*
inamidare *to starch.*
inappuntabile *irreproachable.*
inaspettatamente *unexpectedly.*
inaspettato *unexpected.*

inavvertenza *inadvertence.*
inaudito *unheard of.*
inaugurare *to inaugurate; to open.*
incantevole *charming.*
incapacità *inability, incapacity.*
incendiare *to set fire to.*
INCENDIO *fire.*
pompa d'incendio *fire pump.*
segnale d'incendio *fire alarm.*
incertezza *uncertainty.*
incerto *uncertain.*
inchiesta *inquiry.*
inchiostro *ink.*
incidente, m. *incident, accident.*
incitare *to incite.*
INCLUDERE *to include.*
incluso *included.*
tutto incluso *everything included.*
incolto *uneducated, uncultivated.*
INCOMINCIARE *to begin; to start.*
incominciando da questo momento *starting from this moment; from this moment on.*
incomodo *uncomfortable.*
dare incomodo *to inconvenience; to disturb.*
incomparabile *incomparable.*
incompatibile *incompatible.*
incompatibilità *incompatibility.*
incompetente, m. *incompetent; (also adj.).*
incompleto *incomplete.*
inconscio *unconscious.*
inconsolabilmente *unconsolably.*
incontentabile *unsatisfiable, exacting.*
INCONTRARE *to meet.*
INCONTRO *meeting, encounter, match.*
un incontro sportivo *a sports match.*
incontro a, adv. *towards, against.*
Andiamogli incontro. *Let's go to meet him.*
Mi venne incontro. *He came towards me.*
inconveniente, m. *inconvenience; (as adj.) inconvenient.*
inconvenienza *inconvenience.*
INCORAGGIARE *to encourage.*
incoraggiarsi *to take courage.*
incorrere *to incur.*
INCREDIBILE *incredible.*
incrociare *to cross; to cruise; to meet.*
incrocio *crossroads.*
incubo *nightmare.*
indebitato *indebted.*
indebolire *to weaken.*
La malattia lo ha indebolito molto. *His illness has made him very weak.*
indecisione, f. *indecision.*
indeciso *undecided.*
indegno *unworthy.*
INDICARE *to indicate; to point out.*
indicare la strada *to show the way.*
indicativo *indicative.*
INDICE, m. *index finger; index.*
INDIETRO *back.*
tornare indietro *to go back.*
volgere lo sguardo indietro *to look back; to look over one's shoulder.*
Quest' orologio va indietro. *This clock is slow.*
indifferente *indifferent.*
Mi è del tutto indifferente. *I am completely indifferent to it.*
indifferenza *indifference, unconcern.*
indigeno *domestic, indigenous; (as noun) native.*
indignato *indignant.*
indignazione, f. *indignation.*
indimenticabile *unforgettable.*
indipendente *independent.*

indipendentemente *independently.*

indipendenza *independence.*

indirettamente *indirectly.*

indiretto *indirect.*

INDIRIZZARE *to address; to direct.*
Le sue parole erano indirizzate a tutti. *His words were directed to everyone.*
Questa lettera non è indirizzata a me. *This letter is not addressed to me.*

indirizzo *address.*

indiscreto *indiscreet.*

indiscrezione, f. *indiscretion.*

individuo *individual* (also adj.).

indivisibile *indivisible.*

indizio *symptom.*

indolente *indolent.*

indossare *to put on; to wear.*

INDOVINARE *to guess; to imagine.*
Indovini un po'. *Just guess.*
Non riesco ad indovinare. *I can't imagine.*

indovinello *enigma, ridicule.*

indubbiamente *undoubtedly.*

indugio *delay.*
Bisogna farlo senza indugio. *It must be done without delay.*

indulgenza *indulgence.*

INDUSTRIA *industry.*

industriale, m. *industrialist;* (as adj.) *industrial.*

industrioso *industrious.*

inesauribile *inexhaustible.*

inesplicabile *inexplicable.*

inevitabile *unavoidable.*

inezia *trifle.*

infallibile *infallible, unfailing.*

infame *infamous.*

infanzia *infancy.*

INFATTI *in fact; in reality.*

infedele *unfaithful.*

infedeltà *infidelity.*

infelice *unhappy.*

infelicità *unhappiness.*

inferiore *inferior.*

inferiorità *inferiority.*
complesso d'inferiorità *inferiority complex.*

infermiera *nurse.*

infilare *to thread.*

INFINE *at last; after all.*

infinito *infinity;* (as adj.) *infinite.*

infliggere *to inflict.*

influenzare *to influence.*

influire *to exert influence over.*
Ha influito sulla mia decisione. *It influenced my decision.*

infondato *unfounded, groundless.*
una paura infondata *a groundless fear.*

informare *to inform.*
Mi ha informato dell'accaduto. *He told me what happened.*

informazione, f. *information.*

infrangere *to shatter; to break.*

INFUORI *out; outwards; outside of.*
all'infuori di *except for.*

ingannare *to deceive.*
Inganno il tempo leggendo. *I kill time reading.*
Mi sono ingannato. *I was mistaken.*

inganno *deceit.*
Mi ha tratto in inganno. *He deceived me.*

ingegnere, m. *engineer.*

ingegno *talent, intelligence.*
una persona d'ingegno *a talented person.*

inghiottire *to swallow.*

inginocchiarsi *to kneel.*

INGIÙ *downwards, down.*

guardare ingiù *to look down.*

ingiustizia *injustice.*

ingiusto *unjust, unfair.*

inglese *English,* (also noun).

ingranaggio *gear.*

ingrassare *to become fat; to grease.*

ingratitudine, f. *ingratitude.*

INGRESSO *entrance, admittance.*
porta d'ingresso *entrance door.*
Ingresso Libero. *No charge for admittance.*
Vietato l'Ingresso! *No Admittance!*

INGROSSO *wholesale.*
vendere all'ingrosso *to sell wholesale.*

INIZIALE, m. *initial* (also adj.).
spesa iniziale *initial outlay.*

iniziare *to start; to initiate.*

iniziativa *initiative.*

inizio *beginning.*
dare inizio allo spettacolo *to begin the performance.*
sin dall'inizio *from the beginning.*

innalzare *to raise.*

innamorare *to charm.*
fare innamorare *to cause to fall in love.*
innamorarsi *to fall in love.*

INNANZI *before.*
innanzi tutto *first of all.*

inno *hymn.*

innocente *innocent.*

innocenza *innocence.*

inoltre *besides.*

inosservato *unobserved.*

inquieto *agitated, restless.*

inquietudine, f. *agitation, restlessness.*

insalata *salad.*
insalata condita *salad with dressing.*

insanguinato *bloody.*

insaponare *to soap; to lather.*

INSEGNA *signboard, flag.*
insegna luminosa *neon sign.*

insegnante *teacher,* m. & f.

insegnare *to teach.*

inseguire *to chase.*

insensato *senseless.*

insensibile *insensible.*

inseparabile *inseparable.*

insidia *snare, trap.*

INSIEME *together.*
mettere tutto insieme *to gather; to put everything together.*
nell'insieme *on the whole.*
uscire insieme *to go out together.*

insignificante *insignificant.*

INSINUARE *to insinuate.*
insinuarsi *to insinuate oneself.*

insistenza *insistence.*

INSISTERE *to insist.*

insolubile *insoluble.*

INSOMMA *in conclusion; in short; well.*
Ma insomma, che cosa facciamo ora? *Well, what are we going to do now?*

insormontabile *unsurmountable.*

insonne *sleepless.*

insperato *unhoped for.*
una gioia insperata *an unhoped for joy.*

installare *to install.*
Si è installato in casa mia. *He installed himself in my home.*

instancabile *untiring.*

INSÙ *up, upwards.*
andare insù ed ingiù *to go up and down.*

insudiciarsi *to become dirty.*

insufficiente *insufficient.*

insufficienza *insufficiency.*
per insufficienza di tempo *for lack of time.*

insulso *insipid.*

insuperabile *insuperable.*

intagliare *to carve.*
legno intagliato *carved wood.*

INTANTO *in the meanwhile; meanwhile.*

intatto *intact.*

integrale *integral.*

intelletto *intellect.*
di scarso intelletto *of poor intellect.*
una persona di grande intelletto *a person of great intellect.*

intellettuale, m. & f. *intellectual;* (also adj.).

intelligente *intelligent.*

intelligenza *intelligence.*

INTENDERE *to intend; to hear; to understand.*
Cerchiamo di intenderci. *Let's try to understand one another.*
Che cosa intende dire? *What do you mean?*
Non ho inteso bene. *I did not hear well.*
Non intendo partire. *I do not intend to leave.*

intenerirsi *to become tender; to be moved to tears.*

intenso *intense.*

intenzione, f. *intention.*
senza intenzione *unintentionally.*
Non ne ho la minima intenzione. *I don't have the slightest intention.*

interamente *entirely.*
Non sono interamente convinto. *I am not entirely convinced.*

interdire *to prohibit.*

interessante *interesting.*

interessare *to interest.*

interesse *interest.*
Non è nel mio interesse farlo. *It is not to my advantage to do it.*

interiore, m. *interior;* (also adj.).
interiori di pollo *chicken giblets.*

intermedio *intermediate.*

internazionale *international.*

interno *interior, inside, internal.*

INTERO *entire, whole.*
il mondo intero *the whole world.*
per intero *wholly, entirely.*

interporre *to interpose.*

interpretare *to interpret.*
interpretare male *to misinterpret.*

interpretazione, f. *interpretation.*

interprete, m. *interpreter.*

interrogare *to question; to ask.*

interruzione, f. *interruption.*

interrompere *to interrupt.*

intervallo *interval.*
l'intervallo fra un'atto e l'altro *between acts; intermission.*

intervista *interview.*
fare un intervista a *to interview someone.*

intervistare *to interview.*

intesa *agreement, understanding.*
secondo la nostra intesa *according to our agreement.*

INTIERO *whole, entire.*

intimazione, f. *order, injunction.*

intimidire *to intimidate; to frighten.*

intimità *intimacy.*
nell'intimità della propria famiglia *in the intimacy of one's own family.*

intimo *intimate.*
un'amico intimo *an intimate friend.*

intitolare *to entitle.*

intollerabile *intolerable.*

intollerante *intolerant.*
intolleranza *intolerance.*
intonazione, f. *intonation.*
intorno *around.*
intraprendere *to undertake.*
intraprendere un viaggio *to embark on a voyage.*
intrattenere *to entertain; to maintain.*
intrigo *plot.*
INTRODURRE *to get in; to put in; to show someone in.*
introdure la chiave nella serratura *to put the key in the lock.*
Si è introdotto in casa mia con una scusa. *He got into my home with an excuse.*
intromettere *to interpose; to interfere with.*
intùito *intuition.*
inumidire *to dampen.*
inutile *useless, unnecessary.*
invadere *to invade.*
invaghirsi *to fall in love.*
invariabile *invariable.*
invariabilmente *invariably.*
invasione, f. *invasion.*
invecchiare *to grow old; to age.*
invece *instead.*
inventare *to invent.*
inventare una scusa *to invent an excuse.*
inventore, m. *inventor.*
invenzione, f. *invention.*
inverno *winter.*
inverso *inverted, inverse.*
invertire *to invert.*
investigare *to investigate; to inquire.*
investimento *investment.*
investire *to invest; to collide with; to run down.*
investire di una carica *to appoint.*
Fui investito da un'automobile. *I was run down by a car.*
inviare *to send.*
invidiare *to envy.*
INVÌO *shipment, mailing.*
invìo di merci *shipment of merchandise.*
l'invìo di posta *the forwarding of mail.*
invisibile *invisible.*
invitare *to invite; to ask.*
INVITO *invitation.*
invocare *to invoke.*
invocare aiuto *to seek help.*
involontario *involuntary.*
involto *parcel, package.*
inzuppare *to soak.*
IO *I.*
iodiu *iodine.*
tintura di iodio *tincture of iodine.*
ipoteca *mortgage.*
IRA *anger, rage.*
con grande ira *with great anger.*
Non posso sfogare la mia ira con nessuno. *I can't give vent to my anger with anyone.*
ironìa *irony.*
l'ironìa del fato *the irony of fate.*
irragionevole *unreasonable.*
irregolare *irregular.*
irreparabile *irreparable.*
irresistibile *irresistible.*
irrigidire *to stiffen.*
irritare *to irritate.*
irritarsi per nulla *to get angry over nothing.*
irritazione, f. *irritation.*
ISOLA *island.*
isolare *to isolate.*
ispettore, m. *inspector.*
ispezionare *to inspect.*

ispezione, f. *inspection.*
ispirazione, f. *inspiration.*
ISTANTANEA *snapshot.*
istantaneo *instantaneous.*
istante, m. *instant.*
istigare *to instigate.*
istintivo *instinctive.*
istinto *instinct.*
per istinto *instinctively.*
istituto *institute, institution.*
istituzione, f. *institution, establishment.*
istruire *to instruct; to teach.*
istruito *educated, learned.*
istruttore, m. *instructor.*
istruzione, f. *education.*
italiano *Italian,* noun & adj.

L

LA 1. *the* (f. sing.).
2. *her, it, you,* personal pronoun obj. (f. sing., and polite form, sing.).
Io la vedo spesso. *I see her often.*
Vediamo la ragazza? Sì, la vediamo. *Do we see the girl? Yes, we see her.*
LÀ *there* (adv.).
LABBRO (labbra, f. pl.) *lip.*
labbro inferiore *lower lip.*
labbro superiore *upper lip.*
Io pendo dalle sue labbra. *I hang on her words.*
laboratorio *laboratory.*
laborioso *laborious.*
laccio *string, knot.*
lacerare *to tear; to rend.*
lacrima *tear.*
scoppiare in lacrime *to burst out into tears.*
ladro *thief.*
LAGGIÙ *down there; there below.*
LAGO *lake.*
lama (lametta) *blade.*
lama di rasoio *razor blade.*
lamentare *to lament; to regret.*
LAMPADA *lamp.*
lampadina *small lamp.*
lampadina elettrica *electric bulb.*
lampadina tascabile *flashlight.*
lampeggiare *to lament; to regret.*
lampo *lightning flash.*
in un lampo *in a flash.*
LANA *wool.*
vestito di lana *woolen suit.*
lanciare *to hurl.*
languire *to languish.*
languore, m. *languor.*
lanterna *lantern.*
lanterna magica *magic lantern.*
lapis, m. *pencil.*
larghezza *width, breadth.*
di questa larghezza *this wide.*
LARGO *wide, broad, large.*
cercare in lungo ed in largo *to seek far and wide.*
su larga scale *on a big scale.*
Fate largo! *Make room!*
LASCIARE *to leave; to quit; to let.*
Ho lasciato detto che sarei tornato alle tre. *I left a message saying I would be back at three.*
Lasciami stare! *Leave me alone!*
Mi ha lasciato una fortuna. *He left me a fortune.*
Ti lascio per sempre. *I'm leaving you forever.*
LASSÙ *up; up there.*
lassù in cima alla montagna *up there at the top of the mountain.*
Guarda lassù. *Look up there.*

lato *side.*
latta *tin.*
lattaio *milkman.*
LATTE, m. *milk.*
latterìa *dairy.*
lattuga *lettuce.*
lavagna *slate, blackboard.*
LAVARE *to wash.*
lavarsi *to wash oneself.*
lavorare *to work.*
lavoratore, m. *workman, worker.*
lavoratrice, f. *workwoman.*
lavoro *work.*
camera del lavoro *trade union.*
lavori forzati *hard labor.*
lavoro drammatico *play.*
lavoro eccessivo *overwork.*
LE 1. *the,* (f. pl.).
2. *them; you* (pl. polite); *to you* (sing. polite); *her, to her.*
leale *loyal.*
lealtà *loyalty.*
leccare *to lick.*
lecito *lawful.*
legale *legal, lawful.*
legare *to tie; to bind.*
un libro legato in pelle *a leather-bound book.*
legatura *binding.*
LEGGE, f. *law.*
approvare una legge *to pass a law.*
fuori legge *outlaw.*
invocare una legge *to invoke a law.*
leggenda *legend.*
La leggenda vuole... *The legend is...*
leggere *to read.*
LEGGERO *light.*
fare un lavoro leggero *to do light work.*
un peso leggero *a lightweight (boxer).*
Egli prende le cose alla leggera. *He takes matters lightly.*
legislazione, f. *legislation.*
legittimo *legitimate.*
legittima difesa *self-defense.*
legno *wood.*
fatto di legno *made of wood.*
legume, m. *vegetable.*
LEI 1. *you* (sing. pol.).
2. *her; to her.*
Noi diamo il libro a lei. *We give her the book.*
lentamente *slowly.*
LENTO *slow.*
lenzuolo, (lenzuola, f. pl.) *sheet.*
cambiare le lenzuola ai letti. *to change the bed sheets.*
leone, m. *lion.*
la parte del leone *the lion's share.*
lepre, m. & f. *hare.*
lesto *nimble, quick.*
lesso *boiled meat.*
LETTERA *letter.*
alla lettera *to the letter.*
lettera di presentazione *letter of introduction.*
lettera maiuscola *capital letter.*
lettera minuscola *small letter.*
lettera per espresso *special-delivery letter.*
lettera raccomandata *registered letter.*
letterario *literary.*
letteratura *literature.*
LETTO *bed.*
letto a doppia piazza *double bed.*
stanza da letto *bedroom.*
lettura *reading.*
LEVARE *to remove; to take off.*

farsi levare un dente   *to have a tooth pulled.*
levare l'incomodo   *to take one's leave.*
levarsi al mattino   *to rise in the morning.*
lezione, f.   *lesson.*
dare lezioni di pianoforte   *to give piano lessons.*
dare una lezione a   *to give a lesson to.*
Lì adv.   *there.*
Lì per lì non ho saputo cosa rispondere.   *At that very moment I didn't know what to answer.*
Metti tutto lì.   *Put everything there.*
Stavo lì lì per farlo.   *I was just about to do it.*
Li   *them.*
Li vedo benissimo.   *I see them clearly.*
libbra   *pound.*
liberale   *liberal.*
liberare   *to free; to liberate.*
liberarsi   *to free oneself.*
Mi sono liberata di un incomodo.   *I got rid of a nuisance.*
libero   *free.*
libertà   *freedom, liberty.*
libraio   *bookseller.*
libreria   *bookshop.*
libro   *book.*
licenza   *license.*
essere in licenza   *to be on leave.*
licenziare   *to dismiss; to fire (from a job).*
Mi sono licenziato.   *I resigned. I quit my job.*
lido   *seashore, beach.*
lieto   *happy.*
Molto lieto di conoscervi.   *Pleased to meet you.*
lievito   *yeast.*
lima   *file.*
limitare   *to limit.*
Se è limitato a un sol bicchiere di vino.   *He limited himself to one glass of wine.*
limite, m.   *limit, bound.*
giungere al limite delle proprie forze   *to reach the end of one's rope.*
È arrivato al limite della sua pazienza.   *He has reached the end of his patience.*
Non c'è limite alla sua insolenza.   *There is no limit to his insolence.*
limone, m.   *lemon.*
succo di limone   *lemon juice.*
linea   *line.*
in linea diretta   *in direct line.*
mettersi in linea   *to get in line.*
Linea Aerea   *Airline.*
Linea Ferroviaria   *Railway Line.*
LINGUA   *tongue, language.*
essere sulla lingua di tutti   *to be a topic for gossip.*
lingua madre   *native tongue.*
parlare bene una lingua   *to speak a language well.*
Il suo nome è sulla punta della mia lingua.   *His name is on the tip of my tongue.*
lino   *linen.*
una tovaglia di lino   *a linen towel.*
liquido   *liquid.*
aver denaro liquido   *to have ready cash.*
liquore, m.   *liquor.*
lista   *menu, list.*
LO   1. *the, (m. sing.).*
   2. *him, it, direct obj. pronoun (m. sing.).*
      Io lo chiamo.   *I call him.*
      Io lo leggo.   *I read it.*
locale   *local.*
locomotiva   *locomotive.*
lodare   *to praise.*
Sia lodato il cielo!   *Heaven be praised!*
logica   *logic.*

logico   *logical.*
la soluzione logica   *the logical solution.*
lontano   *distant, far.*
LORO   1. *they; you (pl. polite), personal pronoun subj.*
   2. *them; to them; you; to you, personal pronoun obj.*
      Io parlo loro francamente.   *I am speaking to you frankly.*
   3. *their, theirs; your, yours (pl. polite) possessive (undeclinable).*
      Also, *il loro; la loro; i loro; le loro.*
      la loro penna   *their pen.*
LOTTARE   *to struggle; to fight.*
lottare contro le avversità   *to struggle against adversity.*
lucidare   *to shine; to sparkle.*
LUCE, f.   *light.*
accendere la luce   *to turn on the light.*
alla luce del sole   *in the sunlight.*
luce elettrica   *electric light.*
spegnere la luce   *to turn off the light.*
venire alla luce   *to come to light.*
luglio   *July.*
lume, m.   *light, lamp.*
luminoso   *luminous.*
luna   *moon.*
lunedì   *Monday.*
lunghezza   *length.*
LUNGO   *long, along.*
a lungo   *for a long time.*
a lungo andare   *in the long run.*
girare in lungo ed in largo   *to wander far and wide.*
lungo la riva del fiume   *along the riverbank.*
lungo un piede   *one foot long.*
La cosa va per le lunghe.   *This matter is taking a long time.*
luogo   *place.*
luogotenente   *lieutenant.*
lupo   *wolf.*
lusinga   *enticement, flattery.*
lusso   *luxury.*
di lusso   *luxurious, de luxe.*
Non mi posso permettere il lusso di comprarlo.   *I can't permit myself the luxury of buying it.*
lussuoso   *luxurious.*
lustrare   *to polish.*
farsi lustrare le scarpe   *to get one's shoes shined.*
lutto   *mourning.*

M

MA   *but, still, however.*
macchia   *spot, stain.*
macchiare   *to spot; to stain.*
MACCHINA   *machine, engine.*
macchina da cucire   *sewing machine.*
macchina lavapiatti   *dishwashing machine.*
macchina per il bucato   *washing machine.*
macellaio   *butcher.*
macelleria   *butchershop.*
macello   *slaughter.*
macinare   *to grind.*
MADRE, f.   *mother.*
maestà   *majesty.*
maestro   *teacher.*
magazzino   *warehouse.*
maggio   *May.*
maggioranza   *majority.*
MAGGIORE   *greater, larger, major.*

di maggior importanza   *of greater importance.*
fratello maggiore   *older brother.*
la maggior parte   *the major part.*
maggiore d'età   *older.*
stato maggiore   *general staff.*
un caso di forza maggiore   *a case of absolute necessity.*
maggiorenne, m. & f.   *of full age.*
magistrato   *magistrate.*
maglia   *stitch, underwear.*
lavoro a maglia   *knitting.*
magnificenza   *magnificence.*
magnifico   *magnificent.*
MAGRO   *thin, lean.*
MAI   *never.*
caso mai   *in case.*
mai e poi mai   *never never.*
mai più   *never again.*
quando mai   *not at all.*
Come mai?   *How come?*
Meglio tardi che mai.   *Better late than never.*
maiale, m.   *pig, pork.*
maiuscolo   *capital.*
lettera maiuscola   *capital letter.*
malamente   *badly.*
MALATO, ill.
MALATTIA   *illness.*
essere colto da malattìa improvvisa   *to become suddenly ill.*
malcontento   *dissatisfied, discontent.*
MALE m.   *evil, harm.*
andare a male   *to spoil.*
di male in peggio   *from bad to worse.*
far male   *to harm; to hurt.*
il minore di due mali   *the lesser of two evils.*
mal d'orecchio   *earache.*
non c'è male   *not too bad.*
Che male fa?   *What harm does it do? What harm is there?*
MALE adv.   *badly.*
capir male   *to misunderstand.*
meno male   *so much the better.*
parlar male di   *to speak ill of.*
star male di salute   *to be in poor health.*
trattar male   *to mistreat.*
È rimasto male.   *He was disappointed.*
Gli affari vanno male.   *Business is poor.*
maledetto   *cursed, abominable.*
maleducato   *ill-bred.*
MALGRADO   *in spite of; notwithstanding.*
mio malgrado   *against my will.*
Malgrado la pioggia siamo usciti.   *We went out, the rain notwithstanding.*
Si è alzato malgrado il divieto del dottore.   *He got up in spite of the doctor's wishes.*
malìa   *charm, enchantment.*
malinteso   *misunderstanding.*
malizia   *malice, cunning.*
malizioso   *malicious, cunning.*
malsano   *unhealthy.*
MALTEMPO   *bad weather.*
maltrattare   *to ill-treat.*
malvagio   *wicked.*
malumore   *ill-humor.*
mamma   *mother.*
MANCANZA   *want, lack.*
in mancanza di meglio   *for lack of something better.*
sentire la mancanza   *to miss.*
una grave mancanza   *a serious fault.*
MANCARE   *to want; to lack; to be absent.*
Egli manca da casa.   *He is away from home.*
Essi hanno mancato.   *They did wrong.*

Manca del denaro dalla cassaforte. *Some money is missing from the safe.*
Mancano cinque minuti alle nove. *It is five minutes to nine.*
Mancano di tutto. *They lack everything.*
mancia *tip.*
mancino *left-handed.*
mandorla *almond.*
mandra *herd.*
MANGIARE *to eat.*
mangiare con gusto *to eat heartily.*
mangiarsi il cuore *to eat one's heart out.*
MANICA *sleeve.*
in maniche di camicia *in shirt sleeves.*
essere di manica larga *to be generous.*
manico *handle.*
aver il coltello dalla parte del manico *to hold the knife by the handle.*
maniera *manner, way.*
in questa maniera *this way.*
in una maniera o nell'altra *in one way or the other.*
manifattura *manufacture.*
manifatturiero *manufacturer.*
manifestare *to manifest.*
maniglia *handle.*
maniglia della porta *door handle.*
MANO, f. *hand.*
a portata di mano *handy.*
cambiar di mano *to change hands.*
dare una mano *to lend a hand.*
fatto a mano *handmade.*
fuori mano *out of the way.*
lavarsi le mani *to wash one's hands.*
star con le mani in mano *to idle.*
stretta di mano *handshake.*
venire alle mani *to come to blows.*
voltare a mano sinistra *to turn to the left.*
mantello *coat, robe.*
MANTENERE *to keep; to maintain.*
mantenere la parola *to keep one's word.*
mantenere una famiglia *to support a family.*
mantenersi calmo *to keep calm.*
mantenersi in contatto con *to keep in contact with.*
mantenersi in vita *to stay alive.*
manzo *steer.*
bollito di manzo *boiled beef.*
marcia *march.*
marciare *to march.*
marcire *to rot; to decay.*
MARE, m. *sea.*
in alto mare *on the high seas.*
mal di mare *seasickness.*
marèa *tide.*
alta marèa *high tide.*
bassa marèa *low tide.*
margherita *daisy.*
margine, m. *margin.*
marina *navy.*
marinaio *sailor.*
marino *marine.*
marito *husband.*
marmellata *marmalade, jam.*
marmo *marble.*
marrone *brown, chestnut.*
martedì *Tuesday.*
martedì prossimo *next Tuesday.*
martedì passato *last Tuesday.*
martello *hammer.*
marzo *March.*
maschera *mask.*
mascherare *to mask.*

mascherarsi *to disguise oneself.*
maschile *masculine, male.*
di genere maschile *of masculine gender.*
di sesso maschile *of male sex.*
maschio, noun *male, boy.*
MASCHIO *manly, virile.*
massa *mass, heap.*
massaia *housewife.*
MASSIMO *greatest.*
al massimo *at best.*
arrivare al massimo della gioia *to reach a peak of happiness.*
peso massimo *heavyweight (boxer).*
masticare *to chew.*
masticare le parole *to mumble.*
matematica *mathematics.*
materasso *mattress.*
materia *matter, substance.*
materiale, m. *material; (also adj.).*
materno *maternal.*
matita *pencil.*
MATRIMONIO *marriage.*
MATTINA *morning.*
matto *mad, crazy.*
È diventato matto. *He went mad.*
Questo bambino mi fa diventare matta. *This child drives me crazy.*
Vado matto per la musica. *I'm crazy about music.*
mattone, m. *brick.*
mattonella *tile.*
maturo *mature, ripe.*
una mela matura *a ripe apple.*
un' uomo di matura età *an aged man.*
ME *me.*
meccanico *mechanic; (as adj.) mechanical.*
medaglia *medal.*
il rovescio della medaglia *the reverse of the medal.*
medesimo *same, alike.*
Portiamo la medesima misura. *We wear the same size.*
media *average.*
una media di *an average of.*
mediante *by means of.*
medicare *to medicate.*
medicina *medicine.*
MEDICO *physician.*
medico chirurgo *surgeon.*
MEDIO *middle, medium.*
di media età *middle-aged.*
dito medio *middle finger.*
Appartiene alla classe media. *He belongs to the middle class.*
Medio Evo *Middle Ages.*
mediocre *mediocre.*
meditare *to meditate.*
meditazione, f. *meditation.*
MEGLIO *better.*
di bene in meglio *better and better.*
quanto c'è di meglio *the best there is.*
sentirsi meglio *to feel better.*
Ci ho pensato meglio. *I thought it over.*
Sarebbe meglio partire ora. *It would be better to leave now.*
MELA *apple.*
melodìa *melody.*
membro *limb, member; **membra, f. pl.** limbs.*
aver le membra stanche *to be tired.*
membri, m. pl. *members.*
memorabile *memorable.*
memoria *memory.*

imparare a memoria *to memorize.*
Ho buona memoria. *I have a good memory.*
menare *to lead.*
MENO *less.*
a meno che *unless.*
fare a meno di *to do without.*
meno gente *fewer people.*
più o meno *more or less.*
venir meno ad una promessa *to break a promise.*
Cinque meno tre fanno due. *Five minus three makes two.*
In meno che non si dica, egli è tornato. *He came back in no time at all.*
Sono le sette meno dieci. *It's ten minutes to seven.*
Sono meno stanca di te. *I am less tired than you.*
mensile, m. *monthly wage; (as adj.) monthly.*
mensilmente *once a month.*
menta *mint, peppermint.*
mentale *mental.*
alienazione mentale *insanity.*
MENTE, f. *mind.*
aver in mente di *to intend.*
malato di mente *mentally ill.*
mente sana in corpo sano *sound mind in sound body.*
tenere a mente *to remember.*
Ho un progetto in mente. *I have a project in mind.*
Un pensiero mi è venuto in mente. *A thought occurred to me.*
mentire *to lie.*
mento *chin.*
MENTRE *while, instead.*
Mi ha detto che sarebbe venuto qui, mentre invece è andato da Maria. *He said he was coming here, but instead he went to Mary's.*
Non m'interrompere mentre sto parlando. *Don't interrupt while I'm speaking.*
menzionare *to mention.*
menzione, f. *mention.*
Non ne far menzione. *Make no mention of it.*
menzogna *falsehood, untruth, lie.*
meraviglia *wonder, amazement.*
mercante, m. *merchant.*
fare orecchio da mercante *to turn deaf ears.*
mercato *market.*
merce, f. *goods, merchandise.*
mercoledì *Wednesday.*
meritare *to deserve.*
merito *merit, worth.*
rendere merito a *to give credit to.*
una persona di grandi meriti *a person of great merit.*
merletto *lace.*
mescolare *to mix.*
MESE *month.*
il mese in corso *the current month.*
il mese passato }
il mese scorso } *last month.*
il mese che viene }
il mese entrante } *next month.*
il mese prossimo }
messa *mass.*
messa solenne *solemn mass.*
messaggero *messenger.*
mestiere, m. *trade.*
ognuno al proprio mestiere *each to his own trade.*
Non faccio questo mestiere. *This is not my trade.*

Qual'è il suo mestiere? *What is your trade?*
meta *goal.*
METÀ *half.*
  a metà paga *at half pay.*
  a metà prezzo *at half price.*
  a metà strada *half way.*
  dividere a metà *to divide in half.*
  fare metà per uno *to give each half.*
metodicamente *methodically.*
metodo *method.*
metropolitana *subway.*
METTERE *to put; to place.*
  mettere fine a *to put an end to.*
  mettere le cose a posto *to put things in order.*
  mettere in libertà *to set free.*
  mettere in moto *to set in motion.*
  mettere in ordine *to tidy.*
  mettersi a *to put oneself to; to begin.*
mezzo, noun *means.*
  con mezzi limitati *with limited means.*
  per mezzo di *by means of.*
MEZZO *half.*
  in mezzo a *in the midst of.*
  mezz' ora *half an hour.*
  un' ora e mezza *one hour and a half.*
mezzogiorno *noon.*
MI *me; to me.*
  Mi dai quel libro per piacere? *Will you please give me that book?*
  Mi scrivono. *They write to me.*
  Mi senti? *Do you hear me?*
mica *not at all.*
microbo *microbe.*
microfono *microphone.*
miele, m. *honey.*
migliaio *thousand.*
  migliàia di persone *thousands of people.*
miglio *mile.*
migliorare *to better; to improve.*
migliore *better.*
milionario *millionaire.*
milione, m. *million.*
militare, m. *soldier.*
MILLE *thousand.*
  duemila *two thousand.*
minacciare *to threaten.*
minaccioso *menacing, threatening.*
miniera *mine.*
minimo *minimum.*
  il minimo che si possa fare *the least that can be done.*
  paga minima *lowest pay.*
  ridurre ai minimi termini *to reduce to the lowest terms.*
  un minimo di *a minimum of.*
ministro *minister.*
minoranza *minority.*
minore *less, lesser, minor.*
  minore d'età *younger.*
  sorella minore *younger sister.*
minorenne, m. & f. *minor; (as adj.) underage.*
minuto *minute.*
  Attenda un minuto. *Wait a minute.*
  Sono le cinque e dieci minuti. *It's ten minutes past five.*
MIO, mio; miei (m. pl.); mie (f. pl.); il mio; la mia; i miei; le mie *my, mine.*
  Questo è il mio libro. *This is my book.*
  Mia zia è arrivata. *My aunt has arrived.*
mira *sight.*
  prendere di mira *to aim at.*
miracolo *miracle.*

mirare *to stare at; to aim at.*
miscuglio *mixture.*
miserabile *miserable.*
miserabilmente *miserably.*
misèria *misery, poverty.*
misericordia *mercy.*
mistero *mystery.*
mistura *mixture.*
misura *measure.*
  misura a nastro *tape-measure.*
  prendere delle misure *to take measures.*
  prendere le misure *to take measurements.*
misurare *to measure.*
mite *mild.*
  clima mite *temperate climate.*
  un carattere mite *a mild character.*
mitragliatrice, f. *machine gun.*
mobilia *furniture.*
mobilità *mobility.*
mobilitazione, f. *mobilization.*
moda *fashion.*
  essere di moda *to be in fashion.*
modella *model.*
modello *pattern, model.*
  essere un modello di virtù *to be a model of virtue.*
moderare *to moderate.*
  moderare i termini *to keep a civil tongue.*
  moderarsi *to moderate oneself.*
moderazione, f. *moderation.*
moderno *modern.*
modèstia *modesty.*
modesto *modest.*
MODO *way, manner.*
  a mio modo di vedere *according to my way of thinking.*
  a modo proprio *in one's own way.*
  in qualche modo *somehow.*
  in questo modo *this way; in this manner.*
  Non è modo d'agire. *That's no way to act.*
modulo *form, blank.*
  riempire un modulo *to fill out a form.*
MOGLIE *wife.*
  chiedere in moglie *to ask in marriage.*
  prendere moglie *to marry.*
mole, f. *bulk.*
molle *soft.*
mollette, f. pl. *tongs.*
mollica *crumb.*
  una mollica di pane *a crumb of bread.*
moltiplicare *to multiply.*
MOLTO *much; molti many.*
  molte persone *many people.*
  molti amici *many friends.*
molto, adv. *very.*
  Ho molto lavoro da fare. *I have much work to do.*
  Molto bene! *Very good!*
  Sono molto stanco. *I am very tired.*
momento *moment.*
  da un momento all'altro *any minute.*
  in questo momento *right now.*
  qualche momento fa *a moment ago.*
monaca *nun.*
monarca, m. *monarch.*
mondano *worldly.*
MONDO *world.*
  andare all'altro mondo *to die.*
  caschi il mondo *come what may.*
  mettere al mondo *to give birth to.*
  venire al mondo *to be born.*
moneta *coin.*
  moneta d'argento *silver coin.*
  moneta d'oro *gold coin.*

  L'ho pagato colla stessa moneta. *I paid him in his own coin.*
  Non ha moneta. *She (he) has no change.*
monotonìa *monotony.*
monotono *monotonous.*
montagna *mountain.*
montare *to go up; to ascend.*
monte, m. *mount, mountain.*
  Il matrimonio è andato a monte. *The wedding was called off.*
monte di pietà *pawnbroker.*
morale *moral.*
morale, f. *morale.*
  Sono un po' giù di morale. *I'm low in spirits.*
morale, f. *moral, morals.*
mordere *to bite.*
morbido *soft.*
morente *dying.*
morire *to die.*
mormorare *to murmur.*
mormorìo *murmur, murmuring.*
morsicare *to bite.*
morso *bite.*
mortalità *mortality.*
mortalmente *mortally.*
  ferito mortalmente *mortally wounded.*
morte, f. *death.*
morto *dead.*
mosca *fly.*
mossa *movement, gesture.*
MOSTRARE *to show; to display.*
  mostrare coraggio *to display courage.*
  mostrare i denti *to bare one's teeth.*
  Cerca di mostrarti più allegra. *Try to appear more cheerful.*
  Mi devi mostrare come si fa. *You must show me how it's done.*
motivare *to motivate.*
motivo *motive, reason, tune.*
  Mi piace il motivo ma non le parole di questa canzone. *I like the tune, but not the words of this song.*
  Non c'è motivo di farlo. *There is no reason to do it.*
moto *motion, impulse.*
  di moto proprio *of one's own volition.*
  essere sempre in moto *to be constantly on the move.*
  mettere in moto l'automobile *to start the car.*
motore, m. *motor, engine.*
movimento *movement.*
mucca *cow.*
mucchio *heap, pile.*
  Ho un mucchio di corrispondenza da sbrigare. *I've a heap of correspondence to attend to.*
muffa *mold, mustiness.*
mugnàio *miller.*
mulino *mill.*
mulo *mule.*
multa *fine, (penalty).*
municipale *municipal.*
municipalità *municipality.*
municipio *municipality.*
  palazzo del municipio *town hall.*
munizione, f. *munition, ammunition.*
muovere *to move.*
mura, f. pl. *walls.*
musèo *museum.*
muratore *mason, bricklayer.*
muro *wall.*
musica *music.*
musicale *musical.*
musicista *musician.*

mutande, f. pl.   shorts (men's).
mutandine, f. pl.   panties.
mutare   to change.
muto   mute.
  sordo-muto   deaf-mute.
mutuo   mutual.

N

napoletano   Neapolitan; (also noun).
narice, f.   nostril.
narrare   to narrate; to tell.
NASCERE   to be born; to originate.
  far nascere dei sospetti   to give rise to suspi-
    cion.
  nascere colla camicia   to be born with a silver
    spoon in one's mouth.
  nascere morto   to be stillborn.
  Non so come sia nato questo malinteso.   I don't
    know how this misunderstanding originated.
nàscita   birth.
  anniversario della mia nàscita   my birthday.
  certificato di nàscita   birth certificate.
NASCONDERE   to hide; to conceal.
  nascondere la verità   to conceal the truth.
  nascondersi   to hide oneself.
  Il gattino si è nascosto sotto il letto.   The
    pussy-cat hid under the bed.
nascosto   hidden.
NASO   nose.
  arricciare il naso   to turn one's nose up at.
  soffiarsi il naso   to blow one's nose.
nastro   ribbon.
  nastro adesivo   adhesive tape.
natale   native.
  città natale   native city.
NATALE   Christmas.
  la vigilia di Natale   Christmas Eve.
  Buon Natale!   Merry Christmas.
nativo   native, noun & adj.
nato   child.
  primo nato   firstborn.
natura   nature.
naturale   natural.
naturalezza   naturalness.
  con naturalezza   without affectation.
naturalmente   naturally; of course.
  Naturalmente!   Naturally!
navale   naval.
navata   aisle, nave.
NAVE, f.   ship.
  a mezzo nave   by ship.
  nave a vapore   steamship.
  nave da carico   cargo ship.
  nave da guerra   warship.
  nave mercantile   merchant ship.
navigare   to navigate.
navigazione, f.   navigation.
nazionale   national.
nazionalità   nationality.
nazionalizzare   to nationalize.
nazione, f.   nation.
  Nazioni Unite.   United Nations.
NE   1. of him; about him; of her; about her; of it;
       about it; of them; about them.
     2. from there.
  Noi ne parliamo spesso.   We often speak of
    him (of her, of them, of it).
  Ne siamo felici.   We are glad of it.
  Ne sono appena tornato.   I've just returned
    from there.
NE, conj.   neither, nor.
  Non desidero ne l'uno ne l'altro.   I wish neither
    one nor the other.

NEANCHE   not even; not either.
  Non l'ho neanche visto.   I didn't even see him.
  Se tu non esci, non esco neanch'io.   If you don't
    go out, I won't go out either.
nebbia   fog.
necessariamente   necessarily.
necessario   necessary.
negare   to deny.
negativa   negative (snapshot).
negativo   negative.
negazione, f.   negation.
negligenza   negligence.
negoziare   to negotiate; to transact business.
negoziazione, f.   negotiation.
negozio   shop.
negro   Negro.
nemico   enemy.
neonato   infant, newborn.
NEPPURE   see neanche.
nero   black.
  Mar Nero   Black Sea.
  d'umore nero   in a dark humor.
nervo   nerve.
nervoso   nervous.
  sistema nervoso   nervous system.
NESSUNO   nobody; no one; no; anyone.
  in nessun modo   in no way.
  È venuto nessuno?   Did anyone come?
  Non c'è nessuno.   There is no one here.
neutrale   neutral.
neve, f.   snow.
nevicare   to snow.
  Nevica.   It's snowing.
nido   nest.
NIENTE   nothing.
  Non c'è niente da fare.   Nothing can be done
    about it.
  Non fa niente.   It doesn't matter.
nipote, m.   nephew, grandson.
nipote, f.   niece, granddaughter.
nitidezza   clearness.
nitido   neat, clear.
NO   no.
  rispondere di no   to answer no.
nobile   noble.
nobiltà   nobility.
nocciola   hazelnut.
nòcciolo   stone, pit.
  il nòcciolo della questione   the very point in
    question.
noce, f.   walnut.
nodo   knot.
  avere un nodo alla gola   to have a lump in one's
    throat.
  fare un nodo   to make a knot.
NOI   we.
  noi stessi   ourselves.
noia   weariness, boredom.
noiosamente   tediously.
noioso   tedious, boring.
noleggiare   to hire.
NOME, m.   name, noun.
  chiamare per nome   to call by name.
  nome comune   common noun.
  nome di famiglia   family name.
nomina   appointment.
nominare   to mention; to appoint.
  Fu nominato ambasciatore.   He was appointed
    ambassador.
  Ti nominiamo spesso.   We mention you often.
NON   not.
  Non ne voglio.   I don't want any.
  Non ti sento.   I don't hear you.

nonna   grandmother.
nonno   grandfather.
nono   ninth.
nonostante   nevertheless.
NORD, m.   north.
  nord-est   northeast.
  nord-ovest   northwest.
  viaggiare verso nord   to travel north.
  America del Nord   North America.
normale   normal.
normalmente   normally.
NOSTRO, -a, -i, -e; (il nostro; la nostra; i nostri;
  le nostre)   our, ours.
  il nostro amico   our friend.
  la nostra casa   our home.
  i nostri genitori   our parents.
  le nostre camere   our rooms.
nota   note.
  degno di nota   noteworthy.
  prendere nota di   to take note of.
NOTARE   to note; to notice.
  farsi notare   to make oneself conspicuous.
  Hai notato come Maria si è invecchiata?   Did
    you notice how Mary has aged?
notevole   remarkable, considerable.
notificare   to notify.
NOTIZIA   news.
  le ultime notizie   the latest news.
  Fammi avere tue notizie.   Let me have news
    of you.
  Non ho notizie di te da molto tempo.   I haven't
    heard from you in some time.
noto   known; well known.
  Il suo nome è noto a tutti.   Everyone knows his
    name.
  Egli è una figura nota nel mondo politico.   He is
    a well known figure in political circles.
NOTTE, f.   night.
  a notte alta   in the middle of the night.
  camicia da notte   nightgown.
  di notte   at night.
  mezzanotte   midnight.
novanta   ninety.
novantesimo   ninetieth.
nove   nine.
  nove volte su dieci   nine times out of ten.
novecento   nine hundred.
novembre   November.
novità   novelty; latest news.
  una novità assoluta   an absolute novelty.
  Avete sentito la novità?   Have you heard the
    latest?
nozione, f.   notion.
nozze, f. pl.   wedding.
nube, f.   cloud.
nubile   unmarried; single (of a woman).
nudo   naked, bare.
  a piedi nudi   barefooted.
  grande abbastanza da vedersi a occhio nudo
    large enough to see with the naked eye.
nulla   see niente.
nullo   null, void.
numerare   to number.
  numero dispari   odd number.
  numero pari   even number.
numeroso   numerous.
nuocere   to harm.
nuora   daughter-in-law.
nuotare   to swim.
  nuotare nell'abbondanza   to be well off.
nuoto   swimming.
nuovo   new.
  di nuovo   again.

nutrimento *nourishment.*
nutrire *to nourish.*
  nutrire rancore *to bear a grudge.*
  Non nutro fiducia in questa impresa. *I have no faith in this enterprise.*
  Si dovrebbe nutrire meglio. *He should have better nourishment.*
nutrizione, f. *nutrition, nourishment.*
nuvola *cloud.*
  una nuvola di fumo *a cloud of smoke.*
  È sempre fra le nuvole. *He's always in the clouds.*
nuvoloso *cloudy.*
nuziale *nuptial.*
  marcia nuziale *wedding march.*
  velo nuziale *bridal veil.*

O

o, od *or.*
  o uno o l'altro *either one or the other.*
  Mi sei amico o nemico? *Are you friend or foe?*
  Scegli questo o quello. *Choose one or the other.*
obbediente *obedient.*
obbedienza *obedience.*
obbedire *to obey.*
obbiettivo *aim, purpose, goal.*
obbligare *to obligate; to compel.*
  Nessuno ti obbliga a pagare. *No one compels you to pay.*
  Sono obbligato a licenziarti. *I am compelled to fire you.*
obbligato *obliged, indebted.*
  Le sono molto obbligato. *I am much obliged to you.*
obbligazione, f. *obligation.*
obbligo *obligation.*
  Non voglio assumere obblighi. *I don't wish to assume obligations.*
obiettare *to object.*
obiettivo *objective.*
obiezione, f. *objection.*
oblìo *forgetfulness.*
oca *goose.*
occasionale *occasional.*
occasionalmente *occasionally; by chance.*
occasione, f. *occasion, opportunity.*
  cogliere l'occasione *to take the opportunity.*
occhiali, m. pl. *eyeglasses.*
occhiata *glance.*
  dare un'occhiata a *to give a glance to.*
occhiello *buttonhole.*
OCCHIO *eye.*
  agli occhi del mondo *in the eyes of the world.*
  a perdita d'occhio *as far as the eye can see.*
  dare nell'occhio *to attract attention.*
  guardare con occhio benigno *to look kindly on.*
  tenere d'occhio *to keep one's eye on.*
occidentale *western; (as noun) westerner.*
occidente, m. *west.*
occorrenza *occurrence.*
occorrere *to happen; to be necessary; to occur.*
occupare *to occupy.*
  Il mio tempo è occupato in altre cose. *My time is taken up by other things.*
  Lei ha occupato il mio posto. *You have occupied my seat.*
  Me ne occupo io. *I'll take care of it.*
occupato *engaged, occupied, busy.*
  Sono molto occupato questa sera. *I'm very busy this evening.*
occupazione, f. *occupation, employment.*
ocèano *ocean.*
odiare *to hate.*

odierno *of today.*
odio *hatred.*
odioso *hateful.*
odorare *to smell.*
odore, m. *smell.*
offendere *to offend.*
offensivo *offensive.*
offensore, m. *offender.*
offerta *offer, offering.*
  Ha respinto la mia offerta di denaro. *He refused my offer of money.*
offesa *offense.*
  recare offesa a *to give offense to.*
officina *workshop.*
offrire *to offer.*
oggettivo *objective.*
oggettivamente *objectively.*
oggetto *object.*
OGGI *today.*
  da oggi in poi *from today on.*
  in data d'oggi *bearing today's date.*
  oggi a otto *a week from today.*
  oggi a quindici *two weeks from today.*
  rimandare dall'oggi al domani *to put off from day to day.*
OGNI *every, each.*
  ogni settimana *every week.*
  Danne uno ad ogni persona presente. *Give one to each person present.*
OGNUNO *everyone, each one.*
  Ognuno di noi è libero di fare ciò che vuole. *Each of us is free to do as he wishes.*
olio *oil.*
  olio d'oliva *olive oil.*
  olio di fegato di merluzzo *cod-liver oil.*
oliva *olive.*
oltraggio *outrage.*
oltraggiosamente *outrageously.*
OLTRE *beside, beyond.*
  andare oltre i limiti *to go beyond the limits.*
  oltre mare *overseas.*
  Gli ho dato dieci dollari, oltre i cinque che gli avevo già dato. *I gave him ten dollars, besides the five I had already given him.*
omaggio *homage, presentation.*
OMBRA *shadow, shade.*
  all'ombra di un' albero *in the shade of a tree.*
  senza neppure l'ombra di un dubbio *without a shadow of a doubt.*
omicidio *murder.*
ombrello *umbrella.*
omettere *to omit.*
  Il mio nome è stato omesso dalla lista degli invitati. *My name was omitted from the guest-list.*
oncia *ounce.*
onda *wave.*
ondata *a wave, surge.*
  un'ondata di freddo *a cold spell.*
ondulare *to wave.*
  farsi ondulare i capelli *to have one's hair waved.*
ondulazione, f. *waving, undulation.*
onesto *honest.*
onorabilità *honorability.*
onorabilmente *honorably.*
onorare *to honor.*
onorario *honorary; (as noun, pl.) wages, fee.*
onorato *honored.*
onore, m. *honor.*
  aver l'onore di chiedere *to have the honor to request.*

  fare onore ai propri impegni *to meet one's obligations.*
  in onore di *in honor of.*
  parola d'onore *word of honor.*
onorevole *honorable.*
opera *opera, work.*
  fare un'opera buona *to do a kind deed.*
  mano d'opera *labor.*
  teatro d'opera *opera house.*
  un'opera d'arte *a work of art.*
operàio *laborer.*
operare *to work.*
  farsi operare *to undergo surgery.*
  Egli opera per il bene di tutti. *He is working for the good of all.*
operazione, f. *operation.*
opinione, f. *opinion.*
  cambiare opinione *to change one's mind.*
  opinione pubblica *public opinion.*
opponente, m. *opponent; (as adj.) opposing.*
opporre *to oppose.*
  opporre resistenza *to resist.*
  opporre un rifiuto *to refuse.*
  opporsi ad un'idea *to oppose an idea; to declare oneself against an idea.*
opportunità *opportunity, opportuneness.*
  Non mi diede l'opportunità di vederlo. *He didn't give me the opportunity of seeing him.*
  Non ne vedo l'opportunità *I can't see that it is opportune.*
opportuno *opportune.*
opposizione, f. *opposition.*
opposto *opposite, facing.*
oppressione, f. *oppression.*
opprimere *to oppress.*
OPPURE *or else.*
opuscolo *pamphlet.*
ORA *hour.*
  fra un'ora *in an hour.*
  le ore lavorative *working hours.*
  ogni ora del giorno *every hour of the day.*
  Che ora è? *What time is it?*
  È ora d'andare a casa. *It's time to go home.*
ORA *now.*
  da ora in poi *from now on.*
  fino ad ora *up until now.*
  ora e per sempre *once and for all.*
  per ora *for the moment.*
orale *oral.*
orario *timetable.*
  arrivare in orario *to arrive on time.*
orario, adj. *per hour.*
  una velocità oraria di trenta chilometri *a speed of thirty kilometers per hour.*
oratore, m. *orator.*
orchestra *orchestra.*
  direttore d'orchestra *conductor.*
ordinare *to order.*
  Ha altro da ordinare? *Have you any further orders?*
  Mi ha ordinato di fare questo lavoro. *He ordered me to do this work.*
  Vuole ordinare la colazione? *Do you wish to order breakfast?*
ordinario *ordinary.*
ordine, m. *order.*
  di prim'ordine *first-rate.*
  fino a nuovo ordine *till a change in orders occurs.*
  mettere in ordine alfabetico *to put in alphabetical order.*
  mettere in ordine una camera *to set a room to rights.*

ordini e contr' ordini *orders and counter-orders.*
per ordine cronologico *in chronological order.*
orecchino *earring.*
ORECCHIO *ear.*
entrare da un orecchio e uscire dall'altro *to go in one ear and out the other.*
essere tutto orecchi *to be all ears.*
fare orecchio da mercante *to make believe one doesn't hear.*
mal all'orecchio *earache.*
prestare orecchio *to lend an ear.*
Non ha orecchio per la musica. *He has no ear for music.*
organo *organ.*
orgoglio *pride.*
orgoglioso *proud.*
orientale *Eastern, Oriental.*
oriente, m. *orient, east.*
l'estremo Oriente *the Far East.*
orientar(si) *to orient oneself.*
originale *original.*
originalità *originality.*
origine, f. *origin.*
dare origine a *to give rise to.*
di comuni origini *of common origin.*
di origine italiana *of Italian descent.*
di umile origine *of humble origin.*
Come ebbe origine il dissidio? *How did the dissension originate?*
orizzonte, m. *horizon.*
orlo *border, edge, hem.*
orma *footprint, footmark.*
Egli segue le orme di suo padre. *He is following in his fathers footsteps.*
ORMAI *now; by now; by this time.*
Ormai tutto è a posto. *Now everything is in order.*
Sara già partito ormai. *He has probably already left by this time.*
ornamento *ornament.*
ORO *gold.*
oro a diciotto *eighteen-carat gold.*
oro zecchino *pure gold.*
riccioli d'oro *golden ringlets.*
Essa vale tant' oro quanto pesa. *She is worth her weight in gold.*
Non è tutt' oro quel che luce. *All that glitters is not gold.*
orologiàio *watchmaker.*
orologio *watch.*
caricare l'orologio *to wind the watch.*
Che ora fa il tuo orologio? *What time is it by your watch?*
Il mio orologio fa le quattro e dieci. *According to my watch, it is ten minutes past four.*
Quest' orologio va avanti venti minuti al giorno. *This watch gains twenty minutes a day.*
orribile *horrible.*
orribilmente *horribly.*
orrore, m. *horror.*
Mi fa orrore. *It horrifies me.*
orso *bear.*
orto *vegetable garden.*
ortografia *spelling.*
OSARE *to dare.*
Come osa fare una cosa simile? *How dare you do such a thing?*
Non oso chiederlo. *I don't dare ask.*
Sarebbe osare troppo. *That would be going too far.*
OSCURARE *to darken; to obscure.*
Il cielo si è improvvisamente oscurato. *The sky darkened suddenly.*

Mi si sta oscurando la vista. *My sight is growing dim.*
oscurità *darkness, obscurity.*
l'oscurità di una notte senza stelle *the darkness of a starless night.*
ospedale, m. *hospital.*
ospitale *hospitable.*
ospitalità *hospitality.*
ospite, m. & f. *guest, host, hostess.*
È stata mia ospite per le vacanze estive. *She was my guest during the summer holidays.*
È un'ospite gradito. *He is a welcome guest.*
I miei ospiti mi hanno gentilmente invitato a tornare a casa loro la settimana prossima. *My hosts have very kindly invited me to return to their home next week.*
osservare *to observe; to notice.*
osservazione, f. *observation, remark.*
Egli ha fatto un' osservazione fuori posto. *He made an uncalled-for remark.*
ossigeno *oxygen.*
OSSO (**ossa** f. pl.) *bone.*
in carne e ossa *in the flesh.*
Ho freddo fino alle ossa. *I'm frozen to the bone.*
Mi sento tutte le ossa rotte. *I'm all aches and pains.*
Si è rotto l'osso del collo. *He broke his neck.*
ostacolare *to hinder.*
ostacolare il cammino di qualcuno *to hinder someone's progress.*
ostacolo *obstacle.*
un ostacolo insormontabile *an insurmountable obstacle.*
oste, m. *host, tavern-keeper.*
ostile *hostile.*
forze ostili *hostile forces.*
ostilità, f. *hostility.*
ostinato *obstinate.*
ostinazione, f. *obstinacy.*
ostrica *oyster.*
ostruzione, f. *obstruction.*
ottanta *eighty.*
ottantesimo *eightieth.*
ottavo *eighth.*
ottenere *to obtain.*
ottenere il permesso *to obtain permission.*
ottimismo *optimism; (as adj.) optimistic.*
ottimista, m. *optimist.*
ottimo *excellent.*
otto *eight.*
oggi a otto *a week from today.*
ottobre *October.*
ottocento *eight hundred.*
nell' ottocento *in the nineteenth century.*
ottone, m. *brass.*
ottoni *brass instruments.*
ovale, m. *oval; (also adj.).*
ovatta *wadding.*
ovazione, f. *ovation.*
OVEST, m. *west.*
ad ovest *to the west.*
OVUNQUE *anywhere, everywhere.*
Stiamo cercando ovunque. *We are looking everywhere.*
Ti seguirò ovunque. *I'll follow you anywhere.*
ovviamente *obviously.*
ovvio *obvious.*
ozio *idleness.*
Verrò a trovarti durante le mie ore d'ozio. *I'll come to see you during my leisure hours.*
ozioso *idle, lazy.*

P

PACCO *package, parcel.*
spedire come pacco postale *to send by parcel post.*
PACE, f. *peace.*
fare la pace col nemico *to make peace with the enemy.*
giudice di pace *justice of the peace.*
lasciare in pace *to leave alone.*
mettere il cuore in pace *to set one's mind at rest.*
trattato di pace *peace treaty.*
Voglio stare in pace. *I want to live in peace.*
pacificare *to pacify; to appease.*
pacifico *peaceful, pacific.*
Pacifico *Pacific.*
padella *frying pan.*
cadere dalla padella nella brace *to fall out of the frying pan into the fire.*
PADRE *father.*
il Santo Padre *the Holy Father.*
padrona *owner, mistress.*
padrona di casa *landlady.*
PADRONE, m. *landlord, owner.*
essere padrone dalla situazione *to have the situation well in hand.*
essere padrone di se *to have self-control.*
Sono padrone di fare quello che mi pare e piace. *I am free to do as I chose.*
poesaggio *landscape.*
PAESE, m. *country; land; small town.*
gente di paese *countryfolk.*
il paese dell' abbondanza *the land of plenty.*
paese di montagna *mountain village.*
paese natio *native land; native town.*
Mi ha mandato a quel paese. *He sent me to the devil.*
Paese che vai, usanza che trovi. *To each country its own customs.*
Siamo del medesimo paese. *We are from the same country.*
paga *pay.*
riscuotere la paga *to collect one's pay.*
pagamento *payment.*
pagamento a rate *payment in installments.*
pagamento in contanti *cash payment.*
PAGARE *to pay.*
da pagarsi alla consegna *C.O.D.*
Quanto mi fa pagare? *How much will you charge me?*
pagato *paid.*
PAGINA *page.*
a piè di pagina *at the foot of the page.*
paglia *straw.*
PAIO (**PAIA**, f. pl.) *pair.*
tre paia di guanti *three pairs of gloves.*
un paio di scarpe *a pair of shoes.*
palato *palate.*
palazzo *palace.*
palazzo municipale *City Hall.*
palco *scaffold, platform, box (theatre).*
palcoscenio *stage.*
palesare *to disclose; to reveal.*
palla *ball.*
pallidezza *paleness.*
pallido *pale.*
pallone, m. *balloon.*
palma *palm.*
palo *pole.*
palo di partenza *starting-post.*
palo telegrafico *telegraph pole.*
saltare di palo in frasca *to stray from the point.*

palpebra *eyelid.*
palpitare *to throb.*
palude, f. *marsh.*
panca *bench.*
PANE, m. *bread.*
pane fresco *fresh bread.*
pane quotidiano *daily bread.*
pane stantìo *stale bread.*
rendere pan per focaccia *to give tit for tat.*
Sono anni che mangia pane a tradimento. *It's years since he's earned his keep.*
panetterìa *bakery shop.*
panettiere, m. *baker.*
pànfilo *yacht.*
pànico *panic.*
paniere, m. *basket.*
rompere le uova nel paniere *to upset one's apple-cart.*
panificio *bakery.*
panino *roll.*
panino imbottito (panino ripieno) *sandwich.*
panna *cream.*
pannello *panel.*
PANNO *cloth, clothes.*
panno di lana *woolen cloth.*
Non vorrei essere nei tuoi panni. *I wouldn't want to be in your shoes.*
panorama, m. *panorama.*
PANTALONI, m. pl. *trousers.*
pantaloni rigati *striped trousers.*
pantofola *slipper.*
papà *dad, father, pop.*
Papa *Pope.*
papavero *poppy.*
pappagallo *parrot.*
paracadute, m. *parachute.*
parafulmine, m. *lightning rod.*
paragonare *to compare.*
paragone, m. *comparison.*
Non c'è paragone. *There's no comparison.*
paragrafo *paragraph.*
paralisi, f. *paralysis.*
paralizzare *to paralyze.*
Mi si è paralizzato il braccio. *My arm has become paralyzed.*
parallelo *parallel; (also adj.).*
parata *parade.*
paravento *screen, wind-screen.*
PARCHEGGIO *parking.*
Vietato il parcheggio! *No Parking.*
parco *park.*
parecchio *a good deal of; a good many; several.*
essere in parecchi *to be several.*
C'erano parecchie persone. *There were a good many people.*
L'ho visto parecchio tempo fa. *I saw him a long time ago.*
PARENTE, m. & f. *relative, kinsman.*
Parenti più stretti *next of kin.*
Egli è senza parenti. *He is without kin.*
parentela *relationship, relatives.*
parentesi, f. *parenthesis.*
fra parentesi *in parenthesis; (fig.) by the way.*
PARERE *to seem.*
A quanto pare... *It seems...*
Mi pare di si. *I think so.*
Mi pare di no. *I think not.*
Pare che sia una buona donna. *She seems to be a good woman.*
Ti pare? *Do you think so?*
parere, m. *opinion, advice, judgment.*
cambiar parere *to change one's opinion.*
Il mio parere è giusto. *My judgment is correct.*

Sono del parere che... *I am of the opinion that...*
PARETE, f. *wall.*
Questo quadro va appeso alla parete. *This picture is to be hung on the wall.*
PARI *equal, even, same.*
numeri pari *even numbers.*
Cammina di pari passo con me. *He walks with even pace with me.*
È arrivato in pari tempo. *He arrived at the same time.*
Egli fu pari alla situazione. *He was equal to the situation.*
Siamo pari. *We are even.*
PARI, noun, m. & f. *peer, equal, par.*
sotto la pari *below par.*
Roma non ha pari. *Rome has no equal.*
Sono i pari del Regno Unito. *They are the peers of the United Kingdom.*
parità *parity, equality.*
a parità di fatti *all things being equal.*
parlamento *Parliament.*
Egli è membro del parlamento. *He is a member of Parliament.*
PARLARE *to speak.*
parlare bene *to speak well.*
parlar male di *to speak ill of.*
Di che parlate? *What are you speaking of?*
La signora ha fatto parlare di se. *The lady has caused much talk.*
Non se ne parli più. *Let us talk no more about it.*
Parliamo di politica! *Let us talk of politics!*
Qui si parla francese. *French is spoken here.*
PAROLA *word.*
Abbiamo avuto parole. *We had words with each other.*
Chiedo la parola. *I ask to speak.*
Do la mia parola. *I give my word.*
Egli è venuto meno alla parola data. *He broke his word.*
Egli s'è rimangiato le parole. *He ate his words.*
È un giuoco di parole. *It is a pun.*
Mi fu tolta la parola. *I was not permitted to speak.*
Non ho parole. *I have no words.*
Rivolgo la parola a te. *I am addressing you.*
parrucca *wig.*
parrucchiere, m. *hairdresser, barber.*
PARTE, f. *part, side, place.*
d'altra parte *on the other hand; on the other side.*
da parte mia *from my point of view; from me.*
da questa parte *on this side; this way.*
la parte del leone *the lion's share.*
parte per parte *bit by bit.*
questa parte del corpo *this part of the body.*
È un caso a parte. *It is a particular case (a thing apart).*
Ha fatto la parte di Othello. *He played the part of Othello.*
Ha messo i libri a parte. *He put the books aside.*
Ha preso la mia parte. *He took my part.*
Ognuno avrà la sua parte. *Each will have his share.*
partecipare *to participate.*
PARTENZA *departure, starting, sailing.*
Ecco il segnale di partenza. *There is the starting signal.*
La mia partenza fu ritardata. *My departure was delayed.*
La partenza del piroscafo è fissata per le tre.

The sailing of the ship is set for three.
particolare *particular, peculiar, special; (also m. noun) detail.*
Ogni particolare è corretto. *It is correct in every detail.*
particolarmente *particularly, in particular.*
PARTIRE *to depart; to set sail; to leave.*
a partire da *beginning from.*
A che ora bisogna partire? *At what time must we leave?*
PARTITA *game, match.*
una partita a scacchi *a game of chess.*
La partita è accomodata. *The question is settled.*
Questa è la partita decisiva. *This is the deciding game.*
PARTITO *party (political).*
il partito del lavoro *the labor party.*
Appartiene al partito d'opposizione. *He belongs to the opposition party.*
È un eccellente partito. *He is an excellent matrimonial prospect.*
prendere un partito *to make up one's mind.*
parziale *partial.*
parzialità *partiality.*
parzialmente *partially.*
pascolo *pastime.*
pasqua *Easter.*
giorno di pasqua *Easter day.*
vacanze di pasqua *Easter holidays.*
vigilia di pasqua *Easter eve.*
passaggio *passage.*
passaporto *passport.*
Mettete il visto sul vostro passaporte. *Have your passport stamped.*
PASSARE *to pass.*
passare attraverso *to pass through.*
passare il peso *to be overweight.*
passare per la bibiloteca *to stop by the library.*
passare un esame *to pass an exam.*
È passato per italiano. *They mistook him for an Italian.*
Il generale passa in rivista le truppe. *The general inspects the troops.*
M'è passato di mente. *It slipped my mind.*
Mio figlio è passato. *My son was promoted (or) my son passed by.*
Non passate i limiti. *Do not overstep the bounds.*
Passate, per favore! *Pass through, please.*
Passiamoci sopra. *Let us dismiss it.*
PASSATO *past; a past time.*
Conosco il suo passato. *I know his (her) past.*
Ha messo una pietra sopra il passato. *He let bygones be bygones.*
Il passato non si distrugge. *The past cannot be undone.*
PASSEGGERO *passenger, traveler.*
PASSEGGERO, adj. *transient, passing.*
È un malessere passeggero. *It is a passing discomfort.*
PASSEGGIARE *to walk.*
Andiamo a passeggio. *Let us go for a walk.*
Me la passeggio tutto il giorno. *I walk all day.*
passeggiata *walk, ride.*
passerella *gangway.*
passero *sparrow.*
passione, f. *passion.*
passivo *passive.*
PASSO *step.*
passo per passo *step by step.*
Bisogna fare passi lunghi. *We must take long steps.*

Essi camminano di pari passo. *They walk at the same pace.*

Non bisogna fare il passo più lungo della gamba. *We must not be over-ambitious.*

Rallentiamo il passo. *Let us slacken our pace.*

Torniamo sui nostri passi. *Let us retrace our steps.*

PASTA *dough, macaroni, pastry.*

pasticcerìa *pastry shop; candy store.*

pasticcio *pie; bungling piece of work; difficulty.*

Non voglio mettermi in un pasticcio. *I don't wish to put myself in a difficult position.*

Questo è un pasticcio. *This is a mess.*

PASTO *meal.*

pasti compresi *meals included.*

E un buon vino da pasto. *It is a good table wine.*

Ho fatto un buon pasto. *I had a good meal.*

Prendiamo i pasti all' osterìa. *We eat our meals at the restaurant.*

PATATA *potato.*

patate lesse *boiled potatoes.*

spirito di patata *poor humor (colloquial).*

patente, f. *patent, diploma, driver's license.*

Ha preso la patente. *He got his license.*

paterno *paternal, fatherly.*

Son tornato alla mia casa paterna. *I returned to my father's home.*

patire *to suffer.*

PATRIA *native country.*

amor di patria *love of mother country.*

ritornare in patria *to go back to one's country.*

patriota, m. *patriot.*

patriottismo *patriotism.*

pattinare *to skate.*

pattino *skate.*

pattino a rotelle *roller-skate.*

PATTO *agreement, term.*

a ressun patto *on no condition; by no means.*

a patto che *on condition that.*

il Patto Atlantico *the Atlantic Pact.*

Facciamo patti chiari. *Let us make clear terms.*

Sono venuti a patti. *They came to terms.*

PAURA *fear, dread, terror, fright.*

aver paura *to be afraid of.*

pausa *pause, rest.*

PAVIMENTO *pavement, floor.*

paziente (adj.) *patient, forbearing; (noun) patient in hospital.*

PAZIENZA *patience.*

mettere a prova la pazienza *to try the patience.*

Abbia pazienza! *Have patience!*

Non perdere la pazienza. *Do not lose your patience.*

Santa Pazienza! *God give me patience!*

pazzo *insane, crazy; (as noun) madman.*

peccato *sin.*

Che peccato! *What a pity!*

pecora *sheep.*

peculiare *peculiar.*

pedale, m. *pedal.*

pedata *kick.*

pedone, m. *pedestrian.*

PEGGIO *worse, worst.*

alla peggio *at the worst.*

Il peggio si è che ... *The worst of it is ...*

Va di male in peggio. *It goes from bad to worse.*

peggiore *worse, worst.*

E il peggiore di tutti. *It is the worst of all.*

pelare *to peel; to strip; to fleece.*

S'è fatto pelare. *He allowed himself to be fleeced.*

PELLE, f. *skin, rind, leather.*

rischiarsi la pelle *to risk one's skin.*

salvarsi la pelle *to save one's skin.*

Ci hanno fatto la pelle. *They killed (skinned, colloq.) him.*

È pelle lucida. *It is patent leather.*

Ha la pelle dura. *He has a thick skin.*

Sono guanti di pelle. *They are kid gloves.*

pelliccia *fur.*

foderato di pelliccia *lined with fur.*

pellicola *film.*

pelo *hair, nap.*

PENA *penalty, punishment, anxiety, pity.*

a mala pena *hardly, scarcely.*

Mi fa pena. *I pity him.*

Vale la pena. *It is worth the trouble.*

pendere *to hang; to hang down; to lean.*

la torre pendente *the leaning tower.*

Pende dalle sue labbra. *He hangs on her words.*

pendìo *the slant; the slope.*

Scende il pendìo. *He goes down the slope.*

PENETRARE *to penetrate; to get into; to enter.*

penisola *peninsula.*

penitenza *penance, penitence.*

Fa penitenza per i suoi peccati. *He is doing penance for his sins.*

PENNA *pen, feather, quill.*

Non sa tenere la penna in mano. *He does not know how to write.*

Mette le penne. *He is growing his feathers.*

pennello *paint brush.*

penoso *painful, difficult.*

PENSARE *to think.*

Pensa agli affari tuoi. *Mind your own business.*

Ripensaci. *Think it over.*

PENSIERO *thought, care.*

È sopra pensiero. *He is worried.*

Ha molti pensieri. *He has many worries.*

Muta pensiero. *Change your mind.*

Non ti dar pensiero. *Don't worry about it.*

Sta in pensiero per qualche cosa. *He is worrying about something.*

PENSIONE, f. *pension; boarding house.*

Quanto si paga per la pensione completa? *How much does one pay for room and board?*

È partita per Roma. *She left for Rome.*

pentir(si) *to repent; to regret.*

pentola *pot, kettle.*

pepe, m. *pepper.*

È pieno di pepe. *He is full of ginger.*

PER *for; by; through; on account of; owing to; to.*

cinque per cento *five per cent.*

una volta e per sempre *once and for all.*

È partita per Roma. *She left for Rome.*

L'ho fatto per te. *I did it for you.*

Lo mando per posta. *I send it by mail.*

Sarò lì per la fine del mese. *I will be there by the end of the month.*

Vado per ferrovìa. *I go by railroad.*

pera *pear.*

percentuale, f. *percentage.*

percepire *to receive; to get.*

PERCHE *why; because; for; as; that; in order that; (as noun) reason.*

Non sa il perchè. *He doesn't know the reason.*

perciò *therefore, so.*

PERDERE *to lose; to miss.*

perdere il treno *to miss the train.*

perdere terreno *to lose ground.*

perdersi *to lose one's self; to be spoiled; to go to ruin.*

perdita *loss, waste.*

PERDONARE *to forgive; to pardon; to excuse.*

È un male che non perdona. *It's an incurable disease.*

Perdonate il distrubo. *Excuse the trouble I'm giving.*

PERDONO *forgiveness, pardon.*

Le chiedo perdono. *I ask your forgiveness.*

perduto *lost, ruined, undone.*

perfetto *perfect.*

PERFEZIONE, f. *perfection, faultlessness.*

Ha raggiunto la perfezione. *He has reached perfection.*

Questo pasto è cotto alla perfezione. *This meal is cooked to perfection.*

perfino *even.*

PERICOLO *danger.*

Si trova in pericolo di vita. *He is in danger of losing his life.*

pericoloso *dangerous.*

periodico *magazine, periodical.*

periodo *period.*

perla *pearl.*

È una perla di marito. *He is the best of husbands.*

permanenza *permanence, stay.*

in permanenza *permanently.*

una lunga permanenza *a long stay.*

PERMESSO *permission, leave, permit, license.*

col vostro permesso *with your permission.*

È in permesso. *He is on leave.*

È permesso. *May I come in?*

permettere *to permit; to allow; to suffer.*

permettersi *to allow oneself; to take the liberty.*

PERO *but, nevertheless, yet, still.*

perossido *peroxide.*

perseguire *to pursue; to continue.*

persistere *to persist.*

PERSONA *person.*

La signora è l'eleganza in persona. *The lady is the personification of elegance.*

Lo conosco in persona. *I know him personally.*

personaggio *character (in a play).*

personale *personal; (as noun, masc.) the staff.*

PERSUADERE *to persuade.*

pesante *heavy.*

PESARE *to weigh.*

Mi pesa sulla coscienza. *It weighs on my conscience.*

Peso le mie parole. *I weigh my words.*

Quel pasto mi pesa sullo stomaco. *The meal weighs on my stomach.*

pesca *peach; the act of fishing.*

pesca della balena *whale-fishing.*

Vado a pesca. *I am going fishing.*

pescare *to fish; to try to find the meaning of.*

Cerco di pescare il significato. *I am trying to find the meaning.*

pescatore, m. *fisherman.*

PESCE, m. *fish.*

Non è nè carne nè pesce. *He is neither fish nor fowl.*

Non so che pesce pigliare. *I don't know which way to turn.*

peso *weight.*

pettegolare *to gossip.*

pettegolo *gossip, tattler.*

pettinare *to comb.*

pettine, m. *comb.*

petto *breast, chest.*

È malato di petto. *He is consumptive.*

Ha un bimbo al petto. *She has a child at her breast.*

PEZZO *piece.*

È tutto di un pezzo. *It's all in one piece.*

L'aspetto da un pezzo. *I've been awaiting for him for some time.*
Lo faccio a pezzi. *I'll break it to pieces.*
PIACERE, m. *pleasure.*
a piacere vostro *as you like it.*
Fammi il piacere... *Do me the kindness...*
Per piacere. *Please.*
PIACERE *to like; to be agreeable.*
Non mi piace. *I do not like it.*
Piace alle masse. *It is liked by the masses.*
PIANGERE *to cry.*
Mi piange il cuore. *My heart cries.*
Piange la morte del suo amico. *He mourns the death of his friend.*
Piange miseria. *He feigns poverty.*
PIANO, noun *piano, plane, plan, floor.*
È un piano orizzontale. *It is an horizontal plane.*
Questo è il mio piano. *This is my plan.*
Sono al secondo piano. *I am on the second floor.*
PIANO, adj. *flat, slow.*
PIANO, adv. *slowly; in a low voice.*
pianoforte, m. *piano.*
pianta *plant.*
piantare *to plant; to place; to leave, quit or abandon.*
Ci piantò. *He left us.*
pianto *weeping, crying.*
pianura *plain.*
piattaforma *platform.*
piattino *saucer.*
piatto *plate; (as adj.) flat.*
PIAZZA *square.*
piazza del mercato *market-place.*
Ha fatto piazza pulita. *He cleared everything away.*
Ha messo tutto in piazza. *He made everything public.*
picche, f. *spade (playing cards).*
picchiare *to beat; to strike.*
PICCOLO *little, small; (as noun) little boy.*
da piccolo *when a little boy.*
PIEDE, m. *foot.*
prendare piede *to gain ground.*
Sto in piedi. *I will stand.*
Tiene il piede in due staffe. *He keeps in with both sides.*
Vado a piedi. *I will walk there.*
Vado a piedi nudi. *I go barefoot.*
piegare *to fold; to bow; to bend.*
pieno *full.*
di pieno inverno *in the heart of winter.*
pieno fino all' orlo *full to the brim.*
PIETA *mercy, pity, piety, devotion.*
pietanza *dish of food.*
pietra *stone.*
pigione, f. *rent.*
pigliare *to take; to catch.*
pigro *lazy.*
pila *pile, battery.*
pillola *pill.*
pinze, f. pl. *tongs.*
pioggia *rain.*
piombatura *filling.*
piombo *lead.*
PIOVERE *to rain.*
Piove a dirotto. *It is raining heavily.*
Sta per piovere. *It is about to rain.*
pipa *pipe.*
piroscafo *steamer.*
piscina *swimming-pool.*
pittore, m. *painter.*
pittura *painting.*

PIÙ *more, most.*
a più non posso *to the utmost.*
mai più *never again.*
molto di più *much more.*
per lo più *for the most part.*
sempre più *more and more.*
tutt'al più *at the most; at most.*
La vidi più volte. *I saw her several times.*
piuma *feather.*
piuttosto *rather.*
pizzicare *to pinch; to prick.*
platea *orchestra seats.*
plurale, m. *plural.*
pneumatico *tire.*
pochino *rather little; very little; short time; little while.*
POCO *little; a short time; a little while.*
fra poco *in a little while.*
poco a poco *little by little.*
poco fa *a short while ago.*
podere, m. *farm.*
poema, m. *poem.*
poesìa *poetry; short poem.*
poeta, m. *poet.*
POI *then, afterwards.*
da ora in poi *from now on.*
prima o poi *now or later.*
E poi? *and then?*
POICHE *for, as, since, because.*
politica *politics.*
politico *political, politic.*
polizìa *police.*
poliziotto *policeman.*
pòlizza *policy.*
pòlizza d'assicurazione contro gl'incendi *fire insurance.*
pòllice *thumb; big toe.*
POLLO *fowl, chicken.*
pollo arrosto *roast chicken.*
brodo di pollo *chicken broth.*
polmonite, f. *pneumonia.*
polso *wrist.*
PÒLVERE, f. *dust, powder.*
caffè in pòlvere *ground coffee.*
pòlvere da fucile *gun powder.*
zucchero in pòlvere *powdered sugar.*
Gettano la pòlvere negli occhi della gente. *They throw dust into the eyes of the people.*
S'innalzò una nube di pòlvere quando partì l'automobile. *A cloud of dust went up as the automobile left.*
pomodoro *tomato.*
salsa di pomodoro *tomato sauce.*
pompelmo *grapefruit.*
pompiere, m. *fireman.*
PONTE, m. *bridge.*
ponte di barche *bridge of boats.*
ponte ferroviario *railway bridge.*
ponte levatoio *draw bridge.*
popolazione, f. *population, people.*
POPOLO *people, mob.*
porco *pig.*
PORGERE *to give; to offer; to hand.*
Mi porge la sua mano. *He offers me his hand.*
Porgimi aiuto. *Give me your aid.*
Porgimi ascolto. *Listen to me. (Lend me your ears.)*
Porgo il mio braccio alla signora. *I offer the lady my arm.*
Se si porge l'occasione, gli parlerò. *If the opportunity arises, I will speak to him.*
porre *to place; to put.*
PORTA *door.*

Accompagnalo alla porta! *See him to the door.*
È entrato dalla porta principale ed è uscito dalla porta secondaria. *He entered by the front door and left by the back door.*
Si chiude una porta, se ne apre un'altra. *One opportunity is lost, but another presents itself.*
portabile *portable.*
portacenere, m. *ashtray.*
portamonete, m. *purse.*
PORTARE *to carry; to bring; to wear; to bear.*
Il passaporto porta la mia firma. *The passport bears my signature.*
Il vecchio porta bene gli anni. *The old man carries his years very well.*
La signora porta bene quel cappotto. *The lady wears that coat well.*
Mi porto abbastanza bene. *I feel rather well.*
Porta il documento con te. *Carry the document with you.*
Porta quest' anello alla signora. *Take (carry) this ring to the lady.*
Una grave malattìa lo portò via. *A serious illness carried him away.*
portata *range.*
a portata di braccio *within arm's length.*
PORTO *harbor, refuge, port, haven.*
porto affrancato *postage prepaid.*
È il Capitano di porto. *He is the harbor-master.*
Cerco un porto di pace. *I seek a haven of rest.*
Condusse in porto la sua missione. *He accomplished his mission.*
portone, m. *gate.*
posare *to place.*
POSITIVO *positive.*
Cio è positivo. *That is for sure.*
POSIZIONE, f. *position, situation.*
La mia casa è in eccellente posizione riguardo il sole. *My house in an excellent situation as far as the sun goes.*
Mi trovo in posizione di reclamare i miei diritti. *I am in a position to demand my rights.*
POSSEDERE *to own; to possess; to have.*
Possiede molto denaro e molte buone qualità. *He has much money and many fine qualities.*
possessione, f. *possession.*
POSSIBILE *possible.*
Al più presto possibile me ne andrò. *At the earliest possible I will go.*
possibilità *possibility, power.*
Si presentano diverse possibilità eppur non abbiamo la possibilità di farlo. *Many possibilities present themselves and yet we don't have the power to carry them out.*
POSTA *post, mail, stall, stake.*
È partito a bella posta. *He left purposely.*
L'animale è nella sua posta. *The animal is in its stall.*
L'ho ricevuto per posta aerea. *I received it by air mail.*
Mandalo per posta. *Send it by mail.*
Parla al direttore delle poste. *Speak to the postmaster.*
Raddoppiate la posta su questa corsa. *Double your stake on this race.*
POSTALE *postal; of the post.*
casella postale *post-office box.*
pacco postale *parcel.*
spese postali *postage.*
timbro postale *postmark.*
ufficio postale *post office.*
vaglia postale *money order.*
Mi mandi una cartolina postale di Roma. *Send me a picture postcard of Rome.*

posterità *posterity.*

postino *postman.*

POSTO *place, spot, space, situation, post, seat.*
Cambiamo posto. *Let's change seats.*
Ecco un posto libero. *Here is a vacant spot.*
Ho un posto riservato. *I have a reserved seat.*
Mi sento fuori posto qui. *I feel out of place here.*
Non c'è posto per tutti e due. *There is no room for both.*
Prendete i vostri posti. *Take your places (seats).*
Ha trovato un ottimo posto a Milano. *He found a fine position (job) in Milano.*

potente *powerful, mighty, influential.*

potenza *power, might.*
Le grandi potenze hanno sempre la grande potenza militare e navale. *The great powers usually have military and naval power.*

POTERE, m. *power.*
Gli hanno accordato pieni poteri. *They have accorded him full powers.*
Ha il potere di un re. *He has the power of a king.*
Il partito che è ora in potere cercherà di restare in potere. *The party that is now in power will seek to remain in power.*

POTERE *to be able; to be allowed; to be permitted; could; may; might.*
Ho tentato a più non posso. *I tried to my utmost.*
Non ne posso più. *I can't stand it anymore.*
Non posso farci nulla. *I can't help it.*
Non potei salvarlo perchè non potei parlare. *I could not save him because I was not permitted to speak.*
può darsi; può essere; potrebbe succedere. *It could happen; it might be; it could occur.*
Spero ch'egli possa arrivare, ma potrebbe aver perso il treno. *I hope he may arrive, but he might have missed the train.*

POVERO *poor, unfortunate, unhappy, humble, late (deceased).*
il mio povero parere *my humble opinion.*
la mia povera sorella *my late sister.*
La nazione è povera di materie prime. *The nation is poor in raw materials.*

povertà *poverty.*

pozzo *well, tank.*

PRANZO *dinner, meal.*
Ho fatto un buon pranzo. *I had a good meal.*

pratica *practice, experience, training.*
Devo fare le pratiche per poter partire. *I must take the necessary steps in order to leave.*
Ha fatto una lunga pratica per diventare avvocato. *He had a long training to become a lawyer.*
Ha molta pratica del suo mestiere. *He knows his job.*
Ho messo in pratica i suoi consigli. *I put your advice into practice.*
La pratica è la migliore maestra. *Practice is the best teacher.*
Mettiamo in pratica le nostre idee. *Let us put our ideas into practice.*
Preferisco la pratica alla teorìa. *I prefer practice to theory.*

pràtico *practical, experienced.*
Non sono pratico di quel luogo. *I do not know that place.*

precauzione, f. *precaution, care, caution.*
Procedi con molta precauzione. *Proceed with great caution.*
Usa Precauzioni! *Use Caution!*

precedente, adj. *preceding, previous, former; (as m. noun) precedent.*
La sua azione è senza precedenti. *His action is without precedent.*

precedere *to precede; to go before.*
Cosa precede? *What goes first?*
Precedimi! *Go first!*

precipizio *precipice.*
Corre a precipizio. *He runs headlong.*
Si troverà sull'orlo del precipizio. *He will find himself on the edge of a precipice.*

preciso *precise, punctual, accurate, exact.*
Bisogna trovare il momento preciso. *We must find the precise moment.*
Egli è preciso nei pagamenti. *He is punctual in his payments.*

prèdica *sermon, lecture.*

predicare *to preach; to lecture.*
Egli prèdica bene e razzola male. *He does not practice what he preaches.*

preferenza *preference.*
Do la preferenza all' aeroplano anzicchè al treno. *I prefer the airplane rather than the train.*
Egli ha la preferenza su tutti gli altri. *He is preferred to all the others.*
Scelgo la rosa a preferenza del garofano. *I pick the rose rather than the carnation.*

PREGARE *to pray; to request; to beg; to ask; to invite.*
Pregate Iddio! *Pray to God!*
Prego! *Please! (or) You are welcome!*
Sono pregati di entrare. *Please enter.*
La prego di considerare. *I beg you to consider.*

preghiera *prayer, entreaty, request.*
Dice le preghiere. *She says her prayers.*
Dopo le mie preghiere, accettò l'invito. *After my entreaties, he accepted the invitation.*
Ho una preghiera da farle. *I have a request to make of you.*

pregio *merit, worth.*

pregiudizio *prejudice.*

prelibato *exquisite.*

PREMERE *to press; to be urgent (or pressing).*
Egli preme la mano della Duchessa. *He presses the Duchess' hand.*
Mi preme molto. *It is of urgent importance to me.*
Non mi preme. *It is of no importance to me.*

PREMIO *prize, premium.*
Gli conferirono il primo premio. *They conferred the first prize on him.*

PREMURA *care; careful attention; kindness; hurry.*
Ho molta premura. *I am in a great hurry.*
Mi fa premura di lasciarlo. *He beseeches me to leave him.*
Non c'è premura! *There is no hurry.*
Una madre ha molte premure per il suo bambino. *A mother has many cares for her child.*
La ringrazio delle sue premure. *I thank you for your kindnesses.*

PRENDERE *to take; to catch; to take lodgings; to seize.*
prendere marito; prendere moglie *to get married.*
prendere volo *to take off.*
Che cosa ti prende? *What is the matter with you?*
Entrò, prese atto e poi prese congedo. *He entered, took notice and then took leave.*
Fu preso dal rimorso. *He was overtaken with remorse.*
L'ha preso in parola e decise di prendere la sinistra. *He took him at his word and decided to turn to the left.*

Lo prese a benvolere. *He took a liking to him.*
Lo prese per il collo e poi per i capelli. *He seized him by the neck and then by the hair.*
Non mi prendo questa libertà. *I will not take this liberty.*
Prende fuoco! *It is catching fire!*
Prendi partito con me o con lui? *Are you siding with me or with him?*
Prendo il treno delle tre. *I am taking the three o'clock train.*
Prese tutto in considerazione. *He took everything into consideration.*
Se la presa col facchino. *He put the blame on the porter.*
Se ti prendo! *If I catch you! (colloq.)*
Sto prendendo un raffreddore. *I am catching a cold.*

PREPARARE *to prepare.*
preparare un pasto, un discorso, un viaggio *to prepare a meal, a speech, a trip.*
prepararsi per un emergenza *to prepare oneself for an emergency.*
Preparati o fai tardi! *Get ready or you'll be late!*

prepotente *tyrannical.*

PRESENTARE *to present; to introduce.*
Egli si presenta bene. *He makes a good impression (presents himself well).*
Il viaggio presenta delle difficoltà. *The trip presents some difficulties.*
Mi fu già presentato. *He has already been introduced to me.*
Presentateglie i miei ossequi. *Give him my best regards.*
Quando si presenta l'occasione, bisogna prenderla. *When the opportunity presents itself, one must take it.*
Questi problemi si presentano più volte. *These problems occur often.*

presente *present.*
tempo presente *present time; present tense.*
tener presente *to bear in mind.*

presenza *presence.*
fare atto di presenza *to put in an appearance.*
Non è qui in presenza attuale ma in presenza di spirito. *He is not here in person but he is here in spirit.*
Non parlò in presenza del presidente. *He did not speak in the presence of the president.*

PRESSO *near, by, beside, with.*
presso a poco *nearby, about.*
presso la fontana *near the fountain.*
qui presso *nearby.*
Il vecchio è presso a morire. *The old man is near death.*
Indirizza la lettera al Signor Berti, presso il Signor Augusti. *Address the letter to Mr. Berti, in care of Mr. Augusti.*
Vivo presso mio zio. *I live with my uncle.*

PRESTARE *to lend; to give; to offer.*
prestare attenzione *to pay attention.*
prestare conforto *to offer comfort.*
Egli si presta volentieri. *He offers himself willingly.*
Non mi presto all'inganno. *I will not consent to this fraud.*

prestito *loan.*

PRESTO *soon, early.*
al più presto possibile *as soon as possible.*
Fa presto! *Hurry up!*
M'alzo presto. *I get up early.*
Presto o tardi lo sapremo. *We'll know sooner or later.*

Si fa presto a dire. *It is easy to say.*
prete *priest.*
pretendere *to pretend; to claim; to exact.*
Cosa pretendete? *What do you want (claim, or exact)?*
Non bisogna pretendere l'impossibile. *One must not exact the impossible.*
Pretende al trono. *He has claims on the throne.*
Pretende d'aver detto il vero. *He claims to have told the truth.*
pretesa *pretension; claim to.*
La moglie ha pretese d'eleganze, mentre il marito non ha pretese affatto. *The wife has pretensions of great elegance, while the husband has no pretensions at all.*
Non bisogna considerare la sua pretesa. *We must not consider his claim.*
pretesto *pretext.*
prevedere *to foresee.*
prezioso *precious.*
PREZZO *price.*
Il listino dei prezzi da il prezzo all' ingrosso, il prezzo al minuto ed il prezzo netto. *The price list gives the wholesale price, the retail and the net price.*
Il prezzo corrente non è prezzo fisso; può diventare prezzo alto o basso. *The current price is not stable; it can go up or down.*
Quella lezione l'ho pagata a caro prezzo. *I learned that lesson the hard way (at a high price).*
prigione, f. *prison.*
PRIMA, noun *first class (in travel); first grade (in school); first performance.*
PRIMA *before, once, formerly, earlier, first.*
per prima cosa *first.*
prima di tutto *first of all.*
Alzati prima. *Get up earlier.*
Avvisatelo prima di arrivare. *Warn him before arriving.*
Da prima mi fece una buona impressione. *At first he made a good impression on me.*
Non sono più quella di prima. *I am no longer my former self.*
Prima o poi ci arriveremo. *Sooner or later we'll get there.*
Quanto prima, viaggeremo in prima. *Pretty soon we will be traveling first class.*
Questa era prima una chiesa e poi una cattedrale. *This was first a church and then a cathedral.*
Siamo più nemici di prima. *We are more enemies than we were.*
primavera *spring, springtime.*
È nella primavera della sua vita. *He is in the springtime (prime) of his life.*
PRIMO *first.*
Arrivò primo. *He arrived first.*
È il primo della classe. *He is the best in the class.*
È il primo in fila. *He is the first in line.*
Fu il primo a partire. *He was the first to leave.*
Ritornerà al primo del mese. *He will return the first of the month.*
principale, adj. *principal, chief, main; (as noun, m.) principal, employer, master.*
principalmente *chiefly, mainly.*
principe, m. *prince.*
PRINCIPIO *beginning, principle.*
dal principio alla fine *from beginning to end.*
È questione di principio. *It's a matter of principle.*
privare *to deprive.*

Mi sono privato di tutto. *I deprived myself of everything.*
Non mi privi del piacere. *Don't deprive me of the pleasure.*
privo *devoid; lacking in.*
privo di mezzi finanziari *lacking financial means.*
privo di senso comune *devoid of common sense.*
Sono privo di notizie da due mesi. *I have been without news for two months.*
prò *profit, advantage, benefit.*
a prò di *for the benefit of.*
A che prò? *What for?*
probabile *probable, likely.*
il costo probabile *the probable cost.*
Non è probabile ch' io venga questa sera. *I am not likely to come tonight.*
probabilmente *probably.*
Probabilmente verrò. *I'll probably come.*
problema, m. *problem.*
un problema di carattere personale *a personal problem.*
PROCEDERE *to proceed; to go on.*
Il lavoro procede molto lentamente. *The work is going on very slowly.*
La neve ci impedisce di procedere. *The snow makes it impossible for us to proceed.*
Procediamo con calma. *Let us proceed calmly.*
procedere, m. *conduct, passing.*
col procedere degli anni *with the passing years.*
Il suo procedere sorprese tutti. *His conduct surprised everyone.*
procedura *procedure.*
procedura legale *legal procedure.*
processo *process, trial.*
processo per assassinio *murder trial.*
L'orfanotrofio è in processo di costruzione. *The orphanage is in the process of construction.*
prodigare *to lavish.*
Mi ha prodigato le sue cure con affetto. *He lavished his cares on me affectionately.*
prodigioso *prodigious.*
PRODOTTO *product.*
prodotti agricoli *agricultural products.*
PRODURRE *to produce; to cause.*
produrre una reazione *to cause a reaction.*
Egli produce articoli di lusso. *He produces luxury items.*
produzione, f. *production.*
professionale *professional.*
professione, f. *profession.*
professore, m. *professor.*
profitto *profit, benefit.*
profondo *deep, profound.*
a notte profonda *in the deep of night.*
cadere in sonno profondo *to fall into a deep sleep.*
profondo rispetto *profound respect.*
profumare *to perfume.*
profumarsi *to put perfume on.*
profumato *scented, sweet-smelling.*
profumo *perfume.*
progettare *to project; to make plans.*
progetto *plan.*
aver in mente un progetto *to have a plan in mind.*
fare progetti *to make plans.*
programma, m. *program.*
in programma *on the program.*
progredire *to make progress.*
progresso *progress.*

Egli sta facendo grandi progressi negli studi. *He is making great progress in his studies.*
proibire *to forbid; to prohibit.*
È proibito l'ingresso. *No admittance.*
Mio madre mi ha proibito di uscire questa sera. *My mother has forbidden me to go out tonight.*
prole, f. *descent, offspring.*
promessa *promise.*
fare una promessa *to make a promise.*
venire meno ad una promessa *to break a promise.*
promettere *to promise.*
prometto di scriverti spesso. *I promise I'll write often.*
prominente *prominent.*
Egli è una figura prominente nel mondo scientifico. *He is a prominent figure in the world of science.*
prominenza *prominence.*
promuovere *to promote; to further.*
pronipote *great-grandchild, m. & f.*
pronome, m. *pronoun.*
prontezza *readiness, promptness.*
prontezza di spirito *presence of mind.*
pronti! (or **pronto!**) *Hello!* (answering phone).
pronto *ready, prompt.*
in attesa di una sua pronta risposta *awaiting your prompt reply.*
Siamo pronti! *We are ready!*
pronunciare *to pronounce; to utter.*
Rimase lì senza pronunciare parola. *He just stayed there without saying a word.*
pronunciare bene *to pronounce well; to have good diction.*
propaganda *advertising.*
far molta propaganda *to advertise well.*
proporre *to propose.*
proporzione, f. *proportion.*
fuori proporzione *out of proportion.*
PROPOSITO *purpose, intention.*
a proposito *by the way.*
di cattivi propositi *with bad intentions.*
di proposito *on purpose.*
A che proposito te ne ha parlato? *In connection with what did he speak to you about it?*
proposta *proposal, proposition.*
proprietà *property, ownership.*
La casa è di sua proprietà. *The house is hers.*
Questo libro è proprietà mia. *This book is my property.*
proprietario *proprietor, owner.*
PROPRIO *own; one's own.*
la propria casa *one's own home.*
nome proprio *proper noun.*
Veste con un gusto che le è proprio. *She dresses with a taste that is all her own.*
PROPRIO, adv. *just, exactly.*
proprio in questo momento *in this very moment.*
proprio mentre *just as.*
proprio ora *just now.*
È proprio come dico io. *It is exactly as I say.*
Proprio! *Exactly!*
prosciutto *ham.*
proseguire *to go on; to continue.*
Da Napoli proseguimmo per Roma. *From Naples we went on to Rome.*
prosperità *prosperity.*
prospero *prosperous.*
PROSSIMO *next, near.*
in un prossimo futuro *in the near future.*
la settimana prossima *next week.*
Siamo prossimi a partire. *We are about to go.*
PROTEGGERE *to protect; to safeguard.*

Ognuno cerca di proteggere i propri interessi. *Everyone tries to protect his own interests.*
Ti protegga Iddio! *May God protect you!*
protesta *protest, protestation.*
fare protesta *to protest; to make a protest.*
proteste d'affetto *protestations of affection.*
protestare *to protest.*
protestare contro *to protest against.*
protetto *protected.*
protezione, f. *protection.*
PROVA *proof, rehearsal, trial.*
fare una prova *to try; to rehearse.*
fino a prova contraria *till there is proof to the contrary.*
fornire le prove *to furnish evidence.*
Ha dato prova di coraggio. *He gave proof of courage.*
provare *to prove; to try; to rehearse.*
provare la verità *to prove the truth.*
Vogliamo provare questa scena? *Shall we rehearse this scene?*
Voglio provare a farlo. *I want to try to do it.*
provenire *to originate; to come from.*
proverbio *proverb, saying.*
come dice il proverbio *as the saying goes.*
provocare *to provoke.*
provvedere *to provide; to supply.*
Bisogna provvedere ai bisognosi. *We must provide for the needy.*
Ci siamo provvisti di tutto il necessario. *We have provided ourselves with all the necessities.*
provvidenza *providence.*
Divina Provvidenza *Divine Providence.*
provvisoriamente *temporarily.*
provvisorio *temporary.*
un alloggio provvisorio *a temporary abode.*
provvista *supply.*
Abbiamo un'ottima provvista di viveri in casa. *We have ample supply of foodstuffs in the house.*
prudente *prudent, wise.*
Non credo sia prudente uscire di casa con questo temporale. *I don't think it wise to go out in this storm.*
prudenza *prudence, wisdom.*
dimostrare prudenza *to display prudence.*
PUBLICARE *to publish.*
pubblico, noun *audience, public.*
esibirsi in pubblico *to appear in public.*
Il pubblico lo applaudì calorosamente. *The audience applauded him warmly.*
PUBBLICO, adj. *public.*
giardino pubblico *park; public garden.*
pugno *fist, punch.*
dare un pugno *to punch.*
di proprio pugno *in one's own handwriting.*
fare a pugni *to fight.*
stringere i pugni *to clench one's fists.*
un pugno di terra *a fistful of earth.*
pulce, f. *flea.*
pulcino *chick.*
PULIRE *to clean.*
pulirsi *to clean oneself.*
pulito *clean.*
con la coscienza pulita *with a clear conscience.*
pulizia *cleanliness.*
fare la pulizia *to do the cleaning.*
PUNGERE *to prick; to sting.*
Mi ha punto un' ape. *A bee stung me.*
Mi sono punta un dito con una spilla. *I pricked my finger with a pin.*

punire *to punish.*
punizione, f. *punishment.*
subire una punizione *to endure punishment.*
PUNTA *point, tip.*
fare una punta a un lapis *to sharpen a pencil.*
Cammino in punta di piedi per non fare rumore. *I'm tiptoeing not to make noise.*
Il suo nome è sulla punta della mia lingua. *His name is on the tip of my tongue.*
punto *stitch, point.*
alle tre in punto *at three o'clock sharp.*
due punti *colon.*
di punto in bianco *all of a sudden.*
fare i punti a mano *to stitch by hand.*
fino a un certo punto *to a certain extent.*
mettere in punto l'orologio *to set one's watch.*
mettere i punti sugl' i *to dot one's i's; to get things straight.*
punto di partenza *point of departure.*
punto di vista *point of view.*
punto e virgola *semicolon.*
punto fermo *period.*
venire al punto *to come to the point.*
puntuale *punctual.*
puntualità *punctuality.*
purchè *provided that.*
PURE *also, too.*
Andiamo pure noi. *We are going too.*
Venga pure! *Do come!*
puro *pure, mere.*
acqua pura *pure water.*
per puro caso *by mere chance.*
PURTROPPO *unfortunately.*

Q

QUÀ *here.*
Vieni quà! *Come here!*
quaderno *notebook.*
quadrato, adj. *square.*
quadri, m. *diamond (playing cards).*
quadro, noun *square picture.*
A quale parete vuole che appenda questo quadro? *On which wall do you want this picture hung?*
QUAGGIÙ *here below; down here.*
Guarda quaggiù, in fondo alla pagina. *Look down here, at the bottom of the page.*
Ti aspetto quaggiù, ai piedi della scala. *I'll wait for you here below, at the foot of the stairs.*
qualche *some, any.*
qualcheduno *someone, somebody.*
qualcuno *somebody, someone, anybody.*
QUALE *which, who, whom.*
Quale scegli? *Which do you choose?*
Le persone alle quali hai esteso l'invito sono arrivate. *The people to whom you have extended an invitation have arrived.*
qualità *quality.*
qualsìasi *any.*
qualunque *whatever, any.*
QUANDO *when, while.*
da quando *since.*
di quando in quando *from time to time.*
quando mai *whenever.*
Quando sei arrivato? *When did you arrive?*
Ti scrissi quand'ero in Italia. *I wrote you while I was in Italy.*
quantità *quantity.*
QUANTO,-A,-I,-E *how much; how many; as many as.*
quanto prima *in a short while.*
Me ne dia quanti ne ha. *Give me as many as you have.*
Quanti ne vuole? *How many do you want?*

Quanto mi fa pagare? *How much will you charge me?*
Quanto tempo? *How long?*
quaranta *forty.*
quarantesimo *fortieth.*
quaresima *Lent.*
quarto *fourth, quarter, half-pint.*
trequarti *three-fourths.*
un quarto di vino *half a pint of wine.*
un quarto d'ora *a quarter of an hour.*
quartiere, m. *quarter, lodging, neighborhood.*
QUASI *almost.*
QUASSÙ *up here.*
quattordicesimo *fourteenth.*
quattordici *fourteen.*
quattro *four.*
quattrocento *four hundred.*
nel Quattrocento *in the fifteenth century (Italian Renaissance).*
quattromila *four thousand.*
quello *that one; that.*
Mi dia quello. *Give me that one.*
Quel libro mi appartiene. *That book belongs to me.*
questione, f. *question, argument.*
questo *this; this one.*
Questo non è affare mio. *This is none of my business.*
questura *police-station.*
QUI *here; in this place.*
Qui non c'è nessuno. *There is no one here.*
Vieni qui! *Come here!*
quietare *to calm; to quiet.*
quietarsi *to become calm; to become quiet.*
quiete, f. *quiet, tranquillity, stillness.*
quieto *quiet, calm, still.*
star quieto *to be still; to be quiet.*
QUINDI *therefore.*
quindicesimo *fifteenth.*
quindici *fifteen.*
quindicimila *fifteen thousand.*
quintale, m. *one hundred kilograms in weight.*
Ho un quintale di lavoro da fare. *I have a tremendous amount of work to do.*
quinto *fifth; (as noun) one fifth.*
quotidiano *daily.*
giornale quotidiano *daily paper.*
pane quotidiano *daily bread.*

R

rabbia *rage, ire.*
rabbioso *irate, wrathful.*
racchiudere *to contain; to enclose.*
raccogliere *to gather; to collect.*
raccolta *harvest, collection.*
raccomandare *to recommend.*
lettera raccomandata *registered letter.*
raccomandarsi a *to appeal to.*
raccontare *to tell; to narrate.*
Mi ha raccontato la storia della sua vita. *He told me the story of his life.*
racconto *story.*
raddolcire *to sweeten.*
raddoppiare *to double.*
Gli hanno raddoppiato lo stipendio. *They doubled his salary.*
radere *to shave.*
farsi radere la barba *to get a shave.*
radice, f. *root, origin.*
radio, f. *radio;* m. *radium.*
radiocopia *X-ray.*
rado *rare.*
di rado *seldom.*

raffinare *to refine.*
  una persona raffinata *a refined person.*
raffreddare *to cool; to chill.*
  raffreddarsi *to catch cold.*
raffreddore, m. *cold.*
ragazza *girl*
  nome di ragazza *maiden name.*
RAGAZZO *boy; young man.*
raggiante *radiant.*
  La sposa era raggiante. *The bride was radiant.*
raggio *ray.*
  un raggio di sole *a ray of sunshine.*
raggiungere *to reach; to arrive; to catch up with.*
  raggiungere una destinazione *to reach a destination.*
  raggiungere una meta *to reach a goal.*
  Era partito prima di me ma l'ho raggiunto. *He had left before me but I caught up with him.*
ragionare *to reason; to discuss logically.*
  Ognuno ragiona a modo proprio. *Each person reasons in his own way.*
  Egli non ragiona. *He is not logical; he has lost his reason.*
RAGIONE, f. *reason.*
  a ragione del vero *in truth.*
  a torto o a ragione *right or wrong.*
  aver ragione *to be right.*
  senza ragione *without reason.*
  Ho le mie buone ragioni. *I have my good reasons.*
  Non ha nessuna ragione di farlo. *He has no reason to do it.*
ragionevole *reasonable.*
ragionevolmente *reasonably.*
ragioniere, m. *bookkeeper.*
ragno *spider.*
rallegrare *to cheer; to make gay.*
  Me ne rallegro! *I am happy about it!*
  Si è rallegrato con me. *Ile extended his felicitations to me. He congratulated me.*
rallentare *to loosen; to slow down.*
  rallentare la stretta *to lessen the grip.*
  rallentare la velocità *to reduce speed.*
rame, m. *copper.*
rammaricar(si) *to grieve.*
rammentare *to remember.*
  Me ne rammento perfettamente. *I remember perfectly well.*
ramo *branch.*
  in ogni ramo della scienza *in every branch of science.*
  ramo d'albero *branch of a tree.*
rancore, m. *resentment.*
  serbar rancore a *to bear a grudge against.*
rannuvolare *to cloud over; to darken.*
  Il cielo si rannuvola. *The sky is clouding.*
  Si è rannuvolato in viso. *His expression darkened.*
ranocchio *frog.*
RAPIDO *rapid, speedy.*
  dare uno sguardo rapido *to give a quick glance.*
  treno rapido *express train.*
rapportare *to report; to repeat.*
  Non è bello rapportare tutto ciò che si vede e si sente. *It is not nice to repeat everything one sees and hears.*
rapporto *report.*
  Mi ha mandato un rapporto sul lavoro compiuto. *He sent me a report on the completed work.*
rappresaglia *reprisal.*
rappresentante, m. *representative.*
rappresentare *to represent.*
rappresentazione, f. *representation, performance.*

È la prima rappresentazione di questo dramma. *This is the first performance of this play.*
raramente *rarely.*
raro *rare; uncommon.*
raso *satin.*
rasoio *razor.*
  lametta da rasoio *razor blade.*
rassegnazione, f. *self-resignation, resignation.*
rassicurare *to reassure.*
  rassicurarsi *to reassure oneself.*
rassicurazione, f. *reassurance.*
rassomiglianza *resemblance.*
rastrello *rake.*
rata *installment.*
rattristare *to sadden.*
rauco *hoarse.*
razionale *rational.*
razione, f. *ration.*
razza *race.*
razzo *rocket.*
re *king.*
reagire *to react.*
reale *royal, real.*
  in vita reale *in real life.*
  la casa reale *the Royal House.*
  un avvenimento reale *a true happening.*
realmente *really.*
reato *crime.*
reazione, f. *reaction.*
recare *to bring.*
recensire *to review (a play, a book, a performance).*
recente *recent.*
recinto *enclosure.*
recipiente, m. *receptacle.*
reciproco *reciprocal.*
recitare *to recite; to play.*
recluta *recruit.*
redazione, f. *editor's office.*
redimere *to redeem.*
reduce, m. *veteran.*
regalare *to make a present.*
regalo *gift, present.*
  fare un regalo a *to give a present to.*
reggimento *regiment.*
reggiseno *brassiere.*
regina *queen.*
regione, f. *region.*
registrare *to register; to record.*
registrazione, f. *registration, recording.*
registro *book, register.*
regno *realm, kingdom.*
regola *rule, regulation.*
  secondo la regola *according to regulations.*
  L'eccezione conferma la regola. *The exception proves the rule.*
regolare *regular.*
regolare *to regulate.*
  regolare un conto *to pay a bill.*
  regolarsi *to behave.*
regolarmente *regularly.*
relativamente *relatively.*
relativo *relative.*
relazione, f. *report, relation.*
  fare una relazione *to make a report.*
  Non c'è relazione fra una cosa e l'altra. *There's no relation between one thing and the other.*
religione, f. *religion.*
religioso *religious.*
remare *to row.*
remo *oar.*
remoto *remote.*

rendere *to render; to make; to return.*
  rendere bene per male *to render good for evil.*
  rendere grazie *to thank.*
  rendere infelice *to make unhappy.*
  Mi ha reso il libro. *He returned the book to me.*
  Questo lavoro non rende molto. *There is little return for this work.*
rene, m. *kidney.*
reparto *department.*
  capo reparto *department head.*
repressione, f. *repression.*
reprimenda *reprimand.*
reprimere *to repress.*
  reprimere uno sbadiglio *to stifle a yawn.*
  reprimersi *to contain oneself.*
  Non riesco a reprimere le lacrime. *I can't hold back the tears.*
repubblica *republic.*
reputazione, f. *reputation.*
  godere di un ottima reputazione *to have a good reputation.*
resa *surrender.*
residente *resident; (also noun, m.).*
residenza *residence.*
  cambiamento di residenza *change of address.*
resistente *resistant.*
resistere *to resist; to withstand.*
  resistere alla prova *to withstand the test.*
  resistere alla avversità *to resist against adversity.*
respingere *to drive back; to reject.*
  respingere il nemico *to drive back the enemy.*
  Ha respinto la mia domanda. *He rejected my application.*
respirare *to breathe; to take a breath.*
  respirare a pieni polmoni *to take a deep breath.*
respiro *breath.*
  avere il respiro corto *to be out of breath.*
  tenere il respiro *to hold one's breath.*
responsabile *responsible.*
responsabilità *responsibility.*
RESTARE *to remain; to stay.*
  restare a pranzo *to stay to dinner.*
  restare indietro *to lag behind.*
  Non restano che due giorni alla partenza. *There are only two days left before our departure.*
restituire *to give back; to return.*
  restituire il saluto *to greet in return.*
  Devo restituire questo libro. *I must return this book.*
RESTO *remainder, rest, change.*
  Il resto del lavoro lo finisco io. *I will finish the remainder of the work.*
  Il resto non conta. *The rest is of no matter.*
  Potete tenere il resto. *You may keep the change.*
restringere *to contract; to shrink.*
rete, f. *net.*
  cadere in una rete *to fall into a trap.*
  rete da tennis *tennis net.*
  rete per i capelli *hair net.*
retrocedere *to go back; to retreat.*
rettificare *to rectify.*
rialzare *to lift up again; to rise.*
  rialzare i prezzi *to raise the prices.*
riassunto *summary.*
ribalta *footlight.*
ribasso *decline, reduction.*
ribelle, m. *rebel.*
ribellione, f. *rebellion.*
ricambiare *to reciprocate; to return.*
ricchezza *wealth.*
riccio *curl.*
ricco *rich, wealthy.*

ricerca   research, demand.
andare alla ricerca di   to go in search of.
Non c'è ricerca per questo articolo.   There is no demand for this article.
RICETTA   prescription, recipe.
Porta questa ricetta al farmacista.   Take this prescription to the druggist.
Questa è la ricetta per fare il ragù.   This is the recipe for making sauce.
RICEVERE   to receive.
ricevere ospiti   to receive guests.
ricevere posta   to receive mail.
ricevimento   reception.
ricevitore, m.   receiver.
staccare il ricevitore   to lift the receiver.
ricevuta   receipt.
richiedente, m.   applicant.
RICHIEDERE   to request; to ask again; to require.
Ho richiesto i soldi che mi deve.   I asked for the money he owes me.
Il signor Alberti richiede l'onore...   Mr. Alberti requests the honor...
Questo lavoro richiede tutto il mio tempo.   This work requires all of my time.
RICHIESTA   request, application.
dietro richiesta di...   at the request of...
fare richiesta d'ammissione   to apply for admission.
RICOMPENSA   reward, recompense.
ricompensare   to reward; to recompense.
È stato ampiamente ricompensato.   He was amply rewarded.
riconciliare   to reconcile.
riconciliazione, f.   reconciliation.
riconoscente   grateful, thankful.
riconoscere   to recognize; to admit.
riconoscere i propri torti   to admit one's fault.
L'ho riconosciuto subito.   I recognized him immediately.
RICORDARE   to remember.
Mi ricordi a sua moglie.   Remember me to your wife.
Non me ne ricordo.   I don't remember it.
RICORDO   remembrance, recollection.
Ho un vago ricordo dei miei primi anni.   I have a vague recollection of my first years.
Lo terrò per tuo ricordo.   I'll keep it as a remembrance of you.
ricorrente   recurrent.
ricorrere   to apply to; to report to.
ricoverare   to shelter; to give shelter.
ricoverarsi   to take shelter; to take refuge.
ricovero   shelter.
ricreare   to create again; to entertain.
RICUPERO   recovery, salvage.
La polizia ha effettuato il ricupero degli oggetti rubati.   The police brought about the recovery of the stolen objects.
RIDERE   to laugh.
ridicolo   ridiculous.
ridotto   reduced.
mal ridotto   in poor shape.
prezzo ridotto   reduced price.
RIDURRE   to reduce.
ridurre le spese   to cut down expenses.
riduzione, f.   reduction.
RIEMPIRE   to fill.
riempire una bottiglia   to fill a bottle.
riempire un modulo   to fill out a blank.
riempirsi   to fill up; to stuff oneself.
rientrare   to come in again; to be included.
riferire   to report; to relate.

Mi ha riferito quanto è accaduto.   He told me what happened.
Non me riferivo a lui.   I was not referring to him.
RIFIUTARE   to refuse; to decline.
Ha rifiutato d'accompagnarmi.   He refused to accompany me.
Sono costretto a rifiutare l'invito.   I am obliged to decline the invitation.
rifiuto   refusal, waste.
riflessione, f.   reflection, consideration.
dopo matura riflessione   upon further consideration.
riflesso   reflection.
Ho visto il mio riflesso nello specchio.   I saw my reflection in the mirror.
riflettere   to reflect; to think.
La luna riflette i raggi del sole.   The moon reflects the sun's rays.
Ho riflettuto bene prima di decidere.   I thought at length before making up my mind.
rifornimento benzina   gas station.
rifugio   refuge, shelter.
RIGA   line, row, ruler.
farsi la riga nei capelli   to make a part in one's hair.
in riga   in a row.
scrivere poche righe   to write a few lines.
stoffa a righe   striped material.
rigido   rigid.
rigore, m.   rigor.
rigoroso   rigorous.
RIGUARDO   regard, respect.
per riguardo a   out of respect for.
senza riguardo   without regard.
Sotto questo riguardo ha perfettamente ragione.   In this respect he is perfectly right.
rilasciare   to leave; to issue; to free.
rilassare   to slacken.
rilassarsi   to relax; to become lax.
rilevare   to point out; to perceive.
RILIEVO   relief.
basso rilievo   bas-relief.
mettere in rilievo   to point out; to emphasize.
riluttante   reluctant.
riluttanza   reluctance.
con riluttanza   reluctantly.
rimandare   to send back; to postpone.
Bisogna rimandare questo appuntamento.   We must postpone this appointment.
Gli ho rimandato il libro che mi aveva prestato.   I sent back the book he lent me.
RIMANERE   to remain; to stay.
Rimane poco tempo.   Little time remains.
rimanere male   to be disappointed.
Siamo rimasti fuori casa per due giorni.   We stayed away from home for two days.
rimaritarsi   to marry again; to take a second husband.
rimborsare   to repay.
rimessa   garage.
RIMETTERE   to put back; to put again; to remit; to lose.
Favorite rimettere la somma di...   Please remit the sum of...
Ho rimesso parecchio in questo affare.   I lost quite a good deal in this business affair.
Ho rimesso tutto a posto.   I put everything back in place.
rimorso   remorse.
rimproverare   to reproach; to scold.
rimprovero   reproach, reprimand.
RIMUOVERE   to remove; to displease.
rinascimento   rebirth.

Rinascimento   Renaissance.
rincorrere   to pursue.
rincrescimento   regret.
rinforzo   reinforcement.
rinfrescare   to cool; to refresh.
rinfrescarsi   to refresh oneself.
rinfresco   refreshment.
ringraziamento   thanks, thanksgiving.
RINGRAZIARE   to thank.
RIPARARE   to repair; to mend.
riparazione, f.   repair, reparation.
RIPARO   shelter.
a riparo da   sheltered from.
ripassare   to look over again.
ripetere   to repeat.
ripetizione, f.   repetition.
RIPOSARE   to rest.
riposo   rest.
riprodurre   to reproduce.
risata   laugh, laughter.
riscaldare   to warm; to heat.
rischiare   to risk.
riscontrare   to check; to examine.
riserbo   discretion, secrecy.
rischio   risk.
RISO   rice, laughter.
riso amaro   bitter laughter.
riso con piselli   rice with peas.
risoluto   determined, resolute.
risoluzione, f.   resolution.
prendere una risoluzione   to resolve.
risorgere   to rise again.
RISPARMIARE   to save.
risparmiare tempo   to save time.
risparmio   saving.
cassa di risparmio   savings bank.
RISPETTARE   to respect.
rispettare le leggi   to respect the laws.
rispetto   respect.
RISPETTOSO   respectful.
RISPONDERE   to answer.
rispondere alla posta   to answer the mail.
rispondere al telefono   to answer the telephone.
RISPOSTA   answer, reply.
ristorante, m.   restaurant.
ristretto   contracted, narrow, limited.
risultare   to result.
risultarne   to result from.
risultato   result.
RISVEGLIARE   to awaken; to reawaken.
RITARDARE   to delay; to be late.
ritardo   delay.
essere in ritardo   to be late.
ritegno   discretion, reservedness.
ritmo   rhythm.
RITORNARE   to return; to go back to.
tornare a casa   to come back home.
È tornata la primavera.   Spring is here.
RITORNO   return.
Attendo con ansia il tuo ritorno.   I anxiously await your return.
Sarò di ritorno alle cinque.   I will be back at five.
RITRATTO   picture.
Questo è un mio ritratto fatto due anni fa.   This is a picture of me, taken two years ago.
ritto   straight.
ritrovo   club.
riunire   to reunite.
RIUSCIRE   to succeed; to be able.
Non riesco a farlo.   I am not able to do it.
È riuscito a far fortuna.   He succeeded in making a fortune.

rivale, m. *rival; (also adj.).*
rivelare *to reveal.*
rivenditore, m. *merchant.*
rivolgere *to turn; to address.*
rivoluzione, f. *revolution.*
roba *thing, goods, stuff.*
roccia *rock.*
romano *Roman; (also noun).*
romantico *romantic.*
romanzo, m. *novel.*
ROMPERE *to break.*
  rompere relazioni con *to break off with.*
  Ho rotto un bicchiere. *I broke a glass.*
rondine, f. *swallow.*
ronzare *to hum; to buzz.*
rosa *rose, (noun & adj.).*
rosso *red.*
  veder rosso *to see red.*
rossore, m. *redness.*
  Il rossore le salì alle guance. *She blushed.*
rotaia *railroad track.*
rotolo *roll, scroll.*
ROTONDO *round.*
rotta *course, rout.*
rotto *broken.*
rovescio *reverse, (noun & adj.).*
  il rovescio della medaglia *the other side of the medal.*
  Si è messo il vestito al rovescio. *He put his suit on wrong side out.*
rovesciare *to overthrow.*
rovina *ruin.*
ROVINARE *to ruin.*
rovinato *ruined.*
rozzo *rough, coarse.*
rubare *to steal.*
  Ha rubato un orologio. *He stole a watch.*
ruggine, f. *rust.*
rugiada *dew.*
RUMORE, m. *noise.*
  far rumore *to make noise.*
rumoroso *noisy.*
RUOTA *wheel.*
rurale *rural.*
russare *to snore.*
russo *Russian; (also noun).*
rustico *rustic.*
ruvido *rough.*

S

sabato *Saturday.*
sabbia *sand.*
sabbioso *sandy.*
saccheggiare *to plunder.*
sacco *bag, sack.*
sacrilegio *sacrilege.*
sacro *sacred.*
  l'osso sacro *sacrum.*
saggio *wise.*
SALA *hall.*
  sala da ballo *ballroom.*
  sala da pranzo *dining room.*
  sala d'aspetto *waiting-room.*
  sala operatoria *operating room.*
salare *to salt.*
salario *wage.*
salato *salty.*
saldo *firm, balanced.*
SALE, m. *salt.*
  aver sale in zucca *to have good sense. (Colloq.)*
  dolce di sale *insipid.*
  Raccontami l'accaduto senza aggiungere nè sale nè pepe. *Tell me what happened without*

adding any trimmings. (Colloq.)
salire *to go up.*
  salire le scale *to go up the stairs.*
  salir su per la montagna *to climb up the hill.*
salita *ascent, ascention, slope.*
  Questa strada è in salita. *This street is on an incline.*
salotto *parlor.*
salsa *sauce.*
salsiccia *sausage.*
SALTARE *to jump; to jump over; to skip.*
  saltar di palo in frasca *to stray from the subject.*
  saltare fuori *to pop up.*
  saltare giù dal letto *to jump out of bed.*
  Bisogna saltare questo fosso. *We have to jump over this hurdle (ditch).*
  Ha saltato una pagina intera. *He skipped a whole page.*
  Non ti far saltare la mosca al naso. *Don't get angry. (Colloq.)*
SALTO *jump.*
  fare un salto nel buio *to take a risk.*
  Faccio un salto a casa di mia madre. *I'll take a quick run over to my mother's house.*
salumeria *grocer.*
SALUTARE *to salute; to greet.*
  Ci siamo salutati alla stazione. *We said goodbye at the station.*
  Mi ha salutato con un cenno della mano. *He waved to me.*
  Mi ha salutato freddamente. *He greeted me coldly.*
salute, f. *health.*
saluto *greetings.*
salvagente, m. *life preserver.*
SALVARE *to save.*
  salvare le apparenze *to keep up appearances.*
  Mi ha salvato dalla rovina. *He saved me from ruin.*
salvezza *salvation, safety.*
SALVO *safe; save for; except for.*
  sano e salvo *safe and sound.*
  trarre in salvo *to conduct to safety; to save.*
  Salvo possibile cambiamenti, tutto rimane come stabilito. *Save for possible changes, everything remains as planned.*
sanabile *curable.*
sanare *to cure; to make well.*
sandalo *sandal.*
sangue, m. *blood.*
  a sangue freddo *in cold blood.*
  dare il proprio sangue *to give one's life.*
  dello stesso sangue *related; of the same family.*
  versare sangue *to shed blood.*
  Il riso fa buon sangue. *Laughter is the best medicine.*
sanguinare *to bleed.*
  Mi sanguina il cuore al pensiero. *My heart bleeds at the thought.*
sanitario *sanitary.*
  leggi sanitarie *sanitary laws.*
SANO *sound, healthy, whole.*
  di principi sani *of sound principles.*
  di sana pianta *entirely.*
  sano di corpo e di mente *sound in mind and body.*
  un'uomo sano *a healthy man.*
santo *saint; (as adj.) saintly.*
santuario *sanctuary.*
sapere, m. *learning, erudition.*
SAPERE *to know.*
  saperla lunga *to be clever.*

  Sa il fatto suo. *He knows his trade.*
sapone, m. *soap.*
saponetta *face soap.*
SAPORE, m. *flavor, taste.*
saporito *flavorful.*
sardina *sardine.*
sarta *dressmaker.*
sarto *tailor.*
sartoria *tailor-shop.*
sasso *small stone; pebble.*
  Egli ha un cuore di sasso. *He is hard-hearted.*
  Siamo rimasti di sasso. *We stood amazed.*
sassolino *pebble.*
satellite, m. *satellite.*
saturare *to saturate.*
  saturare la mente *to fill one's mind.*
SAVIO *wise, learned.*
SAZIARE *to satiate; to satisfy.*
  saziare la fame *to satisfy hunger.*
  saziare la sete *to quench thirst.*
  saziarsi di *to fill oneself with.*
sazio *satiated, satisfied.*
sbadato *heedless, inadvertent.*
sbadigliare *to yawn.*
sbadiglio *yawn.*
sbagliare *to mistake; to be mistaken.*
SBAGLIO *error.*
sbalordire *to amaze; to astonish.*
sbalzare *to thrust; to bounce.*
sbalzo, (balzo) *bounce.*
  cogliere la palla al balzo *to catch a ball on the bounce; to take advantage of an opportunity.*
sbarazzar(si) *to get rid of.*
sbarbare *to shave; to pull out by the roots.*
  sbarbarsi *to shave oneself.*
sbarcare *to disembark; to go ashore.*
  sbarcare il lunario *to make ends meet.*
sbarrare *to bar; to obstruct.*
sbattere *to slam.*
  Ha sbattuto la porta e se n' è andato. *He slammed the door and left.*
sbiadito *faded.*
sbottonare *to unbutton.*
sbrigare *to dispatch; to expedite.*
sbucciare *to peel; to skin.*
scacchiera *chess-board.*
scadere *to fall due.*
scala *stairway, stairs.*
  farsi scala di *to use as a stepping stone.*
  scala a chiocciola *spiral staircase.*
  scala mobile *escalator.*
  È faticoso fare le scale tutto il giorno. *It is tiresome going up and down stairs all day.*
scalo *call, landing-place.*
scaltro *astute, clever.*
scalzo *barefooted.*
scambiare *to exchange.*
scampagnata *picnic.*
scampare *to escape from danger.*
  Dio ci scampi e liberi! *Heaven preserve us!*
scappare *to run away; to escape.*
SCARICARE *to unload.*
  scaricare una nave *to unload a ship.*
  scaricare un fucile *to unload a gun; to fire all the rounds of a gun.*
scarico *unloaded.*
SCARPA *shoe.*
scarso *scarce, lacking.*
  di scarso valore *of little value.*
  scarso d'ingegno *unintelligent.*
scartare *to reject; to discard.*
SCATOLA *box.*
scavare *to dig; to dig up; to excavate.*

andare a scavare   to try and find out.
scavare la propria fossa   to be the cause of
one's own ruin.
SCEGLIERE   to choose.
scelto   chosen.
scemare   to diminish; to lessen.
scena   scene.
SCENDERE   to descend.
Scendo subito!   I'll be right down!
scheletro   skeleton.
scherzare   to jest; to joke.
schiena   back.
Ho un dolore alla schiena.   I have a pain in my
back.
schiuma   froth, foam.
schizzo   sketch, splash.
sciagura   misfortune, ill-luck.
sciarpa   scarf.
scienza   science.
scimmia   monkey.
sciocchezza   nonsense.
fare una sciocchezza   to do something silly.
sciocco   silly, nonsensical.
SCIOGLIERE   to untie; to melt; to release.
sciogliere da una promessa   to release from a
promise.
sciogliere la neve   to melt snow.
sciogliere un nodo   to untie a knot.
sciolto   loose, untied.
sciopero   strike.
SCIUPARE   to spoil; to damage; to waste.
sciupare il tempo inutilmente   to waste time.
sciupare la salute   to damage one's health.
Mi ha sciupato tutto il vestito.   He spoiled my
dress completely.
scivolare   to slip; to glide.
scoiattolo   squirrel.
scolaro   pupil, student.
scolorare, (scolorire)   to fade; to lose color.
scomodare   to inconvenience.
scomodo   uncomfortable, inconvenient.
SCOMPARIRE   to disappear; to vanish.
scompartimento   division, compartment.
sconosciuto   unknown; (as noun) stranger.
scontrino   check, ticket.
scontro   collision.
sconvolto   upset.
SCOPA   broom.
scopare   to sweep.
scoperta   discovery.
scoperto   uncovered.
SCOPO   aim, intent, scope.
lo scopo della mia vita   my aim in life.
A che scopo?   To what intent?
scoppiare   to burst; to explode.
SCOPRIRE   to discover; to uncover.
scoraggiare   to discourage.
scordare   to forget.
scorretto   incorrect, improper.
scorso   last, past.
scortese   impolite.
scorza   peel.
scorza d'arancia   orange peel.
scossa   shake, shock.
scottare   to burn; to scald.
scrittore, m. scrittrice, f.   writer.
scrittura   writing.
scrivania   desk.
SCRIVERE   to write; to spell.
scucire   to rip (a seam).
SCUOLA   school.
frequentare la scuola   to go to school; to attend
school.

scuotere   to shake.
scuro   dark (in color).
scusa   excuse.
fare le scuse   to excuse oneself.
scusare   to excuse.
Scusi (or mi scusi).   Excuse me.
sdegno   indignation.
sdraiare   to lay.
sdraiarsi   to lie; to lie down.
sdrucciolare   to slip.
Sdrucciolosa Quando Bagnata.   Slippery When
Wet.
SE   if.
anche se   even if.
come se   as if.
se posso   if I can.
se vuoi   if you wish.
SÈ   her, him, them, herself, himself, themselves.
Egli è fuori di sè.   He has no control of himself.
Essi pensano solo a sè.   They think only of
themselves.
Maria non sta in sè dalla gioia.   Mary is beside
herself with joy.
SE   of it; from it; for it.
Se ne liberò.   He got rid of it.
Se ne pentì.   She was sorry for it.
seccare   to dry, to bother.
seccato   bored, angry.
secchio   pail.
secco   dry.
secolo   century.
secondo   second, noun & adj.
secondo, adv.   according to.
secondo il mio giudizio   according to my way of
thinking.
sedano   celery.
SEDERE   to sit.
sedersi a tavola   to sit at table.
SEDIA   chair.
sedici   sixteen.
sedicesimo   sixteenth.
seduto   seated.
sega   saw.
SEGNO   sign, indication.
dare segni di vita   to give signs of life.
perdere il segno   to lose one's place in a book.
È buon segno.   It's a good sign.
segretaria   secretary, f.
segretario   secretary, m.
segreto   secret, noun & adj.
seguente   following, ensuing.
Egli ha fatto la seguente dichiarazione.   He
made the following statement.
seguire   to follow.
sei   six.
seicento   six hundred.
seimila   six thousand.
selvatichezza   wildness.
SEMBRARE   to seem.
Egli sembra impazzito.   He seems to be insane.
Mi sembra strano.   It seems strange to me.
Sembra impossibile!   It seems impossibile!
seme, m.   seed.
semi- (prefix)   half-, semi-.
semicerchio   semicircle.
semivivo   half-alive.
seminare   to sow.
semplice   simple, easy.
SEMPRE   always.
per sempre   forever.
senno   sense.
sensibile   sensitive, impressionable.
SENSO   sense, meaning.

espressione a doppio senso   an ambiguous expression.
senso unico   one-way (street).
usare un po' di buon senso   to use common sense.
sentimentale   sentimental.
sentenza   judgment.
SENTIRE   to hear; to feel.
non sentire dolore   to feel no pain.
sentire freddo   to feel cold.
sentire odore   to smell.
sentire rimorso   to feel remorse.
Come si sente?   How do you feel?
Con tutto questo rumore non riesco a sentire
niente.   With all this noise, I can't hear a
thing.
Mi sento bene.   I feel well.
Sentiamo fame.   We are hungry.
Sentite!   Hear!
SENZA   without.
senza considerazione   inconsiderately, inconsiderate.
senza dar fastidio a nessuno   without bothering
anyone.
senz'altro   right away; without delay.
SEPARARE   to separate; to part.
la distanza che ci separa   the distance that
separates us.
separarsi da   to separate from.
Ci siamo separati a malincuore.   We parted reluctantly.
SEPARATO   separate.
separazione, f.   separation, parting.
SERA   evening, night.
Buona sera.   Good evening.
SERATA   evening.
Passeremo una serata in compagnìa.   We will
spend the evening in company.
serenamente   serenely.
sereno   serene, clear.
una giornata serena   a clear day.
serie, f.   series.
una serie di articoli   a series of articles.
serio   serious, grave.
sul serio   seriously.
serpente, m.   snake, serpent.
serpente a sonagli   rattlesnake.
serra   greenhouse, hothouse.
SERRARE   to close; to shut.
con i pugni serrati   with clenched fists.
serrare le file   to close ranks.
serratura   lock.
serva   maid, servant.
SERVIRE   to serve.
servirsi da   to patronize.
A che serve?   What is it used for?
In che cosa la posso servire?   What can I do for
you?
No, grazie, mi servo da me.   No, thanks, I'll
help myself.
Noi ci serviamo dal negozio vicino casa nostra.
We patronize (buy from) the shop near our home.
Non serve!   It's of no use!
Potete servire il pranzo.   You may serve dinner.
Vuole che le serva la carne?   Shall I serve you
the meat?
servitù, f.   servants, servitude.
SERVIZIO   service, set.
fuori servizio   off duty.
in servizio   on duty.
rendere un servizio a   to render a service.
servizio da tavola   dinner set; dinner service.
servizio militare   military service.
Il servizio è pessimo in quest'albergo.   The

service is very poor in this hotel.
servo servant (male).
sessanta sixty.
sessantesimo sixtieth.
sesto sixth.
seta silk.
  seta cruda pongee.
  seta greggia raw silk.
SETE, f. thirst.
  aver sete to be thirsty.
settanta seventy.
settantesimo seventieth.
sette seven.
settecento seven hundred.
  nel Settecento in the eighteenth century.
settembre, m. September.
settentrionale northern; (as noun, m.) northerner.
  Italia settentrionale northern Italy.
SETTIMANA week.
  di settimana in settimana from week to week.
  fra una settimana in a week.
  la settimana prossima (entrante) next week.
  una settimana fa a week ago.
settimanale weekly; (also noun, m.).
  un settimanale a weekly publication.
settimo seventh.
settore, m. sector.
severamente severely.
severo severe, strict.
sezione, f. section.
sfaccendato idle, unemployed.
sfarzo pomp, magnificence.
  fare le cose con sfarzo to do things in grand style.
sfarzoso gorgeous, magnificent.
sfasciare to remove the bandages; to break into pieces.
sfavorevole unfavorable.
sfavorevolmente unfavorably.
sfera sphere.
  la sfera dell'orologio the face of the clock.
sfibbiare to unbuckle.
sfida challenge.
sfidare to challenge; to dare.
  sfidare le intemperie to face (to challenge) the inclemency of the weather (the storms).
  Sfido io! Of course!
  Ti sfido a farlo. I dare you to do it.
sfiducia distrust.
  Nutro una grande sfiducia verso di lui. I distrust him very much.
sfilare to unthread; to unstring (beads); to march.
  una calza sfilata a ripped stocking.
  I soldati sfilano. The soldiers march.
sfinire to exhaust; to wear down.
  Mi sento sfinito. I feel exhausted.
  Questo lavoro mi ha sfinito. This work has exhausted me.
sfogare to vent; to give vent to.
  sfogarsi con to confide in.
  Ha sfogato la sua ira su di me. He vented his wrath on me.
sfoggiare to show off; to make a display.
sfondo background.
sfortuna bad luck; misfortune.
  per mia sfortuna unfortunately for me.
  La sfortuna lo perseguita. Misfortune dogs his footsteps.
sfortunatamente unfortunately.
sfortunato unlucky.
  sfortunato al giuoco unlucky at cards (at games).
  sfortunato in amore unlucky in love.
sforzare to strain; to force.

sforzarsi to strain oneself; to try hard.
SFORZO effort.
  fare uno sforzo to make an effort.
  senza sforzo without effort.
  Non mi costa sforzo. It is no effort to me.
sfrangiare to fray; to unravel.
  Questo cappotto si è sfrangiato. This coat is frayed.
sfrattare to dispossess; to evict.
sfratto eviction.
sfrontato shameless, bold.
sfruttamento exploitation.
sfruttare to exploit.
  sfruttare al massimo to exploit fully; to get the most out of.
sfuggire to run away; to escape.
sgabello stool.
sgarbatamente rudely.
sgarbato rude.
  Mi ha trattato in maniera molto sgarbata. He treated me with great rudeness.
sgarbo rudeness; act of rudeness.
  fare uno sgarbo a qualcuno to be rude towards someone; to commit an act of rudeness towards someone.
sgelare to melt; to thaw.
sgombrare to clear; to clear out of.
  sgombrare il passo to make way; to get out of the way.
sgombro clear, free.
  La stanza è sgombra. The room is free.
sgomento dismay.
sgonfiare to deflate.
  Si è sgonfiata una gomma alla mia automobile. My car has a flat tire.
sgonfio deflated; not swollen.
sgorgare to gush out; to overflow.
sgradevole unpleasant, disagreeable.
sgradito unpleasant, disagreeable, unwelcome.
SGRIDARE to scold; to reprimand.
sgridata scolding.
  Mi ha fatto una sgridata per nulla. He gave me a scolding over nothing.
sgualcire to rumple.
  Questa veste è tutta sgualcita. This dress is all wrinkled.
SGUARDO look, glance.
  con sguardo severo with a stern look.
  dare uno sguardo a to glance at.
  Mi ha lanciato uno sguardo di sottocchio. He glanced at me furtively.
sgusciare to shell; to slip away.
  sgusciare dalle mani to slip out of one's hands; to slip away.
  sgusciare i piselli to shell the peas.
SI oneself, himself, herself, itself, themselves, we, they, one; one another; each other.
  Non si è sempre lieti. We are not always glad.
  Si dice che... They (one says) say that...
  Si è messo a piovere. It has started to rain.
  Si è messo a sedere. He sat (himself) down.
  Si sono divertiti. They enjoyed themselves.
  Si sono finalmente rivisti. They finally saw each other again.
sì, adv. yes.
  dire di sì to say yes.
  Mi pare di sì. I think so.
  Sì davvero! Yes indeed!
sia ...sia whether ...or...
  sia che ti piaccia, sia che non ti piaccia whether you like it or not.
sibilare to hiss.
sibilo hiss, hissing.

  il sibilo del vento the hissing of the wind.
sicchè so; so that.
  Sicchè hai deciso di venire? So you've decided to come?
siccome as; inasmuch as.
  Siccome era già partito, non ho potuto dargli la tua imbasciata. Inasmuch as he had already left, I wasn't able to give him your message.
siciliano Sicilian; (also noun).
sicuramente certainly, surely.
  Verrà sicuramente. He will surely come.
sicurezza safety, security.
  per maggior sicurezza for greater safety.
  rasòio di sicurezza safety razor.
  spilla di sicurezza safety-pin.
sicuro safe, secure, sure.
  essere sicuro di to be sure of.
  mettersi al sicuro to place oneself in safety.
  Sicuro! Certainly!
siepe, f. hedge.
siesta siesta.
sigaretta cigarette.
sigaro cigar.
sigillare to seal.
sigillo seal.
significante significant.
significare to mean; to signify.
  Che cosa intendeva significare con quel gesto? What did you wish to signify with that gesture?
  Che cosa significa questa parola? What does this word mean?
  Che significa tutto ciò? What is the meaning of all this?
significato meaning, significance.
SIGNORA Mrs.; lady.
  È una vera signora. She is a real lady.
SIGNORE, m. Mr.; gentleman.
  Questo signore desidera vederla. This gentleman wishes to see you.
  Signor Rossi Mr. Rossi.
signorile gentlemanly, ladylike.
signorilmente refinedly.
SIGNORINA Miss; young lady.
SILENZIO silence.
silenziosamente silently.
silenzioso silent.
sillaba syllable.
simboleggiare to symbolize.
simbolo symbol.
similarità similarity.
SIMILE like, similar, such.
  il tuo simile thy neighbor; thy fellow creature.
  Non ho mai visto una cosa simile. I've never seen such a thing.
  Questa borsetta è simile alla mia. This handbag is like mine.
simmetria symmetry.
simmetrico symmetrical.
simpatia liking.
  aver simpatia per to have a liking for.
simpatico nice, pleasant.
  riuscire simpatico to be liked.
simulare to feign; to pretend.
simultaneamente simultaneously.
simultaneo simultaneous.
sinceramente sincerely, truly.
SINCERO sincere, candid.
  un amicizia sincera a sincere friendship.
  Dammi la tua sincera opinione. Give me your candid opinion.
sindaco mayor.
sinfonia symphony.
singhiozzare to sob.

Si è messa a singhiozzare. *She started to sob; she burst into sobs.*

singhiozzo *sob, hiccup.*

Ho il singhiozzo. *I have the hiccups.*

singolare *singular, peculiar.*

SINISTRA *left hand.*

voltare a sinistra *to turn to the left.*

sinistro *left, sinister.*

lato sinistro *left side.*

Quell'uomo ha un'aspetto sinistro. *That man has a sinister look.*

sinonimo *synonymous; (as noun) synonym.*

sintetico *synthetic.*

sintomo *symptom.*

sipario *curtain.*

SISTEMA, m. *system.*

sistema nervoso *nervous system.*

sistema solare *solar system.*

sistemare *to arrange; to settle.*

sistemarsi *to settle; to settle down.*

sistematico *systematic.*

situazione, f. *situation, position.*

slanciar(si) *to fling oneself; to jump on.*

sleale *disloyal, unfair.*

slealmente *unfairly; disloyally.*

slealtà *disloyalty.*

slegare *to unbind.*

slitta *sleigh, sled.*

slogare *to dislocate.*

slogarsi una caviglia *to sprain an ankle.*

smacchiare *to remove stains from; to clean.*

smacchiatura *cleaning.*

smalto *enamel.*

SMARRIRE *to lose.*

smarrirsi *to lose one's way.*

smarrito *lost, bewildered.*

smentire *to belie; to deny.*

smeraldo *emerald.*

SMETTERE *to stop.*

Smettila! *Stop it!*

Smetto di lavorare alle sei. *I stop working at six.*

SMONTARE *to dismount; to get out; to take apart.*

È smontato da cavallo. *He dismounted from his horse.*

Ho dovuto smontare l'orologio. *I had to take the clock apart.*

smorto *pale, dull.*

sobborgo *suburb.*

SOCCORSO *help, aid, succor.*

chiedere soccorso *to ask for help.*

prestare i primi soccorsi *to render first aid.*

pronto soccorso *first aid.*

società di mutuo soccorso *mutual aid society.*

società *society, company.*

in società con *in partnership with.*

società anonima *joint-stock company.*

società di beneficenza *charitable organization.*

socievole *sociable, companionable.*

SOCIO *associate, partner, member.*

socio in affari *business associate.*

Siamo tutti e due soci del medesimo circolo. *We are both members of the same club.*

soddisfacente *satisfactory.*

soddisfacentemente *satisfactorily.*

soddisfare *to satisfy.*

soddisfatto *satisfied.*

soddisfazione, f. *satisfaction.*

con mia grande soddisfazione *to my great satisfaction.*

sode *boiled.*

sodo *solid, substantial.*

dormir sodo *to sleep soundly.*

uovo sodo *hard-boiled egg.*

sofa m. *sofa.*

sofferente *suffering, unwell.*

sofferenza *suffering, pain.*

sofferto *suffered, endured.*

SOFFIARE *to blow.*

soffiarsi il naso *to blow one's nose.*

SOFFICE *soft.*

soffio *puff, breath.*

in un soffio *in a moment.*

senza un soffio d'aria *without a breath of air.*

un soffio di vapore *a puff of steam.*

un soffio di vento *a breeze.*

soffitta *garret, attic.*

soffitto *ceiling.*

soffocante *suffocating, oppressive.*

SOFFOCARE *to choke; to suffocate; to smother; to stifle.*

Egli cerca di soffocare ogni impulso generoso. *He tries to stifle every generous impulse.*

L'emozione la soffoca. *She is choked with emotion.*

soffocazione, f. *suffocation.*

Morì di soffocazione durante un incendio. *He suffocated during a fire.*

soffribile *endurable, bearable.*

SOFFRIRE *to suffer; to bear.*

Egli soffre di mal di cuore. *He is suffering from heart trouble.*

Non posso soffrire quella gente. *I can't bear those people.*

Se non ti concedi un po' di riposo, la tua salute ne soffrirà. *If you don't take some rest, your health will suffer.*

soggettivamente *subjectively.*

soggettivo *subjective.*

SOGGETTO *subject.*

essere soggetto a *to be subject to.*

un pessimo soggetto *a very bad specimen (of mankind).*

soggezione, f. *uneasiness, awe, embarrassment.*

Egli mi da soggezione. *He makes me uneasy.*

Provo soggezione a parlarne. *It embarrasses me to speak of it.*

soggiorno *stay, sojourn.*

Il nostro soggiorno a Parigi sarà della durata di due settimane. *Our sojourn in Paris will be two weeks long.*

soglia *threshold.*

SOGNARE *to dream, to fancy.*

sognatore, m. *dreamer.*

sogno *dream.*

neanche per sogno *by no means.*

SOLAMENTE *only, merely.*

Se potessi solamente vederla! *If I could only see her!*

solco *furrow.*

SOLDATO *soldier.*

fare il soldato *to be a soldier.*

soldo *cent.*

SOLE, m. *sun.*

bagno di sole *sun bath.*

raggio di sole *ray of sun.*

solenne *solemn.*

solido *solid, substantial.*

solitario *solitary.*

SOLITO *usual.*

contro il mio solito *contrary to my custom.*

più presto del solito *earlier than usual.*

sollecitare *to hasten; to entreat.*

sollecito *prompt, speedy, solicitous.*

sollecita della salute dei suoi bambini *solicitous of her children's health.*

una risposta sollecita *a prompt reply.*

solleticare *to tickle.*

SOLLEVARE *to lift; to raise; to comfort.*

sollevare gli occhi *to lift one's eyes.*

sollevare una nuvola di polvere *to raise a cloud of dust.*

sollevare un peso *to lift a weight.*

Mi solleva il pensiero del tuo prossimo ritorno. *I am comforted by the thought of your impending return.*

Molte voci si sollevarono in protesta. *Many voices were raised in protest.*

sollevato *lifted, raised; in good spirits.*

sollievo *relief, comfort.*

SOLO *alone, only.*

Sono completamente sola al mondo. *I am completely alone in the world.*

Sono i soli rimasti. *They are the only ones left.*

SOLTANTO *only.*

Eravamo soltanto in due. *We were only two.*

soluzione, f. *solution.*

SOMIGLIARE *to resemble.*

SOMMA *sum, amount.*

fare una somma *to make an addition; to add; to total.*

sommesso *subdued.*

sommità *summit, top.*

sommo *chief, greatest, highest.*

sommossa *rising, riot.*

sommosso *troubled, excited.*

sonaglio *bell, rattle.*

serpente a sonagli *rattlesnake.*

sonnambulo *sleepwalker.*

sonnecchiare *to doze.*

sonnellino *nap.*

SONNO *sleep.*

aver sonno *to be sleepy.*

malattia del sonno *sleeping sickness.*

sonno leggero *light sleep.*

sonno profondo *deep sleep.*

sontuoso *sumptuous.*

soppressione, f. *suppression.*

soppresso *suppressed, abolished.*

sopprimere *to suppress; to abolish.*

SOPRA *on; on top of; above.*

al piano di sopra *on the floor above.*

andar di sopra *to go upstairs.*

la signora di sopra ricordata *the above-mentioned lady.*

sopra coperta *on deck.*

sopra tutto *above all.*

sopra zero *above zero.*

Posa quel libro sopra il tavolo. *Put that book on the table.*

soprannome, m. *surname, nickname.*

sopraffare *to overwhelm.*

soprano *soprano.*

soprappiù *extra.*

per soprappiù *in addition.*

soprascarpa *overshoe;* **soprascarpe**, f. pl. *overshoes.*

soprassalto *start, jolt.*

svegliarsi di soprassalto *to wake with a start.*

sopravvivere *to survive; to remain in existence.*

sopravvivere a *to outlive.*

SORBIRE *to swallow; to sip.*

sorbire una tazza di caffè *to sip a cup of coffee.*

sordità *deafness.*

SORDO *deaf.*

fare il sordo *to turn a deaf ear.*

sordo da un orecchio *deaf in one ear.*

sordomuto *deaf-mute.*

sorella *sister.*

SORGENTE, f. *spring, source.*
 sorgente di ricchezza *a source of wealth.*
 una sorgente d' acqua minerale *a mineral spring.*
sorgere *to rise; to arise.* (Also noun, m.)
 al sorgere del sole *at sunrise.*
 far sorgere dei dubbi *to give rise to doubt.*
 È sorto un malinteso. *A misunderstanding arose.*
sormontabile *surmountable.*
sormontare *to surmount; to overcome.*
 Abbiamo sormontato tutti gli ostacoli. *We have surmounted all the obstacles.*
 Non riesce a sormontare le difficoltà della vita. *He can't succeed in overcoming life's difficulties.*
sornione *sly, sneaking.*
 gatto sornione *tabby-cat.*
sorpassare *to surpass.*
 La produzione di quest'anno ha sorpassato quella dell'anno precedente. *This year's production surpassed last year's.*
sorpassato *surpassed, old-fashioned, out-dated.*
 È un'usanza sorpassata. *It's an out-dated custom.*
sorprendente *surprising, astonishing.*
SORPRENDERE *to surprise.*
 sorprendersi *to be surprised.*
 sorpresi in atto *caught in the act.*
 La tua condotta mi sorprende. *Your behavior surprises me.*
 Siamo stati sorpresi da una tempesta. *We were overtaken by a storm.*
SORPRESA *surprise.*
 con mia grande sorpresa *much to my surprise.*
 di sorpresa *by surprise.*
 fare una sorpresa a *to surprise.*
 prendere di sorpresa *to take by surprise; to catch someone unawares.*
sorpreso *surprised, astonished.*
 Siamo tutti molto sorpresi. *We are all very surprised.*
 Sono rimasta sorpresa nel sentire. *I was surprised to hear it.*
SORRIDERE *to smile.*
 La fortuna mi sorride. *Fortune smiles on me.*
SORRISO *smile.*
 con sorriso amaro *with a bitter smile.*
 fare un sorriso a *to smile at.*
sorso *sip, gulp.*
 tutto d'un sorso *all in a gulp.*
 un sorso d'acqua *a sip of water; a drop of water.*
sorta *kind, lot.*
 di ogni sorta *of all kinds; all kinds of.*
SORTE, f. *lot, destiny, fate.*
 le sorti del paese *the destiny of the country.*
 tirare a sorte *to draw lots.*
 La sorte gli fu avversa. *Fate was against him.*
 Non era mia sorte vincere. *It was not my lot to win.*
sorveglianza *superintendence, watch, surveillance.*
 mantener sorveglianza *to keep watch.*
 sotto sorveglianza *under surveillance.*
sorvegliare *to oversee; to watch; to watch over.*
 sorvegliare i lavori *to oversee the work.*
 Il malato fu sorvegliato con cura. *The patient was watched over with care.*
sorvolare *to fly over; to pass over.*
 L'aereo ha sorvolato la mia casa. *The plane flew over my house.*
 Sorvoliamo questi dettagli di poca importanza. *Let's pass over these unimportant details.*
sospendere *to suspend; to adjourn; to hang.*

Bisogna sospendere i lavori. *The work must be stopped.*
 La seduta fu sospesa. *The meeting was adjourned.*
sospeso *suspended, hung.*
 con animo sospeso *with anxious mind.*
 sospeso ad un chiodo *hanging on a nail.*
 sospeso in aria *hanging in mid-air.*
 tener in sospeso *to keep in suspense.*
SOSPETTARE *to suspect.*
 Non sospettavo di nulla. *I suspected nothing.*
sospetto *suspicion.*
 fare sorgere dei sospetti *to create suspicion.*
 sotto sospetto di *on suspicion of.*
sospettosamente *suspiciously.*
sospettoso *suspicious.*
sospirare *to sigh.*
sospiro *sigh.*
 sospiro di sollievo *a sigh of relief.*
sossopra *upside down; head over heels.*
 mettere sossopra una stanza *to turn a room upside down.*
SOSTA *halt, stay.*
 fare una sosta breve *to stop for a short while.*
 senza sosta *without pause; without stops.*
 Divieto di Sosta. *No Parking.*
sostanza *substance.*
 dare sustanza a *to give substance to.*
 in sostanza *on the whole.*
sostanziale *substantial.*
sostanzialmente *substantially.*
sostare *to stay; to stop.*
sostegno *support, mainstay.*
 senza sostegno alcuno *completely without support.*
 Sono il sostegno della mia famiglia. *I am the mainstay of my family.*
SOSTENERE *to support; to sustain; to hold up; to maintain.*
 Io sostengo il contrario. *I maintain the contrary.*
 Mi sostengo come meglio posso. *I support myself as well as I can.*
 Si è sostenuto al muro. *He leaned (supported himself) against the wall.*
 Sostienila perchè sta per venire meno. *Hold her up because she is about to faint.*
sostenuto *sustained, played, tolerated.*
SOSTITUIRE *to substitute; to replace; to take the place of.*
 essere sostituito da *to be replaced by.*
sostituto *substitute.*
sostituzione, f. *substitution, replacement.*
 Mi hanno dato questo paio di guanti in sostituzione di quelli difettosi. *They gave me this pair of gloves in place of the defective ones.*
SOTTANA *skirt, underskirt.*
sottanino *petticoat.*
sotterfugio *subterfuge.*
sottinteso *understood, implied.*
sotterra *underground.*
sotterare *to bury.*
sottile *subtle, thin.*
SOTTO *under.*
 al di sotto di *below, beneath.*
 sott' acqua *underwater.*
 sotto forma di *in the shape of; in the guise of.*
 sotto l'influenza di *under the influence of.*
 sotto piego separato *under separate cover.*
 sottosopra *upside down.*
 sotto sospetto *under suspicion.*
 sotto terra *underground.*
 sotto zero *below zero.*
sottomesso *submissive, subdued.*

sottomettere *to submit; to subdue.*
sottoporre *to submit to; to place under.*
sottorraneo *underground.*
 ferrovìa sottorranea *subway.*
sottoscritto *signed; (as noun) undersigned.*
sottoveste *slip.*
SOTTOVOCE *in a whisper.*
SOTTRARRE *to subtract; to steal.*
 sottrarsi a *to get out of; to avoid.*
sottrazione, f. *subtraction, theft.*
SOVENTE *often, frequently.*
soverchio *excessive; (as noun) surplus.*
sovrana (sovrano) *sovereign.*
sovraporre *to superimpose.*
sovvertire *to overthrow.*
spaccare *to cleave; to split.*
 spaccare la legna *to chop wood.*
spaccio *shop.*
 spaccio di sale e tabacchi *tobacco and salt shop.*
spada *sword.*
spaghetti, m. pl. *spaghetti.*
spagnuolo *Spanish, noun & adj.* (Also *Spaniard.*)
spago *string.*
spaiato *unmatched.*
spalancare *to throw open.*
 spalancare la porta *to throw open the door.*
spalancato *wide-open.*
 finestra spalancata *wide-open window.*
SPALLA *shoulder.*
 scrollare le spalle *to shrug one's shoulders.*
spalliera *back (of a chair); back-rest.*
spalmare *to spread.*
 spalmare il burro sul pane *to spread butter on the bread.*
spandere *to spread; to spill.*
sparare *to shoot; to fire.*
sparecchiare *to clear away.*
 Ho sparecchiato la tavola. *I cleared the table.*
SPARGERE *to spread; to shed.*
 spargere sangue *to shed blood.*
 La notizia si è sparsa rapidamente. *The news was spread quickly.*
SPARIRE *to disappear; to vanish.*
sparizione, f. *disappearance.*
sparso *scattered.*
spasimo *spasm.*
spassionato *dispassionate, impartial.*
 giudizio spassionato *impartial judgment.*
spavaldo *bold, defiant; (as noun) braggart.*
SPAVENTARE *to frighten.*
 spaventarsi *to become frightened.*
spavento *fright, terror, fear.*
 provare spavento *to feel fear.*
spaventoso *frightening, fearful.*
SPAZIO *space.*
 nello spazio di un giorno *in a day's time.*
 spazio bianco *blank space.*
 Non c'è spazio. *There is no room.*
spazioso *spacious, broad.*
spazzaneve, m. *snowplow.*
spazzare *to sweep; to sweep away.*
SPAZZOLA *brush.*
spazzolino *small brush.*
 spazzolino da denti *tooth brush.*
SPECCHIO *mirror.*
SPECIALE *special.*
specialista, m. *specialist.*
specialità *specialty.*
 la specialità della casa *the specialty of the house.*
specialmente *specially, especially.*
specie, f. *species, kind, sort.*

di ogni specie   *of every kind.*

specificare   *to specify.*

specifico   *specific.*

speculare   *to speculate.*

speculatore, m.   *speculator.*

speculazione, f.   *speculation.*

SPEDIRE   *to send; to mail.*

Ho già spedito la lettera.   *I have already mailed (sent) the letter.*

spedito   *sent, unconstrained, quick.*

spedizione, f.   *shipment.*

SPEGNERE   *to extinguish; to blow out.*

spegnere la luce   *to turn off the light.*

spegnersi   *to die.*

spellare   *to skin.*

SPENDERE   *to spend.*

Chi più spende meno spende.   *The best is always the cheapest. (Who spends more, spends less.)*

spensieratamente   *thoughtlessly, lightheartedly.*

spensierato   *lighthearted; without cares; happy-go-lucky.*

spento   *extinguished.*

a luce spenta   *with the lights out.*

uno sguardo spento   *a lifeless expression.*

SPERANZA   *hope.*

perdere ogni speranza   *to lose all hope.*

senza speranza   *hopeless.*

SPERARE   *to hope.*

sperare in vano   *to hope in vain.*

Spero di vederti domani.   *I hope to see you tomorrow.*

SPESA   *expense, expenditure.*

a spese mie   *at my expense.*

fare la spesa   *to go shopping; to do the shopping.*

Si tratta di una spesa troppo grande.   *It's too great an expense.*

SPESSO   *thick, dense.*

SPESSO, adv.   *often.*

Ci vediamo spesso.   *We see each other often.*

spessore, m.   *thickness.*

spettabile   *respectable.*

SPETTACOLO   *spectacle, performance, sight.*

spettacolo di gala   *gala performance.*

uno spettacolo triste   *a sad sight.*

Egli ha dato spettacolo di se.   *He made a spectacle of himself.*

spettacoloso   *spectacular.*

spettare   *to belong; to be one's duty.*

L'eredità spetta al figlio del defunto.   *The inheritance belongs to the son of the deceased.*

Spetta all'uomo di casa mantenere la propria famiglia.   *It is the duty of the man of the house to support his own family.*

spettatore, m.; **spettatrice,** f.   *spectator.*

spettro   *ghost, spectre.*

spezie, f. pl.   *spices.*

spezzar(si)   *to break.*

Mi si spezza il cuore.   *My heart is breaking.*

Si è spezzato.   *It broke.*

spiacere   *to displease; to be disagreeable; to be sorry for; to regret.*

spiacevole   *unpleasant.*

spiacevolmente   *unpleasantly.*

SPIAGGIA   *shore, beach.*

spianare   *to smooth; to level.*

spianare la fronte   *to smooth one's brow.*

spianare la via   *to level the way.*

spiantato   *uprooted, ruined, broke.*

spiccato   *detached, pronounced, marked.*

spicchio   *segment, clove.*

spicciare   *to dispatch.*

spicciarsi   *to hurry.*

spicciolo   *small.*

avere spiccioli   *to have change.*

moneta spicciola   *small change.*

SPIEGARE   *to explain; to unfold.*

spiegare le ali   *to spread out; to try one's wings; to unfold one's wings.*

Spiegami che cosa significa questa parola.   *Explain the meaning of this word.*

spiegazione, f.   *explanation.*

spietato   *merciless, pitiless.*

spiga   *ear.*

spiga di grano   *ear of corn.*

SPILLA   *pin, brooch.*

cuscinetto per spille   *pincushion.*

spilla di diamanti   *diamond brooch.*

spilla da balia }

spilla di sicurezza }   *safety pin.*

spilorcio   *miserly, stingy.*

spina   *thorn.*

spina dorsale   *spinal column.*

spinaci, m.pl.   *spinach.*

SPINGERE   *to push; to drive.*

spingersi   *to drive oneself; to push forward.*

Non spingere!   *Don't push!*

Sono stata spinta a farlo.   *I was driven to do it.*

spinoso   *thorny.*

un problema spinoso   *a thorny problem.*

spinta   *push, shove.*

dare una spinta   *to shove; to give a push forward.*

spintone, m.   *violent push.*

spiraglio   *opening, air-hole.*

spirare   *to blow; to die; to expire.*

Egli è spirato fra le braccia di sua madre.   *He died in his mother's arms.*

Spira aria cattiva per me.   *An ill wind is blowing for me.*

Il tempo per fare i pagamenti spira domani.   *The time for making payments expires tomorrow.*

SPIRITO   *spirit, ghost, wit.*

senza spirito   *without spirit.*

un uomo di spirito   *a witty man.*

spiritoso   *witty.*

spirituale   *spiritual.*

splendente   *shining, resplendent.*

splendere   *to shine.*

splendidamente   *splendidly.*

splendido   *splendid.*

splendore, m.   *splendor.*

spogliare   *to undress; to strip.*

spogliarsi   *to undress oneself.*

spogliatòio   *dressing room.*

spolverare   *to dust.*

sponda   *bank (of a river).*

spontaneamente   *spontaneously.*

spontaneità   *spontaneity, spontaneousness.*

spontaneo   *spontaneous.*

SPORCARE   *to dirty.*

sporcarsi   *to get dirty; to become dirty.*

sporcizia   *dirt.*

sporco   *dirty.*

sporgente   *protruding.*

denti sporgenti   *protruding teeth.*

sporgere   *to put out; to stretch out; to lean out.*

Si è sporto dalla finestra.   *He leaned out the window.*

Ha sporto la mano dal finestrino dell'automobile.   *He put his hand out of the car window.*

sportello   *window, booth.*

sportello dei biglietti   *ticket window.*

SPOSA   *bride.*

sposalizio   *wedding.*

sposare   *to marry.*

sposarsi   *to get married.*

spossato   *weary, fatigued.*

spostare   *to move; to shift.*

Si è spostato da un paese all'altro.   *He moved from one country to the other.*

Sposta quel libro all'altra parte del tavolo.   *Shift that book to the other side of the table.*

sprecare   *to waste.*

spreco   *waste.*

spregevole   *despicable.*

spremere   *to squeeze; to wring out.*

spremere un arancio   *to squeeze an orange.*

spremuta   *squeezing.*

una spremuta di arancio   *an orange juice.*

sprofondare   *to sink; to collapse.*

sproporzionatamente   *disproportionately.*

sproporzionato   *disproportionate.*

sproposito   *mistake, blunder.*

spugna   *sponge.*

spuma   *foam, lather.*

spuntare   *to appear; to break through.*

spuntino   *snack.*

fare un spuntino   *to have a snack.*

sputare   *to spit.*

squadra   *team.*

squilibrio   *lack of balance.*

squilibrio mentale   *mental unbalance.*

squillare   *to resound; to ring.*

squisitamente   *exquisitely.*

squisito   *exquisite.*

sradicare   *to uproot.*

sregolato   *disordered, irregular.*

stàbile   *stable, steady.*

stabilimento   *factory, establishment.*

stabilire   *to establish; to settle.*

Si è stabilito in Italia.   *He settled in Italy.*

Stabiliamo prima dove c'incontreremo.   *Let's settle first where we are going to meet.*

staccare   *to detach.*

staccarsi da   *to part from.*

stadio   *stadium.*

staffa   *stirrup.*

Ha perduto le staffe.   *He lost his temper. (He lost his stirrups.)*

stagione, f.   *season.*

stagnante   *stagnant.*

stagnare   *to cover with tin; to stop (the flow of a liquid); to be stagnant.*

Le acque stagnano.   *The waters are stagnant.*

stagno   *tin.*

stagnola   *tinfoil.*

stalla   *stable.*

stampa   *print, press.*

errore di stampa   *misprint.*

libertà di stampa   *freedom of the press.*

stampare   *to print.*

stampatore, m.   *printer.*

STANCARE   *to tire.*

stancarsi   *to get tired.*

stanchezza   *tiredness.*

stanco   *tired.*

STANOTTE   *tonight.*

STANZA   *room, chamber.*

prendere una stanza all'albergo   *to take a room in an hotel.*

prenotare una stanza all'albergo   *to reserve a room at a hotel.*

stanza da bagno   *bathroom.*

stanza da letto   *bedroom.*

Si Affitta Stanza.   *Room to Let.*

STARE *to stay.*
non stare in se *to be beside oneself.*
stare a sentire *to listen to.*
stare attento *to be careful.*
stare bene *to feel well.*
stare di casa a *to live at.*
stare in piedi *to stand up.*
Che cosa stai facendo? *What are you doing?*
Come stanno le cose? *How do things stand?*
Lasciami stare! *Let me be!*
Stai qui finchè torno. *Stay here till I come back.*
Sto preparando il pranzo. *I'm preparing dinner.*
starnutire *to sneeze.*
starnuto *sneeze.*
STASERA *this evening; tonight.*
STATO *state.*
affari di stato *affairs of state.*
in cattivo stato *in bad shape; in poor condition.*
Gli Stati Uniti *The United States.*
Lo stato della sua salute mi preoccupa. *The state of his health worries me.*
Questo stato di cose non può durare. *This state of affairs cannot last.*
statua *statue.*
STAZIONE, f. *station.*
stazione balneare *beach resort; seaside resort.*
stazione climatica *health resort.*
stazione ferroviaria *railroad station.*
stecchino *toothpick.*
STELLA *star.*
portare alle stelle *to praise someone to the skies.*
stellato *starry, star-studded.*
stelo *stem, stalk.*
stemma, m. *emblem; coat of arms.*
stendere *to stretch out.*
stendere i panni *to hang the clothes.*
Mi ha steso la mano. *He offered his hand.*
stento *difficulty, fatigue.*
STESSO *self, selves.*
egli stesso *himself.*
essa stessa *herself.*
me stessa *myself,* f.
noi stessi *ourselves.*
STESSO, adj. *same.*
dello stesso sangue *of the same blood; kindred.*
sempre lo stesso *always the same.*
stile, m. *style.*
stilla *drop.*
stilla a stilla *drop by drop.*
stima *esteem, evaluation.*
degno di stima *worthy of esteem.*
fare una stima *to evaluate; to make an appraisal.*
stimare *to appraise; to consider; to esteem.*
Ho fatto stimare il mio anello. *I had my ring appraised.*
Lo stimerei un onore. *I would consider it an honor.*
Non mi stimo degno di questo onore. *I don't consider myself worthy of this honor.*
stimolare *to stimulate.*
L'odore d'arrosto stimola il mio appetito. *The smell of roast whets (stimulates) my appetite.*
stipendio *salary, wage.*
stipo *cabinet.*
STIRARE *to iron.*
far stirare *to have ironed.*
stirar(si) *to stretch.*
stiva *hold.*
stivale, m. *boot.*
stizza *grudge, pique.*
stoffa *material.*

fatto di stoffa buona *made with good material.*
stola *stole.*
stolto *foolish, silly.*
stomaco *stomach.*
mal di stomaco *stomach-ache.*
stonato *out of tune.*
stordire *to stun.*
stordito *dizzy.*
STORIA *story, tale, history.*
raccontare una storia *to tell a story.*
La storia insegna. . . *History teaches us. . .*
storico *historical; (as noun) historian.*
storpio *crippled.*
storto *crooked.*
stracciare *to tear.*
straccio *rag.*
carta straccia *wrapping paper; wastepaper.*
STRADA *street, road.*
farsi strada *to make headway; to get on.*
per istrada *on the road.*
strada di campagna *country road.*
strada facendo *on the way.*
strada maestra *main street.*
È sulla mia strada. *It's on my way.*
Non mi ha detto che strada prendere. *He did not tell me which road to take.*
STRANIERO *foreign; (as noun) foreigner.*
Egli parla una lingua straniera. *He speaks a foreign language.*
strano *strange, queer, odd.*
Mi sembra strano. *It seems strange to me.*
straordinario *extraordinary.*
strapazzo *overwork, disorder.*
strappare *to snatch; to tear.*
strato *layer.*
strato su strato *layer upon layer.*
uno strato di pòlvere *a layer of dust.*
stravolto *altered, troubled.*
strega *witch.*
stregare *to bewitch.*
strepito *noise.*
STRETTA *grasp, grip, hold.*
rallentare la stretta *to relax the grip.*
una stretta di mano *handshake.*
STRETTO *narrow, tight; (as noun) strait.*
La strada è molto stretta. *The street is very narrow.*
Lo Stretto di Messina. *The Strait of Messina.*
Questo vestito è troppo stretto per me. *This dress is too tight for me.*
stridente *shrill, sharp.*
stridere *to screech; to shriek.*
strillare *to scream; to shout.*
strillo *cry, shriek.*
strillone, m. *newsboy, newsman.*
STRINGERE *to tighten.*
far stringere i freni *to have the brakes tightened.*
stringere amicizia con *to make friends with.*
stringere la mano *to shake hands.*
Il tempo stringe. *Time presses; time is drawing short.*
striscia *strip, stripe.*
a strisce *striped.*
strisciare *to creep; to slide.*
strizzare *to wring out; to squeeze.*
strizzare i panni *to wring clothes out.*
strizzare un occhio *to wink.*
strofinare *to rub.*
strofinarsi *to rub oneself.*
strumento *tool, implement, instrument.*
studente, m.; **studentessa,** f. *student.*
STUDIARE *to study.*

studio *study.*
stufa *stove.*
stufare *to stew.*
stufarsi *to grow weary.* (Colloq.)
stufato *stew.*
stufo *weary, tired.*
stupendo *stupendous.*
stupidamente *stupidly.*
stupido *stupid; (as noun) fool.*
stupire *to astonish.*
stupirsi *to be astonished.*
stupore, m. *astonishment, stupor.*
SU *up, above, on.*
andar su per le scale *to go up the stairs.*
sulla panca *on the bench.*
sullo scaffale *on the shelf.*
su per giù *more or less.*
più su *further up.*
subire *to endure; to feel.*
SUBITO *immediately; at once.*
subito dopo *right after.*
subito prima *just before.*
Bisogna farlo subito. *It must be done right away.*
Torno subito. *I'll be right back.*
Vieni subito! *Come quickly!*
sublime *sublime.*
SUCCEDERE *to happen; to follow.*
Che cosa è successo? *What happened?*
La calma succede alla tempesta. *Calm follows the storm.*
successione, f. *succession.*
successivamente *successively.*
successivo *successive, following.*
la settimana successiva *the following week.*
successo *success.*
aver successo *to be successful.*
successore, m. *successor.*
SUCCHIARE *to suck.*
succo *juice.*
succursale, f. *branch; branch office.*
SUD, m. *south.*
a sud di *south of.*
sud-est *southeast.*
sud-ovest *southwest.*
sudare *to perspire; to sweat.*
suddetto *above-mentioned.*
suddito *subject.*
sudicio *dirty.*
sudore, m. *perspiration, sweat.*
sufficiente *sufficient.*
sufficienza *sufficient quantity.*
a sufficienza *more than enough.*
suggerire *to suggest; to prompt.*
sughero *cook.*
sugo *juice, gravy.*
SUO, sua, suoi, sue (il suo; la sua; i suoi; le sue) *his, her, its.*
la sua maestra *his teacher; her teacher.*
suo padre *his father; her father.*
Metti questo libro al posto suo. *Put this book in its place.*
Vive coi suoi. *He lives with his parents (family).*
SUOCERA *mother-in-law.*
SUOCERO *father-in-law.*
suolo *soil, ground.*
il patrio suolo *native soil.*
SUONARE *to sound; to ring; to play.*
suonare il campanello *to ring the bell.*
suonare il pianoforte *to play the piano.*
suonare l'allarme *to sound the alarm.*
SUONO *sound.*

a suon di   *to the tune of.*
suora   *nun, sister.*
SUPERARE   *to surpass; to excel; to exceed.*
   superare gli esami   *to pass one's examinations.*
   superare in numero   *to surpass in number.*
   Mi supera per ingegno.   *He has greater talent than I.*
superbo   *proud.*
superficiale   *superficial.*
superficie, f.   *surface.*
superfluo   *superfluous.*
superiore   *superior; (also noun, m.).*
superiorità   *superiority.*
superlativo   *superlative.*
superstizione, f.   *superstition.*
superuomo   *superman.*
suppergiù   *approximately, about.*
supplire   *to substitute; to be enough.*
supporre   *to suppose.*
supposizione, f.   *supposition.*
supposto   *supposed.*
supremo   *supreme.*
   la Corte Suprema   *the Supreme Court.*
suscettibile   *susceptible, touchy.*
suscettibilità   *susceptibility.*
   offendere la suscettibilità di   *to hurt the feelings of.*
suscitare   *to rouse; to provoke; to give rise to.*
   suscitare l'ira di qualcuno   *to rouse someone's anger.*
   suscitare uno scandalo   *to provoke a scandal.*
susurrare   *to murmur; to mutter.*
Suvvia!   *Come on!*
svagare   *to distract.*
   Mi voglio svagare un po'.   *I want to amuse myself (distract myself) a little.*
svago   *amusement, recreation.*
SVANIRE   *to vanish.*
svanito   *vanished.*
SVEGLIA   *alarm clock.*
SVEGLIARE   *to wake.*
   svegliar(si)   *to wake up.*
sveglio   *awake, alert, quick-witted.*
   È una ragazza molto sveglia.   *She is a very bright girl.*
   Sono sveglio dalle sette di questa mattina.   *I've been awake since seven this morning.*
svelare   *to reveal.*
   svelare un segreto   *to reveal a secret.*
sveltamente   *quickly.*
sveltezza   *quickness.*
svelto   *quick, rapid, swift.*
   Bisogna agire alla svelta.   *We must act quickly.*
svenire   *to faint.*
sventura   *misfortune.*
sventuratamente   *unfortunately.*
sventurato   *unfortunate, unlucky.*
svenuto   *unconscious; in a faint.*
svestire   *to undress.*
   svestirsi   *to undress oneself.*
sviare   *to mislead; to lead astray.*
sviluppo   *development, growth.*
svista   *oversight.*
   Fu una svista da parte mia.   *It was an oversight on my part.*
svitare   *to unscrew.*
svizzero   *Swiss; (also noun).*
svogliato   *indifferent.*
svolgere   *to develop; to unfold.*
svolta   *turn; turning point.*

T

tabaccaio   *tobacco-shop owner.*

tabacco   *tobacco.*
tacchino   *turkey.*
tacciare   *to accuse; to charge with.*
tacco   *heel.*
taccuino   *notebook.*
TACERE   *to be silent.*
   far tacere   *to silence.*
tacitamente   *silently, tacitly.*
tacito   *tacit, silent.*
taciturno   *taciturn.*
taffetà   *taffeta.*
taglia   *size, ransom.*
   della stessa taglia   *of the same size.*
tagliacarte, m.   *paper-knife.*
TAGLIARE   *to cut.*
   essere tagliato per   *to be cut out for.*
   farsi tagliare i capelli   *to get a haircut.*
   tagliare i panni addosso a   *to speak ill of.*
tagliatelle, f.   *noodles.*
tagliente   *cutting, sharp.*
taglio   *cut.*
   Il taglio di questo vestito non mi si addice.   *The cut of this suit is not good for me.*
talco   *talc.*
TALE   *such.*
   di uno splendore tale   *of such splendor.*
   il signor Tal di Tale   *Mr. So-and-So.*
   quel tale   *that certain party.*
   tale e quale   *exactly the same.*
talento   *talent, intelligence.*
tallone, m.   *heel.*
talmente   *so; so much.*
talvolta   *sometimes.*
tamburo   *drum.*
tana   *den, lair.*
tanfo   *odor, stench, smell.*
   C'è un tanfo di muffa in questa stanza.   *There is a musty smell in this room.*
tangibile   *tangible.*
tangibilmente   *tangibly.*
TANTO   *so; so much.*
   di tanto in tanto   *from time to time.*
   ogni tanto   *every so often.*
   tanto meglio   *so much the better.*
   tanto per cominciare   *to begin with.*
   tanto quanto   *as much as.*
   una volta tanto   *once in a while.*
   Si vogliono tanto bene.   *They love each other so much.*
tappa   *halting place.*
   a piccole tappe   *in small stretches.*
tappare   *to stop; to stop up; to cork.*
   tappare una bottiglia   *to cork a bottle.*
tappetino   *small rug; scatter rug.*
tappeto   *rug, carpet.*
tappezzeria   *tapestry, wall-paper.*
tappezziere, m.   *upholsterer.*
tappo   *stopper, cork.*
TARDARE   *to delay; to be late.*
   Ho tardato tanto a scrivere perchè sono stata male.   *I delayed so long in writing because I've been ill.*
   Non tarderanno molto a venire.   *They will not be very late coming.*
TARDI   *late.*
   fare tardi   *to be late.*
   meglio tardi che mai   *better late than never.*
   presto o tardi   *sooner or later.*
   Si sta facendo tardi.   *It's getting late.*
targa   *plate, nameplate.*
   targa dell' automobile   *license plate.*
tariffa   *rate, tariff.*
tarma   *moth.*

tarmare   *to become moth-eaten.*
tartagliare   *to stutter; to stammer.*
tartaruga   *tortoise, turtle.*
tasca   *pocket.*
tassa   *tax, duty.*
   tassa d'ammissione   *entrance fee.*
   tassa sul reddito   *income tax.*
tassare   *to tax.*
tassativo   *positive, explicit.*
tassì, m.   *taxi.*
tastare·   *to feel; to touch.*
tastiera   *keyboard.*
tasto   *key (of musical instruments).*
tattica   *tactics.*
   seguire la tattica sbagliata   *to go about things in the wrong manner.*
TAVOLA   *table, board, plank.*
   apparecchiare la tavola   *to set the table.*
   sparecchiare la tavola   *to clear the table.*
   una tavola di legno   *a wooden board.*
TAZZA   *cup.*
   tazza da tè   *teacup.*
   tazza di tè   *cup of tea.*
te   *you, sing.*
   Parlo di te.   *I am speaking of you.*
tè, m.   *tea.*
teatrale   *theatrical.*
TEATRO   *theatre.*
tecnica   *technique.*
tecnicamente   *technically.*
tecnico   *technical; (as noun) technician.*
tedesco   *German; (also noun).*
tediare   *to tire; to weary; to bore.*
   tediarsi   *to get weary; to get tired; to be bored.*
tedio   *weariness, tediousness.*
tedioso   *tedious, weary.*
tegame, m.   *pan.*
tegola   *tile.*
teiera   *teapot.*
tela   *cloth, linen.*
telefonare   *to telephone.*
telefonata   *telephone call.*
telefonicamente   *by telephone.*
telefonico   *telephonic.*
   cabina telefonica   *telephone booth.*
telefonista, m. & f.   *telephone operator.*
telefono   *telephone.*
telegrafare   *to telegraph; to wire.*
telegrafia   *telegraphy.*
telegraficamente   *telegraphically.*
telegrafico   *telegraphic.*
   ufficio telegrafico   *telegraph office.*
telegrafista, m. & f.   *telegraphist.*
telegrafo   *telegraph.*
telegramma   *telegram, wire, cable.*
telepatia   *telepathy.*
   telepatia mentale   *mental telepathy.*
telescopio   *telescope.*
televisione, f.   *television.*
tema, m.   *theme.*
tema, f.   *fear.*
   per tema di   *for fear of.*
temerario   *rash.*
TEMERE   *to fear; to be afraid; to dread.*
   Non temo di nulla.   *I fear nothing.*
temibile   *dreadful.*
temperamatite, m.   *pencil sharpener.*
temperante   *temperate, sober, tempering.*
temperatura   *temperature.*
temperino   *penknife.*
tempesta   *storm, tempest.*
   una tempesta in un bicchier d'acqua   *a storm in a teacup.*

tempestivo *timely.*

tempestoso *tempestuous.*

tempia *temple (side of head).*

tempio *temple (cathedral).*

TEMPO *time, weather.*

cattivo tempo *bad weather.*

di questi tempi *in these times.*

di tempo in tempo *from time to time.*

nello stesso tempo *at the same time.*

perdere tempo *to lose time.*

tempo fà *some time ago.*

tempo presente *present tense.*

Che tempo fa? *How is the weather?*

Chi ha tempo non aspetti tempo. *Never put off till tomorrow what can be done today.*

Da quanto tempo non ci vediamo! *How long it has been since we've seen each other!*

È tempo di... *It's time to ...*

temporale, m. *storm.*

temporaneamente *temporarily.*

temporaneo *temporary.*

tenace *tenacious, persevering.*

tenacemente *tenaciously.*

tenacia *tenaciousness.*

tenda *tent, curtain.*

tendenza *tendency.*

tendere *to tend to; to stretch out; to hold out.*

tenente, m. *lieutenant.*

teneramente *tenderly.*

TENERE *to keep; to hold.*

tenere a mente *to remember; to keep in mind.*

tenere compagnia a *to keep someone company.*

tenere d'occhio *to keep an eye on.*

tenere gli occhi aperti *to keep one's eyes open.*

tenere il broncio verso *to keep a grudge against.*

tenere il fiato *to hold one's breath.*

tenere le mani in mano *to be idle.*

tenersi a destra *to keep to the right.*

tenersi in contatto con *to keep in contact with.*

Non ci tengo. *I don't care about it.*

tenerezza *tenderness.*

tenero *tender, affectionate.*

tenore, m. *tenor.*

tensione, f. *tension.*

tensione nervosa *nervous tension.*

TENTARE *to attempt.*

tentativo *attempt, endeavor.*

tentazione, f. *temptation.*

resistere alla tentazione *to resist temptation.*

tentennare *to sway; to hesitate.*

tenuta *estate, country farm.*

teorìa *theory.*

tergere *to wipe; to dry.*

terme, f. pl. *hot springs.*

TERMINARE *to finish; to end.*

Appena ho terminato questo lavoro, ti raggiungo. *I'll join you as soon as I finish this work.*

termine, m. *term, limit, boundary.*

allo scadere del termine fissato *at the end of the established term.*

aver termine *to end.*

fissare un termine *to fix a date; to set a date.*

porre termine a *to put an end to.*

ridurre ai minimi termini *to reduce to the lowest terms.*

secondo i termini stabiliti in precedenza *according to the terms previously agreed to.*

termòmetro *thermometer.*

termos, m. *thermos bottle.*

termosifone, m. *radiator (heating).*

TERRA *earth.*

cader per terra *to fall to the ground.*

per terra *on the ground.*

scendere a terra *to go ashore.*

terra madre *motherland; native land.*

terra nativa *native land.*

terrazza *balcony, terrace.*

terreno *earthly; (as noun) earth.*

a pian terreno *on the ground floor.*

perdere terreno *to lose ground.*

terribile *terrible.*

terribilmente *terribly.*

territorio *territory.*

terrore, m. *terror.*

terrorizzare *to terrorize.*

TERZA *third class.*

fare la terza elementare *to be in the third grade in elementary school.*

mettere in terza *to shift to high gear.*

viaggiare in terza *to travel third class.*

TERZO *third; (also noun).*

teso *stretched out; tightened.*

tesoro *treasure.*

tessera *card, ticket.*

tessere *to weave.*

tessuto *cloth, fabric.*

TESTA *head.*

alla testa di *at the head of.*

giramento di testa *dizzy spell.*

mal di testa *headache.*

perdere la testa *to lose one's head.*

testardaggine, f. *stubbornness.*

testardamente *stubbornly.*

testardo *stubborn, headstrong.*

teste, m. & f. *witness.*

testimone, m. & f. *witness.*

testimone oculare *eye-witness.*

testimonianza *testimony.*

testimoniare *to witness.*

testo *text.*

libro di testo *textbook.*

testuale *exact, precise.*

le mie testuali parole *my very words.*

tetro *gloomy, dismal.*

TETTO *roof.*

TI *you; to you; yourself.*

Che cosa ti ha detto? *What did he tell you?*

Questo libro ti appartiene. *This book belongs to you.*

Ti sei guardato allo specchio? *Did you look at yourself in the mirror?*

tiara *tiara.*

tiepido *tepid, lukewarm.*

tifone, m. *typhoon.*

tifoso *typhus patient; fan.*

un tifoso del cinema *movie fan.*

un tifoso del pugilato *boxing fan.*

tignola (tignuola) *moth.*

tigre, f. *tiger, tigress.*

timbro *stamp.*

timbro postale *postmark.*

timidamente *timidly.*

timidezza *timidity, shyness.*

tìmido *timid, shy.*

TIMORE, m. *fear.*

aver timore di *to be afraid of.*

per timore di *for fear of.*

tìmpano *eardrum.*

tìngere *to dye; to tint.*

tingere di nero *to dye black.*

tingersi i capelli *to dye one's hair.*

tinta *dye.*

a forti tinte *sensational.*

tintore, m. *dyer.*

tipicamente *typically.*

tìpico *typical.*

tipo *type.*

tiranno *tyrant.*

TIRARE *to draw; to pull.*

tirare a scherma *to fence.*

tirare a sorte *to draw lots.*

tirare avanti *to keep going.*

tirare un colpo *to fire a shot.*

tirar per le lunghe *to go on and on.*

tirarsi da una parte *to stand aside.*

tirarsi indietro *to draw back.*

una carrozza tirata da quattro cavalli *a coach drawn by four horses.*

tiretto *drawer.*

tiro *trick.*

tirocinio *apprenticeship.*

titolato *titled.*

titolo *title.*

titubante *hesitant, irresolute.*

titubanza *hesitancy, irresoluteness.*

titubare *to hesitate; to waver.*

TOCCARE *to touch.*

toccare il cuore *to touch one's heart.*

toccare sul vivo *to touch a sore spot.*

A chi tocca? *Whose turn is it?*

Mi tocca rifare la strada. *I have to retrace my footsteps.*

Tocca alla madre educar bene i propri figli. *It's a mother's duty to educate her children.*

TOGLIERE *to take; to take off; to remove.*

togliere di mano *to snatch.*

togliersi di mezzo *to get out of the way.*

togliersi il cappello ed il cappotto *to remove one's hat and coat.*

togliersi la vita *to commit suicide.*

Chi ha tolto il libro che era qui? *Who took the book that was here?*

toletta *toilet, toilette.*

tollerabile *tolerable.*

tollerante *tolerant.*

tolleranza *tolerance.*

tomba *grave, tomb.*

tondo *round.*

cifra tonda *round sum.*

dire chiaro e tondo *to speak plainly.*

tonico *tonic, noun & adj.*

tonnellata *ton.*

tonno *tuna.*

tono *tone, tint.*

con tono aspro *with a sharp tone.*

Non permetto che mi si parli in quel tono di voce. *I will not be spoken to in that tone of voice.*

Questi sono tutti toni diversi del medesimo colore. *These are different tints of the same color.*

tonsilla *tonsil.*

tonsillite, f. *tonsillitis.*

topazio *topaz.*

topo *mouse.*

Topolino. *Mickey Mouse (little mouse).*

torbido *muddy; not clear.*

torcere *to twist.*

torcia *torch.*

torcicollo *stiff neck.*

torlo *yolk; egg yolk.*

tormenta *blizzard.*

tormentare *to torment.*

tormentarsi *to torment oneself; to worry.*

tormento *torment, torture.*

TORNARE *to return.*

tornare a casa *to come home.*

tornare in se *to come to one's senses.*

tornare sui propri passi *to retrace one's foot-steps.*

Il conto non torna. *The account is incorrect.*

Torna indietro! *Come back!*

tornèo *tournament.*

toro *bull.*

torpedone, m. *bus, motor-coach.*

torre, f. *tower.*

la Torre di Pisa *the Tower of Pisa (the Leaning Tower).*

torrente, m. *torrent, stream.*

Piove a torrenti. *It's raining in torrents.*

torso *trunk, torso.*

torta *cake, pastry.*

torta di frutta *pie.*

TORTO *wrong.*

a torto o a ragione *right or wrong.*

aver torto *to be wrong.*

essere dalla parte del torto *to be in the wrong.*

fare un torto a *to wrong someone.*

tortuoso *tortuous, winding.*

tosse, f. *cough.*

tosse convulsiva *whooping cough.*

un colpo di tosse *a coughing fit; a coughing spell.*

Ho la tosse. *I have a cough.*

TOSSIRE *to cough.*

tosto *hard.*

aver la faccia tosta *to have cheek; to be impudent.*

uovo tosto *hard-boiled egg.*

tosto, adv. *soon.*

totale, m. *total; (also adj.).*

totalmente *totally.*

TOVAGLIA *tablecloth.*

tovagliolo *napkin.*

traballare *to stagger; to reel.*

traboccare *to overflow.*

traccia *trace, track, trail.*

mettersi sulle tracce di *to follow in the trail of.*

perdere traccia di *to lose track of.*

seguire la traccia di *to follow the track of.*

Non ne rimane neppure una traccia. *There is not a trace of it left.*

tracciare *to trace; to mark out; to draw.*

tracciare una linea *to make a line.*

tradimento *betrayal, treason.*

colpevole di alto tradimento *guilty of high treason.*

TRADIRE *to betray; to deceive; to be unfaithful to.*

tradire la propria moglie *to be unfaithful to one's wife.*

tradirsi *to betray oneself; to give oneself away.*

Egli ha tradito la patria. *He betrayed his country.*

La sua espressione tradiva il suo terrore. *Her expression betrayed her terror.*

traditore, m.; **traditrice,** f. *traitor.*

tradizionale *traditional.*

traducibile *translatable.*

tradurre *to translate.*

tradurre dall'italiano all'inglese *to translate from Italian to English.*

traduttore, m.; **traduttrice,** f. *translator.*

traduzione, f. *translation.*

trafficare *to trade; to traffic.*

traffico *traffic.*

tragedia *tragedy.*

traghetto *ferry, ferryboat.*

tragicamente *tragically.*

tragico *tragic; (as noun) tragedian.*

tragicomico *tragicomic.*

tragitto *journey, passage.*

tralasciare *to leave out; to omit.*

senza tralasciare nulla *without leaving anything out.*

tralucere *to be transparent; to shine through.*

tram, m. *trolley-car.*

tramandare *to hand down.*

Questa usanza fu tramandata da padre in figlio. *This custom was handed down from father to son.*

TRAMONTARE *to go down; to set; to fade.*

al tramontar del sole *at sundown.*

La sua gloria non tramonterà mai. *His glory will never fade.*

tramonto *setting.*

tramonto del sole *sunset.*

trampolino *springboard.*

trampolo *stilt.*

camminare sui trampoli *to walk on stilts.*

tramutamento *change.*

tramutare *to transmute; to turn.*

La sua gioia si è tramutata in dolore. *His joy turned to sorrow.*

tranello *trap, snare.*

tendere un tranello *to trap; to ensnare.*

TRANNE *save, but, except.*

tutti tranne uno *all save one; all but one.*

Ha invitato tutti tranne Maria. *She invited everyone except Mary.*

tranquillamente *peacefully.*

tranquillizzare *to quiet; to calm.*

tranquillizzarsi *to calm down; to calm oneself.*

tranquillità *tranquillity, peace.*

tranquillo *peaceful.*

mare tranquillo *a calm sea.*

Lasciami tranquillo. *Leave me in peace.*

transazione, f. *transaction.*

transigere *to yield; to come to terms.*

Su questioni di denaro io non trinsigo. *On financial matters I do not yield.*

transitare *to pass through.*

Molte persone transitano per questa strada. *Many people pass through this street.*

trànsito *transit.*

La merce è in trànsito. *The merchandise is in transit.*

Vietato il Trànsito! *No Through Traffic!*

transitorio *transitory, temporary.*

transizione, f. *transition.*

tranvài, m. *streetcar; trolley car.*

trapiantare *to transplant.*

trappola *trap, snare.*

cadere in trappola *to be caught in a trap.*

trapunta *quilt.*

trarre *to draw; to draw out.*

trarre in inganno *to deceive.*

trarre ispirazione da *to draw inspiration from.*

trarre vantaggio da *to benefit from.*

trarsi in disparte *to draw aside.*

trasalire *to start.*

Un rumore improvviso mi ha fatto trasalire. *A sudden noise made me start (startled me).*

trasandato *careless.*

trascinare *to drag.*

trascinare per terra *to drag about the floor.*

trascinarsi *to drag oneself.*

trascorrere *to spend; to pass.*

trascorrere il tempo leggendo *to spend the time reading.*

Abbiamo trascorso un'estate meravigliosa in campagna. *We spent a marvelous summer in the country.*

Sono trascorsi molti anni dall'ultima volta che lo vidi. *Many years have gone by since the last time I saw him.*

trascrivere *transcribe.*

trascrizione, f. *transcription.*

trascurabile *negligible.*

TRASCURARE *to neglect.*

trascurare il proprio dovere *to neglect one's duties.*

trascurarsi *to neglect oneself.*

trascuratamente *carelessly.*

trascuratezza *carelessness, neglect.*

trascurato *careless.*

trasferimento *transfer.*

trasferire *to transfer.*

trasferirsi *to move.*

Fu trasferito da una città all'altra. *He was transferred from one city to the other.*

trasformare *to transform.*

trasformarsi *to transform oneself.*

trasformazione, f. *transformation.*

trasfusione, f. *transfusion.*

trasfusione di sangue *blood transfusion.*

trasgredire *to transgress.*

traslocare *to move; to change address.*

trasloco *removal.*

furgone per traslochi *moving van.*

trasmettere *to transmit.*

trasmettere per radio *to broadcast.*

trasmettitore, m. *transmitter.*

trasmissione, f. *transmission, broadcast.*

trasognato *dreamy; lost in reverie; lost in day-dreams.*

trasparente *transparent.*

trasparire *to shine through; to be transparent.*

traspirare *to perspire.*

traspirazione, f. *perspiration.*

trasportare *to transport; to convey.*

trasportare per mare *to transport by sea.*

trasportare per terra *to transport by land.*

trasportato *transported.*

trasporto *transportation, transport.*

Non vi sono mezzi di trasporto. *There is no means of conveyance.*

trastullare *to amuse; to toy with.*

trasvolare *to fly across; to fly.*

trasvolata *flight.*

tratta *draft.*

pagare una tratta *to pay a draft.*

tratta bancaria *bank draft.*

trattabile *tractable, treatable.*

trattamento *treatment.*

TRATTARE *to treat; to deal (with).*

trattare bene *to treat well.*

trattare male *to treat badly.*

trattare un argomento *to deal with a subject.*

trattarsi *to be a question of.*

Di che si tratta? *What is it all about?*

Si tratta della prossima festa. *It's about the coming party.*

trattative, f. pl. *negotiations.*

condurre a termine le trattative *to carry out negotiations.*

essere in trattative *to be negotiating.*

Abbiamo dovuto interrompere le trattative. *Negotiations had to be interrupted.*

trattato *treaty.*

trattato di pace *peace treaty.*

TRATTENERE *to withhold; to restrain; to keep.*

trattenere il respiro *to hold one's breath.*

trattenere le lacrime *to restrain one's tears.*

Mi dispiace non potermi trattenere più a lungo

con voi. *I'm sorry I can't stay with you any longer.*

Riesco a stento a trattenermi. *I can hardly restrain myself.*

Si è trattenuta la somma che gli dovevo. *He withheld the sum I owed him.*

trattenimento *entertainment.*

Vorrei organizzare un piccolo trattenimento in casa mia domani sera. *I would like to organize a small party at my house tomorrow night.*

trattenuta *deduction.*

trattino *hyphen, dash.*

TRATTO *stroke, gesture.*

a grandi tratti *by leaps and bounds.*

da un tratto all'altro *from one moment to the other.*

tutto d'un tratto *all of a sudden.*

un tratto di spirito *a joke; a witty remark.*

un tratto di strada *a part of the way.*

trattore, m. *tractor.*

trattorìa *restaurant; eating place.*

travaglio *labor, toil, anxiety.*

trave, f. *beam, rafter.*

TRAVERSARE *to cross.*

traversare una strada *to cross a street.*

traversata *crossing.*

travestimento *disguise.*

travestire *to disguise.*

travisare *to distort; to misrepresent.*

Egli ha travisato completamente i fatti. *He completely distorted the facts.*

travolgere *to sweep away.*

TRE *three.*

treccia *braid.*

portare le trecce *to wear one's hair in braids.*

trecento *three hundred.*

tredicesimo *thirteenth,* noun & adj.

tredici *thirteen.*

tregua *truce.*

senza tregua *unrelentingly.*

TREMARE *to tremble; to shake.*

tremar di freddo *to shiver with cold.*

tremar di paura *to shake with fear.*

tremarella *trembling.*

aver la tremarella *to have the shakes.*

tremendamente *tremendously.*

tremito *trembling, tremble.*

TRENO *train.*

perdere il treno *to miss the train.*

prendere il treno *to take the train.*

treno direttissimo *express train.*

treno diretto *fast train.*

treno merci *freight train.*

trenta *thirty.*

trentesimo *thirtieth.*

trepidante *anxious, apprehensive, trembling.*

triangolare *triangular.*

triangolo *triangle.*

tribolare *to trouble; to worry; to suffer.*

tribolazione, f. *worry, suffering, tribulation.*

tribù, f. *tribe.*

tribunale, m. *tribunal, court.*

tributare *to give; to render.*

tributare omaggio *to pay homage.*

tributario *tributary.*

tributo *tribute.*

triciclo *tricycle.*

trifoglio *clover.*

trilingue *trilingual.*

trimestrale *quarterly.*

trimestre, m. *quarter.*

trio *trio.*

trionfale *triumphal.*

trionfalmente *triumphantly.*

trionfante *triumphant.*

trionfare *to triumph.*

trionfare di *to triumph over.*

trionfo *triumph.*

triplice *threefold.*

triplo *triple.*

trippa *tripe.*

trisillabo *trisyllable.*

TRISTE *sad, sorrowful.*

uno sguardo triste *a sad look.*

tristemente *sadly, sorrowfully.*

tristezza *sadness, sorrow.*

tristo *wicked.*

tritacarne, m. *meat grinder.*

tritare *to mince; to hash.*

trito *trite, common.*

tritolare *to crush.*

triviale *trivial, vulgar.*

trivialità *triviality.*

trivialmente *trivially; vulgarly.*

trofèo *trophy.*

tromba *trumpet.*

troncare *to cut off; to break off.*

tronco *trunk (tree).*

trono *throne.*

tropicale *tropical.*

TROPPO *too; too much.*

parlare troppo *to talk too much.*

troppi *too many.*

troppo forte *too loud; too strong.*

troppo spesso *too often.*

trottare *to trot.*

trotto *trot.*

mettere a trotto *to put to a trot.*

TROVARE *to find.*

trovarsi come a casa propria *to feel at home.*

Come l'hai trovato? *How did you find it?*

Come ti trovi qui? *How do you feel here?*

Mi trovo molto bene, grazie. *I feel quite well, thank you.*

Ti verrò a trovare. *I'll come to see you.*

trovata *invention, contrivance, expedient.*

trovatello *foundling.*

ospizio dei trovatelli *foundling hospital; foundling home.*

truccare *to make up; to apply make-up.*

truccarsi *to make oneself up.*

truccarsi da pagliaccio *to make up as a clown.*

truffa *swindle.*

truffare *to cheat; to swindle.*

truffatore, m. *cheat, cheater, swindler.*

truppa *troop.*

TU *you,* fam. sing.

tubare *to coo.*

tubatura *piping; plumbing pipes.*

tubercolare *tubercular.*

tubercolosi, f. *tuberculosis.*

tuberosa *tuberose.*

tubo *pipe, tube.*

tubo del gas *gas pipe.*

tubo di scarico *exhaust pipe.*

tubolare *tubular.*

tuffare *to plunge.*

tuffarsi *to dive.*

tuffata *dive.*

tuffo *dive.*

bombardiere a tuffo *dive bomber.*

sentire un tuffo al cuore *to feel one's heart skip a beat.*

tugurio *hovel.*

tumulto *tumult, uproar.*

tumultuoso *tumultuous.*

tunnel, m. *tunnel.*

TUO, tua, tuoi, tue (il tuo; la tua; i tuoi; le tue) *your, yours.*

Il tuo libro è qui. *Your book is here.*

Questo libro è tuo. *This book is yours.*

tuorlo *yolk.*

turacciolo *cork.*

turare *to stop; to cork; to fill.*

turare un dente *to fill a tooth.*

turarsi gli orecchi *to stop one's ears.*

turba *mob, crowd.*

turbamento *agitation, commotion.*

turbante, m. *turban.*

turbare *to trouble; to disturb; to agitate.*

turbarsi *to become agitated.*

Questo pensiero mi turba molto. *This thought disturbs me a great deal.*

turbato *troubled, agitated.*

avere un aria turbata *to have a troubled air.*

turbinare *to whirl.*

turbine, m. *hurricane, whirlwind.*

un turbine di pólvere *a whirl of dust.*

turbolento *turbulent, troubled.*

turbolenza *turbulence.*

turchese, f. *turquoise.*

turchino *dark blue.*

turismo *touring.*

turista, m. *tourist.*

turistico *touring, tourist.*

classe turistica *tourist class.*

turno *turn.*

essere di turno *to be on duty.*

lavorare a turni *to work by turns.*

medico di turno *doctor on duty.*

tuta *overall.*

tutela *tutelage, guardianship.*

sotto la tutela di *under the wardship of.*

tutelare *to protect; to defend.*

tutore, m. *guardian, protector.*

TUTTAVIA *still, yet, however, nevertheless.*

Non lo vedo da molti anni, tuttavìa credo che lo riconoscerei subito. *I haven't seen him in many years, yet I think I would recognize him right away.*

TUTTO *all, whole, every.*

del tutto *quite, completely.*

essere tutti d'accordo *to be all in agreement.*

in tutto e per tutto *all and for all.*

tutte le sere *every night.*

tutti i giorni *every day.*

tutti insieme *all together.*

tutto ciò che *all that.*

tutto fatto *all done.*

tutto il giorno *all day.*

tutto il mondo *all the world; the whole world.*

Essa conosce tutta la mia famiglia. *She knows all my family.*

U

ubbidire *to obey.*

ubbidiente *obedient.*

ubbriaco (ubriaco) *drunk, inebriated.*

ubriacare *to make drunk; to intoxicate.*

ubriacarsi *to become drunk; to become intoxicated.*

ubriacatura *intoxication.*

ubriachezza *drunkenness.*

ubriacone, m. *drunkard.*

UCCELLO *bird.*

uccello di mal augurio *bird of ill omen.*

UCCIDERE *to kill; to slay.*

uccidersi *to commit suicide; to kill oneself.*

uccisione, f. *killing, murder.*

ucciso *killed, slain.*

uccisore, m. *killer.*

udibile *audible.*

udienza *audience, hearing.*
chiedere un'udienza *to ask an audience.*
L'udienza è rinviata. *Court is adjourned.*

UDIRE *to hear.*
Egli fu udito entrare a mezzanotte. *He was heard coming in at midnight.*
Non ho udito bene. *I didn't hear well.*
Odo un rumore strano. *I hear a strange noise.*

udito *hearing.*
aver l'udito fine *to have a good hearing.*

uditore, m.; **uditrice,** f. *hearer, listener.*

uditorio *auditory; (as noun) audience.*

ufficiale, noun, m. *official, officer.*
ufficiale della marina *navy officer.*

ufficiale *official.*
comunicato ufficiale *official communiqué.*
L'Italiano è la lingua ufficiale dell'Italia. *Italian is the official language in Italy.*

ufficiare *to officiate.*

UFFICIO *office.*
per i buoni uffici di *by the good offices of; through the courtesy of.*
ufficio postale *post office.*
ufficio telegrafico *telegraph office.*

uggia *dislike, annoyance.*
L'ho in uggia dal giorno che l'ho conosciuto. *I've disliked him since the very day I met him.*

uggioso *dull, tiresome.*
una giornata uggiosa *a boring day; a dull day.*

ugola *uvula.*

uguale *equal, same.*
Dividilo in parti uguali. *Divide it in equal parts.*
Il prezzo dei due abiti è uguale. *The price of the two dresses is the same.*
La legge è uguale per tutti. *The law is the same for everyone.*

uguaglianza *equality.*

uguagliare *to equal.*
Nessuna ti uguaglia in bellezza. *No one equals you in beauty.*

ugualmente *equally; all the same.*
Devi essere ugualmente gentile con tutti. *You must be equally courteous with everyone.*
Preferirei restare in casa questa sera, ma dovrò uscire ugualmente. *I would prefer to remain at home this evening, but I will have to go out all the same.*

ulcera *ulcer.*

ulcerare *to ulcerate.*

ulcerato *ulcerated.*

ulteriore *further, ulterior.*
Ti darò ulteriori informazioni domani. *I will give you further information tomorrow.*

ulteriormente *ulteriorly; later on.*

ultimamente *ultimately.*

ultimare *to finish; to complete.*
I lavori furono ultimati soltanto ieri. *The work was completed only yesterday.*
a lavoro ultimato *upon completion of the work.*

ultimatum *ultimatum.*

ULTIMO *latest, last.*
le ultime notizie *the latest news.*
l'ultima volta che ci siamo visti *the last time we saw each other.*
ultima moda *latest fashion.*
Fui l'ultima ad arrivare. *I was the last to arrive.*

ultramoderno *ultrafashionable.*

ultravioletto *ultraviolet.*

ululare *to howl.*
Il vento ulula. *The wind is howling.*

ululato (ululo) *howl, howling.*

umanamente *humanly, humanely.*
trattare umanamente *to treat humanely.*
Non è umanamente possibile. *It is not humanly possible.*

umanità, f. *humanity, mankind, humaneness.*

umanitario *humanitarian.*

umanizzare *to humanize.*
umanizzarsi *to become humane.*

umano *human, humane.*
la natura umana *human nature.*
ogni essere umano *every human being.*

umidità *humidity, dampness, moisture.*
l'umidità dell'aria *the humidity of the air.*

umido *damp, moist.*

umile *humble.*
di umile origine *of humble origin; of humble birth.*

umiliante *humiliating, mortifying.*

umiliare *to humiliate; to mortify.*
umiliarsi *to humble oneself.*

umiliato *humbled, humiliated.*

umiliazione, f. *humiliation.*

umilmente *humbly.*

umiltà *humility, humbleness.*

UMORE, m. *humor, temper.*
di cattivo umore *bad-tempered, moody.*
d'umore nero *in bad humor.*

umorismo *humor.*
Non è il caso di fare dell'umorismo. *It's not a matter to joke about.*

umorista, m. *humorist.*

umoristico *humorous.*

un *see uno.*

unanime *unanimous.*

unanimemente *unanimously.*

unanimità *unanimity.*
all'unanimità *unanimously.*

uncinetto *crochet hook.*
lavoro all'uncinetto *crochet.*

undicesimo *eleventh, noun & adj.*

undici *eleven.*

ungere *to grease; to smear.*
ungere le ruote *to oil the wheels; to make things go more smoothly.*

unghia *nail, hoof.*
le unghie del cavallo *the horse's hooves.*
pulirsi le unghie *to clean one's nails.*
spazzolino da unghie *nail brush.*

unguento *unguent, ointment.*

unicamente *only, solely.*

UNICO *only, sole, unique.*
l'unico motivo della mia visita *the sole reason for my visit.*
Ha un talento unico al mondo. *He has a unique talent.*

unificare *to unify.*

unificazione, f. *unification.*

uniformare *to conform.*
Mi sono uniformato ai suoi voleri. *I complied with his wishes.*

uniforme, f. *uniform.*
indossare l'uniforme militare *to don military uniform.*

uniforme *uniform.*

uniformità *uniformity.*

unione, f. *union.*

UNIRE *to unite; to join; to enclose.*
unire in matrimonio *to join in marriage.*

Mi sono unito a lui in questa impresa. *I joined him in this endeavor.*
In questa mia lettera unisco una fotorafìa del mio bambino. *I am enclosing in my letter a photograph of my baby.*

unisono *unison, harmony.*
Hanno risposto tutti all'unisono. *They all answered in unison.*

unità *unity.*

unito *united.*

universale *universal.*

universalità *universality.*

universalmente *universally.*

università *university.*

universitario *of a university; (as noun) university student.*
diploma universitario *university degree.*

universo *universe; (as adj.) universal.*

UNO (UN, UNA) *one, a, an, someone.*
l'un l'altro *each other; one another.*
una ragazza *a girl; one girl.*
un'idea *an idea; one idea.*
uno ad uno *one by one.*
uno alla volta *one at a time.*
uno dopo l'altro *one after the other.*
uno sciocco *a fool; one fool.*
un ragazzo *a boy; one boy.*
Ne desidero uno di qualità migliore. *I want one of better quality.*
Uno mi ha detto... *Someone told me...*
Uno non sa mai quando può succedere una disgrazia. *One never knows when an accident might happen.*

unto *greasy.*

untuoso *oily, unctuous.*

unzione, f. *unction.*

UOMO *man.*
un bell'uomo *a handsome man.*
un'uomo d'affari *a business man.*
un'uomo di mezz'età. *a middle-aged man.*
un'uomo di parola *a man of his word.*
un'uomo fatto *a grown man.*

UOVO *egg; (le uova eggs).*
uovo fresco *fresh egg.*
uovo sodo *hard-boiled egg.*
Meglio l'uovo oggi, che la gallina domani. *A bird in the hand is worth two in the bush.*

urbano *urban, urbane.*

urgente *urgent.*
aver bisogno urgente *to have urgent need.*

urgentemente *urgently.*

urgenza *urgency.*
Il medico è stato chiamato d'urgenza. *The doctor was called in a hurry.*

urgere *to be urgent.*
Urge la sua presenza. *Your presence is urgently needed.*

urlare *to shout; to howl.*

urlo *shout, cry.*

urna *urn.*

urtante *irritating.*

urtare *to knock against; to annoy.*
Ho urtato contro lo stipite della porta. *I knocked against the doorpost.*
Mi urta il suo modo di fare. *His manner irritates me.*

urto *push, shove.*

USANZA *usage, custom.*
un'usanza antica *an old custom.*
un'usanza comune *a common custom.*

USARE *to use; to make use of.*
usare giudizio *to use common sense; to exercise judgment.*

I cappelli a larghe falde si usano molto quest'-
anno. *Wide-brimmed hats are very fashionable
this year.*
Mia madre usava raccontarmi delle storielle delle
fate. *My mother used to tell me fairy stories.*
Posso usare la sua penna per un momento? *May
I use your pen for a moment?*
usato *second-hand, used, usual.*
mobili usati *second-hand furniture.*
non più usato *obsolete.*
più dell'usato *more than usual.*
usciere, m. *usher, bailiff.*
ùscio *door.*
sull'ùscio di casa *on the doorstep.*
USCIRE *to go out; to come out.*
Desidero uscire da questa situazione penosa.
I wish to get out of this unhappy situation.
Esco di casa ogni mattina alle otto. *I leave
the house (go out of the house) every morning
at eight.*
La Signora esce questa sera? *Is the lady going
out this evening? Will the lady be out this
evening?*
Usciamo a fare una passeggiata! *Let's go out
for a walk!*
USCITA *coming out; getting out; exit; outlay.*
Dov'è l'uscita del palazzo? *Where is the exit
of the building?*
Gli attori furono applauditi alla loro uscita.
The actors were applauded upon coming out.
Le uscite sono grandi e le entrate sono
piccole. *The expenditures are great and the
income is small.*
Non abbiamo via d'uscita. *We have no avenue
of escape.*
USO *use, custom.*
fare uso di *to make use of.*
pagare per l'uso di *to pay for the use of.*
Non è mio uso comportarmi male. *It is not my
custom to behave badly.*
uso *accustomed.*
Egli non è uso a fare lavori pesanti. *He is not
accustomed to doing heavy work.*
usuale *usual, customary.*
usualmente *usually, generally.*
usufruire *to take advantage of; to benefit by.*
Usufruisco soltanto degli interessi sul capitale.
I benefit only by the interest on the capital.
usura *usury.*
Mi ha ricompensato ad usura. *He repaid me
with interest (abundantly; generously).*
utensile, m. *utensil.*
utensili di cucina *kitchen utensils.*
ÙTILE *useful.*
utilità *utility, usefulness.*
È un oggetto bello, ma non ha utilità. *It is a
beautiful object, but it is of no use.*
utilizzare *to utilize.*
utilmente *usefully, profitably.*
uva *grapes.*
un grappolo d'uva *a bunch of grapes.*
uva passa *raisins.*

V

vacante *vacant, unfilled.*
VACANZA *vacation, holiday.*
Dove passa le vacanze di Natale? *Where are
you spending the Christmas holidays?*
vacca *cow.*
vaccinare *to vaccinate.*
vaccinazione, f. *vaccination.*
vaccino *vaccine.*

vacillante *vacillating, wavering, hesitating.*
vacillare *to vacillate; to waver; to hesitate.*
vagabondo *vagabond, wanderer.*
vagamente *vaguely.*
rispondere vagamente *to answer in a vague
manner.*
vagante *wandering, rambling.*
vagare *to wander; to ramble.*
vagire *to whimper.*
Il neonato vagiva nella sua culla. *The infant
was whimpering in his cradle.*
vagito *whimper.*
vaglia, f. *worth, merit.*
una persona di vaglia *a person of merit.*
vaglia, m. *postal money-order; check.*
vagliare *to sift; to consider.*
vagliare una proposta *to consider a proposal.*
vago *vague, lovely, desirous.*
una vaga fanciulla *a lovely girl.*
vago di gloria *desirous of glory.*
Ne ho una vaga idea. *I have a vague idea of it.*
vagone, m. *truck, van, car (of train).*
valanga *avalanche.*
È scesa una valanga di neve. *An avalanche of
snow came down.*
valente *clever; of worth.*
valentìa *cleverness, skill.*
VALERE *to be worth.*
vale a dire *that is to say; namely.*
A che vale? *What good is it?*
La salute vale più del denaro. *Health is worth
more than wealth.*
Mi sono valso dei miei diritti. *I took advantage
of my rights.*
Non vale la pena parlarne. *It isn't worth
speaking of.*
Per quanto tempo vale questo biglietto? *For
how long is this ticket good?*
Questo diamante vale diversi milioni. *This
diamond is worth several millions.*
valevole *good, usable, effective.*
È un rimedio valevole. *It is an effective
remedy.*
Il biglietto è valevole per dieci giorni. *The
ticket is good for ten days.*
valicare *to pass over; to cross.*
Bisognerà valicare i monti, per giungere al nostro
paese. *We'll have to cross the mountains
before arriving in our country.*
validamente *validly.*
validità *validity.*
valido *valid, strong.*
Egli ha una mente valida. *He has an untiring
mind.*
Questo contratto non è valido. *This contract is
not valid.*
valigerìa *luggage shop.*
valigia *suitcase.*
vallata (also **valle,** f.) *valley.*
VALORE, m. *value, valor.*
secondo il valore che egli da alle sue parole
*according to the value (meaning) he gives his
words.*
È un' artista di gran valore. *He is a great
artist.*
Il valore di queste gemme è inestimabile. *The
value of these gems is inestimable.*
I nostri soldati hanno dimostrato gran valor.
Our soldiers displayed great valor (courage).
I valori morali sono molto cambiati negli ultimi
decenni. *Moral values have changed a great
deal in the last decades.*
valorosamente *bravely, valiantly.*

Hanno combattuto valorosamente. *They fought
valiantly.*
valoroso *brave, valiant.*
valuta *value; monetary value; currency.*
valuta d'una cambiale *face value of a promissory note.*
valuta estera *foreign currency.*
VALUTARE *to appraise; to estimate.*
Sarà difficile valutare il tempo che ci vorrà per
finire questo lavoro. *It will be difficult to
estimate the time it will take to finish this
work.*
Valutò l'anello cento mila lire. *He appraised
the ring at one hundred thousand lire.*
valutazione, f. *estimate, appraisal.*
valvola *valve.*
valvola di sicurezza *safety valve.*
valzer, m. *waltz.*
Vuol ballare questo valzer con me? *Will you
dance this waltz with me?*
vampa *sudden wave of intense heat; passion;
flush.*
vampeggiare *to throw off gusts of great heat; to
blaze.*
Il fuoco vampeggiava. *The fire was blazing.*
vanagloria *vainglory.*
vanaglorioso *vainglorious.*
vanamente *vainly; in vain.*
Decantava vanamente le proprie virtù. *He was
vainly extolling his own virtues.*
Ti ho atteso vanamente. *I waited for you in
vain.*
vaneggiamento *raving.*
vaneggiare *to rave.*
vanga *spade.*
vangare *to dig; to turn over the earth.*
Vangèlo *Gospel.*
vaniglia *vanilla.*
vanigliato *flavored with vanilla.*
vanità *vanity.*
vano *room, noun.*
un appartamento di quattro vani *a four-room
apartment.*
VANO *vain, useless, empty.*
È perito nel vano tentativo di salvare sua figlia
dalle fiamme. *He died trying vainly to save
his daughter from the fire.*
VANTAGGIO *advantage, odds.*
Egli ha il vantaggio su di me. *He has the advantage over me.*
Mi ha dato dieci punti di vantaggio. *He gave
me a ten-point advantage over him.*
vantaggioso *advantageous.*
VANTARE *to boast of; to boast.*
vantarsi *to brag.*
Egli ha agito male e se ne vanta. *He behaved
poorly and he brags about it.*
Egli vanta le sue ricchezze. *He boasts about
his wealth.*
vantatore, m. *braggart.*
vanto *honor, merit.*
Egli si dava vanto dei suoi successi. *He was
priding himself on his successes.*
vanvera (a) *at random; without thought.*
parlare a vanvera *to talk nonsense.*
vaporare *to evaporate.*
vaporazione, f. *evaporation.*
vapore, m. *vapor, steam.*
bagno a vapore *steam bath (Turkish bath).*
bastimento a vapore *steamship.*
vaporizzare *to vaporize.*
vaporizzatore, m. *vaporizer.*
vaporoso *vaporous, vague.*

varare *to launch.*
varare una nave *to launch a ship.*

varcare *to cross; to go beyond.*
varcare la soglia di casa *to cross the threshold.*
varcare una frontiera *to pass a frontier.*
Essa ha varcato i quarant' anni. *She has passed her fortieth year.*

varco *passage, way.*
aspettare al varco *to lie in wait for.*
aprirsi un varco *to clear a path.*

variabile *variable, changeable.*
Il suo umore è variabile. *His mood is changeable.*

variare *to vary.*
tanto per variare *just for a change.*
La temperatura varia da una stanza all'altra.
The temperature varies from room to room.

variato *varied, various.*

variazione, f. *variation, change.*

varicella *chicken pox.*

varietà *variety.*
teatro di varietà *music hall; vaudeville house.*

vario *various, different, several.*
Ho da fare varie cose. *I have various things to do.*
Gli è successo varie volte. *It has happened to him several different times.*

vasca *basin, tub.*
vasca da bagno *bathtub.*
vasca di marmo *marble basin.*
vasca per pesci *fish pond.*

vaselina *vaseline.*

vaso *pot, vase.*
vaso da fiori *flowerpot.*

vassòio *tray.*

vastamente *widely, vastly.*

vastità *vastness.*

vasto *wide, vast.*
le vaste distese dell' ovest *the vast plains of the West.*

Vaticano *Vatican.*

ve *there.*
Ve ne sono appena tornato. *I have just returned from there.*

vecchiàia *old age.*
pensioni per la vecchiàia *old-age pensions.*

VECCHIO *old; (as noun) old man.*
i vecchi *the aged.*
Il vecchio camminava a stento. *The old man could hardly walk.*
Questo vestito è troppo vecchio per essere messo. *This suit is too old to wear.*

vece, f. *stead.*
fare le veci di *to act as.*
Vai tu in vece mia. *You go in my place.*

VEDERE *to see.*
dare a vedere *to make one believe.*
essere ben visto *to be popular; to be well liked.*
Il bimbo ha visto la luce il 3 Marzo, 1956. *The child was born March 3, 1956.*
Lo vidi tre settimane fà. *I saw him three weeks ago.*
Non mi può vedere. *He can't stand me (see me).*
Non ne vedo la necessità. *I don't see the necessity of it.*
Non si fa vedere da un pezzo. *He hasn't shown up for some time.*
Non vedo l'ora di finire. *I can hardly wait to finish.*

vedetta *lookout, watch.*
far da vedetta *to act as lookout.*

vedova *widow.*

vedovanza *widowhood.*

vedovare *to widow.*

vedovato *widowed.*

vedovo *widower.*

VEDUTA *view.*
Da questa finestra c'è un ottima veduta del mare. *From this window there is a lovely view of the sea.*
Ognuno ha le proprie vedute. *Everyone has his own views.*

vegetale, m. *vegetable; (also adj.)*

vegetare *to vegetate.*

vegetariano *vegetarian, noun & adj.*

vegetazione, f. *vegetation.*

vègeto *strong, vigorous.*

veglia *waking; watch; evening party.*
fare la veglia *to keep vigil.*
fra veglia e sonno *between slumber and waking.*

vegliante *waking, watching.*

VEGLIARE *to sit up; to remain awake.*
vegliare presso un ammalato *to sit up with a patient; to watch over a patient.*

veicolo *vehicle.*

vela *sail.*
barca a vela *sailboat.*
Tutto procede a gonfie vele. *Everything is going very well.*

velare *to veil.*

velatamente *covertly.*

velato *veiled.*
con voce velata *in a disguised voice.*
una velata minaccia *a veiled threat.*

veleno *poison.*

velenoso *poisonous, venomous.*

velìvolo *airplane.*

vellutato *velvety.*

velluto *velvet.*

velo *veil.*
stendere un velo sopra *to draw a veil over.*

veloce *swift, rapid.*

velocemente *swiftly, rapidly.*

velocità *velocity, speed.*
ad una velocità media di *at an average speed of.*
a grande velocità *at great speed.*
a tutta velocità *at full speed.*
la velocità del suono *the speed of sound.*

velocìpede, m. *velocipede.*

vena *vein.*
essere in vena *to be in the mood.*
vena artistica *an artistic vein.*

venale *venal.*

venalità *venality.*

venatorio *of hunting.*
stagione venatoria *hunting season.*

vendemmia *grape harvest.*

VENDERE *to sell.*
vendere a buon mercato *to sell cheap.*
vendere all'ingrosso *to sell wholesale.*
vendere al minuto *to sell retail.*
vendere bene *to sell at a good price; to sell well.*

vendetta *revenge.*

vendibile *saleable.*

vendicare *to avenge.*

vendicativo *revengeful.*

vendita *sale.*
in vendita *on sale.*

venditore, m. *seller.*
venditore ambulante *peddler.*

venduto *sold.*

venerabile *venerable.*

venerabilità *venerability.*

venerare *to venerate; to revere.*

venerazione, f. *veneration.*

venerdì *Friday.*

Veneziano *Venitian; (also noun).*

veniente *coming, next.*
la settimana veniente *the coming week.*

VENIRE *to come.*
venir bene *to turn out well.*
venire ai fatti *to get down to facts.*
venire alle mani *to come to blows.*
venire meno *to faint.*
venire meno ad una promessa *to break a promise.*
Egli viene da famiglia umile. *He comes from a humble family.*
Mi è venuta un' idea! *I just got an idea!*
Mi venne in aiuto. *He came to my aid.*
Mi venne incontro. *He came to meet me.*
Mi vien male. *I feel sick.*
Non mi viene in mente il suo nome. *I can't remember his name.*
Vieni su! *Come up!*

ventaglio *fan.*

ventata *gust; rush of wind.*
una ventata di freddo *a gust of cold air.*

ventesimo *twentieth, noun & adj.*

venti *twenty.*

venticello *light wind; breeze.*

ventilare *to ventilate.*
ventilare una stanza *to air a room.*

ventilato *airy, ventilated.*

ventilatore, m. *ventilator.*

ventilazione, f. *ventilation.*

VENTO *wind.*
farsi vento *to fan oneself.*
parlare al vento *to talk into deaf ears.*
vento contrario *contrary wind.*
vento favorevole *fair wind.*
Tira vento. *It's windy.*

ventoso *windy.*

ventrìloquo *ventriloquist.*

ventura *luck.*
andare alla ventura *to trust to chance.*
augurare buona ventura *to wish good luck.*
per mia buona ventura *luckily for me.*

venturo *next, future, coming.*
la settimana ventura *next week.*
le generazioni venture *the coming generations; the future generations.*

venturoso *lucky, fortunate.*

venusto *beautiful, lovely.*

VENUTA *coming, arrival.*
La sua venuta fu una sorpresa per tutti. *His coming was a surprise to everyone.*

verace *veracious, true.*

veramente *truly, really.*
Mi ha fatto veramente piacere. *I was really pleased.*
Veramente? *Really?*

veranda *veranda.*

verbale, m. *minutes.*
leggere il verbale *to read the minutes.*

verbale *verbal.*

verbo *verb.*

VERDE *green.*
essere al verde *to be penniless.*

verdechiaro *light green.*

verdecupo *dark green.*

verdetto *verdict.*

verdura *verdure, vegetables, greens.*
Fa bene mangiare un po' di verdura. *It is good for one to eat some vegetables.*

minestra di verdura *vegetable soup.*
vergogna *shame, disgrace.*
vergognarsi *to be ashamed.*
vergognosamente *shamefully.*
vergognoso *shameful.*
verifica *inspection, examination.*
  verifica dei conti *inspection of the accounts.*
  verifica dei passaporti *examination of pass-*
  ports.
verificare *to verify; to inspect.*
  verificarsi *to occur; to happen.*
  Si è verificato un increscioso incidente. *An un-*
  fortunate incident happened.
verismo *realism.*
VERITÀ *truth.*
  dire la verità *to tell the truth.*
  in verità *in truth.*
  la verità dei fatti *the truth of the matter.*
verme, m. *worm.*
vermiglio *vermilion, red.*
vermut, m. *vermouth.*
vernacolo *vernacular, dialect.*
vernice, f. *varnish.*
verniciare *to varnish.*
VERO, noun *truth.*
  a dire il vero *to tell the truth.*
  Non c'è una parola di vero in quanto mi ha raccontato. *There isn't a word of truth in what*
  he told me.
VERO *true.*
  Non è vero. *It's not true.*
  Venite con noi, è vero? *You are coming with*
  us, isn't that so?
verosimile *likely, probable.*
VERSARE *to pour; to spill; to shed.*
  versare lacrime *to shed tears.*
  versare una somma *to pay a sum.*
  versare un bicchiere d'acqua *to pour a glass of*
  water.
  Si è versato il caffè addosso. *He spilled the*
  coffee over himself.
versatile *versatile.*
versatilità *versatility.*
versione, f. *version.*
  versione in italiano *Italian version; Italian*
  translation.
  una versione nuova *a new version.*
  Ognuno mi ha dato una versione diversa dell'
  accaduto. *Everyone gave me a different*
  version of what happened.
VERSO *verse. line.*
  per un verso o per l'altro *one way or the other.*
  scrivere dei versi *to write verses (poetry).*
  versi sciolti *blank verse.*
  Questo dramma è scritto in versi. *This drama is*
  written in verse.
VERSO *toward.*
  verso la fine del mese *towards the end of the*
  month.
  verso nord *northward.*
  Egli viene verso di me. *He is coming toward*
  me.
vertenza *quarrel, question.*
  risolvere una vertenza *to settle a quarrel.*
verticale *vertical.*
verticalmente *vertically.*
vertigine, f. *dizzy spell; dizziness.*
vertiginoso *dizzy.*
  un altezza vertiginosa *a dizzy height.*
vescovo *bishop.*
vespa *wasp.*
vespaio *wasps' nest.*
vestaglia *dressing gown.*

VESTE, f. *dress, gown.*
  in veste di *in the guise of.*
  veste da camera *dressing gown.*
  veste da sposa *bridal gown.*
vestiario *clothes.*
vestibolo *hall.*
vestigio *trace, vestige.*
VESTIRE *to dress.*
  vestire bene *to dress well.*
  vestirsi *to dress oneself.*
VESTITO *suit, dress.*
  vestiti da sera *evening clothes.*
veterano *veteran.*
veterinario *veterinary, noun & adj.*
veto *veto.*
vetràio *glass blower; glazier.*
vetrame *glassware.*
vetrato *glazed.*
vetrina *shop window.*
VETRO *glass.*
  vetro colorato *stained glass.*
vetta *summit.*
vettovaglie, f. pl. *food provisions.*
vettura *carriage, coach.*
  l'ultima vettura *the last coach.*
  In vettura! *All aboard!*
vetturino *driver, cabbie.*
vezzo *charm, coaxing.*
VI *there.*
  Non ho desiderio di andarvi. *I don't wish to go*
  there.
  Vi andrò se potrò. *I'll go there if I can.*
VI *you; to you; both sing. & pl.*
  Vi restituirò il libro domani. *I will give the*
  book back to you tomorrow.
  Vi rivedo con piacere. *I am pleased to see you*
  again.
VIA *street, road, way.*
  in via *on the way.*
  la via più breve *the shortest way.*
  per via di *by way of.*
  Via Veneto *Veneto Street.*
VIA *away, off.*
  andar via *to go away.*
  e così via *and so forth.*
  mandar via *to send away.*
viadotto *viaduct.*
viaggetto *trip.*
VIAGGIARE *to travel.*
  viaggiare in prima *to travel first class.*
viaggiatore, m.; **viaggiatrice**, f. *traveler, pas-*
  senger.
VIAGGIO *journey, voyage.*
  essere in viaggio *to be traveling; to be on the*
  way.
  fare un viaggio *to take a voyage; to take a trip.*
  mettersi in viaggio *to set out; to start out.*
  Buon viaggio! *Happy journey! Bon Voyage!*
viale, m. *avenue.*
  viali alberati *tree-lined avenues.*
viandante, m. *passer-by, pedestrian.*
viavai *coming and going; hustle and bustle.*
  C'è un viavai continuo in questa casa. *There*
  is a continuous hustle and bustle in this house.
vibrare *to vibrate.*
  vibrare un colpo *to strike a blow.*
vice *vice.*
  vicepresidente *vice-president.*
  vicedirettore *assistant director.*
vicenda *vicissitude, event.*
  a vicenda *in turn.*
  le vicende della vita *the vicissitudes of life.*
  volersi bene a vicenda *to love one another.*

vicendevole *mutual.*
vicendevolmente *mutually, reciprocally.*
viceversa *vice versa; on the contrary.*
  Se viceversa vuole rimanere qui, faccia pure.
  If on the other hand you prefer to remain here,
  do so.
vicinanza *nearness, proximity, vicinity, neigh-*
  borhood.
  essere in vicinanza di *to be close to; to be*
  approaching.
  La mia casa è nelle vicinanze della sua. *My*
  home is near his.
  La sua vicinanza è un gran conforto per me.
  His nearness is a great comfort to me.
vicinato *neighborhood.*
vicino, noun *neighbor.*
  La mia vicina mi ha salutato dalla finestra. *My*
  neighbor greeted me from the window.
VICINO *near.*
  vicino casa mia *near my home.*
  Siamo vicini alla fine del lavoro. *We are close to*
  the end of the work.
VIETARE *to forbid; to prohibit.*
  Il medico mi ha vietato di fumare. *The doctor*
  has forbidden me to smoke.
VIETATO *forbidden, prohibited.*
  Vietato l'Ingresso! *No Admittance!*
  Vietato Fumare! *No Smoking!*
  Vietata la Sosta! *No Parking!*
  Vietata l'Affisione! *Post No Bills!*
vigente *in force.*
  leggi vigenti *laws in force.*
vigere *to be in force.*
  Questa legge vige ancora. *This law is still in*
  force.
vigilante *vigilant.*
vigilanza *vigilance.*
vigilare *to watch over; to guard.*
vigile, m. *policeman.*
  vigile del fuoco *fireman.*
vigilia *eve, vigil.*
  la vigilia di capodanno *New Year's Eve.*
  la vigilia di Natale. *Christmas Eve.*
vigliacco *coward.*
vigna *vineyard.*
vignetta *vignette.*
vigore, m. *vigor, strength.*
  con vigore instancabile *with untiring strength.*
  in pieno vigore *in full strength.*
  Questa legge non è ancora in vigore. *This law*
  in not in force yet.
vigorosamente *vigorously.*
vigoroso *vigorous, strong.*
vile *low, mean, cowardly.*
villa *villa; country house.*
villanamente *rudely, roughly.*
villanìa *rudeness.*
villano *an unrefined man; a peasant.*
villeggiatura *holiday, country vacation.*
  luogo di villeggiatura *vacation spot.*
villino *cottage.*
vilmente *cowardly, meanly.*
viltà *cowardice.*
vinaio *wine merchant.*
vincente *winning; (as noun) winner.*
  il numero vincente *the winning number.*
  Il vincente riceverà un premio. *The winner*
  will receive a prize.
VINCERE *to win; to overcome; to get the better*
  of.
  vincere una battaglia *to win a battle.*
  vinto dalla stanchezza *overcome by fatigue.*
  Non voglio lasciarmi vincere dalla collera. *I*

don't want to let my anger get the better of me.
vincitore, m.; **vincitrice,** f. *winner.*
vincolare *to bind.*
  vincolarsi *to bind oneself.*
vincolo *tie, bond.*
  vincolo di sangue *blood tie.*
VINO *wine.*
  vino bianco *white wine.*
  vino leggero *light wine.*
  vino rosso *red wine.*
  vino spumante *sparkling wine.*
VINTO *won, overcome, conquered.*
  darsi per vinto *to give up; to give in.*
  È un uomo vinto dalle sventure. *He is a man who has been overcome by misfortune.*
  Non te la do vinta. *I won't let you have your own way.*
viola *violet, noun & adj.*
violare *to violate.*
violazione, f. *violation.*
violentemente *violently.*
violento *violent.*
violenza *violence.*
violinista, m. *violinist.*
violino *violin.*
vipera *viper.*
virgola *comma.*
  punto e virgola *semicolon.*
virgolette, f. pl. *quotation marks.*
virile *manly, virile.*
virilmente *manfully.*
virtù, f. *virtue.*
  in virtù di *in virtue of.*
virtuoso *virtuous.*
virus, m. *virus.*
visibile *visible.*
visibilità *visibility.*
visibilmente *visibly.*
visiera *visor.*
visione, f. *vision.*
VISITA *visit.*
  biglietto da visita *visiting card.*
  fare una visita a *to pay a visit to.*
  farsi fare una visita medica *to submit to a medical examination.*
VISITARE *to visit; to call on somebody.*
  visitare un amico *to visit a friend.*
visivo *visual.*
VISO *face.*
visone, m. *mink.*
  una pelliccia di visone *a mink coat.*
vispo *lively.*
  un bimbo vispo *a lively child (boy).*
VISTA *sight, view.*
  a prima vista *at first sight.*
  aver la vista buona *to have good eyesight.*
  aver la vista corta *to be short-sighted.*
  conoscere di vista *to know by sight.*
  in vista *in sight.*
  perdere di vista *to lose sight of.*
  punto di vista *point of view.*
  una vista panoramica *a panoramic view.*
visto, m. *visa.*
vistoso *showy, gaudy.*
VITA *life, waist.*
  essere corta di vita *to be short-waisted.*
  essere lunga di vita *to be long-waisted.*
  intorno alla vita *around the waist.*
  in vita *alive.*
  pieno di vita *full of life.*
vitale *vital.*
vitalità *vitality.*
vitamina *vitamin.*

vite, f. *screw, vine.*
vitello *calf.*
  cotoletta di vitello *veal cutlet.*
  fegato di vitello *calves' liver.*
vittima *victim.*
VITTO *food.*
  vitto e alloggio *food and lodging.*
  Il prezzo della camera comprende anchè il vitto. *The price of the room includes meals.*
vittoria *victory.*
vittoriosamente *victoriously.*
vittorioso *victorious.*
vivace *lively, vivacious.*
vivacemente *vivaciously.*
vivacità *vivacity, liveliness.*
vivamente *keenly, deeply.*
vivanda *food.*
vivente *living.*
  Non ho parenti viventi. *I have no living relatives.*
VIVERE *to live.*
  Egli vive alla giornata. *He lives from hand to mouth.*
viveri, m. pl. *victuals; food supplies.*
vivido *vivid.*
VIVO *alive, living.*
  argento vivo *quicksilver.*
  con suo vivo dolore *with great sorrow on his part.*
  I miei genitori sono ancora vivi. *My parents are still alive.*
viziare *to spoil.*
viziato *spoiled.*
vizio *fault, vice.*
vocabolario *vocabulary.*
vocabolo *word, term.*
vocale *vocal; (also noun, f.) vowel.*
  corde vocali *vocal cords.*
VOCE, f. *voice.*
  abbassare la voce *to lower one's voice.*
  alzar la voce *to shout.*
  a voce alta *in a loud voice.*
  a voce bassa *in a low voice.*
  Corre voce che... *There is a rumor that...*
voga *fashion, vogue.*
  essere in voga *to be in fashion.*
vogare *to row.*
VOGLIA *wish, desire.*
  Hai voglia di fare una passeggiata? *Do you feel like going for a walk?*
  Non ho voglia di uscire questa sera. *I don't wish to go out this evening.*
VOI *you, pl. familiar; also formal.*
volante, m. *wheel.*
  Ero al volante quando è avvenuto lo scontro. *I was at the wheel when the crash occurred.*
volante *flying.*
VOLARE *to fly.*
volata *flight.*
volente *willing.*
  volente o nolente *willing or not.*
volentieri *willingly.*
  mal volentieri *unwillingly.*
volere, m. *will.*
  il volere di Dio *the will of God.*
  il volere del popolo *the will of the people.*
VOLERE *to want; to wish.*
  voglia o non voglia *whether he wishes or not.*
  voler dire *to mean.*
  Non voglio mangiare ora. *I don't want to eat now.*
  Vorrei riposare un po'. *I would like to rest a while.*

volgare *vulgar.*
volgarità *vulgarity.*
volgarmente *vulgarly.*
VOLGERE *to turn.*
  volgere al termine *to come to an end; to draw to a close.*
  volgere gli occhi insù *to look up.*
  volgere intorno lo sguardo *to look about; to look around.*
  volgere le spalle a *to turn one's back to.*
volo *flight.*
volontà *will.*
  di spontanea volontà *of one's free will.*
  le ultime volontà del defunto *the last will of the deceased.*
volontariamente *voluntarily.*
volontario *voluntary.*
volpe, f. *fox.*
  volpe argentata *silver fox.*
volpone, m. *old fox.*
VOLTA *time.*
  di volta in volta *from time to time.*
  due per volta *two at a time.*
  la prossima volta *next time.*
  qualche volta *sometimes.*
  questa volta *this time.*
  una alla volta *one at a time.*
  una volta e per sempre *once and for all.*
  C'era una volta... *Once upon a time...*
  Ora è la mia volta! *Now it's my turn!*
VOLTARE *to turn.*
  voltare a destra *to turn to the right.*
  voltare una pagina *to turn a page.*
  voltarsi *to turn around.*
voltata *turn, turning.*
  la seconda voltata a sinistra *the second turn to the left.*
voltato *turned.*
  Gli occhi di tutti erano voltati verso di lui. *All eyes were turned toward him.*
volto *face.*
volume, m. *volume.*
VOSTRO, -a, -i, -e (il vostro; la vostra; i vostri; le vostre) *your, yours.*
  il vostro amico *your friend.*
  vostro padre *your father.*
  Questo libro è il vostro. *This book is yours.*
votare *to vote.*
votato *consecrated.*
voto *vow, vote.*
  dare il proprio voto a *to cast one's vote for.*
  fare un voto *to make a vow.*
vulcano *volcano.*
vulnerabile *vulnerable.*
vulnerabilità *vulnerability.*
vuotare *to empty.*
  vuotare il sacco *to get something off one's chest (to empty the sack).*
vuoto, noun *emptiness; empty space; vacuum.*
  andare a vuoto *to come to nothing.*
VUOTO *empty.*
  a tasche vuote *with empty pockets; penniless.*
  Non posso andare a mani vuote. *I can't go empty-handed.*
  Questo fiasco è vuoto. *This bottle is empty.*

Z

zabaione, m. *eggnog.*
zafferano *saffron.*
zaffiro *sapphire.*
zaino *knapsack, pack.*
  collo zaino a tracollo *with a knapsack on his back.*

zampa paw.
zampillare to gush; to spring.
 La fontana zampillava. The fountain was gushing.
zampillo jet, squirt, stream.
zanna tusk, fang.
zanzàra mosquito.
zappa hoe.
zappare to hoe; to dig.
zàttera raft.
zebra zebra.
zebrato zebra-striped.
zecca mint.
 nuovo di zecca brand-new.
zèffiro breeze.
zelante zealous.
zelantemente zealously.
zelo zeal.
zènzero ginger.
zeppo full.
 Questa valigia è piena zeppa. The suitcase is quite full.
zero zero.
 sopra zero above zero.

 sotto zero below zero.
zeta z.
 dall'A alla Z from start to finish.
ZIA aunt.
zibellino sable.
zigomo cheekbone.
 aver gli zigomi alti to have high cheekbones.
zimarra robe.
zimbello laughingstock.
zinco zinc.
zingaro gypsy.
ZIO uncle.
zitella maid.
zitellona old maid; spinster.
zittire to hush; to shush.
ZITTO silent.
 stare zitto to keep quiet.
 Zitto! Quiet!
zoccolo wooden shoe; hoof.
 gli zoccoli del cavallo the horse's hooves.
zodìaco zodiac.
zolfo sulphur.
zolla clod, sod.
zolletta lump (of sugar).

zona zone.
zoologìa zoology.
zoologico zoological.
 giardino zoologico zoo.
zoppicare to limp.
zoppo lame.
 essere zoppo to be lame.
 sedia zoppa wobbly chair.
zucca pumpkin, pate.
 aver la zucca pelata to be bald-headed.
 aver sale in zucca to be sensible.
 semi di zucca pumpkin seeds.
zuccherare to sugar; to sweeten.
zuccherato sugared, sweetened.
ZUCCHERO sugar.
 due zollette di zucchero two lumps of sugar.
 zucchero di canna cane sugar.
 zucchero in pòlvere powdered sugar.
zucchino squash.
zuccone, m. blockhead.
zufolare to whistle.
zuppa soup.
zuppiera soup tureen.

GLOSSARY OF PROPER NAMES

Adriana *Adriane.*
Alberto *Albert.*
Alessandro *Alexander.*
Alfredo *Alfred.*
Alice *Alice.*
Andrèa *Andrew.*
Anita *Anita.*
Antonio *Anthony.*
Arnoldo *Arnold.*
Arrigo *Harry.*
Arturo *Arthur.*

Beatrice *Beatrice.*
Bernardo *Bernard.*
Bertrando *Bertrand.*
Bianca *Blanche.*

Carlo *Charles.*
Carlotta *Charlotte.*
Carolina *Carol.*
Caterina *Katherine.*

Daniele *Daniel.*
Davide *David.*
Donato *Donald.*

Editta *Edith.*
Edmondo *Edmund.*
Edoardo *Edward.*

Eleonora *Eleanor.*
Elizabetta *Elizabeth.*
Emilia *Emily.*
Emmanuele *Emanuel.*
Enrichetta *Henrietta.*
Enrico *Henry.*
Evelina *Evelyn.*

Federico *Frederick.*
Ferdinando *Ferdinand.*
Francesca *Frances.*
Francesco *Francis.*

Gabriele *Gabriel.*
Gianna *Jean, Jane.*
Gilberto *Gilbert.*
Giorgio *George.*
Giovanna *Joan.*
Giovanni *John.*
Giuditta *Judith.*
Giulia *Julia.*
Giuliano *Julian.*
Giuseppe *Joseph.*
Gregorio *Gregory.*
Guglielmo *William.*
Guido *Guy.*

Irene *Irene.*
Isabella *Isabel.*

Liliana *Lillian.*
Lorenzo *Lawrence.*
Lucìa *Lucy.*
Luigi *Lewis, Louis.*
Luisa *Louise.*

Marìa *Mary.*
Maurizio *Maurice.*
Michele *Michael.*

Paolo *Paul.*
Pietro *Peter.*
Peppino *Joe.*

Raffaele *Ralph.*
Raimondo *Raymond.*
Riccardo *Richard.*
Roberto *Robert.*
Rosa *Rose.*

Silvia *Sylvia.*

Teresa *Theresa.*
Tommaso *Thomas.*

Vincenzo *Vincent.*
Violetta *Violet.*
Viviana *Vivian.*

GLOSSARY OF GEOGRAPHICAL NAMES

Adriatico *Adriatic.*
Africa *Africa.*
Alpi, f. pl. *Alps.*
America *America.*
  America del Nord *North America.*
  America del Sud *South America.*
  America Centrale *Central America.*
Argentina *Argentina.*
Asia *Asia.*
Atlantico *Atlantic.*
Australia *Australia.*

Belgio *Belgium.*
Bermude, f. pl. *Bermuda.*
Brasile *Brazil.*
Brusselles *Brussels.*

Canadà *Canada.*
Cina *China.*

Danimarca *Denmark.*
Dover *Dover.*

Egitto *Egypt.*
Europa *Europe.*

Firenze *Florence.*
Francia *France.*

Galles *Wales.*
Germania *Germany.*
Genova *Genoa.*
Giappone *Japan.*
Ginevra *Geneva.*
Gran Bretagna *Great Britain.*
Grecia *Greece.*

India *India.*
Inghilterra *England.*
Irlanda *Ireland.*
Islanda *Iceland.*
Italia *Italy.*

Lisbona *Lisbon.*
Londra *London.*

Messico *Mexico.*
Milano *Milan.*
Mosca *Moscow.*

Napoli *Naples.*
Norvegia *Norway.*
Nuova Zelanda *New Zealand.*

Olanda *Holland.*

Pacifico *Pacific.*
Padova *Padua.*

Parigi *Paris.*
Persia *Persia.*
Polonia *Poland.*
Portogallo *Portugal.*
Prussia *Prussia.*

Reno *Rhine.*
Roma *Rome.*
Rumanìa *Roumania.*
Russia *Russia.*

Sardegna *Sardinia.*
Scozia *Scotland.*
Siberia *Siberia.*
Sicilia *Sicily.*
Sorrento *Sorrento.*
Spagna *Spain.*
Stati Uniti *United States.*
Svezia *Sweden.*
Svizzera *Switzerland.*

Toscana *Tuscany.*
Turchìa *Turkey.*

Ungherìa *Hungary.*

Venezia *Venice.*
Vesuvio *Vesuvius.*
Vienna *Vienna.*

English-Italian DICTIONARY

A

a (an)   uno, un, una.
abandon (to)   abbandonare.
abbreviate (to)   abbreviare.
abbreviation   abbreviazione, f.
ability   abilità, talento.
able (to be)   potere; essere capace di; avere la
  forza di.
able (adj.)   abile, capace.
aboard   a bordo.
abolish (to)   abolire.
about   circa; a proposito di (with reference to);
  in giro (in circulation).
  about the end of the month   verso la fine del
  mese.
  What's it about?   Di che si tratta?
above   sopra; in alto.
  above all   sopratutto.
abroad   all' estero.
absence   assenza.
absent   assente.
absent-minded   distratto.
absolute   assoluto.
absorb (to)   assorbire.
abstain from   astenersi dal.
abstract   astratto.
absurd   assurdo.
abundance   abbondanza.
abundant   abbondante.
abuse   abuso.
abuse (to)   abusare.
academy   accademia.
accelerate (to)   accelerare.
accelerator   acceleratore, m.
accent   accento.
accent (to)   accentare, accentuare.
accept (to)   accettare.
accident   accidente, m.; incidente, m.
accidental   accidentale, casuale.
accidentally   accidentalmente.
accommodate (to)   accomodare.
accommodation   accomodamento; alloggio (lodging).
accompany (to)   accompagnare.
accomplish (to)   compi(e)re, finire, perfezionare.
accord   accordo.
according to   secondo.
account   conto; resoconto; relazione, f. (report).
  on account of   a causa di.
accuracy   esattezza, accuratezza.
accurate   esatto.
accuse (to)   accusare.
accustom (to)   abituare, abituarsi a.
ace   asso.
ache   dolore, m.
  headache   mal di testa.
ache (to)   dolere; fare male.
  It hurts me.   Mi fa male. (Mi duole.)
achieve (to)   compiere; raggiungere.
achievement   compimento, successo.
acid   acido.
acknowledge (to)   riconoscere, convenire.
acquaintance   conoscenza.
  to make someone's acquaintance   fare la
  conoscenza di qualcuno.
acquire (to)   acquistare.
across   attraverso.
act   atto.
act (to)   agire; rappresentare (represent).
  to act as   fare da.
action   azione, f.
active   attivo.
activity   attività.

actor   attore,
actual   reale, vero.
acute   acuto.
adapt (to)   adattare.
add (to)   aggiungere; fare la somma; addizionare.
addition   addizione, f.
  in addition to   oltre a.
address   indirizzo (street, location); discorso
  (speech).
address (to)   indirizzare.
  to address oneself to   rivolgersi a.
adequate   sufficiente, adeguato.
adhesive tape   nastro adesivo.
adjective   aggettivo.
adjoining   vicino, confinante.
  adjoining rooms   stanze contigue.
administer (to)   amministrare.
administration   amministrazione, f.
admiral   ammiraglio.
admiration   ammirazione, f.
admire (to)   ammirare.
admission   ammissione, f.
  ticket of admission   biglietto d'ingresso.
admit (to)   riconoscere, ammettere.
admittance   ammissione, f.; permesso d'entrare.
  Free admittance   Entrata libera.
  No admittance   Vietato l'ingresso.
adopt (to)   adottare.
  adopted child   figlio adottivo.
adult   adulto.
advance   progresso, avanzata.
  in advance   in anticipo.
advance (to)   progredire.
advantage   vantaggio.
adventure   avventura.
adverb   avverbio.
advertise (to)   avvisare; fare della pubblicità.
advertisement   avviso, annunzio, pubblicità.
advice   consiglio.
  to take someone's advice   seguire il consiglio
  di qualcuno.
advise (to)   consigliare.
affair   affare, m.
affect (to)   influire, concernere, riguardare.
affected   affettato, studiato.
affection   affezione, f.; affetto.
affectionate   affettuoso.
affirm (to)   affermare.
afloat   a galla.
  to be afloat   galleggiare.
afraid   pauroso, intimorito.
after   dopo; in seguito; più tardi.
afternoon   pomeriggio; dopo pranzo.
afterwards   dopo.
again   di nuovo.
  never again   mai più.
against   contro.
age   epoca; età (of a person).
  of age   maggiorenne.
  under age   minorenne.
age (to)   invecchiare.
agency   agenzia.
agent   agente, rappresentante, m.
aggravate (to)   aggravare.
ago   fa.
  five years ago   cinque anni fa.
  long ago   molto tempo fa.
agree (to)   consentire; essere d'accordo.
agreeable   convenevole, ameno.
agreed   inteso, d'accordo.
agreement   patto, accordo.
  as by agreement   come si è convenuto.
agricultural   agricolo.

agriculture   agricoltura.
ahead   in avanti.
  to get ahead of   oltrepassare.
aid   assistenza, aiuto.
aid (to)   assistere, aiutare.
  first aid   pronto soccorso.
aim   mira, fine, m.; intento.
aim (to)   prendere di mira; mirare.
air   aria.
  by air   per via aerea.
air mail   posta aerea.
airplane   aeroplano.
air raid   incursione aerea.
aisle   corridoio; passaggio; navata (of a church).
alarm   allarme, m.
alarm (to)   allarmare; dare l'allarme.
alien   straniero.
alike   simile.
alive   vivo.
  more dead than alive   più morto che vivo.
all   tutto.
all (adj.)   tutto, tutta, tutti, tutte.
  all day   tutto il giorno.
allow (to)   permettere.
allowed   permesso.
ally   alleato.
almost   quasi.
alone   solo.
along   lungo.
aloud   ad alta voce.
also   anche.
alter (to)   alterare, cambiare.
alternate (to)   alternare.
alternately   a vicenda; alternamente.
although   benchè, sebbene.
altitude   altitudine, f.
always   sempre.
amaze (to)   stupire.
amazed (to be)   essere sorpreso; essere stupefatto.
amazement   stupore, m.
ambassador   ambasciatore, m.
ambitious   ambizioso.
amend (to)   correggere, modificare.
amends   riparazione, f.
American   americano.
among   fra; nel mezzo.
amount   somma.
amount (to)   ammontare.
ample   ampio, vasto.
amuse (to)   intrattenere, divertire.
amusement   intrattenimento, divertimento.
amusing   divertente.
analyze (to)   analizzare.
ancestor   antenato.
anchor   àncora.
ancient   antico.
and   e.
anecdote   aneddoto.
angel   angelo.
anger   collera.
angry   irato, collerico.
  to get angry   adirarsi.
animal   animale, m.
animate (to)   animare.
annihilate (to)   annientare.
anniversary   anniversario.
announce (to)   annunziare.
annoy   infastidire, disturbare, contrariare.
annual   annuale.
annul (to)   annullare.
anonymous   anonimo.

another un altro, un'altra.
 in another hour un'ora più tardi.
answer risposta.
answer (to) rispondere.
anterior anteriore.
anticipate (to) anticipare.
antique antico.
anxiety ansia.
anxious ansioso; desideroso (eager).
any qualunque, qualche, del.
anybody chiunque, qualcuno.
anyhow comunque.
anyone chiunque, qualcuno.
anything qualunque cosa; qualche cosa.
anyway in qualunque modo.
anywhere dovunque.
apart a parte.
apartment appartamento.
apiece ciascuno; per uno.
apologize (to) scusarsi.
apparent evidente.
appeal (to) rivolgersi a; ricorrere a.
appear (to) apparire.
appearance aspetto; apparizione, f.
appease (to) placare.
appendix appendice, f.
appetite appetito.
applaud (to) applaudire.
applause applauso.
apple mela.
application domanda; richiesta (request);
 assiduità (diligence).
apply (to) essere adatto (to be suitable);
 sollecitare (to apply for); rivolgersi a (to apply to).
appoint (to) nominare, stabilire.
appointment appuntamento; nomina (to a position).
appreciate (to) apprezzare.
appreciation apprezzamento.
approach (to) avvicinare.
appropriate appropriato, adatto.
approval approvazione, f.
approve (to) approvare.
April aprile.
apron grembiule, m.
arbitrary arbitrario.
arcade arcata.
architect architetto.
architecture architettura.
ardent ardente.
area area, spazio.
argue (to) discutere.
argument discussione, f.; argomento.
arise (to) levarsi, sorgere.
arm braccio.
 arm in arm a braccetto.
army esercito.
around in giro (in circulation); intorno a.
arouse (to) svegliare, sollevare, aizzare.
arrange (to) aggiustare, assettare, stabilire.
arrangement disposizione, f; accordo (agreement).
arrest arresto, cattura.
arrest (to) arrestare, catturare.
arrival arrivo.
arrive (to) arrivare.
art arte, f.
 Fine Arts Belle Arti, f.
article articolo, oggetto.
artificial artificiale.
artist artista, m & f.
artistic artistico.
as come (like); mentre (while).
 as... as... così... come...
 as it were per così dire.

as little as tanto poco quanto.
as long as finchè.
as much altrettanto.
as much... as ... tanto... quanto...
ascertain (to) constatare.
ash cenere, f.
ashamed vergognoso.
 to be ashamed of aver vergogna di.
ash tray portacenere, m.
aside a parte.
ask (to) chiedere, domandare.
 to ask a question fare una domanda.
asleep addormentato.
 to fall asleep addormentarsi.
aspire (to) aspirare.
aspirin aspirina.
assault assalto.
assemble (to) riunire.
assign (to) assegnare.
assist (to) assistere, aiutare.
assistance assistenza, soccorso.
associate socio.
associate (to) associare.
assume (to) assumere.
assurance sicurezza.
 self-assurance confidenza in se stesso.
assure (to) assicurare.
astonish (to) stupire.
astounded stupefatto.
astounding stupefacente.
at a.
 at first in principio; dapprima.
 at last finalmente.
 at once immediatamente, subito.
 at the same time nel stesso tempo.
athlete atleta, m.
athletic atletico.
athletics sports, m. pl.
atmosphere atmosfera.
attach (to) attaccare, aderire (a).
attack assalto, attacco.
attack (to) assalire, attaccare.
attain (to) ottenere, conseguire, raggiungere.
attempt tentativo.
attempt (to) tentare.
attend (to) assistere.
 to attend to occuparsi di.
attention attenzione, f.
attic soffitta.
attitude atteggiamento.
attorney avvocato.
attract (to) attirare.
attraction attrazione, f.; attrattiva.
attractive seducente.
audience udienza, uditorio.
August agosto.
aunt zia.
author autore, m.
authority autorità.
authorize (to) autorizzare.
automatic automatico.
automobile automobile, f.; vettura.
autumn autunno.
available utilizzabile, disponibile.
average media, f.; medio (adj.).
avoid (to) evitare.
awake sveglio.
awake (to be) essere sveglio.
awaken (to) svegliare, destare.
award premio.
away assente, lontano.
 to go away andar via.
awful spaventoso.

awhile per qualche tempo.
awkward goffo.

B

baby bambino, bambina.
back (noun) dorso (in body); spalliera (of piece
 of furniture); fondo (of room or place).
 to be back essere di ritorno.
back (adv.) indietro; di dietro.
background sfondo.
backwards indietro.
bacon lardo.
bad cattivo; malo; guasto (spoiled).
badge segno, insegna.
badly male.
bag sacco, borsa.
baker panettiere.
bakery panetterìa.
balance equilibrio.
bald calvo.
ball palla; ballo (dance).
balloon pallone, m.
banana banana.
band orchestra, banda.
bandage benda.
banister balaustrata.
bank banca; sponda (river).
 bank account deposito in banca.
bank note biglietto di banca.
bankruptcy bancarotta, fallimento.
 to go bankrupt fare fallimento.
banquet banchetto.
bar bar, m.
barber barbiere, m.; parrucchiere, m.
barbershop barberìa.
bare nudo.
bargain affare, m.
barge barchetta.
barn capanna, granaio.
barrel barile, m.
barren sterile, arido.
base fondamento.
bashful timido.
basin bacino, catinella.
basket paniere, m.; canestro; cesto.
bath bagno.
bathe (to) bagnare.
 bathing suit costume da bagno, m.
bath-tub vasca.
battle battaglia.
be (to) essere.
 (to) be ahead essere in capo.
 (to) be hungry aver fame.
 (to) be right aver ragione.
 (to) be sleepy aver sonno.
 (to) be sorry dispiacersene.
 (to) be thirsty aver sete.
 (to) be wrong aver torto.
 (to) be tired sentirsi stanco.
beach spiaggia.
beaming raggiante.
bean fagiuolo.
bear (to) sostenere; soffrire con rassegnazione
 (morally).
beat (to) battere.
beautiful bello.
beauty bellezza.
because perchè.
 because of a causa di.
become (to) diventare.
 to become accustomed abituarsi.
becoming confacente.

This dress is becoming to me. Questo vestito mi sta bene.
bed letto.
bedclothes coperte, f. pl.
bedroom camera da letto.
beef manzo, vaccina.
beefsteak bistecca.
beer birra.
beet bietola.
before prima; davanti; prima che.
the day before la vigilia.
beg (to) mendicare.
beggar mendicante, m. & f.
begin (to) incominciare.
beginning principio, inizio.
behave (to) comportarsi, condursi.
behavior condotta; maniere, f. pl.
behind di dietro; dietro a.
Belgian belga, m.
belief credenza, opinione, f.
believe (to) credere.
bell campana, campanello.
belong (to) appartenere; essere di.
below di sotto; in basso.
belt cintura.
bench panca.
bend (to) piegare, curvare.
beneath al di sotto; inferiore a.
benefit beneficio, vantaggio.
benefit (to) beneficare, giovare.
beside presso; accanto a.
besides a parte; inoltre.
best il migliore; il meglio.
bet scommessa.
bet (to) scommettere.
betray (to) tradire.
better migliore, meglio.
between fra.
beyond oltre; al di là.
bicycle bicicletta.
bid offerta.
big grande.
bill conto.
to pay the bill pagare il conto.
bill of fare menu, m.; lista.
billion bilione, m.
bind (to) legare.
bird uccello.
birth nascita.
birthday compleanno.
biscuit biscotto.
bishop vescovo.
bit pezzetto.
bit (a) un po'.
bite morsicatura; boccone, m.
bite (to) mordere.
bitter amaro.
bitterness amarezza.
black nero.
blackbird merlo.
blade lama; lametta (razor).
blame colpa, biasimo.
blame (to) incolpare.
blank (noun) modulo (form).
blank (adj.) in bianco.
blanket coperta.
bleed (to) sanguinare.
bless (to) benedire.
blessing benedizione, f.
blind (noun) tendina (for window).
blind cieco.
blind (to) accecare.
block blocco; caseggiato (a city square).

block (to) ostacolare, sbarrare.
blood sangue m.
blotter carta sugante.
blouse camicia, camicetta.
blow colpo.
blow (to) soffiare.
blue blu, azzurro, turchino.
blush rossore, m.
blush (to) arrossire.
board vitto e alloggio (food and lodging); asse, f. (plank).
boarding house pensione, f.
boast (to) vantare.
boat barca, battello.
sailboat barca a vela.
rowboat barca a remi.
boil (to) bollire.
boiler caldaia.
bold ardito.
bomb bomba.
atomic bomb bomba atomica.
bond legame, m.
bone osso.
book libro.
bookseller libraio.
bookstore libreria.
border frontiera.
boring noioso.
born (to be) nascere.
borrow (to) pigliare in prestito.
both ambedue, entrambi.
bother noia.
bother (to) annoiare.
Don't bother. Non disturbatevi.
bottle bottiglia.
bottle opener apribottiglia.
bottom fondo.
bottom (adj.) ultimo; in fondo.
bounce (to) saltare.
boundary limite, m.; confine, m.
boundless sconfinato, illimitato.
bowl scodella.
box scatola.
boy ragazzo.
bracelet braccialetto.
braid treccia.
brain cervello.
brake freno.
branch ramo; succursale, f. (business).
brassiere reggiseno, m.
brave coraggioso, bravo.
bread pane, m.
break (to) rompere.
to break out irrompere.
breakfast colazione, f.
to have breakfast far colazione.
breath soffio, respiro.
breathe (to) respirare.
breeze brezza.
bribe (to) corrompere.
brick mattone, m.
bride sposa.
bridge ponte, m.
brief breve.
bright chiaro, vivo.
brighten (to) brillare.
brilliant brillante.
bring (to) portare, condurre.
bring together (to) avvicinare.
bring up (to) educare.
British inglese, britannico.
broad largo.
broil (to) arrostire.

broiled sulla graticola.
broken rotto.
brook ruscello.
broom scopa.
brother fratello.
brother-in-law cognato.
brown marrone.
bruise (to) ammaccare.
brush spazzola.
brute bruto.
bubble bolla.
buckle fibbia.
bud bocciuolo.
budget bilancio.
buffet buffet.
build (to) costruire, fabbricare.
building costruzione, f.; palazzo, edifizio.
bulletin bollettino.
bundle pacco.
burn (to) bruciare.
burst eruzione, f.; scoppio.
burst (to) scoppiare.
bus autobus, m.
bush cespuglio, macchia.
business affare, m.; commercio.
businessman uomo d'affari; commerciante (dealer).
busy occupato.
but ma.
butcher macellaio.
butcher shop macelleria.
butter burro.
button bottone, m.
buy (to) comprare.
buyer compratore, m.
by per, a.
by and by più in là; fra poco.
by day di giorno.
by then allora.

C

cab tassì, m.
cabbage cavolo.
cab driver autista, m.
cabinet gabinetto, armadio.
cable (to) mandare un cablogramma.
cablegram cablogramma, m.
cage gabbia.
cake torta.
cake of soap pezzo di sapone.
calendar calendario.
calf vitello.
call chiamata, visita, grido.
call (to) chiamare.
to call back richiamare.
to call forth evocare.
to call out gridare.
to call on (someone) visitare.
calm sereno.
camera macchina fotografica.
camp campo.
camp (to) accampare.
can scatola, latta.
can potere (to be able).
cancel (to) annullare.
candidate candidato.
candle candela.
can-opener apriscatola.
cap berretto.
capacity capacità.
capital capitale, f. (city); capitale, m. (money).
capital (adj.) capitale, principale.
capricious capriccioso.
captain capitano.

captive prigioniero.
capture (to) catturare.
car automobile, f.; vettura (wagon).
carbon paper carta copiativa.
card carta.
    game of cards partita a carte.
care cura.
    in care of presso (on a letter).
    take care of prendere cura di.
care (to) curare.
    to care for amare.
    to care to desiderare.
    I don't care. Non me ne curo.
career carriera.
careful cauto, attento.
careless incauto, trascurato.
cares noie, f. pl.
carpenter falegname, m.
carpet tappeto.
carry (to) portare.
carry out (to) eseguire.
carve (to) tagliare, scolpire.
case caso; recipiente, m. (container); cassa or cassetta (box).
    in that case in tal caso.
cash contanti, m. pl.
cash (to) incassare.
cashier cassiere, m.
cast (to) gettare (throw).
castle castello.
cat gatto.
catch (to) afferrare.
category categorìa.
Catholic cattolico.
cattle bestiame, m.
cause causa.
cause (to) causare.
cavalry cavallerìa.
cease (to) cessare.
ceiling soffitto.
celebrate (to) celebrare.
cellar cantina.
cement cemento.
cemetery cimitero.
cent centesimo.
center centro.
central centrale.
century secolo.
cereal cereale, m.
ceremony cerimonia.
certain certo.
certainty certezza.
certificate certificato, atto.
    birth certificate atto di nascita.
chain catena.
chain (to) incatenare.
chair sedia.
chairman presidente, m.
chalk gesso.
challenge sfida.
challenge (to) sfidare.
champagne champagne, m.
champion campione, m.
chance caso, azzardo, sorte, f.
    to take a chance correre il rischio.
change cambiamento; trasformazione; resto (money).
change (to) cambiare.
chapel cappella.
chapter capitolo.
character carattere, m.; personaggio (in a play).
characteristic caratteristica.

charge (to) far pagare; mettere a carico di; accusare (to accuse).
charitable caritatevole.
charity carità.
charm fascino.
charm (to) affascinare.
charming affascinante.
chase (to) inseguire.
chat (to) chiacchierare.
cheap a buon mercato.
cheat (to) ingannare, truffare.
check freno; assegno (bank).
check (to) verificare (verify); reprimere (hold back).
cheek guancia.
cheer (to) rallegrare, acclamare, rianimare.
cheerful allegro, gaio.
cheese formaggio.
chemical sostanza chimica.
chemist chimico.
cherish (to) amare teneramente.
cherry ciliegia.
chest petto (body); cassa (box).
    chest of drawers stipo; armadio.
chestnut castagna.
chew (to) masticare.
chicken pollo.
chief capo.
chief (adj.) principale.
child bambino, bambina, fanciullo, fanciulla.
chime cariglione, m.
chimney camino; focolare, m. (hearth).
chin mento.
china porcellana.
chip scheggia.
chocolate cioccolato.
choice scelta; (adj.) scelto.
choir coro.
choke (to) strangolare.
choose (to) scegliere.
chop cotoletta (cut of meat).
Christian cristiano (noun & adj.).
Christmas Natale.
    Christmas Eve Vigilia di Natale.
    Merry Christmas! Buon Natale!
church chiesa.
cigar sigaro.
circle cerchio.
circular rotondo.
circulation circolazione, f.
circumstances circostanze, f. pl.
citizen cittadino.
city città.
city hall municipio.
civil civile.
civilization civilizzazione, f.; civiltà.
civilize (to) civilizzare, incivilire.
claim diritto, reclamo.
claim (to) reclamare, affermare.
clamor clamore, m.; strepito.
clap (to) applaudire, battere le mani.
class classe, f.
classify (to) classificare.
clause clausola.
clean pulito.
clean (to) pulire.
    (to) dry clean pulire a secco.
cleanliness pulizia.
clear chiaro.
clear (to) chiarire.
clearly chiaramente.
clerk commesso.
clever scaltro.

climate clima, m.
climb (to) arrampicarsi.
clip (to) attaccare, appuntare.
cloak mantello.
clock orologio.
close vicino (near).
close (to) chiudere.
closed chiuso.
closet armadio.
cloth stoffa.
clothe (to) vestire.
clothes vestiti, indumenti.
    clothes hanger attaccapanni, m.
cloud nuvola.
cloudy nuvoloso.
clover trifoglio.
club circolo (organization); bastoni, f. (playing cards).
coal carbone, m.
coarse ruvido.
coast costa.
coat cappotto (overcoat).
cocoa cacao.
code codice, m.
coffee caffè, m.
    coffee with cream caffè con panna.
coffin bara.
coin moneta.
cold freddo.
    to be cold aver freddo; far freddo (weather).
coldness freddezza.
collaborate (to) collaborare.
collar collare, m.; colletto.
collect (to) raccogliere.
collection collezione, f.; raccolta.
collective collettivo.
college università.
colonial coloniale.
colony colonia.
color colore, m.
color (to) colorare.
column colonna.
comb pettine, m.
comb (to) pettinare.
combination combinazione, f.
combine (to) combinare.
come (to) venire.
    to come about accadere.
    to come back ritornare.
    to come by passare per.
    to come down scendere.
    to come for venire a prendere.
    to come in entrare.
    to come out uscire.
comedy commedia.
comet cometa.
comfort conforto, agio.
comfort (to) consolare, rassicurare.
comfortable confortevole.
comma virgola.
command comando.
command (to) comandare.
commander comandante, m.
commerce commercio.
commercial commerciale.
commission commissione, f.
commit (to) commettere.
common comune.
communicate (to) comunicare.
communication comunicazione, f.
community comunità.
companion compagno, compagna.
company compagnìa (firm); invitati (guests).

compare (to) paragonare, confrontare.
comparison paragone, m.
compete (to) competere.
competition competizione, f.
complain (to) lagnarsi.
complaint lagnanza.
complete completo.
complex complesso (noun & adj.).
complexion carnagione, f.
complicate (to) complicare.
complicated complicato.
compliment complimento.
compose (to) comporre.
composer compositore, m.
composition composizione, f.
comprehend (to) comprendere, includere.
compromise compromesso.
compromise (to) compromettere.
comrade camerata, m.
conceit vanagloria.
conceive (to) concepire, immaginare.
concentrate (to) concentrare.
concern ditta (business); ansietà (anxiety).
concern (to) concernere, riguardare.
concert concerto.
conclusion conclusione, f.; fine, f.
concrete (adj.) concreto.
condemn (to) condannare.
condense (to) condensare.
condition condizione, f.
conduct condotta.
conduct (to) condurre, dirigere.
conductor conduttore, m.; direttore, m.
confess (to) confessare.
confession confessione, f.
confidence confidenza.
confident confidente, sicuro.
confidential confidenziale.
confirm (to) confermare.
confirmation conferma.
congratulate (to) congratulare.
congratulation congratulazione, f.
connect (to) unire.
connection connessione, f.; relazione, f.
conquer (to) conquistare.
conquest conquista.
conscience coscienza.
conscientious coscienzioso, scrupoloso.
conscious conscio, consapevole.
consent consenso.
consent (to) acconsentire.
conservative conservativo.
consider (to) considerare.
considerable considerabile.
consideration considerazione, f.
consist (to) consistere.
consistent consistente.
console (to) consolare.
constant costante.
constitution costituzione, f.
constitutional costituzionale.
construct (to) costruire.
consul console, m.
contagious contagioso.
contain (to) contenere.
container recipiente, m.
contemporary contemporaneo.
contend (to) contendere.
content (to) accontentare.
content (to be) essere contento.
content(s) contenuto.
continent continente, m.
continual continuo.

continue (to) continuare.
contract contratto.
contract (to) contrattare.
contractor contrattante, m.; contraente, m.
contradict (to) contradire, smentire.
contradiction contradizione, f.
contradictory contradittorio.
contrary contrario.
  on the contrary contrariamente; al contrario.
contrary (adj.) contrario.
contrary to contrario a.
contrast contrasto.
contrast (to) contrastare.
contribute (to) contribuire.
contribution contributo.
control controllo; potere, m. (power or ability).
control (to) controllare.
controversy controversia.
convenience convenienza.
  at your convenience a vostro agio.
convenient conveniente.
convention convenzione, f.
conversation conversazione, f.
converse (to) conversare.
convert (to) convertire.
convict (to) condannare.
conviction convinzione, f.
convince (to) convincere.
cook cuoco, cuoca.
cook (to) cucinare.
cool fresco.
cool (to) rinfrescare, raffreddarsi.
copy copia.
copy (to) copiare.
cork sughero.
cork (to) tappare, turare.
corkscrew cavaturaccioli, m.
corn grano.
corner angolo.
corporation corporazione, f.
correct corretto.
correct (to) correggere.
correction correzione, f.
correspond (to) corrispondere.
correspondence corrispondenza.
correspondent corrispondente, m. & f.
corresponding corrispondente.
corrupt corrotto.
corruption corruzione, f.
cost prezzo, costo.
  at any cost a qualunque costo.
cost (to) costare.
costume costume, m.
cottage capanna.
cotton cotone, m. (cotton thread, material);
  ovatta (wadding).
couch divano.
cough tosse, f.
cough (to) tossire.
count conte, m. (title); conto, m. (computation,
  reckoning).
count (to) contare.
counter banco (store).
countess contessa.
countless innumerevole.
country campagna; patria (fatherland).
country-house casa di campagna.
countryman compatriota; contadino (farmer).
couple coppia.
courage coraggio.
course corso.
  of course naturalmente; s'intende.
court corte, f., tribunale, m.

courteous cortese.
courtesy cortesia.
courtship corte, f.
courtyard cortile, m.
cousin cugino, cugina.
cover coperchio, (lid); coperta (for a bed).
cover (to) coprire.
cow mucca, vacca.
crack fessura.
crack (to) crepare, fendere.
cradle culla.
crash scontro, fracasso.
crash (to) fracassare.
crazy folle, pazzo.
cream crema.
create (to) creare.
creature creatura.
credit credito, fiducia.
creditor creditore, m.
cricket grillo.
crime delitto.
criminal delinquente, m. (Also adj.)
crisis crisi, f.
crisp croccante.
critic critico.
criticism critica.
crooked storto; disonesto (morally).
crop raccolta.
cross croce, f.
cross (adj.) adirato; di cattivo umore.
cross (to) traversare.
crossing passaggio.
crossroads bivio, crocevia, m.
crouch (to) appiattarsi.
crow corvo.
crowd folla.
crowd (to) affollare, ingombrare.
cruel crudele.
cruelty crudeltà.
cruise crociera.
crumb mollica, briciola.
crumble (to) sgretolarsi.
crust crosta.
crutch gruccia, stampella.
cry grido.
cry (to) piangere, gridare.
cuff manichino, polsino.
cunning scaltrezza.
cup tazza.
cure cura.
cure (to) curare.
curiosity curiosità.
curious curioso.
curl riccio.
curl (to) arricciare.
current corrente, f.
current (adj.) corrente; in corso.
curtain tendina; sipario (theater).
curve curva.
cushion cuscino.
custom usanza.
customary abituale.
customer cliente, m. & f.
customhouse dogana.
customs official doganiere, m.
cut taglio.
cut (to) tagliare.

D

dagger pugnale, m.
daily quotidiano.
dainty delicato.
dairy latteria.

dairy products latticini, m. pl.
dam diga.
damage danno.
damage (to) danneggiare.
damp umido.
dance danza.
dance (to) ballare, danzare.
danger pericolo.
dangerous pericoloso.
dark buio; oscuro; scuro (color).
darkness oscurità.
dash (to) precipitarsi.
date data.
date (to) datare.
daughter figlia.
daughter-in-law nuora.
dawn alba.
day giorno.
  all day tutto il giorno.
  day after tomorrow dopo domani; l'indomani, m.
  day before giorno prima.
  day before yesterday avantieri; ieri l'altro.
dazzle (to) abbagliare.
dead morto, morta.
deaf sordo. (Also deaf person.)
deaf and dumb sordomuto, sordomuta.
deal affare, m.
dealer mercante, m.; venditore, m.
dear caro.
death morte, f.
debatable discutibile.
debate discussione, f.
debate (to) discutere.
debris rovine, f. pl.
debt debito.
debtor debitore, m.
decanter caraffa.
decay decadenza.
decay (to) decadere, appassire.
deceased defunto.
deceit inganno.
deceive (to) ingannare.
December dicembre.
decent decente.
decide (to) decidere.
decidedly decisamente.
decision decisione, f.
decisive decisivo.
deck ponte, m.
declare (to) dichiarare.
decline decadenza, abbassamento.
decline (to) declinare.
decrease diminuzione, f.
decrease (to) diminuire.
decree decreto.
dedicate (to) dedicare.
deed atto.
deep profondo.
deer cervo.
defeat sconfitta.
defeat (to) sconfiggere.
defect difetto.
defend (to) difendere.
defense difesa.
defiance sfida, disfida.
define (to) definire.
definite definitivo.
defy (to) sfidare.
degree grado.
delay ritardo.
delay (to) ritardare.
delegate delegato.
delegate (to) delegare.

deliberate (adj.) deliberato.
deliberate (to) deliberare.
deliberately deliberatamente.
delicacy delicatezza.
delicate delicato.
delicious delizioso.
delight delizia.
delight (to) dilettare.
deliver (to) rimettere, consegnare.
deliverance liberazione, f.
delivery liberazione, f.; consegna (package).
demand domanda, richiesta.
demand (to) domandare, richiedere.
demonstrate (to) dimostrare.
demonstration dimostrazione, f.
denial diniego, rifiuto.
denounce (to) denunziare.
dense denso.
density densità.
dental dentale.
dentifrice dentifricio.
dentist dentista, m.
deny (to) negare.
department dipartimento, reparto.
depend (to) dipendere.
dependence dipendenza.
dependent (adj.) dipendente.
deplore (to) deplorare.
deposit deposito.
deposit (to) depositare.
depot deposito.
depress (to) deprimere.
depression depressione, f.
deprive (to) privare.
depth profondità.
derive (to) derivare.
descend (to) discendere, scendere.
descent discesa.
describe (to) descrivere.
description descrizione, f.
desert deserto.
desert (to) abbandonare.
deserve (to) meritare.
design disegno.
design (to) disegnare (to draw).
designed (for) destinato a.
desirable desiderabile.
desire desiderio.
desire (to) desiderare.
desirous desideroso.
desk scrivanìa.
desolate desolato.
desolation desolazione, f.
despair disperazione, f.
despair (to) disperare.
desperate disperato.
despise (to) dispregiare, sdegnare.
despite malgrado.
despondent abbattuto.
dessert frutta e dolci.
destiny destino.
destitute indigente.
destroy (to) distruggere.
destruction distruzione, f.
detach (to) staccare, separare.
detail dettaglio, particolare, m.
detain (to) trattenere.
detect (to) notare.
determination determinazione, f.
determine (to) determinare, fissare, stabilire.
detest (to) detestare.
detour svolta.
detract from (to) detrarre, denigrare.

detriment detrimento.
develop (to) sviluppare.
development sviluppo.
device espediente, m.
devil diavolo.
devise (to) immaginare.
devoid of privo di.
devote (to) dedicare.
devour (to) divorare.
dew rugiada.
dial quadrante (clock).
dialect dialetto.
dialogue dialogo.
diameter diametro.
diamond diamante, m.; quadri, m. pl. (playing cards).
diary diario.
dictate (to) dettare.
dictionary dizionario, vocabolario.
die (to) morire.
diet dieta.
differ (to) differire.
difference differenza.
different diverso.
difficult difficile.
difficulty difficoltà.
dig (to) scavare.
digest (to) digerire.
dignity dignità.
dim oscuro, annebbiato, debole.
dimension dimensione, f.
diminish (to) diminuire.
dine (to) pranzare.
dinner pranzo.
dip (to) immergere, intingere.
diplomacy diplomazìa.
diplomat diplomatico.
direct (to) dirigere.
direction direzione, f.; senso.
  in all directions in tutte le direzioni.
director direttore, m.
directory elenco, direttorio.
dirt sudiciume, m.
dirty sudicio, sporco.
disability incapacità.
disabled incapacitato, mutilato.
disadvantage svantaggio.
disagree (to) differire; non essere d'accordo.
disagreeable contrario, sgradevole.
disagreement differenza, disaccordo.
disappear (to) sparire.
disappearance sparizione, f.; scomparsa.
disappoint (to) deludere l'aspettativa di.
disapprove (to) disapprovare.
disaster disastro.
disastrous disastroso.
discharge congedo (from army or a position); scarica (of a gun).
discharge (to) congedare (military); licenziare (from a position); scaricare (firearm).
discipline disciplina.
disclaim (to) negare, rinunziare.
disclose (to) svelare, palesare.
disclosure rivelazione, f.; palesamento.
discomfort disagio.
discontent malcontento.
discontented scontento.
discontinue (to) cessare.
discord discordia, dissenso, dissidio.
discount sconto.
discourage (to) scoraggiare.
discouragement scoraggiamento.
discover (to) scoprire.
discovery scoperta.

discreet discreto.
discretion discrezione, f.
discuss (to) discutere.
discussion discussione, f.
disdain sdegno.
disdain (to) disdegnare.
disease malattìa.
disgrace vergogna, disonore, m.
disguise travestimento.
in disguise travestito.
disgust disgusto.
disgusted disgustato.
disgusting disgustante.
dish piatto.
dishonest disonesto.
disk disco.
dislike avversione, f.; antipatìa.
dislike (to) sentire avversione; sentire antipatìa; non amare.
dismiss (to) congedare, licenziare.
dismissal congedo.
disobey (to) disobbedire.
disorder disordine, m.
dispense (to) dispensare, distribuire.
display esposizione, f.
display (to) esporre.
displease (to) dispiacere.
disposal disposizione, f.; vendita (sale).
dispose (to) disporre.
dispute disputa, contesa.
dispute (to) disputare, contestare.
dissolve (to) dissolvere, disfare.
distance distanza.
distant lontano, distante.
distinct distinto, chiaro.
distinction distinzione, f.
distinguish (to) distinguere.
distort (to) storcere, deformare.
distract (to) distrarre.
distress afflizione, f.; affanno, imbarazzo.
distress (to) affliggere.
distribute (to) distribuire.
distribution distribuzione, f.
district quartiere, m.
distrust sfidùcia.
distrust (to) non aver fiducia.
disturb (to) disturbare.
disturbance disturbo, disordine, m.
ditch fosso.
dive (to) tuffarsi.
divide (to) dividere, separare.
divine divino.
division divisione, f.
divorce divorzio.
divorce (to) divorziare.
dizziness vertigine, f.
dizzy stordito.
do (to) fare.
dock darsena.
doctor dottore, m.
doctrine dottrina.
document documento.
dog cane, m.
dome cupola.
domestic domestico.
dominate (to) dominare.
door porta.
next door accanto.
dose dose, f.
dot punto.
double doppio.
doubt dubbio.
doubt (to) dubitare.

doubtful dubbioso.
doubtless senza dubbio.
dough pasta.
down giù, in basso.
downwards in giù.
dozen dozzina.
draft corrente, f. (air); leva (military); cambiale, f. (bank).
draft (to) reclutare (military); fare la pianta (make a plan).
drag (to) strascinare.
drain (to) seccare, fognare.
drama dramma, m.
draw (to) disegnare.
drawback svantaggio.
draw back (to) indietreggiare.
drawer tiretto, cassetto.
drawing room salone, m.
dread terrore, m.; paura.
dread (to) temere.
dreaded terribile, formidabile.
dream sogno.
dream (to) sognare.
dreamer sognatore, m.
dress abito, vestito, veste, f.
dress (to) vestirsi, vestire.
drink bevanda.
drink (to) bere.
drip (to) sgocciolare.
drive (to) guidare (car); spingere (to force or induce).
driver conducente, m.
drop goccia (of water); caduta (a fall).
drop (to) lasciare cadere.
drown (to) annegare.
drug droga.
druggist farmacista, m.
drugstore farmacìa.
drum tamburo.
drunk ubriaco, ebbro.
dry asciutto, secco.
dry (to) asciugare, seccare.
dryness aridità.
duchess duchessa.
due dovuto.
duke duca, m.
dull fosco (color); ottuso (stupid).
dumb muto (mute); stupido (stupid).
during durante.
dust polvere, f.
dust (to) spolverare.
dusty polveroso.
duty dazio (customs tolls); dovere (obligation).
dwell (to) dimorare, abitare.
dwelling dimora, abitazione, f.
dye tintura.
dye (to) tingere.

E

each ciascuno, ciascuna, ogni.
each other si; ci; l'un l'altro.
each time ogni volta.
eager ansioso; desideroso di.
eagle aquila.
ear orecchio.
early presto; di buon'ora.
earn (to) guadagnare.
earnest zelante, fervido, sincero.
earth terra.
ease agio.
ease (to) alleviare, mitigare.
easily facilmente.
east est, m.; oriente, m.

Easter Pasqua.
eastern orientale.
easy facile.
eat (to) mangiare.
echo eco, m. & f.
economical economico.
economize (to) fare delle economìe; economizzare.
economy economìa.
edge bordo, orlo.
edition edizione, f.
editor editore, m.; redattore, m.
editorial articolo di fondo; (adj.) editoriale.
education educazione, f.; istruzione, f.
effect effetto.
effect (to) effettuare, compiere.
effective efficace.
efficiency efficienza.
effort sforzo.
egg uovo.
hard-boiled egg uovo sodo.
scrambled eggs uova strapazzate.
egoism egoismo.
eight otto.
eighteen diciotto.
eighteenth diciottesimo.
eighth ottavo.
eightieth ottantesimo.
eighty ottanta.
either ... or ... sia ... che ...
either ... or ... o ... o ...
either one l'uno o l'altro.
either one of the two qualunque dei due.
elastic elastico (noun & adj.).
elbow gomito.
elder anziano, maggiore.
elderly anziano.
eldest il più anziano; il maggiore.
elect scegliere, eleggere.
election elezione, f.
elector elettore, m.
electric(al) elettrico.
electricity elettricità.
elegant elegante.
element elemento, fattore, m.
elementary elementare.
elephant elefante, m.
elevator ascensore, m.
eleven undici.
eleventh undicesimo.
eliminate (to) eliminare.
eloquence eloquenza.
eloquent eloquente.
else altro.
or else altrimenti.
someone else qualche altro.
elsewhere altrove.
elude (to) eludere.
embark (to) imbarcare, imbarcarsi.
embarrass (to) imbarazzare.
embarrassing imbarazzante.
embarrassment imbarazzo.
embassy ambasciata.
embody (to) incarnare.
embroider (to) ricamare.
embroidery ricamo.
emerge (to) emergere.
emergency emergenza.
eminent eminente.
emotion emozione, f.
emperor imperatore.
emphasis enfasi, f.
emphasize (to) accentuare.

emphatic enfatico.
empire impero.
employ (to) impiegare.
employee impiegato.
employer datore di lavoro, m.
employment impiego.
empty vuoto.
empty (to) vuotare.
enable (to) rendere abile; mettere in condizione di.
enamel smalto.
enclose (to) rinchiudere.
enclosed rinchiuso.
encourage (to) incoraggiare.
encouragement incoraggiamento.
end fine, f.
end (to) finire.
endeavor sforzo, tentativo.
endeavor (to) tentare; sforzarsi di.
endorse (to) firmare (a check); sottoscrivere a (an idea).
endure (to) durare (last); sopportare (bear).
enemy nemico, nemica.
energetic energico.
energy energìa.
enforce (to) imporre.
engage (to) impegnare.
engagement impegno (social); fidanzamento (romantic).
engine macchina, motore, m.
engineer ingegnere, m.; macchinista, m. (railway).
English inglese (noun & adj.).
engrave (to) intagliare.
enjoy (to) godere.
enjoyment godimento.
enlarge (to) ingrandire.
enlist (to) arrolare, arrolarsi.
enormous enorme.
enough abbastanza.
   Enough! Basta!
enrich (to) arricchire.
enter (to) entrare.
entertain (to) intrattenere.
entertainment intrattenimento.
enthusiasm entusiasmo.
enthusiastic entusiastico.
entire intero.
entitle (to) intitolare (title); dare diritto di (give the right to).
entrance entrata.
entrust (to) affidare.
enumerate (to) enumerare.
envelope busta.
envious invidioso.
envy invidia.
episode episodio.
equal uguale.
equal (to) uguagliare.
equality uguaglianza.
equilibrium equilibrio.
equip (to) fornire; equipaggiare (ship, army).
equipment fornimento; equipaggiamento (army).
equity equità.
era era.
erase (to) cancellare.
eraser gomma,
erect diritto, eretto.
erect (to) erigere.
err (to) errare.
errand commissione, f.
error errore, m.
escalator scala mobile.

escape fuga.
escape (to) fuggire.
escort scorta, guida.
escort (to) scortare, accompagnare.
especially specialmente.
essay composizione, f. (school); tentativo (attempt).
essence essenza.
essential essenziale.
establish (to) stabilire.
establishment stabilimento.
estate beni, m. pl.; proprietà.
esteem stima.
esteem (to) stimare.
esthetic estetico.
estimate valutazione, f.; preventivo.
estimate (to) valutare.
estimation valutazione, f.; estimazione, f.
eternal eterno.
eternity eternità.
ether etere, m.
European europeo (noun & adj.).
evade (to) evadere.
evasion evasione, f.
eve vigilia.
   on the eve of la vigilia di.
even pari, uguale.
even (adv.) anche.
evening sera, serata.
   tomorrow evening domani sera.
   yesterday evening ieri sera.
   Good evening! Buona sera!
event avvenimento.
ever sempre.
every ogni.
everybody tutti, tutte.
everyone ognuno, ognuna.
everything tutto.
everywhere ovunque, dappertutto.
evidence evidenza.
evident evidente.
evil male, m.
evil (adj.) cattivo.
evoke (to) evocare.
evolve (to) evolvere.
exact preciso.
exaggerate (to) esagerare.
exaggeration esagerazione, f.
exalt (to) esaltare.
exaltation esaltazione, f.
examination esame, m.
   to take an examination fare un esame.
examine (to) esaminare.
example esempio.
exceed (to) eccedere, oltrepassare.
excel (to) eccellere.
excellence eccellenza.
excellent eccellente.
except eccetto, salvo.
except (to) eccettuare.
exception eccezione, f.
exceptional eccezionale.
exceptionally eccezionalmente.
excess eccesso.
exchange cambio.
excite (to) eccitare.
excitement eccitamento.
exclaim (to) esclamare.
exclamation esclamazione, f.
exclamation mark punto esclamativo.
exclude (to) escludere.
exclusive esclusivo.
excursion escursione, f.

excuse scusa.
excuse (to) scusare.
   Excuse me. Mi scusi.
execute (to) eseguire (to carry out); giustiziare (a prisoner).
execution esecuzione, f.
exempt esente.
exercise esercizio.
exercise (to) esercitare, esercitarsi.
exert (to) adoprarsi.
exertion sforzo.
exhaust (to) sfinire, esaurire.
exhaustion esaurimento.
exhibit (to) esibire.
exhibition esibizione, f.; mostra.
exile esilio.
exile (to) esiliare.
exist (to) esistere.
existence esistenza.
exit uscita.
expand (to) espandere.
expansion espansione, f.
expansive espansivo.
expect (to) attendere, aspettare, aspettarsi.
expectation aspettativa.
expedition spedizione, f.
expel (to) espellere.
expense spesa.
expensive costoso, caro.
experience esperienza.
experience (to) provare.
experiment esperimento.
expert esperto.
expire (to) spirare, morire.
explain (to) spiegare.
explanation spiegazione, f.
explode (to) esplodere.
exploit gesta, f. pl.
exploit (to) sfruttare.
explore (to) esplorare.
explosion esplosione, f.
export esportazione, f.
export (to) esportare.
expose (to) esporre.
express espresso (noun & adj.).
express (to) esprimere.
expression espressione, f.
expressive espressivo.
expulsion espulsione, f.
exquisite squisito.
extend (to) estendere.
extensive estensivo.
extent estensione, f.; limite, m.
   to some extent fino ad un certo punto.
exterior esteriore.
exterminate (to) sterminare.
external esteriore.
extinct estinto.
extinction estinzione, f.
extinguish (to) estinguere.
extra in più; supplementare.
extract estratto.
extract (to) estrarre.
extraordinary straordinario.
extravagance stravaganza.
extravagant stravagante.
extreme estremo.
extremely estremamente.
extremity estremità.
eye occhio.
eyebrow ciglio.
eyeglasses occhiali, m. pl.
eyelid palpebra.

F

fable favola.
face viso, faccia.
face (to) affrontare.
facilitate (to) facilitare.
facility facilità.
fact fatto.
 in fact infatti.
factory fabbrica.
faculty facoltà.
fade (to) sbiadire.
fail fallo, mancanza.
 without fail senz' altro; senza fallo.
fail (to) fallire, mancare.
faint fievole (sound, voice); debole; fioco.
faint (to) svenire.
fair giusto; equo; biondo (blond).
faith fede, f.
faithful fedele.
faithfulness fedeltà.
fall caduta; cascata (of water).
fall (to) cadere.
false falso.
fame fama, reputazione, f.
familiar noto.
family famiglia.
famine carestìa.
famous famoso.
fan ventaglio.
 electric fan ventilatore elettrico.
fancy fantasìa, capriccio.
fantastic fantastico.

far lontano.
 far away molto lontano.
farce farsa.
fare prezzo della corsa.
farm fattorìa, podere, m.
farmer agricoltore, m.
farming agricoltura.
farther più lontano.
farthest il più lontano.
fashion moda.
 old-fashioned passato di moda; fuori di moda.
fashionable di moda.
fast veloce, fisso.
fasten (to) attaccare.
fat grasso (noun & adj.).
fatal fatale.
fate destino.
father padre, m.
father-in-law suocero.
faucet rubinetto.
fault colpa.
favor favore, m.; cortesìa.
favor (to) favorire, preferire.
favorable favorevole.
favorite favorito (noun & adj.).
fear timore, m.; paura.
 to be afraid aver paura.
fearless intrepido.
feather piuma.
feature caratteristica, lineamento.
February febbraio.
federal federale.
fee onorario, paga.
feeble debole.
feed (to) nutrire.
feel (to) sentire; tastare (to touch).
 to feel well sentirsi bene.
feeling sensibilità, sentimento.
fellow compagno, camerata, m.
fellowship compagnia, società.

fellow-worker collega, m. & f.
female femmina.
feminine femminile.
fence siepe, f.; chiusura, steccato.
fencing scherma.
fender parafango.
ferocious feroce.
ferry chiatta.
 ferry-boat nave-traghetto.
fertile fertile.
fertilize (to) fertilizzare.
fertilizer fertilizzante, m.
fervent fervente.
fervor fervore, m.
festival festa, festival.
fetch (to) andare a cercare.
fever febbre, f.
few pochi, poche, m. & f. pl.
fiber fibra.
fiction finzione, f.; invenzione, f.; romanzo.
field campo.
fierce violento.
fiery focoso.
fifteen quindici.
fifteenth quindicesimo.
fifth quinto.
fiftieth cinquantesimo.
fifty cinquanta.
fig fico.
fight lotta.
fight (to) lottare, combattere.
figure forma (form); cifra (number).
file lima (tool); fascicolo (papers).
file (to) limare.
fill (to) riempire.
film pellicola.
filthy sudicio.
final finale.
finance finanza.
financial relativo alle finanze; finanziario.
find (to) trovare.
 to find out scoprire.
fine multa.
fine (adj.) fine (not coarse); bello.
 Fine! Bene!
finger dito.
finish (to) terminare, completare.
fire fuoco, incendio.
firearms armi da fuoco.
fireplace focolare, m.
firm ditta.
firm (adj.) fermo, fisso.
first (adj.) primo.
 for the first time per la prima volta.
first (adv.) prima.
 at first dapprima; da principio.
fish pesce, m.
fish (to) pescare.
fisherman pescatore, m.
fist pugno.
fit (noun) attacco; crisi, f. (illness).
fit (adj.) idoneo, capace.
fit (to) essere idoneo; essere della stessa misura.
fitness convenienza; attitudine, f.; proporzione, f.
five cinque.
fix (to) accomodare, aggiustare.
flag bandiera.
flame fiamma.
flank fianco, lato.
flash baleno.
flashlight lampadina tascabile; pila.
flat appartamento (living quarters); bemolle, m. (in music).

flat (adj.) piatto, piano.
flatter (to) adulare.
flattery adulazione, f.
flavor gusto.
fleet flotta.
flesh carne, f.
flexibility flessibilità.
flexible flessibile.
flight volo (in air); fuga (escape).
fling (to) gettare.
flint pietra focaia.
float (to) galleggiare.
flood inondazione, f.
flood (to) inondare.
floor pavimento.
flourish (to) prosperare.
flow (to) scorrere.
flower fiore, m.
fluid fluido.
fly mosca.
fly (to) volare.
foam schiuma.
foam (to) fare la schiuma.
fog nebbia.
fold piega.
fold (to) piegare.
foliage fogliame, m.
follow (to) seguire.
following seguente.
fond (to be) sentire tenerezza.
fondness tenerezza.
food nutrimento, cibo.
fool sciocco (noun & adj.).
foolish sciocco.
foot piede, m.
football gioco del calcio.
footstep passo.
for per.
 for example per esempio.
 for the first time per la prima volta.
 for the most part per la maggior parte.
 for the present per il momento.
forbid (to) vietare.
force forza.
force (to) obbligare.
ford guado.
foreground primo piano.
forehead fronte, f.
foreign straniero.
foreigner straniero.
forest foresta.
forget (to) dimenticare.
forgetfulness oblìo, dimenticanza.
forgive (to) perdonare.
forgiveness perdono.
fork forchetta.
form forma.
form (to) formare.
formal formale.
formation formazione, f.
former precedente.
formerly precedentemente.
formula formula.
forsake (to) abbandonare.
fort forte, m.
fortunate fortunato.
fortunately fortunatamente.
fortune fortuna.
fortieth quarantesimo.
forty quaranta.
forward avanti.
forward (to) spedire (goods, letters).
foster (to) nutrire, proteggere.

found trovato.
found (to) fondare.
foundation fondazione, *f. (society or order);* fondamento *(base).*
founder fondatore, *m.*
fountain fontana.
four quattro.
fourteen quattordici.
fourteenth quattordicesimo.
fourth quarto.
fowl uccello, pollo.
fox volpe, *f.*
fragment frammento.
fragrance fragranza, profumo.
fragrant fragrante, profumato.
frail fragile.
frame cornice, *f.*
frame (to) incorniciare.
frank franco.
frankness franchezza.
free libero *(without restraint);* gratuito *(gratuitous).*
free (to) liberare.
freedom libertà.
freeze (to) gelare.
freight merce, *f.;* carico.
  freight train treno merci.
French francese *(noun & adj.).*
frequent frequente.
frequently frequentemente.
fresh fresco.
friction frizione, *f.*
Friday venerdì.
friend amico, amica.
  to be friends with essere in buoni rapporti.
friendly amichevole.
friendship amicizia.
frighten (to) spaventare.
frightening spaventoso.
fringe frangia.
frivolity frivolezza.
frog rana.
from da.
front (in front of) davanti a.
fruit frutto, frutta.
fry (to) friggere.
frying pan padella.
fuel combustibile, *m.*
fugitive fuggitivo.
fulfill (to) adempire.
full pieno.
fully pienamente.
fun divertimento.
  to have fun divertirsi.
function funzione, *f.*
function (to) funzionare.
fund fondo.
fundamental fondamentale.
funds fondi, *m. pl.*
funny buffo.
fur pelliccia *(coat).*
furious furioso.
furnace fornace, *f.*
furnish (to) fornire *(provide);* ammobigliare *(a house).*
furniture mobilia.
furrow solco, fosso.
further più lontano; ulteriore.
fury furia.
future futuro, avvenire.
  in the future nel futuro.

G

gaiety gaiezza.
gain guadagno.
gain (to) guadagnare.
gallant galante.
gallery gallerìa.
gallop (to) galoppare.
gamble (to) giuocare.
game partita.
gang banda.
gangplank passerella.
garage rimessa, autorimessa.
garbage rifiuti, *m. pl.*
garden giardino.
gardener giardiniere, *m.*
garlic aglio.
gas benzina *(for car);* gas *(chemical).*
gate cancello.
gather (to) raccogliere, riunire.
gathering riunione, *f.*
gay gaio.
gem gemma.
gender genere, *m.*
general generale *(noun & adj.).*
generality generalità.
generalize (to) generalizzare.
generation generazione, *f.*
generosity generosità.
generous generoso.
genius genio.
gentle gentile, tenero.
gentleman gentiluomo, signore.
  Gentlemen. Signori.
  Ladies and gentlemen. Signore e signori.
gentleness gentilezza.
genuine genuino, autentico.
geographical geografico.
geography geografìa.
germ germe, *m.*
German tedesco *(noun & adj.).*
gesture gesto.
get (to) ottenere, diventare.
  Get down! Scenda! Scendete! Scendi!
  Get up! Si alzi! Alzatevi! Alzati!
giant gigante, *m.*
gift dono; talento *(talent).*
gifted dotato; con talento *(talented).*
girdle fascia.
girl fanciulla; ragazza.
give (to) dare, donare.
give back (to) restituire, rendere.
give up (to) abbandonare.
glad felice.
gladly volentieri.
glance (to) intravedere; dare un 'occhiata; gettare uno sguardo.
glass bicchiere, *m.;* vetro.
  glasses occhiali, *m. pl.*
  looking glass specchio.
glitter splendore, *m.*
glitter (to) splendere, brillare.
globe globo.
gloomy lugubre, fosco.
glorious glorioso.
glory gloria.
glove guanto.
go (to) andare.
  (to) go away partire.
  (to) go back ritornare.
  (to) go down discendere.
  (to) go forward avanzare.
  (to) go out uscire.

(to) go to bed coricarsi.
(to) go to sleep addormentarsi.
(to) go up salire.
(to) go with accompagnare.
God Dio.
gold oro.
golden d'oro.
good buono.
  Good! Bene!
  Good afternoon. Buon pomeriggio.
  Good evening. Buona sera.
  Good morning. Buon giorno.
  Good night. Buona sera; buona notte.
good-bye arrivederci, addio.
goodness bontà.
goods merce, *f.*
good will buona volontà.
goose oca.
gossip pettegolezzo.
gossip (to) pettegolare.
govern (to) governare.
governess governante, *f.*
government governo.
grace grazia.
graceful grazioso.
grade grado.
grain grano.
grammar grammatica.
  grammar school scuola elementare.
grand grandioso.
  Grand! Magnifico!
grandchild nipote, *m. & f.*
grand-daughter nipote, *f.*
grandfather nonno.
grandmother nonna.
grandson nipote, *m.*
grant concessione, *f.;* dono.
grant (to) concedere, accordare.
  Granted! D'accordo!
grape uva.
grapefruit pompelmo.
grasp (to) afferrare *(seize);* comprendere *(understand).*
grass erba.
grateful riconoscente, grato.
gratitude riconoscenza, gratitudine, *f.*
grave tomba.
grave (adj.) grave, serio.
graveyard cimitero.
gravel ghiaia.
gray grigio.
grease grasso.
great grande *(person);* enorme *(size);* lungo *(time).*
greatness grandezza.
greedy avido.
green verde.
greet (to) salutare.
greeting saluto.
grief pena.
grieve (to) penare.
grin (to) sogghignare.
grind (to) macinare.
groan gemito.
groan (to) gemere.
grocer venditore di generi alimentari.
grocery store negozio di generi alimentari.
gross grosso.
ground terra.
group gruppo.
group (to) raggruppare.
grouping raggruppamento.
grow (to) crescere.
growth crescita.

grudge   rancore, m.
 hold a grudge against   volerne a.
guard   guardia.
guard (to)   fare la guardia a.
guardian   guardiano.
guess   congettura.
guess (to)   indovinare.
guide   guida.
guilt   colpa.
guilty   colpevole.
gum   gengiva (of the teeth).
 chewing gum   gomma (da masticare).
gun   fucile, m.; schioppo.
gush   getto.

H

habit   abitudine, f.
 to be in the habit of   aver l'abitudine di.
habitual   abituale.
hail   grandine, f.
hair   capello.
hairdo   pettinatura.
hairpin   forcina.
hairdresser   parrucchiere, m.
half (noun)   metà.
half (adj.)   mezzo.
half-hour   mezz'ora.
hall   sala.
ham   prosciutto.
hammer   martello.
hand   mano, f.
 hand-made   fatto a mano.
hand (to)   consegnare, passare.
handbag   borsetta.
handful   manata.
handkerchief   fazzoletto.
handle   manico.
handle (to)   maneggiare, toccare.
handsome   bello.
handy   destro, abile (person); conveniente (thing).
hang (to)   appendere.
happen (to)   succedere, avvenire.
happening   avvenimento.
happiness   felicità.
happy   felice.
harbor   porto (ship); rifugio (refuge).
hard   difficile (difficult); duro (not soft).
harden (to)   indurire.
hardly   appena.
hardness   durezza.
hardship   privazione, f.
hardware   chincaglia.
hardware store   chincaglierìa.
hare   lepre, m. & f.
harm   male, m.; danno.
harm (to)   nuocere; fare del male a.
harmful   nocivo.
harmless   innocuo.
harmonious   armonioso.
harmony   armonìa.
harsh   aspro.
harvest   raccolta.
haste   fretta.
hasten (to)   affrettarsi.
hat   cappello.
hate   odio.
hate (to)   odiare.
hateful   odioso.
hatred   odio.
haughty   altero.
have (to)   avere.
 to have a bath   fare un bagno.
haven   asilo, rifugio.

hay   fieno.
he   egli.
head   testa; capo (leader or chief).
headache   mal di testa.
heal (to)   guarire; cicatrizzarsi (a wound).
health   salute, f.
healthy   sano.
heap   mucchio.
heap up (to)   ammucchiare.
hear (to)   udire, sentire.
 to hear from   ricevere notizie da.
hearing   udito.
heart   cuore, m.; cuori, m. pl. (playing cards).
 by heart   a memoria.
heaven   cielo.
heavy   pesante.
hedge   siepe, f.
heed (to)   badare.
heel   calcagno, tallone, m.
height   altezza.
heir   erede, m. & f.
helm   elmo, timone, m.
help   aiuto, soccorso.
help (to)   aiutare, soccorrere.
 I cannot help it.   Non ci posso nulla.
helper   aiutante, m.; assistente, m.
helpful   utile.
hem   orlo.
hen   gallina.
henceforth   d'ora in poi.
her (pron.)   lei, la, le.
 to her   a lei.
her (adj.)   il suo; la sua; i suoi; le sue.
herb   erba.
herd   branco, mandra, gregge, m.
here   qui.
 Here!   Ecco! Tenga! Tenete! Tieni!
herewith   con ciò.
hero   eroe, m.; protagonista, m. (theater).
heroine   eroina.
herring   aringa.
hers   il suo; la sua; i suoi; le sue.
herself   se stessa; ella stessa.
hesitant   esitante.
hide (to)   nascondere; nascondersi (oneself).
hideous   mostruoso.
high   alto.
higher   più in alto.
hill   collina.
him (pron.)   lui, lo, gli.
 to him   a lui.
himself   se stesso; egli stesso.
hinder (to)   ostacolare.
hinge   cardine, m.
hint   allusione, f.; accenno.
hint (to)   alludere.
hip   fianco.
hire (to)   affittare; noleggiare; prendere in
 servizio (person).
his   il suo; la sua; i suoi; le sue.
hiss (to)   sibilare; fischiare (a play).
historian   storico.
historic   storico.
history   storia.
horn   tromba (musical); corno (animal).
horrible   orribile.
horror   orrore, m.
horse   cavallo.
horseback (on)   a cavallo.
hosiery   calze.
hospitable   ospitale.
hospital   ospedale, m.
host   ospite, m.

hostess   ostessa.
hostile   ostile.
hot   caldo.
hotel   albergo.
hour   ora.
house   casa.
household   famiglia (family).
housekeeper   massaia.
housemaid   donna di servizio.
how   come.
how long   quanto tempo.
how many   quanti, quante.
how much   quanto.
how often   quante volte.
however   comunque.
How are you?   Come sta? Come state? Come stai?
How beautiful!   Com' è bello!
howl   ululato, ululo.
howl (to)   ululare.
human   umano.
humane   umano.
humanity   umanità.
humble   umile.
hoarse   rauco.
hoe   zappa.
hold   presa.
hold (to)   tenere.
 to hold back   trattenere.
hole   buco.
holiday   giorno di festa.
holiness   santità.
hollow   vuoto.
holy   santo.
homage   omaggio.
home   casa.
 at home   a casa.
home town   città nativa.
honest   onesto.
honesty   onestà.
honey   miele, m.
honor   onore, m.
honor (to)   onorare.
honorable   onorevole.
hood   cappuccio.
hoof   zoccolo.
hook   gancio.
hope   speranza.
hope (to)   sperare.
hopeful   fiducioso.
hopeless   disperato.
horizon   orizzonte, m.
horizontal   orizzontale.
humid   umido.
humiliate (to)   umiliare.
humility   umiltà.
humor   umore, m.; spirito.
hundred   cento.
hundreth   centesimo.
hunger   fame, f.
hungry (to be)   aver fame.
hunt   caccia.
hunt (to)   andare a caccia.
hunter   cacciatore, m.
hurry   fretta.
 to be in a hurry   aver fretta.
hurry (to)   affrettarsi.
hurt (to)   far male.
husband   marito.
hyphen   tratto d'unione.
hypocrisy   ipocrisìa.
hypocrite   ipocrita, m.
hypothesis   ipotesi, f.

I

I io.
ice ghiaccio.
ice cream gelato.
icy ghiacciato.
idea idea.
ideal ideale, *m.* (Also *adj.*)
idealism idealismo.
idealist idealista, *m.*
identical identico.
identity identità.
idiot idiota *(noun & adj.).*
idle pigro, inattivo.
idleness ozio.
idol idolo.
if se.
ignoble ignobile.
ignorance ignoranza.
ignorant ignorante.
ignore (to) ignorare.
ill malato.
  to become ill ammalarsi.
illness malattìa.
illusion illusione, *f.*
illustrate (to) illustrare.
illustration illustrazione, *f.*
image immagine, *f.*
imaginary immaginario.
imagination immaginazione, *f.*
imagine (to) immaginare.
imitate (to) imitare.
imitation imitazione, *f.*
immediate immediato.
immediately immediatamente.
imminent imminente.
immobility immobilità.
immoral immorale.
immorality immoralità.
immortal immortale.
immortality immortalità.
impartial imparziale.
impatience impazienza.
impatient impaziente.
imperfect imperfetto.
impertinence impertinenza.
impertinent impertinente.
impetuosity impetuosità.
impetuous impetuoso.
impious empio, irreligioso.
import importazione, *f.*
import (to) importare.
importance importanza.
  of the utmost importance della massima
  importanza.
important importante.
imposing imponente.
impossible impossibile.
impress (to) imprimere.
impression impressione, *f.*
  to be under the impression that avere l'impressione che.
imprison (to) imprigionare.
improve (to) migliorare.
improvement miglioramento.
improvise (to) improvvisare.
imprudence imprudenza.
imprudent imprudente.
impulse impulso, slancio.
impure impuro.
in in, dentro.
inadequate inadeguato.
inaugurate (to) inaugurare.

incapable incapace, inabile.
incapacity incapacità.
inch pollice, *m.*
incident incidente, *m.*
include (to) includere, comprendere.
included incluso.
income rendita, entrata.
  income tax imposta sul reddito.
incomparable incomparabile.
incompatible incompatibile.
incompetent incompetente.
incomplete incompleto.
incomprehensible incomprensibile.
inconvenience inconveniente, *m.*
inconvenient inconveniente, incomodo.
incorrect non corretto, scorretto.
increase aumento.
increase (to) aumentare.
incredible incredibile.
indebted indebitato, obbligato.
indecision indecisione, *f.*
indecisive indecisivo, indeciso.
indeed infatti.
independence indipendenza.
independent indipendente.
index indice, *m.*
index finger indice, *m.*
indicate (to) indicare.
indicative indicativo.
indifference indifferenza.
indifferent indifferente.
indignant indignato.
indignation indignazione, *f.*
indirect indiretto.
indirectly indirettamente.
indiscretion indiscrezione, *f.*
indispensable indispensabile.
individual individuo.
individual *(adj.)* individuale.
indivisible indivisibile.
indolence indolenza.
indolent indolente.
indoors in casa; dentro.
  to go indoors rientrare.
indorse (to) girare, approvare.
induce (to) indurre.
induct (to) iniziare, installare.
indulge (to) favorire, concedere, essere
  indulgente.
indulgence indulgenza.
indulgent indulgente.
industrial industriale.
industrious industrioso.
industry industria.
ineffective inefficace.
inexhaustible inesauribile.
inexplicable inesplicabile.
inexpressible inesprimibile.
infallible infallibile.
infamous infame.
infancy infanzia.
infant neonato, *m.*; neonata, *f.*
infantry fanterìa.
infection infezione, *f.*
infer (to) inferire, dedurre.
inference inferenza, deduzione, *f.*
inferior inferiore.
infernal infernale.
infinite infinito.
infinity infinità.
inflict (to) infliggere.
influence influenza.
influence (to) influenzare.

inform (to) informare; far sapere.
information informazione, *f.*; notizia.
ingenious ingegnoso.
ingenuity ingegno, ingegnosità.
ingratitude ingratitudine, *f.*
inhabit (to) abitare.
inhabitant abitante, *m.*
inherit (to) ereditare.
inheritance eredità.
inhuman inumano.
initial iniziale, *f.* (Also *adj.*)
initiate (to) iniziare.
initiative iniziativa.
injurious offensivo.
injury danno, ingiuria.
injustice ingiustizia.
ink inchiostro.
inkwell calamaio.
inland interno.
inn albergo, osteria.
innate innato.
inner interno.
innkeeper albergatore, *m.*
innocence innocenza.
innocent innocente.
inquire (to) domandare, ricercare.
inquiry inchiesta, indagine, *f.*
inscription iscrizione, *f.*
insect insetto.
insensible insensibile.
inseparable inseparabile.
inside di dentro; all'interno.
insight percezione, *f.*
insignificant insignificante.
insincere non sincero; falso.
insinuate (to) insinuare.
insist (to) insistere.
insistence insistenza.
insoluble insolubile.
inspect (to) esaminare, ispezionare.
inspection ispezione, *f.*; esame, *m.*
inspiration ispirazione, *f.*
install (to) installare.
installment installazione, *f.*; rata *(payment).*
instance esempio.
instant istante, *m*; attimo.
instantaneous istantaneo.
instantly all'istante; istantaneamente.
instead of invece di.
instigate (to) istigare.
instinct istinto.
instinctive istintivo.
institute istituto.
institute (to) istituire.
institution istituzione, *f.*
instruct (to) istruire.
instruction istruzione, *f.*
instructor istruttore, *m.*
instrument strumento.
insufficiency insufficienza.
insufficient insufficiente.
insult insulto, offesa.
insult (to) insultare, offendere.
insuperable insuperabile.
insurance assicurazione, *f.*
insure (to) assicurare.
integral integrale.
intellect intelletto.
intellectual intellettuale, *m.* (Also *adj.*)
intelligence intelligenza.
intelligent intelligente.
intend (to) intendere.
intense intenso.

intensity intensità.
intention intenzione, f.
interest interesse, m.
interesting interessante.
interfere (to) interferire, intromettersi.
interference interferenza.
interior interiore, m.; interno. (Also adj.)
intermediate intermediaro. (Also noun.)
international internazionale.
interpose (to) interporre.
interpret (to) interpretare.
interpretation interpretazione, f.
interpreter interprete, m.
interrupt (to) interrompere.
interruption interruzione, f.
interval intervallo.
interview intervista, colloquio.
intimacy intimità.
intimate intimo.
intimidate (to) intimidire.
into entro, dentro.
intolerable intollerabile.
intolerance intolleranza.
intolerant intollerante.
intonation intonazione, f.
introduce (to) presentare.
introduction presentazione, f.
    letter of introduction lettera di presentazione.
intuition intuito, intuizione, f.
invade (to) invadere.
invariable invariabile.
invasion invasione, f.
invent (to) inventare.
invention invenzione, f.
inventor inventore, m.
invert (to) invertire.
invest (to) investire.
investment investimento.
invisible invisibile.
invitation invito.
invite (to) invitare.
invoice fattura.
invoke (to) invocare.
involuntary involontario.
involve (to) implicare.
iodine iodio.
iron ferro; ferro da stiro (for pressing).
iron (to) stirare.
irony ironia.
irregular irregolare.
irreparable irreparabile.
irresistible irresistibile.
irritate (to) irritare.
irritation irritazione, f.
island isola.
isolate (to) isolare.
issue emissione, f.
it lo, la, esso, essa.
    it is è.
    it's here. È qui.
    it's late. È tardi.
Italian italiano (noun & adj.).
item dettaglio (detail); articolo.
its il suo; la sua; i suoi, le sue.
itself se stesso; se stessa; da se.
ivy edera.

J

jacket giacca (for a suit).
jail prigione, f.
jam marmellata.
jar vaso.
jaw mascella.

jealous geloso.
jealousy gelosìa.
jelly marmellata.
jest scherzo.
Jew ebreo (noun & adj.).
jewel gioiello.
job impiego (occupation); lavoro (work).
join (to) unire.
joint giuntura.
joke burla.
joke (to) burlare, scherzare.
jolly allegro.
journal giornale, m.
journalism giornalismo.
journalist giornalista, m.
journey viaggio.
joy gioia.
joyous gioioso.
judge giudice, m.
judge (to) giudicare.
judgment giudizio, discernimento.
judicial giudiziario.
juice succo.
July luglio.
jump salto.
jump (to) saltare.
June giugno.
junior più giovane; minore.
just giusto (adj.); appena (adv.).
    just now proprio ora.
justice giustizia.
justify (to) giustificare.

K

keen acuto.
keep (to) tenere.
    (to) keep back tenere indietro.
    (to) keep from impedire (prevent); astenersi
    (refrain).
    (to) keep quiet tacere.
    (to) keep in mind tener conto di; ricordare.
    (to) keep still star fermo.
kernel gheriglio; nocciolo (of a discussion).
kettle pentola.
key chiave, f.
keyhole buco della serratura.
kick calcio.
kick (to) dare un calcio.
kid capretto (leather).
kidney rene, m.
kill (to) uccidere.
kin parente, m. & f.
kind (noun) sorta, qualità.
kind (adj.) benigno, gentile, amabile.
kindly benignamente.
    Will you kindly... Volete avere la bontà di ...
kindness bontà.
king re, m.
kingdom regno.
kiss bacio.
kiss (to) baciare.
kitchen cucina.
kite aquilone, m.
knee ginocchio.
    on one's knees in ginocchio.
kneel (to) inginocchiarsi.
knife coltello.
    penknife temperino.
knight cavaliere, m.
knit (to) lavorare a maglia.
knock bussata.
knock (to) bussare.

knot nodo.
know (to) sapere, conoscere.
knowledge conoscenza, sapere, m.
known conosciuto.

L

label etichetta.
labor lavoro, fatica.
laboratory laboratorio.
lace merletto.
lack mancanza.
lack (to) mancare.
ladder scala a piuoli.
lady signora.
    the lady of the house la padrona di casa.
    Ladies. Signore.
    Ladies and gentlemen. Signore e signori.
lake lago.
lamb agnello.
lame zoppo.
lamp lampada.
land terra, terreno.
land (to) sbarcare (ship); atterrare (airplane).
landscape paesaggio.
language linguaggio.
languish (to) languire.
languor languore, m.
lantern lanterna.
large grande.
last ultimo.
    at last finalmente.
    last month il mese scorso.
    last night ieri sera.
last (to) durare.
lasting duraturo.
latch saliscendi, m.
late tardi.
lately ultimamente, poco fa.
latter ultimo.
laugh (to) ridere.
    to laugh at ridere di.
laughter risata, riso.
laundry lavanderìa.
lavish prodigo, profuso.
lavish (to) prodigare.
law legge, f.
lawful legale.
lawn prato.
lay (to) deporre, collocare.
layer strato.
lazy pigro.
lead piombo.
lead (to) condurre, guidare.
leader capo; duce, m.
leadership direzione, f.
leaf foglia (of a tree); foglio, m.
leak (to) gocciolare.
lean (to) appoggiarsi.
leap salto.
leap (to) saltare.
learn (to) apprendere, imparare.
learned erudito, colto.
learning cultura, erudizione, f.
lease (to) affittare.
least minore.
    at least almeno.
leather cuoio.
leave congedo, permesso.
leave (to) abbandonare (desert); lasciare (quit).
lecture conferenza.
left sinistra (noun & adj.).
    left-handed mancino.
    to the left a sinistra.

leg gamba.
legal legale.
legend leggenda.
legislation legislazione, f.
legitimate legittimo.
leisure agio, ozio.
lemon limone, m.
lemon juice succo di limone.
lemonade limonata.
lend (to) prestare.
length lunghezza; durata (of time).
lengthen (to) allungare.
less meno.
lesson lezione, f.
let (to) lasciare, permettere; affittare (rent).
To Let. Si Affitta.
to let alone lasciare tranquillo.
letter lettera.
level livello.
liable responsabile.
liar mentitore, m.; bugiardo.
liberal liberale.
liberty libertà.
library biblioteca.
license licenza, permesso.
lick (to) leccare.
lie menzogna.
lie (to) mentire (tell a falsehood); sdraiarsi (lie down); coricarsi (go to bed).
lieutenant tenente (first lieutenant); sottotenente (second lieutenant).
life vita.
lift (to) sollevare, alzare.
light luce, f.; lume, m.
light (adj.) chiaro; leggero (in weight).
light (to) accendere.
lighten (to) alleggerire.
light up (to) illuminare.
lighthouse faro.
lighting illuminazione, f.
lightning fulmine, m.
like simile (adj.); come (adv.).
like (to) voler bene a; piacere.
Would you like to go? Le piacerebbe andare?
likely probabile.
likeness somiglianza.
likewise altrettanto.
liking piacere, m.; gusto.
limb membro, estremità.
limit limite, m.
limit (to) limitare.
limp fiacco.
limp (to) zoppicare.
line linea.
line up (to) allineare.
linen lino (textile); biancheria.
linger (to) indugiarsi, indugiare.
lining fodera.
link anello (in a chain).
link (to) concatenare, legare.
lion leone.
lip labbro.
liquid liquido (noun & adj.).
liquor liquore, m.
list lista, elenco.
listen (to) ascoltare.
literary letterario.
literature letteratura.
little piccolo.
little by little poco a poco.
little (a) un po' di; poco.
live vivo.
live (to) vivere.

lively vivace.
liver fegato.
load carico.
load (to) caricare.
loan prestito.
loan (to) prestare.
local locale.
locate (to) situare.
location situazione, f.; sito.
lock serratura.
lock (to) chiudere a chiave.
locomotive locomotiva.
log tronco.
logic logica.
logical logico.
loneliness solitudine, f.
lonely solitario.
long lungo.
a long time lungo tempo.
before long quanto prima.
long ago tempo fa; molto tempo fa.
longing desiderio.
look sguardo; aspetto (appearance).
look (to) guardare; sembrare (seem).
Look out! Attenzione!
loose sciolto, slegato.
loosen (to) sciogliere, slegare.
lord signore, m.; padrone, m.; Iddio (God).
lose (to) perdere.
loss perdita.
lost perduto.
lot (a) molto, tanto.
a lot of money molto denaro.
a lot of people molta gente.
loud forte.
Speak louder. Parlate più forte.
love amore, m.
love (to) amare.
lovely amabile, bello.
low basso.
lower (to) abbassare.
loyal leale.
loyalty lealtà.
luck fortuna.
lucky fortunato.
luggage bagaglio.
luminous luminoso.
lump massa.
lunch colazione, f.
lung polmone, m.
luxe lusso.
de luxe di lusso.
luxurious lussuoso.
luxury lusso.

M

macaroni maccheroni, m. pl.
machine macchina.
mad folle, irato.
madam signora.
madness follia.
magazine periodico, rivista.
magistrate magistrato.
magnificent magnifico.
maid cameriera, serva.
mail posta.
mail (to) impostare.
main principale.
main road via principale.
main street strada principale.
maintain (to) mantenere.
maintenance mantenimento.
majesty maestà.

major maggiore, m. (Also adj.)
majority maggioranza.
make (to) fare.
male maschio.
malice malizia.
man uomo.
manage (to) gestire, amministrare.
management gestione, f.; amministrazione, f.
manager amministratore, m.
mankind umanità.
manner maniera, modo.
good manners buone maniere.
manufacture manifattura.
manufacture (to) fabbricare.
manufacturer fabbricante, m.
manuscript manoscritto. (Also adj.)
many molti, molte.
map carta.
March marzo.
march (to) marciare.
margin margine, m.
marine marino.
mark segno.
mark (to) segnare; prendere nota (heed).
market mercato.
marriage matrimonio.
marry (to) sposare.
marvel meraviglia.
marvelous meraviglioso.
masculine maschile, virile.
mask maschera.
mask (to) mascherare.
mason muratore, m.
mass massa (quantity); messa (religious rite).
mast albero.
master padrone, m.
master (to) dominare.
masterpiece capolavoro.
match fiammifero, cerino; incontro (sports); unione, f. (marriage).
match (to) agguagliare.
material materiale, m. (Also adj.)
maternal materno.
mathematics matematica.
matter affare, m.; cosa, materia.
matter (to) importare.
mattress materasso.
mature maturo.
maximum massimo.
May maggio.
may potere (to be able).
mayor sindaco.
me me, mi.
meadow prateria.
meal pasto.
mean cattivo.
mean (to) voler dire; significare.
meaning significato.
means mezzo; mezzi (resources).
meanwhile frattanto.
in the meanwhile nel frattempo.
measure misura.
measure (to) misurare.
meat carne, f.
mechanic meccanico (noun & adj.).
mechanically meccanicamente.
medal medaglia.
meddle (to) intromettersi.
mediate (to) intervenire.
medical medico.
medicine medicina.
mediocre mediocre.
mediocrity mediocrità.

meditate (to)   meditare.
meditation   meditazione, f.
medium   mezzo; intermedio; medio (adj.).
meet (to)   incontrare.
meeting   incontro; riunione, f. (reunion).
melt (to)   squagliare, liquefare, sciogliersi.
member   membro.
memorize (to)   imparare a memoria.
memory   memoria.
mend (to)   rappezzare, rattoppare.
mental   mentale.
mention   menzione, f.
mention (to)   menzionare.
merchandise   merce, f.
merchant   mercante, m.; commerciante, m.
merciful   clemente.
merciless   inclemente.
mercury   mercurio.
mercy   clemenza, misericordia.
merit   merito.
merry   allegro.
message   messaggio, imbasciata.
messenger   messaggero, fattorino.
metal   metallo.
metallic   metallico.
method   metodo.
metropolis   metropoli, f.
microphone   microfono.
middle   in mezzo; intermedio.
  in the middle of the night   durante la notte.
  Middle Ages   Medio Evo.
midnight   mezzanotte, f.
might   forza, potere, m.
mild   mite.
mildness   mitezza.
military   militare.
milk   latte, m.
milkman   lattaio.
mill   mulino.
miller   mugnaio.
million   milione, m.
millionaire   milionario (noun & adj.).
mind   mente, f.
mind (to)   fare attenzione.
  Do you mind?   La disturba?
mine   miniera (coal or steel).
mine   il mio; la mia; i miei; le mie.
miner   minatore, m.
mineral   minerale, m. (Also adj.)
minimum   minimo.
minister   ministro.
ministry   ministero.
mink   visone, m.
minor   minore; più giovane.
minority   minoranza.
minute   minuto.
  Any minute now.   Da un momento all'altro.
  Just a minute!   Un minuto!
  Wait a minute.   Attenda un minuto.
miracle   miracolo.
mirror   specchio.
miscellaneous   vario, miscellaneo.
mischief   cattiveria, malizia.
mischievous   cattivo, malizioso.
miser   avaro.
miserable   miserabile.
miserably   miseramente.
misery   miseria.
misfortune   sfortuna, disgrazia.
mishap   infortunio, accidente, m.
misprint   errore (di stampa), m.
Miss   Signorina.
miss (to)   mancare; sentire la mancanza di.

mission   missione, f.
missionary   missionario.
mist   rugiada.
mistake   errore, m.
mistake (to)   sbagliare, errare.
Mister   Signore.
  Mr. Rossi   Signor Rossi.
mistrust   diffidenza.
mistrust (to)   diffidare.
mistrustful   diffidente.
misunderstand (to)   capire male.
misunderstanding   malinteso.
misuse   abuso.
misuse (to)   abusare.
mix (to)   mischiare.
mixture   miscuglio; mistura (liquids and drugs).
mob   folla.
mobility   mobilità.
mobilization   mobilitazione, f.
mobilize (to)   mobilitare.
mock (to)   deridere.
mockery   derisione, f.
mode   moda.
model   modello (noun & adj.).
model (to)   modellare.
moderate   moderato.
moderate (to)   moderare.
moderation   moderazione, f.
modern   moderno.
modest   modesto.
modesty   modestia.
modification   modifica.
modify (to)   modificare.
moist   umido.
moisten (to)   inumidire.
moment   momento.
  any minute now   da un momento all'altro.
  Just a moment!   Un momento!
monarchy   monarchìa.
monastery   monastero.
Monday   lunedì.
money   denaro.
monk   monaco.
monkey   scimmia.
monologue   monologo.
monopoly   monopolio.
monotonous   monotono.
monotony   monotonìa.
monster   mostro.
monstrosity   mostruosità.
monstrous   mostruoso.
month   mese, m.
  last month   il mese passato.
  next month   il mese prossimo.
monthly   mensile.
monument   monumento.
monumental   monumentale.
mood   umore, m.
moody   di cattivo umore.
moon   luna.
  honeymoon   luna di miele.
moonlight   chiaro di luna.
moral   morale, f. (both fable and morality).
morale   morale, m.
moralist   moralista, m.
morality   moralità.
more   di più.
morning   mattina.
  this morning   stamane.
mortal   mortale, m. (Also adj.)
mortgage   ipoteca.
mortgage (to)   ipotecare.
mosquito   zanzara.

most   il più; la più; i più; le più.
mostly   in gran parte; la maggior parte.
moth   tignola.
mother   madre.
mother-in-law   suocera.
motion   movimento, mozione, f.
motionless   immobile.
motivate (to)   motivare.
motive   motivo.
motor   motore, m.
motor (to)   andare in auto.
motorist   automobilista, m.
mount   monte, m.
mount (to)   montare.
mountain   montagna.
mountainous   montagnoso.
mourn (to)   lamentare.
mournful   triste, lugubre.
mourning   lutto.
mouse   topo.
mouth   bocca.
movable   movibile, mobile.
move   movimento.
move (to)   muovere, muoversi; sloggiare (household).
movement   movimento.
movies   cinema, m.
moving   commovente (touching).
Mr.   Signore.
Mrs.   Signora.
much   molto.
mud   fango.
muddy   fangoso.
mule   mulo.
multiple   molteplice (numerous).
multiply (to)   moltiplicare.
multitude   moltitudine, f.
mumble (to)   borbottare.
municipal   municipale.
municipality   municipalità.
munitions   munizioni, f.
murder   omicidio.
murder (to)   assassinare.
murmur   mormorìo.
murmur (to)   mormorare.
muscle   muscolo.
museum   musèo.
mushroom   fungo.
music   musica.
musical   musicale.
musician   musicista, m.
must (have to)   dovere.
mustard   mostarda.
mute   muto.
mutter   mormorìo, borbottamento.
mutter (to)   mormorare, borbottare.
mutton   montone, m.; carne di castrato, f.
my   il mio; la mia; i miei; le mie.
myself   io stesso; me stesso.
mysterious   misterioso.
mystery   mistero.

N

nail   unghia (finger-); chiodo (carpentry).
nail (to)   inchiodare.
naive   ingenuo.
naked   nudo.
name   nome, m.
  first name   nome.
  last name   cognome.
  What is your name?   Come si chiama?
  My name is...   Mi chiamo...
name (to)   nominare, chiamare.

nameless senza nome; anonimo.
namely specialmente, cioè.
nap sonnellino.
napkin salvietta, tovagliolo.
narrow stretto.
narrow (to) restringere.
nasty offensivo, spiacevole.
nation nazione, f.
national nazionale.
nationality nazionalità.
nationalization nazionalizzazione, f.
nationalize (to) nazionalizzare.
native nativo, indigeno.
natural naturale.
naturalness naturalezza.
nature natura.
  human nature natura umana.
naughty birichino.
naval navale.
navy marina.
Neapolitan napoletano.
near vicino.
nearly quasi.
neat nitido; ben tenuto.
neatness nitidezza.
necessarily necessariamente.
necessary necessario.
necessity necessità.
neck collo.
necklace collana.
necktie cravatta.
need bisogno.
need (to) aver bisogno.
needle ago.
needless inutile.
needy bisognoso.
negative negativa (denial or film).
negative (adj.) negativo.
neglect negligenza.
neglect (to) trascurare.
negotiate (to) trattare.
negotiation trattativa.
Negro negro.
neighbor vicino.
neighborhood rione, m.; vicinato.
neither nessuno.
  neither one nè l'uno, nè l'altro.
  neither...nor... nè...nè...
nephew nipote.
nerve nervo.
  What a nerve! Che sfacciato!
nervous nervoso.
nest nido.
net rete, f.
net (adj.) netto.
neuter neutro.
neutral neutrale, m. (Also adj.)
never mai.
nevertheless ciò nonostante.
new nuovo.
news notizia.
newsdealer giornalaio.
newspaper giornale, m.
next prossimo.
nice piacevole.
nickname nomignolo, soprannome, m.
niece nipote.
night notte, f.; sera.
nightmare incubo.
nine nove.
nineteen diciannove.
nineteenth diciannovesimo.
ninetieth novantesimo.

ninety novanta.
ninth nono.
no nò.
  no longer non più.
  No Smoking! Vietato Fumare!
nobility nobiltà.
noble nobile.
nobody nessuno.
nod cenno, saluto.
noise rumore, m.
noisy rumoroso.
nominate (to) nominare.
nomination nomina.
none nessuno.
  She has none. Non ne ha.
nonsense assurdità, sciocchezza.
noon mezzogiorno.
nor nè...non...
  neither...nor... nè...nè...
normal normale.
north nord.
northern a nord; settentrionale.
northwest nord-ovest.
nose naso.
nostril narice, f.
not non.
note nota, biglietto.
note (to) notare.
noted conosciuto.
nothing niente.
notice avviso.
  Notice to the public. Avviso al pubblico.
notice (to) notare.
notify (to) notificare.
notion nozione, f.
noun nome, m.
nourish (to) nutrire.
nourishment nutrimento.
novel romanzo (literary).
novel (adj.) nuovo.
novelty novità.
November novembre.
now ora.
  now and then di tanto in tanto.
  nowadays di questi tempi.
  nowhere in nessun posto.
nude nudo.
nuisance seccatura.
null nullo, invalido.
numb insensibile, addormentato.
number numero.
number (to) numerare.
nun monaca.
nurse infermiera.
nursery giardino d'infanzia.
nut noce, f.

O

oak quercia.
oar remo.
oat avena.
oath giuramento.
obedience obbedienza.
obedient obbediente.
obey (to) obbedire.
object oggetto; scopo (aim).
object (to) opporsi, obbiettare.
objection obbiezione, f.
  I see no objection to it. Non ho nulla da
    obbiettare.
objective obbiettivo (noun); oggettivo (adj.).
objectively oggettivamente.
objectivity oggettivismo.

obligation obbligo.
obligatory obbligatorio.
oblige (to) obbligare.
obliging gentile, cortese.
oblique obliquo.
obscure oscuro.
obscurity oscurità.
observation osservazione, f.
observatory osservatorio.
observe (to) osservare.
observer osservatore, m.
obstacle ostacolo.
obstinacy ostinazione, f.
obstinate ostinato.
obvious ovvio.
obviously ovviamente.
occasion occasione, f.
occasion (to) cagionare, causare.
occasionally occasionalmente.
occupation impiego.
occupy (to) occupare.
occur (to) avvenire.
occurrence avvenimento.
ocean oceano.
October ottobre.
odd dispari (numbers); disuguale (not matched);
    bizzarro (strange).
odor odore, m.
of di.
  of course certo.
offend (to) offendere, insultare.
offense offesa.
offensive offensiva (military).
offensive (adj.) offensivo.
offer offerta.
offer (to) offrire.
offering offerta.
office ufficio.
officer ufficiale, m.
official funzionario; ufficiale, m. (Also adj.)
often sovente, spesso.
  How often? Quante volte?
oil olio; petrolio (mineral).
old vecchio.
  He is two years old. Ha due anni.
old age vecchiaia.
old man vecchio.
olive oliva.
  olive oil olio d'oliva.
on su, sopra.
once una volta.
  all at once d'un tratto.
  at once immediatamente.
  once a year una volta l'anno.
  once in a while di tanto in tanto.
one (pron.) uno, qualcuno, si.
one (adj.) uno, un, una.
oneself se stesso; si.
onion cipolla.
only soltanto, solamente.
open (adj.) aperto.
  in the open all'aperto.
open (to) aprire.
opening apertura.
opera opera.
operate (to) operare.
operation operazione, f.
opinion opinione, f.
opponent opponente, m.
opportune opportuno.
opportunity opportunità.
oppose (to) opporre.
opposite opposto.

opposition opposizione, f.
oppress (to) opprimere.
oppression oppressione, f.
optimism ottimismo.
optimist ottimista, f.
optimistic ottimista.
or o
  either...or... o...o...
oral verbale, orale.
orange àrancia, arancio.
orator oratore, m.
oratory oratoria.
orchard orto, frutteto.
orchestra orchestra.
ordeal prova.
order ordine, m.
  in order to per.
  to put in order mettere in ordine.
order (to) ordinare.
ordinary ordinario.
organ organo.
organization organizzazione, f.
organize (to) organizzare.
Orient (the) Oriente, m.
oriental orientale.
origin origine, f.
originality originalità.
originate (to) creare.
ornament ornamento.
orphan orfano, orfana.
ostentation ostentazione, f.
other altro, altra, altri, altre.
ought dovere.
ounce oncia.
our(s) il nostro; la nostra; i nostri; le nostre.
ourselves noi stessi, noi stesse.
out fuori.
  out of danger fuori pericolo.
outcome conseguenza, risultato.
outdo (to) sorpassare.
outer esteriore.
outfit corredo (clothes, trousseau); equipaggiamento.
outlast (to) sopravvivere.
outlaw proscritto, bandito.
outlaw (to) proscrivere.
outlay spesa.
outlet sbocco.
outline delineazione, f.; schizzo.
outline (to) delineare; tracciare le grandi linee.
outlook prospettiva.
output rendimento, produzione, f.
outrage oltraggio.
outrageous oltraggioso.
outside fuori.
oval ovale, m. (Also adj.)
oven forno.
overcoat cappotto.
overcome (to) sormontare.
overflow (to) inondare, traboccare.
overhead in alto.
overlook (to) trascurare.
overpower (to) sopraffare.
overrule (to) dominare, respingere.
overrun (to) invadere.
overseas oltre mare.
overshoes soprascarpe, f. pl.
oversight inavvertenza.
overtake (to) raggiungere, sorpassare.
overthrow (to) rovesciare.
overwhelm (to) sopraffare.
owe (to) dovere.
own proprio.
own (to) possedere.

owner proprietario.
ox bue.
oxygen ossigeno.
oyster ostrica.

P

pace passo.
pacific pacifico.
pack (to) imballare, impaccare.
package pacco.
pact patto.
page pagina.
pain dolore, m.
pain (to) far male; addolorare.
painful doloroso.
paint pittura, colore, m.
  Wet paint. Pittura fresca.
paint (to) dipingere.
painter pittore, m.
painting pittura, quadro.
pair paio.
pale pallido.
pamphlet libretto.
pan padella.
pancake frittella.
pane vetro.
panel pannello.
panic panico.
panorama panorama, m.
panties mutandine, f. pl.
pants pantaloni, m. pl.
paper carta.
parachute paracadute, m.
parade parata.
paragraph paragrafo.
parallel parallelo.
paralysis paralisi, f.
paralyze (to) paralizzare.
parcel pacco.
pardon perdono.
pardon (to) perdonare.
parent genitore, m.; genitrice, f.; parente, m.
parenthesis parentesi, f.
park parco; giardino pubblico.
park (to) parcare.
  No parking! Divieto di sosta!
parkway autostrada.
parliament parlamento.
part parte, f.
part (to) separarsi.
partial parziale.
partially parzialmente; in parte.
particular particolare, m. (Also adj.)
particularity particolarità.
particularly particolarmente.
partner socio, socia, (business); compagno di giuoco (in games).
party partito (political); ricevimento (social); partita (sports).
pass permesso (permission).
pass (to) passare.
passage passaggio.
passenger passeggero.
passion passione, f.
passive passivo.
past passato. (Also noun.)
  half-past seven le sette e mezzo.
  past ten o'clock le dieci passate.
  the past year l'anno passato.
past (prep.) oltre (beyond).
paste colla (glue); conserva (preserve).
paste (to) incollare.

pastry paste, f. pl.; dolci, m. pl. (sweets).
pastry shop pasticceria.
patch pezza; rappezzo; benda (bandage).
patch (to) rattoppare.
patent brevetto, patente, f.
paternal paterno.
path sentiero.
pathetic patetico.
patience pazienza.
patient paziente, m. or f. (Also adj.)
patriot patriota, m.
patriotism patriottismo.
patron patrono.
patronize (to) patrocinare.
pattern modello; campione, m.; disegno.
pause pausa.
pause (to) fare una pausa; arrestarsi.
pave (to) pavimentare.
pavement selciato.
paw zampa.
pay stipendio.
pay (to) pagare.
  to pay in cash pagare in contanti.
payment pagamento, ricompensa.
pea pisello.
peace pace, f.
peaceful pacifico, tranquillo.
peach pesca.
peak cima.
pear pera.
pearl perla.
peasant contadino, contadina.
pebble sassolino, sasso.
peculiar peculiare, strano.
pecuniary pecuniario.
pedal pedale, m.
pedantic pedante.
pedestrian pedone, m.
peel buccia, corteccia.
peel (to) spellare, sbucciare.
pen penna.
  fountain pen penna stilografica.
penalty pena, multa.
pencil lapis, m.; matita.
penetrate (to) penetrare.
peninsula penisola.
penitence penitenza.
pension pensione, m.
people gente, f.; popolo.
pepper pepe, m.
peppermint menta.
perceive (to) scorgere, capire.
per cent percento.
percentage percentuale, f.
perfect perfetto.
perfect (to) perfezionare.
perfection perfezione, f.
perfectly perfettamente.
perform (to) compiere; eseguire; rappresentare (in a play).
performance compimento; esecuzione; rappresentazione (of a play).
perfume profumo.
perfume (to) profumare.
perhaps forse.
peril pericolo.
period punto fermo (punctuation); epoca (era).
periodical periodico (also adj.).
perish (to) perire.
permanent permanente, f. (Also adj.)
permission permesso.
permit permesso, licenza.
permit (to) permettere, concedere.

peroxide acqua ossigenata; perossido.

perplex (to) confondere; rendere perplesso.

persecute (to) perseguitare.

persecution persecuzione, f.

perseverance perseveranza.

persist (to) persistere, perseverare.

person persona.

personal personale.

personality personalità.

personnel personale, m.

perspective prospettiva.

persuade (to) persuadere.

pertaining appartenente, riferendosi a.

petty meschino.

pharmacist farmacista.

pharmacy farmacìa.

phenomenon fenomeno.

philosopher filosofo.

philosophical filosofico.

philosophy filosofìa.

photograph fotografìa.

  to take a photograph fare una fotografìa.

photostatic copy copia fotostatica.

phrase frase, f.

physical fisico.

physician medico.

piano pianoforte, m.

pick (to) scegliere (choose); rompere col piccone (to break up with a pick); mangiucchiare (nibble on food); sottrarre da (a pocket).

pick up (to) raccogliere.

picnic merenda all'aperto; campagnata.

picture ritratto, disegno, dipinto, quadro.

  to take a picture fare una fotografìa.

picturesque pittoresco.

pie torta di frutta;

piece pezzo.

pig maiale, m.

pigeon piccione, m.

pile ammasso, mucchio.

pile (to) ammassare.

pill pillola.

pillar colonna.

pillow guanciale, m.

pilot pilota, m.

pin spilla.

pinch (to) pizzicare.

pink (adj.) rosa.

pious pio.

pipe pipa (for smoking); tubo (plumbing); zampogna (musical).

pitiful pietoso.

pity pietà.

  What a pity! Che peccato!

place luogo, località, posto.

  in my place al mio posto.

  to lose one's place perdere il segno.

  to take place aver luogo.

place (to) mettere.

plain (adj.) chiaro (clear); semplice (simple).

plan progetto, piano.

plan (to) progettare.

plane aeroplano, areo (airplane); pialla (carpenter's tool).

plant pianta.

plant (to) piantare.

plaster empiastro (medical); intonaco; gesso (walls).

plate piatto.

platform piattaforma.

platter largo piatto.

play gioco; lavoro teatrale (theatrical).

play (to) giocare; recitare (to act); sonare (musical instruments).

player giocatore, m.

plea causa, processo, supplica.

plead (to) perorare (court case); dichiararsi (plead guilty or innocent).

plead with (to) supplicare.

pleasant piacevole.

please (to) piacere, accontentare.

  if you please per piacere.

pleased contento, soddisfatto.

pleasure piacere, m.

pledge pegno, garanzìa.

pledge (to) garantire.

plenty abbondanza.

plenty (adj.) abbondante.

plot complotto (conspiracy); pezzo di terra (of ground); intreccio (of a play).

plough aratro.

plough (to) arare.

plum prugna.

plunder (to) saccheggiare.

plural plurale, m. (Also adj.)

plus più.

pneumonia polmonite, f.

pocket tasca.

poem poesìa, poema, m.

poet poeta, m.

poetic poetico.

poetry poesìa.

point punto.

point (to) indicare.

pointed appuntito (sharp); acuto (incisive).

poise equilibrio.

poison veleno.

poison (to) avvelenare.

poisoning avvelenamento.

polar polare.

police polizìa.

policeman vigile urbano; poliziotto.

policy politica; linea di condotta.

polish lucido, vernice, f.

polish (to) lucidare, lustrare.

polite cortese.

politeness cortesìa.

political politico.

politics politica.

pond stagno, laghetto.

poor povero.

popular popolare.

population popolazione, f.

pork carne di maiale, f.

port porto.

porter facchino.

portrait ritratto.

position posizione, f.; situazione, f.

positive positivo.

possess (to) possedere.

possession possesso.

possibility possibilità.

possible possibile.

post palo (pole or support); posta (mail).

postage affrancatura.

  postage stamp francobollo.

poster manifesto, affisso, cartellone, m.

posterity posterità.

post office posta; ufficio postale.

pot pentola, vaso, recipiente, m.

potato patata.

pound libbra.

pour (to) versare.

  It's pouring! Piove a dirotto!

poverty povertà.

powder polvere, f.

  face-powder cipria.

power potere, m.; forza.

powerful potente.

practical pratico.

practice pratica, abitudine, f.; esercizio.

practice (to) esercitarsi, esercitare, praticare.

praise elogio, lode, f.

praise (to) elogiare.

prank scherzo.

pray (to) pregare.

prayer preghiera.

preach (to) predicare.

precaution precauzione, f.

precede (to) precedere.

preceding precedente.

precept precetto.

precious prezioso.

precise preciso.

precision precisione, f.

predecessor predecessore, m.

preface prefazione, f.

prefer (to) preferire.

preference preferenza.

prejudice pregiudizio.

preliminary preliminare.

prepare (to) preparare.

prescribe (to) prescrivere.

presence presenza.

present dono (gift); presente (present time).

present (adj.) presente, attuale.

present (to) presentare.

preserve (to) preservare, conservare.

preside (to) presiedere.

president presidente, m.

press stampa.

press (to) stirare (iron clothes); premere; comprimere.

pressing urgente.

pressure pressione, f.

prestige prestigio.

presume (to) presumere.

pretend (to) pretendere, fingere.

pretext pretesto.

pretty (adj.) bello, grazioso.

pretty (adv.) quanto.

  pretty nearly quasi.

  pretty soon quanto prima.

prevail (to) prevalere.

prevent (to) impedire.

prevention prevenzione, f.; impedimento.

previous precedente.

  the previous year l'anno precedente.

prey preda.

price prezzo, costo.

pride orgoglio.

priest prete.

prime primo, principale.

prince principe.

princess principessa.

principal principale.

principle principio.

print (to) stampare.

prison prigione, f.

prisoner prigioniero, prigioniera.

private privato.

privilege privilegio.

prize premio.

prize (to) stimare molto.

probable probabile.

probably probabilmente.

problem problema, m.

procedure procedura.

proceed (to) procedere.
process processo.
procession processione, f.
proclaim (to) proclamare.
produce (to) produrre.
product prodotto.
production produzione, f.
productive produttivo.
profession professione, f.
professional professionale.
professor professore, m.
profile profilo.
profit profitto, utile, m.
profit (to) trarre profitto.
profits profitti, utili.
program programma, m.
progress progresso.
progress (to) progredire.
prohibit (to) vietare.
prohibition divieto, proibizione, f.
project progetto.
project (to) progettare.
promise promessa.
promise (to) promettere.
promotion promozione, f.
prompt pronto.
promptness prontezza.
pronoun pronome, m.
pronounce (to) pronunciare, pronunziare.
proof prova.
proper proprio, corretto.
property proprietà (country home); beni, m. pl. (estate, in legal sense).
proportion proporzione, f.
proposal proposta.
propose (to) proporre.
prosaic prosaico.
prose prosa.
prospect prospetto, (business); prospettiva, (panorama).
prosper (to) prosperare.
prosperity prosperità.
prosperous prospero.
protect (to) proteggere.
protection protezione, f.
protector protettore, m.
protest protesta.
protest (to) protestare.
Protestant protestante, m. (Also adj.)
proud orgoglioso, fiero.
prove (to) provare.
proverb proverbio.
provide (to) provvedere.
provided that purchè.
province provincia.
provoke (to) provocare.
proximity prossimità.
prudence prudenza.
prune prugna secca.
psychological psicologico.
psychology psicologìa.
public pubblico (also adj.).
publication pubblicazione, f.
publish (to) pubblicare.
publisher editore, m.
pull (to) tirare.
pulpit pulpito.
pulse polso.
pump pompa.
punish (to) punire.
punishment punizione, f.
pupil allievo, allieva; pupilla (eye).
purchase acquisto.

purchase (to) acquistare.
pure puro.
purity purezza.
purpose scopo.
purse borsa.
pursue (to) inseguire.
pursuit' inseguimento.
push (to) spingere.
put (to) mettere.
  (to) put away mettere via.
  (to) put off rimandare; rinviare.
  (to) put on indossare (clothes).
  (to) put out spegnere (light).
puzzle perplessità, indovinello, cruciverba, m.
puzzle (to) render perplesso; indovinare.

Q

quaint strano, disusato.
qualify (to) essere adatto.
quality qualità.
quantity quantità.
quarrel litigio.
quarrel (to) litigare.
quarter quarto; quartiere (district).
queen regina.
queer strano, bizzarro.
quench (to) dissetare (thirst); estinguere (flame).
question questione, f.; domanda.
question (to) domandare, interrogare.
quick rapido.
quickly rapidamente.
Come quickly! Venga subito!
quiet (adj.) quieto, tranquillo.
Keep quiet. Stai zitto.
quiet (to) calmare, tranquillizzare.
quit (to) abbandonare, lasciare.
quite completamente; del tutto; proprio.
quite good proprio buono.
quote (to) citare.

R

rabbit coniglio; lepre, m. & f.
race corsa (horse race, etc.); razza (of people).
radio radio, f.
rag cencio, straccio.
ragged cencioso.
rail rotaia (train); sbarra (wood or iron); cancellata (fence).
railroad ferrovia.
railroad station stazione ferroviaria.
rain pioggia.
rain (to) piovere.
rainbow arcobaleno.
rainy piovoso.
raise aumento (in pay).
raise (to) sollevare (lift); innalzare, produrre (produce).
raisin uva secca.
rake rastrello.
rally (to) riunire insieme.
range estensione, f.; catena (mountains).
range (to) percorrere, disporre.
rank grado, fila.
ransom riscatto.
rapid rapido.
rapidity rapidità.
rapidly rapidamente.
rapture estasi, f.
rare raro.
rat topo.
rate velocità (of speed); tariffa (fare).

first rate di prim' ordine.
rate (to) valutare.
rather piuttosto.
  rather good piuttosto buono.
  rather than piuttosto che.
  I'd rather go. Preferirei andare.
ration razione, f.
rational razionale, ragionevole.
rave (to) delirare.
raw crudo.
ray raggio.
razor rasoio.
razor blade lametta.
reach portata, estensione, f.
reach (to) stendere; arrivare; raggiungere; allungare (with the arm).
react (to) reagire.
reaction reazione, f.
read (to) leggere.
reading lettura.
ready pronto.
  to get ready prepararsi.
real reale, vero.
realization realizzazione, f.; comprensione, f.
realize (to) rendersi conto di.
really in verità; veramente.
rear di dietro.
rear (to) crescere (children).
reason ragione, f.
reasonable ragionevole.
reasoning ragionamento.
reassure (to) rassicurare.
rebel ribelle, m. (Also adj.)
rebel (to) ribellarsi.
rebellion ribellione, f.
recall richiamo.
recall (to) richiamare, ricordare.
receipt ricevuta.
receive (to) ricevere.
receiver ricevitore, m. (telephone).
recent recente.
reception accoglienza; ricevimento (social).
recess recesso; sospensione del lavoro (rest period).
reciprocal reciproco.
recite (to) recitare.
recognize (to) riconoscere.
recollect (to) richiamare alla mente; ricordare.
recollection ricordo.
recommend (to) raccomandare.
recommendation raccomandazione, f.
reconcile (to) riconciliare.
reconstitute (to) ricostituire.
record disco (phonograph); registro (file); primato (sports).
recover (to) ritrovare (find); guarire (from illness).
recovery guarigione, f.
recruit recluta.
rectangle rettangolo.
red rosso.
Red Cross Croce Rossa.
redeem (to) redimere, riscattare.
redouble (to) raddoppiare.
reduce (to) ridurre.
reduction riduzione, f.
reed canna.
refer (to) riferire, alludere.
reference riferimento, referenza, allusione, f.
referring to con riferimento.
refine (to) raffinare.
refinement raffinatezza.
reflect (to) riflettere.
reflection riflesso.

reform   riforma, miglioramento.

reform (to)   formare di nuovo; riformare.

refrain   ritornello.

refrain (to)   trattenersi.

refresh (to)   rinfrescare.

refreshment   rinfresco.

refrigerator   frigorifero.

refuge   rifugio.

to take refuge   rifugiarsi.

refund (to)   rimborsare.

refusal   rifiuto.

refuse (to)   rifiutare.

refute (to)   confutare.

regard   riguardo, stima.

in regard to   a proposito di.

regime   regime, m.

regiment   reggimento..

region   regione, f.

register   registro.

register (to)   registrare, iscriversi.

regret   rimpianto, rammarico.

regret (to)   rimpiangere, rammaricarsi di.

regular   regolare.

regulate (to)   regolare.

regulation   regola.

rehearsal   prova.

rehearse (to)   provare.

reign   regno.

reign (to)   regnare.

reinforce (to)   rinforzare.

reject (to)   respingere, rifiutare.

rejoice (to)   gioire, rallegrarsi.

relapse   ricaduta.

relate (to)   raccontare.

relation   relazione, f.; rapporto.

in relation to   in riferimento a.

relationship   rapporto, parentela.

relative (noun)   parente, m. & f.

relative (adj.)   relativo, affine.

relax (to)   rilassarsi; rallentare; riposare (rest); calmarsi (calm).

relaxation   diminuzione, f.; rallentamento; ricreazione, f.

release   liberazione, f.; scarico.

relent (to)   cedere; divenire meno severo.

relentless   inflessibile.

relevant   pertinente.

reliable   degno di fiducia; fidato.

reliance   fiducia.

relic   reliquia.

relief   sollievo, soccorso.

relieve (to)   sollevare.

religion   religione, f.

religious   religioso.

relinquish (to)   abbandonare, cedere.

relish   gusto, sapore, m.

relish (to)   trovar piacevole.

reluctance   riluttanza.

reluctant   riluttante.

rely upon (to)   fare assegnamento su (di).

remain (to)   rimanere.

remainder   resto, residuo.

remark   osservazione, f.

remark (to)   osservare, notare.

remarkable   notevole, straordinario.

remedy   rimedio.

remember (to)   ricordare.

remembrance   ricordo.

remind (to)   richiamare alla mente.

remorse   rimorso.

remote   remoto.

removal   rimozione, f.

remove (to)   rimuovere.

renew (to)   rinnovare.

rent   affitto.

rent (to)   dare in affitto; prendere in affitto.

repair   riparazione, f.

repair (to)   riparare.

repeat (to)   ripetere.

repent (to)   pentirsi.

repetition   ripetizione, f.

reply   risposta.

reply (to)   rispondere.

report   notizia, resoconto, rapporto.

represent (to)   rappresentare.

representation   rappresentazione, f.

representative   rappresentante, deputato.

repress (to)   reprimere.

reprimand   rimprovero.

reprimand (to)   rimproverare.

reprisal   rappresaglia.

reproach   rimprovero.

reproach (to)   rimproverare.

reproduce (to)   riprodurre.

republic   repubblica.

reputation   riputazione, f.

request   domanda, richiesta.

request (to)   richiedere.

require (to)   esigere; aver bisogno di; chiedere.

rescue   salvezza, soccorso.

rescue (to)   salvare, soccorrere.

research   ricerca.

resemble (to)   rassomigliare.

resent (to)   offendersi di.

resentment   risentimento.

reservation   riserva; prenotazione (for tickets, etc.).

reserve   riserva.

reserve (to)   riservare; prenotare (tickets, tables, etc.).

resign (to)   dimettersi; dare le dimissioni.

resignation   dimissione, f. (from a position); rassegnazione, f. (acquiescence).

resist (to)   resistere.

resistance   resistenza.

resolute   risoluto.

resolution   soluzione, f. (solution or explanation); risoluzione, f. (determination).

resolve (to)   risolvere.

resort   stazione climatica.

resort (to)   ricorrere.

resource   risorsa.

respect   rispetto.

respect (to)   rispettare.

respectful   rispettoso.

respective   rispettivo.

respite   tregua.

responsibility   responsabilità.

responsible   responsabile.

rest   riposo.

rest (to)   riposare.

restaurant   ristorante, m.

restless   inquieto, irrequieto.

restoration   restaurazione, f.

restore (to)   restaurare.

restrain (to)   reprimere, trattenere.

restraint   restrizione, f.; controllo.

restrict (to)   restringere, limitare.

restriction   restrizione, f.

result   risultato, esito.

result (to)   risultare, risolversi.

resume (to)   riprendere.

retail   vendita al minuto.

retail (to)   vendere al minuto.

retain (to)   trattenere, ritenere.

retaliate (to)   vendicarsi di; ritorcere.

retaliation   rappresaglia.

retire (to)   ritirarsi.

retirement   ritiro, isolamento.

retract (to)   ritrarre.

retreat   ritirata.

return   ritorno.

return (to)   ritornare; restituire (give back).

reveal (to)   rivelare.

revelation   rivelazione, f.

revenge   vendetta.

revenue   entrata, reddito.

reverence   riverenza.

reverend   reverendo.

reverse   inverso, contrario. (Noun & adj.)

reverse (to)   rovesciare, invertire, rivoltare.

revert (to)   tornare indietro; spettare (go to, as in a will).

review   rivista (periodical).

review (to)   recensire (a book, play, etc.).

to pass in review (as troops)   passare in rivista.

revise (to)   rivedere, emendare.

revision   revisione, f.

revive (to)   fare rivivere; rianimare; risvegliare (memories).

revoke (to)   revocare.

revolt (to)   ribellarsi (rebel); disgustare (disgust or offend).

revolution   rivoluzione, f.

revolve (to)   roteare (rotate); meditare (think, consider).

reward   ricompensa.

reward (to)   ricompensare.

rhyme   rima.

rib   costola.

ribbon   nastro.

rice   riso.

rich   ricco.

richness   ricchezza.

rid (to get)   sbarazzarsi.

to get rid of something   sbarazzarsi di qualche cosa.

riddle   enigma, indovinello.

ride   corsa (in a car); galoppata (on horseback); passeggiata.

ride (to)   andare.

to ride a horse   andare a cavallo.

to ride a bicycle   andare in bicicletta.

to ride in a car   andare in auto.

to go for a boatride   andare in barca.

to go for a plane ride   andare in aeroplano.

ridiculous   ridicolo.

rifle   fucile, m.

right   destra, bene, m.

to have a right to   aver il diritto di.

to be right   aver ragione.

to the right   a destra.

Right!   Bene!

right (adj.)   corretto, diritto, esatto, giusto.

righteous   giusto, retto.

righteousness   giustizia, rettitudine, f.

rightful   giusto, legittimo.

rigid   rigido.

rigor   rigore, m.

rigorous   rigoroso.

ring   anello (finger); cerchio (circle); recinto (enclosure); suono (of a bell).

ring (to)   sonare.

rinse (to)   sciacquare.

riot   tumulto, rivolta.

ripe   maturo.

ripen (to)   maturare.

rise   ascesa, salita.

rise (to)   alzarsi, levarsi, sollevarsi

risk   rischio.

risk (to)   rischiare; mettere in pericolo.

rite   rito.

ritual   rituale, m. (Also adj.)

rival   rivale, m. & f. (Also adj.)

rivalry   rivalità.

river   fiume, m.

road   strada, via.

roar   ruggito (of an animal); rombo (of cannon, motor).

roar (to)   ruggire.

roast   arrosto.

roast (to)   arrostire.

rob (to)   derubare.

robber   ladro.

robbery   furto.

robe   mantello.

robust   robusto.

rock   roccia, scoglio.

rock (to)   dondolare, cullare.

rocky   roccioso.

rod   bacchetta, asta.

roll   rotolo; rullìo (drums); panino (bread).

roll (to)   rotolare.

Roman   romano, romana. (Noun & adj.)

romantic   romantico.

romanticism   romanticismo.

roof   tetto.

room   camera (of a house); spazio (space or area).

make room for   fare largo.

There's no room.   Non c'è spazio.

root   radice, f.

rope   corda.

rose   rosa.

rot (to)   marcire; languire (in prison).

rough   ruvido, rozzo.

round (adj.)   rotondo.

round (adv.)   attorno; in giro.

round   ripresa (in boxing); giro (inspection); ronda (patrol).

round off (to)   arrotondire.

route   via, percorso.

row   fila.

row (to)   remare.

royal   reale.

rub (to)   strofinare.

rubber   gomma (also tire); cauccíù (also overshoes).

rubbish   scarti, m.pl; rifiuti, m.pl.

rude   rude; grossolano; scortese (impolite).

ruffle   increspatura.

ruffle (to)   increspare.

ruin   rovina.

ruin (to)   rovinare.

rule   regola, dominio.

rule (to)   regolare, governare.

ruler   governante (boss); sovrano (of a country); riga (for drawing lines).

rumor   diceria; voce generale, f.

run (to)   correre.

to run away   fuggire.

rural   rurale.

rush   assalto, impeto.

rush (to)   precipitarsi.

Russian   russo, russa. (Noun & adj.)

rust   ruggine, f.

rustic   rustico.

rusty   arrugginito.

rye   segala.

S

sacred   sacro.

sacrifice   sacrificio.

sacrifice (to)   sacrificare.

sacrilege   sacrilegio.

sad   triste.

sadden (to)   rattristare.

saddle   sella.

sadness   tristezza.

safe   salvo, sicuro.

safe (to be)   essere al sicuro.

safely   sicuramente.

safety   sicurezza.

sail   vela.

sail (to)   salpare, navigare.

sailor   marinaio.

saint   santo, m.; santa, f. (Also adj.)

sake   amore, motivo, scopo.

for my sake   per amor mio.

for the sake of   per amor di.

salad   insalata.

salary   stipendio.

sale   vendita.

salt   sale, m.

salt (to)   salare.

salute   saluto.

salute (to)   salutare.

salvation   salvezza.

same   medesimo, stesso.

all the same   lo stesso.

sample   campione, m.

sanctuary   santuario.

sand   sabbia.

sandal   sandalo.

sandwich   panino ripieno.

sandy   sabbioso.

sane   sano.

sanitary   sanitario.

sap   linfa.

sarcasm   sarcasmo.

sarcastic   sarcastico.

sardine   sardina.

satiate (to)   saziare.

satin   raso.

satisfaction   soddisfazione, f.

satisfactory   soddisfacente.

satisfy (to)   soddisfare.

saturate (to)   saturare.

Saturday   sabato.

sauce   salsa.

saucer   piattino.

sausage   salsiccia.

savage   selvaggio (noun & adj.).

save (prep.)   tranne, eccetto.

save (to)   salvare (person); fare delle economìe (money).

to save time   guadagnar tempo.

savings   risparmi, m. pl.

savior   salvatore, m.

say (to)   dire.

scales   bilancia.

scalp   cuoio capelluto.

scan (to)   scandire, scrutare.

scandal   scandalo.

scanty   scarso, ristretto.

scar   cicatrice, f.

scarce   scarso, raro.

scarcely   appena, scarsamente.

scare (to)   spaventare.

scarf   sciarpa.

scatter (to)   spargere.

scene   scena.

scenery   paesaggio (landscape); scenario (theater).

sceptic(al)   scettico (noun & adj.)

schedule   tabella, lista, inventario.

scheme   disegno, piano.

scholar   dotto, erudito.

school   scuola.

science   scienza.

scientific   scientifico.

scientist   scienziato.

scissors   forbici, f. pl.

scold (to)   rimproverare.

scope   scopo, campo, prospettiva.

scorn   sdegno.

scorn (to)   sdegnare.

scornful   sdegnoso.

scrape   grattare.

scratch (to)   graffiare.

scream   urlo, grido.

scream (to)   gridare, urlare.

screen   paravento; schermo (movie).

screw   vite, f.

screwdriver   cacciavite, m.

scribble (to)   scribacchiare.

scruple   scrupolo.

scrupulous   scrupoloso.

scrutinize (to)   scrutare.

sculpture   scultura.

sea   mare, m.

seal   sigillo.

seal (to)   sigillare.

seam   cucitura.

search   ricerca.

search (to)   ricercare.

seashore   spiaggia.

seasickness   mal di mare, m.

season   stagione, f.

season (to)   condire.

seat   sedile, m.; posto.

seat (to)   sedere.

second   secondo (unit of time).

second (adj.)   secondo (numeral).

secondary   secondario.

secret   segreto (noun & adj.).

secretary   segretario, segretaria.

sect   setta.

section   sezione, f.

secure (adj.)   sicuro.

secure (to)   procurarsi, ottenere, (get or obtain); assicurare (make secure).

security   sicurezza.

see (to)   vedere.

seed   seme, m.

seek (to)   cercare; sforzarsi di.

seem (to)   sembrare.

seize (to)   afferrare, catturare.

seldom   raramente.

select (to)   scegliere, selezionare.

selection   scelta, assortimento.

self   stesso, stessa.

self-confidence   fiducia in se stesso.

selfish   egoista, egoistico.

selfishness   egoismo.

sell (to)   vendere.

semi-   mezzo, metà.

semicolon   punto e virgola.

senate   senato.

senator   senatore, m.

send (to)   inviare.

senior   maggiore, m. or f.; anziano. (Also adj.)

sensation   sensazione, f.

sense   senso.

senseless   insensibile.

sensibility   sensibilità.

sensible   sensibile, ragionevole.

sensitive   sensibile, sensitivo.

sensitiveness   sensibilità.

sentence proposizione, f.; sentenza.
sentiment sentimento.
sentimental sentimentale. *(Also used as noun.)*
separate separato.
separate (to) separare.
separately separatamente.
separation separazione, f.
September settembre.
sergeant sergente, m.
series serie, f.
serious serio.
seriously seriamente.
sermon sermone, m.; predica.
servant servo, m.; serva, f.
serve (to) servire.
service servizio.
session sessione, f.
set serie, f.; assortimento.
set *(adj.)* fisso, stabilito.
set (to) mettere a posto.
settle (to) fissare, stabilire.
settlement sistemazione, f.; accomodamento; colonizzazione, f. *(colonization).*
seven sette.
seventeen diciassette.
seventeenth diciassettesimo.
seventh settimo.
seventieth settantesimo.
seventy settanta.
several diversi, parecchi.
 several times diverse volte.
severe severo.
severity severità.
sew (to) cucire.
sewer fogna.
sex sesso.
shabby meschino, logoro.
shade ombra.
shade (to) ombreggiare.
shadow ombra.
shady ombreggiato.
shake (to) scuotere; agitare; tremare *(tremble).*
shallow poco profondo.
shame vergogna.
shame (to) gettar vergogna su.
shameful vergognoso.
shameless impudente.
shape forma.
shape (to) formare.
shapeless informe; senza forma.
share parte, f.; porzione, f.; azione, f. *(of stock).*
share (to) dividere.
shareholder azionista, m.
sharp diesis, m. *(in music).*
sharp *(adj.)* tagliente.
sharpen (to) affilare.
shave (to) radersi.
she essa, ella, lei.
shed capannone, m.
shed (to) versare; spandere; perdere *(leaves).*
sheep pecora.
sheer puro; sottile *(thin).*
sheet lenzuolo.
shelf scaffale, m.
shell guscio.
shelter ricovero.
shelter (to) ricoverare.
shepherd pastore, m.
shield scudo.
shield (to) proteggere.
shift cambiamento.
shift (to) cambiare, trasferire, spostarsi.
shine splendore, m. *(of the sun);* lucidatura.

shine (to) brillare.
ship nave, f.
ship (to) spedire.
shipment imbarco, spedizione, f.
shirt camicia.
shiver brivido.
shiver (to) rabbrividire, tremare.
shock scossa.
shock (to) urtare, sbalordire.
shoe scarpa.
shoemaker calzolaio.
shoot (to) sparare.
shooting sparata, sparatoria.
shop bottega.
shop (to) fare delle spese; fare delle compre.
shore riva.
short corto, breve.
shortly fra poco.
shorten (to) abbreviare.
shorthand stenografia.
shorts mutande, f. pl.
shot colpo.
shoulder spalla.
shout grido.
shout (to) gridare.
shove (to) spingere.
shovel pala, paletta.
show spettacolo.
show (to) mostrare.
shower doccia.
shrill stridente.
shrimp gambero.
shrink (to) ritirarsi.
shrub arbusto.
shun (to) evitare.
shut *(adj.)* chiuso.
shut (to) chiudere.
shy timido.
sick infermo, malato.
sickness infermità, malattia.
Sicilian siciliano, siciliana. *(Noun & adj.)*
side lato, parte.
 side dish contorno.
sidewalk marciapiede, m.
siege assedio.
sigh sospiro.
sigh (to) sospirare.
sight vista.
sign segno, simbolo, targa.
sign (to) firmare.
signal segnale, m.
signature firma.
significance significato.
signify (to) significare.
silence silenzio.
silence (to) far tacere.
silent silenzioso.
silk seta.
silken di seta; delicato *(soft).*
silly sciocco.
silver argento.
silvery argentato.
similar simile.
similarity somiglianza.
simple semplice.
simplicity semplicità.
simply semplicemente.
simulate (to) simulare.
simultaneous simultaneo.
sin peccato.
sin (to) peccare.
since da quando.
sincere sincero.

sincerely sinceramente.
 Yours sincerely Vostro sincero amico.
sincerity sincerità.
sing (to) cantare.
singer cantante, m. & f.
single solo; celibe *(unmarried man);* nubile *(unmarried woman).*
singular singolare.
sinister sinistro.
sink lavandino *(kitchen).*
sink (to) affondare.
sinner peccatore, m.; peccatrice, f.
sip (to) centellinare.
sir signore.
 Thank you, sir! Grazie, signore!
sister sorella.
sister-in-law cognata.
sit (to) sedere.
site sito, luogo.
situation situazione, f.
six sei.
sixteen sedici.
sixteenth sedicesimo.
sixth sesto.
sixtieth sessantesimo.
sixty sessanta.
size misura.
skate (to) pattinare.
skates pattini, m. pl.
skeleton scheletro.
sketch schizzo, abbozzo.
ski (to) sciare.
skill destrezza.
skillful destro, abile.
skin pelle, f.
skirt sottana, gonna.
skull teschio.
sky cielo.
slander calunnia.
slap schiaffo.
slate lavagna.
slaughter macello.
slave schiavo, schiava.
slavery schiavitù.
sleep sonno.
sleep (to) dormire.
sleeve manica.
slender snello.
sleigh slitta.
slice fetta.
slide (to) scivolare.
slight lieve, esile.
slight (to) disprezzare.
slip (to) scivolare.
slipper pantofola.
slippery sdrucciolevole.
slope pendìo.
slot fessura.
slovenly disordinato.
slow lento.
slowness lentezza.
slumber sonno.
slumber (to) sonnecchiare, dormire.
sly furbo.
small piccolo.
smart elegante; abile *(skillful);* piccante.
smash (to) fare a pezzi.
smear macchia.
smear (to) lordare, macchiare.
smell odore, m.
smell (to) odorare, fiutare.
smile sorriso.

smile (to) sorridere.

smoke fumo.

smoke (to) fumare.

smoker fumatore, m.

smooth liscio.

smother (to) soffocare.

smuggle (to) far entrare di contrabbando.

snake serpente, m.; rettile, m.

snapshot istantanea.

snatch frammento (fragment).

sneer (to) sogghignare.

sneeze (to) starnutire.

snore (to) russare.

snow neve, f.

snow (to) nevicare.

so (thus) così.

 and so on e via di seguito.

soak (to) mettere a bagno.

soap sapone, m.

sob singhiozzo.

sober sobrio.

sociable socievole.

social sociale.

society società.

sock calzino.

socket orbita.

soft morbido.

soften (to) ammorbidire.

soil (to) sporcare.

soldier soldato.

sole unico, solo.

solemn solenne.

solemnity solennità.

solicit (to) sollecitare.

solid solido.

solitary solitario.

solitude solitudine, f.

solution soluzione, f.

solve (to) risolvere.

some del; qualche; alcuni, m. pl.; alcune, f. pl.

somebody qualcuno.

somehow in un modo o in un'altro.

someone qualcuno, m.; qualcuna, f.

something qualche cosa.

sometime un tempo; qualche volta.

sometimes talvolta; delle volte.

somewhat alquanto.

somewhere in qualche luogo.

son figlio.

song canzone, f.

son-in-law genero.

soon presto.

soot fuliggine, f.

soothe (to) calmare.

sore piaga.

sorrow dolore, m.

sorry dispiacente.

 to be sorry about essere dispiacente di.

 I am sorry. Mi dispiace.

sort sorta; genere, m.

sort (to) assortire.

soul anima.

sound suono.

sound (to) suonare.

soup minestra, brodo.

sour acido (milk, etc.); acerbo (fruit); amaro (bitter).

source fonte, f.

south sud, m.; meridione, m.

southern meridionale (also noun, m.); al sud.

southwest sudovest, m.

sovereign sovrano, sovrana. (Also adj.)

sow (to) seminare.

space spazio.

space (to) spaziare.

spacious spazioso.

spade vanga; badile, m.; picche, f. (playing cards).

spaghetti spaghetti.

Spanish spagnuolo. (Noun & adj.)

spare disponibile; di ricambio (said of a tire).

spare (to) risparmiare, disporre.

spark scintilla.

sparkle (to) scintillare.

sparrow passero.

speak (to) parlare.

speaker oratore, m.; parlatore, m.

special speciale, particolare.

specialty specialità.

specific specifico.

specify (to) specificare.

spectacle spettacolo.

spectator spettatore, m.

speculate (to) speculare.

speech discorso.

speed velocità.

speedy rapido, veloce.

spell incanto.

spell (to) compitare, scrivere.

 How do you spell this word? Come si scrive questa parola?

spelling ortografia.

spend (to) spendere.

sphere sfera.

spice spezie, f. pl.

spider ragno.

spill (to) versare; far cadere.

spin (to) filare.

spirit spirito.

spiritual spirituale.

spit (to) sputare.

spite dispetto.

spite (to) contrariare.

spiteful dispettoso.

splash (to) schizzare.

splendid splendido.

splendor splendore, m.

split (to) fendere, spaccare.

spoil (to) guastare, sciupare.

sponge spugna.

spontaneous spontaneo.

spoon cucchiaio.

spoonful cucchiaiata.

sport sport, m.; giuoco.

spot luogo determinato (location); punto; macchia (stain).

spread (to) stendere, spandere.

spring primavera (season); balzo (leap); molla (machine); sorgente, f. (of water).

spring (to) saltare; balzare; provvenire da; far scattare (a trap).

sprinkle (to) spruzzare, aspergere, cospargere.

sprout (to) germogliare.

spry vivace, attivo.

spur (to) spronare.

spurn (to) respingere, disprezzare.

spy spia.

spy (to) spiare.

squadron squadrone, m.

squander (to) sprecare.

square quadrato; piazza (city).

squeeze (to) spremere.

squirrel scoiattolo.

stabilize (to) stabilizzare.

stable stalla.

stable (adj.) stabile.

stack catasta, mucchio.

stack (to) ammucchiare.

stadium stadio.

staff bastone, m.; stato maggiore (military).

stage palcoscenico.

stain macchia.

stain (to) macchiare.

stairs scale, f. pl.

stammer balbuzie, f.

stammer (to) balbettare, balbuziare.

stamp francobollo (postage); marchio (seal).

stand banco (newsstand); leggio (music).

stand (to) stare in piedi; subire (endure).

star stella.

stare (to) fissare.

start (to) sobbalzare, trasalire, cominciare.

starve (to) morir di fame.

state stato.

state (to) affermare, dichiarare.

stately imponente.

statement dichiarazione, f.

stateroom cabina.

station stazione, f.

 first aid station pronto soccorso.

statistics statistiche, f. pl.

statue statua.

statute statuto.

stay permanenza.

stay (to) restare.

steady fermo, saldo.

steak bistecca.

steal (to) rubare.

steam vapore, m.

steamer piroscafo; vapore, m.

steel acciaio.

steep ripido.

steeple campanile, m.

steer (to) dirigire, guidare.

stem ramo, stelo.

stenographer stenografa, f.; stenografo, m.

stenography stenografia.

step gradino.

step (to) camminare.

sterile sterile.

sterilized sterilizzato.

stern severo.

stew stufato.

stew (to) cuocere a stufato.

steward dispensiere, m.; cameriere, m. (on a ship).

stick bacchetta.

stick (to) conficcare, appiccicare.

stiff rigido.

stiffen (to) irrigidire.

stiffness rigidezza.

still (adj.) quieto, calmo.

 Keep still! Sta' quieto!

still (adv.) ancora, sempre.

stimulate (to) stimolare.

stimulus stimolo.

sting puntura.

sting (to) pungere.

stinginess tirchieria.

stingy tirchio.

stir (to) agitare, incitare, muoversi.

stitch punto; puntura (of pain).

stock bestiame, m. (cattle); merce, f. (wares).

stocking calza.

stomach stomaco.

stone pietra.

stool sgabello.

stop fermata.

stop (to) fermare, arrestare, smettere.

store   negozio.
stork   cicogna.
storm   tempesta.
story   storia.
stove   stufa.
straight   diritto.
straighten (to)   raddrizzare.
strain   sforzo, tensione, f.
strange   strano.
stranger   straniero.
strap   cinghia.
straw   paglia.
strawberry   fragola.
stream   corrente, f.; fiume, m.
street   strada.
streetcar   tranvài, m.
strength   forza.
strengthen (to)   rafforzare.
strenuous   strenuo.
stress   pressione, f.; forza; enfasi, f.
stretch   stiramento; sforzo (effort); tratto (of road).
stretch (to)   stendere, allargare.
strict   stretto, rigido, severo.
stride   passo lungo; andatura.
stride (to)   camminare a gran passi.
strife   contesa, conflitto.
strike   sciopero.
strike (to)   colpire, battere.
string   spago.
strip (to)   spogliare.
stripe   striscia.
strive (to)   sforzarsi, lottare.
stroke   colpo, tocco.
stroll   breve passeggiata.
stroll (to)   andare a passeggio.
strong   forte.
structure   struttura, edificio.
struggle   lotta, sforzo.
struggle (to)   lottare.
stubborn   ostinato.
student   studente, m.; studentessa, f.
studious   studioso.
study   studio.
study (to)   studiare.
stuff   stoffa.
stuff (to)   imbottire.
stumble (to)   inciampare.
stump   ceppo.
stun (to)   stordire.
stunt   ostentazione di forza, f.
stupendous   stupendo.
stupid   stupido.
stupidity   stupidità.
stupor   stupore, m.
sturdy   forte, tenace.
stutter (to)   balbettare.
style   moda (fashion); stile, m.
subdue (to)   soggiogare.
subject   soggetto.
subject (to)   sottoporre, assoggettare.
subjective   soggettivo.
subjugate (to)   soggiogare.
subjunctive   congiuntivo.
sublime   sublime.
submission   sottomissione, f.
submissive   sottomesso.
submit (to)   sottomettere, sottoporre.
subordinate   subordinato, subalterno.
subscribe (to)   sottoscrivere.
subscription   sottoscrizione, f.
subside (to)   abbassarsi.
subsidy   sovvenzione, f.

subsist (to)   sussistere.
substance   sostanza.
substantial   sostanziale.
substantive   sostantivo.
substitute   sostituto.
substitute (to)   sostituire.
substitution   sostituzione, f.
subtle   sottile, fine.
subtract (to)   sottrarre.
subtraction   sottrazione, f.
suburb   sobborgo.
subway   ferrovia sotterranea; metropolitana.
succeed (to)   succedere, seguire, riuscire.
success   successo.
successful   fortunato.
succession   successione, f.
successor   successore, m.
such   tale.
sudden   improvviso.
suddenly   improvvisamente.
sue (to)   chiamare in giudizio.
suede   daino.
suffer (to)   soffrire.
suffering   sofferenza.
sufficient   sufficiente.
sugar   zucchero.
suggest (to)   suggerire.
suggestion   suggerimento.
suicide   suicidio.
suit   vestito, (clothes); petizione, f. (lawsuit).
suit (to)   adattare.
suitable   adatto.
sulk (to)   essere di cattivo umore.
sullen   imbronciato.
sum   somma.
summary   riassunto.
summer   estate, f.
summit   sommità.
summon (to)   citare, convocare.
sumptuous   sontuoso.
sum up (to)   fare la somma; fare un riassunto.
sun   sole, m.
sunbeam   raggio di sole.
Sunday   domenica.
sunny   solatìo.
sunrise   sorgere del sole, m.
sunset   tramonto.
sunshine   luce di sole, f.; sole, m.
superb   superbo.
superficial   superficiale.
superfluous   superfluo.
superintendent   sovrintendente, m.
superior   superiore, m. (Also adj.)
superiority   superiorità.
superstition   superstizione, f.
supervise (to)   sorvegliare.
supper   cena.
supplement   supplemento.
supplementary   supplementare.
supply   provvista.
supply (to)   fornire.
support   sostegno.
support (to)   sostenere.
suppose (to)   supporre.
suppress (to)   sopprimere.
supreme   supremo.
sure   sicuro.
surety   sicurezza.
surface   superficie, f.
surgeon   chirurgo.
surgery   chirurgìa.
surmount (to)   sormontare.
surname   cognome, m.

surpass (to)   sorpassare.
surplus   eccedenza; soprappiù, m.
surprise   sorpresa.
surprise (to)   sorprendere.
surrender   resa.
surrender (to)   arrendersi.
surround (to)   circondare.
surroundings   dintorni, m. pl.
survey   esame, m.; ispezione, f.
survey (to)   esaminare.
survive (to)   sopravvivere.
susceptibility   suscettibilità.
susceptible   suscettibile.
suspect   sospetto.
suspect (to)   sospettare.
suspense   sospensione d'animo, f.
suspension   sospensione, f.
suspicion   sospetto.
suspicious   sospettoso.
sustain (to)   sostenere.
swallow (to)   inghiottire.
swamp   palude, f.
swan   cigno.
sway (to)   oscillare.
swear   bestemmiare (curse); giurare (take an oath).
sweat   sudore, m.
sweat (to)   sudare.
sweep (to)   scopare, spazzare.
sweet   dolce.
sweetness   dolcezza.
swell (to)   gonfiarsi.
swift   veloce, rapido.
swim (to)   nuotare.
swindler   truffatore, m.
swing (to)   dondolare.
switch   interruttore, m. (electric).
sword   spada.
syllable   sillaba.
symbol   simbolo.
symbolic   simbolico.
symbolize (to)   simboleggiare.
symmetrical   simmetrico.
symmetry   simmetrìa.
sympathetic   tenero, sensibile.
sympathy   compassione, f.
symptom   sintomo.
syrup   sciroppo.
system   sistema, m.
systematic   sistematico.

T

table   tavola, tavolo.
tablecloth   tovaglia.
tacit   tacito.
tacitly   tacitamente.
taciturn   taciturno.
tact   tatto.
tactfully   con tatto.
tail   coda.
tailor   sarto.
take (to)   prendere.
tale   storia, racconto.
talent   talento.
talk (to)   parlare, chiacchierare, discorrere.
talkative   ciarliero.
tall   alto.
tame   mansueto, addomesticato, domato.
tangle (to)   ingarbugliare.
tank   serbatoio; cisterna (cistern); carro armato (army).
tapestry   tappezzerìa, arazzo.
tar   catrame, m.
tardy   lento, tardino.

target bersaglio.

tarnish (to) appannare; rendere opaco.

task compito.

taste gusto.

taste (to) assaggiare.

tax tassa, imposta.

taxi tassì.

tea tè.

teach (to) insegnare.

teacher insegnante, *m. & f.*

team squadra.

tear (to) strappare.

tease (to) molestare, tormentare.

teaspoon cucchiaino.

technical tecnico.

technique tecnica.

tedious tedioso.

telegram telegramma, *m.*

telegraph telegrafo.

telegraphic telegrafico.

telephone telefono.

telephone operator telefonista, *m. & f.*

telephone (to) telefonare.

tell (to) dire.

temper umore, *m. (mood);* temperamento *(disposition).*

temperance temperanza.

temperate temperato, moderato.

temperature temperatura.

tempest tempesta.

temple tempio.

temporary temporaneo.

tempt (to) tentare.

temptation tentazione, *f.*

ten dieci.

tenacious tenace.

tenant inquilino.

tend (to) tendere.

tendency tendenza.

tender tenero.

tennis tennis, *m.*

tense tempo *(grammar).*

tense *(adj.)* teso.

tension tensione, *f.*

tent tenda.

tenth decimo.

tepid tiepido.

term termine, *m.*

terrace terrazzo.

terrible terribile.

terrify (to) atterrire.

territory territorio.

terror terrore, *m.*

test prova, esame, *m.*

test (to) provare; esaminare *(school).*

testify (to) attestare, deporre.

testimony testimonianza.

text testo.

textbook libro di testo.

than di; che; di quello che; di quanto che.

thank (to) ringraziare.

thanks grazie, *f. pl.;* ringraziamenti, *m. pl.*

that *(pron.)* quello, quella, ciò, quelle, quelli.

   that is vale a dire.

   That's it. È così.

that *(adj.)* quel, quello, quella, quelle, quei, quelli, quegli.

thaw disgelo.

thaw (to) disgelare.

the il, lo, la, i, gli, le.

theater teatro.

their il loro; la loro; i loro; le loro.

theirs il loro; la loro; i loro; le loro; di loro.

them essi, esse, loro, li, le, quelli, quelle, coloro.

theme tema, *m.*

themselves essi stessi; esse stesse; se stessi; se stesse; sè; si.

then allora, perciò, dunque.

theoretical teorico.

theory teoria.

there là, lì.

   there is c'è.

   there are ci sono.

thereafter d'allora in poi.

thereupon in conseguenza di ciò.

thermometer termometro.

these queste, questi.

thesis tesi, *f.*

they essi, esse, loro.

thick spesso.

thicken (to) ingrossare *(make larger);* far restringere *(a gravy or sauce).*

thickness spessore, *m.*

thief ladro.

thigh coscia.

thimble ditale, *m.*

thin sottile; magro *(referring to people).*

thing cosa.

think (to) pensare, credere, ritenere.

third terzo.

thirst sete, *f.*

thirteen tredici.

thirteenth tredicesimo.

thirtieth trentesimo.

thirty trenta.

this questo, questa.

thorn spina.

thorough intero, completo.

though sebbene, quantunque, però.

thought pensiero.

thoughtful pensieroso.

thoughtless spensierato.

thousand mille.

thread filo.

thread (to) infilare.

threat minaccia.

threaten (to) minacciare.

three tre.

threshold soglia.

thrift economia.

thrifty economico.

thrill palpito, tremito.

thrill (to) elettrizzare.

thrilling emozionante.

throat gola.

throb (to) pulsare.

throne tròno.

throng folla, ressa.

through attraverso.

throughout per tutta la durata di.

throw lancio, tiro.

throw (to) lanciare, gettare.

thumb pollice, *m.*

thunder tuono.

thunder (to) tuonare.

thunderbolt fulmine, *m.*

Thursday giovedì.

thus così; in tal modo.

ticket biglietto.

ticket window biglietterìa; sportello del biglietti.

tickle solletico.

ticklish sensitivo, delicato.

tide marèa.

tidiness pulizia, accuratezza, ordine, *m.*

tidy ordìnato.

tie cravatta.

tie (to) legare.

tiger tigre, *f.*

tight stretto.

tile mattonella.

till (to) coltivare.

till fino a; finchè.

tilt (to) inclinare.

timber legname da costruzione, *m.*

time tempo

   behind time in retardo.

   from time to time di volta in volta.

   in time a tempo.

   to have a good time divertirsi.

   What time is it? Che ora è?

timid timido.

timidity timidezza.

tin stagno.

tinkle tintinnìo.

tiny piccolo.

tip punta; mancia *(money).*

tip (to) dare la mancia.

tip over (to) far ribaltare.

tire pneumatico, gomma.

tire (to) stancare, stancarsi.

tired stanco.

tireless instancabile.

tiresome stanchevole, noioso.

title titolo.

to a, ad, verso.

toad rospo.

toast pane abbrustolito; pane tostato.

toast (to) brindare *(drink to);* tostare *(bread).*

tobacco tabacco.

tobacco store tabaccherìa.

today oggi.

toe dito del piede.

together insieme.

toil fatica.

toil (to) faticare.

toilet toletta, gabinetto.

token segno; simbolo; pegno *(of affection).*

tolerable tollerabile.

tolerance tolleranza.

tolerant tollerante.

tolerate (to) tollerare.

toll (to) suonare a rintocco.

tomato pomodoro.

tomb tomba.

tomorrow domani, *m.*

ton tonnellata.

tone tono.

tongs mollette, *f. pl. (tool);* pinze, *f. pl. (tweezers, pincers).*

tongue lingua.

tonight stasera.

too anche *(also);* pure.

too much troppo.

tool strumento; arnese, *m.;* utensile, *m.*

tooth dente, *m.*

toothache mal di dente.

toothbrush spazzolino dei denti.

toothpaste dentifricio.

toothpick stuzzicadenti, *m.*

toothpowder polvere dentifricia.

top sommità, cima.

topic soggetto.

torch torcia, fiaccola.

torment tormento.

torture tortura.

toss (to) lanciare; agitarsi *(in sleep).*

total totale, *m.* (Also *adj.)*

totally totalmente.
touch tocco.
touch (to) toccare.
touching commovente.
touchy suscettibile.
tough duro, rude.
tour viaggio *(journey)*; giro.
tour (to) fare un viaggio.
tourist turista, *m.* or *f.*
tourist agency agenzia di viaggi.
tournament tornèo, gara.
toward verso.
towel asciugamani.
tower torre, *f.*
town città.
town hall palazzo municipale.
toy giocattolo.
trace traccia.
trace (to) tracciare.
track orma; binario *(railroad)*; traccia.
trade commercio; mestiere, *m. (occupation).*
trade union camera del lavoro.
tradition tradizione, *f.*
traditional tradizionale.
traffic traffico.
tragedy tragedia.
tragic tragico.
trail sentiero, traccia.
trail (to) seguire le tracce di; strisciare.
train treno.
freight train treno merci.
train (to) ammaestrare, allenarsi.
training esercitazione, *f.*; allenamento.
traitor traditore, *m.*; traditrice, *f.*
trample (to) calpestare.
tranquil tranquillo.
tranquillity tranquillità.
transaction affare, *m.*; trattamento.
transfer trasferimento.
transfer (to) trasferire.
transition transizione, *f.*
transitory transitorio.
translate (to) tradurre.
translation traduzione, *f.*
translator traduttore, *m.*
transmission trasmissione, *f.*
transmit (to) trasmettere.
transparent trasparente.
transport trasporto.
transport (to) trasportare.
transportation trasportazione, *f.*; trasporto.
transverse trasverso.
trap trappola.
trap (to) prendere in trappola.
trash rifiuto.
travel viaggio.
travel (to) viaggiare.
travel agency agenzia di viaggi.
traveler viaggiatore, *m.*; viaggiatrice, *f.*
tray vassoio.
treacherous proditorio, sleale.
treachery tradimento.
treason tradimento.
treasure tesoro.
treasurer tesoriere, *m.*
treasury tesoro.
treat cosa offerta; gioia; festa.
treat (to) trattare.
treatment trattamento; cura *(medical).*
treaty trattato.
tree albero.
tremble (to) tremare.
trembling tremito.

trembling *(adj.)* tremulo.
tremendous tremendo.
trench trincèa.
trend tendenza.
trial prova; esperimento; processo *(court).*
triangle triangolo.
tribe tribù, *f.*
tribulation tribolazione, *f.*
tribunal tribunale, *m.*
tribute tributo.
trick stratagemma, *m.*
trick (to) ingannare.
trifle inezia.
trifling insignificante.
trim (to) guarnire.
trimming guarnizione, *f.*
trip viaggio; gita; incespicamento *(fall).*
trip (to) inciampare.
triple triplice.
triumph trionfo.
triumph (to) trionfare.
triumphant trionfante.
trivial insignificante.
trolley car tranvài, *m.*
trophy trofèo.
trot trotto.
trot (to) trottare; mettere al trotto.
trouble disturbo, incomodo.
trouble (to) importunare, disturbare.
Don't trouble yourself. Non si disturbi.
troup truppa.
trousers calzoni, *m. pl.*
truck carro, autocarro.
true vero.
truly veramente, sinceramente.
yours truly suo devotissimo, *m.*
sua devotissima, *f.*
trump briscola.
trump (to) giocare una briscola.
trumpet tromba.
trunk tronco *(tree)*; baule, *m. (luggage)*;
proboscide, *f. (elephant's).*
trust fiducia.
trust (to) aver fiducia in.
trusting fidente.
trustworthy fidato.
truth verità.
truthful sincero.
truthfully sinceramente.
truthfulness sincerità.
try tentativo.
try (to) tentare.
Try to come. Cerchi di venire.
Try to be on time. Cerchi di arrivare in tempo.
tube tubo.
tumble (to) cadere, precipitare.
tumult tumulto.
tune aria, tono, melodìa.
tune (to) accordare.
tunnel gallerìa.
turf terreno erboso.
turkey tacchino.
turmoil tumulto.
turn giro, turno.
turn (to) voltare, rivoltare.
Left turn. Voltare a sinistra.
turnip rapa.
twelfth dodicesimo.
twelve dodici.
twentieth ventesimo.
twenty venti.
twenty-five venticinque.
twenty-four ventiquattro.

twenty-six ventisei.
twice due volte.
twilight crepuscolo.
twin gemello, *m.*; gemella, *f.*
twist torcere, contorcere, torcersi.
two due.
type tipo.
type (to) dattilografare.
typewriter macchina da scrivere.
tyranny tirannìa.
tyrant tiranno.

U

ugliness bruttezza.
ugly brutto.
ulterior ulteriore.
ultimate ultimo, finale.
ultimately finalmente; in definitiva.
umbrella ombrello.
umpire arbitro.
unable to (to be) essere incapace di.
unanimity unanimità.
unanimous unanime.
unanimously unanimemente.
unaware (to be) essere inconsapevole.
unbearable insopportabile.
unbelievable incredibile.
unbutton (to) sbottonare.
uncertain incerto.
uncertainty incertezza.
unchangeable immutabile.
uncle zio.
uncomfortable scomodo.
uncommon raro; non comune.
unconscious inconscio; privo di sensi; sub-
cosciente.
unconsciously inconsciamente.
uncouth goffo, sgraziato, grossolano.
uncover (to) scoprire.
undecided indeciso.
undefinable indefinibile.
undeniable innegabile.
under sotto.
undergo (to) subire; sottomettersi a.
underground sotterra.
underhand *(adj.)* clandestino, subdolo.
underline (to) sottolineare.
underneath sotto; al disotto.
understand (to) comprendere.
understanding comprensione, *f.*; intesa; accordo.
undertake (to) intraprendere.
undertaker direttore di pompe funebri, *m.*
undertaking impresa.
undesirable non desiderabile.
undignified non dignitoso.
undo (to) disfare.
undress (to) svestirsi.
uneasiness inquietudine, *f.*; ansia.
uneasy inquieto; non comodo.
unemployed non impiegato; disoccupato.
unequal ineguale.
uneven ineguale; dispari *(numbers).*
uneventful tranquillo; senza importanti avveni-
menti.
unexpected inaspettato, imprevisto.
unexpectedly inaspettatamente, improvvisamente.
unfailing immancabile.
unfair ingiusto.
unfaithful infedele.
unfamiliar non familiare; poco noto.
unfavorable sfavorevole.
unfit inadatto.
unfold (to) spiegare, stendere, svelare.

unforeseen impreveduto, imprevisto.
unforgettable indimenticabile.
unfortunate sfortunato.
unfortunately sfortunatamente.
ungrateful ingrato.
unhappily infelicemente.
unhappiness infelicità.
unhappy infelice.
unharmed incolume.
unhealthy non sano.
unheard (of) inaudito.
unhesitatingly senza esitazione.
unhoped for insperato.
unhurt illeso, incolume.
uniform uniforme, f. (Also adj.)
uniformity uniformità.
uniformly uniformemente.
unify (to) unificare.
unimportant insignificante.
unintentional involontario.
unintentionally involontariamente.
uninviting non invitante.
union unione, f.
unique unico.
unit unità.
unite (to) unire.
united unito, congiunto.
unity unità.
universal universale.
universe universo.
university università.
unjust ingiusto.
unjustifiable ingiustificabile.
unkind poco gentile; scortese.
unknown sconosciuto.
unlawful illegale, illecito.
unless a meno che.
unlikely improbabile.
unlimited illimitato.
unload (to) scaricare.
unluckily sfortunatamente, disgraziatamente.
unmistakably chiaramente.
unnecessary non necessario.
unoccupied non occupato; disponibile; libero.
unofficial non ufficiale.
unpack (to) disfare le valigie.
unpleasant spiacevole, doloroso, sgradevole.
unpublished inedito.
unquestionably indubitatamente.
unravel (to) dipanare.
unreal irreale.
unreasonable irragionevole.
unrecognizable irriconoscibile.
unreliable immeritevole di fiducia.
unrest inquietudine, f.
unrestrained sfrenato.
unrestricted libero; sfrenato; senza restrizioni.
unroll (to) svolgere, distendere.
unsafe pericoloso.
unsatisfactory non soddisfacente.
unsatisfied insoddisfatto.
unscrupulous senza scrupoli.
unseemly sconvenevole.
unseen (adj.) inosservato.
unselfish disinteressato.
unspeakable indicibile.
unsteady instabile, incostante.
unsuccessful senza successo.
unsuitable inadatto.
unthinkable impensabile.
untidy disordinato.
untie (to) sciogliere, slegare.
until fino a; finchè.

until now fino ad ora.
untrimmed senza guarnizione.
untrue falso, infedele.
untrustworthy indegno di fiducia.
untruth menzogna.
unusual insolito, raro.
unwell indisposto, sofferente.
unwholesome malsano, nocivo.
unwilling non disposto; mal disposto.
unwise non saggio; insensato.
unworthy indegno, immeritevole.
up su; sopra; in alto; in piedi.
upheaval sollevamento.
uphold (to) sostenere, mantenere.
upkeep mantenimento, sostentamento.
upon sopra.
upper superiore.
upright diritto; in piedi; retto.
uprising rivolta, insurrezione, f.
uproar tumulto, clamore, m.
upset capovolgimento, rovesciamento.
upset (to) capovolgere, sconvolgere.
upside down sottosopra.
upstairs al piano superiore; sopra.
upward in su; in alto.
urge (to) esortare.
urgency urgenza.
urgent urgente.
us noi, ci.
use uso, usanza.
use (to) usare; servirsi di.
used to abituato.
useful utile.
useless inutile.
usual solito, usuale.
usually usualmente.
utensil utensile, m.
utility utilità.
utilize (to) utilizzare.
utter estremo, assoluto.
utter (to) emettere.
utterly estremamente, totalmente.

V

vacancy vacanza.
vacant vuoto; non occupato.
vacation vacanze, f.
vague vago.
vain vano, vanitoso.
in vain in vano.
valiant valoroso, intrepido.
valid valido.
validity validità.
valley valle, f.
valuable costoso, prezioso.
value valore, m.
value (to) valutare, stimare.
valued stimato, apprezzato.
valve valvola.
vanilla vaniglia.
vanish (to) svanire.
vanity vanità.
vanquish (to) vincere, conquistare.
vapor vapore, m.
variable variabile.
variation variazione, f.
varied vario, variato.
variety varietà; varietà, m. (show).
various diverso, vario.
varnish vernice, f.
varnish (to) verniciare.

vary (to) variare, mutare.
vase vaso.
vast vasto.
vault volta; sepoltura in sotterraneo (church or
  cemetery).
veal vitello.
vegetable legume, m.; verdura.
vehemence veemenza.
vehicle veicolo.
veil velo.
veil (to) velare.
vein vena.
velocity velocità.
velvet velluto.
venerable venerabile.
venerate (to) venerare.
veneration venerazione, f.
Venetian veneziano. (Noun & adj.)
vengeance vendetta.
venom veleno.
ventilation ventilazione, f.
ventilator ventilatore, m.
venture (to) azzardare, osare.
verb verbo.
verdict verdetto.
verge limite; punto estremo.
verification verifica.
verify (to) verificare.
versatile versatile.
versatility versatilità.
verse verso.
version versione, f.
vertical verticale.
very molto.
vessel recipiente, m. (container); vascello;
  nave, f.
vest panciotto.
veterinarian veterinario.
vex (to) irritare.
via via.
vibrate (to) oscillare; far vibrare.
vice vizio, difetto.
vice-president vice presidente, m.
vice-versa viceversa.
vicinity vicinanza.
victim vittima.
victor vincitore, m.
victorious vittorioso.
victory vittoria.
victuals vettovaglie, f. pl.
view vista, veduta.
view (to) guardare, considerare.
vigor vigore, m.
vigorous vigoroso.
vile abbietto.
village villaggio.
villain furfante, m.
vindicate (to) rivendicare.
vindictive vendicativo.
vine vigna.
vinegar aceto.
violence violenza.
violent violento.
violet viola, mammola.
violin violino.
virile virile.
virtue virtù, f.
virtuous virtuoso.
visibility visibilità.
visible visibile.
visibly visibilmente.
vision visione, f.; vista (eyesight).
visit visita.

visitor visitatore, *m.*; ospite, *m.*
visual visivo.
visualize (to) immaginare, raffigurarsi.
vital vitale.
vitality vitalità.
vivacious vivace.
vivid vivido.
vocabulary vocabolario.
vocal vocale.
vocation vocazione, *f.*
vogue voga.
voice voce, *f.*
void non valido; privo; nullo.
volubility fluidità, abbondanza.
voluble volubile.
volume volume, *m.*
voluminous voluminoso.
voluntary volontario.
vote voto.
vote (to) votare.
vow voto.
vow (to) far voto di.
vowel vocale, *f.*
vulgar volgare.
vulnerable vulnerabile.

W

wager scommessa.
wager (to) scommettere.
wages salario.
waist vita, cintura.
wait (to) attendere.
waiter cameriere.
wake (to) svegliarsi.
walk cammino, passeggiata.
walk (to) camminare.
** to go for a walk** fare una passeggiata.
wall muro.
wallet portafogli, *m.*
walnut noce, *f.*
wander (to) vagabondare, divagare.
want bisogno.
want (to) volere; desiderare; aver bisogno.
war guerra.
ward pupillo *(person)*; corsìa *(hospital)*.
wardrobe guardaroba, corredo.
ware, wares merce, *f.*; merci, *f. pl.*
warehouse magazzino.
warfare guerra.
warm caldo.

to be warm (hot) { aver caldo *(a person)*.
essere caldo *(an object)*.
far caldo *(the weather)*.

warm (to) riscaldare.
warmth calore, *m.*
warn (to) mettere in guardia; avvertire.
warning avvertimento, ammonimento.
warrant autorizzazione, *f.*; mandato.
warrant (to) assicurare, giustificare.
warrior guerriero.

wary cauto, guardingo.
wash bucato.
wash (to) lavare.
washroom lavandino.
waste sperpero, spreco.
waste (to) consumare; sperperare; deperire *(waste away)*.
watch guardia *(guard)*; orologio *(clock)*; veglia *(vigil)*.
watch (to) stare in guardia; guardare.
watchful guardingo.
water acqua.

fresh water acqua dolce.
waterfall cascata d'acqua; cataratta.
waterproof impermeabile.
wave onda.
wave (to) ondeggiare *(speaking of sea)*; far segno *(to signal)*; mettere in piega *(set hair)*.
waver (to) vacillare.
wax cera.
way via, modo, maniera.
we noi.
weak debole.
weaken (to) indebolire.
weakly debolmente.
weakness debolezza.
wealth ricchezza.
wealthy ricco.
weapon arma.
wear (to) portare; indossare; consumare *(consume)*.
weariness stanchezza.
weary stanco.
weather tempo.
weave (to) tessere.
wedding sposalizio.
Wednesday mercoledì.
weed erbaccia.
week settimana.
weekend fine settimana.
weekly settimanalmente.
weep (to) piangere.
weigh (to) pesare.
weight peso.
welcome benvenuto.
Welcome! Benvenuto!
You're welcome. { Prego.
Non c'è di che.
welfare benessere, *m.*
well pozzo.
Well! Bene!
west ovest.
western occidentale.
wet bagnato.
whale balena.
what quale; quali; che; ciò che; quello che, *etc.*; *(interrog.)* come?; che cosa?
What? Come?
What is it? Che cos'è?
whatever qualunque cosa; tutto ciò che.
wheat grano.
wheel ruota.
when quando.
whenever ogni qual volta.
where dove.
wherever dovunque.
whether se; sia che.
which quale, *sing.*; quali, *pl.*
while mentre.
Wait a while. Attenda un po'.
whim capriccio.
whine (to) piagnucolare.
whip frusta.
whip (to) frustare.
whirlwind turbine, *m.*
whisper bisbiglio, mormorìo.
whisper (to) bisbigliare.
whistle fischio.
whistle (to) fischiare.
white bianco.
who chi; che; il quale; la quale; i quali; le quali; colui che; colei che.
whoever chiunque.
whole (the) il tutto.
whole *(adj.)* tutto, intero.

wholesale all'ingrosso.
wholesome sano, salubre.
whom See *who*.
whose di chi; di cui.
why perchè.
Why not? Perchè no?
wicked cattivo.
wide largo.
widen (to) allargare.
widow vedova.
widower vedovo.
width larghezza.
wife moglie.
wig parrucca.
wild selvaggio.
wilderness deserto.
wildness selvatichezza.
wile astuzia, inganno.
will volontà.
will (to) volere; lasciare per testamento *(bequeath)*.
willful volontario, premeditato.
willing disposto, pronto.
willingly volentieri.
win (to) vincere.
wind vento.
wind (to) attorcigliare; caricare *(a watch)*.
windmill mulino a vento.
window finestra.
windy ventoso.
wine vino.
wing ala.
wink strizzatina d'occhio.
winner vincitore, *m.*; vincitrice, *f.*
winter inverno.
wipe (to) asciugare, pulire.
wire filo metallico *(metal)*; telegramma, *m. (telegram)*.
wire (to) telegrafare.
wisdom saggezza.
wise saggio.
wish desiderio.
wit senso, spirito.
witch strega.
with con.
withdraw (to) ritirarsi.
withdrawal ritirata.
wither (to) disseccare, inaridirsi, appassire.
within di dentro.
without senza.
witness testimone, *m.*
witty spiritoso.
woe dolore, *m.*
wolf lupo.
woman donna.
wonder meraviglia.
wonder (to) meravigliarsi, domandarsi.
wonderful meraviglioso.
Wonderful! Meraviglioso!
wood legno.
woods bosco.
work lavoro.
work (to) lavorare.
worker lavoratore, *m.*; lavoratrice, *f.*
workman lavoratore, *m.*; operaio.
work of art lavoro d'arte.
workshop laboratorio; officina.
world mondo.
worldliness mondanità.
worldly mondano.
worm verme, *m.*
worry preoccupazione, *f.*; inquietudine, *f.*
worry (to) essere inquieto; preoccuparsi.

Don't worry. Non si preoccupi.
worse peggiore, peggio.
worship adorazione, *f.*; culto.
worship (to) adorare, venerare.
worst il peggiore; il peggio.
worth valore, *m.*; merito.
worthless senza valore; immeritevole.
worth degno, meritevole.
wound ferita.
wound (to) ferire.
wounded ferito.
wrap (to) avvolgere, coprirsi.
wrath ira.
wrathful irato.
wreath ghirlanda, corona.
wreck rovina; naufragio *(ship).*
wreck (to) rovinare; demolire *(a building);* naufragare *(ship).*
wrestle (to) lottare.
wrestler lottatore, *m.*
wrestling lotta.
wretched miserabile, misero.
wring (to) torcere, spremere, estorcere.
wrinkle ruga, grinza.
wrinkle (to) produrre rughe o grinze; corrugare.
wrist polso.
write (to) scrivere.

writer scrittore, *m.*; scrittrice, *f.*
writing scrittura.
in writing per iscritto.
written scritto.
wrong torto, ingiustizia.
wrong (adj.) erroneo, sbagliato.
wrong (to) fare torto; offendere; giudicare erroneamente.

X

x-ray radiografia.

Y

yacht panfilo.
yard cortile, *m.*; recinto; cantiere, *m. (shipyard).*
yarn filato.
yawn sbadiglio.
yawn (to) sbadigliare.
year anno.
yearly annualmente *(adv.);* annuale *(adj.)*
yearn for (to) aver desiderio di; bramare.
yearning desiderio.
yeast lievito.
yell (to) urlare.
yellow giallo.
yes sì.

yesterday ieri, *m.*
yet ancora, tuttora.
yield (to) produrre *(produce);* cedere *(give in);* arrendersi *(surrender).*
yoke giogo, vincolo.
yolk torlo *(egg).*
you voi; vi; tu; te; ti; lei; la; loro; le; li.
young giovane, *m. & f.* (Also *adj.)*
young lady signorina.
young man giovanetto.
your(s) il vostro; la vostra; i vostri; le vostre; il tuo; la tua; i tuoi; le tue; il suo; la sua; i suoi; le sue.
yourself voi stesso; tu stesso; te stesso; lei stesso.
youth giovinezza.
youthful giovanile.
youthfulness giovinezza.

Z

zeal zelo.
zealous zelante.
zero zero.
zone zona.
zoo giardino zoologico.
zoology zoologia.

GLOSSARY OF PROPER NAMES

Adrian   Adriana.
Albert   Alberto.
Alexander   Alessandro.
Alfred   Alfredo.
Alice   Alice.
Andrew   Andrèa.
Anita   Anita.
Anthony   Antonio.
Arnold   Arnoldo.
Arthur   Arturo.

Beatrice   Beatrice.
Bernard   Bernardo.
Bertram   Bertrando.
Blanche   Bianca.

Carol   Carolina.
Charles   Carlo.
Charlotte   Carlotta.

Daniel   Daniele.
David   Davide.

Edith   Editta.
Edmond   Edmondo.
Edward   Edoardo.

Eleanor   Eleonora.
Emily   Emilia.
Evelyn   Evelina.

Ferdinand   Ferdinando.
Frances   Francesca.
Francis   Francesco.
Frederick   Federico.

Gabriel   Gabriele.
George   Giorgio.
Gertrude   Gertrude.
Gregory   Gregorio.
Guy   Guido.

Harriet   Enrichetta.
Harry   Enrico.
Henry   Enrico.
Hugh   Ugo.

Irene   Irene.

Jane   Gianna.
Jerome   Geronimo.
Joan   Giovanna.
Judith   Giuditta.

Julian   Giuliano.

Lawrence   Lorenzo.
Lewis   Luigi.
Lucy   Lucìa.

Mary   Marìa.
Maurice   Maurizio.
Michael   Michele.

Paul   Paolo.
Peter   Pietro.

Ralph   Raffaele.
Richard   Riccardo.
Robert   Roberto.

Sylvia   Silvia.

Theresa   Teresa.
Thomas   Tommaso.

Vincent   Vincenzo.
Vivian   Viviana.

William   Guglielmo.

GLOSSARY OF GEOGRAPHICAL NAMES

Africa   Africa.
Alps   Alpi.
America   America.
  North America   America del Nord.
  Central America   America Centrale.
  South America   America del Sud.
Argentina   Argentina.
Asia   Asia.
Atlantic   Atlantico.
Australia   Australia.
Austria   Austria.

Belgium   Belgio.
Bermuda   Bermude.
Brazil   Brasile.
Brussels   Brusselle.

Canada   Canadà.
Chile   Cile.
China   Cina.
Czechoslovakia   Cecoslovacchia.

Denmark   Danimarca.
Dover   Dover.

Egypt   Egitto.
England   Inghilterra.
Europe   Europa.

Florence   Firenze.

Geneva   Ginevra.
Genoa   Genova.
Germany   Germania.
Greece   Grecia.

Hamburg   Amburgo.
Holland   Olanda.
Hungary   Ungherìa.

Iceland   Islanda.
India   India.
Ireland   Irlanda.
Ischia   Ischia.
Italy   Italia.

Japan   Giappone.
Jugoslavia   Iugoslavia.

Lisbon   Lisbona.
London   Londra.

Mexico   Messico.
Milan   Milano.
Moscow   Mosca.

Naples   Napoli.
New Zealand   Nuova Zelanda.
Norway   Norvegia.

Pacific   Pacifico.

Palermo   Palermo.
Persia   Persia.
Poland   Polonia.
Prussia   Prussia.

Rhine   Reno.
Rome   Roma.
Roumania   Romanìa.
Russia   Russia.

Sardinia   Sardegna.
Scotland   Scozia.
Siberia   Siberia.
Sicily   Sicilia.
Spain   Spagna.
Sweden   Svezia.
Switzerland   Svizzera.

Tuscany   Toscana.
Turkey   Turchìa.

United States   Stati Uniti.

Vatican   Vaticano.
Venice   Venezia.
Vienna   Vienna.

Wales   Galles.

COMMON USAGE DICTIONARY

Portuguese–English
English–Portuguese

By **Oscar Fernández**, Director Portuguese Program,
New York University

Based on the Method Devised by
Ralph Weiman
Formerly Chief of Language Section,
U.S. War Department

---

*CONTAINING OVER 18,000 BASIC TERMS, WITH
MEANING ILLUSTRATED BY SENTENCES, AND
1,000 ESSENTIAL WORDS SPECIALLY INDICATED*

INTRODUCTION

The Portuguese Common Usage Dictionary lists the most frequently used Portuguese words, gives their most important meanings, and illustrates their use.

1. The *basic* words are indicated by capitals. These are the words generally considered essential for any reasonable command of the language.

2. Only the most important meanings are given.

3. These meanings are illustrated, wherever necessary, by means of everyday phrases and sentences. Where there is no close English equivalent for a Portuguese word or where the English equivalent has several different meanings, the context of the illustrative sentences helps to make the meanings clear.

4. Each important word is followed by the everyday expression and/or sentences in which it most frequently occurs. The Common Usage Dictionary serves accordingly as a phrase book or conversation guide: it contains thousands of everyday sentences that are of practical importance (for traveling, correspondence, etc.) or that serve as illustrations of the grammatical features of current written and spoken Portuguese. The Common Usage Dictionary should, therefore, prove helpful both to beginners who are building up their vocabulary and to advanced students who want to perfect their command of colloquial Portuguese.

5. In translating the Portuguese phrases and sentences, an attempt has been made to give not a mere translation but an equivalent— that is, what an English speaker would say in the same situation. (Literal translations have been added to help the beginner.) The user is thus furnished with numerous examples of how common Portuguese expressions (particularly the very idiomatic and the very colloquial ones) can best be translated into English. This feature makes the Common Usage Dictionary especially useful for translation work.

6. The English-Portuguese part contains the most common English words and their Portuguese equivalents. By consulting the sentences given under the Portuguese word in the Portuguese-English part, the reader can observe whether the Portuguese word always translates the English one or whether it does so only in certain cases.

EXPLANATORY NOTES

1. For differences between Brazilian and Continental Portuguese, consult Section 7 of the Introduction to the Conversation Manual.

2. Differences in Portugal in spelling, in accent marks, or other variants, are given in parentheses:

   DIRETOR (DIRECTOR) m. *director*.
   Antônio (António) *Anthony*.
   govêrno (governo) m. *government*.

3. If more than one form is used they are given:

   toicinho
   toucinho, m. *bacon*.

4. Ⓑ will be used to indicate a particularly Brazilian term or meaning, and Ⓟ a Continental Portuguese one:

   suéter m. *sweater* Ⓑ.

garage Ⓑ, **garagem** f. *garage*.
ALMÔÇO (ALMOÇO) m. *lunch*.
   Primeiro almoço. *Breakfast* Ⓟ.
   Pequeno almoço. *Breakfast* Ⓟ.

5. The pronunciation of *x* between vowels is indicated: **abacaxi** ($x = sh$); **exame** ($x = z$); **próximo** ($x = s$); **táxi** ($x = ks$).

6. A few literal translations are given in quotation marks: o Rio de Janeiro ("the river of January").

7. Usually only the masculine, singular form of an adjective is given.

8. Abbreviations used: *adj.* adjective; *adv.* adverb; *conj.* conjunction; *f.* feminine; *fam.* familiar; *fig.* figurative; *ind.* indefinite; *m.* masculine; *n.* noun; *pro.* pronoun; *prep.* preposition.

Portuguese-English DICTIONARY

A

A *to, in, at, by, for, the, her, it, on, with.*
Vou à cidade. *I'm going to the city.*
A tempo. *In time.*
A que horas? *At what time?*
Um a um. *One by one.*
A janela está aberta. *The window is open.*
Não a vimos. *We did not see her.*
Êle (Ele) a comprou ontem. *He bought it (fem.) yesterday.*
Vamos a pé. *We're going on foot.*

abacate *m. avocado.*
abacaxi (*x = sh*) (**ananás**) *m. pineapple; difficult situation, mess* Ⓑ.
abafado *adj. stuffy, close, sultry, hidden, oppressed; annoyed, very busy, swamped* Ⓑ.
abaixar (*x = sh*) *to lower, to bring down, to humiliate.*
abaixar-se (*x = sh*) *to stoop down, to humble oneself.*
ABAIXO (*x = sh*) *below, under.*
Abaixo e acima. *Up and down.*
abalado *shaken, loose; moved, touched (fig.).*
abanar *to fan, to shake.*
Êle (Ele) abanou a cabeça. *He shook his head.*
abandonado *adj. abandoned, forsaken; friendless.*
abandonar *to abandon, to give up, to leave.*
Êle (Ele) abandonou a família. *He abandoned his family.*
abandono *m. abandonment, desertion; neglect, destitution.*
abanico *m. a small fan.*
abarcar *to comprise, to enclose, to contain, to grasp.*
Quem muito abarca, pouco aperta. *To bite off more than one can chew.*
abastado *adj. wealthy, rich, well-off.*
abastar *to supply, to provide.*
abastecer *to provide, to supply.*
abastecimento *m. supplies, provisions.*
abatido *adj. depressed, discouraged.*
abatimento *m. decrease, reduction, discount; low spirits, depression.*
abdicar *to abdicate, to renounce, to resign.*
abdome, abdômen (abdómen) *m. abdomen.*
abecedário *m. the alphabet; primer.*
abelha *f. bee.*
abençoado *adj. blessed; happy.*
abençoar *to bless; to make happy.*
abertamente *openly, frankly, plainly.*
ABERTO *adj. open, opened; frank.*
A loja está aberta? *Is the store open?*
João não tinha aberto as janelas. *John had not opened the windows.*
abertura *f. opening.*
abismo *m. abyss, chasm.*
abjurar *to renounce, to repudiate.*
aboliçao *f. abolition.*
abolir *to abolish, to revoke, to cancel.*
abominável *adj. abominable.*
abonado *adj. trustworthy, creditable; wealthy, well-off* Ⓑ.
abonar *to guarantee, to vouch for; to advance (money) to.*
abono *m. loan; warranty, surety.*
abordar *to go aboard, to board; to accost, to broach.*
Ela não quis abordar o assunto. *She did not wish to broach the subject.*
aborrecer *to hate, to detest; to annoy, to bother.*
Tudo isto nos aborrece. *All this annoys us.*
aborrecido *adj. annoyed, bored, worried.*
aborrecimento *m. annoyance, nuisance, bore.*
abotoar *to button; to bud.*

abraçar *to embrace, to hug; to encompass.*
Os dois amigos se abraçaram. *The two friends embraced each other.*
ABRAÇO *m. embrace, hug.*
Receba um abraço do seu amigo. *Receive a hug from your friend (In a letter, a complimentary close, "Cordially yours," or equivalent.)*
abreviar *to shorten, to abbreviate, to summarize.*
abreviatura *f. abbreviation.*
abricó, abricote, albricote *m. apricot.*
abridor *m. opener.*
abrigar *to shelter, to protect.*
ABRIGO *m. shelter, protection, sanctuary.*
ABRIL *m. April.*
ABRIR *to open; to unclock; to begin; to turn on.*
Faça o favor de abrir a porta. *Please open the door.*
Não abra a torneira. *Don't turn on the faucet.*
abrupto *adj. abrupt, sudden.*
abscesso *m. abscess.*
absoluto *adj. absolute, complete, independent.*
absolver *to absolve, to acquit, to pardon.*
absolvido *adj. absolved, acquitted, pardoned.*
absorto *adj. absorbed, enraptured.*
abster *to abstain, to refrain, to repress.*
abstinência *f. abstinence; fasting.*
absurdo *adj. absurd, foolish; n. m. absurdity, nonsense.*
abundância *f. abundance, plenty.*
abundante *adj. abundant, plentiful.*
abundar *to abound.*
abusar *to abuse, to take advantage of.*
O oficial abusou de sua autoridade. *The officer abused his authority.*
abuso *m. abuse, misuse.*
abutre *m. vulture.*
ACABADO *adj. finished, complete; exhausted.*
ACABAR *to finish, to complete, to end; to have just (with de).*
Você já acabou o trabalho? *Did you already finish the work?*
Acabamos de jantar. *We have just had dinner.*
acabrunhar *to oppress, to distress, to afflict.*
academia *f. academy, school; learned society.*
acalmar *to calm, to appease, to soothe.*
Eu vou acalmá-lo. *I'm going to calm him down.*
acampar *to camp, to pitch camp.*
acanhado *adj. shy, bashful, timid; miserly; close, narrow.*
AÇÃO (ACÇÃO) *f. action, act, deed; share of stock.*
Houve muito falar e pouca ação. *There was much talk and little action.*
acariciar *to caress, to pet; to cherish.*
ACASO *by chance, perhaps, possibly; m. chance, accident.*
Por acaso. *By chance.*
Escolhemos ao acaso. *We picked at random.*
Foram os acasos da fortuna. *They were the hazards of fortune.*
aceder *to accede, to assent, to agree.*
ACEITAÇÃO *f. acceptance.*
ACEITAR *to accept, to take.*
Aceitam cheque de viagem? *Will you accept a traveler's check?*
ACEITÁVEL *adj. acceptable.*
ACEITE *m. acceptance; adj. accepted.*
ACEITO *adj. accepted.*
acelerador *adj. accelerating; m. accelerator.*
acelerar *to accelerate, to speed up.*
ACENDER *to light (up), to ignite, to turn on (a light); to animate.*
Deixe-me acender um fósforo. *Let me light a match.*

ACENTO *m. accent, accent mark.*
Escreva o acento circunflexo, e não o agudo. *Write a circumflex accent, not an acute one.*
acentuar *to accent, to stress.*
acepção *f. acceptation, meaning, sense.*
acêrca (acerca) de *about, concerning.*
Escrevemos-lhe acêrca de nossa viagem. *We wrote him about our trip.*
acercar *to approach, to enclose.*
acertado *adj. proper, right.*
ACERTAR *to hit the mark, to be right, to accomplish, to set right.*
Acertamos no alvo. *We hit the mark.*
Tenho que acertar o relógio. *I have to set my watch.*
acêrto (acerto) *m. hit; discretion.*
Com acêrto. *Properly.*
acessório *adj. accessory, additional; n. m. accessory.*
ACHAR *to find, to discover; to think, to believe.*
Não achei o livro. *I did not find the book.*
Acho que êle não vem. *I believe he is not coming.*
Acho que sim. *I think so.*
acidental *adj. accidental, incidental.*
ACIDENTE *m. accident.*
Foi um acidente. *It was an accident.*
ácido *adj. acid, sour; n. m. acid.*
ACIMA *above, up.*
Êles (Eles) foram pela rua acima. *They went up the street.*
Acima de tudo. *Above all.*
acionista (accionista) *m. and f. stockholder, shareholder.*
aclamar *to acclaim, to proclaim, to applaud.*
aclarar *to explain, to make clear, to clear up; to illuminate.*
aclimar *to acclimate.*
aço *m. steel.*
acolá *there, to that place.*
Cá e acolá. *Here and there.*
ACOLHER *to receive, to welcome; to heed.*
ACOLHIDA *f. welcome, reception.*
Todos tiveram boa acolhida. *They all received a good welcome.*
acomodar *to accommodate.*
ACOMPANHAR *to accompany, to escort, to attend.*
Queremos que êle (ele) nos acompanhe. *We want him to accompany us.*
ACONSELHAR *to advise, to recommend.*
Êles (Eles) me aconselham estudar mais. *They advise me to study more.*
ACONTECER *to happen, to take place.*
Não aconteceu nada. *Nothing happened.*
ACONTECIMENTO *m. event, happening.*
ACORDAR *to awake; to come to an agreement.*
Êle (Ele) ainda não acordou. *He didn't wake up yet.*
acordeão *m. accordion.*
ACÔRDO (ACORDO) *m. agreement, accord.*
Chegamos a um acôrdo com êles (eles). *We came to an agreement with them.*
ACOSTUMADO *adj. accustomed, used to; usual.*
Estamos acostumados a deitar-nos tarde. *We are used to going to bed late.*
ACOSTUMAR *to accustom, to be in the habit of.*
AÇOUGUE *butcher's shop, meat market.*
AÇOUGUEIRO *m. butcher.*
acre *adj. sour, bitter; n. m. acre.*
ACREDITAR *to believe; to believe in.*
Não acredito nisso. *I don't believe in that.*
Você acredita? *Do you believe it?*
AÇÚCAR *m. sugar.*
açucena *f. Easter lily.*
açude *m. dam, reservoir.*

acudir *to assist, to help, to run to help.*

acumulador *m. storage battery, accumulator.*

acumular *to accumulate, to collect.*

acusação *f. accusation, charge, indictment.*

acusado *adj. accused, charged.*

acusar *to accuse, to charge; to acknowledge.*
Acusamos o recebimento de sua carta. *We acknowledge the receipt of your letter.*

adaptação *f. adaptation.*

adaptar *to adapt, to adjust.*

adequado *adj. adequate, proper.*

aderente *adj. adherent, attached.*

aderir *to adhere; to unite, to join.*

adestramento *m. training.*

adestrar *to train, to instruct.*

ADEUS *good-by, farewell.*

adiantado *adj. advanced, ahead.*

ADIANTAR(-SE) *to advance, to get ahead; to be fast (of clock).*
Meu relógio (se) adianta. *My watch is fast.*
Não adianta. *It doesn't do any good.*

ADIANTE *ahead, forward.*
Adiante! *Go on!*

adiar *to postpone, to defer.*

adição *f. addition, sum; bill, check (restaurant).*

adicional *adj. additional.*

adido *m. attaché.*

adivinha *f. puzzle, riddle; fortuneteller.*

adivinhar *to guess, to find out; to predict.*
Acho que você nunca adivinha. *I think you'll never guess.*

adivinho *m. fortuneteller.*

adjetivo (adjectivo) *m. adjective.*

adjunto *adj. joined; n. m. adjunct, assistant, deputy.*

administração *f. administration.*

administrador *m. administrator, manager.*

administrar *to administer, to manage.*

admiração *f. admiration, wonder, surprise.*

admirador *m. admirer.*

admirar *to admire; to be surprised.*
Não é de admirar. *It's not surprising.*

admirável *adj. admirable, wonderful.*

ADMISSÃO *f. admission, entrance.*
Exame de admissão. *Entrance examination.*

ADMITIR *to admit, to accept, to grant.*

adoção *f. adoption.*

adoecer *to become ill.*

adolescência *f. adolescence.*

adoração *f. adoration, worship.*

adorar *to adore, to worship; to like very much.*

adorável *adj. adorable.*

ADORMECER *to put to sleep; to fall asleep.*

adornar *to adorn, to dress, to ornament.*

adotar (adoptar) *to adopt.*

adquirir *to acquire, to get.*

aduaneiro *adj. customs, of customs; n. m. customhouse officer.*

adulador *m. flatterer.*

adular *to flatter.*

adultério *m. adultery.*

adulto *adj. adult; n. m. adult.*

advérbio *m. adverb.*

adversário *adj. adverse; n. m. opponent, adversary.*

adversidade *f. adversity.*

advertência *f. warning, notice.*
Você recebeu a advertência? *Did you receive the warning?*

advertir *to warn, to advise.*

advogado *m. lawyer, attorney.*

aéreo *adj. aerial, air.*
Por via aérea. *By airmail.*

aeródromo *m. airport.*

aeronáutica *f. aeronautics.*

aeroplano *m. airplane.*

aeroporto *m. airport.*

afã *m. anxiety, toil.*

afanar *to work hard; to steal* Ⓑ.

afastado *adj. apart, distant.*

afastar *to separate, to remove.*

afeção, afecção (afecção) *f. affection, disease.*

afeição *f. affection, fondness.*

afetar (afectar) *to affect, to pretend.*

afeto (afecto) *adj. affectionate, friendly; n. m. affection, friendship.*

afetuoso (afectuoso) *adj. affecionate, kind.*

afiar *to sharpen; to make pointed.*

aficionado *adj. fond, enthusiastic; n. m. fan (sports), follower.*

afilhado *m. godchild, protégé.*

afiliado *adj. affiliated.*

afiliar *to affiliate.*

afinal *finally, at last.*
Afinal de contas. *After all.*

afirmação *f. affirmation.*

afirmar *to affirm, to state.*

afirmativamente *affirmatively.*

afixar *(x = ks) to fix, to fasten, to post (posters, etc.).*

aflição *f. affliction, distress, grief, agony.*

afligir-se *to grieve, to worry.*
Não se aflija. *Don't worry.*

aflito *adj. grieved, worried, distressed.*

afogar (-se) *to drown, to suffocate, to stifle.*
Êle se afoga em pouca água. *It doesn't take much to bother him.*

aforismo *m. maxim, aphorism.*

AFORTUNADAMENTE *fortunately, luckily.*

AFORTUNADO *adj. fortunate, lucky, happy.*

afrontar *to affront, to insult; to strike, to meet.*

afundamento *m. sinking.*

afundar *to sink.*

agarrar *to grasp, to hold, to seize.*

agasalhar *to receive, to welcome, to shelter.*

agência *f. agency, bureau, office.*

agenda *f. agenda, memorandum, memorandum notebook.*

agente *adj. acting; n. m. agent.*

ágil *adj. agile, quick.*

agir *to act, to do.*

agitação *f. agitation, commotion, trouble.*

agitar *to agitate, to disturb, to shake.*

agonia *f. agony, great grief, suffering.*

AGORA *now, at the present time.*
Vamos agora. *We are going now.*
Agora mesmo. *Right now.*
Agora não. *Not now.*

AGÔSTO (AGOSTO) *m. August.*

AGRADAR *to please, to like.*
Isso não me agrada. *I don't like that.*

AGRADÁVEL *adj. pleasant, agreeable, nice.*
Ela é muito agradável. *She is very nice.*

AGRADECER *to be grateful (for), to thank.*
Agradeço muito a sua bondade. *I thank you for your kindness.*

AGRADECIDO *adj. grateful, thankful.*
Fico-lhe muito agradecido. *I am very grateful to you.*

agradecimento *m. gratitude, thanks.*

agrado *m. pleasure, liking, satisfaction.*

agravar *to aggravate, to make worse.*

agregar *to bring together, to accumulate.*

agressão *f. aggression, offense.*

agressivo *adj. aggressive.*

agressor *m. aggressor.*

agrícola *adj. agricultural.*

agricultor *m. farmer.*

agricultura *f. agriculture, farming.*

agrupamento *m. grouping, group.*

agrupar *to group, to gather.*

ÁGUA *f. water.*
Água corrente. *Running water.*
Água doce. *Fresh water.*
Água mineral. *Mineral water.*
Água potável. *Drinking water.*
Água gelada. *Ice water.*

aguaceiro *m. shower (rain).*

agua-marinha *f. (pl. águas-marinhas) aquamarine.*

aguardar *to wait for, to expect, to observe (laws).*
Aguardo a sua resposta. *I'm waiting for your answer.*

aguardente *m. brandy, a strong drink.*

agudo *adj. sharp; acute; witty.*

agüentar (aguentar) *to stand, to bear, to put up with.*
Não agüento mais. *I can't stand any more.*

águia *f. eagle; m. talented person; an untrustworthy person* Ⓑ.

AGULHA *f. needle.*
Isso é procurar agulha em palheiro. *That's like looking for a needle in a haystack.*

ah! *ah! oh!*

ai! *oh! (exclamation of surprise, pain, etc.).*
Ai de mim! *Poor me!*

Aí *there, over there (near you).*
Aí mesmo. *Right there.*
Ponha-o aí. *Put it there.*
Por aí. *That way. Over there.*

AINDA *still, yet.*
Êle (Ele) ainda nos escreve. *He still writes us.*
Êle chegou? Ainda não. *Did he arrive? Not yet.*

AINDA QUE *although.*

aipo *m. celery.*

ajoelhar(-se) *to kneel.*

AJUDA *f. help, assistance.*

ajudante *m. and f. assistant, helper.*

AJUDAR *to help, to assist, to aid.*
Você quer que ajude? *Do you want me to help?*

ajustar *to arrange, to fix, to settle.*
Vamos ajustar contas. *Let's settle accounts.*

ala *f. wing, row.*

alarde *m. show, display, parade.*

alargar *to enlarge, to widen.*

alarma *f. alarm.*

alarmar *to alarm.*

alarmar-se *to become frightened.*

alarme *m. alarm.*

alavanca *f. lever.*

albergue *m. inn, shelter.*

albricoque *m. apricot.*

álbum *m. album.*

alcachôfra (alcachofa, alcachofra) *f. artichoke.*

alcançar *to reach, to attain, to catch up with, to be enough.*
Não o alcancei. *I did not catch up with him.*

alcance *m. extent, reach, scope.*
Está ao alcance de todos. *It is within reach of all.*

alçar *to raise, to lift.*

alcatrão *m. tar, pitch.*

álcool *m. alcohol.*

Alcorão *m. the Koran.*

alcunha *f. nickname.*

aldeia *f. village.*

aldraba, aldrava *f. latch, knocker (of door).*

alecrim *m. rosemary.*

alegação f. allegation, claim.

alegar to allege, to claim.

alegrar to cheer, to make happy.

alegre adj. cheerful, happy, gay.

alegria f. gaiety, joy.

aleijado adj. lame, crippled.

aleijar to cripple, to maim.

ALÉM beyond, besides, farther.
   Além disso. Besides, furthermore.
   Muito além. Much farther.

alemão adj. German; n. m. German.

alento m. breath, courage.

alerta adj. alert, vigilant.

alfabeto m. alphabet.

alface f. lettuce.
   Salada de alface. Lettuce salad.

alfaiataria f. tailor shop.

alfaiate m. tailor.

alfândega f. customhouse.

alfinête (alfinete) m. pin.
   Alfinete de gravata. Tiepin.

algarismo m. number, figure.

algibeira f. pocket.

algo some, something; adv. somewhat.

ALGODÃO m. cotton.
   Tecido de algodão. Cotton fabric.

ALGUÉM somebody, someone.
   Alguém entrou. Somebody came in.

ALGUM adj. some, any; pl. a few.
   Alguma coisa. Something.
   Algum dia. Some day.
   Algumas vêzes (vezes). Sometimes.
   Quero alguns. I want a few.

alheio adj. belonging to somebody else; foreign; alienated.

alho m. garlic.

ALI there, over there (away from person spoken to).
   Está ali. It's over there.
   Ali mesmo. Right there.
   Êle desapareceu por ali. He disappeared that way.

aliança f. alliance, association; wedding ring.

aliás however, besides.

alicate m. pliers.

ALIMENTO m. food, nourishment.

alisar to smooth (out).

alistar to enlist, to enroll.

aliviar to alleviate, to mitigate.

ALMA f. soul, heart, spirit, essence.
   Não apareceu nenhuma alma. Not a soul (person) appeared.
   Êle (Ele) tem boa alma. He has a good heart (is kind).

almanaque m. almanac.

almirante m. admiral.

ALMOÇAR to have lunch.
   Sempre almoçamos ao meio-dia. We always have lunch at noon.

ALMÔÇO (ALMOÇO) m. lunch.
   Primeiro almoço. Breakfast Ⓟ.
   Pequeno almoço. Breakfast Ⓟ.

almôndega f. meatball.

almotolia f. oil can.

alô! hello!

alojamento m. lodging.

alojar to lodge, to billet.

alparca, alpargata, alpercata f. sandal.

alteração f. alteration, change, disturbance.

alterar to alter, to change, to disturb.

alternar to alternate.

alternativa f. alternative, choice.

altitude f. altitude.

altivo adj. haughty, proud, lofty.

ALTO adj. high, tall; loud; n. m. top, height.
   Êle (Ele) é alto e magro. He is tall and thin.
   Aconteceu no alto mar. It happened on the high seas.
   Fale mais alto, por favor. Speak louder, please.
   A vida tem muitos altos e baixos. Life has many ups and downs.

alto! halt! stop!

alto-falante m. loudspeaker.

altura f. height, point (of time).
   Não sei a altura. I don't know its height.
   Nessa altura. At that point.

aludir to allude to.

ALUGAR to rent, to hire.
   Aluguei a casa para o verão. I rented the house for the summer.
   Alugam-se quartos. Rooms for rent.

ALUGUEL m. rent, hiring.
   Quanto é o aluguel? How much is the rent?

alumiado adj. illuminated, light.

alumiar to illuminate, to light (up).

alumínio m. aluminum.

ALUNO m. pupil, student.
   Você conhece êsse (esse) aluno? Do you know that student?

alva f. dawn.

alvo m. target, aim, white.
   Êle (Ele) deu no alvo. He hit the target.

ama f. housekeeper, nursemaid, governess.

AMABILIDADE f. amiability, kindliness.

amado adj. loved, beloved.

amador adj. loving; n. m. amateur, fan.

amadurecer to ripen.

amaldiçoado adj. cursed, damned.

amaldiçoar to curse, to damn.

AMANHÃ m. tomorrow.
   Êles (Eles) chegam amanhã. They are arriving tomorrow.
   Vou depois de amanhã. I'm going the day after tomorrow.
   Até amanhã. See you tomorrow.

amanhecer to dawn.

amante m. and f. lover.

AMAR to love, to like.

AMARELO yellow.

amargo bitter.

amarra f. chain, cable.

amarrar to tie (up), to fasten, to moor.

amassar to knead, to mix, to beat.

AMÁVEL adj. kind, amiable.
   O senhor é muito amável. You are very kind.

ambição f. ambition.

ambicioso adj. ambitious.

ambiente m. atmosphere, milieu.

AMBOS both.
   Fico com ambos. I'll take both.

ambulância f. ambulance.

ameaça f. threat.

ameaçar to threaten.

ameixa (x = sh) f. plum.

ameixa (x = sh) **passada** or **preta** f. prune.

amêndoa f. almond.

amendoim m. peanut.

ameno adj. pleasant, gentle, mild.

AMERICANO adj. American; n. m. American.

amido, âmido (amido) m. starch.

AMIGO m. friend.
   Apresento(-lhe) o meu amigo, João. I introduce my friend John (to you).
   Meu caro amigo: My dear friend:
   Você é amigo da onça! You're a fine friend! (disapprovingly).

amiúde often.

amizade f. friendship.

amo m. master.

amolação f. sharpening; bother, annoyance Ⓑ.
   Desculpe a amolação. Please excuse the bother.

amolar to sharpen; to bother, annoy Ⓑ.
   Não me amole com isso! Don't bother me with that!

AMOR m. love, affection, a lovely person or thing.
   O amor é cego. Love is blind.
   Julieta é um amor. Julie is a lovely person.

amostra f. sample.
   Êle (Ele) me deu (deu-me) uma amostra. He gave me a sample.

amparar to protect, to shelter.

ampliação f. amplification, enlargement.

ampliar to amplify, to enlarge.

amplo adj. ample.

ampola f. blister.

amputar to amputate, to cut off.

analfabeto m. illiterate.

analisar to analyse.

análise f. analysis.

ananás (abacaxi Ⓑ **)** m. pineapple.

anão m., **anã** f. dwarf.

anatomia f. anatomy.

âncora f. anchor.

ANDAR to walk, to go, to be.
   Andamos à casa de João. We walked to John's house.
   Anda! Get going!
   Não ando muito bem hoje. I don't feel very well today.

andorinha f. swallow.

anedota f. anecdote.

anel m. ring, link.
   Êle (Ele) esqueceu o anel de casamento. He forgot the wedding ring.

ângulo m. angle, corner.

angústia f. anguish, distress.

animado adj. lively, animated.
   Desenho animado. Animated cartoon.

animal m. animal.

animar to animate, to encourage.

ânimo m. courage, mind.

aniversário m. anniversary, birthday.
   Quando é o seu aniversário? When is your birthday?

anjo m. angel.

ANO m. year.
   Quantos anos você tem? How old are you?
   Tenho vinte e dois anos. I am twenty-two years old.
   Quando você faz anos? When is your birthday?
   Ano bissexto. Leap year.
   Ano bom. New Year.
   Ano nôvo (novo). New Year.
   Feliz ano nôvo (novo)! Happy New Year!
   Em que ano aconteceu? In what year did it happen?
   Vamos todos os anos. We go every year.
   Êles (Eles) não vão no ano que vem. They are not going next year.
   Elas foram no ano passado. They went last year.

anoitecer to become dark.
   Ao anoitecer. At nightfall.

anônimo (anónimo) adj. anonymous.

anormal adj. abnormal.

anotar to note, to record, to comment.

ânsia f. anxiety, anguish, sorrow.

ansiedade f. anxiety, care, concern, yearning.

ansioso adj. anxious, desirous.
   Estamos muito ansiosos para fazer a viagem. We are very anxious to take the trip.

ante before.

antecedente *adj., antecedent; n. m. antecedent.*

antecessor *m. predecessor.*
 Antecessores. *Ancestors.*

antecipação *f. anticipation.*

antecipado *adj. anticipated, expected.*

antecipar *to anticipate, to expect, to precipitate.*

antemão, de antemão *beforehand.*

antena *f. antenna.*

anteontem *day before yesterday.*

antepassado *adj. past; -ados n. pl. ancestors.*

anterior *adj. anterior; previous, former, preceding.*

ANTES *before, rather.*
 Quanto antes. *As soon as possible.*
 Telefone-me antes de partir. *Phone me before you leave.*
 Antes tarde do que nunca. *Better late than never.*

ANTIGO *adj. old, ancient; former.*
 Lisboa antiga. *Old Lisbon.*

antiguidade *f. antiquity, ancient times.*

antipatia *f. antipathy.*

antipático *adj. unpleasant.*

antiquado *adj. old, obsolete.*

anual *adj. yearly.*

anular *to cancel, to void.*

ANUNCIAR *to announce, to advertise.*
 Anunciaram-no ontem. *They announced it yesterday.*

ANÚNCIO *m. announcement, notice, sign, advertisement.*
 Sempre leio os anuncios nos jornais. *I always read the ads in the papers.*

AO *(contr. of* **a** + **o***) to the, at the; on, when.*
 Vamos ao teatro. *We are going to the theatre.*
 Ao anoitecer. *At nightfall.*
 Ao contrário. *On the contrary.*
 Ao chegarem, disseram-nos tudo. *When they arrived they told us everything.*

AONDE *where.*
 Aonde foram? *Where did you go?*

apagador *m. extinguisher, eraser.*

apagar *to extinguish, to erase.*

apaixonado *(x = sh) adj. in love.*

apaixonar-se *(x = sh) to fall in love.*
 Apaixonaram-se. *They fell in love.*

apanhar *to catch, to get, to take, to pick.*
 Apanhei um resfriado. *I caught a cold.*
 Êles (Eles) foram apanhados dois dias mais tarde. *They were caught two days later.*

aparador *m. sideboard, buffet.*

APARECER *to appear, to show up, to turn up.*
 Êle (Ele) não apareceu ontem. *He didn't show up yesterday.*

aparelho *m. apparatus, device; phone* (B).
 Não tenho aparelho de rádio. *I don't have a radio set.*
 Quem está no aparelho? (B) *Who is on the phone?*

aparência *f. appearance.*

aparentar *to seem, to appear, to feign.*

aparente *adj. apparent, evident.*

apartado *adj. apart, remote.*

apartamento *m. apartment, separation.*

apartar *to separate, to set apart.*

apelar *to appeal.*

apelido *m. surname, nickname.*

apenas *only, hardly.*
 Êle (Ele) apenas me falou. *He hardly spoke to me.*

aperitivo *m. apéritif.*

apertado *adj. tight, close.*

APESAR DE *in spite of.*
 Apesar de ser tarde, vamos. *In spite of the fact that it is late, we are going.*

apetecer *to long for, to have an appetite for.*

apetite *m. appetite, hunger.*
 Quando ouvi isso, perdi o apetite. *When I heard that, I lost my appetite.*

apinhar *to crowd.*

apitar *to whistle.*

apito *m. whistle.*

aplaudir *to applaud.*

aplauso *m. applause.*

aplicação *f. application, use.*

aplicado *adj. applied; industrious, studious*

aplicar *to apply.*

aplicar-se *to apply oneself, to be diligent.*

apoderar-se de *to take possession of.*

apôdo (apodo) *m. nickname.*

apoiar *to support, to favor, to defend, to aid, to lean.*

apoio *m. support.*

apólice *f. policy, bond, share.*
 Apólice de seguro. *Insurance policy.*

apontar *to sharpen; to point out, to indicate.*

aportuguesar *to render in Portuguese.*

após *after, behind.*

aposentar *to lodge, to pension; to dwell.*

aposta *f. bet.*

apostar *to bet.*
 Quanto você apostou? *How much did you bet?*

apóstrofo *m. apostrophe.*

aprazer *to please.*

apreciar *to appreciate, to value.*

apreço (apreço) *appreciation, esteem.*

APRENDER *to learn.*
 Paulo não aprendeu muito português. *Paul did not learn very much Portuguese.*
 Ela o aprenderá de cor. *She will learn it by heart.*

APRESENTAR *to present, to introduce.*
 Apresento(-lhe) os meus cumprimentos. *I send you my regards.*
 Vou apresentar(-lhe) o meu amigo Carlos Costa. *I'm going to introduce my friend Carlos Costa to you.*

apressar-se *to hurry.*

apropriar *to appropriate.*

aprovação *f. approval, praise; passing grade.*

aprovado *adj. approved; passed (in an examination).*
 João não foi aprovado. *John did not pass (was not passed.)*

aprovar *to approve; to pass (a student in an examination).*

aproveitar *to make good use of, to profit.*
 Êle (Ele) aproveita tudo. *He makes good use of everything.*

aproveitar-se de *to take advantage of, to make good use of.*
 Êle (Ele) se aproveitou da oportunidade para escapar. *He took advantage of the opportunity to escape.*

aprovisionar *to supply.*

aproximar *(x = s) to approach.*

aptidão *f. aptitude, ability.*

apto *adj. apt, able.*

apunhalar *to stab.*

apurar *to improve, to select, to settle.*

apuro *m. precision, elegance; plight.*
 Êle (Ele) se veste com apuro. *He dresses very well.*
 Agora estamos em apuros. *We're in a mess now.*

aquarela *f. watercolor.*

aquecedor *m. heater.*

aquecer *to heat, to warm.*

aquecimento *m. heating.*

AQUELA *that, that one; the former.*
 Aquela jovem dança muito bem. *That girl*

dances very well.
 Esta cadeira é mais nova que aquela. *This chair is newer than that one.*

AQUÊLE (AQUELE) *that, that one; the former.*
 Não quero aquêle prefiro êste. *I don't want that one (over there); I prefer this one.*
 José e Eduardo chegaram ontem. Êste (Eduardo) me telefonou, mas aquêle (José) ainda não comunicou comigo. *Joseph and Edward arrived yesterday. The former has not communicated with me yet, but the latter telephoned me.*

AQUI *here, in this place.*
 Ficamos aqui? *Do we stay here?*
 Aqui mesmo. *Right here.*
 Daqui a nove dias. *In nine days.*
 Venha por aqui. *Come this way.*

aquilo *that (neuter form).*

AR *m. air, wind; aspect, look.*
 Vamos sair ao ar livre. *Let's go out into the open air.*
 Quero quarto com ar condicionado. *I want an air-conditioned room.*
 Êle (Ele) tem ar de inteligente. *He has an intelligent look.*

arado *m. plow.*

arame *m. wire.*

aranha *f. spider.*

arar *to plow.*

arbitrar *to arbitrate.*

árbitro *m. arbiter, umpire, referee.*

arbusto *m. bush, shrub.*

arca *f. arc, chest.*

arcar *to arch, to bow.*

arcebispo *m. archbishop.*

arco *m. arc, arch.*

arco-íris *rainbow.*

arder *to burn, to glow.*

área *f. area, region.*

areia *f. sand.*

arengar *to harangue.*

argamassa *f. mortar.*

argola *f. ring; door knocker.*

argumento *m. argument, reason, topic, plot.*
 Êsse (Esse) argumento não me convence. *That argument does not convince me.*

árido *adj. arid, dry.*

aritmética *f. arithmetic.*

arma *f. weapon, arm.*
 Não temos armas de fogo. *We have no firearms .*

armada *f. fleet.*

armamento *m. armament.*

armar *to arm.*

armário *m. cupboard, closet.*

armazém *m. grocery store, warehouse.*

armistício *m. armistice.*

arquiteto (arquitecto) *m. architect.*

arquitetura (arquitectura) *f. architecture.*

arquivo *m. record, filing cabinet.*

arrancar *to pull out, to tear out, to start (as a motor).*
 O motor não arrancava. *The motor wouldn't start.*

arranha-céu *m., pl.* **arranha-céus**, *skyscraper.*
 Há muitos arranha-céus em Nova Iorque. *There are many skyscrapers in New York.*

arranhar *to scratch.*

ARRANJAR *to arrange.*
 Não se preocupe, nós arranjamos tudo. *Don't worry, we'll arrange everything.*

arranjo *m. arrangement.*

arrastar *to haul, to drag.*

arrebatar *to grab, to carry off.*

arrebentar *to burst, to explode.*

arredores *m. pl. outskirts, suburbs.*

arregalar *to open the eyes wide, to stare.*

arrendar *to rent, to hire.*

arrepender-se *to repent, to be sorry for.*

arrepiar *to frighten, to terrify.*

arriba *up.*

arribar *to arrive, to put in to port.*

arriscar *to risk, to dare.*
  Quem não arrisca, não petisca. *Nothing ventured, nothing gained.*

arrogante *adj. arrogant.*

arroio *m. brook.*

arrojar *to throw, to hurl.*

arrolhar *to cork.*

arroz *m. rice.*

arruinar *to ruin, to destroy.*

arrumar *to arrange, to put in order.*
  Ainda não arrumaram as malas? *Haven't you packed your bags yet?*
  Ela arruma tudo. *She keeps everything in order.*

arte *f. art, skill; way.*
  É uma verdadeira obra de arte. *It is a true work of art.*
  Belas artes. *Fine arts.*

ártico (árctico) *adj. arctic.*

artigo *m. article.*
  Não gostei do artigo de fundo. *I did not like the main editorial (or main article).*

artista *m. and f. artist.*

árvore *f. tree; shaft.*
  Árvore de Natal. *Christmas tree.*
  O tronco da árvore. *The trunk of a tree.*
  A árvore não tem fôlhas (folhas). *The tree doesn't have any leaves.*

ás *m. ace.*

asa *f. wing.*
  Vamos cortar-lhe as asas. *We're going to clip his wings.*

ascender *to rise.*

ascensão *f. ascension, elevation.*

ascensor *m. elevator.*

asfalto *m. asphalt.*

asilo *m. asylum, shelter.*

asneira *f. foolish thing, nonsense.*
  Mas isso é asneira! *But that's nonsense!*

asno *m. ass, fool.*

aspas *f. pl. quotation marks.*

aspecto, aspeto (aspecto, aspeito) *m. aspect, appearance.*

aspirador de pó *m. vacuum cleaner.*

aspirante *m. and f. aspirant, candidate; m. cadet.*
  Aspirante de marinha. *Midshipman.*

aspirina *f. aspirin.*

assado *adj. roast, roasted, baked.*
  Frango assado. *Roast chicken.*
  Assado de carneiro. *Roast lamb.*

assaltar *to assault, to attack.*

assalto *m. assault, attack.*

assar *to roast, to broil, to burn.*

assassinar *to assassinate, to murder, to kill.*

assassinato *m. assassination, murder.*

assassínio *m. assassination, murder.*

assassino *m. assassin, murderer.*

asseado *adj. clean, neat.*

assear *to clean, to tidy up.*

assear-se *to be neat, to dress well.*

assegurar *to insure; to secure, to fasten; to assure; to affirm, to assert.*

assembléia (assembleia) *f. assembly, meeting.*
  Assembléia legislativa. *Legislative assembly.*

assemelhar-se *to be similar, to resemble.*

assentar *to set, to place, to seat, to adjust.*

assento *m. seat, chair; place; record, entry.*

ASSIM *so, thus, in this manner, therefore, so that.*
  Assim espero. *I hope so.*
  Você deve fazê-lo assim. *You should do it this way.*
  Não é assim, asseguro-lhe. *I assure you that's not so.*
  Assim, assim. *So-so.*
  Assim que êle chegar, falaremos. *We'll talk as soon as he arrives.*

assinado *adj. signed.*

assinar *to sign, to assign, to subscribe.*
  Faça o favor de assinar o cheque. *Please sign the check.*

assinatura *f. subscription, signature.*
  Quero uma assinatura anual. *I would like a year's subscription.*

assistir *to attend, to be present; to help, to assist.*
  Êle (Ele) não assistiu à aula. *He did not attend (the) class.*

assoar *to blow the nose.*

assobiar *to whistle.*

assobio *m. whistle, whistling.*

associação *f. association, company, society, club.*

assomar *to arise, to appear.*

assomar-se *to become angry.*

assombrado *adj. astonished, frightened.*

assombrar *to astonish, to frighten.*

assombro *m. astonishment, fright.*

ASSUNTO *m. subject, matter, business.*
  Preciso de mais detalhes sôbre (sobre) êste (este) assunto. *I need more information on this matter.*
  Conheço a fundo o assunto. *I am thoroughly acquainted with the matter.*
  Qual é o assunto dessa peça? *What is that play about?*

assustar *to startle, to frighten.*

asterisco *m. asterisk.*

astro *m. star.*

astucioso *adj. cunning, astute.*

atacado *adj. attacked.*
  Por atacado. *Wholesale.*

atacar *to attack, to assail.*

ataque *m. attack.*

atar *to tie, to tighten.*

atarefado *adj. busy, occupied.*

atas *f. pl. proceedings, minutes (of a meeting).*

ataúde *m. coffin, tomb.*

ATÉ *until; as far as; up to; also, even.*
  Até logo. *So long. See you later.*
  Até a vista. *See you soon. See you later.*
  Até amanhã. *See you tomorrow.*
  Até breve. *See you soon.*
  Até segunda. *See you Monday.*
  Fomos até o parque. *We went as far as the park.*
  O elevador sobe até o quinto andar. *The elevator goes up to the fifth floor.*
  Até onde vai êste (este) caminho? *How far does this road go?*

ATENÇÃO *f. attention.*
  Quero chamar a sua atenção para isto. *I want to call your attention to this.*
  Em atenção a sua carta. *With regard to your letter.*
  Atenção! *Watch out!*

atencioso *adj. attentive, thoughtful, polite.*

atender *to attend (to), to take care of; to answer (the telephone).*
  Maria, atenda o telefone, por favor. *Mary, please answer the telephone.*

atentar *to attempt.*

atento *adj. attentive, courteous.*
  Êle (Ele) é muito atento. *He is very attentive.*

  Atento e obrigado. *Very truly yours.*

aterragem *f. landing (aircraft).*

aterrar *to cover with earth; to frighten.*

aterrissagem *f. landing (aircraft).*

aterrissar *to land (aircraft).*

aterrorizar *to terrify, to frighten.*

atestar *to attest.*

atinar *to hit upon, to find out.*

atingir *to attain, to reach.*

atitude *f. attitude, position.*

atividade (actividade) *f. activity.*
  Em plena atividade. *In full swing (activity).*

ativo (activo) *adj. active.*

atlântico *adj. Atlantic.*

atleta *m. and f. athlete.*

atlético *adj. athletic.*

atmosfera *f. atmosphere.*

ATO (ACTO) *m. act, action, deed; meeting.*
  No primeiro ato não acontece nada. *Nothing happens in the first act.*

átomo *m. atom.*

átono *adj. atonic, unaccented.*

ator (actor) *m. actor.*

atormentar *to torment.*

atração (atracção) *f. attraction.*

atracar *to come alongside, to tie up (a ship).*

atraente *adj. attractive.*

atrair *to attract.*

ATRÁS *behind, backward; past; ago.*
  Eu fiquei atrás. *I stayed behind.*
  Êles (Eles) tiveram que voltar para atrás. *They had to turn back.*
  Que há atrás da caixa? (x = sh) *What's behind the box?*

atrasado *adj. behind, backward, late.*
  Os meninos vão chegar atrasados. *The children are going to be late.*
  Parece que meu relógio está atrasado. *It seems my watch is slow.*

atrasar(-se) *to hold back, to delay, to run slow (watch).*

atraso *m. delay.*

atrativo (atractivo) *adj. attractive.*

atravessar *to cross, to pass over; to hinder.*

atrever-se *to dare.*
  Alfredo não se atreveu a fazê-lo. *Alfred did not dare to do it.*

atrevido *adj. daring, bold.*

atribuir *to attribute.*

atriz (actriz) *f. actress.*

atroar *to thunder, to roar.*

atrocidade *f. atrocity.*

atropelar *to step on, to trample, to run over; to abuse.*
  Êle foi atropelado por um automóvel. *He was run over by an automobile.*

atropêlo (atropelo) *m. trampling, running over.*

atroz *adj. atrocious, cruel.*

atuação (actuação) *f. performance, acting.*

ATUAL (ACTUAL) *adj. actual, present.*

atualidade (actualidade) *f. the present, today.*

ATUALMENTE (ACTUALMENTE) *today, nowadays, at the present time.*
  Atualmente êles (eles) estão em São Paulo. *At the present time they are in São Paulo.*

atuar (actuar) *to act, to put into action.*

atum *m. tuna.*

aturdido *adj. bewildered.*

audácia *f. audacity, boldness, presumption.*

audacioso *adj. bold, audacious.*

audição *f. audition.*

auditório *m. auditorium, audience.*

auge *m. height, summit.*

augusto *adj. august, venerable.*

aula *f. class, recitation.*
Hoje não tenho aulas. *I don't have any classes today.*

aumentar *to increase, to augment, to enlarge.*

aumento *m. increase.*
Aumento de preços sem aumento de ordenado, não adianta. *An increase in prices without an increase in salary doesn't help.*

áureo *adj. golden, brilliant.*

aurora *f. dawn, daybreak.*

ausência *f. absence.*

ausentar-se *to be absent, to be away.*

AUSENTE *adj. absent.*

autêntico *adj. authentic, true.*

auto *m. automobile, auto; document; public act; short dramatic work.*

autocarro *m. bus* (P).

automático *adj. automatic.*

automóvel *m. automobile.*

autor *m. author.*

autoridade *f. authority.*

autorização *f. authorization.*

autorizar *to authorize.*

auxiliar (x = s) *to aid, to help; adj. auxiliary.*

auxílio (x = s) *m. help, aid, assistance.*

avaliar *to evaluate, to judge.*

avançado *adj. advanced.*

avançar *to advance, to go ahead, to progress.*

avante *forward.*
Avante! *Forward!*

avaria *f. damage, loss.*

avariado *adj. damaged.*

avariar *to damage.*

avaro *adj. miserly, greedy.*

ave *f. bird, fowl; hail!*
Ave, Maria, cheia de graça. *Hail, Mary, full of grace.*

aveia *f. oat, oats.*

avenida *f. avenue.*

avental *m. apron.*

aventura *f. adventure.*

averiguar *to inquire, to find out, to investigate.*
Averigúe a que horas o trem sai. *Find out (at) what time the train leaves.*

avêsso (avesso) *adj. opposite, contrary.*

avestruz *m. and f. ostrich.*

aviação *f. aviation.*

aviador *m. aviator.*

avião *m. airplane.*

aviar *to get ready, to prescribe (medicine), to supply.*
Numa farmácia aviam receitas. *In a pharmacy they fill prescriptions.*

avisado *adj. notified, advised.*

avisar *to inform, to notify, to let know; to warn.*
Eu o avisarei assim que souber. *I'll notify you as soon as I know.*

aviso *m. notice, warning.*

avistar *to sight, to see.*

avô *m. grandfather.*

avó *f. grandmother.*

azar *m. chance, hazard.*

azeite *m. oil.*
Êle (Ele) sempre deita azeite no fogo. *He's always adding fuel to the fire.*

azeiteira (almotolia) *f. oil can.*

azeitona *f. olive.*

AZUL *blue.*
Gosto mais do vestido azul. *I like the blue dress better.*
Tudo azul! *Everything's fine!*

azulejo *m. glazed tile.*

B

babá *f. nursemaid* (B).

bacalhau *m. codfish.*

bacharel *m. bachelor (school graduate).*

bacia *f. basin.*

báculo *m. staff, rod.*

badalada *f. sound, stroke (of a bell).*

badalar *to ring, to toll.*

bagagem *f. baggage, luggage.*
Onde posso deixar (x = sh) a bagagem? *Where can I leave my luggage?*

bagatela *f. bagatelle, trifle.*

bagunça *f. confusion, mess* (B).

baía *f. bay.*

bailar *to dance.*

baile *m. dance.*

bairro *m. district, neighborhood, suburb.*
Moro no bairro residencial. *I live in the residential district (suburb).*

baixa (x = sh) *f. fall, depreciation (price); casualty.*

BAIXAR (x = sh) *to go (come down); to get (bring) down; to get off; to lower, let down; to drop (fever, temperature, etc.).*
Baixo agora. *I'm coming down now.*
Quando vocês vão baixar os preços? *When are you going to lower prices?*

BAIXO (x = sh) *adj. low; under, below; short.*
Êle (Ele) é baixo e gordo. *He is short and fat.*
Fale mais baixo. *Speak a little more softly.*

bala *f. bullet.*

balança *f. balance, scale; justice.*
Balança de plataforma. *Platform scale.*

balanço *m. swinging, balancing, balance.*
Diga-me o balanço para êste (este) mês. *Give me the balance for this month.*

balar *to bleat.*

balbuciar *to stutter, to stammer.*

balbúrdia *f. disorder, confusion.*

balcão *m. balcony; counter.*

balde *m. pail, bucket.*

baldear *to bail (water); to tranship; to transfer; to change trains.*
Temos que baldear antes de chegar ao Rio? *Do we have to change trains before we arrive in Rio?*

baleia *f. whale.*

balneário *m. bathhouse, health resort.*

baluarte *m. bulwark, stronghold; shelter.*

bambu *m. bamboo.*

banal *adj. banal, trite, commonplace.*

banana *f. banana.*

banca *f. table, desk, stand; board (examining).*
Comprei na banca (no quiosque) de jornais. *I bought it at the newsstand.*

banco *m. bank (commercial); bank, bar, reef; bench.*
Hoje o banco está fechado. *Today the bank is closed.*
Elas se sentaram no banco. *They sat down on the bench.*

banda *f. band; strip, stripe.*
Aqui vem uma banda de música. *Here comes a brass band.*

bandeira *f. flag, pennant, banner; colonial exploratory expedition* (B).

bandeirante *m. member of a bandeira* (B).

bandeja *f. tray, platter.*

bandido *m. bandit, robber.*

bando *m. band, gang; flock.*

banhar(-se) *to bathe, to wash.*

banheira *f. bathtub.*

BANHEIRO *m. bathroom* (B).

BANHO *m. bath, bathing.*
Gosto tomar banho de chuveiro. *I like to take a shower.*
Casa de banho (P). *Bathroom.*

banir *to banish, to forbid.*

banqueiro *m. banker.*

bar *m. bar, tavern.*

baralhar *to shuffle (cards); to mix up.*

barata *f. cockroach.*

BARATO *adj. cheap, inexpensive.*

barba *f. chin; beard.*
Eu ainda não fiz a barba. *I haven't shaved yet.*
Pincel de barba. *Shaving brush.*

bárbaro *adj. barbaric, coarse, brutal.*

barbear *to shave* (**barbeio**, *etc.*).

barbear-se *to shave (oneself)* (**barbeio-me**, *etc.*).
Primeiro vou barbear-me. *First I'm going to shave.*
Sempre me barbeio antes de sair de casa. *I always shave before leaving home.*

barbearia *f. barbershop.*

barbeiro *m. barber.*

barbudo *adj. heavily bearded.*

barca *f. boat, barge.*

barco *m. boat, ship, vessel.*
Barco a motor. *Motorboat.*
Barco a vapor. *Steamship.*
Barco a vela. *Sailboat.*

barômetro (barómetro) *m. barometer.*

barquinha *f. small boat; log (of ship).*

barra *f. bar, ingot; strip, band; sandbar.*

barraca *f. hut, tent, shelter.*

barragem *f. dam, barrier.*

barranco *m. ravine, gully; precipice.*

barrar *to make metal bars; to bar, to obstruct.*

barreira *f. barrier, bar, obstruction.*

barriga *f. belly, stomach.*

barril *m. barrel, cask.*

barro *m. mud, clay.*

barulho *m. noise.*
Meninos, isso é muito barulho. *Children, that's too much noise.*

base *f. base, basis.*

basear *to base.*

básico *adj. basic.*

basquetbol *m. basketball.*

BASTANTE *enough, sufficient; rather.*
Êle (Ele) não tem bastante dinheiro. *He does not have enough money.*
Acho bastante caro. *I think that's rather expensive.*

bastão *m. cane, walking stick.*

BASTAR *to suffice, to be enough.*
Isso basta. *That's enough.*
Basta! *Enough! Stop!*

bata *f. dressing gown; smock.*

batalha *f. battle, combat, fight.*

batalhão *m. battalion.*

batalhar *to battle, to fight, to struggle.*

batata *f. potato.*
Batatas fritas. *Fried potatoes.*
Purê de batatas. *Mashed potatoes.*
Batata-doce. *Sweet potato.*

BATER *to beat, to strike; to knock.*
Quem bate à porta? *Who's knocking at the door?*

bateria *f. battery.*
Bateria de cozinha. *Kitchen utensils.*

batida *f. blow, knock; collision; a mixed drink with a brandy base* (B).

batismo (baptismo) *m. baptism, christening.*

batizar (baptizar) *to baptise, to christen.*

batuque *m. Afro-Brazilian dance* (B).

baú m. *trunk, chest.*

baunilha f. *vanilla.*

bazar m. *bazaar, store.*

bebê (bebé) m. *baby.*

bêbedo adj. *drunk, intoxicated; m. drunkard.*

BEBER *to drink.*

bebida f. *drink, beverage.*
Êle (Ele) se deu à bebida. *He took to drink.*

beco m. *alley, lane, side street.*
Beco sem saída. *Blind alley.*

beijar *to kiss.*

beijo m. *kiss.*

beira f. *brink, edge, bank.*

beira-mar f. *seashore, coast.*

beleza f. *beauty.*

bélico adj. *bellicose, warlike.*

belicoso adj. *bellicose, warlike; hostile.*

BELO adj. *beautiful.*
Ela é bela! *She is beautiful!*
O belo sexo (x = ks). *The fair sex.*
As belas artes. *The fine arts.*

BEM *well, right; m. loved one, darling.*
Você está bem? *Are you all right?*
Muito bem, obrigado. *Very well, thank you.*
Não muito bem. *Not very well.*
Passe bem. *Good luck. Good-by.*
Está bem. *All right. O.K.*
Bem educado. *Well brought up.*
É bem longe. *It's quite far.*
É bem pouco. *It's not very much.*
Por que chora, meu bem? *Why are you crying, my darling?*

bem-estar m. *well-being, welfare.*

bênção f. *blessing, benediction.*

bendito adj. *blessed.*

bendizer *to praise; to bless.*

beneficiar *to benefit, to profit.*

beneficiário adj. *beneficiary.*

benefício m. *benefit, profit, advantage.*

benfeitor m. *benefactor.*

bengala f. *cane, walking stick.*

benigno adj. *kind.*

bens m. pl. *property, possessions.*

bento adj. *blessed, holy.*

benzer *to bless.*

benzer-se *to make the sign of the cross.*
Ela se benzeu ao entrar na igreja. *She made the sign of the cross on entering the church.*

berço m. *cradle, crib; birthplace, birth.*
Desde o berço até à morte, o estado entra na nossa vida. *The state enters our life, from birth to death.*

berinjela f. *eggplant.*

berrar *to roar, to shout.*

berro m. *roar, shout.*

bêsta (besta) f. *beast; fool.*

besteira f. *foolish thing, nonsense.*
Êles (Eles) só dizem besteiras. *They speak nothing but nonsense.*

beterraba f. *beet.*

bexiga (x = sh) f. *bladder; smallpox.*

bezerro m. *calf.*

Bíblia f. *Bible.*

bibliografia f. *bibliography.*

biblioteca f. *library.*

bicarbonato m. *bicarbonate.*

bicho m. *animal, insect, worm; unpleasant person; crafty person.*
Êle (Ele) é um bicho. *He's a sharp fellow.*
Jôgo (Jogo) do bicho. *A type of lottery in Brasil.*

bicicleta f. *bicycle.*

bico m. *beak, bill, point.*

bife m. *steak, beefsteak.*

bigode m. *moustache.*

bilhar m. *billiards.*

BILHETE m. *ticket, note.*
Quero bilhete de ida e volta. *I want a round-trip ticket.*
Ontem Carlos recebeu o bilhete azul. *Charles was fired yesterday.*
Bilhete postal. *Postcard.*

bilheteria (bilheteira) f. *ticket office.*

binóculo m. *binoculars, opera glasses.*

biombo m. *screen.*

bis *again; encore!*

bisavô m. *great-grandfather.*

bisavó *great-grandmother.*

biscoito m. *biscuit, cookie, cracker.*

bisneto m. *great-grandson.*

bispo m. *bishop.*

bissexto adj. *bissextile.*
Ano bissexto. *Leap year.*

bitola f. *gauge (railroad); measure.*

blindado adj. *armored.*

blindar *to armor, to cover.*

bloco m. *block; tablet.*
Compre-me um bloco de papel. *Buy me a writing tablet.*

BOA adj. f. *of bom.*

boas-vindas f. pl. *welcome.*

bobagem f. *nonsense, foolishness.*

bôbo (bobo) adj. *foolish, silly; m. fool, clown.*

BÔCA (BOCA) f. *mouth.*

bocadinho m. *a bit.*
Espere um bocadinho. *Wait a bit.*

bocado m. *bite, piece; short while.*

bocejar *to yawn.*

bochecha f. *cheek.*

boda f. *wedding.*

bofetada f. *slap in the face, blow.*

boi m. *ox, bull.*

BOLA f. *ball, globe; wits.*
Bola de tênis (ténis). *Tennis ball.*
Ora bolas! *Baloney! Nuts!*

boletim m. *bulletin, report.*

bôlo (bolo) m. *cake; stake, kitty.*

BÔLSA (BOLSA) f. *purse, bag; stock exchange.*

BÔLSO (BOLSO) m. *pocket.*
Esta é uma edição de bôlso. *This is a pocket edition.*

BOM adj. *good; kind; satisfactory; suited, fit; well.*
Bom dia. *Good morning.*
Boa tarde. *Good afternoon. Good evening.*
Boa noite. *Good night.*
É uma boa idéia (ideia). *That's a good idea.*
Eu acho muito bom. *I think that's fine.*
Êle (Ele) está bom. *He's well.*
Nós lhe fizemos uma boa! *We played a fine trick on him!*

bomba f. *pump; fire engine; bomb.*

bombeiro m. *fireman; plumber.*

bombom m. *bonbon, candy.*

BONDADE f. *goodness, kindness.*
Tenha a bondade de sentar-se. *Please sit down.*

bonde m. *streetcar* Ⓑ.

bondoso adj. *kind.*

boné m. *cap.*

bonitão m., bonitona f. adj. *good-looking.*

bonito adj. *pretty, good.*

borboleta f. *butterfly.*

bordar *to embroider; to edge.*

bordo m. *board (ship); border; course, tack (boat).*
Peço licença para ir a bordo. *I ask permission to go aboard.*

borracha f. *rubber; eraser.*

borrasca f. *storm.*

bosque m. *forest, woods.*

bosquejo m. *sketch, draft.*

bossa nova f. *type of Brazilian popular music.*

bota f. *boot.*

botão m. *button; bud.*

BOTAR *to cast, to throw; to put, to place* Ⓑ.
Bote fora! *Throw it out!*
Botou cinco dólares no balcão. *He put five dollars on the counter.*

bote m. *boat.*

botica f. *pharmacy.*

boticário m. *pharmacist, druggist.*

boxe (x = ks) m. *boxing.*

boxeador (x = ks) m. *boxer.*

boxear (x = ks) *to box.*

BRAÇO m. *arm.*
Êles (Eles) ficaram com os braços cruzados. *They stayed there with their arms folded.*

bradar *to roar, to shout.*

BRANCO *white, pale, blank.*
Quero seis camisas brancas. *I want six white shirts.*
Você pode deixar (x = sh) em branco. *You can leave it blank.*
Verso branco. *Blank verse.*

brando adj. *soft, smooth.*

brasa f. *live coal, ember.*
Êles (Eles) estão sôbre (sobre) brasas. *They're very worried about it.*

BRASIL m. *Brazil.*

BRASILEIRO adj. *Brazilian.*

bravo adj. *brave, wild; bravo!*

BREVE *brief, short, soon, shortly.*
Até breve. *See you soon.*
Em breve. *Soon.*
Faça o mais breve possível! *Do it as soon as possible!*

brevidade f. *briefness, brevity.*

briga f. *quarrel, fight.*

brigada f. *brigade.*

brigar *to quarrel, to fight.*

brilhante adj. *brilliant, sparkling; n. m. diamond.*

brilhar *to shine, to sparkle.*

brincadeira f. *joke; jest, prank.*
Chega de brincadeiras! *That's enough joking!*

brincar *to joke; to play.*
Os meninos estão brincando. *The children are playing.*
Mas êle (ele) só estava brincando! *But he was only joking!*

brindar *to toast.*

brinde m. *toast; offering.*

brinquedo m. *toy.*

brisa f. *breeze.*

broche m. *clasp; brooch.*

brochura f. *brochure, pamphlet; paperback.*

bronze m. *bronze, brass.*

brotar *to bud; to produce; to burst out.*

brusco adj. *brusque, rude, rough.*

brutal adj. *brutal, rough.*

bruto adj. *brutal; rude.*
Foi um ato (acto) muito bruto. *It was a very brutal act.*

bruxaria (x = sh) f. *witchcraft.*

bruxo (x = sh) m. bruxa f. *sorcerer, medicine man; witch.*

bufão m. *braggart, joker.*

bufete m. *buffet, sideboard, dresser.*

bugia f. *wax candle.*

bugigangas f. pl. *trinkets, knickknacks.*

buraco m. *hole, opening.*
Buraco de fechadura. *Keyhole.*
burla f. *joke; trick; deceit.*
burlar *to joke, to jest; to trick; to deceive.*
burro m. *donkey, ass.*
busca f. *search, pursuit.*
Êle (Ele) vai em busca de fama. *He's in pursuit of fame.*
buscar *to look for, to go for.*
busto m. *bust.*
buzina f. *horn.*
buzinar *to blow a horn.*

C

CÁ *here, this way.*
Venha cá! *Come here!*
cabana f. *hut, cabin.*
CABEÇA f. *head.*
Tenho dor de cabeça. *I have a headache.*
Dos pés à cabeça. *From head to foot.*
Isso não tem pés nem cabeça. *That doesn't make sense.*
cabeceira f. *head of a bed, table or list.*
Mesa de cabeceira. *Bedside table.*
CABELO m. *hair.*
caber *to fit into; to have enough room; to contain.*
Não cabe mais nada no baú. *There's no more room in the trunk.*
cabide m. *coat hanger, hatrack, peg.*
cabina, cabine f. *cabin, booth.*
Cabina telefônica (cabine telefónica). *Telephone booth.*
cabo m. *tip, extremity, end; cape; rope; corporal.*
Ao cabo do dia. *At the end of the day.*
Ele (Ele) nunca leva nada ao cabo. *He never finishes anything.*
Cabo da Boa Esperança. *Cape of Good Hope.*
caboclo m. Ⓑ. *backwoodsman; Brazilian Indian, half-breed; adj. copper-colored.*
cabra f. *she-goat;* m. Ⓑ *half-breed; bandit; ruffian.*
caça f. *hunting; game.*
caçador m. *hunter.*
caçar *to hunt, to chase.*
cacarejar *to cackle; to chatter.*
caçarola f. *saucepan, casserole.*
cacau m. *cocoa, cacao.*
cacête (cacete) m. *club, stick; adj. unpleasant, boring* Ⓑ.
cachaça f. *Brazilian rum or brandy drink.*
cachimbo m. *pipe.*
cachoeira f. *waterfall.*
cachorro m. *dog.*
Cachorro quente. *Hot dog.*
caçoar *to tease, to make fun of.*
CADA adj. m. and f. *each, every.*
Cada hora. *Each hour.*
Cada qual. *Each one. Every one.*
Cada vez que êle (ele) vem. *Each time he comes.*
Dar a cada um. *To give each one.*
Cada dia êle fala português melhor. *Every day he speaks Portuguese better.*
cadáver m. *corpse, cadaver.*
cadeia f. *chain.*
CADEIRA f. *chair.*
caderno m. *notebook.*
cadete m. *cadet.*
CAFÉ m. *coffee; coffeehouse.*
Uma xícara (x = sh) de café. *A cup of coffee.*
Café com leite. *Coffee with milk.*
Café prêto (preto). *Black coffee.*
CAFÉ DA MANHÃ m. *breakfast* Ⓑ.
Tomo o café da manhã às nove. *I have breakfast at nine o'clock.*
cafeteira f. *coffeepot.*

CAFÈZINHO m. *small cup of black coffee* Ⓑ.
caída f. *fall, downfall.*
caído adj. *fallen.*
CAIR *to fall; to tumble down; to drop; to become, to fit.*
Caía chuva no telhado. *Rain was falling on the roof.*
Êsse (Esse) vestido lhe cai bem. *That dress becomes you.*
O aniversário de João cai no mesmo dia que o meu. *John's birthday falls on the same day as mine.*
cais m. *dock, pier.*
CAIXA (x = sh) f. *box, case; chest; cabinet.*
Essa caixa é muito pequena. *That box is too small.*
Faça o favor de pagar na caixa. *Please pay the cashier.*
caixão (x = sh) m. *large box, chest; coffin.*
caixeiro (x = sh) m. *salesman, clerk.*
cajadada f. *blow with a stick.*
caju m. *cashew.*
cal m. *lime.*
calabouço m. *jail, prison.*
calado adj. *quiet, silent, reserved.*
calamidade f. *calamity.*
calar *to keep quiet, to be silent; to conceal.*
Cale-se! *Be quiet!*
calçada f. *sidewalk; pavement.*
calçado m. *footwear, shoes.*
calção m. *shorts, trunks.*
Calção de banho. *Bathing trunks.*
calçar *to put on (shoes, socks, etc.); to tread on.*
calças f. pl. *trousers; panties.*
calcular *to calculate, to estimate, to presume.*
cálculo m. *computation, estimate; calculus.*
caldo m. *soup, broth; juice.*
calefação (calefacção) f. *heat, heating system.*
calendário m. *calendar, almanac.*
calibre m. *caliber; bore; gauge.*
caligrafia f. *penmanship, handwriting.*
calmo adj. *calm, quiet.*
calo m. *corn, callus.*
CALOR m. *heat, warmth.*
Sempre faz calor no verão. *It's always warm in the summer.*
calouro m. *beginner, freshman, greenhorn.*
calúnia f. *calumny, slander.*
caluniar *to slander.*
calvície f. *baldness.*
calvo adj. *bald; bare, barren.*
CAMA *bed; couch; layer.*
Fazer a cama. *To make the bed.*
Êle (Ele) foi para a cama às dez. *He went to bed at ten.*
câmara f. *chamber; room; camera.*
Câmara municipal. *City council.*
Câmara cinematográfica. *Movie camera.*
camarada m. and f. *friend, companion.*
camarão m. *shrimp, prawn.*
camareira f. *chambermaid.*
camareiro m. *steward; room servant (hotel).*
camarote m. *box (theatre); cabin (ship).*
cambiar *to change, to exchange.*
câmbio m. *change, exchange.*
Câmbio exterior. *Foreign exchange.*
Eu perdi no câmbio. *I lost in the exchange.*
caminhão m. *truck.*
CAMINHAR *to walk; to march; to move along.*
CAMINHO m. *road, way, highway.*
Qual é o caminho mais curto para a cidade? *Which is the shortest way to the city?*
Todos os caminhos levam a Roma. *All roads lead to Rome.*

CAMISA f. *shirt, chemise.*
Ela me comprou três camisas. *She bought me three shirts.*
Eu prefiro trabalhar em mangas de camisa. *I prefer to work in shirt sleeves.*
camisaria f. *haberdashery; shirt factory.*
camisola f. *nightgown; undershirt* Ⓟ.
campainha f. *bell, buzzer.*
campeão m. *champion.*
campestre adj. *rural, rustic, country.*
campo m. *field, country; space.*
cana f. *cane, reed.*
Cana-de-açúcar. *Sugar cane.*
canal m. *canal; channel.*
Passamos pelo canal do Panamá. *We went through the Panama Canal.*
canalha m. *rascal, scoundrel;* f. *rabble, mob.*
canário m. *canary.*
CANÇÃO f. *song.*
cancelar *to cancel.*
câncer m. *cancer, sign of the zodiac.*
cancioneiro m. *songbook.*
cancro m. *cancer, chancre, canker.*
candeeiro m. *lamp; chandelier.*
candeia f. *oil lamp, lamp.*
candelabro m. *candelabrum.*
candidato m. *candidate.*
candidatura f. *candidacy.*
candidez f. *candor; simplicity.*
cândido adj. *candid, frank.*
caneca f. *mug.*
canela f. *cinnamon; shin.*
Gabriela, Cravo e Canela. *Gabriela, Clove and Cinnamon. (Title of a novel by Jorge Amado.)*
caneta f. *penholder, pen.*
Caneta esferográfica. *Ballpoint pen.*
Caneta-tinteiro. *Fountain pen.*
cânfora f. *camphor.*
cangaceiro m. *outlaw, bandit* Ⓑ.
canhão m. *cannon, gun; canyon.*
caniço m. *reed, rod.*
canino adj. *canine.*
Estou com uma fome canina. *I'm terribly hungry.*
canivete m. *penknife, pocketknife.*
canja f. *chicken soup with rice; a cinch, easy* Ⓑ.
É canja! *That's a cinch! That's easy!*
cano m. *pipe, tube.*
canoa f. *canoe.*
cansaço m. *weariness, fatigue.*
CANSADO adj. *tired, weary; tedious; annoying.*
Ficamos muito cansados. *We are very tired.*
cansar *to tire; to annoy, to bore.*
cansar-se *to get tired, to get annoyed, to become bored.*
cantador m. *singer (of popular songs).*
CANTAR *to sing.*
cântaro m. *pot, jar, pitcher.*
cantarolar *to hum.*
cântico m. *song, hymn.*
cantiga f. *popular song, ballad.*
cantina f. *canteen.*
canto m. *song; corner, nook.*
cantor m. *singer.*
CÃO m. *dog.*
Quem não tem cão, caça com gato. *One does the best he can. To make the best of things.*
capa f. *cape, cloak, coat; cover.*
Capa de chuva. *Raincoat.*
Capa de livro. *Book cover, binding.*
capacidade f. *capacity.*
capataz m. *foreman, boss.*
capaz adj. *capable, able.*

Êle (Ele) é capaz de fazê-lo. *He's capable of doing it.*

capela *f. chapel.*

capelão *m. chaplain.*

capital *adj. principal, main; m. principal (money); capital (stock); f. capital (city).*
Quanto capital precisa para essa emprêsa (empresa)? *How much capital do you need for that undertaking?*
Qual é a capital do estado? *What is the capital of the state?*

capitão *m. captain.*

capitólio *m. capitol.*

capítulo *m. chapter.*

capote *m. cape, cloak, overcoat.*

captar *to capture, to catch.*

capturar *to capture, arrest.*

CARA *f. face, look, appearance.*
Encontraram-se cara a cara. *They met face to face.*
Êle (Ele) tem boa cara. *He looks like a good fellow.*
Você tem cara de fome. *You have a starved look.*
Cara ou coroa? *Heads or tails?*

caranguejo *m. crab.*

caráter (carácter) *m. character.*

carbono *m. carbon; carbon paper.*

cárcere *m. jail, prison.*

cardápio *m. menu.*

cardeal *adj. cardinal; n. m. cardinal.*
Pontos cardeais. *Cardinal points.*

cardinal *adj. cardinal, principal.*
Números cardinais. *Cardinal numbers.*

careca *adj. bald; n. m. bald person.*

CARECER *to lack, to need.*

carga *f. load, burden, freight, cargo.*
O asno é animal de carga. *The donkey is a beast of burden.*
Tôda (toda) a carga chegou? *Did all the load arrive?*

cargo *m. obligation, charge, responsibility; employment.*
Alberto assumiu o cargo. *Albert took on the responsibility.*

carícia *f. caress.*

caridade *f. charity, pity.*

carimbar *to stamp, to seal.*

carinho *m. love, affection.*

carinhoso *adj. affectionate, kind.*

CARIOCA *adj. of the city of Rio de Janeiro; m. and f. inhabitant of Rio de Janeiro.*
Êle (Ele) é carioca da gema. *He's a real carioca.*

caritativo *adj. charitable.*

CARNAVAL *m. carnival.*
É um samba de carnaval. *It's a carnival samba.*

CARNE *f. meat; flesh; pulp (of fruit).*
Gosto mais de carne de vaca. *I like beef better.*
Carne de carneiro. *Mutton.*
Carne de vitela. *Veal.*
Carne de porco. *Pork.*
Nem carne nem peixe. *Neither fish nor fowl.*

carneiro *m. sheep.*

CARO *adj. expensive; dear (cherished).*
Tudo é muito caro. *Everything is quite expensive.*
Meu caro amigo: *My dear friend:*
Minha cara metade não concorda. *My better half does not agree.*

carpinteiro *m. carpenter; woodpecker.*

carregado *adj. loaded, heavy.*

carregar *to load, to burden.*

carreira *f. career, race (running).*

carrêta (carreta) *f. cart, wagon.*

carro *m. car, automobile; cart.*
Carro-restaurante. *Dining car.*
Carro eléctrico. *Streetcar* (P).

carroça *f. cart.*

CARTA *f. letter; map, chart; charter; playing card.*
Nem uma carta recebi dêle (dele) *I didn't receive even one letter from him.*
Cartaregistrada(registada). *Registered letter.*
Carta expressa. *Special delivery letter.*
Carta de crédito. *Letter of credit.*
Carta de naturalização. *Naturalization papers.*

cartão *m. cardboard; card; calling card.*
Êle (Ele) me mandou (mandou-me) vários cartões (bilhetes) postais. *He sent me several postcards.*
Deixei (x = sh) meu cartão. *I left my calling card.*

cartaz *m. poster, placard.*

carteira *f. wallet, pocketbook; portfolio; license.*
Roubaram-me a carteira. *They stole my wallet.*
Carteira de motorista. *Driver's license.*

carteiro *m. mailman, postman.*

cartilha *f. primer.*

carvalho *m. oak tree.*

carvão *m. coal, charcoal.*

CASA *f. house, home; firm, concern; room* (P).
Ela mora na casa da tia. *She lives in her aunt's home.*
Vamos para casa. *Let's go home.*
Estarei em casa o dia todo. *I'll be home all day.*
Êles (Eles) estão em casa de João. *They're at John's house.*
A casa editôra (editora) ainda não me escreveu. *The publishing house did not write me yet.*
O Presidente mora na Casa Branca. *The President lives in the White House.*
Casa de banho (P). *Bathroom.*

casado *adj. married.*

casal *m. couple; married couple.*

casamento *m. marriage, wedding.*

casar *to marry.*

CASAR-SE *to get married.*
Ela se casou com o filho do prefeito (B). *She married the mayor's son.*

casca *f. peel, husk, shell, bark.*

caseiro *adj. pertaining to the home, domestic.*
É um remédio caseiro. *It's a home remedy.*

casimira *f. cashmere, woolen cloth.*

CASO *case, event.*
É um caso raro! *It's a strange case!*
Bem, vamos ao caso. *Well, let's get to the point.*
Êle (Ele) não faz caso de nada. *He doesn't pay attention to anything.*

caspa *f. dandruff.*

castanha *f. chestnut.*
Castanha-do-Pará. *Brazil nut.*

castiço *adj. pure; of good birth.*

castigar *to punish.*

castigo *m. punishment, penalty.*

casual *adj. accidental, casual.*

casualidade *f. chance, coincidence, accident.*
Eu o encontrei por casualidade. *I met him by chance.*

catálogo *m. catalog.*

catarata *f. cataract; waterfall.*

catedral *f. cathedral.*

catedrático *m. professor (especially of a university).*

categoria *f. category, class.*

catolicismo *m. Catholicism.*

católico *adj. Catholic.*

CATORZE *fourteen, fourteenth.*

caução *f. bond, bail, security.*

cauda *f. tail; end; extremity.*
Piano de cauda. *Grand piano.*

caudilho *m. chief, leader.*

CAUSA *f. cause, motive.*
Por causa disto, ninguém veio. *For that reason, nobody came.*

causar *to cause.*
Causou muito dano. *It caused great damage.*

cautela *f. caution, prudence.*

cauto *adj. cautious.*

cavala *f. mackerel.*

cavalaria *f. cavalry.*

cavaleiro *m. horseman, rider.*

cavalheiro *m. gentleman.*

cavalo *m. horse; knight (chess); jack (cards).*

cavar *to dig.*

caverna *f. cavern, cave.*

cavidade *f. cavity.*

cear *to eat supper (ceio, etc.).*

cebola *f. onion.*

ceder *to grant; to give in, to yield.*

CEDO *early, soon.*
Ainda é muito cedo. *It's still too early.*
Mais cedo ou mais tarde. *Sooner or later.*

cedro *m. cedar.*

cédula *f. certificate, bill, promissory note.*

cego *adj. blind; n. m. blind person.*

cegonha *f. stork.*

cegueira *f. blindness.*

ceia *f. supper.*

CELEBRAR *to celebrate; to praise; to commemorate.*
Vamos celebrar a ocasião com uma festa no sábado. *We are going to celebrate the occasion with a party on Saturday.*

célebre *adj. famous; celebrated.*

célula *f. cell.*

CEM *hundred.*
Custa mais de cem dólares. *It costs more than a hundred dollars.*

cemento *m. cement.*

cemitério *m. cemetery.*

cena *f. scene; stage.*
Não gostei nada da primeira cena da peça. *I didn't like the first scene of the play at all.*

cenário *m. stage, setting, scenery.*

cenoura *f. carrot.*

censura *f. censorship; censure.*

censurar *to censor; to censure.*

CENTAVO *m. centavo; cent.*

centeio *m. rye.*

centelha *f. spark.*

centena *f. hundred, about a hundred.*

centenário *m. centenary.*

centésimo *adj. hundredth.*

centígrado *adj. centigrade.*

CENTO *hundred.*
Vasco da Gama chegou à Índia em mil quatrocentos e noventa e oito. *Vasco da Gama reached India in 1498.*

CENTRAL *adj. central; f. main office.*
América Central. *Central America.*
Onde é a central do correio? *Where is the main post office?*

CENTRO *m. center, middle; core; club, social circle.*

cepilho *m. plane (carpenter's).*

cêra (cera) *f. wax.*

cêrca (cerca) *f. fence, hedge; enclosed land.*

cêrca (cerca) de *about, approximately.*
Acho que vi cêrca de quarenta quadros mo-

dernos. *I believe I saw about forty modern paintings.*

cercar *to fence in, to enclose, to surround; to besiege.*

cereal m. *cereal.*

cérebro m. *brain, mind.*

cereja f. *cherry.*

cerejeira f. *cherry tree.*

cerimônia (cerimónia) f. *ceremony; formality.*

ceroulas f. pl. *long underwear, drawers.*

cerração f. *fog, mist.*

cerrado adj. *thick; dense; closed.*

cerrar *to close, to lock; to enclose.*

cêrro (cerro) m. *small hill.*

certeza f. *certainty.*
  Temos certeza de que êle (ele) não vem hoje. *We are sure that he is not coming today.*
  Com certeza. *Of course.*

certidão f. *certificate.*
  É preciso apresentar a certidão de nascimento. *You must bring your birth certificate.*

certificado m. *certificate.*

certificar *to certify, to attest.*

CERTO adj. *sure, certain; right; true.*
  Eu estou certo disso. *I'm sure of that.*
  Está certo. *That's right.*
  Certo amigo me disse isso. *A certain friend told me that.*

cerveja f. *beer, ale.*

cervejaria f. *brewery; beer hall.*

cervo m. *deer.*

cessar *to stop, to cease.*

cêsto (cesto) m. *basket.*

cetim m. *satin.*

céu m. *sky; heaven.*

cevada f. *barley.*

CHÁ m. *tea.*
  Quer café ou prefere chá? *Do you want some coffee or do you prefer tea?*
  Colher de chá. *Teaspoon.*

chácara f. *country house* Ⓑ.

chaleira f. *teakettle; m. and f. flatterer* Ⓑ.

chama f. *flame.*

chamada f. *call.*
  Chamada interurbana. *Long-distance call.*
  O professor sempre faz a chamada. *The teacher always calls the roll.*

CHAMAR *to call; to appeal; to name; to send for.*
  O senhor chamou? *Did you call?*
  Chamar pelo telefone. *To phone.*
  Chame um táxi (x = ks), por favor. *Please call a taxi.*

CHAMAR-SE *to be called, to be named.*
  Como se chama êle (ele)? *What is his name?*
  Êle se chama (chama-se) João Costa. *His name is John Costa.*

chaminé f. *chimney.*

chão m. *floor, ground.*

chapa f. *plate, license plate.*

CHAPÉU m. *hat.*
  Não sei onde deixei (x = sh) o chapéu. *I don't know where I left my hat.*
  Chapéu de fêltro (feltro). *Felt hat.*
  Quando ela entrou, êle (ele) tirou o chapéu. *When she entered he took off his hat.*

charlatão m. *quack, impostor.*

charque m. *jerked beef* Ⓑ.

charuto m. *cigar.*

chatear *to bore, to annoy.*

chato adj. *flat; boring.*
  Êle (Ele) é muito chato. *He's a big bore.*

CHAVE f. *key; wrench.*
  Não posso abrir a porta sem a chave. *I can't open the door without the key.*
  Chave de parafusos. *Screwdriver.*

Chave inglêsa (inglesa). *Monkey wrench.*

chávena f. *cup, teacup.*

chefe m. and f. *chief, director.*

CHEGADA f. *arrival.*

CHEGAR *to arrive, to come; to be enough.*
  Quando chegaram? *When did you arrive?*
  Chega para hoje. *That's enough for today.*
  Êle (Ele) chegou a ser presidente da firma. *He got to be president of the firm.*

CHEIO adj. *full.*
  Foi um dia bem cheio. *It was quite a full day.*

cheiro m. *odor, smell.*

cheque m. *check.*
  Quando viajo sempre levo comigo cheques de viagem. *When I travel I always take travelers' checks with me.*

chiada f. *squeaking, chirping.*

chiado m. *squeaking.*

chiar *to squeak, to screech, to chirp.*

chifre m. *horn.*

chinela f. *house slipper.*

chinelo m. *slipper.*

chique adj. *chic, stylish.*

chiqueiro m. *pigpen.*

chispa f. *spark.*

chiste m. *joke, wisecrack.*

chita f. *calico, cotton cloth.*

choça f. *hut, shack.*

chocolate m. *chocolate.*

chofer m. *driver, chauffeur.*
  Chofer de praça. *Cabman, cabby.*

chope m. *draft beer* Ⓑ.
  Chope-duplo. *A double-sized glass of draft beer; double-decked bus* Ⓑ.

choque m. *jolt, shock, collision.*

choramingar *to whimper, to whine.*

CHORAR *to cry, to weep, to mourn, to lament.*
  Quando ouviram a notícia, choraram. *When they heard the news they cried.*
  Quem não chora não mama. *The squeaky wheel gets the most grease.*

chôro (choro) m. *crying, weeping; type of Brazilian popular music.*

CHOVER *to rain.*
  Se chover não vamos. *If it rains we won't go.*

chumbo m. *lead.*

CHUVA f. *rain, rainfall, shower.*
  Há muita chuva em março (Março). *There is much rainfall in March.*

chuveiro m. *shower.*

chuviscar *to drizzle.*

chuvisco m. *drizzle.*

cicatriz f. *scar.*

cicerone m. and f. *guide.*

ciclista m. and f. *cyclist.*

ciclone m. *cyclone.*

cidadania f. *citizenship.*

cidadão m. *citizen.*

CIDADE f. *city.*
  Rio de Janeiro, cidade maravilhosa. *Rio de Janeiro, marvelous city.*
  Em que cidade o senhor nasceu? *In what city were you born?*

cidra f. *cider; citron.*

ciência f. *science.*

ciente adj. *aware, cognizant.*

científico adj. *scientific.*

cifra f. *figure, cipher, number; code.*

cigano m. *gypsy.*

cigarra f. *locust, cicada.*

cigarreira f. *cigarette case.*

CIGARRO m. *cigarette.*

cilindro m. *cylinder, roller.*

cima f. *top, highest part.*
  O livro está em cima da mesa. *The book is on top of the table.*

cimento m. *cement.*

CINCO *five.*

CINEMA m. *movies; movie theater.*
  Vamos ao cinema todos os domingos. *We go to the movies every Sunday.*

CINQÜENTA (CINQUENTA) *fifty.*

cinta f. *belt, girdle, band.*

cinto m. *belt, sash.*

cintura f. *waist.*

cinza f. *ash, powder; adj. gray, ashen.*

cinzeiro m. *ashtray.*

cinzento adj. *gray, ashen.*

cipreste m. *cypress.*

circo m. *circus, ring.*

circulação f. *circulation.*

circular *to circulate.*

círculo m. *circle.*

circunflexo (x = ks) adj. *circumflex.*

circunstância f. *circumstance.*

cirurgião m. *surgeon.*

cismar *to think about, to ponder, to meditate.*
  "Em cismar sòzinho à noite." *At night, alone, as I meditate.*

cisne m. *swan.*

cita f. *quotation, citation.*

citação f. *quotation, citation.*

citar *to quote, to cite.*

ciúme m. *jealousy.*
  Acho que êle (ele) tem ciumes dela. *I believe he is jealous of her.*

ciumento adj. *jealous.*
  Êle (Ele) é muito ciumento. *He is very jealous.*

civil adj. *civil, civilian; courteous.*

civilização f. *civilization.*

clamar *to shout, to cry out.*

claridade f. *clearness; light; distinctness.*

clarim m. *bugle, trumpet.*

clarinete m. *clarinet.*

CLARO adj. *clear, bright; evident, intelligible, obvious; plain, frank; transparent, pure; light (color); n. m. blank, space.*
  Escreva claro. *Write clearly.*
  Claro! *Of course!*
  Claro que sim! *Of course!*
  Claro que não! *Of course not!*

CLASSE f. *class; kind; sort; order.*
  É obra de primeira classe. *It's a topnotch work.*

clérigo m. *clergyman, priest.*

clero m. *clergymen, clergy.*

cliente m. and f. *client; customer; patient.*

clima m. *climate.*

clínica f. *clinic.*

cloaca f. *sewer, cesspool, latrine.*

clorofórmio m. *chloroform.*

clube m. *club.*

cobertor m. *blanket.*

cobra f. *snake.*

cobrador m. *collector.*

COBRAR *to charge, to collect, to receive (money).*
  Quanto cobraram? *How much did they charge?*
  Êle (Ele) está cobrando ânimo. *He is feeling much encouraged.*

cobre m. *copper.*

COBRIR *to cover.*

coçar *to scratch; to thrash.*

coceira f. *itching.*

côche (coche) m. *coach, carriage.*

cochichar *to whisper.*

cochicho m. *whispering, whisper.*

cochilo m. *nap, dozing; oversight* Ⓑ.

côco (coco) m. *coconut.*

cócoras, *in de cócoras squatting.*

codorniz *f. quail.*

coelho m. *rabbit.*
  Matar dois coelhos com uma só cajadada. *To kill two birds with one stone.*

cofre m. *safe, chest.*

coincidência *f. coincidence.*
  Encontramo-nos por coincidência. *We met by chance.*

coincidir *to coincide.*

COISA COUSA, *f. thing, matter.*
  Não há tal coisa. *There is no such thing.*
  Alguma coisa. *Something.*
  O senhor deseja outra coisa? *Do you wish something else?*
  É a mesma coisa. *It's the same thing.*
  Será coisa de três dias. *It will take about three days.*
  Como vão as coisas? *How are things?*

coitado adj. *poor, unfortunate; n. m. poor fellow, poor thing.*

cola *f. glue.*

colaboração *f. collaboration.*

colaborar *to collaborate.*

colar m. *necklace, collar.*

colcha *f. bedspread.*

colchão m. *mattress.*

coleção (colecção) *f. collection.*

colecionar (coleccionar) *to collect.*

colégio m. *school (below college level—elementary or secondary).*

cólera *f. anger; cholera.*

colete (colete) (m.) *vest.*

colheita *f. crop, harvest.*

COLHER *f. spoon.*
  Você esqueceu as colheres. *You forgot the spoons.*
  Colher de café. *Coffee spoon.*
  Colher de chá. *Teaspoon.*
  Colher de sopa. *Soup spoon. Tablespoon.*

COLHER (COLHER) *to gather; to take, to obtain; to harvest; to pick.*
  Quer colher-me algumas flôres (flores)? *Would you pick some flowers for me?*

colibri m. *hummingbird.*

colina *f. hill.*

colmeia *f. beehive.*

colo m. *lap, neck.*

colocar *to place; to give employment to.*
  Coloque tudo em seu lugar. *Put everything in its place.*
  Meu pai o colocou numa casa de comércio. *My father got him a position in a business firm.*

colónia (colónia) *f. colony.*

colonial adj. *colonial.*

coluna *f. column, pillar.*
  Quinta coluna. *Fifth column.*

COM *with.*
  Nós vamos com êle (ele). *We are going with him.*
  Com muito prazer. *Gladly. With much pleasure.*
  Estamos com pressa. *We are in a hurry.*
  Êles (Eles) o prepararam com cuidado. *They prepared it carefully.*
  Estou com frio. *I am cold.*

comandante m. *commander; captain of a ship.*

comando m. *command.*

comarca *f. district.*

combate m. *combat, military action.*
  Pôr fora de combate. *To put out of action.*

combatente adj. *fighting; m. fighter, combatant.*
  Não combatente. *Noncombatant.*

combater *to combat, to fight.*

combinação *f. combination; slip (lady's garment).*

combinar *to combine.*

comboio m. *convoy; train* Ⓟ.

combustível m. *fuel.*

COMEÇAR *to begin, to commence.*
  A que horas começa o programa? *At what time does the program begin?*

começo (começo) m. *beginning, start.*

comédia *f. comedy.*

comemoração *f. commemoration, celebration.*

comemorar *to commemorate, to celebrate.*

comentar *to comment on, to discuss.*
  Êle (Ele) gosta de comentar as notícias. *He likes to comment on the news.*

comentário m *comment.*

COMER *to eat.*
  Os meninos comem demais. *The children eat too much.*

comerciante m. *businessman.*

comerciar *to trade, to do business.*

comércio m. *business, trade, commerce.*

comestíveis m. pl. *food.*

cometer *to commit.*
  Todos cometemos êrros (erros). *We all make mistakes.*

cometida *f. attack.*

cômico (cómico) adj. *comic, funny.*

comida *f. food.*
  Comida e bebida. *Food and drink.*
  Quarto e comida. *Room and board.*

comigo *with me.*
  Quer ir comigo? *Do you want to go with me?*

comissão *f. commission, committee.*

comissário m. *commissioner.*

comite (comité) m. *committee.*

comitiva *f. train, retinue.*

COMO *how, how much; as, like.*
  Como vai o senhor? *How are you?*
  Como se chama ela? *What is her name?*
  Como o senhor quiser. *As you wish.*
  Êle (Ele) entrou como se estivesse em casa. *He came in as if he were in his own home.*

cômoda (cómoda) *f. dresser, chest of drawers.*

comodidade *f. comfort, ease; convenience.*
  Éste (Este) apartamento tem tôdas (todas) as comodidades. *This apartment has all conveniences.*

cômodo (cómodo) adj. *comfortable, convenient.*

compadecer *to pity, to sympathize with.*

compaixão (x = sh) *f. compassion, pity, sympathy.*

companheiro m. *companion, comrade, colleague.*
  Êle (Ele) é meu companheiro de quarto. *He's my roommate.*
  Êles (Eles) sempre têm sido bons companheiros. *They have always been good companions.*

companhia *f. company; business firm.*
  Gomes & Cia. *Gomes and Co.*

comparação *f. comparison.*

COMPARAR *to compare.*

comparecer *to appear.*

compartilhar *to share.*

compartimento m. *compartment; room.*

compatível adj. *compatible.*

compatriota m. and f. *compatriot.*

compensação *f. compensation.*

compensar *to compensate, to pay.*

competência *f. competence, ability; competition.*

competente adj. *competent, fit.*

competição *f. competition, rivalry; contest.*

competir *to compete, to contend; to behoove.*
  Compete a êles (eles) começar. *It is up to*

them to begin.

complacente adj. *accommodating, agreeable, pleasing.*

complemento m. *complement.*

COMPLETAMENTE *completely.*

COMPLETAR *to complete, to finish.*
  Completar um trabalho. *To finish a task (job).*

COMPLETO adj. *complete, finished, full.*
  Por completo. *Completely.*

complicado adj. *complicated.*

complicar *to complicate.*

compor *to compose, to constitute.*
  Êle (Ele) compôs dois poemas épicos. *He composed two epic poems.*

comportamento m. *behavior.*

comportar *to allow, to stand, to include.*

comportar-se *to behave, to act.*

composição *f. composition.*

compositor m. *composer; typesetter.*

composto adj. *composed, compound; n. m. compound, combination.*

compostura *f. composure; composition; falsity.*

compota *f. compote, preserves, stewed fruit.*

COMPRA *f. purchase.*
  Hoje vamos de compras. *We are going shopping today.*

comprador m. *buyer.*

COMPRAR *to buy.*
  Comprar a crédito. *To buy on credit.*
  Comprar a dinheiro. *To buy for cash.*
  Comprar a prestações. *To buy on installments.*
  Comprar por atacado. *To buy wholesale.*
  Eu comprei tudo muito barato. *I bought everything very cheap.*

COMPREENDER *to understand; to comprise, to include.*
  Compreende o que estou dizendo (a dizer)? *Do you understand what I am saying?*
  Não compreendi nada. *I didn't understand a thing.*

compreendido adj. *understood; including.*

compreensão *f. comprehension, understanding.*

compreensível adj. *comprehensible.*

compreensivo adj. *comprehensive.*

comprido adj. *long.*

comprimento m. *length.*

comprimir *to compress, to restrain, to repress.*

comprometer-se *to commit oneself.*

compromisso m. *compromise; engagement, commitment.*

comprovante adj. *confirming.*

comprovar *to prove, to confirm.*

compulsório adj. *compulsory.*

computar *to compute.*

COMUM adj. *common.*
  Em comum. *In common.*
  De comum acôrdo (acordo). *By mutual consent.*
  Senso comum. *Common sense.*

comunicação *f. communication.*
  Telefonista, ponha-me em comunicação com o número...*Operator, connect me with number...*

comunicar *to communicate, to announce, to inform.*

comunidade *f. community.*

comunismo m. *communism.*

comunista m. *communist.*

conceber *to conceive.*

conceder *to grant.*

conceito m. *concept, idea.*

concelho m. *council of a municipality.*

concentrar *to concentrate.*

concepção f. conception, idea.
concernir to concern.
concêrto (concerto) m. concert.
concessão f. concession.
concha f. shell.
conciliação f. conciliation.
conciliar to conciliate, to reconcile.
conciso adj. concise.
concluir to conclude, to finish; to settle.
conclusão f. conclusion.
Todos chegaram à mesma conclusão. They all arrived at the same conclusion.
concordância f. agreement, harmony.
concordar to agree.
concorrência f. competition.
concorrer to compete; to concur.
concreto adj. concrete.
concurso m. contest, competition.
conde m. count.
condecoração f. decoration, medal.
condenado adj. condemned.
condenar to condemn, to convict; to disapprove.
Êle (Ele) foi condenado ontem. He was convicted yesterday.
condição f. condition.
Êles (Eles) aceitaram sob a condição de que êle (ele) não voltasse. They accepted on condition that he not return.
Tudo está em boas condições. Everything is in good order.
condicionado adj. conditioned.
Com ar condicionado. Air conditioned.
condicional adj. conditional.
condimentar to season.
condiscípulo m. classmate.
condolência f. condolence; sympathy.
Aceite as minhas condolências. Please accept my condolences.
condor m. condor.
conduta f. conduct, behavior.
conduto m. conduit, pipe; canal.
condutor m. conductor.
CONDUZIR to drive; to conduct; to carry; to lead.
Êste (Este) caminho conduz ao lago. This road goes to the lake.
confeitaria f. confectionary, candy store.
conferência f. conference; lecture.
conferencista m. and f. lecturer.
conferir to confer, to bestow.
confessar to admit, to confess.
Confesso que não pensei nisso. I admit I didn't think of that.
confiança f. confidence, faith; familiarity.
Êle (Ele) é digno de confiança. He is reliable.
Eu lhe digo isto em confiança. I'm telling you this in confidence.
Todos têm confiança nêle (nele). Everybody has confidence in him.
confiar to confide; to trust.
confidência f. confidence.
confidencial adj. confidential.
confirmação f. confirmation.
confirmar to confirm, to ratify.
confissão f. confession; acknowledgment.
conflito m. conflict, strife.
conformar to conform; to fit; to agree; to comply with.
conformar-se com. to be satisfied with.
CONFORME according to; agreed.
Estar conforme. To be in agreement.
conformidade f. conformity; resemblance.
De conformidade com. In accordance with.
confortante adj. comforting.

confortar to comfort.
confortável adj. comfortable.
confôrto (conforto) m. comfort, ease.
confundir to confuse; to mistake.
confundir-se to become confused; to be perplexed.
confusão f. confusion, perplexity.
confuso adj. confused.
congelar to freeze.
congestão f. congestion.
congratulação f. congratulation.
congratular to congratulate.
congregação f. congregation.
congresso m. congress; assembly; conference.
conhaque m. cognac, brandy.
CONHECER to know, to understand, to be acquainted with.
Você conhece Maria? Do you know Maria?
Não a conheço. I don't know her.
Vocês se conhecem? Do you know each other?
Muito prazer em conhecê-lo. Very glad to know you.
conhecido adj. known; n. m. acquaintance.
A obra dêle (dele) é bem conhecida. His work is well known.
conhecimento m. knowledge, understanding, acquaintance.
Tudo chegou ao conhecimento de nossos amigos. All came to the knowledge of our friends.
Tomar conhecimento de. To take notice of.
conjetura (conjectura) f. conjecture, guess.
conjeturar (conjecturar) to conjecture, to guess.
conjugação f. conjugation.
conjugar to conjugate.
conjunção f. conjunction.
conjunto adj. joint, united; n. m. whole.
conjuração f. conspiracy.
conquista f. conquest.
conquistar to conquer, to win over.
consciência f. conscience.
consciente adj. conscious, aware.
conseguinte adj. consequent; consecutive.
Por conseguinte, perdemos. Consequently we lost.
CONSEGUIR to obtain, to attain, to get, to succeed in.
Será difícil consegui-lo. It will be difficult to get it.
Não consegui convencê-lo. I did not succeed in convincing him.
conselheiro m. member of a board (council); adviser; counselor.
conselho m. advice; council, advisory board.
Seguirei seu conselho. I shall follow your advice.
Conselho de ministros. Cabinet.
Conselho de guerra. War council. Court-martial.
consentimento m. consent.
consentir to consent; to agree, to be willing; to tolerate.
Você consente em isso? Do you agree to that?
Não consinto nunca. I'll never consent.
conseqüência (consequência) f. consequence.
Em conseqüência. Therefore. As a result.
Você terá que aceitar as conseqüências. You will have to accept the consequences.
consertar to fix, to repair.
O senhor pode consertar meu relógio? Can you fix my watch?
consêrto (conserto) m. repair, mending.
conservação f. conservation.
conservador adj. conservative; n. m. conservative.

conservar to conserve, to keep, to preserve.
Ela não conserva nada. She doesn't keep anything.
Conserve a sua direita. Keep to the right.
conservas f. preserves; canned food.
consideração f. consideration, regard.
considerar to consider, to take into account.
considerável adj. considerable, large.
consignar to consign, to assign.
consigo with him, with her, with you, with them.
Êles (Eles) o levaram consigo. They took it with them.
consistência f. consistency; stability; firmness.
consistente adj. consistent, solid, firm.
consistir to consist, to be composed of.
consoante f. consonant.
consolação f. consolation.
consolar to console, to comfort.
conspícuo adj. conspicuous.
constante adj. constant.
constar to be evident; to consist of.
Consta que êles (eles) nunca o fizeram. The fact is that they never did it.
constipação f. a cold.
constituição f. constitution.
constituir to constitute.
construção f. construction, building.
CONSTRUIR to construct, to build.
cônsul m. consul.
consulado m. consulate.
consulta f. consultation.
consultar to consult, to seek advice.
Você deve consultar um médico. You should consult a doctor.
consultório m. doctor's office.
consumidor m. consumer.
consumir to consume, to use.
consumo m. consumption; expenditure.
Artigos de consumo. Consumer goods.
CONTA f. count; account; statement; bill; bead.
Traga-me a conta, por favor. Please bring me the bill.
Ponha tudo na minha conta. Charge it all to my account.
Conta corrente. Current account.
Dar conta de. To give an account of, to report.
Tenha em conta que êle (ele) não sabe nada disto. Keep in mind that he knows nothing about this.
Afinal de contas, que mais poderia eu ter feito? After all, what more could I have done?
contabilidade f. bookkeeping, accounting.
contador m. accountant; purser; meter (gas, etc.).
contagiar to infect, to contaminate.
contagioso adj. contagious.
conta-gotas m. dropper.
contaminar to contaminate.
CONTAR to count; to tell.
Você tem alguma coisa que me contar? Do you have something to tell me?
Vocês podem contar comigo. You can count on me.
contemplação f. contemplation.
contemplar to contemplate, to consider, to have in view.
contemporâneo adj. contemporary; n. m. contemporary.
contenda f. quarrel, dispute, fight.
contentamento m. contentment.
contentar to please; to satisfy.
CONTENTE adj. content, happy, pleased.
Ela está muito contente. She is very happy.
conter to contain, to include, to hold.

conter-se *to refrain, to restrain oneself.*

contestação *f. answer, reply.*

contestar *to contest; to reply.*

conteúdo *m. contents.*

contigo *with you (fam. sing.).*

contíguo *adj. contiguous; close, near.*

continente *m. continent.*

continuação *f. continuation.*

CONTINUAR *to continue.*

CONTO *m. story, tale; a thousand cruseiros or escudos.*
  Conto de fadas. *Fairy tale.*
  Conto policial. *Detective story.*

CONTRA *against, contrary to, counter to.*
  Êle (Ele) o fêz (fez) contra a sua vontade. *He did it against his will.*
  Eu sou contra isso. *I am against that.*

contrabando *m. contraband; smuggling.*

contradição *f. contradiction.*
  Êle (Ele) diz o contrário do que sente. *He says the opposite of what he thinks.*
  Ao contrário. *On the contrary.*

contradizer *to contradict.*

contrafazer *to counterfeit.*

contrafeito *adj. counterfeit.*

contrariar *to contradict; to annoy, to vex.*

contrariedade *f. mishap; disappointment; vexation.*

contrário *adj. contrary, opposite; n. m. opponent.*
  Aconteceu-me o contrário. *The opposite happened to me.*

contra-senha *f. countersign; password.*

contrastar *to contrast.*

contraste *m. contrast.*

contratar *to engage, to hire; to bargain, to trade; to contract.*

contratempo *m. mishap, setback; disappointment.*

contrato *m. contract.*

contribuição *f. contribution; tax.*

contribuir *to contribute.*

controlar *to control* Ⓑ.

contrôle *m. control* Ⓑ.

contudo *nevertheless, however.*

conturbar *to trouble, to disturb.*

contusão *f. bruise, contusion.*

convalescença *f. convalescence.*

convenção *f. convention, agreement; pact.*

convencer *to convince.*

convencido *adj. convinced.*

conveniência *f. convenience, fitness.*

conveniente *adj. convenient, suitable.*

convento *m. convent.*

CONVERSA *f. conversation, talk, chatter.*
  Acho que é conversa demais. *In my opinion that's enough chatter.*
  Conversa mole. *Idle chatter.*

CONVERSAÇÃO *f. conversation, talk.*

CONVERSAR *to chatter, to converse.*
  Tenho que conversar com você. *I have to talk to you.*

converter *to convert, to change.*

convés *m. deck (ship).*

convicção *f. conviction, belief, certainty.*

convidado *adj. invited; m. guest.*

convidar *to invite.*

convir *to suit; to agree.*

convite *m. invitation.*

cooperação *f. cooperation.*

cooperar *to cooperate.*

coordenar *to coordinate.*

copa *f. pantry; crown (hat); pl. hearts (cards).*

cópia *f. copy.*
  É uma cópia. *It's a copy.*

copiar *to copy.*

COPO *m. glass (drinking); goblet, cup.*
  Por favor, um copo dágua. *A glass of water, please.*

coqueiro *m. coconut palm; palm tree.*

coquete *adj. coquettish; n. f. coquette.*

coquetel *m. cocktail, cocktail party* Ⓑ.

CÔR (COR) *f. color.*
  Esta côr está na moda. *This color is very stylish.*
  Esta côr vai bem com essa. *This color goes well with that one.*
  Côr fixa (x = ks). *Fast color.*
  Côr viva. *Bright color*
  Côr de laranja. *Orange.*
  Um homem de côr. *A colored man.*
  Ela vê tudo côr de rosa. *She sees everything through rose-colored glasses.*

CORAÇÃO *m. heart; core.*
  Com todo o meu coração. *With all my heart.*
  Mãos frias, coração quente. *Cold hands, warm heart.*

coragem *f. courage.*
  Coragem! *Have courage! Cheer up!*

corcovado *adj. humped; hunchbacked.*

corda *f. cord, rope; string; spring (watch).*
  Esqueci dar corda ao relógio. *I forgot to wind my watch.*
  Cordas vocais. *Vocal cords.*

cordão *m. cord, string, lace.*
  Cordões de sapato. *Shoelaces.*

cordeiro *m. lamb.*

cordel *m. twine, string, cord.*

cordial *adj. cordial, affectionate.*

cordilheira *f. mountain range.*

cordura *f. good sense.*

corneta *f. bugle, horn.*

côrno (corno) *m. horn, antler.*

côro (coro) *m. choir, chorus.*

coroa *f. crown; wreath, garland.*

coroar *to crown; to complete.*

coronel *m. colonel.*

CORPO *m. body; corps.*
  Corpo e alma. *Body and soul.*
  Corpo diplomático. *Diplomatic corps.*
  Corpo de Paz. *Peace Corps.*

corredor *m. corridor; runner.*

correia *f. leather strap, leash, thong.*

CORREIO *m. mail; post office.*
  A que horas sai o correio? *At what time does the mail leave?*
  Correio aéreo. *Airmail.*

corrente *adj. current, present (month); f. current; stream; draft (air).*
  Conta corrente. *Current account.*
  Recebi (a) sua estimada carta de 15 do corrente. *I have received your letter of the 15th of this month.*
  Sinto uma corrente de ar. *I feel a draft.*
  Estar ao corrente. *To be acquainted with. To be up-to-date on.*
  Corrente alternada. *Alternating current.*
  Corrente contínua. *Direct current.*
  Água corrente. *Running water.*

CORRER *to run; to flow; to elapse; to blow (wind); to draw (curtains).*
  Êles (Eles) vêm correndo. *They come running.*
  Corra as cortinas. *Draw the curtains.*

correspondência *f. correspondence, mail.*
  Eu estou em correspondência com êles (eles). *I am in correspondence with them.*

correspondente *adj. corresponding.*

corresponder *to correspond.*

correto (correcto) *adj. correct.*

corrida *f. run, race, course.*
  Corrida de cavalos. *Horse race.*

corrigir *to correct.*

corroborar *to corroborate.*

corromper *to corrupt.*

corrupção *f. corruption.*

corrupto *adj. corrupt.*

CORTAR *to cut; to cut off, to shorten.*
  Esta faca não corta. *This knife doesn't cut.*
  Vou cortar o cabelo. *I'm going to get a haircut.*

corte *m. cut; edge (knife).*

côrte (corte) *f. court, house of parliament, assembly; courting.*

cortejar *to court; to flatter.*

cortês *adj. courteous, gentle, polite.*
  Êle (Ele) é muito cortês. *He's very polite.*

cortesia *f. courtesy, politeness.*

cortiça *f. cork; bark.*

cortiço *m. beehive; tenement.*

cortina *f. curtain, screen.*
  Cortina de ferro. *Iron curtain.*
  Faça o favor de correr as cortinas. *Please draw the curtains.*

coruja *f. owl.*

corvo *m. crow, raven.*

coser *to sew.*

cosmético *adj. cosmetic.*

COSTA *f. coast, shore; pl. back.*
  A costa atlântica. *The Atlantic coast.*
  As costas da mão. *The back of the hand.*
  Êle (Ele) me deu as costas. *He turned his back on me.*

costela *f. rib; wife, fam.*

costeleta *f. chop.*
  Costeleta de porco. *Pork chop.*

costumado *adj. customary.*

costumar-se *to become accustomed.*

costume *m. custom, habit, practice.*

costura *f. sewing.*
  Máquina de costura. *Sewing machine.*

cotidiano *adj. daily.*

cotovêlo (cotovelo) *m. elbow.*

couraçado *adj. armored; n. m. battleship.*

couro *m. leather; hide; skin.*

cousa *f. see COISA.*

couve-flor *f. cauliflower.*

cova *f. cave, cavern.*

covarde *m. coward.*

cozer *to cook, to bake, to boil.*

cozinha *f. kitchen; cuisine.*

cozinhar *to cook.*

cozinheiro *m. cook, chef.*

crânio *m. skull, cranium.*

cravo *m. nail, tack.*
  Você deu no cravo. *You hit the nail on the head.*

crédito *m. credit; credence; reputation, standing.*
  Comprar a crédito. *To buy on credit.*
  Vender a crédito. *To sell on credit.*
  Dar crédito. *To give credit.*
  Carta de crédito. *Letter of credit.*

creme *m. cream.*

CRER *to believe, to think.*
  Creio que sim. *I think so.*
  Creio que não. *I think not.*
  Ver é crer. *Seeing is believing.*

crescer *to grow; to increase.*

crescimento *m. growth, increase.*

criada *f. servant.*

criado *m. servant.*

CRIANÇA *f. child.*

criar *to create, to produce; to nurse; to rear; to bring up.*

criatura *f. creature, person.*

crime *m. crime.*

criminal *adj. criminal.*

criminoso *adj. criminal; n. m. outlaw, criminal.*

crioulo *adj. native; creole; n. m. creole.*

crise *f. crisis; depression.*

cristal *m. crystal.*

cristão *m. Christian.*

cristianismo *m. Christianity.*

critério *m. criterion.*

crítica *f. criticism, judgment, comment; review.*
   A crítica não gostou da peça. *The critics did not like the play.*

criticar *to criticize, to judge.*

crônica (crónica) *f. chronicle; newspaper article or column.*

cronista *m. and f. chronicler; columnist.*

croquete *m. croquette.*

cruz *f. cross;*

cruzar *to cross; to cruise.*

CRUZEIRO *m. Brazilian monetary unit; large cross; cruise; cruiser (ship).*
   Custa duzentos cruzeiros. *It costs 200 cruzeiros.*
   Cruzeiro do Sul. *Southern Cross.*

cubano *adj. Cuban; m. Cuban.*

cubo *m. cube.*

cuecas *f. pl. men's shorts (underwear).*

CUIDADO *m. care, attention; anxiety, worry.*
   Cuidado! *Be careful!*
   Ter cuidado. *To be careful.*
   Cuidado com o cachorro! *Look out for the dog!*
   Ao cuidado de ... *Care of ...*

cuidadoso *adj. careful.*

cuidar *to care, to take care, to mind, to look after.*
   Quem cuida do jardim? *Who takes care of the garden?*
   Cuide-se. *Take care of yourself.*

cujo *whose, of which, of whom.*
   O professor Cândido, cujo livro sôbre (sobre) a literatura brasileira acaba de sair ... *Professor Cândido, whose book on Brazilian literature has just come out ...*

culpa *f. fault, guilt; sin.*

culpável *adj. guilty.*

cultivar *to cultivate; to till; to improve.*
   No Brasil se cultiva (cultiva-se) muito o café. *Much coffee is grown in Brazil.*

cultivo *m. farming, cultivation, tillage.*

culto *adj. well-educated; polished; n. m. worship, cult, religion.*
   Êle (Ele) é um homem culto. *He is a well-read man.*

cultura *f. culture; refinement.*

cultural *adj. cultural.*

cumprimentar *to greet; to congratulate.*

cumprimento *m. greeting, compliment.*
   Meus cumprimentos. *My regards.*

cumprir *to carry out, to fulfill; to behoove.*
   Êle (Ele) sempre cumpre a palavra. *He always keeps his word.*
   Êles (Eles) cumpriram o curso em três anos. *They completed the course in three years.*
   Cumpre-me avisá-lo ... *I am pleased (it behooves me) to inform you ... (business letter).*

cunha *f. wedge.*

cunhada *f. sister-in-law.*

cunhado *m. brother-in-law.*

cura *f. cure; m. priest.*

curar *to cure, to heal.*

curável *adj. curable.*

curiosidade *f. curiosity; oddity.*

curioso *adj. curious, inquisitive; strange, odd.*
   Estou curioso por sabê-lo. *I'm anxious to know (it).*

cursar *to cross, to travel; to study at a university.*

curso *m. course, direction; current; course of studies.*
   João fará o curso de filosofia. *John will study philosophy.*

curva *f. curve.*

custa *f. cost.*
   À custa de. *At the cost of.*

CUSTAR *to cost.*
   Quanto custam êstes (estes) sapatos? *How much do these shoes cost?*
   Custa-me trabalho crê-lo. *It's hard for me to believe it.*
   Custe o que custar. *Cost what it may.*

custear *to defray expenses.*

custo *m. cost, price; difficulty.*
   A todo custo. *At all costs.*

custódia *f. custody, guard.*

custodiar *to guard, to take into custody.*

custoso *adj. costly, expensive.*

cútis *f. skin, complexion.*

D

DA *(contr. of de + a) of the, from the.*
   O irmão da menina. *The girl's brother.*
   Feche a porta da sala. *Close the door of the room.*

dactilógrafa *f. typist.*

dactilógrafo *m. typist.*

dádiva *f. gift, present.*

dadivoso *adj. liberal, generous.*

DAÍ *from there, of there; therefore.*
   Daí a pouco. *A little later.*

dalém *from beyond.*
   Dalém mar. *Beyond the sea, overseas.*

DALI *from there, of there; therefore.*
   Saiu dali. *It came from over there.*
   Dali a pouco. *A little later.*

dália *f. dahlia.*

dama *f. lady, dame.*
   Jôgo (jogo) de damas. *Checkers.*

damasco *m. apricot; damask.*

danado *adj. spoiled, damaged.*

danar *to damage, to hurt.*

dança *f. dance.*

dançar *to dance.*

daninho *adj. harmful.*

dano *m. damage, loss; hurt, harm.*

DAQUELA *(contr. of de + aquela) f. of that, from that.*
   Não conheço nenhum professor daquela escola. *I don't know any teacher of that school.*

DAQUELE *(contr. of de + aquêle) m. of that, from that.*
   O chapéu é daquele senhor. *The hat belongs to that man.*

DAQUI *(contr. of de + aqui) from here, of here.*
   Êle (Ele) não é daqui. *He's not from this area.*
   Daqui a oito dias. *In a week.*

DAQUILO *(contr. of de + aquilo) of that, from that.*

DAR *to give; to show; to strike (hour); to hit; to take (a walk).*
   Faça o favor de me dar (dar-me) o seu endereço (endereço). *Please give me your address.*
   Eu lhe dou quatro dólares por êsse (esse) livro. *I'll give you four dollars for that book.*
   Vamos dar um passeio. *Let's take a walk.*
   Vamos dar uma volta. *Let's go for a walk.*
   Eu lhe dou (dou-lhe) as boas-vindas. *I welcome you.*
   O relógio acaba de dar seis horas. *The clock has just struck six.*
   Êle (Ele) me deu as costas. *He turned his back on me.*

Vamos dar fim a todo isso. *We're going to put an end to all that.*
   Isso me dá cuidado. *That worries me.*
   Êles (Eles) se dão muito bem. *They get along very well.*
   Eu lhe dou (dou-lhe) a minha palavra. *I give you my word.*
   É preciso dar corda ao relógio. *You must wind the watch.*
   Você dá as cartas. *You deal.*
   Êles vão dar uma festa no sábado. *They are going to have a party on Saturday.*
   Eu dei com êles ontem. *I met (came upon) them yesterday.*
   A mãe deu pancadas ao filho. *The mother struck her son.*
   Dê-se pressa! *Hurry up!*
   Dar um jeito. *To find a way.*
   Dar-se conta de. *To realise.*
   Dar à luz. *To give birth.*
   Dar gritos. *To cry out.*
   Dar os parabéns. *To congratulate.*
   Dar a conhecer. *To make known.*
   Tudo deu em nada. *It all came to naught.*
   Dar de comer. *To feed.*
   Dar de beber. *To give water to.*
   Dar aula. *To conduct a class.*
   Dá licença? *May I?*

dardo *m. dart.*

data *f. date.*

datar *to date.*

DE *of; from; for; by; on; to; with.*
   Essa é a casa de meu amigo. *That's my friend's house.*
   De quem é êste (este) livro? *Whose book is this?*
   O que é feito dêle (dele)? *What has become of him?*
   O livro é dela. *The book is hers.*
   Êle (Ele) é do Brasil. *He's from Brasil.*
   Eu sou de Lisboa. *I'm from Lisbon.*
   Um copo dágua. *A glass of water.*
   Uma casa de pedra. *A stone house.*
   Uma xícara (x = sh) de café. *A cup of coffee.*
   Máquina de costura. *Sewing machine.*
   Está na hora do jantar. *It's time for dinner.*
   De dia. *During the day.*
   De noite. *At night.*
   De nada. *Don't mention it.*
   Ela está vestida de azul. *She is dressed in blue.*
   De vez em quando. *From time to time.*
   Aquela jovem de olhos azuis. *That girl with the blue eyes.*
   Êles (Eles) e 'tão de pé. *They are standing.*
   Carlos está de cama. *Charles is sick in bed.*

deão *m. dean.*

DEBAIXO *(x = sh) under, underneath.*
   A carta estava debaixo dos papéis. *The letter was under the papers.*

debate *m. debate.*

debater *to debate, to discuss.*

débil *adj. feeble, weak.*

debilidade *f. feebleness, weakness.*

debilitar *to weaken, to debilitate.*

débito *m. debt.*

debruçar *to lean.*

debuxo *(x = sh) sketch.*

década *f. decade.*

decadência *f. decay, decadence; decline.*

decair *to decay, to decline, to die down.*

decano *m. dean.*

decente *adj. decent, honest; neat.*

decepção *f. disappointment.*

decidido *adj. decided; firm; determined.*

DECIDIR *to decide, to resolve, to determine.*

DECIDIR-SE *to decide, to make up one's mind.*

decifrar *to decipher, to decode.*

decímetro *m. decimeter.*

décimo *adj. tenth; n. m. tenth.*

Décimo primeiro. *Eleventh.*
Décimo segundo. *Twelfth.*
Décimo terceiro. *Thirteenth.*
Décimo quarto. *Fourteenth.*
Décimo quinto. *Fifteenth.*
Décimo sexto. *Sixteenth.*
Décimo sétimo. *Seventeenth.*
Décimo oitavo. *Eighteenth.*
Décimo nono. *Nineteenth.*
decisão *f. decision, determination.*
decisivo *adj. decisive.*
declaração *f. declaration.*
declarar *to declare, to state; to testify.*
Tem alguma coisa a declarar? *Do you have anything to declare (customs)?*
declinar *to decline.*
decoração *f. decoration; stage scenery.*
decorar *to decorate; to learn by heart, to memorize.*
decôro (decoro) *m. decency, decorum, honor.*
decotado *adj. low-necked.*
decrescente *adj. decreasing.*
decrescer *to decrease.*
decrescimento *m. decrease.*
decretar *to decree.*
decreto *m. decree.*
dedal *m. thimble.*
dedicação *f. dedication.*
dedicado *adj. dedicated, devoted.*
dedicar *to dedicate; to devote.*
Êle (Ele) se dedicou à pintura. *He devoted himself to painting.*
dedicatória *f. dedication.*
DEDO *m. finger; toe.*
Dedo mínimo. *Little finger.*
Dedo indicador. *Index finger.*
Dedo polegar. *Thumb.*
Dedo médio. *Middle finger.*
Dedo anular. *Ring finger.*
dedução *f. deduction.*
deduzir *to deduce, to understand.*
defeito *m. fault, defect.*
defeituoso *adj. defective.*
defender *to defend.*
defensiva *f. defensive.*
defensor *m. supporter, defender.*
defesa *f. defense.*
deficiência *f. deficiency.*
deficit *m. shortage, deficit.*
definição *f. definition, explanation.*
definido *adj. definite.*
definir *to define, to determine.*
definitivo *adj. definitive.*
deformação *f. deformation.*
deformar *to deform.*
deformidade *f. deformity.*
defraudar *to defraud, to swindle.*
defronte *facing.*
defunto *adj. deceased; n. m. deceased; dead person.*
degêlo (degelo) *m. thawing; thaw.*
degeneração *f. degeneration.*
degenerar *to deteriorate, to degenerate.*
degradante *adj. degrading.*
degradar *to degrade.*
degrau *m. step; rung (ladder); degree.*
degredar *to banish, to exile.*
DEITAR *to throw, to cast, to lay.*
Isso é deitar lenha no fogo. *That's adding fuel to the fire.*
DEITAR-SE *to lie down, to go to bed.*
Nós nos deitamos às dez. *We go to bed at ten.*
DEIXAR *(x = sh) to leave, to let; to quit, to give up.*

Deixe-me vê-lo. *Let me see it.*
Não nos deixaram entrar. *They did not let us enter.*
Posso deixar meus livros aqui? *May I leave my books here?*
Deixe para amanhã. *Leave it for tomorrow.*
Deixe-me em paz! *Leave me alone!*
Êle (Ele) deixou de escrever-me. *He stopped writing me.*
Êle deixou seu emprêgo (emprego). *He gave us his job.*
Isso deixa muito a desejar. *That leaves much to be desired.*
Não deixe de telefonar-me. *Don't fail (be sure) to telephone me.*
delegação *f. delegation.*
delegacia *f. delegacy*
Delegacia de polícia. *Police headquarters.*
delegado *m. delegate, deputy, commissioner.*
deleitar *to please, to delight.*
deleite *m. delight, pleasure.*
delgado *adj. thin, slender.*
deliberação *f. deliberation.*
deliberar *to deliberate.*
delicado *adj. delicate; dainty, nice; exquisite; fragile.*
delícia *f. delight, pleasure.*
delicioso *adj. delicious, delightful.*
A sobremesa está deliciosa. *The dessert is delicious.*
delinquente (delinquente) *m. delinquent, offender.*
delirar *to rave, to be delirious.*
delírio *m. delirium, raving; enthusiasm; frenzy.*
delito *m. misdemeanor, offense, crime.*
DEMAIS *other; rest; too much, too many.*
Custa demais. *It costs too much.*
Você bebe demais. *You drink too much.*
Dois é bom; três é demais. *Two is company, three is a crowd.*
Os demais. *The others; the rest.*
demanda *f. claim, demand, request; lawsuit.*
demandar *to demand, to claim; to take legal action; to enter a claim; to sue.*
demarcação *f. demarcation.*
demasiado *too much; too; excessive.*
demência *f. insanity, madness.*
demente *adj. insane, crazy.*
demissão *f. dismissal; firing; resignation.*
demitido *adj. dismissed; fired.*
demitir *to dismiss, to fire.*
demitir-se *to resign.*
democracia *f. democracy.*
democrata *m. ard f. democrat.*
democrático *adj. democratic.*
demolição *f. demolition.*
demolir *to demolish.*
demônio (demónio) *m. devil, demon.*
Como um demônio. *Like the devil.*
demonstração *f. demonstration.*
demonstrar *to demonstrate, to prove, to show.*
demora *f. delay.*
Sem mais demora. *Without further delay.*
demorar(-se) *to delay, to tarry; to stay.*
Você se demorou muito. *You are quite late.*
denegar *to refuse, to deny.*
denominação *f. denomination.*
denominar *to name.*
denotar *to denote, to indicate, to express.*
densidade *f. density.*
denso *adj. dense, thick.*
dentadura *f. denture, set of teeth.*
dental *adj. dental.*
DENTE *m. tooth.*
Escôva (escova) de dentes. *Toothbrush.*
Dente molar. *Molar.*

Dor de dentes. *Toothache.*
Dentes postiços. *False teeth.*
dentifrício *adj. dentifrice; tooth; n. m. dentifrice.*
dentista *m. and f. dentist.*
DENTRO *within, inside.*
Dentro de alguns dias. *Within a few days.*
Dentro em pouco. *In a short while.*
Que está acontecendo (a acontecer) lá dentro? *What's going on inside there?*
denuncia *f. denunciation; accusation.*
denunciar *to denounce, to accuse; to give notice; to inform.*
departamento *m. department.*
dependência *f. dependence, dependency; annex.*
DEPENDER *to depend, be dependent on.*
Muito depende do que você faça. *A great deal depends on what you do.*
deplorar *to deplore, to be sorry, to regret*
Deploro muito o acontecido. *I'm sorry about what happened.*
deplorável *adj. deplorable.*
DEPOIS *after, afterward, later.*
Dois dias depois. *Two days later.*
Depois de pagar a conta êle (ele) saiu. *After he payed the bill he left.*
Depois de amanhã. *Day after tomorrow.*
deportar *to deport.*
depositar *to deposit, to place; to put in a safe place; to entrust.*
Êles (Eles) depositaram o dinheiro. *They deposited the money.*
depósito *m. deposit; depot; warehouse; reservoir; tank.*
Depósito de bagagem. *Baggage room.*
Depósito de água. *Water reservoir.*
DEPRESSA *fast; rapidly; in haste.*
Mais depressa! *Faster!*
Depressa! *Hurry!*
depressão *f. depression.*
deprimir *to depress.*
deputado *m. deputy, congressman.*
derivar *to derive.*
derramamento *m. spilling, shedding.*
derramar *to spill; to shed; to scatter; to spread.*
derredor *around, about.*
derreter *to melt, to dissolve.*
derribamento *m. knocking down, felling.*
derribar *to demolish, to knock down, to bring down.*
derrocar *to overthrow; to demolish; to destroy.*
derrota *f. defeat, rout; ship's course.*
derrotar *to rout, to defeat.*
derrubar *to knock down, to bring down, to overthrow.*
desabafar *to free, to uncover; to unburden oneself.*
desabitado *adj. uninhabited, unoccupied.*
desabitar *to vacate.*
desabotoar *to unbutton.*
desabrido *adj. rude, insolent.*
desabrigado *adj. uncovered; without shelter, exposed.*
desabrigar *to uncover; to leave without shelter.*
desabrigo *m. lack of shelter.*
desabrochar *to unbutton; to unclasp, to unfasten.*
Desabrochar-se. *To free oneself.*
desacêrto (desacerto) *m. mistake, error.*
desacôrdo (desacordo) *m. disagreement.*
desacreditar *to discredit.*
desafiar *to challenge, to defy.*
desafinar *to get out of tune, to play out of tune.*
desafio *m. challenge; competition.*
desafogar-se *to unburden oneself.*
desafôgo (desafogo) *m. ease, relief.*
desafortunado *adj. unlucky, unfortunate.*

desagradar *to displease.*

desagradável *adj. unpleasant, disagreeable.*
Tudo isso foi muito desagradável. *It was all very unpleasant.*

desagradecer *to be ungrateful.*

desagradecido *adj. ungrateful.*

desagrado *m. displeasure, discontent.*

desagravar *to vindicate, to avenge.*

desagravo *m. amends, vindication.*

desaguamento *m. drainage, draining.*

desaguar *to drain.*

desairoso *adj. clumsy, awkward.*

desalentar *to discourage.*

desalento *m. discouragement, dismay.*

desalojar *to dispossess, to evict; to dislodge; to drive out.*

desalugado *adj. vacant, unrented.*
Atualmente o apartamento está desalugado. *At present the apartment is vacant.*

desalugar *to vacate.*

desamparado *adj. abandoned.*

desanimado *adj. discouraged.*

desanimar *to discourage.*

desânimo *m. discouragement.*

desaparecer *to disappear.*
Meu cachorro desapareceu. *My dog disappeared.*

desapercebido *adj. unprepared, not ready.*

desaprovar *to disapprove of.*

desaproveitar *to misuse, not to make good use of.*

desarmado *adj. unarmed.*

desarmar *to disarm; to dismount, to take apart.*

desarrolhar *to uncork.*

desassossegar *to disturb.*

desassossêgo (desassossego) *uneasiness, restlessness.*

desastre *m. disaster, calamity.*

desatar *to untie, to loosen.*

desatento *adj. inattentive, thoughtless, negligent.*

desatino *m. lack of tact; folly, madness.*

desbaratar *to thwart, to upset (a plan); to destroy; to disperse, to rout, to spoil, to run.*

descabelado *adj. disheveled; hairless; impetuous.*

descalabro *m. calamity, great loss.*

descalçar *to take off shoes, gloves.*
Ela se sentou e se descalçou. (Ela sentou-se e descalçou-se) *She sat down and took her shoes off.*

descalço *adj. barefoot.*

descamisado *adj. shirtless.*

DESCANSAR *to rest.*
O senhor não quer descansar um pouco? *Don't you want to rest a little?*

descanso *m. rest, calm, support.*

descarado *adj. brazen, impudent.*

descarga *f. discharge, unloading.*

descargo *m. discharge of an obligation.*

DESCARREGAR *to unload, to discharge; to fire (a gun).*
Vão descarregar o navio amanhã. *They will unload the ship tomorrow.*

descarrilamento *m. derailing.*

descarrilar *to become derailed.*

descartar *to discard, to dismiss.*

descendência *f. descent, origin.*

descendente *adj. descendent; n. m. and f. descendant.*

descender *to descend from.*

descenso *m. descent.*

DESCER *to descend, to go down; to drop.*
Desçam já! *Come down right away!*

descoberta *f. discovery.*

descoberto *adj. discovered, uncovered; bareheaded.*

descobrimento *m. discovery.*

DESCOBRIR *to discover, to uncover; to find out; to disclose.*
Descobrimos que não era verdade. *We found out that it was not true.*
O Brasil foi descoberto em mil e quinhentos. *Brazil was discovered in 1500.*

descolorido *adj. discolored, faded*

descomedido *adj. immoderate; excessive; impolite; rude.*

descompor *to discompose, to disarrange.*

descompor-se *to become upset.*

descomposto *adj. out of order; upset.*

desconcertante *adj. disconcerting; confusing.*

desconcertar *to disturb, to confuse, to baffle.*

desconfiança *f. distrust.*

desconfiar *to distrust, to suspect.*
Nós desconfiamos dêles (deles). *We distrust them.*

desconhecer *not to recognize, not to know; to ignore.*

desconhecido *adj. unknown; n. m. stranger.*
Quem é aquêle (aquele) desconhecido? *Who is that stranger?*

desconhecimento *m. ignorance; ingratitude.*

desconsiderado *adj. thoughtless, inconsiderate.*

desconsolação *f. disconsolation.*

desconsolador *adj. disheartening, sad.*

descontar *to discount, to deduct.*

descontentamento *m. discontent, dissatisfaction.*

descontente *adj. discontented.*

descortês *adj. discourteous, impolite.*

descoser *to unstitch, to rip.*

descrédito *m. discredit.*

DESCREVER *to describe.*

descrição *f. description.*

descuidado *adj. careless; negligent; slovenly.*

descuidar *to neglect, to overlook.*
Não descuide de preparar a lista. *Don't neglect to prepare the list.*

descuido *m. negligence, carelessness; omission, oversight.*

desculpa *f. excuse, apology.*

desculpar *to excuse, to pardon.*

DESCULPE! *Excuse me! Pardon me! I'm sorry!*

DESDE *since, after, from.*
Ela está de cama desde ontem. *She's been (sick) in bed since yesterday.*
Desde então. *Since then.*
Desde criança. *From childhood.*
Desde agora. *From now on.*
Desde já *Immediately, from now on.*

desdém *m. disdain, scorn, contempt.*

desdenhar *to disdain, to scorn.*

desdita *f. misfortune, calamity, unhappiness.*

desditado *adj. wretched; unfortunate; unhappy.*

desdizer *to retract, to deny, to contradict.*

DESEJAR *to desire, to wish.*
Não desejo nada. *I don't want anything.*
João deseja falar com você. *John wants to talk to you.*
Eu lhe desejo felicidade. *I wish you happiness.*

desejável *adj. desirable.*

DESEJO *m. desire, wish.*
Êsses (esses) são (os) meus desejos. *Those are my wishes.*

desejoso *adj. desirous.*

desembaraçar *to free, to disentangle.*

desembaraçar-se *to get rid of.*

desembarcadouro *m. landing place, dock.*

desembarcar *to disembark, to go ashore.*

desembarque *m. landing.*

desembolsar *to pay out, to disburse.*

desembôlso (desembolso) *m. disbursement.*

desempacotar *to unpack.*

desempenhar *to perform; to accomplish; to carry out; to redeem, to take out of pawn; to free from debt.*
O ator principal desempenhou bem seu papel. *The main actor (the male lead) played his part well.*

desemprêgo (desemprego) *m. unemployment.*

desencantar *to disappoint, to disillusion.*

desenfreado *adj. unbridled, unrestrained.*

desenganado *disappointed, disillusioned.*

desenganar *to disappoint, to disillusion.*

desengano *m. disappointment, disillusionment.*

desenhar *to design, to sketch.*

desenho *m. design, sketch.*

desenlace *m. outcome, result, dénouement.*
O desenlace da peça é muito fraco. *The play's dénouement is very weak.*

desenredar *to disentangle.*

desenrêdo (desenredo) *m. outcome, result, dénouement.*

desenrolar *to unwind, to unroll.*

desentender *to misunderstand.*

desentendido *adj. not understanding; misunderstood.*

desentoar *to be out of tune.*

desenvoltura *f. ease, boldness; impudence.*

DESENVOLVER *to develop, to grow; to unfold.*

desenvolvido *adj. developed.*

desenvolvimento *m. development.*

desequilibrar *to unbalance.*

desertar *to desert.*

deserto *adj. deserted; n. m. desert.*
A cidade ficou deserta. *The city remained deserted.*

desertor *m. deserter.*

desesperação *f. desperation, despair; fury.*

desesperado *adj. hopeless; desperate; furious.*

desesperar *to despair; to exasperate.*
Isso me desespera. *That exasperates me.*

desespêro (desespero) *m. desperation, despair; fury.*

desfalecer *to faint; to weaken.*

desfalecimento *m. faint; weakness.*

desfazer *to undo; to take apart; to dissolve.*
Foi preciso desfazer a maior parte do que elas tinham feito. *It was necessary to undo most of what they had done.*

desfeito *adj. destroyed; in pieces; undone.*

desfiar *to ravel, to fray.*

desfigurar *to disfigure; to misshape; to distort.*

desfilar *to parade, to march in review.*

desfile *m. parade, review.*

desfolhar *to strip (as of leaves)*

desfrutar *to enjoy; to make fun of.*

desgastar *to wear out.*

desgaste *m. wear and tear.*

desgostar *to displease.*

desgôsto (desgosto) *m. displeasure; sorrow.*
Ela sofreu muitos desgostos. *She suffered many sorrows.*

desgraça *f. misfortune, sorrow.*
Que desgraça! *What a misfortune!*
Por desgraça. *Unfortunately.*
Nunca uma desgraça vem só. *It never rains but it pours.*

desgraçado *adj. unfortunate, unlucky; unhappy; m. poor fellow, wretch.*
Êle (Ele) é um desgraçado. *He's a poor (unfortunate) fellow.*

designar *to designate, to appoint.*

desígnio *m. design; plan.*

desigual *adj. uneven.*

desigualar *to make uneven.*

desigualdade *f. inequality; unevenness.*

desilusão *f. disillusion.*

desinfestar *to disinfest.*

desinfetante *adj. disinfectant; n. m. disinfectant.*

desinfetar *to disinfect.*

desinterêsse (desinteresse) *m. disinterest.*

desistir *to desist.*

desleal *adj. unfaithful; disloyal.*

deslealdade *f. unfaithfulness; disloyalty.*

desligado *adj. disconnected; off (light, radio, etc.).*

desligar *to disconnect; to turn off.*
> Faça o favor de desligar êsse (esse) televisor. *Please turn that TV set off.*
> Espere um momento; não desligue. *Wait a minute; don't hang up (telephone).*

deslizar *to slip, to slide.*

deslize *m. slip, slipping.*

deslocação *f. dislocation; displacement.*

deslocar *to dislocate; to displace.*

deslumbramento *m. dazzling (great) light.*

deslumbrar *to dazzle, to daze.*

desmaiar *to faint, to turn pale.*

desmaio *m. faint, fainting spell; paleness.*

desmedido *adj. immoderate, excessive.*

desmemoriado *adj. forgetful.*

desmentir *to deny, to contradict.*

desmobiliar (desmobilar) *to remove the furniture.*

desmontar *to dismount; to take apart (a machine, etc.).*

desmoralizado *adj. demoralized.*

desmoralizar *to demoralize.*

desnatar *to skim (milk).*

desnudar *to undress, to bare.*

desnudo *adj. naked.*

desobedecer *to disobey.*

desobediência *f. disobedience.*

desobediente *adj. disobedient.*

desocupado *adj. not busy; unemployed.*
> Eu lhe falarei quando você estiver desocupado. *I'll speak to you when you are not busy.*

desocupar *to vacate, to empty.*

desonesto *adj. dishonest; indecent.*

desonra *f. dishonor; disgrace.*
> Ser pobre não é desonra. *Poverty is no disgrace.*

desonrar *to dishonor; to disgrace.*

desonroso *adj. dishonorable; disgraceful.*

desordem *f. disorder.*

desordenado *adj. disorderly, unruly.*
> A vida do Eduardo é bastante desordenada. *Edward's life is quite wild.*

desorganizar *to disorganize.*

desorientar *to lead astray; to confuse.*

despachar *to dispatch, to forward, to expedite, to send.*

despedaçar *to tear or break into bits.*

despedida *f. farewell; dismissal.*
> A despedida foi uma ocasião muito triste. *The farewell was a very sad occasion.*
> Jantar de despedida. *Farewell dinner.*

despedir *to send away, to dismiss.*

despedir-se *to say farewell, to say good-by to; to take leave.*
> Despedimo-nos dêles (deles) na estação. *We said good-by to them at the station.*

despeito *m. spite.*
> A despeito de. *In spite of.*

despejar *to empty; to throw out.*

despensa *f. pantry.*

desperdiçar *to waste.*

desperdício *m. waste.*

despertador *m. alarm clock.*

despertar *to awaken; to wake up.*

desperto *adj. awake.*

DESPESA *f. expense, cost.*
> Cada ano tenho ainda mais despesas. *Each year I have even more expenses.*
> Sempre há despesas imprevistas. *There are always some unforeseen expenses.*

DESPIR *to undress; to strip.*
> Ela se despiu e deitou-se. *She undressed and went to bed.*

despistar *to throw off the track, to mislead.*

despojar *to despoil; to strip.*

desposar *to marry.*

déspota *m. and f. despot.*

desprazer *to displease; displeasure.*

desprender *to unpin; to unfasten; to separate.*

desprendido *adj. unfastened; generous.*

despreocupado *adj. unconcerned.*

despreocupar *not to worry.*

desprezar *to despise, to scorn; to slight; to look down on.*

desprêzo (desprezo) *m. contempt, scorn.*
> Todos o trataram com desprêzo. *They all treated him with contempt.*

desproporcionado *adj. disproportionate, unequal.*

despropósito *m. nonsense, absurdity; excessive amount.*

desprovido *adj. lacking.*

desqualificar *to disqualify.*

desquitar *to free; to separate, to divorce.*

desquitar-se *to separate, to divorce.*

desquite *m. separation, divorce.*
> O casamento terminou por desquite. *The marriage ended in separation (divorce).*

destacamento *m. detachment.*

destacar *to detach, to stand out.*

destapar *to uncover, to open.*

desterrado *adj. exiled, banished; n. m. exile.*

desterrar *to exile, to banish, to deport.*
> Alguns dos chefes foram desterrados. *Some of the leaders were exiled.*

destinar *to appoint; to destine.*

destinatário *m. addressee.*
> Escreva no envelope o nome do destinatário. *Write the name of the addressee on the envelope.*

destino *m. fate, destiny; destination.*
> Com destino a Lisboa. *Bound for Lisbon.*

destreza *f. skill.*

destro *adj. skillful, adroit.*

destróier (destruidor) *m. destroyer (ship).*

destruição *f. destruction.*

destruidor *adj. destructive; n. m. destroyer.*

destruir *to destroy.*
> É mais fácil destruir (do) que construir. *It is easier to destroy than to build.*

desumanidade *f. inhumanity.*

desumano *adj. inhumane, inhuman.*

desvanecer *to vanish; to dispel.*

desvantagem *f. disadvantage.*

desvantajoso *adj. disadvantageous.*

desvão *m. attic; hiding place.*

desvelar *to keep awake; to watch over; to unveil.*

desvêlo (desvelo) *m. watching over; solicitude.*

desventurado *adj. unfortunate.*

desviar *to divert, to deviate, to dissuade.*
> Êle (ele) se desviou do assunto. *He digressed from the subject.*

desvio *m. deviation; detour.*

detalhe *m. detail.*
> Conte-me em detalhe o que aconteceu. *Tell me in detail what happened.*
> Detalhes biográficos. *Biographical data.*

detective Ⓑ *m. detective.*

detenção *f. detention.*

DETER *to detain, to hold back, to stop.*
> Meu amigo me deteve. *My friend detained me.*

DETER-SE *to hold oneself back; to delay; to stop.*

detergente *adj. n. m. detergent.*

deteriorar *to deteriorate.*

determinação *f. determination, decision, courage.*
> Êle (ele) sempre fala com determinação. *He always speaks with conviction.*

determinado *adj. determined, resolute.*

determinar *to determine, to decide.*

determinar-se *to resolve, to make up one's mind.*

detestar *to detest, to abhor.*

detestável *adj. detestable.*

detido *adj. detained; arrested.*
> O ladrão foi detido pela polícia. *The thief was arrested by the police.*

DETRÁS *behind.*
> Detrás da porta. *Behind the door.*
> Falam dêle (dele) por detrás. *They talk about him behind his back.*

DEUS *God.*
> Meu Deus! *Good Lord! Heavens!*
> Se Deus quiser! *God willing.*
> Pelo amor de Deus! *For heaven's sake!*
> Deus me livre! *Heaven forbid!*
> Graças a Deus! *Thank God!*
> O homem propõe e Deus dispõe. *Man proposes and God disposes.*
> Deus lhe pague! *God bless you!*

DEVAGAR *slow, slowly.*
> Devagar se vai ao longe. *Easy does it.*
> Faça o favor de falar mais devagar. *Please speak more slowly.*

devastação *f. devastation.*

devastar *to devastate, to ruin.*

DEVER *to owe; should, must, ought; m. duty, task.*
> Quanto lhe devo? *How much do I owe you?*
> Devemos ir já. *We should go now.*
> Você devia comer mais. *You should eat more.*
> Que devemos fazer? *What should we do?*
> Êle (Ele) sempre cumpre o seu dever. *He always does his duty.*

deveras *really, truly.*

devido *adj. due; owing to, on account of; proper.*
> Devido à hora, não esperemos mais. *Owing to the time, let's not wait any longer.*

devoção *f. devotion.*

devolução *f. restitution, return.*

devolver *to return, to give back.*
> João nunca me devolveu o dinheiro. *John never returned the money to me.*

devorar *to devour, to consume.*

devoto *adj. devout, pious; devoted.*

DEZ *ten, tenth.*

DEZANOVE *nineteen, nineteenth* Ⓟ.

DEZASSEIS *sixteen, sixteenth* Ⓟ.

DEZASSETE *seventeen, seventeenth* Ⓟ.

DEZEMBRO *December.*

DEZENOVE *nineteen, nineteenth* Ⓑ.

DEZESSEIS *sixteen, sixteenth* Ⓑ.

DEZESSETE *seventeen, seventeenth* Ⓑ.

DEZOITO *eighteen, eighteenth.*

DIA *m. day.*
> Bom dia! *Good morning!*
> Que dia é hoje? *What day is it?*
> Daqui a cinco dias. *Five days from now.*
> Estarei em casa o dia todo. *I'll be home all day.*

Eu o vejo todos os dias. *I see him every day.*
De dia. *During the day.*
Um dia sim um dia não. *Every other day.*
No dia seguinte. *On the following day.*
De dia em dia. *From day to day.*
Dia feriado. *Holiday.*
Dia de trabalho. *Work day.*
Dia útil. *Work day. Week day.*
Dia de Ano Bom. *New Year's Day.*
De quatro em quatro dias. *Every four days.*
O dia todo. *All day long.*

diabete, diabetes m. and f. *diabetes.*

diabo m. *devil.*
Pobre diabo! *Poor devil! Poor fellow!*
Pintar o diabo. *To raise the devil.*

diagnóstico adj. *diagnostic;* n. m. *diagnosis.*

diagrama m. *diagram, chart.*

dialeto (dialecto) m. *dialect.*

diálogo m. *dialogue.*

diamante m. *diamond.*

diâmetro m. *diameter.*

DIANTE *before, in front, in the presence of.*
Êle (ele) está esperando diante do clube. *He is waiting in front of the club.*
Daqui em diante. *From now on.*

dianteira f. *front, lead.*

dianteiro adj. *leading, front;* m. *forward (sports).*

DIÁRIO adj. *daily;* n. m. *daily, daily newspaper; diary.*
O diário ainda não chegou. *The paper did not arrive yet.*
Eu gostaria de ver o diário dela. *I'd like to see her diary.*

diarréia (diarreia) f. *diarrhea.*

dicionário m. *dictionary.*

dieta f. *diet.*

difamação f. *defamation.*

difamar *to defame.*

DIFERENÇA f. *difference.*
Partir a diferença. *To split the difference.*

DIFERENTE adj. *different.*

diferir *to defer, to put off; to differ.*

DIFÍCIL adj. *difficult.*
A lição é muito difícil. *The lesson is very difficult.*

dificuldade f. *difficulty.*

dificultar *to make difficult, to obstruct.*

dificultoso adj. *difficult.*

difteria f. *diphtheria.*

difundir *to diffuse; to divulge; to broadcast.*

difusão f. *diffusion; broadcasting.*

digerir *to digest.*

digestão f. *digestion.*

dignar-se *to deign, to condescend.*

dignidade f. *dignity.*

digno adj. *deserving, worthy; honorable.*
Digno de confiança. *Trustworthy.*

digressão f. *digression.*

dilação f. *delay.*

dilatar *to put off, to delay; to expand.*

dilema m. *dilemma.*

dileto adj. *loved, beloved.*

diligência f. *diligence; legal arrangement; stagecoach.*

diligente adj. *diligent; active.*

diluir *to dilute.*

dilúvio m. *flood.*

dimensão f. *dimension.*

diminuir *to diminish, to decrease.*

diminutivo adj. *diminutive.*

diminuto adj. *diminutive, minute.*

dinamite f. *dynamite.*

dínamo m. *dynamo.*

dinheirão m. *large amount of money.*

DINHEIRO m. *money, currency.*
Dinheiro em caixa (x = sh). *Cash on hand.*
Estou sem dinheiro. *I'm broke.*
Dinheiro é um bom companheiro mas mal conselheiro. *Money is a good friend but a bad master.*

diploma m. *diploma.*

diplomacia f. *diplomacy.*

diplomático adj. *diplomatic.*

DIREÇÃO (DIRECÇAO) f. *direction; guidance; management; administration.*
O volante de direção. *Steering wheel.*
Em direção a. *Toward.*

DIREITO adj. *straight, direct; proper;* n. m. *law, justice; claim, title; right; royalty; duty (import), tax.*
À direita. *To the right. On the right.*
A mão direita. *The right hand.*
Faculdade de direito. *Law school.*
É preciso proteger os direitos do indivíduo. *One must protect the rights of the individual.*
Siga sempre direito. *Continue straight ahead.*
O senhor não tem direito a queixar-se (x = sh). *You have no right to complain.*
Direitos. *Rights. Fees. Duties.*

diretivo (directivo) adj. *directive.*

DIRETO (DIRECTO) adj. *direct, straight; nonstop, frank.*
Êste trem (este comboio) é direto? *Is this a through train?*

DIRETOR (DIRECTOR) adj. *directing, managing;* n. m. *director, manager, administrator.*
Diretor de escola. *Principal (school).*
Diretor geral. *General manager.*

diretório m. *directory, directorate.*

DIRIGIR *to direct; to address; to conduct, to control, to guide; to drive.*
Vou dirigir-lhe uma carta. *I am going to write a letter to him.*
Ela sabe dirigir (um) automóvel? *Does she know how to drive a car?*

dirigir-se *to address oneself to, to speak to; to apply.*
A quem devo dirigir-me? *To whom should I apply?*
O senhor se dirige a nós? *Are you speaking to us?*

dirigível m. *dirigible.*

discar Ⓑ *to dial (telephone).*

discernante adj. *discerning, discriminating.*

discernimento m. *discernment.*

discernir *to discern; to distinguish.*

disciplina f. *discipline.*

discípulo m. *disciple, follower; student.*

disco m. *disk; record (phonograph); dial (telephone).*

discordante adj. *discordant.*

discórdia f. *discord, disagreement; dissension.*

discrepância f. *discrepancy.*

discrepar *to disagree, to differ.*

discreto adj. *discreet.*

discurso m. *speech.*
Fazer um discurso. *To make a speech.*

discussão f. *discussion; dispute.*

DISCUTIR *to discuss; to argue.*

disenteria f. *dysentery.*

disfarçar-se *to disguise.*

disfarce m. *disguise; mask.*

díspar adj. *unequal.*

disparar *to shoot, to fire, to discharge.*

disparatado adj. *nonsensical, absurd.*

disparatar *to blunder; to talk nonsense.*

disparate m. *nonsense.*

disparo m. *discharge, shot.*

dispendioso adj. *expensive, costly.*

dispensar *to dispense, to exempt; to bestow, to extend.*

dispensário m. *dispensary.*

disperso adj. *dispersed, scattered.*

disponível adj. *available.*

dispor *to dispose, to arrange, to provide for; to determine; to prepare;* m. *disposal.*
Eu estou ao seu dispor. *I'm at your disposal.*
Disponho de pouco tempo. *I have very little time now.*
O homem põe, Deus dispõe. *Man proposes, God disposes.*

disposição f. *disposition; service; state of mind, condition.*
Estou à sua disposição. *I'm at your disposal.*
Ela está com disposição a aceitar. *She is inclined to accept.*

disposto adj. *disposed, ready, inclined; arranged.*
Êles (eles) estão dispostos para fazê-lo. *They are inclined to do it.*
Eu estou bem disposto. *I feel fine.*

disputa f. *dispute, quarrel; contest.*

disputar *to dispute, to quarrel.*

disseminar *to disseminate; to scatter.*

dissenção f. *dissension, strife.*

dissidente adj. *dissident;* n. m. *dissenter; nonconformist.*

dissimulação f. *dissimulation; pretense.*

dissimular *to pretend; to disguise.*

dissolver *to dissolve; to melt; to break up.*

dissuadir *to dissuade; to deter.*

DISTÂNCIA f. *distance.*
É a pouca distância. *It's not far.*

DISTANTE adj. *far, distant.*

distinção f. *distinction; discrimination; difference.*
Êle (ele) é um homem de grande distinção. *He is a very distinguished man.*
Aqui é preciso fazer distinção. *It is necessary to make a distinction here.*

distinguir *to distinguish; to discriminate; to tell apart.*
Não posso distinguir um do outro. *I can't tell one from the other.*

distinguir-se *to distinguish oneself.*

DISTINTO adj. *distinct; different; distinguished.*
Um homem distinto. *A man of distinction.*

distração (distracção) f. *distraction; absentmindedness.*

distraído adj. *inattentive, absentminded.*

distrair *to distract; to entertain.*

distrair-se *to enjoy oneself.*
Ela se distraiu na festa. *She had a good time at the party.*

distribuição f. *distribution.*

distribuidor adj. *distributing;* n. m. *distributor.*

distribuir *to distribute; to divide; to allot, to allocate.*

distrito m. *district; region.*

disturbar *to disturb.*

distúrbio m. *disturbance.*

ditado m. *dictation; saying, proverb.*

ditador m. *dictator.*

ditar *to dictate.*
Escreva o que vou ditar. *Write what I am going to dictate.*

dito adj. *said;* n. m. *saying.*
Dito e feito. *No sooner said than done.*

ditongo m. *diphthong.*

divã m. *divan, couch.*

divagação f. *wandering, digression.*

divergência f. *divergence.*

diversão f. *diversion, amusement, recreation.*

diversidade f. *diversity, variety.*

DIVERSO adj. *different, diverse;* pl. *several, various.*

Eu o vi em diversas ocasiões. *I saw him on several occasions.*

DIVERTIDO *adj. entertaining, amusing; funny.*
Tudo isto é muito divertido. *This is all very amusing.*

divertimento *m. diversion, amusement; sport.*

DIVERTIR *to amuse, to divert, to entertain.*

DIVERTIR-SE *to amuse oneself, to have a good time.*
Nós nos divertimos na festa. *We had a good time at the party.*
Divirta-se! *Have a good time!*

dívida *f. debt.*
Ela pagou tôdas (todas) as dívidas. *She paid all her debts.*
Dívida ativa (activa). *Outstanding debt.*
Contrair dívidas. *To contract debts.*

dividendo *m. dividend.*

DIVIDIR *to divide.*

divindade *f. divinity.*

divino *adj. divine; heavenly.*

divisa *f. motto, slogan; emblem.*

divisão *f. division; partition, compartment; section.*

divisar *to perceive, to catch sight of.*

divorciar *to divorce.*

divorciar-se *to get a divorce, to be divorced.*

divórcio *m. divorce.*

divulgar *to divulge, to disclose.*

DIZER *to say; to speak; to tell; m. saying.*
Dígame, por favor. *Please tell me.*
Pode dizer-me onde é a estação? *Can you tell me where the station is?*
Eu lhe direi. *I'll tell him.*
Não me diga! *You don't say!*
Que quer dizer esta palavra? *What does this word mean?*
Dizer adeus. *To say good-by.*
Dizer bem (mal) de alguém. *To speak well (ill) of someone.*
Para dizer a verdade... *To tell the truth...*
Ouvi dizer que... *I heard that...*

DO (contr. of **de** + **o**) *of the, with the, from the.*
Qual é a capital do estado? *What is the capital of the state?*
Ele (ele) é do norte. *He's from the north.*

dó *m. do (music); pity; mourning.*

doação *f. donation, gift.*

doar *to give, to donate.*

DOBRAR *to turn; to double; to fold; to bend; to dub.*
Dobrar (Virar) a esquina. *To turn the corner. Dobre bem a carta. Fold the letter well.*

doca *f. dock.*

DOCE *adj. sweet; agreeable, pleasant; n. m. candy; sweet.*

dócil *adj. docile; obedient; gentle.*

documentação *f. documentation.*

documento *m. document.*

doçura *f. sweetness; gentleness.*

DOENÇA *f. illness; malady.*
Apanhar uma doença. *To catch a disease.*
Doença contagiosa. *Contagious disease.*

DOENTE *adj. ill, sick; n. m. and f. sick person.*
Ela está doente. *She is ill.*

doer *to ache, to pain.*

doido *adj. crazy, mad; n. m. madman; fool.*

doirado *adj. golden, gilded.*

DOIS *two; second.*
Dois a dois. *Two by two.*
De dois em dois meses. *Every two months.*
Dois é bom, três é demais. *Two is company, three's a crowd.*

DÓLAR *m. dollar.*

dolência *f. sorrow, grief.*

dolorosa *f. bill (for a meal) (slang).*

doloroso *adj. painful.*

dom *m. gift; talent; dom (title).*
Dom Pedro I foi o primeiro imperador do Brasil. *Dom Pedro I was the first emperor of Brasil.*

domar *to tame; to break in.*

doméstico *adj. domestic; n. m. servant.*

domicílio *m. residence, domicile.*

dominação *f. domination.*

dominante *adj. dominant.*

dominar *to dominate.*

DOMINGO *m. Sunday.*
Domingo de Ramos. *Palm Sunday.*
Domingo de Páscoa. *Easter Sunday.*

domínio *m. dominion; command; control.*

DONA *f. lady; title (used with the first name) meaning Mrs. or Miss.*
Dona da casa. *Lady of the house.*
Dona Ana. *Miss (or Mrs.) Anne.*

donaire *m. grace; elegance; witty saying.*

donativo *m. gift, donation.*

DONDE (contr. of **de** + **onde**) *from where, from which.*
Donde é o senhor? *Where are you from?*

dono *m. owner.*

DOR *f. ache, pain, sorrow.*
Dor de cabeça. *Headache.*
Dor de dente(s). *Toothache.*
Dor de garganta. *Sore throat.*

dormente *adj. dormant, sleeping; n. m. beam (house); crosstie (railroad).*

DORMIR *to sleep.*
Dormiu bem? *Did you sleep well?*
Eu não pude dormir. *I couldn't sleep.*
Dormir como uma pedra. *To sleep like a log.*
Dormir a sesta. *To take a nap.*

dormitar *to doze.*

dormitório *m. dormitory; bedroom* Ⓑ.

dose *f. dose.*

dotação *f. endowment; allocation.*

dotar *to allocate; to endow.*

dote *m. dowry; talent.*

dourado *adj. golden, gilded.*

doutor *m. doctor.*

doutrina *f. doctrine.*

DOZE *twelve; twelfth.*

drama *m. drama.*

dramalhão *m. melodrama.*

dramático *adj. dramatic.*

dramatizar *to dramatize.*

dramaturgo *m. dramatist, playwright.*

drástico *adj. drastic.*

droga *f. drug.*

drogaria *f. drugstore, pharmacy.*

DUAS *f. of dois, two.*
Duas semanas. *Two weeks.*
Às duas horas. *At two o'clock.*

duelo *m. duel.*

duende *m. ghost; goblin.*

duo *m. duo, duet.*

duodécimo *twelfth.*

duplicado *adj. duplicate; n. m. duplicate, copy.*

duplicar *to duplicate; to repeat; to double.*

duplo *adj. double; duplicate; n. m. double.*

duque *m. duke; deuce (cards).*

duquesa *f. duchess.*

duração *f. duration.*

duradouro *adj. durable; lasting.*

DURANTE *during.*
Durante o dia. *During the day.*
Durante a noite. *During the night.*
Durante algum tempo. *For some time.*

DURAR *to last; to continue; to wear well.*
A viagem durou quatro dias. *The trip lasted*

four days.

durável *adj. durable, lasting.*

dureza *f. hardness; harshness.*

DURO *adj. hard; difficult; firm; difficult; n. m. Spanish peso.*
A vida dêle (dele) foi muito dura. *His life was a very difficult one.*
Não seja duro com êle (ele). *Don't be hard on him.*
Pão duro. *Stale bread.*

DÚVIDA *f. doubt.*
Sem dúvida. *Without a doubt.*
Pôr em dúvida. *To doubt.*

DUVIDAR *to doubt; to hesitate.*
Duvidamos que ela venha. *We doubt she will come.*

duvidoso *adj. doubtful; uncertain.*

DUZENTAS *f. two hundred.*

DUZENTOS *m. two hundred.*

DÚZIA *f. dozen.*
Por dúzia. *By the dozen.*

E

e (pron. as Eng. e in be) *and*
Maria e João chegaram tarde. *Mary and John arrived late.*

ébrio *adj. intoxicated, drunk.*

economia *f. economy, thrift.*
Economia política. *Political economy.*

econômico (económico) *adj. economic; economical.*

economizar *to economise; to save.*

edição *f. edition, issue; publication.*

edificar *to construct, to build.*
Vão edificar uma nova escola. *They are going to build a new school.*

edifício *m. building.*
Êste (este) edifício é um edifício público. *This building is a public building.*

editar *to edit; to publish.*

editor *adj. publishing; n. m. publisher.*
Casa editôra. *Publishing house.*
O editor não aceitou o livro. *The publisher did not accept the book.*

editorial *adj. editorial; n. m. newspaper editorial; n. f. publishing house.*

educação *f. education; upbringing; training.*
Êle (ele) é um senhor de boa educação. *He is a man of good manners.*

educar *to educate; to bring up; to train.*
Êle (ele) é muito mal educado. *He is very ill-bred.*

educativo *adj. educational, instructive.*

EFEITO *m. effect, result, consequence; impression; pl. effects, assets, goods, belongings.*
As palavras causaram mau efeito. *The words had a bad effect.*
Com efeito, ela não sabe nada. *In fact, she doesn't know anything.*
Levar a efeito. *To carry out. To put into practice.*
Sem efeito. *Without effect.*

efetivo (efectivo) *adj. effective; real; actual.*

eficaz *adj. effective; efficient.*

eficiente *adj. effective; efficient.*

égua *f. mare.*

eis *behold; here is; there is.*
Eis a razão. *That's the reason.*
Eis porque não fomos. *That's why we didn't go.*

eixo (x = sh) *m. axle; axis.*

ELA *she; her; it.*
Ela não sabe nada. *She doesn't know anything.*
O vestido é para ela. *The dress is for her.*

elaboração *f. elaboration.*

elaborado *adj. elaborate.*

elaborar *to elaborate; to work out.*

ELAS *f. they; them.*
  Elas são irmãs. *They are sisters.*

elasticidade *f. elasticity.*

elástico *adj. elastic; n. m. elastic; rubber band.*

ÊLE (ELE) *he; him; it.*
  Êle vem amanhã. *He's coming tomorrow.*
  A carta é para êle. *The letter is for him.*

electricidade Ⓟ **(eletricidade** Ⓑ**)** *f. electricity.*

eléctrico Ⓟ **(elétrico** Ⓑ**)** *adj. electric.*

elefante *m. elephant.*

eleger *to elect; to choose.*

eleição *f. election; choice.*

eleito *adj. elected; selected.*
  Carlos foi eleito presidente do clube. *Charles was elected president of the club.*

elementar *adj. elementary; elemental.*

elemento *m. element; pl. rudiments, first principles.*

elenco *m. cast (theater); catalogue; list; index.*
  A peça é boa mas o elenco é muito ruim. *The play is good but the cast is very bad.*

ÊLES (ELES) *m. they; them.*
  Êles gostaram muito do filme. *They liked the film very much.*
  Eduardo partiu com êles. *Edward left with them.*

eletricidade (electricidade) *f. electricity.*

elétrico (eléctrico) *adj. electric.*

elevação *f. elevation.*

elevador *m. elevator; lift.*
  O prédio tem elevador? *Does the building have an elevator?*

elevar *to elevate; to lift up.*

eliminação *f. elimination.*

eliminar *to eliminate.*

elo *m. link; tie.*

elogiar *to praise.*

elogio *m. praise, eulogy.*

eloqüência (eloquência) *f. eloquence.*

elucidação *f. elucidation, explanation.*

eludir *to elude, to evade.*

EM *in, into, on, at, by.*
  Eu o tenho na mão. *I have it in my hand.*
  O senhor chegou em boa hora. *You arrived at the right time.*
  Entremos nesta loja. *Let's go into this store.*
  Em que dia? *On what day?*
  Ela está em casa. *She is home.*
  Tudo foi em vão. *It was all in vain.*
  Em geral. *In general. Generally.*
  Em vez de. *Instead of.*
  Em tôda (toda) a parte. *Everywhere.*
  Em meio de. *In the middle (midst) of.*
  Em breve. *Soon.*
  Em fim. *Finally.*
  Em verdade. *In truth. Truly.*
  Eu estava pensando nisso. *I was thinking about that.*

emagrecer *to become thin.*

embaixada *(x = sh) f. embassy.*

embaixador *(x = sh) m. ambassador.*

embaixo *(x = sh) below, under.*
  Lá embaixo. *Down there.*

embandeirar *to deck out or decorate with flags.*

embaraçar *to embarrass; to hinder.*

embaraço *m. embarrassment; difficulty.*

embaralhar *to shuffle (cards); to mix.*

embarcação *f. vessel, ship, boat; embarkation.*

embarcar *to embark, to go aboard.*
  Vamos embarcar em vinte minutos. *We are going aboard in twenty minutes.*

embargar *to embargo; to hinder.*
  Sem embargo. *Nevertheless.*

embarque *m. embarkation; shipment.*

emblema *m. emblem, symbol.*

EMBORA *although; away.*
  Vamos embora! *Let's go!*
  Embora não tivéssemos (tínhamos) dinheiro saímos de casa. *Although we did not have any money we went out of the house.*

emborrachar-se *to become drunk.*

emboscada *f. ambush, trap.*

emboscar *to ambush.*

embriagar *to intoxicate; to enchant.*

embriagar-se *to become intoxicated; to become enchanted.*

embrulhar *to wrap up; to confuse; to disturb.*

embrulho *m. package; parcel; trick, swindle* Ⓑ.
  Deixei *(x = sh)* os embrulhos na mesa. *I left the packages on the table.*

embrutecer *to brutalize; to make coarse.*

embrutecer-se *to be or to become stupid or coarse.*

embuste *m. lie; trick.*

embusteiro *m. liar; deceiver; cheater.*

embutido *adj. inlaid; n. m. inlaid work; mosaic.*

emendar *to amend, to correct.*

ementa *f. menu* Ⓟ.

emergência *f. emergency.*

emigração *f. emigration.*

emigrante *adj. emigrant; n. m. and f. emigrant.*

eminente *adj. eminent.*

emissor *adj. issuing; n. m. transmitter.*

emissora *f. broadcasting station.*

emitir *to emit, to send forth; to issue (bonds); to utter; to broadcast.*

emoção *f. emotion.*

emocionante *adj. moving, touching.*

emocionar *to move, to excite.*

empachar *to stuff; to overload.*

empacotar *to package; to pack.*

empalmar *to palm; to pilfer.*

empanada *f. meat pie.*

empapar *to soak.*
  Ficamos empapados. *We were soaked.*

emparelhar *to pair; to join.*

empatar *to tie (score); to tie up (money).*
  Os quadros empataram. *The teams tied.*

empate *m. tie, draw.*

empeçar *to entangle.*

empecilho *m. hindrance; difficulty.*

empenhar *to pawn; to pledge; to engage.*
  Eu empenhei minha palavra. *I pledged (gave) my word.*

empenho *m. pledge, obligation; pawning; determination; persistence.*
  Elas estudam com empenho. *They study diligently.*

empertigado *adj. haughty.*

empolgante *adj. thrilling, gripping.*

empório *m. trading center; grocery store* Ⓑ.

empreender *to undertake.*

empregado *adj. used, occupied; n. m. employee; servant.*
  Isso foi bem empregado. *That was put to good use.*
  Ela tem um empregado e duas empregadas. *She has one male servant and two maids.*

EMPREGAR *to employ, to hire; to use; to spend.*
  Em que o senhor empregou a tarde? *How did you spend the afternoon?*
  Empregamos dois dias em fazê-lo. *It took us two days to do it.*

EMPRÊGO (EMPREGO) *m. employment, job, occupation; use.*
  Mário tem um bom emprêgo. *Mario has a good job.*

emprêsa (empresa) *f. undertaking; enterprise; company.*

empresário *m. impresario; contractor; manager.*

emprestar *to lend.*
  Emprestar de. *To borrow* Ⓑ.
  Pedir emprestado. Tomar emprestado. *To borrow.*

empréstimo *m. loan.*

empurrar *to push, to shove.*

enamorar-se *to fall in love.*

encabeçar *to head, to direct; to start.*
  Quem encabeçou a revolução? *Who headed the revolution?*

encadear *to chain; to link.*

encadernado *adj. bound (book).*
  Eu prefiro o livro encadernado. *I prefer the book bound.*

encaixar *(x = sh) to fit; to inlay; to box, to put in a box; to come in handy.*
  Isto encaixa sem dificuldade. *This fits easily.*

encalhar *to run aground; to stick.*

encaminhar *to guide, to direct.*

encaminhar-se *to take the road to; to set out for.*

encanamento *m. plumbing; pipelines.*

encanecer *to turn gray; to grow old; to mature.*

encantado *adj. charmed; delighted, enchanted.*

encantador *adj. charming, delightful, enchanting.*

encantamento *m. charm; delight; fascination; enchantment; marvel.*

encanto *m. charm; enchantment; delight; spell.*
  Como por encanto. *As if by magic.*
  Ela é um encanto de menina. *She is a delightful little girl.*

encarar *to face; to look straight at.*
  Temos que encarar o problema. *We have to face the problem.*

encarcerar *to imprison.*

encarecer *to raise the price; to entreat.*

encargo *m. charge; duty; tax.*
  Os meus encargos vão crescendo. *My duties are growing.*

encarnado *adj. red; scarlet.*

encarregado *adj. in charge; n. m. person in charge.*

encarregar *to put in charge, to charge (with).*

encarregar-se de *to take charge of, to take care of.*
  Eu me encarrego de tudo. *I'll take care of everything.*

encenação *f. staging.*

encenador *m. director (theatre); producer (theatre).*

encenar *to stage (play); to display.*

enceradeira *f. floor waxer.*

encerar *to wax; to polish.*

encerrar *to close in; to enclose; to confine; to contain.*

encetar *to start; to begin.*
  Encetar um assunto. *To broach a subject.*

encharcar *to drench; to soak.*

enchente *f. flood.*
  As enchentes causam muito dano. *The floods cause great damage.*

ENCHER *to fill, to fill up.*
  Encha o tanque. *Fill it up (fill up the tank).*

enchova *f. anchovy.*

enciclopédia *f. encyclopedia.*

encoberto *adj. covered; hidden.*
  O céu está encoberto. *The sky is overcast.*

encobrir *to cover; to conceal.*

encolher *to shrink; to contract.*
  Encolher os ombros. *To shrug the shoulders.*

encomenda *f. an order (purchase); commission.*

encomendar *to order; to commission.*
  Ela encomendou os cinco volumes. *She ordered the five volumes.*

ENCONTRAR *to find; to meet; to meet by chance.*
O senhor encontrou o que procurava? *Did you find what you were looking for?*
Êles (eles) devem nos encontrar aqui. *They are to meet us here.*

ENCONTRAR-SE *to find oneself; to be; to meet.*
Eu me encontrei sòzinho. *I found myself all alone.*
Vamos encontrar-nos amanhã. *We are going to meet tomorrow.*

ENCONTRO *m. meeting; encounter.*

encrenca *f. difficulty; obstacle.*
Deixe-me de encrencas. *I don't want any trouble.*

encrespar *to curl; to frizzle.*

encruzilhada *f. crossroads.*

endereçar *to address; to direct.*
Um momento. Vou endereçar esta carta. *Just a moment. I'm going to address this letter.*

enderêço (endereço) *m. address.*

endossar *to endorse.*

endurecer *to harden.*

energia *f. energy, power.*

enérgico *adj. energetic, active.*

enfadar *to irk, to annoy.*

enfado *m. displeasure; annoyance.*

enfartar *to glut; to stuff.*

ênfase *f. emphasis.*

enfático *adj. emphatic.*

enfeitar *to adorn, to decorate.*

enfermar *to become ill.*
Se ela continua assim vai enfermar. *If she continues that way she is going to become ill.*

enfermeira *f. nurse.*

enfermeiro *m. male nurse; hospital orderly.*

enfêrmo (enfermo) *adj. sick; n. m. patient, sick person.*

ENFIM *finally, at last; in short.*

enforcar *to hang (a person).*

enfrear *to curb; to brake.*
É preciso enfrear nas colinas. *You have to use your brakes on the hills.*

enfrentar *to face; to confront.*
Temos que enfrentar o problema hoje. *We have to face the problem today.*

enfurecer *to become angry; to become furious.*

engaiolar *to cage; to lock up.*

engalanar *to decorate, to adorn.*

enganar *to deceive, to fool.*

enganar-se *to deceive oneself; to be mistaken.*
Sinto muito! Enganei-me. *I'm very sorry! I was mistaken.*

enganchar *to hook.*

engano *error, mistake; deceit.*

enganoso *adj. misleading; deceiving.*

engarrafar *to bottle.*

engendrar *to engender.*

engenharia *f. engineering.*

engenheiro *m. engineer; owner of a mill* Ⓑ.

engenho *m. ingenuity; skill; wit; mill.*
Engenho de açúcar. *Sugar mill.*

engolir *to swallow; to gulp down.*
Engula a pílula! *Swallow the pill!*
Faça o favor de falar mais alto e de não engolir as palavras. *Please speak louder and do not swallow your words.*

engomar *to starch.*

engordar *to fatten; to grow fat.*

ENGRAÇADO *adj. amusing; funny.*
Não acho muito engraçado. *I don't think it's very funny.*

engraxar *(x = sh) to wax; to shine shoes, to grease.*

engraxate (engraxador) *(x = sh) bootblack.*

engrenagem *f. gear.*

enguia *f. eel.*

enjoado *adj. nauseated; carsick; seasick.*

enjoar *to nauseate; to feel nausea.*

enjôo (enjoo) *m. nausea; seasickness; car sickness.*

enlaçar *to join, to connect; to bind; to tie.*

enlace *m. union; marriage.*
Enlace matrimonial. *Marriage.*

enlatado *adj. canned.*

enlatar *to can (food).*

enlouquecer *to go mad; to drive mad.*

enojar *to nauseate; to feel nausea; to disgust.*

enôjo (enojo) *m. nausea; disgust.*

ENQUANTO *while.*
Enquanto nós estudávamos êles (eles) escreviam cartas. *While we studied they wrote letters.*
Por enquanto. *For the time being.*

enredar *to entangle; to catch with a net.*

enrêdo (enredo) *m. plot (of book); story; complication.*
O enrêdo (enredo) do romance é muito fraco. *The novel's plot is quite weak.*

enriquecer *to enrich; to become rich.*

enrolar *to wind; to roll up; to wrap up.*

ensaboar *to soap; to lather.*

ensaiar *to try; to rehearse; to test.*

ensaio *m. trial; rehearsal; essay.*
Balão de ensaio. *Trial balloon.*

ensejo *m. opportunity; occasion.*
Aproveitamos o ensejo para ... *We take this opportunity to ...*

ensinamento *m. teaching, instruction.*

ENSINAR *to teach; to show; to train.*
Quer que lhe ensine? *Would you like me to teach you?*

ensino *m. teaching, instruction; training.*

ensurdecer *to deafen; to stun.*

ensurdecimento *m. deafness; deafening.*

ENTANTO *meanwhile.*
No entanto. *Nevertheless. However.*

ENTÃO *then; in that case; at that time.*
Então o senhor não quer ir comigo. *Then you don't want to go with me.*
Desde então. *Since that time.*

ENTENDER *to understand.*
Não entendi nada. *I didn't understand a thing.*
João entende disso. *John is familiar with that.*
Entendi mal. *I misunderstood.*
Ela me deu a entender que já era tarde. *She led me to believe that it was already too late.*
Não posso me entender com elas. *I can't come to an understanding with them.*
Agora nos entendemos. *Now we understand each other.*

entendimento *m. understanding.*

enternecer *to soften; to move to pity.*

enterrar *to bury.*

entêrro (enterro) *m. burial; interment; funeral.*

entidade *f. entity.*

entoação *f. intonation; tone.*

entoar *to tune; to intone; to be in tune.*

ENTRADA *f. entrance; entry; admission; ticket; entree.*
Quanto é a entrada? *How much is the admission?*
A entrada é gratuita. *(The) admission is free.*
Devemos comprar as entradas agora. *We should buy the tickets now.*
É proibida a entrada. *No admittance.*
Meia entrada. *Half-price ticket.*

ENTRAR *to enter; to go in; to fit.*

Entre! *Come in!*
Que não entre ninguém. *Don't let anybody in.*
Entramos no cinema às três. *We went into the movie theatre at three.*
Entrar com o pé direito. *To have a good start.*
Ela entrou na universidade no ano passado. *She entered the university last year.*
Entrar por um ouvido e sair pelo outro. *To go in one ear and out the other.*

ENTRE *between; among.*
Fizeram-no entre os dois. *They did it between the two of them.*
Procure entre os papéis. *Look among the papers.*
Entre nós. *Between ourselves.*
Entre a espada e a parede. *Between the devil and the deep blue sea.*

entreato (entreacto) *m. intermission.*

entrega *f. delivery; surrender.*
Entrega urgente. *Special delivery (mail).*

ENTREGAR *to deliver; to hand over.*
A quem entregou a carta? *To whom did you deliver the letter?*

entregar-se *to surrender; to give oneself up; to devote oneself (to).*
O criminoso se entregou à polícia. *The criminal gave himself up to the police.*
Entregar os pontos. *To give up.*

entregue *adj. delivered.*

entrementes *meanwhile.*

entremeter *to insert; to place between.*

ENTRETANTO *meanwhile; however.*

entretenimento *m. entertainment, amusement.*

entrevista *f. interview; conference.*

entrevistar *to interview.*

entristecer *to become sad.*

entusiasmar *to fill with enthusiasm.*

entusiasmar-se *to become enthusiastic.*

entusiasmo *m. enthusiasm.*

entusiasta *adj. enthusiastic; n. m. and f. enthusiast, fan.*

entusiástico *adj. enthusiastic.*

envasar *to bottle; to put in pots (flowers).*

envelhecer *to make old; to grow old.*

envelope *m. envelope.*
Não esqueça de escrever o endereço (endereço) no envelope. *Don't forget to write the address on the envelope.*

envenenar *to poison.*

ENVIAR *to send; to dispatch.*
Envie-me uma dúzia. *Send me a dozen.*

envio *m. shipment; shipping.*

enviuvar *to become a widow or widower.*

envolver *to wrap up; to make into a package; to envelop; to surround.*

enxaguar *(x = sh) to rinse.*

época *f. epoch, age, era.*

equipagem *f. equipment; ship's crew.*

equipar *to equip; to furnish.*

equipe *f. team (sports).*

equivocação *f. mistake.*

equivocado *adj. mistaken.*

equivocar *to make a mistake; to mistake.*

equívoco *adj. equivocal; n. m. mistake; pun; misunderstanding.*
Acho que tudo foi um equívoco. *I believe it was all a misunderstanding.*

era *f. era; age; period.*

ereto (erecto) *adj. erect; upright.*

erguer *to erect, to raise.*

erigir *to erect, to build.*

errado *adj. wrong, in error.*

ERRAR *to err, to make a mistake.*
Erramos o caminho. *We lost our way.*

errata *f. erratum, error in writing or printing.*

ÊRRO (ERRO) *m. error, mistake.*

erudição *f. erudition, learning.*

erudito *adj. erudite, learned; n. m. scholar, erudite person.*

erva *f. herb, plant.*
Erva-mate. *Paraguay tea; mate.*

ervilha *f. pea.*

esbelto *adj. slim, slender; elegant.*

esbôço (esboço) *m. sketch; outline.*

escabroso *adj. rough; uneven; difficult.*

escada *f. stairs; staircase; ladder.*
Escada de incêndio. *Fire escape.*
Escada de mão. *Stepladder.*
Escada de serviço. *Service stairway.*
Escada rolante. *Escalator.*

escala *f. scale; ladder; stop.*
Em grande escala. *On a large scale.*
Pôrto (porto) de escala. *Port of call.*

escapar *to escape, to flee.*

escape *m. escape.*

escapo *adj. escaped; free.*

escarmentar *to punish; to reprimand.*

escárnio *m. scorn.*

escasso *adj. scarce, scanty.*

esclarecer *to clarify; to enlighten.*

escoamento *m. drainage.*

escoar *to drain; to flow.*

ESCOLA *f. school.*
Escola elementar. *Elementary school.*
Escola secundária. *Secondary school.*

ESCOLHER *to choose, to pick.*

escolhido *adj. chosen, select.*

escolta *f. escort.*

escoltar *to escort.*

escombros *m. pl. ruins.*

esconder *to hide, to conceal.*

escondido *adj. hidden.*

escorrer *to trickle; to drip.*

escoteira *f. girl scout.*

escoteiro *m. boy scout.*

ESCÔVA (ESCOVA) *f. brush.*
Escôva de cabelo. *Hairbrush.*
Escôva de dentes. *Toothbrush.*
Escôva de roupa. *Clothes brush.*

escovar *to brush, to scrub.*

escravatura *f. slavery.*

escravidão *f. slavery.*

escravo *m. slave.*

ESCREVER *to write.*
Escreva claramente. *Write clearly.*
Como se escreve esta palavra? *How do you write (spell) that word?*
Prefiro que escreva a carta à máquina. *I prefer that you type the letter.*
Máquina de escrever. *Typewriter.*

escrito *adj. written; n. m. something written, writing.*
Escrito à mão. *Handwritten.*
Escrito à máquina. *Typewritten.*
Pôr por escrito. *To put in writing.*

escritor *m. writer, author.*

escritório *m. office; study.*

escritura *f. writing; writ; document; deed.*

escrivão *m. notary, scribe.*

escrutínio *m. scrutiny; balloting; voting.*

ESCUDO *m. shield; Portuguese monetary unit, worth approximately 3 1/2 cents.*
Comprei-o por quarenta escudos. *I bought it for forty escudos.*

escurecer *to grow dark.*

escuridão *f. darkness.*

escusa *f. excuse.*

ESCUTAR *to listen; to heed.*
Escute! *Listen!*

esfera *f. sphere.*

esforçar *to strengthen; to encourage.*

esforçar-se *to try hard, to endeavor, to strive.*

esfôrço (esforço) *m. effort; endeavor.*

esfregar *to rub; to scrub; to scratch.*

esfriar *to cool off; to grow cold.*

esgotado *adj. exhausted; sold out; out of print.*
Essa edição já está esgotada. *That edition is already sold out.*

esgotar *to drain; to exhaust.*

esgrima *f. fencing (sport).*

eslavo *adj. Slavic; Slav; n. m. Slav.*

esmagar *to overcome; to smash; to crush.*

esmaltar *to enamel.*

esmalte *m. enamel.*
Esmalte de unhas. *Nail polish.*

esmerado *adj. carefully done; accomplished.*

esmerar *to do with great care; to perfect.*

esmêro (esmero) *m. care; perfection; neatness.*

esmola *f. alms.*

espaço *m. space, room.*
Aqui não há espaço. *There's no room here.*

espada *f. sword.*

espalda *f. back of a chair.*

espaldar *m. back of a chair.*

espalhar *to spread; to scatter; to disseminate.*

espanhol *Spanish.*

espantar *to frighten, to drive away.*

espanto *m. fright.*

espantoso *adj. frightful.*

esparadrapo *m. adhesive tape.*

espargo *m. asparagus.*

espátula *f. spatula; paper knife.*

especial *adj. special.*

especialidade *f. specialty.*

especiarias *f. pl. spices.*

espécie *f. species; kind; sort.*

espetáculo ℗ (espetáculo Ⓑ) *m. spectacle, show.*

especulação *f. speculation.*

ESPELHO *m. mirror; looking glass.*
Espelho retrovisor. *Rearview mirror.*

espera *f. wait, waiting.*
Onde é a sala de espera? *Where is the waiting room?*

esperança *f. hope.*

ESPERAR *to wait for; to expect; to hope.*
Assim o espero. *I hope so.*
Espero que não. *I hope not.*
Espero que sim. *I hope so.*
Espere-me. *Wait for me.*
Diga-lhe que espere. *Tell him to wait.*
Espere um momento. *Wait a moment.*

esperto *adj. smart; alert; clever.*
Ela é muito esperta. *She's very smart.*

espêsso (espesso) *adj. thick, dense.*

espetáculo (espectáculo) *m. spectacle, show.*

espiar *to spy on.*

espiga *f. spike; ear (corn).*

espinafre *m. spinach.*

espingarda *f. shotgun, rifle.*

espinha *f. spine; fishbone.*

espinho *m. thorn.*

espírito *m. spirit; mind; wit; soul.*
Espírito prático. *Practical mind.*
Êle (Ele) é uma pessoa de espírito. *He is a man of wit.*
Espírito Santo. *Holy Spirit. Holy Ghost.*

espiritual *adj. spiritual.*

espirrar *to sneeze; to burst out.*

espirro *m. sneeze, sneezing.*

esplêndido *adj. splendid; excellent.*

esplendor *m. splendor, magnificence.*

esponja *f. sponge; parasite.*

esporte *m. sport.*

ESPÔSA (ESPOSA) *f. wife, spouse.*

ESPÔSO (ESPOSO) *m. husband, spouse.*

espreguiçadeira *f. chaise longue, easy chair.*

espreguiçar-se *to stretch oneself out.*

espuma *f. foam, froth.*
Espuma de sabão. *Lather. Soapsuds.*

esquadra *f. squadron; squad; police station ℗.*

ESQUECER *to forget; to neglect.*
Não esqueça o que lhe disse. *Don't forget what I told you.*

ESQUECER-SE *to forget.*
Ela se esqueceu de chamar. *She forgot to call.*

esquema *m. scheme, drawing.*

ESQUERDA *f. left, left side.*
À esquerda. *To the left.*
Esquerda, volver! *Left, face! (Military command).*

ESQUERDO *adj. left.*

esqui *m. ski.*

esquilo *m. squirrel.*

ESQUINA *f. corner.*
Dobrar (Virar) a esquina. *To turn the corner.*
A loja está na esquina. *The shop is on the corner.*

esquisito *adj. peculiar; odd; strange; unusual.*

esquivança *f. disdain, contempt.*

ESSA *f. that; that one; pl. those.*
Essa senhora. *That lady.*
Vamos por essa rua. *Let's go down that street.*
Essas coisas não me interessam. *Those things don't interest me.*
Prefiro estas a essas. *I prefer these to those.*
Ora essa! *Come now!*

ÊSSE (ESSE) *m. that; that one; pl. those.*
Êsse senhor. *That man.*
Êsses meninos. *Those boys.*
Não quero êsses; prefiro êstes (estes). *I don't want those; I prefer these.*

essência *f. essence.*

essencial *adj. essential.*

essoutro *that (other) one.*

ESTA *f. this; this one; pl. these.*
Esta senhora e aquêle (aquele) homem são irmãos. *This lady and that man are brother and sister.*
De quem é esta casa? *Whose house is this?*
Não gosto destas. *I don't like these.*

estabelecer *to establish.*

estabelecimento *m. establishment.*

estábulo *m. stable.*

ESTAÇÃO *f. station; season.*
Onde é a estação? *Where is the station?*
O inverno (Inverno) é a estação mais fria do ano. *Winter is the coldest season of the year.*

estacionamento *m. parking.*
Estacionamento proibido. *No parking.*

estacionar *to park; to stop.*

estada *f. stay; stop.*

estádio *m. stadium; stage, phase.*

ESTADO *m. state; condition.*
Em bom estado. *In good condition.*
Homem de estado. *Statesman.*
Estado-maior. *General staff.*
Estado de guerra. *State of war.*
Estados Unidos do Brasil. *United States of Brasil.*
Estados Unidos da América. *United States of America.*

estágio *m. period, phase; apprenticeship.*

estalagem *f. inn.*

estalar *to burst, to explode; to crack; to snap.*

estampa *f. picture; print.*

estampar *to stamp; to print.*

estampilha *f. small stamp; revenue stamp Ⓑ.*

estampilhar *to stamp; to put stamps on.*

estancar *to check; to stop.*

estância f. dwelling, residence; station; stay..

estanho m. tin.

estante f. bookcase; lectern.

ESTAR to be.
Estamos prontos. We are ready.
Elas estão cansadas. They are tired.
Que está fazendo? What are you doing?
Eles (eles) estão estudando. They are studying.
Êles estão a estudar (P). They are studying.
Onde está o seu irmão? Where is your brother?
Êle (ele) está no teatro. He is at the theater.
Devemos estar lá antes das nove. We should arrive before nine.
A janela está aberta. The window is open.
Ela está de pé. She is standing.
Estou certo. I am sure.
Nós estamos de acôrdo (acordo). We agree.
Ela está doente. She is sick.
Estou para sair de viagem. I am about to leave on a trip.
Está bem. Very well. Fine.
Está na hora de partir. It's time to leave.
Estou com pressa. I'm in a hurry.

estátua f. statue.

estatura f. stature.

estatuto m. statute, law.

este m. east.

ÊSTE (ESTE) m. this; this one; pl. these.
Êste senhor. This man.
Êstes livros. These books.
Êste é o meu. This one is mine.
Não quero êstes. I don't want these.

estender to extend; to stretch out.

estenógrafa f. stenographer.

estenógrafo m. stenographer.

estiagem f. dry weather, drought.

esticar to stretch.

estilo m. style.

estima f. esteem; appreciation.

estimar to esteem; to value.

estimular to stimulate.

estímulo m. stimulus.

estio (Estio) m. summer.

estirar to stretch, to extend.

estirpe f. stock; ancestry.

estivador m. stevedor, longshoreman.

estôjo (estojo) m. kit; case, box; set.
Estôjo de barba. Shaving set.

estômago m. stomach.

estoque m. stock, supply (B).

estorvar to disturb; to hinder.

estourar to burst; to explode.

ESTRADA f. road, highway.
Estrada de rodagem. Highway.
Estrada de ferro. Railway.

ESTRANGEIRO adj. foreign; n. m. foreigner, alien; stranger.
Ela está no estrangeiro. She is abroad.

estranhar to be surprised; to find strange.

estranheza f. strangeness; surprise.

estranho adj. strange; unusual; odd.
Êle (Ele) é um pouco estranho. He's somewhat strange.

estratégia f. strategy.

estratégico adj. strategic.

estrear to try or use for the first time; to make one's debut; to open (play).

estréia (estreia) f. opening, première; first showing.
A estréia da peça vai ser na sexta. The play will open on Friday.

estreito adj. narrow; n. m. strait.

estrêla (estrela) f. star.

estremecer to shake, to tremble.

estremecimento m. shaking, quiver.

estribo m. stirrup; running board.

estropiar to cripple; to deform.

estrutura f. structure.

estudante m. and f. student.

ESTUDAR to study.
Os meus filhos não estudam bastante. My children don't study enough.

estudioso adj. studious.

ESTUDO m. study.
Bôlsa (bolsa) de estudos. Scholarship.

estufa f. stove; hothouse.

estupendo adj. stupendous; wonderful.

estupidez f. stupidity.

estúpido adj. stupid; n. m. stupid person.

éter m. ether.

eternidade f. eternity.

eterno adj. eternal.

ética f. ethics.

ético adj. ethic, ethical.

etiquêta (etiqueta) etiquette; ceremony.

europeu adj. European.

evacuação f. evacuation.

evacuar to evacuate.

evadir to evade.

evangelho m. the Gospel.

evaporar to evaporate.

evasão f. evasion; escape.

evasivo adj. evasive.

evento m. event, happening.

evidência f. evidence; indication.

evidente adj. evident, obvious.

EVITAR to avoid.
Quero evitar essa situação, se puder. I should like to avoid that situation if I can.

evitável adj. avoidable.

evocar to evoke.

evolução f. evolution.

exageração (x = s). f. exaggeration.

exagerar (x = s) to exaggerate.

exagêro (exagero) (x = s). m. exaggeration.

exaltação (x = s). f. exaltation.

exaltar (x = s) to exalt, to praise.

exame (x = s) m. examination.
Exame de admissão. Admission examination.
Exame médico. Medical examination.

examinar (x = s) to examine; to inquire into; to investigate.

exasperação (x = s) f. exasperation.

exasperar (x = s) to exasperate.

exatidão (exactidao) (x = s) f. exactitude, exactness.

EXATO (EXACTO) (x = s) adj. exact; correct.
Exatamente. Exactly.

exceção f. exception.

exceder to exceed.

excelência f. excellence.
Vossa Excelência. Your Excellency.

excelente adj. excellent; fine.

excelentíssimo adj. most excellent.

excelso adj. eminent; exalted.

excepcional adj. exceptional; unusual.

excessivo adj. excessive; too much.

excesso m. excess.
Em excesso. In excess. Excessively.

exceto (excepto) except.

excetuar (exceptuar) to except; to exempt; to exclude.

excitação f. excitation; excitement.

excitante adj. exciting.

excitar to excite; to stimulate.

excitável adj. excitable.

exclamação f. exclamation.

exclamar to exclaim.

excluir to exclude; to keep out; to rule out.

exclusão f. exclusion.

exclusivo adj. exclusive.

excursão f. excursion, trip.

execução (x = s) f. execution; performance.

executar (x = s) to execute; to carry out.

executivo (x = s) adj. executive.

exemplar (x = s) adj. exemplary; n. m. copy; model.
Eu lhe mandarei um exemplar. I'll send you a copy.

EXEMPLO (x = s) m. example; pattern.
Por exemplo. For example.

exercer (x = s) to exercise; to carry out; to practice.
Exercer a medicina. To practice medicine.

exercício (x = s) m. exercise; drill.
Fazer exercício. To exercise.

exército (x = s) m. army.

exibição f. exhibition.

exibir (x = s) to exhibit.

exigência (x = s) f. exigency, urgent need.

exigente (x = s) adj. exigent, demanding.
Não seja tão exigente. Don't be so demanding.

exigir (x = s) to demand; to require; to exact.
As circunstâncias o exigem. The situation requires it.

exilar (x = s) to exile.

exílio (x = s) m. exile.

existência (x = s) f. existence; stock of goods (P).

existente (x = s) adj. living, existent.

EXISTIR (x = s) to exist, to be.
Não existe tal coisa. No such thing exists.

ÊXITO (x = s) m. success; result; outcome.
Êles (eles) tiveram bom êxito. They were a big success.

exortar (x = s) to exhort; to urge.

expandir to expand; to spread out.

expansão f. expansion.

expectativa f. expectation; hope.

expedição f. expedition; shipment.

expediente adj. expeditious; n. m. expedient; office hours.

expedir to expedite; to dispatch, to send.

expelir to expel.

experiência f. experience; trial.

experimentar to experience; to experiment.

experimento m. experience; experiment.

experto adj. expert; n. m. expert.

expirar to expire; to die; to exhale.

explicação f. explication.

EXPLICAR to explain.
Deixe-me explicá-lo. Let me explain it.

explicativo adj. explanatory.

explicável adj. explainable.

explícito adj. explicit.

exploração f. exploration.

explorador m. explorer.

explorar to explore.

explosão f. explosion; outburst.

expoente m. and f. exponent.

expor to expound; to explain; to make clear; to expose.

exportação f. export.

exportador adj. exporting; n. m. exporter.
Casa exportadora. Exporting firm.

exportar to export.

exposição f. exposition, show, exhibition; exposure.

expositor m. exhibitor; expositor.

exposto adj. exposed; liable to.
Está exposto das dez às quatro horas. It is being shown from ten to four o'clock.

expressão f. expression.

expresso adj. express; clear; n. m. express (train); special delivery.

exprimir to express.

expulsão f. expulsion.

expulsar to expel, to eject, to throw out.

expulso adj. expelled, expulsed.

extensão f. extension; extent.

Em tôda (toda) extensão. In every sense.

extensivo adj. extensive; far-reaching.

extenso adj. extensive; vast.

extenuação f. extenuation.

extenuar to extenuate.

exterior adj. exterior; foreign.

extinguir to extinguish, to put out.

extra extra.

extrair to extract, to pull out.

extra-oficial adj. unofficial; off the record.

extraordinário adj. extraordinary.

É um caso extraordinário. It's an unusual case.

extratar to extract.

extrato (extractor) m. extract.

extravagância f. folly, extravagance.

extravagante adj. extravagant; odd.

extraviado adj. lost, missing; astray.

extraviar to mislead; to mislay.

extravio m. loss; deviation; straying.

extremidade f. extremity; very end.

extremo adj. extreme; last; n. m. extreme; end.

F

fá n. musical note.

fã m. and f. fan (follower).

fábrica f. factory; mill; plant.

Preço de fábrica. Factory price.

Marca de fábrica. Trademark.

fabricação f. manufacturing; manufacture.

fabricante m. and f. manufacturer; maker.

fabricar to manufacture, to make; to build.

fábula f. fable; story, tale.

fabuloso adj. fabulous; incredible.

FACA f. knife.

Faca de papel. Paper knife.

façanha f. deed; accomplishment.

fação Ⓑ **facção** Ⓑ and Ⓟ, f. faction.

face f. face; side.

O negócio tem duas faces. There are two sides to the matter.

fachada f. façade.

FÁCIL easy.

Parece fácil mas é difícil. It looks easy but it's difficult.

Fàcilmente. Easily.

É fácil de aprender. It's easy to learn.

facilidade f. ease, facility.

facilitar to facilitate, to make easy.

FACTO Ⓟ **(FATO** Ⓑ**)** m. fact; occurrence.

faculdade f. faculty.

Faculdade de direito. Law school.

fada f. fairy.

Conto de fadas. Fairy tale.

fadista m. and f. singer and player of fados; ruffian.

FADO m. fate, destiny; Portuguese popular folk song.

faina f. task, chore.

faixa (x = sh) f. sash; strip.

faixar (x = sh) to bind; to tie up.

fala f. speech; language.

falador adj. talkative; n. m. talker; gabbler.

FALAR to speak, to talk.

O senhor fala português? Do you speak Portuguese?

Eu falo português. I speak Portuguese.

Aqui se fala inglês. English spoken here.

Fale! Speak!

Fale mais devagar. Speak more slowly.

Desejo falar com o gerente. I wish to speak to the manager.

Gostaria de falar-lhe sôbre (sobre) um assunto importante. I should like to speak to you about an important matter.

Fale mais alto. Speak louder.

De que estão falando? What are you talking about?

Falemos nisso agora mesmo. Let's talk about that right now.

falecer to die.

Êle (ele) faleceu no ano passado. He died last year.

falha f. fault, flaw.

falhar to fail; to miss.

falho adj. faulty; defective.

falsear to falsify; to distort.

falsidade f. falsehood; untruth.

falsificação f. falsification; forgery.

falsificar to falsify.

falso adj. false; incorrect.

Alarme falso. False alarm.

Chave falsa. Skeleton key.

FALTA f. need, lack; absence; fault, defect; mistake.

Temos que desculpar as faltas dêle (dele). We must excuse his faults.

Eu corrigirei as faltas. I'll correct the mistakes.

Sem falta. Without fail.

Estamos com falta dágua. We are short of water.

Perdemos tudo por falta de dinheiro. We lost everything for lack of money.

FALTAR to need, to lack; to be absent; to fail.

Aqui faltam três livros. Three books are missing here.

Ela faltou à aula hoje. She missed class today.

Era o que faltava! That's the last straw!

Faltam vinte minutos para as duas. It's twenty minutes to two.

Êle (ele) nunca falta à palavra. He never goes back on his word.

falto adj. lacking, wanting.

fama f. fame, reputation; rumor, report.

FAMÍLIA f. family.

familiar adj. familiar; m. and f. close friend; relative.

faminto adj. hungry, famished.

famoso adj. famous.

fanático adj. fanatic.

fanfarrão adj. boasting, bragging; n. m. braggart.

fantasia f. fantasy, fancy; fancy dress Ⓑ.

fantasma m. ghost, phantasm.

fantástico adj. fantastic.

fantoche m. puppet.

farda f. uniform.

fardo m. bale; parcel; bundle.

faringe f. pharynx.

farinha f. flour, meal.

Farinha de trigo. Wheat flour.

farmacêutico m. pharmacist, druggist.

farmácia f. pharmacy, drugstore.

faro m. lighthouse; sense of smell (animal).

farofa f. a dish made of manioc meal, meat, eggs, vegetables, etc.

farol m. lighthouse; beacon; headlight.

Farol verde. Green light.

Farol vermelho. Red light. Stoplight.

farrapo m. rag; ragamuffin.

farroupilha m. ragamuffin.

farsa f. farce.

farsante m. and f. actor, actress in farces; joker.

farsista adj. joking; n. m. and f. joker, clown.

fartar to fill with, to satiate.

farto adj. satiate, full; abundant.

fascinar to fascinate, to charm.

fase f. phase; aspect.

fastidioso adj. boring, annoying.

fastígio m. apex, summit.

fastio m. boredom; lack of appetite.

fatal adj. fatal.

fatalidade f. fate, destiny; fatality.

fatia f. slice.

Uma fatia de pão. A slice of bread.

fatigador adj. tiring; boring.

fatigante adj. tiring.

fatigar to tire; to annoy.

FATO (FACTO) m. fact, occurrence; **fato** man's suit Ⓟ.

De fato. As a matter of fact.

O fato é que já é tarde. The fact is that it is already too late.

fator (factor) m. factor; agent.

fátuo adj. fatuous; foolish.

fatura (factura) f. invoice, bill.

Aqui tem a fatura. Here is the invoice.

faturar (facturar) to bill, to invoice.

fauna f. fauna.

fausto adj. happy; fortunate; n. m. pageantry.

FAVA f. bean.

Mandar às favas. To send to the devil.

favela f. slum Ⓑ.

favelado m. slum-dweller Ⓑ.

FAVOR m. favor; service; good graces; letter.

É um grande favor que me faz. It's a great favor you are doing me.

Por favor. Please.

Faça o favor de chamar-me às sete. Please call me at seven.

Recebemos seu favor de 5 do corrente. We are in receipt of your favor (letter) of the 10th instant.

favorável adj. favorable.

favorecer to favor; to help.

favorito adj. favorite.

fazenda f. farm; plantation; estate; cloth, material.

Fazenda de café. Coffee plantation.

Fazenda de lã. Woolen cloth.

fazendeiro m. farmer, planter; owner of **fazenda**.

FAZER to make; to do; to cause; to be (cold, etc.)

Faça o favor de dar-me o mapa. Please give me the map.

Permite-me fazer-lhe algumas perguntas? May I ask you some questions?

Fazem bom pão aqui. They make good bread here.

Que faço? What shall I do?

Faça como quiser. Do as you wish.

Que está fazendo (a fazer)? What are you doing?

Que hemos de fazer? What are we to do?

Que hemos de fazer? What are we to do?

Já está feito. It's already done.

O navio faz água. The ship leaks.

Hoje faço vinte anos. I am twenty years old today.

Faço a barba com gilete. I shave with a safety razor.

Ela faz a cama tôdas (todas) as manhãs. She makes her bed every morning.

Faça chamar o médico. Have the doctor called.

Vamos fazer uma viagem no verão (Verão). We're going on a trip in the summer.

O deputado fêz (fez) um discurso. The congressman made a speech.

Fazer gazeta. To play hookey (from school).

Fazer greve. *To go on strike.*
Fazer a chamada. *To call the roll.*
Fazer caso de. *To pay attention to.*
Fazer o papel. *To play the part.*
Fazer mal. *To do evil, harm.*
Fazer compras. *To go shopping.*
Fazer economias. *To save.*
Fazer exercício. *To exercise.*
Fazer frio. *To be cold (weather).*
Fazer calor. *To be warm (weather).*
Faz bom tempo. *The weather is good.*
Faz mau tempo. *The weather is bad.*
Fazer falta. *To need. To be lacking.*
Fazer alto. *To stop.*
Fazer parte de. *To belong to; to take part in.*
Fazer fila. *To stand in line.*
Não faz mal. *Never mind.*
Fazer um passeio. *To go for a walk.*

FÉ *f. faith; certificate.*
Ela o fêz (fez) de boa fé. *She did it in good
faith.*
Êle (ele) o disse de má fé. *He said it in bad
faith (deceitfully).*
A fé católica. *The Catholic religion.*

febre *f. fever.*
Febre amarela. *Yellow fever.*

FECHADO *adj. closed; shut; finished.*
A porta não está fechada. *The door is not
closed.*

FECHAR *to close; to shut; to finish.*
Amanhã vou fechar a conta. *Tomorrow I am
going to close my account.*
Feche a porta à chave. *Lock the door.*

fecundo *adj. fruitful, productive, fecund.*
feder *to smell bad, to stink.*
federação *f. federation.*
FEIJÃO *m. bean, beans.*
feijoada *f. a popular dish made of black beans,
meat, vegetables, etc.*
feio *adj. ugly; unpleasant.*
feira *f. fair; market.*
feiticeira *f. witch.*
feiticeiro *m. witch doctor.*
feitio *m. pattern; style; workmanship.*
FEITO *adj. made; done; finished; n. m. act;
fact; deed.*
Mal feito. *That was wrong. Poorly done
(made).*
Bem feito. *Well done.*
Dito e feito. *No sooner said than done.*
Feito! *Agreed!*
Já feito. *Already made. Ready-made.*
Feito sob medida. *Tailor-made.*
Feito à mão. *Handmade.*
Feito à máquina. *Machine-made.*

feitor *m. administrator; manager; foreman.*
feitura *f. workmanship; work.*
felicidade *f. happiness.*
felicitação *f. congratulation.*
Felicitações! *Congratulations!*
felicitar *to congratulate, to felicitate.*
FELIZ *adj. happy; fortunate.*
Feliz Ano Nôvo (Novo)! *Happy New Year!*
Feliz Natal! *Merry Christmas!*
Foi o dia mais feliz da minha vida. *It was
the happiest day of my life.*
Somos muito felizes. *We are very happy.*
Felizmente. *Happily. Fortunately.*

fêmea *f. female.*
feminino *adj. feminine.*
fenômeno (fenómeno) *m. phenomenon.*
fera *f. wild beast.*
féria *f. weekday; workday; wages; pl. holidays,
vacations.*
Vamos passar as férias nas montanhas. *We
going to spend our vacation in the
mountains.*
feriado *m. holiday.*
ferido *adj. wounded, injured; n. m. wounded
person.*

Êle (ele) foi ferido no braço. *He was
wounded in the arm.*
O ferido está muito melhor. *The wounded
man is much better.*
ferir *to wound, to injure, to hurt.*
fermentação *f. fermentation; ferment.*
fermentar *to ferment; to leaven.*
fermento *leaven, yeast.*
fero *adj. fierce.*
feroz *adj. ferocious, fierce; cruel.*
ferradura *f. horseshoe.*
ferramenta *f. tool.*
ferreiro *m. blacksmith.*
férreo *adj. iron, ferrous.*
FERRO *m. iron; electric iron.*
Passar a ferro. *To iron (clothes).*
Estrada de ferro. *Railroad.*
ferrovia *f. railroad.*
ferroviário *adj. railroad.*
ferrugem *f. rust.*
fértil *adj. fertile, fruitful.*
ferver *to boil; to seethe.*
fervor *m. fervor, zeal.*
FESTA *f. feast; party; celebration; holiday.*
Dona Maria vai dar uma festa no sábado.
*Dona Maria is going to give a party on
Saturday.*
Boas Festas! *Merry Christmas! Happy New
Year!*
festejar *to celebrate; to praise.*
festividade *f. festival.*
festivo *adj. festive, gay, merry.*
FEVEREIRO *m. February.*
O segundo mês do ano é fevereiro (Fevereiro). *February is the second month of
the year.*
fiado *adj. on credit.*
Ela não gosta de comprar fiado. *She
doesn't like to buy on credit.*
fiador *m. guarantor; bondsman.*
fiambre *m. cold meats.*
fiança *f. bail, bond; security; deposit.*
fiar *to trust, to confide; to sell on credit;
to spin, to weave.*
Todos nós fiamos dêle (dele). *All of us.
trust him.*
fibra *f. fiber; filament.*
FICAR *to remain, to stay; to be; to become.*
Não quero ficar mais aqui. *I don't want to
stay here any longer.*
João ficou com os tios. *John stayed with
his aunt and uncle.*
Quando lhe expliquei a situação êle (ele)
ficou convencido. *When I explained the
situation to him he was convinced.*
Ela ficou pálida. *She turned pale.*
Eu fico com êste (este). *I'll take this one.*
Ficamos sem dinheiro. *We ran out of money.*
Hoje ela ficou em casa. *Today she stayed
home.*
Fique com o trôco (troco). *Keep the change.*
Ela ficou doente. *She became ill.*
ficção *f. fiction.*
ficha *f. index card, file card; chip (poker).*
fichar *to record, to file.*
fichário *m. file cabinet; card index.*
fidelidade *f. fidelity; loyalty.*
De alta fidelidade. *High fidelity.*
fiel *adj. faithful, loyal; accurate.*
fígado *m. liver; courage.*
figo *m. fig.*
figueira *f. fig tree.*
figura *f. figure, form, appearance; image.*
figurar *to figure; to appear.*
fila *f. line; row; rank.*
Em fila. *In line. In a row.*
Fazer fila. *To line up. To stand in line.*

Primeira fila. *First row. Front rank.*
filar *to seise, to grasp; to sponge, to mooch.*
filé *m. fillet (meat, fish).*
fileira *f. line, row; tier; rank.*
filête (filete) *m. fillet; thread; thread (screw).*
FILHA *f. daughter, child.*
Êles (eles) têm três filhas e um filho.
They have three daughters and one son.
FILHO *m. son, child; pl. children.*
Não temos filhos. *We don't have any children.*
Tal pai, tal filho. *Like father, like son.*
filiação *f. filiation; relationship.*
filial *adj. filial; n. f. branch office or store.*
filipino *Philippine.*
filmar *to film.*
FILME *m. film; movie.*
Não gostei do filme. *I didn't like the film.*
filosofia *f. philosophy.*
filósofo *m. philosopher.*
filtrar *to filter, to strain.*
filtro *m. filter, strainer.*
FIM *end; object, purpose, aim.*
No fim do mês. *At the end of the month.*
Em fins de junho (Junho). *Toward the end of
June.*
Dar fim a. *To finish.*
Por fim. *Finally. At last.*
Sem fim. *Endless.*
A fim de. *In order that.*
No fim das contas. *After all.*
finado *adj. deceased; n. m. deceased.*
Dia de Finados. *All Souls' Day.*
FINAL *adj. final; n. m. end.*
Parte final. *Last part.*
No final das contas. *After all. In the end.*
Finalmente. *Finally.*
finalizar *to finish, to conclude.*
finanças *f. pl. finances; public funds.*
financeiro *adj. financial; n. m. financier.*
findar *to finish, to end.*
fineza *f. fineness; delicacy; courtesy.*
Agradeço muito a sua fineza. *I appreciate
your courtesy very much.*
fingir *to pretend.*
finlandês *Finnish.*
fino *adj. fine, delicate; cunning; keen; polite.*
fio *m. thread, string; filament; edge (knife).*
Fio de pérolas. *String of pearls.*
Dias a fio. *Days on end.*
Ela perdeu o fio da conversa. *She lost the
thread of the conversation.*
FIRMA *f. firm; business concern; signature.*
Ela trabalha com uma firma norteamericana. *She works for an American (North
American) firm.*
firmar *to sign, to endorse; to make firm; to
secure.*
firme *adj. firm, fast, stable, secure, resolute.*
Êle se mantém firme. *He holds his ground..*
fiscal *adj. fiscal; n. m. inspector; controller.*
física *f. physics.*
físico *adj. physical; n. m. physicist; physique.*
Êle (Ele) tem um defeito físico. *He has a
physical defect.*
fisiologia *f. physiology.*
fisionomia *f. appearance; look.*
FITA *f. ribbon; movie film; tape.*
Fita de máquina de escrever. *Typewriter
ribbon.*
fitar *to share at.*
fixar *(x = ks) to fix, to fasten; to determine; to
stare.*
fixo *(x = ks) adj. fixed, set; fast (of color).*
flagrante *adj. flagrant; red-handed; n. m. snapshot.*
Em flagrante. *In the act. Red-handed.*
flamejar *to flame.*

flamengo *adj. Flemish; n. m. Fleming; flamingo.*

flâmula *f. small flame; pennant; streamer.*

flanela *f. flannel.*

flauta *f. flute.*

flecha *f. arrow, dart.*

flertar *to flirt.*

flexível *adj. flexible, pliable.*

FLOR *f. flower, blossom.*
  Estar em flor. *To be in bloom.*
  Na flor da idade. *In the prime of life.*

florescer *to blossom, to bloom.*

floresta *f. forest.*

florista *m. and f. florist.*

fluente *adj. fluent, flowing.*

fluido *adj. fluid; fluent; n. m. fluid.*

fluminense *adj. of the State of Rio de Janeiro; m. and f. native of the State of Rio de Janeiro.*

flutuar *to float; to fluctuate.*

foca *f. seal, sea lion.*

focalizar *to focus, to focalise.*

focinho *m. snout; nose.*

foco *m. focus.*
  Em foco. *In focus.*

fogão *m. stove, heater.*

FOGO *m. fire.*
  Abrir fogo. *To open fire.*
  Pegar fogo. *To catch fire.*
  Armas de fogo. *Firearms.*
  Fogos de artifício. *Display of fireworks.*
  Não há fumaça sem fogo. *Where there's smoke there's fire.*

fogoso *adj. fiery, impetuous.*

fogueira *f. bonfire; blaze.*

foguete *m. rocket; missile; firecracker; lively person* Ⓑ.

fôlego *m. breath, wind.*
  Sem tôlego. *Out of breath.*

folga *f. rest, leisure.*
  Dia de folga. *Day off.*

folgar *to rest; to take it easy; to amuse oneself.*

FÔLHA (FOLHA) *f. leaf; sheet; blade.*
  A árvore não tem mais fôlhas (folhas). *The tree has no more leaves.*
  Virar a fôlha (folha). *To change the subject.*
  Fôlha de estanho. *Tinfoil.*
  Uma fôlha de papel. *A sheet of paper.*
  Fôlha de faca. *Knife blade.*

folhagem *f. foliage.*

folhear *to thumb through, to glance at.*

folhetim *m. serial publication.*

folheto *m. pamphlet.*

folia *f. gaiety, merrymaking.*

fólio *m. folio.*

FOME *f. hunger.*
  Estou com fome (Tenho fome). *I am hungry.*
  Estar com (Ter) uma fome canina. *To be terribly hungry.*
  Estou morrendo (a morrer) de fome. *I'm starving.*

fomentar *to foment, to encourage.*

fonética *f. phonetics.*

fonógrafo *m. phonograph, record player.*

FONTE *f. spring, fountain; source.*
  Eu sei de boa fonte. *I have it on good authority.*

FORA *outside, out.*
  Há mais gente fora do que dentro. *There are more people outside than inside.*
  Fora! *Get out!*
  Estar fora. *To be absent. To be out.*
  Fora disso. *Besides that.*
  Fora de si. *Beside oneself. Frantic.*
  Deite fora. *Throw it away.*

forasteiro *adj. foreign; strange; n. m. foreigner; stranger.*

FÔRCA (FORÇA) *f. force, strength, power.*
  À fôrça. *By force.*
  À fôrça de. *By dint of.*
  Fôrça motriz. *Motive power.*
  Fôrças armadas. *Armed forces.*

forçar *to force, to compel, to oblige.*

forçoso *adj. forceful; compelling; compulsory.*

FORMA *f. form, shape; manner, way.*
  A forma desta caixa (x = sh) é interessante. *The shape of this box is interesting.*
  Em forma de "U." *U-shaped.*
  De nenhuma forma! *By no means!*
  Desta forma. *In this way.*
  Fora de forma! *Dismissed! (Military.)*
  Última forma! *As you were! (Military.)*

fôrma (forma) *f. mold; pattern.*

formação *f. formation.*

formal *adj. formal.*

formalidade *f. formality.*

formar *to form, to shape.*
  Os alunos formaram um círculo. *The students formed a circle.*

formar-se *to graduate.*
  O filho dela se formou em direito. *Her son graduated in law.*

formatura *f. graduation, commencement.*

formidável *adj. formidable; excellent; wonderful.*
  Ela é formidável. *She's wonderful.*

formiga *f. ant.*

formoso *adj. beautiful; handsome; lovely; fine.*

formosura *f. beauty.*

fórmula *f. formula; blank form; recipe.*
  Faça o favor de preencher esta fórmula. *Please fill out this form.*

formular *to formulate.*

formulário *m. blank form, application form.*
  Primeiro é preciso preencher êste (este) formulário. *First you must fill out this form.*

fornalha *f. oven; furnace.*

fornecer *to furnish, to provide.*

forno *m. oven; furnace.*

forrar *to line (a garment, etc.); to cover.*
  O sobretudo está forrado. *The overcoat is lined.*

fôrro (forro) *adj. free, freed; m. lining; padding.*

fortalecer *to fortify.*

fortaleza *f. fortress, stronghold; fortitude, strength.*

FORTE *adj. strong, powerful; n. m. fort; strong point.*
  Caixa-forte (x = sh). *Strongbox. Safe.*
  Ele (ele) sempre joga forte. *He always plays hard.*
  O irmão dela é muito forte. *Her brother is very strong.*

fortidão *f. strength.*

fortificação *f. fortification.*

fortificar *to fortify, to strengthen.*

fortuito *adj. fortuitous, accidental.*

fortuna *f. fortune.*
  Boa fortuna. *Good luck.*
  Por fortuna. *Fortunately.*

fósforo *m. phosphorous; match (to light with).*

fossa *f. pit, hole.*

fotografar *to photograph.*

fotografia *f. photography; photograph, photo, picture.*

foz *f. mouth (of a river).*

fracalhão *m. weakling, coward.*

fração (fracção) *f. fraction.*

fracassar *to fail.*

fracasso *m. failure.*

fraco *adj. lean, thin; weak; n. m. weakling; weakness.*

frade *m. friar, monk.*

fragate *f. frigate.*

frágil *adj. fragile, brittle; weak, frail.*

fragmento *m. fragment.*

fragrância *f. fragrance, pleasing odor.*

fragrante *adj. fragrant.*

frágua *f. forge.*

framboesa *f. raspberry.*

francês *adj. French; n. m. Frenchman; French language.*

FRANCO *adj. frank, free, open, plain; n. m. franc.*
  Êle (ele) não foi franco conosco. *He was not frank with us.*
  Porto franco. *Free port.*
  Franco de porte. *Postpaid.*
  Entrada franca. *Admission free.*

frango *m. chicken.*
  Frango assado. *Roast chicken.*

franqueado *adj. franked; free.*

franquear *to frank, to free from charges; to prepay; to facilitate.*
  Franqueou as cartas? *Did you put stamps on the letters?*
  Franquear a passagem. *To clear the way.*

franqueza *f. frankness, sincerity.*
  Fale com franqueza. *Speak frankly.*

franquia *f. franchise; exemption from duties (taxes).*

fraqueza *f. weakness.*

frasco *m. flask, bottle.*

frase *f. phrase, sentence.*
  Frase feita. *Idiom. Common expression.*

fraternidade *f. fraternity, brotherhood.*

fraude *f. fraud.*

FREAR Ⓑ *to put on the brakes; to slow down; to curb.*
  Freie! *Put on the brakes!*

freguês *m. customer, client.*

frei *m. friar.*

FREIO *m. brake; check, curb; bit.*
  Freio de mão. *Hand brake.*
  Freio de emergência. *Emergency brake.*

freira *f. nun, sister.*

freire *m. friar, monk.*

frenético *adj. mad, frantic.*

FRENTE *f. front; façade; appearance.*
  Na frente de. *In front of.*
  Frente a frente. *Face to face.*
  Bem em frente. *Straight ahead.*
  Porta da frente. *Front door.*

frequência (frequência) *f. frequency.*
  Êles (eles) se viam com frequência. *They saw one another frequently.*

frequente (frequente) *adj. frequent.*

FRESCO *adj. cool; fresh; wet (paint); n. m. fresh air; fresco (painting).*
  A água está fresca. *The water is cool.*
  Tomar o fresco. *To go out for some fresh air.*
  Tinta fresca. *Wet paint.*
  Ar fresco. *Fresh air.*

frescura *f. freshness; coolness.*

fretar *to freight; to charter.*

frete *m. freight; cargo.*

fricassé *m. fricassee.*

fricção *f. friction, rubbing.*

friccionar *to rub, to massage.*

frigir *to fry; to bother.*

frigorífico *m. refrigerator, freezer.*

FRIO *adj. cold, cool; n. m. cold.*
  Estou com frio (Tenho frio). *I am cold.*
  Está frio hoje. *It's cold today.*
  Sangue frio. *Cold blood.*
  Tempo frio. *Cold weather.*

friorento *adj. sensitive to cold.*

fritada *f. fried dish.*

fritar *to fry.*

frito *adj. fried.*
Batatas fritas. *Fried potatoes.*
Estou frito. *I'm in trouble. I'm in a mess* Ⓑ.
fronha *f. pillowcase; pillow.*
fronte *f. forehead; front.*
fronteira *f. frontier, border.*
frota *f. fleet.*
Frota mercante. *Merchant fleet.*
frouxo (*x = sh*) *adj. loose; slack; flabby.*
frugal *adj. frugal, thrifty.*
frustrar *to frustrate.*
FRUTA *f. fruit.*
frutífero *adj. fruitful.*
frutificar *to bear fruit.*
FRUTO *m. fruit; result; profit.*
Em dois anos vai dar fruto. *In two years.*
it will show results.
fubá *m. Brasilian cornmeal.*
fuga *f. escape, flight.*
Em fuga. *In flight.*
Pôr em fuga. *To put to flight. To rout.*
fugaz *adj. fleeting, transitory.*
fugir *to flee, to escape, to run away.*
fugitivo *adj. fugitive; n. m. fugitive.*
fulano *m. person; So-and-So; John Doe.*
Fulano de Tal. *So-and-So. John Doe.*
Fulano, Beltrano e Sicrano. *Tom, Dick, and*
Harry.
fulgir *to glow, to shine.*
fulgor *m. brilliance, glow.*
fumaça *f. smoke.*
Não há fumaça sem fogo. *Where there's*
smoke there's fire.
fumador *adj. smoking; n. m. smoker.*
FUMAR *to smoke.*
Ela fuma demais. *She smokes too much.*
fumo *m. smoke; tobacco* Ⓑ; *fumes.*
Quero fumo para cachimbo. *I want some pipe*
tobacco.
função *f. function, performance.*
funcionar *to function; to work; to run (machine).*
Esta máquina não funciona. *This machine*
doesn't work.
Funcionar bem. *To be in good working*
condition.
funcionário *m. functionary; employee.*
Funcionário público. *Government employee.*
fundação *f. foundation.*
fundador *m. founder.*
fundamental *adj. fundamental.*
fundamento *m. foundation, base, ground; reason.*
Sem fundamento. *Groundless.*
Faltar de fundamento. *To be without founda-*
tion or reason.
fundar *to found, to base.*
Foi fundada em 1965. *It was founded in 1965.*
fundear *to anchor.*
fundição *f. foundry; casting, melting.*
fundir *to melt; to fuse.*
FUNDO *adj. deep; bottom; base; background;*
n. m. pl. funds.
Fundo duplo. *Double bottom.*
Artigo de fundo. *Main article in a newspaper.*
Conhecer a fundo. *To know well.*
Fundos públicos. *Public funds.*
fúnebre *adj. funereal; sad.*
funeral *adj. funeral, funereal; m. funeral.*
funesto *adj. fatal; fateful.*
funil *m. funnel.*
furacão *m. hurricane.*
furar *to penetrate, to break through.*
Furar uma festa. *To crash a party.*
furgão *m. baggage car; van.*
fúria *f. fury, rage, fit of maaness.*
furioso *adj. furious, mad, frantic.*

furor *m. fury.*
furtar *to steal; to cheat.*
Furtar-se ao dever. *To shirk one's respon-*
sibility.
Não furtarás. *Thou shalt not steal.*
furto *m. theft.*
fusão *f. fusion; union.*
fusível *m. fuse.*
fuso *m. spindle, spool; screw; zone (time).*
futebol *m. soccer.*
futebolista *m. and f. soccer fan; soccer player.*
fútil *adj. futile.*
FUTURO *adj. future; n. m. future; fiancé.*
Em futuro próximo. *In the near future.*
Ela nos apresentou seu futuro. *She*
introduced her fiancé to us.
fuzil *m. rifle.*

G

gabardina *f. gabardine.*
gabinete *m. cabinet; study; laboratory; ministry.*
Gabinete de leitura. *Reading room.*
gado *m. cattle, livestock.*
gaiola *f. cage.*
gaita *f. fife; harmonica; "dough," money* Ⓑ,
useless things Ⓑ.
Não tenho gaita. *I don't have any money.*
Gaita galega. *Bagpipe.*
gaiteiro *m. player of fife, harmonica or bagpipe.*
gaivão *m. swift (bird).*
gaivota *f. sea gull, gull; fool* Ⓑ.
gala *f. gala occasion; fine or formal dress.*
De gala. *Full or formal dress.*
Fazer gala de. *To boast of; to show off.*
galã *m. main romantic lead (theatre); lover.*
galantaria *f. gallantry; politeness.*
galante *adj. gallant; polite.*
galantear *to court; to compliment.*
galão *m. gallon; stripe (uniform).*
galego *adj. Galician; n. m. Galician;*
a Portuguese person in Brazil (not complimen-
tary) Ⓑ.
galeria *f. gallery; arcade.*
galgo *m. greyhound.*
Correr como um galgo. *To rush. To hurry.*
along.
galhardete *m. pennant, streamer, banner.*
galho *m. branch (tree).*
galhofa *f. something funny; joke; fun.*
galicismo *m. gallicism.*
galinha *f. chicken, hen; coward* Ⓑ.
Deitar-se com as galinhas. *To go to bed with*
the chickens. To retire early.
Muita galinha e poucos ovos. *Much talk and*
little action.
galinheiro *m. chicken coop; gallery (theatre).*
galo *m. rooster, cock.*
Ao cantar do galo. *At dawn.*
Missa do galo. *Midnight mass.*
galocha *f. galochas, rubber overshoes.*
galopar *to gallop.*
galope *m. gallop.*
gamão *m. backgammon.*
gamo *m. deer, stag.*
gana *f. desire, craving; hate.*
gancho *m. hook; hairpin.*
ganhador *adj. winning; n. m. winner.*
GANHAR *to gain; to earn; to win; to reach.*
Como ganhar amigos. *How to win friends.*
Quanto dinheiro ganhou? *How much money*
did you earn?
Não ganhamos. *We did not win.*
Êle (ele) não pode ganhar a vida. *He can't*
make a living.

ganho *adj. gained, earned; n. m. profit, gain.*
ganso *m. goose, gander.*
garage Ⓑ, **garagem** *f. garage.*
garantia *f. guarantee; guaranty; security.*
Garantia por escrito. *Written guarantee.*
garantir *to guarantee; to vouch for.*
garção *m. waiter* Ⓑ.
gardénia (gardénia) *f. gardenia.*
GARFO *m. fork.*
gargalhada *f. burst of laughter.*
GARGANTA *f. throat; gorge.*
Dor de garganta. *Sore throat.*
Estou com êle (ele) pela garganta.
I've had enough of him.
garôta (garota) *f. young girl* Ⓑ.
garôto (garoto) *m. boy; urchin.*
garra *f. claw; finger; hand.*
GARRAFA *f. bottle.*
Uma garrafa de cerveja. *A bottle of beer.*
gás *m. gas.*
Gas lacrimogêneo (lacrimogénio). *Tear gas.*
gasolina *f. gasoline.*
gasosa *f. soda pop.*
gasoso *adj. gaseous.*
GASTAR *to spend; to wear out; to use.*
Gastei todo o dinheiro que me deu. *I spent*
all the money you gave me.
Não gaste o tempo com ela. *Don't waste your*
time with her.
Os meninos gastam tudo em pouco tempo.
The children wear everything out in a short
time.
GASTO *adj. spent; worn out; n. m. cost,*
expense.
Todo o dinheiro foi gasto em dois meses.
All the money was spent in two months.
Houve muitos gastos. *There were many ex-*
penses.
gata *f. cat.*
gatilho *m. trigger.*
gatinha *f. kitten.*
Andar de gatinhas. *To crawl on all fours.*
GATO *m. cat; clever person; a slip, error.*
Não dê carne ao gato. *Don't give the cat*
meat.
Não compre gato por lebre. *Don't buy a pig*
in a poke.
Êles (Eles) vivem como cão e gato. *They*
fight like cat and dog.
Quem não tem cão, caça com gato. *To make*
the best of things.
Ela cometeu um gato. *She pulled a boner.*
gauchesco *adj. Gaucho* Ⓑ.
gaúcho *adj. of Rio Grande do Sul in Brazil; n.*
m. native of Rio Grande do Sul; also type of
cowboy of Uruguay and of Argentina.
gaveta *f. drawer (desk).*
A carta está na gaveta da mesa. *The letter*
is in the drawer of the table.
gavião *m. hawk; sly person* Ⓑ; *ladies' man* Ⓑ;
children's game Ⓟ.
gazeta *f. gazette, newspaper.*
geladeira *f. icebox, refrigerator.*
gelado *adj. frozen; icy; cold; n. m. sherbet; ice*
cream; cold drink.
gelar *to freeze; to frighten.*
gelatina *f. gelatin; jelly.*
geléia (geleia) *jelly, jam.*
gêlo (gelo) *m. ice; indifference.*
Gêlo sêco (seco). *Dry ice.*
gema *f. yolk (egg); core.*
Carioca da gema. *A true carioca (native of*
the city of Rio de Janeiro).
gêmeo (gémeo) *m. twin.*
gemer *to moan; to creak.*
gemido *m. groan; sigh.*

general m. general (mil. rank).

GÊNERO (GÉNERO) m. class, kind, sort; gender; pl. goods.
O gênero humano. Mankind.
Gêneros alimentícios. Foodstuffs.

generosidade f. generosity.

generoso adj. generous, liberal.

gengibre m. ginger.

gengiva f. gum (mouth).

gênio (génio) m. genius; talent; nature, disposition; temperament.
Êle (ele) tem mau gênio. He has a bad temper.

genro m. son-in-law.

GENTE f. people; personnel; one, they, we.
Há muita gente today. There are many people (here) today.
A gente não faz isso. One doesn't do that.

gentil adj. kind; polite; courteous.

gentileza f. kindness; courtesy.
Agradeço muito a sua gentileza. I am very grateful for your kindness.

gentio adj. and n. m. gentile, pagan, heathen.

genuíno adj. genuine, real.

geografia f. geography.

geometria f. geometry.

geração f. generation.

gerador adj. generating; n. m. generator.

GERAL adj. general.
Em geral. In general. Generally.
Minas Gerais. Minas Gerais ("General Mines"), name of a state in Brazil.

gerânio m. geranium.

gerar to generate.

gerência f. management, administration.

gerente m. manager, administrator.

gerigonça f. jargon; slang.

germânico adj. Germanic.

germe m. germ.

germinar to germinate.

gerúndio m. gerund.

gesticular to gesticulate.

gesto m. gesture.

gigante adj. giant; n. m. giant.

gilete f. safety razor.
Não uso navalha; só gilete. I don't use a straight razor; just a safety razor.

ginásio m. high school; gymnasium.

girar to rotate, to turn; to circulate.

girassol m. sunflower.

gíria f. slang; jargon.

giro m. turn; stroll.

giz m. chalk.
Sem giz não se pode escrever no quadro-negro. We can't write on the blackboard without chalk.

glacial adj. glacial; cold.

globo m. globe, ball.

glória f. glory; fame.

gloriar to glorify.

glorioso adj. glorious.

glosa f. comment; criticism.

goiaba f. guava.

goiabada f. guava paste.

goiano adj. and n. m. of the state of Goiás in Brazil.

gol m. goal (sports).

gola f. collar; throat.

gôlfe (golfe) m. golf.
Tacos de gôlfe. Golf clubs.

gôlfo (golfo) m. gulf.
Gôlfo do México. Gulf of Mexico.

GOLPE m. blow; coup.
De golpe. Suddenly. All at once.

De um só golpe. At one stroke. With one blow.
Um golpe de sorte. A lucky blow or stroke.
Golpe de estado. Coup d'état.
Golpe de mestre. Master stroke.
Golpe de mar. Surf. Heavy sea.

goma f. gum; starch.
Goma de mascar. Chewing gum.

GORDO adj. fat; n. m. fat person.
O pai dêle (dele) é muito gordo. His father is very fat.

gordura f. fat; grease; stoutness.

gorila m. gorilla.

gorjear to warble.

gorjeta f. tip (money).

gorro m. cap.

GOSTAR to like; to taste.
Gosto muito dêle (dele). I like him very much.
Gosto mais dêste (deste). I prefer this one.
Eu gostaria de ver a peça. I should like to see the play.

GÔSTO (GOSTO) m. liking; taste; pleasure.
Ela tem bom gôsto. She has good taste.
Isto é muito a meu gôsto. This is very much to my taste.

gostoso adj. tasty, delicious.

gota f. drop (liquid); gout.
Gota a gota. Drop by drop.
Elas se parecem como duas gotas d'água. They are as alike as two peas in a pod.
Essa foi a gota d'água que fêz (fez) transbordar o copo. That was the straw that broke the camel's back.

gotejar to trickle, to drip.

governador m. governor.

governante adj. governing, ruling; n. m. ruler; governor.

governar to govern, to rule; to control.
E ela quem governa em casa. She rules the house.

govêrno (governo) m. government; control.
O novo govêrno é forte. The new government is strong.

gozar to enjoy.
Elas gozam de boa saúde. They enjoy good health.

gôzo (gozo) m. joy; enjoyment.

gozoso adj. joyful, merry.

GRAÇA f. grace; favor; pardon; wit; charm; name; pl. thanks.
Graças a Deus. Thank God.
Eu terminei tudo, graças à sua ajuda. I finished everything, thanks to your help.
Não acho graça nisso. I don't think that's funny.
Tem graça. That's funny.
Qual é sua graça? What is your name?

gracejar to joke.
Êle (ele) sempre está gracejando (está a gracejar). He's always joking.

gracioso adj. gracious; witty.

grade f. grating; grille; latticework.

gradual adj. gradual.

graduar to grade, to classify; to graduate.

graduar-se to graduate (school).

gráfica f. writing; spelling.

gráfico adj. graphic; n. m. graph; chart.

gralha f. crow; jay; magpie; chatterbox, gossip, misprint.

grama f. grass; gram.

gramática f. grammar.

grampear to staple; to clip.
Máquina de grampear. Stapler.

grampo m. staple; clip; pin; cramp.

granada f. grenade.

GRANDE adj. great, large, tall.
A casa dêle (dele) é muito grande. His house is very large.
Êle (ele) é um grande artista. He is a great artist.

grandeza f. greatness.

grandioso adj. grandiose, magnificent.

granizar to hail.

granizo m. hail.

granja f. farm.

grão m. grain; kernel.

gratidão f. gratitude.

gratificação f. gratuity, tip.

gratificar to reward; to tip.

grátis free.

grato adj. grateful; pleasant.
Fico-lhe muito grato. I remain gratefully yours. I am very grateful to you.

gratuito adj. free.

grau m. degree.
Dez graus abaixo (x = sh) de zero. Ten degrees below zero.
Por graus. By degrees.

gravado adj. engraved; recorded.

gravador adj. engraving; recording; n. m. engraver; recorder; tape recorder.

gravar to engrave; to record.
O professor gravou duas fitas. The professor recorded two tapes.

GRAVATA f. necktie.
Vou levar seis gravatas na mala. I'm going to take six neckties in my bag.
Eu prefiro gravata-borboleta. I prefer a bow tie.

grave adj. grave, serious.
Foi muito grave. It was very serious.
Acento grave. Grave accent mark.

gravidade f. seriousness, gravity.

gravura f. etching; engraving; picture.

graxa (x = sh) f. grease; shoe polish.

graxento (x = sh) adj. greasy.

grego adj. Greek.

grelha f. grill.

grelhar to grill, to broil.

grêmio (grémio) m. guild, society.

greve f. strike.
Os operários entraram em greve. The workers went on strike.

grevista m. and f. striker.

grifo m. italics.
Leia a parte em grifo. Read the part in italics.

grilo m. cricket.

gripe f. grippe, influenza.

grisalho adj. grayish; grizzly.

gritar to shout, to scream.
Quem gritou? Who cried out?

gritaria f. shouting; hubbub.

grito m. shout, scream.
Grito de guerra. Battle cry.

groselha f. currant; gooseberry.

grosseiro adj. coarse, rude, impolite.

grosso adj. thick; coarse.

grou m. crane (bird).

grua f. crane (bird); crane, derrick.

grudar to glue, to stick together.

grude m. glue, paste.

grunhido m. grunt.

grunhir to grunt.

GRUPO m. group.
Vamos dividi-los em quatro grupos diferentes. We are going to divide them into four different groups.

gruta f. grotto, cave.

guarda m. and f. guard; watch; guardian; watchman.
Guarda de honra. Guard of honor.
Quem está de guarda? Who is on duty?
guarda-chuva m. umbrella.
Hoje não precisamos de guarda-chuva. We don't need an umbrella today.
guarda-livros m. and f. bookkeeper.
guarda-marinha m. midshipman.
guardanapo m. napkin.
GUARDAR to keep; to guard; to take care of.
Guarde o dinheiro no banco. Keep your money in the bank.
Ela não sabe guardar segrêdo (segredo). She doesn't know how to keep a secret.
guarda-roupa m. wardrobe; cloakroom.
guarnecer to trim; to garnish; to garrison.
guarnição f. trim; garrison; crew.
Todos os membros da guarnição estão a bordo. All the members of the crew are aboard.
guatemalteco adj. and n. m. Guatemalan.
GUERRA f. war.
Fazer guerra. To wage war.
Guerra civil. Civil war.
Guerra atômica (atómica) Atomic war.
Guerra fria. Cold war.
guerreiro adj. warlike; m. warrior.
GUIA m. guide, leader; guidebook; directory; f. guidance; permit, bill.
Gostaria dos serviços dum guia. I'd like to have the services of a guide.
Não tem guia da cidade? Don't you have a guidebook of the city?
guianês adj. Guianan; n. m. Guianan.
guiar to guide, to direct; to drive.
O senhor sabe guiar? Do you know how to drive?
guichê (guichet, guiché) m. window (ticket, information).
Guichê de informações. Information window.
guisa f. guise.
À guisa de. Like.
guisado m. stew.
guisar to stew.
guitarra f. guitar.
guitarrista m. and f. guitarist.

H

há ha!
hábil adj. able; clever; capable.
Êle (ele) é muito hábil. He is very clever.
habilidade f. ability, skill.
habilitado adj. able; qualified.
habilitar to qualify; to enable.
habitação f. dwelling, residence.
habitante m. and f. inhabitant, resident.
É uma cidade de vinte mil habitantes. It is a city of twenty thousand inhabitants.
habitar to inhabit.
hábito m. habit, custom; dress, garb.
Êle (ele tinha o hábito de levantar-se cedo. He was in the habit of getting up early.
Ela tinha êsse (esse) mau hábito. She had that bad habit.
O hábito não faz o monge. Clothes don't make the man.
habituar to accustom.
habituar-se to become accustomed.
haitiano adj. and n. m. Haitian.
hálito m. breath.
Mau hálito. Bad breath.
hangar m. hangar.
harmonia f. harmony.
harpa f. harp.

haste f. pole, rod.
hastear to hoist (flag).
havaiano adj. Hawaiian; n. m. Hawaiian.
havana m. and f. Havana cigar.
HAVER to have (auxiliary verb; however, today "ter" is replacing it in this use); to be, to exist; there to be.
Há. There is. There are.
Havia. There was. There were.
Houve. There was. There were.
Haverá. There will be.
Haveria. There would be.
Haja. There may be.
Que haja. Let there be.
Houvesse. There might be.
Se houvesse. If there were.
Há havido. There has (have) been.
Havia havido. There had been. There would have been.
Haveria havido. There would have been.
Há que. It is necessary.
Haverá que. It will be necessary.
Houve que. It was necessary.
Há de ser. It must be.
Hei de partir amanhã. I'm to leave tomorrow.
Há pouco tempo. A short while ago.
Ela havia escrito a carta? Had she written the letter?
Ontem não houve aulas. There were no classes yesterday.
Deve haver cartas para mim. There must be some letters for me.
Há uma semana que a vi. I saw her a week ago.
Que há de nôvo (novo)? What's new?
O que é que há? What's the matter?
Haja o que houver. Come what may.
Não há remédio. It can't be helped.
Vai haver muita gente lá. There will be many people there.
Não há de quê. Don't mention it.
hebreu adj. Hebrew; n. m. Hebrew.
hectare m. hectare.
hediondo adj. hideous, repugnant.
hélice m. and f. propeller.
hemisfério m. hemisphere.
hera f. ivy.
herança f. inheritance, legacy, heritage.
herdar to inherit.
herdeiro m. heir.
hereditário adj. hereditary.
herói m. hero.
heróico adj. heroic.
hesitar to hesitate.
Ela hesitou em fazê-lo. She hesitated in doing it.
hidráulico adj. hydraulic.
hidroavião m. seaplane.
hidrofobia f. hydrophobia, rabies.
hiena f. hyena.
hífen m. hyphen.
higiene f. hygiene.
higiênico (higiénico) adj. hygienic, sanitary.
hino m. hymn; anthem.
Hino nacional. National anthem.
hipnotismo m. hypnotism.
hipnotizar to hypnotize.
hipocrisia f. hypocrisy.
hipócrita adj. hypocritical; n. m. and f. hypocrite.
hipódromo m. racetrack, hippodrome.
hipopótamo m. hippopotamus.
hipoteca f. mortgage.
hipotecar to mortgage.
hispánico adj. Hispanic.
hispano-americano adj. Spanish-American; n. m.

Spanish-American.
Literatura hispano-americana. Spanish-American literature.
HISTÓRIA f. history; story.
História antiga. Ancient history.
História moderna. Modern history.
Não me conte mais histórias! Don't tell me any more stories!
historiador m. historian.
histórico adj. historic.
HOJE m. today.
Hoje é segunda-feira. Today is Monday.
Qual é o programa de hoje? What's today's program?
De hoje em diante. From now on.
Hoje em dia. Nowadays.
De hoje a oito dias. In a week.
Hoje à noite. Tonight. This evening.
Hoje à tarde. This afternoon.
holandês adj. Dutch; n. m. Dutch.
holofote m. searchlight.
HOMEM m. man.
Homem de bem. Honest man.
Homem do mundo. Man of the world.
Homem de letras. Man of letters.
Homem de negócios. Businessman.
Homem de Estado. Statesman.
O homem põe e Deus dispõe. Man proposes, God disposes.
homenagem f. homage, honor, respects.
Prestar homenagem. To render homage to.
homenzarrão m. very large man.
hondurenho adj. Honduran; n. m. Honduran.
honesto adj. honest; sincere.
honra f. honor, respect.
Em honra de. In honor of.
honradez f. honesty, integrity.
honrar to honor.
HORA f. hour; time.
Que horas são? What time is it?
São duas horas e meia. It's two thirty.
À que horas começa a festa? At what time does the party begin?
Está na hora de jantar. It's time for dinner.
Hora de verão. Daylight-saving time.
Êle (ele) chegou na hora. He arrived on time.
horário m. schedule; timetable.
horizontal adj. horizontal.
horizonte m. horizon.
horrível adj. horrible.
horror m. horror.
horroroso adj. horrible, frightful, dreadful.
horta f. vegetable garden.
hospedagem f. lodging; board.
hospedar to lodge.
hóspede m. and f. guest.
hospício m. an asylum.
hospital m. hospital.
hospitalizar to hospitalize.
hóstia f. Host.
hostil adj. hostile.
hostilidade f. hostility.
hostilizar to antagonize.
hotel m. hotel.
hoteleiro m. hotelman, innkeeper.
humanidade f. humanity, mankind.
humanitário adj. humanitarian, philanthropic.
HUMANO adj. human, humane; n. m. man, human being.
Um ser humano. A human being.
humildade f. humility.
humilde adj. humble.
humilhado adj. humiliated.
humilhante adj. humiliating.
humilhar to humiliate; to humble.

HUMOR m. humor; disposition.
Estar de bom humor. To be in a good mood.
Estar de mau humor. To be in a bad mood.
humorado adj. humored.
humorista m. and f. humorist.
húngaro adj. Hungarian; n. m. Hungarian.
hurra! hurrah!

I

iaiá f. missy, miss Ⓑ.
iate m. yacht.
ibérico adj. Iberian; n. m. Iberian.
ibero adj. Iberian; n. m. Iberian.
içar to hoist.
Içar a bandeira. To hoist the flag.
ida f. departure; one-way (ticket).
Bilhete de ida e volta. Round-trip ticket.
IDADE f. age; time, period.
Idade de ouro. Golden Age.
Idade Média. Middle Ages.
Certidão de idade. Birth certificate.
Que idade o senhor tem? How old are you?
ideal adj. ideal; n. m. ideal.
idealizar to idealize.
idear to think of, to conceive; to devise; to plan.
IDÉIA (IDEIA) f. idea.
Não tenho a minima idéia. I haven't the slightest idea.
É uma boa idéia. It's a good idea.
Mais tarde ela mudou de idéia. Later she changed her mind.
idem the same, ditto.
idêntico adj. identical, the same.
identidade f. identity.
O senhor tem os seus documentos de identidade? Do you have your identification papers?
identificação f. identification.
identificar to identify.
idioma m. language.
idiota adj. idiotic; n. m. and f. idiot, fool.
idiotice f. foolishness, foolish thing.
idiotismo m. idiom.
ídolo m. idol.
idoso adj. aged, old.
ignomínia f. infamy; disgrace.
ignorância f. ignorance.
ignorante adj. ignorant; unaware; n. m. ignoramus, ignorant person.
Ela estava ignorante do que acontecia. She was unaware of what was happening.
Êle (Ele) é um ignorante. He's an ignoramus.
ignorar to be ignorant of, not to know, to be unaware.
Ignoro seu nome. I don't know his name.
IGREJA f. church.
IGUAL adj. equal; similar, like; even.
Vamos dividi-lo em partes iguais. We'll divide it in equal parts.
Não ter igual. To be matchless. To have no equal.
Nunca vi coisa igual. I never saw anything like it.
Cada qual com seu igual. Birds of a feather flock together.
igualar to equalize, to make even; to compare.
igualdade f. equality.
Igualdade de condições. Equal terms.
ilegal adj. illegal.
ilegítimo adj. illegitimate.
ilegível adj. illegible.
ileso adj. unharmed, safe.
iletrado adj. illiterate; n. m. illiterate.
ilha f. island, isle.
ilimitado adj. unlimited.

iludir to deceive.
iluminação f. illumination.
iluminar to illuminate.
ilusão f. illusion.
ilusivo adj. illusive.
ilustração f. illustration.
ilustrar to illustrate; to explain.
ilustrar-se to acquire knowledge; to become distinguished.
ilustre adj. illustrious, celebrated.
imagem f. image, figure.
imaginação f. imagination.
IMAGINAR to imagine, to think, to suspect.
Imagine! Just imagine!
Não posso imaginar tal coisa! I can't imagine such a thing!
imbecil adj. imbecile; n. m. imbecile.
imediação f. immediacy; pl. environs.
imediatamente immediately.
imediato adj. immediate; near; m. second in command.
imenso adj. immense.
imigração f. immigration.
imigrante adj. immigrant; n. m. immigrant.
imigrar to immigrate.
imitação f. imitation.
imitar to imitate; to mimic.
imoderado adj. immoderate.
imoral adj. immoral.
imortal adj. immortal.
imóvel adj. immobile; n. m. real estate Ⓑ.
impaciência f. impatience.
impacientar to make impatient, to exasperate.
impaciente adj. impatient, restless.
ímpar adj. odd, uneven (number).
Número ímpar. Uneven number.
imparcial adj. impartial, unbiased.
impávido adj. fearless.
impedimento m. impediment, hindrance, obstacle.
impedir to hinder, to prevent.
A linha está impedida Ⓟ. The line (telephone) is busy.
impenetrável adj. impenetrable.
imperador m. emperor.
imperativo adj. imperative; n. m. imperative.
imperfeito adj. imperfect, faulty; n. m. imperfect (tense).
império m. empire, domain.
Império Romano. Roman Empire.
impermeabilizar to waterproof.
impermeável adj. waterproof; n. m. raincoat.
Hoje vou levar o impermeável. I'm going to take my raincoat today.
impertinente adj. impertinent.
impessoal adj. impersonal.
ímpeto m. impetus.
impetuoso adj. impetuous.
ímpio adj. wicked, impious; n. m. impious person.
implicar to implicate; to imply.
implícito adj. implicit.
implorar to implore.
imponente adj. imposing.
IMPOR to impose; to command.
Impor respeito. To command respect.
Impor condições. To impose conditions.
Impor um impôsto (imposto). To levy a tax.
importação f. importation, import.
IMPORTÂNCIA f. importance.
Não tem importância. It doesn't matter.
Sem importância. Unimportant.
IMPORTANTE adj. important.
Isto é importante. This is important.

IMPORTAR to import; to matter, to be important; to amount to.
Esta casa importa café do Brasil. This firm imports coffee from Brazil.
Que importa? What does it matter?
Não importa. It doesn't matter. Never mind.
Importa muito. It matters a lot. It's very important.
Não me importa. It makes no difference to me.
Em quanto importa a conta? How much is the bill? How much does the bill come to?
importunar to annoy, to bother.
imposição f. imposition.
impossibilidade f. impossibility.
impossibilitar to make impossible, to preclude.
IMPOSSÍVEL adj. impossible.
É impossível. It's impossible. It can't be done.
impôsto (imposto) adj. imposed, set; n. m. tax, duty.
Impôsto de renda. Income tax.
Isento de impôsto. Tax-free.
impreciso adj. vague, not clear.
imprensa f. press.
impressão f. impression; printing, edition.
impressionar to impress; to move; to affect.
impresso adj. printed; n. m. printed document.
imprevisto adj. unforeseen, unexpected; sudden.
Êle (ele) chegou de imprevisto. He arrived unexpectedly.
imprimir to print, to imprint.
impróprio adj. improper, unfit; unbecoming.
improvável adj. unlikely, improbable.
improvisar to improvise.
improviso adj. unexpected; impromptu.
De improviso. Unexpectedly.
imprudência f. imprudence, lack of prudence.
impulsionar to impel; to drive; to urge.
impulso m. impulse.
impunidade f. impunity.
impureza f. impurity, contamination.
impuro adj. impure, contaminated.
imputar to impute, to attribute.
imunizar to immunize.
imutável adj. fixed, unchangeable.
inaceitável adj. inadmissible; unacceptable.
inadaptável adj. not adaptable.
inadequado adj. inadequate.
inadmissível adj. inadmissible.
inadvertido adj. inadvertent.
inalterável adj. unalterable, unchangeable.
inativo (inactivo) adj. inactive.
inauguração f. inauguration.
inaugurar to inaugurate, to begin.
incansável adj. untiring.
incapacidade f. incapacity, inability, incompetence.
incapaz adj. incapable, incompetent.
Ela é incapaz de fazê-lo. She is incapable of doing it.
incendiar to set on fire.
incêndio m. fire.
incerteza f. uncertainty.
incerto adj. uncertain.
incessante adj. incessant, continual, ceaseless.
inchar to swell, to puff up.
incidente adj. incident; n. m. incident.
incisão f. incision.
inciso adj. incised, cut.
incitar to incite, to stimulate.
inclemência f. inclemency.
A inclemência do tempo não nos permitiu sair. The bad weather kept us at home.
inclinação f. inclination, tendency.

inclinar *to incline, to bend.*
inclinar-se *to incline; to bow..*
INCLUIR *to include, to enclose.*
Está incluído o vinho? *Is the wine included?*
inclusive *inclusively.*
inclusivo *adj. inclusive.*
incluso *adj. included; enclosed.*
incoerente *adj. incoherent.*
incógnito *adj. incognito; unknown.*
incombustível *adj. incombustible.*
incomodar *to disturb, to inconvenience, to bother.*
Não se incomode. *Don't bother.*
incômodo (incómodo) *adj. uncomfortable, inconvenient.*
incomparável *adj. matchless, without equal.*
incompatível *adj. incompatible.*
incompetência *f. incompetency.*
incompleto *adj. incomplete, unfinished.*
incompreensível *adj. incomprehensible.*
inconcebível *adj. inconceivable, unthinkable.*
incondicional *adj. unconditional.*
inconfidência *f. disloyalty.*
incongruência *f. incongruity.*
inconsciência *f. unconsciousness; lack of conscience.*
inconsciente *adj. unconscious; unaware.*
inconstância *f. inconstancy, fickleness.*
inconstitucional *adj. unconstitutional.*
inconveniente *adj. unseemly, inopportune; n. m. inconvenience, difficulty.*
incorporar *to incorporate.*
incorreto (incorrecto) *adj. incorrect, inaccurate, wrong, improper.*
incorrigível *adj. incorrigible.*
incredulidade *f. incredulity, disbelief.*
incrédulo *adj. incredulous; n. m. unbeliever.*
incremento *m. increment, increase.*
increpar *to reproach, to rebuke.*
incrível *adj. incredible, unbelievable.*
Mas isso é incrível! *But that's incredible!*
incubadora *f. incubator.*
incubar *to incubate, to hatch.*
inculcar *to inculcate.*
inculpar *to blame.*
inculto *adj. uncultivated; uncultured.*
incumbência *f. duty, charge, mission.*
incumbir *to commit, to entrust.*
incurável *adj. incurable.*
indagar *to inquire, to investigate.*
indecente *adj. indecent, shameful.*
indecisão *f. indecision, vacillation.*
indeciso *adj. undecided, vacillating, hesitant.*
indefeso *adj. defenseless.*
indefinido *adj. indefinite.*
indelével *adj. indelible.*
indenização *f. indemnity, reparation.*
indenizar *to indemnify, to reimburse.*
independência *f. independence.*
Dia da Independência. *Independence Day.*
independente *adj. independent.*
indesejável *adj. undesirable; n. m. and f. undesirable.*
indeterminado *adj. indeterminate; undecided.*
indevido *adj. improper.*
índex *m. index; index finger; pl. índices.*
indianista *adj. Indianist; n. m. and f. Indianist.*
indiano *adj. Indian; n. m. and f. Indian.*
INDICAR *to indicate, to point out.*
Faça o favor de me indicar o caminho. *Please show me the way.*
índice *m. index, table of contents.*
Índice de preços. *Price index.*

Índice de mortalidade. *Death rate.*
indício *m. indication, sign, mark, clue.*
indiferença *f. indifference.*
indiferente *adj. indifferent.*
indígena *adj. native; n. m. and f. na*
indignar *to irritate, to annoy, to anger.*
indigno *adj. unworthy, undeserving, shameful.*
índio *adj. Indian; n. m. Indian.*
indireto (indirecto) *adj. indirect.*
indiscreto *adj. indiscreet.*
indiscrição *f. indiscretion.*
indiscutível *adj. unquestionable.*
indispensável *adj. indispensable, essential.*
indispor *to indispose, to upset.*
indisposição *f. indisposition.*
individual *adj. individual.*
indivíduo *m. individual, person.*
índole *f. disposition.*
indulgência *f. indulgence.*
indulgente *adj. indulgent.*
indústria *f. industry.*
industrial *adj. industrial; n. m. and f. industrialist.*
induzir *to induce, to influence.*
ineficácia *f. inefficacy.*
ineficaz *adj. inefficacious, ineffectual.*
inegável *adj. undeniable.*
inépcia *f. ineptitude.*
inepto *adj. inept.*
inequívoco *adj. unmistakable, clear.*
inércia *f. inertia.*
inerte *adj. inert; inactive.*
inesgotável *adj. inexhaustible.*
inesperado *adj. unexpected.*
Inesperadamente. *Suddenly. Unexpectedly.*
inesquecível *adj. unforgettable.*
inevitável *adj. inevitable, unavoidable.*
inexatidão (inexactidão) *f. inaccuracy.*
inexato (inexacto) *adj. inexact, inaccurate.*
inexperto *adj. inexpert, inexperienced.*
inexplicável *adj. inexplicable.*
infalível *adj. infallible.*
infamar *to defame, to malign.*
infame *adj. infamous.*
infâmia *f. infamy.*
infância *f. childhood.*
infantaria *f. infantry.*
infante *adj. infant; n. m. and f. infant.*
infantil *adj. infantile, childish.*
infatigável *adj. tireless.*
infecção *f. infection.*
infeccionar, infecionar (infeccionar) *to infect, to contaminate.*
infeliz *adj. unhappy; unfortunate; n. m. unhappy, unfortunate person.*
Êle (ele) é infeliz. *He is unhappy.*
Infelizmente. *Unfortunately.*
inferior *adj. inferior, lower; subordinate; n. m. inferior person; subordinate.*
É uma fazenda de qualidade inferior. *The material is of inferior quality.*
inferioridade *f. inferiority.*
inferir *to infer, to conclude.*
inferno *m. hell, inferno.*
infestar *to infest; to overrun.*
infiel *adj. unfaithful.*
ínfimo *adj. lowest.*
infinidade *f. infinity.*
infinito *adj. infinite.*
inflação *f. inflation.*
inflamação *f. inflammation.*
inflamar *to inflame.*

inflamável *adj. inflammable.*
inflar *to inflate.*
influência *f. influence.*
Êle (ele) tem muita influência no govêrno (governo). *He is quite influential in the government.*
influenciar *to influence.*
INFLUIR *to influence, to inspire.*
INFORMAÇÃO *f. information; inquiry, investigation.*
Eu não recebi essa informação. *I did not receive that information.*
informalidade *f. informality.*
INFORMAR *to inform; to report.*
Ela não me informou disso. *She did not inform me about that.*
informe *adj. formless; n. m. information.*
infortunado *adj. unfortunate.*
infração, infracção (infracção) *f. infraction, infringement.*
infreqüência (infrequência) *f. infrequence.*
infreqüente (infrequente) *adj. infrequent.*
infringir *to infringe, to violate.*
infrutuoso *adj. unsuccessful, fruitless.*
infundado *adj. unfounded, groundless.*
infundir *to infuse, to instill.*
ingênuo (ingénuo) *adj. ingenuous.*
INGLÊS *adj. English; n. m. Englishman; English language.*
Fala-se inglês. *English spoken here.*
Ela não fala inglês. *She does not speak English.*
Êle (ele) é inglês. *He is English.*
ingratidão *f. ingratitude.*
ingrato *adj. ungrateful.*
ingressar *to enter.*
ingresso *m. entry, entrance; admission ticket* Ⓑ
inicial *adj. initial; n. f. initial.*
iniciar *to initiate, to begin.*
iniciativa *f. initiative.*
Tomar a iniciativa. *To take the initiative.*
início *m. beginning*
De início. *At first.*
inimigo *adj. enemy; n. m. enemy.*
iniqüidade (iniquidade) *f. iniquity, wickedness.*
injúria *f. insult; injury; offense.*
injustiça *f. injustice.*
injusto *adj. unjust, unfair.*
inocência *f. innocence.*
inocente *adj. innocent.*
inodoro *adj. odorless.*
inofensivo *adj. inoffensive, harmless.*
inolvidável *adj. unforgettable.*
inoportuno *adj. inopportune, untimely.*
inovar *to innovate.*
inquebrantável *adj. unbreakable; tenacious, unyielding.*
inquérito *m. inquiry; inquest.*
inquietar *to disturb, to cause anxiety.*
inquieto *adj. restless, uneasy.*
Ela passou tôda (toda) a noite inquieta. *She was restless all night.*
inquirir *to inquire.*
insalubre *adj. unsanitary, unhealthful.*
insano *adj. insane, mad.*
inscrever *to inscribe; to register; to sign up.*
inscrever-se *to register (at a school, etc.), to sign up.*
inscrição *f. inscription, registration.*
inseguro *adj. uncertain; insecure.*
insensatez *f. foolishness.*
insensato *adj. foolish; insane.*
insensível *adj. insensitive, impassive.*
inseparável *adj. inseparable.*

inserir *to insert; to introduce.*
inseticida (insecticida) *f. insecticide.*
inseto (insecto) *m. insect.*
insidioso *adj. insidious, treacherous.*
insigne *adj. famous, noted.*
insígnia *f. badge; pl. insignia.*
insignificante *adj. insignificant.*
insinuar *to insinuate, to hint.*
insipidez *f. insipidity; lack of flavor (taste); flatness.*
insípido *adj. insipid; tasteless.*
insistência *f. insistence, persistence.*
insistir *to insist.*
  Insistimos em que ela venha. *We insist that she come.*
insolação *f. sunstroke.*
insolência *f. insolence, rudeness.*
insolente *adj. insolent, rude.*
insolvente *adj. insolvent.*
insônia (insónia) *f. insomnia.*
inspeção (inspecçao) *f. inspection*
inspecionar (inspeccionar) *to inspect, to examine.*
inspetor (inspector) *m. inspector, supervisor.*
inspiração *f. inspiration.*
inspirar *to inspire; to inhale.*
  Êle (ele) inspira confiança. *He inspires confidence.*
instalação *f. installation; pl. fixtures.*
instalar *to install, to set up.*
instância *f. instance; request.*
  Em última instância. *As a last resort.*
instantâneo *adj. instantaneous, immediate; n. m. snapshot.*
INSTANTE *adj. instant; urgent; n. m. instant, moment.*
  Espere um instante. *Wait a minute.*
  A cada instante. *Every minute. All the time.*
instar *to urge, to press.*
instaurar *to establish, to restore.*
instinto *m. instinct.*
instituição *f. institution.*
instituir *to institute, to establish.*
instituto *m. institute.*
instrução *f. instruction; education.*
  Instrução pública. *Public education.*
  Instrução primária. *Elementary education.*
  Instrução secundária. *Secondary education.*
  Instruções de manejo. *Operating instructions.*
instruir *to instruct, to teach.*
instrumento *m. instrument.*
  Que instrumento você toca? *What instrument do you play?*
  Instrumento de sôpro (sopro). *Wind instrument.*
instrutivo *adj. instructive.*
instrutor *m. instructor, teacher.*
insubordinado *adj. insubordinate.*
insubordinar-se *to rebel, to revolt.*
insuficiência *f. insufficiency.*
insuficiente *adj. insufficient.*
insultar *to insult.*
insulto *m. insult, offense.*
insuperável *adj. insuperable, insurmountable.*
intato (intacto) *adj. intact, untouched.*
integral *adj. integral, whole.*
  Pão integral. *Whole wheat bread.*
integrar *to integrate.*
integridade *f. integrity.*
íntegro *adj. entire, whole; upright, honest.*
inteirar *to complete.*
inteirar-se *to become informed.*
inteiro *adj. entire, complete.*

inteletual (intelectual) *adj. intellectual; n. m. and f. intellectual.*
inteligência *f. intelligence; understanding.*
INTELIGENTE *adj. intelligent, bright.*
  Ela é muito inteligente. *She is very intelligent.*
inteligível *adj. intelligible.*
intemperado *adj. intemperate.*
intempérie *f. rough or bad weather.*
INTENÇÃO *f. intention, intent.*
  Êle (ele) tinha segundas intenções. *He had ulterior motives.*
  Ter boas intenções. *To have good intentions. To mean well.*
  Ter más intenções. *To have bad intentions. Not to mean well.*
  Ter a intenção de. *To intend to.*
intendência *f. quartermaster (corps); administration.*
intendente *m. quartermaster; superintendent.*
intensidade *f. intensity.*
intenso *adj. intense.*
intentar *to try, to attempt; to intend.*
intento *adj. intent, purpose.*
intercalar *to intercalate, to insert.*
intercâmbio *m. interchange, exchange.*
interceder *to intercede, to plead (in another's behalf).*
interceptar *to intercept; to block.*
INTERESSANTE *adj. interesting.*
  Êste (este) romance é muito interessante. *This novel is very interesting.*
INTERESSAR *to interest, to concern.*
  Isso não me interessa. *That doesn't interest me.*
INTERESSAR-SE *to be concerned; to become interested.*
  Não me interesso por isso. *I'm not interested in that.*
INTERÊSSE (INTERESSE) *m. interest.*
  Êle (ele) não mostra o menor interêsse. *He doesn't show the slightest interest.*
interino *adj. provisional, temporary, acting.*
INTERIOR *adj. interior, internal; n. m. interval, inside; country (rural)* Ⓑ.
  Ministério do Interior. *Department of the Interior.*
intermediar *to intermediate.*
intermediário *adj. intermediary, n. m. intermediary.*
intermédio *adj. intermediate; n. m. intermediary; intervention; interlude.*
internacional *adj. international.*
internar *to intern.*
interno *adj. internal, interior; n. m. intern; boarding student.*
  Para uso interno. *For internal use.*
interpor *to interpose.*
interpretação *f. interpretation.*
interpretar *to interpret.*
  Acho que o senhor interpretou mal. *I believe you misunderstood.*
intérprete *m. and f. interpreter.*
interrogação *f. interrogation, questioning; question; inquiry; question mark.*
interrogar *to interrogate, to question.*
  Não me interrogue mais. *Don't question me any longer.*
interrogatório *m. interrogation, examination.*
INTERROMPER *to interrupt.*
  Foi preciso interromper o trabalho. *It was necessary to interrupt the work.*
interrupção *f. interruption.*
  Sem interrupção. *Without stopping.*
interruptor *m. switch (electric).*
interurbano *adj. interurban; n. m. long-distance telephone call.*

intervalo *m. interval; intermission.*
  Podemos falar no intervalo. *We can talk during the intermission.*
intervir *to intervene, to mediate.*
intestino *adj. intestinal, internal; n. m. intestine.*
intimar *to summon; to order; to inform.*
intimidade *f. intimacy, closeness, friendship.*
intimidar *to intimidate, to frighten.*
íntimo *adj. intimate, close.*
  Eles (eles) eram amigos íntimos. *They were very close friends.*
intitular *to entitle, to give a name to.*
intolerância *f. intolerance.*
intolerante *adj. intolerant.*
intolerável *adj. intolerable, unbearable.*
intoxicação *(x = ks) f. intoxication, poisoning.*
intranqüilo (intranquilo) *adj. restless.*
intransigência *f. intransigence.*
intransigente *adj. intransigent, uncompromising, unyielding.*
intransitável *adj. impassable.*
intratável *adj. hard to deal with, stubborn, unsociable.*
intrepidez *f. intrepidity, courage.*
intrépido *adj. intrepid, fearless.*
intricado *adj. intricate, complicated.*
intriga *f. intrigue, plot.*
  Fazer intriga. *To plot.*
intrigante *adj. intriguing, scheming; n. m. and f. intriguer, schemer.*
introdução *f. introduction.*
introduzir *to introduce (not people; see apresentar), to initiate.*
  O professor introduziu uma nova teoria. *The professor introduced (brought out) a new theory.*
intromissão *f. interference.*
intruso *adj. intrusive; n. m. intruder.*
intuição *f. intuition.*
inumano *adj. inhuman, cruel.*
inundar *to flood, to run over, to overflow.*
INÚTIL *adj. useless; fruitless; futile.*
  É inútil fazer a viagem. *There's no use (in) taking the trip.*
  Êle (ele) é um homem inútil. *He's good for nothing. He can't do anything.*
inutilidade *f. uselessness, inutility.*
inutilizar *to spoil, to ruin, to disable.*
INÙTILMENTE *uselessly, in vain.*
  Fizemos a viagem inùtilmente. *We took the trip in vain.*
invadir *to invade.*
  Portugal foi invadido nos primeiros anos do século dezenove (dezanove). *Portugal was invaded in the early years of the nineteenth century.*
invalidar *to invalidate, to nullify; to render void.*
inválido *adj. invalid, disabled; n. m. invalid.*
invariável *adj. invariable, constant.*
invasão *f. invasion.*
inveja *f. envy.*
invejar *to envy.*
invenção *f. invention.*
inventar *to invent.*
inventário *m. inventory.*
invento *m. invention.*
invernar *to spend the winter, to hibernate.*
INVERNO *m. winter.*
  Não gosto nada do inverno (Inverno). *I don't like winter at all.*
inverossímil *adj. unlikely, improbable.*
inverter *to invert, to reverse; to invest.*
investigação *f. investigation.*
investigar *to investigate.*

invisível adj. invisible; n. m. the invisible; lady's fine hair net; fine hairpin.

iôdo (iodo) m. iodine.

IR to go; to move; to be.
Vamos! Let's go!
Já vou! I'm coming!
Vou para casa. I'm going home.
Vá embora! Go away!
Não posso ir. I can't go.
Como vai? How are you?
Vou bem, obrigado. I'm fine, thank you.
Como vão as coisas? How are things? How is everything?
Ela vai muito melhor. She is much better.
Vamos ver. Let's see.
Vamos, chega. Come now, that's enough.
A situação vai de mal a pior. The situation is going from bad to worse.
Ir a pé. To walk. To go on foot.
Ir a cavalo. To ride. To go on horseback.
Ir de carro. To drive. To go by car.
Ir de avião. To fly. To go by plane.
Ir a bordo. To go aboard.
João foi à cidade. John went downtown.
O chapéu lhe vai bem. The hat is becoming to you.
Acho que vai chover. I believe it's going to rain.
Ir à francêsa (francesa). To take French leave.
Devagar se vai ao longe. Easy does it.
Água vem, água vai. Easy come, easy go.

ira f. anger, rage.
Acesso de ira. Fit of rage.

iracundo adj. irascible.

irlandês adj. Irish; n. m. Irishman.

IRMÃ f. sister.
Êle (ele) tem duas irmãs. He has two sisters.

IRMÃO m. brother.

ironia f. irony.

irônico (irónico) adj. ironic.

irradiar to irradiate; to broadcast.

irreal adj. unreal.

irreflexão (x = ks) f. thoughtlessness.

irregular adj. irregular.

irresponsabilidade f. irresponsibility.

irresponsável adj. irresponsible.

irrigar to irrigate.

irritar to irritate, to exasperate.

irrompível adj. unbreakable.

isentar to exempt, to free.

isolado adj. isolated.

isolar to isolate, to separate.

isqueiro m. cigarette lighter.

ISSO that.
Isso mesmo. That's it.
Por isso. Therefore.
Que é isso? What's that?
Isso não me importa. That makes no difference to me.
Nem por isso. Don't mention it. Not at all.
Só faltava isso. That's the last straw.

ISTO this.
Que é isto? What's this?
Para que serve isto? What's this for?
Tudo isto é muito interessante. All this is very interesting.
Por isto. Therefore.
Com isto. Herewith.
Isto é. That is. Namely.
Além disso. Besides. Furthermore.

italiano Italian.

itinerário m. itinerary.

iugoslavo n. and adj. Yugoslav.

J

JÁ already; now, immediately; ever.
Já me falaram nisso. They already spoke to me about that.
Venha já. Come right now.
Já esteve na capital? Were you ever in the capital?
Já não. No longer.
Já vou! I'm coming!
Já que. Since. Inasmuch as.
Desde já. Immediately.

jaça f. fault, imperfection.

jacaré m. alligator.

jacente adj. lying, recumbent.

jacinto m. hyacinth.

jactância f. boasting.

jactar-se to boast, to brag.

jamais never.

JANEIRO m. January; years.
Ela tem sessenta janeiros. She is sixty years old.

JANELA f. window.
A janela de meu quarto é grande. The window in my room is large.

jangada f. raft; sailing raft used in northeastern Brasil.

JANTAR m. dinner; to have dinner, to dine.
Jantamos às sete. We dine at seven.
Sala de jantar. Dining room.
Jantar fora. To dine out.
O jantar está na mesa. Dinner is served.

japonês Japanese.

jaqueta f. jacket.

jaquetão m. double-breasted jacket.

jarda f. yard (36 inches).

JARDIM m. garden.
Jardim botânico. Botanical garden.
Jardim da infância. Kindergarten.
Jardim público. Public park.
Jardim zoológico. Public park.

jardineira f. woman gardener; small table; small bus Ⓑ.

jardineiro m. gardener.

jarra f. jar, vase.

jarro m. pitcher, jug.

jato, jacto (jacto) jet, stream.
Jato de luz. Flash of light.
Avião a jato. Jet plane.

javali m. wild boar.

jazer to lie.
Aquí jaz. Here lies.

jazida f. mineral deposit, bed; resting place.

JEITO m. manner, way; aptitude; special knack or ability.
Ela tem jeito para professôra (professora). She is especially talented for teaching.
Com jeito. Skillfully. Adroitly.
Dar um jeito. To find a way.

jejuar to fast.

jejum m. fast, fasting.
Dia de jejum. Fast day.
Em jejum. Fasting.

jérsei m. jersey (sweater) Ⓑ.

jesuíta m. Jesuit.

Jesus, Jesus Cristo m. Jesus, Jesus Christ.

jibóia f. boa constrictor.

joalharia, joalheria (joalharia) f. jewelry store.

jocoso adj. jocose, funny.

JOELHO m. knee.
De joelhos. On one's knees. Kneeling.
Pôr-se de joelhos. To kneel.

jogada f. play, move (in a game); throwing, casting.
Foi uma boa jogada. It was a good play (in a game).

jogador m. player; gambler.

JOGAR to play (game); to gamble; to cast, to throw.
No Brasil e em Portugal jogam futebol. In Brasil and in Portugal they play soccer.
Êle perdeu todo o dinheiro jogando. He lost all his money gambling.
Jogue isso fora! Throw that out!

JÔGO (JOGO) m. game; play; gambling; set.
Jôgo de cartas. Card game.
Jôgo de azar. Game of chance.
Jôgo de damas. Checkers.
Jôgo do bicho. Brazilian lottery, numbers game Ⓑ.
Jôgo de palavras. Play on words.
Casa de jôgo. Gambling house.

joguête (joguete) m. toy, plaything.

jóia f. jewel, gem; pl. jewelry.

jornada f. journey; short trip.

JORNAL m. newspaper; diary; journal.
Banca de jornais. Newsstand Ⓑ.

jornaleiro m. day laborer; newsboy.

jornalismo m. journalism.

jornalista m. and f. journalist; newspaper man or woman.

jôrro (jorro) m. torrent, outpouring.
A jorros. In torrents.

JOVEM adj. young; n. m. young man; n. f. young lady.
Quem é essa jovem? Who's that young lady?
Não conheço êsse (esse) jovem. I don't know that young man.

jubilação f. jubilation, rejoicing; retirement of a teacher.

jubilar to rejoice; to retire.

judeu adj. Jewish; n. m. Jew.

judicial adj. judicial.

juiz m. judge; arbiter; referee; umpire.
Juiz de paz. Justice of the peace.
Juiz de direito. District judge.

juízo m. judgment; opinion; decision; good judgment; mind.
Você perdeu o juízo? Have you lost your mind?
Êle (ele) é um homem de juízo. He's a man of good judgment.
Chamar a juízo. To summon to court.
Dia de juízo. Judgment day.

julgado adj. tried; sentenced; n. m. judicial district.

julgamento m. judgment, sentence; trial.

julgar to judge; to suppose, believe.
Julgo que será assim. I believe that's the way it will be.

JULHO m. July.

jumento m. donkey.

JUNHO m. June.

júnior adj. junior.

junta f. board, council, junta, committee; junction, union, coupling; joint.
A que horas foi a junta? What time did the meeting take place?
Junta administrativa. Administrative council.
Junta de comércio. Board of trade.
Junta universal. Universal joint.

JUNTAR to join, to unite; to assemble, to gather; to amass.
Os dois exércitos juntaram fôrças (forças). The two armies joined forces.

junto adj. joined; close.
Deixe (x = sh) tudo junto à porta. Leave it all by the door.
Fizemos o trabalho juntos. We did the work together.
Junto de. Next to. Near.

juramento m. oath, vow.

jurar to swear, to take an oath.
Juro que sim. I swear it is so.

júri m. jury.

juro m. interest.
Juros compostos. Compound interest.

justiça f. justice; fairness; law.
Fazer justiça. To do justice. To be just.
Levar à justiça. To bring to justice.

justificar to justify.

JUSTO adj. just; fair; exact; tight; close-fitting.
Isso não é justo. That's not fair.

Êste (este) chapéu é muito justo. *This hat is too tight.*
Uma parte justa. *A fair share.*

juventude *f. youth.*

L

la *it, her, you (after verb form; see Grammar Summary, section 20, item 5).*

LÁ *over there, there.*

LÃ *f. wool.*

LÁBIO *m. lip.*
Lamber os lábios. *To smack one's lips.*

laborar *to work, to cultivate.*

laboratório *m. laboratory.*

laborioso *adj. laborious; hardworking.*

lacerar *to lacerate, to mangle.*

laço *m. lasso; loop; trap; tie.*
Cair no laço. *To fall into a trap.*

lacônico (lacónico) *adj. laconic, brief.*

ladear *to be or go alongside; to dodge.*
Êle (ele) ladeou a questão. *He dodged the issue.*

ladeira *f. slope; hillside.*
Ladeira abaixo (x = sh). *Downhill.*
Ladeira acima. *Uphill.*

ladino *adj. shrewd, crafty, cunning.*

LADO *m. side; party, faction.*
Sente-se a meu lado. *Sit next to me.*
Ao outro lado da rua. *Across the street. On the other side of the street.*
Ela mora na casa ao lado. *She lives next door.*
Por outro lado. *On the other hand.*
Não cabe de lado. *It won't fit sideways.*
Trabalharam lado a lado. *They worked side by side.*
Olhar de lado. *To look askance at. To look down at.*
De todos os lados. *From all sides. From all directions.*
Conheço muito bem seu lado fraco. *I know his weakness very well.*
Eu estou do lado de você. *I am on your side.*

ladrão *m. thief, robber.*

ladrar *to bark.*

ladrido *m. barking, bark.*

lagarta *f. caterpillar.*

lagarto *m. lizard.*

lago *m. lake, pond.*

lagoa *f. lagoon, pond.*

lagosta *f. lobster.*

LÁGRIMA *f. tear; drop.*
Lágrimas de alegria. *Tears of joy.*
Lágrimas de crocodilo. *Crocodile tears.*

laguna *f. lagoon.*

lama *f. mud.*

lamentar *to lament, to regret, to deplore.*

lamentável *adj. lamentable, regrettable, deplorable.*
É lamentável. *It's regrettable.*

lâmina *f. lamina, blade.*

LÂMPADA *f. lamp; bulb.*
Lâmpada de mesa. *Table lamp. Desk lamp.*
Lâmpada néon. *Neon bulb.*
Lâmpada elétrica (eléctrica). *Electric light bulb.*
Lâmpada de rádio. *Radio tube.*

lançamento *m. launching; throwing, casting.*

LANÇAR *to launch; to throw; to cast; to eject.*
Lançar à água. *To launch (a ship).*
Lançar fora. *To throw out.*
Êle (ele) se lançou aos pés dela. *He threw himself at her feet.*
Lançar um livro. *To publish a book.*
Lançar mão de. *To take hold of. To resort to.*

lance *m. throwing, casting; incident; predicament.*

lancha *f. launch, motorboat.*

lânguido *adj. languid, listless.*

lanterna *f. lantern.*
Lanterna elétrica (eléctrica) de mão. *Flashlight.*

lápide *f. a flat stone with an inscription; tombstone.*

LÁPIS *m. pencil.*

lapso *m. lapse; slip.*

lar *m. hearth; home.*

LARANJA *f. orange.*

laranjada *f. orangeade.*

laranjeira *f. orange tree.*

lareira *f. hearth, fireplace.*

largar *to release; to cast off.*

LARGO *adj. wide; ample.*
Um metro de largo. *A meter wide. One meter in width.*

largura *f. width; extent.*

laringe *m. and f. larynx.*

laringite *f. laryngitis.*

lástima *f. pity, compassion.*
É uma lástima! *That's too bad!*
Que lástima! *What a pity!*

lastimar *to feel sorry for; to regret.*

lastimável *adj. lamentable, deplorable.*

lastro *m. ballast.*

LATA *f. tin; tin can.*
Lata de lixo (x = sh). *Garbage can.*
Latas de conservas. *Canned goods.*
Abridor de latas. *Can opener.*

lateral *adj. lateral.*

latido *m. barking, bark.*

latifúndio *m. large landed estate.*

latim *m. Latin.*

latino *adj. Latin.*

latino-americano *adj. Latin-American; n. m. Latin-American.*

latir *to bark, to yelp.*

latitude *f. latitude.*

lavadeira *f. washerwoman; washing machine.*

lavagem *f. washing; wash.*

lavanderia *f. laundry.*

LAVAR *to wash; to bathe; to clean.*
Lave as mãos antes de jantar. *Wash your hands before dinner.*
Lavar a sêco (seco). *To dry-clean.*

lavatório *m. lavatory; washbasin.*

lavável *adj. washable.*

lavrador *m. farmer.*

lavrar *to cultivate, to till; to cut; to work.*

laxante *(x = sh) adj. laxative; n. m. laxative.*

lazer *m. leisure.*

leal *adj. loyal*

lealdade *f. loyalty.*

leão *m. lion.*

lebre *f. hare.*
Comprar gato por lebre. *To buy a pig in a poke.*

lecionar (leccionar) *to teach, to give lessons; to lecture.*

legal *adj. legal; all right, permissible.*

legalizar *to legalize; to validate.*

legar *to bequeath; to delegate.*

legenda *f. legend; inscription.*

legendário *adj. legendary.*

legião *f. legion.*

legislação *f. legislation.*

legislar *to legislate.*

legislatura *f. legislature.*

legitimar *to legitimate, to legalize.*

legítimo *adj. legitimate, authentic.*

legível *adj. legible.*

légua *f. league (measure of distance).*

legume *m. vegetable.*

LEI *f. law, act; rule.*
Lei das médias. *Law of averages.*
Lei de oferta e procura. *Law of supply and demand.*

leitão *m. suckling pig.*

LEITE *m. milk.*
Leite condensado. *Condensed milk.*
Leite magro. *Skim milk.*
Tirar leite de vaca morta. *To cry over spilled milk.*

leiteiro *m. milkman.*

leiteria *f. dairy.*

leito *m. bed.*

leitor *m. reader.*

leitura *f. reading; reading matter.*

lema *m. motto; slogan.*

LEMBRANÇA *f. remembrance; reminder; souvenir; pl. regards, greetings.*
Lembranças à sua irmã! *Give my regards to your sister!*

LEMBRAR *to remember, to recall; to remind.*

LEMBRAR-SE *to remember, to recall.*
Não me lembro. *I don't remember.*
Ela não se lembra disso. *She doesn't remember that.*

leme *m. rudder, helm.*

LENÇO *m. handkerchief.*

lençol *m. sheet (bed).*

lenda *f. legend, tale.*

lenha *f. firewood.*
Deitar lenha ao fogo. *To add fuel to the fire.*

lenhador *m. woodcutter.*

lenho *m. tree trunk.*

lentamente *adv. slowly.*

lente *m. teacher, professor; lens.*

lentidão *f. slowness*

LENTO *adj. slow.*

leoa *f. lioness*

leopardo *m. leopard.*

LER *to read.*
Leia em voz alta. *Read aloud.*
Você leu êste (este) romance? *Did you read this novel?*

lesão *f. lesion, injury; wrong.*

lesar *to hurt; to wound; to injure; to wrong.*

leste *m. east.*

LETRA *f. letter; lyrics; handwriting.*
Letra maiúscula. *Capital letter.*
Letra minúscula. *Small letter.*
Não me lembro da letra dessa canção. *I don't remember the lyrics of that song.*
Ela tem boa letra. *She has a good handwriting.*
Ao pé da letra. *Literally.*
Letra de câmbio. *Bill of exchange.*

letrado *adj. learned, erudite; n. m. scholar; lawyer.*

letreiro *m. inscription; sign; label; poster.*

levantamento *m. raising; uprising, revolt.*

LEVANTAR *to raise, to lift, to pick up; to suspend.*
Levantar a voz. *To raise the voice.*
Levantar o pano. *To raise the curtain (theatre).*
Levantar a mão. *To raise one's hand.*
Levantar a mesa. *To clear the table.*
Levantar os ombros. *To shrug the shoulders.*
Levantar a sessão. *To adjourn the meeting.*

LEVANTAR-SE *to get up.*
A que horas se levanta? *At what time do you get up?*
Levanto-me às sete. *I get up at seven.*

LEVAR *to carry, to take; to wear; to bear; to need.*
Leve-me ao seu chefe. *Take me to your leader.*

Leve êste (este) livro a seu pai. *Take this book to your father.*
Quanto tempo vai levar? *How long will it take?*
Levar a cabo. *To carry out. To bring about.*
Êles (eles) levam boa vida. *They lead a good (easy) life.*
Levar em conta. *To take into account.*
Levar pau. *To fail (an examination).*
Levar à fôrça (força). *To take by force.*
leve *adj. light (weight); slight.*
leviano *adj. frivolous; imprudent.*
léxico (x = ks) m. *lexicon.*
lha (*contr. of* lhe + a) *it to him, to her, to you, etc.*
LHE *to him, to her, to you, to it.*
lho (*contr. of* lhe + o) *it to him, to her, to you, etc.*
liar *to tie, to bind.*
liberação *f. liquidation, discharge.*
liberal *adj. liberal; n. m. and f. liberal.*
liberar *to release.*
LIBERDADE *f. liberty, freedom.*
Tomar a liberdade. *To take the liberty.*
libertador *adj. liberating; n. m. liberator.*
libertar *to liberate, to free.*
libra *f. pound.*
LIÇÃO *f. lesson.*
Dar lições. *To give lessons.*
LICENÇA *f. permission; leave; license; permit.*
Com licença. *Excuse me. May I?*
Dá licença? *Excuse me. May I?*
Pedir licença. *To ask for leave. To ask for permission.*
Licença de motorista. *Driver's license.*
licenciado m. *person holding a master's degree.*
licenciar *to license; to allow; to grant leave of absence.*
lícito *adj. lawful; licit.*
licor m. *liqueur, liquor.*
lidar *to combat, to fight.*
líder m. *leader* Ⓑ.
lido *adj. read; well-read.*
liga *f. league.*
Liga das Nações. *League of Nations.*
LIGAR *to join, to connect; to tie, to bind; to turn on (radio, etc.).*
A ferrovia liga as duas cidades. *The railroad joins the two cities.*
Ligue-me com... *Connect me with...*
Faça o favor de ligar o rádio. *Please turn on the radio.*
ligeireza *f. lightness; quickness.*
LIGEIRO *adj. light (weight); quick, swift.*
lilás *adj. lilac; n. m. lilac.*
lima *f. file (tool); lime.*
Lima de unhas. *Nail file.*
limão m. *lemon.*
limar *to file, to make smooth; to polish.*
limitação *f. limitation, limit.*
limitado *adj. limited.*
limitar *to limit; to restrain; to border on.*
limite m. *limit; boundary, border.*
Tudo tem os seus limites. *There's a limit to everything.*
limoeiro m. *lemon tree.*
limonada *f. lemonade.*
LIMPAR *to clean, to cleanse; to clear.*
Limpar a garganta. *To clear the throat.*
limpeza *f. cleaning; cleanliness.*
LIMPO *adj. clean; neat; clear.*
Quero uma toalha limpa. *I want a clean towel.*
Estou limpo. *I'm broke.*
linácea *f. flax.*
lince m. *and f. lynx.*

linchar *to lynch.*
lindar *to delimit; to border.*
linde m. *.limit; boundary.*
LINDO *adj. pretty, beautiful.*
Como ela é linda! *How pretty she is!*
líneo *adj. linen.*
LÍNGUA *f. tongue; language.*
Língua portuguêsa (portuguesa). *Portuguese language.*
Língua materna. *Mother tongue.*
Língua românica. *Romance language.*
Tenho na ponta da língua. *I have it on the tip of my tongue.*
linguagem *f. language.*
lingüista (linguista) m. *and f. linguist.*
LINHA *f. line; row; string, thread.*
Linha, por favor. *Line, please (telephone).*
Linha interurbana. *Long-distance line.*
Linha ferroviária. *Railway.*
Linha aérea. *Airline.*
Manter em linha. *To keep in line.*
Linha reta. *Straight line.*
linimento m. *liniment.*
linóleo m. *linoleum.*
linotipista m. *and f. linotypist.*
linotipo m. *linotype.*
liqüidação (liquidação) *f. liquidation.*
liqüidar (liquidar) *to liquidate.*
líquido, líqüido (líquido) *adj. liquid; net (profit, etc.); n. m. liquid.*
lírico *adj. lyric.*
lírio m. *lily.*
LISBOETA *adj. of Lisbon; n. m. and f. person from Lisbon.*
liso *adj. smooth, even.*
Cabelo liso. *Straight hair.*
lisonja *f. praise, flattery.*
lisonjear *to praise, to flatter; to please.*
lisonjeiro *adj. flattering; pleasing; n. m. flatterer.*
LISTA *f. list; stripe; directory; menu.*
Lista telefônica (telefónica). *Telephone book.*
Lista negra. *Blacklist.*
literário *adj. literary.*
literato m. *man of letters.*
literatura *f. literature.*
litigar *to litigate.*
litígio m. *litigation, lawsuit.*
litoral *adj. coastal; n. m. coastline.*
litro m. *liter.*
lituano *adj. Lithuanian; n. m. Lithuanian.*
livrar *to free.*
Deus me livre! *Heaven forbid!*
livraria *f. bookstore.*
LIVRE *adj. free.*
Quando você estiver livre falaremos. *When you are free we'll talk.*
Livre a bordo. *Free on board.*
Ao ar livre. *In the open air.*
Tradução livre. *Free translation.*
Verso livre. *Free verse.*
livreiro m. *bookseller.*
LIVRO m. *book.*
Livro brochado. *Paperback.*
Livro caixa (x = sh). *Cash book.*
Livro de bôlso (bolso). *Pocketbook.*
Livro de consulta. *Reference book.*
lixo (x = sh) m. *garbage.*
lo (*form taking the place of pronoun* o *after a verb form ending in* r, s *or* z) *him, you, it.*
lôbo (lobo) m. *wolf.*
lôbrego (lobrego) *adj. murky, dark; sad.*
lóbulo m. *lobule, lobe.*
local *adj. local; m. place.*
localidade *f. locality, place.*

localizar *to localise, to locate.*
loção *f. lotion, wash.*
locomoção *f. locomotion.*
locutor m. *speaker, announcer.*
lôdo (lodo) m. *mud, mire.*
lógico *adj. logical, reasonable.*
LOGO *right away, immediately; soon; shortly.*
Até logo. *So long. See you soon.*
Desde logo. *At once.*
Logo depois. *Soon after.*
Logo que. *As soon as.*
lograr *to obtain, to get; to attain; to manage; to succeed.*
Elas lograram fazê-lo. *They managed to do it.*
LOJA *f. shop, store; lodge.*
Loja americana. *Five- and-ten-cent store.*
Loja de miudezas. *Notions shop.*
lona *f. canvas.*
londrino *adj. of London; n. m. Londoner.*
LONGE *far, distant.*
É muito longe! *It's too far!*
É longe daqui? *Is it far from here?*
Devagar se vai ao longe. *Easy does it. Haste makes waste.*
Bem longe. *Quite far.*
Longe disso. *Far from it.*
longitude *f. longitude.*
longo *adj. long.*
lotação *f. capacity; small bus* Ⓑ.
lotado *adj. filled full (capacity).*
lotar *to fill to capacity.*
lote m. *lot, piece of land; share.*
loteria *f. lottery.*
louça *f. dishes, chinaware.*
louco *adj. crazy, mad, insane; n. m. madman.*
Êle (ele) está louco. *He's crazy.*
Êle está louco por ela. *He's crazy about her. He's madly in love with her.*
loucura *f. madness, insanity; folly.*
Isso é uma loucura. *That's absurd. That's crazy.*
louro *adj. blond.*
louvar *to praise.*
LUA *f. moon.*
Lua nova. *New moon.*
Lua de mel. *Honeymoon.*
luar m. *moonlight.*
lubrificante *adj. lubricating; n. m. lubricant.*
lubrificar *to lubricate.*
lucrativo *adj. lucrative, profitable.*
lucro m. *profit, gain.*
Lucros e perdas. *Profits and losses.*
LUGAR m. *place, site; seat; occasion.*
Ponha as coisas em seu lugar. *Put things in their places.*
Eu em seu lugar não iria. *If I were you (in your place) I would not go.*
A que horas terá lugar? *What time will it take place?*
Em lugar de. *Instead of.*
Dar lugar a. *To give cause for. To give occasion for.*
Em primeiro lugar. *In the first place.*
lume m. *fire; light.*
luminoso *adj. shining, luminous.*
lunático *adj. lunatic, n. m. lunatic.*
lusíada *adj. and n. m. and f. Lusitanian, Portuguese.*
LUSITANO *adj. and n. m. Lusitanian, Portuguese.*
LUSO *adj. and m. Lusitanian, Portuguese.*
Luso-brasileiro. *Luso-Brasilian, Portuguese-Brasilian.*
lustrar *to polish, to shine.*
lustre m. *luster, gloss; splendor.*

luta *f. fight, struggle, battle.*
   A luta pela vida. *The struggle for existence.*
lutador *m. fighter, wrestler.*
lutar *to fight, to wrestle, to struggle.*
luto *m. mourning; grief, sorrow.*
   De luto. *In mourning.*
LUVA *f. glove; coupling.*
   Assentar como uma luva. *To fit like a glove.*
luxo (x = sh) *m. luxury.*
   Edição de luxo. *De luxe edition.*
luxuoso (x = sh) *adj. luxurious, de luxe.*
LUZ *f. light.*
   Acenda a luz. *Turn the light on.*
   Apague a luz. *Put the light out. Turn the light off.*
   Luz elétrica (eléctrica). *Electric light.*
   Dar a luz. *To give birth to. To publish.*
luzir *to shine, to brighten.*

M

ma *(contr. of* me + a*) it to me, her to me, you to me.*
MÁ *adj. f. bad, evil.*
   Má fama. *Ill repute.*
   De má vontade. *Unwillingly.*
MAÇÃ *f. apple.*
   Maçã-de-Adão. *Adam's apple.*
macaco *m. monkey; jack (for lifting).*
macarrão *m. macaroni.*
machacaz *adj. cunning, sly.*
machado *m. ax.*
machete *m. machete; small guitar.*
macho *adj. male, masculine; vigorous; n. m. male, male animal.*
machucar *to pound; to bruise.*
maciço *adj. massive; compact; solid; firm.*
macio *adj. soft, smooth; gentle.*
mácula *f. stain, spot; dishonor.*
macumba *f. voodoo ceremony of Brazil* Ⓑ.
MADEIRA *f. wood, lumber, timber.*
   A caixa (x = sh) é de madeira. *The box is made of wood.*
madeireiro *m. lumber dealer.*
madeirense *adj. of the island of Madeira; n. m. and f. person from the island of Madeira.*
madeixa (x = sh) *f. lock of hair; skein.*
madrasta *f. stepmother.*
madre *f. nun.*
madressilva *f. honeysuckle.*
madrileno *adj. of Madrid; n. m. person from Madrid.*
madrinha *f. godmother; sponsor; maid of honor.*
madrugada *f. dawn, early morning.*
   De madrugada. *At dawn.*
madrugador *m. early riser.*
madrugar *to get up early; to get ahead of.*
   A quem madruga, Deus ajuda. *The early bird catches the worm.*
madurar *to ripen, to mature.*
madureza *f. maturity, ripeness.*
maduro *adj. ripe, mature.*
   A fruta ainda não está madura. *The fruit isn't ripe yet.*
MÃE *f. mother.*
magia *f. magic.*
mágico *adj. magic; marvelous.*
magistério *m. teaching profession; teaching position.*
magistrado *m. magistrate.*
magnânimo *adj. magnanimous.*
magnésia *f. magnesia.*
magnético *adj. magnetic.*
magnífico *adj. magnificent, excellent, wonderful.*
magnitude *f. magnitude.*

magno *adj. great.*
magnólia *f. magnolia.*
mago *adj. magic; m. magician; wizard.*
   Os Reis Magos. *The Wise Men.*
mágoa *f. sorrow; anguish.*
MAGRO *adj. thin.*
MAIO *m. May.*
maionese *f. mayonnaise.*
MAIOR *adj. greater, greatest; bigger, larger; adult, of age.*
   A maior parte. *Most. The majority.*
   Êste (este) é maior do que aquêle (aquele). *This one is larger than that one.*
   Maior de idade. *Of age.*
   Estado maior. *General staff (military).*
maioria *f. majority, plurality.*
MAIS *more; any more; besides; n. m. rest; most.*
   Mais ou menos. *More or less.*
   Deseja mais alguma coisa? *Would you like something else?*
   Quer mais café? *Would you like more coffee?*
   Nada mais? *Is that all? Nothing else?*
   Não há mais. *There is (there are) no more.*
   Não tenho mais. *I don't have any more.*
   Ela é mais inteligente (do) que êle (ele). *She is more intelligent than he.*
   É a coisa mais fácil do mundo. *It's the easiest thing in the world.*
   Mais adiante. *Further on.*
   A casa é mais longe. *The house is farther.*
   São mais de dez horas. *It's after ten o'clock.*
   Mais depressa! *Faster!*
   Mais devagar! *Slower!*
   Fale mais alto, por favor. *Speak louder, please.*
   Os mais dos alunos não estudam bastante. *Most students don't study enough.*
   O mais cedo possível. *As soon as possible.*
   Tenho mais de quinze. *I have more than fifteen.*
   Vou trabalhar mais dez anos. *I'm going to work ten more years.*
   Mais tarde. *Later. Later on.*
   Não querem estudar mais. *They don't want to study any longer.*
   Nunca mais. *Never again.*
maiúscula *adj. capital (letter); n. f. capital letter.*
majestade *f. majesty.*
majestoso *adj. majestic, imposing.*
MAL *badly, poorly; hardly; as soon as; n. m. evil; harm; disease, illness.*
   O livro está mal escrito. *The book is poorly written.*
   De mal a pior. *From bad to worse.*
   Fazer mal. *To do harm. To do wrong.*
   Estar mal de saúde. *To be ill.*
   Não faz mal. *It doesn't matter. Don't bother.*
   O paletó me fica mal. *The jacket doesn't fit right.*
   Eu me sinto mal hoje. *I don't feel well today.*
   Ela mal me falou. *She hardly spoke to me.*
   Mal-agradecido. *Ungrateful.*
   Menos mal. *Not so bad.*
mala *f. suitcase, bag; trunk.*
   Fazer as malas. *To pack.*
malária *f. malaria.*
malbaratar *to squander; to sell at a loss.*
malcriado *ill-mannered, impolite.*
maldade *f. wickedness.*
maldição *f. curse.*
maldizer *to damn; to curse.*
malefício *m. evil act; witchcraft.*
maleita *f. malaria.*
mal-estar *m. indisposition; discomfort.*
maleta *f. handbag, suitcase.*
malfalante *adj. slandering; n. m. and f. slanderer.*
malfeitor *m. malefactor, criminal.*

malgastar *to squander, to waste.*
malhar *to hammer, to beat.*
   Malhar o ferro enquanto está quente. *To strike while the iron is hot.*
mal-humorado *adj. ill-humored, peevish.*
malícia *f. malice; cunning.*
malicioso *adj. malicious; cunning.*
malignar *to corrupt.*
maligno *adj. malignant.*
mal-intencionado *adj. evil-minded.*
malsão *adj. unhealthy, unhealthful.*
maltratar *to treat roughly, to mistreat, to abuse; to harm.*
maltrato *m. ill-treatment.*
maluco *adj. crazy, insane; m. madman.*
malvado *adj. wicked.*
mamã *f. mamma, mother; wet nurse* Ⓑ.
MAMÃE *f. mommy, mother* Ⓟ.
mamar *to suck; to take the breast.*
mamífero *adj. mammalian; m. mammal.*
mana *f. sis, sister.*
manancial *m. fountain, spring; source.*
manar *to flow, to ooze.*
mancha *f. stain, spot, blemish.*
   Mancha solar. *Sunspot.*
manchar *to stain, to spot, to soil.*
manchete *f. headline* Ⓑ.
manco *adj. crippled, lame; n. m. cripple.*
mandado *m. order, command; writ.*
   A mandado de. *By order of.*
MANDAR *to send; to order, to command; to govern.*
   Mande-o à minha casa. *Send it to my home.*
   Mandei que chamassem o médico. *I had them call the doctor.*
   Quem manda aqui? *Who's in charge here?*
   Mandar às favas. *To send to the devil.*
   Mandar aviar uma receita. *To have a prescription filled.*
mandatário *adj. mandatory; n. m. attorney; agent; proxy.*
mandato *m. mandate, order.*
mandíbula *f. jaw.*
mandioca *f. manioc, cassava.*
mando *m. command, authority, control.*
mandolina *f. mandolim m. mandolin.*
MANEIRA *f. manner, way, method.*
   Faça desta maneira. *Do it this way.*
   Faça de qualquer maneira. *Do it any way you can.*
   Não há maneira de fazê-lo. *There's no way to do it.*
   De maneira que o senhor não vem? *So you're not coming?*
   De maneira alguma. *By no means.*
   Escreva-o de maneira que se possa ler. *Write it so that it can be read.*
   Da mesma maneira. *In the same way.*
   Boas maneiras. *Good manners.*
manejar *to handle; to manage; to govern.*
manejo *m. management; handling.*
MANGA *f. sleeve; glass funnel; water spout.*
   Em mangas de camisa. *In shirt sleeves.*
MANHÃ *f. morning, forenoon.*
   Ontem de manhã. *Yesterday morning.*
   Amanhã de manhã. *Tomorrow morning.*
   Hoje de manhã. *This morning.*
   Tôdas (todas) as manhãs. *Every morning.*
manhoso *adj. skillful, cunning.*
mania *f. mania; whim; obsession.*
maníaco *adj. maniacal; n. m. maniac; crackpot.*
manicômio (manicómio) *m. insane asylum.*
manifestação *f. manifestation, demonstration.*
manifestar *to manifest; to state; to reveal.*
manifesto *adj. manifest, clear; obvious.*
manipulação *f. manipulation, handling.*

manipular *to handle, to manipulate; to manage.*
manivela *f. crank; lever; handle.*
manjar *m. food.*
mano *m. brother.*
mansão *m. mansion.*
manso *adj. tame, gentle, meek.*
manta *f. blanket; cloak; neckerchief.*
MANTEIGA *f. butter; flattery.*
  Pão e manteiga. *Bread and butter.*
mantel *m. tablecloth.*
manter *to maintain, to support; to keep up; to uphold.*
  Manter a ordem. *To maintain order.*
  Manter correspondência. *To keep up a correspondence.*
  Manter palavra. *To keep one's word.*
manter-se *to carry on, to remain, to keep.*
  Manter-se firme. *To remain firm.*
mantimento *m. maintenance, support.*
manto *m. mantle, cloak.*
manual *adj. manual; n. m. manual, handbook.*
manuelino *adj. of D. Manuel I of Portugal, esp. referring to the architecture of the period, early 16th century.*
manufaturar (manufacturar) *to manufacture.*
manuscrito *adj. handwritten; n. m. manuscript.*
manutenção *f. support, maintenance.*
MÃO *f. hand; forefoot; paw; coat (of paint).*
  Ter à mão. *To have at hand.*
  Ter na mão. *To have in the hand.*
  Apertar a mão. *To shake hands.*
  Apêrto (aperto) de mão. *Handshake.*
  Mão esquerda. *Left hand.*
  Mão direita. *Right hand.*
  Pedir a mão de. *To ask for the hand of (in marriage).*
  Estar em boas mãos. *To be in good hands.*
  Vir às mãos. *To come to blows.*
  Lavar as mãos. *To wash one's hands.*
  De boa mão. *From good authority.*
  As mãos cheias. *Liberally. Abundantly.*
  Feito à mão. *Made by hand.*
  De primeira mão. *First-hand.*
  Mãos à obra! *Let's get to work!*
  Dar a mão a. *To shake hands with.*
maometano *adj. Mahommedan; n. m. Mahommedan.*
mapa *m. map, chart.*
mapa-múndi *m. world map.*
MÁQUINA *f. machine, engine.*
  Máquina de escrever. *Typewriter.*
  Máquina de lavar. *Washing machine.*
  Máquina de lavar louça. *Dishwasher.*
  Máquina fotográfica. *Camera.*
maquinaria *f. machinery.*
maquinista *m. machinist; engineer.*
MAR *m. sea.*
  Fazer-se ao mar. *To sail. To put to sea.*
  Por mar. *By sea.*
maracá *m. maraca (musical instrument).*
maranha *f. entanglement.*
maranhense *adj. and n. m. and f. of the state of Maranhão, in Brazil.*
maravilha *f. marvel, wonder.*
maravilhoso *adj. marvelous, wonderful.*
  Cidade maravilhosa. *Marvelous city.*
marca *f. mark; brand; make; sign.*
  Marca registrada (registada). *Registered trademark.*
MARCAR *to mark; to brand.*
  Vamos marcar a data. *Let's set the date.*
  Marquemos a hora. *Let's decide on a time.*
marceneiro *m. cabinetmaker.*
marcha *f. march.*
marchar *to march.*
marco *m. window frame, doorframe; boundary mark; mark (German monetary unit).*

MARÇO *m. March.*
maré *f. tide.*
mareado *adj. seasick.*
marear *to get seasick.*
marfim *m. ivory.*
margarida *f. daisy, marguerite.*
margarina *f. margarine.*
margem *f. margin, border, edge; shore, bank (river).*
marido *m. husband.*
marinha *f. navy.*
  Marinha mercante. *Merchant marine.*
  Marinha de guerra. *Navy.*
marinheiro *m. sailor, seaman.*
mariposa (mariposa) *f. moth; butterfly.*
marítimo *adj. maritime.*
marmelada *f. marmalade.*
marmita *f. dinner pail; mess kit.*
mármore *m. marble.*
marquês *m. marquis.*
marrom *adj. brown* Ⓑ; *n. m. brown color* Ⓑ.
martelar *to hammer.*
martelo *m. hammer.*
mártir *m. and f. martyr.*
MAS *but, yet, however.*
  Eu esperei duas horas mas ela não chegou. *I waited for two hours but she did not arrive.*
  Ela é não só bela mas também inteligente. *She is not only pretty but also intelligent.*
  Nem mas nem meio mas. *No ifs, ands or buts.*
mascar *to chew.*
máscara *f. mask, disguise.*
mascote *f. mascot.*
masculino *adj. masculine.*
  Gênero (género) masculino. *Masculine gender.*
massa *f. dough; mass.*
mastigar *to chew.*
mata *f. forest, woods.*
mata-borrão *m. blotting paper.*
matadouro *m. slaughterhouse.*
matança *f. slaughter.*
MATAR *to kill, to murder.*
  Matar o tempo. *To kill time.*
  Matar a fome. *To satisfy one's hunger.*
mate *m. maté, mate (tea).*
matemática *f. mathematics.*
matemático *m. mathematician.*
matéria *f. matter, material; subject.*
  Matéria-prima. *Raw material.*
material *adj. material; n. m. material, equipment.*
materializar *to materialize.*
maternal *adj. maternal.*
maternidade *f. maternity.*
materno *adj. maternal, motherly.*
matiz *m. shade of color.*
mato *m. woods, forest, thicket; country (rural).*
matrícula *f. matriculation, registration.*
matricular *to matriculate, to register.*
  Em que universidade se matriculou? *At what university did you register?*
matrimonial *adj. matrimonial.*
matrimônio (matrimónio) *m. marriage, matrimony.*
matuto *m. backwoodsman, hillbilly.*
MAU (f. MÁ) *adj. bad, wicked; ill; poor.*
  Não é má idéia (ideia). *That's not a bad idea.*
  Mau tempo. *Bad weather.*
  Êle (Ele) é mau. *He's bad.*
  Mau humor. *Bad humor.*
mausoléu *m. mausoleum.*
máximo *(x = ss) adj. maximum, highest, greatest; n. m. maximum.*
  Máxima altura. *Highest point. Peak.*

  Qual é o preço máximo? *What is the top price?*
  Até o máximo. *To the utmost.*
maxixe *(x = sh) m. gherkin; Brazilian dance.*
ME *me; to me; myself.*
  João me deu o livro. *John gave me the book.*
  Dê-me o enderêço (endereço), por favor. *Give me the address, please.*
  Eu me levanto às seis. *I get up at seven.*
  Primeiro vou lavar-me. *First I'm going to wash (myself).*
meão *(f. meã) adj. average, mean.*
mecânico *adj. mechanical; n. m. mechanic.*
mecanismo *m. mechanism, machinery.*
mecha *f. wick, fuse.*
medalha *f. medal.*
mediação *f. mediation, intervention.*
mediador *m. mediator, go-between.*
mediano *adj. median, medium.*
mediante *by means of, by virtue of.*
mediar *to mediate, to intercede.*
medicina *f. medicine, remedy.*
médico *adj. medical; n. m. physician, doctor.*
MEDIDA *f. measure, measurement; rule.*
  Medida padrão. *Standard measure.*
  Tomaram-se as medidas necessárias. *The necessary measures were taken.*
  Feito sob medida. *Tailor-made. Made to order.*
  À medida que êle (ele) falava, ela escrevia o que êle dizia. *As he spoke, she wrote what he said.*
médio *adj. mean, medium, average; n. m. halfback.*
  Classe média. *Middle class.*
  Médio direito. *Right halfback.*
mediocre *adj. mediocre.*
mediocridade *f. mediocrity.*
medir *to measure.*
  Medir as palavras. *To measure one's words.*
meditação *f. meditation.*
meditar *to meditate.*
mêdo (medo) *m. fear, dread.*
  Ela está com mêdo Ⓑ. *She is afraid.*
  Elas têm mêdo dêle (dele). *They are afraid of him.*
medula *f. medulla, marrow; pith, essence.*
MEIA *f. stocking; sock.*
  Quer meias de lã ou de algodão? *Do you want wool or cotton stockings?*
MEIO *adj. and adv. half, halfway, mean; n. m. sing. and pl. means.*
  Quero meio quilo de café. *I want half a kilo of coffee.*
  Às duas e meia. *At two thirty.*
  Meio irmão. *Half brother.*
  Está meio cheio. *It's half full.*
  Meio dólar. *Half dollar.*
  Meios legais. *Legal means.*
  Por meio de. *By means of.*
  Meio de transporte. *Means of transportation.*
  Por qualquer meio. *By any means.*
MEIO-DIA *m. noon.*
  Ao meio-dia. *At noon.*
mel *m. honey.*
  Lua de mel. *Honeymoon.*
melaço *m. molasses.*
melancia *f. watermelon.*
melancólico *adj. melancholic, sad.*
melão *m. melon.*
MELHOR *adj. and adv. better, best.*
  Sinto-me melhor. *I feel better.*
  Êle (ele) é o melhor aluno de todos. *He's the best student of all.*
  Ela fala português melhor do que êle (ele). *She speaks Portuguese better than he does.*
  Talvez isso seja melhor. *Perhaps that would be better.*

Eu fiz o melhor que pude. *I did the best I
could.*

Eu farei o melhor possível. *I'll do the best I
can.*

Tanto melhor! *So much the better!*

Tanto melhor se ela não vem. *So much the
better if she doesn't come.*

Êle está um tanto melhor. *He's somewhat
better.*

Cada vez melhor. *Better and better.*

Êle e o meu melhor amigo. *He's my best
friend.*

melhora *f. improvement.*

melhorar *to improve.*
O tempo está melhorando (está a melhorar).
The weather is getting better.
Melhorar de saúde. *To get better (health).*

melodia *f. melody.*

membrana *f. membrane, tissue.*

membro *m. member; part.*

memorável *adj. memorable.*

MEMÓRIA *f. memory; memoir; memorandum.*
Ela tem uma memória extraordinária. *She has
an extraordinary memory.*
Eu não tenho boa memória. *I don't have a
good memory.*
Aprenda-o de memória. *Learn it by heart.*
Em memória de. *In memory of.*

menção *f. mention.*

mencionar *to mention.*

mendigar *to beg.*

mendigo *m. beggar.*

menear *to move; to stir; to shake; to wag.*

MENINA *f. child, girl, young lady.*
Menina, onde você mora? *Little girl, where
do you live?*

MENINO *m. child, boy, young man.*
Êle (ele) é um menino muito inteligente.
He's a very intelligent boy.

MENOR *adj. smaller; younger; least; n. m. and
f. minor.*
Êle (Ele) é menor. *He's a minor. He's underage.*

MENOS *adj. and adv. less; least; minus; except.*
É mais ou menos a mesma coisa. *It's more
or less the same thing.*
Todos foram menos eu. *Everyone went but
me.*
Estaremos lá às sete menos um quarto. *We'll
be there at a quarter to seven.*
Não irei a menos que você me acompanhe. *I
won't go unless you go with me (accompany
me).*
Pelo menos. *At least.*
Menos mal. *Not so bad. It could be worse.*
Estarei em casa em menos de dez minutos. *I
shall be home in less than ten minutes.*
Mais dia, menos dia. *Sooner or later.*
Cada vez menos. *Less and less.*
Menos que nunca. *Less than ever.*

menoscabo *m. disdain, contempt; belittlement.*

menosprezar *to belittle, to disparage; to disdain.*

menosprêzo (menosprezo) *m. belittlement; scorn.*

mensageiro *m. messenger.*

mensagem *f. message.*
Eu não recebi mensagem alguma. *I didn't receive any message at all.*

mensal *adj. monthly.*

mensalidade *f. monthly allowance; monthly payment.*

menta *f. mint.*

mental *adj. mental.*

mentalidade *f. mentality.*

MENTE *f. mind, understanding.*
Tenha-o sempre em mente. *Always bear it in
mind.*

mentecapto *adj. crazy.*

mentir *to lie.*

mentira *f. lie, falsehood.*

mentiroso *adj. lying, false, deceitful; n. m.
liar.*

menu *m. menu.*

mercado *m. market, marketplace.*
Mercado de valores. *Stock market.*

mercador *m. merchant, dealer.*

mercadoria *f. commodity, merchandise, goods.*

mercante *adj. merchant, commercial; n. m.
merchant*
Navio mercante. *Merchant ship.*
Marinha mercante. *Merchant marine.*

mercê *f. favor; reward; mercy.*
Estar à mercê de. *To be at the mercy of.*

mercearia *f. grocery store.*

mercenário *adj. mercenary.*

merecer *to deserve, to merit.*

merecido *adj. deserved.*

merenda *f. light lunch, snack.*

merendar *to have a snack, to eat a light lunch.*

merengue *m. meringue.*

mergulhar *to dive, to plunge.*

meridiano *adj. meridian; n. m. meridian.*

mérito *m. merit, worth, value.*

mero *adj. mere, only, pure, simple.*

MÊS *m. month.*
Há dois meses. *Two months ago.*
O mês que vem. *Next month.*
O mês passado. *Last month.*
Todos os meses. *Every month.*

MESA *f. table; board, committee.*
Ponha a mesa. *Set the table.*
Maria vai servir à mesa. *Mary is going to
wait on table.*
Os convidados se sentaram à mesa. *The
guests sat down at the table.*

mesclar *to mix, to blend, to mingle.*

MESMA *adj. f. same, equal, self.*
Ela mesma o disse. *She herself said so.*
Êle (ele) já não é a mesma pessoa. *He's no
longer the same person.*
Somos da mesma idade. *We're of the same
age.*

MESMO *adj. and adv. same.*
O mesmo dia. *The same day.*
É o mesmo homem que vi ontem. *He's the
same man I saw yesterday.*
Eu mesmo o farei. *I'll do it myself.*
Agora mesmo. *Right now.*
Ali mesmo. *Right there. In that very place.*
Eu espero aqui mesmo. *I'll wait right here.*
Mesmo assim, não vou. *Even so, I won't go.*
Hoje mesmo o faço. *This very day I'll do it.*
Não é o mesmo. *It's not the same (thing).*
Ao mesmo tempo. *At the same time.*
É mesmo? *Is that so?*
É isso mesmo! *That's it (exactly)!*
Para mim é o mesmo. *It's all the same to me.*
Por isso mesmo não vamos. *For that very
reason we're not going.*

mesquinho *adj. niggardly, stingy.*

mestiço *adj. and n. m. of mixed blood, mestizo.*

mestre *m. and f. teacher; master; expert.*

meta *f. goal; end, object, aim.*

metade *f. half; middle, center.*
Dê-me a metade. *Give me half.*
Cara metade. *Better half. Wife.*
Eu fui só a metade do caminho a pé. *I went
only one half of the way on foot.*

metal *m. metal.*

metálico *adj. metallic.*

METER *to put; to put in, to insert.*
Meter a mão no bôlso (bolso). *To put one's
hand in one's pocket.*
Não consigo meter a chave na fechadura. *I
can't get the key in the lock.*
Meter-se com. *To get mixed up with. To interfere.*

Meter-se em camisa de onze varas. *To get
into a difficult situation.*

metódico *adj. methodic.*

método *m. method.*

metralhadora *f. machine gun.*

METRO *m. meter (39.37 inches).*

metrópole *f. metropolis.*

MEU *adj. and pro. m. my, mine; pl. meus.*
Meu livro. (O meu livro). *My book.*
Meus livros. (Os meus livros.) *My books.*
Êste (este) lenço não é meu. *This handker-
chief is not mine.*
Êles (eles) são amigos meus. *They're friends
of mine.*
Isto é meu. *This is mine. This belongs to
me.*
O prazer é todo meu. *The pleasure is all
mine.*
Meus senhores: *Gentlemen:*
A meu ver. *In my opinion.*

mexer (x = sh) *to stir; to disturb.*

mexer-se (x = sh) *to stir, to move.*

mexicano (x = sh) *adj. m. Mexican; n. m. Mexican.*

micróbio *m. microbe, germ.*

microscópio *m. miscroscope.*

migalha *f. crumb; bit.*

migrar *to migrate.*

MIL *adj. thousand; n. m. thousand.*
Mil novecentos e sessenta e seis. *1966.*
Dois mil dólares. *Two thousand dollars.*
Duas mil casas. *Two thousand houses.*

milagre *m. miracle, marvel.*

milagroso *adj. miraculous.*

milésimo *adj. thousandth; n. m. thousandth.*

milha *f. mile.*
Quantas milhas são daqui a Chicago? *How
many miles is it from here to Chicago?*

milhão *m. million.*

MILHO *m. corn.*
Milho-pipoca. *Popcorn.*

miligrama *m. milligram.*

milímetro *m. millimeter.*

milionário *adj. millionaire; n. m. millionaire.*

militante *adj. militant.*

militar *adj. military; n. m. military man, soldier.*
Serviço militar. *Military service.*
Escola militar. *Military academy.*

mil-réis *m. former monetary unit of Brasil, replaced by the cruzeiro* Ⓑ

MIM *me, myself (after a prep.)*
Para mim. *For me.*
Para mim tanto faz. *It's all the same to me.*
Ai de mim! *Poor me!*

mimar *to pamper, to spoil (person).*

mina *f. mine.*

mineral *adj. mineral; n. m. mineral.*

mingau *m. a soft, mushy food.*

MINHA (*f. of meu) adj. and pro. my, mine; pl.
minhas.*
Esta gravata é minha. *This tie is mine. This
is my tie.*
Ela é uma amiga minha. *She is a friend of
mine.*
Minhas senhoras: *Ladies:*
Minha casa é sua. *Make yourself at home.
You're always welcome here.*

miniatura *f. miniature.*

mínimo *adj. minimum, least, smallest; n. m.
minimum.*
Não tenho a mínima idéia (ideia). *I haven't
the slightest idea.*
Êste (este) é o preço mínimo. *This is the
lowest price.*

MINISTÉRIO *m. cabinet; ministry; a department
of the government.*
Ministério de Educação e Saúde. *Department
of Education and Welfare.*

Ministério da Guerra. *War Department.*
Ministério da Marinha. *Navy Department.*
Ministério da Aeronáutica. *Air Department.*
Ministério da Fazenda. *Treasury Department.*
MINISTRO m. *minister; secretary (of government department).*
Ministro da Agricultura. *Secretary of Agriculture.*
minoria f. *minority.*
minuta f. *note, memorandum.*
MINUTO m. *minute.*
Espere um minuto! *Wait a minute!*
miolo m. *brain; core, interior.*
míope adj. *myopic, nearsighted.*
mirar *to look, to behold, to gaze at.*
miserável adj. *miserable, wretched; miserly.*
miséria f. *misery; destitution.*
Êles (eles) vivem na miséria. *They live in abject poverty.*
misericórdia f. *mercy.*
MISSA f. *mass.*
Missa cantada. *High mass.*
Missa do galo. *Midnight mass (Christmas).*
Ouvir missa. *To attend mass.*
missão f. *mission.*
missionário m. *missionary.*
mistério m. *mystery.*
misterioso adj. *mysterious.*
misto adj. *mixed.*
Colégio misto. *Coeducational school.*
mistura f. *mixture.*
misturar *to mix.*
mitigar *to mitigate, to ease.*
mito m. *myth.*
mitologia f. *mythology.*
miudeza f. pl. *details; odds and ends; notions.*
Loja de miudezas. *Notions shop.*
miúdo adj. *small; n. m. small change; pl. small children* Ⓟ.
Trôco (troco) miúdo. *Small change.*
mo (contr. of **m + o**) *it to me, you to me, him to me.*
Ela escreveu-mo. *She wrote it to me.*
Êles (eles) mos mandaram. *They sent them to me.*
mobilar, mobiliar (**mobilar**) *to furnish (furniture).*
mobília f. *furniture.*
mobiliário adj. *of furniture; n. m. furniture.*
MOÇA f. *girl, young lady.*
moção f. *motion, movement; parliamentary motion.*
mochila f. *knapsack.*
mocidade f. *youth.*
MOÇO m. *boy, young man.*
Moço de recados. *Messenger.*
moda f. *fashion, style; manner.*
Os chapéus de palha estão fora de moda? *Are straw hats out of style?*
Estar na moda. *To be in style.*
A última moda. *The latest style.*
modalidade f. *modality; form.*
modêlo (**modelo**) m. *model; pattern.*
moderação f. *moderation.*
moderado adj. *moderate.*
moderar *to moderate; to restrain.*
MODERNO adj. *modern.*
Métodos modernos. *Modern methods.*
Arte moderna. *Modern art.*
modéstia f. *modesty.*
modesto adj. *modest.*
módico adj. *moderate, reasonable.*
E um preço módico. *It's a reasonable price.*
modificar *to modify, to alter.*
modismo m. *idiom.*
modista m. and f. *popular singer; f. dressmaker.*

MODO m. *mode, method, manner; mood.*
É o melhor modo de fazê-lo. *It's the best way to do it.*
Dêste (deste) modo. *This way.*
De modo que. *So that.*
Fale de modo que todos possam ouvir. *Speak so that all can hear.*
De nenhum modo. *By no means. In no way. Not at all.*
Do mesmo modo. *In the same way.*
Modo condicional. *Conditional mood.*
moeda f. *money; coin.*
Papel moeda. *Paper currency. Bills.*
Pagar na mesma moeda. *To give tit for tat.*
mofa f. *mockery, derision.*
mofar *to mock, to deride.*
mofino adj. *unfortunate, unhappy.*
mogno, mógono m. *mahogany.*
moído adj. *ground, crushed; worn out, exhausted.*
moinho m. *mill.*
mola f. *spring; motivating force.*
Mola de relógio. *Watch spring.*
molde m. *mold, pattern, model.*
moldura f. *molding; picture frame.*
molecada f. *a gang of boys, street urchins.*
moleque m. *urchin; Negro boy* Ⓑ.
molestar *to disturb, to trouble, to bother, to annoy; to tease.*
moléstia f. *illness; discomfort.*
molesto adj. *bothersome; uncomfortable; annoying.*
molhar *to wet, to moisten, to dampen.*
Molhar a garganta. *To wet one's whistle.*
môlho (**molho**) m. *gravy, sauce.*
Môlho de salada. *Salad dressing.*
molusco m. *mollusk, shellfish.*
momentâneo adj. *momentary.*
MOMENTO m. *moment, instant.*
Não tenho mem um momento livre. *I don't have a free moment.*
Espere um momento. *Wait a moment.*
A qualquer momento. *At any moment.*
De um momento para outro. *From one moment to the next.*
monarca m. and f. *monarch.*
monarquia f. *monarchy.*
mondar *to weed; to prune.*
monge m. *monk.*
monólogo m. *monologue.*
monopólio m. *monopoly.*
monopolizar *to monopolize.*
monotonia f. *monotony.*
monótono adj. *monotonous.*
monstro m. *monster.*
monstruosidade f. *monstrosity.*
monstruoso adj. *monstrous.*
monta f. *amount, total.*
De pouca monta. *Of little importance.*
montanha f. *mountain.*
montar *to mount; to ride (horseback); to amount to; to assemble; to set (a precious stone).*
Montar a cavalo. *To ride (a horse).*
A quanto monta a conta? *How much does the bill come to?*
Monte esta máquina. *Assemble this machine.*
monte m. *mountain, hill; pile.*
montra f. *shopwindow, showcase.*
monumental adj. *monumental.*
monumento m. *monument.*
morada f. *dwelling, residence.*
morador m. *resident, inhabitant.*
moral adj. *moral; n. m. morality; morale; n. f. morals, ethics.*
morango m. *strawberry.*
MORAR *to dwell, to reside, to live.*
Onde o senhor mora? *Where do you live?*

mordedura f. *bite.*
morder *to bite.*
morena adj. *dark-complexioned; n. f. brunette.*
moreno adj. *dark-complexioned; n. m. brunet.*
moribundo adj. *dying.*
MORRER *to die.*
Êle (ele) morreu de fome. *He died of hunger.*
morro m. *hill, mound.*
Morro abaixo (x = sh). *Downhill.*
Morro acima. *Uphill.*
mortal adj. *mortal, fatal.*
mortalidade f. *mortality, death rate.*
MORTE f. *death.*
Morte súbita. *Sudden death.*
morteiro m. *mortar.*
mortificação f. *mortification.*
mortificar *to humiliate, to mortify; to vex.*
MORTO adj. *dead; m. dead person.*
Estou morto de fome. *I'm famished. I'm starved.*
Êle (ele) está morto. *He is dead.*
môsca (**mosca**) f. *fly; a bore.*
moscatel m. *muscatel (grape or wine).*
moscovita adj. and n. m. and f. *Muscovite, Russian.*
mosquito m. *mosquito.*
mostarda f. *mustard.*
mostra f. *exhibition, show; pl. gestures.*
À mostra. *On view.*
mostrador m. *counter, showcase.*
MOSTRAR *to show; to exhibit; to prove.*
Ela me mostrou as costas. *She turned her back on me.*
mostruário m. *showcase.*
motivar *to motivate.*
motivo m. *motive, reason; motif.*
Sem motivo. *Groundless. Unfounded.*
motocicleta f. *motorcycle.*
MOTOR m. *motor, engine.*
Não chegamos a' tempo porque o motor falhou. *We didn't arrive on time because the motor stalled.*
motorista m. and f. *motorist, driver.*
MÓVEL adj. *movable; n. m. a piece of furniture; motive.*
MOVER *to move.*
movimentar *to move, to get moving.*
movimento m. *movement, motion; traffic.*
Há muito movimento nesta rua. *There is much traffic on this street.*
Pôr em movimento. *To set in motion.*
mucama, mucamba both Ⓑ f. *Negro servant, mammy.*
muda f. *change, move.*
mudança f. *change, moving out.*
MUDAR *to change, to alter; to remove; to move out or away.*
Eu mudei de parecer. *I've changed my mind.*
Vamos mudar de casa. *We're going to move.*
Mudar de roupa. *To change clothes.*
Quando ela chegou êles (eles) mudaram de conversa. *When she arrived they changed the subject.*
mudo adj. *dumb, mute, silent.*
mugir *to moo; to roar.*
MUITO adj. and adv. *much, very much, very; pl. many, too many.*
Muito dinheiro. *A lot of money.*
Ela escreve muito. *She writes a great deal.*
Muito mais barato. *Much cheaper.*
Muitos livros. *Many books.*
Isto é muito melhor. *This is much better.*
Com muito prazer. *Gladly. With much pleasure.*
Agradeço muito. *I appreciate it very much.*
Há muito tempo. *A long time ago.*
Está muito frio hoje. *It's very cold today.*

Não muito. *Not much.*
Ainda falta muito. *There's still a lot missing. There's still a lot to be done.*
Muito bem! *Fine! Excellent!*
Muitas vêzes (vezes). *Often. Frequently.*
Muito obrigado. *Thank you very much.*
mula *f. she-mule.*
muleta *f. crutch.*
MULHER *f. woman, wife.*
Mulher de casa. *Housewife.*
mulo *m. mule.*
multa *f. fine, penalty.*
multar *to fine.*
multidão *f. multitude, crowd.*
multiplicar *to multiply.*
multiplicidade *f. multiplicity.*
múltiplo *adj. multiple.*
MUNDO *m. world; multitude; great quantity.*
Ela quer ver o mundo. *She wants to see the world.*
Tenho que comprar um mundo de coisas. *I have to buy a lot of things.*
Todo o mundo quer ir. *Everybody wants to go.*
O mundo todo. *The whole world.*
munheca *f. wrist.*
munição *f. ammunition.*
municipal *adj. municipal.*
municipalidade *f. municipality; city council.*
município *m. municipality.*
muralha *wall; rampart.*
murmurar *to murmur; to whisper; to gossip.*
murmúrio *m. murmur, whisper.*
muro *m. wall.*
murro *m. blow, punch.*
músculo *m. muscle.*
museu *m. museum.*
Que dias o museu está aberto? *What days is the museum open?*
O Museu de Arte Moderna. *The Museum of Modern Art.*
MÚSICA *f. music.*
Música clássica. *Classical music.*
Música popular. *Popular music.*
Música de dança. *Dance music.*
musical *adj. musical.*
músico *adj. musical; n. m. musician.*
mutável *adj. changeable.*
mutilar *to mutilate.*
mútuo *adj. mutual.*

N

NA (contr. *of* em + a) *in the, on the, at the.*
Na cidade. *In the city.*
na *(form of object pronoun a when used after a verb ending in a nasal sound), it, her, you.*
Compraram-na. *They bought it.*
nabo *m. turnip.*
NAÇÃO *f. nation.*
Nações Unidas. *United Nations.*
nacional *adj. national.*
nacionalidade *f. nationality.*
NADA *nothing; not at all.*
Não desejo nada. *I don't want anything.*
Nada de novo. *Nothing new.*
Nada mais. *Nothing more. Nothing else.*
De nada. *Don't mention it.*
Não vale nada. *It's worthless.*
Nada disso. *None of that. Not at all.*
Não sei nada disso. *I know nothing about it. I don't know a thing about it.*
Antes de mais nada. *First of all.*
Nada de queixas (x = sh). *(No complaints. Let's have no complaints.*
Eu não tenho nada com isso. *I have nothing to do with that.*
Ou tudo ou nada. *All or nothing.*
nadador *m. swimmer.*

nadar *to swim, to float.*
Ela sabe nadar? *Does she know how to swim?*
nado *m. swimming.*
Nado de peito. *Breast stroke.*
naipe *m. suit (cards).*
namorado *adj. in love; m. lover, suitor, boy-friend.*
namorar *to court, to make love to.*
namôro (namoro) *m. love affair, courtship.*
NÃO *no not.*
Não falo espanhol. *I don't speak Spanish.*
Eu tive que dizer que não. *I had to say no.*
Ainda não. *Not yet.*
Não sei. *I don't know.*
Não a conheço. *I don't know her.*
Não quer sentar-se? *Won't you have a seat? Won't you sit down?*
Não há ninguém na sala. *There's no one in the room.*
Não tenho mais. *I don't have any more.*
Já não. *No longer. Not any more.*
Não tenho muito tempo. *I don't have much time.*
Não há de quê. *Don't mention it. You're welcome.*
Não importa. *It doesn't matter.*
Não me diga! *You don't say! Don't tell me!*
A não ser que. *Unless.*
Não obstante. *Nevertheless.*
Acho que não. *I don't think so.*
Ela não disse palavra. *She didn't say anything.*
Não? *or* Não é? *or* Não é verdade? *Isn't that so?*
Não faz mal. *Don't bother. It's all right.*
Pois não! *Certainly! Of course!*
napolitano *adj. Neapolitan; n. m. Neapolitan.*
NAQUELA (contr. *of* em + aquela) *f. in that, on that, in that one, on that one.*
Não há ninguém naquela sala. *There is no one in that room.*
NAQUELE (contr. *of* em + aquêle, aquele) *m. in that, on that, in that one, on that one.*
Naquele ano. *In that year.*
NAQUILO (contr. *of* em + aquilo) *in that, on that.*
narcótico *adj. narcotic; n. m. narcotic.*
NARIZ *m. nose.*
Nariz aquilino. *Aquiline nose.*
Ele (Ele) mete o nariz em tudo. *He pokes his nose into everything.*
Torcer o nariz. *To turn up one's nose.*
Limpar o nariz. *To blow one's nose.*
narração *f. account, narration, story.*
narrar *to narrate, to relate.*
NASCER *to be born; to bud; to rise (sun); to originate.*
Ele (ele) nasceu em São Paulo mas os pais dêle (dele) nasceram em Lisboa. *He was born in São Paulo but his parents were born in Lisbon.*
nascimento *m. birth; origin, source.*
nata *f. cream; the best part.*
natação *f. swimming.*
natal *adj. natal, native; n. m. Christmas.*
natalício *adj. natal.*
nativo *adj. native.*
natural *adj. natural, native; n. m. native.*
Isto é natural. *This is quite natural.*
NATURALMENTE *of course, naturally.*
natureza *f. nature.*
naturismo *m. naturalism; back-to-nature movement.*
naturista *m. naturalist; believer in back-to-nature movement.*
naufragar *to be shipwrecked; to fail.*
naufrágio *m. shipwreck; failure.*
náusea *f. nausea; seasickness.*
náutica *f. navigation.*

náutico *adj. nautical.*
naval *adj. naval.*
navalha *f. razor; knife.*
navegação *f. navigation; shipping.*
navegador *m. navigator, sailor.*
navegante *m. navigator, sailor.*
navegar *to navigate; to sail.*
navegável *adj. navigable.*
navio *m. ship.*
Navio mercante. *Merchant ship.*
Navio de guerra. *Warship.*
neblina *f. fog, mist.*
NECESSÁRIO *adj. necessary.*
É necessário fazê-lo hoje. *It must be done today.*
NECESSIDADE *f. necessity; need.*
Não há necessidade de registrar a carta. *It's not necessary to register the letter.*
A necessidade faz lei. *Necessity knows no law.*
necessitado *adj. poor, needy; n. m. person in need.*
NECESSITAR *to need; to be in need.*
Necessita mais alguma coisa? *Do you need anything else?*
necrologia *f. necrology, obituary.*
nefasto *adj. ill-fated; ominous.*
NEGAR *to deny; to refuse; to disown.*
Não o negue. *Don't deny it.*
Não o nego. *I don't deny it.*
Ele (ele) se negou a fazê-lo. *He refused to do it.*
negativa *f. refusal.*
negativo *adj. negative.*
Uma resposta negativa. *A negative answer. An answer in the negative.*
negligência *f. negligence, neglect.*
negligente *adj. negligent, careless.*
negociante *m. merchant, trader, businessman.*
negociar *to negotiate.*
NEGÓCIO *m. business; affair; transaction.*
Fazer bons negócios. *To do good business.*
Fazer mau negócio. *To drive a bad bargain.*
Abandonar os negócios. *To retire from business.*
Homem de negócios. *Businessman.*
NEGRO *adj. black; gloomy; n. m. Negro.*
Vestir-se de negro. *To dress in black.*
Ele (Ele) vê tudo negro. *He always looks on the dark side. He takes a gloomy view of everything.*
NELA (contr. *of* em + ela) *f. in it, on in, on her, in her.*
NÊLE (NELE) (contr. *of* em + êle, ele) *m. in it, on it, in him, on him.*
NEM *neither, either, nor, not.*
Não vou nem com voce nem com êle. *I won't go either with you or with him.*
Nem meu irmão nem eu fomos. *Neither my brother nor I went.*
Nem sempre. *Not always.*
Nem sequer. *Not even.*
Nem mais nem menos. *Exactly. Neither more nor less.*
Nem peixe (x = sh) nem carne. *Neither fish nor fowl.*
NENHUM *not any, no, none, any.*
Nenhum homem. *No man.*
De modo nenhum. *By no means.*
A nenhum preço. *Not at any price.*
Nenhuma das meninas. *None of the girls.*
Nenhum de nós. *None of us.*
Estar a nenhum. *To be broke* (B).
nervo *m. nerve.*
Nervo ótico (óptico). *Optic nerve.*
Ela é uma pilha de nervos. *She's a bundle of nerves.*
nervoso *adj. nervous.*

NESSA (*contr. of* em + essa) *f. in that, on that, in that one, on that one.*
Ponha o livro nessa mesa. *Put the book on that table.*

NESSE (*contr. of* em + êsse, esse) *m. in that, on that, in that one, on that one.*
Nesse caso eu não vou. *In that case I'll not go.*

NESTA (*contr. of* em + esta) *f. in this, on this, in this one, on this one.*
Não foram a outra cidade; ficaram nesta. *They did not go to another city; they stayed here (in this one).*

NESTE (*contr. of* em + êste, este) *m. in this, on this, in this one, on this one.*
Não está nesse, está neste. *It's not in that one, it's in this one.*

neto *m. grandchild.*

neurastenia *f. neurasthenia.*

neurótico *adj. neurotic.*

neutral *adj. neutral.*

neutro *adj. neutral, neuter; n. m. neuter.*

nevar *to snow.*
Está nevando (a nevar). *It's snowing.*

neve *m. snow.*

nevoeiro *m. fog.*

nicaraguano *adj. Nicaraguan; n. m. Nicaraguan.*

nicotina *f. nicotine.*

NINGUÉM *nobody, anybody, no one, anyone, none.*
Ninguém veio. *Nobody came.*
Êle (ele) nunca fala mal de ninguém. *He never says anything bad about anyone.*
Um joão-ninguém. *A nobody.*

ninho *m. nest.*

NISSO (*contr. of* em + isso) *in that, of that; at that moment.*

NISTO (*contr. of* em + isto) *in this, of this; at this moment.*

nítido *adj. clear, bright, sharp.*

nível *m. level.*

NO (*contr. of* em + o) *in the, on the, at the.*
No livro. *In the book.*

no (*form of object pronoun* o *when used after a verb ending in a nasal sound*) *it, him, you.*
Viram-no ontem. *They saw him yesterday.*

nó *m. knot; tie; joint; knuckle.*

nobre *adj. noble; n. m. nobleman.*

nobreza *f. nobility.*

noção *f. notion, idea.*

nocivo *adj. harmful.*

nogueira *f. walnut.*

NOITE *f. night, evening.*
Boa noite. *Good evening. Good night.*
Hoje à noite. *Tonight.*
Ontem à noite. *Last night.*
Tôdas (Todas) as noites. *Every night.*
De noite. *At night. In the evening.*
À meia-noite. *At midnight.*

noivado *m. engagement; wedding.*

noivar *to court; to go on a honeymoon.*

noivo *m. sweetheart, boyfriend, fiancé, bridegroom.*
Os noivos. *The newlyweds.*

nojo *m. nausea; disgust.*

NOME *m. name; noun.*
Ponha aqui o nome e o endereço (endereço). *Put your name and address here.*
Eu a conheço de nome. *I know her by name.*
Nome de batismo (baptismo). *Baptismal name.*
Nome de família. *Family name. Last name.*
Qual é o seu nome? *What is your name?*
Nome coletivo (colectivo). *Collective noun.*

nomeação *f. nomination, appointment.*

nomear *to appoint, to nominate; to name.*
Êle (ele) foi nomeado diretor (director). *He was appointed director.*

nono *adj. ninth; n. m. ninth.*

nora *f. daughter-in-law.*

nordeste *adj. northeast; n. m. northeast.*

norma *f. norm, rule, standard, model.*

normal *adj. normal.*

normalidade *f. normality, normalcy.*

noroeste *adj. northwest; n. m. northwest.*

NORTE *adj. north; n. m. north.*
Norte América. *North America.*

norte-americano *adj. North American; n. m. North American.*

norueguês *adj. Norwegian; n. m. Norwegian.*

NOS *us, to us, ourselves.*
Levantamo-nos imediatamente. *We got up immediately.*
Elas não nos disseram nada. *They didn't say anything to us.*
Êles (eles) não nos deixaram entrar. *They did not let us enter.*

NÓS *we, us.*
Nós vamos hoje; elas vão amanhã. *We are going today; they are going tomorrow.*
Êstes (estes) livros são para nós? *Are these books for us?*

NOSSO *our.*
Nossa cidade. *Our town.*
Nossa irmã. *Our sister.*
Nosso irmão. *Our brother.*
De quem é? É nossa. *Whose is it? It's ours.*

NOTA *f. note; grade, mark.*
Tomar nota. *To take note.*
Nota promissória. *Promissory note.*
O aluno recebeu boas notas. *The student received good grades.*
Digno de nota. *Noteworthy.*

notar *to note, to notice.*
Não notei nada. *I didn't notice anything.*

notário *m. notary.*

notável *adj. notable; worthy of notice.*
Êle (ele) é um homem notável. *He's an outstanding man.*

NOTÍCIA *f. a piece of news, information; notice; pl. news.*
Boa notícia. *A piece of good news.*
As notícias do dia. *The news of the day.*
Más notícias. *Bad news.*

notificação *f. notification.*

notificar *to notify, to inform.*

notório *adj. well-known, evident.*

noturno (nocturno) *adj. nocturnal, night, in the night.*

novato *m. novice, beginner.*

NOVE *adj. nine; n. m. nine.*

novela *f. novelette, novel.*

novelista *m. and f. novelist.*

NOVEMBRO *m. November.*

noventa *adj. ninety; n. m. ninety.*

noviço *m. novice, apprentice.*

NOVIDADE *f. novelty; news.*
Há alguma novidade? *Anything new?*
Não há novidade. *Nothing new.*
A última novidade. *The latest thing.*
Cheio de novidades. *Full of airs.*

NÔVO (NOVO) *adj. m.* NOVA *f.*
Êsse (Esse) chapéu é nôvo? *Is that hat new? Is that a new hat?*
Que há de nôvo? *What's new?*
É preciso fazê-lo de nôvo. *It's necessary to do it again. It has to be done again.*
Feliz Ano Nôvo! *Happy New Year!*
O irmão mais nôvo. *The younger brother.*

noz *f. nut.*

nu *adj. naked, nude, bare.*

nublado *adj. cloudy.*

nublar *to become cloudy, to cloud.*

nuca *f. nape (neck).*

nulidade *f. nullity; nonentity; incompetent person.*

nulo *adj. null, void; n. m. worthless person.*

NUM (*contr. of* em + um) *in a, on a, to a.*
Num livro. *In a book.*

NUMA (*contr. of* em + uma) *in a, on a, to a.*
Numa mesa. *On a table.*

numerar *to number.*

NÚMERO *m. number, figure.*
O número de meu telefone é ... *My telephone number is ...*
Escreva o número. *Write the number.*
Números arábicos. *Arabic numerals.*
Números pares. *Even numbers.*
Números ímpares. *Odd numbers.*
Número cardinal. *Cardinal number.*
Número ordinal. *Ordinal number.*
Sem número. *Countless. Endless.*

NUNCA *never, ever.*
Nunca! *Never!*
Nunca vou ao cinema. *I never go to the movies.*
Quase nunca. *Hardly ever.*
Nunca mais. *Never more.*
Mais vale tarde do que nunca. *Better late than never.*

nupcial *adj. nuptial.*

núpcias *f. pl. nuptials, wedding.*

nutrição *f. nutrition, nourishment.*

nutrir *to nourish, to feed.*

nutritivo *adj. nutritious, nourishing.*

nuvem *f. cloud.*

O

O *m. the; it, him.*
O livro. *The book.*
Comprei-o. *I bought it.*
Eu não o vi. *I didn't see him.*
Nós não os vimos. *We did not see them.*
Os alunos estão na escola. *The children are in school.*

obcecado *adj. stubborn; blind.*

obedecer *to obey.*
Êle (ele) sempre obedece. *He always obeys.*

obediência *f. obedience.*

obediente *adj. obedient.*

obeso *adj. obese, fat.*

objetar (objectar) *to object, to oppose.*

OBJETO (OBJECTO) *m. object, thing; purpose, aim.*
Por fim êle (ele) logrou seu objeto. *Finally he reached his goal.*
Objeto direto (directo). *Direct object.*

oblíquo *adj. oblique.*

OBRA *f. work; book; deed; action.*
É uma obra em quatro volumes. *The work is in four volumes.*
Obra-prima. *Masterpiece.*
Obras públicas. *Public works.*
Obra de arte. *Work of art.*
Obra de consulta. *Reference book. Reference work.*
Obra dramática. *Dramatic work. Play.*
Mãos à obra! *Let's get to work! To work!*

obrar *to work; to act; to operate; to defecate.*

obreiro *m. worker, workman.*

obrigação *f. obligation, duty.*

OBRIGADO *adj. obliged, thankful; thanks, thank you.*
Muito obrigado. *Thank you very much.*

obrigar *to oblige.*

obrigatório *adj. obligatory.*

obscurecer *to darken, to grow dark.*

obscuridade *f. obscurity.*

obscuro *adj. obscure, dark.*
Uma noite obscura. *A dark night.*

obsequiar *to obl... o favor.*

obséquio *m. favor, kindness.*
Agradeço muito o seu obséquio. *Thank you for your kindness.*

observar *to observe, to notice; to obey.*
É preciso observar as regras. *One must follow the rules.*
observatório *m. observatory.*
obsessão *f. obsession.*
obstáculo *m. obstacle.*
obstinado *adj. obstinate.*
obstruir *to obstruct, to block.*
Obstruir o tráfico. *To block traffic.*
obtenção *f. attainment.*
OBTER *to obtain, to get; to attain.*
Êle (ele) obteve um bom emprêgo (emprego). *He got a good job.*
obturador *m. shutter (camera); plug, stopper.*
obtuso *adj. obtuse, blunt.*
obus *m. howitzer.*
óbvio *adj. obvious, evident.*
OCASIÃO *f. occasion, opportunity.*
Eu perdi uma boa ocasião. *I missed a good opportunity.*
Eu irei na primeira ocasião que tiver. *I shall go the first chance I have.*
Em outra ocasião. *Some other time.*
Por ocasião de. *On the occasion of.*
ocasionar *to cause, to bring about.*
ocaso *m. setting (sun); decline.*
oceano *m. ocean.*
Oceano Atlântico. *Atlantic Ocean.*
Oceano Pacífico. *Pacific Ocean.*
ocidental *adj. western, occidental.*
ócio *m. idleness, leisure.*
ociosidade *f. idleness, leisure.*
ocioso *adj. idle; lazy.*
ocorrência *f. event.*
ocorrer *to happen, to occur.*
Não me ocorreu. *It didn't occur to me.*
oculista *m. and f. oculist.*
óculo *m. spyglass; pl. eyeglasses.*
Usar óculos. *To wear glasses.*
ocultar *to conceal, to hide.*
oculto *adj. concealed, hidden.*
ocupação *f. occupation, business; occupancy.*
OCUPADO *adj. busy; occupied; engaged.*
Estou muito ocupado. *I am very busy.*
OCUPAR *to occupy; to take possession of.*
Os móveis ocupam muito lugar. *The furniture takes up a lot of space.*
odiar *to hate.*
ódio *m. hatred.*
odioso *adj. hateful.*
OESTE *m. west.*
ofender *to offend.*
ofensa *f. offense.*
ofensiva *f. offensive.*
Tomar a ofensiva. *To take the offensive.*
OFERECER *to offer; to present.*
Êle (Ele) me ofereceu dois dólares pelo livro. *He offered me two dollars for the book.*
oferecimento *m. offer.*
oferta *f. offer, offering; gift.*
É a última oferta. *It's the last (final) offer.*
Oferta e procura. *Supply and demand.*
oficial *adj. oficial; n. m. official, officer.*
oficina *f. workshop.*
ofício *m. job, occupation.*
oh *oh.*
oitavo *adj. eighth; n. m. eighth.*
OITENTA *adj. and m. eighty; eightieth.*
OITO *adj. and n. m. eight; eighth.*
De hoje a oito dias. *A week from today.*
olá *hello!*
óleo *m. oil.*
Óleo de amendoim. *Peanut oil.*
Óleo combustível. *Fuel oil.*

olfatar *to smell.*
olfato *m. sense of smell, smell.*
olhada *f. glance, look.*
Dar uma olhada. *To take a look.*
olhadela *f. glimpse, glance, look.*
OLHAR *to look at, to glance at, to watch; n. m. glance, look.*
Êle (ele) olhou para ela. *He looked at her.*
Olhar com bons olhos. *To look upon with favor.*
ÔLHO (OLHO) *m. eye; attention, care.*
Eu tenho os olhos cansados de tanto ler. *My eyes are tired from reading so much.*
Ôlho de agulha. *Eye of a needle.*
Num abrir e fechar de olhos. *In the twinkling of an eye.*
Quatro olhos vêem mais que dois. *Two heads are better than one.*
oliva *f. olive.*
olor *m. fragrance, odor.*
oloroso *adj. fragrant.*
olvidar *to forget.*
olvido *m. forgetfulness.*
ombro *m. shoulder.*
Encolher os ombros. *To shrug the shoulders.*
omeleta *f. omelet.*
omissão *f. omission.*
omitir *to omit, to leave out.*
Você omitiu a primeira parte. *You left out the first part.*
onça *f. ounce; wildcat.*
Tempo da onça. *Long ago.*
Amigo da onça. *False friend.*
onda *f. wave.*
Onda curta. *Shortwave (radio).*
Onda sonora. *Sound wave.*
ONDE *where.*
Onde está a tinta? *Where is the ink?*
Onde vendem romances brasileiros? *Where do they sell Brasilian novels?*
De onde (or donde) é o seu professor? *Where is your teacher from?*
ondular *to wave.*
ônibus (ónibus, autocarro) *m. bus.*
ONTEM *yesterday.*
Êles (eles) chegaram ontem. *They arrived yesterday.*
ONZE *adj. eleven; n. m. eleven.*
ôpa! *wow!*
opaco *adj. opaque; dull.*
opção *f. option, choice.*
ópera *f. opera.*
operação *f. operation.*
operar *to operate (medical); to produce, to work.*
operário *m. worker, workman.*
opinar *to give an opinion.*
opinião *f. opinion.*
Esta é a opinião de todos. *Everyone is of this opinion.*
Eu mudei de opinião. *I changed my opinion.*
opor *to oppose.*
opor-se *to oppose.*
Eu me oponho a essa resolução. *I am against that resolution.*
oportunidade *f. opportunity.*
Esta é uma boa oportunidade. *This is a good opportunity.*
oportuno *adj. opportune.*
oposição *f. opposition.*
opositor *adj. opposing; n. m. opponent, competitor.*
oposto *adj. opposed, opposite, contrary.*
opressão *f. oppression.*
opressivo *adj. oppressive.*
opressor *m. oppressor.*
oprimir *to oppress.*

optar *to choose.*
óptico, ótico (óptico) *adj. optic, optical; m. optician.*
ora *now, but, however.*
Ora! *Well! Come now!*
Por ora. *For the time being.*
oração *f. prayer; speech; clause, sentence.*
orador *m. speaker, orator.*
oral *adj. oral.*
orar *to pray; to ask for.*
orçamento *m. budget.*
ORDEM *f. order; method; rule.*
Às suas ordens. *At your service.*
Por ordem de. *By order of.*
Chamar à ordem. *To call to order.*
Em ordem. *In order.*
A ordem do dia. *The order of the day.*
Fora de ordem. *Out of order.*
ordenado *m. salary.*
ordenança *f. ordinance; m. and f. orderly (military).*
ordenar *to order, to command; to ordain; to arrange.*
ordenhar *to milk.*
ordinal *adj. ordinal.*
ordinário *adj. ordinary, common.*
orelha *f. ear.*
Orelha dum livro. *Flap of a book.*
órfão *m. orphan.*
orgânico *adj. organic.*
organismo *m. organism.*
organização *f. organization.*
organizar *to organise, to form, to arrange.*
órgão *m. organ.*
orgulho *m. pride.*
orgulhoso *adj. proud, haughty.*
oriental *adj. oriental, eastern; n. m. Oriental.*
orientar *to orient.*
orientar-se *to orient oneself, to get one's bearings.*
É difícil orientar-se nesta cidade. *It is difficult to get one's bearings in this city.*
ORIENTE *m. orient, east.*
origem *f. origin, source.*
original *adj. original.*
originalidade *f. originality.*
originar *to cause, to originate.*
ornamento *m. ornament, decoration.*
ornar *to adorn.*
orquestra *f. orchestra.*
ortografia *f. orthography, spelling.*
orvalho *m. dew.*
osso *m. bone.*
Em carne e osso. *In the flesh, In person.*
ostentar *to display, to show off, to boast.*
ostra *f. oyster.*
ótico *adj. otic, auricular.*
otimismo (optimismo) *m. optimism.*
otimista (optimista) *m. optimist.*
ótimo (óptimo) *adj. excellent, wonderful.*
Ótimo! *Excellent! Wonderful!*
OU *or, either.*
Compre-me dois ou três. *Buy me two or three.*
OURO *m. gold, money; pl. diamonds (cards).*
Sim, tenho um relógio de ouro. *Yes, I have a gold watch.*
ousar *to dare.*
OUTONO *m. autumn, fall.*
outorgar *to grant; to agree to.*
OUTRO *adj. other, another.*
Não quero êste (este), quero o outro. *I don't want this one, I want the other one.*
Prefiro os outros. *I prefer the other ones.*
Outro dia. *Another day.*

No outro dia. *The other day.*
Outra garrafa de cerveja! *Another bottle of beer!*
Outra vez. *Again.*
Outras vêzes (vezes). *Other times.*

OUTUBRO m. *October.*

OUVIDO m. *hearing; ear.*
Dor de ouvido. *Earache.*
Ela tem ouvido para música. *She has a good ear for music.*
Entrar por um ouvido e sair pelo outro. *To go in one ear and out the other.*

ouvinte m. and f. *listener; auditor.*

OUVIR *to hear, to listen.*
Não ouço nada. *I can't hear a thing.*
Não ouvi o despertador. *I didn't hear the alarm clock.*
Ouvir missa. *To hear mass.*
Ouvimos dizer que ela é atriz. *We heard that she's an actress.*

ovação f. *ovation.*

oval adj. *oval.*

ovelha f. *sheep.*

ÔVO (OVO) *egg.*
Ovos duros. *Hard-boiled eggs.*
Ovos estrelados. *Fried eggs.*
Ovos mexidos (x = sh). *Scrambled eggs.*
A clara do ôvo. *The white of the egg.*
A gema do ôvo. *The yolk of the egg.*

oxalá *God grant; I hope so!*

P

pá f. *shovel, spade; blade (propeller).*
Pá de hélice. *Propeller blade.*

pacato adj. *quiet, peaceful.*

paciência f. *patience.*
Tenha paciência. *Be patient. Have patience.*
Estou perdendo (a perder) a paciência. *I'm losing my patience.*

paciente adj. *patient;* n. m. and f. *patient.*

pacífico adj. *peaceful; mild.*

PACOTE m. *package, bundle.*

pacto m. *pact, agreement.*

pactuar *to reach an agreement, to sign a pact.*

padaria f. *bakery.*

padecer *to suffer, to bear.*

padecimento m. *suffering.*

padeiro m. *baker.*

padrão m. *standard.*
Padrão de vida. *Standard of living.*

padrasto m. *stepfather.*

padre m. *priest, father.*
Padre-nosso. *Our Father, The Lord's Prayer.*
Padre Tomás. *Father Thomas.*

padrinho m. *godfather; best man; sponsor.*

paga f. *payment; pay, wages, fee.*

pagador m. *payer, paymaster, teller.*

pagamento m. *payment; pay.*
Pagamento adiantado. *Payment in advance.*
Dia de pagamento. *Payday.*
Pagamento a (em) prestações. *Payment in installments.*

pagão adj. *pagan;* n. m. *pagan.*

PAGAR *to pay, to pay for.*
Quanto lhe pagaram? *How much did they pay you?*
Pagar na mesma moeda. *To pay back in the same coin.*
Pagar uma visita. *To pay a visit.*
Pagar a prestações. *To pay in installments.*
Pagar caro. *To pay dear.*

PÁGINA f. *page (book).*
Em que página está? *On what page is it?*

pago adj. *paid;* m. *pay, wages.*

PAI m. *father; pl. parents.*
Tal pai, tal filho. *Like father, like son.*

pai-de-santo m. *voodoo priest; medicine mar* ⓑ.

painel m. *panel.*

pairar *to hover.*

país m. *country (nation).*

paisagem f. *landscape, view.*

paisano adj. *civilian;* m. *civilian; fellow countryman.*

paixão (x = sh) f. *passion.*

palácio m. *palace.*

paladar m. *palate; taste.*

PALAVRA f. *word; promise.*
Que quer dizer esta palavra? *What does this word mean?*
Êle (Ele) me tirou a palavra da bôca (boca). *He took the words right out of my mouth.*
Não falte à sua palavra. *Don't go back on your word.*
Peço a palavra. *May I have the floor?*
Êle me deu a sua palavra. *He gave me his word.*
Em poucas palavras. *In short. In a few words.*
Cumprir a palavra. *To keep one's word.*
Em tôda (toda) a extensão da palavra. *In the full sense of the word.*
Não dizer sequer uma palavra. *Not to say a word.*

palavrão m. *a curse word, an ugly word.*

palco m. *stage.*

palestino adj. *Palestinian;* n. m. *Palestinian.*

palestra f. *talk, conversation; address.*

PALETÓ n. *man's jacket, coat.*

palha f. *straw.*
Chapéu de palha. *Straw hat.*

palhaço m. *clown.*

pálido adj. *pale.*

palito m. *toothpick.*

palma f. *palm; pl. applause.*
Bater palmas. *To applaud. To clap hands.*

palmada f. *slap.*

palmeira f. *palm tree.*

palmo m. *span (of the hand).*

palpável adj. *palpable, evident.*

pálpebra f. *eyelid.*

palpitar *to beat, to throb, to palpitate.*

palrar *to chatter.*

paludismo m. *malaria.*

pampa f. *pampa, treeless plain.*

panamenho adj. *Panamanian;* n. m. *Panamanian.*

pança f. *paunch, belly.*

pancada f. *blow; drubbing.*

pandeireta f. *small tambourine.*

pandeiro m. *tambourine.*

pane f. *breakdown (due to motor).*

panela f. *pot, pan.*

panfleto m. *pamphlet.*

pânico adj. *panic;* n. m. *panic.*

PANO m. *cloth, material; curtain (theatre).*
Pano de mesa. *Tablecloth.*

panorama m. *panorama, landscape, view.*

panqueca f. *pancake.*

pantalha f. *lampshade; screen.*

pântano m. *swamp, marsh.*

panteísmo m. *pantheism.*

pantomima f. *pantomime.*

panturrilha (pantorrilha) f. *calf (of leg).*

PÃO m. *bread.*
Pão com manteiga. *Bread and butter.*
O pão nosso de cada dia. *Our daily bread.*

pãozinho m. *roll (bread).*

PAPA m. *Pope.*

PAPÁ m. *papa, daddy.*

papagaio m. *parrot; kite.*

PAPAI m. *papa, daddy.*

Papai Noel. *Santa Claus.*

PAPEL m. *paper; role.*
Preciso duma folha de papel. *I need a sheet of paper.*
Escreva-o neste papel. *Write it on this paper.*
Há papel de escrever na gaveta. *There's some writing paper in the drawer.*
Papel moeda. *Paper currency. Bills.*
Papel de sêda (seda). *Tissue paper.*
Papel carbono. *Carbon paper.*
Papel de embrulho. *Wrapping paper.*
Papel em branco. *Blank paper.*
Saco de papel. *Paper bag.*
Desempenhar um papel. *To play a role.*

papelão m. *cardboard.*

papelaria f. *stationery shop.*

paquête (paquete) m. *steamship.*

PAR adj. *equal; par; even (number);* n. m. *pair, couple; peer.*
O cruzeiro e o escudo estavam ao par. *The cruzeiro and the escudo were at par.*
Um par de luvas. *A pair of gloves.*
Números pares e ímpares. *Even and odd numbers.*
Ela é uma senhora sem par. *There's nobody like her.*

PARA *for, to, until, about, in order to, toward.*
Para quê? *What for? For what purpose?*
Para quem é isto? *For whom is this?*
Esta carta é para o senhor. *This letter is for you.*
Para que serve isto? *What's this for? What's this good for?*
Deixemos (x = sh) para amanhã. *Let's leave (it) for tomorrow.*
Ela tem talento para a música. *She has a gift for music.*
Vou agora para não chegar tarde. *I'm leaving now in order not to arrive late.*
Quando sai o trem (comboio) para a capital? *When does the train for the capital leave?*
Para sempre. *For ever.*
Para onde foram? *Where did they go?*
Para cá e para lá. *To and fro.*

parabéns m. pl. *congratulations.*

parábola f. *parable; parabola.*

pára-brisa m. *windshield.*

pára-choque m. *bumper (car).*

PARADA f. *stopping place; stop, halt; pause; parade; wager.*
Ponto de parada (paragem). *Stopping place.*
Parada de ônibus (Paragem de autocarro). *Bus stop.*
Cinco minutos de parada. *Five minutes' stop.*

paradeiro m. *stopping place.*

parado adj. *stopped, still.*

paradoxo (x = ks) m. *paradox.*

paraense adj. and n. m. and f. *of the state of Pará in Brasil.*

parafuso m. *screw.*
Chave de parafuso. *Screw driver.*

PARAGEM f. *stopping place; stop.*
Paragem de autocarro ⓟ (Parada de ônibus ⓑ). *Bus stop.*

parágrafo m. *paragraph.*

paraguaio adj. *Paraguayan;* n. m. *Paraguayan.*

paraibano adj. and n. m. *of the state of Paraíba in Brasil.*

paraíso m. *paradise.*

paralelo adj. and m. *parallel.*

paralisar *to paralyze.*

paralisia f. *paralysis.*

paralítico adj. and m. *paralytic.*

paranaense adj. and n. m. and f. *of the state of Paraná in Brasil.*

parapeito m. *parapet, rampart; windowsill.*

pára-quedas m. *parachute.*

pára-quedista m. *parachutist.*

PARAR *to stop, to halt, to stay; to bet.*
Por que paramos aqui? *Why do we stop here?*
Pare em frente da estação. *Stop in front of the station.*
(O) meu relógio parou. *My watch stopped.*
Quando vai parar de chover? *When is it going to stop raining?*
Em que hotel pararam? *At what hotel did you stay?*
Sem parar. *Continuously.*
pára-raios m. *lightning rod.*
parasita m. *and f. parasite.*
pára-sol m. *parasol.*
parceiro m. *partner.*
parcela f. *parcel, portion.*
parcelado adj. *divided.*
parcelar *to parcel out.*
parceria f. *partnership.*
parcial adj. *partial.*
parcialidade f. *partiality, bias.*
parco adj. *economical, thrifty.*
pardo adj. *brown, dark n. m. mulatto.*
PARECER *to appear, to seem, to look; m. opinion; appearance.*
Que lhe parece? *What do you think (of it)?*
Parece-me muito caro. *It seems too expensive to me.*
Ao que parece. *Apparently.*
Parece que vai chover. *It looks as if it's going to rain.*
Dê-me o seu parecer. *Give me your opinion.*
Eu também sou do mesmo parecer. *I'm also of the same opinion.*
Ela se parece muito com a tia. *She looks very much like her aunt.*
parecido adj. *similar, like.*
PAREDE f. *wall.*
As paredes têm ouvidos. *The walls have ears.*
Estar entre a espada e a parede. *To be between the devil and the deep blue sea.*
parelha f. *matching item, pair.*
parelho adj. *similar.*
PARENTE m. *relative, relation.*
Não tenho parentes nesta cidade. *I don't have any relatives in this city.*
parêntese m. *parenthesis.*
parêntesis m. *sing. and pl. parenthesis, parentheses.*
Parêntesis quadrado. *Bracket.*
parir *to give birth.*
parisiense adj. *and n. m. and f. of the city of Paris, Parisian.*
parlamento m. *parliament.*
paróquia f. *parish.*
paroquiano m. *parishioner.*
parque m. *park.*
Parque de diversões. *Amusement park.*
Parque infantil. *Playground.*
parreira f. *trellised grapevine.*
parreiral m. *grape arbor; arbor.*
PARTE f. *part, portion, share; side; role; party (dispute).*
Em que parte da cidade mora? *In what part of the city do you live?*
Cada um pagou a sua parte. *Each one paid his share.*
Trago isto da parte do senhor Nunes. *This is from Mr. Nunes.*
Cumprimente João da minha parte. *Give John my regards.*
Li a maior parte do livro. *I read most of the book.*
O senhor o viu (viu-o) em alguma parte? *Did you see him anywhere?*
Em nenhuma parte. *Nowhere.*
Em parte. *In part. Partly.*
Em grande parte. *Largely. In large part.*
Em tôda (toda) parte. *Everywhere.*

Dar parte. *To inform. To notify.*
Por tôda parte. *Everywhere.*
Por minha parte. *For my part. As far as I'm concerned.*
participação f. *participation; share; announcement.*
Participação de casamento. *Marriage announcement.*
participar *to participate, to take part; to share; to announce, to inform, to notify.*
Vocês participaram no jôgo (jogo)? *Did you take part in the game?*
Não poderemos participar da festa. *We won't be able to attend the reception.*
particípio m. *participle.*
Particípio passado. *Past participle.*
Particípio presente. *Present participle.*
particular adj. *particular, private; m. pl. particulars, details.*
Em particular. *In private, In particular.*
Escola particular. *Private school.*
particularidade f. *particularity, peculiarity.*
PARTIDA f. *departure; item, entry; game, match.*
Ponto de partida. *Starting point. Point of departure.*
Uma partida de xadrez (x = sh.). *A game of chess.*
Partida dobrada. *Double entry (account).*
partidário adj. *and n. m. partisan, follower, supporter.*
Ser partidário de. *To be in favor of.*
Máquina partidária. *Party machinery.*
PARTIDO adj. *divided, split, broken; n. m. party; advantage; side.*
Está partido! *It's broken!*
Que partido vamos tomar? *What course are we going to take?*
O Partido Democrático. *The Democratic party.*
O Partido Republicano. *The Republican party.*
O Partido Trabalhista. *The Labor party.*
PARTIR *to divide, to split; to leave; to cut; to break.*
O avião está para partir. *The plane is about to leave.*
Vamos partir na sexta. *We are going to leave on Friday.*
Preciso duma faca para partir o pão. *I need a knife to cut the bread.*
A partir de hoje. *From today on.*
parto m. *childbirth.*
parvo adj. *small, little; foolish.*
Páscoa f. *Easter; Passover.*
pasmar *to bewilder; to wonder.*
passa f. *raisin.*
passadiço m. *corridor, passageway.*
PASSADO adj. *past, done; n. m. past; past tense; pl. ancestors.*
O ano passado. *Last year.*
A semana passada. *Last week.*
Esqueçamos o passado. *Let's forget the past.*
Um bife bem passado. *A well-done steak.*
Mal passado. *Rare.*
passageiro adj. *passing, transitory; m. passenger; traveler.*
passagem f. *passage; fare.*
Passagem de ida e volta. *A round-trip ticket.*
Quanto custa a passagem? *What is the fare?*
passaporte m. *passport.*
PASSAR *to pass, to go by, to go across; to come over, to come in; to spend (time); to approve; to happen.*
Passe-me o sal, por favor. *Please pass the salt.*
Passe por aqui. *Come this way.*
Pode passar por meu escritório amanhã? *Can you drop by my office tomorrow?*
Êle (Ele) passa por brasileiro mas é ameri-

cano. *He passes for a Brasilian but he's an American.*
Os anos passam ràpidamente. *The years pass quickly.*
Passe bem. *Good-by.*
Passar por alto. *To overlook. To omit.*
Passar a ferro. *To iron. To press (clothes).*
Muitos dias êle (ele) passava fome. *Many days he would go hungry.*
Passar um telegrama. *To send a telegram.*
Como tem passado? *How have you been?*
pássaro m. *bird.*
Mais vale um pássaro na mão que dois voando (a voar). *A bird in the hand is worth two in the bush.*
passatempo m. *pastime, amusement.*
passe m. *pass, permit; free ticket.*
PASSEAR *to walk, to take a walk; to ride.*
PASSEIO m. *walk, stroll; ride; trip.*
Dar um passeio. *To go for a walk.*
passivo adj. *passive; n. m. liability.*
PASSO m. *step; pass; passageway; gait.*
Está a dois passos daqui. *It's only a few steps from here.*
Passo a passo. *Step by step.*
A cada passo. *At every step. Frequently.*
Ao passo que. *While. As.*
Quem vai dar o primeiro passo? *Who will take the first step?*
pasta f. *paste; briefcase.*
Pasta de dente(s). *Toothpaste.*
pastagem f. *pasture.*
pastel m. *pastry; pastel.*
pastelaria f. *pastry shop.*
pasteleiro m. *pastrycook.*
pastilha f. *lozenge, drop.*
pasto m. *pasture; food.*
pastor m. *shepherd; pastor.*
pata f. *paw; foot; goose; duck.*
Pata anterior. *Foreleg.*
Pata posterior. *Hind leg.*
Meter a pata. *To put one's foot in. To make a blunder.*
patente adj. *patent, obvious; f. patent; privilege.*
patife adj. *knavish; n. m. knave, rascal.*
patim m. *skate.*
Patins de rodas. *Roller skates.*
Patins de gêlo (gelo). *Ice skates.*
patinar *to skate.*
pátio m. *patio, courtyard, yard.*
pato m. *drake, gander.*
patranha f. *lie, fib.*
patrão m. *master; skipper; employer; boss; landlord.*
pátria f. *fatherland, native country.*
patriota m. *and f. patriot.*
patriotismo m. *patriotism.*
patrocinar *to patronise, to sponsor.*
patrono m. *patron, sponsor.*
patrulha f. *patrol.*
PAU adj. *boring; n. m. pole, stick, club; wood.*
Pau de bandeira. *Flagpole.*
A meio pau. *At half-mast.*
Êle (Ele) levou pau. *He failed (an examination)* Ⓑ.
paulista adj. *and m. and f., of the state of São Paulo in Brasil; Paulist.*
paulistano adj. *and n. m., of the city of São Paulo in Brasil.*
pausa f. *pause.*
pauta f. *guidelines; ruled lines.*
pavão m. *peacock.*
pavilhão m. *pavilion; tent; pennant; bell.*
pavimento m. *pavement.*
pavio m. *wick.*
Pavio de vela. *Candlewick.*
De fio a pavio. *From beginning to end.*

pavor m. fear, terror.

PAZ f. peace.
Por que não fazem as pazes? Why don't you make up? Why don't you bury the hatchet?
Em paz. In peace.
Deixe-me (x = sh) em paz! Leave me alone!

PÉ m. foot; footing; base; basis.
A pé. On foot.
Ao pé da colina. At the foot of the hill.
De (or em) pé. Standing. On foot.
Ao pé da letra. Literally.
Pôr-se em pé. To stand up.
Ficar de pé. To remain standing. To stand (including agreements, etc.).
Isso não tem pés nem cabeça. I can't make head or tail of that.
Êle (ele) se levantou (levantou-se) com o pé esquerdo. He got up on the wrong side of the bed.

peão m. pedestrian; peon; pawn (chess).

PEÇA f. piece, part; room; article; joke, trick; play (drama).
Peça por peça. Piece by piece.
Quantas peças (divisões) tem o apartamento? How many rooms does the apartment have?
A peça é em três atos (actos). The play has three acts.
Pregar uma peça. To play a trick or practical joke.

pecado m. sin.

pecar to sin, to err.

pecuário adj. of cattle; n. m. cattleman.

peculiar adj. peculiar, individual.

peculiaridade f. peculiarity.

PEDAÇO m. bit, piece; attractive woman (slang) (B).
Fazer em pedaços. To break into pieces.

pedagogo m. pedagogue, teacher.

pedal m. pedal.

pedestal m. pedestal, support.

pedestre adj. pedestrian; n. m. and f. pedestrian.

pedido adj. ordered; asked for; n. m. order, demand, request.
O pedido chegou ontem. The order arrived yesterday.
Fazer um pedido. To order (goods). To place an order.
A pedido de. At the request of.

PEDIR to ask for; to demand; to order (goods); to beg.
Ela me pediu que lhe fizesse um favor. She asked me to do her a favor.
Pedir licença. To ask permission.
Peço a palavra. May I have the floor?
Pedir informações. To inquire. To ask for information.
Pedir desculpas. To apologize.
Pedir emprestado. To borrow.

PEDRA f. stone, rock; blackboard; gem.
Pedras preciosas. Precious stones.
Duro como uma pedra. Hard as (a) stone.
Não deixar pedra sôbre (sobre) pedra. To leave no stone unturned.

pedreiro m. bricklayer; stonemason.

PEGAR to glue; to stick; to grasp, to take hold of; to catch.
Êle (ele) pegou na pasta e saiu. He took his brief case and left.
Ela já pegou no sono. She's already fallen asleep.
Pegar fogo. To catch fire.
Pegue e pague. Cash and carry.

PEITO m. chest; breast, bosom; heart, courage.
Não o tome a peito. Don't take it to heart.
Êle (ele) é um homem de peito. He is a courageous man.

PEIXE (x = sh) m. fish.

pelado adj. plucked, bare, bald; penniless.

pelar to peel, to skin; to rob; to grow bald.

pele f. skin; hide; fur.
Salvar a pele. To save one's skin.

peleja f. fight, struggle.

pelejar to fight, to struggle.

peleteria f. furrier's, fur shop.

película f. film.

PELO (contr. of por + o) for the, through the.
Pelo amor de Deus. For the love of God.
Pelo contrário. On the contrary.

pêlo m. fur, fuzz.
Montar em pêlo. To ride bareback.
Em pêlo. Naked.

pelota f. pellet; soccer ball.

pelotão m. platoon; group.

PENA f. feather; writing pen; penalty, punishment; grief, sorrow.
Desenho a bico de pena. Pen-and-ink drawing.
Pena de morte. Death sentence.
É (uma) pena! That's too bad!
Ter pena de. To feel sorry for.
Que pena! What a pity!
Não vale a pena. It's not worthwhile. It's not worth the trouble.

penal adj. penal.

penalidade f. penalty.

penalizar to distress, to pain.

pendão m. pennant, flag.

pendente adj. pendent, hanging; pending; n. m. pendant, earring.

pender to hang; to be pending.

pendurar to hang, to suspend; to pawn (B); to put on the cuff (B).

penetrador adj. penetrating, piercing.

penetrar to penetrate; to comprehend.

penha f. rock, cliff, bluff.

penhor m. pawn, pledge.
Dar em penhor. To pawn. To pledge.
Casa de penhôres (penhores). Pawnshop.

península f. peninsula.

penitência f. penitence; penance.

penitente adj. penitent; n. m. and f. penitent.

penoso adj. painful, distressing; arduous.

pensador adj. thinking; n. m. thinker.

pensamento m. thought, idea.

pensão f. pension; board; boardinghouse.

PENSAR to think; to consider; to intend.
Pense antes de falar. Think before you speak.
Sem pensar. Without thinking.
Ela está pensando (a pensar) nas férias. She's thinking about her vacation.
Pensamos estar no cinema às oito. We expect to be in the movie theatre at eight.

pensativo adj. pensive, thoughtful.

pensionista m. and f. pensioner, boarder.

PENTE m. comb.

penteado m. coiffure, hairdo, hairstyle.
Que penteado prefere? Which hairstyle do you prefer?

pentear to comb.

penúltimo adj. penultimate, last but one.

penúria f. penury, poverty.

pepino m. cucumber.

PEQUENO adj. little, small; n. m. child.
Êle (Ele) é muito pequeno. He's quite small.
Como estão os pequenos? How are the children?

PÊRA (PERA) f. pear; goatee.

peral m. pear orchard.

perante before, in the presence of.

percal m. percale.

perceber to perceive, to understand, to get.
Dar a perceber. To imply.
Percebemos o que queriam fazer. We understood what they wanted to do.

percentagem f. percentage.

percepção f. perception.

percha f. perch, pole.

percorrer to go through; to examine.

perda f. loss; damage; waste.
A perda foi grande. The loss was heavy. It was a great loss.
Perda total. Total loss.

perdão f. pardon.
Perdão! I'm sorry! Excuse me!

PERDER to lose; to spoil; to miss.
Perdi a caneta. I lost my pen.
Estamos perdendo (a perder) tempo. We're losing time. We're wasting time.
Perder de vista. To lose sight of.
Você perdeu uma boa oportunidade. You missed a good opportunity.
Perdemos a paciência. We lost patience. We lost our patience.
Êle (ele) perdeu o avião. He missed the plane.
Depressa! Não há tempo a perder. Hurry! There's no time to lose.
Perder a vez. To lose one's turn.

perdição f. perdition; ruin.

perdido adj. los.; ruined.

perdiz f. partridge.

PERDOAR to excuse, to pardon, to forgive.
Perdoe-me. Pardon me. Excuse me.
Perdoe a demora. Pardon the delay.

perdurar to last a long time; to endure.

perecer to perish, to die.
O menino pereceu de fome. The child died of hunger.

peregrino m. pilgrim.

perfeição f. perfection, excellence.

PERFEITO adj. perfect; excellent.
É um trabalho perfeito. It's a perfect piece of work.

perfídia f. perfidy, treachery.

perfil m. profile; outline.

perfumaria f. perfume shop.

perfume m. perfume; scent, fragrance.

perfurar to perforate, to penetrate.

PERGUNTA f. question.
Fazer perguntas. To ask questions.

PERGUNTAR to ask, to inquire.
Por que me pergunta isso? Why do you ask me that?
Ela lhe perguntou (perguntou-lhe) alguma coisa? Did she ask you something?
Quem perguntou por mim? Who asked for me?

perícia f. skill.

perigo m. danger, peril.
Não há perigo. There's no danger.

perigoso adj. dangerous.

periódico adj. periodic, periodical; n. m. periodical.

periodista m. and f. journalist, newspaper writer.

período m. period, span of time.

perito adj. expert, experienced, skillful; n. m. expert; appraiser.

permanecer to remain, to stay; to continue.
Quanto tempo vai permanecer fora da cidade? How long will you be out of town?

permanência f. permanence; stay.

PERMANENTE adj. permanent.

permeável adj. permeable.

PERMISSÃO f. permission; permit; authorization; consent.
Ter permissão. To have permission.

PERMITIR to permit, to let, to allow.
Permita-me. Allow me.
Permite que lhe faça uma pergunta? May I ask you a question?

permuta f. permutation; exchange; barter.

PERNA f. leg.

Estirar as pernas. *To stretch one's legs.*

pernambucano *adj. and n. m. of the state of Pernambuco in Brazil.*

pernicioso *adj. pernicious, injurious, harmful.*

pérola *f. pearl.*

perpendicular *adj. and n. f. perpendicular.*

perpetrar *to perpetrate.*

perpetuar *to perpetuate.*

perpetuidade *f. perpetuity.*

perpétuo *adj. perpetual, everlasting.*

perplexidade (x = ks) *f. perplexity, bewilderment.*

perplexo (x = ks) *adj. perplexed, bewildered, puzzled.*
Fico perplexo. *I'm puzzled.*

perro *adj. stubborn, stuck.*

persa *adj. Persian; n. m. and f. Persian.*

perscrutar *to scrutinize, to scan.*

perseguição *f. persecution; pursuit.*

perseguir *to persecute; to pursue; to harass.*

perseverança *f. perseverance.*

perseverar *to persevere, to persist.*

persignar-se *to cross oneself, to make the sign of the cross.*

persistencia *f. persistence.*

persistente *adj. persistent, firm.*

persistir *to persist.*

personagem *m. and f. personage; character (in book, play).*

personalidade *f. personality.*

perspetiva, perspectiva (perspectiva) *f. perspective.*

perspicácia *f. perspicacity.*

perspicaz *adj. perspicacious, acute.*

perspirar *to perspire.*

persuadir *to persuade, to convince.*

persuasão *f. persuasion.*

pertencer *to belong.*
Não me pertence. *It doesn't belong to me.*

pertinente *adj. pertinent.*

PERTO *near.*
Fica perto. *It's close. It's nearby.*
Fica perto da escola. *It's near the school.*

perturbar *to perturb, to disturb.*

peru *m. turkey.*

peruano *adj. Peruvian; n. m. Peruvian.*

perversão *f. perversion.*

perversidade *f. perversity.*

perverso *adj. perverse, wicked.*

perverter *to pervert.*

pesadelo *m. nightmare.*

pesado *adj. heavy; tedious, tiresome.*
O ferro é pesado. *Iron is heavy.*
É um trabalho pesado. *It's hard work.*

pêsames *m. pl. condolences.*

PESAR *to weigh; to cause regret or sorrow; n. m. grief, sorrow; regret.*
Quanto pesa a caixa (x = sh)? *How much does the box weigh?*
Pesar as palavras. *To weigh one's words.*
É com grande pesar que lhe escrevo. *It is with great sorrow that I write you.*

pesca *f. fishing; catch.*

pescado *m. catch of fish; fish.*

pescar *to fish; to catch.*
Pescar em águas turvas. *To fish in troubled waters.*

pescaria *f. fishing.*

pescoço *m. neck.*

pêso (peso) *m. weight; burden; importance; peso (money).*
Pêso líquido. *Net weight.*
Pêso bruto. *Gross weight.*
Pêso pesado. *Heavyweight (boxing).*

pesquisa *f. research, investigation.*

pêssego *m. peach.*

pessimismo *m. pessimism.*

pessimista *adj. pessimistic; n. m. and f. pessimist.*

péssimo *adj. very bad, terrible.*

PESSOA *f. person.*
Ela é muito boa pessoa. *She's a very nice person. She's a wonderful person.*
Pessoa de bem. *Fine person.*
Ela apareceu em pessoa. *She was there in person.*

pessoal *adj. personal, private; n. m. personnel.*

pestana *f. eyelash; fringe, edging. .*
Queimar as pestanas. *To burn the midnight oil.*

peste *f. plague, pestilence; pest.*

petição *f. petition; claim.*

petróleo *m. petroleum.*

pia *f. washbasin; sink; font.*
Pia da cozinha. *Kitchen sink.*

piada *f. joke, wisecrack.*

pianista *m. and f. pianist.*

piano *m. piano.*

piar *to chirp.*

picada *f. sting; prick; dive (airplane).*

picante *adj. hot, highly seasoned; sharp; caustic; n. m. appetizer.*

pica-pau *m. woodpecker.*

picar *to bite, to sting; to prick; to itch; to chop; to nibble; to spur; to be hot (pepper, etc.); to dive (airplane).*
Picou-me uma abelha. *A bee stung me.*
Picar carne. *To chop (up) meat.*

pícaro *adj. crafty, roguish.*

pico *m. peak, summit; spine; thorn; sting; a bit.*
Subiram ao pico mais alto. *They climbed to the highest peak.*
Ficaram lá um mês e pico. *They stayed there a little more than a month.*

piedade *f. piety; pity; mercy.*

pigarrear *to clear the throat.*

pigarro *m. a frog in the throat.*

pijama *m. and f. pajama.*

pilar *m. pillar, column, post.*

pilha *f. pile, heap; robbery; battery.*
Pilha sêca (seca). *Dry battery.*

pilhéria *f. joke, gag.*

pilôto (piloto) *m. pilot.*
Pilôto de provas. *Test pilot.*

pílula *f. pill.*

pimenta *f. pepper.*

pincel *m. brush.*

pindorama *m. country of palms* Ⓑ

pingar *to drip, to leak.*

pingue-pongue *m. Ping-Pong.*

pinha *f. pinecone; sweetsop, sugar apple* Ⓑ

pinheiro *m. pine tree.*

pinho *m. pine (wood).*

pino *m. peg; pin; apex.*
Pino mestre. *Kingpin.*
No pino de. *At the peak of.*

pinta *f. spot; mole, beauty mark.*

pintado *adj. painted; spotted, speckled, freckled.*

pintar *to paint; to describe.*
Que está pintando (a pintar)? *What are you painting?*
Pintar a óleo. *To paint in oil.*
Pintar o sete. *To raise the devil.*

pintor *m. painter.*

pintura *f. painting.*
Pintura a óleo. *Oil painting.*

pio *adj. pious; n. m. peep, chirp.*

piolho *m. louse.*

pioneiro *m. pioneer.*

PIOR *adj. and adv. worse, worst.*
Êle (ele) está pior. *He's worse.*
Isso é o pior. *That's the worst of it.*
Ainda pior. *Worse yet.*
A situação vai de mal a pior. *The situation is going from bad to worse.*
Cada vez pior. *Worse and worse.*

piorar *to worsen.*

piquenique *m. picnic.*

pirâmide *f. pyramid.*

pirata *m. pirate.*

pires *m. sing. and pl. saucer, saucers.*

pisada *f. footstep; footprint.*

pisar *to tread, to step on; to press; to walk.*

piscar *to wink, to blink.*
Êle (ele) piscou para ela. *He winked at her.*

piscina *f. swimming pool.*

piso *m. floor, ground; tread; gait.*

pista *f. track; landing strip; trail, clue.*
Seguir a pista. *To follow the trail.*
Pista de corridas. *Race track.*

pistão *m. piston; cornet.*

pistola *f. pistol, gun.*

pitoresco *adj. picturesque.*

placa *f. plate; plaque; badge.*
Placa de licença. *License plate.*

placar *to placate, to appease; n. m. placard, poster; badge.*

plaina *f. carpenter's plane.*

plana *f. category, class.*

planalto *m. plateau.*

planejar *to plan.*

planêta (planeta) *m. planet.*

planície *f. plain.*

plano *adj. smooth, even; n. m. plane; plan.*
Primeiro plano. *Foreground.*
Último plano. *Background.*
Geometria plana. *Plane geometry.*

planta *f. plant; plan.*
Planta anual. *Annual plant.*

plantação *f. plantation; planting.*

plantar *to plant; to drive in the ground.*
Vamos plantar algumas árvores perto da casa. *We're going to plant some trees near the house.*

plástica *f. plastic art; plastic surgery.*

plástico *adj. plastic; n. m. plastic.*

plataforma *f. platform.*

plátano *m. plane tree; sycamore.*

platéia (plateia) *f. orchestra section (theatre); audience.*

platina *f. platinum.*

platino *adj. of the River Plate region.*

pleito *m. lawsuit; dispute.*

PLENO *adj. full, complete.*
Plenos poderes. *Full powers.*
Em pleno dia. *In broad daylight.*

pluma *f. feather, plume; pen.*

plural *adj. plural; n. m. plural.*

pneu *m. short form of* **pneumático.**

pneumático *adj. pneumatic; n. m. rubber tire.*

pó *m. dust; powder.*
Pó de arroz. *Face powder.*

POBRE *adj. poor; n. m. and f. poor person; beggar.*
Êle (ele) é muito pobre. *He is very poor.*
Pobre homem! *Poor man! Poor fellow!*

pobreza *f. poverty, need.*

poço *m. well, pit.*
Poço de petróleo. *Oil well.*

podar *to prune.*

PODER *to be able; can; may; n. m. power; authority; command.*
Em que posso servi-lo? *What can I do for you?*

Não posso ir. *I can't go.*
Não pode ser! *That can't be! That's impossible.*
Eu fiz o melhor que pude. *I did the best I could.*
Quem tem o poder nesse país? *Who has the power in that country?*
Poder executivo. *Executive power.*
Plenos poderes. *Full powers.*
Não posso com êles (eles). *I can't do anything with them.*
Posso entrar? Pode. *May I come in? You may.*

poderoso *adj. mighty, powerful.*
podre *adj. rotten; corrupt.*
podridão *f. rottenness; corruption.*
poeira *f. dust.*
poema *m. poem.*
poesia *f. poetry.*
poeta *m. poet.*
POIS *as, since; so; well; then; why; now; indeed.*
Pois faça-o. *Then do it.*
Pois vamos. *Then let's go.*
Pois bem. *Well then.*
Pois é. *That's it. Of course.*
Pois não! *Of course! Certainly!*
polaco *adj. Polish; n. m. Pole.*
polar *adj. polar.*
Estrêla (estrela) polar. *North Star.*
polca *f. polka.*
polcar *to dance the polka.*
polegada *f. inch.*
polegar *m. thumb; big toe.*
poleiro *m. perch; top gallery of theatre* Ⓑ.
polêmica (polémica) *f. polemics; controversy.*
polêmico (polémico) *adj. polemic, polemical.*
polícia *f. police force; m. policeman.*
Polícia Militar. *Military police.*
policial *adj. police; n. m. policeman, officer.*
Romance policial. *Detective story.*
polido *adj. polished, bright.*
polígamo *adj. polygamous; n. m. polygamist.*
polimento *m. polishing; polish.*
poliomielite *f. poliomyelitis.*
polir *to polish.*
política *f. politics; political science; policy.*
A Política de Boa Vizinhança. *The Good Neighbor Policy.*
político *adj. political; n. m. politician.*
Ter influência política. *To have good political connections.*
Economia política. *Political economy.*
pólo *pole; polo.*
polonês *adj. Polish; n. m. Polish.*
poltrona *f. easy chair; orchestra seat.*
pólvora *f. powder, gunpowder.*
pomada *f. pomade.*
pomar *m. orchard.*
pombo *m. pigeon, dove.*
Pombo de barro. *Clay pigeon.*
pômulo (pómulo) *m. cheek.*
ponche *m. punch (drink).*
ponderação *f. consideration, reflection.*
ponderar *to ponder, to weigh.*
PONTA *f. point; tip.*
Ter na ponta da língua. *To have on the tip of the tongue.*
Nas pontas dos pés. *On tiptoe.*
pontapé *m. kick.*
pontaria *f. aim, aiming.*
ponte *f. bridge.*
Ponte suspensa. *Suspension bridge.*
Ponte levadiça. *Drawbridge.*
ponteiro *m. pointer; hand (clock).*
pontiagudo *adj. pointed, sharp.*

PONTO *m. point; dot; period; place; stitch; prompter.*
Ponto de partida. *Starting point. Point of departure.*
Ponto final. *Period.*
Ponto e vírgula. *Semicolon.*
Dois pontos. *Colon.*
Ponto por ponto. *Point by point.*
Estarei lá às sete horas em ponto. *I'll be there at seven o'clock sharp.*
Ponto cardeal. *Cardinal point.*
Ponto culminante. *Climax.*
Ponto fraco. *Weakness. Weak point.*
Estávamos a ponto de sair quando chegaram. *We were about to leave when they arrived.*
Até certo ponto é verdade. *To a certain extent it is true.*
pontual *adj. punctual.*
pôpa (popa) *f. stern.*
À pôpa. *Aft.*
De proa à pôpa. *From stem to stern.*
popular *adj. popular.*
É uma canção popular. *It's a popular song.*
popularidade *f. popularity.*
pôquer Ⓑ *m. poker.*
POR *for; by; through; about.*
Por correio aéreo. *By airmail.*
Ganharam por dois pontos. *They won by two points.*
Dom Casmurro foi escrito por Machado de Assis. *Dom Casmurro was written by Machado de Assis.*
Entrem pela porta principal. *Enter through the main door.*
Pode pasar pela casa? *Can you pass by the house?*
Por mês. *By the month.*
Por muito tempo. *For a long time.*
Pela manhã. *In the morning.*
Pela tarde. *In the afternoon.*
Pela noite. *In the evening.*
Por agora. *For the present.*
Por dentro. *On the inside.*
Por fora. *On the outside.*
Por conseguinte. *Consequently.*
Por fim. *Finally.*
Por quê? *Why?*
Por tôda (toda) parte. *Everywhere.*
Por Deus! *Heavens! For heaven's sake!*
Por outro lado. *On the other hand.*
Por exemplo (x = z). *For example.*
Por volta (de). *Around. About.*
Por pouco. *Almost. Nearly.*
Por meio de. *By means of.*
Por atacado. *Wholesale.*
Por aqui. *This way.*
Por acaso. *By chance.*
Por favor. *Please.*
Eu não votei por êle (ele). *I didn't vote for him.*
PÔR *to put; to set (table); to put on; to lay (eggs).*
Ponha o livro na mesa. *Put the book on the table.*
Pôr a mesa. *To set the table.*
Pôr ovos. *To lay eggs.*
Pôr à prova. *To put to the test.*
Pôr em execução (x = z). *To carry out. To execute.*
Pôr em dúvida. *To doubt. To question.*
Pôr mãos à obra. *To get to work.*
Pôr em liberdade. *To free.*
Pôr uma gravata. *To put on a tie.*
Pôr por escrito. *To put in writing.*
Pôr os pontos nos ii. *To dot the i's and cross the t's.*
Pôr mel em bôca (boca) de asno. *To cast pearls before swine.*
O homem põe e Deus dispõe. *Man proposes and God disposes.*
pôr-se *to start, to begin, to get.*
Pôr-se a falar. *To begin to speak.*
Pôr-se de joelhos. *To get on one's knees.*

porão *m. hold (ship), basement* Ⓑ.
porca *f. sow; nut (for bolt).*
porção *f. portion, part, share; many, much* Ⓑ.
Dividir em porções. *To divide. To share.*
porcelana *f. porcelain; chinaware.*
porco *adj. dirty, filthy; n. m. pig, pork.*
porém *however, but, nevertheless.*
porfia *f. insistence, obstinacy.*
porfiado *adj. stubborn, obstinate.*
porfiar *to persist.*
pormenor *m. detail.*
PORQUE *because, on account of, for, as, since.*
Ela não veio porque estava ocupada. *She didn't come because she was busy.*
Porque era tarde ficamos em casa. *Since it was late we stayed home.*
porquê *m. reason, the why, why.*
Não sei porquê. *I don't know why.*
porqueiro *m. swineherd.*
PORTA *f. door, doorway; gate.*
Abra a porta. *Open the door.*
Feche a porta. *Close the door.*
Feche a porta à chave quando sair. *Lock the door when you leave.*
Porta principal. *Main entrance. Main door.*
Porta giratória. *Revolving door.*
porta-aviões *m. aircraft carrier.*
portador *m. bearer, carrier; porter, messenger.*
portal *m. portal, doorway.*
portão *m. large door, gate.*
portar *to carry; to reach a port; to arrive.*
portar-se *to behave.*
Portar-se mal. *To behave badly.*
portaria *f. reception desk.*
portátil *adj. portable.*
Máquina de escrever portátil. *Portable typewriter.*
porte *m. transportation; freight cost; deportment; postage.*
Quanto é o porte? *How much is the postage?*
Porte pago. *Postpaid.*
porteiro *m. doorman; janitor.*
portenho *adj. and n. m. of the city of Buenos Aires.*
portento *m. wonder, portent, prodigy.*
portentoso *adj. prodigious, marvelous.*
pôrto (porto) *m. port, harbor; port (wine).*
Pôrto de escala. *Port of call.*
portuense *adj. and n. m. of the city of Pôrto (Porto) in Portugal.*
PORTUGUÊS *adj. Portuguese; n. m. Portuguese.*
Eu falo português. *I speak Portuguese.*
Uma gramática de português. *A Portuguese grammar.*
Êle (Ele) é português mas ela não é portuguêsa (portuguesa). *He is Portuguese but she is not Portuguese.*
porvir *m. future.*
pós-guerra *m. and f. period after a war.*
POSIÇÃO *f. position, place, situation.*
Posição firme. *A firm stand. A firm position.*
positivo *adj. positive, sure, certain.*
posse *f. possession; pl. possessions; wealth.*
Homem de (grandes) posses. *A man of wealth.*
possessão *f. possession.*
possibilidade *f. possibility.*
POSSÍVEL *adj. possible.*
Não será possível fazê-lo. *It won't be possible to do it.*
Farei quanto me fôr (for) possível. *I'll do as much as I can.*
O mais cedo possível. *As soon as possible.*
possuir *to possess, to have.*
posta *f. slice; post, mail.*
Posta-restante. *General delivery.*

postal adj. postal; n. m. postal card, postcard.
Cartão postal. (Bilhete postal). Postcard.

posteridade f. posterity.

posterior adj. posterior, rear, back.

PÔSTO (POSTO) adj. put, placed; set (table, sun); n. m. place, post, station.
Pôsto de gasolina. A filling station.
Pôsto militar. Military post.
Pôsto naval. Naval station.
Pôsto policial (esquadra). Police station.

póstumo adj. posthumous.

postura f. posture, position.

potável adj. potable.

potência f. power, strength, force.
As grandes potências. The Great Powers.

potentado m. potentate, ruler.

potente adj. potent, powerful, mighty.

potro m. colt.

POUCO adj. and adv. little; small; scanty; n. m. a little, a small part; pl. a few.
Quer um pouco de café? Would you like some coffee?
Ela sabe um pouco de tudo. She knows a little about everything.
Fica-me muito pouco dinheiro. I have very little money left.
Êle (ele) chegará dentro de pouco (tempo). He'll be here shortly.
Poucas vêzes (vezes). A few times.
Gosto um pouco. I like it a bit.
Aos poucos. Little by little.
Acho um pouco caro. I think it's rather (a little) expensive.
Há pouco. A short while ago.
Tenho uns poucos. I have a few.

poupar to save, to economise.
Vou poupar o meu dinheiro. I'm going to save my money.

pousar to set down; to put; to stay, to lodge.

POVO m. people; public.
O povo português. The Portuguese people.

povoação f. population; town.

povoar to populate; to stock.

PRAÇA f. plaza, square; market; enlisted man.
Vamos dar uma volta pela praça. Let's take a stroll around the square.
Carro de praça. Taxi.

prado m. meadow, pasture, field.

praga f. plague; curse.

praia f. beach, shore.

pranto m. weeping, crying.

prata f. silver; silverware.

prateleira f. shelf.

prática f. practice; exercise; talk.
A prática faz o mestre. Practice makes perfect.

praticante adj. practicing; n. m. practitioner; apprentice.

praticar to practice; to do.

prático adj. practical; skilled; experienced worker; n. m. harbor pilot.

PRATO m. dish, plate; course (meal).
Êste (este) prato é gostoso. This dish is delicious.
Qual é o prato do dia? What's today's special?
Prato fundo. Soup plate.
Prato raso. Dinner plate.
Do prato à bôca (boca) se perde a sopa. There's many a slip between the cup and the lip.

praxe (x = sh) f. custom, habit.
De praxe. Usual. Customary.

PRAZER f. pleasure; m. pleasure, enjoyment.
Tenho muito prazer em conhecê-lo. I am very glad to know you.
O prazer é todo meu. The pleasure is all mine.

Foi um prazer vê-lo de nôvo (novo). It was a pleasure to see you again.

prazo m. term; period of time.
Comprar a prazo. To buy on time. To buy on the installment plan.
Prazo de entrega. Time of delivery.

preâmbulo m. preamble, introduction.
É um preâmbulo interessante. It's an interesting preface.
Deixe (x = sh) de preâmbulos e diga o que quer. Stop beating around the bush and tell me what you want.

precário adj. precarious.

precaução f. precaution.

precaver to forewarn, to caution.

precedência f. precedence.

precedente adj. preceding; n. m. precedent.

preceder to precede.

preceito m. precept, rule.

preciosidade f. preciousness; precious or beautiful thing.

precioso adj. precious, dear.
Pedras preciosas. Precious stones.

precipício m. precipice.

precipitação f. precipitation.

precipitado adj. precipitate, hasty.

precipitar to precipitate; to hurry; to rush on.

precisão f. precision, accuracy; necessity.
Instrumento de precisão. Precision instrument.

PRECISAR to need; to specify.
Preciso duma dúzia. I need a dozen.
Precisamos (de) estudar mais. We must study more.

PRECISO adj. necessary; exact.
É preciso pagar hoje. It is necessary to pay today.
É preciso que cheguemos antes das seis. It is necessary that we arrive before six.
Não é preciso. It's not necessary.

PREÇO m. price; value.
Por que preço? At what price?
Preço fixo. Fixed price.
Preço de fábrica. At cost.
A qualquer preço. At any price.
Preço de ocasião. Bargain price.
Preço de varejo. Retail price.
Abaixar (x = sh) o preço. To lower the price.

preconceito m. prejudice.
Preconceito de raça. Race prejudice.

predição f. prediction.

predicar to preach.

predileção f. predilection, preference.
Ter predileção por. To have a fondness for. To have a preference for.

prédio m. building, house; land.
É um prédio de dois andares. It's a building with two floors.

predisposto adj. predisposed, inclined.

predizer to predict, to foretell.

predominar to predominate, to prevail.

preencher to fill (out).
Faça o favor de preencher êste (este) formulário. Please fill out this blank form.
Preencher uma vaga. To fill a vacancy.

prefácio m. preface, introduction.

prefeito (administrador do concelho) m. mayor, administrator.

prefeitura (câmara municipal) f. city hall.

preferência f. preference, choice.
De preferência. Preferably.
Ter preferência. To have preference. To have priority.

preferente adj. preferable, preferring.

PREFERIR to prefer.
Qual prefere? Which do you prefer?
Prefiro êste (este). I prefer this one.

preferível adj. preferable.

É preferível ir pessoalmente. It's better to go in person.

prefixo (x = ks) m. prefix.

prega f. crease, fold.

pregar to nail; to fasten; to stick; to preach.
Pregar um prego. To drive a nail in.
Pregar uma peça. To play a trick.
Não preguei os olhos. I didn't sleep a wink.

prego m. nail.

preguiça f. laziness.

preguiçoso adj. lazy.
O João é muito preguiçoso. John is very lazy.

pré-histórico adj. prehistoric.

prejuízo m. harm, damage; loss.

preliminar adj. preliminary.

prelo m. printing press.

prelúdio m. prelude.

prematuro adj. premature.

premeditação f. premeditation.

premeditar to premeditate.

premiar to reward.

PRÊMIO (PRÉMIO) m. prize, reward; premium.
Ela ganhou o prêmio. She won the prize.

prenda f. gift, present; talent.

prendar to present with.

prendedor m. clasp; fastener; arrester.
Prendedor de gravata. Tie clip.

PRENDER to fasten; to catch; to arrest.
Quem prendeu o ladrão? Who arrested (caught) the thief?

prenhe adj. pregnant.

prensa f. printing press; press.
Prensa hidráulica. Hydraulic press.

preocupação f. preoccupation, concern, worry.

preocupar to preoccupy, to concern.
Êles (eles) estão muito preocupados. They are quite concerned.

preparação f. preparation.

preparado adj. prepared; preparation (medicinal).

PREPARAR to prepare, to get ready.
Primeiro temos que preparar a lição. First we have to prepare the lesson.

preparativo adj. preparative; n. m. pl. preparations.
Estamos fazendo (a fazer) os preparativos para a viagem. We're making preparations for the trip.

preparatório adj. preparatory.

preponderância f. preponderance.

preponderar to prevail.

preposição f. preposition.

prêsa (presa) f. prey, capture; dam; prisoner; fang; claw.

prescindir to do without, to dispense with.

prescrever to prescribe.

presença f. presence.
Presença de espírito. Presence of mind.

presenciar to be present; to witness, to see.
Acabamos de presenciar... We've just witnessed...

PRESENTE adj. present; n. m. gift, present; present time; present tense.
Presente! Present! Here!
Presente de aniversário. Birthday gift.
A presente serve para dizer-lhe... (in a letter) This is to inform you...

presépio m. stable; crèche, Nativity scene.

preservação f. preservation.

preservar to preserve; to maintain; to keep.

presidência f. presidency.

presidente m. president; chairman.

presidiário m. convict.

presídio m. penitentiary, prison.

presidir to preside, to direct.

prêso (preso) adj. imprisoned, arrested; n. m. prisoner, convict.
 Prêso em flagrante. Caught in the act.
 Êle (ele) foi prêso como cúmplice. He was arrested as an accomplice.
PRESSA f. haste, speed, hurry.
 Estou com pressa. (Tenho pressa). I'm in a hurry.
 Sem pressa. Leisurely.
 Por que tanta pressa? Why such a hurry?
pressagiar to predict, to foretell.
presságio m. prediction; omen.
pressentimento m. presentiment.
prestar to lend; to aid; to pay (attention).
 Prestar atenção. To pay attention.
 Você me prestou um bom serviço. You rendered me a great service.
 Não presta para nada. It's not good for anything.
prestes adj. ready.
presteza f. quickness, speed, promptness.
prestígio m. prestige.
prestigioso adj. famous; influential.
presumido adj. vain, conceited; n. m. conceited person.
 Ela é muito presumida. She's very conceited.
presumir to presume, to assume; to be conceited.
presunção f. presumption; conceit.
presunto m. ham.
pretendente adj. pretending; n. m. and f. pretender, candidate; n. m. suitor.
pretender to pretend; to intend.
 Pretendemos visitar o Brasil. We intend to visit Brasil.
pretensão f. pretension.
pretensioso adj. pretentious; n. m. pretentious person.
pretexto m. pretext.
PRÊTO (PRETO) adj. black; dark; difficult; n. m. Negro.
 Vestir de prêto. To wear black.
prevalecer to prevail.
prevenção f. prevention; prejudice.
prevenir to prevent; to warn.
 Estamos prevenidos. We're ready. We've been warned.
 Um homem prevenido vale por dois. Forewarned is forearmed.
prever to foresee; to anticipate.
 Êle (Ele) previu essa dificuldade. He expected (foresaw) that difficulty.
prévio adj. previous, prior.
 Aviso prévio. Previous notice.
 Questão prévia. Previous question (parliamentary procedure).
previsão f. foresight, prevision.
previsto adj. foreseen, expected.
prezado adj. dear, esteemed.
 Prezado Senhor: Dear Sir:
primário adj. primary.
 Escola primária. Elementary school. Primary school.
PRIMAVERA f. spring (season).
PRIMEIRO adj. and n. m. first; foremost.
 Traga-nos primeiro a sopa. Bring us the soup first.
 Bilhete de primeira. First-class ticket.
 Êles (eles) moram na primeira casa. They live in the first house.
 De primeira ordem. First-rate.
 A primeira vez. The first time.
 O primeiro do mês. The first of the month.
 Primeiro andar. First floor.
 Em primeiro lugar. In the first place.
 Primeiro ministro. Prime minister.
 Primeiro prêmio (prémio). First prize.
 Primeiros socorros. First aid.
 O romance está escrito na primeira pessoa.

 The novel is written in the first person.
 Primeiro plano. Foreground.
primitivo adj. primitive.
primo adj. prime; n. m. cousin.
 Número primo. Prime number.
 Obra prima. Masterpiece.
 Ela é prima de João. She is John's cousin.
primor m. beauty; excellence.
princesa f. princess.
PRINCIPAL adj. principal, main, chief; n. m. principal.
 Quem tem o papel principal? Who has the main role?
 O principal é acabar êste (este) trabalho antes da sexta. The main thing (most important) is to finish this work before Friday.
príncipe m. prince.
principiante adj. beginning; n. m. and f. beginner.
PRINCÍPIO m. beginning, origin; principle.
 No princípio parecia-me fácil. It seemed easy to me at first.
 Pagam no princípio do mês. They pay the first part of the month.
 Em princípio não me parece má idéia (ideia). In principle it doesn't seem to be a bad idea.
prioridade f. priority.
prisão f. imprisonment; prison.
prisioneiro m. prisoner.
privação f. privation, want.
privada f. toilet.
privado adj. private, confidential.
 Vida privada. Private life.
privar to deprive.
privilegiado adj. privileged.
privilégio m. privilege.
pró m. pro; argument for.
 Os prós e os contras. The pros and cons.
 Em pró de. In favor of.
proa f. bow (ship).
probabilidade f. probability.
PROBLEMA m. problem.
procaz adj. insolent, impudent, bold.
procedência f. origin, source; validity.
procedente adj. coming or proceeding from; logical.
proceder to proceed; to act, to behave; m. behavior, conduct.
 Êle (ele) procedeu corretamente (correctamente). He acted properly.
 Proceda com muito cuidado. Proceed very carefully.
procedimento m. procedure; method.
processar to sue; to indict.
processo m. process, procedure; lawsuit.
proclamação f. proclamation.
proclamar to proclaim; to promulgate.
 Nesse mesmo dia proclamaram a paz. Peace was declared on that very day.
procriar to procreate.
procura f. search; demand.
 Oferta e procura. Supply and demand.
 Ela está à procura duma boa gramática de português. She is looking for a good Portuguese grammar.
PROCURAR to look for, to seek; to try.
 Estou procurando (a procurar) o chapéu. I'm looking for my hat.
 Procure estar na esquina às nove. Try to be on the corner at nine.
prodígio m. wonder, marvel.
prodigioso adj. prodigious, marvelous.
produção f. production, output.
produtivo adj. productive.
produto m. product, yield.

 Produtos alimentícios. Foodstuffs. Food products. Food.
PRODUZIR to produce, to turn out; to bear; to yield.
 Essa fábrica produz automóveis. That factory produces (turns out) automobiles.
proeza f. prowess; accomplishment.
profanação f. profanation.
profanar to profane.
profano adj. profane, irreverent; worldly.
profecia f. prophecy.
proferir to utter, to say.
 Êle (ele) proferiu um discurso. He delivered an address.
professar to profess, to declare openly; to teach.
professor m. professor, teacher.
 Professor particular. Private tutor.
profeta m. prophet.
profético adj. prophetic.
profissão f. profession; declaration.
 Seu nome e profissão, por favor. Your name and profession, please.
profissional adj. professional.
profundidade f. profundity, depth.
 200 metros de profundidade. 200 meters deep.
PROFUNDO adj. profound, deep; intense.
 Silêncio profundo. Deep silence.
 O poço é muito profundo. The well is very deep.
prognosticar to prognosticate, to forecast.
prognóstico adj. prognostic; n. m. prognostication, forecast.
PROGRAMA m. program; plan.
 O program não foi muito bom. The program was not very good.
progredir to progress, to advance.
progresso m. progress.
 Ordem e progresso. Order and progress.
proibição f. prohibition.
proibido adj. prohibited, forbidden.
 É proibido fumar. No smoking.
 É proibida a entrada. No admittance.
PROIBIR to prohibit, to forbid.
 Proibo-lhe fazer isso. I forbid you to do that.
projetado (projectado) adj. projected, planned.
projetar (projectar) to project, to plan.
projetil, projétil (projéctil) m. projectile, missile.
projeto (projecto) m. project, plan.
proletariado m. proletariat.
proletário adj. proletarian.
prólogo m. prologue.
prolongação f. prolongation, extension.
prolongar to prolong, to extend.
promessa f. promise.
PROMETER to promise.
 Mas você prometeu fazê-lo. But you promised to do it.
 Êle (Ele) nunca cumpre o que promete. He never does what he promises.
prometido adj. promised; m. promise; fiancê.
 Cumprir o prometido. To keep a promise.
promoção f. promotion.
promover to promote, to advance.
promulgar to promulgate, to publish.
pronome m. pronoun.
prontidão f. promptness; swiftness.
PRONTO adj. ready, prepared.
 Estamos prontos. We are ready.
prontuário m. handbook.
pronúncia f. pronunciation.
 Ela tem uma boa pronúncia. She has a good pronunciation. Her pronunciation is good.
pronunciar to pronounce; to utter; to give (a speech).

A senhora pronuncia muito bem o português. *You pronounce Portuguese very well.* Pronunciar (uma) sentença. *To pronounce sentence.*

propagação *f. propagation, dissemination.*

propaganda *f. propaganda.*

propagandista *m. and f. propagandist.*

propagar *to propagate; to spread (news, etc.).*

propender *to tend, to incline to.*

propensão *f. propensity, tendency.*

propenso *adj. inclined, disposed.*

propício *adj. propitious, favorable.* Um momento propício. *A favorable moment.*

proponente *adj. proponent; n. m. and f. proponent.*

propor *to propose; to suggest.* Proponho ir vê-lo. *I intend to go to see him.* O homem propõe, Deus dispõe. *Man proposes, God disposes.*

proporção *f. proportion.*

proporcionar *to provide, to supply; to proportion, to adjust.*

proposição *f. proposition, proposal.*

propósito *m. purpose, intention.* Fizemos isso de propósito. *We did it on purpose.* A propósito. *By the way.* A propósito de. *Regarding. With regard to.*

proposta *f. proposal, proposition.*

proposto *adj. proposed.*

propriedade *f. property; ownership; propriety.* Acabo de comprar essa propriedade. *I've just bought that property.* Propriedade literária. *Copyright.*

proprietário *m. proprietor, owner, landlord.*

PRÓPRIO *adj. own; proper, fit, suitable.* Essas foram suas próprias palavras. *Those were his very words.* Êsse (esse) é um jôgo (jogo) próprio de meninos. *That's a game (suitable) for children.*

prorrogação *f. prorogation, extension.*

prorrogar *to extend (time), to prolong.*

prorromper *to break out, to burst out.*

prosa *f. prose; chatter, idle talk* Ⓑ.

prosaico *adj. prosaic.*

prosista *m. and f. prose writer; chatterer* Ⓑ.

prosperar *to prosper, to thrive; to be successful.*

prosperidade *f. prosperity.*

próspero *adj. prosperous; successful.* Próspero ano novo! *Prosperous New Year!*

prospeto (prospecto) *m. prospectus; prospect.*

prosseguir *to pursue, to carry on, to go on, to continue, to proceed.* Prossiga! *Continue!*

prostrar *to prostrate.*

protagonista *m. and f. protagonist.*

proteção (protecção) *f. protection; support.*

proteger *to protect; to support.*

protestante *adj. protesting, protestant; n. m. and f. protestor; Protestant.*

protestar *to protest.*

protesto *m. protest, objection; expression.* Sob protesto. *Under protest.* Com os protestos de minha alta consideração. *Sincerely yours.*

protetor (protector) *m. protector.*

PROVA *f. proof; test, examination; proof sheet; fitting (of garments).* Recebi duas provas. *I received two proofs.* À prova de fogo. *Fireproof.* Prova oral. *Oral test.* Prova escrita. *Written test.*

provado *adj. proved, tried.*

PROVAR *to try; to taste; to prove; to try on.* Prove êste (este) vinho. *Try this wine.*

PROVÁVEL *adj. probable, likely.* É pouco provável. *It's not likely.* É provável que venha amanhã. *It's likely that he will come tomorrow.*

PROVEITO *m. profit; benefit, advantage.* Tirar proveito. *To derive profit from. To turn to advantage.* Bom proveito! *(said at meals). May you enjoy it! Hearty appetite!*

proveitoso *adj. profitable, beneficial.*

prover *to provide, to furnish, to supply.*

provérbio *m. proverb.*

providência *f. providence, precaution; pl. steps, measures.* Tomar providências. *To take steps. To take measures.*

província *f. province.*

provir *to derive from, to come from.*

provisão *f. provision, supply; pl. provisions.* Provisões de guerra. *Munitions.*

provisional *adj. provisional, temporary.*

provisório *adj. provisional, temporary.*

provocação *f. provocation.*

provocador *adj. provoking; n. m. provoker, troublemaker.*

provocar *to provoke, to vex.*

PRÓXIMO *(x = s) adj. near, next, neighboring; m. neighbor, fellowman.* Na próxima semana. *Next week.* Amor o próximo. *To love one's neighbor.*

prudência *f. prudence, moderation.*

prudente *adj. prudent, cautious.*

pseudônimo (pseudónimo) *m. pseudonym.*

psicologia *f. psychology.*

psicólogo *m. psychologist.*

psiquiatra *m. and f. psychiatrist.*

psiquiatria *f. psychiatry.*

psiu! *pst! hush!*

pua *f. sharp point, prong; bit (drill).*

publicação *f. publication.*

publicar *to publish, to announce.* Êle (ele) publicou uma série de artigos sôbre (sobre) a literatura brasileira. *He published a series of articles about Brasilian literature.*

publicidade *f. publicity.*

PÚBLICO *adj. public; n. m. public; audience.* Biblioteca pública. *Public library.* Em público. *In public.* O público não gostou da peça. *The audience did not like the play.*

pudim *m. pudding.*

pudor *m. modesty, shyness; propriety.*

pugilista *m. pugilist, boxer.*

pugna *f. struggle, fight.*

pular *to jump.*

pulcro *adj. pulchritudinous, beautiful.*

pulga *f. flea.* Andar com a pulga atrás da orelha. *To be suspicious. To be uneasy.*

pulmão *m. lung.*

pulmonia *f. pneumonia.*

pulo *m. jump, skip.* Quando ela ouviu a notícia deu pulos de alegria. *When she heard the news she jumped with joy.* Em dois pulos. *Right away. With little delay.*

pulôver Ⓑ *m. pullover, sweater.*

pulsar *to pulsate; to beat.*

pulseira *f. bracelet.* Relógio-pulseira. *Wristwatch.*

pulso *m. pulse; wrist; force, strength.* Deixe-me tomar-lhe o pulso. *Let me take your pulse.*

pum! *Bang! Boom!*

puncionar *to punch, to puncture.*

pundonor *m. dignity, honor, decorum.*

pungente *adj. pungent, acute.*

pungir *to prick, to pierce; to torment; to incite.*

punhado *m. handful, a few.* Um punhado de soldados defenderam a posição. *A few soldiers defended the position.*

punhal *m. dagger.*

punhalada *f. a stab.*

punho *m. fist, wrist; cuff; handle.* De próprio punho. *In one's own handwriting.*

punição *f. punishment.*

punir *to punish.*

pupilo *m. ward; protegé.*

purê (puré) *m. purée.* Purê de batatas. *Mashed potatoes.*

pureza *f. purity.*

purga *f. purge; laxative.*

purgação *f. purgation.*

purgante *adj. purgative; n. m. purgative.*

purgar *to purge; to cleanse.*

purgatório *m. purgatory.*

purificar *to purify.*

puro *adj. pure, clean; plain.* É a pura verdade. *That's the plain truth.*

púrpura *f. crimson, purple.*

pusilânime *adj. cowardly; n. m. and f. coward.*

pútrido *adj. rotten.*

putrificar *to putrefy, to rot.*

puxa! *(x = sh) Well now! Come now!*

puxar *(x = sh) to pull; to haul; to take after, to resemble.* Puxar conversa. *To strike up a conversation.* Puxa-saco. *Apple-polisher* Ⓑ.

Q

quadra *f. square area; quatrain; series of four; quarter; block (of street)* Ⓑ; *court (sports).*

quadrado *adj. square.* Um metro quadrado. *One square meter.*

quadrilha *f. a squadron; a gang; a square dance.* Uma quadrilha de ladrões. *A gang of thieves.*

quadro *m. picture; painting; team; board.* Quadro negro. *Blackboard.* Quadro a óleo. *Oil painting.* Quadro de avisos. *Bulletin board.*

QUAL *which; what; which one; like; as.* Qual prefere o senhor? *Which (one) do you prefer?* Quais são os do senhor? *Which (ones) are yours?* Cada qual. *Each one.*

qualidade *f. quality; kind; grade.*

qualquer *adj. any.* A qualquer hora. *At any time.* Êle (ele) é capaz de qualquer coisa. *He is capable of anything.* De qualquer maneira. *By any means. Anyhow.*

QUANDO *when.* Quando vai partir? *When are you going to leave?* Quando o senhor quiser. *Whenever you wish.* Até quando? *Until when?* De quando em quando. *From time to time.* De vez em quando. *From time to time.* Quando ela chegou, êle já tinha partido. *When she arrived, he had already left.*

quantia *f. quantity, amount.*

quantidade *f. quantity, amount.*

QUANTO *how much; how; as much as; all that.* Quanto? *How much?* Quantos? *How many?* A quantos do mês estamos? *What day of the month is it?* Quanto é? *How much is it?*

Compre quantos livros você quiser. *Buy as many books as you like.*

Quanto mais lhe dou, mais me pede. *The more I give him, the more he asks for.*

Quanto antes. *As soon as possible.*

Quanto a mim, não irei nunca. *As for me', I'll never go.*

quão *adv. how, as.*

QUARENTA *adj. and n. m. forty; fortieth.*

quaresma *f. Lent.*

QUARTA, QUARTA-FEIRA *f. Wednesday.*

quarteirão *m. city block.*

quartel *m. barracks; quarter.*

Quartel-general. *General headquarters.*

QUARTO *adj. fourth, quarter; m. quarter, fourth; room, bedroom.*

Estarei lá as dez menos um quarto. *I'll be there at a quarter to ten.*

Às quatro e um quarto. *At a quarter past four.*

Quarto de solteiro. *Single bedroom.*

Quarto para casal. *Double bedroom.*

QUASE *almost, nearly.*

Quase nunca leio o jornal. *I hardly ever read the newspaper.*

Quase sempre. *Almost always.*

Quase nunca. *Hardly ever.*

QUATRO *adj. and n. m. four; fourth.*

São quatro horas. *It's four o'clock.*

quatrocentos *adj. four hundred; n. m. four hundred.*

QUE *what, how; that, which; who, whom; than.*

Que deseja? *What do you want?*

Que é isto? *What's this?*

Que horas são? *What time is it?*

Por que me chamou? *Why did you call me?*

De que está falando (a falar)? *What are you talking about?*

Que pena! *What a pity!*

Não sei o que disseram. *I don't know what they said.*

Isso é o que eu digo. *That's what I say.*

Maria disse que o faria. *Mary said she would do it.*

Vale mais do que o senhor pensa. *It's worth more than you think.*

Espero que sim. *I hope so.*

Ela é mais inteligente (do) que êle (ele). *She is more intelligent than he is.*

Temos que partir. *We have to leave.*

quê (used as an interjection or as an interrogative when it stands alone or in final position) *what! why! why? something.*

Por quê? *Why? (For what reason?)*

Para quê? *Why? (For what purpose?)*

Não há de quê. *Don't mention it. You're welcome.*

quebra *f. break; crash; bankruptcy.*

quebradiço *adj. fragile, brittle.*

quebrado *adj. broken; ruptured; m. fraction.*

quebra-luz *m. lampshade.*

quebrantar *to break; to violate.*

QUEBRAR *to break; to burst; to weaken.*

Quebrar a palavra. *To break one's word.*

queda *f. fall; inclination.*

Queda de água. *Waterfall.*

Ela tem queda para as letras. *She has a bent for literature.*

quedar *to stay.*

quefazer *m. chore, task.*

QUEIJO *m. cheese.*

queimado *adj. burned.*

Cheira a queimado. *It smells of burning.*

queimar *to burn; to parch; to sell at reduced prices; to get angry.*

Queimar as pestanas. *To burn the midnight oil.*

queixa (x = sh) *f. complaint; protest.*

Apresentar queixa. *To lodge a complaint.*

Ter motivo de queixa. *To have grounds for complaint.*

queixar-se (x = sh) *to complain.*

Êles (eles) se queixaram das condições nas escolas. *They complained about school conditions.*

queixo (x = sh) *m. chin; jaw.*

queixoso (x = sh) *adj. complaining.*

QUEM *who, whom; he who.*

Quem é êle (ele)? *Who is he?*

Quem são os outros convidados? *Who are the other guests?*

Quem fala? *Who's speaking?*

Para quem é esta caixa (x = sh)? *Who is this box for?*

De quem é? *Whose is it?*

Quem fala assim não conhece o problema. *Whoever (he who) says that doesn't know the problem.*

QUENTE *warm, hot.*

Está muito quente hoje. *It's very hot today.*

quer *whether, or.*

Quer êle (ele) aceite quer não aceite, eu vou continuar. *Whether he accepts or not, I'm going to continue.*

Quer sim, quer não. *Whether yes or no.*

querença *f. affection, fondness; wish, desire*

QUERER *to wish, to want, to desire; to like.*

Que quer o senhor? *What do you want? What would you like?*

O senhor quer ver o apartamento? *Do you want (would you like) to see the apartment?*

Eu não o quero. *I don't want it.*

Se o senhor quiser. *If you wish.*

Faça como quiser *Do as you wish.*

Como quiser. *As you wish.*

Quero comprar um relógio. *I want to buy a watch.*

Não quero mais. *I don't want any more.*

Que quer dizer esta palavra? *What does this word mean?*

Sem querer. *Unintentionally.*

Queira Deus. *God willing.*

Querer é poder. *Where there's a will, there's a way.*

querido *adj. dear, beloved.*

Querida filha. *Beloved daughter.*

QUESTÃO *f. question; dispute; matter.*

Êles (eles) resolveram a questão. *They settled the matter.*

Eis a questão. *That's the point.*

questionar *to question.*

questionável *adj. questionable, debatable.*

quiçá *perhaps.*

QUIETO *adj. quiet, still.*

Fique quieto! *Be quiet!*

quilate *m. carat; excellence.*

quilha *f. keel.*

quilo *m. kilo, kilogram.*

quilociclo *m. kilocycle.*

quilograma *m. kilogram.*

quilômetro (quilómetro) *m. kilometer.*

química *f. chemistry.*

químico *adj. chemical; m. chemist.*

quimono *m. kimono.*

quinhentos *adj. and m. five hundred.*

quinina *f. quinine.*

QUINTA *f. fifth; Thursday; farm; country house.*

QUINTA-FEIRA *f. Thursday.*

quintal *m. backyard.*

QUINTO *adj. fifth.*

O quinto andar. *The fifth floor.*

A quinta coluna. *The fifth column.*

quintuplicar *to quintuplicate.*

quíntuplo *adj. quintuple, fivefold.*

QUINZE *adj. and n. m. fifteen; fifteenth.*

Dentro de quinze dias. *Within fifteen days. In two weeks.*

quinzena *f. period of fifteen days, two weeks.*

quiosque *m. kiosk, stand (for newspapers, etc.).*

quitanda *f. vegetable market or shop.*

quitandeiro *m. greengrocer, operator of a quitanda.*

quitar *to free, to release.*

quite *adj. even, clear.*

Estamos quites. *We're even.*

quota *f. quota.*

R

rã *f. frog.*

rábano *m. radish.*

rabi *m. rabbi.*

rabo *m. tail.*

De cabo a rabo. *From head to tail. From end to end.*

raça *f. race; breed.*

Raça humana. *Human race.*

Cavalo de raça. *Thoroughbred horse.*

ração *f. ration.*

racemo *m. bunch (grapes).*

raciocinar *to reason.*

raciocínio *m. reasoning.*

racional *adj. rational; reasonable.*

racionar *to ration.*

racista *m. and f. racist.*

radar *m. radar.*

radiação *f. radiation.*

radiador *m. radiator.*

radiar *to radiate; to shine.*

radical *adj. radical; n. m. and fem. radical.*

RÁDIO *m. radio; radius; radium.*

Aparelho de rádio. *Radio set.*

Rádio portátil. *Portable radio.*

radioatividade (radioactividade) *f. radioactivity.*

radiodifusão *f. radiobroadcasting; radiobroadcast.*

radioemissora *f. broadcasting station.*

radiografia *f. radiography; X-ray photography.*

radiograma *m. radiogram.*

radiotelefonia *f. radiotelephony.*

radiotelegrafia *f. radiotelegraphy.*

radiouvinte *m. and f. radio listener.*

raia *f. line; ray.*

Passar as raias. *To go too far.*

raiar *to line; to radiate, to shine; to dawn.*

Estaremos lá no raiar do dia. *We'll be there at dawn.*

rainha *f. queen.*

RAIO *m. ray, beam; spoke (wheel); lightning; thunderbolt; misfortune; radius.*

Raio de sol. *A ray of sunlight.*

Raios X. *X-rays.*

Como um raio. *Like a flash.*

Raio de ação (acção). *Sphere of action.*

raiva *f. anger, rage; rabies.*

Ela estava pálida de raiva. *She was livid with rage.*

raivar *to be furious, to be angry, to rage.*

Raivar por. *To be extremely eager or anxious for something.*

raivoso *adj. furious, angry; mad.*

raiz *f. root.*

Lançar raízes. *To take root.*

Raiz quadrada. *Square root.*

raja *f. stripe, streak.*

rajado *adj. striped, streaked.*

ralar *to grate; to annoy.*

ralhar *to scold; to nag; to get angry.*

rama *f. branches; foliage.*
Algodão em rama. *Raw cotton.*

ramal *m. branch, line, extension.*

ramificação *f. ramification.*

ramo *m. branch; limb; bunch (flowers).*
Não sei nada dêsse (desse) ramo da família. *I don't know anything about that branch of the family.*
Domingo de Ramos. *Palm Sunday.*

rampa *f. ramp, slope.*

rancho *m. mess (military); hut; a group of strollers.*

ranço *adj. rancid.*

ranger *to gnash; to creak.*
Quando ouviu isso, êle (ele) rangeu os dentes. *When he heard that he gnashed his teeth.*

rapado *adj. scraped; close-cropped.*

rapariga *f. girl.*

RAPAZ *m. young man; fellow.*
Quem é êsse (esse) rapaz? *Who is that fellow?*

rapidez *f. rapidity, swiftness.*

RÁPIDO *adj. rapid, fast, swift; n. m. express train; messenger service; rapids.*
Vou tomar o rápido. *I'm going to take the express.*

rapôsa (raposa) *f. fox.*
Cova de rapôsa. *Foxhole.*

rapôso (raposo) *m. fox.*

raptar *to abduct, to kidnap; to rob.*

rapto *m. kidnapping; abduction; robbery.*

raqueta *f. racket (tennis).*

rareza *f. rarity.*

raridade *f. rarity.*

raro *adj. rare, unusual.*
Êle (ele) é um homem muito raro. *He's a very unusual man.*
Raras vêzes (vezes). *Rarely. Seldom.*

rascante *adj. bitter, sour.*

rascar *to scratch.*

rascunho *m. draft, preliminary copy.*

rasgadura *f. rent, tear, rip.*

rasgão *m. rent, tear, rip.*

rasgar *to tear, to rend, to rip.*
Rasgar em pedaços. *To tear to pieces.*

rasgo *m. tear, rip; flash of wit; noble deed.*
Rasgo de eloqüência (eloquência). *Burst of eloquence.*

raso *flat, even, level; n. m. flat land.*
Soldado raso. *Private (military).*

raspar *to scrape; to rasp; to ease.*

rasteiro *adj. low; creeping.*
Planta rasteira. *Creeping plant.*

rasto *m. track, trail; trace, sign, clue; footprint.*
Andar de rasto. *To crawl.*

rata *f. rat; blunder.*

ratificação *f. ratification.*

ratificar *to ratify, to sanction.*

rato *m. rat, mouse; thief.*
Calado como um rato. *Quiet as a mouse.*

ratoeira *f. mousetrap; trick.*

ratoneiro *m. petty thief.*

RAZÃO *f. reason; cause; rate; right.*
Ter razão. *To be right.*
Não ter razão. *To be wrong.*
O senhor tem razão. *You are right.*
Ela não tem razão. *She's wrong.*
À razão de. *At the rate of.*
Dar ouvidos à razão. *To listen to reason.*
Idade da razão. *Age of discretion.*
Perder a razão. *To lose one's reason.*

razoamento *m. reasoning.*

razoar *to reason, to argue.*

razoável *adj. reasonable, fair.*

ré *f. female criminal; stern.*
Marcha à ré. *Reverse speed.*
À ré. *Astern.*

reabastecer *to replenish, to restock.*

reabilitar *to rehabilitate.*

reação (reacção) *f. reaction.*

reacionário (reaccionário) *adj. and m. reactionary.*

real *adj. real; actual; royal; n. m. monetary unit.*

realçar *to enhance; to intensify.*

realidade *f. reality; fact.*
Na realidade. *Actually. In fact.*

realismo *m. realism.*

realista *adj. realistic; royalist; n. m. and f. realist; royalist.*

realizar *to realise, to accomplish, to fulfill.*
Ele (ele) realizou e que tinha projetado (projectado). *He accomplished what he had planned.*

reaparecer *to reappear.*

reator (reactor) *m. reactor.*

rebaixamento (x = sh) *m. reduction, lowering.*

rebaixar (x = sh) *to reduce, to lower, to diminish.*
Esta semana rebaixaram os preços. *This week they lowered prices.*

rebanho *m. flock, herd.*

rebater *to repel; to refute; to discount (note); to return (sports).*

rebelar *to rebel; to revolt.*

rebelde *adj. rebellious; defiant; n. m. and f. rebel.*

rebelião *f. rebellion.*

rebentar *to burst.*

rebocador *m. plasterer; tugboat.*

reboque *m. tow, towing; trailer.*
Levar a reboque. *To take in tow.*

rebuçar *to hide; to muffle up.*

rebuscar *to search; to glean.*

recado *m. message; errand; pl. greetings.*
Tem algum recado para mim? *Do you have a message for me?*
Dê-lhe meus recados. *Give him my regards.*

recaída *f. relapse.*

recair *to fall back; to relapse.*

recalcar *to trample, to read; to repress.*

recalcitrar *to oppose, to resist.*

recanto *m. nook; retreat.*

recatado *adj. prudent, modest, sober.*

recatar-se *to be cautious.*

recato *m. caution.*

RECEAR *to fear.*
Receio que êle (ele) não venha. *I'm afraid he won't come.*

RECEBER *to receive, to accept.*
Hoje recebi duas cartas. *I received two letters today.*

receio *m. fear; doubt.*

receita *f. prescription; recipe; receipts; income.*
Aviar uma receita. *To fill a prescription.*
Receita bruta. *Gross income.*
Receita líquida. *Net income.*

receitar *to prescribe.*

recém-chegado *adj. newly arrived; n. m. newcomer.*

RECENTE *adj. recent, new, fresh; modern.*
Um acontecimento recente. *A recent event.*
Recentemente. *Recently.*

recepção *f. reception.*

receptor *m. receiver.*

rechonchudo *adj. fat, chubby.*

recibo *m. receipt.*

Pode me dar (dar-me) um recibo? *Can you give me a receipt?*

recife *m. reef.*
Recife de coral. *Coral reef.*

recinto *m. enclosed area; enclosure.*

recipiente *adj. recipient, receiving; m. receiver, container.*

reciprocar *to reciprocate.*

reciprocidade *f. reciprocity.*

recíproco *adj. reciprocal, mutual.*
Reciprocamente. *Reciprocally.*

récita *f. recital.*

recitar *to recite, to relate.*

reclamação *f. reclamation, complaint.*

reclamante *m. and f. claimant.*

reclamar *to complain, to protest.*

reclamo *m. claim, complaint.*

recluso *adj. confined; n. m. recluse; convict.*

recobrar *to recover, to regain.*
Recobrar a saúde. *To regain one's health.*

RECOLHER *to pick up; to gather; to collect.*
Ela recolheu todos os documentos. *She gathered all the documents.*

recomendação *f. recommendation.*
Carta de recomendação. *Letter of recommendation.*

RECOMENDAR *to recommend, to advise; to command; to entrust.*
Aquêle (aquele) amigo que você recomendou recebeu o emprêgo (emprego). *That friend you recommended received the job.*

recomendável *adj. recommendable.*

recompensa *f. reward, compensation.*

recompensar *to recompense, to reward.*

reconciliação *f. reconciliation.*

reconciliar *to reconcile.*

RECONHECER *to recognise; to admit; to examine; to appreciate.*
O senhor reconhece esta letra? *Do you recognise this handwriting?*
Reconheço que tudo é como êle (ele) indicou. *I admit that everything is as he indicated.*

reconhecimento *m. recognition; acknowledgment; appreciation, gratitude; reconnaissance.*

reconstituinte *m. tonic.*

reconstrução *f. reconstruction.*

reconstruir *to reconstruct, to rebuild.*

recopilar *to compile, to collect.*

recordação *f. remembrance.*

recordar *to remember, to recall.*
Não posso recordar o nome dêle (dele). *I don't recall his name.*

recorde *m. record (sports, etc.)* Ⓑ
Êle (ele) bateu o recorde. *He broke the record.*

reco-reco *m. Brazilian musical instrument of bamboo.*

recorrer *to go over, to look over; to appeal to.*
Recorremos a todos os meios. *We tried everything.*

recortar *to cut, to trim, to clip, to shorten.*

recorte *m. clipping; outline.*
Eu lhe mandei um recorte do jornal. *I sent him a newspaper clipping.*

recostar *to lean against.*

recostar-se *to lean back, to recline, to lie down.*

recreação *f. recreation, diversion, amusement.*

recrear *to entertain, to amuse, to delight.*

recrear-se *to have a good time.*

recreio *m. recreation, diversion, amusement.*

recruta *m. recruit, new member.*

recrutar *to recruit.*

recuar *to recede, to back away.*

recuperar *to recuperate, to recover.*
    Recuperar as fôrças (forças). *To recover one's strength.*
    Temos que recuperar o tempo perdido. *We have to make up for lost time.*

recurso *m. recourse; appeal; resource; pl. resources, means.*
    Sem recursos. *Without means.*

recusar *to refuse, to deny; to reject; to prohibit.*
    Recusamos o projeto (projecto). *We turned down the plan.*

redação *f. editing; editorial office.*

redator (redactor) *m. editor.*

rêde (rede) *f. net; network; trap.*
    Rêde ferroviária. *Railroad system.*
    O animal caiu na rêde. *The animal was trapped. The animal fell into the trap.*

rédea *f. reins; control.*
    À rédea sôlta (solta). *At full tilt, at full speed; unrestrained.*

redenção *f. redemption.*

redigir *to write, to compose.*

REDONDO *adj. round; chubby.*
    A mesa é redonda. *The table is round.*
    Em números redondos. *In round numbers.*

redor *m. circle, circuit; environs.*
    Em redor. *Around. All around.*
    Ao redor. *Around. All around.*

redução *f. reduction.*

redundância *f. redundance.*

redundante *adj. redundant.*

redundar *to redound, to result.*

reduzir *to reduce, to cut down.*
    De hoje em diante vou reduzir as minhas despesas. *From now on I'll cut down on my expenses.*
    Reduzir a cinzas. *To reduce to ashes.*

reeleger *to reelect.*

reeleição *f. reelection.*

reembolsar *to reimburse.*

reembôlso (reembolso) *m. reimbursement, refund.*

refazer *to make over, to redo.*

refeição *f. meal.*
    Fazer uma refeição. *To have a meal.*

referência *f. reference.*
    Com referência a. *With regard to.*

referente *adj. referring, relating.*

referir *to refer.*

refinado *adj. refined, polished.*

refinar *to refine, to improve.*

refinaria *f. refinery.*

refletir (reflectir) *to reflect.*

refletor (reflector) *adj. reflecting; n. m. reflector, headlight.*

reflexão (x = ks) *f. reflection, thought.*

reflexionar (x = ks) *to think over, to reflect.*

reflexivo (x = ks) *adj. reflexive.*

reflexo (x = ks) *adj. reflected; n. m. reflex.*
    Ação (Acçao) reflexa. *Reflex action.*

reforçar *to reinforce, to strengthen.*

reforma *f. reform, reformation; alteration; remodeling.*

reformar *to reform;to correct; to alter; to remodel;to retire.*

reformar-se *to retire.*
    Depois de quarenta anos de serviço militar, o general se reformou (reformou-se). *After forty years of military service the general retired.*

reformatório *m. reformatory.*

refrão *m. refrain; chorus; saying, proverb.*

refrear *to curb, to restrain, to refrain.*

refrega *f. fight, skirmish, fray.*

refrescante *adj. cooling.*

refrescar *to refresh; to cool.*
    Refrescar a memória. *To refresh one's memory.*

refrêsco (refresco) *m. refreshment; cold drink.*

refrigerador *adj. refrigerating, cooling; n. m. refrigerator, icebox.*

refrigerar *to refrigerate, to cool.*

refugiado *m. refugee.*

refugiar-se *to take refuge; to take shelter.*

refúgio *m. refuge, shelter, haven.*

regadeira *f. shower; gutter; irrigation ditch.*

regador *adj. irrigating; n. m. sprinkler, watering can.*

regalado *adj. regaled; pleased.*
    Êle (ele) leva uma vida regalada. *He leads an easy life.*

regalar *to regale; to enjoy.*

regalo *m. regalement; pleasure; gift; muff (as fur muff).*

regar *to water, to irrigate.*

regata *f. boat race, regatta.*

regatear *to bargain, to haggle; to stint.*

regateio *m. haggling.*

regeneração *f. regeneration.*

regenerar *to regenerate.*

regente *m. regent; leader; conductor.*

reger *to rule, to govern.*

região *f. region; district.*
    Região campestre. *Country. Countryside.*

regime, regimen *m. regime; diet.*
    Eu estou fazendo (a fazer) regime. *I'm on a diet.*
    O país mudou de regime. *The country had a change of government.*

regimento *m. regiment.*

régio *adj. royal, regal.*

regional *adj. regional, local.*

registrar, registar *to register, to put on record.*
    As compras se registram (registram-se) neste livro. *Purchases are entered in this book.*
    Registrar uma carta. *To register a letter.*

registro, registo *m. registration; register; record.*
    Registro de nomes. *Directory of names.*

REGRA *f. rule; ruler (for measuring).*
    O passaporte está em regra? *Is the passport in order?*
    Tudo está em regra. *Everything is in order.*
    Estas são as regra do jôgo (jogo). *These are the rules of the game.*
    Não há regra sem exceção (excepção). *There is an exception to every rule.*

regressar *to return, to go back, to come back.*
    Regressarei na sexta. *I'll be back Friday.*

regresso *m. return.*

regulamento *m. rule, regulation, law.*

REGULAR *to regulate; to adjust; adj. regular, ordinary; fair, moderate; fairly good.*
    Regular o tráfico. *To regulate traffic.*
    João recebe um salário regular. *John receives a moderate salary.*

rei *m. king.*

reimprimir *to reprint.*

reinado *m. reign.*

reinar *to reign; to predominate, to prevail.*
    O rei reinou durante vinte anos. *The king reigned twenty years.*

reino *m. kingdom, reign.*

reintegrar *to restore.*

réis *m. pl. former monetary unit of Brazil.*

reiterar *to reiterate.*

reitor *m. rector; dean.*

rejeitar *to reject.*

RELAÇÃO *f. relation, connection; report; pl. connections.*
    Não há relação entre estas duas coisas. *There is no relation (connection) between these two things.*
    Nós estamos em boas relações com êles (eles). *We are on good terms with them.*

relacionado *adj. acquainted; related.*

relacionar *to relate; to connect.*

relâmpago *m. lightning.*

relampejar *to lighten (lightning).*

relatar *to relate, to tell.*

relativo *adj. relative.*
    Relativo a. *With reference to.*

relato *m. account, statement; story.*
    Êle (ele) fêz (fez) um relato do que tinha acontecido. *He gave an account of what had happened.*

relatório *m. report; statement.*

reler *to reread.*

relêvo (relevo) *m. relief, projection.*

religião *f. religion.*

religioso *adj. religious.*

RELÓGIO *m. clock, watch.*
    Relógio de bôlso (bolso). *Pocket watch.*
    Relógio-pulseira Wristwatch.
    Dar corda ao relógio. *To wind the watch.*
    O relógio está adiantado. *The watch is fast.*
    O relógio está atrasado. *The watch is slow.*

relojoaria *f. watchmaking; watchmaker's shop.*

relojoeiro *m. watchmaker.*

reluzir *to shine, to sparkle.*
    Nem tudo que reluz é ouro. *All that glitters is not gold.*

remar *to row, to paddle.*

rematar *to complete; to put the finishing touches on.*

remate *m. end, conclusion, finish.*

remediar *to remedy; to make good; to help.*
    Isso não se pode remediar. *That can't be helped.*

REMÉDIO *m. remedy; medicine.*
    Isto não tem remédio. *There's no remedy for this. This can't be helped.*
    Não há remédio. *It can't be helped.*
    Sem remédio. *Inevitable.*
    Remédio caseiro. *Household remedy.*

remendar *to mend, to patch.*

remessa *f. remittance; shipment.*

remetente *adj. sending; n. m. and f. sender.*

remeter *to remit, to send.*
    Faça o favor de remeter (as) minhas cartas a êste (este) endereço (endereço). *Please forward my mail to this address.*

remir *to redeem.*

remitente *adj. remittent.*

remitir *to remit, to forgive; to abate.*

remo *m. oar, paddle.*
    Remo de duas pás. *Double-bladed paddle.*

remodelar *to remodel.*

remoinhar *to spin, to whirl.*

remontar *to remount, to repair; to go up; to go back.*

remorso *m. remorse.*

remover *to remove; to take away.*

remuneração *f. remuneration; reward.*

remunerar *to remunerate, to reward.*

renascença *f. renaissance, rebirth; Renaissance.*

renascer *to be reborn; to grow again.*

renascimento *m. rebirth.*

RENDA *f. income, revenue; rent; lace.*
Imposto (imposto) de renda. *Income tax.*
Renda bruta. *Gross income.*
render *to subdue; to surrender; to produce, to yield; to tire out.*
Êste (este) negócio rende pouco. *This business is not very profitable.*
Render homenagem. *To pay homage.*
rendição *f. surrender.*
rendido *adj. split; submissive; overcome.*
rendimento *m. income, return; surrender.*
Rendimento bruto. *Gross income.*
renegado *m. renegade.*
renegar *to deny; to reject.*
renhido *adj. hard-fought; furious.*
renome *m. renown, fame.*
renomeado *adj. renowned, famous.*
renovação *f. renovation, renewal.*
renovar *to renovate, to renew; to reform.*
rente *adj. close; even with.*
Cortar bem rente. *To cut quite close.*
renúncia *f. renunciation; resignation.*
renunciar *to renounce; to reject, to resign.*
Eu renunciei o emprêgo (emprego). *I resigned the position.*
Renunciar um direito. *To give up a right.*
reorganização *f. reorganisation.*
reorganizador *adj. reorganizing, reforming; n. m. reorganiser.*
reorganizar *to reorganise.*
reparação *f. reparation, repair; amends; satisfaction.*
reparador *adj. reparative; compensating; n. m. repairer.*
reparar *to repair; to notice.*
Reparei em que todos olhavam para ela. *I noticed that they were all looking at her.*
reparo *m. repair; notice; remark.*
repartição *f. partition; department.*
repartidor *adj. sharing; n. m. sharer.*
repartir *to distribute, to divide.*
Repartiram os lucros. *They divided the profits.*
repassar *to go over, to review; to soak.*
Vamos repassar a lição. *Let's review the lesson.*
repelir *to repel; to reject.*
repente *m. sudden act or movement.*
De repente. *Suddenly. All of a sudden.*
repentino *adj. sudden.*
repercussão *f. repercussion; reaction.*
repercutir *to echo; to reverberate; to have a repercussion.*
repertório *m. repertory; repertoire; list, index.*
repetente *adj. repeating; n. m. and f. repeater (student).*
repetição *f. repetition.*
O relatório está cheio de repetições *The report is full of repetitions.*
REPETIR *to repeat.*
Faça o favor de repetir o que disse. *Please repeat what you said.*
Repito que eu não vou. *I repeat that I'm not going.*
repicar *to pierce; to ring, to peal, to toll; to mince, to chop.*
repleto *adj. full, replete.*
O ônibus (autocarro) está repleto. *The bus is full.*
réplica *f. reply, answer.*
Não gostamos (gostámos) de (da) sua réplica. *We didn't like your answer*
replicar *to reply, to retort.*
Não me repliques! *Don't answer back! Don't talk back to me!*

repor *to replace; to restore.*
reportagem *f. reporting, report.*
reportar *to go back in time; to moderate.*
repórter *m. and f. reporter.*
repositório *m. repository.*
repreender *to reprimand, to reprehend.*
reprêsa (represa) *f. dam.*
representação *f. representation; performance.*
representante *adj. representative; n. m. and f. representative, agent.*
representar *to represent; to act, perform.*
Que casa representa? *Which firm do you represent?*
Eu vi a peça; ela representou muito mal. *I saw the play; she performed very badly. I saw the play; her acting was very bad.*
repressão *f. repression.*
reprimir *to repress, to check, to hold in check.*
Não me pude reprimir por mais tempo. *I couldn't contain myself any longer.*
reprodução *f. reproduction.*
reproduzir *to reproduce.*
reprovar *to reprove; to fail.*
O aluno foi reprovado. *The student failed.*
reptil, réptil (réptil) *m. reptile.*
república *f. republic.*
republicano *adj. republican; n. m. republican.*
repudiar *to repudiate; to disavow.*
repugnância *f. repugnance; dislike.*
repugnante *adj. repugnant, distasteful.*
repugnar *to be distasteful, to be repugnant; to dislike, to detest; to reject; to oppose.*
Isso me repugna. *I detest it.*
repulsa *f. repulsion, aversion.*
repulsar *to repulse; to repeal.*
reputação *f. reputation, name.*
Ele (ele) tem uma boa reputação. *He has a good reputation.*
requerer *to require, to request.*
Isso requer muita atenção. *That requires a lot of attention.*
requisito *m. requisite, requirement.*
rés *adj. level; close.*
Rés-do-chão. *Ground floor.*
resenha *f. report; list; summary.*
resenhar *to report; to list.*
reserva *f. reserve; reservation; privacy.*
Reserva mental. *Mental reservation.*
Sem reserva. *Without reservation. Unreservedly.*
De reserva. *Extra. Spare. In reserve.*
Fundo de reserva. *Reserve fund.*
reservado *adj. reserved; cautious; confidential.*
reservar *to reserve; to keep.*
Queremos que nos reserve um lugar. *We want you to reserve a place (to make a reservation) for us.*
resfriado *m. a cold.*
Apanhei um resfriado. *I caught a cold.*
resfriar *to cool.*
resgatar *to redeem; to release.*
resgate *m. redemption; release.*
resguardar *to protect; to guard.*
resguardo *m. protection; guard.*
residência *f. residence.*
residencial *adj. residential.*
residente *adj. residing, resident; n. m. and f. resident, inhabitant.*
residir *to reside, to live.*
Resido na Rua da Alfândega. *I live on Alfândega Street.*
resíduo *adj. residual; n. m. residue, remainder.*
resignação *f. resignation; patience.*
resignar *to resign.*
resignar-se *to resign oneself, to be resigned.*

resistência *f. resistance.*
resistente *adj. resistant; hardy.*
resistir *to resist, to endure.*
Resistir à tentação. *To resist temptation.*
Resistir à prova. *To stand the test.*
resmungar *to grumble, to mumble.*
resolução *f. resolution; determination; decision; solution.*
É preciso tomarmos uma resolução *We must come to some decision.*
resoluto *adj. resolute.*
resolver *to resolve, to determine, to decide; to solve; to dissolve; to settle.*
Resolvi fazê-lo eu mesmo. *I determined to do it myself.*
Êste (este) problema é difícil de resolver. *This problem is difficult to solve.*
respeitar *to respect, to honor.*
respeitável *adj. respectable.*
RESPEITO *m. relation; respect; reference; regard.*
Com respeito a. *With regard to. Concerning.*
A respeito de. *With regard to. Concerning.*
Falta de respeito. *Disrespect.*
respeitoso *adj. respectful, polite.*
respiração *f. respiration, breathing.*
Falta de respiração. *Shortness of breath.*
respirar *to breathe.*
Deixe-me (x = sh) respirar. *Give me a chance to catch my breath.*
respiro *m. breath, breathing; respite.*
resplandecer *to shine.*
RESPONDER *to answer, to respond; to be responsible for.*
Êle (ele) nem sequer me respondeu. *He didn't even answer me.*
Quem responde por êle (ele)? *Who stands up (is responsible) for him?*
responsabilidade *f. responsibility.*
responsável *adj. responsible, liable.*
RESPOSTA *f. answer, reply, retort, response.*
Resposta favorável. *Favorable reply.*
Resposta negativa. *Negative reply. Refusal.*
ressaltar *to rebound; to stand out; to stress.*
ressentir-se *to resent; to feel.*
Ela se ressentiu por nada. *She became offended over a trifle.*
ressoar *to resound.*
ressonância *f. resonance.*
ressonar *to resound.*
ressurgimento *m. resurgence.*
ressurgir *to resurge; to reappear.*
ressuscitar *to resuscitate.*
restabelecer *to reestablish; to restore.*
restante *adj. remaining; n. m. remainder.*
Posta-restante. *General delivery.*
restar *to remain, to be left.*
Restam-me cinco dólares. *I have five dollars left.*
restauração *f. restoration.*
restaurante *m. restaurant.*
restaurar *to restore.*
restituição *f. restitution.*
restituir *to restore.*
RESTO *m. rest, remainder; pl. remains; leftovers.*
A cozinheira sabe aproveitar os restos. *The cook knows how to make good use of leftovers.*
De resto. *Besides.*
restrição *f. restriction.*
restringir *to restrain; to curtail; to restrict, to limit.*
RESULTADO *m. result.*
Qual foi o resultado? *What was the result?*
resultar *to result.*

Resultou-nos muito caro. *It was very expensive for us.*

resumido *adj. condensed; abridged.*

resumir *to abridge, to cut short; to summarize.*
Resumir um discurso. *To cut a speech short.*

resumo *m. summary.*

retaguarda *f. rear guard.*

retalho *m. piece, scrap.*
A retalho. *At retail.*
Colcha de retalhos. *Crazy quilt.*

retângulo (rectângulo) *m. rectangle.*

retardamento *m. delay.*

retardar *to retard, to delay.*

reter *to retain; to withhold; to keep; to remember.*
A polícia o reteve (reteve-o). *The police detained him.*
Não posso reter tanta informação. *I can't retain so much information.*

reticência *f. reticence.*

retificar (rectificar) *to rectify, to correct.*

retina *f. retina.*

retirada *f. retreat, withdrawal.*

retirado *adj. withdrawn; retired.*

retirar *to withdraw; to retire; to take back.*
O general retirou as tropas. *The general withdrew his troops.*

retirar-se *to leave; to retire.*
Ela se retirou (retirou-se) ao seu quarto. *She retired to her room.*

retiro *m. retreat.*

reto (recto) *adj. straight; just, upright; erect.*
Êle (ele) é um homem reto. *He is an upright man.*
Ângulo reto. *Right angle.*
Linha reta. *Straight line.*

retocar *to retouch.*

retoque *m. retouch.*

retorcer *to twist.*

retornar *to return; to restore.*

retôrno (retorno) *m. return; exchange.*

retorsão *f. retortion; twisting.*

retraído *adj. withdrawn, reserved.*
Êle (ele) é muito retraído. *He is quite withdrawn.*

retraimento *m. reserve; retreat; seclusion.*

retrair *to retract, to hold back.*

retratar *to portray; to show.*

retrato *m. portrait; photograph; picture.*
Tirar o retrato. *To have one's picture taken.*
Ele (ele) é o retrato fiel de seu pai. *He's the living image of his father.*

retrete *f. toilet; lavatory.*

retribuição *f. reward.*

retribuir *to pay back; to reward.*

retrocedente *adj. retrocedent, retroceding.*

retroceder *to back up; to draw back; to fall back; to grow worse.*
Êle (ele) não pôde retroceder na sua decisão. *He could not reverse his decision.*

retrospecção, retrospeção (retrospecção) *f. retrospection.*

retumbar *to resound.*

réu *m. defendant; convict.*

reumatismo *m. rheumatism.*

reunião *f. reunion; meeting.*
Haverá uma reunião às cinco. *There will be a meeting at five o'clock.*

reunir *to gather; to collect; to bring together.*
O professor reuniu os alunos numa festa. *The teacher brought his students together at a party.*

reunir-se *to get together; to meet; to join.*
A que horas podíamos reunir-nos? *At what time could we get together?*

Reunem-se de dois em dois anos. *They get together every two years.*

revelação *f. revelation.*

revelar *to reveal, to show; to disclose; to develop (photography).*
Revelar um segrêdo (segredo). *To reveal a secret.*
O autor revelou grande talento nesse livro. *The author showed great talent in that book.*

revendedor *m. dealer; retailer.*

revender *to resell; to retail.*

reverência *f. reverence; bow.*
Fazer uma reverência. *To bow.*

reverso *adj. reverse, opposite; n. m. reverse.*
O reverso da medalha. *The other side of the coin. The other side of the question.*

revés *m. reverse; backhand; misfortune.*
Ao revés. *Upside down. Inside out.*

revisão *f. revision; review.*

revisar *to look over; to revise; to review.*
Revisar os livros. *To audit the books.*

revisor *m. conductor; reviewer; proofreader.*

REVISTA *f. review; magazine; musical comedy.*
Ainda não recebi êsse (esse) número da revista. *I haven't received yet that number of the magazine.*

reviver *to revive.*

revocação *f. revocation, repeal.*

revocar *to revoke, to repeal; to evoke.*

revolta *f. revolt.*

revoltoso *adj. rebellious.*

revolução *f. revolution.*

revolucionário *adj. revolutionary; n. m. revolutionist.*

revolver *to revolve; to turn; to stir.*
Revolver céu e terra. *To move heaven and earth.*

revólver *m. revolver.*

rezar *to pray; to read, to say.*
Ela reza todos os dias. *She prays (says her prayers) every day.*
Reza aqui que ... *It says here that ...*

riacho *m. brook.*

ribeira *f. bank (river); shore.*

ribeiro *m. stream, brook.*

RICO *adj. rich, wealthy.*
Se eu fôsse rico não trabalharia tanto. *If I were rich I wouldn't work so much.*

ridente *adj. smiling; gay.*

ridicularizar *to ridicule.*

ridículo *adj. ridiculous, foolish; n. m. ridiculous thing; ridiculous person.*
Fazer-se ridículo. *To make a fool of oneself.*

rifa *f. raffle.*

rifar *to raffle.*

rifle *m. rifle.*

rigidez *f. rigidity; sternness.*

rígido *adj. rigid; severe; hard; stern.*

rigor *m. rigor.*

rigoroso *adj. rigorous, severe, strict.*

rijo *adj. rigid.*

rim *m. kidney.*

rima *f. rhyme.*

rinha Ⓑ *f. cockfight; fight.*

rinoceronte *m. rhinoceros.*

RIO *m. river.*
Rio abaixo (x = sh). *Down the river. Downstream.*
O Rio de Janeiro. *Rio de Janeiro ("the river of January").*

rio-grandense-do-norte *adj. and n. m. of the state of Rio Grande do Norte of Brazil.*

rio-grandense-do-sul *adj. and n. m. of the state of Rio Grande do Sul of Brazil.*

riqueza *f. riches, wealth.*

RIR *to laugh.*
Rir às gargalhadas. *To laugh out loud. To laugh heartily.*

RIR-SE *to laugh.*
Por que se ri dêle (dele)? *Why do you laugh at him?*

risada *f. laughter.*

risco *m. risk.*
Correr um risco. *To run a risk. To take a chance.*

RISO *m. laughter, laugh.*
Um frouxo (x = sh) Ⓑ de riso. *A fit of laughter.*
Isso não é motivo de riso. *That's no laughing matter.*

risonho *adj. smiling, pleasing.*

ritmo *m. rhythm.*

rito *m. rite, ceremony.*

rival *adj. rival; n. m. and f. rival.*

rivalidade *f. rivalry.*

rivalizar *to vie, to compete, to rival.*

roble *m. oak.*

robusto *adj. robust, strong.*
Êle (ele) é muito robusto. *He is very strong.*

roca *f. rock.*

roça *f. country, backwoods; plot of cleared land.*

rocha *f. stone, boulder.*
Rocha calcária. *Limestone.*

rochoso *adj. rocky.*

rociar *to bedew.*

rocio *m. dew.*
O Rocio. *Famous square in Lisbon.*

RODA *f. wheel, circle.*
Roda da sorte. *Wheel of fortune.*
Roda sobressalente. *Spare wheel.*

rodagem *f. set of wheels.*
Estrada de rodagem. *Highway.*

rodante *adj. rolling.*
Material rodante. *Rolling stock.*

rodapé *m. valance; baseboard; newspaper article at bottom of the page.*

rodar *to roll; to revolve; to rake.*

rodeio *m. rodeo; evasion.*
Deixe (x = sh) de rodeios e responda claramente. *Stop beating around the bush and give a straight answer.*

rodovia *f. highway* Ⓑ.

rodoviário *adj. highway* Ⓑ.

roer *to gnaw; to nibble; to erode.*

rogar *to pray, to beg, to entreat, to request.*
Rogo-lhe que ... *I beg you to ... Please ....*

rôgo (rogo) *m. request, petition; plea.*

rol *m. roll, list.*

rolante *adj. rolling.*
Escada rolante. *Escalator.*

rolar *to roll, to revolve.*

rôlha (rolha) *f. cork, stopper.*
Saca-rôlhas. *Corkscrew.*

rôlo (rolo) *m. roll; roller.*

romance *m. novel; romance.*

romanceiro *m. collection of songs, poems, etc.*

romano *adj. Roman; n. m. Roman.*

romanticismo *m. romanticism.*

romântico *adj. romantic; n. m. romantic.*

romantismo *m. romanticism.*

romaria *f. pilgrimage, excursion, tour.*

romeiro *m. pilgrim.*

ROMPER *to break; to smash; to tear; to rip; to fracture; to start, to begin.*
De repente ela rompeu o silêncio. *Suddenly she broke the silence.*
Nos rompemos com êles (eles). *We broke with them.*

roncar *to snore; to boast; to roar.*

ronco *m. snore; roar.*

ronda *f. watch, patrol; rounds.*

rondar *to watch, to patrol.*

ronha *f. scabies; malice, ill will.*

rosa *f. rose.*
Não há rosa sem espinhos. *No rose without a thorn.*

rosal *m. rose garden; rosary.*

rosário *m. rosary.*

rôsca (rosca) *f. ring (bread or cake); thread (of a screw).*

roseira *f. rosebush.*

ROSTO *m. face.*

rota *f. rout; route; course.*

roteiro *m. itinerary, schedule.*

rotina *f. routine; habit; rut.*

roubar *to rob, to steal.*
Roubaram-me a carteira. *They stole my wallet.*

roubo *m. robbery, theft.*

ROUPA *f. wearing apparel, clothing, clothes.*
Tenho que mudar de roupa. *I have to change my clothes.*
Roupa feita. *Ready-made clothes.*
Roupa de cama. *Bed linen.*

roupão *m. bathrobe; dressing gown.*

rouxinol (*x* = *sh*) *m. nightingale.*

roxo (*x* = *sh*) *adj. purple.*

RUA *f. street.*
Rua de uma mão. *One-way street.*
Rua principal. *Main street.*

rubi *m. ruby.*

rubo *m. brier, bramble.*

ruborizar *to redden, to blush.*

rude *adj. rude; rough; harsh.*

rudez, rudeza *f. rudeness; roughness, harshness.*

rugido *adj. roaring; n. m. roar.*

rugir *to roar; to bellow.*

ruído *m. noise.*

ruim *adj. bad; terrible; inferior.*
Eu achei o filme muito ruim. *I thought the film was terrible.*

ruína *f. ruin; downfall; pl. ruins.*

ruinoso *adj. ruinous.*

rumar *to steer; to head (for).*

rumo *m. course; route; direction.*
Vamos tomar outro rumo. *We'll take another course (road).*
Sem rumo. *Adrift. Without direction.*

rumor *m. rumor; noise.*

ruptura *f. rupture; break.*

rural *adj. rural, rustic.*

russo *adj. Russian; n. m. Russian.*

rústico *adj. rustic, rural.*

S

SÁBADO *m. Saturday.*

SABÃO *m. soap.*

sabedoria *f. learning, knowledge, wisdom.*

SABER *to know; to know how; to be able to; to taste; to find out.*
O senhor sabe a que horas abrem as lojas? *Do you know at what time the stores open?*
O senhor sabe nadar? *Do you know how to swim?*
Sei lá! *I don't know! How should I know?*
Quem sabe! *Who knows!*
Ela não sabe nada. *She doesn't know anything.*
Como se sabe. *As is known. As one knows.*
Que eu saiba. *Not as far as I know.*

Pelo que sei. *As far as I know.*
Saber de cor. *To know by heart.*

sabiá *m. thrush, bird of Brazil.*

sábio *adj. wise, learned; n. m. scholar, sage.*

SABONETE *m. toilet soap.*

sabor *m. taste, flavor.*

saborear *to flavor; to savor; to relish.*

saboroso *adj. delicious, tasty; pleasant.*
O jantar foi muito saboroso. *The dinner was delicious.*

sabotagem *f. sabotage.*

sabotar *to sabotage.*

sabre *m. saber.*

saca *f. bag, sack.*

sacar *to draw out.*

saca-rôlhas (saca-rolhas) *m. corkscrew.*

saciar *to satiate.*

SACO *m. sack; bag; purse.*
O que há neste saco de papel? *What's in this paper bag?*

sacramento *m. sacrament.*

sacrificar *to sacrifice.*

sacrifício *m. sacrifice.*

sacrilégio *m. sacrilege.*

sacristão *m. sexton.*

sacristia *f. sacristy, vestry.*

sacro *adj. sacred, holy.*

sacrossanto *adj. sacrosanct.*

sacudida *f. shock, shake, shaking; beating.*

sacudidela *f. shock; shake, shaking; beating.*

sacudidura *f. shaking.*

sacudir *to shake.*
Sacudir a cabeça. *To shake the head.*

sadio *adj. sound, healthy.*

sagacidade *f. sagacity, shrewdness.*

sagaz *adj. sagacious; shrewd; clever.*

sagrado *adj. sacred.*

saia *f. skirt.*

SAÍDA *f. departure; exit; outlet; loophole.*
Saída de emergência. *Emergency exit.*
Um beco sem saída. *A blind alley.*
Rua sem saída. *Dead-end street.*

sainete *m. short comedy or farce.*

SAIR *to go out; to leave; to depart; to appear; to come out.*
Ela já saiu. *She's already left.*
Ela sai à sua mãe. *She takes after her mother.*
A família saiu de viagem. *The family left on a trip.*
Vou sair ao ar livre. *I'm going out into the open air.*
Tudo saiu bem. *It all came out fine.*
Sair da linha. *To get out of line.*
Sair à francesa. *To take French leave.*
Sair caro. *To end up costing a lot.*

SAL *m. salt; wit.*
Sal e pimenta. *Salt and pepper.*

SALA *f. room.*
Quantos alunos há na sala de aula? *How many students are there in the classroom?*
Sala de espera. *Waiting room.*
Sala de jantar. *Dining room.*

salada *f. salad.*

salão *m. large room; hall; salon; parlor.*
Salão de beleza. *Beauty parlor.*
Salão de baile. *Dance hall. Ballroom.*

salário *m. salary, wages.*

salazarista *adj. of Salazar; n. m. follower of Salazar.*

saldar *to settle.*

saldo *m. balance, remainder.*
Saldo negativo. *Debit balance.*
Saldo positivo. *Credit balance.*

saleiro *adj. salt, salty; n. m. salt shaker.*

salgado *adj. salty, salted; witty.*

salientar *to make clear, to point out.*

saliente *adj. salient, prominent.*

saliva *f. saliva.*

salmão *m. salmon.*

salmo *m. psalm.*

salpicar *to sprinkle (with).*

salpico *m. sprinkle; speck; a drop or dash of something.*

salsa *f. parsley; sauce.*

salsicha *f. sausage.*

SALTAR *to jump, to leap; to hop; to skip; to omit.*
Você pode saltar a parede? *Can you jump over the wall?*
Ela saltou várias palavras. *She skipped several words.*
Saltar do ônibus (autocarro). *To get off the bus.*
Saltar da cama. *To jump out of bed.*

saltear *to assault, to attack.*

SALTO *m. jump, leap; heel.*
Dar saltos. *To jump. To leap.*
Salto de borracha. *Rubber heel.*

salubre *adj. salutary, healthy.*

salva *f. salvo; volley; tray.*
Uma salva de aplausos. *Thunderous applause.*

salvação *f. salvation.*

salvamento *m. salvage; rescue.*

salvar *to save; to salvage; to jump over; to salvo.*
O médico perdeu a esperança de salvá-lo. *The doctor gave up hope of saving him.*
Salvar com vinte e um tiros. *To salvo with twenty-one guns.*

salva-vidas *m. life preserver; lifeboat.*

salvo *adj. safe, saved; prep. besides, except.*
São e salvo. *Safe and sound.*
Em salvo. *Safe.*
Todos vieram salvo êle (ele). *Everyone came except him.*

salvo-conduto *m. safe-conduct, pass.*

samba *m. samba, Brazilian music and dance.*

sanar *to cure, to heal; to recover.*

sanatório *m. sanatorium, sanitarium.*

sanção *f. sanction.*

sancionar *to sanction; to confirm.*

sandália *f. sandal.*

sanduíche *m. sandwich.*

saneamento *m. sanitation.*

sanear *to make sanitary; to repair.*

sangrar *to bleed; to drain.*

sangrento *adj. bloody, sanguinary.*

SANGUE *m. blood.*
A sangue e fogo. *Without mercy.*
A sangue frio. *In cold blood.*
Ter o sangue quente. *To be hot-blooded.*

sanha *f. anger, fury.*

sanitário *adj. sanitary, hygienic.*

SANTO *adj. saintly, holy; n. m. saint.*
Semana Santa. *Holy Week (Easter).*
Santo Antônio (António). *Saint Anthony.*
Santa Bárbara. *Saint Barbara.*
Despir um santo para vestir outro. *To rob Peter to pay Paul.*

SÃO *adj. sound, healthy; sane; safe; n. m. saint.*
Regressou são e salvo. *He returned safe and sound.*
São Pedro. *Saint Peter.*

sapataria *f. shoe store; shoe-repair shop.*

sapateiro *m. shoemaker.*

SAPATO *m. shoe.*
Um par de sapatos. *A pair of shoes.*
Onde aperta o sapato? *Where does the shoe pinch?*
Sapatos de tênis (ténis). *Tennis shoes. Sneakers.*

Sapatos de salto alto. *High-heeled shoes.*
Calçar os sapatos. *To put one's shoes on.*
Descalçar os sapatos. *To take the shoes off.*

sapo *m. toad, frog.*

saque *m. bank draft; serve (tennis); sack, sacking, plunder.*

saquear *to sack, to loot, to pillage.*

sarampo *m. measles.*

sarar *to cure, to heal; to correct.*

sarcasmo *m. sarcasm.*

sardinha *f. sardine.*

sargento *m. sergeant.*

sarna *f. scabies, itch.*

satanás *m. Satan, devil.*

satélite *m. satellite.*

sátira *f. satire.*

satírico *adj. satiric.*

SATISFAÇÃO *f. satisfaction; pleasure; apology.*
Eu tive a satisfação de conhecê-lo. *I had the pleasure of meeting him.*
Isso foi uma grande satisfação para mim. *That gave me great satisfaction.*
Dar satisfações. *To apologise.*

satisfatório *adj. satisfactory.*

SATISFAZER *to satisfy; to please; to pay (a debt).*
O trabalho dêle (dele) não me satisfaz. *His work doesn't satisfy me.*
Satisfazer uma dívida. *To pay a debt.*

SATISFEITO *adj. satisfied, content; fulfilled.*
Quermos que todos estejam satisfeitos. *We want everyone to be satisfied.*
Estou satisfeito. *I'm satisfied.*

SAUDADE *f. longing, yearning; pl. regards, greetings; longing.*
Ter saudades de. *To miss. To long for.*
Tenho saudades de minha terra. *I'm homesick (for my country, district).*

saudar *to greet, to salute.*
Êle (ele) a saudou (saudou-a) muito afetuosamente (afectuosamente). *He greeted her affectionately.*

saudável *adj. healthful, good for the health; salutary; beneficial.*

SAÚDE *f. health.*
Ela está de boa saúde. *She is in good health.*
Ela está bem de saúde. *She is in good health.*
Êle (Ele) está mal de saúde. *He is in bad health.*
Estamos gozando de boa saúde. *We are enjoying good health.*
À sua saúde! *Good luck! To your health! (a toast).*

saudoso *adj. longing, yearnirg, homesick.*

sazão *f. season; time.*
Em sazão. *At the proper time. In season.*

sazonar *to season; to mature, to ripen.*

SE *(third person reflexive pronoun; also used as reciprocal pronoun and for the passive voice) himself, herself, themselves, etc.*
O menino não se lavou antes de sentar-se à mesa. *The boy did not wash before sitting at the table.*
Cale-se! *Be quiet! Be still!*
Diz-se que... *It's said that...*
Sabe-se que... *It's known that...*
Êles (Eles) se conhecem (conhecem-se). *They know each other.*
Escrevem-se todos os dias. *They write each other every day.*
Como se chama o senhor? *What is your name?*
Fala-se português. *Portuguese spoken (here).*

SE *conj. if, whether.*
Se o senhor quiser. *If you wish.*
Se tivesse o dinheiro eu o compraria. *If I*

had the money I would buy it.
Se ela chegar antes das oito iremos ao cinema. *If she arrives before eight we'll go to the movies.*
Se bem que ... *Although ...*
Se não. *If not.*

sé *f. see.*
A Santa Sé. *The Holy See.*

sêca (seca) *f. drought, dry spell.*

secante *adj. drying, boring; n. m. drying agent; bore.*

secão, secção (secção) *f. section; division; department; cutting, portion.*
Em que seção trabalha? *In what section do you work?*

SECAR to dry.
Ela pôs a roupa a secar ao sol. *She put the clothes out to dry in the sun.*

SÊCO (SECO) *adj. dry, withered; lean; curt; rude.*
Tenho a garganta sêca. *My throat is dry.*
Ele (ele) é um homém sêco. *He is a very curt ("dry") person.*
Clima sêco. *Dry climate.*
Vinho sêco. *Dry wine.*

secretaria *f. secretariat; office.*

secretária *f. secretary; desk.*

secretário *m. secretary.*

secreto *adj. secret; private.*
Serviço secreto. *Secret service.*

século *m. century; age; a long time.*
Estamos no século vinte. *We are in the twentieth century.*
Há um século que não o vejo. *I haven't seen you for ages.*

secundar *to second; to support; to aid.*
Ela o secunda em tudo. *She supports him in everything.*

secundário *adj. secondary.*

sêda (seda) *f. silk.*
Bicho da sêda. *Silkworm.*
Papel de sêda. *Tissue paper.*
Gravata de sêda. *Silk tie.*

sede *f. seat, headquarters.*

SÊDE (SEDE) *f. thirst; desire, craving.*
Estou com sêde. (Tenho sede). *I'm thirsty.*

sedento *adj. thirsty.*

sedição *f. sedition; rebellion.*

sedimento *m. sediment.*

sedução *f. seduction, enticement.*

sedutor *adj. seductive, enticing; n. m. seducer.*

seduzir *to seduce; to tempt; to fascinate.*

segador *m. harvester; mower.*

segar *to reap; to mow; to harvest.*

segrêdo (segredo) *m. secret; secrecy; mystery.*
Você pode guardar o segrêdo? *Can you keep the secret?*

segregacionismo *m. segregation.*

segregacionista *m. and f. segregationist.*

segregar *to segregate; to separate.*

seguido *adj. continued; following.*
Em seguida. *Right away. Immediately.*

SEGUINTE *adj. following, next.*
No dia seguinte êle (ele) partiu. *The following day he left.*
Não gosto de todos; mande-me só os seguintes: *I don't like all of them; send me only the following:*

SEGUIR *to follow; to pursue; to continue, to go on, to keep on.*
Siga-me. *Follow me.*
Seguirei os seus conselhos. *I'll follow your advice.*
Siga bem em frente. *Continue straight ahead.*
Que segue depois? *What comes afterwards?*
Como segue: *As follows:*
É preciso seguir as instruções. *One must follow the directions.*
Quem segue? *Who's next?*

SEGUNDA *f. Monday.*

SEGUNDA-FEIRA *f. Monday.*

SEGUNDO *adj. second; n. m. second; prep. according to.*
Ela mora no segundo andar. *She lives on the second floor.*
Desejo o segundo volume. *I want the second volume.*
Em segundo lugar. *In second place.*
Um bilhete de segunda. *A coach ticket. ("A second-class ticket.")*
De segunda mão. *Secondhand.*
Segundo o relatório. *According to the report.*

segurança *f. security; safety; certainty; protection.*
Com segurança. *Assuredly.*
Freio de segurança. *Emergency brake.*
Alfinête (alfinete) de segurança. *Safety pin.*

segurar *to secure; to assure; to insure.*

SEGURO *adj. secure, sure, safe, certain; insured; n. m. insurance; security.*
Você não está seguro? *Aren't you sure?*
Companhia de seguros. *Insurance company.*
Apólice de seguro. *Insurance policy.*
Seguro de vida. *Life insurance.*
Seguro contra acidentes. *Accident insurance.*

seio *m. breast, bosom.*

SEIS *adj. and n. m. six; sixth.*

seiscentos *adj. and n. m. six hundred; six hundredth.*

selar *to seal; to stamp; to saddle.*
Faça o favor de selar estas cartas. *Please put stamps on these letters.*

seleção (selecção) *f. selection, choice.*

selecionar (seleccionar) *to select, to choose.*

SÊLO (SELO) *m. seal; stamp; postage stamp.*
Sêlo postal. *Postage stamp.*

selvagem *adj. savage, wild; n. m. and f. savage.*

SEM *without, besides.*
Iremos sem êle (ele). *We'll go without him.*
Não posso ler sem os meus óculos. *I can't read without my glasses.*
Eu fiz sem pensar. *I did it without thinking.*
Sem falta. *Without fail.*
Sem dúvida. *Without a doubt. Undoubtedly.*
Sem fim. *Endless.*
Sem mais nem menos. *Without further ado.*

SEMANA *f. week.*
Irei a semana que vem. *I'll go next week.*
Ela virá a próxima semana. *She'll come next week.*
A semana passada. *Last week.*
Numa semana mais ou menos. *In a week or so.*
Semana Santa. *Holy Week.*
Fim de semana. *Weekend.*

semanal *adj. weekly.*
Uma revista semanal. *A weekly magazine.*

semanário *adj. weekly; n. m. weekly (publication).*

semblante *m. countenance, face; look, aspect.*
Você tem bom semblante hoje. *You look well today.*

semear *to sow, to seed; to scatter, to spread.*

semelhança *f. similarity, resemblance, likeness.*

semelhar *to resemble, to be like.*

semente *f. seed.*

semestre *m. semester.*

seminarista *m. seminarist.*

semítico *adj. Semitic.*

sem-par *adj. unequaled, peerless.*

SEMPRE *always, ever.*
Êle (ele) sempre chega tarde. *He's always late.*
Como sempre. *As always. As usual.*
Para sempre. *Forever.*

senado *m. senate.*

senador *m. senator.*

senão *conj. if not, otherwise.*

senda *f. path.*

senha *f. signal; sign; password; readmission theatre ticket, pass.*

SENHOR *m. mister, sir; gentleman; o senhor you.*
Bom dia, senhor Silva. *Good morning, Mr. Silva.*
O senhor Silva não estará aqui hoje. *Mr. Silva won't be here today.*
Muito obrigado, senhor. *Thank you, sir.*
O senhor é americano? *Are you an American?*
Não conheço êsse (esse) senhor. *I don't know that gentleman.*
Caro Senhor: *Dear Sir:*
Sim, senhor. *Yes, sir.*

SENHORA *f. Mrs., madam, lady; wife; a senhora you.*
A senhora Silva está em casa? *Is Mrs. Silva in?*
A senhora não está em casa. *The lady of the house is not at home.*
A senhora é americana? *Are you an American?*
Não conheço essa senhora. *I don't know that lady.*
Prezada Senhora: *Dear Madam:*
Sim, senhora. *Yes, madam.*
Minhas senhoras e meus senhores: *Ladies and gentlemen.*

senhoria *f. lordship, ladyship.*
Vossa Senhoria. *Your lordship. Your ladyship.*

SENHORINHA *f. miss, young lady* Ⓑ.

SENHORITA *f. miss; young lady.*

senil *adj. senile.*

sensação *f. sensation.*

sensacional *adj. sensational.*

sensatez *f. good sense, discretion.*

sensato *adj. sensible, discreet.*

sensibilidade *f. sensibility; sensitivity.*

sensível *adj. sensitive; appreciable.*
Os olhos são sensíveis à luz. *The eyes are sensitive to light.*

senso *m. sense.*
Senso comum. *Common sense.*

sensual *adj. sensual.*

sensualidade *f. sensuality.*

sentado *adj. seated.*
Ela estava sentada à minha esquerda. *She was seated on my left.*

sentar *to sit, to seat.*

SENTAR-SE *to sit (down).*
Os convidados se sentaram (sentaram-se) à mesa. *The guests sat at the table.*
Sentemo-nos. *Let's sit down.*

sentença *f. sentence; verdict; maxim.*

sentenciar *to sentence.*

SENTIDO *adj. felt; experienced; offended; sad; n. m. sense; meaning; direction.*
Ela ficou muito sentida. *She was very offended.*

sentimental *adj. sentimental, romantic.*

sentimentalismo *m. sentimentalism.*

sentimento *m. sentiment, feeling.*
Sentimentos nobres. *Noble sentiments.*
Sentimento de culpa. *Guilty feeling.*

SENTIR *to feel; to be sorry; to hear; to sense; to be (happy, cold, etc.); to appreciate; m. feeling; opinion.*
Sinto muito. *I'm very sorry.*
Sinto não poder ir. *I'm sorry I can't go.*
Agora sinto frio. *Now I'm cold.*
Sentimos falta dela. *We miss her.*
Sentimos que você não pudesse vir. *We are sorry you could not come.*

sentir-se *to feel.*
Ela se sente (sente-se) muito bem. *She feels very well.*

separação *f. separation.*

separar *to separate.*
Uma cortina separa as duas salas. *A curtain separates the two rooms.*

separar-se *to separate, to part company.*
Decidiram separar-se. *They decided to separate.*

sepulcro *m. sepulcher, grave, tomb.*

sepultar *to bury, to inter; to hide.*

sepultura *f. burial; grave, tomb.*

seqüência (sequência) *f. sequence; series; order.*

sequer *adv. at least, so much as, even.*
Nem sequer. *Not even.*

seqüestrar (sequestrar) *to kidnap; to confiscate.*

SER *to be.*
Quem é? *Who is it?*
É o João. *It's John.*
Quem será? *Who can it be?*
O senhor é o senhor Smith? *Are you Mr. Smith?*
Donde é o senhor? *Where are you from?*
Sou de Boston. *I'm from Boston.*
Somos brasileiros. *We are Brasilians.*
De quem é êste (este) lápis? *Whose pencil is this?*
É meu. *It's mine.*
É de João. *It's John's.*
Esta caixa (x = sh) é de madeira. *This box is made of wood.*
Ela é bonita. *She is pretty.*
Sou escritor. *I'm a writer.*
Que é isso? *What is that?*
Quanto é? *How much is it?*
Que horas são? *What time is it?*
É uma hora. *It's one o'clock.*
São duas (horas). *It's two o'clock.*
Ainda é cedo. *It's still early.*
É tarde. *It's late.*
Quando será a boda? *When will the wedding take place?*
Que dia é hoje? *What day is today?*
Hoje é segunda-feira. *Today is Monday.*
É fácil. *It's easy.*
É difícil. *It's difficult.*
É verdade? *Is it true?*
Não é verdade. *It's not true.*
Pode ser. *That may be.*
Farei quanto puder. *I'll do what I can.*
Fôsse quem fôsse (Fosse quem fosse). *Whoever it might be.*
Que é feito dêle (dele)? *What has become of him?*
A carteira foi achada na rua. *The wallet was found in the street.*
Era uma vez. *Once upon a time.*
É isso mesmo! *That's it exactly!*

serenar *to calm down, to pacify.*

serenata *f. serenade.*

serenidade *f. serenity, coolness.*

sereno *adj. serene, calm; clear; n. m. dew; open air.*
Foi uma noite serena. *It was a calm evening.*

série *f. series.*

seriedade *f. seriousness, gravity.*

seringa *f. syringe.*

seringueira *f. rubber tree.*

seringueiro *m. rubber worker.*

SÉRIO *adj. serious, earnest.*
Tomar a sério. *To take seriously.*
Você está sério? *Are you serious?*

sermão *m. sermon; lecture.*

serpente *f. serpent, snake.*

serpentina *f. paper streamer.*

serpentino *adj. serpentine.*

serra *f. saw; range of mountains, sierra.*
A serra não corta bem. *The saw doesn't cut well.*
Serra de cadeia. *Chain saw.*

serrar *to saw.*

sertanejo *adj. of the sertão, of the backwoods; m. backwoodsman.*

sertão *m. backwoods, interior.*

SERVIÇO *m. service, favor; set.*
Serviço de mesa. *Table service.*
Você me prestou (prestou-me) um grande serviço. *You rendered me a great service.*
O serviço neste hotel é muito ruim. *The service in this hotel is terrible.*
Êle (ele) está de serviço. *He's on duty.*
Serviço militar. *Military service.*

servidão *f. servitude.*

servidor *m. servant, server.*
Servidor público. *Public servant.*

SERVIR *to serve; to do a favor; to do, to be useful; to serve at the table; to wait on table.*
Em que posso servi-lo? *What can I do for you?*
Pode me servir (servir-me) um pouco de vinho? *Can you serve me a little wine?*
Servir à mesa. *To wait on table.*
Para que serve esta máquina? *What's this machine for?*
Não serve. *It's no good.*
Não serve para nada. *It's no good. It's good for nothing.*
Ela pode servir de intérprete. *She can act as interpreter.*

servitude *f. servitude.*

sessão *f. session, meeting.*
Estar em sessão. *To be in session.*

SESSENTA *adj. and n. m. sixty; sixtieth.*

sesta *f. siesta, nap.*

seta *f. arrow; hand (clock).*

SETE *adj. and n. m. seven; seventh.*
Pintar o sete. *To have a wild time.*
Sete de setembro (Setembro). *September 7, Brazilian Independence Day.*

setecentos *adj. and n. m. seven hundred; seven hundredth.*

SETEMBRO *m. September.*

SETENTA *adj. and n. m. seventy; seventieth.*

setentrional *adj. northern.*

sétimo *adj. seventh; n. m. seventh.*

setuagenário *adj. septuagenarian; n. m. septuagenarian.*

SEU *m. adj. and pron. your, his, her, its, their.*
João, onde deixou (x = sh) o seu livro? *John, where did you leave your book?*
Os meus filhos estão com os seus avós. *My children are with their grandparents.*
Êste (este) procedimento tem as suas vantagens e desvantagens. *This procedure has its advantages and its disadvantages.*

severidade *f. severity, strictness.*

severo *adj. severe, strict.*

sexagenário (x = ks) *adj. sexagenarian; n. m. sexagenarian.*

sexo (x = ks) *m. sex.*

SEXTA *f. Friday.*

SEXTA-FEIRA *f. Friday.*

sexto *adj. sixth.*

si *yourself, himself, herself, themselves, itself.*
Ela o quer para si mesma. *She wants it for herself.*

sibilo *m. whistle; hiss.*

sicrano *m. Mr. So and So.*
Fulano, Beltrano e Sicrano. *Tom, Dick and Harry.*

sidra *f. cider.*

significação *f. meaning, significance.*

significado *m. meaning, significance.*

significante *adj. significant.*

significar *to mean, to signify.*
Que significa isso? *What's the meaning of that?*

significativo *adj. significant.*

signo m. sign (zodiac).

sílaba f. syllable.

silêncio m. silence.
Silêncio! Silence!
Guardar silêncio. To remain silent.
Sofrer em silêncio. To suffer in silence.
O silêncio vale ouro. Silence is golden.

silencioso adj. silent, noiseless; n. m. muffler (auto).
Quero uma máquina de escrever silenciosa. I want a silent typewriter.

silvar to whistle, to hiss.

silvestre adj. wild, rustic.
Plantas silvestres. Wild plants.

SIM adv. yes; indeed; n. m. consent, assent.
Sim senhor. Yes, sir.
Eu lhe disse que sim. I told him yes.
Acho que sim. I think so.
Um dia sim, um dia não. Every other day.
Pois sim! Fine! All right! or Oh, yeh!
Come now! (depends on inflection).
Dar o sim. To say yes. To give consent.

simbolizar to symbolise.

símbolo m. symbol.

simetria f. symmetry.

simétrico adj. symmetrical.

similar adj. similar.

similitude f. similitude, similarity, resemblance.

simpatia f. sympathy.
Ter simpatia por. To sympathise with. To have sympathy for.

simpático adj. nice, pleasant, sympathetic.
Ela é muito simpática. She's very nice.

simpatizar to sympathise.

SIMPLES adj. simple; plain; n. m. and f. simpleton.
É muito simples. It's quite simple.
Simplesmente. Simply.
Juros simples. Simple interest.

simplicidade f. simplicity.

simplificação f. simplification.

simplificar to simplify.

simulação f. simulation; sham.

simulacro m. sham; imitation.

simular to simulate, to feign.

simultâneo adj. simultaneous.

SINAL m. sign; mark; signal; token; beauty spot; deposit.
Ponha um sinal nessa página. Put a mark on that page.
Ela deu sinal de alarma. She sounded the alarm.
Sinal de perigo. Danger signal.
Sinal aberto. Green light.
Sinal fechado. Red light.
Ela fêz (fez) o sinal da cruz. She made the sign of the cross.

sinalar to mark; to signal; to point out; to indicate.
É preciso sinalar o dia da reunião. The date of the meeting must be set.

sinceridade f. sincerity.

sincero adj. sincere.
Ele (ele) é um amigo sincero. He's a true friend.

síncope f. syncope; fainting spell.

sincronizar to synchronise.

sindical adj. pertaining to a trade union; syndical; union.

sindicato m. labor union; trade union.

sinfonia f. symphony.

sinfônico (sinfónico) adj. symphonic.

singelo adj. simple; sincere; single.

singular adj. singular; unusual; individual; odd.
"Lápis" é singular e plural: o lápis, os lápis. "Lápis" is singular and plural: the pencil, the pencils.
É um caso singular. It's a strange case.

singularidade f. singularity; peculiarity.

sinhá f. miss, missy Ⓑ.

sinistra f. left hand.

sinistro adj. left; sinister; unfortunate; n. m. accident, loss.
Lado sinistro. Left side.
Tem um aspecto sinistro. It looks sinister.
Onde aconteceu o sinistro? Where did the accident occur?

sino m. bell.

sinônimo (sinónimo) adj. synonymous; n. m. synonym.

sinopse f. synopsis, summary.

sintaxe (x = ks) f. syntax.

síntese f. synthesis.

sintético adj. synthetic.

sintoma m. symptom.

sintonizar to syntonise; to tune in (radio).
O aparelho de rádio está mal sintonizado. The radio set is not properly tuned.

sirena f. siren, nymph.

siri m. crab.

sisal m. sisal, sisal hemp.

sistema m. system.
Sistema métrico. Metric system.
Sistema decimal. Decimal system.

sistemático adj. systematic.

sisudo adj. pensive; prudent; calm.

sitiar to besiege.

sítio m. place, site, location; siege.

SITUAÇÃO f. situation; position; circumstances; site, location.
Êle (ele) está em má situação. He's in a bad situation.

situar to place, to locate, to situate.

smoking m. tuxedo, dinner jacket Ⓑ.

SÓ adj. alone; single; adv. only.
O senhor está só? Are you alone?
Só para adultos. Adults only.
Sòmente. Only.

soalho m. floor.

SOAR to sound; to ring.
O sino soou. The bell rang.

sob prep. under, below.
Sob juramento. Under oath.
Sob medida. Made-to-order.

soberania f. sovereignty.

soberano adj. sovereign; n. m. sovereign.

soberbo adj. proud, haughty; magnificent.

sobra f. excess, surplus; pl. leftovers.
Tenho tempo de sobra. I've plenty of time.

sobrado adj. left over; plenty; n. m. wooden floor; house of two or more stories Ⓑ; plantation owner's large home Ⓑ.

sobrancelha f. eyebrow.
Franzir as sobrancelhas. To frown.

sobrar to be more than enough; to be left over.
Sobrou muito alimento. A great deal of food was left over.
Parece-me que aqui sobro. It seems to me that I'm not needed here.
Sobram seis. There are six too many.

SÔBRE (SOBRE) on; over; above; about.
Ponha o copo sôbre a mesa. Put the glass on the table.
Êle (ele) escreveu um livro sôbre Portugal. He wrote a book about Portugal.
Sôbre que falaram? What did they talk about?

sobrecarga f. overload; overcharge.

sobrecarregar to overload; to overcharge.

sobremaneira adv. excessively, greatly.

SOBREMESA f. dessert.

sobrenatural adj. supernatural; n. m. supernatural.

sobrenome m. surname.

sobrepor to superimpose, to place over; to overlay; to overlap.

sobressair to stand out; to excel.

sobressalente adj. spare; salient.
Pneu sobressalente. Spare tire.

sobressaltar to frighten; to startle; to surprise.

sobressalto m. fright; surprise; shock.

sobretudo adv. above all, especially; n. m. overcoat.

sobreviver to survive.

sobriedade f. sobriety, temperance, moderation.

sobrinho m. nephew.

sóbrio adj. sober, temperate.

socar to strike, to hit, to beat, to punch, to pound.

social adj. social.
Assistência social. Social work
Ordem social. Social order.
Quem representa esta razão social? Who represents this firm?

socialismo m. socialism.

socialista adj. socialistic; n. m. and f. socialist.

socializar to socialise.

sociável adj. sociable.

sociedade f. society; community; company; corporation; partnership.
A alta sociedade. High society.
Formaram uma sociedade. They formed a partnership.
Sociedade anônima (anónima). Corporation.

sócio m. partner, associate; member.
O senhor é sócio dêsse (desse) clube? Are you a member of that club?
Sócio principal. Senior partner.

sociologia f. sociology.

sociólogo m. sociologist.

socorrer to aid, to help, to assist; to rescue.
Ninguém quer socorrê-lo. Nobody wants to help him.

socorro m. succor, aid, help.

soda f. soda.

sofá m. sofa, couch.

sofrer to suffer, to stand.

sofrido adj. patient.

sofrimento m. suffering.

soga f. rope, lariat.

sogro m. father-in-law.

SOL m. sun, sunshine.
Tomar banho de sol. To have a sunbath.
Nascer do sol. Sunrise.
Pôr do sol. Sunset.
De sol a sol. From sunrise to sunset.
Queimadura de sol. Sunburn.

sola f. sole (of the foot, of shoe).

solar to sole (shoe); to play a solo; adj. solar, manorial; n. m. mansion, manor house.
Ano solar. Solar year.
Mancha solar. Sunspot.

soldado m. soldier.
Soldado raso. Buck private.
Soldado Desconhecido. Unknown Soldier.

soldar to solder; to weld.

solene adj. solemn; serious, grave; religious.

solenidade f. solemnity.

soletrar to spell; to read slowly; to read badly.

solicitação f. solicitation, request.

solicitador adj. soliciting; n. m. solicitor.

solicitar to solicit; to ask; to apply for.
Ele (ele) solicita um emprego (emprego). He's applying for a position.

solícito adj. solicitous, concerned.

solicitude f. solicitude, concern.

solidão f. solitude.

solidariedade f. solidarity.

solidário adj. solidary; joint; mutual.

solidez f. solidity, firmness, soundness.

sólido adj. solid, sound; strong; firm; n. m. solid.

Tem uma base muito sólida. *It has a very solid base.*

solitário *adj. solitary, lonely; n. m. hermit.*

solo *m. soil; ground; solo.*

soltar *to untie, to loosen; to set free; to let out; to let go.*
Soltaram o prêso (preso). *They set the prisoner free.*
Soltaram as amarras. *They loosened the cables.*
De repente êle (ele) soltou uma gargalhada. *Suddenly he burst into laughter.*
Soltar o cabelo. *To let one's hair down.*

soltar-se *to get loose.*
Ela soltou um grito. *She cried out.*

solteirão *m. confirmed bachelor.*

solteiro *adj. single, unmarried, bachelor; n. m. bachelor.*
O senhor é casado ou solteiro? *Are you married or single?*
Ainda sou solteiro. *I'm still a bachelor.*

solteirona *f. old maid, spinster.*

sôlto (solto) *adj. loose; free; licentious.*
Verso sôlto. *Blank verse.*
Ela tem a língua muito sôlta. *She has a very loose tongue.*

SOLUÇÃO *f. solution; answer; dénouement, outcome; payment.*
Isto não tem solução. *There's no solution to this.*
Essa é a melhor solução. *That's the best solution.*

soluço *m. sob.*

solúvel *adj. soluble; solvable.*

solvência *f. solvency.*

solvente *adj. solvent.*

solver *to solve; to resolve.*

SOM *m. sound; tone; noise; manner, way.*
Sem tom nem som. *Without rhyme or reason.*
À prova de som. *Soundproof.*
Em alto e bom som. *Loud and clear.*

soma *f. sum, amount, addition.*
Quanto é a soma total? *What's the total amount?*
Em soma. *In short. In all.*

somar *to add, to sum up.*
Você sabe usar máquina de somar? *Do you know how to use an adding machine?*

SOMBRA *f. shadow; shade; darkness.*
Ela se sentou (sentou-se) à sombra duma árvore. *She sat down in the shade of a tree.*
Não há nem sombra de verdade no que êle (ele) diz. *There isn't an iota of truth in what he says.*

sombrinha *f. parasol.*

sombrio *adj. shady; gloomy; somber.*

SÒMENTE *solely, only.*
Aprendi sòmente um pouco de português. *I learned only a little Portuguese.*

sonâmbulo *m. sleepwalker.*

sonata *f. sonata.*

sondagem *f. sounding.*

sondar *to sound, to sound out.*
Estavam sondando (a sondar) a baía. *They were sounding the bay.*

soneca *f. nap (short sleep).*
Ele (ele) está tirando (a tirar) uma soneca. *He is taking a nap.*

sonêto (soneto) *m. sonnet.*

sonhador *m. dreamer.*

sonhar *to dream.*
Ela sonha com dias passados. *She dreams of days gone by.*

sonho *m. dream.*
Tudo parece um sonho. *It all seems a dream.*

SONO *m. sleep.*
Você está com sono? (Você tem sono?) *Are you sleepy?*
Êle (ele) pegou no sono. *He fell asleep.*

sonoridade *f. sonority.*

sonoro *adj. sonorous.*
Um filme sonoro. *A sound film, a film with sound.*

SOPA *f. soup; easy, simple* (B).
Quer mais sopa? *Do you want more soup?*
Isto é sopa. *This is easy. There's nothing to this.*

sopapo *m. blow, slap.*

soprano *m. and f. soprano.*

soprar *to blow; to whisper.*

sôpro (sopro) *m. blowing; breath; puff.*
Instrumento de sôpro. *Wind instrument.*

sôro (soro) *m. serum; whey (milk).*

sorrir *to smile.*
Todos sorriram. *They all smiled.*

sorriso *m. smile.*

SORTE *f. chance, lot, fortune, luck; fate; manner; kind.*
Boa sorte! *Good luck!*
Ela tem muita sorte. *She is very lucky.*
Deitemos sortes. *Let's cast lots.*
Má sorte. *Bad luck.*
Quem tirou a sorte grande? *Who won the grand prize?*

sortear *to cast lots; to raffle.*

sorteio *m. raffle; drawing of lots.*

sortir *to supply; to mix.*

sorver *to sip; to absorb; to swallow.*

sorvete *m. ice cream; sherbet.*

soslaio *m. slant.*
De soslaio. *Askance.*

sossegado *adj. calm, quiet.*

sossegar *to calm, to quiet.*
Quando você sossegar, falaremos. *When you calm down we'll talk.*

sossêgo (sossego) *m. peace, calm, quiet.*
Não tivemos um minuto de sossêgo. *We didn't have a moment's peace.*

sótão *m. attic.*

sotaque *m. accent, foreign accent.*
Ela fala português com um sotaque espanhol. *She speaks Portuguese with a Spanish accent.*

soviético *adj. Soviet.*

sòzinho *adj. alone, all alone.*

SUA *f. adj. and pron. your, his, her, its, their, yours, hers, theirs.*
José, onde está (a) sua irmã? *Joseph, where is your sister?*
Ela está com (a) sua amiga Maria. *She is with her friend Mary.*

suar *to sweat, to perspire.*

suave *adj. soft; mild; gentle; mellow; sweet.*
Ele (ele) tem maneiras suaves. *He has gentle manners.*

suavidade *f. softness, gentleness.*

suavizar *to soften, to soothe.*

subalterno *adj. and n. m. subaltern, subordinate.*

subarrendar *to sublet, to sublease.*

subconsciente *adj. subconscious; n. m. subconscious.*

subdiretor (subdirector) *m. subdirector, assistant director.*

subdivisão *f. subdivision.*

SUBIR *to go up, to ascend, to rise; to climb; to mount; to raise.*
Subamos. *Let's go up.*
Suba ao quarto andar. *Go up to the fourth floor.*
Ela já subiu para o trem. *She has already boarded the train.*
Os preços vão subindo. *Prices keep going up.*

súbito *adj. sudden.*
De súbito. *Suddenly. All of a sudden.*

subjetividade (subjectividade) (subjectividade) *f. subjectivity.*

subjetivo (subjectivo) *adj. subjective.*

subjugar *to subjugate, to overpower.*

subjuntivo *adj. subjunctive; n. m. subjunctive.*

sublevação *f. insurrection, uprising.*

sublevar *to stir up, to rebel.*

sublime *adj. sublime.*

sublinhar *to underline; to emphasize.*

submarino *adj. submarine; n. m. submarine.*

submeter *to submit; to subdue.*
Submeter à votação. *To put to a vote.*

subordinado *adj. subordinate.*

subordinar *to subordinate.*

subornar *to bribe.*

subôrno (suborno) *m. bribe, bribery.*

subscrever *to subscribe.*
O senhor quer subscrever a esta revista? *Would you like to subscribe to this magazine?*

subscrição *f. subscription.*

subscritor *m. subscriber.*

subsecretário *m. undersecretary.*

subseqüente (subsequente) *adj. subsequent.*

subsidiar *to subsidize, to aid.*

subsídio *m. subsidy, aid.*

subsistência *f. subsistence.*

subsistir *to subsist; to exist; to last.*

substância *f. substance; essence.*
Em substância. *In substance. In short.*

substancial *adj. substantial.*

substanciar *to substantiate.*

substancioso *adj. substantial; nourishing.*

substantivo *adj. substantive; n. m. substantive, noun.*

substituição *f. substitution.*

substituir *to substitute.*
Ele (ele) substituiu o seu amigo. *He substituted for his friend.*

substituto *m. substitute.*

subterrâneo *adj. subterranean, underground.*

subtítulo *m. subtitle.*

subtração *f. subtraction.*

subúrbio *m. suburb.*

subvenção *f. subsidy, grant.*

subvencionar *to subsidize.*

subversão *f. subversion.*

suceder *to happen; to succeed.*
Que sucedeu depois? *What happened then (next)?*
Suceda o que suceda, eu estarei aqui. *No matter what happens, I'll be here.*
Crê-se que o filho dêle (dele) lhe sucederá. *It is believed that his son will succeed him.*

sucessão *f. succession.*

sucessivo *adj. successive.*

sucesso *m. event, incident; result; success.*
A peça teve grande sucesso. *The play was a hit.*

sucessor *m. successor.*

suco *m. juice; sap.*
Suco de laranja. *Orange juice.*

sucumbir *to succumb; to die; to yield.*

sucursal *adj. branch; n. m. branch.*

sudeste *adj. southeast; n. m. southeast.*

sudoeste *adj. southwest; n. m. southwest.*

sueco *adj. Swedish; n. m. Swede; Swedish.*

suéter *m. sweater* (B).

suficiência *f. sufficiency, adequacy.*

suficiente *adj. sufficient, enough.*
Isso não é suficiente. *That's not enough.*

sufixo *(x = ks) m. suffix.*

sufocar *to suffocate; to strangle.*

sufrágio *m. suffrage, voting.*

sugerir *to suggest, to hint.*

Que me sugere o senhor? *What do you suggest (to me)?*

sugestão *f. suggestion; hint.*
Essa foi uma boa sugestão. *That was a good suggestion.*

sugestivo *adj. suggestive.*

suicida *m. and f. suicide (person).*

suicidar-se *to commit suicide.*

suicídio *m. suicide.*

suíço *adj. Swiss; n. m. Swiss.*

sujeitar *to subject; to subdue.*

SUJEITO *adj. subject; liable; n. m. subject; theme; fellow, guy.*
Estar sujeito a. *To be subject to.*
Quem é êsse (esse) sujeito? *Who is that fellow?*

sujo *adj. dirty, soiled; foul.*

SUL *adj. south, southern; n. m. south.*
Cruzeiro do Sul. *Southern Cross.*

sulcar *to plow.*

súlfur *m. sulfur.*

sulista *adj. southern; n. m. southerner.*

sumário *m. summary.*

sumir, sumir-se *to disappear, to fade away.*

sumo *adj. great, high, supreme; n. m. juice; top.*
Ao sumo. *At the most.*

suntuosidade *f. sumptuousness.*

suntuoso *adj. sumptuous, magnificent.*

suor *m. sweat, perspiration; hard work.*

superabundância *f. superabundance, oversupply.*

superabundante *adj. superabundant, very abundant.*

superar *to exceed, to excel, to surpass; to overcome.*
Êsse (esse) trabalho supera tôdas (todas) as expectativas. *That work exceeds all expectations.*

superficial *adj. superficial.*

superficialidade *f. superficiality.*

superfície *f. surface, area.*
Superfície da terra. *Surface of the earth.*

supérfluo *adj. superfluous.*

superintendente *m. superintendent, supervisor.*

superior *adj. superior; higher; better; n. m. superior.*
Ele (ele) é um homem superior. *He's a great man.*
Este (este) é um vinho superior. *This is an excellent wine.*

superioridade *f. superiority.*

superlativo *adj. superlative.*

super-mercado *m. supermarket.*

supernumerário *adj. supernumerary.*

superprodução *f. overproduction.*

superstição *f. superstition.*

supersticioso *adj. superstitious.*

suplantar *to supplant, to displace.*

suplemento *m. supplement.*

suplente *adj. substituting, alternate; n. m. substitute, alternate.*

súplica *f. request, entreaty, petition.*
Ele (ele) não cedeu às súplicas dela. *He did not give in to her pleas.*

suplicar *to beg, to implore, to beseech, to entreat.*
Suplico-lhe que o perdone. *I entreat (beg) you to forgive him.*

suplício *m. ordeal; torment; torture; execution.*
Êle (ele) passou pelo suplício de ... *He went through the ordeal of ...*

supor *to suppose, to imagine, to presume.*
Você bem pode supor o que aconteceu. *You can well imagine what happened.*

suportar *to support; to bear.*

suportável *adj. supportable, bearable.*

suposição *f. supposition, conjecture, assumption.*

suposto *adj. supposed, presumed.*

supremacia *f. supremacy.*

supremo *adj. supreme, highest.*
A Côrte (Corte) Suprema. *The Supreme Court.*

supressão *f. suppression.*

suprimir *to suppress; to eliminate; to omit.*

surdo *adj. deaf; muffled; n. m. deaf person.*

surgir *to arise, to emerge.*

surpreendente *adj. surprising.*

surpreender *to surprise.*
A chegada dêle (dele) surpreendeu a todos. *His arrival surprised everybody.*

surpreendido *adj. surprised.*

surprêsa (surpresa) *f. surprise.*

surprêso (surpreso) *adj. surprised.*

surrar *to beat, to thrash.*

surtir *to cause.*

suscetibilidade (susceptibilidade) *f. susceptibility.*

suscetível (susceptível) *adj. susceptible, sensitive.*

suscitar *to stir up, to excite.*

suspeita *f. suspicion, doubt.*

suspeitar *to suspect, to distrust.*
Suspeito dêle (dele). *I'm suspicious of him. I suspect him.*

suspeito *adj. suspected; suspect; n. m. suspect.*

suspeitoso *adj. suspicious, doubtful.*

suspender *to suspend; to postpone; to put off; to discontinue; to stop; to adjourn.*
Suspendeu-se a publicação da revista. *The publication of the magazine was suspended.*
Suspender os pagamentos. *To stop payment.*
Suspender a sessão. *To adjourn the meeting.*

suspensão *f. suspension, cessation.*

suspensivo *adj. suspensive.*

suspenso *adj. suspended, hanging.*
Em suspenso. *In suspense. Pending.*
Deixar (x = sh) em suspenso. *To hold over. To hold in abeyance.*

suspirar *to sigh; to long for.*
Suspirar por. *To long for.*

suspiro *m. sigh.*

sussurrar *to whisper, to murmur.*

sussurro *m. whisper, murmur.*

substância, sustância *f. substance.*

sustentar *to support; to sustain; to assert.*
Devemos sustentar as artes. *We should support the arts.*

sustento *m. maintenance, support.*

suster *to support, to sustain.*

susto *m. fright.*

sutil, subtil (subtil) *adj. subtle.*

sutileza, subtilezza (subtileza) *f. subtleness.*

T

ta *(contr. of te + a) it to you (fam.), her to you.*

tabacaria *f. tobacco shop.*

tabaco *m. tobacco.*
Tabaco em fôlha (folha). *Leaf tobacco.*

taberna *f. tavern, inn, bar.*

taberneiro *m. tavern keeper, innkeeper.*

tabique *m. partition wall, partition.*

tablado *m. stage, platform; scaffold.*

tábua *f. table (of information); board, plank.*
Tábua de multiplicação. *Multiplication table.*
Tábua de mesa. *Leaf of a table.*

taça *f. cup; trophy.*

tacanho *adj. stingy, miserly; narrow-minded; short.*

tacão *m. shoe heel.*

tacha *f. tack, nail; blemish, fault.*

tachar *to criticise; to stain.*

tácito *adj. tacit.*

taciturno *adj. taciturn.*

taco *m. golf club; billiard cue; bite.*

tagarelar *to chatter, to gossip.*

TAL *adj. such, so, as.*
Que tal? *What do you think about it?*
Que tal uma cerveja? *How would you like a beer?*
Não permitirei tal coisa. *I won't allow such a thing.*
Um tal Smith o disse (disse-o). *A certain Smith said it.*
Fulano de tal. *John Doe.*
Tal pai, tal filho. *Like father, like son.*

talão *m. heel; check; stub; receipt.*
Talão de bagagem. *Baggage check.*

talco *m. talcum, talc.*

talento *m. talent, ability.*
Êle (ele) é um escritor de grande talento. *He's a very talented writer.*

talhar *to carve; to engrave; to cut.*

talhe *m. shape, figure.*

talher *m. table setting for one person.*

TALHO *m. butcher's shop, meat market* (P).

TALVEZ *perhaps, maybe.*
Talvez aconteça como você disse. *Perhaps it will turn out as you said.*

tamanho *adj. such, so great, so big; n. m. size, dimensions.*
Nunca vi tamanho mêdo (medo). *I never saw such fear.*
Qual é o tamanho? *What size is it?*
De grande tamanho. *Very large.*

tâmara *f. date.*

TAMBÉM *also, too; as well; likewise.*
Eu também. *I also.*
Ela também comprou dois romances. *She also bought two novels.*

tambor *m. drum; drummer; barrel.*

tampa *f. cover, lid; cap.*

tampar *to cover, to cap.*

tampouco *neither.*
Êle (ele) não quer vê-la. Nem eu tampouco. *He doesn't want to see her. Neither do I.*

tanger *to play (musical instrument), to pluck (strings), to ring (a bell).*

tangerina *f. tangerine.*

tangível *adj. tangible.*

tango *m. tango.*

tanque *m. tank, vat.*
Tanque de gasolina. *Gasoline tank.*
Encher o tanque. *To fill the tank.*

TANTO *adj. so much, as much; pl. so many; adv. so, in such a manner, so much; n.m. some.*
Não beba tanto. *Don't drink so much.*
Por que tanta pressa? *Why the hurry?*
Tanta gente. *So many people.*
Ter tantos anos de idade. *To be so many years old.*
Custou tanto? *Did it cost so much?*
A tanto o metro. *So much a meter.*
Algum tanto. *A little. Somewhat.*
Outro tanto. *Just as much. As much more.*
Outros tantos. *Just as many.*
Tanto um como outro. *One as well as the other. Both of them.*
Quanto mais lhe dou, tanto mais pede. *The more I give him, the more he asks for (wants).*
Tanto melhor. *So much the better.*
Tanto pior. *So much the worse.*
Tantas vêzes (vezes). *So often.*
Estou um tanto cansado. *I'm somewhat tired.*

TÃO *adv. so, as, such.*
Por que voltou tão cedo? *Why did you return so soon?*

Êle (ele) é tão alto quanto o pai. *He's as tall as his father.*
Tão bem. *So well. As well.*
Tão mal. *So bad. As bad.*

tapar *to cover; to conceal, to hide.*

tapeçaria *f. tapestry; upholstery.*

tapête (tapete) *m. carpet, rug, mat.*

tapioca *f. tapioca.*

taquígrafa *f. stenographer.*

taquigrafia *f. shorthand.*

taquígrafo *m. stenographer.*

tardança *f. delay, slowness.*
Perdoe a minha tardança. *Pardon my delay.*

tardar *to delay; to be late.*
Não tarde. *Don't be long. Don't take too long.*
Não tardarei em voltar. *I'll be back before long.*

TARDE *adv. late; n. m. afternoon.*
Boa tarde! *Good afternoon!*
Hoje à tarde. *This afternoon.*
Mais tarde. *Later.*
Amanhã à tarde. *Tomorrow afternoon.*
Ontem à tarde. *Yesterday afternoon.*
É tarde. *It's late.*
Fazer-se tarde. *To grow late.*
Antes tarde do que nunca. *Better late than never.*

tardio *adj. tardy; slow; late.*

tarefa *f. job; task, chore.*
A tarefa está concluída. *The job is finished.*

tarifa *f. tariff; table of rates.*

tartamudear *to stammer, to stutter.*

tartamudo *adj. stammering, stuttering; n. m. stammerer, stutterer.*

tartaruga *f. turtle.*

tatear *to feel; to feel one's way; to probe.*

tática *f. tactics.*

tático (táctico) *adj. tactic, tactical; n. m. touch.*

tato (tacto) *m. sense of touch; tact.*
Êle (ele) é um homem de muito tato. *He's a very tactful man.*
É suave ao tato. *It feels soft. ("It's soft to the touch.")*

tatuagem *f. tattoo; tattooing.*

tatuar *to tattoo.*

taxa *(x = sh) f. tax, duty, toll; rate.*
Taxa de exportação. *Export duty.*
Taxa de juro. *Rate of interest.*

taxar *(x = sh) to tax; to price.*

TÁXI *(x = ks) m. taxi, taxicab.*

taxímetro *(x = ks) m. taximeter.*

te *to, for you (fam.)*

teatral *adj. theatrical.*

TEATRO *m. theatre.*
Peça de teatro. *Play.*

teatrólogo *m. playwright.*

tecer *to spin, to weave; to intrigue.*

tecido *adj. woven; n. m. textile, fabric.*
Tecido de algodão. *Cotton fabric.*

tecla *f. key (piano, typewriter, etc.).*

teclado *m. keyboard (piano, typewriter, etc.).*

técnica *f. technique.*

técnico *adj. technical; n. m. technician.*

tédio *m. boredom, tediousness.*

tedioso *adj. tiresome, tedious.*

teia *f. cloth, material; web.*
Teia de aranha. *Cobweb.*

teimar *to persist, to insist.*

tela *f. network, web; canvas (painting); screen (for viewing).*
Tela de cinema. *Movie screen.*

telão *drop curtain (theatre).*

TELEFONAR *to telephone.*
Telefone-me às cinco. *Give me a ring at five.*

TELEFONE *m. telephone.*

telefonema *m. telephone call.*

telefônico (telefónico) *adj. telephonic, telephone.*
Lista telefônica. *Telephone directory.*
Cabine (or cabina) telefônica. *Telephone booth.*

telegrafar *to telegraph, to wire.*
Teremos que telegrafar-lhe. *We'll have to wire him.*

telegrafista *m. and f. telegraph operator.*

telégrafo *m. telegraph; telegraph office.*
Onde é o telégrafo? *Where is the telegraph office?*

telegrama *m. telegram.*
Quero passar um telegrama. *I want to send a telegram.*

telepatia *f. telepathy.*

telescópio *m. telescope.*

teletipo *m. teletype.*

televisão *f. television.*
Aparelho de televisão. *Television set.*

televisor *m. television set.*

televisora *f. television station.*

telha *f. tile (roofing).*

telhado *m. roof.*

tema *m. theme, subject; written composition.*

TEMER *to fear, to dread, to be afraid.*
Temo que seja muito tarde. *I'm afraid it's too late.*

temerário *adj. reckless, rash.*

temeroso *adj. afraid, fearful.*

temido *adj. fearful, feared.*

temível *adj. fearful.*

temor *m. fear, dread.*

temperamento *m. temperament, nature.*

temperatura *f. temperature.*
Ver a temperatura. *To take one's temperature.*

têmpero *m. seasoning.*

tempestade *f. tempest, storm.*

TEMPO *m. time, tense; weather; tempo.*
Por muito tempo. *For a long time.*
Há muito tempo. *It's been a long time (long time ago).*
Há pouco tempo. *Lately. Not long ago.*
Há quanto tempo você mora aqui? *How long have you been living here?*
Quanto tempo? *How long?*
Há tempo de sobra. *There's plenty of time.*
Não tenho tempo. *I have no time.*
A tempo. *In time.*
Perder tempo. *To lose time. To waste time.*
Bom tempo. *Good weather.*
Mau tempo. *Bad weather.*
O tempo está péssimo. *The weather is terrible.*
Fora de tempo. *Out of season.*
O tempo é dinheiro. *Time is money.*

temporada *f. season, period.*
Esta peça é a melhor da temporada. *This play is the best of the season.*

tenacidade *f. tenacity.*

tenaz *adj. tenacious, stubborn; n. f. tongs.*

tencionar *to intend.*
Tencionamos visitá-lo mais tarde. *We intend to visit him later.*

tenda *f. tent; stall, booth.*

tendência *f. tendency, leaning, trend.*

tender *to spread out; to tend.*

tenebroso *adj. dark, gloomy.*

tenente *m. lieutenant.*

tênis (ténis) *m. tennis.*
Jogar tênis. *To play tennis.*

tenor *m. tenor.*

tenro *adj. soft, tender.*

tensão *f. tension, pressure.*

tenso *adj. tense, tight.*

tentação *f. temptation.*
Não nos deixeis cair em tentação. *Lead us not into temptation.*

tentar *to try, to attempt; to tempt.*
Vou tentá-lo hoje. *I'm going to try it today.*

tentativa *f. attempt.*

tentativo *adj. tentative.*

teor *m. meaning; content.*
Teor alcoólico. *Alcohol content.*

teoria *f. theory.*

teórico *adj. theoretical.*

TER *to have, to possess; to keep; to hold; to contain; to take; to be (hungry, tired, etc.).*
Que tem na mão? *What do you have in your hand?*
Você terá que partir hoje. *You will have to leave today.*
Não tenho muito tempo. *I haven't much time.*
Tenho muito que fazer antes de partir. *I have a lot to do before I leave.*
Não tenho trôco (troco). *I haven't any change.*
Não tenho mais. *I don't have any more.*
Que idade tem Maria? *How old is Mary?*
Quantos anos tem Maria? *How old is Mary?*
Mary tem dezoito anos. *Mary is eighteen years old.*
Aqui tem um livro interessante. *Here's an interesting book.*
Que é que você tem? *What's the matter with you?*
Não tenho nada. *There's nothing the matter with me.*
Tenho fome. *I'm hungry.*
Tenho sêde (sede). *I'm thirsty.*
Tenho vontade de almoçar agora. *I feel like having lunch now.*
Tenho muito frio. *I'm very cold.*
Tenho dor de cabeça. *I have a headache.*
Ela tem sono. *She is sleepy.*
Elas têm razão. *They are right.*
Elas não têm razão. *They are wrong.*
Tenha cuidado! *Be careful!*
Ter sorte. *To be lucky.*
Ter pressa. *To be in a hurry.*
Ter lugar. *To take place. To happen.*
Ter em conta. *To bear in mind.*
Ter em muito (em pouco). *To think much (little) of.*
Ter jeito. *To have a special skill or talent.*
Ter saudades de. *To miss. To long for.*
Ter notícias de. *To hear from.*
Tenha a bondade de repetir. *Please repeat.*
Não tem importância. *It doesn't matter.*
Quando eu cheguei, êles (eles) já tinham partido. *When I arrived, they had already left.*

TÊRÇA (TERÇA) *adj. third; n. f. Tuesday.*

TÊRÇA-FEIRA (TERÇA-FEIRA) *f. Tuesday.*

TERCEIRO *adj. third; n. m. third person, mediator, intermediary.*
O terceiro capítulo. *The third chapter.*
A terceira lição. *The third lesson.*
Êle (ele) serviu de terceiro nas negociações. *He was an intermediary in the negotiations.*

TÊRÇO (TERÇO) *m. third.*

terminação *f. termination, ending.*

terminal *adj. terminal.*

terminante *adj. terminating; decisive.*

TERMINAR *to end, to terminate, to finish.*
Quase terminei. *I'm almost finished.*
A reunião terminou às três. *The meeting ended at three o'clock.*

término *m. terminus, end; boundary, limit.*

terminologia *f. terminology.*

termo *m. Thermos.*

têrmo (termo) *m. term; limit; span; end.*
Pôr têrmo a. *To put an end to.*
Têrmos técnicos. *Technical terms.*

termômetro (termómetro) *m. thermometer.*

termóstato *m. thermostat.*

terno adj. tender, affectionate; n. m. trio, group of three; man's suit Ⓑ

ternura f. tenderness, fondness.

TERRA f. earth; soil; ground; land, country.
Viajar por terra. To travel by land.
Terra natal. Fatherland. Native land.
Terra Santa. Holy Land.
Descer à terra. To land. To go ashore.
Minha terra. My land. My country.

terraço m. terrace.

terremoto m. earthquake.

terreno m. land, soil, piece of ground; field.
Partiram o terreno em vários lotes. They divided the land into several lots.
Sondar o terreno. To sound out the situation.
Perder terreno. To lose ground.

terrestre adj. ground, terrestrial.

território m. territory.

TERRÍVEL adj. terrible, dreadful.

terror m. terror.

tertúlia f. social or cultural gathering.

tese f. thesis.

têso (teso) adj. tense, tight.

tesoura, tesoira f. scissors, shears.

tesouraria, tesoiraria f. treasury, bursar's office.

tesoureiro, tesoireiro m. treasurer, bursar.

tesouro, tesoiro m. treasury.

testa f. forehead, brow; front.
Pôr-se à testa de. To put oneself at the head of.
Testa de ferro. Figurehead. Straw man.

testar to will; to bequeath; to testify.

teste m. test, examination; trial.

testemunha f. witness.

testemunhar to testify; to witness.

testemunho m. testimony; proof.

testificar to testify, to declare.

teto (tecto) m. ceiling; roof.
Preço teto. Ceiling price.

teu m. adj. and pron. your, yours (fam.).

têxtil adj. textile.

texto m. text.

tez f. complexion; skin.
Ela tem uma tez muito suave. Her skin is very smooth.

ti you (fam.) (used after a preposition).

tíbia f. tibia, shinbone.

tíbio adj. lukewarm, indifferent.

tico m. a bit; tic.

tifo m. typhoid fever.

tifóide adj. typhoid.
Febre tifóide. Typhoid fever.

tigela f. bowl, dish; cup.

tigre m. tiger; student repeater.

tijolo m. brick.

til m. tilde (wavy line over a nasal vowel; **não**).

timbre m. stamp; seal; timbre, tone.

time m. team Ⓑ

timidez f. timidity, shyness.

tímido adj. timid, shy.
Maria é muito tímida. Mary is very shy.

timoneiro m. helmsman.

tina f. vat, tub.

tingir to dye, to tinge.

tino m. judgment, prudence, discretion.

tinta f. ink; paint.
Não há tinta no tinteiro. There's no ink in the inkwell.
Tinta fresca! Wet paint!

tinteiro m. inkwell.

tinto adj. dyed, colored; red.
Vinho tinto. Red wine.

tintura f. dye, dyeing.

tinturaria f. cleaner's, dry-cleaning shop.

tintureiro m. (dry) cleaner; dyer.

TIO m. uncle.
Os meus tios. My uncle and aunt.
O tio Sam. Uncle Sam.
Ela foi ao cinema com a tia. She went to the movies with her aunt.

típico adj. typical, characteristic.

tipo m. type, class; fellow, "character."
Tipo negrito. Boldface type.
Tipo grifo. Italic type.
Ele (ele) é um tipo esquisito. He's a "character."

tipografia f. printing; printing shop.

tipógrafo m. printer, typographer, typesetter.

tique-taque m. tick-tock.

tique-tique m. tick-tock.

tira f. band, strip.

tirada f. drawing; tirade.

tiragem f. printing, circulation; drawing, draft.

tirania f. tyranny.

tirano m. tyrant.

tirante adj. pulling, drawing.

TIRAR to take, to take out, to withdraw; to deduct; to remove; to drag; to win; to draw out; to pull; to throw.
Ela tirou um lápis da gaveta. She took a pencil out of the drawer.
O professor tirou a sorte grande. The teacher won the grand prize.
A mãe retirou o filho da escola. The mother withdrew her son from school.
Ao entrar na igreja ele (ele) tirou o chapéu. On entering the church he took off his hat.
Tiramos (Tirámos) proveito do negócio. We benefited from the business.
Tirar a prova. To check (a computation)
Tirar uma fotografia. To take a photograph.

tiritar to shiver.

tiro m. shot; shooting; drawing, hauling.
O tiro errou. The shot missed.
Ao sairmos de casa depois de jantar, ouvimos um tiro. On leaving home after dinner, we heard a shot.
Tiro ao alvo. Target practice.

tirotear to fire, to volley.

tiroteio m. firing, volley.

tísica f. tuberculosis, consumption.

tísico adj. consumptive; n. m. consumptive, person with tuberculosis.

tisnar to blacken.

titã m. titan.

títere m. puppet, marionette.

titubear to hesitate; to stagger.
A testemunha respondia sem titubear. The witness answered without hesitation.

titular to title, to entitle; adj. titular; n. m. and f. titular, head.

título m. title; degree; inscription; bond.
Qual é o título do livro? What is the title of the book?
Título honorífico. Honorary title.

to (contr. of te + o) it, him to you (fam.).

toada f. tune, air; sound.

TOALHA f. towel; cloth.
Toalha de rosto. Face towel.
Toalha de banho. Bath towel.
Toalha de mesa. Tablecloth.

toar to sound; to be in tune with.

toca-discos m. record player.

tocador m. player (music).

tocante adj. touching, affecting, regarding.
No tocante a. Concerning. Regarding.

TOCAR to touch; to play (music); to concern, to interest; to ring (bells); to be one's turn; to be one's share; to call (at a port).
Não toque! Don't touch! Hands off!
Tocar o violão. To play the guitar.
Tocar bem. To play well.
Tocar mal. To play badly.

A orquestra está tocando (a tocar) um samba. The orchestra is playing a samba.
A quem lhe toca agora? Whose turn is it now?
Agora toca a êle. It's his turn now.
O navio tocou em Lisboa. The ship called (stopped) at Lisbon.
Pelo que me toca. As far as I'm concerned.
Tocar de ouvido. To play by ear.
Tocar o piano. To play the piano.

tocha f. torch, large candle.

todavia adv. however, yet.

TODO adj. each, every; all; n. m. all, whole; pl. all, everyone.
Ele (ele) perdeu todo o seu dinheiro. He lost all his money.
Ela estudou tôda (toda) a manhã. She studied all morning.
Todos dizem o mesmo. They all say the same thing.
Todo o dia. All day.
O dia todo. All day long.
Todos os dias. Every day.
Tôda (toda) a família. All the family.
Todo o mundo. Everybody.
Todos de uma vez. All at once. All at the same time.
Todos nós. All of us.
Em todo caso. In any case.
Todo homem. Every man.
A cidade tôda (toda). All the city.

tôldo (toldo) m. awning.

tolerância f. tolerance.

tolerante adj. tolerant.

tolerar to tolerate.
Não podemos tolerar tal barulho. We can't tolerate such noise.
Não posso tolerá-lo. I can't stand him.

tolerável adj. tolerable.

tolice f. foolishness, nonsense.
Que tolice! What nonsense!
Não diga tolices. Don't speak foolishness.

tolo adj. foolish; crazy; n. m. fool.
Não seja tolo. Don't be a fool.

tom m. tone; sound; color.
Sem tom nem som. Without rhyme or reason.

TOMAR to take; to get; to seize; to have (drink, food).
Que quer tomar? What will you have (to drink)?
Nunca tomo vinho. I never drink wine.
Tome o remédio às horas indicadas. Take the medicine at the times indicated.
Tomemos um táxi (x = ks). Let's take a taxi.
Aconselho-lhe tomar o trem (comboio) das oito. I advise you to take the eight o'clock train.
Tomar nota de. To take note of.
Tomaram as medidas necessárias. They took the necessary measures.
Tomar emprestado. To borrow.
Não quer tomar uma bebida? Don't you want a drink?
É preciso tomar uma decisão. One must come to a decision.
Tomar a palavra. To take the floor.
Tomar em conta. To take into account.
Tomar banho. To take a bath.
Não o tome a mal. Don't take it wrong. Don't take it in the wrong way.
Tomar a peito. To take to heart.
Tomar o pulso. To take the pulse.
Tomar posse de. To take possession of.
Eu o tomei (tomei-o) por outro. I took (mistook) you for somebody else.

tomara I hope. Would that Ⓑ.
Tomara! I hope so!
Tomara que não! I hope not!

tomate m. tomato.

tombar to fell, to bring down; to fall.

tomo m. volume (book).
É uma obra em três tomos. It's a three-volume work.

tonelada f. *ton.*

tônico (tónico) *adj. stressed; tonic; n. m. tonic.*

tono m. *tone; tune.*

tonsilite f. *tonsillitis.*

tontear *to act foolishly, to talk nonsense; to feel dizzy.*

tonto *adj. silly, foolish; dizzy; n. m. fool.*

topar *to meet by chance.*
Topei com êle (ele) no cinema. *I met him (came across him) at the movies.*

topázio m. *topas.*

tope m. *top, summit; clash, collision.*

topête (topete) m. *forelock; "nerve."*

tópico *adj. topical.*

topografia f. *topography.*

topógrafo m. *topographer.*

toque m. *touch; bugle call.*
Toque de alvorada. *Reveille.*
Toque de silêncio. *Taps.*

tora f. *portion; nap* Ⓑ.
Tirar uma tora. *To take a nap (slang)* Ⓑ.

tórax (x = ks) m. *thorax.*

torcedura f. *twisting; sprain.*

torcer *to twist; to sprain; to distort.*
Torcer o nariz. *To turn up one's nose.*
João torceu o tornozelo. *John sprained his ankle.*

torcida f. *group of rooters, cheering section.*

torcido *adj. twisted, crooked.*

tormenta f. *storm, tempest.*

tormento m. *torment, distress.*

tormentoso *adj. stormy.*

tornar *to come back; to change;* **tornar a** *to do again.*
Ela tornou a cantar. *She sang again.*

tornar-se *to become.*
José se tornou (tornou-se) chefe do grupo. *Joseph became leader of the group.*

torneio m. *tournament.*

torneira f. *faucet, spigot.*
Abrir a torneira. *To turn the faucet on.*
Fechar a torneira. *To turn the faucet off.*

tôrno (torno) m. *lathe; vise; faucet.*

tornozelo m. *ankle.*

toronja f. *grapefruit.*

torpe *adj. base, lowly.*

torpedeiro m. *torpedo boat.*

torpedo m. *torpedo.*

torrada f. *toast (bread).*

torrado *adj. toasted, roasted.*

tôrre (torre) f. *tower; turret; belfry; castle (chess).*
Tôrre de igreja. *Steeple.*

torrente f. *torrent.*

tórrido *adj. torrid.*

torta f. *pie, tart, cake.*
Torta de maçã. *Apple pie.*

tortilha f. *tortilla.*

torto *adj. twisted, crooked.*
A torto e a direito. *By hook or by crook.*

tortura f. *torture.*

torturar *to torture.*

torvar *to disturb, to upset.*

torvelinho, torvelino m. *whirlwind, eddy.*

tosar *to shear.*

tôsco (tosco) *adj. rough, clumsy, coarse.*

tosquiar *to shear.*
Ir buscar lã e vir tosquiado. *To go for wool and return shorn.*

tosse f. *cough.*

tossir *to cough.*

tostão m. *former Portuguese coin; Brazilian coin.*
Não vale um tostão. *It's not worth anything. It's worthless.*

tostar *to toast, to brown, to tan.*

total *adj. and n. m. total, whole.*
Quantos há no total? *How many are there in all?*

totalidade f. *totality, all.*

touca f. *bonnet, cap, coif.*

toucador m. *vanity, dressing table; dressing room.*

toucar *to dress the hair; to adorn.*

toucinho, toicinho m. *bacon, pork fat.*

tourada, toirada f. *bullfight.*
As touradas em Madrid. *The bullfights in Madrid.*

tourear, toirear *to fight bulls.*

toureiro, toireiro m. *bullfighter.*

touro, toiro m. *bull.*

tóxico (x = ks) *adj. toxic, poisonous; n. m. poison.*

trabalhador *adj. hard-working, industrious; n. m. worker, laborer.*
O filho dêle (dele) é muito trabalhador. *His son is very industrious.*

TRABALHAR *to work, to labor.*
Alberto trabalha como um mouro. *Albert works like a Trojan.*
Acho que êle (ele) não trabalha muito. *I believe he doesn't work very hard.*

TRABALHO m. *work, labor; job; product, result.*
Garantimos o trabalho. *We guarantee the work.*
Tudo isto é trabalho perdido. *All this is wasted effort.*
Sem trabalho. *Unemployed. Out of work.*
Trabalho de noite. *Night work.*
Trabalhos forçados. *Hard labor.*

trabalhoso *adj. difficult.*

traçar *to draw, to sketch; to outline; to plan.*
Traçar uma linha. *To draw a line.*
Os engenheiros traçaram os planos para uma nova ponte. *The engineers drew up the plans for a new bridge.*

tracejar *to trace, to outline.*

tradição f. *tradition.*

tradicional *adj. traditional.*

tradução f. *translation.*
Tradução literal. *Literal translation.*
Tradução livre. *Free translation.*

tradutor m. *translator.*

traduzir *to translate.*
Traduza esta carta para o inglês. *Translate this letter into English.*
Não há maneira de traduzi-lo. *There's no way to translate it.*

tráfego m. *traffic; trading, trade.*
Sinal de tráfego. *Traffic light.*

traficante *adj. dishonest; n. m. swindler.*

traficar *to traffic, to trade; to swindle.*

tráfico m. *traffic, trade.*

tragar *to swallow; to devour.*

tragédia f. *tragedy.*

trágico *adj. tragic.*

trago m. *swallow, swig, drink.*
Vamos tomar um trago. *Let's have a drink.*

traição f. *treason, treachery.*

traidor *adj. treacherous; n. m. traitor.*

trair *to betray; to divulge.*

traje, trajo m. *clothing, suit, dress.*
Traje de banho (fato de banho). *Bathing suit.*

trama f. *weft (weaving); n. m. and f. web; plot, conspiracy.*

tramar *to weave; to plot, to scheme.*

tranca f. *crossbar; bar; obstacle.*

tranqüilidade (tranquilidade) f. *tranquillity, peace.*

tranqüilo (tranquilo) *adj. tranquil, quiet, calm.*
Este (este) lugar é muito tranqüilo. *This place is very quiet.*

transação (transacção) f. *transaction.*

transatlântico *adj. transatlantic; n. m. ocean liner.*

transbordar *to overflow.*

transcendental *adj. transcendental.*

transcendente *adj. transcendent.*

transcender *to transcend.*

transcorrer *to pass, to elapse (time).*

transcrever *to transcribe.*

transcurso m. *course, lapse (time).*

transeunte m. *and f. pedestrian, passerby.*

transferência f. *transference, transfer.*

transferir *to transfer; to defer.*

transformação f. *transformation.*

transformador *adj. transforming; n. m. transformer.*

transformar *to transform.*
A cidra se transformou (transformou-se) em vinagre. *The cider turned into vinegar.*

transfusão f. *transfusion.*

transgredir *to transgress.*

transição f. *transition, passage.*

transigir *to compromise, to agree.*

transistor m. *transistor.*

trânsito m. *passage, transit, transition; traffic.*
Trânsito impedido. *No thoroughfare.*

transitório *adj. transitory.*

transmissão f. *transmission, broadcast.*

transmissor *adj. transmitting; n. m. transmitter.*

transmissora f. *transmitter.*

transmitir *to transmit, to send, to convey.*

transparente *adj. transparent; clear.*

transpiração f. *transpiration; perspiration.*

transpirar *to transpire; to perspire; to become known.*

transpor *to transpose, to cross over.*

transportar *to transport, to convey; to transpose.*
Não sei se podem transportar tanta bagagem. *I don't know whether they can carry so much baggage.*

transporte m. *transport, transportation.*
Transporte pago. *Carriage paid.*

transtornar *to overturn; to upset, to disturb.*

trapalhada f. *predicament, mess.*
Que trapalhada! *What a mess!*

trapo m. *rag; pl. old clothes.*
Boneca de trapos. *Rag doll.*

TRÁS *after, behind.*
Ir para trás. *To go back, backwards.*
Um trás outro. *One after the other.*

traseiro *adj. back, rear.*
A porta traseira dá para o jardim. *The back door opens out into the garden.*

trasladar *to transport, to move, to transfer; to postpone; to transcribe, to translate.*

traslado m. *transfer; transcript; translation; copy.*

traspassar *to cross; to transfer; to trespass.*
Traspassar de um lado a outro. *To cross from one side to the other.*
Traspassar um negócio. *To transfer a business.*

traste m. *household item of little value.*

tratado m. *treaty.*

tratamento m. *treatment; form of address.*

TRATAR *to treat, to deal with; to discuss.*
De que se trata? *What's it all about?*
Trata-se dum assunto importante. *The matter in question is important.*
De que trata êste (este) artigo? *What's this article about?*
Este livro trata da vida de Camões. *This book is about the life of Camões.*
Prefiro tratar com pessoas sérias. *I prefer to deal with serious people.*

Tratam mal (os) seus empregados. *They don't treat their employees well.*

trato *m. treatment; form of address; contract, agreement.*
Tenho tido pouco trato com êles (eles). *I haven't had much to do with them.*
Façamos um trato. *Let's make a deal.*

trator (tractor) *m. tractor.*

travar *to join, to unite, to bind, to link.*
Travar conversa. *To open a conversation.*
Travar amizade. *To make friends.*
Travar conhecimento. *To make someone's acquaintance. To strike up an acquaintance.*

través *m. bias, slant.*
Ao través. *Across. Through.*
Olhar de través. *To look sideways. To look out of the corner of one's eyes.*

travessa *f. crosspiece, crossbeam; alley.*

travessão *m. crosspiece, crossbeam; dash (mark).*

travesseiro *m. pillow, pillowcase.*

travessia *f. ocean crossing, sea voyage, crossing; strong wind.*

travessura *f. mischief, prank, trick.*

TRAZER *to bring, to carry; to wear.*
Traga-me uma cerveja. *Bring me a beer.*
Trouxeram (z = s) tudo o que lhes pedi. *They brought everything I asked for.*
Você trouxe (z = s) consigo (or com você)? *Did you bring it with you?*
Ela traz um chapéu nôvo (novo). *She is wearing a new hat.*

trecho *m. distance, interval.*
A trechos. *At intervals.*

trégua *f. truce, respite.*

treinador *m. trainer, coach.*

treinamento *m. training, coaching.*

treinar *to train, to coach.*

TREM *m. train* Ⓑ; *retinue, luggage.*
A que horas sai o trem (comboio) para São Paulo? *At what time does the train for São Paulo leave?*
Êste (este) trem pára em tôdas (todas) as estações? *Does this train stop at all stations?*
Vamos tomar o trem das oito. *Let's take the eight o'clock train.*

tremendo *adj. tremendous, dreadful, awful.*

tremer *to tremble, to shake.*

trenó *m. sled, sleigh.*

trepar *to climb.*

TRÊS *adj. and n. m. three, third.*
As duas por três. *Two out of three times.*
Dois é bom, três é demais. *Two's company, three's a crowd.*

trevas *f. pl. darkness.*

trevo *m. clover.*
Trevo de quatro fôlhas (folhas). *Four-leaf clover.*

treze *adj. and n. m. thirteen, thirteenth.*

trezentos *adj. and n. m. three hundred, three hundredth.*

triângulo *m. triangle.*

tribo *f. tribe.*

tribuna *f. tribune, platform.*

tribunal *m. tribunal (of justice).*

tributar *to pay taxes; to pay tribute; to tax, to assess.*

tributo *m. tribute, tax.*

tricotar *to knit.*

trigésimo *adj. thirtieth; n. m. thirtieth.*

trigo *m. wheat.*
Farinha de trigo. *Wheat flour.*

trigonometria *f. trigonometry.*

trilhar *to thresh; to tread.*

trilho *m. trail, way; track, rail* Ⓑ.

trimestre *m. trimester; quarter (of a year).*

trinar *to warble.*

trincar *to bite, to chew.*

trinchar *to carve (meat).*

trincheira *f. trench, ditch.*

trindade *f. trinity, Trinity.*

TRINTA *adj. and n. m. thirty, thirtieth.*

trio *m. trio.*

tripa *f. tripe, intestines.*

triplicar *to triple, to treble.*

triplo *adj. triple; n. m. triple.*

tripulação *f. crew.*

tripulante *m. and f. member of a crew.*

TRISTE *adj. sad, gloomy.*
Ele (ele) faz um papel triste. *He cuts a sorry figure.*
Isto é muito triste. *That's (this is) very sad.*
Ao ouvir a notícia ela ficou muito triste. *She became very sad when she heard the news.*

tristeza *f. sadness, grief, gloom.*
Tristeza não tem fim. *There's no end to sadness.*

triunfante *adj. triumphant.*

triunfar *to triumph, to succeed.*

triunfo *m. triumph.*

trivial *adj. trivial.*

troada *f. thunder; roaring.*

troar *to thunder; to roar.*

troça *f. mockery, derision; joke.*
Fazer troça de. *To make fun of.*

trocadilho *m. pun, play on words.*

trocar *to change, to exchange, to barter.*
Trocar dinheiro. *To change money.*
Trocar uma coisa por outra. *To exchange one thing for another.*
Trocar roupa. *To change clothes.*

troçar *to joke; to ridicule.*

trocista *m. and f. joker; mocker.*

trôco (troco) *m. change (money); exchange.*
Fique com o trôco. *Keep the change.*

trombada *f. crash, collision.*

trombeta *f. trumpet, horn.*

trombone *m. trombone.*

trompa *f. horn; tube.*

tronar *to thunder; to roar.*

tronco *m. trunk (wood, body); stem.*

trono *m. throne.*

tropa *f. troop.*

tropeçar *to stumble, to trip; to make a mistake.*

tropêço (tropeço) *m. stumbling, tripping; obstacle.*

tropical *adj. tropical.*

trópico *m. tropic.*
Trópico de Câncer. *Tropic of Cancer.*

trotar *to trot.*

trote *m. trot.*

trovão *m. thunder.*

trovoar *to thunder.*

truta *f. trout.*

tu *you (fam.).*

tua *f. adj. and pron. your (fam.).*

tuberculose *f. tuberculosis.*

tuberculoso *adj. tubercular; n. m. tubercular.*

tubo *m. tube, pipe.*

TUDO *all, everything.*
Ou tudo ou nada. *All or nothing.*
Ele (ele) sabe um pouco de tudo. *He knows a little about everything.*
Tudo está pronto. *Everything is ready.*
Antes de tudo. *First of all.*
Tudo quanto lhe digo é verdade. *Everything I'm telling you is the truth.*
Apesar de tudo. *Nevertheless.*

tule *m. tulle, silk net.*

tulipa (tulipa, túlipa) *f. tulip.*

tumba *f. tomb, grave.*

tumor *m. tumor.*

túmulo *m. tomb, grave, vault.*

túnel *m. tunnel.*

tupi *adj. and n. m. Tupi, Indian tribes of Brazil.*

tupi-guarani *adj. and n. m. of the Tupi-Guarani tribes.*

turba *f. mob, rabble, crowd.*

turbação *f. disturbance.*

turbante *m. turban.*

turbar *to disturb, to upset; to darken, to muddy.*

turbina *f. turbine.*

turbulência *f. turbulence, disturbance.*

turbulento *turbulent.*

turco *adj. Turkish; n. m. Turk.*

turismo *m. touring, tourism.*
Agência de turismo. *Travel agency.*

turista *m. and f. tourist.*
No ano passado houve muitos turistas em Portugal. *Last year there were many tourists in Portugal.*

turma *f. group, gang; class (division of a school, as the first class).*
Turma de noite (or noturna). *Night shift.*

turno *m. turn; shift; school period.*
Por turnos. *By turns.*

turquesa *f. turquoise.*

turrão *adj. stubborn.*

turvar *to confuse, to upset; to darken, to muddy.*

tutear *to address someone in the familiar form, to use the "tu" form.*

tutela *f. guardianship, tutelage.*

tutor *m. tutor, guardian.*

U

ufa! *whew!*

ufanar-se *to be proud, to boast.*

ufano *adj. proud, haughty.*

ui! *oh!*

uísque *m. whiskey* Ⓑ.

uivo *m. howl.*

úlcera *f. ulcer.*

ulterior *adj. ulterior.*

ultimato *m. ultimatum.*

ÚLTIMO *adj. last, latest; final, ultimate.*
José foi último em (a) chegar. *Joseph was the last one to arrive.*
Por último. *Finally. At last.*
No último momento. *At the last moment.*
Ultimamente. *Recently.*

ultramar *m. overseas lands or areas.*

ultramarino *adj. overseas.*

ulular *to howl, to cry out.*

UM, UMA *(ind. article) a, an.*
Um homem. *A man.*
Uma mulher. *A woman.*
Um pouco. *A little.*
Uma vez. *Once.*
Vou comprar sômente um livro. *I'm going to buy only one book.*
Um dia sim, um dia não. *Every other day.*

umbral *m. threshold, doorway.*

umedecer *to moisten, to dampen.*

umidade *f. humidity, dampness, moisture.*

úmido *adj. humid, moist, damp.*

unânime *adj. unanimous.*

unanimidade *f. unanimity.*

undécimo *adj. eleventh; n. m. eleventh.*

ungüento (unguento) *m. unguent, ointment.*

UNHA *f. fingernail, toenail; claw; hoof.*
Fazer as unhas. *To trim the nails.*

união *f. union, unity; coupling.*
A união faz a fôrça (força). *In union there is strength.*
Traço de união. *Hyphen.*

único *adj. only, only one, unique, singular.*
Essa foi a única vez que êle (ele) me falou. *That was the only time he spoke to me.*
unidade *f. unity; unit.*
unido *adj. united, joined.*
unificar *to unify.*
uniforme *adj. uniform; n. m. uniform.*
uniformidade *f. uniformity.*
unir *to unite, to join together, to put together.*
Vamos fazer tudo possível para uni-los. *We're going to do everything possible to unite them.*
unir-se *to come together, to unite, to join.*
As duas firmas se uniram (uniram-se). *The two firms merged.*
universal *adj. universal.*
universidade *f. university.*
universitário *adj. of a university, academic; n. m. university faculty member or student.*
universo *m. universe.*
uno *adj. one, only one.*
untar *to grease, to anoint.*
urânio *m. uranium.*
urbanidade *f. urbanity, good manners, politeness.*
urbano *adj. urban; urbane, refined, polite.*
urdir *to warp; to scheme, to plot.*
urgência *f. urgency, pressure.*
Com urgência. *Urgently.*
A urgência dos negócios. *The pressure of business.*
urgente *adj. urgent.*
Entrega urgente. *Special delivery (mail).*
É urgente que você venha amanhã às oito horas. *It's urgent that you come tomorrow at eight o'clock.*
urgir *to urge, to press, to be urgent, to be pressing.*
urna *f. urn; ballot box.*
urrar *to roar, to howl.*
urro *m. roar, howl.*
urso *m. bear; distinguished student; rude individual.*
Urso-branco. *Polar bear.*
Amigo urso. *False friend.*
Ursa Maior. *Great Bear.*
urubu *m. black vulture.*
uruguaio *adj. Uruguayan; n. m. Uruguayan.*
usança *f. usage, custom.*
USAR *to use; to be accustomed to; to wear.*
Usar o telefone. *To use the telephone.*
Sempre uso óculos para ler. *I always wear (use) glasses to read.*
No verão uso camisa de manga curta. *In the summer I wear short-sleeved shirts.*
useiro *adj. usual, customary.*
usina *f. factory, mill.*
Usina de aço. *Steel mill.*
Usina de açúcar. *Sugar mill.*
Usina hidrelétrica (hidroeléctrica). *Hydroelectric power station.*
USO *m. use; usage; custom; wear.*
Para uso externo. *For external use.*
Em uso. *In use.*
Fora de uso. *Out of use.*
USUAL *adj. usual, customary.*
Isso é muito usual. *That's very common.*
O usual. *The usual. That which is customary.*
usura *f. usury.*
usurário *m. usurer.*
usurpação *f. usurpation.*
usurpador *m. usurper.*
usurpar *to usurp.*
utensílio *m. utensil.*
Utensílios de cozinha. *Kitchen utensils.*
ÚTIL *adj. useful, profitable; n. m. utility.*

Você o encontrará útil. *You'll find it very useful.*
Dias úteis. *Workdays. Weekdays.*
utilidade *f. utility, usefulness.*
utilizar *to utilise.*
Utopia *f. Utopia, utopia.*
uva *f. grape.*

V

VACA *f. cow; pooling of resources, pool.*
Carne de vaca. *Beef.*
vacante *adj. vacant; in abeyance.*
vacar *to vacate; to be vacant; to be free.*
vacilação *f. vacillation, hesitation.*
vacilante *adj. vacillating, wavering, uncertain, hesitating.*
vacilar *to vacillate, to waver, to hesitate.*
Êles (eles) não vacilaram em fazê-lo. *They did not hesitate to do it.*
vacina *f. vaccination; vaccine.*
vacinar *to vaccinate.*
vadear *to ford.*
vadiar *to waste time, to loaf.*
vadio *adj. lazy, idle; n. m. idler, loafer.*
vaga *f. vacancy.*
vagabundo *adj. vagabond, vagrant; inferior; n. m. idler, vagabond, tramp.*
vagão *m. coach, car; wagon; freight car.*
Vagão restaurante. *Dining car.*
vagar *to rove, to roam; to vacate, to be vacant; to idle.*
vagem *f. string bean, green bean.*
vago *adj. vague, indefinite; vacant; vagrant.*
Horas vagas. *Spare time.*
vaia *f. hoot, boo, hiss, jeer.*
vaiar *to hoot, to boo, to hiss, to jeer.*
vaidade *f. vanity.*
Ela o faz (fá-lo) por vaidade. *She does it out of vanity.*
vaidoso *adj. vain, conceited.*
vaivém *m. coming and going; vicissitude.*
Os vaivéns da sorte. *The ups and downs of life (of fortune).*
vale *m. IOU, voucher; valley.*
Vale postal. *Postal money order.*
O jogador assinou o vale. *The gambler signed the IOU.*
valente *adj. brave, valiant.*
valentia *f. valor, courage, bravery.*
VALER *to be worth, to amount to; to cost; to merit; to assist; to be of use.*
Quanto vale? *How much is it worth?*
Não vale nada. *It's worthless. It isn't worth anything.*
Acho que êste (este) vale mais (do) que êsse (esse). *I believe this one is better than that one.*
Mais vale tarde do que nunca. *Better late than never.*
Valer a pena. *To be worthwhile.*
Valha-me Deus! *God help me!*
validar *to validate.*
validez *f. validity.*
válido *adj. valid; sound.*
O passaporte é válido por um ano. *The passport is valid (good) for a year.*
valioso *adj. valuable, worthy.*
valise *f. valise, grip, traveling bag.*
VALOR *m. value; price; worth; valor, courage; pl. securities.*
De pouco valor. *Of little value.*
Sem valor. *Of no value. Worthless.*
Dar valor a. *To value.*
Valor nominal. *Face value. Par value.*
Bôlsa (bolsa) de valores. *Stock exchange.*
valorizar *to value, to appraise; to increase in value.*

valsa *f. walts.*
válvula *f. valve.*
Válvula de segurança. *Safety valve.*
VAMOS! *Come! Come now! Let's go! Hurry up!*
vanguarda *f. vanguard.*
vantagem *f. advantage; profit; odds (games); handicap (sports).*
Este (este) procedimento tem as suas vantagens e desvantagens. *This procedure has its advantages and disadvantages.*
Levar vantagem. *To have the advantage. To gain the upper hand.*
vão *adj. (vã fem.) vain; futile; n. m. space, opening.*
Tôda (toda) tentativa foi em vão. *Every attempt was in vain.*
vapor *m. vapor, steam; steamship.*
A todo vapor. *At full steam.*
Cavalo-vapor. *Horsepower.*
vaqueiro *m. cowboy.*
vara *f. rod, pole, stick, wand; judgeship; jurisdiction; measurement of 43.3 inches.*
varanda *f. veranda, balcony.*
varão *adj. male; n. m. man, male.*
varar *to pierce, to stick; to beat with a stick; to ford (a stream); to beach (a boat).*
varejo *m. retail (B); search, raid.*
Vender a varejo. *To sell at retail.*
variação *f. variation, change.*
Sem variação. *Unchanged.*
variado *adj. varied.*
variante *adj. varying, variant; f. variant, variation.*
variar *to vary, to change.*
Não varia nada. *It doesn't change (vary) a bit.*
variável *adj. variable, changeable.*
varicela *f. chicken pox.*
variedade *f. variety.*
VÁRIO *adj. different, changeable; pl. several, some.*
Hoje comprei vários livros sôbre (sobre) Portugal e o Brasil. *Today I bought several (some) books about Portugal and Brasil.*
varíola *f. smallpox.*
varonil *adj. manly, virile.*
varredor *adj. sweeping; n. m. sweeper.*
varrer *to sweep.*
várzea *f. meadow, plain.*
vaselina *f. Vaseline.*
vasilha *f. vessel (for liquids).*
vaso *m. vase, bowl, vessel.*
Vaso de flôres (flores). *Flowerpot. Vase for flowers.*
vassoura, vassoira *f. broom.*
vastidão *f. vastness.*
vasto *adj. vast.*
vatapá *m. a seasoned Brasilian dish (B).*
vaticano *adj. Vatican; n. m. Vatican.*
vau *m. river crossing, ford; opportunity.*
vazar *to empty; to flow out; to drain.*
vazio *adj. empty, vacant; n. m. void, vacuum.*
veado *m. deer.*
vedar *to prohibit, to stop.*
vedeta *f. advanced guard, sentry; star (movies, theatre).*
vegetação *f. vegetation.*
vegetal *adj. vegetal; n. m. vegetable.*
veia *f. vein.*
Veia artéria. *Pulmonary artery.*
veículo *m. vehicle.*
veio *m. grain (wood), streak, vein.*
vela *f. candle; sail; watch.*
Apagar as velas. *To blow out the candles.*
Vela de cêra (cera). *Wax candle.*

Vela de ignição. *Spark plug.*
Barco à vela. *Sailboat.*

velar *to watch; to keep vigil; to veil.*

veleiro *m. sailboat.*

velhaco *adj. knavish, tricky; n. m. knave, rogue, crook.*

velhice *f. old age; old people.*

VELHO *adj. old; ancient; worn-out; old man.*
Somos velhos amigos. *We're old friends.*
A mãe dela é muito velha. *Her mother is very old.*
Êsse (esse) velho é rico. *That old man is rich.*
Mais velho. *Older. Senior.*
Meu velho. *Old fellow. My friend* Ⓑ.

velocidade *f. velocity, speed; gear.*
Primeira, segunda, e terceira velocidade. *First, second, and third gear.*
Passaram a tôda (toda) velocidade. *They went by at full speed.*

veloz *adj. swift, fast.*

veludo *adj. hairy, shaggy, velvety; n. m. velvet; something smooth.*

vencer *to conquer, to vanquish, to win.*

vencido *adj. defeated; due, outstanding.*
Dar-se por vencido. *To give up.*

venda *f. sale; store; blindfold.*

vendar *to blindfold.*

vendedor *m. seller, trader, dealer.*

VENDER *to sell; to trade; to betray.*
Não vendemos a varejo; só por atacado. *We don't sell retail; only wholesale.*
Também não vendemos a crédito (or fiado); só a dinheiro. *We also don't sell on credit; only cash.*

veneno *m. venom, poison.*

venenoso *adj. poisonous.*

veneração *f. veneration.*

venerar *to venerate.*

venezuelano *adj. Venezuelan; n. m. Venezuelan.*

venta *f. nostril.*

ventilação *f. ventilation.*

ventilador *m. ventilator, electric fan.*

ventilar *to ventilate, to air.*

VENTO *m. wind; breeze, air.*
Ir de vento em pôpa (popa). *To get along very well. To be progressing.*

ventre *m. stomach, belly, paunch.*

ventura *f. happiness; fortune, chance; venture; risk.*
Por ventura. *By chance. Perchance.*

venturoso *adj. lucky, fortunate, happy.*

VER *to see; to look at; to visit; to meet; n. m. sense of sight; opinion.*
De!xe-me (x = sh) ver. *Let me see.*
Vamos ver. *Let's see.*
Que quadros deseja ver? *What paintings do you wish to see?*
Veja esta carta. *Look at this letter.*
Não ter nada que ver com. *To have nothing to do with.*
A meu ver. *In my view. As I see it.*
Tenha a bondade de ver quem é. *Please see who it is.*
Já se vê. *It is clear. It is evident.*
Agora estou vendo. *I see now. I understand.*
Vamos vê-los no sábado. *We're going to see them Saturday.*
Veja só! *Just imagine!*
Quatro olhos vêem melhor que dois. *Two heads are better than one.*
Ver para crer. *Seeing is believing.*

ver-se *to see oneself, to find oneself, to be.*

VERÃO *m. summer.*

veras *f. pl. truth, reality.*
Com tôdas (todas) as veras. *Truthfully.*

verba *f. item; entry; appropriation*

verbal *adj. verbal, oral.*

verbete *m. entry; note.*

verbo *m. verb.*

VERDADE *f. truth.*
Diga a verdade. *Tell the truth.*
Quero saber se é verdade. *I want to know if it is true.*
Você chegou tarde, não é verdade? *You arrived late; didn't you?*
É verdade. *That's right. That's true.*
De verdade? *Really?*
Para dizer a verdade. *To tell the truth.*

verdadeiro *adj. true; real; sincere.*

VERDE *adj. green; not ripe; immature; n. m. green.*

verdugo *m. executioner, hangman; unkind person.*

verdura *f. greenness; pl. vegetables, greens.*

vereador *m. alderman, councilman.*

vereda *f. path, footpath, trail.*

veredicto *m. verdict.*

vêrga (verga) *f. stick, switch.*

vergar *to bend, to curve; to stoop.*

vergonha *f. shame, disgrace; timidity, embarrassment.*
Não tem vergonha? *Aren't you ashamed?*
Que vergonha! *What a shame!*
Sem vergonha. *Shameless.*
É uma vergonha. *It's a shame.*

vergonhoso *adj. shameful, disgraceful.*

verídico *adj. truthful, veracious.*

verificação *f. verification.*

verificar *to check, to verify.*
Verifique tudo. *Check everything.*

verificar-se *to take place.*

verme *m. worm, vermin, larva.*

VERMELHO *adj. red; n. m. red.*
A Cruz Vermelha. *The Red Cross.*

verminose *f. verminosis, disease caused by worms.*

verniz *m. varnish.*

verossímil (verosímil) *adj. verisimilar.*

verossimilhança (verosimilhança) *f. verisimilitude.*

versão *f. version, rendition.*
Cada um dêles (deles) deu a sua versão. *Each one of them gave his own version.*

versar *to deal with; to be about; to examine; to put into verse.*

versátil *adj. versatile, fickle.*

verso *m. verse; back side.*
Verso branco. *Blank verse.*

vértebra *f. vertebra.*

vertedor *m. water pitcher, jug.*

verter *to pour; to spill; to translate.*
Verter lágrimas. *To weep. To shed tears.*

vertical *adj. vertical.*

vértice *m. vertex, apex, top.*

vertigem *f. dizziness; fainting.*

vesgo *adj. cross-eyed; n. m. cross-eyed person.*

vesguear *to squint.*

vespa *f. wasp, hornet.*

véspera *f. eve.*
Véspera de Natal. *Christmas Eve.*

vespertino *m. evening newspaper.*

vestiário *m. checkroom, cloakroom.*

vestíbulo *m. vestibule, lobby, hall.*
Encontramo-nos (Encontramo-nos) vestíbulo do teatro às oito. *We met in the lobby of the theatre at eight.*

VESTIDO *adj. dressed; n. m. dress; garment; clothing.*
Ela estava bem vestida. *She was well dressed.*
Vestido de baile. *Evening dress.*

vestígio *m. vestige, trace.*

VESTIR *to dress, to put on.*
Êle (ele) veste bem. *He dresses well.*
A mãe está vestindo (a vestir) os filhos.

The mother is dressing her children.

VESTIR-SE *to dress oneself, to get dressed.*
Os meninos ainda não se vestiram. *The children haven't dressed yet.*

vestuário *m. wardrobe; clothing, apparel.*

veterano *adj. veteran; n. m. veteran.*

veterinário *m. veterinarian.*

veto *m. veto.*

vetusto *adj. old, ancient.*

vexar (x = sh) *to vex, to annoy.*

VEZ *f. time, turn.*
Uma vez. *Once.*
Duas vêzes (vezes). *Twice.*
Outra vez. *Again.*
Repetidas vêzes. *Again and again.*
De uma vez para sempre. *Once (and) for all.*
Raras vêzes. *Seldom.*
Muitas vêzes. *Often.*
Cada vez. *Each time. Every time.*
Cada vez mais. *More and more.*
De vez em quando. *Now and then.*
Algumas vêzes. *Sometimes.*
Fazer as vêzes de. *To take the place of.*
Duas vêzes três são seis. *Two times three are six.*
É minha vez. *It's my turn.*

via *f. road, way; manner; via; track.*
Por via de regra. *As a general rule.*
Via dupla. *Double track.*
Via férrea. *Railroad. Railway.*
Via aérea. *By airmail.*
Via pública. *Public road. Thoroughfare.*
Via expressa. *Express highway.*

viação *f. traffic; transit system.*

viaduto *m. viaduct.*

viageiro *adj. traveling; n. m. traveler, passenger, voyager.*

VIAGEM *f. trip, voyage, journey, travel.*
Boa viagem! *Pleasant journey!*
Estar de viagem. *To be on a trip.*
Viagem de ida e volta. *Round trip.*

viajante *adj. traveling; n. m. and f. traveler.*
Caixeiro-viajante. *Traveling salesman.*

VIAJAR *to travel.*
Viajar de trem (comboio). *To go by train.*
Eu viajei por Portugal. *I traveled through Portugal.*

viatura *f. vehicle.*

víbora *f. viper.*

vibração *f. vibration.*

vibrar *to vibrate, to throb; to brandish; to touch, to sound (stringed instrument).*

vice-almirante *m. vice admiral.*

vice-cônsul *m. vice-consul.*

vice-presidente *m. vice-president.*

vice-versa *adv. vice versa.*

viciar *to vitiate, to corrupt; to make void; to falsify.*

vício *m. vice; bad habit; defect.*

vicissitude *f. vicissitude, fluctuation.*

VIDA *f. life, living.*
Ganhar a vida. *To earn a living.*
Assim é a vida. *That's life. Such is life.*
Seguro de vida. *Life insurance.*
Custo de vida. *Cost of living.*

vidente *m. and f. seer.*

vidraça *f. windowpane.*

vidro *m. glass; bottle.*
Vidro de aumento. *Magnifying glass.*
Fábrica de vidro. *Glassworks.*

vienense *adj. Viennese; n. m. and f. Viennese.*

viga *f. beam, girder.*

vigário *m. vicar.*
Conto do vigário. *Swindle, fraud.*

vigésimo *adj. twentieth; n. m. twentieth.*

vigiar *to watch; to stand guard.*

vigilância *f. vigilance.*

vigília *f. vigil.*

vigor m. *vigor, strength.*
Em vigor. *In force.*
vigoroso adj. *vigorous, strong.*
vil adj. *mean, low, vile, despicable.*
vila f. *village; villa.*
vilão adj. *villainous; rustic; n. m. villain, scoundrel; peasant.*
vime m. *wicker.*
Cadeira de vime. *Wicker chair.*
vinagre m. *vinegar.*
vinda f. *arrival.*
Eu lhe dou as boas vindas. *I welcome you.*
vindicar *to vindicate.*
vingador adj. *avenging, vindictive; n. m. avenger.*
vingança f. *vengeance, revenge.*
vingar *to avenge, to take vengeance.*
vingativo adj. *vindictive.*
vinha f. *vineyard, vine.*
vinho m. *wine.*
Vinho branco. *White wine.*
Vinho tinto. *Red wine.*
Vinho do Pôrto (Porto). *Port.*
VINTE adj. and n. m. *twenty, twentieth.*
vintém m. *former coin of Portugal and Brazil.*
Eu estou sem um vintém. *I am broke.*
viola f. *guitar; viola.*
violação f. *violation, breach.*
violão m. *guitar.*
violar *to violate; to offend.*
violência f. *violence.*
violento adj. *violent.*
violeta adj. *violet; n. m. violet (color); n. f. violet (flower).*
violinista m. *violinist, fiddler.*
violino m. *violin, fiddle.*
violoncelo m. *violoncello, cello.*
VIR *to come, to approach.*
Venha cá! *Come here!*
O mês que vem. *Next month.*
Venha o que vier. *Come what may.*
Vem a ser a mesma coisa. *It's all the same.*
Êles (eles) vieram do sul do país. *They came from the southern part of the country.*
virar *to turn; to upset.*
Vire à esquerda. *Turn to the left.*
Virar as costas. *To turn one's back on.*
viravolta f. *turnabout, sudden change.*
vírgula f. *comma.*
viril adj. *virile, manly.*
virilidade f. *virility.*
virtude f. *virtue.*
Em virtude de. *By virtue of.*
virtuoso adj. *virtuous.*
virulência f. *virulence.*
virulento adj. *virulent.*
visar *to endorse; to visa; to aim at.*
viscosidade f. *viscosity.*
viscoso adj. *viscous, sticky.*
visibilidade f. *visibility.*
VISITA f. *visit, call; visitor.*
Temos visitas. *We have company.*
Fazer uma visita. *To call on.*
Cartão de visita. *Calling card.*
VISITAR *to visit, to call on.*
Eu os visito (visito-os) de vez em quando. *I visit them from time to time.*
VISTA f. *sight, view; glance, look; scenery.*
Conheço-o de vista. *I know him by sight.*
Não o perca de vista. *Don't lose sight of him.*
À primeira vista. *At first sight.*
Em vista de. *In view of. Considering.*
Ponto de vista. *Point of view.*
Vista curta. *Nearsightedness.*
Até a vista. *So long. See you soon.*

visto adj. *seen; visaed; n. m. visa.*
Está visto. *It's obvious. It's evident.*
Visto que. *Considering that.*
vistoso adj. *showy, colorful, attractive.*
visual adj. *visual.*
vital adj. *vital.*
vitalício adj. *lifelong.*
vitalidade f. *vitality.*
vitalizar *to vitalise.*
vitamina f. *vitamin.*
vitela f. *calf; veal.*
vitelo m. *calf.*
vítima f. *victim.*
vitória f. *victory.*
Vitória moral. *Moral victory.*
vitorioso adj. *victorious.*
vitrina f. *show window.*
vitupério m. *vituperation, shame, insult.*
viuvez f. *widowhood.*
viúvo m. *widower.*
Êle (ele) é viúvo e tem três filhos. *He's a widower and has three children.*
viva! *Hurrah! Long live!*
Viva o Brasil! *Long live Brazil!*
vivacidade f. *vivacity.*
vivaz adj. *lively, spirited; perennial.*
viveiro m. *plant nursery; hatchery; aquarium.*
VIVER *to live, to exist; n. m. life, living.*
Êle (ele) vive só. *He lives alone.*
Êles (eles) vivem bem. *They live well. They lead a good life.*
Comer para viver e não viver para comer. *To eat to live and not to live to eat.*
víveres m. pl. *foodstuffs, food.*
viveza f. *liveliness, vivacity.*
vivificar *to vivify, to animate.*
VIVO adj. *living, alive; lively; smart, bright.*
Êle (ele) está vivo. *He's alive.*
De viva voz. *By word of mouth.*
Côr (cor) viva. *Bright color.*
Os vivos e os mortos. *The quick and the dead.*
vizinhança f. *vicinity, neighborhood.*
vizinho adj. *neighboring, next; n. m. neighbor.*
Um bom vizinho. *A good neighbor.*
VOAR *to fly; to flee; to blow up.*
As horas voaram. *The hours flew (by).*
vocabulário m. *vocabulary.*
vocábulo m. *word, term.*
vocação f. *vocation.*
vocal adj. *vocal, oral.*
VOCÊ *you; pl. vocês.*
Você tem razão. *You are right.*
vociferar *to vociferate, to shout, to cry out.*
vodu m. *voodoo.*
vo-la (contr. of vos + a, direct object) *it to you, her to you.*
volante adj. *flying, mobile; n. m. steering wheel; balance wheel (watch); shuttlecock.*
volátil adj. *volatile, changeable.*
vo-lo (contr. of vos + o, direct object) *it to you, her to you.*
VOLTA f. *turn, turning; return; curve; change; walk.*
Estar de volta. *To be back.*
Dar uma volta. *To take a walk. To go for a stroll.*
Passagem de ida e volta. *Round-trip ticket.*
Meia volta, volver! *About, face!*
VOLTAR *to turn; to return; to change.*
Volte amanhã. *Come back tomorrow.*
Ela ainda não voltou. *She hasn't returned yet.*
Voltar as costas. *To turn one's back.*

volume m. *volume; bulk; tome; piece of luggage; package.*
volumoso adj. *voluminous, bulky.*
voluntário adj. *voluntary, willing; volunteer.*
voluptuoso adj. *voluptuous, sensual.*
volver *to turn, to revolve.*
À direita, volver! *Right, face!*
Volver a si. *To regain consciousness.*
vomitar *to vomit.*
vômito (vómito) m. *vomiting.*
VONTADE f. *will; desire; intention.*
Esteja à vontade. *Make yourself at home. Make yourself comfortable.*
Estou com vontade de ir ao cinema. *I feel like going to the movies.*
Ela o fará de boa vontade. *She will do it willingly.*
vôo m. *flight, flying.*
Levantar vôo. *To take off. To take flight.*
voracidade f. *voracity, greediness.*
voragem f. *vortex, whirlpool.*
vórtice m. *vortex, whirlpool.*
vos *direct and indirect object, fam. pl. you, to you.*
vós fam. pl. *you.*
vosso fam. pl. *your.*
Vossa Excelência. *Your Excellency.*
Vossa Senhoria. *In formal correspondence or announcements it is often used to translate "you."*
votação f. *voting.*
Votação secreta. *Ballot. Secret vote.*
votante m. and f. *voter, elector.*
votar *to vote; to vow.*
Eu não votarei por êle (ele). *I'll not vote for him.*
voto m. *vote; ballot; vow; wish.*
Voto de confiança. *Vote of confidence.*
VOZ f. *voice; outcry; word; rumor.*
À meia voz. *In an undertone. In a whisper.*
Em voz alta. *Aloud.*
Em voz baixa (x = sh). *In a low tone.*
Levantar a voz. *To raise one's voice.*
A voz do povo. *Public opinion.*
vulcanizar *to vulcanise.*
vulgar adj. *vulgar, common, ordinary.*
vulgo m. *the people.*
vulnerável adj. *vulnerable.*
vulto m. *form, figure; bulk; important person.*

X

xadrez (x = sh) m. *chess.*
xale (x = sh) m. *shawl.*
xampu (x = sh) m. *shampoo.*
xaropada (x = sh) f. *cough syrup.*
xarope (x = sh) m. *syrup, remedy.*
xavante (x = sh) adj., n. m. and f. *Chavante, Indian tribe of Brazil.*
xelim (x = sh) m. *shilling.*
XÍCARA (x = sh) f. *cup.*
Uma xícara de chá. *A cup of tea.*
xingar (x = sh) *to call names, to abuse.*

Z

zagal m. *shepherd.*
zangado adj. *angry.*
zangar *to anger, to annoy.*
zangar-se *to get angry.*
Zangaram-se quando ouviram as palavras do rapaz. *They got angry when they heard the young man's words.*
zarpar *to weigh anchor, to sail.*
zebra (zebra) f. *zebra.*
zéfiro m. *zephyr.*
zelador m. *caretaker.*

zelar *to watch over, to take care of.*
zêlo (zelo) *m. zeal, devotion.*
zeloso *adj. zealous, dedicated; jealous.*
zênite (zénite) *m. zenith.*
ZERO *m. zero, nothing.*
  Acima de zero. *Above zero.*

ziguezague *m. zigzag.*
ziguezaguear *to zigzag.*
zinco *m. zinc.*
zoar *to hum, to buzz.*
zona *f. zone, area, region.*

Zona temperada. *Temperate zone.*
Zona de silêncio. *Quiet zone.*
zorro *m. fox.*
zumbido *m. buzzing, hum.*
zumbir *to buzz, to hum.*

GLOSSARY OF PROPER NAMES

Adolfo Adolph.
Afonso Alphonse.
Alberto Albert.
Alexandre Alexander.
Alfredo Alfred.
Alice Alice.
Ana Ann, Anne, Anna.
André Andrew.
Antônio (António) Anthony.
Artur Arthur.
Augusto Augustus.
Aurélio Aurelius.

Bárbara Barbara.
Beatriz Beatrice.
Bernardo Bernard.

Camilo Camillus.
Carlos Charles.
Carlota Charlotte.
Carolina Caroline.
Cecília Cecilia.
Cláudio Claude, Claudius.

Diogo James.
Dorotéia (Doroteia) Dorothy.

Edmundo Edmund.
Eduardo Edward.
Emília Emily.
Ernesto Ernest.
Ester Esther.
Eugênio (Eugénio) Eugene.
Eva Eve.

Fernando Ferdinand.
Filipe Philip.
Francisco Francis.
Frederico Frederic(k).

Gertrudes Gertrude.
Gil Giles.
Glória Gloria.
Guilherme William.
Gustavo Gustavus.

Heitor Hector.

Henrique Henry.

Inácio Ignatius.
Inês Agnes, Inez.
Isabel Elizabeth.

Jesus Jesus.
João John.
Joaquim Joachim.
Jorge George.
José Joseph.
Josefa Josephine.
Josefina Josephine.
Júlio Julius.

Leonardo Leonard.
Leonor Eleanor.
Lúcia Lucy.
Luís Louis.
Luísa Louise.

Manuel Emanuel, Manuel.
Margarida Margaret.

Maria Mary.
Mário Mario, Marius.
Marta Martha.
Maurício Maurice, Morris.
Miguel Michael.

Paulo Paul.
Pedro Peter.

Raimundo Raymond.
Raquel Rachel.
Ricardo Richard.
Roberto Robert.
Rodolfo Rudolph, Ralph.
Rodrigo Roderic.
Rosa Rose.

Sebastião Sebastian.

Teresa Theresa.
Tomás Thomas.

Vicente Vincent.

GLOSSARY OF GEOGRAPHICAL NAMES

Açôres (Açores) Azores.
África Africa.
Alemanha Germany.
Alpes Alps.
América America.
América do Norte North America.
América do Sul South America.
América Espanhola Spanish America.
Andes Andes.
Angola Angola.
Argentina Argentina.
Ásia Asia.
Atenas Athens.
Atlântico Atlantic.
Austrália Australia.

Barcelona Barcelona.
Belém Belem, Bethlehem.
Bélgica Belgium.
Bolívia Bolivia.
Brasil Brazil.
Brasília Brasilia.
Bruxelas (x = sh) Brussels.
Buenos Aires Buenos Aires.

Checoslováquia Czechoslovakia.
Chile Chile.
China China.
Coimbra Coimbra.
Colômbia Colombia.
Costa Rica Costa Rica.
Cuba Cuba.

Dinamarca Denmark.

Egito (Egipto) Egypt.
El Salvador El Salvador.
Equador Ecuador.
Escandinávia Scandinavia.
Escócia Scotland.

Espanha Spain.
Estados Unidos (da América) United States (of America).
Estados Unidos do Brasil United States of Brazil.
Europa Europe.

Filipinas Philippines.
Finlândia Finland.
França France.

Galiza Galicia.
Genebra Geneva.
Grã-Bretanha Great Britain.
Grécia Greece.
Guatemala Guatemala.

Haiti Haiti.
Havaí Hawaii.
Havana Havana.
Hispano-América Hispanic America.
Holanda Holland.
Honduras Honduras.
Hungria Hungary.

Inglaterra England.
Irlanda Ireland.
Israel Israel.
Itália Italy.
Iugoslávia (Jugoslávia) Yugoslavia

Japão Japan.

Lisboa Lisbon.
Londres London.

Macau Macao.
Madeira Madeira.
Madrid Madrid.
Mediterrâneo Mediterranean.
México (x = sh) Mexico.

Moçambique Mozambique.
Moscou, Moscóvia (Moscovo) Moscow.

Nicarágua Nicaragua.
Noruega Norway.
Nova Iorque New York.
Nova Zelândia New Zealand.

Oceânia Oceania.

Pacífico Pacific.
Países Baixos (x = sh) Low Countries, Netherlands.
Paraguai Paraguay.
Paris Paris.
Peru Peru.
Pireneus (Pirenéus) Pyrenees.
Polônia (Polónia) Poland.
Pôrto (Porto) Oporto.
Pôrto (Porto) Rico Puerto Rico.
Portugal Portugal.

República Dominicana Dominican Republic.
Rio de Janeiro Rio de Janeiro.
Roma Rome.
Romênia (Roménia) Romania.
Rússia Russia.

São Paulo São Paulo, St. Paul.
Sicília Sicily.
Suécia Sweden.
Suíça Switzerland.

Timor Timor.
Turquia Turkey.

Uruguai Uruguay.

Vaticano Vatican.
Viena Vienna.

English-Portuguese DICTIONARY

A

a (an) um, uma.
ability capacidade, habilidade; aptidão, talento.
able *adj.* capaz.
able (be) poder.
abnormal anormal.
aboard a bordo.
abolish abolir, suprimir.
about cêrca (cerca) de, quase, mais ou menos; sôbre (sobre); em volta de.
above sôbre (sobre), acima de; acima.
abroad no estrangeiro, para o exterior, fora de casa.
absence susência.
absent ausente.
absent-minded distraído.
absolute absoluto.
absorb absorver, incorporar.
absurd absurdo, ridículo.
abundant abundante.
abuse abuso.
abuse (to) abusar, maltratar.
academic acadêmico (académico).
academy academia, colégio.
accent acento.
accent (to) acentuar.
accept aceitar, receber; reconhecer.
acceptance aceitação.
accident acidente.
accommodate acomodar.
accommodations acomodações, alojamento.
accompany acompanhar.
accomplish efetuar (efectuar), realizar.
according to segundo, conforme.
account conta; relato, narrativa.
accuracy exatidão (exactidão) *(x = s)*, precisão.
accusative acusativo.
accuse acusar, denunciar.
accustomed acostumado.
ache dor.
achieve conseguir, realizar, ganhar.
acid ácido *(n. and adj.)*.
acknowledge reconhecer, admitir; acusar recebimento de.
acknowledgment reconhecimento; confirmação.
acquaintance conhecimento; conhecido (person).
acre acre.
across através; através de.
act ato (acto); ação (acção).
act (to) agir, atuar (actuar) (to do); potar-se, comportar-se, conduzir-se (to behave); representar (theatre).
action ação (acção).
active ativo (activo).
activity atividade (actividade).
actor ator (actor).
actual real, verdadeiro.
add adicionar, aumentar.
address endereço (endereço).
address (to) dirigir-se a.
adequate adequado.
adjective adjetivo (adjectivo).
adjoining contíguo, adjacente, vizinho.
administrative administrativo.
admiral almirante.
admiration admiração.
admire admirar.
admirer admirador.
admission admissão, entrada.
  Admission free. Entrada gratuita.
admit admitir, conceder; reconhecer.

admittance admissão, entrada.
  No admittance. Entrada proibida.
admonish advertir, prevenir; repreender.
adopt adotar (adoptar).
adoption adoção (adopção); aceitação.
adult adulto.
advance adiantamento, antecipação; avanço.
advance (to) avançar, adiantar.
advantage vantagem, benefício, proveito.
advantageous vantajoso, proveitoso.
adventure aventura.
adverb advérbio.
adversity adversidade.
advertise anunciar, publicar, fazer propaganda.
advertisement anúncio, aviso.
advice conselho.
advise aconselhar, recomendar.
affair assunto; negócio.
affected afetado (afectado), comovido.
affection afeição; amor.
affectionate afetuoso (afectuoso), carinhoso.
  Affectionately yours. Afetuosamente.
affirm afirmar, confirmar.
affirmative afirmativo.
after depois de, após; atrás de; depois que.
afternoon tarde.
  Good afternoon! Boa tarde!
afterwards depois, mais tarde.
again outra vez, de nôvo (novo).
against contra.
age idade.
age (epoch) época.
age (to) envelhecer.
agency agência.
aggravate agravar, piorar; irritar.
aggressive agressivo.
ago
  a long time ago há muito tempo.
  How long ago? Quanto tempo há?
  Há quanto tempo?
agony angústia, agonia.
agree concordar, estar de acôrdo (acordo).
agreeable agradável; satisfatório.
agreed combinado; de acôrdo (acordo).
agreement convênio (convénio), acôrdo (acordo).
agricultural agrícola.
agriculture agricultura, lavoura.
ahead avante, adiante.
  straight ahead; bem em frente.
aid ajuda, auxílio *(x = s)*.
aim propósito, intenção.
air ar.
  open air ar livre.
air-conditioning condicionamento de ar.
airfield campo de aviação.
airmail correio aéreo.
airplane avião.
aisle passagem, corredor.
alarm alarme.
alarm (to) alarmar.
alarm clock despertador.
album álbum.
alcohol álcool.
alight (to) desmontar, descer.
alike parecido, semelhante.
alive vivo.
all todo; tudo.
  all day o dia todo.
  all right está bem.
  after all afinal de contas.
  not at all de modo algum.
allied aliado.

allow permitir, deixar (x = sh).
  Allow me. Permita-me.
allowed permitido.
ally aliado.
almond amêndoa.
almost quase.
alone só, sòzinho.
along ao longo de, ao lado de.
  along with junto com, com.
  all along sempre, continuamente.
  to get along arranjar-se, avançar.
  to go along with acompanhar.
also também, além disso.
alternate (to) alternar.
alternately alternativamente.
although embora, ainda que, pôsto (posto) que.
always sempre.
ambassador embaixador (x = sh).
amber âmbar.
ambition ambição.
ambitious ambicioso.
amen amém, âmen (ámen).
amend emendar.
amends indenização (indemnização), compensação.
America América.
  North America América do Norte.
American americano, norte-americano.
among entre.
amount quantia, quantidade, soma.
ample amplo.
amuse divertir.
amusement divertimento.
amusing divertido; engraçado.
analyze analisar.
anchor âncora.
ancient antigo.
and e.
anecdote anedota.
angel anjo.
anger raiva, ira.
anger (to) irritar.
angry zangado, irado.
  to get angry zangar-se.
animal animal.
animate animar.
ankle tornozelo.
annex anexo (x = ks).
annex (to) anexar (x = ks).
anniversary aniversário.
announce anunciar.
annoy aborrecer, irritar.
annual anual.
anonymous anônimo (anónimo).
another outro.
answer resposta, contestação.
answer (to) responder.
ant formiga.
anxious ansioso.
any qualquer, algum, alguma.
anybody qualquer pessoa, alguém.
anyhow de qualquer maneira, de qualquer forma.
anyone qualquer pessoa, alguém.
anything qualquer coisa, alguma coisa.
anyway de qualquer maneria, em qualquer caso.
anywhere em qualquer parte, em qualquer lugar.
apart à parte; separado.
apartment apartamento.
apiece cada um.
apologize desculpar-se, apresentar desculpas, pedir desculpas.
apology desculpa.

apparatus aparelho.

appeal apelação (law); súplica, apêlo (apelo) (request); atração (atracção), simpatia (attraction).

appear aparecer, comparecer; parecer (seem).

appetite apetite.

applaud aplaudir, aclamar, bater palmas.

applause aplauso.

apple maçã.

applicable aplicável.

applicant pretendente, requerente, candidato.

application aplicação; requerimento, solicitação, petição (application for something).
  to fill out an application preencher um requerimento (or uma petição).

apply (to) usar; aplicar (put on).
  to apply for solicitar, pedir.

appreciate apreciar, prezar.

appreciation apreciação, gratidão, reconhecimento.

approach acesso (access); maneira de aproximação (x = s)

approach (to) aproximar-se (x = s) de (to come near); abordar (a subject).

approval aprovação, autorização.

approve (to) aprovar, autorizar.

April abril (Abril).

apron avental.

arbitrary arbitrário.

arcade arcada.

architect arquiteto (arquitecto).

architecture arquitetura (arquitectura).

area área, superfície, região.

Argentinean, Argentine argentino.

argument argumento; discussão.

arid árido, sêco (seco).

arm braço (part of body).

armed forces fôrças (forças) armadas.

army exército (x = z).

around em tôrno (torno) de, em redor de, em volta de.

arrange (to) arranjar, preparar.

arrangement arranjo.

arrival chegada.

arrive chegar.

article artigo.

artificial artificial.

artist artista.

artistic artístico.

as como
  as ... as ... tão ... como ...
  as it were por assim dizer.
  as much tanto.
  as much as tanto quanto, tanto como.
  as many as tantos quanto.

ascertain averiguar, indagar, verificar.

ashamed envergonhado.

aside à parte, de lado.

ask perguntar (a question); pedir (request).

asleep adormecido.
  He's asleep. Êle (ele) está dormindo (a dormir).
  to fall asleep adormecer, cair no sono.

aspire aspirar, ansiar.

aspirin aspirina.

assemble reunir (to gather); montar, armar (a machine); ajuntar, acumular (to collect).

assembly assembléia (assembleia), reunião.

assets ativo (activo); bens.

assign designar, nomear.

assimilate assimilar.

assist ajudar, auxiliar (x = s).

assistance ajuda, auxílio (x = s).

associate sócio, associado.

associate (to) associar, associar-se a.

assume assumir, supor.

assumption suposição.

assurance segurança, certeza.

assure assegurar, convencer, garantir.

astonish assombrar, surpreender muito

astounded perplexo (x = ks), surpreendido.

astounding assombroso, surpreendente.

at a, em.
  at all events em qualquer caso.
  at first a princípio
  at last finalmente.
  at once imediatamente.
  at the same time ao mesmo tempo, à vez.
  at two o'clock as duas (horas).
  at that time naquele tempo
  We were at John's. Estávamos na casa de João.
  at work trabalhando.

athlete atleta.

athletic atlético.

athletics atletismo.

atmosphere atmosfera; ambiente.

atom átomo.

atom bomb bomba atômica (atómica).

attach afixar (x = ks), unir, juntar.

attack ataque.

attack (to) atacar.

attempt tentativa, ensaio.

attempt (to) tentar, procurar; experimentar.

attend assistir, estar presente; cuidar, tomar conta de; prestar atenção.

attention atenção.

attentive atento, atencioso.

attic sótão.

attitude atitude.

attorney advogado.

attract atrair.

attraction atração (atracção).

attractive atrativo (atractivo).

audience audiência; platéia (plateia) (in theatre); público.

August agôsto (Agosto).

aunt tia.

author autor.

authority autoridade.

authorize autorizar.

automobile automóvil.

autumn outono (Outono).

available disponível, acessível.

avenue avenida.

average média.

avoid evitar.

awake adj. acordado.

awake (to) acordar.

aware inteirado, ciente.

away ausente, fora, longe.
  to go away ir-se embora.

awful terrível, horrível; tremendo.

awkward desajeitado; embaraçoso, difícil (embarrassing, difficult).

ax, axe machado.
  to have an ax to grind ter interêsse (interesse) pessoal.

B

babble balbuciar, palrar.

baby bebê (bebé); nenê (nené).

bachelor solteiro.

back costas (of the body); posterior; atrás, para trás; reverso, verso; espaldar, encôsto (encosto) (of a chair).
  behind one's back nas costas.
  back door porta dos fundos.

  to go back voltar.
  to be back estar de volta.

background fundo (scenery, painting, etc.); educação (education); experiência.

backward atrasado, retrógrado; acanhado.
  to go backwards ir para trás, ir de costas.

backwoods sertão Ⓑ; interior Ⓑ.

bacon toicinho, toucinho.

bad adv. mal; adj. mau.

badge insígnia, emblema.

bag saco, saca; bôlsa (bolsa).

baggage bagagem.

bait isca.

baker padeiro.

bakery padaria.

balance balança; equilíbrio; saldo (account).

bald calvo, careca.

ball bola.

balloon balão; globo.

ball-point pen caneta esferográfica.

banana banana.

band banda.

bandage bandagem, atadura.

banister corrimão.

bank banco; margem (of river).

bankruptcy bancarrota.

baptize batizar (baptizar)

bar bar (where liquor is served); barra (of metal, etc.); tribunal.

barber barbeiro.

barbershop barbearia.

bare nu, despido.

barefoot descalço.

bargain contrato, negócio; coisa barata.

barge barcaça.

bark cortiça, casca (of a tree); latido (of a dog).

barley cevada.

barn celeiro; estábulo.

barrel barril.

barren estéril.

base base.

baseball basebol.

basic básico.

basin bacia.

basis base.

basket cêsto (cesto), cesta.

bath banho.

bathe (to) banhar; banhar-se; tomar banho.

bathing suit roupa de banho.

battery bateria, pilha.

battle batalha, luta.

be (to) ser; estar; ficar.
  to be hungry estar com fome, ter fome.
  to be right ter razão.
  to be sleepy estar com sono, ter sono.
  to be slow ser lento; estar atrasado (of a watch).
  to be sorry sentir.
  to be thirsty estar com sêde (sede), ter sêde.
  to be used to estar acostumado.
  to be wrong não ter razão.

beach praia.

beam viga; raio (of light).

beaming radiante, brilhante.

bean feijão, fava.

bear urso.

bear (to) agüentar (aguentar), suportar, sofrer (to endure, to suffer); carregar, levar (to carry); parir, dar à luz (children, etc.); produzir (fruit, etc.).
  to bear a grudge ter ressentimento.

to bear in mind gardar na memória, ter em mente.

beard barba.

bearer portador.

beat (to) palpitar (heart); bater, dar pancadas em (strike); tocar (a drum); bater (eggs, etc.); vencer, derrotar (in a game).

beating surra, açoitamento (whipping); palpitação, pulsação (heart).

beautiful belo, formoso.

beauty beleza.

because porque.

because of devido a, por causa de.

become tornar-se, vir a ser, fazer-se (to come to be); sentar bem, ficar bem (to be becoming).

becoming conveniente (appropriate); cair bem, assentar bem, ficar bem (to be becoming, as a hat, etc.).

bed cama.

bedclothes roupa de cama.

bed linen roupa de cama.

bedroom quarto de dormir.

bee abelha.

beech faia.

beef carne de vaca.

beehive cortiço, colmeia.

beer cerveja.

beet beterraba.

before antes; antes que; diante de; na frente de; anterior.

beforehand de antemão, anteriormente.

beg pedir, rogar.

beggar mendigo.

begin principiar, começar.

beginning princípio, começo (começo).

behind atrás, detrás.

Belgian belga.

belief crença, opinião.

believe crer, acreditar, pensar, achar.

bell campainha, sino.

belong pertencer, ser de.

below abaixo (x = sh), debaixo (x = sh).

belt cinto.

bench banco; tribunal (court).

bend dobrar, curvar; dobrar-se, inclinar-se.

beneath debaixo (x = sh), abaixo (x = sh).

benefit benefício.

benefit (to) beneficiar.

beside ao lado de.

besides além disso, também; além de.

best melhor.

bet aposta.

bet (to) apostar.

better *adj.* melhor.

better half cara-metade, espôsa (esposa).

between entre, no meio de.

beyond mais longe, além; além de.

Bible Bíblia.

bicycle bicicleta.

big grande.

bill conta, nota (check, account); fatura (factura).

bill of fare menu, cardápio.

billiards bilhar.

billion bilhão.

bind (to) atar, unir; encadernar (book).

binding encadernação (book).

birch vidoeiro.

bird pássaro, ave.

birth nascimento.

to give birth dar à luz.

birthday data de nascimento, aniversário.

biscuit biscoito.

bishop bispo.

bit (a) bocado, pouquinho (small amount).

bite mordedura.

bite (to) .morder.

bitter amargo.

bitterness amargor, amargura.

black prêto (preto), negro.

blackbird melro.

blackboard quadro-negro, lousa.

blacken enegrecer; escurecer.

blade lâmina.

blame culpa.

blame (to) culpar, acusar.

blank (em) branco.

blanket cobertor.

blank form formulário (em branco).

bleed sangrar.

bless benzer, abençoar.

blessing bênção.

blind *adj.* cego.

blind (to) cegar.

blindness cegueira.

blister empôla (empola), bôlha (bolha).

block (city) quadra, quarteirão.

block up obstruir, tapar.

blood sangue.

blotter mata-borrão.

blouse blusa.

blow golpe, pancada.

blow (to) soprar.

blue azul.

blush rubor.

blush (to) ruborizar.

board tábua (wood); pensão (food); junta, conselho (of directors, etc.); tabuleiro (for games).

on board a bordo.

boarder pensionista.

boardinghouse pensão.

boast jactância.

boast (to) jactar-se, vangloriar-se.

boat bote, barco, embarcação; navio.

body corpo.

boil furúnculo.

boil (to) ferver.

boiler caldeira.

boiling *adj.* fervendo, fervente.

bold corajoso, valente.

Bolivian boliviano.

bomb bomba.

bond união, laço, ligação; título (stocks).

bone osso.

book livro.

bookseller livreiro.

bookstore livraria.

boot bota.

border fronteira, limite (boundary); beira, margem.

bore (to) aborrecer, amolar; furar, perfurar (to make holes).

boring aborrecido, tedioso.

born nascido.

born (be) nascer.

borrow pedir emprestado, tomar emprestado.

boss chefe, patrão.

both ambos, os dois.

bother amolação, incômodo (incómodo).

bother (to) aborrecer, amolar.

bottle garrafa.

bottom fundo.

bound atado, amarrado.

bound for com destino para, em viagem para.

boundless ilimitado.

bow saudação, reverência (greeting); arco (weapon, bow of a violin); proa (ship).

bow (to) saudar, fazer uma reverência (to bow in reverence); ceder, submeter-se (to submit or yield).

bowl tijela, bacia.

bow tie (gravata) borboleta.

box caixa (x = sh).

box office bilheteria (bilheteira).

boy menino, garôto (garoto), moço, jovem.

bracelet bracelete, pulseira.

braid trança.

brain cérebro.

brake freio.

bran farelo.

branch ramo, galho (of tree); ramal (railroad, etc.); filial, sucursal (local office, etc.)

brand marca (of goods).

brave bravo, corajoso, valente.

Brazilian brasileiro.

bread pão.

break ruptura, quebra.

break (to) romper, quebrar.

breakfast café-da-manhã (pequeno almoço, primeiro almoço).

breakfast (to) tomar o café-da-manhã (tomar o pequeno almoço, tomar o primeiro almoço).

breath respiração, fôlego.

breathe respirar.

breeze brisa.

bribe subôrno (suborno).

bribe (to) subornar.

bride noiva.

bridegroom noivo.

bridge ponte.

brief breve, curto.

briefcase pasta.

briefly brevemente.

bright claro (opposite of dark); radiante (radiant); inteligente; vivo (lively).

brighten clarear, tornar claro (to make clearer); alegrar, animar (to make cheerful).

brilliant brilhante, luminoso.

brim aba (hat).

bring trazer.

to bring together juntar, unir, reunir.

to bring toward aproximar (x = s), trazer

to bring up educar, criar (to rear); trazer a baila (a matter, etc.).

bringing up educação, criação.

British britânico.

broad largo.

broadcast radiodifusão, emissão.

broil grelhar, assar (meat).

brook riacho.

broom vassoura.

brother irmão.

brother-in-law cunhado.

brotherly fraternal.

brown castanho.

bruise contusão, machucadura.

bruise (to) machucar.

brush escôva (escova).

clothesbrush escôva de roupa.

toothbrush escôva de dentes.

brushwood mato.

brute bruto.

bubble bôlha (bolha).

buckle fivela.

bud botão; brôto Ⓑ.

budget orçamento.

buffet aparador, bufete (dresser).

bug inseto (insecto), bicho.
build construir.
building edifício.
bulb (electric) lâmpada.
bull touro, toiro.
bulletin boletim.
bullfighter toureiro.
bundle pacote, embrulho.
burden carga, pêso (peso).
bureau cômoda (cómoda) (in a bedroom); escritório (an office); departamento.
burglar ladrão.
burial entêrro (enterro).
burn queimadura.
burn (to) queimar.
　to burn up queimar-se, consumir-se.
burst estouro, explosão.
burst (to) estourar, explodir, rebentar.
　to burst out laughing cair na gargalhada.
bury enterrar.
bus ônibus (ónibus, autocarro).
bush arbusto.
bushel alqueire.
business trabalho, ocupação; negócio.
businessman negociante, comerciante, homem de negócios.
busy ocupado.
but mas.
butcher açougueiro.
butcher's shop açougue (talho).
butter manteiga.
button botão.
buy comprar.
buyer comprador.
by por, a, em, de, para; junto a, perto de (near).
　by and by daqui a pouco, logo.
　by and large de modo geral.
　by hand à mão.
　by reason of por causa de.
　by the way a propósito.
　by virtue of em virtude de.
　Finish it by Sunday. Termine-o antes do domingo.
　Send it by airmail. Envie-o por correio aéreo.

C

cab táxi (x = ks).
cabbage repôlho (repolho), couve.
cabin cabana; cabina, camarote (ship).
cabinet gabinete.
cable cabo.
cadet cadete.
café café, restaurante; bar.
cage gaiola.
cake bôlo (bolo); sabonete (soap).
calendar calendário.
calf bezerro.
call chamada (act of calling); telefonema (telephone); visita (visit).
call (to) chamar; convocar (a meeting); citar (to summon); visitar (to call upon).
　to call (someone) back chamar, fazer voltar.
　to call out gritar, bradar.
calling card cartão de visita.
calm adj. calmo, quieto, tranqüilo (tranquilo).
calm n. calma, silêncio.
camera câmara; máquina fotográfica.
camp acampamento.
camp (to) acampar.
campaign campanha.
can lata.
can poder (to be able); saber (to know how); enlatar (to put in a can)
canal canal.

candidate candidato.
candle vela.
candy bala, doce, bombom.
can opener abridor de lata.
cap boné, gorro.
capable capaz.
capital capital.
capitalism capitalismo.
capital letter letra maiúscula.
captain capitão; comandante (skipper of ship); capitão de mar-e-guerra (navy captain).
capture (to) capturar.
car carro; automóvel.
card cartão; carta (playing card).
cardboard cartão, papelão.
care cuidado.
　to take care ter cuidado, tomar cuidado.
　to take care of cuidar de, tomar conta de.
　in care of (c/o) ao cuidado de (a/c).
care (to) interessar-se, importar-se.
　I don't care to go. Não me interessa ir.
　He doesn't care a hang. Não lhe importa nada.
　I don't care. Não me importa.
career carreira.
careful cuidadoso.
　Be careful! Cuidado!
careless desquidado.
carnival carnaval.
carpenter carpinteiro.
carpet tapête (tapete).
carry levar, conduzir, carregar.
　to carry away levar.
　to carry out levar a cabo (finish).
　to carry on continuar (continue).
cart carrêta (carreta), carroça.
carve trinchar, cortar (meat), esculpir, entalhar (marble, wood, etc.).
case caso (a particular instance; grammar, etc.); estôjo (estojo) (kit); caixa (x = sh) (case of beer, etc.).
　in case of em caso de.
cash dinheiro disponível, dinheiro em caixa (x = sh).
　cash on hand dinheiro em caixa.
　cash payment pagamento à vista.
cash (to) cobrar (a check).
cashier o caixa (x = sh).
cask barril, tonel.
castle castelo.
casual casual.
casually casualmente.
cat gato.
catch (to) apanhar, agarrar.
　to catch cold pegar um resfriado.
　to catch on compreender, dar-se conta.
　to catch (on) fire pegar fogo.
　to catch up alcançar (overtake).
catholic católico.
cattle gado.
cause causa, motivo, razão.
cause (to) causar.
caution cautela.
cavalry cavalaria.
ceiling teto.
celebrate celebrar.
celebration celebração, comemoração.
celery aipo.
cellar adega; porão Ⓑ.
cement cimento.
cemetery cemitério.
cent centavo.
center centro.
century século.
ceremony cerimônia (cerimónia).

certain seguro, certo; claro, evidente.
certainly certamente, sem dúvida, seguramente.
certificate certidão, certificado, atestado.
chain cadeia.
chain (to) encadear.
chair cadeira.
chairman presidente (of a meeting).
chalk giz.
chance azar, acaso, casualidade (happening by chance); oportunidade (opportunity); probabilidade (probability); risco (risk).
　by chance por casualidade, por acaso.
　to take a chance arriscar-se.
chance (to) aventurar, arriscar.
change trôco (troco) (money).
change (to) trocar (money); cambiar.
channel canal.
chapel capela.
chapter capitulo.
character caráter (carácter).
characteristic adj. característico, típico.
charge carga (load; quantity of powder, electricity, etc.); ordem, comando (order); custo, preço (price); acusação (accusation); carga, ataque (attack).
　in charge encarregado.
charge (to) carregar (a battery, etc.; to load); cobrar (a price); acusar (to accuse).
　How much do you charge for this? Quanto cobra por isto?
charges despesas (expenses); instruções (to a jury, etc.).
charitable caridoso, caritativo, generoso.
charity caridade.
charm encanto.
charming encantador.
chart carta (for the use of navigators); mapa (outline, map); quadro, gráfico (graph).
chase (to) perseguir.
chat (to) conversar; bater papo Ⓑ.
cheap barato.
check cheque (banking); talão (claim check); conta, nota (in a restaurant); xeque (x = sh) (chess); contrôle Ⓑ, supervisão (control); restrição (restraint); obstáculo, empecilho (hindrance); verificação (verification).
check (to) investigar (to investigate); verificar (to verify); frear, reprimir (to restrain); depositar, enviar (baggage); dar xeque pôr em xeque (x = sh) (chess).
cheek bochecha.
cheer n. alegria, bom humor; pl. vivas, aplausos (applause).
cheerful alegre, animado.
cheese queijo.
chemical químico.
chemist químico.
cherish apreciar, estimar (to hold dear).
cherished estimado (dear); caro (dear).
cherry cereja.
chest peito (body); arca, caixa (x = sh), caixão (x = sh).
chestnut castanha.
chew (to) mastigar, mascar.
chicken galinha, frango.
chief adj. principal.
chief n. chefe.
child criança; menino (m.); menina (f.).
childhood infância, meninice.
Chilean chileno.
chimney chaminé.
chin queixo (x = sh).
china louça, porcelana.
chocolate chocolate.
choice adj. seleto (selecto), escolhido.

choice *n.* escolha, seleção (selecçao).
choir côro (coro).
choke sufocar, afogar.
choose escolher, eleger.
chop costeleta (cut of meat).
chop (to) cortar (wood, etc.); picar (meat).
chore tarefa.
Christian cristão.
Christmas Natal.
church igreja.
cider sidra.
cigar charuto.
cigarette cigarro.
cigarette lighter isqueiro.
cinnamon canela.
circle círculo.
circulation circulação.
citizen cidadão.
city cidade.
city hall prefeitura (câmara municipal).
civil civil.
civilization civilização.
civilize civilizar.
civil rights direitos civis.
claim pretensão, reclamação, título, direito.
claim (to) reclamar, pretender.
clam marisco.
clamor clamor, gritaria, tumulto.
clap aplaudir, bater palmas.
class classe.
class (to) classificar.
clause cláusula.
claw garra.
clay argila.
clean *adj.* limpo.
clean (to) limpar.
cleanliness asseio, limpeza.
clear claro.
clear (to) aclarar (to make clear); melhorar (to clear up, referring to the weather); absolver (of blame, guilt); liqüidar (liquidar), pagar (to settle a debt, account, etc.); tirar (levantar) a mesa (a table).
clearly claramente.
clerk caixeiro (x = sh); escrivão.
clever destro, hábil; inteligente.
climate clima.
climb (to) subir, trepar.
cloak capa, manto.
clock relógio.
close (near) perto;
close by muito perto.
close (to) fechar (to shut, to shut down); terminar (to end); encerrar (a meeting); fechar (a deal).
closed fechado.
closet armário (clothes, food, etc.); guarda-roupa (clothes).
cloth tecido, fazenda, pano.
clothe (to) vestir.
clothes roupa.
clothes brush escôva (escova) de roupa.
clothes dryer secador de roupa.
clothes hanger cabide.
clothing roupa.
cloud nuvem.
cloudy nublado, nebuloso.
clover trevo.
club clube, sociedade, associação; (association); cacête (cacete), porrete (stick).
coach côche (coche), carruagem.
coal carvão.

coast costa.
coat paletó, casaco; sobretudo.
cocktail coquetel.
coconut côco (coco).
code código.
coffee café.
coffin caixão (x = sh).
coin moeda.
coincidence coincidência.
by coincidence por casualidade.
cold frio.
cold cuts frios.
coldness frialdade.
cold war guerra fria.
collaborate colaborar.
collar colarinho.
collect (to) colecionar (coleccionar); cobrar (money due).
collection coleção (colecção).
collective coletivo (colectivo).
college escola de estudos universitários (university); colégio (of cardinals, etc.).
Colombian colombiano.
colonial colonial.
colony colônia (colónia).
color côr (cor).
color (to) colorir, dar côr (cor) a.
colored de côr (cor).
colt potro.
column coluna.
comb pente.
combination combinação.
combine combinar.
come vir.
to come back voltar.
to come forward adiantar; apresentar-se.
to come across dar com, encontrar-se com.
to come for vir por.
to come in entrar.
to come down descer, baixar *(z = sh).*
to come up subir.
Come on! Vamos!
comedy comédia.
comet cometa.
comfort confôrto (conforto), comodidade; consôlo (consolo) (consolation).
comfort (to) confortar, consolar.
comfortable cômodo (cómodo), confortável.
comma vírgula.
command ordem (order); mandado, comando (authority to command).
command (to) mandar, comandar.
commence começar, iniciar.
commercial comercial.
commission comissão.
commit cometer.
committee comissão, comitê Ⓑ.
common comum.
common sense senso comum.
communicate comunicar.
communism comunismo.
communist comunista.
community comunidade.
companion companheiro.
company companhia; hóspedes, visitas (guests).
compare comparar.
comparison comparação.
by comparison em comparação.
compete with competir com.
competition concurso; concorrência, competição.
complain queixar-se (x = sh), lamentar-se.
complaint queixa (x = sh).

complete completo.
complete (to) completar, acabar.
complex complexo (x = ks).
complexion cútis, tez (skin); aspecto (appearance).
complicate complicar.
complicated complicado.
complication complicação.
compliment cumprimento.
compliment (to) cumprimentar.
compose compor.
composition composição.
comprise compreender, abranger.
compromise compromisso, acôrdo (acordo).
compromise (to) transigir, fazer concessão (to settle by mutual concessions); resolver, ajustar (a difference between parties); comprometer (to endanger).
comrade camarada.
conceit presunção, vaidade.
conceive (to) conceber.
concentrate (to) concentrar.
concentration concentração.
concern assunto, negócio (business, affair); interêsse (interesse); firma, emprêsa (empresa) comercial (a business organization); ansiedade, inquietação (worry).
concern (to) concernir; interessar, preocupar.
concert concêrto (concerto).
conclusion conclusão.
concrete *adj.* concreto.
concrete *n.* concreto.
condemn condenar.
condense condensar.
condition condição.
conduct conduta, comportamento (behavior); condução, direção (direcção) (direction).
conduct (to) conduzir, guiar (to lead); comportar-se (to conduct oneself).
conductor condutor.
cone cone.
confer conferir (to grant); conferenciar (to hold a conference); consultar (to consult, to compare views).
confidence confiança.
confident *adj.* seguro, confiado.
confidential confidencial, de confiança, secreto.
confirm confirmar, verificar.
confirmation confirmação.
conflict conflito.
confusion confusão.
congeal congelar.
congratulate felicitar, congratular.
congratulation felicitação, parabéns.
Congratulations! Parabéns!
congress congresso.
congressman congressista; deputado; senador.
conjunction conjunção.
connect ligar, juntar.
connection ligação, união, conexão (x = ks).
conquer conquistar, vencer.
conquest conquista.
conscience consciência.
conscientious consciencioso, escrupuloso.
conscious consciente.
consent consentimento, permissão.
consent (to) consentir.
consequence conseqüência (consequência).
consequently por conseguinte, portanto.
conservative conservador.
consider considerar.
considerable considerável.

consideration consideração.
consist consistir, constar.
consistent constante (in ideas, etc.); congruente (congruous); consistente.
consonant consoante.
constable guarda, policial.
constant constante.
constitution constituição.
constitutional constitucional.
construct construir.
consul cônsul.
consume consumir.
consumer consumidor.
consumption consumo (use of goods); consumpção, consunção (consumpção) (med.).
contagion contágio.
contagious contagioso.
contain conter.
container recipiente.
contemplation contemplação.
contemporary contemporâneo.
contend sustentar, afirmar (to assert, to maintain); contender, disputar, competir (to strive, to compete).
content *adj.* contente.
contents conteúdo.
continent continente.
continuation continuação.
continue (to) continuar.
contract contrato.
contract (to) contratar.
contractor contratante.
contradict contradizer.
contradiction contradição.
contradictory contraditório.
contrary contrário.
   on the contrary ao contrário, pelo contrário.
contrast contraste.
contrast (to) contrastar, fazer contraste.
contribute contribuir.
contribution contribuição.
control contrôle (B); domínio, direção (direcção).
control (to) controlar (B); dominar, dirigir.
convenience conveniência.
   at your conveinence quando quiser, à vontade.
convenient conveniente.
   if it's convenient for you se fôr (for) conveniente para você.
convent convento.
convention convenção, assembléia (assembleia).
conversation conversação, conversa.
converse (to) conversar.
convert (to) converter.
conviction convicção.
convince convencer.
cook cozinheiro.
cook (to) cozinhar.
cool fresco.
cooperation cooperação.
cooperative cooperativo.
copy cópia; exemplar (x = z) (of a book).
copy (to) copiar.
cordial cordial.
cork cortiça; rôlha (rolha) (stopper).
corn milho.
corner esquina (street); canto (nook, corner of a room).
corporation corporação, sociedade anônima (anônima).
correct correto (correcto).

correct (to) corrigir.
correction correção (correcção).
correspond corresponder.
correspondence correspondência.
correspondent correspondente.
corresponding correspondente.
corrupt corrupto, corruto (corrupto)
corrupt (to) corromper.
cost custo, preço.
cost (to) custar.
Costa Rican costarriquense, costarriquenho.
cost of living custo de vida.
costume traje, costume.
cottage casa pequena, casa de campo.
cotton algodão.
couch sofá, divã.
cough tosse.
cough (to) tossir.
cough drop pastilha para a tosse.
council conselho, junta, concelho.
counsel conselho.
count conde (title).
count (to) contar.
counter balcão (in a store).
countess condêssa (condessa).
countless incontável, sem conta, sem número.
country país (nation); região rural, campo (opposed to city); pátria (fatherland).
country house casa de campo.
countryman compatriota; camponês.
couple casal; par.
courage coragem, valentia.
course curso; pista (racing); prato (of a meal); rumo (route).
court tribunal (law).
courteous cortês.
courtesy cortesia.
courtyard pátio, quintal.
cousin primo.
cover cobertura, tampa.
cover (to) cobrir; tampar (to place a lid on); percorrer (a distance); incluir, compreender (to include).
cow vaca.
cowboy vaqueiro.
crab caranguejo.
crack quebra, fenda (split).
crack (to) fender, rachar, quebrar, estalar.
cradle berço.
cramp *n.* cãibra, cãimbra (cãibra).
crash estrépito, estrondo (noise); quebra, ruína (business); colisão (collision).
crash (to) estalar; colidir; espatifar-se (a plane, etc.).
crazy louco, demente, doido.
cream creme, nata.
create criar; causar.
creation criação.
credit *n.* crédito.
creditor credor.
cricket grilo (insect).
crime crime, delito.
crisis crise.
critic crítico.
criticism criticismo, crítica.
criticize criticar, censurar.
crook ladrão (thief).
crooked torcido (bent).
crop colheita (harvest).
cross cruz (symbol).
cross (to) cruzar, atravessar (a street); riscar, cancelar (to cross out).

   to make the sign of the cross fazer o sinal da cruz, persignar-se.
   to cross one's mind ocorrer-lhe, ver-lhe a idéia (ideia).
   to cross over atravessar.
cross-examination interrogatório.
cross-eyed vesgo, estrábico.
crossing cruzamento, travessia; viagem; encruzilhada (intersection).
crouch (to) agachar-se.
crow corvo.
crowd multidão.
crowded apinhado, cheio.
crown coroa.
crown (to) coroar.
cruel cruel.
cruelty crueldade.
cruise cruzeiro, viagem.
crumb migalha.
cry grito; chôro (choro) (weeping).
cry (to) gritar (shout); chorar (weep).
crystal cristal.
Cuban cubano.
cube cubo.
cucumber pepino.
cuff punho.
culture cultura.
cup xícara (x = sh), chávena.
cure cura.
cure (to) curar.
curiosity curiosidade.
curious curioso.
curl caracol de cabelo.
curl (to) enrolar, encaracolar.
current *adj.* corrente.
current *n.* corrente.
curtain cortina.
curve curva.
cushion almofada.
custom costume.
customer freguês.
customhouse alfândega.
customs (duties) direitos aduaneiros.
customs officer oficial alfandegário.
cut corte.
cut (to) cortar.

D

dagger punhal, adaga.
daily *adj.* diário, cotidiano.
   daily newspaper jornal diário, diário.
dainty delicado.
dairy leitaria.
dam açude, reprêsa (represa) (dique).
damage dano, prejuízo.
damp úmido.
dampness umidade.
dance baile.
dance (to) dançar.
dancer dançarino, bailarino.
dandruff caspa.
danger perigo.
dangerous perigoso.
Danish dinamarquês.
dare atrever-se, ousar (venture); desafiar (challenge).
dark escuro.
darkness escuridão.
darling querido, amado; caro.
darn cerzir.
data dados, fatos (factos).

date encontro, compromisso (rendezvous); data (time); datil, tâmara (fruit).

date (to) datar, pôr data em.

daughter filha.

daughter-in-law nora.

dawn alvorada, madrugada.
  at dawn ao amanhecer, de madrugada.

day dia
  day after tomorrow depois de amanhã.
  day before véspera.
  day before yesterday anteontem.
  every day todos os dias.

daze ofuscação, confusão, entorpecimento.

dead morto.

deadly mortal, fatal.

deaf surdo.

deal negócio, negociação, acôrdo (accord).

dealer negociante, mercador.

dear querido, amado, caro, prezado.

death morte.

debatable contestável, discutível.

debate debate, discussão.

debate (to) discutir, disputar.

debt dívida.

debtor devedor.

decade década.

decadence decadência.

decay decadência (decadence); declínio (decrease); podridão (rot).

decay (to) decair, declinar (decline); deteriorar (deteriorate); apodrecer (fruit); cariar (teeth).

deceit engano.

deceive enganar.

December dezembro (Dezembro).

decency decência.

decent decente, decoroso.

decide decidir; resolver, solucionar (a dispute).

decidedly decididamente.

decision decisão.

decisive decisivo.

deck convés (of ship), baralho (of cards).

declaration declaração.

declare declarar, afirmar.

decrease diminuição, redução.

decrease (to) diminuir, minguar.

decree n. decreto.

dedicate dedicar.

deduct deduzir, diminuir.

deduction dedução, redução, desconto.

deep fundo, profundo.

deeply profundamente.

defeat derrota.

defeat (to) derrotar, vencer.

defect defeito.

defective defectivo, defeituoso.

defend defender, proteger.

defender defensor.

defense defesa.

defer diferir (to put off).

defiance deasfio.

definite definido, definito, preciso.

definition definição.

defy desafiar.

degenerate degenerar.

degree grau.

delay tardança, demora, atraso.

delay (to) tardar, demorar, atrasar.

delegate delegado.

delegate (to) delegar.

delegation delegação.

deliberate adj. circunspeto (circunspecto), acautelado (careful); deliberado, considerado (carefully thought out).

deliberate (to) deliberar.

delicacy delicadeza (finesse); guloseima, gulodice (food).

delicate delicado.

delicious delicioso, saboroso.

delight delícia, encanto, alegria, prazer.

delight (to) encantar, deleitar.

delinquency delinqüência (delinquência).

deliver entregar (hand over); livrar de (deliver from); pronunciar, proferir (a speech).

delivery entrega (of goods); distribuição (mail).

de luxe de luxo (x = sh).

demand demanda.

demand (to) demandar, exigir.

democracy democracia.

democrat democrata.

democratic democrático.

demonstrate demonstrar.

demonstration demonstração, exibição (x = z).

denial negativa, denegação.

denounce denunciar.

dense denso.

density densidade.

dentist dentista.

deny negar; recusar (to refuse to grant).

depart partir.

department departamento.

depend (to) depender.

dependable de confiança, seguro.

dependence dependência.

dependent adj. dependente, pendente, sujeito.

dependent n. dependente.

deplore deplorar, lamentar.

deposit depósito.

deposit (to) depositar.

depth profundidade.

descend (to) descer, baixar (x = sh).

descendant descendente.

descent descida.

describe descrever.

description descrição.

desegregate dessegregar.

desegregation dessegregação.

desert deserto.

desert (to) desertar, abandonar.

deserve merecer.

desirable desejável.

desire desejo.

desire (to) desejar.

desirous desejoso, ansioso.

desk escrivaninha, secretária.

desolation desolação.

despair desespêro (desespero).

despair (to) desesperar.

desperate desesperado.

despite apesar de, a despeito de.

dessert sobremesa.

destiny destino, sorte, fado.

destroy destruir.

destruction destruição.

detach (to) separar, despegar (to separate); destacar (soldiers).

detail detalhe, pormenor.

detain deter.

determination determinação.

determine determinar.

detour desvio.

develop desenvolver; revelar (photography).

development desenvolvimento; revelação (photography).

devil diabo, demônio (demónio).

devilish diabólico, satânico.

devote dedicar.

devotion devoção.

devour devorar, engolir.

dew orvalho, rocio.

dial (clock) face.

dialogue diálogo.

diameter diâmetro.

diamond diamante; ouros (cards).

dictate ditar.

dictator ditador.

dictionary dicionário.

die morrer, falecer.

diet regime, dieta.

differ diferençar (to stand apart); dissentir, não estar de acôrdo (acordo).

difference diferença.

different diferente, distinto.

difficult difícil.

difficulty dificuldade.

diffuse difundir.

dig cavar, escavar.

digest digerir.

digestion digestão.

dignity dignidade.

dim escuro, pouco claro.

dimple covinha.

dine jantar.

dinner jantar.

diplomacy diplomacia.

diplomat diplomata.

diplomatic diplomático.

direct direito, em linha reta (recta).

direct current corrente contínua.

direction direção (direcção).

directly diretamente (directamente).

director diretor (director).

directory lista, catálogo.
  telephone directory lista telefônica (telefónica).

dirt sujeira, imundície.

dirty sujo.

disadvantage desvantagem.

disagree discordar, não concordar.

disagreeable desagradável.

disappear desaparecer.

disappearance desaparição.

disappoint desapontar.

disappointment desapontamento, decepção.

disapprove desaprovar.

disarm desarmar.

disaster desastre.

disastrous desastroso.

discipline disciplina.

discontent descontente.

discord discórdia, desacôrdo (desacordo).

discourage desanimar, dissuadir.

discouragement desânimo.

discover descobrir.

discoverer descoobridor.

discovery descoberta, descobrimento.

discreet discreto.

discretion discrição, prudência.

discuss discutir, tratar de.

discussion discussão.

disease doença.

disgrace desonra, vergonha, desgraça.

disgust repugnância, asco.

disgust (to) repugnar, desagradar, enojar.

disgusting repugnante, disgostoso.

dish prato.

dishonest desonesto.

disk disco.

dismal lúgubre, triste, funesto.

dismiss despedir.

disobey desobedecer.

disorder desordem.

dispatch despacho, mensagem.

dispatch (to) despachar, enviar.

display desfile (of troops); exibição (x = z) (show); ostentação.

display (to) exibir (x = z), mostrar (to show); ostentar.

displease desagradar.

dispute disputa.

dispute (to) disputar, discutir.

dissolve dissolver.

distance distância.

distinct distinto, claro.

distinction distinção.

distinguish distinguir.

distinguished distinguido.

distort falsear, corromper, torcer.

distract distrair.

distraction distração (distracção).

distribute distribuir, repartir.

distribution distribuição.

district distrito, bairro.

disturb perturbar, incomodar.

disturbance perturbação, desordem.

dive mergulho (into water); picada (a plane).

dive (to) mergulhar; dar picada, descer a pique (aviation).

divide dividir.

dividend dividendo.

divine divino.

diving board trampolim.

division divisão.

divorce divórcio, separação.

divorce (to) divorciar, separar-se de.

dizzy vertiginoso, aturdido.

do fazer
How do you do? Como vai? Como está?
to do one's best fazer o possível.
to do without passar sem.
to have to do with ter que ver com.
That will do. Chega. Basta. Isto serve.
Do you believe it? Você crê? Você acredita? Você acha?

dock (pier) doca, cais.

doctor doutor, médico.

doctrine doutrina.

document documento.

dog cão, cachorro.

dogma dogma.

doll boneca.

dollar dólar.

dome cúpula.

domestic adj. doméstico (pertaining to the household); caseiro (homemade); do país, nacional (trade, etc.).

Dominican dominicano.

don dom.

door porta.

double duplo.

doubt dúvida.

doubt (to) duvidar.

doubtful duvidoso.

doubtless sem dúvida, certo.

dough massa de farinha, pasta.

down abaixo (x = sh), para baixo (x = sh).
to go down baixar (x = sh), descer.
to come down baixar (x = sh), descer.

downstairs em baixo (x = sh), para baixo (x = sh); no andar-térreo.

downtown na cidade, para a cidade.

dozen dúzia.

draft corrente de ar (air); saque, letra de câmbio (bank); sorteio (military); desenho, esbôço (esboço), rascunho (sketch, outline).

draft (to) rascunhar, esboçar.

drag arrastar.

drama drama.

dramatist dramaturgo.

draw (to) debuxar (x = sh), desenhar (to sketch); tirar (money, liquids, etc.); correr (curtains); sacar (bank draft); ganhar, receber (a salary); formular, escrever (to draw up).

drawer gaveta.

drawing desenho.

dread (to) temer.

dreaded temido.

dreadful terrível, horrível.

dream sonho.

dreamer sonhador.

dress vestido, traje, roupa.

dress (to) vestir-se (to get dressed); limpar, medicar (a wound).

dresser cômoda (cómoda) (furniture).

dressmaker modista, costureira.

drink bebida.

drink (to) beber, tomar.

drip (to) pingar, gotejar.

drive volta, passeio (a ride in a car, etc.); passeio, estrada (a road); campanha (to raise money, etc.).

drive (to) conduzir, dirigir (a car, etc.); cravar (a nail); expulsar, expelir (to drive away).

driver motorista, chofer (B).

driver's license carteira de chofer (B), carteira de motorista.

drop gôta (gota) (liquid); queda, caída (fall).
cough drops pastilhas para tosse.

drop (to) soltar, deixar (x = sh) cair (to release, to let fall); pingar, gotejar (fall in drops); abandonar, renunciar, desistir de, deixar (to let go).
to drop in visitar.
to drop a subject mudar de assunto.

drown afogar, afogar-se.

drug droga.

druggist farmacêutico, droguista.

drugstore farmácia, drogaria.

drum tambor.

drunk bêbedo, ébrio.

drunkard bêbedo, ébrio.

drunkenness embriaguez, ebriedade.

dry sêco (seco).

dry (to) secar.

dry cleaning lavagem a sêco (seco).

dryness sêca (seca), secura, aridez.

duchess duquesa.

duck pato.

due devido; pagável (payable); suficiente, bastante (enough).

duke duque.

dull opaco; apagada (color); pesado, aborrecido, grosseiro (slow, boring); estúpido (stupid).

dumb mudo; estúpido (stupid).

durable durável.

during durante.

dusk crepúsculo, escuridão.

dust pó, poeira.

dust (to) tirar o pó, limpar do pó.

dusty poeirento, empoeirado, coberto de pó.

Dutch holandês.

duty dever.

dwelling morada, habitação, residência.

dye tintura, tinta.

dye (to) tingir, corar.

E

each cada.
each one cada um.
each other mùtuamente, um ao outro, uns aos outros.

eager ansioso.

eagle águia.

ear ouvido (the organ of hearing, the internal ear); orelha (the external ear); espiga (of corn).

early cedo.

earn ganhar.

earnest sério (serious); ansioso (eager).
in earnest a sério, de boa fé.

earth terra.

earthquake tremor de terra, terremoto.

ease tranqüilidade (tranquilidade), alívio; facilidade (with ease); à vontade (at ease).

ease (to) aliviar, mitigar.

easily fàcilmente.

east este, leste oriente.

Easter Páscoa.

eastern oriental.

easy fácil.

eat comer.

economic econômico (económico).

economics economia.

economy economia.

Ecuadorian equatoriano.

edge beira, margem (of a stream, etc.); canto (of a table); gume, fio (of a blade).

edition edição.

editor redator (redactor), diretor (director).

educate educar, ensinar.

education educação.

eel enguia.

effect efeito.

effect (to) efetuar (efectuar).

efficiency eficiência, eficácia.

effort esfôrço (esforço).

egg ôvo.

eggplant berinjela.

eggshell casca de ôvo.

egoism egoísmo.

eight oito.

eighteen dezoito.

eighteenth décimo-oitavo.

eighth oitavo.

eighty oitenta.

either ou; qualquer.
one or the other um ou o outro.
either of the two qualquer dos dois.

elastic elástico.

elbow cotovêlo (cotovelo).

elder adj. mais velho.

elderly idoso, de idade avançada.

eldest o mais velho.

elect (to) eleger.

elected eleito.

election eleição.

elector eleitor.

electric elétrico (eléctrico).

electricity eletricidade (electricidade).

electronics eletrónica (electrónica).

elegance elegância.

elegant elegante.

element elemento.

elementary elementar.

elephant elefante.

elevation elevação, altura.

elevator elevador, ascensor.

eleven onze.

eleventh undécimo, décimo-primeiro.
eligible elegível.
eliminate eliminar.
eloquence eloqüência (eloquência).
eloquent eloqüente (eloquente).
else outro, mais, além disso.
  nothing else nada mais.
  something else mais alguma coisa.
  or else senão, ou então.
  nobody else ninguém mais.
elsewhere em qualquer outra parte, noutra
  parte.
elude eludir, evitar.
embark embarcar.
embarrass embaraçar, atrapalhar.
embarrassing embaraçante, embaraçoso.
embassy embaixada (x = sh).
embody encarnar, incorporar.
embrace abraço.
embrace (to) abraçar.
embroidery bordado.
emerge emergir, surgir.
emergency emergência, urgência.
emigrant emigrante.
emigrate emigrar.
emigration emigração.
eminent eminente.
eminently eminentemente.
emotion emoção.
emphasis ênfase.
emphasize acentuar, dar ênfase.
emphatic enfático.
empire império.
employ empregar.
employee empregado.
employer empregador, patrão.
employment emprêgo (emprego).
empty vazio.
empty (to) esvaziar, evacuar.
enclose (to) cercar (ground, etc.); incluir.
enclosed anexo (x = ks), incluso.
encourage animar, estimular.
encouragement encorajamento, estímulo.
end fim; extremidade; conclusão.
end (to) acabar, terminar.
endeavor esfôrço (esforço).
endeavor (to) esforçar-se.
endorse endossar.
endow dotar.
endure suportar, resistir, agüentar (aguentar).
enemy inimigo.
energetic enérgico.
energy energia.
enforce fazer cumprir, executar (x = z) (a law);
  forçar, compelir (to compel).
engage empregar, contratar (services); alugar
  (a room).
engagement compromisso, encontro (date);
  noivado (for marriage); contrato (for employment).
engine motor, máquina.
engineer engenheiro.
English inglês.
engrave gravar.
enjoy gozar, gostar de.
  to enjoy oneself divertir-se.
enjoyment gôzo (gozo).
enlarge aumentar, ampliar.
enlargement ampliação, aumento.
enlist alistar, alistar-se.
enlistment alistamento.
enough bastante, suficiente.
enrich enriquecer.

enroll, enrol matricular, registrar, registar.
entangle enredar, complicar.
enter entrar (a house, etc.); anotar, registrar
  (in a register, etc.); ingressar, matricular-se
  (a school).
entertain divertir, entreter; considerar (ideas).
entertainment entretenimento, diversão.
enthusiasm entusiasmo.
enthusiastic entusiástico.
entire inteiro, todo.
entirely completamente.
entitle intitular; autorizar.
entrance entrada.
entrust confiar.
entry entrada (entrance); registro, entrada
  (books, records); verbete (dictionary).
enumerate enumerar.
envelope n. envelope.
enviable invejável.
envious invejoso.
envy inveja.
episode episódio.
epoch época, era.
equal igual.
equal (to) igualar.
equality igualdade.
equator equador.
equilibrium equilíbrio.
equip equipar, guarnecer.
equipment equipamento.
equity eqüidade (equidade), igualdade.
era era, época.
erase apagar, riscar, extinguir.
eraser apagador, borracha.
err (to) errar, enganar-se.
errand recado, mandado, mensagem.
error êrro (erro).
escape fuga, escape.
escape (to) escapar, fugir.
escort escolta (a body of soldiers, etc.);
  acompanhante (an individual).
escort (to) escoltar, acompanhar.
especially especialmente, particularmente.
essay ensaio, composição.
essence essência.
essential essencial, indispensável.
establish estabelecer.
establishment estabelecimento.
estate bens, propriedade (properties, possessions); fazenda (a country estate).
esteem estima, aprêço (apreço).
esteem (to) estimar.
estimable estimável.
estimate cálculo; avaliação.
estimate (to) calcular, avaliar.
eternal eterno.
eternity eternidade.
ether éter.
European europeu.
evacuate evacuar.
eve véspera.
even adj. par (not odd); plano, liso (level).
  to be even with estar quite com.
even adj. ainda, até, mesmo.
  even if mesmo que.
  even so mesmo assim.
  even that até isso.
  not even that nem sequer isso.
evening tarde, noite.
  Good evening! Boa tarde! Boa noite!
  yesterday evening ontem à noite.
event acontecimento.
  in the event that no caso de.

ever sempre.
  as ever como sempre.
  ever so much muito, muitíssimo.
  ever since desde então.
  not ... ever nunca.
  nor ... ever nem nunca.
every cada.
  every bit inteiramente.
  every day todos os dias.
  every other day um dia sim, um dia não.
  every one cada um, todos êles (eles).
  every once in a while de vez em quando.
everybody todos, todo o mundo.
everyone todos, todo o mundo.
everything tudo.
everywhere em tôda (toda) parte.
evidence evidência, prova, testemunho.
evident evidente, claro.
evil adj. mau.
evil n. mal.
evoke evocar.
exact exato (exacto) (x = z), preciso.
exaggerate exagerar (x = z).
exaggeration exageração, exagêro (exagero).
  (x = z).
exalt exaltar (x = z).
examination exame (x = z).
examine examinar (x = z).
example exemplo (x = z).
exasperate exasperar (x = z), irritar.
excavate escavar, cavar.
exceed exceder, superar.
excel exceder, superar.
excellence excelência.
excellent excelente.
except exceto (excepto), menos, a menos que,
  a não ser que.
except (to) excetuar (exceptuar), excluir.
exception exceção (excepção).
exceptional excepcional.
exceptionally excepcionalmente.
excess excesso.
excessive excessivo.
exchange câmbio, troca.
  in exchange for em troca de.
exchange (to) cambiar, trocar.
excite excitar.
excitement excitação, agitação.
exclaim exclamar.
exclamation exclamação.
exclude excluir, eliminar.
exclusive exclusivo.
excursion excursão.
excuse escusa.
excuse (to) escusar, dispensar, desculpar.
execute executar (x = z).
executive executivo (x = z).
exempt isentar, eximir (x = z).
exercise exercício (x = z).
exercise (to) exercer (x = z); fazer exercícios
  (x = z).
exhaust esgotar.
exhausted esgotado, exausto (x = z).
exhausting exaustivo (x = z).
exhibition exibição (x = z).
exile exílio (x = z), destêrro (desterro),
  degrêdo (degredo).
exile (to) exilar (x = z), desterrar.
exist existir (x = z).
existence existência (x = z).
existentialism existencialismo (x = z).
exit saída.
expand expandir, espalhar, desenvolver.

expansion expansão.
expansive expansivo.
expect esperar, aguardar
expectation expetação Ⓑ, expectação, esperança.
expel expelir, expulsar.
expense despesa.
   at one's expense à custa de.
expensive caro.
experience experiência.
experience (to) experimentar.
experiment experimento.
experiment (to) experimentar.
experimental experimental.
expert perito, experto.
expire expirar.
explain explicar.
explanation explicação.
explanatory explicativo.
explode explodir, estourar.
exploit façanha, proeza.
exploit (to) explorar, utilizar.
exploration exploração.
explore explorar.
explorer explorador.
explosion explosão, estouro (estoiro).
export exportação.
export (to) exportar.
expose expor.
express adj. expresso.
express (to) expressar, exprimir.
expression expressão.
expulsion expulsão.
extend estender.
extension extensão.
extensive extensivo.
extent extensão.
   to a certain extent até certo ponto.
exterior exterior.
exterminate exterminar.
external externo.
extinguish extinguir.
extra extra.
extract extrato (extracto).
extract (to) extrair.
extraordinary extraordinário.
extravagance extravagância.
extravagant extravagante.
extreme extremo.
extremely extremamente, sumamente.
extremity extremidade.
eye ôlho.
eyebrow sobrancelha.
eyeglasses óculos.
eyelash pestana.
eyelid pálpebra.

F

fable fábula.
fabulous fabuloso.
face face, rosto, cara.
fact fato (facto).
   in fact de fato.
factory fábrica.
faculty faculdade.
fade murchar, enfraquecer.
fail (to) fracassar (in an undertaking); ser reprovado (in an examination); faltar (to fail to do something);
   Don't fail to do it. Não deixe de fazê-lo.
failure fracasso; falha, falta (fault, defect); quebra (bankruptcy); avaria (motor).

faint (to) desmaiar, desfalecer.
fair adj. louro (loiro) (hair); branco (complexion); claro (clear); justo (just); regular (moderate); bom (weather).
fair n. feira.
fairness justiça, eqüidade (equidade).
fairy tale conto de fadas.
faith fé.
faithful fiel, leal.
fall caída, queda; outono (Outono) (autumn).
fall (to) cair.
false falso.
fame fama.
familiar familiar.
familiarity familiaridade, confiança.
family família.
famine fome.
famous famoso, célebre.
fan leque; ventilador (electric fan); fã, aficionado (of sports, etc.).
fancy fantasia, capricho.
fantastic fantástico.
far longe.
   How far? A que distância?
   far away muito longe.
   so far até agora.
   As far as I'm concerned. Quanto a mim.
fare passagem.
farewell despedida.
farmer fazendeiro, agricultor (lavrador).
farming lavoura, agricultura.
farther mais longe, mais distante.
fashion moda, uso.
fashionable à moda, da moda; elegante, de bom gôsto (gosto).
fast ràpidamente, depressa.
fasten prender, fixar (x = ks), segurar.
fat adj. gordo.
fat n. gordura, graxa (x = sh).
fate fado, destino, sorte, fortuna.
father pai.
fatherhood paternidade.
father-in-law sogro.
fatherland pátria.
fatten engordar.
faucet torneira.
fault falta.
favor favor, serviço.
favor (to) favorecer.
favorable favorável.
favorite favorito.
fear mêdo (medo), temor, receio.
fear (to) temer, recear.
fearless intrépido.
feast festa.
feather pena, pluma.
feature traço, característica.
February fevereiro (Fevereiro).
federal federal.
fee paga, remuneração, honorários.
feeble débil, fraco; delicado.
feed alimentar, dar de comer a.
feeding alimentação.
feel (to) sentir; tocar (touch).
feeling tato (tacto) (tact); sentimento (sentiment); sensibilidade (sensitiveness).
fellow sujeito, tipo; rapaz; companheiro.
   fellow student condiscípulo.
   fellow traveler companheiro de viagem.
   fellow worker companheiro de trabalho, colega.
female fêmea.
feminine feminino.

fence cêrca (cerca), grade, cercado.
ferment fermentar.
fermentation fermentação.
ferry barco de passagem, barca.
fertile fértil, fecundo.
fertilize fertilizar, fecundar.
fertilizer fertilizante, adubo.
fervent fervente.
fervor fervor.
festival festa, festival.
fever febre.
feverish febril, febricitante.
few poucos.
   a few alguns, algumas.
   quite a few muitos.
fewer menos.
fiber fibra.
fiction ficção.
field campo; campanha, campo de batalha (military); especialidade, ramo Ⓑ (specialty).
fierce feroz.
fiery veemente, impetuoso.
fifteen quinze.
fifteenth décimo quinto.
fifth quinto.
fifty cinqüenta (cinquenta).
fig figo, figueira.
fight luta, batalha, peleja, briga.
fight (to) lutar, batalhar, pelejar, brigar.
figure figura.
file lima (for nails, etc.,); arquivo, fichário (for papers, etc.).
file (to) limar (with an instrument); arquivar (papers, etc.).
file cabinet arquivo, fichário.
file card ficha.
Filipino filipino.
fill encher.
filling station pôsto (posto) de gasolina.
film filme, fita, película.
filthy sujo, imundo.
final final.
finally finalmente.
finance finança, finanças.
financial financial, financeiro.
find (to) achar, encontrar.
find adj. fino, bom, magnífico, excelente.
   Fine! Ótimo! Muito bem!
fine n. multa, penalidade, pena.
finger dedo.
fingernail unha.
fingernail polish esmalte de unhas.
finish (to) terminar, acabar.
fire fogo; incêndio.
fire (to) incendiar, queimar (burn); disparar (a gun); demitir, despedir (an employee).
firm adj. seguro, firme.
firm n. firma, emprêsa (empresa) (business).
firmness firmeza.
first primeiro.
   first of all antes de mais nada.
   the first time a primeira vez.
   in the first place em primeiro lugar.
   first floor primeiro andar.
firstly primeiramente, em primeiro lugar.
fish peixe (x = sh).
fish (to) pescar.
fisherman pescador.
fishing pesca.
fist punho.
fit adj. conveniente, bom, justo, digno.
   to see fit achar conveniente.
fit (to) ajustar, adaptar, assentar (to fit a

dress, etc.); cair bem (to fit well, to look good).
   to fit into encaixar (x = sh).
   It fits you well. Assenta muito bem.
   It fits badly. Assenta mal. Não lhe cai bem.
fitness aptidão.
fitting (be) ser apropriado.
five cinco.
five hundred quinhentos.
fix (to) fixar (x = ks), consertar.
flag bandeira.
flagrant flagrante.
flame chama.
flannel flanela.
flash n. jato (jacto) de luz; relâmpago, clarão (lightning).
flashlight lanterna elétrica (eléctrica).
flat plano, liso; chato, insípido (taste, etc.).
flatten nivelar, alisar, achatar.
flatter lisonjear, adular.
flattery lisonja, adulação.
flavor sabor, gôsto (gosto).
flavor (to) sazonar, condimentar.
flax linho.
flea pulga.
fleet frota, armada.
flesh carne; polpa (fruit).
flexibility flexibilidade (x = ks).
flexible flexível (x = ks).
flight vôo (in the air); fuga (escape).
flint pederneira; pedra (of lighter).
float (to) flutuar.
flood enchente, inundação.
flood (to) inundar.
floor chão, soalho (of room); andar (of building, second floor, etc.).
flour farinha.
flow (to) fluir, correr.
flower flor.
flowery florido.
fluid fluido.
fly môsca (mosca).
fly (to) voar.
foam espuma.
foam (to) espumar.
focus foco.
fog nevoeiro, névoa, cerração.
fold prega, dobra.
fold (to) preguear, dobrar.
foliage folhagem.
folks parentes, família; gente.
follow (to) seguir.
following seguinte.
food alimento, comida.
fool tolo.
foolish tolo, ridículo.
foolishness tolice.
foot pé.
   on foot a pé.
football futebol.
for para, por.
   This is for her. Isto é para ela.
   for example por exemplo (x = z).
   for the first time pela primeira vez.
   for the present por agora.
forbid proibir.
forbidden proibido.
force fôrça (força).
force (to) forçar, obrigar.
forced forçado, obrigado.
ford vau.
ford (to) vadear.
forecast prognóstico, previsão.

forecast (to) prognosticar, prever.
forehead fronte, testa.
foreign estrangeiro, alheio, estranho.
foreigner estrangeiro, forasteiro.
foresee prever.
forest floresta, selva.
forever para sempre.
forget esquecer, esquecer-se.
forgetfulness olvido, esquecimento.
forgive perdoar.
forgiveness perdão.
fork garfo.
form forma.
form (to) formar.
formal formal, cerimonioso, solene.
formality formalidade, cerimônia (cerimónia).
formation formação.
former anterior
former (the) aquêle (aquele), aquela, aquêles (aqueles).
formerly antigamente, em tempos passados.
formula fórmula.
forsake deixar (x = sh), abandonar.
fortieth quadragésimo.
fortunate afortunado.
fortunately afortunadamente.
fortune fortuna, sorte.
fortuneteller adivinho, cartomante, quiromante.
fortunetelling adivinhação, cartomancia, quiromancia.
forty quarenta.
forward adv. adiante, avante.
forward (to) expedir, enviar, transmitir.
found encontrado, achado.
found (to) fundar.
foundation fundação.
founder fundador.
fountain fonte.
fountain pen caneta-tinteiro.
four quatro.
fourteen catorze, quatorze Ⓑ.
fourteenth décimo quarto.
fourth quarto.
fowl ave, ave doméstica.
fragment fragmento.
fragrance fragrância, aroma.
fragrant fragrante, aromático.
frail débil, delicado, frágil.
frame quadro, moldura (of a picture, etc.); armação, estrutura (structure).
   frame of mind disposição de espírito.
frame (to) enquadrar, emoldurar (a picture, etc.)
frank franco, sincero.
frankly francamente.
frankness franqueza.
free adj. livre; gratuito, grátis.
   free of charge grátis.
free (to) livrar, libertar.
freedom liberdade.
freeze gelar, congelar.
freight carga, frete.
French francês.
frequent freqüente (frequente).
frequent (to) freqüentar (frequentar).
frequently freqüentemente (frequentemente).
fresh fresco.
Friday sexta-feira, sexta.
friend amigo.
friendly amigável, amistoso, cordial.
friendship amizade.
frighten aterrar, assustar.

frightening alarmante, assustador.
frivolity frivolidade.
frivolous frívolo.
frog rã.
from de, desde.
   from a distance de longe.
   from memory de memória.
front adj. anterior, dianteiro, da frente.
front frente.
   in front of à frente de.
frown cenho, olhar carrancudo.
frown (to) franzir as sobrancelhas.
fruit fruta.
fry fritar.
frying pan frigideira.
fuel combustível.
fugitive fugitivo.
fulfill cumprir.
full cheio; lotado.
fully completamente.
fun divertimento, diversão.
   to have fun divertir-se.
   to make fun of fazer troça de, ridicularizar.
function função.
function (to) funcionar.
fundamental fundamental.
funds fundos.
funeral funeral, entêrro (enterro).
funny engraçado, divertido, cômico (cómico).
fur pele.
furious furioso.
furnace fornalha, forno.
furnish mobiliar (mobilar) (a room, house, etc.); suprir, fornecer (supply, provide).
furniture mobília, móveis.
furrow sulco.
further adv. mais longe, mais distante; além, ademais.
   further on mais adiante.
fury fúria, furor.
future futuro.
   in the future no futuro.

G

gaiety alegria.
gain ganho.
gain (to) ganhar.
Galician galego.
gallant galante.
gamble (to) jogar.
game jôgo (jogo); partida; caça (hunting); a game of chess uma partida de xadrez. (x = sh).
garage garagem, garage Ⓑ.
garbage lixo (x = sh).
garden jardim.
gardener jardineiro.
gargle (to) gargarejar, fazer gargarejo.
garlic alho.
garment peça de roupa, vestido, roupa.
garter liga.
gas gás; gasolina (gasoline).
   gas station pôsto (posto) de gasolina.
gasoline gasolina.
gasoline pump bomba de gasolina.
gas tank tanque de gasolina.
gate portão, porta.
gather (to) reunir, juntar, recolher.
gay alegre.
gear engrenagem.
gem pedra preciosa, jóia.
gender gênero (género).
general adj. geral.
   in general em geral.

general *n.* general.
generality generalidade.
generalize generalizar.
generally geralmente.
generation geração.
generosity generosidade.
generous generoso.
genius gênio (génio).
gentle suave; amável, bondoso (of a person).
gentleman cavalheiro.
    gentlemen sennores; prezados senhores (in a letter).
gentleness bondade, delicadeza.
gently suavemente, bondosamente.
genuine genuíno, autêntico.
geographic geográfico.
geography geografia.
geometric geométrico.
geometry geometria.
gem germe, micróbio.
German alemão.
gesture *n.* gesto, ademã.
get (to) conseguir, obter, adquirir, receber.
    to get ahead adiantar.
    to get away partir, ir-se embora, fugir.
    to get back voltar, regressar.
    to get home chegar a casa.
    to get in entrar.
    to get married casar-se.
    to get off descer, saltar, desmontar.
    to get on subir, montar.
    to get out sair.
    to get up levantar-se; subir.
giant gigante.
gift presente.
gifted talentoso, dotado.
gin gim Ⓑ, genebra.
ginger gengibre.
girdle cinta.
girl menina, moça.
girl friend noiva, amiguinha.
girl scout escoteira.
give (to) dar.
    to give in ceder.
    to give up desistir, dar-se por vencido.
    to give a gift presentear.
giver doador.
glad contente, alegre.
glance olhadela.
glance (to) dar uma olhada, dar uma olhadela.
glass vidro; copo (for drinking).
    looking glass espelho.
    drinking glass copo.
glimpse *n.* olhadela.
glitter (to) brilhar, resplandecer.
globe globo.
gloomy triste, sombrio, melancólico.
glorious glorioso.
glory glória.
glove luva.
glue *n.* cola, grude.
go (to) ir.
    to go away ir-se embora, partir.
    to go back regressar, voltar.
    to go down descer, baixar.
    to go forward adiantar, ir adiante.
    to go out sair; apagar-se (a light, fire, etc.).
    to go up subir.
    to go with acompanhar.
    to go without passar sem.
goal meta, objetivo (objectivo), fim; gol (sports).
    to reach one's goal conseguir o objetivo (objectivo).
God Deus.

godchild afilhado.
godfather padrinho.
godmother madrinha.
godparents padrinhos.
gold ouro.
golf gôlfe (golfe).
golf club taco de gôlfe (golfe).
good bom.
    good morning bom dia.
    good afternoon boa tarde.
    good night boa noite.
good-by adeus.
goodness bondade.
    Goodness! Goodness gracious! Meu Deus!
    Goodness knows! Quem sabe!
goods mercadorias, fazendas, tecidos.
goodwill boa vontade.
goose ganso.
gossip tagarelice, tagarela, mexerico (x = sh).
gossip (to) tagarelar.
govern governar.
government govêrno (governo).
governor governador.
gown vestido, beca.
grab (to) agarrar, arrebatar.
grace *n.* graça.
graceful gracioso.
gracious bondoso, afável, cortês.
grade grau.
gradual gradual.
gradually gradualmente.
graduate pessoa graduada.
graduate (to) graduar-se, formar-se.
grain grão.
grammar gramática.
grammar school escola primária.
grammatical gramatical.
grand grande, grandioso, magnífico.
grandchild neto.
granddaughter neta.
grandfather avô.
grandmother avó.
grandparents avós.
grandson neto.
grant concessão.
grant (to) conceder, outorgar.
    to take for granted tomar por certo, achar natural.
    granting (granted) that admitido que.
grape uva.
grapefruit toranja.
grasp (to) agarrar, apertar, pegar; compreender, entender.
grass erva, grama.
grasshopper gafanhoto.
grateful agradecido.
gratefully agradecidamente, gratamente.
gratis gratuito, grátis.
gratitude gratidão, agradecimento.
grave *adj.* grave, sério.
grave *n.* túmulo, sepultura.
gravity gravidade.
gravy môlho (molho).
gray cinza Ⓑ, cinzento.
grease graxa (x = sh).
great grande.
    a great man um grande homem.
    a great many muitos.
    a great deal muito.
    Great! Estupendo! Magnífico!
greatness grandeza.
greedy ganancioso, cobiçoso.
green verde.

greet cumprimentar.
greeting cumprimento.
grief pesar, dor.
grieve (to) afligir-se, sofrer.
grill (to) grelhar, assar.
grin sorriso.
grin (to) sorrir.
grind moer.
groan gemido.
groan (to) gemer.
grocer merceeiro.
groceries comestíveis, secos e molhados.
grocery store mercearia, armazém.
groove ranhura.
grope tatear (tactear).
ground *n.* terra, terreno; chão.
group grupo.
group (to) agrupar.
grow (to) crescer.
    to grow old envelhecer.
    to grow dark escurecer.
    to grow better melhorar.
    to grow worse piorar.
growth crescimento.
grudge rancor, ressentimento.
gruff áspero, grosseiro.
grumble (to) grunhir, resmungar, murmurar.
guarantee garantia.
guarantee (to) garantir.
guard guarda.
guard (to) guardar, vigiar.
    to guard against guardar-se de.
Guatemalan guatemalteco.
guess conjetura (conjectura), suposição.
guess (to) adivinhar, conjeturar (conjecturar).
    to guess right acertar.
guest hóspede, convidado, visita.
guide guia.
guide (to) guiar, conduzir.
guidebook guia de viagem.
guilt culpa.
guilty culpado.
guitar violão.
gulf gôlfo (golfo).
gum gengiva (teeth).
    chewing gum goma de mascar.
gun arma de fogo, revólver, pistola, fuzil (rifle).
gymnasium ginásio.
gypsy cigano.

H

haberdashery camisaria, loja de artigos para homens.
habit costume, hábito.
    to be in the habit of costumar, ter o hábito de.
habitual habitual, costumeiro.
habitually habitualmente, comumente.
hail granizo (during storm); viva, salve (cheering, greeting).
hail (to) granizar (in a thunderstorm); saudar (to greet).
hair cabelo.
    hairbrush escôva (escova) para cabelo.
    haircut corte de cabelo.
    hairdye tintura para o cabelo.
    hairpin grampo para o cabelo.
hairdo penteado.
half meio; metade.
    half and half meio a meio; metades iguais.
    half past two duas (horas) e meia.
    half-hour meia hora.
half brother meio-irmão.
half sister meia-irmã.

halfway a meio caminho.

hall vestíbulo (entrance, foyer); salão (assembly room); corredor.

halt alto, parado (paragem).

halt (to) parar, deter, deter-se.
Halt! Alto!

ham presunto.

hammer martelo.

hammer (to) martelar.

hand mão; ponteiro (of a watch).
by hand à mão, manual.
in hand em mão.
on hand à mão, em estoque (em existência).
on the one hand por um lado.
on the other hand por outro lado.

hand (to) passar (pass).
to hand over entregar.

handbag mala, maleta (for travel); bôlsa (bolsa) (purse).

handbook manual.

handful punhado.

handkerchief lenço.

handle asa, cabo.

handmade feito à mão.

handshake apêrto (aperto) de mãos.

hang pendurar.

hanger (clothes) gancho, suporte; cabide.

happen acontecer.

happening acontecimento.

happiness felicidade.

happy feliz, contente.

harbor pôrto (porto).

hard duro, difícil.
hard luck má sorte.
hard work trabalho difícil.
to rain hard chover a cântaros.

harden endurecer.

hardly apenas, mal, quase.

hardness dureza.

hardware ferragens.

hardware store loja de ferragens.

hardy forte, robusto.

hare lebre.

harm n. mal, prejuízo, dano.

harmful prejudicial, nocivo.

harmless inofensivo.

harmonious harmonioso.

harmonize harmonizar.

harmony harmonia.

harness n. arreios.

harsh áspero, severo.

harshness aspereza.

harvest n. colheita.

haste pressa.
in haste à pressa, às pressas.

hasten apressar-se, acelerar.

hastily apressadamente.

hasty apressado.

hat chapéu.

hatch (to) incubar.

hate ódio.

hate (to) odiar.

hateful odioso.

hatred ódio.

haughty soberbo, arrogante.

Havana Havana.

have (to) ter (to possess), possuir (to possess).
to have in mind ter em mente, lembrar.
to have to ter que, ter de.
to have a mind to estar disposto a.

hay feno.

he êle (ele).

head cabeça; chefe (chief).

head (to) encabeçar.

headache dor de cabeça.

heading título, cabeçalho.

headline título, cabeçalho, manchete Ⓑ.

headquarters quartel-general.

heal curar; recobrar a saúde.

health saúde.
to be in good health estar bem de saúde.

healthful saudável.

healthy são.

heap montão, pilha.

heap (to) acumular, amontoar.

hear (to) ouvir.
to hear from ter notícias de.

heart coração.
by heart de memória.
at heart no fundo, em realidade.
to take to heart tomar a sério.

heart attack ataque cardíaco.

hearth lareira, lar.

hearty cordial (warm), entusiástico.

heat calor.

heat (to) aquecer.

heater aquecedor.

heating aquecimento.

heaven céu.
Heavens! Céus!

heavy pesado.

hedge cêrca (cerca) viva, sebe viva.

heel calcanhar (of foot); salto (of shoe).

height altura.

heir herdeiro.

helicopter helicóptero.

hell inferno.

Hello! Alô! Olá!

help ajuda, auxílio (x = s).

help (to) ajudar.
to help oneself to servir-se.

helper ajudante.

helpful útil, proveitoso.

hemisphere hemisfério.

hen galinha.

her a, dela, a ela, seu, sua, lhe.

herb erva.

here aqui; cá.
Here it is. Aqui está.
Come here. Venha cá.
around here por aqui.
near here perto daqui.

hereafter daqui em diante.

herein incluso, anexo (x = ks).

herewith com isto, incluso.

hero herói.

heroic heróico.

heroine heroína.

heroism heroísmo.

herring arenque.

hers seu, sua, dela; o seu, a sua, os seus, as suas.

herself ela mesma, si mesma; se, si.
by herself sòzinha.
she herself ela mesma.

hesitant hesitante, indeciso.

hesitate hesitar, vacilar.

hesitation hesitação, indecisão.

hidden escondido, oculto.

hide (to) ocultar, esconder, esconder-se.

hideous horrível, horrendo.

high alto, elevado; caro (price).
to be so high ter tanto de altura.
It is two meters high. Tem dois metros de altura.

higher mais alto; superior.

high fidelity alta fidelidade.

highway rodovia, estrada de rodagem.

hill colina, morro.

him o, êle (ele), lhe.

himself êle (ele) mesmo; si mesmo; se, si.

hinder (to) impedir, estorvar.

hindrance impedimento, estôrvo (estorvo), obstáculo.

hinge dobradiça, gonzo.

hint insinuação, alusão, sugestão.

hint (to) insinuar.
to take the hint compreender.

hip quadril, anca.

hire (to) alugar.

his seu, sua, seus, suas, o seu, a sua, os seus, as suas, dêle (dele).

Hispanic hispânico.

hiss (to) silvar, chiar.

historian historiador.

historic histórico.

history história.

hit golpe, pancada.

hit (to) bater, dar pancadas.

hive cortiço, colmeia.

hoarse rouco.

hoe enxada (x = sh).

hog porco.

hold (to) ter (in one's hands, arms, etc.); agarrar, segurar (to grasp, hold); caber, conter (to contain); ter, ocupar (a job, etc.).
to hold a meeting realizar uma reunião.
to hold one's own manter-se.

hole buraco.

holiday feriado.

Hollander holandês.

holy santo.

homage homenagem.

home casa, lar, residência.
at home em casa.

homely feio.

homemade caseiro, feito em casa.

Honduran hondurenho.

honest honesto, honrado.

honesty honestidade.

honey mel.

honeymoon lua de mel.

honor honra.

honor (to) honrar.

honorable honroso, honrado.

hoof casco, pata.

hook n. gancho, anzol (for fishing).

hope esperança.

hope (to) esperar.

hopeful esperançoso.

hopeless desesperado; incorrigível.

horizon horizonte.

horizontal horizontal.

horn chifre (of animals); buzina (of car); corneta, trompa (music).

horrible horrível.

horror horror.

horse cavalo.
on horseback a cavalo.

hosiery meias.

hospitable hospitaleiro.

hospital hospital.

hospitality hospitalidade.

host hospedeiro, anfitrião.

hostess hospedeira; dona da casa; recepcionista (receptionist).

hot quente.

hot dog cachorro-quente.

hotel hotel.

hour hora.

house casa.

household família, casa.
housekeeper governanta.
housemaid empregada.
housewife dona de casa.
how como; que; quanto.
  How do you do? Como vai? Como está?
  How many? Quantos?
  How much? Quanto?
  How far? A que distância?
  How long? Quanto tempo?
  How pretty! Que linda!
  How old is she? Quantos anos ela tem?
however porém, todavia.
huge imenso, enorme.
human humano.
  human race raça humana.
humane humano, humano, humanitário.
humanity humanidade.
humble humilde.
humiliate humilhar.
humiliation humilhação.
humility humildade.
humor humor.
humorous cômico (cómico), humoroso.
hundred cem.
  two hundred duzentos.
hundredth centésimo.
hunger fome.
hungry (be) estar com fome, ter fome.
hunt caça.
hunt (to) caçar.
hunter caçador.
hunting caça.
hurry pressa.
  to be in a hurry estar com pressa, ter pressa.
hurt (to) machucar, ferir; ofender (one's feelings).
husband marido, espôso (esposo).
hydrant hidrante.
hygiene higiene.
hymn hino.
hyphen hífen.
hypnotism hipnotismo.
hypnotize hipnotizar.
hypocrisy hipocrisia.
hypocrite hipócrita.
hysteria histeria.
hysterical histérico.

I

I eu.
Iberian ibero, ibérico.
ice gêlo (gelo).
icebox geladeira, refrigerador.
ice cream sorvete.
ice skate (to) patinar (sôbre o gêlo) (sobre o gelo).
idea idéia (ideia).
ideal ideal.
idealism idealismo.
identical idêntico.
identification identificação.
identify identificar.
identity identidade.
idiom idiotismo.
idiot idiota, imbecil.
idle ocioso.
idleness ociosidade, ócio.
if se.
  if not senão.
  even if ainda que, mesmo que.
  If I may. Com licença.
ignorance ignorância.

ignorant ignorante.
ignore não saber; não fazer caso de.
ill doente, (sick); mau; mal.
  ill breeding falta de educação, má educação, más maneiras.
  ill will má vontade.
illegal ilegal.
illegible ilegível.
illiteracy analfabetismo.
illiterate analfabeto.
illness doença.
illogical ilógico, absurdo.
illuminate iluminar, alumiar.
illumination iluminação.
illusion ilusão.
illustrate ilustrar.
illustration ilustração, gravura.
image imagem.
imagery imaginação, fantasia.
imaginary imaginário.
imagination imaginação.
imaginative imaginativo.
imagine imaginar, supor.
  Just imagine! Imagine!
imitate imitar.
imitation imitação.
immediate imediato.
immediately imediatamente.
immense imenso.
immigrant imigrante.
immigrate imigrar.
immigration imigração.
imminent iminente.
immoderate imoderado, excessivo.
immoral imoral.
immorality imoralidade.
immortal imortal.
immortality imortalidade.
impartial imparcial.
impatience impaciência.
impatient impaciente.
imperative imperativo.
imperceptible imperceptível.
imperfect imperfeito.
impersonal impessoal.
impertinence impertinência.
impertinent impertinente.
impetuous impetuoso, impulsivo.
implement instrumento, utensílio, ferramenta.
implied implícito.
imply implicar, querer dizer, significar.
impolite descortês.
import (to) importar.
importance importância.
important importante.
importation importação.
importer importador.
impose impor; abusar de (impose upon).
imposing imponente.
impossibility impossibilidade.
impossible impossível.
impress impressionar.
impression impressão.
  to have the impression ter a impressão.
impressive impressionante.
imprison encarcerar.
improbable improvável.
improper impróprio.
improve melhorar, aperfeiçoar; adiantar, progredir; melhorar-se, restabelecer-se (health).
improvement melhora, melhoria, progresso, aperfeiçoamento.

improvise improvisar.
imprudence imprudência.
imprudent imprudente.
impure impuro.
in em.
  in fact de fato (de facto).
  in the afternoon de tarde, pela tarde.
  in a week daqui a uma semana, daqui a oito dias.
  to be in estar em casa, estar no escritório.
  in general em geral.
  in part em parte.
  in reality na verdade.
  in spite of apesar de.
  in vain em vão.
  in writing por escrito.
inability inabilidade, inaptidão, incapacidade.
inaccessible inacessível.
inaccuracy inexatidão (inexactidão) (x = z).
inaccurate inexato (inexacto) (x = z), incorreto (incorrecto).
inactive inativo (inactivo).
inadequate inadequado.
inaugurate inaugurar.
incapability incapacidade.
incapable incapaz.
incapacity incapacidade.
inch polegada.
incident incidente.
inclination inclinação.
include incluir, abranger, compreender.
inclusive inclusivo.
incoherent incoerente.
income renda.
income tax impôsto (imposto) de renda.
incomparable incomparável.
incompatible incompatível.
incomprehensible incompreensível.
inconsistent inconsistente.
inconvenience inconveniência.
inconvenience (to) incomodar.
inconvenient inconveniente.
incorrect incorreto (incorrecto).
increase aumento.
increase (to) aumentar.
incredible incrível.
incurable incurável.
indebted endividado, em dívida; reconhecido, obrigado (for kindness shown).
indecent indecente, imoral.
indeed realmente, na verdade, de fato (facto), certamente, naturalmente.
indefinite indefinido.
independence independência.
independent independente; autosuficiente.
indescribable indescritível.
index índice, índice.
index finger dedo indicador, índice, index.
indicate indicar.
indifference indiferença.
indifferent indiferente.
indigestion indigestão.
indignant indignado, furioso.
indignation indignação, raiva.
indirect indireto (indirecto).
indiscreet indiscreto, imprudente.
indispensable indispensável.
indisputable indisputável.
indistinct indistinto.
individual *adj.* individual, particular.
individual n. indivíduo.
individuality individualidade.
individually individualmente.

indivisible indivisível.
indolence indolência, preguiça.
indolent indolente, preguiçoso.
indoors dentro de casa, em casa.
indulge tolerar, favorecer; entregar-se a (to indulge in).
indulgence indulgência, tolerância.
indulgent indulgente.
industrial industrial.
industrious industrioso, trabalhador, diligente.
industry indústria.
inequality desigualdade.
inevitable inevitável.
inexcusable indesculpável, imperdoável.
inexhaustible inesgotável.
inexpensive barato.
inexperience inexperiência.
inexperienced inexperiente, sem experiência.
infallible infalível.
infant criança, bebê (bebé).
infantry infantaria.
infection infecção.
infectious infeccioso, contagioso.
infer inferir, deduzir, concluir.
inference inferência, dedução.
inferior inferior.
inferiority inferioridade.
infinite infinito.
infinitive infinitivo.
infinity infinidade, infinito.
influence influência.
influence (to) influenciar, influir.
influential influente.
influenza influenza, gripe.
information informação.
　information desk guichê (guichet) de informações.
infrequent infreqüente (infrequente), raro.
infrequently infreqüentemente (infrequentemente), raramente.
ingenious engenhoso.
ingenuity engenho, talento.
ingratitude ingratidão.
inhabit habitar, ocupar, morar.
inhabitant habitante.
inherit herdar.
inheritance herança.
initial inicial.
initiative iniciativa.
injure injuriar, ofender; ferir.
injurious injurioso, prejudicial.
injury ferimento, dano; injúria, insulto.
injustice injustiça.
ink tinta.
inkwell tinteiro.
inland interior.
inn hospedaria, estalagem, pousada.
innate inato.
inner interno, interior.
innkeeper hospedeiro, estalajadeiro.
innocence inocência.
innocent inocente.
insane insano, demente, louco.
insanity demência, loucura.
inscribe inscrever.
inscription inscrição, dedicatória.
insect inseto (insecto).
insecticide inseticida (insecticida).
insecure inseguro.
insecurity insegurança, inseguridade.
insensible insensível.
inseparable inseparável.

insert (to) inserir, introduzir.
insertion inserção.
inside dentro; interior.
　on the inside por dentro.
　toward the inside para dentro.
　inside out às avessas.
insignificance insignificância.
insignificant insignificante, sem importância.
insincere insincero, não sincero.
insincerity insinceridade, falta de sinceridade.
insist insistir.
insistence insistência.
insolence insolência.
insolent insolente, arrogante.
inspect inspecionar (inspeccionar), examinar (x = z).
inspection inspeção (inspecção).
inspector inspetor (inspector).
inspiration inspiração.
install instalar, acomodar, colocar.
installation instalação.
instance instância; exemplo (x = z); caso.
　for instance por exemplo.
　in this instance neste caso.
instead of em lugar de, em vez de.
instinct instinto.
institute instituto.
institute (to) instituir, estabelecer.
institution instituição.
instruct instruir, ensinar; informar.
instruction instrução, ensino, educação.
instructive instrutivo.
instructor instrutor.
instrument instrumento.
insufficiency insuficiência, deficiência.
insufficient insuficiente, deficiente.
insult insulto.
insult (to) insultar.
insulting insultante.
insuperable insuperável.
insurance seguro.
intact intato (intacto).
integral integral.
intellectual inteletual (intelectual).
intelligence inteligência.
intelligent inteligente.
intend intentar, tencionar.
　to be intended for ter por finalidade.
intense intenso, enérgico.
intensity intensidade.
intention intenção, propósito, finalidade.
intentional intencional.
intentionally intencionalmente.
interest interêsse (interesse).
interest (to) interessar.
interesting interessante.
interior interior, interno.
intermission intervalo, intermissão.
internal interno.
international internacional.
interpose interpor.
interpret interpretar.
interpretation interpretação.
interpreter intérprete.
interrupt interromper, suspender.
interruption interrupção, suspensão.
interval intervalo.
intervention intervenção.
interview entrevista.
intestines intestino.
intimacy intimidade.
intimate íntimo.

intimidate intimidar.
into em, dentro, para dentro.
intonation entoação.
intoxicate embriagar; intoxicar (to poison) (x = ks).
intoxicating inebriante; intoxicante (x = ks).
intoxication embriaguez; intoxicação (x = ks) (poison).
intricate intricado, complicado, complexo (x = ks).
intrigue intriga, trama.
intrinsic intrínseco.
introduce introduzir; apresentar (a person).
　to introduce a person apresentar uma pessoa.
introduction introdução; apresentação.
intruder intruso.
intuition intuição.
invade invadir.
invalid adj. inválido, doente (person); não válido, nulo (void).
invalid n. inválido.
invasion invasão.
invent inventar.
invention invenção.
inventor inventor.
invert inverter, virar.
invest investir; inverter.
investigate investigar.
investigation investigação, inquérito.
investment investimento.
investor pessoa que faz investimento.
invisible invisível.
invitation convite.
invite convidar.
invoice fatura (factura).
involuntary involuntário.
involve implicar, comprometer.
iodine iôdo (iodo).
iris íris.
iron ferro (metal, and for ironing).
iron (to) passar a ferro (clothes).
ironic, ironical irônico (irónico).
ironing ação (acção) de passar a ferro.
irony ironia.
irregular irregular.
irresolute irresoluto, indeciso.
irresponsible irresponsável.
irrigate irrigar, regar.
irrigation irrigação.
irritable irritável.
irritate irritar, exasperar (x = z).
irritation irritação.
island ilha.
isolation isolação, isolamento.
issue edição, tiragem (books, etc.); assunto, tema (subject).
issue (to) publicar, lançar (books, etc.); distribuir.
it êle (ele), ela, o, a, lhe; isto, êste (este), esta. ("It" is not translated in phrases like "it's raining" **chove**, "it's late" **é tarde**, (it's two o'clock" **são duas horas**, etc.).
　I have it. Tenho. Tenho-o (m.).
　I have it. Tenho. Tenho-a (f.).
　I said it. Eu o disse. Disse-o.
　Isn't it? Não é verdade? Não é?
　That's it. Isso é.
Italian italiano.
itinerary itinerário.
its seu, sua, seus, suas, dêle (dele), dela, dêles (deles), delas.
itself si mesmo, si, si próprio, se.
　by itself por si, por si mesmo.

ivory marfim.
ivy hera.

J

jack macaco (tool).
jacket paletó, jaqueta; sobrecapa, capa (book); camisa, revestimento (covering).
jail cadeia, cárcere; xadrez (x = sh) Ⓑ.
jam geléia (geleia); apêrto (aperto) (a fix); congestionamento (traffic).
janitor porteiro, zelador de prédio.
January janeiro (Janeiro).
Japanese japonês.
jar n. jarro, cântaro, vaso.
jaw queixo (x = sh).
jealous ciumento, cioso.
jealousy ciúme.
jelly geléia (geleia); gelatina.
jerk (to) arrancar, sacudir.
jest pilhéria, galhofa, graça, brincadeira.
jest (to) galhofar, caçoar, troçar, gracejar, brincar.
Jesuit jesuíta.
jet jato (jacto).
  jet plane avião a jato.
Jew judeu, hebreu, israelita.
jewel jóia, pedra preciosa.
jewelry jóias, pedras preciosas.
jewelry store joalheria.
Jewess judia.
Jewish judeu, judaico, hebreu, israelita.
job emprêgo (emprego), trabalho; tarefa (task).
John Doe Fulano de Tal.
join unir, juntar (to put together); unir-se, associar-se (to unite); ingressar em, incorporar-se a (an organization).
joint juntura, junção, união.
joke anedota, piada, pilhéria, troça, brincadeira.
  to play a joke on pregar peça em.
joke (to) gracejar, brincar, troçar.
jolly adj. alegre, jovial, convival.
jostle empurrar, acotovelar.
journal diário, jornal.
journalist jornalista, periodista.
journalistic journalístico.
journey viagem.
jovial jovial.
joy alegria, felicidade.
joyful alegre, feliz.
judge juiz.
judge (to) julgar.
judgment julgamento.
judicial judicial, judiciário.
juice suco, sumo.
juicy suculento; picante, vivo.
July julho (Julho).
jump salto, pulo.
jump (to) saltar, pular.
June junho (Junho).
junior adj. júnior, mais jovem, mais nôvo (novo), mais moço; subordinado.
  junior partner sócio mais nôvo.
jurisprudence jurisprudência.
juror jurado.
jury júri.
just adj. justo.
  It's not just. Não é justo.
just adv. justamente, exatamente (exactamente) (x = z), sòmente.
  just as no momento em que, neste momento.
  just as I came in no memento em que eu entrava.

just a moment um momento.
just now agora mesmo.
I just wanted to eu sòmente queria.
to have just acabar de.
I have just come. Acabo de chegar.
It is just two o'clock. São exatamente (exactamente) duas horas.
Just as you please. Como você quiser.
justice justiça.
justifiable justificável.
justification justificação.
justify justificar.
juvenile adj. juvenil, jovem adolescente.
juvenile n. jovem, adolescente.

K

keen agudo.
keep (to) guardar, manter.
  to keep away manter afastado.
  to keep back (retain) deter, reter.
  to keep from impedir (hinder); abster-se (refrain).
  to keep quiet calar-se, ficar quieto.
  to keep in mind ter em mente.
  to keep one's word cumprir (a) sua promessa.
  to keep a secret guardar um segrêdo (segredo).
  keep to the right conserve (a) sua direita.
kernel semente, grão.
kerosene querosene.
kettle caldeirão, chaleira.
key chave.
keyboard teclado.
kick pontapé, patada.
kick (to) dar pontapé.
kidney rim.
kill (to) matar.
kilo quilo.
kilogram quilograma.
kilometer quilômetro (quilómetro).
kin família, parentes.
kind adj. bom, amável, bondoso.
kind n. classe, espécie, gênero (género), qualidade.
kindergarten jardim de infância, jardim-escola.
kind-hearted bondoso, de bom coração.
kindly amàvelmente, cordialmente.
  Kindly do it. Tenha a bondade de fazê-lo.
kindness bondade, amabilidade.
king rei.
kiss beijo.
kiss (to) beijar.
kitchen cozinha.
kite papagaio de papel.
kitten gatinho.
knee joelho.
kneel ajoelhar(-se).
knife faca.
knit tricotar.
knock golpe, pancada; batida.
knock (to) dar pancadas, bater.
knot nó.
know (to) saber; conhecer (be acquainted with).
knowledge conhecimento.
knuckle nó dos dedos.

L

label rótulo, etiquêta (etiqueta).
labor labor, trabalho.
laboratory laboratório.
laborer trabalhador, operário.
lace n. renda.
lack falta, carência, deficiência, necessidade.
lack (to) carecer de, faltar, necessitar.

ladder escada de mão.
lady senhora.
  Ladies. Senhoras.
  Ladies and gentlemen. Senhoras e senhores.
  Meus senhores e minhas senhoras.
lake lago.
lamb cordeiro.
lamb chop costeleta de carneiro.
lame coxo (x = sh), manco, aleijado.
lame (be) coxear (x = sh).
lameness coxeadura (x = sh).
lament (to) lamentar.
lamentation lamento, lamentação.
lamp lâmpada.
land terra (ground); terreno (terrain); país (country).
land (to) desembarcar (ship); aterrar, pousar (plane).
landing n. desembarque (from a ship); aterrissagem, pouso (of an airplane); patamar (a staircase).
landlady estalajadeira, proprietária.
landlord estalajadeiro, proprietário, patrão.
landscape paisagem.
language língua, idioma.
languid lânguido.
languish languir.
languor langor, languidez.
lantern lanterna, farol.
lap colo, regaço.
lard toucinho, banha.
large grande.
  at large livre, livremente, à vontade.
large-scale em grande escala.
lark cotovia.
larynx laringe.
last último; passado.
  lastly por fim, finalmente, por último.
  at last finalmente.
  last night ontem à noite.
  last week a semana passada.
  last year o ano passado.
last (to) durar.
lasting duradouro, durável.
latch trinco, aldrava.
late adj. tarde.
  to be late chegar tarde.
  late in the year no fim do ano.
  How late? Até que horas?
lately ùltimamente, recentemente, há pouco tempo.
lateness atraso, demora.
later mais tarde.
latest último.
  lastest styles últimos estilos, últimos modelos.
  at the latest o mais tardar.
lather espuma.
Latin adj. latino.
Latin n. latim.
Latin American latino-americano.
laudable laudável, louvável.
laugh riso, risada.
laugh (to) rir, rir-se.
  to make someone laugh fazer rir.
laughable risível, ridículo.
laughter riso, risada, gargalhada.
launder lavar e passar roupa.
laundress lavadeira, lavandeira.
laundry lavanderia (laundry shop); roupa para lavar (clothes to be washed); roupa lavada (laundered clothes).
lavish pródigo, generoso.
lavish (to) ser generoso, dissipar.
law lei; jurisprudência (legal science); direito.

(body of laws); regra (rule).
law school escola de direito.
international law direito internacional.
lawful legal, lícito.
lawn gramado.
lawyer advogado.
laxative laxante (x = ch).
lay (to) pôr.
to lay aside pôr de lado.
to lay hold of agarrar.
to lay off despedir.
laziness preguiça.
lazy preguiçoso.
lead (metal) chumbo.
lead (to) conduzir, guiar.
to lead the way mostrar o caminho.
leader líder Ⓑ, condutor, chefe; guia (guide); diretor (director).
leadership direção (direcção), chefia, comando.
leading principal, primeiro.
leading article artigo de fundo.
leading man (theatre) galã, ator principal.
leaf fôlha (folha).
lean (to) inclinar-se.
to lean back encostar-se.
to lean over inclinar-se.
leaning inclinação, propensão, tendência.
leap salto, pulo.
leap (to) saltar, pular.
learn aprender (to acquire knowledge, skill); enterar-se de, saber de (to find out about).
learned adj. douto, erudito.
learning erudição, saber.
lease contrato, arrendamento.
lease (to) arrendar, alugar.
least mínimo, o mínimo, menor, menos.
at least pelo menos, ao menos.
not in the least de maneira alguma, de modo algum.
the least possible o menos possível.
leather couro.
lecture n. conferência, discurso, preleção (prelecção) (a speech); repreensão (reprimand).
lecturer conferencista.
left adj. esquerdo.
left hand mão esquerda.
to the left à esquerda.
left-handed canhoto.
left n. esquerda.
left (be) ficar, restar.
leg perna.
legal legal, lícito.
legend lenda, legenda.
legible legível.
legislation legislação.
legislator legislador.
legislature legislatura.
leisure lazer, folga, ócio, horas vagas.
lemon limão.
lemonade limonada.
lend (to) emprestar, dar emprestado.
to lend an ear prestar atenção.
to lend a hand ajudar.
length comprimento.
at length finalmente; detalhadamente.
at full length ao comprido, em tôda (toda) a extensão.
less menos.
more or less mais ou menos.
less and less cada vez menos.
lessen reduzir, diminuir.
lesson lição.
let (to) deixar (x = sh), permitir (to allow); alugar, arrendar (to rent).
Let's go. Vamos.

Let's see. Vejamos. Vamos ver.
Let them go. Que se vão.
to let alone deixar em paz.
to let go soltar.
to let in deixar entrar.
to let know avisar.
letter carta; letra (of the alphabet).
letters (literature) letras.
homem de letras man of letters, writer.
lettuce alface.
level adj. plano, raso, igual, nivelado.
level nível.
level off (to) nivelar.
liable sujeito, exposto (exposed to); responsável por (accountable); capaz de (liable to do, etc.).
liar mentiroso.
liberal liberal.
liberty liberdade.
library biblioteca.
license licença, autorização.
lick lamber.
lid tampa.
lie mentira (falsehood).
lie (to) mentir (tell a falsehood); deitar-se, jazer (to lie down, to lie).
lieutenant tenente.
life vida.
life preserver salva-vidas.
lifeboat barco salva-vidas.
life insurance seguro de vida.
lifetime a vida tôda (toda), existência.
lift alçar, levantar.
light luz, lume, claridade, iluminação.
light adj. leviano, ligeiro (in weight); claro (color).
light-hearted despreocupado, alegre.
light (to) acender (a cigarette); iluminar (to illuminate).
light bulb lâmpada elétrica (eléctrica).
lighten aliviar, mitigar.
lighthouse farol.
lighting iluminação.
lightness leveza.
lightning relâmpago, raio.
like parecido, semelhante (similar).
in like manner da mesma maneira, do mesmo medo.
to be like ser semelhante.
like (to) querer, gostar de.
I like him very much. Gosto muito dêle (dele).
As you like. Como você quiser.
Do you like it? Você gosta?
I like it. Gosto.
I don't like it. Não gosto.
She looks like her mother. Ela se parece com a mãe.
likely provável.
likeness semelhança.
likewise igualmente, do mesmo modo.
liking afeição, simpatia, gôsto (gosto).
limb membro.
lime cal.
limit limite.
limit (to) limitar.
limp (to) coxear (x = sh).
line linha.
line (to) traçar linhas, alinhar.
to line up alinhar, alinhar-se.
linen linho.
lining fôrro (forro).
link elo.
link (to) unir, ligar.
lip lábio.
lipstick batom.

liquid líquido.
liquor licor, bebida alcoólica.
lisp cicio.
list lista.
listen escutar.
literal literal, ao pé da letra.
literally literalmente, ao pé da letra.
literary literário.
literature literatura.
little pequeno (size); pouco (amount).
a little um pouco.
very little muito pouco.
the little ones os pequenos, as crianças.
little by little pouco a pouco.
live adj. vivo.
live (to) viver.
lively vivo, animado.
liver fígado (body organ).
living adj. vivo.
to make a living ganhar a vida.
living room sala de estar.
load carga.
load (to) carregar.
loaf pão.
loan empréstimo.
lobby vestíbulo.
lobster lagosta.
local local.
locate colocar, situar.
location sítio, situação (place, locality); posição.
lock fechadura.
lock (to) fechar à chave, trancar.
locomotive locomotiva.
locust locusta.
lodging alojamento.
lodging house hospedaria, pensão.
log toro, lenho.
log book diário de bordo, barquilha.
logic lógica.
logical lógico.
lonely solitário, só.
long adj. comprido, longo.
It's five meters long. Tem cinco metros de comprido.
a long time ago há muito tempo.
long distance call telefonema interurbano.
long adv. muito tempo, muito.
long ago há muito tempo.
all day long o dia todo.
not long ago há pouco tempo.
How long ago? Quanto tempo há?
How long? Quanto tempo?
longer adj. mais comprido.
longer adv. mais tempo.
How much longer? Quanto tempo mais?
no longer não mais; já não.
to long for anelar por, ter saudades de.
longing ânsia, desejo, saudade.
look olhar, olhada.
look (to) ver, olhar.
Look! Olhe!
to look for procurar, buscar.
to look after cuidar de.
to look like parecer-se com.
to look forward to esperar.
to look into examinar (x = z).
to look as though it's going to rain parecer que vai chover.
to look out ter cuidado (be careful).
Look out! Cuidado!
to look over (review) repassar.
loose sôlto (solto), frouxo (x = sh).
loosen (to) desatar, soltar.
Lord Senhor, Deus.
lose (to) perder.

loss perda.
  at a loss perplexo (x = ks), confuso.
lot (a) muito.
  a lot of money muito dinheiro.
loud alto.
love amor.
  to be in love estar apaixonado (x = sh).
love (to) amar, querer.
lovely encantador, bonito.
low baixo (x = sh).
lower mais baixo (x = sh), inferior.
  lower case letras minúsculas.
lower (to) baixar (x = sh), abaixar (x = sh), reduzir; arriar (sails).
loyal leal, fiel.
loyalty lealdade.
luck sorte, fortuna, destino.
  good luck boa sorte.
  to have luck estar com sorte, ter sorte.
luckily afortunadamente, felizmente.
lucky afortunado.
luggage bagagem.
lukewarm môrno (morno), tépido; indiferente.
lumber madeira.
luminous luminoso.
lunch almôço (almoço).
lunch (to) almoçar.
lung pulmão.
Lusitanian lusitano.
de luxe de luxo (x = sh).
luxurious luxuoso (x = sh).
luxury luxo (x = sh).

M

machine máquina.
machinery maquinaria.
mad louco, demente, doido, tolo.
made feito, fabricado.
madness loucura, demência.
magazine revista.
magic *adj.* mágico.
magic n. magia.
magistrate magistrado.
magnanimous magnânimo, generoso.
magnet magnete ímã.
magnetic magnético.
magnificent magnífico.
magnify aumentar, exagerar (x = z), magnificar.
magnifying glass lente de aumento.
maid empregada, criada.
mail correio.
mailbox caixa (x = sh) de correio.
mailman carteiro.
main principal.
  main street rua principal.
  main reason motivo principal, razão principal.
mainly principalmente.
maintain manter, sustentar, conservar.
maintenance manutenção, sustentação, conservação.
majestic majestoso, grandioso.
majesty majestade.
major *adj.* maior, principal.
major n. major (military).
majority maioria.
make (to) fazer, fabricar, produzir.
  to make sad entristecer, tornar triste.
  to make happy alegrar, tornar alegre.
  to make a living ganhar a vida.
  to make possible fazer possível.
  to make ready preparar.
  to make room for fazer lugar para.
  to make known dar a conhecer.

to make a hit ser um sucesso.
to make a mistake errar, enganar-se.
to make a stop parar, fazer uma parada.
to make friends fazer amizade com.
to make fun of fazer troça de, rir-se de.
to make haste apressar-se.
to make headway progredir, avançar.
to make into converter.
to make no difference não importar.
to make out compreender, decifrar (understand); sair bem, sair mal (well or badly).
to make sick tornar doente; irritar, aborrecer (to annoy).
to make the best of tirar o maior proveito de, tirar o melhor partido de.
to make tired cansar.
to make up one's mind decidir-se, resolver-se.
maker fabricante, criador.
malady doença.
male macho, masculino.
malice malícia.
malicious malicioso, maligno.
malted milk leite maltado.
man homem.
  young man jovem.
  Men (as on a sign) Senhores. Homens. Cavalheiros.
manage (to) administrar, governar, dirigir; conseguir, sair bem (to get along, to succeed).
management administração, direção.
manager administrador, diretor (director), gerente.
manifest (to) manifestar.
mankind humanidade, gênero (género) humano.
manly viril, varonil.
manner maneira, modo.
manners maneiras, costumes, conduta.
mansion mansão.
manual manual.
manufacture (to) manufaturar (manufacturar), fabricar.
manufacturer fabricante.
manuscript manuscrito.
many muitos.
  many times muitas vêzes (vezes).
  as many as tantos quanto, tantos como.
  How many? Quantos?
map mapa.
maple bôrdo (bordo).
marble mármore; bolinha de gude (for children).
March março (Março).
march marcha.
march (to) marchar.
margin margem.
marine marinho.
mark marca.
mark (to) marcar.
market mercado.
marriage matrimônio (matrimónio), casamento.
marry (to) casar-se, casar.
  to get married casar-se.
marvel (to) maravilhar-se, admirar-se, estranhar.
marvel n. maravilha, prodígio.
marvelous maravilhoso.
marvelously maravilhosamente.
masculine masculino.
mashed potatoes purê (puré) de batatas.
mask máscara.
mason pedreiro.
mass massa; missa (religious).
massage massagem.
massage (to) fazer massagem, dar massagem.
massive maciço, sólido.
mast mastro.

master dono, amo, senhor; mestre.
masterpiece obra prima.
mat esteira.
match fósforo (to light with); partida, jôgo (jogo) (sports); companheiro, parelha (a pair); aliança, casamento (marriage).
match (to) emparelhar, igualar; combinar (colors); casar (marry).
material material.
maternal materno, maternal.
mathematical matemático.
mathematics matemática.
matinee matinê Ⓑ, vesperal.
matter matéria; coisa (thing); assunto, questão (question).
  an important matter um assunto importante.
  What's the matter? O que há? Que aconteceu? Que tem você?
matter (to) importar.
  It doesn't matter. Não importa. Não tem importância.
mattress colchão.
mature *adj.* maduro.
mature (to) madurar, amadurecer.
maturity maturidade, madureza.
maximum máximo (x = s).
May maio (Maio).
may poder, ser possível.
  It may be. Pode ser. É possível.
  It may be true. Pode ser verdade.
  May I? Com licença. O senhor permite?
maybe talvez.
mayonnaise maionese.
mayor prefeito (administrador do concelho, presidente da câmara municipal).
maze labirinto.
  to be in a maze estar confuso.
meadow prado.
meal refeição.
mean *adj.* baixo (x = sh), vil, desprezível.
mean (to) significar, querer dizer, tencionar.
  What do you mean? O que você quer dizer?
meaning propósito, intenção (intent); sentido, significado.
means meio, meios, recursos.
  by all means sem dúvida, certamente.
  by no means de nenhuma maneira.
  by some means de alguma maneira, de algum jeito.
  by this means por esta maneira.
meantime entretanto, entrementes.
meanwhile entretanto, entrementes.
measure medida.
  in a great measure em grande parte.
  to take measures tomar providências.
measure (to) medir.
  to measure up to estar à altura de.
measurement medida, medição.
meat carne.
mechanic mecânico.
mechanical mecânico.
mechanically mecânicamente, maquinalmente.
mechanism mecanismo.
medal medalha.
meddle (to) intrometer-se, meter-se.
mediate mediar.
medical médico.
  medical school escola de medicina, faculdade de medicina.
medicine medicina (in general), remédio (particular remedy).
medieval medieval.
meditate meditar.
meditation meditação, contemplação.
Mediterranean Mediterrâneo.
medium *adj.* médio, mediano.

medium-sized de tamanho médio.

meet (to) encontrar, encontrar-se, dar com (to come across); conhecer (to get to know); reunir-se (to get together).
  to go to meet ir receber.
  Glad to meet you. (Tenho muito) prazer em conhecê-lo.
  I hope to meet you again. Espero ter o prazer de vê-lo de nôvo (novo) (tornar a vê-lo).
  Till we meet again. Até a vista.

meeting n. reunião, sessão.

melancholy adj. melancólico.

melody melodia.

melon melão.

melt (to) derreter, dissolver; fundir (metals).

member membro, sócio.

memorable memorável.

memorandum memorando.

memory memória.

mend emendar, consertar; corrigir-se (mend one's ways).

mental mental.

mention menção, alusão.

mention (to) mencionar.

menu menu, cardápio (ementa).

merchandise mercadoria.

merchant comerciante, negociante.

merciful misericordioso, compassivo.

merciless impiedoso, cruel.

mercury mercúrio.

mercy misericórdia.

merit mérito.

merry alegre.

message mensagem, recado.

messenger mensageiro.

metal adj. metálico.

metal n. metal.

meter metro (measurement); medidor (for gas, etc.).

method método.

methodic(al) metódico.

methodically metòdicamente.

metric métrico.
  metric system sistema métrico.

metropolis metrópole.

metropolitan metropolitano.

Mexican mexicano (x = sh).

midday meio-dia.

middle adj. médio.
  Middle Ages Idade Média.
  middle-aged de meia idade.
  middle-class da classe média.

middle n. meio, centro.
  in the middle no meio, no centro.

midnight meia-noite.

might poder, fôrça (força).

mighty potente, forte.

mild suave, brando, meigo; moderado (moderate); macio.

mile milha.

military militar.

milk leite.

milkman leiteiro.

milk shake batida de leite com sorvete.

mill moinho; fábrica (factory); usina (steel mill, etc.) engenho.

miller moleiro.

million milhão.

millionaire milionário.

mind mente.
  to have in mind ter em mente, pensar em.
  to change one's mind mudar de opinião.

mine pron. meu, minha, meus, minhas, o meu, a minha, os meus, as minhas.

  a friend of mine um amigo meu.
  your friends and mine (os) seus amigos e os meus.

mine n. mina.

miner mineiro.

mineral mineral, minério.

miniature miniatura.

minimum mínimo.

minister ministro.

minor adj. menor, secundário.

minor n. menor (de idade).

minority minoria, menoridade.

mint menta (plant); casa da moeda (money).

minus menos.

minute minuto (time).
  minute hand ponteiro dos minutos.
  Just a minute, please. Um minuto, por favor.
  Um momento, por favor.
  any minute de minuto em minuto.
  Wait a minute! Aguarde um momento!

miracle milagre.

miraculous milagroso, miraculoso.

mirror espelho.

mirth alegria, jovialidade.

misbehave portar-se mal.

misbehavior mau comportamento, má conduta.

mischief travessura, diabrura.

mischievous travêsso (travesso).

miser avarento.

miserable miserável, infeliz.

misfortune infortúnio, má sorte.

Miss senhorita, senhorinha.

miss (to) ter saudades de (someone or something); perder, não alcançar (bus, etc.); errar, não acertar (mark, etc.).
  to miss the point não compreender o verdadeiro sentido.

mission missão.

missionary missionário.

mistake êrro (erro), equívoco, engano.

mistake (to) errar, enganar-se.
  to be mistaken enganar-se.

mister senhor.

mistrust desconfiança.

mistrust (to) desconfiar de, suspeitar de.

misunderstand entender mal, compreender mal.

misunderstanding equívoco, engano, desentendimento.

mix (to) misturar, mesclar.

mixture mistura, mescla.

moan gemido, lamento.

moan (to) gemer, lamentar-se.

mobilization mobilização.

mobilize mobilizar.

mockery escárnio, mofa; esfôrço (esforço) vão.

mode modo.

model modêlo (modelo).

moderate adj. moderado.

moderate (to) moderar.

moderately moderadamente.

moderation moderação.

modern moderno.

modernism modernismo.

modern languages línguas modernas.

modest modesto.

modesty modéstia.

modify modificar.

moist úmido.

moisten umedecer.

moisture umidade.

moment momento.
  Just a moment! Um momento!

momentary momentâneo.

momentous momentoso, importante.

monarch monarca.

monarchy monarquia.

Monday segunda-feira, segunda.

money dinheiro.

monk monge, frade.

monkey macaco.

monologue monólogo.

monopoly monopólio.

monosyllable monossílabo.

monotonous monótono.

monotony monotonia.

monster monstro.

monstrous monstruoso.

month mês.

monthly mensal.

monument monumento.

monumental monumental.

moon lua.

moonlight luar.

moral adj. moral, ético.

morale moral, disposição de ânimo.

morbid mórbido.

more mais.
  more or less mais ou menos.
  one more outra vez, mais uma vez.
  no more não mais.
  the more ... the better quanto mais ... tanto melhor.

moreover além disso.

morning manhã.
  Good morning! Bom dia!

morsel bocado.

mortal mortal.

mortgage n. hipoteca.

mosquito mosquito.

moss musgo.

most o mais, os mais, o maior número, a maior parte, a maioria.
  at most quando muito.
  for the most part em geral, na maior parte.
  most of us quase todos nós, a maior parte de nós.

moth traça.

mother mãe.

mother-in-law sogra.

motion movimento; moção, proposta.

motion picture filme, fita.

motive motivo.

motor n. motor.

mount n. monte, colina, montanha (hill, mountain); base, montagem (base); suporte (for instruments, etc.).

mount (to) montar, colocar.

mountain montanha.

mountainous montanhoso.

mourn lamentar.

mournful triste, pesaroso.

mourning lamento, lamentação, dor, luto.
  in mourning de luto.

mouse camundongo; rato.

mouth bôca (boca).

mouthful bocado.

movable móvel, móbil.

move (to) mover, pôr em movimento (to set in motion), mudar-se (to another house), afastar, deslocar (to change place), jogar, fazer uma jogada (in a game).

movement movimento.

movie filme.

movies cinema.

moving adj. comovente, tocante (emotionally).

moving picture filme (cinematográfico).

Mr. senhor.

Mrs. senhora.

much muito.

    as much tanto.

    as much as tanto...quanto, tanto...como.

    How much? Quanto?

    too much demais, demasiado.

    much the same quase o mesmo, mais ou menos o mesmo.

    much money muito dinheiro.

    so much the better tanto melhor.

    so much the worse tanto pior.

mud lama, lôdo (lodo), barro.

muddy turvo, barrento.

mule mulo, mula.

multiple múltiplo.

multiplication multiplicação.

multiply multiplicar.

murder assassínio.

murder (to) assassinar, matar.

murderer assassino.

murmur n. murmúrio.

muscle músculo.

museum museu.

music música.

musical musical, músico.

musician músico.

must ter que, ter de, dever, precisar.

    I must go. Tenho que ir. Preciso ir.

    It must be. Deve ser.

mustache bigode.

mustard mostarda.

mutton carne de carneiro.

mutual mútuo.

my meu, minha, meus, minhas, o meu, a minha, os meus, as minhas.

myself eu mesmo, me, para mim.

mysterious misterioso.

mystery mistério.

N

nail unha.

nail (to) cravar, pregar.

nail polish esmalte de unhas.

naïve ingênuo (ingénuo), simples.

naked nu, despido.

name nome.

    Christian name, first name nome de batismo (baptismo), prenome.

    surname sobrenome, apelido.

    What is your name? Qual é o seu nome? Como se chama?

    My name is chamo-me.

namely isto é, a saber.

nap n. soneca, cochilo.

napkin guardanapo.

narration narração.

narrative n. narrativa.

narrow estreito.

nation nação.

national nacional.

nationality nacionalidade.

nationalization nacionalização.

nationalize nacionalizar, naturalizar.

native adj. nativo, indígena.

    native land terra natal, pátria.

natural natural.

naturalist naturalista.

naturally naturalmente, claro.

naturalness naturalidade.

nature natureza; caráter (carácter), índole.

    good nature boa índole.

naughty mau, travêsso (travesso), malicioso.

naval naval.

navigable navegável.

navigator navegador, navegante.

navy marinha de guerra, armada.

near perto, perto de.

nearby perto, à mão.

nearly quase, por pouco.

nearsighted míope.

nearsightedness miopia.

nearsighted person míope.

neat limpo, asseado, esmerado; em ordem, arrumado.

neatness asseio, limpeza.

necessarily necessàriamente.

necessary necessário, preciso.

    to be necessary ser necessário.

necessitate necessitar, precisar.

necessity necessidade.

    of necessity necessàriamente.

neck pescoço, colo.

necklace colar.

necktie gravata.

need necessidade.

need (to) necessitar, precisar de; faltar.

    to be in need of ter necessidade de, precisar de.

    to be in need estar necessitado.

needle agulha.

negative adj. negativo.

    a negative answer uma resposta negativa.

negative n. negativa; negativo (photography).

neglect descuido, negligência.

neglect (to) descuidar.

Negro negro.

neighbor vizinho.

neither conj. nem; adj. nenhum, nenhum dos dois; pron. nenhum.

    neither...nor nem...nem.

    neither this one nor that one nem um nem outro, nem êste (este) nem aquêle (aquele).

    neither one nem um nem outro.

nephew sobrinho.

nerve nervo.

nervous nervoso.

nest ninho.

net n. rêde (rede).

neuter neutro.

neutral neutral, imparcial, neutro.

never nunca, jamais.

nevertheless não obstante, todavia.

new nôvo (novo).

    new moon lua nova.

    New Year ano nôvo (novo).

news notícia, notícias.

newsboy jornaleiro (ardina).

newspaper jornal, diário.

newsstand banca de jornais, quiosque.

New York Nova Iorque.

next seguinte, próximo (x = s).

    the next day no dia seguinte.

    (the) next week a semana que vem.

    (the) next time a próxima vez.

    next to ao lado de, junto a.

    Who's next? Quem segue?

nice agradável, simpático, amável; bonito, lindo.

nickname alcunha, apelido.

niece sobrinha.

night noite.

    by night de noite.

    good night boa noite.

    last night ontem à noite.

night club boîte, cabaré.

nightfall anoitecer.

nightmare pesadelo.

nighttime noite.

nine nove.

nine hundred novecentos.

nineteen dezenove (dezanove).

ninety noventa.

ninth nono, nona parte.

no não; nenhum, nenhuma.

    no other nenhum outro.

    no one ninguém.

    no longer já não.

    no more não mais.

    no matter não importa.

    by no means de nenhuma maneira, de forma alguma.

    No admittance. É proibida a entrada.

    No smoking. É proibido fumar.

nobility nobreza.

noble nobre.

nobody ninguém.

    nobody else ninguém mais.

nod (to) inclinar a cabeça, acenar com a cabeça; dormitar (to doze), cabecear (become sleepy).

noise barulho, ruído.

noisy barulhento, ruidoso.

nominative nominativo.

none ninguém, nenhum, nada.

    none of us nenhum de nós.

nonsense tolice, asneira.

noon meio-dia.

nor nem.

    neither...nor... nem...nem...

normal normal.

normally normalmente.

north norte.

North America América do Norte.

North American norte-americano.

northeast nordeste.

northern do norte, setentrional.

nose nariz.

nostril narina.

not não; nem.

    if not se não.

    not any nenhum.

    not one nem um.

    not a word nem uma palavra.

    not at all de nenhuma maneira, de modo algum.

    not even nem sequer.

notable notável.

note nota, bilhete; cédula (bank note).

note (to) anotar, notar; observar.

notebook caderno.

nothing nada.

    nothing doing nada disso, não pode ser.

    It's nothing. Não é nada.

    nothing much pouca coisa.

    for nothing grátis; em vão (in vain).

notice aviso, anúncio.

notice (to) notar, observar, perceber.

notwithstanding não obstante, apesar de, embora, ainda que.

noun nome, substantivo.

nourish alimentar, nutrir.

nourishment alimento, nutrição.

novel romance, novela.

novelist romancista, novelista.

novelty novidade, inovação.

November novembro (Novembro).

now agora, pois bem.

    until now até agora.

    now and then de vez em quando.

    Is it ready now? Já está pronto?

nowadays hoje em dia.

nowhere em nenhuma parte, em lugar algum.

number número.

numerous numeroso.

nun freira, monja.
nurse n. enfermeira (f.), enfermeiro (m.).
nursery quarto de crianças.
nut noz; amêndoa; porca (for a screw).

O

oak carvalho.
oar remo.
oat aveia.
oath juramento.
oatmeal farinha de aveia.
obedience obediência.
obedient obediente.
obey obedecer.
object objeto (objecto), objetivo (objectivo);
complemento (grammar).
object (to) opor-se, objetar (objectar).
objection objeção (objecção).
objective objetivo (objectivo), propósito.
obligation obrigação.
oblige obrigar, forçar.
oblique oblíquo.
obscure obscuro, escuro; pouco conhecido.
observation observação.
observatory observatório.
observe observar, notar, perceber.
observer observador.
observing observador, atento.
obstacle obstáculo.
obstinacy pertinácia, obstinação.
obstinate obstinado, persistente.
obstruct obstruir.
obstruction obstrução, impedimento.
obtain obter, conseguir.
obvious óbvio.
occasion ocasião, oportunidade.
occasional ocasional, casual (casual); pouco
freqüente (frequente).
occasionally de vez em quando,
ocasionalmente.
occidental ocidental.
occupation ocupação, emprêgo (emprego), profissão.
occupy ocupar.
occur ocorrer, acontecer.
occurrence ocorrência, acontecimento.
ocean oceano.
ocean liner vapor, transatlântico.
o'clock horas.
  at nine o'clock às nove (horas).
  It's ten o'clock. São dez (horas).
October outubro (Outubro).
oculist oculista.
odd ímpar (number); raro, estranho (strange).
odds and ends miudezas.
of de, do, da.
  to taste of ter gôsto (gosto) de.
  to think of pensar em.
  of course naturalmente, claro.
  of himself por si mesmo.
  It's twenty of two. Faltam vinte para as
    duas. É uma hora e quarenta minutos.
  That's very kind of you. O senhor é muito
    amável.
off longe, distante, fora; desligado (disconnected); de folga (as day off).
  off and on de vez em quando.
  The meeting is off. Cancelaram a reunião.
  off the coast perto da costa.
  a day off um dia de folga, dia de descanso.
  to take off tirar.
offend ofender.
offended (be) ressentir-se.
offense ofensa, injúria.

offensive adj. ofensivo, desagradável.
offensive n. ofensiva, ataque.
offer oferta, oferecimento, proposta.
offer (to) oferecer, propor.
offering n. oferecimento; oferenda, oblação
(gift, oblation).
office escritório, repartição (a building, a room,
etc.); cargo, posição, pôsto (posto) (position).
officer oficial.
official adj. oficial.
often muitas vêzes (vezes), freqüentemente
(frequentemente).
oil óleo, petróleo; azeite (olive or vegetable).
  oil painting pintura a óleo.
ointment ungüento (unguento).
old velho, antigo.
  to be twenty years old ter vinte anos.
  old man velho.
  old age velhice.
  old maid solteirona.
olive azeitona, oliva.
  olive oil azeite (de oliva).
  olive tree oliveira.
omelette omeleta.
omission omissão.
omit omitir.
omnibus ônibus (ónibus, autocarro).
on sôbre (sobre), em cima de, em; a, ao; com,
baixo (x = sh); por; ligado (connected).
  on the table sôbre a mesa.
  on the train no trem (comboio).
  on that occasion naquela ocasião.
  on the left à esquerda.
  on board a bordo.
  on foot a pé.
  on credit a crédito.
  on time na hora.
  on my part de minha parte.
  on the average em média.
  on the contrary pelo contrário.
  on the whole geralmente, em geral.
  on Monday na segunda.
  The radio is not on. O rádio não está ligado.
once uma vez.
  once and for all uma vez por tôdas (todas).
  at once imediatamente.
  all at once de repente, sùbitamente.
one (numeral) um, uma.
one se, um.
  one by one um por um.
  this one êste (este).
  the blue one o azul.
oneself si, se, si mesmo.
one-way de uma só mão (de um sentido, sentido
único) (traffic).
onion cebola.
only adj. só, único.
only adv. só, sòmente, apenas.
opaque opaco.
open aberto.
  open air ar livre.
open (to) abrir.
opening abertura.
opera ópera.
operate (to) funcionar, operar; fazer funcionar.
operation operação.
opinion opinião.
  in my opinion a meu ver.
opponent oponente, antagonista.
opportune oportuno.
opportunity oportunidade.
oppose opor-se, resistir.
opposite oposto, contrário.
opposition oposição.
oppress oprimir.
oppression opressão.
optic óptico, ótico (óptico).

optician óptico, ótico (óptico).
optimism otimismo (optimismo).
optimistic otimista (optimista).
or ou.
oracle oráculo.
oral oral, verbal.
orange laranja.
oratory oratória.
orchard pomar.
orchestra orquestra.
order ordem, pedido (of goods).
  in order that a fim de que, para que.
order (to) mandar, comandar; pedir, encomendar
(goods).
ordinal ordinal.
  ordinal number número ordinal.
ordinarily ordinàriamente, geralmente.
ordinary ordinário, usual.
organ órgão.
organic orgânico.
organism organismo.
organization organização.
organize organizar.
organizer organizador.
orient oriente.
oriental oriental.
origin origem, princípio.
original original.
originality originalidade.
originate (to) originar, criar.
ornament ornamento, adôrno (adorno).
orphan órfão.
ostentation ostentação, pompa.
other outro, outra, outros, outras.
  the other day o outro dia.
  the others os outros.
  Give me the other one. Dê-me o outro.
ought dever.
  You ought not to do it. Você não devia
    fazê-lo.
ounce onça.
our, ours nosso, nossa, nossos, nossas,
o nosso, a nossa, os nossos, as nossas.
out fora.
  out of breath sem fôlego, esbaforido.
  out of date antiquado, fora de moda.
  out of doors ao ar livre.
  out of order desarranjado, enguiçado.
  out of place fora do seu lugar, deslocado;
    inoportuno.
  out of print esgotado.
  out of respect for por respeito a.
  out of style fora de moda.
  out of work sem trabalho, desempregado.
outcome resultado.
outdoor(s) ao ar livre.
outline esbôço (esboço), esquema, contôrno
(contorno), croqui Ⓑ.
outline (to) esboçar, delinear.
output produção, rendimento.
outrage n. ultraje.
outrageous ultrajante, excessivo.
outside externo, exterior; fora, fora de.
outstanding saliente, eminente, extraordinário;
pendente, a pagar (to be paid).
outward externo, exterior; aparente.
  outward bound rumo ao exterior.
oven forno.
over sôbre (sobre), por cima de; ao outro lado;
mais de; por; em.
  overnight durante a noite.
  to stay over the weekend passar o fim de
    semana.
  to be over ter passado; acabar-se;
    terminar-se.
  all over por tôda (toda) parte.

all the world over (over the whole world) por todo o mundo.
over again outra vez, mais uma vez.
over and over repetidas vêzes (vezes).
overcoat sobretudo.
overcome (to) vencer, superar, conquistar.
overflow (to) transbordar.
overseas ultramarino, de ultramar.
oversight inadvertência, descuido.
overtake alcançar.
overwhelm subjugar, dominar, esmagar.
overwhelming esmagador, irresistível.
overwork trabalho excessivo, trabalho em excesso.
overwork (to) trabalhar demais, fazer trabalhar demais.
owe dever.
owing to devido a.
owl coruja.
own próprio.
This is your own. Isto é o seu.
I'll do it on my own. Eu farei por minha própria conta.
our own (o) nosso próprio.
own (to) possuir, ter, ser dono de.
owner dono, proprietário.
ox boi.
oyster ostra.

P

pace passo.
pack (to) empacotar, carregar, fazer a mala.
package pacote, embrulho.
packing n. embalagem.
paddle remo de tipo para canoa.
paddle (to) remar.
page página.
pail balde.
pain n. dor.
painful doloroso, penoso.
paint pintura, tinta de pintar.
paint (to) pintar.
painter pintor.
painting pintura, quadro.
pair n. par; casal; parelha.
pajamas pijama.
palace palácio.
palate palato, paladar.
pale adj. pálido.
to turn pale empalidecer.
paleness palidez, palor.
palm palma (of the hand).
palm tree palmeira.
pamphlet panfleto.
pan panela, caçarola.
pancake panqueca.
pane vidraça.
panel painel.
panic pânico.
pant (to) ofegar, palpitar.
pantry copa, despensa.
pants calças.
papa papai, papá.
paper papel.
writing paper, papel de escrever.
newspaper jornal, diário.
paperback brochura, livro brochado.
parade parada, desfile.
paradise paraíso.
paragraph parágrafo.
parallel adj. paralelo.
paralysis paralisia.
paralyze paralisar.

parcel pacote, embrulho.
parcel post encomenda postal.
pardon perdão.
I beg your pardon. Perdoe(-me). Desculpe(-me).
pardon (to) perdoar, desculpar.
parentheses parêntese, parêntesis.
parents pais.
parish paróquia, freguesia.
park parque.
park (to) estacionar.
parking estacionamento.
parliament parlamento.
parliamentary parlamentar.
parlor sala, salão.
parrot papagaio.
parsley salsa.
part parte.
a great (large) part of, most of a maior parte de.
for my part de minha parte.
he did his part êle (ele) cumpriu com o seu dever.
to play the part (role) of desempenhar o papel de.
partial parcial.
partiality parcialidade.
partially parcialmente.
participant participante.
participle particípio.
particular adj. particular.
particularly particularmente.
partly em parte, parcialmente.
partner sócio, companheiro.
party partido (political); festa, recepção (social, entertainment).
pass passagem; passe (permit).
pass (to) passar; ser aprovado (in an exam).
passage passagem.
passenger passageiro, viajante.
passerby transeunte.
passion paixão (x = sh).
passive passivo.
passport passaporte.
past prep. além de, depois de.
half past two as duas e meia.
past adj. passado.
the past year o ano passado.
past n. passado.
paste pasta, massa; cola, grude (for sticking).
pastime passatempo, diversão.
pastry pasteleria.
past tense pretérito, pretérito perfeito.
patent patente.
paternal paternal, paterno.
path caminho, senda, trilha.
patience paciência.
patient adj. paciente.
patient n. paciente.
patriot patriota.
patriotic patriótico.
patriotism patriotismo.
pave pavimentar.
to pave the way abrir caminho.
pavement pavimento.
pavilion pavilhão.
paw pata.
pawn (to) penhorar, empenhar.
pawnshop casa de penhores.
pay pagamento, paga, ordenado, salário.
pay (to) pagar; prestar (attention); fazer (a visit).
to pay attention prestar atenção.
to pay a call fazer uma visita.

to pay in installments pagar a prestações.
to pay on account pagar por conta.
to prepay pagar adiantado.
to pay dear (dearly) pagar caro.
payment pagamento, paga.
pea ervilha.
peace paz.
peach pêssego, pessegueiro.
peanut amendoim.
pear pêra, pereira (tree).
pearl pérola.
peasant camponês.
peculiar peculiar.
peddler vendedor ambulante, bufarinheiro, mascate Ⓑ.
pedestal pedestal, base.
pedestrian pedestre.
peel cascar.
peel (to) descascar, pelar.
peg cavilha, prego de madeira.
pen pena de escrever, caneta.
penalty pena; multa (fine).
pencil lápis.
penetrate penetrar.
penetration penetração.
peninsula península.
pension pensão.
pensive pensativo.
people gente, povo.
many people muita gente.
people say dizem, diz-se.
pepper pimenta.
perceive perceber.
per cent por cento.
percentage percentagem, porcentagem.
perfect adj. perfeito.
perfection perfeição.
perform executar (x = z), levar a cabo, realizar.
performance execução (x = z), cumprimento; representação (theatre).
perfume perfume.
perfume (to) perfumar.
perhaps talvez, quiçá.
period período; ponto (punctuation).
periodical periódico.
perish perecer.
permanent permanente.
permanently permanentemente.
permission permissão, licença.
permit (to) permitir.
perpendicular perpendicular.
persecute perseguir, oprimir.
persecution persecução, perseguição, opressão.
persistent persistente.
person pessoa.
personal pessoal.
personality personalidade.
personally pessoalmente.
personnel pessoal.
persuade persuadir.
persuasion persuasão.
persuasive persuasivo.
pertaining pertencente, relativo.
pessimist pessimista.
pessimistic pessimista.
petal pétala.
petition petição.
petroleum petróleo.
petty insignificante, trivial, pequeno.
petty cash dinheiro para despesas menores.
pharmacist farmacêutico.
pharmacy farmácia.

phase fase.
phenomenon fenômeno (fenómeno).
philosopher filósofo.
philosophical filosófico.
philosophy filosofia.
phone n. telefone.
phone (to) telefonar.
phonograph fonógrafo.
photograph fotografia.
photograph (to) fotografar.
   to take a photograph tirar uma fotografia.
physical físico.
physician médico.
physics física.
piano piano.
pick picareta (tool); escolha (choice).
pick (to) escolher (choose).
   to pick up pegar, apanhar; acelerar (speed); melhorar, convalescer (health); arrumar (tidy up); captar, sintonizar (radio).
   to have a bone to pick with ter conta a ajustar com.
   to pick on atormentar, perseguir.
pickle pepino em escabeche, picles pl. Ⓑ.
picnic piquenique.
picture quadro, foto, fotografia.
   She is the picture of her mother. Ela é a imagem da mãe.
   to take a picture tirar uma fotografia.
picturesque pitoresco.
pie pastel, torta.
piece pedaço, parte.
pier cais, molhe.
pig porco.
pigeon pombo.
pill pílula.
pillow travesseiro.
pilot pilôto (piloto).
pin n. alfinête (alfinete).
pinch beliscar.
pineapple abacaxi (ananás).
pink côr (cor) de rosa.
pipe cachimbo (smoking); tubo, cano.
pistol pistola.
pitch piche (tar); inclinação.
pitcher jarro, cântaro (for water, etc.); lançador (baseball).
pitiful lastimável.
pity pena, piedade, compaixão (x = sh).
   It's a pity. É pena. É uma pena.
   What a pity! Que pena!
   to feel pity for compadecer-se de.
pity (to) ter pena de, compadecer-se de.
place lugar, posição.
   in the first place em primeiro lugar.
   in the next place em segundo lugar.
   in place no seu lugar.
   in place of em lugar de, em vez de.
   out of place fora do seu lugar.
   to take place ter lugar.
place (to) colocar, pôr.
plain plano, liso; simples; franco.
   the plain truth a pura verdade.
plan plano, projeto (projecto).
plan (to) planejar, projetar (projectar).
planet planêta (planeta).
plant planta.
plant (to) plantar.
plantation plantação.
planter plantador, fazendeiro, lavrador.
plaster embôço (emboço); gêsso (gesso).
plastic plástico.
plate prato (food); chapa, lâmina (metal in sheets); chapa (photography).
   a plate of soup um prato de sopa.

plateau planalto.
platform plataforma.
play jôgo (jogo) (game); peça (theatre).
play (to) jogar (sports); tocar (music); brincar (games, recreation); representar (theatre).
   to play a part representar, fazer um papel.
   to play a game jogar uma partida.
   to play a joke on pregar uma peça em.
player jogador.
playful brincalhão.
playground pátio de recreio.
plea rôgo (rogo), apêlo (apelo), argumento, pleito (law).
plead (to) rogar, suplicar; pleitear (law).
pleasant agradável, amável.
please (to) agradar, dar prazer a.
   I'm pleased. Estou satisfeito. Estou contente.
   It pleases me. Agrada-me.
   It doesn't please me. Não me agrada.
   He was quite pleased. Êle (ele) ficou contente.
   please faça o favor de (de), tenha a bondade (de), queira.
   Please tell me. Faça o favor de me dizer (dizer-me).
   Pleased to meet you. Prazer em conhecê-lo.
pleasing agradável, amável.
pleasure prazer, gôsto (gosto).
plenty abundância.
plot n. conspiração, intriga (scheme); lote ⒷⒷ, pedaço de terra (land), trama, enrêdo (enredo) (novel, etc.).
plow arado.
plug tomada (electric plug).
plum ameixa (x = sh).
plumber bombeiro, encanador.
plumbing encanamento.
plump gordo, rechonchudo.
plural plural.
plus mais.
pocket bôlso (bolso) (algibeira).
poem poema.
poet poeta.
poetic poético.
poetry poesia.
point ponto; ponta (of a pin, etc.).
   point of view ponto de vista.
   cardinal points pontos cardeais.
point (to) apontar, indicar.
pointed pontudo, agudo.
poise porte, equilíbrio.
poison veneno.
poison (to) envenenar.
poisonous venenoso.
polar polar.
pole poste, vara; pólo (of the earth).
police polícia.
policeman polícia, policial, guarda.
police station pôsto (posto), policial (esquadra).
policy política (of a government); costume, plano; apólice (insurance).
polish polimento, lustro; graxa (x = sh) (for shoes).
   shoe polish graxa para sapatos.
polish (to) polir, lustrar; engraxar (x = sh) (shoes).
polite cortês.
political político.
politician político.
politics política.
pond lagoa.
pool piscina (for swimming).
poor pobre.
pope papa.

poppy papoula.
popular popular.
population população.
porch pórtico, varanda.
pork carne de porco.
pork chop costeleta de porco.
port pôrto (porto), vinho do Pôrto (Porto).
portable portátil.
porter porteiro (of building); carregador.
portion porção, parte.
portrait retrato.
Portuguese português.
position posição.
positive positivo.
positively certamente, positivamente.
possess possuir.
possession possessão, posse.
   to take possession of tomar posse de.
possessor possessor.
possibility possibilidade.
possible possível.
   as soon as possible o mais cedo possível.
possibly possìvelmente, talvez.
post n. poste; correio (mail); pôsto (posto) guarnição (military).
   postcard cartão postal, bilhete postal.
   post office correio.
postage porte.
postage stamp sêlo (selo) postal.
posterity posteridade.
postman carteiro.
postscript pós-escrito.
pot panela, pote, caçarola.
potato batata.
   fried potatoes batatas fritas.
   mashed potatoes purê (puré) de batatas.
pound libra.
pour verter, vazar, despejar; chover a cântaros (rain).
poverty pobreza.
powder pó; pó de arroz (for face); pólvora (gunpowder).
power poder, fôrça (força), potência.
   electric power fôrça elétrica (eléctrica).
   horsepower cavalo-vapor.
   the great powers as grandes potências.
   power of attorney procuração.
powerful poderoso.
practicable praticável.
practical prático.
practice prática; uso, costume (usage); desempenho (of a profession).
practice (to) praticar; desempenhar (a profession).
praise elogio, louvor.
praise (to) elogiar, louvar.
prank peça, brincadeira, travessura.
pray rezar, orar; suplicar.
prayer oração; súplica.
precede preceder.
precedent precedente.
preceding precedente.
precept preceito.
precious precioso, de grande valor.
precipice precipício.
precise preciso, exato (exacto) (x = z).
precisely precisamente, exatamente (exactamente) (x = z).
precision precisão.
precocious precoce.
predecessor antecessor.
predicament apuro.
predict predizer, profetizar.

prediction predição, profecia.
predominant predominante.
preface prefácio.
prefer preferir.
preferable preferível.
preferably preferívelmenta, de preferência.
preference preferência.
prejudice n. preconceito.
preliminary preliminar.
premature prematuro.
preparation preparação.
prepare preparar.
preposition preposição.
prescribe prescrever; receitar (medicine).
prescription receita (medicine).
presence presença.
present presente, oferta.
   at present atualmente (actualmente).
   for the present por agora.
   present participle particípio presente.
   present-day atual (actual).
   the present month o corrente.
   to give a present fazer presente, dar de presente.
   to be present estar presente.
present (to) apresentar (introduce); dar de presente, ofertar.
presentation apresentação.
presentiment pressentimento.
preservation preservação, conservação.
preserve preservar, conservar.
preside presidir.
president presidente.
press prensa, imprensa.
   in the press no prelo.
press (to) apertar; passar a ferro (clothes); insistir, urgir (to urge).
pressing adj. urgente.
pressure pressão.
prestige prestígio.
presumable presumível.
presume presumir, supor.
pretend fingir, pretender.
pretense pretensão, pretexto, simulação.
   under the pretense of sob o pretexto de.
   under false pretenses sob falsos pretextos.
pretension pretensão, pretexto.
preterit, preterite pretérito.
pretext pretexto.
pretty adj. belo, bonito, lindo.
pretty adv. um tanto, bastante, um pouco.
   pretty tired um tanto cansado.
   pretty good bastante bom.
   pretty much quase (almost).
   pretty much the same quase o mesmo.
prevail (to) prevalecer, predominar.
   to prevail over vencer, triunfar.
   to prevail upon persuadir, convencer.
prevent prevenir, impedir.
prevention prevenção, impedimento.
previous prévio.
previously prèviamente, antes.
   previous to antes de.
price preço.
pride orgulho.
priest padre, sacerdote.
primarily principalmente, em primeiro lugar.
primary primário, principal (first, principal); elementar (elementary).
   primary color côr (cor) primária.
   primary school escola primária.
prince príncipe.
principal principal.
principally principalmente.

principle princípio.
   in principle em princípio.
print (to) imprimir, publicar.
printed impresso, publicado.
   printed matter impressos.
printer impressor, tipógrafo.
prior adj. anterior, precedente, prévio.
   prior to antes de.
prison prisão, cadeia, cárcere.
prisoner prisoneiro, prêso (preso).
private privado, particular, pessoal, confidencial, reservado, secreto.
   private office escritório particular.
   private secretary secretária particular.
   in private em segrêdo (segredo), secretamente.
privately em segrêdo (segredo), confidencialmente.
privilege privilégio.
prize prêmio (prémio).
pro pro.
probability probabilidade.
probable provável.
probably provàvelmente.
problem problema.
procedure procedimento.
proceed seguir, prosseguir, continuar.
process processo, procedimento, método (method); curso, marcha (of time); citação (law).
   in the process of no decurso de.
procession procissão, cortejo.
proclaim proclamar.
proclamation proclamação.
produce produzir, fabricar, render.
product produto.
production produção.
productive produtivo.
profession profissão.
professional profissional.
professor professor.
proficient proficiente, competente.
profile perfil.
profit benefício, ganho, lucro.
profit (to) tirar proveito, ganhar.
profitable proveitoso, lucrativo.
program programa.
progress progresso.
progressive progressivo.
prohibit proibir.
prohibition proibição.
project projeto (projecto), plano.
project (to) projetar (projectar), planejar.
prolong prolongar.
prominent proeminente, saliente.
promise promessa.
promise (to) prometer.
promote promover, elevar (in grade); fomentar, incentivar (industry, etc.).
promotion promoção, elevação; fomento.
prompt pronto, preparado; pontual.
promptly prontamente.
promptness prontidão, pontualidade.
pronoun pronome.
pronounce pronunciar.
pronunciation pronúncia.
proof prova.
propaganda propaganda.
propeller hélice.
proper próprio, correto (correcto), apropriado.
properly pròpriamente, corretamente (correctamente).
property propriedade; bens.

prophecy profecia, predição.
prophesy profetizar, predizer.
proportion proporção.
   in proportion em proporção.
   out of proportion fora de proporção, desproporcionado.
proposal proposta, oferta.
propose propor, sugerir.
proprietor proprietário, dono.
prosaic prosaico.
prose prosa.
prosper prosperar.
prosperity prosperidade.
prosperous próspero.
protect proteger.
protection proteção (protecção).
protector protetor (protector).
protest protesto.
protest (to) protestar.
Protestant protestante.
proud orgulhoso, soberbo.
prove estabelecer, provar, demonstrar; revelar-se, mostrar-se (to turn out).
proverb provérbio, rifão.
provide prover, fornecer.
   to provide oneself with prover-se de.
   provided that sempre que, contanto que.
providence providência.
province província.
provincial provinciano.
provisions mantimentos, víveres.
prudence prudência.
prudent prudente.
psychologic psicológico.
psychology psicologia.
public público.
publication publicação.
publicity publicidade.
publish publicar.
publisher editor.
publishing house casa editôra (editora).
pudding pudim.
pull (to) tirar, puxar (x = sh).
   to pull in chegar, entrar (train).
   to pull out sair, partir (train).
   to pull apart separar, romper.
   to pull through sair bem.
pulpit púlpito.
pulse pulso.
pump bomba.
punctual pontual.
punctuate pontuar.
punctuation pontuação.
puncture n. punctura (puntura).
punish castigar, punir.
punishment castigo, punição.
pupil aluno (school); pupila (eye).
purchase compra.
purchase (to) comprar.
purchaser comprador.
pure puro.
purely puramente, simplesmente.
purple púrpura.
purpose propósito, fim, finalidade, objetivo (objectivo), intenção.
   on purpose de propósito.
   to no purpose inùtilmente, em vão.
   for the purpose of com o fim de.
   With what purpose? Com que finalidade?
purse bôlsa (bolsa).
pursue perseguir, prosseguir.
pursuit perseguição, procura.
push empurrar.

put (to) pôr, colocar.
  to put away guardar, pôr de lado.
  to put in order pôr em ordem.
  to put off adiar.
  to put up for sale pôr à venda.
  to put up with suportar, agüentar (aguentar).
  to put on vestir, pôr.
  to put out apagar (a light); publicar (a book).
  to put to bed pôr na cama, fazer deitar.
  to put to sleep pôr na cama, fazer dormir.
  to put together juntar.
  to put to a vote submeter a votação.
puzzle n. enigma, problema; quebra-cabeça.
puzzled (be) estar perplexo (x = ks).

Q

quaint curioso, raro, singular.
qualify qualificar.
quality qualidade.
quantity quantidade.
quarrel briga, disputa.
quart quarto.
quarter quarto, quarta parte.
  a quarter hour um quarto de hora.
quarters alojamento; quartel (military).
queen rainha.
queer estranho, esquisito, raro.
quell esmagar, sufocar.
quench apagar, reprimir.
question pergunta.
  to ask a question fazer uma pergunta.
  to be a question of tratar-se de, ser uma questão de.
  question mark ponto de interrogação.
  What's the question? De que se trata?
  without any question sem dúvida.
  to be out of the question ser impossível.
quick ligeiro, rápido.
quickly ràpidamente, depressa.
quiet quieto, sossegado, tranqüilo (tranquilo).
quietly quietamente, tranqüilamente (tranquila-mente).
quietness quietude.
quilt colcha, acolchoado.
quinine quinina.
quit deixar (x = sh), parar, cessar, desistir.
  to quit work deixar de trabalhar.
quite completamente, muito, realmente, bem.
  quite good muito bom.
  quite soon bem cedo.
  quite difficult bem difícil.
  quite well done muito bem feito.
  She seems quite different. Ela parece outra.
quotation citação, cotação.
  quotation marks aspas.
quote (to) citar.

R

rabbit coelho.
race raça (ethnic); corrida, carreira.
racial racial.
radiance brilho, esplendor.
radiant radiante, brilhante.
radiator radiador.
radio rádio.
radio set aparelho de rádio.
radio station estação de rádio, radioemissora.
radish rabanete.
radium rádio.
rag trapo, farrapo.
rage raiva, ira.
ragged esfarrapado, surrado.
rail barreira, barra; trilho (train).
railroad estrada de ferro (caminho de ferro), ferrovia.
  railroad coach vagão.

rain chuva.
rain (to) chover.
rainbow arco-íris.
raincoat impermeável.
rainfall chuva.
rainy chuvoso.
raise aumento.
raise (to) levantar, elevar; aumentar, subir (prices, salary); criar (bring up); cultivar (a crop).
  to raise an objection levantar uma objeção (objecção), objetar (objectar).
  to raise Cain provocar desordem.
  to raise money arranjar dinheiro.
raisin passa de uva.
rake ancinho.
rake (to) usar ancinho.
ranch fazenda, estância.
range alcance, raio de ação (acção); cadeia (mountains).
rank pôsto (posto) (military, etc.); fileira (line of soldiers); posição.
  rank and file soldados rasos; gente comum.
rapid rápido.
rapidly ràpidamente.
rare raro.
rarely raramente.
rascal velhaco.
rash adj. precipitado, temerário.
rash n. erupção.
rat rato.
rate preço, taxa (x = sh).
  at the rate of à razão de.
  rate of exchange taxa de câmbio.
  at any rate de qualquer maneira.
rather um pouco, antes, muito, um tanto.
  rather expensive um tanto caro, muito caro.
  rather than em vez de.
ratio proporção, razão.
ration ração.
rational racional.
raw cru.
  raw materials matérias primas.
ray raio.
rayon sêda (seda) artificial.
razor navalha; gilete (safety razor).
  razor blade lâmina (de navalha).
reach alcance (range).
  out of reach fora do alcance.
  within reach ao alcance.
reach (to) alcançar, chegar a, chegar até.
  to reach the end terminar, chegar ao fim, conseguir o objetivo (objectivo).
  to reach out one's hand estender a mão.
react reagir.
reaction reação (reacção).
reactionary reacionário (reaccionário).
read (to) ler.
readable legível.
reader leitor.
reading leitura.
reading room gabinete de leitura.
ready pronto, disposto.
ready-made feito, já feito.
ready-made clothes roupa feita.
real real, verdadeiro.
  real estate bens imóveis.
realist realista.
reality realidade.
realization realização; compreensão.
realize (to) dar-se conta de, compreender; realizar, conseguir (obtain, achieve), levar a cabo.
  to realize a danger dar-se conta do perigo.
  to realize a project levar a cabo um projeto (projecto).

  to realize a profit tirar proveito, tirar lucro.
really de fato (facto), realmente.
reap segar, colher (colher).
rear adj. traseiro, posterior.
rear n. parte traseira, fundo.
reason razão, motivo, causa.
  by reason of por causa de.
  for this reason por isto.
  without reason sem razão.
reason (to) raciocinar, pensar.
reasonable razoável, módico.
reasonably razoàvelmente, moderadamente.
reasoning raciocínio.
rebel rebelde.
rebel (to) rebelar-se, revoltar-se.
rebellion rebelião, revolta.
rebellious rebelde, revoltoso.
recall (to) lembrar, recordar.
receipt recibo, recebimento.
  to acknowledge acusar o recebimento.
receipts receitas, entradas.
receive receber.
receiver recebedor, destinatário.
recent recente.
recently recentemente.
reception recepção, recebimento, acolhimento.
recipe receita.
recite recitar.
reckless temerário, imprudente.
recklessly temeràriamente, imprudentemente.
recline reclinar, recostar.
recognition reconhecimento.
recognize reconhecer.
recollect recordar, lembrar (to remember).
recollection recordação, lembrança.
recommend recomendar.
recommendation recomendação.
reconcile reconciliar, harmonizar.
reconciliation reconciliação.
record n. registro; disco (phonograph); recorde Ⓑ (sports); evidência.
  on record registrado.
records arquivo, anais.
recover recuperar, recobrar.
recovery recuperação, cura.
recreation recreio, divertimento, passatempo.
recuperate recuperar-se, restabelecer-se.
red vermelho.
  Red Cross Cruz Vermelha.
reduce reduzir, diminuir.
reduction redução, abatimento desconto (prices).
refer referir.
reference referência.
  reference book livro de consulta.
refine refinar.
refinement refinação, cultura.
reflect refletir (reflectir), pensar.
reflection reflexão (x = ks), reflexo (x = ks).
reflexive reflexivo (x = ks).
reform reforma.
reform (to) reformar, corrigir.
refrain (from) abster-se de.
refresh refrescar.
  to refresh one's memory trazer à memória, lembrar-se de.
refreshment refrêsco (refresco).
refrigerator refrigerador, geladeira.
refuge refúgio, asilo, amparo.
refugee refugiado.
refusal recusa.
refuse recusar, negar.
refute refutar.

regard consideração, respeito, estima.
  in regard to com referência a.
  in this regard a êsse respeito, neste respeito.
  with regard to com referência a.
  without any regard to sem nenhuma consideração para.
regard (to) considerar, estimar, julgar.
regarding com respeito a, quanto a.
regardless of embora, ainda que, não obstante.
regards lembranças, cumprimentos.
  lembranças a regards to.
regime regime.
regiment regimento.
region região, área.
register registro.
register (to) registrar, registar, inscrever.
  registered letter carta registrada.
regret pesar, pena, arrependimento.
regret (to) sentir, deplorar, lamentar.
  I regret it very much. Sinto(-o) muito.
  I regret that Sinto que.
regular regular.
regularity regularidade.
regularly regularmente.
regulation regulamento, regra, ordem.
rehearsal ensaio.
rehearse ensaiar.
reign reinado, reino.
reign (to) reinar.
reject rejeitar, repelir, recusar.
rejection rejeição, recusa.
rejoice alegrar, regozijar.
rejoicing regozijo, alegria, júbilo.
relate relatar, narrar, contar; relacionar.
  everything relating to quanto se relaciona com.
relation relação; parente (a relative).
relationship relação; parentesco (family).
relative adj. relativo, concernente.
relative parente (family).
release (to) soltar, libertar, permitir (publication, etc.).
reliability confiança.
reliable de confiança.
relief alívio (from pain); socorro, auxílio (aid).
religion religião.
religious religioso.
relish (to) gostar de; condimentar.
reluctance relutância, resistência.
reluctant relutante, hesitante.
reluctantly de má vontade, relutantemente.
rely on (to) confiar em, contar com.
remain ficar, permanecer, restar.
  to remain silent ficar quieto, calar.
  to remain undone ficar por fazer.
remains restos.
remark observação, comentário.
  to make a remark fazer um comentário.
remark (to) observar, comentar, notar.
remarkable notável, extraordinário.
remarkably notàvelmente.
remedy remédio.
remedy (to) remediar, corrigir.
remember lembrar, lembrar-se, recordar.
  I don't remember. Não me lembro.
  Remember me to him. Dê-lhe (as) minhas lembranças.
remembrance lembrança.
remind lembrar.
reminder lembrança.
remit remeter.
remorse remorso.
removal remoção, demissão.

remove mudar (to another place); demitir (from a job).
renew renovar, recomeçar.
  to renew a subscription renovar uma assinatura.
rent aluguel, renda.
  for rent aluga-se.
rent (to) alugar.
repair consêrto (conserto).
  in good repair em bom estado.
repair (to) consertar.
repeal (to) revogar, anular.
repeat repetir.
repeatedly repetidamente.
repetition repetição.
reply resposta, réplica.
reply (to) responder, replicar.
report relatório, informação.
report (to) informar, comunicar, fazer relatório; denunciar (to the police).
  it is reported diz-se que, dizem que.
reporter repórter, jornalista.
represent representar.
representation representação.
representative representante, agente, deputado.
reproach censura, repreensão.
reproach (to) censurar, repreender.
reproduce reproduzir.
reproduction reprodução.
reptile réptil.
republic república.
republican republicano.
reputation reputação, renome, fama.
request pedido, petição.
request (to) pedir, rogar.
rescue salvamento.
rescue (to) salvar, socorrer.
resemblance semelhança.
resemble (to) parecer-se com.
  Êle (ele) se parece com o pai. He looks like his father.
resent ressentir-se.
reservation reserva, reservação; restrição.
reserve reserva.
  without reserve sem reserva.
reserve (to) reservar.
reside morar, residir, viver.
residence residência, domicílio.
resident residente.
resign demitir-se; resignar-se (to resign oneself).
resignation resignação, renúncia, demissão.
resist resistir, opor-se.
resistance resistência, oposição.
resolute resoluto, determinado.
resolution resolução, solução.
resolve resolver, determinar, decidir.
resource recurso.
respect respeito.
  in this respect neste respeito.
  with respect to com respeito a.
  with due respect com todo respeito.
  in all respects em todo sentido, sob todos os pontos de vista.
  in every respect em todo sentido.
respect (to) respeitar, estimar.
respectable respeitável.
respectful respeitoso.
  respectfully yours atenciosamente.
respective respectivo.
response resposta, réplica.
responsibility responsabilidade.
responsible responsável, de confiança.

a responsible person uma pessoa de confiança.
rest resto (what is left over); descanso, repouso (when tired).
rest (to) descansar, repousar.
restaurant restaurante.
restful sossegado, tranquilo (tranquilo).
restless inquieto, impaciente.
restore (to) restaurar, restabelecer.
restrict limitar, confinar.
result resultado, consequência (consequência).
result (to) resultar.
  to result in acabar em, terminar em, resultar em.
retail venda a retalho, venda a varejo.
retire (to) retirar, retirar-se, reformar-se; deitar-se (to go to bed).
retail (to) vender a retalho, vender a varejo.
return volta.
  in return for em troca de.
  by return mail à volta do correio.
  return trip viagem de volta.
  Many happy returns! Felicitações!
return (to) voltar, regressar; devolver (to return something).
  to return a book devolver um livro.
  to return a favor retribuir um favor.
  to return home voltar para casa.
review revista; revisão, repasso (going over); exame (x = z).
review (to) rever, revisar, repassar; criticar (criticism).
revise revisar.
revision revisão.
revive ressucitar, restaurar, animar.
revolt revolta, sublevação.
revolt (to) revoltar(-se), rebelar(-se).
revolution revolução.
reward recompensa, prêmio (prémio).
reward (to) recompensar, premiar.
rhyme rima.
rhythm ritmo.
rib costela (of the body).
ribbon fita.
rice arroz.
rich rico; sazonado (food).
riches riquezas, bens.
riddle adivinha, enigma.
ride passeio, viagem.
ride (to) montar a cavalo passear a cavalo (on horseback); viajar.
ridiculous ridículo.
rifle rifle.
right adj. direito; justo (just); correto (correcto); adequado.
  the right man o homem certo.
  right hand mão direita.
  the right time a hora certa.
  right or wrong com razão ou sem razão.
  right side lado direito.
  Is this right? Está certo?
  It's right. Está certo.
  to be right ter razão.
right direito.
  to be in the right ter razão.
  to the right à direita.
  keep to the right conserve a sua direita.
  to have a right ter direito.
  by rights de direito.
right adv. bem; certo; certamente; justamente; perfeitamente; mesmo.
  right here aqui mesmo.
  right away imediatamente, já.
  right now agora mesmo.
  all right está bem, bem.
  Everything is all right. Tudo vai bem.
  Go right ahead. Siga sempre em frente.

right along sem parar.
to know right well saber perfeitamente bem.
ring anel (for finger).
ring (to) tocar, soar (bells).
riot motim, desordem, revolta.
riot (to) levantar-se, amotinar-se, revoltar-se.
ripe maduro.
ripen amadurecer.
rise n. subida, aumento.
sunrise nascer do sol, levantar do sol.
rise (to) subir; levantar-se (to get up); sair (sun); revoltar-se (revolt); aumentar (salary).
risk risco, perigo.
to run a risk correr um perigo, arriscar.
risk (to) arriscar.
river rio.
road estrada, caminho.
main road estrada principal, caminho principal.
roar rugido, berro.
roar (to) rugir, berrar.
roast assado.
roast beef rosbife.
roast (to) assar.
rob roubar.
robber ladrão.
robbery roubo, furto.
rock rocha, rochedo, pedra.
rock (to) balançar, embalar (to sleep).
rocket foguete, projetil, projétil (projéctil).
rocking chair cadeira de balanço.
roll rôlo (rolo); pão, pãozinho (bread).
roll (to) enrolar, rolar.
romance romance, novela; aventura amorosa.
romantic romântico.
roof teto (tecto).
room sala, quarto, peça (divisão).
to make room dar lugar, fazer lugar.
There's not enough room. Não há bastante espaço.
There's not enough room in the trunk for all my clothes. Tôda (toda) (a) minha roupa não cabe no baú.
There's no room for doubt. Não cabe dúvida.
dining room sala de jantar.
rooster galo.
root raiz.
rooted enraizado, radicado.
rope corda.
to be at the end of one's rope estar numa situação difícil, estar sem recursos, estar na última.
rose rosa.
rosebush roseira.
rotary giratório, rotativo.
rotary press rotativa.
rouge ruge, carmim.
rough áspero.
rough draft rascunho.
round adj. redondo.
a round table uma mesa redonda.
round number número redondo.
round trip viagem de ida e volta.
all year round o ano todo.
route rota, rumo, caminho, curso.
routine rotina.
row fila, fileira (rank, file); desordem, agitação, briga (brawl).
row (to) remar.
rub (to) esfregar, friccionar.
rubber borracha.
rude rude, descortês.
rudeness rudeza, grosseria.
rug tapête (tapete).
ruin ruína.

rule regra, norma; reinado, domínio (reign).
as a rule em regra.
to be the rule ser regra, ser uso.
rule (to) governar, mandar (to govern); determinar (court).
to rule out excluir, eliminar.
to rule over governar.
ruler governador, administrador; régua (for drawing lines).
rumor rumor.
run correr; andar, funcionar (a watch, a machine, etc.).
to run across encontrar, dar com.
to run into encontrar-se com.
to run away escapar, fugir.
to run the risk of correr o risco de, arriscar.
to run up and down correr de cá para lá (acolá).
to run a business dirigir um negócio.
rural rural.
rush pressa (haste).
in a rush depressa.
rush (to) ir depressa, apressar-se.
to rush in entrar correndo, entrar precipitadamente.
to rush through fazer depressa.
Russian russo.
rusty ferrugento, enferrujado.
rye centeio.

S

Sabbath dia de descanso.
saccharine sacarina.
sack saco, saca.
sacred sagrado, sacro.
sacrifice sacrifício.
sacrifice (to) sacrificar.
sad triste.
saddle sela.
sadly tristemente.
sadness tristeza.
safe cofre, caixa (x = sh) forte.
safe adj. seguro; salvo, ileso (unhurt); sem perigo (safe from danger); sem risco (safe from risk).
safe and sound são e salvo.
Safe trip. Feliz viagem. Boa viagem.
safely a salvo.
safety segurança.
safety razor aparelho para fazer a barba, gilete.
sail vela; barco a vela, veleiro.
sail (to) velejar, fazer à vela, navegar.
sailor marinheiro, marujo.
saint santo, são.
Saint Paul São Paulo.
Saint Barbara Santa Bárbara.
Saint Andrew Santo André.
sake causa, motivo, amor, bem, consideração.
for your sake para seu próprio bem.
for the sake of por, por amor a, por causa de.
for the sake of brevity por brevidade.
for the sake of mercy por misericórdia.
for God's sake, for the love of God por Deus, pelo amor de Deus.
salad salada.
salary salário, ordenado.
sale venda.
for sale à venda.
salesgirl caixeira, vendedora.
salesman caixeiro, vendedor.
traveling salesman caixeiro viajante.
salmon salmão.
salt sal.
salt (to) salgar, pôr sal.
saltcellar saleiro.

same mesmo, próprio, igual.
the same o mesmo, os mesmos.
It's all the same to me. Tanto faz. Para mim é o mesmo.
much the same quase o mesmo.
the same as o mesmo que, os mesmos que.
sample amostra.
sand areia.
sandpaper lixa (x = sh).
sandwich sanduíche.
sandy arenoso.
sane são.
sanitarium sanatório.
sanitary sanitário.
sanitation saneamento.
sanity sanidade mental, juízo, razão.
sap seiva; sapa (military).
sarcasm sarcasmo.
sarcastic sarcástico.
sardine sardinha.
Satan satã, satanás, diabo.
satisfaction satisfação.
satisfactorily satisfatòriamente.
satisfactory satisfatório.
satisfy satisfazer.
Saturday sábado.
sauce môlho (molho).
saucer pires.
sausage salsicha, lingüiça (linguiça).
savage selvagem.
save prep. salvo, exceto (excepto); conj. a não ser.
save (to) salvar, livrar (a person); economizar, poupar (money).
to save appearances (face) salvar as aparências.
savings economias, dinheiro economizado.
savings bank caixa (x = sh) econômica (económica).
saw serra, serrote.
say dizer.
that is to say quer dizer, isto é.
it is said diz-se, dizem.
saying dito, provérbio, rifão.
as the saying goes como diz o provérbio, como se costuma dizer.
scale n. escala; prato (the dish of a balance); escama (of fishes, etc.).
scales balança.
scalp escalpo.
scandal escândalo.
Scandinavian escandinavo.
scanty escasso, pouco, insuficiente.
scar n. cicatriz.
scarce raro, escasso.
scarcely apenas, escassamente; mal, com dificuldade.
scarcity escassez, falta.
scarf cachecol.
scarlet escarlate.
scene cena.
scenery cenário, decoração (theatre); paisagem, vista (view).
scent cheiro, aroma, odor.
schedule horário (time table); lista, programa.
scheme plano, projeto (projecto), esquema.
school escola.
schoolteacher professor.
schoolbook livro escolar.
schoolmate condiscípulo, colega.
schoolroom sala de aula.
science ciência.
scientific científico.
scientist cientista.

scissors tesoura.
scold ralhar, repreender.
score contagem, pontos; partitura (music).
score (to) fazer pontos, marcar os pontos; criticar, repreender (admonish).
scorn desdém, desprêzo (desprezo).
scorn (to) desdenhar, desprezar.
scornful desdenhoso.
Scotch escocês.
scrape (to) raspar (on a surface).
scratch arranhadura, arranhão (on the hand, etc.); raspadura (on a table, etc.).
scratch (to) arranhar (with the nails); rasgar (a table, etc.); cancelar, apagar (eliminate).
scream (to) berrar, gritar.
screen n. biombo (partition); tela (windows, movies); cortina, barreira.
screw parafuso.
screw (to) parafusar, apertar parafuso.
scruple escrúpulo.
sculptor escultor.
sculpture escultura.
sea mar, oceano.
seal sêlo (selo).
seal (to) selar; lacrar.
seam costura.
search busca, procura (act of looking for); pesquisa, investigação (research. investigation).
  in search of em procura de, em busca de.
search (to) procurar, buscar (to search for); pesquisar, investigar (to do research, to investigate); explorar (to explore).
  to search after indagar, perguntar por.
  to search for procurar, buscar.
seasick enjoado.
season estação (of the year)
  in season em voga, em época, em tempo.
  out of season fora de época, fora de tempo.
season (to) sazonar, condimentar (food).
seat n. assento.
  to take a seat sentar-se, tomar assento.
  front seat assento dianteiro.
  back seat assento traseiro.
second segundo.
  second class de segunda classe.
  second year o segundo ano.
  Wait a second! Espere um momento!
  on second thought depois de pensá-lo bem.
  second to none sem par.
secondary secundário.
secondary school escola secundária.
secondhand de segunda mão, usado.
secondly em segundo lugar.
secrecy segrêdo (segredo), reserva, silêncio.
secret secreto.
  in secret em segrêdo (segredo), secretamente.
secretary secretário, secretária.
section seção (secção).
secure seguro, certo, firme.
secure (to) assegurar; garantir; conseguir (obtain).
securely seguramente, certamente.
security segurança; garantia.
see (to) ver.
  See? Sabe? Compreende?
  I see. Já estou compreendendo. Já estou vendo.
  Let's see. Vamos ver.
  to see about averiguar, indagar.
  to see someone off despedir-se.
  to see someone home acompanhar para casa.
  to see the point perceber, compreender.
  to see a thing through terminar, levar a cabo.

to see fit achar conveniente.
  to see one's way clear ver o modo de fazer alguma coisa.
  to see to cuidar de, encarregar-se de.
seed semente.
seeing vista, ver.
  seeing that visto que, desde que.
seek (to) procurar, buscar.
seem (to) parecer.
  it seems to me parece-me.
  it seems parece.
seize agarrar (to grasp); pegar, apanhar (to get hold of, to take); apoderar-se de (to take possession of); dar-se conta de, compreender (to understand).
seldom raramente.
select adj. seleto (selecto), escolhido.
select (to) escolher, selecionar (seleccionar).
selection seleção (selecção).
self mesmo, por si mesmo; si, se.
  myself eu mesmo.
  I said to myself. Disse para mim. Eu me disse.
  yourself você mesmo; o senhor mesmo.
  himself êle (ele) mesmo.
  He said to himself. Êle (ele) disse para si. Êle se disse.
  She said to herself. Ela disse para si. Ela se disse.
  ourselves nós mesmos.
  yourselves vocês mesmos; os senhores mesmos.
  themselves êles (eles) mesmos.
  Wash yourself. Lave-se. (Láva-te. fam.).
  by himself por si mesmo.
self-conceited presunçoso.
self-confidence confiança em si mesmo.
self-defense defesa pessoal.
self-determination autodeterminação.
self-evident evidente, claro.
selfish egoísta.
selfishness egoísmo.
self-taught autodidata (autodidacta).
sell (to) vender.
semester semestre.
senate senado.
senator senador.
send (to) enviar, mandar, expedir, transmitir.
  to send away despedir, mandar embora.
  to send word mandar recado, mandar dizer.
  to send back devolver.
  to send in mandar entrar.
  to send for mandar buscar.
senior mais velho, mais antigo, superior.
sense n. sentido, senso.
  common sense senso comum.
  to be out of one's senses ter perdido o juízo.
sensible sensato, razoável, sensível.
sensibly sensatamente, sensivelmente.
sentence sentença, frase (grammar); sentença, julgamento (court).
sentence (to) sentenciar, condenar.
sentiment sentimento.
sentimental sentimental.
separate adj. separado, distinto.
  under separate cover em separado.
separate (to) separar, afastar.
separately separadamente.
separation separação.
September setembro (Setembro).
serene sereno.
sergeant sargento.
serial adj. em série, serial.
series série.
serious sério.

seriously sèriamente.
seriousness seriedade, gravidade.
sermon sermão.
servant empregado, criado.
serve (to) servir.
  to serve the purpose servir.
  to serve notice notificar, fazer saber, avisar.
  to serve one right ser bem feito, ser merecido.
  to serve as servir de.
service serviço.
  at your service às suas ordens.
  to be of service ser útil, servir.
session sessão.
set adj. fixo (x = ks), estabelecido, determinado.
  set price preço fixo.
set n. jôgo (jogo).
  set of dishes jôgo de copos.
set (to) pôr.
  to set aside pôr de lado.
  to set back impedir; atrasar (watch).
  to set free liberar.
  to set in order pôr em ordem.
  to set on fire incendiar.
  to set to work começar a trabalhar.
settle arranjar, arrumar (arrange); pagar, liquidar, saldar (an account, a debt); fixar residência, estabelecer-se (to settle down); pousar, assentar (to go down, as liquids).
  to settle an account saldar uma conta.
settlement acôrdo (acordo), entendimento (adjustment, agreement); colônia (colónia), povoação (village); colonização (colonization).
seven sete.
seventeen dezessete (dezassete).
seventeenth décimo sétimo.
seventh sétimo.
seventy setenta.
several vários, alguns.
  several times várias vêzes (vezes).
severe severo.
severity severidade, gravidade.
sew coser, costurar.
sewing costura.
sewing machine máquina de costura.
sex sexo (x = ks).
sexual sexual (x = ks).
shade sombra.
shade (to) sombrear.
shadow sombra.
shady sombroso.
shake sacudida, tremor; apêrto (aperto) de mãos (handshake); batida (drink).
shake (to) sacudir; tremer (to tremble); apertar a mão (shake hands); acenar (com a cabeça) (to nod).
shall, will (auxiliary) the future tense of the indicative is formed by adding -ei, (-ás) -á, -emos, (-eis), -ão to the infinitive.
  I shall go irei.
  you will go (fam.) (irás).
  he will go irá.
  we shall go iremos.
  you will go (ireis).
  they will go irão.
shame vergonha.
shame (to) envergonhar.
shameful vergonhoso, escandaloso.
shameless desavergonhado, sem vergonha.
shampoo xampu (x = sh), lavagem de cabeça.
shampoo (to) fazer xampu (x = sh), lavar a cabeça.
shape forma, figura, vulto.
shape (to) formar, dar forma.

share porção, parte; ação (acção) (stock).

share (to) partilhar, repartir (to apportion); participar, tomar parte em (to share in).

shareholder acionista (accionista).

sharp agudo, afiado, pontudo (sharp-pointed); cortante (sharp-edged).
   a sharp pain uma dôr (dor) aguda.
   a sharp curve uma curva fechada.
   sharp-witted esperto, inteligente.
   at two o'clock sharp as duas horas em ponto.

sharpen afiar, aguçar; apontar, fazer a ponta (a pencil).

shatter destruir, espatifar.

shave (to) barbear, fazer a barba.

shaving para fazer a barba.
   shaving brush pincel de barba.
   shaving cream creme de barbear.

shawl xale (x = sh).

she ela.

shears tesoura, tesourão.

shed coberta, abrigo, barracão.

shed (to) verter, derramar (tears, etc.).

sheep carneiro, ovelha.

sheet lençol (bed); fôlha (folha) (paper).

shelf estante, prateleira.

shell concha, carapaça; casca (egg, nut); granada, bomba (military).

shelter refúgio, abrigo.
   to take shelter abrigar-se.
   to give shelter abrigar, proteger.

shelter (to) abrigar, proteger, dar asilo.

shepherd pastor.

sheriff xerife (x = sh).

sherry xerez (x = sh).

shield escudo, defesa.

shield (to) proteger, defender, servir de escudo.

shift mudança; turma, grupo.

shift (to) mudar, cambiar.

shine (to) brilhar, iluminar; polir, lustrar (shoes, etc.).

shining brilhante, reluzente, lustroso.

shiny lustroso, brilhante.

ship navio, vapor.
   merchant ship navio mercante.

ship (to) embarcar, despachar, enviar, mandar.

shipment embarque, despacho, carregamento.

shipwreck naufrágio.

shipyard estaleiro.

shirt camisa.
   shirt store camisaria.
   sport shirt camisa-esporte.

shiver tremor, arrepio, calafrio.

shiver (to) tremer (from cold), tiritar.

shock choque, golpe.

shock (to) chocar, abalar, surpreender.

shoe sapato.
   shoe store sapataria.
   shoelaces cordões de sapato.
   shoe polish graxa (x = sh) para sapato.

shoehorn calçadeira.

shoemaker sapateiro.

shoot (to) atirar, disparar.

shop loja.

shore costa, litoral, margem.

short curto (not long); baixo (x = sh) (not tall); breve, conciso (brief); com falta de (of goods).
   short cut atalho.
   short circuit curto-circuito.
   short story conto.
   in short em resumo.
   to be short faltar-lhe dinheiro, estar sem dinheiro.

   in a short while dentro de pouco.
   a short time ago há pouco tempo.

shorten (to) encurtar, abreviar.

shorts calças curtas.

shot tiro, descarga.

should, would deve, deveria, devia.
   I should go. Eu devia ir.
   I would go eu iria.
   if I should go se eu fôsse (fosse).
   The window should be open. A janela devia estar aberta.

shoulder ombro.
   shoulder to shoulder ombro a ombro.

shout grito, berro.

shout (to) gritar, berrar.

shovel pá.

show exposição (exhibition); espetáculo (espectáculo) (spectacle); entretenimento (entertainment).
   show window vitrina (montra).

show (to) mostrar, ensinar, provar, demonstrar.
   to show someone in mandar entrar.
   to show to the door acompanhar até a porta.
   to show off exibir-se.
   to show up apresentar-se, aparecer, comparecer.

shower aguaceiro, chuveiro.
   shower bath banho de chuveiro.

shrewd astuto, sagaz, esperto.

shrimp camarão.

shrink encolher-se, contrair-se.

shrub arbusto.

shut (to) fechar.
   to shut in encerrar, confinar.
   to shut out excluir.
   to shut up calar, fazer calar.

shutter veneziana; obturador (photography)

shy tímido, acanhado.

sick doente.
   to feel sick sentir-se mal, sentir-se doente.

sickness doença.

side lado.
   side by side lado a lado.
   on this side dêste (deste) lado.
   on that side dêsse (desse) lado.
   on the other side de outro lado.
   (the) wrong side out ao revés.

sidewalk calçada.

sieve peneira.

sigh suspiro.

sigh (to) suspirar.

sight vista, aspecto.
   at first sight à primeira vista.
   to keep in sight não perder de vista.

sightseeing (to go) ver as coisas de interêsse (interesse), visitar os lugares notáveis.

sign sinal (mark); letreiro, tabuleta (as over a shop).
   sign of the cross sinal da cruz.

sign (to) assinar.
   to sign a check assinar um cheque.

signal sinal, aviso.

signal (to) fazer sinal, fazer sinais, comunicar por meio de sinais.

signature assinatura.

significance significado, importância.

significant significante, importante.

silence silêncio.

silence (to) silenciar, fazer calar.

silent silencioso, calado.

silently silenciosamente.

silk sêda (seda).

silly tolo, bôbo (bobo).

silver prata.

silverware prataria, utensílios de prata.

similar semelhante, similar.

similarity semelhança, similaridade.

simple simples.

simplicity simplicidade.

simplification simplificação.

simplify simplificar.

simply simplesmente, meramente.

sin pecado.

sin (to) pecar.

since adj. desde então, depois, após.
   since then desde então.

since conj. já que, desde que, visto que.

since prep. desde, depois de, após.

sincere sincero.

sincerely sinceramente.
   sincerely yours de Vossa Senhoria, atento e obrigado.

sincerity sinceridade.

sing cantar.

singer cantor.

single só, único; solteiro (unmarried).
   not a single word. nem uma só palavra.
   single room quarto de solteiro.

singly individualmente, separadamente.

singular singular.

sink pia, bacia.

sink (to) afundar, ir a pique.

sinner pecador.

sip sôrvo (sorvo), golinho.

sip (to) sorver, beber em golinhos.

sir senhor.
   Dear Sir (My dear Sir) Prezado Senhor.

siren sirena (whistle); sereia.

sister irmã.

sister-in-law cunhada.

sit sentar, sentar-se.
   to sit down sentar-se.

sitting room sala de estar.

situated situado.

situation situação.

six seis.

sixteen dezesseis (dezasseis).

sixteenth décimo-sexto.

sixth sexto, sexta parte.

size tamanho, medida.

skate patim.
   ice skate patim para o gêlo (gelo).
   roller skate patim de rodas.

skate (to) patinar.

skeleton esqueleto.

sketch esbôço (esboço), desenho.

sketch (to) esboçar.

skill destreza, habilidade.

skillful destro, hábil.

skin pele.

skinny magro.

skirt saia.

skull crânio, craveira.

sky céu.
   sky blue azul-celeste.

slander calúnia.

slang gíria, calão.

slap bofetada, palmada, tapa.

slap (to) dar tapa, dar bofetada, esbofetear.

slate ardósia, lousa.

slaughter n. matança.

slave escravo.

slavery escravidão.

slay matar, assassinar.

sleep sono.
   to go to sleep deitar-se, adormecer.

sleepy sonolento.
   to be sleepy estar com sono, ter sono.

sleeve manga.
slender delgado, magro, esbelto.
slice fatia.
slice (to) cortar, cortar em fatias.
slide escorregar, deslizar.
slight adj. ligeiro, leve.
slight (to) desprezar.
slightly ligeiramente, levemente.
slim delgado, fraco, esbelto.
sling funda.
slip escorregadura, escorregadela (slipping).
slip (to) escorregar, deslizar.
  to slip one's mind escapar à memória.
  to slip away fugir, escapulir(-se).
slippers chinelos.
slippery escorregadio, escorregadiço,
  resvaladiço.
slope inclinação, declive.
slow lento, devagar.
  to be slow (as watch) atrasar-se.
slow down (to) reduzir a velocidade.
slowly lentamente, devagar.
  Drive slowly. Dirija devagar.
  Go slowly. Vá devagar.
slowness lentidão.
slumber sono leve, soneca.
slumber (to) dormir, dormitar, tirar soneca.
slums bairros pobres; favelas Ⓑ.
sly astuto.
small pequeno.
  small change trôco (troco).
smallness pequenez.
smart inteligente (clever), astuto.
smash (to) esmagar, quebrar, destruir.
smell cheiro, odor.
smell (to) cheirar.
smile sorriso.
smile (to) sorrir.
smoke fumaça, fumo; cigarro (a cigarette).
  Have a cigarette. Tome um cigarro.
smoke (to) fumar (tobacco); fumegar.
  No smoking. É proibido fumar.
smoker fumante (fumador).
smooth liso, plano, suave.
snail caracol.
snake cobra, serpente.
snatch (to) arrancar, arrebatar.
sneeze espirro.
snore (to) espirrar.
snore (to) roncar (resonar).
snow neve.
snow (to) nevar.
snowflake floco de neve.
snowy nevoso, coberto de neve.
so adj. assim, tal; de modo que, de maneira
  que.
  That is so. Assim é.
  so and so Fulano de Tal.
  so much tanto.
  at so much a meter a tanto o metro.
  so that para que, de modo que.
  so so regular; mais ou menos; assim,
    assim.
  Is that so? Realmente? É verdade?
  I think so. Acredito. Acho que sim.
  not so expensive as não tão caro quanto.
soak saturar.
soap sabão, sabonete (cake of soap).
sob soluço.
sob (to) soluçar.
sober sóbrio, sério, solene.
sociable sociável, agradável.
social social.
socialism socialismo.

society sociedade.
socket cavidade; tomada (electric).
  eye socket órbita de ôlho (olho).
socks · meias curtas, meias (peúgas).
soda soda.
  soda water água gasosa, água de soda.
sofa sofá.
soft brando, suave, macio.
  soft-boiled eggs ovos quentes.
soften amolecer, suavizar.
softness moleza, maciez, brandura.
soil terra (ground).
soil (to) sujar, manchar.
soiled sujo.
solar solar.
sold vendido.
  sold out esgotado.
soldier soldado.
sole adj. só, único.
sole n. sola.
solemn solene.
solemnity solenidade.
solid sólido.
solidity solidez.
solidly sòlidamente.
solitary solitário.
solitude solidão.
so long até logo.
soluble solúvel.
solution solução.
solve solver, resolver.
some um pouco; algum, alguns, alguma,
  algumas, uns, umas.
  Some (people) think so. Há quem pensa
    assim.
  at some time or other em qualquer ocasião.
  Bring me some cigars. Traga-me alguns
    charutos.
  There are some left. Ainda ficam alguns.
  some of his books alguns dos seus livros.
  some two hundred uns duzentos.
somebody alguém, algum.
  somebody else alguém mais, algum outro.
somehow de algum modo, de alguma maneira.
something alguma coisa.
  something else? mais alguma coisa?
sometime algum dia, alguma vez.
sometimes algumas vêzes (vezes), às vêzes.
somewhat um pouco, um tanto.
  somewhat busy um tanto ocupado.
somewhere em alguma parte.
  somewhere else em outra parte.
son filho.
  son-in-law genro.
song canto, canção.
soon cedo, breve.
  as soon as logo que, assim que.
  as soon as possible o mais cedo possível.
  sooner or later mais cedo ou mais tarde.
  the sooner the better quanto antes melhor.
  How soon will you finish? Quanto tempo
    domorará em terminar?
soothe (to) aliviar, acalmar, suavizar.
sore adj. dolorido, doído.
  sore throat dor de garganta.
sore n. chaga (on the body).
sorrow dor, tristeza, pesar.
sorry triste, penalizado; arrependido.
  to be sorry sentir.
  I'm very sorry. Sinto muito.
sort espécie, classe, maneira, sorte.
  all sorts of people tôda (toda) classe de
    gente.
  a sort of uma espécie de.
  nothing of the sort nada disso.
soul alma.

sound adj. são, firme.
  safe and sound são e salvo.
  sound sleep sono profundo.
sound n. som.
soup sopa.
  soup plate prato de sopa, prato fundo.
  vegetable soup sopa de legumes.
sour acre, ácido.
source fonte.
south sul.
  South America América do Sul.
  South American sul-americano.
southern meridional, sulista.
souvenir lembrança.
soviet adj. soviético.
sow (to) semear.
space espaço.
spacious espaçoso, amplo, vasto.
spade pá.
Spaniard espanhol.
Spanish espanhol.
  Spanish America América Espanhola,
    Hispano-América.
  Spanish American hispano-americano.
spare adj. de sobra; sobressalente de reserva.
  spare time horas vagas, tempo livre.
  spare money dinheiro de reserva.
  spare room quarto para hóspedes.
  spare parts peças sobressalentes.
  spare tire pneu sobressalente.
spare (to) poupar, economizar (to save)
  perdoar (to forgive).
sparingly frugalmente.
spark faísca.
spark (to) faiscar.
sparrow pardal.
speak falar.
  to speak for falar em favor de, falar em
    nome de.
  to speak for itself ser evidente, ser claro.
  to speak one's mind dizer o que se pensa.
  to speak out falar claramente.
  to speak to falar a.
  to speak up falar, dizer.
speaker orador, locutor.
spear lança.
spearmint hortelã.
special especial.
  special delivery entrega urgente.
specialist especialista.-
specialize especializar.
specially especialmente.
specialty especialidade, ramo especializado.
specific específico.
specifically especìficamente.
specify especificar.
specimen espécime, amostra.
spectacle espetáculo (espectáculo).
spectacles (glasses) óculos.
spectator espectador.
speculation especulação.
speech fala; discurso; língua.
  to make a speech fazer um discurso.
speechless mudo, sem fala.
speed velocidade.
  at full speed a tôda (toda) velocidade.
  speed limit velocidade máxima (x = s).
speed (to) acelerar, apressar-se, ir em alta
  velocidade.
spell (to) soletrar.
spelling soletração, ortografia.
spend gastar.
  to spend time passar tempo.
  to spend the night passar a noite.
  I'll spend the winter in the south.
    Vou passar o inverno (Inverno) no sul.

spice n. especiaria.

spicy condimentado, picante.

spider aranha.

spin giro, volta; parafuso (aviation).

spin (to) fiar (thread, etc.); girar, virar, rodar.

spinach espinafre.

spine espinha, espinha dorsal.

spiral espiral.

spirit espírito.

spiritual espiritual.

spit espêto (espeto).

spit (to) cuspir.

spite n. rancor, despeito, malevolência.
in spite of apesar de.

spiteful rancoroso, vingativo.

splash (to) salpicar, chapinhar.

splendid esplêndido, ótimo (óptimo), magnífico.

splendor esplendor.

split adj. fendido, partido, dividido.

split (to) fender, partir, dividir, repartir.
They split the difference. Repartiram a diferença.
to split hairs perder-se em minúcias.

spoil (to) danificar, arruinar, estragar; apodrecer (to rot).

spoke n. raio de roda (of a wheel).

sponge esponja.

sponsor patrocinador, padrinho.

spontaneity espontaneidade.

spontaneous espontâneo.

spool carretel, bobina.

spoon colher.
teaspoon colher de chá.
tablespoon colher de sopa.

spoonful colherada.

sport adj. esportivo, de esporte.
sport shirt camisa-esporte.

sports esportes.

spot mancha (strain); borrão (of ink, paint); lugar, ponto (place); dificuldade (difficulty).
on the spot no lugar, no mesmo lugar; imediatamente; em dificuldades (in trouble).

sprain torcedura, distensão.

sprain (to) torcer, deslocar.

spray (to) pulverizar, borrifar.

sprayer pulverizador.

spread difusão, extensão.

spread (to) espalhar, propagar, difundir (news, etc.); estender, distribuir.

spring primavera (Primavera) (season); manancial, fonte (water); salto, pulo (jump); mola (of wire, etc.).
spring mattress colchão de molas.

spring (to) saltar, pular.
to spring at lançar-se sôbre (sobre).

sprinkle rociar, regar; chuviscar.

sprout brotar, germinar.

spy espião.

spy (to) espiar, espionar.

squad esquadra, turma.

squadron esquadra, esquadrão, esquadrilha.

square quadrado; praça (town).

squash n. abóbora.

squeeze (to) espremer, apertar.

squirrel esquilo.

stab punhalada.

stab (to) apunhalar.

staff pau (pole); bastão, bengala (rod, stick); pessoal (personnel); estado-maior (military).
office staff pessoal de escritório.
editorial staff redação.
staff officer oficial de estado-maior.

stage palco, tablado (theatre).
by stages por etapas.

stage (to) representar, encenar (theatre).

stain mancha.

stain (to) manchar.

stair escada, degrau.

stake estaca, poste (for driving into the ground).
at stake arriscado, em perigo.

stake (to) estacar, estaquear (into the ground); apostar, arriscar (money).

stammer tartamudear, gaguejar.

stamp sêlo (selo), timbre, carimbo.
postage stamp sêlo de correio.

stand n. pôsto (posto), banca (quiosque) (stall); tribuna, plataforma (platform); posição, opinião (opinion); resistência (defense).
newstand banca (quiosque) de jornais.

stand (to) colocar, pôr em pé (to set); levantar-se, pôr-se em pé, estar em pé (to stand, be standing); resistir, sustentar, agüentar (aguentar); parar (to stop moving).
Stand up! Levante-se!
I'm up. I'm standing. Estou em pé.
I can't stand him. Não o posso aguentar (aguentar).
to stand a chance ter uma probabilidade.
to stand by estar presente, estar de prontidão.
to stand for estar por, favorecer, aprovar; significar, querer dizer (to mean); agüentar (aguentar), tolerar, permitir (to tolerate).
to stand in line fazer fila.
to stand off manter-se à distância.
to stand on one's own feet ser independente.
to stand one's ground resistir, manter-se firme.
to stand out salientar-se, distinguir-se.
to stand up levantar-se, pôr-se em pé.

standard norma, padrão, modêlo (modelo); estandarte, bandeira (flag).
standard of living padrão de vida.
standard time hora oficial.

standpoint ponto de vista.

star estrêla (estrela), astro.

starch amido, goma.

start princípio, começo (começo) (beginning); partida, começo, saída (starting point, departure); arranque (of car, engine).

start (to) principiar, começar (to begin); partir, sair (to start out); arrancar (an engine).

starvation fome, sofrimento de fome, morte de fome.

starve morrer de fome.

state n. estado, condição, situação.

state (to) dizer, exprimir, declarar, explicar, afirmar.

statement declaração, afirmação; relatório (report); extrato (extracto) de contas, conta (of account, bill).

stateroom camarote (ship), cabina.

statesman estadista.

station estação.
railroad station estação ferroviária.

stationary estacionário, parado.

stationery papel de carta, artigos de papelaria.

stationery store papelaria.

statistical estatístico.

statistics estatística.

statue estátua.

stay estadia, permanência; suspensão (legal).

stay (to) ficar, permanecer, morar, residir, parar; suspender (to put off).
to stay in ficar em casa.
to stay in bed ficar na cama.
to stay away estar ausente, não voltar.

steadily constantemente.

steady firme, fixo (x = ks), estável, constante.

steak bife.

steal roubar, furtar.

steam vapor.

steamboat barco a vapor.

steam engine máquina a vapor.

steamer navio a vapor, vapor.

steamship navio a vapor.
steamship line companhia de navegação.

steel aço.

steep íngreme, escarpado.

steer (to) guiar, dirigir, governar, pilotar.

steering wheel volante.

stem talo, tronco; raiz (grammar).

stenographer taquígrafo, estenógrafo.

stenography taquigrafia, estenografia.

step passo, degrau (stair).
step by step passo por passo.
in step em cadência.
out of step fora de cadência.
steps, stairway escada.

step (to) dar um passo, pisar, andar, caminhar.
to step aside dar passagem.
to step back retroceder.
to step down descer.
to step in entrar; intervir (intervene).
to step on pisar.
to step out sair; descer (down).

stepbrother meio-irmão.

stepchild enteado.

stepdaughter enteada.

stepfather padrasto.

stepmother madrasta.

stepsister meia-irmã.

stepson enteado.

stern adj. austero, severo.

stew cozido, guisado.

steward camareiro, aeromoço.

stewardess camareira, aeromoça.

stick pau, vara; bastão, bengala (cane).

stick (to) apunhalar (to stab); transpassar, perfurar (to penetrate); colar, grudar (to glue); fixar (x = ks).
to stick by manter-se fiel a.
to stick out pôr para fora; salientar.
to stick it out aguentar (aguentar) perseverar.
to stick up for defender, tomar a defesa de.
to stick to perseverar, sustentar, manter, aderir a.

stiff adj. têso (teso), duro, rijo; afetado (not natural in manners); cerimonioso (formal); fôrte (wind, drink); caro (of prices).
stiff collar colarinho engomado.
stiff neck torcicolo.

stiffen endurecer, fortalecer; obstinar-se.

stiffness rigidez, dureza.

still adj. quieto, imóvel, tranqüilo (tranquilo).
to stand still ficar quieto.
still life natureza morta.
Be still! Cale-se!

still adv. ainda, não obstante, entretanto.
She's still at home. Ela ainda está em casa.

stillness calma, quietude, silêncio.

sting picada.

sting (to) picar.

stir (to) agitar, misturar, revolver.
to stir the fire atiçar o fogo.
to stir up comover, excitar.

stirrup estribo.

stock estoque (existência), mercadoria (supply of goods); ações (acções) (stocks, shares); gado (animals); origem, raça (race, background).
stock market bôlsa (bolsa).

stock company sociedade anônima (anónima).
in stock em estoque (em existência).
out of stock esgotado.
stockings meias.
stomach estômago.
stone pedra.
stool banquinho, banco, tamborete.
stop parada (paragem).
stop (to) parar, deter, deter-se; parar, ficar (to stay).
to stop raining deixar (x = sh) de chover.
Stop! Alto!
Stop that! Basta! (That's enough!).
Stop a minute. Fique um momento.
store loja, armazém.
department store armazém, loja.
stork cegonha.
storm tempestade, temporal.
stormy tempestuoso, tormentoso.
story história, conto (tale); andar (building); mentira (lie).
short story conto.
as the story goes conforme consta, segundo consta.
stout corpulento, gordo.
stove fogão, estufa.
straight direito, reto (recto).
straight line linha reta.
Go straight ahead. Siga bem em frente.
straighten endireitar, pôr em ordem.
straightforward *adj.* direito; reto (recto); franco (frank); honesto, honrado (honest).
strain tensão (tension); esfôrço (esforço).
strain (to) coar (through a strainer); cansar (the eyes, etc.); esforçar-se (to make an effort).
to stand the strain agüentar (aguentar) o esfôrço (esforço).
strange estranho, raro (unusual); desconhecido (not known).
strangeness estranheza, singularidade.
stranger estrangeiro, estranho, desconhecido.
strap correia.
strategic estratégico.
strategy estratégia.
straw palha.
straw hat chapéu de palha.
to be the last straw a útima gôta (gota), o cúmulo.
strawberry morango.
stream *n.* corrente, rio.
street rua.
street crossing cruzamento.
streetcar bonde Ⓑ (but disappearing in Brazil) (carro eléctrico).
strength fôrça (força).
strengthen fortalecer(-se), reforçar(-se).
stress fôrça (força) (force); esfôrço (esforço) (effort); tensão (strain); pressão (pressure); acento (accent); ênfase (emphasis); importância (importance).
stress (to) acentuar, dar ênfase a.
stretch (to) estirar, estender, espreguiçar-se.
stretcher padiola.
strict estrito (estricto), rigoroso, severo.
strike greve (of workers).
strike (to) bater, dar pancada, golpear; entrar em greve (workers).
to strike at atacar.
to strike a match acender um fósforo.
to strike against chocar-se contra, colidir com.
to strike back devolver golpe por golpe.
to strike home acertar, acertar no alvo.
striking surpreendente, extraordinário.
string barbante, fio, cordel, corda.

stripe lista.
stroll passeio, volta.
to go for a stroll dar uma volta.
stroll (to) passear.
strong forte, poderoso.
stronghold fortaleza, baluarte.
structure estrutura, construção.
struggle luta.
struggle (to) lutar.
stubborn teimoso, obstinado.
student estudante, aluno.
studious estudioso.
study estudo.
study (to) estudar.
stuff *n.* fazenda, pano (cloth, material); coisa (thing), coisas, trastes, bugigangas (miscellaneous things); bobagem, tolice (foolishness).
stumble tropeçar.
stump tôco (toco), toro, cepa.
stupid estúpido.
to be stupid ser estúpido.
stupidity estupidez.
stupor estupor, letargia.
style estilo, maneira, modo; moda (fashion).
subdue subjugar.
subject sujeito; matéria, assunto, tema (subject matter).
subject (to) sujeitar, submeter.
submarine submarino.
submission submissão.
submit submeter, submeter-se.
subordinate subordinado.
subscribe subscrever.
subscriber assinante, subscritor.
subscription subscrição, assinatura.
subsequent subseqüente (subsequente), seguinte, ulterior.
substance substância.
substantial substancial.
substitute substituto.
substitute (to) substituir.
substitution substituição.
subtract subtrair, tirar, deduzir.
suburb subúrbio.
succeed sair bem, suceder, ter sucesso, ter êxito (x = z); lograr.
success sucesso, êxito (x = z).
successful feliz, bem sucedido, próspero.
successive sucessivo, consecutivo.
successor sucessor, herdeiro.
such tal, semelhante.
such as tais como.
in such a way de tal modo, de tal maneira.
sudden *adj.* repentino, súbito.
all of a sudden de repente.
suddenly repentinamente, sùbitamente.
suffer (to) sofrer.
suffering *n.* sofrimento, padecimento.
suffice ser suficiente, bastar.
sugar açúcar.
suggest sugerir.
suggestion sugestão.
suicide suicídio.
to commit suicide suicidar-se.
suit terno (fato), traje completo.
processo (court); naipe (cards).
suit (to) acomodar, adaptar (to make suitable); cair bem, ficar bem (to be becoming); satisfazer, agradar (to please, to satisfy); vestir (to clothe).
suitable adequado, apropriado.
suitably adequadamente, apropriadamente.
sulfur enxôfre (enxofre).

sum soma, adição.
summary sumário.
summer verão (Verão).
summer resort lugar de veraneio.
summit cume; cúmulo.
summon citar, convocar, chamar, convidar.
summons citação (to court).
sun sol.
sunbath banho de sol.
to take a sunbath tomar banho de sol.
sunbeam raio de sol.
sunburn queimadura de sol.
sunburnt queimado pelo sol.
Sunday domingo.
sunlight luz do sul.
sunny de sol, ensolarado; alegre, jovial (disposition).
sunrise nascer do sol, levantar do sol.
sunset pôr do sol.
sunshine luz solar.
superb soberbo, magnífico, esplêndido.
superfluous supérfluo.
superintendent superintendente.
superior superior.
superiority superioridade.
superstition superstição.
superstitious supersticioso.
supper ceia, jantar.
supplement suplemento.
supply abastecimento; estoque (existência).
supply and demand oferta e procura.
supply (to) abastecer, fornecer, prover.
support apoio, sustento; manutenção (act of providing for).
support (to) apoiar, sustentar; manter (to provide for).
suppose supor.
supposition suposição, conjetura (conjectura).
suppress suprimir.
suppression supressão.
supreme supremo, sumo.
Supreme Court Côrte (Corte) Suprema.
sure certo, seguro.
to be sure estar certo.
be sure to não deixe (x = sh) de.
surely seguramente, certamente.
surface superfície.
surgeon cirurgião.
surgery cirugia.
surname apelido, sobrenome.
surprise surprêsa (surpresa).
surprise (to) surpreender.
surprising surpreendente.
surprisingly surpreendentemente.
surrender rendição, entrega.
surrender (to) render(-se), entregar(-se).
surround cercar, rodear.
surrounding circundante, cercante.
surroundings arredores, vizinhança; meio, ambiente (atmosphere).
survey exame (x = z), estudo; inspeção (inspecção) (inspection); levantamento topográfico.
survey (to) examinar (x = z), estudar; inspecionar (inspeccionar) (to inspect); levantar um plano (in surveying).
survival sobrevivência.
survivor sobrevivente.
susceptible suscetível (susceptível).
suspect suspeito, pessoa suspeita.
suspect (to) suspeitar.
suspend suspender.
suspenders suspensórios.

suspicion suspeição, suspeita.

suspicious suspeito, suspeitoso, desconfiado.

swallow andorinha (bird).

swallow (to) engolir.

swamp pântano.

swan cisne.

swarm enxame (x = sh).

swarm (to) enxamear (x = sh).

swear jurar, prestar juramento.
to swear by jurar por.

sweat suor.

sweet doce.
sweet potato batata doce.
to have a sweet tooth ser guloso.

sweetheart noivo, noiva.

sweetness doçura.

swell *adj.* (*slang*) excelente, magnífico, estupendo.

swell (to) inchar; subir, crescer.

swift rápido, veloz.

swiftly ràpidamente, velozmente.

swim (to) nadar.
My head's swimming. Minha cabeça gira.

swimmer nadador.

swimming pool piscina.

swing balanço, balanceio, oscilação.
in full swing em plena atividade (actividade).

swing (to) balançar, oscilar, fazer girar.

switch chave (key); interruptor, comutador (electric switch); agulha (railroad).

switch (to) ligar, desligar (to turn electric switch on or off); desviar (railroad); cambiar (to change, to shift); açoitar (to whip).

sword espada.

syllable sílaba.

symbol símbolo.

sympathetic simpático.

sympathize simpatizar, compadecer-se.

sympathy simpatia.

symphony sinfonia.
symphony orchestra orquestra sinfônica (sinfónica).

symptom sintoma.

synthetic sintético.

syrup xarope (x = sh).

system sistema.

systematic sistemático, metódico.

T

table mesa; tabela (of measures, etc.).
to set the table pôr a mesa.

tablecloth toalha de mesa.

table lamp lâmpada de mesa.

tablespoon colher de sopa.

tablet tablete, comprimido (of aspirin, etc.); bloco de papel (for writing); tábua, chapa, placa (with an inscription).

tableware utensílios de mesa.

tact tato (tacto).

tactful de tato (tacto), diplomático.

tactical tático (táctico).

tactics tática (táctica).

tactless sem tato (tacto), indelicado, indiscreto.

tail rabo, cauda.

tailor alfaiate.

take (to) tomar; colher, agarrar (to grasp).
to take a bath tomar banho, banhar-se.
to take a picture tirar uma fotografia, tirar uma foto.
to take a walk dar um passeio, dar uma volta.
to take a nap tirar uma soneca.
to take a trip fazer uma viagem.

to take an oath prestar juramento.
to take apart desarmar (a machine).
to take a step dar um passo.
to take away levar.
to take back levar de volta, receber de volta.
to take into account levar em conta.
to take advantage of aproveitar-se de.
to take advice tomar conselho.
to take care ter cuidado.
to take charge of encarregar-se de.
to take into consideration levar em consideração.
to take to heart levar a sério.
to take it easy ir com calma.
to take leave despedir-se.
to take notes tomar notas.
to take notice observar, notar.
to take out tirar; levar para fora.
to take after (resemble) parecer-se com.
to take off (plane) decolar, levantar vôo.
to take one's clothes off despir-se, desnudar-se.
to take one's shoes off descalçar-se.
to take the hat, etc. off tirar o chapéu.
to take part tomar parte.
to take place acontecer.
to take possession tomar posse.
to take refuge refugiar-se.
to take upon oneself encarregar-se de.

talcum talco.

talcum powder talco em pó.

tale conto, história, narrativa.

talent talento.

talk conversa, conversação (conversation); palestra, conferência, discurso (speech); rumor (rumor).

talk (to) falar, conversar, dizer.
to talk back retrucar.
to talk over discutir.
to talk to falar a.

talkative falador.

tall alto.

tame *adj.* domesticado, manso.

tame (to) domar, domesticar.

tan *n.* côr (cor) bronzeada, côr morena.

tan *adj.* bronzeado, moreno.

tan (to) bronzear, amorenar; curtir (hides).

tank tanque, cisterna, depósito, piscina.

tape fita.
tape measure fita métrica.
tape recorder gravador de fita.

tapestry tapeçaria, tapête (tapete).

tar breu, alcatrão.

target alvo, objetivo (objectivo).
to hit the target dar no alvo.

task tarefa, dever, trabalho.

taste gôsto (gosto), sabor.
in bad taste de mau gôsto.
in good taste de bom gôsto.
to have a taste for ter gôsto por.

taste (to) sentir o gôsto (gosto), saborear, provar; ter gôsto de.
The soup tastes of onion. A sopa tem gôsto de cebola.

tavern taverna.

tax taxa (x = sh), impôsto (imposto).
income tax impôsto de renda.

tax (to) taxar (x = sh), impor impôsto (imposto), cobrar impôsto.

taxi taxi (x = ks).

tea chá.

teach ensinar.

teacher professor.

teacup xícara de chá, chávena de chá.

teakettle chaleira.

team junta, parelha (horses, etc.); equipe, time (B).

teamwork trabalho de equipe, trabalho coordenado.

teapot bule.

tear (from weeping) lágrima.
in tears em pranto, chorando.

tear (to) rasgar, dividir, partir, romper.
to tear down derrubar, demolir.
to tear to pieces despedaçar, rasgar.
to tear one's hair arrancar-se os cabelos.

tease cacetear, arreliar.

teaspoon colher de chá.

technical técnico.

technique técnica.

tedious tedioso, cansativo.

teeth dentes.
false teeth dentes postiços, dentadura postiça.
set of teeth dentadura.

telegram telegrama.

telegraph telégrafo.

telegraph (to) telegrafar.

telephone telefone.
telephone booth cabina telefônica (telefónica).
telephone call telefonema, chamada telefônica.
telephone exchange estação telefônica.
telephone operator telefonista.
telephone directory lista telefônica.

telephone (to) telefonar.

telescope telescópio.

television set televisor, aparelho de televisã

tell dizer; contar, narrar.
to tell a story contar uma história.
Who told you so? Quem lhe disse isso?

temper têmpera, temperamento, disposição, humor.
bad temper mau humor.
to lose one's temper perder a paciência.

temperament temperamento, disposição.

tempest tempestade, temporal.

temple templo; fonte (of the head).

temporarily temporàriamente.

temporary temporário, provisário.

tempt tentar, provocar.

temptation tentação.

tempting tentador.

ten dez.

tenacious tenaz, obstinado, firme.

tenant inquilino, habitante, ocupante.

tendency tendência.

tender *adj.* tenro, macio; carinhoso.
tender-hearted compassivo.

tennis tênis (ténis).
tennis court quadra de tênis.

tense tenso.

tension tensão.

tent tenda, barraca.

tentative tentativa.

tenth décimo.

term têrmo (termo), prazo; condições (terms).
to be on good terms with ter boas relações com.
to come to terms chegar a um acôrdo (acordo).

terminal *adj.* terminal, final, último.

terminal término, fim; estação final, terminal.

terrace terraço.

terrible terrível.

terribly terrivelmente, excessivamente.

territory território.

terror terror, pavor.

terse conciso, breve, sucinto.

terseness concisão, brevidade.

test prova, ensaio, exame (x = z), análise.

test (to) ensaiar, experimentar, examinar (x = z).

testify testificar, testemunhar, afirmar.

text texto, livro escolar.

textbook livro escolar.

than que, do que.
　more than that mais (do) que isso.
　fewer than menos que, menos de.
　He is richer than I am. Êle (ele) é mais rico (do) que eu.

thank (to) agradecer.
　Thank you. Obrigado.

thankful agradecido, reconhecido.

thanks obrigado.
　thanks to graças a.

that êsse (esse), essa, isso, aquêle (aquele), aquella, aquilo *(dem. adj. and pron.); que,* quem, o qual, a qual *(rel. pron.).*
　that man aquêle, êsse homem.
　that woman aquela, essa mulher.
　That's it. Isso é. Isso mesmo.
　That's to say. Isto é.
　That may be. É possível. Talvez.
　That's all. É tudo.
　That way. Por ali.
　That's how. Assim é como se faz.

that *adv.* tão.
　not that far não tão longe.

that *conj.* que, para que.
　so that de modo que, para que.
　in order that para que, de maneira que.

the o, a, os, as.
　the man o homem.
　the men os homens.
　the woman a mulher.
　the women as mulheres.
　the sooner the better quanto antes melhor.

theatre teatro.

theatrical teatral.

their seu, sua, seus, suas, dêles (deles), delas.

them os, as, lhes, êles (eles), elas.

theme tema.

themselves êles (eles) mesmos, elas mesmas, si mesmos, se.

then então, nesse tempo.
　now and then de vez em quando.
　and then e então.
　just then nesse mesmo momento.
　by then naquela altura.
　what then? e então?

theoretical teórico.

theory teoria.

there ali, aí (near the person addressed), lá, acolá (more remote).
　Put it there. Ponha-o aí.
　I was there. Eu estive ali.
　Go there. Vá lá.
　Over there. Por ali. Lá.
　there is há.
　there are há.

thereabouts por aí, por ali.

thereafter depois disso, daí em diante.

there are há.

thereby assim, dêsse (desse) modo.

therefore portanto, por essa razão, por conseguinte.

there is há.
　There's plenty. Há bastante.

thermometer termômetro (termómetro).

these êstes (estes), estas.

thesis tese.

they êles (eles), elas.

thick grosso, denso; estúpido.
　three inches thick três polegadas de grossura.
　thick-headed cabeçudo, estúpido.

thickness grossura, espessura.

thief ladrão.

thigh coxa (x = sh).

thimble dedal.

thin magro, delgado, esbelto.

thing coisa, objeto (objecto).
　something alguma coisa.
　anything qualquer coisa.

think (to) pensar, ácreditar, crer, achar.
　to think of pensar em.
　to think well of pensar bem de.
　As you think fit. Como você quiser.
　to think it over pensá-lo.
　to think nothing of não ligar a mínima importância.
　to think twice pensar bem.
　I don't think so. Não acredito. Não acho.
　Acho que não.
　I think so. Acredito. Acho que sim.

thinness delgadeza, magreza.

third terceiro, terceira parte.
　a third person um terceiro.
　thirdly em terceiro lugar.

thirst sêde (sede).
　to be thirsty estar com sêde, ter sêde.

thirteen treze.

thirteenth décimo terceiro.

thirty trinta.

this êste (este), esta.
　this man êste homem.
　this woman esta mulher.
　this evening hoje à noite.
　this one and that one êste e aquêle.
　this and that isto e aquilo.

thorn espinho.

thorough *adj.* completo, inteiro, perfeito.

thoroughfare via pública.

thoroughly completamente.

those aquêles, aquelas.

though embora, ainda que, todavia.
　as though como se.

thought pensamento.
　to give thought to pensar em.

thoughtful pensativo, atento; atencioso, solícito.

thoughtfully atenciosamente, pensativamente.

thoughtfulness reflexão (x = ks), meditação, atenção.

thoughtless descuidado, imprudente.

thoughtlessly descuidadamente, sem reflexão (x = ks).

thousand mil, milhar.

thread linha, fio.

thread (to) enfiar.

threat ameaça, perigo.

threaten ameaçar, intimidar.

three três.

threefold triplo, triplicado.

threshold limiar, soleira.

thrift economia, frugalidade.

thrifty frugal, econômico (económico).

thrill emoção, sensação.

thrill (to) emocionar(-se), excitar, estremecer.

throat garganta.
　sore throat dor de garganta.

throne trono.

through *adj.* contínuo, direto (directo).
　a through train um trem direto (um comboio directo).

through *adv.* de uma parte a outra, de lado a lado, completamente, totalmente.
　through and through completamente.
　to be through ter terminado.
　to be through with cortar relações com, ter acabado com.

through *prep.* por, através de, por meio de, devido a, por causa de.
　through the door pela porta.

through his influence devido à sua influência.

throughout *prep.* durante todo, por todo, em todo; *adv.* por tôda (toda) parte, completamente.

throw atirar, lançar.
　to throw out deitar fora, jogar fora.
　to throw light on esclarecer.

thumb polegar.

thumbnail unha do polegar.

thumbtack percevejo.

thunder trovão.

thunder (to) trovejar.

thunderbolt raio.

thundershower aguaceiro com raios e trovões.

Thursday quinta-feira, quinta.

thus assim, dêste (deste) modo, como segue.
　thus far até aqui, até êste (este) ponto.

ticket bilhete.
　round-trip ticket bilhete de ida e volta.
　ticket window guichê (guichet), bilheteria (bilheteira).

tickle (to) titilar, fazer cócegas.

tide maré.
　high tide maré cheia.
　low tide maré baixa (x = sh).

tie gravata (necktie); laço (bond); nó (knot); dormente (of railroad); empate, jôgo (jogo) empatado (tie game).

tie (to) atar, amarrar.

tiger tigre.

tight apertado, justo, firme; bêbedo (drunk).

tighten apertar.

tile telha (for roof), azulejo.

till *prep.* até, até que.
　till now até agora.

till (to) cultivar, lavrar.

timber madeira.

time tempo; hora; vez; época; prazo.
　What time is it? Que horas são?
　the first time a primeira vez.
　on time a tempo, na hora.
　a long time ago há muito tempo.
　at the same time ao mesmo tempo.
　any time a qualquer hora, quando você quiser.
　at no time nunca.
　one at a time um à vez.
　at this time agora.
　at this time (of the day) a estas horas.
　at times às vêzes (vezes).
　for the time being por agora.
　from time to time de vez em quando.
　in no time imediatamente, num instante.
　in an hour's time em uma hora.
　to be on time estar na hora.
　Have a good time! Divirta-se!
　spare time horas de folga.

timely *adv.* oportunamente.

timely *adj.* oportuno, conveniente.

timetable horário.

timid tímido.

timidity timidez.

tin lata.
　tin can lata.
　tinfoil fôlha (folha) de estanho.

tincture tintura.
　tincture of iodine tintura de iôdo (iodo).

tint matiz, toque.

tip ponta, extremidade (point, end); gorjeta (gratuity); palpite, aviso, informação secreta (secret information); sugestão (suggestion).

tip (to) inclinar (to slant); dar uma gorjeta (to give a gratuity); informar, aconselhar, dar palpite (to give information).

tire pneu, pneumático.
　flat tire pneu furado.

tire (to) cansar, fatigar; aborrecer (to bore).

tireless incansável, infatigável.
tissue tecido (skin, etc.); gaze (gauze).
 tissue paper papel de sêda (seda).
title título.
 title page frontispício.
to a, para, de, por, até, que.
 to give to dar a.
 to go to ir a.
 ready to go pronto para ir-se embora.
 It's time to leave. Está na hora de partir.
 from house to house de casa em casa.
 to be done por fazer.
 letters to be written cartas por escrever.
 to this day até agora.
 in order to para, a fim de.
 to and fro para cá e para lá.
 I have to go. Tenho que ir-me. Tenho de
 ir-me.
 I have something to do. Tenho alguma coisa
 para fazer.
 It's twenty (minutes) to three. São três menos
 vinte. Faltam vinte para as três. São duas
 horas e quarenta minutos.
toad sapo.
toast torrada.
toast (to) torrar, tostar.
toaster torrador, torradeira.
tobacco tabaco, fumo.
 tobacco shop tabacaria.
today hoje.
 a week from today daqui a oito dias.
toe dedo do pé.
together juntos; juntamente; ao mesmo tempo.
 Let's go together. Vamos juntos.
 together with junto com.
 to call together reunir.
toil trabalho pesado, fadiga.
toilet banheiro, privada; toilette, toalete (combing the hair, bathing, etc.).
 toilet soap sabonete.
 toilet paper papel higiênico (higiénico).
 toilet water (cologne) água-de-colônia
 (colônia).
tolerance tolerância.
tolerant tolerante.
tolerate tolerar.
tomato tomate.
 tomato juice suco de tomate.
tomb túmulo, sepultura.
tomcat gato.
tomorrow amanhã.
 day after tomorrow depois de amanhã.
 tomorrow morning amanhã de manhã.
ton tonelada.
tone tom.
tongs tenaz.
tongue língua.
 to hold one's tongue calar-se.
tonic tônico (tónico).
tonight hoje à noite, esta noite.
tonsil amígdala.
tonsilitis tonsilite, amigdalite.
too demais (too much), também (also).
 too much demais, muito.
 too many demais, muitos.
 It's too bad. É (uma) pena.
 It's too early. É cedo demais.
 That's too much. That's the last straw.
 É o cúmulo.
 me (I) too eu também.
 I am only too glad to do it. Eu o farei com
 muito prazer.
 one dollar too much um dólar demais.
 That's too little. Isso é muito pouco.
tool ferramenta.
tooth dente.
 toothache dor de dente(s).
 toothbrush escôva (escova) de dentes.

 toothpaste pasta de dentes.
 toothpick palito.
top pico, cume; parte superior; superfície; pião
 (toy).
 the top of the mountain o cume da montanha.
 at top speed a tôda (toda) velocidade.
 from top to bottom de cima para baixo (x =
 sh).
 from top to toe da cabeça aos pés.
topcoat sobretudo.
torch tocha.
torment tormento.
torrent torrente.
torrid tórrido.
 torrid zone zona tórrida.
tortoise tartaruga.
torture tortura, tormento.
torture (to) torturar, atormentar.
total total.
touch toque, contato (contacto).
 to be in touch with estar em contato com.
touch (to) tocar.
touching adj. patético, comovente, tocante.
tough duro, forte; difícil.
toughen endurecer(-se).
tour viagem, viagem de turismo.
tour (to) percorrer, viajar por.
touring turismo.
tourist turista.
 tourist agency agência de turismo.
 tourist guide guia de turismo.
tournament torneio.
toward para, para com, em direção a.
 to go toward a place ir para um lugar.
 his attitude toward me a atitude dêle (dele)
 para comigo.
towel toalha.
 face towel toalha de rosto.
 bath towel toalha de banho.
tower tôrre (torre).
town cidade.
 town hall prefeitura (câmara municipal).
toy brinquedo.
trace indício, rasto.
trace (to) seguir pelo rasto, investigar; traçar,
 esboçar (to mark out).
track rasto, pista; trilho (rail); pista (race).
trade comércio.
 trademark marca registrada, marca de fábrica.
 trade union sindicato.
trading comércio.
tradition tradição.
traditional tradicional.
traffic tráfico, tráfego, trânsito.
tragedy tragédia.
tragic trágico.
train trem (comboio).
train (to) treinar, instruir.
training treinamento, treino.
traitor traidor.
tramp vagabundo.
tranquil tranqüilo (tranquilo).
transatlantic transatlântico.
transfer transferência; passagem, bilhete (bus,
 etc.); transporte.
transfer (to) transferir, transportar.
translate traduzir.
translation tradução.
translator tradutor.
transparent transparente.
transport transporte.
transport (to) transportar.
transportation transportação, transporte.
trap armadilha.

trap (to) apanhar, capturar.
travel (to) viajar.
traveler viajante.
tray bandeja.
treacherous traiçoeiro.
treachery traição.
tread passo.
tread (to) pisar.
treason traição.
treasure tesouro.
treasure (to) prezar, apreciar.
treasurer tesoureiro.
treasury tesouraria.
treat (to) tratar; convidar (with food, etc).
 to treat a patient tratar de um paciente.
 to treat well (badly) dar bom (mau) tratamento.
treatment tratamento.
treaty tratado.
tree árvore.
tremble tremer, estremecer.
trembling adj. trêmulo (trémulo).
trembling n. tremor, estremecimento.
tremendous tremendo, enorme, extraordinário.
trench trincheira.
trend tendência, direção (direcção), rumo.
trial prova, ensaio, tentativa; julgamento (law).
triangle triângulo.
tribe tribo.
tribunal tribunal.
trick artifício, ardil, engano, travessura.
 to do the trick resolver o problema.
 to play a trick pregar uma peça.
trifle bagatela, insignificância.
trim (to) cortar, aparar (hair); podar (trees);
 adornar, decorar (clothes).
trimming adôrno (adorno), decoração.
trinket bugiganga, berloque.
trip n. viagem (voyage); tropeço (stumble).
 one-way trip viagem de ida.
 round trip viagem de ida e volta.
trip (to) tropeçar, fazer tropeçar.
triple triplo.
triumph triunfo.
triumph (to) triunfar.
triumphant triunfante.
trivial insignificante, trivial.
trolley car bonde (carro eléctrico).
troops tropas.
trophy troféu.
tropic trópico.
tropical adj. tropical.
trot (to) trotar.
trouble dificuldade (difficulty); aborrecimento
 (bother); desordem (disorder); doença (illness).
 to be in trouble estar em apuros.
 not to be worth the trouble não valer a pena.
 It's no trouble at all. Incômodo (incómodo)
 nenhum.
trouble (to) aborrecer, importunar.
troubled preocupado, perturbado.
troublesome importuno, difícil, desagradável.
trousers calças.
trout truta.
truck caminhão.
true certo, exato (exacto) (x = z), verdadeiro,
 fiel, leal.
 It's true. É verdade.
trunk tronco (tree); baú, mala (for packing).
trust confiança.
 on trust fiado, a crédito.
 in trust em depósito.
trust (to) confiar em, ter confiança em.
 I trust her. Confio nela.

trustworthy digno de confiança.

truth verdade.

truthful verdadeiro, verídico.

truthfulness veracidade, autenticidade.

try (to) tentar, experimentar, provar, procurar.
to try on clothes provar roupa.
Try to do it. Tente fazê-lo.

tub tina.
bathtub banheira.

tube tubo, cano.

Tuesday têrça-feira, têrça (terça).

tune toada, melodia.
to be out of tune estar desafinado.

tune (to) afinar; sintonizar (radio).

tunnel túnel.

turkey peru.

turn turno, período, vez (time, order); volta,
giro (motion); favor (favor).
by turns alternativamente.
in turn em sua vez.
to take turns cada uma ter a sua vez.
It's my turn now. Agora é a minha vez.

turn (to) girar, rodar (to turn); dobrar, virar (to
turn direction); tornar-se (to become pale,
etc.).
to turn around virar.
to turn down recusar, rejeitar (to refuse);
abaixar (x = sh), diminuir (lights, etc.).
to turn into transformar, converter.
to turn off fechar, desligar (radio, etc.).
to turn off the light apagar a luz.
to turn on the light acender a luz.
to turn on ligar (radio, etc.).
to turn back (return) voltar.
to turn one's back on dar as costas a.
to turn over transferir (to transfer) entregar,
dar (to hand over); ponderar, considerar (to
think about); fazer girar (motor).
to turn sour azedar.
to turn up aparecer.

turnip nabo.

turtle tartaruga.

twelfth duodécimo, décimo segundo,

twelve doze.

twentieth vigésimo.

twenty vinte.

twice duaz vêzes (vezes).

twilight crepúsculo.

twin gêmeo (gémeo).
twin brother irmão gêmeo.

twist (to) torcer, retorcer.

two dois, duas.

type tipo.

typewrite (to) escrever à máquina.

typewriter máquina de escrever.
portable typewriter máquina de escrever
portátil.
typewriter ribbon fita de máquina de
escrever.

typical típico.

typist dactilógrafo.

tyrannical tirânico.

tyranny tirania.

tyrant tirano.

U

ugly feio.

ulcer úlcera.

umbrella guarda-chuva.

umpire árbitro, juiz.

unable incapaz.
I was unable to do it. Não pude fazê-lo.
Foi-me impossível.

unanimous unânime.

unaware desapercebido, inconsciente.

unbearable insuportável.

unbutton desabotoar.

uncertain incerto.

uncertainty incerteza.

unchangeable imutável, permanente.

uncle tio.

uncomfortable incômodo (incómodo), desagradável.

unconquered invicto, indomado.

undecided indeciso.

under debaixo (x = sh), em; menos; sob.
under the table debaixo da mesa.
under consideration em consideração, objeto
(objecto) de estudo.
under penalty of sob pena de.
underage menor de idade.
under contract conforme o contrato.
under the circumstances em tais circunstâncias.
under obligation dever favores.
under one's nose nas barbas.

underclothes roupa branca.

undergo agüentar (aguentar), passar por, sofrer,
submeter-se.
to undergo an operation submeter-se a uma
operação.

underground subterrâneo.

underline sublinhar.

underneath embaixo, debaixo (in both x = sh)
sob.

understand compreender, entender.
Compreende? Do you understand?

understanding entendimento, acôrdo (acordo).
to come to an understanding chegar a um
acôrdo.

undertake empreender, encarregar-se de.

undertaking emprêsa (empresa), compromisso,
promessa (promise).

undo desfazer, desatar; anular.

undress despir-se.

uneasiness inquietude, desassossêgo
(desassossego).

uneasy inquieto, desassossegado.

unequal desigual.

uneven desigual, irregular; ímpar (number).

unexpected inesperado.

unfair injusto.

unfaithful infiel, desleal.

unfavorable desfavorável.

unfinished inacabado, incompleto.

unfit inadequado, impróprio.

unfold (to) desdobrar, estender, abrir, revelar,
esclarecer.

unforeseen imprevisto.

unforgettable inolvidável.

unfortunate desventurado, infeliz.

unfortunately infelizmente.

unfurnished desmobiliado (desmobilado), sem
móveis.
unfurnished apartment apartamento sem
móveis.

ungrateful ingrato.

unhappy infeliz, infortunado.

unhealthy doentio, malsão.

unheard of inaudito, desconhecido.

unhurt ileso.

uniform uniforme.

union sindicato.

unit unidade, grupo.

unite unir(-se).

united unido.
United States. Estados Unidos.

unity unidade.

universal universal.

universality universalidade.

universe universo.

university universidade.

unjust injusto.

unkind cruel, desapiedado.

unknown desconhecido.

unless a menos que, a não ser que, se não.

unlike diferente, dessemelhante, distinto.

unlikely inverossímil (inverosímil), improvável.

unload descarregar.

unlucky desgraçado, desafortunado, infeliz.

unmarried solteiro.
bachelor, unmarried man solteiro.
unmarried woman solteira.

unmoved impassível, indiferente, frio.

unnecessary desnecessário.

unpaid sem pagar, não pago.

unpleasant desagradável.

unquestionable indiscutível, indisputável.

unreasonable irracional, excessivo.

unrest desassossêgo (desassossego), inquietação.

unruly ingovernável, rebelde.

unsatisfactory insatisfatório, inadequado.

unseen não visto, inobservado.

unselfish desinteressado.

unsettled desarranjado, desordenado; variável,
inconstante (not stable); não pago, não
saldado (not paid).

unsteady instável, inconstante, inseguro.

unsuccessful sem êxito (x = z), malogrado,
infeliz.

unsuitable impróprio, inadequado, inconveniente.

until até.

untiring incansável, infatigável.

unusual extraordinário, raro, fora do comum.

unwelcome mal acolhido, mal recebido.

unwilling relutante, sem vontade.

unwillingly de má vontade.

unwise imprudente.

unworthy indigno.

unwritten não escrito, em branco.

up para cima, para o alto; em pé, de pé.
up and down para cima e para baixo
(x = sh), de um lado para outro.
to go up subir.
to go upstairs subir.
What's up? Que (se) passa? O que é que há?
She's not up yet. Ela ainda não se levantou.
up to até.
up-to-date moderno, contemporâneo.

upon sôbre (sobre), em cima de.
upon my word sob minha palavra.

upper superior, mais alto.
upper floor andar superior.
upper lip lábio superior.

upright vertical; direito, justo (character).

upset (to) transtornar, perturbar.

upside down invertido; de cabeça para baixo
(x = sh).

upstairs andar superior; em cima, para cima.
to go upstairs subir.

upstart n. pessoa arrogante, pessoa preten-
siosa.

upward para cima.

urgency urgência.

urgent urgente.

Uruguayan uruguaio.

use uso.
to make use of utilizar, servir-se de.
in use em uso.
of no use inútil, não servir para nada.
It's no use. Não adianta. É inútil.
What's the use? Para quê? É inútil.
Não adianta.

use (to) usar, servir-se de, utilizar; habituar,
acostumar (to be in the habit of).
to use up gastar, esgotar, consumir.

I'm used to it. Estou acostumado.
I used to see her every day. Eu acostumava vê-la todos os dias. Eu a via (via-a) todos os dias.
used usado, de segunda mão.
useful útil.
useless inútil, vão.
usher porteiro; indicador (theatre, etc.).
usual usual, habitual, costumeiro.
 as usual como de costume.
usually usualmente, geralmente.
 I usually get up early. Geralmente eu me levanto (levanto-me) cedo.
utensil utensílio.
 kitchen utensils utensílios de cozinha.
utility utilidade.
utilize utilizar, empregar.
utmost extremo, sumo, máximo (x = s).
utterly inteiramente, totalmente, completamente.

V

vacancy vacância, vagância; quarto para alugar, apartamento para alugar.
vacant vago, desocupado.
vacation férias.
vaccinate vacinar.
vaccine vacina.
vacuum vácuo, vazio.
vacuum cleaner aspirador de pó.
vague vago.
vain vão.
 in vain em vão.
vainly inùtilmente, fùtilmente.
valid válido.
valise valise, mala de mão.
valley vale.
valuable valioso, de valor.
value valor, valia; preço (price); aprêço (apreço), estima (regard).
value (to) avaliar, estimar (to estimate the value); apreciar, estimar (to think highly of).
valve válvula.
vanilla baunilha.
vanish desaparecer.
vanity vaidade.
variable variável.
variety variedade.
various vários, diversos, variados.
varnish verniz.
vary variar.
vaseline vaselina.
vast vasto, imenso, enorme, amplo.
veal vitela, came de vitela.
 veal cutlet costeleta de vitela.
vegetable legume, verdura.
vegetation vegetação.
vehement veemente.
vehicle veículo.
veil véu.
vein veia (body), veio (mineral).
velvet veludo.
vendor vendedor, mascate.
Venezuelan venezuelano.
vengeance vingança.
ventilate ventilar.
ventilation ventilação.
veranda varanda, terraço.
verb verbo.
verdict veredicto, julgamento.
verse verso.
vertical vertical.
very muito.

very much muito, muitíssimo.
very many muitíssimos, muitíssimas.
very much money muito dinheiro.
(Very) much obliged. Muito agradecido.
Very well, thank you. Muito bem, obrigado.
the very same man o mesmo homem.
vessel vaso, vasilha (for liquids); navio, embarcação (ship).
vest colête (colete).
veteran veterano.
veterinary veterinário.
vex vexar (x = ks), irritar, aborrecer, amolar.
vexation amolação, irritação.
vibration vibração.
vice vício.
vice-president vice-presidente.
vice versa vice versa.
vicinity vizinhança.
vicious vicioso, malvado, malévolo.
 vicious circle círculo vicioso.
victim vítima.
victor vencedor.
victorious vitorioso.
victory vitória.
view vista, panorama, paisagem.
 in view of em vista de.
 point of view ponto de vista.
 What a view! Que vista! Que paisagem!
view (to) olhar, ver, contemplar.
vigil vigília.
vigilant vigilante.
vigor vigor, fôrça (força), vitalidade.
vigorous vigoroso.
vile vil, baixo (x = sh).
villa casa de campo.
village aldeia, povoação.
villager aldeão.
villain vilão.
vine vinha, videira.
vinegar vinagre.
vineyard vinha.
violate violar.
violation violação.
violence violência.
violent violento.
violet violeta.
violin violino.
violinist violinista.
violoncello violoncelo.
virgin virgem.
virtue virtude.
virtuous virtuoso.
visa visto.
visible visível.
vision visão.
visit visita.
 to pay a visit visitar, fazer uma visita.
visitor visitante, visita.
visual visual.
vital vital, essencial.
vitamin vitamina.
vivid vívido, vivo, animado.
vocal vocal, oral.
 vocal cords cordas vocais.
voice voz.
void adj. vazio, inválido, nulo.
void n. vazio, vácuo.
volcano vulcão.
volt volt (vóltio).
volume volume, tomo (book).
voluntary voluntário.
volunteer voluntário.
vomit vômito (vómito).

vomit (to) vomitar.
vote voto, sufrágio.
vote (to) votar.
voter votante, eleitor.
vow voto, promessa, juramento.
vow (to) jurar, fazer voto, fazer promessa.
voyage viagem.
voyager viajante, viageiro.
vulgar vulgar, comum.
vulture abutre.

W

wade vadear.
 to wade entrar na água.
 to wade into (something) pôr mãos à obra, dedicar-se a.
wage (to) travar, empreender, promover.
 to wage war fazer guerra.
wager aposta.
wager (to) fazer aposta.
wages salário, ordenado.
wagon carro, carroção, vagão.
waist cíntura.
wait (to) esperar, aguardar.
 Wait for me. Espere-me.
 to keep waiting fazer esperar.
 to wait on servir.
waiter garção, garçom (empregado).
waiting espera.
 waiting room sala de espera.
waitress garçonete (empregada).
wake (to) acordar, despertar.
 to wake up acordar, despertar.
 I woke up at seven Acordei às sete.
waken acordar, despertar.
walk passeio.
 to take a walk dar um passeio.
walk (to) andar, caminhar.
 to walk away from afastar-se.
 to walk down descer.
 to walk up subir.
 to walk out sair.
 to walk out on abandonar, desertar.
walking passeio, andar.
 to go walking dar um passeio.
 walking cane bengala.
wall muro, parede, muralha.
 wallpaper papel de parede.
walnut noz, nogueira.
waltz valsa.
waltz (to) valsar, dançar uma valsa.
wand vara, varinha.
wander vagar; perder-se, desviar-se (to go astray).
want necessidade, falta, escassez.
 to be in want estar necessitado.
 for want of por falta de.
want (to) necessitar, ter necessidade de (to need); querer, desejar (to desire).
 What do you want? Que deseja o senhor?
 Don't you want to come? Não quer vir?
 Cook wanted. Procura-se uma cozinheira.
wanting insuficiente, deficiente; necessitado, destituído.
 to be wanting faltar.
war guerra.
 War Department Ministério de Guerra.
 to wage war fazer guerra.
ward sala, divisão (hospital); bairro, distrito (city); pupilo, tutelado (under a guardian).
warden diretor (director) (school); administrador (prison).
ward off (to) aparar, parar, desviar, repelir.
wardrobe guarda-roupa.
 wardrobe trunk mala-armário.
warehouse armazém.

wares mercadorias.
warfare guerra, combate.
warlike bélico, belicoso, marcial.
warm quente.
  It's warm. Está quente.
  I am warm. Estou com calor. Tenho calor.
  warm water água quente.
warm (to) aquecer.
warmly calorosamente, ardentemente.
warn advertir, prevenir, avisar.
warning advertência, admoestação, aviso.
  to give warning advertir.
warrant autorização; mandado (legal).
warrior guerreiro.
wash lavagem, roupa para lavar, roupa lavada.
  washbasin lavatório, bacia.
  washing machine máquina de lavar roupa.
wash (to) lavar.
  to wash one's hands lavar as mãos.
waste desperdício, perda, estrago.
waste (to) gastar, desgastar, destruir, perder.
  to waste one's time perder o tempo.
wastebasket cêsto (cesto) para papéis.
wastepaper papéis usados.
watch relógio; guarda (guard).
  wristwatch relógio-pulseira.
  to wind up (a watch) dar corda a.
watch (to) velar, guardar, vigiar.
  to watch out ter cuidado.
  to watch over guardar, vigiar.
watchful alerta, vigilante, atento.
watchmaker relojoeiro.
watchman guarda, vigia.
watchword senha, lema.
water água.
  fresh water água doce.
  hot water água quente.
  mineral water água mineral.
  running water água corrente.
  soda water água gasosa.
  water faucet torneira.
  waterpower fôrça (força) hidráulica.
  to make one's mouth water fazer água na bôca (boca).
water (to) regar (to sprinkle); irrigar, molhar, aguar.
waterfall cachoeira, queda d'água.
watermelon melancia.
waterproof impermeável, à prova d'água.
wave onda, ondulação.
  shortwave onda curta.
  longwave onda longa.
  sound wave onda sonora.
  wavelength comprimento de onda.
wave (to) ondular; fazer sinais (to signal by waving); agitar (a handkerchief).
  to wave one's hand fazer sinais com a mão.
waver (to) vacilar, hesitar.
wavering adj. vacilante, hesitante.
wavy ondulado.
wax cêra (cera).
  wax candle vela de cêra.
  wax paper papel encerado.
wax (to) encerar.
way caminho, via, rumo; modo, maneira (manner).
  way in entrada.
  way out saída.
  by way of via.
  by the way a propósito.
  in such a way de tal maneira.
  in this way dêste (deste) modo.
  any way de qualquer modo.
  in no way de nenhum modo, de maneira alguma.
  this way assim, desta maneira.
  Go this way. Vá por aqui.
  on the way to a caminho para, rumo de.

out of the way fora do caminho; longe; raro.
  across the way em frente.
  Which way? Por onde?
  Step this way. Venha por aqui. Venha cá
  in some way or other de um modo ou de outro.
  under way a caminho, em marcha.
  the other way around ao contrário.
  all the way todo o caminho.
  to give way ceder, dar lugar.
we nós.
  the five of us nós cinco.
weak débil, fraco.
weaken debilitar(-se), enfraquecer(-se).
weakness debilidade, fraqueza.
wealth riqueza, bens.
wealthy rico, abastado.
weapon arma.
wear (to) usar, vestir.
  to wear down cansar, aborrecer (to annoy), vencer (to overcome).
  to wear off gastar-se.
  to wear out gastar-se.
  to wear well durar (to last).
weariness cansaço, fadiga.
wearing apparel roupa.
weary adj. cansado, fatigado.
weary (to) cansar(-se), fatigar(-se).
weather tempo.
  bad weather mau tempo.
  nice weather bom tempo.
weave tecer.
web teia, tecido.
  spider web teia de aranha.
wedding boda, casamento.
  wedding dress vestido de noiva.
  wedding ring aliança.
wedge cunha.
Wednesday quarta-feira, quarta.
weed erva daninha.
week semana.
  weekday dia útil.
  last week a semana passada.
  next week a semana que vem.
weekend fim de semana.
weekly adj. semanal.
  weekly publication semanário.
weekly adv. semanalmente.
weep chorar.
  to weep for, to weep over chorar por.
weigh pesar; levantar ferro (to weigh anchor).
weight pêso (peso).
  gross weight pêso bruto.
  net weight pêso líquido.
  weights and measures pesos e medidas.
weighty pesado; momentoso, importante.
welcome adj. bem-vindo.
  Welcome! Bem-vindo!
  You're welcome (answer to "Thank you."). De nada.
welcome n. boas-vindas.
welcome (to) dar as boas-vindas.
welfare bem-estar.
  welfare work obra de beneficência social.
well poço.
well adj. bom; adv. bem.
  to be well sentir-se bem.
  very well muito bem.
  I don't feel well. Não me sinto bem.
  well-being bem-estar.
  well-bred bem educado.
  well-done bem feito.
  well-to-do rico, abastado, próspero.
  well-known bem conhecido.
  well-timed oportuno.
  as well as assim como, tanto como, tanto quanto.
  Well then? E agora?

Very well! Fine! Está bem!
west oeste, ocidente.
western ocidental.
wet adj. molhado, úmido.
  to get wet molhar-se.
wet (to) molhar.
wharf cais.
what que, o que.
  What's that? Que é isso?
  What's the matter? Que é que há?
  What else? Que mais?
  What for? Para quê?
whatever qualquer que, tudo quanto.
  whatever you like o que você quiser.
wheat trigo.
wheel roda.
  sterring wheel volante.
  wheelchair cadeira de rodas.
wheelbarrow carrinho de mão.
when quando.
  Since when? Desde quando?
whenever quando, sempre que, quando quer que.
  whenever you like quando você quiser.
where onde.
  Where is it? Onde está?
  Where are you from? Donde (de onde) é o senhor?
  Where are you going? Para onde vai?
whereby pelo qual, por médio de que, por médio do qual.
wherever onde quer que.
whether se, quer, ou.
  I doubt whether duvido que.
  whether he like it or not quer queira quer não.
which qual, que, o qual, a qual.
  Which book? Que livro?
  Which way? Por onde? Por que caminho?
  Which of these? Qual dêstes (destes)?
  all of which todo o qual, todos dos quais.
  both of which ambos.
whichever qualquer.
while n. momento, tempo.
  a little while um pouco tempo.
  a little while ago há pouco tempo.
  for a while por algum tempo.
  once in a while de vez em quando.
  to be worthwhile valer a pena.
while conj. enquanto, ao passo que.
whip chicote, açoite, látego.
whip (to) chicotear açoitar; bater (cream, eggs, etc.).
  whipped cream nata batida.
whirl giro, rodopio.
whirl (to) girar, rodopiar, dar voltas.
whirlpool remoinho de água, vórtice.
whirlwind remoinho de vento, furacão.
whisper sussurro, cochicho, murmúrio.
whisper (to) sussurrar, cochichar, murmurar.
  in a whisper em voz baixa (x = sh).
whistle apito, assobio.
whistle (to) apitar, assobiar.
white branco.
  white of egg clara de ôvo (ovo).
  white lie mentira inofensiva.
  White House Casa Branca.
whiten (to) branquear.
who quem, que, qual, o qual, a qual, os quais, as quais, aquêle (aquele), aquela.
  Who is it? Quem é?
whoever quem quer que, qualquer que.
  whoever it may be quem quer que fôr (for), seja quem fôr.
whole todo, inteiro, completo.
  the whole of Portugal todo Portugal.
  whole wheat bread pão integral.
  on the whole em geral.
  whole number número inteiro.

wholehearted sincero, dedicado.

wholesale por atacado.

wholesome são, salubre.

wholly totalmente, inteiramente.

whom quem, que.

whose cujo, de quem.

why por que.
Why not? Por que não?

wicked mau, malvado.

wickedness maldade.

wide largo, vasto, amplo, extenso.
two inches wide duas polegadas de largura.
wide open aberto de par em par.

wide-awake desperto, alerta, vivo.

widely muito, extensamente.
widely different completamente diferente.
widely used muito usado.
widely known muito conhecido.

widen alargar, estender, ampliar.

widespread muito difundido, muito espalhado.

widow viúva.

widower viúvo.

width largura.

wife espôsa (esposa), mulher, senhora.

wig cabeleira postiça, peruca.

wild selvagem (savage); silvestre (plants);
não domesticado (not tamed); bárbaro;
desenfreado, precipitado (unruly).

wilderness deserto, selva.

will vontade; testamento (legal).
at will à vontade.
against one's will contra a vontade.

will (to) querer, desejar; legar.
Will you tell me the time? Quer ter a
bondade de me dizer (dizer-me) que horas
são?
Will you do me a favor? Quer me fazer
(fazer-me) um favor?
I'll not go. Não irei. Não quero ir.

willing disposto, pronto, inclinado.
to be willing estar disposto, querer.
God willing. Se Deus quiser.

willingly de boa vontade, voluntàriamente.

willingness boa vontade.

win (to) ganhar, vencer, triunfar.
to win out sair bem, triunfar.

wind vento.
wind instrument instrumento de sôpro
(sopro).

wind (to) enrolar, dar corda a (a watch).

windmill moinho de vento.

window janela.
windowpane vidro, vidraça.

windshield pára-brisa.

windy ventoso.

wine vinho.
red wine vinho tinto.
white wine vinho branco.

wing asa.

wink piscadela.

wink (to) piscar.

winner vencedor.

winter inverno (Inverno).

wintry invernal.

wipe (to) limpar; secar, enxugar (x = sh)
(to dry).
to wipe out eliminar, destruir.

wire n. arame (metal); telegrama (telegram).
barbed wire arame farpado.

wire (to) telegrafar.

wisdom sabedoria, prudência, bom senso.
wisdom tooth dente do siso.

wise adj. sábio, inteligente.

wish desejo.

wish (to) desejar, querer.

wit engenho, agudeza, capacidade mental.

witch bruxa (x = sh).

with com, de, a, em, por meio de, contra.
coffee with milk café com leite.
to touch with the hand tocar com a mão.
She came with a friend. Ela veio com um
amigo.
to identify oneself with identificar-se com.
to struggle with (against) lutar contra.
with respect to com respeito a.
the young girl with the red dress a jovem
de vestido vermelho.
That always happens with friends. Isso
sempre acontece entre amigos.
with (by) much study por meio de muito
estudo.

withdraw (to) retrair, tirar, remover.

withdrawal retirada.

within dentro de, dentro, a pouco de.
within a week dentro de uma semana.
within a short distance a pouca distância.

without sem; adj. fora, por fora.
coffee without sugar café sem açúcar.
without fail sem falta.
without doubt sem dúvida.
without thinking it over well sem pensá-
lo bem.

witness testemunha.

witness (to) presenciar, ver, testemunhar.

witty engenhoso, gracioso.

wolf lôbo (lobo).

woman mulher.
young woman jovem.

wonder maravilha.
no wonder não é de admirar.

wonder (to) admirar-se, surpreender-se,
perguntar-se.
I wonder whether it's true. Eu me pergunto
(pergunto-me) se será verdade. Será
verdade?
to wonder at admirar-se de.

wonderful maravilhoso, admirável, magnífico,
estupendo.
wonderful city cidade maravilhosa.

wood madeira; floresta, selva, mato (woods);
lenha (firewood).

woodwork madeiramento, trabalho de madeira.

wool lã.

woolen de lã.

word palavra.
word for word palavra por palavra.
in other words em outras palavras.
by word of mouth oralmente, verbalmente.
upon my word palavra de honra.
to leave word deixar (x = sh) recado.

work trabalho, obra.
to be at work estar ocupado, estar
trabalhando (a trabalhar).
out of work desempregado.
work of art obra de arte.

work (to) trabalhar; funcionar, andar (a
machine); cultivar.
to work out resolver (a problem).
the radio is not working o rádio não
está funcionando (a funcionar).

worker trabalhador, operário.

working trabalho, funcionamento.
working day dia útil, dia de trabalho.

workman trabalhador, operário.

workshop oficina.

world mundo.
all over the world por todo o mundo.
worldwide mundial.
World War Guerra Mundial.

worm verme, bicho, gusano.

worn-out gasto, estragado, batido.

worry preocupação, cuidado, ansiedade.
Don't worry. Não se preocupe.
to be worried estar preocupado.

worse pior.
to get worse piorar.
so much the worse tanto pior.
worse and worse, from bad to worse de mal
a pior.
to take a turn for the worse piorar.

worship adoração, culto.

worship (to) adorar, venerar, idolatrar.

worst o pior.
the worst o pior.
at worst no pior dos casos.
if worst comes to worst se acontecer o
pior.

worth valor, mérito.
What's it worth? Quanto vale?
It's not worth that much. Não vale
tanto.
to be worthwhile valer a pena.

worthless inútil, sem valor.

worthwhile que vale a pena, de valor.

worthy digno, merecedor.

would querer. The conditional tense is
generally expressed by adding -ia, (-ias),
-ia, íamos, (-íeis), -iam to the infinitive of
the verb. The imperfect indicative is also
used in this sense, especially in conversation. The verbs of the second and third
conjugations (infinitives ending in -er, -ir)
add the above endings to the stem of the infinitive to make the imperfect indicative
tense. Verbs of the first conjugation
(infinitive ending in -ar) add -ava, (-avas),
-ava, -ávamos, (-áveis), -avam to the stem of
the infinitive.
I would go eu iria, eu ia.
I would like to go. Gostaria de ir.
Gostava de ir.
I would go if I could. Eu iria (ia) se
pudesse.
She wouldn't come. Ela não quis vir.
I wish she would come. Oxalá (x = sh)
que venha.
I would like to ask you a favor.
Gostaria de lhe pedir (pedir-lhe) um
favor.

wound ferida, ferimento.

wound (to) ferir.

wounded ferido.

wrap (to) enrolar, envolver, embrulhar.

wrapper envoltório, embalagem, empacotamento.

wrapping paper papel de embrulho.

wreath grinalda, coroa.

wreck destruição, ruína, naufrágio
(shipwreck).

wreck (to) arruinar, destruir, naufragar (ship).

wrench arranco, torcedura; chave inglêsa
(inglesa) (tool).

wrench (to) torcer, deslocar, arrancar.

wrestle (to) lutar corpo a corpo.

wring torcer, retorcer.

wrinkle ruga, prega.

wrinkle (to) enrugar(-se), franzir.
she wrinkled her brow ela franziu a testa.

wrist pulso, munheca.
wristwatch relógio-pulseira.

write (to) escrever.

writer escritor, autor.

writing escrita, escrito, escritura.
in writing por escrito.
writing desk escrivaninha, secretária.
writing paper papel de escrever.

written escrito.

wrong n. mal; dano (harm); injúria, injustiça;
êrro (erro); transgressão, infração (infracção);
adj. mau, incorreto (incorrecto), falso, errado,
injusto; adv. mal.
to do wrong fazer mal.
You are wrong. Você não tem razão. Você
está errado.

to get out on the wrong side of the bed
levantar-se com o pé esquerdo.
That's wrong. Está mal escrito (written).
Está mal feito (done).
Something is wrong with the engine. O motor
não funciona bem.
wrong side out do lado do avêsso (avesso).
What's wrong with him? O que há com êle?

X

X-rays raios X.

Y

yard yarda (measurement); pátio.
yawn bocejo.
yawn (to) bocejar.
year ano.
last year o ano passado.
next year o ano que vem.
many years ago há muitos anos.
every year todos os anos.
all year long o ano todo.
yearbook anuário.
yearly *adj.* anual.

yearly *adv.* anualmente.
yeast levedura, fermento.
yell grito, berro.
yell (to) gritar, berrar.
yellow amarelo.
yes sim.
yesterday ontem.
the day before yesterday anteontem.
yet *adv.* ainda; *conj.* porém, todavia, não
obstante.
not yet ainda não.
as yet até agora.
I don't know yet. Ainda não sei.
yield rendimento, renda, produção, produto.
yield (to) render, produzir; ceder (to give in).
yoke jugo.
yolk gema.
you (tu) (*fam.*); você (friendly); o senhor, os
senhores, a senhora, as senhoras (polite).
young jovem.
young man jovem, moço.
young lady jovem, moça.
young people jovens.
your, yours (teu, tua, teus, tuas) (*fam.*); seu,
sua, seus, suas, de você, de vocês, do senhor,

dos senhores, da senhora, das senhoras.
This book is yours. Êste (este) livro é seu.
Yours sincerely De Vossa Senhoria atento e
obrigado.
yourself você mesmo, o senhor mesmo, a senhora mesma, se.
Wash yourself. Lave-se.
yourselves vocês mesmos, os senhores mesmos, as senhoras mesmas.
youth juventude, adolescência, mocidade.
youthful jovem, juvenil.

Z

zeal zêlo (zelo), fervor, ardor.
zealous zeloso, ardoso.
zero zero.
zest entusiasmo, gôsto (gosto).
zigzag ziguezague.
zinc zinco.
zone zona.
zoo jardim zoológico.
zoological zoológico.
zoology zoologia.

GLOSSARY OF PROPER NAMES

Adolph Adolfo.
Alexander Alexandre.
Alfred Alfredo.
Alice Alice.
Alphonse Afonso.
Andrew André.
Ann, Anna Anne Ana.
Anthony Antônio (António).
Arthur Arturo.
Augustus Augusto.

Barbara Bárbara.
Beatrice Beatriz.
Bernard Bernardo.

Caroline Carolina.
Cecilia Ceoflia.
Charles Carlos.

Charlotte Carlota.

Dorothy Dorotéia (Doroteia).

Edward Eduardo.
Eleanor Leonor.
Elizabeth Isabel.
Emily Emflia.
Ernest Ernesto.
Esther Ester.
Eugene Eugênio (Eugénio).

Francis Francisco.
Frederic(k) Frederico.

George Jorge.
Gertrude Gertrudes.
Gloria Glória.

Helen Helena.
Henry Henrique.

Inez Inês.

John João.
Joseph José.
Josephine Josefa, Josefina.
Julius Júlio.

Leonard Leonardo.
Louis Luís.
Louise Luísa.
Lucy Lúcia.

Manuel Manuel.
Margaret Margarida.
Martha Marta.

Mary Maria.
Michael Miguel.

Paul Pablo.
Peter Pedro.
Philip Filipe.

Raymond Raimundo.
Richard Ricardo.
Robert Roberto.
Rose Rosa.

Theresa Teresa.
Thomas Tomás.

Vincent Vicente.

William Guilherme.

GLOSSARY OF GEOGRAPHICAL NAMES

Africa África.
Alps Alpes.
America América.
Andes Andes.
Angola Angola.
Argentina Argentina.
Asia Asia.
Athens Atenas.
Atlantic Ocean Oceano Atlântico.
Australia Austrália.
Azores Açôres (Açores).

Barcelona Barcelona.
Belgium Bélgica.
Bolivia Bolívia.
Brasilia Brasília.
Brazil Brasil.
Brussels Bruxelas (x = sh).
Buenos Aires Buenos Aires.

Chile Chile.
China China.
Coimbra Coimbra.
Colombia Colômbia.
Costa Rica Costa Rica.
Cuba Cuba.
Czechoslovakia Checoslováquia.

Denmark Dinamaroa.
Dominican Republic República Dominicana.

Ecuador Equador.
Egypt Egito (Egìpto).
El Salvador. El Salvador.
England Inglaterra.
Europe Europa.

Finland Finlândia.
France França.

Galicia Galiza.

Geneva Genebra.
Germany Alemanha.
Great Britain Grã Bretanha.
Greece Grécia.
Guatemala Guatemala.

Haiti Haiti.
Havana Havana.
Hawaii Havaí.
Hispanic America Hispano América.
Holland Holanda.
Honduras Honduras.
Hungary Hungria.

Ireland Irlanda.
Israel Israel.
Italy Itália.

Japan Japao.

Lisbon Lisboa.
London Londres.
Low Countries Países Baixos (x = sh).

Macao Macau.
Madeira Madeira.
Madrid Madrid.
Mediterranean Sea Mar Mediterrâneo.
Mexico México (x = sh).
Moscow Moscovo, Moscóvia.
Mozambique Moçambique.

Netherlands Países Baixos (x = sh), Holanda.
New York Nova Iorque.
New Zealand Nova Zelândia.
Nicaragua Nicarágua.
North America America do Norte.
Norway Noruega.

Oceania Oceânia.

Pacific Ocean Oceano Pacífico.
Panama Panamá.
Paraguay Paraguai.
Paris Paris.
Peru Peru.
Philippines Filipinas.
Poland Polônia (Polónia).
Portugal Portugal.
Puerto Rico Pôrto (Porto) Rico.
Pyrenees Pirenéus.

Rio de Janeiro Rio de Janeiro.
Romania Romênia (Roménia).
Rome Roma.
Russia Rússia.

Sao Paulo, St. Paul São Paulo.
Scandinavia Escandinávia.
Scotland Escócia.
Sicily Sioflia.
South America América do Sul.
Spain Espanha.
Spanish America América Espanhola, Hispano-América.
Sweden Suécia.
Switzerland Suíça.

Timor Timor.
Turkey Turquia.

United States of America Estados Unidos da América.
United States of Brazil Estados Unidos do Brasil.
Uruguay Uruguai.

Vatican Vaticano.
Venezuela Venezuela.
Vienna Viena.

COMMON USAGE DICTIONARY

Russian-English
English-Russian

BY **Aron Pressman**

BASED ON THE METHOD DEVISED BY
RALPH WEIMAN
FORMERLY CHIEF OF LANGUAGE SECTION
U. S. WAR DEPARTMENT

*CONTAINING OVER 15,000 BASIC TERMS WITH
MEANINGS ILLUSTRATED BY SENTENCES AND
1000 ESSENTIAL WORDS ESPECIALLY INDICATED*

INTRODUCTION

The *Russian Common Usage Dictionary* lists the most frequently used Russian words, gives their most important meaning, and illustrates their use.

1. The *basic* Russian words are indicated by the use of a • to their left.

2. Only the most important meanings are given.

3. These meanings are illustrated, wherever necessary, by means of everyday phrases and sentences. Where there is no close English equivalent for a Russian word, or where the English equivalent has several different meanings, the context of the illustrative sentences helps make the meaning clear.

4. Each important word is followed by the everyday expressions in which it most frequently occurs. The *Common Usage Dictionary* serves accordingly as a phrase book or conversation guide; it contains thousands of everyday sentences which are of practical importance (for traveling, correspondence, etc.) or which serve as illustrations of the grammatical features of current written and spoken Russian. The Common Usage Dictionary should, therefore, prove helpful both to beginners who are building up their vocabulary and to advanced students who want to perfect their command of colloquial Russian.

5. In translating the Russian phrases and sentences, an attempt has been made to give not a mere translation, but an equivalent — that is, what an English speaker would say in the same situation. (Literal translations have been added to help the beginner.) The user is thus furnished with numerous examples of how common Russian expressions (particularly the very idiomatic and colloquial ones) can best be translated into English. This feature makes the *Common Usage Dictionary* especially useful for translation work.

6. The English-Russian part contains the most common English words and their Russian equivalents. By consulting the sentences given under the Russian word in the Russian-English part, the student can observe how the word is used in practical cases.

Russian-English DICTIONARY

A

●а but, and, or (first letter of alphabet)
  Вот перо́, а вот бума́га. Here is a pen and here is paper.
  не он, а его́ сестра́ not he, but his sister
  Спеши́, а то опозда́ешь. Hurry, or you'll be late.
абажу́р lampshade
абрико́с apricot
абсолю́тный absolute
абстра́ктный abstract
абсу́рд absurdity
  довести́ до абсу́рда to carry to an absurdity
абсу́рдный absurd
абсце́сс abscess
ава́нс advance
  де́лать ава́нсы to make advances or overtures
  плати́ть ава́нсом to pay on account
  получа́ть ава́нс в счёт зарпла́ты to receive an advance on salary
авантю́ра adventure
а́вгуст August
  в а́вгусте in August
авиа́тор aviator, pilot
авиа́ция aviation, aircraft
●аво́сь perhaps, maybe
  идти́ на аво́сь to take a chance
  на аво́сь on the off-chance
автобиогра́фия autobiography
●авто́бус bus
автокра́тия autocracy
●автома́т automatic machine
автомати́ческий automatic
  автомати́ческий телефо́н dial telephone
●автомоби́ль (m.) automobile
●автоно́мия autonomy
●а́втор author
●авторите́т authority
  по́льзоваться авторите́том to use one's authority
а́вторские royalties (to an author)
  а́вторское пра́во copyright
●авторучка fountain pen
аге́нт agent, factor
аге́нтство agency
агита́тор instigator
агита́ция agitation, propaganda
аго́ния agony
агресси́вный aggressive
агре́ссия aggression
агрикульту́ра agriculture
агробиоло́гия agricultural biology
ад hell
адвока́т lawyer
адвокату́ра legal profession, the bar
  занима́ться адвокату́рой to be a practicing attorney

●администра́тор administrator
администра́ция administration, management
●а́дрес address
адресова́ть to address, direct
ажита́ция agitation
аза́ртно recklessly
  аза́ртно игра́ть to gamble
●а́збука alphabet
азо́т nitrogen
  за́кись азо́та nitrous oxide
  о́кись азо́та nitric oxide
акаде́мия academy
акваре́ль (f.) water color
  аквapeли́ст water-color painter
акко́рд chord
аккордео́н accordion
аккура́тность (f.) accuracy, carefulness, punctuality
аккура́тный careful, neat, punctual
акт act
  выпускно́й акт graduation exercise
  обвини́тельный акт indictment
актёр actor
●акти́вно actively
актри́са actress
аку́ла shark
акуше́р, акуше́рка obstetrician (m., f.), midwife
акце́нт accent
акционе́р stockholder
а́кция share
  а́кции па́дают shares go down (in value)
а́лгебра algebra
●алкого́ль (m.) alcohol
  алкого́льный напи́ток alcoholic beverage, strong drink
алкало́ид alkaloid
алле́я avenue, path
алта́рь (m.) altar
алфави́т alphabet
  по алфави́ту in alphabetical order
альбо́м album
альтруи́зм altruism, unselfishness
алюми́ний aluminum
амби́ция ambition, self-love, pride
амбулато́рия clinic
Аме́рика America
америка́нец, америка́нка American (m. f.)
америка́нский American
●ана́лиз analysis, test
  сде́лать ана́лиз кро́ви to make a blood test
анало́гия analogy
анана́с pineapple
анато́мия anatomy
а́нгел angel
англи́йский English
  англи́йская була́вка safety pin
  по-англи́йски in English
англича́нин (m.) Englishman

англича́нка (f.) Englishwoman
анекдо́т anecdote, joke
анке́та questionnaire
  запо́лнить анке́ту to fill in a form
ано́нс announcement (usually theatrical, concert)
антагони́ст antagonist
антагонисти́ческий antagonistic
антипа́тия antipathy, aversion
  пита́ть антипа́тию к чему́-нибудь.. to feel an aversion for something
  почу́вствовать антипа́тию к кому́-нибудь to take a dislike to someone
антрополо́гия anthropology
анчо́ус anchovy
аншла́г the "sold out" notice
  Пье́са идёт с аншла́гом. The house (play) is sold out every night.
апельси́н orange
аплоди́ровать to applaud, cheer
●аппара́т apparatus, instrument
  фотографи́ческий аппара́т camera
●аппети́т appetite
  прия́тного аппети́та *bon appétit*
аппети́тный appetizing, tempting
апре́ль (m.) April
апте́ка drugstore, pharmacy
аранжи́ровать to arrange
арбу́з watermelon
аргуме́нт argument
  ве́ский аргуме́нт significant or telling argument
аре́нда lease
  взять в аре́нду to take on lease
●аре́ст arrest
  взять под аре́ст to arrest
●арифме́тика arithmetic
●а́рмия army
аром́ат aroma, fragrance, perfume
арома́тный aromatic, scented
арти́ст, арти́стка artist, master, actor (m., f.)
артисти́ческий artistic
археоло́гия archeology
архите́ктор architect
аспира́нт post-graduate student
аспири́н aspirin
ассортиме́нт selection, assortment
ассоциа́ция association
  по ассоциа́ции by association of ideas
а́тлас atlas
атле́т athlete
атмосфе́ра atmosphere
ато́мный atomic
  ато́мная эне́ргия atomic energy
аукцио́н auction
  продава́ть с аукцио́на to sell by auction
афи́ша poster, bill, placard
ах! oh!, ah!

áхать (áхнуть) to exclaim, gasp, sigh

он и áхнуть не успéл before he knew where he was (he didn't even have time to gasp)

аэродрóм airfield

аэроплáн airplane

Б

бáбочка butterfly

•бáбушка grandmother

багáж baggage

ручнóй багáж hand or small luggage

úмственный багáж store of knowledge

бáза base, basis

подводúть бáзу под чтó-нибýдь to give good grounds for something

сырьевáя бáза source of raw materials

экономúческая бáза economic basis

•базáр market

устрóить базáр to create an uproar

базúровать(ся) (imp.) to be based on, rest on, depend

бакалéйный grocer

бакалéйная лáвка grocery store

бакалáвр holder of Bachelor of Arts degree

стéпень бакалáвра Bachelor of Arts degree

баклажáн eggplant

бактериолóгия bacteriology

•бал dance, ball

балáнс balance

балéт ballet

•балкóн balcony

балóванный spoiled (by indulgence)

•баловáть to spoil, indulge

бáловень pet

быть общим бáловнем to be a general favorite

банáн banana

•банк bank

•бáнка jar

барабáн drum

барабáнная перепóнка eardrum

•барáнина mutton, lamb

барáнина жáреная roast lamb

бáрхат velvet

барьéр barrier

бассéйн basin

бассéйн для плáвания swimming pool

бассéйн рекú river basin

•бастовáть to strike, go on strike

•башмáк shoe

быть под башмакóм у женû to be henpecked

•бéгать, бежáть to run

бежáть бегóм to hurry

Егó глазá бéгают. He has roving eyes.

бéгло fluently, superficially

Он бéгло говорúт по-рýсски. He speaks Russian fluently.

Я бéгло просмотрéл кнúгу. I looked the book over superficially.

бегóм running, double-quick

Бегú бегóм! Hurry! (Come on the double!)

•бедá misfortune, trouble

Быть бедé! Look out for trouble!

В том то и бедá. That's just the trouble.

Не бедá. It doesn't matter.

беднéть (обеднéть) to become poor

•бéдность (f.) poverty

Бéдность не порóк. Poverty is not a vice.

бéдность пóчвы poverty of the soil

бéдный poor, unfortunate

беднûга, беднûжка poor fellow, poor thing (m., f.)

•бедóвый mischievous, naughty

бедóвый человéк daredevil

бедрó thigh

•бéдствие calamity, disaster

•без without (prep. with gen.)

безбéдно comfortably

жить безбéдно to be fairly well off financially

безболéзненный painless

безвúнный innocent, guiltless

безвкýсие lack of taste

безвкýсный tasteless

безвóлие lack of will

безврéдный harmless, innocuous

безврéменно untimely

безврéменье hard times

•безгрáмотность illiteracy

безгрáмотный illiterate

бездáрно untalented

бездáрность (f.) mediocrity, lack of talent

бездéйствие inactivity

бездéльничать (imp.) to idle, loaf

бездýшный heartless, callous

безжúзненный lifeless, insipid

•беззабóтный carefree, lighthearted

беззакóнный lawless, unlawful

беззастéнчивый shameless, impudent

беззащúтный defenseless, unprotected

беззвýчный soundless, silent

беззлóбие kindliness

•безнадëжность (f.) hopelessness

безнадзóрность (f.) neglect

•безнрáвственность (f.) immorality

безнрáвственный immoral, dissolute

•безобрáзие outrage, disgrace

Там творûтся безобрáзия. Disgraceful things are going on there.

Что за безобрáзие! It's scandalous!

•безопáсность (f.) safety, security

безотвéтственность (f.) irresponsibility

•безрабóтица unemployment

•безразлúчие indifference

•безразлúчно indifferently

Мне совершéнно безразлúчно. It's all the same to me.

безýмец madman

безýмие folly, insanity

любúть до безýмия to be madly in love

безýмно madly, terribly

быть безýмно устáлым to be terribly tired

любúть безýмно to love madly

•безуслóвно undoubtedly, absolutely

безуспéшно unsuccessfuly

безыскýсственный unaffected, simple

бекóн bacon

•бéлка squirrel

беллетрúст fiction writer

беллетрúстика fiction

белокýрый blond, fairhaired

белокýрая жéнщина blonde (woman)

•бéлый white

бельë linen

нúжнее бельë underwear

постéльное бельë bedclothes

бензúн benzine, gasoline

бéрег shore, coast, bank

берëза birch tree

берéменная pregnant

•берéчь (сберéчь) to guard, save, take care of

берéчь своë врéмя to make the most of one's time

берéчь своë здорóвье to take care of one's health

берéчь тáйну to keep a secret

бес demon, devil

бесéда conversation, talk

бесéдовать (imp.) to converse, talk

бесконéчно infinitely, endlessly

бесконéчность (f.) endlessness, eternity

беспáмятность (f.) forgetfulness

беспáмятство unconsciousness, frenzy

•бесплáтно free of charge, gratis

бесподóбный matchless, incomparable

•беспокóить to worry, to disturb

беспокóиться to be anxious, to worry about

Не беспокóйтесь. Don't trouble yourself. Don't worry.

беспокойный troubled, uneasy
бесполезность (f.) uselessness
•беспомощность helpless
•беспорядок disorder, confusion
беспричинно without cause, without
  reason
беспутный dissipated, dissolute
бессердечность (f.) heartlessness,
  callousness
бессильный feeble, weak, helpless
бессмертный immortal
бессмысленно senselessly, foolishly
бессовестный dishonest, unscrupulous
бесстыдный shameless
бестактный tactless
бесцельный aimless
бесценный priceless, invaluable, beloved
бесчестить (обесчестить) to disgrace,
  dishonor
бесчувственный unfeeling, insensible
  бесчувственный человек unfeeling
    person
  находиться в бесчувственном со-
    стоянии to be unconscious
бешенство fury, rage
  довести до бешенства to drive
    wild
библиотека library
библия Bible
бикарбонат bicarbonate
билет ticket
биллион billion
бинокль binoculars
бинт bandage
бинтовать (забинтовать) to bandage
•биография biography
биолог biologist
биология biology
биохимия biochemistry
биполярность (f.) bipolarity
биржа stock exchange, stock market
бирюк lone wolf, morose fellow
  смотреть бирюком to look sullen
бис encore
бисульфат bisulphate
•бить (побить) to beat, hit, struggle
  against
  бить в цель to hit the mark
  бить в ладоши to clap hands
  бить ключом to be in full swing
  бить на эффект to strike for
    -effect
  бить тревогу to sound the alarm
биться to fight with, hit, strike, beat
  биться над задачей to struggle
    with a problem
  как он ни бился no matter how
    he tried
  Сердце сильно бьётся. The heart
    is beating hard.

•бифштекс steak
  бифштекс натуральный regular
    steak
  бифштекс рубленый chopped steak
благо blessing, good
  Желаю вам всех благ. I wish you
    every happiness.
•благодарить (поблагодарить) to
  thank
благодарность (f.) gratitude, thanks
благодарный grateful
благодаря thanks to (with dat.)
  благодаря тому, что thanks to the
    fact that
благодушие good humor, placidity
благонравие good behavior
•благополучно all right, well
  Всё кончилось благополучно.
    Everything ended happily.
благословение blessings
благотворитель (m.) philanthropist,
  benefactor
блаженство bliss, felicity
  на верху блаженства in perfect
    bliss
бледнеть (побледнеть) to grow pale
  бледнеть от страха to blanch with
    terror
•бледность (f.) pallor, colorlessness
блеск lustre, brilliance
•блеснуть flash, make a brilliant
  display
  Блеснула молния. Lightning
    flashed.
  У меня блеснула мысль. An idea
    flashed across my mind.
  Он любит блеснуть своим умом.
    He likes to show off his wit.
•блестеть shine, glitter, sparkle
  глаза блестят eyes sparkle
  Он ничем не блещет. He does not
    shine in anything.
блестяще brilliantly
  Дела идут блестяще. Things are
    going excellently.
•близ near (prep. with gen.)
близиться to draw near, to approach
•близкий near, similar (to)
  близкий родственник near relation
  близкий по духу человек kindred
    spirit
•близко (от) near
близнецы twins
•близорукий nearsighted
блинчики pancakes
•блондин, блондинка blonde, or
  fairhaired person (m., f.)
блузка blouse
блюдо dish, course
  его любимое блюдо his favorite
    dish
  обед из трёх блюд three-course
    dinner

•бог god
  ради бога for goodness' sake
богатеть (разбогатеть) to grow rich
богатство wealth
  естественные богатства natural
    resources
•богатый rich, wealthy
•бодрый cheerful, brisk
божественный divine
•бойкий smart, sharp, ready
  бойкая улица busy street
  бойкий ум ready wit
•бойко говорить по-русски to speak
  Russian fluently
•бок side
  сбоку from the side
  на боку sideways
•более more
•больница hospital
•больно painful
  Ему больно. He is in pain.
  ему больно, что it grieves him
    that
•больной sick
  больное воображение morbid
    imagination
  больной вопрос sore subject
•больше more
  больше всего most of all
  больше никогда never again
  Он больше не живёт там. He
    doesn't live there any more.
болезнь (f.) illness, disease
•болеть (заболеть) to ache, hurt
  У меня болит голова. I have a
    headache.
  У него болят зубы. His teeth ache.
    He has a toothache.
•болтать to chatter, babble
  болтать глупости to talk nonsense
болтун, болтунья chatterbox (m., f.)
боль (f.) pain, heartache
  душевная боль mental suffering
•большинство majority
большой big
  Большое спасибо. Thanks a lot.
бормотать (пробормотать) to
  mutter, mumble
борный boric
  борная кислота boric acid
•борода beard
•бороться to fight, contend, struggle
  бороться с самим собой to
    struggle with oneself
•борьба struggle, fight, wrestling
•босиком barefooted
босяк hobo
•ботинок boot
боязнь (f.) dread, fear
•бояться to fear
  Боюсь сказать. I am afraid to say.
  Боюсь, что он не придёт. I am
    afraid he won't come.

Не бо́йся. Don't worry. Don't be
afraid
●брак marriage, wedlock, defective
goods
●брат brother
двою́родный брат first cousin
●брать (взять) to take
брать взаймы́ to borrow
брать на себя́ сме́лость to take the
liberty
брать себя́ в ру́ки to pull oneself
together
Это берёт у него́ мно́го вре́мени.
It takes him a lot of time.
бра́ться (взя́ться) to undertake,
begin
бра́ться за чте́ние to begin to read
Он взя́лся за э́ту рабо́ту. He
undertook the work.
бриллиа́нт diamond
бри́тва razor
бри́тый clean-shaven
●бри́ть-ся (побри́ть-ся) to shave
(oneself)
бровь (f.) eyebrow
броди́ть to wander, roam, rove (only
by foot)
бром bromide
бро́мистый ка́лий potassium
●броса́ть (бро́сить) to throw, cast
броса́ть взгляд to cast a look
броса́ть ка́мни to throw stones
броса́ть кури́ть to give up smoking
броса́ть семью́ to desert one's
family
броса́ться (бро́ситься) to throw
oneself, to dash
броса́ться на по́мощь to rush to
help
броса́ться на ше́ю кому́-нибудь
to throw one's arms around someone's neck
брошю́ра pamphlet
●брю́ки trousers
●брюне́т, брюне́тка dark-haired
person, brunet, brunette
●бу́дет that will do, that's enough
Бу́дет тебе́ пла́кать! Stop crying!
буди́льник alarm clock
●буди́ть (разбуди́ть) to awaken
●бу́дто as if, as though,
apparently
Говоря́т, бу́дто он уе́хал. It seems
(they say) that he has gone
away.
У вас тако́й вид, бу́дто вы не
по́няли. You look as if you did
not understand.
бу́дущее (noun) the future
в бу́дущем in the future
бу́дущий future
на бу́дущей неде́ле next week
●бу́ква letter (of the alphabet)

буква́льно literally, word for word
●бу́лка roll (bread)
бульва́р avenue, boulevard
●бума́га докумснт, paper
бума́жник wallet
бума́жный cotton, paper
бума́жная матє́рия cotton material
бу́рный stormy
●бу́ря tempest, bad storm
●бутербро́д sandwich
●буты́лка bottle
●быва́ть to be sometimes
быва́ет, что it happens that
Ве́чером он быва́ет до́ма. He is at
home in the evenings.
Он когда́-то ча́сто быва́л у них.
At one time he visited them often.
●бы́вший former
бы́вший президе́нт former
president
●бы́стро rapidly
быстрота́ speed
●бы́стрый quick, rapid
●быть to be

В

●в to, into—direction (with acc.)
in, at—location (with prep.)
в 1944 году́ in 1944
в слу́чае, е́сли if, in case
в три часа́ at three o'clock
в четве́рг on Thursday
в январе́ in January
Я иду́ в го́род. I am going to the
city.
Я живу́ в го́роде. I live in the
city.
●ваго́н railway car
ва́жничать to put on airs
●ва́жно importantly
Ва́жно, что он пойдёт. It is important that he go.
●ва́жный important, pompous
ва́за vase, bowl
●вака́нсия vacancy
вальс waltz
●ва́нна bath
приня́ть ва́нну to take a bath
ва́нная bathroom
●варёный boiled, cooked
●варе́нье jam, preserves
вариа́ция variation
●вари́ть (свари́ть) boil, cook
вари́ться (свари́ться) to be cooking
●ваш, ва́ша, ва́ше, ва́ши your, yours
вая́тель (m.) sculptor
вбира́ть (вобра́ть) to absorb
введе́ние introduction, preface
●вводи́ть (ввести́) to introduce
ввести́ зако́н в де́йствие to implement a law
вводи́ть кого́-нибудь в заблужде́ние
to lead someone astray

вводи́ть мо́ду to introduce a
fashion
●вдво́е double, twice
вдво́е бо́льше twice as much
вдво́е ме́ньше half as much
Мы вдвоём пошли́. The two of us
went.
вдова́ widow
вдове́ц widower
●вдоль along (prep.. with gen.)
вдохнове́ние inspiration
●вдруг suddenly
вду́мчивость (f.) thoughtfulness
●ве́жливость (f.) politeness,
courtesy
ве́жливый polite, courteous
●везде́ everywhere
●век century, epoch
Век живи́, век учи́сь. You have to
study as long as you live.
ве́ксель (m.) promissory note, bill
of exchange
●вели́кий great, big
●великоду́шно generously, magnani-
mously
●великоле́пно splendidly, fine
●велосипе́д bicycle
●ве́на vein
вентиля́тор ventilator, fan
●венча́ть (повенча́ть) to marry
●ве́ра faith, belief
●верёвка rope, cord, string
●ве́рить (пове́рить) to believe, trust
●ве́рно right, correctly
ве́рно говори́ть to be right
ве́рно петь to sing on key
соверше́нно ве́рно quite right
●верну́ть(ся)—see возвраща́ть(ся)
ве́рный correct, right, faithful
ве́рный друг true friend
У вас ве́рные часы́? Is your watch
right?
вероя́тность (f.) probability
по всей вероя́тности in all probability
вертика́льно vertically
●верх top, head
е́здить верхо́м to ride horseback
одержа́ть верх to gain the upper
hand
верши́на top, summit
●вес weight, influence
изли́шек ве́са overweight
име́ть большо́й вес to be very
influential
приба́вить в ве́се to put on weight
уде́льный вес specific weight or
gravity
весели́ться to enjoy oneself
●весёлый cheerful, gay
●весна́ spring
весно́й in the spring

•вести, водить (повести) to lead,
conduct
вести войну to carry on a war
вести собрание to conduct a
meeting
Куда ведёт эта дорога? Where
does this road lead?
Он очень дурно ведёт себя. He
behaves badly.
•весь, вся, всё, все all, the whole
во весь голос at the top of one's
lungs
всего хорошего all of the best
всё же all the same
всё-таки nevertheless
весьма very, extremely
•ветер wind, breeze
•ветхий decrepit, dilapidated
ветхое платье threadbare clothes
•вечер evening, evening party
вечером in the evening
•вечеринка evening party
•вечный eternal, everlasting
вечное перо fountain pen
•вешалка clothes stand, hanger
•вешать (повесить) to hang up
вешать голову to hang one's head,
be dejected
•вещь (f.) thing
Вот это вещь! That's something
like it!
Это хорошая вещь. That's a good
thing.
взад и вперёд to and fro
взаимно mutually
взаимная помощь mutual aid
взаперти locked up
жить взаперти to live in seclusion
взволнованно with emotion, with
agitation
•взгляд look, stare, glance
бросить взгляд to cast a glance
на мой взгляд in my opinion
на первый взгляд on first sight
•вздор nonsense
вздох deep breath, sigh
•вздыхать (вздохнуть) to breathe,
heave a sigh, yearn for
•взрослый grownup, adult
взрыв explosion, outburst
взрыв смеха outburst of laughter
•взять—see брать
•вид appearance, view
вид из окна view from the window
имейте в виду to keep in mind,
take notice
У вас усталый вид. You look tired.
•видеть (увидеть) to see
видно apparently
•видно evidently, apparently
всем было видно, что it was clear
to everyone, that

визит call, visit
прийти с визитом к кому-нибудь
to pay someone a visit
•вилка fork
электрическая вилка electric plug
•вина fault, guilt
Ваша вина. It's your fault.
свалить вину на кого-либо to put
the blame on someone
•вино wine
•виноватый guilty
Я виноват. It's my fault.
виноград grapes
•висеть to hang, be suspended
Пальто висит в шкафу. The coat
is hanging in the closet.
витрина display window
•вишня cherry
•вкладывать (вложить) to put in,
insert
вкладывать в конверт to enclose in
an envelope
вкладывать всю душу во что-либо
to put one's whole soul into something
вложить кому-либо в уста to put
into someone's mouth
•включать (включить) to include,
insert
включать радио to switch
on the radio
•вкус taste
быть горьким на вкус to taste
bitter
одеваться со вкусом to dress
tastefully
человек со вкусом a man of taste
Это не по моему вкусу. That's
not to my taste.
вкусный tasty
владеть to own, possess
владеть аудиторией to hold one's
audience
владеть своей темой to be master
of one's subject
владеть собой to control oneself
•власть (f.) power, authority, rule
•влияние influence, authority
влиять (повлиять) to influence
влюблённый in love
влюблённая пара loving couple
•влюбляться (влюбиться) to fall in
love
вместе together
•вместо instead of (prep. with gen.)
вмешивать-ся (вмешать-ся) to
interfere, implicate
вмешиваться в чужие дела to
meddle with other people's
business
•вначале at first, in the beginning

•вне outside (prep. with genitive)
вне закона illegal
вне себя от радости beside oneself with joy
вне сомнения without a doubt
•внешний outward, outer
внешний вид outer appearance
внешняя политика foreign policy
•вниз down, downward
спускаться вниз to go down,
descend
внизу below
Он внизу. He is down below.
•внимание attention
обратить внимание to pay
attention
внимательно carefully, attentively
•внук grandson
внутренний inner, internal
внутренние болезни internal
diseases
внутренние причины intrinsic
causes
•внутри inside, within (prep. with
gen.)
•во время during (prep. with gen.)
вовремя on time
•вовсе quite
вовсе... не not at all
•вода water
как с гуся вода like water off a
duck's back
•водить, вести (повести) to lead,
conduct
•водка vodka
водоворот whirlpool
водород hydrogen
возбуждать (возбудить) to excite,
arouse
возбуждать аппетит to stimulate
the appetite
возбуждать надежды to raise
hopes
возбуждённый excited
•возвращать (вернуть) to return,
give back
возвращаться (вернуться) to return,
come back
•воздух air
воздушный airy
воздушные замки castles in the air
воздушный шарик balloon
•везти, возить to carry, transport
(by conveyance)
•возможно possible, it may be
likely
возможно скорее as soon as
possible
сколько возможно as much as
possible
возможность (f.) possibility,
opportunity

материа́льные возмо́жности means (financial)

возраст age

  одного́ во́зраста of the same age

•война́ war

  «Война́ и Мир» "War and Peace"

•войти́—see входи́ть

•вокза́л railway station

•вокру́г round, around (prep. with gen.)

  говори́ть вокру́г да о́коло to beat about the bush

•волна́ wave

волне́ние agitation, emotion

  быть в волне́нии to be agitated

  На о́зере волне́ние. The lake is rough.

•во́лосы hair

•во́льность (f.) liberty, freedom

  позволя́ть себе́ во́льности to take liberties

  поэти́ческая во́льность poetic license

вольфра́м tungsten

•во́ля will

  име́ть си́лу во́ли to have will power

  Он на во́ле. He is free.

  по до́брой во́ле voluntarily

•вообража́ть (вообрази́ть) to imagine, fancy

воображе́ние imagination

вообрази́ть—see вообража́ть

•вообще́ in general, altogether

  вообще́ говоря́ generally speaking

  Он вообще́ тако́й. He is always like that.

•вопро́с question

  вопро́с жи́зни и сме́рти matter of life or death

  Вопро́с не в э́том. That is not the question.

  оста́ться под вопро́сом to remain undecided

  спо́рный вопро́с moot point

•воро́та gates

•воротни́к collar

восемна́дцать eighteen

восемна́дцатый eighteenth

во́семь eight

восклица́ть (воскли́кнуть) to exclaim

воскресе́ние resurrection

•воскресе́нье Sunday

•воспита́ние upbringing, training

воспи́тывать (воспита́ть) to bring up, educate, train

воспо́льзоваться to take advantage of, profit by

  воспо́льзоваться слу́чаем to take advantage of the opportunity

воспомина́ние recollection, reminiscence

  Оста́лось одно́ воспомина́ние. All that is left is memory.

воспреща́ть(ся) (воспрети́ть) to prohibit

  вход воспреща́ется no admittance

  кури́ть воспреща́ется no smoking

восто́к east

восто́рг delight, enthusiasm

  быть в восто́рге to be in raptures

•восхити́тельный delightful, exquisite

восьмидеся́тый eightieth

восьмо́й eighth

•вот here is, here are

  Вот как! Is that so!

  вот почему́ that's why

  Вот приме́р. Here is an example.

впервы́е for the first time, first

•вперёд forward, in the future

  плати́ть вперёд to pay in advance

  Часы́ иду́т вперёд. The clock is fast.

впереди́ in front, before

  У него́ ещё це́лая жизнь впереди́. His whole life is before him.

•впечатле́ние impression, effect

вполго́лоса in an undertone, under one's breath

•вполне́ quite, fully

  вполне́ доста́точно quite enough

  вполне́ заслужи́ть fully deserve

  вполне́ успоко́енный fully reassured

впуска́ть (впусти́ть) to let in, admit

•враг enemy, foe

•врач physician, doctor

•вре́дно harmful, injurious

  Ему́ вре́дно кури́ть. It's bad for him to smoke.

•вре́мя time

  во́время on time

  во все времена́ at all times

  вре́мя го́да season

  Вре́мя пока́жет. Time will tell.

  всё вре́мя all the time

  в ско́ром вре́мени soon

  за после́днее вре́мя lately

всевозмо́жный all kinds of, every possible sort

  всевозмо́жные сре́дства every possible means

•всегда́ always

всерьёз seriously, in earnest

всё-таки all the same, nevertheless

вска́кивать (вскочи́ть) to jump onto, leap up

  вскочи́ть на́ ноги to jump to one's feet

вскипа́ть (вскипе́ть) to boil up

•вслух aloud

•вспомина́ть (вспо́мнить) to recollect, recall

вспо́мнить—see вспомина́ть

вспоте́ть—see поте́ть

встава́ть (встать) to get up, rise

Встал вопро́с. The question arose.

  встать гру́дью за что́-нибудь to stand up staunchly for something

  встать на́ ноги to become independent

•встать—see встава́ть

•встре́ча meeting, reception

  при встре́че с ке́м-нибудь on meeting someone

  оказа́ть раду́шную встре́чу to give a hearty welcome to

встре́тить (ся)—see встреча́ть (ся)

встреча́ть-ся (встре́тить-ся) to meet

  встреча́ть госте́й to welcome one's guests

  встреча́ть ла́сковое отноше́ние to meet with kindness

  встреча́ться с затрудне́ниями to meet with difficulties

  Их взо́ры встре́тились. Their eyes met.

•вступа́ть (вступи́ть) to enter, join

  вступа́ть в до́лжность to assume office

  вступа́ть в спор to enter into an argument

  вступа́ть в си́лу to come into effect

  вступа́ть в шко́лу to enter school

вступи́ть—see вступа́ть

•вся́кий any, every

  во вся́кое вре́мя at any time

  во вся́ком слу́чае at any rate

  Вся́кое быва́ет. Anything is possible.

  вся́кий раз each time

  на вся́кий слу́чай just in case

вта́йне in secret

вта́лкивать (втолкну́ть) to push, shove

втолкну́ть—see вта́лкивать

•вто́рник Tuesday

  во вто́рник on Tuesday

  по вто́рникам every Tuesday, on Tuesdays

•второ́й second

•вход entrance

  пла́та за вход admission fee

•входи́ть (войти́) to enter, go or come in (on foot)

  войти́ в исто́рию to go down in history

  входи́ть в долги́ to get into debt

  входи́ть в привы́чку to become a habit

  входи́ть в соглаше́ние to enter into an agreement

  Это е́ле вхо́дит. It is a tight fit.

•вчера́ yesterday

  иска́ть вчера́шнего дня to run a wild goose chase

въезд entrance, entry

въезжа́ть (въе́хать) to drive in, enter (by vehicle)

въе́хать—see (въезжа́ть)

•вы you (plural, or polite form)

•выбира́ть (вы́брать) to choose, select

выбра́ть—see выбира́ть

вы́бор choice, selection

У него́ нет вы́бора. He has no choice.

выбра́сывать (вы́бросить) to throw out, reject

вы́бросить из головы́ to put out of one's head

вы́бросить това́р на ры́нок to throw goods on the market

вы́годно advantageously, it is profitable

выдава́ть (вы́дать) to distribute, give out

выделе́ние isolation (chem.)

выделя́ть (ся)—see выделя́ть (ся)

выделя́ть-ся (вы́делить-ся) to single out, to isolate

вы́держать—see выде́рживать

выде́рживать (вы́держать) to sustain, endure

вы́держать экза́мен to pass an examination

вы́держать хара́ктер to stand firm

Он не вы́держал и запла́кал. He broke down and cried.

Он не мог э́того бо́льше вы́держать. He could not stand it any longer.

•вы́держка self-control, endurance

вы́думанный made-up, invented

выду́мывать (вы́думать) to invent, fabricate

вы́звать—see вызыва́ть

•вызыва́ть (вы́звать) to call, send for, challenge

вы́звать на дуэ́ль to challenge to a duel

вызыва́ть из ко́мнаты to call out of the room

вы́звать любопы́тство to provoke curiosity

вы́играть—see выи́грывать

•выи́грывать (вы́играть) to win

вы́играть де́ло to win one's case

вы́играть па́ртию to win a game

От э́того он то́лько вы́играет. He will only benefit from that.

вы́йти—see выходи́ть

вы́кройка sewing pattern

вылива́ть (вы́лить) to pour out, empty

вы́лить—see вылива́ть

вынима́ть (вы́нуть) to pull out, draw out

вы́нуть—see вынима́ть

вы́нудить—see вынужда́ть

вынужда́ть (вы́нудить) to compel, make

вынужда́ть призна́ние to force admission or recognition

выпа́ривание evaporation, steaming

вы́парить—see па́рить

вы́пить—see пить

выполне́ние fulfillment, realization

вы́полнить—see выполня́ть

•выполня́ть (вы́полнить) to carry out, fulfill

выполня́ть жела́ния to fulfill wishes

выполня́ть свои́ обя́занности to carry out one's duties

выраба́тывать (вы́работать) to manufacture, work out

вы́работать—see выраба́тывать

•выража́ться (вы́разить-ся) to express (oneself), voice

выража́ть слова́ми to put into words

Мне тру́дно выража́ться по-ру́сски. It is difficult to express myself in Russian.

мя́гко выража́ясь to put it mildly

выраже́ние expression

идиомати́ческое выраже́ние idiomatic expression

Он знал по выраже́нию её лица́. He knew by her look.

вы́разить (ся)—see выража́ть (ся)

выраста́ть (вы́расти) to grow up, increase

выраста́ть на 20% to increase by 20%

вы́расти—see выраста́ть

выска́кивать (вы́скочить) to jump out, leap out

вы́скочить— see выска́кивать

высо́кий high, tall

высо́кий челове́к tall fellow

высо́кие це́ли lofty aims

•высоко́ high

высота́ height

вы́ставка exposition, display

вы́стирать— see стира́ть

вы́стрел shot

высу́шивать (вы́сушить) to dry

вы́сушить—see высу́шивать

•вы́сший highest

вы́тереть— see вытира́ть

•вытира́ть (вы́тереть) to wipe dry

вы́учивать (вы́учить) to learn, teach

вы́учить наизу́сть to learn by heart

вы́учить студе́нтов ру́сскому языку́ to teach students the Russian language

вы́учить—see вы́учивать

•вы́ход exit, way out, coming out

вы́ход на у́лицу exit to street

по́сле вы́хода кни́ги after the book had appeared

У него́ не́ было друго́го вы́хода. He had no other way out.

•выходи́ть (вы́йти) to go out (on foot)

вы́йти из мо́ды to go out of fashion

вы́йти в отста́вку to resign, retire

вы́йти за́муж to get married (of women)

выходи́ть и́з дому to go out of the house

Из э́того ничего́ не вы́йдет. Nothing will come of it.

Кни́га уже́ вы́шла. The book was already published.

Окно́ выхо́дит в сад. The window faces the garden.

выходно́й день day off

вычита́ние subtraction

вяза́ть (связа́ть) to knit, crochet, bind up

вя́ло limply, sluggishly

Г

га́дость (f.) filth, muck

сде́лать га́дость кому́-либо to play a dirty trick on someone, double-cross

газ gas, gauze, gossamer

•газе́та newspaper

газоли́н gasoline

гала́нтный gallant

газо́н lawn, grass

га́йка nut (screw)

галере́я gallery

галло́н gallon

•гало́ша overshoes, rubbers

•га́лстук necktie

гара́ж garage

гаранти́ровать to guarantee

•гара́нтия guarantee, security

гардеро́б wardrobe

•гармо́ния harmony

гармони́ст accordion player

гарни́р garnish, vegetables served with main course

•где where—location

где́-то somewhere

где́-нибудь anywhere

гениа́льность (f.) genius, greatness

•ге́ний (noun—m.) genius

геогра́фия geography

геоме́трия geometry

•геро́й (noun—m.) hero

ги́бкий flexible, pliant

•ги́бнуть (поги́бнуть) to perish

гига́нтский gigantic

дви́гаться гига́нтскими шага́ми to progress at a great rate

- гита́ра guitar
- глава́ head, chief

  глава́ прави́тельства head of the government

  стоя́ть во главе́ to be at the head of

  глава́ chapter
- гла́вный main, chief
- глаго́л verb
- гла́дить (погла́дить) to iron, press, caress

  гла́дкий smooth, even, sleek

  гла́дкая доро́га smooth road

  гла́дкий материа́л solid-color material
- глаз eye
- глота́ть to swallow, gulp

  глота́ть слёзы to choke down one's tears

  глото́к one swallow, mouthful
- глубо́кий deep

  занима́ться до глубо́кой но́чи to work until late at night

  глубо́кая печа́ль deep sorrow

  глубо́кая таре́лка soup plate

  глубоко́ deeply, profoundly
- глу́пость (f.) foolishness

  глу́пый foolish, stupid
- глухо́й deaf

  глухо́й лес dense forest

  глуха́я ночь still night

  Он глух к мои́м про́сьбам. He is deaf to my entreaties.

  Он соверше́нно глух. He is completely deaf.

  гляде́ть (погляде́ть) to look at, gaze at, look like

  гляде́ть геро́ем to look like a hero

  гнев anger, ire

  гнездо́ nest

  гнуть (согну́ть) to bend, drive

  гнуть спи́ну перед ке́м-либо to kowtow to someone

  Я ви́жу, куда́ он гнёт. I see what he is driving at.
- говори́ть (сказа́ть) to say, tell

  говори́ть по-ру́сски to speak Russian

  говоря́т they say

  Он говори́т, что он бо́лен. He says he is ill.

  Он сказа́л, что он бо́лен. He said he is ill.
- год year

  годи́ться to be fit for, serve

  ни на что́ не годи́тся not fit for anything

  Он не годи́тся в учителя́. He is not suited to be a teacher.

  годовщи́на anniversary
- голова́ head, mind

  Мне пришла́ в го́лову мысль. A thought occurred to me.

  потеря́ть го́лову to lose one's head

  челове́к с головой a man with sense
- го́лод hunger

  умира́ть с го́лоду to starve to death

  голо́дный hungry
- го́лос voice

  в оди́н го́лос unanimously

  пра́во го́лоса the right to vote
- го́лый naked, bald

  го́лые но́ги bare legs

  спать на го́лом полу́ to sleep on the bare floor

  гоня́ть to drive, chase
- гора́ mountain

  ходи́ть по гора́м to climb mountains
- гора́здо much, by far

  гора́здо лу́чше much better

  го́рдый proud
- го́ре grief, misfortune
- горе́ть to burn, shine

  горе́ть в жару́ to burn with fever

  горе́ть жела́нием to burn with desire

  Дом гори́т. The house is burning.

  горизонта́льно horizontally
- го́рло throat

  во всё го́рло at the top of one's lungs
- го́род town, city

  за́ город out of town (direction)

  за го́родом out of town (location)

  горо́шек peas

  горчи́ца mustard
- го́рький bitter
- горя́чий hot, passionate (objects or emotions)

  горя́чее жела́ние ardent wish

  горя́чий ко́фе hot coffee

  горя́чее сочу́вствие heartfelt sympathy

  го́спиталь (m.) hospital

  господи́н Mr., sir

  госпожа́ Mrs., lady

  гости́ная living room

  гости́ница hotel
- гость (m.) guest

  У нас сего́дня го́сти. We have company today.

  ходи́ть в го́сти to visit

  госуда́рство state
- гото́вить (пригото́вить) to prepare, make ready, cook

  гото́вить кни́гу к печа́ти to prepare a book for the press

  гото́вить уро́к to do a lesson

  Она́ хорошо́ гото́вит. She is a good cook.

  гото́виться (пригото́виться) to prepare oneself

  гото́вый ready, prepared

  гото́вое пла́тье ready-made clothes

  Обе́д гото́в. Dinner is ready.

  Он гото́в на всё. He is ready to do anything.

  гра́дус degree

  у́гол в 60 гра́дусов angle of 60 degrees

  Сего́дня 10 гра́дусов тепла́. The temperature is 10 degrees above zero today.

  граждани́н, гражда́нка citizen (m.,f.)

  грамма́тика grammar

  гра́мотность (f.) literacy

  грани́ца boundary, border

  вы́йти из грани́ц to overstep the limits

  за грани́цу abroad

  грацио́зный gracefully

  гребешо́к comb
- греть (согре́ть) to warm up, heat

  греть суп to warm up the soup
- грех sin

  гре́шный sinful

  грибы́ mushrooms
- гроза́ thunderstorm, tempest

  гро́зный terrible, threatening

  грома́дный enormous
- гро́мкий loud
- гро́мко loudly

  гру́бый rough, coarse

  гру́бая мате́рия coarse material

  гру́бая оши́бка flagrant error

  гру́бый вкус bad taste

  гру́бое сло́во rude word
- грудь (f.) breast, chest, bosom

  гру́ппа group
- грусти́ть to be sad, melancholy

  гру́стный sad, melancholy

  У него́ гру́стное настрое́ние. He is in low spirits.

  гру́ша pear

  гря́зный dirty, muddy
- грязь (f.) dirt, filth
- губа́ lip
- гуля́ть (погуля́ть) to walk, take a stroll

  гуманита́рный humanitarian
- густо́й thick, dense

  густы́е бро́ви bushy eyebrows

  густо́й лес dense forest

  густы́е сли́вки heavy cream

  густо́й тума́н heavy fog

Д

- да yes

  да and, but

  да ещё and what is more

  он да я he and I

  Он охо́тно сде́лал бы э́то, да у него́ нет вре́мени. He would gladly do it, but he has no time.

давáй, давáйте let us (with inf.)
•давáть (дать) to give, allow
  давáть своё соглáсие to give one's consent
  дать концéрт to give a concert
  дать мéсто to make room for
  Емý не дáли говорить. They didn't let him speak.
давлéние pressure
  высóкое давлéние high pressure
  окáзывать давлéние to put pressure on
  под давлéнием under pressure
•давнó long ago, for a long time
  давны́м давнó long ago
  Ужé давнó порá уходить. It is high time to go.
•дáже even
далёкий distant, remote
  далёкое прóшлое remote past
  Они далёкие друг дрýгу лю́ди. They have little in common.
•далекó far
  далекó за пóлночь long after midnight
  Он далекó не дурáк. He is far from being a fool.
•дальнозóркий farsighted
•дáльше farther
•дáма lady
дар gift
дарить (подарить) to give a present
•дáром gratis, in vain
  Весь день дáром пропáл. The whole day has been wasted.
  Он э́того и дáром не возьмёт. He wouldn't have it as a gift.
•дать—see давáть
•дáча country house, summer cottage
  éхать на дáчу to go to the country
  на дáче in the country
два, две two
  кáждые два дня every other day
  ни два ни полторá neither fish nor fowl
двáдцать twenty
двадцáтый twentieth
двенáдцать twelve
двенáдцатый twelfth
•дверь (f.) door
  политика откры́тых дверéй open door policy
  при закры́тых дверя́х in private, closed hearing
двéсти two hundred
двигатель (m.) motor
•двигать-ся (двинуть-ся) to move, set in motion
•движéние motion, movement, traffic
  мнóго движéния на дорóге a lot of traffic on the road

Он вéчно в движéнии. He is always on the move.
рабóчее движéние working class movement
двинуть (ся)—see двигать (ся)
двóе two (collective)
  Их двóе. There are two of them.
двойнóй double, twofold
двою́родный брат, двою́родная сестрá first cousin (m., f.)
двуспáльная кровáть double bed
•дéвочка little girl
•дéвушка young girl (unmarried)
девянóсто ninety
девянóстый ninetieth
девятнáдцать nineteen
девятнáдцатый nineteenth
•дéвять nine
девятьсóт nine hundred
девя́тый ninth
•дéдушка (m.) grandfather
  дéдушка морóз Santa Claus or Grandfather Frost
•дéйствие action, act, effect
  Дéйствие происхóдит в Москвé. The action takes place in Moscow.
  окáзывать дéйствие to have an effect on
  приводить в дéйствие to put into action
  пьéса в трёх дéйствиях play in three acts
•действительно really, actually
дéйствовать (подéйствовать) to act operate, function
  дéйствовать на нéрвы to get on one's nerves
  Как дéйствовать дáльше? What is to be done next?
  Лекáрство ужé дéйствует. The medicine is already taking effect.
декáбрь (m.) December
декольтé low-necked (dress)
•дéлать (сдéлать) to do, make
  дéлать вид, что to pretend
  дéлать визит to pay a visit
  дéлать доклáд to make a report
  дéлать когó-либо счастливым to make someone happy
  дéлать рабóту to do work
  дéлать шля́пы to make hats
  нéчего дéлать nothing to do
дéлаться (сдéлаться) to become, grow
  Дéлается хóлодно. It is getting cold.
  Там дéлаются стрáнные вéщи. Strange things happen there.
  Что с ним сдéлалось. What has happened to him.
делéние division
деликáтность (f.) gentleness, tact

•делить (раздели́ть) to divide
  делить пополáм to divide in half
  раздели́ть сýмму, двáдцать на пять to divide twenty by five
дели́ться (раздели́ться) to divide (into), share
  дели́ться впечатлéниями to share impressions, compare notes
  Онá во всём дéлится со мной. She shares everything with me.
  Рекá дéлится на два рукавá. The river divides into two arms.
•дéло matter, business
  В том то и дéло. That's the point.
  В чём дéло? What's the matter?
  говорить по дéлу to speak about business
  дéло в том, что the fact is, that
  дéло мира cause of peace
  Как делá? How are things?
  на сáмом дéле as a matter of fact
  У меня́ мнóго дел. I have many things to do.
  Это моё дéло. That is my affair.
•день (m.) day
  в два часá дня two o'clock in the afternoon
  в один прекрáсный день one fine day
  день рождéния birthday
  днём in the daytime (р. м.)
  со дня на день from day to day
  чéрез дéнь every other day
•дéньги (pl.) money
деревéнский village, country (adj.)
•дерéвня village, country
  в дерéвне in the country
•дéрево tree
деревя́нный wooden
•держáть to hold, keep
  держáть в тáйне to keep a secret
  держáть когó-нибудь зá руку to hold someone by the hand
  держáть пари to make a bet
  держáть слóво to keep one's word
  держáть экзáмен to take an exam
держáться (imp.) to hold on, stick to
  держáться на ногáх to keep on one's feet
  держáться тогó взгля́да to hold to the opinion
  Держись! Hold steady!
  Пýговица дéржится на ниточке. The button is hanging by a thread.
  Такóе положéние не мóжет дóлго держáться. This state of affairs can't last long.
•дéрзкий impudent, insolent, daring, fresh
дéрзость (f.) impudence, insolence
десéрт dessert
•дéсять ten

деся́тый tenth
●дета́ль (f.) detail
дета́льно in detail
●де́ти children
де́тский child's, children's
  де́тский сад kindergarten
●де́тство childhood
  впада́ть в де́тство to be in one's
    second childhood
  с де́тства from childhood
дефе́кт defect, blemish
●дёшево cheaply
  дёшево отде́латься to get off
    cheap
  Это дёшево сто́ит. It is worth
    little.
дешёвый inexpensive
джентльме́н gentleman
диа́гноз diagnosis
диагона́льно diagonally
диале́кт dialect
дива́н divan, sofa
ди́кий wild, savage
дикто́вка dictation
  писа́ть дикто́вку to take dictation
ди́ктор announcer
●дире́ктор director, manager
дирижёр conductor of an orchestra
дирижи́ровать to conduct an
  orchestra
диску́ссия discussion, debate
●дисципли́на discipline
●дие́та diet
  соблюда́ть дие́ту to keep to a diet
●длина́ length
дли́нный long (distance)
●для for, intended for (prep. with
  gen.)
дно bottom
●до as far as, until, up to, before
  (with genitive)
  до сих пор until this time
  до свида́ния good-by
  от … до … from … to …
доба́вить—see добавля́ть
добавле́ние addition, supplement
●добавля́ть (доба́вить) to add to,
  supplement
●добро́ good
  де́лать кому́-либо добро́ to be
    good to someone
  Он жела́ет вам добра́. He wishes
    you well.
●доброво́лец volunteer
доброво́льно voluntarily, by one's
  own will
доброде́тель (f.) virtue
●доброду́шный good-natured
доброта́ kindness, goodness
●до́брый good, kind
  бу́дьте добры́ would you be so
    kind
  всего́ до́брого all the best

до́брый ве́чер good evening
до́брый день good afternoon
до́брое у́тро good morning
●дове́рие faith, confidence, trust
дове́рить—see доверя́ть
дове́рчивость (f.) trustfulness
деверя́ть (дове́рить) to entrust,
  commit
●дово́льно enough, rather
  Дово́льно! Enough! That will do.
  Он дово́льно хорошо́ говори́т. He
    speaks rather well.
дово́льный satisfied, pleased with
догада́ться—see дога́дываться
●дога́дываться (догада́ться) to
  guess, surmise
●догна́ть—see догоня́ть
договори́ться (perf.) to come to an
  understanding
●догово́р agreement, contract,
  treaty
догоня́ть (догна́ть) to catch up,
  gain on
●доезжа́ть (дое́хать) to get as far
  as, reach (by vehicle)
  Он не дое́хал до го́рода. He
    didn't reach the city.
дое́хать—see доезжа́ть
●дождеви́к raincoat
●дождь (m.) rain
  Дождь идёт. It is raining.
до́за dose
доказа́ть—see дока́зывать
доказа́тельство proof, evidence
доказа́ть—see дока́зывать
●дока́зывать (доказа́ть) to prove,
  show
  счита́ть дока́занным to take for
    granted
  Это дока́зывает его́ вину́. This
    proves his guilt.
●докла́д lecture, paper, report
  де́лать докла́д to make a report,
    give a talk
●до́ктор doctor
●долг debt
  брать в долг to borrow
  входи́ть в долги́ to get into debt
  долг че́сти debt of honor
  плати́ть долг to pay a debt
●до́лго for a long time
●до́лжен, должна́, должно́, должны́
  to owe, have to, be obliged to, must
  должно́ быть probably
  Ско́лько мы вам должны́? How
    much do we owe you?
  Я должна́ написа́ть пи́сьма. I must
    write letters.
до́ллар dollar
●дом house, home
до́ма at home
домо́й homeward (direction
  toward)

и́з дому out of the house
дополни́тельный additional,
  supplementary
●доро́га road, way
  в доро́ге on a trip
  да́льняя доро́га long journey
  желе́зная доро́га railroad
  Нам с ва́ми по доро́ге. We go the
    same way.
  по доро́ге туда́ on the way there
до́рого expensively
●дорого́й dear, expensive
  дорого́й мой my dear
  Она́ ему́ дорога́. She is dear to
    him.
доса́да vexation, annoyance
  с доса́ды out of vexation
доска́ board, blackboard
  от доски́ до доски́ from cover to
    cover
  чёрная доска́ black list
●достава́ть (доста́ть) to get,
  obtain, reach
доста́точно enough
доста́ть—see достава́ть
достига́ть (дости́гнуть) to reach
  attain (with genitive)
  достига́ть бе́рега to reach land
  достига́ть свое́й це́ли to attain
    one's objectives
дости́гнуть—see достига́ть
●достиже́ние achievement
●досто́инство dignity, value
  моне́та ма́лого досто́инства a coin
    of small denomination
  чу́вство со́бственного досто́инства
    self-respect
досто́йный deserving, worthy
досу́г leisure
  на досу́ге at leisure
до́сыта to one's heart's content
  нае́сться до́сыта to eat one's fill
●дохо́д profit, return
●дочь (f.) daughter
драгоце́нность (f.) jewel, treasure
драгоце́нный precious
●дра́ма drama
●дра́ться (imp.) to fight
дрема́ть to dose, drowse
дрова́ (pl.) firewood
●дрожа́ть (imp.) to quiver, shake
  дрожа́ть за кого́-либо to tremble
    for someone's safety
  дрожа́ть от ра́дости to thrill with
    joy
  дрожа́ть от хо́лода to shiver with
    cold
●друг friend
  друг дру́га each other
  друг дру́гу to each other
  друг о дру́ге about each other
●друго́й other, another, different
  други́ми слова́ми in other words

и тот и друго́й both
оди́н за други́м one after another
Он мне каза́лся други́м. He
  seemed different to me.
с друго́й стороны́ on the other
  hand
•дру́жба friendship
дру́жеский friendly
  по-дру́жески in a friendly way
•ду́мать (поду́мать) to think,
  believe
•дура́к fool
ду́рно badly
  Ему́ ду́рно. He feels faint.
дурно́й evil, ill
•дуть (imp.) to blow
  Ве́тер ду́ет. It's windy.
  Здесь ду́ет. There's a draft here.
•дух spirit, courage
  быть не в ду́хе to be out of
    spirits
  злой дух evil spirit
  не в моём ду́хе not to my taste
  па́дать ду́хом to lose courage
духи́ perfume, scent
духо́вка oven
духо́вный spiritual
  духо́вная жизнь spiritual life
душ shower
•душа́ soul
  в глубине́ души́ at heart
  всей душо́й with all one's heart
    and soul
  говори́ть с душо́й to speak with
    feeling
  ско́лько душе́ уго́дно to one's
    heart's content
•ду́шно stuffy
ду́эт duet
•дым smoke
  Нет ды́ма без огня́. Where there's
    smoke there's fire.
ды́ня melon
дыра́, ды́рка hole
дыха́ние breathing
•дыша́ть (imp.) to breathe
•дю́жина dozen
•дя́дя (m.) uncle

Е ё

европе́йский European
•его́, её, его́ his, hers, its
•еда́ food
  во вре́мя еды́ while eating
•едва́ hardly, just
  Он едва́ на́чал говори́ть. He had
    just begun to speak.
  Он едва́ не упа́л. He nearly fell.
  Он едва́ подня́л э́то. He could
    hardly lift it.
единообра́зие uniformity

еди́нственно only
  еди́нственно возмо́жный спо́соб
    the only possible way
•еди́нственный only, sole
ежего́дно annually
ежедне́вно daily
•е́здить, е́хать (imp.) to go (ride,
  travel)
ёлка fir tree, Christmas tree
ерунда́ nonsense!
•е́сли if
•есте́ственный natural
•есть (съесть) to eat
  Я хочу́ есть. I want to eat.
•есть to be (present tense), is
е́хать—see е́здить
•ещё more, still yet
  Ещё бы! And how!
  ещё по стака́нчику another glass
    each
  ещё раз once again
  Он ещё не ел. He hasn't eaten yet.
  Он пока́ ещё оста́нется здесь.
    He'll stay here for the time
    being.
  Хоти́те ещё ко́фе? Would you like
    more coffee?
  Что ещё? What else?

Ж

жа́дный greedy
жа́жда thirst, craving
  возбужда́ть жа́жду to make
    thirsty
  жа́жда зна́ний thirst for
    knowledge
•жале́ть (пожале́ть) to regret, be
  sorry
жа́лкий pitiful, wretched
жа́лоба complaint
жа́лованье salary
•жа́ловаться (пожа́ловаться) to
  complain
жа́лость (f.) pity
  жаль It is a pity.
  Ему́ жаль куска́ хле́ба. He
    grudges a bit of bread.
  Как жаль! What a shame!
  О́чень жаль. It's a great pity.
жар heat, fever
  говори́ть с жа́ром to speak with
    fire
  У него́ жар. He has a fever.
жара́ heat
жа́реный fried
жа́рить (ся) (imp.) to fry
жа́ркий hot, ardent
  жа́ркий кли́мат hot climate
  жа́ркий спор heated discussion
•жа́рко hot (of weather or room
  temperature)

жарко́е roast meat, pot roast
•ждать (подожда́ть) to wait
  Вре́мя не ждёт. There's no time
    to be lost.
  Она́ его́ ждёт. She is waiting for
    him.
жела́ние desire, wish
•жела́ть (пожела́ть) to wish, covet
железа́ glands
•желе́зный ferrous
  желе́зная доро́га railroad
  желе́зная дисципли́на iron discip-
    line
желе́зо iron
желто́к egg yolk
жёлтый yellow
желу́док stomach
жёмчуг pearl
•жена́ wife
•жена́тый married (of men)
•жени́ться (пожени́ться) to marry
же́нский feminine, womanish
•же́нщина woman
же́ртва sacrifice, victim
жест gesture
жесто́кий cruel, brutal
жесто́кость (f.) cruelty
жечь (сжечь) to burn (down, up)
жи́во vividly, with animation
•живо́й live, animated, vivacious
  жив и здоро́в safe and sound
  живо́й ум lively wit
  живо́й язы́к living language
  живы́е кра́ски vivid colors
  живы́е цветы́ natural flowers
жи́вопись (f.) painting
живо́тное (noun) animal
жи́дкий liquid, fluid (adj.)
жи́дкость (f.) liquid, fluid
жи́зненность (f.) vitality
•жизнь (f.) life
  борьба́ за жизнь struggle for
    existence
  вопро́с жи́зни и сме́рти question
    of life or death
  о́браз жи́зни way of life
  проводи́ть что́-либо в жизнь to
    put something into practice
•жили́ще dwelling, living quarters
жир fat, grease
•жи́рный fat, greasy, rich
  жи́рная земля́ rich soil
  жи́рное пятно́ grease spot
жи́тель inhabitant, resident
•жить to live
жре́бий fate, destiny, lot
  Жре́бий пал на него́. The lot fell
    to him.
  тяну́ть жре́бий to draw lots
жу́лик rogue, swindler
журна́л periodical, magazine
журнали́ст journalist

З

● **за** for, behind, beyond—direction (with acc.) behind, beyond, after, for—location (with instrumental)

бежа́ть за ке́м-либо to run after someone

боро́ться за свобо́ду to fight for freedom

быть за мир to be for peace

день за днём day after day

за ва́ше здоро́вье to your health (toast)

за обе́дом during dinner

за после́днее вре́мя recently

Ко́шка была́ за шка́фом. The cat was behind the bureau.

купи́ть за де́сять рубле́й to buy for ten rubles

Она́ пошла́ за у́гол. She went around the corner.

Она́ сиди́т за столо́м. She is sitting at the table.

Он сча́стлив за неё. He is happy for her sake.

Он уе́хал за́ город. He went out of town.

Они́ живу́т за́ городом. They live out of town.

посла́ть за до́ктором to send for the doctor

сади́ться за стол to sit down at the table

забава amusement

заба́вный amusing, funny

забасто́вка strike

● **заблуди́ться** to get lost, lose oneself

заблужда́ться to err, be mistaken

● **заболе́ть** (perf.) to fall ill

забота anxiety, trouble

● **забыва́ть** (забы́ть) to forget

забы́ть—see забыва́ть

заве́довать to manage, to head

Он заве́дует шко́лой. He heads the school.

зави́довать (позави́довать) to envy

Я не зави́дую вам. I don't envy you.

зави́сеть (от) to depend (on)

Это зави́сит от обстоя́тельств. It depends on circumstances.

зави́симость (f.) dependence

зави́стливый envious

за́висть (f.) envy

завлека́ть (завле́чь) to entice, seduce

завле́чь—see завлека́ть

● **заво́д** plant, works

● **за́втра** tomorrow

● **за́втрак** breakfast

второ́й за́втрак lunch

на за́втрак for breakfast

за́втракать (поза́втракать) to have breakfast or lunch

завяза́ть—see завя́зывать

● **завя́зывать** (завяза́ть) to tie up, knot

● **зага́дка** riddle

зага́р suntan, sunburn

за́говор plot, conspiracy

заговори́ть (perf.) to start to talk

загоре́ть (perf.), загора́ть (impf.) to become tanned, bake in the sun

● **заграни́ца** foreign countries

● **задава́ть** (зада́ть) to give, set

задава́ть вопро́с to ask a question

задава́ть тон to set the fashion

зада́ть—see задава́ть

зада́ние task, mission

● **зада́ча** problem

задержа́ть—see заде́рживать

● **заде́рживать** (задержа́ть) to detain, delay

Его́ задержа́ли. He was delayed.

задержа́ть дыха́ние to hold one's breath

задержа́ть упла́ту to hold back payment

● **за́дний** back, hind

задо́лго long in advance

заду́мчивость (f.) pensiveness

заду́маться (perf.) to become thoughtful

заже́чь—see зажига́ть

зажива́ть (зажи́ть) to heal

● **зажига́ть** (заже́чь) to light, set fire to

зажига́лка cigarette lighter

зажи́ть—see зажива́ть

заинтересова́ться (perf.) to become interested in

зайти́—see заходи́ть

● **зака́з** order

● **зака́зывать** (заказа́ть) to order something to be made or done

заказа́ть—see зака́зывать

● **зака́т** sunset

закипа́ть (закипе́ть) to begin to boil

закипе́ть—see закипа́ть

заключа́ть (заключи́ть) to conclude, infer

заключа́ть догово́р to conclude a treaty

заключа́ть речь to finish a speech

из ва́ших слов, я заключа́ю from what you say I can conclude

Из чего́ вы заключа́ете? What makes you think that?

заключа́ться to consist in

тру́дность заключа́ется в том, что the difficulty lies in the fact that

заключе́ние conclusion; inference

заключи́ть—see заключа́ть

● **зако́н** ruling, law

вне зако́на unlawful

Её сло́во для него́ зако́н. Her word is law with him.

по зако́ну according to law

зако́нный legal, legitimate

закружи́ть (perf.) to turn, send whirling

закружи́ть кому́-либо го́лову to turn someone's head

закружи́ться—see кружи́ться

● **закрыва́ть** (закры́ть) to shut, close

закры́ть лицо́ рука́ми to cover one's face with one's hands

закры́ть на ключ to lock

закры́ть собра́ние to close the meeting

закры́ть шко́лу to close down the school

закры́ть—see закрыва́ть

закры́тый closed

заку́пка purchase

де́лать заку́пки to buy supplies

закури́ть (perf.) to light up a cigarette or pipe

заку́сывать (закуси́ть) to have a bite to eat

закуси́ть—see заку́сывать

зал hall, reception room

зама́нчивый tempting, alluring

● **заме́на** replacement, substitution

замени́ть—see заменя́ть

● **заменя́ть** (замени́ть) to substitute

замени́ть мета́лл де́ревом to substitute wood for metal

Не́кому его́ замени́ть There is no one to take his place.

● **замерза́ть** (замёрзнуть) to freeze

Река́ замёрзла. The river has frozen up.

замёрзнуть—see замерза́ть

● **замести́тель** (m.) substitute

замести́ть—see замеща́ть

заме́тить—see замеча́ть

● **заме́тно** noticeably, it is noticeable

Заме́тно, как он постаре́л. It is noticeable how he has aged.

Он заме́тно постаре́л. He looks much older.

● **замеча́ние** remark, observation, reproof

сде́лать замеча́ние to reprove

● **замеча́тельно** remarkably, out of the ordinary

замеча́тельный remarkable

замеча́ть (заме́тить) to notice, observe

замеща́ть (замести́ть) to act as substitute for

замо́к lock

запере́ть на замо́к to lock up

●замолчать (замолкнуть) to become silent

замолкнуть—see замолчать

замороженный frozen

  замороженные продукты frozen foods

●замуж married (of women)

  быть замужем за кем-либо to be married to someone

  выйти замуж за кого-либо to get married to someone

  замужем to be married

занавес curtain

●занимать (занять) to occupy, take up, borrow

  Его занимает вопрос. He is preoccupied with the question.

  занимать должность to fill a position

  занимать квартиру to occupy an apartment

  занимать много места to take up a lot of room

  занимать первое место to take first place

●заниматься (заняться) to be occupied with, to study

  заниматься спортом to go in for sports

  заниматься хозяйством to be occupied with one's household duties

  Она занимается. She is studying.

заночевать (perf.) to spend the night

●занятие occupation, employment

занятый busy

занять (ся)—see занимать (ся)

заострить—see заострять

заострять (заострить) to sharpen, emphasize

  заострить карандаш to sharpen a pencil

  заострять противоречия to emphasize the contradictions

запад west

западный western

●запас fund, supply

  большой запас слов large vocabulary

  быть в запасе to be in the military reserve

  проверять запас to take stock

●запах smell, odor

запереть—see запирать

●запирать (запереть) to lock

●записка note

  записки notes, memoirs

записать-ся (записать-ся) to write down, record

  записаться в кружок to join a club

  записаться к врачу to make an appointment with the doctor

записывать голос to record

  записывать лекцию to take notes on a lecture

записать(ся)—see записывать(ся)

заплакать (плакать) (perf.) to burst into tears, begin to cry

заплатить— see платить

заполнять (заполнить) to fill in, occupy

  заполнять анкету to fill in a questionnaire

  заполнять время to occupy time

заполнить—see заполнять

запоминать (запомнить) to memorize

запомнить—see запоминать

запретить—see запрещать

●запрещать (запретить) to forbid, prohibit

  запрещается it is forbidden

●зарабатывать (заработать) to earn

  зарабатывать много денег to earn a lot of money

заработать—see зарабатывать

●заранее beforehand

зарезать—see резать

заря daybreak, dawn

заслуживать (заслужить) to deserve, merit

  заслужить чье-либо доверие to earn someone's confidence

заслужить—see заслуживать

засмеяться (perf.) to burst out laughing

заснуть—see засыпать

заставить—see заставлять

●заставлять (заставить) to force, compel

  Он заставил его замолчать. He silenced him.

  Он заставил нас ждать. He made us wait.

застенчивость (f.) shyness, bashfulness

застенчивый shy, bashful

засчитать—see засчитывать

засчитывать (засчитать) to take into consideration

●засыпать (заснуть) to fall asleep

●затем thereupon, subsequently

  затем что because

затерянный lost

●зато on the other hand

●затруднение difficulty, embarrassment

  выйти из затруднения to get out of difficulty

  денежное затруднение financial difficulty

заходить (зайти) to call on, drop in, stop in on the way

захотеть to begin wanting something, suddenly want to, get a desire to

захотеться—see хотеться

●зачем why, wherefore, what for

зачеркивать (зачеркнуть) to cross out

заштопать—see штопать

защитить—see защищать

●защищать (защитить) to defend, protect

  защищать диссертацию to defend one's thesis

●звать (imp.) to call

  Как вас зовут? What is your name?

  звать на помощь to cry for help

●звезда star

  звезда первой величины star of the first magnitude

  звезда экрана film star

  падающие звёзды falling stars

звёздочка asterisk, little star

●зверь (m.) wild animal, beast

звон peal, ringing

  звон в ушах ringing in the ears

●звонить (позвонить) to ring

  Вы не туда звоните. You've got the wrong number.

  звонить по телефону to telephone

звонкий ringing, clear

●звонок ring

  дать звонок to ring the bell

  Я жду вашего звонка. I am waiting for your phone call.

●звук sound

  гласный звук vowel

  не издавать ни звука never utter a sound

  пустой звук merely a name

  согласный звук consonant

звучно loudly, sonorously

●здание building

●здесь here

здешний of this place, local

  Он не здешний. He is a stranger here.

●здороваться (поздороваться) to to greet, to say, "How do you do?"

здорово well done! magnificently

  Мы здорово поработали. We have done good work.

●здоровый healthy, strong

  здоровый климат healthful climate

  здоровая пища wholesome food

  Он здоровый мальчик. He's a healthy youngster.

●здоровье health

  пить за здоровье кого-либо to drink to someone's health

●здравствуйте how do you do, hello

зевать (зевнуть) to yawn

зевнуть—see зевать

зелёный green

зелень (f.) greens, vegetables

●земля earth, land, soil

●зе́ркало mirror
зерно́ grain, seed, kernel
●зима́ winter
  зимо́й in the winter
  Ско́лько лет, ско́лько зим!
    I haven't seen you for ages!
зли́ться (imp.) to be in a bad
  temper, to be angry
зло evil, harm
злой wicked, vicious, angry
змея́ snake, serpent
●знак sign, symbol
  вопроси́тельный знак question
    mark
  дать знак to give a signal
  де́нежный знак banknote
  знак ра́венства sign of equality
●знако́миться (познако́миться) to
  become acquainted with
знако́мый (noun or adj.)
  acquaintance or familiar
  Он мой знако́мый. He is an
    acquaintance of mine.
  У него́ знако́мое лицо́. He has a
    familiar face.
знамени́тый famous
зна́ние knowledge
знато́к expert
●знать to know
  дава́ть себя́ знать to make itself
    felt
  дать знать кому́-либо to let
    someone know
  знать в лицо́ to know by sight
  наско́лько я зна́ю as far as
    I know
  не знать поко́я to know no rest
значе́ние significance, meaning
  име́ть ва́жное значе́ние to have
    particular importance
значи́тельно considerably,
  significantly
зна́чить to mean, signify
  Что э́то зна́чить? What does that
    mean?
зо́лото gold
золото́й golden, gilded
зо́нтик umbrella
зре́ние sight
  по́ле зре́ния field of vision
  сла́бое зре́ние weak eyesight
  то́чка зре́ния point of view
●зуб tooth
зубно́й dental
  зубно́й врач dentist

И Й

●и and, also
  и . . . и . . . both...and...
  и так да́лее and so forth

иго́лка needle
  сиде́ть как на иго́лках to be on
    pins and needles
●игра́ game, acting performance
  аза́ртная игра́ game of chance
  за игро́й at play
  игра́ приро́ды freak of nature
●игра́ть (сыгра́ть) to play, perform
  игра́ть в ка́рты, в мяч to play
    cards, play ball
  игра́ть на роя́ле, на скри́пке to
    play the piano, the violin
  игра́ть роль to play a part
  Э́то не игра́ет ро́ли.
    It is of no importance.
●игру́шка toy
идеалисти́ческий idealistic
идеа́льный perfect, ideal
иде́йный lofty, high-principled
●иде́я idea, conception
  гениа́льная иде́я brilliant idea
  иде́я рома́на theme of a novel
  навя́зчивая иде́я fixed idea
●идти́, ходи́ть to go, walk
  Вот он идёт. Here he comes.
  Де́ло хорошо́ идёт. Business is
    going well.
  Дождь идёт. It is raining.
  идти́ как по ма́слу to go
    swimmingly
  идти́ пешко́м to go by foot
  Иду́т перегово́ры. Negotiations
    are going on.
  Лес идёт до реки́. The forest goes
    as far as the river.
  О чём идёт речь? What are you
    talking about?
  По́езд идёт в пять. The train leaves
    at five o'clock.
  Фильм идёт. A movie is playing.
  Э́тот цвет вам идёт. That color
    becomes you.
●из from, out of (with gen.)
из-за because of, from behind
из-под from under
из страха́ out of fear
лу́чший из всех best of all
оди́н из его́ друзе́й one of his
  friends
пить из стака́на to drink from
  a glass
приезжа́ть из Москвы́ to arrive
  from Moscow
сде́лано из де́рева made of wood
изба́вить—see избавля́ть
избавля́ть (изба́вить) to save,
  deliver from
  Изба́ви Бог! God forbid!
  избавля́ть от сме́рти to save from
    death
  Изба́вьте меня́ от ва́ших замеча́ний.
    Spare me your remarks.
избало́ванный spoilt (child)

избега́ть (избе́гнуть) to avoid, shun
избе́гнуть—see избега́ть
избра́ние election
и́збранный selected
изве́стие news, information
изве́стно it is known
  ему́ изве́стно he is aware
  наско́лько мне изве́стно as far as
    I know
изве́стность (f.) reputation, fame
изве́стный well-known, famous
извине́ние apology
извини́ть (ся)— see извиня́ть(ся)
●извиня́ть-ся (извини́ть-ся) to
  forgive, pardon (apologize)
  Она́ извини́лась. She excused
    herself.
издава́ть (изда́ть) to publish
и́здали from far away
изда́ние publication, edition
изда́ть—see издава́ть
издёрганный harried, worried,
  run-down
●из-за from behind
  встать из-за стола́ to get up from
    the table
  из-за до́ма from behind the house
  Из-за ле́ни она́ не ко́нчила рабо́ту.
    Out of laziness she didn't finish
    her work.
излече́ние recovery, cure
  на излече́нии undergoing medical
    treatment
изле́чивать (излечи́ть) to cure
излечи́ть— see изле́чивать
изли́шек surplus, excess
изли́шество over-indulgence
изло́манный broken
измене́ние change, alteration
измени́ть—see изменя́ть
изменя́ть (измени́ть) to change,
  alter, betray
изнаси́ловать—see наси́ловать
изобража́ть (изобрази́ть) to depict,
  portray, imitate
изобрази́ть—see изобража́ть
изоли́рованный isolated
и́зредка now and then, seldom
изуми́тельный amazing, wonderful
изумле́ние amazement, consternation
изуча́ть (изучи́ть) to study, learn
изучи́ть—see изуча́ть
изю́м raisins
изя́щный refined, elegant, graceful
ико́на icon, sacred image
икра́ roe, caviar
икс-лучи́ X rays
●и́ли or
  и́ли . . . и́ли . . . either...or...
иллю́зия illusion
иллюстра́тор illustrator
имби́рь (m.) ginger
име́ние estate

и́менно namely, exactly, just
Вот и́менно! Exactly!
Вот и́менно э́то он и говори́л.
That's exactly what he was
saying.
и́менно потому́ just because
• име́ть to have, bear (in mind)
име́йте в виду́, что don't forget
that
име́ть большо́е значе́ние to matter
very much
име́ть бу́дущность to have a
future
име́ть возмо́жность to be a
possibility
име́ть де́ло с ке́м-либо to have
to do with someone
име́ть успе́х to make a success
иму́щество property, belongings
• и́мя name
и́мя прилага́тельное adjective
имя существи́тельное noun
челове́к с и́менем a well-known
man
• и́наче differently, otherwise
инде́йка turkey
индивидуали́ст individualist
индивидуа́льность (f.) individuality
инжене́р engineer
инжи́р fig
• иногда́ sometimes
ино́й different, other
ины́ми слова́ми in other words
не кто ино́й, как no other than
тот и́ли ино́й one or another
иностра́нец foreigner
институ́т institute
инстру́ктор instructor
инструме́нт instrument
интеллиге́нтный cultured, educated
интере́с interest
интере́сный interesting, attractive
Она́ о́чень интере́сная же́нщина.
She is a very attractive woman.
интересова́ться (заинтересова́ться)
to be interested in
инти́мность (f.) intimacy
иро́ния irony
• иска́ть to seek, search
исключа́ть (исключи́ть) to exclude,
eliminate
исключе́ние exception
исключи́тельно exceptionally
исключи́ть—see исключа́ть
ископа́емое fossil, mineral
и́скра spark
и́скренний sincere, frank,
unaffected
искуси́тель (m.) tempter
искуси́ть—see искуша́ть
иску́ственный artificial
иску́сство art, skill

искуша́ть (искуси́ть) to tempt,
seduce
испа́нец, испа́нка Spaniard (m., f.)
испа́нский Spanish
испари́ться to evaporate
и́споведь (f.) confession
исполне́ние fulfillment, execution
испо́лнить—see исполня́ть
исполня́ть (испо́лнить) to carry out,
fulfill
испо́ртить(ся)—see по́ртить(ся)
испо́рченный spoiled, rotten
испра́вить(ся)—see исправля́ть(ся)
исправля́ть (испра́вить) to correct,
repair
• испу́г fright, scare
испуга́ть(ся)—see пуга́ть(ся)
иссле́дование investigation,
research
иссле́довать (imp.) to investigate,
explore
и́стина truth
и́стинно truly
истори́ческий historical
• исто́рия history, story, tale
истра́тить—see тра́тить
исчеза́ть (исче́знуть) to disappear,
vanish
исче́знуть—see исчеза́ть
италья́нец, италья́нка Italian (m., f.)
италья́нский Italian (adj.)
и т. п. (и тому́ подо́бное) and the
like, etc.
• их their, theirs, them (gen. and
acc. of они́)
ию́ль (m.) July
ию́нь (m.) June

К

• к to, towards, for (with dat.)
заходи́ть к кому́-либо to call on
someone
к ва́шим услу́гам at your service
к сожале́нию unfortunately
к сча́стью fortunately
к тому́ же moreover
Он добр к ней. He is kind to her.
он нашёл к свое́й ра́дости, что he
found to his joy that
Это ни к чему́. It's of no use.
кабине́т study, consulting room
каблу́к heel
быть у кого́-либо под каблуко́м
be under someone's thumb
каблу́к ту́фли heel of a shoe
кавале́р partner, admirer
кавы́чки quotation marks
• ка́ждый every, each
• каза́ться (показа́ться) to seem,
appear

Ка́жется, бу́дет дождь. It looks
like rain.
каза́лось бы one would think
ка́жется, что it seems that
мне ка́жется it seems to me
Он ка́жется у́мным. He seems to
be clever.
• как how, what, as, like
Бу́дьте как до́ма. Make yourself
at home.
Вот как! Is that so!
как бу́дто бы as if
как бы не так nothing of the sort
Как вас зову́т? What is your
name?
как ви́дно as can be seen
как до́лго how long
Как он э́то сде́лал? How did he
do it?
как то́лько as soon as
с тех пор, как since
широ́кий как мо́ре wide as the sea
Это как раз то, что мне ну́жно.
That's exactly what I need.
• как-нибудь somehow, anyhow
• како́й what, what a, what kind of
Кака́я краси́вая де́вушка! What a
pretty girl!
Како́й он у́мный! How clever he is!
како́й-то a certain
Каку́ю кни́гу вы чита́ете? What
book are you reading?
• ка́к-то somehow
Он ка́к-то устро́ился. He arranged
it somehow.
календа́рь (m.) calendar
ка́менный stony, hard
ка́мень (m.) stone, rock
драгоце́нный ка́мень precious
stone
моги́льный ка́мень tombstone
се́рдце как ка́мень heart of stone
У него́ ка́мень лежи́т на се́рдце. A
weight lies heavy on his heart.
ка́мерный chamber
ка́мерная му́зыка chamber music
ками́н fireplace, chimney
кандида́т candidate
кани́кулы (only pl.) vacation, school
holiday
кану́н eve
кану́н но́вого го́да New Year's Eve
канцеля́рия office
капита́л capital
капита́н captain
• ка́пля drop
похо́жи как две ка́пли воды́ as
like as two peas
после́дняя ка́пля the last straw
капри́з whim, caprice
капри́зничать (imp.) to be naughty,
be cranky

●капу́ста cabbage
цветна́я капу́ста cauliflower
●каранда́ш pencil
карма́н pocket
ка́рта card, map, chart
коло́да карт pack of playing cards
карти́на picture
●карто́фель (m.) potatoes
карто́фельное пюре́ mashed
potatoes
ка́рточка card, photograph
ка́рточка вин wine list
карье́ра career
●каса́ться (косну́ться) to touch,
concern
что каса́ется меня́ as far as I am
concerned
Это его́ не каса́ется. That is not
his business.
ка́сса box office, cashier's office
кастрю́ля pot, pan, saucepan
катало́г catalogue
ката́ться (поката́ться) to ride, drive
(for pleasure)
ката́ться на конька́х to skate
категори́чески categorically
катего́рия category
кача́ние rocking, swinging
кача́ть (качну́ть) to rock, swing
Ве́тер кача́ет дере́вья. The wind
shakes the trees.
Он кача́л голово́й. He shook his
head.
ка́чество quality, virtue
в ка́честве наблюда́теля in the
capacity of an observer
высо́кого ка́чества of high quality
качну́ть—see кача́ть
●ка́ша cereal, porridge, jumble
гре́чневая ка́ша buckwheat cereal
завари́ть ка́шу to stir up trouble
У него́ ка́ша во рту́. He mumbles.
ка́шель (m.) cough
●ка́шлять to cough
квадра́т square
квалифика́ция qualification
кварта́л block, quarter of the year
●кварти́ра apartment
кекс cake
ке́пка cap
кероси́н kerosene
киломе́тр kilometer
кино́ movies
кио́ск kiosk, stand
кни́жный кио́ск book stand
кипе́ние boiling
то́чка кипе́ния boiling point
кипе́ть (imp.) to boil, seethe
кипе́ть зло́бой to boil with hatred
Рабо́та кипи́т. Work is in full
swing.
кипято́к boiling water

кисе́ль (m.) jelly-like pudding
dessert
кислоро́д oxygen
кислота́ sourness, acid
ки́слый sour
кита́ец, китая́нка Chinese (m., f.)
кита́йский Chinese (adj.)
кичли́вый conceited
кла́дбище cemetery
кла́няться (поклони́ться) to bow,
greet
класс class
классифика́ция classification
класси́ческий classical
●класть (положи́ть) to lay, put (in
a horizontal position)
класть на ме́сто to put something
in its place
класть са́хар в чай to put sugar
in one's tea
класть фунда́мент to lay a
foundation
положи́ть коне́ц чему́-либо to put
an end to something
положи́ть себе́ на таре́лку to help
oneself to food
клевета́ slander
кле́ить to glue, paste
кле́йкий sticky
кли́мат climate
клуб club
клубни́ка strawberry
клю́ква cranberry
ключ key, clue
●кни́га book
ковёр rug
●когда́ when
когда́-нибудь sometime
когда́-то once, formerly
ко́е-как haphazardly
ко́жа skin
коке́тка coquette
коке́тничать (imp.) to coquette, pose,
show off
ко́лба retort (chemical)
●колбаса́ sausage
коле́но knee
колесо́ wheel
коли́чество quantity, number,
amount
колле́га colleague
колле́дж college
ко́локол bell
●колхо́з collective farm
колхо́зник collective farmer
колыбе́ль (f.) cradle
кольцо́ ring
кольцо́ ды́ма ring of smoke
обруча́льное кольцо́ wedding ring
колю́чий prickly, thorny
кома́ндовать to give orders,
command
комбина́ция combination

коме́дия comedy (play)
коми́ссия committee, commission
●ко́мната room
комо́д chest of drawers
компа́ния company
весёлая компа́ния lively crowd
компенса́ция compensation
комплиме́нт compliment
компози́тор composer
компо́т compote
компроми́сс compromise
конве́рт envelope
●коне́ц end
в конце́ дня at the close of the day
в конце́ концо́в in the end
о́стрый коне́ц point
приходи́ть к концу́ to come to an
end
Пришёл коне́ц. It was the end. The
end came.
своди́ть концы́ с конца́ми to make
both ends meet
●коне́чно of course, certainly
конкре́тный concrete, specific
конкуре́нт rival, competitor
конкуре́нция competition
консервати́вный conservative
конспе́кт summary, synopsis
конститу́ция constitution
конструкти́вный constructive
ко́нсул consul
ко́нсульство consulate
консульта́нт consultant
контине́нт continent
конто́ра office
контра́кт contract, agreement
контра́ст contrast
контро́ль (m.) control
под контро́лем under the control
Это не поддаётся контро́лю. It is
uncontrollable.
конфе́та candy
конфирма́ция confirmation
конфли́кт conflict
конфу́зиться (сконфу́зиться) to
become embarrassed
концентра́т concentrated product
пищевы́е концентра́ты food
concentrates
конце́рт concert
концерта́нт concert performer
●конча́ть (ко́нчить) to end, finish
конча́ть рабо́ту to finish one's
work
конча́ть университе́т to finish
college, to graduate
пло́хо ко́нчить to come to a bad
end
●конча́ться (ко́нчиться) to end, finish
ко́нчиться ниче́м to come to
nothing
на э́том всё и ко́нчилось and that
was the end of it

Шкóла кончáется в середи́не мáя. School closes in the middle of May.

кóнчено enough, finished

Всё кóнчено. All is over.

кóнчик tip

кóнчить(ся)—see кончáть(ся)

конь (m.) horse, steed

Дарёному коню́ в зу́бы не смóтрят. Never look a gift horse in the mouth.

конькú (pl.) skates

коньяк cognac

•копéйка kopeck

до послéдней копéйки to the last penny

копéйка в копéйку exactly

копи́рка carbon paper

копи́ровать (скопи́ровать) to copy, imitate

кóпия duplicate, copy

снимáть кóпию чегó-либо to make a copy of something

корá crust, bark

корáбль (m.) ship, vessel

•кóрень (m.) root

в кóрне fundamentally

вырывáть с кóрнем to tear up by the roots

квадрáтный кóрень square root

краснéть до корнéй волóс to blush to the roots of one's hair

пусти́ть кóрни to take root

смотрéть в кóрень чегó-либо to get at the root of something

корзи́на basket

корзи́на для бумáги wastepaper basket

коридóр corridor

кори́чневый brown

корми́ть (накорми́ть) to feed

Здесь хорошó кóрмят. The food is good here.

корми́ть обещáниями to feed with promises

корóбка box

корóва cow

корóнка crown

стáвить корóнку на зуб to put a crown on a tooth

•корóткий short

в корóткий срок in a short time

корóткая волнá short wave

корóткий путь short cut

корóтко briefly

корóтко говоря́ in short

хотя́ бы корóтко if only briefly

корóче shorter

кóрпус body

дипломати́ческий кóрпус diplomatic corps

подáться всем кóрпусом вперёд lean forward

коррéктор proofreader

корреспондéнт correspondent, reporter

корсéт corset, stays

корыстолю́бие self-interest, greed

корьíто trough

коря́вый rough, uneven

косá braid, scythe

заплетáть кóсу to braid one's hair

космéтика cosmetics

космети́ческий кабинéт beauty parlor

коснýться—see касáться

косóй slanting, oblique, cross-eyed

костёр bonfire, campfire

кость (f.) bone

игрáть в кóсти to play or throw dice

промóкнуть до костéй to get drenched to the skin

слонóвая кость ivory

костю́м suit

костя́к skeleton

кот tomcat

котёнок kitten

котлéта cutlet

•котóрый which, who

в котóром часý at what time

егó мать, котóрая живёт далекó his mother who lives far off

котóрый из них which of them

Котóрый раз я тебé э́то говори́л? How often have I told you that?

Котóрый час? What time is it?

кни́га, котóрая лежи́т на столé the book which is lying on the table

кóфе coffee

кофéйник coffeepot

кóфта woman's jacket

кóфточка blouse

кóшка cat

кошмáр nightmare

крáжа theft, larceny

край (m.) border, edge

на сáмом краю́ on the very brink

по края́м along the edges

пóлный до краёв filled to the brim

крáйне (adv.) extremely

•крáйний extreme, the last

в крáйнем слýчае at the worst

крáйности extremes

крáйняя необходи́мость urgency

по крáйней мéре at least

красá beauty

красáвец, красáвица handsome man, handsome woman

краси́вый beautiful, handsome

крáсить-ся (покрáсить-ся) to color, paint

крáска paint, dye

акварéльная крáска water colors

мáсляная крáска oil paint

писáть крáсками to paint

краснéть (покраснéть) to redden, blush

крáсный red

красотá beauty

красть (украсть) to steal

крáткий short, brief

крахмáл starch

крáшеный painted, colored

кревéтка shrimp

крем cream

крем для бритья́ shaving cream

Кремль Kremlin

•крéпкий strong, firm

крéпкое здорóвье robust health

крéпкая ткань strong cloth

крéпкий чай strong tea

крéпко fast, strong

Держи́тесь крéпко! Hold tight!

крéпко задýматься to fall into deep thought

крéпко спать to sleep soundly

крéсло armchair

крест cross

крести́ть (окрести́ть) to baptize

кривóй crooked, curved

кри́зис crisis

крик cry, shout

послéдний крик мóды last word in fashion

кри́кнуть—see кричáть

кристáлл crystal

кристаллизáция crystallization

кри́тика criticism

ни́же вся́кой кри́тики beneath criticism

крити́ческий critical

•кричáть (кри́кнуть) to shout, scream

кров shelter

кровáть (f.) bed

кровь (f.) blood

•крóме besides, except (with gen.)

крóме тогó besides that

крóме шýток joking aside

круг circle

в семéйном кругý in the family circle

круг знакóмых circle of acquaintances

плóщадь крýга area of a circle

прави́тельственные кругú government circles

крýглый round

в крýглых ци́фрах in round numbers

крýглый год the whole year round

кругóм (adv.) around, round

Вы кругóм виновáты. You alone are to blame.

Он кругóм дóлжен. He owes money all around.

повернýться кругóм to turn around

кружи́ться (закружи́ться) to spin, go round
   У него́ кру́жится голова́. He feels dizzy.
кру́пный large-scale, big
крути́ть to twist, roll up
круто́й steep
крыло́ wing
   подреза́ть кры́лья кому́-либо to clip someone's wings
крыльцо́ porch
кры́тый sheltered, covered
   кры́тый мост covered bridge
кры́ша roof
кста́ти (adv.) by the way, opportunely
   Замеча́ние бы́ло сде́лано кста́ти. The remark was to the point.
   Кста́ти, как его́ здоро́вье? By the way, how is he?
•кто who
   кто́-нибудь anyone
   кто́-то someone
ку́бики children's playing blocks
•куда́ where, in which direction, where to (answer should be in accusative case)
кудря́вый curly
кузе́н, кузи́на cousin (m., f.)
ку́кла doll
   теа́тр ку́кол puppet show
кукуру́за corn
кула́к fist
•культу́ра culture
культу́рный educated, cultured
купа́льный bathing
   купа́льный костю́м bathing suit
•купа́ться (искупа́ться) to bathe
   купа́ться в зо́лоте to roll in money
купи́ть—see покупа́ть
куре́ние smoking
кури́ть (imp.) to smoke
ку́рица hen, chicken
куро́рт health resort
курс course
куса́ть (imp.) to bite off, sting
•кусо́чек, кусо́к piece
ку́хня kitchen
•ку́шать to eat or take some food
   Пожа́луйста, ку́шайте пиро́г. Please have some pie.
   Пожа́луйте ку́шать. Dinner is served.
куше́тка couch

Л

лаборато́рия laboratory
ла́вка shop, store
лавр laurel
   лавро́вый лист bay leaf
   пожина́ть ла́вры to reap laurels
   почи́ть на ла́врах to rest on one's laurels

ла́герь (m.) camp
•ла́дно very well, all right
лакони́ческий laconic, short-spoken
ла́мпа lamp
ла́ндыш lily of the valley
ла́ска caress, endearment
ласка́тельный caressing, endearing
   ласка́тельное и́мя pet name (diminutive)
ласка́ть (imp.) to caress, fondle, pet
   ласка́ть себя́ наде́ждой to flatter oneself with hope
ла́сковый affectionate, tender, sweet
ла́ять (imp.) to bark
лгать (imp.) to lie
лев lion
•ле́вый left-hand
   встать с ле́вой ноги́ to get out of bed on the wrong side
•лёгкий light, easy
   лёгкая инду́стрия light industry
   лёгкая просту́да slight cold
   лёгкая рабо́та light work
   лёгкий слог easy style
легко́ lightly, easily
   Он легко́ отде́лался. He got off easy.
легкомы́сленно thoughtlessly, light-mindedly
легкомы́сленность (f.) lightness, thoughtlessness
ле́гче easier, lighter
лёд ice
   Лёд разби́т. The ice is broken.
ледени́ть (imp.) to freeze, chill
ле́дник refrigerator, icebox
•лежа́ть (imp.) to lie
   Го́род лежи́т на берегу́ мо́ря. The town is by the seashore.
   Он лежи́т в посте́ли. He stays in bed.
лека́рство medicine
ле́ктор lecturer
ле́кция lecture
лени́вый lazy
ле́нта ribbon
ленти́й, лентя́йка lazy person (m., f.)
лень (f.) laziness, idleness
лес forest, woods
ле́стница stairway, stairs, ladder
ле́стный flattering, complimentary
лесть (f.) flattery
лета́ years
   Они́ одни́х лет. They are the same age.
   Ско́лько вам лет? How old are you?
•лета́ть, лете́ть (полете́ть) to fly
   лете́ть на всех пара́х to rush at full speed
ле́тний summer (adj.)
•ле́то summer
   ле́том in the summer

   на всё ле́то for the whole summer
лету́чий flying (adj.)
   лету́чая мышь bat
лётчик pilot
лече́ние medical treatment
лечи́ть (imp.) to treat medically
лечь—see ложи́ться
ли whether, if
   ли... ли... whether ... or ...
   сего́дня ли, за́втра ли whether today or tomorrow
   Он не по́мнит, ви́дел ли он его́. He doesn't remember whether he has seen him.
   Посмотри́, там ли де́ти. Go and see if the children are there.
ли́бо or
   ли́бо... ли́бо... either ... or ...
лигату́ра alloy
ли́лия lily
лило́вый lilac, violet (color)
лимо́н lemon
   лимо́нная кислота́ citric acid
лине́йка ruler
ли́ния line
   крива́я ли́ния curved line
   ли́ния поведе́ния line of policy
   по ли́нии наиме́ньшего сопротивле́ния on the line of least resistance
лири́ческий lyrical
лист leaf, sheet
   дрожа́ть как лист to tremble like a leaf
   загла́вный лист title page
литера́тор writer, man of letters
литерату́ра literature
•лить (нали́ть) to pour, run (of liquid)
   Дождь льёт как из ведра́. The rain is coming down in buckets.
   лить слёзы to shed tears
лифт elevator
ли́фчик brassière
лихора́дочный feverish
•лицо́ face
   в лице́ кого́-либо in the person of someone
   де́йствующие ли́ца cast (of a play)
   знать в лицо́ to know by sight
   исче́знуть с лица́ земли́ to disappear from the face of the earth
   Это ему́ к лицу́. This becomes him.
ли́чно personally
ли́чность (f.) personality
   переходи́ть на ли́чности to become personal
ли́чный personal
лиша́ть (лиши́ть) to deprive, rob
   лиша́ть кого́-либо насле́дства to disinherit someone

Он лишён чувства меры. He lacks a sense of proportion. He doesn't know when to stop.

лишение deprivation

лишить—see лишать

лишний extra, superfluous, unnecessary

лоб forehead

•ловить (поймать) to catch
ловить каждое слово to devour every word
ловить момент to seize an opportunity
ловить рыбу to fish

ловкий adroit, deft

логический logical

лодка boat

ложиться (лечь) to lie down
ложиться спать to go to bed
На него ложится обязанность. It is his duty.

ложка spoon
столовая ложка tablespoon
чайная ложка teaspoon

ложь (f.) lie, falsehood

локоть (m.) elbow

ломать (сломать) to break

лопаться (лопнуть) to break, burst
чуть не лопнуть со смеху to burst one's sides laughing

лопнуть—see лопаться

лососина salmon

лотерея lottery

лошадь (f.) horse

луг meadow

лужа puddle, pool
сесть в лужу to get into a mess, to blunder

лужайка lawn

лук onion

луна moon

луч ray, beam

•лучше better
как нельзя лучше never better
лучше всего best of all
Лучше остаться здесь. It is better to stay here.
Мне лучше. I am better.
тем лучше so much the better

лучший better, best
всего лучшего all the best
к лучшему for the better

лыжи skis

лысина bald spot

лысый bald, bald-headed

любезность (f.) courtesy, kindness

любезный polite, amiable, obliging

любимец pet, favorite

любимый favorite, loved one

любитель (m.) amateur, fancier
любительский спектакль amateur performance

Он любитель цветов. He loves flowers.

любить (imp.) to like, to love
Масло не любит тепла. Heat is not good for butter.
Он её любит. He loves her.
Он любит, когда она поет. He likes her to sing.

любоваться (imp.) to admire

любовный loving, amorous

•любовь (f.) love

любознательный inquisitive, curious

любой every, any
в любое время at any time

любопытство curiosity

любопытный curious

любящий loving, affectionate

•люди (nom. pl. of человек) people, men and women

люстра chandelier

лягушка frog

М

•магазин store, shop
магазин готового платья ready-made clothing store
универсальный магазин department store

магнит magnet

магнитофон tape recorder

мазать (imp.) to grease, lubricate, spread
мазать губы to put on lipstick
мазать хлеб маслом to butter the bread

мазь (f.) ointment

•май (m.) May

майонез mayonnaise

максимальный maximum, highest possible

максимум maximum, upper limit
выжать максимум из to get the most out of

маленький small, little

малина raspberries

•мало little, few
мало известный little-known
мало народу few people
мало того moreover
мало того, что it is not enough that
Мы его мало видим. We see little of him.

малодушие faintheartedness

малоизвестный little-known, not popular

малолетний juvenile, under-age

мало-помалу gradually, little by little

малый small
Знания его слишком малы. His knowledge is scanty.
малый ростом short
самое малое the least

•мальчик boy, lad

•мама mama

манера manner, style
У него хорошие манеры. He has good manners.

марка stamp, mark

мармелад fruit jelly

март March

маршрут route, itinerary

маслина olive

•масло butter, oil
Всё идёт, как по маслу. Things are going swimmingly.
писать маслом to paint in oils

масса mass, a large amount
в массе as a whole
масса работы a lot of work

мастер master
быть мастером своего дела to be an expert at one's job

мастерски (adv.) skillfully

математик mathematician

математика mathematics

материал material, stuff, fabric
строительные материалы building materials
Это хороший материал для кинокартины. That would be good stuff for a film.

материализм materialism

материя cloth, fabric

матрас mattress

матрос sailor

мать (f.) mother

махать (махнуть) to wave, flap
махнуть рукой to give up as hopeless
Он махнул мне рукой. He waved his hand to me.

махнуть—see махать

машина machine, engine

машинально absent-mindedly, mechanically

машинистка typist (woman)

машинка typewriter

машинописный typewritten

машиностроение mechanical engineering

мгла haze

мгновение instant, moment

мебель (f.) furniture

меблированный furnished

мёд honey

медведь (m.) bear

медицина medicine (field of)

медленно slowly

медлить (imp.) to linger, hesitate, be slow

медный copper (adj.)

медовый honeyed
медовый месяц honeymoon
медовые речи honeyed words

медсестра nurse

медь (f.) copper

• ме́жду between, among (with inst.)

ме́жду двумя́ и тремя́ between two and three o'clock

ме́жду на́ми говоря́ just between us

ме́жду о́кнами between the windows

ме́жду про́чим by the way

ме́жду тем meanwhile

чита́ть ме́жду строк to read between the lines

междунаро́дный international

мезони́н attic

мел chalk

меланхоли́ческий melancholy (adj.)

меланхо́лия melancholy

ме́лкий small, petty, shallow

ме́лкие де́ньги small change

ме́лкий дождь drizzling rain

ме́лкий челове́к petty person

мелоди́ческий melodious

мело́дия melody

ме́лочность (f.) meanness, pettiness

ме́лочь (f.) small things, small change, details

мель (f.) shoal, shallow

мелька́ть (мелькну́ть) to flash, gleam

У него́ мелькну́ла мысль. An idea flashed across his mind.

мелькну́ть—see мелька́ть

ме́нее less

бо́лее и́ли ме́нее more or less

Ему́ ме́нее сорока́ лет. He is not yet forty.

ме́нее всего́ least of all

тем не ме́нее nevertheless

• ме́ньше smaller, less

не бо́льше не ме́ньше как neither more nor less than

ме́ньший lesser, younger

ме́ньшая часть lesser part

меньшинство́ minority

меню́ menu

меня́ть-ся (поменя́ть-ся) to change

меня́ть де́ньги to change one's money

меня́ть пла́тье to change one's clothes

меня́ть своё мне́ние to change one's opinion

меня́ться роля́ми to switch roles

ме́ра measure

в значи́тельной ме́ре in a large measure

ме́ры длины́ linear measure

не знать ме́ры to be immoderate, to know no limits

по кра́йней ме́ре at least

реши́тельные ме́ры drastic measures

соблюда́ть ме́ру to keep within limits

мерза́вец villain

мёрзлый frozen

мёрзнуть (imp.) to freeze

ме́рить (приме́рить, сме́рить) to measure

приме́рить пла́тье to try on a dress

сме́рить взгля́дом to measure with one's eyes, to give a dirty look

мёртвый dead, lifeless

мёртвая тишина́ dead silence

мёртвая то́чка standstill

мёртвый язы́к dead language

спать мёртвым сном to be sound asleep, to sleep like a rock

ме́стный local

ме́стный жи́тель inhabitant

• ме́сто place, seat, locality

знать своё ме́сто to know one's place

иска́ть ме́ста to look for a job

Нет ме́ста. There is no room.

уступа́ть ме́сто кому́-либо to give up one's place to someone

хоро́шее ме́сто для до́ма an excellent site for a house

местоиме́ние pronoun

• ме́сяц month, moon

мета́лл metal

металлу́рг metallurgist

металлу́ргия metallurgy

метла́ broom

ме́тод method

мето́дика methods

методи́ческий systematic, methodical

метр meter

метро́ subway

механиза́ция mechanization

механизи́рованный mechanized

меха́ник engineer

меха́ника mechanics

механи́ческий mechanical

меч sword

меч-ры́ба swordfish

мечта́ daydream

мечта́тельный dreamy, pensive

мечта́ть (imp.) to daydream

• меша́ть (помеша́ть) to hinder

е́сли ничто́ не помеша́ет if nothing interferes

мешо́к bag, sack

Костю́м сиди́т на нём мешко́м. His clothes are baggy.

мешки́ под глаза́ми bags under one's eyes

миг instant, moment

ми́гом in a flash

мига́ть (мигну́ть) to blink, wink

мигну́ть кому́-либо to wink at someone

мигну́ть—see мига́ть

микроско́п microscope

микрофо́н microphone

милиционе́р policeman

мили́ция police station

миллиа́рд billion

миллио́н million

милосе́рдие mercy, clemency

ми́лость (f.) favor, grace

быть в ми́лости у кого́-либо to be in someone's good graces

из ми́лости out of charity

ми́лости про́сим welcome

Сде́лайте ми́лость. Do me a favor.

• ми́лый dear, lovely

ми́ля mile

ми́мо past, by (prep. with gen.)

мимолётный fleeting

ми́на mine

минда́ль (m.) almond

минера́л mineral

ми́нимум minimum

минова́ть (imp.) to escape, pass

Ему́ э́того не минова́ть. He cannot escape it.

Опа́сность минова́ла. The danger is past.

Чему́ быть, того́ не минова́ть. What will be, will be.

• мину́та minute

под влия́нием мину́ты on the spur of the moment

Подожди́те мину́ту. Wait a minute.

сию́ мину́ту this very minute

• мир peace, world

литерату́рный мир literary world

Мир победи́т войну́. Peace will triumph over war.

со всего́ ми́ра from every corner of the globe

мири́ться (помири́ться) to reconcile

помири́ться с кем-ли́бо to be reconciled with someone

примири́ться со свои́м положе́нием to reconcile oneself to one's situation

ми́рный peaceful

мировоззре́ние world outlook

ми́ска basin, soup tureen

мла́дший younger, junior

мне́ние opinion

быть о себе́ сли́шком высо́кого мне́ния to think too much of oneself

Я того́ мне́ния. I am of that opinion.

мно́гие many

во мно́гих отноше́ниях in many respects

• мно́го much, many, a lot

мно́го рабо́ты much work

о́чень мно́го very much

прошло́ мно́го вре́мени a long time passed

многозначи́тельно significantly

многокра́тно repeatedly

многообра́зие variety, diversity

многосторо́нний versatile, many-sided

многоуважа́емый respected

многоуго́льник polygon

мно́жество great number

Их бы́ло мно́жество. There were many of them.

моги́ла grave

мо́да fashion, vogue

быть оде́тым по мо́де to be fashionably dressed

модерни́зм modernism

мо́дный fashionable, stylish

мо́жет быть perhaps

Не мо́жет быть. It is impossible.

•мо́жно one may, it is possible

е́сли мо́жно if possible

Здесь мо́жно кури́ть. One may smoke here.

как мо́жно скоре́е as soon as possible

Мо́жно откры́ть окно́? May I open the window?

мозг brain

•мой, моя́, моё, мой my

мо́кнуть (imp.) to become wet

мо́кро it is wet

На у́лице мо́кро. It is wet outside.

мо́крый wet, moist

моле́кула molecule

молекуля́рный вес molecular weight

моли́тва prayer

моли́ть (imp.) to pray, entreat

мо́лния lightning

молодёжь (f. collective) youth, young people

•молоде́ц fine fellow

вести́ себя́ молодцо́м to behave oneself magnificently

Молоде́ц! Well done!

молодо́й young, youthful, new

мо́лодость (f.) youth

не пе́рвой мо́лодости not in one's first youth

молоко́ milk

мо́лот hammer, mallet

мо́лча (adv.) silently, without a word

молчали́вый taciturn, silent

молча́ние silence

молча́ть (imp.) to be silent

моль (f.) moth

моме́нт moment, instant

момента́льно instantly

моне́та coin

зво́нкая моне́та hard cash

плати́ть кому́-либо той же

моне́той to pay someone in his own coin

приня́ть за чи́стую моне́ту to take at its face value

моното́нность (f.) monotony

мора́ль (f.) moral

мора́льный moral, ethical

мо́ре sea

морко́вь (f.) carrot

моро́женое ice cream

моро́женый frozen, chilled

моро́з frost, freezing weather

морска́я сви́нка guinea pig

морщи́на wrinkle (facial)

москви́ч inhabitant of Moscow

моски́т mosquito

моско́вский Moscow (adj.)

мост bridge

мото́р motor, engine

•мочь (смочь) to be able

мо́жет быть perhaps

мрак gloom, darkness

мра́мор marble

мра́чный gloomy, somber

мсти́тельность (f.) vindictiveness, revengefulness

мстить (отомсти́ть) to revenge oneself

мудре́ц sage, wise man

му́дрость (f.) wisdom

му́дрый wise, sage

•муж husband

•му́жеский (grammatical) masculine

му́жество courage, fortitude

мужско́й male, masculine

мужско́й портно́й men's tailor

•мужчи́на (m.) man

музе́й museum

му́зыка music

музыка́льный musical

музыка́нт musician

му́ка torment, torture

мука́ flour

му́мия mummy

мураве́й ant

му́скул muscle

му́сор rubbish, refuse

мусоросжига́тельная печь incinerator

му́тный dull, cloudy, muddy

лови́ть ры́бу в му́тной воде́ to fish in troubled waters

му́ха fly

де́лать из му́хи слона́ to make mountains out of molehills

Кака́я му́ха его́ укуси́ла? What's troubling him?

муче́ние torture, torment

му́чить (imp.) to torment, worry

Э́то му́чит мою́ со́весть. It lies heavy on my conscience.

•мы we

мы́ло soap

мы́сленно mentally

мы́слить to think, reflect

мысль (f.) thought, idea

Мысль пришла́ ему́ в го́лову. A thought occurred to him.

предвзя́тая мысль preconceived idea

мы́слящий thinking, intellectual

•мы́ть-ся (помы́ть-ся, вы́мыть-ся) to wash (oneself)

мышь (f.) mouse

лету́чая мышь bat

мя́гкий soft, gentle

мя́гкий звук mellow sound

мя́гкий кли́мат mild climate

мя́гкое движе́ние gentle movement

мя́гкое се́рдце soft heart

мя́гко softly, mildly

мя́гкость (f.) softness, gentleness

мягчи́ть (imp.) to soften

мя́со meat

мяч ball

игра́ть в мяч to play ball

Н

•на on, onto,—direction (with acc.); for—extent of time (with acc.); on in, at—location (with prep.)

говори́ть на иностра́нном языке́ to speak in a foreign language

е́хать на по́езде to ride on the train

име́ть что́-либо на свое́й со́вести to have something on one's conscience

Кни́га лежи́т на столе́. The book is lying on the table.

на э́той неде́ле this week

на се́вер to the north

на се́вере in the north

Он прие́хал на неде́лю. He came for a week.

переводи́ть на друго́й язы́к to translate into a different language

помно́жить пять на три to multiply five by three

ре́зать на куски́ to cut into pieces

сесть на по́езд to take the train

уро́к на за́втра lesson for tomorrow

Я положи́л кни́гу на стол. I put the book on the table.

на, на́те here, here you are, take it (familiar, polite)

набира́ться (набра́ться) to accumulate, acquire

набра́ться но́вых сил to find new strength

набра́ться ума́ to acquire wisdom

наблюда́тель (m.) observer

наблюдать (imp.) to observe, keep one's eye on, control

набожность (f.) devotion, piety

набраться—see набираться

набросок sketch, outline

навек, навеки forever

•наверно surely, most likely

наверх up, upward (motion toward)

наверху above, upstairs

наволочка pillowcase

навсегда forever

навстречу to meet
  идти навстречу кому-либо to go to meet someone

навыворот inside out

нагибать (нагнуть) to bend

наглость (f.) impudence, insolence

наглядеться (perf.) to see enough
  не наглядеться на кого-либо never to be tired of looking at someone

нагнуть—see нагибать

наготове in readiness, at call
  держать наготове to keep in readiness

награда reward, prize

нагревать (нагреть) to warm, heat

нагреть—see нагревать

•над above, over (with inst.)
  висеть над столом to hang over the table
  засыпать над книгой to fall asleep over a book
  работать над темой to work at a subject
  смеяться над кем-либо to laugh about someone

надежда hope
  в надежде in the hope of
  питать надежды to cherish hopes
  подавать надежды promise well

надёжность (f.) reliability

надёжный reliable, thrustworthy

наделить—see наделять

наделять (наделить) to allot, provide

•надеяться (imp.) to hope
  надеяться на кого-либо to rely on someone
  Я надеюсь увидеть вас сегодня. I hope to see you today.

•надо it is necessary, one must
  мне надо I must

надобность (f.) necessity
  в случае надобности in case of need
  Нет никакой надобности. There is no need whatever.

надоедать (надоесть) to pester, bore
  Он мне до смерти надоел. He bored me to death.

надоесть—see надоедать

надолго for a long time

надписать see надписывать

н..дписывать (надписать) to inscribe

надпись (f.) inscription

надувать (надуть) to inflate, puff out
  надуть губы to pout

надуть—see надувать

наедаться (наесться) to eat one's fill

наезд flying visit
  бывать наездом to pay a flying visit

наесться—see наедаться

нажатие pressure

нажать—see нажимать

нажимать (нажать) to press, put pressure on

нажиться (perf.) to make a fortune

•назад back, backwards
  смотреть назад to look back
  тому назад ago
  много лет тому назад many years ago
  шаг назад a step backward

название name (inanimate things)

назвать (ся)—see называть (ся)

назначать (назначить) to appoint, fix, set
  назначать день to set a day
  назначать цену to fix a price

назначить—see назначать

называть (назвать) to call, name
  Девочку нельзя назвать красавицей. The girl cannot be called a beauty.
  Его называют Ваней. They call him Vanya.

называть вещи своими именами to call a spade a spade

наиболее most
  наиболее удобный most convenient

наизусть by heart
  знать наизусть to know from memory

найти (сь)—see находить (ся)

наказ order, instruction

наказание punishment

накануне on the eve of

наклонение inclination, mood (gram.)

наклонность (f.) inclination, leaning
  иметь наклонность к чему-либо to have an inclination for something

наконец at last, finally

накормить—see кормить

накрахмаленный starched stiff

накрывать (накрыть) to cover
  накрывать стол скатертью to cover the table with a cloth
  накрыть стол to set the table

накрыть—see накрывать

налево to the left

•наливать (налить) to pour out, fill
  налить чашку чая to pour out a cup of tea

налить—see наливать

наличный available, on hand
  наличные (деньги) cash on hand

налог tax

намёк hint
  понять намёк to take a hint
  сделать намёк to drop a hint

намекать (намекнуть) to hint at, imply

намекнуть—see намекать

намерение intention, purpose

намеренный intentional, deliberate

наметить—see намечать

намётка basting

намечать (наметить) to plan, outline

намокать (намокнуть) to get wet

намокнуть—see намокать

нанимать (нанять) to rent, hire

нанять—see нанимать

наоборот on the contrary

напевать (напеть) to hum

напеть—see напевать

напечатать—see печатать

написание spelling

написать—see писать

напиток drink, beverage

наполнить—see наполнять

наполнять (наполнить) to fill

напоминание reminder

напоминать (напомнить) to remind
  напомним, что we would remind you that
  Он напоминает свою мать. He resembles his mother.

напомнить—see напоминать

направить—see направлять

направление direction, trend
  во всех направлениях in all directions
  литературное направление literary school

направлять (направить) to direct, turn
  Меня направили к вам. I was directed to you.
  направлять внимание to direct attention
  направлять свои шаги to direct one's steps

направо to the right

напрасно in vain, to no purpose, wrongly
  вы напрасно так думаете you are mistaken if you think that
  Его напрасно обвинили. He was wrongly accused.

Напрáсно ждать чегó-либо от негó.
It is useless to expect anything
of him.

напримéр for instance

напрокáт for hire (only object, not
person)

взять напрокáт to hire

•напрóтив on the contrary

напрягáть (напрéчь) to strain

напряжéние effort, tension

высóкое напряжéние high tension

напряжённый strained, tense

напрéчь—see напрягáть

напúсано it is written

напýганный frightened, scared

напугáть (perf.) to frighten

напугáться (perf.) to become
frightened

напýдриться—see пýдриться

напускáть (напустúть) to fill

напустúть воды́ в вáнну to fill
a bathtub

напустúть—see напускáть

нараспéв in a singsong voice

нарезáть (нарéзать) to slice, to cut
into pieces

нарéзать—see нарезáть

нарисовáть see рисовáть

•нарóд nation, people

мнóго нарóду crowd, many people

нарóдность (f.) nationality

нарóдный folk, national

нарóчно purposely

как нарóчно as luck would have it

нарýжно outwardly

нарýжность (f.) appearance,
exterior

нарушáть (нарýшить) to break,
disturb

нарушáть покóй to disturb the
peace

нарушáть слóво to break one's
promise

нарушéние breach, violation

нарýшить—see нарушáть

наря́д attire, smart clothes

наря́дно smartly (dressed)

нарядý side by side, at the same
time

нарядý с э́тим at the same time

насекóмое insect

населéние population

насúлие violence, coercion

насúловать (изнасúловать) to force,
violate, rape

насúльно by force, under compulsion

насквóзь through, throughout

вúдеть когó-либо насквóзь to see
through someone

насквóзь промóкнуть to get wet
through

нaскóлько how much, as far as

наскóлько мне извéстно as far as
I know

Наскóлько он стáрше вас? How
much older is he than you?

нáскоро hastily, carelessly

дéлать чтó-либо нáскоро to do
something carelessly

наскýчить (perf.) to bore, annoy

Мне наскýчило э́то. I am bored
by this.

насладúться—see наслаждáться

наслаждáться (насладúться) to take
pleasure in, enjoy

наслаждáться мýзыкой to enjoy
the music

наслаждéние delight, enjoyment

наслéдник heir, successor

наслéдовать (imp.) to inherit,
succeed

наслéдственный hereditary

наслéдство inheritance, legacy

насмехáться (imp.) to mock, deride

насмéшка mocking

нáсморк head cold

насолúть—see солúть

насóс pump

настáивать (настоя́ть) to insist on,
persist

настáивать на своём to insist on
having one's own way

нáстежь (adv.) wide

Окна бы́ли нáстежь откры́ты. The
windows were wide open.

настигáть (настúгнуть) to overtake

настúгнуть—see настигáть

настóйчивость (f.) persistence,
insistence

настóйчивый persistent, urgent

настóлько so, this much

настоя́тельность (f.) urgency

настоя́ть—see настáивать

настоя́щее the present (noun)

настоя́щий present, real, genuine

настоя́щее врéмя present tense

настоя́щий друг true friend

настоя́щий мужчúна real man,
"he-man"

настроéние mood, frame of mind

быть в настроéнии to be in good
spirits

У меня́ нет для э́того настроéния.
I am not in the mood for that.

наступáть (наступúть) to come
(of time)

Наступúла веснá. Spring came.

Наступúло корóткое молчáние.
A brief silence ensued.

наступúть—see наступáть

наступлéние coming, approach,
offensive attack (military)

насчёт as regards, concerning

насчёт э́того so far as that matter
is concerned

насы́пать—see насыпáть

насыпáть (насы́пать) to pour, fill
(dry products)

насы́тить—see насыщáть

насыщáть (насы́тить) to saturate,
satiate

насы́щенность (f.) saturation

насы́щенный saturated

натýра nature

Он по натýре óчень дóбрый
человéк. He is a kind man by
nature.

платúть натýрой to pay in kind

рисовáть с натýры to paint from
life

Это стáло у негó вторóй натýрой.
It became second nature with
him.

натурáльный natural

в натурáльную величинý life-size

натурáльный шёлк genuine silk

нáука science, study

занимáться наýкой to be a scientist

тóчные наýки exact sciences

научúть (perf.) to teach

научúть когó-либо англúйскому
языкý to teach someone English

научúться (perf.) to learn something

наýчно scientifically

наýчно-исслéдовательский
scientific research

наýчный scientific

нахáльство impudence, to be fresh

•находúть (найтú) to find, discover

Егó нахóдят ýмным. He is
considered clever.

находúть утешéние to find
comfort

Он никáк не мог найтú причúну
э́того. He never managed to
discover the cause of it.

находúться (найтúсь) to be found
or situated

Дом нахóдится в пáрке. The
house is in a park.

Он всегдá найдётся. He is never
at a loss.

Рабóта для всех найдётся. We will
find work for everyone.

нахмýриться—see хмýриться

националистúческий nationalistic

национáльность (f.) nationality

нáция nation

•начáло beginning

в начáле гóда in the beginning of
the year

для начáла to start with

с начáла from the beginning

начáльный elementary, initial

начáльные глáвы ромáна opening
chapters of the novel

начáльная шкóла elementary
school

начáть—see начинáть
• начинáть (начáть) to begin, start
начáть пить to take to drink
начинáть день прогýлкой to begin
the day with a walk
Он нáчал рабóтать. He began
working.
начúнка filling, stuffing
• нáш, нáша, нáше, нáши our
нашивáть (нашúть) to sew on
нашúть—see нашивáть
нашумéть (perf.) to make much
noise
• не not
не́ на когó положúться no one to
rely on
не тóлько not only
не трýдный, но не простóй not
difficult but not simple
Он не мóжет читáть. He cannot
read.
Это не вáша кнúга. It is not your
book.
Это не так. That is not so.
Это не шýтка. It is no joke.
не- negative prefix with adjectives,
"un-"
неаккурáтный inaccurate,
unpunctual, messy
небéсный celestial, heavenly
неблагодáрность (f.) ingratitude
неблагоразýмие imprudence
неблагосклóнность (f.) unfavorable
attitude
• нéбо sky, heaven
быть на седьмóм нéбе to be in
seventh heaven
под открытым нéбом in the open
air
небоскрёб skyscraper
небóсь it is most likely, one must be
Он, небóсь, устáл. He must be
tired.
• небрéжность (f.) carelessness,
negligence
небрéжный careless, slipshod
небрúтый unshaven
небывáлый unprecedented,
fantastic
небьющийся unbreakable
небьющееся стеклó safety glass
невáжно never mind, it is
unimportant
невáжно poorly, indifferently
Он себя невáжно чýвствует. He
doesn't feel well.
Рабóта сдéлана невáжно. The
work is poorly done.
невéдение ignorance
находúться в невéдении to be in
ignorance
невéдомый unknown, mysterious
невéжливый impolite, rude

невéрно incorrectly
невероятно incredibly, inconceivably
невероятность (f.) incredibility
невесóмость (f.) weightlessness
невéста (f.) fiancée, bride
невзгóда adversity
невúдимый invisible
невúнность (f.) innocence, naïveté
невúнный innocent, harmless
невкýсный not tasty
невнимáтельный inattentive,
careless
невозврáтность (f.) irrevocability
невоздéржанность (f.) lack of self-
control
невозмóжно impossible, it is
impossible
невóльно involuntarily,
unintentionally
невоспúтанный unmannerly
невредúмый safe, unharmed
невыгодно disadvantageously, it is
not advantageous
стáвить в невыгодное положéние
to place at a disadvantage
• нéгде there is nowhere (plus
infinitive)
Нéгде сесть There is nowhere to
sit.
негóдность (f.) unfitness,
worthlessness
негодовáние indignation
негодяй scoundrel, villain
негрáмотность (f.) illiteracy
неграциóзный ungraceful
• недáвно recently, not long ago
• недалекó not far
Им недалекó идтú. They have a
short way to go.
недалекó то врéмя, когдá the time
is not far distant when
недалёкость (f.) narrow-mindedness,
dull-wittedness
недáром not without reason, not in
vain
недáром говорят not without
reason it is said
неделикáтный indelicate, rough
• недéля week
кáждую недéлю every week
чéрез недéлю in a week
недёшево at a considerable price
Это емý недёшево достáлось. It
cost him dearly.
недовéрие distrust
недовéрчивый distrustful
недовóльный dissatisfied
недовóльство dissatisfaction,
discontent
недоедáние malnutrition
недокóнченный unfinished

недóлго not long
недóлго дýмая without a second
thought
недооцéнивать (недооценúть) to
underestimate, undervalue
недооценúть—see недооцéнивать
недоразумéние misunderstanding
недоставáть (недостáть) to lack, be
missing
емý недостаёт слов, чтóбы
вырáзить . . . he cannot find
words to express . . .
Нам óчень недоставáло вас. We
missed you very much.
Чегó вам недостаёт? What do you
lack?
недостáток shortage, defect
за недостáтком чегó-либо for want
of something
имéть серьёзные недостáтки to
have serious shortcomings
недостáточно insufficiently
недостáть—see недоставáть
недостижúмый unattainable
недостóйный unworthy
недоумéние bewilderment,
perplexity
недохóдный unprofitable
недружелюбный unfriendly
недýрно not bad!, rather well
неестéственный unnatural, affected
неженáтый unmarried (of a man)
нéжность (f.) tenderness
нéжный tender, delicate, loving
нéжный вóзраст tender age
нéжное здорóвье delicate health
нéжный сын loving son
незабывáемый unforgettable
независимость (f.) independence
независимый independent
незакóнный illegal
незакономéрный irregular
незакóнченный incomplete,
unfinished
незамéтно imperceptible, not
noticeable
незамýжняя unmarried (of women)
незаслýженный undeserved
нездорóвый unwell, indisposed
незнакóмец stranger
незначúтельный negligible,
unimportant
незрéлый unripe, immature
неизвéстно it is not known
неизвéстный unknown, obscure
нейскренний insincere
нейскренность (f.) insincerity
неискушённый inexperienced,
unsophisticated
неквалифицúрованный unskilled

● нéкоторый some
  до нéкоторой стéпени to a certain
  extent
  нékоторое врéмя some time
  нékоторые из них some of them
некрасивый unattractive, ugly
некультýрный uncivilized,
  uncultured
нелéпость (f.) absurdity
нелéпый ridiculous, incongruous
нелицемéрный sincere, frank
нелóвкий awkward, clumsy,
  inconvenient
  нелóвкое молчáние awkward
  silence
  оказáться в нелóвком положéнии
  to find oneself in an awkward
  situation
● нельзя it is impossible, one cannot
  Здесь курить нельзя. Smoking is
  not permitted here.
  как нельзя лýчше in the best way
  possible
  Никогдá нельзя знать, где он мóжет
  быть. You never know where to
  find him (he may be).
  Там нельзя дышáть. It is
  impossible to breathe there.
нелюбéзность (f.) coldness,
  discourtesy
нелюбéзный ungracious,
  discourteous
нелюдимый unsociable
немéдленно immediately
нéмец, нéмка German (m., f.)
немéцкий German (adj.)
немилосéрдный merciless,
  unmerciful
неминýемо inevitably, unavoidably
● немнóго a little, a few
немнóжко a trifle, a very little
немóй mute, deathly still
  немóе обожáние mute adoration
  немóй dumb man
ненавидеть (imp.) to hate, detest
нéнависть (f.) hatred
ненадёжный unreliable,
  untrustworthy
ненадóлго for a short while
ненамéренно unintentionally
необразóванный uneducated
● необходимо it is necessary
  Необхóдимо кóнчить рабóту. It
  is necessary to finish the work.
необходимость (f.) necessity
необходимый necessary,
  indispensable
необыкновéнный unusual
неограниченный unlimited
неодобрительный disapproving
неодушевлённый inanimate
неожиданно unexpectedly

неожиданность (f.) suddenness,
  unexpectedness
неоправданный unjustified
неопределённый indefinite,
  indeterminate
неóпытный inexperienced
неорганический inorganic
  (chemistry)
неотвратимость (f.) inevitability
неотчётливый vague, indistinct
неохóта reluctance
неохóтно unwillingly, reluctantly
неплодорóдный barren, infertile
неплохóй not bad, quite good
неподвижно motionless
неподвижный immovable, stationary
неподкýпный incorruptible, someone
  who can't be bought
неподходящий unsuitable,
  inappropriate
неполноцéнность (f.) inferiority
непóлный incomplete, imperfect
непонимáние incomprehension,
  misunderstanding
непорядочный dishonorable,
  ungentlemanly
непосильный beyond one's strength
● непрáвда untruth, falsehood
непрáвильно irregularly,
  erroneously, incorrectly
● непремéнно certainly, without fail
непреодолимый insurmountable,
  unconquerable
непрерывно uninterruptedly,
  continuously
непрерывность (f.) continuity
непривéтливый unfriendly,
  ungracious
непривлекáтельный uninviting,
  unpleasant
неприличный indecent, unseemly
  Какóе неприличное поведéние!
  What disgraceful behavior!
непринуждённо without
  embarrassment, nonchalantly
  чýвствовать себя непринуждённо
  to feel at ease
непринуждённый natural, free and
  easy
  непринуждённая пóза natural
  attitude, poise
неприятно unpleasant, it is
  unpleasant
неприятность (f.) trouble,
  annoyance
неприятный unpleasant, disagreeable
непростительный unpardonable,
  inexcusable
непрямóй indirect, hypocritical
нерáвенство inequality
неразлýчный inseparable
неразýмие foolishness, unreason
неразýмный unreasonable, unwise

нерасчётливость (f.) extravagance
нерасчётливый extravagant,
  wasteful
нерв nerve
  дéйствовать комý-либо на нéрвы
  to get on someone's nerves
страдáть нéрвами to have a nervous
  disease
нéрвничать (imp.) to be nervous
нéрвный nervous
нерешительность (f.) indecision
нерóвный uneven, rough
несвязно incoherently
несгорáемый fireproof
● нéсколько several, some, a few
нескрóмный immodest, indiscreet
неслóжный simple, uncomplicated
неслышный inaudible
несмотря на то, что despite the fact
  that
неснóсный unbearable, intolerable
несовершéнный imperfect,
  incomplete
несовместимый incompatible
несоглáсие dissent, disagreement,
  difference of opinion
несомнéнно undoubtedly, beyond all
  question
неспокóйный restless, uneasy
неспосóбный incapable, incompetent
несправедливость (f.) injustice,
  unfairness
несправедливый unjust, unfair
несравнéнно incomparably,
  matchlessly
несравнимый incomparable,
  unmatched
нестерпимый unbearable, intolerable
● нести, носить (imp.) to bear, carry
  нести отвéтственность to bear the
  responsibility
несчастливый unfortunate
несчáстный unhappy, unfortunate
несчáстье misfortune
  к несчáстью unfortunately
несъедóбный uneatable
● нет no, there is (are) not
  Бýдет он там или нет? Will he be
  there or not?
  Егó нет дóма. He is not at home.
  ещё нет not yet
  Почемý нет? Why not?
  совсéм нет not at all
  Там никогó нет. There is no one
  there.
нетерпеливо impatiently
нетерпеливый impatient
нетерпéние impatience
нетерпимый intolerant
нетрéбовательный unpretentious,
  modest
неуважительно disrespectfully

неуве́ренный uncertain, hesitating
неуго́дный undesirable
неуда́ча failure
неуда́чный unsuccessful, unfortunate
неудо́бный uncomfortable, inconvenient
неудо́бство inconvenience, discomfort
неудовлетвори́тельный unsatisfactory, inadequate
неудово́льствие displeasure
•неуже́ли! Really! Is it possible!
неуклю́жий clumsy, awkward
неутоми́мый tireless
неую́тный bleak, not cosy
не́хотя unwillingly, reluctantly
•неча́янно accidentally
нече́стный dishonest
нечи́стый unclean, impure
  нечи́стая со́весть guilty conscience
  нечи́стое де́ло suspicious affair
•ни not a
  Не мог найти́ ни одного́ приме́ра. He could not find a single example.
  ни за что́ for no reason at all
  Ни ка́пли не упа́ло. Not a single drop fell.
  ни... ни... neither ... nor ...
  Ни ра́зу не ви́дела его́. She never saw him.
•нигде́ nowhere
•ни́жний lower
ни́жний to lower
  ни́жнее бельё underwear
  ни́жний эта́ж ground floor
•ни́зкий low, short, inferior
  ни́зкий го́лос deep voice
  ни́зкое ка́чество poor quality
•ника́к in no way
  Ника́к нельзя́. It is quite impossible.
  Он ника́к не мог откры́ть я́щик In no way could he open the box.
•никогда́ never
  никогда́ бо́льше never again
  никогда́ в жи́зни never in one's life
  почти́ никогда́ hardly ever
•никто́ no one
•никуда́ nowhere
  никуда́ не годи́тся won't do at all
  никуда́ не го́дный челове́к good-for-nothing
•ниско́лько not at all, not in the least
  Это ниско́лько не тру́дно. It is not difficult at all.
ни́тка thread
  вдева́ть ни́тку в иго́лку to thread a needle

•ничего́ nothing, never mind, it doesn't matter
  Ничего́! It's nothing! No harm done.
  Ничего́ не ви́дел. He saw nothing.
  Ничего́ не поде́лаешь. There's nothing to be done.
  ничего́ подо́бного nothing of the sort
  Это ему́ ничего́. It is nothing to him.
  Это ничего́ не зна́чит. It means nothing.
ничто́жный insignificant, worthless
•но but
нова́торство innovation
новомо́дный new-fashioned, modern
новосе́лье housewarming
но́вость (f.) news
•но́вый new, modern
  Что но́вого? What's new?
•нога́ foot, leg
  вверх нога́ми upside down
  встать с ле́вой ноги́ to get out of bed on the wrong side
  идти́ в но́гу to keep pace
  со всех ног as fast as one can run
  стать на́ ноги to become independent
но́готь (m.) fingernail, toenail
•нож knife
•но́жницы scissors
•но́мер number
но́рма standard, norm
•норма́льно normally
норма́льный normal, sane
  норма́льные усло́вия normal conditions
•нос nose
  говори́ть в нос to speak nasally
  не ви́деть да́льше своего́ но́са to see no farther than one's nose
  носово́й плато́к handkerchief
  перед но́сом under one's nose
  сова́ть нос во что́-либо to pry into something
  уткну́ться но́сом во что́-либо to bury oneself in something
•носи́ть (imp.) to carry (by hand), wear (clothes)
носи́ться (imp.) to wear
  Эта мате́рия бу́дет хорошо́ носи́ться. This material will wear well.
носо́к, носки́ sock, socks
но́ты music (printed music)
  игра́ть без нот to play without music
ночева́ть (imp.) to spend the night
•ночь (f.) night
  но́чью at night
  споко́йной но́чи good night
ноя́брь (m.) November

нрав disposition, temper
  У него́ весёлый нрав. He has a cheerful disposition.
  Это ему́ не по нра́ву. It goes against his grain.
•нра́виться (понра́виться) to please
  Ему́ нра́вится её лицо́. He likes her face.
  Она́ стара́ется нра́виться ему́. She tries to make him like her.
  Это ему́ не понра́вилось. He did not like it.
нра́вственный moral
нра́вы (pl.) customs, morals and manners
•ну! Well! now
  Ну, и что же да́льше? Well, and what then?
  Ну, коне́чно. Why, of course.
  Ну так что́ же? Well, what of it?
нужда́ need
  в слу́чае нужды́ in case of need
нужда́ться (imp.) to need, want
•ну́жно it is necessary, one should
  мне ну́жно I need
  Это ну́жно сде́лать. It must be done.
ну́жный necessary
нуль (m.) zero, nought
  своди́ть к нулю́ to bring to nothing
ны́не the present
ны́нче today
ню́хать (поню́хать) to smell, sniff
ня́ня nursemaid, nurse

О

•о, об about, concerning (with prep.)
  ду́мать о ко́м-либо to think of someone
  кни́га об а́томной эне́ргии a book about atomic energy
о́ба, о́бе both (m. and n., f.)
обвине́ние charge, accusation
обвини́ть—see обвиня́ть
обвиня́ть (обвини́ть) to accuse, charge
обгоре́лый burnt
обду́манно after long consideration, deliberately
обду́мать—see обду́мывать
обду́мывать (обду́мать) to consider, think over
обе́д dinner
•обе́дать (пообе́дать) to dine
обедне́вший impoverished
обезья́на monkey
обеща́ние promise
обеща́ть (imp.) to promise
обже́чь—see обжига́ть
обжига́ть (обже́чь) to burn, scorch
обжо́ра glutton

обзо́р survey, review
оби́деть (ся)—see обижа́ть (ся)
оби́дно offensively
обижа́ть-ся (оби́деть-ся) to offend,
hurt someone's feelings
Не обижа́йтесь. Don't be offended.
Они́ его́ оби́дели. They have
offended him.
оби́женный bearing a grudge
оби́лие abundance, plenty
оби́льный abundant, plentiful
о́блако cloud
о́бласть (f.) sphere, province
о́бласть зна́ний field of knowledge
облегча́ть (облегчи́ть) to facilitate,
make easier, relieve
облегчи́ть—see облегча́ть
обма́н fraud, deception
обману́ть—see обма́нывать
обма́нчивый deceptive, delusive
обма́нывать (обману́ть) to deceive,
swindle
обме́н exchange
о́бморок fainting fit
упа́сть в о́бморок to faint
обнима́ть (обня́ть) to embrace
обнима́ть умо́м to comprehend
обня́ть—see обнима́ть
обогати́ть—see обогаща́ть
обогаща́ть (обогати́ть) to enrich
обогати́ть свой о́пыт to enrich
one's expierence
обогрева́ть (обогре́ть) to warm
обогре́ть—see обогрева́ть
ободре́ние encouragement
ободри́ть—see ободря́ть
•ободря́ть (ободри́ть) to encourage,
reassure
обожа́ние adoration
обожа́ть (imp.) to adore, worship
обознача́ться (обозна́читься) to
show, appear
обозна́читься—see обознача́ться
обойти́—see обходи́ть
обою́дно mutually
обраба́тывать (обрабо́тать) to work
up, process
обрабо́тать—see обраба́тывать
обра́доваться—see ра́доваться
•о́браз image, shape, form
гла́вным о́бразом most importantly
о́браз жи́зни way of living
таки́м о́бразом in this way
•образова́ние education, formation
дать образова́ние to educate
образова́ние слов word formation
образо́ванный (well)-educated
обрати́ть—see обраща́ть
•обра́тно back
идти́ обра́тно to return, go back
туда́ и обра́тно round trip, to and
fro
обра́тный reverse

в обра́тную сто́рону in the
opposite direction
обраща́ть (обрати́ть) to turn, direct
обраща́ть внима́ние to pay
attention
обрати́ть в шу́тку to turn into
a joke
обруче́ние betrothal
обслу́живание service, maintenance
обслу́живать (обслужи́ть) to attend,
serve
обслужи́ть—see обслу́живать
обста́вить—see обставля́ть
обставля́ть (обста́вить) to furnish,
arrange
обстано́вка furniture
обстоя́тельство circumstance
ни при каки́х обстоя́тельствах
under no circumstances
смягча́ющие вину́ обстоя́тельства
extenuating circumstances
обсуди́ть—see обсужда́ть
обсужда́ть (обсуди́ть) to discuss
обходно́й roundabout
общежи́тие dormitory
обще́ственный public, social
обще́ственное мне́ние public
opinion
обще́ственный строй social system
о́бщество society
о́бщий general, common
не име́ть ничего́ о́бщего to have
nothing in common
о́бщее де́ло common cause
о́бщее собра́ние general meeting
объе́кт object, objective
объекти́вный objective (adj.)
объём volume, size
объяви́ть—see объявля́ть
объявле́ние announcement,
declaration
объявля́ть (объяви́ть) to declare,
announce
объясне́ние explanation
объясни́ть—see объясня́ть
объясня́ть (объясни́ть) to explain
объя́тие embrace
обыкнове́нно usually, as a rule
обыкнове́нный usual, ordinary
обы́чай custom, usage
по обы́чаю according to custom
обы́чно usually
обя́занность (f.) duty, responsibility
исполня́ть свои́ обя́занности to
attend to one's duties
обя́занный obliged
быть обя́занным кому́-либо to be
indebted to someone
быть обя́занным что́-либо сде́лать
to be obliged to do something
•обяза́тельно certainly, without fail
обяза́тельный obligatory,
compulsory

о́вощи vegetables
овра́г ravine
овца́ sheep
оглуши́тельный deafening
огово́рка reservation
с огово́ркой with reserve
оголённый nude
•ого́нь (m.) fire
огоро́д vegetable garden
ограбле́ние robbery
ограниче́ние limitation, restriction
ограни́ченность (f.) scantiness,
narrow-mindedness
ограни́чивать (ограни́чить) to limit,
restrict
ограни́чить—see ограни́чивать
огро́мный huge, enormous
•огуре́ц cucumber
о́да ode
одева́ть-ся (оде́ть-ся) to dress
(oneself)
оде́жда clothes
оде́ть (ся)—see одева́ть (ся)
одея́ло blanket, quilt
•оди́н, одна́, одно́, одни́ one, alone,
only (m., f., n., plural)
оди́н за други́м one after other
оди́н из них one of them
Оди́н он мо́жет сде́лать э́то. Only
he can do it.
оди́н раз once
Одно́ бы́ло ему́ я́сно. One thing
was clear to him.
Он был совсе́м оди́н. He was quite
alone.
Они́ живу́т в одно́м до́ме. They
live in the same house.
одни́м сло́вом in a word
Там была́ одна́ вода́. There was
nothing but water.
одина́ково equally
одина́ковый identical
оди́ннадцать eleven
оди́ннадцатый eleventh
одино́кий solitary, lonely
одино́чество solitude, loneliness
•одна́жды once
одна́ко however, but
одновре́менно simultaneously
однозву́чный monotonous (sound)
однообра́зие monotony
однообра́зный monotonous
одолжа́ть (одолжи́ть) to lend,
borrow
одолже́ние favor
одолжи́ть—see одолжа́ть
одушеви́ть (ся)—see одушевля́ть (ся)
одушевле́ние animation
одушевлённый animated
одушевля́ть-ся (одушеви́ть-ся) to
animate (to become animated)

ожере́лье necklace
оживи́ть(ся)—see оживля́ть(ся)
оживлённо animatedly
оживля́ться (ожива́ть-ся) to enliven, revive
ожида́ние expectation
●ожида́ть (imp.) to wait for, expect, anticipate
озабо́ченный preoccupied, anxious, worried
озаря́ть (озари́ть) to illuminate, light up
его́ озари́ло it dawned on him
озари́ть—see озаря́ть
●о́зеро lake
озлобле́ние bitterness, animosity
ознако́миться—see ознакомля́ться
ознакомля́ться (ознако́миться) to familiarize oneself (with)
оказа́ть (ся)—see ока́зывать (ся)
оказа́ть-ся (оказа́ть-ся) to render, show
оказа́лось, что it turned out that
ока́зывать влия́ние to exert influence
ока́зывать предпочте́ние to show a preference
ока́зывать услу́гу to render (do) a service
Трево́га оказа́лась напра́сной. There proved to be no ground for alarm.
ока́нчивать (око́нчить) to finish, end
око́нчить университе́т to graduate from the university
океа́н ocean
окисле́ние oxidation
оклика́ть (окли́кнуть) to hail, call (to)
окли́кнуть—see оклика́ть
●окно́ window
●о́коло near, approximately, about (with gen.)
говори́ть вокру́г да о́коло to beat about the bush
Никого́ нет о́коло. There is no one around.
О́коло го́рода есть о́зеро. There is a lake near the town.
Сейча́с о́коло трёх часо́в. It is now about three o'clock.
У меня́ о́коло трёх до́лларов. I have approximately three dollars.
оконча́ние termination, finishing, ending
оконча́тельный final, definitive
око́нчить—see ока́нчивать
окрести́ть—see крести́ть
окре́стность (f.) environs, neighborhood
окружа́ть (окружи́ть) to surround, encircle

окружи́ть—see окружа́ть
окру́жность (f.) circumference
октя́брь (m.) October
ола́дьи pancakes
ома́р lobster
омле́т omelette
●он he (used when referring to any masculine noun, animate or inanimate)
●она́ she (used to refer to any feminine noun)
●они́ they (used to refer to any plural noun)
●оно́ it (used when referring to any neuter noun, animate or inanimate)
опа́здывать (опозда́ть) to be late
Извини́те, что я опозда́л. Pardon me for being late.
опозда́ть на по́езд to miss a train
Часы́ опа́здывают на пять мину́т. The watch is five minutes slow.
опасе́ние fear, apprehension
опа́сно dangerously
опа́сность (f.) danger, peril
опа́сный dangerous, perilous
●о́пера opera
из друго́й о́перы quite a different matter
●опера́ция operation
перенести́ опера́цию to undergo an operation
описа́ние description
описа́ть—see опи́сывать
●опи́сывать (описа́ть) to describe, portray
опозда́ние delay, tardiness
опозда́ть—see опа́здывать
оправда́ние justification, excuse
оправда́ть (ся)—see опра́вдывать (ся)
опра́вдывать (оправда́ть) to justify, excuse
опра́вдывать дове́рие кого́-либо to justify someone's confidence
опра́вдываться (оправда́ться) to justify oneself, excuse
опра́вдываться пе́ред ке́м-либо to put oneself right with someone
Тео́рия оправда́лась. The theory proved to be correct.
определе́ние determination, definition
определённо definitely
определённо знать что́-либо to know something definitely
определённый specific, definite
определи́ть—see определя́ть
определя́ть (определи́ть) to define, determine
оптими́ст optimist
опубликова́ть—see публикова́ть
опуха́ть (опу́хнуть) to swell
опу́хнуть—see опуха́ть
о́пыт experiment, test, experience

о́пытный experienced
опя́ть again
ора́нжевый orange (color)
о́рган organ
о́рганы ре́чи organs of speech
о́рганы вла́сти organs of government
орга́н organ (musical instrument)
организо́ванный organized
органи́ческий organic
органи́ческая хи́мия organic chemistry
орёл eagle
оре́х nut
оригина́льный original, eccentric, unusual
орке́стр orchestra
ору́дие instrument, tool
осве́домить—see осведомля́ть
осведомля́ть (осве́домить) to inform
освежа́ть (освежи́ть) to refresh
освежи́ть—see освежа́ть
освети́ть—see освеща́ть
освеща́ть (освети́ть) to illuminate, light up
освеще́ние lighting, illumination
освободи́ть—see освобожда́ть
освобожда́ть (освободи́ть) to liberate, release
освобожде́ние liberation, release
осво́ить to master, assimilate
осво́иться to make oneself familiar with
о́сень (f.) autumn
о́сенью in the autumn
оскорби́тельный insulting, abusive
оскорби́ть (ся)—see оскорбля́ть (ся)
оскорбле́ние insult, outrage
оскорбля́ть (оскорби́ть) to insult, outrage
оскорбля́ться (оскорби́ться) to take offense
ослабе́ть—see слабе́ть
ослепи́тельный dazzling, blinding
ослепи́ть—see ослепля́ть
ослепля́ть (ослепи́ть) to blind, dazzle
осле́пнуть (pf.) to lose one's sight
осложне́ние complication
осма́тривать (осмотре́ть) to examine, survey
осме́ивать (осмея́ть) to ridicule
осмея́ть—see осме́ивать
осмотре́ть—see осма́тривать
осно́ва base, foundation, basis
на осно́ве чего́-либо on the basis of something
приня́ть за осно́ву to assume as a basis
основа́тель (m.) founder
основно́й fundamental, basic
осо́бенно especially, particularly

особенность (f.) peculiarity
в особенности in particular
оставаться (остаться) to remain, stay
  До шести остаётся несколько минут. A few minutes remain until six (o'clock.)
  оставаться на ночь to stay the night
  Перо осталось на столе. The pen remained on the desk.
  Это навсегда останется в моей памяти. It will always remain in my memory.
оставить—see оставлять
оставлять (оставить) to leave, abandon
  Оставляет желать лучшего. It leaves much to be desired.
  оставлять вопрос открытым to leave the question unsettled
  оставлять надежду to give up hope
  оставлять в покое to leave alone
остальной remaining, the rest of
останавливать (остановить) to stop
•останавливаться (остановиться) to stop, come to a stop
  внезапно остановиться to stop short
  ни перед чем не останавливать(ся) to stop at nothing
остановить(ся)—see останавливаться
остановка stop, bus or trolley stop
остаться—see оставаться
остолбенеть (perf.) to be dumbfounded
•осторожно carefully, cautiously
осторожность (f.) care, caution
осторожный careful, wary
остричься—see стричься
остро sharply, keenly
остров island
острота sharpness, pungency
остроумный witty
острый sharp, acute
  Он остёр на язык. He has a sharp tongue.
  острая боль acute pain
  острый нож sharp knife
  острый соус piquant, hot sauce
остудить—see студить
•от from (with gen.)
  близко от города near the town
  Он получил письмо от сестры. He received a letter from his sister.
  Он узнал это от него. He learned it from him.
  от города до станции from the town to the station
  от имени on behalf of

страдать от болезни to suffer from an illness
ответ answer, reply
ответить—see отвечать
ответсвенность (f.) responsibility
•отвечать (ответить) to answer, reply
  отвечать за себя to answer for oneself
  отвечать на письмо to answer a letter
  отвечать на чьё-либо чувство to return someone's feeling
отвыкать (отвыкнуть) to become unaccustomed, grow out of a habit
отвыкнуть—see отвыкать
отгадать—see отгадывать
отгадывать (отгадать) to guess
•отдавать (отдать) to give back, give up
  отдавать должное кому-либо to render someone his due
  отдавать свою жизнь to devote one's life
отдать—see отдавать
отдел section, department
отделение separation, section, department
отделить (ся)—see отделять (ся)
отдельно separately
отдельный separate
отделять-ся (отделиться) to separate, detach
отдохнуть—see отдыхать
отдых rest, relaxation
отдыхать (отдохнуть) to rest
•отец father
отечество native land, fatherland
отживший obsolete
отказ refusal, rejection
отказаться—see отказываться
•отказываться (отказаться) to refuse, decline
  отказываться выслушать кого-либо to refuse to listen to someone
  отказываться от борьбы to give up the struggle
  отказываться от своих слов to retract one's words
откровенно frankly, openly
откровенность (f.) frankness
откровенный frank, outspoken
•открывать (открыть) to open, discover
  открывать прения to open the debate
  открыть душу кому-либо to open one's heart to someone
  открыть кран to turn on a faucet
•открытка postcard
открыто openly, plainly

открытый open, frank
  на открытом воздухе in the open air
  открытое море open sea
  открытое платье low-necked dress
  с открытой душой open-heartedly
открыть—see открывать
•откуда where from, whence
  Откуда вы? Where are you from?
  Откуда вы это знаете? How do you come to know about it?
откусить (perf.) to bite off
отличать (отличить) to distinguish
отличаться (отличиться) to differ from, be notable for
отличие difference, distinction
отличить (ся)—see отличать (ся)
отлично excellently, it is excellent
  отлично понимать to understand perfectly
отличный excellent, perfect
  отличное здоровье perfect health
  отличное настроение high spirits
отложить (perf.) to set aside
  отложить в долгий ящик to shelve
  отложить решение to suspend one's judgment
отметить—see отмечать
отметка mark
  хорошие отметки high grades
отмечать (отметить) to mark, note, mention
относительно relatively, concerning
  Она говорила мне относительно брата. She spoke to me about her brother.
относиться (imp.) to treat, regard
  Как вы относитесь к моему плану? What do you think of my plan?
  хорошо относиться к кому-либо to treat someone well
  Это к нему не относится. That's none of his business. It doesn't concern him.
отношение attitude, relationship
  быть в хороших отношениях с кем-либо to be on good terms with someone
  в прямом отношении in direct ratio
  в этом отношении in this respect
  иметь отношение к чему-либо to have a bearing on something
отойти—see отходить
отомстить—see мстить
отопление heating system
отпаривать (отпарить) to steam
отпарить—see отпаривать
отпертый unlocked
отпереть—see отпирать
отпирать (отпереть) to unlock
отплата repayment

отплати́ть—see отпла́чивать

отпла́чивать (отплати́ть) to pay back

    отплати́ть кому́-либо за услу́гу to repay someone for his service

    отплати́ть кому́-либо той же моне́той to pay someone in his own coin

отпра́виться—see отправля́ться

отправля́ться (отпра́виться) to set out, start

    отпра́виться в путь to set out on a trip

    По́езд отправля́ется в пять часо́в. The train leaves at five o'clock.

о́тпуск leave, vacation

отпуска́ть (отпусти́ть) to let go, set free

    отпуска́ть во́лосы to let one's hair grow long

    отпуска́ть сре́дства to allot resources, to budget

отпусти́ть—see отпуска́ть

отра́да delight, joy

отре́зок piece, segment

отрица́ние denial, negation

отрица́тельно negatively

отрица́тельный negative, unfavorable

    отрица́тельное влия́ние bad influence

    отрица́тельные ти́пы в рома́не negative characters in a novel

    отрица́тельный отве́т negative answer

отрица́ть (imp.) to deny, disclaim

отстава́ть (отста́ть) to lag, be slow

    Часы́ отста́ют. The watch (clock) is slow.

    Этот учени́к отстаёт. This pupil lags behind.

отставно́й retired

отста́ть—see отстава́ть

отсу́тствие absence, lack

    в моё отсу́тствие in my absence

    за отсу́тствием де́нег for lack of money

отсу́тствовать (imp.) to be absent

•отсю́да from here, hence

отте́нок nuance, inflection, trace

    отте́нок значе́ния shade of meaning

•отту́да from there, thence

отхо́д departure

•отходи́ть (отойти́) to go away from, move away, leave, diverge

отча́яние despair

отча́янно desperately

отчёркивать (отчеркну́ть) to mark off

отчеркну́ть—see отчёркивать

отчётливость (f.) distinctness

отчётливый distinct

отъе́зд departure

официа́нт waiter

охо́тник hunter

охо́тно willingly, readily

охрани́ть—see охраня́ть

охраня́ть (охрани́ть) to guard, protect

оцара́пать (perf.) to scratch

оцени́ть—see цени́ть

очарова́ние charm, fascination

очаро́ванный charmed, taken with

очарова́тельный charming, fascinating

очарова́ть (perf.) to charm, fascinate

очеви́дно obviously, apparently, it is obvious

•о́чень very, very much, greatly

о́чередь (f.) turn

    по о́череди in turn

    стоя́ть в о́череди to stand in line

очки́ (only pl.) eyeglasses

ошиба́ться (ошиби́ться) to err, make a mistake

ошиби́ться—see ошиба́ться

•оши́бка mistake, error

о́щупью gropingly, by sense of touch

ощути́ть—see ощуща́ть

ощуща́ть (ощути́ть) to feel, sense

ощуще́ние sensation

П

•па́дать (упа́сть) to fall, slump, diminish

    во́лосы па́дают на лоб hair falls across the forehead

    Отве́тственность за э́то па́дает на вас. The responsibility for this falls on you.

    па́дать ду́хом to lose courage

паке́т parcel, package

пакт pact

пала́тка tent, marquee

•па́лец finger, toe

    обвести́ кого́-либо вокру́г па́льца to twist someone around one's finger

    Он па́льцем никого́ не тро́нет. He wouldn't hurt a fly.

па́лка stick, cane

    па́лка о двух конца́х double-edged weapon

па́луба deck

пальто́ (not declined) coat, overcoat

па́мятник memorial, monument

па́мятный memorable

па́мять (f.) memory

    люби́ть кого́-либо без па́мяти to love someone to distraction

    подари́ть на па́мять to give as a keepsake

    Это вы́пало у него́ из па́мяти. It slipped his memory.

пансио́н boarding school, boarding-house

•па́па papa, daddy

папиро́са cigarette

папиро́сница cigarette case

пар steam

па́ра pair, couple

    на па́ру слов for a few words

    па́ра сапо́г pair of boots

    хоро́шая па́ра fine couple

пара́д parade

параллелепи́пед parallelipiped

паралле́льный parallel

па́рень (m.) fellow, lad, chap

пари́ bet

    держа́ть пари́ to make a bet

пари́жский Parisian

парикма́хер barber

парикма́херская barbershop

па́рить (вы́парить) to steam, stew

парк park

парохо́д steamship

па́ртия party

партнёр partner

па́рус sail

па́смурно it is cloudy, dull

па́смурный cloudy, dull, gloomy

    па́смурная пого́да dull weather

па́спорт passport

пассажи́р, пассажи́рка passenger (m.,f.)

пасси́вный passive

    пасси́вный бала́нс unfavorable balance

    пасси́вный хара́ктер passive temperament

па́ста paste

    зубна́я па́ста toothpaste

па́стбище pasture

патети́чный pathetic

па́уза pause, interval

пау́к spider

паути́на cobweb

па́хнуть to smell (of)

    Па́хнет бедо́й. This means trouble.

    Па́хнет от него́ вино́м. He smells of wine.

пацие́нт patient

па́чка package

певе́ц, певи́ца singer (m., f.)

пейза́ж landscape

пека́рня bakery

пе́карь baker

пе́ние singing

пе́нсия pension

пе́пельница ashtray

пе́рвенство superiority

первокла́ссный first-rate

первонача́льно originally, at first

первонача́льный primary, original
первонача́льная причи́на first cause

• пе́рвый first, earliest
Он зна́ет э́то из пе́рвых рук. He has firsthand information.
пе́рвая по́мощь first aid
пе́рвого января́ on the first of January
пе́рвый эта́ж ground floor
с пе́рвого взгля́да at first sight

перева́ривать (перевари́ть) to overcook, digest
перевари́ть—see перева́ривать
перево́д translation
перевести́—see переводи́ть
переводи́ть (перевести́) to translate, interpret, transfer
перево́дчик translator, interpreter
перегиба́ться (перегну́ться) to lean over
перегну́ться—see перегиба́ться
переговори́ть (perf.) to discuss, talk over
перегово́ры negotiations
вести́ перегово́ры to carry on negotiations

• пе́ред before, in front of (place or time) (with inst.)
Они́ ничто́ перед ним. They are nothing compared to him.
Перед на́ми больша́я зада́ча. There is a great task before us.
пе́ред обе́дом before dinner
Стул стои́т перед столо́м. The chair is standing in front of the table.

передава́ть (переда́ть) to pass, give
передава́ть по ра́дио to broadcast
Переда́йте, пожа́луйста, соль. Please pass the salt.
переда́ть приве́т to send regards
переда́ть—see передава́ть
передвига́ть (передви́нуть) to move, shift
Стол на́до передви́нуть. The table should be moved.
передви́нуть—see передвига́ть
переде́лать (perf.) to do again, alter
переде́лать пла́тье to alter a dress
пере́дник apron
пере́дняя entrance room, foyer
передово́й headmost, forward, progressive
передова́я статья́ editorial
передова́я те́хника advanced technique
переду́мать (perf.) to change one's mind
переезжа́ть (перее́хать) to move

переезжа́ть на но́вую кварти́ру to move to a new apartment
перее́хать—see переезжа́ть
пережа́ренный overcooked
пережива́ние experience
пережива́ть (пережи́ть) to experience, endure, outlive
тяжело́ пережива́ть что́-либо to feel something keenly
пережи́ть—see пережива́ть
перейти́—see переходи́ть
пе́рекись водоро́да hydrogen peroxide
перелиста́ть—see перели́стывать
перели́стывать (перелиста́ть) to turn over pages, leaf through
переломи́ть (perf.) to break
переме́на change
перемени́ть—see меня́ть
перемудри́ть (perf.) to be too clever
перенапряже́ние overstrain, overexertion
перенасы́щенный oversaturated
перенести́—see переноси́ть
переноси́ть (перенести́) to endure, bear, bring over (by hand)
перено́сный portable
в перено́сном смы́сле figuratively
переночева́ть (perf.) to spend the night
переоде́ть (ся) (perf.) to change (one's) clothes
перепеча́тать (perf.) to reprint, type again
переписа́ть—see перепи́сывать
перепи́ска correspondence
перепи́сывать (переписа́ть) to copy over
перепи́сываться (imp.) to correspond
переплати́ть—see перепла́чивать
перепла́чивать (переплати́ть) to overpay
переплёт binding (book cover)
перепо́лнить—see переполня́ть
переполня́ть (перепо́лнить) to overfill
перереша́ть (перереши́ть) to solve
перереша́ть все зада́чи to solve all the problems
переры́в interruption, intermission
переста́ть (perf.) to stop, cease
переступа́ть (переступи́ть) to overstep, transgress
переступа́ть грани́цы to overstep the limits
переступи́ть—see переступа́ть
переу́лок lane, alley
переутомле́ние overstrain
перехо́д crossing, transition
переходи́ть (перейти́) to cross, get over, pass on to

переходи́ть грани́цу to cross the frontier
переходи́ть к друго́му владе́льцу to change hands
перехо́дный transitional
пе́рец pepper
пери́од period, spell
периоди́ческий periodical
перо́ pen
перпендикуля́рно perpendicular
пе́рсик peach
перспекти́ва perspective, outlook
перча́тка glove
пёс dog

• пе́сня song
тяну́ть всё ту же пе́сню to harp on one theme
Это ста́рая пе́сня. It's the same old story.
песо́к sand
са́харный песо́к granulated sugar
пёстрый many-colored
пе́тля loop, buttonhole

• петь (спеть) to sing, chant
петь ба́сом to sing in a bass voice
петь сла́ву to sing the praises
печа́ль (f.) grief, sorrow
печа́льный sad, wistful, mournful
печа́тать (напеча́тать) to print, type
печа́ть (f.) press, seal
быть в печа́ти to be in print
свобо́да печа́ти freedom of the press
печёнка liver
печёный baked
пече́нье baking, pastry, cookie
печь stove, oven
печь (imp.) to bake
пешко́м on foot
ходи́ть пешко́м to go on foot
пиани́но upright piano
пиани́ст, пиани́стка pianist (m., f.)
пи́во beer
пиджа́к suit coat
пижа́ма pajamas
пика́нтный piquant, savory
пика́нтный анекдо́т spicy story
пикни́к picnic
пи́кули pickles
пилю́ля pill
пирами́да pyramid
пиро́г pie, cake
пиро́жное pastry, fancy cake
писа́ние writing
писа́тель (m.) writer, author

• писа́ть (написа́ть) to write, paint
Перо́ хорошо́ пи́шет. The pen writes well.
писа́ть карти́ны to paint pictures
писа́ть под дикто́вку to take dictation
писа́ть разбо́рчиво to write plainly
писа́ть стихи́ to write verse

писа́ться (imp.) to be spelled
Как э́то сло́во пи́шется? How do you spell that word?
пи́сьменно in writing
пи́сьменный written
пи́сьменная рабо́та written work
пи́сьменный стол desk
письмо́ letter
пита́ние nourishment
пита́ть (imp.) to feed, nourish
пита́ть больно́го to nourish a patient
пита́ть симпа́тию to have a friendly feeling for
пита́ть чу́вство to entertain a feeling
•пить (вы́пить) to drink
Мне хо́чется пить. I'm thirsty.
пи́ща food
горя́чая пи́ща hot meal
дава́ть пи́щу слу́хам to feed rumors
духо́вная пи́ща spiritual nourishment
пла́вание swimming, sailing
пла́вать (imp.) to swim, sail
Всё плывёт пе́редо мной. Everything is swimming before my eyes.
пла́кать (imp.) to cry, weep
го́рько пла́кать to weep bitterly
Хоть плачь! It is enough to make one cry!
план plan, scheme
пласти́нка phonograph record, plate
пласти́ческий plastic
•плати́ть (imp.) to pay
плати́ть в рассро́чку to pay in installments
плати́ть добро́м за зло to return good for evil
•плато́к shawl, kerchief
носово́й плато́к handkerchief
платфо́рма platform
•пла́тье dress, clothes
племя́нник, племя́нница nephew, niece
•плечо́ shoulder
выноси́ть на свои́х плеча́х to endure, carry on one's shoulders
пожима́ть плеча́ми to shrug one's shoulders
с плеча́ straight from the shoulder
плодоро́дность (f.) fertility
пло́ский flat
пло́ская пове́рхность plane surface
пло́ская шу́тка flat joke
пло́скость (f.) flatness
пло́тник carpenter
•пло́хо badly, poorly
пло́хо обраща́ться to ill-treat

пло́хо себя́ чу́вствовать to feel ill
плохо́й bad, poor
плоха́я пого́да bad weather
плохо́е здоро́вье poor health
пло́щадь (f.) square, public square, area
плыть—see пла́вать
плюс plus
пляж beach
•по along, down, about, on, according to, by (with dat.)
говори́ть по-ру́сски to speak in Russian
е́хать по у́лице to ride along the street
идти́ по траве́ to walk on the grass
Кни́ги разло́жены по всему́ столу́. Books are lying all over the table.
по-мо́ему in my opinion
по оши́бке by mistake
по приро́де by nature
по по́чте by mail
по пять рубле́й at five rubles each
побе́да victory
победи́ть—see побежда́ть
побежда́ть (победи́ть) to conquer, win a victory
побли́зости near at hand
побо́льше somewhat larger, somewhat more
побужде́ние motive, incentive
пова́льно without exception
по́вар cook, chef
по-ва́шему in your opinion
поведе́ние conduct, behavior
поверну́ть—see поверя́ть
поверну́ть(ся)—see повора́чивать(ся)
•пове́рх over (with gen.)
пове́рх пла́тья на ней бы́ло наде́то пальто́ She wore a coat over her dress
пове́рхностно superficially
пове́рхность (f.) surface
поверя́ть (пове́рить) to trust, entrust, verify
по́весть (f.) narrative, story
по-ви́димому apparently
пови́нность (f.) duty, obligation
повора́чивать (поверну́ть) to turn, change
повора́чиваться (поверну́ться) to turn around
поворо́т bend, curve, turn
поврежде́ние damage, injury
повсю́ду everywhere
повторе́ние repetition
повторя́ть—see повторя́ть
повторя́ть (повтори́ть) to repeat
повы́сить—see повыша́ть

повыша́ть (повы́сить) to raise, heighten
повы́сить го́лос to raise one's voice
повыша́ть по слу́жбе to advance in one's work
повыша́ть усло́вия жи́зни to raise the standards of living
повы́ше a little higher
погиба́ть (поги́бнуть) to perish
поги́бельный (ги́бельный) disastrous, fatal
поги́бнуть—see погиба́ть
погла́дить—see гла́дить
погляде́ть—see гляде́ть
поговори́ть (perf.) to have a talk
•пого́да weather
погуля́ть (гуля́ть) to walk a while
•под under—location (with inst.) under—direcion (with acc.)
Он пошёл под де́рево. He went under the tree.
Он стоя́л под де́ревом. He stood under the tree.
под аре́стом under arrest
подава́ть (пода́ть) to give, serve
подава́ть мяч to serve the ball
подава́ть наде́жду to give hope
подава́ть на стол to wait on the table
пода́ть проше́ние to forward a petition
пода́ть ру́ку to offer one's hand
подари́ть—see дари́ть
пода́рок gift
в пода́рок as a gift
подборо́док chin
подва́л basement
подгото́вить to prepare
подгото́вить по́чву to pave the way
подержа́ть—see подде́рживать
подде́рживать (поддержа́ть) to support, maintain
поддержа́ть разгово́р to keep up the conversation
поддержа́ть мора́льно to encourage
подде́ржка backing, support
подде́йствовать—see де́йствовать
поде́ржанный secondhand, used
поджа́рить (perf.) to fry, roast, grill
подже́чь (perf.) to set on fire
поджо́г arson
подкла́дка lining
подкрепле́ние confirmation, reinforcement
•по́дле beside (prep. with gen.)
подле́ц villain
подли́вка sauce, gravy
по́длость (f.) meanness, baseness
подмести́—see подмета́ть

подметáть (подмести́) to sweep

•поднимáть (подня́ть) to lift, raise

подымáть всех нá ноги to raise an alarm

поднимáть рýку to raise one's hand

подня́ть вопрóс to raise a question

поднимáться (подня́ться) to rise, climb

поднимáться нá гору to climb a mountain

поднимáться нá ноги to rise to one's feet

Тéсто поднялóсь. The dough has risen.

Цéны подня́ли́сь. Prices went up.

поднóс tray

подня́ть (ся)—see поднимáть (ся)

подóбно like, similarly

подóбный like, similar

и томý подóбное. (и т. п.) and so on, and so forth

ничегó подóбного nothing of the kind

Он ничегó подóбного не ви́дел. He has never seen anything like it.

•подождáть (pf.) to wait for

подозвáть (pf.) to call up, beckon

подозревáть (imp.) to suspect

подозрéние suspicion

подозри́тельно suspiciously

подойти́—see подходи́ть

подóл hem (of a skirt)

подписáться (perf.) to sign, subscribe

подпи́ска subscription

пóдпись signature

подражáние imitation

подражáть (imp.) to imitate

подрóбно in detail, at length

подрóбность (f.) detail

вдавáться в подрóбности to go into detail

подрóбный detailed

•подрýга female friend

по-дрýжески in a friendly way

подружи́ться (perf.) to make friends

•подря́д in succession

пять часóв подря́д five hours in succession

подсказáть (perf.) to prompt

подслýшать (perf.) to eavesdrop

подýмать—see дýмать

подýшка pillow, cushion

подхóд approach, point of view

подхóд к вопрóсу approach to the problem

•подходи́ть (подойти́) to come up to, approach, fit

подходи́ть к концý to come to an end

Это емý не подхóдит. This won't do for him.

подходя́щий suitable, appropriate

подчёркивать (подчеркнýть) to underline, emphasize

подчеркнýть—see подчёркивать

подчини́ться—see подчиня́ться

подчиня́ться (подчини́ться) to obey, submit to

подшивáть (подши́ть) to sew underneath, hem

подши́вка hem, hemming

подши́ть—see подшивáть

подъём ascent, raising, instep

•пóезд train

поéздка journey

•поéхать (perf.) to set off, depart (by vehicle)

Поéхали! Come along! Let's start!

пожалéть—see жалéть

пожáловаться—see жáловаться

пожáлуй perhaps, very likely

Пожáлуй, вы прáвы. You may be right.

Пожáлуй, он придёт. I think he will come.

•пожáлуйста please, don't mention it

Дáйте мне, пожáлуйста, воды́. Give me some water, please.

Спаси́бо. Пожáлуйста. Thank you. Don't mention it.

пожáр accidental fire

пожáрная комáнда fire brigade

пожáть—see пожимáть

пожелáние wish, desire

пожелáть—see желáть

поживáть to get along, fare

Как поживáете? How are you?

пожилóй elderly

пожимáть (пожáть) to press

вмéсто отвéта пожáть плечáми to shrug off the question

пожимáть плечáми to shrug one's shoulders

пожимáть рýки to shake hands

пóза pose, attitude

позави́довать—see зави́довать

позавчерá the day before yesterday

•позади́ behind (adv.), behind (prep. with gen.)

Всё тяжёлое остáлось позади́. Hard times are past.

Позади́ столá стои́т стул. A chair is standing behind the table.

позвáть—see звать

позволéние permission, leave

проси́ть позволéния to ask permission

э́тот, с позволéния сказáть, дом this so-called house

позвóлить—see позволя́ть

позволя́ть (позвóлить) to allow, permit

позволя́ть себé to indulge, afford

позволя́ть себé вóльность to take liberties

позвони́ть—see звони́ть

пóздний late, tardy

пóздний гость late arrival

спать до пóзднего утрá to sleep late in the morning

•пóздно late, it is late

Лýчше пóздно, чем никогдá. Better late than never.

поздорóваться—see здорóваться

поздрáвить—see поздравля́ть

поздравлéние congratulation

поздравля́ть (поздрáвить) to congratulate

поздравля́ть с днём рождéния to congratulate someone on his birthday

пóзже later, later on

познакóмиться—see знакóмиться

позóр shame, disgrace

поймáть—see лови́ть

пои́стине indeed, in truth

пойти́ (идти́) to set out, go, start

•покá while, for the time being

Покá всё. That is all for the time being.

покá... не until

Он ждал покá онá не вы́шла. He waited until she came out.

покá что meanwhile

показáтельный model, demonstration (adj.)

показáть—see покáзывать

покáзывать (показáть) to show, point to, display

показáть себя́ to put one's best foot forward

покáзывать хрáбрость to display courage

Часы́ покáзывают дéсять. The clock is set at ten.

показáться—see казáться

покатáться—see катáться to go for a short drive

покачáть (imp.) to rock, swing

Покачáй ребёнка. Swing the child.

покачáть головóй to shake one's head

поки́нутый abandoned, deserted

поки́нуть (perf.) to abandon, forsake

поклóн bow

Передáйте емý поклóн. Give him my regards.

поклони́ться—see кла́няться

поклóнник admirer, worshiper

покóй (m.) rest, peace

не давáть покóя to give no rest, to haunt

оста́вить в поко́е to leave alone
поко́йно quietly
поко́йник the deceased
поколе́ние generation
поко́рно humbly, obediently
поко́рный submissive, obedient, resigned
   поко́рный судьбе́ resigned to one's fate
покра́сить (ся)—see кра́сить (ся)
покрасне́ть—see красне́ть
покрови́тельство patronage, protection
покрыва́ло shawl, veil, bedspread
покрыва́ть (покры́ть) to cover, coat, roof
   покрыва́ть себя́ сла́вой to cover oneself with glory
   покры́ть та́йной to shroud in mystery
покры́ть—see покрыва́ть
покры́шка covering
•покупа́ть (купи́ть) to buy
поку́пка purchase
   де́лать поку́пки to go shopping
покури́ть (perf.) to have a smoke
•пол floor
   Она́ сиде́ла на полу́. She was sitting on the floor.
пол sex
   же́нского и́ли мужско́го по́ла female or male sex (gender)
   прекра́сный пол the fair sex
полага́ть to suppose, think
   Полага́ют, что он в Москве́. He is believed to be in Moscow.
полага́ться (положи́ться) to rely on
   Здесь не полага́ется кури́ть. One is not supposed to smoke here.
   полага́ется one is supposed
   Положи́тесь на меня́. Depend on me.
   Так полага́ется. It is the custom.
полго́да half a year
по́лдень midday, noon
•по́ле field
   по́ле зре́ния field of vision
   спорти́вное по́ле playground
поле́зно healthful, useful
поле́зный useful, healthy
по́лзать (imp.) to creep, crawl
полете́ть—see лета́ть
ползти́ (imp.) to crawl, creep
   По́езд ползёт. The train is crawling.
   Тума́н ползёт. A fog is creeping up.
политехни́ческий polytechnic
поли́тика politics
полице́йский policeman
по́лка shelf
   кни́жные по́лки bookshelves

полне́ть (пополне́ть) to become fat, put on weight
полно́ brimful
по́лно enough!, that will do!
по́лностью completely, in full
по́лночь midnight
•по́лный full, complete, stout
   В ко́мнате полно́ наро́ду. The room is full of people.
   по́лная луна́ full moon
   по́лное разоре́ние utter ruin
   по́лное собра́ние сочине́ний complete works
полови́на half
положе́ние position, situation, condition
   будь он в ва́шем положе́нии if he were in your place
   Он челове́к с положе́нием. He is a man of high standing.
   по положе́нию by one's position
поло́женный fixed, prescribed
положи́м let us assume
положи́тельно positively, absolutely
положи́тельный positive, sedate
   положи́тельная сте́пень сравне́ния positive degree (grammatical)
   положи́тельный отве́т affirmative answer
•положи́ть (класть) to lay down, put down, put in a horizontal position
·положи́ться—see полага́ться to rely on
   не́ на кого положи́ться no one to rely on
полоса́ stripe, strip
полоте́нце towel
полтора́ one and a half
полу gives meaning of semi- or half
полугра́мотный semi-literate
полуоде́тый half-dressed
полусве́т twilight
•получа́ть (получи́ть) to receive, get, obtain
   получа́ть пре́мию to receive a prize
   получи́ть интере́сные вы́воды to obtain valuable conclusions
получа́ться (получи́ться) to come, arrive, turn out
   Результа́ты получи́лись блестя́щие. The results were brilliant.
получи́ть (ся)—see получа́ть (ся)
полчаса́ half-hour
по́льза use, benefit
   в по́льзу in favor of
   обще́ственная по́льза public benefit
   приноси́ть по́льзу to be of use
   Что по́льзы говори́ть об э́том? What's the use of talking about that?

по́льзоваться (imp.) to use
   по́льзоваться дове́рием to enjoy someone's confidence
   по́льзоваться слу́чаем to take the opportunity
   по́льзоваться успе́хом to be a success
по́льский Polish (adj.)
полюби́ть (perf.) to fall in love
пома́да pomade
   губна́я пома́да lipstick
пома́зать—see ма́зать
поме́длить—see ме́длить
поме́ньше somewhat less, somewhat smaller
поменя́ть—see меня́ть
помести́ть (ся)—see помеща́ть (ся)
помеща́ть (помести́ть) to place, locate
помеща́ться (imp.) to be located, accommodated
   Стул туда́ помеща́ется. The chair fits in there.
помеще́ние location, lodging
поме́щик landowner, landlord
помидо́р tomato
поми́ловать (perf.) to pardon, forgive
поми́луй, поми́луйте for goodness' sake
•поми́мо besides, apart from (with gen.)
   поми́мо други́х соображе́ний apart from other considerations
   Там бы́ло мно́го наро́ду поми́мо них. There were many people besides them.
помину́тно every minute
помири́ться—see мири́ться
•по́мнить (imp.) to remember, keep in mind
   Он по́мнит об э́том. He remembers it.
помога́ть (помо́чь) to help, assist
по-мо́ему in my opinion
помо́чь—see помога́ть
помо́щник, помо́щница assistant, helper (m., f.)
по́мощь (f.) help, aid, relief
помы́ть (ся)—see мыть (ся)
понаде́яться (perf.) to count on
по-настоя́щему in the right way, as it should be
понево́ле against one's will
понеде́льник Monday
понемно́гу a little at a time, little by little
пониже́ние lowering, reduction
понима́ние understanding, comprehension
•понима́ть (поня́ть) to understand comprehend
поно́шенный shabby, worn

понра́виться—see нра́виться

понужде́ние compulsion

понюхать—see нюхать

поня́тие idea, concept

Поня́тия не име́ю. I have no idea.

поня́тно understandable, it is clear

поня́тный clear, understandable

поня́ть—see понима́ть

пообе́дать—see обе́дать

поощри́ть—see поощря́ть

поощря́ть (поощри́ть) to encourage

попада́ть (попа́сть) to get somewhere (by chance), to find oneself

Как попа́сть на вокза́л? How does one get to the railroad station?

попа́сть на по́езд to catch a train

попа́сть в цель to hit the mark

попа́сть—see попада́ть

попола́м in halves

пополне́ть—see полне́ть

поправиться—see поправля́ться

поправля́ть (попра́вить) to repair, mend, correct

поправля́ть де́нежные дела́ to better one's financial situation

поправля́ть причёску to smoothe one's hair

поправля́ться (попра́виться) to recover, get well, gain weight, improve

попре́жнему as before, as usual

попрёк reproach

попрека́ть (попрекну́ть) to reproach

попро́бовать—see про́бовать

попроси́ть—see проси́ть

попроща́ться—see проща́ться

попуга́й parrot

повторя́ть как попуга́й to parrot someone's words

популя́рный popular

попыта́ться—see пыта́ться

попы́тка attempt, endeavor

•пора́ time

Давно́ пора́. It is high time.

до сих пор until now

Пора́ идти́. It is time to go.

с каки́х пор since when

поража́ть (порази́ть) to startle, strike, stagger

поража́ться—(порази́ться) to be' surprised, astonished

порази́тельный striking, startling

порази́тельное схо́дство striking likeness

порази́ть (ся)—see поража́ть (ся)

поре́зать (perf.) to cut

Он поре́зал себе́ па́лец. He cut his finger.

поро́г threshold

поро́к vice, defect

порт port, harbor

по́ртить (испо́ртить) to spoil, corrupt

Не по́ртите себе́ не́рвы. Don't worry. Don't take it to heart.

по́ртить аппети́т to spoil one's appetite

по́ртиться (испо́ртиться) to deteriorate, decay, become corrupt, to become spoiled

портни́ха dressmaker

портно́й tailor

портре́т portrait

портфе́ль (m.) briefcase

по-ру́сски Russian, in Russian

поруче́ние commission, errand

по́рция portion, helping

поры́в gust, rush

в поры́ве ра́дости in a burst of joy

•поря́док order

алфави́тный поря́док alphabetical order

быть не в поря́дке to be out of order (not working)

Всё в поря́дке Everything is well.

в спе́шном поря́дке quickly (rush order)

приводи́ть в поря́док to put in order

ста́рый поря́док old regime, order

поря́дочно honestly, decently

поря́дочный sizable, honest, respectable

поса́дочный тало́н boarding stub (airport)

по-сво́ему in one's own way

посети́тель (m.) visitor

посети́ть—see посеща́ть

посеща́ть (посети́ть) to call on, visit

поскака́ть—see скака́ть

поско́льку so far as

поско́льку ему́ изве́стно as far as he knows, as long as he knows

поскоре́е somewhat quicker, quick!, make haste!

поскрипе́ть—see скрипе́ть

посла́ть—see посыла́ть

•по́сле after (time, with gen.) also: adverb—later, afterwards

Он придёт по́сле рабо́ты. He will come after work.

Это мо́жно сде́лать по́сле. You can do it afterward.

•после́дний last, latest

за после́днее вре́мя of late, lately

после́дние изве́стия latest news

после́дний сорт the worst kind

послеза́втра the day after tomorrow

посло́вица proverb

послужи́ть—see служи́ть

послу́шать—see слу́шать

посме́ть—see сметь

посмотре́ть—see смотре́ть

посове́товать—see сове́товать

посо́л ambassador

посо́льство embassy

поспа́ть (perf.) to have a nap

поспе́шно hastily

поспо́рить—see спо́рить

поспе́шный hasty, thoughtless

сде́лать поспе́шное заключе́ние to draw a hasty conclusion

•посреди́ in the middle of (prep. with gen.)

посре́дством by means of

поста́вить—see ста́вить

постара́ться—see стара́ться

по-ста́рому as before, as of old

посте́ль (f.) bed

постепе́нно gradually

постила́ть (постла́ть) spread

постила́ть ковёр to spread a carpet

постила́ть посте́ль to make the bed

постла́ть—see постила́ть

посторо́нний strange, outside, outsider

постоя́нно constantly, always

постоя́нный constant, permanent

пострада́ть—see страда́ть

постро́енный built

постро́ить—see стро́ить

поступа́ть (поступи́ть) to act, join

поступа́ть в произво́дство to go into production

поступа́ть в университе́т to enter the university

поступа́ть на вое́нную слу́жбу to join (enlist) in the army

поступа́ть пло́хо с ке́м-либо to treat someone badly

поступи́ть—see поступа́ть

постуча́ть (perf.) to knock, rap

посу́да dishes

посчита́ться—see счита́ться

посыла́ть—(посла́ть) to send, dispatch

пот perspiration

потемне́ть—see темне́ть

поте́рянный lost, embarrassed, perplexed

потеря́ть (ся)—see теря́ть (ся)

поте́ть (вспоте́ть) to perspire, to become misty with steam

Окна поте́ют. The windows are misty.

потихо́ньку slowly, silently, stealthily

потоло́к ceiling

•пото́м then, afterwards

пото́мство posterity

потолсте́ть—see толсте́ть

потому́ that is why

Потому́ он и прие́хал неме́дленно. That's why he came immediately.

потому́ что because
потре́бность (f.) want, necessity
потре́бовать—see тре́бовать
потрево́жить—see трево́жить
потуши́ть—see туши́ть
потяну́ть (ся)—see тяну́ть (ся)
поу́жинать—see у́жинать
похвали́ть—see хвали́ть
похва́стать (ся)—see хва́стать (ся)
походка walk, step
  лёгкая похо́дка light step
похо́жий resembling, like
  На что вы похо́жи! Just look at
    yourself!
  Они́ о́чень похо́жи друг на дру́га.
    They are very much alike.
  Похо́же на то, что пойдёт дождь.
    It looks as if it will rain.
похорони́ть—see хорони́ть
похороше́ть—see хороше́ть
похуде́ть—see худе́ть
поцелова́ть (ся)—see целова́ть (ся)
поцелу́й kiss
по́чва soil, ground
  не теря́ть по́чвы под нога́ми to
    stand on sure ground
  плодоро́дная по́чва fertile soil
  подгото́вить по́чву to pave the way
• почему́ why
  почему́-то for some reason or
    other
по́черк handwriting
почеса́ться—see чеса́ться
почи́стить—see чи́стить
по́чта post office, mail
почте́ние respect, consideration
• почти́ almost, nearly
почти́тельный respectful, deferential
  на почти́тельном расстоя́нии at a
    respectful distance
почу́вствовать—see чу́вствовать
пощади́ть—see щади́ть
пощекота́ть—see щекота́ть
пощёчина slap in the face
по́эзия poetry
поэ́т poet
поэ́тому therefore
появи́ться—see появля́ться
появля́ться (появи́ться) to appear,
  emerge
по́яс belt, waistband
• пра́вда truth
  иска́ть пра́вды to seek justice
  не пра́вда ли? isn't that so?
пра́вило rule
пра́вильно correctly, you are right
пра́вильный correct, right, regular
прави́тельство government
пра́вить (imp.) to drive, govern
пра́во right, license, law
  води́тельские права́ driver's
    license

обы́чное пра́во common law
  по пра́ву by right
• пра́вый right, correct
пра́здник holiday
пра́здновать (imp.) to celebrate
пра́ктика practice, experience
пребыва́ние stay, sojourn
превосхо́дный excellent, magnificent
пре́данный devoted, staunch
предви́дение foresight
преде́л limit, end
предисло́вие preface, foreword
предлага́ть (предложи́ть) to offer,
  propose, suggest
предло́г preposition, pretense
предложе́ние offer, suggestion,
  proposal
предложе́ние sentence, clause
предложи́ть—see предлага́ть
предме́т object, subject, theme
преднаме́ренный premeditated
предполага́емый supposed,
  conjectured
предполага́ть (предположи́ть) to
  suppose, conjecture
предположе́ние supposition
предположи́ть—see предполага́ть
предпосле́дний next to the last
предпоче́сть—see предпочита́ть
предпочита́ть (предпоче́сть) to
  prefer
предпочте́ние preference
предрассу́док prejudice
председа́тель (m.) chairman,
  president
предсказа́ние prophecy, prediction
предсказа́ть (perf.) to foretell,
  predict
представи́тель (m.) representative
представи́ть—see представля́ть
представля́ть (прдста́вить) to
  present, offer
  представи́ть кого́-либо to introduce
    someone
  представля́ть на рассмотре́ние to
    submit for consideration
  представьте себе́ моё удивле́ние
    imagine my astonishment
  Что он собо́й представля́ет?
    What kind of person is he?
  Это не представля́ет тру́дности.
    It offers no difficulty.
предупреди́ть—see предупрежда́ть
предупрежда́ть (предупреди́ть) to
  notify, forewarn, prevent, anticipate
предупрежде́ние notice, warning
предыду́щий previous
• пре́жде earlier, before (of time),
  formerly
президе́нт president
презира́ть (презре́ть) to despise
презре́ние contempt, disdain
презре́ть—see презира́ть

презри́тельный contemptuous,
  scornful
преиму́щество advantage,
  preference, priority
прекра́сно fine, excellently,
  beautifully
прекра́сный excellent, beautiful
  в оди́н прекра́сный день one fine
    day
преле́стный charming, delightful,
  lovely
пре́лесть (f.) charm, fascination
пре́мия premium, bonus, prize
премье́р prime minister, premier
преобража́ть (преобрази́ть) to
  transform, change
преображе́ние transformation
преобрази́ть—see преобража́ть
преодолева́ть (преодоле́ть) to
  overcome, surmount
преодоле́ть—see преодолева́ть
преподава́ние teaching
преподава́тель, преподава́тельница
  teacher (m., f.)
преподава́ть (imp.) to teach
препя́тствие obstacle, hindrance,
  barrier
прерва́ть—see прерыва́ть
прерыва́ть (прерва́ть) to interrupt
  прерыва́ть заня́тия to interrupt
    one's studies
  прерыва́ть молча́ние to break the
    silence
  прерыва́ть разгово́р to interrupt a
    conversation
преры́висто in a broken way
пресле́дование persecution
пресле́довать (imp.) to pursue,
  haunt
  пресле́довать цель to pursue one's
    object
  Эта мысль пресле́дует меня́. This
    thought haunts me.
пре́сный fresh, sweet, insipid
  пре́сная вода́ fresh water
престо́л throne
преступа́ть (преступи́ть) to
  transgress, violate
преступи́ть—see преступа́ть
преступле́ние crime, offense
престу́пник criminal
прете́нзия claim, pretension
преувеличе́ние exaggeration,
  overstatement
преувели́ченный exaggerated
преувели́чивать (преувели́чить) to
  exaggerate
преувели́чить—see преувели́чивать
преуменьша́ть (преуме́ньшить) to
  underestimate
преуменьше́ние underestimation

преуме́ньшить—see приуменьша́ть

• при in the presence of, at, by (with prep.)

Он э́то сказа́л при свое́й ма́тери. He said it in his mother's presence.

при дневно́м све́те by daylight

при Петре́ Пе́рвом during the reign of Peter the First

При университе́те нахо́дится це́рковь. There is a church in the university.

приба́вить—see прибавля́ть

приба́вка addition, supplement

прибавля́ть (приба́вить) to add, increase

приба́вочный additional, supplementary

прибежа́ть (perf.) to approach running

приближа́ть (прибли́зить) to draw nearer

прибли́зить кни́гу к глаза́м to bring the book closer to one's eyes

приближа́ться (прибли́зиться) to approach, draw near, approximate

приближа́ться к и́стине to approximate the truth

Шум прибли́зился. The noise drew nearer.

приблизи́тельно approximately

приблизи́тельный approximate

прибли́зить (ся)—see приближа́ть (ся

прибо́р device, apparatus

привезти́—see привози́ть

привести́—see приводи́ть

приве́т greeting

приве́тливость (f.) affability

приве́тливый friendly

преве́тствие greeting, salutation

приве́тствовать (imp.) to greet, welcome

привиде́ние ghost, specter

привлека́тельный attractive, alluring, inviting

привлека́ть (привле́чь) to attract, draw to

привле́чь—see привлека́ть

приводи́ть (привести́) to bring

приводи́ть в поря́док to put in order

приводи́ть кого́-либо в чу́вство to bring someone to his senses

привози́ть (привезти́) to bring

привыка́ть (привы́кнуть) to become accustomed

Он уже́ привы́к к тому́. He has already become used to it.

Ребёнок привы́к к ба́бушке. The child became accustomed to his grandmother.

привы́кнуть—see привыка́ть

привы́чка habit

по привы́чке by force of habit

привя́занность (f.) attachment

привя́занный attached

привяза́ть—see привя́зывать

привя́зывать (привяза́ть) to attach, to fasten

пригласи́ть—see приглаша́ть

приглаша́ть (пригласи́ть) to ask, invite

приглаше́ние invitation

при́город suburb

пригото́вить—see гото́вить

приготовле́ние preparation

приготовля́ть-ся (пригото́вить-ся) to prepare (oneself), also of cooking

приду́мать—see приду́мывать

приду́мывать (приду́мать) to devise, invent

прие́зд arrival

приезжа́ть (прие́хать) to arrive

приём reception

приёмный receiving, reception

приёмная мать foster mother

приёмные часы́ office hours (of a doctor)

прие́хать—see приезжа́ть

прижима́ть (прижа́ть) to press, clasp

прижима́ть к груди́ to clasp to one's breast

прижа́ть—see прижима́ть

призва́ние vocation, calling

признава́ть (призна́ть) to acknowledge, recognize

признава́ть свои́ оши́бки to admit one's mistakes

при́знак sign, indication

призна́ние acknowledgement, recognition

призна́ть—see признава́ть

прийти́ (сь)—see приходи́ть (ся)

прика́з order, command

приказа́ть—see прика́зывать

прика́зывать (приказа́ть) to order, command

приле́жный diligent

прили́чие decency, decorum

прили́чно decently, properly

прили́чный decent, proper, becoming

• приме́р example

брать приме́р с кого́-либо to follow someone's example

наприме́р for example, for instance

подава́ть приме́р to set an example

приме́рить—see ме́рить

приме́рить—see примеря́ть

приме́рно exemplarily, approximately

приме́рно вести́ себя́ to be an example, to conduct oneself exemplarily

примеря́ть (приме́рить) to try on, fit

Семь раз приме́рь, а оди́н отре́жь. Try it on seven times, cut once. Look before you leap.

примеча́ние note, comment

примире́ние reconciliation

примиря́ться (imp.) to become reconciled, to put up with

принадлежа́ть (imp.) to belong

принести́—see приноси́ть

• принима́ть (приня́ть) to take, admit

за кого́ вы меня́ принима́ете? Whom do you take me for?

принима́ть ва́нну to take a bath

принима́ть во внима́ние to take into consideration

принима́ть в шко́лу to admit to the school

принима́ть госте́й to receive guests

принима́ть как до́лжное to accept as one's due

принима́ть на себя́ что-либо to take something on oneself

принима́ть реше́ние to come to a decision

принима́ть чью́-либо сто́рону to take someone's side

приня́ть гражда́нство to become a citizen

приня́ть уча́стие to take part

приноси́ть (принести́) to bring, fetch

приноси́ть дохо́д to make profit

приноси́ть обра́тно to bring back

Э́то не принесло́ ему́ по́льзы. He got no benefit from it.

прину́дить—see принужда́ть

принужда́ть (прину́дить) to compel, coerce

принуждённый constrained, forced

при́нцип principle

при́нятый accepted, adopted

приня́ть—see принима́ть

приобрести́—see приобрета́ть

приобрета́ть (приобрести́) to acquire gain

припа́док fit, attack

припра́ва seasoning, flavoring

• приро́да nature

Он лени́в от приро́ды. He is lazy by nature.

явле́ние приро́ды natural phenomenon

прислу́га servant

присоедине́ние addition, joining

присоединиться—see присоединяться

присоединяться (присоединиться) to join, add

пристально fixedly, intently

пристальный fixed, intent

присутствие presence

присутствовать to be present

приход coming, arrival

приходить (прийти) to come, arrive

приходить в голову to come into someone's mind

приходить в себя to come to one's senses

приходить к заключению to come to the conclusion

приходиться (прийтись) to have to, fit

Ему пришлось уехать. He had to leave.

Он приходится мне двоюродным братом. He is my cousin.

Причём тут я? What have I to do with it?

причесать (ся)—see причёсывать (ся)

причёска coiffure, hair-do

причёсывать-ся (причесать-ся) to comb (one's own) hair

причина cause, reason

приятель, приятельница friend (m., f.)

•приятно (adv.) pleasantly, it's pleasant

приятный pleasant, agreeable

•про about, concerning (with acc.)

Он слышал про это. He has heard about it.

про себя to oneself

проба test, trial

пробегать (пробежать) to run past, run through

пробирка test tube

пробка cork, stopper, plug

проблема problem

пробовать (попробовать) to attempt, try, taste

пробуждение awakening

пробыть (perf.) to stay, remain

Он пробыл там три дня. He stayed there three days.

проверить—see проверять

проверять (проверить) to verify, check

провести—see проводить

провод wire, conductor

проводить (провести) to spend time

Мы хорошо провели время. We had a good time.

проводить—see провожать

провожать (проводить) to accompany, see someone off

провожать глазами to follow with

one's eyes

провожать до угла to accompany to the corner

программа program

театральная программа playbill

учебная программа curriculum

прогресс progress

прогулка walk, outing

на прогулку for a walk, outing

•продавать (продать) to sell

продажа selling, sale

идти в продажу to be put up for sale

проданный sold

продать—see продавать

•продолжать (продолжить) to continue

продолжение continuation, sequel

продолжительный long, prolonged

продолжить—see продолжать

продукты provisions, foodstuffs

продумать (perf.) to think over

проезд passage, thoroughfare

проезжать (проехать) to pass, go by, cover a distance

проезжий traveler, passer-by

проехать—see проезжать

проза prose

прозвание nickname

прозрачный transparent

проиграть (perf.) to lose (at playing)

произведение work, production

избранные произведения selected works

музыкальное произведение musical composition

произвести—see производить

производить (произвести) to carry out, make, manufacture

производить впечатление to make an impression

производить опыты to conduct experiments

производство production, manufacture

произнести—see произносить

произносить (произнести) to pronounce, utter

произносить речь to deliver a speech

произношение pronunciation

произойти—see происходить

происходить (произойти) to happen, occur, be going on, be descended from

Что здесь происходит? What's going on here?

происхождение origin, descent

по происхождению by birth

пройти—see проходить

прокат hire

взять на прокат to rent, to hire

проклятый cursed, damned

проливать (пролить) to spill, shed

проливать свет to throw light

проливать слёзы to shed tears

пролить—see проливать

промедлить (perf.) to linger, delay

промелькнуть (perf.) to flash, pass quickly

промелькнуть в голове to flash through one's mind

Промелькнули две недели. Two weeks flew by.

промышленность (f.) industry

пронзительно (adv.) shrilly, stridently

пронзительный shrill, sharp, piercing

пропадать (пропасть) to be lost, be wasted

Весь день пропал у меня. The whole day has been wasted.

Где вы пропадали? Where on earth have you been?

Я пропал! I am lost!

пропасть—see пропадать

пропорционально (adv.) in proportion

обратно пропорционально inversely

пропорция proportion, ratio

пропускать (пропустить) to let go, let pass, miss, leave out

не пропускать воду to be waterproof

Пропускайте подробности. Omit the details.

пропустить лекцию to cut a lecture

пропустить строчку to skip a line

пропустить—see пропускать

пророк prophet

просвещение enlightenment

•просить (попросить) to ask, beg, request

просматривать (просмотреть) to look over, run through

просмотреть—see просматривать

проснуться—see просыпаться

•простить—see прощать

просто simply, it is simple

Ему очень просто это сделать. It costs him nothing (It is very simple for him) to do it.

Он просто ничего не знает. He simply doesn't know anything.

простодушие openheartedness, artlessness

простодушный openhearted, unsophisticated

● простой simple, common, plain
  простое любопы́тство mere curiosity
  просты́е ·лю́ди unpretentious people
  просты́е мане́ры unaffected manners
простота́ simplicity
просту́да cold, chill
простуди́ться (pf.) to catch cold
просыпа́ться (просну́ться) to wake up
● про́сьба request
  У меня́ к вам про́сьба. I have a favor to ask of you.
● про́тив against, opposite, opposed to (with gen.)
  друг про́тив дру́га face to face
  Он ничего́ не име́ет про́тив э́того. He has nothing against it. He doesn't mind.
  про́тив его́ ожида́ний contrary to his expectations
  про́тив тече́ния against the current
  спо́рить про́тив чего́-либо to argue against something
проти́вный opposite, contrary, adverse, nasty, repulsive
  в проти́вном слу́чае otherwise
  проти́вная сторона́ opposite party
противополо́жность (f.) contrast, opposition
противоре́чие contradiction, opposition
противоре́чить (imp.) to contradict
профе́ссия profession, occupation
профе́ссор professor
прохла́да coolness
прохлади́ться—see прохлажда́ться
прохла́дно (adv.) cool, chilly, it is cool
прохла́дный fresh, cool
прохлажда́ться (прохлади́ться) to refresh oneself
● проходи́ть (пройти́) to pass, go by, pass through
  Доро́га прохо́дит че́рез лес. The road lies through a wood.
  Его́ боле́знь прошла́. His illness has passed.
  Не прошло́ ещё и го́да. A year has not yet passed.
  пройти́ курс to study a course
  пройти́ ми́мо to go past
проходно́й connecting
процеду́ра procedure
проце́нт percentage, rate
проце́сс process
про́чий other
  все про́чие the others
  и про́чее (и проч.) et cetera

ме́жду про́чим by the way
прочесть—see чита́ть
прочита́ть—see чита́ть
● прочь away, off
  Прочь отсю́да! Get out of here!
  Ру́ки прочь! Hands off!
проше́дший past
  проше́дшее вре́мя past tense
про́шлое the past
  в недалёком про́шлом not long ago
про́шлый last, past
  в про́шлом году́ last year
  Де́ло про́шлое. Let bygones be bygones.
проща́й, проща́йте good-by, farewell
проща́льный parting
● проща́ть (прости́ть) to forgive, pardon
  Прости́те! Forgive me!
проща́ться (попроща́ться) to say good-by, take leave
про́ще simpler, plainer
проще́ние forgiveness, pardon
проэкзаменова́ть—see экзаменова́ть
прояви́ть—see проявля́ть
проявле́ние manifestation, development
проявля́ть (прояви́ть) to display, reveal, develop
  проявля́ть плёнку to develop film
  проявля́ть ра́дость to show joy
  проявля́ть себя́ to show one's worth
  проявля́ть си́лу to display strength
проясне́ть (perf.) to clear up, brighten up
  Не́бо проясне́ло. The sky cleared up.
пруд pond
пры́гать (пры́гнуть) to jump, spring, leap
пры́гнуть—see пры́гать
прыжо́к jump, spring
● пря́мо straight, exactly
  держа́ться пря́мо to hold oneself erect
  Он пря́мо геро́й. He is a real hero.
  попада́ть пря́мо в цель to hit the mark
  пря́мо к де́лу straight to the point
  сказа́ть пря́мо to say frankly
прямоду́шный straightforward
прямо́й straight, upright, sincere
прямоуго́льник rectangle
прямоуго́льный rectangular, right-angled
пря́ник gingerbread
пря́ность (f.) spice
пря́ный spicy
пря́тать-ся (спря́тать-ся) to hide, conceal (oneself)

психиа́тр psychiatrist
психо́з psychosis
психо́лог psychologist
психоло́гия psychology
● пти́ца bird, fowl
пу́блика public, audience
публикова́ть (опубликова́ть) to publish
публи́чно (adv.) publicly, openly
пуга́ть (испуга́ть) to frighten, intimidate
пуга́ться (испуга́ться) to be frightened, to take fright
пу́говица button
пу́дра powder
пу́дреница powder case, compact
пу́дриться (напу́дриться) to powder one's face
пузы́рь (m.) bubble, blister, bladder
пульс pulse
пункт point, station
  медици́нский пункт dispensary
  нача́льный пункт starting point
  по пу́нктам paragraph after paragraph
пунктуа́льно (adv.) punctually
пурга́ blizzard
● пуска́ть (пусти́ть) to allow, permit, set free, put in action
  Не пуска́йте его́ сюда́. Don't allow him to enter.
  пуска́ть во́ду to turn on the water
  пуска́ть маши́ну to start an engine
  пуска́ть слух to spread a rumor
пусти́ть—see пуска́ть
пусто́й empty, hollow
  пуста́я болтовня́ idle talk
  пусты́е мечты́ castles in air
пустота́ emptiness, void
пусты́ня desert, wilderness
● пусть let (him, her, them)
  Пусть он идёт. Let him go.
пу́таный confused, tangled
пу́тать (imp.) to tangle, confuse, mix-up
путеше́ственник traveler
путеше́ствовать (imp.) to travel
пу́тник traveler
● путь (m.) trip, road, path
  Друго́го пути́ нет. There is no other way.
  дыха́тельные пути́ respiratory tract
  по пути́ on the way
  стоя́ть на чьём-либо пути́ to stand in someone's way
пу́хленький plump, chubby
пу́хнуть (imp.) to swell
пчела́ bee
пыл ardor, passion
пылесо́с vacuum cleaner

пы́лкий ardent, passionate
   пы́лкая речь fervent speech
пыль (f.) dust
пыта́ться (попыта́ться) to attempt,
   try, endeavor
пы́шность (f.) splendor,
   magnificence
пье́са play
   дава́ть пье́су to give a play
   ста́вить пье́су to stage a play
пья́ница drunkard
пья́ный drunk, tipsy
пятна́дцать fifteen
пя́тка heel
пятна́дцать fifteen
пятна́дцатый fifteenth
●пя́тница Friday
   в пя́тницу on Friday
пятно́ spot, stain, blotch
●пять five
пятьдеся́т fifty
пятьсо́т five hundred
пя́тый fifth

Р

раб slave
●рабо́та work, working
   ажу́рная рабо́та openwork,
     tracery
   дома́шняя рабо́та homework
   лепна́я рабо́та stucco work
   Она́ за рабо́той. She is at work.
   нау́чная рабо́та scientific work
●рабо́тать to work
   рабо́тать над кни́гой to work at
     a book
   рабо́тать по на́йму to work for
     hire
   Телефо́н не рабо́тает. The
     telephone is out of order.
●рабо́чий workingman
ра́бство slavery
●ра́венство equality
●равно́ (adv.) alike, in like manner
   Всё равно́. It makes no
     difference. It is all the same.
   Он всё равно́ придёт. He will
     come anyway.
   Он поступа́ет равно́ со все́ми. He
     treats everyone alike.
равнобе́дренный треуго́льник
   isosceles triangle
равноду́шие indifference
равноду́шный indifferent
равноме́рно (adv.) uniformly,
   evenly
равноси́льный equivalent
ра́вный equal
   на ра́вных усло́виях on equal
     conditions
   относи́ться к кому́-либо как к
     ра́вному to treat someone as
     one's equal

ра́вное коли́чество equal quantity
равня́ть (сравня́ть) to equalize,
   compare
●рад, ра́да, ра́до, ра́ды glad
●ра́ди for the sake of (prep. with
   gen.)
радика́льный drastic
ра́дио radio, wireless
ра́доваться (обра́доваться) to be
   glad, rejoice
ра́достный glad, joyous
ра́дость (f.) gladness, joy
ра́душно cordially, invitingly
●раз time (occasion)
   ещё раз once again
   как раз just exactly
   ни раз many a time
   ни ра́зу not once
   раз в год once a year
разбива́ть (разби́ть) to smash,
   break, divide
разби́ть—see разбива́ть
разбира́ть (разобра́ть) to take
   apart, sort out, discuss
   Он не мо́жет разобра́ть её по́черк.
     He cannot make out her hand-
     writing.
   разбира́ть пробле́му to discuss the
     problem
разбо́йник robber, bandit
разбо́р analysis, critique
разбуди́ть—see буди́ть
разбо́рчивый fastidious
●ра́зве can it be that, really
   (usually used in amazement)
развива́ть (разви́ть) to develop,
   untwist
разви́тие development
развито́й developed
разви́ть—see развива́ть
развлека́ть (развле́чь) to entertain,
   divert
развлече́ние entertainment,
   amusement
развле́чь—see развлека́ть
развод divorce
разводи́ть (imp.) to breed or
   cultivate
●разгова́ривать (imp.) to converse,
   speak with
разгово́р conversation, talk
   И разгово́ра не́ было об э́том.
     There was no question of that.
   перемени́ть разгово́р to change
     the subject
разгово́рчивый talkative
раздава́ть (разда́ть) to distribute,
   give out
разда́ть—see раздава́ть
раздева́ть-ся (разде́ть-ся) to
   undress (oneself), strip
разделе́ние division
раздели́ть (ся)—see дели́ть (ся)

разде́льно (adv.) separately
разделя́ть-ся (раздели́ть-ся) to
   divide, separate
раздели́ть (ся)—see разделя́ть (ся)
разде́ть (ся)—see раздева́ть (ся)
раздража́ть (раздражи́ть) to irritate,
   annoy, exasperate
раздраже́ние irritation
раздражённый angry, irritated
раздражи́ть—see раздража́ть
разду́мье meditation, thoughtful
   mood
различа́ть (различи́ть) to differ,
   distinguish
различа́ться (imp.) to differ
   Различа́ется длино́й. It differs in
     length.
разли́чие distinction
различи́ть—see различа́ть
разли́чный different
разложе́ние expansion,
   decomposition
разложи́ться—see раскла́дываться
разме́р size, dimension
размышле́ние reflection, meditation
●ра́зница difference
разногла́сие difference, discordance
   (of opinion)
разнообра́зие variety, diversity
разнообра́зный various, diverse
ра́зность (f.) difference
ра́зный different, various
разобра́ть—see разбира́ть
разойти́сь—see расходи́ться
разочарова́ние disappointment
разочаро́ванный disappointed
разочарова́ться (perf.) to be
   disappointed in
разреша́ть (разреши́ть) to allow,
   permit, authorize, solve
разреше́ние permission, solution
разреши́ть—see разреша́ть
разруша́ть (разру́шить) to destroy,
   demolish
разруше́ние destruction, demolition
разру́шить—see разруша́ть
разры́в break, rupture
   Ме́жду ни́ми произошёл разры́в.
     They have come to a breaking
     point.
ра́зум reason, intelligence
●разуме́ется of course
   Само́ собо́й разуме́ется. It goes
     without saying.
рай paradise
райо́н region, district
ра́ма frame
ра́на wound
ра́неный wounded
ра́нний early
   ра́нним у́тром early in the morning
   с ра́ннего де́тства from early
     childhood

•ра́но (adv.) early, it is early

ра́ньше earlier, formerly
  как мо́жно ра́ньше as early as possible
  Ра́ньше здесь помеща́лась шко́ла. There was a school here formerly.

раскла́дываться (разложи́ться) to unpack

раскрыва́ть (раскры́ть) to open, reveal, disclose

раскры́ть—see раскрыва́ть

расписа́ние timetable, schedule

распи́ска receipt

расплати́ться—see распла́чиваться

распла́чиваться (расплати́ться) to pay off, get even with

распра́вить—see расправля́ть

расправля́ть (распра́вить) to straighten, smooth out

распрода́жа sale

распростране́ние spreading, diffusion

распространи́ть—see распространя́ть

распространя́ть (распространи́ть) to spread, disseminate

рассве́т dawn, daybreak

рассерди́ться (perf.) to become angry

рассе́янно (adv.) absently, absent-mindedly

рассе́янность (f.) absent-mindedness, distraction

рассе́янный scattered, diffused, absent-minded

расска́з story, tale

рассказа́ть—see расска́зывать

•расска́зывать (рассказа́ть) to tell, narrate, relate

рассма́тривать (рассмотре́ть) to consider, examine, look over

рассмотре́ть—see рассма́тривать

расстёгивать (расстегну́ть) to unfasten, unbutton

расстегну́ть—see расстёгивать

расстоя́ние distance, space
  держа́ться на почти́тельном рас-стоя́нии to keep aloof
  на не́котором расстоя́нии at some distance

рассу́дочный rational

рассчи́танный deliberate, calculated, designed

рассчи́тывать to calculate,
  не рассчита́ть свои́х сил to over-rate one's strength

растя́ять—see та́ять

раство́р solution

растёрянный confused, embarrassed, perplexed

•расти́ (imp.) to grow, grow up

растере́ть—see растира́ть

растира́ть (растере́ть) to grind

растя́гивать (растяну́ть) to stretch, strain, sprain

растя́гивать удово́льствие to prolong a pleasure

растяну́ть себе́ му́скул to strain a muscle

растя́нутый stretched, long-drawn-out

растяну́ть—see растя́гивать

•расхо́д expense, expenditure

расходи́ться (разойти́сь) to separate, disperse
  Мне́ния расхо́дятся. Opinions vary.
  На́ши пути́ разошли́сь. Our ways have parted.
  Он разошёлся со свое́й жено́й. He separated from his wife.

расцвести́—see расцвета́ть

расцвета́ть (расцвести́) to blossom, bloom, flourish

•расчёт calculation, estimate
  по его́ расчёту according to his calculations
  принима́ть в расчёт to take into consideration

расчётливо (adv.) prudently, economically

расчётливость (f.) economy, thrift

расши́рить—see расширя́ть

расширя́ть (расши́рить) to enlarge, widen, expand

расши́тый embroidered

•рвать (imp.) to tear, rend, pull out
  рвать зу́бы to extract teeth
  рвать на себе́ во́лосы to tear out one's hair
  рвать отноше́ния to break off relations
  рвать цветы́ to pick flowers

реаге́нт reagent

реа́кция reaction

реалисти́ческий realistic

•ребёнок baby, infant

ребро́ rib

•ребя́та children, boys

ревни́вый jealous

ревнова́ть (imp.) to be jealous

революцио́нный revolutionary

регистри́роваться (imp.) to register

регуля́рный regular

редакти́ровать (imp.) to edit

реда́ктор editor

ре́дкий rare, uncommon, sparse

•ре́дко (adv.) seldom, rarely

ре́дкость (f.) rarity, curiosity

режиссёр producer, director

•ре́зать (заре́зать) to cut, slice

•рези́на rubber, elastic

рези́нка eraser

ре́зкий sharp, harsh
  ре́зкая кри́тика severe criticism
  ре́зкие слова́ sharp words

ре́зкий ве́тер cutting wind

ре́зкое измене́ние пого́ды sharp change in the weather

ре́зко (adv.) sharply, abruptly

результа́т result, outcome

•река́ river, stream

рекла́ма advertisement, publicity

реклами́ровать (imp.) to advertise, publicize, boost

рекомендова́ть (imp.) to advise, recommend
  Тако́й спо́соб не рекоменду́ется. This method is not recommended.

религио́зный religious

рели́гия religion

ремесло́ trade, handicraft, profession

ремо́нт remodeling, repairs

репертуа́р repertoire

репута́ция reputation
  по́льзоваться хоро́шей репута́цией to have a good reputation

рестора́н restaurant

рето́рта retort (chemical)

рефо́рма reform

реце́нзия review, theater notice

реце́пт recipe, prescription

ре́чка river

речно́й river (adj.)

речь (f.) speech, oration
  дар ре́чи gift of speech
  засто́льная речь dinner speech
  О чём идёт речь? What are you talking about?
  ча́сти ре́чи parts of speech

•реша́ть (реши́ть) to decide, make up one's mind, settle
  Он реши́л уе́хать. He decided to go.
  реша́ть зада́чу to solve a problem
  Э́то реша́ет вопро́с. That settles the question.

реше́ние decision

реши́тельно (adv.) resolutely, decidedly, positively

реши́тельный decisive, resolute, firm

реши́ть—see реша́ть

рис rice

риск risk

рискну́ть—see рискова́ть

рискова́ть (рискну́ть) to risk, venture, take a chance

рисова́ть (нарисова́ть) to draw, paint

рису́нок drawing, picture

ритм rhythm

ри́фма rhyme

ро́бкий shy, timid

•ро́вно (adv.) equally, exactly

ро́вный flat, even, plane
  ро́вный счёт balanced account
  ро́вный хара́ктер even-tempered

•род family, kin, origin, sort, gender

вся́кого ро́да of all kinds

из ро́да в род from generation to generation

му́жеского ро́да masculine gender

•ро́дина native country

•роди́тели (pl.) parents, father and mother

роди́ть (imp. and perf.) to give birth to

роди́ться (imp. and perf.) to be born

•родно́й native, own

родно́й брат brother by birth

родно́й язы́к native tongue

ро́дственник relative, kinsman

рожде́ние birth

день рожде́ния birthday

рождество́ Christmas

ро́за rose

ро́зовый pink

роль (f.) role, part

рома́н novel, romance

рома́нс song (art song)

романти́ческий romantic

роня́ть (урони́ть) to drop, let fall, shed

роса́ dew

ро́скошь (f.) luxury, splendor

рост growth, development, height

ро́стбиф roast beef

•рот mouth

роя́ль (m.) grand piano

игра́ть на роя́ле to play the piano

•руба́шка shirt

рубе́ж boundary, borderline

руби́ть (imp.) chop, hack, slash

ру́бленый minced, chopped

рубль (m.) ruble

руга́ть (imp.) to scold, abuse

руга́ться (imp.) to swear, call names

Они́ постоя́нно руга́ются. They are always abusing each other. They are always quarreling with each other.

ружьё gun

•рука́ hand, arm

брать себя́ в ру́ки to pull oneself together

быть в хоро́ших рука́х to be in good hands

держа́ть на рука́х to hold in one's arms

из рук в ру́ки from hand to hand

пода́ть ру́ку по́мощи to lend a helping hand

под руко́й near at hand, handy

предлага́ть ру́ку кому́-либо to offer someone one's hand in marriage

Ру́ки прочь! Hands off!

умы́ть ру́ки to wash one's hands of it

У него́ ру́ки че́шутся. His fingers itch (plus infinitive).

Э́то не его́ рука́. That is not his writing.

рука́в sleeve

руководи́тель (m.) leader

руководи́ть (imp.) to lead, guide

руково́дство guidance, guiding principle

под руково́дством under the leadership

ру́копись (f.) manuscript

•ру́сский, ру́сская Russian (m., f.) (n. and adj.)

руча́тельство guarantee

руче́й brook, stream

•ру́чка handle, arm, penholder

автомати́ческая ру́чка fountain pen

ручно́й hand (adj.), tame

•ры́ба fish

лови́ть ры́бу в му́тной воде́ to fish in troubled waters

ни ры́ба ни мя́со neither fish nor fowl

рыда́ние sobbing

рыда́ть (imp.) to sob

ры́жий red-haired

ры́нок market

ры́сью (adv.) at a trot

ры́царь (m.) knight

рю́мка wineglass

ряд row, line

•ря́дом (adv.) side by side, beside

сиде́ть ря́дом с ке́м-либо to sit side by side with someone

Э́то совсе́м ря́дом. It is close by.

С

•с from, off, since (with gen.) with, together with, and (with inst.)

Брат с сестро́й ушли́. Brother and sister went away.

Он её не ви́дел с про́шлого го́да. He hasn't seen her since last year.

Он пришёл с детьми́. He came with the children.

прие́хать с рабо́ты to come from work

с доса́ды out of vexation

с пе́рвого взгля́да at first sight

с удово́льствием with pleasure

упа́сть с кры́ши to fall off the roof

Что с тобо́й? What's the matter with you?

•сад garden

де́тский сад kindergarten

•сади́ться (сесть) to sit down, take a seat

Он сел на по́езд. He took the train.

Он сел на стул. He sat down on a chair.

сади́ться в лу́жу to get into a fix

са́жа soot

сала́т lettuce, salad

сала́тник salad bowl

са́ло fat, lard

салфе́тка napkin

са́льный greasy

•сам, сама́, само́, са́ми self (m., f., n., pl.)

Он сам хоте́л э́то сде́лать. He wanted to do it himself.

Э́то говори́т само́ за себя́. It speaks for itself.

Я сам себе́ хозя́ин. I am my own master.

самова́р samovar

самоде́льный homemade

самоде́ятельность (f.) spontaneous activity, amateur stage

самодово́льный self-satisfied

самодово́льство self-satisfaction, complacency

самозва́нец imposter

самолёт airplane

самолюби́вый proud, touchy

самолю́бие self-respect, pride

ло́жное самолю́бие false pride

самооблада́ние self-control, composure

самостоя́тельно (adv.) independently

самостоя́тельный independent

самоуби́йство suicide

самоуве́ренно (adv.) with self-confidence

самоуве́ренность (f.) self-confidence, self-assurance

самоуправле́ние self-government

•са́мый the very, the same

в са́мом де́ле! indeed!, really!

в са́мом нача́ле at the very beginning

в то же са́мое вре́мя, когда́ just when

до са́мого до́ма all the way home

на са́мом де́ле actually

та же са́мая кни́га the same book in superlatives:

са́мая хоро́шая кни́га the best book

са́мый тру́дный most difficult

са́ни (only pl.) sleigh

сапо́г high boot

сара́й shed, barn

•са́хар sugar

са́харница sugarbowl

сближа́ться (сбли́зиться) to draw together, approach, become good friends

сбли́зиться—see сближа́ться

сбо́ку (adv.) from one side, on one side

сборник collection
свадьба wedding
сведение information
свежий fresh
  свежая рыба fresh fish
  свежий воздух fresh air
  свежо в памяти fresh in one's mind
сверкать (imp.) to sparkle, twinkle, glitter, glare
сверкнуть (pf.) to flash
  Сверкнула молния. Lightning flashed.
сверх over, besides, beyond (with gen.)
  сверх ожидания beyond expectation
  Сверх платья она надела пальто. She put on a coat over her dress.
  сверх программы in addition to the program
•сверху (adv.) from above, on top
  вид сверху view from above
  пятая строка сверху fifth line from the top
  сверху донизу from top to bottom
•свет light
  бросать свет на что-либо to throw light on something
  дневной свет daylight
  представлять что-либо в выгодном свете to show something to best advantage
  при свете луны by moonlight
•свет world, society
  весь свет the whole world
  выпускать в свет to publish
  высший свет society
  ни за что на свете not for the world
  тот свет the next world
светить (ся) (imp.) to shine
  Его глаза светились от радости. His eyes shone with joy.
  Луна светит. The moon is shining.
светло (adv.) it is light, brightly
  На дворе светло. It is daylight.
•светлый light
  светлая комната light room
  светлый ум bright spirit
  светлое платье light-colored dress
светский secular, worldly
  светская женщина woman of the world
  светское общество society
свеча candle
•свидание meeting, appointment
  до свидания good-by
  до скорого свидания see you soon
свидетель (m.) witness
свидетельство evidence, certificate, license
свинина pork

свинья pig, swine
свист whistle
свистать (свистеть) to whistle, pipe
свитер sweater
свобода freedom, liberty
  выпускать на свободу to set free
  предоставлять кому-либо полную свободу действий to give someone a free hand
  свобода печати freedom of the press
свободно (adv.) freely, fluently, with ease
  говорить свободно to speak fluently
свободный free
  свободное время free time
  свободные деньги spare cash
своевременно (adv.) in good time, opportunely
•свой, своя, своё, свои one's own (m., f., n., pl.)
  Всё придёт в своё время. Everything comes in its time.
  Он признаёт свои недостатки. He acknowledges his faults.
  Он там свой человек. He is quite at home there.
свойство property, characteristics
связанный combined, constrained
связать—see связывать
связывать (связать) to bind, tie together, connect
  связывать обещанием to bind by a promise
  Этот вопрос тесно связан с другими. This problem is bound up with others.
связь (f.) tie, bond, connection, relation
  в этой связи in this connection
  причинная связь causal relationship
  с хорошими связями with good ties
священник priest
сгибаться (согнуться) to bend down, stoop
сгорать (сгореть) to burn (down)
  Дом сгорел. The house burned down.
  сгорать от стыда to burn with shame
сгореть—see сгорать
•сдача surrender, renting, deal (in cards)
  Ваша сдача. It's your deal.
  дать сдачу to give change
  сдача в аренду to lease
сделано finished
сделать (ся)—see делать (ся)

сдержанно (adv.) with restraint, with discretion
сдержанность (f.) restraint, reserve
сдержать (ся)—see сдерживать (ся)
сдерживать (сдержать) to hold in, restrain, contain
  сдержать своё слово to keep one's word
сдерживаться (сдержаться) to control oneself
сдружиться (pf.) to become friends with
•себя self, oneself (reflexive pronoun)
север north
северный northern
•сегодня today
  сегодня вечером this evening
  сегодня утром this morning
сегодняшний today's
седина gray hair
  Седина в бороду, а бес в ребро. The later love comes, the more it burns. (Gray hair in the beard and a devil in the ribs.)
седой gray (only of hair)
  Он седой. He has gray hair.
седьмой seventh
•сейчас now, presently, right away
  Где он сейчас живёт? Where does he live now?
  сейчас же immediately, at once
секрет secret
  по секрету secretly, in confidence
  секрет успеха secret of success
секретарша secretary
секретно secretly, covertly
секунда second
селёдка herring
село village
  ни к селу ни к городу neither here nor there
сельдерей celery
сельский rural
  сельская жизнь country life
сельскохозяйственный agricultural
семидесятый seventieth
семейный domestic, family
  семейные связи family ties
  семейный человек family man
семестр term, semester
семнадцать seventeen
семнадцатый seventeenth
семь seven
семьдесят seventy
семьсот seven hundred
•семья family
сено hay
сентиментальный sentimental
сентябрь (m.) September

сердечный cordial, hearty, of the heart
сердечная болезнь heart disease
сердечный привет hearty greetings
сердитый angry
сердиться (imp.) to get angry, be cross
• сердце heart
доброе сердце kind heart
от всего сердца from the bottom of one's heart
принимать что-либо к сердцу to take something to heart
С глаз долой, из сердца вон. Out of sight, out of mind.
У него отлегло от сердца. He felt relieved.
У него сердца нет. He has no heart.
У него сердце упало. His heart sank.
серебро silver
серебряный silver (adj.)
серебряная посуда silverplate
• середина middle
в самой середине in the very middle
золотая середина golden mean
серия series
серный sulphuric
серная кислота sulphuric acid
серый gray
серая жизнь dull life
серьга earring
серьёзно (adv.) seriously, earnestly
серьёзный serious, earnest
• сестра sister
двоюродная сестра cousin
медицинская сестра (медсестра) nurse
сесть—see садиться
сжечь—see жечь
сжимать (сжать) to squeeze, compress
сжимать губы to compress one's lips
сжимать кулаки to clench one's fists
сжать—see сжимать
сзади (adv.) from behind
вид сзади view from behind
пятый вагон сзади fifth car from the end
толкать сзади to push from behind
сигара cigar
сигнал signal
• сидеть (imp.) to sit, be perched, fit
Платье хорошо сидит. The dress fits well.
сидеть в тюрьме to be imprisoned
сидеть дома to stay at home

сидеть за столом to sit at the table
• сила strength, force
брать силой to take by force
быть ещё в силах to be still vigorous enough
входить в силу to come into force
изо всех сил with all one's strength
лошадиная сила horsepower
морские силы naval force
сила воли will power
сила привычки force of habit
сила тяжести gravity
Это сверх сил. This is beyond one's powers.
сильно (adv.) strongly, very, violently, greatly
сильно нуждаться to be in extreme need
сильно пить to drink heavily
Сильно сказано! That's going too far!
сильно чувствовать to feel keenly
• сильный strong, powerful, keen, intense, heavy
силён в математике good at mathematics
сильная страсть violent passion
сильный запах strong smell
символ symbol
симпатический sympathetic
симпатичный likable
симфония symphony
синий dark blue
сирота orphan
система system
систематичный systematic
сито strainer, sieve
ситуация situation
• сказать—see говорить to say, tell
Легче сказать, чем сделать. Easier said than done.
правду сказать to tell the truth
Сказано—сделано. No sooner said than done.
Трудно сказать. It's hard to say.
сказка fairy tale, story
скакать (поскакать) to skip, jump, hop
скамья bench
посадить на скамью подсудимых to put into the dock
со школьной скамьи since school days
скандал scandal
Какой скандал! What a disgrace!
скатерть (f.) tablecloth
скверно (adv.) badly
Пальто скверно сидит на нём. The coat fits him badly.
пахнуть скверно to smell bad

скверно чувствовать себя to feel badly
скверный bad, nasty
сквозить (imp.) to blow through, go through
Здесь сквозит. There is a draft here.
Свет сквозит через занавеску. Light is shining through the blind.
• сквозь through (with acc.)
говорить сквозь зубы to speak through clenched teeth
Как сквозь землю провалился. He disappeared without leaving a trace (as though through the earth).
скептический skeptical
скидка rebate, reduction, discount
делать скидку to give a reduction
со скидкой with rebate, with discount
складка fold, pleat, crease, wrinkle
складной folding, collapsible, portable
склонность (f.) inclination, bent, disposition
сковорода frying pan
скользить (скользнуть) to slip, slide
скользкий slippery
говорить на скользкую тему to be on slippery ground
скользкая дорога slippery road
скользнуть—see скользить
• сколько how much, how many
не столько... сколько... not so much... as...
Сколько мы вам должны? How much do we owe you?
Сколько с меня? How much do I owe?
Сколько стоит? How much does it cost?
сколько угодно as much as you like
сконфуженный abashed, disconcerted, embarrassed
сконфузить (ся)—see конфузить (ся)
скончаться (pf.) to pass away, die
скопировать—see копировать
скорбный sorrowful, mournful
скорбь (f.) sorrow, grief
скорее rather, sooner, quicker
как можно скорее as soon as possible
Он скорее умрёт, чем сдастся. He would rather die than surrender.
• скоро (adv.) quickly, soon
Он скоро придёт. He will come soon.
скоропортящийся perishable

скóрость (f.) speed, rate
максимáльная скóрость top speed
скóрость движéния rate of
movement
скóрый fast, rapid
в скóром врéмени soon, before
long
До скóрого свидáния. See you
soon.
скóрая пóмощь first aid
скóрый пóезд fast train, express
скóрый шаг quick step
скот cattle
скреплять (скрепить) to fasten
together, strengthen
скрипáч violinist
скрипéть (поскрипéть) to squeak,
creak
скрипка violin
игрáть на скрипке to play the
violin
скрóмность (f.) modesty
лóжная скрóмность false modesty
скрóмный modest, frugal,
unpretentious
скрывáть (скрыть) to hide, conceal,
keep back
не скрывáть тогó, что to make no
secret of the fact that
Он засмеялся, чтобы скрыть своё
беспокóйство. He laughed to
cover his anxiety.
скрывáться (скрыться) to hide
oneself
скрытый secret, latent
скрыть (ся)—see скрывáть (ся)
скýка boredom, tedium
скýльптор sculptor
скýпо (adv.) stingily, sparingly
скупóй stingy, miserly
скýпость (f.) stinginess, miserliness
скучáть (imp.) to be bored, to miss
Я скучáла по тебé. I missed you.
скýчно (adv.) boring, dull
Мне скýчно. I am bored.
скýчный boring, tiresome
слабéть (ослабéть) to grow
weak, grow feeble, slack off
слáбо faintly, weakly
слáбость (f.) weakness, feebleness
слáбый weak, faint, feeble
слáбое оправдáние lame excuse
слáбые глазá weak eyes
слáбый учени́к poor pupil
слáва glory, fame
слáвный famous, renowned, nice
слáвный мáлый nice fellow
слáдкий sweet, honeyed
на слáдкое for dessert
спать слáдким сном to be fast
asleep
слáдостный sweet, delightful

слáдость (f.) sweetness, delight
слегкá (adv.) somewhat, slightly
Он слегкá устáл. He is somewhat
tired.
слегкá трóнуть to touch gently
след track, trace, sign, vestige
следить (imp.) to watch, follow
внимáтельно следить to watch
closely
следить глазáми за кéм-либо to
follow someone with one's eyes
следить за детьми́ to look after
children
следить за чьи́ми-либо мы́слями
to follow the thread of someone's
thoughts
слéдовательно consequently,
therefore, it follows that
слéдовать (послéдовать) to follow,
come next
во всём слéдовать отцý to take
after one's father in everything
как слéдует из скáзанного as
appears from the above
Лéто слéдует за веснóй. Summer
follows spring.
обращáться кудá слéдует to apply
to the proper quarter
слéдующий following, next
слéдующий день the next day
слезá tear
до слёз бóльно enough to make
anyone cry
слезáть (слезть) to get off, get
down
слезть—see слезáть
слéпо (adv.) blindly
слепóй blind
слепóе подражáние blind imitation
слепóй мéтод touch system
слепотá blindness
сли́ва plum
сли́вки cream
сли́шком (adv.) too, too much
словáрь (m.) dictionary,
vocabulary
слóво word
давáть слóво to give the floor,
promise
другими словáми in other words
одни́м слóвом in a word
Помяни́те моё слóво! Mark my
words!
сдержáть слóво to keep one's
word
слóво в слóво word for word
чéстное слóво word of honor
сложéние adding, addition, build
слóжно (adv.) in a complicated
manner, it is complicated
слóжный complicated, intricate

слой layer
сломáть (ся)—see ломáть (ся)
слон elephant
служáнка maid
служáщий employee
служба service, work
быть на воéнной службе to be in
the military service
искáть службу to look for work
служить (послужить) to serve, be
in use
служить во флóте to serve in the
navy
служить кому́-либо вéрой и прáвдой
to serve someone faithfully
служить примéром to serve as an
example
служить цéли to serve a purpose
Чем могу́ служить? What can I
do for you?
Это пальтó служит ему́ два гóда.
He has had this coat for two
years.
слух hearing, rumor
игрáть по слýху to play by ear
Не всякому слýху верь. Believe
only half of what you hear.
Ни слýху ни дýху. Nothing has
been heard.
óрган слýха organ of hearing
по слýхам it is rumored
пустить слух to set a rumor
going
слýчай (m.) event, chance, case
во всяком слýчае at any event
воспóльзоваться удóбным слýчаем
to seize an opportunity
на всякий слýчай in case
на слýчай in case of
несчáстный слýчай accident
ни в кóем слýчае on no account
по слýчаю чегó-либо on the
occasion of something
при всяком удóбном слýчае with
every opportunity
случáйно by chance, accidently
Вы случáйно не знáете егó? Do
you know him, by any chance?
не случáйно, что it is no mere
chance that
случáйный accidental, fortuitous
случáться (случиться) to happen, to
take place
Как это случи́лось? How did it
happen?
случиться—see случáться
слýшать (послýшать) to listen, pay
attention
слы́шать (услы́шать) to hear
слы́шно (adv.) audibly, one can
hear, it is said

Слышно как муха пролетит. You might have heard a pin drop. (One can hear how a fly flies.)

Что слышно? What's the news?

слюни saliva

У него слюни текут. His mouth is watering.

смело (adv.) boldly, bravely, daringly, fearlessly

говорить смело to speak boldly

я могу смело сказать I can safely say

смелость (f.) boldness, courage, daring

смелый bold, courageous, daring (adj.)

смерить—see мерить

смерть (f.) death

быть между жизнью и смертью to be between life and death

надоедать до смерти to pester to death

сметана sour cream

сметь (посметь) to dare

смех laughter

Ему не до смеху. He is in no mood for laughter.

Смех да и только. It's simply absurd.

смешанный mixed, compound

смешать—see смешивать

смешивать (смешать) to mix, mix together, blend

смешно (adv.) it is ridiculous, it makes one laugh, in a funny manner, comically

смешной funny, ridiculous

В этом нет ничего смешного. There is nothing to laugh at.

Как он смешон. How absurd he is.

•смеяться (imp.) to laugh

смеяться исподтишка to laugh up one's sleeve

смеяться над кем-либо to make fun of someone

Хорошо смеётся тот, кто смеётся последним. He who laughs last laughs best.

смирение humility, humbleness

смолкать (смолкнуть) to grow silent, fall silent

смолкнуть—see смолкать

смолоду since one's youth

смородина currant

•смотреть (посмотреть) to look, look at

Как вы на это смотрите? What do you think of it?

смотреть в оба to be on one's guard

смотреть за порядком to keep order

смотря по according to

смотри!, смотрите! look out!, take care!

смочь—see мочь

смуглый swarthy, dark (complexion)

смутно (adv.) vaguely, dimly, not clearly

смутный vague, dim

смутное время troubled times

смущение confusion, embarrassment

смущённый confused, embarrassed

смысл sense, meaning

в полном смысле этого слова in the full sense of the word

В этом нет смысла. There's no point in it.

здравый смысл common sense

Не имеет никакого смысла. It makes no sense at all.

прямой смысл literal meaning

смягчаться (смягчиться) to soften, relent, grow mild, ease off

снаружи from the outside

•сначала (adv.) from the beginning, at first

снег snow

•снизу from below

•снимать (снять) to take, take off, remove, take pictures

снимать квартиру to rent an apartment

снимать копию с чего-либо to make a copy of something

снимать шляпу to take off one's hat

снимок photograph, snapshot

снисходительный condescending, lenient

сниться (присниться) to dream

ему снилось, что he dreamed that

Ему это даже и не снилось. He had never even dreamed of it.

снова (adv.) anew, afresh, again

начинать снова to begin again

снова сесть to resume one's seat

сновидение dream

снять—see снимать

собака dog

•собирать (собрать) to gather, assemble, collect

собирать свои вещи to collect one's belongings

собрать всё своё мужество to pluck up one's courage

собрать мысли to collect one's thoughts

собираться (собраться) to gather together, assemble, make up one's mind

Он собирается ехать в Москву. He intends to go to Moscow.

собираться в путь to prepare for a journey

соблазнитель (m.) tempter, seducer

соблазнить (pf.) to entice, allure, tempt, seduce

собор cathedral

собрание meeting, gathering

собрать(ся)—see собирать(ся)

собственно (adv.) properly

собственно говоря as a matter of fact, strictly speaking

собственность (f.) property

личная собственность personal property

собственный own, personal

чувство собственного достоинства self-respect

событие event

текущие события current events

Это было большим событием. It was a great event.

совершать (совершить) to accomplish, perform

совершать подвиг to accomplish a feat, or deed

совершать сделку to strike a bargain

•совершенно (adv.) absolutely, quite, totally, utterly

совершенно верно quite so, of course

совершенно незнакомый человек total stranger

совершённый absolute, perfect

совершенство perfection

совершить—see совершать

совесть (f.) conscience

по совести говоря honestly speaking

•совет council, advice, counsel

советовать (посоветовать) to advise, counsel

советский Soviet

Советский Союз Soviet Union,

совместно (adv.) commonly, jointly

совместный joint, combined

совместное обучение coeducation

совпадать (совпасть) coincide, concur

совпадение coincidence

совпасть—see совпадать

современный contemporary, modern

•совсем (adv.) quite, entirely, totally

совсем не not in the least

совсем не то nothing of the kind

согласие consent, assent

согласиться—see соглашаться

согласно (adv.) in accord, according, in harmony

согласный agreeable

быть согласным to agree with something

●соглашáться (согласи́ться) to
consent, agree, concur
соглашéние agreement,
understanding
согнýться—see сгибáться
согревáть (согрéть) to warm, heat
согрéть—see согревáть
содержáние maintenance, upkeep,
contents
быть на содержáнии у когó-либо
to be supported by someone
содержáние кислорóда в вóздухе
content of oxygen in the air
содержáние кни́ги subject matter
of a book
содержáнка kept woman
содержáть (imp.) to support,
maintain, contain
соединéние joining, combination
соединённый united
Соединённые Штáты United States
соедини́ть (ся)—see соединя́ть (ся)
соедини́ть-ся (соедини́ть-ся) to join,
unite, connect, combine
●сожалéние regret, pity
к сожалéнию unfortunately
сожи́тель (m.) roommate
создавáть (создáть) to create, found,
originate
создавáть иллю́зию to create an
illusion
создавáть мóщную промы́шленность
to create a powerful industry
создáть—see создавáть
сознáтельно (adv.) consciously,
deliberately, conscientiously
сойти́—see сходи́ть
сок juice, sap
сократи́ть—see сокращáть
сокращáть (сократи́ть) to shorten,
curtail, abbreviate
Придётся сократи́ться. We'll have
to tighten the purse-strings.
сокращéние shortening, abbreviation
сокращённый brief, abbreviated
солдáт soldier
солёный salty, salted
соли́дность (f.) solidity, reliability
соли́дный solid, strong, reliable
соли́дный журнáл reputable
magazine
соли́дный человéк reliable man
сóлнечный sunny, solar
●сóлнце (n.) sun
солони́на corned beef
●соль (f.) salt
англи́йская соль Epsom salts
соль земли́ salt of the earth
●сомневáться (imp.) to doubt, have
doubts
Сомневáюсь в егó и́скренности.
I doubt his sincerity.
я не сомневáюсь I don't doubt

сомнéние doubt
сомни́тельно (adv.) doubtfully, it
is doubtful
●сон dream, sleep
ви́деть сон to have a dream
во снé in one's sleep
крéпкий сон sound sleep
сóнный sleepy, drowsy
сообщáть (сообщи́ть) to report,
communicate, inform
сообщéние report, information
сообщи́ть—see сообщáть
сопéрник rival
сопéрничать (imp.) to compete with
сопровождáть (imp.) to accompany,
escort
сопротивля́ться (imp.) to resist,
oppose
сопýтствовать (imp.) to travel with
сорвáть (ся)—see срывáть (ся)
сóрок forty
сороковóй fortieth
сорт sort, kind
●сосéд, сосéдка neighbor (m., f.)
сосéдний neighboring, adjacent
соси́ска sausage (hot dog)
соскáкивать (соскочи́ть) to jump
down, jump off
соскочи́ть—see соскáкивать
соснá pine tree
сосредотóчивать (сосредотóчить) to
concentrate, focus
состáв composition, structure
состáвить (ся)—see составля́ть (ся)
составля́ть (состáвить) to compose,
compile, formulate
состáвить спи́сок to make up a list
составля́ть план to formulate a
plan
составля́ться (состáвиться) to be
formed
состоя́ние state, condition, fortune
в хорóшем состоя́нии in good
condition
получи́ть состоя́ние to come into
a fortune
состоя́ние здорóвья state of
health
состоя́ть to consist in, of
Кварти́ра состои́т из трёх кóмнат.
The apartment consists of three
rooms.
рáзница состои́т в том, что . . . the
difference consists of . . .
сосýд vessel
сострадáние compassion
сóтый hundredth
сóус sauce, gravy
софá sofa
сóхнуть (imp.) to dry, get dry
сохранéние preservation,
conservation

сохрани́ть—see сохраня́ть
●сохраня́ть (сохрани́ть) to keep,
preserve, retain
сохрани́ть на пáмять to keep as a
souvenir
сохрани́ть хладнокрóвие to keep
one's head
социали́зм socialism
●сочинéние composition, work
пóлное собрáние сочинéний
Пýшкина complete works of
Pushkin
сочини́ть—see сочиня́ть
сочиня́ть (сочини́ть) to write,
compose, make up
сóчный juicy, succulent
сóчное я́блоко juicy apple
сóчный стиль rich style
сочýвствие sympathy
сочýвствовать (imp.) to sympathize
(with), feel (for)
●сою́з union, alliance
спáльный sleeping
спáльный вагóн sleeping car
●спáльня bedroom
спáржа asparagus
●спасáть (спасти́) to save, rescue
спасти́ жизнь to save the life
спасти́ положéние to save the
situation
спасáться (спасти́сь) to save oneself,
escape
спасéние rescue, salvation
●спаси́бо thanks, thank you
большóе спаси́бо many thanks
спасти́ (сь)—see спасáть (ся)
●спать (imp.) to sleep
ложи́ться спать to go to bed
Он спит как уби́тый. He is sound
asleep. He sleeps like a log.
спектáкль (m.) play, performance
спéлый ripe
первá (adv.) at first, firstly
спéреди (adv.) from the front
спеть—see петь
специали́ст specialist, expert
специáльно (adv.) especially
●специáльный special
●спеши́ть (поспеши́ть) to hurry,
hasten
Егó часы́ спешáт на дéсять минýт.
His watch is ten minutes fast.
спéшно (adv.) in haste, hastily
спéшный urgent, pressing
в спéшном поря́дке quickly, rush
●спинá back
спи́сок list
спи́чка match
сплéтник, сплéтница gossip, talebearer (m., f.)
сплéтничать (imp.) to gossip, talk
scandal

сплошной continuous, entire
    сплошная масса solid mass
    сплошное удовольствие sheer joy
●сплошь (adv.) entirely, everywhere
    сплошь и рядом very often
    сплошь одни цветы flowers
       everywhere
спокойно (adv.) quietly
●спокойный quiet, peaceful, tranquil
    Будьте спокойны. Don't worry.
    спокойное море calm sea
    Спокойной ночи. Good night.
спор argument, debate
●спорить (поспорить) to argue,
    dispute
спорный questionable, debatable,
    moot, controversial
●спорт sport
спортивный sporting, athletic
способ way, method
    способ выражения manner of
       expressing oneself
    таким способом in this way
●способность (f.) ability, faculty
способный able, clever, gifted,
    capable
справедливость (f.) justice, fairness
справедливый just, fair
справочник reference book,
    information book, guidebook
●спрашивать (спросить) to ask a
    question, demand, inquire
спрос demand
    в большом спросе in great
       demand
    спрос и предложение demand and
       supply
спросить—see спрашивать
спрятать (ся)—see прятать (ся)
спускать (спустить) to let down,
    lower
    не спускать глаз not to take one's
       eyes off
    спускать флаг to lower the flag
спускаться (спуститься) to descend,
    go down
    спуститься по лестнице to go
       downstairs
спустить (ся)—see спускать (ся)
●спустя (adv.) after, later
    несколько дней спустя several,
       days later
спутник fellow-traveler, satellite,
    one who travels with
    Луна спутник Земли. The moon is
       the earth's satellite.
●сравнение comparison
    по сравнению in comparison
    степени сравнения degrees of
       comparison
сравнивать (сравнить) to compare
сравнительно (adv.) comparatively,
    in comparison

сравнительный comparative
сравнить—see сравнивать
●сразу (adv.) at once, right away
среда Wednesday
    в среду on Wednesday
●среди amongst, amidst (with gen.)
    среди комнаты in the middle of
       the room
    среди нас among us
средний middle, medium, average
    мужчина средних лет middle-aged
       man
    ниже среднего below average
    средние способности average
       ability
    средняя школа secondary school
средство means
    жить не по средствам to live
       beyond one's means
    местные средства local resources
    средства к существованию means
       of existence
    средства производства means of
       production
сровнять—see равнять
срывать (сорвать) to tear away,
    tear off
    сорвать маску с кого-либо to tear
       the mask from someone
срываться (сорваться) to break loose,
    break away
ссориться (поссориться) to quarrel
    (with), fall out (with)
●ставить (поставить) to set, place,
    put in a vertical position
    высоко ставить кого-либо to think
       highly of someone
    поставить пьесу to produce a play
    ставить всё на карту to stake all
    ставить кому-либо препятствия
       to put obstacles in one's way
    ставить проблему to raise a
       problem
    ставить условия to lay down
       conditions
    ставить часы to set the clock
стадион stadium
стадо herd, flock
●стакан drinking glass
сталкиваться (столкнуться) to
    collide, run into
    Автомобили столкнулись. The cars
       collided.
    Интересы их столкнулись. Their
       interests clashed.
    Мы вчера случайно столкнулись.
       We ran into each other yesterday.
стало быть so, thus, consequently, it
    follows that
сталь (f.) steel
стандарт standard

стандартный standard (adj.)
    стандартный дом prefabricated
       house
●становиться (стать) to become, grow
    Его не стало. He has passed away.
    Становится холодно. It is getting
       cold.
    стать учителем to become a
       teacher
станция station
старательно (adv.) diligently,
    assiduously
стараться (постараться) to endeavor,
    try
    стараться впустую to waste one's
       efforts
    стараться изо всех сил to do one's
       utmost
●старик old man
старина olden times
старинный ancient, antique
старомодный old-fashioned
старость (f.) old age
●старуха old woman
●старший older, senior
    старший врач head physician
    старший сын oldest son
●старый old
    Всё по-старому. Everything is the
       same (all as of old).
    старая дева old maid
стать (pf.) to begin, come to be
    Он стал читать. He began to
       read.
стать—see становиться
статься (pf.) to become, happen
    Что с ним сталось? What has
       become of him?
статья article
    передовая статья editorial
    Это особая статья. That's another
       matter.
●стекло glass
    оконное стекло window glass
стеклянный glass (adj.)
●стена wall
стенографистка stenographer (f.)
●степень (f.) degree, extent
    возводить во вторую степень to
       raise to the second power
    До какой степени? To what
       extent?
    до последней степени to the last
       degree
    степени сравнения degrees of
       comparison
    степень доктора doctorate, Ph.D.
степь (f.) steppe
стереть—see стирать
стеречь (imp.) to guard, watch over
стесняться to feel shy, be ashamed
    of

Он стесняется сказать вам. He is ashamed to tell you.

стиль (m.) style

  возвышенный стиль grand style

стимул incentive, stimulus

стипендия stipend, scholarship

стирать (стереть) to wipe, clean, erase

  стирать пыль to dust

стирать (выстирать) to wash, launder

стих verse

стихотворение poem

сто hundred

●**стоить** (imp.) to cost

  ничего не стоит to be worthless

  Сколько это стоит? How much does it cost?

  Стоит прочесть это. It is worth reading.

  Это стоило ему большого труда. This cost him much trouble.

●**стол** table

  личный стол personnel office

  накрывать на стол to set the table

  письменный стол desk

  стол и квартира room and board

столетие century

столица capital city

столкновение collision, clash

столкнуться—see **сталкиваться**

столовая dining room

столовый table (adj.)

  столовая ложка tablespoon

  столовое вино table wine

●**столько** (adv.) so much, so many

  столько времени so much time

  столько сколько as much as

стонать (imp.) to moan, groan

сторож watchman, guard

●**сторона** side

  брать чью-либо сторону to take someone's side

  иметь свои хорошие стороны to have one's good points

  откладывать в сторону to put aside

  родственник со стороны отца relative on one's father's side

  с другой стороны on the other hand

  с моей стороны for my part

  уклоняться в сторону to deviate

  шутки в сторону joking aside

●**стоять** to stand

  Перед ним стоит выбор. He is faced with a choice.

  Солнце стоит высоко на небе. The sun is high in the heavens.

  стоять на коленях to kneel

  стоять на якоре to be at anchor

  Часы стоят. The watch has stopped.

страдание suffering

страдать (пострадать) to suffer

страна country

страница page

●**странно** (adv.) strangely, in a strange way

странный strange, queer, odd, funny

страстно (adv.) passionately

страстный ardent, fervent, passionate

страсть (f.) passion

страх fear, fright

страховка insurance

●**страшно** (adv.) it is terrible, terribly, awfully

страшный terrible, frightful, fearful

стрелка pointer, hand (of a clock)

стричься (остричься) to have one's hair cut

строгий strict, severe

строго (adv.) strictly, severely

строить (построить) to build, construct

строй system, order, formation

стройный well-proportioned, well-composed

строка line

  читать между строк to read between the lines

студент, студентка student (m., f.)

студень aspic

студить (остудить) to cool off

студия studio, workshop

стук knock, tap, noise

стукать (стукнуть) to knock, rap, pound

стукнуть—see **стукать**

●**стул** chair

●**стучать** (imp.) to knock, rap

  Стучит в висках. The blood is pounding in my temples.

  стучать в дверь to knock at the door

стыд shame

стыдливо (adv.) shamefacedly, bashfully, shyly

●**стыдно** it is a shame, it is disgraceful

  Как вам не стыдно! You ought to be ashamed of yourself.

  Мне стыдно. I am ashamed.

суббота Saturday

  в субботу on Saturday

суд law court, justice, judgment

судить (imp.) to try, referee, judge

  насколько он может судить to the best of one's judgment

  судить по внешнему виду to judge by appearances

судьба fate, destiny, fortune

  искушать судьбу to tempt one's fate

судья judge

сумасшедший mad

  сумасшедшая скорость breakneck speed

  Это будет стоить сумасшедших денег. It will cost an enormous sum.

суматоха bustle, turmoil

сумбур confusion

●**суметь** (pf.) to know how, be able, succeed

  Он не сумеет этого сделать He will not be able to do it.

сумка handbag, pouch, pocketbook

сумма sum

сумрак twilight, dusk

сундук trunk, box, chest

сунуть (perf.) to poke, thrust, shove

  сунуть свой нос to pry

  сунуть что-либо в карман to slip something in one's pocket

суп soup

супруг, супруга spouse (m., f.)

сурово (adv.) severely, sternly

суровый severe, stern

сутки twenty-four hours, day

сухо (adv.) it is dry, dryly

●**сухой** dry, arid

  сухой климат dry climate

  сухой приём cold reception

сушить (высушить) to dry

существо being, creature

существование existence

существовать (imp.) to be, exist

  существуют люди, которые there are people who

  Это существует. It exists.

сфера sphere, realm

  сфера влияния sphere of influence

  Это вне его сферы. It is out of his line.

сфинкс sphinx

схватить—see **хватать**

●**сходить (сойти)** to go down, get off, alight

  Краска сошла со стены. The paint came off the wall.

  сходить с ума to go mad

сходный similar, suitable

сходство likeness, resemblance

сцена stage, scene

  устраивать сцену to make a scene

●**счастливый** happy, fortunate

  Счастливого пути! Have a good trip!

счастье luck, happiness

  к счастью fortunately

счесть—see **считать**

●**счёт** calculation, score, bill

  на счёт on account

  На этот счёт вы можете быть покойны. You may be easy on that score.

открыть счёт to open an account
по его счёту by his reckoning
принять что-либо на свой счёт to take something as referring to oneself
сводить старые счёты to pay off old scores
●считать (счесть) to count, consider
Он считает его честным человеком. He considers him an honest man.
считать по пальцам to count on one's fingers
считать себя to consider oneself (to be)
считаться (посчитаться) to consider, take into consideration, reckon
Он считается хорошим учителем. He is considered a good teacher.
считается, что it is considered that
Это не считается. It does not count.
сшить—see шить
съедобный edible
съезд congress, convention, conference
съесть—see есть
сыграть—see играть
сын son
сыр cheese
сыро (adv.) damply, it is damp
●сырой damp, raw, uncooked
сырая погода damp weather
сырое мясо raw meat
сырой материал raw material
сырость (f.) dampness
сытый satisfied, replete
сэкономить—see экономить
●сюда here, hither
Идите сюда. Come this way. Come here.
сюжет subject, topic, plot
сюрприз surprise, unexpected present
сюртук frock coat

Т

табак tobacco
таблица table, chart
таблица логарифмов table of logarithms
таинственный mysterious, secret
таить (imp.) to hide, conceal
нечего греха таить it must be confessed
таить злобу против кого-либо to bear malice, have a grudge against someone
таиться (imp.) to be hidden, be concealed, hide oneself

Не таись от меня. Don't conceal anything from me.
тайком (adv.) secretly, surreptitiously
●тайна mystery, secret, secrecy
выдавать тайну to betray a secret
держать что-либо в тайне to keep something secret
не тайна, что it is no secret that
под покровом тайны under the veil of secrecy
тайно (adv.) secretly, underhandedly
тайный secret, covert, clandestine
●так so, thus, in this way
Вот так. That's the right way.
если так, if that's the case
Здесь что-то не так. There is something wrong here.
именно так just so
и так далее (и т. д.) and so forth, etc.
Как бы не так. Nothing of the sort.
не так ли? isn't it so?
Она так же красива как её сестра. She is just as pretty as her sister.
Он говорил так, как будто она не знала. He spoke as though she did not know.
Сделайте так, чтобы она не знала. Do it so that she won't know.
так важно so important
Так вы его знаете! So you know him!
так давно so long ago
Так ему и надо. It serves him right.
так или иначе in any event
так как она уже уехала since she has already left
Так ли это? Is that really so?
так называемый so-called
так себе so-so, middling
Я так и сказал ему. I told him so in so many words.
●также also, in addition, either
Он также поедет в Москву. He will also go to Moscow.
Он также не поедет в Москву. He will not go to Moscow either.
●такой such, such a
в такой-то час at such and such an hour
Вы всё такой-же. You are just the same.
таким образом in this way
такой же как the same as
Что такое? What is the matter?
Что это такое? What is that?
такси (n., not declined) taxi

такт tact, bar (in music)
отсутствие такта tactlessness
человек с тактом a man of tact
тактично tactfully, with tact
талант talent, gift
талантливо (adv.) ably, finely
талантливость (f.) talent, gifted nature
талантливый gifted, talented
талия waist
●там there
танец dance
пойти на танцы to go to a dance
танцовать (imp.) to dance
●тарелка plate
таскать (тащить) to drag, pull, lag
тащить—see таскать
таять (растаять) to melt, thaw
Его силы тают. His strength is dwindling.
Звуки тают. The sounds are fading away.
твёрдость (f.) hardness, solidity, firmness
твёрдый hard, firm, steadfast
стать твёрдой ногой где-либо to secure a firm footing somewhere
твёрдые цены fixed prices
твёрдое убеждение firm conviction
●твой, твоя, твоё, твои your, familiar (m., f., n., pl.)
творческий creative
т. е. (то есть) that is
театр theater
театральный theatrical, melodramatic
текст text
телевидение television
телевизор television set
телеграмма telegram
телефон telephone
звонить по телефону to telephone
тело body
жидкое тело liquid ⎫ physics
твёрдое тело solid ⎭
постороннее тело foreign body
телятина veal
тем the (not as an article)
тем не менее nevertheless
тем хуже so much the worse
Чем больше, тем лучше. The more the better.
тема subject, topic, theme
темнеть (потемнеть) to grow dark
Краски потемнели. The colors have darkened.
Темнеет. It is getting dark.
У него потемнело в глазах. Everything went dark before his eyes.
темно (adv.) dark, it is dark
●темнота darkness, intellectual ignorance
●тёмный dark, obscure

темп rate, speed, pace

температу́ра temperature

тенде́нция tendency, purpose
основна́я тенде́нция underlying purpose
проявля́ть тенде́нцию to exhibit a tendency

те́ннис tennis
игра́ть в те́ннис to play tennis

•тень (f.) shade, shadow
боя́ться со́бственной те́ни to be afraid of one's own shadow
держа́ться в тени́ to remain in the background
От него́ оста́лась одна́ тень. He is a shadow of his former self.

теоре́ма theorem

теорети́чески (adv.) in theory, theoretically

тео́рия theory

•тепе́рь now, at present, nowadays

•тепло́ (adv.) warmly, it is warm
оде́ться тепло́ to dress warmly
тепло́ встре́тить кого́-либо to give someone a hearty welcome

теплота́ warmth, cordiality

тёплый warm, cordial, kindly
тёплая компа́ния rascally crew
тёплые кра́ски warm colors
тёплый приём cordial welcome

тере́ть (imp.) to rub, polish, grind

термо́метр thermometer

терпели́во (adv.) patiently, with patience

•терпели́вость (f.) patience, endurance

терпели́вый patient

терпе́ние patience, endurance, forbearance
выводи́ть кого́-либо из терпе́ния to try someone's patience
вы́йти из терпе́ния to lose patience

терпе́ть (imp.) to suffer, endure, undergo, bear
Вре́мя те́рпит. There's no hurry.
Он не мо́жет э́того бо́льше терпе́ть. He can't stand it any longer
терпе́ть нужду́ to suffer privation

терпи́мый tolerant, indulgent

•теря́ть (потеря́ть) to lose

теря́ться (потеря́ться) to be lost, get lost, lose one's self possession

те́сно (adv.) narrowly, tightly, it is crowded

те́сный cramped, tight, small, close
те́сная дру́жба intimate friendship
те́сная связь close connection
те́сные объя́тия tight embrace

те́сто dough

тетра́дь (f.) notebook, copybook

•тётя aunt

те́хник technician

те́хника technic, technique

те́хникум technical school

техни́ческий technical

тече́ние current (as of water), course, trend, tendency
в тече́ние неде́ли in the course of the week, during the week

течь (imp.) to flow (as of water), run, glide, leak
Вре́мя течёт бы́стро. Time flies.
Здесь течёт. There's a leak here.
Река́ течёт. The river is flowing.
У него́ слю́нки теку́т. His mouth is watering.

ти́гель (m.) crucible

тип type, model, species

ти́хий quiet, still, low, gentle, faint

ти́хо (adv.) quietly, faintly, gently, it is calm

ти́ше quieter, hush!

•тишина́ quiet, silence, peace
наруша́ть тишину́ to disturb the silence
соблюда́ть тишину́ to make no noise

•то then, in that case, that
Е́сли вы не пойдёте, то я пойду́. If you don't go, (then) I will.
Не то, что́бы мне не хоте́лось ... It is not that I don't want to ...
то́ есть (т. е.) that is

•това́рищ comrade, close friend

•тогда́ then, at that time
тогда́ же at the same time

тогда́шний of that time

•то́же also, too, likewise, as well
Он то́же пойдёт. He is going, too (as well).
Он то́же не зна́ет. He does not know either.
То́же хоро́ш! You are a nice one, to be sure.
Я то́же не бу́ду. Neither shall I.

толка́ть (толкну́ть) to push, shove

толкну́ть—see толка́ть

толко́вый intelligible, clear, sensible

толпа́ crowd, throng

толсте́ть (потолсте́ть) to become fat

•то́лстый fat, thick, heavy, stout

•то́лько only, merely, solely
Где то́лько он не быва́л! Where has he not been!
как то́лько as soon as
Он то́лько хоте́л узна́ть. He only wanted to know.
то́лько в после́днюю мину́ту not until the last moment
то́лько что just now
Ты то́лько поду́май! Just think!

том volume

томи́тельно (adv.) it is wearisome

томи́тельный wearisome, tedious, trying, painful

томи́ть (imp.) to weary, tire, wear out
Его́ томи́т жара́. He is exhausted by the heat.

тон tone
Не говори́те таки́м то́ном. Don't use that tone of voice.
то́ном вы́ше in more excited tones, a tone higher

то́ненький slender, slim

•то́нкий thin, fine, delicate, slender
Где то́нко, там и рвётся. The strength of the chain is determined by its weakest link.
то́нкая фигу́ра slender figure
то́нкие черты́ лица́ delicate features
то́нкий вкус delicate taste
то́нкий намёк gentle hint
то́нкий слой thin layer
то́нкий слух keen ear
то́нкое разли́чие subtle distinction

то́нко (adv.) thinly, subtly

то́нкость (f.) thinness, delicacy, subtlety, fine point

тону́ть (утону́ть) to sink, drown

топи́ть (утопи́ть) to sink, drown (something else)
топи́ть го́ре в вине́ to drown one's sorrows in drink
топи́ть су́дно to sink a ship

топи́ться (утопи́ться) to drown oneself

топо́р ax

торгова́ться (imp.) to bargain

торго́вец merchant, dealer

торго́вля trade, commerce

торже́ственный solemn, festive, triumphant

торжество́ festival, celebration, triumph

торжествова́ть (imp.) to celebrate, triumph, exult

то́рмоз brake, drag, hindrance

тормози́ть to brake, hinder

торопи́ться (поторопи́ться) to hurry, be in a hurry
На́до торопи́ться. You must hurry.
не торопя́сь leisurely
торопи́ться в теа́тр to hurry to the theater

торт cake

тоска́ melancholy, depression, tedium, yearning
тоска́ по ро́дине homesickness
У него́ тоска́ на се́рдце. His heart is heavy.
Э́та кни́га — одна́ тоска́. This book is very boring.

тост toast

•тот, та, то, те that, those (m., f., n., pl.)

вмéсте с тем at the same time
дéло в том, что the fact is that
и томý подóбное (и т. п.) and so
on
крóме тогó besides that
к томý же moreover
несмотря́ на то, что in spite of the
fact that
ни с тогó, ни с сегó for no reason
at all
пóсле тогó, как after
с тех пор since then
•тóчка point, dot, spot, period
попáсть в тóчку to strike home,
hit the nail on the head
тóчка зрéния point of view
тóчка с запятóй semicolon
тóчно (adv.) exactly, precisely,
accurately
тóчно так just so, exactly
тóчность (f.) exactness, precision,
accuracy
тошни́ть (imp.) to be nauseous
Егó тошни́т. He feels sick.
Меня́ тошни́т. I feel nauseous.
от э́того тошни́т. It is sickening.
травá grass
трагéдия tragedy
траги́чески (adv.) tragically
траги́ческий tragic
траги́ческий актёр tragedian
тради́ция tradition
трáктор tractor
трамвáй (m.) streetcar
éздить на трамвáе to go by
streetcar
•трáтить (истрáтить) to spend,
expend
трáур mourning
трéбование demand, request, claim
трéбовательный exacting,
fastidious, particular
трéбовать (потрéбовать) to demand,
urge, require
тревóга alarm, anxiety, uneasiness
лóжная тревóга false alarm
тревóжить (потревóжить) to disturb,
harrass, make uneasy
трéзво soberly
трéзвый sober (sensible), abstinent
трепетáние trembling, trepidation
трепетáть (imp.) to tremble, quiver,
thrill
трепетáть от рáдости to thrill with
joy
трепетáть при мы́сли to tremble at
the thought
трéснуть—see трещáть
трéтий third
треугóльник triangle
трещáть (трéснуть) to crack,
crackle
три three

тривиáльный banal, trite
три́дцать thirty
тридцáтый thirtieth
трина́дцать thirteen
тринáдцатый thirteenth
три́ста three hundred
трóгательно (adv.) pathetically,
touchingly
трóгательный touching, moving,
affecting, pathetic
•трóгать (трóнуть) to touch,
disturb, trouble
Не тронь егó! Leave him alone!
Это не трóгает егó. It does not
move him.
троллéйбус trolley bus
трóнуть—see трóгать
тротуáр sidewalk
трубá pipe, chimney, smokestack
•труд labor, difficulty, work
без трудá without effort
жить свои́м трудóм to live by one's
own labor
Он с трудóм её понимáет. He
understands her with difficulty.
сли́шком мнóго трудá too much
trouble, too much work
трýдно (adv.) with difficulty, it is
difficult
трýдный difficult, hard, arduous
трýдный вопрóс difficult question
трýдный ребёнок unmanageable
child
труп corpse, dead body
трус coward
трусли́во (adv.) apprehensively, in a
cowardly manner
трусли́вый cowardly, timid
трущóба slum
трáпка rag, duster, spineless
creature
трясти́сь (imp.) to shake, tremble,
shiver
Он весь трясётся. He is trembling
all over.
трясти́сь от хóлода to shiver with
cold
•тудá there, thither
биле́т тудá и обрáтно round-trip
ticket
Тудá емý и дорóга. It serves him
right.
тудá и сюдá here and there
тумáн mist, fog, haze
быть как в тумáне to be in a fog
напусти́ть тумáну to obscure
Тумáн рассéялся. The fog has
cleared.
тумáнно (adv.) hazily, obscurely,
vaguely
тумáнный misty, foggy, obscure
тумáнный смысл hazy meaning

тупи́к dead end street, blind alley
найти́ вы́ход из тупикá to find a
way out of an impasse
тупóй blunt, dull, stupid
тупóе зрéние dim sight
тупóй учени́к dunce
тýпость (f.) bluntness, dullness,
stupidity
тури́ст tourist
тýсклый dim, dull, lusterless
тýсклая жизнь dreary life
тýсклый свет dim light
тýсклый стиль lifeless style
•тут here
не тýт-то бы́ло nothing of the
sort
тýт же there and then
тýфля shoe, slipper
тýча storm cloud, swarm
смотрéть тýчей to lower (look
very angry)
тýча мух swarm of flies
тушёный stewed
туши́ть (потуши́ть) to put out, quell,
stew
туши́ть газ to turn off the gas
туши́ть свет to put out the light
тщáтельный careful, painstaking
тщéтно (adv.) vainly, in vain
тщéтный vain, futile
•ты you (sing., familiar)
ты́сяча thousand
ты́сячный thousandth
тюрьмá prison
тяжелó (adv.) heavily, seriously,
gravely
Емý тяжелó. It is hard for him.
тяжелó бóлен dangerously ill
тяжелó вздыхáть to sigh heavily
•тяжёлый heavy, severe, difficult,
serious
тяжёлая болéзнь serious illness
тяжёлая рабóта hard work
тяжёлое наказáние severe
punishment
тяжёлые временá hard times
У негó тяжёлый харáктер. He is
hard to get along with.
тя́жесть (f.) weight, gravity
тянýть (потянýть) to pull, draw,
drag
Егó тя́нет домóй. He longs to go
home.
Не тяни́! Hurry up! Don't drag it
out.
тянýть всё ту же пéсню to harp on
the same string
тянýть жрéбий to draw lots
тянýть когó-либо за рукáв to pull
someone by the sleeve
тянýть нóту to sustain a note
тянýться (потянýться) to stretch,
extend

Дни тя́нутся однообра́зно. The days drag on monotonously.

Равни́на тя́нется на сто киломе́тров. The plain extends for 100 kilometers.

Цвето́к тя́нется к со́лнцу. The flower turns towards the sun.

у

•у by, at, near, at the home of, possession (with gen.)

Он был у меня́. He was at my house.

стоя́ть у две́ри to stand near, by the door

у меня́ есть I have

Я э́то взял у неё. I took it from her.

убавить—see убавля́ть

убавля́ть (уба́вить) to diminish, reduce, lessen

Он убавля́ет себе́ го́ды. He makes himself out younger than he is.

уба́вить в ве́се to lose weight

убавля́ть це́ну to lower the price

убеди́тельный convincing, persuasive

убега́ть (убежа́ть) to run away

убеди́ть—see убежда́ть

убежа́ть—see убега́ть

убежда́ть (убеди́ть) to convince, persuade

убежде́ние persuasion, conviction

Все убежде́ния бы́ли напра́сны. All persuasion was in vain.

де́йствовать по убежде́нию to act according to one's convictions

убива́ть (уби́ть) to kill, slay

убива́ть вре́мя to kill time

убива́ть мо́лодость to waste one's youth

Хоть убе́й не зна́ю. I couldn't tell you to save my life.

уби́йство murder, assassination

уби́йца killer

•убира́ть (убра́ть) to remove, take away

убира́ть ко́мнату to clean a room

убира́ть со стола́ to clear the table

уби́ть—see убива́ть

•убо́рная lavatory, dressing room

убра́ть—see убира́ть

уважа́емый respected

•уважа́ть (imp.) to respect, esteem

глубоко́ уважа́ть to hold in high respect

уважа́ть себя́ to have self-respect

уваже́ние respect, esteem

из уваже́ния in deference

Он досто́ин уваже́ния. He is worthy of respect.

по́льзоваться глубо́ким уваже́нием to be held in high respect

увеличе́ние increase, extension, expansion, enlargement

увели́чивать (увели́чить) to increase, enlarge, extend

увеличи́тельный magnifying

увели́чить—see увели́чивать

увере́ние assurance, protestation

уве́ренно (adv.) confidently, with confidence

уве́ренность (f.) confidence

с уве́ренностью with confidence

уве́ренность в себе́ self-reliance

•уве́ренный sure, assured, positive, confident

бу́дьте уве́рены you may be sure

уве́ренная рука́ sure hand

уве́ренный шаг confident step

уве́рить—see уверя́ть

уверя́ть (уве́рить) to assure, convince

уверя́ю вас, что I assure you that

уви́деть—see ви́деть

увлека́тельный fascinating, captivating

увлека́ть (увле́чь) to fascinate, captivate, allure, entice

увлече́ние enthusiasm, animation

говори́ть с увлече́нием to speak with enthusiasm

его́ ста́рое увлече́ние an old flame of his

увле́чь—see увлека́ть

увы́! alas!

угада́ть—see уга́дывать

уга́дывать (угада́ть) to guess, divine

углублённый deep, profound, absorbed

угова́ривать (уговори́ть) to try to persuade, talk into

угова́риваться (уговори́ться) to arrange (with), agree

Они́ уговори́лись встре́титься в библиоте́ке. They arranged (agreed) to meet at the library.

уговори́ть (ся)—see угова́ривать (ся)

уго́дно (adv.) willingly, obligingly

Задава́йте каки́е уго́дно вопро́сы. Ask any questions you like.

как вам уго́дно as you please

как уго́дно anyhow

кто уго́дно anybody

ско́лько душе́ уго́дно to one's heart's content

у́гол corner, angle

в углу́ in the corner

за угло́м around the corner

за́гнутые углы́ dog-eared pages

име́ть свой у́гол to have a home of one's own

под прямы́м угло́м at right angles

у́голь coal

угости́ть—see угоща́ть

•угоща́ть (угости́ть) to treat, entertain

угоще́ние treating, refreshments

угрю́мый sullen, gloomy, morose

удалённый remote

удали́ться—see удаля́ться

удаля́ться (удали́ться) to move off, away

удаля́ться от бе́рега to move away from the shore

удаля́ться от те́мы to wander from the subject

уда́р blow, stroke

одни́м уда́ром уби́ть двух за́йцев to kill two birds with one stone

со́лнечный уда́р sunstroke

Это для него́ тяжёлый уда́р. It is a hard blow for him.

ударе́ние accent, stress, emphasis

уда́рить—see ударя́ть

•ударя́ть (уда́рить) to hit, strike

Мо́лния уда́рила. Lightning struck.

уда́рить кого́-либо по карма́ну to cost someone a pretty penny

ударя́ть по столу́ to bang on the table

уда́ться (perf.) to turn out well, be a success

Ему́ удало́сь найти́ э́то. He succeeded in finding it.

Мы хоте́ли пое́хать, но нам не удало́сь. We wanted to go, but it didn't work out.

уда́ча good luck, success

Ему́ всегда́ уда́ча. He always has luck.

уда́чи и неуда́чи ups and downs

уда́чно (adv.) successfully, well

•уда́чный successful, apt

уда́чная попы́тка successful attempt

уда́чное выраже́ние apt expression

уде́льный specific

уде́льный вес specific gravity

удиви́тельно (adv.) amazingly, astonishingly, it is strange

не удиви́тельно, что no wonder that

удиви́тельный astonishing, surprising, striking, amazing, wondrous

удиви́ть (ся)—see удивля́ть (ся)

удивле́ние astonishment, surprise, wonder, amazement

разину́ть рот от удивле́ния to be open-mouthed with astonishment

удивля́ть (удиви́ть) to astonish, surprise, amaze

удивля́ть-ся (удиви́ть-ся) to be surprised, wonder at

Вот онá удивѝтся. She will be so surprised.

удóбно (adv.) comfortably, conveniently

Ему́ удóбно. He feels comfortable.

éсли ему́ э́то удóбно if it is convenient for him

● удóбный comfortable, handy, convenient

удóбное крéсло comfortable armchair

удóбный момéнт opportune moment

удóбный слу́чай opportunity

удóбство comfort

удовлетворéние satisfaction, gratification

находѝть удовлетворéние to find satisfaction

получѝть пóлное удовлетворéние to be fully satisfied

удовлетворѝтельно (adv.) satisfactorily

удовлетворѝтельный satisfactory, satisfying

удовлетворѝть—see удовлетворя́ть

удовлетворя́ть (удовлетворѝть) to satisfy, content, comply with

удовóльствие   pleasure

жить в своё удовóльствие to enjoy one's life

получѝть удовóльствие от чегó-либо to enjoy something

с удовóльствием with pleasure, gladly

уединéние solitude, seclusion

уединённо (adv.) solitarily

уезжáть (уéхать) to leave, go away, depart (by conveyance)

уéхать—see уезжáть

у́жас terror, horror

быть в у́жасе to be horrified

Какóй у́жас! How terrible!

У́жас как хóлодно. It is terribly cold.

● ужáсно (adv.) terribly, horribly, awfully, it is terrible

ужáсный terrible, horrible

● ужé already, no longer

Он ужé не ребёнок. He is no longer a child.

Он ужé кóнчил. He has already finished.

ужé давнó, как it is a long time since

ужé не раз more than once

● у́жин supper

за у́жином at supper

у́жинать (поу́жинать) to have supper

у́зел knot, bundle

завя́зывать у́зел to tie a knot

● у́зкий narrow, tight

у́зкие взгля́ды narrow views

● узнавáть (узнáть) to recognize, find out

Он узнáл её по гóлосу. He knew her by her voice.

Он узнáл мнóго нóвого. He learned much that was new to him.

Узнáйте по телефóну когдá начáло спектáкля. Find out by telephone when the play begins.

узнáть—see узнавáть

уйтѝ—see уходѝть

укáз decree, edict

указáтельный indicating, indicatory

указáтельный пáлец forefinger

указáть—see укáзывать

укáзывать (указáть) to show, indicate, point out

уклáдываться (уложѝться) to pack

укрáсть—see красть

укрепѝть—see укрепля́ть

укреплéние strengthening, fortifying

укрепля́ть (укрепѝть) to fortify, strengthen

у́ксус vinegar

уку́с bite, sting

укусѝть (perf.) to bite, sting

Какáя му́ха егó укусѝла? What possessed him?

улáдить (perf.) to settle, arrange

улáдить спóрный вопрóс to settle a controversial question

● у́лица street

на у́лице on the street, out of doors

уложѝться—see уклáдываться

улóженный packed

улучшáть-ся (улу́чшить-ся) to improve (itself), make better

Егó здорóвье улу́чшилось. His health has improved.

улу́чшить (ся)—see улучшáть (ся)

● улыбáться (улыбну́ться) to smile

Жизнь ему́ улыбáлась. Life smiled on him.

не улыбáясь unsmilingly

улы́бка smile

улыбну́ться—see улыбáться

● ум mind, wit, intellect

в здрáвом умé in one's right senses

ему́ пришлó на ум it occurred to him

сходѝть с умá to go mad

Ум хорошó, а два лу́чше. Two heads are better than one.

уменьшáть-ся (умéньшить-ся) to diminish, decrease, lessen

уменьшѝтельный diminutive

умéньшить (ся)—see уменьшáть (ся)

умéренность (f.) moderation, temperance

умéренный moderate, temperate

умерéть—see умирáть

● умéть (imp.) to know how, be able

Он сдéлает э́то как умéет. He'll do it to the best of his ability.

умирáть (умерéть) to die

умирáть от ску́ки to be bored to death

умнó (adv.) cleverly, wisely, sensibly

умножéние multiplication, increase

● у́мный clever, intelligent

умолкáть (умóлкнуть) to fall silent

умóлкнуть—see умолкáть

умоля́ть (imp.) to entreat, implore

умоля́ющий pleading, suppliant

у́мственный mental, intellectual

умывáть-ся (умы́ть-ся) to wash (oneself)

умы́ть (ся)—see умывáть (ся)

унестѝ—see уносѝть

универсáльный universal

университéт unversity

унижéние humiliation

уничтожáть (уничтóжить) to destroy, crush, wipe out

Огóнь всё уничтóжил. The fire has destroyed all.

уничтóжить—see уничтожáть

уносѝть (унестѝ) to take away, carry off

Воображéние унеслó егó далекó. He was carried away by his imagination.

уны́ло despondently, dolefully

уны́лый sad, dismal, despondent

упáдок decline, breakdown

приходѝть в упáдок to fall into decay

упáдок ду́ха low spirits

упакóван packed

упáсть—see пáдать

упоéние rapture, ecstasy

упоминáть (упомяну́ть) to mention, refer to

упоминáть вскользь to mention in passing

упомяну́ть—see упоминáть

упóрный persistent, stubborn

употребѝтельный common, generally used

употребѝть—see употребля́ть

употребля́ть (употребѝть) to make use of

употребѝть власть to exercise one's authority

употребѝть все усѝлия to exert every effort

употребля́ться (употребѝться) to be in use

широкó употребля́ться to be in common usage

упрáвиться—see управля́ться

управле́ние management, control, conducting

управля́ть-ся (упра́вить-ся) to govern, rule, manage, conduct

упражне́ние exercise

упражня́ть (imp.) to exercise

упражня́ться to practice

упрёк reproach, reproof

упрека́ть (упрекну́ть) to reproach, upbraid

упрекну́ть—see упрека́ть

упроще́ние simplification

упря́мство stubbornness, obstinacy

•упря́мый obstinate, stubborn

уравне́ние equalization, equation (math.)

ура́внивать (уровня́ть) to equalize, level

урага́н hurricane

у́ровень (m.) level, standard
  жи́зненный у́ровень living standard
  у́ровень воды́ water level

уровня́ть—see ура́внивать

•уро́к lesson

ус, усы́ (pl.) mustache, whiskers
  мота́ть что́-либо себе́ на ус to observe something silently

усе́рдие zeal, diligence

усе́рдный zealous, diligent

уси́лие effort

ускори́ть—see ускоря́ть

ускоря́ть (ускори́ть) to hasten, quicken, expedite

усла́ть—see усыла́ть

•усло́вие condition, term
  ни при каки́х усло́виях under no circumstances
  обяза́тельное усло́вие indispensable condition
  при усло́вии, что on condition that
  усло́вия догово́ра terms of the treaty
  усло́вия жи́зни conditions of life
  ста́вить усло́вия to lay down terms

усложне́ние complication

услу́га service, good turn
  к ва́шим услу́гам at your service
  ока́зывать кому́-либо услу́гу to do someone a service
  Услу́га за услу́гу. One good turn deserves another.

услу́живать (услужи́ть) to render a service, do a good turn

услужи́ть—see услу́живать

услы́шать—see слы́шать

усмотре́ние discretion, judgment

•успе́ть (pf.) to have time
  Ему́ уже́ не успе́ть на по́езд. He cannot be in time for the train.
  Он успе́л ко́нчить уро́к. He had time to finish the lesson.

•успе́х success, good luck
  де́лать успе́хи to make progress
  Жела́ю вам успе́ха. I wish you good luck.
  по́льзоваться успе́хом to be a success

успе́шно (adv.) successfully

успе́шный successful

успока́ивать-ся (успоко́ить-ся) to calm, soothe, appease
  успока́ивать свою́ со́весть to salve one's own conscience
  Успоко́йтесь. Compose yourself. Calm yourself.

успоко́ить (ся)—see успока́ивать (ся)

•устава́ть (уста́ть) to get tired

уста́лость (f.) tiredness, weariness, fatigue

уста́лый tired, weary, фати́гued
  У вас уста́лый вид. You look tired.

уста́ть—see устава́ть

у́стный oral, verbal

устра́ивать (устро́ить) to arrange, organize, establish
  устра́ивать сканда́л to make a row
  устра́ивать свои́ дела́ to settle one's affairs
  устро́ить так, что́бы to arrange so as to
  устро́ить ребёнка в шко́лу to get a child into school
  Это меня́ вполне́ устра́ивает. That suits me completely.

устра́иваться (устро́иться) to settle
  Всё устро́илось. Everything has turned out all right.
  Он хо́чет устро́иться в Москве́. He wants to settle in Moscow.
  устра́иваться в но́вой кварти́ре to settle in a new apartment

устремле́ние aspiration

у́стрица oyster

устро́ить (ся)—see устра́ивать (ся)

усту́пка concession
  идти́ на усту́пки to make concessions

усыла́ть (усла́ть) to send away

утверди́тельно (adv.) affirmatively

утверди́ть—see утвержда́ть

утвержда́ть (утверди́ть) to affirm, maintain, assert, confirm

утвержде́ние assertion, statement

утере́ть—see утира́ть

утеша́ть (уте́шить) to comfort, console

утеше́ние comfort, consolation

утеши́тельный comforting, consoling

уте́шить—see утеша́ть

утира́ть (утере́ть) to wipe, dry

у́тка duck

утоми́тельный tiresome, tiring, wearing

утоми́ть—see утомля́ть

утомле́ние tiredness, weariness

утомля́ть (утоми́ть) to tire, weary

утону́ть—see тону́ть

утопи́ть (ся)—see топи́ть (ся)

у́тренний morning (adj.)
  у́тренний за́втрак breakfast

•у́тро morning
  в де́вять часо́в утра́ at nine o'clock in the morning
  До́брое у́тро. Good morning.
  у́тром in the morning
  С до́брым у́тром. Good morning.

утю́г iron (for clothes), flatiron

уха́живать (imp.) to nurse, look after, court
  уха́живать за ребёнком to tend to a child

•у́хо ear
  влюби́ться по́ уши to be head over heels in love
  в одно́ у́хо вошло́, в друго́е вы́шло in one ear and out the other
  Он уша́м не ве́рил. He could not believe his ears.

•уходи́ть (уйти́) to leave, depart (on foot)
  Все си́лы ухо́дят на э́то. One's whole energy is spent on it.
  От э́того не уйдёшь. You can't get away from it.
  уходи́ть в отста́вку to retire
  уходи́ть в себя́ to withdraw into oneself

уча́ствовать (imp.) to take part in, participate

уча́стие participation, collaboration
  принима́ть уча́стие в чём-либо to take part in something

уче́бник textbook, manual

уче́бный educational, school
  уче́бное заведе́ние educational institution
  уче́бный год school year

уче́ние studies, learning
  ко́нчить уче́ние to finish one's studies

•учени́к, учени́ца student (m., f.)

учёный learned, learned person, scholar, scientist

учи́тель, учи́тельница teacher (m., f.)

•учи́ть (imp.) to learn, study, teach
  Она́ у́чит му́зыку. She is studying music.
  Он у́чит её му́зыке. He teaches her music.

учи́ться (imp.) to learn, study
  Век живи́—век учи́сь. You have to study as long as you live.
  учи́ться в университе́те to attend the university
  учи́ться на со́бственных оши́бках to profit by one's own mistakes

уют comfort, cosiness
уютно (adv.) comfortably, cosily
ую́тный cozy, comfortable
  ую́тная ко́мната cozy room

Ф

фа́брика factory, mill
фабрика́т manufactured product
фабри́чный industrial,
  manufacturing
  фабри́чная ма́рка trademark
  фабри́чный го́род industrial city
фа́була plot, story
фа́за phase, period
  фа́зы луны́ phases of the moon
факт fact
  го́лые фа́кты bare facts, naked
    facts
  факт тот, что the fact is that
  Фа́кты — упря́мая вещь. You can't
    fight facts.
факти́чески (adv.) practically,
  actually, in fact
факти́ческий actual, factual, virtual
фа́ктор factor
  вре́менные фа́кторы transitory
    factors
факульте́т department of a university
  быть на юриди́ческом факульте́те
    to be a student in the law school
  медици́нский факульте́т medical
    school
фальсифици́рованный counterfeited,
  forged, adulterated
фальши́вый false, artificial,
  counterfeit
  фальши́вая но́та false note
  фальши́вые зу́бы false teeth
фами́лия surname, family name
фамилья́рно (adv.) unceremoniously
фамилья́рный unceremonious
  familiar
фанати́ческий fanatic
фантази́ровать (imp.) to daydream,
  dream, let one's imagination run
фанта́зия fancy, fantasy, imagination
фантасти́ческий fantastic, fabulous
Фаренге́йт Fahrenheit
фа́ртук apron
фарфо́р porcelain, china
фарш stuffing
фарширо́ванный stuffed
  фарширо́ванная ры́ба gefilte fish
фасо́н fashion, style
  на друго́й фасо́н in a different
    fashion
  снять фасо́н to copy a dress
фата́льный fatal
февра́ль (m.) February
федера́ция federation
феномена́льный phenomenal

фе́рма farm
  моло́чная фе́рма dairy
фе́рмер farmer
фе́тровый felt
  фе́тровая шля́па felt hat
фехтова́ние fencing
фиа́лка violet
фи́га fig
фигу́ра figure
  кру́пная фигу́ра outstanding
    figure
  представля́ть собо́ю жа́лкую фигу́-
    ру to cut a poor figure
  У неё хоро́шая фигу́ра. She has a
    good figure.
фигу́рка statuette, figurine
фи́зик physicist
фи́зика physics
физи́ческий physical
  физи́ческая си́ла physical strength
  физи́ческий кабине́т physics
    laboratory
фикти́вный fictitious
фи́кция fiction
филантро́п philanthropist
филантропи́ческий philanthropic
филе́ sirloin, fillet
филиа́л subsidiary, branch office
филосо́ф philosopher
филосо́фски (adv.) philosophically
филосо́фия philosophy
фильм film
  снима́ть фильм to make a film
  цветно́й фильм color film
фина́л finale
фина́нсовый financial
фина́нсы finances, financial position
фи́ник date (fruit)
фиоле́товый violet (color)
фи́рма firm, company
флаг flag
фланель (f.) flannel
фле́йта flute
  игра́ть на фле́йте to play the flute
фли́гель (m.) wing of a building,
  outbuilding
флиртова́ть (imp.) to flirt
флот fleet, the navy
  возду́шный флот air force
фойе́ (n., not declined) foyer,
  lobby
фо́кус trick, focus
фона́рь (m.) lantern, lamp
  подста́вить фона́рь кому́-либо to
    give someone a black eye
  у́личный фона́рь street light
  электри́ческий фона́рь flashlight
фонд fund, stock, reserve
  фо́ндовая би́ржа stock exchange
фонта́н fountain
  фонта́н красноре́чия fount of
    eloquence

фо́ра odds
  дать фо́ру to give odds
•фо́рма form, shape, uniform
  в пи́сьменной фо́рме in written
    form
  в фо́рме ша́ра in the form of a
    globe
  граммати́ческие фо́рмы gram-
    matical forms
  надева́ть фо́рму to wear a uniform
  оде́тый не по фо́рме not properly
    dressed
форма́льность (f.) formality
фо́рмула formula
фортепиа́но upright piano
фотографи́ровать (imp.) to take a
  photograph
фотогра́фия photography
фра́за phrase, sentence
  пусты́е фра́зы mere words
франт dandy
францу́з, францу́женка Frenchman
  (m., f.)
францу́зский French
фрукт fruit
фунда́мент foundation, groundwork
фундамента́льный fundamental,
  solid, substantial
фуникулёр funicular (railway)
функциона́льный functional
фу́нкция function
фунт pound
фуро́р furor
  произвести́ фуро́р to create a
    furor
фут foot
  длино́ю в два фу́та two feet long
футбо́л football, soccer
  футболи́ст football player
футуристи́ческий futuristic
фуфа́йка jersey, sweater
фы́ркать (фы́ркнуть) to snort, sniff
  презри́тельно фы́ркнуть to sniff
    scornfully
фы́ркнуть—see фы́ркать

Х

хала́т dressing gown, bathrobe
хандра́ the blues
  На него́ напа́ла хандра́. He has
    the blues.
ха́ос chaos
•хара́ктер disposition, temper,
  character
  име́ть тве́рдый хара́ктер to have a
    strong will or character
  тяжёлый хара́ктер difficult nature
характери́стика characteristics
хара́ктерно (adv.) characteristically
характе́рный typical, distinctive,
  characteristic

хáта hut
Моя́ хáта с крáю. It's no concern of mine. (My hut is on the outskirts.)

• **хвали́ть (похвали́ть)** to commend, praise

хвáстать-ся (похвáстать-ся) to brag, boast

хватáть (схвати́ть) to snatch, seize, grasp, grab
хватáть когó-либо зá руку to seize someone by the hand
хватáть чтó-либо на летý to be very quick at something
хватáться за соло́минку to catch at a straw

хватáть (хвати́ть) to suffice, be enough, last out
Емý хвати́ло врéмени. He had the time.
На сегóдня хвáтит. That will do for today.
Этого емý хвáтит на мéсяц. It will last him for a month.

хвати́ть—see хватáть

хвост tail, train
бить хвостóм to lash the tail
стоя́ть в хвостé за чéм-либо to stand in a line for something
хвост комéты tail of a comet

хи́мик chemist
хими́ческий chemical
хи́мия chemistry
хиру́рг surgeon
хи́тро (adv.) slyly, cunningly

• **хи́трый** cunning, artful, sly

хладнокрóвие coolness, composure, equanimity
сохрани́ть хладнокрóвие to keep one's head

хладнокрóвный cool, composed

• **хлеб** bread, grain
жить на чужи́х хлебáх to live at someone else's expense
зарабáтывать себé на хлеб to earn one's living
отби́ть у когó-либо хлеб to take the bread out of someone's mouth

хлéбница breadbasket
хлеб-соль hospitality (bread and salt)

хлопотáть (похлопотáть) to bustle about, take trouble, solicit
Не хлопочи́те! Don't trouble!
хлопотáть о мéсте to seek a job

хлóпоты trouble, cares, fuss
несмотря́ на все егó хлóпоты in spite of all the trouble he has taken
Не стóит хлопóт. It is not worth the trouble.

хму́риться (нахму́риться) to frown, lower, be overcast

хму́рый gloomy, sullen

• **ход** motion, run, course, speed, entry
быть в ходý to be in vogue
зáдний ход backward motion
знать все ходы́ и вы́ходы to know all the ins and outs
лóвкий ход clever move
ти́хий ход slow speed
ход мы́слей train of thought
ход собы́тий course of events

• **ходи́ть (imp.)** to go, walk (habitual action)
Пóезд хóдит кáждый день. There is a train every day.
Слýхи хóдят. Rumors are afloat.
Тýчи хóдят по нéбу. Storm clouds are drifting across the sky.
ходи́ть вокрýг да óколо to beat about the bush
ходи́ть в шкóлу to attend school
ходи́ть на лы́жах to ski
ходи́ть по магази́нам to go shopping
ходи́ть пóд руку to walk arm in arm

ходьбá walking
полчасá ходьбы́ half an hour's walk

• **хозя́ин** master, boss, proprieter, owner, host, landlord
Он хорóший хозя́ин. He is thrifty and industrious.
хозя́ин положéния master of the situation

хозя́йка mistress, owner, hostess, landlady
домáшняя хозя́йка housewife

• **хозя́йничать (imp.)** to keep house, manage a household, play the boss

хозя́йство economy, household
занимáться хозя́йством to keep house
плáновое хозя́йство planned economy
сéльское хозя́йство agriculture

холм hill, mound
хóлод coldness
холодéц jellied meat
холоди́льник refrigerator
хóлодно (adv.) coldly, it is cold
Мне хóлодно. I am cold.
хóлодно встрéтить когó-либо to receive someone coldly

• **холóдный** cold, cool
холостóй unmarried (of men)
холостя́к bachelor
хор chorus
хорони́ть (похорони́ть) to bury
хорóшенький pretty, nice
хорóшенькая истóрия a pretty kettle of fish

хорошéть (похорошéть) to grow prettier, better-looking

• **хорóший** good
Всегó хорóшего. Good-by. (All of the best.)
Онá хорошá собóй. She is good-looking.
хорóшая погóда good weather
Что хорóшего? What's new?
Это дéло хорóшее. That's a good thing.

• **хорошó (adv.)** good, well, nice
Вот хорошó. That's fine.
Вы хорошó сдéлаете, éсли придёте. You would do well to come.
Емý хорошó здесь. He is comfortable here.
óчень хорошó very well
хорошó скáзано well said
Хорошó то, что хорошó кончáется. All's well that ends well.

• **хотéть (захотéть)** to wish, want
как хоти́те just as you like
Он не хóчет мне злá. He means no harm to me.
Он óчень хóчет её ви́деть. He wants to see her very much.
хотéть спать to want to sleep
хóчешь, не хóчешь willy-nilly

хотéться (захотéться) to want, feel like
Емý хóчется поговори́ть с вáми. He wants to talk with you.
Мне хóчется пить. I am thirsty.
не так, как хотéлось бы not as one would like it

• **хоть** even, if you wish, at least
Емý нýжно хоть два дня. He ought to have at least two days.
Не могý сдéлать э́то, хоть убéй. I can't do it for the life of me.
Хоть бы он поскорéе пришёл. If only he would come.
хоть сейчáс at once if you like

хотя́ although, though
Мы должны́ говори́ть хотя́ бы на двух языкáх. We should speak at least two languages.
хотя́ бы if only, even if
хотя́ бы и так even if it were so

хохотáть (imp.) to laugh boisterously

хрáбрый brave, valiant, gallant
храни́тель (m.) keeper, guardian
храни́ть (imp.) to keep, retain
храни́ть в пáмяти to keep in one's memory
храни́ть в тáйне to keep something secret
храни́ть дéньги в сберкáссе to keep one's money in a savings bank

храпéть (imp.) to snore

хребет spinal column, backbone
хрен horseradish
христианство Christianity
хромать (imp.) to limp
    хромать на правую ногу to be
        lame in the right leg
    У него хромает орфография. His
        spelling is poor.
хромой lame, limping
хронический chronic
хрусталь (m.) cut glass, crystal
худенький slender, slim
худеть (похудеть) to grow thin
худо (adv.) ill, badly
художественный art, artistic
художество art
художник artist
•худой lean, thin, bad, worn-out
    на худой конец if worst comes
        to worst
•хуже worse
    Погода сегодня хуже, чем вчера.
        The weather is worse today than
        yesterday.
    тем хуже so much the worse
    хуже всего worst of all

Ц

царапать (царапнуть) to scratch,
    claw, scribble
царапина scratch, abrasion
царапнуть—see царапать
царить (imp.) to reign
    Царил мрак. Darkness reigned.
•цвет color
    Какого цвета? What color?
    цвет лица complexion
цветной colored
цветок flower
целиком (adv.) as a whole, wholly
целовать-ся (поцеловать-ся) to kiss
    (each other)
•целый whole, entire, intact
    по целым неделям for weeks on
        end
    целая дюжина a whole dozen
    цел и невредим safe and sound
    целые числа whole numbers
•цель (f.) aim, goal, object, purpose
    достичь цели to achieve one's
        goal
    отвечать цели to answer the
        purpose
    попасть в цель to hit the mark
    с какой целью? for what purpose?
•цена price, worth, cost
    знать себе цену to know one's own
        value
    любой ценой at any price
    твёрдые цены fixed prices

Это не имеет цены. It is worthless.
цензура censorship
ценить (оценить) to value, estimate,
    appreciate
    высоко ценить себя to think much
        of oneself
    Его не ценят. He is not
        appreciated.
ценный valuable
цент cent
центр center
центральный central
цепь (f.) chain, bonds
    горная цепь mountain range
    спустить с цепи to let loose
церемониться (imp.) to stand on
    ceremony
    без церемоний informally
церковь (f.) church
цивилизация civilization
циник cynic
цинический cynical
цинк zinc
цирк circus
цитата quotation
цитировать to quote, cite
цифра figure, cipher
цыганский gypsy

Ч

•чай (m.) tea
чайка seagull
чайник teapot
чайная ложка teaspoon
чайная роза tea rose
•час hour
    в котором часу at what time
    в час дня at 1:00 P.M.
    Который час? What time is it?
    приёмные часы reception or
        visiting hours
    через час in an hour
часовой clock, watch (adj.), sentry
    (noun)
    двигаться по часовой стрелке to
        move clockwise
    часовая оплата payment by the
        hour
частица fraction, little part
частный private
•часто (adv.) often, frequently
часть (f.) part, share, portion
    большая часть greater part
    большей частью for the most part
    запасные части spare parts
    по частям in parts
    части тела parts of the body
часы (plural only) watch, clock,
    timepiece

поставить часы to set a watch
Часы отстают. The watch is slow.
Часы спешат. The clock is fast.
чахотка consumption
чашка cup
•чаще more often
чаяние expectation, hope
    сверх чаяния beyond expectation
•чей, чья, чьё, чьи whose (m., f.,
    n., pl.)
чек check
•человек (pl. люди) man, person,
    human being
человеческий human
    человеческая природа human
        nature
человечество humanity, mankind
•чем than
    меньше чем less than
    Чем больше, тем лучше. The more,
        the better.
    Чем писать, вы бы раньше спросили.
        You'd better ask first and write
        afterward.
чемодан valise
чемпион champion
чепуха nonsense
    говорить чепуху to talk nonsense
чередовать (ся) (imp.) to take
    turns, alternate
•через over, across, through (with
    acc.)
    перейти через дорогу to walk
        across the room
    писать через строчку to write on
        every other line
    через неделю in a week
череп skull
чересчур too
    чересчур много much too much
    Это уже чересчур. That's going
        too far.
черешня cherry
чернила (pl.) ink
•чёрный black
    на чёрный день against a rainy
        day
    ходить в чёрном to wear black
    чёрные мысли gloomy thoughts
    чёрный как смоль jet-black,
        pitch-black
    чёрный рынок black market
черта trait, line
    черты лица features
    Это фамильная черта. It is a
        family trait.
чертёнок imp
чесаться (почесаться) to scratch
    oneself, itch
    У него чешется нос. His nose
        itches.
    У неё руки чешутся это сделать.
        Her fingers itch to do it.

чеснóк garlic

чéстно (adv.) honestly, fairly, frankly

чéстность (f.) honesty

•чéстный honest, fair
дать чéстное слóво to give one's word of honor
Чéстное слóво! Upon my word!

честолюбúвый ambitious

честь (f.) honor
в честь когó-либо in honor of someone
дéло чéсти matter of honor
Не имéю чéсти знать вас. I do not have the honor of knowing you.
Считáю за честь. I consider it an honor.
Это дéлает емý честь. It does him credit.

четвéрг Thursday
в четвéрг on Thursday

четвертáк a quarter (25 kopecks)

чéтверть (f.) one-fourth, a quarter
чéтверть часá a quarter of an hour

четвёртый fourth

четы́ре four

четы́реста four hundred

четы́рнадцать fourteen

четы́рнадцатый fourteenth

чин rank, grade

чинúть (починúть) to repair, mend

чинóвник official, functionary

•числó number, date
в большóм числé in great numbers
в пéрвых чúслах ию́ня in the first days of June
Какóе сегóдня числó? What is today's date?
неизвéстное числó unknown quantity

чúстить (почúстить) to clean, scour, scrub

чúсто (adv.) cleanly, neatly, purely, it is clean

чистотá cleanliness, purity

•чúстый clean, neat, tidy, pure
бриллиáнт чúстой воды́ a diamond of the first water
чúстая рабóта neat job
чúстое безýмие sheer madness
чúстый бары́ш clear profit
чúстый вес net weight
чúстый слýчай pure chance

•читáть (прочитáть, прочéсть) to read
читáть лéкцию to give a lecture

чихáть (чихнýть) to sneeze

чихнýть—see чихáть

•чúще cleaner

член member, limb
член парлáмента member of parliament

член уравнéния term of an equation

чорт devil, deuce
Какóго чóрта он там дéлает? What the blazes is he doing there?
Чорт возьмú! The devil take it!

чрезвычáйно (adv.) extraordinarily, extremely

чрезвычáйный extraordinary, extreme

чтéние reading

•что what, that
всё, что он знал all that he knew
Мне чтó-то не хóчется. I somehow don't feel like it.
Ну и чтó же? Well, what of it?
потомý что because
Что вы! You don't say so!
Что дéлать? What is to be done?
Что знáчит э́то слóво? What does this word mean?
чтó-нибудь anything
Что с вáми? What is the matter with you?
чтó-то something, somehow

•чтóбы that, in order that
Невозмóжно, чтóбы он сказáл это. It is impossible that he should have said it.
Он говорúл грóмко, чтóбы все слы́шали. He spoke loudly so that all would hear.
Он не мóжет написáть ни стрóчки без тогó, чтóбы не сдéлать ошúбки. He can't write a line without making a mistake.
Он рáно встал, чтóбы быть там вó-время. He got up early in order to be there on time.
Он хотéл, чтóбы онá слы́шала. He wanted her to hear.

чувствúтельность (f.) sensitivity, perceptibility, sentimentality

чувствúтельный sensible, perceptible, painful, sensitive

•чýвство sense, feeling
обмáн чувств delusion, illusion
прийтú в чýвство to come to one's senses
пять чувств the five senses
чýвство мéры sense of proportion
чýвство прекрáсного feeling for the beautiful
чýвство ю́мора sense of humor

•чýвствовать (почýвствовать) to feel, sense
Как вы себя́ чýвствуете? How do you feel?
чýвствовать гóлод to be hungry
чýвствовать рáдость to feel joy
чýвствовать свою́ винý to feel one's guilt

чýдно (adv.) beautifully, wonderfully, it is beautiful

чýдный wonderful, marvelous, beautiful

чýдо miracle, wonder, marvel

чужóй someone else's, strange, alien
в чужúе рýки into strange hands
на чужóй счёт at someone else's expense
под чужúм úменем under an assumed name
чужúе краù foreign lands

чулóк stocking

чумáзый dirty-faced, smudgy

чýткий sensitive, keen, tactful, delicate
чýткий подхóд tactful approach
чýткий сон light sleep

чýткость (f.) sensitiveness, keenness, tactfulness, delicacy

•чуть hardly, slightly, just
Он чуть ды́шит. He can hardly breathe.
Он чуть не упáл. He nearly fell.
чуть-чуть a little

Ш

•шаг step, stride, footstep
в двух шагáх a few steps away
лóвкий шаг clever move
на кáждом шагý at every step
сдéлать пéрвый шаг to take the first step
шаг за шáгом step by step
шáгом at a walking pace

•шалúть (imp.) to play pranks, be naughty

шалýн, шалýнья playful person, mischievous child (m., f.)

шаль (f.) shawl

шампáнское champagne

шанс chance
имéть мнóго шáнсов to have many chances
ни малéйшего шáнса not the ghost of a chance

•шáпка cap

•шар ball, sphere, globe
воздýшный шар balloon

шарф scarf, muffler

шáткий unsteady, shaky, tottering

шáхматы chess
игрáть в шáхматы to play chess

швéдский Swedish

швéйный sewing
швéйная машúна sewing machine

швейцáрский Swiss

швея́ seamstress

шевелúть (шевельнýть) to stir, move
Он пáльцем не шевельнёт. He won't stir a finger.

шевельну́ть—see шевели́ть
шёлк silk
шёлковый silken
  Он стал, как шёлковый. He has
    become as meek as a lamb.
шепну́ть—see шепта́ть
шепта́ть (шепну́ть) to whisper
шерсть wool
шерстяно́й woolen
шестидеся́тый sixtieth
шестна́дцать sixteen
шестна́дцатый sixteenth
шесто́й sixth
шесть six
шестьдеся́т sixty
шестьсо́т six hundred
ше́я neck
  броса́ться кому́-либо на ше́ю to
    throw one's arms around
    someone's neck
  получи́ть по ше́е to get it in the
    neck
  по ше́ю up to the neck
  сиде́ть у кого́-либо на ше́е to be
    a burden to someone
шика́рный chic, smart
ши́на tire
шине́ль (f.) overcoat (uniform)
ши́ре broader, wider
ширина́ width, breadth
• широ́кий wide, broad
  в широ́ком смы́сле in the broad
    sense
  жить на широ́кую но́гу to live in
    grand style
  широ́кая пу́блика general public
  широ́кое обобще́ние sweeping
    generalization
широко́ (adv.) widely, broadly
  смотре́ть широко́ to take a broad
    view of things
  широко́ толкова́ть to interpret
    loosely
широта́ width, breadth, latitude
  широта́ ума́ breadth of mind
шить (сшить) to sew
шитьё sewing, needlework
шкаф cupboard, closet, wardrobe
• шко́ла school
  вы́сшая шко́ла college, university
  нача́льная шко́ла elementary
    school
  романти́ческая шко́ла литерату́ры
    romantic school of literature
  сре́дняя шко́ла secondary,
    high school
  ходи́ть в шко́лу to attend school
  челове́к ста́рой шко́лы man of the
    old school
шку́ра skin, hide
  дрожа́ть за свою́ шку́ру to tremble
    for one's life

спаса́ть свою́ шку́ру to save one's
  own skin
Я не хоте́л бы быть в его́ шку́ре.
  I would not like to be in his place.
шля́па hat
  Де́ло в шля́пе. It's in the bag.
шнур cord
шокола́д chocolate
шо́пот whisper
  шо́потом in a whisper, under
    one's breath
шо́рох rustle
шотла́ндский Scottish
шофёр chauffeur, driver
шпага́т string, cord, twine
шпи́лька hairpin
шпина́т spinach
шприц syringe
шрифт print, type
штаны́ (pl.) trousers, breeches
штат state
шта́тский civil
што́пать (зашто́пать) to darn
што́пор corkscrew
што́ра blind, shade
  спусти́ть што́ры to draw the blinds
штраф fine, penalty
шту́ка piece, thing
  Вот так шту́ка! That's a fine
    thing!
  В том то и шту́ка! That's just the
    point.
  штук де́сять about ten pieces
шту́чный piece
  шту́чная рабо́та piecework
шуба fur coat
шу́лер cheat, cardsharp
• шум noise, uproar
  мно́го шу́ма из ничего́ much ado
    about nothing
  шум и гам hue and cry
шуме́ть (imp.) to make a noise,
  be noisy
шу́мный noisy, loud
шурша́ние rustling
шурша́ть (imp.) to rustle
шути́ть (пошути́ть) to joke, jest
  Не шути́! Don't trifle with this!
  Он не шу́тит. He is serious.
• шу́тка joke, jest
  в шу́тку in jest
  шу́тки в сто́рону joking aside
  Это не шу́тки. It is not a laughing
    matter.
шутя́ (adv.) in jest, for fun, easily
  не шутя́ seriously

Щ

щади́ть (пощади́ть) to spare
  Не щади́те расхо́дов. Do not spare
    expenses.

не щадя́ себя́ without sparing
  oneself
щади́ть чью́-либо жизнь to spare
  someone's life
ще́дрость (f.) generosity, liberality
ще́дрый generous, liberal
  ще́дрой руко́й lavishly
щека́ cheek
щекота́ть (пощекота́ть) to tickle
  У меня́ в го́рле щеко́чет. My
    throat tickles.
  щекота́ть чьё-либо самолю́бие to
    tickle someone's vanity
щекотли́вый ticklish, delicate
  щекотли́вый вопро́с ticklish
    point
щено́к puppy
щётка brush
  зубна́я щётка toothbrush

Э

эволюцио́нный evolutionary
эгои́зм selfishness
эго́ист egoist, selfish person
эгоисти́ческий selfish, egotistical
экза́мен examination
  вы́держать экза́мен to pass an
    exam
  держа́ть экза́мен to take an exam
  провали́ться на экза́мене to fail at
    an exam
экзаменова́ть (проэкзаменова́ть) to
  examine
экземпля́р copy, specimen
экипа́ж carriage, crew
эконо́мика economics
эконо́мист economist
эконо́мить (сэконо́мить) to
  economize, save
экономи́ческий economical
эконо́мия economy
  для эконо́мии вре́мени to save
    time
  полити́ческая эконо́мия political
    economy
  соблюда́ть эконо́мию to save,
    economize
экра́н screen
экску́рсия excursion, trip
экспанси́вный effusive
экспа́нсия expansion
экспеди́ция expedition
экспериме́нт experiment
эксперимента́льный experimental
экспе́рт expert
экспе́ртный expert (adj.)
эксплуата́ция exploitation
э́кспорт export
экспресси́вный expressive
экспре́ссия expression
экста́з ecstasy

экстенси́вный extensive
экстрава́гантный extravagant
экстра́кт extract
э́кстренно urgently
эксцентри́ческий eccentric
эксце́сс excess
элева́тор elevator
элега́нтность (f.) elegance
элега́нтный elegant
эле́гия elegy
•электри́ческий electric
электри́чество electricity
элеме́нт element (chemistry)
элемента́рный elementary
эликси́р elixir
эма́левый enamel (adj.)
эма́ль (f.) enamel
эмансипа́ция emancipation
эмоциона́льный emotional
эмо́ция emotion
эмфати́ческий emphatic
энерги́чный energetic
эне́ргия energy
энтузиа́зм enthusiasm
энциклопе́дия encyclopedia
эпиде́мия epidemic
эпо́ха age, era, epoch
э́ра era
эроти́ческий erotic
эскала́тор escalator
эски́з sketch, study, outline
эстети́ческий aesthetic
•эта́ж floor, story
•эта́кий such, like this
  по́сле э́такой неуда́чи after such
    a failure
  Эта́кий дура́к! What a fool!
э́тика ethics
эти́ческий ethical
•э́то this, it, that
  как э́то возмо́жно? How is it
    possible?
  Кто э́то? Who is that?
  по́сле э́того after that
  при всём э́том in spite of all this
  Что э́то? What is that?
  Это моя́ кни́га. This is my book.
  Это хорошо́. That's good.
•э́тот, э́та, э́то, э́ти this, these (m.,
  f., n., pl.)
этю́д study sketch
эффе́кт effect
эффе́ктный spectacular, effective
э́хо echo

Ю

юбиле́й anniversary, jubilee
ю́бка skirt
юг south
ю́жный southern
ю́мор humor
  чу́вство ю́мора sense of humor
юмористи́ческий humorous, comic
ю́ность (f.) youth
ю́ноша (m.) youth, lad
юриди́ческий juridical, legal
юри́ст lawyer

Я

•я I
  я́блоко apple
я́блочный apple (adj.)
  я́блочный пиро́г apple pie
яви́ться—see явля́ться
явле́ние appearance, occurrence
  обы́чное явле́ние everyday
    occurrence
  явле́ние приро́ды natural
    phenomenon
явля́ться (яви́ться) to appear,
present oneself, occur
  как то́лько я́вится подходя́щий
    слу́чай as soon as an opportunity
    presents itself
  У него́ яви́лась мысль. An idea
    occurred to him.
  явля́ться в указа́нное вре́мя to
    present oneself at a fixed time
  явля́ться кста́ти to arrive
    opportunely
я́вно (adv.) it is evident, evidently,
obviously
я́вный evident, obvious, manifest
я́года berry
  одного́ по́ля я́годы birds of a
    feather
яд poison, venom
  яд его́ рече́й the venom of his
    words
ядови́тый poisonous, toxic
я́зва ulcer, sore
•язы́к language, tongue
  владе́ть каки́м-то языко́м to know
    a language

  копчёный язы́к smoked tongue
  литерату́рный язы́к literary
    language
  о́бщий язы́к common language
  о́стрый язы́к sharp tongue
  показа́ть язы́к to stick out one's
    tongue
  родно́й язы́к mother tongue
  ру́сский язы́к Russian language
  У него́ отня́лся язы́к. He became
    speechless. (His tongue failed
    him.)
  чеса́ть язы́к to wag one's tongue
  Язы́к до Ки́ева доведёт. You can
    get anywhere if you know how
    to use your tongue. (The tongue
    will take you as far as Kiev.)
языково́й linguistic
язы́ческий heathen, pagan
яи́чница omelet
  яи́чница-болту́нья scrambled eggs
яи́чный egg (adj.)
•яйцо́ egg
  яйцо́ в мешо́чек poached egg
  яйцо́ всмя́тку soft-boiled egg
я́корь (m.) anchor
я́мочка dimple
янва́рь (m.) January
янта́рь (m.) amber
япо́нский Japanese
я́ркий bright, vivid, brilliant
  я́ркое описа́ние vivid description
  я́ркий приме́р striking example
  я́ркий свет bright light
я́рко brightly, strikingly, vividly
я́ркость (f.) brightness, brilliance,
vividness
я́рмарка fair
я́рость (f.) fury, rage
  вне себя́ от я́рости beside oneself
    with rage
•я́сно (adv.) clearly, distinctly, it is
clear
  ко́ротко и я́сно to put it in a
    nutshell (short and clear)
я́сность clearness, lucidity
я́сный clear, lucid, distinct
я́щик box, drawer, chest
  откла́дывать в до́лгий я́щик to
    shelve, procrastinate

GLOSSARY OF PROPER NAMES

Ага́фья	Agatha	Карл	Carl
Агне́са	Agnes	Кла́вдия	Claudia
Адела́йда, Аде́ль	Adelaide	Константи́н	Constantine
Алексе́й	Alexis	Лавре́нтий	Laurence
Алекса́ндр	Alexander	Лёв	Leo
Али́са	Alice	Леони́д	Leonidas
Альфре́д	Alfred	Луи́за	Louise
Анаста́сия	Anastasia	Лука́	Luke
Анато́лий	Anatole	Любо́вь	Amy
Андре́й	Andrew	Людми́ла	Ludmilla
Анна	Anna	Мака́р	Macarius
Анто́н	Anthony	Макс	Maxim
Аполло́н	Apollo	Маргари́та	Margaret
Арту́р	Arthur	Мари́я	Marie, Mary
Бори́с	Boris	Ма́рфа	Martha
Валенти́н	Valentine	Матве́й	Matthew
Ва́льтер	Walter	Михаи́л	Michael
Варва́ра	Barbara	Наде́жда	Hope
Васи́лий	Basil	Ната́лия	Natalia
Ве́ра	Vera	Ники́та	Nikita
Ви́ктор	Victor	Никола́й	Nicholas
Вильге́льм	William	Оле́г	Oleg
Влади́мир	Vladimir	О́льга	Olga
Гео́ргий	George	Па́вел	Paul
Ге́рман	Herman	Пётр	Peter
Григо́рий	Gregory	Самуи́л	Samuel
Дави́д	David	Святосла́в	Sviatoslaff
Дани́ла	Daniel	Серге́й	Sergius
Дими́трий	Demetrius	Симео́н	Simon
Дороте́я	Dorothy	Соломо́н	Solomon
Ева	Eva	Софи́я	Sofia
Евге́ний	Eugene	Суса́нна	Susan
Екатери́на	Catherine	Тимофе́й	Timothy
Еле́на	Helen	Фёдор	Theodore
Елизаве́та	Elizabeth	Фили́пп	Philip
Заха́р	Zacharias	Фома́	Thomas
Ива́н	John	Шарло́тта	Charlotte
Ида	Ida	Эдуа́рд	Edward
Илья́	Elias	Элеоно́ра	Eleanor
Ио́сиф	Joseph	Ю́лия	Julia
Ири́на	Irene	Яков	Jacob, James

GLOSSARY OF GEOGRAPHICAL NAMES

Австралия Australia
Австрия Austria
Адриатическое море Adriatic Sea
Азербайджанская Советская
  Социалистическая Республика
    Azerbaijan Soviet Socialist
    Republic
Азия Asia
Албания Albany
Алжир Algeria
Альпы The Alps
Аляска Alaska
Америка America
Англия England
Аравия Arabia
Аргентина Argentina
Астрахань Astrakhan
Атлантический Океан Atlantic Ocean
Африка Africa
Байкал Baikal (Lake)
Баку Baku
Белорусская Советская
  Социалистическая Республика
    Byelorussian Soviet Socialist
    Republic
Бельгия Belgium
Болгария Bulgaria
Бонн Bonn
Бостон Boston
Бразилия Brazil
Брюссель Brussels
Вашингтон Washington
Великобритания Great Britain
Венгрия Hungary
Владивосток Vladivostok
Волга Volga (River)
Гамбург Hamburg
Германия Germany
Горький Gorky (City)
Грузинская Советская
  Социалистическая Республика
    Georgian Soviet Socialist
    Republic
Дания Denmark
Детройт Detroit
Днепр Dnieper (River)
Дон Don (River)
Дунай Danube (River)
Европа Europe
Египет Egypt
Женева Geneva
Иерусалим Jerusalem
Индия India
Иордань Jordan
Ирак Iraq
Иран Iran
Ирландия Ireland
Испания Spain
Италия Italy
Кавказ The Caucasus (Mountains)

Карпатские Горы Carpathian
  Mountains
Каспийское Море Caspian Sea
Киев Kiev
Китай China
Копенгаген Copenhagen
Корея Korea
Крым Crimea
Ламанш English Channel
Ленинград Leningrad
Лондон London
Лос Анжелос Los Angeles
Магнитогорск Magnitogorsk
Мадрид Madrid
Мексика Mexico
Москва Moscow
Мюнхен Munich
Нева Neva (River)
Нидерланды The Netherlands
Норвегия Norway
Нью-Йорк New York
Одесса Odessa
Палестина Palestine
Панамский Канал Panama Canal
Париж Paris
Пиренеи Pyrenees (Mountains)
Польша Poland
Португалия Portugal
Рейн Rhine (River)
Рим Rome
Российская Советская Федеративная
  Социалистическая Республика
    Russian Soviet Federative
    Socialist Republic
Россия Russia
Сан-Франциско San Francisco
Северная Америка North America
Сена Seine (River)
Сибирь Siberia
Сирия Syria
Скалистые Горы Rocky Mountains
Соединённые Штаты Америки
  United States of America
Союз Советских Социалистических
  Республик Union of Soviet
    Socialist Republics
Средиземное Море Mediterranean
  Sea
Сталинград Stalingrad
Стокгольм Stockholm
Таджикская Советская
  Социалистическая Республика
    Tajik Soviet Socialist Republic
Ташкент Tashkent
Тбилиси Tbilisi
Темза Thames (River)
Тихий Океан Pacific Ocean
Токио Tokyo
Турция Turkey
Узбекская Советская
  Социалистическая Республика

Uzbek Soviet Socialist Republic
Укра́инская Сове́тская
Социалисти́ческая Респу́блика
Ukrainian Soviet Socialist
Republic
Ура́л Urals (Mountains)
Филаде́льфия Philadelphia
Финля́ндия Finland
Фра́нция France
Хе́льсинки Helsinki

Чёрное Мо́ре Black Sea
Чехослова́кия Czechoslovakia
Чика́го Chicago
Чи́ли Chile
Швейца́рия Switzerland
Шве́ция Sweden
Шотла́ндия Scotland
Югосла́вия Yugoslavia
Южная Аме́рика South America
Япо́ния Japan

English-Russian DICTIONARY

A

abandon (to) оставлять, покинуть
abbreviate (to) сокращать
abbreviation сокращение
ability способность (f.)
able (to be) мочь
able способный
about о (prep.), около (gen.), про (acc.)
above наверху, над (inst.)
abruptly резко
absence отсутствие
absent (to be) отсутствовать
absent-minded рассеянный
absent-mindedly машинально, рассеянно
absolute абсолютный, совершенный
absolutely безусловно, совершенно
absorb (to) всасывать, впитывать
absorbed углубленный
abstain (to) воздерживаться
abstinent трезвый
abstract абстрактный
absurd абсурдный
absurdity абсурд, нелепость (f.)
abundant обильный
abuse (to) ругать
abusive оскорбительный
academy академия
accent акцент
accepted принятый
accident несчастный случай
accidental случайный
accidentally нечаянно, случайно
accommodate (to) приспособлять, давать пристанище
accommodated (to be) помещаться
accompany (to) провожать, сопровождать, аккомпанировать
accomplish (to) совершать, выполнять
according согласно, по (dat.)
accumulate (to) набирать (ся)
accuracy аккуратность (f.), точность (f.)
accusation обвинение
accuse (to) обвинять
accustomed (to become) привыкать
ache (to) болеть
achievement достижение
acknowledge (to) признавать
acknowledgment признание
acquaintance знакомый
acquainted (to become) знакомиться
acquire (to) приобретать
across через (acc.)
act (to) действовать, играть (on stage)
act акт (of a play), документ (deed)
action действие

actively активно
actor актёр, артист
actress актриса, артистка
actual фактический
actually действительно, фактически
acute острый
add (to) прибавлять, присоединять
add to (to) добавлять, прибавлять
addition сложение; добавление, прибавка
additional дополнительный, прибавочный
address (to) адресовать, обращаться, выступать
address адрес
adjacent соседний
administration администрация
administrator администратор
admire (to) любоваться
admirer кавалер, поклонник
admit (to) впускать, принимать
adopted принятый
adoration обожание
adore (to) обожать
adroit ловкий
adult взрослый
advance аванс
advantage преимущество
to take advantage of воспользоваться
advantageously выгодно
adventure приключение
adversity невзгода
advertise (to) рекламировать
advertisement реклама
advice совет
advise (to) рекомендовать, советовать
affected неестественный
affectionate ласковый, любящий
affirm (to) утверждать
affirmatively утвердительно
afresh снова
after за (inst.), после (gen.)
afterward после, потом, спустя
again опять
against против (gen.)
age возраст
agency агентство
agent действующая сила, агент, представитель
aggression агрессия
aggressive агрессивный
agitation агитация, волнение
ago тому назад
long ago давно
agony агония
agree (to) соглашаться
agreeable приятный, согласный
agreement договор, контракт, соглашение

agriculture агрикультура
ah! ах
ahead вперёд, впереди
aid помощь (f.)
aim цель (f.)
aimless бесцельный
air воздух
airfield аэродром
airplane аэроплан, самолёт
airy воздушный
alarm тревога
alarm clock будильник
alas! увы!
album альбом
alcohol алкоголь (m.)
algebra алгебра
alien чужой
alike равно
all весь (вся, всё, все)
alley переулок
alliance союз
allot (to) наделять
allow (to) позволять, пускать, разрешать
allure (to) увлекать, соблазнить
alluring привлекательный, заманчивый
ally (to) соединяться
almond миндаль
almost почти
alone один, одинокий
to leave alone оставить в покое
along вдоль (gen.) по (dat.)
alongside рядом
aloud вслух
alphabet азбука, алфавит
already уже
also и, тоже, также
altar алтарь (m.)
alter (to) изменять, переделать
alteration изменение
alternate (to) чередовать (ся)
although хотя
altitude высота
altruism альтруизм
always всегда
amaze (to) удивлять
amazement удивление, изумление
amazing изумительный, удивительный
ambassador посол
amber янтарь (m.)
ambition амбиция
ambitious честолюбивый
America Америка
American американский
amiable любезный
among между (inst.), среди (gen.)
amorous любовный
amount количество
amusement забава, развлечение

analysis разбо́р, ана́лиз
anatomy анато́мия
anchor я́корь (m.)
ancient стари́нный
and и, да
anew сно́ва
angel а́нгел
anger гнев
angle у́гол
angry (to be) зли́ться, рассерди́ться, серди́ться
angry злой, раздражённый, серди́тый
animal живо́тное
animated живо́й, одушевлённый
animatedly оживлённо, жи́во
animation одушевле́ние, увлече́ние
animosity озлобле́ние
anniversary годовщи́на
announce (to) объявля́ть
announcement объявле́ние
announcer ди́ктор (radio or T. V.)
annoy (to) раздража́ть
annoyance доса́да, неприя́тность (f.)
annually ежего́дно
another друго́й
answer (to) отвеча́ть
answer отве́т
ant мураве́й
anticipate (to) ожида́ть
antique стари́нный
anxiety трево́га, забо́та
anxious озабо́ченный
any вся́кий, любо́й
anybody кто уго́дно, кто́-нибудь
anyhow как уго́дно, ка́к-нибудь
apartment кварти́ра
apology извине́ние
apparatus аппара́т
apparently ви́дно, очеви́дно, повиди́мому
appear (to) обознача́ться, появля́ться, явля́ться
to appear to каза́ться
appearance вид, нару́жность, явле́ние
appease (to) успока́ивать
appetite аппети́т
appetizing аппети́тный
applaud (to) аплоди́ровать
apple я́блоко
appoint (to) назнача́ть
appreciate (to) цени́ть
approach (to) бли́зиться, подходи́ть, приближа́ться
approach подхо́д
approximate (to) приближа́ться
approximate приблизи́тельный
approximately о́коло (gen.), приблизи́тельно
apricot абрико́с
April апре́ль (m.)
apron пере́дник, фа́ртук

architect архите́ктор
ardent жа́ркий, пы́лкий, стра́стный
ardor пыл
area пло́щадь (f.)
argue (to) спо́рить
argument спор, аргуме́нт
arid сухо́й
arithmetic арифме́тика
arm рука́
armchair кре́сло
army а́рмия
aroma арома́т
aromatic аромати́ческий
around вокру́г (gen.), круго́м
arouse (to) возбужда́ть
arrange (to) аранжи́ровать, ула́дить, устра́ивать
arrangement устро́йство, расположе́ние
arrest аре́ст
to arrest взять под аре́ст
arrival прие́зд, прихо́д
arrive (to) приезжа́ть, приходи́ть
arson поджо́г
art иску́сство, худо́жество
article статья́
artificial фальши́вый, иску́сственный
artist худо́жник
artistic артисти́ческий, худо́жественный
as как
as if как бу́дто
as far as до
as soon as как то́лько
as though бу́дто
ascent подъём
ash tray пе́пельница
ashamed (to be) стесня́ться
ask (to) проси́ть, спра́шивать
asleep (to fall) засыпа́ть
asparagus спа́ржа
aspiration устремле́ние
aspirin аспири́н
assemble (to) собира́ть (ся)
assent согла́сие
assert (to) утвержда́ть, дока́зывать
assertion утвержде́ние
assimilate (to) осво́ить
assist (to) помога́ть
assistant помо́щник
association ассоциа́ция
assortment ассортиме́нт
assurance увере́ние
assure (to) уверя́ть
assured уве́ренный
asterisk звёздочка
astonish (to) удивля́ть
astonished (to be) поража́ться
astonishment удивле́ние
at в (prep.), у (gen.)
at first внача́ле
at last наконе́ц
athlete атле́т

athletic спорти́вный
atlas а́тлас
atmosphere атмосфе́ра
atomic а́томный
attach (to) привя́зывать
attached привя́занный
attachment привя́занность, приспособле́ние
attack припа́док
attain (to) достига́ть
attempt (to) про́бовать, пыта́ться
attempt попы́тка
attend (to) прису́тствовать
attention внима́ние
attentively внима́тельно
attic мезони́н, черда́к
attitude отноше́ние
attract (to) привлека́ть
attractive интере́сный, привлека́тельный
auction аукцио́н
audibly слы́шно
audience пу́блика
August а́вгуст
aunt тётя
author а́втор, писа́тель
authority авторите́т, власть, влия́ние
autobiography автобиогра́фия
autocracy автокра́тия
automatic автомати́ческий
automobile автомоби́ль (m.)
autonomy автоно́мия
autumn о́сень (f.)
available нали́чный, предоста́вленный в распоряже́ние
avenue бульва́р
aversion антипа́тия
aviation авиа́ция
avoid (to) избега́ть
awaken (to) разбуди́ть, просну́ться
awakening пробужде́ние
away! прочь!
awfully стра́шно, ужа́сно
awkward нело́вкий, неуклю́жий

B

baby ребёнок
bachelor холостя́к
back спина́
back за́дний (adj.), обра́тно, наза́д (adv.)
backbone хребе́т
backing подде́ржка
backward наза́д
bacon беко́н
bad плохо́й, скве́рный
badly ду́рно, пло́хо, скве́рно
bag мешо́к
baggage бага́ж
bake (to) печь
baked печёный
balance бала́нс
balcony балко́н

bald (headed) лы́сый
ball мяч, шар
ballet бале́т
banana бана́н
bandage (to) бинтова́ть
bank банк (savings)
bar (to) устра́ивать препя́тствие,
    прегражда́ть
bar полоса́, брусо́к
barber парикма́хер
barbershop парикма́херская
bare (to) обнажа́ть, раскрыва́ть
bare го́лый
bargain (to) торгова́ться
bark (to) ла́ять
bark кора́
barren неплодоро́дный
barrier барье́р
base осно́ва, ба́зис
basement подва́л
baseness по́длость (f.)
bashful засте́нчивый
bashfulness засте́нчивость
basin, ми́ска
basis ба́за, осно́ва
basket корзи́на
bath ва́нна
bathe (to) купа́ться
bathrobe хала́т
bathroom ва́нная
be (to) быть, быва́ть (to be some-
    times)
beach пляж
beam луч
bear (to) носи́ть, терпе́ть
bear медве́дь
beard борода́
beast зверь (m.)
beat (to) бить, би́ться
beautiful краси́вый, прекра́сный
beauty краса́, красота́
because потому́ что
beckon (to) подозва́ть
become (to) де́латься, станови́ться,
    ста́ться
bed крова́ть (f.), посте́ль (f.)
bedroom спа́льня
bee пчела́
beer пи́во
beet свёкла
before впереди́ (adv.), до (gen.)
    пе́ред (inst.)
beforehand зара́нее
beg (to) проси́ть
begin (to) начина́ть, стать
beginning нача́ло
    from the beginning снача́ла
behavior поведе́ние
behind за (acc. and inst.), позади́
    (gen.), позади́ (adv.)
belief ве́ра
believe (to) ве́рить, ду́мать
bell ко́локол

belong (to) принадлежа́ть
below внизу́
belt по́яс
bench скамья́
bend (to) гнуть, нагиба́ть
bend поворо́т
berry я́года
beside по́дле (gen.), ря́дом с (inst.)
besides кро́ме (gen.), поми́мо (gen.),
    сверх (gen.)
best лу́чший
betray (to) изменя́ть
better лу́чший (adj.), лу́чше (adv.)
between ме́жду (inst.)
beyond по ту сто́рону, по́зже
Bible би́блия
bicarbonate бикарбона́т
bicycle велосипе́д
big большо́й, кру́пный
bill счёт, законопрое́кт
billion биллио́н, миллиа́рд
bind (to) свя́зывать
binding переплёт
biography биогра́фия
biologist био́лог
biology биоло́гия
birch tree берёза
bird пти́ца
birth рожде́ние
birthday день рожде́ния
bite (to) куса́ть, укуси́ть
bite уку́с
bitter го́рький
bitterness озлобле́ние
black чёрный
blanket одея́ло
blend (to) сме́шивать
blessing благослове́ние
blind слепо́й
blindness слепота́
bliss блаже́нство
blizzard пурга́
block кварта́л
blood кровь (f.)
bloom расцвета́ть
blouse блу́зка, ко́фточка
blow дуть
blow уда́р
blue голубо́й, си́ний
blush (to) красне́ть
board, blackboard доска́
boarding house пансио́н
boat ло́дка
body ко́рпус, те́ло
boil (to) кипе́ть
boiled варёный
bold сме́лый
bone кость (f.)
book кни́га
bookstore кни́жный магази́н
bore (to) наску́чить, надоеда́ть
bored (to be) скуча́ть
boring ску́чный

born (to be) роди́ться
borrow (to) одолжа́ть
both о́ба (m., n.), о́бе (f.)
bottle буты́лка
bottom дно
boulevard бульва́р
boundary грани́ца, рубе́ж
bow (to) кла́няться
box коро́бка, сунду́к, я́щик
boy ма́льчик
brag (to) хва́стать (ся)
braid коса́
brain мозг
brake (to) тормози́ть
brake то́рмоз
brassiere ли́фчик
brave хра́брый
bravely сме́ло
bread хлеб
break (to) лома́ть, наруша́ть
break разры́в, перело́м
breakfast за́втрак
    to have breakfast за́втракать
breast грудь (f.)
breathe (to) вздыха́ть, дыша́ть
breeze ве́тер
bridge мост
brief кра́ткий, сокращённый
briefcase портфе́ль
bright я́ркий, све́тлый
brighten (to) проясне́ть
brilliance блеск
brilliantly блестя́щее
bring (to) приводи́ть, привози́ть,
    приноси́ть
brisk бо́дрый, живо́й
broad широ́кий
broken ло́манный, сло́манный
brook руче́й
broom метла́, ве́ник
brother брат
brown кори́чневый
brush щётка, кисть
brutal жесто́кий
bubble пузы́рь (m.)
build (to) стро́ить
building зда́ние
bundle у́зел, паке́т
burn (to) горе́ть, жечь, сгора́ть
burst (to) ло́паться
bury (to) хорони́ть
bus авто́бус
bus stop остано́вка (авто́буса)
business де́ло
busy за́нятый
but а, да, но, одна́ко
butter ма́сло
butterfly ба́бочка
button пу́говица
buttonhole пе́тля
buy (to) покупа́ть
by у (gen.), по (dat.), ми́мо (gen.)
    by the way кста́ти

C

cab наёмный экипа́ж, та́кси
cabbage капу́ста
cake кекс, торт
calamity бе́дствие
calculate (to) рассчи́тывать
calculation расчёт, счёт
calendar календа́рь
call (to) звать, оклика́ть
 to call on заходи́ть
calm (to) успока́ивать
camp ла́герь (m.)
can (to be able) мочь
candidate кандида́т
candle свеча́
candy конфе́та
cane па́лка
cap ке́пка, ша́пка
capable спосо́бный
capacity объём, вмести́мость
capital city столи́ца
capitalist капитали́ст
captain капита́н
card ка́рточка
care забо́та, осторо́жность
career карье́ра
carefree беззабо́тный
careful аккура́тный, осторо́жный,
 тща́тельный
carefully внима́тельно, осторо́жно
careless небре́жный,
 невнима́тельный
caress (to) ласка́ть
caress ла́ска
carpenter пло́тник
carrots морко́вь (f.)
carry (to) вози́ть (by conveyance),
 носи́ть (on foot)
carry out (to) исполня́ть,
 производи́ть
case слу́чай (m.)
cashier касси́р
cat ко́шка
catch (to) лови́ть, пойма́ть
category катего́рия
cathedral собо́р
cattle скот
cause причи́на
 without cause беспричи́нно
cautiously осторо́жно
caviar икра́
cease (to) переста́ть
ceiling потоло́к
celebrate (to) пра́здновать
celery сельдере́й
cemetery кла́дбище
censorship цензу́ра
cent цент
center центр
central центра́льный
century век, столе́тие
cereal ка́ша

ceremony церемо́ния
certain уве́ренный, определённый
certainly коне́чно, непреме́нно,
 обяза́тельно
chain цепь (f.)
chair стул
chairman председа́тель (m.)
chalk мел
challenge (to) вызыва́ть
champagne шампа́нское
champion чемпио́н
chance слу́чай, шанс
 by chance случа́йно
change (to) изменя́ть, меня́ть (ся),
 преобража́ть
 to change one's clothes пере-
 оде́ть (ся)
 to change one's mind переду́мать
change измене́ние, переме́на,
 ме́лочь (f.) (money)
chapter глава́
character хара́ктер
characteristics характери́стика
charge (to) обвиня́ть, назнача́ть
 це́ну (a price)
charge обвине́ние
charm очарова́ние, пре́лесть (f.)
charming очарова́тельный,
 преле́стный
chart ка́рта
chat (to) болта́ть
cheap дешёвый
cheat шу́лер (at cards), обма́нщик
check (to) проверя́ть
check чек
cheek щека́
cheerful весёлый
cheese сыр
chemical хими́ческий
chemist хи́мик
chemistry хи́мия
cherry ви́шня, чере́шня
chess ша́хматы
chest грудь (f.) (part of the body);
 сунду́к, я́щик, комо́д
chic шика́рный
chicken ку́рица
chief глава́
chief (adj.) гла́вный
child ребёнок; дитя́
children де́ти, ребя́та
chimney труба́
chin подборо́док
china фарфо́р
chocolate шокола́д
choice вы́бор
choose (to) выбира́ть
chop (to) руби́ть
chopped ру́бленый
chord акко́рд
chorus хор
Christianity христиа́нство
Christmas рождество́

church це́рковь
cigar сига́ра
cigarette папиро́са
cigarette case папиро́сница,
 портсига́р
circle круг
circumstance обстоя́тельство
circus цирк
citizen граждани́н (m.),
 гражда́нка (f.)
city го́род
civil шта́тский
civilization цивилиза́ция
claim прете́нзия, тре́бование
clap (to) аплоди́ровать
class класс
classical класси́ческий
classification классифика́ция
clause предложе́ние (gram.)
clean (to) стира́ть, чи́стить
clean чи́стый
cleanliness чистота́
clear зво́нкий, я́сный
clear up (to) проясня́ть
clever у́мный
climate кли́мат
climb поднима́ться
clinic амбулато́рия, кли́ника
clock часы́
close (to) закрыва́ть
close те́сный
close бли́зко от
closed закры́тый
cloth мате́рия
clothes оде́жда
cloud о́блако, ту́ча
cloudy па́смурный
club клуб
clumsy неуклю́жий, нело́вкий
coal у́голь
coarse гру́бый
coat пальто́
cobweb паути́на
coffee ко́фе
coffeepot кофе́йник
cognac конья́к
coin моне́та
coincide (to) совпада́ть
coincidence совпаде́ние
cold на́сморк, просту́да, холо́дный
 to catch cold простуди́ться
coldness хо́лод
collar воротни́к
colleague колле́га
collect (to) собира́ть (ся)
collection сбо́рник
college ко́лледж
collide (to) ста́лкиваться
collision столкнове́ние
color (to) кра́сить
color цвет
colored кра́шеный, цветно́й
comb (to) причёсывать (ся)

comb гребешо́к
combination комбина́ция, соедине́ние
combine (to) объединя́ть, сочета́ть
combined свя́занный, совме́стный
comedy коме́дия
comfort (to) утеша́ть
comfort удо́бство, утеше́ние, ую́т
comfortable удо́бный, ую́тный
comic смешно́й, юмористи́ческий
command (to) кома́ндовать,
  прика́зывать
command прика́з
commerce торго́вля, комме́рция
commission поруче́ние
commit (to) доверя́ть, соверша́ть
committee коми́ссия
common о́бщий, просто́й
communicate (to) сообща́ть
compact пу́дреница
company компа́ния, фи́рма
compare (to) сра́внивать
comparison сравне́ние
compel (to) принужда́ть, заставля́ть
compensation компенса́ция
compete (to) сопе́рничать
competition конкуре́нция
compile (to) составля́ть
complain (to) жа́ловаться
complaint жа́лоба
complete по́лный
complexion цвет лица́
complicated сло́жный
complication осложне́ние,
  усложне́ние
compliment комплиме́нт
compose (to) сочиня́ть
composer компози́тор
composition сочине́ние
composure хладнокро́вие
compote компо́т
compromise компроми́сс
compulsory обяза́тельный
comrade това́рищ
conceal (to) пря́тать (ся),
  скрыва́ть (ся), таи́ть (ся)
conceited кичли́вый
concentrate (to) сосредото́чивать
concept иде́я, поня́тие
concern (to) каса́ться
concerning относи́тельно, насчёт,
  о (prep.) про (acc.)
concert конце́рт
conclude (to) заключа́ть
conclusion заключе́ние
condition положе́ние, состоя́ние,
  усло́вие
conduct (to) води́ть (lead),
  дирижи́ровать (orchestra),
  управля́ть (rule)
conduct поведе́ние
conductor дирижёр (orchestra),
  проводни́к (wire, train)
confession и́споведь

confidence дове́рие, уве́ренность
confident уве́ренный
confirm (to) утвержда́ть
conflict конфли́кт
confused пу́танный, расте́рянный,
  смущённый
confusion смуще́ние, сумбу́р
congratulate (to) поздравля́ть
congratulation поздравле́ние
connect (to) свя́зывать,
  соединя́ть (ся)
connection связь
conquer (to) побежда́ть
conscience со́весть (f.)
conscious сознаю́щий, созна́тельный
consciously созна́тельно
consent (to) соглаша́ться
consent согла́сие
conservation сохране́ние
conservative консервати́вный
consider (to) засчи́тывать,
  обду́мывать, счита́ть (ся)
consist (to) заключа́ться, состоя́ть
constant постоя́нный
constitution конститу́ция
constructive конструкти́вный
consul ко́нсул
consulate ко́нсульство
consultant консульта́нт
consumption чахо́тка, туберкулёз
contain (to) содержа́ть
contemporary совреме́нный
contempt презре́ние
contemptuous презри́тельный
content (to) удовлетворя́ть
contents содержа́ние
continent контине́нт
continuation продолже́ние
continue (to) продолжа́ть
continuity непреры́вность
continuously непреры́вно
contract контра́кт
contradict (to) противоре́чить
contradiction противоре́чие
contrary проти́вный
  on the contrary наоборо́т,
  напро́тив
contrast контра́ст,
  противополо́жность (f.)
control контро́ль
control oneself (to) сде́рживаться
convenient удо́бный
convention съезд
conversation бесе́да, разгово́р
converse (to) бесе́довать,
  разгова́ривать
conviction убежде́ние
convince (to) уверя́ть, убежда́ть
cook (to) гото́вить
cook по́вар
cookie пече́нье
cool прохла́дный, хладнокро́вный
  (person)

copper медь
copy (to) копи́ровать, перепи́сывать
copy ко́пия, экземпля́р
coquette коке́тка
cord верёвка, шнур, шпага́т
cordial серде́чный, тёплый
cork про́бка
corkscrew што́пор
corn кукуру́за, мозо́ль
corned beef солони́на
corner у́гол
corpse труп
correct (to) исправля́ть, поправля́ть
correct ве́рный, пра́вильный
correspond (to) перепи́сываться
correspondence перепи́ска
correspondent корреспонде́нт
corridor коридо́р
corset корсе́т
cosmetics косме́тика
cost (to) сто́ить
cost цена́
cotton бума́жный
couch куше́тка
cough (to) ка́шлять
counsel (to) сове́товать
counsel сове́т
country дере́вня, страна́
  country house да́ча
couple па́ра
courage дух, му́жество, сме́лость,
  (f.), хра́брость (f.)
courageous сме́лый
course курс
courteous ве́жливый
courtesy ве́жливость, (f.),
  любе́зность (f)
cousin кузе́н (m.), кузи́на (f.),
  двою́родный брат, двою́родная
  сестра́
cover (to) накрыва́ть, покрыва́ть
covered кры́тый
covering покры́шка
cow коро́ва
coward трус
cozy ую́тный
crackle (to) треща́ть
cradle колыбе́ль
cranberry клю́ква
cranky капри́зный
  to be cranky капри́зничать
craving жа́жда, жела́ние
creak (to) скрипе́ть
cream крем, сли́вки
crease скла́дка
create (to) создава́ть
creative тво́рческий
creep (to) по́лзать
crime преступле́ние
criminal престу́пник
crisis кри́зис
critical крити́ческий
criticism кри́тика

crooked кривой
cross (to) переходи́ть
  to cross out зачёркивать
cross крест
crossing перехо́д
crowd толпа́
crown коро́на, коро́нка (dental)
cruel жесто́кий
cruelty жесто́кость (f.)
crush (to) уничтожа́ть
crust кора́
cry (to) пла́кать
cry крик
cucumber огуре́ц
cultural интеллиге́нтный,
  культу́рный
culture культу́ра
cunning хи́трый
cup ча́шка
cupboard шкаф
cure (to) излечивать
cure излече́ние, сре́дство
curiosity любопы́тство
curious любозна́тельный,
  любопы́тный
curly кудря́вый
current тече́ние, ток (electric)
cursed прокля́тый
curtail (to) сокраща́ть
curtain за́навес
curved криво́й
cushion поду́шка
custom нра́вы, обы́чай
cut (to) нареза́ть, ре́зать, поре́зать
cutlet котле́та
cynic ци́ник
cynical цини́ческий

D

daily ежедне́вно
dam плоти́на
damage поврежде́ние
damned прокля́тый
damp сыро́й
dampness сы́рость (f.)
dance (to) танцева́ть
dance бал, та́нец
danger опа́сность (f.)
dangerous опа́сный
dare (to) сметь
daring де́рзкий, сме́лый
dark тёмный
darken (to) темне́ть
darkness темнота́
darn (to) што́пать
date число́, (of time); фи́ник (fruit)
daughter дочь (f.)
dawn заря́, рассве́т
day день, (m.), су́тки (24 hours)
  day after tomorrow послеза́втра
  day before yesterday позавчера́
daydream (to) фантази́ровать,
  мечта́ть

daydream мечта́
dazzle (to) ослепля́ть
dazzling ослепи́тельный
dead мёртвый
deaf глухо́й
dealer торго́вец
dear дорого́й, ми́лый
death смерть
debate дискуссия, спор
debt долг
decay (to) по́ртиться
deceased (the) поко́йник
deceive (to) обма́нывать
December дека́брь (m.)
decency прили́чие
decent поря́дочный, прили́чный
deceptive обма́нчивый
decide (to) реша́ть
decision реше́ние
deck па́луба
declaration заявле́ние, деклара́ция
decline (to) отка́зываться
decline упа́док
decrease (to) уменьша́ть
decree ука́з, прика́з
deep глубо́кий
defect дефе́кт, недоста́ток, брак
defend (to) защища́ть
defenseless беззащи́тный
define (to) определя́ть
definite определённый
definition определе́ние
deft ло́вкий
defy (to) вызыва́ть
degree гра́дус, сте́пень (f.) (extent)
delay (to) заде́рживать, ме́длить
delay опозда́ние
delegate делега́т
deliberate наме́ренный,
  рассчи́танный
delicacy то́нкость (f.), чу́ткость (f.)
delicate то́нкий, чу́ткий
delicious вку́сный
delight восто́рг, отра́да, наслажде́ние
delightful восхити́тельный,
  преле́стный
demand (to) тре́бовать
demand спрос, тре́бование
denial отрица́ние
dense густо́й
dental зубно́й
deny (to) отрица́ть
depart (to) пойти́, пое́хать, уходи́ть,
  уезжа́ть
department отде́л, отделе́ние,
  факульте́т (of a university)
departure отхо́д, отъе́зд
depend on (to) бази́ровать, зави́сеть
  (от)
dependable положи́тельный
dependence зави́симость (f.)
deposit (to) отлага́ть
deprivation лише́ние

deprive (to) лиша́ть
depth глубина́
descend (to) происходи́ть,
  спуска́ться
descent происхожде́ние
despise (to) презира́ть
description описа́ние
desert пусты́ня
deserted поки́нутый
deserve (to) заслу́живать
deserving досто́йный
desire жела́ние
desk пи́сьменный стол
despair отча́яние
desperately отча́янно
despise (to) презира́ть
dessert десе́рт, сла́дкое
destiny жре́бий, судьба́
destroy (to) разруша́ть, уничтожа́ть
destruction разруше́ние
detach (to) отделя́ть
detail дета́ль (f.), подро́бность (f.),
  ме́лочь
detailed подро́бный
detain (to) заде́рживать
determination определе́ние
determine (to) определя́ть
detest (to) ненави́деть
develop (to) проявля́ть, развива́ть
development проявле́ние, разви́тие,
  рост
device прибо́р
devil бес, чорт, дья́вол
devise (to) приду́мывать
devotion на́божность (f.),
  пре́данность (f.)
dew роса́
diagnosis диа́гноз
dial цифербла́т
dialect диале́кт
diameter диа́метр
diamond бриллиа́нт, алма́з
dictionary слова́рь (m.)
die (to) сконча́ться, умира́ть
diet дие́та
differ (to) отлича́ться,
  различа́ть (ся)
difference ра́зница, разногла́сие (of
  opinion), ра́зность (f.)
different друго́й, разли́чный, ра́зный
difficult тру́дный
difficulty затрудне́ние
dig (to) копа́ть, рыть
digest (to) перева́ривать
digestion пищеваре́ние
dignity досто́инство
diligence усе́рдие
diligent приле́жный, усе́рдный
dim нея́сный, сму́тный
dimension разме́р
diminish (to) па́дать, убавля́ть,
  уменьша́ть
dimple я́мочка

dine (to) обе́дать
dining room столо́вая
dinner обе́д
diplomacy диплома́тия
direct (to) направля́ть, обраща́ть,
　руководи́ть, управля́ть
direct (adj.) прямо́й
direction направле́ние
director дире́ктор, режиссёр
　(theater)
dirt грязь (f.)
dirty гря́зный, чума́зый
disadvantage невы́года
disagreeable неприя́тный, неуго́дный
disappear (to) исчеза́ть
disappoint (to) разочарова́ть
　to be disappointed быть
　разочаро́ванным
disappointed разочаро́ванный
disappointment разочарова́ние
disapproving неодобри́тельный
disaster бе́дствие
disastrous поги́бельный
discipline дисципли́на
disclose (to) раскрыва́ть
discomfort неудо́бство
discontent недово́льство
discount ски́дка
discourage (to) обескура́живать,
　отбива́ть охо́ту
discourteous нелюбе́зный
discourtesy нелюбе́зность (f.)
discover (to) находи́ть, открыва́ть
discovery откры́тие
discretion осторо́жность (f.),
　усмотре́ние
discuss (to) обсужда́ть, переговори́ть,
　разбира́ть
discussion диску́ссия,
　обсужде́ние
disdain презре́ние
disease боле́знь (f.)
disgrace позо́р
disgust отвраще́ние
dish блю́до (course)
dishes посу́да
dishonest нече́стный
disk диск, круг
disorder беспоря́док
display (to) пока́зывать
displeasure неудово́льствие
disposition нрав, скло́нность (f),
　хара́ктер
dispute (to) спо́рить
disrespectfully неуважи́тельно
dissatisfaction недово́льство
dissatisfied недово́льный
distance расстоя́ние
distant далёкий
distinct отчётливый, я́сный
distinction отли́чие, разли́чие
distinguish (to) отлича́ть,
　различа́ть

distraction рассе́янность
distribute (to) выдава́ть, раздава́ть
district райо́н
distrust (to) не доверя́ть
distrust недове́рие
distrustful недове́рчивый
disturb (to) беспоко́ить, меша́ть,
　наруша́ть, трево́жить
divide (to) дели́ть (ся), разделя́ть
　(ся)
divine боже́ственный
division деле́ние, разделе́ние
divorce разво́д
dizzy (to be) чу́вствовать голово-
　круже́ние
do (to) де́лать
doctor врач, до́ктор
doctrine уче́ние, доктри́на
document бума́га, докуме́нт
dog пёс, соба́ка
doll ку́кла
dollar до́ллар
domestic семе́йный, (family),
　ме́стный
door дверь (f.)
dose до́за
double вдво́е, двойно́й
doubt (to) сомнева́ться
doubt сомне́ние
dough те́сто
down вниз
　to get down слеза́ть, спуска́ться
　сходи́ть
downstairs вниз, внизу́
doze (to) дрема́ть
dozen дю́жина
draft чертёж, план, отбо́р для
　специа́льной це́ли
drag (to) таска́ть, тяну́ть
drag то́рмаз
drama дра́ма
drastic радика́льный
draw (to) рисова́ть (paint)
draw out (to) вынима́ть
drawer я́щик
dread боя́знь (f.), стра́шный (adj.)
dream (to) сни́ться
dream сон, сновиде́ние
dress (to) одева́ть (ся)
dress пла́тье
dressing-gown хала́т
dressmaker портни́ха
drink (to) пить
drink напи́ток
drive (to) гоня́ть, ката́ться (pleasure)
　пра́вить
driver шофёр
drop (to) роня́ть
drop ка́пля
drown (to) тону́ть, топи́ть
　(something else) топи́ться (oneself)
drugstore апте́ка
drum бараба́н

drunk пья́ный
drunkard пья́ница
dry (to) суши́ть, утира́ть, со́хнуть
dry сухо́й
duck у́тка
due (adj.) сле́дуемый
duet дуэ́т
dull му́тный, па́смурный, тупо́й
dumb глу́пый (stupid) немо́й
　deaf and dumb глухонемо́й
during во-вре́мя
dust пыль (f.)
duty обя́занность (f.) пови́нность
　(f.)
dwelling жили́ще
dye кра́ска

E

each ка́ждый
eagle орёл
ear у́хо
early ра́нний, ра́но (adv.)
earn (to) зараба́тывать
earnest серьёзный
earring серьга́
earth земля́
east восто́к
eastern восто́чный
easy лёгкий
eat (to) есть, ку́шать
echo э́хо
economically экономи́ческий
economize (to) эконо́мить
economy расчётливость (f.)
edge край (m.)
edit (to) редакти́ровать
edition изда́ние
editor реда́ктор
educate (to) воспи́тывать, дава́ть
　образова́ние
educated интеллиге́нтный,
　культу́рный, образо́ванный
education образова́ние
effect впечатле́ние, де́йствие
effective эффе́ктный
efficient де́йственный
effort уси́лие
egg яйцо́
egoist эгои́ст
eight во́семь
eighteen восемна́дцать
eighteenth восемна́дцатый
eighth восьмо́й
eightieth восьмидеся́тый
either та́кже, тот и́ли друго́й
　either . . . or и́ли . . . и́ли
elastic (n.) рези́на
elbow ло́коть (m.)
elder ста́рший
elderly пожило́й
election избра́ние, вы́боры

electric электрический
electricity электричество
elegant изящный, элегантный
element элемент
elementary начáльный,
   элементáрный
elephant слон
elevator лифт, элевáтор
eleven одиннадцать
eleventh одиннадцатый
eliminate (to) исключáть
else (adv.) ещё, крóме
   No one else has come. Никтó
   бóльше не приходил.
elsewhere где-нибудь в другóм
   мéсте
embarrassed сконфýженный,
   смущённый
   to become embarrassed
   сконфýзиться
embarrassment затруднéние,
   смущéние
embassy посóльство
embrace (to) обнимáть
embroidered расшитый
emerge (to) появляться
emergency крáйняя необходимость
emigrant эмигрáнт
eminent выдающийся, знаменитый
emotion волнéние, эмóция
emphasize (to) подчёркивать,
   заострять
emphatic эмфатический
employ (to) давáть рабóту,
   нанимáть
employee слýжащий
employment занятие, рабóта,
   слýжба
empty (to) выливáть
empty пустóй
enamel эмáль (f.)
enclose (to) окружáть, вклáдывать
encore бис
encourage (to) ободрять, поощрять
encouragement ободрéние
end (to) кончáть (ся), окáнчивать
end конéц, предéл, окончáние
endeavor (to) пытáться, старáться
endeavor попытка
endurance выдержка, терпéние
endure (to) выдéрживать,
   переносить, терпéть
enemy враг
energy энéргия
engine машина, мотóр
engineer инженéр, механик
English английский
enjoy (to) веселиться (oneself),
   наслаждáться
enjoyment наслаждéние
enlarge (to) увеличивать
enormous громáдный, огрóмный
enough достáточно, довóльно

enter (to) входить, вступáть (on
   foot), въезжáть (by vehicle)
entertain (to) развлекáть, угощáть
entertainment развлечéние
enthusiasm востóрг, энтузиáзм
entire цéлый, сплошнóй
entirely совсéм
entrance вход, въезд
entrust (to) поверять, доверять
envelope конвéрт
envious завистливый
envy (to) завидовать
envy зáвисть (f.)
equal рáвный
equality рáвенство
equalize (to) урáвнивать
equilibrium равновéсие
era эпóха, э́ра
erase (to) стирáть
eraser резинка
err (to) заблуждáться, ошибáться
errand поручéние
error ошибка
escalator эскалáтор
escape (to) избежáть, спастись
escort (to) сопровождáть
especially осóбенно, специáльно
establish (to) устрáивать
estate имéние
esteem (to) уважáть
esteem уважéние
estimate (to) оцéнивать, составлять
   смéту
estimate оцéнка, смéта
eternal вéчный
eternity вéчность (f.)
ether эфир
ethics э́тика
European европéйский
evacuate (to) очищáть,
   эвакуировать
eve канýн
even (adj) глáдкий, рóвный
even (adv.) дáже, хоть
evening вéчер
   in the evening вéчером
event случай (m.), событие
ever всегдá
   forever навсегдá
   ever since с тех пор
   hardly ever почти никогдá
every всякий, кáждый, любóй
everyone кáждый
everything всё
everywhere вездé, повсюду
evidence доказáтельство,
   свидéтельство
evident я́вный
evidently видно
evil (n.) зло
evil (adj.) дурнóй, злой
exact тóчный, аккурáтный
exacting трéбовательный

exactly именно, тóчно
exaggerate (to) преувеличивать
exaggerated преувеличенный
exaggeration преувеличéние
examination экзáмен
examine (to) осмáтривать,
   рассмáтривать, экзаменовáть
example примéр
   for example напримéр
exceed (to) превышáть, переходить
   границы
excel (to) превосходить
excellent отличный, прекрáсный
except (prep.) крóме (gen.)
exception исключéние
exceptionally исключительно
excess излишек
excessive чрезмéрный
exchange (to) обмéнивать
exchange обмéн
excite (to) возбуждáть
excitement волнéние
exclaim (to) áхнуть, воскликнуть
exclude (to) исключáть
excursion экскýрсия
excuse (to) извинять, прощáть
   Excuse me. Извините, простите
excuse оправдáние
execution исполнéние (of an idea)
exercise (to) упражнять
exercise упражнéние
exertion напряжéние, усилие
exhaust (to) вытягивать, изнурять
exhibition выставка
exist (to) существовáть
existence существовáние
exit выход
expand (to) расширять (ся),
   увеличивать (ся)
expansion разложéние, экспáнсия,
   увеличéние
expect (to) ожидáть
expectation ожидáние, чáяние
expel (to) исключáть
expense расхóд
expensive дорогóй
experience (to) переживáть
experience óпыт, эксперимéнт
experienced óпытный
experimental прóбный,
   эксперментáльный
expert знатóк, специалист
explain (to) объяснять
explanation объяснéние
explode (to) взрывáть
exploit (to) эксплуатировать
explore (to) исслéдовать
explosion взрыв
export э́кспорт
expose (to) разоблачáть,
   раскрывáть
express oneself (to) выражáть (ся)
expression выражéние

expressive экспресси́вный,
вырази́тельный
exquisite преле́стный
extend (to) выта́гивать, тяну́ться
extensive обши́рный, экстенси́вный
extent сте́пень (f.)
exterior вне́шний (adj.),
нару́жность (noun, f.)
external вне́шний
extinguish (to) туши́ть
extra осо́бенно, сверх, э́кстра
extraordinary чрезвыча́йный
extravagant нерасчётливый,
экстраваѓа́нтный
extreme кра́йний, чрезвыча́йный,
(adj.), кра́йность (noun, f.)
extremely весьма́, кра́йне
eye глаз
eyebrow бровь (f.)
eyeglasses очки́ (pl.)
eyelid ве́ко
eyesight зре́ние

F

fabric материа́л, мате́рия
face лицо́
face to face лицо́м к лицу́
facilitate (to) облегча́ть
facility лёгкость (f.)
fact факт
factory фа́брика
factual факти́ческий
faculty спосо́бность (f.), преподава́-
тельский персона́л
fade (to) вя́нуть, блёкнуть
fail (to) провали́ться (exam.),
слабе́ть
failure неуда́ча
faint (to) упа́сть в о́бморок
faint-hearted малоду́шие
fair справедли́вый, че́стный
faith ве́ра, дове́рие
faithful ве́рный
fall (to) па́дать
to let fall урони́ть
false фальши́вый
falsehood ложь (f.), непра́вда
fame изве́стность (f.), сла́ва
familiar знако́мый
to become familiar with ознако́-
миться
family семе́йный (adj.), семья́ (noun)
famous знамени́тый
fan вентиля́тор
fancy (noun) фанта́зия, воображе́ние
fantastic фантасти́ческий
far далёкий (adj.), далеко́ (adv.)
from far away и́здали
not far недалеко́
fare (to) пожива́ть
fare (carfare) пла́та за прое́зд
farewell проща́ние (n.)
Farewell! Проща́й! До свида́ния

farm фе́рма
farmer фе́рмер
farther да́льше
fascinating очарова́тельный,
увлека́тельный
fashion фасо́н, мо́да
fashionable мо́дный
fast кре́пкий, ско́рый (of speed)
fasten (to) привя́зывать
to fasten together скрепля́ть
fastidious разбо́рчивый
fat жир (noun), жи́рный,
то́лстый (adj.)
fatal поги́бельный, фата́льный
fate жре́бий (noun), судьба́
father оте́ц
fatherland оте́чество
faucet кран
fault вина́
favor ми́лость (f.), одолже́ние
favorite люби́мец (noun), люби́мый
(adj.)
fear (to) боя́ться
fear боя́знь (f.), страх
February февра́ль (m.)
federation федера́ция
fee вознагражде́ние, пла́та
feeble бесси́льный, сла́бый
feed (to) корми́ть, пита́ть
feel (to) ощуща́ть, чу́вствовать
feeling чу́вство
fellow па́рень (m.)
feminine же́нский
fencing фехтова́ние
fertility плодоро́дность (f.)
fervent пы́лкий, стра́стный
fetch (to) доста́ть, приноси́ть
fever жар
feverish лихора́дочный
few ма́ло, немно́го, не́сколько
fewer ме́ньше
fiber фи́бра, волокно́
fiction беллетри́стика, фи́кция
fictitious фикти́вный, вообража́емый
field по́ле
fifteen пятна́дцать
fifteenth пятна́дцатый
fifth пя́тый
fiftieth пятидеся́тый
fifty пятьдеся́т
fig инжи́р, фи́га
fight (to) боро́ться, дра́ться
fight борьба́, дра́ка
figure фигу́ра, ци́фра (number)
file (to) приня́ть к выполне́нию
зака́з, регистри́ровать и храни́ть
file напи́льник, картоте́ка
fill (to) наполня́ть
to fill in заполня́ть
fillet (meat) филе́
film фильм
filthy гря́зный
final оконча́тельный

finally наконе́ц
finances фина́нсы
financial фина́нсовый
find (to) находи́ть
to find out узнава́ть
fine (penalty) штраф
fine то́нкий
fine fellow! молоде́ц!
fine point то́нкость (f.)
finger па́лец
fingernail но́готь (m.)
finish (to) конча́ть (ся), ока́нчивать
finished ко́нчено, сде́лано
fire ого́нь (m.), пожа́р
fireplace ками́н
fireproof несгора́емый
firewood (pl.) дрова́
firm фи́рма (company), кре́пкий,
твёрдый (adj.)
first пе́рвый
at first сперва́
first-rate первокла́ссный
for the first time впервы́е
fish ры́ба
fist кула́к
fit (to) сиде́ть, подходи́ть
fit припа́док (attack)
five пять
fix (to) исправля́ть, починя́ть
flag флаг
flame пла́мя
flap (to) маха́ть
flash (to) блесну́ть, мелька́ть,
сверкну́ть
flashlight ручно́й электри́ческий
фона́рь
flat пло́ский, ро́вный
flattering ле́стный
flattery лесть (f.)
flavor арома́т
fleet флот
flesh сыро́е мя́со
flexible ги́бкий
flight бе́гство, отступле́ние, полёт
flirt (to) флиртова́ть
float (to) пла́вать
flood пото́к, наводне́ние
floor пол, эта́ж (story)
flour мука́
flourishing здоро́вый, цвету́щий
flow (to) течь
flower цвето́к
fluently бе́гло, свобо́дно
fluid жи́дкость, жи́дкий (noun, f.)
(adj.)
fly (to) лета́ть
fly му́ха
flying летучий
focus (to) сосредото́чивать,
наводи́ть на фо́кус
focus фо́кус
fog тума́н
fold (to) скла́дывать

fold скла́дка
folk (adj.) наро́дный
follow (to) следи́ть, сле́довать
following сле́дующий
fond не́жный, лю́бящий
food еда́, пи́ща
fool дура́к
foolish глу́пый
foolishness глу́пость (f.)
foot нога́, фут (of length)
  on foot пешко́м
football футбо́л
footstep шаг
for для (gen.), за (acc., inst.), на (extent of time)
  for the sake of ра́ди (gen.)
forbid (to) запреща́ть
force (to) заставля́ть, принужда́ть
force си́ла
forehead лоб
foreign иностра́нный
foreigner иностра́нец
foresight предви́дение
forest лес
forever наве́ки, навсегда́
forewarn (to) предупрежда́ть
forged фальсифици́рованный
forget (to) забыва́ть
forgetfulness забы́вчивость (f.)
forgive (to) извиня́ть, проща́ть
forgiveness проще́ние
fork ви́лка
form о́браз, фо́рма
formality форма́льность (f.)
formation строй
formed (to be) составля́ть (ся)
former бы́вший
formerly пре́жде, ра́ньше
formula фо́рмула
forsake (to) поки́нуть
fortieth сороково́й
fortunate счастли́вый, уда́чный
fortunately к сча́стью
fortune сча́стье, уда́ча, судьба́
forty со́рок
forward вперёд (adv.), передово́й (adj.)
found (to) создава́ть
foundation фунда́мент
founder основа́тель (m.)
fountain фонта́н
fountain pen авторуч́ка
four четы́ре
fourteen четы́рнадцать
fourteenth четы́рнадцатый
fourth четвёртый
fowl дома́шняя пти́ца
foyer пере́дняя, фойе́ (n. not decl.)
fragment кусо́к, отры́вок
fragrance арома́т
fragrant арома́тный
frame ра́ма
frank и́скренний, открове́нный

frankness открове́нность (f.)
fraud обма́н
free беспла́тно (gratis), свобо́дный
freedom во́льность (f.), свобо́да
freely свобо́дно
freeze (to) замерза́ть, замора́живать, ледени́ть, мёрзнуть
French францу́зский
frequently ча́сто
fresh све́жий
Friday пя́тница
fried жа́реный
friend друг (m.), подру́га (f.), прия́тель,-ница
friendly дру́жеский, приве́тливый
friendship дру́жба
fright испу́г, страх
frighten (to) пуга́ть, напуга́ть
  to become frightened испуга́ться
frightening стра́шный
frog лягу́шка
from из (gen.), от (gen.), с (gen.)
  from behind из-за
front фаса́д (noun), пере́дняя (adj.)
frost моро́з
frown (to) хму́риться
frozen мёрзлый, заморо́женный
fruit фрукт
fry (to) жа́рить (ся)
frying pan сковорода́
fuel горю́чее, то́пливо
fugitive бе́глый
fulfill (to) выполня́ть, исполня́ть
fulfillment выполне́ние, исполне́ние
full по́лный
fully вполне́
fun весе́лье, шу́тка (joke)
  to have fun весели́ться
function (to) де́йствовать
function фу́нкция
fund запа́с, фонд
fundamental основно́й, фундамента́льный
funeral по́хороны
funny заба́вный, смешно́й
fur мех
  fur coat шу́ба
furnace горн, печь, то́пка
furnish (to) обставля́ть
furniture ме́бель (f.), обстано́вка
fury бе́шенство, я́рость (f.)
fuss хло́поты, суета́
futile тще́тный
future бу́дущий (adj.), бу́дущее (noun)

G

gain (to) вы́играть (win)
  to gain weight полне́ть
gain дохо́ды
gallant гала́нтный
gallery галлере́я
gallon галло́н
gamble (to) игра́ть в аза́ртные и́гры

game игра́
garage гара́ж
garbage му́сор
garden сад
garlic чесно́к
garment предме́т оде́жды, пла́тье
gas газ
gasoline бензи́н, газоли́н
gates воро́та
gather (to) собира́ть (ся)
gauze газ, ма́рля
gay весёлый
gender род
general (adj.) о́бщий
  in general вообще́
generality неопределённость
generally обы́чно, вообще́, широко́
generation поколе́ние
generosity ще́дрость (f.)
generous ще́дрый
genius гениа́льность (f.), ге́ний
gentle мя́гкий
gentleman джентльме́н
genuine настоя́щий
geography геогра́фия
geometry геоме́трия
germ микро́б
German (adj.) неме́цкий
gesture жест
get (to) достава́ть (fetch), получа́ть (receive)
  to get along пожива́ть
  to get even with распла́чиваться
  to get up встава́ть
ghost привиде́ние
gift дар (talent), пода́рок
gifted спосо́бный, тала́нтливый
gigantic гига́нтский
girl де́вочка (little girl), де́вушка (young girl, unmarried)
give (to) дава́ть
  to give a present дари́ть
  to give back возвраща́ть, отдава́ть
  to give out выдава́ть, раздава́ть
glad рад, ра́достный
gladly охо́тно
glance взгляд
glands железа́, же́лезы
glass стака́н (drinking), стекло́, стекля́нный (adj.)
glasses очки́
gleam (to) мелька́ть
glimpse мелька́ние, мимолётное впечатле́ние
glitter (to) блесте́ть, сверка́ть
globe гло́бус, шар
gloom мрак
gloomy мра́чный, угрю́мый
glory сла́ва
glove перча́тка
glue (to) кле́ить
go (to) идти́, ходи́ть (on foot), е́хать, е́здить (by conveyance)

goal цель (f.)
God Бог
gold золото
golden золотой
good добро (noun), добрый,
  хороший (adj.)
  good morning доброе утро
  good day добрый день
  good evening добрый вечер
  good night спокойной ночи
good-by до свидания
good-looking красивый
good-natured добродушный
goodness доброта
gossip (to) сплетничать
gossip сплетник, сплетница (m., f.)
govern (to) править, управлять
government правительство,
  управление
grace милость (f.)
graceful грациозный, изящный
gradually мало-помалу, постепенно
grammar грамматика
grand грандиозный, великолепный
granddaughter внучка
grandfather дедушка
grandmother бабушка
grandson внук
grant (to) соглашаться, давать
  субсидию
grapes виноград
grasp (to) хватать
grass трава
grateful благодарный
gratitude благодарность (f.)
gratis бесплатно, даром
grave могила
gravely тяжело
gravity тяжесть (f.)
gravy подливка, соус
gray серый
  gray-haired седой
grease (to) мазать, смазывать
grease жир
greasy сальный, жирный
great великий
greatly очень, сильно
greedy жадный
green зелёный
greet (to) здороваться,
  приветствовать
greeting привет, приветствие
grief горе, печаль (f.),скорбь (f.)
grieve (to) горевать
grind (to) растирать, тереть
groan (to) стонать
grocery store бакалейная лавка
ground земля, фундамент
groundwork фундамент
group группа
grow (to) делаться (become) расти,
  становиться (become)
  to grow up вырастать

grownup взрослый
growth развитие, рост
grumble (to) ворчать, жаловаться
guarantee (to) гарантировать
guarantee гарантия, ручательство
guard (to) охранять, стеречь
guard сторож
guardian хранитель
guess (to) догадываться, отгадывать
guess догадка, предположение
guest гость (m.)
guidance руководство
guide (to) руководить
guidebook справочник
guilt вина
guilty виноватый
guitar гитара
gulp (to) глотать
gulp глоток
gum десна, резина
gun ружьё
gust порыв
gypsy цыганский

H

habit привычка
habitual обычный
hair волосы
  to cut hair остричь волосы
haircut стрижка
hair-do причёска
hairdresser парикмахер
hairpin шпилька
half половина
  by halves пополам
  half-hour полчаса
  half a year полгода
  halfway на полпути, возможный
  компромисс
hall зал
halt привал, стой (команда)
ham ветчина
hammer молот
hand рука, стрелка (of a clock),
  ручной (adj.)
handbag сумка
handicraft ремесло, ручная работа
handkerchief носовой платок
handle ручка
handmade ручной работы
handshake рукопожатие
handsome красивый
handwriting почерк
handy удобный, сподручный
hang (to) висеть
  to hang up вешать
hanger вешалка
haphazardly кое-как
happen (to) происходить, случаться
happiness счастье
happy счастливый
harbor порт

hard твёрдый (firm), трудный
  (difficult)
harden (to) твердеть
hardly едва, чуть
hardness твёрдость (f.)
harm (to) вредить
harm зло, вред
harmful вредный
harmless безвредный
harmonious гармонический
harmony гармония
harsh резкий, грубый
harvest урожай
haste торопливость (f.)
hasten (to) ускорять
hastily поспешно, спешно
hasty поспешный
hat шляпа
hate (to) ненавидеть
hatred ненависть (f.)
haughty высокомерный
haunt (to) преследовать
have (to) иметь
  to have to должен (а, о, ы),
  приходиться
hay сено
hazy туманный
he он
head глава (chief), голова
head (to) заведовать, возглавлять
headache головная боль
headmost передовой
heal (to) заживать
health здоровье
healthful полезный
healthy здоровый
hear (to) слышать
hearing слух
heart сердце
  by heart наизусть
  of the heart сердечный
heartless бездушный
heat (to) греть, нагревать
  heating system отопление
heat жара
heaven небо
heavenly небесный
heavy сильный (strong), тяжёлый,
  толстый
  to grow heavy толстеть
heel каблук
height высота, рост
heir наследник
hell ад
hello здравствуйте
help (to) помогать
help помощь (f.)
helpless беспомощный, бессильный
hem (to) подшивать
hem подол, подшивка
hen курица
her её, ей
herd стадо

here здесь, сюда, тут
  here are (is) вот
  here you are на (s.), наѣте (pl.)
  from here отсюда
hero герой
heroine героиня
herring селёдка
hers её
herself она сама
hesitate (to) колебаться
hide (to) прятать (ся),
  скрывать (ся), таить (ся)
hideous ужасный
high высокий
  high-principled идейный
highest высший
highway большая дорога
hill холм
him его
himself он сам
hinder (to) мешать
hint намёк
hint at (to) намекать
hip бедро
hire (to) взять напрокат, нанимать
  for hire давать напрокат
his его
historical исторический
history история
hit (to) бить, ударять
hoarse хриплый
hold (to) держать (ся)
  to hold in сдержаться
  to hold out выдерживать
hole дырка
holiday праздник
hollow пустой
holy святой
home дом
  at home дома
  to go home идти домой
homemade самодельный, домашний
honest порядочный, честный
honesty честность (f.)
honey мёд
honeymoon медовый месяц
honor (to) почитать
honor честь (f.)
hook крюк
hope (to) надеяться
hope надежда, чаяние
hopeful надеющийся
hopeless безнадёжный
horizon горизонт
horizontal горизонтально
horn рог
horrible ужасный
horror ужас
horse конь (m.), лошадь (f.)
  horseback верхом
hospitable гостеприимный
hospital больница, госпиталь (m.)
hospitality гостеприимность,

хлеб-соль (bread and salt)
host хозяин
hostess хозяйка
hot горячий (objects, emotions),
  жаркий
hotel гостиница
hour час
house дом
housemaid горничная
housewarming новоселье
how как
  how much, many сколько
however однако
huge огромный
hum (to) напевать
human человек (noun),
  человеческий (adj.)
humanitarian гуманитарный
humanity человечество
humble скромный
humiliate (to) унижать
humility смирение
humor юмор
humorous юмористический
hundred сто
hundredth сотый
hunger голод
hungry голодный
hunter охотник
hunting охота
hurricane ураган
hurry (to) спешить, торопиться
hurt (to) болеть, сделать больно
husband муж
hush (to) молчать
hyphen дефис, тире
hypocrite лицемер
hysterical истерический

I

I я
ice лёд
ice cream мороженое
icon икона
icy ледяной
idea идея, мысль (f.), понятие
ideal идеальный
idealistic идеалистический
identical одинаковый
identity личность (f.)
idiot идиот
idle ленивый
idleness лень (f.)
if если
ignorance неведение, темнота
ignorant невежественный
ignore (to) игнорировать
ill больной
  to fall ill заболеть
illegal незаконный
illiteracy безграмотность
illiterate безграмотный
illness болезнь (f.)
illuminate (to) освещать

illumination освещение
illusion иллюзия
illustrate (to) иллюстрировать,
  пояснять
illustration пояснение, рисунок
imaginary воображаемый
imagination воображение, фантазия
imagine (to) воображать
imitate (to) изображать, подражать
imitation подражание
immature незрелый
immediate прямой, спешный
immediately немедленно, сразу
immense безмерный, огромный
imminent близкий
immobility неподвижность (f.)
immodest нескромный
immoral безнравственный
immorality безнравственность (f.)
immortal бессмертный
immortality бессмертие, вечность
  (f.)
immovable неподвижный
imp чертёнок
impartial беспристрастный
impatience нетерпение
impatient нетерпеливый
imperfect дефектный, неполный,
  бракованый
impersonal безличный
impertinence дерзость (f.) наглость
  (f.)
implore (to) умолять
imply (to) намекать
impolite невежливый
important важный
impossible невозможно, нельзя
imposter самозванец
impoverished обедневший
impression впечатление
imprison (to) заключать в тюрьму
improve (to) поправлять (ся),
  улучшать (ся)
improvement улучшение
improvise (to) импровизировать
imprudent неблагоразумный
impudence дерзость (f.), нахальство
impudent дерзкий
impulse импульс
impure нечистый
in в (prep.), на (асс., prep.)
  in case на всякий случай, в случае
  in fact фактически
inaccurate неаккуратный
inactivity бездействие
inadequate неудовлетворительный,
  недостаточный
inanimate неодушевлённый
inappropriate неподходящий
inaudible неслышный
incapable неспособный
incentive побуждение
inch дюйм

incident случай
inclination наклонение
include (to) включать
income доход
incomparable бесподобный
   несравнимый
incompatible несовместимый
incompetent неспособный,
   некомпетентный
incomplete неполный,
   несовершённый
inconvenient неудобный
incorrect неправильный
incorruptible неподкупный
increase (to) возрастать,
   прибавлять, увеличивать
increase умножение, увеличение
incredible невероятный
incredibility невероятность (f.)
indecent неприличный
indecision нерешительность (f.)
indeed поистине
indefinite неопределённый
independence независимость (f.)
independent независимый,
   самостоятельный
index индекс, оглавление
index finger указательный палец
indicate (to) указывать
indication признак
indifference безразличие,
   равнодушие
indifferent равнодушный
indignant негодующий
indignation негодование
indirect непрямой, побочный
indiscreet неосторожный,
   нескромный
indispensable необходимый
individual индивидуальный, личный
indoors в доме, внутри
induce (to) убеждать
indulge (to) позволять себе
   удовольствие, злоупотреблять
indulgence терпимость (f.)
indulgent терпимый
industrial фабричный
industrious прилежный
industry промышленность (f.)
inedible несъедобный
inefficient неспособный
inequality неравенство
inexpensive дешёвый
inexperienced неопытный
infancy раннее детство,
   младенчество
infant ребёнок
infection заражение
inferior низший
inferiority неполноценность (f.)
infinite безграничный, бесконечный
infinitive неопределённое
   наклонение, инфинитив

infinity бесконечность (f.)
influence (to) влиять
influence вес, влияние
inform (to) сообщать
informally без церемоний
information известие (news),
   сведение
ingenious остроумный
ingratitude неблагодарность (f.)
inhabit (to) жить
inhabitant житель (m.)
inherit (to) наследовать
inheritance наследство
inhuman бесчувственный, жестокий,
   бесчеловечный
initial начальный
initiate (to) вводить
initiative инициатива
injection вспрыскивание
injurious вредно
injury повреждение
injustice несправедливость (f.)
ink чернила
inn гостиница
inner внутренний
innocence невинность (f.)
innocent безвинный (guiltless)
   невинный (harmless)
inquire (to) спрашивать
inquiry вопрос, справка
inquisitive любознательный
insane безумный, сумасшедший
insanity безумие
inscription надпись
insect насекомое
insensible бесчувственный
inseparable неразлучный
insert (to) вкладывать
inside внутри
   inside out навыворот
insight интуиция, понимание
insignificant ничтожный
insincere неискренний
insincerity неискренность (f.)
insist (to) настаивать
insistence настойчивость (f.)
inspect (to) рассматривать,
   проверять
inspiration вдохновение
install (to) помещать, устанавливать
instance пример, случай
   for instance например
instant мгновение, миг, момент
instantly моментально
instead of вместо (gen.)
instep подъём
instinct инстинкт
institute институт
instruct (to) учить
instruction наказ (order), обучение
instructor инструктор
instrument инструмент, орудие
insufficient недостаточный

insult (to) оскорблять
insult оскорбление
insulting оскорбительный
insurance страховка
insure (to) страховать (ся)
intact целый
intellect ум
intellectual интеллектуальный,
   мыслящий
intelligence разум, ум
intelligent умный
intense сильный
intensity интенсивность (f.)
intention намерение
intentional намеренный
interest (to) интересовать,
   заинтересовать
interest интерес
interested (to become)
   интересоваться
interesting интересный
interfere (to) вмешивать (ся)
interior внутренность (f.)
intermission перерыв
internal внутренний
international международный
interpret (to) переводить
interpretation перевод, взгляд
interpreter переводчик
interrupt (to) прерывать
interval пауза, перерыв
intimacy интимность (f.)
intimate интимный
into в (acc.)
intolerable несносный, нестерпимый
intolerant нетерпимый
intoxicate (to) опьянять, возбуждать
intoxication опьянение
intricate сложный
intrigue интрига
introduce (to) вводить,
   представлять (a person)
introduction введение
   представление
intuition интуиция
invalid больной, нетрудоспособный
invaluable бесценный
invent (to) выдумывать, изобретать
   придумывать
invented выдуманный
investigate (to) исследовать
investigation исследование
invisible невидимый
invitation приглашение
invite (to) приглашать
inviting привлекательный
involuntary невольно
iodine иод
Irish ирландский
iron (to) гладить
iron железо, утюг (for ironing),
   железный (adj.)
irony ирония

irregular незакономе́рный, непра́вильный
irresistible неотрази́мый
irresponsibility безотве́тственность (f.)
irritate (to) раздража́ть
irritation раздраже́ние
island о́стров
isolate (to) изоли́ровать, отделя́ть
isolated изоли́рованный
issue изда́ние
it оно́
Italian италья́нский
itch (to) чеса́ться
itinerary маршру́т
its его́
ivory слоно́вая кость
ivy плющ

J

jacket жаке́т
jail тюрьма́
jam варе́нье
January янва́рь (m.)
Japanese япо́нский
jar ба́нка
jaw че́люсть (f.)
jealous ревни́вый
    to be jealous ревнова́ть
jealousy за́висть, ре́вность (f.)
jelly желе́
jewel драгоце́нность (f.)
Jewish евре́йский
job рабо́та
join (to) присоединя́ться, соединя́ться
joint суста́в, ме́сто соедине́ния, совме́стный (adj.)
joke (to) шути́ть
joke анекдо́т, шу́тка
jokingly шутя́
journalist журнали́ст
journey пое́здка
joy отра́да, ра́дость (f.)
joyous ра́достный
judge (to) суди́ть
judge судья́
judgment суд (legal), усмотре́ние
juice сок
juicy со́чный
July ию́ль (m.)
jumble ка́ша (fig.)
jump (to) пры́гать, скака́ть
    to jump off соска́кивать
    to jump out выска́кивать
jump прыжо́к
June ию́нь (m.)
junior мла́дший
just справедли́вый (adj.)
just (hardly) едва́, чуть
justice справедли́вость (f.), суд
justification оправда́ние
justify (to) опра́вдывать (ся)
juvenile малоле́тний

K

keen си́льный (strong), чу́ткий
keep (to) держа́ть, сохраня́ть, храни́ть
kernel зерно́
kerosene кероси́н
key ключ
kick (to) ударя́ть ного́й, брыка́ться (animal)
kidney по́чка
kill (to) убива́ть
killer уби́йца
kin род, родство́
kind сорт (n.), до́брый (adj.)
kindly до́брый, тёплый
kindness любе́зность (f.)
king коро́ль (m.)
kiss (to) целова́ть (ся)
kiss поцелу́й
kitchen ку́хня
knee коле́но
kneel (to) стоя́ть на коле́нях
knife нож
knight ры́царь
knit (to) вяза́ть
knock (to) стуча́ть
knock стук
knot (to) завя́зывать
knot у́зел
know (to) знать
    it is known изве́стно
    it is not known неизве́стно
    little known малоизве́стный
    to know how уме́ть
    well-known изве́стный
knowledge зна́ние
kopeck копе́йка
Kremlin Кремль

L

label ярлы́к
labor труд
laboratory лаборато́рия
laborer рабо́чий
lace шнуро́к
lack (to) недостава́ть
lack недоста́ток, отсу́тствие
ladder ле́стница
lady да́ма
lag (to) отстава́ть
lake о́зеро
lamb бара́нина
lame хромо́й
lamp ла́мпа, фона́рь (m.) (lantern)
lampshade абажу́р
land земля́
landlord хозя́ин
landscape пейза́ж
language язы́к
lantern фона́рь (m.)
lard са́ло

large большо́й, кру́пный
last (to) продолжа́ться (continue), хвата́ть (last out)
last (adj.) после́дний, про́шлый
late по́здний
    to be late опа́здывать
lately за после́днее вре́мя
later по́зже
    two days later два дня спустя́
laugh (to) смея́ться
    to burst out laughing засмея́ться
    to laugh boisterously хохота́ть
laughter смех
launder (to) стира́ть
lavatory убо́рная
lavish ще́дрый
law зако́н, пра́вило, пра́во
    law court суд
lawful зако́нный
lawless беззако́нный
lawn лужа́йка
lawyer адвока́т, юри́ст
lay (to) класть, положи́ть
layer слой
lazy лени́вый
    lazy person лентя́й (m.), -ка (f.)
lead (to) води́ть, руководи́ть
leader руководи́тель (m.)
leadership руково́дство
leaf лист
leak (to) течь
lean (to) наклоня́ться, опира́ться
    to lean over перегиба́ться
leap (to) пры́гать, скака́ть
leap прыжо́к, скачо́к
learn (to) учи́ть (ся), вы́учить (ся)
learned учёный
learning уче́ние
least наиме́ньший
    at least по кра́йней ме́ре
leather ко́жа
leave (to) оставля́ть, уезжа́ть, уходи́ть
    to leave out пропуска́ть
leave о́тпуск (vacation)
lecture докла́д, ле́кция
lecturer ле́ктор
left ле́вый
    to the left нале́во
leg нога́
legal зако́нный, юриди́ческий (profession)
legislation законода́тельство
legitimate зако́нный
leisure досу́г
lemon лимо́н
lend (to) одолжа́ть
length длина́
lengthen (to) удлиня́ть (ся)
less ме́ньше
lessen (to) убавля́ть, уменьша́ть
lesson уро́к

let (to) дава́ть, позволя́ть, пуска́ть
  let us дава́й, дава́йте (plus
    infinitive)
letter бу́ква (alphabet), письмо́
  (correspondence)
lettuce сала́т
level у́ровень (m.)
liable отве́тственный
liar лгун
liberal либера́льный, ще́дрый
  (lavish)
liberate (to) освобожда́ть
liberty во́льность (f.), свобо́да
library библиоте́ка
license пра́во, разреше́ние
  driver's license води́тельские
    права́
lie (to) лгать (falsify), лежа́ть (rest)
  to lie down ложи́ться
lie ложь (f.)
life жизнь (f.)
lifeless безжи́зненный
lift (to) поднима́ть
light (to) зажига́ть
  to light up освеща́ть
light лёгкий (adj.), све́тлый (bright)
  (adj.), свет (noun)
lighten (to) светле́ть (make
  brighter), облегча́ть (in weight)
lighter зажига́лка
lighting освеще́ние
lightning мо́лния
likable симпати́чный
like (to) люби́ть, нра́виться
like как (as), подо́бный, похо́жий
  (similar)
likely возмо́жно, наве́рно
likeness схо́дство
likewise то́же
limb член, коне́чность
limit (to) ограни́чивать
limit грани́ца, ограниче́ние, преде́л
limp (to) хрома́ть
line ли́ния, ряд (row), строка́ (of a
  page)
linen бельё (household or
  underwear), полотно́
linger (to) ме́длить
lingerie да́мское бельё
linguistic языково́й
lining подкла́дка
link (to) свя́зывать, соединя́ть
link связь (f.), звено́
lion лев
lip губа́
lipstick губна́я пома́да
liquid жи́дкий (adj.), жи́дкость
  (noun, f.)
liquor спиртно́й напи́ток
list спи́сок
listen (to) слу́шать
literacy гра́мотность (f.)

literally буква́льно
literary литерату́рный
literature литерату́ра
little ма́ленький
  a little ма́ло, немно́го
live (to) жить
live живо́й
lively живо́й
liver печёнка
living room гости́ная
load груз, тя́жесть
loaf (to) безде́льничать
loaf (of bread) це́лый хлеб
loan заём
lobby прихо́жая, фойе́
lobster ома́р
local зде́шний, ме́стный
locality ме́сто
locate (to) находи́ть (find),
  поселя́ться
location помеще́ние
lock (to) запира́ть
  locked up взаперти́
lock замо́к
locomotive локомоти́в, парово́з
logic ло́гика
logical логи́ческий, логи́чный
loneliness одино́чество
lonely одино́кий, уединённый
long (to) тоскова́ть
long дли́нный (distance), до́лго
  (time)
  long ago давно́, давны́м-давно́
  not long недо́лго
longing жела́ние
look (to) гляде́ть, смотре́ть
  to look for иска́ть
  to look over просма́тривать
  Look! посмотри́те!
  Look out! осторо́жно!
look взгляд
loop пе́тля
loose свобо́дный
lose (to) теря́ть, проигра́ть (at
  playing)
  to lose one's self-possession
    теря́ться
loss поте́ря
lost зате́рянный, поте́рянный
  to get lost заблуди́ться
lot (a) мно́го
loud гро́мкий
love (to) люби́ть
  in love влюблённый
  to fall in love влюбля́ться
love любо́вь (f.)
loved люби́мый
lovely ми́лый
loving лю́бящий, не́жный
low ни́зкий (height), ти́хий (faint)
lower (to) спуска́ть
loyal ве́рный
loyalty ве́рность (f.), лоя́льность

luck сча́стье
lucky счастли́вый, уда́чный
luggage бага́ж
luminous све́тлый
lump глы́ба, кусо́к (small piece)
lunch за́втрак
lung лёгкое
luster блеск
luxurious роско́шный
luxury ро́скошь (f.)
lyrical лири́ческий

M

machine маши́на
mad сумасше́дший
madam госпожа́, мада́м
made сде́ланный
madman безу́мец
madness сумасше́ствие, безу́мие
magazine журна́л
magistrate судья́
magnet магни́т
magnificent великоле́пный,
  превосхо́дный
magnifying увеличи́тельный
maid служа́нка
mail по́чта
main гла́вный
maintain (to) содержа́ть
maintenance содержа́ние (support),
  обслу́живание (service)
majority большинство́
make (to) де́лать
male (adj.) мужско́й
man мужчи́на (m.), челове́к
  (person)
manage (to) заве́довать, управля́ть
management администра́ция,
  управле́ние
manager дире́ктор, заве́дующий
mankind челове́чество
manner мане́ра, нра́вы (customs)
manufacture (to) произво́дство
  manufactured product фабрика́т
manuscript ру́копись (f.)
many мно́гие, мно́го
marble мра́мор
March март
margin по́ле
mark (to) отмеча́ть
  to mark off отчёркивать
mark пятно́ (spot), ме́тка
market база́р, ры́нок
marriage брак
marry (to) жени́ться (men),
  выходи́ть за́муж (women)
marvel (to) удивля́ться
marvel чу́до
marvelous чуде́сный
masculine мужско́й
mask (to) скрыва́ть
mask ма́ска

mass ма́сса
master (to) овладе́ть, вы́учить
master ма́стер, хозя́ин
match (to) подходи́ть
match спи́чка
matchless беспод́обный
material материа́л
maternal матери́нский
mathematician матема́тик
mathematics матема́тика
matter вещество́
  a matter of course я́сное де́ло
mattress матра́ц
mature взро́слый, зре́лый
maximum ма́ксимум
May май (m.)
may мочь, мо́жно
mayonnaise майоне́з
me меня́ (acc.), мне (dat.)
meadow луг
mean (to) зна́чить
mean (adj.) скро́мный, захуда́лый, неприя́тный
meaning значе́ние, смысл (sense)
meanness ме́лочность (f.), ни́зость (f.)
means сре́дства
  by means of посре́дством
meanwhile ме́жду тем
measure (to) ме́рить
measure ме́ра
meat мя́со
mechanic меха́ник
mechanical механи́ческий
mechanically машина́льно
mechanized механизи́рованный
medicine лека́рство, медици́на (the profession)
  medical treatment лече́ние
mediocre посре́дственный
mediocrity посре́дственность (f.)
meditate (to) размышля́ть
meditation размышле́ние
medium середи́на (noun), сре́дний (adj.)
meet (to) встреча́ть
  I'm very happy to meet you. Óчень прия́тно с ва́ми познако́миться.
meeting встре́ча, свида́ние, собра́ние (gathering)
melancholy меланхоли́я (n.), меланхоли́ческий (adj.)
melodious мелоди́чный
melody мело́дия
melon ды́ня
melt (to) та́ять
member член
memorable па́мятный
memorize (to) запомина́ть
memory па́мять (f.)
mend (to) исправля́ть, чини́ть
mental у́мственный

mention (to) отмеча́ть, упомина́ть
menu меню́
merchandise това́ры
merchant купе́ц, торго́вец
merciful милосе́рдный
merciless немилосе́рдный
mercy милосе́рдие
merit (to) заслу́живать
merit заслу́га
merry весёлый
message сообще́ние
messenger курье́р, посы́льный
metal мета́лл
metallic металли́ческий
metallurgy металлу́ргия
method ме́тод, спо́соб
microphone микрофо́н
microscope микроско́п
midday по́лдень (m.)
middle середи́на (noun), сре́дний (adj.)
  in the middle of посреди́ (gen.)
midnight по́лночь (f.)
midway полпути́
might си́ла
mighty грома́дный (huge), си́льный (strong)
mild мя́гкий
mildness мя́гкость (f.)
mile ми́ля
milk молоко́
mill ме́льница, фа́брика
million миллио́н
mind (to) следи́ть, забо́титься
  I don't mind. Я ничего́ не име́ю про́тив.
mind голова́ (head), ум
mineral ископа́емый, минера́л
minimum ми́нимум
minister мини́стр (state), свяще́нник (church)
mirror зе́ркало
minority меньшинство́
minute мину́та
  this very minute сию́ мину́ту
  Wait a minute. Подожди́те мину́ту.
miracle чу́до
miscellaneous разнообра́зный
mischief беда́, вред, ша́лость
mischievous зло́бный, шаловли́вый
miser скупо́й, бедня́га
miserable жа́лкий, несча́стный
miserliness ску́пость (f.)
miserly скупо́й
misfortune беда́, го́ре, несча́стье
miss (to) скуча́ть, пропуска́ть (leave out)
Miss, Mrs. Госпожа́ (for foreigners); гражда́нка, това́рищ (among Soviet people)
mission поруче́ние, зада́ние, делега́ция

mist тума́н
mistake оши́бка
  to be mistaken заблужда́ться
  to make a mistake ошиба́ться
Mister, Mr. господи́н, (for foreigners); граждани́н, това́рищ (among Soviet people)
mistrust (to) не доверя́ть
misty тума́нный
misunderstand (to) непра́вильно поня́ть
misunderstanding недоразуме́ние
mix (to) сме́шивать
  to mix up (confuse) пу́тать
mixed сме́шанный
moan (to) стона́ть
mob толпа́
mobile подвижно́й
mobilize (to) мобилизова́ть
mock (to) насмеха́ться
mocking насме́шка
mode мо́да
model моде́ль, тип, показа́тельный (adj.)
moderate уме́ренный
moderation уме́ренность (f.)
modern новомо́дный, но́вый, совреме́нный
modernism модерни́зм
modest скро́мный
modesty скро́мность (f.)
modification видоизмене́ние
modify (to) видоизменя́ть
moist сыро́й
moisten (to) увлажня́ть
moment мгнове́ние, миг, моме́нт
Monday понеде́льник
money де́ньги
monkey обезья́на
monotonous однозву́чный (tone), однообра́зный
monotony однообра́зие
monstrous чудо́вищный
month ме́сяц
monthly ежеме́сячный
monument па́мятник
mood настрое́ние
moody угрю́мый
moon луна́, ме́сяц
mop швабра́
moral мора́ль (noun, f.) мора́льный, нра́вственный (adj.)
more бо́льше, ещё
moreover к тому́ же, кро́ме того́
morning у́тро (noun), у́тренний (adj.)
  in the morning у́тром
morose угрю́мый
morsel кусо́чек
mortal сме́ртный
mortality сме́ртность (f.)
mortgage закла́д, закладна́я
Moscow Москва́, моско́вский (adj.)

mosquito москит
most наибо́льший
mostly гла́вным о́бразом
moth моль (f.)
mother мать (f.)
motion движе́ние, ход
motionless неподви́жный
motivate (to) побужда́ть,
   мотиви́ровать
motive побужде́ние, моти́в
motor дви́гатель (m.), мото́р
mound холм
mount (to) влеза́ть, поднима́ться
mountain гора́
mourn (to) опла́кивать, се́товать
mournful печа́льный, ско́рбный
mourning тра́ур
mouse мышь (f.)
mouth рот
   mouthful глото́к
move (to) дви́гаться, переезжа́ть
   (a household)
   to move off удаля́ться
movement движе́ние
movies кино́
moving тро́гательный
much гора́здо, мно́го
   how much ско́лько
mud грязь (f.)
muddy гря́зный, му́тный
multiplication умноже́ние
multiply (to) увели́чивать,
   размножа́ться, умножа́ть (arith.)
mumble (to) бормота́ть
municipal городско́й
murder (to) убива́ть
murder уби́йство
murderer уби́йца
murmur (to) жужжа́ть, журча́ть
muscle му́скул
museum музе́й
mushrooms грибы́
music му́зыка
musical музыка́льный
musician музыка́нт
must до́лжен (а́, о́, ы́)
mustache усы́
mustard горчи́ца
mute немо́й
mutter (to) бормота́ть
mutton бара́нина
mutually взаи́мно, обою́дно
my мой (моя́, моё, мой)
myself я сам; себя́, меня́, самого́
mysterious неве́домый
   таи́нственный
mystery та́йна

N

nail гвоздь (hardware), но́готь (m.),
   ко́готь
naïve наи́вный
naked го́лый

name (to) называ́ть, дава́ть и́мя
name и́мя, назва́ние (inanimate
   things), фами́лия (surname)
   What is your name? Как вас
   зову́т?
named (to be) называ́ть
namely и́менно, то есть (т.е.)
nap (to) поспа́ть
napkin салфе́тка
narrate (to) расска́зывать
narrow у́зкий
nasty проти́вный
nation на́ция
national наро́дный
nationalistic националисти́ческий
nationality наро́дность (f.),
   национа́льность (f.)
native родно́й
   native country ро́дина
natural есте́ственный, натура́льный
naturally есте́ственно, натура́льно,
   коне́чно (of course)
nature нату́ра, приро́да
naughty дурно́й, капри́зный
   to be naughty капри́зничать
navy флот
near близ, о́коло, у́ (prep. with
   gen.), бли́зко (adv.), бли́зкий (adj.)
   near at hand побли́зости
   to draw near бли́зиться,
   приближа́ться
nearly почти́
nearsighted близору́кий
neat аккура́тный, чи́стый
necessary необходи́мый, ну́жный
   it is necessary на́до, необходи́мо,
   ну́жно
necessity на́добность (f.)
   необходи́мость (f.)
neck ше́я
necklace ожере́лье
necktie га́лстук
need (to) нужда́ться
   I need мне ну́жно
need нужда́
needle иго́лка
needless изли́шний, нену́жный
negation отрица́ние
negative отрица́тельный
neglect (to) пренебрега́ть
neglect небре́жность (f.)
negotiations перегово́ры
Negro негр
neighbor сосе́д, -ка
neighborhood окре́стность (f.)
neighboring сосе́дний
neither никако́й
   neither . . . nor ни . . . ни
nephew племя́нник
nerve нерв
nervous не́рвный
   to be nervous не́рвничать

nest гнездо́
neuter сре́дний (adj.), сре́днего
   ро́да
neutral нейтра́льный
never никогда́
   Never mind. Ничего́, Нева́жно.
nevertheless всё-таки, несмотря́ на
new но́вый
news изве́стие, но́вость (f.)
newspaper газе́та
next сле́дующий
nice прия́тный, сла́вный
nickname прозва́ние
niece племя́нница
night ночь (f.)
   at night но́чью
   Good night. Споко́йной но́чи.
nightmare кошма́р
nine де́вять
nineteen девятна́дцать
nineteenth девятна́дцатый
ninetieth девяно́стый
ninety девяно́сто
ninth девя́тый
no нет
nobody никто́, ничто́жество
noise шум
   to make noise шуме́ть
noisy шу́мный
nominate (to) назнача́ть, называ́ть
nomination назначе́ние
none никако́й, ни оди́н
nonsense вздор, ерунда́
   to talk nonsense говори́ть чепуху́
noon по́лдень (m.)
no one никто́
nor та́кже не
norm но́рма
normal норма́льный
north се́вер
northern се́верный
nose нос
not не, ни
   not at all ниско́лько
   there is not нет
note (to) отмеча́ть
note запи́ска, примеча́ние
notebook тетра́дь (f.)
nothing ничто́, ничего́
notice (to) замеча́ть
notice предупрежде́ние
noticeably заме́тно
notify (to) предупрежда́ть, сообща́ть
notion иде́я
noun и́мя существи́тельное
nourish (to) пита́ть
nourishment пита́ние
novel рома́н
novelty новизна́
November ноя́брь (m.)
now сейча́с, тепе́рь
nowadays тепе́рь

nowhere нигде (location), никуда
  (direction)
nuance оттенок
nude нагой, обнажённый
nuisance неудобство, неприятность
numb онемелый
number номер, число
numerous многочисленный
nurse медсестра (for the sick),
  няня (for children)
nursery детская, ясли
nut гайка (hardware), орех

O

oak дуб
oar весло
oath присяга
oats овёс
obedience послушание
obedient покорный, послушный
obey (to) подчиняться
object (to) протестовать, быть
  против
objection возражение
objective объективный
obligation обязательство, повинность
  (f.)
oblige (to) обязывать
obliging любезный
obscure мрачный, неясный,
  неизвестный (unknown)
obscurity мрак, тьма
observation замечание (remark),
  наблюдение
observe (to) замечать (notice),
  наблюдать
observer наблюдатель (m.)
obsolete отживший
obstacle препятствие
obstetrician акушер-ка
obstinacy упрямство
obstinate упрямый
obtain (to) доставать
obvious очевидный, ясный
obviously очевидно
occasion случай
occasional редкий, случайный
occasionally изредка, от времени до
  времени
occupation занятие
occupy (to) занимать (ся)
occur (to) происходить, случаться
occurrence происшествие, случай
ocean океан
October октябрь (m.)
odd странный
ode ода
odor запах
of из, от (gen.)
  of course конечно, разумеется
  out of из-за
off с (gen.)
  Off! Прочь!

to get off слезать, сходить
offend (to) обижать
offended обиженный
offense оскорбление, преступление
  (legal) наступление (military)
  to take offense оскорбляться
offensive оскорбительный
offer (to) предлагать, представлять
offer предложение
office канцелярия, контора
official официальный (adj.), (pl.)
  чиновник (noun)
often часто
oil масло, нефть
ointment мазь (f.)
old старый
  old age старость (f.)
  olden times старина
  old-fashioned старомодный
  old man старик
  old woman старуха
olive маслина
omelet омлет, яичница
on на (acc. and prep.)
once однажды
  at once сейчас же
  once in a while иногда
  once more ещё раз
one один (одна, одно)
  one and a half полтора
oneself себя
onion лук
only единственный (adj.), только
  (adv.)
open (to) открывать, расскрывать
open откровенный, открытый
open-hearted простодушный
opening отверстие (hole), открытие
  (season)
opera опера
operate (to) оперировать
operation операция
opinion мнение
  in my opinion по-моему
opponent противник
opportunely кстати, своевременно
opportunity удобный случай,
  возможность (f.)
oppose (to) сопротивляться
opposed to против (gen.)
opposite против (gen.)
opposition противоположность (f.),
  противоречие
oppress (to) притеснять
oppression притеснение
optician оптик
optimism оптимизм
optimist оптимист
optimistic оптимистический
or а, или, либо
  either . . . or или . . . или,
  либо . . . либо
oral устный

orange апельсин (noun), оранжевый
  (color)
orator оратор
orchard фруктовый сад
orchestra оркестр
ordeal тяжёлое испытание
order (to) заказать (commercial),
  приказать (command)
order порядок (neatness), заказ
  (commercial order), приказ
  (command), строй (system)
  out of order не работать
  to put in order приводить в
    порядок
ordinarily обыкновенно
ordinary обыкновенный
organ орган (musical), орган
  (anatomy)
organization организация,
  устройство
organize (to) устраивать
organized организованный
Orient восточные страны, Восток
origin происхождение
original оригинальный,
  первоначальный
originality оригинальность (f.)
ornament украшение
orphan сирота
other другой, иной
  on the other hand зато, с другой
    стороны
otherwise иначе
ounce унция
our наш (а, е, и)
ourselves (мы) сами
out из (gen.)
outburst взрыв
outcome результат
outing прогулка
outlast (to) переживать
outlet выходное отверстие,
  электрический штепсель
outline (to) намечать
outline очертание, эскиз, контур
outlook вид, перспектива
output продукция
outrage безобразие, оскорбление
outside вне (prep. with gen.),
  посторонний (adj.)
outward внешний
oven духовка, печь (f.)
over над (inst.), сверх (gen.),
  через (across) (acc.)
overcoat пальто (not declined)
  шинель (m.)
overcome (to) преодолевать
overcooked пережаренный,
  переваренный
overdue просроченный
overeat (to) переедать
overestimate (to) переоценивать
overflow (to) переливаться

overlook (to) не замечать, смотреть сквозь пальцы
overpay (to) переплачивать
overseas за морем
overshoes галоши
overstep (to) переступать
overstrain (to) переутомлять, перенапрягать
overstrain переутомление
overtake (to) настигать
overthrow (to) опрокидывать, свергать
owe (to) быть должным
own (to) владеть
own родной, собственный, свой (свой, своё, свой)
owner владелец, хозяин
oxygen кислород
oyster устрица

P

pace темп
pacific мирный
pack (to) укладываться
package пакет, пачка
pact пакт
page страница
pain боль (f.)
painful чувствительный
painfully больно
painless безболезненный
paint (to) красить, рисовать (artistic)
paint краска
painting живопись (f.)
pair пара
pajamas пижама
pale бледный
    to grow pale бледнеть
pamphlet брошюра
pan кастрюля
pancakes блинчики, оладьи
pane оконное стекло, грань
panel панель; тонкая доска для живописи; распределительная доска
panic паника
pants брюки, штаны
paper бумага
parade парад
paradise рай
paragraph абзац, параграф
parallel параллельный
paralysis паралич
parcel пакет
pardon (to) извинять, прощать помиловать
pardon прощение
parenthesis скобки
parents родители (pl.)
Parisian парижский
park парк
parrot попугай

part (to) прощаться, расстаться, разделять
part роль (f.) (acting), часть (f.)
    little part частица
partial частичный, пристрастный (favoring)
    partial to неравнодушный
participate (to) участвовать
participation участие
particular требовательный
particularly особенно
partner партнёр
party вечер, вечеринка (social), партия
pass (to) проезжать (by conveyance) проходить (on foot), передавать (give), выдержать (examination)
passage проезд, проход
passenger пассажир,-ка
passion пыл, страсть (f.)
passionate горячий, пылкий, страстный
passionately страстно
passive пассивный
passport паспорт
past прошлое (noun), прошедший прошлый (adj.), мимо (prep. with gen.)
paste (to) клеить
paste паста
pastry печенье, пирожное
patch заплата
path тропинка
pathetic патетичный
patience терпение
patient пациент (noun), терпеливый (adj.)
patriot патриот
patriotism патриотизм
patron покровитель (m.)
patronage покровительство
pattern (sewing) выкройка, шаблон
pause пауза
paw лапа
pay (to) платить
    to pay off расплачиваться
payment уплата
peace мир, тишина (quiet), покой (quiet)
peaceful мирный, спокойный
peach персик
peak вершина
peanut земляной орех
pear груша
pearl жемчуг
peas горошек
pebble галька
peculiar особенный
peculiarity особенность (f.)
peel (to) снимать кору, снимать кожицу

peel корка
pen перо
    fountain pen авторучка
penalty штраф
pencil карандаш
penetrate (to) проникать внутрь
peninsula полуостров
pension пенсия
pensive мечтательный
people народ, нация, люди
pepper перец
perceive (to) замечать, ощущать
per cent на сотню, %
percentage процент
perfect идеальный, совершённый
perfection совершенство
perfectly вполне, совершенно
perform (to) играть (on stage), исполнять
performance игра, спектакль
perfume духи
perhaps может быть
peril опасность (f.)
period период, точка (punctuation)
periodical журнал (magazine), периодический (adj.)
perish (to) погибать
perishable скоропортящийся
permanent постоянный
permission разрешение, позволение
permit (to) позволять, пускать, разрешать
perpendicular перпендикуляр
perpetual вечный, бесконечный
persecute (to) преследовать
persecution преследование
perseverance настойчивость (f.)
persist (to) настаивать
persistent настойчивый, упорный
person лицо, человек
personal личный, собственный
personality личность (f.)
perspective перспектива
perspiration пот
perspire (to) потеть
persuade (to) убеждать, уговаривать
pet (to) ласкать
petroleum нефть, петролеум, керосин
petticoat нижняя юбка
petty мелкий
pharmacy аптека
phase фаза
phenomenon необыкновенное явление
philanthropist благотворитель (m.) филантроп
philosopher философ
philosophically философски
philosophy философия
phone телефон
photograph (to) снимать, фотографировать

photograph ка́рточка, сни́мок
photography фотогра́фия
phrase фра́за
physical физи́ческий
physician врач
physicist фи́зик
physics фи́зика
pianist пиани́ст, -ка
piano роя́ль (m.), пиани́но
pick (to) срыва́ть
    to pick out выбира́ть
    to pick up поднима́ть
picnic пикни́к
picture карти́на, рису́нок
pie пиро́г
piece кусо́к, кусо́чек, шту́ка, (noun), шту́чный (adj.)
piercing пронзи́тельный
pig свинья́
pigeon го́лубь
pile ку́ча
pill пилю́ля
pillow поду́шка
pillowcase на́волочка
pilot авиа́тор, лётчик
pin була́вка
pinch (to) ущипну́ть
pineapple анана́с
pine tree сосна́
pink ро́зовый
pious набо́жный
pipe труба́, тру́бка (for tobacco)
pistol револьве́р, пистоле́т
pitiful жа́лкий
pity жа́лость (f.), сожале́ние
    It's a great pity. Очень жаль.
place (to) помеща́ть
place ме́сто
plain просто́й
plan (to) составля́ть план
plan план
plane ро́вный
planet плане́та
plant (to) сажа́ть
plant заво́д (factory), расте́ние (botany)
plaster штукату́рка
plastic пласти́ческий
plate таре́лка
plateau плато́, плоского́рье
platform платфо́рма
play (to) игра́ть
play спекта́кль (m.), пье́са
plead (to) проси́ть, умоля́ть
pleasant прия́тный
please (to) нра́виться
please пожа́луйста
pleasure удово́льствие
pleat скла́дка
pledge обеща́ние
plentiful оби́льный
plenty оби́лие (noun), доста́точно (adv.)

plot за́говор (conspiracy), сюже́т, фа́була (of a story)
plug про́бка, заты́чка
plum сли́ва
plumber водопрово́дчик
plump пу́хленький
plus плюс
pneumonia воспале́ние лёгких
pocket карма́н
pocketbook су́мка
poem поэ́ма, стихотворе́ние
poet поэ́т
poetic поэти́ческий
poetry поэ́зия
point (to) пока́зывать, ука́зывать
point о́стрый коне́ц, пункт, то́чка
pointed остроконе́чный
pointer стре́лка
poison яд
poisonous ядови́тый
pole столб, шест, по́люс
police поли́ция
policeman полице́йский
policy поли́тика, страхово́й по́лис (insurance)
polish (to) наводи́ть гля́нец, полирова́ть
polish гля́нец
Polish по́льский
polite ве́жливый, любе́зный
politeness ве́жливость (f.)
political полити́ческий
politics поли́тика
pond пруд
pool лу́жа, прудо́к
poor бе́дный
    to become poor бедне́ть
Pope ри́мский па́па
popular наро́дный, популя́рный
population населе́ние
porch крыльцо́
pork свини́на
port порт
portable перено́сный, складно́й
porter носи́льщик
portion по́рция
portrait портре́т
portray (to) изобража́ть, опи́сывать
pose по́за
position положе́ние
positive уве́ренный
possess (to) облада́ть, владе́ть
possibility возмо́жность (f.)
possible возмо́жно, мо́жно
post по́чта
postage stamp почто́вая ма́рка
post card откры́тка
poster афи́ша
posterity пото́мство
post office по́чта
postpone (to) отложи́ть
pot кастрю́ля
potato карто́фель (m.)

pound фунт
pour (to) налива́ть (a liquid), насыпа́ть (dry products)
    to pour out вылива́ть, высыпа́ть
poverty бе́дность (f.)
powder (to) пу́дриться
powder пу́дра
power власть (f.)
powerful си́льный
practical практи́чный
practice (to) упражня́ться
practice пра́ктика
praise (to) хвали́ть
prank вы́ходка
pray (to) моли́ть
prayer моли́тва
precaution предосторо́жность (f.)
precede (to) предше́ствовать
precious драгоце́нный
precise то́чный
precisely то́чно
precision то́чность (f.)
predicament затрудни́тельное положе́ние
predict (to) предсказа́ть
preface предисло́вие
prefer (to) предпочита́ть
preference предпочте́ние
pregnant бере́менная
prejudice предрассу́док
preliminary предвари́тельный
premature преждевре́менный
premeditated преднаме́ренный
preparation приготовле́ние
prepare (to) приготовля́ть
prepared гото́вый
prepay (to) плати́ть вперёд
preposition предло́г
prescribe (to) предпи́сывать
prescription реце́пт
presence прису́тствие
present (to) представля́ть
present настоя́щее (noun), ны́не (adv.), настоя́щий (adj.)
    at present тепе́рь
preservation сохране́ние
preserve (to) сохраня́ть
preserves варе́нье
president председа́тель (m.), президе́нт
press (to) нажима́ть, гла́дить (clothes)
press печа́ть (f.) (journalism)
pressing спе́шный
pressure давле́ние, нажа́тие
prestige прести́ж
presume (to) предполага́ть
pretend (to) притворя́ться, де́лать вид
pretension прете́нзия
pretty (adj.) хоро́шенький
    to grow pretty хороше́ть
    pretty (adv.) дово́льно

prevent (to) предупреждáть
prevention предупреждéние
previous предыдýщий
price ценá
pride самолюбие
priest свящéнник
primary первичный, основнóй
prime minister премьéр
principal глáвный
principle принцип
print (to) печáтать
prison тюрьмá
private чáстный
privilege привилéгия
prize (to) ценить
prize нагрáда, приз
probably вероятно
problem задáча, проблéма
procedure процедýра
proceed (to) продолжáть
process процéсс
proclamation воззвáние,
    официáльное объявлéние
produce (to) вырабáтывать
producer режиссёр
product продýкт
production произведéние,
    произвóдство (manufacture)
profession профéссия, ремеслó
professor профéссор
profile прóфиль
profit (to) приносить пóльзу
    to profit by воспóльзоваться
profit дохóд, пóльза
profound углублённый
program прогрáмма
progress (to) продвигáться,
    развивáться
progress прогрéсс
progressive передовóй,
    прогрессивный
prohibit (to) воспрещáть (ся),
    запрещáть
prohibition запрещéние
project (to) бросáть, проектировать
project проéкт
prolong (to) растягивать
prolonged продолжительный
promise (to) обещáть
promise обещáние
prompt (to) подсказáть
prompt быстрый
pronoun местоимéние
pronounce (to) произносить
pronunciation произношéние
proof доказáтельство
proofreader коррéктор
propaganda агитáция, пропагáнда
proper приличный (decent)
property имýщество, сóбственность
    (f.)
prophecy предсказáние

prophesy (to) прорóчить,
    предскáзывать
prophet прорóк
proportion пропóрция
proposal предложéние
propose (to) предлагáть
prose прóза
prospect вид, надéжда
prosper (to) процветáть
prosperity процветáние
prosperous процветáющий, богáтый
protect (to) защищáть
protection защита
protector защитник
protest протéст
proud гóрдый
prove (to) докáзывать
proverb послóвица
provide (to) обеспéчивать
province óбласть (f.)
provisions продýкты (pl.)
provoke (to) возбуждáть,
    провоцировать
prudence благоразýмие
prudent благоразýмный
prune чернослив
psychiatrist психиáтр
psychologist психóлог
psychology психолóгия
public пýблика (noun)
    общéственный (adj.)
publication издáние
publicity реклáма
publicize (to) реклами́ровать
publish (to) издавáть (books)
    публиковáть (to announce)
publishing house издáтельство
publisher издáтель (m.)
puddle лýжа
puff out (to) надувáть
pull (to) тянýть, таскáть
pulse пульс
pump насóс
punctual аккурáтный, пунктуáльный
puncture прокóл
pungency остротá
pungent óстрый, éдкий
punish (to) накáзывать
punishment наказáние
pupil учени́к, учени́ца (f.)
puppy щенóк
purchase (to) покупáть
purchase покýпка
pure чистый
purity чистотá
purpose цель (f.), намéрение
purposely нарóчно
purse кошелёк
pursue (to) преслéдовать
push (to) толкáть
put (to) класть, положи́ть,
    (horizontally); стáвить (vertically)

to put away убирáть
to put down подавля́ть,
    запи́сывать
to put forth проявля́ть, пускáть
to put forward выдвигáть,
    предлагáть
to put in вставля́ть,
    вклáдывать, всóвывать
to put off отклáдывать
to put on надевáть, принимáть
    вид
to put out выгоня́ть, удаля́ть
to put through выполня́ть
to put up поднимáть, стрóить,
    воздвигáть
pyramid пирами́да
puzzle загáдка

Q

quaint необы́чный, стрáнный
qualification квалифи́кáция
qualify (to) квалифици́ровать (ся)
quality кáчество
quantity коли́чество
quarrel (to) ссóриться
quarter чéтверть, четвертáк (25c)
queer стрáнный
quench (to) туши́ть, утоля́ть (thirst)
question (to) спрáшивать
question вопрóс
questionable сомни́тельный,
    спóрный
questionnaire анкéта
quick быстрый, скóрый
quicken (to) ускоря́ть
quiet тишинá (noun), спокóйный,
    ти́хий (adj.)
quietly спокóйно, ти́хо
quit (to) оставля́ть рабóту (leave),
    перестáть (stop)
quite вóвсе, вполнé, совсéм
quiver (to) дрожáть
quotation цитáта
quotation marks кавы́чки
quote (to) цити́ровать

R

rabbit крóлик
race рáса (species); скáчки, бегá
    (horseraceş)
radiator радиáтор
radio рáдио
rag тря́пка
rage бéшенство, я́рость (f.)
ragged понóшенный, рвáный
railroad желéзная дорóга
    railroad car вагóн
    railroad station вокзáл
rain дождь
rainbow рáдуга

raincoat дождеви́к
rainy дождли́вый
raise (to) повыша́ть, поднима́ть (lift)
raisin изю́м
rank чин
rap (to) стуча́ть
rapid бы́стрый, ско́рый
rapidly бы́стро
rapture упое́ние, экста́з
rare ре́дкий
rarity ре́дкость (f.)
rash сыпь (noun, f.) (skin), стреми́тельный (adj.) (hasty)
raspberries мали́на
rate (to) оце́нивать, счита́ть
rate проце́нт (per cent), темп (speed), ско́рость (f.) (speed)
rather дово́льно, скоре́е, слегка́
ratio пропо́рция
rational рассу́дочный
rave (to) бре́дить, восторга́ться
raw сыро́й
ray луч
razor бри́тва
reach (to) достава́ть, достига́ть, доезжа́ть
react (to) реаги́ровать
reaction реа́кция
read (to) чита́ть
readily охо́тно
reading чте́ние
ready гото́вый
in readiness нагото́ве
ready-made гото́вые изде́лия
real настоя́щий
realistic реалисти́ческий
realization осозна́ние, реализа́ция
realize (to) представля́ть себе́, понима́ть я́сно
really действи́тельно, неуже́ли, ра́зве
realm сфе́ра
rear (to) воспи́тывать (bring up)
rear за́дний
reason (to) рассужда́ть
reason причи́на (cause), ра́зум (intelligence)
reasonable разу́мный
reassure (to) успока́ивать
rebel (to) восстава́ть
rebel бунтовщи́к
rebellion восста́ние
recall (to) вспомина́ть
receipt распи́ска
receive (to) получа́ть, принима́ть
receiver получа́тель (m.), приёмник
recent неда́вний, но́вый
recently неда́вно
reception приём (noun), приёмный (adj.)
recess переры́в
recipe реце́пт

reciprocal взаи́мный
recite (to) деклами́ровать
recklessly аза́ртно, сломя́ го́лову
recognition призна́ние
recognize (to) признава́ть, узнава́ть
recollect (to) вспомина́ть
recollection воспомина́ние
recommend (to) рекомендова́ть
recommendation рекоменда́ция
reconcile (to) примиря́ть
reconciliation примире́ние
record (to) запи́сывать
record за́пись, протоко́л
phonograph record пласти́нка
recover (to) поправля́ться
recovery излече́ние
rectangle прямоуго́льник
red кра́сный
Red Cross Кра́сный Крест
red-haired ры́жий
reduce (to) убавля́ть (weight), уменьша́ть
reduction сниже́ние, ски́дка (price)
refer (to) ссыла́ться, упомина́ть
reference рекоменда́ция
in reference to относи́тельно
reference book справо́чник
refine (to) очища́ть, усоверше́нствовать
refined изя́щный
refinement изы́сканность (f.)
reflect (to) отража́ть, мы́слить, размышля́ть
reflection отраже́ние, размышле́ние (thought)
reform (to) улучша́ть
reform рефо́рма, улучше́ние
refrain (to) сде́рживать, возде́рживаться
refresh (to) освежа́ть
refreshment оживле́ние, освежа́ющий напи́ток
refrigerator ле́дник, холоди́льник
refuge убе́жище
refugee эмигра́нт, бе́женец
refund (to) возвраща́ть
refund упла́та
refusal отка́з
refuse (to) отка́зывать
regard уваже́ние
regime режи́м
regiment полк
region райо́н
register (to) регистри́ровать (ся)
regret (to) жале́ть
regret сожале́ние
regular пра́вильный, регуля́рный
regulate (to) регули́ровать
regulation пра́вило
rehearsal репети́ция
rehearse (to) репети́ровать
reign (to) цари́ть
reinforce (to) подкрепля́ть

reject (to) отклоня́ть, отка́зывать
rejoice (to) ра́доваться
relate (to) расска́зывать
relation отноше́ние, связь (f.)
relationship отноше́ние
relative ро́дственник
relaxation о́тдых, развлече́ние
release (to) освобожда́ть
release освобожде́ние
relent (to) смягча́ться
reliable надёжный, соли́дный
reliability надёжность (f.)
relief облегче́ние
relieve (to) облегча́ть
religion рели́гия
religious религио́зный
reluctance неохо́та
reluctantly неохо́тно, не́хотя
rely (to) полага́ться
remain (to) остава́ться
remainder оста́ток
remaining остально́й
remark (to) замеча́ть
remark замеча́ние
remarkable замеча́тельный
remedy сре́дство от боле́зни, лека́рство
remember (to) по́мнить, вспомина́ть
remembrance воспомина́ние
remind (to) напомина́ть
reminder напомина́ние
remodeling переде́лка, ремо́нт
remorse раска́яние
remote далёкий, удалённый
remove (to) снима́ть, убира́ть
render (to) ока́зывать
renew (to) обновля́ть
renewal возобновле́ние
rent (to) нанима́ть
rent аре́ндная пла́та
repair (to) исправля́ть, поправля́ть, починя́ть
repairs ремо́нт
repay (to) заплати́ть, отпла́чивать
repayment отпла́та
repeat (to) повторя́ть
repeatedly многокра́тно
repent (to) раска́иваться
repertoire репертуа́р
repetition повторе́ние
replacement заме́на
reply (to) отвеча́ть
reply отве́т
report (to) сообща́ть
report докла́д, сообще́ние
reporter корреспонде́нт
represent (to) представля́ть
representation представи́тельство
representative представи́тель (m.)
repress (to) подавля́ть
repression подавле́ние
reprimand вы́говор
reproach (to) попрека́ть, упрека́ть

reproach попрёк, упрёк
reproduction репродукция
republic республика
reputation известность (f.)
   репутация
request (to) просить
request просьба, требование
require (to) нуждаться
required потребный, обязательный
requirement требование
rescue (to) спасать
research исследование
resemblance сходство
resembling похожий
resent (to) негодовать
resentment негодование
reservation оговорка, место,
   заказанное заранее
reserve фонд, запас
reservoir хранилище, резервуар
residence местожительство,
   проживание
resident житель (m.)
resign (to) отказываться, уходить
   в отставку
resignation отказ, отставка
resigned покорный
resist (to) сопротивляться
resistance сопротивление
resolute решительный, твёрдый
resolution решительность (f.)
resolve (to) решать (decide),
   разрешать (a problem)
resort курорт
resource средство
respect (to) уважать
respect почтение, уважение
respected уважаемый
respectful почтительный
responsibility обязанность (f.)
   ответственность (f.)
responsible ответственный
rest (to) отдыхать
rest отдых, покой
restaurant ресторан
restless беспокойный
restoration восстановление
restore (to) восстанавливать
restrain (to) сдерживать
restraint сдержанность (f.)
   with restraint сдержанно
restrict (to) ограничивать
restriction ограничение
result (to) следовать
result результат
resume (to) продолжать
retain (to) сохранять, удерживать
retaliate (to) отплачивать
retaliation отплата
retire (to) выходить в отставку
retired отставной
retreat (to) отступать
return (to) возвращать (ся)

return возвращение
reveal (to) проявлять, раскрывать
revelation откровение
revenge (to) мстить
revenge реванш, месть
reverse (to) перевернуть
reverse обратный
review обзор, рецензия (theater)
revise (to) проверять, изменять
revive (to) оживлять (ся)
revoke (to) отменять
revolt (to) восставать
revolt восстание
revolution революция
revolutionary революционный
revolve (to) вращаться
reward (to) вознаграждать
reward награда
rhyme рифма
rhythm ритм
rib ребро
ribbon лента
rice рис
rich богатый
   to grow rich богатеть
richness богатство
rid of (to get) избавлять (ся) от
riddle загадка
ride (to) ездить, кататься (for
   pleasure)
ridicule (to) осмеивать
ridiculous нелепый, смешной
right верный, правильный (adj.)
   (correct), правый (adj.) (position),
   право (noun)
   all right хорошо
   to the right направо
rigid негибкий, неподвижный
ring (to) звонить
ring кольцо
   wedding ring обручальное кольцо
ring звонок (sound)
rinse (to) полоскать
ripe спелый
ripen (to) зреть
rise (to) подниматься (increase,
   mount), вставать (get up),
   восходить (sun)
rise повышение, подъём
risk (to) рисковать
risk риск
ritual ритуал
rival конкурент, соперник
rivalry соперничество
river река (noun), речной (adj.)
road дорога
roar (to) реветь
roam (to) бродить (only on foot)
roast (to) жарить
roast жареное
   roast beef ростбиф
rob (to) грабить

robber разбойник
robbery ограбление
robe халат
robust крепкий, здоровый
rock (to) качать
rock камень (m.)
rocket ракета
rocky каменистый, скалистый
rogue жулик
role роль (f.)
roll (to) катиться
roll булка (bread), связка, катушка
romance роман
romantic романтический
roof крыша
room комната
   no room (space) нет места
root корень (m.)
rope верёвка
rose роза
rot (to) портить (ся), гнить
rotten испорченный, гнилой
rough грубый, неделикатный
   (crude), неровный
round вокруг (gen.), кругом (adv.),
   круглый (adj.)
roundabout обходный
rouse (to) будить, возбуждать
   (anger)
route маршрут
routine рутина
row ряд
royalties (author's) авторские
rub (to) тереть
rubber резина
ruble рубль (m.)
rude невежливый
rug ковёр
ruin (to) разрушать
ruin гибель (f.)
rule (to) править, управлять
rule закон, правило
ruler линейка
rumor слух
run (to) бегать, течь (water)
   running бегом
   run down издёрганный
rupture разрыв
rural сельский
rush (to) торопиться
Russian русский (noun and adj.)
   in Russian по-русски
rust (to) ржаветь
rusty заржавленный
rye рожь

S

sack мешок
sacred священный
sacrifice (to) жертвовать
sacrifice жертва

sad гру́стный, печа́льный
  to be sad грусти́ть
safe невреди́мый
safety безопа́сность (f.)
sail (to) пла́вать
sail па́рус
sailing пла́вание
sailor матро́с
sake (for the —— of) ра́ди
salad сала́т
salad bowl сала́тник
salary жа́лованье
sale распрода́жа
salesman продаве́ц
saleswoman продавщи́ца
salmon лососи́на
salt соль (f.)
salty солёный
salute (to) приве́тствовать
salvation спасе́ние
same са́мый (ая, ое, ый)
  all the same всё-таки
  it's all the same всё равно́
sample образе́ц
samovar самова́р
sand песо́к
sandal санда́лия
sandwich бутербро́д
sandy песо́чный
sane норма́льный
sanitary санита́рный
sap сок
sarcasm сарка́зм
sarcastic саркасти́ческий
satellite спу́тник, приспе́шник
satiate (to) насыща́ть
satin атла́с
satisfaction удовлетворе́ние
satisfactory удовлетвори́тельный
satisfied дово́льный, сы́тый
satisfy (to) удовлетворя́ть
saturate (to) насыща́ть
saturation насы́щенность (f.)
Saturday суббо́та
sauce подли́вка, со́ус
saucepan кастрю́ля
sausage колбаса́
savage ди́кий (adj.), дика́рь (noun)
save (to) спаса́ть, избавля́ть
say (to) говори́ть, сказа́ть
scale весы́ (weight), га́мма
  (musical)
scalp скальп
scan (to) разгля́дывать
scandal сканда́л
  to talk scandal спле́тничать
scanty ску́дный, ограни́ченный
scar шрам
scarce недоста́точный, ре́дкий
scarcely едва́, то́лько что
scare (to) пуга́ть
scare испу́г
scarf шарф

scarlet а́лый
scattered рассе́янный
scene сце́на
scented арома́тный
schedule расписа́ние
scheme схе́ма, прое́кт
scholar учёный
scholarship стипе́ндия
school шко́ла
schoolteacher преподава́тель, -ница
science нау́ка
scientific нау́чный
  scientific research нау́чно-
    иссле́довательский
scientist учёный
scissors но́жницы
scold (to) руга́ть
scorch (to) обжига́ть
score счёт
scorn (to) презира́ть
scornful презри́тельный
Scottish шотла́ндский
scoundrel негодя́й
scrape (to) скрести́
scratch (to) цара́пать, чеса́ться
  (oneself)
scratch цара́пина
scream (to) крича́ть
scream крик
screen экра́н (movies), ши́рма
screw винт
scribble (to) писа́ть небре́жно
scrupulous щепети́льный
scrutinize (to) рассма́тривать
sculptor ску́льптор
sculpture скульпту́ра
sea мо́ре
seagull ча́йка
seal (to) запеча́тывать, опеча́тывать
seal печа́ть (m.)
seam шов
seamstress швея́
search (to) иска́ть, иссле́довать
search по́иски
seashore морско́й бе́рег
season вре́мя го́да, сезо́н (events)
seasoning припра́ва
seat (to) сесть (oneself)
seat ме́сто
second второ́й (number), секу́нда
  (noun)
secondhand поде́ржанный
secret секре́т, та́йна (noun)
  таи́нственный
  in secret вта́йне (adj.)
secretary секрета́рша
sect се́кта
section отде́л, отделе́ние
secure (to) обеспе́чивать
secure уве́ренный (in something),
  безопа́сный (not dangerous)
security гара́нтия, безопа́сность
seduce (to) соблазня́ть

see (to) ви́деть
seed зерно́
seem (to) каза́ться
segment отре́зок
seize (to) хвата́ть, захва́тывать
seldom и́зредка, ре́дко
select (to) выбира́ть
selected и́збранный
selection ассортиме́нт, вы́бор
self сам (а, о, и), себя́ (reflex. pron.)
self-confidence самоуве́ренность (f.)
self-control вы́держка
self-government самоуправле́ние
selfish эгоисти́ческий
selfishness эгои́зм
self-satisfied самодово́льный
sell (to) продава́ть
semester семе́стр
semicolon то́чка с запято́й
senate сена́т
senator сена́тор
send (to) посыла́ть, усыла́ть (away)
senior ста́рший
sensation ощуще́ние
sense (to) ощуща́ть, чу́вствовать
sense чу́вство, смысл (meaning)
senseless бессмы́сленный
sensibility здравомы́слие
sensible здравомы́слящий
sensitive чу́ткий, чувстви́тельный
sensitivity чу́ткость,
  чувстви́тельность (f.)
sensual сладостра́стный
sensuality сладостра́стность (f.)
sentence пригово́р (legal), фра́за,
  предложе́ние (grammar)
sentiment чу́вство
sentimental сентимента́льный
separate (to) отделя́ть (ся),
  разделя́ть (ся), расходи́ться
separate отде́льный
separation отделе́ние, разделе́ние
September сентя́брь (m.)
serene споко́йный
series се́рия
serious серьёзный
seriously всерьёз
servant прислу́га, служа́нка
  (female)
serve (to) подава́ть (meals),
  служи́ть, обслу́живать
service обслу́живание
  (maintenance), слу́жба (work),
  услу́га (good turn)
set (to) ста́вить, класть, назнача́ть
  (determine), тверде́ть (harden),
  заходи́ть (sun)
  to set aside отложи́ть
  to set free пуска́ть
set прибо́р
settle (to) ула́дить, реша́ть (decide),
  устра́ивать (in a new place)

settlement упла́та, расчёт, населе́ние (people)

seven семь

seventeen семна́дцать

seventeenth семна́дцатый

seventh седьмо́й

seventy се́мьдесят

seventieth семидеся́тый

several не́сколько

severe стро́гий, суро́вый, тяжёлый (heavy)

sew (to) шить
to sew on нашива́ть

sewing шитьё
sewing machine швейная маши́на

sex пол, род

shabby поно́шенный

shade тень (f.), што́ра (window)

shadow тень (f.)

shake (to) дрожа́ть, трясти́ (сь)

shaky ша́ткий

shallow ме́лкий

shame стыд, позо́р (disgrace)

shameful позо́рный

shameless бессты́дный

shape фо́рма

share (to) дели́ть (ся), разделя́ть

share до́ля, часть (f.), а́кция (stock)

shareholder акционе́р

sharp о́стрый, ре́зкий

sharpen (to) заостря́ть, точи́ть

sharpness острота́

shave (to) брить (ся)

shawl шаль (f.)

she она́

shed (to) роня́ть, теря́ть

sheep овца́

sheer прозра́чный, лёгкий

sheet простыня́ (bed), лист (paper)

shelf по́лка

shell скорлупа́

shelter (to) приюти́ть, прикрыва́ть

shelter кров

shepherd пасту́х

shield (to) защища́ть

shield щит

shift (to) передвига́ть

shine (to) блесте́ть, свети́ть (ся), чи́стить

ship (to) грузи́ть, отправля́ть

ship кора́бль (m.)

shipment погру́зка, перево́зка

shirt руба́шка

shiver (to) дрожа́ть, вздра́гивать

shiver дрожь (f.)

shock (to) потряса́ть, шоки́ровать (behavior)

shock уда́р

shoe башма́к, ту́фля

shoot (to) стреля́ть

shop ла́вка, магази́н

shore бе́рег

short коро́ткий, ни́зкий

shortage недоста́ток

shorten (to) сокраща́ть

shorthand стеногра́фия

shot вы́стрел

shoulder плечо́

shout (to) крича́ть

shout крик

shove (to) су́нуть (ся), толка́ть

shovel лопа́та

show (to) пока́зывать, дока́зывать

show вы́ставка, представле́ние

shower душ (bath)

shrill пронзи́тельный

shrimp креве́тка

shrink (to) сади́ться

shun (to) избега́ть

shut (to) закрыва́ть

shut закры́тый

shy засте́нчивый, ро́бкий
to be shy стесня́ться

sick больно́й

sickness боле́знь (f.)

side бок (physical), сторона́

sidewalk тротуа́р

sideways на боку́

sieve си́то

sigh (to) вздыха́ть

sigh вздох

sight вид (view), зре́ние

sign (to) подписа́ться

sign знак

signal (to) сигнализи́ровать

signal сигна́л

signature по́дпись

significance значе́ние

significant многозначи́тельный

significantly многозначи́тельно

signify (to) зна́чить

silence молча́ние, тишина́

silent молчали́вый
to be silent молча́ть
to become silent замолча́ть

silk шёлк

silken шёлковый

silly глу́пый

silver серебро́

similar похо́жий, подо́бный

similarity схо́дство

simple просто́й, несло́жный

simplicity простота́

simplification упроще́ние

simply про́сто

simulate (to) симули́ровать

simultaneous одновре́менный

sin (to) греши́ть

sin грех

since с (prep., gen.), так как

sincere и́скренний, нелицеме́рный

sincerity и́скренность (f.)

sinful гре́шный

sing (to) петь

singer певе́ц, певи́ца

singing пе́ние

single еди́нственный, оди́н

singular еди́нственное число́ (grammar), необыча́йный (unusual)

sinister злове́щий

sink (to) тону́ть, топи́ть (something else)

sink ра́ковина

sinner гре́шник

sip (to) потя́гивать

sip ма́ленький глото́к

sir суда́рь

sister сестра́

sit (to) сиде́ть, сесть (down)

site местоположе́ние

situated (to be) находи́ться

situation положе́ние, ситуа́ция

six шесть

sixteen шестна́дцать

sixteenth шестна́дцатый

sixth шесто́й

sixtieth шестидеся́тый

sixty шестьдеся́т

size величина́, разме́р

skate (to) ката́ться на конька́х

skates коньки́

skeleton скеле́т

skeptical скепти́ческий

sketch (to) рисова́ть эски́зы

sketch эски́з, набро́сок

skill иску́сство, мастерство́

skillful иску́сный, уме́лый

skillfully мастерски́

skin ко́жа

skip (to) скака́ть, пропуска́ть (miss)

skirt ю́бка

skis лы́жи

skull че́реп

sky не́бо

skyscraper небоскрёб

slander (to) клевета́ть

slander клевета́

slang жарго́н

slanting косо́й

slap пощёчина

slaughter убива́ть

slave раб

slavery ра́бство

sleep (to) спать

sleep сон

sleepy со́нный

sleeve рука́в

sleigh са́ни (only in pl.)

slender то́нкий

slice (to) ре́зать, нареза́ть

slice ло́мтик

slide (to) скользи́ть

slight лёгкий

slightly слегка́, чуть

slim то́нкий, стро́йный

slip (to) скользи́ть

slip оши́бка (error), ни́жняя ю́бка (underwear)
slippery ско́льзкий
slope накло́н
slow ме́дленный
  to be slow ме́длить. отстава́ть (clock)
slowly ме́дленно, потихо́ньку
sly хи́трый
small ма́ленький, ме́лкий
  small things, change ме́лочь (f.)
smart у́мный (clever), наря́дный (clothes)
smash (to) разбива́ть
smear (to) ма́зать
smell (to) ню́хать (sniff), па́хнуть (of)
smell за́пах
smile (to) улыба́ться
smile улы́бка
smoke (to) кури́ть
smoke дым
smoking куре́ние
smooth гла́дкий
smother (to) души́ть, туши́ть
smudgy чума́зый
snake змея́
snapshot сни́мок
snatch (to) хвата́ть
sneer (to) насме́шливо улыба́ться
sneeze (to) чиха́ть
snore (to) храпе́ть
snow снег
snowstorm мете́ль
so так
  and so on и так да́лее (и т. д.)
  just so и́менно так
  so much сто́лько
soak (to) мо́кнуть, впи́тывать (up)
soap мы́ло
sob (to) рыда́ть
sobbing рыда́ние
sober тре́звый
social обще́ственный
socialism социали́зм
society о́бщество, свет
sock носо́к (pl. носки́)
sofa дива́н, софа́
soft мя́гкий
soften (to) смягча́ться
soil (to) па́чкать (ся)
soil по́чва, земля́
soiled гря́зный
sold про́данный
soldier солда́т
sole подо́шва, еди́нственный (adj.) (only)
solemn торже́ственный
solemnity торжество́
solicit (to) проси́ть
solid соли́дный, твёрдый
solidity твёрдость (f.)

solitary уединённый, одино́кий (lonely)
solitude уедине́ние, одино́чество
solution разреше́ние (answer), раство́р (chemical)
solve (to) разреша́ть
somber мра́чный
some не́который
somebody кто́-то, кто́-нибудь
somehow ка́к-то, ка́к-нибудь
something что́-то, что́-нибудь
sometimes иногда́
somewhat слегка́
somewhere где́-то, куда́-то (direction)
son сын
song пе́сня
soon ско́ро
soot са́жа
soothe (to) успока́ивать, утеша́ть, облегча́ть (pain)
sore ра́на, я́зва (noun), чувстви́тельный, боле́зненный (adj.)
sorrow печа́ль (f.), скорбь (f.), го́ре
sorry (to feel) жале́ть
  I'm sorry. Мне жа́лко.
sort (to) разбира́ть
sort сорт, род
soul душа́
sound (to) звуча́ть
sound звук
soundless беззву́чный
soup суп
sour ки́слый
  sour cream смета́на
source исто́к, ключ
south юг
southern ю́жный
Soviet сове́тский
Soviet Union Сове́тский Сою́з
sow (to) се́ять
space простра́нство, расстоя́ние
Spanish испа́нский
spare (to) щади́ть, бере́чь
spare запасно́й, ли́шний (extra)
spark и́скра
sparkle (to) блесте́ть, сверка́ть
sparrow воробе́й
speak (to) говори́ть
special специа́льный
specialist специали́ст
specialty специа́льность (f.)
species тип, разнови́дность
specific определённый, характе́рный
spectacle спекта́кль (m.), зре́лище
spectator зри́тель (m.)
speech речь (f.)
speed ско́рость (f.), быстрота́
speedy бы́стрый, ско́рый
spell (to) писа́ть, писа́ться (is spelled)
spell заклина́ние

spelling написа́ние
spend (to) тра́тить
  to spend time проводи́ть вре́мя
sphere шар (ball), сфе́ра, о́бласть (f.)
sphinx сфинкс
spice (to) приправля́ть
spice пря́ность (f.)
spicy пря́ный
spider пау́к
spill (to) пролива́ть, просы́пать
spin (to) кружи́ться
spinach шпина́т
spine спинно́й хребе́т
spirit дух
spiritual духо́вный
spit (to) плева́ть
spite зло́ба
  in spite of несмотря́ на то
splash (to) забры́згивать
splendid великоле́пный, роско́шный
splendor ро́скошь (f.), пы́шность (f.)
split (to) тре́скаться
split тре́щина
spoil (to) по́ртить (ся), балова́ть (a child)
spoiled испо́рченный, избало́ванный (child)
sponge гу́бка
spontaneous самопроизво́льный
spoon ло́жка
sport спорт
spot пятно́
spouse супру́г, -а
spread (to) распространя́ть (ся), разма́зывать (bread)
spring (to) пры́гать
spring весна́, (season), прыжо́к, (jump), исто́чник (source)
spur шпо́ра
spurn (to) отверга́ть с презре́нием
square квадра́т, пло́щадь (f.)
squeak (to) скрипе́ть
squeeze (to) сжима́ть
squirrel бе́лка
stabilize (to) стабилизи́ровать
stable сто́йкий, усто́йчивый
stack (to) скла́дывать в стог, в ку́чу
stack стог, ку́ча
stadium стадио́н
staff штат слу́жащих, штаб, но́тные лине́йки (music)
stage сце́на
stain (to) па́чкать (ся)
stain пятно́
stairs ле́стница
stammer (to) занка́ться
stamp ма́рка (postage), штамп
stand (to) стоя́ть
standard станда́рт, у́ровень (m.), но́рма
standard станда́ртный

star звезда́
starch крахма́л
stare (to) смотре́ть при́стально
stare взгляд
start (to) начина́ть
  to start out (on a trip)
  отправля́ться
start нача́ло
starve (to) умира́ть от го́лода,
  голода́ть
state (to) заявля́ть
state штат, госуда́рство (government),
  состоя́ние (condition)
statement утвержде́ние, заявле́ние
station ста́нция
stationary неподви́жный
stationery канцеля́рские
  принадле́жности
statistics стати́стика
statue ста́туя
staunch пре́данный
stay (to) остава́ться, пробы́ть
stay пребыва́ние
steady усто́йчивый
steak бифште́кс
steal (to) красть
steam (to) па́рить
steam пар
steamship парохо́д
steel сталь (f.)
steep круто́й
steer (to) управля́ть
stem ствол
stenographer стенографи́стка
step похо́дка, шаг
stern стро́гий, суро́вый
stew (to) туши́ть (ся), вари́ть (ся)
stew туше́ное мя́со
stick (to) втыка́ть, прикле́ивать
stick па́лка
sticky кле́йкий
stiff туго́й, ги́бкий
stiffen (to) де́лать неги́бким,
  тверде́ть
still (to) успока́ивать
still ти́хий, споко́йный (adj.), ещё
  (yet) (adv.)
stimulant возбужда́ющее сре́дство,
  сти́мул
stimulate (to) побужда́ть
sting (to) куса́ть, ужа́лить, укуси́ть
sting уку́с
stinginess ску́пость (f.)
stingy скупо́й
stipend стипе́ндия
stir (to) шевели́ть (ся), меша́ть
stitch (to) шить
stitch стежо́к
stock фонд, запа́с
  stock market фо́ндовая би́ржа
stockholder акционе́р
stocking чуло́к

stomach желу́док
stone ка́мень (m.)
stony ка́менный
stool скаме́ечка, табуре́тка
stoop (to) сгиба́ться
stop (to) остана́вливать (ся),
  конча́ть (finish)
stopper про́бка
store ла́вка, магази́н
storm бу́ря
stormy бу́рный
story расска́з, по́весть (f.),
  исто́рия, эта́ж (floor)
stout по́лный
stove печь (f.)
straight прямо́й
straighten (to) выпрямля́ть,
  приводи́ть в поря́док (straighten
  up)
straightforward прямоду́шный
strain напряже́ние
strange чужо́й, стра́нный (queer)
stranger незнако́мец
strap реме́нь (m.)
straw соло́ма
strawberry клубни́ка
stream пото́к, река́ (river)
street у́лица
streetcar трамва́й
strength си́ла
strengthen (to) укрепля́ть
strenuous си́льный, энерги́чный
stress давле́ние, ударе́ние
stretch (to) тяну́ть (ся), растя́гивать
strict стро́гий
stride большо́й шаг
strike (to) ударя́ть (hit), бастова́ть
strike забасто́вка
string верёвка, шпага́т
strip (to) сдира́ть, разде́ть (ся)
  (clothes)
stripe полоса́
stroll (to) гуля́ть
stroll прогу́лка
stroke уда́р
strong си́льный, кре́пкий
structure зда́ние, соста́в, строе́ние,
  структу́ра
struggle борьба́
struggle with (to) би́ться, боро́ться
stubborn упо́рный, упря́мый
student студе́нт, -ка; учени́к
  учени́ца
studies уче́ние
studio сту́дия
studious приле́жный
study (to) учи́ться, изуча́ть,
  занима́ться
study кабине́т (room), эски́з, этю́д
  (sketch)
stuff (to) набива́ть, заполня́ть
stuffing фарш
stuffy ду́шный

stumble (to) спотыка́ться
stun (to) оглуша́ть
stunt по́двиг
stupendous изуми́тельный
stupid глу́пый, тупо́й
stupidity глу́пость (f.)
stupor оцепене́ние
sturdy си́льный, кре́пкий
stutter (to) заика́ться
style фасо́н, стиль (m.)
stylish мо́дный
subdue (to) подчиня́ть
subject те́ма, предме́т, сюже́т
  (theme)
subjugate (to) покоря́ть
submission подчине́ние
submissive поко́рный
submit (to) подчиня́ться
subordination подчине́ние
subscribe (to) подпи́сывать (ся)
subscription подпи́ска
subsequently зате́м, впосле́дствии
subsidiary филиа́л
subsist (to) существова́ть
substance су́щность (f.), содержа́ние
substantial реа́льный, значи́тельный,
  фундамента́льный
substitute (to) замеща́ть (for)
substitute замести́тель (m.)
substitution заме́на
subtle то́нкий
subtract (to) вычита́ть
subtraction вычита́ние
suburb при́город
subway метро́, тонне́ль
succeed (to) насле́довать (to title
  or office), удава́ться, достига́ть це́ли
success уда́ча, успе́х
successful уда́чный, успе́шный
succession после́довательность (f.)
  in succession подря́д
successor насле́дник
such тако́й, э́такий
sudden внеза́пный, неожи́данный
suddenly вдруг
suddenness неожи́данность (f.)
suffer (to) страда́ть, терпе́ть
  (endure)
suffering страда́ние
suffice (to) хвата́ть
sufficient доста́точно
sugar са́хар
  sugar bowl са́харница
suggest (to) предлага́ть
suggestion предложе́ние
suicide самоуби́йство
suit костю́м
suitable подходя́щий
sulk (to) ду́ться
sullen угрю́мый
sulphur се́ра
sum су́мма
summary конспе́кт

summer ле́то, ле́тний (adj.)
summit верши́на
summon (to) вызыва́ть
sumptuous роско́шный, пы́шный
sum up (to) резюми́ровать
sun со́лнце (n.)
sunburn зага́р
Sunday воскресе́нье
sunny со́лнечный
sunrise восхо́д
sunset захо́д, зака́т
suntan зага́р
superb прекра́сный
superficial пове́рхностный
superfluous изли́шний, ли́шний
superior ве́рхний, лу́чший
superiority превосхо́дство,
  пе́рвенство
superstition суеве́рие
supervise (to) наблюда́ть
supper у́жин
  to eat supper у́жинать
supplement добавле́ние, приба́вка
supplementary дополни́тельный
supply (to) снабжа́ть
supply запа́с
support (to) подде́рживать,
  содержа́ть
support подде́ржка
suppose (to) полага́ть, предполага́ть
supposition предположе́ние
supreme верхо́вный, вы́сший
suppress (to) подавля́ть
sure ве́рный, уве́ренный
surely коне́чно, наве́рно
surface пове́рхность (f.)
surgeon хиру́рг
surgery хирурги́я
surmise (to) дога́дываться
surmount (to) преодолева́ть
surname фами́лия
surpass (to) превосходи́ть
surplus изли́шек
surprise (to) удивля́ть (ся) (be
  surprised)
surprise сюрпри́з
surprising удиви́тельный
surrender (to) сдава́ться
surround (to) окружа́ть
surroundings окре́стности
survey (to) осма́тривать
survey осмо́тр, обзо́р (review)
survive (to) пережи́ть
susceptibility впечатли́тельность (f.)
susceptible впечатли́тельный
suspect (to) подозрева́ть
suspense неизве́стность (f.)
suspicion подозре́ние
suspicious подозри́тельный
sustain (to) выде́рживать
swallow (to) глота́ть
swallow глото́к
swamp боло́то

swarthy сму́глый
swear (to) кля́сться, руга́ться
sweat (to) поте́ть
sweat пот
sweater сви́тер
Swedish шве́дский
sweep (to) подмета́ть
sweet сла́дкий
sweetness сла́дость (f.)
swell (to) пу́хнуть, опуха́ть
swift бы́стрый, ско́рый
swim (to) пла́вать
swimming пла́вание
swindle (to) обма́нывать
swindler моше́нник, жу́лик
swing кача́ть
swinging кача́ние
Swiss швейца́рский
switch выключа́тель (m.)
sword меч
swordfish меч-ры́ба
syllable слог
symbol си́мвол
symbolic символи́ческий
symmetrical симметри́чный
sympathetic сочу́вствующий
sympathize (to) сочу́вствовать
sympathy сочу́вствие
symphony симфо́ния
symptom симпто́м, при́знак
synthetic иску́сственный
syringe шприц
syrup сиро́п
system систе́ма, строй (order)
systematic методи́ческий,
  системати́ческий

T

table стол, табли́ца
  tablespoon столо́вая ло́жка
  to set the table накры́ть стол
tablecloth ска́терть
taciturn молчали́вый
tact делика́тность (f.), такт
tactfully такти́чно
tactless беста́ктный
tail хвост
tailor портно́й
take (to) брать, принима́ть
  (medicine, advice)
  to take away убра́ть
  to take leave проща́ться
  to take off снима́ть
tale исто́рия, расска́з
talent тала́нт
talk (to) говори́ть (in general),
  разгова́ривать
    to talk over переговори́ть
talk бесе́да, разгово́р
talkative разгово́рчивый
tall большо́й, высо́кий
tame (to) прируча́ть

tame ручно́й
tangle (to) запу́тывать
tank бак, танк (military)
tap стук
tape тесьма́, ле́нта
  tape recorder магнитофо́н
tar дёготь
tardy по́здний
target цель (f.)
tarnish (to) тускне́ть
task зада́ние
taste (to) про́бовать
taste вкус
tasteless безвку́сный
tasty вку́сный
tax нало́г
taxi такси́ (not declined)
tea чай (m.)
  teapot ча́йник
  teaspoon ча́йная ло́жка
teach (to) преподава́ть, учи́ть
teacher преподава́тель, -ница;
  учи́тель, -ница
team брига́да (work), кома́нда (sport)
tear (to) (cut) рвать, срыва́ть
tear слеза́ (teardrop)
tease (to) дразни́ть
technical техни́ческий
  technical school те́хникум
technician те́хник
technique те́хника
tedious ску́чный
teeth зу́бы
telegram телегра́мма
telegraph (to) телеграфи́ровать
telephone (to) звони́ть по телефо́ну
telephone телефо́н
telescope телеско́п
television телеви́дение
  television set телеви́зор
tell (to) расска́зывать
temper темпера́мент, нрав
  to lose one's temper вы́йти из себя́
temperate уме́ренный
temperature температу́ра
tempest бу́ря
temple висо́к (part of body), храм
temporary вре́менный
tempt (to) привлека́ть, соблазня́ть
temptation искуше́ние
ten де́сять
tenacious упо́рный, це́пкий
tenacity упо́рство во́ли, це́пкость
tendency тенде́нция
tender ла́сковый, не́жный,
  чувстви́тельный (feeling)
tennis те́ннис
  to play tennis игра́ть в те́ннис
tense напряжённый, вре́мя (noun)
  (grammar)
tension напряже́ние
tent пала́тка
tentative про́бный, усло́вный

tenth деся́тый

tepid теплова́тый

term срок, семе́стр (school)

terminal заключи́тельный, коне́чный вокза́л (noun)

terrible гро́зный, стра́шный, ужа́сный

terrify (to) ужаса́ть (ся)

territory террито́рия

terror у́жас

test о́пыт, про́ба

testify (to) свиде́тельствовать

testimony доказа́тельство

text текст

textbook уче́бник

than чем

thank (to) благодари́ть

  Thank you. Спаси́бо.

  thanks to благодаря́ тому́

  thanks a lot большо́е спаси́бо

thankful благода́рный

that тот (та, то), что (conj.)

  in order that чтобы

  that is то́ есть (т.е.)

thaw (to) та́ять

the—no article in Russian

theater теа́тр

  theater notice реце́нзия

theatrical театра́льный

theft кра́жа

their, theirs их

them их, им

theme те́ма

themselves са́ми

then пото́м, тогда́, то

theory тео́рия

there там (location), туда́ (direction)

  from there отту́да

thereafter с э́того вре́мени

thereby посре́дством э́того

therefore поэ́тому, сле́довательно

thermometer термо́метр

these э́ти

thesis диссерта́ция, те́зис

they они́

thick густо́й (dense), то́лстый

thief вор

thigh бедро́

thimble напёрсток

thin худо́й

  to grow thin худе́ть

thing вещь (f.), шту́ка

think (to) ду́мать, мы́слить

  to think over обду́мать, проду́мать

third тре́тий

thirst жа́жда

thirteen трина́дцать

thirteenth трина́дцатый

thirtieth тридца́тый

thirty три́дцать

this э́тот, (э́та, э́то)

  this is э́то

thorn колю́чка, шип

thorough по́лный, соверше́нный

thoroughfare прое́зд

though хотя́

thought мысль (f.)

thoughtful внима́тельный, забо́тливый

thoughtless легкомы́сленный, необду́манный

thousand ты́сяча

thousandth ты́сячный

thrash (to) бить

thread ни́тка

threat угро́за

threaten (to) угрожа́ть

threatening гро́зный

three три

threshold поро́г

thrift бережли́вость (f.)

thrifty бережли́вый

thrill глубо́кое волне́ние, тре́пет

thrive (to) процвета́ть

thriving цвету́щий

throat го́рло

throb (to) си́льно би́ться

throne престо́л, трон

throng толпа́

through сквозь (acc.), че́рез (acc.)

throughout наскво́зь

throw (to) броса́ть (ся)

  to throw out выбра́сывать

thumb большо́й па́лец

thunder (to) греме́ть

thunder гром

thunderstorm гроза́

Thursday четве́рг

thus так, таки́м о́бразом

ticket биле́т

  ticket window ка́сса

tickle (to) щекота́ть

ticklish щекотли́вый

tide морско́й прили́в (incoming) и отли́в (receding)

tidiness аккура́тность (f.)

tidy аккура́тный

tie (to) свя́зывать

tie связь (f.) (bond), га́лстук (necktie)

tiger тигр

tight те́сный, у́зкий

till до (gen.)

timber лесоматериа́л

time вре́мя, раз (occasion)

  on time во́время

  It is time to go. Пора́ идти́.

  to have time успе́ть

  What time is it? Кото́рый час?

timepiece часы́ (m. pl.)

timid ро́бкий

timidity ро́бкость (f.)

tin о́лово

tiny о́чень ма́ленький

tip ко́нчик

  to give a tip дать на чай

tipsy пья́ный

tire (to) устава́ть, утомля́ть (ся)

tire ши́на

tired уста́лый

tireless неутоми́мый

tiresome надое́дливый, ску́чный

title загла́вие, назва́ние

to в (acc.), к (dat.) на (acc.)

toast тост

tobacco таба́к

today ны́не, сего́дня

toe па́лец

toenail но́готь (m.)

together вме́сте (adv.)

  to draw together сближа́ться

toil труди́ться

toilet туале́т, убо́рная

token знак

tolerable сно́сный

tolerance терпи́мость (f.)

tolerant терпи́мый

tolerate (to) выноси́ть, терпе́ть

tomato (sing. and pl.) помидо́р

tomb моги́ла

tomorrow за́втра

ton то́нна

tone тон

tongue язы́к

tonight сего́дня ве́чером

too то́же (also), сли́шком, чересчу́р (much)

tool инструме́нт, ору́дие

tooth зуб

  toothbrush зубна́я щётка

  toothpaste зубна́я па́ста

  tooth powder зубно́й порошо́к

top верши́на, верх

torch фа́кел

torment (to) му́чить

torment му́ка, муче́ние

torture (to) пыта́ть, му́чить

torture пы́тка, муче́ние

toss (to) кида́ть

total це́лое

totally соверше́нно

touch (to) тро́гать

touching тро́гательный

touchy оби́дчивый, чувстви́тельный

tough жёсткий

tour (to) путеше́ствовать

tour путеше́ствие, объе́зд

tourist тури́ст

tournament турни́р

toward к (dat.)

towel полоте́нце

tower ба́шня

town го́род

toy игру́шка

trace (to) черти́ть (draw), проследи́ть

trace след

track след

tractor тра́ктор

trade торго́вля

tradition традиция
traditional традиционный
traffic движение
tragedy трагедия
tragic трагический
train (to) воспитывать, тренировать
train поезд
training воспитание, тренировка
trait черта
traitor изменник
trample (to) топтать
tranquil спокойный
tranquility спокойствие
transaction сделка, дело
transfer (to) переносить, передавать
transform (to) преображать
transformation преображение
transgress (to) переступать
transit проход, проезд, переход
transitional переходный
translate (to) переводить
translation перевод
translator переводчик
transmission передача
transmit (to) передавать
transparent прозрачный
transport (to) перевозить
transportation перевозка; пути
    сообщения
trap (to) ловить
trap ловушка
trash отбросы
travel (to) путешествовать
travel путешествие
traveler путешественник, путник
tray поднос
treacherous предательский
treachery предательство
treason измена
treasure драгоценность (f.)
treasurer казначей
treasury государственное
    казначейство
treat (to) обращаться, относиться
    to treat medically лечить
treat наслаждение
treatment обращение, обработка,
treaty договор
tree дерево
tremble (to) трепетать
trembling трепетание
tremendous громадный
trend направление, течение
    (direction)
trial проба, суд
triangle треугольник
tribe племя
tribute дань (f.)
trick фокус
trifle мелочь
    a trifle немножко
trifling пустячный

trim (to) подстригать (hair),
    украшать (decorate)
trimming украшение
trip (to) споткнуться
trip путь, экскурсия
triple тройной
triumph (to) победить (win),
    торжествовать
triumph торжество, триумф
trivial тривиальный
trolley bus троллейбус
tropical тропический
trot (to) ехать рысью
trouble (to) беспокоиться,
    хлопотать
trouble беда, забота, хлопоты (fuss)
troubled беспокойный
trousers брюки
truck грузовик
true верный (faithful), правильный
    (correct)
truly поистине, точно
trunk чемодан, сундук
trust (to) верить, доверять
trust вера, доверие
trustworthy надёжный
truth истина, правда
thruthful правдивый
try (to) пробовать, пытаться,
    стараться, судить (in court)
    to try on примерять
Tuesday вторник
tumble (to) падать
tumult шум и крики
tune мелодия
tunnel туннель
turkey индюк
turmoil суматоха
turn (to) поворачивать (ся)
    to turn around переворачиваться
    to turn out получаться
    to turn pages перелистывать
turn поворот (rotation), очередь,
    (chance)
twelfth двенадцатый
twelve двенадцать
twentieth двадцатый
twenty двадцать
twice дважды, вдвое
twilight полусвет, сумрак
twin двойной
twins близнецы
twist (to) крутить
two два (m.), две (f.)
type (to) печатать
typewriter пишущая машинка
typical характерный
typist машинистка (f.)
tyranny деспотизм
tyrant тиран, деспот

U

ugly безобразный
ultimate максимальный
umbrella зонтик
umpire посредник, рефери
unable неспособный, неумеющий
unaffected безыскусственный
unanimous единогласный
unattainable недостижимый
unattractive некрасивый
unaware неожиданно
unbearable несносный, нестерпимый,
    невыносимый
unbelievable невероятный
unbreakable небьющийся
unbutton (to) расстёгивать
uncertain неопределённый
    (indefinite), неуверенный (unsure)
uncle дядя
uncomfortable неудобный
uncommon редкий
unconscious бессознательный
unconsciousness беспамятство
uncover (to) раскрывать
undecided нерешённый
undeniable несомненный
under под (inst.—location; acc.—
    direction)
underestimate (to) недооценивать
undergo (to) испытывать
underline (to) подчёркивать
underneath под (under)
understand (to) понимать
understandable понятный
understanding соглашение,
    понимание
    to come to an understanding
    договориться
undertake (to) предпринимать
undertaker гробовщик
underwear нижнее бельё
undeserved незаслуженный
undesirable нежелательный
undo (to) развязывать
undoubtedly безусловно
undress (to) раздевать (ся)
uneasiness тревога
uneasy неспокойный
uneducated необразованный
unemployed незанятый, безработный
unemployment безработица
unequal неравный
uneven неровный
unexpectedly неожиданно
unfair несправедливый
unfaithful неверный
unfavorable отрицательный
unfeeling бесчувственный
unfinished недоконченный
unforeseen непредвиденный
unforgettable незабываемый
unfortunate несчастный, неудачный

unfortunately к сожалéнию
unfriendly недружелю́бный
ungentlemanly непоря́дочный
ungraceful неграцио́зный
ungrateful неблагода́рный
unhappy несчастли́вый, несча́стный
unharmed невреди́мый
unhealthy боле́зненный
unheard of неслы́ханный
uniform фо́рма (noun),
    однообра́зный (adj.)
uniformity единообра́зие
unify (to) объединя́ть
unimportant нева́жный
unintentionally нево́льно
union сою́з, соедине́ние
unit едини́ца, едини́ца измере́ния
unite (to) соединя́ть
united соединённый
    United States Соединённые
    Шта́ты
universal универса́льный
universe ко́смос
university университе́т
unjust несправедли́вый
unkind недо́брый
unknown неизве́стный
unlawful беззако́нный
unless éсли . . . не
unlike неправдоподо́бный,
    непохо́жий
unlimited неограни́ченный
unlock (to) отпира́ть
unlocked о́тпертый
unluckily к сожале́нию
unmarried нежена́тый, холосто́й (of
    men), незаму́жняя (of women)
unmerciful немилосе́рдный
unnatural неесте́ственный
unnecessary нену́жный
unoccupied незаня́тый, свобо́дный
unpack (to) раскла́дываться
unpleasant неприя́тный
unpleasantness неприя́тность (f.)
unprecedented небыва́лый
unprofitable недохо́дный
unprotected беззащи́тный
unpublished неи́зданный
unquestionably несомне́нно,
    бесспо́рно
unravel (to) распу́тывать
unreal ненастоя́щий
unreasonable неразу́мный
unreliable ненадёжный
unrestrained несде́ржанный
unripe незре́лый
unroll (to) развёртывать
unsafe опа́сный
unsatisfactory
    неудовлетвори́тельнный
unsatisfied неудовлетворённый
unscrupulous бессо́вестный

unselfish бескоры́стный
unsociable нелюди́мый
unsophisticated простоду́шный
unsteady неусто́йчивый
unsuccessful неуда́чный
unsuitable неподходя́щий
untidy неаккура́тный
untie (to) развя́зывать
until до (gen.)
untrue ло́жный, непра́вильный,
    неве́рный (faithless)
unusual необыкнове́нный
unwell нездоро́вый
unwilling несклонный
unwillingly неохо́тно, не́хотя
unwise неблагоразу́мный
unworthy недосто́йный
up, upward наве́рх
uphold (to) подде́рживать
upkeep содержа́ние
upper ве́рхний
upright прямо́й
uprising восста́ние
upset (to) опроки́дывать,
    беспоко́ить
upside down вверх дном
upstairs наверху́
urge (to) наста́ивать на, убежда́ть
urgency настоя́тельность (f.)
urgent насто́йчивый, спе́шный
us нас, нам
use (to) по́льзоваться, употребля́ть
use по́льза, употребле́ние
used to (to become) привыка́ть
useful поле́зный
useless бесполе́зный
usual обыкнове́нный
usually обыкнове́нно, обы́чно
utility поле́зность (f.), вы́годность
    (f.)
utilize (to) испо́льзовать
utmost са́мый отдалённый, кра́йний
utter (to) произноси́ть
utterly чрезвыча́йно

V

vacant неза́нятый, свобо́дный
vacation о́тпуск, кани́кулы
vaccination приви́вка
vacuum пустота́
vacuum cleaner пылесо́с
vaguely неотчётливо, сму́тно
vain тщесла́вный
    in vain напра́сно, да́ром, тще́тно
valiant хра́брый
valid действи́тельный, име́ющий
    си́лу
validity действи́тельность (f.)
valise чемода́н
valley доли́на
valuable це́нный
value (to) цени́ть

value це́нность (f.)
valve ве́нтиль, кла́пан
vanilla вани́ль
vanish (to) исчеза́ть
vanity суета́
vanquish (to) побежда́ть
vapor пар
variable изме́нчивый, переме́нный
variation измене́ние, вариа́ция
varied разли́чный
variety разнообра́зие
various ра́зный, разнообра́зный
varnish (to) лакирова́ть
vary (to) меня́ть (ся)
vase ва́за
vast грома́дный
veal теля́тина
vegetables зе́лень, о́вощи
vehicle пово́зка, теле́га
veil (to) закрыва́ть покрыва́лом,
    скрыва́ть (hide)
veil покрыва́ло
vein ве́на
velvet ба́рхат
venerable почте́нный
venerate (to) благогове́ть перед
    ке́м-либо
veneration почита́ние
vengeance месть (f.)
ventilation прове́тривание,
    вентиля́ция
ventilator вентиля́тор
venture (to) рискова́ть
verb глаго́л
verbal у́стный
verdict при́говор, сужде́ние
verge край
verification подтвержде́ние
verify (to) проверя́ть
versatile многосторо́нний
verse стих
version перево́д (translation),
    ве́рсия
vertical вертика́льный
very о́чень
vest жиле́т
vexation доса́да
vibrate (to) вибри́ровать
vibration вибра́ция
vice поро́к
vice versa наоборо́т
vicinity бли́зость (f.), окре́стности
vicious злой
victim же́ртва
victorious победоно́сный
victory побе́да
view вид
viewpoint подхо́д, то́чка зре́ния
vigorous энерги́чный
vile по́длый
village село́, дере́вня
villain подле́ц
vinegar у́ксус

violate (to) преступа́ть
violation наруше́ние
violence наси́лие
violent бе́шеный
violet фиа́лка
violet фиоле́товый
violin скри́пка
violinist скрипа́ч
virtue доброде́тель, ка́чество
virtuous доброде́тельный
visa ви́за
visible ви́димый
vision зре́ние
visit (to) посеща́ть
visit визи́т, посеще́ние
visitor гость (m.), посети́тель (m.)
visual зри́тельный
vital жи́зненный, роково́й
vitality жи́зненность (f.)
vitamin витами́н
vivacious живо́й
vivid я́ркий
vocabulary словарь (m.), запа́с
    слов
vocal голосово́й
vocation призва́ние
vodka во́дка
vogue мо́да
voice го́лос
void пустота́ (noun), пусто́й,
    недействи́тельный (invalid)
volt вольт
volume том
voluntary доброво́льный
volunteer доброво́лец
vote (to) голосова́ть
vote го́лос
vow кля́тва
vowel гла́сный
voyage путеше́ствие
vulgar гру́бый, вульга́рный
vulnerable уязви́мый

W

wager (to) держа́ть пари́
wager пари́
wages зарпла́та
waist та́лия
wait (to) ждать
    to wait for (expect) ожида́ть
    waiting room приёмная
waiter официа́нт, -ка
wake up (to) просыпа́ться
walk (to) идти́, ходи́ть
walk прогу́лка
wall стена́
wallet бума́жник
waltz вальс
wander (to) броди́ть
want (to) хоте́ть
want недоста́ток (lack), нужда́
    (need)

war война́
wardrobe шкаф, гардеро́б
wares това́ры, проду́кты
warm (to) греть, согрева́ть
warm тёплый
warmth теплота́
warn (to) предупрежда́ть
warning предупрежде́ние
wash (to) мыть (ся), умыва́ть (ся),
    стира́ть (clothes)
waste (to) расточа́ть
wasteful нерасчётливый
watch (to) наблюда́ть, сторожи́ть
watch часы́ (pl.)
watchful бди́тельный
watchman сто́рож
water вода́
waterfall водопа́д
water color акваре́ль (f.)
watermelon арбу́з
waterproof водонепроница́емый
wave (to) маха́ть
wave волна́
wax воск
way доро́га, путь (road), спо́соб
    (manner)
we мы
weak сла́бый, бесси́льный
weaken (to) слабе́ть, ослабля́ть
weakness сла́бость (f.)
wealth бога́тство
wealthy бога́тый
weapon ору́жие
wear (to) носи́ть
weariness уста́лость (f.), утомле́ние
wearing утоми́тельный
weary (to) утомля́ть
weary уста́лый, утомлённый
weather пого́да
weave (to) ткать
web ткань, паути́на
wedding сва́дьба
Wednesday среда́
weed со́рная трава́
week неде́ля
    week end коне́ц неде́ли
weekly еженеде́льный
weep (to) пла́кать
weigh (to) взве́шивать (ся)
weight вес
welcome (to) приве́тствовать
    Welcome! Добро́ пожа́ловать!
welcome приве́тствие, раду́шный
    приём
welfare благосостоя́ние
well хорошо́, благополу́чно
west за́пад
western за́падный
westward на за́пад
wet мо́крый
what как, что
    what a, what kind of како́й
wheel колесо́

when когда́
whenever когда́ бы ни
where где (location), куда́
    (direction)
    where . . . from отку́да
whereas так как
whether ли
    I don't know whether he is here.
    Я не зна́ю здесь ли он.
which кото́рый (ая, ое, ые)
whichever како́й уго́дно, како́й бы
    ни
while пока́
whim капри́з
whiskers усы́
whisper (to) шепта́ть
    in a whisper шо́потом
whistle (to) свиста́ть
whistle свист
white бе́лый
who кто, кото́рый (inter. pron.)
whole весь (вся, всё все), це́лый
    as a whole целико́м, в це́лом
wholesale о́птом
wholesome здоро́вый, поле́зный
wholly вполне́
whom кого́, кому́, о ко́м
whose чей (чья, чьё, чьи)
why почему́, заче́м
wicked злой
wide широ́кий, на́стежь (adv.)
widen (to) расширя́ть
widow вдова́
widower вдове́ц
width ширина́
wife жена́
wild ди́кий
wilderness пусты́ня, ди́кое ме́сто
will во́ля, завеща́ние (legal)
willing гото́вый
willingly охо́тно
win (to) вы́играть, побежда́ть
    (a victory)
wind (to) ви́ться
wind ве́тер
window окно́
windy ве́треный
wine вино́
    wineglass рю́мка
wing крыло́
wink (to) мига́ть
winter зима́
wipe (to) вытира́ть, уничтожа́ть
    (wipe out)
wire про́волока, про́вод
wisdom му́дрость (f.)
wise му́дрый
wish (to) жела́ть
wish жела́ние
wit ум, ра́зум
witch ве́дьма
with с (inst.)
wither (to) вя́нуть, со́хнуть

within внутри (adv. and prep., gen.)
without без (gen.), снаружи (adv.), (outside)
 without fail непременно, обязательно
witness (to) быть свидетелем
witness свидетель (m.)
witty остроумный
woe горе
wolf волк
woman женщина
wonder (to) желать знать, удивляться (be surprised)
wonder чудо, удивление (surprise)
wonderful изумительный, чудный
wood дерево
wooden деревянный
woods лес
wool шерсть
woolen шерстяной
word слово
work (to) работать
work труд, работа, сочинение (composition)
worker рабочий
works (plant) завод
world мир, свет
 world outlook мировоззрение
wordly светский
worried озабоченный, издёрганный
worry (to) беспокоить (ся)
 Don't worry. Не беспокойтесь.
worry тревога, забота
worse хуже

worship (to) бывать в церкви, молить (ся) (pray), обожать (adore)
worst наихудший
worth цена, достоинство
worthless негодный, недостойный
worthy достойный
wound (to) ранить
wound рана
wounded раненый
wrap (to) обёртывать, завёртывать
wrath гнев, ярость
wreck (to) разрушать
wreck авария, крушение
wrench (tool) гаечный ключ
wretched жалкий, несчастный
wring (to) выжимать, скручивать
wrinkle складка, морщина (facial)
write (to) писать
writer писатель (m.)
writing писание (noun), письменный (adj.)
 in writing письменно
wrong неправильный

X, Y, Z

X rays икс-лучи

yacht яхта
yard двор (courtyard)
yarn нить
yawn (to) зевать

yawn зевота
year год
 years лета
yearly ежегодный
yearn (to) тосковать
yearning тоска, желание
yeast дрожжи
yell (to) кричать
yellow жёлтый
yes да
yesterday вчера
yet ещё
yield (to) производить
yield (harvest) урожай
you вы, ты, (pl. and polite, sing.) вас, тебя, (acc. pl. and polite sing), вам, тебе (dat., pl. and polite, sing.)
young молодой
younger младший
your, yours ваш (а, е, и) (pl. and polite), твой (твоя, твоё, твой) (sing.)
youth юность (f.), молодёжь (f., coll.) (young people), юность (f.) (early years)

zeal усердие
zealous усердный
zero нуль
zinc цинк
zipper застёжка-молния
zone зона, пояс
zoo зоопарк
zoology зоология

GLOSSARY OF PROPER NAMES

Adelaide Аделаи́да, Аде́ль	John Ива́н
Agatha Ага́фья	Joseph Ио́сиф
Agnes Агне́са	Julia Ю́лия
Alexander Алекса́ндр	Laurence Лавре́нтий
Alexis Алексе́й	Leo Лёв
Alfred Альфре́д	Leonidas Леони́д
Alice Али́са	Louise Луи́за
Amy Любо́вь	Ludmilla Людми́ла
Anastasia Анаста́сия	Luke Лука́
Anatole Анато́лий	Macarius Мака́р
Andrew Андре́й	Marie, Mary Мари́я
Anna Анна	Margaret Маргари́та
Anthony Анто́н	Martha Ма́рфа
Apollo Аполло́н	Matthew Матве́й
Arthur Арту́р	Maxim Макс
Barbara Варва́ра	Michael Михаи́л
Basil Васи́лий	Natalia Ната́лия
Boris Бори́с	Nicholas Никола́й
Carl Карл	Nikita Ники́та
Catherine Екатери́на	Oleg Оле́г
Charlotte Шарло́тта	Olga Ольга
Claudia Кла́вдия	Paul Па́вел
Constantine Константи́н	Peter Пётр
Daniel Дани́ла	Philip Фили́пп
David Дави́д	Samuel Самуи́л
Demetrius Дими́трий	Sergius Серге́й
Dorothy Дороте́я	Simon Симео́н
Edward Эдуа́рд	Sofia Со́фия
Eleanor Элеоно́ра	Solomon Соломо́н
Elias Илья́	Susan Суса́нна
Elizabeth Елизаве́та	Sviatoslaff Святосла́в
Eugene Евге́ний	Theodore Фёдор
Eva Ева	Thomas Фома́
George Гео́ргий	Timothy Тимофе́й
Gregory Григо́рий	Valentine Валенти́н
Helen Еле́на	Vera Ве́ра
Herman Ге́рман	Victor Ви́ктор
Hope Наде́жда	Vladimir Влади́мир
Ida Ида	Walter Ва́льтер
Irene Ири́на	William Вильге́льм
Jacob, James Я́ков	Zacharias Заха́р

GLOSSARY OF GEOGRAPHICAL NAMES

Adriatic Sea Адриати́ческое мо́ре
Africa Африка
Alaska Аля́ска
Albany Алба́ния
Algeria Алжи́р
Alps, The Альпы
America Аме́рика
Arabia Ара́вия
Argentina Аргенти́на
Asia Азия
Astrakhan Астрахань
Atlantic Ocean Атланти́ческий Океан
Australia Австра́лия
Austria Австрия
Azerbaijan Soviet Socialist Republic
  Азербайджа́нская Сове́тская
  Социалисти́ческая Респу́блика
Baikal (Lake) Байка́л
Baku Баку́
Belgium Бе́льгия
Black Sea Чёрное Мо́ре
Bonn Бонн
Boston Босто́н
Brazil Брази́лия
Brussels Брюссе́ль
Bulgaria Болга́рия
Byelorussian Soviet Socialist Republic
  Белору́сская Сове́тская
  Социалисти́ческая Респу́блика
Carpathian Mountains Карпа́тские
  Го́ры
Caspian Sea Каспи́йское Мо́ре
Caucasus The, (Mountains) Кавка́з
Chicago Чика́го
Chile Чи́ли
China Кита́й
Copenhagen Копенга́ген
Crimea Крым
Czechoslovakia Чехослова́кия
Danube (River) Дуна́й
Denmark Да́ния
Detroit Детро́йт
Dnieper (River) Днепр
Don (River) Дон
Egypt Еги́пет
England Англия
English Channel Лама́нш
Europe Евро́па
Finland Финля́ндия
France Фра́нция
Geneva Жене́ва
Georgian Soviet Socialist Republic
  Грузи́нская Сове́тская
  Социалисти́ческая Респу́блика
Germany Герма́ния
Gorky (City) Го́рький
Great Britain Великобрита́ния
Hamburg Га́мбург
Helsinki Хе́льсинки
Hungary Ве́нгрия
India Индия

Iran Ира́н
Iraq Ира́к
Ireland Ирла́ндия
Italy Ита́лия
Japan Япо́ния
Jerusalem Иерусали́м
Jordan Иорда́нь
Kiev Ки́ев
Korea Коре́я
Leningrad Ленингра́д
London Ло́ндон
Los Angeles Лос Анжелос
Madrid Мадри́д
Magnitogorsk Магнитого́рск
Mediterranean Sea Средизе́мное
  Мо́ре
Mexico Ме́ксика
Moscow Москва́
Munich Мю́нхен
The Netherlands Нидерла́нды
Neva (River) Нева́
New York Нью-Йорк
North America Се́верная Аме́рика
Norway Норве́гия
Odessa Оде́сса
Pacific Ocean Ти́хий Океа́н
Palestine Палести́на
Panama Canal Пана́мский Кана́л
Paris Пари́ж
Philadelphia филаде́льфия
Poland По́льша
Portugal Португа́лия
Pyrenees (Mountains) Пирене́и
Rhine (River) Рейн
Rocky Mountains Скали́стые Го́ры
Rome Рим
Russia Росси́я
Russian Soviet Federative Socialist
  Republic Росси́йская Сове́тская
  Федерати́вная Социалисти́ческая
  Респу́блика
San Francisco Сан-Франци́ско
Scotland Шотла́ндия
Seine (River) Се́на
Siberia Сиби́рь
South America Южная Аме́рика
Spain Испа́ния
Stalingrad Сталингра́д
Stockholm Стокго́льм
Sweden Шве́ция
Switzerland Швейца́рия
Syria Си́рия
Tajik Soviet Socialist Republic
  Таджи́кская Сове́тская
  Социалисти́ческая Респу́блика
Tashkent Ташке́нт
Tbilisi Тбили́си
Thames (River) Те́мза
Tokyo То́кио
Turkey Ту́рция

Ukrainian Soviet Socialist Republic
Укра́инская Сове́тская
Социалисти́ческая Респу́блика
Union of Soviet Socialist Republics
Сою́з Сове́тских
Социалисти́ческих Респу́блик
United States of America
Соединённые Шта́ты Аме́рики

Urals (Mountains) Ура́л
Uzbek Soviet Socialist Republic
Узбе́кская Сове́тская
Социалисти́ческая Респу́блика
Vladivostok Владивосто́к
Volga (River) Во́лга
Washington Вашингто́н
Yugoslavia Югосла́вия

COMMON USAGE
DICTIONARY

Spanish-English
English-Spanish

BY **Ralph Weiman**   FORMERLY CHIEF
OF LANGUAGE SECTION, U.S. WAR DEPARTMENT

AND **O. A. Succar**

REVISED AND ENLARGED BY **Robert E. Hammarstrand**, Ph.D.
ASSISTANT PROFESSOR OF EDUCATION, HUNTER COLLEGE

---

*CONTAINING OVER 20,000 BASIC TERMS WITH
MEANINGS ILLUSTRATED BY SENTENCES AND
1000 ESSENTIAL WORDS SPECIALLY INDICATED*

INTRODUCTION

The Spanish Common Usage Dictionary lists the most frequently used Spanish words, gives their most important meanings and illustrates their use.

1. The *basic* words are indicated by capitals. These are the words generally considered essential for any reasonable command of the language.

2. Only the most important meanings are given.

3. These meanings are illustrated, wherever necessary, by means of everyday phrases and sentences. Where there is no close English equivalent for a Spanish word or where the English equivalent has several different meanings, the context of the illustrative sentences helps to make the meanings clear.

4. Each important word is followed by the everyday expression and sentences in which it most frequently occurs. The Common Usage Dictionary serves accordingly as a phrase book or conversation guide: it contains thousands of everyday sentences which are of practical importance (for traveling, correspondence, etc.) or which serve as illustrations of the grammatical features of current written and spoken Span-

ish. The Common Usage Dictionary should, therefore, prove helpful both to beginners who are building up their vocabulary and to advanced students who want to perfect their command of colloquial Spanish.

5. In translating the Spanish phrases and sentences an attempt has been made to give not a mere translation but an equivalent—that is, what an English speaker would say in the same situation. (Literal translations have been added to help the beginner.) The user is thus furnished with numerous examples of how common Spanish expressions (particularly the very idiomatic and the very colloquial ones) can best be translated into English. This feature makes the Common Usage Dictionary especially useful for translation work.

6. The English-Spanish part contains the most common English words and their Spanish equivalents. By consulting the sentences given under the Spanish word in the Spanish-English part the reader can observe whether the Spanish word always translates the English one or whether it does so only in certain cases.

EXPLANATORY NOTES

Literal translations are in quotation marks.
Very colloquial phrases and sentences are marked *coll.*
Expressions used in Latin America are marked *Amer.*
Expressions used in a particular country are followed by an abbreviation of the name of the country (*Mex., Arg.,* etc.).

Spanish-English DICTIONARY

A

A *to, in, at, on, by, for.*

Voy a Barcelona. *I'm going to Barcelona.*

¿A quién quiere Ud. escribir? *Who(m) do you want to write to?*

Dígaselo a él. *Tell it to him.*

A la derecha. *To the right. On the right.*

A las cinco y cuarto. *At a quarter past five.*

A veces. *At times.*

A la vista. *At sight.*

A tiempo. *In time.*

A pie. *On foot.*

Uno a uno. *One by one.*

ABAJO *down, below, under; downstairs.*

Está abajo. *He's downstairs.*

De arriba abajo. *From top to bottom. From top to toe. From head to foot.*

Calle abajo. *Down the street.*

abandonado *adj. abandoned, given up; untidy; careless.*

abandonar *to abandon, to give up, to leave.*

Después de cinco años lo abandonó. *He gave it up after five years.*

abandono *m. abandonment; slovenliness.*

abanico *m. fan.*

abarcar *to embrace, include, contain; to cover (a subject); to reach, extend to.*

La tienda abarca toda la cuadra. *The store occupies the whole block.*

abarrotes *m. groceries; grocery (store).*

Tienda de abarrotes. *Grocery.*

abastecer *to supply, to provide.*

abastecimiento *m. supply.*

abdomen *m. abdomen.*

abecedario *m. the alphabet; primer (book).*

abeja *f. bee.*

abiertamente *openly, frankly, plainly.*

ABIERTO *adj. open; frank.*

¿Hasta qué hora está la tienda abierta? *How late does the store stay open? Till what time does the store stay open?*

Ha dejado Ud. abierta la ventana. *You've left the window open.*

abogado *m. lawyer, attorney; mediator.*

abonado *adj. reliable, rich; m. subscriber; commuter.*

Guía de abonados. *Telephone directory.*

abonar *to credit to; to pay; to fertilize (the soil).*

abonarse *to subscribe to.*

abono *m. allowance; subscription; commutation ticket; fertilizer.*

aborrecer *to despise, to hate, to dislike.*

aborrecimiento *m. hatred, abhorrence.*

abotonar *to button.*

Abotónese el chaleco. *Button your vest.*

abrazar *to embrace, to hug.*

abrazo *m. hug, embrace.*

abrelatas *m. can opener.*

abreviar *to abbreviate.*

abreviatura *f. abbreviation.*

abridor *m. opener.*

abrigar *to shelter, to protect; to make or keep warm.*

abrigarse *to take shelter; to cover oneself; to dress warmly.*

ABRIGO *m. shelter; protection; overcoat.*

ABRIL *m. April.*

ABRIR *to open, to unlock.*

Abra la ventana. *Open the window.*

abrochar *to button; to fasten.*

absceso *m. abscess.*

ABSOLUTAMENTE *absolutely.*

absoluto *adj. absolute.*

absolver *to absolve, to acquit.*

abstenerse *to abstain, to refrain.*

abstinencia *f. abstinence, temperance.*

absuelto *adj. absolved, acquitted.*

absurdo *adj. absurd.*

Es un cuento absurdo. *It's an absurd story.*

abuela *f. grandmother.*

abuelo *m. grandfather.*

abundancia *f. abundance.*

abundante *adj. abundant.*

abundar *to abound.*

aburrido *adj. weary, bored, tiresome.*

aburrimiento *m. weariness, boredom.*

aburrir *to bore; to annoy.*

aburrirse *to be (get) bored.*

abusar *to abuse; to take advantage of.*

Abusa de su bondad. *He's taking advantage of your kindness.*

abuso *m. abuse, misuse.*

¡Esto es un abuso! *That's taking advantage!*

ACÁ *here, this way.*

¡Ven acá! *Come here!*

¿De cuándo acá? *Since when?*

ACABAR *to finish, to complete, to end.*

¿Consiguió Ud. acabar su trabajo? *Did you manage to finish your work?*

Acabar de. *To have just.*

Acabo de comer. *I've just eaten.*

El tren acaba de llegar. *The train has just arrived.*

academia *f. academy.*

acaecer *to happen, to take place.*

acaecimiento *m. event, incident.*

acampar *to camp, to encamp.*

acaparamiento *m. monopoly; hoarding.*

acaparar *to monopolize; to control the market; to hoard.*

acariciar *to caress, to pet; to cherish.*

acarrear *to carry, to transport; to cause.*

acarreo *m. carrying, transportation; carriage, cartage.*

ACASO *by chance, perhaps; m. chance, accident.*

Acaso preferiría usted ir en persona. *Perhaps you would prefer to go in person.*

Por si acaso va Ud. allí. *If you happen to go there.*

Llevemos paraguas por si acaso llueve. *Let's take umbrellas in case it rains.*

acatarrarse *to catch cold.*

Estoy acatarrado. *I've caught a cold. I have a cold.*

acceder *to accede, to agree, to consent.*

accesorio *adj. accessory, additional.*

accidental *adj. accidental.*

ACCIDENTE *m. accident.*

El accidente ocurrió aquí mismo. *The accident happened right here.*

Fué un accidente. *It was an accident.*

ACCION *f. action, act, deed, feat; share; stock.*

Sus acciones contradicen sus palabras. *His actions contradict his words.*

¿Tiene Ud. acciones de la compañía X.? *Have you any shares of the X company?*

Acciones ferroviarias. *Railway stocks (bonds).*

accionista *m. and f. stockholder, shareholder.*

aceitar *to oil, to lubricate.*

aceite *m. oil.*

Aceite de olivo. *Olive oil.*

aceitera *f. oil cruet (glass bottle set on the table); oil can.*

aceituna *f. olive.*

acelerador *m. accelerator.*

acelerar *to accelerate, to hasten, to hurry.*

ACENTO *m. accent; accent mark.*

Habla con acento español. *He speaks with a Spanish accent.*

acentuar *to accent; to accentuate, to emphasize.*

aceptación *f. acceptance; approval.*

ACEPTAR *to accept.*

¿Aceptan ustedes cheques de viajeros? *Do you accept travelers' checks here?*

acera *f. sidewalk.*

ACERCA *about, concerning, in regard to.*

Le escribimos acerca de su viaje. *We wrote to him concerning your trip.*

¿Qué opina Ud. acerca de eso? *What do you think of (about) that?*

acercar *to approach; to bring near.*

Acerque Ud. esa silla. *Pull up that chair. Bring that chair closer.*

acercarse *to approach, to come near.*

¡Acérquese! *Come nearer!*

El invierno se acerca. *It will soon be winter. ("Winter is approaching.")*

acero *m. steel.*

acertadamente *opportunely, fitly, wisely.*

Lo ha dicho Ud. acertadamente. *That's well said (put).*

acertado *adj. fit, apt, proper, to the point.*

Su observación fué muy acertada. *His remark was to the point.*

Eso es lo más acertado. *That's the best thing to do.*

ACERTAR *to hit the mark, to guess right; to succeed.*

Es difícil acertar quien va a ganar. *It's difficult to guess who's going to win.*

Acertaba a pasar por la casa cuando salía. *I happened to be passing by the house when she came out.*

Acertó con la casa. *He succeeded in finding the house.*

ácido *m. acid.*

ácido *adj. sour.*

acierto *m. good hit; skill; tact.*

Obrar con acierto. *To act wisely.*

aclaración *f. explanation, clarification.*

aclarar *to explain, to make clear; to clear up; to rinse (clothes).*

¿Aclarará hoy el tiempo? *Will the weather clear up today?*

Va aclarando. *It's clearing up.*

aclimatar *to acclimatize, to acclimate.*

acoger *to receive, to welcome.*

Le acogieron cordialmente. *They received him cordially.*

Le acogimos como a un familiar. *We gave him a warm welcome. ("We welcomed him as a relative.")*

acogida *f. reception; welcome.*

Una calurosa acogida. *A warm welcome.*

acomodador *m. usher.*

acomodar *to accommodate, to suit; to arrange, to place.*

Haga Ud. lo que le acomode. *Do as you please.*

acompañante *chaperon, companion.*

acompañar *to accompany, to escort, to attend.*

No puedo persuadirla que nos acompañe. *I can't get (persuade) her to come with us.*

Le acompañaré hasta la esquina. *I'll go with you as far as the corner.*

Si Ud. me permite la acompañaré a su casa. *If you don't mind I'll take you home.*

Acompaño a usted en el sentimiento. *I'm very sorry to hear about your loss.*

acongojarse *to become sad, to grieve.*

aconsejable *adj. advisable.*

aconsejar *to advise.*

¿Qué me aconseja Ud. que haga? *What do you advise me to do?*

acontecer *to happen, to take place.*

acontecimiento *m. event, happening.*

acorazado *m. battleship.*

acordar *to agree; to resolve; to remind.*
Tenemos que acordar la hora de salida. *We have to agree on the time of departure.*

ACORDARSE *to come to an agreement; to remember, to keep in mind.*
Se acordó enviarle un telegrama. *It was decided to send him a telegram.*
No me acuerdo de su nombre. *I don't recall his name.*

acortar *to shorten, to cut short.*

ACOSTARSE *to go to bed, to lie down.*

acostumbrar *to accustom, to be accustomed.*
Estoy acostumbrado a acostarme tarde. *I'm used to going to bed late.*

acreditar *to credit; to accredit.*

acreedor *m. creditor.*

acrobacia *f. acrobatics.*

acróbata *m. and f. acrobat.*

acta *f. minutes, record of proceedings; certificate.*
Acta de matrimonio. *Marriage certificate.*

actitud *f. attitude.*

actividad *f. activity.*
En plena actividad. *In full swing.*

activo *adj. active; m. assets.*

ACTO *m. act, action, deed; meeting.*
En el acto. *At once.*
Acto seguido. *Then. Immediately afterwards.*
Primer acto. *First act.*

actor *m. actor, performer.*

actriz *f. actress.*

actuación *f. way of acting; role; record (of a person); play, work (of a team); pl. proceedings.*

ACTUAL *adj. present, existing. (The equivalent of "actual" is real, verdadero.)*
La moda actual. *The present-day fashion. The fashion now.*
El cinco del actual. *The fifth of this month.*

actualidad *f. present time.*
En la actualidad. *At present.*

actualmente *at present, at the present time, nowadays. ("Actually" is realmente.)*
Está actualmente en Madrid. *He's at present in Madrid.*

actuar *to act, to put into action.*

acuatizar *to land on water (a plane).*

ACUDIR *to rush to, to come to; to turn to; to attend.*
No sé a quién acudir. *I don't know who(m) to turn to.*
Un policía acudió en nuestra ayuda. *A policeman came to our aid.*

acueducto *m. aqueduct.*

ACUERDO *m. agreement, accord, understanding; resolution.*
No estoy de acuerdo con Ud. *I don't agree with you.*
Llegar a un acuerdo. *To come to an understanding. To reach an agreement.*
De común acuerdo. *By mutual consent (agreement).*
De acuerdo. *All right.*

acumulador, *m. battery.*

acusación *f. accusation.*

acusado *m. defendant.*

acusar *to accuse, to prosecute; to acknowledge (receipt).*
Acusar recibo. *To acknowledge receipt.*

adaptable *adj. adaptable.*

adaptar *to adapt, to fit.*

adaptarse *to adapt oneself.*

adecuado *adj. adequate, fit, suited.*

ADELANTADO *adj. anticipated, advance, in advance.*
Pagar adelantado. *To pay in advance.*
Por adelantado. *Beforehand. In advance.*

adelantar *to advance; to pay in advance; to be fast (a watch).*
Mi reloj adelanta. *My watch is fast.*
Poco se adelanta con eso. *Little can be gained by that. That won't get one (you) very far.*

adelantarse *to take the lead, to come forward.*

ADELANTE *ahead, farther on, forward, onward.*
¡Adelante! 1. *Go on!* 2. *Come in!*
De hoy en adelante. *From today on.*
En adelante. *Henceforth. From now on.*
Más adelante se lo explicaré. *I'll explain it to you later on.*

adelanto *m. progress, improvement; advance payment.*
Adelantos modernos. *Modern improvements.*

adelgazar *to make thin; to become slender, to lose weight.*
Me parece que usted ha adelgazado un poco. *I think you've gotten a little thinner.*

ademán *m. gesture, motion.*

ADEMAS *moreover, besides, furthermore, too.*
Además de eso. *Moreover. Besides that.*

ADENTRO *inside, within, inwardly.*
Vaya adentro. *Go in.*
Decir a sus adentros. *To say to oneself.*

adeudar *to owe; to pay (duty or freight).*

adeudarse *to get into debt.*

adherente *m. follower, supporter (of a party, society, etc.).*

adherirse *to become a member, to join.*

adhesión *f. adhesion; belonging to.*

adición *f. addition.*

ADICIONAL *adj. additional.*

adiestramiento *m. training.*

adiestrar *to train, to instruct, to teach.*

adinerado *adj. rich, wealthy.*

ADIÓS *m. Goodby.*

adivinanza *f. riddle, puzzle, guess.*

adivinar *to guess, to foretell.*

adjetivo *m. adjective.*

adjuntar *to enclose, to attach.*

adjunto *adj. enclosed, attached, annexed: m. assistant.*

administración *f. administration, management; office of an administrator.*

administrador *m. administrator, manager.*

administrar *to administer, to manage.*

admirable *adj. admirable.*

admirablemente *admirably.*

admiración *f. admiration, wonder; exclamation mark.*

admirador *m. admirer.*

admirar *to admire.*

admirarse *to wonder, to be amazed, to be surprised.*

admisión *f. admission, acceptance.*

ADMITIR *to admit, to accept, to grant.*

ADONDE *where, whither.*
¿Adónde? *Where?*
¿Adónde va Ud.? *Where are you going?*

adopción *f. adoption.*

adoptar *to adopt.*

adoquinado *m. pavement.*

adorable *adj. adorable.*

adoración *f. adoration.*

adorar *to adore, to worship.*

adormecimiento *m. drowsiness; numbness.*

adornar *to trim, to adorn, to decorate.*

adquirir *to acquire.*

adquisición *f. acquisition.*

adrede *purposely, on purpose.*
Lo hizo adrede. *He did it on purpose.*

aduana *f. customhouse, customs.*

aduanero *m. customs official.*

adulador *m. flatterer.*

adular *to flatter.*

adulón *adj. and m. flatterer.*

adulterio *m. adultery.*

adulto *adj. and n. adult.*

adverbio *m. adverb.*

adversario *m. adversary, enemy.*

adversidad *f. adversity.*

advertencia *f. warning, admonition, notice, advice.*

advertir *to warn, to give notice, to let know; to take notice of.*

aéreo *adj. aerial, by air, air.*
Por correo aéreo. *By air mail.*

aeródromo *m. airdrome, airport.*

aeronáutica *f. aeronautics.*

aeronave *f. airship.*

aeroplano *m. airplane.*

aeropuerto *m. airport.*

afán *m. anxiety, eagerness.*

afanarse *to be uneasy, to be anxious; to act eagerly, to work hard or eagerly, to take pains.*
No se afane tanto. *Don't work so hard. Take it easy.*

afección *f. affection, fondness.*

afectar *to affect, to concern.*

afecto *m. affection, fondness, love.*
Afecto a. *Fond of.*
En prueba de mi afecto. *As a token of my affection (esteem).*

afeitado *adj. shaven.*

afeitar *to shave.*
Hojas de afeitar. *Razor blades.*

afeitarse *to shave oneself.*

afición *f. fondness; hobby.*

aficionado *adj. fond of; m. fan, amateur.*
¿Es Ud. un aficionado a los deportes? *Are you a sports fan? Are you fond of sports?*

afilar *to sharpen.*

afiliado *adj. affiliated; m. member (of a society).*

afiliarse *to affiliate oneself, to join, to become a member (of a society).*

afinidad *f. affinity, analogy, resemblance.*

afirmación *f. affirmation, assertion, statement.*

afirmar *to affirm, to assert; to fasten, to make fast.*

afirmativamente *affirmatively.*

aflicción *f. affliction, sorrow, grief.*

afligirse *to grieve, to become despondent, to worry.*
No hay porque afligirse. *There's no reason to worry.*

aflojar *to loosen; to slacken; to become lax.*

afortunadamente *fortunately, luckily.*

afortunado *adj. fortunate, lucky.*
¡Qué afortunado es Ud.! *How fortunate (lucky) you are!*

afrenta *f. affront, insult, outrage.*

afrontar *to confront, to face.*

AFUERA *out, outside; f. pl. suburbs, outskirts.*
Salgamos afuera. *Let's go outside.*
¡Afuera! *Get out of the way!*
La fábrica está en las afueras de la ciudad. *The factory is on the outskirts of the city.*

agacharse *to bend down, to stoop.*

agarrar *to grasp, to seize.*

agarrarse *to clinch; to grapple, to hold on.*

agasajar *to entertain, to receive and treat hospitably.*

agencia *f. agency.*

agenda *f. notebook, memorandum book.*

agente *m. agent.*

ágil *adj. agile, light, fast.*

agitación *f. agitation, excitement.*

agitar *to agitate, to stir, to shake up.*
Agítese antes de usarse. *Shake well before using.*

agonía *f. agony.*

agonizar *to be dying; to tantalize.*

AGOSTO *m. August.*

agotamiento *m. exhaustion.*

AGOTAR *to drain, to exhaust, to run out of.*
Estoy agotado. *I'm exhausted.*
Se me agotó la gasolina. *I ran out of gas.*
Esta edición está agotada. *This edition is out of print.*
Se han agotado las localidades. *All the seats are sold out.*

AGRADABLE *adj. agreeable, pleasant, pleasing.*
Pasamos un rato muy agradable. *We had a very pleasant time.*

AGRADAR *to please, to like.*
Esto me agrada más. *I like this (one) better. This (one) pleases me more.*

AGRADECER *to give thanks, to be grateful.*
Se lo agradezco mucho. *I appreciate this very much.*
Le estoy muy agredecido. *I'm very much obliged to you.*

agradecimiento *m. gratitude, gratefulness.*

agrado *m. liking, pleasure.*
Ser del agrado de uno. *To be to one's taste (liking).*

agravarse *to grow worse.*

agregar *to add; to aggregate, to heap together; to assign temporarily.*

agresión *f. aggression.*

agresor *m. aggressor.*

agriarse *to turn sour.*

agricultor *m. farmer.*

agricultura *f. farming, agriculture.*

agrietarse *to crack; to chap.*

AGRIO *adj. sour.*

agrupación *f. gathering, crowd; association.*

agrupar *to bring together; to group, to come together in a group.*

AGUA *f. water.*
Agua corriente. *Running water.*
Agua fresca. *Cold water.*
Agua mineral. *Mineral water.*
Agua potable. *Drinking water.*
Agua tibia. *Lukewarm water.*

aguacate *m. alligator pear, avocado.*

aguacero *m. downpour, heavy shower.*

aguantar *to bear, to endure; to resist.*
Lo siento pero no la puedo aguantar. *I'm sorry but I can't stand her.*

AGUARDAR *to expect; to wait for; to allow time for.*
Estoy aguardando a un amigo. *I'm expecting (waiting for) a friend.*
Podemos aguardar en la sala. *We can wait in the living room.*
¡Aguarda un momento! *Wait a minute!*
¡Aguárdame! *Wait for me!*

águila *f. eagle.*

aguinaldo *m. Christmas or New Year's gift.*

AGUJA *f. needle.*
Pasar la hebra por el ojo de la aguja. *To thread a needle.*

agujerear *to bore, to make holes.*

agujero *m. hole.*

¡ah! *ah! oh!*
¡Ah, se me olvidaba! *Oh, I almost forgot!*

ahí *there (near the person addressed).*
¿Qué tiene Ud. ahí? *What have you got there?*
Ponlo ahí. *Put it there.*
¡Ahí viene! *There he comes!*
Por ahí. *Over there. That way.*
De ahí que. *Hence. Therefore. As a consequence.*

ahijado *m. godchild; protégé.*

ahogado *adj. drowned.*

ahogar *to drown; to choke.*

ahogarse *to drown; to be suffocated.*

AHORA *now, at present.*
Vámonos ahora. *Let's go now.*
Ahora me toca a mí. *It's my turn now.*
Ahora mismo. *Right now. This very moment.*
Venga Ud. ahora mismo. *Come right away (this moment).*

ahorcar *to hang (to suspend by the neck).*

ahorita *in a little while, just now, this minute.*
Ahorita mismo. *Right away.*
Ahorita pasará el autobús. *The bus will pass by in a little while.*
Libreta de la Caja de Ahorros. *Bankbook.*

ahorrar *to save, to economize; to spare.*
Ahorrar algo para el día de mañana. *To lay something aside for a rainy day.*

ahorro *m. savings; thrift.*

AIRE *m. air, wind; aspect, look.*
Una corriente de aire. *A draft ("current of air").*
Voy a salir a tomar un poco de aire. *I'm going out for some fresh air.*
¿Qué aires lo traen a Ud. por acá? *"What good wind blows you here?"*
Tiene un aire muy severo. *He has a very severe (stern) look.*
Estar en el aire. *To be up in the air.*
Al aire libre. *In the open. Outdoors.*
Aire popular. *Folk music. Folk song.*

ajedrez *m. chess.*

ajeno *another's, of others, other people's, foreign, strange.*
Estoy completamente ajeno de ello. *I'm completely unaware of it. I know absolutely nothing about it.*
Ajeno al asunto. *Foreign to the subject. Having nothing to do with the subject.*
Lo ajeno. *That which belongs to others.*
Bienes ajenos. *Other people's goods (property).*

ají *m. chili.*

ajo *m. garlic.*

ajustar *to adjust; to fit; to settle (an account, matter, etc.).*

AL *(contraction of a + el) to the, at the; on, when. See also a and el.*
Aviso al público. *Notice to the public.*
Al contrario. *On the contrary.*
Al amanecer. *At dawn (daybreak).*
Al anochecer. *At dusk (nightfall).*
Al fin y al cabo. *At last. In the end. At length. After all. In the long run.*
Al saberlo. *When I learned that.*
Se rieron mucho al oír eso. *They laughed a lot when they heard that.*

ala *f. wing; brim (of a hat).*

alabar *to praise.*

alabarse *to praise oneself, to boast.*

alacena *f. kitchen closet, cupboard.*

alacrán *m. scorpion.*

alambrado *m. wire fence, wire net.*

alambre *m. wire.*

alameda *f. public walk lined with trees.*

alarde *m. ostentation, showing off, boasting.*
Hacer alarde de. *To boast of (about).*

alargar *to lengthen; to stretch, to extend; to prolong, to drag on; to hand over, to pass.*
Alargar el paso. *To walk faster.*

alargarse *to become or grow longer.*
Se alargan los días. *The days are growing (getting) longer.*

alarma *f. alarm.*

alarmarse *to become alarmed; to be alarmed.*

alba *f. dawn.*
Al rayar el alba. *At daybreak.*

albañil *m. mason, bricklayer.*

albaricoque *m. apricot.*

albóndiga *f. meatball.*

alborotarse *to become excited.*

alboroto *m. excitement; disturbance.*

álbum *m. album.*

alcachofa *f. artichoke.*

alcalde *m. mayor.*

alcance *m. reach, range; scope; ability, intelligence.*
De gran alcance. *Far-reaching.*
Estar al alcance de. *To be within the reach of. To be within someone's means.*
Dar alcance. *To catch up with. To catch (arrest).*
Es un hombre de pocos alcances. *He's not very intelligent.*

alcancía *f. money box, a small bank.*

alcanfor *m. camphor.*

alcanzar *to overtake, to catch up with; to catch; to reach; to obtain, to attain, to get; to be enough; to be sufficient; to hand, to pass; to affect.*
Los alcanzaremos con nuestro coche. *We'll overtake them with our car.*
¿Pudieron alcanzar el tren? *Were they able to catch the train?*
No alcanza para todos. *There's not enough for everybody.*
Tenga la bondad de alcanzarme el salero. *Please pass me the saltshaker.*
Alcanzar a comprender. *To understand. To make out.*
Poco se le alcanza. *He doesn't understand it very well. He doesn't care very much about it.*
Alcanzar con la mano. *To reach with one's hand.*

alcoba *f. bedroom.*

alcohol *m. alcohol.*

aldaba *f. door knocker, latch.*

aldea *f. small village.*

alegrar *to gladden, to make glad, to enliven.*

ALEGRARSE *to rejoice, to be glad, to be happy.*
Me alegro muchísimo. *I'm very glad. I'm delighted.*
Me alegro de que esté usted mejor. *I'm very glad you're better.*
Me alegro de saberlo. *I'm happy to know it.*

alegre *adj. glad, merry, happy.*

alegría *f. merriment, gaiety, delight, rejoicing, joy.*
Está llena de alegría. *She's very happy.*

alejar *to remove, to take away; to hold off (at a distance).*

alejarse *to go far away; to move away.*

alemán *adj. and n. German.*

alfabeto *m. alphabet.*

alfiler *m. pin.*

alfombra *f. carpet, rug.*

ALGO *some, something, anything, somewhat.*
  Algo que comer. *Something to eat.*
  En algo. *In some way. Somewhat.*
  Por algo. *For some reason.*
  ¿Hay algo de particular? *Is there anything special?*
  ¿Necesita Ud. algo más? *Do you need anything else?*
  ¿Tiene Ud. algo que hacer esta tarde? *Do you have anything to do this afternoon?*
  ¿Quiere Ud. tomar algo? *Do you want anything to drink?*
  Quiero comer algo ligero. *I want something light to eat.*
  Tengo algo que decirle. *I have something to tell you.*
  Lo encuentro algo caro. *I find it somewhat expensive.*
  Comprendo algo. *I understand a little.*
algodón *m. cotton.*
alguacil *m. constable.*
ALGUIEN *somebody, someone.*
  Alguien llama a la puerta. *Someone's knocking at the door.*
  ¿Aguarda Ud. a alguien? *Are you waiting for someone?*
algún *adj. (used only before a masculine noun) some, any.*
  ¿Tiene Ud. algún libro para prestarme? *Have you a (any) book to lend me?*
  Algún día se lo contaré. *I'll tell you some day.*
  Durante algún tiempo. *For some time.*
ALGUNO *adj. some, any.*
  En modo alguno. *In any way.*
  Alguna cosa. *Anything.*
  En alguna parte. *Anywhere.*
  ¿Hay alguna farmacia cerca de aquí? *Is there a drugstore near here?*
  Lo habré leído en alguno que otro periódico. *I probably read it in some newspaper or other.*
  Déjeme ver algunas camisas. *Let me see some shirts.*
  Conozco a algunas personas aquí pero no a todas. *I know some (several) people here but not everyone.*
  Alguna que otra vez. *Once in a while. Occasionally.*
alhaja *f. jewel.*
alianza *f. alliance.*
alicates *m. pliers, pincers.*
aliento *m. breath; courage.*
  Sin aliento. *Out of breath.*
  Dar aliento. *To encourage.*
alimentación *f. feeding, food.*
alimentar *to feed, to nourish; to cherish.*
alimento *m. food, nourishment.*
alistar *to enlist; to get ready.*
alistarse *to enlist; to get ready.*
  Se estaba alistando para salir. *He was getting ready to go out (leave).*
  Se alistó en el ejército. *He enlisted in the army.*
aliviar *to lighten; to make things easier; to get better.*
  ¡Que se alivie pronto! *I hope you'll get better soon.*
alivio *m. relief, ease.*
  ¡Qué alivio! *What a relief!*
ALMA *f. soul.*
  No hay ningún alma viviente en este lugar. *There's not a living soul in this place.*
  Con toda mi alma. *With all my heart.*
  Lo siento en el alma. *I deeply regret it. I'm*

extremely sorry about it.
almacén *m. warehouse; store, shop.*
  Tener en almacén. *To have in stock.*
  Almacenes. *Department store.*
almacenar *to store; to hoard.*
almanaque *m. almanac, calendar.*
almeja *f. clam.*
almendra *f. almond.*
almendro *m. almond tree.*
almidón *m. starch.*
almidonar *to starch.*
almirante *m. admiral.*
almohada *f. pillow, bolster.*
almohadón *m. large cushion or pillow.*
almorzar *to lunch; to breakfast (Mex.).*
ALMUERZO *m. lunch.*
alojamiento *m. lodging; billeting (soldiers).*
alojar *to lodge; to billet (soldiers).*
alpargata *f. hemp sandal.*
ALQUILAR *to rent, to hire.*
  Se alquila. *To let (a room, a house, etc.). For rent.*
  La casa está por alquilar. *The house is for rent.*
ALQUILER *m. rent, rental, the act of hiring or renting.*
  ¿Cuánto es el alquiler? *How much is the rent?*
ALREDEDOR *around; pl. outskirts, surroundings.*
  Tengo alrededor de veinte dólares. *I have about twenty dollars.*
  Un viaje alrededor del mundo. *A trip around the world.*
  Vive en los alrededores de Madrid. *He lives in the outskirts of Madrid.*
altavoz *m. loudspeaker.*
alterarse *to become angry, to get annoyed.*
altercado *m. quarrel.*
alternar *to alternate.*
alternativa *f. alternative.*
ALTO *adj. high, tall; loud; halt, stop.*
  Es muy alto para su edad. *He's very tall for his age.*
  Haga el favor de hablar más alto. *Please speak louder.*
  No puedo alcanzarlo, está muy alto. *I can't reach it; it's too high.*
  Hacer alto. *To halt.*
  ¡Alto! *Stop!*
  ¡Alto ahí! *Stop there!*
  Se me pasó por alto. *I overlooked it. I didn't notice it.*
  A altas horas de la noche. *Late at night.*
altoparlante *m. loudspeaker.*
altura *f. height, altitude.*
aludir *to allude, to refer to.*
alumbrado *m. lighting, illumination.*
alumbrar *to light, to illuminate.*
aluminio *m. aluminum.*
alumno *m. pupil, student.*
alza *f. rise, increase (price, stocks, etc.); sight (on a gun, on instruments).*
ALZAR *to raise, to lift up.*
  Alce eso. *Lift that.*
  Alzar cabeza. *To get on one's feet again. ("To raise one's head.")*
ALLÁ *there, over there (away from the speaker); in other times, formerly.*
  Más allá. *Farther on. Beyond.*
  Más allá de. *Beyond.*
  Vaya Ud. allá. *Go there.*
  ¡Allá voy! *I'm coming!*
  Allá en España. *Over there in Spain.*
  Allá en el sur. *Down South.*

Allá en mis mocedades. *In the days of my youth.*
  Eso allá él. *It's his own business.*
ALLÍ *there, in that place.*
  De allí. *From there. From that place.*
  Allí mismo. *Right there. In that very place.*
  Lléveme allí. *Take me there.*
  Vive allí, en la casa de la esquina. *He lives in the corner house over there.*
  Esté Ud. allí a las nueve. *Be there at nine o'clock.*
  Por allí. *That way. Over there.*
ama *f. mistress of the house, landlady.*
  Ama de llaves. *Housekeeper.*
AMABILIDAD *f. amiability, affability, kindness.*
  ¿Tendría Ud. la amabilidad de decirme la hora? *What time is it, please? Can you please tell me the time?*
  Le agradezco mucho su amabilidad. *Thanks for your kindness.*
AMABLE *adj. amiable, kind.*
  Ud. es muy amable. *You're very kind. That's very kind of you.*
AMANECER *m. daybreak, dawn.*
  Al amanecer. *At dawn (daybreak).*
amante *adj. loving; m. and f. lover, sweetheart.*
  Ser amante de. *To be fond of.*
AMAR *to love.*
AMARGO *adj. bitter.*
AMARILLO *adj. yellow.*
amarrar *to tie, to fasten; to moor.*
amartillar *to hammer; to cock (a gun).*
amasar *to knead, to mold.*
ambición *f. ambition.*
ambicioso *adj. ambitious; greedy.*
ambiente *m. environment; atmosphere.*
AMBOS *adj. both.*
  Ambos hermanos vinieron a la fiesta. *Both brothers came to the party.*
  Ambos a dos. *The two together.*
ambulancia *f. ambulance.*
amenaza *f. menace, threat.*
amenazar *to menace, to threaten.*
ameno *adj. pleasant, agreeable, pleasing; light, entertaining (reading).*
americana *f. man's coat, jacket; an American (woman).*
americano *m. American.*
ametralladora *f. machine gun.*
amigablemente *amicably, in a friendly manner.*
amígdala *f. tonsil.*
AMIGO *m. friend.*
  Somos amigos íntimos. *We're close friends.*
  Vino a vernos con su amiga. *He came to see us with his girl friend.*
  Ser amigo de. *To be fond of.*
amistad *f. friendship.*
amistosamente *amicably, in a friendly manner.*
amistoso *adj. friendly.*
amo *m. master, lord; proprietor, owner; boss.*
amontonar *to heap, to pile up.*
AMOR *m. love.*
  De mil amores. *With great pleasure.*
amparar *to shelter, to protect, to help.*
ampliación *f. enlargement.*
ampolla *f. blister; ampule.*
amputar *to amputate.*
amueblar *to furnish.*
analfabeto *adj. illiterate.*
análisis *m. analysis.*
anatomía *f. anatomy.*
anciano *m. old man.*
ancla *f. anchor.*

ANCHO adj. broad, wide; m. width, breadth.
Estos zapatos me vienen muy anchos. These shoes are too wide for me.
Dos pies de ancho. Two feet wide.
A todo el ancho. Full-width.
Estoy a mis anchas aquí. I'm very comfortable here.
anchura f. width, breadth.
ANDAR to walk; to go; to be.
Andar a pie. To go on foot.
Es demasiado lejos para ir andando. It's too far to walk.
¿Anda bien su reloj? Does your watch keep good time?
Ando mal de dinero. I'm short of money.
Andar triste. To be sad.
Andar en mangas de camisa. To go around in one's shirt sleeves.
Andar en cuerpo. To go outdoors without an overcoat.
Andando el tiempo. In the course of time.
¡Andando! Let's get going!
¡Anda! Go on! Come on!
andén m. platform of a railroad station, track.
anécdota f. anecdote.
anemia f. anemia.
anfitrión m. host.
ángel m. angel.
angosto adj. narrow.
anguila f. eel.
ángulo m. angle.
angustia f. anguish, distress, affliction.
anhelar to long for, to yearn.
anhelo m. desire, longing.
anillo m. ring, band.
animal animal; brute.
¡No seas animal! Don't be stupid!
animar to animate, to encourage, to cheer up, to enliven.
animarse to become lively, to feel encouraged, to cheer up.
ÁNIMO m. courage; mind, feeling.
No me animo a hacerlo. I wouldn't dare to do it.
Los ánimos están excitadísimos. Feeling is running very high.
¡Ánimo! Cheer up!
aniversario m. anniversary.
ANOCHE last night.
¿Se divertieron Uds. anoche? Did you have a good time last night?
anochecer to grow dark.
Anochecía (se hacía de noche) cuando llegamos a Madrid. It was getting dark when we arrived in Madrid.
Al anochecer. At dusk (nightfall).
anormal adj. abnormal.
anotar to annotate, to make notes; to write down.
ansia f. anxiety, eagerness, longing.
ansiedad f. anxiety.
ansioso adj. anxious, eager.
ANTE before, in the presence of.
Ante todo. Above all. First of all.
ante m. suede.
ANTEAYER the day before yesterday.
antebrazo m. forearm.
antecedente m. antecedent; pl. data, references, record (of a person).
antecesores m. ancestors.
antemano beforehand.
antena f. antenna, aerial.
ANTENOCHE night before last.
anteojos m. pl. glasses.

antepasado adj. past, last; m. pl. ancestors, forefathers.
anterior adj. anterior, previous, former, preceding.
anteriormente previously.
ANTES before.
Cuanto antes. As soon as possible.
Hágalo cuanto antes. Do it as soon as possible.
Agítese antes de usarse. Shake well before using.
Haga antes un borrador. Make a rough copy first.
Antes de tiempo. Ahead of time.
anticipación f. anticipation, foretaste.
Si vienes, avísame con anticipación. Let me know in advance if you come.
anticipar to anticipate; to advance (money).
Me anticipó veinte pesos. He gave me twenty pesos in advance.
anticiparse to anticipate; to act or occur before the regular or expected time.
Se anticiparon media hora. They arrived half an hour earlier.
anticipo m. advance payment, advance.
anticuado adj. old fashioned.
anticuario m. antiques dealer, antiquarian.
ANTIER day before yesterday.
antifaz m. mask.
antiguamente formerly, in ancient times.
antigüedad f. antiquity; antique; seniority.
Tienda de antigüedades. Antique shop.
ANTIGUO adj. antique, ancient, old.
Ese es un dicho muy antiguo. That's a very old saying.
antipatía f. antipathy, dislike, aversion.
antipático adj. displeasing, not congenial.
Me es muy antipático. I don't find him at all congenial. I don't like him.
antiséptico adj. and n. antiseptic.
antojarse to desire, to long for, to crave.
Tiene cuanto se le antoja. She has everything she could wish for.
Que haga lo que se le antoje. Let him do as he pleases.
antojo m. desire, caprice, whim.
anual adj. yearly, annual.
anular to void, to annul, to make void.
ANUNCIAR to announce; to advertise.
Lo acaban de anunciar en la radio. They just announced that on the radio.
La tienda anuncia un saldo. The store is advertising a sale.
ANUNCIO m. announcement, notice, sign, advertisement.
anzuelo m. fishhook; bait.
AÑADIR to add.
Añádalo a mi cuenta. Add it to my bill.
AÑO m. year.
¿En qué año ocurrió? (In) What year did it happen?
Hace dos años que vivo aquí. I've been living here for two years.
Todo el año. All year. All year round.
El año pasado. Last year.
El año que viene. Next year.
¡Feliz año nuevo! Happy New Year!
¿Cuántos años tiene Ud.? How old are you? ("How many years do you have?")
Tengo treinta años. I am thirty years old. ("I have thirty years.")
apagar to quench, to extinguish, to put out.
Apague la luz. Turn off the light. Put out the light.
apagarse to go out (of a light, fire, etc.).

Se apagaron las luces. The lights went out.
aparador m. sideboard, cupboard.
aparato m. apparatus, device; ostentation.
APARECER to appear, to show up, to turn up.
No apareció en todo el día. He didn't show up all day.
Apareció como por ensalmo. He appeared as though by magic.
aparentar to pretend, to affect.
Aparenta ser rico. He seems to be rich.
aparentemente apparently.
Aparentemente es así. Apparently it's so.
apariencia f. appearance, looks, aspect.
Las apariencias engañan. Appearances are deceiving.
Al juzgar por las apariencias. To judge by appearances.
apartado adj. separated, distant; m. post-office box.
Apartado de correos. Post-office box.
apartamento m. apartment. (also written **apartamiento**.)
Casa de apartamentos. Apartment house.
¿Tienen apartamentos por alquilar? Do you have any vacancies? Are there any apartments for rent?
apartamiento m. separation; a distant place; apartment.
apartar to separate, to lay aside.
apartarse to keep away, to get out of the way.
Apártese del fuego. Get away from the fire.
Se apartó de nosotros. He kept away from us.
APARTE aside, separately.
Ponga este paquete aparte. Put this package aside.
Esa es una cuestión aparte. That's another question.
apearse to get off.
Quiero apearme en la próxima parada. I want to get off at the next stop.
apellido m. surname, last name, family name.
Escriba su nombre y apellido. Write down your first and last names.
APENAS scarcely, hardly; no sooner than, as soon as.
Apenas puedo creerlo. I can hardly believe it.
Apenas podía moverse. He could scarcely move.
Las dos apenas. Not quite two o'clock. A little before two.
apetecer to long for, to desire.
apetito m. appetite.
apio m. celery.
aplaudir to applaud.
aplauso m. applause, praise; approbation.
aplazar to put off, to postpone, to defer, to convene, to adjourn.
Han aplazado el viaje hasta el mes que viene. They've put off the trip until next month.
aplicado adj. studious, industrious, diligent.
aplicarse to apply oneself, to devote oneself to; to study.
apoderarse to take possession of.
apodo m. nickname.
apostar to bet; to post (soldiers, etc.).
¿Cuánto apuestas? How much do you bet?
Apuesto cualquier cosa a que no lo dice. I'll bet anything he won't say it.
apoyar to favor, to back up, to support, to defend, to aid; to lean.
Apóyalo contra la pared. Lean it against the wall.
Apoyar una moción. To second a motion.
apreciación f. estimation, appreciation.
apreciar to estimate, to value, to appreciate, to esteem.

aprecio *m. appreciation, esteem, regard.*
Le tengo mucho aprecio. *I have a high regard for him.*
apremiante *adj. urgent, pressing.*
apremiar *to urge, to press.*
APRENDER *to learn.*
Aprendí solamente un poco de español. *I learned only a little Spanish.*
Apréndaselo de memoria. *Learn it by heart.*
apresurarse *to hurry, to hasten.*
Apresúrese si no quiere perder el tren. *Hurry up if you don't want to miss the train.*
apretado *adj. tight.*
apretar *to tighten, to press, to compress, to squeeze.*
Estos zapatos me aprietan un poco. *These shoes are a little tight for me.*
aprieto *m. difficulty, fix, spot.*
Estoy en un verdadero aprieto. *I'm in a tough spot. I'm in a bad fix.*
Ya saldremos de aprietos. *We'll get out of these difficulties.*
APRISA *fast, swiftly, promptly.*
Vaya lo más aprisa posible. *Go as quickly as you can.*
aprobación *f. approval.*
aprobar *to approve, to approve of; to pass (an examination).*
¿Ha sido aprobado el plan? *Has the plan been approved?*
Apruebo su conducta. *I approve of his conduct.*
No me aprobaron en historia. *I failed in history.*
aprovechar *to be useful or beneficial; to profit; to make use of.*
Hay que aprovechar la ocasión. *We must take advantage of the opportunity.*
Esta cocinera sabe aprovechar los restos. *This cook knows how to make good use of the leftovers.*
Aprovechar el tiempo. *To make good use of one's time.*
No deje que se aprovechen de Ud. *Don't let people take advantage of you.*
¡Que aproveche! *I hope you enjoy it (said when entering a room where people are eating).*
aprovecharse *to take advantage of, to derive profit from, to make use of.*
aprovisionamiento *m. supply.*
aproximadamente *approximately.*
aproximarse *to approach, to come near.*
aptitud *f. aptitude, fitness, ability; pl. qualifications.*
apuesta *f. bet, wager.*
La gané la apuesta. *I won the bet from him.*
apuntar *to aim; to indicate, to point out; to write down.*
Apunte la dirección para que no se le olvide. *Write down the address so you won't forget it.*
Apúntelo en mi cuenta. *Charge it to my account.*
apuñalar *to stab.*
apurarse *to hurry; to worry, to fret; to exert oneself.*
¡Apúrese! *Hurry up!*
No se apure Ud. que ya saldremos de aprietos. *Don't worry, we'll get out of these difficulties.*
apuro *m. want; affliction; plight; fix, difficulty, scrape.*
¿Salió Ud. del apuro? *Did you manage to get out of that difficulty?*
Estar en apuros. *To be in difficulties.*
AQUEL *that, that one; the former.*
Mire aquel avión. *Look at that plane.*

Aquel negocio le arruinó. *That business ruined him.*
En aquel mismo momento llegó. *He arrived at that very moment.*
En aquel entonces. *At that time.*
No quería éste sino aquél. *I didn't want this one but the one over there.*
aquella *(f. of aquel) that, that one.*
Aquella muchacha baila muy bien. *That girl (over there) dances very well.*
Esta silla es más cómoda que aquélla. *This chair is more comfortable than that one.*
aquellas *(pl. of aquella) those.*
Mira aquellas chicas que van allá. *Look at those girls walking over there.*
aquello *(neuter) that (referring to an idea).*
Aquello fué horrible. *That was horrible.*
Ya pasó aquello. *That's gone (past) and forgotten. That's water under the bridge.*
aquellos *(pl. of aquel) those.*
¿Te acuerdas de aquellos tiempos? *Do you remember the good old days?*
¿Cuáles prefieres, éstos o aquéllos? *Which do you prefer, these or those?*
AQUÍ *here, in this place.*
¿Paramos aquí? *Do we stop here?*
¿Vive Ud. aquí? *Do you live here?*
¿Se puede telefonear desde aquí? *Can we phone from here?*
¿Qué demonios hace Ud. aquí? *What on earth are you doing here?*
Venga Ud. por aquí. *Come this way.*
¿Cuánto hay de aquí a Zaragoza? *How far is it from here to Zaragoza?*
Está muy lejos de aquí. *It's quite a distance from here.*
Aquí tiene lo que ha pedido. *Here's what you ordered (asked for).*
De aquí en adelante. *From now on.*
araña *f. spider; chandelier.*
arañazo *m. a long, deep scratch.*
árbol *m. tree; mast; shaft.*
La raíz del árbol. *The root of a tree.*
El tronco del árbol. *The trunk of a tree.*
archipiélago *m. archipelago.*
archivar *to keep in an archive, to file.*
archivo *m. archives; file, files; records.*
arco *m. arch.*
arcón *m. chest.*
arder *to burn.*
ardilla *f. squirrel.*
arena *f. sand; arena.*
argumento *m. reason; argument; plot (of a novel, play, etc.).*
No me convencen sus argumentos. *His arguments don't convince me.*
No me gustó el argumento de la película. *I didn't like the plot of the film.*
aritmética *f. arithmetic.*
arma *f. weapon, arm.*
armamento *m. armament.*
armario *m. closet, cabinet.*
armisticio *m. armistice.*
aroma *m. aroma.*
arquitecto *m. architect.*
arquitectura *f. architecture.*
arrabal *m. suburb.*
arrancar *to tear out by the roots, to tear off; to start (car, etc.).*
arranque *(or **arrancador**) m. starter.*
arrastrar *to drag, to haul.*
arreglar *to arrange; to settle; to regulate; to fix.*
Todo está arreglado. *Everything has been ar-*

ranged.
Arreglar una cuenta. *To settle an account.*
¿Cuánto pide Ud. para arreglar una radio? *How much do you charge to fix a radio?*
arreglarse *to make up, to get ready; to manage; to be settled; to come up.*
Arréglate un poco y vámonos al cine. *Get yourself ready and we'll go to the movies.*
arreglárselas *to manage (oneself).*
Me las arreglé para escaparme. *I managed to escape.*
arrendamiento *m. rental, lease, renting.*
arrendar *to rent, to lease, to hire.*
arrepentirse *to repeat, to regret.*
Te arrepentirás de esto. *You'll be sorry for this.*
ARRIBA *up, above, over, overhead, upstairs.*
Vamos arriba. *Let's go upstairs.*
Patas arriba. *Upside down.*
De arriba abajo. *From top to bottom. From head to foot.*
arriendo *m. renting, lease, rental.*
arrimar *to approach, to draw near; to lay aside.*
arrimarse *to lean against; to draw near.*
Arrímese a la estufa. *Draw up (come closer) to the stove.*
arrodillarse *to kneel down.*
arrojar *to throw, to hurl; to show, to leave (a balance).*
arte *m. and f. art; skill.*
Bellas artes. *Fine arts.*
artículo *m. article; clause.*
Artículo de fondo. *Editorial.*
Artículos de tocador. *Toilet articles.*
artificial *adj. artificial.*
artista *m. and f. artist.*
arzobispo *m. archbishop.*
as *m. ace.*
asa *f. handle, haft.*
asado *adj. roasted; m. roast meat.*
asador *m. spit (for roasting meat).*
asalto *m. assault; holdup.*
asamblea *f. assembly.*
asar *to roast.*
ascender *to ascend, to climb; to amount to; to be promoted.*
La cuenta asciende a cien pesos. *The bill amounts to one hundred pesos.*
ascenso *m. promotion.*
ascensor *m. elevator.*
aseado *adj. clean, neat.*
asear *to clean, to make neat.*
asegurar *to insure; to secure, to fasten; to assure; to affirm, to assert.*
Le aseguro que estaré allí dentro de una hora. *I assure you that I'll be there in an hour.*
El equipaje está asegurado. *The baggage is insured.*
aseo *m. cleanliness, neatness.*
aserrar *to saw.*
asesinar *to assassinate, to murder.*
asesinato *m. assassination, murder.*
asesino *m. assassin, murderer.*
asfalto *m. asphalt.*
ASÍ *so, thus, in this manner, therefore, so that.*
Así lo espero. *I hope so.*
Lo debe Ud. hacer así. *You must (have to) do it this way.*
No es así, se lo aseguro. *I assure you that's not so.*
Así, así. *So, so.*
Más vale así. *It's better this way.*
Así que llegue le avisaré. *As soon as I arrive I'll*

notify you.

Así que hubo hablado se marchó. *He left as soon as he'd finished speaking.*

asiento *m.* seat, chair; entry, registry; bottom.

¿Está tomado este asiento? *Is this seat taken?*

Tome Ud. asiento. *Take a seat. Have a seat.*

asignar *to assign; to appoint; to allot.*

asignatura *f.* subject (in school).

asilo *m.* asylum; refuge.

asimismo *likewise, exactly so.*

asir *to grasp, to hold, to grip.*

asirse de *to avail oneself of; to hold to; to take hold of.*

asistir *to attend; to assist, to help; to be treated by (a doctor).*

No asistió a clase hoy. *He did not attend class today.*

¿Asistió Ud. a la reunión? *Did you attend the meeting?*

Un médico famoso asiste a mi mujer. *My wife is being treated by a famous doctor.*

asno *m.* donkey, ass.

asociación *f.* association.

asomar *to loom, to become visible, to begin to appear.*

asomarse *to look out of, to lean out (of a window, etc.).*

Asómese Ud. a la ventana. *Look out (lean out) of the window.*

¡Prohibido asomarse! *Don't lean out of the window!*

asombro *m.* amazement, astonishment.

Figúrese mi asombro. *Imagine my amazement.*

No salgo de mi asombro. *I can't get over it.*

aspecto *m.* aspect, appearance, look.

Ud. no tiene mal aspecto. *You don't look ill.*

Trate de mejorar su aspecto. *Try to improve your appearance.*

aspirina *f.* aspirin.

astuto *adj.* cunning, sly.

ASUNTO *m.* subject, matter, business.

Necesito más detalles sobre este asunto. *I need more information on this matter.*

Conozco a fondo el asunto. *I'm thoroughly acquainted with the matter.*

¿Cuál es el asunto de esa comedia? *What's the subject of that play?*

asustar *to frighten.*

asustarse *to be frightened.*

¿De qué te asustas? *What are you afraid of?*

atacar *to attack.*

ataque *m.* attack.

atar *to bind, to tie, to fasten.*

Atese los zapatos. *Tie your shoelaces.*

atardecer *to grow late (toward the end of the afternoon).*

ataúd *m.* coffin.

atemorizar *to frighten, to intimidate.*

ATENCIÓN *f.* attention.

Quisiera llamar la atención de Ud. sobre este punto. *I'd like to bring this point to your attention.*

Muchas gracias por su atención. *Thanks for your attention.*

Le estoy muy reconocido por sus atenciones. *I'm grateful for your kindness.*

En atención a. *Considering. In view of.*

atender *to attend, to pay attention; to look after; to wait on.*

atenta *f. "Your esteemed (letter)."*

Su atenta. *Your ("esteemed") letter.*

atentado *m.* attempt.

atentar *to try, to attempt.*

atento *adj.* attentive, courteous.

Su atento y seguro servidor. *Very truly yours.*

aterrizaje *m.* landing (of an airplane).

aterrizar *to land (an airplane).*

atestado *adj.* crowded.

atestiguar *to depose, to testify.*

atinar *to guess right, to hit on.*

atlántico *m.* Atlantic.

atleta *m. and f.* athlete.

atlético *adj.* athletic.

atmósfera *f.* atmosphere.

átomo *m.* atom.

atornillar *to screw.*

atracar *to dock, to moor; to hold up.*

atraco *m.* assault, holdup.

atractivo *adj.* attractive, appealing.

atraer *to attract.*

ATRÁS *behind, backwards, past; ago.*

Quedarse atrás. *To remain behind.*

Volverse atrás. *To go back on one's word. To retract.*

Hacerse atrás. *To move backward. To back up. To recoil.*

Tres días atrás. *Three days ago.*

atrasar *to retard, to delay; to be in arrears; to be slow (a watch).*

atrasarse *to remain behind; to be late; to get behind (in payment).*

Mi reloj atrasa. *My watch is slow.*

Nos estamos atrasando en el trabajo. *We're getting behind in our work.*

Esto atrasará mucho mi viaje. *This will delay my trip a long time.*

Atrasarse en los pagos. *To fall behind in one's payments.*

atravesar *to cross, to move across; to lay a thing across; to pierce.*

Atravesemos la calle. *Let's cross the street.*

atrayente *adj.* attractive.

atreverse *to dare, to venture.*

atrevido *adj.* bold, daring; fresh.

atribuir *to attribute, to impute.*

atrocidad *f.* atrocity.

¡Qué atrocidad! *What a horrible (awful) thing!*

atropellar *to trample, to run over; to abuse, to insult.*

Fué atropellado por un coche. *He was run over by a car.*

atropello *m.* trampling, abuse, outrage.

atroz *adj.* atrocious, outrageous; enormous.

Tengo un hambre atroz. *I'm famished. ("I have an enormous hunger.")*

atún *tuna fish.*

aturdido *adj.* bewildered, stunned, dizzy.

aturdir *to stun.*

audición *f.* audition.

auditorio *m.* audience.

aumentar *to augment, to enlarge, to increase.*

aumentarse *to grow larger.*

aumento *m.* increase.

Aumento de precios. *Price increase. Increase in prices.*

Aumento de salario. *Salary increase.*

AUN *yet, still; even (written aún when it follows a verb).*

Aun no lo sabe. *He doesn't know yet.*

Tengo que escribir aún otra carta. *I've still got another letter to write.*

Aun cuando. *Although. Even though.*

AUNQUE *though, notwithstanding, even if.*

aurora *f.* dawn, daybreak.

ausencia *f.* absence.

AUSENTARSE *to be absent, to be away.*

AUSENTE *adj.* absent.

auténtico *adj.* authentic, genuine.

auto *m.* automobile, motor car; sentence, edict.

¿Le parece a Ud. que demos un paseo en auto? *How would you like to take a ride?*

autobús *m.* bus.

¿Dónde para el autobús? *Where does the bus stop?*

¿Dónde queda la parada del autobús? *Where's the bus stop?*

autocar *m.* bus (in Spain).

automático *adj.* automatic.

automóvil *m.* automobile.

autor *m.* author.

autoridad *f.* authority.

autorización *f.* authorization.

autorizar *to authorize.*

autorretrato *m.* self-portrait.

auxiliar *to aid, to help; adj.* auxiliary.

auxilio *m.* help, aid, assistance.

avance *m.* advance, progress.

avanzar *to advance, to go ahead, to progress.*

ave *f.* bird; fowl.

Aves de corral. *Fowl. Poultry.*

avena *f.* oats.

avenida *f.* avenue.

aventura *f.* adventure.

aventurarse *to venture, to risk, to take a chance.*

No se aventure usted. *Don't take the risk. Don't take a chance.*

avergonzarse *to be ashamed.*

avería *f.* damage, loss.

averiguar *to inquire, to find out, to investigate.*

Averigüe a que hora sale el tren. *Find out (at) what time the train leaves.*

aviación *f.* aviation.

aviador *m.* aviator.

avión *m.* airplane.

avisar *to inform, to notify, to let know; to warn.*

Avíseme con tiempo. *Notify me in time.*

Ya le avisaré. *I'll let you know.*

aviso *m.* notice; advertisement; warning.

Aviso al publico. *Public Notice. Notice to the Public.*

AYER *yesterday.*

Ayer por la tarde. *Yesterday afternoon.*

ayuda *f.* help, assistance, aid.

ayudante *m. and f.* assistant; adjutant (in the army).

AYUDAR *to aid, to assist, to help.*

¿Permítame que le ayude? *May I help you? Allow me to help you.*

ayuntamiento *m.* city hall.

azadón *m.* hoe.

azahar *m.* orange or lemon blossom.

azar *m.* chance; hazard.

Al azar. *At random.*

azotar *to whip.*

azote *m.* whip; whipping, spanking.

azotea *f.* flat roof; roof garden.

AZÚCAR *m.* sugar.

AZUL *adj.* blue.

Azul celeste. *Sky blue.*

Azul marino. *Navy blue.*

B

bacalao *m.* codfish.

bagatela *f.* bagatelle, trifle.

bahía *f.* bay, harbor.

bailar *to dance.*

baile *m.* dance, ball.

baja *f.* fall, depreciation (price); casualty.

BAJAR *to go (come) down; to get (bring) down; to get off; to lower, let down; to drop (fever, temperature, etc.).*
   Bajaré dentro de unos minutos. *I'll come (be) down in a few minutes.*
   Bajaron del tranvía. *They got off the streetcar.*
   Haga Ud. que bajen los baúles. *Have them get (bring) the trunks down.*
BAJO *low; under, below.*
   El es algo más bajo que yo. *He's a little bit shorter than I am.*
   Hable un poco más bajo. *Speak a little lower.*
   Tenemos diez grados bajo cero. *It's ten degrees below zero.*
bala *f. bullet.*
balance *m. balance.*
balde *m. bucket.*
   De balde. *Free. For nothing.*
   Trabajó de balde. *He worked for nothing. He didn't get paid for his work. He did the work free.*
   En balde. *In vain. With no result. To no purpose.*
   Trabajó en balde. *He worked in vain.*
ballena *f. whale.*
banana *f. banana.*
banano *m. banana tree.*
banco *m. bench; bank.*
banda *f. band; sash, ribbon; gang.*
bandeja *f. tray.*
bandera *f. flag, banner.*
bandido *m. bandit, outlaw.*
banquero *m. banker.*
BAÑO *m. bath; bathroom; bathtub.*
BARATO *adj. cheap.*
barba *f. chin; beard.*
   En sus barbas. *To his face.*
   Por barba. *A head. Apiece.*
barbería *f. barbershop.*
barbero *m. barber.*
barca *f. small boat.*
barco *m. boat, vessel, ship.*
barniz *m. varnish.*
barómetro *m. barometer.*
barranco *m. ravine, gully.*
barrer *to sweep.*
barriada *f. district, ward, suburb.*
barriga *f. belly.*
barril *m. barrel.*
barrio *m. district, ward, suburb.*
barro *m. mud.*
báscula *f. platform scale.*
base *f. base, basis.*
básico *adj. basic.*
basquetbol *m. basketball.*
BASTANTE *enough, sufficient.*
   Tiene bastante dinero. *He has enough money.*
   Bastante bien. *Pretty well. Rather well.*
BASTAR *to suffice, be enough.*
   Eso basta por ahora. *That's enough for now.*
   ¡Basta, ya! *That's enough!*
bastón *m. cane, walking stick.*
basura *f. refuse, garbage.*
bata *f. robe, gown.*
   Bata de baño. *Bathrobe.*
   Bata de dormir. *Nightgown.*
batalla *f. battle, combat, fight.*
batallar *to battle, to fight.*
batallón *m. battalion.*
batería *f. battery.*
   Batería de cocina. *Kitchen utensils.*
batir *to beat.*
baúl *m. trunk, chest.*

bautizar *to baptize, christen.*
bautizo *m. baptism. christening.*
bebé *m. baby.*
BEBER *to drink.*
   ¿Le gustaría beber algo? *Would you like something to drink?*
bebida *f. drink, beverage.*
becerro *m. calf; calfskin.*
belleza *f. beauty.*
BELLO *adj. beautiful.*
   Una mujer bella. *A beautiful woman.*
   Las bellas artes. *The fine arts.*
   ¡Qué bello! *How beautiful!*
bendecir *to bless.*
   ¡Dios le bendiga! *God bless you!*
bendición *f. blessing; benediction.*
bendito *adj. blessed; m. simpleton.*
   Es un bendito. *He's a simpleton.*
beneficiar *to benefit, to profit.*
beneficio *m. benefit, profit.*
berenjena *f. eggplant.*
berro *m. watercress.*
besar *to kiss.*
beso *m. kiss.*
bestia *f. beast.*
betún *m. shoepolish.*
biberón *m. nursing bottle.*
bibliografía *f. bibliography.*
biblioteca *f. library; bookcase.*
bicarbonato *m. bicarbonate.*
bicicleta *f. bicycle.*
bicho *m. insect; vermin; a ridiculous person (coll.). (Not to be used in Puerto Rico.)*
   Es un mal bicho. *He's a bad egg.*
   Es un bicho raro. *He's very odd. He's a queer person.*
BIEN *well, right.*
   ¿Está Ud. bien? *Are you all right?*
   Muy bien, gracias. *Very well, thank you.*
   No muy bien. *Not so well.*
   ¡Qué lo pase Ud. bien! *Good luck to you!*
   Está bien. *All right. O.K.*
bienes *m. pl. property, estate, possessions.*
bienestar *m. well-being, welfare.*
bienvenida *f. welcome.*
BILLETE *m. ticket; bank note. (See boleto.)*
   ¿Dónde puedo sacar mis billetes? *Where can I buy my tickets?*
   ¿Puede usted cambiarme un billete de diez dólares? *Can you change a ten-dollar bill for me?*
   Billete de ida y vuelta. *Round-trip ticket.*
billetera *f. wallet, pocketbook.*
biombo *m. screen.*
blanco *adj. white; m. mark, target.*
   Dar en el blanco. *To hit the mark.*
blando *adj. soft, smooth.*
blondo *adj. blond.*
bobo *adj. foolish, silly; m. fool, simpleton.*
boca *f. mouth.*
bocacalle *f. street intersection.*
bocadillo *m. a snack; sandwich.*
bocado *m. mouthful, a bite (to eat).*
   No he probado bocado desde ayer. *I haven't had a bite to eat since yesterday.*
bocina *f. horn (of a car).*
boda *f. wedding.*
bodega *f. wine-cellar; hold (of a ship); storeroom, grocery store.*
bofetada *f. a slap in the face.*
   Soltar una bofetada. *To slap in the face.*
boina *f. beret.*
bola *f. ball, globe.*

BOLETO *m. ticket. (See billete.)*
bolsa *f. purse; bag; stock exchange.*
bolsillo *m. pocket.*
bolso *m. change purse; bag.*
bomba *f. pump; fire engine; bomb.*
bombilla *f. flashbulb.*
bombón *m. candy, bonbon.*
bombonera *f. candy box.*
bondad *f. goodness, kindness.*
   Tenga la bondad de servirse. *Please help yourself.*
   Tenga Ud. la bondad de sentarse. *Please sit down.*
bonito *adj. pretty, good, graceful; m. bonito (a kind of fish).*
bordo, a *on board.*
   Todo el pasaje estaba a bordo. *All the passengers were on board.*
borracho *adj. drunk, intoxicated; m. drunkard.*
borrador *m. eraser; rough draft.*
borrar *to strike or cross out, to erase.*
borrón *m. blot, stain.*
bosque *m. wood, forest.*
bostezar *to yawn, to gape.*
botar *to launch (a ship); to bounce; to throw (Amer.).*
bote *m. boat; jar, can, container.*
   Bote salvavidas. *Lifeboat.*
   Un bote de mermelada. *A jar of marmalade.*
BOTELLA *f. bottle.*
botica *f. drugstore.*
boticario *m. druggist.*
botiquín *m. medicine cabinet, medicine chest.*
botón *m. button; bud.*
botones *m. hotel page, bellboy.*
boxeador *m. boxer.*
boxear *to box.*
boxeo *m. boxing.*
bravo *adj. brave.*
¡Bravo! *Bravo!*
brazalete *m. bracelet.*
BRAZO *m. arm.*
   Puede llevar el paquete debajo del brazo. *You can carry the package under your arm.*
   Iban del brazo. *They were walking arm in arm.*
BREVE *adj. brief, short.*
   En breve. *Shortly. In a little while.*
brevedad *f. briefness, brevity.*
brigada *f. brigade.*
brillante *adj. brilliant, sparkling; m. diamond.*
brillar *to shine, to sparkle.*
brindar *to toast; to offer; to invite.*
brindis *m. toast, drinking someone's health.*
brisa *f. breeze.*
brocha *f. brush.*
   Brocha para afeitar. *Shaving brush.*
broche *m. clasp; brooch; hook-and-eye.*
broma *f. joke, jest.*
   En broma. *As a joke. Jestingly.*
   Tomar a broma. *To take as a joke.*
bromear *to joke, to have fun.*
   ¡Ud. bromea! *You're joking! You're kidding!*
bromista *m. and f. joker.*
bronce *m. bronze, brass.*
bruma *f. fog, mist.*
brusco *adj. brusque, rude, rough.*
brutal *adj. brutal, brutish.*
bruto *adj. brutal; rude.*
   En bruto. *In the rough. In a rough state. In the raw state.*
   Peso bruto. *Gross weight.*
BUEN *(contraction of bueno; used only before a masculine noun).*

Pasamos un buen rato en el cine. *We had a good time at the movies.*

¡Buen viaje! *Bon voyage! Have a pleasant trip!*

Tuve un buen día. *I spent a pleasant day.*

Hace muy buen tiempo. *The weather's very nice.*

En buen estado. *In good condition.*

Un buen hombre. *A good man.*

BUENO *adj. good; kind; satisfactory; suited, fit; well.*

¡Buenos días! *Good morning!*

¡Buenas tardes! *Good afternoon! Good evening!*

¡Buenas noches! *Good night!*

Esa es una buena idea. *That's a good idea.*

He pasado muy buena noche. *I've had a very good night's rest.*

¿Tiene Ud. algo de bueno? *Have you anything good (to eat)?*

¡Sé buena! *Be good!*

Se pasa de bueno. *He's too good.*

¡Tanto bueno por aquí! *Look who's here! I'm glad to see you.*

¡Eso sí que está bueno! *That's a pretty how-do-you-do!*

De buena gana. *Willingly.*

buho *m. owl.*

buitre *m. vulture.*

bujía *f. candle; spark plug.*

bulla *f. noise, fuss.*

No metan tanta bulla. *Don't make so much noise.*

bullicio *m. noise, bustle, tumult.*

bulto *m. bundle, parcel, package.*

¿Cabrán estos bultos en su coche? *Will these packages fit in your car?*

Compré todos sus muebles a bulto. *I bought all his furniture for a lump sum.*

buñuelo *m. bun, cruller, fritter.*

buque *m. ship, vessel, steamer.*

burla *f. mockery, scoffing, sneering, fun.*

Le hicimos burla de su sombrero. *We made fun of her hat.*

¿Se burla usted de mí? *Are you making fun of me?*

burlón *adj. mocking, bantering; m. mocker, jester, scoffer.*

burro *m. ass, donkey.*

BUSCAR *to seek, look for, search; to fetch, get.*

¿Qué busca Ud.? *What are you looking for?*

¿A quién busca Ud.? *Who(m) do you wish to see? Who(m) are you looking for?*

Está buscando una colocación. *He's looking for a job.*

Voy a buscar mis libros. *I'm going to get my books.*

¿Quién la va a buscar? *Who's going to get her? Who's going after her?*

Enviaron a buscar al médico. *They sent someone for the doctor.*

búsqueda *f. search.*

busto *m. bust.*

butaca *f. easy chair; orchestra seat (in a theater).*

Siéntese Ud. en esta butaca. *Sit down in this armchair.*

Sacaré tres butacas. *I'll buy three orchestra seats.*

butifarra *f. kind of sausage.*

buzón *m. mailbox.*

Eche Ud. la carta en el buzón. *Put the letter in the mailbox.*

C

¡cá! *Oh, no!*

¡Cá! ¡Por supuesto que no! *No, indeed! Non-*sense! Of course not!

cabalgar *to ride on horseback.*

caballa *f. mackerel.*

caballería *f. cavalry; riding horse.*

caballero *m. gentleman; knight; horseman.*

Es todo un caballero. *He's a perfect gentleman.*

caballo *m. horse; knight (in chess); queen (cards).*

cabaña *f. hut, cabin.*

cabaret *m. cabaret, night club.*

cabecera *f. head of a bed or table.*

Sentarse a la cabecera. *To take one's place (to sit) at the head of the table.*

CABELLO *m. hair.*

CABER *to fit into; to have enough room; to contain.*

El libro no cabe en el estante. *The book won't fit on the shelf.*

No cabe más en el baúl. *The trunk won't hold any more. There's no more room in the trunk.*

No me cabe la menor duda. *I haven't the slightest doubt.*

Todo cabe en él. *He's capable of anything.*

Eso cabe en lo posible. *It's possible.*

CABEZA *f. head.*

Me duele la cabeza. *I've a headache.*

¿Le lavo la cabeza? *Do you want a shampoo? ("Shall I wash your hair?")*

Tiene mala cabeza. *He's reckless.*

Pagar a tanto por cabeza. *To pay so much per head.*

De pies a cabeza. *From head to foot.*

cabina *f. cabin, booth.*

Cabina telefónica. *Telephone booth.*

cable *m. cable; rope, line.*

cablegrafiar *to cable.*

CABO *m. tip, extremity, end; cape; rope; corporal.*

Al cabo de día. *At the end of the day.*

Leyó el libro de cabo a rabo. *She read the book from cover to cover.*

Al fin y al cabo. *At last. In the end. At length. After all. In the long run.*

Al cabo y a la postre. *At last. In the end. At length. After all. In the long run.*

Llevar a cabo. *To accomplish. To carry through.*

cabra *f. goat.*

cacahuate *m. peanut.*

cacao *m. cocoa; cocoa tree.*

cacería *f. hunt, hunting.*

cacerola *f. casserole, pan.*

cacharro *m. coarse earthen pot, piece of junk.*

cachetada *f. a slap in the face.*

cachimba *f. pipe (for smoking).*

CADA *adj. every, each.*

Cada hora. *Every hour.*

Cada cual. *Each one.*

Cada vez que viene. *Every time he comes.*

Dar a cada uno lo suyo. *To give everyone his due.*

Cada día se pone más delgada. *She's growing thinner day by day.*

cadáver *m. corpse, cadaver.*

cadena *f. chain.*

cadera *f. hip.*

cadete *m. cadet.*

CAER *to fall; to tumble down; to drop; to become, fit; to realize.*

Por poco me caigo. *I almost (nearly) fell down.*

Cayó enfermo ayer. *He fell ill yesterday. He got sick yesterday.*

¿Qué se le ha caído a Ud.? *What have you dropped?*

Yo caigo en ello. *I catch on. I see. I get it.*

No había caído en cuenta. *I didn't realize what you meant.*

Caer bien con. *To match. To match well with.*

Ese vestido le cae muy bien. *That dress fits her very well.*

La ventana cae al río. *The window overlooks the river.*

La pascua cae en marzo este año. *Easter falls (comes) in March this year.*

caerse *to fall down.*

Me caí. *I fell down.*

café *m. coffee; café.*

Una taza de café. *A cup of coffee.*

Café con leche. *Coffee with cream.*

Café solo. *Black coffee.*

Tomemos una cerveza en este café. *Let's have some beer in this café.*

cafetera *f. coffeepot.*

caída *f. fall, downfall.*

calambre *m. cramp.*

CAJA *f. box, case; coffin; chest; cash.*

Quiero una caja de galletas surtidas. *I want a box of assorted cookies.*

En caja. *Cash. Cash on hand.*

Pague en la caja. *Pay the cashier.*

Caja registradora. *Cash register.*

Caja de ahorros. *Savings bank.*

Caja fuerte. *A safe. ("Strong box.")*

Caja de caudales. *A safe.*

cajero *m. cashier.*

cajón *m. drawer; box, case (made of wood).*

calabaza *f. pumpkin, squash.*

¿Te dieron calabazas? *Didn't you pass (an exam)? Did you fail?*

Ella le dió calabazas. *She refused him (a suitor). She gave him the air.*

calabozo *m. dungeon, prison, cell.*

calamar *m. squid.*

calamidad *f. calamity, misfortune.*

calavera *f. skull; m. madcap.*

Es un calavera. *He leads a wild life.*

calcetín *m. sock.*

calcular *to calculate, estimate.*

cálculo *m. computation; estimate; calculus.*

caldo *m. broth.*

Caldo de gallina. *Chicken broth.*

calefacción *f. heating.*

calendario *m. almanac, calendar.*

calentador *m. heater.*

calentar *to warm, heat.*

calentarse *to grow warm, to warm oneself; to become excited, to get angry.*

No quiero calentarme la cabeza por éso. *I don't want to worry my head about that.*

calentura *f. fever.*

calibre *m. caliber; bore; gauge.*

calidad *f. quality; condition, capacity.*

CALIENTE *adj. warm, hot.*

Prefiero la leche fría a la caliente. *I prefer cold milk to warm.*

El sol está muy caliente. *The sun's very hot.*

calificación *f. qualification; mark (in an examination).*

calificar *to qualify; to rate; to describe; to authorize; to attest.*

caligrafía *f. calligraphy, handwriting.*

calma *f. calm, calmness, slowness.*

Tómelo con calma. *Take it easy.*

Debemos mirar este asunto con más calma. *We must look at this matter more calmly.*

calmante *m. sedative.*

calmar *to calm, to quiet.*

calmarse *to quiet down.*

¡Cálmese! *Calm yourself!*

CALOR *m. heat, warmth; thick (of a fight).*

Tengo calor. *I'm warm. I'm hot.*

Hace mucho calor. *It's very hot.*

calumniar *to calumniate, to slander.*

caluroso *adj. warm, hot.*

Es un día caluroso. *It's a hot day.*

calva *f. bald head.*

calvicie *f. baldness.*

calvo *adj. bald; barren.*

calzada *f. causeway, highway.*

calzado *m. footwear.*

calzador *m. shoe horn.*

calzar *to put on shoes; to wedge.*

calzoncillos *m. shorts.*

callado *adj. quiet; silent; discreet, reserved.*

callar *to keep quiet, to be silent; to conceal.*

¡Cállate! *Keep quiet!*

En este caso vale más callar. *In this case it's better to keep quiet (to say nothing).*

callarse *to be quiet, to shut up.*

CALLE *f. street; lane.*

Atravesemos la calle. *Let's cross the street.*

¿Qué calle es ésta? *What street is this?*

¿Cómo se llama esta calle? *What's the name of this street?*

¿Cuál es la calle próxima? *What's the street after this? What's the next street?*

Esta calle es de dirección única. *This is a one-way street.*

Al otro lado de la calle. *Across the street.*

Echar a la calle. *To throw out. To put out. ("To throw out into the street.")*

Quedarse en la calle. *To be left penniless.*

callejón *m. alley.*

Callejón sin salida. *Blind alley.*

callo *m. corn, callus.*

CAMA *f. bed; couch; litter; layer.*

Hacer la cama. *To make the bed.*

Guardar cama. *To be confined to bed. To stay in bed.*

camarada *m. and f. comrade.*

camarera *f. waitress, chambermaid.*

camarero *m. waiter; steward.*

camarote *m. cabin, stateroom.*

CAMBIAR *to barter, to exchange; to change.*

¿Puede Ud. cambiarme un billete de diez dólares? *Can you change a ten-dollar bill for me?*

He cambiado mi reloj por uno nuevo. *I've exchanged my watch for a new one.*

¿En qué estación cambiamos de tren? *At what station do we change trains?*

¿Ha cambiado Ud. de idea? *Have you changed your mind?*

Cambiemos de tema. *Let's change the subject.*

Cambiar la velocidad. *To shift gears.*

CAMBIO *m. barter, exchange; rate of exchange; change.*

No tengo cambio. *I haven't any change.*

¿A cuánto está el cambio? *What's the rate of exchange?*

En cambio. *On the other hand. In return.*

Cambio de velocidad (de marchas). *Gearshift.*

camilla *f. small bed; stretcher.*

CAMINAR *to walk; to march; to move along.*

CAMINO *m. road, way, highway.*

¿Dónde va este camino? *Where does this road lead to?*

¿Es éste el camino a Lima? *Is this the road to Lima?*

¿Voy bien por este camino? *Am I on the right road? Am I going the right way?*

Indíqueme el camino. *Show me the way.*

camión *m. truck; bus (Mex.).*

CAMISA *f. shirt, chemise.*

En mangas de camisa. *In one's shirt sleeves.*

camisería *f. haberdashery; haberdashery store; shirt factory.*

camiseta *f. undershirt.*

camisón *m. nightshirt, nightgown.*

camote *m. sweet potato.*

campamento *m. camp, encampment.*

campana *f. bell.*

¿Tocó Ud. la campanilla? *Did you ring the bell?*

Parece ser una persona de muchas campanillas. *He seems to be a very important person.*

campeón *m. champion.*

campeonato *m. championship.*

campesino *m. peasant.*

campo *m. field, country; space.*

cana *f. gray hair.*

canal *m. channel, canal.*

canario *m. canary.*

canasta *f. basket, hamper.*

canasto *m. large basket.*

cancelar *to cancel; to annul.*

cáncer *m. cancer.*

CANCIÓN *f. song.*

cancha *f. sports grounds, playing field.*

candado *m. padlock.*

candelero *m. candlestick.*

candidato *m. candidate.*

candidatura *f. candidacy.*

candidez *f. candor, simplicity.*

cándido *adj. candid, simple.*

canela *f. cinnamon.*

cangrejo *m. crab, crawfish.*

canjear *to exchange.*

canoa *f. canoe.*

CANSADO *adj. tired; tedious; annoying.*

cansancio *m. fatigue.*

cansar *to tire; to annoy, to bore.*

cansarse *to get tired, to get annoyed, to become bored.*

cantante *m. and f. singer.*

CANTAR *to sing; to reveal a secret.*

cantidad *f. quantity; amount; sum (of money).*

cantina *f. barroom, saloon; canteen.*

canto *m. singing; song; border; edge; front edge of a book; back of a knife; pebble, stone.*

caña *f. cane, reed; leg, upper part of a boot.*

Caña de pescar. *Fishing rod.*

Caña de azúcar. *Sugar cane.*

cañada *f. ravine.*

cañaveral *m. reed field, sugar cane plantation.*

cañería *f. conduit, piping; water pipe; main (gas).*

caño *m. pipe, tube, spout.*

cañón *m. cannon, gun; gorge, canyon; tube; funnel (of a chimney).*

caoba *f. mahogany.*

capa *f. cape, cloak; layer; coat, coating.*

capacidad *f. capacity.*

capataz *m. foreman, overseer.*

CAPAZ *adj. capable, able; liable, apt; spacious, having plenty of room.*

Es capaz de cualquier cosa. *He's capable of anything.*

capital *adj. principal, main; m. principal (money invested); capital (stock); f. capital (metropolis).*

capitán *m. captain; commander; ringleader.*

capítulo *m. chapter.*

CARA *f. face; front, façade.*

Su cara no me es desconocida. *Your face is familiar.*

Tiene Ud. muy buena cara. *You look very well.*

Hacer cara a. *To face. To cope with. To meet.*

Echar en cara. *To reproach. ("To throw in someone's face.")*

De cara. *Facing.*

Sacar la cara por uno. *To take someone's part. To defend someone.*

¿Cara o cruz? *Heads or tails?*

¡caray! *Good gracious! Goodness! Gosh!*

carbón *m. coal; charcoal; carbon.*

Papel carbón. *Carbon paper.*

carcajada *f. hearty laughter.*

Reírse a carcajadas. *To laugh uproariously. To split one's sides laughing.*

Soltar una carcajada. *To burst out laughing.*

Se ríe a carcajadas. *He has a hearty laugh.*

cárcel *f. prison, jail.*

CARECER *to lack, to be in want.*

Carecemos del dinero suficiente para eso. *We lack (don't have) enough money for that.*

Lo que dijo carece de lógica. *His words aren't logical. ("What he said lacks logic.")*

carestía *f. lack, scarcity; famine; high price.*

carga *f. freight; load; cargo; burden.*

cargado *adj. loaded; strong (tea).*

Estaba cargado de razón. *He was absolutely right.*

No quiero el té cargado. *I don't want my tea strong.*

cargamento *m. cargo; load.*

cargar *to load; to charge; to carry a load.*

Cargar en cuenta. *To charge to an account.*

caricia *f. caress.*

caridad *f. charity.*

cariño *m. fondness, love, affection; pl. regards.*

Tomar cariño a. *To become attached to.*

Poner cariño a alguna cosa. *To take a liking to something.*

Dar cariños. *To give one's regards.*

cariñoso *adj. affectionate, loving.*

caritativo *adj. charitable.*

carnaval *m. carnival.*

CARNE *f. flesh; meat; pulp (of fruit).*

Carne asada. *Roast meat.*

Carne de vaca. *Beef.*

Ser carne y uña. *To be like two peas in a pod. To be hand in glove with each other. To be bosom friends.*

carnero *m. mutton.*

carnet *m. booklet; membership book, membership card.*

carnet de conducir *driver's license.*

carnicería *f. butcher shop, meat market; slaughter.*

carnicero *m. butcher.*

CARO *adj. dear; expensive.*

Es muy caro. *It's too expensive (dear).*

Un amigo caro. *A dear friend.*

Lo pagará Ud. caro. *You'll pay dearly for it.*

¡Qué caro se vende Ud.! *How seldom you come to see us!*

Cara mitad. *Better half.*

carpintero *m. carpenter.*

carrera *f. career; race.*

carreta *f. heavy cart, wagon.*

carrete *m. spool, reel, bobbin, coil; kind of hat (Mex.).*

carretel *m. spool, bobbin, reel.*

carretera *f. road, highway, drive.*

¿Dónde va esta carretera? *Where does this highway lead?*

carretilla *f. wheelbarrow.*

carrillo *m. cheek.*

Echar carrillos. *To grow fat in the cheeks.*
Comer a dos carrillos. 1. *To draw benefits from two sides.* 2. *To eat like a horse.*
carro *m. cart; car, motorcar (Amer.).*
carruaje *m. any kind of vehicle or carriage.*
CARTA *f. letter; map, chart; charter; playing card.*
¿Cómo tengo que dirigir la carta? *How shall (do) I address the letter?*
Eche Ud. la carta en el buzón. *Put the letter in the mailbox.*
¿A qué hora reparten las cartas? *When is the mail delivered?*
Carta certificada. *Registered letter.*
Carta urgente. *Special delivery letter.*
Carta de crédito. *Letter of credit.*
Carta de naturaleza. *Naturalization papers.*
Tomar cartas. *To take part. To take sides.*
Vamos a jugar a las cartas. *Let's play cards.*
cartel *m. placard, poster, cartel.*
cartera *f. portfolio; pocketbook, wallet.*
Le han robado la cartera. *They've stolen his wallet.*
carterista *m. pickpocket.*
cartero *m. mailman, letter carrier.*
cartilla *f. primer (book).*
cartón *m. cardboard.*
CASA *f. house, home; firm, concern.*
Vive en esa casa que hace esquina. *He lives in the corner house.*
Mándemelo a casa. *Send it to my house.*
Vamos a mudarnos de casa pronto. *We're going to move soon.*
¿Cuándo viene Ud. por mi casa? *When are you coming to my place?*
Estaré en casa todo el día. *I'll be (at) home all day.*
Está en la casa de Juan. *He's at John's house.*
Aquí tiene Ud. su casa. *Come again.* ("This is your home.")
"Su casa." *"Your house."* (A polite form of giving one's address, implying my house is yours or at your disposal.)
Esta casa goza de buena fama. *This firm has a good reputation.*
Casa de huéspedes. *Boarding house.*
Casa de apartamentos. *Apartment house.*
casado *adj. married.*
casamiento *m. marriage, wedding.*
casar *to marry; to match.*
casarse *to get married.*
cascanueces *m. nutcracker.*
cáscara *f. peel, husk, shell, bark.*
caserío *m. row of houses, hamlet.*
casero *adj. pertaining to the home, domestic.*
No hay nada como la comida casera. *There's nothing like home cooking.*
Remedios caseros. *Home remedies.*
CASI *almost, nearly.*
Casi he terminado. *I'm almost finished.*
La comida está casi lista. *Dinner is about ready.*
Casi nunca leo los periódicos. *I hardly ever read the newspapers.*
casilla *f. small house; post-office box (Amer.).*
casino *m. casino.*
CASO *m. case, event, accident.*
¿Qué caso tan singular! *What a strange case!*
Bien, vamos al caso. *Well, let's get to the point.*
Hacer caso. *To pay attention to. To mind.*
No le haga caso. *Pay no attention to him. Don't mind him.*
castañuela *f. castanet.*
castellano *adj. Castilian; m. Spanish language.*

castigar *to punish.*
castigo *m. punishment, penalty.*
castizo *adj. pure Spanish without foreign influence.*
casual *adj. accidental, casual.*
casualidad *f. chance, coincidence, accident.*
Me lo encontré de pura casualidad. *I met him by chance.*
¿Qué casualidad! *What a coincidence!*
catálogo *m. catalog.*
catarata *f. waterfall, cascade; cataract (of the eye).*
catarro *m. a cold.*
Tengo un catarro terrible. *I have a bad cold.*
catedral *f. cathedral.*
catedrático *m. professor of a university.*
categoría *f. category, class.*
catolicismo *m. Catholicism.*
católico *adj. Catholic.*
CATORCE *fourteen; fourteenth.*
catre *m. cot.*
caudillo *m. leader, chieftain.*
CAUSA *f. cause, motive; lawsuit.*
No vino a causa de la lluvia. *He didn't come on account (because) of the rain.*
Sin causa. *Without cause. Without a reason.*
causar *to cause.*
Causa horror. *It's horrible!*
Causar daño. *To do harm. To cause damage. To injure.*
cautela *f. caution, prudence.*
cauto *adj. cautious, prudent.*
cavar *to dig up, to excavate.*
caverna *f. cave, cavern.*
cavidad *f. cavity.*
cavilar *to ponder.*
caza *f. hunting; game.*
cazador *m. hunter.*
cazar *to hunt, to chase.*
cazuela *f. casserole.*
cebada *f. barley.*
cebo *m. bait; priming.*
cebolla *f. onion.*
ceder *to grant; to give in, yield.*
cedro *m. cedar.*
cédula *f. warrant, certificate.*
Cédula de vecindad (cédula personal). *Identification papers.*
ceguera *f. blindness.*
ceja *f. eyebrow.*
celda *f. cell.*
CELEBRAR *to celebrate; to be glad; to praise; to hold, take place.*
Lo celebro mucho. *I'm very happy to hear it.*
Celebro que le haya ido bien. *I'm glad he's done well (that things have gone well with him).*
¿Cuándo se celebra la reunión? *When will the meeting take place?*
célebre *adj. famous, renowned.*
celeste *adj. light blue.*
celos *m. pl. jealousy.*
celoso *adj. jealous.*
célula *f. cell.*
cementerio *m. cemetery.*
cemento *m. cement.*
CENA *f. supper, dinner.*
cenar *to have supper, to dine.*
cenicero *m. ash tray.*
ceniza *f. ashes.*
censura *f. censorship; reproach.*
censurar *to censure; to reproach; to criticize.*
CENTAVO *m. cent.*
centena *f. a hundred, about a hundred.*
centenar *m. a hundred, about a hundred.*

A centenares. *By the hundreds.*
centenario *m. centenary.*
centeno *m. rye.*
centésimo *adj. hundredth.*
centígrado *adj. centigrade.*
centímetro *m. centimeter.*
céntimo *m. centime; a hundredth part of a peseta (Spain).*
CENTRAL *adj. central; f. main office.*
América Central. *Central America.*
¿Dónde está la central telefónica? *Where is the telephone exchange?*
CENTRO *m. center, middle; core; club, social circle.*
ceñirse *to limit oneself to.*
ceño *m. frown.*
cepillar *to brush; to plane, to polish.*
cepillo *m. brush; carpenter's plane.*
Cepillo de dientes. *Toothbrush.*
cera *f. beeswax, wax; wax candle.*
CERCA *near, about, close by; f. fence.*
¿Hay alguna farmacia cerca de aquí? *Is there a drugstore near here?*
Está muy cerca. *It's quite near.*
Esto me toca de cerca. *This concerns me very much.*
Por aquí cerca. *Near here. Somewhere around here.*
cercanías *f. vicinity, neighborhood.*
cercano *adj. nearby.*
cercar *to fence, inclose, surround; to besiege.*
cerciorarse *to ascertain, to make sure.*
cerco *m. fence; siege.*
cerdo *m. hog, pig.*
cereal *m. cereal.*
cerebro *m. brain.*
ceremonia *f. ceremony; formality.*
cereza *f. cherry.*
cerezo *m. cherry tree.*
cerilla *f. match (wax match).*
cero *m. zero; nought.*
Tenemos diez grados bajo cero. *It's ten degrees below zero.*
Ser un cero a la izquierda. *To be a nobody.*
cerrado *adj. closed, shut; stupid.*
Cerrado por reformas. *Closed for repairs.*
Las tiendas estarán cerradas mañana. *The stores will be closed tomorrow.*
Se trató el asunto a puerta cerrada. *The matter was discussed privately.*
cerradura *f. lock.*
CERRAR *to close, lock, shut; to turn off.*
Cierre la puerta. *Close (shut) the door.*
Cerrar con llave. *To lock.* ("To close with a key.")
Haga el favor de cerrar el grifo. *Please turn the water off.*
cerro *m. hill.*
cerrojo *m. bolt, latch.*
certeza *f. certainty, conviction.*
certidumbre *f. certainty.*
certificado *m. certificate.*
certificar *to certify; to register (a letter, etc.).*
Quisiera certificar esta carta. *I'd like to register this letter.*
cervecería *f. brewery, beer saloon.*
cerveza *f. beer, ale.*
cesante *adj. unemployed; dismissed, fired.*
CESAR *to cease, stop; to leave (a job).*
Quédese aquí hasta que cese la lluvia. *Stay here until the rain stops.*
Ha cesado en su cargo. *He left his job.*
césped *m. grass, lawn.*

cesta f. *basket, hamper.*
cesto m. *hand basket.*
cicatriz f. *scar.*
ciclista m. *and* f. *bicyclist.*
ciclón m. *cyclone.*
ciego adj. *blind;* m. *a blind person.*
cielo m. *sky; heaven.*
CIEN (*contraction of* **ciento;** *used before nouns*), *one hundred.*
  ¿Le bastará a usted con cien pesos? *Will one hundred pesos be enough for you?*
ciencia f. *science.*
científico adj. *scientific.*
CIENTO adj. *and* n. *one hundred; one hundredth.*
CIERTO adj. *certain.*
  Es cierto. *It's certain. It's true.*
  Eso no es cierto. *That's not certain. That's not true.*
  Lo dimos por cierto. *We assumed that it was true.*
  Hasta cierto punto eso es verdad. *That's true to a certain extent.*
  Esto me lo dijo cierta persona. *A certain person told me that.*
  ¡Sí, por cierto! *Yes, indeed!*
ciervo m. *deer.*
cifra f. *number; cipher, code.*
cigarrera f. *woman who makes or sells cigars; cigarette case.*
  Le regalaron una cigarrera. *They gave him a cigarette case as a present.*
CIGARRILLO m. *cigarette.*
cigarro m. *cigar; cigarette* (*Mex.*).
cigüeña f. *stork.*
cilindro m. *cylinder.*
cima f. *summit, top.*
  Dar cima. *To carry through successfully.*
  Dió cima a su proyecto. *He concluded his project successfully.*
cimiento m. *foundation, base.*
CINCO adj. *and* n. *five; fifth.*
CINCUENTA adj. *and* n. *fifty; fiftieth.*
cincuentavo m. *fiftieth* (*part*).
CINE m. *movies, motion picture, cinema.*
cinema m. *movies, cinema.*
cinematógrafo m. *movie, motion picture.*
cinta f. *ribbon; tape; film.*
  Cinta magnetofónica. *Tape* (*for a tape recorder*).
cintura f. *waist.*
cinturón m. *belt.*
ciprés m. *cypress.*
circo m. *circus.*
circulación f. *circulation; traffic.*
circular adj. *circular.*
circular *to circulate.*
círculo m. *circle; circuit; club.*
circunferencia f. *circumference.*
circunstancia f. *circumstance.*
  Lo exigen las circunstancias. *The circumstances demand it. The situation requires it.*
ciruela f. *plum, prune.*
cirujano m. *surgeon.*
cisne m. *swan.*
CITA f. *appointment, date; summons; quotation.*
  Deseo hacer una cita con Ud. *I'd like to make an appointment with you.*
  Nunca llega a tiempo a sus citas. *He's never on time for his appointments.*
  Tengo una cita esta noche con mi novia. *I've a date tonight with my girl.*
citar *to cite; to make an appointment; to summon.*
  Me he citado con él para el lunes. *I've made an appointment with him for next Monday.*

Citó una porción de casos semejantes. *He cited a number of similar cases.*
CIUDAD f. *city.*
  Ciudad natal. *Home town. City in which one is born.*
ciudadanía f. *citizenship.*
ciudadano m. *citizen.*
civil adj. *civil; courteous, polite.*
civilización f. *civilization.*
civilizar *to civilize.*
clara f. *white of an egg.*
claridad f. *clearness; light; distinctness, plainness.*
  Escriba Ud. la dirección con claridad. *Write the address clearly.*
  Hablar con claridad. *To speak clearly* (*plainly*).
clarín m. *bugle; bugler.*
clarinete m. *clarinet; clarinetist.*
CLARO adj. *clear; intelligible; obvious, evident; plain, frank; transparent, pure* (*water, etc.*); *light* (*color*); *bright* (*room, etc.*); m. *skylight; space* (*in writing*); *gap.*
  Escriba claro. *Write clearly.*
  Poner en claro. *To make* (*something*) *clear. To clarify. To clear* (*something*) *up. To set right.*
  Claro que lo haré. *Certainly I'll do it. Of course I'll do it.*
  ¡Claro que sí! *Certainly! Of course!*
  ¡Claro que no! *Of course not!*
  Decir las cosas claras. *To speak plainly.*
  Pasé la noche en claro. *I couldn't sleep a wink all night.*
CLASE f. *class; kind; sort; classroom; lesson.*
  Clase de español. *Spanish class.*
  Tomó clases de español pero no adelantó mucho. *He took Spanish lessons but he didn't get very far* (*make much progress*).
  Es el primero de la clase. *He's at the head of his class.*
  El niño no asistió hoy a clase. *The child didn't attend school today.*
  ¿Qué clase de fruta es esa? *What kind of fruit is that?*
  La clase obrera. *The working class.*
clásico m. *classic, typical.*
  Este es un caso clásico. *This is a typical case.*
clavar *to nail, fasten; to drive in, to pierce; to cheat.*
  Clavar la vista en. *To stare at.*
CLAVE f. *key; cipher, code.*
clavel m. *carnation.*
clavo m. *nail; clove.*
  Por fin ha dado Ud. en el clavo. *At last you've hit the nail on the head.*
clero m. *clergy.*
cliente m. *and* f. *client; customer.*
clientela f. *clientele, customers.*
clima m. *climate.*
clínica f. *clinic; dispensary.*
cloaca f. *sewer.*
cloroformo m. *chloroform.*
club m. *club.*
cobarde adj. *timid, cowardly;* m. *coward.*
cobija f. *bed cover, blanket.*
cobrador m. *conductor* (*bus, streetcar, etc.*); *collector.*
COBRAR *to collect, receive* (*money*); *to charge* (*price*).
  Quisiera cobrar este cheque. *I'd like to have this check cashed.*
  Cobre Ud. de este dólar. *Take it out of this dollar.*
  Cobramos a primero de mes. *We're paid on the first of the month.*

  ¿Cuánto cobra Ud. por la hechura de un abrigo? *How much do you charge for making a coat?*
  Cobrar ánimo. *To take courage.*
cobre m. *copper.*
cocer *to cook, boil, bake.*
cocido m. *dish made of boiled meat and vegetables.*
cocina f. *kitchen; cuisine.*
cocinar *to cook.*
cocinero m. *chef, cook.*
coco m. *coconut tree; coconut.*
COCHE m. *coach, carriage; car.*
  Vaya Ud. por un coche. *Call a cab* (*taxi*).
  Coche comedor. *Dining car. Diner.*
  Coche cama. *Sleeping car. Sleeper.*
  Coche de fumar. *Smoking car.*
  Coche salón. *Parlor car.*
codazo m. *a shove with the elbow.*
  Me dió un codazo. *He gave me a shove* (*with his elbow*).
codiciar *to covet, to desire eagerly.*
codicioso adj. *covetous, greedy; diligent.*
codo m. *elbow.*
  Hablar hasta por los codos. *To be a chatterbox.*
codorniz f. *quail.*
COGER *to catch, to take hold of; to gather; to take, to seize; to have room or capacity for.* (*It's a bad word in Argentina or Uruguay. In those countries use "tomar."*)
  Coja Ud. bien la pluma. *Hold your pen properly.*
  Coja Ud. un lápiz y escriba. *Take a pencil and write.*
  He cogido un resfriado. *I've caught a cold.*
  Esa pregunta me ha cogido de sorpresa. *That question took me by surprise.*
  Esta alfombra no cogerá toda la sala. *This carpet won't cover the whole room.*
  Los niños desbarataron todo lo que cogen. *Children destroy everything they get hold of* (*lay their hands on*).
  Ha cogido mi sombrero en vez del suyo. *He took my hat instead of his own.*
  Le cojo la palabra. *I'll take you up on that.*
cogote m. *neck.*
cohecho m. *bribery.*
cohete m. *rocket.*
coincidencia f. *coincidence.*
  Nos encontramos por una simple coincidencia. *We met by pure chance* (*coincidence*).
coincidir *to coincide.*
cojear *to limp.*
  Sé de que pie cojea. *I know his weakness.*
cojera f. *lameness.*
cojo adj. *lame.*
cola f. *tail; rear of a train; glue; line* (*of people*).
  Hacer cola. *To stand in line.*
colaboración f. *collaboration.*
colaborar *to collaborate.*
colar *to strain.*
colcha f. *bedspread.*
colchón m. *mattress.*
colección f. *collection.*
coleccionar *to collect.*
colecta f. *collection, collect.*
colectar *to collect; to solicit.*
colegio m. *school; association* (*means "college" only in the sense of a body of persons having common interests or corporate functions; for example, the electoral college or college of cardinals*).
  No ha debido aprender gran cosa en el colegio. *I don't think he learned much at school.*

Colegio de abogados. *Lawyers association. The bar.*

Colegio de médicos. *Medical association.*

El colegio de cardinales. *The College of Cardinals.*

Colegio electoral. *Electoral college.*

cólera *f. anger, fit of temper, rage; m. cholera.*

Se le pasó la cólera fácilmente. *He got over his fit of temper easily.*

COLGAR *to hang, to suspend.*

Colgaron al criminal. *The criminal was hanged. ("They hanged the criminal.")*

Cuelgue su abrigo en la percha. *Hang your coat on the clothes-rack.*

¡No cuelgue Ud.! *Don't hang up!*

Cuelgue el receptor. *Hang up the receiver.*

cólico *m. colic.*

coliflor *f. cauliflower.*

colilla *f. cigar or cigarette stub.*

colina *f. small hill.*

colmena *f. beehive.*

colmillo *m. eyetooth, canine tooth, premolar.*

colmo *m. heap; climax, limit.*

¡Es el colmo! *That's the limit! That's the last straw!*

colocación *f. employment, situation; arrangement.*

Anda buscando una colocación. *He's looking for a job.*

Ha obtenido una buena colocación. *He has a good job. He got a good job.*

colocar *to place, to give employment to; to dispose of, to sell; to invest.*

Colóquelo en su lugar. *Put it back in its place.*

Se ha colocado en una casa de comercio. *He got a job in a business firm.*

colonia *f. colony; residential section in the outskirts of a town.*

colonial *adj. colonial.*

COLOR *m. color; paint; tendency, policy; aspect; pretext.*

Es un color muy de moda. *It's a very stylish color.*

Este color va bien con el verde. *This color goes well with green.*

Color firme (solido). *Fast Color. Color that doesn't fade.*

Color vivo. *Bright color.*

Color claro. *Light color.*

Color muerto. *Dull (dead) color.*

De color. *Colored.*

¿Qué color tiene ese periódico? *What's that newspaper's policy? How does that newspaper stand politically?*

colorado *adj. red.*

Ponerse colorado. *To blush.*

colorete *m. rouge.*

colorido *m. colorful.*

columna *f. column, pillar.*

columpiar *to swing.*

columpio *m. swing.*

collar *m. necklace, collar.*

coma *f. comma.*

comadre *f. term applied both to the godmother and to the mother of a child; a gossip.*

comadrear *to gossip.*

comadrona *f. midwife.*

comandante *m. commander, commandant.*

comarca *f. territory, district.*

combate *m. combat.*

Poner fuera de combate. *To knock out.*

combatiente *noun and adj. combatant, fighter.*

No combatiente. *Noncombatant.*

combatir *to combat, fight.*

combinación *f. combination; a slip (for women).*

combinar *to combine.*

combustible *m. combustible, fuel.*

comedia *f. comedy, play; farce.*

La comedia agradó mucho al auditorio. *The audience liked the play very much.*

Es una comedia. *It's a farce.*

comediante *m. comedian.*

comedor *m. dining room.*

Coche comedor. *Diner. Dining car.*

comensal *m. and f. guest (at the table); boarder.*

comentar *to comment.*

comentario *m. comment, commentary.*

Comentarios del día. *News commentary.*

Eso se entiende sin comentarios. *That's a matter of course. That's very clear (obvious, self-evident). ("It's clear without any comments; it needs no comments.")*

COMENZAR *to begin, to commence.*

¿A qué hora comienza la función? (At) *What time does the play begin?*

COMER *to eat, to dine.*

¿Qué tiene Ud. de comer? *What do you have to eat?*

¿Qué quiere Ud. comer? *What do you want (would you like) to eat?*

¿Come Ud. con gana? *Are you enjoying your food? How do you like the food?*

Tengo ganas de comer. *I'm hungry.*

No tengo ganas de comer ahora. *I don't feel like eating just now.*

Dar de comer. *To feed.*

Ser de buen comer. *To have a hearty appetite.*

Se ha comido Ud. una línea. *You've omitted a line.*

Se comen el uno al otro. *They fight like cats and dogs.*

Ud. se come las palabras. *You don't enunciate clearly. You swallow half of your words.*

comerciar *to deal, to trade.*

comercio *m. commerce, trade.*

comestible *adj. edible; m. pl. food, groceries.*

cometer *to commit; to make (a mistake).*

Todos cometemos errores. *We all make mistakes. Anyone can make a mistake.*

cometido *m. mission, trust, task; duty.*

Yo he cumplido con mi cometido. *I've done my duty.*

Desempeñó su cometido muy bien. *He carried out his mission faithfully. He fulfilled his obligation (commitment) faithfully.*

comezón *f. itching, itch.*

cómico *adj. comic, comical.*

COMIDA *f. food; meal; dinner.*

La comida es muy sabrosa. *The food's very tasty.*

No debe Ud. tomar nada entre comidas. *You mustn't eat anything between meals.*

No hay nada como la comida casera. *There's nothing like home cooking.*

¿Está la comida? *Is dinner ready?*

La comida está servida. *Dinner's served. Dinner's on the table.*

comienzo *m. beginning, start.*

comillas *f. quotation marks.*

comisaría *f. police station.*

comisario *m. commissioner.*

comisión *f. commission.*

comité *m. committee.*

COMO *how; as, like.*

¿Cómo lo pasa Ud.? *How do you do? How are you getting along?*

¿A cómo estamos? *What's the date?*

¿Cómo se llama Ud.? *What's your name?*

¿A cómo se venden estas medias? *How much are these stockings?*

¿Cómo no? *Why not?*

¡Cómo no! *Yes, of course.*

Como Ud. quiera. *As you wish (like).*

Habla español tan bien como ella. *He speaks Spanish as well as she.*

El pasaje en autobús cuesta tanto como en tranvía. *It costs as much to ride on a bus as it does on a streetcar.*

Hace como que trabaja para que no la regañen. *She pretends to work so they won't scold her.*

Como si tal cosa. *As if nothing had happened.*

Según y como. *It all depends.*

cómoda *f. chest of drawers, a dresser.*

comodidad *f. comfort; convenience.*

Para su comodidad. *For your convenience.*

Esta casa tiene muchas comodidades. *This house has many (modern) conveniences.*

Comodidades de la vida moderna. *Modern conveniences.*

cómodo *adj. comfortable; convenient, handy.*

Estoy muy cómodo aquí. *I'm very comfortable here.*

Esta silla es un poco más cómoda. *This chair's a bit more comfortable.*

compadecer *to pity, to sympathize with.*

Le compadezco. *I pity him. I sympathize with him.*

compadre *m. term applied both to the godfather and to the father of a child; friend, pal, buddy (coll.).*

compañero *m. companion, comrade, pal; fellow member.*

En poco tiempo pasó a sus compañeros de estudios. *In a short time he was doing better than his fellow students.*

Es mi compañero de cuarto. *He's my roommate.*

compañía *f. company; partnership, society.*

Suárez y Cía. *Suárez and Co.*

comparación *f. comparison.*

En comparación con. *In comparison with.*

COMPARAR *to compare.*

compartir *to share.*

compás *m. compasses, dividers; compass; time (in music).*

compasión *f. pity, sympathy.*

compatible *adj. compatible, consistent with.*

compatriota *m. and f. countryman, countrywoman.*

compensación *f. compensation, reward.*

compensar *to compensate, to reward.*

competencia *f. competition; competence.*

competente *adj. competent, fit.*

competir *to compete, to contend.*

complacer *to please, to accommodate.*

Uno no puede complacer a todo el mundo. *One can't please everybody.*

Lo siento, pero no puedo complacerle. *I'm sorry but I can't accommodate you.*

complacerse *to be pleased.*

Se complace mucho en lo que hace. *He's very pleased (satisfied) with what he's doing.*

complaciente *adj. accommodating, agreeable, pleasing.*

complemento *m. complement, object (grammar).*

COMPLETAR *to complete.*

Completar un trabajo. *To complete a job (task).*

COMPLETO *adj. full; complete, finished.*

El autobús va completo. *The bus is full.*

Hay un lleno completo esta noche. *There's a full house tonight.*

Por completo. *Completely.*
complicado *adj. complicated.*
complicar *to complicate.*
cómplice *m. and f. accomplice.*
complot *m. conspiracy, plot, intrigue.*
componer *to repair, to mend; to manage; to compose.*
Quiero que me compongan los zapatos. *I'd like to have my shoes repaired.*
Quiero que componga Ud. esta radio. *I'd like you to fix this radio.*
Ya sabré componérmelas. *I'll know how to manage. I'll manage all right (one way or another).*
comportamiento *m. behavior.*
comportar *to suffer, to tolerate.*
comportarse *to behave.*
composición *composition.*
compositor *m. composer; typesetter.*
compostura *f. repair; neatness; modesty; composure.*
compota *f. preserves, stewed fruit.*
COMPRA *f. purchase, shopping.*
Ir de compras. *To go shopping.*
Tengo que hacer unas compras. *I want to make a few purchases. I want to buy a few things.*
comprador *m. buyer, purchaser; customer.*
COMPRAR *to buy, to shop.*
Comprar a crédito. *To buy on credit.*
Comprar al fiado. *To buy on credit.*
Comprar al contado. *To buy for cash.*
Comprar de ocasión. *To buy secondhand.*
COMPRENDER *to understand; to comprise, to include.*
¿Me comprende Ud. bien? *Do you understand me ("all right")?*
Le entiendo perfectamente. *I understand you perfectly.*
¡Se comprende! *That's understood. That's clear. That's a matter of course.*
comprendido *adj. understood; including.*
comprensible *comprehensible.*
comprensión *f. comprehension, understanding.*
comprensivo *adj. comprehensive.*
comprimir *to compress; to repress, to restrain.*
comprimirse *to restrain oneself, to control oneself.*
comprobante *m. proof, voucher.*
comprobar *to prove, to verify.*
comprometerse *to commit oneself; to become engaged.*
compromiso *m. compromise; jeopardy; engagement; pledge, commitment.*
compuesto *adj. and n. compound.*
compulsorio *adj. compulsory.*
computar *to compute.*
COMÚN *adj. common.*
Sentido común. *Common sense.*
En común. *In common. Jointly.*
Por lo común. *Generally.*
De común acuerdo. *By mutual consent.*
comunicación *f. communication.*
Telefonista, nos ha cortado la comunicación. *Operator, we've been cut off.*
Por favor, póngame en comunicación con el número . . . *Kindly connect me with number . . .*
comunicar *to announce; to communicate; to inform.*
comunidad *f. community.*
CON *with, by.*
Se viene con nosotros. *She's coming with us.*
Con mucho gusto. *With ("great") pleasure. Gladly.*
No sea duro con él. *Don't be hard on him.*

Con tal. *Provided that.*
Con que. *And so. So. Then. Well then.*
¿Con que esas tenemos! *So that's the story!*
Con todo. *Notwithstanding. Nevertheless. However. Even so.*
Tratar con. *To do business with. To deal with.*
Dar con. *To find. To meet. To come across.*
Con tal que. *On (the) condition that. Provided that.*
concebir *to conceive.*
conceder *to grant.*
concentración *f. concentration.*
concentrar *to concentrate.*
concepto *m. concept, idea.*
concernir *to concern.*
Eso no le concierne a Ud. *That doesn't concern you.*
concesión *f. concession.*
conciencia *f. conscience, consciousness.*
concierto *m. concert; agreement.*
conciliación *f. conciliation.*
conciliar *to conciliate, to reconcile.*
conciso *adj. concise.*
concluir *to conclude; to finish; to close (a deal).*
conclusión *f. conclusion.*
concluso *adj. ended, concluded, closed.*
concordancia *f. concordance; harmony, agreement.*
concordarse *to agree.*
concretar *to make concrete, reduce to its simplest form.*
concretarse *to limit or confine oneself (to a subject).*
Concrétese a la pregunta. *Stick to the point. Answer the question.*
concreto *adj. concrete.*
En concreto. *In short.*
concurrencia *f. audience, attendance; coincidence; competition.*
concurrir *to concur; to attend.*
concurso *m. competition, contest.*
concha *f. shell.*
conde *m. count (title).*
condecoración *f. decoration, medal.*
condena *f. sentence, penalty.*
condenar *to condemn, to convict; to disapprove.*
Se le condenó a muerte. *He was condemned to death.*
Condeno su proceder. *I disapprove of his behavior.*
condición *f. condition, state; term.*
A condición que. *On (the) condition that. Provided that.*
Convengo en sus condiciones. *I agree to your terms.*
¿Está todo en buenas condiciones? *Is everything in good order?*
condicional *adj. conditional.*
condimentar *to season (food).*
condimento *m. seasoning, condiment.*
condiscípulo *m. fellow student, schoolmate.*
condonar *to forgive, to pardon.*
cóndor *m. condor.*
CONDUCIR *to drive; to conduct; to carry; to lead.*
¿Sabe Ud. conducir? *Do you know how to drive?*
Este camino nos conducirá al lago. *This road will take us to the lake.*
conducirse *to conduct oneself, to behave.*
conducta *f. conduct, behavior.*
conductor *m. conductor, driver.*
conejo *m. rabbit.*
confeccionar *to make, to prepare.*
conferencia *f. conference, lecture; call (long distance).*

Asistimos a la conferencia del lunes. *We attended Monday's lecture.*
Conferencia a larga distancia. *Long distance call.*
Conferencia interurbana. *Long distance call (Spain).*
conferenciante *m. and f. lecturer.*
conferir *to confer, to bestow.*
confesar *to admit, to confess.*
¿Confiesa Ud. su falta? *Do you admit your guilt?*
confesión *f. confession, acknowledgment.*
confianza *f. confidence; faith; familiarity.*
Digno de confianza. *Reliable. Trustworthy.*
En confianza. *In confidence.*
Tener confianza en. *To trust.*
confiar *to confide; to trust in, to entrust.*
confidencia *f. confidence.*
confidencial *adj. confidential.*
confidente *adj. confident.*
confirmación *f. confirmation.*
confirmar *to confirm. to ratify.*
confite *m. candy.*
conflicto *m. conflict, strife; predicament.*
conformar *to conform; to fit, to agree; to comply with.*
Conformarse con. *To agree with. To be satisfied with.*
CONFORME *alike; according to; O.K., correct.*
Conforme a. *According to.*
Estar conforme. *To be in agreement.*
conformidad *f. conformity, resemblance.*
De conformidad con. *In accordance with.*
confort *m. comfort.*
confortable *adj. comfortable.*
confortante *adj. comforting.*
confortar *to comfort, to cheer.*
confundir *to confuse; to mistake.*
confundirse *to become confused; to be perplexed.*
confusión *f. confusion, perplexity.*
confuso *adj. confused.*
congelar *to freeze.*
congeniar *to be congenial.*
congestión *f. congestion.*
congratulación *f. congratulation.*
congratular *to congratulate.*
congregación *f. congregation.*
congregar *to congregate, to assemble.*
conjetura *f. conjecture, guess.*
conjeturar *to conjecture, to guess.*
conjugación *f. conjugation.*
conjugar *to conjugate.*
conjunción *f. conjunction.*
conjunto *adj. joint, united; m. the whole.*
En conjunto. *On the whole. In all. Altogether.*
conmemoración *f. commemoration.*
conmemorar *to commemorate.*
conmigo *with myself, with me.*
¿Quiere Ud. hablar conmigo? *Do you want to speak with (to) me?*
Venga Ud. conmigo. *Come (along) with me.*
conmoción *f. commotion, tumult, disturbance.*
conmutador *m. electric switch; telegraph key.*
CONOCER *to know, to understand, to be acquainted with.*
¿Conoce Ud. a María? *Do you know Mary?*
No la conozco. *I don't know her.*
¿Se conocen Uds.? *Have you met? Do you know each other?*
¿No se conocen Uds.? *Don't you know each other?*
No tengo el gusto de conocerle. *No, I haven't had the pleasure (of meeting him).*

Sí, ya nos conocemos. *Yes, we've already met.*
Dar a conocer. *To make known.*
conocido *adj. well-known; m. acquaintance.*
Es un antiguo conocido nuestro. *He's an old acquaintance of ours.*
conocimiento *m. knowledge, understanding, acquaintance; bill of lading.*
Poner en conocimiento. *To inform. To let know.*
Llegar a conocimiento de. *To come to the knowledge of.*
Tomar conocimiento de. *To take notice of.*
conque *and so, so then, well then.*
Conque ¿te vas? *So you're leaving.*
conquista *f. conquest; winning somebody's affection, ingratiating oneself.*
conquistar *to conquer, to win over.*
consciente *adj. conscious.*
consecuencia *f. consequence.*
No es de ninguna consecuencia. *It's of no consequence.*
Como consecuencia. *In consequence. As a consequence.*
En consecuencia. *Therefore. In consequence.*
CONSEGUIR *to obtain, to attain, to get.*
Será difícil conseguirlo. *It'll be difficult to get it.*
No pude conseguir ningún dinero. *I couldn't get (obtain) any money.*
consejero *m. member of a board (council); counselor, advisor.*
consejo *m. advice; council, advisory board.*
Seguiré sus consejos. *I'll follow your advice.*
Consejo de ministros. *Cabinet (government).*
Consejo de guerra. *Court-martial.*
consentimiento *m. consent.*
consentir *to consent; to agree, to be willing to; to tolerate; to spoil (a child).*
¿Consentirá Ud. en ello? *Will you consent to it?*
Nunca consentiré tal cosa. *I'll never tolerate such a thing.*
conserje *m. and f. janitor, concierge.*
conserva *f. preserve, canned food; convoy (of ships).*
conservación *f. conservation, upkeep, maintenance.*
conservador *adj. and n. preserver; conservative.*
CONSERVAR *to preserve, to keep, to conserve.*
Lo conservé como recuerdo. *I kept it as a souvenir.*
considerable *adj. considerable, large.*
consideración *f. consideration, regard; importance.*
considerar *to consider, to take into account; to treat well.*
consigna *f. watchword; check room.*
Dejaré esta maleta en la consigna. *I'll check this bag. I'll leave this suitcase in the check room.*
consigo *with oneself; with himself; with herself; with yourself, yourselves.*
¿Lo trajo consigo? *Did you bring it with you?*
Lléveselo consigo. *Take it along with you.*
consiguiente *adj. consequent, consecutive; consistent, logical.*
Por consiguiente. *Consequently.*
consistencia *f. consistence, consistency; stability, solidity, firmness.*
consistente *adj. consistent, solid, firm.*
consistir *to consist, to be composed of.*
consolación *f. consolation.*
consolar *to console, to comfort, to cheer.*
conspicuo *adj. conspicuous.*
constante *adj. constant.*

constitución *constitution.*
constituir *to constitute.*
construcción *f. construction, building.*
CONSTRUIR *to construct, to build.*
cónsul *m. consul.*
consulado *m. consulate.*
consulta *f. consultation.*
consultar *to consult, to seek advice.*
Vaya Ud. a consultar al médico. *Go and consult the doctor.*
¿Ha consultado Ud. a un médico? *Have you seen a doctor?*
Consultar algo con la almohada. *To sleep on something. ("To consult with one's pillow.")*
consultorio *m. doctor's office; bureau of information.*
consumidor *m. consumer.*
consumir *to consume, to use.*
consumo *m. consumption; demand (goods).*
Artículo de consumo. *Staple.*
contabilidad *f. bookkeeping, accounting.*
contado *adj. rare, scarce; m. cash.*
Por de contado. *Of course. As a matter of course.*
Vendemos sólo al contado. *We sell only for cash.*
Se lo pagaré al contado. *I'll pay cash for it.*
contador *m. accountant, purser; meter (gas, electric, etc.).*
contagiar *to infect, to contaminate.*
contagioso *adj. contagious.*
contaminar *to contaminate.*
CONTAR *to count; to tell.*
¿Contó Ud. su cambio? *Did you count your change?*
¿Tiene Ud. algo que contarme? *Have you anything to tell me?*
¿Qué cuenta Ud.? *What's new?*
¡Me lo cuenta a mí! *You're telling me!*
¿Puedo contar con Ud.? *Can I count (depend) on you?*
contemplación *f. contemplation.*
contemplar *to contemplate, to consider, to have in view.*
CONTENER *to hold, to contain.*
Esta botella contiene vino. *This bottle contains wine. There's wine in this bottle.*
contenerse *to refrain, to restrain oneself.*
No puede contenerse. *He can't restrain himself.*
contenido *m. contents.*
contentar *to please, to satisfy.*
contentarse *to be pleased, to be contented.*
No se contentará con palabras nada más. *He won't be satisfied with mere words.*
CONTENTO *adj. glad, happy, pleased; m. contentment.*
Parecía contenta. *She looked happy.*
Estamos contentos de su trabajo. *We're pleased with his work.*
contestación *f. answer, reply.*
CONTESTAR *to answer, to reply; to attest; to dispute.*
Le hice una pregunta y no supo contestarme. *I asked him a question and he didn't know the answer.*
Debe Ud. contestar su carta. *You ought to reply to his letter.*
No contestan. *They don't answer.*
contigo *with you (familiar, singular).*
contiguo *adj. contiguous; close, near.*
continente *adj. moderate; m. continent.*
continuación *f. continuation.*

CONTINUAR *to continue.*
continuo *adj. continuous.*
De continuo. *Continually.*
Sesión continua. *Continuous performance.*
CONTRA *against, contrary to, counter to.*
Lo hizo contra su voluntad. *She did it against her will.*
Apóyalo contra la pared. *Lean it against the wall.*
¿Sabe Ud. de algún remedio contra el mareo? *Do you know of a remedy for seasickness?*
contrabandista *m. and f. smuggler.*
contrabando *m. contraband, smuggling.*
contradecir *to contradict.*
contradicción *f. contradiction.*
contraer *to contract.*
Contraer matrimonio. *To get married.*
Contraer deudas. *To run into debt.*
contrahacer *to counterfeit.*
contrahecho *adj. counterfeit; deformed.*
contrariar *to contradict; to annoy, to vex.*
contrariedad *f. mishap; disappointment; vexation.*
¡Qué contrariedad! *What a disappointment!*
contrario *adj. contrary, opposite; m. opponent.*
A mí me pasa lo contrario. *With me it's the opposite.*
Dice lo contrario de lo que siente. *He says the opposite of what he thinks.*
Al contrario. *On the contrary.*
contraseña *f. watchword; countersign, check.*
contrastar *to contrast.*
contraste *m. contrast; assayer.*
contrata *f. contract.*
contratar *to engage, to hire; to bargain, to trade; to contract.*
contratiempo *m. mishap, setback, disappointment.*
contrato *m. contract.*
contribución *f. contribution; tax.*
contribuir *to contribute.*
contrincante *m. opponent, competitor.*
control *m. control.*
controlar *to control.*
contusión *f. bruise, contusion.*
convalecencia *f. convalescence.*
convaleciente *adj. and n. convalescent.*
convencer *to convince.*
conveniencia *f. convenience; fitness, advantage.*
conveniente *adj. convenient, suitable; advantageous.*
convenio *m. pact, agreement, covenant.*
CONVENIR *to agree; to suit, to be advisable.*
Eso me conviene. *That suits me.*
No me conviene. *It doesn't suit me. It won't do.*
Convengo con Ud. *I agree with you. I'm of your opinion.*
No convenimos en el precio. *We didn't agree on the price.*
Hágalo Ud. como más le convenga. *Do it in the way that's most convenient for you.*
Al tiempo y en el lugar convenidos. *At the time and place agreed on.*
convento *m. convent.*
conversación *f. conversation, chat, talk.*
Su conversación es agradable. *It's pleasant to talk with her. ("Her conversation is pleasant.")*
conversar *to converse, to chat.*
convertir *to convert, to change.*
convicción *f. conviction, belief, certainty.*
convicto *adj. guilty; convicted.*
convidado *adj. invited; m. guest.*
convidar *to invite, to treat.*

convoy m. convoy.

cónyugue m. and f. husband or wife.

coñac m. cognac, brandy.

cooperación f. cooperation.

cooperar to cooperate.

coordinar to coordinate.

copa f. goblet, top of a tree; crown of a hat.

copia f. copy, transcript; abundance.

   Sacar una copia. To make a copy.

copiar to copy.

coqueta f. flirt, coquette.

coquetear to flirt.

coraje m. courage; anger.

CORAZÓN m. heart; core.

   Poner el corazón en algo. To set one's heart on something.

corbata f. necktie.

corcho m. cork.

cordel m. cord, rope.

cordero m. lamb.

cordial adj. cordial, effectionate.

cordillera f. mountain range.

cordón m. cord, string, lace.

cordura f. prudence, judgment, common sense.

corona f. crown; wreath; tonsure.

corral m. yard, court; corral.

correa f. leather strap, leash, thong.

corredor m. runner; broker.

corregir to correct.

CORREO m. post office; mail.

   ¿Hay una oficina de correos cerca? Is there a post office near by?

   ¿A qué hora sale el correo? (At) What time does the mail leave?

   ¿Ha echado Ud. mi carta al correo? Have you mailed my letter?

   A vuelta de correo. By return mail.

   Por correo aéreo. By air mail.

   Lista de correos. General delivery.

   Apartado de correos. Post-office box.

CORRER to run; to flow; to elapse; to blow (wind); to draw (curtains, etc.).

   Fuimos allí a todo correr. We rushed there.

   Corre mucho aire. There's a good breeze.

   Corra las cortinas. Draw the curtains.

   ¿Le corre a Ud. mucha prisa el trabajo? Are you in a hurry for the work?

   No corre prisa. There's no hurry.

   Esto corre de mi cuenta. This is on me. This will be at my own expense.

   Corrió mucho riesgo. He took quite a chance. He ran a great risk.

correrse to slide over, move away; to make rash promises; to act or speak with undue haste; to overpay; to gutter (of a candle).

   Córrase un poco. Move away a little.

   La vela se corre. The candle's guttering.

correspondencia f. correspondence, mail.

   Estar en correspondencia con. To correspond with.

   Mantener correspondencia con. To correspond with.

   Llevar la correspondencia. To be in charge of the correspondence. To take care of the mail.

correspondiente adj. corresponding.

corresponsal m. correspondent.

corrida f. run, race, course.

   Corrida de toros. Bullfight.

corriente adj. current, present (month or year); ordinary, common; f. current; stream; draft (air).

   Cuenta corriente. Current account.

   Salgo el quince del corriente. I'm leaving on the fifteenth of this month.

   Hay una corriente de aire. There's a draft.

   Quítese Ud. de la corriente. Get out of the draft.

   Estar al corriente. To be acquainted with. To be familiar with. To be abreast of.

   Poner al corriente. To inform. To acquaint with.

   Tener al corriente. To keep informed.

   Corriente alterna. Alternating current (A. C.).

   Corriente continua. Direct current (D. C.).

   Seguir la corriente. To go with the tide. To follow the crowd.

corroborar to corroborate.

corromper to corrupt.

corrupción f. corruption.

cortaplumas m. penknife.

cortar to cut; to cut off; to shorten.

   Me he cortado. I've cut myself.

   Este cuchillo no corta. This knife doesn't cut well.

   Telefonista, nos ha cortado. Operator, I've been cut off ("you've cut us off").

   Barbero, córteme el pelo. ("Barber,") Give me a haircut.

   Se ha cortado la leche. The milk has turned sour.

corte cut; edge (of a knife, etc.); court; pl. congress (Spain).

   Corte de pelo. Haircut.

   Las Cortes. The Spanish congress.

   Llamar a Cortes. To convoke the Cortes.

   Hacer la corte. To court.

cortejar to court.

cortés adj. courteous, gentle, polite.

   El es muy cortés. He's very polite.

cortesía f. courtesy, politeness.

corteza f. bark; peel; crust.

   Corteza del árbol. Bark of a tree.

cortina f. curtain, screen.

CORTO adj. short; shy; stupid; backward.

   Las mangas son muy cortas. The sleeves are very short.

   Es muy corto de genio. He's very shy.

   A la corta o larga. Sooner or later.

   Cuento corto. Short story.

   Es corto de vista. He's near-sighted.

cortocircuito m. short circuit.

COSA f. thing; matter.

   No hay tal cosa. There's no such thing.

   ¡Qué cosa más preciosa! What a beautiful thing!

   Ninguna cosa. Nothing.

   ¿Desea Ud. alguna otra cosa? Would you like anything else?

   Es poco más o menos la misma cosa. It's more or less the same thing.

   Venga Ud. aquí, tengo que decirle una cosa. Come here, I want to tell you something.

   Como si tal cosa. As if nothing had happened.

   No es cosa de risa. It's no laughing matter.

   Hace cosa de dos meses. It was about two months ago.

   Cosa rara. A strange thing.

   Eso es cosa suya. That's his business.

cosecha f. harvest, crop; harvest time.

cosechar to reap, to gather in the crop.

coser to sew.

   Máquina de coser. Sewing machine.

cosmético m. cosmetic.

cosquillas f. pl. tickling.

cosquillear to tickle.

cosquilloso adj. ticklish, easily offended.

costa f. coast, shore; cost, expense.

   A toda costa. At all costs. By all means.

   A lo largo de la costa. Coastwise. Along the coast.

costado m. flank; side.

COSTAR to cost.

   ¿Cuánto cuestan estos zapatos? How much do these shoes cost?

   ¿Cuánto me costará más o menos? About how much will it cost?

   Me cuesta trabajo creerlo. It's hard for me to believe it.

   Cueste lo que cueste. Whatever it costs. At all costs.

   Costar un ojo de la cara. To cost a fortune.

costear to pay the expenses; to sail along the coast.

costilla f. rib; wife; stave.

COSTO m. cost, expense, price.

   Precio de costo. Cost price.

costoso adj. dear, expensive.

costumbre f. custom; habit.

   De costumbre. Usually.

   Como de costumbre. As usual.

   Tener costumbre de. To be used to. To be in the habit of.

costura f. sewing; needlework; seam.

   Alta costura. High fashion.

costurera f. seamstress.

cotejar to confront, to check.

cotejo m. comparison, collation.

cotidiano adj. daily, everyday.

cotización f. quotation (of prices).

cotizar to quote (prices).

coyuntura f. articulation, joint; opportunity.

coz f. kick.

cráneo m. skull, cranium.

crear to create; to establish, to set up.

CRECER to grow; to increase.

crecimiento m. increase, growth, increment.

credencial f. credential.

crédito m. credit; credence; reputation, standing.

   Comprar a crédito. To buy on credit.

   Vender a crédito. To sell on credit.

   Dar crédito. To give credit.

   Carta de crédito. Letter of credit.

creencia f. credence, belief.

CREER to believe; to think.

   Creo que es una buena idea. I think it's a good idea.

   Creo que sí. I believe so. I think so.

   Creo que no. I don't think so.

   Ya lo creo. I should think (say) so! Of course! Naturally!

   Ver y creer. Seeing is believing.

crema f. cream.

   Crema de noche. Night cream.

   Crema dentrífica. Toothpaste.

criada f. maid, servant.

criado m. a manservant; valet.

criar to create, to produce; to nurse; to rear, to bring up.

criatura f. creature; baby, child.

cribar to sift.

cribo m. sieve.

crimen m. crime; guilt.

criminal m. and f. criminal.

criollo adj. and n. Creole (one born in Spanish America of European parents).

crisantemo m. chrysanthemum.

crisis f. crisis.

cristal m. crystal; glass.

cristianismo m. Christianity.

cristiano adj. and n. Christian.

criterio m. *criterion, judgment, opinion.*
Lo dejo a su criterio. *I leave it up to you.*
crítica f. *criticism, review.*
criticar *to criticize.*
crítico m. *critic.*
crónica f. *chronicle.*
cronista m. *reporter.*
croqueta f. *croquette.*
cruce m. *crossing; crossroads.*
crucero m. *crossing; cruiser.*
crudo adj. *raw, crude.*
cruel adj. *cruel, hard.*
crueldad f. *cruelty.*
cruz f. *cross.*
cruzar *to cross; to cruise.*
cuaderno m. *notebook; memoranaum book.*
cuadra f. *stable; block (of houses).*
cuadrado adj. *square.*
cuadrilla f. *gang, crew.*
cuadro m. *painting, picture; frame; scene (in a play).*
CUAL *which; what; like; as;* **el cual** (m.); **la cual** (f.); **los cuales** (m. pl.); **las cuales** (f. pl.) *who, which.*
¿Cuál de ellos prefiere Ud.? *Which one do you prefer (like best)?*
¿Cuáles son los últimos modelos? *What are the latest styles?*
Por lo cual. *For that reason.*
Cada cual. *Each one.*
Tal para cual. *Tit for tat. Two of a kind.*
cualquier *any (used immediately before a noun). See also* **cualquiera.**
A cualquier hora. *At any time.*
En cualquier momento. *At any moment.*
Es capaz de cualquier cosa. *He's capable of anything.*
cualquiera *any; anyone; anybody.* (**Cualquiera** and **cualquier** *do not change for gender.*)
Cualquiera de los hombres. *Any of the men.*
Cualquiera puede hacer eso. *Anybody can do that.*
Tome Ud. cualquiera que le guste. *Take anyone (whichever one) you like.*
Un cualquiera. *A nobody.*
cuan *how, as (used only before adjectives or adverbs).*
¡Cuán lejos! *How far!*
¡Cuán hermoso! *How pretty!*
CUANDO (written **cuándo** *when interrogative*), *when.*
¿Cuándo se marcha Ud.? *When are you leaving?*
Cuando Ud. guste. *Whenever you say. Whenever you wish.*
¿Hasta cuándo? *Until when?*
¿De cuándo acá? *Since when? How come? How is that?*
De cuando en cuando. *From time to time.*
De vez en cuando. *Once in a while.*
Cuando más (mucho). *At best. At most.*
Cuando menos. *At least.*
CUANTO *as much as, as many as.*
Compre cuantas naranjas encuentre. *Buy as many oranges as you can find.*
Avíseme en cuanto esté libre. *Let me know as soon as it's free.*
Cuanto más se lo doy, tanto más me pide. *The more I give him, the more he asks for.*
Cuanto más gaste tanto menos tendrá. *The more you spend, the less you'll have.*
Cuanto antes mejor. *The sooner the better.*
Se quedó con tanto cuanto quiso. *He kept*

for himself as much as he wanted.
Cuanto antes. *As soon as possible.*
Por cuanto. *Whereas. Inasmuch as.*
En cuanto a. *In regard to.*
Cuanto Ud. quiera. *All (as much as) you wish.*
CUÁNTO *how much; how long; how far; how;* pl. *how many.*
¿Cuánto? *How much?*
¿Cuántos? *How many?*
¿A cuántos estamos? *What's the date?*
¿Cuánto es? *How much is it?*
¿Cuánto vale? *How much is it worth?*
¿Cuánto hay de aquí a Zaragoza? *How far is it from here to Zaragoza?*
¿Cuánto tiempo se tarda en aeroplano? *How long does it take by airplane?*
¡Cuánto me alegro! *I'm very glad. ("How glad I am!")*
¡Cuánto ha cambiado Ud.! *You have changed a lot! How (much) you've changed!*
CUARENTA adj. and n. *forty; fortieth.*
cuartel m. *quarter; barracks; district of a city.*
Cuartel general. *Headquarters.*
CUARTO adj. *fourth, quarter;* m. *room.*
Le daré la cuarta parte. *I'll give you a fourth of it.*
A las once menos cuarto. *At a quarter to eleven.*
A las cinco y cuarto. *At a quarter past five.*
¿Tiene Ud. un cuarto para dos personas? *Do you have a double room?*
Es mi compañero de cuarto. *He's my roommate.*
CUATRO adj. and n. *four; fourth.*
Son las cuatro. *It's four o'clock.*
Soltar cuatro frescas. *To give (someone) a piece of one's mind.*
cuatrocientos adj. and n. *four hundred.*
Cuba f. *Cuba.*
cubano adj. and n. *Cuban.*
cubeta f. *small barrel; pail, bucket; mercury cup (of a barometer).*
cubierta f. *cover; deck of a ship.*
cubierto m. *cover; place at a table; table d'hôte; shelter.*
cubo m. *bucket; tub; hub of a wheel.*
cubrecama f. *bedspread.*
CUBRIR *to cover; to roof.*
cucaracha f. *cockroach.*
CUCHARA f. *spoon.*
cucharada f. *spoonful.*
cucharadita f. *teaspoonful.*
cucharetear *to stir with a spoon; to meddle in other people's affairs.*
cucharilla f. *teaspoon.*
cucharita f. *teaspoon.*
cucharón m. *ladle; large spoon.*
cuchichear *to whisper.*
cuchicheo m. *whispering.*
cuchilla f. *large knife.*
cuchillo m. *knife.*
cuello m. *neck; collar.*
CUENTA f. *count; account; statement; bill; bead.*
Tráigame Ud. la cuenta. *Let me have the bill.*
¿Cuál es el saldo de mi cuenta? *What's the balance of my account?*
Apúntelo en mi cuenta. *Charge it to my account.*
Caer en la cuenta. *To notice.*
Ya caigo en la cuenta. *Now I see the point.*
Abonar en cuenta. *To credit with.*
Cuenta corriente. *Current account.*
Cuenta pendiente. *Unpaid balance. Balance*

due.
Dar cuenta de. *To report on.*
Darse cuenta. *To realize.*
Tener en cuenta. *To bear in mind. To take into account (consideration).*
Tomar por su cuenta. *To take upon oneself. To assume responsibility for.*
cuentagotas m. *medicine dropper.*
cuento m. *story, tale; gossip.*
Cuento de hadas. *Fairy tale.*
Cuento corto. *Short story.*
Traer a cuento. *To bring up. To turn the conversation to a certain point.*
Venir a cuento. *To be to the point. To be pertinent.*
Esto no viene a cuento. *That's beside the point. That's not the case.*
Dejarse de cuentos. *To stop beating around the bush.*
cuerda f. *cord, rope; spring (of a watch).*
Quiero un mozo de cuerda. *I want a porter.*
¿Le ha dado Ud. cuerda a su reloj? *Have you wound (up) your watch?*
Lo hizo por debajo de cuerda. *He did it in an underhand way.*
cuerdo adj. *in one's senses; wise, prudent.*
cuerno m. *horn.*
cuero m. *leather; hide; skin.*
CUERPO m. *body; element; corps.*
cuervo m. *crow, raven.*
cuesta f. *slope, grade; hill; collection for charity.*
Ir cuesta abajo. *To go downhill.*
Ir cuesta arriba. *To go uphill.*
Cuesta arriba. *With great trouble and difficulty. Painfully.*
A cuestas. *On one's back.*
CUESTIÓN m. *question; dispute, quarrel; problem.*
cuestionable adj. *questionable, problematical.*
cuestionar *to question.*
cueva f. *cave; cellar.*
CUIDADO m. *care, attention; anxiety, worry.*
¡Cuidado! *Be careful!*
Tener cuidado. *To be careful.*
¡Tenga cuidado! *Be careful!*
Me tiene sin cuidado. *I don't care.*
¡No tenga Ud. cuidado! *Don't worry!*
Estar con cuidado. *To be worried.*
cuidadoso adj. *careful.*
cuidar *to care, to take care, to mind, to look after.*
¡Cuídese Ud.! *Take good care of yourself.*
Cuidar de. *To take care of.*
culebra f. *snake.*
culpa f. *fault, guilt; sin.*
¿Quién tiene la culpa? *Whose fault is it?*
Yo no tengo la culpa. *It isn't my fault.*
Es culpa mía. *It's my fault.*
Echar la culpa a. *To blame.*
Tener la culpa de. *To be to blame. To be at fault.*
culpable adj. *guilty.*
culpar *to accuse, to blame.*
cultivar *to cultivate; to till; to improve.*
En Canadá se cultiva mucho el trigo. *They grow a lot of wheat in Canada.*
Este terreno me parece que está cultivado. *This ground appears to be cultivated.*
cultivo m. *farming, cultivation; tillage.*
culto adj. *well-educated; polished;* m. *worship; cult, religion.*
Es un hombre culto. *He's a well-read (cultured) man.*
cultura f. *culture; urbanity.*
cultural adj. *cultural.*

cumpleaños m. birthday.
cumplido adj. courteous, polite; full, abundant; m. compliment, attention, courtesy.
No gaste Ud. cumplidos. Don't stand (so much) on ceremony.
cumplimiento m. compliment; accomplishment; compliance, fulfillment, carrying out.
No se ande Ud. en cumplimientos conmigo. You don't have to stand on ceremony with me.
Ofrecer algo por cumplimiento. To offer something out of courtesy.
CUMPLIR to carry out, to fulfill, to keep one's word; to expire.
Siempre cumple con su deber. He always does his duty. He always fulfills his obligations.
El plazo se ha cumplido. The time has expired.
Al cumplir los veinte y un años será mayor de edad. He'll be of age when he's twenty-one.
Cumplir años. To have a birthday.
cuna f. cradle; family, lineage.
cuña f. wedge.
cuñada f. sister-in-law.
cuñado m. brother-in-law.
cuota f. share; quota.
cura m. parson; priest; f. cure; curing; preserving.
Los casó el cura. The priest married them.
Este mal tiene cura. This sickness is curable.
curable adj. curable.
curación f. healing, cure.
curar to cure; to heal.
curiosear to pry into other people's affairs, to be a busybody.
curiosidad f. curiosity; neatness, cleanliness.
curioso adj. curious.
curso m. course, direction; succession; current.
curva f. curve.
cúspide f. summit, top.
custodia f. custody, guard; escort.
custodiar to guard, to take into custody.
cutis m. complexion; skin.
cuya (f. of **cuyo**) whose, of which, of whom (pl. cuyas).
La señora a cuya hija le he presentado, es amiga de su padre. The lady whose daughter I introduced you to is a friend of your father's.
cuyo whose, of which, of whom (pl. cuyos).
Era un pequeño pueblo, cuyo nombre no recuerdo. It was a small town, the name of which I don't remember.

CH

chabacano adj. coarse, unpolished; m. kind of apricot (Mex.).
chacal m. jackal.
chacota f. noisy merriment; fun.
Hacer chacota de. To make fun of. To ridicule.
chacra f. farm (Arg.).
chal m. shawl.
chaleco m. vest.
chalet m. chalet; cottage.
chalupa f. sloop; small canoe.
chambón adj. awkward, clumsy.
chambonada f. blunder.
champaña m. champagne.
champú m. shampoo.
chancear to joke, to fool.
chanclos m. pl. galoshes, rubbers.
chancho adj. dirty, unclean; m. hog, pig.
chantaje m. blackmailing.
chantajista m. and f. blackmailer.

chanza f. jest, joke.
chaqueta f. jacket, coat.
charco m. pond, puddle.
charla f. chat, chatter.
charlar to chat, to chatter.
charlatán m. quack, charlatan; babbler, one who is always talking.
chasco m. disappointment; joke.
chasis m. chassis.
chato adj. flat, flat-nosed.
chelín m. shilling.
cheque m. check (money).
chicle m. chicle; chewing gum.
chica f. little girl; girl.
Es una chica encantadora. She's a charming girl.
chico adj. small, little; m. boy; pl. youngsters.
Es un chico muy obediente. He's a very obedient boy.
chicharrón m. crisp fried bacon or pork fat.
chichón m. lump on the head.
chiflado adj. silly, crazy.
chillar to scream, to screech; to squeak, to creak.
chillido m. scream.
chillón adj. loud, gaudy (color); m. bawler, screamer.
chimenea f. chimney; fireplace.
chinche f. thumbtack; bedbug; boring person.
chinela f. slipper.
chiquero m. pigsty, pigpen.
chiquillada f. childishness, childish action.
chiquillo m. little boy; f. little girl.
chiquito adj. small, tiny; m. little boy, f. little girl.
chiripa f. fluke; lucky chance; bargain.
De chiripa. By mere chance. By a fluke.
chirriar to hiss; to squeak.
chisme m. gossip.
chismear to gossip, to tattle.
chismorreo m. gossip.
chismoso adj. talebearing, gossiping; m. talebearer, tattletale, one who gossips.
chispa f. spark.
Echar chispas. To get raving mad.
Ser chispa. To be full of life. To sparkle.
chistar to mutter, to mumble.
Ni siquiera chistó. He didn't say a word. He didn't open his mouth.
chiste m. joke.
chistoso adj. witty, humorous.
¡Chito! ¡Chitón! Hush! Silence!
chivo m. kid, goat.
chocar to collide; to strike; to disgust; to shock.
choclo m. cob. green ear of corn.
chocolate m. chocolate.
chófer m. chauffeur.
choque m. collision; clash; shock.
chorizo m. sausage.
chorro m. gush, spurt, jet of water.
choza f. hut, hovel.
chubasco m. squall.
chuchería f. trinket, gewgaw, trifle.
chuleta f. cutlet; chop.
Chuleta de cordero. Lamb chop.
Chuleta de puerco. Pork chop.
Chuleta de ternera. Veal chop.
chupar to suck, to absorb; to sponge on.
churro m. a kind of doughnut, fritter (Spain).
chusco adj. droll, amusing, funny.

D

dactilógrafo m. typist.
dádiva f. gift, present.
dadivoso adj. liberal, generous.

dados m. pl. dice.
dama f. lady, dame; king (in checkers).
Primera dama. Leading lady.
Jugar a las damas. To play checkers.
daga f. dagger.
dalia f. dahlia.
danzón m. a Cuban dance.
dañado adj. spoiled, damaged.
dañar to damage, to hurt; to spoil.
dañino adj. harmful.
daño m. damage, loss; hurt, harm.
¿Te has hecho daño? Did you get hurt?
¿Le ha hecho daño la comida? Did the food disagree with you?
Causar daño. To do harm or damage.
DAR to give; to deal (cards); to show (a picture); to strike (hours); to hit; to take (a walk).
Dénos algo de comer. Give us something to eat.
Déme un poco de pan. Give me some bread.
¿En cuánto me lo da Ud.? How much will you sell ("give") it to me for?
Le doy dos pesetas por el libro. I'll give you two pesetas for the book.
¿A quién le toca dar? Whose turn is it to deal?
Ud. da las cartas. You deal (cards).
La radio dió la noticia. The news came over the radio.
¿Dónde dan esa película? Where are they showing that picture (film)?
Este reloj da las horas y las medias horas. This clock strikes the hours and the half-hours.
Acaban de dar las tres. It's just struck three.
Dar un paseo. To take a walk.
Vamos a dar un paseo. Let's take a walk.
Dar memorias. Dar recuerdos. To give one's regards.
Le doy la razón. I admit you are right.
Dar palmadas. To clap one's hands.
Dar a entender. To insinuate. ("To give to understand.")
Dar el golpe. To make a hit. To create a sensation.
Dar a conocer. To make known.
Dar en el clavo. To hit the nail on the head.
Dar razón de. To inform about.
Dar que decir. To give cause for criticism.
Dar de comer. To feed.
Dar prestado. To lend.
Dar los buenos días. To say good morning. To greet. To pass the time of day.
Dar fiado. Dar a crédito. To give credit.
Dar con. To meet. To come across.
Dar a la calle. To face the street.
Dar a luz. To give birth.
Dar parte. To report.
Dar la mano. To shake hands.
Dar marcha atrás. To put in reverse (a car).
Dar en el blanco. To hit the mark. To hit the bull's-eye.
Darse prisa. To hurry.
Darse cuenta. To realize.
dátil m. date (fruit).
dato m. datum.
DE of; from; for; by; on; to; with.
La casa de mi amigo. My friend's house.
¿De quién es este libro? Whose book is this?
No sé que ha sido de él. I don't know what's become of him.
Estoy escaso de dinero. I'm short of money.
El libro es de ella. The book is hers.
¿De dónde es usted? Where are you from?
Soy de Madrid. I'm from Madrid.
La chica del sombrero verde. The girl with

the green hat.
Un reloj de oro. A gold watch.
Un vaso de vino. A glass of wine.
Una taza de café. A cup of coffee.
Tres pies de largo. Three feet long.
Máquina de coser. Sewing machine.
Hora de comer. Time to eat. Dinnertime.
De pie. Standing.
De puntillas. On tiptoes.
De prisa. In a hurry.
De buena gana. Willingly.
De todo un poco. A little of everything.
Un día de estos. One of these days.
De hoy en adelante. From now on.
De día. In the daytime.
De noche. At night.
De nada. Don't mention it.
DEBAJO under, underneath.
Debajo de los papeles estaba la carta. The letter was under these papers.
Lo hizo por debajo de cuerda. He did it in an underhanded way.
debate m. debate.
debatir to debate, to discuss.
deber m. obligation, duty.
DEBER to owe; to be obliged; must; ought.
¿Qué se debe hacer? What can one do? What can be done? What ought (should) one do?
Debemos irnos. We must (have to) go.
Ud. debiera comer más. You should eat more.
Debe Ud. aprovechar esta ocasión. You should take advantage of this opportunity.
El debe de haber recibido mi carta ya. He must have received my letter already.
¿Cuánto le debo a Ud.? How much do I owe you?
No me debe Ud. nada. You don't owe me anything.
Siempre cumple con su deber. He always does his duty. He always fulfills his obligations.
debido adj. due, owing to, on account of; proper.
Debido a la lluvia no pude venir ayer. I couldn't come yesterday on account of the rain.
Redacte Ud. la instancia en debida forma. Draw up the petition in proper form.
débil adj. feeble, weak.
debilidad f. feebleness, weakness.
debilitar to weaken, to debilitate.
débilmente weakly.
débito m. debt; duty.
debut m. debut, first (public) appearance.
década f. decade.
decadencia f. decay, decadence, decline.
decaer to decay, to decline, to die down.
decano m. dean; senior.
decapitar to decapitate, to behead.
decena f. ten.
decente adj. decent; honest; neat.
decepción f. disappointment.
décididamente decidedly.
decidido adj. decided, firm, determined.
Es una persona muy decidida. He's a very determined person.
DECIDER to decide, to resolve, to determine.
DECIDIRSE to decide, to make up one's mind.
No me he decidido todavía. I haven't decided yet. I haven't made up my mind yet.
decímetro m. decimeter.
décimo adj. tenth.
décimoctavo adj. eighteenth.
décimocuarto adj. fourteenth.
décimonono adj. nineteenth.
décimonoveno adj. nineteenth.
décimoquinto adj. fifteenth.

décimoséptimo adj. seventeenth.
décimosexto adj. sixteenth.
décimotercero adj. thirteenth.
décimotercio adj. thirteenth.
deciocheno adj. eighteenth.
decir m. saying.
Es sólo un decir. It's just a saying.
DECIR to speak; to say, to tell.
Dígame, por favor. Please tell me.
Dígame dónde está la estación. Tell me where the station is.
Dígaselo a él. Tell it to him.
Se lo diré. I'll tell him.
Dice Ud. bien. You're right. That's correct. You've said the right thing.
¡No me diga! You don't say (so)! ("Don't tell me!")
¡Diga! ¿Quién habla? Hello! Who's speaking?
Decir las cosas claras. To speak plainly.
Querer decir. To mean.
¿Qué quiere decir esta palabra? What does this word mean?
¿Qué me quiere Ud. decir? What do you want to tell me? What do you mean?
Por decirlo así. As it were. So to speak.
decisión f. decision, determination.
decisivo adj. decisive.
declaración f. declaration.
declarar to declare; to state; to testify.
¿Tiene Ud. algo que declarar? Do you have anything to declare (customs)?
Declararse en huelga. To go on strike. To declare a strike.
Juan se declaró a María. John proposed to Mary.
declinar to decline; to decay.
decoración f. decoration; stage scenery.
decorado m. decoration; stage scenery; adj. decorated.
decorar to decorate.
decoro m. decency; decorum; honor.
decrecer to decrease.
decreciente adj. decreasing.
decremento m. decrease.
decretar to decree.
decreto m. decree.
dedal m. thimble.
dedicar to dedicate; to devote.
La mañana la dedicamos a visitar los alrededores de la población. We spent the morning visiting the suburbs of the town.
Se dedica a los negocios. He's a businessman. He's engaged in business.
Se dedicó a la pintura. He devoted himself to painting.
dedicatoria f. dedication.
dedillo m. little finger.
Saber al dedillo. To have at one's fingertips.
Me sé la lección al dedillo. I know the lesson by heart. ("I have it on my fingertips.")
DEDO m. finger; toe.
Dedo meñique. Little finger.
Dedo índice. Index finger.
Dedo pulgar. Thumb.
Dedo del corazón. Middle finger.
Dedo anular. Ring finger.
Los zapatos me aprietan los dedos. The shoes are tight around the toes.
Está a dos dedos de la tumba. He's on the brink of death.
deducción f. deduction.
deducir to deduce; to gather, to understand.
Deduzco de su carta que no es muy feliz. I

gather from his letter that he's not very happy.
defecto m. fault, defect.
Conozco sus defectos. I know his faults.
Tiene un defecto físico. He has a physical defect.
Poner defectos. To find fault.
defectuoso adj. defective.
defender to defend.
defensa f. defense.
defensiva f. defensive.
defensor m. supporter, defender; lawyer, counsel.
deferencia f. deference, respect, regard.
deficiencia f. deficiency.
deficiente adj. deficient.
déficit m. shortage, deficit.
definición f. definition, explanation.
definido adj. definite.
definir to define, to determine.
definitivamente definitely.
definitivo adj. definitive.
deformación f. deformation.
deformar to deform.
deforme adj. deformed; ugly.
deformidad f. deformity; ugliness.
defraudar to defraud, to swindle.
defunción f. death.
Acta de defunción. Death certificate.
degenerado adj. and n. degenerate.
degollar to slash the throat; to decapitate.
degradante adj. degrading.
degradar to degrade.
dejadez f. laziness; negligence.
dejado adj. lazy, negligent, sloppy.
dejamiento m. carelessness, indolence, self-neglect.
DEJAR to leave, to let; to quit, to give up.
Déjeme verlo. Let me see it.
Déjemelo en menos. Can you let me have it cheaper? ("Give it to me for less.")
No se nos dejó entrar. They didn't let us come in.
¿Puedo dejarle un recado? May I leave a message for him?
Déjelo para mañana. Leave it for tomorrow. Put it off until tomorrow.
Déjeme en paz. Let me alone. ("Leave me in peace.")
Dejar de. To stop.
¿Por qué ha dejado Ud. de visitarnos? Why have you stopped visiting us?
Dejó su empleo por otro mejor. He gave up his job for a better one.
Dejó a su mujer y a sus hijos. He abandoned his wife and children.
Le dejaron plantado. They left him in the lurch.
No puedo dejar de creerlo. I can't help believing it.
Déjese enfriar y sírvase. ("Let") Cool and serve.
dejarse to abandon oneself to; not to take care of oneself, to let oneself go.
dejo m. accent (in speech); taste, aftertaste; end; effect.
DEL (contraction of de + el) of the.
La casa del médico. The doctor's house.
Del principio al fin. From (the) beginning to (the) end.
No del todo. Not quite.
delantal m. apron.
DELANTE before; in front; in the presence of.
Nos aguarda delante del club. He's waiting for us in front of the club.
Firmó el testamento delante de testigos. He signed his will before witnesses.
No digas eso delante de ella. Don't say that in

front of her (in her presence).
delantera *f. front; start, lead.*
delegación *f. delegation.*
delegado *m. delegate, deputy, proxy.*
deleitar *to please, to delight.*
deleite *m. delight, pleasure; lust.*
deletrear *to spell.*
deletreo *m. spelling.*
delgado *adj. thin, slender.*
deliberación *f. deliberation.*
deliberar *to deliberate.*
delicado *adj. delicate; dainty, nice; exquisite, delicious; in poor ("delicate") health, having a weak constitution.*
delicia *f. delight, pleasure.*
delicioso *adj. delicious, delightful.*
  El postre está delicioso. *The dessert is delicious.*
  Hemos pasado un rato delicioso. *We had a delightful time.*
delincuente *m. delinquent, offender.*
delinquir *to commit an offense against the law, to violate the law.*
delirar *to rave; to be delirious.*
  Está delirando. *He's talking nonsense. He's raving.*
delirio *m. delirium; raving; wild excitement; nonsense.*
  El delirio le duró toda la noche. *The delirium lasted all night.*
  La quiere con delirio. *He's madly in love with her. He's head over heels in love with her.*
delito *m. misdemeanor, offense, crime.*
demacrarse *to become emaciated.*
demanda *f. claim, demand, request; inquiry.*
  No atendieron su demanda. *They didn't pay any attention to his claim.*
  Hay mucha demanda de este artículo. *There's a great demand for this article.*
demandante *m. and f. plaintiff.*
DEMANDAR *to demand, to claim; to take legal action, to enter a claim, to start a suit.*
demarcación *f. demarcation.*
DEMÁS *other; remaining, rest; los (m.) demás; las (f.) demás others; the others.*
  Lo demás se lo contaré luego. *I'll tell you the rest later.*
  Por lo demás me parece bien. *Aside (apart) from that (otherwise), it seems all right to me.*
  Pensé que estaba por demás decírselo. *I didn't think it was necessary to mention it to you.*
  Esperemos a los demás. *Let's wait for the others.*
DEMASIADO *excessive; too; too much.*
  Es demasiado. *It's too much.*
  Cuesta demasiado. *It costs too much.*
  Es demasiado temprano aún. *It's too early yet.*
  Este chaleco me aprieta demasiado. *This vest is too tight for me.*
demencia *f. insanity, madness.*
demente *adj. insane, crazy.*
democracia *f. democracy.*
demócrata *m. and f. democrat.*
democrático *adj. democratic.*
demoler *to demolish.*
demolición *f. demolition.*
demonio *m. demon, devil.*
  Se puso hecho un demonio. *He became very angry.*
  ¿Para qué demonio lo querrá (coll.)? *What the devil does he need it for?*
  ¿Qué demonios hace Ud. aquí (coll.)? *What on earth are you doing here?*
demostración *f. demonstration.*

demostrar *to demonstrate, to prove, to show.*
  Demuéstrelo Ud. *Prove it.*
  Demostró que tenía razón. *He proved he was right.*
  No demuestra el menor interés. *He doesn't show the slightest interest.*
demora *f. delay.*
  Sin demora. *Without delay.*
demorar *to delay; to remain.*
  Se demoraron en el camino. *They were delayed on the road.*
demovilizar *to demobilize.*
denegar *to refuse, to deny.*
denigrante *adj. defamatory, slanderous.*
denigrar *to blacken, to defame.*
denominación *f. denomination.*
denominar *to name.*
denotar *to denote, to indicate, to express.*
densidad *f. density.*
denso *adj. dense, thick.*
dentadura *f. set of teeth.*
dental *adj. dental.*
dentífrico *adj. and n. dentifrice.*
  Pasta dentífrica. *Toothpaste.*
  Polvo dentífrico. *Toothpowder.*
dentista *m. dentist.*
DENTRO *within, inside.*
  Le espero dentro. *I'll wait for you inside.*
  Hay más gente fuera que dentro. *There are more people outside than inside.*
  El tren sale dentro de cinco minutos. *The train will leave in five minutes.*
  Vuelva dentro de media hora. *Come back in half an hour.*
  Dentro de poco. *Shortly.*
  Hacia dentro. *Toward the inside.*
  Por dentro. *On the inside.*
denuncia *f. complaint; denunciation.*
denunciar *to denounce; to give notice; to inform.*
departamento *m. department; apartment.*
dependencia *f. dependence, dependency; sales staff, personnel of an office, employees; branch office or store.*
DEPENDER *to depend, be dependent on.*
  Mucho depende de lo que Ud. haga. *A great deal will depend on what you do.*
  Depender de. *To depend on. To count on. To rely on.*
dependiente *m. clerk; subordinate; dependent.*
deplorable *adj. deplorable, pitiful.*
deplorar *to deplore, to be sorry, to regret.*
  Deploro mucho lo ocurrido. *I'm sorry about what happened.*
deportar *to deport.*
deporte *m. sport.*
deportista *m. sportsman; f. sportswoman.*
deportivo *adj. having to do with sport(s).*
depositar *to deposit; to place; to put in a safe place; to entrust.*
  Depositaron su dinero en el banco. *They deposited their money in the bank.*
  Deposité en él toda mi confianza. *I placed all my trust in him.*
depositario *m. trustee; depositary.*
depósito *m. deposit; depot; warehouse; bond; reservoir; tank (of gasoline).*
  Estos edificios son los depósitos de la fábrica. *These buildings are the warehouses of the factory.*
  Lléneme el depósito. *Fill the tank up.*
  En depósito. *As a deposit. In bond.*
depresión *f. depression.*
deprimir *to depress.*

DERECHA *f. right side; right hand.*
  A la derecha. *To the right.*
  Es su mano derecha. *He's his right-hand man ("He's his right hand.")*
  Pertenece a un partido de derecha. *He belongs to a conservative party.*
  No hace nada a derechas. *He doesn't do anything right.*
DERECHO *m. law, justice; claim, title; right; straight; direct.*
  Es estudiante de derecho. *He's a law student.*
  Obrar conforme a derecho. *To act according to law.*
  Ud. no tiene derecho de quejarse. *You have no right to complain. You have no grounds for complaint.*
  Siga derecho. *Keep straight ahead. Go straight ahead.*
  Perdió el brazo derecho en la guerra. *He lost his right arm in the war.*
  Fíjese que esté del derecho. *Make sure it's right side out.*
  Ya es un hombre hecho y derecho. *He's now fully grown-up. He's now a man.*
  Derechos de autor. *Copyright. Royalties.*
  Derechos. *Rights. Fees. Duties.*
deriva *f. deviation; drift (of a ship or airplane).*
derogar *to annul; to repeal.*
derramamiento *m. spilling, shedding.*
derramar *to spill; to shed; to scatter; to spread.*
derrame *m. leakage; discharge (med.).*
derredor *m. circumference.*
  Al derredor. (En derredor.) *About. Around.*
  Mire en derredor suyo. *Look around you.*
derretir *to melt, to dissolve.*
derribar *to demolish; to knock down; to overthrow.*
  Han derribado muchas casas viejas. *Many old houses have been torn down.*
  De un golpe lo derribó al suelo. *He knocked him down with one punch (blow).*
derrocar *to overthrow.*
derrochador *m. spendthrift, squanderer.*
  Es un derrochador. *He's a spendthrift. Money burns a hole in his pocket.*
derrochar *to squander; to waste away.*
derrota *f. ship's course; rout, defeat.*
derrotar *to rout, to defeat.*
derrotero *m. charts; course.*
derrumbamiento *m. collapse; landslide.*
derrumbar *to throw down, to demolish.*
desabotonar *to unbutton.*
desabrido *adj. insipid, tasteless.*
desabrigado *adj. uncovered; without shelter; without enough clothes on.*
desabrigar *to uncover; to leave without shelter.*
  Desabrigase. *To uncover. To take off one's coat or hat.*
desabrochar *to unbutton, to unclasp, to unfasten.*
desacierto *m. error, blunder.*
desacreditar *to discredit.*
desacuerdo *m. disagreement.*
desafiar *to challenge, to defy.*
desafío *m. challenge; competition.*
desafortunado *adj. unlucky, unfortunate.*
desagradable *adj. disagreeable, unpleasant.*
desagradar *to displease.*
desagradecido *adj. ungrateful.*
desagrado *m. displeasure, discontent.*
desagraviar *to vindicate; to give satisfaction.*
desagravio *m. vindication, justice.*
desaguar *to drain.*
desagüe *m. drainage.*
desahogarse *to find relief (from heat, fatigue, etc.);*

to free oneself from debt; to open one's heart.

desahogo *m. ease, relief.*

desahuciar *to give up as hopeless.*

El médico ha desahuciado al enfermo. *The doctor has given up hope for the patient.*

desairar *to slight, to snub.*

No quiero desairarle. *I don't want to slight him.*

desaire *m. slight, snub.*

desalentar *to discourage.*

desaliento *m. discouragement; dismay.*

desalojar *to disposses, to evict; to dislodge, to drive out.*

desalquilado *adj. vacant (for rent).*

desalquilar *to move out; to ask someone to vacate (a rented place).*

desamparado *adj. abandoned.*

desamueblado *adj. unfurnished.*

desamueblar *to remove the furniture, to take the furniture out.*

desangrar *to bleed.*

desanimado *adj. discouraged; dull.*

La fiesta estuvo muy desanimada. *The party was very dull.*

desanimar *to discourage.*

desánimo *m. discouragement.*

desaparecer *to disappear.*

desapercibido *adj. unprepared, not ready; unnoticed.*

desaprobar *to disapprove of.*

desaprovechar *to misuse, not to make good use of.*

Desaprovechó la oportunidad. *He didn't make (good) use of the opportunity.*

desarmado *adj. unarmed.*

desarmar *to disarm; to dismount, to take apart.*

desarme *m. disarmament.*

desarraigar *to uproot, to extirpate.*

desarreglado *adj. immoderate; slovenly; disarranged, in disorder.*

desarreglar *to derange; to disarrange.*

desarreglo *m. disorder, derangement; irregularity.*

DESARROLLAR *to develop; to grow; to evolve; to unfold. (See* revelar *for "to develop" applied to film, etc.)*

desarrollo *m. development; evolution; growth.*

desaseado *adj. unclean, untidy.*

desaseo *m. slovenliness, untidiness, uncleanliness.*

desasosiego *m. uneasiness, restlessness.*

desastre *m. disaster, calamity.*

desatar *to untie, to loosen.*

desatender *to neglect; to disregard, to pay no attention, to take no notice of; to slight.*

desatento *adj. rude, not attentive.*

desatinar *to talk nonsense; to become confused.*

desatino *m. lack of tact; blunder; nonsense.*

desautorizar *to deprive of authority.*

desavenencia *f. disagreement, discord, misunderstanding.*

desayunarse *to breakfast.*

¿Se ha desayunado Ud. ya? *Have you had your breakfast yet?*

desayuno *m. breakfast.*

Sírveme el desayuno. *Serve my breakfast.*

desbarrar *to act or talk foolishly; to slip out.*

desbarajuste *m. confusion, disorder.*

desbaratar *to thwart, to upset (a plan); to talk nonsense; to destroy; to disperse, to route (an army); to spoil, to ruin.*

desbocarse *to run away (a horse); to use vile language.*

descabellado *adj. crazy, wild, unrestrained.*

¡Qué ideas tan descabelladas tienes! *What crazy ideas you have!*

descalabro *m. calamity, great loss.*

descalificar *to disqualify.*

descalzarse *to take off one's shoes and stockings.*

descalzo *adj. barefoot(ed).*

DESCANSAR *to rest; to sleep.*

¿No quiere Ud. descansar un rato? *Don't you want to rest a little?*

¡Qué descanse Ud. bien! (¡Qué Ud. descanse!) *Good night, may you sleep well. I hope you sleep well.*

descanso *m. rest; quiet; landing (of a staircase); intermission (in Spain.)*

Le santará muy bien un descanso. *A rest will do him good.*

descapotable *m. convertible (car).*

descarado *adj. brazen, impudent.*

descarga *f. discharge; unloading.*

descargar *to unload; to discharge; to acquit.*

descaro *m. boldness; impudence.*

descarrilamiento *m. derailment, running off the rails.*

descarrilar *to derail.*

descartar *to discard; to dismiss.*

Hay que descartar esa posibilidad. *You must discard that possibility.*

Me he descartado de un rey. *I discarded the king (at cards).*

descendencia *f. descent, origin.*

descender *to descend, to come down; to drop; to decrease.*

descendiente *adj. and n. descendant.*

descenso *m. descent; decline, fall.*

descifrar *to decipher; to decode.*

No pude descifrarlo. *I couldn't figure it out. I couldn't make head or tail (out) of it.*

descolgar *to take down; to lift up, to pick up (the receiver).*

descolorido *adj. discolored, faded.*

descomedido *adj. immoderate; excessive; impolite; rude.*

Es un muchacho muy descomedido. *He's very impolite.*

descomponer *to spoil, to break; to set at odds; to decompose; to disarrange.*

descomponerse *to rot; to be indisposed; to lose one's temper; to change for the worse (weather).*

Parece que el tiempo se descompone. *It looks as though the weather will change (for the worse).*

descompuesto *adj. out of order; spoiled (food); impolite, brazen.*

desconcertante *adj. confusing, baffling, disconcerting.*

desconcertar *to disturb, to confuse, to baffle.*

desconectar *to disconnect.*

desconfianza *f. distrust.*

desconfiar *to distrust, to mistrust.*

No tiene Ud. razón para desconfiar de él. *You have no reason to mistrust him.*

El médico desconfiaba de poder salvarlo. *The doctor had little hope of saving him.*

desconocer *not to recognize; to disavow; to ignore.*

desconocido *adj. unknown; m. stranger.*

Se la acercó un desconocido. *A stranger approached him.*

La cara de Ud. no me es desconocida. *Your face is familiar.*

desconocimiento *m. ignorance; ingratitude.*

desconsiderado *adj. thoughtless, inconsiderate.*

desconsolador *adj. disheartening; sad.*

desconsuelo *m. affliction, grief.*

descontar *to discount, to deduct; to take for*

granted.

descontento *adj. not pleased, unhappy; m. discontent, dissatisfaction, disgust.*

descorrer *to draw (a curtain); to retrace one's steps.*

descortés *adj. discourteous, impolite.*

descortesía *f. lack of politeness, rudeness.*

descoser *to unstitch, to rip out the seams.*

descote *m. having a low neck (of a dress).*

descrédito *m. discredit.*

DESCRIBIR *to describe.*

descripción *f. description.*

descubierto *adj. discovered, uncovered; bareheaded; m. overdraft; deficit.*

Estar en descubierto. *To have overdrawn a bank account.*

descubrimiento *m. discovery.*

DESCUBRIR *to discover, to find out; to disclose, to bring to light.*

Descubrimos que todo era mentira. *We found out (discovered) that it was all a lie.*

descubrirse *to take off one's hat.*

descuento *m. discount.*

descuidado *adj. negligent, careless, slovenly.*

descuidar *to neglect, to overlook; to relieve from care.*

No descuide Ud. sus asuntos. *Don't neglect your business.*

Descuide Ud. que no le pasará nada. *Don't worry, nothing will happen to her!*

descuido *m. negligence, carelessness, omission, oversight.*

DESDE *since, after, from.*

Se siente enfermo desde ayer. *He's been feeling sick since yesterday.*

¿Se puede telefonear desde aquí? *Can we phone from here?*

Estoy llamando desde hace rato. *I have been ringing quite a while.*

Desde entonces. *Since then. From then (that time) on.*

Desde luego. *Of course.*

Desde que. *Ever since.*

Desde niño. *From childhood.*

desdecirse *to retract, to go back on one's word; to gainsay.*

desdén *m. disdain, scorn, contempt.*

desdeñar *to scorn, to disdain.*

desdicha *f. misfortune, calamity, unhappiness.*

desdichado *adj. wretched; unfortunate; unhappy; m. an unfortunate person, a poor fellow.*

Es un desdichado. *He's a poor devil.*

deseable *adj. desirable.*

DESEAR *to wish, to desire.*

¿Qué desea Ud.? *What do you want (wish)? What would you like?*

¿Desea Ud. alguna otra cosa? *Do you wish anything else? Would you like anything else?*

Desearía hablar dos palabras con Ud. *I'd like to have a few words with you. I'd like to speak with you a few minutes.*

Le deseo muchas felicidades. *Lots of luck! ("I wish you much happiness.")*

desechar *to discard, to throw away, to scrap; to reject; to dismiss; to depreciate.*

Desecharon su propuesta. *They rejected his proposal.*

desecho *m. remainder, residue; refuse; leftovers.*

desembarazarse *to rid oneself of difficulties or hindrances.*

desembarcadero *m. wharf, pier, landing place.*

desembarcar *to disembark, to go ashore.*

desembarco *m. landing, disembarkment; unloading.*

desembarque m. landing, unloading.

desembolsar to pay out, to disburse.

desembolso m. expenditure, disbursement.

desembragar to release the clutch.

desempacar to unpack.

Tengo que desempacar el equipaje. I have to unpack the baggage.

desempaquetar to unpack.

desempeñar to perform, to accomplish; to carry out; to redeem, to take out of pawn; to free from debt.

Desempeñó muy bien su cometido. He carried out his mission very well. He fulfilled his obligation (commitment) faithfully.

desencantar to disappoint, to disillusion.

desencanto m. disappointment, disillusion.

desenfrenado adj. unbridled, wild.

desengañado adj. disappointed; disillusioned.

desengañar to disappoint, to become disillusioned; to disabuse, to rid of a false notion.

desengaño m. disappointment, disillusionment.

desengrasar to take out (remove) the grease; to scour.

desenlace m. outcome, result.

desenmascarar to unmask.

desenredar to disentangle.

desenredo m. disentanglement.

desenrollar to unwind, to unroll.

desentenderse to shirk; to ignore, to pay no attention.

desentendido adj. unaware; unmindful.

No se haga Ud. el desentendido. Don't pretend you don't notice it. Don't pretend you don't know it.

desenterrar to disinter, to dig up.

desentonado adj. out of tune.

desentonar to be out of tune.

desenvoltura f. ease; self-possession; boldness; impudence.

desenvolver to unwrap, to unfold; to unravel; to develop.

DESEO m. wish, desire.

No puede refrenar sus deseos. He has no self-control. He can't restrain his desires.

Tener deseo de. To desire to.

Tengo muchos deseos de conocerla. I'm very eager to meet her.

deseoso adj. desirous.

desequilibrado adj. unbalanced.

desequilibrio m. lack of balance; state of being unbalanced (mind).

desertar to desert.

desertor m. deserter.

desesperación f. despair, desperation; fury.

desesperado adj. hopeless, desperate; raving mad.

desesperarse to despair, to lose hope; to exasperate.

Eso me desespera. That exasperates me.

desfalcar to embezzle.

desfalco m. embezzlement; diminution.

desfallecer to faint; to pine, to languish.

desfallecimiento m. fainting; languor.

desfigurar to disfigure; to misshape; to distort.

desfiladero m. defile, gorge.

desfilar to march in review; to parade.

desfile m. review, parade.

desganarse to lose interest; to lose one's appetite; to become disgusted.

desgañitarse to scream, to bawl.

desgarrar to tear, to rend.

desgastar to consume, to wear out; to waste.

desgastarse to lose strength; to wear out.

desgaste m. wear and tear; wastage.

desgracia f. misfortune; sorrow; accident. (Desgracia never means "disgrace." See vergüenza,

deshonra.)

¡Qué desgracia! What a misfortune!

Por desgracia. Unfortunately.

Por desgracia no lo supimos a tiempo. Unfortunately we didn't know it in time.

Acaba de ocurrir una desgracia en la calle. There just was an accident outside ("in the street").

Caer en desgracia. To lose favor.

desgraciadamente unfortunately.

desgraciado adj. unhappy, unfortunate, unlucky; m. wretch, poor fellow.

Es un desgraciado. He's a poor devil. He's unlucky (unhappy, unfortunate).

deshabitado adj. deserted, uninhabited; vacant.

deshabitar to move out.

deshacer to undo; to unwrap; to take apart; to melt; to break up (a party); to liquidate (a business); to rout (an army).

¿Quieres deshacer el paquete? Would you please unwrap the package?

Hemos deshecho el negocio. We've liquidated the business.

Deshacer el equipaje. To unpack.

deshacerse to do one's best; to get rid of; to get out of order; to grow feeble; to be impatient; to grieve; to vanish.

¿Se deshizo Ud. de su automóvil? Did you sell (get rid of) your car?

Deshacerse en lágrimas. To burst into tears.

Deshacerse como el humo. To vanish into thin air. ("To vanish like smoke.")

deshecho adj. wasted; in pieces; destroyed; undone; melted.

deshelar to melt, to thaw.

desheredar to disinherit.

deshielo m. thaw, thawing.

deshilar to ravel, to fray.

deshilvanado adj. incoherent; disconnected.

deshojar to strip off the leaves.

deshonesto adj. dishonest; immodest; indecent.

deshonor m. dishonor; disgrace.

deshonra f. dishonor; disgrace.

El ser uno pobre no es deshonra. Poverty is no disgrace.

Tiene a deshonra el saludarme. He thinks it beneath him to greet me.

deshonrar to dishonor; to disgrace.

deshonroso adj. dishonorable; disgraceful.

deshora f. inconvenient time.

Viene siempre a deshora. He always comes at the wrong time.

desidia f. idleness, indolence.

desierto adj. deserted; solitary; m. desert, wilderness.

designar to appoint; to designate.

designio m. intention, design, purpose.

desigualdad f. inequality; unevenness.

El terreno era muy desigual. The ground was very uneven.

desilusión f. disillusion.

desilusionar to disillusion.

desinfectante adj. disinfecting; m. disinfectant.

desinfectar to disinfect.

desinflar to deflate.

desinterés m. disinterestedness, unselfishness.

desistir to desist; to waive (one's right).

Desistió de hacer el viaje. He called off the trip. He didn't make the trip.

desleal adj. disloyal.

deslealtad f. disloyalty.

desligar to untie, to unbind; to free (from an obligation).

deslindar to demarcate, to mark off the limits.

deslinde m. demarcation.

desliz m. slip, lapse.

deslizar to slide; to slip; to lapse (in speech or conduct).

Desliz de la lengua. Slip of the tongue.

deslumbramiento m. glare, overpowering luster or brilliance; bewilderment.

deslumbrar to dazzle; to bewilder.

desmayarse to faint; to become dismayed.

desmayo m. swoon; faint; dismay.

desmedido adj. immoderate; out of proportion.

desmejorarse to grow worse, to decay.

El enfermo está muy desmejorado hoy. The patient is much worse today.

desmemoriado adj. forgetful.

desmentir to deny; to contradict.

Lo desmintió rotundamente. He denied it flatly.

desmontar to dismount; to clear (a wood); to take apart (a machine, etc.).

desmoralizado adj. demoralized.

desmoralizar to demoralize.

desnatar to skim milk.

desnivel m. unevenness (of ground).

desnudarse to undress, to take one's clothes off.

desnudo adj. naked, nude.

desobedecer to disobey.

desobediencia f. disobedience.

desobediente adj. disobedient.

desocupación f. unemployment; idleness.

desocupado adj. not busy; unemployed.

Hablaré con Ud. cuando esté desocupado. I'll speak with you when you're not busy.

desocupar to vacate; to empty.

Tenemos que desocupar la casa antes del mes próximo. We must vacate the house before next month.

Voy a desocupar este armario para que Ud. lo use. I'll empty this cabinet so that you can use it.

desoír to turn a deaf ear; to pretend not to hear; not to heed, to disregard.

desorden m. disorder; excess.

desordenado adj. disorderly; irregular; unruly.

Lleva una vida desordenada. He lives a very wild (irregular) life.

desorganizar to disorganize.

desorientar to lead astray, to confuse.

despabilado adj. wakeful, vigilant; lively.

despabilar to brighten up.

despabilarse to wake up; to snap out of.

Despabílese. Wake up. Snap out of it.

Ud. verá como se despabila. You'll see how he'll brighten up.

despachar to dispatch, to forward, to expedite, to send; to sell; to wait on; to attend to (the mail); to ship; to clear (at the customhouse).

¿Quiere Ud. despacharme? Will you wait on me?

Despacharon un vagón de géneros. They shipped out a wagonload of merchandise.

No he despachado todavía la correspondencia de hoy. I still haven't attended to ("sent out") today's correspondence (mail).

despacho m. dispatch; cabinet; office; shipment.

Estaré en mi despacho entre las ocho y las nueve. I'll be at my office between eight and nine.

Acaban de recibir un despacho de la embajada. They've just received a dispatch from the embassy.

Esto lo despacho en un minuto. I'll finish this in a minute.

Despacho de localidades. *Box office.*
Despacho de billetes. *Ticket office.*
Despacho de equipajes. *Baggage room.*
DESPACIO *adj. slowly.*
Hable un poco más despacio. *Speak a little slower. Speak more slowly.*
Camine despacio. *Walk slowly.*
desparramar *to scatter, to squander.*
despecho *m. spite.*
despedazar *to tear or break into bits.*
despedir *to fire, to dismiss; to see off; to say good-by.*
despedirse *to take leave; to say good-by; to see off.*
despegar *to unglue, to detach; to take off.*
El sello se despegó. *The stamp came off.*
Acaba de despegar el avión. *The plane just took off.*
Se pasó la noche sin despegar los labios. *She didn't open her mouth ("lips") all night long.*
despegue *m. take-off (aviation).*
despeinar *to dishevel.*
despejado *adj. self-possessed; cloudless; smart, bright.*
No creo que llueva, el cielo está despejado. *I don't think it will rain. The sky is clear.*
¡Qué muchacho tan despejado! *What a smart boy!*
despejarse *to cheer up; to clear up (weather).*
Me parece que el tiempo se está despejando. *I think it's clearing up.*
despensa *f. pantry, provisions.*
desperdiciar *to waste; to squander.*
desperdicio *m. waste.*
desperezarse *to stretch oneself.*
desperfecto *m. slight damage; defect.*
despertador *m. alarm clock.*
Ponga el despertador a las siete. *Set the alarm for seven.*
DESPERTAR *to awaken; to wake up.*
¿Se acordará Ud. de despertarme? *Will you remember to wake me?*
despertarse *to wake up.*
Me desperté temprano. *I awoke early.*
despierto *adj. awake; vigilant, lively.*
despilfarrar *to squander, to waste.*
despilfarro *m. slovenliness; waste.*
despistar *to throw off the track; to confuse.*
desplazar *to displace.*
desplegar *to unfold, to unfurl; to hoist (the flag).*
desplomarse *to collapse; to fall flat on the ground.*
despoblado *adj. depopulated; m. deserted, uninhabited place.*
despojar *to despoil, to strip.*
Le han despojado hasta del último centavo. *They took everything he had down to the last penny.*
Despójese Ud. de esas ideas. *Forget those ideas.*
desposar *to marry.*
déspota *m. despot.*
despreciable *adj. despicable, contemptible.*
despreciar *to despise; to look down on.*
desprecio *m. contempt, scorn.*
Lo trataron con desprecio. *They treated him with contempt.*
desprender *to unfasten, to separate.*
desprenderse *to extricate oneself; to be inferred; to give away; to get rid of.*
Se ha desprendido de toda su fortuna. *He gave away his whole fortune.*
desprendido *adj. generous.*
despreocupado *adj. unconcerned; unconventional, free from prejudice.*

despreocuparse *to become unbiased; not to worry; to ignore, to forget, to pay no attention.*
desproporcionado *adj. disproportionate, out of proportion.*
despropósito *m. absurdity, nonsense.*
desprovisto *adj. unprovided.*
DESPUÉS *after, afterward, later.*
¿Qué pasó después de eso? *What happened after that?*
Llegó media hora después. *He arrived half an hour later.*
Mas bien antes que después. *"Rather before than after."*
desquitarse *to get even.*
desquite *m. revenge; making up for, getting even.*
destacamento *m. detachment (of troops).*
destacar *to detach (troops); to emphasize.*
destajo *m. piecework.*
Trabajamos a destajo. *We do piecework.*
destapar *to uncover; to open, to uncork.*
desteñirse *to fade (color).*
desternillarse *to split one's sides with laughter.*
Desternillarse de risa. *To split with laughter.*
Me desternillé de risa. *I split my sides laughing.*
desterrado *adj. exiled; m. exile.*
desterrar *to exile.*
destinar *to appoint; to allot; to assign; to station; to intend for; to address to.*
La carta venía destinada a mí. *The letter was addressed to me.*
destinatario *m. addressee.*
destino *m. destiny; destination; assignment; position.*
Salió con destino a Buenos Aires. *He was bound for Buenos Aires.*
No sé que destino le van a dar a ese edificio. *I don't know what they'll use that building for.*
destornillador *m. screwdriver.*
destornillar *to unscrew.*
destreza *f. skill.*
destróyer *m. destroyer (ship).*
destrozar *to destroy; to smash.*
destrucción *f. destruction.*
destruir *to destroy.*
desvanecerse *to vanish; to faint; to swell, to become puffed up (with pride).*
desvelar *to keep awake.*
desvelo *m. lack of sleep; anxiety.*
desventaja *f. disadvantage.*
desventajoso *adj. disadvantageous.*
desventurado *adj. unfortunate.*
desvergonzado *adj. impudent, unashamed, brazen.*
desvergüenza *f. impudence, brazenness.*
desvestirse *to undress.*
desviación *f. deviation; deflection.*
desviar *to divert; to deviate; to dissuade.*
Desviar la mirada. *To turn one's head away.*
desvío *m. deviation; detour.*
desvivirse *to long for; to be dying for.*
desyerbar *to weed.*
detallar *to detail; to retail.*
detalle *m. detail; retail.*
Comprar al detalle. *To buy at retail.*
Vender al detalle. *To sell at retail.*
detallista *m. retailer.*
detective *m. detective.*
detención *f. detention, arrest; delay.*
detener *to detain; to retain; to withhold; to stop.*
DETENERSE *to stay, stop over; to stop; to pause.*
Nos tendremos que detener en Panamá dos días. *We'll have to stop in Panama for two days.*

Se detuvo un momento para pensarlo. *He paused a moment to think about it.*
detenidamente *slowly, carefully.*
detenido *adj. under arrest.*
detenimiento *m. detention; care.*
deteriorar *to deteriorate.*
deterioro *m. damage, deterioration.*
determinación *f. determination; daring.*
Tomar la determinación. *To resolve. To make the (a) decision.*
determinado *adj. determined, resolute.*
determinar *to determine, to decide.*
determinarse *to resolve, to make up one's mind.*
¿Se determinó a hacer el viaje? *Has he decided to take the trip?*
detestable *adj. detestable.*
detestar *to detest, to abhor.*
DETRÁS *behind; behind one's back.*
Detrás de la puerta. *Behind the door.*
Vienen detrás. *They're following behind.*
Por detrás hablaba mal de él. *He talked about him behind his back.*
deuda *f. debt.*
Pagó todas sus deudas. *He paid all his debts.*
Deuda pendiente. *An unpaid balance.*
Contraer deudas. *To incur debts.*
deudo *m. relative, kin, kindred.*
deudor *m. debtor.*
devastación *f. devastation.*
devastar *to devastate, to ruin.*
devoción *f. devotion.*
devolución *f. restitution.*
devolver *to restore; to return.*
devorar *to devour, to consume.*
devoto *adj. devout, pious; devoted.*
DÍA *m. day.*
¡Buenos días! *Good morning!*
¿Qué día es hoy? *What's today?*
¿En qué día del mes estamos? *What day of the month is it?*
Dentro de ocho días. *In (within) a week ("eight days").*
Estaré en casa todo el día. *I'll be (at) home all day.*
La veo todos los días. *I see her every day.*
¿Cuál es el plato del día? *What's today's special? ("What's the plate of the day?")*
De día. *In the daytime.*
Un día sí y otro día no. *Every other day.*
Al día siguiente. Al otro día. *On the following day.*
Un día tras otro. *Day after day.*
De día en día. *From day to day.*
Día festivo. *Holiday.*
Día de trabajo. (Día laborable.) *Weekday. ("Working day.")*
Día entre semana. *Weekday.*
diabetes *f. diabetes.*
diablo *m. devil.*
¡Qué diablos! *What the devil!*
¿En dónde diablos te metiste? *Where on earth did you go? ("Where the devil did you hide yourself?")*
diagnóstico *m. diagnosis.*
diagrama *f. diagram.*
dialecto *m. dialect.*
diálogo *m. dialogue.*
diamante *m. diamond.*
Diamante en bruto. *Diamond in the rough.*
diámetro *m. diameter.*
diapositiva *f. slide.*
DIARIO *adj. and n. daily; diary; daily newspaper.*
He leído el diario sólo por encima. *I just*

glanced at (scanned) the paper.

Nos veíamos a diario. *We see each other every day.*

Los cuartos en este hotel no bajarán de diez pesos diarios. *The rooms in this hotel will cost at least ("won't cost less than") ten pesos a day.*

diarrea *f. diarrhea.*

dibujante *m. and f. draftsman, designer.*

dibujar *to draw, to design; to sketch.*

dibujo *m. drawing, design.*

diccionario *m. dictionary.*

DICIEMBRE *m. December.*

dictado *m. dictation.*

dictador *m. dictator.*

dictar *to dictate; to issue, to pronounce.*

Escriba Ud. Yo le dictaré. *Take this down. I'll dictate.*

El juez dictó sentencia. *The judge pronounced sentence.*

dicha *f. happiness; good luck.*

¡Qué dicha! *What luck!*

dicho *adj. said; m. saying.*

Niega que lo haya dicho. *He denies that he said it.*

Lo dicho, dicho. *I stick to what I've said. I'll (I'd) say it again.*

Dicho y hecho. *No sooner said than done. ("Said and done.")*

Es un dicho. *It's a saying.*

Tiene unos dichos muy graciosos. *She makes some very witty remarks.*

dichoso *adj. happy; fortunate.*

¡Dichosos los ojos que lo ven a Ud.! *What a pleasure (how nice) to see you! ("Happy are the eyes that see you.")*

DIECINUEVE *adj. and n. nineteen; nineteenth.*

diecinueveavo *adj. nineteenth.*

dieciochavo *adj. eighteenth.*

DIECIOCHO *adj. and n. eighteen; eighteenth.*

DIECISEIS *adj. and n. sixteen; sixteenth.*

dieciseisavo *adj. sixteenth.*

DIECISIETE *adj. and n. seventeen; seventeenth.*

diecisieteavo *adj. seventeenth.*

DIENTE *m. tooth.*

Tener buen diente. *To have a hearty appetite ("To have a good tooth.")*

Cepillo de dientes. *Toothbrush.*

Diente molar. *Molar.*

Diente de leche. *Milk tooth.*

Hablar entre dientes. *To mumble. To mutter. ("To speak between one's teeth.")*

DIESTRA *f. right hand.*

diestro *adj. and n. skillful, bullfighter.*

dieta *f. diet; doctor's fee.*

Estoy a dieta. *I'm on a diet.*

DIEZ *adj. and n. ten; tenth.*

difamación *f. defamation.*

difamar *to defame.*

DIFERENCIA *f. difference.*

Partir la diferencia. *To split the difference.*

DIFERENTE *adj. different.*

diferir *to defer, to put off; to differ.*

Telegrama diferido. *Night letter.*

DIFÍCIL *adj. difficult, hard.*

No es nada difícil. *It isn't difficult at all.*

Todo es difícil al principio. *Everything is hard in the beginning.*

Este escritor es difícil. *This author is difficult to understand.*

dificultad *f. difficulty.*

dificultar *to make difficult, to obstruct.*

dificultoso *adj. difficult; hard to please.*

difteria *f. diphtheria.*

difundir *to diffuse, to divulge; to broadcast.*

difunto *adj. deceased, dead; late; m. corpse.*

difusión *f. diffusion; broadcasting.*

digerir *to digest.*

digestión *f. digestion.*

dignarse *to deign, to condescend.*

dignidad *f. dignity.*

digno *adj. deserving, worthy; dignified.*

Digno de confianza. *Trustworthy.*

digresión *f. digression.*

dilación *f. delay.*

dilatar *to put off, to delay; to expand.*

dilección *f. love, affection.*

dilecto *adj. loved, beloved.*

dilema *m. dilemma.*

¡Vaya un dilema! *What a dilemma! What a difficult situation!*

diligencia *f. diligence; haste; business, errand.*

Estudia con diligencia sus lecciones. *He studies his lessons diligently.*

Hacer una diligencia. *To attend to some business. To do an errand.*

Hacer diligencias. *To try. To endeavor.*

Hay que resolverlo con toda diligencia. *You must solve it quickly.*

diligente *adj. diligent; prompt, swift.*

diluir *to dilute.*

diluviar *to rain heavily.*

Seguía diluviando cuando partimos. *It was still pouring when we left.*

dimensión *f. dimension.*

diminutivo *adj. diminutive.*

diminuto *adj. diminutive, minute.*

dimisión *f. resignation (from a position, society, etc.)*

dimitir *to resign, to retire.*

dinamita *f. dynamite.*

dínamo *f. dynamo.*

dineral *m. large amount of money.*

DINERO *m. money, currency.*

Ando mal de dinero. *I'm short of money.*

Dinero contante. *Ready money. Cash payment.*

Persona de dinero. *A well-to-do person.*

DIOS *m. God.*

¡Dios mío! *My God! Dear me!*

Dios mediante. *God willing. With the help of God.*

¡Por Dios! *For heaven's sake!*

¡Válgame Dios! *Goodness! My heavens! Good gracious!*

¡No, por Dios! *Good heavens, no!*

¡Vaya Ud. con Dios! *Good-by.*

¡Sabe Dios! *God knows!*

¡Qué Dios le oiga! *God grant it!*

diploma *m. diploma.*

diplomacia *f. diplomacy.*

diplomático *adj. diplomatic; m. diplomat.*

diptongo *m. diphthong.*

diputado *m. deputy; delegate; representative.*

DIRECCIÓN *f. address; direction, way; control, management, administration; manager's office.*

¿En qué dirección va Ud.? *Which way are you going?*

En esa dirección. *In that direction.*

Escriba la dirección. *Write (down) the address.*

Calle de dirección única. *One-way street.*

directamente *directly.*

directivo *adj. managing; f. governing board, board of directors.*

directo *adj. direct; straight; nonstop.*

¿Es éste un tren directo o tiene uno que cam-

biar? *Is that an express or must one change?*

director *adj. and n. directing; manager, director; chief editor; principal (of a school).*

Director de orquesta. *Orchestra conductor.*

directorio *m. directory; board of directors; executive committee.*

Presidente del directorio. *Chairman of the Board.*

dirigente *adj. leading, directing; m. leader.*

dirigible *m. dirigible, airship.*

DIRIGIR *to address; to direct; to conduct, to control; to guide; to drive.*

¿Cómo tengo que dirigir la carta? *How shall I address the letter?*

dirigirse *to apply to; to be bound for; to address.*

¿A quien tengo que dirigirme? *To whom shall I apply?*

Hágame el favor de dirigirme a. *Please direct me to.*

¿Se dirige Ud. a nosotros? *Are you speaking to us?*

El lugar hacia el cual se dirigen está aún muy lejos. *The place you're going to is still a good way off.*

discerniente *adj. discerning, discriminating.*

discernimiento *m. discernment.*

discernir *to discern; to distinguish.*

disciplina *f. discipline.*

disciplinar *to discipline.*

discípulo *m. disciple; pupil.*

disco *m. disk, record; telephone dial.*

discordante *adj. discordant.*

discordia *f. discord; disagreement; dissension.*

discreción *f. discretion; keenness; sagacity.*

A discreción. *At one's discretion. Left to one's discretion. Optional.*

discrepancia *f. discrepancy.*

discrepar *to disagree; to differ from.*

discreto *adj. discreet.*

disculpa *f. excuse, apology.*

disculpar *to excuse.*

discurrir *to wander about; to think over; to flow (a liquid.)*

Discurramos un poco más sobre esto. *Let's consider that a little longer.*

discurso *m. speech.*

Hacer un discurso. *To make a speech. To deliver an address.*

discusión *f. discussion.*

discutible *adj. debatable.*

DISCUTIR *to discuss.*

diseminar *to disseminate; to scatter.*

disensión *f. dissension, strife.*

disentería *f. dysentery.*

diseñar *to draw, to design, to sketch.*

diseño *m. drawing; sketch, outline.*

disfraz *m. disguise; mask.*

disfrazar *to disguise.*

DISFRUTAR *to enjoy.*

Disfrutaremos más si vamos en grupo. *We'll have more fun if we all go together.*

Disfruta de muy buena salud. *He's enjoying good health.*

disfrute *m. enjoyment.*

disgustar *to displease, to disgust; to offend.*

¿Le disgusta que fume? *Do you mind my smoking? Do you mind if I smoke? Does my smoking bother you?*

disgustarse *to be displeased, to get angry; to quarrel.*

¿No se disgustará Ud? *Won't you be angry?*

disgusto *m. displeasure, disgust, annoyance; quarrel.*

A disgusto. *Against one's will. Not at ease.*

Llevarse un disgusto. *To be disappointed.*
disidente *adj. and n. dissident; dissenter.*
disimulación *f. dissimulation.*
disimulado *adj. dissembling.*
   A lo disimulado. *Dissemblingly.*
disimular *to dissimulate; to overlook.*
disimulo *m. dissimulation; pretense; tolerance.*
dislocación *f. dislocation.*
dislocarse *to sprain; to dislocate.*
disminución *f. lessening, diminishing.*
disminuir *to diminish, to decrease.*
disolver *to melt; to dissolve; to break up (a crowd).*
dispar *adj. different, unlike.*
disparar *to shoot; to fire.*
disparatado *adj. nonsensical, absurd.*
disparatar *to ramble, to talk nonsense; to blunder.*
disparate *m. nonsense; blunder.*
disparo *m. discharge, shot.*
DISPENSAR *to excuse; to dispense; to exempt.*
   Dispénseme. *Excuse me.*
   Dispense Ud. *I beg your pardon.*
   Dispénseme, ¿qué hora es? *Excuse me, what time is it?*
   Está dispensado. *You're excused.*
dispensario *m. dispensary.*
disperso *adj. dispersed; scattered.*
disponer *to dispose; to arrange; to provide for; to prepare; to determine.*
   Disponga Ud. lo que quiera. *Decide whatever you like (wish).*
   Me dispongo a salir mañana. *I'm determined to leave tomorrow.*
   Dispongo de muy poco tiempo. *I have very little time now ("at my disposal").*
disponible *adj. available.*
disposición *f. service; disposition; state of mind; regulation, order.*
   Estoy a su disposición. *I'm at your service.*
   Tiene muy buena disposición. *She has a very pleasant disposition.*
   Había que sujetarse a la nueva disposición. *We had to submit to the new regulation.*
dispuesto *adj. disposed; ready, arranged; inclined; willing (to).*
   Bien dispuesto. *Favorably disposed (inclined).*
   Mal dispuesto. *Unfavorably disposed (inclined).*
   ¿Tiene Ud. algo dispuesto para esta noche? *Do you have anything arranged for tonight?*
   Estamos dispuestos a todo. *We're prepared for anything.*
   La casa está bien dispuesta. *The house is nicely arranged.*
disputa *f. dispute; contest; quarrel.*
disputar *to dispute; to quarrel.*
DISTANCIA *f. distance.*
   ¿Qué distancia hay a Madrid? *How far is it to Madrid?*
   Hemos recorrido toda la distancia a pie. *We've walked the whole way.*
   Conferencia a larga distancia. *Long distance call.*
DISTANTE *adj. distant, far off.*
distar *to be distant, to be far.*
   ¿Dista mucho de aquí? *Is it far from here?*
   Distaba mucho de ser cierto. *It was far from certain.*
distinción *f. distinction; discrimination; difference.*
   Hay que hacer una distinción entre los dos sonidos. *It's necessary to make a distinction between the two sounds.*
   Era un hombre de mucha distinción. *He was a very distinguished man.*
   A distinción. *In contradistinction.*

distinguido *adj. distinguished, eminent.*
distinguir *to distinguish; to discriminate; to tell (apart); to show regard for.*
   ¿Cómo puede distinguirlos? *How do (can) you tell them apart?*
distinguirse *to distinguish oneself, to excel.*
distintivo *adj. distinctive; m. badge, insignia.*
DISTINTO *adj. distinct; different.*
distracción *f. oversight; distraction; absence of mind; entertainment, recreation, pastime.*
   La lectura es su distracción favorita. *Reading is his favorite diversion.*
   El cine es su distracción favorita. *Going to the movies is his favorite entertainment (diversion).*
   Lo hizo por distracción. *He did it absent-mindedly.*
distraer *to distract; to entertain.*
   Ese ruido me distrae. *That noise distracts me.*
distraerse *to enjoy oneself, to have fun; to be absent-minded.*
   ¿Se ha distraído en la fiesta? *Did you have a good time at the party?*
distraído *adj. inattentive; absent-minded.*
distribución *f. distribution.*
distribuidor *adj. distributing; m. distributer.*
distribuir *to distribute; to divide; to allot, to allocate.*
distrito *m. district; region.*
disturbar *to disturb.*
disturbio *m. disturbance.*
disuadir *to dissuade.*
disuasión *f. dissuasion.*
divagación *f. wandering, digression.*
divagar *to wander.*
diván *m. couch.*
divergencia *f. divergence.*
divergente *adj. divergent.*
diversidad *f. diversity; variety.*
diversión *f. amusement, diversion, recreation.*
diverso *adj. diverse; various, several.*
   Le he visto en diversas ocasiones. *I've seen him on several occasions.*
divertido *adj. entertaining, amusing, funny.*
   Este libro es muy divertido. *This book is very entertaining.*
   Todo esto es muy divertido. *All this is very amusing.*
   Es una muchacha divertidísima. *She's lots of fun.*
divertimiento *m. diversion, amusement, sport, pastime.*
divertir *to distract; to divert; to amuse.*
   Nos contó unos chistes que nos divertieron mucho. *He told us some jokes which amused us very much (a lot).*
DIVERTIRSE *to amuse oneself, to have a good time, to have fun.*
   ¡Que se divierta! *Have a good time! Enjoy yourself!*
dividendo *m. dividend.*
DIVIDIR *to divide.*
divinamente *splendidly; divinely, heavenly; very well.*
   Canta divinamente. *She sings beautifully ("divinely"). She has a beautiful voice.*
   Este sombrero le sienta divinamente. *This hat is most becoming to you.*
divinidad *f. divinity.*
divino *adj. divine; excellent; heavenly.*
divisa *f. motto; badge; emblem.*
divisar *to perceive, to catch sight of.*
división *f. division; partition, compartment.*
divorciarse *to get a divorce, to be divorced.*

divorcio *m. divorce.*
divulgar *to divulge, to publish; to disclose.*
dobladillo *m. hem.*
doblar *to turn; to double; to fold; to bend.*
   Doble a la derecha. *Turn to the right.*
   Doblar la esquina. *To turn the corner.*
   Doble bien la carta antes de meterla en el sobre. *Fold the letter well before putting (enclosing) it in the envelope.*
doble *adj. double, twofold; two-faced, deceitful.*
   No se fíe Ud. de él, es muy doble. *Don't trust him, he's very deceitful.*
   Esto tiene doble sentido. *This has a double meaning.*
   Al doble. *Doubly.*
doblement *doubly; deceitfully.*
doblez *m. fold; crease; duplicity, double dealing.*
DOCE *adj. and n. twelve; twelfth.*
DOCENA *f. dozen.*
   Por docena. *By the dozen.*
dócil *adj. docile; obedient; gentle.*
doctor *m. doctor.*
doctrina *f. doctrine.*
documentación *f. documentation, documents, papers.*
documento *m. document.*
dólar *m. dollar.*
dolencia *f. ailment; disease.*
DOLER *to ache, to cause pain, to hurt.*
   ¿Dónde le duele? *Where does it hurt you?*
   Me duele la cabeza. *I've a headache.*
   El pie me duele muchísimo. *My foot hurts a lot.*
   Me duelen los ojos. *My eyes hurt.*
   Me duele una muela. *My tooth aches.*
   Me duele la garganta. *I have a sore throat.*
dolerse (de) *to be sorry (for); to regret; to pity; to complain (of).*
DOLOR *m. ache, pain; sorrow.*
   Tener dolor. *To have a pain.*
   Tener dolor de cabeza. *To have a headache.*
   Dolor de muelas. *Toothache.*
   Dolor de garganta. *A sore throat.*
doloroso *adj. sorrowful, afflicted; painful.*
domar *to tame; to subdue.*
   Sin domar. *Untamed.*
doméstico *adj. domestic.*
domicilio *m. residence, domicile; home; address.*
dominación *f. domination.*
dominante *adj. dominant.*
dominar *to dominate; to master.*
dominarse *to control oneself.*
DOMINGO *m. Sunday.*
dominio *m. dominion; command, control.*
   Tiene un buen dominio del español. *He has an excellent command of Spanish.*
   Tenía un gran dominio sobre sí mismo. *He had great self-control. He had great control over himself.*
don *m. Don (title of respect used only before Christian names); natural gift.*
   Dirija Ud. la carta a Don Antonio Sucre. *Address the letter to Mr. Antonio Sucre.*
   Tiene el don de hacer amigos. *She has the gift of making friends.*
   Don de gentes. *Pleasant manners. Social graces. Savoir-faire.*
donación *f. gift, donation; grant.*
donaire *m. grace; elegance; witty saying.*
donar *to donate, to give as a gift, to make a gift to someone.*
donativo *m. gift, donation.*
DONDE *where.*
   ¿Dónde vive? *Where do you live?*

¿Dónde está el teléfono? *Where is the telephone?*

Iremos donde a Ud. le plazca. *We'll go wherever you like.*

¿De dónde? *From where?*

¿Hacia dónde? *In what direction?*

¿Por dónde? *Which way?*

dondequiera *anywhere; wherever.*

Iré dondequiera que me mande. *I'll go wherever you send me.*

doña (*f. of* **don**) *lady; madam.*

dorado *adj. gilt, gilded.*

dormilón *adj. fond of sleeping; m. sleepyhead.*

DORMIR *to sleep.*

¿Ha dormido Ud. bien? *Did you sleep well?*

No he podido dormir. *I couldn't sleep.*

DORMIRSE *to fall asleep.*

Debo haberme dormido. *I must have been asleep.*

Se ha quedado dormido. *He's fallen asleep.*

dormitar *to doze, to be half asleep.*

dormitorio *m. dormitory; bedroom.*

DOS *adj. and n. two; second (day of the month).*

Dos a dos. *Two by two.*

De dos en dos. *Two abreast.*

En un dos por tres. *In the twinkling of an eye.*

Para entre los dos. *Between you and me.*

Son las dos. *It's two o'clock.*

Las dos hermanas se parecen. *Both sisters look alike.*

¿Tiene Ud. un cuarto para dos personas? *Do you have a double room?*

Está a dos pasos de aquí. *It's only a few steps from here.*

DOSCIENTOS *m. pl. two hundred.*

dosis *f. dose.*

dotación *f. crew; equipment; allocation.*

dotar *to provide (with); to allocate; to give a dowry; to endow with.*

dote *m. and f. dowry; pl. gifts, talents.*

drama *m. drama.*

dramático *adj. dramatic.*

dramatizar *to dramatize.*

drástico *adj. drastic.*

droga *f. drug.*

droguería *f. drugstore.*

ducha *f. shower (bath).*

DUDA *f. doubt.*

Lo pongo en duda. *I doubt it.*

No me cabe la menor duda. *I haven't the slightest doubt.*

Sin duda. *Without a doubt. Undoubtedly.*

DUDAR *to doubt.*

Lo dudo. *I doubt it.*

Dudo que venga. *I doubt if he'll come.*

Nadie lo duda. *Nobody doubts it.*

dudoso *adj. doubtful; uncertain.*

duelo *m. duel; mourning; grief; affliction.*

duende *m. ghost.*

dueña *f. owner; landlady; mistress.*

dueño *m. owner; landlord; master.*

Hacerse dueño. *To take possession.*

Dueño de sí mismo. *Self-controlled. ("Master of oneself.")*

DULCE *adj. sweet; agreeable; m. candy.*

dulcería *f. candy store.*

dulzura *f. sweetness; gentleness.*

dúo *m. duo, duet.*

duodécimo *adj. twelfth.*

duplicado *m. duplicate; copy.*

duplicar *to duplicate, to repeat.*

duque *m. duke.*

duquesa *f. duchess.*

durable *adj. durable; lasting.*

¿Es durable esta tela? *Will this cloth wear well?*

duración *f. duration.*

duradero *adj. durable; lasting.*

DURANTE *during, for.*

Durante el día. *During the day.*

Durante la noche. *During the night.*

Durante algún tiempo. *For some time.*

DURAR *to last; to continue; to wear well.*

¿Cuánto dura la película? *How long does the picture last?*

Este abrigo me ha durado mucho tiempo. *This overcoat has lasted me a long time.*

El viaje en barco durará cinco días. *The voyage will take five days.*

Todavía le dura el enfado. *He's still angry.*

durazno *m. peach (Amer.).*

dureza *f. hardness; harshness.*

Dureza de oído. *Hardness of hearing.*

durmiente *adj. sleeping; m. sleeper.*

DURO *adj. hard; unbearable; obstinate; stingy; harsh; m. peso, dollar (Spain).*

No sea duro con él. *Don't be hard on him.*

Este pan es tan duro que es difícil cortarlo. *This bread is so hard that it's difficult to cut ("it").*

¿Me puede Ud. cambiar un billete de veinte duros? *(Spain) Can you change a twenty-dollar bill for me?*

A duras penas. *Scarcely. Hardly. With difficulty.*

E

e *and (used before words beginning with i or hi).*

Padre e hijo. *Father and son.*

ebanista *m. cabinetmaker.*

ebrio *adj. intoxicated, drunk.*

economía *f. economy, economics, saving.*

Economía política. *Political economy.*

económico *adj. economic; economical, not too expensive.*

economizar *to economize; to save.*

ECHAR *to throw; to throw out; to fire; to sprout; to shoot; to lay down; to start to.*

Eche esto a la basura. *Throw this in the garbage.*

Lo echaron de su empleo por holgazán. *They fired him because he was too lazy.*

Eche un poco de agua caliente en la tetera. *Pour some hot water in the teapot.*

Eche Ud. la carta al buzón. *Put this letter in the mailbox.*

Echó la carta al correo. *He mailed the letter.*

Lo echaron a patadas. *They kicked him out.*

Eche la llave al salir. *Lock the door when you go out.*

¿Quiere Ud. echar una partida de damas? *Would you like to play a game of checkers?*

Echar de ver. *To notice. To perceive.*

Echar mano a. *To grab. To get hold of. To arrest.*

Echar a correr. *To start to run.*

Echar a perder. *To spoil.*

Echar la culpa a alguno. *To blame someone.*

Echar de menos. *To miss.*

Echar tierra a. *To forget.*

Echarla de. *To pretend. To claim to be.*

Echar el guante. *To arrest.*

Echar raíces. *To take root.*

Echar el ancla. *To drop anchor.*

ECHARSE *to lie down; to throw oneself, to plunge; to rush, to dash.*

Se echó en la cama. *He lay down on the bed.*

Se echó a reír. *He burst out laughing.*

EDAD *f. age; era, epoch, time.*

¿Qué edad tiene Ud? *How old are you? What's your age?*

Somos de la misma edad. *We're (of) the same age.*

Ser menor de edad. *To be a minor.*

Mayor de edad. *Of age.*

Es un hombre de edad. *He's well along in years.*

Edad media. *Middle Ages.*

edición *f. edition, issue; publication.*

edificar *to construct, to build.*

Van a edificar una nueva escuela. *They are going to build a new school.*

edificio *m. building.*

Este edificio es bonito por fuera. *This building looks (is) nice from the outside.*

editor *adj. and n. publishing; m. publisher.*

Casa editora. *Publishing house.*

Fui a ver a un editor. *I went to see a publisher.*

editorial *adj. editorial; f. publishing house.*

educación *f. education; bringing up, breeding.*

Es un hombre sin educación. *He's ill-bred. He has no breeding.*

educar *to educate; to bring up; to train.*

Es muy mal educado. *He has no breeding.*

Es una chica muy bien educada. *She's a very well-bred girl.*

educativo *adj. educational, instructive.*

efectivo *adj. effective, certain, real, actual; m. cash.*

Pagar en efectivo. *To pay in cash.*

Efectivo en caja. *Cash on hand.*

Valor efectivo. *Real value.*

Hacer efectivo. *To make effective. To put into effect. To cash (a check, etc.).*

Medidas efectivas. *Effective measures.*

EFECTO *m. effect, result, consequence; impression; pl. effects, assets, goods, belongings.*

Sus palabras causaron mal efecto. *His words made a bad impression.*

En efecto, no sabe nada. *In fact, he doesn't know anything.*

A tal efecto. *For this purpose.*

A cuyo efecto. *For the purpose of which. To which end.*

Por efecto de. *As a result of.*

Llevar a efecto. *To carry out. To put into practice (effect).*

Dejar sin efecto. *To cancel. To annul. To make (declare) void.*

Efectos personales. *Personal belongings.*

Efectos en cartera. *Securities in hand.*

Efectos públicos. *Public securities.*

eficaz *adj. effective, efficient.*

eficiente *adj. effective, efficient.*

eje *m. axle, axis.*

ejecución *f. execution, carrying out, performance.*

ejecutar *to execute, to carry out, to perform.*

ejecutivo *adj. executive.*

ejemplar *adj. exemplary, serving as an example; m. copy; sample.*

No pude conseguir otro ejemplar del libro. *I couldn't get another copy of the book.*

EJEMPLO *m. example; pattern.*

Por ejemplo. *For example.*

ejercer *to exercise, to perform, to practice.*

Ejercer la medicina. *To practice medicine.*

ejercicio *m. exercise; drill.*

Ejercicio de tiro. *Target practice.*

ejército *m. army.*

EL *(article m.) the.*

El libro. *The book.*

¿No le gusta el frío? *Don't you like the cold?*
¿Cuál es el mejor hotel? *Which is the best hotel?*
Hasta el lunes. *See you Monday.*
ÉL (*pronoun m.*) *he, him.*
¿Qué dijo él? *What did he say?*
Dígaselo a él. *Tell it to him.*
elaboración *f. elaboration, working out.*
elaborado *adj. elaborate; manufactured.*
elaborar *to elaborate; to work out; to manufacture.*
elasticidad *f. elasticity.*
elástico *adj. and n. elastic.*
ele *f. name of the letter l.*
elección *f. election; choice.*
Hoy se celebran las elecciones. *Elections will be held today.*
Hizo una buena elección. *He made a good choice.*
electricidad *f. electricity.*
eléctrico *adj. electric.*
Luz eléctrica. *Electric light.*
elefante *m. elephant.*
elegancia *f. elegance; refinement.*
Viste con elegancia. *She dresses neatly.*
elegante *adj. elegant, refined, well dressed.*
elegir *to elect; to choose.*
elemental *adj. elementary; elemental.*
elemento *m. element; pl. elements, rudiments, first principles.*
elenco *m. catalogue, list, table, index.*
elevación *f. elevation.*
elevador *m. elevator; hoist.*
elevar *to elevate; to lift up.*
elevarse *to rise; to be elated, to be conceited.*
eliminación *f. elimination.*
eliminar *to eliminate.*
elocuencia *f. eloquence.*
elocuente *adj. eloquent.*
elogiar *to praise.*
elogio *m. praise, eulogy.*
elucidación *f. elucidation.*
eludir *to elude, to evade.*
Deje de eludir la cuestión; vamos al grano. *Stop evading the issue; let's get to the point.*
ELLA (*f. of* **él**) *she, her.*
¿Cómo es ella? *What does she look like?*
¿Cómo se llama ella? *What's her name?*
ELLAS (*pl. of* **ella**) *they, them.*
¿Quiénes son ellas? *Who are they?*
Ellas son mis hermanas. *They are my sisters.*
ELLO (*neuter of* **él** *and* **ella**) *it.*
No doy en ello. *I don't get it.*
Ello podrá ser verdad, pero no lo creo. *It may be true but I don't believe it.*
Hablemos de ello. *Let's talk about that.*
Para ello. *For the purpose.*
Ello es que. *The fact is (that).*
ELLOS (*pl. of* **él**) *they, them.*
Ellos se van, pero yo me quedo. *They're leaving but I'll stay.*
Ninguno de ellos tiene dinero. *None of them has money.*
embajada *f. embassy.*
embajador *m. ambassador.*
embalaje *m. packing; putting in bales; packing-box.*
embalar *to pack in bales; to pack.*
embarcación *f. vessel, ship, boat; embarkation.*
embarcadero *m. wharf, place of embarkation.*
embarcar *to embark.*
embarcarse *to go on board a ship, to embark.*
embargo *m. embargo.*
Sin embargo. *Nevertheless.*
embarque *m. embarkation, shipment, shipping.*
embestida *f. assault, attack.*

emborrachar *to intoxicate.*
emborracharse *to get drunk.*
emboscar *to ambush.*
emboscarse *to lie in ambush.*
embotellar *to bottle.*
embrollo *m. jumble, tangle; fix, jam.*
No sé como salir de este embrollo. *I don't know how to get out of this fix (tight spot, jam).*
embrutecerse *to become stupid or coarse, to become brutalized.*
embustero *m. liar, fibber.*
embutido *m. inlaid work; sausage.*
emergencia *f. emergency.*
emigración *f. emigration.*
emigrante *m. emigrant.*
emigrar *to emigrate.*
eminente *adj. eminent.*
emisora *f. broadcasting station.*
emitir *to emit, to send forth; to issue (bonds, etc.); to utter, to express; to broadcast (news, etc.).*
emoción *f. emotion.*
emocionante *adj. touching.*
emocionar *to move, to arouse the emotions.*
emocionarse *to be moved.*
Se emociona fácilmente. *He's easily moved. He's very emotional.*
empacar *to pack.*
empachar *to cause indigestion; to overeat, eat too much, to cram; to embarrass.*
empacho *m. indigestion; embarrassment.*
Sin empacho. *Without ceremony. With ease.*
empalmar *to join; to splice.*
empanada *f. meat pie.*
empañar *to swaddle; to blur; to sully.*
empapar *to soak.*
empaparse *to be soaked, to be drenched.*
empapelar *to paper.*
• **empaquetar** *to pack.*
emparedado *m. sandwich.*
emparentado *adj. related.*
emparentar *to become related.*
empastar *to paste; to bind (books); to fill (a tooth).*
empatar *to equal, to tie.*
Los dos equipos empataron. *The game ended in a tie. ("The two teams tied.")*
empeñar *to pawn; to pledge; to engage.*
Empeñé mi palabra. *I gave (pledged) my word.*
Está empeñado hasta los ojos. *He's up to his neck in debt. He's head over heels in debt.*
empeñarse *to bind oneself; to get into debt.*
Se empeñó en venir conmigo. *He (she) was determined to come with me. He (she) insisted on coming with me.*
empeño *m. pledge, obligation; determination; earnest desire; persistence.*
Estudia con empeño. *He's studying diligently.*
Tener empeño en. *To be bent on.*
EMPEZAR *to begin.*
empinar *to raise.*
Empinar el codo. *To drink like a fish.*
empinarse *to stand on tiptoe; to stand on the hind legs; to rise high; to zoom (aviation).*
empleado *m. employee, clerk.*
EMPLEAR *to employ; to hire; to use; to spend.*
¿En qué empleó Ud. la tarde? *How did you spend the afternoon?*
Empleamos dos días en hacerlo. *It took us two days to do it.*
Estoy empleado en su casa. *I work in his firm.*
Se acaba de emplear. *He just got a job.*
Emplearon un centenar de obreros esta mañana. *They hired a hundred workers*

this morning.
EMPLEO *m. employment, job, occupation; use.*
Tiene un buen empleo. *He has a good job.*
El empleo de esa palabra no es correcto. *That word is not used correctly.*
emprender *to undertake, to take up, to set off.*
empresa *f. undertaking; enterprise; company.*
empresario *m. impresario, contractor, manager.*
empréstito *m. loan.*
empujar *to push.*
¡No me empuje! *Don't push me!*
empuje *m. push; impulse.*
Es un hombre de empuje. *He's an energetic man.*
empujón *m. push; shove.*
A empujones. *By fits and starts.*
EN *in, into, on, at, by.*
Lo tengo en la mano. *I have it in my hand.*
En buen estado. *In good condition.*
Entremos en esta tienda. *Let's go into this store.*
Métase en la cama. *Get into bed.*
He venido en avión. *I came by plane.*
¿En qué fecha? *On what date?*
En casa. *At home.*
En vano. *In vain.*
En general. *In general.*
En adelante. *From now on.*
En cambio. *On the other hand.*
En vez (lugar) de. *Instead of.*
En todas partes. *Everywhere.*
En medio de. *In the middle (midst) of.*
En seguida. *right away.*
enamorado *adj. in love.*
enamorarse *to fall in love.*
enano *m. dwarf; midget.*
encabezar *to write a heading; to register, to enroll; to head.*
encadenar *to chain, to link together.*
encajar *to fit in; to gear; to inlay; to sock, to hit; to palm, to pass off.*
encaje *m. lace.*
encaminar *to guide; to direct.*
encaminarse *to be on the way; to take the road to.*
encanecer *to turn gray, to grow old.*
encantador *adj. charming.*
Es una chica encantadora. *She's charming. She's a charming girl.*
encantar *to enchant; to delight; to fascinate.*
Me encantan las flores. *I love (am fond of) flowers.*
Quedaré encantado. *I shall be delighted.*
encanto *m. charm; delight; fascination.*
Es un encanto de criatura. *She's a charming girl.*
encapricharse *to become stubborn; to be infatuated; to indulge in whims.*
encarcelar *to imprison.*
encarecer *to raise the price; to entreat, to beg.*
Le encarezco que lo haga con cuidado. *Please (I beg you to) do it carefully.*
Ha encarecido el precio de la carne. *The price of meat has gone up.*
encargado *m. person in charge; agent.*
encargar *to ask, to have someone go on an errand; to entrust; to undertake; to instruct.*
Le encargué que me lo comprara. *I asked her to buy it for me.*
encargarse *to take charge, to take care.*
¿Quién se encargará de los niños? *Who'll take care of the children?*
encargo *m. request; errand; order, charge.*
encarnado *adj. red; m. flesh color.*
Se puso encarnada. *She blushed.*

encendedor m. cigarette lighter.

encender to kindle; to light; to incite.

Haga el favor de encender la luz. *Please put on the light.*

encerar to wax.

encerrar to close in, to shut up, to confine; to contain.

encerrarse to lock oneself in; to live in seclusion.

encía f. gum (of the teeth).

ENCIMA above, over, at the top.

Encima de la mesa. *On the table.*

Encima de los árboles. *Above the trees.*

Por encima. *Superficially.*

Por encima de todo. *Above all.*

Estar muy por encima de. *To be far and away above.*

¿Cuánto dinero lleva Ud. encima? *How much money do you have with you?*

encina f. evergreen oak.

encolar to glue.

encomendar to recommend; to commend; to entrust; to praise, to extol.

encomendarse to commit oneself, to place oneself into the hands of.

encomienda f. parcel; parcel post (Amer.).

encono m. irritation; soreness; animosity, rancor, bitter resentment.

ENCONTRAR to find; to meet.

¿Encontraste lo que buscabas? *Did you find what you were looking for?*

¿Cómo encuentra Ud. el trabajo? *How do you find the work?*

Debían encontrarnos aquí. *They were supposed to meet us here.*

ENCONTRARSE to meet, to come across; to clash; to differ with; to be, to feel.

¿Cómo se encuentra Ud.? *How do you feel? How are you?*

Hoy me encuentro mejor. *I feel better today.*

encorvado adj. bent; curved.

encrespar to curl; to frizzle.

encresparse to become rough (sea); to be involved (in an affair).

encubrir to hide, to conceal.

ENCUENTRO m. meeting; encounter.

encharcar to form puddles; to inundate.

enchilada f. a Mexican corn-flour pancake with chili.

enchufar to plug in; to fit one tube into another; to telescope.

enchufe m. plug, socket; coupling, joint (for pipes).

enderezar to straighten; to set right.

endeudarse to get into debt.

endosar to endorse.

endurecer to harden, to make hard.

ene f. name of the letter n.

enemigo adj. unfriendly, hostile; m. enemy, foe.

Es enemigo del tabaco. *He has an aversion to tobacco. He's against the use of tobacco.*

enemistad f. enmity; hatred.

energía f. energy, power.

enérgico adj. energetic.

ENERO m. January.

enfadar to vex, to annoy, to make someone angry.

enfadarse to get angry, to become angry.

enfado m. vexation, anger.

enfermar to get ill; to fall sick.

Ud. va a acabar por enfermarse. *You'll end by getting sick.*

enfermizo adj. infirm, not healthy, sickly.

enfermo adj. ill, sick; m. patient.

Me siento enfermo. *I feel ill. I don't feel well.*

Está gravemente enfermo. *He's very ill.*

¿Cómo sigue el enfermo? *How is the patient getting along?*

enfocar to focus.

enfrentar to face, to confront.

ENFRENTE in front of, opposite.

El automóvil está parado enfrente de aquel edificio. *The car's parked in front of that building.*

Viven en la casa de enfrente. *They live in the house across the street.*

enfriamiento m. cooling; refrigeration; cold.

Enfriamiento por aire. *Air cooling.*

enfriar to cool.

enfriarse to cool off, to get cool.

enfurecer to infuriate, to enrage.

enfurecerse to become furious.

enganchar to hook; to get caught; to hitch; to couple; to recruit.

engañar to deceive, to fool.

engañarse to deceive oneself.

Ud. se engaña. *You're deceiving (fooling) yourself.*

Se le engaña fácilmente. *He's easily fooled (taken in).*

engañoso adj. deceitful; tricky.

engendrar to bring into existence; to produce, to create.

engordar to fatten; to grow fat.

engranaje m. gear.

engrasar to grease, to lubricate.

engrase m. lubrication.

engreído conceited, haughty.

engreír to spoil (a child, etc.).

engreírse to become conceited, to become haughty.

engrudo m. paste, glue.

enhebrar to thread a needle.

enhorabuena f. congratulation.

¡La enhorabuena! *Congratulations!*

enjabonar to soap; to wash with soap.

enjaular to cage; to imprison.

enjuagar to rinse.

enjugar to dry; to wipe off.

enlace m. connection; marriage; liaison, wedding, joining.

El enlace de trenes es excelente en esta estación. *The train connections are excellent at this station.*

Un feliz enlace. *A happy marriage.*

enlazar to join, to bind, to connect; to catch with a lasso.

enmendar to correct, to amend, to reform.

enmudecer to silence.

enmudecerse to become dumb; to be silent.

enojado adj. angry, cross.

Estar enojado. *To be angry.*

enojar to irritate, to make angry.

enojarse to get angry.

enredar to entangle; to make trouble; to upset.

enredarse to become entangled.

enredo m. entanglement.

enriquecer to enrich; to improve.

enriquecerse to get rich.

ENROLLAR to roll, to coil, to wind.

enronquecer to make hoarse.

enronquecerse to become hoarse.

ensalada f. salad.

ensanchar to widen, to enlarge.

ENSAYAR to try, to rehearse, to test.

ensayarse to train, to practice.

ensayo m. trial; rehearsal.

enseñanza f. teaching, instruction.

ENSEÑAR to teach; to point out, to show.

¿Quiere Ud. enseñarme a hablar español?

Would you like to teach me to speak Spanish?

Enseñe Ud. el camino al señor. *Show this gentleman the way.*

No se lo enseñe a ella. *Don't show it to her.*

enseñarse to accustom oneself.

ensordecer to deafen.

ensordecerse to become deaf.

ensordecimiento m. deafness.

ensuciar to dirty, to soil.

ensuciarse to get dirty; to lower oneself.

entender m. understanding; opinion.

A mi entender. *In my opinion.*

ENTENDER to understand.

¿Entiende Ud. español? *Do you understand Spanish?*

No pude entender lo que decían. *I couldn't understand what they were saying.*

Entendido. *It's understood.*

Es un obrero muy entendido en su oficio. *He's very skilled in his trade.*

No darse por entendido. *To ignore. Not to take notice.*

Según tenemos entendido. *As far as we know.*

Entender de. *To be an expert in. To be familiar with.*

Entender en. *To be in charge of. To deal with. To attend to.*

Entendido. *Understood, right.*

entenderse to understand one another; to come to an understanding, to agree, to arrange; to be understood; to be meant.

Entenderse con. *To have to do with. To deal with. To come to an understanding with. To arrange with.*

entendimiento m. understanding.

enteramente entirely, completely, quite, fully.

enterar to inform, to acquaint.

Estamos enterados de sus planes. *We know what his plans are.*

enterarse to learn, to find out.

Entérate de cuándo sale el tren. *Find out when the train leaves.*

Acabo de enterarme de la noticia. *I've just heard the news.*

enternecer to soften; to move, to touch.

enternecerse to pity; to be affected with emotion, to be moved.

ENTERO adj. entire, whole, complete.

Por entero. *Entirely. Completely.*

Color entero. *Solid color.*

enterrar to bury.

entidad f. entity.

entierro m. interment, burial, funeral.

entonación f. intonation; tone.

entonar to tune, to intone.

ENTONCES then, at that time.

Era entonces un niño. *He was a child then.*

Por entonces. *At the time.*

Desde entonces. *Since then. From then on.*

entornar to leave ajar.

ENTRADA f. entrance; entry; admission; ticket; entree.

¿Cuánto cuesta la entrada? *How much is the admission?*

Debemos comprar las entradas ahora mismo. *We have to buy the tickets right away.*

¿Qué desea Ud. como entrada? *What would you like as an entree?*

"Se prohibe la entrada." *"No admittance."*

Entrada libre. *Admission free.*

entrante adj. entering; coming; next (day, week, month, etc.); m. next month.

ENTRAR *to enter, to go in; to fit in.*
¿Se puede entrar? *May I come in?*
Que no entre nadie. *Don't let anyone come in.*
El zapato no me entra, es muy pequeño. *I can't get my foot into this shoe; it's too small.*
ENTRE *between; in; among.*
Lo hicieron entre los dos. *They did it between the two of them.*
Mire entre los papeles. *Look among the papers.*
Parta Ud. 300 entre 3. *Divide 300 by 3.*
Reírse entre sí. *To laugh to oneself.*
Entre manos. *In hand.*
Entre tanto. *Meanwhile.*
Por entre. *Through.*
entreacto *m. intermission.*
entredós *m. insertion (of lace, etc.).*
entrega *f. delivery; surrender.*
entregar *to deliver; to surrender.*
¿A quién ha entregado Ud. la carta? *Who(m) did you give the letter to?*
No han entregado la mercancía todavía. *They haven't delivered the goods yet.*
entregarse *to take to, to abandon oneself to; to give oneself up.*
El criminal se entregó a la policía. *The criminal gave himself up to the police.*
Se ha entregado a la embriaguez. *He's taken to drink.*
entremeter *to place between, to insert.*
entremeterse *to meddle, to intrude, to interfere.*
entremetido *m. meddler, busybody, intruder.*
entrenador *m. coach, trainer.*
entrenamiento *m. training.*
entrenar *to train, to coach.*
entresuelo *m. mezzanine.*
ENTRETANTO *meanwhile.*
ENTRETENER *to entertain, to amuse; to put off, to delay.*
entretenido *adj. pleasant, amusing.*
entretenimiento *m. amusement, entertainment.*
entrevista *f. interview, conference.*
entristecer *to grieve, to be unhappy.*
entristecerse *to be sad, to become sad.*
entrometer. *See entremeter.*
enturbiar *to make muddy; to muddle.*
entusiasmar *to fill with enthusiasm; to elate.*
entusiasmarse *to become enthusiastic.*
entusiasmo *m. enthusiasm.*
entusiasta *adj. enthusiastic; m. and f. enthusiast.*
envasar *to can; to barrel; to bottle.*
envejecer *to make old; to grow old.*
envenenar *to poison.*
ENVIAR *to send; to dispatch.*
¿Puede Ud. enviar mi equipaje al hotel? *Can you send my luggage to the hotel?*
Se lo enviaré hoy mismo. *I'll send it to him today ("this very day.").*
Enviaron a buscar al médico. *They sent someone for the doctor.*
envidia *f. envy.*
envidiable *adj. enviable.*
envidiar *to envy.*
envidioso *adj. envious, jealous.*
envío *m. sending, remittance, shipment.*
enviudar *to become a widow or a widower.*
envoltorio *m. bundle.*
envolver *to wrap up, to make into a package; to surround, to envelop; to disguise.*
época *f. epoch, age, era, period.*
equipaje *m. baggage; equipment; crew (of a ship).*
Coche de equipaje. *Baggage car.*
Equipaje de mano. *Hand luggage.*

equipar *to equip, to furnish.*
equipo *m. equipment; team (sports).*
equis *f. name of the letter x.*
equivocación *f. mistake.*
EQUIVOCADO *adj. mistaken, wrong.*
Estoy equivocado. *I'm mistaken. I'm wrong.*
Ud. está muy equivocado. *You're entirely mistaken.*
equivocar *to mistake.*
EQUIVOCARSE *to be wrong, to make a mistake.*
Se equivoca Ud. *You're wrong. You're making a mistake.*
era *f. era; threshing-floor; garden patch for vegetables.*
ere *f. name of the letter r.*
erario *m. public funds.*
erección *f. erecting, establishment.*
erguir *to erect, to raise.*
erigir *to erect, to build; to establish.*
ERRAR *to err, to go wrong, to make a mistake, to miss; to wander.*
Todos somos susceptibles de errar. *We are all liable to make mistakes. ("We are all subject to error.")*
Errar el tiro. *To miss the target.*
errata *f. erratum, error in writing or printing.*
erre *f. name of the letter rr.*
ERROR *m. error, fault, mistake.*
erudición *f. erudition, learning.*
erudito *adj. erudite, learned; m. scholar, erudite person.*
ESA *(f. of ese) that; pl. esas those.*
Esa mujer. *That woman.*
Vamos por esa calle. *Let's go down that street.*
Esas mujeres. *Those women.*
No se ocupe Ud. de esas cosas. *Don't pay any attention to such things. Don't bother about such things.*
ÉSA *(f. of ése) that, that one, that person, that thing; pl. ésas those.*
Ésa es su mujer. *That (woman) is his wife.*
Deme ésa. *Give me that one.*
En ésa. *In that place. In your town.*
Ni por ésas. *Not even so. Not even for that.*
esbelto *adj. slim, slender; elegant.*
escabeche *m. pickle; pickled fish.*
escabroso *adj. rugged, harsh.*
escala *f. stepladder; scale; port of call.*
Hacer escala en. *To stop. To call at a port.*
escalera *f. staircase; ladder.*
escalofrío *m. chill.*
Tengo escalofríos. *I have the chills.*
escamoteo *m. juggling; swindling.*
escampar *to stop raining; to clear up.*
Si no escampa no iré. *I won't go if it doesn't stop raining.*
escapar *to escape, to flee.*
escaparate *m. show window, glass case; cupboard; cabinet.*
escape *m. escape.*
escarabajo *m. beetle.*
escarbar *to scratch (as fowls); to dig; to poke (fire); to probe.*
escarcha *f. frost.*
escarmentar *to learn by experience, to take warning; to make an example of.*
Ud. debe de escarmentar de eso. *That should be a lesson to you. You ought to profit from that.*
escaso *adj. scarce, scanty; short of.*
Estoy escaso de dinero. *I'm short of money.*
escena *f. stage; scene; view; episode.*
Poner en escena. *To stage (produce) a play.*

escenario *m. stage (theater).*
escenográfico *adj. scenic.*
escéptico *adj. skeptical; m. a skeptic.*
esclavitud *f. slavery.*
esclavo *m. slave.*
escoba *f. broom.*
ESCOGER *to choose, to pick out.*
escogido *adj. selected, choice.*
escolta *f. escort.*
escoltar *to escort.*
escombro *m. debris, rubbish.*
esconder *to hide, to conceal.*
esconderse *to hide, to remain hidden.*
escondido *adj. hidden.*
escopeta *f. shotgun.*
escribano *m. notary.*
ESCRIBIR *to write.*
Escriba claro. *Write clearly.*
¿Cómo se escribe esa palabra? *How is that word written (spelled)? How do you write that word?*
Escriba Ud. a estas señas. *Address it this way. Write this address.*
Escribir a máquina. *To typewrite.*
escrito *adj. written; m. writing; manuscript; communication.*
Por escrito. *In writing. In black and white.*
escritor *m. writer, author.*
escritorio *m. writing desk.*
escritura *f. writing; deed.*
Escritura social. *Deed of a partnership.*
escrutinio *m. scrutiny; election returns.*
escuadra *f. fleet; squad; square (instrument).*
ESCUCHAR *to listen; to heed.*
Escúcheme Ud. *Listen to me.*
No quiere escuchar razones. *He won't listen to reason.*
ESCUELA *f. school; schoolhouse.*
escupir *to spit.*
"Prohibido escupir." *"No spitting."*
escurrir *to drain; to wring; to slip; to glide.*
ese *f. name of the letter s.*
ESE *(demonstrative adjective m.) that; pl. esos those.*
Ese hombre. *That man.*
Esos hombres. *Those men.*
ÉSE *(demonstrative pronoun m.) that, that one, that person, that thing; pl. ésos those.*
Dígale a ése que no venga. *Tell that man not to come.*
Ésos no saben lo que dicen. *Those men don't know what they're talking about.*
Ése ya es otro cantar. *That's a different matter. That's something else (again).*
esencia *f. essence.*
esencial *adj. essential.*
esfera *f. sphere.*
esforzar *to strengthen; to force, to strain.*
esforzarse *to try hard, to endeavor, to strive, to make an effort.*
esfuerzo *m. effort; endeavor.*
Es inútil hacer mayores esfuerzos. *It's useless to continue trying ("to make further efforts").*
esgrima *f. fencing.*
eslabón *m. link (of a chain).*
esmalte *m. enamel.*
esmaltar *to enamel.*
esmeradamente *with the greatest care; nicely.*
esmerado *adj. done with care, carefully done.*
esmeralda *f. emerald.*
esmerar *to polish.*
esmerarse *to do one's best.*
Se esmera en todo. *She tries her hardest in*

everything (she does).

esmeril m. emery.

ESO (neuter of ese and ése) it; that, that thing.
Eso es. That's it.
No es eso. That's not it.
Eso de. That matter of.
A eso de. At about. Towards.
Por eso. Therefore. For that reason.
¿Cómo es eso? How's that?
Eso no me gusta. I don't like that.
Eso no me importa. That makes no difference to me. That doesn't matter to me.

ESPACIO m. space, room; distance.
Un pequeño espacio de terreno. A small piece of land.
Anduvimos por espacio de dos horas. We walked for two hours.

espada f. sword; spade (cards); m. bullfighter who uses a sword, matador.

ESPALDA f. back.
¿Siente Ud. dolor en la espalda? Does your back ache?
A espaldas. Behind one's back.
Dar la espalda. To turn one's back.

espantar to frighten; to chase out.

espantarse to be frightened.

espanto m. fright.

espantosamente frightfully.

espantoso adj. frightful.

España f. Spain.

español adj. and n. Spanish; Spaniard; m. Spanish language.
Yo soy español. I'm a Spaniard.
Aquí se habla español. Spanish spoken here.

esparadrapo m. adhesive tape.

esparcir to scatter; to divulge, to make public.

especial adj. special, particular.
En especial. Especially. Specially. In particular.

especialidad f. specialty.

especie f. species; motive; kind, sort.

espectáculo m. spectacle, show.

espectador m. spectator.

especulación f. speculation.

especular to speculate.

espejo m. looking glass, mirror.
Mírese Ud. al espejo. Look at yourself in the mirror.

espera f. waiting; pause; adjournment.
¿Dónde está la sala de espera? Where's the waiting room?

esperanza f. hope.

ESPERAR to hope; to expect, to wait for.
Así lo espero. I hope so.
Espero que no. I hope not.
Espéreme. Wait for me.
Dígale que espere. Ask him to wait.
¿Espera Ud. visitas? Do you expect company?
Espero volver a verle. I hope I'll see you again.

espeso adj. thick, dense.

espía m. and f. spy.

espiga f. ear (of corn, wheat, etc.); peg.

espina f. thorn; splinter; fishbone; spine.

espinaca f. spinach.

espíritu m. spirit, soul.

espiritual adj. spiritual.

espléndido adj. splendid, magnificent; brilliant.

esplendor m. splendor, magnificence.

ESPOSA f. wife.

esposas f. pl. handcuffs.

ESPOSO m. husband.

espuela f. spur; incentive.

espuma f. foam, froth.

esquela f. note, slip of paper.

esquí m. ski.

ESQUINA f. corner.
La farmacia de la esquina. The drugstore on the corner.
Doblar la esquina. To turn the corner.
A la vuelta de la esquina. Around the corner.

ESTA (f. of este) this; pl. **estas** these.
Esta mujer y aquel hombre son hermanos. This woman and that man are brother and sister.
¿De quién es esta casa? Whose house is this?
Hágalo de esta manera. Do it this way. Do it in this manner.
Esta mañana. This morning.
Esta noche. Tonight.
A estas horas. At the present time. By now.

ESTA (f. of éste) this, this one, the latter; pl. **éstas** these.
En ésta no hay novedad. There's nothing new here.
Ésta y aquélla. This one and that one.

establecer to establish.

establecerse to establish oneself, to set up in business.
Un nuevo médico acaba de establecerse en esta calle. A new doctor has just opened his office ("established himself") on this street.
Esto es lo que establece la ley. This is what the law provides.

establo m. stable.

ESTACIÓN f. station; railroad station; season of the year.
¿Dónde está la estación? Where is the station?
El invierno es la estación más fría del año. Winter is the coldest season of the year.

estacionamiento m. parking.

estacionar to stop; to park.

ESTADO m. state; condition.
¿Cómo sigue el estado del enfermo? How is the patient's condition?
En buen estado. In good condition.
Estado de cuenta. Statement (of an account).
Hombre de estado. Statesman.
Ministerio de Estado. State Department.
Estado Mayor. General Staff.
Estado de guerra. State of war.
Estados Unidos de América m. pl. United States of America.

estafa f. fraud, trick, swindle.

estampa f. picture; print; stamp.

estampilla f. postage stamp (Amer.).

estancia f. stay; ranch (in Latin America).

estanco adj. tight, water-tight; m. cigar store (Spain); monopoly.

estanque m. pond; reservoir.

estante m. shelf.
Estante para libros. Bookcase.

estaño m. tin (metal).

ESTAR to be.
¿Cómo está Ud? How are you?
Estoy bien, gracias. I'm well, thank you.
Estoy cansado. I'm tired.
Estamos listos. We're ready.
¿Qué está haciendo? What are you doing?
Estoy afeitándome. I'm shaving.
¿Dónde está Juan? Where's John?
Está en la oficina. He's at the office.
He estado en Washington. I've been in Washington.
¿Dónde está el correo? Where's the post office?
Está cerca. It's near.
Está en la calle de Alcalá. It's on Alcala Street.
Boston está en los Estados Unidos. Boston is in the United States.

Hay que estar allí a las nueve. We must be there at nine.
Estaré de vuelta a las cinco. I'll be back at five o'clock.
¿A cuánto estamos? What's the date?
Hoy estamos a diez. Today's the tenth.
La ventana está abierta. The window's open.
Está muy nublado. It's very cloudy.
Estar de viaje. To be on a journey.
Estar de prisa. To be in a hurry.
Estar de pie. To stand. To be on one's feet.

estatua f. statue.

estatura f. stature, height of a person.

estatuto m. statute, law, by-law.

ESTE m. east.
Esa calle está al este de la ciudad. This street is on the east side of the city.

ESTE (demonstrative adj. m.) this; pl. **estos** these.
Este hombre. This man.
Estos libros. These books.

ESTE (demonstrative pron. m.) this, this one; pl. **éstos** these.
Éste es el mío y aquél es el tuyo. This one is mine and that one is yours.
Éstos y aquéllos. These and those.
Éstos no saben lo que dicen. These men don't know what they're talking about.

estenógrafa f. stenographer.

estibador m. stevedore, longshoreman.

estilar to be customary, to be in the habit of.

estilarse to be in style.
Ese modelo ya no se estila. That model is not worn any more (is not in style any longer).

ESTILO m. style, manner; method, way.
Por el estilo. Of the kind. Like that. In that manner.
Y así por el estilo. And so forth.

estilográfica f. fountain pen.

estima f. esteem, respect; dead reckoning (navigation).

estimación f. estimation, valuation.

estimar to esteem; to estimate.
Era muy estimado de cuantos le conocían. He was held in esteem by all who knew him.
Se estima que este trabajo costará mil dólares. It's estimated that this work will cost a thousand dollars.

estimular to stimulate.

estímulo m. stimulus.

estirar to stretch; to pull.

estirarse to stretch, to put on airs.

estirpe f. race, stock, origin.

ESTO (neuter) this; this thing.
¿Qué es esto? What's this?
¿Para qué sirve esto? What's this for?
Esto es mío. This belongs to me.
Todo esto es muy divertido. All this is very amusing.
Esto es todo cuanto tengo que decir. This is all I have to say.
Por esto. For this. Hereby. Therefore. For this reason. On account of this.
En esto. At this time. At this juncture.
Con esto. Herewith.
Esto es. That is. Namely.

estocada f. stab, thrust.

estofado m. stew; stewed meat.

estorbar to hinder, to be in the way.
¿Le estorba a Ud. esta maleta? Is this suitcase in your way?

estómago m. stomach.

estornudar to sneeze.

estornudo m. sneeze.

estrategia f. strategy.
estratégico adj. strategic.
estrechar to tighten; to narrow; to squeeze.
  Estrechar la mano. To shake hands.
estrechez f. tightness, narrowness.
estrecho adj. tight, narrow.
estrella f. star.
estrellar to dash, to hurl, to shatter; to fry (eggs).
  Por poco nos estrellamos. We had a narrow escape.
  ¿Quiere los huevos estrellados? Do you want your eggs fried?
estremecer to shake, to tremble.
estremecerse to shudder, to tremble, to shake.
estremecimiento m. tremor; shudder; trembling, shaking; thrill.
estrenar to wear or put on something for the first time; to show for the first time.
  Estrené este traje ayer. I wore this suit for the first time yesterday.
estrenarse to appear for the first time, to make one's debut.
estreno m. première, first public performance.
estreñimiento m. constipation.
estribo m. stirrup; running board.
  Perder los estribos. To lose one's temper.
estricto adj. strict.
estropear to ruin, to damage, to spoil.
estructura f. structure.
estruendo m. loud noise, din, clatter; turmoil; ostentation.
estrujar to squeeze, to press.
estuche m. case, small box, kit; sheath.
estudiante m. and f. student.
ESTUDIAR to study.
ESTUDIO m. study; examination; consideration; survey; office; studio.
  Están haciendo un estudio de la situación. They're making a survey of the situation.
  Estar en estudio. To be under consideration (study).
  El estudio del profesor. The professor's office (study).
  El estudio del pintor. The painter's studio.
estudioso adj. studious.
estufa f. stove; heater.
  Arrímese a la estufa. Draw up (come closer) to the stove.
estupendo adj. stupendous, wonderful, terrific, great.
estupidez f. stupidity.
estúpido adj. stupid.
etapa f. daily ration, a day's march; stage, halt, stop.
etcétera f. et cetera.
éter m. ether.
eternidad f. eternity.
eterno adj. eternal, everlasting, endless.
ética f. ethics.
ético adj. ethical, moral.
etiqueta f. etiquette; label.
  Vestido de etiqueta. Evening dress.
  ¿Qué dice la etiqueta de la botella? What does the label on the bottle say?
evacuación f. evacuation.
evacuar to evacuate; to quit; to vacate; to dispose of.
evadir to evade; to avoid.
evaluación f. evaluation.
evaluar to appraise, to value.
evalúo m. appraisal.
evangelio m. gospel.
evaporar to evaporate.

evasión f. evasion, escape.
evasiva f. pretext, excuse; subterfuge.
evasivo adj. evasive.
evento m. event.
eventual adj. eventual.
evidencia f. evidence.
  Poner en evidencia. To make evident (clear, obvious). To make conspicuous. To display, reveal, show. To demonstrate.
evidente adj. evident.
evitable adj. avoidable.
EVITAR to avoid; to spare.
  Evitar un disgusto. To avoid an unpleasant situation.
evocar to evoke.
evolución f. evolution.
exactamente exactly.
exactitud f. accuracy.
EXACTO adj. exact, just, accurate, correct.
exageración f. exaggeration.
exagerar to exaggerate.
exaltación f. exaltation.
exaltar to exalt, to praise.
exaltarse to become excited.
examen m. examination; test.
EXAMINAR to examine, to investigate, to look into, to study.
exasperación f. exasperation.
exasperar to exasperate.
excedente adj. excessive.
exceder to exceed.
excederse to overstep, to go too far.
excelencia f. excellence.
EXCELENTE adj. excellent.
excelso adj. lofty, exalted.
excepción f. exception.
excepcional adj. exceptional, unusual.
excepto except that, excepting.
exceptuar to except, to exempt.
excesivo adj. excessive, too much.
exceso m. excess, surplus.
  En exceso. In excess.
  Exceso de equipaje. Excess luggage.
excitable adj. excitable.
excitación f. excitement.
excitante adj. exciting.
excitar to excite, to stir up.
exclamación f. exclamation.
exclamar to exclaim.
excluir to exclude, to keep out; to rule out.
exclusión f. exclusion.
exclusiva f. exclusive (right); refusal, rejection.
exclusivamente exclusively.
exclusive exclusively.
excursión f. excursion, trip.
excusa f. excuse, apology.
excusable adj. excusable.
excusado adj. excused, exempted; m. toilet.
excusar to excuse; to apologize; to exempt.
  Excusamos decir. It's needless to say.
  Excusarse de. To apologize for.
exención f. exemption.
exento adj. exempt, free; duty free.
  Estar exento de. To be exempt from. To be free from.
exhalar to exhale.
exhibición f. exhibition.
exhibir to exhibit.
exhortar to exhort, to admonish.
exigencia f. urgent need; demand for immediate action or attention, exigency.
exigente adj. demanding, hard to please.
  Es muy exigente. He's a very hard person to

please.
  No seas tan exigente. Don't be so difficult (demanding, hard to please, particular).
exigir to demand; to require; to exact.
  Lo exigen las circunstancias. The situation requires it.
exiguo adj. small, scanty, exiguous.
eximir to exempt, to excuse.
existencia f. existence; stock, supply.
  En existencia. In stock.
  Agotarse las existencias. To be out of stock.
existente adj. existing, existent.
EXISTIR to exist, to be.
  En mi opinión existen pruebas bastante claras de ello. There are, it seems to me, pretty strong proofs of it.
ÉXITO m. end, outcome; success.
  Buen éxito. Success.
  Le felicito por el éxito obtenido. I congratulate you on your success.
expedición f. expedition; shipment.
  Gastos de expedición. Shipping expenses.
expedidor m. dispatcher; sender.
expediente m. expedient; document, dossier; proceedings.
  Incoar expediente. To start proceedings.
EXPEDIR to expedite; to dispatch, to send, to forward; to issue; to make out (a check, etc.).
expeler to expel.
expendedor m. dealer, retailer, seller.
expensas f. pl. expenses, charges, costs.
  A expensas de. At the expense of.
experiencia f. experience; trial.
experimentar to experience; to experiment.
experimento m. experiment.
experto adj. experienced; able; m. expert.
explicable adj. explainable.
explicación f. explanation.
EXPLICAR to explain.
  Déjeme Ud. que se lo explique. Let me explain it to you.
explicarse to explain oneself; to account for.
  No podemos explicárnoslo. We can't make it out (account for it).
explicativo adj. explanatory.
explícito adj. explicit.
exploración f. exploration.
explorador m. explorer, scout.
explorar to explore.
explosión f. explosion, outburst.
  Hacer explosión. To explode.
explotar to exploit; to operate; to profiteer.
exponente m. and f. exponent; exhibitor.
exponer to expound, to explain; to make clear; to expose.
exponerse to expose oneself; to run a risk.
exportación f. export.
exportador adj. exporting; m. exporter.
  Casa exportadora. Export house (firm).
exportar to export.
exposición f. exposition, show, exhibition; explanation; peril, risk, exposure; statement.
expositor m. exhibitor; expounder, expositor.
expresar to express; to set forth, to state.
expresarse to express oneself.
expresión f. expression.
expresivo adj. expressive.
expreso adj. express; clear; m. express (train); special delivery.
exprimidor m. squeezer; wringer.
exprimir to squeeze.
  Exprimir un limón. To squeeze a lemon.
expuesto adj. explained, stated; exposed (to);

liable (to).

Lo expuesto. *What has been stated.*

Todos estamos expuestos a equivocarnos. *Anyone is liable (apt) to make a mistake.*

expulsar *to expel, to eject, to throw out.*

expulsión *f. expulsion.*

exquisito *adj. exquisite, excellent, choice.*

extender *to extend, to stretch out; to make out (a check, a document).*

extensión *f. extension, extent.*

En toda su extensión. *To the full extent. In every sense.*

extensivo *adj. extensive, ample, far-reaching.*

extenso *adj. extensive, vast.*

extenuación *f. extenuation.*

extenuar *to extenuate.*

exterior *adj. exterior; foreign.*

Comercio exterior. *Foreign trade.*

externo *adj. external, on the outside.*

extinguir *to extinguish; to put out.*

extra *extra.*

extractar *to extract, to abridge, to summarize.*

extracto *m. extract, abridgment, summary.*

extraer *to extract, to pull out.*

EXTRANJERO *adj. foreign; m. foreigner, alien.*

Estar en el extranjero. *To be abroad.*

Ir al extranjero. *To go abroad.*

extrañar *to wonder at, to find strange.*

No es de extrañar que. *It's not surprising that.*

extrañarse *to be surprised.*

Me extraña su conducta. *I'm surprised at his behavior.*

extrañeza *f. wonder, surprise.*

extraño *strange, rare, odd, queer.*

Es un hombre extraño. *He's a queer fellow.*

extraoficial *adj. unofficial, off the record.*

extraordinario *adj. extraordinary.*

Tiene una memoria extraordinaria. *He has an extraordinary memory.*

extravagancia *f. folly; extravagance.*

extravagante *adj. queer, extravagant.*

extraviado *adj. astray; missing; mislaid.*

extraviar *to mislead; to mislay.*

extraviarse *to go astray; to get lost.*

extravío *m. straying; deviation, misplacement; misguidance.*

extremadamente *extremely, exceedingly.*

extremar *to go to extremes.*

extremarse *to exert oneself to the utmost.*

extremidad *f. extremity; very end.*

extremo *adj. and n. extreme, last, very end.*

En caso extremo. *As a last resort.*

Al extremo de que. *To such an extent that.*

De extremo a extremo. *From end to end.*

En extremo (Por extremo). *Extremely.*

F

fa *m. fa, F (fourth note in the musical scale).*

fabada *f. dish of pork and beans.*

fábrica *f. factory, mill, plant; fabrication; structure, building.*

Precio de fábrica. *Factory price.*

Marca de fábrica. *Trade mark.*

fabricación *f. manufacturing.*

fabricante *m. manufacturer.*

fabricar *to manufacture, to make; to build.*

fábula *f. fable, story, tale.*

fabuloso *adj. fabulous; incredible.*

FÁCIL *adj. easy.*

Parece fácil pero es difícil. *It looks easy but it's difficult.*

Es la cosa más fácil del mundo. *It's the easiest thing in the world.*

Nada hay más fácil que eso. *Nothing could be easier than that.*

facilidad *f. ease, facility.*

Con facilidad. *Easily. With ease.*

Facilidad de pagos. *Easy terms. Easy payments.*

facilitar *to facilitate, to make easy; to supply, to provide.*

Facilitar dinero. *To supply (provide) money.*

fácilmente *easily.*

A mí no se me engaña tan fácilmente. *You can't fool me that easily.*

No puedo expresarme fácilmente. *I can't express myself easily.*

factor *m. factor, element; agent; baggage master.*

factura *f. invoice, bill.*

¿A cuánto monta la factura? *What does the bill amount to?*

La factura sube a mil pesetas. *The invoice amounts to one thousand pesetas.*

facturar *to bill, to invoice; to check (baggage).*

Tendrá que facturar el baúl. *You'll have to check the trunk.*

facultad *f. faculty.*

facultar *to authorize, to empower.*

facultativo *adj. optional; m. physician.*

facha *f. appearance, look.*

fachada *f. façade; bearing (of a person).*

faena *f. work, task, labor.*

faja *f. band; girdle.*

fajar *to swaddle; to girdle.*

fajo *m. bundle; roll (bills).*

falda *f. skirt; the lap; slope (of a hill).*

falsear *to falsify; to forge, to distort, to adulterate.*

falsedad *f. falsehood, untruth.*

falsificación *f. falsification; forgery.*

falso *adj. false; incorrect; deceitful; counterfeit.*

Esta noticia es falsa. *This news is false.*

Me han dado una moneda falsa. *They've given me a counterfeit coin.*

FALTA *f. fault; defect; need; lack; absence, mistake.*

Tenemos que disculpar sus faltas. *We must excuse his faults.*

Yo le corregiré las faltas. *I'll correct the mistakes.*

Hacer falta. *To be needed. To be necessary.*

¿Qué le hace falta? *What do you need?*

No hace falta. *It's not necessary. It's not needed.*

Sin falta. *Without fail.*

Tener falta de. *To be in need of.*

Por falta de. *For lack of. Owing to the shortage of.*

Falta de pago. *Non-payment.*

FALTAR *to be lacking; to be absent; to miss (classes); to fail; not to fulfill one's promise; to offend, to be rude.*

Aquí faltan tres libros. *Three books are missing here.*

Ud. faltó a su palabra. *You didn't keep your word.*

Faltó a la oficina esta mañana. *He wasn't (present) at the office this morning.*

Faltó a su padre. *He was rude to his father.*

No faltes a clase. *Don't miss school.*

Faltar a la verdad. *To lie.*

No faltaba más. *That's the last straw.*

falto *adj. wanting, lacking, short of.*

Estar falto de. *To be short of.*

Falto de peso. *Underweight. Lacking the proper weight.*

falla *f. failure; fault.*

fallar *to deliver a verdict, pronounce a sentence; to fail.*

fallecer *to die.*

Falleció repentinamente. *He died suddenly.*

fallo *m. sentence, verdict, judgment, finding, decision.*

El juez dió el fallo. *The judge gave the verdict.*

fama *f. fame; reputation; rumor.*

FAMILIA *f. family; household.*

familiar *adj. familiar; m. close friend, relative.*

famoso *adj. famous; excellent.*

fanático *adj. fanatic.*

fanfarrón *adj. boasting; m. bully, boaster, braggart.*

fanfarronada *f. boast, bragging, bluff.*

fanfarronear *to boast, to brag.*

fango *m. mire, mud.*

fangoso *adj. muddy.*

fantasía *f. fantasy, fancy.*

fantasma *m. phantom; scarecrow; ghost.*

fantástico *adj. fantastic.*

fantoche *m. puppet; ridiculous fellow.*

fardo *m. bale of goods, parcel, bundle.*

faringe *f. pharynx.*

farmacéutico *m. pharmacist, druggist.*

farmacia *f. pharmacy, drugstore.*

faro *m. lighthouse; beacon; headlight.*

farol *m. lantern; street lamp; light.*

Farol delantero. *Headlight.*

Farol trasero (de cola). *Taillight.*

farolero *adj. conceited, showing-off; m. a lamplighter.*

farsa *f. farce.*

farsante *adj. and n. impostor.*

fascinar *to fascinate, to charm; to allure.*

fase *f. phase; aspect.*

fastidiar *to annoy, to disgust.*

fastidio *m. disgust, annoyance; boredom.*

fastidioso *adj. squeamish; annoying, disgusting; tiresome.*

fatal *adj. fatal.*

fatiga *f. tiredness, fatigue, weariness, toil.*

fatigado *adj. tired, fatigued.*

fatigar *to tire; to annoy.*

fatigoso *adj. tiring; tiresome.*

fatuo *adj. fatuous, stupid, silly.*

fauna *f. fauna.*

fausto *adj. happy, fortunate; m. splendor.*

FAVOR *m. favor, good turn, service; good graces.*

Me hace Ud. un gran favor. *You're doing me a great favor (service).*

¡Es mucho favor que me hace! *You're flattering me!*

Por favor. *Please.*

Me hace Ud. el favor. *Please. If you please.*

Hágame Ud. el favor de. *Please ("Do me the favor of").*

Hágame el favor de ir con él. *Please go with him.*

Haga el favor de pasarme la sal. *Please pass me the salt.*

Haga el favor de indicarme el camino. *Please show me the way.*

Por favor, póngame en comunicación con el número . . . *Please connect me with number . . .*

Haga el favor de repetir lo que dijo. *Please repeat what you said.*

A favor de. *In favor of.*

favorable *adj. favorable.*

favorecer *to favor; to help.*

favorito *adj. favorite.*

faz *f. face, front.*

FE *f. faith; credit.*

Lo hizo de buena fe. *He did it in good faith.*

Lo dijo de mala fe. *He said it deceitfully.*

La fe católica. *The Catholic religion.*
La fe de bautismo. *Birth certificate.*
Dar fe. *To attest. To certify. To give credit.*
A fe mía. *Upon my word.*
FEBRERO m. *February.*
fecundo adj. *fruitful, productive, fecund, fertile, prolific.*
FECHA f. *date.*
¿Qué fecha es hoy? *What's the date today? What's today's date?*
¿En qué fecha estamos? *What day of the month is it?*
Hasta la fecha. *To date. Up to today.*
Para estas fechas. *By this time.*
A dos meses de la fecha. *Two months from today.*
fechar *to date (a letter).*
La carta está fechada el seis del corriente. *The letter is dated the sixth of this month.*
fechoría f. *misdeed, a wicked action.*
federación f. *federation.*
felicidad f. *happiness.*
¡Muchas felicidades! *Congratulations!*
felicitación f. *congratulation.*
felicitar *to congratulate, to felicitate.*
Le felicito a Ud. *Congratulations! ("I congratulate you.")*
FELIZ adj. *happy, fortunate.*
¡Feliz año nuevo! *Happy New Year!*
¡Feliz cumpleaños! *Happy birthday. Many happy returns of the day.*
¡Que las tenga Ud. muy felices! *Many happy returns of the day.*
Fué el día más feliz de mi vida. *It was the happiest day of my life.*
Vivían felices. *They lived happily.*
Feliz idea. *Clever (happy) idea.*
femenino adj. *feminine.*
fémur m. *femur, thigh bone.*
fenómeno m. *phenomenon.*
feo adj. *ugly, unpleasant.*
feria f. *fair, show.*
feriado adj. *relating to a holiday.*
Día feriado. *Holiday.*
fermentación f. *fermentation.*
fermentar *to ferment.*
fermento m. *ferment; leaven.*
feroz adj. *ferocious, fierce, cruel.*
férreo adj. *iron, ferrous.*
ferretería f. *hardware; hardware store.*
ferrocarril m. *railway, railroad.*
Por ferrocarril. *By railway.*
fértil adj. *fertile, fruitful.*
fervor m. *fervor, zeal.*
festejar *to celebrate.*
festividad f. *festivity; holiday.*
festivo adj. *festive, gay, merry.*
Día festivo. *Holiday.*
fiado adj. *on credit.*
Comprar al fiado. *To buy on credit.*
Dar fiado. *To give credit. To sell on credit.*
Se lo podemos dar fiado. *We can let you have it on credit.*
fiador m. *guarantor; stop, catch.*
fiambre m. *cold meat, cold cuts, cold lunch.*
fianza f. *guarantee, security, bail, bond.*
fiar *to trust, to confide; to sell on credit.*
Se lo puedo fiar. *I can sell it to you on credit.*
No me fío de él. *I don't trust him.*
Puede Ud. fiarse de su palabra. *You may rely (depend) on his word.*
fibra f. *fiber.*
ficha f. *chip (used in games); card, token.*

fideo m. *vermicelli, noodle.*
fiebre f. *fever; rush, excitement.*
fiel adj. *faithful, loyal; true, right; m. pointer, needle (of a balance, scale).*
fiera f. *wild beast.*
fiero adj. *fierce, cruel.*
fierro m. *iron (Amer.).*
FIESTA f. *feast, party; holiday.*
¡Qué fiesta más agradable! *What a lovely party!*
Mañana es día de fiesta. *Tomorrow is a holiday.*
figura f. *figure, form, appearance, image.*
Tiene muy linda figura. *She has a nice figure.*
figurar *to figure; to appear.*
No figura en la lista de invitados. *His name was not on the guest list.*
figurarse *to imagine, to fancy.*
¡Figúrese! *Just imagine!*
figurín m. *costume; (fig) elegant person.*
fijar *to fix, set (a date); to post (a notice).*
"Prohibido fijar carteles." *"Post no bills."*
fijarse *to look at, to take notice, to pay attention to.*
Fíjese en la hora. *Look at the time. Look what time it is! Watch the time!*
¿Por qué no se fija Ud. mejor en lo que hace? *Why don't you pay more attention to what you're doing?*
fijo adj. *fixed, firm, fast; permanent.*
Precio fijo. *Fixed price.*
fila f. *row, line, rank.*
En fila. *In line. In a row.*
Una fila de sillas. *A row of chairs.*
filete m. *fillet, hem; tenderloin, filet mignon.*
filiación f. *relationship; file, record, description (of a person).*
filial adj. *filial; f. branch.*
film m. *film, picture, movie.*
filmadora m. *movie camera.*
filmar *to film, to make a moving picture.*
filosofía f. *philosophy.*
filósofo m. *philosopher.*
filtrar *to filter, to strain.*
filtrarse *to leak out, to leak through.*
filtro m. *filter.*
FIN m. *end; object, aim, purpose.*
A fin de mes. *At the end of the month.*
A fines de año. *In the latter part of the year. Towards the end of the year.*
Dar fin a. *To finish.*
Por fin. *Finally.*
Al fin. *At last.*
Sin fin. *Endless.*
Al fin y al cabo. *At last. In the end. At length. After all. In the long run.*
Con el fin de. *For the purpose of. With the object of.*
A fin de. *In order that.*
Con este fin. *To this end. With this end (purpose) in view.*
finado m. *deceased, late.*
FINAL adj. *final, last; m. end; pl. finals (in a contest).*
La letra final de una palabra. *The last letter of a word.*
Punto final. *Period. Full stop.*
Al final. *At the end. At the foot (of a page).*
Al final de la calle. *At the end of the street.*
El final de la línea. *The end of the line (streetcar, bus, etc.).*
Final de trayecto). *Last stop.*
finalizar *to finish; to conclude, to expire.*
Al finalizar el contrato. *When the contract expires.*

FINALMENTE *finally, at last.*
financiero adj. *financial; m. financier.*
finca f. *farm; real estate, property.*
fineza f. *fineness; delicacy; courtesy.*
fingir *to feign, to pretend.*
fino adj. *fine, delicate; cunning, keen; polite.*
Esta es una tela muy fina. *This is a very fine material.*
Es un niño muy fino. *He's a very polite boy.*
FIRMA f. *signature; firm; business concern.*
Trabaja con una firma norteamericana. *He works for a North American firm.*
El documento es nulo si no lleva la firma del cónsul. *The document isn't valid without the consul's signature.*
firmar *to sign.*
firme adj. *firm, fast, stable, secure, resolute.*
Mantenerse firme. *To stand one's ground.*
Color firme. *Fast color.*
fiscal adj. *fiscal; m. public prosecutor.*
física f. *physics.*
físico adj. *physical, m. physicist, face; physique.*
Tiene un defecto físico. *He has a physical defect.*
fisiología f. *physiology.*
fisonomía f. *features, physiognomy.*
flaco adj. *lean, thin, weak; m. weak point.*
flagrante adj. *flagrant.*
En flagrante. *In the very act. Red-handed.*
flamear *to flame; to flutter (flag).*
flan m. *custard.*
flaqueza f. *weakness, feebleness.*
flauta f. *flute.*
fleco m. *fringe, purl; bang (hair) (Mex.).*
flecha f. *arrow, dart.*
fletar *to charter (a ship, etc.).*
flete m. *freight, freightage.*
flexible adj. *flexible, pliable; docile.*
flirtear *to flirt.*
flojo adj. *lax, slack, lazy; loose; not tight; light.*
Es un hombre flojo. *He's a lazy man.*
La cuerda está floja. *The string's loose.*
Vino flojo. *Light wine.*
flor f. *flower.*
¿Cómo se llama esta flor? *What's the name of this flower?*
Estar en flor. *To be in blossom.*
Echar (decir) flores. *To flatter (a woman).*
florecer *to blossom; to bloom.*
florero m. *flower vase, flower stand.*
florista m. *and f. florist.*
flota f. *fleet.*
flote m. *floating.*
A flote. *Afloat.*
Sostenerse a flote. *To keep afloat.*
flúido adj. *fluid, fluent; m. fluid.*
foca f. *seal.*
foco m. *focus.*
fogón m. *fireplace; cooking stove.*
fogonazo m. *flash (of a gun).*
fogoso adj. *fiery, impetuous.*
folio m. *leaf of a book, folio.*
folklore m. *folklore.*
folletín m. *feuilleton, a novel in installments, serial story in a newspaper.*
folleto m. *pamphlet.*
fomenta *to foment, to encourage.*
fonda f. *inn, hotel, boarding house.*
fondear *to cast anchor.*
FONDO m. *bottom; background; fund.*
Artículo de fondo. *Editorial.*
En el fondo del pozo. *At the bottom of the well.*
Los dibujos son de color pero el fondo es

blanco. *The designs are in color (are colored) but the background is white.*

Conocer a fondo. *To know well. To be thoroughly acquainted with.*

En el fondo. *At heart. At bottom. Basically. As a matter of fact.*

Irse a fondo. *To sink. To go to the bottom.*

Fondos de reserva. *Reserve funds.*

fonética *f. phonetics.*

fonógrafo *m. phonograph.*

forastero *adj. foreign, strange; m. stranger, foreigner.*

forjar *to forge; to frame.*

FORMA *f. form, shape; mold; manner, way.*

La forma de esta caja es interesante. *The shape of this box is interesting.*

No hay forma de hacerlo. *There's no way of doing it.*

¿De qué forma se gana la vida? *How does he make a living?*

En forma de. *In the shape of.*

En forma. *In due form.*

De forma que. *In order that. In such a manner that.*

formación *f. formation.*

formal *adj. formal, proper, serious.*

formalidad *f. formality.*

formar *to form; to shape.*

La parada se formará a las doce. *The parade will form at twelve o'clock.*

Formaron una sociedad. *They formed a society.*

formarse *to take form, to develop, to grow.*

Formarse una idea. *To get an idea.*

formidable *adj. formidable.*

fórmula *f. formula; recipe.*

formular *to formulate.*

formulario *m. formulary; form, blank.*

Llene este formulario. *Fill out this application blank.*

forrar *to line (clothes, etc.); to cover (books).*

El abrigo está forrado por dentro. *The coat is lined inside.*

fortalecer *to fortify, to strengthen.*

fortaleza *f. fortress, stronghold; strength, fortitude.*

fortificación *f. fortification.*

fortificar *to fortify, to strengthen.*

fortitud *f. strength, fortitude.*

fortuito *adj. fortuitous, accidental.*

Un caso fortuito. *An accident.*

fortuna *f. fortune.*

Por fortuna. *Fortunately.*

forzar *to force, to compel, to oblige.*

forzosamente *necessarily, of necessity.*

forzoso *adj. compulsory, compelling.*

forzudo *adj. strong, robust.*

fosa *f. pit, hole; grave.*

fósforo *m. phosphorus; match (to light with).*

¿Tiene Ud. fósforos? *Do you have some matches?*

foto *f. (abbreviation of* **fotografía**) *photo, picture.*

Las fotos salieron bien. *The pictures came out all right.*

fotografía *f. photography; photograph, photo, picture.*

fotografiar *to photograph.*

fotógrafo *m. photographer.*

frac *m. dress coat.*

fracasar *to fail, to come out badly.*

fracaso *m. failure.*

La función fué un fracaso. *The play was a failure.*

fracción *f. fraction.*

fragancia *f. fragrance, pleasing odor.*

fragante *adj. fragrant.*

frágil *adj. fragile, brittle; weak, frail (morally).*

fragmento *m. fragment.*

fragua *f. forge.*

fraguar *to forge; to scheme, to plot.*

fraile *m. friar.*

frambuesa *f. raspberry.*

francamente *frankly, openly.*

francés *adj. French; m. Frenchman; French language, f. Frenchwoman.*

FRANCO *adj. frank, free, open, plain; m. French franc.*

Puerto franco. *Free port.*

Franco de porte. *Freight prepaid.*

franela *f. flannel.*

franquear *to put a stamp on a letter, to prepay postage; to clear from obstacle; to free (a slave).*

¿Ha franqueado las cartas? *Did you put stamps on the letters?*

Franquear el paso. *To clear the way.*

franqueo *m. postage.*

franqueza *f. frankness, sincerity.*

Hable con franqueza. *Speak frankly.*

franquicia *f. franchise; exemption from duties (taxes).*

frasco *m. flask, bottle.*

frase *f. sentence.*

Esta frase no está bien escrita. *This sentence isn't well written.*

fraternidad *f. fraternity, brotherhood.*

frazada *f. blanket.*

frecuencia *f. frequency.*

Se veían con frecuencia. *They saw one another frequently.*

frecuentar *to frequent, to visit often.*

Este bar es muy frecuentado por mis amigos. *My friends go to this bar a lot.*

frecuente *adj. frequent.*

frecuentemente *often, frequently.*

fregar *to scrub; to wash dishes; to annoy.*

freír *to fry.*

frejol *m. kidney bean. See frijol.*

FRENAR *to put on the brakes, to slow up or stop by using a brake; to bridle; to curb.*

¡Frene! *Put on the brakes!*

frenético *adj. mad, frantic.*

freno *m. brake; bridle, bit, curb.*

Quite el freno. *Release the brake.*

FRENTE *f. forehead; face; m. front; façade.*

En frente. *In front. Opposite. Across the way.*

Estar al frente de. *To be in charge of.*

Hacer frente a. *To face. To cope with.*

Frente a frente. *Face to face.*

fresa *f. strawberry.*

fresco *adj. cool; fresh; recent; bold; forward; m. fresco (painting); fresh air, breeze; a fresh person.*

El agua está fresca. *The water is cool.*

Ese es un fresco. *He's very fresh. He's a very impudent person.*

Tomar el fresco. *To go out for some fresh air.*

Aire fresco. *Fresh air.*

Un fresco agradable. *A nice breeze.*

frescura *f. freshness.*

fricasé *m. fricassee.*

fricción *f. friction, rubbing.*

frijol *m. kidney bean.*

FRÍO *adj. and n. cold.*

Tengo mucho frío. *I'm very cold.*

Hace frío. *It's cold (of the weather).*

Está frío. *It's cold (of an object).*

Sangre fría. 1. *Cold blood.* 2. *Sang-froid. Presence of mind.*

Le mataron a sangre fría. *They killed him in*

cold blood.

friolento *adj. allergic to cold.*

friolera *f. trifle.*

fritada *f. dish of fried fish or meat.*

frito *adj. fried.*

frontera *f. frontier, border.*

frontón *m. handball court; the wall of a handball court.*

frotar *to rub.*

fructífero *adj. fruitful.*

fructificar *to bear fruit; to yield profit.*

frugal *adj. frugal, thrifty.*

fruncir *to pleat; to knit (the brows).*

Fruncir las cejas. *To knit one's brows. To frown. To scowl.*

frustrar *to frustrate.*

fruta *f. fruit.*

frutería *f. fruit store.*

frutilla *f. strawberry (Chile, Arg., Peru).*

FUEGO *m. fire.*

No deje apagarse el fuego. *Don't let the fire go out.*

Prender fuego a. *To set fire to.*

Hacer fuego. *To fire (a gun).*

Armas de fuego. *Firearms.*

Fuegos artificiales. *Fireworks.*

FUENTE *f. spring, fountain, source; platter, large shallow dish.*

Lo sé de buena fuente. *I have it from a reliable ("good") source. I have it on good authority.*

FUERA *out, outside.*

Hay más gente fuera que dentro. *There are more people outside than inside.*

¡Fuera! *Get out!*

Estar fuera. *To be absent. To be out.*

Por fuera. *On the outside.*

Hacia fuera. *Outwards. Towards the outside.*

Fuera de eso. *Besides. Moreover. In addition (to that).*

Fuera de sí. *Frantic. Beside oneself.*

FUERTE *adj. strong; powerful; excessive; heavy (meal); loud (voice); deep (breath); hard; violent (quarrel); firm, fast; m. forte, strong point; fort, fortress.*

No hable tan fuerte. *Don't speak so loud.*

Este boxeador es más fuerte que el otro. *This boxer is stronger than the other one.*

Es una tela muy fuerte. *This material is very strong.*

Le pegó muy fuerte. *He hit him very hard.*

Respire Ud. fuerte. *Breathe deeply.*

Hubo un fuerte altercado. *There was a violent quarrel.*

Comer fuerte. *To eat too much. To have a heavy meal.*

La música es su fuerte. *Music is his forte.*

FUERZA *f. force, strength, power.*

De por fuerza. *Forcibly. Necessarily. By force.*

Por fuerza. *By force.*

A fuerza de. *By dint of.*

A viva fuerza. *By main force.*

A la fuerza. *By sheer force.*

Por fuerza mayor. *Owing to circumstances beyond one's control. Act of God.*

Fuerza motriz. *Motive power.*

Fuerzas armadas. *Armed forces.*

fuga *f. escape; flight.*

Poner en fuga. *To put to flight. To rout.*

fugarse *to escape, to run away, to flee.*

fugaz *adj. short-lived, passing soon, not lasting, transient.*

fugitivo *adj. and n. fugitive.*

FULANO *m. So-and-so, What's-his-name.*

El señor fulano de tal. *Mr. So-and-So. Mr. What's-his-name.*
fumador *m. smoker.*
fumar *to smoke (cigarettes, etc.).*
Se prohibe fumar. *No smoking.*
función *f. function, performance, play.*
funcionar *to function; to work, to run (a machine).*
Esta máquina no funciona. *This machine doesn't work.*
Funcionar bien. *To be in good working condition.*
funcionario *m. official, officer, person who holds a public position.*
funda *f. pillowcase; sheath; case (of a pistol).*
Funda de almohada. *Pillowcase.*
fundación *f. foundation.*
fundador *m. founder.*
fundamental *adj. fundamental.*
fundamento *m. foundation, base, ground, cause.*
Sin fundamento. *Groundless.*
Carecer de fundamento. *To be without foundation, logic or reason.*
fundar *to found, to base.*
Han fundado una nueva sociedad. *They've founded a new society.*
fundarse *to base something on.*
¿En qué funda Ud. sus esperanzas? *On what do you base your hopes?*
fundición *f. foundry, casting, melting.*
fundir *to melt, fuse; to burn out (a bulb).*
fúnebre *adj. mournful, sad.*
funeral *adj. funeral, funereal; m. pl. funeral.*
furgón *m. baggage car; freight car.*
furia *f. fury, rage, fit of madness.*
furioso *adj. furious, mad, frantic.*
furor *m. fury.*
fusible *m. fuse (electricity).*
fusil *m. rifle.*
fusilar *to shoot.*
fútbol *m. football.*
FUTURO *adj. future; m. future; fiancé, husband.*
En un futuro próximo. *In the near future.*
En lo futuro. *In the future.*
Nos presentó a su futuro. *She introduced her fiancé to us.*

G

gabán *m. overcoat.*
gabardina *f. gabardine.*
gabinete *m. cabinet; study, studio, laboratory.*
Gabinete de lectura. *Reading room.*
gaceta *f. gazette, official government journal; newspaper.*
gacetilla *f. a newspaper column, newspaper squib.*
gachas *f. pl. porridge, mush, pap.*
Hacerse unas gachas. *To be very affectionate.*
A gachas. *On all fours.*
gafa *f. grapple hook; spectacles, eyeglasses.*
gaita *f. bagpipe.*
gaitero *m. piper.*
gajo *m. branch of a tree; each section or piece of an orange or lemon; part of a bunch of grapes.*
gala *f. gala occasion, gala affair; full dress.*
De gala. *Full dress.*
Hacer gala de. *To boast of.*
galán *m. leading man (theater); gallant, lover.*
Primer galán. *Leading man.*
galante *adj. gallant; generous.*
galantear *to court, to make love.*
galantería *f. gallantry, politeness and attention to women; elegance; generosity.*
galería *f. gallery.*
gales *m. Prince of Wales pattern.*

galgo *m. greyhound.*
galicismo *m. gallicism.*
galón *m. stripe (on uniform); gallon.*
galopar *to gallop.*
galope *m. gallop.*
galvanizar *to galvanize.*
gallardo *adj. gallant, brave, daring; handsome, spruce.*
galleta *f. cookie, biscuit; hardtack.*
gallina *f. hen; coward.*
Es un gallina. *He's a coward. He's yellow.*
gallinero *m. chicken coop; top gallery (in a theater).*
gallo *m. cock, rooster.*
gamo *m. buck, male of fallow deer.*
gamuza *f. suede, chamois.*
GANA *f. appetite, hunger; desire, inclination, will.*
No tengo ganas de comer ahora. *I'm not hungry now. I don't feel like eating now.*
De buena gana. *Willingly. With pleasure.*
De mala gana. *Unwillingly. Reluctantly.*
Trabajó de mala gana. *He worked unwillingly (against his will, reluctantly).*
Comer con gana. *To eat with an appetite.*
No me da la gana. *I don't want to. I don't feel like. I won't.*
Hace siempre lo que le da la gana. *She always does what she pleases.*
Tener ganas de. *To desire. To want to. To feel like. To have a mind to.*
Dan ganas de. *One feels inclined to. One feels like.*
ganadería *f. cattle raising, cattle ranch; livestock.*
ganadero *m. cattleman, cattle dealer; rancher.*
ganado *m. cattle, livestock.*
ganador *m. winner.*
ganancia *f. gain, profit.*
Ganancias y pérdidas. *Profit and loss.*
Sacar ganancia. *To make a profit.*
GANAR *to gain; to earn; to win; to reach.*
¿Cuánto quiere Ud. ganar? *What salary do you want? ("How much do you want to earn?")*
Le gané la apuesta. *I won the bet from him.*
Ganaron por dos tantos a cero. *They won two to nothing.*
No es capaz de ganarse la vida (ganarse el pan). *He's not capable of earning his living.*
El prófugo ganó la frontera en pocas horas. *The fugitive reached the border in a few hours.*
gancho *m. hook; hairpin; clip.*
gandul *m. tramp, loafer, vagabond.*
ganga *f. bargain; bargain sale.*
A precio de ganga. *At a bargain price.*
gangoso *adj. snuffling, speaking through the nose or with a nasal tone.*
ganso *m. gander, goose; a slow (clumsy) person; a simpleton.*
Hacer el ganso. *To try to be funny.*
Hablar por boca de ganso. *To be like a parrot. To repeat mechanically what other people say.*
ganzúa *f. picklock, skeleton key; thief, burglar.*
garaje *m. garage.*
¿Me puede decir dónde hay un garaje cerca? *Can you please tell me where there's a garage near here?*
garantía *f. guarantee; guaranty, bond.*
garantizar *to vouch, to guarantee.*
gardenia *f. gardenia.*
garganta *f. throat; neck; gorge; instep.*
Tengo dolor de garganta. *I have a sore throat.*
Me llegaba el agua a la garganta. *The water was up to my neck.*
gárgara *f. gargle; gargling.*

Hacer gárgaras. *To gargle.*
garra *f. claw, talon; clutch.*
garrafa *f. carafe, decanter.*
garrapata *f. tick (insect).*
garrocha *f. good; stock; pole (for jumping).*
Salto a la garrocha. *Pole vaulting.*
garrote *m. cudgel, club; garrote.*
garza *m. heron.*
Garza real. *Purple heron.*
gas *m. gas.*
Estufa de gas. *Gas stove.*
gasa *f. gauze.*
gasolina *f. gasoline.*
Me he quédado sin gasolina. *I've run out of gas.*
Estación de gasolina. (Puesto de gasolina.) *Gas station.*
gasolinera *f. gasoline pump or station (in Spain).*
GASTAR *to spend, to wear out; to waste; to wear, to use.*
Gastó más de cien pesos. *He spent more than a hundred pesos.*
Gastar bromas. *To make jokes. To joke.*
Nunca gasto sombrero en verano. *I never wear a hat in summer.*
Gasta muy buena salud. *He's always in good health.*
Gastar palabras en vano. *To waste words.*
GASTO *m. expense, cost; expenditure; consumption.*
Gastos menudos. *Petty cash. ("Small expenses.")*
Gastos generales. *General expenses, overhead.*
Gasto adicional. *Additional expense.*
gata *f. she-cat.*
A gatas. *On all fours.*
gatillo *m. trigger.*
gato *m. cat, tomcat; jack.*
El gato me ha arañado la mano. *The cat scratched my hand.*
Nos hace falta un gato para levantar el coche. *We need a jack to raise the car.*
gaucho *m. gaucho, cowboy (Arg.).*
gaveta *f. drawer (of a desk); locker.*
gavilán *m. sparrow-hawk.*
gavilla *f. sheaf (of wheat, etc.); a gang of thugs.*
gaviota *f. seagull.*
ge *f. name of the letter g.*
gelatina *f. gelatine, jelly.*
gema *f. gem; bud.*
gemelo *m. twin; pl. binoculars; cufflinks.*
gemido *m. groan, moan.*
gemir *to groan, to moan, to howl.*
generación *f. generation.*
GENERAL *adj. general, usual; m. general.*
Por lo general. *As a rule. Usually.*
En general. *In general. On the whole.*
Es general. *He's a general.*
generalmente *generally.*
GÉNERO *m. cloth, material, stuff; class, kind, sort; gender, sex; pl. goods.*
Género para vestidos. *Dress material.*
Género humano. *Mankind.*
generosidad *f. generosity.*
generoso *adj. generous, liberal.*
genial *adj. outstanding, brilliant, gifted; genial, pleasant.*
Tiene un carácter genial. *He's a pleasant person.*
Es una idea genial. *It's a brilliant idea.*
genio *m. genius; nature, disposition, temper.*
Es un verdadero genio. *He's a real genius.*
Tiene muy mal genio. *He has a bad temper.*
GENTE *f. people, crowd.*
Aquí hay mucha gente. *There are many people here.*

Don de gentes. *Pleasant manners. Social graces. Savoir-faire.*

gentil *adj. courteous; graceful; m. gentile, heathen.*

gentileza *f. politeness, courtesy, kindness.*

gentío *m. crowd.*

genuino *adj. genuine, real.*

geografía *f. geography.*

geometría *f. geometry.*

geranio *m. geranium.*

gerencia *f. management.*

gerente *m. manager.*

gerigonza *f. gibberish.*

germen *m. germ.*

germinar *to germinate, to sprout, to start growing or developing.*

gerundio *m. gerund, present participle.*

gesticular *to gesticulate, to make gestures.*

gestión *f. management; negotiation; attempt to obtain or accomplish.*

Encárguese Ud. de esa gestión. *You attend to that matter.*

Está haciendo gestiones para conseguir un puesto. *He's trying to get a job.*

¿Cuáles fueron los resultados de la gestión? *What were the results of the negotiations?*

gestionar *to manage; to negotiate; to try, to take the necessary steps to obtain or accomplish something; to attend to.*

Están gestionando la solución de la huelga. *They're trying to find a way to settle the strike.*

gesto *m. gesture; grimace; facial expression.*

gigante *adj. gigantic; m. giant.*

gimnasia *f. gymnastics, exercise.*

Hacer gimnasia. *To exercise.*

gimnasio *m. gymnasium.*

ginebra *f. gin (liquor); Geneva (Switzerland).*

GIRAR *to rotate, turn; to draw (a draft, etc.); to operate.*

La tierra gira alrededor del sol. *The earth rotates around the sun.*

Esta casa gira bajo la razón social de. *This firm does business (operates) under the name of.*

Girar contra. *To draw on.*

girasol *m. sunflower.*

GIRO *m. turn; rotation; course (of events); draft; money order.*

Giro postal. *Money order.*

Giro bancario. *Bank draft.*

El giro de los acontecimientos. *The course of events.*

Tomar otro giro. *To take another turn (course).*

Tomar mal giro. *To take a turn for the worse.*

gitano *m. gypsy.*

glacial *adj. glacial, icy.*

Corre un viento glacial. *There's an icy wind.*

global *global, total.*

globo *m. globe; balloon.*

En globo. *In bulk. In a lump.*

gloria *f. glory; pleasure, delight.*

Esta comida sabe a gloria. *This food's delicious (wonderful).*

gloriarse *to be proud of, to boast, to take delight in.*

glorioso *adj. glorious.*

glosa *f. gloss, comment.*

glotón *m. a n. gluttonous; glutton.*

goal *m. goal (at games).*

gobernación *f. administration, government. See* gobierno.

Ministerio de la gobernación. *Department of the Interior.*

gobernador *m. governor.*

gobernante *m. ruler.*

gobernar *to govern, to rule; to control, to steer; to regulate; to direct.*

Gobernar un barco. *To steer a ship.*

gobierno *m. government; control.*

Para su gobierno. *For your guidance.*

Hombre de gobierno. *Statesman.*

goce *m. enjoyment; possession.*

golf *m. golf.*

golfo *m. gulf; idler, tramp.*

golondrina *f. swallow (bird).*

golosina *f. dainty, delicacy, tidbit.*

goloso *adj. fond of sweets, having a sweet tooth.*

GOLPE *m. blow, stroke, hit; knock; shock.*

Eso fué un golpe muy fuerte. *That was a heavy blow.*

De golpe. *Suddenly. All at once.*

De golpe y porrazo. *Unexpectedly. All of a sudden.*

Golpe de estado. *Coup d'état.*

Golpe de gracia. *Coup de grâce. Finishing stroke.*

Golpe de fortuna. *Stroke of fortune.*

De un golpe. *With one blow.*

Golpe de mar. *Surf. Heavy sea.*

golpear *to strike, to hit, to beat; to knock; to pound.*

Deje de golpear la mesa. *Stop pounding the table.*

goma *f. gum, glue; rubber; eraser.*

Tacones de goma. *Rubber heels.*

Goma de mascar. *Chewing gum.*

gordo *adj. fat, stout; big; m. lard, suet; first prize in a lottery.*

Es un hombre muy gordo. *He's a fat man. He's very fat.*

Dedo gordo. *Thumb.*

gordura *f. stoutness, obesity.*

gorila *m. gorilla.*

gorra *f. cap (for the head).*

De gorra. *Sponging. At someone else's expense.*

gorrión *m. sparrow.*

gorro *m. cap, hood.*

gota *f. drop (of liquid); gout.*

Gota a gota. *Drop by drop.*

gotear *to drip, to dribble; to leak.*

gotera *f. drip, leak; gutter.*

GOZAR *to enjoy; to have, to possess.*

Goza de buena salud. *He enjoys good health.*

Goza de muy buena reputación. *He has a very good reputation.*

gozarse *to rejoice; to find pleasure (in).*

Se goza en . . . *He finds pleasure in . . . He takes pleasure in . . .*

gozo *m. joy, pleasure.*

No cabe en sí de gozo. *He's very happy. ("He can't contain himself for joy.")*

gozoso *adj. cheerful, glad, merry.*

grabado *m. picture, illustration; engraving.*

grabar *to engrave; to impress upon the mind.*

GRACIA *f. grace; favor; pardon; wit, humor; name (of a person); pl. thanks.*

Muchas gracias. *Thank you very much.*

Gracias a Dios. *Thank God.*

Un millón de gracias. *Thanks a lot. ("A million thanks.")*

Dar gracias. *To thank.*

¿Cuál es su gracia? *What's your name?*

Eso tiene gracia. *That's funny.*

Eso no me hace gracia. *I don't think that's funny.*

Caer en gracia. *To take one's fancy.*

Tener gracia. *To be amusing (funny).*

Hacer gracia. *To amuse.*

gracioso *adj. graceful; witty, funny.*

Un dicho gracioso. *A witty remark.*

grada *f. step (of a staircase).*

GRADO *m. degree, rank; grade; will; pleasure.*

Tenemos diez grados bajo cero. *It's ten degrees below zero.*

Acaba de recibir el grado de doctor. *He has just received his doctor's degree.*

Tenía un grado superior en el ejército. *He held a high rank in the army.*

Está en el cuarto grado. *He's in the fourth grade.*

De buen grado. *Willingly. With pleasure.*

Mal de su grado. *Unwillingly. Much to one's regret.*

En alto grado. *In the highest degree.*

gradual *adj. gradual, by degrees.*

graduar *to graduate; to give military rank to; to adjust.*

graduarse *to graduate, to receive a degree.*

gráfico *adj. graphic; vivid; m. graph, diagram.*

gramática *f. grammar.*

GRAN *(contraction of* grande*) big, great.*

Me hace Ud. un gran favor. *You're doing me a great favor.*

Es un hombre de gran talento. *He's a man of great talent.*

Es un gran embustero. *He's a big liar.*

granada *f. pomegranate; grenade, shell.*

GRANDE *adj. great, large, huge; m. grandee, a Spanish nobleman.*

Separe Ud. los grandes de los pequeños. *Separate the large ones from the small.*

Vive en una casa muy grande. *She lives in a very large house.*

Estos zapatos me quedan muy grandes. *These shoes are too big for me.*

Este jarrón es un poco más grande. *This vase is a little larger.*

En grande. *On a large scale.*

grandeza *f. greatness.*

grandioso *adj. grand, magnificent.*

granero *m. granary, barn.*

granizar *to hail.*

Graniza. (Está granizando.) *It's hailing.*

granizo *m. hail.*

granja *f. grange, farm; country house.*

granjear *to gain, to win (somebody's affection or goodwill).*

granjearse *to gain the goodwill of another.*

grano *m. grain; cereal bean (of coffee); pimple.*

Vamos al grano. *Let's get to the point. Let's get down to brass tacks.*

grasa *f. grease, fat.*

grasiento *adj. greasy.*

grasoso *adj. greasy.*

gratamente *gratefully.*

gratificación *f. gratuity, tip, reward; allowance.*

gratificar *to reward, to gratify, to tip.*

gratis *adj. gratis, free.*

La entrada será gratis. *Admission will be free.*

gratitud *f. gratitude, thankfulness, gratefulness.*

GRATO *adj. pleasing, gratifying, pleasant.*

Me es grato. *I'm pleased to.*

Me será grato hacerlo. *I'll be glad to do it.*

Su grata del 5 de mayo. *Your letter ("favor") of May the 5th.*

gratuito *adj. gratis, free.*

grave *adj. grave; serious.*

gravedad *f. gravity, seriousness.*

gremio *m. trade union, guild.*

grieta *f. crevice, crack, fissure; chap (skin).*

grifo *m. faucet; griffin.*

Haga Ud. el favor de cerrar el grifo. *Please turn the water off.*

grillo m. *cricket (insect).*

grillos pl. *fetters, shackles.*

gringo m. *name given to Americans and Englishmen in Latin America.*

gripe f. *grippe, influenza.*

gris adj. *gray.*

gritar *to shout, to scream.*

No grites tanto. *Don't shout so. Don't scream like that.*

grito m. *cry, scream, shout.*

Llamó a gritos. *He yelled (screamed). He called out loud.*

Poner el grito en el cielo. *To complain bitterly. To make a big fuss. ("To cry to heaven.")*

Estar en un grito. *To be in agony.*

grosella f. *currant (fruit).*

grosería f. *coarseness, rudeness.*

grosero adj. *coarse, rude, impolite.*

grúa f. *crane, derrick, hoist.*

gruesa f. *gross (144).*

GRUESO adj. *thick, coarse, bulky.*

Una tajada gruesa. *A thick slice.*

El tronco de ese árbol es muy grueso. *This tree has a very thick trunk.*

grulla f. *crane (bird).*

gruñido m. *grunt.*

gruñir *to grumble, to grunt.*

grupo m. *group.*

gruta f. *grotto, cavern.*

guano m. *guano, manure of sea birds, fertilizer.*

guante m. *glove.*

Echar el guante. *To catch. To arrest.*

guapo adj. *good-looking, pretty, handsome; courageous, bold, brave (Amer.).*

¿Es guapa la hija? *Is the daughter pretty?*

Es guapísima. *She's very pretty.*

guarda f. and m. *guard, watchman, keeper; custody, guardianship.*

guardapelo m. *locket.*

GUARDAR *to keep, to guard, to take care of.*

Guarde su dinero en la caja fuerte. *Keep your money in the safe.*

No le guardo ningún rencor. *I don't bear him any grudge.*

Ha tenido que guardar cama. *He had to stay in bed. He was confined to bed.*

guardarse *to be on guard; to guard against; to abstain from.*

guardarropa f. *wardrobe; m. cloakroom, the cloakroom attendant.*

guardia f. *guard (a body of soldiers); watch (on a ship); m. guard (a person), policeman.*

Cualquier guardia puede indicarle el camino. *Any policeman can direct you (show you the way).*

Está de guardia. *He's on duty.*

guarecer *to shelter, to protect.*

guarnecer *to trim, to garnish; to garrison.*

guarnición f. *trimming, garniture; setting (in gold, silver, etc.); garrison; pl. harness.*

guasa f. *nonsense; dullness; joke, fun.*

guasón adj. *humorous, playful; m. teaser, joker.*

guayaba f. *guava (fruit).*

GUERRA f. *war; trouble.*

Estar en guerra. *To be at war.*

Hacer guerra. *To wage war.*

Estos chicos dan mucha guerra. *These children are a lot of trouble.*

guerrero adj. *warlike; m. warrior.*

GUÍA m. *guide; cicerone; f. guidebook; directory.*

¿Dónde puedo encontrar un guía que me acompañe? *Where can I get a guide to accompany me?*

Guía telefónica. *Telephone directory.*

Servir de guía. *To serve as a guide.*

guiar *to guide, to direct; to drive.*

¿Sabe Ud. guiar? *Do you know how to drive?*

guijarro m. *pebble.*

guillotina f. *guillotine.*

guinda f. *kind of cherry.*

guiñar *to wink; to deviate (a ship).*

guión m. *hyphen; guidon (small flag).*

guisado m. *ragout, a stew of meat and vegetables.*

guisante m. *pea.*

guisar *to cook.*

guiso m. *stew.*

guitarra f. *guitar.*

gusano m. *worm.*

GUSTAR *to taste; to like.*

¿Le gusta a Ud. la fruta? *Do you like fruit?*

A mí no me gusta el café. *I don't like coffee.*

¿Le gusta a Ud. eso? *Do you like that?*

No me gusta. *I don't like it.*

Nos gustó la comida. *We enjoyed the food.*

Me gusta más el vino. *I like wine better.*

Si Ud. gusta. *If you please. If you wish.*

Como Ud. guste. *As you please.*

Me gustaría mucho ir a España. *I'd like very much to go to Spain.*

GUSTO m. *taste; pleasure; liking.*

Esto tiene un gusto extraño. *This has a strange (funny) taste.*

Con (mucho) gusto. *With (much) pleasure.*

Tengo mucho gusto en conocerle. *I'm glad to have met you. Glad to know you.*

A mi gusto. *To my liking.*

Se lo haré a su gusto. *I'll do it the way you want.*

Estar (encontrarse, sentirse) a gusto. *To feel at home. To be comfortable.*

Me siento a gusto aquí. *I feel at home here.*

Dar gusto. *To please.*

Tener gusto en. *To take pleasure in.*

gustoso adj. *tasty; glad, willing, with pleasure.*

Aceptamos gustosos la invitación. *We accept your invitation with pleasure.*

gutapercha f. *gutta-percha.*

H

¡ha! *ah! alas!*

haba f. *broad bean.*

habano m. *Havana cigar.*

haber m. *credit (bookkeeping); assets.*

HABER *to have (as an auxiliary verb); to be, to exist.*

Hay. *There is. There are.*

Había. *There was. There were.*

Hubo. *There was. There were.*

Habrá. *There will be.*

Habría. *There would be.*

Haya. *There may be.*

Que haya. *Let there be.*

Hubiera (hubiese). *There might be.*

Si hubiera (hubiese). *If there were. If there should be.*

Ha habido. *There has (have) been.*

Había (hubo) habido. *There had been.*

Habría habido. *There should (would) have been.*

Hay que. *It's necessary.*

Habrá que. *It will be necessary.*

Hubo que. *It was necessary.*

Ha de ser. *It must be.*

He de hacer un largo viaje. *I have (I've got) to make a long trip.*

He aquí. *Here is.*

Poco ha. *A little while ago.*

¿Ha escrito la carta? *Has she written the letter?*

No la ha escrito todavía. *She hasn't written it yet.*

No he estado allí. *I haven't been there.*

Pudo haber sucedido. *It might have happened.*

Debían haber llegado anoche. *They were supposed to have come last night.*

Ayer hubo clase. *There was school yesterday.*

De haber sido Ud. no lo hubiera hecho. *If I had been you, I wouldn't have done it.*

Debe haber cartas para mí. *There must be some letters for me.*

¿Habrá alguien en la estación esperándome? *Will there be someone at the station to meet me?*

¿Qué distancia hay? *How far is it?*

Habrá unas cinco millas de aquí. *That must be about five miles from here.*

Hemos de ir el martes a su casa. *We must go (we have to go) to his (her) house on Tuesday.*

No habíamos comido desde hacía muchas horas. *We hadn't eaten for many hours.*

Así que hubo hablado se marchó. *He left as soon as he'd finished speaking.*

Me alegro de haberle visto. *I'm glad to have seen you.*

Dede haber hecho fortuna en América. *He must have made a fortune in America.*

Debe haber habido un edificio aquí en otros tiempos. *There must have been a building here formerly (in the past).*

Hace una semana que la vi. *I saw her a week ago.*

¿Qué se ha hecho? *What happened to her?*

¿Hábrase visto cosa igual? *Did you ever see such a thing?*

Habérselas con. *To have to deal with. To cope with. To contend with.*

haberes m. pl. *possessions, property.*

habichuela f. *bean; kidney bean.*

Habichuelas verdes. *String beans.*

HÁBIL adj. *able; clever; skillful; capable.*

Es muy hábil. *He's very clever.*

Día hábil. *Working day.*

habilidad f. *ability, skill.*

habilitado m. *paymaster.*

habilitar *to qualify; to enable, to provide; to supply with.*

habitación f. *room; dwelling; place to live in.*

¿Cuántas habitaciones tiene el apartamento? *How many rooms does the apartment have?*

habitante m. and f. *inhabitant; tenant.*

habitar *to inhabit, to live in, to reside.*

¿Qué tal es el piso que habitan? *What kind of an apartment do you live in?*

hábito m. *habit, custom; cowl, habit (worn by members of a religious order).*

Tenía el hábito de levantarse temprano. *He was in the habit of getting up early.*

Colgó los hábitos. *He threw off the cowl.*

habituar *to accustom.*

habituarse *to become accustomed.*

habla f. *speech, talk.*

Perdió el habla. *He was speechless.*

Ponerse al habla con. *To get in touch with. To have a talk with.*

hablador adj. *talkative; m. gossip, chatterbox, talker.*

HABLAR *to speak, to talk.*

¿Habla Ud. español? *Do you speak Spanish?*

Yo no hablo español. *I don't speak Spanish.*

Aquí se habla español. *Spanish is spoken here.*

¡Hable! *Speak!*

¿Quién habla? *Who's speaking (telephone)?*

¡Diga! (¡Holá!) ¿Quién habla? *Hello! Who's this (telephone)?*

Hable más despacio. *Speak slower.*

Nunca habla mal de nadie. *He never says anything bad about anyone.*

Hablando en serio, eso no está bien. *Joking apart, that's wrong. Seriously, that's not right.*

Hablar con. *To speak with.*

Hablar por demás. *To talk too much. Not to talk to the point.*

Hablar por hablar. *To talk for the sake of talking.*

Hablar hasta por los codos. *To chatter. To talk constantly. To be a chatterbox.*

hacendado *m. rancher, landowner (Amer.).*

hacendoso *adj. diligent; industrious.*

Es una chica muy hacendosa. *She's a very industrious girl.*

HACER *to make; to do; to cause; to be (cold, warm, etc.).*

Hágame Ud. el favor de. *Please.*

Me hace Ud. el favor de. *Please.*

¡Haga el favor de pasarme la sal! *Please pass me the salt.*

¿Me permite que le haga una pregunta? *May I ask you a question?*

Hacen muy buenos pasteles aquí. *They make very good pies here.*

He mandado hacer un traje a la medida. *I'm having a suit made to order.*

Hicimos los planes de común acuerdo. *We made (laid) the plans by mutual agreement.*

Hágame un poco de sitio. *Make a little room for me.*

¿Tiene Ud. algo que hacer esta tarde? *Have you anything to do this afternoon?*

Tengo mucho que hacer hoy. *I've a lot to do today.*

¿Qué hago? *What shall I do?*

Haga Ud. lo que quiera. *Do as you please (like).*

¿Qué hace Ud.? *What are you doing?*

¿Qué hemos de hacer? *What are we to do?*

Hágalo Ud. de esta manera. *Do it this way.*

Hace lo que puede. *He does what he can. He does his best.*

Queda mucho por hacer. *Much still remains to be done.*

Me ha dado mucho que hacer. *He's given me a lot of trouble.*

Ya está hecho. *It's already done (finished).*

Dicho y hecho. *No sooner said than done.*

¿Le ha hecho daño la comida? *Did the food disagree with you?*

Ropa hecha. *Ready-made clothes.*

Yo le hacía en España. *I thought you were in Spain.*

Le hacíamos rico. *We thought he was rich.*

Haga Ud. por venir. *Try to come.*

Haga Ud. memoria. *Try to remember.*

Salió hace un rato. *He left a while ago.*

No hace mucho. *Not long ago.*

Hace cosa de dos meses. *It was about two months ago.*

Se va haciendo tarde. *It's getting late.*

Hace frío. *It's cold.*

Hace calor. *It's warm.*

Hace sol. *It's sunny.*

Hace viento. *It's windy.*

Hace mal tiempo. *The weather's bad. It's nasty out.*

Hacer falta. *To need. To be lacking.*

No hace falta. *It's not necessary.*

Hacer caso. *To pay attention.*

Hacer burla. *To make fun.*

Hacer alto. *To halt.*

Hacer un paréntesis. *To pause.*

Hacer de las suyas. *To be up to one's old tricks again.*

Hacer de cuenta. *To pretend.*

Hacer gimnasia. *To exercise.*

Hacer una convocatoria. *To call a meeting.*

Hacer cola. *To stand in line.*

Hacer frente a. *To face. To resist.*

Hacer ver. *To show.*

Hacer volver. *To send back.*

Hacer esperar. *To keep waiting.*

Hacer saber. *To make known. To inform.*

Hacer juego. *To match.*

Hacer por la vida. *To eat something.*

Hacer mal. *To do harm.*

Hacerlo bien (mal). *To do it well (badly).*

Hacer gasto. *To spend.*

Hacer fuego. *To fire. To shoot.*

Hacer cuentas. *To figure. To reckon.*

Hacer la corte. *To court. To woo.*

HACERSE *to become; to accustom oneself; to pretend; to be able to.*

¿Puede Ud. hacerse entender en inglés? *Can you make yourself understood in English?*

Juan está en camino de hacerse rico. *John's getting rich. ("John's on the way to becoming rich.")*

Se hacía más loco de lo que era. *He pretended to be crazier than he really was.*

La muñeca se hizo pedazos. *The doll broke into pieces.*

Me hice un lío. *I was all mixed up.*

Hacerse rogar. *To like to be coaxed.*

Hacerse cargo de. *To take charge of. To take into consideration.*

Hacerse atrás. *To fall back.*

Hacerse una sopa. *To become drenched. To get soaked to the skin.*

Hacerse a. *To become accustomed (used) to.*

Hacerse a la vela. *To set sail.*

Hacerse de. *To obtain. To get.*

Hacerse con alguna cosa. *To get hold of something. To obtain something.*

Hacerse el tonto. *To play the fool.*

¡Hazte allá! *Move on! Make way! Get out of the way!*

HACIA *toward, in the direction of.*

Péineme el pelo hacia atrás. *Comb my hair back.*

Iba hacia su casa. *He was going towards his house.*

El edificio está hacia el sur. *The building faces (the) south.*

Se dirigieron hacia la puerta. *They went towards the door.*

Hacia abajo. *Downwards.*

Hacia arriba. *Upwards.*

Hacia acá. *Over here. Towards this place.*

Hacia allá. *Over there. Towards that place.*

Hacia adelante. *Forward. Onward. Toward the front.*

hacienda *f. property, lands, ranch, plantation, large estate (Amer.); fortune, wealth; treasury; finance.*

Ministerio de Hacienda. *The Treasury.*

hacha *f. ax, hatchet.*

hache *f. name of the letter h.*

hada *f. fairy.*

Cuentos de hadas. *Fairy tales.*

hado *m. destiny, fate.*

halagar *to please, to flatter.*

halago *m. flattery, excessive praise.*

halagüeño *adj. pleasing, nice; flattering, attractive.*

halar *to pull (Amer.).*

Hale la cuerda. *Pull the rope.*

HALLAR *to find, to meet with.*

Hallé muchas faltas en esta carta. *I found many mistakes in this letter.*

No lo hallo en ninguna parte. *I can't find it anywhere.*

Lo hallará en el escritorio. *You'll find it on the desk.*

hallarse *to find oneself, to be.*

Se halla muy bien. *He's very well. He's fine.*

Me hallo sin dinero. *I find myself without any money.*

hallazgo *m. finding; thing found.*

hamaca *f. hammock.*

HAMBRE *m. hunger.*

Tengo hambre. *I'm hungry.*

No tengo hambre. *I'm not hungry.*

Me estoy muriendo de hambre. *I'm starving.*

hambriento *adj. hungry; starved; greedy.*

hangar *m. hangar.*

haragán *adj. and n. lazy; indolent; loafer.*

harapo *m. tatter; rag.*

harina *f. flour.*

hartarse *to stuff oneself, to gorge.*

Tomó helado hasta hartarse. *He stuffed himself with ice cream.*

harto *adj. satiated, full; fed up; enough.*

Estoy harto de todo esto. *I'm fed up with all this.*

HASTA *until; as far as; up to; also, even.*

Hasta luego. *So long. See you later.*

Hasta después. *I'll see you later.*

¡Hasta la vista! *Till we meet again! I'll be seeing you soon! See you soon!*

Hasta muy pronto. *I'll see you soon. See you later.*

Hasta mañana. *Until tomorrow. See you tomorrow.*

Hasta el lunes. *Until Monday.*

Fuimos andando hasta el parque. *We walked as far as the park.*

Hay ascensor hasta el quinto piso. *There is an elevator to the fifth floor.*

¿Hasta dónde va el camino? *How far does the road go?*

Estoy calado hasta los huesos. *I'm soaking wet. ("I'm soaked to the bones.")*

Hasta cierto punto. *To a certain extent.*

Hasta ahora. *Up to now. Up to this time.*

HAY *(see haber) there is, there are.*

¿Hay vino? *Is there any wine?*

No hay vino. *There is no wine.*

¿Hay cartas? *Are there any letters?*

¿Hay algo para mí? *Is there anything for me?*

¿Qué hay de bueno? *What's new?*

No hay novedad. *Nothing new. The same old thing. The same as usual.*

¿Qué hay? *What's the matter? What's up?*

¡No hay de qué! *Don't mention it! You're welcome!*

Hay un hombre esperándole. *There's a man waiting for you.*

Hay que ver lo que se puede hacer por ella. *We must see what can be done for her.*

haz *m. sheaf; fagot; f. face; right side (of a cloth);*

surface (of the earth).

hazaña f. prowess, feat, exploit.

he look here, take notice (used with aquí, ahí, allí, and me, te, la, le, lo, las and los).

He aquí las razones. *These are the reasons (indicating what follows).*

He ahí las razones. *Those are the reasons (indicating what precedes).*

Héme aquí. *Here I am.*

¿Dónde está mi libro?—Hélo aquí. *Where's my book?—Here it is.*

hebilla f. buckle.

hebra f. thread; fiber.

Pasar la hebra por el ojo de la aguja. *To thread a needle.*

hectárea f. hectare (10,000 square meters).

hectólitro m. hectoliter.

hechicero adj. fascinating, charming; m. wizard.

Tiene un semblante hechicero. *She has a fascinating face.*

hechizar to fascinate, to charm, to bewitch.

HECHO adj. made, done; m. fact; deed; action; event.

Mal hecho. *That's wrong. Poorly made.*

Bien hecho. *Well done.*

Ropa hecha. *Ready-made clothes.*

El hecho es . . . *The fact is . . .*

Los hechos demostraron otra cosa. *The facts proved otherwise.*

Dicho y hecho. *Said and done.*

Hecho y derecho. *Perfect in every respect.*

De hecho. *In fact. Actually.*

De hecho y de derecho. *"By act and right."*

hechura f. workmanship, making, cut, shape, form.

heder to stink.

helada f. frost.

helado adj. frozen; icy; astonished, amazed, astounded; m. ice cream.

Traiga dos helados de chocolate. *Bring two orders of chocolate ice cream.*

La noticia me dejó helado. *The news astounded me.*

helar to freeze; to astonish.

hélice f. propeller.

hembra f. female; woman; eye of a hook.

hemisferio m. hemisphere.

hendedura f. fissure, crevice.

heno m. hay.

heredad f. property, land, farm.

heredar to inherit.

heredera f. heiress.

heredero m. heir.

hereditario adj. hereditary.

herencia f. inheritance, heritage, legacy.

herida f. wound, injury.

herido adj. wounded, injured; m. wounded man.

Fué herido en el brazo. *He was wounded in the arm.*

El herido sigue mejor. *The wounded man is improving.*

herir to wound, to hurt.

HERMANA f. sister.

hermanastro m. stepbrother.

HERMANO m. brother.

HERMOSO adj. beautiful; lovely, fine.

¡Qué paisaje tan hermoso! *What beautiful scenery! What a lovely landscape!*

¡Qué día más hermoso! *What a beautiful day!*

hermosura f. beauty.

héroe m. hero.

heroico adj. heroic.

hervir to boil.

Hierva el agua antes de beberla. *Boil the water*

before you drink it.

Agua hirviendo. *Boiling water.*

herradura f. horseshoe.

herramienta f. tool; set of tools.

herrero m. blacksmith.

hidrofobia f. hydrophobia; rabies.

hidroplano m. seaplane.

hiedra f. ivy.

hiel f. gall, bile.

hielo m. ice; frost; indifference.

hiena f. hyena.

hierba f. herb; weed; grass.

hierbabuena f. mint (plant).

hierro m. iron; poker.

Remueva la lumbre con el hierro. *Stir the fire with the poker.*

hígado m. liver.

higiene f. hygiene.

higiénico adj. hygienic, sanitary.

higo m. fig.

higuera f. fig tree.

HIJA f. daughter.

hijastro m. stepchild.

HIJO m. son; pl. children.

¿Tiene Ud. hijos? *Do you have any children?*

Tal padre, tal hijo. *Like father, like son.*

hilar to spin.

hilero f. row, file.

HILO m. thread; string; linen; wire.

Pañuelo de hilo. *Linen handkerchief.*

No puedo seguir el hilo de la conversación. *I can't follow the conversation.*

Perder el hilo. *To lose the thread (of what one is saying, etc.).*

Sin hilos. *Wireless.*

Carrete (carretel) de hilo. *Spool of thread. Spool of cotton.*

hilván m. tacking, basting.

hilvanar to tack, to baste; to do a thing hurriedly.

himno m. hymn.

hincapié m. unyielding.

Hacer hincapié. *To insist on. To emphasize. To dwell on. To stand firm.*

hinchado adj. swollen.

hinchar to swell, to inflate.

hincharse to swell; to become arrogant.

hinchazón m. swelling; vanity.

hipnotismo m. hypnotism.

hipo m. hiccough.

hipocresía f. hypocrisy.

hipócrita adj. and n. hypocritical, not sincere; hypocrite.

hipódromo m. racetrack; hippodrome.

hipoteca f. mortgage.

hipotecar to mortgage.

hipótesis f. hypothesis.

hispano adj. Hispanic, Spanish.

hispanoamericano adj. Spanish American.

histérico adj. hysterical.

historia f. history; story.

Me vino con una larga historia. *He came to me with a long story.*

historiador m. historian.

histórico adj. historic.

historieta f. short story; anecdote.

hocico m. snout; muzzle.

Meter el hocico en todo. *To be nosy. To poke one's nose into everything.*

hogar m. fireplace; home.

hoguera f. bonfire; blaze.

HOJA f. leaf; blade; sheet.

En otoño caen las hojas. *The leaves fall in autumn.*

Doblemos la hoja. *Let's change the subject.*

Hoja en blanco. *Blank sheet.*

Hoja de servicio. *Service record.*

Hoja de afeitar. *Razor blade.*

Hoja de lata. *Tin plate.*

hojalata f. tin plate.

hojear to turn the leaves or glance at a book; to look over hastily.

holgar to rest; to be idle; to go on strike.

Huelga decir. *Needless to say.*

holgarse to be pleased with, to take pleasure in, to amuse oneself.

holgazán adj. lazy, idle; m. a lazy person, idler.

¡hola! Hello!

hombre m. man.

Es hombre de mundo. *He's a man of the world.*

Hombre de bien. *An honest man.*

Hombre de Estado. *Statesman.*

HOMBRO m. shoulder.

Se lastimó el hombro. *He hurt his shoulder.*

Arrimar el hombro. *To give a hand.*

Encogerse de hombros. *To shrug one's shoulders.*

homenaje m. homage, honor, respect.

Rendir homenaje. *To pay homage to.*

hondo adj. profound; deep.

honesto adj. decent, honest.

honor m. honor.

Dió su palabra de honor. *He gave his word of honor.*

Honores Militares. *Military honors.*

honra f. honor, respect.

Tener a honra. *To regard as an honor. To consider it an honor. To be proud of.*

A mucha honra. *I (we) consider it an honor. I (we) are honored. I'm (or we're) proud of it.*

honradez f. honesty, integrity.

honrado adj. honest, honorable.

Era un hombre honrado. *He was an honest man.*

honrar to honor.

honrarse to deem something an honor, to be honored.

HORA f. hour; time.

¿Qué hora es? *What time is it?*

¿Qué hora será? *I wonder what time it is.*

¿A qué hora empieza la función. (At) *What time does the show begin?*

¿A qué hora sale el correo? (At) *What time does the mail leave?*

Ya es hora de levantarse. *It's ("already") time to get up.*

Este reloj da las horas y las medias horas. *This clock strikes the hours and the half hours.*

Llegó media hora después. *He arrived half an hour later.*

A la hora. *On time.*

A la hora en punto. *On the dot.*

A la misma hora. *At the same time.*

A estas horas. *By this time. By now.*

horario adj. hourly; m. hour-hand; timetable.

horca f. gallows; pitchfork.

horizontal adj. horizontal.

horizonte m. horizon.

horma f. form, model, mold; shoe last.

Horma para zapatos. *Shoe last.*

hormiga f. ant.

hormigón m. concrete (for building).

hornada f. batch (of bread).

hornillo m. portable stove; burner; blast hole.

horno m. oven; furnace.

hortaliza f. vegetables (for cooking), garden greens.

horrible adj. horrible.

horror m. horror.

horroroso adj. horrible, frightful, dreadful.
hosco adj. sullen, gloomy; dark-colored.
hospedaje m. lodging; board.
hospedar to lodge; to entertain (guests).
hospicio m. orphan asylum; poorhouse.
hospital m. hospital.
hospitalizar to hospitalize; to be taken to the hospital.
hostèlero m. innkeeper, tavern keeper.
hostia f. host (in the Catholic Church).
hostil adj. hostile.
hostilizar to harass, to antagonize.
HOTEL m. hotel; villa; cottage.
  ¿Dónde queda el hotel más próximo? Where's the nearest hotel?
HOY today.
  ¿Qué día es hoy? What day is today? What's today?
  ¿Cuál es el programa de hoy? What's today's program?
  De hoy en adelante. From now on. Henceforth.
  Hoy por hoy. Hoy día. Nowadays.
hoyo m. hole, pit, excavation.
hoz f. sickle.
hueco m. hole, hollow, empty space.
huelga f. strike (of workers).
huelguista m. striker, a workman on strike.
huella f. track, footprint, trail.
  Huellas digitales. Fingerprints.
huérfano m. orphan.
  Quedarse huérfano. To be left an orphan.
huerta f. orchard; irrigated land.
huerto m. small orchard; vegetable garden.
hueso m. bone; stone (of fruit); drudgery.
  A otro perro con ese hueso. Tell it to the marines. You expect me to believe that? ("Give that bone to another dog.")
huésped m. and f. guest; lodger; innkeeper, host.
  Casa de huéspedes. Boarding house.
HUEVO m. egg.
  ¿Cómo quiere Ud. los huevos? How do you like your eggs?
  Huevos y tocino. Bacon and eggs.
  Huevos fritos. Fried eggs.
  Huevos pasados por agua. Soft-boiled eggs.
  Huevos revueltos. Scrambled eggs.
huida f. flight, escape.
huir to flee, to escape; to run away.
hule m. oilcloth; linoleum; India rubber.
humanidad f. mankind, humanity.
humanitario adj. humanitarian, philanthropic.
HUMANO adj. human; humane; m. man, human being.
  Eso fué un acto humano. That was a humane act. That was a very humane thing to do.
  Un ser humano. A human being.
humear to smoke (chimneys, etc.).
humedad f. humidity, dampness, moisture.
humedecer to moisten, to dampen.
húmedo adj. humid, moist, damp.
humildad f. humility, humbleness.
humilde adj. poor; humble; unaffected.
humillación f. humiliation; affront.
humillante adj. humiliating.
humillar to humiliate, to lower.
humo m. smoke; fume; pl. airs, conceit.
HUMOR m. humor; disposition; temper.
  Estar de buen humor. To be in a good mood.
  Estar de mal humor. To be in a bad mood. To have the blues.
humorada f. joke, witty remark, humorous saying.
humorista m. and f. humorist.

hundimiento m. sinking, scuttling; collapse, downfall.
hundir to sink; to submerge.
hundirse to sink; to cave in; to collapse.
huraño shy, not sociable.
hurtadillas (a) by stealth, on the sly.
  Me miró a hurtadillas. He looked at me out of the corner of his eye.
  Lo hizo a hurtadillas. He did it on the sly.
hurtar to steal, to rob.
  Hurtar el cuerpo. To shy away.
hurto m. stealing; theft.
¡hurra! Hurrah!
husmear to smell, to scent; to pry into; to begin to smell (meat).

I

ida f. going; one-way trip, trip to a place.
  Billete de ida. One-way ticket.
  Billete de ida y vuelta. Round-trip ticket.
IDEA f. idea; mind.
  No tengo la menor idea. I haven't the least idea.
  Creo que es una buena idea. I think it's a good idea.
  No es mala idea. That's not a bad idea.
  ¿Ha cambiado Ud. de idea? Have you changed your mind?
ideal adj. and n. ideal.
idealizar to idealize.
idear to think of, to conceive; to devise; to plan.
  Ideó un juego divertidísimo. He thought up a very amusing game.
  Idear nuevos métodos. To devise new methods.
idem the same, ditto.
idéntico adj. identical, the same.
identidad f. identity.
  ¿Tiene Ud. sus documentos de identidad? Do you have your identification papers?
identificación f. identification.
identificar to identify.
idioma m. language.
idiota adj. idiotic; m. and f. idiot.
ídolo m. idol.
iglesia f. church.
ignominia f. infamy; disgrace.
ignorancia f. ignorance.
IGNORANTE adj. ignorant; unaware; m. ignoramus, ignorant person.
  Estaba ignorante de lo que ocurría. He was unaware of what was happening.
  Es un ignorante. He's an ignorant man. He's an ignoramus.
IGNORAR to be ignorant of, not to know; to be unknown.
  Ignoro su nombre. I don't know his name.
  Se ignora su paradero. His whereabouts are unknown.
IGUAL adj. equal; similar, like; even.
  Mi corbata es igual que la suya. My tie is like yours.
  Me es igual. It's all the same to me. It makes no difference (to me).
  Al igual que los demás. The same as the others.
  Igual a la muestra. Like the sample.
  Por igual. Equally. In a like manner.
  No tener igual. To be matchless. To have no equal.
igualar to equalize; to compare, to liken; to make even.
igualarse to put oneself on the same level with someone else.

igualdad f. equality.
  En igualdad de condiciones. On equal terms.
ilegal adj. illegal, unlawful.
ilegible adj. illegible.
ilegítimo adj. illegitimate, spurious.
ileso adj. unhurt, unscathed, not harmed.
ilimitado adj. unlimited.
iluminación f. illumination.
iluminar to illuminate.
ilusión f. illusion.
ilustración f. illustration.
ilustrado adj. illustrated; m. well-educated person.
ilustrar to illustrate; to explain.
ilustrarse to acquire knowledge.
ilustre adj. illustrious, celebrated.
imagen f. image, figure.
imaginación f. imagination.
IMAGINAR to imagine, to think, to suspect.
IMAGINARSE to imagine.
  ¡Imagínese Ud.! You can imagine!
  Me imagino lo que pensaría de mí. I can imagine what he thought of me.
imán m. magnet.
imbécil adj. and n. imbecile.
imbecilidad f. imbecility, stupidity.
imitación f. imitation.
imitar to imitate; to mimic.
impaciencia f. impatience.
impacientar to vex, to irritate, to make someone impatient.
impacientarse to become impatient.
impaciente adj. impatient, restless.
impar adj. odd, uneven.
  Números impares. Odd numbers.
imparcial adj. impartial, unbiased.
impedimento m. impediment, hindrance, obstacle; inability to act.
IMPEDIR to hinder, to prevent, to keep from.
  El ruido me impidió dormir. The noise kept me from sleeping. The noise kept me awake.
impenetrable adj. impenetrable; inscrutable, mysterious.
imperativo adj. and n. imperative.
imperdible m. safety pin.
imperfecto adj. imperfect, faulty; m. imperfect (tense).
imperio m. empire; dominion.
impermeabilizar to make waterproof.
impermeable adj. impermeable, waterproof; m. raincoat.
impersonal adj. impersonal.
impertinente adj. impertinent, out of place; importunate.
ímpetu m. impulse, impetus.
impetuoso adj. impulsive, impetuous.
impío adj. wicked; impious, ungodly.
implicar to implicate; to imply.
implícito adj. implicit.
implorar to implore; to beg.
imponer to impose; to acquaint with; to have personal knowledge of; to command (respect).
imponerse to assert oneself, to command respect.
importación f. import; importation.
IMPORTANCIA f. importance.
IMPORTANTE adj. important.
IMPORTAR to import; to matter; to cost, to amount to.
  Esta casa importa café del Brasil. This firm imports coffee from Brazil.
  Este libro importa un dólar. This book costs a dollar.
  ¿Cuánto importa la cuenta? What does the bill amount to?

¿Que importa? *What difference does it make?*
No importa. *Never mind. It doesn't matter.*
Importa mucho. *It matters a lot. It's very important.*
No se meta en lo que no le importa. *Mind your own business.*
importe *m. amount; value, cost.*
importunar *to importune, to annoy.*
imposibilidad *f. impossibility.*
imposibilitar *to make impossible.*
IMPOSIBLE *adj. impossible.*
imposición *f. imposition.*
impostor *m. impostor, deceiver.*
impotencia *f. inability, impotence.*
impotente *adj. powerless, helpless, impotent.*
impracticable *adj. impracticable, not practical.*
imprenta *f. printing; printing plant.*
impresión *f. impression; print, printing.*
impresionante *adj. impressive.*
impresionar *to impress; to move; to affect.*
impreso *adj. printed; stamped; m. printed matter.*
impresor *m. printer.*
imprevisto *adj. unforeseen, unexpected; sudden.*
Llegó de imprevisto. *He arrived unexpectedly.*
imprimir *to print; to imprint.*
improbable *adj. unlikely, improbable.*
impropio *adj. improper, not correct, unfit; unbecoming.*
improvisar *to improvise, to extemporize; to make or do something offhand; to make for the occasion.*
improviso *adj. unexpected.*
De improviso. *Unexpectedly.*
imprudencia *f. lack of prudence, imprudence.*
imprudente *adj. imprudent; indiscreet.*
impuesto *adj. imposed; informed; m. impost, tax, duty.*
Estar impuesto de. *To be informed of (about).*
impulsar *to impel; to drive; to urge.*
impulso *m. impulse; spur; urge.*
Dar impulsos a. *To get something going (started).*
impunidad *f. impunity.*
impureza *f. impurity; contamination.*
impuro *adj. impure, not pure, adulterated.*
imputar *to impute, to blame, to attribute.*
inaceptable *adj. not acceptable.*
inactivo *adj. inactive, idle.*
inadaptable *adj. not adaptable.*
inadecuado *adj. inadequate, not adequate.*
inadmisible *adj. inadmissible, objectionable.*
inadvertido *adj. unnoticed.*
inalámbrico *adj. wireless.*
inalterable *adj. unalterable, changeless.*
inauguración *f. inauguration.*
inaugurar *to inaugurate; to begin.*
incansable *adj. untiring.*
incapacidad *f. incapacity, inability; incompetence, disability.*
incapaz *adj. incapable, inefficient, incompetent.*
Es incapaz de hacerlo. *He's incapable of doing it.*
incautación *f. seizure, taking over.*
incautarse *to take over, to seize.*
incendiar *to set on fire.*
incendio *m. fire.*
incertidumbre *f. uncertainty.*
incesante *adj. incessant, continual.*
Un ruido incesante. *A continual noise.*
incidente *adj. incidental; m. incident.*
incierto *adj. uncertain.*
incisión *f. incision.*
inciso *adj. incised, cut; m. partial meaning of a clause, parenthetic clause; comma.*

incitar *to incite, to stimulate.*
inclemencia *f. inclemency; severity.*
La inclemencia del tiempo no nos permitió salir. *The bad weather kept us at home.*
inclinación *f. inclination; leaning, tendency; bank (of an airplane).*
inclinar *to incline, to bend.*
inclinarse *to incline, to tend to, to lean towards.*
INCLUIR *to include; to enclose.*
¿Está incluído el vino? *Is wine included?*
Incluya su nombre en la lista. *Include his name on the list.*
Incluí el recibo en la carta. *I enclosed the receipt in the letter.*
inclusive *adj. inclusive, including.*
incluso *adj. enclosed; including.*
incógnito *adj. unknown; incognito.*
Viajó de incógnito. *He traveled incognito.*
incoherente *adj. incoherent; disconnected.*
incombustible *adj. incombustible.*
incomodar *to disturb, to inconvenience, to bother.*
Si eso no le incomoda. *If it doesn't inconvenience you.*
incómodo *adj. uncomfortable; inconvenient.*
incomparable *adj. matchless, without equal.*
incompatible *adj. incompatible.*
incompetencia *f. incompetency.*
incompleto *adj. incomplete, unfinished.*
incomprensible *adj. incomprehensible, impossible to understand.*
incomunicado *adj. incommunicado.*
incomunicar *to isolate, to hold someone incommunicado.*
inconcebible *adj. inconceivable, unthinkable, incredible.*
incondicional *adj. unconditional.*
incongruencia *f. incongruity, being out of place, being inconsistent.*
inconsciencia *f. unconsciousness.*
inconsciente *adj. unconscious.*
inconstancia *f. inconstancy, unsteadiness, fickleness.*
inconveniente *adj. inconvenient.*
Tener inconveniente en. *To object to.*
No tener inconveniente en. *Not to mind. Not to object to.*
incorporar *to incorporate; to join.*
incorporarse *to sit up or rise from a lying position.*
incorrección *f. incorrectness; inaccuracy.*
incorrecto *adj. incorrect, inaccurate, wrong, improper.*
incorregible *adj. incorrigible.*
incredulidad *f. incredulity, lack of belief.*
incrédulo *adj. incredulous.*
increíble *adj. incredible.*
incremento *m. increment, increase.*
Tomar incremento. *To increase.*
increpar *to reproach, to rebuke.*
incubadora *f. incubator.*
inculcar *to inculcate, to impress by repetition.*
inculpar *to inculpate, to involve, to blame.*
inculto *adj. uncultivated; uncultured, uneducated, boorish.*
incumbencia *f. duty, concern.*
Eso no es de mi incumbencia. *It doesn't concern me.*
incumbir *to concern, to pertain.*
Esto te incumbe a tí. *This concerns you.*
incumplimiento *m. nonfulfillment.*
incurable *adj. incurable; hopeless.*
incurrir *to incur, to run or get into; to make (a mistake).*
Incurrir en deudas. *To get into debt.*

Ha incurrido en una falta terrible. *He's made a terrible mistake.*
indagar *to inquire, to investigate.*
indebidamente *improperly, unduly, wrongly.*
indebido *adj. improper; wrong; undue; illegal.*
indecente *adj. indecent; unbecoming.*
indecisión *f. indecision, hesitation.*
indeciso *adj. undecided, hesitant.*
indefenso *adj. defenseless.*
indefinido *adj. indefinite.*
indeleble *adj. indelible.*
indemnización *f. indemnity, indemnification, compensation.*
indemnizar *to indemnify, to make good, to compensate.*
independencia *f. independence.*
independiente *adj. independent.*
indeseable *adj. undesirable.*
indeterminado *adj. indeterminate; doubtful; undecided.*
indiano *m. a Spaniard who returns to his birthplace after a long residence in Spanish America.*
indicación *f. indication, hint, sign; suggestion; pl. instructions.*
Eso era una buena indicación. *That was a good sign.*
Lo hizo por indicación de su amigo. *He did it at his friend's suggestion.*
Una indicación de Ud. es bastante. *A hint from you is enough.*
Siguió las indicaciones del médico. *He followed the doctor's instructions.*
Para usarlo, siga las indicaciones siguientes. *To use it, follow these instructions.*
indicador *m. indicator, pointer, gauge.*
INDICAR *to indicate; to point out.*
Haga el favor de indicarme el camino. *Please show me the way.*
índice *m. index; hand (of a clock, etc.).*
Dedo índice. *Index finger.*
indicio *m. indication, mark, clue.*
indiferencia *f. indifference.*
indiferente *adj. indifferent.*
Me es indiferente. *It makes no difference to me.*
indígena *adj. native.*
indigencia *f. poverty, indigence.*
indigente *adj. poor, indigent.*
indigestión *f. indigestion.*
indigesto *adj. hard to digest.*
indignación *f. indignation, anger.*
indignar *to irritate, to annoy, to anger.*
indignidad *f. indignity.*
indigno *adj. unworthy, undeserving; unbecoming; disgraceful.*
índio *m. Indian; Hindu.*
indirecta *f. hint.*
indirecto *adj. indirect.*
indiscreción *f. indiscretion.*
indiscreto *adj. indiscreet, imprudent.*
indiscutible *adj. unquestionable, indisputable.*
indispensable *adj. indispensable, essential.*
indisponer *to indispose; to become ill; to cause enmity or quarrels.*
¿Está Ud. indispuesto? *Are you ill (indisposed)?*
indisposición *f. indisposition.*
individual *adj. individual.*
individualmente *individually.*
individuo *m. individual, person.*
índole *f. disposition, character; kind, class.*
inducir *to induce; to persuade.*
indudable *adj. indubitable, certain.*
indulgencia *f. indulgence.*
indulgente *adj. indulgent, lenient.*

indultar *to pardon (a prisoner, etc.).*
indulto *m. pardon.*
indumentaria *f. clothing, clothes, outfit.*
industria *f. industry; diligence.*
industrial *adj. industrial, manufacturing; m. industrialist.*
ineficacia *f. inefficiency.*
ineficaz *adj. inefficient.*
ineludible *adj. unavoidable.*
ineptitud *f. ineptitude, inability, unfitness.*
inepto *adj. inept, incompetent; unfit.*
inequívoco *adj. unmistakable.*
inerte *adj. inert; slothful, sluggish.*
inesperadamente *unexpectedly.*
inesperado *adj. unexpected, unforeseen.*
inevitable *adj. inevitable, unavoidable.*
inexactitud *f. inaccuracy.*
inexacto *adj. inexact, inaccurate.*
inexperto *adj. inexperienced; inexpert.*
inexplicable *adj. inexplicable, impossible to explain.*
infalible *adj. infallible.*
infamar *to disgrace, to dishonor, to defame.*
infame *adj. infamous, shameful.*
infamia *f. infamy, disgrace.*
infancia *f. childhood.*
infantería *f. infantry.*
infantil *adj. infantile; childish.*
> Parálisis infantil. *Infantile paralysis.*
infatigable *adj. tireless, untiring.*
infección *f. infection.*
infectar *to infect, to spread disease.*
infectarse *to become infected.*
infeliz *adj. unhappy; unfortunate; m. a naïve (good-hearted, gullible) person.*
INFERIOR *adj. inferior; lower; subordinate; m. an inferior, a subordinate.*
> Es una tela de calidad inferior. *This material is of inferior quality.*
> Trata muy bien a sus inferiores. *He treats his subordinates well.*
> Labio inferior. *Lower lip.*
inferioridad *f. inferiority.*
inferir *to infer; to imply; to inflict (wounds, injuries, etc.).*
infiel *adj. unfaithful.*
> Si no me es infiel la memoria. *If my memory doesn't fail me. If I remember correctly.*
infierno *m. hell, inferno.*
ínfimo *adj. lowest; least.*
> No lo quiero vender a precio tan ínfimo. *I don't want to sell it at such a low price. I don't want to sell it for so little.*
infinidad *f. infinity; too many, a vast number.*
> Hay infinidad de gente que no piensa así. *There are many (a lot of) people who don't think so.*
infinitamente *infinitely, immensely.*
infinitivo *m. infinitive (grammar).*
infinito *adj. infinite.*
inflamable *adj. inflammable.*
inflamación *f. inflammation.*
inflamar *to catch fire; to inflame.*
> Tenga Ud. cuidado porque se inflama fácilmente. *Be careful, it's inflammable.*
> Tiene los ojos inflamados. *His eyes are inflamed.*
inflar *to inflate.*
influencia *f. influence.*
influenza *f. influenza, grippe, flu.*
INFLUIR *to influence.*
> La propaganda influye mucho en el público. *Advertising has a great influence on the public. ("Advertising influences the public very much.")*

> Influya usted para que . . . *Use your influence to . . .*
INFORMACIÓN *f. information; inquiry; investigation.*
> ¿Dónde queda la ventanilla de información? *Where is the information window (in a railway station)?*
informal *adj. unreliable, not to be depended on; not serious; unbusinesslike.*
informalidad *f. informality; lack of reliability, not being dependable.*
informar *to report, to inform, to let know; to plead (law).*
informarse *to find out, to learn.*
> Acabo de informarme del asunto. *I've just learned about the matter.*
informe *adj. shapeless; m. information; report; plea, allegation; pl. references.*
> Dar un informe. *To give information. To make a report.*
informes *m. information.*
infortunado *adj. unlucky, unfortunate.*
infracción *f. infraction, violation, infringement.*
infranqueable *adj. insurmountable.*
infrecuente *adj. infrequent, unusual.*
infringir *to infringe, to violate.*
infructuoso *adj. unsuccessful, vain, fruitless.*
infundado *adj. unfounded, groundless, without cause or reason.*
infundir *to give (courage), to command (respect), to make (someone suspicious).*
> Infundir ánimo. *To give courage.*
> Infunde respeto. *It commands respect.*
> Me infunde sospechas. *His actions make me suspect him.*
ingeniería *f. engineering.*
ingeniero *m. engineer.*
ingenio *m. ingenuity; talent; mill.*
> Fué un escritor de mucho ingenio. *He was a very talented writer.*
> Mi hermano trabaja en un ingenio de azúcar. *My brother works at a sugar mill.*
ingenioso *adj. ingenious, clever.*
ingenuidad *f. naïveté, simplicity.*
ingenuo *adj. naïve, simple.*
ingerir *to insert; to ingest, to take food.*
INGLÉS *adj. and n. English; Englishman; English language.*
> Se habla inglés. *English spoken here.*
> Habla muy mal el inglés. *He speaks English very badly.*
> El señor es inglés. *The gentleman is an Englishman (is English).*
ingratitud *f. ingratitude, lack of gratitude.*
ingrato *adj. ungrateful.*
ingresar *to enter.*
ingreso *m. entry (bookkeeping); money received; pl. f. income, revenue, returns.*
> Ingresó en el ejército como soldado. *He joined the army as a private.*
> Hubo más gastos que ingresos. *There were more expenses than profits.*
íngrimo *adj. alone (Amer.).*
> Estaba íngrimo. *He was all alone.*
inhábil *adj. incapable; unfit, unqualified.*
inhalar *to inhale.*
inhospitalario *adj. inhospitable.*
inhumación *f. burial.*
inhumano *adj. inhuman, cruel, hard-hearted.*
inicial *adj. initial; f. initial.*
iniciar *to initiate; to begin.*
iniciativa *f. initiative.*
> Tomar la iniciativa. *To take the initiative.*

inicuo *adj. wicked.*
iniquidad *f. wickedness, iniquity.*
injerto *m. graft (of trees).*
injuria *f. insult, injury, offense.*
injustamente *unjustly.*
injusticia *f. injustice.*
injusto *adj. unjust, unfair.*
> Eso es injusto. *That's not fair. That's unjust.*
inmediación *f. contiguity, nearness; vicinity.*
INMEDIATAMENTE *immediately.*
inmediato *adj. immediate; contiguous.*
inmejorable *adj. the very best, unsurpassable.*
inmensamente *immensely.*
inmenso *adj. immense, huge, vast.*
inmerecido *adj. undeserved.*
inmesurable *adj. boundless, immeasurable.*
inmiscuir *to mix.*
inmiscuirse *to meddle, to interfere.*
inmoderado *adj. immoderate, not moderate.*
inmoral *adj. immoral.*
inmortal *adj. immortal.*
inmóvil *adj. immovable, firmly fixed; deathlike.*
inmovilizar *to immobilize.*
inmueble *m. property; real estate.*
inmundicia *f. filth, dirt.*
inmundo *adj. filthy, dirty, unclean.*
inmutable *adj. unchangeable, immutable, never-changing.*
innecesario *adj. unnecessary, not necessary.*
innegable *adj. undeniable, unquestionable.*
inocencia *f. innocence.*
inocente *adj. innocent.*
inodoro *adj. odorless; m. toilet.*
> ¿Dónde está el inodoro? *Where's the toilet?*
inofensivo *adj. inoffensive, harmless.*
inoportuno *adj. inopportune, untimely; said or done at the wrong time.*
> No sea Ud. inoportuno. *Don't come at the wrong time (do things at the wrong time, say the wrong things).*
inquebrantable *adj. tenacious, unyielding.*
inquietar *to disturb, to cause anxiety.*
inquietarse *to become anxious or worried; to be uneasy or restless.*
inquieto *adj. restless, uneasy, worried.*
> Pasó toda la noche inquieto. *He was restless all night.*
inquietud *f. uneasiness, anxiety, restlessness.*
inquilino *m. tenant.*
inquirir *to inquire.*
insalubre *adj. unhealthful.*
insano *adj. insane, mad.*
inscribir *to inscribe; to register, to record.*
inscribirse *to register (at a school, etc.).*
inscripción *f. inscription.*
insecticida *adj. insecticide.*
> Polvo insecticida. *Insect powder. Insecticide.*
insecto *m. insect.*
inseguro *adj. uncertain.*
insensatez *f. foolishness, stupidity.*
insensato *adj. stupid, foolish.*
insensible *adj. not sensitive, unfeeling, heartless.*
inseparable *adj. inseparable.*
insertar *to insert; to introduce.*
inservible *adj. useless, good-for-nothing.*
insidioso *adj. insidious, sly.*
insigne *adj. famous, noted.*
insignia *f. badge; pl. insignia.*
insignificante *adj. insignificant.*
insinuar *to insinuate, to hint.*
insipidez *f. insipidity; lack of flavor (taste).*
insípido *adj. insipid, tasteless.*
insistencia *f. insistence, persistence.*

insistir *to insist.*
insolación *f. sunstroke.*
insolencia *f. insolence, rudeness.*
insolente *adj. insolent, rude.*
insolvente *adj. insolent, not able to pay, broke.*
insomnio *m. insomnia, sleeplessness.*
inspección *f. inspection.*
inspeccionar *to inspect, to examine.*
inspector *m. inspector; superintendent.*
inspiración *f. inspiration.*
inspirar *to inspire; to inhale.*
  Le inspiró mucha simpatía. *He found her very congenial.*
instalación *f. installation; fixtures.*
  Instalación eléctrica. *Electrical fixtures.*
instalar *to install; to set up.*
  Todavía no han instalado la luz eléctrica. *They haven't yet installed the electric lights.*
instancia *f. instance; request.*
  A instancia de. *At the request of.*
instantánea *f. snapshot.*
instantáneamente *instantly, at once.*
  Contestó instantáneamente. *He answered at once (right away).*
INSTANTE *m. instant.*
  Aguárdame un instante. *Wait for me a moment.*
  Me contestó al instante. *He answered me right away.*
instar *to urge, to press.*
instaurar *to establish, to restore.*
instintivamente *instinctively.*
instinto *m. instinct.*
institución *f. institution, establishment.*
instituir *to institute, to establish.*
instituto *m. institute; high school.*
institutriz *f. governess.*
instrucción *f. instruction; education; pl. directions.*
  Instrucción pública. *Public education.*
  ¿Tiene Ud. las instrucciones para el manejo de esta máquina? *Do you have the directions for the use of this machine?*
instructivo *adj. instructive.*
instructor *m. instructor, teacher.*
instruir *to instruct, to teach.*
instrumento *m. instrument.*
  ¿Qué instrumento toca Ud.? *What instrument do you play?*
insubordinado *adj. insubordinate.*
insubordinarse *to rebel; to mutiny.*
insuficiencia *f. insufficiency.*
insuficiente *adj. not enough, insufficient.*
insufrible *adj. unbearable.*
insultar *to insult.*
insulto *m. insult, offense.*
insuperable *adj. insuperable, insurmountable.*
intacto *adj. intact, untouched, whole.*
intachable *adj. irreproachable, faultless.*
integral *adj. integral; whole.*
  Pan integral. *Whole-wheat bread.*
integrar *to integrate.*
integridad *f. integrity.*
ÍNTEGRO *adj. entire, whole, in full; upright, honest.*
  Es un hombre íntegro. *He's an honest man. He's very upright.*
  La suma íntegra. *The amount in full.*
  Se comió un pan íntegro. *He ate a whole loaf of bread.*
intelectual *adj. and n. intellectual.*
inteligencia *f. intelligence; understanding.*
  En la inteligencia de que. *With the understanding that.*
INTELIGENTE *adj. intelligent.*

inteligible *adj. intelligible.*
intemperie *f. rough or bad weather.*
  A la intemperie. *Outdoors. In the open.*
INTENCIÓN *f. intention, mind, meaning.*
  ¿Cuál es su intención? *What does he intend to do?*
  Lo dijo con segunda intención. *What he said had a double meaning.*
  Tener buena intención. *To mean well.*
  Tener mala intención. *Not to mean well.*
  Tener la intención de. *To intend to.*
intendencia *f. administration, management; quartermaster (corps).*
intendente *m. quartermaster (officer); superintendent.*
intensidad *f. intensity.*
intenso *adj. intense.*
intentar *to try, to attempt, to intend, to endeavor.*
  Es inútil que intente. *It's useless to try.*
intento *m. intent, purpose.*
  No lo hice de intento. *I didn't do it on purpose.*
intercalar *to intercalate, to put in between.*
intercambio *m. interchange; exchange.*
interceder *to intercede, to plead in another's behalf.*
interceptar *to intercept; to block.*
INTERÉS *m. interest.*
  No demuestra el menor interés. *He doesn't show the slightest interest.*
  Pone interés en hacerlo bien. *He tries hard to do it well.*
  Devengar intereses. *To pay interest.*
interesado *adj. interested, concerned.*
INTERESANTE *adj. interesting.*
  Es una novela poco interesante. *It's not a very interesting novel.*
INTERESAR *to interest, to concern.*
  No me interesa. 1. *It doesn't interest me.* 2. *I don't care for him (her, it, etc.).*
INTERESARSE *to be concerned; to become interested.*
  Se interesó mucho en el negocio. *He became very interested in the business.*
interino *adj. provisional, temporary, acting.*
INTERIOR *adj. interior, internal; m. interior; inside.*
  Un cuarto interior. *An inside room.*
  Lo dijo para su interior. *He said it to himself.*
  El comercio interior. *Domestic trade.*
  El Ministerio de lo Interior. *Department of the Interior.*
  Ropa interior. *Underwear.*
  Navegación interior. *Inland navigation.*
intermediar *to mediate.*
intermediario *adj. and n. intermediary.*
intermedio *adj. intermediate; m. interval, recess.*
internacional *adj. international.*
internar *to intern, to confine.*
interno *adj. internal; interior; m. boarding student; intern.*
  Para uso interno. *For internal use.*
interponer *to interpose.*
interpretación *f. interpretation, meaning, acting.*
interpretar *to interpret; to understand.*
  Interpretar bien. *To understand correctly.*
  No interpretar bien. *To misunderstand.*
intérprete *m. and f. interpreter.*
intervalo *m. interval.*
intervenir *to intervene; to mediate.*
interrogación *f. interrogation, questioning; question, inquiry; question mark.*
  Signo de interrogación. *Question mark.*
interrogar *to interrogate, to question.*
interrogatorio *f. cross examination.*

INTERRUMPIR *to interrupt.*
  Dispense Ud. que le interrumpa. *Pardon me for interrupting you.*
interrupción *f. interruption; stop.*
  Sin interrupción. *Without stopping.*
interruptor *m. switch (electricity).*
intestino *adj. intestinal; domestic, internal; m. pl. intestines.*
intimar *to intimate, to hint; to order; to become intimate.*
intimidad *f. intimacy, close friendship.*
intimidar *to intimidate, to frighten.*
íntimo *adj. intimate, close.*
  Eran amigos íntimos. *They were very close friends.*
  Tuvimos una conversación íntima. *We had an intimate conversation. We had a tête-à-tête.*
intolerable *adj. intolerable, unbearable.*
intolerancia *f. intolerance.*
intolerante *adj. intolerant.*
intoxicación *f. intoxication, poisoning.*
intranquilo *adj. restless.*
intransigencia *f. uncompromisingness, intransigence.*
intransigente *adj. uncompromising, unyielding, die-hard, intransigent.*
intransitable *adj. impassable.*
intratable *adj. hard to deal with; hidebound; not sociable.*
intrepidez *f. intrepidity, courage.*
intrépido *adj. intrepid, fearless.*
intriga *f. intrigue, plot.*
intrigante *adj. intriguing; m. intriguer.*
intrincado *adj. intricate, entangled, complicated.*
introducción *f. introduction. See* presentación *and* recomendación.
introducir *to introduce, to put in. See* presentar.
  Introduje la carta en el buzón. *I put the letter in the mailbox.*
intromisión *f. interference.*
intruso *adj. intruding; m. and f. intruder.*
intuición *f. intuition.*
inundar *to inundate, to flood.*
INÚTIL *useless; fruitless; unnecessary.*
  Es inútil que se lo pida. *There's no use (in) asking him.*
  Es un hombre inútil. *He's good-for-nothing. He can't do anything.*
inutilidad *f. inutility, uselessness.*
inutilizar *to spoil, to ruin, to disable.*
INÚTILMENTE *uselessly, in vain.*
  Hicimos el viaje inútilmente. *We made the trip in vain.*
invadir *to invade.*
invalidar *to invalidate, to nullify, to render void.*
inválido *adj. invalid, null; crippled; m. an invalid; a cripple.*
invariable *adj. unchangeable, invariable.*
invasión *f. invasion.*
invención *f. invention.*
inventar *to invent.*
inventario *m. inventory.*
invento *m. invention.*
inverisímil *adj. See* inverosímil.
invernar *to winter, to spend the winter.*
  Fueron a invernar a California. *They went to spend the winter in California.*
inverosímil *adj. improbable, unlikely; incredible.*
  Me pareció inverosímil el relato. *The story seemed improbable to me.*
invertir *to invert, to turn upside down; to spend, to take (time); to invest (money).*
investigación *f. investigation.*

investigar *to investigate.*
INVIERNO *m. winter.*
invisible *adj. invisible.*
invitación *f. invitation.*
INVITADO *adj. invited; m. guest.*
  Estamos invitados a una reunión mañana. *We are invited to go to a meeting tomorrow.*
  Hoy tendremos invitados. *We're having guests today.*
INVITAR *to invite.*
inyección *f. injection.*
inyectar *to inject.*
iodo *m. iodine. See* **yodo.**
IR *to go; to be; to concern, to have to do with.*
  ¡Vámonos! *Let's go!*
  ¡Voy! *I'm coming!*
  Me voy. *I'm going away. I'm leaving.*
  Voy a mi casa. *I'm going home.*
  Debemos irnos. *We must go.*
  ¡Váyase! *Go away!*
  ¡Qué se vaya! *Let him go!*
  No se vaya Ud. *Don't go away.*
  No puedo ir. *I can't go.*
  ¿Cómo le va? (¿Cómo vamos?) *How are you? How are you getting along?*
  ¿Cómo van los negocios? *How's business?*
  El paciente va mucho mejor. *The patient is much better.*
  Van a dar las doce. *It will soon be twelve.*
  Vamos a ver. *Let's see.*
  Vamos a dar un paseo. *Let's take a walk.*
  Vamos, Juan, dígamelo Ud. *Go on, John, tell it to me.*
  Vamos, déjame ya. *Come on, let me alone (don't bother me).*
  ¡Qué se le ha de hacer! *It can't be helped!*
  Vamos al grano. *Let's get to the point.*
  ¿Quién va? *Who's there?*
  ¡Vaya! *Go on! I don't believe it!*
  ¡Vaya una ocurrencia! *What an idea!*
  ¡Vaya Ud. con Dios! *Good-by! Good luck to you! ("Go with God.")*
  ¡Vaya Ud. a paseo! *Go to the dickens! Go to blazes!*
  ¡Vaya por Dios! *Good gracious!*
  Váyase con la música a otra parte. *Go away, don't bother me.*
  ¡Qué va! *Nonsense!*
  Ahora va de veras. *Now it's really serious.*
  ¡Ahí va eso! *Here it comes! Catch!*
  Ahí van dos dólares a que yo llego. *I bet you two dollars that I'll get there first.*
  La situación va en peor. *The situation is getting worse and worse (is going from bad to worse).*
  Eso no me va ni me viene. *It (that) doesn't concern me in the least.*
  Eso no va conmigo. *That doesn't concern me.*
  Va de punta en blanco. *She's all dressed up.*
  El buque se fué a pique. *The ship sank.*
  Ir a pie. *To walk. To go on foot.*
  Ir a caballo. *To ride. To go on horseback.*
  Ir en coche. *To drive.*
  Ir de brazo. *To walk arm-in-arm.*
  Ir a medias. *To go half-and-half. To share equally.*
ira *f. anger, fury, rage.*
  Tuvo un repente de ira. *He had a fit of temper.*
iracundo *adj. irate, angry; enraged.*
  Estaba iracunda por lo que dije. *She was furious at what I said.*
ironía *f. irony.*
irónico *adj. ironical.*

irradiar *to irradiate.*
irreal *adj. unreal.*
irreflexivo *adj. thoughtless, rash.*
irregular *adj. irregular.*
irrespetuoso *adj. disrespectful, showing no respect.*
irresponsabilidad *f. irresponsibility, lack of responsibility.*
irresponsable *adj. irresponsible.*
irrigar *to irrigate.*
irritado *adj. irritated, angry.*
irritar *to irritate, to exasperate.*
  Ella le irrita. *She exasperates him.*
irrompible *adj. unbreakable.*
isla *f. isle, island.*
italiano *adj. and n. Italian.*
itinerario *adj. and n. itinerary; route; timetable, schedule.*
  ¿Qué itinerario seguirán? *Which route will you take?*
  Quisiera un itinerario de trenes. *I'd like a timetable.*
IZQUIERDO *adj. left; left-handed; f. left hand.*
  A la izquierda. *To the left.*
  Estaba sentado a mi izquierda. *He was sitting on my left.*
  Es un cero a la izquierda. *He doesn't count. He's a nonentity.*

J

jabalí *m. wild boar.*
jabón *m. soap.*
jabonar *to soap.*
jabonera *f. soapdish.*
jaca *f. nag, pony.*
jacinto *m. hyacinth.*
jactancia *f. boasting.*
jactarse *to boast, to brag.*
  Se jacta de haber viajado mucho por el mundo. *He boasts of having traveled all over the world.*
jalea *f. jelly.*
jalear *to encourage (a dancer); to sic (a dog).*
jaleo *m. clapping of hands to encourage a dancer; Andalusian dance; noisy party, revelry, racket.*
jalón *m. pole; surveying staff.*
JAMÁS *never.*
  Jamás he visto una corrida de toros. *I've never seen a bull fight.*
  Jamás lo hubiera hecho yo. *I'd never have done it.*
  Nunca jamás. *Never. Never again.*
  Para siempre jamás. *For ever and ever.*
  Jamás de los jamases. *Never again.*
jamón *m. ham (smoked or cured).*
jaque *m. check (in chess); boaster.*
  Jaque mate. *Checkmate.*
jaqueca *f. migraine, headache.*
  Tengo jaqueca. *I have a very bad headache.*
jarabe *m. syrup.*
  Jarabe para la tos. *Cough syrup.*
  Jarabe tapatío. *A typical Mexican dance.*
jardín *m. garden.*
jardinero *m. gardener.*
jarra *f. jug, pitcher.*
  En jarras. *With arms akimbo.*
jarro *m. pitcher, pot, jug; babbler.*
jarrón *m. vase, large jar.*
jaula *f. cage.*
jazmín *m. jasmine.*
jazz *m. jazz.*
jefatura *f. headquarters; leadership; office of a chief.*

  Jefatura de Policía. *Police headquarters.*
JEFE *m. chief; head, principal; leader; boss, employer.*
  Jefe de taller. *Foreman.*
  El jefe del gobierno. *The head of the government.*
  El jefe de la oficina. *The office manager.*
  Jefe de estación. *Stationmaster.*
jerarquía *f. hierarchy.*
jerez *m. sherry wine.*
jeringa *f. syringe.*
Jesucristo *m. Jesus Christ.*
jesuíta *m. Jesuit; hypocrite.*
Jesús *m. Jesus.*
  ¡Jesús! *Good heavens! God bless you (said when someone sneezes)!*
jilguero *m. linnet (bird).*
jinete *m. horseman, rider.*
JIRA *f. outing, excursion, picnic; tour.*
  Jira campestre. *Picnic.*
  Jira de inspección. *Tour of inspection.*
jirafa *f. giraffe.*
jornada *f. journey, trip; day's travel; one day's work.*
  Una jornada de cinco días. *A five days' journey (trip).*
  Los obreros trabajan jornadas de ocho horas. *The laborers work eight hours a day.*
jornal *m. day's pay; wages.*
  Trabaja a jornal. *He works by the day.*
  Gana un buen jornal. *He earns good wages.*
jornalero *m. day laborer.*
joroba *f. hump.*
jorobado *m. hunchback.*
jorobar *to importune, to annoy.*
jota *f. name of the letter j; a typical Spanish dance.*
  No saber una jota. *To be very ignorant.*
JOVEN *adj. young; m. young man; f. young lady.*
  Todavía es muy joven. *She's still very young.*
  ¿Quién es esa joven? *Who's that young lady?*
  Es un joven muy simpático. *He's a very nice young man.*
jovial *adj. jovial, merry.*
joya *f. jewel, gem; precious, wonderful.*
  Llevaba unas lindas joyas. *She wore very beautiful jewels.*
  Esa muchacha es una joya. *She's a wonderful girl.*
joyas *f. jewelry*
jubilar *to pension off, to retire from service.*
judía *f. bean; string bean; Jewess.*
  Déme una libra de judías. *Give me a pound of beans.*
  Estas judías verdes son excelentes. *These string beans are excellent.*
judío *adj. Jewish; m. Jew.*
JUEGO *m. play, game; gambling; set; play, movement.*
  ¿Qué juego prefiere? *Which game do you like best?*
  Este sombrero no hace juego con mi vestido. *This hat doesn't match my dress.*
  Ya te veo el juego. *I see what your intentions are. I see what you're driving (getting) at.*
  Compró un juego de loza. *She bought a set of dishes.*
  Juego de té. *Tea set.*
  Juego de azar. *Game of chance.*
  Juego de naipes (cartas). *Card game.*
  Juego de prendas. *A game of forfeits.*
  Hacer juego. *To match.*
  Estar en juego. *To be at stake.*
  Poner en juego. *To bring to bear upon. To put into play.*

JUEVES m. Thursday.

juez m. judge.

Juez de paz. Justice of the peace.

jugada f. play; move (chess); turn (cards); mean trick.

Jugada de bolsa. Stock market speculation.

jugador m. gambler; player.

JUGAR to play; to gamble; to stake; to take part.

Juega bien al tenis. He plays tennis well.

Ha jugado todo su dinero. He's gambled all his money.

Juega su última carta. He's playing his last card. That's his last card.

jugarreta f. bad play; bad turn, nasty trick.

jugo m. juice.

jugoso adj. juicy.

juguete m. toy, plaything; laughing stock.

Le regalaron un juguete. They gave him a toy as a present.

Está sirviendo de juguete. He's being made a laughingstock.

juicio m. judgment; mind; opinion; wisdom, good judgment; lawsuit, trial.

¿Ha perdido Ud. el juicio? Have you lost your mind?

Es un hombre de juicio. He's a man of good judgment. He has good judgment.

A mi juicio. In my opinion.

Someter a juicio. To bring to trial.

Pedir en juicio. To sue (at law).

juicioso adj. prudent, sensible, wise, well-behaved.

JULIO m. July.

JUNIO m. June.

junta f. board, council, junta, committee; meeting; joint, coupling, union, junction.

¿A qué hora fué la junta? What time did the meeting take place?

Junta directiva. Board of directors. Executive committee.

Junta de comercio. Board of trade.

Junta de acreedores. Creditors' meeting.

Junta de sanidad. Board of health.

Junta remachada. Riveted joint.

JUNTAR to join, to unite; to assemble, to gather; to pile up (money); to leave ajar (door).

Junte toda la ropa y póngala en la maleta. Get all the clothes together and put them in the suitcase.

Junte la puerta. Leave the door ajar (open).

Juntar dinero. To pile up money.

JUNTARSE to get together, to meet; to join, to associate with, to keep company.

Se junta con mala gente. He keeps bad company.

Se juntó mucha gente para oír al orador. Quite a crowd gathered to hear the speaker.

No me gusta con quien se junta. I don't like the people you associate with.

JUNTO near, close to; together.

Déjalo junto a la puerta. Leave it near the door.

Pasar por junto de. To pass near. To pass by.

Emprenderemos el negocio juntos. We're going into this business together.

Si Ud. quiere, vamos juntos. If you wish, we'll go together.

jura f. oath of allegiance.

jurado m. jury, juryman, juror.

jurar to swear, to take oath.

No se lo creo aunque me lo jure. I won't believe you even if you swear that it's true.

justicia f. justice; fairness; law.

Hacer justicia. To do justice. To be just.

Hacerse justicia por sí mismo. To take the law into one's hands.

La justicia. The police.

justificación f. justification.

justificar to justify.

JUSTO adj. just; fair; exact, to the point; scarce; tight; m. a just and pious man.

Eso no es justo. That's not fair.

Al año justo de. Just a year after.

El peso justo. The exact weight.

El sombrero me está muy justo. My hat is very tight.

Vivimos muy justos. We live from hand to mouth.

juvenil adj. juvenile, youthful.

juventud f. youth, youthfulness.

juzgado m. tribunal, court (of justice).

JUZGAR to judge; to think.

Lo ha juzgado Ud. mal. You have judged it wrongly.

¿Lo juzga Ud. conveniente? Do you think it's advisable?

K

ka f. name of the letter k.

kermese f. charity festival; bazaar.

kilo m. kilo, kilogram (2.2046 pounds).

Déme un kilo de azúcar. Give me a kilogram of sugar.

kilogramo m. kilogram.

kilometraje m. mileage.

kilométrico kilometric; mileage (ticket).

kilómetro m. kilometer.

kimono m. kimona, dressing gown.

kiosco m. kiosk, newsstand.

kodak m. Kodak.

L

LA (f. article) the; m. pl. los; f. pl. las the. See los.

La muchacha. The girl.

Las muchachas. The girls.

Las dos hermanas se parecen. Both sisters look alike.

Los padres. The parents.

LA (f. direct object pronoun) you, her, it; pl. las them, you. See los and les.

¿La vió Ud. en la fiesta? Did you see her at the party?

No la vi. I didn't see ner.

Me alegro de verla. I'm glad to see you (a woman).

Dámela. Give it (f.) to me.

Traduzca estas palabras al español y léalas en voz alta. Translate these words into Spanish and read them aloud.

la m. la, A (sixth note of the musical scale)..

labia f. sweet, winning talk.

Tiene mucha labia para vender. He has a good sales talk.

LABIO m. lip.

Lápiz de labios. Lipstick.

labor f. labor, task; needlework, embroidery.

laborable adj. workable; working.

Día laborable. Working day.

laborar to labor; to work; to till.

laboratorio m. laboratory.

laborioso adj. laborious; hardworking.

labrador m. farmer, peasant.

labranza f. farming; farm.

labrar to till, to cultivate (land); to carve (wood, etc.).

labriego m. peasant.

lacerar to lacerate; to mangle.

lacio adj. withered; languid; straight (hair).

lacónico adj. laconic, brief.

lacrar to communicate (a disease); to seal (with wax).

lacre m. sealing wax.

ladear to tilt, to incline; to skirt.

ladino adj. shrewd; crafty, cunning.

LADO m. side; party, faction.

Siéntese a mi lado. Sit next to me. Sit beside me.

Al otro lado de la calle. Across the street. On the other side of the street.

Vive en la casa de al lado. She lives next door. She lives in the next house.

Ese edificio queda al otro lado del parque. That building's on the other side of the park.

Nos quedamos a este lado del lago. We'll stay on this side of the lake.

Por un lado. On the one hand. On one side.

Por un lado me gusta, pero por el otro no. On the one hand I like it, on the other I don't.

¡Mire Ud. al otro lado! Look on the other side!

¿Quiere hacerse a un lado? Please move aside.

No cabe de lado. It won't fit sideways.

Trabajaron lado a lado. They worked side by side.

Mirar de lado. To look askance. To look out of the corner of one's eye. To look down on.

Dejemos esto a un lado. Let's put this aside.

Conozco muy bien su lado flaco. I know his weakness (weak side) very well.

ladrar to bark.

ladrido m. barking; criticism; calumny.

ladrillo m. brick, tile.

ladrón m. thief, robber.

lagartija f. small lizard.

lagarto m. lizard; alligator (Amer.).

lago m. lake.

lágrima f. tear; drop.

laguna f. pond; gap, blank.

lamentable adj. regrettable, deplorable.

Es lamentable. It's regrettable.

lamentar to regret, to deplore; to mourn.

Lo lamento mucho. I'm very sorry.

Lamento mucho lo ocurrido. I regret what happened. I'm sorry about what happened.

lamer to lick.

lámina f. plate, sheet of metal; engraving, print, picture.

lámpara f. lamp.

lana f. wool.

lance m. hazard; trouble, accident; quarrel.

De lance. Secondhand. At a bargain.

Libros de lance. Secondhand books. Used books.

lancha f. launch, boat.

langosta f. locust; lobster.

lánguido adj. languid, faint, weak.

lanzallamas m. flame thrower.

lanzamiento m. launching (of a ship); throwing; dispossessing.

lanzar to throw; to launch; to dispossess.

lapicero m. pencil holder.

lápida f. a flat stone with an inscription; gravestone.

LÁPIZ m. pencil; crayon.

Lápiz de labios. Lipstick.

lapso m. lapse (of time).

larga f. delay, adjournment.

A la larga. In the long run.

Dar largas a. To put off. To quibble. To delay.

largar to loosen; to let go; to heave (a ship).

Largarse. To leave. To go away.

¡Lárguese de aquí! Get out of here (not polite)!

LARGO adj. long; lengthy; m. length.

Tiene los brazos muy largos. He has very long arms.

Tiene cinco pies de largo. *It's five feet long.*
Conferencia a larga distancia. *Long distance call.*
No ponga Ud. esa cara tan larga. *Don't pull such a long face.*
Tres horas largas. *Three whole hours.*
¿Entró Ud. en casa de Juan?—No, pasé de largo. *Did you stop in at John's house?—No, I (just) passed by.*
A lo largo. 1. *In the distance.* 2. *Lengthwise.*
A lo largo de. *Along.*
A la corta o a la larga. *Sooner or later.*
A lo más largo. *At most.*
¡Largo de aquí! *Get out of here!*
Largo de mano. *Light-fingered.*
laringe *f. larynx.*
laringitis *f. laryngitis.*
larva *f. larva.*
las *f. pl. See la the.*
LÁSTIMA *f. pity; compassion.*
Es lástima. *It's a pity.*
¡Qué lástima! *What a pity! It's too bad! What a shame!*
Me da mucha lástima. *I feel very sorry for him.*
lastimar *to hurt; to injure.*
¿Se ha lastimado Ud.? *Have (did) you hurt yourself?*
Me lastimé una pierna al caer. *I hurt my leg when I fell (down).*
lastre *m. ballast.*
lata *f. tin; tin can; nuisance.*
lateral *adj. lateral.*
latido *m. beat; throbbing.*
latigazo *m. lash; crack (of a whip).*
látigo *m. whip.*
latín *m. Latin.*
latino *adj. Latin.*
latir *to palpitate, to beat.*
latoso *adj. tiresome; boring.*
lava *f. lava.*
lavable *adj. washable.*
lavabo *m. washstand; washroom.*
lavadero *m. laundry, washing-place.*
lavado *m. washing.*
Lavado y planchado. *Laundry. ("Washing and ironing.")*
lavandera *f. laundress, washwoman.*
lavandería *f. laundry.*
lavaplatos *m. and f. dishwasher.*
lavar *to wash; to launder.*
Láveme estos calcetines. *Wash these socks for me.*
¿Le lavo la cabeza? *Do you want a shampoo? ("Do you want to have your hair washed?")*
lavarse *to wash oneself.*
Lavarse las manos. *To wash one's hands.*
¿Quiere lavarse antes de comer? *Do you want to wash up before eating?*
lavativa *f. enema.*
laxante *adj. and n. laxative.*
lazo *m. bow; lasso, loop.*
Corbata de lazo. *Bow tie.*
LE *him, her, it; to him, to her, to it. See les.*
¿Qué le pasa? *What's the matter with him (her)?*
Le conozco. *I know him.*
Le di el libro (a ella). *I gave her the book.*
Le hablé hace un momento. *I spoke to him a little while ago.*
Le expliqué el caso a mi esposa. *I explained the matter to my wife.*
leal *adj. loyal.*
lealtad *f. loyalty.*
lección *f. lesson.*

lector *adj. reader.*
lectura *f. reading.*
LECHE *f. milk.*
lechería *f. dairy.*
lechero *m. milkman.*
lecho *m. bed; bed of a river; stratum.*
lechón *m. little pig, suckling pig.*
lechuga *f. lettuce.*
lechuza *f. owl.*
LEER *to read.*
Puedo leer español pero no lo puedo hablar. *I can read Spanish but I can't speak it.*
legajo *m. bundle of papers.*
legal *adj. legal, lawful; standard.*
Peso legal. *Standard weight.*
legalizar *to legalize.*
legar *to bequeath; to delegate.*
legendario *adj. legendary.*
legible *adj. legible.*
legión *f. legion.*
legislación *f. legislation.*
legislar *to legislate.*
legislatura *f. legislature.*
legitimar *to make legitimate, to legalize.*
legítimo *adj. legitimate; authentic.*
legua *f. league (measure of distance—about three miles).*
legumbre *f. vegetable.*
leído *adj. well-read, well-educated.*
Es un hombre muy leído. *He's a well-read man.*
lejano *adj. distant, remote, far.*
Un país lejano. *A distant country.*
LEJOS *far, far away, distant.*
¿Es muy lejos de aquí? *Is it very far from here?*
¿Queda lejos el hotel? *Is the hotel far from here?*
Está muy lejos de aquí. *It's very far from here. It's a long way from here. It's quite a distance from here.*
Algo lejos. *Rather far.*
Más lejos. *Further. Farther. More distant.*
A lo lejos. *In the distance.*
Desde (de) lejos. *From afar. From a distance.*
lema *m. motto.*
lencería *f. linen goods, linen shop; linen trade.*
LENGUA *f. tongue; language.*
Lengua española. *Spanish language.*
Lengua madre. *Mother tongue.*
Tirar de la lengua. *To draw one out.*
No morderse la lengua. *Not to be afraid to talk.*
Morderse la lengua. *To hold one's tongue. ("To bite one's tongue.")*
Irsele a uno la lengua. *To speak out of turn.*
Pegarse la lengua al paladar. *To be speechless with excitement or fear.*
lenguaje *m. language; style.*
LENTAMENTE *slowly.*
lente *m. lens; pl. eyeglasses.*
lenteja *f. lentil.*
lentitud *f. slowness.*
LENTO *adj. slow; sluggish.*
leña *f. firewood.*
A falta de carbón quemaremos leña. *If there's no coal, we'll burn wood.*
Echar leña al fuego. *To add fuel to the fire.*
leñador *m. woodcutter.*
leño *m. log, block.*
león *m. lion.*
leona *f. lioness; brave woman.*
leopardo *m. leopard.*
lepra *f. leprosy.*
LES *to them; to you (pl.); them, you (pl.). See le.*
Les escribiré. *I'll write to them.*
Les estimo mucho. *I have a high regard for*

them (you, pl.).
Les querrás mucho. *You'll like them a lot.*
Les encantará (a Uds.). *You (pl.) will love it. You'll be charmed by it.*
lesión *f. lesion, injury, wound.*
lesionar *to hurt; to wound; to injure.*
LETRA *f. letter; handwriting; printing type; words of a song; draft, bill (of exchange).*
Tiene buena letra. *She has a good handwriting.*
A la letra. *To the letter. Literally. Verbatim.*
letrado *adj. learned, erudite; m. lawyer.*
letrero *m. inscription; sign; label.*
No me había fijado en el letrero. *I didn't notice the sign.*
letrina *f. latrine.*
levadura *f. leaven, yeast.*
levantamiento *m. raising, uprising, revolt.*
LEVANTAR *to raise, to lift, to pick up; to remove, to clear (the table); to draw (a map).*
¿Puede Ud. levantar ese peso? *Can you lift that weight?*
Levante la mesa. *Clear the table.*
Levanta ese papel del suelo. *Pick up that paper from the floor.*
Levantar cabeza. *To raise one's head again. To get on one's feet again.*
Empezó a levantar la voz. *He began to raise his voice.*
Levantar un plano. *To draw a map (of a place).*
Llegamos en el momento de levantar el telón. *We arrived just as the curtain was going up.*
Levantar la vista. *To lift one's eyes. To look up.*
LEVANTARSE *to rise, to get up.*
¿A qué hora se levanta Ud.? *What time do you get up?*
Me levanto temprano. *I get up early.*
Es hora de levantarse. *It's time to get up.*
leve *adj. light (weight); slight.*
levita *f. frock coat.*
léxico *m. lexicon.*
LEY *f. law, act; legal standard of quality, weight or measure.*
Proyecto de ley. *Bill (of Congress).*
La ley fué aprobada en el senado. *The law was passed in (by) the Senate.*
De ley. *Standard (gold, etc.).*
leyenda *f. legend; inscription (on coins, metals, etc.).*
lezna *f. awl.*
liar *to tie, to bind; to enbroil.*
liberación *f. liberation.*
liberal *adj. and n. liberal.*
liberar *See libertar.*
libertad *f. liberty, freedom.*
libertador *adj. liberating; m. liberator.*
libertar *to liberate, to free.*
libertino *adj. and n. dissolute, licentious; libertine.*
libra *f. pound.*
Déme media libra de café. *Give me half a pound of coffee.*
Libra esterlina. *Pound sterling.*
libranza *f. draft; money order.*
LIBRE *adj. free.*
Avíseme en cuanto esté libre. *Let me know as soon as he's free.*
Libre a bordo. *Free on board (F.O.B.).*
Entrada libre. *Admission free.*
librería *f. bookstore; library; bookcase.*
librero *m. bookseller.*
libreta *f. memorandum book; loaf of bread weighing one pound (in Madrid).*
Libreta de apuntes. *Notebook.*
Libreta de depósitos. *Bankbook.*
LIBRO *m. book.*

Libro en rústica. *Paper-bound book.*

Libro de caja. *Cashbook.*

Libros de lance. *Secondhand books.*

Firme en el libro de registro. *Sign the register.*

licencia *f. license; leave, furlough; permit; certificate; degree.*

licenciado *m. license; lawyer.*

licenciar *to license; to allow; to discharge (a soldier).*

licitador *m. bidder.*

lícito *adj. licit, lawful, just, fair.*

licor *m. liquor.*

licorería *f. liquor store.*

líder *m. leader.*

lidiar *to combat, to fight; to contend.*

liebre *f. hare.*

Donde menos se piensa salta la liebre. *Things happen unexpectedly. ("The hare leaps from the bush where we least expect her.")*

lienzo *m. linen cloth; canvas (painting).*

liga *f. garter; birdlime; league; alloy.*

ligar *to bind, to tie; to alloy.*

ligereza *f. lightness; fickleness; hastiness.*

LIGERO *adj. quick, swift, light (weight); hasty.*

Hágalo ligero. *Do it quickly.*

Es muy ligero de cascos. *He's very silly (feather-brained, light-headed).*

lija *f. sandpaper; dogfish.*

lila *f. lilac; lilac color.*

lima *f. lime (fruit); file (tool).*

limar *to file (with a tool); to polish.*

limitación *f. limitation, limit.*

limitado *adj. limited.*

limitar *to limit; to restrain.*

Limitarse a decir. *To say only. To confine oneself to.*

límite *f. limit, boundary, border.*

Todo tiene sus límites. *There's a limit to everything. One must draw the line somewhere.*

limón *m. lemon.*

limonada *f. lemonade.*

limosna *f. alms, charity.*

Pedir limosna. *To beg.*

limpiabotas *m. bootblack.*

limpiador *m. cleaner; cleanser.*

limpiar *to clean, to cleanse; to mop up.*

Quiero que me limpie en seco este traje. *I'd like this suit dry-cleaned.*

Quiero que me limpien los zapatos. *I want my shoes shined. I want a shoeshine.*

limpiaúñas *m. nail cleaner.*

limpieza *f. cleaning; cleanliness; honesty.*

LIMPIO *adj. clean; neat; pure.*

Tiene su casa muy limpia. *She keeps her house very clean.*

Tráigame una toalla limpia. *Bring me a clean towel.*

Poner en limpio. *To make a good (final, "clean") copy.*

Sacar en limpio. *To make out. To conclude. To infer.*

Jugar limpio. *To play fair. To deal fairly.*

linaza *f. linseed; flaxseed.*

lince *adj. keen, sharp-sighted; m. lynx.*

linchar *to lynch.*

lindar *to adjoin, to border.*

linde *m. limit, boundary; landmark.*

lindero *adj. adjoining, bordering; m. boundary.*

LINDO *adj. pretty; neat.*

¡Qué muchacha tan linda! *What a pretty girl!*

Nos divertimos de lo lindo. *We had a wonderful time. ("We enjoyed ourselves wonderfully.")*

LÍNEA *f. line.*

Tire Ud. una línea recta. *Draw a straight line.*

La línea está ocupada. *The line is busy.*

Escribir cuatro líneas. *To write a few lines. To drop someone a note.*

Línea telefónica. *Telephone line.*

Línea férrea. *Railway.*

Línea aérea. *Air line.*

En toda la línea. *All along the line.*

lingote *m. ingot.*

lingüista *m. and f. linguist.*

linimento *m. liniment.*

lino *m. flax; linen.*

linóleo *m. linoleum.*

linotipia *f. linotype.*

linotipista *m. linotype operator.*

linterna *f. lantern; flashlight.*

lío *m. bundle, parcel; row, fix, mess.*

Me hice un lío. *I was all mixed up.*

En buen lío nos hemos metido. *We got ourselves in quite a fix.*

Armar un lío. *To start a row.*

liquidación *f. liquidation.*

liquidar *to liquidate.*

LÍQUIDO *adj. liquid; clear, net; m. liquid, fluid.*

Producto líquido. *Net proceeds.*

lírico *adj. lyric, lyrical.*

lirio *m. lily.*

lisiado *adj. maimed, crippled.*

liso *adj. smooth, even; plain.*

Tela lisa. *Plain cloth.*

lisonja *f. flattery.*

lisonjear *to flatter; to please.*

lisonjero *adj. flattering, pleasing; n. flatterer.*

El habla de Ud. de una manera muy lisonjera. *He speaks well of you. ("He speaks of you in a very flattering manner.")*

LISTA *f. list; roll, muster; menu; strip of cloth; stripe.*

Tráigame la lista de vinos. *Bring me the wine list.*

Aquí está la lista de platos. *Here is the menu.*

Pasar lista. *To call the roll.*

Tela a listas. *Striped cloth.*

Lista de correos. *General delivery.*

listado *adj. striped.*

listín *m. telephone book.*

LISTO *adj. ready; quick; bright, clever, smart, cunning.*

¿Está Ud. listo? *Are you ready?*

Todo está listo. *Everything's ready.*

No crea, es más listo de lo que parece. *Don't get the wrong idea; he's smarter than he looks.*

litera *f. litter.*

literario *adj. literary.*

literato *adj. learned man: writer.*

literatura *f. literature.*

litigio *m. litigation, lawsuit.*

litografía *f. lithography.*

litoral *adj. littoral; m. coast; seacoast.*

litro *m. liter.*

liviano *adj. light (weight); fickle; lewd.*

Es liviano; Ud. puede alzarlo facilmente. *It's light; you can lift it easily.*

lívido *adj. livid; pale.*

Se puso lívido. *He became pale.*

LO *(neuter article) the.*

Lo más hermoso. *The prettiest.*

Lo mejor. *The best.*

Lo peor. *The worst.*

Lo dicho. *What's said.*

Lo mío y lo tuyo. *Mine and yours. What's mine and what's yours.*

Lo demás importa poco. *The rest doesn't matter a great deal. The rest is not very important.*

Eso es lo que quiero. *That's what I want.*

A lo lejos. *At a distance. In the distance.*

A lo sumo. *At the most.*

LO *(m. and neuter direct object pronoun) it, him, you.*

¿Quién lo quiere? *Who wants it?*

¿Me lo das? *Will you give it to me?*

Démelo. *Give it to me.*

No me lo diga Ud. *Don't tell it to me.*

Dígaselo a ella. *Tell it to her.*

¿Están Uds. listos? —Lo estamos. *Are you ready? —We are.*

No lo conozco. *I don't know him.*

Se lo llevaron a casa. *They took (carried) him home.*

No lo puedo remediar. *I can't help it.*

¿Por qué no se lo pides? *Why don't you ask him for it?*

No lo suelte Ud. *Hold it. Don't let it go.*

lobo *m. wolf.*

lóbulo *m. lobule, lobe.*

lóbrego *adj. murky, dark; sad.*

local *adj. local; m. place; quarters.*

Costumbre local. *Local custom.*

Este local es muy pequeño. *This place (hall, etc.) is very small.*

localidad *f. locality, place; seat (theater).*

localizar *to localize, to locate.*

loción *f. lotion, wash.*

loco *adj. mad, insane, crazy; m. madman.*

Volverse loco. *To lose one's mind. To become insane.*

Estar loco. *To be crazy.*

Está loco por ella. *He's head over heels in love with her. He's crazy about her.*

Hablar a tontas y a locas. *To tell idle stories (tales).*

locomoción *f. locomotion.*

locuaz *adj. loquacious, talkative.*

locura *f. insanity, madness, folly.*

Eso es una locura. *That's a crazy thing to do. That's absurd.*

lodo *m. mud, mire.*

lógica *f. logic.*

Carece de lógica y de sentido común. *It lacks logic and common sense.*

lógico *adj. logical, reasonable.*

LOGRAR *to obtain, to get; to attain; to manage, to succeed.*

Por fin logró lo que quería. *He finally got what he wanted.*

Debe haber algún medio de lograrlo. *There must be some way of getting it (of obtaining it).*

Lograron hacerlo. *They managed to do it.*

Hemos logrado que nos paguen. *We have succeeded in getting them to pay us.*

Nada lograba influenciarle. *Nothing could influence him.*

logro *m. gain; attainment; achievement.*

loma *f. hillock, little hill.*

lombriz *f. earthworm.*

lomo *m. loin; back (of a book); ridge (agriculture).*

Llevar a lomo. *To carry on one's back.*

lona *f. canvas.*

longaniza *f. a kind of sausage.*

longitud *f. longitude.*

lonja *f. slice, rasher; exchange market.*

loro *m. parrot.*

LOS *(pl. of el) the. See la, lo.*

Los hombres. *The men.*

Los dos. *Both. The two of them.*

Los míos. *My people. My family. My folks.*

Lávese las manos. *Wash your hands.*

Límpiate los dientes. *Brush your teeth.*

LOS *(pl. direct object pronoun) they, them; you (pl.).* See **le** and **les.**

¿Cómo los quiere Ud.? *How do you want them?*

Los aguardábamos (a Uds.). *We were waiting for you (pl.).*

Se los daré mañana. *I'll give them to you (them) tomorrow.*

Ya no los queremos. *We don't want them any longer.*

¿Ve Ud. a los soldados?—Los veo. *Do you see the soldiers?—I see them.*

lote *m. lot; portion, share.*

loza *f. chinaware; crockery.*

lozanía *f. vigor; exuberance, liveliness.*

lozano *adj. healthy; sprightly, lively.*

lubricación *f. lubrication.*

lubricante *adj. lubricating; m. lubricant.*

lubricar *to lubricate.*

lucidez *f. lucidity, clearness.*

lúcido *adj. lucid, brilliant.*

luciérnaga *f. glowworm, firefly.*

lucir *to shine; to show off.*

lucirse *to outshine; to show off.*

lucrativo *adj. lucrative, profitable.*

lucro *m. gain, profit.*

lucha *f. fight, struggle, strife.*

La lucha por la vida. *The struggle for existence.*

luchador *wrestler, fighter.*

luchar *to fight, to wrestle, to struggle.*

LUEGO *immediately, soon, afterwards, then, later.*

¡Hasta luego! *See you later. So long.*

¿Qué haremos luego? *What will we do afterwards?*

Cenaremos y luego iremos al teatro. *We'll have dinner and then we'll go to the theater.*

Quiero que lo hagas muy luego. *I want you to do it right away.*

Lo haré luego. *I'll do it later.*

Desde luego. *Of course.*

Avíseme luego que lo reciba. *As soon as you receive it, let me know.*

LUGAR *m. place; time; occasion; motive, cause.*

Nos encontraremos en el lugar de costumbre. *We'll meet at the usual place.*

Ponga las cosas en su lugar. *Put the things in their place. Put everything in its place.*

Yo en su lugar, no iría. *If I were you (in your place) I wouldn't go.*

¿A qué hora tendrá lugar la boda? *What time will the wedding take place?*

En lugar de. *Instead of.*

Dar lugar a. *To give cause for. To give occasion for. To lead up to.*

lugarteniente *m. deputy, substitute, lieutenant.*

lujo *m. luxury.*

Edición de lujo. *De luxe edition.*

lujoso *adj. luxurious.*

lujuria *f. lust; excess.*

LUMBRE *f. fire, light.*

Déme lumbre. *Give me a light.*

Sentémonos junto a la lumbre. *Let's sit near the fire.*

luminoso *adj. shining, luminous.*

LUNA *f. moon; glass plate for mirrors.*

Hay luna esta noche. *The moon is out tonight.*

Luna de miel. *Honeymoon.*

lunático *adj. lunatic, mad, eccentric.*

LUNES *m. Monday.*

lustrar *to polish, to shine.*

lustre *m. luster, gloss; splendor.*

luto *m. mourning; grief, sorrow.*

De luto. *In mourning.*

LUZ *f. light, daylight.*

Encienda la luz. *Put the light on.*

Apaque la luz. *Turn the light off. Put the light out.*

Se apagaron las luces. *The lights went out.*

Luz eléctrica. *Electric light.*

Dar a luz. 1. *To give birth.* 2. *To publish.*

Salir a luz. *To be published. To appear (a book).*

A todas luces. *In every respect.*

LL

llaga *f. ulcer, wound.*

llama *f. flame; llama (animal).*

llamada *f. call; marginal note.*

Llamada telefónica. *Phone call.*

llamamiento *m. calling; call; appeal.*

LLAMAR *to call; to appeal; to name; to send for; to knock (at the door).*

¿Ha llamado Ud.? *Did you call?*

Llamar por teléfono. *To phone.*

Llámeme por teléfono. *Give me a ring. Phone me. ("Call me on the telephone.")*

Llame Ud. un taxi, por favor. *Please call a taxi.*

Llaman a la puerta. *Somebody's knocking at the door. Someone's at the door.*

Llama a la criada y pide café y tostadas. *Ring for the maid and order coffee and toast.*

Mandar a llamar. *To send for.*

Mande a llamar al doctor. *Send for the doctor.*

Llamar la atención. *To call attention to.*

Llamar a gritos. *To call out loud. To yell for someone.*

LLAMARSE *to be called or named.*

¿Cómo se llama Ud.? *What's your name?*

Me llamo . . . *My name is . . .*

¿Cómo se llama esta calle? *What's the name of this street?*

llamarada *f. blaze; flushing (of the face).*

llamativo *adj. conspicuous, striking, attractive, showy.*

llanamente *simply, plainly, clearly; sincerely, frankly.* Hable llanamente. *Speak plainly (simply). Speak frankly.*

llaneza *f. simplicity, plainness.*

llano *adj. even, smooth, flat; frank; m. plain, flatland.*

Un campo llano. *A smooth terrain.*

llanta *f. rim; tire.*

llanto *m. weeping, crying.*

llanura *f. plain, flatlands.*

LLAVE *f. key; wrench; faucet, spigot.*

¿Dónde está la llave de mi cuarto? *Where's the key to my room?*

Cerrar con llave. *To lock.*

Cierre la puerta con llave cuando salga. *Lock the door when you leave.*

Llave inglesa. *Monkey wrench.*

llavero *m. key-ring.*

llegada *f. arrival, coming.*

Avíseme de su llegada. *Let me know when you'll (he'll) arrive.*

LLEGAR *to arrive; to come; to reach, to succeed; to amount.*

¿A qué hora llega el tren? *(At) What time does the train arrive?*

El tren llega con dos horas de retraso. *The train is two hours late.*

Llegué ayer. *I came home yesterday. I got back (here) yesterday.*

¿Llegó Ud. a tiempo? *Were you in time?*

¿Cuándo llegamos a la frontera? *When will we reach the border?*

Llegó a hacerlo. *He managed to do it.*

Llega Ud. de improviso. *You've come rather unexpectedly.*

Tenía prisa por llegar a la hora. *He was in a hurry to get there on time.*

Ha llegado a mis oídos que . . . *I've heard that . . .*

Llegar a ser. *To become.*

Llegar a las manos. *To come to blows.*

LLENAR *to fill, to stuff; to occupy; to satisfy; to fulfill.*

Llene la botella de vino. *Fill the bottle with wine.*

La noticia la llenó de alegría. *The news made her very happy. The news filled her with joy.*

Al verla se llenó de gozo. *He was glad to see her. ("He was very happy when he saw her.")*

No me llena su explicación. *His explanation doesn't satisfy me.*

Llenar completamente. *To fill up (completely).*

LLENO *adj. full; complete; m. fullness, abundance; full house (theater).*

Estoy lleno. *I'm full. I've had enough.*

El vaso está lleno. *The glass is full.*

Hay un lleno completo esta noche. *There's a full house tonight.*

llevadero *adj. bearable, tolerable.*

LLEVAR *to carry, to take; to take away; to set (a price); to wear (clothes); to be (older, late, etc.).*

Lléveme allí. *Take me there.*

Taxi, lléveme a la estación. *Taxi, take me to the station.*

Lleve estas cartas al correo. *Take these letters to the post office.*

Lleve Ud. este paquete a mi casa. *Take this package to my house.*

¿Llevamos paraguas? *Shall we take umbrellas?*

No llevo bastante dinero. *I don't have enough money on me. ("I'm not carrying enough money on me.")*

Ayúdeme a llevar este hombre en la camilla. *Help me carry this man on the stretcher.*

¿Cuánto le llevó el tendero por esto? *How much did the storekeeper charge you for this?*

Me lo llevo si me lo deja en tres dólares. *I'll take it if you'll let me have it for three dollars.*

Llevamos un tanto por ciento de interés. *We charge so much (per cent) interest.*

Hace una semana que llevo este traje. *I've worn this suit for a week.*

Llevar al revés. *To wear on the wrong side. To wear wrong side out.*

¿Cuánto tiempo lleva Ud. esperándome? *How long have you been waiting for me?*

El tren lleva una hora de retraso. *The train is an hour late.*

Le llevo cinco años. *I'm five years older than he.*

Llevar a cuestas. *To carry on one's shoulders.*

Llevar a cabo. *To carry out. To bring about. To put through.*

Llevar consigo. *To carry along with one. To carry with it. To imply.*

Llevar la delantera. *To lead. To be ahead.*

Llevar los libros. *To keep books (bookkeeping).*

Llevar la correspondencia. *To take care of the correspondence.*

Llevar lo mejor. *To get the best. To get the best part of.*

llevarse to take or carry away; to get along.
  Llévese Ud. estos libros. *Take these books away.*
  Se llevó la palma. *He carried the day. He carried off the laurels.*
  Llevarse bien. *To get along well (together).*
  Llevarse mal. *To be on bad terms.*
  Llevarse un chasco. *To suffer a bitter disappointment.*
llorar to weep, to cry; to lament.
lloro m. weeping, crying.
LLOVER to rain, to shower.
  Está lloviendo. *It's raining.*
  Parece que va a llover. *It looks as if it's going to rain.*
  Llueve a cántaros. *It's pouring. It's raining cats and dogs.*
  Eso ya es llover sobre mojado. *That's adding insult to injury.*
llovizna f. drizzle.
lloviznar to drizzle.
LLUVIA f. rain, shower.

M

macana f. (Arg.) blunder, nonsense, joke.
  Déjate de macanas. *Stop talking nonsense. Stop doing foolish things.*
macanear (Arg.) to do silly things, to talk nonsense.
macanudo adj. (Amer.) fine, excellent, grand, dandy, first-rate.
macarrones m. pl. macaroni.
maceta f. flowerpot; mallet.
macizo adj. solid; massive; firm.
machacar to pound; to crush; to harp; to dwell (on a subject).
machete m. machete.
macho adj. male; masculine; vigorous; m. male animal; he-mule.
machucar to pound, to bruise.
madama f. madam.
madeja f. hank, skein; lock of hair.
MADERA f. wood; lumber; timber.
  Esto es de madera. *This is made of wood.*
maderero m. dealer in lumber.
madero m. beam; timber; piece of lumber.
madrastra f. stepmother.
madre f. mother; bed (of a river).
madreselva f. honeysuckle.
madriguera f. burrow; den.
madrina f. godmother; bridesmaid; sponsor, patroness.
madrugada f. dawn; early morning.
  De madrugada. *At dawn.*
  En la madrugada. *In the early morning.*
  Telegrama de madrugada. *Night letter.*
madrugador adj. early riser.
  ¡Ud. es muy madrugador! *You're an early bird!*
madrugar to get up early; to get ahead of.
  Caray, tú, sí que has madrugado. *My, but you're up early!*
  A quien madruga Dios le ayuda. *The early bird catches the worm.*
madurar to ripen; to mature.
madurez f. maturity; ripeness.
maduro adj. ripe; mature.
  La fruta todavía no está madura. *The fruit isn't ripe yet.*
maestro adj. masterly, master; m. teacher; skilled craftsman; master.
  Una obra maestra. *A masterpiece.*
  Es un maestro. *He's a teacher.*
  Maestro de obras. *Builder.*
magia f. magic.
mágico adj. magic; marvelous.

magisterio m. teaching profession; teachers (as a class).
magistrado m. magistrate.
magnánimo adj. magnanimous.
magnesia f. magnesia.
magnético adj. magnetic.
magnífico adj. magnificent, fine, splendid, wonderful.
  Habrá que felicitarle por su magnífica labor. *We ought to (must) congratulate him on his wonderful achievement.*
  Tenemos un magnífico surtido de corbatas. *We have a fine selection of ties.*
magnitud f. magnitude; importance, greatness.
magno adj. great.
  Alejandro Magno. *Alexander the Great.*
  Es una obra magna. *It's an excellent piece of work.*
magnolia f. magnolia.
mago m. magician, wizard.
maguey m. maguey (fruit), American aloe.
mahometano adj. and n. Mohammedan.
maicena f. corn flour.
maíz m. maize, Indian corn.
maizal m. corn field.
majadero adj. and n. silly; bore, pest.
majestad f. majesty.
majestuoso adj. majestic, imposing.
MAL adj. (shortening of malo used before masc. nouns) bad; adv. badly, poorly; m. evil; harm; disease; illness.
  Hace mal tiempo. *The weather's bad.*
  Está de muy mal humor. *He's in a very bad mood.*
  Ud. no tiene mal aspecto. *You don't look ill.*
  No está mal pensado. *It's (that's) not a bad idea.*
  No está mal. *Not bad. It's not bad.*
  Este libro está mal escrito. *This book is badly written.*
  Ando mal de dinero. *I'm short of money.*
  El enfermo va mal. *The patient is getting worse.*
  De mal en peor. *Worse and worse. From bad to worse.*
  Hacer mal. *To do harm. To do wrong. To act wrongly.*
  Eso no puede hacerle mal. *That can't hurt him.*
  Este abrigo me está mal. *This coat doesn't fit me.*
  Mal hecho. *Badly done.*
  Mal que le pese. *In spite of him.*
  Mal de su grado. *Unwillingly.*
  El bien y el mal. *Right and wrong. Good and evil.*
  Tomemos del mal el menos. *Let's choose the lesser of the two evils.*
  Mal de garganta. *Sore throat.*
  Este mal tiene cura. *This sickness (disease) is curable.*
malagradecido adj. ungrateful.
malaria f. malaria; paludism.
malbaratar to undersell; to squander.
malcriado adj. ill-bred; naughty.
maldad f. wickedness.
maldecir to damn, to curse.
maldición f. curse.
maldito adj. wicked; damned; cursed.
malecón m. sea wall, jetty.
maleficio m. witchcraft, enchantment.
malestar m. indisposition, discomfort.
  Sentir un malestar. *To be indisposed.*
maleta f. valise, suitcase.
  Lleve estas maletas, por favor. *Please carry these suitcases.*

maleza f. underbrush, thicket.
malgastar to squander, to waste.
malhablado adj. foul-mouthed.
malhechor m. malefactor, criminal.
malhumorado adj. ill-humored, peevish.
malicia f. malice; suspicion.
malicioso adj. malicious, suspicious.
maligno adj. malignant.
malintencionado adj. evil-minded, ill-disposed.
MALO adj. bad; wicked; ill; difficult; poorly.
  No es mala idea. *That's not a bad idea.*
  ¿Qué hay de malo en eso? *What harm is there in that? What's wrong with it?*
  ¿Te sientes malo? *Do you feel ill?*
  Está muy malo. *He's very sick.*
  Es un escritor bastante malo. *He's a very poor writer.*
  ¿Tiene Ud. los ojos malos? *Are your eyes sore?*
  Ese niño es muy malo. *This child is very bad.*
  Estos huevos están malos. *These eggs are bad.*
  Lo dijo de mala fe. *He said it deceitfully.*
  Lo malo es que no tengo tiempo. *The trouble is that I've no time.*
  Llevaba muy mala vida. *He led a very dissolute life.*
  Tiene mala cabeza. *He's reckless.*
  Trabajó de mala gana. *He worked unwillingly.*
  Hoy ando de malas. *I have no luck today.*
  Tener malas pulgas. *To be hot-tempered. To be hot-headed (hot-blooded).*
  Por malas o por buenas. *Willingly or unwillingly. Willy-nilly.*
malsano adj. unhealthy, unhealthful.
  Es un clima muy malsano. *It's a very unhealthful climate.*
maltratar to treat roughly, to mistreat, to abuse; to harm.
maltrato m. ill-treatment.
malvado adj. wicked.
mamá f. mamma.
mamar to suck; to cram.
mamarracho m. daub; ridiculous thing.
mamey m. mamee (tree and its fruit).
mamífero adj. mammalian; m. pl. mammals.
manantial m. spring, source.
manar to flow; to ooze.
manco adj. one-handed; one-armed; crippled.
mancomún (de) adj. jointly, in common; by mutual consent.
mancomunar to associate; to subject; to joint liability.
mancha f. stain, spot; blemish.
manchado adj. stained, spotted.
manchar to stain, to spot, to soil.
mandadero m. messenger; errand boy.
mandado m. errand.
  ¿Puede Ud. hacerme un mandado? *Will (can) you do (run) an errand for me?*
mandamiento m. mandate; commandment.
MANDAR to send; to will, bequeath; to order; to command; to govern.
  Mándamelo a casa. *Send it to my house.*
  Mande el paquete a estas señas. *Send the package to this address.*
  Quiero mandar un telegrama (cable). *I want to send a telegram (cable).*
  ¿Me ha mandado Ud. llamar? *Did you send for me? Have you sent for me?*
  Le mandé venir inmediatamente. *I had him come immediately.*
  Mande por una ambulancia. *Send for an ambulance.*
  ¿Qué ha mandado Ud. a pedir para comer?

What have you ordered for dinner?
He mandado hacer un traje a la medida. *I'm having a suit made to order.*
Lo he hecho porque Ud. me lo ha mandado. *I did it because you told me to.*
Si no manda Ud. otra cosa, me retiro. *If you don't need anything else, I'll leave now. If you'll excuse me, I'll leave now.*
Mandar decir. *To send word.*
mandarina *f. mandarin, tangerine.*
mandatario *m. attorney; agent; proxy.*
mandato *m. mandate, order.*
mandíbula *f. jaw, jawbone.*
mando *m. command, authority, control.*
mandolina *f. mandolin.*
mandón *adj. domineering, bossy.*
manecilla *f. small hand; hand of a clock or watch.*
manejar *to handle; to drive; to govern; to manage.*
¿Sabe Ud. manejar? *Do you know how to drive?*
manejo *m. management; handling.*
MANERA *f. manner, way, method.*
Hágalo Ud. de esta manera. *Do it this way.*
Hágalo de cualquier manera. *Do it any way you can. Do it any old way.*
No hay manera de traducirlo. *There's no way to translate it.*
No tiene buenas maneras. *He has no manners.*
Lo dijo de mala manera. *He said it in a rude way.*
¿Qué manera es ésa de contestar? *Is that the way to answer?*
¿De manera que no viene Ud.? *So you're not coming?*
Le alabó en gran manera. *He praised him very highly.*
En cierta manera. *To a certain extent.*
De ninguna manera. *By no means.*
De todas maneras iremos. *We'll go in any case.*
De manera que. *So then. So as to. In such a manner as to.*
Escríbalo de manera que se pueda leer. *Write it so that it can be read (that one can read way.*
manga *f. sleeve; hose; (for water); waterspout.*
Tener manga ancha. *To be broad-minded.*
En mangas de camisa. *In shirt sleeves.*
mangante *m. sponger.*
mango *m. handle, haft; mango (tree and its fruit).*
mangonear *to sponge; to loaf; to meddle, to pry.*
mangoneo *m. meddling; pettifogging; sponging.*
manía *f. mania, frenzy, whim.*
maniático *adj. and n. maniac.*
manicomio *m. insane asylum.*
manicura *f. manicure.*
manifestación *f. manifestation, demonstration.*
manifestar *to manifest; to state; to reveal.*
manifiesto *adj. manifest; clear, obvious.*
maniobra *f. maneuver; handiwork.*
manipulación *f. handling, manipulation.*
manipular *to handle, to manipulate; to manage.*
maniquí *m. mannikin.*
manivela *f. crank.*
Manivela de arranque. *Crank for starting.*
manjar *m. dish, food; victuals.*
MANO *f. hand; forefoot; coat (of paint, etc.); first hand (cards).*
Lo tengo en la mano. *I have it in my hand.*
Dénse la mano. *Shake hands.*
Le dió la mano al verle. *He shook hands with him when he saw him.*
Mano izquierda. *Left hand.*
Mano derecha. *Right hand.*
El es mi mano derecha. *He's my right-hand*

man. *("He's my right hand.")*
Pidió la mano de mi hermana. *He asked for my sister's hand (in marriage).*
Dejo el asunto en sus manos. *I leave the matter in your hands. I leave it up to you.*
¡Manos a la obra! *Get it started! Get to work! Let's start (it)!*
Suelte Ud. las manos. *Let go!*
Vinieron a las manos. *They came to blows.*
Se lavó las manos como Pilatos. *He washed his hands of the affair. ("He washed his hands like Pontius Pilate.")*
Bajo mano. (Debajo de manos.) *Underhandedly. In an underhand manner.*
De buena mano. *On good authority. From a reliable source.*
A manos llenas. *Liberally. Abundantly.*
Mano a mano. *Even. On equal terms.*
A mano. 1. *At hand. Near-by.* 2. *By hand.*
Hecho a mano. *Made by hand. Hand-made.*
De primera mano. *First-hand.*
manojo *m. handful, bunch.*
manosear *to handle; to feel; to rumple.*
mansión *f. mansion; residence.*
manso *adj. tame; gentle.*
manta *f. blanket.*
manteca *f. lard; fat; butter.*
mantecado *m. vanilla ice cream; buttercake.*
mantel *m. tablecloth.*
mantener *to feed, to support, to maintain; to keep up; to uphold (an opinion).*
Tiene que mantener dos familias. *He has to support two families.*
Mantener correspondencia. *To keep up a correspondence.*
Mantener una opinión. *To hold to (maintain) an opinion.*
mantenerse *to support oneself, to earn one's living; to stick to; to hold one's own; to remain; to stay.*
En este termos el agua se mantiene fresca. *The water stays cold in this thermos bottle.*
El barco se mantuvo a flote depués de torpedeado. *The ship remained afloat after being torpedoed.*
Me mantengo en lo dicho. *I maintain (stick to) what I've said.*
Se mantuvieron firmes hasta el fin. *They held their ground till the very end.*
mantenimiento *m. maintenance, support.*
MANTEQUILLA *f. butter.*
mantequillera *f. butter dish.*
manto *m. mantle, cloak.*
mantón *m. large shawl.*
manual *adj. manual; m. handbook; manual.*
manufacturar *to manufacture.*
manuscrito *adj. written by hand; m. manuscript.*
manutención *f. support, maintenance.*
manzana *f. apple; block of houses.*
manzanilla *f. camomile (plant); manzanilla (a strong white wine).*
manzano *m. apple tree.*
maña *f. dexterity, skill, cunning; knack, trick, habit.*
mañana *f. morning, forenoon; tomorrow.*
Esta mañana. *This morning.*
Hasta mañana. *See you tomorrow. Until tomorrow.*
Mañana por la mañana. *Tomorrow morning.*
Pasado mañana. *The day after tomorrow.*
mañoso *adj. handy, skillful; cunning.*
mapa *m. map, chart.*
mapamundi *m. map of the world.*

máquina *f. machine; engine.*
Máquina de escribir. *Typewriter.*
A máquina. *By machine.*
maquinaria *f. machinery.*
maquinilla *f. small machine.*
Maquinilla de afeitar. *Safety razor.*
maquinista *m. machinist; engineer, engine driver.*
MAR *m. and f. sea.*
Iremos por mar. *We'll go by sea.*
Viaje por mar. *Sea voyage.*
En el mar. *At sea.*
maraca *m. maraca (musical instrument).*
maraña *f. entanglement, perplexity, puzzle.*
maravilla *f. marvel, wonder.*
A maravilla. *Marvelously.*
maravillarse *to marvel, to admire.*
maravilloso *adj. marvelous, wonderful.*
Pasamos un tiempo maravilloso. *We had a wonderful time.*
marca *f. mark; brand; make.*
Es una marca renombrada. *It's a well-known brand.*
marcar *to mark; to brand; to register.*
El termómetro marca treinta grados a la sombra. *The thermometer registers thirty degrees in the shade. It's thirty degrees in the shade.*
Marcar un número. *To dial (a number).*
marco *m. frame.*
marcha *f. march.*
marchante *m. customer; client.*
MARCHAR *to go; to go off; to leave; to march.*
¿Se marcha Ud. ya? *Are you leaving already?*
Tengo que marcharme en seguida. *I have to go immediately.*
Se marcha al extranjero. *He's going abroad.*
Las cosas marchan viento en popa. *All's well. Everything's going nicely.*
Al negocio marcha a pedir de boca. *Business is progressing splendidly.*
El sargento marchaba delante de la compañía. *The sergeant was marching in front of the company.*
marchitar *to wither, to fade.*
marchito *adj. faded, withered.*
marea *f. tide.*
mareado *adj. seasick.*
marearse *to get seasick.*
mareo *m. seasickness.*
marfil *m. ivory.*
margarina *f. margarine.*
margen *m. and f. margin, border; bank (of a river).*
marido *m. husband.*
Marido y mujer. *Husband and wife.*
marina *f. navy.*
marinero *adj. seaworthy; m. sailor.*
marino *m. seaman.*
mariposa *f. butterfly; rushlight.*
marítimo *adj. maritime.*
marmita *f. kettle.*
mármol *m. marble.*
marqués *m. marquis.*
marquesa *f. marchioness.*
MARTES *m. Tuesday.*
martillar *to hammer.*
martillazo *m. a hammer blow.*
martillo *m. hammer.*
mártir *m. martyr.*
MARZO *m. March.*
marrano *m. hog, pig; dirty person.*
MAS *conj. but, yet, however.*
Parecen distintos mas no lo son. *They seem different but they're not.*
MÁS *adv. more; most; over; besides; plus.*

Más o menos. *More or less.*

¿Cuánto me costará, más o menos? *About how much will it cost?*

¿Desean algo más? *Will you have anything more?*

¿Quiere Ud. más ensalada? *Would you like some more salad?*

¿Nada más? *Is that all? Nothing else?*

No se me ocurre nada más. *I can't think of anything else.*

No hay más. *There are (there is) no more.*

No tengo más. *I haven't got any more.*

¿A quién quiere Ud. más? *Who(m) do you like (love) the best (more)?*

La madre es más bonita que la hija. *The mother's prettier than the daughter.*

Cinco más dos son siete. *Five plus two are seven.*

Es la cosa más fácil del mundo. *It's the easiest thing in the world.*

Más adelante se lo explicaré. *Later on, I'll explain it to you.*

Más acá del río. *On this side of the river.*

La casa está más allá. *The house is further on.*

Son más de las diez. *It's after ten o'clock.*

Corre más que yo. *He runs faster than I do.*

¡Qué papel más malo! *What bad (poor, awful) paper!*

¡Más vale así! *So much the better!*

Eso es lo más acertado. *That's the best thing to do.*

No faltaba más que eso. *That's all we needed. That's the limit.*

Acérquese un poco más al micrófono. *Come a little closer to the microphone.*

Las más de las veces. *Most of the time.*

Lo más pronto. *As soon as possible.*

A lo más. *At most.*

Más tarde o más temprano. *Sooner or later.*

A más tardar. *At the latest.*

Más de. *More than. Over.*

De más. *Too much. Too many.*

Sin más ni más. *Without much ado.*

Más bien. *Rather.*

masa f. *dough; mass; crowd.*

En masa. *In bulk.*

masaje m. *massage.*

Dar un masaje. *To massage. To give a massage.*

masajista m. and f. *masseur, masseuse.*

mascar to chew.

máscara f. *mask; disguise.*

mascota f. *mascot.*

masculino adj. *masculine.*

Género masculino. *Masculine gender.*

masón m. *Freemason.*

masonería f. *Freemasonry.*

masticar to chew, to masticate.

Mastique bien la comida. *Chew your food well.*

mástil m. *mast, post.*

mata f. *plant, shrub.*

matadero m. *slaughterhouse.*

matanza f. *slaughter, massacre.*

matar to kill, to murder.

No matarás. *Thou shalt not kill!*

Matar el tiempo. *To kill time.*

Me ha matado con su pelmacería. *He's so dull he bores me to death.*

mate adj. dull (finish); m. *checkmate; maté, Paraguay tea; dull color.*

matemáticas m. *mathematics.*

matemático m. *mathematician.*

materia f. *matter; material; subject.*

Materia prima. *Raw material.*

material adj. *material; m. material; equipment.*

Ese material no sirve. *This material is no good.*

Material rodante. *Rolling stock.*

materializar to materialize; to realize.

maternal adj. *maternal.*

maternidad f. *maternity.*

materno adj. *maternal, motherly.*

matiz m. *shade of color.*

matón m. *bully.*

matorral m. *thicket, bushes.*

matrícula f. *register; list; matriculation.*

matricular to matriculate, to register.

¿En qué escuela te has matriculado? *At what school did you register?*

matrimonio m. *marriage, matrimony; married couple.*

mausoleo m. *mausoleum.*

máxima f. *maxim, rule; proverb.*

máximo adj. *maximum, highest, largest, chief, principal.*

Máxima altura. *Highest point. Peak.*

El precio máximo es de diez dólares. *The maximum price is ten dollars.*

MAYO m. *May.*

mayonesa f. *mayonnaise.*

MAYOR adj. *greater, greatest; larger, largest; elder, eldest; m. major.*

Fué Mayor en el ejército. *He was a major in the army.*

¿Cuál es la ciudad mayor del mundo? *What is the largest city in the world?*

¿Es su hermana mayor o menor que Ud.? *Is your sister older or younger than you?*

Ser mayor de edad. *To be of age.*

Este asunto es del mayor interés. *This matter is of the greatest interest.*

La mayor parte de la gente lo cree. *Most (of the) people believe it.*

Pasé la mayor parte de la noche en vela. *I stayed awake most of the night.*

Viven en la calle Mayor. *They live on Main Street.*

Sólo vendemos al por mayor. *We sell wholesale only.*

mayordomo m. *majordomo, steward, butler; administrator.*

mayoría f. *majority; plurality.*

Así piensan la mayoría de los hombres. *Most men think that way.*

Fué electo por una gran mayoría. *He was elected by a large majority.*

mayúscula f. *capital letter.*

mazapán m. *marzipan.*

mazorca f. *cob of corn.*

Déme unas mazorcas de maíz. *Give me some corn on the cob.*

ME pron. *me; to me; myself.*

Me lo dió. *He gave it to me.*

Dámelo. *Give it to me.*

Vino a verme. *He came to see me.*

Me es indiferente. *It makes no difference to me.*

Me ha convencido Ud. *You've convinced me.*

Me duele la cabeza. *I have a headache.*

Me he cortado. *I've cut myself.*

Me dije para mis adentros. *I said to myself.*

mecánica f. *mechanics; kitchen police (military).*

mecánico adj. *mechanical; m. mechanic.*

mecanismo m. *mechanism.*

mecanógrafa f. *typist.*

Se necesita una mecanógrafa. *Typist wanted.*

mecanógrafo m. *typist.*

mecedora f. *rocking chair.*

mecha f. *wick; fuse; lock of hair.*

mechar to lard.

mechón m. *lock of hair.*

medalla f. *medal.*

media f. *stocking; mean (mathematics).*

¿Quiere Ud. medias de seda o de nilón? *Do you want silk or nylon stockings?*

Media diferencial. *Arithmetical mean.*

mediación f. *mediation, intervention.*

mediador mediator, go-between.

mediados about the middle.

A mediados de marzo. *About the middle of March.*

mediano adj. *medium, middling, not so good, mediocre.*

medianoche f. *midnight.*

A medianoche. *At midnight.*

mediante by means of, by virtue of.

Lo obtuve mediante su ayuda. *I got it through his help.*

Dios mediante. *God willing.*

mediar to mediate, to intercede.

medicina m. *medicine; remedy.*

médico adj. *medical; m. physician, doctor.*

MEDIDA f. *measure; measurement.*

Medida patrón. *Standard measure.*

Se tomaron las medidas necesarias en contra de la epidemia. *They took the necessary measures against the epidemic.*

Esta chaqueta me queda como a la medida. *This jacket fits me perfectly.*

A la medida. *Made to order (suit, dress, etc.).*

A medida de su deseo. *According to your wish.*

A medida que reciba la mercadería, envíemela. *Send me the goods as you receive them.*

Escriba estos números a medida que se los vaya diciendo. *Write these numbers down as I give them to you.*

MEDIO adj. and adv. *half; half-way; midway; means; average; m. middle, center; way, method; pl. means.*

Déme media libra de café. *Give me half a pound of coffee.*

A las dos y media. *At half past two.*

Una hora y media. *An hour and a half.*

La clase media. *The middle class.*

En un término medio. *On an average.*

Los telegramas diferidos se pagan a media tasa. *You pay only half rate for a night letter.*

Estoy medio muerto de cansancio. *I'm exhausted. I'm half dead.*

Hicimos el trabajo a medias. *We did the work between (the two of) us.*

La criada viene día por medio a hacer la limpieza. *The maid comes every other day to do the cleaning.*

Lo puso de vuelta y media. *He gave him a dressing down.*

¡Quítese de en medio! *Get out of the way!*

No había medio de saberlo. *There was no way of finding out.*

Vive según sus medios. *He lives according to his means.*

Media vuelta. *About face. Right about-face.*

En medio. *In the middle.*

Medio en broma, medio en serio. *Half in fun, half in earnest.*

Medio muerto de hambre. *Half-starved.*

A medio vestir. *To be half dressed.*

Medio asado. *Medium (of roasted meat). ("Half roasted.")*

mediocre adj. *mediocre.*

mediocridad f. *mediocrity.*

mediodía m. *midday, noon; south.*

Al mediodía. *At noon.*

medir *to measure.*

meditación *f. meditation.*

meditar *to meditate.*

médula *f. medulla, marrow; pitch.*

mejilla *f. cheek.*

Mejillas rosadas. *Rosy cheeks.*

MEJOR *adj. and adv. better; rather.*

Me siento mejor. *I feel better.*

Es el mejor hombre del mundo. *He's the best man alive. ("He's the best man in the world.")*

Esta es la mejor señal de mejoría. *That's the best sign of improvement.*

Escribe el español mejor que yo. *He writes Spanish better than I do.*

Tal vez eso sea mejor. *Perhaps that would be better.*

Hice lo mejor que pude. *I did the best I could.*

Tanto mejor. *All the better. So much the better.*

Tanto mejor si no viene. *So much the better if he doesn't come.*

Cuanto antes mejor. *The sooner the better.*

A lo mejor mañana no llueve. *Perhaps it won't rain tomorrow.*

Mejor que escribir ponga Ud. un telegrama. *It would be better to send a telegram than to write.*

Mejor que mejor si Ud. puede venir. *So much the better (all the better) if you can come.*

mejora *f. improvement.*

Eso es una gran mejora. *That's a great improvement.*

mejorar *to improve; to outbid.*

Sigue mejorando. *He's improving.*

El tiempo ha mejorado. *The weather has improved.*

mejoría *f. improvement; recovery.*

melaza *f. molasses.*

melocotón *m. peach.*

melodía *f. melody.*

melón *m. melon.*

mella *f. notch; dent; gap; impression.*

Hacer mella. *To make an impression. To impress.*

mellizo *adj. twin.*

membrete *m. letterhead; memorandum, note.*

membrillo *m. quince (tree and its fruit).*

memorable *adj. memorable.*

MEMORIA *f. memory; memoir, report; pl. regards, compliments.*

Tiene una memoria extraordinaria. *He has an extraordinary memory.*

Si la memoria no me es infiel. *If my memory doesn't fail me. If I remember correctly.*

Déle Ud. memorias mías. *Give her my regards.*

Apréndaselo de memoria. *Learn it by heart.*

Haga Ud. memoria. *Try to remember.*

Hágame Ud. memoria de ello mañana. *Remind me of it tomorrow.*

menaje *m. household goods, furnishings, furniture.*

Menaje de casa. *Household goods. Furniture.*

mencionar *to mention.*

mendigar *to beg, to ask charity.*

mendigo *m. beggar.*

mendrugo *m. a piece of bread.*

menear *to move, to stir; to wag.*

menester *m. need; occupation.*

Es menester que lo hagamos. *We must do it. It's necessary that we do it.*

menesteroso *adj. needy.*

mengua *f. decrease; decline; poverty; disgrace.*

menguar *to decay; to diminish, to wane.*

MENOR *adj. less; smaller; younger; m. minor,*

---

a person under age.

No me cabe la menor duda. *I haven't the slightest doubt.*

No le hicieron el menor caso. *They didn't pay the slightest attention to him.*

El es menor que ella. *He's younger than she is.*

Es menor de edad. *She's a minor (underage).*

MENOS *adj. and adv. less; least; minus; except.*

Es poco más o menos la misma cosa. *It's more or less the same thing.*

Tengo cinco pesetas de menos. *I'm five pesetas short.*

Eso es lo de menos. *That's the least of it.*

Todos fueron menos yo. *Everyone went but me.*

A las once menos cuarto. *At a quarter to eleven.*

Echar de menos a. *To miss someone or something.*

¿Echa Ud. de menos algo? *Is anything missing? Do you miss anything?*

No puedo menos que hacerlo. *I can't help doing it.*

No pude menos de reirme de él. *I couldn't help laughing at him.*

Menos mal que no le vió. *It's a good thing that he didn't see you.*

Tiene a menos hablarles. *He considered it beneath him to speak to them.*

¡Si yo tuviera veinte años menos! *If only I were twenty years younger!*

Tiene poco más o menos treinta años. *He's about thirty.*

No iré a menos que Ud. me acompañe. *I won't go unless you go with me (accompany me).*

Su familia ha ido muy a menos. *His family has become poor.*

Es lo menos que puede Ud. hacer. *It's the least you can do.*

menoscabo *m. damage, loss; detriment.*

Con menoscabo de. *To the detriment of.*

menospreciar *to underrate; to despise, to slight.*

menosprecio *m. underrating; scorn, contempt.*

mensaje *m. message.*

Quisiera enviarle un mensaje. *I'd like to send him a message.*

mensajero *m. messenger.*

mensual *adj. monthly.*

mensualidad *f. monthly salary; monthly allowance.*

menta *f. mint, peppermint.*

mental *adj. mental.*

mentalidad *f. mentality.*

mentar *to mention.*

Lo mentó en el discurso. *He mentioned it in his speech.*

MENTE *f. mind, understanding.*

Téngalo siempre en mente. *Always bear it in mind.*

mentecato *adj. silly, stupid; m. fool.*

mentir *to lie, to tell lies.*

mentira *f. lie, falsehood.*

mentiroso *adj. lying, false, deceitful; m. liar.*

menudeo *m. detail; retail trade.*

menudillos *m. pl. giblet (of fowl).*

MENUDO *adj. small; minute; m. change (money); entrails (of animals).*

¿Tiene Ud. menudo? *Do you have any change?*

Déjese Ud. ver más a menudo. *Come around more often.*

Sucede a menudo. *It happens very often.*

Gente menuda. *Children.*

meñique *m. little finger.*

El dedo meñique. *The little finger.*

mercader *m. merchant, dealer.*

---

mercadería *f. commodity, merchandise, goods.*

mercado *m. market; marketplace.*

La sirvienta fué de compras al mercado. *The maid went to the market to do the shopping.*

mercancía *f. merchandise, goods.*

mercante *adj. merchant, mercantile.*

Barco mercante. *Merchant ship.*

Marina mercante. *Merchant Marine.*

merced *f. gift, favor; mercy.*

Hacer merced. *To do someone a favor.*

Tener merced. *To show mercy. To be merciful.*

Merced a. *Thanks to.*

A la merced de. *At the mercy of.*

Estar a merced de. *To be at someone's mercy.*

mercenario *adj. mercenary.*

mercería *f. haberdashery; sort of five-and-ten.*

merecer *to deserve, to merit.*

Se lo merece. *He deserves it.*

merecido *m. deserved punishment.*

merendar *to lunch, to eat a light meal.*

merengue *m. meringue (pastry).*

meridiano *adj. and n. meridian.*

merienda *f. lunch, light meal.*

mérito *m. merit, worth; value.*

merma *f. decrease; waste; drop, loss.*

mermar *to decrease, to dwindle, to diminish.*

mermelada *f. marmalade.*

mero *adj. mere, only, pure, simple.*

Es una mera broma. *It's only a joke.*

Por mera casualidad. *By a mere coincidence.*

MES *m. month; monthly wages.*

¿Qué día del mes tenemos? *(¿En qué día del mes estamos?) What day of the month is it?*

Hace cosa de dos meses. *It was about two months ago.*

El mes que viene. *Next month.*

El mes pasado. *Last month.*

A últimos de mes. *Toward the end of the month.*

A principios del mes que viene. *In the early part of next month.*

MESA *f. table; chair, chairman and other officers of an assembly.*

¿Quién va a servir a la mesa? *Who's going to wait on the table?*

Levante la mesa. *Clear the table.*

Ponga la mesa. *Set the table.*

Los invitados se sentaron a la mesa. *The guests sat around the table. The guests sat down to eat.*

meseta *f. plateau; landing (of staircase).*

mestizo *adj. and n. half-breed; mestizo.*

mesura *f. moderation; politeness.*

meta *f. object, end, goal.*

Alcanzó la meta. *He reached his goal.*

metal *m. metal.*

metálico *adj. metallic.*

METER *to put in; to smuggle; to insert.*

Meter la mano en el bolsillo. *To put one's hand in one's pocket.*

Meta Ud. el dinero en el bolsillo. *Put the money in your pocket.*

No atino a meter la llave en la cerradura. *I can't get the key in the lock.*

Haga el favor de meter un poco las costuras de la chaqueta. *Please take in the seams of the jacket a little.*

Meter bulla. *To make a lot of noise.*

Meter la pata. *To put one's foot in it.*

METERSE *to meddle; to interfere; to become; to choose a profession or trade; to pick (a quarrel); to give oneself to; to get oneself in.*

No quiero meterme en líos. *I don't want to get myself involved in difficulties.*

En buen lío nos hemos metido. *We got ourselves in quite a fix.*

No se meta en lo que no le importa. *Mind your own business. Don't meddle in other people's affairs.*

Mete las narices en todo. *He's a busybody.*

No se meta Ud. de por medio. *Don't interfere in this.*

Meterse en vidas ajenas. *To meddle in other people's affairs.*

Se metió a cura. *He became a priest.*

Jamás se me metió en la cabeza idea semejante. *Such an idea never entered my head.*

¿Por qué se mete Ud. conmigo? *Why do you pick on me?*

Meterse en la cama. *To get into bed.*

¿En dónde diablos se ha estado metido Ud.? *Where on earth have you been?*

Este frío se le mete a uno hasta los huesos. *This cold's very penetrating. This cold goes right through you ("goes to the bones").*

metódico *adj. methodical.*

método *m. method.*

metralla *f. grape-shot, shrapnel.*

metro *m. meter (39.37 inches), subway (in Spain.)*

metrópoli *f. metropolis.*

mezcla *f. mixture, blending; mortar (for holding bricks or stones together).*

Sin mezcla. *Unmixed. Pure.*

mezclar *to mix, to blend, to mingle.*

No mezcle estas cosas. *Don't mix these things.*

mezquino *adj. stingy; mean; petty.*

MI *(possessive adj.) my; pl. mis.*

Mi libro. *My book.*

Mis libros. *My books.*

Siéntese a mi lado. *Sit next to me. ("Sit at my side.")*

MÍ *(pron. used after a preposition) me.*

Para mí. *For me.*

Me llaman a mí. *They're calling me.*

¡Me lo cuenta a mí! *You're telling me!*

MÍA *(f. of mío) mine; pl. mías.*

Esta corbata es mía. *This tie is mine. This is my tie.*

Es una amiga mía. *She's a friend of mine.*

Son amigas mías. *They're friends of mine.*

¡Querida mía! *My darling!*

Muy señora mía (in a letter). *Dear Madam.*

miaja *f. crumb, small piece.*

microbio *m. microbe.*

microscópico *adj. microscopic.*

microscopio *m. microscope.*

miedo *m. fear, dread.*

Tener miedo. *To be afraid.*

No tengas miedo. *Don't be afraid.*

miedoso *adj. fearful, easily frightened.*

miel *f. honey.*

Luna de miel. *Honeymoon.*

miembro *m. member, limb.*

MIENTRAS *in the meantime, while.*

Entró mientras leía. *He came in while I was reading.*

Mientras tanto. *Meantime. In the meantime. In the meanwhile.*

¿Qué hizo mientras tanto? *What did he do in the meantime?*

MIÉRCOLES *m. Wednesday.*

Miércoles de ceniza. *Ash Wednesday.*

miga *f. crumb, fragment, bit.*

Hacer buenas migas. *To be in perfect harmony.*

MIL *m. thousand.*

Su carta está fechada el veintitres de mayo de mil novecientos cuarenta y seis. *Your letter is dated May the twenty-third, nineteen hundred and forty-six.*

De mil amores. *With great pleasure.*

Lo hizo a las mil maravillas. *He did it wonderfully.*

Mil gracias. *Many thanks. ("A thousand thanks.")*

milagro *m. miracle, wonder.*

milagroso *adj. miraculous, marvelous.*

milésimo *adj. and n. thousandth.*

miligramo *m. milligram.*

milímetro *m. millimeter.*

militante *adj. militant.*

militar *adj. military; m. military man, soldier.*

milla *f. mile.*

¿Cuántas millas hay de aquí a Madrid? *How many miles is it from here to Madrid?*

Madrid dista veinte millas de aquí. *Madrid está a veinte millas de aquí. Madrid is twenty miles from here.*

millar *m. thousand; pl. a great number.*

millón *m. million.*

millonario *adj. and n. millionaire.*

mimado *adj. spoiled.*

Es un niño mimado. *He's a spoiled child.*

mimar *to spoil (a child).*

mina *f. mine.*

mineral *adj. and n. mineral.*

minería *f. mining, working of a mine.*

miniatura *f. miniature.*

mínimo *adj. minimum; least, smallest.*

La cosa más mínima. *The smallest thing.*

Una suma mínima. *A very small sum.*

Este es el precio mínimo. *This is the lowest price.*

ministerio *m. cabinet, ministry; secretary's office.*

ministro *m. Secretary (Cabinet); minister.*

minorista *m. retailer (Arg.).*

minuta *f. minutes (record); memorandum.*

minutero *m. minute hand.*

minuto *m. minute (of an hour).*

¡Espere un minuto! *Wait a minute!*

Estará listo dentro de unos minutos. *It will be ready in a few minutes.*

MÍO *mine; pl. míos.*

Este pañuelo no es mío. *This handkerchief is not mine.*

Son amigos míos. *They're friends of mine.*

Esto es mío. *This is mine. This belongs to me.*

Lo que es mío es suyo. *What's mine is yours.*

El gusto es mío, señor. *The pleasure is mine, sir.*

Hijo mío. *My son.*

Muy señor mío (in a letter). *Dear Sir.*

miope *adj. and n. nearsighted.*

¿Es Ud. miope? *Are you nearsighted?*

mirada *f. glance, look.*

Mirada triste. *A sad look.*

Mirada fija. *A fixed look.*

mirado *adj. looked at.*

Es una persona bien mirada. *He's very respected (well-considered).*

MIRAR *to look, to behold; to observe; to watch; to consider.*

¡Mire Ud! *Look!*

¡Mírelo, ahí está! *Look at it, there it is!*

Déjeme mirarle bien. *Let me take a good look at you.*

Mire Ud. donde pisa. *Watch where you're going. Watch your step.*

Mire Ud. bien lo que hace. *Consider carefully ("well") what you're doing.*

¿No tienen a nadie que mire por ellos? *Don't they have anyone to look after them?*

Dos de las habitaciones miran a la calle. *Two of the rooms face the street.*

Miraba lo que estábamos haciendo. *He watched what we were doing.*

Mirar de reojo. *To look askance. To look out of the corner of one's eye.*

Bien mirado. 1. *Carefully considered.* 2. *Well-considered. Respected.*

mirarse *to look at oneself; to look at each other.*

Mírese Ud. al espejo. *Look at yourself in the mirror.*

misa *f. mass.*

miserable *adj. miserable, wretched; miserly, avaricious.*

Vive una vida miserable. *He leads a miserable life.*

miseria *f. misery, destitution; stinginess; trifle.*

misericordia *f. mercy.*

misión *f. mission, errand.*

misionero *m. missionary.*

MISMA *(f. of mismo) same; similar; equal; self.*

Ella misma lo dice. *She says it herself.*

No es ya la misma persona. *He's no longer the same person. He's changed a great deal.*

Somos de la misma edad. *We're (of) the same age.*

MISMO *adj. same; similar; equal; self.*

El mismo día. *The same day.*

Es el mismo hombre que ví ayer. *He's the same man I saw yesterday.*

No es ya lo mismo. *It's no longer the same (thing).*

Yo mismo lo ví. *I myself saw it.*

Yo mismo lo haré. *I'll do it myself.*

Soy del mismo parecer. *I'm of the same opinion.*

No piensa sino en sí mismo. *He only thinks of himself.*

Ahora mismo. *Right now.*

Allí mismo. *In that very place.*

Te espero aquí mismo. *I'll wait for you right here.*

Ayer mismo. *Only yesterday.*

Mañana mismo. *Tomorrow for sure. Tomorrow without fail.*

Mañana mismo voy. *I'll come tomorrow without fail.*

Te estás engañando a tí mismo. *You're fooling yourself.*

Me da lo mismo. *It's all the same to me. It makes no difference to me.*

Siempre me pasa lo mismo. *The same thing always happens to me.*

Lo mismo que si. *Just as if.*

Pienso precisamente lo mismo. *I think exactly the same thing (the same way).*

misterio *m. mystery.*

misterioso *adj. mysterious.*

MITAD *f. half; middle, center.*

Déme la mitad. *Give me half.*

Mi cara mitad. *My better half.*

Fuí la mitad del camino a pie y la otra mitad a caballo. *I went one half of the way on foot and the other half on horseback.*

mitigar *to mitigate; to quench.*

mitin *m. meeting.*

mito *m. myth.*

mitología *f. mythology.*

mixto *adj. mixed, mingled.*

Ese es un tren mixto. *That's both a passenger and a freight train. That train carries both passengers and freight.*

Una escuela mixta. *A mixed school (for both boys and girls). Co-educational school.*

mobiliario m. *furniture.*

mocedad f. *youth.*

moción f. *motion.*

  Ambas mociones fueron rechazadas. *Both motions were rejected.*

mochila f. *knapsack.*

moda f. *fashion, style.*

  ¿Están aún de moda los sombreros de paja? *Are straw hats still worn? Are straw hats still in style?*

  Es un color muy de moda. *It's a fashionable color. You see that color worn a lot now.*

  Estar de moda. *To be in style.*

  Ya no está de moda. *To be out of style.*

  La última moda. *The latest style.*

modales m. pl. *manners, breeding.*

  Este niño tiene muy buenos modales. *This child has very good manners.*

  Sus modales le hacen odioso. *His manners make people dislike (hate) him.*

modalidad f. *modality; form.*

modelo m. *model, pattern; style.*

  ¿Cuáles son los últimos modelos? *What are the latest styles?*

  Ese modelo ya no se estila. *That model isn't worn any more (any longer).*

moderación f. *moderation.*

moderado adj. *moderate; mild.*

moderar *to moderate, to restrain; to slow up.*

  Modere la velocidad. *Slow up. Slow down.*

modernista m. and f. *modernist.*

MODERNO adj. *modern.*

  Métodos modernos. *Modern methods.*

  Adelantos modernos. *Modern improvements.*

modestia f. *modesty.*

modesto adj. *modest.*

módico adj. *moderate; m. reasonable price.*

  Es un precio módico. *It's a reasonable price.*

modificar *to modify, to alter.*

modismo m. *idiom.*

modista f. *modiste, dressmaker; milliner.*

MODO m. *mode; method, manner; mood.*

  Es el mejor modo de hacerlo. *It's the best way to do it.*

  De este modo. *In this way.*

  No me parece bien su modo de hablar. *I don't approve of (like) his manner of speaking.*

  De modo que. *So that.*

  Hable de modo que se le pueda oír. *Speak so that they can hear you (you can be heard).*

  Hágalo de cualquier modo. *Do it any way.*

  De todos modos. *Anyway.*

  De todos modos iré a su casa. *I'll go to his house anyway (anyhow).*

  De ningún modo. *By no means. In no way. Not at all.*

mofa f. *mockery; scoff, sneer.*

mofarse *to mock, to scoff, to jeer.*

mojar *to wet; to moisten; to dampen.*

  Las calles están mojadas. *The streets are wet.*

  Eso ya es llover sobre mojado. *That's adding insult to injury.*

molde m. *mold; pattern, model.*

  En letras de molde. *In print.*

moldura f. *molding.*

moler *to grind; to mill; to bore; to pound.*

molestar *to disturb, to trouble, to bother, to annoy; to tease.*

  No se moleste Ud. *Don't trouble yourself. Don't bother.*

  Siento mucho molestarle. *I'm sorry to bother you.*

  ¿Le molesta a Ud. el humo? *Does the smoke*

bother you?

  No se moleste Ud., lo haré yo mismo. *Don't bother, I'll do it myself.*

  Deje Ud. de molestarme. *Stop bothering me.*

molestia f. *trouble, bother, annoyance.*

  No es ninguna molestia. *Why, it's no bother. It's no trouble at all.*

  Siento darle a Ud. tanta molestia. *I'm sorry to trouble you so much.*

  Este asunto me ha ocasionado muchas molestias. *This business has given me a great deal of trouble.*

  Tomarse la molestia de. *To take the trouble to.*

molesto adj. *bothersome; uncomfortable; annoying, boring.*

  Visitas tan largas son molestas. *Such long visits become annoying.*

  ¡Qué molesto es! *How annoying he is!*

  No tenía porque sentirse molesto. *He had no reason to be annoyed.*

molino m. *mill.*

momentáneo adj. *momentary.*

MOMENTO m. *moment.*

  No tengo ni un momento libre. *I don't have a free moment.*

  Un momento, que suena el teléfono. *Just a moment, the phone is ringing.*

  Le ví abajo hace un momento. *I saw him downstairs a moment ago.*

  Le espero de un momento a otro. *I expect him any minute now.*

  Estamos en un momento crítico. *We are at the critical point now.*

  Por el momento. *For the moment. For the present.*

  En cualquier momento. *At any moment.*

  Al momento. *In a moment. Immediately.*

monarca m. *monarch.*

monarquía f. *monarchy.*

mondadientes m. *toothpick.*

mondadura f. *peeling.*

mondar *to clean; to husk, to remove the bark; to peel.*

moneda f. *coin; money.*

monja f. *nun.*

monje m. *monk.*

mono adj. *pretty, cute, nice; m. monkey, ape.*

  ¡Qué mono! ¿Verdad? *Isn't it cute! It's cute, isn't it?*

  Tiene dos hijas muy monas. *He has two very pretty daughters.*

  He conseguido un apartamento monísimo. *I found the coziest apartment.*

monólogo m. *monologue, soliloquy.*

monopolio m. *monopoly.*

monopolizar *to monopolize.*

monotonía f. *monotony.*

monótono adj. *monotonous.*

monstruo m. *monster.*

monstruosidad f. *monstrosity.*

monstruoso adj. *monstrous; huge.*

monta f. *amount, total sum.*

  De poca monta. *Of little importance.*

montacargas m. *hoist.*

montaña f. *mountain.*

montar *to mount; to ride; to amount to; to set (a diamond); to put together, to fit together, to assemble.*

  ¿Monta Ud. a caballo? *Can you ride (a horse)?*

  ¿Monta Ud. en bicicleta? *Can you ride a bicycle?*

  ¿A cuánto monta la cuenta? *How much does the bill come to?*

  Monte esta máquina. *Assemble this machine.*

  Put this machine together.

monte m. *mountain; wood, forest; monte (card game).*

montón m. *heap, mass.*

montura f. *mount, saddle horse; saddle and trappings.*

monumental adj. *monumental.*

monumento m. *monument.*

mora f. *delay; mulberry; blackberry.*

morada f. *dwelling, abode.*

morado adj. *purple.*

morador m. *resident, inhabitant.*

moral adj. *moral; f. ethics; morale; m. mulberry tree; blackberry bush.*

morar *to inhabit, to reside.*

mordedura f. *bite.*

morder *to bite.*

mordisco m. *bite; biting; a piece bitten off.*

morena f. *brunette.*

moreno adj. *brown; dark, swarthy.*

morera f. *white mulberry tree.*

moribundo adj. *dying.*

MORIR *to die.*

  Murió de pena. *She died of a broken heart.*

  Morirse de hambre. *To starve.*

  Morirse de frío. *To freeze to death.*

morral m. *nosebag; knapsack.*

mortadela f. *bologna sausage.*

mortaja f. *shroud, winding sheet.*

mortal adj. *mortal, fatal.*

mortalidad f. *mortality; death rate.*

mortero m. *mortar.*

mortificación f. *mortification, humiliation.*

mortificar *to humiliate, to vex.*

mosca f. *fly; dough, money (coll.).*

moscatel m. *muscatel (grape or wine).*

mosquito m. *mosquito.*

mostaza f. *mustard; mustard seed.*

mosto m. *must, grape juice; new wine.*

mostrador m. *counter.*

MOSTRAR *to show; to exhibit; to prove.*

  ¿Me lo puede mostrar? *Can you show it to me?*

  ¿Puede mostrarnos como hacerlo? *Can you show us how to do it?*

motivo m. *motive, reason; motif.*

  No tiene motivo para quejarse. *You have no reason to complain. You have no grounds for complaint.*

  No hay motivo para preocuparse tanto. *There's no need to be so worried.*

  Sus afirmaciones dieron motivo a una seria disputa. *His statements led to a serious quarrel.*

motocicleta f. *motorcycle.*

motociclista m. and f. *motorcyclist.*

motor m. *motor; engine.*

  El motor no funciona. *The motor doesn't work.*

MOVER *to move; to stir up; to shake.*

  No mueva la mesa. *Don't shake the table.*

  No dejó piedra que no moviese. *He left no stone unturned. He searched high and low.*

  Apenas podía hablar ni moverse. *He could scarcely talk or move.*

móvil adj. *movable; mobile; m. motive.*

movilización f. *mobilization.*

movilizar *to mobilize.*

movimiento m. *movement, motion; traffic.*

moza f. *girl; maid, servant.*

mozo adj. *young; m. young man; waiter; porter.*

  ¡Vaya con el mozo! *What a man!*

  Mozo, tráigame una cerveza. *Waiter, bring me a (glass of) beer.*

  El mozo le subirá la maleta al tren. *The porter*

will put your suitcase on the train.
Quiero un mozo de cuerda. *I want a porter.*
MUCHA *adj. (f. of mucho) much, very much, a great deal, a lot; very; pl. many, a great many, too many.*
Mucha agua. *A lot of water.*
Había mucha gente. *There was a big crowd.*
Muchas veces. *Many times.*
Muchas cosas. *Many things.*
Esto y muchas otras cosas más. *This and many other things.*
Muchísimas gracias. *Thank you very much.*
MUCHACHA *m. girl; servant, maid.*
¡Qué muchacha tan encantadora! *What a lovely girl! What a charming girl!*
MUCHACHO *m. boy; lad.*
Es un muchacho muy inteligente. *He's a very intelligent boy.*
muchedumbre *f. multitude; crowd.*
MUCHO *adj. much, very much, a great deal of, a lot; very; long (time); pl. many, a great many, too many; very.*
Mucho dinero. *A lot of money.*
Escribe mucho. *He writes a great deal.*
Mucho más grande. *Much larger.*
Muchos libros. *Many books. A lot of books.*
Tiene muchos amigos. *He has a lot of friends.*
Esto es mucho mejor. *This is much better.*
Mucho menos lejos. *Much nearer.*
Tengo mucho que hacer hoy. *I've a lot to do today.*
Con mucho gusto. *Gladly. With (much) pleasure.*
Lo celebro mucho. *I'm very happy to hear it.*
Hace mucho tiempo. *It's been a long time. A long time ago.*
Hace mucho frío. *It's very cold.*
Se lo agradezco muchísimo. *Thank you very much.*
Tengo muchísimo trabajo. *I have a great deal of work to do.*
Lo cuidaré mucho. *I'll take good care of it.*
muda *f. change of clothes, change of linen; molting.*
mudanza *f. change; moving out.*
MUDAR *to change; to alter; to remove; to molt.*
He mudado de parecer. *I've changed my mind.*
MUDARSE *to change (clothes); to move (household).*
Tengo que mudarme de ropa. *I have to change my clothes.*
Mi amigo se ha mudado de casa. *My friend has moved.*
Vamos a mudarnos de casa pronto. *We're going to move soon.*
mudo *adj. dumb, mute, silent.*
MUEBLE *m. piece of furniture.*
Con muebles. *Furnished.*
Una habitación sin muebles. *An unfurnished room.*
mueca *f. grimace, wry face.*
muela *f. millstone; molar tooth.*
muelle *adj. tender, soft; easy (life); m. pier, quay, dock, wharf; spring (metal).*
MUERTE *f. death.*
Se le condenó a muerte. *He was condemned to death.*
Muerte repentina. *Sudden death.*
muerto *adj. dead; languid; m. corpse.*
Muerto de hambre. *Starved.*
Muerto de cansancio. *Dead tired.*
Medio muerto. *Half dead.*
Estar muerto por alguna persona. *To be madly in love with someone.*
muestra *f. sample; specimen.*

muestrario *m. collection of samples.*
MUJER *f. woman; wife.*
¡Qué mujer más hermosa! *What a beautiful woman!*
Su mujer es joven. *His wife is young.*
mula *f. she-mule.*
muleta *f. crutch; stick on which the matador displays his red cape.*
mulo *m. mule.*
multa *f. fine, penalty.*
multar *to mulct; to fine.*
múltiple *adj. multiple.*
multiplicar *to multiply.*
multitud *f. multitude; crowd.*
MUNDO *m. world; multitude; great quantity.*
Quiere ver el mundo. *He (she) wants to see the world.*
Tengo que comprar un mundo de cosas. *I have to buy a lot of things.*
Todo el mundo quiere ir. *Everyone wants to go.*
Critica a todo el mundo. *He criticizes everybody.*
Este hombre se ríe de todo el mundo. *He ("this man") laughs at (ridicules) everybody.*
Tener mundo. *To be a man of the world.*
munición *f. ammunition.*
municipal *adj. municipal.*
municipalidad *f. municipality; town hall.*
municipio *m. municipality.*
muñeca *f. wrist; doll; figure (in dressmaking).*
muñeco *m. puppet; doll; pl. comics, funnies.*
Nunca se cansa de leer los muñecos. *She never gets tired of reading the comics (funnies).*
muralla *f. wall; rampart.*
murmuro *m. murmur, whisper.*
murmurar *to murmur, to whisper.*
muro *m. wall; rampart.*
músculo *m. muscle.*
museo *m. museum.*
¿Qué días está abierto el museo? *What days is the museum open?*
música *f. music.*
Tiene talento para la música. *She has a gift for music.*
Váyase con la música a otra parte. *Go away, don't bother me.*
musical *adj. musical.*
músico *m. musician.*
muslo *m. thigh.*
mutilar *to mutilate.*
mutuo *adj. mutual.*
Se detestan mutuamente. *They detest each other.*
MUY *very; greatly.*
Muy bien, gracias. *Very well, thank you.*
No muy bien. *Not so well. Not very well.*
Muy mal. *Very bad.*
Ese vestido le cae muy bien. *That dress fits her very well.*
Vino muy de mañana. *He came very early in the morning.*
Estoy muy molesto. *I'm very much annoyed.*
Es muy española. *She's very Spanish. She's a typical Spanish woman (girl).*
Está muy lejos de aquí. *It's a long way from here. It's very far from here.*

N

nabo *m. turnip.*
NACER *to be born; to sprout; to rise (sun); to originate.*

Nació en Madrid. *He was born in Madrid.*
nacimiento *m. birth; origin; source.*
Partida de nacimiento. *Birth certificate.*
nación *f. nation.*
nacional *adj. national.*
nacionalidad *f. nationality.*
NADA *nothing; by no means.*
No quiero nada. *I don't want anything.*
Nada de particular. *Nothing special. Nothing in particular.*
Nada más que una taza de café negro. *Just a cup of black coffee.*
De nada. *Don't mention it.*
No es nada. *It's nothing at all.*
No importa nada. *It doesn't matter at all.*
No vale nada. *It's worthless.*
¿Nada más? *Is that all?*
Nada de eso. *None of that. Nothing of the sort.*
No sé nada de eso. *I know nothing about it. I don't know a thing about it.*
Por nada. *For nothing. Under no circumstances.*
¿No se puede hacer nada? *Can't something be done?*
¿Qué tiene Ud.?—No tengo nada. *What's the matter (with you)?—Nothing's the matter.*
No quiero nada con él. *I don't want to have any dealings with him. I don't want to have anything to do with him.*
No me acuerdo de nada. *I don't remember it at all. I don't remember anything.*
Déme un poquito, nada más. *Give me just a little.*
Antes que nada. *First of all. Before anything else.*
nadador *m. swimmer.*
nadar *to swim, to float.*
Sabe nadar muy bien. *She swims very well.*
Se me nadan los pies en los zapatos. *These shoes are much too big for me. ("My feet are swimming in these shoes.")*
NADIE *nobody, anybody, no one, anyone, none.*
Nadie lo duda. *Nobody doubts it.*
Eso no lo cree nadie. *Nobody believes it.*
Nunca habla mal de nadie. *He never says anything bad about anyone.*
No teme a nadie. *He's not afraid of anyone.*
Importa a Ud. más que a nadie. *It concerns you more than anyone else.*
No le gusta rozarse con nadie. *She doesn't like to have anything to do with anybody.*
nado (a) *swimming.*
Pasar el río a nado. *To swim across a (the) river.*
naipe *m, playing card.*
naranja *f. orange.*
naranjada *f. orangeade.*
naranjo *m. orange tree.*
narcótico *adj. and n. narcotic.*
NARIZ *f. nose; nostril.*
Nariz parfilada. *A straight nose.*
Nariz aguileña. *An aquiline nose.*
Nariz chata. *A flat nose.*
Mete las narices en todo. *He's a busybody.*
Le dieron con la puerta en las narices. *They slammed the door in his face ("nose").*
Tener de (por) las narices. *To have someone under control. To lead someone by the nose.*
narración *f. account, narration; story.*
narrar *to narrate; to relate.*
nata *f. cream; best part.*
Es de la flor y nata. *He's crème de la crème. He's in the highest society.*
natación *f. swimming.*

natal *adj. natal, native.*

natalidad *f. birth rate.*

nativo *adj. native.*

natural *adj. and n. natural; native.*
Eso es muy natural. *That's quite natural.*
Dibujar del natural. *To draw from life.*
Son naturales de esta isla. *They're natives of this island.*

naturaleza *f. nature.*

NATURALMENTE *of course, naturally.*
Naturalmente que lo haré. *Of course I'll do it.*
¿Estará Ud. allí?—Naturalmente. *Will you be there?—Naturally.*

naturismo *m. vegetarianism; nudism.*

naturista *m. and f. nature-lover; vegetarian; nudist.*

naufragar *to be shipwrecked; to fail.*

naufragio *m. shipwreck; failure.*

náusea *f. nausea, nauseousness.*

náutica *f. navigation.*

naval *adj. naval.*

nave *f. ship, vessel.*

navegable *adj. navigable.*

navegación *f. navigation; shipping.*

navegante *m. navigator.*

navegar *to navigate; to sail.*

navidad *f. Nativity; Christmas.*
Por navidad. *For Christmas.*
¡Felices Navidades! ¡Felices Pascuas! *Merry Christmas!*

naviero *adj. shipping; m. shipowner.*

navío *m. warship, ship.*

neblina *f. mist, light fog.*

necesariamente *necessarily.*

NECESARIO *adj. necessary.*
Es necesario hacer esto inmediatamente. *It's necessary to do this right away.*
¿Cree Ud. que tendrá los medios necesarios? *Do you think you'll have the necessary means?*
Carecemos de lo más necesario. *We lack even the essentials.*

NECESIDAD *f. necessity; need, want.*
No hay necesidad de certificar la carta. *It's not necessary to register the letter.*
Tengo necesidad de ir al banco. *I have (need) to go to the bank.*
Tienen muchas necesidades. *They need many things.*
Verse en la necesidad de. *To be in need of. To be compelled to.*

necesitado *adj. very poor; needy; m. person in need.*
Está necesitado. *He's in want. He's down and out.*

NECESITAR *to need; to be in need; to want.*
¿Necesita Ud. algo más? *Do you need anything else (in addition)?*
Necesito un nuevo par de zapatos. *I need a new pair of shoes.*
Necesita tomar un taxi para ir al aeropuerto. *He has to take a taxi to get to the airport.*
Le prestaré el dinero que necesita. *I'll lend you the money you need.*
Se necesita una mecanógrafa. *Typist wanted.*

necio *adj. ignorant, stupid; fool.*

necrología *f. necrology, obituary.*

nefasto *adj. ill-fated; unlucky.*
Día nefasto. *Unlucky day.*

NEGAR *to deny; to refuse; to disown.*
No lo niegue Ud. *Don't deny it.*
No lo niego. *I don't deny it.*
Lo negó de plano. *He denied it flatly.*

Ella se negó a aceptarlo. *She refused to accept it.*
Le niega hasta el saludo. *He even refused to greet her.*

negativa *f. refusal.*

negativo *adj. negative.*
Una respuesta negativa. *A negative answer. An answer in the negative.*

negligencia *f. negligence, neglect.*

negligente *adj. negligent, careless.*

negociado *m. bureau, department.*
Preséntese Ud. al negociado de inmigración. *Report to the Immigration Department.*

negociante *m. merchant, trader, businessman.*
Es un negociante muy hábil. *He's a clever (good) businessman.*

negociar *to negotiate.*

NEGOCIO *m. business; affair; transaction.*
¿A qué negocio se dedica Ud.? *What business are you in?*
¿Qué tal van sus negocios? *How's business?*
Se dedica a los negocios. *He's a businessman.*
Hacer negocios. *To do (conduct) business.*
Retirarse de los negocios. *To retire from business.*

NEGRO *adj. black; gloomy; m. Negro.*
Vestirse de negro. *To dress in black.*

nervio *m. nerve.*
Tengo los nervios de punta. *My nerves are on edge.*

nervioso *adj. nervous.*

neto *adj. neat, pure; net.*
Peso neto. *Net weight.*

neumático *m. tire.*
Se me ha pinchado un neumático. *I have a flat (tire). One of my tires blew out.*

neurastenia *f. neurasthenia.*

neurótico *adj. neurotic.*

neutral *adj. neutral.*

nevar *to snow.*
Está nevando. *It's snowing.*

nevera *f. icebox.*

NI *neither, either, nor.*
Ni come ni bebe. *He doesn't eat or drink.*
No iré ni con Ud. ni con ellos. *I won't go either with you or with them.*
Ni mi hermano ni yo le podíamos ayudar. *Neither my brother nor I could (were able to) help him.*
Ni siquiera eso. *Not even that.*
Ni aún viene a verme. *She doesn't even come to see me.*
Ni por asomo creí volver a verlo. *I never dreamed I would see him again.*

nicho *m. niche.*

nicotina *f. nicotine.*

nido *m. nest.*

niebla *f. fog, haze.*
Hay niebla. *It's foggy.*

nieta *f. granddaughter.*

nieto *m. grandson.*

nieve *f. snow.*

nilón *m. nylon.*

NINGÚN *adj. (shortening of ninguno used only before a masculine noun) no, none, any.*
Ningún hombre. *No man.*
De ningún modo. *By no means. In no way.*
A ningún precio. *Not at any price.*

NINGUNA *adj. (f. of ninguno) no, none, any, no one, nobody.*
Ninguna de las chicas. *None of the girls.*
No he visto a ninguna de las chicas. *I haven't seen any of the girls.*

Al presente no tenemos ninguna noticia. *At present we have no news (haven't any news).*
No quiero ir a ninguna parte esta noche. *I don't want to go anywhere tonight.*
De ninguna manera. *By no means. In no way.*

NINGUNO *adj. no, none, not one, any; indefinite pronoun none, no one, nobody.*
No tengo ninguno. *I haven't any.*
Ninguno ha venido. *Nobody has come.*
Ninguno de nosotros. *None of us.*

NIÑA *f. girl; pupil (of the eye).*

niñez *f. childhood, infancy.*

NIÑO *m. child; pl. children.*

níquel *m. nickel (metal).*

NO *no, not.*
No fumo. *I don't smoke.*
No, gracias. *No, thank you.*
Le tuve que decir que no. *I had to say no to him.*
Ciertamente que no. *Certainly not.*
¡Por supuesto que no! *No, indeed!*
Todavía no. *Not yet.*
No sé. *I don't know.*
No la conozco. *I don't know her.*
¿Cómo dice? No oigo nada. *What are you saying? I can't hear anything.*
¿No quiere Ud. sentarse? *Won't you take a seat (sit down)?*
No hay nadie aquí. *There's no one here.*
No tengo más. *I haven't got any more. I don't have any more.*
No está mal. *It's not bad.*
No corre prisa. *There's no hurry.*
Ya no. *No longer.*
No del todo. *Not quite. Not altogether.*
No tengo mucho tiempo. *I haven't much time.*
No hay de que. *Don't mention it.*
¡No importa! *It doesn't matter!*
¡No me diga! *You don't say (so)! Don't tell me!*

noble *adj. noble; m. nobleman.*

nobleza *f. nobleness, nobility.*

noción *f. notion, idea.*
No tenía noción de que fuera posible. *I had no idea that it would be possible.*

nocivo *adj. harmful.*

nocturno *adj. nocturnal, night, in the night.*
Trabajo nocturno. *Night work.*

NOCHE *f. night.*
¡Buenas noches! *Good night!*
Esta noche. *Tonight.*
Mañana por la noche. *Tomorrow night.*
¿Sale Ud. todas las noches? *Do you go out every night?*
Se hace de noche. *It's getting dark.*
Ya es de noche. *It's dark.*
Hace una noche deliciosa. *It's a delightful evening.*
Por la noche. *At night.*
Durante la noche. *During the night.*
A medianoche. *At midnight.*
A altas horas de la noche. *Late at night.*
Que pase Ud. buena noche. *I hope you have a good night's sleep (rest).*
Pasar la noche. *To spend the night.*

nochebuena *f. Christmas Eve.*
Esta noche es nochebuena. *Tonight's Christmas Eve.*

nombramiento *m. nomination; appointment.*

nombrar *to appoint; to nominate; to name.*
Fué nombrado gobernador de la isla. *He was appointed Governor of the island.*
Al niño le nombraron José. *They named the child Joseph.*

NOMBRE m. name; noun.

¿Su nombre y profesión, por favor? *Your name and occupation?*

Ponga el nombre y las señas del remitente en el reverso del sobre. *Put the sender's name and address on the back of the envelope.*

La conozco de nombre. *I know her by name.*

No conozco a nadie con ese nombre. *I don't know anyone by that name.*

Salúdele en mi nombre. *Remember me to him.*

Va a poner a su hijo el nombre de Antonio. *He's going to name his son Anthony.*

nómina f. payroll.

norma f. rule, standard, model.

normal adj. normal; f. normal school.

normalidad f. normality.

NORTE m. north.

norteamericano adj. and n. North America; American (restricted to persons or things from the United States).

NOS we; us; to us.

Nos hace falta dinero. *We need money.*

Nos reuníamos todos los lunes a cierta hora. *We used to meet at a certain hour every Monday.*

Dénoslo. *Give it to us.*

No nos dejaron entrar. *They didn't let us in.*

El mismo nos lo dijo. *He told us so himself.*

NOSOTRAS (f. of nosotros) we; us; ourselves.

(Nosotras) Somos sus hermanas. *We're his sisters.*

Nosotras las mujeres. *We women.*

NOSOTROS we; us; ourselves.

(Nosotros) Somos vecinos. *We're neighbors.*

Lo haremos nosotros mismos. *We'll do it ourselves.*

Quiere venir con nosotros. *She wants to come with us.*

Nosotros los norteamericanos. *We Americans.*

nostalgia f. nostalgia, homesickness.

NOTA f. note.

Tomar nota. *To take note.*

Cuaderno de notas. *Notebook.*

Nota marginal. *Marginal note.*

Nota musical. *Musical note.*

The notes of the scale in Spanish are: *do* C, *re* D, *mi* E, *fa* F, *sol* G, *la* A, *si* B.

Do agudo. *Upper C.*

Do grave. *Lower C.*

Do sostenido. *C sharp.*

Re bemol. *D flat.*

Redonda. *Semibreve.*

Blanca. *Minim.*

Negra. *Crochet.*

Corchea. *Quaver.*

Semicorchea. *Semiquaver.*

Fusa. *Demisemiquaver.*

Semifusa. *Semidemisemiquaver.*

notable adj. notable; worthy of notice.

Es un hecho notable. *It's an outstanding fact.*

Es un hombre notable. *He's an outstanding man.*

notar to note; to notice.

¿Notó Ud. algo raro? *Did you notice anything strange?*

notario m. notary.

NOTICIA f. piece of news; information; notice; pl. news.

La radio dió la noticia. *The news came over the radio.*

Las noticias del día. *The news of the day.*

Hay buenas noticias. *There's good news. Good news!*

No he tenido noticias de mi familia. *I haven't heard from my family.*

notificación f. notification.

notificar to notify; to inform.

notorio adj. well-known, evident.

novato adj. novice, beginner.

novecientos adj. and n. nine hundred.

NOVEDAD f. novelty; latest news or fashion.

¿Qué hay de novedad? *What's new?*

Sin novedad. *As usual. Nothing new.*

Llegamos a Toluca sin novedad. *We arrived in Toluca safely.*

Ultima novedad. *Latest style.*

novela f. novel.

novelista m. and f. novelist.

noventa adj. and n. ninety.

novia f. sweetheart, girl friend; fiancée; bride.

noviazgo m. engagement, betrothal.

novicio adj. novice; apprentice.

novio m. sweetheart, boy friend; fiancé; bridegroom.

Los novios. *The newlyweds.*

nube f. cloud; film (on the eyeball).

Hay muchas nubes. *There are many clouds. It's cloudy.*

nublado adj. cloudy.

Está nublado. *It's cloudy.*

nuca f. nape, back of the neck.

nudo m. knot.

nuera f. daughter-in-law.

NUESTRA (f. of nuestro) our, ours; pl. nuestras.

Nuestra hermana. *Our sister.*

Nuestras hermanas. *Our sisters.*

Ella es vecina nuestra. *She's a neighbor of ours.*

La nuestra. *Ours.*

NUESTRO our; ours; pl. nuestros.

Nuestro amigo. *Our friend.*

Nuestros derechos. *Our rights.*

Nuestro deber. *Our duty.*

Es un antiguo conocido nuestro. *He's an old acquaintance of ours.*

Es en nuestro beneficio. *It's to our advantage (benefit).*

El nuestro. *Ours.*

Lo nuestro. *Ours. What's ours.*

Los nuestros. *Our folks (people).*

NUEVE adj. and n. nine.

NUEVO adj. new.

¿Es nuevo ese sombrero? *Is that hat new? Is that a new hat?*

¿Qué hay de nuevo? *What's new?*

¿Sabe Ud. algo de nuevo? *Have you heard anything new?* ("Do you know anything new?")

¿Tiene Ud. alguna obra nueva? *Have you any recent books?*

Hágalo Ud. de nuevo. *Do it again.*

¡Feliz año nuevo! *Happy New Year!*

nuez f. walnut; nut; Adam's apple.

nulidad f. nullity; nonentity; incompetent person.

nulo adj. null, void; not binding.

numerar to number.

número m. number; figure; issue (of a magazine), act.

¿Qué número es el de su casa? *What's your house number? What's your address?*

¿Cuál es su número de teléfono? *What is your telephone number?*

Escriba el número. *Write the number.*

Por favor, póngame en comunicación con el número . . . *Kindly connect me with number . . .*

En números redondos. *In round numbers (figures).*

No me gustó ese número. *I didn't like that act.*

NUNCA never, ever.

¡Nunca! *Never!*

Nunca tomo café. *I never take coffee.*

Nunca lo consentiré. *I'll never consent (agree to it).*

Casi nunca leo los periódicos. *I hardly ever read the newspapers.*

Más vale tarde que nunca. *Better late than never.*

nupcial adj. nuptial.

nupcias f. pl. nuptials, wedding.

nutrición f. nutrition, nourishment.

nutrir to nourish, to feed.

nutritivo adj. nutritious, nourishing.

Ñ

ñame m. yam (plant).

ñato adj. flat-nosed.

O

O or, either.

Más o menos. *More or less.*

Más tarde o más temprano. *Sooner or later.*

Le he visto o en Roma o en París. *I saw him either in Rome or in Paris.*

obcecado adj. stubborn, obdurate.

obedecer to obey.

Quiero que me obedezcan. *I expect to be obeyed.*

Eso obedece a otras razones. *This is due to other reasons.*

obediencia f. obedience.

obediente adj. obedient.

obeso adj. obese, extremely fat.

obispo m. bishop; ray (fish).

objetar to object, to oppose.

objetivo m. objective, aim.

OBJETO m. object, thing, article; purpose, aim.

No tengo objetos de valor que declarar. *I have nothing ("no articles of value") to declare.*

Por fin logró su objeto. *Finally he reached his goal.*

Al objeto de. *For the purpose of.*

Ser objeto de. *To be the cause of. To be the object of.*

Ser objeto de burla. *To be the laughingstock.*

Llenar su objeto. *To suit one's purpose.*

Objetos de escritorio. *Office equipment.*

oblicuo adj. oblique.

obligación f. obligation; duty; pl. liabilities.

obligar to oblige; to compel; to obligate.

Me veré obligado a dar parte a la policía. *I'll have (be compelled) to report it to the police.*

Me dió un resfriado terrible que me obligó a guardar cama por una quincena. *I caught a bad cold which kept me in bed for two weeks.*

obligatorio adj. obligatory, compulsory.

OBRA f. work; labor; book; play (theater); building; repairs (in a house); means; deed, action.

¿Dan ya esa obra? *Are they giving that play yet?*

Es una obra de tres tomos. *The work is in three volumes.*

Toda obra importante requiere trabajo. *All important work requires labor.*

Obra maestra. *Masterpiece.*

Obras públicas. *Public works.*

Poner en obra. *To put into practice. To set into operation.*

Obra de arte. *Work of art.*

obrar *to work; to act; to do things.*
No me gusta su modo de obrar. *I don't like the way he does things.*
Obrar conforme a derecho. *To act in accordance with the law.*
obrero *m. worker, workman.*
obscurecer *to darken; to grow dark.*
obscurecerse *to get dark.*
Está obscureciendo. *It's getting dark.*
obscuridad *f. obscurity; darkness.*
obscuro *adj. obscure; dark.*
Una noche obscura. *A dark night.*
obsequiar *to entertain, to treat; to make a present, to give a gift.*
Le obsequiamos con motivo de su cumpleaños. *We entertained him on his birthday.*
Me han obsequiado un libro. *They gave me a book (as a gift).*
obsequio *m. entertainment; gift, present.*
Le agradezco mucho su obsequio. *Thank you very much for your present.*
En obsequio de. *For the sake of.*
observación *f. observation; remark.*
observar *to observe, to notice; to keep, to follow (the law, etc.); to make a remark; to look.*
observatorio *m. observatory.*
obsesión *f. obsession.*
obstáculo *m. obstacle.*
obstante *(preceded by no) notwithstanding, in spite of.*
No obstante. *Notwithstanding. Regardless.*
obstinación *f. obstinacy, stubbornness.*
obstinado *adj. obstinate.*
obstinerse *to be obstinate; to persist.*
obstruir *to obstruct, to block.*
Obstruir el tráfico. *To block traffic.*
obtención *f. attainment; accomplishment.*
OBTENER *to obtain, to get; to attain.*
Ha obtenido una buena colocación. *He got a good job.*
obturador *m. shutter (of a camera); plug, stopper.*
obtuso *adj. obtuse, blunt.*
obús *m. howitzer, shell (of a gun).*
obvio *adj. obvious, evident.*
OCASIÓN *f. occasion; opportunity.*
He perdido una buena ocasión. *I lost (missed) a good opportunity.*
Iré a Bolivia en la primera ocasión. *I'll go to Bolivia at the first opportunity.*
Celebro la ocasión de conocerla. *I'm very happy to know you.*
Dar ocasión a. *To give rise to.*
Aprovechar la ocasión. *To take advantage of the occasion (opportunity).*
De ocasión. *Secondhand.*
Con (en) ocasión de. *On the occasion of.*
ocasionar *to cause; to bring about.*
occidental *adj. western, occidental.*
occidente *m. occident, west.*
océano *m. ocean.*
Océano Atlántico. *Atlantic Ocean.*
Océano Pacífico. *Pacific Ocean.*
ocio *m. idleness, leisure; pastime.*
ociosidad *f. idleness, leisure.*
ocioso *adj. idle, useless.*
octavo *adj. eighth.*
OCTUBRE *m. October.*
oculista *m. and f. oculist.*
ocultar *to conceal; to hide.*
No se pueden ocultar las penas. *It's impossible to conceal one's troubles (sorrows, grief).*
No se le ocultará a Ud. que . . . *You must be aware that . . .*

oculto *adj. concealed, hidden.*
ocupación *f. occupation, business, trade.*
¿Cuál es su nombre y ocupación? *What is your name and occupation?*
OCUPADO *adj. occupied; busy; engaged.*
Ultimamente he estado muy ocupado. *I've been very busy lately.*
La línea está ocupada. *The line is busy.*
Ese taxi está ocupado. *That cab is taken.*
OCUPAR *to occupy; to take possession of; to give work to; to hold a position.*
¿Está este asiento ocupado? *Is this seat taken (occupied)?*
Ocupa un puesto muy importante. *He holds a very important position.*
Han ocupado más obreros en la fábrica. *They have employed (taken on) more workers at the factory.*
Nuestras tropas han ocupado la ciudad. *Our troops have occupied the city.*
El edificio ocupa toda una manzana. *The building occupies an entire block.*
OCUPARSE *to pay attention to; to be concerned about; to attend to; to be encouraged in; to have as one's business.*
No se ocupe Ud. de esas cosas. *Don't bother about such things. Don't pay attention to such things.*
Se ocupaba poco de aquellos rumores. *He paid little attention to those rumors.*
Ocuparse de. *To look into. To take care of.*
El asunto que nos ocupa. *The matter in question.*
¿En qué se ocupa Ud.? *What's your occupation?*
ocurrencia *f. occurrence, incident; wisecrack, joke.*
Fué una ocurrencia desgraciada. *It was an unfortunate incident.*
¡Qué ocurrencia! 1. *What an idea!* 2. *What a joke!*
Siempre dice muchas ocurrencias. *He's always telling jokes.*
OCURRIR *to occur, to happen.*
¿Qué ocurre? *What's the matter? What's happening? What's up?*
No ha ocurrido nada de nuevo. *Nothing new has happened.*
¿Cuando ocurrió eso? *When did that happen?*
El accidente ocurrió aquí mismo. *The accident happened right here (in this very place).*
ocurrirse *to occur to one, to strike one (an idea).*
Se me ocurre una idea. *An idea occurred to me. I have an idea.*
No se me ocurrió ponerles un telegrama. *I didn't think of sending them a telegram. It didn't occur to me to send them a telegram.*
OCHENTA *adj. and n. eighty.*
OCHO *adj. and n. eight.*
Dentro de ocho días. *A week from today.*
odiar *to hate.*
odio *m. hatred.*
odioso *adj. hateful.*
OESTE *m. west.*
ofender *to offend.*
ofenderse *to take offense, to be offended.*
Se ofende por nada. *He (she) gets offended over (takes offense at) the least little thing (over trifles).*
ofensa *f. offense.*
ofensiva *f. offensive.*
Tomar la ofensiva. *To take the offensive.*
oferta *f. offer; offering, gift.*
Es su última oferta. *That's his last (final) offer.*

Oferta y demanda. *Supply and demand.*
oficial *adj. official; m. officer, official; trained worker.*
oficialmente *officially.*
oficina *f. office; workshop.*
¿Cuál es la dirección de su oficina? *What's your office address?*
oficinista *m. and f. office worker.*
oficio *m. occupation, work, trade, business; written communication.*
¿Qué oficio tiene? *What's your profession? What do you do for a living?*
OFRECER *to offer; to present.*
Ofrézcales un poco. *Offer them some.*
Nos ofreció su ayuda. *He offered us his help. He offered to help us.*
¿Qué se le ofrece? *What would you like? What can I do for you?*
Me ofreció dos dólares por el libro. *He offered me two dollars for the book.*
ofrecimiento *m. offer.*
oh! *Oh!*
OÍDO *m. hearing; ear.*
Tengo dolor de oído. *I have an earache.*
Tiene oído para la música. *He has a good ear for music.*
Le dijo algo al oído y se marchó. *He whispered something in his ear and left.*
Ha llegado a mis oídos que . . . *I've heard that . . .*
OIR *to hear; to listen.*
¡Oye! (¡Oiga! ¡Oígame!) *Say! Say there! Listen! Look here!*
¿Cómo dice? No oigo nada. *What are you saying? I can't hear a thing.*
No oí el despertador. *I didn't hear the alarm clock.*
¿Ha oído Ud. la última noticia? *Have you heard the latest news?*
¡Qué Dios le oiga! *Let's hope so! ("God grant it!")*
ojal *m. buttonhole.*
¡Ojalá! *God grant (it)! Would that . . .*
¡Ojalá que venga! *I wish she would come.*
¡Ojalá fuera así! *I wish it were so! Would that it were so!*
OJO *m. eye; attention, care; keyhole.*
Tengo los ojos cansados de tanto leer. *My eyes are tired from reading so much.*
No pude pegar los ojos en toda la noche. *I couldn't sleep a wink ("close my eyes") all night.*
Hay que tener mucho ojo. *One should be very careful.*
Le costó un ojo de la cara. *It cost him a mint of money. It cost him a small fortune.*
ola *f. wave (of water).*
OLER *to smell.*
Huelo algo. *I smell something.*
Me huele a quemado. *I smell something burning.*
Esto no me huele bien. *There's something fishy about it.*
Oler a soga. *To deserve to be hanged.*
Huele a chamusquina. *It looks like a fight.*
olfatear *to smell.*
olfato *m. sense of smell.*
oliva *f. olive.*
Aceite de oliva. *Olive oil.*
olivo *m. olive tree.*
olor *m. scent, odor.*
oloroso *adj. fragrant.*
OLVIDAR *to forget.*
Olvidé los guantes. *I forgot my gloves.*
Se me olvidó el paraguas. *I forgot my umbrella.*

Siempre se me olvida su nombre. *I always forget his name.*

¡Ah, se me olvidaba! *Oh, I almost forgot!*

Olvidemos lo pasado. *Let bygones be bygones.*

olvido *m. forgetfulness; oversight.*

Nos ha echado al olvido. *He's forgotten us.*

Fué un olvido. *It was an oversight.*

olla *f. pot.*

ombligo *m. navel; center, middle.*

omisión *f. omission.*

omitir *to omit, to leave out.*

Ud. ha omitido varias frases. *You've omitted several sentences.*

ómnibus *m. bus.*

¿Dónde para el ómnibus? *Where does the bus stop?*

¿Dónde queda la parada del ómnibus? *Where is the bus stop?*

ONCE *adj. and n. eleven.*

onda *f. wave; ripple.*

Onda corta. *Short wave.*

Onda larga. *Long wave.*

onza *f. ounce.*

opaco *adj. opaque; dull; not transparent.*

opción *f. option, choice.*

ópera *f. opera.*

operación *f. operation.*

operar *to operate; to act, to take effect; to operate on.*

La medicina empieza a operar. *The medicine is beginning to take effect.*

Hay que operar al enfermo. *It's necessary to operate on the patient.*

operario *m. worker; operator.*

opinar *to give an opinion.*

Opino que debes hacerlo. *I think you should do it ("It's my opinion that . . .")*

¿Qué opina Ud. de esto? *What do you think of that? What's your opinion about that?*

opinión *f. opinion.*

Esta es la opinión de todos. *Everyone is of that opinion.*

He cambiado de opinión. *I've changed my mind.*

oponer *to oppose, to go against.*

No opuso la menor dificultad. *He didn't raise any difficulties.*

oponerse *to be against, to object to.*

Me opongo a eso. *I'm against that.*

oportunamente *opportunely, in good time.*

oportunidad *f. opportunity, good chance.*

oportuno *adj. opportune.*

oposición *f. opposition; competition for a position.*

opositor *m. opponent; competitor.*

opresión *f. oppression.*

opresivo *adj. oppressive.*

opresor *m. oppressor.*

oprimir *to press, to squeeze; to oppress.*

optar *to choose, to pick up.*

Optar por. *To choose.*

óptico *adj. optic, optical; m. optician.*

optimismo *m. optimism.*

optimista *m. and f. optimist.*

opuesto *adj. opposed, opposite, contrary.*

ora *whether; either; now, then.*

Ora esto, ora estotro. *Now this (one), now that (one).*

oración *f. prayer; sentence (grammar).*

orador *m. orator, speaker.*

oral *adj. oral.*

orar *to pray.*

ORDEN *m. order, arrangement; f. order, command; brotherhood, society, order.*

A sus órdenes. *At your service.*

Por orden de. *By order of.*

Llamar al orden. *Call to order.*

En orden. *In order.*

Dar orden. *To instruct.*

Hasta nueva orden. *Until further instructions. Until further orders. Until further notice.*

La orden del día. *The order of the day.*

El orden del día. *Agenda.*

Mantener el orden público. *To preserve the ("public") peace.*

ordenanza *f. order; statute, ordinance; m. orderly.*

ordenar *to arrange; to order; to command; to ordain.*

ordeñar *to milk.*

ordinariamente *ordinarily.*

ORDINARIO *adj. ordinary; vulgar, unrefined; m. carrier, mailman; delivery boy; daily household expense.*

Es una mujer ordinaria. *She's vulgar.*

De ordinario. *Usually. Ordinarily.*

oreja *f. ear (external); flange, lug.*

Enseñar la oreja. *To let the cat out of the bag.*

orfandad *f. orphanage.*

orgánico *adj. organic.*

organillo *m. barrel organ.*

organismo *m. organism.*

organización *f. organization.*

organizar *to organize; to form; to arrange.*

órgano *m. organ; means, agency.*

orgullo *m. pride; haughtiness.*

orgulloso *adj. proud; haughty.*

oriental *adj. oriental, eastern; m. oriental.*

orientar *to orient.*

orientarse *to find one's bearings, to find one's way around.*

Es difícil orientarse en una ciudad desconocida. *It's difficult to find one's way around in a strange city.*

ORIENTE *m. orient, east.*

origen *m. origin, source.*

original *adj. and n. original.*

originalidad *f. originality.*

originar *to cause, to originate.*

Los gastos originados. *The cost.*

orilla *f. border, edge; shore; bank (of a river).*

ornamento *m. ornament, decoration.*

ornar *to adorn.*

ORO *m. gold; pl. diamonds (at cards).*

Perdí mi reloj de oro. *I lost my gold watch.*

orquesta *f. orchestra, band.*

ortografía *f. orthography, spelling.*

oruga *f. caterpillar; rocket (planet).*

os *(dative and accusative of vos and vosotros) you, to you.*

oscuro *m. dark.*

oso *m. bear.*

ostentar *to display; to show off, to boast.*

OTOÑO *m. autumn, fall.*

otorgar *to consent, to agree to; to grant.*

Quien calla otorga. *Silence gives consent. ("Whoever keeps silent, consents.")*

OTRA *(f. of otro) other, another; pl. otras.*

Déme otra manzana. *Give me another apple.*

Mi otra hija. *My other daughter.*

Sus otras fincas. *His other estates.*

¿Desea alguna otra cosa? *Would you like anything else?*

Y otras muchas cosas. *And many other things.*

Parece otra. *She looks quite different. She looks changed.*

Otra vez. *Again. Once more.*

Otras veces. *Other times.*

OTRO *adj. other, another; pl. otros.*

¡Otro vaso de cerveza! *Another glass of beer!*

Busco otro. *I'm looking for another (one).*

Busco el otro. *I'm looking for the other (one).*

Queremos otros. *We want some others.*

Queremos los otros. *We want the others.*

Otro tanto. *As much more.*

Otros tantos. *As many more.*

¿Quiénes son los otros invitados? *Who are the other guests?*

Debe haber otros dos. *There must be two more.*

Al otro lado de la calle. *Across the street.*

Algún otro. *Someone else.*

Otro día. *Another day.*

El otro día. *The other day.*

De otro modo. *Otherwise.*

Si no manda Ud. otra cosa, me retiro. *If you don't need anything else, I'll leave (go) now.*

ovación *f. ovation.*

oval *adj. oval.*

oveja *f. sheep.*

oyente *m. and f. hearer; listener; pl. audience, listeners.*

P

pabellón *m. pavilion; flag, colors.*

pacer *to pasture; to graze.*

paciencia *f. patience.*

Tenga paciencia. *Be patient. Have patience.*

Estoy perdiendo la paciencia. *I'm losing my patience.*

paciente *adj. patient; m. patient.*

pacífico *adj. peaceful; mild.*

pactar *to reach an agreement, to sign a pact, to agree upon.*

pacto *m. pact, agreement.*

padecer *to suffer; to be liable to.*

¿Qué es lo que Ud. padece? *What seems to be the matter with you?*

Ha padecido mucho. *He's suffered a lot.*

Padezco mucho de dolores de cabeza. *I suffer from headaches a lot.*

padecimiento *m. suffering.*

padrastro *m. stepfather.*

PADRE *m. father; pl. parents.*

De tal padre, tal hijo. *Like father, like son.*

padrino *m. godfather; best man (at a wedding); second (in a duel); sponsor.*

paella *f. a popular Valencian dish.*

paga *f. payment; pay, wages, fee.*

pagadero *adj. payable.*

pagador *m. payer; paymaster; paying teller.*

pagaduría *f. paymaster's office.*

pagano *m. pagan, heathen.*

PAGAR *to pay, to pay for; to return (a visit, a favor).*

¿Nos pagarán hoy? *Will they pay us today?*

Pagar al contado. *To pay cash.*

Pagar en la misma moneda. *To pay back in the same coin.*

Pagar una visita. *To return a visit.*

Me la pagará. *I'll make him pay for it.*

Pagar el pato. *To be blamed for something. To take the blame for something.*

Pagarse de. *To be pleased with. To be fond of. To be conceited.*

Está muy pagado de sí. *He has a high opinion of himself.*

pagaré *m. promissory note, I.O.U.*

PÁGINA *f. page (of a book, etc.).*

La página siguiente. *The following page.*

pago *m. payment; reward.*

En pago de. *In payment of.*

Suspender los pagos. *To stop payment.*

país *m. country (nation).*

paisaje m. *landscape, view.*

paisano adj. *coming from the same country;* m. *fellow countryman; civilian.*
Somos paisanos. *We are fellow countrymen.*
Iba vestido de paisano. *He was dressed in civilian clothes.*

paja f. *straw.*

pájaro m. *bird.*

PALABRA f. *word; promise.*
¿Qué quiere decir esta palabra? *What does this word mean?*
No entiendo palabra. *I don't understand a word.*
Desearía hablar dos palabras con Ud. *I should like to have a few words with you.*
Me quitó la palabra de la boca. *He took the words right out of my mouth.*
No falte a su palabra. *Don't break your promise.*
Pido la palabra. *May I have the floor?*
Esas son palabras mayores. *That's no joking matter.*
Dió su palabra de honor. *He gave his word of honor.*
Le cojo la palabra. *I'll take you up on that.*
Libertad de palabra. *Freedom of speech.*
De palabra. *By word of mouth.*
Dirigir la palabra. *To address.*
Palabra de matrimonio. *Promise of marriage.*
El que lleva la palabra. *The spokesman.*
Empeñar la palabra. *To give one's word.*

palacio m. *palace.*

paladar m. *palate; taste.*

palanca f. *lever; crowbar.*

palangana f. *washbowl; basin.*

palco m. *grandstand; box (in a theater).*

palidecer to *turn pale.*

pálido adj. *pale.*

palillo m. *toothpick;* pl. *chopsticks; castanets; drumsticks.*

paliza f. *spanking; beating.*

palma f. *palm tree; palm leaf; palm (of the hand).*
Llevarse la palma. *To carry the day. To carry off the laurels.*

palmada f. *pat, clap; clapping.*
Dar palmadas. *To clap one's hands.*

palmo m. *span, measure of length.*
Palmo a palmo. *Inch by inch.*

palo m. *stick; cudgel; timber; blow; suit (of cards).*
Palo de escoba. *Broomstick.*
De tal palo tal astilla. *A chip off the old block. Like father, like son.*

paloma f. *pigeon; dove.*
Paloma mensajera. *Homing pigeon. Carrier pigeon.*

palomar m. *pigeon house, dovecot.*

palpable adj. *palpable, evident.*

palpar to *feel, to touch.*

palpitar to *beat, to throb, to palpitate.*

paludismo m. *paludism; malaria.*

pampa f. *pampas, vast treeless plain.*

PAN m. *bread; loaf.*
Pan con mantequilla. *Bread and butter.*
¿Tienen Uds. bastante pan? *Have you (pl.) enough bread?*
Se comió un pan entero. *He ate a whole loaf.*

panadería f. *bakery.*

panadero m. *baker.*

panal m. *honeycomb; hornet's nest.*

pandereta f. *tambourine.*

pandilla f. *gang.*

panecillo m. *roll (bread).*

panera f. *breadbasket; granary.*

pánico adj. *panic;* m. *panic.*

panorama m. *landscape, view.*

panorámico adj. *panoramic.*

pantalón m. *trousers.*

pantalla f. *lamp shade; screen.*

pantano m. *marsh, swamp.*

pantera f. *panther.*

pantomima f. *pantomime.*

pantorrilla f. *calf (of the leg).*

panza f. *paunch, belly.*

pañal m. *swaddling cloth; diaper.*

paño m. *woolen material, cloth, fabric; (by extension) ar.y woven material.*
¿Le queda a Ud. bastante paño para hacer otro traje? *Have you enough material left to make another suit?*
Paños menores. *Underwear.*

pañuelo m. *handkerchief.*

papa f. *potato;* m. *Pope.*

papá m. *papa, daddy.*

papagayo m. *parrot.*

papel m. *paper; role; part (in a play).*
¿Quiere darme un pliego de papel? *Will you please give me a sheet of paper?*
Escríbalo en este papel. *Write it on this paper.*
Hay papel de escribir en el cajón. *There's some writing paper in the drawer.*
Hizo el papel de tonto. *He played the fool.*
Hacer un papel. *To play a part. To play a role.*
Papel moneda. *Paper money (currency).*
Papel secante. *Blotting paper. Blotter.*
Papel para calcar. *Tracing paper.*
Papel de estraza. *Wrapping paper.*
Papel de seda. *Tissue paper.*
Papel de fumar. *Cigarette paper.*

papelera f. *writing desk; (paper) folder.*

papelería f. *stationery store.*

PAQUETE m. *package; parcel.*
Mande el paquete a estas señas. *Send the package to this address.*

PAR adj. *equal; par (value); even (number);* m. *pair, couple; team; peer.*
Es una mujer sin par. *There's nobody like her.*
La peseta estaba a la par. *The peseta was at par value.*
La puerta estaba abierta de par en par. *The door was wide open.*
Un par de zapatos. *A pair of shoes.*
Llegará dentro de un par de días. *He'll arrive in a couple of days.*
¿Toma Ud. pares o nones? *Do you take odds or evens?*

PARA *for, to, until, about, in order to, toward.*
¿Para qué? *What for? For what purpose?*
¿Para quién es esto? *For whom is this?*
Esta carta es para Ud. *This letter is for you.*
¿Para quién es este libro? *Who's this book for?*
¿Para qué sirve esto? *What's this for? What's this good for?*
Tengo una cita para las cuatro. *I have an appointment for four o'clock.*
Déjelo para mañana. *Leave it until tomorrow.*
Tiene talento para la música. *She has a gift for music.*
Me abrigo para no tener frío. *I dress warmly so as not to be cold.*
Bueno para comer. *Good to eat.*
Dije para mí. *I said to myself.*
Está para llover. *It's going to rain.*
Estoy para salir. *I'm about to leave.*
El tren está para partir. *The train is about to leave.*
Quisiera algo para leer. *I'd like something to read.*

Trabajar para comer. *To work for a living.*
Estudia para médico. *He's studying to be a doctor.*
Para siempre. *Forever.*
Para entre los dos. *Between ourselves.*

parabién m. *congratulation.*

parábola f. *parable; parabola.*

parabrisa m. *windshield.*

paracaídas m. *parachute.*

paracaidista m. *parachutist.*

parada f. *stop; pause; halt; parade; wager.*
¿Dónde está la parada más cerca del tranvía? *Where is the nearest streetcar stop?*
Cinco minutos de parada. *Five minutes' stop.*
La parada se formará a las doce. *The parade will form at twelve o'clock.*

paradero m. *whereabouts; terminus; end.*

parado adj. *stopped, at a standstill; closed (a factory); unemployed; standing up (Amer.).*

paradoja f. *paradox.*

PARAGUAS m. *umbrella.*
¿Llevamos paraguas? *Shall we take (our) umbrellas?*

paraíso m. *paradise.*

paraje m. *place, spot.*

paralelo adj. *and n. parallel.*

parálisis f. *paralysis.*

paralítico adj. *paralytic.*

paralizar to *paralyze; to bring to a standstill; to impede, to hinder.*

PARAR to *stop, to halt, to stay; to bet; to stand (Amer.).*
¿Por qué para el tren? *Why is the train stopping?*
¿Paramos aquí? *Do we stop here?*
Pare Ud. en frente de la estación. *Stop in front of the station.*
Mi reloj se paró. *My watch stopped.*
No para de llover desde ayer. *It hasn't stopped raining since yesterday.*
Con estas cartas yo voy a parar cincuenta pesos. *With these cards I'm going to bet fifty pesos.*
¿En qué hotel pararán sus amigos? *At what hotel will your friends stay?*
Paró la oreja para oír lo que decíamos. *He pricked up his ears to hear what we were saying.*
No paró bien aquel negocio. *That business didn't end very well.*
¿Dónde irá a parar todo esto? *How's all this going to end?*

pararse to *stop; to stand up (Amer.).*
Se pararon (Amer.) al verla llegar. *They stood up when they saw her coming.*
Párese (Amer.) en esta esquina que ahorita pasará el autobús. *Stand on this corner; the bus will pass by in a little while.*

pararrayos m. *lightning rod.*

parásito m. *parasite.*

parcela f. *parcel; piece of land.*

parcial adj. *partial.*

parcialidad f. *partiality, bias.*

parcialmente *partially, partly.*

pardo adj. *brown; dark.*

PARECER to *appear, to show up, to turn up; to seem, to look, to be like, to resemble;* m. *opinion; appearance.*
¿Qué le parece? *What do you think of it? How do you like it? How does it seem to you?*
Léalo Ud. despacio y dígame lo que le parece. *Read it carefully and let me know what you think of it.*
¿Le parece que vayamos al cine? *What do you say to our going to the movies?*

Me parece barato a ese precio. *I think it's cheap at that price.*

Está enfermo, pero no lo parece. *He's sick but he doesn't look it.*

Al parecer vendrá la semana próxima. *Apparently he's coming next week.*

Parece que va a a llover. *It looks as if it's going to rain.*

Déme Ud. su parecer. *Give me your opinion (about it).*

¿Cuál es su parecer respecto a eso? *What's your opinion about that?*

También soy yo del mismo parecer. *I'm also of the same opinion.*

No me gusta su parecer. *I don't like his appearance.*

parecerse *to look alike, to resemble.*

Este niño se parece a su padre. *This child looks like his father.*

Las dos hermanas se parecen. *Both sisters look alike.*

Se parecen como dos gotas de agua. *They are as alike as two peas in a pod.*

PARECIDO *adj. like, similar, resembling; (good or bad) looking; m. likeness.*

Yo tengo un traje muy parecido al suyo. *I have a suit very much like yours.*

Los dos trabajos son muy parecidos. *The two jobs are very similar.*

Su hijo es muy bien parecido. *Your son is very good-looking.*

PARED *f. wall.*

Apóyalo contra la pared. *Lean it against the wall.*

Entre la espada y la pared. *Between the devil and the deep blue sea.* *("Between the wall and the sword.")*

pareja *f. pair; couple; team (of horses); dancing partner.*

paréntesis *m. parenthesis.*

PARIENTE *m. relative, relation.*

¿Tiene Ud. parientes en esta ciudad? *Do you have any relatives in this town?*

Fuí a visitar a unos parientes. *I went to visit some relatives.*

parir *to give birth.*

parlamento *m. parliament; parley.*

paro *m. unemployment; stoppage of work.*

Paro forzoso. *Lockout.*

párpado *m. eyelid.*

parque *m. park.*

parra *f. grapevine.*

párrafo *m. paragraph.*

Echar un párrafo. *To have a chat.*

parrilla *f. gridiron, broiler.*

parroquia *f. parish; clientele, customers.*

parroquiano *m. parishioner; customer.*

Somos sus parroquianos. *We're his (your) customers.*

PARTE *f. part; portion; share; side; role; party; m. report, communication, dispatch.*

¿Qué parte del pollo le gusta más? *What part of the chicken do you like best?*

¿En qué parte de la ciudad vive Ud.? *In what part of the city do you live?*

Hagamos el trabajo por partes iguales. *Let's divide the work equally.* *("Let's do the work in equal parts.")*

Cada uno pagó su parte. *Each one paid his share.*

Traigo esto de parte del señor Sucre. *This is from Mr. Sucre.*

Salude a Juan de mi parte. *Give John my re-*

gards.

Recibimos felicitaciones de ambas partes. *We received congratulations from both sides.*

He leído la mayor parte del libro, pero no todo. *I've read most of the book, but not all.*

No tengo arte ni parte en el asunto. *I've nothing to do with the matter.*

¿Le ha visto en alguna parte? *Have you seen him anywhere?*

No lo hallo en ninguna parte. *I can't find it anywhere.*

No iremos a ninguna parte. *We won't go anywhere.*

¿Ha leído Ud. el parte de guerra? *Have you read the communiqué?*

En todas partes. *Everywhere.*

En parte. *In part.*

En gran parte. *Largely.*

De algún tiempo a esta parte. *For some time past.*

De cinco días a esta parte. *Within the(se) last few days.*

Haré todo de mi parte. *I'll do all in my power.*

Parte de la oración. *Part of the speech.*

Dar parte. *To inform. To notify.*

Le he dado parte de mi llegada. *I've sent him word of my arrival.*

Por mi parte. *As far as I'm concerned. For my part.*

Por una parte. *On one hand.*

Por otra parte. *On the other hand. Besides.*

La parte interesada. *The party concerned. The interested party.*

¿De parte de quién? *Who's calling?*

participación *f. participation, share.*

participar *to participate, to take part, to share; to inform, to notify.*

No se crea que yo participo de sus ideas. *Don't think that I share his views.*

Le participo mi decisión. *I'm informing you of my decision.*

¿Participaron Uds. en el juego? *Did you take part in the game?*

particular *adj. particular, unusual, peculiar; m. private citizen; individual.*

Eso no tiene nada de particular. *There's nothing unusual about it.*

¿Qué tiene de particular? *What's there strange about it? What's so strange about it?*

¿Hay algo de nuevo?—Nada de particular. *Anything new?—Nothing in particular.*

En particular. *In particular.*

particularidad *f. particularity, peculiarity.*

particularmente *particularly, especially.*

partida *f. departure; entry, item (in an account); lot; one game; certificate (birth, etc.).*

Punto de partida. *Point of departure. Starting point.*

Partida de nacimiento. *Birth certificate.*

Echemos una partida de ajedrez. *Let's play a game of chess.*

Partida doble. *Double entry.*

partidario *adj. and n. partisan, follower, supporter.*

Soy partidario de los paseos al aire libre. *I like to take walks in the fresh air.*

Es partidario de la política del buen vecino. *He's in favor of the Good-Neighbor Policy.*

partido *adj. divided, split; broken; m. party; advantage; game.*

Ese vaso está partido. *That glass is broken.*

La tabla esta partida. *The board is split.*

¿Qué partido tomaremos? *What course shall we take?*

No sabía que partido tomar. *I didn't know what to do.*

Pertenecen al mismo partido. *They belong to the same party.*

¿Quiere Ud. ver el partido de fútbol? *Would you like to see the football game?*

¿Cuál fué el resultado del partido? *What was the final score of the game?*

PARTIR *to divide, to split; to leave; to cut; to break.*

El tren está para partir. *The train is about to leave.*

Partiremos el primero del mes. *We'll leave on the first of the month.*

Seguía diluviando cuando partimos. *It was still pouring when we left.*

Necesito un cuchillo para partir este pan. *I need a knife to cut this bread.*

La tabla se ha partido en dos. *The board broke in two.*

Partió la manzana en dos. *He divided (split) the apple in two.*

Parta Ud. 300 entre 3. *Divide 3 into 300.*

Partieron el terreno en varios lotes. *They divided the land into several lots.*

Al partirse el hielo cayeron al agua. *When the ice broke, they fell into the water.*

Partir la diferencia. *To split the difference.*

parto *m. childbirth.*

parvo *adj. small, little.*

párvulo *m. child.*

Escuela de párvulos. *Kindergarten.*

pasa *f. raisin.*

PASADO *m. past; past tense.*

Pasados dos días. *After two days.*

Lo pasado. *The past.*

El martes pasado, tres de marzo. *Last Tuesday, March the third.*

Pasado mañana. *The day after tomorrow.*

pasaje *m. passage; fare; strait.*

¿Cuánto cuesta el pasaje? *What's the fare?*

pasajero *adj. passing, transitory; m. passenger.*

pasaporte *m. passport.*

PASAR *to pass, to go by, to go across; to come over, to come in, to call (visit); to spend (the time); to get along; to be taken for; to put on, to pretend; to overlook; to surpass; to happen.*

Pásame la sal, por favor. *Pass the salt, please.*

Pase Ud. y siéntese. *Come in and sit down.*

Pase Ud. por aquí. *Come this way.*

Pase por aquí otro día. *Drop in again some time.*

¿Puede Ud. pasar por mi oficina mañana? *Can you call at my office tomorrow?*

Pasamos el río a nado. *We swam across the river.*

Ya pasó el tren. *The train has already passed.*

Pasó el rápido a las nueve. *The express went by at nine.*

Pasaron por aquí hace poco. *They went by this place a moment ago.*

Pasamos por la calle de Arenal. *We passed through Arenal Street.*

Pasa por norteamericano, pero no lo es. *He passes for an American but he isn't really.*

Los años se pasan rapidamente. *The years pass quickly.*

¿Cómo se llama este pueblo que acabamos de pasar? *What's the name of the village we just passed?*

Se pasó todo el día leyendo. *She spent the whole day reading.*

Se pasa la vida refunfuñando. *He's always grumbling about something.*

¿Qué pasa? *What's the matter?*

¿Cómo lo pasa Ud.? *How are you getting along? How are things with you?*

Ud. lo pase bien. *Good-by! Have a good time.*

¿Qué le pasa a Ud.? *What's the matter with you?*

Que pase Ud. buena noche. *I hope you have a good night's sleep (rest). Sleep well.*

Lo pasa uno bien allí. *Life is pleasant there.*

Yo no sé lo que le pasa. *I don't know what's the matter with him.*

Ud. no sabe lo que ha pasado. *You don't know what has happened.*

Sólo Dios sabe qué pasará. *(Only) God knows what will happen.*

Esta lluvia pasará pronto. *The (this) rain will stop soon.*

Ya se le pasará. *He'll get over it.*

Ya pasó aquello. *That's gone (past) and forgotten.*

Eso ha pasado de moda. *That's gone out of style.*

Se pasa de buena. *She's too good.*

El papel se pasa. *The paper blots.*

Se me pasó por alto. *I overlooked it. I didn't (take) notice.*

Voy a pasar lista a la clase. *I'm going to call the class roll.*

Estamos pasando el rato. *We're killing time. We're having fun.*

pasatiempo *m. pastime, amusement.*

Pascua *f. Christmas; Easter; Passover.*

¡Felices Pascuas! *Merry Christmas!*

Está como unas pascuas. *He's as merry as a cricket.*

pase *m. pass, permit; thrust.*

paseante *m. stroller.*

PASEAR *to walk; to ride; to take a walk.*

Vamos a pasear. *Let's go for a walk.*

Saca los niños a pasear. *Take the children out for a walk.*

pasearse *to go for a walk.*

PASEO *m. walk, stroll; ride; drive; avenue or road bordered by trees.*

Demos un paseo. *Let's take a walk.*

Vamos a dar un paseo en coche. *Let's go for a drive.*

Hay muchos árboles en el paseo de Recoletos. *There are a lot of trees on Recoletos Avenue.*

pasillo *m. corridor; aisle; hall; basting stitch.*

Iré al pasillo para llamar por teléfono. *I'll go out into the hall to phone.*

pasión *f. passion.*

pasivo *adj. passive; m. liabilities.*

PASO *m. step; pass; passage; place; gait.*

Está a dos pasos de aquí. *It's only a few steps from here.*

Los pasos que sentí no parecían de mujer. *The steps I heard didn't sound like a woman's.*

Tuvimos que abrirnos paso por entre la multitud. *We had to make our way through the crowd.*

Este caballo tiene un paso excelente. *This horse has a fine gait.*

Apretemos el paso para llegar a tiempo. *Let's hurry so that we'll get there on time.*

De paso. *By the way. Incidentally.*

Salir de paso. *To get out of a difficulty.*

Dar los pasos necesarios. *To take the necessary steps.*

Paso a paso. *Step by step.*

Llevar el paso. *To keep in step.*

Marcar el paso. *To mark time.*

"Prohibido el paso." *"Keep out." "No trespassing."*

pasta *f. paste; dough; binding (of a book).*

Pasta dentífrica. *Toothpaste.*

pastel *m. pie, cake.*

pastelería *f. pastry shop; pastry.*

pastelero *m. pastry cook; a temporizer.*

pastilla *f. drop, lozenge; cake (of soap).*

Pastillas de menta. *Mint drops.*

Pastillas para la tos. *Cough drops.*

pastor *m. shepherd; pastor.*

pata *f. foot and leg of an animal; leg (of a table, chair, etc.); duck.*

Ha roto la pata de la mesa. *He broke the leg of the table.*

A pata (coll.). *On foot.*

Patas arriba. *Upside down.*

Meter la pata. *To make a blunder. To put one's foot in it.*

patalear *to stamp (the foot).*

patata *f. potato.*

patente *adj. patent, obvious; f. patent; grant, privilege.*

Hacer patente. *To make clear.*

patín *m. skate.*

Patín de ruedas. *Roller skates.*

patinar *to skate; to skid.*

patio *m. patio; yard; pit (theater).*

pato *m. drake, duck.*

Pagar el pato. *To be made the scapegoat.*

patraña *f. falsehood, fib.*

patria *f. native country, fatherland.*

patriota *m. patriot.*

patriótico *adj. patriotic.*

patriotismo *m. patriotism.*

patrocinar *to patronize.*

patrón *m. master, skipper (of a ship); employer, boss; pattern; standard (gold).*

patrono *m. employer; patron saint.*

patrulla *f. patrol.*

paulatinamente *slowly, by degrees.*

paulatino *adj. slow, gradual.*

pausa *f. pause.*

pauta *f. paper ruler; guide lines; example, model.*

pava *f. turkey hen.*

Pelar la pava. *To flirt.*

PAVIMENTO *m. pavement.*

pavo *m. turkey.*

Pavo real. *Peacock.*

pavor *m. fear, terror.*

payaso *m. clown.*

PAZ *f. peace.*

¿Por qué no hacen las paces? *Why don't they bury the hatchet? Why don't they make up?*

En paz. *Even. Quits. On even terms.*

Déjeme en paz. *Let me alone. ("Leave me in peace.")*

pe *f. name of the letter p.*

De pe a pa. *Entirely. Thoroughly. From top to bottom. From beginning to end.*

peatón *m. pedestrian.*

pecado *m. sin, trespass.*

pecar *to sin.*

peculiar *adj. peculiar.*

peculiaridad *f. peculiarity.*

PECHO *m. chest; breast; bosom.*

Me duele el pecho. *My chest hurts me.*

Es un hombre de pelo en pecho. *He's a daring (bold, brave, aggressive) fellow.*

No lo tome Ud. a pecho. *Don't take it to heart.*

Dar el pecho. *To suckle.*

pechuga *f. breast (of a fowl).*

pedagogo *m. pedagogue, teacher.*

pedal *m. pedal, treadle.*

PEDAZO *m. bit, piece, morsel.*

Sírvame otro pedazo de carne. *May I have another piece of meat? ("Serve me another piece of meat.")*

Hágame el favor de un pedazo de papel. *May I have a piece of paper?*

Hacer pedazos. *To break into pieces.*

¡Pedazo de alcornoque! *Blockhead!*

pedestal *m. pedestal; support.*

pedido *m. order (for goods); request.*

No podemos servir el pedido. *We can't fill the order.*

Hacer un pedido. *To order (goods). To place an order.*

A pedido de. *At the request of.*

PEDIR *to ask for; to beg; to demand; to wish; to order (goods).*

Me ha pedido que le haga un favor. *He asked me to do him a favor.*

¿Ya pidió Ud. el desayuno? *Have you ordered breakfast?*

Tengo que pedirle permiso. *I have to ask his permission.*

Pido la palabra. *May I have the floor?*

Coma lo que le pida el cuerpo. *Eat whatever you like.*

El negocio marcha a pedir de boca. *Business is going splendidly. Business is excellent.*

Pidió socorro a voces. *She cried out for help.*

El público entusiasmado pidió la repetición. *The enthusiastic audience called for an encore.*

Pedir informes. *To ask for information. To inquire.*

pegajoso *adj. sticky, viscous; contagious.*

pegar *to paste, to glue; to sew on; to hit, to beat; to stop.*

Pegue las etiquetas. *Paste the labels on.*

Pegar a una persona. *To hit (beat up) a person.*

Pégueme un botón a esta camisa. *Sew a button on this shirt.*

Pegar fuego a. *To set fire to.*

No pude pegar los ojos en toda la noche. *I couldn't sleep a wink all night.*

peinado *m. hairdressing; hair style, coiffure, hairdo.*

¿Qué peinado prefiere? *What hair style do you prefer?*

peinar *to comb.*

Péineme el pelo hacia atrás. *Comb my hair back.*

peinarse *to do or to comb one's hair.*

Ella se peina muy bien. *She does her hair very nicely.*

Sólo me falta peinarme. *I just (only) have to comb my hair.*

PEINE *m. comb.*

peineta *f. dress comb.*

pelado *adj. plucked, bare, bald; penniless, broke (Amer.).*

pelar *to peel; to cut somebody's hair; to pluck, to rob, to cheat.*

Péleme esa manzana. *Peel that apple for me.*

Es duro de pelar. *He's (it's) a hard nut to crack.*

peldaño *m. step (of staircase).*

pelea *f. fight, struggle.*

pelear *to fight.*

peletería *f. furrier's, fur shop.*

película *f. film.*

La película resultó muy aburrida. *The picture was dull.*

¿Qué película dan esta noche? *What's showing*

tonight? ("What film are they giving tonight?")
peligro m. peril, danger.
No hay peligro. There's no danger.
peligroso adj. dangerous.
PELO m. hair.
Quiero que me corten el pelo. I want a haircut.
¡No me tome Ud. el pelo! Don't make fun of me! Don't kid me! Don't tease me!
Para más pelos y señales. In more detail.
pelota f. ball.
peluca f. wig.
peluquería f. barber shop.
Peluquería de señoras. Beauty parlor.
peluquero m. barber; wigmaker.
pellejo m. skin; peel; rawhide.
pellizcar to pinch.
pena f. penalty, punishment; grief, sorrow, hardship, toil.
Murió de pena. She died of a broken heart.
Ha sufrido muchas penas. He has been through many hardships.
Lo hizo a duras penas. He did it with great difficulty.
No vale la pena hacerlo. It's not worth while doing.
So pena de. Under penalty of.
Pena capital. Capital punishment. Death penalty.
penal adj. penal; m. prison.
penalidad f. hardship; penalty.
penar to suffer; to be in agony.
pender to hang; to be pending.
pendiente adj. pendent; pending; m. earrings. f. slope.
Cuestión pendiente. An open question. A question still pending.
Eso queda pendiente. That's still pending.
Deuda pendiente. Balance due.
Lleva unos pendientes muy bonitos. She's wearing very pretty earrings.
Bajar una pendiente. To descend (go down) a hill.
penetrante adj. penetrating, piercing.
penetrar to penetrate; to fathom, to comprehend.
península f. peninsula.
penitente adj. and n. penitent.
penoso adj. painful; difficult, arduous; distressing.
pensado adj. deliberate; thought out.
Está muy bien pensado. It's (very) well thought out.
Tengo pensado comprarlo. I intend to buy (buying) it.
pensador m. thinker; thinking.
pensamiento m. thought; idea; pansy.
PENSAR to think; to consider, to intend.
Piense antes de hablar. Think before you speak.
Lo hice sin pensar. I did it without thinking.
¿En qué piensa Ud.? What are you thinking about?
Esto me da en que pensar. This gives me something to think about. This gives me food for thought.
Pienso igual que Ud. I think the way you do. I think the same as you. I agree with you.
Pensaban estar aquí para el lunes. They planned to be here about Monday.
¿Cuándo piensa Ud. marcharse? When do you intend to leave?
¿En qué hotel piensa Ud. parar? At what hotel do you expect to stop.
pensativo adj. pensive, thoughtful.
pensión f. pension; board; boarding house.

pensionista m. and f. pensioner; boarder.
penúltimo adj. penultimate, last but one.
peña f. rock, large stone; circle (of friends).
peñón m. large rock; cliff; rocky mountain.
El peñón de Gibraltar. The rock of Gibraltar.
peón m. peon; pawn (in chess); pedestrian; (spinning) top.
PEOR adj. and adv. worse; worst.
Sigue peor. He's getting worse.
Eso es lo peor. That's the worst of it.
Tanto peor. All the worse. So much the worse.
Llevar la peor parte. To get the worst of it.
El mes pasado fué el peor de todos. Last month was the worst of all.
La situación va (sigue) de mal en peor. The situation is going from bad to worse.
pepinillos m. pl. pickles.
pepino m. cucumber.
pequeñez f. a trifle; pettiness.
Discutieron sobre una pequeñez. They argued over a trifle.
PEQUEÑO adj. little, small, tiny; young; m. child.
Su hijo es muy pequeño. His child is very young.
Tiene los dientes blancos y pequeños. She has small white teeth.
¿Cómo están los pequeños? How are the children?
PERA f. pear.
Partir peras con alguno. To treat a person familiarly. To be on familiar terms with someone.
peral m. pear tree.
percal m. percale.
percance m. misfortune, mishap, accident.
percepción f. perception.
perceptible adj. perceptible, perceivable.
percibir to perceive, to get.
No percibo bien lo que dice. I don't quite get what he's saying.
Percibe un sueldo de cien pesos. He has (receives) a salary of a hundred dollars a month.
percha f. perch, pole, staff.
PERDER to lose.
He perdido mi cartera. I've lost my wallet.
No tengo tiempo que perder. I haven't any time to lose.
Estuvo a punto de perder la vida. He nearly lost his life.
Han echado a perder el jardín. They've spoiled the garden.
Está echado a perder. He's spoiled.
No lo pierdas de vista. Don't lose sight of him.
He perdido una buena ocasión. I missed a good opportunity.
Lo hice a ratos perdidos. I did it in my spare moments (time).
Está borracho perdido. He's dead drunk.
¿Este color no pierde? Is this a fast color? ("Does this color fade?")
Ha perdido la razón. He's lost his reason (mind).
Perdió la vista. He lost his eyesight.
Perdió la vergüenza. To lose all sense of shame.
Perder el respeto. To lose respect for.
Perder el habla. To become speechless. ("To lose one's tongue.")
perderse to get lost; to spoil, to get spoiled; to go astray.
La comida se va a perder si no se come hoy. The food will spoil if it's not eaten today.

Perderse en el bosque. To get lost in the woods.
perdición f. perdition; ruin.
pérdida f. loss; damage; leakage.
Reparar una pérdida. To recover a loss.
perdidamente desperately.
Está perdidamente enamorado. He's head over heels in love.
perdiz f. partridge.
perdón m. pardon.
¡Perdón! Pardon me!
PERDONAR to excuse, to pardon, to forgive.
Perdóneme Ud. Excuse me.
Le suplico a Ud. que me perdone. Please excuse me.
Perdone mi tardanza. Pardon my lateness.
Esta vez te lo perdono. This time I forgive you.
No perdonar una fiesta. Not to miss a party.
No perdonar ni un detalle. To leave nothing untold. To tell every detail.
perecer to perish, to die.
Perecer ahogado. To drown.
peregrino adj. migratory; odd, strange.
perejil m. parsley.
pereza f. laziness, idleness.
perezoso adj. lazy, indolent.
perfección f. perfection, improvement, perfecting.
perfeccionar to make perfect, to improve.
perfeccionarse to improve oneself, to increase one's knowledge.
PERFECTO adj. perfect.
Es un trabajo perfecto. It's a perfect piece of work.
perfidia f. perfidy, treachery, foul play.
perfil m. profile; outline.
perfume m. perfume; scent, fragrance
perfumería f. perfume store.
pericia f. skill; knowledge.
perilla f. knob, doorknob.
Déle vuelta a la perilla. Turn the knob.
Eso me viene de perilla. That just fits the purpose.
periódico adj. periodic(al); m. newspaper, magazine, periodical.
periodismo m. journalism.
periodista m. and f. journalist, newspaperman, newspaperwoman.
período m. period, time.
perito adj. experienced, skillful; m. expert; appraiser.
perjudicar to damage, to injure, to hurt.
perjudicial adj. prejudicial, harmful.
perjuicio m. prejudice; damage, harm.
perjuro adj. perjured; m. perjurer.
perla f. pearl.
permanecer to remain, to stay.
¿Cuánto tiempo permanecerá Ud. fuera de la ciudad? How long will you be (remain) out of town?
permanencia f. permanence; stay.
PERMANENTE adj. and n. permanent.
Un lugar permanente. A permanent place.
Ondulado permanente. Permanent wave.
permeable adj. permeable.
PERMISO m. permission; permit, authorization, consent.
Tener permiso de. To have permission to.
Con su permiso. If I may. With your permission ("by your leave").
No lo haga Ud. sin mi permiso. Don't do it without my permission.
Permiso de llevar armas de fuego. A permit to carry firearms.
Permiso para guiar. A driving license.
permitir to permit, to let, to allow.

¿Me permite Ud. que fume? *May I smoke? Do you mind if I smoke?*

¿Me permite que le haga una pregunta. *May I ask you a question?*

No permitiré tal cosa. *I won't allow such a thing.*

Permítame Ud. que le presente a mi amigo. *Allow me to introduce you to my friend.*

permuta f. permutation; exchange; barter.

permutar to permute; to barter, to exchange.

pernicioso adj. pernicious, injurious, harmful.

PERO but, yet, except; m. defect, fault.

Ud. no querrá ir, pero yo sí. *You may not want to go, but I do.*

Quisiera ir, pero no puedo. *I'd like to go, but I can't.*

Pero no es así. *But it's not so. But that's not the case.*

Pero él dice otra cosa. *But he tells a different story.*

¡Pero qué calor hace! *How hot it is! It's certainly hot!*

Es hermoso sin pero. *It's very beautiful. ("It's beautiful with no buts about it.")*

No hay pero que valga. *No buts.*

Poner peros. *To find fault.*

perpendicular adj. and n. perpendicular.

perpetuar to perpetuate.

perpetuidad f. perpetuity.

perpetuo adj. perpetual, everlasting.

perplejo adj. perplexed, bewildered, puzzled.

Me siento perplejo. *I'm perplexed (puzzled).*

perra f. bitch; drunkenness; copper coin (Spain).

Perra gorda. *Ten centime copper coin (Spain).*

Perra chica. *Five centime copper coin (Spain).*

PERRO m. dog.

persecución f. persecution.

perseguir to persecute; to pursue; to harass.

perseverancia f. perseverance.

perseverar to persevere, to persist.

persiana f. window blind; pl. Venetian blind.

persistencia f. persistence, obstinacy.

persistente adj. persistent, firm.

persistir to persist.

PERSONA f. person.

Es muy buena persona. *He's a very nice person.*

Esto me lo dijo cierta persona. *A certain person told me that.*

En este salón caben más de cien personas. *This hall can accommodate over a hundred people.*

personaje m. personage; character (in a play).

personal adj. personal; m. personnel, staff.

Estos artículos son de mi uso personal. *These articles are for my personal use.*

personalidad f. personality.

perspectiva f. perspective.

perspicacia f. perspicacity.

perspicaz adj. perspicacious, acute, sagacious, quick-sighted.

persuadir to persuade; to convince.

persuasión f. persuasion.

pertenecer to belong.

Esto pertenece a . . . *This belongs to . . .*

Esa pluma me pertenece. *That pen belongs to me.*

Pertenece al Cuerpo de Sanidad. *He belongs to (is in) the Medical Corps.*

pertinente adj. pertinent.

perturbar to perturb, agitate.

perversidad f. perversity, wickedness.

perversión f. perversion.

perverso adj. perverse.

pervertir to pervert.

pesadilla f. nightmare.

pesado adj. heavy; tedious; tiresome; m. bore.

El hierro es pesado. *Iron is heavy.*

Es un pesado. *He's a bore.*

pésame m. condolence; message of condolence.

PESAR to weigh, to be of weight; to cause regret; m. grief, sorrow; regret.

¿Cuánto pesa Ud.? *How much do you weigh?*

¿Pesa demasiado la carta? *Does the letter weigh too much?*

Antes de entrar en el avión hay que pesarse. *Before boarding the plane you have to be weighed.*

Vale lo que pesa. *It's worth its weight in gold.*

Me pesa mucho haberle ofendido. *I'm sorry I offended him.*

Aunque me pese no puedo menos que hacerlo. *Although I regret it, I can't help doing it.*

Lo haremos a pesar de todo. *We'll do it in spite of everything.*

pesca f. fishing; fishery.

PESCADO m. fish (after it is caught; see **pez**).

pescar to fish; to catch.

pesebre m. crib, manger.

peseta f. peseta (Spanish silver coin).

pesimismo m. pessimism.

pesimista adj. pessimistic; m. and f. pessimist.

pésimo adj. very bad.

peso m. weight; weighing; scales; importance; burden; peso (standard monetary unit in some Spanish American countries).

Las ramas se doblan bajo el peso de la fruta. *The branches are bending under the weight of the fruit.*

Le presté cinco pesos. *I lent him five pesos.*

Ponga Ud. esto en el peso. *Put that on the scales.*

Me han quitado un peso de encima. *That took a load off my mind.*

Sobre nosotros cayó todo el peso de la lucha. *We bore the brunt of the struggle.*

Eso cae de su peso. *That goes without saying.*

Peso neto. *Net weight.*

Peso bruto. *Gross weight.*

De peso. *Of weight. Of importance.*

pestaña f. eyelash; fringe, edging.

peste f. plague; pestilence.

pestillo m. door latch.

petición f. petition; claim; demand; plea.

petróleo m. petroleum; mineral oil.

pez m. fish (in the water; see **pescado**); f. pitch, tar.

pezuña f. hoof.

piadoso adj. pious; merciful.

pianista m. and f. pianist.

piano m. piano.

picadillo m. hash; minced meat.

picadura f. prick; puncture; bite (of an insect or snake); cut tobacco.

picante adj. hot, highly seasoned; cutting, sarcastic, pungent (wit).

picaporte m. latch.

picar to bite, to sting; to prick; to itch; to chop; to nibble; to spur; to be hot (pepper, etc.).

Me ha picado una abeja. *I was stung by a bee.*

Me pica la espalda. *My back itches.*

Picar la carne. *To chop (up) meat.*

Esta pimienta pica mucho. *This pepper is very hot (strong).*

El sol pica. *The sun is scorching.*

Picar el caballo. *To spur a horse.*

Picar alto. *To aim too high.*

picarse to begin to rot (fruit); to decay; to be piqued; to be moth-eaten; to become choppy (sea).

El vino empieza a picarse. *The wine is turning sour (fermenting).*

Tengo un diente picado. *I have a cavity in one of my teeth.*

picardía f. knavery; deceit, malice.

pícaro adj. roguish; mischievous; m. and f. rogue, rascal, scoundrel.

Tiene trazas de ser un pícaro. *He looks like a rascal.*

pico adj. odd, left over; m. beak, bill; pick; spout; peak.

Subieron al pico más alto de la sierra. *They climbed to the highest peak of the mountain ridge.*

Tiene mucho pico. *She's a chatterbox.*

Son las once y pico. *It's a little after eleven.*

Veinte dólares y pico. *Twenty dollars and some odd cents.*

picor m. itching.

PIE m. foot, leg; footing, basis.

Me duele mucho el pie. *My foot hurts a lot.*

Esta mesa tiene seis pies de largo. *This table is six feet long.*

A pie. *On foot.*

Nos fuimos a pie al hotel. *We walked to the hotel.*

Al pie del cerro. *At the foot of the hill.*

A los pies de Ud., señora. *At your service, madam. ("At your feet, madam.")*

De (en) pie. *Standing (up).*

Al pie de la letra. *Literally. To the letter.*

Ponerse en pie. *To stand up.*

Quedar en pie. *To hold good. To be (still) pending.*

No tiene pies ni cabeza. *It doesn't make any sense.*

Tiene buenos pies. *She's a good walker.*

Ha nacido de pie. *He was born with a silver spoon in his mouth.*

piedad f. mercy; pity.

piedra f. stone; gravel; hail.

Piedras preciosas. *Precious stones.*

Este pan es duro como una piedra. *The bread's hard as a rock.*

No dejar piedra por mover. *To leave no stone unturned. To move heaven and earth.*

PIEL f. skin; hide; fur.

Tiene la piel como seda. *She has very soft skin. Her skin is soft as silk.*

Abrigo de pieles. *Fur coat.*

Quiero este libro encuadernado en piel de Rusia. *I want this volume bound in Russian leather.*

PIERNA f. leg.

Dormir a pierna tendida. *To sleep soundly.*

PIEZA f. piece; part; room; a play.

Esta pieza tiene dos ventanas. *This room has two windows.*

Géneros de pieza. *Piece goods. Yard goods.*

Piezas de repuesto. *Spare parts.*

pijamas m. pl. pajamas.

pila f. stone trough or basin; fountain; holy-water basin, font; sink (kitchen, etc.); pile, heap; battery.

Pila de cocina. *Kitchen sink.*

Una pila de leña. *A pile of wood.*

Pila seca. *Dry cell (battery).*

Nombre de pila. *Christian name. ("Baptismal name.")*

pilar m. pillar, column, post.

píldora f. pill.

piloto m. pilot; first mate.

pillo m. rogue, rascal.

pimentón m. ground red pepper; paprika.

pimienta f. pepper.

pimiento m. pepper, pimento.

pincel m. artist's brush.

pinchar to prick, to puncture.

Se pinchó el dedo. He pricked his finger.

Se me ha pinchado un neumático. I have a flat tire. One of my tires blew out.

pinchazo m. puncture; flat tire; prick.

pino m. pine.

pintado adj. painted; spotted; just right, exact.

Ese traje le queda como pintado. That dress fits her just right.

Pintado de rojo. Painted red.

No puedo verle ni pintado. I can't stand the sight of him.

pintar to paint; to describe; to begin to ripen.

¿Qué pinta Ud.? What are you painting?

Pinte de azul la pared. Paint the wall blue.

Empiezan a pintar las uvas. The grapes are becoming (getting) ripe.

pintor m. painter.

pintura f. painting.

La pintura no está seca. The paint is still wet ("isn't dry").

Pintura al óleo. Oil painting.

Esa es una pintura histórica. That's an historical painting.

piña f. pineapple.

piojo m. louse.

pipa f. tobacco pipe; cask, barrel (wine).

pique (a) sink (used with the verb echar and ir).

El buque se fué a pique. The ship sank.

Echar a pique. To sink. To send to the bottom.

pirámide f. pyramid.

pirata m. pirate.

piropear to flatter (a girl or a woman).

pisada f. footstep; footprint.

pisar to tread, to step on; to press; to cover.

Mire Ud. donde pisa. Watch your step. Watch where you're going.

Pise el acelerador. Step on the gas ("accelerator").

piscina f. swimming pool.

PISO m. floor; pavement; story, apartment.

¿Se alquila este piso? Is this apartment for rent?

¿Cuántos roperos tiene este piso? How many closets are there in this apartment?

Ella vive en el segundo piso. She lives on the second floor.

Suban Uds. un piso más. Walk up another flight.

pisotear to tread, to trample; to step on someone's foot.

pisotón m. tread; stepping on someone's foot.

Me dió un pisotón. He stepped on my foot.

pista f. trail, track, footprint; trace, clue; race-track.

Seguir la pista. To follow the trail.

Le estamos siguiendo la pista. We're on his trail (track).

pisto m. a dish made of fried peppers, tomatoes and eggs.

Darse pisto. To show off.

pistola f. pistol.

pitillera f. cigarette case.

pitillo m. cigarette.

No tengo ni pitillos ni cerillas. I have neither cigarettes nor matches.

pito m. whistle.

Eso no vale un pito. It isn't worth a hang. It isn't worth a tinker's dam.

pívote m. pivot.

pizarra f. slate; blackboard.

pizca f. mite, bit; pinch.

Tiene su pizca de gracia. It has its funny side.

placa f. plate; plaque, tablet; badge.

Una placa fotográfica. A photographic plate.

Una placa metálica. A metal plate.

PLACER to please; m. pleasure, enjoyment.

Iremos donde a Ud. le plazca. We'll go wherever you like.

Es un placer conversar con ella. It's a pleasure to talk to (with) her.

Tener placer en. To take pleasure in.

Tendré mucho placer en hacerlo. I'll be very pleased (happy) to do it.

Me será un gran placer conocerle. I'd be very happy ("it would be a great pleasure for me") to meet him (you).

plaga f. plague; epidemic.

plan m. plan; scheme; drawing.

plana f. page; plain (land).

Lo leí en primera plana. I read it on the first page of the newspaper.

La plana mayor del regimiento. The regimental staff.

plancha f. plate (metal); iron (for clothes); blunder; gangplank.

La plancha está muy caliente. The iron is very hot.

Plancha de acero. Steel plate.

Hizo una plancha. He made a blunder. He put his foot in it.

planchado m. ironing; linen to be ironed.

Lavado y planchado. Washed and ironed laundry.

planchar to iron, to press (clothes).

Quiero que me planchen el traje. I'd like to have my suit pressed.

Ella misma lava y plancha la ropa. She washes and irons the clothes herself.

planeta m. planet.

planicie f. plain (land).

plano adj. level, flat; m. plane, map; plan.

Lo negó de plano. He denied it flatly.

Quisiera un plano de la ciudad. I'd like a map of the city.

Levantar un plano. To draw a map (of a place).

planta f. plant; sole (of the foot).

La planta ha echado raíces. The plant has taken root.

He alquilado un cuarto en la planta baja. I've rented a room on the ground floor.

plantación f. plantation; planting.

plantar to plant; to drive in (the ground); to hit, to punch; to throw out.

Van a plantar unos árboles en el jardín. They're going to plant some trees in the garden.

Lo dejaron plantado. They left him in the lurch.

Se plantó en Guadalajara en dos horas. It took him two hours to get to Guadalajara.

Plantar una bofetada. To slap in the face.

Lo plantaron en la calle. They threw him out. They put him out on the street.

plantilla f. insole; payroll; pattern.

plástico adj. plastic.

PLATA f. silver; silver coin.

¿Tiene Ud. dinero en plata? Have you any silver (money)?

Plata fina. Sterling silver.

plátano m. banana.

platillo m. saucer; cymbal; pan of a balance.

platino m. platinum.

PLATO m. dish, plate, course.

Este plato está a pedir de boca. This dish is delicious.

¿Cuál es el plato del día? What's today's special? ("What's the plate of the day?")

Hay que secar los platos. We have to dry the dishes.

¿Puedo repetir de este plato? May I have a second helping?

Pagar los platos rotos. To be made the scapegoat. To be blamed for everything.

Plato hondo (sopero). Soup plate.

Plato llano (de mesa). Dinner plate.

Ser plato de segunda mesa. To play second fiddle.

playa f. shore, beach.

PLAZA f. plaza, square; market; fortified place.

Vamos a dar una vuelta por la plaza. Let's take a stroll around the square.

Hoy no habían naranjas en la plaza. There weren't any oranges in the market today.

Plaza de toros. Bull-ring.

Plaza fuerte. Stronghold. Fortress.

plazo m. term, time; credit.

¿En cuántos plazos debo pagar este automóvil? How many payments do I have to make on this car?

A plazos. On credit. On the installment plan.

Comprar a plazos. To be on the installment plan.

Pagar a plazos. To pay in installments.

El plazo se ha cumplido. The time has expired.

plegable adj. folding; pliable.

plegar to fold; to plait.

pleito m. litigation; lawsuit; dispute, quarrel.

Tuvo un pleito con él. He had a quarrel with him.

plenamente fully, completely.

plenitud f. plenitude, fullness.

PLENO adj. full, complete.

Plenos poderes. Full powers.

Sesión plena. Joint session.

En pleno. In full. As a whole.

pliego m. sheet of paper; letter or document sealed in an envelope.

¿Quiere darme un pliego de papel? Will you please give me a sheet of paper?

Pliego de valores declarados. Sealed envelope containing money.

pliegue m. plait; crease; fold.

plomo m. lead; a bore, a dull person.

El plomo se funde fácilmente. Lead melts easily.

Ande con pies de plomo. Proceed cautiously.

pluma f. pen; feather.

plural adj. and n. plural.

población f. population; town.

poblado m. town, village, inhabited place.

poblar to populate, to inhabit, to colonize; to bud, to put forth leaves.

POBRE adj. poor; m. a poor person; a beggar.

Es un hombre muy pobre. He's a very poor man.

El pobre no da pie en bola. The poor fellow can't do anything right.

El pobre ha venido muy a menos. The poor fellow has come down in the world.

¡Pobrecito! Poor little thing!

¡Qué de pobres hay en esta ciudad! What a lot of beggars there are in this city!

pobreza f. poverty.

POCO adj. and adv. little; small; scanty; m. a lit-

prefecto *m. prefect, chief administrative official of a county or province.*

prefectura *f. office, jurisdiction, territory and official residence of a prefect; prefecture.*

preferencia *f. preference, choice.*

La tratan con preferencia. *She's given preferential treatment. She's treated with favoritism.*

preferente *adj. preferable, preferring.*

preferible *adj. preferable.*

Es preferible ir personalmente. *It's preferable to go in person.*

PREFERIR *to prefer, to like best.*

¿Prefiere vino o cerveza? *Do you prefer wine or beer?*

Prefiero el vino a la cerveza. *I prefer wine to beer?*

¿Cuál de estos colores prefiere Ud.? *Which one of these colors do you like best?*

prefijo *m. prefix.*

pregonar *to proclaim in public, to make known.*

PREGUNTA *f. question.*

¿Me permite que le haga una pregunta? *May I ask you a question?*

Estar a la cuarta pregunta. *To be penniless. To be broke.*

PREGUNTAR *to ask, to inquire.*

¿Por qué me lo preguntas? *Why do you ask me?*

¿Le preguntó a Ud. algo? *Did he ask you anything?*

¿Quién pregunta por mí? *Who's asking for me?*

Alguien pregunta por Ud. *Someone's asking for you.*

preguntarse *to wonder.*

preguntón *m. inquisitive person.*

prehistórico *adj. prehistoric.*

prejuicio *m. prejudice, bias.*

preliminar *adj. and n. preliminary.*

preludio *m. prelude, introduction.*

Ser el preludio de. *To lead to.*

prematuro *adj. premature.*

premeditación *f. premeditation.*

premeditar *to premeditate, to think out.*

premiar *to reward, to remunerate.*

premio *m. prize; reward.*

premura *f. haste, hurry, urgency.*

prenda *f. pledge, security, pawn; piece of jewelry; garment; forfeit; a very dear person; token; pl. qualities, talents.*

Prendas de vestir. *Articles of clothing.*

Juego de prendas. *Forfeits. The game of forfeits.*

Es un hombre de buenas prendas. *He's a man of fine qualities.*

prendar *to pledge, to give or take something as security; to ingratiate oneself.*

prendarse *to take a fancy to, to be taken with (the beauty of something, etc.), to become fond of, to fall in love.*

prendedor *m. clasp; breastpin, brooch.*

PRENDER *to clasp, to grasp; to catch; to arrest; to take root (a plant); to burn.*

Prender con alfileres. *To fasten with pins.*

¿Quién prendió al ladrón? *Who arrested (caught) the thief?*

La leña no prende. *The wood won't burn.*

La planta ha prendido. *The plant has taken root.*

PRENSA *f. press (newspaper).*

preñada *adj. pregnant.*

preocupación *f. preoccupation, concern, worry.*

preocupar *to preoccupy; to prejudice; to cause concern.*

Está algo preocupado. *He has something on his mind.*

preocuparse *to be worried, to care about, to be concerned.*

No se preocupe tanto. *Don't worry so much.*

Se preocupa por la suerte de su hija. *He's concerned (worried) about his daughter.*

preparación *f. preparation.*

preparado *adj. prepared; m. (medicinal) preparation.*

PREPARAR *to prepare, to get ready.*

Nos preparamos a partir. *We're getting ready to start.*

Prepare Ud. su billete. *Get your ticket ready.*

Tenme preparada la comida. *Have dinner ready for me.*

prepararse *to prepare oneself, to be prepared.*

Prepárese. *Get ready.*

Prepararse para un viaje. *To get ready (prepare) for a trip.*

preparativo *m. preparation.*

Estamos haciendo los preparativos para el viaje. *We're making preparations for the trip.*

preparatorio *adj. preparatory.*

preponderancia *f. preponderance.*

preponderar *to prevail.*

preposición *f. preposition.*

presa *f. capture; prey; dam.*

presagiar *to predict, to give warning.*

presagio *m. omen, prediction.*

prescindir *to do without, to dispense with, to do away with.*

prescribir *to prescribe.*

prescripción *f. prescription.*

presencia *f. presence.*

Se exige su presencia. *His presence is required. It's necessary that he be present.*

Lo dije en su presencia. *I said it in his presence.*

Hacer acto de presencia. *To put in an appearance.*

Presencia de ánimo. *Presence of mind.*

presenciar *to be present, to witness, to see.*

Acabamos de presenciar . . . *We've just witnessed . . .*

PRESENTAR *to present; to introduce; to show.*

No la conozco, preséntemela. *I don't know her. Will you introduce me? (Introduce her to me.)*

Le presento a mi prometido. *I'd like you to meet my fiancé.*

Presente este talón al reclamar su equipaje. *Present this check when you claim your baggage.*

Presentaron una queja a la dirección. *They complained to the management.*

presentarse *to put in an appearance, to show up.*

Se presentó inesperadamente. *He showed up unexpectedly.*

PRESENTE *adj. present; m. gift; present.*

¡Presente! *Present (in a roll call)!*

Al presente no tenemos ninguna noticia. *At present we have no news.*

Tengo presente lo que me dijo. *I'm bearing in mind what he told me.*

Tendré siempre presente su bondad. *I shall always remember your kindness.*

"La presente es para saludarle y decirle . . ." (in a letter). *"This is to greet you and to say . . ."*

Lo dije en voz alta a fin de que lo oyesen todos los presentes. *I said it out loud, so that everyone present could hear it.*

Un presente de valor. *An expensive (valuable) gift.*

presentimiento *m. presentiment.*

presentir *to have a presentiment.*

preservación *f. preservation.*

preservar *to preserve; to maintain; to keep.*

presidencia *f. presidency; (presidential) chair; chairmanship.*

Ocupar la presidencia. *To preside. ("To occupy the chair.")*

presidente *m. president; chairman.*

presidiario *m. convict.*

presidio *m. penitentiary, prison.*

presidir *to preside; to direct, to lead.*

presión *f. pressure.*

preso *adj. and n. imprisoned, prisoner.*

prestado *adj. lent, loaned.*

Vino a pedirme prestado un libro. *He came to borrow a book from me.*

Dar prestado. *To lend.*

Tomar (pedir) prestado. *To borrow.*

prestamista *m. and f. money lender; pawnbroker.*

préstamo *m. loan.*

PRESTAR *to lend, to aid; to pay (attention).*

Me prestó un libro muy interesante. *He lent me a very interesting book.*

Le presté cinco pesos. *I lent him five dollars.*

¿Quiere Ud. prestarnos su ayuda? *Will you give (lend) us a hand?*

Prestar atención. *To pay attention.*

Se ruega prestar atención. *May I have your attention? ("Your attention is requested.")*

Me ha prestado Ud. un gran servicio. *You've done (rendered) me a great service.*

prestarse *to offer to; to be apt to, to lend itself to.*

Se prestó a ayudarnos. *He offered to help us.*

Eso se prestará a malas interpretaciones. *That is apt to be misinterpreted.*

presteza *f. quickness, speed, haste.*

Con presteza. *Quickly..*

prestigio *m. prestige; good name.*

prestigioso *adj. famous.*

PRESTO *adj. quick, prompt; ready; adv. quickly; soon.*

Estamos prestos para salir. *We're ready to go out.*

Vístete presto. *Get dressed quickly.*

De presto. *Promptly. Swiftly.*

presumido *adj. and n. vain, conceited; conceited person.*

Es muy presumida. *She's very conceited.*

presumir *to presume; to assume; to be conceited.*

Presume ser listo. *He thinks he's smart.*

Era de presumir que . . . *It was to be expected that . . . It was to be presumed . . .*

presunción *f. presumption; presumptuousness, conceit.*

presunto *adj. presumed; apparent.*

Presunto heredero. *Heir apparent.*

presuntuoso *adj. presumptuous, vain.*

presuponer *to presuppose, to take for granted in advance, to assume beforehand.*

presupuestar *to estimate, to make an estimate, to make a budget.*

presupuesto *m. budget; estimate.*

pretencioso *adj. presumptuous, conceited.*

pretender *to pretend; to apply for; to try, to endeavor.*

Pretender un empleo. *To apply for a job.*

Pretende su mano. *He's asking for her hand in marriage.*

Pretendió convencerme. *He tried to convince me.*

pretendiente *adj. and n. pretender; suitor; candidate.*

pretensión *f. pretension; contention.*

pretexto *m. pretext.*

prevalecer *to prevail.*

prevención *f. prevention; foresight; prejudice.*

prevenir *to prepare; to prevent; to foresee; to forewarn, to warn.*

Estámos prevenidos. *We're prepared (on guard).*

Le prevengo a Ud. que no lo haga. *I warn you not to do it.*

prever *to foresee, to see ahead, to anticipate, to provide for.*

Prevemos el éxito. *We anticipate success.*

Es de prever. *It's to be expected.*

previamente *previously.*

prévio *adj. previous; prior to.*

Una cuestión previa. *Previous question (parliamentary procedure).*

Previo pago de. *Upon payment of.*

previsto *adj. foreseen.*

En las condiciones previstas en el acuerdo . . . *Under (In) the conditions which have been provided for in the agreement . . .*

prima *f. first string (in musical instruments); premium; female cousin.*

Prima de seguro. *Insurance premium.*

María es mi prima. *Mary is my cousin.*

primario *adj. primary.*

Escuela primaria. *Elementary school. Primary school.*

PRIMAVERA *f. spring (the season).*

PRIMER *(a shortening of* **primero** *used before a noun) first.*

Primer galán. *Leading man.*

En primer lugar. *In the first place.*

El primer año. *The first year.*

Este es mi primer vuelo en avión. *This is my first flight.*

primeramente *first, firstly, in the first place.*

PRIMERO *adj. and n. first; former.*

Tráiganos primero un poco de sopa. *Bring us some soup first.*

Es el primero de la clase. *He ranks highest in his class.*

Veamos primero la hora que es. *Let's first see what time it is.*

Sírvase Ud. darme dos billetes de primera para Madrid. *Two pullman ("first class") tickets to Madrid, please.*

Es un nadador de primera. *He's an excellent swimmer.*

Primera velocidad. *First gear.*

Primera dama. *Leading lady.*

La primera casa. *The first house.*

La primera vez. *The first time.*

Primera enseñanza. *Primary education.*

De primera clase. *First class.*

De primera. *Of superior quality. Highest grade.*

Al primero del mes que viene. *On the first of next month.*

A primeros del mes que viene. *In the early part of next month.*

Primeros auxilios. *First aid.*

De buenas a primeras. *All of a sudden.*

primitivo *adj. primitive.*

primo *m. cousin; a fool (coll.).*

Primo hermano. *First cousin.*

primor *m. beauty, exquisiteness; dexterity, skill.*

Ese bordado es un primor. *That embroidery is very lovely.*

princesa *f. princess.*

PRINCIPAL *adj. principal, main, chief, most important; m. capital; head (of a concern); first floor.*

Este es uno de los argumentos principales de su tesis. *This is one of the main arguments of*

his thesis.

Vivimos en el princpal. *We live on the first floor.*

príncipe *m. prince; ruler.*

principiante *adj. and n. beginner, apprentice.*

principiar *to begin, to commence.*

Van a principiar la construcción. *They're beginning to build.*

PRINCIPIO *m. beginning; origin; principle.*

Al principio me parecía fácil. *It seemed easy to me at first.*

Le pagarán a principios del mes que viene. *They'll pay you the early part of next month.*

Al principios de la semana entrante. *Early next week.*

Al principio. *At the beginning. At first.*

Dar principio. *To begin.*

¿En qué principio basa Ud. su teoría? *On what principle do you base your theory?*

En principio no me parece mal la idea. *That idea doesn't seem bad in principle.*

prioridad *f. priority.*

PRISA *f. haste, hurry; urgency.*

Tengo mucha prisa. *I'm in a great hurry.*

No corre prisa. *There's no hurry.*

Siempre anda de prisa. *He's always in a hurry.*

¡Démonos prisa, que es tarde! *Let's hurry, it's late.*

¿Por qué tanta prisa? *Why such a hurry?*

Déle Ud. prisa. *Make him (get him to) hurry up.*

prisión *f. imprisonment; prison.*

prisionero *m. prisoner.*

privación *f. privation, want.*

privado *adj. private, intimate; personal.*

Vida privada. *Private life.*

En privado. *Confidentially.*

Carta privada. *Personal letter.*

privar *to deprive; to forbid.*

Privarse de. *To do without.*

No se priva de nada. *He doesn't deprive himself of anything.*

Privado del conocimiento. *Unconscious.*

privilegiado *adj. privileged.*

privilegio *m. privilege.*

pro *m. and f. profit, advantage; pro.*

En pro de. *In favor of.*

El pro y el contra. *The pros and the cons.*

proa *f. prow, bow (of a ship).*

probabilidad *f. probability, likelihood.*

PROBABLE *adj. probable, likely.*

Es poco probable. *It's not likely.*

Es más que probable. *It's more than probable.*

PROBABLEMENTE *probably, likely.*

probado *adj. proved, tried.*

Eso está probado. *That's been proved.*

PROBAR *to try; to taste; to prove; to try on.*

Pruebe Ud. este vino, a ver si le gusta. *Taste this wine and see if you like it.*

Me probaré estos zapatos. *I'll try these shoes on.*

Pruebe otra vez. *Try again. Try once more.*

PROBLEMA *m. problem.*

procaz *adj. insolent, impudent, bold.*

procedencia *f. origin; place of sailing.*

procedente *adj. coming or proceeding from; according to law, rules or practices.*

PROCEDER *to proceed; to act, to behave; m. behavior, conduct.*

Procedió correctamente. *He acted properly.*

Procede con mucho tiento. *He uses a great deal of tact.*

Lo que procede hacer. *The correct and proper thing (to do).*

Proceder a. *To proceed with.*

Proceder de. *To come from.*

Proceder contra. *To proceed against. To take action against.*

No me gusta su proceder. *I don't like his behavior.*

procedimiento *m. procedure; method.*

procesado *adj. indicted; m. and f. defendant.*

procesar *to sue; to indict.*

procesión *f. procession, parade.*

proceso *m. legal proceedings, (legal) process, lawsuit.*

proclamación *f. proclamation.*

proclamar *to proclaim; to promulgate.*

La República Española fué proclamada el 14 de abril de 1931. *The Spanish Republic was proclaimed on April 14th, 1931.*

Se ha proclamado la ley marcial. *Martial law has been proclaimed.*

procrear *to procreate.*

PROCURAR *to endeavor, to try.*

Procuraré estar a tiempo. *I'll try to be on time.*

Procuró levantarse pero no pudo. *He tried to get up but he couldn't.*

Procure no faltar. *Don't fail to come (do it, etc.). Try your best to come (do it, etc.).*

prodigar *to squander, to lavish.*

prodigio *m. wonder, marvel.*

prodigioso *adj. prodigious, marvelous.*

pródigo *adj. prodigal, wasteful, lavish.*

producción *f. production; output.*

PRODUCIR *to produce; to yield, to bear; to bring as evidence (law).*

Producen 200 aeroplanos al día. *They turn out (produce) 200 planes per day.*

Todo aquello le producía risa. *That made him laugh.*

producirse *to be produced.*

productivo *adj. productive.*

producto *m. product; amount.*

Productos alimenticios. *Foodstuffs. Food products. Food.*

profanación *f. profanation.*

profanar *to profane.*

profano *adj. profane; secular; irreverent.*

profecía *f. prophecy.*

proferir *to utter, to say.*

profesar *to profess; to declare openly.*

profesión *f. profession.*

¿Su nombre y profesión, por favor? *Your name and profession?*

profesional *adj. professional.*

profesor *m. professor, teacher.*

profeta *m. prophet.*

profético *adj. prophetic.*

prófugo *adj. fugitive; m. draft dodger, slacker.*

profundamente *deeply; soundly (sleep).*

Lo siento profundamente. *I regret it deeply.*

Anoche, dormí profundamente. *I slept soundly last night.*

profundidad *f. profundity, depth.*

¿Qué profundidad tiene ese lago? *What's the depth of this lake?*

200 pies de profundidad. *200 feet deep.*

profundizar *to deepen; to delve into, to fathom.*

PROFUNDO *adj. profound, deep, intense.*

Dolor profundo. *Intense pain.*

Es un pozo muy profundo. *It's a very deep well.*

Nos perdimos en lo más profundo del bosque. *We were lost in the depths of the woods.*

programa *m. program, plan; curriculum.*

¿Cuál es el programa de hoy? *What is today's program?*

¿Hasta qué punto del programa han estudiado? *How far did they get in the curriculum?*

progresar *to progress, to make progress.*

progreso *m. progress.*

Hacer progresos. *To progress. To make progress.*

prohibición *f. prohibition.*

prohibido *adj. forbidden.*

"Prohibido fumar." *"No smoking."*

"Prohibido por la ley." *"Prohibited by law."*

"Prohibido pasar." *"No thoroughfare." "Do not pass beyond here." "No trespassing."*

"Prohibido el tráfico." *"Closed to traffic."*

"Prohibida la entrada." *"No admittance."*

PROHIBIR *to prohibit, to forbid.*

Le prohibo hacer eso. *I forbid you to do that.*

Está prohibido llevar perros en los autobuses. *Dogs are not allowed on the busses.*

"Se prohibe la entrada.". *"No admittance."*

"Se prohibe fumar." *"No smoking."*

prójimo *m. fellow man, neighbor.*

proletariado *m. proletariat, working class.*

proletario *adj. proletarian; of the working class.*

La clase proletaria. *The working class.*

prolijo *adj. prolix, too long, using too many words.*

prólogo *m. prologue, preface, introduction.*

prolongación *f. prolongation, lengthening.*

prolongar *to prolong, to extend.*

promedio *m. average, mean.*

promesa *f. promise, assurance.*

PROMETER *to promise.*

¿Por qué no me ha escrito Ud. como me prometió? *Why haven't you written to me as you promised?*

Nunca cumple lo que promete. *He never does what he promises.*

Este negocio no promete mucho. *This business is not very promising.*

prometido *adj. promised; m. fiancé; f. fiancée.*

Cumplir lo prometido. *To keep a promise.*

Mi prometido. *My fiancé.*

prominencia *f. prominence; protuberance.*

prominente *adj. prominent; conspicuous.*

Ocupa un puesto prominente en el gobierno. *He occupies a prominent position in the government.*

promover *to promote; to advance.*

promulgar *to promulgate, to publish.*

pronombre *m. pronoun.*

pronosticar *to forecast.*

pronóstico *m. forecast, prediction; prognosis.*

Pronóstico del tiempo. *Weather forecast.*

prontitud *f. promptness, swiftness.*

PRONTO *adj. prompt, quick; ready; adv. promptly, quickly; soon; m. impulse, fit (of temper).*

Hasta muy pronto. *So long. I'll see you soon.*

¡Venga pronto! *Come quickly! Come right away!*

Mientras más pronto mejor. *The sooner the better.*

Hizo muy pronto el trabajo. *He did the work very quickly.*

Me dijo que estaría de vuelta pronto. *She told me she would be back soon.*

Su respuesta fué muy pronta. *He replied (very) promptly. ("His reply was very prompt.")*

Estoy pronto para empezar. *I'm ready to begin.*

Está arrepentido de aquel pronto que tuvo. *He still regrets that sudden impulse.*

De pronto. *Suddenly. All of a sudden.*

De pronto ocurrió algo. *All of a sudden something happened.*

Por de pronto. *For the time being.*

pronunciación *f. pronunciation.*

pronunciar *to pronounce; to utter; to deliver (a speech).*

Ud. pronuncia muy bien el español. *You pronounce Spanish very well.*

Pronunciará un discurso sobre historia contemporánea. *He's going to give a lecture on Modern History.*

Pronunciar sentencia. *To pronounce sentence.*

propagación *f. propagation, dissemination.*

propaganda *f. propaganda.*

propagandista *m. and f. propagandist.*

propagar *to propagate; to spread (news, knowledge, etc.).*

propasarse *to take undue liberties; to exceed one's authority.*

propender *to tend, to incline to.*

propensión *f. propensity, inclination.*

propenso *adj. inclined to, disposed to.*

Está propenso a hacerlo. *He's inclined to do it.*

propiamente *properly.*

propicio *adj. propitious, favorable.*

Una ocasión propicia. *A favorable opportunity.*

propiedad *f. ownership; property.*

Esas casas son de su propiedad. *Those houses belong to him (are his property).*

El jabón tiene la propiedad de quitar la mugre. *Soap has the property of removing dirt.*

Acabo de comprar esa propiedad. *I've just bought that property.*

propietario *m. proprietor, owner, landlord.*

propina *f. tip, gratuity.*

PROPIO *adj. own, self; proper, fit, suitable.*

Sus propias palabras. *His own words.*

Le deseo lo propio. *I wish you the same. The same to you.*

Eso es un juego propio de niños. *It's a game suitable for children.*

Eso sería lo propio. *That would fit the case.*

Estimación propia. *Self-respect.*

Amor propio. *Self-conceit.*

proponer *to propose; to suggest; to move.*

Me propongo ir a verle. *I intend to go to see him.*

Propongo que vayamos todos a casa. *I suggest we all go home.*

Señor presidente, propongo que se levante la sesión. *Mr. Chairman, I move that the meeting be adjourned.*

Le será difícil llevar a cabo lo que se propone. *It will be hard to carry out what you have in mind (intend).*

proporción *f. proportion.*

proporcional *adj. proportional.*

proporcionar *to provide, to furnish, to supply; to proportion, to fit.*

proposición *f. proposition; proposal, motion.*

PROPÓSITO *m. purpose, intention.*

Lo hizo de propósito. *He did it on purpose.*

A propósito. *By the way.*

Fuera de propósito. *Not to the point. Irrelevant. Foreign to the subject.*

A propósito de. *With regards to. Regarding.*

propuesta *f. proposal, offer; nomination.*

Aceptaron nuestra propuesta. *They accepted our proposal.*

prórroga *f. extension of time, renewal.*

Dar prórroga. *To extend the time of payment. To grant an extension.*

prorrogar *to extend (time), to prolong.*

prosa *f. prose.*

prosaico *adj. prosaic.*

proseguir *to pursue, to carry on, to go on, to continue, to proceed.*

prosista *m. prose writer.*

prospecto *m. prospectus, catalogue.*

prosperar *to prosper, to thrive, to be successful, to get rich.*

próspero *adj. prosperous.*

protagonista *m. and f. protagonist.*

protección *f. protection, support.*

protector *m. protector.*

proteger *to protect; to support.*

protesta *f. protest.*

protestante *adj. and n. protesting; Protestant.*

protestar *to protest.*

PROVECHO *m. profit; benefit, advantage.*

Ser de provecho. *To be useful.*

Sacar provecho. *To derive profit from. To turn to advantage.*

En su provecho. *In your favor. To your advantage.*

¡Buen provecho (said at meals)! *I hope you enjoy your food. Hearty appetite!*

provechoso *adj. profitable, beneficial.*

proveer *to provide; to furnish, to supply; to dispose.*

Proveer de fondos. *To provide with funds.*

Proveerse de. *To supply oneself with.*

provenir *to be due to; to derive from, to come from.*

Eso puede provenir de un resfrío. *That can come from (be caused by) a cold.*

proverbio *m. proverb.*

providencia *f. providence; pl. dispositions, measures.*

Tomar providencias. *To take measures.*

provincia *f. province.*

provisión *f. provision; stock, supply.*

Provisiones alimenticias. *Foodstuffs. Food.*

provisional *adj. provisional, temporary.*

provisionalmente *provisionally, temporarily.*

provisto *adj. provided for, supplied.*

La tienda está muy bien provista de mercaderías. *The store is well stocked with merchandise.*

provocación *f. provocation.*

provocador *m. trouble maker.*

provocar *to provoke, to vex, to make angry.*

PROXIMO *adj. near, next, neighboring.*

La próxima estación. *The next station.*

La semana próxima. *Next week.*

¿Cuál es la calle próxima? *What's the street after this?*

proyecto *m. project; plan, scheme; design.*

prudencia *f. prudence; moderation.*

prudente *adj. prudent, cautious.*

PRUEBA *f. proof; test; fitting (of garments).*

Existen pruebas bastante claras de ello. *There are pretty strong proofs of it.*

Me han sacado dos pruebas. *I had two proofs made.*

Sala de pruebas. *Fitting room.*

A prueba de fuego. *Fireproof.*

psicología *f. psychology.*

psicológico *adj. psychological.*

psicólogo *m. psychologist.*

psiquiatra *m. psychiatrist.*

psiquiatría *m. psychiatry.*

púa *f. sharp point, prong.*

Alambre de púas. *Barbed wire.*

publicación *f. publication.*

publicar *to publish; to announce.*

Acaba de publicarse este libro. *This book has just been published.*

Va a publicar un artículo en el periódico de mañana. *He's going to publish an article in tomorrow's paper.*

Publíquese y ejecútese. *Let it be made public and put into effect. ("Let it be published and enforced.")*

publicidad *f. publicity.*

PÚBLICO *adj. public, not private; m. public, crowd, audience.*

Sacarán la casa a pública subasta. *They'll sell the house at public auction.*

En público. *Publicly. In public.*

"Aviso al público." *"Notice to the public."*

El público silbó la comedia. *The audience booed the comedy.*

puchero *m. earthen pot; dish of stewed vegetables and meats.*

pudiente *adj. powerful; wealthy, rich.*

pudín *m. pudding.*

pudor *m. modesty, shyness.*

pudrir *to rot.*

Las manzanas se están pudriendo. *The apples are spoiling (rotting).*

PUEBLO *m. village, town; population; people.*

¿Qué pueblo es éste? *What town is this?*

Pueblo natal. *Native town.*

El pueblo español. *The Spanish people.*

puente *m. bridge.*

puerco *adj. nasty, filthy, dirty; m. hog.*

PUERTA *f. door; doorway; gate.*

Abra la puerta. *Open the door.*

Cierre la puerta. *Shut the door.*

Cierre la puerta con llave cuando salga. *Lock the door when you leave.*

La puerta trasera da al jardín. *The back door opens out into the garden.*

puerto *m. port, harbor; haven; pass through the mountains.*

Puerto franco. *Free port.*

Puerto de destino. *Port of destination.*

PUES *as, since; so; well; then; why; now; indeed.*

Pues hágalo Ud. *Then do it.*

Pues vamos. *Then let's go.*

¿Pues qué quiere? *What do you want?*

¡Pues sí! *Yes, indeed!*

¡Pues hombre! *Why, man!*

¡Pues mira, chico! *Now look here, pal!*

Pues vámonos ya. *Let's run along.*

¡Pues no faltaba más! *Well, that's the last straw!*

Pues, como no fumo, no compro tabaco. *Since I don't smoke, I don't buy tobacco.*

Pues bien. *Well, then.*

¿Y pues? *What of it? So what?*

¿Pues qué? *Why not?*

¿Pues y qué? *So what?*

Pues no. *Not at all.*

¡Pues bien, iré! *All right then, I'll go!*

Pues no puede ser. *But it can't be. But it's impossible.*

puesta *f. set, setting; laying (eggs).*

La puesta del sol. *The sunset.*

PUESTO *adj. put, placed; on; set (table); m. place; stand; post; position, employment.*

La mesa está puesta. *The table is set.*

Esto está mal puesto. *This is in the wrong place.*

Llevaba puesto su traje nuevo. *He had his new suit on.*

Puesto que. *Since. Inasmuch as.*

Le compré en un puesto del mercado. *I bought it at a stand in the market.*

¿Dónde habrá un puesto de gasolina? *Where do you suppose there's a filling station?*

Tiene un buen puesto. *He has a good position.*

Puesto militar. *Military post*

Puesto a bordo. *Free on board.*

Puesto en Neuva York. *Delivered free in New York.*

púgil, pugilista *m. prizefighter.*

pugna *f. struggle.*

pulcro *adj. neat, tidy*

pulga *f. flea.*

Tiene malas pulgas. *He's bad-tempered.*

pulgada *f. inch.*

pulgar *m. thumb.*

pulir *to polish.*

pulmón *m. lung.*

pulmonía *f. pneumonia.*

pulpa *f. pulp.*

pulsera *f. bracelet.*

pulso *m. pulse; steadiness of the hand; tact.*

Déjeme tomarle el pulso. *Let me feel your pulse.*

Obra con gran pulso. *He acts with great circumspection.*

punta *f. point; tip; edge; cape, headland.*

La punta del lápiz. *Pencil point.*

Sáquele punta al lápiz. *Sharpen the pencil.*

Tengo los nervios de punta. *My nerves are on edge.*

Va de punta en blanco. *She's all dressed up.*

puntada *f. stitch.*

puntapié *m. kick.*

puntería *f. aim, aiming, marksmanship.*

puntiagudo *adj. sharp-pointed.*

puntilla *adj. narrow lace edging.*

De puntillas. *On tiptoe.*

PUNTO *m. point; dot; period; place; stitch; loop (in knitting); net (cloth material); hole (in a stocking).*

Punto de partida. *Starting point. Point of departure.*

¿Donde está el punto en esta máquina de escribir? *Where's the period on this typewriter?*

Punto y coma. *Semicolon.*

Dos puntos *Colon.*

Ganó por pocos puntos. *He won by a few points.*

Nos veremos en el mismo punto. *We'll meet at the same place.*

Punto por punto. *Point by point.*

Ha dado Ud. en el punto. *You've put your finger on it.*

Llevaba un traje de puntos blancos. *She wore a dress with white polka dots.*

Un vestido de punto. *A knitted dress.*

Hay que poner punto final a esto. *We must put a stop to this.*

Estábamos a punto de salir cuando llegaron. *We were just about to leave (on the point of leaving) when they arrived.*

A la hora en punto. *On the dot.*

Estaré a la una en punto. *I'll be there at one o'clock sharp.*

Hasta cierto punto es verdad. *To a certain extent it's true.*

Desde cierto punto de vista Ud. tiene razón. *You're right from a certain standpoint.*

Estuvo a punto de perder la vida. *He nearly lost his life.*

Su cólera subía de punto. *He became angrier by the minute.*

No sé a punto fijo. *I don't know for certain.*

La comida está en su punto. *The food is just right.*

Punto cardinal. *Cardinal point.*

En punto a. *In regard to.*

Punto menos que imposible. *Almost impossible.*

puntuación *f. punctuation.*

Signos de puntuación *Punctuation marks.*

puntual *adj. punctual, prompt, on time; exact.*

Sea Ud. puntual. *Be on time. Be punctual.*

puntualizar *to give a detailed account of; to emphasize.*

puntualmente *punctually, on time.*

punzada *f. puncture, prick; acute pain.*

punzante *sharp.*

punzar *to prick, to puncture, to stick.*

puñado *m. handful; a few.*

Un puñado de soldados defendieron la posición. *A few soldiers defended the position.*

puñal *m. dagger.*

puñetazo *m. a punch*

puño *m. fist; cuff; hilt (of a sword); haft (of a tool); handle (of an umbrella); head (of a cane).*

Firmado de mi puño y letra. *Signed by me.*

pupila *f. pupil (of the eye).*

pupilo *m. ward (under someone's guardianship); boarder; a day student.*

pupitre *m. writing desk.*

puré *m. puree, thick soup.*

Puré de guisantes. *Pea soup.*

Puré de patatas (papas). *Mashed potatoes.*

pureza *f. purity.*

purga *f. purge, physic.*

purgante *m. laxative; purgative.*

purgatorio *m. purgatory.*

Está pasando las penas del purgatorio. *He's suffering many hardships. ("He's going through purgatory.")*

purificar *to purify.*

PURO *adj. pure; clean; plain; m. cigar.*

Aire puro. *Pure air.*

Le digo a Ud. la pura verdad. *I'm telling you the plain truth.*

Me lo encontré de pura casualidad. *I met him by ("pure") chance.*

Pruebe estos puros. *Try these cigars.*

pútrido *adj. putrid, rotten.*

Q

QUE *(rel. pron.) that, which, who, whom; conj. that, than, whether.*

El que. *He who, the one which.*

La que. *She who, the one which.*

Los que *(m. pl.). They who, those who, the ones who.*

Las que *(f. pl.). They who, those who, the ones who.*

Lo que. *That which, which, that, what.*

Yo fuí la que lo dijo. *It's I who said it. I was the one who said it.*

El que está hablando. *The one who's speaking. The one speaking.*

Yo no sé lo que le pasa. *I don't know what's the matter with him.*

Eso es lo que yo digo. *That's what I say.*

Alguno que otro. *Someone or another.*

Dice que lo hará. *He said he'd (he'll) do it.*

Vale mucho más de lo que se figuran. *It's worth much more than they imagine.*

Que le guste o no. *Whether he likes it or not.*

Que no entre nadie. *Don't let anyone come in.*

Q.E.S.M. (Que estrecha su mano). *Yours truly. ("Who shakes your hand.")*

QUÉ *(interrogative pron.) what; how.*

¿Por qué? *Why?*

¿Por qué se apura Ud.? *What are you worrying about?*

¿Qué es esto? *What's this?*

¿Qué hora es? *What time is it?*

¿Qué busca Ud.? *What are you looking for?*
¿Qué pasa? *What's going on?*
¿Qué van a tomar Uds.? *What are you going to have?*
¿Qué hora será? *I wonder what time it is?*
¿Pues y qué? *So what?*
No sé qué hacer. *I don't know what to do.*
¿De qué está hablando? *What's he talking about?*
¿En qué quedamos? *How do we stand?*
¡Qué va! *Nonsense!*
¡Qué barbaridad! *How awful!*
¿Qué sé yo? *How do I know?*
¡Qué gracia! *How amusing!*
¡Ay qué risa! *How funny! What a joke!*
¡Qué hombre! *What a man!*
No hay de qué. *Don't mention it. You're welcome.*

quebrada f. *ravine, gorge.*
quebradizo adj. *brittle, fragile.*
quebrado adj. *broken; bankrupt; ruptured; m. fraction (math.).*
quebradura f. *fissure; fracture; rupture, hernia.*
quebrantado adj. *tottering, broken down; failing (health).*
Salud quebrantada. *Failing health.*
quebrantamiento m. *breaking, breach (of law, promise, etc.)*
quebrantar *to break, to crash; to trespass; to violate (the law).*
quebranto m. *weakness; failure; great loss, severe damage; grief.*
QUEBRAR *to break; to rupture (hernia); to become bankrupt.*
Al caer se quebró un brazo (Amer.). *He broke his arm when he fell.*
El negocio quebró. *The business failed.*
QUEDAR *to remain; to stop; to be; to fit; to be left; to agree.*
¿Cuántos dólares le quedan? *How many dollars do you have left?*
¿Queda lejos el hotel? *Is the hotel far from here?*
Este traje le queda como mandado a hacer. *This suit fits you as if it were made to order.*
Me quedan un poco estrechos. *They're a little tight for me.*
Todo quedó muy mal. *Everything came off (turned out) badly.*
Quedó más pobre que una rata. *He became poorer than a church mouse.*
No le queda a Ud. mucho tiempo. *You haven't much time left.*
Quedaron en hacer el trabajo. *They agreed to do the work.*
Quédese sentado. *Remain seated. Keep your seats.*
Nuestro amigo se quedó en Europa. *Our friend stayed in Europe.*
Me quedaré aquí un ratio. *I'll stay here (for) awhile.*
Me quedaré hasta el viernes. *I'll stay until Friday.*
¿En qué quedamos? *How do we stand? What's the final agreement?*
Esto queda entre los dos. *This is just between the two of us.*
Quedarse con. *To keep. To take.*
Se quedó con el libro. *He kept the book. He didn't return the book.*
Me quedo con esta camisa. *I'll take (buy) this shirt.*

Quedarse sin dinero. *To be left penniless.*
quehacer m. *occupation, work.*
Quehaceres domésticos. *Housework.*
queja f. *complaint; resentment; groan.*
quejarse *to complain.*
Ella se queja de Ud. *She complains (is complaining) about you.*
Se queja de dolor de cabeza. *She complains of a headache.*
Eso le dará motivo para quejarse. *That will give him grounds for complaint.*
quejoso adj. *complaining; plaintive.*
quemado adj. *burnt.*
Huele a quemado. *I smell something burning. ("It smells burnt.")*
quemadura f. *burn; scald.*
QUEMAR *to burn; to scald; to parch; to be very hot.*
Cuidado con quemarse. *Be careful, don't burn yourself.*
Por poco me quemo la lengua. *I nearly (almost) burned my tongue.*
Este teatro se ha quemado dos veces. *This theater has burned down twice.*
El sol quema hoy. *The sun's scorching today.*
¡Que te quemas! *You're warm! (i.e. You've almost found or guessed it.)*
querella f. *complaint; quarrel.*
querellarse *to complain.*
querencia f. *affection, fondness.*
QUERER *to wish, to want, to desire; to like; to love.*
¿Qué quiere Ud.? *What do you want? What would you like?*
¿Quiere Ud. ver el piso? *Do you want (would you like) to see the apartment?*
¿Quiere Ud. callarse? *Will you keep quiet?*
¿Lo quiere? *Do you want it?*
Yo no lo quiero. *I don't want it.*
Si Ud. quiere. *If you like.*
Haz lo que quieras. *Do as you please.*
Pide lo que quieras. *Order whatever you want.*
Iremos donde quieras. *We'll go wherever you wish.*
Como quieras. *As you like.*
¿A quién quieres más? *Who (m) do you love most? Who (m) do you love the best?*
La quiere mucho. *He loves her very much.*
Quisiera un helado. *I'd like some ice cream.*
Yo quisiera un vaso de vino tinto. *I would like a glass of red wine.*
Quiero comprar un reloj. *I want to buy a watch.*
Hubiera querido ver aquella película. *I should like to have seen that film. ("I should have liked to see . . .")*
No quiero nada más. *I don't care for anything more.*
¿Qué quiere decir esta palabra? *What does this word mean?*
Sin querer. *Without wanting (wishing) to.*
Querer es poder. *Where there's a will there's a way.*
Como Ud. quiera. *As you wish (like).*
Si Ud. quiere. *If you like.*
querido adj. *beloved, dear; m. lover; f. mistress.*
Querido amigo. *Dear friend.*
queso m. *cheese.*
¡quiá! *Come now! Not at all! No, indeed!*
quicio m. *hinge.*
Estar fuera de quicio. *To be out of one's mind. To be unbalanced. ("To be unhinged.")*
Sacar de quicio. *To drive one crazy. To exasperate. ("To unhinge.")*

QUIEN *who, which; pl.* quienes.
¿Quién es Ud.? *Who are you?*
¿Quiénes son los otros invitados? *Who are the other guests?*
¿Quién habla? *Who's speaking?*
¿Quién lo quiere? *Who wants it?*
¿De quién es este sombrero? *Whose hat is this?*
¿Para quién es? *For whom is it?*
¿Quién va? *Who's there?*
¿A quién busca Ud.? *Who(m) are you looking for?*
Quien así piensa se equivoca. *Whoever thinks so is wrong.*
¡Quién sabe! *Who knows! Heaven knows!*
¿A quién de ellos conoce Ud.? *Which one of them do you know?*
quienquiera *whoever.*
QUIETO adj. *quiet, still.*
¡Estése quieto! *Be quiet!*
quietud f. *quietness, quiet, tranquillity.*
quilla f. *keel.*
química f. *chemistry.*
químico adj. *chemical,* m. *chemist.*
quimono m. *kimona.*
QUINCE adj. *and n.* fifteen; fifteenth.
Hace quince días estaba aquí. *He was here two weeks ago.*
quincena f. *fortnight, period of two weeks, fifteen days; semi-monthly pay.*
Nos pagan por quincena. *They pay us every two weeks.*
quincenal *biweekly, fortnightly.*
quinientos adj. *and n.* five hundred.
quinina f. *quinine.*
quinta f. *country house; levy, draft.*
quintal m. *quintal, hundredweight.*
quinto adj. *and n.* fifth; m. *drafted soldier.*
quintuplicar *to quintuplicate.*
quíntuplo adj. *quintuple, fivefold.*
quiosco m. *kiosk, stand.*
Quiosco de periódicos. *Newspaper stand.*
quirúrgico adj. *surgical.*
quisquilloso adj. *touchy, too sensitive, difficult.*
QUITAR *to remove; to take away; to rob.*
Quite esa silla de aquí. *Take this chair away.*
Quita los pies de la silla. *Take your feet off the chair.*
Me han quitado el reloj. *They have stolen my watch.*
Esta crema quita las pecas. *This cream removes freckles.*
Quite el freno. *Release the brake.*
quitarse *to get rid of; to take off.*
Al entrar en la iglesia se quitó el sombrero. *He took his hat off when he entered the church.*
Ya se me quitó el resfriado. *I've gotten rid of my cold.*
Quitarse a uno de encima. *To get rid of someone.*
QUIZÁ, QUIZÁS *perhaps, maybe.*
Quizá sea verdad lo que dice. *Perhaps what he says is true.*
Quizá lo haga. *I might do it. Maybe I'll do it.*

R

rábano m. *radish.*
rabia f. *rabies, hydrophobia; rage, anger.*
Me da rabia. *It makes me angry (mad).*
rabiar *to be furious, to rage, to be angry.*
Rabiar por. *To be extremely eager (anxious) for something.*

rabioso *adj. furious, mad.*
Perro rabioso. *Mad dog.*
rabo *m. tail.*
racimo *m. bunch (grapes), cluster.*
ración *f. ration.*
racional *adj. rational, reasonable.*
racionar *to ration.*
radiador *m. radiator.*
radiar *to radiate; to broadcast.*
radical *adj. and n. radical.*
RADIO *m. radius; radium; f. radio.*
radiodifusión *f. broadcasting.*
radioemisora *f. broadcasting station.*
radioescucha *m. and f. radio listener.*
radiografía *f. radiography, X-ray photography.*
radiograma *m. radiogram.*
radiooyente *m. and f. radio listener.*
radiotelefonía *f. radiotelephony.*
radiotelegrafía *f. radiotelegraphy.*
raid *m. raid.*
raíz *f. root; foundation.*
El árbol fué arrancado de raíz. *The tree was uprooted.*
Echar raíces. *To take root.*
rajar *to split, to cleave.*
rejarse *to crack; to back out.*
rallador *m. grater.*
rallar *to grate.*
Queso rallado. *Grated cheese.*
rama *f. branch; chase (printing).*
Tabaco en rama. *Leaf tobacco.*
Algodón en rama. *Cotton wool. Raw cotton.*
Andarse por las ramas. *To beat around the bush.*
ramal *m. strand (of a rope); halter; branch, line (railway); ramification.*
ramificación *f. ramification.*
ramillete *m. bouquet.*
ramo *m. branch, line; bunch; bouquet.*
Esa clase de mercancía no es de nuestro ramo. *That type of merchandise is not in our line.*
Le obsequió un ramo de flores. *He gave her a bouquet of flowers.*
rampa *f. ramp, slope.*
rana *f. frog.*
rancio *adj. rancid, stale.*
ranchero *m. mess attendant; rancher.*
rancho *m. mess; hut; hamlet; ranch.*
Sirvieron el rancho a las doce. *Mess was served at twelve.*
Tiene un rancho muy grande. *He has a big ranch.*
rango *m. rank; position.*
ranura *f. slot, groove.*
RAPIDAMENTE *rapidly.*
rapidez *f. rapidity, swiftness.*
RAPIDO *adj. rapid; fast; swift; quick; m. express train.*
Fué una opercaión rápida. *It was a swift move.*
¿Es este tren rápido? *Is this an express train?*
Será mejor que tomemos el rápido. *It would be better if we took the express.*
rapiña *f. robbery, plundering.*
raptar *to abduct, to kidnap.*
rapto *m. kidnapping, abduction.*
raqueta *f. racket (tennis).*
raramente *seldom.*
Raramente vamos a su casa. *We rarely go to his house.*
rareza *f. rarity; queer habit, queer way.*
Ese chico tiene muchas rarezas. *That boy has many queer habits.*
RARO *adj. rare; unusual; odd, queer, strange.*
Es muy raro que haya mosquitos en esta época

del año. *It's strange there should be mosquitos at this time of the year.*
Es un hombre muy raro. *He's a very queer person.*
Era raro el día que no recibía cartas. *Hardly a day would go by without her getting a letter.*
Se equivoca raras veces. *He seldom makes a mistake.*
rascacielos *m. skyscraper.*
rascar *to scratch.*
rasgadura *f. tent, tear.*
rasgar *to tear, to rend, to rip.*
rasgo *m. dash, stroke (in writing); feature, characteristic; deed, feat.*
Rasgo de pluma. *A stroke of the pen.*
Rasgo característico. *Outstanding feature.*
Un rasgo heroico. *A heroic action.*
A grandes rasgos. *In bold strokes. Broadly. In outline.*
rasguño *m. scratch.*
raso *adj. clear; flat; plain; m. satin.*
Cielo raso. *Ceiling.*
Un soldado raso. *Private. Buck private.*
Pasamos la noche al raso. *We spent the night in the open air.*
raspador *m. scraper; eraser.*
raspar *to scrape; to rasp; to erase.*
rastrillo *m. rake; hackle.*
rastro *m. track; trail; trace, sign; harrow, rake; slaughterhouse (Amer.); a junkyard (Madrid).*
Ni encontrar rastro de. *Not to find any trace of.*
rata *f. rat.*
ratero *m. petty thief; pickpocket.*
ratificación *f. ratification.*
ratificar *to ratify, to sanction.*
RATO *m. little while, short time.*
¿No quiere Ud. descansar un rato? *Won't you take a little rest? Don't you want to rest awhile?*
Salió hace un rato. *He left for a little while ago.*
Lo haré a ratos perdidos. *I'll do it in my spare time.*
ratón *m. mouse.*
ratonera *f. mousetrap.*
raya *f. dash; stripe, line; part (hair).*
Prefiero esa camisa de rayas. *I'd rather have that striped shirt.*
Tener (poner) a raya. *To hold at bay (at a distance). To keep within limits.*
rayado *adj. striped.*
Tela rayada. *Striped material (cloth).*
rayar *to draw lines; to rule (paper); to dawn.*
Al rayar el alba. *At daybreak.*
rayo *m. ray, beam; spoke (of wheel); thunderbolt; flash of lightning.*
Rayo de sol. *Sunbeam.*
Rayos X. *X-rays.*
raza *f. race (of people, animals, etc.).*
RAZON *f. reason; cause; rate; right.*
Tener razón. *To be right.*
No tener razón. *To be wrong.*
Tiene Ud. razón. *You're right.*
No tiene razón. *He's wrong.*
No tener razón de ser. *To be without foundation. To have no raison d'être.*
Atender a razones. *To listen to reason.*
Por razones. *For reasons.*
A razón de. *At the rate of.*
Ponerse en razón. *To be reasonable.*
Dar razón de. *To give an account of. To account for. To give information about.*

Dar la razón. *To agree with.*
En razón a. *Concerning. As regards. In regard to.*
Perder la razón. *To lose one's reason.*
Razón social. *Firm. Name of a concern. Firm name.*
Aquí no hay quien dé razón. *There's no one here to give any information.*
¡Con razón! *I can see it now!*
razonable *adj. reasonable, fair.*
razonamiento *m. reasoning.*
razonar *to reason; to argue.*
re *m. D, re (musical note).*
reacción *f. reaction.*
reaccionar *to react.*
Reaccionó violentamente al oír esas palabras. *He reacted violently when he heard that ("those words").*
reaccionario *adj. reactionary.*
reacio *adj. obstinate, stubborn.*
REAL *adj. real, actual; royal; m. a silver coin.*
realidad *f. reality; truth.*
En realidad. *In reality. Really. Actually.*
realismo *m. realism.*
realizar *to realize, to sell out; to accomplish, to fulfill; to materialize.*
realmente *in reality, really, actually.*
reanudar *to renew; to resume.*
Reanudar un negocio. *To resume a business.*
reaparecer *to reappear.*
rebaja *f. reduction; deduction; abatement, diminution.*
¿Puede Ud. hacerme una rebaja en el precio? *Can you let me have it cheaper?*
rebajar *to reduce; to lower; to diminish.*
Han rebajado un poco los precios. *They've reduced the prices a little.*
rebajarse *to lower oneself.*
rebanada *f. a slice of bread.*
rebanar *to slice.*
rebaño *m. flock, herd of cattle.*
rebatir *to repel; to refute.*
rebelarse *to rebel; to revolt.*
rebelde *adj. hard to manage, rebellious; stubborn; m. rebel.*
rebelión *f. rebellion.*
rebosar *to muffle up; to dip into batter; to overflow.*
rebotar *to bounce; to rebound.*
rebuscar *to search; to glean.*
recado *m. message; gift; compliment; daily marketing; errand.*
Lo mandaron a un recado. *They sent him on an errand.*
¿Tiene Ud. algún recado para mí? *Have you a message for me?*
recaer *to fall back; to relapse; to devolve.*
Recayó a los pocos días de haberse levantado. *He had a relapse a few days after he got up (got out of bed).*
recaída *f. relapse.*
recalcar *to emphasize, to stress.*
recalentar *to heat again; to overheat.*
recámara *f. dressing room; breech (of a gun).*
recapacitar *to think over, to recollect, to recall.*
recargado *adj. overloaded; strong; heavy.*
recargar *to overcharge; to overload; to make an additional charge; to increase (a sentence).*
recargo *m. overload; extra charge; overcharge; additional tax; new charge or accusation; increase (of sentence).*
recatado *adj. circumspect, prudent, cautious.*
recatarse *to act carefully, to be cautious.*
recaudación *f. collection (of rent, taxes, etc.); col-*

lector's office.
recaudar to collect (rent or taxes).
recelar to suspect, to distrust.
recelo m. misgiving, suspicion, mistrust.
receloso adj. suspicious, apprehensive.
recepción f. reception.
receptor m. receiver.
　Descuelgue el receptor. Pick up the receiver.
　Cuelgue el receptor. Hang up the receiver.
receta f. prescription; recipe.
　¿Puede Ud. prepararme esta receta? Can you
　　fill this prescription for me?
　Receta de cocina. Recipe.
recetar to prescribe a medicine.
RECIBIR to receive; to accept.
　Recibí hoy una carta de mi hermano. I re-
　　ceived a letter from my brother today.
recibirse to graduate (as a doctor, lawyer, etc.).
recibo m. receipt.
　Acusar recibo. To acknowledge receipt.
recién (used immediately before past participles)
　　recently; lately.
　Recién casado. Newly wed.
　El recién llegado. The newcomer.
RECIENTE adj. recent, new, fresh; modern.
　Un acontecimiento reciente. A recent event.
RECIENTEMENTE recently.
　Falleció recientemente. He died recently.
recinto m. precinct; inclosure; place.
recio adj. strong, vigorous; loud (voice); coarse,
　　thick; severe (weather).
　Hombre de recia constitución. A man of strong
　　constitution.
　Hablar recio. To talk in a loud voice.
　De recio. Strongly. Violently.
recipiente adj. receiving; m. container.
reciprocar to reciprocate.
recíproco adj. reciprocal, mutual.
　A la recíproca. Reciprocally.
　Deben Uds. ayudarse recíprocamente. You
　　should help each other.
reclamación f. reclamation; complaint.
reclamante m. and f. claimant.
reclamar to reclaim, to claim.
reclamo m. advertisement; decoy bird; claim.
recluir to shut up, to confine.
recluso adj. imprisoned; m. recluse; convict.
recluta f. recruiting; m. recruit.
reclutar to recruit.
recobrar to recover; to regain.
　Recobrar la salud. To regain one's health.
RECOGER to pick up; to call for someone; to
　　gather; to collect; to shelter.
　Recoja Ud. eso que se le ha caído. Pick up what
　　you dropped.
　Puedes venir a recogerme a las seis. You can
　　come to pick me up at six o'clock.
recogerse to retire, to go home, to take a rest.
　Se recoge temprano. He goes to bed early.
recolección f. gathering; compilation; harvest; sum-
　　mary.
recolectar to gather, to harvest.
recomendable adj. recommendable.
recomendación f. recommendation; praise.
　Carta de recomendación. Letter of introduction.
　　Letter of recommendation.
RECOMENDAR to recommend; to commend; to
　　advise.
　La persona a quien me recomendó Ud. me ha
　　prometido un empleo. The person you rec-
　　ommended me to has promised me a job.
　Le recomiendo a Ud. que lo haga de prisa. I
　　advise you to do it quickly.

recompensa f. reward, compensation.
　En recompensa. In return.
recompensar to recompense, to reward, to make up
　　for.
reconciliación f. reconciliation, bringing together
　　again.
reconciliar to reconcile, to make friends again.
RECONOCER to recognize; to admit; to inspect, to
　　reconnoiter; to consider; to appreciate.
　¿Reconoce Ud. esta letra? Do you recognize
　　this handwriting?
　Fué necesario reconocer todo el equipaje. All
　　the baggage had to be inspected.
　Le estoy muy reconocido por sus atenciones.
　　I'm grateful to you for your attention.
reconocimiento m. recognition, acknowledgment;
　　appreciation, gratitude; reconnoitering, re-
　　connaissance.
reconstituyente m. tonic (medicine).
reconstrucción f. reconstruction.
reconstruir to reconstruct, to rebuild.
recopilar to compile, to collect.
record m. record (sports, etc.).
　Batir el record. To break the record.
recordar to remind.
　No puedo recordar su apellido. I don't recall
　　his name.
　Se lo recordaré. I'll remind you of it.
recordatorio m. reminder.
recorrer to travel over; to go over; to look over.
　Ayer recorrimos diez millas. Yesterday we
　　covered ten miles.
　Esta mañana recorrimos casi todas las tiendas.
　　This morning we went to nearly all the stores.
recorrido m. distance traveled; run, way, line.
　¿Es éste el final del recorrido? Is this the end
　　of the line (streetcar, bus, etc.)?
recortar to cut, to trim, to clip; to shorten.
recorte m. clipping; outline; pl. cuttings, trimmings.
　Le envié un recorte del periódico. I sent him
　　a newspaper clipping.
recostar to lean against.
recostarse to lean back, to recline.
recreación f. recreation, diversion, amusement.
recrear to entertain, to amuse, to delight.
recrearse to have a little distraction, to have a good
　　time.
recreo m. recreation, diversion, amusement.
rectángulo m. rectangle.
rectificar to rectify; to correct.
rectitud f. rectitude, straight-forwardness, honesty.
RECTO adj. straight; just, upright; erect.
　Trace una linea recta. Draw a straight line.
　Era un hombre recto. He was a very upright
　　man.
rector m. rector, the head of a college or university.
recuento m. checking, recount, inventory.
recuerdo m. recollection; memory; souvenir.
　Este pañuelo es un recuerdo. This handkerchief
　　is a souvenir.
　Déle recuerdos de mi parte. Remember me to
　　him. Give him my regards.
recuperar to recuperate, to recover.
recurrir to recur, to appeal; to resort to, to turn
　　to.
　Tuvimos que recurrir a su ayuda. We had to
　　turn to him for help.
recurso m. recourse; appeal; resource; pl. means.
　Sin recursos. Without means.
rechazar to repulse, to reject, to refuse.
red f. net; network; trap, snare.
　Los pescadores tendieron la red. The fisher-
　　men spread out the net.

　Cayó en las redes que le tendieron. He fell
　　into the trap they set for him.
　Red ferroviaria. Railroad system.
redacción f. wording; editing.
redactar to edit; to word, to write.
　Redactar una carta. To word a letter.
　El manuscrito estaba bien redactado. The
　　manuscript was well written.
redactor m. editor.
rededor m. surroundings.
　Al rededor. Around. Roundabout.
　Al rededor de. Around. About. More or less.
　　Nearly.
redención f. redemption; recovery.
redimir to redeem, to recover, to buy back.
rédito m. interest; revenue, yield of invested capi-
　　tal.
redoblar to double, to redouble; to clinch (a nail);
　　to roll (a drum); to toll (bells).
redonda f. neighborhood; semibreve (music).
　Tres millas a la redonda. Three miles around.
　A la redonda. Roundabout.
REDONDO adj. round.
　La mesa es redonda. The table is round.
　En números redondos. In round numbers.
　Boleto de viaje redondo (Mex.). Round-trip
　　ticket.
reducción f. reduction, decrease.
REDUCIR to reduce; to cut down; to make smaller;
　　to subdue.
　De hoy en adelante reduciré mis gastos. From
　　now on I'll cut down on my expenses.
　Todo se redujo a nada. It didn't amount to any-
　　thing.
　Reducir la marcha. To slow down.
　Reducir a polvo. To pulverize.
redundancia f. redundance.
redundante adj. redundant.
redundar to redound, to turn to, to result.
　Redundará todo en nuestro beneficio. Every-
　　thing will turn out to be to our advantage.
reelección f. re-election.
reelegir to re-elect.
reembolsar to get one's money back, to get a re-
　　fund.
reembolso m. refund.
reemplazar to replace; to restore.
reemplazo m. replacement; substitution.
reexpedir to forward.
　Tenga la bondad de reexpedir mi correspon-
　　dencia a esta dirección. Please forward my
　　mail to this address.
referencia f. reference; account, report.
　¿Quién puede dar referencia de Ud.? Who(m)
　　can you give as reference?
　El asunto de referencia. The matter in question.
referente adj. referring, relating.
REFERIR to refer; to relate; to report.
referirse to refer to.
　¿A qué se refiere Ud.? What are you referring
　　to?
refinado adj. refined; polished.
refinería f. refinery.
reflector adj. reflecting; m. searchlight.
reflejar to reflect.
　Eso refleja su carácter. That reflects his char-
　　acter.
reflejo m. reflex; glare.
　Es un fiel reflejo de la verdad. It's an exact
　　account. This is the (plain) truth. ("It's an
　　exact reflection of the truth.")
reflexión f. reflection; thinking something over
　　carefully.

reflexionar *to think over, to think carefully, to meditate; to reflect.*
Reflexiónelo bien. *Think it over carefully.*
Tengo que reflexionar sobre eso. *I have to think about that. I have to think that over.*

reflexivo *adj. reflexive.*

reforma *f. reform; reformation; alteration.*
Cerrado por reformas. *Closed for alterations (repairs).*

reformar *to reform; to correct; to alter.*
Hay que reformar esta americana. *This coat has to be altered.*

reformatorio *adj. reforming; m. reformatory.*

reforzar *to reinforce; to strengthen.*

refrán *m. proverb, saying.*

refrenar *to curb, to restrain, to refrain.*

refrendar *to legalize; to countersign, to authenticate.*

refrescar *to refresh; to cool; to brush up.*

refresco *m. refreshment; cold drink.*

refriega *f. fray, skirmish, strife.*

refrigerador *adj. refrigerating; m. refrigerator.*

refrigerar *to refrigerate, to cool.*

refuerzo *m. reinforcement.*

refugiado *adj. and n. refugee.*

refugiar *to shelter.*

refugiarse *to take shelter (refuge).*

refugio *m. refuge, shelter, haven.*

refunfuñar *to growl, to grumble.*
No refunfuñe tanto. *Don't grumble so much.*

regadera *f. sprinkler; watering pot.*

regalado *adj. free, given away for nothing; cheap; easy.*
Hace una vida muy regalada. *He leads an easy life.*

regalar *to make a gift; to entertain; to treat; to caress.*
Le regalaré este libro. *I'll make him a present of this book. I'll give him this book as a gift.*
Es muy amigo de regalarse. *He's very fond of good living.*

REGALO *m. gift, present; comfort, good living.*
Ese regalo es para Ud. *This present is for you.*
Recibió un bonito regalo. *He received a nice gift.*
Vivía con mucho regalo. *He lived in luxury.*

regañar *to scold; to quarrel; to growl.*
La regañaron por llegar tarde. *They scolded her for being late.*
Ese hombre se pasa la vida regañando. *That man is always quarreling.*

regaño *m. reprimand, scolding.*

regañón *adj. and n. growling; growler; a scolding person.*

regar *to water, to irrigate.*

regata *f. boat race, regatta.*

regatear *to bargain; to haggle; to stint; to dodge, to evade.*

regateo *m. haggling.*

regeneración *f. regeneration.*

regenerar *to regenerate.*

regente *m. regent; foreman (printing press); registered pharmacist.*

régimen *m. regime; diet.*
El médico me ha puesto a régimen. *The doctor has put me on a diet.*
El país cambió de régimen. *The country changed its government. The country has a new regime.*

regimiento *m. regiment.*

regio *adj. royal, regal; splendid, magnificent.*

región *f. region.*

regional *adj. regional, local.*

REGIR *to rule, to govern; to go by; to prevail; to*
be in force (law, etc.).
Regía los destinos del pueblo. *He governed ("ruled the destinies of") the people.*
¿Por qué método se rige Ud.? *What method (system) do you use? What rules do you go by?*
Aún rige ese decreto. *That decree is still in effect.*
Los precios que rigen. *The prevailing prices.*

registrar *to inspect, to examine; to search; to register, to put on record.*
Es preciso registrarse en el Consulado. *You have to register at the Consulate.*
En este libro se registran las compras y ventas. *Purchases and sales are entered in this book.*
La policía registró su casa. *The police searched his house.*
¿Dónde registrarán el equipaje? *Where will they examine the baggage?*

registro *m. inspection; search; record, register.*
Firme en el libro de registro. *Sign the register.*

REGLA *f. ruler; rule; principle.*
¿Puede dejarme la regla? *Can you let me have the ruler?*
¿Tiene Ud. el pasaporte en regla? *Is your passport in order?*
Todo está en regla. *Everything is in order.*
Estas son las reglas del juego. *These are the rules of the game.*
Por regla general. *As a general rule.*

reglamentario *adj. according to regulations; usual, customary.*

reglamento *m. rules and regulations, by-laws.*

regocijar *to make glad (happy).*

regocijarse *to rejoice, to be glad.*
Se regocijó mucho por la noticia. *The news made him very glad. He was very happy at the news.*

regocijo *m. rejoicing, pleasure.*

REGRESAR *to return, to go or come back.*
Regresará por Navidad. *He'll come back for Christmas.*
Regresaré a España en junio. *I'll go back to Spain in June.*

regreso *m. return, coming back.*
En nuestro viaje de regreso. *On our voyage back. On our return voyage.*
A mi regreso. *On my return.*

REGULAR *to regulate; to adjust; adj. regular, ordinary; fair, moderate; medium in size, quality, grade, etc.*
Regular el tráfico. *To regulate traffic.*
Estoy regular. *I'm so, so. Can't complain!*
Disfrutaba de un salario regular. *He received a moderate salary.*
De tamaño regular. *Of medium size.*
Por lo regular le veía todos los días. *Ordinarily I used to see him every day.*

regularmente *regularly.*

rehabilitación *f. rehabilitation.*

rehabilitar *to rehabilitate; to restore.*

rehacer *to make over; to refit.*

rehacerse *to recover, to regain strength; to rally (military).*

rehuir *to withdraw; to shun, to avoid; to refuse.*
Siempre rehuye verme. *He always avoids me.*

rehusar *to refuse; to reject.*
Rehusó la invitación. *He refused the invitation.*

reimprimir *to reprint.*

reina *f. queen.*

reinado *m. reign.*

reinar *to reign; to predominate, to prevail, to exist.*
La reina Victoria reinó durante sesenta años.
Queen Victoria reigned sixty years.
Reina un malestar general. *There's a general unrest.*

reincidir *to relapse, to fall back into a former state or way of acting, to backslide.*

reino *m. kingdom, reign.*

reintegrar *to restore; to refund.*
Hay que reintegrar la suma. *We have to make good (replace) the sum.*
Le reintegrarán el importe. *They'll refund your money.*

reintegrarse *to recuperate; to return.*
Reintegrarse al trabajo. *To return to work.*

reintegro *m. restitution; refund.*

REÍR *to laugh.*
Se echó a reír. *He burst out laughing.*
Reír a carcajadas. *To laugh uproariously. To laugh out loud.*

reírse *to scoff, to make fun, to laugh.*
¿Por qué se ríe de él? *Why are you laughing at him?*
Se ríe por nada. *The least little thing makes him laugh. ("He laughs over nothing.")*
Reírse entre sí. *To laugh up one's sleeve.*

reiterar *to reiterate.*

reja *f. plowshare; grate; railing, iron fence; iron bars.*

rejuvenecer *to rejuvenate.*

RELACIÓN *f. relation, connection; report, account; pl. connections; relations.*
No hay relación entre estas dos cosas. *There's no relation (connection) between these two things.*
Hizo una relación del suceso. *He gave an account of what happened.*
Tiene muy buenas relaciones. *He has very good connections.*
Relaciones diplomáticas. *Diplomatic relations.*

relacionado *adj. acquainted, related, well-connected.*
Está muy bien relacionado. *He has very good connections.*

relacionar *to relate; to connect; to be acquainted.*
Estamos relacionados con la firma. *We do business (have dealings) with the firm.*

relacionarse *to associate oneself with, to get acquainted, to make connections.*
Se relaciona mucho con artistas y escritores. *He associates a lot with artists and writers.*
Cuanto se relaciona con. *Everything which relates to.*
Entiende todo cuanto se relaciona con la mecánica. *He understands everything that has to do with mechanics.*

relámpago *m. lightning.*

relampaguear *to lighten (lightning).*
Relampaguea (Está relampagueando). *It's lightning.*

relatar *to relate, tell.*

relativo *adj. relative.*
Relativo a. *With regard to. With reference to.*

relato *m. account, statement; story.*
Hizo un relato de lo que ocurrió. *He gave an account of what had happened.*

releer *to read over again.*

relieve *m. relief.*

religión *f. religion.*

religioso *adj. religious.*

RELOJ *m. clock, watch.*
Reloj de bolsillo. *Pocket watch.*
Reloj de pulsera. *Wristwatch.*
Reloj de pared. *Clock.*

relojero *m. watchmaker.*

relucir *to shine, to sparkle, to glitter; to excel, to be brilliant.*

Sacó a relucir aquella vieja cuestión. *He brought up that old question (problem) again.*

relumbrar *to shine, to sparkle, to glisten.*

rellanar *to refill; to stuff; to pad.*

relleno *adj. stuffed; filled; m. stuffing.*

Pimientos rellenos. *Stuffed peppers.*

remar *to row, to paddle.*

rematar *to complete, to put the finishing touches on; to sell at auction.*

remate *m. end, conclusion; auction.*

De remate. *Utterly, Irremediably.*

Por remate. *Finally.*

remedar *to imitate; to mimic.*

remediar *to remedy; to make good; to help; to avoid.*

No lo puedo remediar. *I can't help it. I can't do anything about it.*

Eso se puede remediar. *That can be remedied.*

Lo que no se puede remediar, se ha de aguantar. *What cannot be cured must be endured.*

REMEDIO *m. remedy; medicine; redress; resource, resort.*

¿Sabe Ud. de algún remedio contra el mareo? *Do you know of any medicine for seasickness?*

Esto no tiene remedio. *There's no remedy for this. This can't be helped. This is hopeless.*

No tuvo más remedio que aceptarlo. *He had no alternative but to accept it. There was nothing he could do—he had to accept it.*

¡No hay más remedio! *There's nothing else to do. Nothing (else) can be done!*

Sin remedio. *Inevitable. Nothing can be done about it.*

Es un caso sin remedio. *It's a hopeless case.*

remendar *to mend, to patch; to darn.*

remesa *f. remittance; shipment.*

remiendo *m. patch; repair.*

remitente *adj. remittent; m. and f. sender, shipper, dispatcher.*

REMITIR *to remit; to send, to forward, to ship.*

Me hace el favor de remitir mis cartas a estas señas. *Please forward my mail ("letters") to this address.*

Le remitimos los géneros. *We sent you the goods.*

remo *m. oar.*

remojar *to soak, to steep, to dip.*

remojo *m. soaking, steeping.*

Ponga las judías en remojo. *Let the beans soak.*

remolcador *m. tugboat; lighter.*

remolcar *to tow; to haul.*

remolino *m. whirlpool; whirlwind; cowlick.*

remolque *m. towing; towline.*

Llevar a remolque. *To tow.*

remontar *to remount; to repair saddles.*

remontarse *to soar, to fly upward, to fly at a great height; to date back.*

Remontarse a. *To date back to.*

remorder *to feel remorse.*

Le remuerde la conciencia. *His conscience is bothering him. He has a guilty conscience.*

remordimiento *m. remorse.*

remover *to remove; to stir; to dismiss.*

remuneración *f. remuneration; reward.*

remunerar *to remunerate, to reward.*

renacer *to be reborn; to grow again.*

rencilla *f. quarrel; grudge.*

rencor *m. rancor, grudge.*

No le guardo ningún rencor. *I don't bear him any grudge.*

rencoroso *adj. resentful, spiteful.*

rendición *f. rendering; surrendering.*

rendido *adj. tired, worn-out, exhausted, overcome.*

Estoy rendido, no puedo andar más. *I'm exhausted. I can't walk any further.*

rendija *f. slit, crevice, crack.*

rendir *to subdue; to surrender; to produce, to yield; to tire out.*

Este negocio rinde poco. *This business is not very profitable.*

rendirse *to give up, to surrender; to be tired.*

Está por rendirse. *He's about to give up.*

Rendirse incondicionalmente. *To surrender unconditionally.*

renegado *m. renegade.*

renglón *m. line (written or printed).*

Le pondré unos renglones. *I'll drop him a few lines.*

Fíjese en el tercer renglón. *Look at the third line.*

Leer entre renglones. *To read between the lines.*

A renglón seguido. *Then. Immediately afterwards.*

renombre *m. renown, fame; surname, family name.*

renovación *f. renovation; renewal.*

renovar *to renovate; to renew; to reform, to transform.*

renta *f. rent, income; profit; rental; revenue, annuity.*

Vive de sus rentas. *He lives on his income.*

renuncia *f. resignation; renunciation, giving up; waiving.*

Presentó su renuncia. *He turned in his resignation.*

renunciar *to renounce, to resign; to waive; to drop (a claim); to refuse.*

Renunciaré a mi empleo. *I'll resign my position.*

Renunciar un derecho. *To give up a right.*

Renunció el ofrecimiento. *He refused (declined) that offer.*

reñir *to quarrel, to fight; to scold.*

Ha reñido con sus suegros. *She quarreled with her in-laws.*

No le riñas al niño. *Don't scold the child.*

reo *m. criminal; defendant.*

reojo *m. (look) askance.*

Mirar de reojo. *To look askance. To look out of the corner of one's eye.*

reorganización *f. reorganization.*

reorganizar *to reorganize.*

reparable *adj. reparable, remediable.*

reparación *f. reparation, repair; amends; satisfaction.*

REPARAR *to repair; to notice; to make up for.*

Hay que reparar la radio. *Our radio needs to be fixed.*

¿Dónde me podrán reparar esto? *Where can I get this repaired (fixed)?*

¿Reparó Ud. en su acento cubano? *Did you notice his Cuban accent?*

reparo *m. remark, hint; consideration; objection; parry (fencing).*

Poner reparo. *To object. To raise an objection.*

Sin ningún reparo. *Without any consideration.*

repartición *f. distribution; partition.*

Repartición de premios. *Distribution of prizes.*

repartidor *m. distributor, delivery-man.*

repartir *to distribute; to divide; to deliver (the mail).*

Se repartieron las ganancias. *They divided the profits between (among) themselves.*

Reparten el correo a eso de las ocho. *The mail is delivered at about eight o'clock.*

reparto *m. distribution; delivery; cast (in a play).*

¿A qué hora se hace el reparto? *At what time is the mail delivered?*

repasar *to check, to look over; to go over; to mend (clothes).*

Repase Ud. esa cuenta detenidamente. *Check that account carefully.*

Repasar la lección. *To go over one's lessons.*

Está repasando la ropa. *She's mending the clothes.*

repaso *m. review (of a lesson); revision.*

repatriar *to repatriate.*

REPENTE *m. sudden movement.*

Tuvo un repente de ira. *She had a fit of temper.*

De repente. *Suddenly. All of a sudden.*

De repente se apagaron todas las luces. *All of a sudden the lights went out.*

repentino *adj. sudden.*

Murió de muerte repentina. *He died suddenly. His death was sudden.*

repercusión *f. repercussion; reaction.*

repercutir *to have a repercussion; to echo, to reverberate.*

Eso repercutirá en la situación. *That will have an effect on the situation.*

repetición *f. repetition, encore.*

El informe estaba lleno de repeticiones. *The report was full of repetitions.*

El público entusiasmando pidió la repetición. *The enthusiastic audience called for an encore.*

REPETIR *to repeat; to have a second helping.*

Haga el favor de repetir lo que dijo. *Please repeat what you said.*

¿Puedo repetir de este plato? *May I have a second helping?*

repisa *f. bracket; shelf.*

REPLETO *adj. full, replete.*

El autobús está repleto. *The bus is full.*

Tiene la cartera repleta de billetes. *His wallet is full of bills.*

La tienda está repleta de mercadería. *The store is well stocked ("is full of merchandise").*

réplica *f. reply, answer.*

Su réplica fué acertadísima. *His reply was very much to the point.*

replicar *to reply; to retort, to talk back.*

¡No me repliques! *Don't answer back! Don't talk back to me!*

reponer *to replace; to restore.*

Repuso los fondos. *He replaced the funds.*

reponerse *to recover; to retrieve.*

No podrá reponerse. *She can't possibly recover.*

Ya me he repuesto de mis pérdidas. *I have already retrieved my losses.*

reporter, reportero *m. reporter.*

reposar *to rest; to lie down.*

Está reposando. *She's resting.*

Reposar la comida. *To rest after eating. To take a nap after lunch (dinner).*

reposarse *to settle (liquids).*

Deja que se repose el café. *Let the coffee settle.*

reposo *m. rest.*

Después de un reposo se sentirá mejor. *You'll feel better after a short rest.*

repostería *f. confectioner's, pastry shop; pantry.*

reprender *to reprimand, to reprehend.*

represión *f. reproof, reproach, reprimand.*

representación *f. representation; play, performance.*

¿A qué hora empieza la representación? *When does the performance (play) begin?*

Ostentó la representación de su país en Rusia. *He went to Russia as his country's representative.*

representante *adj. representing; m. and f. representative, agent.*

representar *to represent; to stage, to play on the stage.*

¿Qué casa representa Ud.? *Which firm do you represent?*

No representa su edad. *She doesn't look her age.*

reprimir *to repress, to check, to hold in check.*

No me pude reprimir por más tiempo. *I couldn't contain myself any longer.*

reprobación *f. reprobation.*

reprobar *to reprove, to condemn, to find fault with.*

reprochar *to reproach; to upbraid.*

reproducción *f. reproduction.*

reproducir *to reproduce.*

reproducirse *to recur.*

reptil *m. reptile.*

república *f. republic.*

republicano *adj. and n. republican.*

repudiar *to repudiate; to disown.*

repuesto *adj. recovered; m. provisions, supply set apart; sideboard; pl. spare parts.*

De repuesto. *Spare. Extra.*

Envíeme Ud. algunas piezas de repuesto. *Send me some spare parts.*

Repuestos. *Spare parts.*

repugnante *adj. repugnant, distasteful.*

repugnar *to be distasteful, to be repugnant; to detest; to act with reluctance.*

Me repugna. *I detest it. It's repugnant to me.*

repulsión *f. repulsion; aversion.*

repulsivo *adj. repulsive, repelling.*

reputación *f. reputation, name.*

Gozar de buena reputación. *To have a good name.*

requerimiento *m. request; summons.*

requerir *to summon; to notify; to require.*

Eso requiere mucha atención. *That requires a lot of attention.*

requisito *m. requisite, requirement.*

Llenar los requisitos. *To meet the requirements.*

res *f. steer, cow, bull (Amer.).*

Carne de res. *Beef.*

resaltar *to rebound; to stand out; to be conspicuous.*

Hacer resaltar. *To emphasize. To call attention to.*

Resaltar a la vista. *To be self-evident. To be very obvious. To stare one in the face.*

resbaladizo *adj. slippery.*

resbalar *to slip, to slide.*

resbalarse *to slip.*

Cuidado con resbalarse. *Watch out you don't slip.*

resbalón *m. slip, slipping.*

resbaloso *adj. slippery.*

La acera está resbalosa. *The sidewalk is slippery.*

rescatar *to ransom; to redeem.*

rescate *m. ransom.*

resentirse *to begin to give way, to fail; to feel the effects of; to resent, to be offended, to feel hurt, to show displeasure; to hurt.*

Está resentida. *She's resentful. She feels hurt.*

Resentirse por nada. *To become offended over trifles. To take offense at unimportant things.*

Se resiente del trabajo pesado que hace. *He's beginning to feel the effects of the hard*

work he's doing.

Tengo el cuerpo resentido. *My body aches all over.*

reseña *f. sketch; brief account.*

reseñar *to outline, to give a brief account.*

reserva *f. reserve; reservation; caution; secret.*

Se lo digo a Ud. en reserva. *I'm telling you this in confidence.*

Con la mayor reserva. *In strict(est) confidence.*

Está en la reserva. *He is in the reserve (Army or Navy).*

Reserva mental. *Mental reservation.*

Sin reserva. *Without reservation. Unreservedly. Openly.*

De reserva. *Extra. In reserve.*

Tengo una reserva en el banco. *I have some money put away in the bank.*

reservadamente *secretly, confidentially.*

reservado *adj. reserved; cautious; confidential.*

Es muy reservado. *He's very reserved.*

reservar *to reserve; to save; to keep; to conceal.*

Queremos que nos reserve un asiento de Pullman. *We want a Pullman reservation.*

Le reservó su habitación hasta su regreso. *He reserved the room for him until his return.*

El Club se reserva el derecho de admisión. *The Club reserves the right of admission.*

Reserve algún dinero para el viaje. *Save some money for the trip.*

Se reservaron una parte de las ganancias. *They kept a share of the profits.*

reservarse *to preserve oneself; to bide one's time; to be cautious.*

resfriado *m. a cold.*

He cogido un resfriado. *I've caught a cold.*

resfriar *to cool; to cool off.*

resfriarse *to catch a cold.*

Se resfrió anoche. *He caught a cold last night.*

El niño va a resfriarse. *The boy is going to catch a cold.*

resfrío *m. a cold.*

Tengo un fuerte resfrío. *I have a bad cold.*

resguardar *to reserve, to keep safe, to protect.*

resguardarse *to take care of oneself; to be on one's guard; to take shelter.*

resguardo *m. voucher; security; safekeeping; guard; customs official.*

Poner a resguardo de. *To keep safe. To preserve from.*

residencia *f. residence.*

residente *adj. residing; resident; m. resident, inhabitant.*

residir *to reside, to live.*

¿En dónde reside su familia actualmente? *Where does your family live at present?*

residuo *m. residue, remainder.*

resignación *f. resignation, patience, state of being resigned.*

resignarse *to be resigned, to resign oneself to.*

resistencia *f. resistance.*

resistente *adj. resistant, strong.*

resistir *to resist, to hold out, to withstand, to endure.*

Resistir la tentación. *To resist temptation.*

Resistir un ataque. *To resist (withstand) an attack.*

Ha resistido la prueba. *It stood the test.*

Esto ya no se puede resistir. *This can't be tolerated any longer.*

resistirse *to offer resistance; to refuse.*

Se resistió a hacerlo. *He refused to do it.*

resolución *f. resolution, determination, decision; solution.*

Tenemos que tomar una resolución. *We must come to some decision.*

resoluto *adj. resolute.*

resolver *to resolve, to determine, to decide; to solve; to dissolve; to settle.*

Estoy resuelto a hacerlo yo mismo. *I'm determined to do it myself.*

Este problema es difícil de resolver. *This problem is hard to solve.*

Puede ser que haya resuelto hacerlo. *It may be that he has decided to do it.*

Es necesario resolver este asunto con toda urgencia. *It's necessary to settle this affair immediately.*

resolverse *to resolve, to make up one's mind, to reach a decision.*

No se resuelve a tomar una decisión. *He couldn't bring himself to the point of making a decision. He couldn't make up his mind.*

resonancia *f. resonance.*

resonante *adj. resonant, resounding.*

resonar *to resound.*

resorte *m. spring (metal); pl. means, resources.*

respaldo *m. back (of a seat); back, reverse (of a sheet of paper); endorsement.*

Al respaldo. *On the back of.*

respectivamente *respectively.*

respectivo *adj. respective.*

RESPECTO *m. relation, respect, reference.*

Con respecto a. *With regards to.*

Al respecto. *Relative to.*

A este respecto. *In regard to this.*

Por todos respectos. *By all means.*

respetable *adj. respectable, honorable.*

respetar *to respect, to honor.*

RESPETO *m. respect, regard, consideration.*

Mis respetos a su señor padre. *My best regards to your father.*

Perder el respeto. *To lose respect for.*

Faltar al respeto. *To be disrespectful.*

Por respeto a. *Out of consideration for.*

Pieza de respeto. *Spare part.*

respetuoso *adj. respectful, polite.*

respiración *f. respiration; breathing.*

Le faltó la respiración. *He was out of breath.*

respirar *to breathe.*

Respire Ud. fuerte. *Breathe deeply.*

Déjeme Ud. respirar. *Give me a chance to get my breath.*

Con aquel dinero pudo respirar un mes más. *With that money he could get by for another month.*

respiro *m. respite, time of relief.*

resplandor *m. splendor; glare.*

RESPONDER *to answer; to respond; to talk back; to correspond; to be responsible for.*

Ni siquiera me respondió. *He didn't even answer me.*

Ese niño siempre responde a sus padres. *That child always talks back to his parents.*

¿Y qué responde Ud. a esto? *And what do you say to that?*

Ha respondido muy bien al tratamiento. *He responded to the treatment very well.*

Respondo de las consecuencias. *I'll answer for the consequences.*

¿Hay alguien que responda por él? *Is there anyone who will stand up for him?*

respondón *adj. saucy, fresh; m. a person who is always answering back.*

responsabilidad *f. responsibility.*

responsable *adj. responsible, liable.*

RESPUESTA f. answer, reply; retort; response.
¿Cuál es su respuesta? What is your answer?
Respuesta favorable. Favorable answer.
Respuesta pagada. Reply prepaid.
resquebrajar to crack, to split.
resta f. subtraction; remainder.
restablecer to re-establish; to restore.
restablecerse to recover.
Restablecerse de una enfermedad. To recover from an illness.
restante adj. remaining; m. remainder.
Hay muchas cosas restantes. There are many things left over (remaining).
restar to subtract; to deduct; to remain; to be left.
Resta dos de cinco. Subtract two from five.
Me restan cinco pesos. I have five pesos left.
No nos resta más que marcharnos. There's nothing left for us to do but leave.
Restan muchas cosas por hacer. Many things remain to be done.
restauración f. restoration.
RESTAURANT, RESTAURANTE m. restaurant.
restaurar to restore; to recover.
restitución f. restitution.
restituir to restore.
Le restituyeron sus propiedades. His property was restored to him.
RESTO m. rest, remainder, residue; pl. remains, left-overs.
Esa cocinera sabe aprovechar los restos. This cook knows how to make good use of left-overs.
Echar el resto. To stake one's all. To bet everything one has.
Le juego mi resto. I bet everything I have.
restricción f. restriction, curtailment.
restringir to restrain; to curtail; to restrict, to limit.
resucitar to resurrect; to revive; to come or bring back.
Resucitar una moda. To revive a style.
resuelto adj. resolute, daring; determined; prompt; settled, resolved.
Es un hombre muy resuelto. He's a very determined person.
Es cosa resuelta. It's (a) settled (matter).
resulta f. result, effect, consequence.
De resultas. As a consequence. Consequently.
RESULTADO m. result; score.
¿Cuál será el resultado? What will be the result?
¿Cuál fué el resultado del partido? What was the final score of the game?
RESULTAR to result, to turn out to be.
No resultó muy bien la combinación. The combination didn't turn out to be a good one.
Si tomamos un cuarto juntos nos resultará más barato. If we take a room together, it will be cheaper for us.
Nos resultó muy caro. It was very expensive for us.
¿Qué traje le ha resultado mejor? Which suit wore better?
La película resultó muy aburrida. The picture was boring.
Resultó herido. He was wounded.
Esto no me resulta. This doesn't suit me.
resumen m. summary, summing up, recapitulation.
resumido adj. abridged.
En resumidas cuentas. In short. To make a long story short.
resumir to abridge, to cut short; to summarize, to sum up.
Resumir un discurso. To cut a speech short.

resurgimiento m. revival.
resurgir to reappear.
retaguardia f. rear guard.
retar to challenge; to reprimand.
retardar to retard; to delay.
¿Qué le ha retardado a Ud.? What made you so late?
retardo m. delay.
Eso fué la causa del retardo. That caused the delay. That was the cause of the delay.
Temo que el retardo sea fatal. I'm afraid that the delay may be fatal.
retazo m. remnant, piece (material, cloth).
retener to retain; to withhold; to hold, to keep; to remember.
Le retuvieron el sueldo aquel mes. They withheld his salary that month.
Retuvieron aquella posición una semana. They held that position for a week.
No puede retener las fechas en la cabeza. He can't remember dates. ("He can't keep dates in his head.")
retina f. retina.
retirada f. retreat, withdrawal.
El enemigo se bate en retirada. The enemy is retreating.
retirar to withdraw; to retire; to take away; to back up (printing).
Quiero retirar cien dólares. I'd like to withdraw a hundred dollars.
Retire un poco la silla para que se pueda pasar. Pull the chair aside a little so there will be room to pass.
Retire esta silla. Take this chair away.
retirarse to go away; to retire; to retreat.
Se ha retirado de los negocios. He has retired from business.
Nuestras fuerzas se retiraron. Our forces withdrew.
Se retiró a su cuarto. He went to his room.
Retírese del fuego. Get away from the fire.
Puede Ud. retirarse. You may go now.
retocar to retouch, to improve.
retoñar to sprout, to reappear.
retoño m. shoot, sprout.
retoque m. retouching; finishing touch.
retorcer to twist; to contort; to distort; to retort.
retornar to return, to shuttle; to give back; to repay; to reciprocate.
retorno m. return; repayment; exchange.
retozar to frisk; to jump and run about playfully, to frolic.
retractar to retract, to withdraw.
retractarse to retract, to go back on one's word.
retraer to dissuade; to draw back.
retraerse to keep aloof; to shy away; to retire, to withdraw from; to live a retired life.
retraído aloof, solitary, not communicative, secretive.
Se muestra retraído. He holds himself aloof. He holds back. He's withdrawn.
Es un hombre retraído. He's not communicative.
retraimiento m. shyness; reserve; retreat, seclusion.
retrasar to retard, to delay, to be slow; to put off; to set back.
Hemos retrasado el viaje. We have put off the trip.
Mi reloj retrasa. My watch is slow.
El tren viene retrasado. The train's late.
retrasarse to be late; to fall behind (in payment); to be backward.

Siento haberme retrasado tanto. I'm sorry to be so late.
Nos hemos retrasado en los pagos. We've fallen behind in our payments.
retraso m. delay.
Habrá un corto retraso. There will be a short delay.
Con retraso. Late.
El tren ha tenido retraso. The train's late.
retratar to portray; to draw a portrait; to photograph, to take a picture.
retrato m. portrait; photograph, picture; image.
Es un retrato muy bien hecho. It's a very good picture.
Este retrato no se parece en nada a ella. This portrait doesn't resemble her at all.
Es el vivo retrato de su padre. He's the living image of his father.
retrete m. toilet, washroom.
retribución f. retribution; reward.
retribuir to pay back; to remunerate.
retroactivo adj. retroactive.
retroceder to back up, to move backward; to draw back, to fall back; to recoil; to grow worse.
El auto retrocedió hasta quedar enfrente de la puerta. The car backed up until it was in front of the door.
Retrocedió unos pasos para reunirse con nosotros. He came back a few steps to join us.
No podía retroceder en su decisión. He couldn't reverse his decision.
retroceso m. recoil, drawing back.
retrógrado adj. retrogressive.
retrospectivo adj. retrospective.
reuma m. rheumatism.
reumatismo m. rheumatism.
reunión f. reunion; meeting, assembly.
Habrá una reunión a las cinco. There will be a meeting at five o'clock.
reunir to gather; to collect, to get (money), to bring together.
Es preciso que Ud. reuna el dinero hoy mismo. You must get the money today.
Reunieron mucho dinero en la función de beneficencia. They collected a lot of money at the benefit.
Reunió a sus amigos en una fiesta. He brought all his friends together at a party.
Se han reunido todos contra él. They've all united against him.
reunirse to get together; to meet; to unite; to join.
¿A qué hora podríamos reunirnos? At what time could we get together?
Se reunen en su casa todos los sábados. They meet at his home every Saturday.
revelación f. revelation.
revelar to reveal, to show, to disclose; to develop (photography).
Revelar un secreto. To reveal a secret.
El autor revela gran talento en este libro. The author shows great talent in this book.
¿Reveló Ud. ya las fotografías? Have you developed the pictures yet?
revendedor m. retailer.
revender to retail; to resell.
reventar to burst, to blow up; to blow out; to break; to sprout, to blossom; to tire, to exhaust, to vex.
Reventar de risa. To burst into laughter.
Reventó el neumático. The tire blew out.
Estoy reventado de tanto caminar. I'm exhausted from walking so much.

Aquel gasto me reventó. *The expense ("that expenditure") just about finished me (left me broke).*

Ese tipo me revienta. *I can't stand that fellow.*

reventarse *to burst.*

Se reventó un neumático en el camino. *We had a blowout on the road.*

reventón *m. bursting; blowout; explosion; steep slope; hard work.*

Tuvo que darse un reventón para terminar el trabajo. *He almost worked himself to death to finish the work.*

reverencia *f. reverence.*

reverso *m. reverse.*

REVÉS *m. reverse; wrong side; backhand slap; misfortune.*

Este es el revés. *This is the wrong side.*

La chaqueta está del revés. *The jacket is wrong side out.*

Llevas puestas las medias al revés. *You're wearing your stockings the wrong side out.*

No es así, precisamente es al revés. *It's not like that, it's just the opposite.*

So lo dije al revés. *I told him just the opposite.*

Todo le salía al revés. *Everything he did went wrong.*

revisar *to look over, to go over; to check; to overhaul; to examine, to audit (accounts).*

Revisar las cuentas. *To audit accounts.*

Hágame el favor de revisar el motor. *Please check the engine.*

revisión *f. checking; verification; overhauling.*

Revisión de cuentas. *Audit.*

revisor *m. overseer; conductor.*

revista *f. review, parade; magazine.*

El general pasó revista a los soldados. *The general reviewed the soldiers.*

Tomaré un ejemplar de esta revista. *I'll take a copy of this magazine.*

revivir *to revive.*

revocación *f. revocation, repeal.*

revocar *to revoke, to repeal, to cancel; to plaster, to cover with plaster.*

revolcar *to knock down, to tread on; to confuse; to floor (an opponent).*

revolcarse *to wallow, to welter.*

revoltoso *adj. rebellious, hard to manage; boisterous; naughty, full of pranks.*

revolución *f. revolution.*

revolucionario *adj. revolutionary; m. revolutionist.*

revolver *to revolve; to turn upside down; to stir up.*

El niño lo revolvía todo en la casa. *The child turned the house upside down.*

Revuélvalo Ud. con una cuchara. *Stir it with a spoon.*

revólver *m. revolver.*

revoque *m. plaster.*

revuelo *m. commotion, sensation.*

revuelta *f. revolt.*

revuelto *adj. turned upside down; scrambled; boisterous, restless.*

Huevos revueltos. *Scrambled eggs.*

rey *m. king.*

reyerta *f. quarrel, brawl.*

rezagado *adj. straggling; m. straggler, someone left behind.*

rezagar *to leave behind; to defer.*

rezagarse *to remain behind; to lag.*

rezar *to pray.*

Rezeba todos los días sus oraciones. *He said his prayers every day.*

Eso no reza conmigo. *That's none of my busi-*

ness. *That's no affair of mine. That has nothing to do with me.*

ría *f. mouth of a river, estuary.*

riachuelo *m. brook, stream, rivulet.*

ribera *f. shore, bank.*

ribete *m. border, trimming; pretense; binding (on seams).*

ricacho, ricachón *m. very rich.*

rícino *m. castor-oil plant.*

Aceite de ricino. *Castor oil.*

RICO *adj. rich, wealthy; delicious.*

Si yo fuera rico no trabajaría tanto. *I wouldn't work so much if I were rich.*

¡Qué sabor más rico el de esta carne! *What a delicious flavor this meat has!*

ridiculizar *to ridicule.*

RIDÍCULO *adj. ridiculous; odd, queer; m. ridicule.*

Es una moda ridícula. *It's a ridiculous fashion.*

Poner en ridículo. *To ridicule.*

Ponerse en ridículo. *To make oneself ridiculous.*

riego *m. irrigation, watering.*

riel *m. rail, track.*

rienda *f. rein; restraint.*

Sujete Ud. bien las riendas. *Hold on to the reins.*

Corrió a rienda suelta. *He ran fast.*

Dar rienda suelta. *To give free rein. To give vent to.*

riesgo *m. risk, danger, hazard.*

Corrió mucho riesgo. *He took a big risk.*

Sin riesgo. *Without risk. Safely.*

rifa *f. raffle; quarrel.*

rifar *to raffle; to quarrel.*

rifle *m. rifle.*

rigidez *f. rigidity, sternness.*

rígido *adj. rigid; severe, hard, stern.*

rigor *m. rigor.*

riguroso *adj. rigorous, severe, strict.*

rima *f. rhyme.*

rincón *m. corner (of a room, etc.); nook; hidden spot, secluded place.*

Ponga Ud. la silla en el rincón. *Put the chair in the corner.*

rinconera *f. corner piece.*

rinoceronte *m. rhinoceros.*

riña *f. quarrel, fray, fight.*

riñón *m. kidney.*

río *m. river.*

El Río Grande. *Rio Grande ("The big river").*

riqueza *f. riches; wealth; fertility.*

RISA *f. laugh, laughter.*

Todo aquello le producía risa. *That ("all that") made him laugh.*

No es cosa de risa. *It's no laughing matter.*

Desternillarse de risa. *To split one's sides laughing.*

¡Ay que risa! *My, how funny! That's very funny!*

risco *m. steep rock; cliff.*

risible *adj. laughable.*

risueño *adj. smiling; pleasing.*

Es un niño muy risueño. *The child is very good-natured ("always smiling").*

ritmo *m. rhythm.*

rito *m. rite, ceremony.*

rival *m. rival.*

rivalidad *f. rivalry.*

rivalizar *to vie, compete.*

rizo *m. curl, frizzle; loop (aviation).*

robar *to rob, to steal; to draw (a card).*

Me han robado. *I've been robbed.*

Me han robado la cartera. *My wallet's been stolen.*

Ahora le toca a Ud. robar. *Now it's your turn to draw (in cards).*

roble *m. oak.*

robo *m. robbery, theft; cards drawn (in certain card games).*

robusto *adj. robust, strong.*

Es de constitución robusta. *He has a strong constitution.*

roca *f. rock.*

roce *m. friction; continual dealing with acquaintances.*

Tiene mucho roce con ellos. *He associates a lot with them.*

rociar *to spray, to sprinkle.*

rocío *m. dew.*

rodada *f. rut, track of a wheel.*

rodar *to roll; to roam around; to shoot (a film).*

Rodó la escalera. *He went rolling down the stairs.*

Ahora rueda el dinero más que nunca. *The money's coming in now hand over fist. ("The money rolls in more than ever now.")*

Desde muy joven empezó a rodar por el mundo. *He began to roam around the world when he was very young.*

Se empezó a rodar la película. *They started shooting the picture.*

rodear *to surround, to encircle; to go around.*

rodeo *m. turn; roundabout way; roundup, rodeo.*

Ese camino da un rodeo muy grande. *That road makes a wide turn.*

Hubo un rodeo la semana pasada. *There was a rodeo last week.*

Déjese de rodeos y conteste claramente. *Stop beating around the bush and give me a straight answer.*

RODILLA *f. knee.*

De rodillas. *On one's knee.*

Ponerse de rodillas. *To kneel.*

rodillo *m. roller; rolling-pin; inking roller (printing).*

roer *to gnaw, to nibble; to pick (a bone); to annoy.*

rogar *to pray, to beg, to entreat, to request.*

Le ruego que . . . *I beg you to . . . Please . . .*

ROJO *adj. red.*

La cruz roja. *The Red Cross.*

rol *m. roll, list, muster roll, crew list; role.*

rollizo *adj. plump; m. log.*

rollo *m. roll.*

Roma *f. Rome.*

romadizo *m. catarrh, cold in the head; hay fever.*

romance *m. romance; ballad.*

romanticismo *m. romanticism.*

romántico *adj. romantic.*

romería *f. pilgrimage; excursion, tour.*

romero *m. rosemary; pilgrim.*

rompecabezas *m. riddle; puzzle.*

rompenueces *m. nutcracker.*

rompeolas *m. breakwater; mole.*

ROMPER *to break; to smash; to tear; to rip; to fracture; to start, to begin.*

¿Ha roto Ud. la botella? *Have you broken (did you break) the bottle?*

Se cayó del caballo y se rompió una pierna. *He fell from his horse and broke a leg.*

Rompió el documento. *He tore up the document.*

Se me ha roto la media. *I've ripped my stocking.*

Romper relaciones. *To break relations.*

Romper con alguno. *To break with someone.*

Al romper el día. *At daybreak.*

ron *m. rum.*

roncar *to snore; to roar; to brag.*

ronco *adj. hoarse.*

roncha f. swelling caused by a bite or by a blow; wheal, welt.

ronda f. night patrol; making the rounds; a round (of drinks, etc.).

rondar to patrol.

ronquido m. snore; roaring.

roña f. scab; filth, dirt; bark of pine trees.

ROPA f. wearing apparel, clothing; clothes.

Tengo que mudarme de ropa. I have to change my clothes.

Quiero que me laven la ropa. I want my clothes washed.

Ropa hecha. Ready-made clothes.

Ropa interior. Underwear.

Ropa sucia. Dirty clothes. Laundry (to be washed).

Ropa limpia. Laundry (washed). Clean clothes (laundry).

ropero m. wardrobe; closet; dealer in clothes.

rosa f. rose.

rosado adj. pink, rosy.

rosal m. rosebush.

rosario m. rosary.

rosca f. ring (bread or cake); thread (of a screw).

Déme Ud. una rosca de esas. Give me one of those rings (bread or cake).

La rosca de un tornillo. The thread of a screw.

rosquilla f. jelly-roll; doughnut.

rostro m. face, countenance.

roto adj. torn; broken; ragged; m. tramp (Chile).

rotular to label.

rótulo m. label; poster, placard.

rotura f. breaking, rupture; crack.

rozar to grub, to clear (the ground); to nibble (grass); to graze.

El avión rozó ligeramente el suelo. The plane grazed the ground.

rozarse to fret, to rub against; to bump one's foot against another; to associate, to rub elbows, to be on familiar terms.

Se roza mucho con ellos. He associates a lot with them.

rubí m. ruby.

rubio adj. blond; f. blonde.

rubor m. blush; bashfulness.

ruborizarse to blush.

rudeza f. coarseness, roughness.

rudimento m. rudiment.

rudo adj. rude, rough; severe.

rueda f. wheel; sunfish.

ruedo m. hem; round mat; bull-ring.

ruego m. request, petition.

Dirigió un ruego a la Cámara. He submitted a petition to the legislature.

A ruego de. At the request of.

rugido m. roar; rumbling.

rugir to roar; to bellow.

RUIDO m. noise.

El ruido me impidió dormir. The noise kept me awake. ("The noise kept me from sleeping.")

Meter (hacer) ruido. To make noise. To create a sensation. To attract attention.

ruin adj. mean, vile, low.

ruina f. ruin; downfall; bankruptcy; pl. ruins.

ruinoso adj. ruinous; in ruins.

ruiseñor m. nightingale.

ruleta f. roulette.

rumba f. rumba (Cuban dance).

rumbo m. course; road, route; pomp, showy display.

Tomaremos otro rumbo. We'll take another course (road).

Con rumbo a. Bound for.

Era un hombre de rumbo. He was a spendthrift.

rumiar to ruminate; to ponder.

rumor m. rumor.

ruptura f. rupture; breaking off.

rural adj. rural, rustic.

ruso adj. and m. Russian.

rustico adj. rustic.

Un libro en rústica. A paper-bound book.

ruta f. route, course.

rutina f. routine, habit; rut.

rutinario adj. according to routine; mechanical.

S

SÁBADO m. Saturday.

sábana f. bedsheet.

sabana f. savanna; grassy plain (Cuba).

sabandija f. small reptile or insect.

sabañón m. chilblain.

saber m. learning, knowledge.

SABER to know; to know how; to be able to; to taste; to hear, to find out. (To know a person or a place = conocer.)

¿Sabe Ud. dónde vive? Do you know where he lives?

¿Sabe Ud. a qué hora abren las tiendas? Do you know at what time the stores open?

¿A ver qué sabe Ud.? Let's see what (how much) you know.

Sabe tanto como su profesor. He knows as much as his teacher (professor).

¿Sabe Ud. lo que pasó? Do you know what happened?

¿Sabe Ud. patinar? Do you know how to skate?

¿Sabe Ud. escribir? Can you write?

¿Sabe Ud. nadar? Can you swim?

Sabe nadar muy bien. She swims very well.

¿Sabe Ud. bailar la conga? Can you dance the conga?

¿Sabe Ud. algo de nuevo? Have you heard anything new?

Celebro saberlo. I'm glad (delighted) to hear it.

¿Le sabe mal? Isn't it all right with you? Don't you like it?

¿Sabe la noticia? Have you heard the news?

¿Cómo ha sabido Ud. eso? How did you find that out (learn that)?

¿Qué sé yo? How do I know? How should I know?

¡Ya lo sé! I know it!

Yo no sé. I don't know.

¡Quién sabe! Who knows!

¿Quién lo sabe? Who knows it?

No se sabe. Nobody knows. It's not known.

No se sabe nunca. One never knows.

¡Sabe Dios! God knows!

Esto sabe mal. This tastes bad.

Esta comida sabe a gloria. This food's delicious. ("This food tastes wonderful.")

Le remitimos los géneros siguientes, a saber: We are sending you the following goods:

Hacer saber. To make known.

Como es sabido. As is known.

Que yo sepa. To my knowledge. As far as I know.

No que yo sepa. Not that I'm aware of.

Saber de sobra. To know well enough.

¿Sabe Ud. una cosa? Do you know what? (Do) You know something?

sabiduría f. learning, knowledge, wisdom.

sabio adj. wise, learned; m. scholar.

sable m. saber; cutlass.

sabor m. savor, taste, flavor.

saborear to flavor; to savor, to relish.

saborearse to relish, to enjoy (eating or drinking); to be delighted.

sabotaje m. sabotage.

sabroso adj. delicious, tasty.

La comida es muy sabrosa. The food is very tasty.

sacacorchos m. corkscrew.

sacamanchas m. cleaning fluid; stain remover.

SACAR to take out, to put out, to bring out, to get out; to draw; to remove, to pull out; to infer; to publish; to win (a prize); to take (a picture); to buy, to get.

Sacar una copia. To make a copy.

¿Cuánto saca por día? How much does he make a day?

Saque Ud. la cuenta. Figure out the bill.

Esta mañana saqué un poco de dinero del banco. I drew some money from the bank this morning.

Saqué un premio en el sorteo. I won a prize at the lottery.

¿Dónde puedo sacar mis billetes? Where can I buy my tickets?

Sacaré tres butacas. I'll buy three orchestra seats.

Saque las manos de los bolsillos. Take your hands out of your pockets.

¿De dónde ha sacado Ud. esa idea? Where did you get that idea?

¿De dónde sacará tanto dinero? Where does he get so much money?

Nos sacó de apuro. He got us out of trouble (out of a difficulty).

Saca los niños a pasear. Take the children out for a walk.

Sacó una moneda de su monedero. She took a coin out of her purse.

Ese hombre saca partido de todo. That man turns everything to profit.

Sacarán la casa a subasta pública. They're going to sell the house at public auction.

Sacar una foto. To take a picture.

Sacar una muela. To pull out a tooth.

Sacar a luz. To print. To publish. To make public.

Sacar en limpio. To infer.

No sacar nada en limpio. Not to be able to make anything out of. Not to be able to make head or tail out of.

saco m. sack, bag; coat (Amer.).

¿Qué hay en este saco? What's in this bag?

El viajero llevaba un saco a cuestas. The traveler carried a bag on his shoulders.

Quítese el saco. Take your coat off.

Caer en saco roto. To come to nothing.

sacramento m. sacrament.

sacrificar to sacrifice.

sacrificio m. sacrifice.

sacrilegio m. sacrilege.

sacristía f. sacristy, vestry.

sacudida f. shock, shake; beating.

Le dió una buena sacudida. He gave him a good beating.

sacudir to shake; to jerk; to beat; to dust; to shake off.

sacudirse to get rid of, to object.

saeta f. arrow; shaft.

sagacidad f. sagacity, shrewdness.

sagaz adj. sagacious, shrewd.

sagrado adj. sacred.

sainete m. farce, burlesque act.

SAL f. salt; wit, humor; charm.

Haga el favor de pasarme la sal. Please pass me the salt.

Tiene mucha sal esta niña. This girl is very witty.

SALA f. living room, parlor; large room; room.

Vamos a la sala a escuchar un poco de música. Let's go to the living room (parlor) and listen to some music.

¿Dónde está la sala de espera? Where is the waiting room?

Sala de pruebas. Fitting room.

Sala de fiestas. Nightclub (in Spain).

salado adj. salty; witty.

Esta carne está muy salada. This meat is very salty.

Es muy salada. She's very witty.

salario m. salary, wages.

salchicha f. sausage.

salchichón m. large sausage.

SALDO m. balance, remainder; sale, bargain.

La tienda anuncia un saldo. The store is advertising a sale.

Queda todavía a mi favor un pequeño saldo. A small sum still remains to my credit.

salero m. salt shaker, saltcellar; gracefulness, charm.

Tenga la bondad de alcanzarme el salero. Please pass me the salt shaker.

Es hermosa y además tiene mucho salero. She's pretty and she's also very charming. .

SALIDA f. departure; exit; outlet; sale; sortie, sally; witty remark; loophole, subterfuge.

Salida y llegada de trenes. Departure and arrival of trains.

¿Dónde está la salida? Where is the exit?

Le veré a la salida. I'll see you on my way out.

Tener salida. To sell well.

Dar salida. To dispose of. To sell.

Salida del sol. Sunrise.

Callejón sin salida. Dead-end street.

SALIR to go out; to leave; to depart; to appear; to come out; to get out; to come off; to turn out; to rise (the sun); to cost; to take after.

¿A qué hora sale el tren? What time does the train leave?

El tren está por salir. The train is about to leave.

¿Piensa Ud. salir esta noche? Are you going out tonight?

Voy a salir a tomar un poco el aire. I'm going out for some air.

Salió hace un rato. He left a while ago.

He salido sin dinero. I left the house without any money.

Me sale a peseta la yarda. It costs me a peseta a yard.

Ella sale a su madre. She takes after her mother.

Mi madre salió de compras hoy. My mother went shopping today.

Eche la llave al salir. Lock the door ("with the key") when you go out.

¡Salga de aquí! Get out!

Muy en breve saldrá el libro. The book will be out (appear) very soon.

El periódico sale todos los días. The paper comes out (appears) every day.

Estas manchas no salen. These spots don't come off.

Se le sale mucho el pañuelo del bolsillo. His handkerchief sticks way out of his pocket.

Salió bien en los exámenes. He passed his examination with good marks.

¿Quién salió ganando? Who was the winner?

Los negocios han salido mal. Business has turned out badly.

Todo le salía al revés. Everything he did went wrong.

Al salir el sol. At sunrise.

El sol sale para todos. The sun shines on the just and on the unjust.

El anillo se me ha salido del dedo. The ring slipped off my finger.

salirse to leak; to overflow.

Esta jarra se sale. This jar is leaking.

¡Cuidado que se sale la leche! Look out, the milk is going to overflow!

Salirse con la suya. To get one's way. To accomplish one's end.

saliva f. saliva.

salmón m. salmon.

salón m. hall; salon; parlor.

¿Hay algún salón de belleza por aquí? Is there a beauty parlor near here?

En este salón caben más de cien personas. This hall can accommodate over a hundred people.

Salón de baile. Dance hall.

salpicar to splash, to spatter.

salsa f. sauce, gravy, dressing.

salsera f. gravy dish.

SALTAR to jump, to leap, to hop; to skip, to omit; to bounce; to fly off.

¿Puede Ud. saltar por encima de esa tapia? Can you jump over that fence?

Al pasar lista saltó mi nombre. When he called the roll he skipped my name.

Esta pelota no salta. This ball doesn't bounce.

Saltó una astilla del leño. A chip flew off the log.

Saltó en su defensa. He sprang to his (her) defense.

Hacer saltar. To blow up.

Saltar a la vista. To be obvious. To stare one in the face.

salteador m. highwayman.

SALTO m. jump, leap; sudden promotion; waterfall, cascade.

Salto de agua. Waterfall.

A saltos. By fits and starts.

Dar saltos. To jump.

De un salto. At one jump.

Salto mortal. A somersault.

SALUD f. health.

Disfruta de muy buena salud. He's enjoying good health.

Bueno para la salud. Good for the health. Healthful.

Estar bien de salud. To be in good health.

Estar mal de salud. To be in poor health.

Bebamos a la salud de nuestro anfitrión. Let's drink to our host ("to the health of our host").

¡Salud! Hello! Good luck! To your health!

¡Salud y pesetas! Here's to health and wealth! ("Health and money!")

saludable adj. healthful, good for the health; salutary, beneficial.

saludar to salute, to greet.

Le saludó muy afectuosamente. He greeted him (her) affectionately.

Y a mí, ¿no me saluda Ud.? (Well,) Aren't you going to say hello to me?

Cuando le vea, salúdele en mi nombre. Remember me to him when you see him.

Salude a Juan de mi parte. Give John my regards.

saludo m. salute, greeting.

Saludos a. Greetings to.

salva f. salvo, volley.

Una salva de aplausos. Thunderous applause.

salvación f. salvation.

salvado m. bran.

salvaje adj. savage; wild.

salvamento m. salvage, rescue.

salvar to salvage; to save; to clear (an obstacle); to avoid (a danger); to jump over (a ditch, etc.), to cover (a distance).

El médico ha perdido la esperanza de salvarle. The doctor has given up hope for him. The doctor has given up hope of saving him.

Salvando pequeños detalles. Apart from minor details.

salvarse to escape from danger; to be saved.

Se salvó por un pelo. He had a narrow escape. He escaped with his skin.

salvavidas m. lifesaver; life preserver; lifeboat, life-belt, life buoy.

salvedad f. reserve, exception, qualification.

SALVO adj. saved, safe; excepted; save, exempting; but, unless.

Todos vinieron salvo él. Everyone came except him.

Salvo los casos imprevistos. Except for unforeseen cases.

Salvo que. Unless.

Poner a salvo. To safeguard. To keep safe.

En salvo. Safe. With safety.

Sano y salvo. Safe and sound.

Ponerse a salvo. To escape.

Quedar a salvo. To be safeguarded.

A su salvo. To one's satisfaction.

salvoconducto m. pass, safe-conduct.

sanar to cure, to heal; to recover.

La herida sanó pronto. The wound healed quickly. The wound soon healed.

sanatorio m. sanatorium, sanitarium.

sanción f. sanction.

sancionar to sanction; to ratify, to confirm.

sandalia f. sandal.

sandía f. watermelon.

saneamiento m. sanitation; surety, bail.

sanear to drain, to improve (lands); to take sanitary measures, to make sanitary; to make good, to indemnify; to give bail.

sangrar to bleed; to drain.

SANGRE f. blood.

A sangre fría. In cold blood.

A sangre y fuego. Without mercy. With fire and sword.

sangriento adj. bloody; sanguinary; cruel.

sanidad f. health; health department.

Sanidad pública. Public health.

Cuerpo de Sanidad. Medical Corps.

sanitario adj. sanitary; hygienic.

SANO adj. sound, healthy; sane; safe.

Está más sano de lo que parece. He's healthier than he looks.

Regresó sano y salvo. He returned safe and sound.

santiamén m. instant, twinkling of an eye, jiffy.

Lo haré en un santiamén. I'll do it in a jiffy (before you can say Jack Robinson).

santiguarse to cross oneself, to make the sign of the cross (on oneself).

santo adj. very good, saintly; saint, holy, sacred.

Esa chica es una santa. She's a very good girl. ("That girl is a saint.")

Semana Santa. *Holy Week (Easter).*
Se ha quedado para vestir santos. *She's going to be (is) an old maid.*
saña *f. rage, fury, anger, passion.*
sapo *m. toad.*
saquear *to sack, to loot, to pillage.*
sarampión *m. measles.*
sarcasmo *m. sarcasm.*
sardina *f. sardine.*
sargento *m. sargeant.*
sarmiento *m. vine shoot.*
sarpullido *m. rash, skin eruption.*
sartén *f. frying pan.*
sastre *m. tailor.*
Lleve este traje al sastre. *Take this suit to the tailor.*
sastrería *f. tailor shop, tailoring.*
Satán, Satanás *m. Satan.*
sátira *f. satire, sarcasm, irony.*
sátirico *adj. satirical.*
SATISFACCIÓN *f. satisfaction; pleasure; apology.*
Tuve la satisfacción de conocerla. *I had the pleasure of meeting her.*
Eso fué una gran satisfacción para mí. *That was a great satisfaction for me.*
El dió un suspiro de satisfacción. *He gave a sigh of relief.*
A satisfacción. *To one's satisfaction. Satisfactorily.*
Dar satisfacciones. *To apologize.*
SATISFACER *to satisfy; to please; to pay (debt); to gratify.*
No me satisface su trabajo. *His work doesn't satisfy me.*
Eso no me satisface. *I'm not satisfied with that. That isn't satisfactory to me.*
Satisfacer una deuda. *To pay a debt.*
satisfactorio *adj. satisfactory.*
SATISFECHO *adj. satisfied, content.*
Deseamos que todos estén satisfechos. *We want everyone to be satisfied.*
Hágalo Ud. de modo que él quede satisfecho. *Do it in a way that will please him.*
No deseo comer más, estoy satisfecho. *I don't want to eat any more, I've had enough.*
sauce *m. willow.*
sazón *f. maturity; seasoning, taste, flavor; opportunity.*
A la sazón estaba yo en Inglaterra. *At that time I was in England.*
En sazón. *In season. Ripe. Seasonably.*
sazonado *adj. seasoned; ripe; expressive.*
Un plato bien sazonado. *A well-seasoned dish.*
sazonar *to season; to mature, to ripen.*
SE *(third person object and reflexive pronoun) to him, to her, to it, to you, etc.; self, oneself, himself, herself, itself, etc. (Se is often used as a reciprocal pronoun and also to introduce the passive form.)*
Se lo diré. *I'll tell it to him.*
Se dice. *It's said.*
¡Figúrese Ud.! *Just imagine!*
Se me figura. *I can imagine.*
Déselo. *Give it to him.*
Lávese. *Wash yourself.*
Se engañan. *They're fooling themselves.*
Se conocen. *They know each other (one another).*
Se aman. *They love each other.*
¿Cómo se llama Ud.? *What's your name?*
Se sabe. *It's known.*
No se sabe. *No one knows.*
Se habla español. *Spanish spoken here.*

Se alquila. *For rent.*
Se prohibe fumar. *No smoking allowed.*
SÉ *(imperative of ser and first person indicative of saber) be; I know.*
Sé bueno. *Be good.*
No lo sé. *I don't know.*
seca *f. drought, dry season.*
Lo dijo a secas. *He told it in a matter-of-fact way ("dryly").*
secante *m. blotter, blotting paper; f. secant.*
¿Dónde está el secante? *Where's the blotter?*
SECAR *to dry, to desiccate; to wipe.*
Hay que secar los platos. *We have to dry the dishes.*
Séquese bien. *Dry yourself well (thoroughly).*
Puso a secar la ropa cerca del fuego. *He put the clothes near the fire to dry.*
sección *f. section; division; department; cutting.*
¿En qué sección trabaja Ud.? *In what section (division) do you work?*
SECO *adj. dry; withered; lean; curt; rude.*
Tengo la garganta seca. *My throat is dry.*
Quiero que me limpie en seco este traje. *I'd like this suit dry-cleaned.*
Era un hombre muy seco. *He was a very curt ("dry") person.*
Consérvese seco. *Keep dry.*
"Consérvese en un lugar seco." *"Keep in a dry place."*
Clima seco. *Dry climate.*
Vino seco. *Dry wine.*
Lavar en seco. *To dryclean.*
secretamente *secretly.*
secretaria *f. woman secretary.*
secretaría *f. secretaryship; secretary's office.*
secretario *m. secretary.*
secreto *adj. secret; private; m. secret; secrecy; mystery.*
Lo he guardado en secreto. *I've kept it a secret.*
Temo que Ud. no guarde el secreto. *I'm afraid you won't keep the secret.*
Era un secreto a voces. *It was an open secret.*
secuestro *m. kidnapping.*
secundar *to second, to back up, to aid.*
Lo secunda en todo y por todo. *He supports him in everything ("and for everything").*
secundario *adj. secondary, subsidiary.*
SED *f. thirst; desire; craving.*
Tengo sed. *I'm thirsty.*
seda *f. silk.*
Tiene la piel como seda. *Her skin is soft as silk.*
Papel de seda. *Tissue paper.*
Ir como seda. *To go smoothly (without a hitch). To work like magic (like a charm). To be smooth sailing.*
sedería *f. silks, silk goods; silk shop.*
sedición *f. sedition, mutiny.*
sediento *adj. thirsty.*
sedimento *m. sediment.*
seducir *to seduce; to tempt, to fascinate; to bribe.*
segadora *f. reaper, harvester (machine).*
segar *to reap; to mow.*
segregar *to segregate, to separate.*
SEGUIDA *f. succession, continuation.*
En seguida. *Right away. Immediately.*
¡Venga en seguida! *Come right away!*
De seguida. *Successively. In succession.*
seguidamente *successively; immediately after, right after that, then.*
seguidilla *f. seguidilla (a lively Spanish dance); the song and music that go with it.*
seguido *adj. continued; straight (ahead).*

Vaya todo seguido y luego tome la bocacalle a la mano derecha. *Go straight ahead and then take the side street to your right.*
SEGUIR *to follow; to pursue; to continue, to go on, to keep on.*
Sígame. *Follow me.*
Le sigo a Ud. *I'll follow you.*
Seguiré sus consejos. *I'll follow your advice.*
¡Siga adelante! 1. *Go straight ahead!* 2. *Go ahead! Continue!*
Siga derecho. *Keep straight ahead.*
¿Qué sigue después? *What comes afterwards?*
Como sigue: *As follows:*
Siga tal como empezó. *Go on just as you started.*
Siguió hablando. *He went on talking. He kept (on) talking.*
La situación sigue de mal en peor. *The situation is going from bad to worse.*
El herido sigue mejor. *The wounded man is improving.*
Seguía diluviando. *It was still pouring.*
Sigo sin comprender. *I still don't understand.*
SEGÚN *according to; in the same way as, just as; it depends.*
Según el informe que me dió. *According to the report he gave me.*
Esto está hecho según los planos. *This was done according to plans.*
Claro que esto es según se mire. *Of course, this depends on how you look at it.*
Según vayan llegando hágalos Ud. entrar. *Have them enter in their order of arrival.*
Según y conforme. *That depends.*
¿Irá Ud.?—Según y cómo. *Will you go?—That all depends.*
SEGUNDO *adj. and n. second; mate (of a ship).*
Espéreme un segundo, ahora vuelvo. *Wait a second, I'll be right back.*
Ella vive en el segundo piso. *She lives on the second floor.*
¿Qué tomo desea Ud., el primero o el segundo? *Which volume do you want, the first or second?*
Segunda velocidad. *Second gear.*
En segundo lugar. *In the second place. Secondly. On second thought.*
Un billete de segunda. *A coach ticket. ("A second-class ticket.")*
De segunda mano. *Secondhand.*
seguramente *certainly, surely.*
Seguramente que sí. *Yes, certainly.*
seguridad *f. security; certainty; safety.*
Puede Ud. tener la seguridad de que lo haré. *You may be sure that I'll do it.*
Con toda seguridad. *With absolute certainty.*
Para mayor seguridad. *For safety's sake. For greater safety.*
SEGURO *adj. secure, sure, safe, certain; m. insurance; safety; stop, safety catch.*
¿No está Ud. seguro? *Aren't you sure?*
Tener por seguro. *To be sure. To consider certain.*
Ir sobre seguro. *To be on safe ground.*
A buen seguro. *Certainly.*
Compañía de seguros. *Insurance company.*
Póliza de seguro. *Insurance policy.*
Prima de seguro. *Insurance premium.*
Seguro de vida. *Life insurance.*
Seguro contra incendios. *Fire insurance.*
Tomar un seguro. *To take out insurance. To take out an insurance policy.*
SEIS *adj. and n. six; sixth.*

seiscientos *adj. and n. six hundred; six hundredth.*

selección *f. selection, choice, digest.*

selecto *adj. select; distinguished.*
Había un público muy selecto. *There was a very distinguished audience.*

selva *f. forest, woods.*

sellar *to seal; to stamp.*
¿Es necesario sellar esta carta con lacre? *Is it necessary to use sealing wax on this letter?*
Selle Ud esas localidades. *Stamp those tickets.*

SELLO *m. seal; stamp; postage stamp.*
El sello se despegó. *The stamp came off.*
Sello de urgencia. Sello de entrega inmediata. *Special delivery stamp.*

semáforo *m. semaphore.*

SEMANA *f. week; week's pay.*
Voy al cine cada semana. *I go to the movies every week.*
Lo veremos la semana que viene. *We'll see him next week.*
Al parecer vendrá la semana próxima. *Apparently he's coming next week. It seems he's coming next week.*
Le semana pasada. *Last week.*
En una semana más o menos. *In a week or so.*
Semana inglesa. *Five-day week.*
Semana Santa. *Holy Week (Easter).*
Un día entre semana. *A weekday.*
A la semana. *Per week.*
Hace una semana. *A week ago.*

semanal *adj. weekly.*
Una revista semanal. *A weekly magazine.*

semanalmente *weekly, by the week, every week.*
Esta revista sale semanalmente. *This magazine appears every week.*

semanario *adj. weekly; m. weekly publication.*

semblante *m. countenance, look; aspect.*
Hoy tiene Ud. muy buen semblante. *You look very well today.*

sembrar *to sow; to scatter, to spread.*

semejante *adj. similar; such; m. fellow man.*
¿Tiene Ud. algo semejante? *Do you have something (anything) similar?*
Los dos relatos son muy semejantes. *The two stories are very similar.*
No creo en semejante cosa. *I don't believe such a thing.*
Piense que son sus semejantes. *Remember that they are your fellow men.*

semejanza *f. similarity, resemblance, likeness.*

semejar *to resemble, to be like.*

semestral *adj. semi-annually.*

semestre *m. space of six months, half-year, semester; half-year's income or pension.*

semi *(prefix) semi, half, partially.*
Semicircular. *Semi-circular.*
Semibreve. *Semi-breve.*

semilla *f. seed.*

seminario *m. seminary.*

seminarista *m. seminarist.*

sempiterno *adj. everlasting.*

senado *m. senate.*

senador *m. senator.*

sencillez *f. simplicity, lack of affectation, plainness; candor.*
Atraía por la sencillez de su carácter. *She attracted people by her lack of affectation.*
Vestía con mucha sencillez. *She dressed very simply.*

SENCILLO *adj. simple; plain; single.*
Era un problema muy sencillo. *It was a very simple problem.*

Aquel trabajo era muy sencillo. *That work (job) was very simple.*
Un vestido sencillo. *A plain dress.*
Le apuesto doble contra sencillo. *I'll bet you two to one.*

senda *f. path, footpath.*

sendero *m. path, footpath.*

senil *adj. senile.*

seno *m. breast, bosom; lap; sinus; womb.*

sensación *f. sensation.*

sensacional *adj. sensational.*

sensatez *f. good sense, discretion.*

sensato *adj. sensible, discreet.*

sensibilidad *f. sensibility; sensitivity.*

SENSIBLE *adj. sensitive; regrettable; f. sensible, seventh note (music).*
Los ojos son sensibles a la luz. *The eyes are sensitive to light.*
Es una chica muy sensible. *She's a very sensitive girl.*
Un corazón sensible. *A tender heart.*
Una pérdida sensible. *A regrettable loss.*

sensual *adj. sensual, voluptuous.*

sensualidad *f. sensuality, lust.*

sentado *adj. seated; judicious; sensible.*
Estaba sentado a mi izquierda. *He was sitting on my left.*
Dar por sentado. *To take for granted.*
Puede esperar sentado. *You'll have to wait for it till doomsday.*

SENTAR *to fit, to be becoming; to agree with one (food, etc.); to seat.*
Este sombrero le sienta divinamente. *This hat is very becoming to you.*
¿No le ha sentado bien el desayuno? *Didn't your breakfast agree with you?*
Le sentará muy bien un descanso. *A rest will do him good.*
Sentar plaza. *To enlist (as a soldier).*
Sentarle a alguien. *To fit (referring to clothing).*

SENTARSE *to sit down, to take a seat.*
Sentémonos aquí. *Let's sit down here.*
¿Dónde me siento? *Where shall I sit?*
Siéntese Ud. en esta butaca. *Sit down in this armchair.*
Los invitados se sentaron a la mesa. *The guests sat at the table.*

sentencia *f. sentence, verdict; maxim.*

sentenciar *to sentence.*

sentencioso *adj. sententious.*

SENTIDO *adj. felt; experienced; offended; disgusted; touchy; m. sense; meaning; understanding; direction.*
Es muy sentida. *She's very touchy.*
Está sentida con ellos. *She's disgusted with them.*
Su muerte fué muy sentida. *His death affected everyone deeply.*
En el sentido de. *In the sense of.*
Sin sentido. *Senseless. Meaningless.*
Carece de lógica y de sentido común. *It lacks logic and common sense.*
No lo tome Ud. en ese sentido. *Don't take it that way. I didn't mean it that way.*
Caminaba en sentido contrario. *He was walking in the opposite direction.*
Pondré mis cinco sentidos al hacerlo. *I'll put everything I've got into it.*
Perder el sentido. *To become unconscious.*

sentimental *adj. sentimental, showing a great deal of feeling.*
Es muy sentimental. *She's very sentimental.*

sentimentalismo *m. sentimentalism.*

sentimiento *m. sentiment, feeling; grief; resentment.*
Era persona de malos sentimientos. *He was a malicious person.*
Le acompaño a Ud. en el sentimiento. *I'm very sorry to hear about your loss.*

SENTIR *to feel; to be sorry; to grieve; to hear; to sense; to be (happy, cold, warm, etc.); m. feeling; opinion.*
Lo siento muchísimo. *I'm very sorry.*
Siento no poder ir. *I'm sorry I can't go.*
Siento haberme retrasado tanto. *I'm sorry to be so late.*
Sentí en el alma la pérdida de tan fiel amigo. *I felt very deeply the loss of such a faithful friend.*
Ahora siento frío. *I'm cold now.*
Siento mucha alegría. *I'm very happy (glad).*
Pasaron las horas sin sentir. *The hours passed without our knowing it. Time passed without our noticing it.*
Siento que viene alguien. *I hear someone coming.*
Díganos cuál es su sentir. *Tell us how you feel (about it).*
Es de sentir. *It's to be regretted. It's regrettable.*
Dar que sentir. *To hurt one's feelings.*

SENTIRSE *to resent; to feel (well, sick, sad, etc.); to ache; to crack (a wall, etc.).*
¿Se siente Ud. mejor? *Do you feel better?*
Me siento mal. *I don't feel well.*
¿Siente Ud. dolor en la espalda? *Do you have a backache?*
Se siente del pecho. *His chest aches.*
No tenía porque sentirse molesto. *He has no reason to feel annoyed.*

SEÑA *f. signal; sign, mark, password; pl. address.*
¿Cuáles son sus señas? *What's your address?*
Escriba Ud. a estas señas. *Write to this address.*
No dejaron ni señas del pastel. *They ate up every bit of the cake. ("They didn't leave a sign of the cake.")*
Hacer señas. *To motion. To signal.*

SEÑAL *f. sign, mark; signal; trace; scar; deposit (paid as a pledge); token.*
Esta es la mejor señal de mejoría. *That's the best sign of improvement.*
Ponga una señal en esa página. *Put a mark on that page. Mark that page.*
La señal de alarma. *The alarm signal.*
Se daba a entender por señales. *He made himself understood by signs.*
¿Quiere Ud. que deje algún dinero en señal? *Do you want me to leave you some money as a deposit?*
Tiene una señal en la cara. *He has a scar on his face.*
Para más pelos y señales. *In more detail.*
En señal de. *As a token of. In proof of.*
Código de señales. *Signal code.*

señalado *adj. distinguished, noted; marked; appointed (time).*
Al (en el) tiempo señalado. *At the appointed time.*

señalar *to mark; to signal; to point out; to set (the date).*
Hay que señalar el día de la reunión. *The date of the meeting must be set.*
Señale Ud. los errores que encuentre. *Point out the errors you find.*
Señalar con el dedo. *To point one's finger at. To point.*

SEÑOR *m. mister, sir; gentleman; master; lord.*

Señor Navarro. *Mr. Navarro (used when addressing the person directly).*

Buenos días, señor Navarro. *Good morning, Mr. Navarro.*

El señor Navarro no podrá venir. *Mr. Navarro will not come (used when speaking of the person).*

Gracias, señor. *Thank you, sir.*

El gusto es mío, señor. *The pleasure is mine, sir.*

El señor es inglés. *The gentleman is an Englishman (is English).*

Hay un señor esperándole. *There's a gentleman waiting for him.*

Los señores de Sucre. *Mr. and Mrs. Sucre.*

SEÑORA *f. Mrs., madam, lady; wife.*

Señora de García. *Mrs. García (direct address).*

La señora de García. *Mrs. García (when speaking of the person).*

¿Puedo hablar con la señora de Navarro? *May I speak to Mrs. Navarro?*

La señora no está en casa. *The lady of the house is not at home.*

Sí, señora. *Yes, madam.*

Mucho gusto en conocer a Ud., señora. *I'm very happy (pleased) to know you, madam.*

A los pies de Ud., señora. *Your humble servant, madam. ("At your feet, madam.")*

Déle una silla a esta señora. *Give this lady a chair.*

¿Cómo está su señora? *How is your wife?*

SEÑORITA *f. miss; young lady.*

Mucho gusto en conocerla, señorita Navarro. *I'm very glad to meet you, Miss Navarro.*

Que pase la señorita Navarro. *Have Miss Navarro come in. Ask Miss Navarro to come in.*

Esta señorita es norteamericana. *This young lady is an American.*

separación *f. separation.*

separar *to separate.*

Separe Ud. los grandes de los pequeños. *Separate the large ones from the small.*

Una cortina separa las dos habitaciones. *A curtain divides the two rooms.*

Separe Ud. un poco la mesa de la pared. *Move the table from the wall a bit.*

separarse *to part company; to get out of the way; to retire (from business, etc.).*

Decidieron separarse legalmente. *They decided to separate legally.*

SEPTIEMBRE *m. September.*

séptimo *adj. seventh.*

septuagenario *adj. and n. septuagenarian.*

sepulcro *m. grave, tomb, sepulcher.*

sepultar *to bury, to inter; to hide.*

sepultura *f. burial; grave; tomb.*

sequedad *f. dryness.*

sequía *f. drought, lack of rain.*

ser *m. being, creature.*

Ser viviente. *Living being. Living creature.*

Seres humanos. *Human beings.*

SER *to be.*

¿Quién es? *Who is it?*

Soy yo. *It's me (I).*

¿Quién será? *Who can it be?*

¿Es Ud. el Sr. Smith? *Are you Mr. Smith?*

¿De dónde es Ud.? *Where are you from?*

Soy de Boston. *I'm from Boston.*

Somos norteamericanos. *We're Americans.*

Somos viejos amigos. *We are old friends.*

¿Qué será de él? *What will become of him?*

¿En qué puedo serle útil? *What can I do for*

you? Can I help you?

¿De quién es este lápiz? *Whose pencil is this?*

Es mío. *It's mine.*

Es de Juan. *It belongs to John.*

¿De quién será esta casa? *Whose house can (could) this be?*

Es la casa de Juan. *It's John's house.*

¿De qué es esta maleta? *What is this suitcase made of?*

Es una maleta de cuero. *It's a leather suitcase. It's made of leather.*

¿Cómo es? *How is it?*

Es algo sordo. *He's rather hard of hearing.*

¿Es guapa la hija? *Is the daughter pretty?*

Es guapísima. *She's very pretty.*

¿Qué es Ud.? *What are you?*

Yo soy escritor. *I'm a writer.*

¿Qué es su hermano? *What is your brother? What does your brother do?*

Es médico. *He is a doctor.*

¿Qué es eso? *What is that?*

¿Cuánto es? *How much is it?*

¿Qué tal ha sido el viaje? *How was the trip?*

¿Qué hora es? *What time is it?*

Es la una. *It's one o'clock.*

Son las dos. *It's two o'clock.*

¿Qué hora será? *I wonder what time it is.*

Ya son las doce pasadas. *It's after twelve. It's past twelve already.*

Son más de las diez. *It's after ten o'clock.*

Es temprano todavía. *It's still early.*

¿Cuándo será la boda? *When will the wedding take place?*

¿Qué fecha es hoy? *What's the date today?*

¿Qué día es hoy? *What day is today?*

Hoy es lunes. *Today is Monday.*

Mañana será otro día. *Tomorrow is another day.*

Es fácil. *It's easy.*

Es difícil. *It's difficult.*

¿Es verdad? *Is it true?*

No es verdad. *It's not true.*

No creo que sea cierto. *I don't believe it's (that's) true.*

¿Será posible? *Would that be possible?*

Puede ser. *That may be. Maybe. Perhaps.*

Eso no puede ser. *That can't be.*

¿Quién quiere ser mano? *Who wants to deal first (cards)?*

Después llegaron a ser buenos amigos. *Afterwards they became good friends.*

Eso no era con Ud. *It wasn't meant for you.*

Haré por Ud. cuanto me sea posible. *I'll do as much as I can for you.*

¿Qué ha sido de su amigo? *What became of your friend?*

Sea Ud. puntual. *Be on time.*

No seas tonto. *Don't be foolish.*

No sea Ud. inoportuno. *Don't come at the wrong time (do things at the wrong time, ¡say the wrong things).*

¡Sé bueno, hijo mío! *Be good, my child!*

Ha llegado a ser gerente. *He became manager.*

Sea quien fuera. *Whoever he might be.*

Son tal para cual. *They're two of a kind.*

serenamente *coolly, calmly.*

serenar *to clear up; to calm down; to pacify.*

Está serenando. *It's clearing up.*

¡Serénese Ud.! *Calm yourself! Calm down!*

serenata *f. serenade.*

serenidad *f. serenity, coolness.*

sereno *adj. serene, calm; clear (sky); m. dew; night watchman.*

Era un hombre sereno. *He was a calm man. He was very calm.*

El cielo está muy sereno. *The sky is very clear.*

Hay mucho sereno en las flores. *There's a lot of dew on the flowers.*

Esta calle no tiene sereno. *This street has no night watchman.*

serie *f. series.*

Pertenece a la serie A. *It belongs to series A.*

seriedad *f. seriousness, reliability; earnestness.*

SERIO *adj. serious; earnest; businesslike.*

Es un hombre serio. *He's businesslike.*

La situación se pone seria. *The situation is becoming serious.*

Lo dijo en serio. *He said it in earnest.*

Hablando en serio, eso no está bien. *Joking apart, that's wrong.*

Tomar en serio. *To take seriously.*

sermón *m. sermon; lecture, reproof.*

serpiente *f. serpent.*

serrano *m. mountaineer.*

serrar *to saw.*

servicial *adj. serviceable; obliging, accommodating.*

SERVICIO *m. service, favor, good turn; set, service.*

Servicio de mesa. *Table service.*

Me ha prestado Ud. un gran servicio. *You've done me a great favor. ("You've rendered me a great service.")*

Ud. podría hacerme un gran servicio. *You could do me a great favor.*

Se quejó del servicio en el hotel. *He complained about the service in the hotel.*

El servicio de trenes es muy malo aquí. *The train service is very bad here.*

Es muy difícil conseguir servicio doméstico. *It's very difficult to get any domestic help.*

Tenemos que tomar en cuenta sus buenos servicios. *We must take into consideration the work he did.*

De servicio. *On duty.*

Estar a servicio de. *To be working for.*

servidor *m. servant, waiter.*

¡Servidor de Ud.! *At your service. ("Your servant.")*

"Quedo de Ud. atento y seguro servidor." *"Sincerely yours."*

Tiene muy buenos servidores. *She has excellent servants.*

servidumbre *f. servants, help; servitude.*

servil *adj. servile, low, mean.*

servilleta *f. napkin.*

SERVIR *to serve; to do a favor; to do for, to be useful, to answer the purpose; to be for; to wait on (the table).*

Para servir a Ud. *At your service.*

¿En qué puedo servirle? *What can I do for you? Can I help you?*

¿Le sirvo a Ud. un poco de vino? *Shall I give (serve) you a little wine?*

Permítame servirle otra taza de café. *Let me give you another cup of coffee.*

La comida está servida. *Dinner is served.*

El camarero sirvió a la mesa. *The waiter waited on the table.*

¿Para qué sirve esta máquina? *What's this machine for?*

Sirvió cuatro años en las fuerzas aéreas. *He was in the Air Corps for four years.*

No lo tire, que puede servir para algo. *Don't throw it away! It may be good for something.*

No sirve. *It's no good.*

No sirve para nada. *It's no good. It's good for nothing. It's worthless.*

El puede servir de intérprete. *He can act as interpreter.*

De nada le servirá escribirles. *Writing to them won't do you any good.*

servirse *to deign, to please; to help oneself (food); to make use of.*

Sírvase venir conmigo. *Please come with me.*

Tenga la bondad de servirse. *Please help yourself.*

Me sirvo del diccionario para traducir. *I use the dictionary for translating.*

SESENTA *adj. and n. sixty.*

sesentón *m. sexagenarian.*

sesgo *adj. sloped, oblique; m. slope; slant, bias.*

Tomar mal sesgo. *To take a bad turn. To take a turn for the worse. To look bad.*

sesión *f. session, meeting.*

En sesión. *In session.*

SESO *m. brain; brains.*

Devanarse los sesos. *To rack one's brains.*

Perder el seso. *To lose one's head.*

No tiene sesos. *He has no brains (coll.).*

seta *f. mushroom.*

setecientos *adj. and n. seven hundred; seven hundredth.*

SETENTA *adj. and n. seventy.*

setentón *m. septuagenarian.*

seudónimo *adj. relating to a pseudonym; m. pseudonym; pen name.*

severidad *f. severity, strictness.*

severo *adj. severe, strict.*

sexo *m. sex.*

sexteto *m. sextet, sextette.*

sexto *adj. sixth.*

SI *conj. if; whether; m. si, B (the seventh note of the musical scale).*

Si Ud. quiere. *If you like.*

Si Ud. gusta. *If you please.*

Si tuviese dinero, lo compraría. *I'd buy it if I had money.*

Si le parece nos citamos para las cuatro. *Let's meet at four o'clock if that's convenient for you.*

Si bien. *Although.*

Si por acaso. *If by any chance. In case.*

¡Si lo acabo de ver! *But I just saw it!*

Si no. *If not. Otherwise.*

SÍ *adv. yes; indeed; refl. pron. himself, herself, itself, oneself, themselves; m. consent, assent.*

Sí señor. *Yes, sir.*

Pues sí. *Yes, indeed.*

¿Sí o no? *Yes or no?*

Le dije que sí. *I told him yes.*

Eso sí que no. *I should say not.*

Creo que sí. *I think so.*

Espero que sí. *I hope so.*

Habla demasiado de sí misma. *She talks too much about herself.*

Lo quiere para sí. *He wants it for himself.*

Todavía no ha vuelto en sí. *He hasn't recovered consciousness yet.*

Estaban fuera de sí. *They were beside themselves (with anger, etc.).*

Reírse entre sí. *To laugh up one's sleeve.*

¡A que sí? *I'll bet I do.*

De sí. *Spontaneously. Of itself (himself, etc.).*

Lo dijo de sí. *He said it spontaneously (of his own accord).*

Dar el sí. *To say yes. To give one's consent. To accept a marriage proposal.*

sidra *f. cider.*

siega. *f. harvest.*

siembra *f. sowing; seedtime; sown ground.*

SIEMPRE *always; ever.*

Siempre llega tarde. *He's always late.*

Es lo de siempre. *It's the same old story.*

Siempre que pueda le escribiré. *I'll write you provided I'm able.*

Para siempre. *For good. Forever.*

Para siempre jamás. *Forever (and ever).*

siempreviva *f. everlasting, immortelle (plant).*

sien *f. temple.*

sierra *f. saw; sierra, mountain range.*

No corta bien la sierra. *The saw doesn't cut well.*

La Sierra Madre está en Mexico. *Sierra Madre is in Mexico.*

siesta *f. siesta, nap.*

¿Va Ud. a dormir la siesta? *Are you going to take your nap?*

SIETE *adj. and n. seven.*

sigilo *m. seal, secrecy; discretion; caution.*

Obra con sigilo. *He acts cautiously.*

sigiloso *adj. secretive; reserved.*

SIGLO *m. century, age; a long time.*

Vivió en el siglo décimo. *He lived in the tenth century.*

Hace un siglo que no le veo. *I haven't seen him for ages.*

El Siglo de Oro. *The Golden Age.*

significación *f. signification; significance, meaning.*

significado *m. significance; meaning.*

¿Cuál es el significado de esta palabra en inglés? *What does that word mean in English?*

SIGNIFICAR *to mean, to signify.*

¿Qué significa eso? *What's the meaning of that? What does that mean?*

No sé qué significa esa palabra. *I don't know what that word means. I don't know the meaning of that word.*

significativo *adj. significant.*

signo *m. sign, mark.*

El signo de la cruz. *The sign of the cross.*

SIGUIENTE *adj. following, next.*

Al día siguiente. *On the following day. On the next day.*

La página siguiente. *The next page.*

La aduana está en la siguiente cuadra. *The customhouse is on the next block.*

Lo siguiente: *The following:*

sílaba *f. syllable.*

silbar *to whistle; to hiss, to boo.*

El público silbó la comedia. *The audience booed the comedy. (Whistling indicates disapproval in Spanish-speaking countries.)*

silbido *m. whistling, whistle; hiss.*

silencio *m. silence; quiet.*

¡Silencio! *Silence!*

Todo estaba en silencio. *Everything was quiet.*

Su silencio me inquieta. *I'm worried because I haven't had any word from her.*

Eso lo pasó Ud. en silencio. *You avoided mentioning that.*

Sufrir en silencio. *To suffer in silence.*

silencioso *adj. silent, noiseless.*

Quiero una máquina de escribir silenciosa. *I want a noiseless typewriter.*

silueta *f. silhouette.*

silvestre *adj. wild, rustic, uncultivated.*

Flores silvestres. *Wild flowers.*

SILLA *f. chair; saddle.*

Ponga la silla aquí. *Put the chair here.*

Ponga al caballo la silla. *Put the saddle on the horse. Saddle the horse.*

sillón *m. armchair.*

simbólico *adj. symbolic.*

simbolizar *to symbolize.*

símbolo *m. symbol.*

simetría *f. symmetry.*

simétrico *adj. symmetrical.*

SIMILAR *adj. similar, resembling. (See parecido.)*

Es un producto similar. *This is a similar product.*

similitud *f. resemblance, similarity, similitude.*

simpatía *f. sympathy, liking.*

Le inspiró mucho simpatía. *He found him (her) very congenial.*

simpático *adj. nice, pleasant, congenial, nice.*

Es muy simpático. *He's very nice. He's very congenial.*

simpatizar *to sympathize; to like.*

SIMPLE *adj. simple; plain; silly, foolish; m. fool; simple (pharm.).*

Por la simple razón. *For the simple reason. A simple vista. At first sight.*

El procedimiento es muy simple. *The system is very simple.*

Es una mujer muy simple. *She's a very simple woman.*

A un simple cualquiera le engaña. *Anyone can cheat a fool.*

simplemente *simply, merely.*

Eso es simplemente un detalle. *That's simply a detail.*

simpleza *f. naivete, foolishness.*

simplicidad *f. simplicity.*

simplificar *to simplify.*

simulación *f. simulation; fake.*

simulacro *m. sham, feign.*

simulado *adj. simulated, sham.*

simular *to simulate, to feign, to sham.*

simultáneo *adj. simultaneous.*

SIN *without, besides.*

Iremos sin él. *We'll go without him.*

No puedo leer sin mis anteojos. *I can't read without my glasses.*

Lo hice sin pensar. *I did it without thinking.*

Lo hice sin querer. *I did it without meaning to. I didn't mean to do it.*

Estaba sin dinero. *He was penniless.*

Es un hombre sin educación. *He's ill-bred.*

Es una mujer sin par. *She's in a class by herself. There's no one like her.*

Me he quedado sin gasolina. *I've run out of gas.*

Sin falta. *Without fail.*

Sin duda. *Without a doubt. Undoubtedly.*

Sin novedad. *Nothing new. The same as usual.*

Sin embargo. *Nevertheless. Notwithstanding.*

Un sin fin de cosas. *A million and one things.*

sinceridad *f. sincerity.*

sincero *adj. sincere.*

Es un amigo sincero. *He's a true friend.*

síncope *f. faint, fainting spell.*

sincronizar *to synchronize.*

sindical *adj. pertaining to a trade union.*

sindicato *m. trade union; syndicate.*

sinfonía *f. symphony.*

sinfónico *adj. symphonic.*

SINGULAR *adj. singular; unusual; exceptional; strange, odd.*

"Niño" es singular, y "niños" es plural. *"Boy" is singular, "boys" plural.*

¡Qué caso tan singular! *What a strange case!*

Es un hombre singular. *He's an exceptional man.*

Es un caso singularísimo. *It's a very singular (unusual) case.*

singularidad *f. singularity; peculiarity.*

siniestro *adj. sinister; unfortunate; m. shipwreck, damage.*

Lado siniestro. *Left side.*

Tiene un aspecto siniestro. *It looks sinister. It has a sinister look.*

¿Dónde ocurrió el siniestro? *Where did the shipwreck occur?*

sinnúmero *m. a great many, too many, numberless, no end.*

SINO *(used after a negative) but, except; only; instead; m. fate, luck.*

No es rojo sino rosado. *It's not red, but pink.*

No iré hoy, sino mañana. *I'll go tomorrow instead of today.*

Nadie puede hacerlo sino tú. *No one but you can do it.*

No piensa sino en sí mismo. *He only thinks of himself.*

Es su triste sino. *It's his hard luck.*

sinónimo *adj. synonymous; m. synonym.*

sintaxis *f. syntax.*

síntesis *f. synthesis.*

sintético *adj. synthetic.*

síntoma *f. symptom.*

sintonizar *to tune in (radio).*

sinvergüenza *m. and f. shameless person.*

SIQUIERA *at least; even; although.*

Siquiera un poquito. *Even a little bit.*

Ni siquiera eso. *Not even that.*

Una vez siquiera. *Once at least.*

Déme siquiera agua fría. *At least give me some cold water.*

Ni me dió las gracias siquiera. *He didn't even thank me.*

sirena *f. siren; whistle; foghorn; mermaid.*

sirviente *m. servant.*

sisa *f. petty theft.*

sisar *to steal small quantities of something; to take in (sewing).*

sistema *m. system.*

Sistema métrico. *Metric system.*

sistemático *adj. systematic.*

sitiar *to besiege.*

SITIO *m. place; space, room; m. siege.*

Ponlo otra vez en su sitio. *Put it back in the same place.*

No hay bastante sitio para todos. *There isn't enough room for everybody.*

Ocupe Ud. su sitio. *Take your seat.*

Me ofreció un sitio en su coche. *He offered me a lift ("seat") in his car.*

Está en algún sitio en la casa. *It's somewhere around the house.*

¿En qué sitio le duele? *Where does it hurt you?*

Hacer sitio. *To make room.*

Poner sitio. *To besiege.*

SITUACIÓN *f. situation; position; circumstances; site, location.*

Está en mala situación. *He's in a bad situation.*

situado *adj. situated, located; m. allowance, annuity.*

situar *to place, to locate; to situate; to allot funds.*

situarse *to place oneself, to settle in a place.*

so *under, below.*

So (capa) pretexto de. *Under the pretext of.*

So pena de. *Under penalty of.*

sobar *to knead; to soften; to pummel; to pet; to beat, to whip.*

soberanía *f. sovereignty.*

soberano *adj. and n. sovereign.*

soberbia *f. pride, haughtiness.*

soberbio *adj. proud, haughty; ill-tempered; superb; magnificent.*

Un edificio soberbio. *A magnificent building.*

Es muy soberbio. *He's very proud.*

sobornar *to suborn, to bribe.*

soborno *m. bribe.*

SOBRA *f. too much, too many, more than is needed; leftover.*

Tengo tiempo de sobra. *I've plenty of time.*

Tengo de sobra con lo que Ud. me dió. *I've more than enough with what you gave me.*

Estar de sobra. *To be superfluous.*

Tiene Ud. razón de sobra. *You're quite right.*

Hay de sobra. *There's more than enough.*

Aproveche las sobras. *Use up the leftovers.*

sobradamente *abundantly.*

Saber sobradamente. *To know only too well.*

sobrante *adj. remaining; m. remainder, surplus; leftover.*

SOBRAR *to be more than enough; to have more than is needed; to remain; to be left.*

Sobró mucha comida. *A great deal of food was left over.*

Nos sobran poquísimas provisiones. *We've got very few supplies (provisions) left.*

Más vale que sobre que no falte. *It's better to have too much than (to have) too little.*

Me parece que aquí sobro. *It seems to me that I'm intruding ("that I'm one too many") here.*

Sobran cinco. *There are five too many.*

SOBRE *on; over; above; about; m. envelope.*

Ponga el vaso sobre la mesa. *Put the glass on the table.*

Desgracia sobre desgracia. *Misfortune on misfortune. Trouble after trouble. Just one thing after another.*

¿Qué opina Ud. sobre esto? *What do you think about this?*

Tengo noticias ciertas sobre su paradero. *I've got reliable information concerning (about) his whereabouts.*

Ha escrito un libro sobre los Estados Unidos. *He has written a book about the United States.*

¿Sobre qué están discutiendo? *What are they discussing?*

Discurramos un poco más sobre esto. *Let's consider that a little longer.*

Tenía un gran dominio sobre sí. *He had great self-control.*

Sobre las tres. *At about three o'clock.*

Tengo sobre cincuenta dólares. *I have about fifty dollars.*

Estar sobre aviso. *To be on guard.*

Sobre todo. *Above all.*

Sobre que. *Besides.*

Déme un sobre. *Give me an envelope.*

sobrealimentación *f. overfeeding.*

sobrealimentar *to overfeed.*

sobrecama *f. bedspread.*

sobrecarga *f. overload; overcharge.*

sobrecargar *to overload; to overcharge.*

sobrecargo *m. purser; supercargo (on a ship).*

sobrecoger *to surprise, to take by surprise.*

sobreentenderse *to be understood, to go without saying.*

Eso se sobreentiende. *That's understood. That goes without saying.*

sobrellevar *to shoulder, to ease (another's burden); to bear; to endure.*

El es el que sobrelleva toda la carga. *He's the one who shoulders the whole burden.*

Sobrelleva sus penas con paciencia. *He endures his difficulties (troubles) patiently.*

sobremanera *excessively, exceedingly.*

sobremesa *f. table cover; dessert; after dinner; after-dinner talk (around the table).*

Después de comer, fuma su cigarro de sobremesa. *After eating he smokes his after-dinner cigar.*

Estuvimos cerca de una hora de sobremesa. *After dinner we sat around the table and talked for about an hour.*

sobrenatural *adj. and m. supernatural.*

sobrepaga *m. extra pay.*

sobrepasar *to exceed, to surpass.*

sobreponer *to place over; to overlay; to overlap.*

sobreponerse *to master, to overcome; to prevail on another; to show (prove) oneself superior to.*

sobresaliente *adj. outstanding; excelling.*

sobresalir *to stand out, to excel.*

sobresaltar *to frighten, to startle; to assail, to fall upon.*

sobresaltarse *to be frightened, to be startled.*

Se sobresalta por la menor cosa. *The least (little) thing frightens her. She gets frightened at the least (little) thing.*

sobresalto *m. start, shock.*

sobresueldo *m. extra pay; bonus.*

sobrevenir *to happen, to take place; to supervene.*

Sobrevino algo inesperado. *Something unexpected happened.*

sobriedad *f. sobriety, temperance, moderation.*

sobrina *f. niece.*

sobrino *m. nephew.*

sobrio *adj. sober, temperate.*

sociable *adj. sociable.*

social *adj. social.*

Tenía muy buen trato social. *He was very agreeable socially.*

Movimiento social. *Social movement.*

¿Quién representa a esta razón social? *Who's the representative of this firm?*

socialismo *m. socialism.*

socialista *adj. socialistic; m. socialist.*

socializar *to socialize.*

sociedad *f. society; social life; company, corporation; partnership.*

Le gustaba frecuentar la buena sociedad. *He liked to move in society.*

Formaron una sociedad. *They formed a partnership.*

Sociedad anónima. *Corporation.*

socio *m. partner, associate; fellow member.*

Le presento a mi socio, Sr. Smith. *Meet my partner, Mr. Smith.*

¿Es Ud. socio de ese club? *Are you a member of that club?*

sociología *f. sociology.*

sociólogo *m. sociologist.*

socorrer *to aid, to help, to assist; to rescue.*

Hay que socorrerlo. *We have to help him.*

socorro *m. succor, aid, help.*

soda *f. soda.*

soez *adj. indecent, obscene; outspoken, rude, coarse.*

sofá *m. sofa.*

sofocante *adj. suffocating.*

sofocar *to suffocate, to stifle, to choke; to vex; to make a person blush; to put out (fire).*

El calor le ha sofocado. *He was suffocated by the heat.*

No se sofoque Ud. *Don't get excited. Don't overexert yourself.*

Sofocar el fuego. *To put out a fire.*

Sofocar una rebelión. *To crush (subdue) a rebellion.*

sofocón *m. chagrin.*

soga *f. rope; halter, cord.*

SOL *m. sun, sunshine; G, sol (the fifth note of the musical scale).*

Hace sol. *The sun's shining. The sun's out.*

Vamos a tomar el sol. *Let's go for a walk in the sun.*

Antes de bañarse estuvieron tomando el sol mucho rato. *They took a long sunbath before bathing.*

Salida del sol. *Sunrise.*

Puesta del sol. *Sunset.*

De sol a sol. *From sunrise to sunset.*

SOLAMENTE *solely, only.*

Aprendí solamente un poco de español. *I learned only a little Spanish.*

Déme Ud. solamente la mitad. *Give me just half.*

solapa *f. lapel.*

solar *m. lot, plot (land); real estate; mansion.*

solas (a) *all alone, by oneself.*

A mis solas. *By myself. All alone.*

A sus solas. *By himself (herself). All alone.*

SOLDADO *m. soldier, private.*

Soldado raso. *Buck private.*

soldar *to solder; to weld.*

Todavía no han soldado la cañería. *They haven't soldered the pipe yet.*

soledad *f. solitude, loneliness.*

solemne *adj. solemn; serious, grave.*

solemnidad *f. solemnity.*

Pobre de solemnidad. *Very poor.*

SOLER *to be unusual, to be accustomed to, to be in the habit of.*

Suele comer despacio. *He usually eats slowly.*

Suele venir los domingos. *He usually comes on Sundays.*

Como suele acontecer. *As often happens. As is apt to be the case.*

solfear *to sing the scale (music).*

SOLICITAR *to solicit; to ask; to apply for.*

Solicita un empleo. *She's applying for a position.*

Hay que solicitar un permiso para visitar ese edificio. *You'll have to ask for a pass to visit that building.*

Solicitó su mano. *He proposed to her.*

solicitud *f. application; request.*

Llene Ud. el pliego de la solicitud. *Fill out the application.*

solidaridad *f. solidarity.*

solidario *adj. jointly responsible.*

solidez *f. solidity, firmness, soundness.*

SÓLIDO *adj. solid, sound, strong, firm; m. solid.*

Tiene una base muy sólida. *It has a very solid base.*

Cuerpo sólido. *Solid substance.*

Tiene una educación sólida. *He has a sound education.*

solitario *adj. solitary, lonely; m. solitary; hermit; solitaire (game).*

SOLO *adj. alone; single; m. solo (music).*

¿Está Ud. solo? *Are you alone?*

Ni una sola palabra. *Not a single word.*

Quiero estar solo. *I want to be alone.*

Vive solo. *He lives alone.*

Estoy muy solo. *I'm very lonely.*

¿Ha venido Ud. solo? *Have you come alone?*

No lo puedo hacer yo solo. *I can't do this all alone (by myself).*

SÓLO *adv. only, solely.*

Sólo tengo dos pesos. *I have only two dollars.*

Sólo para adultos. *Adults only.*

Hace sólo un rato que almorcé. *I had breakfast only a little while ago.*

Sólo Dios sabe lo que pasará. *(Only) God knows what will happen.*

SOLTAR *to untie, to loosen; to set free; to let out; to let go.*

Soltaron al preso. *They set the prisoner free.*

¡No lo suelte Ud! *Hold it! Don't let go!*

Soltaron las amarras. *They loosened the cables.*

De repente soltó una carcajada. *Suddenly he burst into laughter (burst out laughing).*

Tengo unas ganas de soltarle cuatro frescas a ése. *I would like to give that fellow a piece of my mind.*

soltarse *to get loose; to become wild; to lose restraint, to become more dexterous; to start.*

Se soltó a correr. *He started to run.*

Soltarse el pelo. *To let one's hair down.*

soltero *adj. single, unmarried; m. bachelor.*

¿Es Ud. casado o soltero? *Are you single or married?*

Todavía soy soltero. *I'm still a bachelor.*

solterón *m. old bachelor.*

solterona *f. old maid.*

soltura *f. ease; ability; agility; release; looseness.*

Bailaba con mucha soltura. *She dances with great ease (gracefully).*

Hablar con soltura. *To speak freely.*

soluble *adj. soluble; solvable.*

SOLUCIÓN *f. solution, answer, way out; denouement, outcome (of a plot in a play, story, etc.).*

Esto no tiene solución. *This doesn't have a solution. There's no solution to this.*

¿Dónde encontraré la solución? *Where can I find the answer?*

Esa es la mejor solución. *That's the best way out. That's the best solution.*

solvencia *f. solvency.*

solvente *adj. solvent.*

sollozar *to sob.*

sollozo *m. sob.*

SOMBRA *f. shade; shadow; darkness.*

El termómetro marca treinta grados a la sombra. *The thermometer registers thirty degrees in the shade.*

Se sentó a descansar a la sombra de un árbol. *He sat down to rest in the shade of the tree.*

Le pusieron a la sombra. *They imprisoned him.*

sombrerera *f. milliner; hatbox.*

sombrerería *f. hat shop; millinery.*

sombrerero *m. hatter.*

SOMBRERO *m. hat.*

Se puso el sombrero y salió. *He put on his hat and left.*

Quítese Ud. el sombrero al entrar. *Take off your hat on entering (when you enter).*

sombrilla *f. parasol.*

sombrío *adj. shady; gloomy.*

Tenía un semblante muy sombrío. *He had a very gloomy face.*

someter *to subject; to subdue; to put (to a test); to submit.*

Fué difícil someter a los rebeldes. *It was difficult to subdue the rebels.*

Someta Ud. esto a un nuevo estudio. *Give it further study.*

somnámbulo *m. sleepwalker, somnambulist. (Also written sonámbulo.)*

SON *m. sound, tune; guise; a Cuban musical rhythm.*

¿A son de qué? *Why? For what reason?*

En son de. *In the guise of. As.*

En son de broma. *As a joke.*

Sin son ni ton. *Without rhyme or reason.*

Bailar uno al son que le tocan. *To adapt oneself to the circumstances.*

sonaja *f. jingles; tambourine.*

sonámbulo *m. sleepwalker.*

SONAR *to sound; to ring; to be mentioned, to sound familiar.*

Esa nota no me suena bien. *That note doesn't sound right.*

Suena el timbre. *The bell's ringing.*

Ese nombre no me suena. *That name doesn't sound familiar to me.*

Suena mucho su nombre para candidato. *His name is often mentioned as a candidate.*

Sonó un disparo. *There was the sound of a shot.*

sonarse *to blow one's nose.*

sonata *f. sonata.*

sondar *(See sondear.)*

sondear *to sound, to fathom; to find out, to learn about.*

Estuvieron sondeando la bahía. *They were sounding the bay.*

Sondee Ud. sus intenciones. *Find out his intentions. Sound him out.*

soneto *m. sonnet.*

sonido *m. sound.*

sonoridad *f. sonority.*

sonoro *adj. sonorous; sounding.*

Tiene una voz muy sonora. *He has a sonorous voice.*

Una película sonora (hablada). *A talking picture. A sound film.*

sonreír *to smile.*

Todos sonrieron satisfechos. *Everyone smiled with satisfaction.*

sonrisa *f. smile.*

Una amable sonrisa. *A pleasant smile.*

sonrojar *to make one blush.*

sonrojarse *to blush.*

Se sonroja por nada. *Anything makes her blush. She blushes at the least little thing.*

sonsacar *to wheedle.*

soñador *m. dreamer.*

SOÑAR *to dream.*

No debería Ud. soñar con tales cosas. *You shouldn't even dream of such things.*

Vive soñando. *His head's in the clouds. ("He lives in a daydream.")*

soñoliento *adj. sleepy, drowsy.*

SOPA *f. soup.*

¿Le sirvo un poco de sopa? *Shall I serve you some soup?*

Estoy hecho una sopa. *I'm soaked to the skin.*

sopapo *m. a blow under the chin, uppercut; slap.*

sopera *f. soup tureen.*

sopetón *m. blow; toasted bread dipped in oil.*

Se presentó de sopetón. *Suddenly he appeared. He appeared all of a sudden.*

soplar *to blow; to inflate; to steal, to rob.*

Soplaba un viento suave. *A very gentle wind was blowing.*

Le soplaron el reloj. *They stole his watch.*

soplo *m. blowing; puff (of wind); hint; denunciation.*

soplón *m. stoolpigeon.*

sopor *m. stupor; drowsiness.*

soportar *to stand, to endure, to bear.*

Ha soportado muchas penas. *He endured*

many hardships.

No puedo soportarlo por más tiempo. *I can't stand it any longer.*

soprano *m. soprano.*

sorber *to sip; to suck; to absorb; to swallow.*

sorbete *m. sherbet.*

sorbo *m. sip, draught, gulp.*

Tómeselo a sorbos. *Sip it.*

sordera *f. deafness.*

SORDO *adj. deaf; not able to hear; not willing to hear; muffled; silent; m. a deaf person.*

Sordo como una tapia. *As deaf as a post.*

Ser sordo a. *To be deaf to.*

sordomudo *adj. and n. deaf and dumb; deaf-mute.*

SORPRENDER *to surprise; to take by surprise.*

No se sorprenda Ud. por eso. *Don't be surprised at that.*

Su llegada nos sorprendió a todos. *His arrival surprised everybody.*

SORPRESA *f. surprise.*

Es una verdadera sorpresa. *This is a real surprise.*

De sorpresa. *By surprise.*

Me ha cogido de sorpresa. *It has taken (it took) me by surprise.*

sortear *to draw lots; to raffle; to avoid, to evade, to dodge.*

sorteo *m. lottery, raffle.*

sortija *f. ring; lock of hair.*

sosa *f. soda.*

Sosa cáustica. *Caustic soda.*

sosegado *adj. calm, quiet.*

sosegar *to appease, to calm; to rest.*

sosegarse *to calm down; to be quiet.*

Cuando Ud. se sosiegue, hablaremos. *We'll talk it over when you calm down.*

sosiego *m. peace, calmness, quiet.*

No tenía un minuto de sosiego. *He hadn't had a moment's peace.*

soslayo *m. slant, askance.*

Mirar de soslayo. *To look askance. To look out of the corner of one's eye.*

soso *adj. insipid, tasteless; uninteresting; simple, homely.*

La comida está sosa. *The food is tasteless.*

Es una chica sosa. *She's an uninteresting girl.*

sospecha *f. suspicion.*

Eso da motivos de sospecha. *That gives ground for suspicion.*

sospechar *to suspect, to have a suspicion.*

Sospecho de él. *I'm suspicious of him. I suspect him.*

sospechoso *adj. suspicious; suspecting.*

Es un individuo sospechoso. *He's a suspicious character.*

sostén *m. support, prop.*

SOSTENER *to support, to sustain; to maintain; to hold; to carry (a conversation).*

Sostenía a su familia. *He supported his family.*

Ahora podemos sostener una conversación en español. *We can now carry on a conversation in Spanish.*

Lo digo y lo sostengo. *I'll stand by what I'm saying. ("I'm saying it and I maintain it.")*

sostenerse *to support oneself, to keep up, to hold out.*

Estaba tan borracho que no podía sostenerse. *He was so drunk, he couldn't stand up.*

sostenido *adj. sustained; m. sharp (music).*

sostenimiento *m. support, maintenance; upkeep.*

sota *f. jack, knave (playing cards).*

sotana *f. cassock.*

sótano *m. cellar.*

soya *f. soy bean. (Also soja.)*

SU *pron. his, her, its, their, your; pl. sus.*

Su libro. *His book.*

Sus libros. *His books.*

Su hermana. *His sister.*

Sus hermanas. *His sisters.*

Su novio. *Her fiancé.*

¿Dónde están sus hijos?—Están con sus abuelos. *Where are your children?—They're with their grandparents.*

Este procedimiento tiene sus ventajas y desventajas. *This procedure has its advantages and disadvantages.*

SUAVE *adj. soft, smooth, mild, gentle, mellow.*

Esta tela es muy suave. *This cloth is very soft.*

Es un vino suave. *This wine is very mellow.*

Tabaco suave. *Mild tobacco.*

suavemente *smoothly, softly, mildly; gently, sweetly.*

suavidad *f. softness; suavity.*

suavizar *to soften; to make smooth.*

subalterno *adj. and n. subaltern, subordinate.*

subarrendar *to sublet.*

subasta *f. auction.*

subconsciente *adj. and n. subconscious.*

subdirector *m. assistant director.*

súbdito *m. subject (of a king, etc.).*

subdivisión *f. subdivision.*

subido *adj. bright, loud, deep (color); high (price).*

Es de un color muy subido. *It's a loud color.*

Es algo subido el precio. *The price is a little high.*

SUBIR *to go up, to walk up; to ascend, to rise; to climb; to mount; to come up; to take up; to bring up; to get on; to raise.*

Suba Ud. a mi cuarto. *Go up to my room.*

Subamos. 1. *Let's go up.* 2. *Let's get on (train, bus, etc.).*

Suban Uds. un piso más. *Walk up another flight.*

Oigo subir a alguien. *I hear someone coming upstairs.*

Me tienes que ayudar a subir el baúl. *You must help me bring the trunk up.*

El mozo le subirá la maleta al tren. *The porter will put your suitcase on the train.*

Subió a lo alto del árbol. *He climbed to the top of the tree.*

El globo subió hasta diez mil pies. *The balloon rose to ten thousand feet.*

Le subió la temperatura. *His temperature rose.*

Los precios suben cada vez más. *Prices are constantly going up (rising).*

Tendrá Ud. que subir un poco la voz, es muy sordo. *You'll have to raise your voice a little; he's very deaf.*

Ha subido muy de prisa ese muchacho. *That boy has made rapid progress.*

¿A cuánto sube la cuenta? *How much is the bill?*

Subir a caballo. *To mount a horse.*

Subir de punto. *To increase. To grow.*

Se le subieron los tragos a la cabeza. *The drinks went to his head.*

SÚBITAMENTE *suddenly.*

SÚBITO *adj. sudden.*

De súbito. *Suddenly. All of a sudden.*

subjefe *m. second in command; chief assistant.*

subjetividad *f. subjectivity.*

subjetivo *adj. subjective.*

subjuntivo *m. subjunctive.*

sublevación *f. insurrection, uprising.*

sublevar *to stir up, to excite to rebellion.*

sublevarse *to revolt.*

sublime *adj. sublime.*

submarino *adj. and n. submarine.*

subordinado *adj. subordinate.*

subordinar *to subordinate.*

subrayar *to underline, to emphasize.*

subsanar *to rectify, to make right, to repair, to make up; to excuse.*

Subsanar un error. *To rectify an error.*

subscribir *to subscribe.*

subscribirse *to subscribe to.*

¿Quiere Ud. subscribirse a esta revista? *Would you like to subscribe to this magazine?*

subscripción *f. subscription.*

subscriptor *m. subscriber.*

subsecretario *m. under secretary; assistant secretary.*

subsecuente *adj. subsequent.*

subsidio *m. subsidy, aid.*

subsistencia *f. subsistence.*

Han subido mucho las subsistencias. *The cost of living has risen (gone up) a great deal.*

Subsistencias alimenticias. *Foodstuffs. Food.*

subsistente *adj. subsistent; subsisting.*

subsistir *to subsist; to exist; to last.*

substancia *f. substance; essence.*

En substancia. 1. *In substance.* 2. *In short. In brief.*

substancial *adj. substantial.*

substanciar *to substantiate.*

substancioso *adj. juicy; nourishing; substantial.*

substantivo *adj. substantive; m. substantive, noun.*

substitución *f. substitution.*

substituir *to substitute.*

substituto *m. substitute.*

substracción *f. subtraction.*

substraer *to subtract.*

subterráneo *adj. subterranean, underground; m. subway (Arg.).*

subtítulo *m. subtitle.*

suburbio *m. suburb.*

subvención *f. subsidy.*

subvencionar *to subsidize.*

subyugar *to subdue, to subjugate.*

SUCEDER *to happen; to succeed; to inherit.*

¿Qué sucedió después? *What happened then (next)?*

¿Qué le ha sucedido? *What happened to you?*

Suceda lo que suceda. yo estaré aquí. *No matter what happens, I'll be here.*

Se cree que su hijo le sucederá. *It's thought that his son will succeed him.*

sucesión *f. succession; estate, inheritance; offspring.*

sucesivamente *successively.*

sucesivo *adj. successive.*

En lo sucesivo. *In the future. Hereafter.*

suceso *m. event; incident.*

Sucesos de actualidad. *Current events. News of the day.*

sucesor *m. successor.*

suciedad *f. dirt, filth.*

sucio *adj. dirty, filthy, nasty.*

Una jugada sucia. *A dirty trick.*

Palabras sucias. *Nasty (dirty) words.*

sucumbir *to die; to succumb; to give way, to yield.*

sucursal *adj. subsidiary; m. branch, annex.*

sud *m. south. (See sur.)*

sudar *to sweat, to perspire; to toil.*

sudeste *m. southeast.*

sudoeste *m. southwest.*

sudor *m. sweat, perspiration, toil, hard work.*

suegra *f. mother-in-law.*

suegro m. *father-in-law.*

suela f. *sole (of shoe); sole leather.*

sueldo f. *salary.*

SUELO m. *soil; ground; floor.*
Levanta ese papel del suelo. *Pick up that paper from the floor.*
Dígale a la criada que barra el suelo. *Tell the servant to sweep the floor.*
El suelo está resbaladizo (resbaloso). *The pavement is slippery.*
Este suelo produce mucho. *This land is very fertile.*
Venirse al suelo. *To fall to the ground.*
Estar por los suelos. *To be very cheap (price).*
Suelo natal. *Native land.*

SUELTO adj. *loose; swift; free; fluent (style); single, odd (copy); m. change (money); newspaper item, short editorial.*
Sus cordones están sueltos. *Your shoelaces are untied (loose).*
Tenemos unos números sueltos de esa revista. *I have some odd copies of that magazine.*
Ese muchacho anda suelto. *That boy's running wild.*
Suelto de lengua. *Outspoken.*
Corrió a rienda suelta. *He ran fast.*
¿Tiene Ud. suelto? *Have you any change?*
No tengo suelto. *I haven't any change.*

SUEÑO m. *sleep; dream.*
¿Tiene Ud. sueño? *Are you sleepy?*
Tengo mucho sueño. *I'm very sleepy.*
Sueño con mucha frecuencia. *I dream very often.*
Todo me parece un sueño. *Everything seems like a dream.*

suero m. *serum.*

SUERTE f. *chance, lot, fortune, luck; manner, way, kind.*
¡Buena suerte! *Good luck!*
Mala suerte. *Bad luck.*
Envidio tu suerte. *I envy your luck.*
Tiene mucha suerte. *He's very lucky.*
Echemos suertes. *Let's draw lots.*
¿A quién le tocó la suerte? *Who won the lottery?*
De la misma suerte. *The same way.*
De suerte que. *So that. So. Thus.*

suficiencia f. *sufficiency, capacity.*

SUFICIENTE adj. *enough; sufficient.*
Eso no es suficiente. *That's not enough.*
Por más que trabaja, nunca gana lo suficiente. *He never earns enough no matter how hard he works.*

sufijo adj. *suffixed; m. suffix.*

sufragar to *pay, to defray; to aid.*
Sufragará todos los gastos del viaje. *He'll pay all the expenses of the trip.*

sufragio m. *suffrage, vote; aid.*

sufrido adj. *patient, enduring; practical (color).*
Es una mujer sufrida. *She's a very patient woman.*
El traje tiene un color sufrido. *The dress is of a practical color.*

sufrimiento m. *suffering.*

sufrir to *suffer, to stand.*
¿De qué dolencia sufre Ud.? *What (illness) are you suffering from? What do you have?*
No puedo sufrirlo por más tiempo. *I can't stand it any more.*

sugerencia f. *suggestion.*

SUGERIR to *suggest, to hint.*
¿Qué me sugiere Ud.? *What do you suggest ("to me")?*

SUGESTION f. *suggestion, hint.*
Esa fué una buena sugestión. *That was a good suggestion.*

sugestionar to *suggest through hypnotism; to influence.*

sugestivo adj. *suggestive.*

suicida m. *and f. suicide (person).*

suicidarse to *commit suicide.*

suicidio m. *(the act of) suicide.*

sujetapapeles m. *paper clip, paper holder.*

SUJETAR to *fasten; to hold; to subdue, to subject.*
Sujete Ud. bien las riendas. *Hold on to the reins.*
No está bien sujeto el cinturón. *The belt isn't fastened well.*
Sujete al perro con una cadena. *Put a leash ("chain") on the dog.*

sujetarse to *submit to, to keep to, to abide by.*
Había que sujetarse a la nueva disposición. *We had to submit to the new regulations.*

SUJETO adj. *subject, liable, likely; m. subject; (coll.) fellow, guy.*
Estar sujeto a. *To be subject to.*
¿Quién es ese sujeto? *Who's that fellow (coll.)?*
Es un buen sujeto. *He's a nice guy (coll.).*

sulfuro m. *sulphide.*

SUMA f. *sum, amount; addition.*
¿Cuánto es la suma total? *What's the total amount?*
Ha menester cincuenta dólares para completar la suma. *Fifty dollars is needed to complete the sum.*
Una suma crecida. *A large sum of money.*
Es hombre de suma cortesía. *He's very (extremely) polite.*
En suma. *In short.*

sumamente *extremely, exceedingly.*
Es Ud. sumamente amable. *You're extremely kind.*

sumar to *add; to sum up.*
Suma muy bien. *He adds accurately.*
Sumarse a. *To join.*
Se sumó al movimiento. *He joined the movement.*

sumario adj. *summary; m. summary; indictment, table of contents.*

sumergir to *submerge.*

sumidero m. *sewer, drain, sink.*

suministrar to *supply, to furnish.*

suministro m. *supply.*

sumisión f. *submission, resignation, obedience.*

sumiso adj. *submissive, obedient, docile.*

SUMO adj. *high, great, supreme.*
Con sumo gusto. *With great pleasure.*
En sumo grado. *In the highest degree.*
A lo sumo. *At the most.*

suntuosidad f. *sumptuousness.*

suntuoso adj. *sumptuous, magnificent.*

supeditar to *subject.*
Estar supeditado a. *To be subject to.*

superabundante adj. *superabundant, very abundant.*

superar to *exceed, to excel, to surpass; to overcome.*

superchería f. *deceit, fraud.*

superficial adj. *superficial.*

superficialidad f. *superficiality.*

superficie f. *surface; area.*

superfluo adj. *superfluous.*

superintendente m. *superintendent; supervisor; quartermaster.*

SUPERIOR adj. *superior; higher, better; above; m. superior.*
Es superior a todo elogio. *It's above all praise.*

Labio superior. *Upper lip.*
Es un hombre superior. *He's a great man.*
Este es un vino superior. *This is an excellent wine.*

superioridad f. *superiority; higher authority.*

superlativo adj. *superlative.*

supernumerario adj. *supernumerary.*

superproducción f. *overproduction.*

superstición f. *superstition.*

supersticioso adj. *superstitious.*

superviviente adj. *and n. survivor; surviving.*

suplantar to *supplant, to displace.*

suplementorio adj. *supplementary.*

suplemento m. *supplementing; supplement, extra (in Spain.)*

suplente adj. *and n. substituting, replacing; alternate, substitute.*

súplica f. *request, entreaty, petition.*
No cedió a sus súplicas. *He didn't give in to her pleas.*

suplicación f. *supplication; request; petition.*

suplicar to *beg, to implore, to beseech, to entreat; to petition.*
Suplico a Ud. que le perdone. *I beg of you (entreat you) to forgive him.*
Le suplicó que le ayudara. *She implored him to help her.*

suplicio m. *ordeal, torment, torture; execution (death penalty).*
Pasó por el suplicio de . . . *He went through the ordeal of . . .*

suplir to *supply; to make up; to substitute.*

SUPONER to *imagine, to suppose, to surmise; to amount to; to expect.*
Ud. podrá suponer lo que ocurrió. *You can imagine what happened.*
¿Cuánto supone todo esto? *What does all this amount to? How important is all this?*
Es de suponer que . . . *It's to be expected that . . .*

suposición f. *supposition, conjecture, assumption; falsehood.*

supremacía f. *supremacy.*

supremo adj. *supreme; highest.*

supresión f. *suppression.*

SUPRIMIR to *suppress; to abolish; to eliminate; to omit, to leave out; to do away with.*
Suprima Ud. los huevos. *Eliminate eggs from your diet.*
Suprimieron los impuestos sobre las diversiones. *The amusement taxes were abolished.*

SUPUESTO adj. *supposed, assumed; m. supposition, assumption.*
Usaba un nombre supuesto. *He used an alias.*
Ud. parte de un supuesto equivocado. *You're starting with a false assumption (from a wrong premise).*
Por supuesto, tendrá Ud. que tener el pasaporte en regla. *Of course, you have to have your passport in order.*
En el supuesto de que. *On the assumption that.*

SUR m. *south. (See sud.)*

surco m. *furrow; wrinkle.*

surgir to *spurt; to arise; to appear.*
Han surgido algunas dificultades. *Some (several) difficulties have arisen.*

surtido adj. *assorted; m. assortment, stock, supply.*
Quiero una caja de galletas surtidas. *I want a box of assorted cookies.*
Hemos recibido un surtido de medias de varios tamaños. *We've received an assortment of stockings of various sizes.*

Un surtido selecto. *A select stock. A selection (of articles, etc.).*

surtidor *m. jet, spout; caterer.*

Surtidor de gasolina. *Filling station (gasoline).*

surtir *to supply, to furnish.*

¿Se ha surtido de todo lo necesario? *Have you supplied yourself with everything necessary?*

SUS *(pl. of su). (See su.)*

susceptibilidad *f. susceptibility.*

susceptible *adj. susceptible, sensitive to.*

suscitar *to stir up, to excite.*

susodicho *adj. above-mentioned; aforesaid.*

SUSPENDER *to suspend; to lay off; to postpone; to put off; to discontinue; to stop (payment); to adjourn.*

La lámpara estaba suspendida del techo. *The lamp was suspended from the ceiling.*

Se ha suspendido la publicación de la revista. *The publication of the magazine was suspended.*

Lo han suspendido de su cargo. *He was laid off from his job.*

Suspendieron el partido por la lluvia. *The game was postponed on account of rain.*

Suspender los pagos. *To stop payment.*

suspensión *f. suspension, cessation, stop.*

suspensivo *adj. suspensive.*

Puntos suspensivos. *Suspension points.*

suspenso *adj. suspended; hung; m. suspense; abeyance.*

El libro lo tiene a uno en suspenso. *The book keeps one in suspense.*

En suspenso. *In suspense. Pending.*

Dejar en suspenso. *To hold over (for future action or consideration). To hold in abeyance.*

suspicacia *f. suspicion; distrust.*

suspicaz *adj. suspicious, distrustful.*

suspirar *to sigh.*

Suspirar por. *To crave. To long for.*

suspiro *m. sigh, breath.*

sustancia *f. (See substancia.)*

sustantivo *m. (See substantivo.)*

sustentar *to support, to feed, to sustain, to assert.*

sustento *m. maintenance, support.*

sustituto *m. (See substituto.)*

sustituir *(See substituir.)*

sustituto *adj. (See substituto.)*

susto *m. fright.*

Dar un susto. *To scare.*

Recuperarse de un susto. *To recover from a shock.*

sustraer *(See substraer.)*

sutil *adj. subtle.*

sutileza *f. subtleness.*

SUYA *(f. of suyo) yours; his; hers; theirs; your own; his own; her own; their own; f. view, way. (See suyo.)*

Mi corbata es igual que la suya. *My tie is like yours.*

Una amiga suya. *A friend of hers.*

Esta pluma es suya. *This pen is yours.*

Ha tomado mi pluma y me ha dado la suya. *He took my pen and gave me his own.*

Ver la suya. *To see one's chance.*

Salirse con la suya. *To have one's way.*

Es una de las suyas. *It's one of his tricks (pranks).*

SUYAS *(pl. of suya). (See suya.)*

Son vecinas suyas. *They're neighbors of yours.*

Estas chicas son amigas suyas. *These girls are friends of hers. These girls are her friends.*

SUYO *yours; his; hers; theirs; one's; your own; his own; her own; their own; its own; sometimes used with the article el, la, lo, los, las. (El suyo, la suya, lo suyo, los suyos and las suyas are equivalent to el de Ud., el de él, el de ella, el de ellos, el de ellas, los de Ud., los de él, los de ella, los de ellos, las de Ud., las de él, las de ellas, las de ellos.)*

¿Es Ud. primo suyo? *Are you his cousin?*

¿Es suyo este lápiz? *Is this pencil yours?*

Me gustaría tener un anillo como el suyo. *I'd like to have a ring like yours.*

Un conocido suyo. *An acquaintance of theirs.*

De suyo. *Of one's own accord. Spontaneously. In itself. Of itself.*

SUYOS *(pl. of suyo). (See suyo.)*

Estos libros son los suyos. *These are your books.*

Unos amigos suyos. *Some friends of yours.*

¿Cómo está Ud. y los suyos? *How are you and your family ("yours")?*

T

tabaco *m. tobacco.*

Tabaco suave (flojo). *Mild tobacco.*

Tabaco en rama. *Leaf tobacco.*

tabaquera *f. snuffbox; tobacco pouch.*

tabaquería *f. cigar store.*

tabaquero *m. tobacconist.*

taberna *f. tavern, inn, bar.*

tabernero *m. tavern keeper.*

tabique *m. partition wall, partition.*

tabla *f. table (of information); board, plank (of wood); pl. stage.*

Con esta tabla haré un banco. *I'll make a bench with this board.*

Tabla de multiplicar. *Multiplication table.*

tablado *m. platform; stage; scaffold.*

tablero *m. panel, board.*

Tablero de damas. *Checkerboard.*

Tablero de ajedrez. *Chessboard.*

tableta *f. tablet.*

tablilla *f. slab, small board; bulletin board.*

tuburete *m. stool; tabouret.*

tacañería *f. stinginess.*

tacaño *adj. stingy, miserly.*

tácito *adj. tacit.*

taciturno *adj. taciturn.*

taco *m. plug, stopper; pad, wad; billiard cue.*

tacón *m. heel; heelpiece of a shoe.*

Tacones de goma. *Rubber heels.*

taconear *to tap with the heels.*

taconeo *m. the act of tapping with the heels.*

táctica *f. tactics.*

tacto *m. touch; tact; skill; feel.*

Es un hombre de mucho tacto. *He's a very tactful man.*

Es suave al tacto. *It feels soft. ("It's soft to the touch.")*

tacha *f. fault, blemish.*

Poner tacha (a). *To find fault. To make objections.*

Sin tacha. *Without fault (blemish).*

tachar *to find fault with; to erase, to cross out; to censure.*

tachuela *f. tack, small nail.*

tafetán *m. taffeta.*

tahona *f. bakery, baker shop.*

tahur *m. gambler; cardsharp.*

tajada *f. slice, cut.*

tajo *m. cut, incision.*

TAL *adj. such, so, as.*

¿Qué tal? *How are you? How are things? What do you say?*

¿Qué tal ha sido el viaje? *How was the trip?*

¿Qué tal está su familia? *How is your family?*

¿Qué tal se porta? *How is she behaving?*

No permitiré tal cosa. *I won't allow such a thing.*

En mi vida nihe visto ni oído tal cosa. *I haven't seen or heard of such a thing in my life.*

Encontramos el país tal como nos lo habíamos imaginado. *We found the country just as we had imagined it to be.*

Tal era el frío que tuvimos que encender la lumbre. *It was so cold that we had to light a fire.*

Como si tal cosa. *As if nothing had happened.*

Lo dejaron todo tal como estaba. *They left everything just as it was.*

Me lo dijo un tal Smith. *A certain Smith told me so.*

Tal vez. *Maybe.*

Con tal que. *Provided that.*

No hay tal. *No such thing.*

Tal para cual. *Two of a kind.*

tala *f. felling of trees; havoc.*

talabartería *f. saddlery, saddler's shop.*

talabartero *m. saddler.*

taladrar *to drill, to bore.*

taladro *m. auger, bit, drill; drill hole, bore.*

talar *to fell trees; to destroy.*

talco *m. talcum, talc; tinsel.*

talego *m. bag, sack; a clumsy person.*

talento *m. talent; cleverness.*

Es un escritor de gran talento. *He's a very talented writer.*

talón *m. heel; check, stub, receipt.*

Presente este talón al reclamar su equipaje. *Present this check when you claim your baggage.*

talonario *m. stub; stub book, checkbook.*

talla *f. stature; size; wood carving; sculpture, engraving.*

Es un hombre de talla media. *He's of medium height.*

tallador *m. engraver.*

tallar *to carve; to engrave.*

tallarín *m. noodle.*

talle *m. waist; size; shape; figure.*

Tiene un talle muy pequeño. *She has a very small waist.*

taller *m. workshop, factory; laboratory.*

Taller de sastre. *Tailor shop.*

Taller de reparaciones. *Repair shop.*

tallo *m. stem; stalk; sprout.*

tamal *m. tamale.*

¿Le gustan los tamales? *Do you like tamales?*

TAMAÑO *adj. of such and such a size; such, so great, so large, so small, etc.; m. size, dimensions.*

Nunca había visto tamaño descaro. *I'd never seen such impudence.*

¿De qué tamaño es? *What size is it?*

¿Tiene Ud. tornillos de este tamaño? *Have you screws of this size?*

Hemos recibido un surtido de medias de varios tamaños. *We've received an assortment of stockings of various sizes.*

De gran tamaño. *Very large.*

De poco tamaño. *Small.*

TAMBIÉN *also, too; as well; likewise.*

Yo también. *I also.*

¿Va Ud. también? *Are you going too?*

También Ud. puede venir. *You may also come. You can come too.*

tambor *m. drum; drummer.*

tamiz *m. fine sieve, sifter.*

tamizar *to sift.*

TAMPOCO *neither (used after a negative).*
A decir verdad, no quiero verle.—Ni yo tampoco. *To tell the truth I don't want to see him.—Neither do I.*
Su mujer tampoco dijo nada. *His wife didn't say anything either.*

TAN *(shortening of tanto) so, as, so much, as well, as much.*
¿Qué le ha hecho volver tan pronto? *What made you return so soon?*
Siendo tan tarde no iré. *Since it's so late, I won't go.*
Tan pronto como sea posible. *As soon as possible.*
Tan largo tiempo. *Such a long time.*
No tan de prisa. *Not so fast.*
Ya es tan alto como su padre. *He's now as tall as his father.*
Habla español tan bien como ella. *He speaks Spanish as well as she.*
Tan bien. *So well. As well.*
Tan mal. *So bad. As bad.*
Además de ser tan encantadora, es inteligente. *She's intelligent as well as charming.*
No le creí tan niño. *I didn't think he was so childish. ("I didn't think him such a child.")*
¿Tan aficionado es su hermano al esquí? *Is your brother that enthusiastic about skiing?*

tanda *f. rotation, turn; (work) shift; batch; team.*

tangible *adj. tangible.*

tango *m. tango.*

tanque *m. tank.*

tantear *to measure; to try, to sound somebody out; to keep the score in a game; to estimate.*

tanteo *m. estimate; sounding (somebody out); score (games).*

TANTO *adj. so much, as much; adv. so, in such a manner; such a long (time); m. point (in games), pl. score.*
Tanto gusto, señora. *I'm very glad (pleased) to know you, Madam.*
¡Lo siento tanto! *I'm so sorry!*
No beba Ud. tanto. *Don't drink so much.*
¡Tanto bueno por aquí! *Look who's here! I'm glad to see you.*
¿Por qué tanta prisa? *Why the hurry? ("Why such a hurry?")*
Tanta gente. *So many people.*
Ciento y tantas libras. *A hundred and some pounds.*
Tener tantos años de edad. *To be so many years old.*
A tantos de mayo. *On such and such a date in May.*
¿Tanto le costó? *Did it cost you as much as that?*
A tanto la yarda. *At so much a yard.*
Algún tanto. *A little. Somewhat.*
Otro tanto. *Just as much. As much more.*
Otros tantos. *Just as many.*
Ni tanto, ni tan poco. *Neither too much nor too little.*
Tanto por tanto. *For the same price.*
Tantos a tantos. *Equal numbers.*
Tanto uno como otro. *The one as well as the other. Both of them.*

Cuanto más le doy, tanto más me pide. *The more I give him, the more he asks for (wants).*
Tanto más cuanto (que). *All the more (because).*
Tanto como. (Tanto cuanto.) *As much as.*
En tanto. (Entre tanto.) *In the meanwhile.*
Hay tanta gente aquí. *There are so many people here.*
Por lo tanto. *Therefore. For the reasons mentioned.*
Estar al tanto de. *To be informed of. To be aware of.*
Tanto mejor. *So much the better.*
Tanto peor. *So much the worse.*

tapa *f. cover, lid, cap.*

tapadera *f. cover, lid.*

tapar *to cover; to conceal, to hide.*

tapia *f. mud wall; fence.*
¿Puede Ud. saltar por encima de esta tapia? *Can you jump over that fence?*
Es sordo como una tapia. *He's deaf as a post.*

tapicería *f. tapestry; upholstery.*

tapioca *f. tapioca.*

tapiz *m. tapestry.*

tapizar *to hang with tapestry; to upholster.*

tapón *m. cork; plug.*

taponar *to plug.*

taquígrafo *m. stenographer.*

taquilla *f. letter file; ticket or key rack; ticket office or window.*
¿Dónde está la taquilla? *Where's the ticket office?*

taquimecanógrafo *m. stenographer-typist.*

tardanza *f. slowness, delay.*
Perdone mi tardanza. *Pardon my lateness.*

TARDAR *to delay; to be late; to be slow.*
No tarde Ud. *Don't be long. Don't take too long. Don't be late.*
No tardaré en volver. *I'll be back before long.*
No creo que tarde mucho. *I don't think he'll be long.*
Tardó una hora en ir allí. *It took him an hour to go (get) there.*
¿Cuánto tiempo se tarda en aeroplano? *How long does it take by airplane?*
Tarda mucho en decidirse. *He's slow in making up his mind. It takes him a long time to decide.*
A más tardar. *At the latest.*

TARDE *f. afternoon; adv. late.*
¡Buenas tardes! *Good afternoon!*
¡Qué hermosa tarde! *What a lovely afternoon!*
¿De modo que pasaron Uds. allí la tarde? *So you spent the afternoon there?*
Esta tarde a las cuatro. *This afternoon at four o'clock.*
En la tarde. *In the afternoon.*
Mañana por la tarde. *Tomorrow afternoon.*
Ya es tarde. *It's late.*
Más vale tarde que nunca. *Better late than never.*
No quiero llegar tarde. *I don't want to be late.*
Puede ser que venga más tarde. *Maybe he'll come later.*
Más tarde o más temprano. *Sooner or later.*
Hacerse tarde. *To grow late.*

tardío *adj. tardy, slow; late.*

tardo *adj. slow; sluggish, dull.*

tarea *f. job, task, work.*
La tarea está concluida. *The job is finished.*

tarifa *f. tariff; fare, rate.*

tarima *f. movable platform; stand.*

tarjeta *f. card.*

Aquí tiene Ud. mi tarjeta. *Here's my card.*
Tarjeta de visita. *Visiting card. Calling card.*
Tarjeta postal. *Postcard.*

tarro *m. jar; can, pot.*

tartamudear *to stammer, to stutter.*

tartamudo *adj. stammering; stuttering; m. stammerer, stutterer.*

tarugo *m. wooden peg.*

tasa *f. assessment; appraisement; measure; standard; rate; valuation.*

tasajo *m. hung beef.*

tasar *to appraise, to assess; to value.*

tatarabuela *f. great-great-grandmother.*

tatarabuelo *m. great-great-grandfather.*

tataranieta *f. great-great-granddaughter.*

tataranieto *m. great-great-grandson.*

tatuaje *m. tattoo; tattooing.*

tatuar *to tattoo.*

tauromaquia *f. bullfighting.*

TAXI *m. taxi, taxicab.*
¿Iremos a pie o en taxi? *Shall we walk or take a taxi?*

taxímetro *m. meter (of a cab).*

TAZA *f. cup; bowl.*
Haga el favor de darme otra taza de café. *Please give me another cup of coffee.*

tazón *m. large bowl.*

TE *pron. (objective and dative cases of tú) you, to you.*
¿Te duele la cabeza? *Do you have a headache?*
¿Qué te parece? *What do you think of it?*
Te lo dió a tí. *He gave it to you.*
Si me escribes te contestaré. *I'll answer you if you write to me.*

te *f. name of the letter t.*

té *m. tea.*
Ya está el té. *Tea is ready.*

teatral *adj. theatrical.*

TEATRO *m. theater; playhouse.*

tecla *f. key (of a piano, typewriter, etc.).*

teclado *m. keyboard (of a piano, typewriter, etc.).*

técnica *f. technique.*

técnico *adj. technical; m. technician, expert.*

techo *m. roof; ceiling.*

tedio *m. boredom, tediousness.*

tedioso *adj. tiresome, tedious.*

teja *f. tile.*
A toca teja. *Cash payment.*

tejado *m. roof, tiled roof.*

tejer *to weave, to knit.*

tejido *m. texture, fabric, web; tissue.*

tela *f. cloth, material; web, fabric.*
Esta tela tiene un metro de ancho. *This material (cloth) is one meter wide.*
¿Se encoge esta tela? *Does this material shrink?*
Ese es el revés de la tela. *That's the wrong side of the material.*

telaraña *f. cobweb.*

TELEFONEAR *to phone.*
Telefonéeme. *Phone me. Give me a ring.*
¿Se puede telefonear desde aquí? *Can we phone from here?*
Telefoneo de parte del Sr. López. *I'm calling for ("in behalf of") Mr. Lopez.*

telefonema *m. telephone message, call.*

telefónico *adj. relating to a telephone.*
¿Dónde está la central telefónica? *Where's the telephone exchange?*
Guía telefónica. *Telephone directory (book).*
Cabina telefónica. *Telephone booth.*

telefonista *m. and f. telephone operator.*

TELÉFONO *m. telephone.*
¿Dónde está el teléfono. *Where's the telephone?*

Llámeme por teléfono. *Phone me. Give me a ring.*

Le llaman por teléfono. *There's a telephone call for you. You're wanted on the phone.*

¿Qué número tiene su teléfono? *What's your phone number?*

Un momento, que suena el teléfono. *Just a minute, the phone is ringing.*

telegrafiar *to telegraph, to wire.*

Tendremos que telegrafiarle. *We'll have to wire him.*

telegráficamente *by telegraph.*

telegrafista *m. and f. telegraph operator.*

telégrafo *m. telegraph.*

¿Dónde está la oficina de telégrafos? *Where's the telegraph office?*

telegrama *m. telegram.*

Quiero mandar un telegrama. *I want to send a telegram.*

Le pondré un telegrama en cuanto llegue. *I'll send you a telegram as soon as I arrive. I'll send you a wire as soon as I get there.*

Telegrama de madrugada. *Night letter.*

telescopio *m. telescope.*

televisión *f. television.*

telón *m. curtain (theater).*

tema *m. theme; subject.*

Cambiemos de tema. *Let's change the subject. Let's talk about something else.*

temblar *to tremble, to shake, to shiver.*

temblor *m. trembling, tremor; earthquake.*

TEMER *to fear, to dread, to be afraid.*

No tiene Ud. nada que temer. *You have nothing to fear. There's nothing to be afraid of.*

Temo que esté enfermo. *I'm afraid he's sick.*

No tema, que no le hará daño. *Don't be afraid, it won't hurt you.*

Temo que sea demasiado tarde. *I'm afraid that it's too late.*

temerario *adj. reckless, rash.*

temeridad *f. temerity, rashness, recklessness; folly.*

temeroso *adj. timid; afraid, fearful.*

temible *adj. dreadful, terrible.*

temor *m. fear, dread.*

temperamento *m. temperament, temper, nature.*

temperatura *f. temperature.*

tempestad *f. tempest, storm.*

templado *adj. moderate, temperate, tempered; lukewarm.*

templo *m. temple; church.*

temporada *f. season; period.*

Este espectáculo es el mejor de la temporada. *This is the best show of the season.*

temporal *adj. temporary; m. storm.*

TEMPRANO *early.*

Salimos por la mañana temprano. *We left early in the morning.*

Me gusta acostarme temprano. *I like to go to bed early.*

Es demasiado temprano aún. *It's too early yet.*

Se sabrá más tarde o más temprano. *It'll become known sooner or later.*

tenacidad *f. tenacity.*

tenaz *adj. tenacious; stubborn.*

tenazas *f. pl. pincers, tongs, pliers; forceps.*

tendencia *f. tendency, leaning; trend.*

tender *to hang (clothes); to stretch out, to spread out, to tend.*

Tengo que tender la ropa para que se seque. *I have to hang the clothes out to dry.*

Los pescadores tendieron la red. *The fisher-*

man spread out the net.

Cayó en las redes que le tendieron. *He fell into the trap they set for him.*

tendero *m. storekeeper.*

tendón *m. tendon.*

tenebroso *adj. dark; gloomy.*

TENEDOR *m. fork; holder.*

Déme un tenedor. *Let me have a fork.*

Tenedor de libros. *Bookkeeper.*

Tenedor de póliza. *Policyholder.*

teneduría *f. keeping (of books).*

Teneduría de libros. *Bookkeeping.*

TENER *to have, to possess; to keep; to hold, to contain; to take; to be (hungry, thirsty, cold, warm, etc.).*

¿Qué tiene Ud. en ese paquete? *What do you have in that package?*

Tendrá que facturar el baúl. *You'll have to check the trunk.*

Tengo que irme ahora. *I have to go now.*

No tengo mucho tiempo. *I haven't much time.*

Tengo mucho que hacer hoy. *I've a lot to do today.*

No tengo suelto. *I haven't any change.*

No tengo más. *I haven't (got) any more. I don't have any more.*

¿Qué tiene Ud. que ver con eso? *What do you have to do with it?*

Aquí tenemos que cambiar de tren. *We have to change trains here.*

Tiene su casa muy limpia. *She keeps her house very clean.*

¿Qué edad tiene Ud.? *How old are you?*

Tengo treinta años. *I'm thirty years old.*

Aquí tiene Ud. un libro interesante. *Here's an interesting book.*

¿Qué día del mes tenemos? *What day of the month is it?*

¿Qué número tiene su teléfono? *What's your phone number?*

¿Qué tiene Ud.? *What's the matter with you?*

No tengo nada. *There's nothing the matter with me.*

No tenga Ud. miedo. *Don't be afraid.*

Tengo hambre. *I'm hungry.*

No tengo ganas de comer ahora. *I don't feel like eating now.*

Tengo sed. *I'm thirsty.*

Tengo mucho frío. *I'm very cold.*

Tengo dolor de cabeza. *I have a headache.*

Tengo dolor de garganta. *I have a sore throat.*

Tengo escalofríos. *I have the chills.*

Tengo un fuerte resfriado. *I have a bad cold.*

¿Tiene Ud. sueño? *Are you sleepy?*

Tenga paciencia. *Be patient. Have patience.*

¡Tenga cuidado! *Be careful! Watch out!*

Tiene buena cara. *It looks very nice. It looks good.*

Tener razón. *To be right.*

¿Quién tiene razón? *Who's right?*

No tener razón. *To be wrong.*

Tiene los brazos muy largos. *He has very long arms.*

Tiene mucha suerte. *He's very lucky.*

Tener prisa. *To be in a hurry.*

Tener lugar. *To take place.*

Tener malas pulgas. *To be hot-tempered. To be hot-headed (hot-blooded).*

Tener buen diente. *To have a hearty appetite.*

Lo tendré en cuenta. *I'll bear it in mind.*

No tengo en mucho a Juan. *I don't think much of John.*

Lo tiene en poco. *He attaches little value to it.*

No puedo tenerme de sueño. *I can't keep awake.*

Tuve un buen día. *I spent a pleasant day.*

¿Con qué ésas tenemos? *So that's the story!*

Tiene mucho pico. *He's a chatterbox.*

No tengo arte ni parte en el asunto. *I've nothing to do with the matter.*

tenis *m. tennis.*

tenor *m. tenor; text; purport.*

tensión *f. tension; voltage.*

tentación *f. temptation.*

tentar *to touch, to feel; to grope; to tempt; to try, to attempt.*

tentativa *f. attempt, try.*

tenue *adj. tenuous, thin, delicate.*

teñir *to dye, to tinge.*

teoría *f. theory.*

teórico *adj. theoretical.*

terapéutica *f. therapeutics.*

TERCER *(shortening of tercero) third.*

Vive en el tercer piso. *He lives on the third floor.*

El tercer día. *The third day.*

TERCERO *adj. third; m. third person; mediator, intermediary.*

La tercera parte. *The third part. A third.*

La tercera lección. *The third lesson.*

El sirvió de tercero en la negociación. *He was an intermediary in the negotiations.*

Ya está en tercera (velocidad). *It's in third (gear).*

tercio *adj. third; m. a third; the Foreign Legion (Spain).*

terciopelo *m. velvet.*

terco *adj. stubborn, headstrong.*

tergiversar *to distort, to misrepresent.*

terminación *f. termination; ending.*

terminal *adj. terminal, final; m. terminal.*

TERMINAR *to end, to terminate; to finish.*

Casi he terminado. *I've almost finished. I'm almost finished.*

La reunión terminó cerca de las diez. *The meeting ended about ten o'clock.*

término *m. term; manner; end; word; boundary.*

¿En qué términos? *On what terms?*

En estos términos. *On these terms. In these words.*

Poner término a. *To put an end to.*

En un término medio. *On an average.*

Me ha hablado en términos lisonjeros de su obra. *She spoke to me in a very flattering way ("in high terms") about your work.*

terminología *f. terminology.*

termómetro *m. thermometer.*

termos *m. thermos bottle.*

ternera *f. veal; heifer.*

Chuletas de ternera. *Veal cutlets.*

ternero *m. calf.*

ternura *f. tenderness, fondness.*

terraplén *m. embankment; mound; banquette.*

terrateniente *m. landowner.*

terraza *f. terrace.*

terremoto *m. earthquake.*

terreno *m. land, soil, field, piece of ground.*

Partieron el terreno en varios lotes. *They divided the land into several lots.*

Sobre el terreno. *On the spot.*

terrestre *adj. ground, terrestrial.*

Fuerzas terrestres. *Ground forces.*

TERRIBLE *adj. terrible, dreadful.*

territorio *m. territory.*

terrón *m. clod; lump.*

Un terrón de azúcar. *A lump of sugar.*

terror *m. terror.*

terruño m. piece of land, native country.

tertulia f. evening party, social gathering, friendly conversation.

tesis f. thesis.

tesorería f. treasury, treasurer's office.

tesorero m. treasurer.

tesoro m. treasure; treasury.

testamento m. testament, will.

testar to make a will; to bequeath.

testarudo adj. headstrong, stubborn, obstinate.
No seas tan testarudo y haz lo que te piden. Don't be so stubborn and do as you are told.

testigo m. and f. witness.

testimonio m. testimony; attestation; affidavit; evidence; deposition.

tetera f. teapot.

textil adj. and n. textile.

texto m. text.
Libro de texto. Textbook.

textual adj. textual.

textualmente textually, according to the text, word for word.

tez f. complexion, skin.
Tiene una tez muy suave. She has a very delicate complexion. Her skin is very smooth.

TI you (prepositional form of tú).
Para ti. For you.
A ti te hablan. They're talking to you.
Te estás engañando a ti mismo. You're fooling yourself.

tía f. aunt.

tibia f. tibia, shinbone.

tibio adj. lukewarm; indifferent.
Agua tibia. Lukewarm water.

tiburón m. shark.

TIEMPO m. time; tense; weather; tempo.
¿Qué tiempo hace? How's the weather? What's the weather like?
Hace muy buen tiempo. Hace un tiempo muy bueno. The weather's fine. The weather's very nice.
Hace mal tiempo. The weather's bad.
El tiempo se pone bueno. The weather's getting very nice.
Parece que el tiempo se descompone. It looks as though the weather will change (for the worse).
El tiempo está muy variable. The weather's very changeable.
El tiempo se está despejando. The weather's clearing up.
Durante algún tiempo. For some time.
Por mucho tiempo. For a long time.
Hace mucho tiempo. It's been a long time.
¿Cuánto tiempo se tarda en aeroplano? How long does it take by airplane?
¿Cuánto tiempo hace que vive Ud. aquí? How long have you been living here?
¡Si hay tiempo de sobra! There's plenty of time. There's time to spare.
Tengo tiempo de sobra. I have plenty of time.
No tengo tiempo. I have no time.
No hay tiempo que perder. There's no time to waste.
Es tiempo de que Ud. hable. It's time for you to speak.
Aprovechar el tiempo. To make good use of one's time.
Darse buen tiempo. To amuse oneself.
Andar con el tiempo. To keep up with the times.
Obedecer al tiempo. To act as circumstances require. To go with the times.
Matar el tiempo. To kill time.
A tiempo. In time.
Fuera de tiempo. Out of season.
A un tiempo. At the same time.
Con tiempo. Timely.
Con el tiempo. In time. In the course of time.
El tiempo es oro. Time is money.

TIENDA f. store, shop; awning; tent.
¿A qué hora abren las tiendas? What time do the stores open?
¿Hasta qué hora está la tienda abierta? Until what time does the store stay open? How late does the store stay open?
Esta tienda anuncia un saldo. This store is advertising a sale.
Poner (abrir) tienda. To open up a store.
Acamparon en tiendas (de campaña). They camped in tents.

tientas (a) in the dark.
Andar a tientas. To feel one's way in the dark. To grope in the dark.
Encienda la luz, no busque a tientas. Turn the light on. Don't look for it in the dark.

tierno adj. tender; soft; affectionate; young.

TIERRA f. earth; soil; land; ground; native country.
Su fortuna consiste en tierras y valores. His fortune consists of land and securities.
Iremos por tierra. We'll go by land (overland).
Iremos a tierra en cuanto atraque el barco. We'll go ashore as soon as the ship docks.
Ver tierras. To see the world. To travel.
Echar tierra. To forget.
Echar a tierra. To bring down.
Tomar tierra. To anchor. To land.
En tierra. On land. Ashore.
Tierra adentro. Inland.
Echar por tierra. To overthrow. To ruin. To destroy.
¡Tierra a la vista! Land in sight!

tieso adj. stiff, hard; firm, strong; solemn; stubborn.
Tenérselas tiesas. To hold to one's opinion. To be stubborn (opinionated).

tiesto m. flowerpot.

tifus m. typhus.

tigre m. tiger.

tijeras f. pl. scissors; shears.

tila f. linden tree; flower of the linden; infusion of linden flowers.

tildar to cross out; to put a tilde over; to brand, to criticize.

tilde f. tilde, a mark (~) used over n; trifle, bit.

timador m. swindler.

timar to swindle, to cheat.

TIMBRE m. stamp, seal; bell, buzzer, tone.
Hay que ponerle un timbre a este certificado. You have to put an official stamp on this certificate.
Tocar el timbre. To ring the bell.
Abrí la puerta luego que sonó el timbre. I opened the door as soon as the bell rang.

timidez f. timidity, shyness.

tímido adj. timid, shy.

tímpano m. kettledrum; tympanum, eardrum; tympan.

tina f. large earthen jar; tub; bathtub; vat.

tinaja f. large earthen jar for water.

tino m. skill, knack; judgment, tact; a good hit.
Sacar de tino. To exasperate. To confound.

tinta f. ink; dye.
La tinta es demasiado espesa, no corre bien. The ink is too thick; it doesn't flow well.
Lo sé de buena tinta. I have that on good authority. I learned that from a reliable source.

tinte m. dye; tint, hue; cleaner's.
Lleve esto al tinte. Take this to the cleaner's.

tintero m. inkstand, inkwell.

tintorería f. cleaner's.

tintorero m. dyer.

tintura f. dyeing; m. tincture; tint; dye.
Tintura para el pelo. Hair-dye.

TÍO m. uncle; (coll.) fellow.
Mis tíos. My uncle and aunt.
¿Quién es ese tío? Who's that fellow?

típico adj. typical, characteristic.

tiple m. and f. treble, soprano.

tipo m. type; rate; standard; class; (coll.) fellow.
¿Cuál es el tipo de cambio hoy? What is the rate of exchange today?
Ese tipo me revienta. I can't stand that fellow.
Ese es un tipo muy malo. He's a bad character.

tipografía f. printing; printing shop; typography.

tipógrafo m. printer, typographer, typesetter.

tira f. strip; stripe.

tirabuzón m. corkscrew; curl of hair.

tirada f. edition, issue; printing; cast, throw; distance; stretch.
De una tirada. At a stretch.

tirador m. marksman, sharpshooter.

tiranía f. tyranny.

tirano m. tyrant.

tirante adj. strained, taut, tight; m. brace, truce; pl. suspenders.

TIRAR to throw, to toss, to cast; to shoot; to pull; to squander; to draw; to print.
No lo tire. Don't throw it away.
Tíremelo. Toss it over to me. Throw it to me.
El niño la tiraba de la falda. The child tugged at her skirt.
Tire una línea recta. Draw a straight line.
Ha tirado su fortuna. He's squandered his fortune.
Han tirado una nueva edición. They've printed a new edition.
Veamos cual de nosotros puede tirar mejor. Let's see which one of us is the better shot.
Tirar a los dados. To shoot dice.
Tirar al blanco. To shoot at a target.
Tira de la cuerda. Pull the cord.
¡Voy tirando! I manage to get along.
Se tiró por la ventana. He threw himself out the window.
Vimos como se tiraban los paracaidistas. We saw the parachutists jump.

tiritar to shiver.

tiro m. shot; report (of a gun); throw, fling; range; reach, mark made by a throw; team (of draft animals); draft of a chimney.
Tiro al blanco. Target practice.
Errar el tiro. To miss the mark.
Matar a tiros a. To shoot to death.
¿Cuántos tiros ha disparado Ud.? How many shots did you fire?

tirón m. tug, pull.
De un tirón. All at once. At one stroke.
Dormí toda la noche de un tirón. I slept all night through.

tiroteo m. shooting.

tísico adj. and n. consumptive; person who has tuberculosis.

tisis f. tuberculosis, consumption.

títere m. puppet.

titiritar to shiver.

titubear to hesitate, to doubt.

El testigo contestaba sin titubear. *The witness answered without hesitation.*

titular *to title; to entitle; adj. and n. titular; head, holder; headline.*

título *m. title, diploma, degree; heading, headline; inscription; pl. shares, securities.*

Recibió el título de abogado. *He became a lawyer.*

A título de. *On the pretense of. Under the pretext of.*

Títulos al portador. *Shares payable to the bearer.*

Títulos ferroviarios. *Railway stock.*

tiza *f. chalk.*

tiznar *to smut, to smudge.*

toalla *f. towel.*

tobillo *m. ankle.*

tocado *adj. touched; tainted; m. headdress, coiffure.*

tocador *m. vanity, dressing table; boudoir, dressing room.*

tocante *adj. touching, respecting, concerning.*

Tocante a. *Concerning. As regards.*

En lo tacante a. *In regard to. Regarding.*

TOCAR *to touch; to play (an instrument); to ring; to toll; to concern, to interest; to be one's turn; to fall to one's share; to call (at a port).*

¡Toque Ud. qué suave es esta tela! *Feel how soft this cloth is.*

¡No tocar! *Don't touch! Hands off!*

Toque el timbre. *Ring the bell.*

¿Qué instrumento toca Ud.? *What instrument do you play?*

La orquesta está tocando un tango. *The band is playing a tango.*

¿A quién le toca ahora? *Whose turn is it now?*

Ahora me toca a mí. *It's my turn now.*

Le toca jugar. *It's your turn to play.*

¿A quién le tocó la suerte? *Who won the lottery?*

Nos tocarán partes iguales. *We'll get equal shares.*

Por lo que toca a mí. *As far as I'm concerned. As regards myself.*

El barco no tocará en Cádiz. *The ship won't call (stop) at Cadiz.*

Tocar a la puerta. *To knock at the door.*

A toca teja. *Cash payment.*

tocayo *m. namesake.*

Es mi tocayo. *He's my namesake. He has the same name I have.*

tocino *m. bacon; salt pork.*

Huevos y tocino. *Bacon and eggs.*

TODAVÍA *yet; still.*

Todavía es temprano. *It's still early.*

Todavía no han dado las diez. *It's not ten o'clock yet.*

¿Terminó la carta?—Todavía no. *Have you finished the letter?—Not yet.*

¿Todavía anda Ud. por aquí? *Are you still around?*

TODO *adj. all, each, every; m. the whole, everything, everyone.*

Todo o nada. *All or nothing.*

Eso es todo. *That's all.*

Estoy todo rendido. *I'm all tired out.*

No estoy del todo satisfecho. *I'm not quite (altogether) satisfied.*

Ha perdido toda su fortuna. *He's lost his whole fortune.*

Todo lo cual no es verdad. *All of which isn't true.*

¡Ya estamos todos! *We're all here!*

Nos han convidado a todos. *They've invited all of us.*

Esta es la opinión de todos. *This is everyone's opinion.*

Todos son uno. *They're all the same.*

Me es todo uno. *It's all the same to me. It makes no difference to me.*

Todos los días. *Every day.*

La veo todos los días. *I see her every day.*

Todo el día. *All day long.*

He esperado todo el día. *I've been waiting all day.*

¿Sale Ud. todas las noches? *Do you go out every night?*

Según parece lloverá toda la tarde. *It looks as if it will rain all afternoon.*

Todo el año. *All year round.*

Espero quedarme todo el otoño. *I hope to stay through the autumn.*

Toda la familia. *The whole family.*

Todo el que. *Whoever. All that. All who.*

Todo el mundo. *Everybody.*

Todo el mundo lo sabe. *Everybody knows it.*

Sabe un poco de todo. *He knows a little about everything.*

Todo cuanto Ud. dice me interesa. *Everything ("all that") you say interests me.*

Le daré todo lo que necesita. *I'll give him everything he needs.*

Todo tiene sus límites. *There's a limit to everything.*

¿Está todo en buenas condiciones? *Is everything in good order?*

Estamos dispuestos a todo. *We're prepared for anything.*

Ella siempre está en todo. *She doesn't miss a thing.*

Todo está arreglado. *Everything has been arranged.*

Fuimos allí a todo correr. *We rushed there.*

Ante todo. *First of all.*

Después de todo. *After all.*

De todos modos. *At any rate. Anyway.*

A toda costa. *By all means. At any price. At all cost. At all hazards.*

Una vez por todas. *Once (and) for all.*

Del todo. *Wholly. Completely. Entirely.*

No del todo. *Not completely. Not quite.*

A toda velocidad. *At full speed.*

Así y todo. *In spite of all.*

Con todo, prefiero no ir. *Still, I prefer not to go. I still would rather not go.*

Jugar el todo por el todo. *To stake or risk all.*

Todo cabe en él. *He's capable of anything.*

Perdido por uno, perdido por todo. *In for a penny, in for a pound.*

toldo *m. awning.*

tolerable *adj. tolerable.*

tolerancia *f. tolerance.*

tolerante *adj. tolerant.*

tolerar *to tolerate.*

No podemos tolerar tal atropello. *We can't tolerate such an outrage.*

No toleraba nunca ninguna intervención de nadie. *He never tolerated any interference from anyone.*

toma *f. seizure, capture; dose (of medicine); tap (of a water main or electric wire); intake (water, gas, etc.).*

TOMAR *to take; to get; to seize; to have (drink or food).*

¿Qué quiere tomar? *What will you have to drink?*

Tomaremos café en lugar de té. *We'll take coffee instead of tea.*

¿Qué toma Ud.? *What will you have (to drink)?*

Tomo vino de vez en cuando. *I drink wine occasionally. I have some (take a little) wine every once in a while.*

Tomemos un bocadillo. *Let's have a bite.*

¿Qué toma Ud. para desayunarse? *What do you eat for breakfast?*

¿Qué tomamos para postre? *What shall we have for dessert?*

Tome la medicina un día sí y otro no. *Take the medicine every other day.*

Tomemos un taxi. *Let's take a taxi.*

Le aconsejo que tome el tren de las ocho. *I advise you to take the eight o'clock train.*

Tome él que más le guste. *Take the one you like best.*

Tomaré un ejemplar de esta revista. *I'll take a copy of this magazine.*

Tomar asiento. *To take a seat. To sit down.*

¿Quiere Ud. tomar asiento? *Would you like to sit down? Won't you sit down?*

Tome dos de ocho. *Take (subtract) two from eight.*

Tomar nota de. *To take note of.*

Lo toman por tonto. *They take him for a fool.*

No lo tome Ud. en ese sentido. *Don't take it that way.*

Tomar a bien. *To take (it) in the right way. To take (it) well.*

Tomar a mal. *To take (it) in the wrong way.*

Tomar a broma. *To take as a joke.*

Esto debe tomarse en consideración. *This should be taken into consideration.*

Tómelo con calma. *Take it easy.*

No lo tome Ud. a pecho. *Don't take it to heart.*

El médico le tomó el pulso. *The doctor took (felt) his pulse.*

Se tomaron las medidas necesarias en contra de la epidemia. *They took the necessary measures against the epidemic.*

No tomaron más tiempo que el necesario para comer. *They only took the time necessary to eat.*

Tomaron la ciudad de noche. *They took (captured) the city during the night.*

Tomar el pelo. *To make fun of. To tease.*

No me tome el pelo. *Don't make fun of me. Don't kid me.*

Voy a salir a tomar un poco el aire. *I'm going out for some air.*

Vamos a tomar el fresco. *Let's go out and get some fresh air.*

Está tomando alas (coll.). *He's putting on airs. He's getting high-hat. He's getting too big for his breeches. ("He's putting on wings.")*

Tomó razón de todo lo que se dijo. *He made a record of all that was said.*

Tomar cariño. *To become attached to. To become fond of. To take a liking to.*

Tomar las once. *To have a light lunch or some appetizers about noon.*

Tomar la responsabilidad. *To assume (the) responsibility.*

Tomar una resolución. *To make a decision. To decide. To resolve.*

La ha tomado conmigo. *He picked a quarrel with me.*

Ya le estoy tomando el gusto a este juego. *I'm beginning to enjoy this game.*

tomate *m. tomato.*

tomo *m. volume (book).*
Es una obra en tres tomos. *The work's in three volumes.*
ton *m. tone.*
Sin ton ni son. *Without rhyme or reason.*
tonel *m. barrel, cask.*
tonelada *f. ton.*
tónico *adj. and n. tonic.*
tono *m. tone; tune; key tone; accent; manner; conceit; shade (color).*
Darse tono. *To show off.*
Gente de buen tono. *Fashionable people.*
tontear *to act foolishly; to talk nonsense.*
tontería *f. foolishness, nonsense.*
No digas tonterías. *Don't talk nonsense. Don't say foolish things.*
TONTO *adj. silly, stupid; m. fool.*
No sea Ud. tonto. *Don't be foolish.*
Es un tonto de cuatro suelas. *He's a downright fool.*
Hablar a tontas y a locas. *To tell idle stories (tales).*
topacio *m. topaz.*
topar *to collide; to run into; to butt.*
tope *m. top, butt; stop (device); buffer (railway); collision, bump.*
topografía *f. topography.*
topógrafo *m. topographer.*
toque *m. touch; ringing, peal; call (bugle).*
tórax *m. thorax.*
torbellino *m. whirlwind; rush, hurly-burly, hurry-scurry.*
torcedura *f. twisting; sprain.*
torcer *to twist; to turn; to sprain; to distort.*
Se me ha torcido el pie. *I've sprained my ankle.*
Tuerza a la derecha. *Turn right.*
torcido *adj. twisted; crooked.*
toreo *m. bullfighting.*
torear *to be a bullfighter; to banter.*
torero *m. bullfighter.*
tormenta *f. storm, tempest.*
tormentoso *adj. stormy.*
tornar *to return; to repeat, to do again; to change.*
tornasol *m. sunflower; litmus.*
torneo *m. tournament.*
tornillo *m. screw.*
La rosca de un tornillo. *The thread of a screw.*
torniquete *m. turnstile; tourniquet.*
torno *m. lathe; winch, windlass; spindle.*
toro *m. bull.*
Vamos a los toros. *Let's go to the bullfight.*
toronja *f. grapefruit.*
torpe *adj. dull, clumsy, slow; awkward.*
torpedero *m. torpedo boat.*
torpedo *m. torpedo.*
torpeza *f. dullness, slowness; awkwardness.*
torre *f. tower; turret; belfry; castle (in chess).*
torrente *m. torrent.*
tórrido *adj. torrid.*
torta *f. cake, tart; font (printing).*
tortilla *f. omelet; a kind of pancake (Mex.).*
Tráigame Ud. una tortilla de cebolla. *Bring me on onion omelet.*
tórtola *f. turtledove.*
tortuga *f. turtle; tortoise.*
tortura *f. torture.*
torturar *to torture.*
tos *f. cough.*
Pastillas para la tos. *Cough drops.*
tosco *adj. rough, coarse, clumsy.*
toser *to cough.*
tostada *f. toast.*

Tráigame una taza de café, tostadas y mantequilla. *Bring me a cup of coffee and some toast and butter.*
tostado *adj. toasted; tanned.*
Pan tostado. *Toast (bread).*
tostar *to toast; to roast; to tan (by exposure to sun).*
TOTAL *adj. and n. total, whole, in all.*
¿Cuál es el importe total? *What's the total amount?*
¿Cuántos hay ahí en total? *How many are there in all?*
Total, ¿qué se adelanta con eso? *In short, where will it get you (what's the good of it)?*
totalitario *adj. totalitarian.*
tóxico *adj. toxic, poisonous; m. poison.*
traba *f. obstacle, hindrance; trammel, hobble, fetter.*
trabajador *adj. hard-working, industrious; m. worker, laborer.*
TRABAJAR *to work; to labor.*
¿En qué trabaja Ud.? *What work do you do?*
Se gana la vida trabajando. *He works for a living.*
TRABAJO *m. work, labor; workmanship; toil, trouble, hardship.*
Se garantiza el trabajo. *The work is guaranteed.*
Este trabajo está hecho a medias. *This work is only halfway done.*
Todo esto es trabajo perdido. *All this work is wasted. This is all wasted effort.*
¡Qué trabajo más bien hecho! *What an excellent piece of work!*
Sin trabajo. *Unemployed. Out of work.*
Costar trabajo. *To be difficult. To require a lot of work (effort).*
Cuesta trabajo creerlo. *It's hard to believe it.*
Día de trabajo. *Working day.*
Tomarse el trabajo de. *To take the trouble to.*
Trabajo nocturno. *Night work.*
Trabajos forzados. *Hard labor. ("Forced labor.")*
trabar *to join, to unite, to bind; to shackle.*
Trabar conversación. *To open a conversation.*
Trabar amistad. *To make friends.*
Trabar conocimiento. *To make someone's acquaintance. To strike up an acquaintance.*
tractor *m. tractor.*
tradición *f. tradition.*
tradicional *adj. traditional.*
traducción *f. translation.*
TRADUCIR *to translate.*
Traduzca esta carta al inglés. *Translate this letter into English.*
No hay manera de traducirlo. *There's no way to translate it.*
traductor *m. translator.*
TRAER *to bring, to carry; to wear.*
¡Mozo! Tráigame una cerveza. *Waiter, bring me a glass of beer.*
¿Me han traído el traje? *Have they brought my suit?*
¿Lo trajo consigo? *Did you bring it with you?*
¿Qué le trae a Ud. acá? *What brings you here?*
¿Qué trae el diario? *What's new in the paper today?*
Todos los días trae un vestido nuevo. *Every day she wears a new dress.*
Traer a cuento. *To bring into the conversation.*
traficante *adj. trading; m. trader.*
traficar *to traffic, to trade, to do business.*
tráfico *m. traffic; trading; trade.*
tragaluz *f. skylight.*

tragar *to swallow; to devour, to glut.*
tragedia *f. tragedy.*
trágico *adj. tragic.*
trago *m. drink, draught.*
Vamos a echarnos un trago. *Let's have a drink.*
Beber a tragos. *To gulp (down).*
tragón *adj. gluttonous; m. glutton.*
traición *f. treason; treachery.*
Hizo traición a su patria. *He betrayed his country.*
traicionar *to betray, to act treacherously.*
traidor *adj. treacherous; m. traitor.*
traje *m. suit; dress; gown.*
Traje de sastre. *Tailored suit.*
Traje hecho. *Ready-made suit.*
Traje de etiqueta. *Evening dress. Formal dress.*
Traje de calle. *Business suit.*
trajinar *to carry, to convey; to travel about.*
trama *f. weft (in weaving), web; plot; conspiracy.*
tramar *to weave; to plot, to scheme.*
Se trama algo. *Something's brewing. Something's in the air.*
tramitar *to conduct, to transact.*
trámite *m. procedure; transaction; pl. formalities.*
trampa *f. trap; fraud; bad debt.*
Trampa para ratones. *Mousetrap.*
tramposo *adj. and n. deceitful; trickster, cheater, deceiver.*
tranca *f. crossbar.*
trance *m. danger; critical moment.*
A todo trance. *By all means. At all costs. To the bitter end.*
tranco *m. a long stride; threshold.*
tranquilidad *f. tranquillity, peace, quietness.*
tranquilizar *to calm, to reassure.*
tranquilo *adj. tranquil, quiet, calm.*
Este es un lugar muy tranquilo. *This is a very quiet place.*
transacción *f. compromise; transaction.*
transatlántico *adj. transatlantic; m. (transatlantic) liner.*
transbordar *to transship; to transfer, to change (trains, busses, etc.).*
transbordo *m. transshipment; transfer.*
transcurso *m. course, lapse (of time).*
transcurrir *to pass, to elapse (time).*
transeúnte *m. and f. passer-by.*
transferencia *f. transference; transfer.*
Déme una tranferencia. *Give me a transfer.*
transformación *f. transformation.*
transformador *adj. transforming; m. transformer.*
transformar *to transform.*
transfusión *f. transfusion.*
transigir *to compromise; to give in.*
transitar *to pass by, to walk along; to travel.*
tránsito *m. passage, transit, transition.*
De tránsito. *In transit.*
transitorio *adj. transitory.*
transmisor *adj. transmitting; m. transmitter.*
transmitir *to transmit, to send, to convey.*
transparencia *f. slide.*
transparente *adj. transparent; m. window shade.*
transpiración *f. perspiration.*
transportar *to transport, to convey; to transpose (music).*
transporte *m. transport; transportation.*
Transporte pagado. *Carriage paid.*
tranvía *m. tramway, street car.*
¿Qué tranvía debo tomar? *Which streetcar should I take?*
¿Dónde está la parada más cerca del tranvía? *Where is the nearest streetcar stop?*
trapecio *m. trapeze.*

trapero m. *junkman, ragman.*

trapo m. *rag;* pl. *old clothes; rags.*
Poner como un trapo. *To reprimand severely. To give someone a dressing down.*
Trapo de limpiar. *Cleaning rag.*

TRAS *after, behind, besides.*
Uno tras el otro. *One after the other.*
Pónlo tras ese biombo. *Put it behind that screen.*
Buscamos en una tienda tras otra. *We tried store after store.*

trascendencia f. *transcendency, importance.*

trascendental adj. *transcendental; very important, far-reaching.*

trascender *to smell; to spread, to pervade; to leak out, to become known.*

trasero adj. *back, rear.*
La puerta trasera da al jardín. *The back door opens out into the garden.*
Asiento trasero. *Back seat.*

trasladar *to move; to transport; to transfer; to postpone; to transcribe, to translate.*
Se trasladaron de casa. *They moved to another house.*
Acaban de trasladarlo a otra sucursal. *He's just been transferred to another branch.*

traslado m. *transfer; notification* (law); *transcript, copy.*

trasmitir (See **transmitir**.)

trasnochador adj. and n. *night owl; one who stays up late, one who keeps late hours.*

trasnochar *to keep late hours, to stay up late, to sit up all night.*

traspasar *to cross; to transfer, to trespass.*
Traspasar de un lado a otro. *To cross from one side to the other.*
Traspasar un negocio. *To transfer a business.*

traspaso m. *transfer; assignment; trespass.*
Acta de traspaso. *Deed of assignment.*

traspié m. *slip; trip.*

trasplantar *to transplant.*

trasquilar *to clip, to shear.*

traste m. *fret* (on a guitar, etc.).
Dar al traste con. *To ruin. To spoil. To destroy.*

trastienda f. *back room* (in a store).

trasto m. *an old piece of furniture; trash.*
Trastos de cocina. *Kitchen utensils.*

trastornar *to upset; to turn upside down; to disturb, to disarrange.*

trastorno m. *upsetting; disturbance.*

trata f. *slave trade.*

tratable adj. *sociable, easy to deal with; amenable.*

tratado m. *treaty; treatise.*

tratamiento m. *treatment; form of address.*
Ha respondido muy bien al tratamiento. *He responded to the treatment very well.*

tratante m. *dealer, trader, merchant.*

TRATAR *to treat; to deal; to try; to discuss.*
¿De qué se trata? *What's it all about? What's it a question of?*
Se trata de un asunto importante. *The matter in question is important.*
De eso se trata. *That's the point. That's what it's about.*
De nada de eso se trató. *That wasn't discussed.*
¿De qué trata este artículo de fondo? *What does this editorial deal with? What's this editorial about?*
Este libro trata de la vida de Washington. *This book deals with* (is about) *the life of Washington.*
Prefiero tratar con personas serias. *I prefer to deal with reliable* (serious) *people.*

Todos los que la tratan la quieren. *She's liked by everyone who meets her.*
Tratan mal a sus empleados. *They don't treat their employees well.*
La trataron como a una hermana. *They treated her like a sister.*
Trató de hacerlo pero no pudo. *He tried to do it but couldn't.*
Trate de ser más puntual en lo futuro. *Try to be more punctual in the future.*
Trataron de un asunto importantísimo. *They discussed a very important matter.*
Le trataron de tonto. *They called him a fool.*
Eso es lo que trataba de decir. *That's what I was trying to say.*
Tratarse con. *To be on friendly terms with. To deal personally with* (someone).
No se tratan desde hace mucho tiempo. *They haven't been on friendly terms for a long time.*
Tratándose de Ud. *In your case.*
Por tratarse de Ud. *In so far as concerns you. In what concerns you.*

trato m. *treatment; form of address; agreement, deal.*
He tenido poco trato con ellos. *I haven't had much to do with them.*
Cerrar el trato. *To close a* (the) *deal.*
Entrar en tratos. *To start a deal. To enter into* (start) *negotiations.*
Hagamos un trato. *Let's make a deal.*
Tener buen trato. *To be pleasant. To be nice.*
Tener mal trato. *To be rude. To be impolite.*

TRAVÉS m. *bias; misfortune; crossbeam; traverse.*
A través de. *Through. Across.*
Mirar de través. *To look sideways. To look out of the corner of one's eyes.*

travesaño m. *crosspiece, crossbeam.*

travesía f. *ocean crossing, sea voyage; crossing.*
Es una larga travesía. *It's a long voyage.*

travesura f. *mischief, prank, trick.*

traviesa f. *tie* (railway).

travieso adj. *mischievous, naughty.*

trayecto m. *distance; stretch; route.*
Final del trayecto. *Last stop.*

trayectoria f. *trajectory.*

traza f. *sketch, outline; appearance.*
Llevar trazas de. *To look like.*
Según todas las trazas. *According to all appearances.*

trazar *to draw, to plan, to outline.*
Trace una línea recta. *Draw a straight line.*
Los ingenieros trazaron los planos para un nuevo muelle. *The engineers drew up plans for a new dock.*

trébol m. *trefoil, clover.*

trece adj. and n. *thirteen; thirteenth.*
Estarse (mantenerse) en sus treces. *To stick to one's opinion.*

trecho m. *distance, stretch.*
A trechos. *At intervals.*

tregua f. *truce; respite.*

TREINTA adj. and n. *thirty.*

tremendo adj. *tremendous, dreadful, awful.*

TREN m. *train; equipment; retinue; ostentation.*
¿A qué hora sale el próximo tren? (At) *What time does the next train leave?*
El tren va a salir. *The train's about to leave.*
¿Dónde va este tren? *Where does this train go?*
¿Para este tren en todas las estaciones? *Does this train stop at all stations?*

trenza f. *braid, tress.*

trenzar *to braid.*

trepar *to climb; to creep* (a plant).

tres adj. *three, third.*

trescientos adj. and n. *three hundred; three hundredth.*

treta f. *trick, wile.*

triángulo m. *triangle.*

tribu f. *tribe.*

tribuna f. *tribune; platform.*

tribunal m. *court* (of justice).

tributar *to pay taxes; to pay tribute, to render homage.*

tributo m. *tribute; tax.*

trigo m. *wheat.*

trigonometría f. *trigonometry.*

trigueña f. *brunette, swarthy.*

trigueño m. *swarthy, having the color of wheat.*

trilla f. *threshing.*

trilladora f. *thresher, threshing machine.*

trillar *to thresh.*

trimestral adj. *quarterly.*

trimestre m. *quarter* (of a year).

trinchar *to carve* (meat).

trinchera f. *trench.*

trineo m. *sleigh, sled, sledge.*

trío m. *trio.*

tripa f. *tripe; intestines; belly* (coll.).

triple adj. *triple, treble.*

triplicar *to triple, to treble.*

tripulación f. *crew.*

tripulante m. and f. *crew member.*

tripular *to man* (a ship); *to equip.*

triquiñuela f. *trickery; dodge.*

TRISTE adj. *sad; gloomy.*
Esto es muy triste. *That's very sad.*
Parecía triste y cansado. *He looked tired and depressed.*
Al oír la noticia se puso muy triste. *She became very sad when she heard the news.*

tristeza f. *sadness, grief, gloom.*
Se muere de tristeza. *She's heartbroken. She's broken-hearted.*

triturar *to grind, to pound.*

triunfal adj. *triumphal.*

triunfante adj. *triumphant.*

triunfar *to triumph, to succeed.*
Triunfó porque era muy determinado. *He succeeded because he was very determined.*

triunfo m. *triumph; trump card.*

trivial adj. *trivial.*
Es algo trivial. *It's a trifling matter. It's a trifle.*

trocar *to change; to barter.*

trofeo m. *trophy; prize.*

trompa f. *trumpet; trunk* (of an elephant).

trompada f. *punch, blow with the fist.*

trompeta f. *trumpet;* m. *trumpeter.*

trompo m. *top, spinning-top.*

tronar *to thunder.*
Por lo que pudiera tronar. *As a precaution. In case of an emergency. In case something happens.*

tronco m. *trunk* (of wood); *log; stem.*

trono m. *throne.*

tropa f. *troop.*

tropezar *to stumble, to trip; to come across, to meet accidentally, to run into; to meet with difficulties.*
Por poco me caigo al tropezar con esa piedra. *I almost tripped over that stone.* ("*I almost fell when I tripped over that stone.*")
¿Ha tropezado Ud. por casualidad con mi libro? *Have you by any chance come across my book?*
Acabo de tropezar con Juan en la calle. *I*

a lot in Europe.

VIAJE m. trip, voyage, journey, travel.

¡Buen viaje! Bon voyage! Pleasant journey!

¡Feliz viaje! A pleasant journey!

Tuvimos una tormenta durante el viaje de ida. We ran into a storm on our way over.

En viaje para. En route for.

Estar de viaje. To be on a trip. To be away traveling.

Viaje redondo. A round trip.

Viaje de novios. Honeymoon.

Viaje de recreo. Pleasure trip.

Viaje de ida. A one-way trip. Trip to a place.

Viaje de vuelta (regreso). A return trip. A trip back.

Viaje de ida y vuelta. A round trip.

VIAJERO m. traveler; passenger.

¡Señores viajeros, al tren! (Passengers.) All aboard!

vianda f. food, viands; pl. vegetables for a Cuban dish called ajiaco.

víbora f. viper.

vibración f. vibration.

vibrar to vibrate, to throb.

vicealmirante m. vice-admiral.

vicecónsul m. vice-consul.

vicepresidente m. vice-president.

viciar to vitiate, to mar; to spoil; to corrupt; to tamper with, to forge; to make void.

El aire aquí está viciado. The air here is impure.

Este manuscrito está viciado. The manuscript has been tampered with.

Las raspaduras vician el documento. The erasures make the document void.

viciarse to give oneself up to vice; to acquire vices.

vicio m. vice; habit; bad habit; defect; exuberance; growth of plants.

Ese niño llora de vicio. That child is always crying.

Este árbol lleva mucho vicio. This tree is rich in foliage.

Dinero para los vicios. Pocket money.

Quejarse de vicio. To complain without cause. To be in the habit of complaining.

Tener el vicio de. To be in the habit of.

Vivir en el vicio. To lead a dissolute life.

vicioso adj. vicious; having bad habits, given to vice.

Es muy vicioso. He has many bad habits.

Círculo vicioso. Vicious circle.

vicisitud f. vicissitude.

víctima f. victim.

victoria f. victory.

victorioso adj. victorious.

VIDA f. life; living.

En mi vida he visto ni oído tal cosa. I've never seen or heard of such a thing in my life.

Me gano la vida escribiendo. I write for a living. I make my living by writing.

Mi vida. My dearest. My darling.

Vida mía. My dearest. My darling.

Buscar la vida. To try to make a living.

Ganarse la vida. To earn (make) a living.

Darse buena vida. To live comfortably.

Dar mala vida. To mistreat. To abuse.

Vida alegre (airada). A merry life.

Pasar la vida. To live frugally. To eke out an existence.

El coste de la vida. The cost of living.

Entre la vida y la muerte. Between life and death.

En su vida. Never.

¡Por mi vida! My word!

Escapar con vida. To have a narrow escape.

vidriera f. showcase; show window.

vidrio m. glass.

Vidrio de aumento. Magnifying glass.

Vidrio tallado. Cut glass.

Pagar los vidrios rotos. To be made the scapegoat.

viejecito m. a little old man.

VIEJO adj. old; worn-out; ancient; m. an old man.

Somos viejos amigos. We're old friends.

Le creí más viejo. I thought you were older.

Su madre es muy vieja. His mother is very old.

Ese viejo tiene muy mal genio. That old man has a bad (vile) temper.

VIENTO m. wind; scent (hunting); airs.

Hace mucho viento. It's very windy.

Corre un viento glacial. There's an icy wind.

Sus negocios van de viento en popa. His business is very successful.

vientre m. belly, stomach.

VIERNES m. Friday.

viga f. beam, rafter, girder.

vigésimo adj. and n. twentieth.

vigilancia f. vigilance.

vigilante adj. vigilant; watchful; m. watchman.

vigilar to watch over, to look after.

vigilia f. vigil; fast; eve; burning the midnight oil.

Pasamos la noche de vigilia. We sat up all night.

Esta novela es el producto de sus vigilias. He spent his nights working on this novel.

Comer de vigilia. To abstain from meat.

vigor m. vigor, strength.

vigoroso adj. vigorous, strong.

vil adj. mean, low, vile, despicable.

vileza f. meanness, infamous deed.

villa f. village; villa.

vinagre m. vinegar.

vinicultura f. viniculture, wine growing.

vinicultor m. wine grower.

VINO m. wine.

¿Le sirvo a Ud. un poco de vino? Shall I pour (serve) you a little wine?

Jerez es famoso por sus vinos. Jerez is famous for its wines.

Vino tinto. Red wine.

Vino blanco. White wine.

Vino espumoso. Sparkling wine.

Vino de Jerez. Sherry.

Vino de Oporto. Port wine.

viña f. vineyard.

viñedo m. vineyard.

violación f. violation, breach.

violar to violate, to infringe, to offend.

violencia f. violence.

violento adj. violent.

violeta f. violet (plant).

violín m. violin.

violinista m. and f. violinist.

violoncelo m. violoncello.

virar to tack, to veer, to change direction, to turn.

Vire a la derecha (izquierda). Turn right (left).

virgen f. virgin.

viril adj. virile, manly.

virilidad f. virility.

virtud f. virtue, a good quality.

En virtud de. By virtue of.

Por virtud de. Because of. On account of.

En tal virtud. In view of which. On account of which.

virtuoso adj. and n. virtuoso.

viruela f. smallpox.

Viruelas locas. Chicken pox.

virulencia f. virulence.

virulento adj. virulent; malignant.

visar to visa, to visé; to O.K.

Deseo hacer visar mi pasaporte para México. I want to get a visa for Mexico.

Tengo mi pasaporte visado. My passport's stamped.

viscosidad f. viscosity.

viscoso adj. viscous, clammy.

visibilidad f. visibility.

visible adj. visible.

visión f. vision, sight; revelation.

VISITA f. visit, call.

Está esperando la visita en la sala. The guest is waiting in the living room.

Tenemos visitas. We have company.

Hacer una visita. To pay a call.

Visita de cumplido. A formal call.

Visita de inspección. Inspection tour.

Pagar una visita. To return a call.

VISITAR to visit; to call on.

¿Por qué ha dejado Ud. de visitarnos? Why have you stopped visiting us? Why have you stopped coming to see us?

Los visito de vez en cuando. I call on them now and then. I go to see them once in a while.

visitarse to call on one another, to be on visiting terms.

víspera f. eve.

Estar en vísperas de. To be on the eve of.

VISTA f. sight; view; glance; looks; trial (law); m. a customhouse officer, a customs official.

¡Hasta la vista! I'll be seeing you! See you soon!

Solamente le conozco de vista. I know him only by sight.

No lo pierdas de vista. Don't lose sight of him.

Bajar la vista. To look down.

Alzar la vista. To look up.

A la vista. On sight.

A primera vista. At first sight.

Corto de vista. Nearsighted.

Cansar la vista. To strain one's eyes.

En vista de. In view of. Considering.

Hacer la vista gorda. To connive.

Echar una vista a. To glance at.

Vista de pájaro. A bird's-eye view.

Hay una hermosa vista desde aquí. There's a nice view from here.

¡Qué vista! What a view!

vistazo m. glance.

Echar un vistazo. To glance.

visto adj. seen; obvious, clear.

Está visto. It's obvious. It's evident.

Nunca visto. Unheard of.

Por lo visto. Evidently. Apparently.

Visto Bueno. (V°.B°.) O.K. All right. Approved.

Visto que. Considering that.

Bien visto. Respected. Highly regarded. Proper. Well considered. On second thought.

Mal visto. Not respected. Looked down on.

vistoso adj. beautiful, showy; dressy.

visual adj. visual.

vital adj. vital.

vitalicio adj. for life; during life.

Renta vitalicia. Life pension.

vitalidad f. vitality.

vitamina f. vitamin.

vitorear to acclaim, to cheer.

vituperio m. vituperation, bitter abuse; infamy, shame.

viuda f. widow; mourning bride (plant).

viudez f. *widowhood.*
viudo f. *widower.*
¡viva! *Long live! Hail! Hurrah!*
  ¡Viva España! *Long live Spain!*
  Es un viva la virgen. *He's a simpleton.*
vivamente *vividly, deeply, very much.*
vivaracho adj. *lively, sprightly, frisky.*
vivaz adj. *lively; vivid; ingenious, bright, witty.*
vivero m. *warren; hatchery; nursery (plants).*
viveza f. *liveliness; vividness; perspicacity, keenness; sparkling (eyes).*
VIVIR *to live; to last; m. life, living.*
  Vive solo. *He lives alone.*
  ¿Dónde vive? *Where do you live?*
  ¿Cuánto tiempo hace que vive Ud. aquí? *How long have you been living here?*
  Se viene a vivir con nosotros. *He's coming to live with us.*
  Ella vive en el segundo piso. *She lives on the second floor.*
  Se vive bien aquí. *One can live well (nicely, comfortably) here.*
  Vive de su pluma. *He makes his living as a writer.*
  Tiene para vivir. *He has enough to live on.*
  Vive soñando. *His head's in the clouds. ("He lives in a daydream.")*
  Vivir para ver. *Live and learn.*
VIVO adj. *living, alive; lively; smart.*
  Está vivo. *He's alive.*
  Copia al vivo. *Facsimile.*
  Es un hombre muy vivo. *He's a very smart man.*
  Color vivo. *Bright color.*
  A lo (al) vivo. *To the life. Like the model. Very like the original.*
  De viva voz. *By word of mouth.*
  Tocar en lo vivo. *To cut to the quick.*
  Los vivos y los muertos. *The quick and the dead.*
vizconde m. *viscount.*
vizcondesa f. *viscountess.*
vocablo m. *word, term.*
vocabulario m. *vocabulary.*
vocación m. *vocation.*
vocal adj. *vocal, oral; f. vowel, m. voter (in an assembly); member of a board of directors.*
vocear *to cry out.*
vocero m. *spokesman; advocate.*
vociferar *to vociferate, to shout, to cry out loudly.*
volandas (en) *in the air; in a jiffy.*
  Lo llevaron en volandas. *They carried him on their shoulders.*
volante adj. *flying; m. steering wheel; balance wheel (watch).*
VOLAR *to fly; to blow up, to blast; to spread, to disseminate (news, a rumor).*
  Volamos desde Madrid a Barcelona. *We flew from Madrid to Barcelona.*
  Las horas vuelan. *The hours flew by.*
  La noticia voló de boca en boca. *The news spread from mouth to mouth.*
  Echar a volar la imaginación. *To let one's imagination run away with one.*
  Sacar (echar) a volar. *To spread. To publish.*
  Volaron el puente. *They blew up the bridge.*
volátil adj. *volatile, changeable.*
volcán m. *volcano.*
volcar *to overturn; to turn upside down; to turn over; to tilt.*
voltear *to turn over (position); to tumble, to roll over (an acrobat).*
voltereta f. *somersault.*

volubilidad f. *volubility.*
voluble adj. *voluble; fickle, changeable.*
volumen m. *volume; size; bulk. (For "volume" in the sense of "volume two of a set," see tomo.)*
voluminoso adj. *voluminous, bulky.*
VOLUNTAD f. *will, desire; disposition, consent; intention.*
  Lo puede hacer pero le falta voluntad. *He can do it but he's unwilling to.*
  Lo hice contra mi voluntad. *I did it against my own will.*
  Mala voluntad. *Bad disposition.*
  De buena voluntad. *With pleasure. Willingly.*
  De mala voluntad. *Unwillingly.*
  A voluntad. *At will.*
  Ultima voluntad. *Last will and testament.*
voluntariamente *voluntarily, of one's own free will.*
voluntario adj. *voluntary, willing; m. volunteer.*
voluptuoso adj. *voluptuous, sensual.*
VOLVER *to come back, to return; to turn; to turn back; to put back.*
  Vuelva mañana. *Come back tomorrow.*
  No ha vuelto todavía. *He hasn't returned yet.*
  Volverá pronto. *He'll come back soon.*
  Se ha marchado para no volver. *He's gone for good.*
  Vuelva la página. *Turn the page.*
  El camino vuelve hacia la izquierda. *The road turns to the left.*
  Vuelve el libro a su sitio. *Put the book back in its place.*
  Volvió a salir. *He went out again.*
  No vuelvas a hacer eso. *Don't do that again.*
  No la volvió a ver más. *He didn't see her again.*
  Vuelva a hacerlo. *Do it again.*
  Volver la cabeza. *To turn one's head.*
  Volver a trabajar. *To resume work.*
  Volver atrás. *To come or go back.*
  Volver en sí. *To recover one's senses.*
  Volver a uno loco. *To drive someone crazy.*
VOLVERSE *to turn, to become.*
  Este papel se ha vuelto amarillo. *This paper has turned yellow.*
  Se ha vuelto loco. *He's become insane.*
  Volverse atrás. *To retract.*
  Volverse la tortilla. *To turn the tables.*
vomitar *to vomit, to throw out.*
vomitivo adj. *and n. emetic.*
vómito m. *vomiting.*
voracidad f. *voracity, greediness.*
vorágine f. *vortex, whirlpool.*
voraz adj. *voracious, greedy.*
vos (pers. pron.) *you (singular and familiar; used in Arg., Costa Rica and Uruguay).*
  Vos y yo. *You and I.*
  Es como vos. *He's like you.*
  Vos tenés que venir mañana. *(Arg.) You have to come tomorrow.*
VOSOTRAS (f. pl. of tú) *you (familiar).*
  Vosotras sois sus hermanas. *You're his sisters.*
  Esto es para vosotras. *This is for you (pl. f.).*
VOSOTROS (m. pl. of tú) *you (familiar).*
  Vosotros sois mis amigos. *You (pl.) are my friends.*
  Vosotros tenéis la culpa. *You're (pl.) to blame.*
  Vosotros os engañais. *You're (pl.) fooling yourselves.*
  Os aguardábamos a vosotros. *We were waiting for you (pl.).*
votación f. *voting.*

  Votación secreta. *Ballot. Secret vote.*
  Poner a votación. *To put to a vote.*
votante m. and f. *voter, elector.*
votar *to vote; to vow.*
  No votaré ni por el uno ni por el otro. *I won't vote for either one.*
voto m. *vote; ballot; vow; wish.*
  Fué elegido por una gran mayoría de votos. *He was elected by a large majority (of votes).*
  Hacemos votos por que obtenga lo que desea. *We hope you'll get your wish.*
  Hacemos votos por su felicidad. *We wish you a lot of happiness.*
  Hago votos por su prosperidad. *I wish you success.*
VOZ f. *voice; outcry; word; rumor.*
  Tiene muy buena voz. *He has a very good voice.*
  El es quien lleva la voz cantante. *He's the spokesman.*
  Pidió socorro a voces. *She cried out for help.*
  Alzar la voz. *To raise one's voice.*
  Anudarse la voz. *To be unable to speak (because of excitement, emotion, etc.).*
  Tener voz y voto. *To have a voice in a (the) matter.*
  Voz de mando. *Word of command.*
  La voz pasiva. *The passive voice (grammar).*
  A media voz. *In an undertone. In a whisper.*
  Dar voces. *To cry. To shout.*
  Corre la voz. *It's rumored. It's said.*
  De viva voz. *By word of mouth.*
  A voz en cuello. *In a very loud voice.*
  En voz alta. *Aloud.*
  En voz baja. *In a low tone.*
  Estar en voz. *To be in voice.*
  A una voz. *Unanimously. ("With one voice.")*
vuelco m. *overturning, tumble.*
vuelo m. *flight; distance flown; frill, ruffle; width, fullness (dress, skirt, etc.).*
  Esta falda tiene mucho vuelo. *There's plenty of fullness in that skirt.*
  Acaban de hacer un vuelo alrededor del mundo. *They have just made a flight around the world.*
  Tomar vuelo. *To grow. To progress.*
  Alzar (levantar) vuelo. *To fly off.*
  A (al) vuelo. *Right away. In a jiffy. In passing. On the fly.*
  Lo entendió al vuelo. *He caught on right away.*
  De alto vuelo. *Of great importance. Of high standing.*
VUELTA f. *turn, turning; return; reverse; back (of a page); a walk; change (money).*
  Estar de vuelta. *To be back. To know beforehand.*
  Me dijo que estaría de vuelta pronto. *She told me she would be back soon.*
  Ya estoy de vuelta de lo que me dice. *I already know what he's telling me.*
  Dar una vuelta. *To take a walk.*
  ¿Le gustaría dar una vuelta después de comer? *Would you like to take a walk after dinner?*
  Dar vueltas. *To turn. To walk back and forth. To keep thinking about the same thing. To hammer on a point.*
  Por más que doy vueltas, no acierto a comprenderlo. *No matter how hard I think about it, I can't understand it.*
  Déme la vuelta. *Give me the change.*
  Quédese con la vuelta. *Keep the change.*
  Eso no tiene vuelta de hoja. *There are no two*

ways about it.

Lo puso de vuelta y media. *She gave him a good dressing-down.*

Billete de ida y vuelta. *Round-trip ticket.*

Viaje de vuelta. *Return trip.*

A la vuelta de la esquina. *Around the corner.*

Dé la vuelta. *Turn around.*

Otra vuelta. *Again. Once more.*

¡Otra vuelta! *Another round (of drinks)!*

A vuelta(s) de. *Around. Approximately.*

A vueltas de Navidad. *Around (about) Christmas.*

A la vuelta. *On the next page. Turn over. Carried over (bookkeeping).*

De la vuelta. *Continued. Brought forward (bookkeeping).*

¡Media vuelta! *Right about-face!*

vuelto m. *change, money returned (Amer.).*

Guarde el vuelto. *Keep the change.*

VUESTRA (f. of vuestro) *your, yours; pl. vuestras.*

Vuestra madre. *Your mother.*

Vuestras hijas. *Your daughters.*

VUESTRO (pers. pron.) *your, yours; pl. vuestros.*

Vuestro amigo. *Your friend.*

Es un amigo vuestro. *He's a friend of yours.*

Vuestros amigos. *Your friends.*

vulcanizar *to vulcanize.*

vulgar adj. *vulgar; common; ordinary.*

vulgaridad f. *vulgarity.*

vulgarmente *vulgarly; commonly.*

vulgo m. *the common people; populace; mob.*

vulnerable adj. *vulnerable.*

W

whiskey m. *whiskey.*

X

x *Most words originally written with x now have j. In Mexico, however, the words Méjico and Mejicano are still spelled with an x: México, Mexicano.*

Rayos X. *X-rays.*

xenofobia f. *hatred of foreigners.*

Y

Y *and.*

Tú y yo. *You and I.*

Hoy y mañana. *Today and tomorrow.*

Pan y queso. *Bread and cheese.*

¿Y después? *What next? What then?*

¿Pero y ella? *But what about her?*

YA *already; now; finally.*

Tengo que irme ya. *I have to go now.*

Ya es tarde. *It's late. It's late now.*

Ya son las doce pasadas. *It's after twelve now.*

Es ya hora de levantarse. *It's time to get up.*

¡Ya voy! *I'm coming.*

Ya está el té. *Tea is ready.*

Ya no lo necesito. *I no longer need it. I don't need it any more.*

El niño ya puede andar. *The child can walk now.*

Lloverá pronto, ya está tronando. *It will rain soon; it's thundering already.*

Pasa ya de los cincuenta. *She's over fifty.*

¡Ya está! *It's all done!*

Ya no puedo más. *I'm worn out. I can't stand it any longer.*

Ya caigo en la cuenta. *Now I see the point.*

¡Ya me las pagará! *I'll get even with him.*

¡Ya lo haré! *I'll do it in time. Certainly I'll do it.*

¡Ya lo creo! *I should think so! Of course! Certainly!*

Ya lo creo que me acuerdo. *Of course I remember (it).*

¡Ya lo decía yo! *Didn't I say so! I had a feeling that it might happen. I was sure of it.*

¡Ya lo ves! *See there! There you are! Now you see it!*

¡Ya veremos! *We'll see.*

yacer *to lie; to be lying (ill in bed); to be lying (in the grave).*

yacimiento m. *bed, layer, deposit (of ore); field (oil).*

Yacimiento petrolífero. *Oil field.*

yanqui adj. and n. *a native of the United States; Yankee.*

yapa f. *lagnappe, something extra given to a customer with a purchase. (See ñapa.)*

yarda f. *yard (a measure).*

yate m. *yacht.*

yedra f. *ivy.*

yegua f. *mare.*

yema f. *bud, shoot; yolk (of an egg); fingertip.*

Me he lastimado la yema del dedo. *I hurt the tip of my finger.*

Este huevo tiene dos yemas. *This egg has two yolks.*

Hay muchas yemas en ese rosal. *There are a lot of buds on that rosebush.*

yerba f. *herb; weed; grass; mate. (See hierba.)*

Yerba mate. *Mate.*

Yerba buena. *Mint.*

yermo adj. *waste, bare; m. desert, wilderness.*

Tierra yerma. *Wasteland.*

yerno m. *son-in-law.*

yerro m. *error, mistake, fault.*

yerto adj. *stiff; motionless.*

yesca f. *tinder.*

yeso m. *gypsum; plaster; cast (of plaster).*

YO *I.*

Soy yo. *It's me (I).*

¡Soy yo mismo! *Yes, it's me. It's me in the flesh.*

Fuí yo el que telefoneó. *I was the one who phoned.*

Yo mismo se lo dí. *I gave it to him myself.*

Yo no sé. *I don't know.*

Yo no hablo español. *I don't speak Spanish.*

yodo m. *iodine.*

yodoformo m. *iodoform.*

yoduro m. *iodine.*

yuca f. *yucca (a plant).*

yugo m. *yoke; bondage, slavery; marriage ties.*

Sacudir el yugo. *To throw off the yoke. To free oneself. To become free.*

yunque m. *anvil.*

yunta f. *yoke (of oxen, horses, etc.); couple, pair.*

Una yunta de bueyes. *A yoke of oxen.*

yute m. *jute.*

yuxtaponer *to juxtapose, to place side by side.*

yuxtapuesto adj. *juxtaposed, side by side.*

Z

zacate m. *grass; hay (Mex., Central America, the Philippines).*

zafar *to disembarrass; to lighten (a ship).*

zafarse *to get rid of; to escape, to get out of; to slip off, to come off; to break loose.*

zafarrancho m. *clearing for action (Navy); row, scuffle.*

zafiro m. *sapphire.*

zafra f. *sugar crop; crop of sugar cane.*

zaga f. *rear, back; load in the rear of a carriage; m. last player (at cards).*

Ella no le va a la zaga. *She's quite as good as he. She's no worse than he is.*

Ir a la zaga. *To lag behind.*

Dejar en zaga. *To leave behind. To outstrip. To do better than.*

Quedarse en zaga. *To be left behind. To be outstripped.*

No ir en zaga. *To be as good as the next one.*

zagal m. *lad, young man; young shepherd.*

zaguán m. *hall, foyer.*

zaguero adj. *laggard; m. backstop (in Basque ballgame).*

zaherir *to blame, to reproach.*

zalamería f. *flattery.*

zalamero adj. *flatterer.*

Es una niña muy zalamera. *She's a flatterer.*

zamba f. *popular South American dance.*

zambo adj. *bowlegged; m. mulatto.*

zambullida f. *dive, plunge.*

zambullir *to duck, to plunge.*

zambullirse *to dive, to plunge (into the water).*

Se zambulló en el río. *He dived into the river.*

zampar *to gulp, to swallow down; to conceal.*

zamparse *to rush in, to barge in.*

Se zampó todo el pastel. *He gulped down the whole pie.*

Se zampó sin más ni más dentro de la casa. *He barged straight into the house.*

zanahoria f. *carrot.*

zanca f. *shank; long leg.*

zancada f. *stride; long step.*

De dos zancadas. *In a jiffy. In no time. ("In two jumps.")*

zanco m. *stilt.*

zancudo adj. *long-legged; wading (bird); m. mosquito; waders, wading birds.*

zángano m. *drone; idler, lazy person.*

zanja f. *ditch.*

zanjar *to ditch, to dig a ditch; to settle in a friendly manner.*

Hay que zanjar ese asunto. *We must settle that matter in a friendly way. That matter has to be settled amicably.*

zapa f. *spade (tool); sap (trench).*

Trabajo de zapa. *Underhanded work.*

zapatazo m. *a blow with a shoe; stamping (with the feet).*

Mandar a zapatazos. *To mistreat. To treat badly.*

zapateado m. *Spanish tap dance.*

zapatear *to tap (with the feet).*

Baile zapateado. *Tap dance.*

zapateo m. *tapping; keeping time with the feet.*

zapatería f. *shoestore; shoemaker's; shoemaking.*

zapatero adj. *poorly cooked (vegetables); m. shoemaker; shoe dealer.*

zapatilla f. *slipper; pump (shoe); washer (ring of leather).*

ZAPATO m. *shoe.*

Un par de zapatos. *A pair of shoes.*

¿Le lastiman los zapatos? *Do your shoes hurt (you)?*

Atese bien los zapatos. *Tie your shoelaces.*

Estos zapatos me vienen anchos. *These shoes are too wide for me.*

Estos zapatos me aprietan mucho. *These shoes are too tight.*

¿Quiere que le limpien los zapatos? *Would you like a shoeshine?*

Quiero que me compongan los zapatos. *I'd like to have my shoes repaired.*

Zapatos de charol. *Patent-leather shoes.*

Zapatos de cabritilla. *Kidskin shoes.*

Zapatos de goma. *Rubbers.*

Encontrarse uno con la horma de su zapato. *To find one's match.*

¡zape! *Scat!*

zaranda *f. screen, sieve (for sand, gravel, coal, etc.).*

zarandear *to sift; to winnow; to shake back and forth.*

zarcillo *m. earring.*

zarco *adj. of a light blue color.*

Ojos zarcos. *Light blue eyes.*

zarpa *f. claw; paw; weighing anchor.*

Echar la zarpa a. *To grab. To grasp.*

zarpar *to weigh anchor, to sail.*

Acaban de dar el último aviso, va a zarpar el barco. *They have just given the last signal. The boat is about to sail.*

zarpazo *m. pawing, stroke with a paw; thud, bang.*

zarrapastroso *adj. ragged, dirty, muddy.*

zarza *f. bramble; brier.*

zarzal *m. a place where there are many thorny bushes or bushes bearing berries.*

zarzamora *f. blackberry (fruit).*

zarzaparrilla *f. sarsparilla.*

zarzuela *f. musical comedy, a typical Spanish operetta.*

¡zaz! *Smack! Slap! Bang!*

zeda *f. name of letter z.*

zigzag *m. zigzag.*

zinc *m. zinc.*

zócalo *m. pedestal, stand.*

zodíaco *m. zodiac.*

zonzo *adj. boresome; stupid; m. a bore; stupid person.*

zoología *f. zoology.*

zopenco *adj. dumbbell, blockhead.*

zoquete *m. block (of wood); morsel (of bread); boor; worm; little, ugly person.*

zorra *f. fox; vixen; streetwalker (coll.); drunkenness.*

zorro *m. fox (male); foxy (cunning, sly, crafty) person.*

zozobra *f. foundering, sinking; anguish, anxiety, worry.*

zozobrar *to be weatherbeaten; to capsize, to sink; to be in great danger; to grieve; to be afflicted.*

zueco *m. wooden shoe, clog.*

zumbar *to buzz; to ring (one's ears); to joke; to hit, to slap.*

El abejarrón zumba. *The bumblebee buzzes.*

Me zumban los oídos. *My ears are ringing.*

Le zumbó una bofetada. *He slapped him.*

zumbido *m. buzzing; ringing (in one's ear).*

zumo *m. juice; profit.*

Zumo de limón. *Lemon juice.*

Zumo de naranja. *Orange juice.*

zurcido *adj. darning; m. a place that has been darned.*

ZURCIR *to darn.*

¿Ha zurcido mis calcetines? *Have you darned my socks?*

zurdo *adj. left-handed.*

zurra *f. tanning (hide, skin); a beating, a whipping, a flogging.*

zurrar *to tan (hide, skin); to whip, to beat, to spank.*

Al llegar a casa su padre le zurró la badana. *When he came home his father gave him a (good) spanking.*

zutano *m. so-and-so; such a one. (See fulano.)*

¿Cómo se llama ese zutano? *What's that fellow's name?*

GLOSSARY OF PROPER NAMES

Alberto Albert.
Alejandro Alexander.
Alfonso Alphonse.
Alfredo Alfred.
Alicia Alice.
Ana Ann, Anne, Anna, Hannah.
Andrés Andrew.
Antonio Anthony.
Arturo Arthur.
Beatriz Beatrice.
Bernardo Bernard.
Carlos Charles.
Carlota Charlotte.
Diego James.
Dorotea Dorothy.
Eduardo Edward.
Elena Ellen, Helen.

Emilia Emily.
Enrique Henry.
Ernesto Ernest.
Ester Esther, Hester.
Eugenio Eugene.
Eva Eve.
Federico Frederic.
Felipe Philip.
Fernando Ferdinand.
Francisco Francis.
Gertrudis Gertrude.
Gustavo Gustavus.
Ignacio Ignatius.
Inés Agnes, Inez.
Isabel Elizabeth.
Javier Xavier.
Jesús Jesus.

Joaquín Joachim.
Jorge George.
José Joseph.
Josefa Josephine.
Josefina Josephine.
Juan John.
Juana Jane, Jennie, Jean, Joan, Joanna.
Julian Julian.
Julio Julius.
León Leo, Leon.
Leonor Eleanor.
Luis Louis.
Luisa Louise.
Manuel Emanuel.
Margarita Margaret.
María Mary, Maria, Miriam.
Marta Martha.

Miguel Michael.
Pablo Paul.
Pedro Peter.
Rafael Raphael.
Raimundo Raymond.
Ramón Raymond.
Ricardo Richard.
Roberto Robert.
Rosa Rose.
Rosalía Rosalie.
Rosario Rosary.
Santiago James.
Susana Susan.
Teresa Theresa.
Vicente Vincent.

GLOSSARY OF GEOGRAPHICAL NAMES

Alemania Germany.
Alpes Alps.
Alsacia Alsace.
Amberes Antwerp.
América del Norte North America.
América del Sur. South America.
América Española Spanish America.
Antillas Antilles, West Indies.
Aragón Aragon.
Argel Algiers.
Argentina Argentina.
Atenas Athens.
Atlántico Atlantic (Ocean).
Bayona Bayonne.
Bélgica Belgium.
Brasil Brazil.
Bolivia Bolivia.
Bretaña Bretagne, Brittany.
Bretaña (Gran) Great Britain.
Bruselas Brussels.
Castilla Castile.
Castilla la Nueva New Castile.
Castilla la Vieja Old Castile.
Cataluña Catalonia.
Chile Chile.
Colombia Colombia.
Costa Rica Costa Rica.
Cuba Cuba.
Ecuador Ecuador.
Egipto Egypt.
El Salvador El Salvador.
Escandinavia Scandinavia.

Escocia Scotland.
España Spain.
Estados Unidos de América United States of America.
Europa Europe.
Filipinas Philippines.
Finlandia Finland.
Flandes Flanders.
Francia France.
Génova Genoa.
Ginebra Geneva.
Gran Bretaña Great Britain.
Grecia Greece.
Guatemala Guatemala.
Habana Havana.
Hispano-América Spanish America.
Holanda Holland.
Honduras Honduras.
Hungría Hungary.
Inglaterra England.
Irlanda Ireland.
Italia Italy.
Japón Japan.
Lisboa Lisbon.
Londres London.
Madrid Madrid.
Marsella Marseilles.
Mediterráneo Mediterranean.
México Mexico.
Moscú Moscow.
Navarra Navarre.
Nicaragua Nicaragua.

Normandía Normandy.
Noruega Norway.
Nueva York. New York.
Nueva Zelandia New Zealand.
Oceanía Oceania, Oceanica.
Pacífico Pacific (Ocean).
Países Bajos Low Countries, Netherlands.
Paraguay Paraguay.
Perú Peru.
Pirineos Pyrenees.
Polonia Poland.
Portugal Portugal.
Prusia Prussia.
Puerto Rico Puerto Rico.
República Dominicana Dominican Republic.
Roma Rome.
Rumania Roumania.
Rusia Russia.
Sevilla Seville.
Sicilia Sicily.
Suecia Sweden.
Suiza Switzerland.
Sur-América South America.
Tejas Texas.
Tolosa Toulouse.
Turquía Turkey.
Uruguay Uruguay.
Valencia Valence (France); Valencia (Spain).
Venezuela Venezuela.
Viena Vienne (France); Vienna (Austria).

English-Spanish DICTIONARY

A

a (an) un, uno, una.
able *adj.* capaz.
able (be) poder.
abolish abolir.
about cerca de; sobre; acerca; tocante a.
above sobre, encima de.
abroad fuera del país, extranjero.
absent ausente.
absolute absoluto.
absorb absorber.
absurd absurdo.
abundant abundante.
abuse abuso.
abuse (to) abusar, maltratar.
academy academia.
accent acento.
accent (to) acentuar.
accept aceptar.
acceptance aceptación.
accident accidente.
accommodate acomodar, ajustar.
accommodations acomodo, alojamiento.
accomplish efectuar, llevar a cabo.
according to según, conforme.
account cuenta; relación, narración.
accuracy exactitud.
accusative acusativo.
accuse acusar.
acid ácido (noun and adj.).
acquaintance conocido (person).
acre acre
across de través; a través de.
act acto, hecho, acción.
act (to) obrar (to work); conducirse (to behave)
    representar (theater).
active activo.
activity actividad.
actor actor, protagonista.
actual real, efectivo.
add añadir.
address dirección, señas.
address (to) dirigir (a letter).
adequate adecuado.
adjective adjetivo.
adjoining contiguo, inmediato.
administrative administrativo.
admiral almirante.
admiration admiración.
admire admirar.
admirer admirador.
admission admisión; entrada.
    Admission free. Entrada gratis.
admit admitir, confesar, reconocer.
admittance entrada.
    No admittance. Se prohíbe la entrada.
admonish amonestar, exhortar.
adopt adoptar.
adoption adopción.
adult adulto.
advance *n.* anticipo; adelanto; avance.
advance (to) avanzar, adelantar.
advantage beneficio, provecho.
advantageous ventajoso.
adventure aventura.
adverb adverbio.
adversity adversidad.
advertise advertir, anunciar.
advertisement aviso, anuncio.
advice consejo.
advise aconsejar.
affected afectado.

affection afecto, cariño.
affectionate cariñoso, afectuoso.
    Affectionately yours. Afectuosamente.
affirm afirmar.
affirmative afirmativo.
afternoon tarde.
    Good afternoon! ¡Buenas tardes!
afterwards después.
again otra vez; de nuevo.
against contra.
age edad.
age (epoch) época.
age (to) envejecer.
agency agencia.
aggravate agravar.
aggressive agresivo.
ago
    a long time ago hace mucho tiempo.
    How long ago? ¿Cuánto tiempo hace?
agony angustia, agonía.
agree acordar, convenir en.
agreeable agradable.
agreed convenido.
agreement convenio, acuerdo.
agricultural agrícola.
agriculture agricultura.
air aire.
air mail correo aéro.
airplane aeroplano, avión.
aisle pasillo.
alarm alarma.
alarm (to) alarmar.
alarm clock despertador.
album álbum.
alcohol alcohol.
alight (to) apearse.
alike igual; semejante.
alive vivo.
all todo.
    all day todo el día.
    all right está bien, bueno.
    all the same igual, lo mismo.
allied aliado.
allow permitir.
    Allow me. Permítame.
allowed permitido.
ally aliado.
almond almendra.
almost casi.
alone solo.
along a lo largo de; al lado de.
    along with junto con, con.
    along the side al costado.
    all along siempre, constantemente.
    to get along hallarse, ir pasando.
    to go along with acompañar.
also también; además.
alternate (to) alternar.
alternately alternativamente.
although aunque, no obstante.
always siempre.
ambassador embajador.
amber ambar.
ambition ambición.
ambitious ambicioso.
amend enmendar.
amends compensación, satisfacción.
America América.
    North America América del Norte.
American americano, norteamericano.
among entre.
amount importe, cantidad, suma.
amount (to) montar, ascender, sumar.

ample amplio.
amuse divertir.
amusement diversión.
analyze analizar.
anchor ancla.
ancient antiguo.
and y.
anecdote anécdota.
angel ángel.
anger cólera, ira.
anger (to) enfadar.
angry enfadado, enojado.
    to get angry enfadarse.
animal animal.
animate animar.
annex anexo.
annex (to) anexionar, anexar.
anniversary aniversario.
annual anual.
anonymous anónimo.
another otro.
answer respuesta, contestación.
answer (to) responder, contestar.
anxious ansioso.
any cualquier, cualquiera, alguno, alguna.
anybody alguno, alguien, quienquiera.
anyhow de cualquier modo, de todos modos.
anyone cualquiera.
anything cualquier cosa, algo.
anyway como quiera, de cualquier modo.
anywhere en cualquier lugar, dondequiera.
apart aparte, separado.
apartment apartamento, piso.
apiece cada uno; por cabeza, por persona.
apologize disculpar; excusarse.
apology excusa, disculpa.
apparatus aparato.
appeal apelación (law); súplica (request); atrac-
    ción, simpatía (attraction).
appeal (to) apelar, recurrir; atraer, interesar,
    llamar la atención (to attract).
appear aparecer.
appetite apetito.
applaud aplaudir.
applause aplauso.
apple manzana.
applicable aplicable, extensivo.
applicant aspirante, candidato.
application aplicación; solicitud (petition).
apply (to) aplicar (put on).
    to apply for solicitar.
appreciate apreciar.
appreciation aprecio, reconocimiento.
approach acceso (access), táctica, manera de
    plantear un asunto o de acercarse a una
    persona.
approach (to) acercarse a (come near); aproxi-
    mar; abordar (a subject).
approval aprobación.
approve (to) aprobar.
April abril.
apron delantal.
arbitrary arbitrario.
arcade arcada.
architect arquitecto.
architecture arquitectura.
Argentina La Argentina.
Argentinian argentino.
argument argumento (to convince or persuade);
    disputa (dispute).
arid árido.
arm brazo (part of body).
arm (to) armar.

armpit axila.
army ejército.
around entorno de, al rededor.
   around here cerca de aquí.
arrangement disposición, arreglo.
arrival llegada.
arrive llegar.
article artículo.
artificial artificial.
artist artista.
artistic artístico.
as como.
   as ... as ... tan ... como ...
   as it were por decirlo así.
   as little as tan poco como.
   as long as mientras, todo el tiempo que.
   as much tanto, tan.
   as much as tanto como.
ascertain aseguarar; asegurarse.
ashes ceniza.
aside aparte; al lado.
ask preguntar (a question); pedir (request).
asleep dormido, durmiendo.
   He's asleep. Está durmiendo.
   to fall asleep dormirse, quedarse dormido.
aspire aspirar.
assemble reunir (to gather); montar, armar (a
   machine); juntar (collect).
assembly asamblea.
assets activo; capital; bienes.
assign asignar.
assimilate asimilar.
assist ayudar, asistir.
assistance asistencia, ayuda.
associate asociado.
associate (to) asociar, asociarse.
assume asumir.
assumption suposición.
assurance seguridad, certeza.
assure asegurar.
astonish asombrar.
astounded atónito.
astounding asombroso, sorprendente.
at a, en.
   at all events a todo trance.
   at first al principio.
   at last al fin, por fin.
   at once inmediatamente, al instante, de una
     vez.
   at the same time a la vez, a un tiempo.
   at two o'clock a las dos.
   at that time en aquel tiempo, entonces.
   We were at John's. Estábamos en la casa de
     Juan.
   at work trabajando.
athlete atléta.
athletic atlético.
athletics atlético.
atmosphere atmósfera, ambiente.
attach prender, unir, adjuntar.
attack ataque.
attack (to) atacar.
attempt intento, tentativa. ·
attempt (to) intentar; tratar de; probar.
attend acudir, asistir, prestar atención.
attention atención.
attentive atento.
attic buhardilla, desván.
attitude actitud.
attorney abogado.
attract atraer.
attraction atracción.
attractive atractivo.

audience auditorio, público.
August agosto.
aunt tía.
author autor.
authority autoridad.
authorize autorizar.
automobile automóvil.
autumn otoño.
avenue avenida.
average promedio.
   on the average por término medio.
avoid evitar.
awake adj. despierto.
awake (to) despertar.
aware enterado, consciente.
away ausente, fuera, lejos.
   to go away marcharse.
awful tremendo; horrible.
awkward torpe; desmañado; embarazoso, difícil
   (embarrassing, difficult).
ax, axe hacha.

B

babble charlar, parlotear.
baby nene, criatura, bebé.
bachelor soltero.
back espalda (of the body); posterior; atrás,
   detrás (behind); respaldo (of a chair).
   behind one's back a espaldas de uno.
   back door la puerta de atrás, puerta trasera.
   to go back volver.
   to be back estar de vuelta (regreso).
background fondo (scenery, painting, etc.); educación (education); antecedentes (of a
   person).
backward atrasado; tardo; retrógrado.
   to go backwards andar de espaldas.
bacon tocino.
bad mal, malo.
badge insignia; placa (of metal).
bag saco; bolsa.
bait cebo.
baker panadero.
bakery panadería.
balance balanza (for weighing); equilibrio (equilibrium); balance (bookkeeping).
bald calvo.
ball bola.
balloon globo.
banana plátano.
band banda.
bandage venda.
banister baranda, barandilla.
bank banco; orilla, ribera (of river).
bank note billete de banco.
bankruptcy quiebra.
baptize bautizar.
bar bar (where liquor is served); barra (of
   metal, etc.).
barber barbero.
barbershop barbería.
bare desnudo.
barefoot descalzo.
bargain trato, negociación; ganga (at a low price).
barge barcaza.
bark corteza (of a tree); ladrido (of a dog).
bark (to) ladrar.
barley cebada.
barn pajar, establo.
barrel barril.
barren estéril.
base base.

basin palangana (bowl).
basis base, fundamento.
basket cesta, canasto.
bath baño.
bathe (to) bañar, bañarse.
battle batalla.
be (to) ser; estar.
   to be hungry tener hambre.
   to be right tener razón.
   to be sleepy tener sueño.
   to be slow ser lento; atrasar, estar atrasado
     (of a watch).
   to be sorry sentir.
   to be thirsty tener sed.
   to be used to estar acostumbrado.
   to be wrong no tener razón.
beach playa.
beam n. viga, madero (of timber, etc.); rayo,
   destello (of light, etc.).
beaming radiante.
bean habichuela, judía, frijol, haba.
bear oso.
bear (to) aguantar, sobrellevar, sufrir (to endure,
   to suffer); soportar (to support); portar (to
   carry); tener (in mind); parir (children, etc.);
   producir (fruit, etc.).
   to bear a grudge guardar rencor.
   to bear in mind tener presente.
bearer portador.
beat (to) latir, palpitar (heart); golpear, pegar
   (strike); tocar (a drum); batir (eggs, etc.);
   ganar (in a game).
beating paliza, zurra (whipping); latido, pulsa-
   ción (heart).
beautiful hermoso; bello.
beauty hermosura, belleza.
because porque.
   because of debido a; a causa de.
become llegar a ser, convertirse (to come to be);
   sentar, quedar bien (to be becoming).
becoming conveniente (appropriate); gracioso,
   mono, que sienta bien (speaking of a dress,
   hat, etc.).
bed cama.
bedclothes ropa de cama.
bedroom alcoba, dormitorio.
bee abeja.
beech haya.
beef carne de vaca (meat).
beehive colmena.
beer cerveza.
beet remolacha.
before antes, antes que; ante, delante de, enfrente de.
beforehand de antemano, previamente.
beg rogar.
beggar mendigo.
begin empezar; comenzar.
beginning principio, comienzo.
behind atrás; detrás.
Belgian belga, bélgico.
Belgium Bélgica.
belief creencia; opinión.
believe creer.
bell campana.
belong pertenecer.
below abajo, debajo; más abajo.
belt cinturón.
bench banco; tribunal (court).
bend doblar; inclinarse.
beneath debajo.
benefit beneficio.
benefit (to) beneficiar.

beside al lado de, contiguo.
besides además de, por otra parte.
best mejor.
bet apuesta.
bet (to) apostar.
better mejor; más bien.
between entre; en medio de.
beyond más allá.
bicycle bicicleta.
big grande.
bill cuenta (check, account); factura (invoice).
bill of fare menú, lista de platos.
billion mil millones.
bind (to) atar, unir; encuadernar (a book).
binding encuadernación (book).
birch abedul.
bird pájaro, ave.
birth nacimiento.
to give birth dar a luz.
birthday cumpleaños.
biscuit bizcocho.
bishop obispo.
bit (a) pizca, pedacito (small amount).
bite mordedura.
bite (to) morder.
bitter amargo.
bitterness amargura.
black negro.
blackbird mirlo.
blacken ennegrecer.
blame culpa.
blame (to) culpar.
blank (en) blanco.
blanket manta, frazada; cobija.
bless bendecir.
blessing bendición.
blind adj. ciego.
blind (to) cegar.
blindness ceguera.
blister ampolla.
block up obstruir.
blotter secante.
blouse blusa.
blow golpe.
blow (to) soplar.
blue azul.
blush rubor.
blush (to) ruborizarse.
board tabla (wood); pensión (food); cartón (pasteboard); junta, consejo (of directors, etc.); tablero (for chess, etc.).
on board a bordo.
boarder pensionista.
boarding house pensión, casa de huéspedes.
boast jactancia.
boast (to) jactarse, hacer alarde.
boat bote, barca; barco, buque.
body cuerpo.
boil grano (on the body).
boil (to) hervir.
boiler caldera.
boiling adj. hirviendo.
bold audaz, temerario.
Bolivia Bolivia.
Bolivian boliviano.
bond bono (stocks).
bone hueso.
book libro.
bookseller librero.
bookshop librería.
boot bota.
border frontera; linde, límite (boundary); borde, ribete (edge).

bore (to) aburrir; taladrar, hacer agujeros (to make holes).
boring aburrido (dull).
born nacido.
born (be) nacer.
borrow tomar prestado.
both ambos.
bother molestia (trouble).
bother (to) molestar.
bottle botella.
bottom fondo.
bound atado, amarrado (tied).
bound for destinado; con rumbo a, con destino a.
boundless ilimitado.
bow saludo, reverencia (greeting); arco (weapon, bow of a violin); proa (ship).
bow (to) saludar, hacer reverencia (to bend in reverence); doblegarse, ceder, someterse (to submit or yield).
bowl escudilla, tazón.
box caja.
boy muchacho, niño; hijo varón (male child).
bracelet pulsera.
braid trenza.
brain cerebro.
brake freno.
bran salvado, afrecho.
branch rama (of tree); ramal (railroad, etc.); sucursal (local office, etc.).
brand marca (of goods).
Brazil Brasil.
Brazilian brasileño.
bread pan.
break ruptura.
break (to) romper.
breakfast desayuno.
breakfast (to) desayunarse.
breaking rompimiento.
breath aliento.
breathe respirar.
breathing respiración.
breeze brisa.
bribe soborno.
bribe (to) sobornar.
bride novia.
bridegroom novio.
bridge puente.
brief breve, corto.
briefly brevemente.
bright claro (opposite of dark); radiante (radiant); inteligente (clever); vivo (lively).
brighten aclarar (to make clearer); alegrar, dar vida, avivarse (to make or become cheerful).
brilliant brillante, luminoso.
brim ala (hat).
bring traer.
to bring together juntar, reunir.
to bring toward acercar.
to bring up educar, criar (to rear); traer a discusión (a matter, etc.); subir (upstairs).
bringing up educación.
Britain La Gran Bretaña.
British británico.
broad ancho.
broil asar (meat).
brook arroyo.
broom escoba.
brother hermano.
brother-in-law cuñado.
brotherly fraternal.
brown café; moreno.
bruise contusión.
bruise (to) magullar.

brush brocha, cepillo.
clothesbrush cepillo para la ropa.
toothbrush cepillo para los dientes.
brush (to) cepillar.
brushwood maleza, zarzal.
brute bruto.
bubble n. burbuja; pompa (soap).
buckle n. hebilla.
bud n. yema, botón, capullo.
buffet aparador (dresser); bufet (counter).
build construir.
building n. edificio.
bulb (electric) bombilla (eléctrica).
bull toro.
bull fighter torero.
bulletin boletín.
bundle atado; bulto.
burden carga; agobio.
bureau tocador (in a bedroom); oficina (an office) negociado (a department).
burial entierro.
burn quemadura.
burn (to) quemar.
to burn up quemarse, consumirse por completo.
burst reventón, estallido.
burst (to) reventar, estallar.
to burst out laughing soltar una carcajada.
bury enterrar.
bus autobús; camión (Mexico); guagua (Cuba).
bush arbusto.
bushel fanega.
business ocupación; negocio.
businessman comerciante.
busy ocupado.
but pero.
butcher carnicero.
butcher's (shop) carnicería.
butter mantequilla.
button botón.
buy comprar.
buyer comprador.
by por, a, en, de, para; junto a, cerca de (near).
by and by poco a poco.
by and large por lo general, de una manera general.
by hand a mano.
by reason of por razón de.
by that time para entonces.
by the way de paso.
by then para entónces.
by virtue of en virtud de.
Finish it by Sunday. Termínelo para el domingo.
Send it by airmail. Envíelo por correo aéreo.

C

cab taxi, coche de alquiler.
cabbage col, repollo.
cabinet gabinete.
cable n. cable.
cage jaula.
cake pastel, torta, pastilla (soap).
calendar calendario.
calf ternera.
call llamada (act of calling, a phone call, etc.); visita (visit).
call (to) llamar (in a loud voice); convocar (a meeting); citar (to summon); visitar (to call upon).
to call back llamar, hacer volver.
to call forth llamar a.

to call out gritar.
calm *adj.* quieto, tranquilo.
calm *n.* calma, silencio.
camp campamento.
camp (to) acampar.
can *n.* lata, bote, tarro.
can poder (to be able); saber (to know how);
    envasar en lata (to put in a can).
canal canal.
candidate pretendiente, candidato.
candle vela, candela.
candy dulce, bombón.
cap gorra, gorro.
capital capital.
captain capitán.
capture (to) capturar.
car carro; automóvil, coche (passenger car).
card tarjeta; naipe, carta (playing card).
cardboard cartón.
care cuidado.
    to take care tener cuidado.
    to take care of cuidar de ocuparse de.
    in care of (c/o) al cuidado de (a/c).
care (to) importar, interesarse, tener cuidado.
    I don't care to go. No me interesa ir.
    He doesn't care a hang. No le importa nada.
    I don't care. No me importa.
    What do I care? ¿Qué me importa?
care about interersarse por, estimar.
    I don't care about him. Me tiene sin cuidado.
    No me importa.
    I don't care about it. Me tiene sin cuidado.
    No me importa.
    He cares about his appearance. Se cuida de
    su aspecto.
career carrera.
care for interesarse por, estimar, querer, gustar,
    desear.
    I don't care for it. No me interesa. No me
    importa nada.
    I don't care for wine. No quiero vino. No me
    gusta el vino.
    Would you care for some dessert? ¿Le gus-
    taría tomar algo de postre?
careful ciudadoso.
    Be careful! ¡Cuidado!
careless descuidado.
carpenter carpintero.
carpet alfombra.
carry llevar, conducir, portar.
    to carry away llevarse.
    to carry out llevar a cabo.
    to carry on continuar (continue), conducir,
    regentear (manage).
cart *n.* carreta, carretón.
carve tajar, trinchar (meat); esculpir, talar
    (marble, wood, etc.).
case caso (a particular instance; grammar, etc.);
    estuche (box for small articles); caja (case
    of wine, etc.).
    in case of en caso de.
cash dinero en efectivo, caja.
    cash on hand efectivo en caja.
    cash payment pago al contado.
cash (to) cobrar o hacer efectivo un cheque, etc.
cashier cajero.
cask tonel.
castle castillo.
casual casual.
casually casualmente.
cat gato.
catch (to) coger, agarrar.
    to catch cold resfriarse.

to catch on caer en la cuenta, comprender.
to catch (on) fire encenderse, prender.
to catch up alcanzar (overtake).
catholic católico.
cattle ganado.
cause causa; razón; motivo.
cause (to) causar.
cavalry caballería.
ceiling techo, cielo raso.
celebrate celebrar.
celebration celebración, conmemoración.
celery apio.
cellar sótano.
cement cemento.
cemetery cementerio.
cent céntimo.
center centro.
century siglo.
ceremony ceremonia, formulismo, cumplido.
certain seguro; cierto, claro, evidente.
certainly ciertamente, sin duda, a buen seguro.
certificate certificado.
chain cadena.
chain (to) encadenar.
chair silla.
chairman presidente (of a meeting).
chalk tiza.
chance azar, acaso, casualidad (happening by
    chance); oportunidad (opportunity); pro-
    babilidad (probability); riesgo (risk).
    by chance por casualidad.
    to take a chance correr un riesgo, aven-
    turarse.
chance (to) aventurar, arriesgar.
chances probabilidades.
change cambio (money).
change (to) cambiar.
chapel capilla.
character carácter.
characteristic *adj.* característico, típico.
charge carga (load; quantity of powder, elec-
    tricity, fuel, etc.); orden, mandato (order);
    costo (price); cargo, acusación (accusation);
    carga, ataque (attack); partida cargada en
    cuenta (bookkeeping).
    in charge encargado; interino.
charge (to) cargar (a battery, etc.; to debit an
    account; to load; to attack); llevar, costar,
    cobrar (a price); acusar (to accuse).
    How much do you charge for this? ¿Cuánto
    cobra Ud. por esto?
charges gastos (expenses); partes (cost of car-
    riage, freight, etc.); instrucciones (to a
    jury, etc.).
charitable caritativo.
charity caridad.
charm encanto.
charm (to) encantar.
charming encantador.
chart carta (for the use of navigators); mapa
    (outline, map); cuadro, gráfico (graph).
chase (to) perseguir.
chat (to) charlar.
cheap barato.
check cheque (banking); talón de reclamo, con-
    traseña (slip of paper); cuenta (in a res-
    taurant); jaque (chess); control, inspección
    (control); restricción (restraint); obstaculo,
    impedimento (hindrance); verificación,
    comprobación (verification).
check (to) examinar (to investigate); verificar (to
    verify); refrenar, reprimir (to curb, to
    restrain); facturar (baggage); dar a guardar,

dejar (to leave for safekeeping); dar jaque
    (chess).
cheek mejilla (part of face).
cheer *n.* alegría, buen humor (gaiety); vivas,
    aplausos (applause).
cheerful alegre, animado.
cheer up animar; animarse, cobrar ánimo.
cheese queso.
chemical químico.
chemist químico.
cherish querer, estimar (to hold dear); acariciar,
    abrigar (a thought, etc.).
cherished estimado (dear); anhelado (longed
    for); caro (dear).
cherry cereza.
chest pecho (body); arca, cajón (box).
chestnut castaña.
chew (to) mascar.
chicken pollo.
chief *adj.* principal.
chief *n.* jefe.
child niño (*m.*); niña (*f*).
childhood infancia, niñez.
Chile Chile.
Chilean chileno.
chimney chimenea.
chin barba.
china porcelana, loza.
chocolate chocolate.
choice *adj.* selecto, escogido.
choice *n.* opción, elección.
choir coro.
choke sofocar, ahogar.
choose escoger; elegir.
chop chuleta (cut of meat).
chop (to) cortar (wood, etc.); picar carne (meat).
Christian cristiano.
Christmas Navidad.
church iglesia.
cider sidra.
cigar cigarro.
cigarette cigarrillo.
cigarette lighter encendedor.
cinnamon canela.
circle círculo.
circulation circulación.
citizen ciudadano.
city ciudad.
city hall ayuntamiento.
civil civil.
civilize civilizar.
claim demanda, petición (demand); pretensión
    (pretension); título, derecho (title, right).
claim (to) demandar (to demand); reclamar (to
    seek, to obtain); sostener, pretender (to
    assert as a fact).
clam almeja.
clamor clamor.
clap aplaudir.
class clase.
class (to) clasificar.
clause cláusula.
claw garra.
clay arcilla.
clean *adj.* limpio.
clean (to) limpiar.
cleanliness aseo, limpieza.
clear claro; neto (net).
clear (to) aclarar, despejar (to make clear);
    aclararse (to clear up); absolver (of blame,
    guilt); liquidar (to settle a debt, account,
    etc.); quitar la mesa (a table).
clearly claramente.

clerk dependiente; escribiente.
clever diestro, hábil; inteligente.
climate clima.
climb (to) trepar.
cloak capa, manto.
clock reloj.
close (near) cerca; junto a.
  close by muy cerca.
close (to) cerrar (to shut, to shut down); terminar (a meeting, etc.); finiquitar, saldar (an account); cerrar (a deal).
closed cerrado.
closet ropero (clothes); alacena (cupboard, kitchen closet).
cloth tela, paño.
clothe (to) vestir.
clothes ropa.
clothesbrush cepillo para la ropa.
cloud nube.
cloudy nublado.
clover trébol.
club club, círculo (association); porra, garrote (stick).
coach coche.
coal carbón.
coast costa.
coat americana, saco; abrigo.
cocoa cacao.
coconut coco.
code código.
coffee café.
coffin ataúd.
coin moneda.
coincidence coincidencia.
  by coincidence por casualidad.
cold frío.
coldness frialdad.
collaborate colaborar.
collar cuello.
collect (to) coleccionar; cobrar (money due).
collection colección.
collective colectivo.
college escuela de estudios universitarios (university); colegio (of cardinals, etc.).
Colombia Colombia.
Colombian colombiano.
colonial colonial.
colony colonia.
color color.
color (to) colorear.
colored de color.
colt potro.
column columna.
comb peine.
comb (to) peinar.
combination combinación.
combine combinar.
come venir.
  to come back volver.
  to come forward adelantar.
  to come across encontrarse con.
  to come for venir por.
  to come in entrar.
  to come down (stairs) bajar.
  to come up (stairs) subir.
  Come on! ¡Vamos! ¡Déjate de tonterías!
comedy comedia.
comet cometa.
comfort confort, comodidad; consuelo (consolation).
comfort (to) confortar, consolar.
comfortable cómodo.
  to be comfortable estar a gusto, estar bien.

comma coma.
command orden (order); mando, commando (authority to command).
command (to) mandar, ordenar.
commerce comercio.
commercial comercial.
commission comisión.
commit cometer.
common común.
communicate comunicar.
community comunidad.
companion compañero.
company compañía; huéspedes, visitas (guests).
compare comparar.
comparison comparación.
  by comparison en comparación.
compete with competir con.
competition concurso (contest); competencia (business).
complain quejarse.
complaint queja.
complete completo.
complete (to) completar, acabar.
complex complejo.
complexion cutis, tez (skin); aspecto (appearance).
complicate complicar.
complicated complicado.
complication complicación.
compliment cumplimiento, cumplido, galantería.
compliment (to) cumplimentar, gastar cumplimientos.
compose componer.
composition composición.
comprise comprender, abarcar.
compromise compromiso.
compromise (to) transigir (to settle by mutual concessions); arreglar, zanjar (a difference between parties); comprometer (to endanger life or reputation).
comrade camarada.
conceit presunción.
conceive (to) concebir.
concentrate (to) concentrar, reconcentrar.
concentration concentración.
concern asunto, negocio (business, affair); interés, incumbencia (interest); empresa, casa de comercio (a business organization); ansiedad, inquietud (worry).
concern (to) importar, concernir; interesarse, preocuparse (to be concerned).
concert concierto.
concrete adj. concreto.
concrete n. hormigón.
  reinforced concrete cemento armado.
condemn condenar.
condense condensar.
conduct conducta (behavior); manejo, dirección (direction).
conduct (to) conducir, manejar, guiar (to lead, to manage); portarse (to conduct oneself).
conductor conductor.
cone cono.
confer conferir (to grant); conferenciar (to hold a conference); tratar, consultar (to compare views).
confidence confianza (trust); confidencia (secret).
confident adj. seguro, cierto, confiado.
confidential confidencial, en confianza.
confirm confirmar, asegurar.
confirmation confirmación.
congeal helar.

congratulate felicitar.
congratulation enhorabuena, felicitación.
  Congratulations! ¡Felicitaciones! ¡La enhorabuena!
congress congreso.
conjunction conjunción.
connect conectar.
connection conexión; relación.
conquer conquistar.
conquest conquista.
conscience conciencia.
conscientious concienzudo, escrupuloso.
conscious consciente.
consent consentimiento, beneplácito.
consent (to) consentir.
consequence consecuencia.
consequently por consiguiente, en consecuencia, por lo tanto.
conservative conservador.
consider considerar.
considerable considerable.
consideration consideración.
consist (of) consistir, constar de, componerse de.
consistent consecuente (in ideas, etc.); congruente (congruous); consistente (solid).
consonant consonante.
constable alguacil, guardia rural.
constant constante.
constitution constitución.
constitutional constitucional.
consume consumir.
consumer consumidor.
consumption consumo (use of goods); consunción, tisis (med.).
contagion contagio.
contagious contagioso.
contain contener; abarcar.
container envase; recipiente.
contemplation contemplación.
contemporary contemporáneo.
contend sostener, afirmar (to assert, to maintain); contender, disputar, competir (to strive, to compete).
content adj. contento.
contents contenido.
continent continente.
continuation continuación.
continue (to) continuar.
contract contrato.
contract (to) contraer; contratar.
contractor contratista.
contradict contradecir.
contradiction contradicción.
contradictory contradictorio.
contrary contrario.
  on the contrary al contrario, por el contrario.
contrast contraste.
contrast (to) contrastar.
contribute contribuir.
contribution contribución.
control control, mando, dirección.
control (to) controlar, dominar, dirigir, verificar.
convenience conveniencia.
  at your convenience cuando le sea cómodo, cuando le venga bien.
convenient conveniente.
  if it's convenient to you si le viene bien.
convent convento.
convention convención, asamblea, junta, congreso.
conversation conversación.
converse (to) conversar.
convert (to) convertir.

conviction convicción.
convince convencer.
cook cocinero.
cook (to) cocinar.
cool fresco.
cool (to) enfriar.
cooperation cooperación.
cooperative cooperativa.
copy copia; ejemplar (of a book).
copy (to) copiar.
cordial cordial.
cork corcho; tapón (stopper).
corn maíz.
corner esquina (street); rincón (nook, corner of a room).
corporation corporación, sociedad anónima.
correct correcto.
correct (to) corregir.
correction corrección.
correspond corresponder.
correspondence correspondencia.
correspondent corresponsal.
corresponding correspondiente.
corrupt corrompido.
corrupt (to) corromper.
cost costo; precio.
cost (to) costar.
Costa Rica Costa Rica
Costa Rican costarricense, costarriqueño.
costume traje, vestido, indumentaria.
cottage hotel, casa de campo.
cotton algodón.
couch diván.
cough tos.
cough (to) toser.
council consejo, junta.
count conde (title).
count (to) contar.
counter mostrador (in a store).
countess condesa.
countless innumerable.
country país (nation); campo (opposed to city); patria (fatherland).
country house casa de campo.
countryman compatriota, paisano.
courage valor.
course curso; marcha (of events); estadio (grounds); plato (of a meal); rumbo (route).
court tribunal (law).
courteous cortés.
courtesy cortesía.
courtyard corral, patio.
cousin primo.
cover cubierta, tapa, tapadera.
cover (to) cubrir; tapar (to place a lid over, to conceal); recorrer (a distance); abarcar (to include).
cow vaca.
crab cangrejo.
crack hendidura, raja (split); chasquido (of a whip); chascarrillo (joke).
crack (to) hender (to split); chasquear (a whip).
cradle cuna.
cramp n. calambre.
crash estrépito, estruendo (noise); quiebra, bancarrota (business); choque (collision).
crash (to) romperse con estrépito (to break); estrellarse (a plane, etc.).
cream nata, crema.
create crear; ocasionar (to cause).
creation creación.
credit n. crédito.
creditor acreedor.

cricket grillo (insect).
crime crimen, delito.
crisis crisis.
critic crítico.
criticism crítica.
criticize criticar.
crooked torcido (bent).
crop cosecha (harvest).
cross cruz (symbol).
cross (to) cruzar, atravesar (a street); tachar, borrar (to cross out).
    to cross one's mind ocurrírsele a uno, pasarle a uno por la imaginación.
    to cross over cruzar, pasar al otro lado.
cross-examination interrogación.
cross-eyed bizco.
crossing cruce; travesía (sea); paso, vado (river).
crossroads encrucijada.
crouch (to) agacharse, agazaparse.
crow cuervo.
crowd gentío, muchedumbre.
crowded apiñado, lleno.
crown corona.
crown (to) coronar.
cruel cruel.
cruelty crueldad.
crumb migaja (a small piece).
crumbling derrumbe.
cry grito; lloro (weeping).
cry (to) gritar (shout); llorar (weep).
crystal cristal.
Cuba Cuba.
Cuban cubano.
cube cubo.
cucumber pepino.
cuff puño, bocamanga.
culture cultura.
cup taza.
cure cura.
cure (to) curar.
curiosity curiosidad.
curious curioso.
curl rizo, bucle.
curl (to) rizar.
current adj. corriente.
current n. corriente.
curtain cortina.
curve curva.
cushion cojín.
custard flan, natilla.
custom costumbre.
customer cliente.
customhouse aduana.
customhouse officer aduanero, vista.
customs (duties) derechos de aduana.
cut corte.
cut (to) cortar.

D

dagger puñal.
daily adj. diario, cotidiano.
    daily newspaper diario, periódico.
dainty delicado.
dairy lechería; quesería (cheese).
dam dique, presa de agua.
damage daño, perjuicio.
damage (to) dañar, perjudicar.
damp húmedo.
dance baile.
dance (to) bailar.
dancer bailarín m.; bailarina f.
danger peligro.

dangerous peligroso.
dare atreverse (venture); desafiar (challenge).
dark obscuro.
darkness obscuridad.
darling amado, querido.
darn zurcir.
date fecha (time); cita (rendezvous); dátil (fruit).
date (to) datar, poner la fecha.
daughter hija.
dawn madrugada, alba, aurora.
    at dawn de madrugada, al amanecer.
day día.
    day after tomorrow pasado mañana.
    day before víspera.
    day before yesterday anteayer.
    every day todos los días.
daze ofuscamiento, atontamiento, aturdimiento
dead muerto.
deadly mortal.
deaf sordo.
dealer vendedor; comerciante.
debatable discutible.
debate debate, discusión.
debate (to) discutir.
debt deuda.
debtor deudor.
decade década.
decay decadencia (decadence); mengua (decrease); podredumbre (rot).
decay (to) decaer, declinar (decline); deteriorarse (deteriorate); pudrirse, dañarse (fruit, etc.); picarse, cariarse (teeth).
deceit angaño.
deceive engañar.
December diciembre.
decency decencia.
decent decente.
decide decidir; resolver, terminar (a dispute, etc.).
decidedly decididamente.
decision decisión.
decisive decisivo.
declaration declaración.
declare declarar, manifestar.
decrease mengua, diminución.
decrease (to) disminuir, menguar.
decree n. decreto.
dedicate dedicar.
deduct deducir, descontar.
deduction deducción, descuento, rebaja.
deep hondo, profundo.
deeply profundamente.
defeat derrota.
defeat (to) derrotar.
defect defecto.
defective defectuoso.
defend defender.
defender defensor.
defense defensa.
defer diferir (to put off).
defiance desafío.
definite definido, preciso.
definition definición.
defy desafiar.
degenerate degenerar.
degree grado.
delay tardanza, demora, retardo.
delay (to) tardar, demorarse (to linger); retardar, diferir (to defer).
delegate delegado.
delegate (to) delegar.
delegation delegación.
deliberate adj. circunspecto, cauto (careful);

pensado, premeditado (carefully thought out).

deliberate (to) deliberar.

delicacy delicadeza (finesse); golosina, bocado exquisito (food).

delicate delicado.

delicious delicioso.

delight deleite, encanto, gusto, placer.

delight (to) encantar, deleitar.

deliver entregar (hand over); librar de (delivery from); pronunciar (a speech).

delivery entrega (of goods); distribución, reparto (mail).

demand demanda.

demand (to) demandar, exigir.

democracy democracia.

demonstrate demostrar.

demonstration demostración, manifestación.

denial negativa, denegación.

denounce denunciar.

dense denso.

density densidad.

deny negar; rehusar (to refuse to grant).

depend (to) depender.

dependence dependencia.

dependent *adj.* dependiente, sujeto, pendiente.

dependent *n.* persona que depende de otra para su manutención.

deplore deplorar, lamentar.

deposit depósito.

deposit (to) depositar.

depth profundidad.

descend (to) descender, bajar.

descendant descendiente.

descent descenso.

describe describir.

description descripción.

desert desierto.

desert (to) desertar, abandonar.

deserve merecer.

desirable de desearse.

desire deseo.

desire (to) desear.

desirous deseoso.

desk escritorio.

desolation desolación.

despair desesperación.

despair (to) desesperar.

desperate desesperado.

despite a pesar de, a despecho de.

dessert postre.

destroy destruir.

destruction destrucción.

detach (to) separar, despegar, desprender (to separate or disunite); destacar (soldiers).

detain detener.

determination determinación.

determine determinar.

detour rodeo.

develop desarrollar; revelar (photography).

development desarrollo; revelamiento (photography).

devil demonio, diablo.

devilish diabólico, endiablado, satánico.

devote dedicar.

devotion devoción.

devour devorar, engullir.

dew sereno, rocío.

dial (clock) esfera.

dialogue diálogo.

diameter diámetro.

diamond diamante; oros (at cards).

dictionary diccionario.

die (to) morir.

diet dieta, régimen.

differ (from) diferenciarse (to stand apart); no estar de acuerdo (to disagree).

difference diferencia; distinción (of persons, etc.).

different diferente, distinto.

difficult difícil.

difficulty dificultad.

diffuse difundir.

dig cavar.

digest digerir.

digestion digestión.

dignity dignidad.

dim obscuro, poco claro, a media luz.

dimple hoyuelo.

dinner comida principal.

diplomacy diplomacia.

diplomat diplomático.

diplomatic diplomático.

direct directo (without deviation); en línea recta (straight line); derecho (straight forward).

direct (to) dirigir.

direction dirección.

directly directamente.

director director.

dirt mugre, suciedad.

dirty sucio.

disadvantage desventaja.

disappear desaparecer.

disappearance desaparición.

disappoint desengañar, desilusionar.

disappointment decepción, desengaño, chasco.

disapprove desaprobar.

disarm desarmar.

disaster desastre.

disastrous desastroso, funesto.

discipline *n.* disciplina.

discontent descontento.

discord discordia.

discourage desanimar, desalentar.

discouragement desaliento, desanimo.

discover descubrir.

discovery descubrimiento.

discreet discreto.

discretion discreción.

discuss discutir (to argue); tratar (to talk over).

discussion discusión.

disease enfermedad.

disgrace afrenta, deshonra.

disgrace (to) deshonrar.

disgust disgusto, asco.

disgust (to) disgustar, repugnar.

disgusting repugnante, odioso.

dish plato.

dishonest deshonesto.

disk disco.

dismal lúgubre, tétrico.

dismiss despedir.

disobey desobedecer.

disorder desorden.

disorder (to) desordenar.

dispatch despacho.

dispatch (to) despachar.

display despliegue (of troops); exhibición (show); alarde, ostentación.

display (to) desplegar; exhibir, mostrar (to show) lucir, hacer ostentación.

displease desagradar.

dispute disputa.

dispute (to) disputar, discutir.

dissolve disolver.

distance distancia.

distinct distinto, claro.

distinction distinción.

distinguish distinguir.

distinguished distinguido.

distort falsear, tergiversar.

distract distraer (divert).

distraction distracción.

distribute distribuir, repartir.

distribution reparto, distribución.

district distrito.

distrust desconfianza.

distrust (to) desconfiar.

disturb estorbar (to interfere with); turbar, inquieta (to disquiet); molestar (to put to inconvenience).

disturbance disturbio.

dive zambullida (into water); picado (a plane).

dive (to) zambullirse, sumergirse (into water), picar (aviation).

divide dividir.

dividend dividendo.

divine divino.

diving board trampolín.

division división.

divorce divorcio.

divorce (to) divorciar.

divorced (to be) divorciarse.

dizzy mareado, aturdido.

do hacer.

How do you do? ¿Cómo le va? ¿Cómo está Ud.? ¿Qué tal?

to do one's best hacer lo posible.

to do without pasarse sin, prescindir de.

to have to do with tener que ver con.

That will do. Eso basta. Eso sirve.

Do you believe it? ¿Lo cree Ud.?

Do come. Venga sin falta.

dock (pier) muelle.

doctor doctor.

doctrine doctrina.

document documento.

dog perro.

dogma dogma.

dome cúpula.

domestic *adj.* doméstico (pertaining to the household); casero (homemade); del país, nacional (domestic trade, etc.).

Dominican Republic República Dominicana.

Dominican dominicano.

door puerta.

double doble.

doubt duda.

doubt (to) dudar.

doubtful dudoso.

doubtless sin duda.

dough masa, pasta.

down abajo; hacia abajo.

to go down bajar.

to come down bajar.

Come down! ¡Baje!

downstairs abajo, en el piso de abajo.

downward descendente, hacia abajo.

dozen docena.

draft corriente de aire (air); letra de cambio, giro (bank); quinta, conscripcion (military); borrador, anteproyecto (sketch or outline).

draft (to) redactar, escribir (a document, etc.); hacer un borrador (a tentative outline).

drag arrastrar.

drama drama.

draw (to) dibujar (with a pencil); sacar (money, liquids, etc.); correr, descorrer (curtains);

librar, girar (a bank draft); cobrar (a salary);
tirar (to putt); redactar, escribir (to draw
up); robar, tomar (a card); sortear (lottery,
etc.).
to draw back reintegrarse de (to get something back); retroceder (to go back).
drawer gaveta, cajón (of a desk, etc.).
drawing dibujo.
dread (to) temer.
dreaded temido.
dreadful horrible.
dream sueño.
dream (to) soñar.
dreamer soñador.
dress vestido, traje.
dress (to) vestirse (to get dressed); vendar (a
wound).
dressmaker modista.
drink bebida (a beverage); trago, copa.
drink (to) beber, tomar.
drip (to) gotear.
drive paseo en coche (a ride in a car, etc.);
paseo, calzada (a road); campaña (to raise
money, etc.).
drive (to) conducir, guiar (a car, etc.); ir en coche
(to take a ride); clavar (a nail); ahuyentar
(to drive away).
driver chófer, conductor (of a çar); maquinista (of
an engine).
drop gota (of water, etc.); caída, baja (fall).
cough drops pastillas para la tos.
drop (to) soltar, dejar caer (to release, to let
fall); verter a gotas (fall in drops); abandonar, desistir de, dejar (to let go).
to drop in on visitar.
to drop a subject cambiar de tema.
drown ahogar.
drug droga.
druggist farmacéutico.
drugstore botica, farmacia.
drum tambor.
drunk borracho, ebrio.
drunkard borracho, borrachín.
drunkenness embriaguez, borrachera.
dry seco.
dry (to) secar.
dryness sequedad.
duchess duquesa.
due debido; pagadero (payable); vencido (at a
given time).
duke duque.
dull opaco, muerto (color); pesado, oburrido, sin
gracia (slow, boring); estúpido (stupid).
dumb mudo (deaf and dumb); estúpido (stupid).
durable duradero.
during durante, mientras.
dusk crepúsculo.
dust polvo.
dust (to) quitar el polvo.
dusty polvoriento.
duty deber.
dwelling habitación, morada.
dye tinte.
dye (to) teñir.

E

each cada.
each one cada uno.
each other mutuamente, el uno al otro, unos
a otros.
eager ansioso.
eagle águila.

ear oído (the organ of hearing or the internal
ear); oreja (the external ear); mazorca (of
corn); espiga (of wheat, rye, etc.).
early temprano.
earn ganar.
earnest serio (serious); ansioso (eager).
in earnest de buena fe, en serio.
earth tierra.
earthquake temblor de tierra, terremoto.
ease tranquilidad, alivio; facilidad (with ease);
con desahogo, cómodamente (at ease).
ease (to) aliviar, mitigar.
easily fácilmente.
east este, oriente.
Easter Pascua florida.
eastern oriental.
easy fácil.
eat comer.
economic económico.
economy economía.
Ecuador Ecuador.
Ecuadorian ecuatoriano.
edge orilla, borde (of a stream, etc.), canto (of a
table, a book); filo (of a blade).
edition edición.
editor redactor.
education educación.
eel anguila.
effect efecto.
effect (to) efectuar.
efficiency eficacia.
effort esfuerzo.
egg huevo.
eggplant berengena.
eggshell cáscara de huevo, cascarón.
egoism egoísmo.
eight ocho.
eighteen dieciocho.
eighteenth decimoctavo.
eighth octavo.
eighty ochenta.
either o, u (*conj.*); uno u otro, el uno o el otro,
cualquiera de los dos, uno y otro, ambos
(*adj.* and *pron.*).
either one el uno o el otro, cualquiera de
los dos.
elastic elástico.
elbow codo.
elder *adj.* mayor, de más edad.
elderly mayor, de edad.
elect (to) elegir.
elected electo, elegido.
election elección.
elector elector.
electric eléctrico.
electricity electricidad.
elegance elegancia.
elegant elegante.
element elemento.
elementary elemental.
elephant elefante.
elevation elevación; altura.
elevator ascensor.
eleven once.
eleventh undécimo, onzavo.
eliminate eliminar.
eloquence elocuencia.
eloquent elocuente.
else otro, más, además.
nothing else nada más.
something else algo más.
or else o bien, o en su lugar, si no.
nobody else ningún otro.

elsewhere en alguna otra parte, en otro lugar.
elude eludir, evitar.
embark embarcar.
embarrass embarazar, poner en aprieto.
embarrassing embarazoso.
in an embarrassing situation en una situación
difícil, en un apuro, en un compromiso.
embassy embajada.
embody encarnar.
embrace abrazo.
embrace (to) abrazar.
embroidery bordado.
emerge surgir.
emergency emergencia, aprieto, apuro, necesidad urgente.
emigrant emigrante.
emigrate emigrar.
emigration emigración.
eminent eminente.
eminently eminentemente.
emotion emoción.
emphasis énfasis.
emphasize hacer hincapié; recalcar.
emphatic enfático, categórico.
empire imperio.
employ emplear.
employee empleado.
employer patrono, patrón.
employment empleo.
empty vacío.
empty (to) vaciar.
enclose (to) cercar (ground, etc.); incluir (in a
letter, etc.).
enclosed adjunto.
encourage animar.
encouragement estímulo, aliento.
end fin; final (of a street); extremidad (tip).
end (to) acabar, terminar.
endeavor esfuerzo.
endeavor (to) esforzarse.
endorse endosar.
endow dotar.
endure soportar, resistir, aguantar.
enemy enemigo.
energetic enérgico.
energy energía.
enforce hacer cumplir, poner en vigor (a law);
forzar, compeler (to compel).
engage ajustar (a servant); emplear (a clerk, etc.);
alquilar (a room, etc.); trabar (in a conversation, etc.).
engagement compromiso, cita (date); promesa
de matrimonio, compromiso (promise of
marriage); contrato (employment for a
stated time).
engineer ingeniero.
English inglés.
engrave grabar.
enjoy gozar, disfrutar.
to enjoy oneself divertirse.
enjoyment goce.
enlarge aumentar, agrandar, ampliar.
enlargement ampliación.
enlist alistarse.
enlistment alistamiento, enganche.
enough bastante, suficiente.
enrich enriquecer.
entangle enredar, embrollar.
enter entrar (a house, etc.); anotar, registrar (in
a register, etc.); entablar (into a conversation); ingresar, matricularse (a school);
afiliarse (a society, etc.).
entertain tener invitados, agasajar (guests);

conversar, entretener (to talk to); acariciar, abrigar (ideas); divertir (to amuse).

entertainment convite (for guests); entretenimiento, diversión (amusement).

enthusiasm entusiasmo.

enthusiastic entusiasta.

entire entero.

entitle titular, poner un título (title); autorizar, dar derecho a (right).

entrance entrada.

entrust confiar a.

entry entrada (entrance); asiento, íngreso (records, bookkeeping).

enumerate enumerar.

envelope n. sobre.

enviable envidiable.

envious envidioso.

envy envidia.

envy (to) envidiar.

episode episodio.

epoch época, era.

equal igual.

equal (to) igualar.

equality igualdad.

equator ecuador.

equilibrium equilibrio.

equip equipar, dotar de.

equipment equipo.

equity equidad.

era era, época.

erase borrar, raspar.

eraser goma de borrar.

err (to) errar, equivocarse.

errand recado, mandado.

error error.

escape fuga.

escape (to) escapar, escaparse de.

escort escolta (a body of soldiers, etc.); acompañante (an individual).

escort (to) escoltar, acompañar.

especially especialmente, particularmente.

essay ensayo; composición (school).

essence esencia.

essential esencial, indispensable.

establish establecer.

establishment establecimiento.

estate bienes, propiedades (properties, possessions); finca, hacienda (a country estate).

esteem estimación, aprecio.

esteem (to) estimar.

estimable estimable.

estimate presupuesto, cálculo.

estimate (to) tasar, calcular.

eternal eterno.

eternity eternidad.

ether eter.

evacuate evacuar.

even adj. par (not odd); parejo, llano, plano (level).

to be even with estar en paz con, estar mano a mano.

even adv. aun, hasta, no obstante.

even as así como.

even if aun cuando.

even so aun así.

even that hasta eso.

not even that ni siquiera eso.

evening tarde.

Good evening! ¡Buenas tardes!

yesterday evening ayer por la tarde.

tomorrow evening mañana por la tarde.

event suceso.

in the event that en el caso de.

ever siempre (always); nunca (never).

as ever como siempre.

ever so much muy, mucho, muchísimo.

ever since desde entonces.

not . . . ever nunca.

nor . . . ever ni nunca.

every cada.

every bit enteramente.

every day todos los días.

every other day un día sí y otro no.

every one cada uno, cada cual.

every once in a while de cuando en cuando.

every time cada vez.

everybody todos, todo el mundo.

everyone todos, todo el mundo.

everything todo.

everywhere en (por) todas partes.

evidence evidencia, prueba, testimonio.

to give evidence dar testimonio, deponer.

evident evidente.

evil adj. malo.

evil n. mal.

evoke evocar.

exact preciso, exacto.

exaggerate exagerar.

exaggeration exageración.

exalt exaltar.

examination examinación.

examine examinar.

example ejemplo.

exasperate exasperar, irritar.

excavate excavar, cavar.

exceed exceder, sobrepujar.

excel sobresalir, descollar.

excellence excelencia.

excellent excelente.

except excepto, menos; sino, a menos que.

except (to) exceptuar, excluir.

exception excepción.

to make an exception hacer una excepción.

exceptional excepcional.

exceptionally excepcionalmente.

excess exceso.

excessive excesivo.

exchange cambio.

in exchange for a cambio de.

exchange (to) cambiar.

excite excitar.

Don't get so excited. No se sofoque Ud.

excitement excitación, conmoción.

exclaim exclamar.

exclamation exclamación.

exclude excluir.

exclusive exclusivo.

excursion excursión.

excuse excusa.

excuse (to) excusar, dispensar, disculpar.

Excuse me. Dispense Ud.

execute ejecutar.

executive ejecutivo.

exempt exentar, eximir.

exercise (to) ejercer; hacer ejercicios (physical exercise); ejercitar (drill).

exhaust agotar.

exhausted agotado, exhausto.

exhausting agotador.

exile adj. exilado, desterrado.

exile destierro, exilio.

exile (to) desterrar.

exist existir.

existence existencia.

exit salida.

expand extender(se), ensanchar(se), dilatar(se),

desarrollar(se).

expansion expansión.

expansive expansivo.

expect esperar, aguardar.

expectation expectativa, esperanza.

expel expulsar.

expense gasto, coste.

at one's expense a costa de uno.

expensive caro, costoso.

experience experiencia, práctica.

experience (to) experimentar; pasar por (undergo).

experiment experimento.

experiment (to) experimentar.

experimental experimental.

expert experto.

expire expirar.

explain explicar.

explanation explicación.

explanatory explicativo.

explode estallar.

exploit hazaña, proeza.

exploit (to) explotar, sacar partido.

exploration exploración.

explore explorar.

explorer explorador.

explosion explosión.

export exportación.

export (to) exportar.

expose exponer.

express adj. expreso.

express (to) expresar.

expression expresión.

expulsion expulsión.

exquisite exquisito.

extend extender.

extensive extensivo.

extent extensión.

to a certain extent hasta cierto punto.

exterior exterior.

exterminate exterminar.

external externo.

extinguish extinguir.

extra extra, extraordinario.

extract extracto.

extract (to) extraer.

extravagance extravagancia.

extravagant extravagante.

extreme extremo.

extremity extremidad.

eye ojo.

eyebrow ceja.

eye glasses anteojos.

eyelash pestaña.

eyelid párpado.

F

fable fábula, ficción.

fabulous fabuloso.

face cara.

fact hecho.

in fact en realidad.

factory fábrica.

faculty facultad.

fade decaer, marchitarse; desteñirse (color).

fail omisión, falta.

without fail sin falta.

fail (to) fracasar, no tener suerte (in an undertaking); salir mal (in an exam); decaer, ir a menos (health); faltar, dejar de (to do something).

not to fail no dejar de.

failure fracaso; falta (fault, defect); quiebra (bankruptcy).
faint (to) desmayarce, desfallecer.
fair *adj.* rubio (hair); blanco (complexion); claro (clear); justo, recto (just); regular, mediano (moderate); bonancible, buen (weather).
fair play juego limpio.
fair weather buen tiempo.
fair *n.* feria (exhibition, place for trade).
fairness justicia, equidad.
fairy tale cuento de hadas.
faith fe.
faithful fiel.
fall caída; otoño (autumn).
fall (to) caer; caerse (fall down).
false falso.
fame fama.
familiar familiar.
familiarity familiaridad, confianza.
family familia.
famine hambre.
famous famoso.
fan abanico; ventilador (electric fan).
fancy fantasía; capricho (whim).
fantastic fantástico.
far lejos.
How far? ¿A qué distancia?
far away muy lejos.
so far hasta aquí, hasta ahora.
As far as I'm concerned. En cuanto a mí toca.
by far con mucho.
fare tarifa, pasaje.
farmer agricultor, labrador.
farming agricultura, cultivo de la tierra.
farther más lejos, más allá; además de.
fashion moda.
fashionable a la moda, de moda, elegante, de buen tono.
fast pronto, de prisa (quickly).
fasten trabar.
fat *adj.* gordo.
fat *n.* manteca, grasa.
fate destino, fatilidad.
father padre.
fatherhood paternidad.
father-in-law suegro.
fatten engordar.
faucet grifo, llave, canilla (Arg.).
fault falta.
favor favor, servicio.
favor (to) hacer un favor, favorecer.
favorite favorito.
fear miedo, temor.
fearless intrépido.
feast fiesta.
feather pluma.
feature rasgo, característica.
February febrero.
federal federal.
fee honorarios.
feeble débil, enfermizo.
feed alimentar, dar de comer.
feeding alimentación.
feel (to) sentir; tocar (touch).
feeling tacto (tact); sentimiento (sentiment); sensibilidad (sensitiveness).
fellow sujeto, individuo.
fellow student condiscípulo.
fellow traveler compañero de viaje.
fellow worker colega, compañero de trabajo.
female hembra.
feminine femenino.

fence valla, cerca.
ferment fermentar.
fermentation fermentación.
ferry ferry, barca de transbordo.
fertile fecundo, fértil.
fertilize fertilizar, fecundar.
fertilizer abono.
fervent ferviente.
fervor fervor.
festival fiesta, festival.
fever fiebre.
feverish febriciente, febril.
few pocos.
a few unos cuantos, unos pocos.
a few days unos pocos días.
fewer menos.
fiber fibra.
fickle veleidoso, caprichoso.
fiction ficción; novela (story, novel).
field campo; campaña (military); ramo, especialidad (specialty).
fierce feroz.
fiery vehemente, furibundo.
fifteenth decimoquinto.
fifth quinto.
fifty cincuenta.
fig higo.
fig tree higuera.
fight riña, pelea, lucha, conflicto.
fight (to) pelear, luchar, combatir.
figure figura.
file lima (for nails, etc.); archivo, fichero (for papers, cards, etc.).
file (to) limar (with an instrument); archivar papers, etc.).
fill llenar.
film película.
filthy sucio, inmundo.
final final.
finally finalmente, por último.
finance hacienda, finanzas.
financial financiero.
find hallar, encontrar.
fine *adj.* fino, buen, magnífico, excelente.
Fine! ¡Muy bien!
fine *n.* multa.
finger dedo.
finish (to) terminar; acabar.
fire fuego.
fire (to) incendiar (burn); disparar (a gun); despedir, dejar cesante (an employee).
firm *adj.* seguro, firme.
firm *n.* firma (business).
firmness firmeza.
first primero.
at first al principio.
at first glance a primera vista.
firstly primeramente.
fish pez (in the water), pescado (when caught).
fish (to) pescar.
fisherman pescador.
fishing pesca.
fist puño.
fit *adj.* apto, idóneo, adecuado, conveniente, a propósito.
to see fit juzgar conveniente.
If you think fit. Si a Ud. le parece.
fit (to) ajustar, adaptar; entallar (to fit a dress, etc.); caer bien, sentar bien (to have the right size or shape).
to fit into encajar en.
That would fit the case. Eso sería lo propio.
The dress fits you well. El vestido le sienta a

Ud. bien (le viene como pintado).
It fits badly. Me sienta mal.
fitness aptitud.
fitting (be) sentar bien, venir bien.
five cinco.
fix (to) arreglar, componer, reparar (to repair).
flag bandera.
flagrant flagrante.
flame llama.
flannel franela.
flash *n.* destello (light); relámpago (lightning).
flashlight linterna.
flat plano, chato; insípido, soso (taste).
flatten aplastar, aplanar.
flatter adular.
flattery adulación, lisonja.
flavor sabor, gusto.
flavor (to) sazonar, condimentar.
flax lino.
flea pulga.
fleet flota, armada.
flesh carne; pulpa (fruit).
flexibility flexibilidad, docilidad.
flexible flexible.
flight vuelo (in the air); fuga (from jail, etc.).
flint pedernal; piedra de encendedor.
float flotar.
flood inundación.
flood (to) inundar.
floor piso.
flow (to) fluir, manar, correr.
flower flor.
flowery florido.
fluid flúido.
fly mosca.
fly (to) volar.
foam espuma.
foam (to) hacer espuma.
focus foco.
fog niebla, neblina.
fold pliegue, doblez.
fold (to) doblar, plegar.
foliage follaje.
follow seguir.
following siguiente.
food comida.
fool tonto, bobo.
foolish tonto, disparatado.
foolishness tontería.
foot pie.
on foot a pie.
football futbol.
for para, por.
This is for her. Esto es para ella.
for example por ejemplo.
for the first time por la primera vez.
for the present por ahora.
for the time being por de pronto.
forbid prohibir.
forbidden prohibido.
force fuerza.
force (to) forzar, obligar.
forced obligado.
ford vado.
ford (to) vadear.
forecast pronóstico, predicción.
forecast (to) pronosticar, vaticinar.
forehead frente.
foreign extraño, extranjero, ajeno.
foreigner extranjero.
foresee prever.
forest selva, monte.
forget olvidar.

forgetfulness olvido.
forgive perdonar.
forgiveness perdón.
fork tenedor.
form forma.
form (to) formar.
formal ceremonioso (ceremonial); oficial (official).
formality formalidad, ceremonia.
formation formación.
former previo, anterior.
former (the) aquél, aquélla, aquéllos, aquéllas, aquello.
formerly antiguamente, en otros tiempos.
formula fórmula.
forsake desamparar, abandonar.
fortunate afortunado.
fortunately afortunadamente.
fortune suerte, fortuna.
fortuneteller adivino.
fortunetelling buenaventura.
forty cuarenta.
forward adv. adelante, en adelante.
forward (to) remitir, reexpedir.
found encontrado.
found (to) fundar.
foundation fundación.
founder fundador.
fountain fuente.
fountain pen estilográfica, pluma fuente.
four cuatro.
fourteen catorce.
fourth cuarto.
fowl volatería, aves de corral.
fragment fragmento.
fragrance fragancia, aroma.
fragrant oloroso, fragante.
frail endeble, frágil.
frame marco (of a picture, door, etc.); armazón, entramado, estructura (structure).
frame of mind estado de ánimo.
frame (to) encuadrar, poner en un marco (a picture, etc.).
France Francia.
frank franco, sincero.
frankness franqueza.
free adj. libre; gratis.
free of charge gratis.
free (to) libertar, librar.
freeze helar, congelar.
freight carga; flete.
French francés.
frequent frecuente.
frequent (to) frecuentar.
frequently frecuentemente.
fresh fresco.
Friday viernes.
friend amigo.
friendly amistoso.
friendship amistad.
frighten asustar.
frightening espantoso.
frivolity frivolidad, trivialidad.
frivolous frívolo.
frog rana.
from de, desde.
from a distance desde lejos.
from memory de memoria.
front adj. anterior, delantero, de frente.
front room cuarto que da a la calle.
front view vista de frente.
front frente.
in front of frente a.

frown ceño, entrecejo.
frown (to) fruncir el ceño.
fruit fruta.
fry freír.
frying pan sartén.
fuel combustible.
fugitive fugitivo.
fulfill cumplir.
full lleno.
fully plenamente, enteramente.
fun broma; diversión.
to have fun divertirse, pasar un buen rato.
to make fun of burlarse de.
funny divertido, cómico.
function función.
function (to) funcionar.
fundamental fundamental.
funds fondos.
funeral funeral, entierro.
fur piel(es).
furious furioso.
furnace horno.
furnish amueblar (a room, house, etc.); suplir (supply); proveer (provide).
furniture muebles.
furrow surco.
further adv. más lejos, más allá; además, aún.
further on más adelante; y además de eso (in speech).
fury furor.
future futuro.
in the future en lo sucesivo, en adelante, en lo futuro.

G

gaiety alegría, alborozo.
gain ganancia.
gain (to) ganar.
gamble (to) jugar por dinero.
game juego; partida, partido; caza (hunting).
a game of chess una partida de ajedrez.
garage garage.
garden jardín.
gardener jardinero.
gargle (to) hacer gárgaras.
garlic ajo.
garment prenda de vestir, vestido.
garter liga.
gas gas; gasolina (gasoline).
gas station puesto de gasolina.
gasoline gasolina.
gasoline station puesto de gasolina.
gate puerta.
gather (to) reunir, juntar.
gay alegre.
gem piedra preciosa.
gender género.
general adj. general.
in general en general, por lo general.
general general.
generality generalidad.
generalize generalizar.
generally generalmente, por lo general.
generation generación.
generosity generosidad.
generous generoso.
genius genio.
gentle suave; amable, delicado (of a person).
gentleman caballero.
gentlemen señores; muy señores nuestros (in a letter).
gentleness ababilidad, delicadeza.

gently suavemente; amablemente.
genuine genuino, auténtico.
geographical geográfico.
geography geografía.
geometric geométrico.
geometry geometría.
germ germen; microbio.
German alemán.
Germany Alemania.
gesture n. gesto, ademán.
get (to) adquirir, obtener, conseguir, recibir.
to get ahead adelantarse.
to get away partir, marcharse; huir.
to get back volver, regresar.
to get home llegar a casa.
to get in entrar.
to get married casarse.
to get off apearse, bajar.
to get on montar, subir.
to get out salir.
to get up levantarse; subir.
giant gigante.
gift regalo, obsequio.
gifted agraciado.
ginger jengibre.
girl chica, niña, muchacha.
give (to) dar.
to give in ceder, acceder.
to give up desistir, darse por vencido.
to give a gift regalar, hacer un regalo.
giver donante.
glad contento, feliz.
to be glad alegrarse de, tener gusto en.
glance ojeada, vistazo.
glance (to) echar un vistazo, dar una ojeada.
to glance at a book hojear un libro.
glass vidrio; vaso (for drinking).
looking glass espejo.
drinking glass vaso.
glimpse n. ojeada, vistazo.
glitter (to) brillar, resplandecer.
globe globo.
gloomy triste, sombrío.
glorious glorioso.
glory n. gloria.
glove guante.
glue n. cola.
go (to) ir.
to go away irse, marcharse.
to go back volverse atrás, retroceder; regresar, volver.
to go down bajar.
to go forward ir adelante, adelantarse.
to go out salir; apagarse (a light, fire, etc.).
to go up subir.
to go with acompañar.
to go without pasarse sin.
goal meta, objetivo, fin.
to reach one's goal alcanzar el objetivo, llegar a la meta, obtener lo que uno se había propuesto.
God Dios.
godfather padrino.
godmother madrina.
gold oro.
golden de oro.
good buen(o).
good morning buenos días.
good evening buenas tardes.
good night buenas noches.
good-by adiós.
goodness bondad.
Goodness! (Goodness gracious!) ¡Válgame

Dios! ¡María santísima!
Goodness knows! ¡Quién sabe!
goods mercancías, géneros, efectos.
goodwill buena voluntad; nombre, reputación, traspaso (business).
goose ganso.
gossip chisme, chismografía, murmuración.
gossip (to) chismear, murmurar.
govern gobernar.
government gobierno.
governor gobernador.
gown vestido de mujer.
grab (to) agarrar, arrebatar.
grace n. gracia.
graceful gracioso.
gracious bondadoso, afable, cortés.
grade grado.
gradual gradual.
gradually gradualmente.
graduate (a) graduado, recíbido de (doctor, etc.).
graduate (to) graduarse, recíbir un título.
graduated (be) graduarse, recíbirse.
grain grano.
grammar gramática.
grammatical gramatical.
grand gran, grandioso, magnífico, espléndido.
Grand! ¡Estupendo! ¡Magnífico!
grandchild nieto.
granddaughter nieta.
grandfather abuelo.
grandmother abuela.
grandparents abuelos.
grandson nieto.
grant concesión.
grant (to) conceder, otorgar.
to take for granted dar por sentado, presuponer.
granting (granted) that supuesto que, concedido que.
grape uva.
grapefruit toronja.
grasp (to) empuñar, asir, agarrar; comprender, percibir.
grass hierba, pasto, césped.
grasshopper saltamontes.
grateful agradecido.
gratefully agradecidamente, gratamente.
gratis gratis, de balde.
gratitude agradecimiento.
grave adj. grave, serio.
grave n. sepultura, tumba.
gravel grava.
gravity gravedad, seriedad.
gravy salsa.
gray gris (color), cano (hair).
gray-haired canoso.
grease grasa.
grease (to) engrasar.
great gran, grande.
a great man un gran hombre.
a great many muchos.
a great deal mucho.
Great! ¡Estupendo! ¡Magnífico!
Great Britain Gran Bretaña.
greatness grandeza, grandiosidad.
green verde.
greet saludar.
greeting saludo.
grief pesar, dolor, pena.
grieve (to) penar, afligirse.
grill (to) asar a la parrilla.
grind moler.
groan gemido.

groan (to) gemir.
grocer abacero; bodeguero (Cuba); abarrotero (Mex.).
groceries comestibles, abarrotes (Amer.).
grocery (store) ultramarinos, tienda de comestibles, abarrotes (Amer.).
groove ranura.
grope andar a tientas.
ground n. tierra, suelo, terreno.
group grupo.
group (to) agrupar.
grow (to) crecer.
to grow old envejecer.
to grow late hacerse tarde.
to grow better ponerse mejor, mejorar.
to grow worse ponerse peor, empeorar.
growth crecimiento.
grudge rencor.
gruff áspero, brusco.
grumble (to) refunfuñar, grunir.
guarantee garantía.
guarantee (to) garantir.
guard guardia; guarda; guardián.
guard (to) guardar, vigilar.
to guard against guardarse de.
Guatemala Guatemala.
Guatemalan guatemalteco.
guess conjetura, suposición.
guess (to) adivinar, conjeturar.
to guess right acertar.
guide guía.
guide (to) guiar.
guidebook guía de viajeros.
guilt culpa.
guilty culpable.
guitar guitarra.
gulf golfo.
gum encía (teeth).
chewing gum chicle.
gun arma de fuego, cañón, fusil, revólver, escopeta.
gymnasium gimnasio.
gypsy gitano.

H

haberdashery camisería, mercería.
haberdashery store camisería.
habit costumbre, hábito.
to be in the habit of estar acostumbrado.
habitual habitual.
habitually habitualmente.
hail granizo (during thunderstorm); viva, vitor (cheering, greeting).
hail (to) granizar (in a thunderstorm); vitorear (to cheer).
hair pelo, cabello.
hairbrush cepillo para la cabeza.
haircut corte de pelo.
hairdye tintura para el pelo.
hairpin horquilla.
half medio; mitad.
half and half mitad y mitad.
half past two las dos y media.
half-hour media hora.
half-year semestre.
half brother hermanastro.
half sister hermanastra.
halfway a medio camino, equidistante..
hall vestíbulo (entrance, foyer); salón (assembly room).
halt alto, parada.
halt (to) parar, detener.

Halt ¡Alto!
ham jamón.
hammer martillo.
hammer (to) martillar.
to hammer on a subject machacar.
hand mano; manecilla (of a watch).
by hand a mano.
in hand entre manos; (dinero) en mano.
offhand improvisadamente, de repente; sin preparación.
on hand disponible, a la mano.
on the other hand por otra parte.
hand (to) pasar.
to hand over entregar.
handbag maleta, bolsa.
handbook manual.
handful puñado.
handkerchief pañuelo.
handle mango, asa.
handle (to) manejar, manipular.
handmade hecho a mano.
handshake apretón de manos.
hang colgar.
hanger (clothes) gancho de ropa, colgador, colgadero, percha.
happen suceder, acontecer.
happening suceso, acontecimiento.
happiness dicha, felicidad.
happy feliz, contento.
harbor puerto.
hard duro; difícil.
hard luck mala suerte.
hard work trabajo difícil.
to rain hard llover a cántaros.
to work hard trabajar duro.
harden endurecer.
hardly apenas, difícilmente, escasamente.
hardness dureza.
hardware ferretería, quincalla.
hardware store ferretería.
hardy fuerte, robusto.
hare liebre.
harm n. mal, prejuicio, daño.
harmful nocivo, dañoso, dañino.
harmless inofensivo.
harmonious armonioso.
harmonize armonizar.
harmony armonía.
harness n. aparejo, arnés.
harsh áspero, tosco; desagradable.
harshness aspereza, rudeza.
harvest n. cosecha.
haste prisa.
in haste de prisa.
hasten darse prisa, acelerar, apresurarse.
hastily apresuradamente, precipitadamente.
hasty apresurado.
hat sombrero.
hatch (to) empollar, incubar.
hatchet hacha pequeña.
hate odio.
hate (to) odiar, detestar.
hateful odioso.
hatred odio, aborrecimiento.
haughty soberbio.
have (to) tener (to possess); haber (auxiliary).
to have in mind tener en cuenta.
to have to tener que.
to have a mind to querer, tener ganas de.
hay heno.
he él.
head cabeza, jefe (chief).
head (to) encabezar.

heading encabezamiento, título.
headache dolor de cabeza.
headline n. encabezamiento, titular.
headquarters cuartel general (Army); oficina principal (main office).
heal curar; recobrar la salud; cicatrizarse (a wound).
health salud.
    tò be in good health estar bien de salud.
healthful saludable.
healthy sano.
heap n. montón.
    in heaps a montones.
heap (to) acumular, apilar.
hear (to) oir.
    to hear from saber de, tener noticias de.
heart corazón.
    heart and soul en cuerpo y alma.
    by heart de memoria.
    to have no heart no tener corazón.
    to take to heart tomar a pecho.
hearth hogar, fogón.
hearty cordial (warm); voraz (appetite).
heat calor.
heat (to) calentar.
heater calentador.
heating calefacción.
heaven cielo.
    Heavens! ¡Cielos!
heavy pesado.
    heavy rain lluvia fuerte, aguacero.
hedge seto.
heel talón (of foot); tacón (shoe).
height altura.
heir heredero.
hell infierno.
Hello! ¡Hola!
help ayuda; auxilio.
help (to) ayudar.
    to help oneself to servirse (comida).
helper asistente, ayudante.
helpful util, provechoso.
hemisphere hemisferio.
hen gallina.
henceforth de aquí en adelante, en adelante, en lo futuro.
her la, le, ella, de ella, a ella, su.
herb hierba, yerba.
here aquí; acá.
    Here it is. Aquí está.
    Come here. Ven acá.
    around here cerca de aquí, por aquí.
    near here cerca de aquí.
hereabout por aquí, por aquí cerca.
hereafter en adelante.
herein aquí dentro, adjunto.
herewith con esto.
hero héroe.
heroic heroico.
heroine heroína.
heroism heroísmo.
herring arenque.
hers suyo, suya, de ella; el suyo, la suya, los suyos, las suyas.
herself ella misma; sí misma; se, sí.
    by herself sola; por sí, por su cuenta.
    she herself ella misma, en persona.
hesitant indeciso, vacilante.
hesitate vacilar.
hesitation vacilación, titubeo.
hidden escondido.
hide (to) esconder; esconderse.
hideous horrible, espantoso.

high alto, elevado; caro (price).
    to be high tener de alto.
    It is five inches high. Tiene cinco pulgadas de alto.
higher más alto; superior.
highway carretera.
hill colina, cerro.
him él, a él, le.
himself el mismo; sí mismo, se, sí.
    by himself solo; por sí, por su cuenta.
    he himself él mismo, en persona.
hinder impedir, estorbar.
hindrance impedimento, estorbo, obstáculo.
hinge gozne.
hint insinuación, indirecta, alusión.
hint (to) insinuar.
    to hint at aludir a.
hip cadera.
hire (to) alquilar.
his su, sus, suyo, suya, el suyo, la suya, los suyos, las suyas, de él.
hiss silbar, sisear.
historian historiador.
historic histórico.
history historia.
hit golpe.
hit (to) golpear.
    to hit the mark dar en el blanco.
hive colmena.
hoarse ronco.
hoe azada, azadón.
hog cerdo, puerco.
hold (to) tener (in one's hands, arms, etc.); coger, agarrar, asir (to grasp); caber, contener (to contain, to have capacity for); tener, desempeñar (a job, etc.).
    to hold good valer, ser válido.
    to hold a meeting celebrar una reunión.
    to hold one's own mantenerse firme, defenderse bien.
    to hold a conversation sostener una conversación.
hole agujero; hueco.
holiday día festivo, día feriado.
holidays vacaciones, asueto.
holy santo.
homage homenaje.
home hogar, casa, domicilio.
    at home en casa.
    home town pueblo natal.
homely feo.
homemade casero, hecho en casa.
Honduras Honduras.
Honduran hondureño.
honest honrado.
honesty honradez.
honey miel.
honor honor.
honor (to) honrar.
honorable honroso; honorable.
hoof casco, pezuña.
hook n. gancho; anzuelo (for fishing).
hope esperanza.
hope (to) esperar.
hopeful lleno de esperanzas, optimista.
hopeless desahuciado, sin remedio.
horizon horizonte.
horizontal horizontal.
horn cuerno (of animals); bocina (of car); corneta de caza (hunting).
horrible horrible, terrible.
horror horror.
horse caballo.

    on horseback a caballo.
hosiery tienda de medias y calcetines (store); géneros de punto (goods knit).
hospitable hospitalario.
hospital hospital.
hospitality hospitalidad.
host anfitrión.
hostess anfitriona.
hot caliente.
hotel hotel.
hour hora.
house casa.
household familia (family); menaje de casa (furniture, etc.).
housekeeper ama (de llaves).
housemaid criada, sirvienta.
housewife ama de casa, madre de familia.
how cómo; qué, cuánto.
    How do you do? ¿Cómo le va? ¿Cómo está Ud.? ¿Qué tal?
    How many? ¿Cuántos?
    How much? ¿Cuánto?
    How far? ¿A qué distancia?
    How early? ¿Cuándo? ¿A qué hora?
    How late? ¿Hasta qué hora? ¿Cuando?
    How long? ¿Cuánto tiempo?
    How soon? ¿Cuándo a más tardar?
however sin embargo.
huge inmenso, enorme.
human humano.
    human race género humano.
humane humanitario, bienhechor.
humanity humanidad.
humble humilde.
humiliate humillar.
humiliation humillación.
humility humildad.
humor humor.
humorous humorista, chistoso, jocoso.
hundred cien, ciento.
hundredth centésimo.
hunger hambre.
hungry (be) tener hambre.
hunt caza.
hunt (to) cazar.
hunter cazador.
hunting caza.
hurry prisa.
    to be in a hurry tener prisa, estar de prisa.
hurry (to) apresurar.
    to hurry up darse prisa.
    Hurry up! ¡Date prisa! (familiar). ¡Dése prisa!
hurt (to) lastimar, herir; ofender (one's feelings).
husband esposo.
hydrant boca de riego.
hygiene higiene.
hyphen guión.
hypnotism hipnotismo.
hypnotize hipnotizar.
hypocrisy hipocresía.
hypocrite hipócrita.
hysteria histeria.
hysterical histérico.

I

I yo.
ice hielo, helado.
ice cream helado.
idea idea.
ideal ideal.
idealism idealismo.
idealist idealista.

identical idéntico.
identification identificación.
identify identificar.
identity identidad.
idiom modismo.
idiot idiota, imbécil.
idle ocioso.
idleness ocio.
if si.
  if not si no.
  even if aun cuando.
  If I may. Con su permiso. Si me permite.
ignorance ignorancia.
ignorant ignorante, inculto.
ignore ignorar, pasar por alto, no hacer caso.
ill enfermo (sick) mal, malo (wrong, bad).
  ill breeding malos modales.
  ill will mala voluntad.
illegal ilegal.
illegible ilegible.
illiteracy analfabetismo.
illiterate analfabeto.
illness enfermedad.
illogical ilógico.
illuminate iluminar, alumbrar.
illumination iluminación, alumbrado.
illusion ilusión.
illustrate ilustrar.
illustrated ilustrado.
illustration ilustración (picture, etc.); ejemplo
  (example).
image imagen.
imaginary imaginario.
imagination imaginación.
imaginative imaginativo.
imagine figurar, imaginar.
  Just imagine! ¡Imagínese!
imitate imitar.
imitation imitación.
immediate inmediato.
immediately inmediatamenta, en seguida, en el
  acto.
immense inmenso.
immigrant inmigrante.
immigrate inmigrar.
immigration inmigración.
imminent inminente.
immoderate inmoderado, excesivo.
immoral inmoral.
immorality inmoralidad.
immortal inmortal.
immortality inmortalidad.
impartial imparcial.
impatience impaciencia.
impatient impaciente.
imperative imperativo.
imperceptible imperceptible.
imperfect imperfecto, defectuoso.
impersonal impersonal.
impertinence impertinencia.
impertinent impertinente.
impetuous impetuoso, arrebatado.
implement herramienta, utensilio.
implied implícito.
imply implicar; querer decir, significar.
impolite descortés.
import (to) importar.
importance importancia.
important importante.
importation importación.
importer importador.
impose imponer; abusar de (impose upon).
imposing imponente; abusivo.

impossibility imposibilidad.
impossible imposible.
impress impresionar.
impression impresión.
  to have the impression tener la impresión.
impressive imponente, grandioso.
imprison encarcelar, aprisionar.
improbable improbable.
improper impropio.
improve mejorar, perfeccionar; adelantar, progresar; aliviarse, mejorarse (health).
improved mejorado, perfeccionado.
improvement mejora, adelanto, progreso, per-
  feccionamiento; alivio, mejoría (health).
improvise improvisar.
imprudence imprudencia.
imprudent imprudente.
impure impuro.
in en.
  in fact en efecto.
  in the morning por la mañana.
  in a week de aquí a una semana, dentro de
    una semana.
  to be in estar en (casa, en la oficina, etc.).
  in front enfrente, delante.
  in general en general, por lo general.
  in part en parte.
  in reality en realidad.
  in spite of a pesar de.
  in turn por turno.
  in vain en vano.
  in writing por escrito.
inability ineptitud, inhabilidad, incapacidad.
inaccessible inaccessible.
inaccuracy inexactitud.
inaccurate inexacto.
inactive inactivo.
inadequate inadecuado.
inaugurate inaugurar.
incapability incapacidad.
incapable incapaz.
incapacity incapacidad.
inch pulgada.
incident incidente.
inclination inclinación, propensión.
include incluir, comprender.
included inclusive, incluso, comprendido.
inclusive inclusivo.
incoherent incoherente.
income renta, ingreso.
incomparable incomparable.
incompatible incompatible.
incomprehensible incomprensible.
inconsistent inconsistente.
inconvenience inconveniencia; molestia.
inconvenience (to) incomodar, molestar.
inconvenient inconveniente; incómodo, molesto.
incorrect incorrecto.
increase aumento.
increase (to) aumentar.
incredible increíble.
incurable incurable.
indebted endeudado, entrampado, lleno de
  deudas; obligado, reconocido (under obligation).
indecent indecente.
indeed verdaderamente, realmente, de veras, a
  la verdad, sí, claro está.
  Indeed? ¿De veras?
  Yes indeed! ¡Claro que sí! ¡Claro está!
  No indeed! ¡Quiá! ¡De ninguna manera!
indefinite indefinido.
independence independencia.

independent independiente; acomodado, ren-
  tista (financially independent).
indescribable indescriptible.
index índice.
index finger índice.
indicate indicar.
indifference indiferencia.
indifferent indiferente.
indigestion indigestión.
indignant indignado.
indignation indignación.
indirect indirecto.
indiscreet indiscreto.
indispensable indispensable.
indisputable indisputable.
indistinct indistinto.
individual adj. individual, particular.
individual n. individuo.
individuality individualidad, personalidad.
individually individualmente.
indivisible indivisible.
indolence indolencia.
indolent indolente.
indoors dentro, en casa.
indorsement endoso.
indulge dar rienda suelta a, darse gusto; entregarse a (to indulge in).
indulgence indulgencia; complacencia (self-
  indulgence).
indulgent indulgente.
industrial industrial.
industrious diligente, trabajador.
industry industria.
inefficient ineficaz.
inequality desigualidad.
inevitable inevitable.
inexcusable inexcusable, imperdonable.
inexhaustible inagotable.
inexpensive barato.
inexperience inexperiencia.
inexperienced sin experiencia, novel.
infallible infalible.
infant infante, niño.
infantry infantería.
infection infección.
infectious infeccioso, contagioso.
infer inferir; colegir.
inference inferencia.
inferior inferior.
inferiority inferioridad.
infinite infinito.
infinitive infinitivo.
infinity infinidad.
influence influencia.
influence (to) influir.
  to influence by suggestion sugestionar.
influential influyente.
influenza influenza.
inform (to) informar, hacer saber, poner al
  corriente.
information información.
  information bureau oficina de información.
infrequent raro, no frecuente.
infrequently raramente.
ingenious ingenioso.
ingenuity ingenio, talento.
ingratitude ingratitud.
inhabit habitar.
inhabitant habitante.
inherit heredar.
inheritance herencia.
initial inicial.
initiative iniciativa.

injure injuriar, agraviar (the feelings, reputation, etc.); dañar, hacer daño, lastimar, (to damage).
injurious nocivo, dañino, perjudicial.
injury daño, avería; perjuicio, mal.
injustice injusticia.
ink tinta.
inkwell tintero.
inland interior, tierra adentro.
  inland navigation navegación fluvial.
inn posada, venta.
innate innato.
inner interior.
innkeeper posadero, ventero.
innocence inocencia.
innocent inocente.
insane loco, demente.
insanity locura.
inscribe inscribir.
inscription inscripción.
insect insecto.
insecticide insecticida.
insecure inseguro.
insecurity inseguridad.
insensible insensible.
inseparable inseparable.
insert (to) insertar, introducir.
insertion inserción.
inside dentro; interior.
  on the inside por dentro.
  toward the inside hacia dentro.
  inside out al revés.
insignificance insignificancia.
insignificant insignificante.
insincere falto de sinceridad, poco sincero.
insincerity falta de sinceridad.
insist insistir.
insistence insistencia.
insolence insolencia.
insolent insolente.
inspect inspeccionar, examinar.
inspection inspección.
inspector inspector.
inspiration inspiración.
install instalar, colocar.
installation instalación.
instance ejemplo; caso.
  for instance por ejemplo.
  in this instance en este caso.
instead of en lugar de, en vez de.
instinct instinto.
institute instituto.
institute (to) instituir.
institution institución.
instruct instruir, enseñar; dar instrucciones.
instruction instrucción, enseñanza.
instructive instructivo.
instructor instructor.
instrument instrumento.
insufficiency insuficiencia.
insufficient insuficiente.
insult insulto.
insult (to) insultar.
insulting insultante.
insuperable insuperable.
insurance seguro.
intact intacto.
integral íntegro.
intellectual intelectual.
intelligence inteligencia.
intelligent inteligente.
intend intentar; tener intención de, proponerse (to have in mind).

  to be intended for tener por objeto.
intense intenso.
intensity intensidad.
intention intención.
intentional intencional.
intentionally intencionalmente.
interest interés.
interest (to) interesar.
interested interesado.
interesting interesante.
interior interior, interno.
intermission intermisión, entreacto (theater).
internal interno.
international internacional.
interpose interponer.
interpret interpretar.
interpretation interpretación.
interpreter intérprete.
interrupt interrumpir.
interruption interrupción.
interval intervalo.
intervention intervención.
interview entrevista.
intestines intestinos.
intimacy intimidad.
intimate íntimo.
intimidate intimidar.
into en, dentro.
intonation entonación.
intoxicate embriagar; intoxicar (to poison).
intoxicated borracho.
intoxicating embriagante.
intoxication embriaguez; intoxicación (poison).
intricate intrincado, enredado, complicado.
intrigue intriga, trama.
intrinsic(al) intrínseco.
introduce introducir; presentar (a person).
  to introduce a person presentar a una persona.
introduction introducción (book); presentación (person).
intruder intruso.
intuition intuición.
invade invadir.
invalid *adj.* inválido (person), nulo (void).
invalid *n.* inválido.
invasion invasión.
invent inventar.
invention invención.
inventor inventor.
invert invertir, volver al revés, trastocar.
invest invertir, colocar (money).
investigate investigar, inquirir.
investigation investigación.
investment inversión.
investor inversionista, persona que invierte dinero.
invisible invisible.
invitation invitación.
invite convidar, invitar.
invoice factura.
involuntary involuntario.
involve comprometer, implicar; enredar.
involved complicado.
iodine yodo.
iris iris.
iron hierro; plancha (for ironing).
iron (to) planchar (clothes).
ironical irónico.
ironing planchado.
irony ironía.
irregular irregular.
irresolute irresoluto.

irresponsible irresponsable.
irrigate regar, irrigar.
irrigation riego.
irritable irritable.
irritate irritar, exasperar.
irritation irritación.
island isla.
isolation aislamiento.
issue edición, tirada (books, etc.); asunto de que se trata.
issue (to) publicar, dar a luz (books, magazines, etc.).
it ello, el, ella; lo, la, le; esto, este, esta. ("It" is not translated in phrases like "it's raining" [llueve] "it's late" [es tarde], "it's two o'clock" [son las dos], etc.).
  I have it. Lo *masc.* tengo.
  I have it. La *fem.* tengo.
  I said it. Yo lo dije.
  Isn't it? ¿No es verdad?
  That's it. Eso es.
Italian italiano.
Italy Italia.
itinerary itinerario.
its su, sus (de él, de ella, de ello, de ellos, de ellas).
itself sí, sí mismo.
  by itself por sí.
ivory marfil.
ivy hiedra.

J

jack gato (tool).
jacket chaqueta (a short coat); camisa, cubierta (covering, casing).
jail cárcel.
jam compota, conserva (of fruit); apuro, aprieto (a fix).
janitor portero, conserje.
January enero.
jar *n.* tarro (for preserves).
jaw quijada.
jealous celoso.
jealousy celos.
jelly jalea.
jerk (to) sacudir.
jest broma.
jest (to) bromear.
Jesuit jesuita.
jewel joya, alhaja.
jewelry joyería.
jewelry shop joyería.
job empleo; tarea.
join unir, juntar (to put together); unirse, asociarse (to unite); afiliarse, adherirse a, ingresar en (an organization).
joint coyuntura, articulación (anatomical); empalme, junta, juntura, ensambladura (the place or part where two things are joined).
joke broma.
joke (to) bromear, embromar.
jolly *adj.* alegre, divertido, jovial.
jostle empellar, rempujar.
journal diario.
journalist periodista.
journalistic periodístico.
journey viaje.
journey (to) viajar.
jovial jovial.
joy alegría, júbilo.
joyful alegre, gozoso.
judge juez.

judge (to) juzgar.
judgment juicio.
judicial judicial.
juice zumo, jugo.
juicy jugoso.
July julio.
jump salto.
jump (to) saltar.
June junio.
junior adj. más joven (younger); hijo (Jr. after a name).
   junior partner socio menos antiguo.
jurisprudence jurisprudencia.
juror jurado (individual).
jury jurado.
just adj. justo.
   It's not just. No es justo.
just adv. justamente, exactamente; solamente, simplemente, no más que.
   just as al momento que, en el mismo instante en que; no bien.
   just as I came in en el mismo instante en que entraba.
   just a moment un momentito.
   just now ahora mismo.
   I just wanted to yo solamente quería.
   to have just acabar de.
   I have just come. Acabo de llegar.
   It is just two o'clock. Son las dos en punto.
   Just as you please. Como Ud. guste.
justice justicia.
justifiable justificable.
justification justificación.
justify justificar.

K

keen agudo.
keep (to) guardar.
   to keep away mantener alejado; no dejar entrar.
   to keep back (retain) detener, retener.
   to keep from impedir (hinder); abstenerse (refrain).
   to keep quiet callar.
   to keep house tener casa puesta.
   to keep in mind recordar, tener presente.
   to keep late hours acostarse tarde.
   to keep one's hands off no tocar, no meterse en.
   to keep one's word tener palabra, cumplir su palabra.
   to keep track of no perder de vista; tener en cuenta.
kernel almendra, pepita.
kerosene kerosen, kerosene, kerosina.
kettle marmita, caldera.
key llave; principal (main).
keyboard teclado.
kick puntapié; patada, coz.
kick (to) patear; cocear.
kidney riñón.
kill (to) matar.
kind adj. bueno, amable, bondadoso.
kind n. clase, calidad.
   a kind of una especie de.
   of the kind semejante.
   nothing of the kind no hay tal, nada de eso.
   of a kind de una misma clase.
kindergarten escuela de párvulos.
kindhearted bondadoso.
kindly bondadosamente; tenga la bondad, haga el favor, sírvase.

Kindly do it. Tenga la bondad de hacerlo.
kindness bondad.
king rey.
kingdom reino.
kiss beso.
kiss (to) besar.
kitchen cocina.
kite cometa.
kitten gatito.
knee rodilla.
kneecap rótula.
kneel arrodillarse.
knife cuchillo.
knit tejer.
knock golpe (blow); llamada (on the door).
knock (to) golpear; tocar, llamar (on the door).
knot nudo.
know (to) saber; conocer (be acquainted with).
knowledge conocimiento.
   to the best of my knowledge según mi leal saber y entender.
known conocido.
knuckle coyuntura, nudillo.
kodak kodak.

L

label etiqueta.
labor trabajo.
laboratory laboratorio.
laborer jornalero, trabajador.
lace n. encaje.
lack falta, escasez, carencia, necesidad.
lack (to) carecer, faltar algo, necesitar.
lacking (be) hacer falta.
ladder escalera de mano.
lady señora.
   Ladies. Señoras.
   Ladies and gentlemen. Señoras y caballeros.
lake lago.
lamb cordero.
   lamb chops chuletas de cordero.
lame cojo (limping); lisiado (crippled); defectuoso, inaceptable (unsatisfactory).
lame (be) cojear (to limp).
lameness cojera.
lament (to) lamentar.
lamentation lamento.
lamp lámpara.
land tierra (ground); terreno (terrain), país (country).
land (to) desembarcar (ship); aterrizar (plane).
landing n. desembarco (from a ship); aterrizaje (of an airplane); meseta, descanso (a staircase).
landlady propietaria, dueña, patrona.
landlord propietario, dueño, casero, patrón.
landscape paisaje, vista.
language lengua, idioma; lenguaje.
languid lánguido.
languish languidecer.
languor languidez.
lantern farol, linterna.
lap falda.
lard manteca, lardo.
large grande.
   at large en libertad, suelto (free, loose); extensamente, sin limitación (widespread); en general, en conjunto (in general).
large-scale en gran escala.
lark alondra.
larynx laringe.
last último; pasado.

lastly al fin, finalmente, por último.
   at last al fin, al cabo, por fin.
   last night anoche.
   last week la semana pasada.
   last year el año pasado.
last (to) durar.
lasting duradero, durable.
latch aldaba, picaporte.
late adj. tarde.
   to be late llegar tarde.
   late in the year a fines de año.
   How late? ¿Hasta que hora?
lately poco ha, no ha mucho, recientemente, últimamente.
lateness tardanza.
later más tarde.
latest último.
   latest style última moda.
   at the latest a más tardar.
lather espuma de jabón, jabonadura.
Latin latino adj.; latín n.
latter (the) éste, último.
laudable laudable, loable.
laugh risa.
   to make someone laugh hacer reír.
laugh (to) reír.
laughable risible, que causa risa, divertido.
laughter risa.
launder lavar y planchar la ropa.
laundress lavandera.
laundry lavandería, establecimiento de la ropa; ropa sucia (clothes to be washed); ropa lavada (washed clothes).
lavish pródigo, gastador.
lavish (to) prodigar.
law ley; jurisprudencia (legal science); derec (body of laws); código (code).
   law school escuela de derecho.
   international law derecho internacional.
lawful legal, conforme a la ley.
lawless ilegal.
lawn césped.
lawyer abogado.
laxative laxante.
lay (to) poner.
   to lay away (aside, by) poner a un lado, guar dar, ahorrar.
   to lay hands on sentar la mano a.
   to lay hold of asir, coger.
   to lay off quitarse de encima; despedir (to fire).
   to lay the blame on echar la culpa a.
laziness pereza.
lazy perezoso.
lead (metal) plomo.
lead (to) conducir, guiar.
   to lead the way mostrar el camino, ir delante.
   to lead up to conducir a.
leader líder, caudillo, conductor, jefe; guía (guide); director (band leader).
leadership dirección.
leading principal, capital.
   leading article editorial.
   leading man cabecilla, jefe.
leaf hoja.
lean (to) inclinar; apoyarse.
   to lean back retreparse, recostarse.
   to lean over reclinarse.
leaning inclinación, propensión, tendencia.
leap salto, brinco.
leap (to) saltar, brincar.
learn aprender (to acquire knowledge, skill); enterarse de, tener noticia de, saber (to find

out about).

learned sabio, docto, erudito.

learning saber, ciencia, erudición.

lease arriendo, contrato de arrendamiento.

lease (to) arrendar, dar en arriendo.

least mínimo, el mínimo, menos.

  at least a lo menos, por lo menos.

  not in the least de ninguna manera, bajo ningún concepto.

  the least possible lo menos posible.

  least of all lo de menos.

leather cuero.

leave (to) dejar (quit); abandonar (desert); salir (go out); irse (go away).

  to leave behind dejar atrás.

  to leave out omitir, excluir.

lecture n. conferencia; disertación (a discourse), regaño (a reprimand).

lecturer conferencianta.

left izquierdo.

  left hand mano izquierda.

  to the left a la izquierda.

  left-handed zurdo.

left (be) quedarse.

leg pierna; pata (of a chicken, etc.); pata, pie (of a table, etc.).

legal legal.

legend leyenda.

legible legible, que puede leerse.

legislation legislación.

legislator legislador.

legislature legislatura.

leisure ocio, holganza, comodidad.

lemon limón.

lemonade limonada.

lend (to) prestar, dar prestado.

  to lend an ear dar oídos, prestar atención.

  to lend a hand arrimar el hombro, dar una mano.

length largo, longitud.

  at length al fin, finalmente; detalladamente (with all the details).

  at full length a lo largo, a todo lo largo.

less menos.

  more or less más o menos.

  less and less cada vez menos.

lessen reducir, disminuir, disminuirse.

lesson lección.

let (to) lejar, permitir; arrendar, alquilar (to rent).

  Let's go. Vamos.

  Let her go que se vaya.

  Let's see Veamos.

  to let alone dejar en paz, no molestar.

  to let be no meterse con.

  to let go soltar.

  to let it go at that dejar pasar, no hacer o decir más.

  to let in dejar entrar, hacer pasar.

  to let know hacer saber, avisar.

letter carta; letra (of the alphabet).

lettuce lechuga.

level adj. plano, llano, igual, parejo nivelado, allanado.

  level crossing paso a nivel.

level nivel.

  to be on the level jugar limpio, ser honrado, no tener dolo.

level off (to) nivelar; planear (a plane).

liable sujeto, expuesto a (exposed to); propenso a, capaz de (liable to think, say, do).

liar embustero.

liberal liberal.

liberty libertad.

library biblioteca.

license licencia, permiso.

lick lamer.

lid tapa, tapadera.

lie mentira (falsehood).

lie (to) mentir (tell a falsehood) reposar, acostarse, echarse (lie down).

lieutenant teniente.

life vida.

  lifesaver salvavidas.

  lifeboat bote salvadidas.

  life insurance seguro sobre la vida.

lifetime toda la vida, duración de la vida.

lift alzar, levantar.

light luz; claridad.

  in the light of según, a la luz de.

  in this light desde este punto de vista.

light adj. liviano, ligero (in weight), claro (color).

  light complexion tez blanca.

  light reading lectura amena.

  light-headed ligero (alegre) de cascos.

light (to) encender (a match, etc.); alumbrar, iluminar (to illuminate).

lighten aligerar, quitar peso.

lighthouse faro.

lighting alumbrado, iluminación.

lightness ligereza.

lightning relámpago.

like parecido, semejante (similar).

  in like manner del mismo modo, análogamente.

  be like ser semejante, parecido.

like (to) querer, gustar, agradar.

  to like someone tener simpatía por.

  I like her very much. La quiero mucho.

  She doesn't like me. Ella no me quiere.

  As you like. Como Ud. quiera (guste).

  Do you like it? ¿Le gusta? ¿Le agrada?

  I like it. Me gusta.

  I don't like it. No me gusta.

likely probable; probablemente.

likeness semejanza.

likewise igualmente, asimismo.

liking afición; simpatía; gusto.

limb miembro.

lime cal.

limit límite.

limit (to) limitar.

limp (to) cojear.

line línea.

line (to) rayar, trazar líneas.

  to line up alinear, alinearse.

linen tela de hilo (goods, material); ropa blanca (bed linen, table linen, etc.).

lining forro.

link eslabón; enlace.

link (to) unir, enlazar, eslabonar, encadenar.

lip labio.

lipstick lápiz para los labios.

liquid líquido.

liquor licor.

lisp (to) cecear, balbucear.

list lista.

list (to) anotar, registrar, poner en lista.

listen escuchar.

literal literal, al pie de la letra.

literally literalmente.

literary literario.

literature literatura.

little pequeño.

  a little un poco, un poquito.

  very little muy poco.

  little boy chico, chiquillo.

  little girl chica, chiquilla.

  a little child un muchachito.

  a little dog un perrito.

  little by little poco a poco.

live adj. vivo.

live (to) vivir.

liver hígado.

living adj. viviente.

living n. vida; mantenimiento.

  to make a living ganarse la vida.

living room sala.

load carga.

load (to) cargar.

loaf pan, panecillo, hogaza (bread).

loan préstamo.

lobby vestíbulo.

lobster langosta.

local local.

locate situar.

located situado.

location sitio, localidad (place, locality); ubicación, situación, posición (site).

lock cerradura.

lock (to) cerrar con llave.

locomotive locomotora.

locust langosta.

log leño, tronco (wood).

  log book cuaderno de bitácora, diario de navegación.

logic lógica.

logical lógico.

lonely solitario, solo.

long adj. largo; de largo.

  It's five inches long. Tiene cinco pulgadas de largo.

  A long time ago. Hace mucho tiempo. Mucho tiempo atrás.

  long distance a large distancia (phone call).

long adj. a gran distancia; mucho, mucho tiempo.

  long ago mucho tiempo ha.

  all day long todo el santo día.

  not long ago no hace mucho.

  How long ago? ¿Cuánto tiempo hace?

  How long? ¿Cuánto tiempo?

  as long as mientras.

longer adj. más largo.

longer adv. más tiempo.

  How much longer? ¿Cuánto tiempo más?

  no longer ya no.

  to long for anhelar.

longing anhelo.

look cara, aspecto (appearance); mirada, ojeada (glance).

look (to) ver, mirar.

  Look! ¡Mire!

  Look in the mirror! ¡Mírate al espejo!

  to look for buscar; esperar.

  to look after cuidar.

  to look alike parecerse.

  to look forward to esperar.

  to look into examinar, estudiar.

  to look like snow parece que va a nevar.

  to look out tener cuidado (be careful).

  Look out! ¡Cuidado!

  to look over repasar, revisar.

loose suelto.

loosen (tc) desatar, soltar.

Lord Señor.

lose (to) perder.

loss pérdida.

at a loss   perdiendo, con pérdida; perplejo (puzzled).
to be at a loss   estar sin saber que hacer.
lot (a)   mucho.
a lot of money   mucho dinero.
loud   ruidoso, fuerte.
a loud laugh   risotada.
love   amor, cariño.
to be in love   estar enamorado.
love (to)   amar, querer.
lovely   encantador, precioso, bonito, hermoso.
low   bajo.
lower   más bajo, inferior.
lower case   letras minúsculas.
lower (to)   bajar; rebajar (price); arriar, abatir (a flag, etc.).
loyal   leal.
loyalty   fidelidad.
luck   suerte, fortuna.
good luck   buena suerte.
to have luck   tener suerte.
luckily   por fortuna, afortunadamente.
lucky   afortunado.
to be lucky   tener suerte.
luggage   equipaje.
lukewarm   tibio, templado.
lumber   madera.
luminous   luminoso.
lunch   merienda, almuerzo.
lunch (to)   almorzar, merendar.
to have lunch   almorzar, merendar.
lung   pulmón.
de luxe   de lujo.
luxury   lujo.
luxurious   lujoso.

M

machine   máquina.
machinery   maquinaria.
mad   loco.
to go mad   volverse loco.
made   hecho, fabricado.
madness   locura.
magazine   revista.
magic adj.   mágico.
magic n.   magia.
magistrate   magistrado.
magnanimous   magnánimo.
magnet   imán.
magnetic   magnético.
magnificent   magnífico.
magnify   aumentar.
magnifying glass   lente (cristal) de aumento, lupa.
mail   correo.
mailbox   buzón.
mailman   cartero.
main   principal, esencial.
the main floor   el principal.
the main issue   la cuestión principal.
main office   casa matriz.
the main point   el punto esencial.
mainly   principalmente, sobre todo.
maintain   mantener, sostener, conservar.
maintenance   mantenimiento; conservación, entretenimiento, reparación (property, equipment).
majestic   majestuoso.
majesty   majestad.
major adj.   mayor, más importante.
major n.   mayor, comandante.
majority   mayoría.
make (to)   hacer; fabricar, producir.

to make sad   poner triste, entristecer.
to make happy   poner alegre, alegrar.
to make a good salary   ganar un buen sueldo.
to make a living   ganarse la vida.
to make possible   hacer posible.
to make ready   preparar.
to make room   hacer lugar.
to make known   dar a conocer.
to make a hit   dar golpe, producir sensación.
to make a mistake   equivocarse.
to make a stop   detenerse.
to make friends   granjearse amigos.
to make fun of   burlarse de.
to make haste   apurarse.
to make headway   progresar, adelantar.
to make into   convertir.
to make for a place   dirigirse a un lugar, encaminarse hacia.
to make no difference   ser indiferente, no importar.
to make out   comprender, descifrar, sacar en limpio; salir bien o mal.
to make sick   causar repugnancia, fastidiar (to annoy).
to make the best of   sacar el mayor provecho de, sacar el mejor partido de.
to make tired   cansar.
to make one's mind up   decidirse, determinarse.
maker   fabricante.
malady   enfermedad.
malice   malicia.
malicious   malicioso.
man   hombre.
young man   joven.
Men (as a sign).   Señores.
manage (to)   administrar; gestionar; arreglárselas.
management   administración, dirección.
manager   administrador, director, gerente.
manifest (to)   manifestar.
mankind   humanidad.
manly   viril, varonil.
manner   manera, modo.
manners   crianza, modales.
mansion   mansión.
manual   manual.
manufacture (to)   manufacturar, fabricar.
manufacturer   fabricante.
manuscript   manuscrito.
many   muchos.
many times   muchas veces.
as many   otros tantos.
as many as   tantos como.
How many?   ¿Cuántos?
map   mapa.
maple   arce, meple.
marble   mármol; canica, bolita (for children).
March   marzo.
march   marcha.
march (to)   marchar.
margin   margen.
marine adj.   marino.
mark   marca, seña, señal.
mark (to)   señalar, marcar.
market   mercado.
marriage   matrimonio.
married   casado.
to get married   casarse.
marrow   meollo, tuétano.
marry   casar; casarse.
marvel n.   maravilla, prodigio.
marvel at (to)   admirarse.
marvelous   maravilloso.

marvelously   maravillosamente.
mask   máscara.
mason   albañil.
mass   masa; misa (religious).
massage   masaje.
massage (to)   dar masaje.
massive   macizo, sólido.
mast   mástil.
master   amo, dueño.
masterpiece   obra maestra.
mat   estera (straw).
match   fósforo, cerilla (to light with); partida, partido (sport); compañero, pareja (a pair); noviazgo, casamiento (marriage).
match (to)   hacer juego (a vase, a picture, etc.); casar (colors).
material   material.
maternal   materno.
mathematical   matemático.
mathematics   matemáticas.
matinee   matiné, función de tarde.
matter   materia; cosa (thing); asunto, cuestión (question).
an important matter   un asunto importante.
What's the matter?   ¿Qué pasa? ¿Qué ocurre?
Nothing's the matter.   No es nada.
matter (to)   importar.
It doesn't matter.   No importa.
mattress   colchón.
mature adj.   maduro.
mature (to)   madurar.
to become mature   madurar; alcanzar la edad madura.
maturity   madurez.
maximum   máximo.
at the maximum   a lo sumo.
May   mayo.
may   poder, ser posible.
It may be.   Puede ser.
It may be true.   Podrá ser verdad.
May I?   ¿Me permite Ud.? Si Ud. me permite. Con su permiso.
May I come in?   ¿Puedo entrar?
maybe   acaso, quizás, tal vez.
mayonnaise   mayonesa.
mayor   alcalde.
maze   laberinto.
to be in a maze   estar perplejo.
meadow   prado.
meal   comida.
mean adj.   bajo, vil, despreciable.
mean (to)   significar, querer decir, dar a entender.
What do you mean?   ¿Qué quiere Ud. decir?
meaning   designio, intención (intent); sentido, significado (of a word, etc.).
means   medio; medios, recursos.
by all means   sin falta.
by no means   de ningún modo.
by some means   de alguna manera.
by this means   por este medio.
meantime   entretanto.
in the meantime   mientras tanto.
meanwhile   mientras tanto, entretanto.
in the meanwhile   mientras tanto.
meanwhile n.   ínterin.
measure   medida.
in a great measure   en gran manera.
in some measure   en cierto modo, hasta cierto punto.
measure (to)   medir.
to measure up   ponerse a la altura de, ser igual.
measurement   medición; medida.

meat carne.
mechanic mecánico.
mechanical mecánico.
mechanically mecánicamente.
mechanism mecanismo.
medal medalla.
meddle (to) intervenir, entremeterse.
mediate mediar.
medical médico.
   medical school escuela de medicina.
medicine medicina.
medieval medieval.
meditate meditar.
meditation meditación.
Mediterranean Mediterráneo.
medium adj. mediano.
medium-sized de tamaño mediano.
meet (to) encontrar, encontrarse (to come across); conocer (to know); pagar, honrar (a bill, etc.); hacer frente a (expenses, etc.); reunirse (to get together, assemble).
   to go to meet salir al encuentro, ir a recibir.
   Glad to meet you. Me alegro de conocerle.
   I hope to meet you again. Espero tener el gusto de verle otra vez.
   Till we meet again. Hasta más ver.
meeting n. mitin, reunión.
melancholy adj. melancólico.
melody melodía.
melon melón.
melt (to) derretir, disolver; fundir (metals).
member miembro.
memorable memorable.
memorandum memorandum.
memory memoria.
mend remendar, componer; enmendarse, corregirse (mend one's ways, etc.).
mental mental.
mention mención.
mention (to) mencionar.
menu menu, lista de platos.
merchandise mercancía.
merchant comerciante, negociante.
merciful misericordioso, compasivo.
merciless desapiadado, sin piedad.
mercury mercurio.
mercy misericordia.
mere mero, puro.
   by mere chance de pura casualidad.
merely meramente, simplemente, puramente.
merit mérito.
merit (to) merecer.
merry alegre.
message mensaje, recado.
messenger mensajero.
metal adj. metálico.
metal n. metal.
meter metro (measurement); medidor, contador (for gas, electricity, etc.).
method método.
methodic(al) metódico.
methodically metódicamente.
metric métrico.
   metric system sistema métrico.
metropolis metrópoli.
metropolitan metropolitano.
Mexican mejicano.
Mexico Méjico.
midday mediodía.
middle adj. medio.
   Middle Ages Edad media.
   middle-aged entrado en años.
   middle-class clase media.

middle medio, centro.
   in the middle en el centro.
   about the middle of March a mediados de marzo.
midnight media noche.
might poder, fuerza.
mighty fuerte, potente.
mild suave (tobacco, etc.); moderado (moderate); leve, ligero (light); apacible, manso (character).
mile milla.
military militar.
milk leche.
milkman lechero.
mill molino; fábrica (factory).
miller molinero.
million millón.
millionaire millonario.
mind mente.
   to have in mind pensar en, tener presente.
   to have on one's mind tener en la mente, preocuparse por.
mine mío, el mío, lo mío.
   a friend of mine un amigo mío.
   your friends and mine sus amigos y los míos.
mine n. mina.
miner minero.
mineral mineral.
miniature miniatura.
minimum mínimo.
   at the minimum lo menos, el mínimum.
minister ministro.
minor adj. menor; secundario.
minor n. menor (age).
minority minoría.
mint menta (plant); casa de la moneda (money).
minus menos.
minute minuto (time).
   minute hand minutero.
   Just a minute, please. Un minuto, por favor.
   any minute de un momento a otro.
   Wait a minute! ¡Aguarde un momento!
miracle milagro.
miraculous milagroso.
mirror espejo.
mirth júbilo, alegría.
misbehave portarse mal.
misbehavior mal comportamiento.
mischief travesura.
mischievous travieso.
miser avaro.
miserable miserable.
misery miseria.
misfortune desgracia.
Miss señorita (title).
miss (to) echar de menos (someone or something); perder (train, etc.); errar (mark, etc.).
   to miss the point desbarrar, no comprender el verdadero sentido.
mission misión.
missionary misionero.
mistake equivocación.
mistake (to) equivocar.
   to be mistaken equivocarse, estar equivocado.
mistrust desconfianza.
mistrust (to) desconfiar de.
misunderstand entender mal una cosa, tomar algo en sentido erróneo.
misunderstanding malentendido, concepto falso, error.
mix (to) mezclar.
mixture mezcla.
moan gemido.

moan (to) gemir.
mobilization movilización.
mobilize movilizar.
mock (to) burlar.
mockery burla.
mode modo.
model modelo.
moderate adj. moderado.
moderate (to) moderar.
moderately moderadamente; módicamente.
moderation moderación.
modern moderno.
modest modesto.
modesty modestia.
modify modificar.
moist húmedo, mojado.
moisten humedecer.
moisture humedad.
moment momento.
   Just a moment! ¡Un momento!
momentary momentáneo.
momentous trascendental, importante.
monarch monarca.
monarchy monarquía.
Monday lunes.
money dinero.
monk fraile, monje.
monkey mono.
monologue monólogo.
monopoly monopolio.
monosyllable monosílabo.
monotonous monótono.
monotony monotonía.
monster monstruo.
monstrous monstruoso, grotesco.
month mes.
monthly mensual.
monument monumento.
monumental monumental.
moon luna.
moonlight luz de la luna.
moral adj. ético, moral.
morale moral, estado de ánimo.
morals conducta, moralidad, ética.
morbid morboso.
more más.
   more or less más o menos.
   once more una vez más.
   no more no más.
   the more . . . the better cuanto más . . . tanto mejor.
moreover además.
morning mañana.
   Good morning! ¡Buenos días!
morsel bocado.
mortal mortal.
mortgage n. hipoteca.
mosquito mosquito.
moss musgo.
most lo más, los más, el mayor número, la mayor parte.
   at most a los más, a lo sumo.
   for the most part generalmente, en su mayor parte.
   most of us casi todos nosotros, la mayor parte de nosotros.
moth polilla.
mother madre.
mother-in-law suegra.
motion movimiento; moción.
motive motivo.
motor n. motor.
mount n. monte (hill); montaje, afuste (artillery);

soporte, trípode (for instruments).
mount (to) montar.
mountain montaña.
mountainous montañoso.
mourn lamentar.
mournful triste, fúnebre.
mourning lamento.
    in mourning de luto.
mouse ratón.
mouth boca.
mouthful bocado.
movable móvil, movible.
move (to) mover, moverse (to set in motion),
    mudar de casa, mudarse (to another
    house), mudar, trasladar; poner en otro
    sitio (to change place, position).
movement movimiento.
movie cine, cinema.
moving adj. conmovedor (emotionally).
Mr. don, señor (abbre. Dn., Sr.).
Mrs. doña, señora, señora de.
much mucho.
    as much tanto.
    as much as tanto . . . como.
    How much? ¿Cuánto?
    too much demasiado.
    much the same casi lo mismo, más o menos
        lo mismo.
    this much more esto más, tanto así más.
    much money mucho dinero.
mud barro, fango, lodo.
muddy turbio.
mule mula.
multiple múltiple.
multiplication multiplicación.
multiply multiplicar, multiplicarse.
murder asesinato, homicidio.
murder (to) asesinar.
murderer asesino.
murmur n. murmuración.
muscle músculo.
museum museo.
music música.
musical musical.
musician músico.
must tener que, haber que, deber.
    I must go. Tengo que irme.
    It must be. Debe ser.
    It must be late. Debe de ser tarde.
    I must confess. Debo confesar. Debo reco-
        nocer.
mustache bigotes, mostacho.
mustard mostaza.
mutton carnero.
mutual mutuo, recíproco.
my mi, mis.
myself yo mismo; me, a mí, mí mismo.
mysterious misterioso.
mystery misterio.

N

nail uña (finger nail); clavo (metal).
nail (to) clavar.
naïve cándido, ingenuo.
naked desnudo.
name nombre.
    Christian name nombre de pila.
    surname apellido.
name (to) nombrar, designar.
namely es decir, a saber.
nap n. siesta.
napkin servilleta.

narration narración.
narrative relato.
narrow estrecho, angosto.
nation nación.
national nacional.
nationality nacionalidad.
nationalization nacionalización.
nationalize nacionalizar.
native adj. nativo, oriundo.
    native country país natal.
natural natural.
naturalist naturalista.
naturally naturalmente.
naturalness naturalidad.
nature naturaleza; carácter, índole.
    good nature buen humor.
    good-natured man bonachón.
naughty malo, granujillo, pílluelo.
naval naval.
navigable navegable.
navigator navegante.
navy armada, marina de guerra.
near cerca de; cerca.
nearby cerca, a la mano.
nearer más cerca.
nearest lo (el, la) más cerca.
nearly casi, cerca de.
nearsighted miope.
nearsighted person miope.
neat esmerado, pulcro (tidy); bonito, lindo (nice).
neatness esmero, pulcritud.
necessarily necesariamente, forzosamente, por
    necesidad.
necessary necesario.
    to be necessary hacer falta, ser necesario.
necessitate necesitar.
necessity necesidad.
    of necessity por necesidad.
neck cuello, garganta, pescuezo.
    neck and neck parejos (in a race).
necklace collar, gargantilla.
necktie corbata.
need necesidad.
need (to) hacer falta, necesitar.
    to be in need of tener necesidad de.
    to be in need estar necesitado.
needle aguja.
negative adj. negativo.
    a negative answer una respuesta negativa.
negative n. negativa; negativo (photography).
neglect descuido, negligencia.
neglect (to) descuidar.
neighbor vecino.
neither conj. ni; adj. ningun, ninguno de los dos;
    pron. ninguno.
    neither . . . nor ni . . . ni.
    neither this one nor that one ni uno ni otro,
        ni éste ni aquél.
    neither one ni el uno ni el otro.
nephew sobrino.
nerve nervio.
nervous nervioso.
nest nido.
net n. red.
neuter neutro.
neutral neutral.
never jamás, nunca.
nevertheless no obstante, sin embargo, con todo.
new nuevo.
    new moon luna nueva.
    New Year año nuevo.
news noticia, noticias.
newsboy vendedor de periódicos.

newspaper diario, periódico.
newsstand puesto de periódicos.
next siguiente, próximo.
    the next day al día siguiente, al otro día.
    (the) next week la semana entrante.
    (the) next time la próxima vez, otra vez.
    next to al lado de, junto a.
    to be next seguir en turno.
    Who's next? ¿Quién sigue?
nice bonito, lindo; gentil, amable; simpático.
nickname apodo, mote.
niece sobrina.
night noche.
    by night de noche.
    good night buenas noches.
    last night anoche.
nightmare pesadilla.
nighttime noche.
nine nueve.
nineteen diez y nueve (diecinueve).
ninety noventa.
ninth noveno.
no no; ningún, ninguno, ninguna.
    no other ningún otro.
    no one nadie.
    no longer ya no.
    no more no más.
    no matter no importa.
    no matter how much por mucho que.
    by no means de ningún modo.
    No admittance. No se permite la entrada.
    No smoking. No se permite fumar.
nobility nobleza.
noble noble.
nobody nadie, ninguno.
    nobody else nadie más, ningún otro.
nod (to) mover, inclinar la cabeza en sentido
    afirmativo; cabecear (become sleepy).
noise ruido.
    to make noise hacer ruido.
noisy ruidoso, bullicioso.
none nadie, ninguno; nada.
    none of us ninguno de nosotros.
nonsense tontería, disparate.
noon mediodía.
nor ni.
    neither . . . nor . . . ni . . . ni . . .
normal normal.
north norte.
    North America. América del Norte.
northern del norte.
nose nariz.
nostril fosa nasal, ventana de la nariz.
not no; ni, ni siquiera.
    if not si no.
    not any ningún, ninguno.
    not one ni uno solo.
    not a word ni una palabra.
    not at all de ninguna manera.
    not even ni siquiera, ni aun.
notable notable.
note nota.
    bank note billete de banco.
note (to) notar.
notebook libreta, libro de apuntes.
nothing nada, ninguna cosa.
    nothing doing nada de eso.
    It's nothing. No es nada.
    nothing much poca cosa.
    for nothing de balde, gratis.
    That's nothing to me. Eso no me importa.
notice aviso.
    Notice to the public. Aviso al público.

notice (to) advertir, notar.
notwithstanding no obstante, a pesar de, aun cuando, aunque, si bien, sin embargo.
noun nombre, substantivo.
nourish alimentar.
nourishment alimento; nutrición.
novel novela.
novelist novelista.
novelty novedad.
November noviembre.
now ahora; ahora bien, ya.
    until now hasta ahora, hasta aquí.
    now and then de vez en cuando.
    Is it ready now? ¿Ya está hecho?
nowadays hoy día.
nowhere en ninguna parte.
number número.
number (to) numerar.
numerous numeroso.
nun monja.
nurse n. enfermera.
nursery cuarto de los niños (room).
nut nuez (for eating); tuerca (for a screw).

O

oak roble.
oar remo.
oat avena.
oath juramento.
obedience obediencia.
obedient obediente.
obey obedecer.
object objeto; complemento (grammar).
object (to) oponer.
objection objeción, reparo.
objective objetivo; acusativo (grammar).
obligation obligación.
oblique oblicuo.
obscure obscuro.
obscure (to) obscurecer.
observation observación.
observatory observatorio.
observe observar; notar.
observer observador.
observing observador, atento.
obstacle obstáculo.
obstinacy porfía, obstinación.
obstinate terco, porfiado.
obstruct obstruir.
obstruction obstrucción.
obtain obtener.
obvious obvio, evidente.
occasion ocasión, oportunidad.
occasional ocasional, accidental, casual (casual); poco frecuente (not frequent).
occasionally a veces, de vez en cuando.
occidental occidental.
occupation ocupación, empleo.
occupy ocupar; emplear (the time).
occur ocurrir, suceder.
occurrence suceso, acaecimiento.
ocean océano.
o'clock
    at nine o'clock a las nueve.
    It's ten o'clock. Son las diez.
October octubre.
oculist oculista.
odd impar (number); raro (strange); suelto, que no hace juego (an odd shoe, etc.).
of de, del.
    to taste of saber a.
    to think of pensar en.

of course naturalmente, por supuesto.
of himself por sí mismo.
    It's ten of one. Faltan diez para la una.
    That's very kind of you. Ud. es muy amable.
off lejos, a distancia, fuera; cerca; quitado, sin; suspendido.
    off and on de vez en cuando.
    The meeting is off. Se ha suspendido la reunión.
    The cover is off. Está destapado.
    off the coast cerca de la costa.
    ten miles off a diez millas de aquí.
    off the track despistado.
    a day off un día libre, un día de asueto.
    to be well off disfrutar de una posición desahogada.
    to take off quitar de; quitarse.
    Take it off the table. Quítelo de la mesa.
    Take your hat off. Descúbrase. Quítese el sombrero.
offend ofender.
offended (be) resentirse, enfadarse.
offense ofensa, agravio; delito.
offensive adj. ofensivo; desagradable (smell, etc.).
offensive n. ofensiva.
offer oferta, ofrecimiento, propuesta.
offer (to) ofrecer.
offering n. ofrenda (gift).
office oficina, despacho (a building, a room, etc.); juesto, cargo (position).
officer oficial.
official adj. oficial.
official n. funcionario.
often muchas veces, frecuentemente, a menudo, con frecuencia.
oil aceite.
    olive oil aceite de oliva.
    oil painting pintura al óleo.
ointment ungüento.
old viejo, antiguo.
    to be twenty years old tener veinte años.
    old man viejo.
    old age vejez.
    old maid solterona.
olive oliva.
    olive oil aceite de oliva.
    olive tree olivo.
omelette tortilla de huevos.
omission omisión.
omit omitir.
omnibus omníbus.
on sobre, encima de, en; a, al; con, bajo; por.
    on the table sobre la mesa.
    on the train en el tren.
    on that occasion en aquella ocasión.
    on the left a la izquierda.
    on my arrival a mi llegada.
    on foot a pie.
    on credit al fiado.
    on time a tiempo, a la hora indicada.
    on my word bajo mi palabra.
    on my part por mi parte.
    on the (an) average por término medio.
    on the contrary por el contrario.
    on the whole en conjunto, en general, por lo general.
    on Saturday el sábado.
on adv. puesto; comenzado.
    with his hat on con el sombrero puesto.
    The show is on. Ya ha empezado la función.
    and so on y así sucesivamente, etcétera.
once una vez.
    once (and) for all una vez por todas.

    at once cuanto antes, en seguida.
    all at once de una vez, de seguida.
    once more otra vez más.
one (numeral) ur, uno.
one se, uno.
    one by one uno a uno, uno por uno.
    one and the same idéntico.
    this one éste.
    the red one el rojo.
onion cebolla.
only adj. sólo, único.
only adv. solamente, únicamente.
    not only . . . but no sólo . . . sino
opaque opaco.
open abierto.
open (to) abrir.
opening abertura.
opera ópera.
operate (to) operar; hacer funcionar (a machine, etc.).
    be operated on operarse.
operation operación.
    to have (undergo) an operation operarse.
opinion opinión.
    in my opinion a mi ver.
opponent antagonista, contendiente.
opportune oportuno.
opportunity oportunidad.
oppose oponer, resistir.
opposite opuesto.
opposition oposición.
oppress oprimir.
oppression opresión.
optic óptico.
optician óptico.
optimism optimismo.
optimistic optimista.
or o, u.
oracle oráculo.
oral oral, verbal.
orange naranja.
oratory oratoria.
orchard huerto.
orchestra orquesta.
order orden; pedido (of goods).
    in order that a fin de, para que.
order (to) ordenar (command); hacer un pedido (goods).
ordinarily ordinariamente.
ordinary ordinario, vulgar.
organ órgano.
organic orgánico.
organism organismo.
organization organización.
organize organizar.
organizer organizador.
orient oriente.
oriental oriental.
origin origen, principio.
original original.
originality originalidad.
originate (to) originarse.
ornament ornamento.
orphan huérfano.
ostentation ostentación.
other otro, otra, otros, otras.
    the other day el otro día, hace poco.
    the others los otros.
    Give me the other one. Déme el otro.
ought deber.
    I ought to Debo.
    you ought not to Ud. no debe.
ounce onza.

our(s) nuestro, nuestra, nuestros, nuestras.
out fuera, afuera.
    out of breath   sin aliento.
    out of date   anticuado.
    out of doors   fuera de casa.
    out of order   descompuesto.
    out of place   fuera de lugar.
    out of print   agotada (una edición).
    out of respect for   por respeto a.
    out of season   que no se da en una estación del año.
    out of style   fuera de moda.
    out of the way   donde no estorbe; apartado.
    out of work   sin trabajo.
outcome resultado.
outdoor(s) fuera de casa; al aire libre, a la intemperie.
outline perfil, contorno; bosquejo, croquis.
outline (to) bosquejar, esbozar, delinear.
output producción, rendimiento.
outrage n. atropello, ultraje.
outrageous atroz.
outside externo, exterior; fuera, afuera; fuera de; ajeno.
outstanding sobresaliente, notable, extraordinario.
outward externo; aparente.
    outward bound   de ida.
oven horno.
over sobre, encima; al otro lado de; más de; mientras, durante; por; en.
    over night   durante la noche.
    to stay over the weekend   pasar el fin de semana.
    to be over   haber pasado; acabarse, terminarse.
    all over   por todas partes.
    all the world over (over the whole world)   por todo el mundo.
    over again   otra vez.
    over and over   repetidas veces.
overcoat gaban, sobretodo, abrigo.
overcome (to) vencer; superar.
overflow (to) rebosar.
overseas ultramar, de ultramar.
oversight inadvertencia, descuido.
overtake alcanzar.
overwhelm abrumar.
overwhelming abrumador, irresistible.
overwork trabajo excesivo.
overwork (to) trabajar demasiado.
owe deber, adeudar.
    owing to   debido a.
owl buho, lechuza.
own propio, mismo.
    to write with one's own hand   escribir con su propio puño.
    my own self   yo mismo.
    This is your own.   Esto es lo suyo.
own (to) poseer, ser dueño de, tener.
owner amo, dueño, propietario.
ox buey.
oxen bueyes.
oyster ostra.

P

pace paso; portante.
pack (to) empacar, empaquetar, hacer el baúl (la maleta), arreglar el equipaje.
package bulto, paquete.
packing n. embalaje.
paddle remo, zagual.
paddle (to) remar.

page página.
pail balde, cubo.
pain n. dolor, dolencia.
painful doloroso.
paint pintura.
paint (to) pintar.
painter pintor.
painting pintura, retrato, cuadro.
pair n. par; pareja.
pajamas pijamas.
palace palacio.
palate paladar.
pale adj. pálido.
    to turn pale   palidecer.
paleness palidez.
palm palma (of the hand).
palm tree palmera.
pamphlet folleto.
pancake panqueque, panquec, tortilla hecha con harina y azúcar.
pane vidrio, cristal de la ventana (glass).
panel panel; painel.
panic pánico.
pant (to) jadear.
pantry despensa.
pants pantalones.
papa papá.
paper papel.
    writing paper   papel de escribir.
    newspaper   diario, periódico.
parade parada.
paradise paraíso.
paragraph párrafo, aparte.
parallel adj. paralelo.
paralysis parálisis.
paralyze paralizar.
parcel paquete.
    Send it parcel post.   Mándelo como paquete postal. Envíelo por encomienda (South Amer.).
pardon perdón.
    I beg your pardon.   Perdone Ud. ¡Dispense! ¡Perdón!
pardon (to) perdonar, dispensar.
    Pardon me.   Perdone Ud. Perdóneme. Dispénseme.
parenthesis (parentheses) paréntesis.
parents padres.
parish parroquia.
park parque.
park (to) estacionar (cars).
parking estacionamiento (cars).
parliament parlamento.
parliamentary parlamentario.
parlor sala.
parrot loro.
parsley perejil.
part parte.
    a great (large) part of   la mayor parte de.
    part of speech   parte de la oración.
    for one's part   por lo que a uno toca.
    to do one's part   cumplir uno con su obligación, hacer uno su parte, hacer lo que pueda.
partial parcial.
partially parcialmente.
participant participante, partícipe.
participle participio.
particular adj. particular.
particularly particularmente.
partly en parte, en cierto modo.
partner socio.
party partido; velada, fiesta (entertainment).
pass paso; pase (permit).

pass (to) pasar; ser aprobado (a student, a bill, etc.).
passage pasaje.
passenger pasajero, viajero.
passer-by transeúnte.
passion pasión.
passionate apasionado.
passive pasivo.
past prep. más allá de.
    past ten o'clock   las diez dadas, más de la diez.
    half-past seven   las siete y media.
past adj. pasado.
    the past year   el año pasado.
past n. pasado.
    in the past   en otros tiempos, anteriormente.
paste pasta.
pastime distracción, diversión, pasatiempo.
pastry pastelería, pasteles, pastas.
past tense pretérito.
patent patente.
paternal paternal.
path senda, sendero.
patience paciencia.
patient adj. paciente.
patient n. enfermo, paciente.
patriot patriota.
patriotic patriótico.
patriotism patriotismo.
pave pavimentar.
    to pave the way   preparar (allanar) el camino.
pavement pavimento.
pavilion pabellón.
paw pata.
pawn (to) empeñar.
pawnshop casa de préstamos (empeños), monte de piedad.
pay paga, sueldo, salario.
pay (to) pagar; prestar (attention); hacer (a visit).
    to pay attention   prestar atención.
    to pay a call   hacer una visita.
    to pay one's respects   presentar (ofrecer) sus respetos.
    to pay on account   pagar a cuenta.
    to pay cash (down)   pagar al contado.
    to pay dearly   costarle a uno caro.
payment pago, paga.
pea guisante; chícharo (Mex.); arveja (Arg., etc.).
peace paz.
peach melocotón, durazno (Amer.).
peanut cacahuate, maní.
pear pera.
pearl perla.
peasant campesino.
peculiar peculiar.
peddler buhonero, vendedor ambulante.
pedestal pedestal.
pedestrian transeúnte, caminante, peatón.
peel cáscara, corteza.
peel (to) pelar, mondar.
peg clavija, estaca.
pen pluma.
penalty pena; multa (fine).
pencil lápiz.
penetrate penetrar.
penetration penetración.
peninsula península.
pension pensión.
pensive pensativo.
people gente; pueblo.
    many people   mucha gente.
    the Spanish people   el pueblo español.
pepper pimienta.
perceive percibir.

per cent por ciento.
percentage porcentaje.
perfect *adj.* perfecto.
   Perfect! ¡Muy bien!
perfection perfección.
perform ejecutar, poner por obra, llevar algo a cabo, desempeñar un cometido.
performance ejecución, actuación, funcionamiento, rendimiento (of a machine); representación, función (theater).
perfume perfume.
perfume (to) perfumar.
perhaps quizá, tal vez, acaso.
period período; punto final (punctuation).
periodical periódico.
perish perecer.
permanent permanente.
permanently permanentemente.
permission permiso.
permit (to) permitir.
perpendicular perpendicular.
perplex (to) confundir, dejar perplejo.
perplexed perplejo.
persecute perseguir.
persecution persecución.
persist persistir, empeñarse, obstinarse.
persistent persistente.
person persona.
personal personal.
personality personalidad.
personally personalmente.
personnel personal, empleados; tripulantes (crew).
persuade persuadir, inducir.
persuasion persuasión.
persuasive persuasivo.
pertaining perteneciente, concerniente, tocante, relativo.
pessimist pesimista.
pessimistic pesimista.
petal pétalo.
petition petición.
petroleum petróleo.
petty insignificante, trivial, sin importancia (trifling).
   petty thief ladronzuelo.
   petty cash dinero para gastos menudos, gastos menores de caja.
pharmacist farmacéutico.
pharmacy farmacia.
phase fase.
phenomenon fenómeno.
philosopher filósofo.
philosophical filosófico.
philosophy filosofía.
phone *n.* teléfono.
phone (to) telefonear.
phonograph fonógrafo, gramófono.
photograph fotografía.
photograph (to) fotografiar, retratar.
   to be photographed retratarse.
physical físico.
physician médico.
physics física.
piano piano.
pick pico.
pick (to) escoger (choose).
   to pick up alzar, levantar (with the fingers), acelerar (speed); tomar incremento (business); restablecerse (to recover).
   to pick a quarrel buscar camorra.
   to have a bone to pick with habérselas con uno.

pickle encurtido, pepinillo.
picnic picnic, jira, partida de campo.
picture retrato, foto, cuadro, pintura, grabado.
   to be in the picture figurar en el asunto.
   to be out of the picture no figurar ya para nada.
picturesque pintoresco.
piece pedazo, trozo.
pier muelle.
pig puerco.
pigeon paloma.
pill píldora.
pillow almohada, almohadón, cojín.
pilot piloto.
pin *n.* alfiler.
pinch pellizcar.
pink rosado.
pipe pipa (smoking); tubo, caño, tubería, cañería (for water, etc.).
pistol pistola.
pitch pez, brea, alquitrán (tar); tono (music).
pitcher jarro, cántaro (for water, etc.); pitcher, lanzador (in baseball).
pitiful lastimoso.
pity lástima, piedad, compasión.
   It's a pity. Es lástima.
   What a pity! ¡Qué lástima!
   Out of pity. Por compasión.
   to have pity tener piedad.
pity (to) compadecer.
place lugar, sitio, parte, local.
   in the first place en primer lugar.
   in the next place luego, en segundo lugar.
   in place en su lugar.
   in place of en lugar de.
   out of place fuera de lugar (propósito).
   to take place tener lugar.
place (to) colocar, poner.
plain llano, simple, sencillo; franco.
   plain speaking hablando con franqueza.
   plain truth la pura verdad.
   plain food alimentos sencillos.
   a plain dress un vestido sencillo.
plan plan; plano (of a city, etc.).
plan (to) proyectar, hacer planes, pensar.
planet planeta.
plant planta.
plant (to) plantar, sembrar.
plantation plantación.
planter sembrador; colono, hacendado (owner of a plantation).
plaster yeso.
plastic plástico.
plate plato (food); plancha, lámina (metal in sheets); estereotipo, clisé (printing); placa (photography).
   a plate of soup un plato de sopa.
plateau meseta.
platform plataforma; andén (railroad station).
play juego (game); drama, representación, función (theater).
play (to) jugar; tocar (to play an instrument); dar, representar, poner en escena (in a theater).
   to play a part representar un papel.
   to play a game jugar una partida (un partido).
   to play a joke hacer una broma.
   to play a trick on someone hacer una mala jugada.
player jugador.
playful juguetón.
playground patio de recreo, campo de deportes.
plea ruego, súplica; alegato (law).
plead (to) rogar, suplicar; alegar, defender una

causa (law).
pleasant agradable; grato; simpático (of a person).
please (to) gustar, agradar; complacer, dar gusto.
   I'm pleased. Estoy satisfecho. Estoy contento.
   It pleases me. Me place. Me agrada.
   It doesn't please me. No me agrada.
   He was quite pleased. Quedó bastante complacido.
   please hágame el favor, por favor.
   Please tell me. Hágame el favor de decirme. Sírvase decirme.
   Pleased to meet you. Mucho gusto de conocerle.
pleasing agradable.
pleasure placer, gusto.
plenty abundancia.
plot *n.* complot, intriga (scheme); solar (of land); trama (of a novel, play, etc.).
plow arado.
plow (to) arar.
plug enchufe (electric plug).
plum ciruela.
plumber plomero.
plumbing plomería, instalación de cañerías.
plump gordo, rollizo.
plural plural.
plus más.
pocket bolsillo.
poem poema.
poetic poético.
poetry poesía.
point punto; punta (of a pin, etc.).
   point of view punto de vista.
   to the point al grano.
point (to) señalar.
   to point out indicar, señalar.
pointed puntiagudo; agudo.
poise porte; aplomo.
poison veneno.
poison (to) envenenar.
poisoning envenenamiento.
poisonous venenoso.
polar polar.
pole polo (north pole, etc.); poste, palo (of wood).
police policía.
policeman policía, agente de policía.
police station comisaría.
policy política (of government, etc.); norma, sistema, costumbre (a settled course); póliza (insurance).
   insurance policy póliza de seguro.
polish pulimento, lustre, pasta o líquido para sacar brillo.
   shoe polish betún.
polish (to) pulir, lustrar.
polished pulido.
polite cortés.
political político.
politician político.
politics política.
pond laguna, charca.
pool piscina (swimming pool).
poor pobre.
pope papa.
poppy adormidera, amapola.
popular popular.
popularity popularidad.
populate (to) poblar.
population población.
porch vestíbulo, portal, porche.
pore poro.
pork puerco, cerdo; carne de puerco (meat).
   pork chops chuletas de puerco.

port puerto (harbor).
portable portátil.
porter mozo; portero (building).
portion porción, parte.
portrait retrato.
   portrait painter retratista.
position posición.
positive positivo.
positively positivamente, ciertamente.
possess poseer.
possession posesión.
   to take possession of posesionarse de.
possessive posesivo.
possessor poseedor.
possibility posibilidad.
possible posible.
   as soon as possible cuanto antes.
possibly quizá, quizás, posiblemente.
post *n.* poste, pilar (pillar, etc.); correo (post
   office); puesto, guarnición (soldiers).
   post card tarjeta postal.
   post office correo, oficina (casa) de correos.
   post office box apartado de correos.
postage franqueo.
postage stamp sello (de correo), estampilla.
postal postal.
postal card tarjeta postal.
posterity posteridad.
postman cartero.
postscript posdata.
pot marmita, puchero, olla.
potato patata, papa (Amer.).
   fried potatoes patatas fritas.
   mashed potatoes puré de patatas (papas).
pound libra.
pour verter, vaciar; llover a cántaros (rain).
poverty pobreza.
powder polvo (for the face, teeth, etc.); pólvora
   (gunpowder).
   tooth powder polvo dentífrico.
   face powder polvos para la cara.
   powder box polvera.
power poder, fuerza, potencia, energía.
   electric power energía eléctrica.
   horse power caballo de fuerza.
   electromotive power fuerza motriz.
   the great powers las grandes potencias.
   power of attorney poder.
   to grant power of attorney dar poder.
   civil power autoridad civil.
powerful poderoso.
practicable practicable.
practical práctico.
practice práctica; regla, uso (usage); costumbre
   (habit); ejercicio (of a profession).
practice (to) practicar; ejercer (a profession).
praise alabanza, elogio.
praise (to) elogiar, alabar, encomiar.
prank travesura.
pray rezar, orar (to God).
prayer rezo, oración, plegaria.
precede (to) anteceder, preceder.
precedent precedente.
preceding precedente, anterior.
   preceding year el año anterior.
precept precepto.
precious precioso.
precipice precipicio.
precise preciso, exacto.
precisely precisamente, exactamente.
precision precisión.
precocious precoz.
predecessor predecesor.

predicament situación difícil, dificultad, apuro.
predict predecir.
prediction predicción.
predominant predominante.
preface preámbulo, prólogo.
prefer preferir.
preferable preferente, preferible.
preferably preferiblemente, preferentemente.
preference preferencia.
preferred preferente, preferido, predilecto.
prejudice *n.* prejuicio.
preliminary preliminar.
premature prematuro.
preparation preparación.
prepare preparar.
preposition preposición.
prescribe prescribir; recetar (medicine).
prescription prescripción, receta.
presence presencia.
present presente; regalo, obsequio (gift).
   at present al presente, ahora.
   for the present por ahora.
   in the present al presente, actualmente.
   present participle participio presente, gerundio.
   present-day actual.
   the present month el actual, el corriente.
   to give a present hacer un regalo, regalar.
   to be present asistir, estar presente.
present (to) presentar, dar a conocer; dar un
   regalo, regalar (to make a gift).
presentation presentación.
presentiment presentimiento.
preservation preservación.
preserve preservar, conservar.
preside presidir.
president presidente.
press prensa (machine, daily press); imprenta
   (printing plant).
   the press la prensa.
press (to) apretar, prensar; planchar (clothes);
   apremiar, instar (to urge).
pressing urgente, apremiante.
pressure presión.
prestige prestigio.
presumable presumible.
presume presumir.
pretend pretender.
pretense pretensión, apariencia, disimulo.
   under pretense of so pretexto de.
   under false pretenses bajo falsas apariencias.
pretension pretensión.
preterite pretérito.
pretext pretexto.
pretty *adj.* bello, bonito, lindo.
pretty *adv.* algo, un poco, algún tanto; bastante.
   pretty tired algo cansado.
   pretty good bastante bueno.
   pretty near bastante cerca.
   pretty well medianamente, así así.
   pretty much casi (almost).
   pretty much the same parecido, casi lo
   mismo.
prevail (to) reinar, prevalecer, predominar.
   to prevail over vencer, triunfar.
   to prevail upon persuadir, convencer.
prevent prevenir, impedir.
prevention prevención.
previous previo.
   previous to antes de.
   previous question cuestión previa.
previously previamente, de antemano.
price precio.

pride orgullo.
   to take pride in preciarse de.
priest sacerdote, cura.
primarily principalmente; en primer lugar.
primary primario, primero, principal (first,
   principal); elemental (elementary).
   primary color color elemental.
   primary school escuela primaria.
prince príncipe.
principal principal.
principally principalmente.
principle principio.
   in principle en principio.
   as a matter of principle como cuestión de
   principios, por principio.
   on general principles por regla general, por
   sistema, por costumbre.
print (to) imprimir.
printed impreso.
   printed matter impresos.
printer impresor.
printing tipografía, imprenta; impresión.
prior *adj.* anterior. precedente, previo.
   prior to antes de.
prison cárcel, prisión.
prisoner preso; prisionero (of war).
private privado, particular, personal, confidencial, reservado, secreto.
   private affair asunto de carácter privado.
   private hearing audiencia secreta.
   private office despacho particular.
   private secretary secretario particular.
   in private en secreto, confidencialmente.
privately en secreto, reservadamente.
privilege privilegio.
prize premio.
pro pro.
probability probabilidad.
probable probable.
probably probablemente.
problem problema.
procedure procedimiento, proceder.
proceed seguir, proseguir, proceder.
process procedimiento, método (method); proceso (of growth, etc.); curso (of time); causa,
   procedimiento (law).
   in the process of en vía de, haciéndose.
   in the process of time con el tiempo, en el
   curso del tiempo.
procession cortejo; procesión.
proclaim proclamar.
proclamation proclama, proclamación.
produce producir, rendir.
product producto.
production producción.
productive productivo.
profession profesión.
professional profesional.
professor profesor.
proficient proficiente, experto.
profile perfil.
profit beneficio, ganancia.
profit (to) sacar provecho, ganar.
   to profit by sacar partido de, sacar provecho
   de, beneficiarse con.
profitable provechoso, útil, lucrativo.
program programa.
progress progreso, adelanto.
progress (to) progresar, adelantar, hacer progresos.
progressive progresivo.
prohibit prohibir.
prohibited prohibido.

prohibited by law prohibido por la ley.
prohibition prohibición.
project proyecto, plan.
project (to) proyectar.
prolong prolongar.
prominent prominente.
  to be prominent sobresalir, ser prominente.
promise promesa.
promise (to) prometer.
promote promover, ascender (in grade); fomentar (industry, etc.).
promotion promoción, ascenso (in grade); fomento (of industry).
prompt pronto.
promptly pronto, prontamente.
promptness prontitud.
pronoun pronombre.
pronounce pronunciar.
pronunciation pronunciación.
proof prueba.
propaganda propaganda.
propeller hélice (of a ship, plane, etc.).
proper propio, conveniente, adecuado (right, fit); correcto, decoroso (correct).
properly propiamente, apropiadamente; correctamente.
property propiedad.
prophecy profecía.
prophesy (to) predecir, profetizar.
proportion proporción.
  in proportion en proporción.
  out of proportion desproporcionado.
proposal propuesta, proposición.
propose proponer.
proprietor dueño, propietario.
prosaic prosaico.
prose prosa.
prosper prosperar.
prosperity prosperidad.
prosperous próspero.
protect proteger.
protection protección.
protector protector.
protest protesta.
protest (to) protestar.
Protestant protestante.
proud orgulloso.
prove establecer, probar; resultar (to turn out).
proverb refrán, proverbio.
provide proveer.
  to provide oneself with proveerse de.
  provided that con tal que, a condición de que.
providence providencia.
province provincia.
provincial provinciano.
provisions provisiones, víveres, comestibles.
prudence prudencia.
prudent prudente.
prune ciruela pasa.
psychological psicológico.
psychology psicología.
public público
publication publicación.
publicity publicidad.
publish publicar.
publisher editor.
publishing house casa editorial, casa editora.
pudding pudín, budín.
pull (to) tirar de, tirar hacia, arrastrar.
  to pull in tirar hacia uno.
  to pull out (off) arrancar.
  to pull up desarraigar.
  to pull apart despedazar, hacer pedazos.

  to pull through salir de un apuro.
pulpit púlpito.
pulse pulso.
pump bomba.
punctual puntual.
punctuate puntuar.
punctuation puntuación.
puncture n. pinchazo.
punish castigar.
punishment castigo.
pupil alumno (school); pupila (eye).
purchase compra.
purchase (to) comprar.
purchaser comprador.
pure puro.
purely puramente, meramente, simplemente.
purple púrpura, cárdeno.
purpose propósito, fin, objeto, intención.
  on purpose intencionadamente, de propósito.
  to no purpose inútilmente.
  for the purpose a propósito, al caso.
  With what purpose? ¿Con qué fin?
purse portamonedas (change purse).
pursue perseguir.
pursuit persecución.
push empujar.
put (to) poner, colocar.
  to put away poner aparte, apartar.
  to put in order arreglar, ordenar.
  to put off diferir, aplazar.
  to put up for sale poner en venta.
  to put up with tolerar, aguantar.
  to put on vestir, ponerse (clothes); ponerse gordo (weight).
  Put on your hat! ¡Cúbrase!
  to put on the spot poner en aprieto.
  to put out apagar (a light, etc.); publicar (a book, etc.).
  to put out of the way quitar, apartar, poner algo donde no estorbe.
  to put to bed acostar.
  to put to sleep hacer dormir.
  to put together juntar; armar (a machine, etc.).
  to put to a vote poner a votación.
puzzle n. enigma, rompecabezas (crossword, etc.).
puzzled (be) (estar) perplejo.

Q

quaint curioso, raro.
qualify calificar.
quality calidad; cualidad (of character).
quantity cantidad.
quart litro, cuarto de galón.
quarter cuarto (fourth).
  a quarter hour un cuarto de hora.
quarters alojamiento; cuartel (for soliders).
queen reina.
queer extraño, raro.
  a queer person un tipo raro.
quell reprimir, sofocar.
quench apagar.
question pregunta.
  to ask a question hacer una pregunta.
  to be a question of tratarse de.
  question mark signo de interrogación.
  What's the question? ¿De qué se trata?
  without any question sin duda.
  to be out of the question ser completamente ajeno al asunto, no haber ni que pensar.
questioning n. interrogatorio.

quick pronto, rápido, presto.
quickly prontamente, rápidamente, con presteza.
  Come quickly. Venga pronto.
quiet quieto, tranquilo.
quiet (to) calmar, tranquilizar.
quietly quietamente, tranquilamente.
quietness quietud, tranquilidad.
quilt edredón, cobertor, colcha.
quinine quinina.
quit dejar, parar, cesar de, desistir de.
  to quit work dejar de trabajar.
quite bastante, más bien; muy.
  quite good bastante bueno.
  quite soon bastante de prisa.
  quite difficult harto difícil.
  quite well done muy bien hecho.
  She seems quite different! ¡Parece otra!
quotation citación, cita, texto citado.
  quotation marks comillas.
quote (to) citar.

R

rabbit conejo.
race n. correra; raza (ethnic).
radiance brillo, esplendor.
radiant radiante, brillante.
radiator radiador
radio radio.
radio station radioemisora, emisora.
radish rábano.
rag trapo.
rage rabia, ira, cólera.
rage (to) rabiar, enfurecerse.
ragged andrajoso, harrapiento.
rail riel, rail (for vehicle).
railroad ferrocarril.
  by railroad por ferrocarril.
railway ferrocarril.
rain lluvia.
rain (to) llover.
rainbow arco iris.
raincoat impermeable.
rainfall cantidad de agua que cae durante un tiempo determinado.
rainy lluvioso.
raise aumento (salary).
raise (to) levantar, alzar, elevar; aumentar, subir (prices, salary); criar (animals); cultivar (a crop).
  to raise an objection objetar, poner una objeción.
  to raise a question suscitar una cuestión.
  to raise a row armar un alboroto, armar un lío.
  to raise money reunir dinero.
raisin pasa.
rake rastrillo.
rake (to) rastrillar.
ranch rancho, hacienda.
range alcance (of a gun, of the voice, etc.); radio de acción (of a plane, etc.); cadena (of mountains).
  range of mountains sierra, cordillera, cadena de montañas.
rank grado (army, etc.); hilera (line of soldiers); posición (social rank).
  rank and file la masa, la base; la tropa (military).
ransom rescate.
rapid rápido.
rapidity rapidez.

rapidly rápidamente.
rare raro.
rarely raramente.
rascal granuja, pícaro, bribón.
rash *adj.* arrebatado, temerario (reckless).
rash *n.* sarpullido.
rat rata.
rate tarifa, precio.
  at the rate of a razón de.
  rate of interest tipo de interés.
  rate of exchange tipo de cambio.
  at any rate de todos modos, sea como fuere.
rather más bien, un poco, algo.
  rather expensive algo caro.
  rather than más bien que, antes que.
ratio proporción, razón.
ration ración.
rational racional.
rationing racionamiento.
raw crudo.
  in a raw state en bruto.
  raw materials materias primas.
ray rayo.
rayon rayón.
razor navaja.
  razor blade hoja de afeitar.
  safety razor maquinilla de afeitar.
reach alcance (range).
  beyond one's reach fuera del alcance de uno.
  within one's reach al alcance de uno, dentro
    del poder de uno.
reach (to) alcanzar, llegar a, llegar hasta (arrive
  at).
  to reach the end terminar, llegar al fin,
    lograr su objeto.
  to reach out one's hand extender la mano.
react reaccionar.
reaction reacción.
reactionary reaccionario.
read (to) leer.
readable legible.
reader lector.
reading lectura.
reading room sala de lectura.
ready listo.
ready-made confeccionado, ya hecho.
ready-made clothes ropa hecha.
real real, verdadero.
  real estate bienes raíces.
reality realidad.
realization realización; comprensión, conciencia
  cierta (understanding, awareness).
realize (to) darse cuenta, hacerse cargo; llevar a
  cabo, realizar, obtener.
  to realize a danger darse cuenta del peligro.
  to realize a project llevar a cabo un proyecto.
  to realize a profit obtener un beneficio,
    lograr un provecho.
really en verdad, realmente, verdaderamente.
  Really! ¡De veras!
reap segar.
rear *adj.* de atrás, trasero, posterior.
rear *n.* parte posterior.
reason razón, juicio, causa.
  by reason of con motivo de, a causa de.
  for this reason por esto.
  without reason sin razón.
reason (to) razonar, raciocinar.
reasonable razonable; módico.
reasonably razonablemente.
reasoning razonamiento.
rebel rebelde.
rebel (to) rebelarse.

rebellion rebelión.
rebellious rebelde, refractario.
recall (to) recordar (remember).
  to recall to mind recapacitar.
receipt recibo.
  to acknowledge receipt acusar recibo.
receipts . ingresos.
receive recibir.
receiver receptor.
recent reciente.
recently recientemente.
reception recepción, acogida.
recipe receta de cocina.
recite recitar.
reckless temerario.
recklessly temerariamente.
recline reclinar.
recognition reconocimiento.
recognize reconocer.
recoil (to) recular, retroceder.
recollect recordar (to remember).
recollection recuerdo, reminiscencia.
recommend recomendar.
recommendation recomendación.
reconcile conciliar, reconciliar.
reconciliation reconciliación.
record *n.* registro; acta; disco (phonograph);
  record (sports); constancia, comprobante
  (voucher, etc.).
  on record registrado, que consta, que hay o
    queda constancia.
records datos, memorias, archivo, anales.
recover recobrar.
  to recover one's health reponerse, recobrar la
    salud.
recovery restablecimiento (of health); recupera-
  ción (of money, etc.).
recreation recreación, recreo.
recuperate restablecerse, recuperarse.
red rojo, colorado.
reduce reducir, rebajar.
reduction reducción, rebaja.
refer referir; recurrir.
  to refer to recurrir a, acudir.
reference referencia.
  reference book libro de referencia, fuente de
    referencia.
referring referente.
refine refinar.
refinement cortesía, cultura, esmero.
reflect reflejar (light); reflexionar (think).
reflection reflejo (light); reflexión (thought).
reform reforma.
reform (to) reformar; reformarse.
refrain (from) refrenarse, abstenerse de.
refresh refrescar.
  to refresh one's memory recordar, refrescar
    la memoria.
  a refreshing drink refresco.
refreshment refresco.
refrigerator refrigeradora, nevera.
refuge refugio, asilo.
refugee refugiado, asilado.
refusal negativa.
refuse rehusar.
refute refutar, rebatir.
regard consideración, respeto.
  in regard to en cuanto a, respecto a, con
    respecto a.
  in this regard en este respecto.
  with regard to con respecto a, a propósito de.
  without any regard to sin miramientos de,
    sin hacer caso de.

regard (to) estimar, considerar, mirar.
regarding relativo a, respecto de, concirniente a.
regardless of a pesar de.
regards recuerdos, memorias, afectos.
  to give (send) one's regards dar memorias,
    dar recuerdos.
regime régimen.
regiment regimiento.
region región.
register registro.
register (to) inscribir, registrar.
  registered letter carta certificada.
regret pesar, pena, remordimiento.
regret (to) sentir, deplorar, lamentar.
  I regret it. Lo siento.
  I regret that. Siento que.
regular regular.
regularity regularidad.
regularly regularmente.
regulation reglamento, regla, regulación, regla-
  mentación.
rehearsal ensayo.
rehearse ensayar (theater).
reign reinado.
reign (to) reinar.
reject rechazar, repeler, negar, desechar.
rejection rechazamiento, repudiación.
rejoice alegrar, regocijarse.
rejoicing regocijo.
relate relatar, contar (tell).
  to be related estar emparentado (kinship);
    relacionarse (be connected with).
  everything relating to cuanto se relaciona
    con.
relation relación; pariente (a relative).
relationship relación; parentesco (family).
relative *adj.* relativo.
relative pariente (family).
release (to) soltar; dar al público (release news);
  exonerar, descargar (from a debt, penalty,
  etc.).
reliability confianza.
reliable digno de confianza.
relief alivio (from pain); socorro (aid); relevo (of
  a sentry, etc.).
relieve aliviar (from pain); socorrer, auxiliar (to
  aid); relevar (a sentry, etc.).
religion religión.
religious religioso.
relish (to) saborear; gustar de.
reluctance renuncia, mala gana, disgusto.
  with reluctance de mala gana.
reluctant reluctante, reacio.
reluctantly de mala gana.
rely on (to) confiar en, contar con.
remain quedar; quedarse, permanecer.
  to remain silent callar, guardar silencio.
  to remain undone quedar sin hacer.
remains restos, sobras.
remark observación, nota.
  to make a remark hacer una observación.
remark (to) observar, advertir, comentar, notar.
remarkable notable, interesante, extraordinario.
remarkably notablemente.
remedy remedio.
remedy (to) remediar.
remember recordar, acordarse.
  I don't remember. No me acuerdo.
  Remember me to him. Déle expresiones
    mías.
remembrance memoria, recuerdo.
remind recordar.
reminder recordatorio, recuerdo; advertencia.

remit remitir.
remorse remordimiento.
removal remoción, acción de quitar; cesantía, deposición (from a position).
remove mudar, trasladar, cambiar (to take to another place); quitar (a stain, etc.); deponer, destituir, dejar cesante (from a job).
renew renovar; extender, prorrogar (to obtain an extension).
renewal renovación; prórroga (extension).
rent renta, alquiler.
   for rent se alquila.
rent (to) alquilar, arrendar.
repair reparación, compostura, remiendo.
repair (to) reparar, componer.
repeal (to) derogar, revocar.
repeat repetir.
repeated repetido, reiterado.
repeatedly repetidamente, repetidas veces.
repetition repetición.
reply respuesta, contestación.
reply (to) contestar, responder.
report relación, informe, parte.
   to give a report dar un informe.
report (to) informar, dar parte; denunciar (to the police).
   to report on the progress of dar cuenta de la marcha de.
   it is reported se dice, corre la voz.
represent representar.
representation representación.
representative representante, agente; diputado (to Congress, etc.).
reproach censura, reproche.
reproach (to) reprochar, censurar.
reproduce reproducir.
reproduction reproducción.
reptile reptil, lagarto.
republic república.
reputation reputación.
request ruego, petición.
request (to) pedir, rogar.
rescue rescate; salvamento.
rescue (to) rescatar; salvar, librar.
resemblance semejanza, parecido.
resemble (to) parecerse a.
   She resembles her mother. Se parece a su madre.
resent resentirse de, ofenderse por.
reservation reservación.
   to make a reservation mandar a reservar.
reserve reserva.
   without reserve sin reserva; con toda franqueza.
   Speak without reserve. Hable con franqueza.
reserve (to) reservar.
reside residir, morar.
residence residencia.
resident residente.
resign resignar, renunciar; resignarse (to resign oneself).
resignation resignación; renuncia (of a position, etc.).
resist resistir; rechazar, oponerse, negarse a (to repel, to refuse).
resistance resistencia.
resolute resuelto.
resolution resolución.
resolve resolver; resolverse.
resource recurso.
respect respecto; respeto (esteem, regard).
   in this respect a este respecto.
   in some respect en cierto sentido.

in (with) respect to tocante a, con respecto a.
   with due respect con todo respeto.
   in all respects en todo sentido, en todos sus aspectos.
   in every respect en todo sentido.
respect (to) respetar.
respectable respetable.
respected considerado.
respectful respetuoso.
respective respectivo.
response respuesta.
responsibility responsabilidad.
   on your (own) responsibility bajo su responsabilidad.
responsible responsable.
rest resto (what is left over), descanso, reposo (when tired).
rest (to) reposar, descansar.
restaurant restaurant.
restful sosegado, tranquilo.
restless inquieto.
restore (to) restaurar, reponer.
result resultado, consecuencia.
result (to) resultar.
   to result in venir a parar, acabar en, conducir a, causar.
retail venta al por menor.
retail (to) vender al por menor.
return vuelta.
   in return a cambio.
   by return mail a vuelta de correo.
   return trip viaje de vuelta.
   Many happy returns! ¡Feliz cumpleaños!
return (to) volver, regresar (to go or come back); devolver (to give back).
   to return a book devolver un libro.
   to return a favor corresponder a un favor.
   to return home regresar a casa.
review revista; examen, análisis (examination); revisión (law).
review (to) revisar; pasar revista, revistar (mil.).
revise revisar.
revision revisión.
revive hacer revivir, resucitar.
revolt rebelión.
revolt (to) rebelarse.
revolution revolución.
reward recompensa.
reward (to) recompensar.
rheumatism reuma, reumatismo.
rhyme rima.
rhythm ritmo.
rib costilla (anatomy).
ribbon cinta.
rice arroz.
   Chicken and rice. Arroz con pollo.
rich rico; muy sazonado, muy fuerte (food).
riches riqueza, riquezas.
riddle acertijo, adivinanza, enigma.
ride paseo en coche (in a car); paseo a caballo (on horseback).
ride (to) cabalgar, montar a caballo (on horseback); ir en coche, pasear en automóvil (in a car).
ridiculous ridículo.
rifle fusil.
right adj. derecho; recto, justo (just); correcto (correct); adecuado (fit).
   the right man el hombre, el hombre que se necesita, el hombre adecuado.
   right hand mano derecha.
   the right time la hora exacta, la hora justa.
   at the right time a buen tiempo, a su debido

tiempo.
   right or wrong bueno o malo, con razón o sin ella.
   right side lado derecho.
   Is this right? ¿Está bien esto?
   It's right. Está bien. Es justo.
   It's not right. No es justo. No está bien.
   to be right tener razón.
right derecho.
   to be in the right tener razón.
   to the right a la derecha.
   to keep to the right seguir por la derecha.
   to have a right tener derecho.
   by rights de (por) derecho, con razón.
right adv. bien; rectamente, justamente, correctamente, perfectamente, propiamente; mismo.
   right here aquí mismo.
   right away inmediatamente, en seguida.
   right now ahora mismo, al instante.
   all right bien, está bien.
   Everything is all right. Todo va bien.
   Go right ahead. Siga todo derecho. Vaya todo seguido.
   right along sin cesar.
   right in the middle en plena actividad, en medio de.
   to know right well saber perfectamente bien.
ring anillo.
ring (to) tocar, sonar.
riot motín.
riot (to) amotinarse, armar motines.
ripe maduro.
ripen madurar.
rise n. subida; alza (prices).
   sunrise salida del sol.
rise (to) subir, ascender (to move upward); levantarse (to stand up, to get up); salir (the sun); sublevarse (to rebel); alzar (prices); aumentar (salary).
risk riesgo.
   to run the risk arriesgar, correr el riesgo.
risk (to) arriesgar.
river río.
road camino.
   main road camino principal.
roar rugido.
roar (to) rugir, bramar.
roast asado.
   roast chicken pollo asado.
roast (to) asar.
   roast beef rosbif, carne de vaca asada.
rob robar.
robber ladrón.
robbery robo.
rock roca, peña, peñasco.
rock (to) mecer.
rocking chair mecedora.
rocky rocoso, peñascoso, rocalloso.
roll rollo; panecillo (bread).
roll (to) rodar; arrollar, enrollar (to roll up).
romance romance; novela (novel).
romantic romántico.
roof techo.
room cuarto, pieza, habitación; lugar, sitio, espacio (space).
   inside room cuarto interior.
   to make room hacer lugar.
   There's not enough room. No hay suficiente sitio.
   There's not enough room in the trunk for all my clothes. No cabe toda mi ropa en el baúl.

There's no room for doubt. No cabe duda.
rooster gallo.
root raíz.
rooted arraigado.
rope cuerda, cordel.
   to be at the end of one's rope estar sin recursos.
rose rosa.
rosebush rosal.
rotary giratorio, rotativo.
   rotary press rotativa.
rouge colorete.
rough áspero, rudo, tosco.
   rough draft borrador.
   rough sea mar alborotado (agitado).
   a rough guess a ojo, a ojo de buen cubero, aproximadamente.
   rough diamond diamante en bruto.
round *adj.* redondo.
   a round table una mesa redonda.
   round number número redondo.
   round sum suma redonda.
   round trip viaje de ida y vuelta; viaje redondo (Mex.).
   all year round todo el año, el año entero.
round tanda, vuelta (of drinks, etc.).
route ruta, vía, camino, curso, itinerario.
routine rutina.
row fila, hilera (rank, file); camorra, trifulca, riña (brawl).
row (to) remar.
rub (to) frotar.
rubber goma, caucho.
   rubber band goma, elástico.
   rubbers chanclos, zapatos de goma.
rude rudo, descortés, tosco, chabacano.
rudeness descortesía, grosería.
rug alfombra, tapete.
ruin ruina.
rule regla, norma; reinado, dominio (reign).
   as a rule por lo general, por regla general.
   to be the rule ser la regla, ser de reglamento.
rule (to) gobernar, mandar (to govern); rayar (to draw lines); disponer, determinar (court); establecer una regla (to establish a rule).
   to rule out descartar, excluir, no admitir.
   to rule over mandar, dominar.
ruler gobernante; regla (for drawing lines).
rumor rumor.
run correr; andar, funcionar (a watch, a machine, etc.).
   to run across tropezar con.
   to run into chocar con, topar con.
   to run away escapar, huir.
   to run the risk of correr el riesgo de, arriesgar.
   to run over derramarse, salirse (a liquid); atropellar (a car, etc.).
   to run up and down correr de una parte a otra.
   to run wild desenfrenarse.
rural rural.
rush prisa (haste).
   in a rush de prisa.
rush (to) ir de presa, apresurarse.
   to rush in entrar precipitadamente.
   to rush through ejecutar de prisa, hacer algo de prisa.
rust moho, herrumbre.
rust (to) enmohecer, enmohecerse, aherrumbrarse.
rusty mohoso, enmohecido, herrumbroso.
rye centeno.

S

Sabbath sábado, día de descanso.
sack saco.
sacred sagrado.
sacrifice sacrificio.
sacrifice (to) sacrificar.
sad triste.
saddle silla de montar.
saddle (to) ensillar.
sadly tristemente.
sadness tristeza.
safe caja fuerte, caja de caudales.
safe *adj.* seguro; salvo, ileso (unhurt); sin peligro (safe from danger); sin riesgo (safe from risk).
   safe and sound sano y salvo.
   Safe trip. Feliz viaje.
safely a salvo.
safety seguridad.
   safety razor maquinilla de afeitar.
   safety zone zona de seguridad.
   safety bolt cerrojo de seguridad.
sail vela; buque de vela, velero (boat).
sail (to) darse a la vela, zarpar; navegar.
saint santo.
   Saint Valentine's Day día de San Valentín.
sake causa, motivo, amor, bien, consideración.
   for your sake por Ud., por su bien; por consideración a Ud.
   for the sake of por causa de. por amor de, por, para mayor.
   for the sake of brevity por brevedad, para mayor brevedad.
   for mercy's sake por misericordia.
   for God's sake por Dios, por amor de Dios.
salad ensalada.
salary sueldo, salario.
sale venta.
   for sale de (en) venta.
salesclerk vendedor, dependiente.
salesgirl vendedora, dependiente.
salesman vendedor.
saleswoman vendedora.
salmon salmón.
salt sal.
salt (to) salar.
saltcellar salero.
salted salado.
same mismo, propio, igual.
   the same lo mismo, el mismo, los mismos; otro tanto.
   all the same todo es uno.
   It's all the same to me. Lo mismo me da, me es igual.
   if it's the same to you si le es a Ud. igual.
   much the same casi lo mismo.
   the same as lo mismo que, el mismo, los mismos que.
sample muestra.
sand arena.
sandpaper papel de lija.
sandwich sandwich, emparedado.
sandy arenoso.
sane sano.
sanitarium sanatorio.
sanitary sanitario.
sanitation saneamiento.
sanity cordura, juicio sano.
sap savia; zapa (trench).
sarcasm sarcasmo.
sarcastic sarcástico.
sardine sardina.
satan satanás.

satin raso.
satire sátira.
satisfaction satisfacción.
satisfactorily satisfactoriamente.
satisfactory satisfactorio.
satisfied satisfecho.
satisfy satisfacer.
Saturday sábado.
sauce salsa.
saucer platillo.
sausage salchicha, chorizo.
savage salvaje; silvestre (growing wild).
save *prep.* salvo, excepto; *conj.* sino, a menos que, a no ser que.
save (to) salvar, librar (a person); economizar, ahorrar (money).
   to save appearances salvar las apariencias.
savings ahorros, economías.
savings bank caja de ahorros.
saw sierra; serrucho (handsaw).
say decir.
   that is to say es decir, esto es.
   it is said se dice.
saying dicho, proverbio, adagio, refrán.
   as the saying goes según el adagio, como dice el refrán.
scale *n.* escala; platillo (the dish of a balance); balanza, báscula (for weights); escama (of fishes, etc.).
scales peso, báscula.
scalp cuero cabelludo.
scandal escándalo.
scanty escaso, escatimado.
scar *n.* cicatriz.
scarce raro, escaso.
scarcely apenas, escasamente, con dificultad.
scarcity escasez.
scarf bufanda, chalina.
scarlet escarlata.
scene escena.
scenery vista, paisaje; decoración (theater).
scent aroma, olor.
schedule *n.* programa, cuadro, lista; horario de trenes (train schedule).
scheme plan, proyecto, designio; ardid, treta.
school escuela.
   schoolteacher maestro de escuela.
   schoolbook texto de escuela.
   schoolmate condiscípulo.
   schoolroom aula.
science ciencia.
scientific científico.
scientist hombre de ciencia.
scissors tijeras.
scold reñir, regañar.
scorn desdén, desprecio.
scorn (to) despreciar.
scornful despreciativo, desdeñoso.
score tantos (in games), partitura (music).
score (to) marcar los tantos, llevar la cuenta (to keep a record in a game, etc.); apuntarse uno un tanto, ganar un tanto (to gain points, etc.).
   to score a point ganar un tanto.
scrape (to) raspar (on a surface).
scratch rasguño, arañazo (on the hand, etc.); raspadura, raya (on a table, etc.).
scratch (to) rascar (from itching), rasguñar, arañar (to cause injury with the claws or nails); rayar (a glass, a table, etc.).
scream (to) chillar, gritar.
screen *n.* biombo, mampara (a portable partition); tela metálica, rejilla (for windows,

etc.); pantalla, cine (movies); cortina (of smoke); barrera (of fire).

screw tornillo; rosca (screw thread).

screw (to) atornillar.

scruple escrúpulo.

sculptor escultor.

sculpture escultura.

sea mar, océano.

seal sello; foca (animal).

seal (to) sellar; lacrar (with wax).

seam costura.

search busca, búsqueda (act of looking for); pesquisa, investigación (scrutiny, investigation); registro (for concealed weapons, etc.).
   in search of en busca de.

search (to) buscar (to search for); registrar (a house, etc.); explorar (to explore); indagar, inquirir, investigar (to inquire, to investigate).
   to search after indagar, preguntar por.
   to search for buscar, procurar.

seasick mareado.

season estación (of the year).
   in season en sazón.
   out of season fuera de sazón.
   to be in season ser de la estación, ser del tiempo.

season (to) sazonar, condimentar (food).

seat n. asiento.
   to take a seat tomar asiento, sentarse.
   front seat asiento delantero.
   back seat asiento trasero.

second segundo.
   second class de segunda clase.
   second year el segundo año.
   Wait a second! ¡Espere un instante!
   on second thought después de pensarlo bien.
   second to none sin segundo, sin par.

secondary secundario.

secondhand de segunda mano, usado.

secondly en segundo lugar.

secrecy secreto, reserva.

secret secreto.
   in secret en secreto.

secretary secretario.
   private secretary secretario particular.

section sección.

secure seguro, firme.

secure (to) asegurar; conseguir (obtain).

securely seguramente, firmemente.

see (to) ver.
   See? ¿Sabe? ¿Comprende?
   Let's see. A ver. Vamos a ver. Veamos.
   to see about averiguar.
   to see someone off ir a despedir a alguien.
   to see someone home acompañar a alguien a casa.
   to see the point caer en la cuenta, comprender el sentido de lo dicho.
   to see a thing through llevar uno hasta el cabo una cosa.
   to see fit creer conveniente.
   to see one's way clear ver el modo de hacer algo.
   to see to atender a, cuidarse de.

seed semilla, simiente.

seeing vista, ver.
   seeing that visto que, puesto que.

seek (to) buscar.
   to seek after tratar de obtener, buscar.

seem (to) parecer, figurarse.
   it seems to me me parece.

it seems parece, a lo que parece.

seize agarrar (to grasp); coger, prender (to apprehend); a poderarse de (to take possession of); darse cuenta de, comprender (to comprehend).

seldom rara vez, raramente.

select adj. selecto, escogido.

select (to) elegir, escoger.

selection selección.

self mismo, por sí mismo; sí, se.
   myself yo mismo, me.
   yourself tu mismo, te.
   himself el mismo, se.
   itself ello mismo, se.
   ourselves nosotros mismos, nos.
   yourselves vosotros mismos, os.
   themselves ellos mismos, se.
   oneself uno mismo, se.
   you yourself tú mismo.
   Wash yourself. Lávate.
   by himself por sí mismo.
   I shave myself. Yo mismo me afeito.

self-conceited presumido, presuntuoso.

self-confidence confianza en sí mismo.

self-defense defensa propia.

self-determination autonomía, independencia.

self-evident patènte.

selfish egoísta.

selfishness egoísmo.

self-sufficient que se basta a sí mismo.

sell (to) vender.

senate senado.

senator senador.

send (to) enviar, despachar, mandar, expedir.
   to send away despedir, echar a la calle.
   to send word mandar recado, avisar, enviar a decir.
   to send back devolver, enviar de vuelta.
   to send in hacer entrar.
   to send for enviar por, mandar a buscar.

sending despacho.

senior mayor, de mayor edad, más antiguo.
   Suarez, Sr. Suarez padre.

sense n. sentido.
   common sense sentido común.
   to be out of one's senses haber perdido el juicio.

sensible sensato, razonable.

sensibly cuerdamente, sensatamente.

sentence oración (grammar); sentencia (court).

sentence (to) sentenciar, condenar.

sentiment sentimiento.

sentimental sentimental.

separate adj. separado, aparte.
   under separate cover por separado.

separate (to) apartar, separar.

separately separadamente.

separation separación.

September septiembre.

serene sereno.

sergeant sargento.

serial adj. de serie, de orden (a number, etc.); por partes, por entregas (publications); en episodios, en serie (a picture).

series serie.
   in series en serie.

serious serio; grave (grave).

seriously seriamente.

seriousness seriedad, gravedad.

sermon sermón.

servant criado, sirviente; criada, sirvienta (maid).

serve (to) servir.
   to serve the purpose venir al caso.

to serve notice notificar, hacer saber, dar aviso.
   It serves you right. Bien se lo merece.
   to serve as servir de.

service servicio.
   at your service servidor, a sus órdenes.
   to be of service ser útil, servir.

session sesión.

set adj. fijo, establecido.
   set price precio fijo.

set n. juego.
   tea set juego de té.
   set of dishes vajilla.

set (to) poner.
   to set aside dar de mano, poner a un lado, apartar; ahorrar (money).
   to set back atrasar.
   to set free poner en libertad.
   to set in order arreglar, poner en orden.
   to set on fire pegar fuego a.
   to set to work poner manos a la obra, poner (se) a trabajar.

settle arreglar, ajustar, saldar (an account, a matter, etc.); instalarse, fijar su residencia, establecerse (to be established); posarse, asentarse (liquids).
   to settle an account saldar una cuenta.

settlement acuerdo, arreglo (adjustment of an account, etc.); colonia, caserío (a small village); colonización (colonization).

seven siete.

seventeen diecisiete.

seventh séptimo.

seventy setenta.

several varios.
   several times varias veces.

severe severo.

severity severidad.

sew coser.

sewing costura.

sewing machine máquina de coser.

sex sexo.

shade sombra.

shade (to) sombrear, dar sombra.

shadow sombra.

shady sombreado, umbroso.

shake sacudida, temblor; apretón de manos (handshake).

shake (to) sacudir; temblar (to tremble); estrechar, darse (shake hands); cabecear, mover (one's head).
   to shake one's head mover la cabeza.
   to shake hands darse la mano.
   to shake in one's shoes temblar de miedo.

shall, will (auxiliary) the future tense of the indicative is formed by adding -é, -ás, -á, -emos, -éis, and -án to the infinitive.
   I shall go iré.
   you will go irás.
   he will go irá.
   we shall go iremos.
   you will go iréis.
   they will go irán.

shame vergüenza.

shame (to) avergonzar.

shameful vergonzoso.

shameless desvergonzado, sin vergüenza.

shampoo champú.

shampoo (to) dar champú, lavar la cabeza.

shape forma, figura.

shape (to) formar, dar forma.

share porción, parte; acción (stock).

share (to) partir, repartir (to apportion); parti-

cipar, tomar parte en (to share in).

to share alike tener una parte igual.

shareholder accionista.

sharp agudo; puntiagudo (sharp-pointed); afilado, cortante (sharp-edged).

a sharp pain un dolor punzante (agudo).

a sharp answer una respuesta tajante (áspera).

a sharp curve una curva muy pronunciada.

sharp-witted perspicaz, de ingenio agudo.

at two o'clock sharp a las dos en punto.

sharpen afilar, aguzar; sacar punta a (a pencil).

shatter destrozar, hacer pedazos, hacer añicos; romperse, hacerse añicos.

shave afeitada.

shave (to) afeitar, rasurar (someone); afeitarse, rasurarse (oneself).

shaving afeitada.

shaving cream crema de afeitar.

shaving brush brocha de afeitar.

shawl chal, mantón.

she ella.

she-cat gata.

she-goat cabra.

shears tijeras grandes, cizallas.

shed cobertizo; cabaña, barraca (a hut).

shed (to) verter, derramar (tears, etc.).

sheep oveja(s).

sheet sábana (bed); hoja, pliego (paper).

shelf estante.

shell concha (of mollusks); cáscara (of nuts, eggs, etc.); granada (artillery).

shelter refugio, abrigo.

to take shelter refugiarse, guarecerse.

to give shelter albergar, dar albergue.

shelter (to) guarecer, albergar, refugiar, poner al abrigo, poner a cubierto.

shepherd pastor.

sheriff jefe de policía de un condado.

sherry jerez.

shield escudo, resguardo, defensa.

shield (to) defender, amparar, resguardar.

shift cambio; tanda (work).

shift (to) cambiar (gears, etc.).

shine (to) brillar; limpiar, lustrar, dar lustre (to shine shoes).

shining brillante, radiante, reluciente.

shiny lustroso, brillante.

ship buque, barco, vapor.

merchant ship buque mercante.

ship (to) embarcar; enviar, despachar (goods).

shipment embarque (act of shipping); envío, despacho (dispatch of goods); cargamento (goods shipped).

shipwreck naufragio.

shipyard astillero.

shirt camisa.

shirt store camisería.

sport shirt camisa de deporte.

shiver escalofrío, temblor.

shiver (to) tiritar.

shock choque; sacudida (shake); sobresalto, emoción (emotion).

shock (to) sacudir, dar una sacudida (to cause to shake); chocar, ofender (to offend); conmover (to move); escandalizar (to scandalize).

shoe zapato.

shoe store zapatería.

shoelaces cordones para los zapatos.

shoe polish betún, crema para los zapatos.

shoehorn calzador.

shoemaker zapatero.

shoot (to) tirar, disparar.

shooting tiro.

shop tienda.

shop (to) hacer compras, ir de tiendas.

to go shopping ir de compras.

shore costa.

short corto (not long); bajo, de escasa estatura (not tall); breve, conciso (brief); falto, escaso (of goods).

short cut atajo.

short circuit corto circuito.

short story cuento corto.

for short para abreviar, para mayor brevedad.

in short en suma, en resumen.

to be short estar escaso, andar escaso (of money, etc.).

in a short while dentro de poco.

a short time ago hace poco.

shorten (to) acortar, abreviar (to make short).

shorts calzoncillos.

shot tiro, disparo, balazo (of a gun).

should, would debe, deberá, debiera, debería.

I should go. Yo debería ir.

I would go yo iría.

if I should go si yo fuese.

The window should be left open. Debe dejarse abierta la ventana.

Things are not as they should be. No están las cosas como debieran estar.

shoulder hombro.

shoulder to shoulder hombro a hombro.

shoulder blade omoplato.

shout grito.

shout (to) gritar, vocear.

shovel pala.

show exposición (exhibition); espectáculo (spectacle); función (theater); apariencia (appearance); ostentación, boato (ostentation).

show window escaparate, vidriera (Amer.).

showcase vitrina.

show (to) mostrar, enseñar; demostrar, probar.

to show someone in hacer entrar.

to show to the door acompañar a la puerta.

to show off hacer alarde.

to show up presentarse, parecer.

shower lluvia, chaparrón, chubasco; ducha (bath).

to take a shower darse una ducha.

shrewd astuto, sagaz.

shrimp camarón.

shrink encogerse; mermar.

to shrink from amilanarse, huir de, apartarse de.

shrub arbusto.

shut adj. cerrado.

shut (to) cerrar.

to shut in encerrar.

to shut out cerrar la puerta a uno; excluir.

to shut up hacer callar, callarse (to be quiet).

shutter persiana (window); obturador (photography).

shy tímido, corto.

sick malo, enfermo.

to feel sick sentirse enfermo.

sickness enfermedad.

seasickness mareo.

side lado, costado.

side by side lado a lado, hombro a hombro, juntos.

on this side de (a, en, por) este lado.

on that side de (a, en, por) ese lado.

on the other side al otro lado, a la otra parte.

(the) wrong side out al revés, del revés.

sidewalk acera, vereda (Arg.).

sieve cedazo, tamiz, criba.

sigh suspiro.

sigh (to) suspirar.

sight vista, aspecto.

at first sight a primera vista.

to be a sight parecer un adefesio.

What a sight! ¡Qué espectáculo!

sight-seeing (to go) ver las cosas de interés, visitar los lugares notables.

sign seña, señal (mark); letrero, rótulo (over a shop); aviso (notice).

sign (to) firmar.

to sign a check firmar un cheque.

signal señal, seña.

signal (to) hacer señas.

signature firma.

significance significación, importancia.

significant significativo, expresivo.

silence silencio.

silence (to) hacer callar.

silent silencioso, callado.

silently silenciosamente.

silk seda.

silly tonto, cándido.

silver plata; monedas de plata (silver money).

silverware vajilla de plata.

similar similar, semejante.

similarity semejanza.

simple simple, sencillo.

simplicity sencillez.

simplification simplificación.

simplify simplificar.

simply sencillamente, puramente, simplemente.

sin pecado.

sin (to) pecar.

since adv. desde entonces, hace.

ever since desde entonces.

not long since hace poco.

since conj. ya que, puesto que, pues que.

since prep. desde, después.

since then desde entonces.

sincere sincero.

sincerely sinceramente.

sincerely yours su seguro servidor (s.s.s.).

sincerity sinceridad.

sing cantar.

singer cantante, cantor, cantora.

single solo, sin compañero; soltero (unmarried).

not a single word ni una sola palabra.

single room habitación individual, habitación para uno.

singly individualmente, separadamente, de uno en uno.

singular singular.

sink lavabo (for washing); fregadero (kitchen sink).

sink (to) hundir, echar a pique, hundirse.

sinner pecador.

sip sorbo.

sip (to) tomar a sorbos.

sir señor, caballero.

Dear Sir (My dear Sir): Muy señor mío:

siren sirena.

sister hermana.

sister-in-law cuñada.

sit sentar, sentarse.

to sit down sentarse.

sitting room sala.

situated situado.

situation situación.

six seis.

sixteen dieciséis.

sixteenth décimo sexto.

sixth sexto.

sixty sesenta.
size tamaño, medida.
skate patín.
  ice skate patín de hielo.
  roller skate patín de ruedas.
skate (to) patinar.
skeleton esqueleto.
sketch bosquejo, dibujo.
sketch (to) bosquejar, esbozar.
skill destreza, habilidad.
skillful diestro, experto, hábil.
skin piel.
skinny flaco, macilento.
skirt falda.
skull cráneo.
sky cielo, firmamento.
  sky blue azul celeste.
slander calumnia.
slang caló, jerga.
slap bofetada.
slap (to) dar una bofetada.
slate pizarra.
slaughter n. matanza.
slave esclavo.
slavery esclavitud.
slay matar.
sleep sueño.
sleep (to) dormir.
  to go to sleep irse a dormir, acostarse.
sleepy soñoliento.
  to be sleepy tener sueño.
sleeve manga.
slender delgado, esbelto.
slice tajada, rebanada.
slice (to) rebanar, cortar en rebanadas.
slide resbalar, deslizarse.
slight adj. ligero, leve.
slight (to) despreciar.
slightly ligeramente.
slim delgado.
sling honda.
slip resbalón.
slip (to) resbalar, resbalarse.
  to slip one's mind irse de la memoria.
  to slip away escabullirse, deslizarse.
slippers zapatillas, babuchas.
slippery resbaladizo, resbaloso.
slope pendiente, declive.
slow lento, despacio.
  to be slow atrasar; ser lento.
slow down (to) reducir la marcha.
slowly lentamente, despacio.
  Drive slowly. Conduzca despacio.
  Go slowly. Vaya despacio.
slowness lentitud, tardanza.
slumber sueño ligero.
slumber (to) dormitar.
slums barrios bajos.
sly astuto.
small pequeño.
  small change suelto.
smallness pequeñez.
smart inteligente (clever).
smash (to) romper, quebrantar.
smell olor.
smell (to) oler.
smile sonrisa.
smile (to) sonreír.
smoke humo; cigarrillo (a cigarette).
  Have a smoke. Sírvase un cigarrillo.
smoke (to) humear; fumar (tobacco).
  No smoking. Se prohíbe fumar.
smoker fumador.

smooth liso, llano, suave.
  smooth wine vino suave.
  smooth surface superficie lisa.
snail caracol.
snake serpiente, culebra.
snatch (to) arrancar, arrebatar.
sneeze estornudo.
sneeze (to) estornudar.
snore (to) roncar.
snoring ronquido.
snow nieve.
snow (to) nevar.
snowflake copo.
snowy nevado.
so adv. así, tal; de modo que.
  That is so. Así es. Eso es.
  and so forth y así sucesivamente, etcétera.
  so and so fulano de tal.
  so much (many) tanto.
  at so much a yard a tanto la yarda.
  so that para que, de suerte que, de modo que.
  so then conque.
  so, so así, así; regular.
  if so si así es.
  Is that so? ¿De veras?
  I think so. Lo creo. Así lo creo.
  I hope so. Así lo espero.
  not so good as no tan bueno como.
  ten dollars or so cosa de diez dólares.
soak empapar.
soap jabón.
  cake of soap pastilla de jabón.
sob sollozo.
sob (to) sollozar.
sober sobrio.
sociable sociable.
social social.
socialism socialismo.
society sociedad.
socket portalámpara (for an electric bulb).
  eye socket órbita.
socks calcetines.
soda soda.
  soda water gaseosa; agua de Seltz (seltzer, carbonated water).
sofa sofá.
soft blando, suave.
  soft-boiled eggs huevos pasados por agua.
soften ablandar.
softness suavidad.
soil tierra (ground).
soil (to) ensuciar.
soiled sucio.
solar solar.
sold vendido.
  sold out agotado.
soldier soldado.
sole adj. único, solo.
sole n. suela (shoe); planta (foot).
solemn solemne.
solemnity solemnidad.
solid sólido.
  solid color color entero.
solidity solidez.
solidly sólidamente.
solitary solitario.
solitude soledad.
soluble soluble.
solution solución.
solve (to) resolver (a problem, etc.).
some algo de; un poco; alguno; unos; unos cuantos.
  Some (people) think so. Hay quienes piensan así.

  at some time or other un día u otro.
  Bring me some cigars. Tráigame unos puros.
  I have some left. Me sobra algo.
  some of his books algunos de sus libros.
  some two hundred unos dos cientos.
somebody alguien, alguno.
  somebody else algún otro.
somehow de algún modo.
something alguna cosa, algo.
  something else otra cosa, alguna otra cosa.
sometime algún día, en algún tiempo.
sometimes algunas veces, a veces.
somewhat algún tanto un poco.
  somewhat busy algo ocupado.
somewhere en alguna parte.
  somewhere else en alguna otra parte.
son hijo.
  son-in-law yerno.
song canto, canción.
soon presto, pronto, prontamente, a poco.
  as soon as tan pronto como, luego que, en cuanto.
  as soon as possible lo más pronto posible.
  sooner or later (más) tarde o (más) temprano.
  the sooner the better mientras más pronto mejor.
  How soon will you finish? ¿Cuánto tiempo tardará Ud. en terminar?
soothe (to) aliviar, calmar, tranquilizar.
sore adj. dolorido, enconado; resentido (offended).
  sore throat dolor de garganta.
sore n. llaga (on the body).
sorrow pesar, tristeza.
sorry triste, afligido.
  to be sorry sentir.
  I'm very sorry. Lo siento muchísimo.
sort especie, clase, manera, suerte.
  all sorts of people toda clase de gentes.
  a sort of una especie de.
  nothing of the sort nada de eso.
  What sort of person is he? ¿Qué tal persona es?
soul alma.
sound adj. sano, robusto.
  sound judgment juicio cabal.
  safe and sound sano y salvo.
  sound sleep sueño profundo.
sound n. sonido.
soup sopa.
  soup plate sopero, plato hondo.
  vegetable soup sopa de legumbres.
sour agrio, ácido.
source fuente.
south sur, sud.
  South America América del Sur. Sudamérica.
  South American sudamericano.
  The South Pole El polo sur.
southern meridional.
sow (to) sembrar.
sowing siembra.
space espacio.
spacious espacioso, amplio, vasto.
spade laya, pala.
Spain España.
Spaniard español.
Spanish español.
  Spanish America Hispanoamérica.
  Spanish American Hispanoamericano.
  Spanish language Castellano.
spare adj. disponible, sobrante; de respeto, de repuesto.
  spare time horas de ocio, ratos perdidos, tiempo desocupado.

spare money   dinero de reserva, ahorros.
spare room   cuarto para huéspedes, cuarto de sobra.
spare parts   repuestos, piezas de repuesto.
spare tire   neumático de repuesto.
spare (to)   ahorrar, economizar (to save); escatimar, ser frugal (to be sparing); perdonar (to forgive); ahorrarse trabajo, molestias (to spare oneself trouble, etc.).
They spared his life.   Le perdonaron la vida.
to have (money, time, etc.) to spare   tener (dinero, tiempo, etc.) de sobra.
I was spared the trouble of   me ahorré la molestia de.
sparingly   escasamente, parcamente, frugalmente; rara vez.
spark   chispa.
spark (to)   echar chispas, chispear.
sparrow   gorrión.
speak   hablar.
to speak for   hablar en favor de, hablar en nombre de.
to speak for itself   ser evidente, hablar por sí mismo.
to speak one's mind   decir uno lo que piensa.
to speak out   decir, hablar claro.
to speak to   hablar a.
to speak up   hablar, decir.
speaker   orador; presidente de (les cortes), la cámara de diputados (congress).
spear   lanza.
spearmint   hierbabuena, menta.
special   especial, particular.
special delivery   entrega inmediata.
special delivery stamp   sello de urgencia.
specialist   especialista.
specialize   especializar, especializarse; tener por especialidad, estar especializado (to be specialized).
specially   especialmente, particularmente, sobre todo.
specialty   especialidad.
specific   específico.
specifically   específicamente.
specify   especificar.
specimen   espécimen, muestra.
spectacle   espectáculo.
spectacles   anteojos, espejuelos, gafas.
spectator   espectador.
speculation   especulación.
speech   habla, palabra; discurso, disertación (address, discourse).
to make a speech   pronunciar un discurso.
speechless   mudo, sin habla.
speed   velocidad, rapidez.
at full speed   a toda velocidad, a todo correr.
speed limit   velocidad máxima, velocidad permitida.
speed (to)   acelerar, apresurar, dar prisa (to speed up); apresurarse, darse prisa (to hasten).
spell (to)   deletrear.
spelling   deletreo; otrografía (orthography).
spelling book   cartilla.
spend   gastar.
to spend time   emplear el tiempo, pasar un tiempo.
to spend the night   pasar la noche, trasnochar.
I'll spend the winter in Florida.   Pasaré el invierno en Florida.
spice n.   especia.
spicy   que tiene especias, picante.
spider   araña.
spin   giro, vuelta (motion); barrena (aviation).

spin (to)   hilar (thread, cotton, wool, etc.); girar, dar vueltas (to turn, to revolve); tornear (on a lathe, etc.).
spinach   espinaca.
spine   espinazo, espina dorsal (backbone).
spiral   espiral.
spirit   espíritu.
spiritual   espiritual.
spit   asador, espeto, espetón (for roasting).
spit (to)   escupir.
spite n.   rencor, despecho, malevolencia.
in spite of   a pesar de, a despecho de.
spiteful   rencoroso, vengativo.
splash   salpicadura, chapoteo.
splash (to)   salpicar, chapotear.
splendid   espléndido, magnífico.
Splendid!   ¡Espléndido!
splendor   esplendor.
split adj.   hendido, partido; dividido (divided).
split (to)   hender, partir, rajar; dividir (to divide).
to split the difference   partir la diferencia.
to split up   repartir, dividir.
to split hairs   pararse en pelillos.
to split one's sides with laughter   desternillarse de risa.
spoil (to)   echar a perder, dañar, estropear (to damage); estropearse, dañarse, echarse a perder (to get spoiled); pudrirse (to rot).
to spoil a child   mimar demasiado a un niño.
spoiled   estropeado, dañado, echado a perder.
a spoiled child   un niño mimado.
spoke n.   rayo de la rueda (of a wheel); travesaño (rung, crossbar).
sponge   esponja.
sponsor   patrocinador; anunciante (radio sponsor).
sponsor (to)   patrocinar, fomentar, apadrinar; costear un programa de radio (radio).
spontaneity   espontaneidad.
spontaneous   espontáneo.
spool   carrete, carretel.
spool of thread   carrete (carretel) de hilo.
spoon   cuchara.
teaspoon   cucharilla, cucharita.
tablespoon   cuchara.
soupspoon   cucharón (ladle).
spoonful   cucharada.
sport adj.   deportivo, de deporte.
sport shirt   camisa de deporte, camisa de cuello abierto.
sports   deportes.
spot   mancha (stain); borron (of ink); sitio, lugar, paraje (place); apuro, aprieto (fix, difficulty).
on the spot   allí mismo, en el mismo lugar; al punto, inmediatamente (at once).
sprain   torcedura, distensión.
sprain (to)   torcerse, distenderse.
spray (to)   pulverizar, rociar.
sprayer   pulverizador.
spread   difusión.
spread (to)   propalar, difundir, divulgar (news, etc.); esparcir, desparramar (to scatter); tender, extender, desplegar, abrir (to stretch out, to unfold, etc.), untar (butter).
spring   primavera (season); manantial, fuente (water); salto (jump), resorte, muelle (of wire, steel, etc.).
bed spring   sommier, resorte, colchón de muelles.
spring (to)   saltar, brincar.
to spring at   lanzarse sobre, saltar.
sprinkle   rociar (liquid); polvorear (powder).
sprout   brotar.

spy   espía.
spy (to)   espiar.
squad   escuadra; pelotón (party).
squadron   escuadrón; escuadra, flotilla (Navy).
square   cuadrado; plaza (town).
squash n.   calabaza.
squeeze (to)   exprimir.
squirrel   ardilla.
stab   puñalada.
stab (to)   apuñalar, dar de puñaladas.
staff   palo, asta (pole); báculo, bastón (rod, stick); bastón de mando (baton); jalón de mira (for surveying); personal (personnel); plana mayor, estado mayor (body of officers).
office staff   personal de oficina.
editorial staff   cuerpo de redacción.
staff officer   oficial de estado mayor.
stage   etapa; escenario, tablas (theater).
by stages   por etapas.
stage (to)   representar, poner en escena (theater).
stain   mancha.
stain (to)   manchar.
stair   escalón, peldaño.
staircase   escalera.
stake   estaca, piquete (for driving into the ground).
at stake   comprometido, envuelto, en peligro.
His life is at stake.   En eso le va la vida. Su vida está en peligro.
stake (to)   estacar, poner estacas; jugar, aventurar, arriesgar (to risk, to put at hazard).
to stake all   jugarse el todo por el todo, echar el resto.
stammer   tartamudear.
stamp   sello, estampilla (for letters); timbre (for documents).
postage stamp   sello de correo.
stamp (to)   estampar, sellar; poner un sello, poner los sellos (a letter).
stand n.   puesto (stall); tribuna (platform); mesita, velador, estante, pedestal, soporte (a piece of furniture).
newsstand   puesto de periódicos.
stand (to)   poner derecho, colocar or poner de pie (to set something on end); ponerse or estar de pie (to take or keep an upright position); resistir, hacer frente (to resist); aguantar, sufrir (pain, etc.); pararse (to stop moving).
Stand back!   ¡Atrás!
Stand up!   ¡Levántese! ¡Póngase de pie!
I am standing.   Estoy de pie.
I can't stand him.   No lo puedo aguantar.
to stand a chance   tener probabilidades.
to stand by   estar listo (ready); estar cerca (near); estar de mirón (to be looking at); atenerse a, sujetarse a (to abide by).
to stand for   estar por, ser partidario de, defender, mantener, aprobar, favorecer; querer decir, significar (to mean); tolerar, aguantar (to tolerate).
to stand in line   hacer cola.
to stand in the way   cerrar el paso, estorbar, ser un estorbo.
to stand off   mantenerse a distancia.
to stand on one's feet   valerse de sí mismo.
to stand one's ground   resistir, mantenerse firme.
to stand out   resaltar, sobresalir, destacarse (to be prominent, conspicuous).
to stand out of the way   hacerse a un lado.
to stand still   no moverse, estarse quieto.
to stand the test   pasar, resistir la prueba.

to stand together   mantenerse unidos, solidarizarse.
to stand up   levantarse, ponerse de pie.
to stand up for   sacar la cara por.
standard   norma, tipo, pauta, patrón, standard; estandarte (flag).
standard of living   nivel de vida.
gold standard   patrón de oro.
standard price   precio corriente.
standpoint   punto de vista.
star   estrella, astro.
starch   almidón.
starch (to)   almidonar.
start   principio, comienzo (beginning); partida, salida (departure); arranque (of a car, an engine).
to get a start   tomar la delantera.
start (to)   comenzar, principiar (to begin); partir, salir, ponerse en marcha (to start out); poner en marcha, arrancar (an engine, etc.).
starvation   hambre.
starve   morir de hambre; matar de hambre (to cause to starve).
state n.   estado, condición, situación.
state (to)   decir, expresar, declarar, exponer, manifestar, afirmar.
statement   declaración, manifestación, exposición, relación; informe, memoria (report); cuenta, estado de cuenta (of an account).
stateroom   camarote.
statesman   estadista, hombre de estado.
station   estación.
railroad station   estación de ferrocarril.
station master   jefe de estación.
stationery   papel para cartas, efectos de escritorio.
stationery store   papelería.
statistical   estadístico.
statistics   estadística.
statue   estatua.
statute   estatuto.
stay   estancia, permanencia, residencia (visit); suspensión temporal de un proceso (court).
stay (to)   quedar, quedarse, parar, detenerse, hospedarse; aplazar, suspender (to put off).
to stay in   quedarse en casa, no salir.
to stay in bed   guardar cama.
to stay away   estar ausente, no volver.
He's staying at the Waldorf Astoria. Para en el Waldorf Astoria.
steadily   constantemente, invariablemente.
steady   firme, fijo, estable, constante.
steak   bistec, biftec.
steal   robar.
They've stolen my watch.   Me han robado el reloj.
steam   vapor.
steamboat   vapor.
steam engine   máquina de vapor.
steamer   buque de vapor.
steamship   buque, vapor.
steamship line   compañía de vapores, compañía de navegación.
steel   acero.
steep   empinado, escarpado.
steer (to)   guiar, conducir, gobernar.
steering wheel   volante.
stem   tallo; raíz (grammar).
stenographer   taquígrafo, estenógrafo.
stenography   taquigrafía, estenografía.
step   paso; escalón, peldaño (stair).
step by step   paso a paso.
to be in step   llevar el paso.

to be out of step   no llevar el paso.
flight of steps   tramo.
step (to)   dar un paso, pisar, andar, caminar.
to step aside   hacerse a un lado.
to step back   retroceder.
to step down   bajar, descender; disminuir (decrease).
to step in   entrar, visitar; meterse, intervenir (take part).
to step on   pisar, poner el pie sobre.
to step out   salir.
stepbrother   hermanastro, medio hermano.
stepchild   hijastro.
stepdaughter   hijastra.
stepfather   padrastro.
stepmother   madrastra.
stepsister   hermanastra.
stepson   hijastro.
stern adj.   austero, severo.
stew   guisado, estofado.
veal stew   guisado de ternera.
steward   camarero (on a ship).
stewardess   camarera.
stick   palo, garrote, bastón (cane).
stick (to)   apuñalar (to stab); clavar, hincar (to thrust); pegar (to glue); fijar, prender (to fasten); perseverar (to keep on).
to stick by   solidarzarse con, apoyar; mantenerse en.
to stick out   sacar; asomar (one's head); perseverar hasta el fin (to put up with until the end).
to stick up   atracar.
to stick up for   defender, sacar la cara por.
to stick to   atenerse a, perseverar, mantenerse en.
stiff   tieso, duro, rígido; estirado, afectado (not natural in manners); ceremonioso (formal); fuerte (strong); caro (of prices).
stiff collar   cuello duro, cuello planchado.
stiff neck   tortícolis.
stiff-necked   cuellierguido; terco, obstinado.
stiff resistance   resistencia obstinada.
stiffen   endurecer(se), atiesar(se), arreciar, enconarse, obstinarse.
stiffness   rigidez, dureza.
still adj.   quieto, inmóvil, tranquilo.
still water   agua estancada.
to stand still   estarse quieto.
still life   naturaleza muerta.
Be still!   ¡Cállate!
still adv.   aun, aún, todavía, hasta ahora, no obstante.
She's still sleeping.   Está durmiendo todavía.
stillness   calma, quietud.
sting   aguijón; picadura (wound).
sting (to)   picar; pinchar (to prick).
stir (to)   agitar; revolver.
to stir the fire   atizar el fuego.
to stir up   conmover, excitar, alborotar, despertar.
stirrup   estribo.
stock   surtido, existencias, mercancías (supply of goods); acción (share); valores, acciones (stocks); caja (of a rifle); raza (race).
stock market   bolsa.
stock company   sociedad anónima.
in stock   en existencia.
out of stock   agotado.
stockings   medias.
stomach   estómago.
stone   piedra.
stool   taburete, banqueta (seat).

stop   parada (of streetcar, etc.).
stop (to)   parar, pararse, detener, detenerse, hacer alto; quedarse (to stay).
to stop raining   dejar (cesar) de llover.
Stop!   ¡Alto!
Stop that now!   ¡Basta!
Stop a minute.   Deténgase un instante.
to stop talking   dejar de hablar.
to stop working   dejar de trabajar.
to stop payment   suspender el pago.
to stop payments   suspender pagos.
to stop at   detenerse en, poner reparo.
to stop short   parar en seco.
to stop over   detenerse durante el viaje; quedarse.
store   tienda (shop).
department store   almacenes, tienda de variedades.
stork   cigüeña.
storm   tempestad, tormenta.
stormy   tempestuoso, borrascoso.
story   historia, cuento, historieta (tale); piso (building); cuento de viejas, embuste (falsehood).
short story   cuento corto.
as the story goes   según se dice, según cuenta la historia.
stout   corpulento, gordo.
stove   estufa.
straight   derecho, recto.
straight line   línea recta.
Go straight ahead.   Vaya todo seguido.
straighten   enderezar, poner en orden.
straightforward adj.   derecho; recto; franco (frank); íntegro, honrado (honest).
strain   tensión (tension); esfuerzo (effort).
strain (to)   colar (through a strainer); cansar (the eyes, etc.); esforzarse (to make an effort).
Don't strain yourself.   No se canse Ud.
to strain the voice   forzar la voz.
strange   extraño, raro (unusual); desconocido (not known).
strange face   cara desconocida.
strangeness   extrañeza, rareza.
stranger   extraño, desconocido, extranjero (foreigner).
strap   correa.
strategic   estratégico.
strategy   estrategia.
straw   paja.
straw hat   sombrero de paja.
the last straw   el colmo, el acabose.
strawberry   fresa.
stream n.   corriente de agua, río, arroyo.
street   calle.
street crossing   cruce de calle.
street intersection   bocacalle.
streetcar   tranvía.
streetcar conductor   cobrador.
strength   fuerza, vigor.
to gain strength   cobrar fuerzas.
on the strength of   fundándose en.
strengthen   fortalecer(se), reforzar.
stress   fuerza (force); esfuerzo (effort); tensión (strain); presión (pressure); acento (accent); énfasis, importancia (importance).
stress (to)   acentuar, dar énfasis.
stretch (to)   estirar, extender, ensanchar; dar de sí (to become longer or wider).
to stretch oneself   desperezarse.
to stretch out   estirar, alargar.
stretcher   camilla.
strict   estricto, riguroso, severo.

strike huelga (of workers).
strike (to) golpear, pegar, chocar.
  to strike at atacar, acometer.
  to strike a match encender un fósforo.
  to strike against chocar con.
  to strike back dar golpe por golpe.
  to strike home dar en el vivo.
  to strike out borrar, tachar (to cross out).
  to strike one as funny hacer gracia.
striking que sorprende, sorprendente; llamativo, que llama la atención (attracting attention).
stripe lista.
stroll paseo, vuelta.
  to go for a stroll dar una vuelta.
stroll (to) pasear(se).
strong fuerte, poderoso.
stronghold fortaleza, fuerte.
structure estructura.
struggle lucha.
struggle (to) luchar.
stubborn obstinado, terco.
student estudiante.
studious estudioso.
study estudio.
study (to) estudiar.
stuff n. tela, paño, género (cloth, material); cosa (thing), cachivaches, chismes, muebles (belongings, furniture).
stumble tropezar.
stump tocón, cepa (of tree).
stupid estúpido.
  to be stupid ser estúpido.
stupidity estupidez.
stupor estupefacción, estupor.
style estilo, modo; moda (fashion).
subdue subyugar.
subject sujeto; materia, asunto, tema (subject matter).
subject (to) sujetar, someter.
submarine submarino.
submission sumisión.
submit someter; someterse.
subordinate subordinado.
subscribe subscribir(se).
subscriber abonado, subscriptor.
subscription subscripción; cantidad subscrita (sum).
subsequent subsiguiente, ulterior.
subsequently posteriormente, subsiguientemente.
substance substancia.
substantial substancial.
substitute substituto.
substitute (to) substituir.
substitution substitución.
subtract quitar, restar, sustraer.
suburb suburbio, arrabal.
succeed salir bien, tener buen éxito (turn out well); suceder (come next after another).
success (buen) éxito, buen resultado.
successful próspero, afortunado.
successive sucesivo.
successor sucesor.
such tal, semejante.
  such as tal como.
  in such a way de tal modo.
  no such (a) thing no hay tal.
sudden adj. repentino, súbito.
  all of a sudden de repente.
suddenly repentinamente, de pronto, súbitamente.
suffer (to) sufrir.
suffering adj. doliente.

suffering n. sufrimiento, padecimiento.
sugar azúcar.
  sugar bowl azucarero.
  sugar cane caña de azúcar.
  sugar mill ingenio.
suggest sugerir, proponer.
suggestion sugestión.
suicide suicidio.
  to commit suicide suicidarse.
suit traje (clothes); causa, pleito (court); palo (in cards).
  ready-made suit traje hecho.
  suit made to order traje a la medida.
  to bring suit entablar juicio.
suit (to) cuadrar, convenir, acomodar (to be suitable); venir or ir bien, sentar (to be becoming); satisfacer, agradar (to please, to satisfy).
suitable adecuado, apropiado.
suitably adecuadamente, convenientemente.
sulphur azufre.
sum suma.
  in sum en suma.
  sum total suma total.
summary sumario.
summer verano.
  summer resort lugar de veraneo.
summit cima, cumbre.
summon citar, emplazar, requerir, convocar.
summons citación, comparendo.
sum up (to) resumir, recapitular.
sun sol.
  sun bath baño de sol.
  to take a sun bath tomar un baño de sol.
sunbeam rayo de sol.
sunburn quemadura de sol.
sunburnt tostado por el sol.
  to get sunburnt tostarse por el sol.
Sunday domingo.
sunlight luz del sol.
sunny de sol, asoleado; alegre, risueño (sunny disposition).
sunrise salida de sol, amanecer.
sunset puesta del sol.
sunshine luz solar.
  in the sunshine al sol.
sunstroke insolación.
superb soberbio, grandioso.
superfluous superfluo.
superintendent superintendente.
superior superior.
superiority superioridad.
superstition superstición.
superstitious supersticioso.
supper cena.
  to have supper cenar.
supplement suplemento.
supply abastecimiento; surtido (stock); oferta (business).
  supply and demand oferta y demanda.
supply (to) abastecer, proveer, surtir.
support apoyo, sostén; sustento, manutención (act of providing for).
support (to) sostener, apoyar; mantener (to provide for).
suppose suponer.
supposition suposición, supuesto.
suppress suprimir.
suppression supresión.
supreme supremo, sumo.
  Supreme Court Corte Suprema, Tribunal Supremo.
sure cierto, seguro.

  to be sure estar seguro, sin duda, ya se ve.
  be sure to no deje de, sin falta.
surely seguramente, ciertamente, indudablemente.
surface superficie.
surgeon cirujano.
surgery cirugía.
surname apellido.
surprise sorpresa, extrañeza.
surprise (to) sorprender.
surprising sorprendente.
surprisingly sorprendentemente.
surrender rendición, entrega.
surrender (to) rendir(se), entregar(se), ceder.
surround cercar, rodear.
surrounding circunvecino.
surroundings inmediaciones, alrededores; medio, ambiente (atmosphere).
survey examen, estudio; inspección (inspection); levantamiento de planos (surveying).
survey (to) examinar, estudiar; reconocer, inspeccionar (to inspect); levantar un plano (in surveying).
survival supervivencia.
survive sobrevivir.
survivor sobreviviente.
susceptible susceptible.
suspect n. persona sospechosa.
suspect (to) sospechar.
suspend suspender.
suspenders tirantes.
suspicion sospecha.
suspicious sospechoso, desconfiado, suspicaz.
swallow golondrina (bird).
swallow (to) tragar.
swamp pantano, ciénaga.
swan cisne.
swarm enjambre.
swarm (to) enjambrar, pulular, bullir, hormiguear.
swear jurar, tomar or prestar juramento.
  to swear by jurar por, poner confianza implícita en.
sweat sudor.
sweat (to) sudar.
sweater sweter, chaqueta de punto.
sweep barrer.
sweet dulce.
  sweet apples manzanas dulces.
  sweet potato batata, patata dulce, boniato (Cuba), camote (Amer.).
  to have a sweet tooth ser goloso.
  She's very sweet. Ella es muy dulce.
sweetheart novio, novia.
sweetness dulzura.
swell adj. excelente, magnífico, estupendo.
swell (to) hinchar(se), subir, crecer (to rise above the level).
swelling hinchazón.
swift rápido, veloz.
swiftly velozmente, rápidamente.
swim (to) nadar.
  My head's swimming. Se me va la cabeza.
swimmer nadador.
swimming pool piscina.
swing columpio (a seat hung from ropes), balanceo, oscilación (movement).
  in full swing en pleno apogeo.
swing (to) columpiar, mecer; mover con soltura los brazos o el cuerpo al andar (to swing one's arms or body when walking).
switch la llave de la luz, el botón de la luz, interruptor, conmutador (electric switch);

cambiavía, aguja de cambio (railroad); cambio (change, shift).

switch (to) dar vuelta la llave de la luz (to turn the switch); desviar, apartar (rails); cambiar (to change, to shift); azotar (to whip).

sword espada.

syllable sílaba.

symbol símbolo.

sympathetic afín, simpático, que simpatiza.

sympathize simpatizar.

sympathy simpatía.

symphony sinfonía.
 symphony orchestra orquesta sinfónica.

symptom síntoma.

synthetic sintético.

syrup almíbar.

system sistema.

systematic metódico, sistemático.

T

table mesa; tabla (of measures, etc.).
 to set the table poner la mesa.

tablecloth mantel.

tablespoon cuchara.

tablet tableta, pastilla (of aspirin, etc.); bloc de papel (for writing); tabla, lápida (with an inscription).

tableware servicio de mesa.

tact tacto.

tactical táctico.

tactics táctica.

tactful cauto, atinado.

tactless falta.

tail cola.

tailor sastre.

take (to) tomar; coger (to grasp).
 to take a bite comer algo.
 to take a bath bañarse.
 to take a picture sacar un retrato.
 to take a walk dar un paseo.
 to take a stroll dar una vuelta.
 to take a nap tomar la siesta.
 to take a look at echar un vistazo a, mirar.
 to take a trip hacer un viaje.
 to take an oath prestar juramento.
 to take apart desarmar (a machine).
 to take a step dar un paso.
 to take away quitar, llevarse.
 to take back retractarse, desdecirse de; devolver; tomar algo devuelto.
 to take account of tomar en cuenta.
 to take advantage of aprovecharse de, abusar de.
 to take a fancy to prendarse de, simpatizar de.
 to take a liking to coger (tomar) cariño a.
 to take advice hacer caso, tomar consejo.
 to take care tener cuidado.
 to take care of cuidar de.
 to take chances correr el riesgo, arriesgar.
 to take down bajar, poner más bajo (to lower); tomar nota (to take note).
 to take for granted tomar por sentado.
 to take charge of encargarse de.
 to take effect surtir efecto.
 to take into consideration tener en cuenta.
 to take to heart tomar pecho.
 to take it easy no apurarse.
 Take it or leave it. ¿Sí o no? Tómelo o déjelo.
 to take from quitar de; restar de (to subtract).
 to take leave despedirse.
 to take note tomar nota.
 to take notice advertir, observar, notar, percatarse de.

to take out sacar, quitar.

to take after salir a, parecerse, ser como.

to take it out on desquitarse con otro, hacer pagar el pato.

to take off despegar (a plane).

to take one's clothes off quitarse la ropa, desnudarse.

to take one's shoes off descalzarse.

Take your hat off. Descúbrase. Quítese el sombrero.

Take my word for it. Créame Ud. Bajo mi palabra.

to take pains cuidar.

to take part tomar parte.

to take place suceder, ocurrir.

to take possession of apoderarse.

to take refuge refugiarse.

to take time tomar tiempo.

to take one's time tomarse tiempo, no darse prisa.

to take up a subject abordar un tema.

to take up room ocupar espacio.

to take upon oneself encargarse de, asumir la responsabilidad, hacerse cargo de.

talcum talco.

talcum powder polvo de talco.

tale cuento; chisme (gossip).

talent talento.

talented talentoso.

talk conversación (conversation); charla (chat); discurso (speech); comidilla (gossip); rumor (rumor).

talk (to) hablar, conversar, charlar.
 to talk back replicar, responder irrespetuosamente.
 to talk over discutir, tratar acerca de.
 to talk to hablar a.

talkative locuaz.

tall alto.

tallness altura, estatura.

tame adj. domesticado, amansado, dócil.

tame (to) domar, domesticar.

tan n. color de canela, color café claro (color).

tan adj. atezado, tostado (skin); de color café claro, de color de canela.

tan (to) curtir; atezarse, tostarse (to become tan).

tank tanque, cisterna; tanque (mil.); depósito, tanque (for gasoline).

tape cinta, tira de tela, de papel o de metal.
 tape measure cinta para medir.
 adhesive tape esparadrapo.

tapestry tapiz, tapicería.

tar brea, alquitrán.

target blanco, objetivo.
 to hit the target dar en el blanco.

task tarea, feana, labor.

taste gusto.
 in bad taste de mal gusto.
 in good taste de buen gusto.
 to have a taste for tener gusto por.

taste (to) gustar, saborear, probar; saber a, tener gusto a (to have a flavor of).
 Taste it. Pruébelo.
 The soup tastes of onïon. La sopa sabe a cebolla.

tavern taberna.

tax impuesto, contribución.
 income tax impuesto sobre la renta.
 tax collector exactor, recaudador de impuestos.
 tax rate tarifa de impuestos.

tax (to) cobrar impuestos, imponer contribuciones.

taxi taxi, coche de alquiler.

tea té.

teach enseñar.

teacher maestro.

teacup taza para té.

teakettle olla para calentar agua.

team pareja, tronco (horses); equipo (sports).
 team work trabajo coordinado, esfuerzo aunado, actuación concertada.

teapot tetera.

tear lágrima.
 in tears llorando.

tear (to) desgarrar, rasgar, romper.
 to tear down demoler.
 to tear to pieces hacer añicos, despedazar.
 to tear one's hair arrancarse los cabellos.

tease tomar el pelo.

technical técnico.

technique técnica.

tedious aburrido, cansado.

teeth dientes.
 false teeth dientes postizos.
 set of teeth dentadura.

telegraph telégrafo.

telegraph (to) telegrafiar.

telephone teléfono.
 telephone booth cabina telefónica.
 telephone call llamada telefónica.
 telephone exchange central telefónica.
 telephone operator telefonista.
 telephone directory guía telefónica, lista de abonados, directorio telefónico.

telephone (to) telefonear.

telescope telescopio.

tell decir; contar, relatar, referir.
 to tell a story contar un cuento.
 Who told you so? ¿Quién se lo dijo?
 Tell it to him. Cuénteselo a él.
 Do what you are told. Haz lo que se te mande.

temper genio, carácter.
 bad temper mal genio.
 to lose one's temper enfadarse, perder la paciencia.

temperament temperamento.

tempest tempestad.

temple templo (for worship); sien (anatomy).

temporarily provisionalmente, temporalmente, transitoriamente.

temporary provisorio, temporal, interino.

temporize (to) contemporizar.

tempt tentar.

temptation tentación.

tempting tentador.

ten diez.

tenacious tenaz, porfiado.

tenant inquilino.

tendency tendencia.

tender adj. tierno.
 tender-hearted compasivo.

tennis tenis.
 tennis court cancha de tenis.

tense tenso.

tension tensión.

tent tienda de campaña.

tentative tentativa.

tenth décimo.

term término; plazo (period of time); especificaciones, condiciones (terms).
 in terms of en concepto de; en función de (math.).
 on no terms por ningún concepto.
 to be on good terms with estar en buenas

relaciones con.

to come to terms llegar a un acuerdo, convenir.

to bring to terms imponer condiciones a, hacer arreglos con.

On what terms? ¿En que términos?

terminal *adj.* terminal, final, último.

terminal término; estación terminal, final de trayecto (station, end of a line); terminal, borne (elec.).

terrace terraza.

terrible terrible, espantoso.

How terrible! ¡Qué espantoso!

terribly espantosamente, terriblemente.

territory territorio.

terror terror, espanto.

terse terso, sucinto, conçiso.

terseness concisión.

test prueba, ensayo, examen, análisis.

test (to) ensayar, probar, analisar.

testify atestiguar, testificar, declarar.

text texto.

textbook libro de texto.

than que.

more than that más que eso.
fewer than menos que.
She's older than I. Ella es mayor que yo.

thank (to) agradecer, dar las gracias.

Thank you. Gracias.

thankful agradecido.

thanks gracias.

thanks to. gracias a.

that ese, esa, eso, aquel, aquella, aquello (*dem. adj.*); ése, ésa, eso, aquél, aquélla, aquello (*dem. pron.*); que, quien, el cual, la cual, lo que, lo cual (*rel. pron.*).

that man ese hombre.
that woman esa mujer.
That's the one. Ese es.
That's it. Eso es.
That's to say. Es decir.
That may be. Es posible. Eso puede ser.
That's all. Eso es todo.
and all that y cosas por el estilo.
That way. Por allí. Por aquel camino.
that's how asi es como es, asi es como se hace.
That's that. Eso es lo que hay. No hay más que decir.
to let it go at that conformarse con eso, dejar correr.

that *adv.* tan, así de.

not that far no tan lejos.
that many tantos.
that much tanto.
that big así de grande.

that *conj.* que, para que.

so that de modo que, de suerte que, para que.
in order that para que, de modo que.
save that salvo que.
in that por cuanto, en que.

the el, la, lo; los, las.

the man el hombre.
the men los hombres.
the woman la mujer.
the women las mujeres.
the sooner the better cuanto más pronto, tanto mejor.
the less . . . the better cuanto menos . . . tanto mejor.

theater teatro.

theatrical teatral.

their su, suyo, suya, de él, de ella; sus, suyos, suyas, de ellos, de ellas.

theirs el suyo, la suya, los suyos, las suyas, de ellos, de ellas.

them los, las, les; ellos, ellas.

theme tema, asunto.

themselves ellos mismos, ellas mismas; sí mismos.

then entonces, en aquel tiempo, a la sazón.

now and then de cuando en cuando, de vez en cuando.
but then si bien es cierto que, sin embargo.
and then y entonces.
just then entonces mismo, en aquel mismo momento.
by then para entonces.
And what then? ¡Y entonces! ¿Pues y qué? ¿Y que pasó después? (What happened then?) ¿Y que pasará después? (What will happen then?)

theoretical teórico.

theory teoría.

there allí, allá, ahí (near the person addressed).

Put it there. Ponlo ahí.
There she goes. Ahí va.
I was there. Yo estuve allí.
She lives there. Ella vive allí.
Go there. Vaya allá.
Over there. Por allí. Allá.
There in Spain. Allá en España.
There you are. Ahí tiene Ud. Para que vea. Eso es todo.
There! ¡Toma! ¡Vaya! ¡Mira!
there is hay.

thereabouts por ahí, por allí, cerca de allí.

thereafter después de eso; conforme.

there are hay.

There are many things. Hay muchas cosas.

thereby por medio de eso; con eso, con lo cual; de tal modo, así.

therefore por lo tanto, por esto, por esa razón; a consecuencia de eso, por consiguiente.

there is hay.

There's plenty (enough). Hay bastante.

thereupon en eso, sobre eso; por lo tanto; inmediatamente después, en seguida, luego.

thermometer termómetro.

these estos, estas; éstos, éstas.

thesis tesis.

they ellos, ellas.

thick espeso (like glue); tupido, denso (dense); grosor, grueso (not thin).

three inches thick tres pulgadas de espesor.
thick-headed torpe.

thickness grueso, espesor, grosor.

thief ladrón.

thigh muslo.

thimble dedal.

thin flaco (lean); delgado (not thick), delgado, esbelto (slender).

thing cosa, objeto.

something algo, alguna cosa.
anything cualquier cosa.

think (to) pensar; creer, opinar (believe).

to think of pensar en, reflexionar acerca de.
to think well of pensar bien de, tener buen concepto de.
As you think fit. Como Ud. quiera, como a Ud. le parezca mejor.
to think it over pensarlo, meditarlo.
to think nothing of no dar importancia a; tener en poco.
to think twice andar con tiento, pensarlo bien, reflexionar mucho.
I don't think so. Creo que no.
I think so. Creo que sí.

thinness delgadez, flacura.

third tercero.

a third person un tercero.
thirdly en tercer lugar.

thirst sed.

to be thirsty tener sed.

thirteen trece.

thirty treinta.

this este, esta; esto; éste, ésta.

this man este hombre.
this woman esta mujer.
this morning esta mañana.
this one and that one éste y aquél.
this and that esto y aquello.

thorn espina.

thorough *adj.* entero, cabal, minucioso, perfecto.

thoroughfare vía pública, calle, carretera.

No thoroughfare. Se prohibe el paso.

thoroughgoing cabal, completo, entero, hasta el final.

thoroughly enteramente, cabalmente.

those aquellos, aquellas.

though aunque, sin embargo, no obstante, si bien, bien que, aun cuando.

as though como si.

thought pensamiento.

to give thought to pensar en.

thoughtful pensativo, meditabundo; precavido (careful); atento, considerado (considerate).

It's very thoughtful of you. Ud. es muy atento.

thoughtfully cuidadosamente, con precaución, con reflexión, con consideración.

thoughtfulness reflexión, meditación, atención, consideración, previsión.

thoughtless inconsiderado, descuidado, insensato.

thoughtlessly descuidadamente, sin reflexión, sin consideración.

thousand mil, millar.

thread hilo.

thread (to) enhebrar.

threat amenaza.

threaten amenazar.

three tres.

threefold triple.

threshold umbral.

thrift economía, frugalidad.

thrifty frugal, económico.

thrill emoción, estremecimiento.

thrill (to) emocionarse, estremecerse, temblar; causar una viva emoción.

throat garganta.

sore throat dolor (mal) de garganta.
I have a sore throat. Me duele la garganta.

throne trono.

through *adj.* continuo, directo.

a through train from Barcelona to Valencia un tren directo de Barcelona a Valencia.

through *adv.* a través, de parte en parte, de un lado a otro; enteramente, completamente.

through and through enteramente, hasta los tuétanos.
I'm wet through and through. Estoy mojado hasta los huesos. Estoy hecho una sopa.
to be through haber terminado.
to be through with no tener más que ver con, haber terminado, no ocuparse ya en.

through *prep.* por, por entre, a través, por medio de, por conducto de; mediante.

through the door por la puerta.
through the strainer a través del colador.
through the trees por entre los árboles.

through his influence mediante su influencia.

throughout *prep.* durante todo, en todo, a lo largo de, por todos lados; *adv.* de parte a parte, desde el principio hasta el fin, en todas partes.

throw echar; tirar (a ball, stone, etc.).

to throw out echar fuera, arrojar.

to throw away tirar, arrojar, botar (Amer.).

to throw light on esclarecer, aclarar.

thumb pulgar.

thumbtack chinche.

thunder trueno.

thunder (to) tronar.

It's thundering. Truena.

thunderbolt rayo, centella.

thunderclap tronada.

thundershower chubasco con truenos y relámpagos.

thunderstorm tronada.

Thursday jueves.

thus así, de este modo, en estos términos, como sigue.

thus far hasta aquí, hasta ahora.

thus much no más, basta, baste esto.

ticket billete, boleto (Amer.).

round-trip ticket billete de ida y vuelta.

season ticket abono, billete de temporada.

ticket window taquilla.

tickle (to) hacer cosquillas.

tickling cosquillas.

ticklish cosquilloso; quisquilloso.

tide marea.

high tide pleamar, plenamar.

low tide bajamar.

tie *n.* corbata (to wear); lazo (bond); atadura, nudo (a knot); traviesa, durmiente (railroad tie).

family ties lazos de familia.

tie (to) atar, amarrar.

tiger tigre.

tight apretado, muy ajustado, bien cerrado.

tighten apretar.

tile azulejo, losa, baldosa; teja (for roof).

tiling azulejos, tejas (tiles); tejado (roof covered with tiles).

till hasta; hasta que.

till now hasta ahora.

till further notice hasta nueva orden.

till (to) cultivar, laborar, labrar.

timber madera.

time tiempo; hora; vez; época; plazo.

What time is it? ¿Qué hora es?

the first time la primera vez.

on time a tiempo.

some time ago tiempo atrás.

a long time ago hace mucho tiempo.

at the proper time a su debido tiempo, en el momento oportuno.

at the same time al mismo tiempo.

any time a cualquier hora; cuando Ud. guste, cuando quiera.

at no time jamás.

one at a time uno a la vez.

at this time ahora, al presente.

at this time (of the day) a estas horas.

at times a veces.

for the time being por ahora, de momento.

time and again una y otra vez.

from time to time de vez en cuando.

in no time en un instante, en un abrir y cerrar de ojos.

in an hour's time en una hora.

Be on time. Sea puntual.

Have a good time! ¡Que se divierta!

We had a good time. Pasamos un buen rato.

to take time tomarse tiempo.

spare time tiempo desocupado, ratos de ocio.

timely oportunamente, a propósito (*adv.*); oportuno, a buen tiempo (*adj.*).

timid tímido.

timidity timidez.

tin lata.

tin can lata.

tin foil hoja de estaño.

tin plate hoja de lata.

tincture tintura.

tincture of iodine tintura de yodo.

tint tinte.

tip punta, extremidad, cabo (point, end); propina (gratuity); soplo, delación (secret information); advertencia (warning).

tip (to) ladear, inclinar (to slant); dar una propina (to give a tip); prevenir, precaver (to warn); delatar, soplar (to tip off).

tire neumático, llanta.

flat tire pinchazo, neumático desinflado.

tire (to) cansar; aburrir (to bore).

to tire out reventar de cansancio.

tired cansado.

tired out rendido de cansancio, agotado.

to become tired cansarse.

tiredness cansancio, fatiga.

tireless incansable, infatigable.

tissue tejido (a mass of cells, skin tissue, etc.); gasa, tisú (cloth).

tissue paper papel de seda.

title título.

title page portada.

to a, para, de, por, hasta, que.

to give to dar a.

to go to ir a.

to speak to hablar a.

ready to go listo para marcharse.

It's time to leave. Es hora de partir.

the road to Madrid la carretera de Madrid.

from house to house de casa en casa.

to be done por hacerse.

letters to be written cartas por escribir.

to this day hasta ahora.

in order to a fin de, para.

to and fro de un lado a otro, de acá para allá.

I have to go. Tengo que irme.

I have something to do. Tengo algo que hacer.

It's five (minutes) to three. Son las tres menos cinco.

toad sapo.

toast tostada.

toast (to) tostar.

toasted tostado.

toaster tostador, parrilla.

tobacco tabaco.

tobacco shop estanco (Spain) cigarrería, tabaquería (Amer.).

today hoy.

a week from today de hoy en ocho días.

toe dedo del pie.

together juntos; juntamente; a un tiempo, simultaneamente.

Let's go together. Vamos juntos.

together with junto con, en compañía de.

to call together reunir, congregar.

toil trabajo, pena, angustia, fatiga, afán.

toilet excusado, retrete, inodoro; tocado (combing the hair, bathing, etc.).

toilet set juego de tocador.

toilet water colonia, agua de colonia.

toilet paper papel higiénico.

tolerance tolerancia.

tolerant tolerante.

tolerate tolerar.

tomato tomate.

tomato juice jugo de tomate.

tomb tumba, sepulcro.

tomcat gato.

tomorrow mañana.

day after tomorrow pasado mañana.

tomorrow morning mañana por la mañana.

tomorrow noon mañana al mediodía.

tomorrow afternoon mañana por la tarde.

tomorrow night mañana por la noche.

ton tonelada.

tone tono.

tongs tenazas, alicates.

tongue lengua; espiga.

to hold one's tongue callarse.

tonic tónico.

tonight esta noche, a la noche.

tonsil amígdala.

tonsilitis amigdalitis.

too demasiado (too much), tambien (also).

too much demasiado, excesivo.

too many demasiados, muchos.

It's too bad. Es lástima.

It's too early. Es demasiado temprano.

It's a little too early. Es un poco temprano.

That's too much. Eso ya es demasiado. Es el colmo.

You have gone a little too far. Ud. se ha excedido un poco.

He's too good. Es muy bueno. Se pasa de bueno.

none (not) too good no muy bueno que digamos, malamente puede llamarse eso bueno.

me (I) too yo tambien.

I am only too glad to do it. Lo haré con muchísimo gusto.

one dollar too much un dollar de más.

That's too little. Eso es muy poco.

tool herramienta.

tooth diente.

tooth powder polvo dentífrico.

toothache dolor de muelas.

toothbrush cepillo de dientes.

toothpaste pasta dentífrica.

toothpick mondadientes, palillo.

top cima, cumbre (of a mountain); copa (of a tree); la parte superior, la parte de arriba, superficie (upper side); cabeza (head), pináculo (pinnacle); trompo (toy).

the top of the mountain la cumbre de la montaña.

top hat chistera, sombrero de copa.

at top speed a todo correr.

at the top a la cabeza, en la cumbre.

from top to bottom de arriba abajo.

from top to toe de pies a cabeza.

on top of encima de, sobre.

top (to) sobrepujar, aventajar, exceder, llegar a la cima.

to top off coronar, rematar, dar cima.

topcoat gabán de entretiempo.

torch antorcha.

torment tormento.

torrent torrente.

torrid tórrido.

torrid zone zona tórrida.

tortoise tortuga.

tortoise shell carey.
torture tortura, tormento.
torture (to) torturar, atormentar.
toss (to) tirar, lanzar.
to toss aside echar a un lado.
to toss up jugar a cara o cruz.
total total.
sum total suma total.
touch contacto.
to be in touch with estar en comunicación con, en relación con.
touch (to) tocar.
touching adj. patético, conmovedor.
touchy quisquilloso.
tough duro, fuerte; difícil, penoso (hard to bear).
toughen endurecer (se).
toughness endurecimiento, rigidez.
tour viaje, gira.
tour (to) recorrer, viajar por.
touring turismo.
touring agency agencia de turismo.
touring car coche de turismo.
touring guide guía de turismo.
tourist turista.
tournament torneo.
tow (to) remolcar (a ship, etc.).
toward(s) hacia, para con, tocante a.
to go towards (a place) ir hacia (un lugar).
His attitude towards me. Su actitud para conmigo.
towel toalla.
face towel toalla para la cara.
hand towel toalla para las manos.
bath towel toalla de baño.
tower torre.
town ciudad, pueblo.
home town ciudad natal.
town hall ayuntamiento.
toy juguete.
trace indicio, huella, pista.
trace (to) trazar (to mark out); seguir la pista (to follow).
track huella; vía, rieles (metal rails); andén (in a railroad station).
trade comercio.
trade mark marca de fábrica.
trade name razón social; nombre de fábrica (for products).
trade union sindicato.
trading comercio.
tradition tradición.
traditional tradicional.
traffic circulación.
tragedy tragedia.
tragic trágico.
train tren.
train conductor cobrador.
train (to) entrenar, adiestrar, instruir.
training preparación, entrenamiento.
traitor traidor.
tramp vago, vagabundo.
tranquil tranquilo.
transatlantic transatlántico.
transfer transferencia; traspaso (a store, a farm, etc.); transbordo (from one train, bus, etc. to another).
transfer (to) transferir (to change hands); transbordar (trains, busses, etc.); trasladar (from one place to another).
translate traducir.
translation traducción.
translator traductor.
transparent transparente.

transport transporte.
transport (to) transportar.
transportation transporte.
trap trampa.
trap (to) atrapar.
travel (to) viajar.
traveler viajero, viajante (salesman).
tray bandeja.
treacherous traidor, alevoso.
treachery traición.
tread pisada.
tread (to) pisar, pisotear.
treason traición.
treasure tesoro.
treasure (to) atesorar, guardar.
treasurer tesorero.
treasury tesorería.
treat (to) tratar; convidar, invitar (with food, drinks, etc.).
to treat a patient tratar a un enfermo.
to treat well (badly) dar buen (mal) trato.
treatment trato; tratamiento (med.).
treaty tratado.
tree árbol.
tremble temblar.
trembling adj. trémulo, tembloroso.
trembling n. temblor.
tremendous tremendo, inmenso.
trench zanja; trinchera (fortification).
trend tendencia, giro, rumbo.
trial prueba, ensayo (test); juicio, vista de una causa (law).
triangle triángulo.
tribe tribu.
tribunal tribunal.
trick treta, artificio, jugada, artimaña; truco, juego de manos (with cards, etc.); maña, destreza (skill).
to do the trick resolver el problema.
He played a trick on me. Me hizo una jugarreta.
trifle friolera, bagatela.
trim (to) adornar (a dress, etc.); podar (a tree); cortar ligeramente (the hair).
trimming adorno, decoración.
trinket dije, chuchería.
trip n. viaje (voyage); traspié, tropezón (stumble); zancadilla (act of catching a person's foot).
one-way trip viaje de ida.
round trip viaje de ida y vuelta.
trip (to) tropezar (to stumble); hacer una zancadilla, (to cause to stumble).
triple triple.
triumph triunfo.
triumph (to) triunfar.
triumphant triunfante.
trivial trivial.
trolley car tranvía.
troops tropas.
trophy trofeo.
tropic trópico.
tropic(al) adj. tropical.
trot (to) trotar.
trouble preocupación, pena (worry); dificultad (difficulty); molestia (bother); apuro, aprieto (distress); disgusto, desavenencia (disagreement) mal, enfermedad (sickness).
to cause trouble causar molestia, dar que hacer.
to be in trouble estar en apuro.
not to be worth the trouble no valer la pena.
It's no trouble at all. No es ninguna molestia.
stomach trouble mal de estómago.

I have stomach trouble. Padezco del estómago.
trouble (to) molestar, importunar.
Don't trouble yourself. No se moleste Ud.
troubled preocupado, afligido.
to be troubled with padecer, sufrir de.
troublesome molesto, embarazoso; importuno, alborotador (person).
trousers pantalones.
trough artesa, pila, cubeta, batea.
trout trucha.
truck camión.
true cierto, exacto, verdadero, fiel.
It's true. Es verdad.
trunk tronco (of a tree), cofre, baúl (for packing).
trust confianza.
on trust al fiado.
in trust en depósito.
trust (to) tener confianza, confiar, fiar.
I trust him. Le tengo confianza.
I don't trust him. No me fío de él.
trustworthy digno de confianza.
truth verdad.
truthful verídico, veraz.
truthfulness veracidad.
try (to) probar, tratar de, esforzarse.
to try on clothes probarse ropa.
Try to do it. Trate de hacerlo.
to try hard hacer lo posible por.
tub cuba, batea.
bathtub baño, bañera.
tube tubo.
Tuesday martes.
tune tonada, tono, melodía.
to be out of tune desafinar.
tune (to) afinar, entonar; sintonizar (radio).
to tune in sintonizar.
tunnel túnel.
turkey pavo.
turn turno (time, order); vuelta, giro (motion); favor (favor).
by turns por turnos.
in turn a su turno, a su vez.
to take turns turnarse.
It's my turn now. Ahora me toca a mí.
turn (to) dar vuelta; dar vueltas, girar (to revolve); volver, doblar, torcer (to change direction); ponerse, volverse (to become pale, etc.).
to turn against predisponer en contra, volverse en contra.
to turn around dar vuelta a.
to turn down rehusar, rechazar (to refuse).
to turn into convertir en, cambiar en.
to turn off cerrar la llave del (gas, steam, etc.).
to turn off the light apagar la luz.
to turn off the water cortar el agua; cerrar el grifo.
to turn off the gas apagar el gas.
to turn on the light encender la luz.
to turn on the water dejar correr el agua, abrir el grifo.
to turn back dar la vuelta, volverse, retroceder.
to turn one's back on voltear la espalda a.
to turn out to be resultar, venir a ser.
to turn over transferir (to transfer), entregar, dar (to hand over); volcar, tumbarse (to tumble); abuñuelar (eggs); dar vuelta, volver (to change in position).
to turn sour agriarse (milk, etc.).
to turn to recurrir a, acudir a; convertir en,

convertirse en.

to turn up   aparecer (to appear), poner más alto, levantar (to give upward turn to); volver (a card, etc.); resultar, acontecer, venir a ser (to occur).

to turn a cold shoulder to   desairar.

to turn upside down   poner patas arriba.

turnip nabo.

turtle tortuga.

twelfth duodécimo, décimo segundo.

twelve doce.

twentieth vigésimo.

twenty veinte.

twice dos veces.

twilight crepúsculo.

twin mellizo, gemelo.

twin brother   hermano gemelo.

twin brothers   mellizos.

twist (to) torcer, retorcer.

two dos.

type tipo.

typewrite (to) escribir a máquina.

typewriter máquina de escribir.

portable typewriter   máquina de escribir portátil.

typewriter ribbon   cinta para la máquina de escribir.

typical típico.

typist mecanógrafa.

tyrannical tiránico.

tyranny tiranía.

tyrant irano.

U

ugliness fealdad.

ugly feo.

ulcer úlcera.

umbrella paraguas.

umbrella stand   paragüero.

unable incapaz.

I was unable to.   No pude. Me fué imposible.

unanimous unánime.

unaware desprevenido, de sorpresa; inadvertidamente, sin pensar.

to take someone unawares   coger a uno de sorpresa.

unbearable insoportable.

unbutton desabrochar.

uncertain incierto.

uncertainty incertidumbre.

unchangeable inmutable.

uncle tío.

uncomfortable incómodo, molesto; indispuesto.

to feel uncomfortable   estar incomodo.

unconquered invicto.

undecided indeciso.

under bajo, debajo de, en; menos; en tiempos de.

under the table   debajo de la mesa.

under consideration   en consideración.

under penalty of   so pena de.

under age   menor de edad.

under contract   bajo contrato; conforme al contrato.

under cover   al abrigo, a cubierto; dentro de un sobre (in an envelope).

under arms   bajo las armas.

under way   en camino, andando, en marcha.

under the circumstances   en las circunstancias.

under an obligation   deber favores.

under one's nose   en las barbas de uno.

underclothes ropa interior.

undergo someterse a, pasar por, sufrir.

to undergo an operation   operarse.

underground subterráneo.

underline subrayar.

underneath bajo, debajo de.

understand comprender, entender; estar de acuerdo.

Do you understand Spanish?   ¿Entiende Ud. español?

That's easy to understand.   Eso se comprende.

understanding entendimiento, modo de ver; acuerdo, inteligencia (agreement).

to come to an understanding   llegar a una inteligencia.

understood entendido, sobreentendido, convenido.

to be understood   sobreentenderse.

be it understood   entiéndase bien.

That's understood.   Está entendido. Por supuesto. Estamos de acuerdo.

undertake emprender; comprometerse a.

undertaking empresa; compromiso, promesa (promise).

undo deshacer, desatar; anular.

undress desnudar (se).

uneasiness malestar, inquietud, desasosiego.

uneasy inquieto, molesto, incómodo, desasosegado.

unequal desigual.

uneven desigual, irregular; non, impar (numbers).

unexpected inesperado.

unfair injusto.

unfaithful infiel.

unfavorable desfavorable.

unfinished incompleto.

unfit inadecuado, impropio; inepto, incapaz de (unable).

unfold (to) desenvolver, desplegar; descubrir, revelar, mostrar (to reveal, to show).

unforeseen imprevisto, inesperado.

unforgettable inolvidable.

unfortunate desgraciado, desdichado.

unfortunately por desgracia, desgraciadamente.

unfurnished sin muebles, desamueblado, no amueblado.

unfurnished apartment   piso sin muebles.

ungrateful ingrato, desagradecido.

unhappy infeliz, desdichado.

unhealthy enfermizo, achacoso; malsano.

unheard of inaudito; que no se ha oído.

unhurt ileso, intacto.

uniform uniforme.

union unión.

unique único.

unit unidad.

unite unir (se).

united unido.

United States   Estados Unidos.

unity unidad.

universal universal.

universe universo.

university universidad.

unjust injusto.

unkind poco amable; despiadado (cruel); tosco, duro (harsh).

unknown desconocido.

unlawful ilegal, ilícito, ilegítimo.

unless a no ser que, a menos que, si no.

unlike diferente, desemejante.

unlikely improbable, inverosímil, inverisímil.

unload descargar.

unlucky desgraciado, desafortunado, de mala

suerte.

unmarried soltero.

unmarried man   soltero.

unmarried woman   soltera.

unmoved impasible, inmutable, frío.

unnecessary innecesario.

unpaid sin pagar, no pagado.

unpleasant desagradable.

unquestionable indiscutible, indisputable.

unreasonable irrazonable, desatinado.

unruly ingobernable.

unsatisfactory que no satisface, inaceptable, poco satisfactorio.

unseen invisible; inadvertido.

unselfish desinteresado.

unsettled revuelto, turbio (liquid); variable, inestable (not stable); sin pagar, pendiente (a bill, etc.).

unsteady instable, inconstante, inseguro.

unsuccessful infructuoso, sin éxito; desafortunado.

unsuitable impropio, inadecuado.

until hasta.

untiring incansable, infatigable.

unusual extraordinario, poco común.

unwelcome mal acogido, malvenido.

unwilling maldispuesto.

to be unwilling   no estar dispuesto.

unwillingly de mala gana.

unwritten no escrito, en blanco.

unworthy indigno.

up arriba, en lo alto, hacia arriba; en pie, de pie.

up and down   arriba y abajo; de un lado a otro.

to go up   subir.

to go upstairs   subir.

to walk up and down   ir de un sitio para otro, dar vueltas.

up the river   río arriba.

one flight up   en el piso de arriba.

Up there!   ¡Alto ahí!

to be up to one   ser asunto de uno, ser cosa de uno.

What's up?   ¿Qué pasa? ¿De qué se trata?

The time is up.   Ya ha vencido el plazo. Ya es tiempo.

She's not up yet.   Todavía no se ha levantado.

this side up   arriba (on cases).

up to   hasta; capaz de (capable of doing); tramando (plotting).

up to anything   dispuesto a todo.

up-to-date   al día moderno.

up to date   hasta la fecha.

upon sobre, encima.

upon my word   bajo mi palabra.

upon which   sobre lo cual.

upper superior, alto.

the upper floor   el piso de arriba.

upper lip   labio superior.

upright vertical; derecho, recto, justo (character).

upset trastornar, perturbar, desarreglar.

upside

upside down   al revés, patas arriba; desconcierto.

upstairs arriba; en el piso de arriba.

to go upstairs   subir.

upstart n. advenedizo.

upwards hacia arriba.

urgency urgencia.

urgent urgente, apremiante.

use uso.

to make use of   utilizar.

in use en uso.
of no use inútil.
to be of no use no servir.
to have no use for no servirle a uno; no tener buena opinión de, tener en poco.
It's no use. Es inútil.
What's the use? ¿Para qué? Es inútil. ¿De qué sirve?
use (to) usar, servirse de, hacer uso de; soler, acostumbrer.
to use one's own judgment obrar uno conforme le parezca.
to use up gastar; agotar.
I'm used to it. Estoy acostumbrado a ello.
I used to see her every day. Solía verla todos los días.
used usado.
used clothes ropa usada.
useful útil.
useless inútil, inservible.
usher acomodador.
usual usual; común, general, ordinario.
as usual como de costumbre.
usually usualmente, ordinariamente, de costumbre, por lo común, por lo general, comunmente.
I usually get up early. Por regla general me levanto temprano.
utensil utensilio.
kitchen utensils batería de cocina.
utility utilidad.
utilize utilizar, emplear.
utmost extremo, sumo.
to the utmost hasta no más.
to do one's utmost hacer cuanto esté de la parte de uno, hacer uno cuanto pueda.
utterly enteramente, del todo.

V

vacancy vacante (unoccupied position); cuarto para alquilar (room); piso para alquilar (apartment).
vacant vacío, desocupado.
vacation vacaciones.
vaccinate vacunar.
vaccine vacuna (med.).
vacuum vacío.
vague vago.
vain vano.
in vain en vano.
vainly vanamente.
valid válido.
valise maleta, saco de viaje.
valley valle.
valuable valioso.
value valor; justiprecio, valuación (estimated value); aprecio, estimación (regard).
value (to) valuar, tasar (to estimate the value); preciar, apreciar, tener en mucho (to think highly of).
valve válvula.
vanilla vainilla.
vanish desvanecerse, desaparecerse.
vanity vanidad.
variable variable.
variety variedad.
various varios; diverso.
varnish (to) barnizar.
vary variar.
vaseline vaselina.
vast vasto, inmenso, enorme, grandísimo.
veal ternera.
veal cutlet chuleta de ternera.

vegetable vegetal, planta.
vegetable man verdulero.
vegetable soup menestra, sopa de legumbres.
vegetables legumbres, verduras, hortalizas.
vegetation vegetación.
vehement vehemente.
vehicle vehículo.
veil velo, mantilla.
vein vena.
velvet terciopelo.
ventilate ventilar.
ventilation ventilación.
verb verbo.
verdict veredicto, sentencia.
verse verso.
vertical vertical.
very muy, mucho, mucha.
very much mucho, muchísimo.
very many muchísimos, muchísimas.
very much money mucho dinero.
(Very) Much obliged. Muy agradecido.
Very well, thank you. Muy bien, gracias.
the very man el mismo hombre.
the very thought el solo pensamiento.
vessel vasija, vaso (container); buque (ship).
vest chaleco.
veteran veterano.
veterinary veterinario.
vex molestar, enfadar.
vexation molestia, enfado.
vexing molesto, importuno.
vibration vibración.
vice vicio.
vice-president vicepresidente.
vice versa viceversa, al contrario.
vicinity vecindad, cercanía.
vicious malvado, depravado.
vicious circle círculo vicioso.
victim víctima.
victor vencedor.
victorious victorioso.
victory victoria.
view vista, perspectiva, panorama.
bird's eye view vista de pájaro.
in view of en vista de.
point of view punto de vista.
What a view! ¡Que vista!
view (to) mirar, ver, contemplar.
vigil vigilia.
vigilant vigilante.
vigor brío, vigor.
vigorous vigoroso.
vile vil, bajo.
villa casa de campo.
village aldea, pueblo, pueblecito.
villager aldeano.
villain villano.
vine parra.
vinegar vinagre.
vineyard viña.
violate violar.
violation violación.
violence violencia.
violent furioso, violento.
violet violeta.
violin violín.
violinist violinista.
violoncello violoncelo.
virgin virgen.
virtue virtud.
virtuous virtuoso.
visa visto bueno, refrendo, visado.
visible visible.

vision visión.
visit visita.
to pay a visit hacer una visita.
visit (to) visitar.
visitor visitante.
visual visual.
vital vital.
vitamin vitamina.
vivid vivo, vívido, gráfico.
vocal vocal.
vocal cords cuerdas vocales.
voice voz.
void adj. vacío; nulo, inválido, sin valor ni fuerza (null).
void n. vacío.
volcano volcán.
volt voltio.
volume volumen; tomo (book).
voluntary voluntario.
volunteer voluntario.
vomit vómito.
vomit (to) vomitar.
vote voto, sufragio.
vote (to) votar.
voter votante.
vow voto.
vow (to) hacer promesa, hacer voto.
voyage viaje.
vulgar vulgar.
vulture buitre.

W

wade vadear.
to wade through the mud andar por el barro.
wage(s) sueldo, paga, jornal.
monthly wages sueldo mensual, salario.
daily wages jornal.
wage earner jornalero, trabajador, obrero.
wage (to) comprender.
to wage war hacer guerra.
wager apuesta.
wager (to) apostar.
wagon carro; furgón (freight car).
wait (to) esperar, aguardar.
Wait for me. Espéreme.
to keep waiting hacer esperar.
to wait on atender a, despachar (in a store, etc.); servir a (to serve).
waiter mozo, camarero.
waiting espera.
waiting room sala de espera.
waitress camarera.
wake (to) despertar(se).
to wake up despertar, llamar; despertarse.
Wake me at seven. Despiérteme a las siete.
I woke up at seven. Me desperté a las siete.
waken despertar.
walk paseo.
to take a walk dar un paseo.
walk (to) andar, caminar.
to walk away marcharse.
to walk down bajar.
to walk up subir.
to walk out salir; declararse en huelga (to go on strike).
to walk arm in arm ir del brazo.
to walk up and down pasearse, ir y venir.
walking paseo, acción de pasear.
to go walking ir de paseo; ir a pié.
walking cane bastón.
wall muro, pared, muralla.
wallpaper papel de empapelar.

walnut nuez (nut); nogal (tree).
waltz vals.
waltz (to) valsar.
wand vara, varita.
wander vagar; perderse, extraviarse (to go astray); divagar, delirar (of the mind).
want necesidad, falta, carencia.
  to be in want estar necesitado.
  for want of por falta de.
want (to) necesitar, tener necesidad de (to need); querer, desear (to desire).
  What do you want? ¿Qué quiere Ud.?
  Don't you want to come? ¿No quiere Ud. venir?
  Cook wanted. Se necesita una cocinera.
wanting defectuoso, deficiente; necesitado, escaso (lacking).
  to be wanting faltar.
war guerra.
  War Department Ministerio de la guerra.
  to wage war hacer la guerra.
ward sala, pabellón (in a hospital); barrio, distrito (of a city); pupilo, menor en tutela (person under the care of a guardian, etc.).
warden guardián, celador; carcelero (of a prison); director (of school, etc.).
ward off (to) parar, detener, desviar.
wardrobe guardarropa, armario, ropero.
  wardrobe trunk baúl ropero.
warehouse almacén, depósito.
wares mercancías, mercadería, géneros or artículos de comercio.
warfare guerra.
warlike belicoso.
warm caliente, cálido, caluroso.
  It's warm. Hace calor.
  I am warm. Tengo calor.
  warm water agua caliente.
warm (to) calentar.
  to warm up calentarse; acalorarse, tomar bríos.
warmly calurosamente, cordialmente.
warn advertir, prevenir, avisar.
warning advertencia, prevención, aviso; lección, escarmiento.
  to give warning prevenir, advertir.
warrant autorización; mandamiento, auto (a written order).
warrior guerrero.
wash lavado; ropa sucia (clothes to be washed); ropa lavada (clothes that have been washed).
  washbasin lavamanos, palangana.
  washing machine máquina de lavar, lavadora mecánica.
  washstand lavabo.
wash (to) lavar.
  to wash one's hands lavarse las manos.
waste despilfarro, derroche; desperdicio.
waste (to) malgastar, desperdiciar; perder, gastar.
  to waste one's time perder uno el tiempo.
wastebasket cesto de los papeles.
wastepaper papel de desecho.
watch reloj; guardia (guard).
  wristwatch reloj de pulsera.
  to be on the watch estar alerta, estar sobre sí.
  to wind up a watch dar cuerda a un reloj.
watch (to) vigilar.
  to watch out tener cuidado con.
  to watch over guardar, vigilar.
  to watch one's step tener cuidado; andarse con tiento.

watchful alerta, vigilante, despierto.
watchmaker relojero.
watchman vigilante, sereno, guardián.
watchword santo y seña; consigna, lema.
water agua.
  fresh water agua fresca.
  hot water agua caliente.
  mineral water agua mineral.
  running water agua corriente.
  soft water agua delgada.
  sea water agua de mar.
  soda water agua de seltz, soda.
  toilet water colonia, agua de colonia.
  water faucet grifo, grifo del agua.
  water front litoral, tierras ribereñas; la sección del puerto.
  water power fuerza hidráulica.
  to make one's mouth water hacer la boca agua.
  water bag bolsa para agua, calientapiés.
water (to) regar (to sprinkle); mojar, humedecer (to wet).
waterfall cascada, catarata.
watermelon sandía.
waterproof impermeable.
wave ola; onda (radio, etc.), ondulación (hair).
  short wave onda corta.
  long wave onda larga.
  sound wave onda sonora.
  wave length longitud de onda.
wave (to) ondular; flotar (in the air); hacer señas (to signal by waving); agitar (a handkerchief, etc.).
  to wave one's hand hacer señas con la mano.
waver (to) vacilar, titubear; cejar, ceder (to give way).
wavering irresoluto, vacilante.
waving n. ondulación.
wavy ondulado.
wax cera.
  wax candle vela de cera.
  wax paper papel encerado.
wax (to) encerar.
way camino, vía, ruta; modo, manera (manner).
  way in entrada.
  way off muy lejos.
  way out salida.
  by way of por la vía de; pasando por.
  by the way a propósito, dicho sea de paso.
  in such a way de tal manera.
  in this way de este modo.
  any way de cualquier modo.
  in no way de ningún modo.
  this way así.
  Go this way. Vaya por aquí.
  on the way en ruta; de camino.
  out of the way fuera de camino; donde no estorbe.
  across the way al otro lado, en frente.
  Which way? ¿Por dónde?
  Get out of the way! ¡Atrás!-
  Step this way. Venga Ud. acá.-
  in some way or other de un modo o de otro.
  under way en camino, en marcha.
  to have (get) one's way salirse con la suya.
  the other way around al contrario, al revés.
  all the way en todo el camino, durante el trayecto; del todo; hasta el fin.
  to give way ceder.
  ways and means medios y arbitrios.
we nosotros, nosotras.
  we Americans nosotros los norteamericanos.
weak débil.

weaken debilitar.
weakness debilidad, flaqueza.
wealth riqueza, bienes.
wealthy rico, adinerado.
weapon arma.
wear uso, desgaste.
wear (to) llevar, usar, llevar puesto, poner.
  to wear down cansar, fastidiar (to tire, annoy); vencer (to overcome).
  to wear off gastarse; borrarse (color).
  to wear out gastarse, apurar mucho (a dress, etc.).
  to wear well durar (to last).
  Which dress will you wear tonight? ¿Qué vestido te vas a poner esta noche?
  I like the blouse she's wearing. Me gusta la blusa que lleva puesta.
weariness cansancio, hastío, aburrimiento.
wearing apparel ropa, prenda de vestir.
weary adj. cansado, hastiado, fastidiado.
weary (to) cansar, hastiar, molestar.
weather tiempo.
  bad weather mal tiempo.
  nice weather buen tiempo.
  The weather is fine. Hace buen tiempo. Hace un tiempo muy bueno.
  weather conditions condiciones meteorológicas.
  weather report boletín meteorológico.
weave tejer.
web tela, tejido.
  spider web tela de araña.
wedding boda, nupcias.
  wedding dress traje de boda.
  wedding present regalo de boda.
wedge cuña.
Wednesday miércoles.
weed maleza, mala hierba.
week semana.
  weekday día de trabajo.
  last week la semana pasada.
  next week la semana que viene.
  a week from tomorrow de mañana en ocho días.
week end fin de semana.
weekly adj. semanario.
  weekly publication semanario.
weekly adv. semalmente, por semana.
weep llorar.
  to weep for llorar por, llorar de.
weigh pesar; levar (anchor).
weight peso.
  gross weight peso bruto.
  net weight peso neto.
  weights and measures pesos y medidas.
weighty de peso, ponderoso, serio, importante.
welcome adj. bienvenido.
  Welcome! ¡Bienvenido!
  You're welcome (answer to "Thank you."). De nada. No hay de qué.
welcome n. bienvenida.
welcome (to) dar la bienvenida.
welfare bienestar.
  welfare work obra de beneficiencia, labor social.
well pozo.
well adj. bueno, bien; adv. bien.
  to be well estar bien.
  very well muy bien.
  I am quite well. Estoy muy bien.
  I don't feel well. No me siento bien.
  to look well tener buena cara.
  well and good la enhorabuena, bien está.

well-being bienestar.
well-bred bien educado.
well done bien hecho.
well-to-do acomodado, rico.
well-known bien conocido.
well-timed oportuno.
as well as asi como, lo mismo que.
well then con que.
Well! ¡Cómo!
Well, well! ¡Vaya! ¡Qué cosa!
Very well! ¡Está bien!
west oeste, occidente.
western occidental.
wet *adj.* mojado; húmedo.
to get wet mojarse.
wet (to) mojar.
whale ballena.
wharf muelle.
what qué.
What's that? ¿Qué es eso?
What's the matter? ¿Qué pasa?
What else? ¿Qué mas?
What for? ¿Para qué?
What about? ¿Qué le parece? ¿Que hay en cuanto a eso? ¿Qué diremos?
What of (about) it? ¿Y eso qué importa?
what if y si, qué será si, qué sucederá si, y qué importa que, aunque.
whatever cualquier cosa que, sea lo que fuere, lo que.
whatever you like lo que Ud. quiera.
whatever reasons he may have sean cuales fueren las razones que tenga.
wheat trigo.
wheel rueda.
steering wheel volante.
wheel chair silla de ruedas.
wheelbarrow carretilla.
when cuando.
Since when? ¿Desde cuándo? ¿De cuándo acá?
whenever cuando quiera, siempre que, en cualquier tiempo que sea.
whenever you like cuando Ud. quiera.
where donde, dónde, adonde, en donde, por donde, de donde.
Where are you from? ¿De dónde es Ud.?
Where are you going? ¿Adónde va?
whereby por lo cual, por el que, por medio del cual, con lo cual.
wherever dondequiera que.
whether si, sea que, que.
I doubt whether dudo que.
whether he likes it or not que quiera, que no quiera.
which cual, que, el que, la cual, lo cual.
Which book? ¿Qué libro?
Which way? ¿Por dónde? ¿Por qué camino?
Which of these? ¿Cuál de éstos?
all of which todo lo cual.
both of which ambos.
whichever cualquiera.
while instante, momento, rato.
a little while un ratito.
a little while ago hace poco rato, no hace mucho.
for a while por algún tiempo.
once in a while de vez en cuando.
to be worth while valer la pena.
while *conj.* mientras, mientras que, a la vez que.
whip látigo, azote.
whip (to) azotar, dar latigazos; batir (cream, eggs, etc.).

whipped cream nata batida.
whirl giro, rotación.
whirl (to) dar vueltas, girar.
whirlpool remolino, vorágine.
whirlwind torbellino.
whisper cuchicheo.
whisper (to) cuchichear, decir al oído.
to whisper in someone's ear decir al oído.
whistle silbido.
whistle (to) silbar.
white blanco.
white of an egg clara de huevo.
white lie mentirilla.
White House Casa Blanca.
whiten (to) blanquear.
who quien, quienes, que, el que, la que, los que, las que; quien.
Who is he? ¿Quién es?
whoever quienquiera, cualquiera.
whoever it may be quienquiera que sea.
whole todo, entero, integral.
the whole todo el.
whole wheat bread pan integral.
on the whole en conjunto, en general.
whole number número entero.
wholehearted sincero, de todo corazón; enérgico, activo.
wholesale (al) por mayor.
wholesome sano.
wholesome food alimento sano, alimento nutritivo.
wholly totalmente, enteramente.
whom a quien, a quienes.
whose cuyo, de quien.
why por qué.
Why not? ¿Por qué no? ¿Pues y qué?
the why and the wherefore el porqué y la razón.
wicked mala, malvado, perverso.
wickedness maldad, iniquidad.
wide ancho, vasto, extenso.
two inches wide dos pulgadas de ancho.
wide open abierto de par en par.
wide-awake muy despierto, alerta, vivo.
widely muy, mucho.
widely different diametralmente opuesto, completamente diferente.
widely used se usa mucho.
widely known muy conocido.
widen ensanchar, extender, ampliar.
widespread divulgado, esparcido.
widow viuda.
widower viudo.
width ancho, anchura.
wife esposa, señora, mujer.
wig peluca.
wild salvaje (savage); silvestre (plants, flowers, etc.); atolondrado, descabellado, desenfrenado (of a person).
wilderness desierto.
will voluntad; testamento.
at will a voluntad, a discreción.
against one's will contra la voluntad de uno.
will (to) querer, desear; testar, hacer testamento (to make a will). (See also *shall.*)
Will you tell me the time? ¿Me hace Ud. el favor de decirme la hora?
Will you do me a favor? ¿Me quiere Ud. hacer un favor?
I won't do it, but she will. Yo no lo haré, pero ella sí.
Will you go? ¿Irá Ud.?
I will not go. No iré. No quiero ir.

willing dispuesto, gustoso, pronto, inclinado.
to be willing estar dispuesto, querer.
God willing Dios mediante.
willingly de buena gana, gustosamente.
willingness buena voluntad, buena gana.
win (to) ganar, vencer, prevalecer, lograr.
to win out salir bien, triunfar.
wind viento.
wind instrument instrumento de viento.
wind (to) enrollar; dar cuerda (a watch).
windmill molino (de viento).
window ventana.
windowpane vidrio (cristal) de la ventana.
window shade transparente, visillo.
window shutter postigo.
windshield parabrisas.
windy ventoso.
to be windy hacer viento.
wine vino.
red wine vino tinto.
white wine vino blanco.
wing ala.
wink guiñada.
not to sleep a wink no pegar los ojos.
wink (to) guiñar.
winner ganador.
winter invierno.
wintry invernal.
wipe (to) limpiar con un trapo, etc. (the floor, etc.); secar, enjugar (to dry).
to wipe out arrasar, extirpar, destruir.
wire *n.* alambre (metal); telegrama (telegram).
barbed wire alambre de púa.
wire (to) telegrafiar.
wisdom sabiduría, juicio; sentido común.
wisdom tooth muela del juicio.
wise sabio; juicioso, prudente.
wish deseo.
wish (to) desear, querer.
to make a wish concebir un deseo, pensar en algo que se quiere.
wit ingenio, agudeza, sal.
witch bruja.
witch hazel loción de carpe, hamamelis.
with con, en compañía de; a, contra, de, en, entre.
coffee with milk café con leche.
to speak with caution hablar con prudencia.
to touch with the hand tocar con la mano.
She came with a friend. Vino con un amigo.
identical with idéntico a.
to struggle with luchar contra.
to fill with llenar de.
with the exception of a excepción de.
with regard to en cuanto a, con respecto a.
with the exception a excepción de.
the girl with the red dress la chica del vestido rojo.
That always happens with friends. Eso ocurre siempre entre amigos.
withdraw (to) retirar, retirarse, replegarse; retractarse de (to retract).
withdrawal retirada, repliegue.
within dentro de; a poco de, cerca de.
within a short distance a poca distancia.
within a week dentro de una semana.
within one's reach al alcance de uno.
from within de adentro.
without sin; *adv.* fuera, afuera, por fuera, de la parte de afuera.
tea without sugar té sin azúcar.
without fail sin falta.
within and without dentro y fuera.

without doubt sin duda.

without noticing it sin advertirlo.

witness testigo.

witness (to) presenciar, ver; declarar, atestiguar, dar testimonio, servir de testigo (to act as a witness).

witty ingenioso, ocurrente, gracioso, salado.

a witty remark una gracia, una agudeza.

She's very witty. Es muy salada.

wolf lobo.

woman mujer.

young woman joven.

wonder maravilla.

No wonder. No es extraño. No es para menos.

wonder (to) admirarse, maravillarse de, preguntarse.

I wonder whether it's true. Yo me pregunto si será verdad. ¿Será verdad?

I wonder what she wants. ¿Qué querrá?

to wonder at maravillarse de.

to wonder about extrañarse, tener sus dudas acerca de; tener curiosidad por.

I wonder why? ¿Por qué será?

I wonder! ¡Si será cierto!

wonderful estupendo, admirable, maravilloso.

wood madera (matinal); monte, bosque (woods).

firewood leña.

woodwork maderaje, maderamen.

wool lana.

woolen de lana.

word palabra.

too funny for words lo más gracioso del mundo.

in so many words en esas mismas palabras, exactamente así, claramente, sin ambages.

word for word palabra por palabra.

in other words en otros términos.

by word of mouth de palabra, verbalmente.

on my word bajo mi palabra.

to leave word dejar dicho, dejar recado.

to send word mandar a decir.

work trabajo, labor.

to be at work estar en el trabajo; estar ocupado, estar trabajando.

out of work sin trabajo.

work of art objeto de arte, obra de arte.

work (to) trabajar; funcionar (machine); explotar (a mine); tallar (a stone); elaborar, fabricar.

to work out resolver (a problem); llevar a cabo (to carry out); salir bien, tener éxito (to come out all right).

The machine doesn't work. La máquina no funciona.

worker obrero, trabajador.

working trabajo, funcionamiento.

working day día de trabajo.

workman obrero, trabajador.

workshop taller.

world mundo.

all over the world por todo el mundo.

world-wide mundial.

World War Guerra mundial.

worm gusano.

worn-out rendido.

worn-out clothes ropa usada.

I'm worn-out. Estoy rendido.

worry preocupación, cuidado ansiedad.

worry (to) preocupar(se), inquietar(se).

Don't worry. No se preocupe. No se apure.

to be worried estar preocupado.

worse peor.

to get worse empeorarse.

so much the worse tanto peor.

worse and worse de mal en peor.

worse than ever peor que nunca.

to take a turn for the worse empeorar.

worship culto, adoración.

worship (to) adorar, venerar.

worst pésimo, malísimo.

the worst lo peor, lo más malo.

at the worst en el peor de los casos.

if worst comes to the worst si sucediera lo peor.

to have the worst of it salir perdiendo, llevar la peor parte.

worth valor, mérito.

What's it worth? ¿Cuánto vale?

It's worth the money. Eso vale su precio. Es una buena compra.

He's worth a lot of money. Tiene mucho dinero.

to be worth while valer la pena.

It's worth while trying. Vale la pena intentarlo.

One dollar's worth in change. Un dólar en calderilla.

worthless inútil, inservible, sin valor.

to be worthless ser inútil.

worth-while que vale la pena.

worthy digno, meredor.

would querer. The future conditional is generally expressed by adding -ía, -ías, -ía, -íamos, -íais, -ían to the infinitive of the verb.

I would go. iría.

I would like to go. Quisiera ir.

I wouldn't go if I could. No iría si pudiera.

She wouldn't come. No quiso venir.

I wish she would come. Querría que viniese. Ojalá que venga.

I would like to ask you a favor. Quisiera pedirle un favor.

Would you do me a favor? ¿Me haría Ud. un favor?

wound herida.

wound (to) herir.

wounded herido.

wrap (to) envolver (to wrap up).

wrapper envoltura.

wrapping adj. de envolver.

wrapping paper papel de envolver.

wreath corona (of flowers, etc.).

wreck naufragio (shipwreck); ruina (ruin).

wreck (to) arruinar; hacer naufragar.

to be shipwrecked irse a pique, naufragar.

wrench torcedura (wrenching), llave de tuercas, llave inglesa (tool).

wrench (to) torcer, dislocar, sacar de quicio.

to wrench one's foot torcerse el pie.

wrestle luchar.

wrestler luchador.

wring torcer, retorcer, estrujar; escurrir (wet clothes, etc.).

to wring out exprimir, escurrir.

wrinkle arruga.

wrinkle (to) arrugar.

wrist muñeca.

wristwatch reloj de pulsera.

write (to) escribir.

to write down poner por escrito, anotar.

writer escritor, autor.

writing escritura, escrito.

in writing por escrito.

to put in writing poner por escrito.

writing desk escritorio.

writing paper papel de escribir.

written escrito.

wrong n. mal; daño (harm); injuria, injusticia (injustice); agravio; adj. mal(o), incorrecto, falso, erróneo, injusto; adv. mal.

the knowledge of right and wrong el conocimiento del bien y el mal.

to do wrong hacer daño, obrar mal.

You are wrong. Ud. no tiene razón. Ud. está equivocado.

to be wrong no tener razón; estar mal hecho.

wrong side out al revés.

That's wrong. Eso está mal. Está mal dicho (said). Está mal escrito (written). Está mal hecho (done).

Something is wrong with the engine. El motor no funciona bien.

Something is wrong with him. Le pasa algo. Tiene algo raro.

I took the wrong road. Erré el camino. Me equivoqué de camino.

X

X-rays rayos X.

Y

yard yarda, vaía (measure); patio (court); corral (around a barn).

Navy yard Arsenal.

yawn bostezo.

yawn (to) bostezar.

year año.

last year el año pasado.

all year round todo el año.

many years ago hace muchos años.

yearbook anuario, anales.

yearly adj. anual.

yearly adv. anualmente, todos los años.

yeast levadura.

yell grito.

yell (to) gritar, chillar.

yellow amarillo.

yes sí.

yesterday ayer.

day before yesterday anteayer.

yet adv. todavía, aún; conj. sin embargo, con todo.

not yet aún no, todavía no.

as yet hasta ahora, hasta aquí.

I don't know it yet. Todavía no lo sé.

yield rendimiento, provecho.

yield (to) rendir, producir; ceder (to give in).

yoke yugo; yunta de bueyes (2 oxen).

yolk yema.

you tú (fam.); usted (polite).

young joven, mozo.

young man joven.

young lady señorita, joven.

young people jóvenes.

to look young verse joven, tener la traza de joven, aparentar poca edad.

your tú, tus, su, sus, vuestro(s), de usted(es).

yours suyo(s), suya(s), tuyo(s), tuya(s), vuestro(s), vuestra(s), el suyo, la suya, el tuyo, la tuya, la vuestra, los (tuyos, suyos, vuestros), las (tuyas, suyas, vuestras), de (usted, ustedes).

This book is yours. Este libro es tuyo (suyo, de usted, vuestro, de ustedes).

a friend of yours un amigo tuyo (suyo, vuestro, de usted, de ustedes).

Yours sincerely Su seguro servidor (S.S.S.), Su

afectísimo y seguro servidor (Su afmo. y s.s.).
yourself usted mismo, tú mismo.
Wash yourself. Lávate. Lávese.
yourselves ustedes mismos, vosotros mismos.
youth juventud.
youthful juvenil.

Z

zeal celo, fervor.
zealous celoso.
zero cero.
zest entusiasmo.

zigzag zigzag.
zinc zinc.
zone zona.
zoo jardín zoológico.
zoological zoológico.
zoology zoología.

GLOSSARY OF PROPER NAMES

Albert Alberto.
Alexander Alejandro.
Alfred Alfredo.
Alice Alicia.
Andrew Andrés.
Ann, Anna Ana.
Anthony Antonio.
Arthur Arturo.
Beatrice Beatriz.
Bernard Bernardo.
Catharine, Catherine Catalina.
Charles Carlos.
Charlotte Carlota.
Dorothy Dorotea.

Edward Eduardo.
Elizabeth Isabel.
Ellen Elena.
Emily Emilia.
Ernest Ernesto.
Esther Ester.
Eugene Eugenio.
Francis Francisco.
Frederic(k) Federico.
George Jorge.
Gertrude Gertrudis.
Helen Elena.
Henry Enrique.
Isabella Isabel.

James Jaime, Diego.
Joan, Joanna Juana.
John Juan.
Joseph José.
Josephine Josefina.
Juliet Julia.
Julius Julio.
Leo León.
Louis Luis.
Louise Luisa.
Margaret Margarita.
Martha Marta.
Mary María.
Michael Miguel.

Paul Pablo.
Peter Pedro.
Philip Felipe.
Raymond Raimundo, Ramón.
Richard Ricardo.
Robert Roberto.
Rose Rosa.
Susan Susana.
Theresa Teresa.
Thomas Tomas.
Vincent Vicente.
William Guillermo.

GLOSSARY OF GEOGRAPHICAL NAMES

Algiers Argel.
Alps Alpes.
Alsace Alsacia.
Andalusia Andalucía.
Antilles Antillas.
Antwerp Amberes.
Aragon Aragón.
Argentina Argentina.
Asturias Asturias.
Athens Atenas.
Atlantic Ocean Océano Atlántico.
Barcelona Barcelona.
Basque Provinces Provincias Vascongadas.
Bayonne Bayona.
Belgium Bélgica.
Bilboa Bilbao.
Biscay Vizcaya.
Bolivia Bolivia.
Brazil Brasil.
Brittany Bretaña.
Brussels Bruselas.
Buenos Aires Buenos Aires.
Castile Castilla.
Catalonia Cataluña.
Chile Chile.
China China.
Colombia Colombia.
Costa Rica Costa Rica.
Cuba Cuba.
Denmark Dinamarca.
Dominican Republic República Dominicana.
Ecuador Ecuador.
Egypt Egipto.
El Salvador El Salvador.
England Inglaterra.

Europe Europa.
Finland Finlandia.
Flanders Flandes.
Florence Florencia.
France Francia.
Galicia Galicia.
Geneva Ginebra.
Genoa Génova.
Germany Alemania.
Greece Grecia.
Guatemala Guatemala.
Havana Habana.
Holland Holanda.
Honduras Honduras.
Hungary Hungría.
Iceland Islandia.
Ireland Irlanda.
Italy Italia.
Japan Japón.
Lima Lima.
Lisbon Lisboa.
London Londres.
Madrid Madrid.
Marseilles Marsella.
Mediterranean Sea Mar Mediterráneo.
Mexico México.
Morocco Marruecos.
Moscow Moscú.
Naples Nápoles.
Navarre Navarra.
Netherlands Países Bajos, Holanda.
New York Nueva York.
New Zealand Nueva Zelandia.
Nicaragua Nicaragua.
Normandy Normandía.

North America América del Norte.
Norway Noruega.
Panama Panamá.
Paraguay Paraguay.
Pacific Ocean Océano Pacífico.
Peru Perú.
Poland Polonia.
Portugal Portugal.
Puerto Rico Puerto Rico.
Prussia Prusia.
Pyrenees Pirineos.
Rome Roma.
Roumania Rumania.
Russia Rusia.
Saragossa Zaragoza.
Scandinavia Escandinavia.
Scotland Escocia.
Seville Sevilla.
Sicily Sicilia.
Spain España.
Spanish America Hispanoamérica.
Sweden Suecia.
Switzerland Suiza.
Texas Tejas.
Toulouse Tolosa.
Turkey Turquía.
United States of America Estados Unidos de América.
Uruguay Uruguay.
Valencia Valencia.
Venezuela Venezuela.
Venice Venecia.
Vienna Viena.